London...

London is a bustling metropolis with some of the best monuments, museums and galleries in the world. There are open-top bus tours of the main sights of central London with the opportunity to get on and off as many times as you like, but the Underground is the quickest way to get around.

The shopping is second to none – Oxford Street and Regent Street are the capital's main shopping arteries. Smart shopping districts include Kensington and Knightsbridge, there are interesting shops around King's Road in Chelsea and Neal Street in Covent Garden, and covered arcades and colourful markets to browse. London's green spaces, a haven from the crowded streets, include eight royal parks. Cultural life encompasses opera, theatre, cinema, street festivals, art exhibitions and much more. The South Bank and the Barbican are arty hot spots.

To help you make the most of your leisure time in London we have provided a useful gazetteer covering a range of attractions from national museums and art galleries, to cinemas and grand theatres featuring everything from opera and classical ballet to West End musicals. As you might expect there are characterful and atmospheric pubs, DJ bars and top-notch clubs catering for all tastes.

Entries are listed alphabetically (ignoring The) under each category heading. The map reference denotes the map page number in the mapping section and the grid square(s) in which the street/road is to be found, not the individual establishments. We have given the street name and post code, telephone and fax numbers and, where possible, email and website details.

Please note: the entries listed in this gazetteer section were provided by a third party and therefore the individual establishments are not necessarily recommended or inspected by the AA.

TOURIST ATTRACTIONS

7 Hammersmith Terrace

The home of Emery Walker, printer, antiquary and mentor to William Morris. A unique arts and crafts domestic interior.

7 Hammersmith Terrace, London W6 9TS
⌁ www.emerywalker.org.uk
⊘ Page 118-D5

BBC Television Centre

A tour of the BBC Television Centre takes almost two hours and features the studios and the BBC News section offering an insight into the functioning of the organisation.

Wood Lane, Shepherds Bush, London W12 7RJ
☎ 0870 603 0304
@ k.barnes@bbc.co.uk
⌁ www.bbc.co.uk
⊘ Page 100-A6

The Banqueting House

The Banqueting House forms part of Whitehall Palace, the sovereign's principal residence from 1530 until 1698 when it was destroyed by fire. The House features Palladian architecture and Rubens' paintings besides a small exhibition and video presentation on Charles I.

Whitehall, Westminster, London SW1A 2ER
☎ 0870 751 5178
⌁ www.hrp.org.uk
⊘ Page 16-E1

Battersea Park

Battersea Park is a large Victorian park, built between 1854 and 1870. Features include a grand riverside promenade, fountains, a large lake (with boating from Easter), lakeside cafe, ornamental and ecological areas, many notable trees, sporting facilities, children's play areas and the Battersea Park Children's Zoo (see following entry).

Queenstown Road, Prince of Wales Drive, London SW11 4NJ
☎ 020 8871 7530
⌁ www.wandsworth.gov.uk/
⊘ Page 140-E1

Battersea Park Children's Zoo

Battersea Park Children's Zoo, in the heart of South London, combines a zoo, animal encounters, play area and cafe. The zoo inmates include ring tailed lemurs, meerkats, otters, pygmy goats, giant rabbits and parrots among others.

Albert Bridge Road, London SW11 4NJ
☎ 020 7924 5826
⌁ www.batterseaparkzoo.co.uk
⊘ Page 140-E2

Bedfont Lakes Country Park

Bedfont Lakes, a water-focussed country park that opened in 1995, has 180 acres of rolling meadows, woodlands and lakes. Over 300 plants and 140 bird species have been recorded in the park. Facilities include an orienteering course, a trim trail, bridlepath, a children's playground and a nature trail.

Clockhouse Lane, Bedfont, London TW14 8QA
☎ 01784 423556
@ bedfont-lakes@cip.org.uk
⌁ www.hounslow.info/bedfontlakes.htm
⊘ Page 152-D6

Bevis Marks Synagogue

Britain's oldest synagogue opened in 1701. The interior retains all its original furnishings, however, several Cromwellian benches come from the place of worship established when Jews first returned to England in the 1650s. The private house where they met was soon outgrown, and Bevis Marks was built.

Bevis Marks, 2 Heneage Lane, London EC3A 5DQ
☎ 020 7626 1274
@ hlh@hiosilver.com
⌁ www.bevismarks.org.uk/
⊘ Page 13-H3

Boston Manor Park

The Boston Manor Park surrounds the Boston Manor House, which was built in 1623 and remained in private ownership until 1924. The park has ornamental lawns and homes a small pond, tennis courts, a basketball court and a children's play area.

Boston Manor Road, Brentford TW8 9JX
☎ 020 8894 2677
@ info@cip.org.uk
⌁ www.hounslow.info
⊘ Page 116-C5

Brent Lodge Park Animal Centre

Brent Lodge Park Animal Centre houses a wide variety of animals including birds and mammals such as rhea and mongooses, domestic species including goats and rabbits and an indoor area with monkeys, reptiles and spiders.

Church Road, Hanwell, London W7 3BL
☎ 020 8825 7529
⌁ www.ealing.gov.uk/
⊘ Page 96-D6

Brompton Cemetery

The cemetery has a formal layout with a central avenue and has been the burial place from all walks of life, including 13 holders of the Victorian Cross, Chelsea Pensioners and the community of West London. It is a haven for wildlife including birds, butterflies, foxes and squirrels.

Fulham Road, Chelsea, London SW10 9UG
☎ 020 7352 1201
⌁ www.royalparks.gov.uk/parks/
⊘ Page 120-A6

Buckingham Palace

Buckingham Palace has served as the official London residence of Britain's sovereigns since 1837. It evolved from a town house that was owned from the beginning of the 18th century by the Dukes of Buckingham. Today it is the Queen's official residence. Although in use for official events and receptions held by the Queen, areas of Buckingham Palace are opened to visitors on a regular basis.

The Mall, St James's, London SW1A 1AA
☎ 020 7766 7300
@ bookinginfo@royalcollection.org.uk
⌁ www.royalcollection.org.uk
▤ 020 7930 9625
⊘ Page 15-K3

Bushy Park

Bushy Park covers 1,100 acres and is home to a large herd of free-roaming deer along with the Arethusa 'Diana' Fountain on the Chestnut Avenue.

The Stockyard Bushy Park, Hampton Court Road, Hampton, London TW12 2EJ
☎ 020 8979 1586
⌁ www.royalparks.gov.uk/parks/bushy_park
⊘ Page 173-J3

Camden Lock

At Camden Lock, the original market of Camden Town, you'll find designer workshops, studios, stalls, shops, cafes, restaurants and bars.

54–56 Camden Lock Place, Chalk Farm Road, Camden, London NW1 8AF
☎ 020 7284 2084
@ info@camdenlockmarket.com
⌁ www.camdenlockmarket.com
⊘ Page 84-A5

Canalside Activity Centre

Canal Close, Ladbroke Grove, London W10 5AY
☎ 020 8968 4500
⌁ www.rbkc.gov.uk
⊘ Page 100-B3

Carew Manor

The Carew Manor dates from around 1500 and offers an insight into its history through tours of the Great Hall with hammer beam roofs, the dovecote with honeycomb structure and the orangery wall.

Church Road, Beddington London SM6 7NH
☎ 020 8647 8349
⌁ www.sutton.gov.uk/leisure/heritage/carewmanor.htm
⊘ Page 210-D1

Carnaby Street

A bustling shopping spot on the edge of Soho.

West End, Soho, London W1
☎ 020 7333 8118
⌁ www.carnaby.co.uk/
⊘ Page 10-A4

Centre for Wildlife Gardening

Home to wildflowers, herbs, pond plants, trees, frogs, grasshoppers and songbirds. The project has an award winning visitors' centre demonstrating innovative environmental building techniques, training courses and activities for visitors.

28 Marsden Road, Peckham, London SE15 4EE
☎ 020 7252 9186
@ lwtwildgarden@cix.co.uk

www.wildlondon.org.uk
Page 143-G4

Chelsea Football Club
Stadium tours most days.

Stamford Bridge, Fulham Road, Fulham, London SW6 1HS
☎ 020 7386 9373
@ tours@chelseavillage.com
www.chelseafc.com
Page 140-A1

Chelsea Physic Garden
The Chelsea Physic Garden was founded in 1673 by the Society of Apothecaries and continues to research the properties, origins and conservation of over 5000 species. A range of events at the garden include Christmas and summer fairs as well as compost clinics.

66 Royal Hospital Road, Chelsea, London SW3 4HS
☎ 020 7352 5646
@ enquiries@
chelseaphysicgarden.co.uk
www.chelseaphysicgarden.
co.uk
Page 120-E6

Chislehurst Caves
Chislehurst Caves are a labyrinth of dark mysterious passageways which have been hewn by hand from the chalk, deep beneath Chislehurst. There are over 20 miles of caverns and passageways, dug over a period of 8,000 years.

Old Hill, Chislehurst, London BR7 5NB
☎ 020 8467 3264
@ enquiries@chislehurstcaves.
co.uk
www.chislehurstcaves.co.uk
Page 185-F4

City Hall
City Hall, a striking rounded glass building on the south bank of the Thames near Tower Bridge, is home to the Mayor of London, the London Assembly and the Greater London Authority. The building hosts regular gallery exhibitions related to life in the capital.

The Queens Walk, Bermondsey, London SE1 2AA
☎ 020 7983 4762/020 7983 4100
@ peoplesquestions@london.
gov.uk
www.london.gov.uk
📄 020 7983 4057
Page 19-H1

Clarence House
Clarence House was built between 1825 and 1827 to the designs of John Nash for Prince William Henry, Duke of Clarence. Today, it is the official London residence of the Prince of Wales, the Duchess of Cornwall and Princes William and Harry. A guided tour of five rooms feature works of art from the Royal Collection as well as other furnishings.

The Mall, London SW1A 1BA
☎ 020 7766 7303
© 020 7766 7303
@ bookinginfo@royalcollection.
org.uk
www.royal.gov.uk
Page 16-B2

The Clock Room
The Clock Room houses collection of historic clocks, watches, and marine timekeepers ranging from 1600 to 1850.

Guildhall Library, Aldermanbury, London EC2P 2EJ
☎ 020 7332 1868
@ keeper@clockmakers.org
www.clockmakers.org
Page 12-D3

County Hall
Located in Lambeth and situated on the River Thames, across from the Houses of Parliament, County Hall is one of London's most recognisable historic buildings. Whether you are looking to explore the ocean depths at the London Aquarium or visit the Dalí Universe art exhibition or one of the temporary attractions and media events, County Hall is a destination with something for everyone.

Westminster Bridge Road, London SE1 7PB
www.londoncountyhall.com
Page 17-G2

Covent Garden Piazza
At the heart of the Covent Garden piazza lies the famous market, designed in 1632 by Inigo Jones and now visited by 30 million people each year. The large glass covered building comprises several arcades of fashionable boutiques, cafes and gift and book shops. In the open piazza jugglers, mime artists, variety acts and musicians delight and amaze the crowds. Restaurants, cafes and

bars line the piazza, offering great views of this daily spectacle.

Covent Garden, London WC2E 8HA
www.coventgarden.uk.com
Page 11-F5

Cranford Countryside Park
The Cranford Countryside Park covers 144 acres and features the relics of a walled garden, icehouse, a restored 18th-century stable block and the medieval St Dunstan's Church and graveyard besides woodlands, wildflower meadows and wetlands.

The Parkway, Cranford, London TW5 9RZ
☎ 020 8573 1443
@ cranford.park@btinternet.com
www.hounslow.info
Page 113-K6

Crofton Roman Villa
Crofton Roman Villa features the remains of ten rooms protected inside a public viewing building along with tiled (tessellated) floors and the under-floor heating system (hypocaust).

Crofton Road, Orpington, Kent BR6 8AE
☎ 020 84601442, 020 8462 4737
@ croftonvilla@aol.com
cka.moon-demon.co.uk/villa.
htm
Page 201-K6

Cutty Sark
The *Cutty Sark* is anchored at Maritime Greenwich overlooking the River Thames and offers an insight into its history through displays of navigational instruments, paintings, figureheads and other maritime memorabilia.

King William Walk, Greenwich, London SE10 9HT
☎ 020 8858 3445
@ enquiries@cuttysark.org.uk
www.cuttysark.org.uk
Page 125-F6

Cutty Sark Conservation Project Visitor Centre
Next to *Cutty Sark* there is an architecturally stunning pavilion where visitors can learn about the Cutty Sark Trust's techniques and plans for the ship which was damaged, during conservation work, in a fire in May 2007.

Cutty Sark Gardens, Greenwich, London SE10 9LW
☎ 020 8858 3445
@ bookings@cuttysark.org.uk
www.cuttysark.org.uk
Page 125-F6

Danson House
Danson House was built *c*1766 in Bexleyheath. It reflects a preoccupation with the golden age of antiquity and is full of the symbolism of classical mythology. It is a revival of Italian villa design from the area around Vicenza in the second half of the 16th century. In the 20th century the house fell into an almost ruinous state. In 1995 English Heritage, which had identified the house as 'the most significant building at risk in London' began ten years of restoration.

Danson Park, Bexleyheath, London DA6 8HL
☎ 020 8303 6699
@ enquiries@dansonhouse.com
www.dansonhouse.com
Page 148-D5

Danson Park
Danson Park occupies more than 180 acres of land which includes a lake and gardens. The park offers recreational facilities and also hosts a wide range of events including open air concerts, fireworks' displays, craft fairs, a dog show and circus.

Danson Road, Bexleyheath, London DA6 8HL
☎ 01322 356879
@ parks&openspaces@bexley.
gov.uk
www.bexley.gov.uk/
Page 148-D5

Dennis Severs' House
The Dennis Severs' House features ten rooms depicting the family life of Huguenot weavers who inhabited the house in early 18th century. The recreated Georgian interiors offer a journey through time with aid of sounds and sights from the bygone period.

18 Folgate Street, Spitalfields, London E1 6BX
☎ 020 7247 4013
@ info@DennisSeversHouse.
co.uk
www.dennissevershouse.co.uk
Page 13-H1

Discover

Discover is a hands-on interactive story trail where children can play, explore, make up new characters and create their own special tales.

1 Bridge Terrace, Stratford, London E15 4BG
☎ 020 8536 5555
@ team@discover.org.uk
⌂ www.discover.org.uk
✎ Page 88-B5

Dr Johnson's House

Dr Johnson's House was built in 1700 and was home and workplace for Samuel Johnson from 1748 until 1759. The interiors feature panelled rooms, a pine staircase and a collection of period furniture, prints and portraits.

17 Gough Square, London EC4A 3DE
☎ 020 7353 3745
@ curator@drjohnsonshouse.org
⌂ www.drjohnsonshouse.org
✎ Page 11-K3

English Heritage: The Albert Memorial

The Albert Memorial, designed by George Gilbert Scott and completed in 1876, is a flamboyant monument to Prince Albert, husband of Queen Victoria. In the middle is Albert holding the catalogue for the 1851 Great Exhibition that he organised. Due to damage caused by the weather and pollution the monument was restored in the 1990s.

The Albert Memorial, Kensington Gardens, London SW7 2AP
☎ 020 7495 0916
⌂ www.english-heritage.org.uk
✎ Page 14-A2

English Heritage: Apsley House

The Apsley House was originally designed and built by Robert Adam between 1771 and 1778 for Baron Apsley and later passed to the Wellesley family in 1807. It was first owned by Richard and then his younger brother Arthur Wellesley, Duke of Wellington. The interiors house an art collection, a statue of Napoleon and the vast collection of silver plate and unique porcelain as trophies from many nations.

Hyde Park Corner, 149 Piccadilly, Mayfair, London W1J 7NT
☎ 020 7495 8525
⌂ www.english-heritage.org.uk
▤ 020 7493 6576
✎ Page 15-G2

English Heritage: Chapter House, Pyx Chamber and Abbey Museum

The Chapter House of Westminster Abbey was originally used in the 13th century by Benedictine monks for their daily meetings. The octagonal building has examples of medieval sculpture, an original floor of glazed tiles and wall paintings. The 11th-century Pyx Chamber also has a medieval tiled floor and was used as a monastic and royal treasury.

Westminster Abbey, East Cloisters, London SW1P 3PE
☎ 020 7654 4834
⌂ www.english-heritage.org.uk
✎ Page 16-E4

English Heritage: Eltham Palace

Eltham Palace was completed in 1936. The exterior of the house was built in sympathy with the older building, but the interior features a 1930s design. The 19 acres of gardens surrounding the palace include both 20th-century and medieval elements. These include a rock garden sloping down to the moat, a medieval bridge, herbaceous borders inspired by modern designer Isabelle Van Groeningen, a sunken rose garden and plenty of picnic areas.

Eltham, London SE9 5QE
☎ 020 8294 2548
⌂ www.elthampalace.org.uk
✎ Page 166-D2

English Heritage: Jewel Tower

The Jewel Tower, or King's Privy Wardrobe, was built in 1365 to house Edward III's treasures and houses Parliament Past and Present, an exhibition about the history of Parliament.

Abingdon Street, Westminster, London SW1P 3JY
☎ 020 7222 2219
⌂ www.english-heritage.org.uk
✎ Page 16-E4

English Heritage: Kenwood House

Kenwood House was remodelled by Robert Adam between 1764 and 1779. Adam transformed the original brick building into a villa for the judge, Lord Mansfield. The house has in its possessions paintings by artists including Rembrandt, Vermeer, Turner, Reynolds and Gainsborough along with Constable's *Hampstead Heath with Pond* and *Bathers*. The first floor houses the Suffolk Collection including portraits of Elizabethan and Stuart men and women by William Larkin, Van Dyck and Lely. The parkland surrounding Kenwood has lakeside walks and meandering woodland paths, which provide a backdrop for the summer concerts.

Hampstead Lane, Highgate, London NW3 7JR
☎ 020 8348 1286/7
⌂ www.english-heritage.org.uk
▤ 020 7973 3891
✎ Page 65-J5

English Heritage: London Wall

London Wall is the remnant of the Roman wall, which once formed part of the eastern defences of Roman Londinium. The Wall was built in AD200 and defined the shape and size of London for over a millennium.

Fenchurch Street, Tower Bridge, London EC3N 4DJ
☎ 020 72221234
⌂ www.english-heritage.org.uk
✎ Page 13-G5

English Heritage: Marble Hill House

Marble Hill is a Palladian villa set in 66 acres of riverside parkland along the River Thames. The villa was built by King George II for his mistress, Henrietta Howard. Inside there is a collection of early Georgian paintings, including portraits of Mrs Howard and her circle. Displays include a hand-painted Chinese wallpaper, designed using historical references and motifs to recreate the wallpaper Henrietta Howard hung in the Dining Room in 1751.

Richmond Road, Twickenham TW1 2NL
☎ 020 8892 5115
⌂ www.english-heritage.org.uk

▤ 020 8607 9976
✎ Page 156-D2

English Heritage: Wellington Arch

Situated at Hyde Park Corner, Wellington Arch was originally commissioned by George IV. It was completed in 1830 by architect Decimus Burton, and moved to its present site in 1882. The bronze sculpture atop the monument depicts the Angel of Peace descending on the Chariot of War.

Hyde Park Corner, Belgravia, London W1J 7JZ
☎ 020 7930 2726
⌂ www.english-heritage.org.uk
▤ 020 7925 1019
✎ Page 15-H2

English Heritage: The Wernher Collection

The Wernher Collection comprises medieval and Renaissance works of art, all purchased by the diamond magnate Sir Julius Wernher (1850–1912). The Collection presents a display of silver and jewels, paintings and porcelain. Nearly 700 works of art are on display, including early religious paintings and Dutch old masters, minute carved Gothic ivories, Renaissance bronzes and silver treasures.

Chesterfield Walk, Greenwich, London SE10 8QX
☎ 020 8853 0035
⌂ www.english-heritage.org.uk
▤ 020 8853 0090
✎ Page 145-G2

English Heritage: Winchester Palace

Part of the Great Hall of Winchester Palace, built in the early 13th century as the London house of the Bishops of Winchester, including the striking rose window which adorns the west gable.

Southwark, London Bridge, London SE1 9DA
☎ 08457 484 950
⌂ www.english-heritage.org.uk
✎ Page 12-E7

Fulham Palace

Bishop's Avenue, Fulham, London SW6 6EA
☎ 020 7736 8140
@ enquiries@fulhampalace.org

www.fulhampalace.org
Page 139-G3

Garrick's Temple to Shakespeare

Garrick's Temple on the Riverside at Hampton was built by the great 18th-century actor-manager David Garrick in 1756 to celebrate the genius of William Shakespeare.

Temple Lawn, Hampton Court Road, Hampton, London TW12 2EN
www.garrickstemple.org.uk
Page 173-H5

Geraldine Mary Harmsworth Park

The park, an impressisve backdrop to the Imperial War Museum, is home of the Peace Garden and has an informal games area and playground for children.

Chatelaine House, 186 Walworth Road, Walworth, London SE17 1JJ
☎ 020 7525 1050
@ parks@southwark.gov.uk
www.southwark.gov.uk
Page 17-K5

The Golden Hinde

The original *Golden Hinde* lay berthed for almost a century on the Thames at Deptford as a visible memorial to Sir Francis Drake. The modern day replica has been interpreted as a small warship of the mid-16th century with three masts, five decks and 18 cannons. Guided tours, workshops and children's activities offer an insight into the ship's history.

Unit 1 & 2, Pickfords Wharf, Clink Street, London SE1 9DG
☎ 0870 011 8700
@ info@goldenhinde.org
www.goldenhinde.org/
📄 0207 407 5908
Page 12-E7

Green Park

Green Park was first recorded in 1554 as the place where a rebellion took place against the marriage of Mary I to Philip II of Spain. It was also a famous duelling site until 1667 when Charles II bought an extra 40 acres and it became known as Upper St James's Park. The park's primary role is as a peaceful refuge for people living, working or visiting Central London, and is

particularly popular for sunbathing and picnics in fine weather.

The Storeyard, Horse Guards Approach, St James's Park, London SW1A 2BJ
☎ 020 7930 1793
@ stjames@royalparks.gsi.gov.uk
www.royalparks.gov.uk/
📄 020 7839 7639
Page 15-K2

Greenwich Park

The park covers 183 acres and supports a small herd of fallow and red deer. Situated on top of a hill, it offers sweeping views across the River Thames to St Paul's Cathedral and beyond.

Blackheath Gate, Charlton Way, Greenwich, London SE10 8QY
☎ 020 8858 2608
@ hq@royalparks.gsi.gov.uk
www.royalparks.gov.uk
Page 145-H1

Griffin Brewery Tours

Griffin Brewery Tours take visitors along cobbled roads and alleyways through the brewery and offers an insight into the brewing process.

Chiswick Lane South, Chiswick, London W4 2QB
☎ 020 8996 2000
@ tours@fullers.co.uk
www.fullers.co.uk
Page 118-C6

HMS Belfast

HMS *Belfast* served throughout World War II, playing a leading part in the destruction of the battle cruiser *Scharnhorst*, and also the Normandy landings. The cruiser hosts exhibitions, talks, lectures and family workshops relating to naval history and life at sea along with guided tours and interactive sessions.

Morgan's Lane, Tooley Street, Bermondsey, London SE1 2JH
☎ 0207 940 6300
hmsbelfast.iwm.org.uk
Page 13-H7

Hall Place and Gardens

Hall Place was built in 1537 for the Lord Mayor of London, Sir John Champneis, and stands at the border of London and Kent. The Hall hosts an array of events including exhibitions and dance workshops to Christmas activities for children.

Bourne Road, Bexley DA5 1PQ
☎ 01322 526574
@ Info@hallplace.com
www.hallplaceandgardens.com
Page 169-K1

Hampstead Heath

West Heath Avenue, Hampstead, London NW11 7QP
☎ 020 8455 5183
@ hampstead.heath@
    corpoflondon.gov.uk
www.cityoflondon.gov.uk
Page 65-J6

Hampton Court Palace

Hampton Court Palace offers an insight into 500 years of royal history through a guided tour featuring the State Apartments, the Tudor Kitchens, the Wolsey Rooms, the Courtyards and Cloisters. The 60 acres of gardens comprise of the Privy Garden, the Knot Garden, an Orangery and a maze.

Hampton Court, London KT8 9AU
☎ 0870 752 7777
@ pressandmarketing@hrp.
    org.uk
hrp.org.uk/hampton
Page 174-A6

Holland House

Situated in historic Holland Park, Holland House was built in 1605 and became a glittering social, literary and political meeting place under the third Lord Holland. Badly damaged by a bombing raid in 1940, the remains of Holland House now create the backdrop for an annual summer season of fine opera performed by Opera Holland Park.

Holland Park, Kensington, London W8
☎ 020 7361 3000
@ information@rbkc.gov.uk
www.rbkc.gov.uk
📄 020 7938 1445
Page 119-J2

Holland Park

The Royal Borough's largest park is near Kensington High Street. There are formal gardens, woodlands, sports facilities and various children's play areas.

Ilchester Place, London W8 6LU
☎ 020 7471 9813
@ leisure.services@rbkc.gov.uk
www.rbkc.gov.uk
Page 119-J2

Honeywood Heritage Centre

Honeywood house dates from the 17th century and is rich in period detail – much of the interior has recently been restored. Honeywood contains displays on the history of the local area including Henry VIII and Nonsuch Palace, the River Wandle, Victorian Carshalton, Edwardian toys and local railways.

Honeywood Walk, Carshalton SM5 3NX
☎ 020 8770 4297
@ lbshoneywood@ukonline.co.uk
www.sutton.gov.uk
Page 209-K2

Hounslow Heath Nature Reserve

The heath is a large area of open heathland and scrub woodland of ecological value and was declared a Local Nature Reserve in 1991. It supports over 132 bird species and several rare insects and plants.

450 Staines Road, Hounslow TW4 5AB
☎ 020 8577 3664
@ hounslow-heath@cip.org.uk
www.hounslow.info/
    hounslowheath.htm
Page 154-D1

The House Mill

References to a watermill in this location date back to the Domesday Book of 1086. However, The House Mill was built in 1776 by Daniel Bisson, on the site of an earlier mill and between two houses occupied by the miller and his family – hence its name. It continued to operate until 1940.

The Miller's House, Three Mill Lane, Bromley-by-Bow, London E3 3DU
☎ 020 8983 1121
www.housemill.org.uk
Page 106-A2

Houses of Parliament

The Houses of Parliament (Palace of Westminster) are home to the House of Commons and the House of Lords and the famous clock tower Big Ben. The new Palace of Westminster was built in the years following the fire of 16 October 1834 which destroyed nearly all the Old Palace. Members of the public can take a tour of the Palace and the Public Galleries, which is known as the Line of Route tour.

Parliament Square, London
SW1A 0AA
☎ 020 7219 3000
@ hcinfo@parliament.uk
🖰 www.parliament.uk
🕮 Page 17-F3

Hungerford Viaduct Arches 150–152

This unique mural depicts the major political world events of the 20th century and the personalities who fashioned them. Six hundred feet long the 'Memoir' is painted on hardboard panels 20-feet high and curves snake-like through railway viaduct arches.

Near Royal Festival Hall, Concert Hall Approach, London SE1 8XU
🕮 Page 17-G1

Hyde Park

Hyde Park is one of London's finest landscapes and covers 350 acres. It provides facilities for many different leisure activities and sports as well as being the focal point for many public events.

Hyde Park, London W2 2UH
☎ 020 7298 2100
@ hyde@royalparks.gsi.gov.uk
🖰 www.royalparks.gov.uk
🕮 Page 8-E7

Jubilee Gardens

Jubilee Gardens was created in 1977 to mark the Queen's Silver Jubilee. It sits at the heart of London's cultural centre, South Bank.

South Bank, London SE1 7XZ
☎ 0870 500 0600
🖰 www.jubileegardens.org.uk/
🕮 Page 17-G1

Kensal Green Cemetery

A 2-hour tour offers an insight into the history, architecture and many famous incumbents of the cemetery.

Kensal Green, Harrow Road, Kensal Green, London W10 4RA
☎ 020 8969 0152
@ fokgc@hotmail.com
🖰 www.kensalgreen.co.uk
🕮 Page 99-G2

Kensington Gardens

Kensington Gardens covers 275 acres and features formal avenues of exotic trees and ornamental flower beds. A bronze statue of *Peter Pan* stands on a pedestal covered with climbing squirrels,

rabbits and mice. The Diana, Princess of Wales' Memorial Playground caters to children of all ages while guided walks and special events are organised frequently at the gardens.

Kensington Gardens, London W8 4PX
☎ 020 7298 2100
🖰 www.royalparks.gov.uk
🕮 Page 120-B1

Kensington Palace State Apartments

Kensington Palace was built in the early 17th century and became the home of King William III and Queen Mary in 1689 when he decided to escape from the oppressive London air to the healthier environment of Kensington. Exhibits include the Royal Ceremonial Dress Collection, the Garden Floor, the Royal Apartments and Orangery.

Kensington Gardens, London W8 4PX
☎ 0870 751 5170
🕽 0870 751 5180
🖰 www.hrp.org.uk
🕮 Page 120-A1

Kew Palace and Queen Charlotte's Cottage

Kew Palace was originally built as a private house for a merchant and later used by George III, Queen Charlotte and their children. Exhibits include the King's collection of artefacts relating to botany, astronomy, architecture, music, art and agriculture. The Queen's cottage was built around 1771 and features 150 framed satirical prints in the Print Room.

Royal Botanic Gardens Kew, Richmond TW9 3AB
☎ 0870 751 5179
@ info@kewpalace.co.uk
🖰 www.hrp.org.uk
🕮 Page 137-F1

Linley Sambourne House

Linley Sambourne House was home to the cartoonist Edward Linley Sambourne and his family from 1874 and features collections of family furnishings and decoratives.

18 Stafford Terrace, London W8 7BH
☎ 020 7602 3316, 07976 060160

@ museums@rbkc.gov.uk
🖰 www.rbkc.gov.uk/ linleysambournehouse
🖶 020 7371 2467
🕮 Page 119-J2

Little Holland House

Little Holland House was designed, built and furnished by Frank Reginald Dickinson (1874–1961). A tour of the house offers an insight into Dickinson's life and works through his paintings, hand-made furniture, furnishings, metalwork and friezes in arts and crafts style.

40 Beeches Avenue, Carshalton SM5 3LW
☎ 020 8770 4781
@ info@sutton.gov.uk
🖰 www.sutton.gov.uk/leisure/ heritage
🕮 Page 209-J5

London Aquarium

The London Aquarium is home to over 350 species in over 50 displays, from sharks, stingrays and clownfish, to moray eels, lionfish and sideways walking crabs.

County Hall, Westminster Bridge Road, Waterloo, London SE1 7PB
☎ 020 7967 8000
@ info@londonaquarium.co.uk
🖰 www.londonaquarium.co.uk
🕮 Page 17-G3

The London Bridge Experience

Housed in the vaults of the world's most famous bridge, The London Bridge Experience is an entertaining, educational and adrenalin-pumping attraction. A stunning combination of special effects, real characters and animation will take you from the bridge's creation in Roman times, right through to the opening of the modern-day bridge. There will be some unexpected shocks, thrills and drama along the way.

2–4 Tooley Street, London SE1 2SY
🕽 0800 434 666
🖰 www.londonbridgeexperience. com
🕮 Page 13-F7

London Butterfly House

Visitors can experience walking among hundreds of free-flying tropical butterflies in a warmed glasshouse environment.

Syon Park, Brentford TW8 8JF
☎ 020 8560 0378.
@ info@londonbutterflyhouse. com
🖰 www.londonbutterflyhouse.com
🕮 Page 136-C2

London Duck Tours

London Duck Tours derives its name from the vehicles, which were used to take the troops ashore for the D-Day landings. The tour starts from Chicheley Street, Waterloo and goes past the London landmarks before launching into the River Thames from the slipway at Vauxhall for the waterborne part of the 75-minute tour of London.

55 York Road, Waterloo, London SE1 7NJ
☎ 020 7928 3132
@ enquiries@londonducktours. co.uk
🖰 www.londonducktours.co.uk
🕮 Page 17-H2

London Dungeon

The London Dungeon, located beneath the paving stones of historic Southwark, brings more than 2,000 years of gruesomely authentic history vividly back to life.

28–34 Tooley Street, Bermondsey, London SE1 2SZ
☎ 020 7403 7221
🖰 www.thedungeons.com
🕮 Page 13-F7

London Eye

The London Eye raises passengers 135 metres above the River Thames, the 30-minute rotation provides stunning panoramic views of the city and reveals parts of London which are not visible from the ground.

Riverside Building, County Hall, Westminster Bridge Road, Waterloo, London SE1 7PB
☎ 0870 990 8883
@ customer.services@londoneye. com
🖰 www.londoneye.com
🖶 0870 990 8884
🕮 Page 17-G2

London Trocadero

The London Trocadero is located in the heart of Piccadilly and offers indoor games and entertainment facilities, which include thrill rides and cinema houses.

13 Coventry Street, Soho, London
W1D 7DH
☎ 09068 881100
@ team@troc.co.uk
⌂ www.londontrocadero.com
🕮 Page 10-C6

London Zoo

London Zoo is home to over 600
species of animals including lions,
tigers, primates, giraffes, reptiles
and birds. A journey around
BUGS (Biodiversity Underpinning
Global Survival), displays over
140 species under one roof while
Into Africa gives an insight into
the wildlife of the continent. The
Zoo also plays host to a series of
scientific meetings, symposia and
special events.

Regent's Park, London NW1 4RY
☎ 020 7449 6228
⌂ www.zsl.org
🕮 Page 3-G2

Madame Tussauds

Madame Tussauds displays a
collection of realistic wax figures
in specially designed settings
which include The Garden Party,
200 Years, Superstars, Sports
Heroes, Famous Actors, The Grand
Hall, The Chamber of Horrors and
The Spirit of London.

Marylebone Road, Regents Park,
London NW1 5LR
☎ 0870 999 0046
@ csc@madame-tussauds.com
⌂ www.madame-tussauds.co.uk
🕮 Page 3-G7

Mansion House

Mansion House is one of the
grandest surviving Georgian
town palaces in London, with
magnificent interiors containing
elaborate plasterwork and carved
timber ornament. It is unique
as the only purpose-built home
of the Lord Mayor of the City of
London, providing not only living
and working space for the Lord
Mayor and his household but
also room for large ceremonial
entertainments and banquets.

Walbrook, London EC4N 8BH
⌂ www.cityoflondon.gov.uk
🕮 Page 12-E4

The Monument

The Monument was designed
by Sir Christopher Wren to
commemorate the Great Fire of
London in 1677. Today, visitors can

climb the 311 steps to the top of
this landmark which offers views
across London.

Monument Street, London
EC3R 8AH
☎ 020 7626 2717
@ enquiries@towerbridge.org.uk
⌂ towerbridge.org.uk
🕮 Page 13-F5

The National Archives

The National Archives of England
and Wales has one of the largest
archival collections in the world.
The records span over 1000
years of British history and range
from Domesday Book of 1086
to government papers recently
released to the public.

Kew, Richmond TW9 4DU
☎ 020 8876 3444
@ marketing@nationalarchives.
gov.uk
⌂ www.nationalarchives.gov.uk
🕮 Page 137-J1

National Trust: Blewcoat
School Gift Shop

Built in 1709 by a local brewer
to provide an education for poor
children and used as a school
until 1926, the venue is now the
National Trust's London Gift Shop
and Information Centre.

23 Caxton Street, Westminster, St
James's Park, London SW1H 0PY
☎ 020 7222 2877
⌂ www.nationaltrust.org.uk
🕮 Page 16-C4

National Trust: Carlyle's
House

Thomas Carlyle lived in this 1708
Queen Anne terraced house, close
to the Thames in Chelsea, from
1834 to 1881. Opened in 1895 as a
literary shrine, the house contains
Carlyle's furniture, books, pictures
and personal possessions, together
with portraits and memorabilia.

24 Cheyne Row, Chelsea, London
SW3 5HL
☎ 020 7352 7087
@ carlyleshouse@nationaltrust.
org.uk
⌂ www.nationaltrust.org.uk
🖨 020 7352 5108
🕮 Page 120-D6

National Trust: Eastbury
Manor House

Eastbury Manor House is an
example of a medium-sized
brick-built Elizabethan manor

house, with early 17th-century
wall paintings. Events at the venue
include visitor days and children's
activities.

Eastbury Square, Barking
IG11 9SN
☎ 020 8724 1002
✆ 020 8724 1000
@ eastburyhouse@lbbd.gov.uk
⌂ www.nationaltrust.org.uk
🖨 020 8724 1003
🕮 Page 91-F6

National Trust: Fenton
House

Fenton House is a late 17th-
century house located on the
winding streets of Hampstead
village. The exhibits include
a collection of porcelain,
17th-century needlework and
Georgian furniture, along with
the Benton Fletcher collection of
early keyboard instruments, most
of which are in working order.
The walled garden features fine
displays of roses, an orchard and
a working kitchen garden.

Windmill Hill, Hampstead, London
NW3 6RT
☎ 020 7435 3471
@ fentonhouse@nationaltrust.
org.uk
⌂ www.nationaltrust.org.uk
🕮 Page 83-G1

National Trust: George Inn

George Inn is a galleried inn
dating from the 17th century when
it was used as a coaching house.

77 Borough High Street,
Southwark, Bermondsey, London
SE1 1NH
☎ 020 7407 2056
⌂ www.nationaltrust.org.uk
🕮 Page 18-E2

National Trust: Ham House

Ham House was built in 1610
and enlarged in the 1670s. The
outbuildings include an orangery,
ice house, still house and dairy
with cast iron 'cows legs'
supporting marble slabs.

Ham Street, Richmond-upon-
Thames, London TW10 7RS
☎ 020 8940 1950
✆ 020 8439 8230
@ hamhouse@nationaltrust.
org.uk
⌂ www.nationaltrust.org.uk
🖨 020 8439 8241
🕮 Page 156-D3

National Trust: Lindsey
House

Lindsey House was built on the
former site of Sir Thomas More's
garden, now part of Cheyne Walk.
The entrance hall, main staircase
to first floor, and front and rear
gardens are open to visitors.

99–100 Cheyne Walk, Chelsea,
London SW10 0DQ
☎ 020 7447 6605
⌂ www.nationaltrust.org.uk
🕮 Page 120-D6

National Trust: Morden Hall
Park

Morden Hall Park covers over 234
acres and features meadows,
wetlands and a network of
waterways. The rose garden has
over 2,000 roses and there is a
kitchen garden.

Morden Hall Road, Morden
SM4 5JD
☎ 020 8545 6852, 020 8545 6850
@ mordenhallpark@
nationaltrust.org.uk
⌂ www.nationaltrust.org.uk
🖨 020 8417 8091
🕮 Page 178-B6

National Trust: Osterley Park
and House

An original redbrick Tudor house,
transformed and remodelled
by Robert Adam between 1760
and 1780 for a wealthy banking
family, the Childs. The interiors
feature Robert Adam architecture
and works by local artists. The
house is set in park and farm
land, complete with pleasure
grounds and neo-classical garden
buildings.

Jersey Road, Isleworth TW7 4RB
☎ 020 8232 5050, 01494 755566
@ osterley@nationaltrust.org.uk
⌂ www.nationaltrust.org.uk
🖨 0 8232 5080
🕮 Page 115-H6

National Trust: Rainham Hall

Rainham Hall, built in 1729 for
merchant and ship owner John
Harle, is a Georgian house in the
Dutch style with wrought-iron
gates, a carved porch and interior
panelling with plasterwork.

The Broadway, Havering, Rainham
RM13 9YN
☎ 020 7447 6605
⌂ www.nationaltrust.org.uk
🕮 Page 111-J3

National Trust: Red House

The Red House was commissioned by William Morris in 1859 and designed by Philip Webb. The Gothic building is constructed of warm red brick, under a steep red-tiled roof. Exhibits include furniture designed by Morris and Webb, as well as wall paintings and stained glass by Burne-Jones.

Red House Lane, Bexleyheath DA6 8JF
☎ 01494 559799
◐ 020 8304 9878
⬧ www.nationaltrust.org.uk
◉ Page 194-B1

National Trust: Roman Bath

Located in the heart of London and restored in the 17th century, the remains of these public baths are believed to have Roman origins.

5 Strand Lane, Holborn, London WC2R 2NA
☎ 020 7641 5264
⬧ www.nationaltrust.org.uk
▤ 020 7641 5215
◉ Page 11-H5

National Trust: Sutton House

Sutton House was built in 1535 by Sir Ralph Sadleir, a rising star at the court of Henry VIII. It became home to successive merchants, Huguenot silk weavers, Victorian schoolmistresses and Edwardian clergy and, although altered over the years, remains a Tudor house. Oak-panelled rooms and carved fireplaces survive intact and an exhibition tells the history of the house and its former occupants.

2–4 Homerton High Street, Hackney, London E9 6JQ
☎ 020 8986 2264
@ suttonhouse@nationaltrust. org.uk
⬧ www.nationaltrust.org.uk
◉ Page 86-E3

Old Bailey

Universally known as the Old Bailey, the Central Criminal Court is the probably the most famous criminal court in the world, and has been London's principal criminal court for centuries. It hears cases remitted to it from all over England and Wales as well as the Greater London area.

Central Criminal Court, Old Bailey, London EC4M 7BH
☎ 020 7248 3277

⬧ www.cityoflondon.gov.uk
◉ Page 12-A3

Old Royal Naval College

Designed by Sir Christopher Wren, the Old Royal Naval College was established by Royal Charter in 1694 for the relief and support of seamen and their dependents. Exhibits include the Painted Hall, Chapel and Visitor Centre, which play host to programmes ranging from film and opera to safari trails and Christmas concerts.

2 Cutty Sark Gardens, Greenwich, London SE10 9LW
☎ 020 8269 4747
@ info@greenwichfoundation. org.uk
⬧ www.oldroyalnavalcollege.org
◉ Page 125-G6

Oxleas Woods

A Site of Special Scientific Interest, the Oxleas woods cover 178 acres and offers guided walks through the woods of oak, silver birch, hornbeam and coppice hazel.

Shooters Hill, London SE9
☎ 020 8856 2232
@ parks@greenwich.gov.uk
⬧ www.greenwich.gov.uk
◉ Page 147-J4

Peter Harrison Planetarium

Royal Observatory Greenwich, Greenwich Park, London SE10 9NF
☎ 020 8858 4422
⬧ www.nmm.ac.uk
◉ Page 145-G1

Petticoat Lane

Petticoat Lane was established over 400 years ago and derives its name from the Huguenots, who came to London from France and sold petticoats and lace. Today the market has ore than 1,000 stalls.

Middlesex Street, Aldgate, Tower Hamlets, London E1 6BD
☎ 020 7377 8963
⬧ www.eastlondonmarkets.com
◉ Page 13-H2

Portobello Road

Portobello Road has been a market since the 1800s but became particularly famous for its antiques in the 1950s. Now there are numerous stalls offering everything from fruit and bread to posters, clothes, ceramics and music.

Portobello Road, Notting Hill, London W11 1LU
☎ 020 7229 8354
@ info@portobelload.co.uk
⬧ www.portobelloroad.co.uk
◉ Page 100-C4

Princess Diana Memorial

Serpentine Bridge, Hyde Park, London W8 4PX
⬧ www.royalparks.gov.uk/parks/ hyde_park/diana_memorial. cfm
◉ Page 14-B1

Queen Elizabeth's Hunting Lodge

Queen Elizabeth's Hunting Lodge was built for King Henry VIII in 1543 and was used as a grandstand. The lodge offers an insight into Tudor times through events ranging from archery days and picnics to family activities and Tudor New Year celebrations.

Rangers Road, Chingford, London E4 7QH
☎ 020 8529 6681
⬧ www.corpoflondon.gov.uk
◉ Page 38-D2

Regent's Park

Regent's Park, designed by John Nash, covers 410 acres and includes rose gardens with more than 30,000 roses of 400 varieties besides a wide range of wildlife species. The Hub is a community sports pavilion for enthusiasts of all abilities and the park hosts art fairs and interactive sessions based on nature and wildlife.

Inner Circle, Regent's Park, London NW1 4NR
☎ 020 7486 7905
@ regents@royalparks.gsi.gov.uk
⬧ www.royalparks.gov.uk
◉ Page 3-G3

Richmond Park

Richmond Park covers 2,500 acres of hills, woodlands, ponds, gardens and grasslands supporting a wide range of wildlife including deer, weasels, rabbits and bats.

Richmond Park, London TW10 5HS
☎ 020 8948 3209
@ richmond@royalparks.gsi. gov.uk
⬧ www.royalparks.gov.uk
◉ Page 157-H5

Rose Theatre

The remains of the Rose Theatre, discovered in 1989, offer an insight into its history between 1587 and 1603. Today it hosts plays, theatres and tours.

21 New Globe Walk, Southwark, London SE1 9AR
☎ 020 7593 0026
@ info@rosetheatre.org.uk
⬧ www.rosetheatre.org.uk
◉ Page 12-C7

Royal Botanic Gardens, Kew

The Royal Botanic Gardens, Kew is a World Heritage Site with botanical collections from round the globe. The gardens contain glasshouses, museums, galleries, temples and other follies dating back to the period of royal ownership in the 18th and early 19th centuries. As a site of research on horticulture and taxonomy, Kew organises conservation programmes on a wide range of endangered and threatened plants and their habitats. There are guided tours and hands-on sessions..

Royal Botanic Gardens, Kew, Richmond TW9 3AB
☎ 020 8332 5655
@ info@kew.org
⬧ www.rbgkew.org.uk
◉ Page 137-F2

Royal Hospital Chelsea

The Royal Hospital, designed by Sir Christopher Wren was completed in 1692 and comprises of accomodation blocks for veteran soldiers. A tour of the establishment takes visitors through the Great Hall, Octagon, Chapel, College and Light Horse Courts and to the museum with displays of artefacts bequeathed by former pensioners.

Royal Hospital Road, Chelsea, London SW3 4SR
☎ 020 7881 5204
@ info@chelsea-pensioners. org.uk
⬧ www.chelsea-pensioners. org.uk
◉ Page 120-E5

The Royal Mews

The Royal Mews at Buckingham Palace allows visitors to see the work of the Royal Household department that provides road transport for the Queen and

members of the royal family. Displays at the Mews include the gold State Coach used for coronations and the carriages used for royal and state occasions, state visits, weddings and the State Opening of Parliament.

Buckingham Palace Road,St James's, London SW1A 1AA
☎ 020 7766 7302
@ buckinghampalace@ royalcollection.org.uk
⌂ www.royal.gov.uk
⊘ Page 15-K4

Royal Observatory Greenwich

The Royal Observatory, founded in 1675, offers an insight into the cellestial world through exhibitions, displays, workshops and public sessions.

National Maritime Museum, Greenwich, London SE10 9NF
☎ 020 8858 4422
⌂ www.rog.nmm.ac.uk
⊘ Page 145-G1

Ruislip Lido Railway

The railway started operatiing around 1945, when short trains were hauled by *Prince Edward* an Atlantic type steam locomotive. Today the railway is operated by the Ruislip Lido Railway Society. Bordering the railway there is a children's play area, a large sandy beach, and an assault course for older children.

Reservoir Road, Ruislip HA4 7TY
☎ 01895 622595, 01895 637400
⌂ www.ruisliplidorailway.org
⊘ Page 58-B1

Ruskin House

Ruskin House is a Georgian townhouse and features Doric columns, a wooden staircase with panelled walls, a tiled fireplace with a statuary marble mantelpiece and french doors leading to the garden.

23 Coombe Road, Croydon CR0 1BD
☎ 020 8688 5339
⌂ www.croydon.org.uk/ruskin
⊘ Page 211-J2

Somerset House

Somerset House, on the banks of the Thames, serves as a cultural centre for London. It houses the Gilbert Collection, Hermitage Rooms and the Courtauld Gallery.

The courtyard at the centre plays host to various cultural events.

Strand, Holborn, London WC2R 1LA
☎ 020 7845 4600
@ info@somerset-house.org.uk
⌂ www.somerset-house.org.uk
⊘ Page 11-G5

Southside House

Southside House offers an insight into the lives and loves of generations of the Pennington Mellor Munthe families. The interiors feature a collection of art and historical objects reflecting the centuries of ownership.

3–4 Woodhayes Road, Wimbledon Common, Wimbledon, London SW19 4RJ
☎ 020 8946 7643
@ info@southsidehouse.com
⌂ www.southsidehouse.com
⊘ Page 177-F2

Spencer House

Spencer House was conceived as a showcase of classical design but it was also designed for pleasure and a festive theme runs through the decoration of the many state rooms which were used for receptions and family gatherings.

27 St James's Place, London SW1A 1NR
☎ 020 7499 8620
⌂ www.spencerhouse.co.uk
🖪 020 7409 2952
⊘ Page 16-A1

St James' Palace

St James's Palace is the senior palace of the sovereign, with a long history as a royal residence. As the home of several members of the royal family and their household offices, it is often in use for official functions and is not open to the public.

Pall Mall, London SW1Y 6
⊘ Page 16-B1

St James's Park

St James's Park covers 57 acres at the heart of London and has a lake with ducks, geese and pelicans. Events at the park include guided tours of the duck island and band concerts.

The Storeyard, Horse Guards Road, St James's Park, London SW1A 2BJ
☎ 020 7930 1793

@ stjames@royalparks.gsi.gov.uk
⌂ www.royalparks.gov.uk
⊘ Page 16-C2

St Paul's Cathedral

A cathedral dedicated to St Paul has overlooked the City of London since AD604. The current cathedral, the fourth to occupy this site, was designed by the court architect Sir Christopher Wren and completed in 1710. As the cathedral of the capital city, St Paul's is the spiritual focus for the nation. This is where people and events of overwhelming importance to the country have been celebrated, mourned and commemorated since the first service in 1697.

The Chapter House, St Paul's Churchyard, London EC4M 8AD
☎ 020 7236 4128
🕔 020 7246 8350
@ chapter@stpaulscathedral. org.uk
⌂ www.stpauls.co.uk
🖪 020 7248 3104
⊘ Page 12-B3

Swaminarayan Temple

105–119 Brentfield Road, Neasden, London NW10 8LD
☎ 020 8965 2651
@ info@mandir.org
⌂ www.mandir.org
🖪 020 8965 6313
⊘ Page 81-F4

Syon Park

Syon House is the residence of the the Duke of Northumberland. Visitors can see the State and Private Apartments, the Great Conservatory and 40 acres of gardens.

Syon Park, Brentford TW8 8JF
☎ 020 8560 0882
@ info@syonpark.co.uk
⌂ www.syonpark.co.uk
⊘ Page 136-D3

Thames Barrier Information Centre

The Thames Barrier, located at Woolwich, was built to stop the River Thames flooding. The information centre uses a range of games, learning activities and information boards to explain the story behind the construction of the Thames Barrier.

1 Unity Way, Woolwich, London SE18 5NJ

☎ 020 8305 4188
@ enquiries@environment-agency.gov.uk
⌂ www.environment-agency. gov.uk
⊘ Page 126-C3

Tower Bridge

Tower Bridge has spanned the River Thames in London since 1894. At the Tower Bridge Exhibition you can enjoy views from the high-level walkways, and learn about how and why the bridge was built. You can visit the Victorian Engine Rooms, home to the original steam engines that once powered the Bridge lifts. Exciting hands-on mechanisms and information panels explain about the ingenuous technology used over the years to keep Tower Bridge in motion.

Tower Bridge, Bermondsey, London SE1 2UP
☎ 020 7403 3761
🕔 020 7407 9191
@ enquiries@towerbridge.org.uk
⌂ www.towerbridge.org.uk
🖪 020 7357 7935
⊘ Page 19-J1

Tower of London

The Tower of London was built by William the Conqueror in 1066–7 and has since played a role as an armoury, royal palace, fortress, prison, place of execution, mint, menagerie and jewel house. The Tower houses exhibitions, hosts concerts and other events besides the regular Ceremony of the Keys.

HM Tower of London, London EC3N 4AB
☎ 0870 756 6060
⌂ hrp.org.uk/TowerOfLondon
⊘ Page 13-J6

Wesley's Chapel and House

John Wesley (1703–1791), the founder of Methodism, built Wesley's Chapel in 1778 as his London base. Wesley's house was built in 1779 and features many of John Wesley's belongings, including his electrical machine and study chair.

49 City Road, London EC1Y 1AU
☎ 020 7253 2262
@ administration@ wesleyschapel.org.uk
⌂ www.wesleyschapel.org.uk
⊘ Page 6-E6

Westminster Abbey

Westminster Abbey is a place of daily worship, a burial place of kings, statesmen, poets, scientists, warriors and musicians. It has been the setting for every coronation since 1066 and for numerous other royal occasions.

20 Dean's Yard, London SW1P 3PA
☎ 020 7222 5152
@ info@westminster-abbey.org
⌂ www.westminster-abbey.org
▤ 020 7233 2072
◉ Page 16-E4

The Wetland Centre

The award-winning London Wetland Centre covers more than 100 acres of created wetlands in the heart of London. It offers visitors the chance to see rare and endangered wetland wildlife and hosts an array of events ranging from wildlife walks and talks to children's activities.

Queen Elizabeth's Walk, Barnes, London SW13 9WT
☎ 020 8409 4400
@ info.london@wwt.org.uk
⌂ www.wwt.org.uk
◉ Page 138-E2

MUSEUMS

Alexander Fleming Laboratory Museum

Penicillin was discovered by Alexander Fleming in a small laboratory at St Mary's Hospital in 1928. The display offers an insight into the life and work of Alexander Fleming.

St Mary's Hospital, Praed Street, London W2 1NY
☎ 020 7886 6528
@ Kevin.Brown@st-marys.nhs.uk
⌂ www.st-marys.nhs.ukl
▤ 020 7886 6739
◉ Page 8-B3

All England Lawn Tennis and Croquet Club

Home to the world's most famous grass tennis club and its museum which offers an insight into the history of lawn tennis in Wimbledon through cinema and three dimensional exhibitions.

Church Road, Wimbledon, London SW19 5AE
☎ 020 8946 6131
@ museum@aeltc.com
⌂ www.wimbledon.org

▤ 020 8944 2257
◉ Page 159-H5

Arsenal Football Club Museum

The Arsenal Museum details the colourful history of this famous north London football club, from its beginings in 1886 when it was founded by a group of munitions workers. The exhibits are wide ranging – from effigies of famous players to the ball used in the club's 1936 FA Cup victory, and the golden boot won by Charlie George for scoring the winning goal in the 1971 cup final.

Northern Triangle Building, Emirates Stadium, Drayton Park, London N5 1BU
☎ 020 7704 4000
@ info@arsenal.co.uk
⌂ www.arsenal.com
◉ Page 85-G2

Bank of England Museum

The museum tells the story of the bank from its foundation in 1694 to its role today as the United Kingdom's central bank. The historical displays include material drawn from the bank's own collections of books, documents, silver, prints, paintings, banknotes, coins and photographs. There is a display of gold, including Roman and modern gold bars, alongside pikes and muskets once used to defend the bank.

Threadneedle Street, London EC2R 8AH
☎ 020 7601 5545
@ museum@bankofengland.co.uk
⌂ www.bankofengland.co.uk
◉ Page 13-F4

Barnet Museum

The museum contains archives, objects, prints, photographs, paintings and maps reflecting the development of Chipping Barnet and the surrounding area, as well as a notable collection of period costumes and accessories, domestic items and lace.

31 Wood Street, Barnet, London EN5 4BE
☎ 020 8440 8066
⌂ www.barnetmuseum.co.uk
◉ Page 20-C5

Benjamin Franklin House

The house offers an insight into the life of Benjamin Franklin through cutting-edge lighting, sound and projection technology.

36 Craven Street, Charing Cross, London WC2N 5NF
☎ 020 7839 2006
@ info@benjaminfranklinhouse.org
⌂ www.benjaminfranklinhouse.org
▤ 020 7930 9124
◉ Page 10-E7

Bethlem Royal Hospital Archives, Museum and Gallery

The archives and museum houses art and historical collections in the field of mental health. The museum holds an outstanding collection of paintings and drawings. The collections contain many other items of historic and artistic significance, including the statues *Raving* and *Melancholy Madness* from the gates of the 17th-century Bethlem Hospital.

Bethlem Royal Hospital, Monks Orchard Road, Beckenham BR3 3BX
☎ 020 8776 4307
☏ 020 8776 4227
@ museum@bethlemheritage.org.uk
⌂ www.bethlemheritage.org.uk
▤ 020 8776 4045
◉ Page 198-D4

Bexley Museum

Hall Place, Bourne Road, Bexley DA5 1PQ
☎ 01322 526574
◉ Page 169-K1

Bramah Museum of Tea and Coffee

The Bramah Museum is in two sections, one tells the story of tea over 400 years, the other tells the story of coffee. Both sections display a collection of ceramics, metalwork and graphic art associated with tea and coffee.

40 Southwark Street, London SE1 1UN
☎ 020 7403 5650
@ bramah@btconnect.com
⌂ www.teaandcoffeemuseum.co.uk
▤ 020 7403 5654
◉ Page 18-D1

Brent Museum

Brent Museum collects and records the history of Brent and the people who live here in the form of objects and oral history.

Willesden Green Library Centre, 95 High Road, London NW10 2SU
☎ 020 8937 3600
@ museum@brent.gov.uk
⌂ www.brent.gov.uk/heritage.nsf
▤ 020 8937 3601
◉ Page 81-K4

Britain At War Experience

The Britain at War Experience recreates the London Blitz in all its fury, with special effects highlighting the sights and sounds, the artefacts and even the dust and smoke of an air raid at its height.

64–66 Tooley Street, London Bridge, Bermondsey, London SE1 2TF
☎ 020 7403 3171
@ info@britainatwar.org.uk
⌂ www.britainatwar.co.uk
▤ 020 7403 5104
◉ Page 19-F1

British Dental Association Museum

The museum offers an insight into all aspects of dental history during the late 19th and early 20th centuries. There are over 5,000 images spanning 500 years of dentistry in Britain offered in digital, print or transparency format.

BDA Headquarters, 64 Wimpole Street, Marylebone, London W1G 8YS
☎ 020 7935 0875
@ museum@bda.org
⌂ www.bda.org/museum
▤ 020 7935 6492
◉ Page 9-J2

The British Museum

Behind its imposing neo-classical facade, the British Museum displays the rich and varied treasures which make it one of the great museums of the world. Founded in 1753, displays cover the works of humanity from pre-historic to modern times. The galleries are the responsibility of eight departments, which include Egyptian, Greek and Roman, Japanese, Prehistory and Europe, Prints and Drawings, and Ethnography. Among the treasures to be seen are the Egyptian

mummies, the sculptures from the Parthenon, the Anglo-Saxon treasure from the Sutton Hoo ship burial and the Vindolanda Tablets from Hadrian's Wall.

Great Russell Street, Bloomsbury, London WC1B 3DG
☎ 020 7323 8000, 020 7323 8299
🕓 020 7323 8181
@ visitorinformation@
thebritishmuseum.ac.uk
🖰 www.thebritishmuseum.ac.uk
✐ Page 10-E2

The British Optical Association Museum
Founded by JH Sutcliffe of the British Optical Association in 1901, the museum houses 10,000 items relating to the history of ophthalmic optics, the human eye and visual aids, as well as the representation of these subjects in art.

The College of Optometrists, 42 Craven Street, Charing Cross, London WC2N 5NG
☎ 020 7766 4353
@ museum@college-
optometrists.org
🖰 www.college-optometrists.org
🖨 020 7839 6800
✐ Page 10-E7

The British Postal Museum and Archive
The museum cares for the visual, written and physical records of over 400 years of postal development.

Freeling House, Phoenix Place, St Pancras, London WC1X 0DL
☎ 020 7239 2570
@ info@postalheritage.org.uk
🖰 www.postalheritage.org.uk
🖨 020 7239 2576
✐ Page 5-H6

Bromley Museum
Bromley Museum has over 20,000 objects relating to the history and archaeology of the London Borough of Bromley. The museum also has permanent displays about the history of the local area.

The Priory, Church Hill, Orpington BR6 0HH
☎ 01689 873826
@ bromley.museum@bromley.
gov.uk
🖰 www.bromley.gov.uk
✐ Page 202-C4

Bruce Castle Museum
Bruce Castle is a 16th-century manor house set in 20 acres of parkland. It was opened as a museum in 1906 and now houses the Borough of Haringey's local history collections and archives.

Lordship Lane, Tottenham, London N17 8NU
☎ 020 8808 8772
@ museum.services@haringey.
gov.uk
🖰 www.haringey.gov.uk/leisure/
brucecastlemuseum
🖨 020 8808 4118
✐ Page 50-A4

The Brunel Museum
The Brunel Museum is a striking piece of 19th-century architecture. It was designed by Sir Marc Brunel to contain the steam engines which drained the celebrated Thames Tunnel between 1825 and 1843. The project was a triumph of ingenuity and perseverance in the face of floods, financial losses, and human disaster.

Railway Avenue, Rotherhithe, London SE16 4LF
☎ 020 7231 3840
@ education@
brunelenginehouse.org.uk
🖰 www.brunelenginehouse.org.uk
✐ Page 123-K2

The Cartoon Museum
The Cartoon Museum exhibits British cartoons, caricature and comic art from the 18th century to the present day.

35 Little Russell Street, Bloomsbury, London WC1A 2HH
☎ 020 7580 8155
@ info@cartoonmuseum.org
🖰 www.cartooncentre.com
✐ Page 10-E2

The Charles Dickens Museum
The museum houses material relating to the Victorian novelist and social commentator, Charles Dickens. On four floors, visitors can see paintings, rare editions, manuscripts and original furniture.

48, Doughty Street, London WC1N 2LX
☎ 020 7405 2127
@ info@dickensmuseum.com
🖰 www.dickensmuseum.com
✐ Page 5-H7

Church Farmhouse Museum
Church Farmhouse has three furnished period rooms. The kitchen, set about 1820, has a huge open fireplace containing a clockwork spit jack, a chimney crane and bread oven. The dining room contains oak panelling dating from the late 17th and 19th centuries.

Greyhound Hill, Hendon, London NW4 4JR
☎ 020 8203 0130
@ info@churchfarm
housemuseum.co.uk
🖰 www.churchfarm
housemuseum.co.uk
✐ Page 45-K6

Churchill Museum and Cabinet War Rooms
The War Rooms were constructed to protect the Prime Minister, his Cabinet and the central core of the military command during World War II. Exhibits include the Map Room, the Cabinet Room and Churchill's suite. The Churchill Museum offers an insight into the life and times of Sir Winston Churchill.

Clive Steps, King Charles Street, Westminster, London SW1A 2AQ
☎ 020 7930 6961
@ cwr@iwm.org.uk
🖰 cwr.iwm.org.uk/
🖨 020 7839 5897
✐ Page 16-D2

The Clink Prison Museum
1 Clink Street, Southwark, London SE1 9DG
☎ 020 7403 0900, 020 7403 9981
🖰 www.clink.co.uk
✐ Page 12-E7

Crystal Palace Museum
Anerley Hill, Crystal Palace, Upper Norwood, London SE19 2BA
☎ 07889 338812
@ info@crystalpalacefoundation.
org.uk
🖰 www.crystalpalacefoundation.
org.uk
🖨 0870 133 7920
✐ Page 181-G2

The Cuming Museum
The museum is home to the collection of the Cuming family and offers a variety of hands-on activities for younger visitors as well as a lively temporary exhibition programme.

151 Walworth Road, Walworth, London SE17 1RS
☎ 020 7525 2000
@ cuming.museum@southwark.
gov.uk
🖰 www.southwark.gov.uk
🖨 020 7525 2345
✐ Page 18-C7

Dartford Borough Museum
The small museum is packed with objects and information relating to the story of Dartford.

Market Street, Dartford DA1 1EU
☎ 01322 224739
@ museum@dartford.gov.uk
🖰 www.dartford.gov.uk
✐ Page 171-H2

Design Museum
The museum was founded in 1989 and offers an insight into innovation in every area of design ranging from industrial design, graphics and multimedia to fashion and architecture.

Shad Thames, Bermondsey, London SE1 2YD
☎ 0870 909 9009
@ info@designmuseum.org
🖰 www.designmuseum.org
🖨 0870 909 1909
✐ Page 19-K1

Erith Museum
Walnut Tree Road, Erith DA8 1RS
☎ 013 2233 6582
@ juliet.oliver@bexley.gov.uk
🖰 www.erithmuseum.org.uk
✐ Page 130-B5

Fan Museum
The museum is home to a collection of more than 3,500 predominantly antique fans from around the world dating from the 11th century to the present day.

12 Crooms Hill, Greenwich, London SE10 8ER
☎ 020 8305 1441, 020 8293 1889
@ admin@fan-museum.org
🖰 www.fan-museum.org
✐ Page 145-F1

Fashion and Textile Museum
The museum explores the changes in contemporary fashion and textile design over the past 50 years, including the disciplines of fashion, textile design and photography.

83 Bermondsey Street, Bermondsey, London SE1 3XF

☎ 020 7407 8664
@ info@ftmlondon.org
🖱 www.ftmlondon.org
🔖 Page 19-H3

Firepower: The Royal Artillery Museum
The museum offers an insight into the history of gunners through the collections and archives.

Royal Arsenal, Woolwich, London SE18 6ST
☎ 020 8855 7755
🖱 www.firepower.org.uk
🖨 020 8855 7100
🔖 Page 127-G3

Florence Nightingale Museum
The Florence Nightingale Museum houses artefacts owned or used by Florence Nightingale, material connected with the Crimean war (1854–56) as well as military, hospital and nursing memorabilia connected with the Nightingale School and St Thomas' Hospital (1860–1910).

St Thomas Hospital, 2 Lambeth Palace Road, Waterloo, London SE1 7EW
☎ 020 7620 0374
@ info@florence-nightingale.co.uk
🖱 www.florence-nightingale.co.uk
🖨 020 7928 1760
🔖 Page 17-G3

The Foundling Museum
The Foundling Museum tells the story of the Foundling Hospital, its campaigning founder the philanthropist Thomas Coram, the artist William Hogarth and the composer George Frideric Handel.

40 Brunswick Square, St Pancras, London WC1N 1AZ
☎ 020 7841 3600
@ enquiries@foundlingmuseum.org.uk
🖱 www.foundlingmuseum.org.uk
🖨 020 7841 3601
🔖 Page 5-F6

Freud Museum
The museum was the home of Sigmund Freud and his family when they escaped Nazi annexation of Austria in 1938. It remained the family home until Anna Freud, the youngest daughter, died in 1982. The centrepiece of the museum is Freud's library and study, preserved just as it was during his lifetime. It contains Freud's collection of antiquities – Egyptian, Greek, Roman and oriental. Almost 2,000 items fill cabinets and are ranged on every surface.

20 Maresfield Gardens, Hampstead, London NW3 5SX
☎ 020 7435 2002, 020 7435 5167
@ info@freud.org.uk
🖱 www.freud.org.uk
🖨 020 7431 5452
🔖 Page 83-G4

The Geffrye Museum
The museum houses furniture, textiles, paintings and decorative arts from 1600 to the present day.

Kingsland Road, Bethnal Green, London E2 8EA
☎ 020 7739 9893
@ info@geffrye-museum.org.uk
🖱 www.geffrye-museum.org.uk
🖨 020 7729 5647
🔖 Page 7-J3

Gilbert Collection
The collection was formed over four decades by the late Sir Arthur Gilbert who first started to collect English silver, attracted by its historical and decorative qualities. His passion for great craftsmanship led him to acquire Italian mosaics, gold boxes, portrait miniatures and Roman enamel mosaics, for which he coined the term micromosaic to evoke the painstaking skill of this demanding technique.

Somerset House, Strand, Holborne, London WC2R 1LA
☎ 020 7420 9400
@ info@gilbert-collection.org.uk
🖱 www.gilbert-collection.org.uk
🔖 Page 11-G5

Grant Museum of Zoology
The museum houses around 32,000 specimens, covering the animal kingdom. Founded in 1827 as a teaching collection, the museum is packed full of skeletons, mounted animals and specimens preserved in fluid as well as glass models made by the Blaschka family in the late 1800s.

Darwin Building, Gower Street, Bloomsbury, London WC1E 6BT
☎ 020 7679 2647
@ zoology.museum@ucl.ac.uk
🖱 www.grant.museum.ucl.ac.uk
🖨 020 7679 7096
🔖 Page 4-C7

Greenwich Heritage Centre
The centre brings together the former Borough Museum and Local History Library to offer a wealth of information and displays about the history of Greenwich. The range of events and activities includes talks and lectures.

Artillery Square, Royal Arsenal, Woolwich, London SE18 4DX
☎ 020 8854 2452
@ heritage.centre@greenwich.gov.uk
🖱 www.greenwich.gov.uk
🔖 Page 127-F5

Guards Museum
The museum contains a wealth of information and artefacts relating to the five regiments of Foot Guards namely Grenadier, Coldstream, Scots, Irish and Welsh Guards.

Wellington Barracks, Birdcage Walk, St James's Park, London SW1A 6HQ
☎ 020 7414 3428, 020 7414 3271
@ guardsmuseum@aol.com
🖱 www.theguardsmuseum.com
🖨 020 7414 3429
🔖 Page 16-B3

Gunnersbury Park Museum
This is the local history museum for the London Boroughs of Ealing and Hounslow. It houses a wide range of objects, paintings and photographs which reflect life here from prehistory to the present day.

Popes Lane, Acton, London W3 8LQ
☎ 020 8992 1612
@ gp-museum@cip.org.uk
🖱 www.hounslow.info
🖨 020 8752 0686
🔖 Page 117-H3

Hackney Museum
The museum was established in 1986 and houses art displays, an education room and object stores relating to the history of Hackney and the worldwide roots of its people.

Technology and Learning Centre, 1 Reading Lane, Hackney, London E8 1GQ
☎ 020 8356 3500
@ hmuseum@hackney.gov.uk
🖱 www.hackney.gov.uk
🖨 020 8356 2563
🔖 Page 86-D4

Hampstead Museum and Burgh House
The museum specialises in the local history of the area. There are permanent displays on the history of Hampstead.

New End Square, Hampstead, London NW3 1LT
☎ 020 7431 0144
@ burghhouse@talk21.com
🖱 www.burghhouse.org.uk
🖨 020 7435 8817
🔖 Page 83-G2

Handel House Museum
The Handel House Museum was home to the baroque composer George Frideric Handel from 1723 until his death in 1759. The museum celebrates Handel's life and works, displaying portraits of Handel and his contemporaries in finely restored Georgian interiors and bringing live music back to his house.

25 Brook Street, Mayfair, London W1K 4HB
☎ 020 7495 1685
📞 020 7399 1953
@ mail@handelhouse.org
🖱 www.handelhouse.org
🖨 020 7495 1759
🔖 Page 9-K5

Harrow Museum
Harrow Museum is based in the historic buildings and grounds of Headstone Manor and offers an insight into 500 years of its existence.

Headstone Manor, Pinner View HA2 6PX
☎ 020 8863 6720, 020 8861 2626
@ museum@harrowarts.com
🖱 www.harrowarts.com/museum
🖨 020 8861 4793
🔖 Page 42-C6

Hogarth's House
Hogarth's House in Chiswick, built around 1700, was the country home of the painter William Hogarth (1697–1764) from 1749 until his death. Hogarth's talents and interests were wide ranging and displays in the house tell the story of his life and works. Two floors of the house include the collection of Hogarth's prints on permanent public display. The panelled rooms also house some replica pieces of 18th-century furniture.

Hogarth Lane, Great West Road,
London W4 2QN
☎ 020 8994 6757
@ info@cip.org.uk
⌐ www.hounslow.info
⌂ Page 118-B6

Horniman Museum and Gardens

The Horniman has a range of
exhibitions, events and activities
which illustrate the cultural and
natural world. The collections of
anthropology, natural history and
musical instruments provide the
inspiration for the programme
of permanent and temporary
exhibitions and events and
activities.

100 London Road, Forest Hill,
London SE23 3PQ
☎ 020 8699 1872
@ enquiry@horniman.ac.uk
⌐ www.horniman.ac.uk
⌂ 020 8291 5506
⌂ Page 163-J3

Household Cavalry Museum

The collection represents over
300 years of military history and
reflects the unique ceremonial and
operational role of the Regiment.
The museum gallery provides
an introduction to the dual role
of today's Household Cavalry
Regiment and traces its origins
and historical development.

Horse Guards, Whitehall,
Westminster, London SW1A 2AX
☎ 020 7414 2392
@ museum@householdcavalry.
co.uk
⌐ www.householdcavalry.co.uk
⌂ 020 7414 2212
⌂ Page 16-D1

Hunterian Museum

The museum offers an insight into
the history of medicine through
displays and exhibitions.

Royal College of Surgeons, 35–43
Lincoln's Inn Fields, Holborn,
London WC2A 3PE
☎ 020 7869 6560
@ museums@rcseng.ac.uk
⌐ www.rcseng.ac.uk/
⌂ 020 7869 6564
⌂ Page 11-H3

Imperial War Museum, London

The Imperial War Museum has
collections covering all aspects
of 20th- and 21st-century

conflict involving Britain and the
Commonwealth. It is also a major
national art gallery, a national
records archive and a research
centre.

Lambeth Road, Kennington,
London SE1 6HZ
☎ 020 7416 5320, 020 7416 5321
@ mail@iwm.org.uk
⌐ london.iwm.org.uk
⌂ 020 7416 5374
⌂ Page 17-K5

Jewish Military Museum

The museum commemorates the
contribution to the Armed Forces
of the Crown made by British Jews,
who loyally served their country for
over two centuries. There are over
1,000 items on display, consisting
of memorabilia, pictures, medals,
uniforms and letters.

Shield House, Harmony Way,
Hendon, London NW4 2BZ
☎ 020 8202 2323
@ headoffice@ajex.org.uk
⌐ www.ajex.org.uk/museum.htm
⌂ 020 8202 9900
⌂ Page 64-A1

Jewish Museum Camden Town

The museum aims to increase
knowledge and understanding
of Jewish history, culture and
religious life, as part of Britain's
diverse heritage. The museum
tells the story of Jewish life
in Britain, through an array of
collections, exhibitions, events and
educational programmes.

Raymond Burton House, 129–131
Albert Street, Camden, London
NW1 7NB
☎ 020 7284 1997
@ admin@jmus.org.uk
⌐ www.jewishmuseum.org.uk
⌂ 020 7267 9008
⌂ Page 3-K1

Jewish Museum Finchley

The museum offers an insight
into Jewish history, culture and
religious life, as part of Britain's
diverse heritage. The collections
include range of documents and
artefacts reflecting the diverse
roots and heritage of Jews in
Britain, as well as an oral history
archive and a photographic
archive.

Sternberg Centre, 80 East End
Road, Finchley, London N3 2SY

☎ 020 8349 1143
@ enquiries@jewishmuseum.
org.uk
⌐ www.jewishmuseum.org.uk
⌂ 020 8343 2162
⌂ Page 46-E5

Keats House

The house, set in the leafy
suburbs of Hampstead, was
home to John Keats from 1818 to
1820. Collections include books,
manuscripts, letters, prints,
paintings and artefacts relating to
the life of the poet, his circle and
the English Romantic movement.

Keats Grove, Hampstead, London
NW3 2RR
☎ 020 7435 2062
@ keatshouse@cityoflondon.
gov.uk
⌐ www.cityoflondon.gov.uk/keats
⌂ Page 83-H2

Kew Bridge Steam Museum

The museum holds special events
and activities ranging from science
activities for children to live steam
model railway show.

Green Dragon Lane, Brentford
TW8 0EN
☎ 020 8568 4757
@ info@kbsm.org
⌐ www.kbsm.org
⌂ 020 8569 9978
⌂ Page 117-G5

Kew Transport Museum

110 North Road, Kew, Richmond
TW9 3QA
☎ 020 8332 0672
⌐ www.londonnet.
co.uk/museums/
kewtransportmuseum.html
⌂ Page 137-H3

Kingston Museum

The museum has three permanent
galleries – Ancient Origins, Town
of Kings and Eadweard Muybridge
– along with an art gallery for
temporary exhibitions. The Local
History Room holds a large and
growing collection of local history
research material.

Wheatfield Way, Kingston upon
Thames KT1 2PS
☎ 020 8547 6460
@ kingston.museum@rbk.
kingston.gov.uk
⌐ www.kingston.gov.uk/
⌂ Page 175-F5

The Lea Valley Experience

10 South Access Road,
Walthamstow, London E17 8AX
☎ 020 8521 1766
⌐ www.leavalleyexperience.co.uk
⌂ Page 69-F4

Leighton House Museum

The museum is the former
studio house of the Victorian
artist Frederic, Lord Leighton
(1830–1896). It offers an insight
into Leighton's private world and
is a venue for the understanding
and appreciation of Victorian art
and architecture.

12 Holland Park Road, Kensington,
London W14 8LZ
☎ 020 7602 3316
@ LeightonHouseMuseum@
rbkc.gov.uk
⌐ www.rbkc.gov.uk/
☎ 020 7371 2467
⌂ Page 119-J3

The Library and Museum of Freemasonry

The museum contains a collection
of objects with Masonic decoration
including pottery and porcelain,
glassware, silver, furniture and
clocks, jewels and regalia. Items
belonging to famous and royal
freemasons including Winston
Churchill and Edward VII are on
display together with examples
of prints and engravings,
photographs and ephemera.

Freemasons Hall, 60 Great Queen
Street, London WC2B 5AZ
☎ 020 7395 9257
@ libmus@ugle.org.uk
⌐ www.freemasonry.london.
museum
⌂ 020 7404 7418
⌂ Page 11-F3

London Brass Rubbing Centre

London Brass Rubbing Centre
offers an insight into the art of
brass rubbing by allowing visitors
to choose from a choice of 90
replica brasses, which include
medieval knights in armour,
costumed ladies, St George and
William Shakespeare.

St Martins-in-the-Fields, Trafalgar
Square, Charing Cross, London
WC2N 4JJ
☎ 020 7766 1100
@ info@smitf.org
⌐ www.st-martin-in-the-fields.org
⌂ Page 10-D6

London Canal Museum

The museum features the history of the ice trade and ice cream as well as the canals.

12–13 New Wharf Road, London N1 9RT
☎ 020 7713 0836
🖰 www.canalmuseum.org.uk
📄 020 7689 6679
🗏 Page 5-F2

London Fire Brigade Museum

Exhibits on display depict the history of firefighting in London from the Great Fire of London in 1666 to the present day. The museum holds information on ex-employees and staff from organisations that preceded the London Fire Brigade, some of which dates back to the 1860s.

Winchester House, 94a Southwark Bridge Road, Southwark, London SE1 0EG
☎ 020 7587 2894
@ museum@london-fire.gov.uk
🖰 www.london-fire.gov.uk
🗏 Page 18-C2

London Motorcycle Museum

The museum is the capital's friendly focus for Britain's biking history and heritage.

Ravenor Farm, Oldfield Lane South, Greenford UB6 9LD
☎ 020 8575 6644
@ thelmm@hotmail.com
🖰 www.motorcycle-uk.com/lmm. htm
🗏 Page 96-C2

The London Sewing Machine Museum

Features a display of antique sewing machines.

308 Balham High Road, London SW17 7AA
☎ 020 8682 7916
@ wimbledon sewingmachine coltd@btinternet.com
🖰 www.sewantique.com
📄 020 8767 4726
🗏 Page 161-G3

London Transport Museum

39 Wellington Street, Covent Garden, London WC2E 7BB
☎ 020 7379 6344
@ enquiry@ltmuseum.co.uk
🖰 www.ltmuseum.co.uk
🗏 Page 11-F5

Manor Park Museum

The museum collections offer an insight into the local history of Newham.

Manor Park Library, Romford Road, Manor Park, London E12 5JY
☎ 020 8514 0274
@ Tom.McAllister@newham. gov.uk
🖰 www.newham.gov.uk
🗏 Page 89-J2

Marylebone Cricket Club Museum

Lord's Cricket Ground, St Johns Wood Road, St Johns Wood, London NW8 8QZ
☎ 020 7616 8656
@ museum@mcc.org.uk
🖰 www.lords.org
📄 020 7616 8659
🗏 Page 2-A5

Museum No 1 at the Royal Botanic Gardens

The museum was designed by Decimus Burton and opened in 1857. The collections highlight the variety of useful plants around the world and celebrates the ingenuity and craft skills in using these riches.

The Royal Botanic Gardens, Kew, Richmond, London TW9 3AB
☎ 020 8332 5655
@ info@kew.org
🖰 www.rbgkew.org.uk
🗏 Page 137-F2

Museum in Docklands

The museum collections include artefacts, objects and documents which offer an insight into the maritime history of the dock.

West India Quay, Canary Wharf, London E14 4AL
☎ 0870 444 3855
🕒 0870 444 3855
@ info@museumindocklands. org.uk
🖰 www.museumindocklands. org.uk
📄 020 7600 1058, 0870 444 3853
🗏 Page 105-J6

The Museum of Brands, Packaging and Advertising

The museum features a display of everyday household products from the Victorian age to present day with a stock over 10,000 consumer goods and reflects how daily life has changed with the arrival of new brands.

2 Colville Mews, Notting Hill, London W11 2AR
☎ 020 7908 0880
@ info@museumofbrands.com
🖰 www.museumofbrands.com
🗏 Page 100-D5

Museum of Croydon

Discover the history of Croydon through exhibits from the 1800s to the present day. Experience the stories behind the exhibits through audio and film clips, and interactive displays.

Katharine Street, Croydon CR9 1ET
☎ 020 8253 1022
@ museum@croydon.gov.uk
🖰 www.museumofcroydon.com
🗏 Page 211-J1

Museum of Domestic Design and Architecture

The Museum of Domestic Design and Architecture (MoDA) is part of Middlesex University. MoDA's varied exhibitions give a vivid picture of domestic life in the first half of the 20th century. MoDA's collections, relate to British domestic design and architecture 1870–1960.

Middlesex University, Cat Hill, Barnet EN4 8HT
☎ 020 8411 5244
@ moda@mdx.ac.uk
🖰 www.moda.mdx.ac.uk
📄 020 8411 6639
🗏 Page 22-A6

Museum of Garden History

The museum is dedicated to the history of gardens and gardening and endeavours to enhance understanding and appreciation of the history and development of gardens and gardening in the UK.

Lambeth Palace Road, London SE1 7LB
☎ 020 7401 8865
@ info@museumgardenhistory. org
🖰 www.museumgardenhistory. org
📄 020 7401 8869
🗏 Page 17-G5

Museum of Great Ormond Street Hospital

The museum is devoted to the history of the hospital and personalities connected with the hospital since its inception in 1852. Part of the Museum and Archive Service, the museum

shows artefacts, artworks, photographs, documents and three book collections.

First Floor, 55 Great Ormond Street, Bloomsbury, London WC1N 3HZ
☎ 020 7405 9200
🖰 www.medicalmuseums.org
🗏 Page 5-F7

Museum of London

Dedicated to the story of London and its people, the Museum of London exists to inspire a passion for London and all who visit it. As well as the permanent collection, the museum has a varied exhibition programme with major temporary exhibitions and topical displays each year.

London Wall, London EC2Y 5HN
☎ 0870 444 3851
🕒 0870 444 3850
@ info@museumoflondon.org.uk
🖰 www.museumoflondon.org.uk
📄 0870 444 3853
🗏 Page 12-C2

Museum of Richmond

The museum celebrates the rich heritage of Richmond, Ham, Petersham and Kew through exhibition and education programmes.

Old Town Hall, Whittaker Avenue, Richmond upon Thames TW9 1TP
☎ 020 8332 1141
@ museumofrichmond@ btconnect.com
🖰 www.museumofrichmond.com
📄 020 8948 7570
🗏 Page 136-E6

Museum of Rugby

The museum houses over 10,000 objects as well as the archive of photographs of team line-ups, players, action and aerial views of various rugby grounds from all around the world.

Twickenham Stadium, Rugby Road, Twickenham, London TW1 1DZ
☎ 0870 405 2001
@ museum@rfu.com
🖰 www.rfu.com/microsites/ museum/index.cfm
📄 0870 405 2002
🗏 Page 155-K1

Museum of the Order of St John

A tour of the priory takes visitors through the North Chapel, the Tudor Gatehouse and the interiors

decorated with collections of painting, furniture and silver.

St John Ambulance, St John's Gate, St John's Lane, London EC1M 4DA
☎ 020 7324 4070
@ museum@nhq.sja.org.uk
🖰 www.sja.org.uk/museum
📖 Page 6-B7

Museum of the Royal Pharmaceutical Society
The society has a collection of around 45,000 items covering all aspects of British pharmacy history. Exhibits include traditional dispensing equipment, drug storage containers, bronze mortars, medical caricatures and photo archive.

Royal Pharmaceutical Society of Great Britain, 1 Lambeth High Street, Kennington, London SE1 7JN
☎ 020 7572 2210
@ museum@rpsgb.org
🖰 www.rpsgb.org
📖 Page 17-G6

The Musical Museum
368 High Street, Brentford TW8 0BD
☎ 020 8560 8108
🖰 www.musicalmuseum.co.uk
📖 Page 116-E6

National Army Museum
The museum offers an insight into the history of Army and the impact it had on Britain, Europe and the world.

Royal Hospital Road, Chelsea, London SW3 4HT
☎ 020 7730 0717
@ info@national-army-museum.ac.uk
🖰 www.national-army-museum.ac.uk
📖 Page 120-E6

National Maritime Museum
The museum collection contains over two million objects related to seafaring, navigation, astronomy and measuring time. Along with these there are oil paintings and memorabilia assiocated with English explorer Matthew Flinders.

Park Row, Greenwich, London SE10 9NF
☎ 020 8312 6565, 020 8858 4422
🖰 www.nmm.ac.uk
📄 020 8312 6632
📖 Page 125-G6

Natural History Museum
First opened in 1881, the Natural History Museum promotes the discovery, understanding, enjoyment, and responsible use of the natural world, with a collection of over 70 million items. The museum's world-renowned collections, exhibitions and cutting-edge research are housed in its landmark buildings, and can also be accessed online.

Cromwell Road, South Kensington, London SW7 5BD
☎ 020 7942 5000
🖰 www.nhm.ac.uk
📖 Page 14-A5

North Woolwich Old Station Museum
The museum collections include carriages, locomotives, a 1920s ticket office and other railway and local history related exhibits.

Pier Road, North Woolwich, London E16 2JJ
☎ 020 7474 7244
@ leisure.heritage@newham.gov.uk
🖰 www.newham.gov.uk
📖 Page 127-F2

Percival David Foundation of Chinese Art
The Percival David Foundation promotes the study and teaching of Chinese art and culture. The collection includes Chinese ceramics from the Song (960–1279) and Yuan (1279–1368) dynasties along with Chinese books on art. There are approximately 1,700 items of Chinese ceramics in the Foundation, reflecting Chinese court taste and dating mainly to the 10th to the 18th centuries.

School of Oriental and African Studies, 53 Gordon Square, Bloomsbury, London WC1H 0PD
☎ 020 7387 3909
@ sp17@soas.ac.uk
🖰 www.pdfmuseum.org.uk
📄 020 7383 5163
📖 Page 4-D6

Petrie Museum of Egyptian Archaeology
The museum was set up as a teaching resource for the Department of Egyptian Archaeology and Philology at University College London. Both the department and the museum

were created in 1892 through the bequest of the writer Amelia Edwards.

University College London, Malet Place, Bloomsbury, London WC1E 6BT
☎ 020 7679 2884
@ petrie.museum@ucl.ac.uk
🖰 www.petrie.ucl.ac.uk
📄 020 7679 2886
📖 Page 4-C7

Polish Institute and Sikorski Museum
20 Princes Gate, South Kensington, London SW7 1PT
📞 020 7589 9249
🖰 www.sikorskimuseum.co.uk
📖 Page 14-B3

Pollock's Toy Museum
The museum takes its name from Benjamin Pollock, the last of the Victorian Toy Theatre printers. Collections include toy theatres, teddy bears, wax and china dolls, board games, optical toys, folk toys, nursery furniture, mechanical toys and doll's houses.

1 Scala Street, London W1T 2HL
☎ 020 7636 3452
@ info@pollockstoymuseum.com
🖰 www.pollockstoymuseum.com
📖 Page 10-B1

Prince Henry's Room
Prince Henry's Room contains the Samuel Pepys exhibition of contemporary items, prints and paintings depicting the diarist and the London of his day.

17 Fleet Street, London EC4Y 1AA
☎ 020 7936 4004
🖰 www.cityoflondon.gov.uk
📄 020 7936 2501
📖 Page 11-J4

Pumphouse Educational Museum, Rotherhithe
The Pumphouse was built in 1929 to regulate the water level in the dock system. When the Surrey Docks closed in 1970, 350 acres became derelict and 270 years of tradition came to an end. The building was refurbished in 1989 and the Heritage Museum opened in 1991.

Lavender Pond and Nature Park, Lavender Road, Rotherhithe, London SE16 5DZ

☎ 020 7231 2976
@ c.marais@thepumphouse.org.uk
🖰 www.thepumphouse.org.uk
📖 Page 124-B1

Ragged School Museum
The museum opened in 1990 in three canalside warehouses in East London. It contains a collection of objects telling the story of life in the East End, past and present.

46–50 Copperfield Road, London E3 4RR
☎ 020 8980 6405
@ enquiries@raggedschoolmuseum.org.uk
🖰 www.raggedschoolmuseum.org.uk
📄 020 8983 3481
📖 Page 105-G3

Redbridge Museum
Central Library, Clements Road, Ilford IG1 1EA
☎ 020 8708 2317
@ gerard.greene@redbridge.gov.uk
🖰 www.redbridge.gov.uk/
📄 020 8708 2431
📖 Page 90-B1

Royal Air Force Museum
The museum houses over 100 aircraft, artefacts, aviation memorabilia, fine art and photographs covering the history of aviation from early balloon flights to the latest jet fighters.

Grahame Park Way, Hendon, Kingsbury, London NW9 5LL
☎ 020 8205 2266
@ hendon@rafmuseum.org
🖰 www.rafmuseum.org/london
📖 Page 45-J5

Royal London Hospital Archives and Museum
The museum is located in the former crypt of a late 19th-century, Early English style church, designed by Arthur Cawston. It offers an insight into the history of the hospital since the 18th century.

The Royal London Hospital, St Augustine with St Philips Church, Newark Street, London E1 2AA
☎ 020 7377 7608
@ jonathan.evans@bartsandthelondon.nhs.uk
🖰 www.bartsandthelondon.nhs.uk
📖 Page 104-D4

St Bartholomews Hospital Archives and Museum

The museum exhibits original and facsimile archives dating back to the 12th century, among them the agreement between Henry VIII and the City of London which refounded the hospital. Objects from the hospital's historical collections are also exhibited, including works of art and surgical and medical equipment used in the hospital.

North Wing, St Bartholomews Hospital, West Smithfield, London EC1A 7BE
☎ 020 7601 8152, 020 7601 8150
@ barts.archives@
   bartsandthelondon.nhs.uk
🖰 www.bartsandthelondon.
   nhs.uk/
✐ Page 12-B2

Science Museum

The origins of the Science Museum lie in the 19th-century movement to improve scientific and technical education. The museum has over 300,000 objects in its care, covering the entire history of Western science, technology and medicine.

Exhibition Road, South Kensington, London SW7 2DD
☎ 0870 870 4868
🖰 www.sciencemuseum.org.uk
✐ Page 14-A5

Shakespeare's Globe

Guides help to bring England's theatrical heritage to life in the recreation of this famous theatre. Discover what an Elizabethan audience would have been like, find out about the rivalry between the Bankside theatres, the bear baiting and the stews, hear about the penny stinkards and find out what a bodger is.

21 New Globe Walk, Bankside, Southwark, London SE1 9DT
☎ 020 7902 1400
@ info@shakespearesglobe.com
🖰 www.shakespeares-globe.org
📄 020 7902 1401
✐ Page 12-B6

Sherlock Holmes Museum

Sherlock Holmes and Dr Watson lived at 221b Baker Street between 1881 and 1904, according to the stories written by Sir Arthur Conan Doyle. The famous 1st floor study overlooking Baker Street is still faithfully maintained as it was kept in Victorian times.

221b Baker Street, Marylebone, London NW1 6XE
☎ 020 7935 8866
@ museumcurator@gmail.com
🖰 www.sherlock-holmes.co.uk
✐ Page 2-F7

Sir John Soane's Museum

Sir John Soane's house, museum and library has been a public museum since the early 19th century. The collections include artefacts acquired between the 1780s and his death in 1837 and range from Egyptian and medieval and renaissance antiquities, 17th- and 18th-century sculpture, stained glass, paintings and picture frames.

13 Lincoln's Inn Fields, Holborn, London WC2A 3BP
☎ 020 7405 2107
@ jbrock@soane.org.uk
🖰 www.soane.org
📄 020 7831 3957
✐ Page 11-G3

The Theatre Museum

The museum houses collections of documents, artefacts and works of art which record the history of the performing arts in Britain from the 16th century to the present.

Russell Street, Covent Garden, London WC2E 7PR
☎ 020 7943 4700
@ tmenquiries@vam.ac.uk
🖰 www.theatremuseum.org.uk
📄 020 7943 4777
✐ Page 11-F5

The Twickenham Museum

The museum houses the archives and artefacts relating to Teddington, Twickenham, Whitton and the Hamptons.

25 The Embankment, Twickenham TW1 3DU
☎ 020 8408 0070
🖰 www.twickenham-museum.
   org.uk
✐ Page 156-B3

Type Museum

100–100A Hackford Road, London SW9 0QU
☎ 020 7735 0055
@ enquiries@typemuseum.org
🖰 www.typemuseum.org
✐ Page 142-A2

UCL, Institute of Archaeology

The institute houses prehistoric ceramics and stone artefacts from many parts of the world as well as collections of Classical Greek and Roman ceramics.

31–34 Gordon Square, London WC1H 0PY
☎ 020 7679 4789
@ i.carroll@ucl.ac.uk
🖰 www.archaeology.museum.
   ucl.ac.uk
📄 020 7679 2572
✐ Page 4-D7

Valence House Museum

The museum houses artefacts and archives offering an insight into the natural history of Barking and Dagenham.

Becontree Avenue, Dagenham RM8 3HT
☎ 020 8270 6865
@ mark.watson@lbbd.gov.uk
🖰 www.barking-dagenham.gov.uk
📄 020 8270 6868
✐ Page 73-K6

Vestry House Museum

Vestry House, a two storey building of brown stock brick, was constructed in 1730 by order of the Vestry. It houses artefacts and archives which offer an insight into the natural history of the area.

Vestry Road, Walthamstow E17 9NH
☎ 020 8509 1917
@ vestry.house@walthamforest.
   gov.uk
🖰 www.walthamforest.gov.uk
✐ Page 69-K1

Victoria and Albert Museum

The V&A holds one of the UKs largest collections in terms of scope and diversity. Discover 3,000 years' worth of artefacts from cultures around the world including ceramics, furniture, fashion, glass, jewellery, metalwork, photographs, sculpture, textiles and paintings.

Cromwell Road, South Kensington, London SW7 2RL
☎ 020 7942 2000
@ vanda@vam.ac.uk
🖰 www.vam.ac.uk
✐ Page 14-B5

The Wallace Collection

The museum displays the works of art collected in the 18th and 19th centuries by the first four Marquesses of Hertford and Sir Richard Wallace, the son of the 4th Marquess. It is probably best known for its paintings by artists such as Titian, Rembrandt, Hals (*The Laughing Cavalier*) and Velazquez and for its superb collections of 18th-century French paintings, porcelain, furniture and gold boxes, probably the best to be found anywhere outside France.

Hertford House, Manchester Square, Marylebone, London W1U 3BN
☎ 020 7563 9500
🖰 www.wallacecollection.org
📄 020 7224 2155
✐ Page 9-G3

The Wandle Industrial Museum

The museum displays the evidence which establishes that the River Wandle was, in its day, the industrialised river in Europe.

The Vestry Hall Annexe, London Road, Mitcham CR4 3UD
☎ 020 8648 0127
@ curator@wandle.org
🖰 www.wandle.org
✐ Page 178-E6

Wandsworth Museum

The Story of Wandsworth is a permanent display telling the story of the area covered by the present borough of Wandsworth from prehistoric times to the present day.

The Courthouse, 11 Garratt Lane, Wandsworth, London SW18 4AQ
☎ 020 8871 7074
@ wandsworthmuseum@
   wandsworth.gov.uk
🖰 www.wandsworth.gov.uk
📄 020 8871 4602
✐ Page 140-A6

Wimbledon Society Museum of Local History

An intimate museum which shows, in pictures, words and objects, the history of Wimbledon over the last 3,000 years.

22 Ridgway, Wimbledon, London SW19 4QN
☎ 020 8296 9914
@ wimbledonmuseum@yahoo.
   co.uk

- www.wimbledonmuseum.org.uk
- Page 177-G2

Wimbledon Windmill Museum

The museum is housed in the windmill on Wimbledon Common. It depicts the history of windmills and milling using working models and the machinery and tools of the trade, with hands-on milling for children. The museum contains many working models of windmills showing how they have developed from early Persian and Greek mills to modern wind farms.

Windmill Road, Wimbledon Common, Merton, London SW19 5NR
- 020 8947 2825
- www.wimbledonwindmill museum.org.uk
- Page 158-F5

ART CENTRES

The Albany

Douglas Way, Deptford, London SE8 4AG
- 020 8692 4446
- aadmin@thealbany.org.uk
- www.thealbany.org.uk
- 020 8469 2253
- Page 144-D1

All Saints Arts Centre

122 Oakleigh Road North, Whetstone, London N20 9EZ
- 020 8445 8388
- arts@allsaints.uk.com
- www.allsaints.uk.com
- Page 33-H4

ArtsDepot

ArtsDepot is committed to providing a diverse range of high quality visual and performance arts for everyone.

5 Nether Street, Tally Ho Corner, North Finchley, London N12 0GA
- 020 8369 5454
- jennie.hammond@artsdepot.co.uk
- www.artsdepot.co.uk
- Page 47-G1

BAC: Battersea Arts Centre

BAC is renowned for creating work that is cutting edge and form-busting. BAC has a reputation for being the venue to see some of London's most innovative and exciting work.

Lavender Hill, Battersea, London SW11 5TN
- 020 7223 6557
- 020 7223 2223
- boxoffice@bac.org.uk
- www.bac.org.uk
- 020 7978 5207
- Page 140-E4

Bernie Grant Arts Centre

Town Hall Approach Road, Tottenham Green, London N15 4RX
- 020 8365 5450
- admin@berniegrantcentre.co.uk
- www.berniegrantcentre.co.uk
- Page 68-B1

Bharatiya Vidya Bhavan

Bharatiya Vidya Bhavan hosts drama, music and classical events and holds courses in music, dance, languages, drama, art and archaeology.

4a Castletown Road, West Kensington, London W14 9HE
- 020 7381 3086, 020 7381 4608
- info@bhavan.net
- www.bhavan.net
- 020 7381 8758
- Page 119-H5

Brady Arts and Community Centre

The centre offers arts courses and workshops including dance, drama, music technology, fashion, film, singing and pottery.

192–196 Hanbury Street, London E1 5HU
- 020 7364 7900
- bradycentre@towerhamlets.gov.uk
- www.towerhamletsarts.org.uk
- 020 7364 7901
- Page 104-C4

Camden Arts Centre

A creative hub which promotes active engagement with art, artists and ideas, through a frequently changing programme of exhibitions and education.

Arkwright Road, London NW3 6DG
- 020 7472 5500
- info@camdenartscentre.org
- www.camdenartscentre.org
- Page 83-G3

Chat's Palace

Chat's Palace is a community arts centre in Hackney in the East End of London.

42–44 Brooksby's Walk, Hackney, London E9 6DF
- 020 8533 0227
- chatspalace@hotmail.com
- www.chatspalace.com
- 020 8985 6878
- Page 87-F3

Christ The Saviour Church

Uxbridge Road, London W5 5JW
- 020 8998 5662
- ealingartgroup@yahoo.co.uk
- www.ealingartgroup.org.uk
- Page 97-K6

Clapham North Arts Centre

Voltaire Road, Clapham, London SW4 6DH
- 020 7769 8595
- Page 141-J4

Compass Theatre and Arts Centre

Compass Theatre and Arts Centre is a place where people can learn drama games, confidence building, theatre craft and acting skills.

Glebe Avenue, Ickenham UB10 8PD
- 01895 632488
- 01895 673200
- compasstheatre@hillingdongrid.org
- www.compasstheatre.co.uk
- Page 76-A2

The Corner House

The Corner House hosts guest productions in dance, drama, comedy and music, and is also the base for a number of in-house initiatives and visual arts.

Douglas Road, Surbiton KT6 7SB
- 020 8296 9012
- info@thecornerhouse.org
- www.thecornerhouse.org
- Page 191-G5

Croydon Clocktower

Croydon Clocktower is an arts and cultural centre with gallery spaces, the interactive Museum of Croydon, the David Lean cinema, music, theatre and comedy performances and a state-of-the-art public library.

Katharine Street, Croydon CR9 1ET
- 020 8253 1030
- ticketoffice@croydon.gov.uk
- www.croydon.gov.uk
- Page 211-J1

Four Corners

Four Corners supports a wide range of filmmakers, photographers and artists and offers facilities for photograpy, film and other forms of visual media.

121 Roman Road, Bethnal Green, London E2 0QN
- 020 8981 6111
- info@fourcornersfilm.co.uk
- www.fourcornersfilm.co.uk
- 020 8983 7866
- Page 105-F1

Harrow Arts Centre

Uxbridge Road, Hatch End, HA5 4EA
- 020 8863 5611
- info@harrowarts.com
- www.harrow.gov.uk
- Page 42-A3

The Horse Hospital

London's premier centre for avant-garde media.

Colonnade, Bloomsbury, St Pancras, London WC1N 1HX
- 020 7833 3644
- popculture@thehorsehospital.com
- www.thehorsehospital.com
- Page 4-F7

ICA: Institute of Contemporary Arts

One of London's leading arts centres presenting contemporary film, exhibitions, talks, club nights, music, dance, and new media events.

The Mall, London SW1Y 5AH
- 020 7930 0493
- 020 7930 3647
- www.ica.org.uk
- Page 10-C7

Inn On The Green

A well-established arts and performance venue and a place for local artists to display their work.

3–5 Thorpe Close, Ladbroke Grove, London W10 5XL
- 0208 962 5757
- info@iotg.co.uk
- www.iotg.co.uk
- Page 100-C5

Islington Arts Factory

2 Parkhurst Road, Holloway, London N7 0SF
- 020 7607 0561
- IAF@islingtonartsfactory.fsnet.co.uk

⌂ www.islingtonartsfactory.
org.uk
⊘ Page 84-E2

Italian Cultural Institute

39 Belgrave Square, London
London SW1X 8NX
☎ 020 7235 1461
@ icilondon@esteri.it
⌂ www.icilondon.esteri.it
▤ 020 7235 4618
⊘ Page 15-H3

Karamel Club

The Karamel Club means to
forge a strong programme of
contemporary live performance,
music, comedy, spoken word,
multimedia and film with particular
focus on showcasing the work of
both new and emerging musicians,
artists and filmmakers alongside
established local and international
artists and companies.

Chocolate Factory 2, 4 Coburg
Road, London N22 6UJ
☎ 07092 387460
⌂ www.karamelclub.co.uk
⊘ Page 49-F5

The Landmark Arts Centre

The Landmark Arts Centre
presents jazz, blues, choral,
classical music, opera and dance
through out the year.

Ferry Road, Teddington TW11 9NN
☎ 020 8977 7558
☏ 020 8977 7558
@ lourda@landmarkartscentre.
org
⌂ www.landmarkartscentre.org
⊘ Page 174-C1

Lantern Arts Centre

Tolverne Road, Raynes Park,
London SW20 8RA
☎ 020 8944 5794
⌂ www.lanternarts.org
⊘ Page 177-F4

Lauderdale House

Lauderdale House is an arts
and education centre based
in Waterlow Park hosting
an extensive programme of
performances, workshops,
outreach projects, classes and
exhibitions.

Highgate Hill, Waterlow Park,
London N6 5HG
☎ 020 8348 8716
⌂ www.lauderdalehouse.co.uk
⊘ Page 66-B5

London Jewish Cultural Centre

Built on the bedrock of the Spiro
Institute, an organisation that has
successfully taught Jewish history,
culture and modern Hebrew for
over 20 years.

Ivy House, 94–96 North End Road,
Hampstead, London NW11 7HU
☎ 020 8457 5000, 020 8455 9900
@ admin@ljcc.org.uk
⌂ www.ljcc.org.uk
▤ 020 8457 5024
⊘ Page 64-E5

Menier Chocolate Factory

Built in the 1870s to house a
chocolate factory, this historical
building has now been converted
in to a leading arts complex which
includes a gallery, restaurant,
theatre and rehearsal space.

51–53 Southwark Street,
Bermondsey, London SE1 1RU
☎ 020 7907 7060
@ info@menierchocolatefactory.
com
⌂ www.menierchocolatefactory.
com
⊘ Page 18-C1

Millfield Arts Centre

Silver Street, Edmonton, Upper
Edmonton, London N18 1PJ
☎ 020 8807 6680
@ info@millfieldtheatre.co.uk
⌂ www.millfieldtheatre.co.uk
▤ 020 8807 3892
⊘ Page 35-K6

Mountview Academy of Theatre Arts

Ralph Richardson Memorial
Studios, Clarendon Road, Wood
Green, London N22 6XF
☎ 020 8881 2201, 020 8826 9210
@ enquiries@mountview.ac.uk
⌂ www.mountview.org.uk
▤ 020 8829 0034
⊘ Page 49-F5

The Orangery

The gallery hosts a wide range of
exhibitions of contemporary art in
the form of photography, paintings
and sculpture.

Holland Park, London W8 6LU
☎ 020 7603 1123, 020 7361 2225
@ museums@rbkc.gov.uk
⌂ www.rbkc.gov.uk
⊘ Page 119-J2

Putney Arts Centre

Ravenna Road, London SW15
6AW
☎ 020 8788 6943
@ mail@putneyartstheatre.
org.uk
⌂ www.putneyartstheatre.org.uk
⊘ Page 139-G5

Redlees Studios

Redlees Park, Worton Road,
Isleworth, London TW7 6DW
☎ 0845 456 2984, 0845 456 2977
@ harkirat.assi@cip.org.uk
⌂ www.hounslow.info/
⊘ Page 136-A4

Rich Mix

The Rich Mix building is a dynamic
cross-cultural arts and media
centre in the heart of the East End.
It houses a three-screen cinema,
recording and music training
studios, a 200-seater performance
venue, a media lab and multimedia
'Newsroom', education and
exhibition spaces, workspaces,
a bar, cafes and a broadcasting
centre for BBC London.

35–47 Bethnal Green Road,
London E1 6LA
☎ 020 7613 7490
@ info@richmix.org.uk
⌂ www.richmix.org.uk
⊘ Page 7-J6

Riverside Studios

Riverside Studios is an arts and
media centre on the banks of
the Thames in Hammersmith,
comprising two main performance
studios, a cinema, a TV studio and
production galleries, rehearsal/
workshop space, numerous offices
and a large contemporary cafe-bar
and terrace.

Crisp Road, Hammersmith,
London W6 9RL
☎ 020 8237 1111, 020 8237 1000
@ online@riversidestudios.co.uk
⌂ www.riversidestudios.co.uk
⊘ Page 119-F5

The Roundhouse

The Roundhouse presents a
varied programme of international
performing arts including music,
theatre, dance, circus and digital
media to reflect the excitement
and diversity of 21st-century
culture.

Chalk Farm Road, London
NW1 8EH

☎ 020 7424 9991
☏ 087 0389 1846
@ info@roundhouse.org.uk
⌂ www.roundhouse.org.uk
▤ 020 7424 9992
⊘ Page 84-A5

The Space

The Space is a multi-arts centre
on the Isle of Dogs, offering
a mixture of theatre, music,
comedy and dance. Converted
from a 19th-century church, with
stained-glass windows, a Steinway
grand piano and flexible seating,
the venue provides a unique and
atmospheric environment.

269 Westferry Road, Isle of Dogs,
London E14 3RS
☎ 020 7515 7799
@ ali@space.org.uk
⌂ www.space.org.uk
⊘ Page 124-D4

Stratford Circus

A contemporary performing arts
venue in the Stratford cultural
quarter in East London. The
centre offers a broad and varied
programme of performances,
events, workshops and education
and training opportunities.

Theatre Square, Stratford, London
E15 1BX
☎ 020 8279 1080
@ info@stratford-circus.com
⌂ www.stratford-circus.com
⊘ Page 88-B4

Trinity Buoy Wharf

64 Orchard Place, Canary Wharf,
London E14 0JW
☎ 020 7515 7153
@ sally.ho@urban-space.co.uk
⌂ www.trinitybuoywharf.com
⊘ Page 106-C6

Watermans

This multipurpose arts centre
overlooking Kew Gardens
comprises a 239-seat theatre,
an intimate 125-seat cinema, a
gallery space, a studio and the
River Terrace Foyer with a cafe,
bar and patio.

40 High Street, Brentford, London
TW8 0DS
☎ 020 8232 1010
@ info@watermans.org.uk
⌂ www.watermans.org.uk
▤ 020 8232 1030
⊘ Page 117-F6

YAA Asantewaa Arts and Community Centre

1 Chippenham Mews, Chippenham Road, Little Venice, London W9 2AN
☎ 020 7286 1656
@ admin@yaaasantewaa.com
🖰 www.yaaasant.demon.co.uk
🖹 020 7266 0377
🏵 Page 100-E3

DANCE AND PERFORMING ARTS

Bar Salsa
The bar features daily salsa lessons.

96 Charing Cross Road, Covent Garden, London WC2H 0JG
☎ 020 7379 3277
@ info@barsalsa.info
🖰 www.barsalsa.info
🖹 020 7240 4066
🏵 Page 10-D4

Cecil Sharp House
Cecil Sharp House is the home of The English Folk Dance and Song Society. It offers a variety of traditional English and Irish dance and music classes as well as folk gigs and workshops.

2 Regents Park Road, Camden, London NW1 7AY
☎ 020 7485 2206
@ info@efdss.org
🖰 www.efdss.org
🏵 Page 84-A6

Central School of Ballet
10 Herbal Hill, Clerkenwell Road, London EC1R 5EG
☎ 020 7837 6332
🖰 www.centralschoolofballet.co.uk
🖹 020 7833 5571
🏵 Page 5-K7

English National Ballet, Markova House
39 Jay Mews, South Kensington, London SW7 2ES
☎ 020 7581 1245
🖰 www.ballet.org.uk
🖹 020 7225 0827
🏵 Page 120-B2

Greenwich Dance Agency
The Borough Hall, Royal Hill, Greenwich, London SE10 8RE
☎ 020 8293 9741
@ info@greenwichdance.org.uk
🖰 www.greenwichdance.org.uk
🏵 Page 145-F1

Laban Theatre
Creekside, Deptford, London SE8 3DZ
☎ 020 8691 8600
@ info@laban.org
🖰 www.laban.org
🏵 Page 144-E1

National Theatre
The National Theatre offers a diverse variety of entertainment events, from music and dance to theatre and comedy.

South Bank, Southwark, London SE1 9PX
☎ 020 7452 3000
@ info@nationaltheatre.org.uk
🖰 www.nationaltheatre.org.uk
🏵 Page 11-H7

The Peacock Theatre
Portugal Street, Holborn, London WC2A 2HT
☎ 020 7863 8198
☏ 0870 737 7737
@ ticket.office@sadlerswells.com
🖰 www.sadlerswells.com/peacock
🏵 Page 11-G4

The Place: Robin Howard Dance Theatre
One of the UK's busiest dance venues. Each year over 100 companies from the UK perform new and experimental works in the 300-seat theatre.

17 Duke's Road, St Pancras, London WC1H 9PY
☎ 020 7387 0031
🖰 www.theplace.org.uk
🖹 info@theplace.org.uk
🏵 Page 4-D5

Purcell Room
As part of the Royal Festival Hall arts complex, the Purcell Room hosts contemporary dance, music theatre, chamber music, solo recitals, world music, poetry events and live art.

South Bank Centre, London SE1 8XX
☎ 0870 380 0400
🖰 www.southbankcentre.co.uk
🏵 Page 17-G1

Queen Elizabeth Hall
The Queen Elizabeth Hall, seating 917, is a part of Royal Festival Hall complex hosting contemporary dance, music theatre, chamber music, solo recitals, world music, poetry events and live art.

South Bank Centre, Belvedere Road, London SE1 8XX
☎ 0870 380 4300
☏ 0870 401 8181
@ customer@rfh.org.uk
🖰 www.rfh.org.uk
🏵 Page 11-G7

The Roundhouse
The Roundhouse presents a varied programme of international performing arts including music, theatre, dance, circus and digital media to reflect the excitement and diversity of 21st-century culture.

Chalk Farm Road, London NW1 8EH
☎ 020 7424 9991
☏ 087 0389 1846
@ info@roundhouse.org.uk
🖰 www.roundhouse.org.uk
🖹 020 7424 9992
🏵 Page 84-A5

Royal Festival Hall
The Royal Festival Hall stands at the heart of Southbank Centre complex. Opened in 1951 as part of the Festival of Britain, the hall is one of the world's leading concert venues, presenting concerts by the finest international orchestras, operas, and a wide spread of contemporary music events, from jazz and world to rock and pop music.

Belvedere Road, London SE1 8XX
☎ 0870 380 4300
@ customer@southbankcentre.co.uk
🖰 www.southbankcentre.co.uk
🖹 0870 163 3898
🏵 Page 17-G1

Royal Opera House
First known as the Theatre Royal in 1728, the reconstructed Royal Opera House opened in December 1999. Apart from its major opera and dance productions, it is now open so that both public and ticketholders can admire the views of London and marvel at the ornate auditorium and the Floral Bar.

Bow Street, Covent Garden, London WC2E 9DD
☎ 020 7304 4000
@ webmaster@roh.org.uk
🖰 www.roh.org.uk
🏵 Page 11-F4

Sadler's Wells
Sadler's Wells is a theatre with a contemporary programme of international and UK dance; from cutting-edge performance to mainstream contemporary dance, tango to tap and flamenco to family shows.

Rosebery Avenue, London EC1R 4TN
☎ 0870 737 7737
@ reception@sadlerswells.com
🖰 www.sadlerswells.com
🏵 Page12-D3

LIVE MUSIC VENUES

The 100 Club
One of London's oldest live music venues, The 100 Club is open every day hosting jazz, blues, indie and rock nights. The club's notable history has seen gigs performed by the Sex Pistols, The Clash, Muddy Waters and The Rolling Stones.

100 Oxford Street, London W1D 1LL
☎ 020 7636 0933
@ info@the100club.co.uk
🖰 www.the100club.co.uk
🏵 Page 10-B3

12 Bar Club
Small but intimate, the 12 Bar Club showcases around four acts a night, from solo performers through to full bands from all over the world with an emphasis on songwriting.

Denmark Street, Covent Garden, London WC2H 8NL
☎ 020 7916 6989
@ 12barclub@btconnect.com
🖰 www.12barclub.com
🏵 Page 10-D4

19 Below
19 New Bridge Street, East Dulwich, London EC4V 6DB
☎ 020 7438 8000
@ loncy.info@ichotelsgroup.com
🖰 www.606club.co.uk
🏵 Page 12-A4

229
229 Great Portland Street, London W1W 5PN
☎ 020 7631 8388
@ info@229thevenue.co.uk
🖰 www.229thevenue.co.uk
🏵 Page 9-K1

606 Club
The 606 Club is a jazz club restaurant offering daily jazz performances.

90 Lots Road, Chelsea, London SW10 0QD
☎ 020 7352 5953
@ jazz@606club.co.uk
🗗 www.606club.co.uk
🖶 020 7349 0655
⊘ Page 140-B1

Ain't Nothin' But... The Blues Bar
Possibly the only authentic club outside of the States providing live blues every night of the week.

20 Kingly Street, Soho, London W1B 5PZ
☎ 020 7287 0514
🗗 www.aintnothinbut.co.uk
⊘ Page 10-A4

Amersham Arms
Live music venue featuring a range of regular rock, metal and indie nights. The club champions up-and-coming original acts from the capital.

388 New Cross Road, London SE14 6TY
☎ 020 8692 1211, 020 8469 1499
@ 590ltd@btconnect.com
🗗 amersham-arms.co.uk
⊘ Page 144-C1

Archway Tavern
Archway Tavern, host to the Tube Club, offers weekly live indie music with DJ support.

1 Archway Close, Archway Road, London N19 3TX
☎ 020 7272 2840
📞 020 7272 2840
@ info@thetubeclub.co.uk
🗗 www.thetubeclub.co.uk
⊘ Page 66-C6

Asian Music Centre
Ground Floor, Unit E, West Point, 33–34 Warple Way, London W3 0RG
☎ 020 8742 9911
@ info@amc.org.uk
🗗 www.amc.org.uk
🖶 020 8749 3948
⊘ Page 118-B2

Astoria 2
The Astoria 2 has a reputation for playing host to some of the freshest and most exciting bands.

165 Charing Cross Road, London WC2 0EN
☎ 020 7434 9592
🗗 www.festivalrepublic.com
⊘ Page 10-D5

BBC Maida Vale Studios
Delaware Road, Maida Vale, London W9 2LG
🗗 www.bbcradioresources.com
⊘ Page 100-F3

Bar Monsta
18 Kentish Town Road, Camden, London NW1 9LJ
☎ 0207 284 2131
🗗 www.barmonsta.com
⊘ Page 84-B4

Bar Music Hall
Situated in the heart of the Shoreditch triangle, the Music Hall offers an up-to-date DJ schedule and live music programme.

134 Curtain Road, London EC2A 3AR
☎ 020 7613 5951, 020 7729 7216
@ events@barmusichall.co.uk
🗗 www.barmusichall.co.uk
⊘ Page 7-G7

Barbican Hall
The Barbican welcomes the world's leading musicians and soloists in both classical and contemporary music. It is the home to the Resident Orchestra, the London Symphony Orchestra, the Associate Orchestra and the BBC Symphony Orchestra among others.

Barbican Centre, Silk Street, London EC2Y 8DS
☎ 020 7638 8891
📞 020 7382 7211
@ music@barbican.org.uk
🗗 www.barbican.org.uk/music
⊘ Page 12-C1

Barden's Boudoir
Barden's Boudoir is a 300-capacity basement venue for gigs and DJ nights.

38–44 Stoke Newington Road, London N16 7XJ
☎ 020 7249 9557
@ info@bardensbar.co.uk
🗗 www.bardensbar.co.uk
⊘ Page 86-B3

Barfly London
A well-established venue in the Camden music scene, the Barfly offers a stage to up-and-coming talent seven days a week.

49 Chalk Farm Road, Camden London NW1 8AN
☎ 020 7691 4244 / 0870 9070999
@ london.info@barflyclub.com
🗗 www.barflyclub.com
⊘ Page 84-A5

Bartok
Innovative, contemporary and classical music. In essence, Bartok, named after the Hungarian composer Bela Bartok, is an expansion of the chill-out room idea, placed in Regency styled surroundings.

78 Chalk Farm Road, Camden London NW1 8AR
☎ 020 7916 0595
🗗 www.bartokbar.com/
⊘ Page 84-A5

Battersea Barge
Nine Elms Lane, London SW8 5BP
☎ 020 7498 0004
@ info@batterseabarge.com
🗗 www.batterseabarge.com
⊘ Page 121-H6

The Bedford
The Bedford hosts an eclectic selection of events and entertainment including comedy, music, dance, poetry and classical events.

77 Bedford Hill, Balham, London SW12 9HD
☎ 020 8682 8940
@ info@thebedford.co.uk
🗗 www.thebedford.co.uk
🖶 020 8682 8959
⊘ Page 161-G4

The Betsey Trotwood
56 Farringdon Road, London EC1R 3BL
☎ 020 7253 4285
🗗 www.plummusic.com
⊘ Page 5-J6

The Big Reunion
Tenterden Street, London W1S 1TD
📞 0870 151 8230
🗗 www.thebigreunion.com
⊘ Page 9-K4

Blackheath Halls
23 Lee Road, Kidbrooke, London SE3 9RQ
☎ 020 8318 9758
@ piershenderson@ blackheathhalls.com
🗗 www.blackheathhalls.com
⊘ Page 145-J4

Boaters Inn
Canbury Park, Lower Ham Road, Kingston KT2 5AU
☎ 020 8541 4672
@ jazz@boaterslivemusic.com
🗗 www.boaterslivemusic.com
⊘ Page 174-E2

Boisdale of Belgravia
Boisdale of Belgravia offers live jazz from the 30s, 40s and 50s by Boisdale Blue Rhythm Band.

15 Eccleston Street, Belgravia, London SW1W 9LX
☎ 020 7730 6922
@ info@boisdale.co.uk
🗗 www.boisdale.co.uk
⊘ Page 15-H5

Boisdale of Bishopsgate
Boisdale of Bishopsgate offers traditional live jazz from the 30s and 40s.

Swedeland Court, 202 Bishopsgate, London EC2M 4NR
☎ 020 7283 1763
@ info@boisdale-city.co.uk
🗗 www.boisdale.co.uk/
🖶 020 7283 1664
⊘ Page 13-H2

The Boogaloo
Boogaloo aims to 'create a bar that would establish itself amongst great rock 'n' roll bars of our time.'

312 Archway Road, London N6 5AT
☎ 020 8340 2928
🗗 www.theboogaloo.co.uk
⊘ Page 65-K2

The Borderline
This renowned music venue is a favourite among record companies both for launching albums and showcasing new acts. Bands of considerable popularity or cult status (Oasis, Lenny Kravitz, PJ Harvey, Ben Harper) can be found here, and as the venue itself is quite small, music fans are treated to what is one of the best 'close up' musical experiences in London. A place for serious, alternative music fans and clubbers.

Orange Yard, off Manette Street, Soho, London W1D 4JB
☎ 020 7734 5547
🗗 www.meanfiddler.com
⊘ Page 10-C3

The Boston Music Room and The Dome

178 Junction Road, Holloway,
London N19 5QQ
☎ 020 7272 8153
🌐 www.the-boston.co.uk
🔖 Page 84-C1

Brick Lane Music Hall

443 North Woolwich Road,
Silvertown, London E16 2DA
☎ 020 7511 6655
@ info@bricklanemusichall.co.uk
🌐 www.bricklanemusichall.co.uk
🖨 020 7476 6333
🔖 Page 126-C1

The Broadway Theatre

Originally opened in 1932 the
venue is a listed Grade II example
of 1930s art deco architecture. The
theatre includes two venues: the
Main Theatre seating 800 and the
Studio Theatre seating 100.

Catford Broadway, Catford,
London SE6 4RU
☎ 020 8690 0002
@ boxoffice@broadwaytheatre.
org.uk
🌐 www.broadwaytheatre.org.uk
🔖 Page 164-E2

Buffalo Bar

An independently run venue in
the heart of Islington offering an
exciting spectrum of live music
performances.

259 Upper Street, London N1 1RU
☎ 020 7359 6191
@ info@buffalobar.co.uk
🌐 www.buffalobar.co.uk
🔖 Page 85-H4

Bull and Gate

A popular music venue for new
and developing acts of all shapes,
sizes and styles. The pub itself
dates back to the 17th century.

389 Kentish Town Road, Kentish
Town, London NW5 2TJ
☎ 020 7738 3184, 020 7093 4820
@ info@bullandgate.co.uk
🌐 www.bullandgate.co.uk
🔖 Page 84-B4

Bull's Head

Since 1959 The Bull's Head has
gained a world-wide reputation
for modern jazz. Musicians from
all over the world can be heard
playing every night of the week
as well as Sunday lunchtimes.
International artists like George

Coleman, Billy Mitchell, Ben
Webster, Coleman Hawkins, Shorty
Rogers, Charles Rouse, Bud Shank,
Al Cohn, Ronnie Scott, Peter King,
Humphrey Lyttelton, Stan Tracey,
Dick Morrisey, Don Weller, and
Art Theman, have all appeared at
The Bull.

373 Lonsdale Road, Barnes,
London SW13 9PY
☎ 020 8876 5241
@ jazz@thebullshead.com
🌐 www.thebullshead.com
🔖 Page 138-C1

Bush Hall

310 Uxbridge Road, Shepherds
Bush, London W12 7LJ
☎ 020 8222 6955
@ notes@bushhallmusic.co.uk
🌐 www.bushhallmusic.co.uk
🔖 Page 118-D1

Cafe 1001

Cool hangout in a bustling
area, 1001 serves up a mix of
dingy lighting, trendy cakes and
pounding hits at the weekend.

1 Dray Walk, 91 Brick Lane,
London E1 6QL
☎ 020 7247 9679
🌐 www.cafe1001.co.uk
🔖 Page 7-J7

The Camden Lock Tavern

This renovated Victorian city pub
holds regular DJ sets and gigs. It
features two bars, a beer garden
and a roof terrace overlooking
Camden Market.

Chalk Farm Road, Camden, London
NW1 8AJ
☎ 020 7482 7163
🌐 www.lock-tavern.co.uk
🔖 Page 84-A5

Cargo

Opened in 2000, Cargo's 800-
capacity venue hosts events
ranging from club nights and
graffiti exhibitions to live
showcases for unsigned bands.

83 Rivington Street, Kingsland
Viaduct, London EC2A 3AY
☎ 020 7749 7840, 020 7739 3440
@ cargomanagers@
cantaloupegroup.co.uk
🌐 www.cargo-london.com
🔖 Page 7-H5

Carling Academy Brixton

211 Stockwell Road, Brixton,
London SW9 9SL

☎ 020 7787 3131
🌐 www.brixton-academy.co.uk
🖨 020 7771 3000
🔖 Page 142-A3

Carling Academy Islington and Bar Academy

Carling Academy Islington is a
purpose-built venue, with a capacity
of 800. Carling Academy 2 Islington
is the adjoining smaller space
re-designed as a stand alone venue
showcasing up-and-coming bands
(capacity 250) and converts to an
extra room for club nights.

21 Parkfield Street, Islington,
London N1 0PS
☎ 020 7288 4400
🌐 www.islington-academy.co.uk
🔖 Page 5-K2

Catch

Catch is a bar and nightclub
located in Shoreditch, bringing
together people and music from
all genres, from DJs and MCs to
signed and unsigned bands.

22 Kingsland Road, Bethnal Green,
London E2 8DA
☎ 020 7729 6097
@ info@thecatchbar.com
🌐 www.thecatchbar.com
🔖 Page 7-H3

Cecil Sharp House

Cecil Sharp House is the home
of The English Folk Dance and
Song Society. It offers a variety of
traditional English and Irish dance
and music classes as well as folk
gigs and workshops.

2 Regents Park Road, Camden,
London NW1 7AY
☎ 020 7485 2206
@ info@efdss.org
🌐 www.efdss.org
🔖 Page 84-A6

CellarDoor

Zero Aldwych, London WC2R 0HT
☎ 020 7240 8848
🌐 www.cellardoor.biz
🔖 Page 11-G4

Charlie Wright's International Bar

45 Pitfield Street, London N1 6DA
☎ 020 7490 8345
🔖 Page 7-G4

Chicago Rock Cafe, Sutton

Chicago Rock Cafe offers a
blend of eating, drinking and
entertainment.

Throwley Road, Sutton SM1 1AD
☎ 020 8643 2606
@ sutton@chicago-rock-cafe.
co.uk
🌐 www.chicago-rock-cafe.co.uk
🖨 020 8770 0145
🔖 Page 209-F3

City Temple

Holborn Viaduct, London EC1A 2DE
☎ 0207 583 5532
🌐 www.city-temple.com
🖨 0207 353 1083
🔖 Page 12-A2

The Clapham Grand

With both modern and retro
design, the plush surroundings
of The Grand offer regular club
nights, a diverse mixture of up-
and-coming bands and comedy.

21–25 St John's Hill, Battersea,
London SW11 1TT
☎ 020 7223 6523
@ info@theclaphamgrand.com
🌐 www.theclaphamgrand.com
🔖 Page 140-C5

Clockwork

Clockwork, positioned on the
Angel high side of Pentonville
Road, hosts some of the best DJs
around with music's bigger names
playing in the clubroom. Also has
some of the finest up-and-coming
live acts on a variety of nights.

96–98 Pentonville Road, London
N1 9JB
☎ 020 7837 5387
@ clockworklondon@gmail.com
🌐 www.clockworkbar.co.uk/
🖨 020 7378 8221
🔖 Page 5-G3

The Club Bar and Dining

The Club Bar and Dining comprises
an informal bar and dining
room on the ground floor, and a
downstairs cocktail lounge bar
with a weekly open-mic acoustic
session.

21 Warwick Street, Soho, London
W1B 5NF
☎ 020 7734 1002
🌐 www.theclubbaranddining.
co.uk
🔖 Page 10-B5

The Cock Tavern

125 Kilburn High Road, London
NW6 6JH
☎ 0207 624 1820
🌐 www.cocktavern.com
🔖 Page 82-E6

The Constitution Pub

42 St Pancras Way, London
NW1 0QT
☎ 020 7387 4805
@ info@cellarbar.co.uk
🖰 Page 84-C5

The Coronet Theatre

26–28 New Kent Road, Elephant
and Castle, London SE1 6TJ
☎ 020 7701 1500
@ info@coronettheatre.co.uk
🖰 www.coronettheatre.co.uk
🖰 Page 18-D6

The Cross Kings

126 York Way, London N1 0AX
☎ 020 7278 8318
@ info@thecrosskings.co.uk
🖰 www.thecrosskings.co.uk
🖰 Page 5-F2

The Dalston Jazz Bar

4 Bradbury Street, Stoke
Newington, London N16 8JN
☎ 020 7254 9728
🖰 Page 86-A3

Darbucka World Music Bar

Darbucka provides a range of
entertainment to suit people
interested in global culture in an
Arabic setting serving a Lebanese
menu. Regular events include
house world music club nights, live
music from around the world and
belly-dancing classes.

182 St John Street, Clerkenwell,
London EC1V 4JZ
☎ 020 7490 8772
@ Darbuckaec1@yahoo.co.uk
🖰 www.darbucka.com
🖰 Page 5-K3

Dex Club

The same site has been a watering
hole for at least 300 years – the
present Prince of Wales art deco
building was constructed in 1938.
Re-launched as The Prince in
2005 and now firmly established
as Brixton's favourite pub with a
great atmosphere, food, drinks
and musical entertainment.

The Prince, 467–469 Brixton Road,
Stockwell, London SW9 8HH
☎ 020 7326 4455
🖰 www.dexclub.co.uk/
🖰 Page 142-B5

Dingwalls

A multipurpose venue that is home
to cafes, bars and a premier live
music and comedy club.

Middle Yard, Camden Lock,
London NW1 8AB
☎ 020 7428 0010
🖰 www.dingwalls.com
🖰 Page 84-B5

Dirty South

Dirty South is a place to party, to
see the buzziest new bands, enjoy
a late weekend night out or even
to come and jam on stage, open
mic style.

162 Lee High Road, Lewisham,
London SE13 5PR
☎ 020 8852 1267
@ info@brixtonjamm.org
🖰 www.dirtysouthlondon.com
🖰 Page 145-H5

Dover Street

The Dover Street Restaurant and
Jazz Bar offers a combination of
French and European cuisine and
nightly live music ranging from
jazz and blues to Latin and soul
with dancing to a resident DJ
until 3am.

8–10 Dover Street, Mayfair,
London W1S 4LQ
☎ 020 7629 9813, 020 7491 7509
🖰 www.doverst.co.uk
📠 020 7491 2958
🖰 Page 9-K6

The Dublin Castle

An internationally famous music
venue noteable for spearheading
various musical movements over
the last couple of decades.

94 Parkway, Camden, London
NW1 7AN
☎ 020 7485 1773, 020 8806 2668
🖰 Page 3-J1

Eel Pie Club

The club preserves and continues
the heritage of Rishmond R'n'B
in the area where it all began in
the 1960s Eel Pie Island. The club
is located above the Cabbage
Patch pub.

67 London Road, Twickenham
TW1 3SZ
☎ 020 8892 3874
🖰 www.eelpieclub.com/
🖰 Page 156-B2

Electric Ballroom

The Electric Ballroom is at the
heart of Camden Town's bustling
community and has been a key
part of it since its early days over
40 years ago. It began as a busy
Irish club playing host to a wide

variety of performers including the
likes of Jim Reeves.

184 Camden High Street, Camden
Town, London NW1 8QP
☎ 020 7485 9006
@ admin@electricballroom.co.uk
🖰 www.electricballroom.co.uk
📠 020 7284 0745
🖰 Page 84-B6

The Epicurean Lounge

10–11 Clerkenwell Green, London
EC1R 0DP
☎ 020 7490 5577
@ office@eplounge.com
🖰 www.eplounge.com
📠 020 7490 5557
🖰 Page 6-A7

Fairfield Halls and Ashcroft Theatre

Park Lane, Croydon, London
CR9 1DG
☎ 020 8681 0821
📞 020 8688 9291
@ boxoffice@fairfield.co.uk
🖰 www.fairfield.co.uk
🖰 Page 211-K1

The Fiddler's Elbow

1 Malden Road, London NW5 3HS
🖰 www.fiddlerselbow.piczo.com
🖰 Page 84-A4

The Fighting Cocks

During the 1950s the club
developed quite a following in jazz
circles, hosting many international
musicians.

56, Old London Road, Kingston
upon Thames KT2 6QA
☎ 020 8974 6469
@ jimbo66@blueyonder.co.uk
🖰 www.the-fighting-cocks.co.uk
🖰 Page 175-G5

Filthy Macnasty's Whiskey Cafe

68 Amwell Street, London
EC1R 1UU
☎ 020 7837 6067
@ veronica@filthymacnastys.com
🖰 www.filthymacnastys.com
🖰 Page 5-J4

Floridita

A Cuban bar with nightly live
music, and a contemporary
restaurant, serving a combination
of Cuban and Latin American
cuisine.

100 Wardour Street, London
W1F 0TN

☎ 020 7314 4000
@ info@floriditalondon.com
🖰 www.floridita.co.uk/london/
🖰 Page 10-B3

The Fly

36–38 New Oxford Street, London
WC1A 1EP
📞 0870 9070999
🖰 www.barflyclub.com
🖰 Page 10-E2

The Forum

9–17 Highgate Road, Kentish
Town, London NW5 1JY
☎ 020 7284 1001
🖰 www.meanfiddler.com
🖰 Page 84-B2

The Foundry

84 Great Eastern Street, London
EC2A 3JL
☎ 020 7739 6900
@ jonathan@foundry.tv
🖰 www.foundry.tv
🖰 Page 7-G6

The Fox & Firkin

316 Lewisham High Street,
Lewisham, London SE13 6JZ
☎ 020 8690 8925
🖰 Page 164-E1

The Gallery

10–11 Austin Friars, London
EC2N 2HG
📞 020 74969900
🖰 Page 13-F3

The Garage

20–22 Highbury Corner, London
N5 1RD
☎ 020 7607 1818
🖰 www.meanfiddler.com
🖰 Page 85-H3

The George Tavern

The George Tavern offers late
night disco with regular live music
and interactive art performances.

373 Commercial Road, Stepney,
London E1 0LA
☎ 020 7790 7335
🖰 Page 104-C5

Ginglik

Ginglik hosts alternative
events including electronic and
underground DJs, musicians
and bands with comedy nights,
film nights, exhibitions and video
installations.

1 Shepherd's Bush Green, Shepherds Bush, London W12 8PH
☎ 020 8749 2310
🖰 www.ginglik.co.uk
🖈 Page 119-F2

The Globe

104 Windmill Road, Brentford TW8 9NA
☎ 020 8580 0086
🖰 www.globemusiclondon.com/
📄 020 8580 2728
🖈 Page 116-D5

The Good Ship

The Good Ship is a bar, pub, club and music venue all rolled into one. Entertainment comes in the form of live bands of all types, pop quiz, general knowledge quiz, and DJs.

289 Kilburn High Road, Kilburn, London NW6 7JR
☎ 07949 008253
@ john@thegoodship.co.uk
🖰 www.thegoodship.co.uk
🖈 Page 82-E5

Gramaphone

Gramaphone is a bar, restaurant, lounge and live music venue.

60–62 Commercial Street, London E1 6LT
☎ 020 7377 5332
@ gramaphone@gmail.com
🖰 www.thegramaphone.co.uk
🖈 Page 13-J2

The Green Dragon

50–60 High Street, Croydon CR0 1NA
☎ 020 8667 0684
🖈 Page 211-J1

Green Note

Green Note offers folk, blues, world, jazz, country and bluegrass music.

106 Parkway, London NW1 7AN
☎ 020 7485 9899
@ mail@greennote.co.uk
🖰 www.greennote.co.uk
🖈 Page 3-J1

The Grey Horse

The Grey Horse hosts live music of all genres.

46 Richmond Road, Kingston upon Thames KT2 5EE
☎ 020 8541 4328
@ richard@grey-horse.co.uk
🖰 www.grey-horse.co.uk
🖈 Page 175-F4

The Grosvenor

As one of South London's premier live music venues, the Grosvenor hosts a scene ranging from rock and reggae, to dance, folk, punk, Brazilian and world music.

17 Sidney Road, Stockwell, London SW9 0TP
☎ 020 7733 1799
🖰 www.thegrosvenorsw9.co.uk/
🖈 Page 142-A3

Hackney Ocean

270 Mare Street, London E8 1HE
☎ 020 8533 0111
🖈 Page 86-D4

The Half Moon

Up-and-coming rock, roots and tribute bands.

10 Half Moon Lane, London SE24 9HU
☎ 0207 274 2733
🕿 0208 761 9078
🖰 www.halfmoonpub.co.uk
🖈 Page 162-E1

Halfmoon Putney

The famous Halfmoon Putney is one of London's longest running and most respected live music venues. Since the early 60s some of the biggest names in the music world have performed here.

93 Lower Richmond Road, London SW15 1EU
☎ 020 8780 9383
@ office@halfmoon.co.uk
🖰 www.halfmoon.co.uk
🖈 Page 139-F4

Halfway House

24 Priests Bridge, Barnes, London SW14 8TA
☎ 020 8878 3961
🖰 www.halfwayhousebarnes.co.uk
🖈 Page 138-B4

Hammersmith Apollo

First opened in 1932, The Hammersmith Apollo hosts large scale touring rock and pop bands as well as theatre productions.

Queen Caroline Street, London W6 9QH
☎ 0870 6063400
🖰 www.hammersmithapollo.net
🖈 Page 119-F5

Hard Rock Cafe London

150 Old Park Lane, Mayfair, London W1K 1QZ

☎ 020 7629 0382
@ London_sales@hardrock.com
🖰 www.hardrock.com
🖈 Page 15-J1

The Hideaway

114 Junction Road, Islington, London N19 5LB
☎ 020 7561 0779
@ info@thehideawaybar.co.uk
🖰 www.thehideawaybar.co.uk
🖈 Page 84-C1

The Hive

Brentford FC, Braemar Road, Brentford London TW8 0NT
☎ 020 8847 2511, 07966 167755
🖰 www.hivemusic.org/index.html
🖈 Page 116-E6

The Honor Oak

1 St German's Road, Forest Hill, London SE23 1RH
☎ 020 8690 8606
🖰 www.thehonoroak.com
🖈 Page 164-B3

Hootananny

Hootananny hosts cutting-edge Ceilidh music. The spotlit stage, candles on the table, wooden floorboards, Jacobite red and brown colours set the scene for the best fiddlers, pipe bands, drums, and Gaelic singers Scotland produces. Comedy nights every month.

95 Effra Road, Brixton, London SW2 1DF
☎ 08719 842688
🖰 www.musicisthebest.org/hoots/
🖈 Page 142-B5

Hope and Anchor

Its 70s pub rock/punk history is well documented as is it's involvement with Stiff Records and Elvis Costello/Clash manager Jake Riviera. A low, low ceiling, drum sound friendly brick back drop and punk rock vibe.

207 Upper Street, Islington, London N1 1RL
☎ 020 7354 1312
🖰 www.bugbearbookings.com/
🖈 Page 5-K2

Hoxton Square Bar & Kitchen

A 450-capacity live music venue, bar and restaurant.

2–4 Hoxton Square, Hoxton, London N1 6NU

☎ 020 7613 0709, 020 7613 1171
@ info@hoxtonsquarebar.com
📄 020 7613 1137
🖈 Page 7-G5

Jazz After Dark

This cocktail bar and restaurant in Soho hosts live jazz, blues and Latin gigs six nights a week.

9 Greek Street, Soho, London W1D 4DQ
🕿 020 7734 0545
🖰 www.jazzafterdark.co.uk
🖈 Page 10-D4

Jazz Cafe

Hosts a variety of live music events, with special emphasis on jazz, hip hop, soul and funk.

5 Parkway, Camden Town, London NW1 7PG
☎ 020 7916 6060
🖰 www.meanfiddler.com/
🖈 Page 84-B6

Jazz Cafe POSK

238–246 King Street, Hammersmith, London W6 0RF
☎ 020 8741 1940
@ jazzcafe@posk.org
🖰 www.jazzcafeposk.co.uk
🖈 Page 118-D4

Jazz at the Crypt

Located in the 300-year-old crypt of St Giles Church, Jazz at the Crypt offers live jazz every Friday.

St Giles Centre, 81 Camberwell Church Street, Camberwell, London SE5 8RB
☎ 020 7701 1016
@ lha@alphaplus.co.uk
🖰 www.jazzlive.co.uk
🖈 Page 142-E2

Kings College London Students' Union (KCLSU)

MacAdam Building, Surrey Street, Holborn, London WC2R 2NS
☎ 020 7848 1588, 020 7848 1566
@ enquiries@kclsu.org
🖰 www.kclsu.org
📄 020 7379 9833
🖈 Page 11-H5

Kingsmeadow

Kingsmeadow Stadium, Jack Goodchild Way, 422a Kingston Road, Kingston upon Thames KT1 3PB
☎ 020 8547 3335
🖰 www.kingsmeadowlive.com
🖈 Page 175-J6

KOKO

The newly renovated KOKO is a versatile, state-of-the-art venue, hosting comedy, rock, cabaret evenings and club nights.

1A Camden High Street, Camden, London NW1 7JE
☎ 0870 432 5527, 020 7334 3922
@ info@koko.uk.com
⌂ www.koko.uk.com
⊘ Page 4-A2

Lark in the Park

60 Copenhagen Street, Islington, London N1 0JW
☎ 0207 2785 781
@ thelark@tiscali.co.uk
⌂ www.larkinthepark.co.uk
⊘ Page 5-H1

Le Quecum Bar

A unique wine bar from a bygone era: pre-war France, with Hot Club gypsy jazz, invented by Django Reinhardt.

42–44 Battersea High Street, Battersea, London SW11 3HX
☎ 020 7787 2227
@ info@quecumbar.co.uk
⌂ www.quecumbar.co.uk
⊘ Page 140-C2

The Lion

27 Wick Road, Teddington TW11 9DN
☎ 020 8977 3199
@ ask@thelionpub.co.uk
⌂ www.thelionpub.co.uk
🖨 020 8977 6631
⊘ Page 174-C3

The Loaded Dog

The Loaded Dog offers showcase music like tributes, original unsigned, cover bands, jazz, R'n'B and also comedy nights.

485 High Road, Leytonstone, London E11 4PG
☎ 020 8556 6695
⌂ www.theloadeddog.co.uk
⊘ Page 88-C1

London Astoria

157 Charing Cross Road, Soho, London WC2 8EN
☎ 020 7434 9592
📞 0870 534 4444
@ astoria@meanfiddler.com
⌂ www.festivalrepublic.com/
⊘ Page 10-D5

Lord Rookwood

314 Cann Hall Road, Leytonstone, Wanstead, London E11 3NN
☎ 020 8519 0785
⊘ Page 88-D2

The Luminaire

311 Kilburn High Road, Kilburn, London NW6 7JR
☎ 020 7372 7123
@ info@theluminaire.co.uk
⌂ www.theluminaire.co.uk
🖨 020 7372 8558
⊘ Page 82-D5

The Macbeth

70 Hoxton Street, Shoreditch, London N1 6LP
☎ 020 7739 5095
⊘ Page 7-G5

Mick Jagger Centre

The Mick Jagger Centre is a live performance facility that aims to programme a high quality range of events and opportunities, in the performance, production and participation of music and the arts for the communities of Dartford and North Kent Region.

Shepherds Lane, Dartford DA1 2JZ
☎ 01322 291101
⌂ www.themickjaggercentre.com
⊘ Page 171-D3

The Miller of Mansfield

96 Snowsfields Road, London Bridge, Bermondsey, London SE1 3SS
☎ 020 7407 2690
@ mail@themiller.co.uk
⌂ www.themiller.co.uk
⊘ Page 18-F2

Millfield Arts Centre

Silver Street, Edmonton, Upper Edmonton, London N18 1PJ
☎ 020 8807 6680
@ info@millfieldtheatre.co.uk
⌂ www.millfieldtheatre.co.uk
🖨 020 8807 3892
⊘ Page 35-K6

Monkey Chews

2 Queens Crescent, Chalk Farm, Camden, London NW5 4EP
☎ 020 7267 6406
@ info@monkeychews.com
⌂ www.monkeychews.com
⊘ Page 84-A4

The Montague Arms

The Montague Arms is an old-fashioned pub that serves food and hosts live music events.

289 Queens Road, New Cross, London SE15 2PA
☎ 020 7639 4923
⊘ Page 143-K2

Monto Water Rats Theatre

328 Grays Inn Road, Kings Cross, St Pancras, London WC1X 8BZ
☎ 020 7813 1079
@ info@themonto.com
⌂ www.themonto.com
⊘ Page 5-F4

Nambucca

596 Holloway Road, London N7 6LB
☎ 020 7272 7366
⊘ Page 85-F2

New Cross Inn

323 New Cross Road, London SE14 6AS
☎ 020 8691 7222, 020 8692 1866
⊘ Page 144-C1

Notting Hill Arts Club

Well-established in London's music scene, the Notting Hill Arts Club specialises in underground and experimental club and music nights.

21 Notting Hill Gate, Kensington, London W11 3JQ
☎ 020 7460 4459
@ info@nottinghillartsclub.com
⌂ www.nottinghillartsclub.com
⊘ Page 100-E6

The O2

The O2 is one of London's largest entertainment venues, centred around its indoor music and sports arena.

Millennium Way, Greenwich, London SE10 0BB
📞 0871 984 0002
⌂ www.theo2.co.uk
⊘ Page 125-H2

Octave

Octave hosts both established and up-and-coming jazz artists.

27–29 Endell Street, Covent Garden, London WC2H 9BA
☎ 0207 836 4616
@ office@octave8.com
⌂ www.octave8.com/index.php
⊘ Page 10-E3

Old Blue Last

39 Great Eastern Street, London EC2A 3ES
☎ 020 7739 7033
⌂ www.theoldbluelast.com
⊘ Page 7-G6

The Old Tiger's Head

351 Lee High Road, Lee Green, London SE12 8RU
☎ 020 8244 2014
@ adrian.straatman@ntlworld.com
⊘ Page 145-H5

Orpington Folk Club

Change of Horses, 87 Farnborough High Street, Farnborough Village, Orpington BR6 7BB
☎ 01689 852949
@ orpingtonfolkclub@hotmail.com
⌂ www.orpingtonfolkclub.fsnet.co.uk
⊘ Page 202-C4

Parker McMillan

Parker McMillan hosts young musicians from The Guildhall School of Music, as well as open mic nights, jam nights and DJ sets.

47 Chiswell Street, London EC1Y 4SB
☎ 020 7256 5883
@ info@parkermcmillan.co.uk
⌂ www.parkermcmillan.co.uk
🖨 020 7256 9532
⊘ Page 12-E1

The Peel

Peelmuzik promotions are committed to providing the best new talent and classic acts in live rock music entertainment. They support the live scene and promote rock punk metal and hardcore bands from the UK and abroad.

160 Cambridge Road, Kingston upon Thames KT1 3HH
☎ 020 8546 3516, 020 8255 8104
⌂ www.peelmuzik.com
🖨 08707 058653
⊘ Page 175-H5

Pigalle Club

The Pigalle Club offers club nights and gigs in the decadent surroundings of a bygone era.

215 Piccadilly, Soho, London W1J 9HN

☎ 020 7734 8142
@ pigalle@vpmg.net
🖳 www.thepigalleclub.com
🖹 020 7494 2022
🌐 Page 10-A7

Pizza Express Jazz Club

Jazz has been a part of the Pizza Express group owing to the love of this music by Company founder Peter Boizot MBE. This acclaimed jazz venue attracts everyone from international stars such as Van Morrison and Diana Krall to up- and-coming national talent.

10 Dean Street, Soho, London W1V 5RL
☎ 020 7734 3220
@ jazz@pizzaexpress.co.uk
🖳 www.pizzaexpresslive.co.uk/
🌐 Page 10-C3

Plan B

418 Brixton Road, London SW9 7AY
☎ 0870 116 5421
@ info@plan-brixton.co.uk
🖳 www.plan-brixton.co.uk
🖹 020 7924 0678
🌐 Page 142-B5

Plastic Red

101 Station Road, Sidcup DA15 7BS
☎ 020 8300 0855
🖳 www.plasticred.com
🌐 Page 168-B4

The Plough Inn

The Plough Inn aims to provide a unique mix of live entertainment including music, comedy, theatre shows and special cinema screenings.

173 Wood Street, Walthamstow London E17 3NU
☎ 020 8503 7419
🖳 www.theploughinne17.co.uk
🌐 Page 52-A6

The Pool

The Pool hosts live music and DJ nights along with regular film screenings.

104–108 Curtain Road, Shoreditch, London EC2A 3AH
☎ 020 7739 9608
@ mail@thepool.uk.com
🖳 www.thepool.uk.com
🌐 Page 7-G7

Portobello Gold

95–97 Portobello Road, Notting Hill, London W11 2QB

☎ 020 7460 4910, 0845 066 0666
@ enquiries@portobellogold.com
🖳 www.portobellogold.com/
🖹 020 7229 2278
🌐 Page 100-C4

Power's Acoustic Room

Intimate live music venue showcasing the very best in up- and-coming new folk, roots, soul and acoustic acts.

332 Kilburn High Road, London NW6 2QN
☎ 020 7372 4598
@ powersacousticroom@ vpmg.net
🖳 www.powersacousticroom.com
🌐 Page 82-E6

Proud, Camden

Hosts landmark photographic shows on historical, musical and political themes. The venue also hosts weekly indie club and band nights.

The Gin House, The Stables Market, Chalk Farm Road, Camden, London NW1 8AH
☎ 020 7482 3867
@ kate@proud.co.uk
🖳 www.proud.co.uk
🌐 Page 84-A5

Punk

14 Soho Street, London W1D 3DN
☎ 020 7734 4004
@ selina@thebreakfastgroup. co.uk
🖳 www.fabbars.com
🌐 Page 10-C3

Purcell Room

As part of the Royal Festival Hall arts complex, the Purcell Room hosts contemporary dance, music theatre, chamber music, solo recitals, world music, poetry events and live art.

South Bank Centre, London SE1 8XX
☎ 0870 380 0400
🖳 www.southbankcentre.co.uk
🌐 Page 17-G1

Purple Turtle Camden

Situated in the heart of London, this venue brings together the best of London's nocturnal talent. A variety of nights ensure that, no matter what your taste, the Turtle has something to offer.

61–65 Crowndale Road, Camden, London NW1 1TN

☎ 020 7383 4976
@ camden@purpleturtlebar.com
🖳 www.purpleturtlebar.com
🌐 Page 4-B2

Queen Charlotte Hall

Parkshot Centre, Parkshot, Richmond upon Thames TW9 2RE
☎ 020 8843 7921
🌐 Page 136-E5

Queen Elizabeth Hall

The Queen Elizabeth Hall, seating 917, is a part of Royal Festival Hall complex hosting contemporary dance, music theatre, chamber music, solo recitals, world music, poetry events and live art.

South Bank Centre, Belvedere Road, London SE1 8XX
☎ 0870 380 4300
📞 0870 401 8181
@ customer@rfh.org.uk
🖳 www.rfh.org.uk
🌐 Page 11-G7

Ram Jam Club

Exciting live music venue.

46 Richmond Road, Kingston upon Thames KT2 5EE
☎ 0208 549 8709
@ ramjamclub@grey-horse.co.uk
🖳 www.grey-horse.co.uk/rjc/
🌐 Page 174-E1

The Redchurch

107 Redchurch Street, Shoreditch, London E2 7DL
☎ 020 7729 8333
@ info@theredchurch.co.uk
🖳 www.theredchurch.co.uk/
🌐 Page 7-J6

The Regal Room at The Distillers

Opened in late 2006, The Regal Room at The Distillers is home to live acoustic music, comedy and other events.

64–66 Fulham Palace Road, London W6 9PH
☎ 020 8748 2834
🖳 www.theregalroom.com
🌐 Page 119-F5

The Roadhouse

35 The Piazza, Covent Garden Market, London WC2E 8BE
☎ 020 7240 6001
@ bookings@roadhouse.co.uk
🖳 www.roadhouse.co.uk
🌐 Page 11-F5

Ronnie Scott's Jazz Club

First opened in 1959, London's famous jazz club offers a varied daily programme of jazz performers, from established international artists to homegrown talent.

47 Frith Street, Soho, London W1D 4HT
☎ 020 7439 0747
@ ronniescotts@ronniescotts. co.uk
🖳 www.ronniescotts.co.uk
🖹 020 7437 5081
🌐 Page 10-C4

The Roundhouse

The Roundhouse presents a varied programme of international performing arts including music, theatre, dance, circus and digital media to reflect the excitement and diversity of 21st-century culture.

Chalk Farm Road, London NW1 8EH
☎ 020 7424 9991
📞 087 0389 1846
@ info@roundhouse.org.uk
🖳 www.roundhouse.org.uk
🖹 020 7424 9992
🌐 Page 84-A5

Royal Albert Hall

The oval-shaped Royal Albert Hall hosts a diverse range of events including classical and rock concerts, conferences, ballroom dancing, poetry recitals, ballet, opera and sporting events such as tennis and boxing. It is most well-known for holding the annual classical music festival The Proms.

Kensington Gore, South Kensington, London SW7 2AP
☎ 020 7838 3110
📞 020 7589 8212
@ access@royalalberthall.com
🖳 www.royalalberthall.com
🌐 Page 14-A3

Royal Festival Hall

The Royal Festival Hall stands at the heart of Southbank Centre complex. Opened in 1951 as part of the Festival of Britain, the hall is one of the world's leading concert venues, presenting concerts by the finest international orchestras, operas, and a wide spread of contemporary music events, from jazz to world, to rock and pop music.

Belvedere Road, London SE1 8XX

☎ 0870 380 4300
@ customer@southbankcentre.
co.uk
🖰 www.southbankcentre.co.uk
🖹 0870 163 3898
🖉 Page 11-G7

Ruskin Arms

Ruskin Arms presents innovative
rock and metal nights for
both live bands and DJ based
performances. Many heavy rock
legends have played here: Iron
Maiden, Genesis, Paul Di'Anno and
many more.

386 High Street North, Manor Park
London E12 6PH
☎ 020 8472 0377, 07957 942242
🖰 www.ruskinarms.co.uk
🖉 Page 89-J4

Ryan's Bar

181 Church Street, London
N16 0UL
☎ 020 7252 7807
🖉 Page 85-K1

Scala

Scala is a popular venue for live
music on week nights.

275 Pentonville Road, Kings Cross,
London N1 9NL
☎ 020 7833 2022
@ reception@scala-london.co.uk
🖰 www.scala-london.co.uk
🖉 Page 5-G3

The Scoop

The Scoop is an open-air sunken
amphitheatre with an events
programme featuring a wide
variety of professional theatre,
street performance, film, music,
dance and visual arts.

More London Riverside,
Bermondsey, London SE1 2DB
☎ 020 7403 4866
@ cbryant-fenn@
morelondonestates.co.uk
🖰 www.morelondon.com/scoop.
html
🖹 020 7403 4867
🖉 Page 19-H1

Shepherd's Bush Empire

Shepherds Bush Green, Shepherds
Bush, London W12 8TT
☎ 020 8354 3300
@ mail@shepherds-bush-empire.
co.uk
🖰 www.shepherds-bush-empire.
co.uk
🖉 Page 119-F2

The Slaughtered Lamb

34–35 Great Sutton Street,
London EC1V 0DX
🖰 www.electroacousticclub.com
🖉 Page 6-B7

Spice of Life

6 Moor Street, Cambridge Circus,
Soho, London W1D 5NA
☎ 020 7437 7013
@ info@spiceoflifesoho.com
🖰 www.spiceoflifesoho.com
🖉 Page 10-D4

The Spitz

The Spitz presents cutting-edge,
cross-genre music from around
the world.

109 Commercial Street, Old
Spitalfields Market, London
E1 6BG
☎ 020 7247 9747, 020 7392 9032
@ mail@spitz.co.uk
🖰 www.spitz.co.uk
🖉 Page 13-J2

The Spotted Dog

38 Willesden High Road, London
NW10 2QD
☎ 02084 592220
🖉 Page 81-K4

St Giles in the Fields Church

A regular series of lunchtime
recitals is arranged by organist
and Director of Music, Jonathan
Bunney for both the Spring and
Autumn. The varied programme
includes both secular and sacred
music.

60 St Giles High Street, Covent
Garden, London WC2H 8LG
☎ 020 7240 2532
@ verger.giles@btopenworld.com
🖰 www.stgilesonline.org
🖉 Page 10-D3

St Martin-in-the-Fields

In addition to daily worship
services, the church holds
lunchtime and evening classical
concerts. The renowned crypt and
cafe holds regular jazz nights.

Trafalgar Square, Charing Cross,
London WC2N 4JJ
☎ 020 776 61100
@ info@smitf.org
🖰 www.st-martin-in-the-fields.org
🖉 Page 10-E6

The Standard

1 Blackhorse Lane, Walthamstow,
London E17 6DS

☎ 020 8503 2523
@ thestandard@btinternet.com
🖰 www.standardmusicvenue.
co.uk
🖉 Page 51-F6

Storm

28a Leicester Square, London
WC2H 7LE
☎ 020 7839 2633
@ info@stormnightclub.co.uk
🖰 www.stormnightclub.co.uk
🖉 Page 10-D6

Stratford Rex

361–373 High Street, Stratford,
London E15 4SB
☎ 020 8215 6003
🖉 Page 88-B5

The Telegraph Pub

Telegraph Road, Putney Heath,
Roehampton, London SW15 3TU
☎ 020 8788 2011
@ telegraph@massivepub.com
🖰 www.massivepub.com
🖉 Page 159-F2

Theatre Royal Stratford East

Gerry Raffles Square, Stratford,
London E15 1BN
☎ 020 8534 7374
📞 0800 183 1188
@ theatreroyal@stratfordeast.
com
🖰 www.stratfordeast.com
🖹 020 8534 8381
🖉 Page 88-B4

Thirst

Live DJs six nights a week.

53 Greek Street, Soho, London
W1D 3DR
☎ 020 7437 1977
@ soho@thirstbar.com
🖰 www.thirstbar.com
🖉 Page 10-D4

Tonky Gorilla

A bar-restaurant with regular club
and live music nights.

539–541 Kingsbury High Road,
Kingsbury, London NW9 9EG
☎ 020 8204 7000
@ info@tonkygorilla.com
🖰 www.tonkygorilla.com
🖉 Page 62-C2

The Troubadour Club

The club hosts a mixed
programme of blues, R'n'B, funk,
indie, and acoustic artists.

263–267 Old Brompton Road,

London SW5 9JA
☎ 020 7370 1434
@ simonandsusie@troubadour.
co.uk
🖰 www.troubadour.co.uk
🖹 020 7341 6329
🖉 Page 120-A5

Troxy

490 Commercial Road, London
E1 0HX
☎ 020 7790 9000
📞 020 7748 2728
@ info@troxy.co.uk
🖰 www.troxy.co.uk
🖉 Page 104-C5

Troy Bar

10 Hoxton Street, London N1 6NG
📞 02077396695
🖉 Page 7-G1

Tufnell's

162 Tufnell Park Road, London
N7 0EE
☎ 020 727 22078
🖉 Page 84-D2

The Turks Head

28 Winchester Road, St Margarets,
Twickenham TW1 1LF
☎ 020 8892 1972
🖉 Page 156-C1

Under The Westway

242 Acklam Road, Westbourne
Studios, Ladbroke Grove, London
W10 5JJ
📞 020 7575 3123
@ info@underthewestway.com
🖰 www.underthewestway.co.uk
🖉 Page 100-D4

The Underworld

This Camden institution provides
a stage for established and up-
and-coming indie, rock and metal
bands, as well as hosting regular
indie club nights.

174 Camden High Street, Camden,
London NW1 0NE
☎ 020 7482 1932
@ contact@theunderworld
camden.com
🖰 www.theunderworldcamden.
co.uk
🖉 Page 4-A1

Union Chapel

The Vestry, Compton Avenue,
London N1 2XD
☎ 020 7226 3750
@ arts@unionchapel.org.uk

⌂ www.unionchapel.org.uk
✎ Page 85-H4

The University of London Union (ULU)

Malet Street, Bloomsbury, London
WC1E 7HY
☎ 020 7664 2000
@ general@ulu.lon.ac.uk
⌂ www.barflyclub.com/
🖹 020 7436 4606
✎ Page 4-C7

The Vera Fletcher Hall

The Vera Fletcher Hall was built in 1887 to commemorate Queen Victoria's Golden Jubilee. The Hall has facilities to host theatre, concert hall and pocket opera by night.

4 Ember Court Road, Thames
Ditton KT7 0LP
☎ 020 8873 7393
℧ 01372 462078
⌂ www.verafletcherhall.co.uk
✎ Page 189-K3

Vibe Bar

The Old Truman Brewery, 91 Brick
Lane, London E1 6QL
☎ 020 7426 0491
@ info@vibe-bar.co.uk
⌂ www.vibe-bar.co.uk
✎ Page 7-J7

Viva Viva

A restaurant and bar with entertainment every night of the week. Each month local musicians and nationally respected artists performing a wide variety of music from all over the world. This includes salsa, latin, jazz, world acoustic and singer song-writer nights.

18 High Street, Hornsey, London
N8 7PB
☎ 020 8341 0999
@ info@viva-viva.co.uk
⌂ www.viva-viva.co.uk
✎ Page 66-E1

Volstead

The Volstead is a lounge bar that re-creates the atmosphere of the swinging 1920s. Mirrored walls, a retro cocktail list and swing music will all help to bring you back to the jazz age.

9 Swallow Street, London
W1R 7HD
☎ 020 7287 1919
⌂ www.volstead.com
✎ Page 10-B6

The Vortex Jazz Club

At it's old location in Stoke Newington, The Vortex was considered by many to be London's oldest jazz club. Despite moving to new premises around the corner, the club hasn't lost its magic and still manages to attract many legendary jazz, blues and soul stars.

11 Gillett Street, Stoke Newington,
London N16 8JN
☎ 020 7254 4097, 020 7993 3643
@ info@vortexjazz.co.uk
⌂ www.vortexjazz.co.uk
✎ Page 86-A3

The Waggon

107 Chase Side, Southgate,
London N14 5HD
@ info@thewaggonsouthgate.co.uk
⌂ www.thewaggonsouthgate.co.uk
🖹 020 8882 0592
✎ Page 34-B2

Walthamstow Assembly Hall

This imposing art deco building set in the Town Hall Complex, hosts concerts, exhibitions and other major events. Its acoustics also make it a venue for recording classical music.

Forest Road, Walthamstow,
London E17 4SY
℧ 020 8496 3000
✎ Page 51-K6

Walthamstow Folk Club

The Plough Inn, 173 Wood Street,
Walthamstow, London E17 3NU
☎ 020 8257 8767
@ info@walthamstowfolk.co.uk
⌂ www.walthamstowfolk.co.uk
✎ Page 52-A6

Wembley Arena

Wembley Arena is one of the most famous indoor concert halls in the world, attracting a variety of superstar performers. Following a £35m refurbishment the Arena reopened in April 2006.

Arena Square, Wembley HA9 0DH
☎ 020 8902 8833
@ contacts@wembley.co.uk
⌂ www.livenation.co.uk/
✎ Page 80-C2

Wembley Stadium

Wembley Stadium has been a world stage for sporting and music

events ever since the 1880s. After a period of renovation starting in 2002, the newly-designed stadium now offers a range of facilities and cutting-edge technologies.

Empire Way, Wembley, London
HA9 0WS
☎ 020 8795 9000
@ info@wembleystadium.com
⌂ www.wembleystadium.com
🖹 020 8795 5050
✎ Page 80-C2

The White Lion

Refurbished pub offering a roster of regular and monthly DJ and band-led evening events.

232 Streatham High Road,
Streatham, London SW16 2BB
☎ 020 8677 3341
⌂ www.thewhitelion.co.uk
✎ Page 161-K6

The Wilmington

With a packed menu for live music, bands play every Thursday, Friday and Saturday nights.

69 Roseberry Avenue, London
EC1R 4RL
☎ 020 7837 1384
⌂ www.upallnightmusic.com/
✎ Page 5-J7

Wimbledon Po Na Na

Wimbledon has built a strong reputation as a venue to hear great music and see high profile DJs. Downstairs you can find a collection of mellow alcoves to chill in before strutting your stuff on the dance floor.

82 The Broadway, Wimbledon,
London SW19 1RH
☎ 020 8540 1616
@ wimbledonpnn@ponana.com
⌂ www.ponana.com/
🖹 020 8540 1617
✎ Page 177-J2

The Windmill

The live music pub has been namechecked over the airwaves by XFMs John Kennedy and Radios 1s Steve Lamacq.

22 Blenheim Gardens, Brixton,
London SW2 5BZ
☎ 020 8671 0700
@ windmillbrixton@yahoo.co.uk
⌂ www.windmillbrixton.co.uk
✎ Page 162-A1

Windsor Castle Pub

358 Carshalton Road, Carshalton
SM5 3PD

☎ 020 8669 1191
@ pam@windsorcastlepub.com
⌂ www.windsorcastlepub.com
✎ Page 209-G3

The Yacht

Temple Pier, Victoria Embankment,
London WC2R 2PN
☎ 020 7836 1566
℧ 0871 332 3603
⌂ www.theyachtclub.co.uk
✎ Page 11-J5

Yates, Leicester Square

Yates is a successful bar chain that holds regular music events.

30 Leicester Square, London
WC2H 7JZ
☎ 020 7839 7967
@ Yates.LeicesterSquare@
laurelpubco.com
⌂ www.yatesinthewestend.com
✎ Page 10-D6

Zavvi

14–16 Oxford Street, London
W1D 1AR
☎ 020 7631 1234
⌂ www.zavvi.co.uk
✎ Page 10-C3

indigO2

State-of-the-art indigO2 venue is part of the multi-million pound redevelopment of The O2, formerly the Millennium Dome. Located in the heart of London, this new 2,350-capacity venue holds large touring music acts as well as regular club nights.

Millennium Way, Greenwich,
London SE10 0AX
℧ 0844 844 0002
⌂ www.theindigo2.co.uk
✎ Page 125-H1

COMEDY CLUBS AND VENUES

The Adelaide

143 Adelaide Road, Primrose Hill,
Hampstead, London NW3 3NL
☎ 020 7633 9539
✎ Page 83-K5

Arts Theatre

A West End venue presenting a variety of music, comedy and theatre.

6–7 Great Newport Street,
Leicester Square, Covent Garden,
London WC2H 7JB

☎ 020 7836 2132
⌁ www.artstheatrelondon.com
⊘ Page 10-D5

Bar FM

184 Hopgood Street, Shepherds
Bush, London W12 7JU
☏ 07870 212189
@ rmajendie@knock2bag.co.uk
⊘ Page 119-F1

Battersea Barge

Nine Elms Lane, London SW8 5BP
☎ 020 7498 0004
@ info@batterseabarge.com
⌁ www.batterseabarge.com
⊘ Page 121-H6

Bearcat Comedy Club at The Turk's Head

Winchester Road, St Margaret's,
Twickenham TW1 1LF
☏ 020 8891 1852
@ jamespunnett@
bearcatcomedy.co.uk
⌁ www.bearcatcomedy.co.uk
⊘ Page 156-C1

The Bedford

The Bedford hosts an eclectic
selection of events and
entertainment including comedy,
music, dance, poetry and classical
events.

77 Bedford Hill, Balham, London
SW12 9HD
☎ 020 8682 8940
@ info@thebedford.co.uk
⌁ www.thebedford.co.uk
▤ 020 8682 8959
⊘ Page 161-G4

The Blue Posts

Stand up comedy is held here
every Monday night, featuring a
top selection of comedians, and
the best newer acts from the
comedy circuit.

18 Kingly Street, Soho, London
W1B 5PX
☏ 07796 171190
@ bp@laughinghorse.co.uk
⌁ www.laughinghorse.co.uk/
oxfordcircus.htm
⊘ Page 10-A4

The Britannia

5 Brewers Lane, Richmond TW9
1HH
☏ 07796 171190
@ brit@laughinghorse.co.uk
⌁ www.laughinghorse.co.uk
⊘ Page 136-E6

The Broadway Theatre

Originally opened in 1932 the
venue is a listed Grade 11 example
of 1930s art deco architecture. The
theatre includes two venues: the
Main Theatre seating 800 and the
Studio Theatre seating 100.

Catford Broadway, Catford,
London SE6 4RU
☎ 020 8690 0002
@ boxoffice@broadwaytheatre.
org.uk
⌁ www.broadwaytheatre.org.uk
⊘ Page 164-E2

Bromley Comedy Club

Churchill Theatre, Studio Bar, High
Street, Bromley BR1 1HA
☎ 020 8291 5259
@ mike@bromleycomedy.com
⌁ www.bromleycomedy.com
▤ 020 8460 3654
⊘ Page 183-K5

The Camden Head

Popular Islington pub dating back
to the 1880s, hosting a wide range
of regular comedy and spoken
word nights upstairs.

2 Camden Walk, Camden Passage,
Camden, London N1 8DY
☎ 020 7359 0851
⊘ Page 6-A2

Canal Cafe Theatre

Based above the Bridge House
Pub, the Canal Cafe is a fringe
theatre venue with a reputation
for comedy and new writing. It
is also home to NewsRevue, the
Guinness World Record Holder for
the world's longest running live
comedy show.

The Bridge House, Delamere
Terrace, London W2 6ND
☎ 020 7289 6056
@ mail@canalcafetheatre.com
⌁ www.canalcafetheatre.com
⊘ Page 101-G4

The Clapham Grand

With both modern and retro decor,
The Grand offers regular club
nights, a diverse mixture of up-
and-coming bands and comedy.

21–25 St John's Hill, Battersea
London SW11 1TT
☎ 020 7223 6523
@ info@theclaphamgrand.com
⌁ www.theclaphamgrand.com
⊘ Page 140-D5

The Coach and Horses

1 Great Marlborough Street, Soho,
London W1F 7HG
☏ 07796 171190
@ canh@laughinghorse.co.uk
⌁ www.laughinghorse.co.uk
⊘ Page 10-A4

The Cock Tavern

125 Kilburn High Road, London
NW6 6JH
☎ 0207 624 1820
⌁ www.cocktavern.com
⊘ Page 82-E6

The Comedy Bunker

The Mill House, Ruislip Golf
Centre, Ickenham Road, Ruislip
HA4 7DQ
☎ 020 8421 1141
@ comedy@comedybunker.co.uk
⌁ www.comedybunker.co.uk
⊘ Page 58-A6

Comedy Cafe

66–68 Rivington Street, London
EC2A 3AY
☎ 020 7739 5706
@ info@comedycafe.co.uk
⌁ www.comedycafe.co.uk
▤ 020 7256 1242
⊘ Page 7-H5

The Comedy Store, London

1a Oxendon Street, St James's,
London SW1Y 4EE
☎ 020 7839 6642
⌁ www.thecomedystore.co.uk
▤ 020 7930 2951
⊘ Page 10-C6

The Comedy Tree at Walkabout Putney

The Comedy Tree opened in 2002
in Putney and was the brainchild
of comics Pete Jonas and Erich
McElroy.

14–16 Putney High Street, Putney,
London SW15 1SL
☎ 020 7938 4355, 020 7736 1446
@ info@thecomedytree.com
⌁ www.thecomedytree.com
⊘ Page 139-H5

Covent Garden Comedy Club

The Covent Garden Comedy
Club prides itself on being the
fastest growing comedy club in
London. The club has twice had
to move to bigger venues to cope
with demand and 40 percent of
every audience are regulars. The
success of the club is perhaps
due to a professional, friendly

and exciting atmosphere. Picking
talent from the international
circuit, many of whom are stars
of radio and television, the
comedians only perform at the
club a few times a year to ensure
every show is different.

The Arches, off Villiers Street,
Charing Cross, London WC2N 6NG
☏ 07960 071340
⌁ www.coventgardencomedy.com
⊘ Page 10-E6

The Cricketers

20 Fairfield South, Kingston upon
Thames KT1 2UL
☎ 020 8296 0479
@ crick@aughinghorse.co.uk
⌁ www.laughinghorse.co.uk
⊘ Page 175-G5

The Cross Kings

126 York Way, London N1 0AX
☎ 020 7278 8318
@ info@thecrosskings.co.uk
⌁ www.thecrosskings.co.uk
⊘ Page 5-F2

Crystal

57b Woodland Road, Crystal
Palace, London SE19 1TS
⊘ Page 181-F1

Downstairs At The King's Head

2 Crouch End Hill, London N8 8AA
☎ 020 8340 1028
@ admin@downstairsat
thekingshead.com
⌁ www.downstairsat
thekingshead.com
⊘ Page 66-D4

EDComedy

EDComedy was set up by a group
of actors who wanted to create a
local theatre in which to perform
and showcase new plays and
playwrights. The comedy club
started as a way of earning funds
to put on these plays. It also
started the All New Stand Up
Show which was a open mic night
where some of the newer comics
learn their trade, and some of the
more established acts come and
try out new material.

The Hob, 7 Devonshire Road,
Forest Hill, London SE23 3HE
☎ 020 8855 0496
@ info@edcomedy.com
⌁ www.edcomedy.com
⊘ Page 164-A2

Ealing Studios
Stage 5, the live venue, hosts comedy evenings.

Ealing Green, London W5 5EP
☎ 020 8567 6655
@ info@ealingstudios.com
🖰 www.ealingstudios.co.uk/
🖹 020 8758 8658
🗺 Page 116-E1

East Dulwich Tavern
1 Lordship Lane, East Dulwich, London SE22 8EW
☎ 020 8693 1316
🗺 Page 163-G1

Essex Serpent
6 King Street, London WC2E 8HN
☎ 020 7240 0302, 0871 984 1253
🖰 www.faucetinn.com
🗺 Page 10-E5

Fairfield Halls and Ashcroft Theatre
Park Lane, Croydon CR9 1DG
☎ 020 8681 0821
☎ 020 8688 9291
@ boxoffice@fairfield.co.uk
🖰 www.fairfield.co.uk
🗺 Page 211-K1

Fitzroy Tavern
Pear Shaped in Fitzrovia (London's Silliest Comedy Club) has been running every week at The Fitzroy Tavern in Central London for the last five years.

16 Charlotte Street, London W1T 2NA
☎ 020 7580 3714
🖰 www.pearshapedcomedy.com
🗺 Page 10-B1

The Fox
413 Green Lanes, Palmers Green, London N13 4JD
☎ 020 8450 4100
🗺 Page 49-F1

The Fym Fyg Bar
231 Cambridge Heath Road, London E2 0EL
☎ 020 7613 1057
🖰 www.thefymfygbar.com
🗺 Page 104-D2

Ginglik
Ginglik hosts alternative events including electronic and underground DJs, musicians and bands with comedy nights, film nights, exhibitions and video installations.

1 Shepherd's Bush Green, Shepherds Bush, London W12 8PH
☎ 020 8749 2310
🖰 www.ginglik.co.uk
🗺 Page 119-G2

Gramaphone
60–62 Commercial Street, London E1 6LT
☎ 020 7377 5332
@ gramaphone@gmail.com
🖰 www.thegramaphone.co.uk
🗺 Page 13-J2

The Grey Goose
Formerly the Smoke Rooms. Hosting the Clapham Comedy Club a friendly and intimate comedy club run by Electric Mouse.

100 Clapham Park Road, Clapham, London SW4 7BZ
☎ 020 7720 8902
@ smokerooms@hotmail.co.uk
🖰 www.smokeroomsclapham.com
🗺 Page 141-J5

Hen and Chickens Theatre
A fringe venue focusing on new theatre writing and comedy.

109 St Pauls Road, Islington, London N1 2NA
☎ 020 7704 2001
@ james@henandchickens.com
🖰 www.henandchickens.com
🗺 Page 85-J4

The Islington Tap
80 Liverpool Road, Islington, London N1 0QD
☎ 07796 171190
@ info@laughinghorse.co.uk
🖰 www.laughinghorse.co.uk
🗺 Page 85-G6

Jongleurs Battersea
49 Lavender Gardens, Battersea, London SW11 1DJ
☎ 0870 011 1965, 0870 787 0707
@ enquiries@jongleurs.com
🖰 www.jongleurs.com
🗺 Page 140-E5

Jongleurs Bow
Bow Wharf, 221 Grove Road, London E3 1AA
☎ 0870 011 1965 , 0870 787 0707
@ enquiries@jongleurs.com
🖰 www.jongleurs.com
🗺 Page 105-G1

Jongleurs Camden
11 East Yard, Camden Lock, Camden, London NW1 8AB
☎ 0870 787 0707, 0870 011 1960

@ enquiries@corporate. jongleurs.com
🖰 www.jongleurs.com
🗺 Page 84-B5

The King's Head
84 Upper Tooting Road, Tooting, London SW17 7PB
☎ 020 8767 6708
🗺 Page 160-E6

LSE Bar
Clare Market Building, Houghton Street, Aldwych, Holborn, London WC2A 2AD
☎ 020 7476 1672
🖰 lse.ac.uk
🗺 Page 11-H4

The Leather Exchange Piano Bar
15 Leathermarket Street, Bermondsey, London SE1 3HN
☎ 020 7407 0295
🖰 www.leather-exchange.com
🗺 Page 19-G3

The Liberties Bar
100 Camden High Street, Camden Town, Camden, London NW1 0LU
☎ 07796 171190
@ lib@laughinghorse.co.uk
🖰 www.laughinghorse.co.uk/
🗺 Page 4-A1

The Long Acre Pub
1–3 Long Acre, Covent Garden, London WC2E 9LH
☎ 020 7520 6920
@ reservations@thelongacre. co.uk
🖰 www.thelongacre.co.uk
🖹 020 7520 6922
🗺 Page 10-E5

Lowdown at the Albany
Comedy and theatre venue.

240 Great Portland Street, London W1W 5QU
☎ 020 7387 5706
@ james@lowdownatthealbany. com
🖰 www.lowdownatthealbany.com
🗺 Page 9-K1

The Miller of Mansfield
96 Snowsfields Road, London Bridge, Bermondsey, London SE1 3SS
☎ 020 7407 2690
@ mail@themiller.co.uk
🖰 www.themiller.co.uk
🗺 Page 19-F2

O'Reilly's
289–291 Kentish Town Road, Camden, London NW5 2JS
☎ 08713 324427
☎ 07932 338203
🖰 www.monkeybusiness comedyclub.co.uk/
🗺 Page 84-B4

The Old English Gentleman
Stand up comedy featuring a selection of comedians and the newer acts from the comedy circuit.

132 Edgware Road, London W2 2DZ
☎ 020 7723 6433
@ OEG@laughinghorse.co.uk
🖰 www.laughinghorse.co.uk/ edgwareroad.htm
🗺 Page 2-A7

The Old Fire Station
55 High Street, Brentford TW8 0AH
☎ 020 8568 5999
@ triple9@the-firestation.co.uk
🖰 www.the-firestation.co.uk
🗺 Page 116-E6

The Quad
Houghton Street, London WC2A 2AD
☎ 020 7955 7136
🗺 Page 11-H4

Red Lion
20 Great Windmill Street, London W1D 7LA
☎ 020 7479 7611
🗺 Page 10-C6

Red Rose Comedy Club
The Red Rose was started in 1987 by the legeadry Ivor Dembina and has played host to numerous comedy stars that will be familiar from TV, radio and their own DVD releases.

129 Seven Sisters Road, Finsbury Park, London N7 7QG
🖰 www.redrosecomedy.co.uk
🗺 Page 85-F1

The Regal Room at The Distillers
Home to live acoustic music, comedy and other events.

64–66 Fulham Palace Road, London W6 9PH
☎ 020 8748 2834
🖰 www.theregalroom.com
🗺 Page 119-F5

The Round Table Pub

25–27 St Martins Court, Charing Cross, London WC2N 4AJ
☎ 020 7836 6436
🖰 www.the99club.co.uk
✆ Page 10-D5

Sir Richard Steele

97 Haverstock Hill, Hampstead, London NW3 4RL
🖰 www.monkeybusiness comedyclub.co.uk
✆ Page 83-K4

Storm

28a Leicester Square, London WC2H 7LE
☎ 020 7839 2633
@ info@stormnightclub.co.uk
🖰 www.stormnightclub.co.uk
✆ Page 10-D5

T Bird

132 Blackstock Road, London N4 2DX
☎ 020 7503 6202
✆ Page 67-A6

The Tattershall Castle

A bar on an old paddle steamer, moored on the Thames hosting comedy nights.

Kings Reach, Victoria Embankment, London SW1A 2HR
☎ 020 7839 6548
📄 020 7839 1139
✆ Page 11-K5

The Tournament

344 Old Brompton Road, Earls Court, London SW5 9JU
☎ 020 7370 2449
@ info@laughinghorse.co.uk
🖰 www.laughinghorse.co.uk
✆ Page 119-K5

Up The Creek Croydon

3 Brighton Road, Croydon, London CR2 6AE
© 020 8680 5363
✆ Page 211-J6

Up The Creek Greenwich

302 Creek Road, Greenwich, London SE10 9SW
☎ 020 8858 4581
🖰 www.up-the-creek.com
✆ Page 125-F6

The Wheatsheaf

25 Rathbone Place, London W1T 1JB

☎ 020 7580 1585
✆ Page 10-C2

The Wibbley Wobbley

Greenland Dock, Rope Street, London SE16 7SZ
☎ 020 7232 2320
🖰 www.wibbleywobbley.co.uk
✆ Page 124-B3

Woolpack

52 High Street, Southgate, London N14 6EB
☎ 020 8886 5051
✆ Page 34-D3

World's End

21–23 Stroud Green Road, London N4 3EF
☎ 020 7281 8679
🖰 www.capitalpubcompany. com/worldsend/index.htm
✆ Page 67-F5

CLASSICAL MUSIC VENUES

The Actors' Church, St Paul's Covent Garden

Bedford Street, Covent Garden, London WC2E 9ED
☎ 020 7836 5221
@ info@actorschurch.org
🖰 www.actorschurch.org
✆ Page 10-E5

All Hallows' Church

Savernake Road, Gospel Oaks, Hampstead, London NW3 2LA
☎ 020 7287 7675
🖰 www.hcschoir.com
✆ Page 83-K2

All Saints Church

Newby Place, London E14 0EY
☎ 020 7538 9198
@ allsaintschurch.poplar@ virgin.net
🖰 www.parishofpoplar.com
✆ Page 106-A6

All Saints Church

All Saints Drive, Blackheath, London SE3 0TH
☎ 020 8852 4280
🖰 www.allsaintsblackheath.org
✆ Page 145-J3

All Souls, Langham Place

All Souls Church, opened in November 1824. The venue conducts courses, organ concerts, choirs, prayers and more.

2 All Souls Place, London W1B 3DA
☎ 020 7580 3522
@ vestry@allsouls.org
🖰 www.allsouls.org
📄 020 7436 3019
✆ Page 9-K2

Asian Music Centre

Ground Floor, Unit E, West Point, 33–34 Warple Way, London W3 0RG
☎ 020 8742 9911
@ info@amc.org.uk
🖰 www.amc.org.uk/
📄 020 8749 3948
✆ Page 118-B2

Barbican Hall

The Barbican welcomes the world's leading musicians and soloists in both classical and contemporary music. It is the home to the Resident Orchestra, the London Symphony Orchestra, the Associate Orchestra and the BBC Symphony Orchestra among others.

Barbican Centre, Silk Street, London EC2Y 8DS
☎ 020 7638 8891
© 020 7382 7211
@ music@barbican.org.uk
🖰 www.barbican.org.uk/music
✆ Page 12-C1

Bartok

Innovative, contemporary and classical music in Regency styled surroundings.

78 Chalk Farm Road, Camden, London NW1 8AR
☎ 020 7916 0595
🖰 www.bartokbar.com/
✆ Page 84-A5

Bloomsbury Central Baptist Church

235 Shaftesbury Avenue, Covent Garden, Bloomsbury, London WC2H 8EP
✆ Page 10-D3

Cadogan Hall

A grand venue, host to many esteemed orchestral societies.

5 Sloane Terrace, Belgravia, London SW1X 9DQ
☎ 020 7730 5744
© 0207 730 4500
@ info@cadoganhall.com
🖰 www.cadoganhall.com
✆ Page 15-G6

Chelsea Old Church

Petyt Hall, 64 Cheyne Walk, Chelsea, London SW3 5LT
☎ 020 7795 1019
@ chelsea.oldchurch@virgin.net
🖰 www.chelseaoldchurch.org.uk
✆ Page 120-D6

Christ Church

Highbury Grove, London N5 1SA
☎ 020 7354 0741
✆ Page 85-H3

Christ Church Southwark

Venue for lunchtime concerts.

27 Blackfriars Road, London SE1 8NY
☎ 020 7928 4707, 020 7928 3970
@ admin@christchurch southwark.org.uk
🖰 www.christchurchsouthwark. org.uk
✆ Page 12-A7

Christ Church Spitalfields

Fournier Street, London E1 6QE
☎ 020 7859 3035
@ friends@christchurch spitalfields.org
🖰 www.christchurch spitalfields.org
📄 020 7859 3037
✆ Page 13-J1

The Church of St Magnus the Martyr

The church hosts regular music recitals.

Lower Thames Street, Pool of London, London EC3R
☎ 020 7623 8022
🖰 www.concertbites.co.uk/ events.php
✆ Page 13-F6

Conway Hall

Hosts a wide variety of lectures, meetings, classes, performances and community events.

25 Red Lion Square, Holborn, London WC1R 4RL
☎ 020 7242 8032
@ conwayhall@ethicalsoc.org.uk
🖰 www.conwayhall.org.uk
📄 020 7242 8036
✆ Page 11-G2

The Dutch Church

7 Austin Friars, London EC2N 2HA
☎ 020 7588 1684
@ info@dutchchurch.org.uk
🖰 www.dutchchurch.org.uk/
📄 020 73740790
✆ Page 13-F3

Fairfield Halls and Ashcroft Theatre

Park Lane, Croydon CR9 1DG
☎ 020 8681 0821
© 020 8688 9291
@ boxoffice@fairfield.co.uk
🖰 www.fairfield.co.uk
◉ Page 211-K1

The Grosvenor Chapel, Mayfair

24 South Audley Street, Mayfair, London W1K 2PA
☎ 020 7499 1684
@ info@grosvenorchapel.force9.co.uk
🖰 www.grosvenorchapel.org.uk
🖩 01923 718870
◉ Page 9-H6

Guildhall School of Music and Drama

Silk Street, Barbican, London EC2Y 8DT
☎ 020 7628 2571
© 020 7638 8891
@ mailing@gsmd.ac.uk
🖰 www.gsmd.ac.uk
◉ Page 12-D1

Handel House Museum

The Handel House Museum was home to the baroque composer George Frideric Handel from 1723 until his death in 1759. Recitals take place every Thursday evening and regularly at the weekends.

25 Brook Street, Mayfair, London W1K 4HB
☎ 020 7495 1685
© 020 7399 1953
@ mail@handelhouse.org
🖰 www.handelhouse.org
🖩 020 7495 1759
◉ Page 9-J5

Henry Wood Hall

Trinity Church Square, London SE1 4HU
☎ 020 7403 0118
@ bookings@hwh.co.uk
🖰 www.hwh.co.uk
🖩 020 7378 8294
◉ Page 18-D4

Holy Trinity Church

The church hosts regular concerts and owns two beautiful organs.

Prince Consort Road, South Kensington, London SW7 2BA
☎ 020/ 581 3493
@ ticketsales@htsk.co.uk
🖰 www.htsk.co.uk/
◉ Page 14-A4

Holy Trinity Sloane Square

Sloane Street, Belgravia, London SW1X 9BZ
☎ 020 7730 7270
@ info@holytrinitysloanesquare.co.uk
🖰 www.holytrinitysloanesquare.co.uk
🖩 020 7730 9287
◉ Page 15-F6

LSO St Lukes

LSO St Luke's is an 18th-century Grade I listed church, and the home of the LSO's community and music education programme LSO Discovery. It houses LSO rehearsals and a diverse mix of evening concerts, as well as free public lunchtime concerts.

161 Old Street, London EC1V 9NG
☎ 020 7638 8891
🖰 www.lso.co.uk
◉ Page 7-G5

Leighton House Museum

The museum is the former studio house of the Victorian artist Frederic, Lord Leighton (1830–1896). Musical recitals.

12 Holland Park Road, Kensington, London W14 8LZ
☎ 020 7602 3316
@ LeightonHouseMuseum@rbkc.gov.uk
🖰 www.rbkc.gov.uk/leightonhousemuseum
🖩 020 7371 2467
◉ Page 119-J3

Middle Temple Hall

Middle Temple Lane, London EC4Y 9AT
☎ 020 7427 4820
🖰 www.templesong.com
🖩 020 7427 4821
◉ Page 11-J5

Millfield Arts Centre

Silver Street, Edmonton, Upper Edmonton, London N18 1PJ
☎ 020 8807 6680
@ info@millfieldtheatre.co.uk
🖰 www.millfieldtheatre.co.uk
🖩 020 8807 3892
◉ Page 35-K6

Morley College

61 Westminster Bridge Road, London SE1 7HT
☎ 020 7928 8501
@ enquiries@morleycollege.ac.uk
🖰 www.morleycollege.ac.uk/
◉ Page 17-K4

National Theatre

The National Theatre offers a diverse variety of entertainment events, from music to dance, theatre to comedy.

South Bank, Southwark, London SE1 9PX
☎ 020 7452 3000
@ info@nationaltheatre.org.uk
🖰 www.nationaltheatre.org.uk
◉ Page 11-H7

The Nave

1 St Paul's Road, London N1 2QN
☎ 020 7704 2158
@ boxoffice@thenave.org
🖰 www.thenave.org
🖩 020 7226 2062
◉ Page 85-J4

Purcell Room

As part of the Royal Festival Hall arts complex, the Purcell Room hosts contemporary dance, music theatre, chamber music, solo recitals, world music, poetry events and live art.

South Bank Centre, London SE1 8XX
☎ 0870 380 0400
🖰 www.southbankcentre.co.uk
◉ Page 17-G1

Queen Charlotte Hall

Parkshot Centre, Parkshot, Richmond upon Thames TW9 2RE
☎ 020 8843 7921
◉ Page 136-E5

Queen Elizabeth Hall

The Queen Elizabeth Hall seating 917, is a part of Royal Festival Hall complex hosting contemporary dance, music theatre, chamber music, solo recitals, world music, poetry events and live art.

South Bank Centre, Belvedere Road, London SE1 8XX
☎ 0870 380 4300
© 0870 401 8181
@ customer@rfh.org.uk
🖰 www.rfh.org.uk
◉ Page 11-G7

Royal Academy of Music

Marylebone Road, Regents Park, London NW1 5HT
☎ 020 7873 7373
🖰 www.ram.ac.uk
🖩 020 7873 7374
◉ Page 3-H7

Royal Albert Hall

The Royal Albert Hall hosts a diverse range of events including classical and rock concerts, conferences, ballroom dancing, poetry recitals, ballet, opera and sporting events. It is most famous for holding the annual classical music festival The Proms.

Kensington Gore, South Kensington, London SW7 2AP
☎ 020 7838 3110
© 020 7589 8212
@ access@royalalberthall.com
🖰 www.royalalberthall.com
◉ Page 14-A3

Royal College of Music

The Royal College of Music is one of the world's leading conservatoires, providing specialised musical education and professional training at the highest international level for performers and composers. Varied programme of events,

Prince Consort Road, South Kensington, London SW7 2BS
☎ 020 7589 3643
@ info@rcm.ac.uk
🖰 www.rcm.ac.uk
🖩 020 7589 7740
◉ Page 14-A4

Royal Festival Hall

The Royal Festival Hall stands at the heart of Southbank Centre complex. It is one of the world's leading concert venues, presenting concerts by the finest international orchestras, operas, and a wide spread of contemporary music events, from jazz to world, to rock and pop music.

Belvedere Road, London SE1 8XX
☎ 0870 380 4300
@ customer@southbankcentre.co.uk
🖰 www.southbankcentre.co.uk
🖩 0870 163 3898
◉ Page 17-G1

St Andrew's Holborn

5 St Andrew's Street, London EC4A 3AB
☎ 020 7520 0330
🖰 www.standrewholborn.org.uk
◉ Page 11-K2

St Anne and St Agnes

Gresham Street, London EC2V 7BX
☎ 020 7606 4986

@ info@StAnnesLutheran
Church.org
🖰 www.stanneslutheran
church.org
⊘ Page 12-C3

St Anne's Lutheran Church

Gresham Street, London EC2V 7BX
🖰 www.stanneslutheranchurch.
org/
⊘ Page 12-C3

St Bride's Church

Bride Lane, Fleet Street, London
EC4Y 8AU
☎ 020 7427 0133
@ info@stbrides.com
🖰 www.stbrides.com/ticket/
index.php
🖺 020 7583 4867
⊘ Page 12-A4

St Dominic's Priory

Southampton Road, London
NW5 4LB
☎ 020 7482 9210
🖰 www.op-london.org
⊘ Page 83-K3

St George's, Bloomsbury

Church in the heart of the West
End in London, that holds regular
Sunday concerts.

7 Little Russell Street, Bloomsbury,
London WC1A 2HR
☎ 020 7405-3044
📞 020 7242 1979
@ stgeorgebloomsbury@hotmail.
com
🖰 www.stgeorgesbloomsbury.
org.uk
⊘ Page 10-E2

St George's, Hanover Square

St George's was built 1721–1724
to the designs of John James,
as one of the Fifty Churches
projected by Queen Anne's Act of
1711. St George's has a full time
professional choir and a strong
choral tradition.

2A Mill Street, Mayfair, London
W1S 1FX
☎ 020 7629 0874
🖰 www.stgeorgeshanoversquare.
org
🖺 020 7629 0874
⊘ Page 9-K5

St George's Cathedral

Cathedral House, Westminster
Bridge Road, London SE1 7HY
☎ 020 7928 5256

@ info@southwark-rc-cathedral.
org.uk
🖰 www.southwark-rc-cathedral.
org.uk
🖺 020 7202 2189
⊘ Page 17-K4

St James's Church Piccadilly

197 Piccadilly, Soho, London
W1J 9LL
☎ 020 7734 4511
@ hugh.valentine@london.
anglican.org
🖰 www.st-james-piccadilly.org
⊘ Page 10-B6

St John the Evangelist, Islington

39 Duncan Terrace, London
N1 8AL
☎ 020 7226 3277
🖰 www.stjohnsislington.org
🖺 020 7704 8988
⊘ Page 6-A2

St John at Hackney

Lower Clapton Road, London
E5 0PD
☎ 020 7613 9525
🖰 www.stjohn-at-hackneychurch.
org.uk
⊘ Page 86-E2

St John's Churchyard

Broadway, Stratford, London
E15 1NG
☎ 020 8503 1913
🖰 www.stjohnse15.co.uk
🖺 020 8503 1620
⊘ Page 88-B4

St John's, Smith Square

Situated in the heart of
Westminster and built in 1728, St
John's hosts regular concerts.

Smith Square, Westminster,
London SW1P 3HA
☎ 020 7222 1061
📞 020 7222 2168
@ info@sjss.org.uk
🖰 www.sjss.org.uk
🖺 020 7233 1618
⊘ Page 16-E5

St John's Church

Waterloo Road, Waterloo, London
SE1 8TY
☎ 020 7928 2003
@ edavis@stjohnswaterloo.co.uk
🖰 www.stjohnswaterloo.co.uk
⊘ Page 17-J1

St Jude's Church

Central Square, London NW11 7AH
☎ 020 8455 8687, 020 8455 7206
@ da.harris@which.net
🖰 www.promsatstjudes.org.uk
🖺 020 8455 7206
⊘ Page 64-E3

St Jude-on-the-Hill

Central Square, Hampstead
Garden Suburb, London
NW11 7AH
☎ 020 8455 7206
🖰 www.promsatstjudes.org.uk
⊘ Page 65-F3

St Lawrence Jewry

Blackwell House, London
EC2V 5AE
☎ 020 7600 9478
⊘ Page 12-D3

St Lawrence, Little Stanmore

Whitchurch Lane, Edgware
HA8 6RB
☎ 020 8952 0019
🖰 www.little-stanmore.org
⊘ Page 44-B3

St Luke's, South Battersea

Ramsden Road, Balham, London
SW12 8RQ
☎ 020 8772 0463
@ parish.office@stlukesonline.
org.uk
🖰 www.stlukesonline.org.uk
⊘ Page 161-F2

St Luke's and Christ Church

Saint Luke's Crypt, Sydney Street,
London SW3 6NH
☎ 020 7351 7365
@ parishoffice@chelseaparish.
org
🖰 chelseaparish.org
🖺 020 7349 0538
⊘ Page 120-D5

St Margaret's, Lee

Brandram Road, London SE13 5EA
☎ 020 8318 9643
@ stmargarets-lee@fish.co.uk
🖰 www.southwark.anglican.
org/parishes/147j.htm
⊘ Page 145-H4

St Martin-in-the-Fields

In addition to daily worship
services, the church holds
lunchtime and evening classical
concerts. The renowned crypt and
cafe hosts regular jazz nights,.

Trafalgar Square, Charing Cross,
London WC2N 4JJ
☎ 020 776 61100
@ info@smitf.org
🖰 www.stmartin-in-the-fields.org
⊘ Page 10-E6

St Mary le Bow

Cheapside, London EC2V 6AU
☎ 020 7248 5139
🖰 www.stmarylebow.co.uk
⊘ Page 12-D4

St Mary le Strand

Strand, London WC2B 1ES
🖰 www.stmarylestrand.org/
⊘ Page 11-G5

St Marylebone

Marylebone Road, London
NW1 5LT
☎ 020 7935 7315
🖰 www.stmarylebone.org.uk
⊘ Page 3-H7

St Mary's Roman Catholic Church

Cadogan Street, Kensington and
Chelsea, London SW3 2QR
☎ 020 7589 5487
🖺 020 7581 5727
⊘ Page 14-E7

St Matthew's, Westminster

20 Great Peter Street,
Westminster, London SW1P 2BU
☎ 020 7222 3704
@ office@stmw.org
🖰 www.stmw.org
🖺 020 7233 0255
⊘ Page 16-C4

St Michael's Church

South Grove, Highgate, London
N6 6BJ
☎ 020 8340 7279
@ office@stmichaelhighgate.org
🖰 www.stmichaelhighgate.org
⊘ Page 66-A5

St Paul's Cathedral

St Paul's Cathedral was designed
by the court architect Sir
Christopher Wren and completed
in 1710. Concerts and events are
held throughout the year.

The Chapter House, St Paul's
Churchyard, London EC4M 8AD
☎ 020 7236 4128
📞 020 7246 8350
@ chapter@stpaulscathedral.
org.uk
🖰 www.stpauls.co.uk

📠 020 7248 3104
🖊 Page 12-C4

St Paul's, Harringay

Wightman Road, Harringay,
London N4 1RW
☎ 020 8533 5722
@ victoriahay@desk64.freeserve.
co.uk
🖊 Page 67-G3

St Peter and St Paul, Chingford

The Green, Chingford E4 7EN
☎ 020 8529 0323
🖳 www.chingfordparish.co.uk
🖊 Page 38-B3

St Peter's Church

119 Eaton Square, Belgravia,
London SW1W 9AL
☎ 020 7235 4482
🖳 www.stpetereatonsquare.
co.uk/
🖊 Page 15-J5

St Stephen's, Walbrook

39 Walbrook, London EC4N 8BN
☎ 020 7606 3998
📞 020 7626 8242
@ martin@ststephenwalbrook.
net
🖳 www.ststephenwalbrook.net
🖊 Page 12-E4

Southwark Cathedral

Southwark Cathedral, situated
on the south bank of the River
Thames, hosts recitals and other
special events.

London Bridge, London SE1 9DA
☎ 020 7367 6700
@ cathedral@southwark.
anglican.org
🖳 www.southwark.anglican.
org/cathedral
☎ 020 7367 6725
🖊 Page 12-E7

Steinway Hall

44 Marylebone Lane, Marylebone,
London W1U 2DB
☎ 020 7487 3391
@ cturner@steinway.co.uk
🖳 www.steinway.co.uk
🖊 Page 9-H3

The Temple Church

The Temple Church was built by
Knights Templar and comprises of
the Round and the Chancel. The
choir organises organ recitals,
concerts and Christmas carol
services.

The Master's House, Temple,
London EC4Y 7BB
☎ 020 7353 3470
@ verger@templechurch.com
🖳 www.templechurch.com
🖊 Page 11-J4

Union Chapel

The Vestry, Compton Avenue,
London N1 2XD
☎ 020 7226 3750
@ arts@unionchapel.org.uk
🖳 www.unionchapel.org.uk
🖊 Page 85-H4

The Vera Fletcher Hall

The Vera Fletcher Hall was built
in 1887 to commemorate Queen
Victoria's Golden Jubilee. The
Hall has facilities to host theatre,
concerts and opera.

4 Ember Court Road, Thames
Ditton KT7 0LP
☎ 020 8873 7393
📞 01372 462078
🖳 www.verafletcherhall.co.uk
🖊 Page 189-K3

The Warehouse

Situated in the heart of London's
South Bank, The Warehouse
offers perfect acoustics and an
intimate atmosphere for concert
performances.

13 Theed Street, London SE1 8ST
☎ 020 7928 9250
🖳 www.thewarehouselondon.
co.uk
🖊 Page 17-J1

Westminster Abbey

Westminster Abbey, a place of
daily worship, has been the setting
for every Coronation since 1066
and for numerous other royal
occasions. Various musical events
are held throughout the year.

20 Dean's Yard, London SW1P 3PA
☎ 020 7222 5152
@ info@westminster-abbey.org
🖳 www.westminster-abbey.org
🖨 020 7233 2072
🖊 Page 16-E4

Westminster Cathedral

Westminster Cathedral, house
of prayer and worship, is a
fascinating example of Victorian
architecture. Hosts musical events
throughout the year.

42 Francis Street, Victoria,
London SW1P 1QW
☎ 020 7798 9055

@ cathedralwebmaster@rcdow.
org.uk
🖳 www.westminstercathedral.
org.uk
🖨 020 7798 9090
🖊 Page 16-A5

Wigmore Hall

Built in 1901 by the Bechstein
piano company, Wigmore Hall is
regarded as one of the world's
great recital halls, attracting
the leading classical musicians
of our time, and often setting
the standard for international
chamber music and song.

36 Wigmore Street, Marylebone,
London W1U 2BP
☎ 020 7258 8200
📞 020 7935 2141
@ info@wigmore-hall.org.uk
🖳 www.wigmore-hall.org.uk
🖨 020 7935 3344
🖊 Page 9-J3

CINEMAS

Apollo Cinema, West End

Luxury cinema in the West End of
London.

19 Regent Street, St James's,
London SW1Y 4LR
☎ 08712 206000
🖳 www.apollocinemas.co.uk
🖊 Page 10-B6

BFI London IMAX Cinema

The BFI London IMAX Cinema is a
477-seat, state-of-the-art, large-
format cinema on the South Bank
in London with the UKs biggest
cinema screen more than 20
metres high and 26 metres wide.

1 Charlie Chaplin Walk, South
Bank, London SE1 8XR
📞 0870 787 2525
🖳 www.bfi.org.uk/incinemas/
imax/
🖊 Page 17-H1

BFI Southbank

BFI Southbank, run by the British
Film Institute, is a repertory
cinema on the South Bank of
the River Thames specialising in
independent, classic and foreign
film.

Belvedere Road, South Bank,
London SE1 8XT
☎ 020 7928 3535
📞 020 7928 3232
@ nft@bfi.org.uk
🖳 www.bfi.org.uk
🖊 Page 17-G2

Barbican Cinema

The Barbican cinemas are all
equipped with state-of-the-art
technology. Cinema 1 was recently
voted London's Most Comfortable
Cinema by BBC Radio 4 Front Row
listeners.

Barbican Centre, Silk Street,
London EC2Y 8DS
☎ 020 7638 4141
📞 020 7638 8891
@ film@barbican.org.uk
🖳 www.barbican.org.uk/film
🖊 Page 12-C1

Belle Vue Cinema

95 High Road, Willesden Green
Library, Willesden, London
NW10 2SF
☎ 020 8830 0823
🖊 Page 81-K5

Boleyn Cinema

7–11 Barking Road, East Ham,
London E6 1PW
☎ 020 8471 4884
🖳 www.boleyncinema.co.uk
🖨 020 8586 0514
🖊 Page 107-H1

Charlotte Street Hotel Screening Room

Venue for the hotel's weekend film
club which includes dinner and the
screening of a film from classics
to the latest releases.

15–17 Charlotte Street, London
W1T 1RJ
☎ 020 7806 2000
🖳 www.firmdale.com/
🖊 Page 10-B1

Chelsea Cinema

Art house cinema chain with five
sites across London.

206 Kings Road, Chelsea, London
SW3 5XP
☎ 020 7351 3742
📞 0870 850 6926
🖳 www.curzoncinemas.com
🖊 Page 120-D5

Cine Lumiere

Launched by Catherine Deneuve
in 1998, the Cine Lumiere is an
independent showcase for French,
European and world cinema.

17 Queensberry Place, South
Kensington, London SW7 2DT
☎ 020 7073 1350
@ box.office@ambafrance.org.uk
🖳 www.institut-francais.org.uk
🖊 Page 14-A6

CineWorld Bexleyheath

28–70 Broadway, Bexleyheath,
London DA6 7LL
☎ 08712 208000
@ customer.services@cineworld.
co.uk
🖰 www.cineworld.co.uk
⊘ Page 149-J5

Cineworld Chelsea

279 Kings Road, Chelsea, London
SW3 5EW
☎ 0870 777 2775
🕓 08712 002000
🖰 www.cineworld.co.uk
⊘ Page 120-C6

Cineworld Enfield

Southbury Leisure Park, 208
Southbury Road, Enfield EN1 1YQ
☎ 0870 777 2775
🕓 08712 002000
🖰 www.ugccinemas.co.uk
⊘ Page 24-C4

CineWorld Feltham

Leisure West, Air Park Way,
Feltham TW13 7LX
☎ 08712 208000
🖰 www.cineworld.co.uk
⊘ Page 154-A4

Cineworld Fulham Road

142 Fulham Road, London
SW10 9QR
☎ 0870 777 2775
🕓 08712 002000
@ customer.services@cineworld.
co.uk
🖰 www.ugccinemas.co.uk
⊘ Page 120-B5

Cineworld Hammersmith

207 King Street, Hammersmith,
London W6 9JT
☎ 0870 777 2775
🕓 08712 002000
@ customer.services@cineworld.
co.uk
🖰 www.cineworld.co.uk
⊘ Page 118-E4

Cineworld Haymarket

63–65 Haymarket, London
SW1Y 4RQ
☎ 0870 777 2775
🕓 08712 002000
@ customer.services@cineworld.
co.uk
🖰 www.cineworld.co.uk
⊘ Page 10-C6

CineWorld Ilford

Clements Road, Ilford IG1 4QR
☎ 08712 208000
🖰 www.cineworld.co.uk
⊘ Page 90-B1

Cineworld Shaftesbury Avenue

Trocadero, 7–14 Coventry Street,
Piccadilly Circus, London
W1D 7DH
☎ 0870 777 2775
🕓 08712 002000
🖰 www.cineworld.co.uk
⊘ Page 10-C5

Cineworld Staples Corner

Staples Corner Retail Park, 7
Geron Way, Dollis Hill, London
NW2 6LW
☎ 0870 777 2775
🕓 08712 002000
🖰 www.cineworld.co.uk
⊘ Page 63-K5

CineWorld Wandsworth

Southside Centre, Wandsworth
High Street, London SW18 4TF
☎ 08712 208000
🖰 www.cineworld.co.uk
⊘ Page 160-A1

Cineworld West India Quay

11 Hertsmere Road, West India
Quay, London E14 4AL
☎ 0870 777 2775
🕓 08712 002000
🖰 www.cineworld.co.uk
⊘ Page 124-D1

CineWorld Wood Green

Wood Green Mall Center, Noel
Park Road, London N22 6LU
☎ 08712 208000
🖰 www.cineworld.co.uk
⊘ Page 49-G5

Clapham Picturehouse

76 Venn Street, Clapham, London
SW4 0AT
☎ 0870 755 0061
@ clapham@picturehouses.co.uk
🖰 www.picturehouses.co.uk/
🖨 020 7498 0490
⊘ Page 141-H5

Covent Garden Hotel Screening Room

Venue for the hotel's weekend film
club which includes dinner and the
screening of a film from classics
to the latest releases.

10 Monmouth Street, Covent
Garden, London WC2H 9HB
☎ 020 7806 1000
🖰 www.firmdale.com/
⊘ Page 10-D4

The Cross Kings

126 York Way, London N1 0AX
☎ 020 7278 8318
@ info@thecrosskings.co.uk
🖰 www.thecrosskings.co.uk
⊘ Page 5-F2

Curzon Mayfair

38 Curzon Street, Mayfair, London
W1J 7TY
🕓 0870 756 4621
@ info@curzoncinemas.com
🖰 www.curzoncinemas.com
⊘ Page 15-J1

Curzon Soho

99 Shaftesbury Avenue, Soho,
London W1D 5DY
☎ 0870 756 4620
@ info@curzoncinemas.com
🖰 www.curzoncinemas.com
⊘ Page 10-D5

David Lean Cinema

A small, intimate, art house-style
cinema presenting the best of
British and World cinema as well
as classic re-releases and recent
favourites. It is centrally situated
within the Croydon Clocktower
complex.

Katharine Street, Croydon CR9 1ET
☎ 020 8253 1030, 07771 837121
@ ticketoffice@croydon.gov.uk
🖰 www.croydon.gov.uk/
clocktower
🖨 020 8760 0871
⊘ Page 211-J1

De Lane Lea

Film studio set up by French
intelligence attache for the British
Government, Major De Lane Lea,
who founded De Lane Lea in 1947
to dub English films into French.

75 Dean Street, Soho, London
W1D 3PU
☎ 020 7432 3800
🖰 www.delanelea.com
🖨 020 7432 3838
⊘ Page 10-C3

The Electric Cinema

This popular, intimate cinema has
a celebrated programme that
comprises a broad range of quality
mainstream and art house films.

191 Portobello Road, Notting Hill,
London W11 2ED
☎ 020 7908 9696
🖰 www.electriccinema.co.uk
🖨 020 7908 9595
⊘ Page 100-D5

Empire Bromley

242 High Street, Bromley BR1 1PG
☎ 08 714 714 714
🖰 www.empirecinemas.co.uk
⊘ Page 183-K6

Empire Ealing

Uxbridge Road, Ealing, London
W5 5AH
☎ 0870 777 2775
🕓 08712 002000
🖰 www.empirecinemas.co.uk
⊘ Page 98-A6

Empire Leicester Square

5–6 Leicester Square, London
WC2H 7NA
☎ 02077 348222
🖰 www.empirecinemas.co.uk
⊘ Page 10-D6

Empire Sutton

St Nicholas Centre, St Nicholas
Way, Sutton SM1 1AZ
☎ 08 714714 714
🖰 www.empirecinemas.co.uk
⊘ Page 209-F3

Everyman Cinema Club

5 Holly Bush Vale, Hampstead,
London NW3 6TX
🕓 0870 066 4777
@ mail@everymancinema.com
🖰 www.everymancinema.com
⊘ Page 83-G2

Four Corners

Four Corners supports a
wide range of filmmakers,
photographers and artists and
offers facilities for photograpy,
film and other forms of visual
media.

121 Roman Road, Bethnal Green,
London E2 0QN
☎ 020 8981 6111
@ info@fourcornersfilm.co.uk
🖰 www.fourcornersfilm.co.uk
🖨 020 8983 7866
⊘ Page 105-F1

Gate Picturehouse

87 Notting Hill Gate, Kensington,
London W11 3JZ
☎ 020 7727 4043
🕓 08707 55 00 63

@ gate@picturehouses.co.uk
⌐ www.picturehouses.co.uk
✆ Page 119-K1

Genesis Cinema

93–95 Mile End Road, Stepney,
London E1 4UJ
☎ 020 7780 2000
☏ 0870 060 6061
@ info@genesis-cinemea.co.uk
⌐ www.genesiscinema.com
✆ Page 104-E3

Goethe Institute

50 Princes Gate, Exhibition Road,
South Kensington, London SW7 2PH
☎ 020 7596 4000
@ info@london.goethe.org
⌐ www.goethe.de/ins/gb/lon/
   enindex.htm
▤ 020 7594 0240
✆ Page 14-B4

Greenwich Picturehouse

180 Greenwich High Road,
Greenwich, London SE10 8NN
☎ 0870 755 0065
@ greenwich@picturehouses.co.uk
⌐ www.picturehouses.co.uk
✆ Page 145-F1

Harrow Safari Cinema

Station Road, Harrow HA1 2TU
☎ 020 8426 0606
⌐ www.safaricinema.com
▤ 02089582141
✆ Page 61-F2

Himalaya Palace Cinema

Luxurious three-screen cinema in
West London. The largest screen
shows Bollywood Blockbusters and
Hollywood movies.

14 South Road, Southall UB1 3RT
☏ 020 8813 8844
⌐ www.himalayapalacecinema.
   co.uk
✆ Page 114-E1

Instituto Cervantes

102 Eaton Square,Belgravia, London
SW1 W9AN
☎ 020 7235 0353
@ cenlon@cervantes.es
⌐ londres.cervantes.es
▤ 020 7235 0329
✆ Page 15-H5

Notting Hill Coronet

103 Notting Hill Gate, Notting Hill,
London W11 3LB
☎ 020 7727 6705
⌐ www.coronet.org
✆ Page 119-K1

Odeon Barnet

Great North Road, Barnet EN5 1AB
☎ 08712 244007
⌐ www.odeon.co.uk
✆ Page 20-E6

Odeon Beckenham

High Street, Beckenham BR3 1DY
☎ 08712 244007
⌐ www.odeon.co.uk
✆ Page 124-C5

Odeon Camden Town

14 The Parkway, Camden, London
NW1 7AA
☎ 08712 244007
⌐ www.odeon.co.uk
✆ Page 182-D5

Odeon Covent Garden

135 Shaftsbury Avenue, London
WC2H 8AH
☎ 08712 244007
⌐ www.odeon.co.uk
✆ Page 10-D4

Odeon Esher

22 High Street, Esher KT10 9RT
☎ 08712 244007
⌐ www.odeon.co.uk
✆ Page 204-B2

Odeon Greenwich

Bugsby Way, Greenwich, London
SE10 0QJ
☎ 0871 22 44 007
⌐ www.odeon.co.uk
✆ Page 125-J4

Odeon Holloway

419–427 Holloway Road, Islington,
London N7 6LJ
☎ 08712 244007
⌐ www.odeon.co.uk
✆ Page 84-E1

Odeon Kensington

Kensington High Street, London
W8 6NA
☎ 08712 244007
⌐ www.odeon.co.uk
✆ Page 119-J3

Odeon Kingston upon Thames

The Rotunda, Clarence Street,
Kingston upon Thames KT1 1QP
☎ 08712 244007
⌐ www.odeon.co.uk
✆ Page 175-F5

Odeon Lee Valley

Lee Valley Leisure Complex, Picketts
Lock Lane, Edmonton N9 0AS

☎ 08712 244007
⌐ www.odeon.co.uk
✆ Page 37-F2

Odeon Leicester Square

24–26 Leicester Square, London
WC2H 7JY
☎ 08712 244007
⌐ www.odeon.co.uk
✆ Page 10-D6

Odeon Marble Arch

10 Edgware Road, Marble Arch,
London W2 2EN
☎ 08712 244007
⌐ www.odeon.co.uk
✆ Page 8-E4

Odeon Muswell Hill

Fortis Green Road, London
N10 3HP
☎ 08712 244007
⌐ www.odeon.co.uk
✆ Page 66-A1

Odeon Panton Street

11–18 Panton Street, London
SW1Y 4DP
☎ 08712 244007
⌐ www.odeon.co.uk
✆ Page 10-D6

Odeon Putney

26 Putney High Street, Putney,
London SW15 1SN
☎ 08712 244007
⌐ www.odeon.co.uk
✆ Page 139-H4

Odeon Richmond

72 Hill Street, Richmond TW9 1TW
☎ 08712 244007
⌐ www.odeon.co.uk
✆ Page 136-E6

Odeon South Woodford

58–66 High Road, South Woodford,
London E18 2QL
☎ 08712 244007
⌐ www.odeon.co.uk
✆ Page 52-E5

Odeon Streatham

47–49 High Road, Streatham,
London SW16 1PW
☎ 08712 244007
⌐ www.odeon.co.uk
✆ Page 161-K5

Odeon Surrey Quays

Surrey Quays Leisure Park, Redriff
Road, Rotherhithe, London
SE16 7LL

☎ 08712 244007
⌐ www.odeon.co.uk
✆ Page 124-A3

Odeon Swiss Cottage

96 Finchley Road, Hampstead,
London NW3 5EL
☎ 08712 244007
⌐ www.odeon.co.uk
✆ Page 83-H5

Odeon Tottenham Court Road

30 Tottenham Court Road, London
W1T 1BX
☎ 08712 244007
⌐ www.odeon.co.uk
✆ Page 10-C2

Odeon West End

40 Leicester Square, London
WC2H 7LP
☎ 08712 244007
⌐ www.odeon.co.uk
✆ Page 10-C6

Odeon Whiteleys

Whiteleys of Bayswater, Queensway,
London W2 4YL
☎ 0871 22 44 007
⌐ www.odeon.co.uk
✆ Page 101-F5

Odeon Wimbledon

The Piazza, The Broadway,
Wimbledon, London SW19 1QB
☎ 08712 244007
⌐ www.odeon.co.uk
✆ Page 177-K3

Peckham Multiplex

95a Rye Lane, Peckham, London
SE15 4ST
☎ 0870 042 9399
⌐ www.peckhamplex.com
✆ Page 143-H3

Phoenix Cinema

52 High Road, East Finchley,
London N2 9PJ
☎ 020 8883 2233
☏ 020 8444 6789
@ management@phoenixcinema.
   co.uk
⌐ www.phoenixcinema.co.uk
✆ Page 65-J1

Prince Charles Cinema

7 Leicester Place, London
WC2H 7BY
☎ 020 7494 3654
@ web@princecharlescinema.com
⌐ www.princecharlescinema.com
✆ Page 10-D5

Renoir Cinema

Brunswick Centre, Brunswick Square, St Pancras, London WC1N 1AW

☎ 020 7837 8402

🖰 www.curzoncinemas.com

🅿 Page 5-F6

Rich Mix

The Rich Mix building is a dynamic new cross-cultural arts and media centre in the heart of the East End with a three-screen cinema.

35–47 Bethnal Green Road, London E1 6LA

☎ 020 7613 7490

@ info@richmix.org.uk

🖰 www.richmix.org.uk

🅿 Page 7-J6

Richmond Filmhouse

3 Water Lane, Richmond TW9 1TJ

☎ 020 8332 0030

© 0870 850 6928

🖰 www.curzoncinemas.com

🅿 Page 136-E6

Rio Cinema

The Rio is an independent, single screen cinema in Hackney restored to its 1930s art deco splendour and now with state of the art digital projector.

107 Kingsland High Street, Hackney, London E8 2PB

☎ 020 7241 9410

@ mail@riocinema.org.uk

🖰 www.riocinema.org.uk

🅿 Page 86-A3

Ritzy Picturehouse

Brixton Oval, Coldharbour Lane, Brixton, London SW2 1JG

☎ 0870 755 0062

@ ritzy@picturehouses.co.uk

🖰 www.picturehouses.co.uk

🅿 Page 142-B5

Riverside Studios

An arts and media centre, on the banks of the Thames in Hammersmith, with a cinema.

Crisp Road, Hammersmith, London W6 9RL

☎ 020 8237 1111, 020 8237 1000

@ online@riversidestudios.co.uk

🖰 www.riversidestudios.co.uk

🅿 Page 118-E5

Rotherhithe Sands Films Studios

119 Rotherhithe Street, Rotherhithe, London SE16 4NF

☎ 020 7231 2209

@ ostockman@sandsfilms.co.uk

🖰 www.sandsfilms.co.uk

🗎 020 7231 2119

🅿 Page 123-K2

Roxy Bar and Screen

128–132 Borough High Street, London SE1 1LB

☎ 020 7407 4057

@ info@roxybarandscreen.com

🖰 www.roxybarandscreen.com

🅿 Page 18-D2

Science Museum IMAX Cinema

Exhibition Road, South Kensington, London SW7 2DD

© 0870 870 4771

@ scimax@nmsi.ac.uk

🖰 www.sciencemuseum.org.uk/imax

🅿 Page 14-A5

The Screen On The Green

Independent cinema chain.

83 Upper Street, London N1 0NP

☎ 020 7226 3520

@ screen.green@btinternet.com

🖰 www.screencinemas.co.uk

🅿 Page 6-A1

Screen On The Hill

203 Haverstock Hill, Hampstead, London NW3 4QG

© 020 7435 3366

🖰 www.screencinemas.co.uk

🅿 Page 83-J3

Screen on Baker Street

96–98 Baker Street, Marylebone, London W1U 6TJ

☎ 020 7486 0036

© 020 7935 2772

🖰 www.screencinemas.co.uk

🅿 Page 9-F1

Showcase Cinema, Newham

Jenkins Lane, Newham IG11 0AD

☎ 020 8477 4500

🖰 www.showcasecinemas.co.uk

🅿 Page 108-C2

Showcase Cinema, Wood Green

Hollywood Green, Wood Green, London N22 6EJ

☎ 0870 162 8960

🖰 www.showcasecinemas.co.uk

🅿 Page 49-G5

The Soho Hotel Screening Room

Venue for the hotel's weekend film club which includes dinner and the screening of a film from classics to the latest releases.

4 Richmond Mews, Soho, London W1D 3DH

☎ 020 7559 3000

🖰 www.firmdalehotels.com/

🅿 Page 10-C4

Soho House Cinema

Small luxury cinema with a lucrative bar and dining area.

21 Old Compton Road, Soho, London W1D 5JJ

☎ 020 7734 5188

🖰 www.sohohouselondon.com/

🗎 020 7292 0170

🅿 Page 10-C4

Soho Screening Rooms

14 D'Arblay Street, Soho, London W1F 8DY

☎ 020 7437 1771

🖰 www.sohoscreeningrooms.co.uk

🅿 Page 10-B4

Stratford Picturehouse

Salway Road, Stratford, London E15 1BX

☎ 0870 755 0064

@ stratfordeast@picturehouses.co.uk

🖰 www.picturehouses.co.uk

🅿 Page 88-B4

Sun & Doves

An independent, quirky venue offering food, drink, art, music and film.

61–63 Coldharbour Lane, Camberwell, London SE5 9NS

☎ 020 77331525

🖰 www.sunanddoves.co.uk/

🅿 Page 142-D3

Tricycle Cinema

269 Kilburn High Road, London NW6 7JR

☎ 020 7372 6611

© 020 7328 1900

@ info@tricycle.co.uk

🖰 www.tricycle.co.uk

🅿 Page 82-D5

Vue Acton

Royale Leisure Park, Western Avenue, Park Royal South, London W3 0PA

☎ 08712 240240

@ guestservices@myvue.com

🖰 www.myvue.com

🅿 Page 98-C3

Vue Croydon Grant's

14 High Street, Croydon, London CR0 1GT

☎ 08712 240240

© 08712 240240

@ guestservices@myvue.com

🖰 www.myvue.com

🅿 Page 196-A6

Vue Croydon Purley Way

Valley Park Leisure Complex, 21 Hesterman Way, Croydon CR0 4YA

☎ 08712 240240

@ customerservices@vuemail.com

🖰 www.myvue.com

🅿 Page 196-A6

Vue Dagenham

Dagenham Leisure Park, Cook Road, Dagenham RM9 6UQ

☎ 08712 240240

@ guestservices@myvue.com

🖰 www.myvue.com

🅿 Page 92-A6

Vue Finchley Road

241–279 O2 Centre, Finchley Road, West Hampstead, London NW3 6LU

☎ 08712 240240

@ customerservices@vuemail.com

🖰 www.myvue.com

🗎 020 7372 9470

🅿 Page 83-G4

Vue Fulham Broadway

Fulham Broadway Retail Centre, Fulham Road, London SW6 1BW

☎ 08712 240240

@ customerservices@vuemail.com

🖰 www.myvue.com

🗎 020 7386 8067

🅿 Page 139-K1

Vue Greenwich (Vue O2)

The O2, Peninsula Square, Greenwich, London SE10 0BB

© 08712 240 240

@ guestservices@myvue.com

🖰 www.myvue.co.uk/

🅿 Page 125-H1

Vue Harrow

St Georges Shopping Centre and Leisure Centre, St Anne's Road, Harrow HA1 1AS

☎ 08712 240240
@ customerservices@vuemail.com
🖰 www.myvue.com
📄 020 8427 1188
📍 Page 60-E3

Vue Islington

36 Parkfield Street, Islington, London N1 0PS
☎ 08712 240240
@ guestservices@myvue.com
🖰 www.myvue.com
📍 Page 5-K2

Vue North Finchley

Great North Leisure Park, Chaplin Square, Finchley, London N12 0GL
☎ 08712 240240
@ customerservices@vuemail.com
🖰 www.myvue.com
📍 Page 47-H3

Vue Romford

1–15 The Brewery, Romford RM1 1AU
☎ 08712 240240
@ customerservices@vuemail.com
🖰 www.myvue.com
📍 Page 75-G2

Vue Shepherd's Bush

West 12 Shopping and Leisure Centre, Shepherds Bush Green, Shepherds Bush, London W12 8PP
☎ 08712 240240
@ customerservices@vuemail.com
🖰 www.myvue.com
📍 Page 119-G2

Vue West End

3 Cranbourn Street, Leicester Square, London WC2H 7AL
☎ 08712 240240
@ customerservices@vuemail.com
🖰 www.myvue.com
📍 Page 10-D5

Watermans

A multipurpose arts centre overlooking Kew Gardens housing an intimate 125-seat cinema.

40 High Street, Brentford TW8 0DS
☎ 020 8232 1010
@ info@watermans.org.uk
🖰 www.watermans.org.uk
📄 020 8232 1030
📍 Page 117-F6

OPERA VENUES

Holland Park Theatre

Holland Park, Kensington High Street, London W8 6LU
☎ 020 7602 7856
🖰 www.operahollandpark.com
📍 Page 119-J2

London Coliseum

St Martin's Lane, Charing Cross, London WC2N 4ES
☎ 020 7632 8300/020 7836 0111
@ box.office@eno.org
🖰 www.eno.org
📄 020 7845 9296
📍 Page 10-E6

National Theatre

South Bank, Southwark, London SE1 9PX
☎ 020 7452 3000
@ info@nationaltheatre.org.uk
🖰 www.nationaltheatre.org.uk
📍 Page 11-H7

Purcell Room

South Bank Centre, London SE1 8XX
☎ 0870 380 0400
🖰 www.southbankcentre.co.uk
📍 Page 17-G1

Queen Charlotte Hall

Parkshot Centre, Parkshot, Richmond upon Thames TW9 2RE
☎ 020 8843 7921
📍 Page 136-E5

Royal College of Music

Prince Consort Road, South Kensington, London SW7 2BS
☎ 020 7589 3643
@ info@rcm.ac.uk
🖰 www.rcm.ac.uk
📄 020 7589 7740
📍 Page 14-A4

Royal Festival Hall

Belvedere Road, London SE1 8XX
☎ 0870 380 4300
@ customer@southbankcentre.co.uk
🖰 www.southbankcentre.co.uk
📄 0870 163 3898
📍 Page 17-G1

Royal Opera House

Bow Street, Covent Garden, London WC2E 9DD
☎ 020 7304 4000
@ webmaster@roh.org.uk
🖰 www.roh.org.uk
📍 Page 11-F4

THEATRES

Acton Community Theatre, West London Trades Union Club

5 Acton High Street, Acton, London W3 6ND
☎ 020 8992 4557
@ wltuc@wltuc.org.uk
🖰 www.wltuc.org
📍 Page 117-K1

Adelphi Theatre

Charing Cross, The Strand, Covent Garden, London WC2R 0NS
☎ 0870 403 0303
🖰 www.adelphi-theatre.com
📍 Page 11-F6

Aldwych Theatre

49 Aldwych, Holborn, London WC2B 4DF
☎ 0870 400 0805
@ info@ticketmaster.co.uk
🖰 www.aldwychtheatre.com
📍 Page 11-G4

Almeida Theatre

Almeida Street, Islington, London N1 1TA
☎ 020 7359 4404
@ info@almeida.co.uk
🖰 www.almeida.co.uk
📍 Page 85-H5

Apollo Theatre

31 Shaftesbury Avenue, Soho, London W1D 7EZ
☎ 0870 040 0085
🖰 www.nimaxtheatres.com
📍 Page 10-C5

Apollo Victoria Theatre

17 Wilton Road, Victoria, London SW1V 1LG
☎ 0870 161 1977
📍 Page 16-A5

Arcola Theatre

27 Arcola Street, Hackney, London E8 2DJ
☎ 020 7503 1646, 020 7503 1645
@ info@arcolatheatre.com
🖰 www.arcolatheatre.com
📍 Page 86-B3

Arts Educational London Schools

Cone Ripman House, 14 Bath Road, Chiswick, London W4 1LY
☎ 0208 987 6655
@ drama@artsed.co.uk,Jules@artsed.co.uk
🖰 www.artsed.co.uk
📍 Page 118-B4

Arts Theatre

6–7 Great Newport Street, Leicester Square, Covent Garden, London WC2H 7JB
☎ 020 7836 2132
🖰 www.artstheatrelondon.com
📍 Page 10-D5

Artszone Theatre

54–56 Market Square, Edmonton Green, London N9 0TZ
☎ 020 8887 9500
@ enfieldarts@btconnect.com
🖰 www.enfieldartspartnership.org
📍 Page 36-D4

Austrian Cultural Forum

28 Rutland Gate, South Kensington, London SW7 1PQ
☎ 020 7584 8653
🖰 www.austria.org.uk/culture/
📄 020 7225 0470
📍 Page 14-C4

Barbican Pit Theatre

Barbican Centre, Silk Street, London EC2Y 8DS
☎ 020 7638 4141
🕓 020 7638 8891
@ theatre@barbican.org.uk
🖰 www.barbican.org.uk/
📍 Page 12-D1

Barbican Theatre

Barbican Centre, Silk Street, London EC2Y 8DS
☎ 020 7638 4141
🕓 020 7638 8891
@ theatre@barbican.org.uk
🖰 www.barbican.org.uk/theatre
📍 Page 12-D1

Barons Court Theatre

28a Comeragh Road, London W14 9HP
☎ 020 8932 4747
@ baronstheatre@hotmail.com
🖰 www.offwestend.com
📍 Page 119-H5

Beck Theatre

Grange Road, Hayes UB3 2UE
☎ 0870 606 3560
🖰 www.becktheatre.org.uk
📍 Page 94-C5

The Bedford

77 Bedford Hill, Balham, London SW12 9HD

☎ 020 8682 8940
@ info@thebedford.co.uk
🖰 www.thebedford.co.uk
🖩 020 8682 8959
🜚 Page 161-G3

The Blue Elephant Theatre

59a Bethwin Road, Camberwell,
London SE5 0XT
☎ 020 7701 0100
@ info@blueelephanttheatre.
co.uk
🖰 www.blueelephanttheatre.co.uk
🜚 Page 142-D1

The Bookshop Theatre

The Calder Bookshop, 51 The Cut,
Waterloo, London SE1 8LP
☎ 020 7633 0599
@ info@godotcompany.com
🖰 www.godotcompany.com
🜚 Page 17-K1

Braithwaite Hall

Croydon Clocktower, Katharine
Street, Croydon CR9 1ET
☎ 020 8253 1030
@ arts@croydon.gov.uk
🖰 www.croydon.gov.uk
🜚 Page 211-J1

The Bridewell Theatre

Bride Lane, Fleet Street, London
EC4Y 8EQ
☎ 020 7353 3331
@ Lucy@stbrideinstitute.org
🖰 www.stbrideinstitute.org/
theatre.html
🖩 020 7353 1547
🜚 Page 12-A4

The Broadway Theatre

Catford Broadway, Catford,
London SE6 4RU
☎ 020 8690 0002
@ boxoffice@broadwaytheatre.
org.uk
🖰 www.broadwaytheatre.org.uk
🜚 Page 164-E2

Broadway Theatre

Broadway, Barking IG11 7LS
☎ 020 8507 5610
🕓 020 8507 5670
@ boxoffice@
thebroadwaybarking.com
🖰 www.thebroadwaybarking.com
🜚 Page 90-C6

Brockley Jack Theatre

410 Brockley Road, Brockley,
London SE4 2DH

☎ 020 8291 6354
🖰 www.brockleyjack.co.uk
🜚 Page 144-B6

Bromley Little Theatre

North Street, Bromley, London
BR1 1SB
☎ 020 8460 3047
@ mail@bromleylittletheatre.
co.uk
🖰 www.bromleylittletheatre.com
🜚 Page 183-K4

The Bush Theatre

Shepherds Bush Green, London
W12 8QD
☎ 020 7610 4224
@ info@bushtheatre.co.uk
🖰 www.bushtheatre.co.uk
🜚 Page 119-F2

Cambridge Theatre

Earlham Street, Covent Garden,
London WC2H 9HU
☎ 020 7494 5200
🖰 www.seetickets.com/useful/
new/venueinfo/cam.asp
🜚 Page 10-E4

Camden People's Theatre

58–60 Hampstead Road, Camden,
London NW1 2PY
☎ 020 7419 4841
@ admin@cptheatre.co.uk
🖰 www.cptheatre.co.uk
🜚 Page 4-A5

Canal Cafe Theatre

The Bridge House, Delamere
Terrace, London W2 6ND
☎ 020 7289 6056
@ mail@canalcafetheatre.com
🖰 www.canalcafetheatre.com
🜚 Page 101-G4

Cannizaro Park Open Air Theatre

Cannizaro Park, Wimbledon,
London SW19 4UE
☎ 0870 400 0882
🜚 Page 177-F1

The Charles Cryer Studio Theatre

39 High Street, Carshalton
SM5 3BB
☎ 020 8770 4950
🕓 020 8770 6990
@ e-mail@charlescryer.org.uk
🖰 www.suttontheatres.co.uk
🜚 Page 210-A2

The Chelsea Theatre

7 World's End Place, Kings Road,
Chelsea, London SW10 0DR
☎ 020 7352 1967
@ admin@chelseatheatre.org.uk
🖰 www.chelseatheatre.org.uk
🜚 Page 140-B1

Chicken Shed Theatre

Chase Side, Southgate, London
N14 4PE
☎ 020 8351 6161
@ info@chickenshed.org.uk
🖰 www.chickenshed.org.uk
🜚 Page 22-A6

Churchill Theatre

High Street, Bromley BR1 1HA
☎ 0870 060 6620
🖰 www.theambassadors.com
🜚 Page 183-K6

Clerkenwell Theatre

24 Exmouth Market, London
EC1R 4QE
☎ 0207 274 4888
🜚 Page 5-K6

Cochrane Theatre

Southampton Row, Bloomsbury,
London WC1B 4AP
☎ 020 7430 2500 / 020 7269
1600, 0207269 1606
@ info@cochranetheatre.co.uk
🖰 www.cochranetheatre.co.uk
🜚 Page 11-G2

Cockpit Theatre

Gateforth Street, St Johns Wood,
London NW8 8EH
☎ 020 7258 2920
@ pound@cockpittheatre.org.uk
🖰 www.cockpittheatre.org.uk
🜚 Page 2-C7

Colour House Children's Theatre

No 3 The Show House, Merton
Abbey Mills, Merton, London
SW19 2RD
☎ 020 8640 5111
@ info@wheelhouse.org.uk
🖰 www.wheelhouse.org.uk
🜚 Page 178-B4

Comedy Theatre

Panton Street, St James's, London
SW1Y 4DN
☎ 0870 060 6637
🖰 www.thecomedytheatre.co.uk
🜚 Page 10-C6

Courtyard Theatre

Hoxton, 40 Pitfield Street, London
N1 6EU
🕓 0870 163 0717
@ tim@thecourtyard.org.uk
🖰 www.thecourtyard.org.uk
🜚 Page 7-G4

Criterion Theatre

2 Jermyn Street, Piccadilly Circus,
St James's, London SW1Y 4XA
☎ 0870 060 2313
@ Admin@criterion-theatre.co.uk
🖰 www.criterion-theatre.com
🜚 Page 10-B6

Dominion Theatre

268–269 Tottenham Court Road,
Bloomsbury, London W1T 7AQ
🕓 0870 169 0116
🖰 www.dominiontheatre.co.uk
🜚 Page 10-D3

Donmar Warehouse

41 Earlham Street, Seven Dials,
Covent Garden, London WC2H 9LX
☎ 020 7240 4882
🕓 0870 060 6624
🖰 www.donmarwarehouse.com
🜚 Page 10-E4

The Drama Centre

Central Saint Martins College
of Art & Design, 10 Back Hill,
London EC1R 5AD
☎ 020 7514 8778, 020 7514 7022
@ drama@arts.ac.uk
🖰 courses.csm.arts.ac.uk/drama
🖩 020 7514 7254
🜚 Page 5-K7

The Drill Hall

16 Chenies Street, Bloomsbury,
London WC1E 7EX
☎ 020 7307 5060
@ admin@drillhall.co.uk
🖰 www.drillhall.co.uk
🖩 020 7307 5062
🜚 Page 10-C1

Duchess Theatre

Catherine Street, Covent Garden,
London WC2B 5LA
☎ 0870 040 0085
🖰 www.nimaxtheatres.com
🜚 Page 11-G5

Duke of York's Theatre

St Martin's Lane, Charing Cross,
London WC2N 4BG
☎ 0870 060 6623
🕓 0870 060 6623

www.theambassadors.com/
dukeofyorks
Page 10-E6

Edward Alleyn Theatre

Dulwich College, Dulwich, London
SE21 7LD
☎ 020 8299 9232
@ boxoffice@dulwich.org.uk
www.dulwich.org.uk
Page 163-F3

Embassy Theatre

Eton Avenue, Hampstead, London
NW3 3HY
☎ 020 7722 8183
@ enquiries@cssd.ac.uk
www.cssd.ac.uk/actors/
productions.htm
Page 83-J5

Emery Theatre

Annabel Close, East India Dock
Road, Poplar, London E14 6DP
www.emerytheatre.co.uk
Page 105-K5

Empire Leicester Square

5–6 Leicester Square, London
WC2H 7NA
☎ 02077 348222
www.empirecinemas.co.uk
Page 10-D5

Erith Playhouse

38–40 High Street, Erith DA8 1QY
© 01322 350345
@ mail@playhouse.org.uk
www.playhouse.org.uk
Page 130-C5

Etcetera Theatre

265 Camden High Street, Camden,
London NW1 7BU
☎ 020 7482 4857
@ etc@etceteratheatre.com
www.etceteratheatre.com
Page 84-B5

**Fairfield Halls and Ashcroft
Theatre**

Park Lane, Croydon CR9 1DG
☎ 020 8681 0821
© 020 8688 9291
@ boxoffice@fairfield.co.uk
www.fairfield.co.uk
Page 211-K1

Finborough Theatre

118 Finborough Road, Chelsea,
London SW10 9ED

☎ 020 7373 3842
@ admin@finboroughtheatre.
co.uk
www.finboroughtheatre.co.uk
Page 120-A6

Finchley Youth Theatre

142 High Road, East Finchley,
London N2 9ED
☎ 020 8359 3540
@ theatre@FYTheatre.org
www.fytheatre.org
Page 47-J6

Fortune Theatre

Russell Street, Holborn, London
WC2B 5HH
☎ 0870 060 6626
www.theambassadors.com
Page 11-F4

The Forum @ Greenwich

Trafalgar Road, Greenwich,
London SE10 9EQ
☎ 020 8853 5212
@ office@forumatgreenwich.org
www.forumatgreenwich.co.uk
▤ 020 8858 1909
Page 125-H5

GBS Theatre at RADA

Malet Street, Bloomsbury, London
WC1E 6ED
☎ 020 7908 4800
www.rada.org
Page 4-C7

Garage

22 Gordon Street, Bloomsbury,
London WC1H 0QB
Page 4-C6

Garrick Theatre

2 Charing Cross Road, Charing
Cross, London WC2H 0HH
☎ 020 7494 5085
© 0870 040 0085
@ general@nimaxtheatres.com
www.nimaxtheatres.com
Page 10-E6

Gate Theatre

11 Pembridge Road, Notting Hill,
London W11 3HQ
☎ 020 7229 0706
@ gate@gatetheatre.co.uk
www.gatetheatre.co.uk
▤ 020 7221 6055
Page 119-K1

Gielgud Theatre

Shaftesbury Avenue, Soho, London
W1D 6AR

☎ 0870 895 5505
www.gielgud-theatre.com/
Page 10-C5

**Greenwich & Lewisham
Young People's Theatre**

Building 18, Royal Arsenal West
Woolwich, London SE18 6ST
☎ 020 8854 1316
@ enquiries@gypt.co.uk
www.gypt.co.uk
Page 127-G3

Greenwich Playhouse

Greenwich Station Forecourt, 189
Greenwich High Road, London
SE10 8JA
☎ 020 8858 9256
@ BoxOffice@Galleontheatre.
co.uk
www.galleontheatre.co.uk
Page 144-E1

Greenwich Theatre

Crooms Hill, Greenwich, London
SE10 8ES
☎ 020 8858 7755, 020 8858 4447
@ info@greenwichtheatre.org.uk
www.greenwichtheatre.org.uk
Page 145-G1

Greenwood Theatre

King's College London, Strand,
Holborn, London WC2R 1LS
☎ 0207 188 3893
www.kcl.ac.uk/iss/av/rooms/
guys/greenwood/
Page 11-G5

Hackney Empire

291 Mare Street, London E8 1EJ
☎ 020 8985 2424
www.hackneyempire.co.uk
Page 86-D4

**Half Moon Young People's
Theatre**

43 Whitehorse Road, London
E1 0ND
☎ 020 7265 8138
© 020 7709 8900
@ admin@halfmoon.org.uk
www.halfmoon.org.uk
▤ 020 7709 8914
Page 105-G4

Hampstead Theatre

Eton Avenue, Swiss Cottage,
London NW3 3EU
☎ 020 7722 9301
@ boxoffice@hampsteadtheatre.
com
www.hampsteadtheatre.com
Page 83-H5

Hampton Hill Playhouse

90 High Street, Hampton Hill,
London TW12 1NY
☎ 020 8979 9499
@ hires@ttc-hhp.org.uk
www.ttc-hhp.org.uk
Page 173-H1

Hen and Chickens Theatre

109 St Pauls Road, Islington,
London N1 2NA
© 020 7704 2001
@ james@henandchickens.com
www.henandchickens.com
Page 85-H4

Her Majesty's Theatre

Haymarket, St James's, London
SW1Y 4QR
☎ 0207 494 5400
www.hermajestys.co.uk
Page 10-D7

Hoxton Hall

130 Hoxton Street, London
N1 6SH
☎ 020 7684 0060
@ info@hoxtonhall.co.uk
www.hoxtonhall.co.uk
▤ 020 7729 3815
Page 7-G2

Incognito Theatre

Holly Park Road, London N11 3HB
☎ 020 8361 8310
© 0791 287 5700
@ enquire@incognitotheatre.com
www.incognitotheatre.com
Page 34-A6

Interchange Studios

Hampstead Town Hall Centre,
213 Haverstock Hill, Hampstead,
London NW3 4QP
☎ 020 7692 5800
@ bookings@interchange.org.uk
www.interchange.org.uk
Page 83-J4

Intermission (St Saviour's)

Walton Place, London SW3 1SA
☎ 020 7589 5747
@ info@intermission.org.uk
www.intermission.org.uk
▤ 020 7589 2247
Page 14-E4

Jacksons Lane Theatre

269a Archway Road, London
N6 5AA
☎ 020 8341 4421
@ Mail@jacksonslane.org.uk
www.jacksonslane.org.uk
Page 66-B3

Jermyn Street Theatre

16b Jermyn Street, St James's,
London SW1Y 6ST
☎ 020 7287 2875/020 7434 1443
@ info@jermynstreettheatre.
co.uk
🖰 www.jermynstreettheatre.co.uk
⊘ Page 10-B6

Kenneth More Theatre

Oakfield Road, Ilford IG1 1BT
☎ 020 8553 4466
@ info@kenneth-more-theatre.
co.uk
🖰 www.kenneth-more-theatre.
co.uk
🖷 020 8553 5476
⊘ Page 90-C1

The King's Head Theatre

115 Upper Street, Islington,
London N1 1QN
☎ 020 7226 8561
📞 020 7226 1916
🖰 www.kingsheadtheatre.org
🖷 020 7226 8507
⊘ Page 85-G6

Kingston College Theatre: Arthur Cotterell Theatre

Kingston Hall Road, Kingston upon
Thames KT1 2AQ
☎ 020 8546 2151
@ info@kingston-college.ac.uk
🖰 www.kingston-college.ac.uk
⊘ Page 174-E6

LAMDA Drama School: Linbury Studio

155 Talgarth Road, Kensington,
London W14 9DA
☎ 020 8834 0500
@ enquiries@lamda.org.uk
🖰 www.lamda.org.uk
⊘ Page 119-H5

Landor Theatre

70 Landor Road, Stockwell,
London SW9 9PH
☎ 020 7737 7276
@ info@landortheatre.co.uk
🖰 www.landortheatre.co.uk
⊘ Page 141-K4

Lilian Baylis Theatre

Rosebery Avenue, London
EC1R 4TN
☎ 020 7863 8198
🖰 www.sadlerswells.com/
whats_on/lilian.asp
⊘ Page 6-A4

Lion & Unicorn

42–44 Gaisford Street, Kentish
Town, London NW5 2EB
☎ 0207 485 9897
🖰 www.actprovocateur.net
⊘ Page 84-C4

The Little Angel Theatre

14 Dagmar Passage, Islington,
London N1 2DN
☎ 020 7226 1787
@ info@littleangeltheatre.com
🖰 www.littleangeltheatre.com
⊘ Page 85-H6

London Palladium

8 Argyll Street, London W1V 1AD
☎ 0207 494 5060
🖰 www.london-palladium.co.uk
⊘ Page 10-A4

Lyceum Theatre

21 Wellington Street, Covent
Garden, London WC2E 7RQ
☎ 0870 606 3441
🖰 www.getlive.co.uk/venues/
venue/lyceum
⊘ Page 11-G5

Lyric Hammersmith

Lyric Square, King Street, London
W6 0QL
☎ 08700 500 511
@ enquiries@lyric.co.uk
🖰 www.lyric.co.uk
⊘ Page 119-F4

Lyric Theatre

Shaftesbury Avenue, Soho, London
W1D 7ES
☎ 020 7494 5045
🖰 www.nimaxtheatres.com
⊘ Page 10-C5

Macowan Theatre

Logan Place, London W8 6QN
☎ 020 8834 0500
@ boxoffice@lamda.org.uk
🖰 www.lamda.org.uk/develop
ment/events/macowan.htm
🖷 020 8834 0501
⊘ Page 119-K4

Menier Chocolate Factory

51–53 Southwark Street,
Bermondsey, London SE1 1RU
☎ 020 7907 7060
@ info@menierchocolatefactory.
com
🖰 www.menierchocolatefactory.
com
⊘ Page 12-B7

Michaelis Theatre

Erasmus House, Roehampton
Lane, London SW15 5PU
☎ 020 8392 3380
@ a.booroff@roehampton.ac.uk
🖰 www.roehampton.ac.uk
⊘ Page 138-D6

Millfield Arts Centre

Silver Street, Edmonton, London
N18 1PJ
☎ 020 8807 6680
@ info@millfieldtheatre.co.uk
🖰 www.millfieldtheatre.co.uk
🖷 020 8807 3892
⊘ Page 35-K6

National Theatre

South Bank, Southwark, London
SE1 9PX
☎ 020 7452 3000
@ info@nationaltheatre.org.uk
🖰 www.nationaltheatre.org.uk
⊘ Page 11-H7

National Theatre: Cottesloe Theatre

South Bank, Southwark, London
SE1 9PX
☎ 020 7452 3000
@ info@nationaltheatre.org.uk
🖰 www.nationaltheatre.org.uk
⊘ Page 11-H7

National Theatre: Lyttelton Theatre

South Bank, Southwark, London
SE1 9PX
☎ 020 7452 3400
📞 020 7452 3000
@ info@nationaltheatre.org.uk
🖰 www.nationaltheatre.org.uk
⊘ Page 11-H7

National Theatre: Olivier Theatre

South Bank, Southwark, London
SE1 9PX
☎ 020 7452 3000
@ info@nationaltheatre.org.uk
🖰 www.nationaltheatre.org.uk
⊘ Page 11-H7

Nettlefold Hall

1a Norwood High Street, West
Norwood, London SE27 9JX
☎ 020 7926 8070
🖰 www.lambeth.gov.uk
⊘ Page 162-C5

Network Theatre

246a Lower Road, Waterloo,
London SE8 5DJ

@ info@networktheatre.org
🖰 www.networktheatre.org
⊘ Page 124-A4

New Ambassadors Theatre

West Street, Covent Garden,
London WC2H 9ND
☎ 0870 060 6627
🖰 www.theambassadors.com/
newambassadors
⊘ Page 10-D4

New End Theatre

27 New End, Hampstead, London
NW3 1JD
☎ 0870 033 2733
@ info@newendtheatre.co.uk
🖰 www.newendtheatre.co.uk
⊘ Page 83-G1

New London Theatre

Drury Lane, Holborn, London
WC2B 5PW
☎ 0870 890 0141
🖰 www.seetickets.com/useful/
new/venueinfo/nln.asp
⊘ Page 11-F3

New Players Theatre

The Arches, Villiers Street,
London WC2N 6NG
☎ 02079306601
@ info@newplayerstheatre.com
🖰 www.newplayerstheatre.com
🖷 08456382102
⊘ Page 11-F7

New Wimbledon Theatre

The Broadway, Wimbledon,
London SW19 1QG
☎ 0870 060 6646
🖰 www.theambassadors.com/
newwimbledon
⊘ Page 177-K3

Noel Coward Theatre

85–88 St Martin's Lane, Charing
Cross, London WC2N 4AH
☎ 0870 950 0920
🖰 www.delfontmackintosh.
co.uk/theatres/albery
⊘ Page 10-E5

Notting Hill Coronet

103 Notting Hill Gate, Kensington,
London W11 3LB
☎ 020 7727 6705
🖰 www.coronet.org
⊘ Page 119-K1

Novello Theatre

Aldwych, Covent Garden, London
WC2B 4LD

☎ 0870 950 0940
✆ 0870 950 0935
@ delfont@delfont-mackintosh.com
🖱 www.delfontmackintosh.co.uk/theatres/novello
📖 Page 11-G5

Old Red Lion Theatre

418 St John Street, London EC1V 4NJ
☎ 020 7837 7816
🖱 www.oldredliontheatre.co.uk
📖 Page 5-K3

Old Royal Observatory Gardens

Greenwich Park, Greenwich, London SE10 9NF
☎ 020 8858 4422
@ Openmuseum@nmm.ac.uk
🖱 www.nmm.ac.uk
📖 Page 145-G1

The Old Vic

103 The Cut, Waterloo, London SE1 8NB
☎ 0870 060 6628
@ info@oldvictheatre.com
🖱 www.oldvictheatre.com
📠 020 7261 9161
📖 Page 17-K2

Open Air Theatre

Inner Circle, Regents Park, London NW1 4NR
☎ 020 7935 5756
@ info@openairtheatre.org
🖱 www.openairtheatre.org
📠 020 7487 4562
📖 Page 3-G5

Orange Tree Theatre

1 Clarence Street, Richmond TW9 2SA
☎ 020 8940 3633
🖱 www.orangetreetheatre.co.uk
📖 Page 137-F5

The Orchard Theatre

Home Gardens, Dartford DA1 1ED
☎ 01322 220000
@ orchard.theatre@dartford.gov.uk
🖱 www.orchardtheatre.co.uk
📖 Page 171-H1

Oval House Theatre

52–54 Kennington Oval, Kennington, London SE11 5SW
☎ 020 7582 7680
@ info@ovalhouse.com
🖱 www.ovalhouse.com
📖 Page 122-B6

Pacific Playhouse

5 Playhouse Court, 62 Southwark Bridge Road, London SE1 0AS
☎ 020 7803 0897
✆ 020 7803 0897
@ info@pacificplayhouse.com
🖱 www.pacificplayhouse.com/index.htm
📠 020 7803 0897
📖 Page 12-D7

Palace Theatre

Shaftesbury Avenue, Soho, London W1D 8AY
✆ 0870 895 5579
🖱 www.palace-theatre.co.uk
📖 Page 10-D5

Paul Robeson Theatre

CentreSpace, Treaty Centre, High Street, Hounslow TW3 1ES
☎ 0845 456 2900
@ info@cip.org.uk
🖱 www.hounslow.info
📖 Page 135-G4

Pentameters Theatre

28 Heath Street, Hampstead, London NW3 6TE
✆ 020 7435 3648
🖱 www.pentameters.co.uk
📖 Page 83-G1

People Show Studios

Pollard Row, Bethnal Green, London E2 6NB
☎ 020 7729 1841
@ people@peopleshow.co.uk
🖱 www.peopleshow.co.uk
📖 Page 104-C2

Phoenix Theatre

Charing Cross Road, Covent Garden, London WC2H 0JP
☎ 0870 060 6629
🖱 www.theambassadors.com
📖 Page 10-D4

Piccadilly Theatre

Denman Street, Soho, London W1D 7DY
☎ 0870 060 6630
🖱 www.theambassadors.com/piccadilly
📖 Page 10-C5

Playhouse Theatre

Northumberland Avenue, Charing Cross, London WC2N 5DE
☎ 0870 060 6631
🖱 www.theambassadors.com
📖 Page 11-F7

Pleasance Theatre

Carpenters Mews, North Road, London N7 9EF
☎ 020 7609 1800
@ info@pleasance.co.uk
🖱 www.pleasance.co.uk
📠 020 7700 7366
📖 Page 84-E4

The Polish Centre

238–246 King Street, London W6 0RF
☎ 020 8742 6401
@ polish.library@posk.org
🖱 www.poskuk.plus.com/posk_eng.html
📖 Page 118-D4

Polka Theatre

240 The Broadway, Wimbledon, London SW19 1SB
☎ 020 8543 4888
@ boxoffice@polkatheatre.com
🖱 www.polkatheatre.com
📠 020 8545 8366
📖 Page 178-A2

The Poor School

242 Pentonville Road, Islington, London N1 9JY
☎ 020 7837 6030
@ acting@thepoorschool.com
🖱 www.thepoorschool.com
📖 Page 5-F3

Prince Edward Theatre

Old Compton Street, Soho, London W1D 4HS
✆ 020 7447 5459
@ delfont@delmack.co.uk
🖱 www.delfont-mackintosh.com
📠 020 7240 3831
📖 Page 10-C4

Prince of Wales Theatre

Coventry Street, St James's, London W1D 6AS
☎ 0870 850 0393
@ powbox@delmack.co.uk
🖱 www.delfont-mackintosh.com
📖 Page 10-C6

Puppet Theatre Barge, Little Venice

Blomfield Road, London W9 2PF
☎ 020 7249 6876
@ puppet@movingstage.co.uk
🖱 www.puppetbarge.com
📠 020 7683 0156
📖 Page 101-G4

Puppet Theatre Barge, Richmond

Buccleuch Gardens, Richmond upon Thames TW10 6UT
☎ 020 7249 6876
@ puppet@movingstage.co.uk
🖱 www.puppetbarge.com
📠 020 7683 0156
📖 Page 156-E1

Queen Charlotte Hall

Parkshot Centre, Parkshot, Richmond upon Thames TW9 2RE
☎ 020 8843 7921
📖 Page 136-E5

Queen's Theatre

51 Shaftesbury Avenue, Soho, London W1D 6BA
☎ 0161 385 1138
✆ 0870 950 0930
@ queensboxoffice@delfont-mackintosh.com
🖱 www.delfont-mackintosh.com
📖 Page 10-C5

Questors Theatre

Mattock Lane, Ealing, London W5 5BQ
☎ 020 8567 0011
✆ 020 8567 5184
@ editor@questors.org.uk
🖱 www.questors.org.uk
📠 020 8567 8736
📖 Page 97-J6

Redbridge Drama Centre

Churchfields, South Woodford, London E18 2RB
☎ 020 8504 5451
@ rdc@redbridgedramacentre.co.uk
🖱 www.redbridgedramacentre.co.uk
📠 020 8505 6669
📖 Page 52-E4

Richmond Theatre

The Green, Richmond upon Thames, London TW9 1QJ
☎ 020 8939 9260
@ richmondboxoffice@theambassadors.com
🖱 www.theambassadors.com/richmond
📖 Page 136-E5

Rose Theatre

21 New Globe Walk, Southwark, London SE1 9AR
☎ 020 7593 0026
@ info@rosetheatre.org.uk
🖱 www.rosetheatre.org.uk
📖 Page 12-C7

Rose Theatre

24–26 High Street, Kingston upon Thames, London KT1 1HL
☎ 020 8546 6983
@ admin@kingstontheatre.org
🖰 www.kingstontheatre.org
▣ Page 174-E5

The Rosemary Branch Theatre

2 Shepperton Road, London N1 3DT
☎ 020 7704 2730
@ cecilia@rosemarybranch.co.uk
🖰 www.rosemarybranch.co.uk
▣ Page 85-K6

Royal Court Theatre

Sloane Square, Chelsea, London SW1 W 8AS
☎ 020 7565 5000
@ info@royalcourttheatre.com
🖰 www.royalcourttheatre.com
▣ Page 15-G7

Royal Festival Hall

Belvedere Road, Waterloo, London SE1 8XX
☎ 0870 380 4300
@ customer@southbankcentre. co.uk
🖰 www.southbankcentre.co.uk
▤ 0870 163 3898
▣ Page 11-G1

St Martin's Theatre

West Street, Cambridge Circus, Covent Garden, London WC2H 9NZ
☎ 020 7836 1443
🖰 www.stmartins-theatre.co.uk
▣ Page 10-D5

Savoy Theatre

Savoy Court, The Strand, Holborn, London WC2R 0ET
☎ 0870 164 8787
🖰 www.theambassadors. com/savoy
▤ 020 7395 1429
▣ Page 11-G6

The Scoop

More London Riverside, Bermondsey, London SE1 2DB
☎ 020 7403 4866
@ cbryant-fenn@ morelondonestates.co.uk
🖰 www.morelondon.com/scoop. html
▤ 020 7403 4867
▣ Page 19-H1

The Secombe Theatre

42 Cheam Road, Sutton SM1 2SS
☎ 020 8770 6990
🖰 www.suttontheatres.co.uk
▣ Page 209-F3

Shaftesbury Theatre

Shaftesbury Avenue, Covent Garden, London WC2H 8DP
✆ 020 7379 5399
🖰 www.shaftesbury-theatre.co.uk
▣ Page 10-E3

Shakespeare's Globe

21 New Globe Walk, Bankside, Southwark, London SE1 9DT
☎ 020 7902 1400
@ info@shakespearesglobe.com
🖰 www.shakespeares-globe.org
▤ 020 7902 1401
▣ Page 12-B6

The Shaw Theatre

100–110 Euston Road, Camden, London NW1 2AJ
☎ 020 7388 2555
✆ 0870 033 2600
@ jjalmond@theshawtheatre. com
🖰 www.theshawtheatre.com
▤ 020 7388 7555
▣ Page 4-D4

Soho Revue Bar

11–12 Walker's Court, Brewer Street, London W1F 0ED
☎ 020 7734 0377
@ cheryl@too2much.com
🖰 www.sohorevuebar.co.uk
▣ Page 10-C5

Soho Theatre

21 Dean Street, Soho, London W1D 3NE
☎ 020 7287 5060
✆ 0870 429 6883
@ mail@sohotheatre.com
🖰 www.sohotheatre.com
▤ 020 7287 5061
▣ Page 10-C3

South London Theatre

2a Norwood High Street, West Norwood, London SE27 9NS
✆ 020 8670 3474
@ info@southlondontheatre. co.uk
🖰 www.southlondontheatre.co.uk
▣ Page 162-D5

Southwark Playhouse

60 Great Suffolk Street, Southwark, London SE1 0BL
✆ 020 7620 3494
@ admin@southwarkplayhouse. co.uk
🖰 www.southwarkplayhouse. co.uk
▤ 020 7261 1072
▣ Page 18-B2

Tabard Theatre

2 Bath Road, Turnham Green, London W4 1LW
☎ 020 8994 5985
✆ 020 8995 6035
@ info@pitchdarktheatre.co.uk
🖰 www.tabardtheatre.co.uk
▤ 020 8747 8256
▣ Page 118-B4

Theatre 503

Latchmere Pub, 503 Battersea Park Road, Battersea, London SW11 3BW
☎ 020 7978 7040
@ mail@theatre503.com
🖰 www.theatre503.com
▣ Page 140-D3

Theatre Royal Drury Lane

Catherine Street, Holborn, London WC2B 5JF
☎ 020 7494 5200
✆ 0870 890 1109
@ hirings@rutheatres.com
🖰 www.theatreroyaldrurylane. co.uk
▤ 020 7434 1217
▣ Page 11-F4

Theatre Royal Haymarket

Haymarket, St James's, London SW1Y 4HT
☎ 020 7930 8890
✆ 0870 901 3356
@ boxoffice@trh.co.uk
🖰 www.trh.co.uk
▣ Page 10-D6

Theatre Royal Stratford East

Gerry Raffles Square, Stratford, London E15 1BN
☎ 020 8534 7374
✆ 0800 183 1188
@ theatreroyal@stratfordeast. com
🖰 www.stratfordeast.com
▤ 020 8534 8381
▣ Page 88-B4

Theatro Technis

26 Crowndale Road, Camden, London NW1 1TT

Theatre Technis

☎ 020 7387 6617
@ info@theatrotechnis.com
🖰 www.theatrotechnis.com
▤ 020 7383 2545
▣ Page 4-B2

Toynbee Studios

28 Commercial Street, London E1 6LS
☎ 020 7247 5102
🖰 www.artsadmin.co.uk/ toynbeestudios
▣ Page 13-J2

Trafalgar Studios

14 Whitehall, Westminster, London SW1A 2DY
☎ 08700 606632
🖰 www.theambassadors.com/ trafalgarstudios
▣ Page 16-E1

Tricycle Theatre

269 Kilburn High Road, Kilburn, London NW6 7JR
☎ 02073 281000
@ info@tricycle.co.uk
🖰 www.tricycle.co.uk
▣ Page 82-D5

Tristan Bates Theatre

1a Tower Street, Covent Garden, London WC2H 9NP
☎ 020 7240 3940
✆ 020 7240 6283
@ act@actorscentre.co.uk
🖰 www.tristanbatestheatre.co.uk
▣ Page 10-E4

The UCL Bloomsbury Theatre

15 Gordon Street, Bloomsbury, London WC1H 0AH
☎ 020 7388 8822
@ blooms.theatre@ucl.ac.uk
🖰 www.thebloomsbury.com
▣ Page 4-C6

Unicorn Theatre

147 Tooley Street, More London, Bermondsey, London SE1 2HZ
☎ 020 7645 0500
✆ 0870 053 4534
@ admin@unicorntheatre.com
🖰 www.unicorntheatre.com
▣ Page 19-H2

Union Theatre

204 Union Street, Southwark, London SE1 0LX
✆ 020 7261 9876
@ sasha@union.co.uk
🖰 www.uniontheatre.org
▣ Page 18-B1

Upstairs at The Gatehouse

The Gatehouse, Highgate Village,
London N6 4BD
☎ 020 8340 3477
© 020 8340 3488
@ events@ovationproductions.
com
⌐ www.upstairsatthegatehouse.
com
▤ 020 8340 3466
❂ Page 66-A4

Vanbrugh Theatre

62–64 Gower Street, London
WC1E 6ED
☎ 020 7636 7076
⌐ www.rada.org
❂ Page 4-C7

Vaudeville Theatre

404 Strand, Covent Garden,
London WC2R 0NH
☎ 0870 040 0085
⌐ home.freeuk.com/
thevaudeville/
❂ Page 11-F5

The Venue

5 Leicester Place, Leicester
Square, London WC2H 7BP
☎ 020 7734 6004
❂ Page 10-D5

Victoria Palace Theatre

Victoria Street, St James's Park,
London SW1E 5EA
☎ 0870 895 5577
⌐ www.victoriapalacetheatre.
co.uk
❂ Page 15-K5

Volupte

9 Norwich Street, London
EC4A 1EJ
☎ 020 7831 1622
@ info@volupte-lounge.com
⌐ www.volupte-lounge.com
❂ Page 11-J3

Waltham Forest Theatre

Lloyd Park, Winns Terrace,
Walthamstow, London E17 5EH
☎ 020 8496 3587
© 020 8521 7111
❂ Page 51-H6

Walworth Road Council Chambers

155–157 Walworth Road,
Walworth, London SE17 1RY
❂ Page 18-C7

Warehouse Theatre

Dingwall Road, Croydon CR0 2NF
☎ 020 8680 4060
@ info@warehousetheatre.co.uk
⌐ www.warehousetheatre.co.uk
❂ Page 196-E6

Watergate School

Lushington Road, Bellingham,
Catford, London SE6 3RJ
☎ 020 8695 6555
⌐ www.lewisham.gov.uk
❂ Page 182-E1

White Bear Theatre

138 Kennington Park Road,
Kennington, London SE11 4RB
☎ 020 7793 9193
@ mkwbear@hotmail.com
⌐ www.whitebeartheatre.co.uk
❂ Page 122-B6

Wilton's Music Hall

Graces Alley, Tower Hamlets,
London E1 8JB
☎ 020 7702 9555
@ info@wiltons.org.uk
⌐ www.wiltons.org.uk
❂ Page 104-C6

Wimbledon Studio Theatre

The Broadway, Wimbledon,
London SW19 1QG
© 0870 060 6646
⌐ www.theambassadors.com/
wimbledonstudio
❂ Page 177-K3

Wyndham's Theatre

Charing Cross Road, Covent
Garden, London WC2H 0DA
☎ 0870 950 0925
© 020 7812 7447
⌐ www.theambassadors.com/
wyndhams/info/index.html
❂ Page 10-D5

Young Vic Theatre

66 The Cut, Waterloo, London
SE1 8LZ
☎ 020 7922 2922
© 020 7922 2922
@ boxoffice@youngvic.org
⌐ www.youngvic.org
❂ Page 17-K2

BARS AND PUBS

101 Bar

101 Bar hosts parties, private and
corporate events with live music.

101 New Oxford Street, Covent
Garden, London WC1A 1DB

☎ 020 7379 3112, 07863 171961
@ info@101bar.com
⌐ www.vpmg.net/101
▤ 020 7379 1905
❂ Page 10-E3

A10 Russian Bar

Underground venue in the heart of
Shoreditch.

267 Kingsland Road, London
E2 8AS
☎ 07809 425905
❂ Page 7-H3

AKA

Next door to the renowned
nightclub The End, AKA London is
a bar venue that holds a variety
of dance nights in its own right as
well as sharing some of its sister-
venue's larger nights. Cocktails
and food also served.

18 West Central Street,
Bloomsbury, London WC1A 1JJ
☎ 020 7836 0110
@ info@akalondon.com
⌐ www.akalondon.com
▤ 020 7419 9099
❂ Page 10-E3

Ace Cafe London

Ace Corner, North Circular Road,
Stonebridge, Park Royal, London
NW10 7UD
☎ 02089 611000
⌐ www.ace-cafe-london.com
▤ 02089 650161
❂ Page 80-C6

Adulis

44-46 Brixton Road, London
SW9 6BT
☎ 020 7587 0055
❂ Page 142-B5

The Alexandra

14 Clapham Common South Side,
Clapham, London SW4 7AA
☎ 020 7627 5102
❂ Page 141-H5

Alphabet Bar

61–63 Beak Street, London
W1F 9SL
☎ 020 7439 2190
@ info@alphabetbar.com
⌐ www.alphabetbar.com
❂ Page 10-A5

Anda de Bridge

42–44 Kingsland Road, Shoreditch,
London E2 8DA

☎ 020 7739 3863
@ info@andadebridge.com
⌐ www.andadebridge.com
❂ Page 7-H3

Anexo

Anexo is Turnmills' 150 capacity,
two-floor DJ bar, restaurant and
venue.

61 Turnmill Street, London
EC1M 5PT
☎ 020 7250 3401
@ anexo@turnmills.co.uk
⌐ www.anexo.co.uk
❂ Page 5-K7

Apt

Complete with chic furnishings
and lounging sofas, the bar won
BEDA's UK Bar of the Year in 2005.

Aldermary House, 10–15 Queen
Street, London EC4N 1TX
☎ 020 7618 9020
@ info@aptbar.co.uk
⌐ www.aptbar.co.uk
❂ Page 12-D4

Archway Tavern

Archway Tavern, host to the Tube
Club, offers weekly live indie music
with DJ support.

1 Archway Close, Archway Road,
London N19 3TX
☎ 020 7272 2840
© 020 7272 2840
@ info@thetubeclub.co.uk
⌐ www.thetubeclub.co.uk
❂ Page 66-C6

The Art Bar

The Artbar nestles not so gently
on the ground floor of a double
fronted thoroughly modernised
pair of houses.

87–89 Walton Street, Chelsea,
London SW3 2HP
☎ 020 7589 8558
@ info@artbar.biz
⌐ www.artbar.biz
❂ Page 14-D6

The Artesian Well

693 Wandsworth Road, Clapham,
London SW8 3JF
☎ 020 7627 3353
@ info@artesianwell.co.uk
⌐ www.artesianwell.co.uk
▤ 020 7627 2850
❂ Page 141-G4

Astria

4 Tooley Street, Bermondsey,
London SE1 2SY

☎ 020 7403 2000
✆ Page 19-G1

Babushka

316–318 Kings Road, Chelsea,
London SW3 5UH
☎ 020 7352 0025
🖨 020 7352 8715
✆ Page 120-C6

Bank Westminster Restaurant and Zander Bar

45 Buckingham Gate, St James's
Park, London SW1E 6BS
☎ 020 7630 6644
@ westminster.reservations@
bankrestaurants.com
🕆 www.bankrestaurants.com/
articles/9
✆ Page 16-A4

Bar 242

242 Blackfriars Road, London
SE1 9UF
☎ 020 7928 8689
🕆 www.bar242.co.uk/
✆ Page 12-A7

Bar Andalucia

A Spanish/South American bar
offering a range of regular events
including tango and salsa dance
classes, and Latin-themed club
nights.

139–143 Whitfield Street, London
W1T 5EN
☎ 020 7388 3369
@ info@barandalucia.co.uk
🕆 www.barandalucia.co.uk
✆ Page 10-B1

Bar Aquarium

The Bar hosts a wide range
of musical entertainment in
conjunction with different
promoters.

256–264 Old Street, London
EC1V 9DD
☎ 020 7253 3558, 07838 360990
@ oj@clubaquarium.co.uk
🕆 www.clubaquarium.co.uk
🖨 020 7253 9885
✆ Page 7-G5

Bar China

292 Haydons Road, Wimbledon,
London SW19 8JZ
☎ 020 8543 3111
@ info@barchina.com
🕆 www.barchina.com
✆ Page 178-A1

Bar Cosa

54 Holloway Road, London N7 8JL
☎ 020 7609 9574
✆ Page 85-F2

Bar M

4 Lower Richmond Road, Putney,
London SW15 1JN
☎ 0208 788 0345
🕆 www.barm.co.uk
🖨 0208 780 2122
✆ Page 139-F4

Bar Rumba

Launched in 1993, Bar Rumba
has a basement capacity of 455
and hosts an eclectic mix of club
nights.

36 Shaftesbury Avenue, Soho,
London W1D 7EP
☎ 020 7287 6933, 020 7287 2715
@ barrumba@thebreakfastgroup.
co.uk
🕆 www.barrumba.co.uk
🖨 020 7287 2714
✆ Page 10-C5

Bar Shu

28 Frith Street, Corner of Romilly
Street, Soho, London W1D 5LG
☎ 0871-223-1808
✆ Page 10-C4

Bar Soho

Bar Soho in Old Compton Street
is a great place for an enjoyable
night out. Relax in the candlelit
rooms while listening to a
selection of 80s and 90s tracks
being spun on the decks by one of
the resident DJs.

23–25 Old Compton Street, Soho,
London W1D 5JL
☎ 020 7439 4089
@ events@barsoho.co.uk
🕆 www.barsoho.co.uk
✆ Page 10-C5

Bar Vinyl

6 Inverness Street, London
NW1 7HJ
☎ 020 7482 5545
🕆 www.barvinyl.co.uk/
✆ Page 84-B6

The Bar and Grill

2–3 West Smithfield, London
EC1A 9JX
☎ 0870 442 2541
@ smithfield@barandgrill.co.uk
🕆 www.blackhousegrills.com
🖨 0870 442 2542
✆ Page 12-A2

The Bath House

96 Dean Street, Soho, London
W1D 3TD
☎ 020 7437 3805
✆ Page 10-C3

The Bedroom Bar

62 Rivington Street, London
EC2A 3AY
☎ 020 7739 5706
🕆 www.bedroom-bar.co.uk
✆ Page 7-H5

Beduin

Beduin is Smithfield's latest late
night bar/club/restaurant with
a decor inspired by a traditional
Moroccan Souk.

57–59 Charterhouse Street,
Smithfield, London EC1M 6HA
☎ 020 7336 6484
@ contact@beduin-london.co.uk
🕆 www.beduin-london.co.uk
🖨 020 7336 6866
✆ Page 12-A2

The Bell On The Green

661 Staines Road, Feltham
TW14 8PA
☎ 020 87511599
✆ Page 152-E3

Belushi's in London Bridge

161–165 Borough High Street,
Southwalk, Bermondsey, London
London SE1 1HR
☎ 0871 332 2975
@ garth.jackson@belushis.com
🕆 www.belushis.com/belushis/
londonbridge.htm
✆ Page 18-D3

Ben Crouches Tavern

77a Wells Street, London
W1P 3RE
☎ 020 7636 0717
🖨 020 7436 2484
✆ Page 10-A2

Bistrotheque

The Bistrotheque bar-restaurant
also houses the PS2 Cabaret Room
which specialises in live, non-DJ
based entertainment.

23–27 Wadeson Street, Bethnal
Green, London E2 9DP
☎ 020 8983 7900
@ info@bistrotheque.com
🕆 www.bistrotheque.com
✆ Page 104-D1

The Bitter End

15 High Street, Romford RM1 1JU

☎ 01708 742923
🕆 www.thebitterendonline.com
✆ Page 75-G2

Black Sheep Bar

68 High Street, Croydon CR0 1NA
☎ 020 8680 2233
@ steph@blacksheepbar.com
🕆 www.blacksheepbar.com
✆ Page 211-J1

Blue Music Venue

Enjoy lazy Sunday afternoons
sitting by the river in the beer
garden listening to cool jazz right
up to the evenings. Also late
nights providing salsa lessons,
live soul, funk R'n'B and Latin jazz
bands, and full on funky house
nights with DJs spinning top tunes
and the occasional live jazzy drum
and bass nights.

222 High Street, Colliers Wood,
London SW19 2BH
☎ 020 85403545
@ info@bluemusicvenue.co.uk
🕆 www.bluemusicvenue.co.uk
✆ Page 178-C3

Bluu, Hoxton

1 Hoxton Square, London N1 6NU
☎ 020 7613 2793
@ hoxton@bluu.co.uk
🕆 www.bluu.co.uk
✆ Page 7-G5

Boulevard Soho

57–59 Old Compton Street, Soho,
London W1D 6HP
☎ 020 7287 0770
@ info@boulevardsoho.com
🕆 www.boulevardsoho.com
🖨 020 7287 2122
✆ Page 10-C5

Brb@The Grove

26 Camberwell Grove,
Camberwell, London SE5 8RE
☎ 020 7703 4553
@ grovecamberwell@youngs.
co.uk
🕆 www.grovecamberwell.co.uk
🖨 020 7703 0624
✆ Page 142-E2

The Bread and Roses

68 Clapham Manor Street,
Clapham, London SW4 6DZ
☎ 020 7498 1779
@ info@breadandrosespub.com
🕆 www.breadandrosespub.com
🖨 020 7978 2472
✆ Page 141-H4

The British Queen

63 New Wanstead, Wanstead,
London E11 2SA
☎ 020 8989 8975
🖰 www.thebritishqueen.com
❂ Page 70-E3

Bullet Bar

147 Kentish Town Road, London
NW1 8PB
☎ 020 7485 6040
@ bar@bulletbar.co.uk
🖰 www.bulletbar.co.uk
❂ Page 84-B4

Bunker

Bunker Beir Hall, 41 Earlham
Street, London WC2H 9LD
☎ 020 7240 0606
@ info@bunkerbar.com
🖰 www.bunkerbar.com
📄 020 7240 4422
❂ Page 10-D4

Calico Bar

67–69 Watling Street, London
EC4M 9DD
☎ 020 7248 0883
@ calico@massivepub.com
🖰 www.massivepub.com
❂ Page 12-C4

The Camden Tup

Bar showing big screen sports
events and serving food all day.

2–3 Greenland Place, London
NW1 0AP
☎ 020 7482 0399
@ camdentup@massivepub.com
🖰 www.massivepub.com
❂ Page 84-B6

The Camel, Fulham

358 Fulham Road, Fulham, London
SW10 9UU
☎ 020 7376 7370
❂ Page 120-C5

The Camel, Waterloo

121 Lower Marsh, Waterloo,
London SE1 7AE
☎ 020 7633 0270, 08713 323086
❂ Page 17-J3

Candy Bar

Candy Bar delivers a world of
uplifting entertainment for gay
girls and their friends every night
of the week.

4 Carlisle Street, Soho, London
W1D 3BJ
☎ 020 7494 4041
🖰 www.candybarsoho.com
❂ Page 10-C4

The Canterbury Arms

8 Canterbury Crescent, Stockwell,
London SW9 7QD
☎ 020 7274 1711
❂ Page 142-B4

The Castle

65 Camberwell Church Street,
Camberwell, London SE5 8TR
☎ 020 7277 2601
@ Bookings@the-castle.co.uk
🖰 www.the-castle.co.uk
❂ Page 142-E2

The Castle

34–35 Cowcross Street, London
EC1M 6DB
☎ 020 7553 7621
❂ Page 12-A1

The Cauliflower

553 High Road, Ilford IG1 1TZ
☎ 020 8553 2300
🖰 www.thecauliflower.co.uk
❂ Page 72-D5

The Cedar Room

235 Upper Street, Islington,
London N1 1RU
☎ 020 7704 6977
@ info@thecedarroom.co.uk
🖰 www.thecedarroom.co.uk
❂ Page 5-K2

The Chancery

314–316 Lillie Road, Fulham,
London SW6 7PS
☎ 020 3080 0982
🖰 thechancerybar.co.uk/
❂ Page 119-G6

The Chapel Bar

The Chapel Bar provides the
ultimate couches, cocktails and
DJs venue and atmosphere in
North London.

29a Penton Street, Islington,
London N1 9PX
☎ 07870 268415
@ info@thechapelbar.co.uk
🖰 www.thechapelbar.co.uk
❂ Page 5-J2

Charlie Wright's International Bar

45 Pitfield Street, London N1 6DA
☎ 020 7490 8345
❂ Page 7-G4

Charlies Bar

9 Crosswall, London EC3N 2JY

☎ 020 7488 1766
@ Charliesclub02@aol.com
🖰 www.charliesnightclub.150m.
com
📄 020 7265 1672
❂ Page 13-J5

Charterhouse

38 Charterhouse Street, London
EC1M 6JH
☎ 020 7608 0858
@ info@charterhousebar.co.uk
🖰 www.charterhousebar.co.uk
📄 020 7608 0859
❂ Page 12-A2

Cheers

Cheers, London, was inspired by
the popular US comedy series, and
incorporates bar, restaurant and
merchandise store. In the evening
it changes from from a bar and
restaurant to London's busiest
dance bar featuring in-house DJs
playing the latest tunes side by
side with classics.

72 Regent Street, Soho, London
W1B 5RJ
☎ 020 7494 3322
🖰 www.cheersbarlondon.com
❂ Page 10-A4

Cherry Jam

58 Porchester Road, London
W2 6ET
☎ 020 7727 9950
@ alan@cherryjam.net
🖰 www.cherryjam.net
❂ Page 101-F5

Chicago Rock Cafe, Sutton

Chicago Rock Cafe offers a
blend of eating, drinking and
entertainment.

Throwley Road, Sutton SM1 1AD
☎ 020 8643 2606
@ sutton@chicago-rock-cafe.
co.uk
🖰 www.chicago-rock-cafe.co.uk
📄 020 8770 0145
❂ Page 209-F3

Cicada

132–136 St John Street, London
EC1V 4JT
☎ 020 7608 1550
@ dariush@cicada.nu
🖰 www.rickerrestaurants.com
📄 020 7608 1551
❂ Page 5-K3

The Claddagh Ring

10 Church Road, Hendon, London
NW4 4EA

☎ 020 8203 2600
@ info@claddagh-ring.co.uk
🖰 www.claddagh-ring.co.uk
📄 020 8203 3368
❂ Page 63-K1

Clapham Boom

167 St Johns Hill, Clapham,
Wandsworth, London SW11 1TQ
☎ 020 7924 3449
@ info@claphamboom.com
📄 020 7924 2092
❂ Page 140-C5

The Clarence

53 Whitehall, Westminster, London
SW1A 2HP
☎ 020 7930 4808
❂ Page 16-E1

Clerkenwell House

Clerkenwell House has lounge and
basement bars with DJ booths
and plenty of room to dance the
night away.

23–27 Hatton Wall, Hatton Garden,
London EC1N 8NJ
☎ 020 7404 1113
🖰 www.clerkenwellhouse.com
❂ Page 11-J1

Cocomo Bar

323 Old Street, London EC1V 9LE
☎ 020 7613 0315
❂ Page 6-C6

The College Arms

18 Store Street, Bloomsbury,
London WC1E 7DH
☎ 020 7436 4697
❂ Page 10-C2

Corks Wine Bar

28 Binney Street, Marylebone,
London W1K 5BW
☎ 020 7408 0100
@ info@corkswinebar.co.uk
🖰 www.corkswinebar.co.uk
❂ Page 9-H5

The Corrib Rest

The Corrib Rest has been
transformed into one of London's
most genuine Irish pubs.

76–80 Salusbury Road, Queens
Park, Kilburn, London NW6 6PA
☎ 020 7625 9585
@ info@claddagh-ring.co.uk
🖰 www.claddagh-ring.co.uk
📄 020 7263 9064
❂ Page 82-C6

☎ 020 8299 9521
✆ Page 163-J1

Home
Home is the laid-back lived-in basement bar that helped Hoxton earn its hip square mile title.

100–106 Leonard Street, London EC2A 4RH
☎ 020 7684 8618
@ mail@homebar.co.uk
🖰 www.homebar.co.uk
🖺 020 7684 1491
✆ Page 7-G6

The Hop Poles
17–19 King Street, Hammersmith, London W6 9HR
☎ 020 8748 1411
✆ Page 118-D4

The Hope
A classic corner house famous for it's sausage and mash as well as a selection of cask conditioned ales.

15 Tottenham Street, London W1T 2AJ
☎ 020 7637 0896
@ hope@reallondonpubs.com
🖰 www.reallondonpubs.com
✆ Page 10-B2

The Hope and Anchor
123 Acre Lane, Brixton, London SW2 5UA
☎ 07985 065224
✆ Page 142-A5

Horse & Groom
28 Curtain Road, London EC2A 3NQ
✆ Page 7-G7

Horse Bar
124 Westminster Bridge Road, Waterloo, London SE1 7XG
☎ 020 7928 6277
@ info@horsebar.co.uk
🖰 www.horsebar.co.uk
🖺 020 7928 5919
✆ Page 17-F3

The Horse and Groom
28 Curtain Road, London EC2A 3NZ
☎ 020 7247 9291
✆ Page 7-G7

ISH (International Student House)
229 Great Portland Street, Regent's Park, London W1W 5PN
☎ 020 7631 8300
@ info@ish.org.uk

🖰 www.ish.org.uk
🖺 020 7631 8307
✆ Page 9-K1

Imbibe
173 Blackfriars Road, Southwark, London SE1 8ER
☎ 020 7928 3693
@ info@imbibe-bar.co.uk
🖰 www.imbibe-bar.com
🖺 020 7620 2092
✆ Page 12-A7

Indo Bar
133 Whitechapel Road, Whitechapel, London E1 1DT
☎ 020 7247 4926
✆ Page 104-C5

Inigo
South London bar with a busy calendar of nights hosted by both guest and resident DJs.

642 Wandsworth Road, London SW8 3JW
☎ 020 7622 4884
@ info@inigobar.com
🖰 www.inigobar.com
✆ Page 141-G4

The International
116 St Martins Lane, Charing Cross, London WC2N 4BF
☎ 020 7257 8626
@ sarah.franklin@cgrestaurants.com
🖰 www.theinternational.uk.com
✆ Page 10-E5

Ion Bar
Renowned international DJs and a new and improved restaurant. Owned by music impresario Vince Power under the VPMG trademark.

161–165 Ladbroke Grove, Notting Hill, London W10 6HJ
☎ 020 8960 1702
🖰 www.vpmg.net
✆ Page 100-B3

The Islington Bar
342 Caledonian Road, London N1 1BB
☎ 020 7609 4917
✆ Page 85-F6

Jam
123 Shoreditch High Street, Shoreditch, London E1 6JE
☎ 020 7613 3554
@ info@jamshoreditch.co.uk
🖰 www.jamshoreditch.co.uk
✆ Page 13-H1

Jamies Bar Charlotte Street
74 Charlotte Street, London W1T 4QH
☎ 020 7636 7556
🖰 www.charlottestreetbar.co.uk/
✆ Page 10-B1

Jamies Bar and Restaurant Mayfair
24–26 Maddox Street, London W1S 1QH
☎ 020 7499 3775
🖰 www.jamiesbars.co.uk/mayfair/
✆ Page 9-K5

Jamm
261 Brixton Road, Stockwell, London SW9 6LH
☎ 020 7274 5537
@ info@brixtonjamm.org
🖰 www.brixtonjamm.org
✆ Page 142-B5

Jerusalem
33–34 Rathbone Place, London W1T 1JN
☎ 020 7255 1120
@ jerusalem@thebreakfastroom.co.uk.
🖰 www.fabbars.com
✆ Page 10-C2

Jewel Bar Covent Garden
Elegant designer bar in the heart of London.

29–30 Maiden Lane, Covent Garden, London WC2E 7JS
☎ 020 7439 4089
@ events@jewelbar.com
🖰 www.jewelbarlondon.co.uk
✆ Page 11-F6

Jewel Bar Piccadilly
Elegant designer bar in the heart of London.

4–6 Glasshouse Street, Soho, London W1B 5DQ
☎ 020 7439 4990
🕾 020 7439 4089
@ events@jewelbar.com
🖰 www.jewelbarlondon.co.uk
✆ Page 10-B6

The Kilburn
307–309 Kilburn High Road, Kilburn, London NW6 7JR
☎ 020 7372 8668
@ kevin@roninnltd.com
🖰 www.thekilburn.com
✆ Page 82-E6

King Eddie's VII
47 Broadway, Stratford, London E15 4BQ
☎ 020 8534 2313
@ enquiries@kingeddie.co.uk
✆ Page 88-B5

The Kings Arms
The Vale, London W3 7JT
☎ 020 8743 2689
✆ Page 118-A1

The Kings Head
214 High Street, Acton, London W3 9NX
☎ 020 8992 0282
✆ Page 117-K1

Kings Head
49 Chiswell Street, London EC1Y 4SA
✆ Page 12-E1

Kinky Mambo
144–145 Upper Street, Islington, London N1 1QY
☎ 020 7704 6868
🖰 www.kinkymambo.co.uk
✆ Page 5-K2

Ku Bar
30 Lisle Street, Leicester Square, London WC2H 7BA
☎ 020 7437 4303
🖰 www.ku-bar.co.uk
✆ Page 10-D5

LHT Urban Bar
176 Whitechapel Road, London E1 1BJ
☎ 020 7247 8978
✆ Page 104-C5

LVPO Bar
LVPO has the ambience of a private members' club but it's open to all. The dark, candlelit environment, with its voluminous velvet drapes and old wooden floorboards creates a cosy atmosphere.

50 Dean Street, Soho, London W1D 5BQ
☎ 020 7434 3399
@ events@lvpo.co.uk
🖰 www.lvpo.co.uk
✆ Page 10-C3

La Luna
438 Mile End Road, Walworth, London E1 4PE

☎ 020 7702 7619
@ info@lalunatapasbar.co.uk
⌂ www.lalunatapasbar.co.uk
⍟ Page 104-E4

The Lamb

94 Lambs Conduit Street,
Bloomsbury, London WC1N 3LZ
☎ 020 7405 0713
⍟ Page 5-G7

The Leather Bottle

277 Kingston Road, Merton,
London SW19 3NW
☎ 0208542 7490
⍟ Page 177-K3

The Legion

348 Old Street, London EC1V 9NQ
☎ 020 7729 4441
@ info@thelegion.co.uk
⌂ www.thelegion.co.uk
⍟ Page 6-C6

The Lion

The Lion has a function room
which doubles as a second
bar hosting a range of local
entertainment from comedy
nights, accoustic sets, bands and
exhibitions.

132 Church Street, Stoke
Newington, London N16 0JX
☎ 020 7249 1318
@ thelion@massivepub.com
⌂ www.massivepub.com/
⍟ Page 68-A6

The Living Room, Islington

Suncourt House, 18–26 Essex
Road, Islington, London N1 8LN
☎ 020 7288 9090
@ islington@thelivingroom.co.uk
⌂ www.thelivingroom.co.uk
▤ 020 7354 3919
⍟ Page 85-J5

Lockside Lounge

A stylish and atmospheric bar
overlooking the canal.

West Yard, Camden Lock, Camden,
London NW1 8AF
☎ 020 7284 0007
@ david@locksidelounge.com
⌂ home2.btconnect.com/
Lockside-Lounge/index.html
⍟ Page 84-B5

The Lodge

226–228 High Street, Harlesden,
London NW10 4TD

☎ 020 8965 3862, 020 8141 9509
@ info@thelodgebar.co.uk
⌂ www.thelodgebar.co.uk
⍟ Page 99-H1

London Bar and Kitchen

Watford Park House Unit 19b,
15–19 Greenhill Crescent, Watford
Business Park, Watford
WD18 8PH
☎ 01923 80 20 88
@ mail@londonbarandkitchen.com
⌂ www.londonbarandkitchen.com
▤ 0871 242 2324
⍟ Page 26-C1

The London Stone

109 Cannon Street, London
EC4N 5AD
☎ 020 7626 8246
⍟ Page 12-C4

Loom Bar

5 Clipstone Street, London
W1W 6BB
☎ 020 7436 0035
@ info@loombar.com
⌂ www.loombar.webitsmart.co.uk
⍟ Page 9-K1

Loop Pool Bar

12 Crown Hill, Croydon, Surrey
CR0 1RZ
☎ 020 8760 7000
⌂ www.looppoolbar.com
⍟ Page 196-D6

The Lord Rook Wood

314 Cannhall Road, Leytonstone,
London E11 3NW
☎ 020 8519 0785
⍟ Page 88-D2

Lorne Arms

64 Queens Road, Walthamstow,
London E17 8PX
☎ 020 8521 1818
⍟ Page 69-H3

Los Locos

A restaurant, cocktail bar and club
with regular dance nights.

24–26 Russell Street, Covent
Garden, London WC2B 5HF
☎ 020 7379 0220
@ info@los-locos.co.uk
⌂ www.los-locos.co.uk
▤ 020 7379 0219
⍟ Page 11-G4

Lost Society

Originally a two-storey barn
dating back to the 16th century,

Lost Society is a late-night bar-
restaurant with a secluded garden.

697 Wandsworth Road, Clapham,
London SW8 3JF
☎ 020 7652 6526
@ info@lostsociety.co.uk
⌂ www.lostsociety.co.uk
⍟ Page 141-G4

Lounge Bar

88–89 Chalk Farm Road, London
W1X 1LB
☎ 020 7485 8222
⍟ Page 84-A5

Lower Ground Bar

269 West End Lane, West
Hampstead, London NW6 1QS
☎ 020 7431 2211, 07801 259307
⌂ www.lowerground.co.uk
⍟ Page 82-E3

Manjaro Bar and Kitchen

Manjaro is a West African
restaurant, bar and entertainment
lounge situated over three floors
with an overall capacity of 200.
In the spacious large basement
lounge guests are entertained by
a variety of sounds ranging from
the West African rhythms of High-
Life, Zouk, chimurenga, kawito,
afrobeats, afro jazz and neo soul.

148 Holloway Road, Islington,
London N7 8DD
☎ 0207 609 2067
⍟ Page 85-F2

Marie Lloyd Bar

The Marie Lloyd Bar, next to the
Hackney Empire in Mare Street, is
the perfect place to meet up prior
to a visit to the Empire.

Hackney Empire, 289 Mare Street,
London E8 1EJ
☎ 020 8510 4500
✆ 020 8985 2424
⌂ www.hackneyempire.co.uk/
bars.php
▤ 020 8510 4530
⍟ Page 86-D4

Market Place

11 Market Place, London W1 8AH
☎ 020 7079 2020
⌂ www.marketplace-london.com
▤ 020 7079 2029
⍟ Page 9-K3

The Marlborough Head

24 North Audley Street, Mayfair,
London W1K 6WB

☎ 020 7629 5981
▤ 020 7495 3396
⍟ Page 10-A3

Mash

19–21 Great Portland Street,
London W1W 8QB
☎ 020 7637 5555
@ book@mashrestaurant.com
⌂ www.mash-bar.co.uk
⍟ Page 9-K1

Masti

576 High Road, Wembley, London
HA0 2AA
☎ 020 8782 2252
@ info@masti-wembley.com
⌂ www.masti-wembley.com
⍟ Page 80-A3

Mau Mau Bar

Live music in a relaxed setting
with friendly down to earth staff
and cosy seating.

265 Portobello Road, Notting Hill,
London W11 1LR
☎ 020 7229 8528
⌂ www.maumaubar.com
⍟ Page 100-C4

McCluskys

4 Bishops Hall, Riverside Walk,
Kingston upon Thames KT1 1QN
☎ 020 8541 1515
@ kingston@mccluskys.com
⌂ www.mccluskys.com
⍟ Page 174-E5

Mera Soho

25 Frith Street, Soho, London
W1D 5LB
⍟ Page 10-C4

The Milan Bar

14–32 High Street, Croydon
CR0 1YA
☎ 020 8603 0870
⍟ Page 211-J1

The Mill Hill Tavern

61 Gunnersbury Lane, London
W3 8ED
☎ 020 8992 1983
⍟ Page 117-J1

Monkey Chews

2 Queens Crescent, Chalk Farm,
Camden, London NW5 4EP
☎ 020 7267 6406
@ info@monkychews.com
⌂ www.monkeychews.com
⍟ Page 84-A4

Montague Pyke

A traditional Westminster pub situated in the heart of London. Venue for the Rushes Soho Short Festival.

105–107 Charing Cross Road, Soho, London WC2H 0DT
☎ 020 7287 6039
⌂ www.jdwetherspoon.co.uk
⌘ Page 10-D5

The Moose

31 Duke Street, Marylebone London W1U 1LG
☎ 0871 426 3857
⌂ www.vpmg.net/moose
⌘ Page 9-H3

Most Cafe Bar

Most is a cafe bar in a unique location within Tower Bridge on the south side of the river.

The Horace Jones Vault, Shad Thames, Bermondsey, London SE1 2UP
☎ 0207 403 6030
⌂ www.mostcafebar.co.uk
⌘ Page 19-K2

NW1

32 Parkway, London NW1 7AH
☎ 020 7485 2815
⌘ Page 84-B6

Nectar

Nectar is a bar, restaurant and club just past Lots Road and only minutes away from Fulham Broadway.

562 Kings Road, London SW6 2DZ
☎ 020 7326 7455, 020 7326 7450
@ info@nectarbar.co.uk
⌂ www.nectarbar.co.uk
▤ 0870 135335
⌘ Page 140-B1

New Globe Bar

359 Mile End Road, Bow, London E3 4QS
☎ 0208 980 6689
@ info@newglobee3.com
⌂ www.newglobee3.com
⌘ Page 105-H2

The New Rose Pub

The New Rose provides great home cooked food and has a good mix of DJs and other entertainment from Thursday to Sunday.

84–86 Essex Road, London N1 8LU
☎ 020 7226 1082
⌂ newrose.co.uk
⌘ Page 85-J5

OH! Bar

111–113 Camden High Street, Camden, London NW1 7JN
☎ 020 7383 0330
⌘ Page 4-A1

The Old Crown

The Old Crown public house is an oasis away from the bustle of the West End.

33 New Oxford Street, London WC1A 1BH
☎ 020 7836 9121
@ ben@theoldcrownpublichouse.com
⌂ www.theoldcrownpublichouse.com
▤ 020 7240 6133
⌘ Page 10-E3

The Old Tiger's Head

351 Lee High Road, Lee Green, London SE12 8RU
☎ 020 8244 2014
@ adrian.straatman@ntlworld.com
⌂ www.theoldtigershead.mysite.wanadoo-members.co.uk
⌘ Page 145-H5

Oporto

168 High Holborn, Covent Garden, WC1V 7AA
☎ 020 7240 1548
@ info@baroporto.com
▤ 020 7379 1417
⌘ Page 11-F3

The Oxford

256 Kentish Town Road, Kentish Town, London NW5 2AA
☎ 020 7485 3521
⌘ Page 84-B4

Oxygen

Oxygen is home to three very different styles of music from past and present chart hits to high tempo mainstream dance.

17–18 Irving Street, Leicester Square, London WC2H 7AZ
☎ 020 7930 0907
@ oxygen@junette.com
⌂ www.oxygenbar.co.uk
▤ 020 7839 7989
⌘ Page 10-D6

Paradise

19 Kilburn Lane, Kensal Green, London W10 4AE
☎ 020 8969 0098
⌂ www.theparadise.co.uk
⌘ Page 100-B2

The Paradise Bar

460 New Cross Road, New Cross, London SE14 6TJ
☎ 020 8692 1530
⌘ Page 144-C1

The Pelican Pub

45 All Saints Road, Notting Hill, London W11 1HE
☎ 020 7792 3073
⌂ www.thepelicanpub.com
⌘ Page 100-D4

The Perseverance

11 Shroton Street, London NW1 6UG
☎ 020 7723 7469
⌘ Page 8-C1

Peter de Wits Cafe

21 Greenwich Church Street, London SE10 9BJ
☎ 0208 305 0048
⌂ www.peterdewitscafe.co.uk
⌘ Page 125-F6

Platinum

Platinum is a lounge bar/club, with room for music, dancing, or just relaxing and talking, against a Moroccan backdrop. The venue is a gentleman's club during the week and hosts DJs at the weekend.

23–25 Paul Street, Shoreditch, London EC2A 4JU
☎ 020 7638 4601, 06452 581198
@ enquiries@platinimbar.co.uk
⌂ www.platinumbar.co.uk
⌘ Page 7-G6

Play Bar

58 Old Street, London EC1V 9AJ
☎ 08713 323061
@ info@playbar.co.uk
⌂ www.playbar.co.uk
⌘ Page 6-C6

The Plough

Museum Street, Bloomsbury London WC1A 1LH
☎ 020 7636 7964
⌘ Page 10-E3

The Pool

The Pool hosts live music and DJ nights along with regular film screenings.

104–108 Curtain Road, Shoreditch, London EC2A 3AH
☎ 020 7739 9608
@ mail@thepool.uk.com
⌂ www.thepool.uk.com
⌘ Page 7-G7

Portobello Gold

95–97 Portobello Road, Notting Hill, London W11 2QB
☎ 020 7460 4910, 0845 066 0666
@ enquiries@portobellogold.com
⌂ www.portobellogold.com/
▤ 020 7229 2278
⌘ Page 100-D6

Potion Bar

28 Maple Street, London W1T 6HP
☎ 020 7580 6474
@ potionbar@btconnect.com
⌂ www.potionbar.co.uk
▤ 020 7436 7983
⌘ Page 10-A1

The Prince Albert

The Prince Albert is a pub that serves a variety of beers, wines and spirits as well as a selection of modern British dishes. Seating on the pavement area is provided and Sky TV showing major sporting events form part of the entertainment.

85 Albert Bridge Road, Battersea, London SW11 4PF
☎ 020 7228 0923
⌘ Page 140-E2

Prince of Wales

186 Battersea Bridge Road, Battersea, London SW11 3AE
☎ 020 7228 0395
⌘ Page 140-D1

The Princess Royal Pub

107 Ealing Road, Brentford TW8 0LF
☎ 020 8847 2018
⌘ Page 117-F6

Prodigal

Love Lane, London EC2V 7JQ
☎ 020 7600 3500
@ prodigal@woodstreet10.fsnet.co.uk
⌘ Page 12-D3

The Prophet Bar

5–11 Worship Street, London EC2A 2BH
☎ 020 7588 8835
@ prophet@lewisandclarke.com
⌂ www.lewisandclarke.com/prophet.html
▤ 020 7588 8312
⌘ Page 7-G7

Public Life

Underground indie venue.

82a Commercial Street, London E1 6LY

☎ 020 7375 1631, 079 0885 9221,
020 7375 1631
@ info@publiclife.org.uk
⌐ www.publiclife.org.uk/
⦿ Page 13-J2

The Puzzle Pub (Victoria)

51 Horseferry Road, Unit 22, Great
Minster, Westminster, London
SW1P 2AA
☎ 020 7802 0047
⦿ Page 16-C5

The Quad

Houghton Street, London
WC2A 2AD
☎ 020 7955 7136
⦿ Page 11-H4

The Quays

471 Holloway Road, London
N7 6LE
☎ 020 7272 3634
@ info@cladddagh-ring.co.uk
⌐ www.claddagh-ring.co.uk/
quays.html
⦿ Page 85-F2

The Queen Adelaide

412 Uxbridge Road, Shepherds
Bush, London W12 0NR
☎ 020 8746 4931
⌐ www.thequeenadelaide.co.uk
⦿ Page 118-D1

The Queen's Head

15 Denman Street, Soho, London
W1D 7HN
☎ 020 7437 1540
⦿ Page 10-B5

The Railway

Pub with a cool and relaxed
atmosphere. There is a steel
fish sculpture hanging from the
exterior of the building.

18 Clapham High Street, London
SW4 7UR
☎ 020 7622 4077
⦿ Page 141-J5

Red Cocktail Bar

This venue, for a stylish, laid-back
crowd, offers friendly service and
unique atmosphere.

5 Kingly Street, Soho, London
W1B 5PF
☎ 020 7434 3417
@ info@redsoho.com
⌐ www.redsoho.com
▤ 020 7434 3418
⦿ Page 10-A4

Red Lion

166 Heath Road, Twickenham
TW1 4BN
☎ 020 8892 5074
⌐ www.redlion-twickenham.co.uk
⦿ Page 156-A3

Red Lion, Isleworth

92–94 Linkfield Road, Isleworth,
London TW7 6QE
☎ 020 8560 1457
@ beverleyturnage@hotmail.com
⌐ www.red-lion.info
⦿ Page 136-A3

Redback Tavern

A leading Australasian live music
venue.

264 High Street, Acton, London
W3 9BH
☎ 020 8896 1458
@ info@redbacktavern.com
⌐ www.redbacktavern.com
▤ 020 8993 4460
⦿ Page 117-K1

The Redchurch

107 Redchurch Street, Shoreditch,
London E2 7DL
☎ 020 7729 8333
@ info@theredchurch.co.uk
⌐ www.theredchurch.co.uk/
⦿ Page 7-J6

Revolution Bar, Clapham

95–97 Clapham High Street,
Clapham, London SW4 7TB
☎ 020 7720 6642
@ clapham@revolution-bars.
co.uk
⌐ www.revolution-bars.co.uk
▤ 020 7622 1387
⦿ Page 141-J5

Revolution Bar, Soho

2 St Annes Court, Soho, London
W1F 0AZ
☎ 020 7434 0330, 020 7434 0363
⌐ www.revolution-bars.co.uk
▤ 020 7434 0356
⦿ Page 10-C4

The River Bar And Brasserie

206–208 Tower Bridge Road,
Bermondsey, London SE1 2UP
☎ 020 7407 0968
⦿ Page 19-H4

The Roebuck

50 Great Dover Street,
Bermondsey, London SE1 4YG
☎ 020 7357 7324
@ info@theroebuck.net
⌐ www.theroebuck.net
▤ 020 7403 4817
⦿ Page 18-E4

The Rose

35 Albert Embankment, London
SE1 7TL
☎ 020 7735 3723
⦿ Page 121-K5

Ruby Blue

Leicester Place, Leicester Square,
London WC2H 7BP
☎ 020 7287 8050
@ info@rubybluebar.co.uk
⌐ www.rubybluebar.co.uk
▤ 020 7287 0100
⦿ Page 10-D5

Salvador and Amanda

Salvador and Amanda offers
respite from the hustle and bustle
of London with authentic tapas and
welcome drinks, and occasional
live events.

8 Great Newport Street, Covent
Garden, London WC2H 7JA
☎ 020 7240 1551
@ salvadorandamanda@
thebreakfastgroup.co.
⌐ www.salvadorandamanda.com
⦿ Page 10-D5

Sand

156 Clapham Park Road, Clapham,
London SW4 7DE
☎ 020 7622 3022
@ enquiries@sandbarrestaurant.
co.uk
⌐ www.sandbarrestaurant.co.uk
▤ 020 7498 4651
⦿ Page 141-J5

Sirocco

34–45 Shaftesbury Avenue, Soho
London W1D 6LA
☎ 020 7437 0847, 020 7255 8615
@ events@sirocco-london.com
⌐ www.sirocco-london.com
⦿ Page 10-C5

Six String Bar

460 New Cross Road, New Cross,
London SE14 6TJ
☎ 0871 223 2870
⦿ Page 144-C1

The Slug and Lettuce
County Hall

5 Chicheley Street, Waterloo
London SE1 7PJ
☎ 020 7803 4790
@ SlugandLettuce.CountyHall@
laurelpubco

⌐ slugandlettuce.co.uk
▤ 020 7803 4791
⦿ Page 17-H2

The Slug and Lettuce
Islington

The oldest 'Slugs' in London,
offering a top-notch service. A
beautiful upstairs bar and lounge,
complete with comfy sofas for
chilling out.

1 Islington Green, London N1 2XH
☎ 020 7226 3864
@ SlugandLettuce.Islington@
laurelpubco
⌐ www.slugandlettuce.co.uk/
▤ 020 7354 8433
⦿ Page 6-A1

Smithy's Wine Bar

A live music and alternative venue,
with Djs, magicians and oher
artists.

The Stables, 15–17 Leeke Street,
St Pancras, London WC1X 9HY
☎ 020 7278 5949
@ info@smithyslondon.com
⌐ www.smithyslondon.com
▤ 020 7837 6898
⦿ Page 5-G4

The Soho Lounge

Spectacularly situated at the hub
of the West End, Soho Lounge is a
chic and intimate lounge bar.

69–70 Dean Street, Soho, London
W1D 3SE
☎ 020 7734 1231, 020 7434 4480
@ info@thesoholounge.co.uk
⌐ www.the-soho-lounge.co.uk
⦿ Page 10-C3

Sosho

2 Tabernacle Street, London
EC2A 4LU
☎ 020 7920 0701
@ bookings@sosho3am.com
⌐ www.sosho3am.com
▤ 020 7920 0702
⦿ Page 7-F7

The Spanish Arch

One of London's most successful
'local' Irish pubs. Warm and
welcoming.

28 Belmont Circle, Kenton Lane,
Harrow HA3 8RF
☎ 020 8909 3269
@ info@claddagh-ring.co.uk
⌐ www.claddagh-ring.co.uk/
▤ 020 8907 7973
⦿ Page 43-H4

Spanish Galleon

Greenwich Church Street,
Greenwich, London SE10 9BL
☎ 020 8293 0949
✆ Page 125-F6

The Sports Cafe, London

Sports bar with regular sports
event screenings and club nights.

80 Haymarket, London SW1Y 4TE
☎ 020 7839 8300
✆ Page 10-C6

The Star

Northolt Road, North Harrow
HA2 0NG
☎ 020 8422 0505
✆ Page 78-B2

Steffanys

262 Old Kent Road, Walworth,
London SE1 5UB
☎ 020 7708 1900
✆ Page 123-J6

Stratford Rex

361–373 High Street, Stratford,
London E15 4SB
☎ 020 8215 6003
✆ Page 88-B5

Strawberry Moons

15 Heddon Street, Mayfair, London
W1B 4BF
☎ 020 7437 7300
@ info@strawberrymoonsbar.
co.uk
🖰 www.strawberrymoonsbar.
co.uk
🖳 020 7437 2391
✆ Page 10-A6

Strongroom Bar

Based within the Strongroom
studio complex, the bar offers a
viable, more relaxing alternative
to the usual hustle and bustle of
Shoreditch.

120–124 Curtain Road, London
EC2A 3SQ
☎ 020 7426 5103
@ mix@strongroom.com
🖰 www.strongroom.com
🖳 020 7426 5102
✆ Page 7-G7

Stylus Bar

58 Camberwell Church Street,
London SE5 8QZ
☎ 020 7326 0055
🖰 www.stylusbar.co.uk
✆ Page 142-E2

Sugar Reef

42–44 Great Windmill Street,
Soho, London W1D 7NB
☎ 020 7851 0800
@ sugarreef@latenightlondon.
co.uk
🖰 www.sugarreef.co.uk
🖳 020 7851 0807
✆ Page 10-C6

Sun & Doves

An independent, quirky venue
offering food, drink, art, music
and film.

61–63 Coldharbour Lane,
Camberwell, London SE5 9NS
☎ 020 7733 1525
🖰 www.sunanddoves.co.uk/index.
php
✆ Page 142-D3

The Sun Tavern

Long Acre, Covent Garden, London
WC2E 9JH
☎ 020 7836 4520
✆ Page 10-E4

Svelte Cocktail Bar and Lounge

80–88 Croydon High Street,
London CR0 1NA
☎ 020 8680 5500
@ info@sveltebar.com
🖰 www.sveltebar.com
✆ Page 211-J1

The Swan

215 Clapham Road, Stockwell,
London SW9 9BE
☎ 020 7978 9778
@ info@theswanstockwell.co.uk
🖰 www.theswanstockwell.co.uk
🖳 020 7738 6722
✆ Page 141-K3

Sway Bar

61–65 Great Queen Street,
Holborn, London WC2B 5BZ
☎ 020 7404 6114
@ info@swaybar.co.uk
🖰 www.swaybar.co.uk
🖳 020 7404 6003
✆ Page 11-F3

The Tabernacle Bar and Grill

55-61 Tabernacle Street,
Shoreditch, London EC2A 4AA
☎ 020 7253 5555
@ thetabernacle@email.com
🖰 www.tabernaclebargrill.com
🖳 020 7253 5747
✆ Page 7-F7

The Taybridge

47–49 Lavender Hill, Battersea,
London SW11 5QN
☎ 020 7978 7682
✆ Page 140-E4

Thirst

Thirst, where the party continues
six nights a week.

53 Greek Street, Soho, London
W1D 3DR
☎ 020 7437 1977
@ soho@thirstbar.com
🖰 www.thirstbar.com
✆ Page 10-D4

Thirteen

13 Gerrard Street, London
W1D 5PS
☎ 020 7494 3223
✆ Page 10-D5

Three Blind Mice

5 Ravey Street, Shoreditch,
London EC2A 4QW
☎ 020 7739 7746
🖰 www.3blindmicebar.com
🖳 0870 460 2531
✆ Page 7-G6

Tonky Gorilla

A bar-restaurant with regular club
and live music nights.

539–541 Kingsbury High Road,
Kingsbury, London NW9 9EG
☎ 020 8204 7000
@ info@tonkygorilla.com
🖰 www.tonkygorilla.com
✆ Page 62-C2

Tooting Tram and Social

46–48 Mitcham Road, Tooting,
London SW17 9NA
☎ 020 8767 0278
🖰 www.antic-ltd.com
✆ Page 178-E1

The Torrington

4 Lodge Lane, High Road, North
Finchley, London N12 8JR
☎ 020 8445 4710
✆ Page 47-G3

Trafik

331 Old Street, London EC1 9LE
☎ 020 7613 0234
@ trafikpr@yahoo.com
🖰 www.trafikinfo.co.uk
✆ Page 6-C6

Trap

201 Wardour Street, Soho,
London W1F 8ZH

☎ 020 7434 3820
🖳 020 7434 3821
✆ Page 10-B3

Trash Palace

11 Wardour Street, Soho, London
W1D 6PG
☎ 020 7734 0522
@ info@trashpalace.co.uk
🖰 www.trashpalace.co.uk
✆ Page 10-B3

TroyBar

10 Hoxton Street, London N1 6NG
☎ 020 7739 6695
🖰 www.troybar.co.uk
✆ Page 7-G1

Umbaba

Umbaba is a nightclub, restaurant
and bar situated in the heart of
Soho.

15–21 Ganton Street, Soho London
W1F 9BN
☎ 020 7734 6696
🖰 www.umbaba.com/
✆ Page 10-A5

The Union Arms

109 Battersea Bridge Road,
Battersea Park, London SW11 3AF
☎ 020 7223 2053
✆ Page 140-D1

University of Greenwich Student Union

Cooper Building, King William
Walk, Greenwich, London
SE10 9JH
☎ 020 8331 7629
🖰 www.suug.co.uk
✆ Page 125-F6

Upstairs At The Crown Pub

64 Brewer Street, Soho, London
W1F 9TR
☎ 0207432 9711
✆ Page 10-B5

The Vauxhall Griffin

8 Wyvil Road, Vauxhall, London
SW8 2TH
☎ 020 7622 0222
@ info@thevauxhallgriffin.com
🖰 www.thevauxhallgriffin.com
✆ Page 141-K1

Vic Naylor

38–42 St John Street, London
EC1M 4AY

☎ 020 7608 2299
🕿 020 7608 2181
@ contact@vicnaylor.com
🖰 www.vicnaylor.com
📠 020 7251 0458
✪ Page 5-K3

The Victoria

Mornington Terrace, Camden,
London NW1 7QD
☎ 020 7387 3804
✪ Page 3-K1

The Village

A firm fixture on Soho's gay scene,
the Village offers a wide range of
drinks, entertainment and music to
a young and trendy crowd.

81 Wardour Street, London
W1D 6QD
☎ 020 7434 2124
🖰 www.village-soho.co.uk
✪ Page 10-B3

Vivo

6 Poland Street, Soho, London
W1F 8PS
☎ 020 7734 3094
@ info@vivosoho.com
🖰 www.alphabetbar.com/vivo/
index.asp
✪ Page 10-B3

Walkabout Islington

56 Upper Street, Islington,
London N1 0NY
☎ 020 7359 2097
@ wbi.islington@walkabout.
eu.com
🖰 www.walkabout.eu.com
✪ Page 5-K2

Walrus Social

172 Westminster Bridge Road,
Waterloo, London SE1 7RW
☎ 020 7928 4368
@ info@walrussocial.com
🖰 www.walrussocial.co.uk
✪ Page 17-F3

The Waterfront

Relaxed and informal atmosphere.

426 Streatham High Road,
Norbury, London SW16 3PX
☎ 020 8764 3985
@ info@waterfrontbar.co.uk
🖰 www.waterfrontbar.co.uk
✪ Page 161-K6

Wax Bar

Leather booths, stylish seating
areas and marble bars.

4 Winsley Street, London
W1W 8HF

☎ 020 7436 4650
@ info@wax-bar.co.uk
🖰 www.wax-bar.co.uk
✪ Page 10-A3

The Westbridge

74–76 Battersea Bridge Road,
Battersea, London SW11 3AG
☎ 020 7228 6482
@ book@thewestbridge.co.uk
🖰 www.thewestbridge.co.uk
📠 020 7228 2554
✪ Page 140-D1

White Hart

1 Mile End Road, Whitechapel,
London E1 4TP
☎ 020 7790 2894
✪ Page 104-E4

The White Horse

An early 18th-century inn, now one
of Brixton's late night venues for
partying, drinking and dining.

94 Brixton Hill, Brixton, London
SW2 1QN
☎ 020 8678 6666
@ info@whitehorsebrixton.com
🖰 www.whitehorsebrixton.com
✪ Page 142-A6

The White Swan

556 Commercial Road, Limehouse,
London E14 7JD
☎ 0207 780 9870
✪ Page 105-G5

William IV

A rambling gastro bar
encompassing five distinct areas.

786 Harrow Road, London
NW10 5JX
☎ 020 8969 5944
🖰 www.elparadorlondon.com
📠 020 8964 9218
✪ Page 99-K2

Winchester Bar

2 Essex Road, Islington, London
N1 8LN
☎ 020 77048789
✪ Page 85-J5

Windsor Castle Pub

358 Carshalton Road, Carshalton
SM5 3PD
☎ 020 8669 1191
@ pam@windsorcastlepub.com
🖰 www.windsorcastlepub.com
✪ Page 209-G3

The Woodstock

Stonecot Hill, Sutton SM3 9HB

☎ 020 86448512/020 8642 5130
✪ Page 193-H5

Yates, Leicester Square

Successful bar chain hosting
regular music events.

30 Leicester Square, London
WC2H 7JZ
☎ 020 7839 7967
@ Yates.LeicesterSquare@
laurelpubco.com
🖰 www.yatesinthewestend.com
✪ Page 10-D6

Zebrano Bar

A lively bar with an extensive
cocktail menu. Regular DJs play
funky house late into the night.

14–16 Ganton Street, Soho,
London W1F 7BT
☎ 020 7287 5267
@ info@zebrano-bar.com
🖰 zebrano-bar.com
✪ Page 10-A5

Zoo Bar

Booths, private bars and amazing
dance spaces.

13–17 Bear Street, Leicester
Square, London WC2H 7AS
☎ 020 7839 4188
@ info@zoobar.co.uk
🖰 www.zoobar.co.uk
📠 020 7839 4479
✪ Page 10-D5

NIGHTCLUBS

The 100 Club

One of London's oldest live music
venues, The 100 Club is open every
day hosting jazz, blues, indie and
rock nights. The club's notable
history has seen gigs by the Sex
Pistols, The Clash, Muddy Waters
and The Rolling Stones.

100 Oxford Street, London
W1D 1LL
☎ 020 7636 0933
@ info@the100club.co.uk
🖰 www.the100club.co.uk
✪ Page 10-B3

12 Acklam Road

A 650-capacity West London
bar, nightclub and concert hall,
situated in the heart of Notting
Hill, an ideal place for a late night
drink and dance.

12 Acklam Road, Ladbroke Grove,
London W10 5QZ
☎ 0208 960 9331

@ info@12acklamroad.co.uk
🖰 www.12acklamroadclub.com
✪ Page 100-D4

333 Mother

This is a large late night venue
with a separate bar upstairs.

333 Old Street, London EC1V 9LE
☎ 020 7739 5949, 020 7739 1800
@ info@333mother.com
🖰 www.333mother.com
📠 02076 130469
✪ Page 6-C6

93 Feet East

Here you'll find three main areas,
the large versatile main hall for a
wide variety of alternative live and
club events, the intimate Gallery
Bar, and the Pink Bar with raised
DJ booth.

150 Brick Lane, London E1 6QL
☎ 020 7247 3293
@ Info@93feeteast.co.uk
🖰 www.93feeteast.co.uk
📠 020 7247 5980
✪ Page 7-K5

A10 Russian Bar

Underground venue in the heart of
Shoreditch.

267 Kingsland Road, London
E2 8AS
☎ 07809 425905
✪ Page 7-H3

AKA

Next door to the renowned
nightclub The End, AKA London is
a bar venue hosting a variety of
dance nights in its own right as
well as sharing some of its sister-
venue's larger nights. Cocktails
and food also served.

18 West Central Street,
Bloomsbury, London WC1A 1JJ
☎ 020 7836 0110
@ info@akalondon.com
🖰 www.akalondon.com
📠 020 7419 9099
✪ Page 10-E3

Abacus

In the heart of the city, Abacus
has three bars and a club over
two floors.

24 Cornhill, London EC3V 3ND
☎ 020 7337 6767
@ info@abucusbar.co.uk
🖰 www.abacusbar.co.uk
📠 020 7337 6760
✪ Page 13-F4

Agenda

A bar, lounge and club in the City, Agenda is popular as a post-work hang out. The venue features a 60-foot bar, boothes and a club playing funky pop and dance classics.

Minster Court, 3 Mincing Lane, London EC3R 7AA
☎ 020 7929 8399
@ info@agendabar.co.uk
🖰 www.agendabar.co.uk
🖹 020 7929 8390
🖉 Page 13-G5

Air and Breathe

This twin scene venue presents resident DJs every Thursday, Friday and Saturday night.

35–37 Essex Road, Dartford DA1 2AU
☎ 01322 222423
@ air&breathe-dartford@ luminar.co.uk
🖰 www.airandbreathe.com
🖹 01322 274224
🖉 Page 171-G1

Alibi

10 Lime Office Court, Shoe Lane, London EC4A 3BQ
☎ 020 7842 0620
@ info@alibi-bar.co.uk
🖰 www.alibi-bar.co.uk
🖹 020 7842 0621
🖉 Page 11-K3

Anda de Bridge

42–44 Kingsland Road, Shoreditch, London E2 8DA
☎ 020 7739 3863
@ info@andadebridge.com
🖰 www.andadebridge.com
🖉 Page 7-H3

The Annexe

9 Brighton Terrace, Brixton, London SW9 8DJ
☎ 020 7737 2095
@ info@substationsouth.co.uk
🖰 www.thebreakfastgroup.co.uk
🖉 Page 142-A5

Arch 269

269 Coldharbour Lane, Brixton, London SW9 8SE
☎ 020 7231 3191, 07950 425296
🖉 Page 142-B5

Arch Angel

11–13 Kensington High Street, London W8 5NP
☎ 020 7938 4137
@ info@baronbars.com

🖰 www.archangelw8.com
🖹 020 7795 6064
🖉 Page 120-A2

Archduke

153 Concert Hall Approach, South Bank, London SE1 8XU
☎ 020 7928 9370
@ manager@thearchduke.co.uk
🖰 www.thearchduke.co.uk
🖹 020 7928 0839
🖉 Page 17-H1

The Arches

51–53 Southwark Street, The Borough, Bermondsey, London SE1 1TE
☎ 020 7403 9643
@ info@xxl-london.com
🖰 www.xxl-london.com/
🖉 Page 12-B7

Area

Area is a gay venue with an exclusive line-up of DJs and the latest in sound and lighting.

67–68 Albert Embankment, London SE1 7TP
☎ 020 7091 0080
@ mail@areaclub.info
🖰 www.areaclub.info
🖉 Page 121-K5

Babalou

Babalou, in the heart of Brixton, is set in a crypt of a converted church. Formerly known as the Bug Bar, it features original crypt architecture, North African style lamps, sturdy wooden tables and sumptuous velvet booths.

The Crypt, St Matthews Church, Brixton Hill, London SW2 1JF
☎ 07974 500 019
🖰 www.babalou.net/home.html
🖉 Page 162-A1

Babble

The City's classic bar and club. Metro-chic furnishings, lounging sofas, sleek bars and luxurious steel and slate finishes.

Lansdowne House, 59 Berkeley Square, London W1X 5DG
☎ 020 7758 8255
@ info@babble-bar.co.uk
🖰 www.babble-bar.co.uk
🖹 020 7758 8254
🖉 Page 9-K6

Bar 512

512 Kingsland Road, Dalston, London E8 4AE
🖉 Page 86-B5

Bar 54

New venue for Bar 54, with a large bar/lounge/club in East London for disco dancing.

438 Mile End Road, London E1 4PE
☎ 0207 790 1005
🖰 www.barfiftyfour.co.uk/
🖉 Page 105-F3

Bar Andalucia

A Spanish/South American bar offering a range of regular events including tango and salsa dance classes, along with Latin-themed club nights.

139–143 Whitfield Street, London W1T 5EN
☎ 020 7388 3369
@ info@barandalucia.co.uk
🖰 www.barandalucia.co.uk
🖉 Page 10-B1

Bar-Eivissa

Bar-Eivissa, a stones throw from the River Thames and close to many top-class restaurants, is widely regarded as the classiest night spot in the area. It plays host to some of the most successfull DJs, performers and promoters in the business.

48 High Street, Kingston upon Thames, London KT1 1HN
☎ 020 8408 4900
@ info@bar-eivissa.com
🖰 www.bar-eivissa.com
🖉 Page 174-E6

Bar Music Hall

Music Hall, at the heart of Shoreditch's buzzing nightlife, has an up-to-date DJ schedule and live music programme.

134 Curtain Road, London EC2A 3AR
☎ 020 7613 5951, 020 7729 7216
@ events@barmusichall.co.uk
🖰 www.barmusichall.com
🖉 Page 7-G7

Bar Rumba

Launched in 1993, Bar Rumba has a basement capacity of 455 and hosts an eclectic mix of club nights.

36 Shaftesbury Avenue, Soho, London W1D 7EP
☎ 020 7287 6933, 020 7287 2715
@ barrumba@thebreakfastgroup. co.uk
🖰 www.barrumba.co.uk
🖹 020 7287 2714
🖉 Page 10-C5

Barcode Soho

3–4 Archer Street, Soho, London W1D 7AP
☎ 020 7734 3342
@ info@barcode.co.uk
🖰 www.bar-code.co.uk
🖹 020 7734 2329
🖉 Page 10-C5

Barcode Vauxhall

Arch 69, Goding Street, London SE11 5AW
☎ 020 7582 4180
@ info@bar-code.co.uk
🖰 www.bar-code.co.uk
🖉 Page 121-K5

Barrio North

45 Essex Road, Islington, London N1 2SF
☎ 020 7688 2882
@ shout@barrionorth.com
🖰 www.barrionorth.com
🖉 Page 85-J5

Bartok

Featuring innovative, contemporary and classical music, Bartok, named after the Hungarian composer Bela Bartok, is an expansion of the chill-out room idea, placed in Regency styled surroundings.

78 Chalk Farm Road, Camden, London NW1 8AR
☎ 020 7916 0595
🖰 www.bartokbar.com/
🖉 Page 84-A5

Battersea Barge

Nine Elms Lane, London SW8 5BP
☎ 020 7498 0004
@ info@batterseabarge.com
🖰 www.batterseabarge.com
🖉 Page 121-H6

Bethnal Green Working Men's Club

First opened in 1953 as a traditional working man's club, the venue now offers a variety of cultural and entertainment events, from wild live music nights in the main functions room, to high-brow art shows in the gallery.

44–46 Pollard Row, Bethnal Green, London E2 6NB
☎ 07940 575 589
@ info@workersplaytime.net
🖰 www.workersplaytime.net
🖉 Page 104-C2

The Big Chill Bar

The Big Chill Bar provides a sumptuous environment with an array of art, oddities, live and DJ based music, multi-media entertainment, and a rich mix of soul food, reflecting the ethos and atmosphere of the festival of the same name.

Dray Walk, Brick Lane, London E1 6QL
☎ 020 7392 9180
@ info@bigchill.net
⌂ www.bigchill.net
♪ Page 7-K7

The Big Chill House

The Big Chill House features three floors of music, a south facing terrace, a balconied dining room and bar, as well as comfortable seating throughout.

257–259 Pentonville Road, King's Cross, London N1 9NL
☎ 020 7427 2540
@ info@bigchill.net
⌂ www.bigchill.net/house.html
♪ Page 5-G3

Bird Nest Pub

32 Deptford Church Street, Deptford, London SE8 4RZ
☎ 020 8692 1928
⌂ www.thebirdsnest.co.uk
♪ Page 144-D1

The Black Cap

Iconic London gay venue with upstairs bar and roof terrace, and large club and performance space at street level. Regular drag shows, resident DJs and late license.

171 Camden High Street, London NW1 7JY
☎ 020 7428 2721
⌂ www.theblackcap.com
♪ Page 4-A1

The Black Gardenia

An atmospheric basement bar featuring a diverse selection of beat tracks and swing classics from the 1940s through to the 1960s.

93 Dean Street, Soho, London W1D 3SZ
☎ 020 7494 4955
♪ Page 10-C3

Blagclub Ladbroke Grove

Duck through the rustic studio door, past the fountain and into a relaxed Asian themed room, characterised by its buddha eyes, woodcarvings and hindu shrines.

Canalot Studios, 222 Kensal Road, London W10 5BN
☎ 020 7243 0123
@ info@blagclub.com
⌂ www.blagclub.com
♪ Page 100-C3

Blagclub Notting Hill Gate

Situated right by Notting Hill Gate tube. Find the front door, stride up the small staircase to discover an exotically serene, Hindu themed lounge room.

68 Notting Hill Gate, Notting Hill, London W11 3HT
☎ 020 7243 0123
@ info@blagclub.com
⌂ www.blagclub.com
♪ Page 119-K1

The Blind Beggar

337 Whitechapel Road, London EC1 1UB
☎ 020 7247 6195
@ info@theblindbeggar.com
⌂ www.theblindbeggar.com
🖷 020 7247 6195
♪ Page 104-C5

Bloomsbury Lanes

Tavistock Hotel, Bedford Way, Bloomsbury, London WC1H 9EU
☎ 020 7691 2610
@ info@bloomsburybowling.com
⌂ www.bloomsburylive.com
🖷 020 7813 1575
♪ Page 4-D7

The Blue Posts

28 Rupert Street, Soho, London W1D 6DJ
☎ 020 7437 1415, 020 7437 5008
♪ Page 10-C6

The BoomBoom Club

Sutton United Football Club, Gander Green Lane, Sutton SM1 2EY
☎ 020 8460 4907, 020 8761 9078
@ webcontact@feenstra.co.uk
⌂ www.boomboomlive.co.uk
♪ Page 208-E2

The Boston Music Room and The Dome

178 Junction Road, Holloway, London N19 5QQ
☎ 020 7272 8153
⌂ www.the-boston.co.uk
♪ Page 84-C1

The Brickhouse

152c Brick Lane, London E1 6RU
♪ Page 7-K5

The Brixton Telegraph

228 Brixton Hill, Brixton, London SW2 1HE
☎ 020 8678 0777
@ telegraphaddress@yahoo.gov.uk
⌂ www.thebrixtontelegraph.co.uk
🖷 020 8678 9066
♪ Page 161-A1

Buffalo Bar

Buffalo Bar is an independently run venue in the heart of Islington offering an exciting spectrum of live music performances.

259 Upper Street, London N1 1RU
☎ 020 7359 6191
@ info@buffalobar.co.uk
⌂ www.buffalobar.co.uk
♪ Page 85-H4

CC Club

13 Coventry Street, London W1D 7DH
☎ 020 7297 3200
⌂ www.cc-club.co.uk
♪ Page 10-C6

Cafe de Paris

4 Coventry Street, Soho, London W1D 6BL
☎ 020 7734 7700
@ reception@cafedeparis.com
⌂ www.cafedeparis.com
♪ Page 10-C6

Camouflage

84–86 Wardour Street, London W1F 0TQ
☎ 020 7287 3834
@ camouflage@vpmg.net
⌂ www.vpmg.net/camouflage
♪ Page 10-B3

Canvas

Located in the heart of the city, Canvas hosts one of the largest sound systems in the country and room for over 2,000 people.

Kings Cross Freight Depot, York Way, London N1 0UZ
☎ 020 7833 8301, 020 7630 6625
@ info@canvaslondon.net
⌂ www.canvaslondon.net
♪ Page 4-F1

Catch

Catch is a bar and nightclub located in Shoreditch, bringing together people and music from all genres, from DJs, MCs to signed and unsigned bands.

22 Kingsland Road, Bethnal Green, London E2 8DA

☎ 020 7729 6097
@ info@thecatchbar.com
⌂ www.thecatchbar.com
♪ Page 7-H3

The Chocolate Lounge

146–148 Newington Butts, Kennington, London SE11 4RN
☎ 020 7735 5306, 08719 714761
@ elaine@thechocolateloungelondon.com
⌂ www.thechocolateloungelondon.com
♪ Page 18-B7

Cirque Hippodrome

10–14 Cranbourne Street, Leicester Square, London WC2H 7JH
♪ Page 10-D5

City Limits

A mix of food, entertainment and lesiure activities combined under one roof.

Collier Row Road, Collier Row, Romford RM5 2BH
☎ 020 8924 2222
⌂ www.citylimits.co.uk
♪ Page 56-B4

Club 414

414–416 Coldharbour Lane, Brixton, London SW9 8LF
☎ 01736 331211, 020 7924 9322
@ info@club414ent.co.uk
⌂ www.club414ent.co.uk
♪ Page 142-B5

Club Aquarium

Club Aquarium opened it doors in 1995 and has played host to a variety of club nights, concerts and video shoots. It also owns Bar Aquarium, a traditional pub next door.

256–264 Old Street, London EC1V 9DD
☎ 020 7253 3558
@ liga@clubaquarium.co.uk
⌂ www.clubaquarium.co.uk
🖷 020 7253 9885
♪ Page 6-C6

Club Boulevard

10 High Street, Ealing, London W5 5JY
☎ 020 8840 0616
@ info@clubboulevard.com
⌂ www.clubboulevard.com
♪ Page 97-K6

Club Colosseum at Market Towers

1 Nine Elms Lane, Vauxhall, London SW8 5NQ
☎ 020 7627 1283, 020 7720 9200
@ info@clubcolosseum.com
🔗 www.clubcolosseum.com
📠 020 7627 1918
📍 Page 141-H1

Club Luca

20–30 London Road, Barking IG11 8AJ
☎ 020 8594 3051
@ info@legendsbarking.com
🔗 www.clubluca.com
📍 Page 90-C5

Club49

49 Greek Street, Soho, London W1D 4EG
☎ 020 7439 4159
@ info@club49soho.com
🔗 www.club49soho.com
📍 Page 10-D4

The Comedy Pub

7 Oxendon Street, Picadilly, St James's, London SW1Y 4EE
☎ 020 7839 7261
📍 Page 10-C6

Copyright Club

110 Pennington Street, Tower Hamlets, London E1 9BB
☎ 020 7488 9000
@ copyrightcontact@aol.com
🔗 www.copyrightnightclub.com
📍 Page 104-D6

Corbet Place Bar and Lounge

Truman Brewery, 91 Brick Lane, London E1 6NH
☎ 020 7770 6100
📍 Page 7-K7

Crash

66 Albert Embankment, London SE11 5AW
☎ 020 7793 9262, 020 7278 0995
@ info@crashlondon.com
🔗 www.crashlondon.com
📍 Page 121-K5

Crazy Larrys

Crazy Larry's is a popular venue on the King's Road, with contemporary, fabulous decor and an upbeat ambience.

533 Kings Road, Chelsea, London SW10 0TZ
☎ 020 7376 5555
@ info@crazylarrys.co.uk
🔗 www.crazylarrys.co.uk/index.htm
📍 Page 140-B1

The Cross

27–31 Arches, York Way, London N1 0BB
☎ 020 7833 4212, 020 7837 0828, 020 8989 6712
🔗 www.the-cross.co.uk
📍 Page 5-F2

The Cross Kings

126 York Way, London N1 0AX
☎ 020 7278 8318
@ info@thecrosskings.co.uk
🔗 www.thecrosskings.co.uk
📍 Page 5-F2

Crystal

57b Woodland Road, Crystal Palace, London SE19 1TS
📍 Page 181-F1

Departure

2 Crutched Friars, Aldgate, London EC3N 2HT
☎ 020 7480 7550
@ info@departurebar.co.uk
🔗 www.departurebar.co.uk
📍 Page 13-H4

Ditch Bar

Ditch Bar is a 330-capacity club and venue with two floors and two bars.

145 Shoreditch High Street, London E1 6JE
☎ 07946 706837, 020 7739 6412
🔗 www.ditchbar.com
📍 Page 7-H5

East Village

DJ Stuart Patterson's venue in the heart of Shoreditch.

89 Great Eastern Street, London EC2A 3HX
☎ 020 7739 5173
@ info@eastvillageclub.com
🔗 www.eastvillageclub.com
📍 Page 7-F6

Eclipse

57 Elderfield Road, London E5 0LF
☎ 020 8986 1591
📍 Page 87-F2

Edge Club

157 Commercial Street, Tower Hamlets, Shoreditch, London E1 6BJ
☎ 020 7247 5123
🔗 www.edgeclub.co.uk/
📍 Page 7-J7

Egg

200 York Way, London N7 9AP
☎ 020 7609 8364
@ rose@egglondon.net
🔗 www.egglondon.net
📠 020 7619 6189
📍 Page 84-E4

Ego @ Southern Pride

Gay and lesbian nightclub with regular event nights.

82 Norwood High Street, West Norwood, London SE27 9NW
☎ 020 8761 5200
@ EgoLondon@SouthernPride.co.uk
🔗 www.ego-southernpride.co.uk/
📍 Page 162-D6

The Elbow Room, Islington

The Islington Elbow Room offers pop and rock music nights, late nights on the weekend, and pool competitions.

88 91 Chapel Market, Islington, London N1 9EX
☎ 020 7278 3244
@ islington@theelbowroom.co.uk
🔗 www.elbow-room.co.uk
📍 Page 5-J2

The Elbow Room, Shoreditch

The Elbow Room offers regular dance-based club nights, late hours on the weekend and pool competitions.

97–113 Curtain Road, Shoreditch, London EC2A 3BS
☎ 020 7613 1316
@ shoreditch@theelbowroom.co.uk
🔗 www.theelbowroom.co.uk
📠 020 7613 1336
📍 Page 7-G7

The Elbow Room, Westbourne Grove

The Elbow Room offers a heady mixture of pool, music, club nights, beer and burgers.

103 Westbourne Grove, London W2 4UW
☎ 020 7221 5211
@ westbournegrove@theelbowroom.co.uk
🔗 www.theelbowroom.co.uk/westbournegrove/index.aspx
📠 020 7221 5512
📍 Page 100-E5

Electrowerkz

7 Torrens Street, London EC1V 1NQ
☎ 020 7837 6419
@ info@electrowerkz.com
🔗 www.electrowerkz.com
📠 020 7278 1437
📍 Page 6-A3

Embargo

Intimate Chelsea club with Champagne bar and VIP room.

533b Kings Road, Chelsea, London SW10 0TZ
☎ 020 7351 5038, 07793 778261
@ info@embargochelsea.com
🔗 www.barclub.com/embargo
📠 020 7352 6526
📍 Page 140-B1

The End

The End has won the prestigious Time Out Live Awards 2005/06 for Best Venue, and resident Laurent Garnier has won the crown for best DJ.

18 West Central Street, Bloomsbury, London WC1A 1JJ
☎ 020 7419 9199
@ info@endclub.com
🔗 www.endclub.com
📠 020 7419 9099
📍 Page 10-E3

The Epicurean Lounge

10–11 Clerkenwell Green, London EC1R 0DP
☎ 020 7490 5577
@ office@eplounge.com
🔗 www.eplounge.com
📠 020 7490 5557
📍 Page 6-A7

The Eve Club

Lower Ground Floor, 3 New Burlington Street, Mayfair, London W1S 2JF
☎ 020 7287 1991
@ info@clubeve.co.uk
🔗 www.clubeve.co.uk
📠 020 7287 9229
📍 Page 10-A5

Excelsior Night Club

191–195 Balham High Road, Balham, London SW12 9BE
📍 Page 161-G3

Fabric

Located opposite the Smithfield Meat Market, Fabric has been a mecca for London clubbers since 1999. With three separate rooms,

each with its own sound system, it manages to squeeze in up to 3,000 people each night for a selection of house, techno, drum and bass, hip hop and breaks from both DJs and live acts.

77a Charterhouse Street, London EC1M 3HN
☎ 020 7336 8898
🖰 www.fabriclondon.com
🖢 Page 12-A2

Faces Nightclub
Faces Nightclub has two rooms of music, six bars and a VIP area playing host to faces from the world of music, show business, sport and fashion.

458 Cranbrook Road, Gants Hill, Ilford IG2 6LE
☎ 020 8554 8899
🖰 www.facesnightclub.co.uk
🖢 Page 72-A4

The Factory
Under the arches club in South London, near other club Crash and performance space Royal Vauxhall Tavern.

65 Goding Street, London SE11 5AW
☎ 020 8386 7421, 0871 971 3827
🖢 Page 121-K5

The Fighting Cocks
During the 50s the club developed a following in jazz circles, hosting many international musicians.

56 Old London Road, Kingston upon Thames KT2 6QA
☎ 020 8974 6469
@ jimbo66@blueyonder.co.uk
🖰 www.the-fighting-cocks.co.uk
🖢 Page 175-F5

Fire
South Lambeth Road, South Lambeth, London SW8 1UQ
☎ 020 7582 9890
🖰 www.fireclub.co.uk
🖢 Page 141-K1

The Forum
9–17 Highgate Road, Kentish Town, London NW5 1JY
☎ 020 7284 1001
🖰 www.meanfiddler.com
🖢 Page 84-B2

The Fridge
1 Town Hall Parade, Brixton Hill, Brixton, London SW2 1RJ

☎ 020 7326 5100
@ info@fridge.co.uk
🖰 www.fridgelondon.com
🖢 Page 162-A1

The Gardening Club at Rock Garden
Established almost 30 years ago, The Rock Garden Restaurant is a dining and party venue in Covent Garden offering dining with an after-dinner lounge bar and nightclub.

6–7 The Piazza, Covent Garden, London WC2E 8HA
☎ 020 7836 4052, 020 7257 8625
@ info@rockgarden.co.uk
🖰 www.rockgarden.co.uk
📄 020 7379 4793
🖢 Page 11-F5

The Ghetto
The Ghetto was started by a group of people who over the years had worked in many different club environments, from the ultra trendy to the cheap and cheerful.

5–6 Falconberg Court, London W1 2AB
☎ 020 7287 3726
@ info@popstarz.org
🖰 www.ghetto-london.co.uk
🖢 Page 10-C3

Guanabara
Guanabara is a Brazilan venue in Covent Garden that features a variety of regular club nights and live bands with a Latin flavour.

Parker Street, Dury Lane, London WC2B 5PW
☎ 020 7242 8600
@ guanabara@evmlondon.com
🖰 www.guanabara.co.uk
🖢 Page 11-F3

Harlem
78 Westbourne Grove, London W2 5RT
☎ 0207985 0900
@ party@harlemsoulfood.com
🖰 www.harlemsoulfood.com
🖢 Page 100-E5

Heaven
Under The Arches, Villiers Street, London WC2N 6NG
☎ 020 7930 2020
@ info@heaven-london.com
🖰 www.heaven-london.com
🖢 Page 11-F7

Herbal
Popular and well-established Shoreditch club playing experimental, urban and electronic music.

10–14 Kingsland Road, Shoreditch, London E2 8DA
☎ 020 7613 4462
@ herbaluk@hotmail.co.uk
🖰 www.herbaluk.com
📄 020 7613 4382
🖢 Page 7-H3

Hidden
100 Tinworth Street, London SE11 5EQ
☎ 020 7820 0788, 07939 486 903
@ amanda@hiddenclub.co.uk
🖰 www.hiddenclub.co.uk
🖢 Page 121-K5

Holland Park Blag Club
Basement, 11 Russell Gardens, London W14 8EZ
☎ 020 7243 0123
@ info@blagclub.com
🖰 www.blagclub.com
🖢 Page 119-H2

Infernos Nightclub
Infernos is a 1970s disco with a piano bar, shooter bar and VIP room. The DJs play disco classics all night.

146 Clapham High Street, Clapham, London SW4 7UH
☎ 020 7720 7633
🖰 www.infernos.co.uk
🖢 Page 141-J5

The Island
180–182 Hungerford Lane, London WC2N 5NG
☎ 020 7389 6622
🖰 www.theisland-london.com
🖢 Page 10-E7

Jrink
62 Frith Street, Soho, London W1D 3JN
☎ 020 7494 9798
@ info@jrinksoho.com
🖰 www.jrinksoho.com
🖢 Page 10-C4

Juno
134–135 Shoreditch High Street, London E1 6JE
☎ 02077292660
🖰 www.junoshoreditch.co.uk
🖢 Page 13-H1

The Key
The Key has two floors with ornate mirrors, squashy leather sofas, eclectic furniture and flowers. It has a capacity of 1,000.

Lazer Road, Kings Cross, Goods Yard, off York Way, London N1 0UZ
☎ 020 7837 1027
@ info@thekeylondon.com
🖰 www.thekeylondon.com
🖢 Page 84-D5

The Kingly Club
The Kingly Club offers an intimate and chic environment. Cocktails are available at the glass bar and private booths and tables are enclosed by dramatic aquariums – all within ultra modern surroundings.

4 Kingly Court, Soho, London W1B 5PW
☎ 020 7287 1331
@ info@kinglyclub.co.uk
🖰 www.kinglyclub.co.uk
🖢 Page 10-B5

Langtry's Nightclub
2–4 High Street, Beckenham BR3 1AZ
☎ 020 8650 1250
@ info@langtrys.co.uk
🖰 www.langtrys.co.uk
🖢 Page 182-D5

The Loop
19 Dering Street, Mayfair, London W1S 1AH
☎ 020 7493 1003
@ info@loopbar.co.uk
🖰 www.theloopbar.co.uk
📄 020 7493 0483
🖢 Page 9-J4

Los Locos
A restaurant, cocktail bar and club with regular dance nights.

24–26 Russell Street, Covent Garden, London WC2B 5HF
☎ 020 7379 0220
@ info@los-locos.co.uk
🖰 www.los-locos.co.uk
📄 020 7379 0219
🖢 Page 11-G4

Madame Jo Jo's
An internationally renowned entertainment venue situated in the heart of London's West End, offering cutting-edge live performances and progressive DJs.

8–10 Brewer Street, Soho, London W1F 0SP

☎ 020 7734 3040
@ paris@madamejojos.com
⌐ www.madamejojos.com
📍 Page 10-B5

Mahiki

1 Dover Street, Mayfair, London
W1S 4LD
☎ 08713 324474, 020 7493 9529
@ jane@mahiki.com
⌐ www.mahiki.com
🖶 0870 746 6011
📍 Page 9-K7

Mass

A club and live music venue set
in the converted St Matthews
Church, located in the Peace
Gardens at the heart of vibrant
Brixton. Hosts new musical talent
crossing every genre.

St Matthews Church, Brixton Hill,
London SW2 1JF
☎ 020 7738 7875
@ info@mass-club.com
⌐ www.mass-club.com
🖶 020 7738 5772
📍 Page 142-A5

Medusa

302–304 Barrington Road, London
SW9 7NN
📍 Page 162-A1

Metro Club

A small basement venue on Oxford
Street hosting a line-up of shows
and clubs almost every night of
the week. It showcases many
up-and-coming bands.

19–23 Oxford Street, Soho,
London W1R 2DN
☎ 020 7437 0964
@ bookings@blowupmetro.com
⌐ www.blowupmetro.com
📍 Page 9-G4

The Ministry of Sound

A nightclub that has famously
been home to electronic music
since 1992. Located in Elephant
and Castle, Ministry of Sound was
one of the key British superclubs
of the 1990s.

103 Gaunt Street, Elephant and
Castle, London SE1 6DP
☎ 020 7378 6528
@ info@ministryofsound.com
⌐ www.ministryofsound.com/
clubbing/
📍 Page 18-B4

The Mission Room

26 Exmouth Market, London
EC1R 4QE
☎ 020 7278 0816
📍 Page 5-K6

Monto Water Rats Theatre

328 Grays Inn Road, London
WC1X 8BZ
☎ 020 7813 1079
@ info@themonto.com
⌐ www.themonto.com
📍 Page 5-F4

Moonlighting

17 Greek Street, Soho, London
W1D 4DR
☎ 020 7437 5782, 020 7734 6308
@ enquiries@Moonlighting
Nightclub.co.uk
⌐ www.moonlightingnightclub.
co.uk
📍 Page 10-D4

Motion

An upbeat party venue overlooking
the Thames, open from lunch and
packed with private booths, snugs
and lounge areas for late nights!

Victoria Embankment, Charing
Cross, London WC2N 6PA
☎ 020 7389 9933
@ info@motion-bar.co.uk
⌐ www.motion-bar.co.uk
🖶 020 7389 9934
📍 Page 11-G6

Movida

8 Argyll Street, Leicester Square,
London W1F 7TA
☎ 020 7292 2788
@ michael@movida-london.com
⌐ www.movida-london.com
📍 Page 10-D6

Nectar

Nectar is a new style bar,
restaurant and club just past Lots
Road and only minutes away from
Fulham Broadway.

562 Kings Road, London SW6 2DZ
☎ 020 7326 7455, 020 7326 7450
@ info@nectarbar.co.uk
⌐ www.nectarbar.co.uk
🖶 0870 135335
📍 Page 140-B1

Notting Hill Arts Club

Well-established in London's
music scene, the Notting Hill Arts
Club specialises in underground
and experimental club and music
nights.

21 Notting Hill Gate, Kensington,
London W11 3JQ
☎ 020 7460 4459
@ info@nottinghillartsclub.com
⌐ www.nottinghillartsclub.com
📍 Page 119-K1

Number One

1 Leicester Square, St James's,
London WC2H 7FB
📍 Page 10-D6

The Old Queens Head

44 Essex Road, Islington, London
N1 8LN
☎ 020 7354 9993
@ shelley@theoldqueenshead.
com
⌐ www.theoldqueenshead.com
📍 Page 85-J5

On Anon

Overlooking Piccadilly Circus, On
Anon is a great multi-room venue
with a room to suit every mood,
from the relaxed Studio Bar to
the feisty Glam bar and the retro
Lodge to the lively Club.

London Pavillion, Piccadilly Circus,
London W1D 7DH
☎ 020 7287 8008
@ info@onanon.co.uk
⌐ www.onanon.co.uk
🖶 020 7287 8100
📍 Page 10-B6

On The Rocks

25 Kingsland Road, London
E2 8AA
☎ 07753 484936
📍 Page 7-H3

The Opera House Nightclub

2 Chesnut Road, Tottenham,
London N17 9EN
☎ 020 8885 2200
⌐ www.clubraunchy.co.uk
📍 Page 50-C6

The Opium Lounge

Inspired by the Far Eastern opium
dens of the 1920s and the lavish
smoking houses of Marrakech.
With its comfortable boudoir
seating and beautiful Moroccan
beds strewn with silk scatter
cushions The Opium Lounge
creates an atmosphere that
screams luxury.

36–38 North Street, Romford
RM1 1BH

☎ 01708 730355
@ paul@opium-lounge.info
⌐ www.opium-lounge.info
📍 Page 75-F1

The Oxford Arms

265 Camden High Street, Camden,
London NW1 7BU
☎ 020 7267 4945
📍 Page 4-A1

Oxygen

Oxygen is home to three very
different bars with three different
styles of music from past and
present chart hits to high tempo
mainstream dance.

17–18 Irving Street, Leicester
Square, London WC2H 7AZ
☎ 020 7930 0907
@ oxygen@junette.com
⌐ www.oxygenbar.co.uk
🖶 020 7839 7989
📍 Page 10-D6

Pacha

Oozing warmth, luxury and
elegance Pacha offers state-of-
the-art sounds.

Terminus Place, Victoria, London
SW1V 1JR
☎ 020 7833 3139
@ info@pachalondon.com
⌐ www.pachalondon.com
📍 Page 15-K5

Pacific Edge

80–84 Market Place, Romford
RM1 3ER
☎ 01708 739 382
@ info@pacificedgeclub.com
⌐ www.pacificedgeclub.com
📍 Page 75-G2

Paper

68 Regent Street, London
W1B 5EL
☎ 020 7439 7770
@ info@paperclublondon.com
⌐ www.paperclublondon.com
🖶 020 7434 0077
📍 Page 10-A4

The Phoenix

37 Cavendish Square, Marylebone,
London W1G 0PP
☎ 020 7493 8003
⌐ www.the-phoenix-cavendish-
sq.co.uk
📍 Page 9-K3

Pier One Nightspot

91 Kingsland High Street, London
E8 2PB

☎ 020 7690 0769
📍 pieronenightspot.com
🔖 Page 86-B4

Pigalle Club

The Pigalle Club offers club nights and gigs in the decadent surroundings of a bygone era.

215 Piccadilly, Soho, London London W1J 9HN
☎ 020 7734 8142
@ pigalle@vpmg.net
🔖 www.thepigalleclub.com
🖩 020 7494 2022
🔖 Page 10-A7

Plan B

418 Brixton Road, London SW9 7AY
☎ 0870 116 5421
@ info@plan-brixton.co.uk
🔖 www.plan-brixton.co.uk
🖩 020 7924 0678
🔖 Page 142-B5

Plastic People

Intimate late night venue in East London .

147–149 Curtain Road, London EC2A 3QE
☎ 07796 302842, 08713 323702
@ info@plasticpeople.co.uk
🔖 www.plasticpeople.co.uk
🔖 Page 7-G7

Platinum Rooms

23 Lewisham Way, New Cross, London SE14 6PP
☎ 020 8694 9644
🔖 Page 144-C3

Powder Monkey

Greenwich premier gay venue.

22 King William Walk, Greenwich, London SE10 9HU
☎ 020 8293 5928
@ info@thepowdermonkey.net
🔖 www.thepowdermonkey.net
🔖 Page 125-F6

Punk

14 Soho Street, London W1D 3DN
☎ 020 7734 4004
@ selina@thebreakfastgroup.co.uk
🔖 www.fabbars.com
🔖 Page 10-C3

Putney Fez

Morrocan-themed bar offering a variety of weekly club nights.

200b Upper Richmond Road, Putney, London SW15 2SH

☎ 020 8780 0123
@ info@putneyfez.com
🔖 www.barclub.com/putneyfez/listings.php
🖩 020 8780 0404
🔖 Page 138-E5

Question

45–47 Dartmouth Road, Forest Hill, London SE23 3HN
☎ 020 8699 5686
@ Questiontmh@aol.com
🔖 www.questionbar.com
🔖 Page 163-J5

The Ram Club

Club for folk and acoustic music that has existed for more than 20 years.

106 Hare Lane, Claygate, Esher KT10 0LZ
☎ 020 8686 9421
@ ramclub@btinternet.com
🔖 www.theramclub.co.uk
🔖 Page 204-E4

The Red Rooms

4 Great Queen Street, Holborn, London WC2B 5DG
☎ 07886 272118
🔖 Page 11-F3

The Refectory

911 Finchley Road, London NW11 7PE
☎ 020 8455 2020
🔖 Page 64-D2

Reflex Nightclub

A friendly gay club, playing music from the 80s and 90s plus the latest dance, pop and house music. The club has two floors and a glass dance floor.

184 London Road, Kingston upon Thames KT2 6QW
☎ 020 8549 9911, 07749 104504
@ info@reflexnightclub.com
🔖 www.reflexnightclub.com
🖩 020 8549 9800
🔖 Page 175-G5

Renaissance Rooms

Miles Street, London SW8 1SD
☎ 020 7498 0004, 020 7720 9140
🔖 Page 121-K6

The Rhythm Factory

A cafe-bar by day with live bands during weekday evenings. At the weekend, the club is host to a variety of nights with DJs playing hip hop, house, breakbeats and

drum'n'bass depending on the night.

16–18 Whitechapel Road, London E1 1EW
☎ 020 7375 3774
@ info@rhythmfactory.co.uk
🔖 www.rhythmfactory.co.uk
🔖 Page 104-C5

The Roadhouse

35 The Piazza, Covent Garden Market, London WC2E 8BE
☎ 020 7240 6001
@ bookings@roadhouse.co.uk
🔖 www.roadhouse.co.uk
🔖 Page 11-F5

Rococo

7–9 Cranbourn Street, Leicester Square, London WC2H 7AG
☎ 020 7287 7773, 020 2877 7773
@ info@rococolondon.com
🔖 www.rococolondon.com/
🖩 020 7287 7774
🔖 Page 10-D5

Room At The Top

197 High Road, Ilford IG1 1LX
☎ 020 8478 5588
@ nightwayltd@aol.com
🔖 www.roomatthetopnightclub.co.uk
🔖 Page 72-B6

The Roxy

3–5 Rathbone Place, London W1T 1HH
☎ 020 7255 1098
@ info@theroxy.co.uk
🔖 www.theroxy.co.uk
🔖 Page 10-C2

Roxy Bar and Screen

128–132 Borough High Street, London SE1 1LB
☎ 020 7407 4057
@ info@roxybarandscreen.com
🔖 www.roxybarandscreen.com
🔖 Page 18-D3

Royal Vauxhall Tavern

Hosts a variety of comedy, cabaret, gay and jazz events plus popular club nights.

372 Kennington Lane, London SE11 5HY
☎ 020 7820 1222
@ info@rvt.org.uk
🔖 www.theroyalvauxhalltavern.co.uk
🔖 Page 122-A5

Ruby-Lo

The Ruby-Lo offers the best cocktails and interior design, along with the raw fun and energy of the best DJs.

23 Orchard Street, Marylebone, London W1H 6HL
☎ 020 7486 3671
@ ruby-lo@ruby.uk.com
🔖 www.ruby.uk.com
🖩 020 7689 1370
🔖 Page 9-G4

The Salmon And Compass

58 Penton Street, Chapel Market Street, London N1 9PZ
☎ 020 7837 3891
@ info@salmonandcompass.com
🔖 www.salmonandcompass.com
🔖 Page 5-J2

Scala

Scala is a multi-purpose venue in the regenerated King's Cross area. The building incorporates four main floors and has three bars, two dance floors and a stage for live performances. It hosts regular weekend club nights and is also a popular venue for live music on week nights.

275 Pentonville Road, Kings Cross, London N1 9NL
☎ 020 7833 2022
@ reception@scala-london.co.uk
🔖 www.scala-london.co.uk
🔖 Page 5-G3

Se One

41–43 St Thomas Street, Bermondsey, London SE1 3QX
☎ 020 7407 1617
@ info@seonelondon.com
🔖 www.seonelondon.com
🖩 020 7378 7463
🔖 Page 19-F1

Sin

144 Charing Cross Road, Covent Garden, London WC2H 0LB
☎ 020 7240 1900
@ reception@sinlondon.com
🔖 www.sinlondon.com
🔖 Page 10-D5

Slimelight

The Slimelight is an alternative club dealing in industrial, power-noise, cyber-synth, cyber-goth, darkwave, traditional and modern goth, plus crossover and related alternative sounds.

7 Torrens Street, Islington,
London EC1 1NQ
☎ 020 7837 6419
@ office@slimelight.net
🖰 www.slimelight.net
📄 020 7278 1437
🖸 Page 6-A3

Smoke Bar Diner
The bar holds club nights every
first Friday night of each month.

14 Trinity Road, Tooting Bec,
London SW17 7RE
☎ 020 8767 3902
@ info@smokebardiner.com
🖰 www.smokeroomsclapham.com
🖸 Page 160-E5

The Social N1
33 Linton Street, Arlington Square,
London N1 7DU
☎ 020 7354 5809
@ managers@thesocialn1.com
🖰 www.thesocial.com/
📄 020 7354 8087
🖸 Page 6-D1

The Social W1
Intimate venue offering a range
of experimental/alternative club
nights as well as a gallery space.

5 Little Portland Street, London
W1W 7JD
☎ 020 7434 0620
@ carl@thesocial.com
🖰 www.thesocial.com
📄 020 7636 4993
🖸 Page 9-K3

Soho Revue Bar
11–12 Walker's Court, Brewer
Street, London W1F 0ED
☎ 020 7734 0377
@ cheryl@too2much.com
🖰 www.sohorevuebar.co.uk
🖸 Page 10-B5

The Soho Spice Cellar Club
Offers all day drinking, dining
and entertainment in stylish
surroundings, right in the heart of
the West End.

124–126 Wardour Street, Soho,
London W1F 0TY
☎ 0207434 0808
@ info@sohospice.co.uk
🖰 www.sohospice.co.uk
🖸 Page 10-B3

Sound
1 Leicester Square, London
WC2H 7NA

☎ 020 7863 7304, 020 72871010
@ info@soundlondon.com
🖰 www.soundlondon.com
🖸 Page 10-D6

South Central
349 Kennington Lane, London
SE11 5QY
☎ 020 7793 0903
🖰 www.southcentrallondon.co.uk
🖸 Page 122-A5

South London Pacific
340 Kennington Road, London
SE11 4LD
☎ 020 7820 9189
@ contact@southlondonpacific.
com
🖰 www.southlondonpacific.com
🖸 Page 17-J7

The Spotted Dog
38 Willesden High Road, London
NW10 2QD
☎ 02084 592220
🖸 Page 81-K4

St Moritz
159 Wardour Street, Soho,
London W1F 8WL
☎ 0871 223 2883
🖰 www.stmoritz-restaurant.co.uk
🖸 Page 10-B3

Storm
28a Leicester Square, London
WC2H 7LE
☎ 020 7839 2633
@ info@stormnightclub.co.uk
🖰 www.stormnightclub.co.uk
🖸 Page 10-D6

Studio 4
Studio 4 is a stylish venue formerly
known as Browns/Cougar Pinks.

4 Greet Queen Street, Holborn,
London WC2B 5DG
☎ 0776 7363 241
🖸 Page 11-F3

Studio 88
88 Chalk Farm Road, Camden
Town, London NW1 8AR
☎ 020 7485 8222
🖸 Page 84-A5

Studio Valbonne
The refurbished and re-vamped
Tantra Club has been transformed
into the hotly anticipated Studio
Valbonne. Based on the venue's
original name, Studio Valbonne
was re-designed to bring back

the classic high end club to the
West End.

62 Kingly Street, Soho, London
W1B 5QN
☎ 0207 434 0888
@ info@studiovalbonne.co.uk
🖰 www.studiovalbonne.co.uk/
home.html
📄 0207 434 0999
🖸 Page 10-A4

Stylus Bar
58 Camberwell Church Street,
London SE5 8QZ
☎ 020 7326 0055
🖰 www.stylusbar.co.uk
🖸 Page 142-E2

The Sun
47 London Road, Romford
RM7 9QA
☎ 01708 743423
🖸 Page 74-C3

T Bar
56 Shoreditch High Street, London
E1 6JJ
☎ 020 7729 2973
@ info@tbarlondon.com
🖰 www.tbarlondon.com
🖸 Page 13-H1

Tennessee Rock n Roll Club
The Tennessee Club is a regular
live rock n roll music venue.

Trent Park Golf Club, Bramley
Road, Southgate, London
N14 4UW
☎ 020 8886 5786
@ ritchiegee@freeuk.com
🖰 www.tennesseeclub.net
🖸 Page 22-C5

Third Base
St Matthews Church, Brixton,
London SW2 1JF
☎ 020 7738 7875
@ info@mass-club.com
🖰 www.mass-club.com
📄 020 7738 5772
🖸 Page 142-A5

Tonky Gorilla
A bar-restaurant with regular club
and live music nights.

539–541 Kingsbury High Road,
Kingsbury, London NW9 9EG
☎ 020 8204 7000
@ info@tonkygorilla.com
🖰 www.tonkygorilla.com
🖸 Page 62-C2

Traffic
Victoria House, 1 Vernon Place,
London WC1A 2EP
☎ 0871 971 6231
@ robbie@x-touch.co.uk
🖰 www.traffic.uk.com/
🖸 Page 11-F2

Troy Bar
10 Hoxton Street, London N1 6NG
🕐 02077396695
🖸 Page 7-G1

Turnmills
63b Clerkenwell Road, London
EC1M 5NP
☎ 020 7250 3409
@ linda@turnmills.com
🖰 www.turnmills.co.uk
📄 020 7250 1046
🖸 Page 5-J7

Twilight Nite Club
21 Peto Street North, Canning
Town, London E16 1DD
☎ 020 7473 2005, 07930 865718
🖸 Page 106-D5

The Two Brewers
114 Clapham High Street, London
SW4 7UJ
☎ 020 7498 4971
@ nfo@the2brewers.com
🖰 www.the2brewers.com
🖸 Page 141-J5

Umbaba
A nightclub, restaurant and bar
situated in the heart of Soho
and located on Ganton Street, a
pedestrian thoroughfare between
Carnaby Street and Kingly Court.

15–21 Ganton Street, Soho,
London W1F 9BN
☎ 020 7734 6696
🖰 www.umbaba.com/
🖸 Page 10-A5

Underbelly
11 Hoxton Square, London N1 6NU
☎ 020 7613 1988
@ office@zigfrid.com
🖰 www.zigfrid.com
🖸 Page 7-G5

The Underworld
This Camden institution provides
a stage for established and up-
and-coming indie, rock and metal
bands, as well as hosting regular
indie club nights.

174 Camden High Street, Camden,
London NW1 0NE

☎ 020 7482 1932
@ contact@theunderworld
camden.co.uk
🏠 www.theunderworldcamden.
co.uk
📍 Page 4-A1

Unit 7

Dark warehouse with a booming
sound system.

Cable Studios, 566 Cable Street,
London E1W 2HB
☎ 0207 4289771
@ info@unitseven.co.uk
🏠 www.unitseven.co.uk/
📍 Page 104-D6

The Vauxhall Griffin

8 Wyvil Road, Vauxhall, London
SW8 2TH
☎ 020 7622 0222
@ info@thevauxhallgriffin.com
🏠 www.thevauxhallgriffin.com
📍 Page 141-K1

The Venue

2a Clifton Rise, New Cross,
London SE14 6JP
☎ 020 8692 4077
@ dance@thevenuelondon.com
🏠 www.thevenuelondon.com
📍 Page 144-B1

Vibe Bar

The Old Truman Brewery, 91 Brick
Lane, London E1 6QL
☎ 020 7426 0491
@ info@vibe-bar.co.uk
🏠 www.vibe-bar.co.uk
📍 Page 7-J7

Victory

55 New Oxford Street,
Bloomsbury, London WC1A 1BS
🏠 www.clubvictory.com
📍 Page 10-E3

Virgo's Nightclub

A contemporary, shared lounge
and dance space, overlooked by
an open stage and intimate VIP
area. Various events are hosted,
including live music and comedy
showcases. Evenings generally
culminate in salsa, R'n'B, soul,
funk and party music.

148 Old Kent Road, Bermondsey,
London SE1 5TY
☎ 020 7703 4480
🏠 www.virgosnightclub.com
📍 Page 19-G7

The Watershed

267 The Broadway, Wimbledon,
London SW19 1SD
☎ 020 8540 0080
@ info@the-watershed.com
🏠 www.the-watershed.com
📍 Page 177-K2

The Wenlock Arms

The Wenlock Arms was built in
1835, and opened as a pub in
January 1836. It survived the
wartime bombing of the district
but still retains much of its original
characteristics.

26 Wenlock Road, London N1 7TA
☎ 020 7608 3406
@ wenlockarms@blueyondes.
co.uk
🏠 www.wenlock-arms.co.uk
📍 Page 6-C3

The Westbury

A sophisticated venue offering
Dim Sum, delicious cocktails and
cracking roast dinners to begin an
evening of the freshest music from
a selection of DJs.

34 Kilburn High Road, Kilburn,
London NW6 5UA
☎ 020 7625 7500
🏠 www.westburybar.com/
📍 Page 82-E6

The White House

The emergence of the Manhattan-
style nightclub across the nightlife
scene in the UK has created a late
night revolution which has been
spearheaded by The White House.

65 Clapham Park Road, London
SW4 7EH
☎ 020 7498 3388
@ info@thewhitehouselondon.
co.uk
🏠 www.thewhitehouselondon.
co.uk
📠 020 7498 5588
📍 Page 141-J5

The Works

1 St James's Road, Kingston upon
Thames KT1 2AH
☎ 020 8541 4411
🏠 www.workskingston.com
📍 Page 174-E5

The Worship

The Worship has two bars and
a terrace to eat out on in good
weather. The venue is cool and
trendy and the decor reflects the
style of its young, urban clientele.

3 Triton Court, Finsbury Square,
London EC2A 1BR
☎ 020 7330 0929
@ info@theworship.co.uk
🏠 www.theworship.co.uk
📠 020 7330 0920
📍 Page 13-F1

Zigfrid

11 Hoxton Square, London N1 6NU
☎ 020 7613 3105
@ office@zigfrid.com
🏠 www.zigfrid.com/
📍 Page 7-G5

SPECIAL EVENTS' VENUES

Alexandra Palace

Alexandra Palace is a venue
for exhibitions, conferences,
hospitality and private
celebrations, from the most
intimate to large-scale events.

Alexandra Palace Way, Wood
Green, London N22 7AY
☎ 020 8365 2121
@ sales@alexandrapalace.com
🏠 www.alexandrapalace.com
📠 020 8883 3999
📍 Page 48-D6

BBC Maida Vale Studios

Delaware Road, Maida Vale,
London W9 2LG
🏠 www.bbcradioresources.
com/locations/maidavale
📍 Page 101-F3

Cabot Place, Canary Wharf

Canary Wharf's central square
offers a variety of free open air
events in the summer months.

North Greenwich, London E14 4QS
🏠 www.mycanarywharf.com
📍 Page 124-D1

Central Hall Westminster

Storeys Gate, St James's Park,
London SW1H 9NH
☎ 020 7222 8010
@ lainsworth@c-h-w.co.uk
🏠 www.c-h-w.com
📠 020 7222 6883
📍 Page 16-D3

Chelsea Old Town Hall

King's Road, Chelsea, London
SW3 5EE
☎ 020 7361 4131
@ hall-let@rbkc.gov.uk
🏠 www.rbkc.gov.uk/
venueschelsea/general
📍 Page 120-D5

County Hall

County Hall plays host to a number
of temporary attractions and
media events, such as Star Wars:
The Exhibition, 2007 Comic Relief
does Fame Academy and the
*Harry Potter and the Order of the
Phoenix* press release.

Westminster Bridge Road, London
SE1 7PB
🏠 www.londoncountyhall.com
📍 Page 17-G2

Earls Court

EC&O Venues – Earls Court,
Olympia and the Brewery – are
iconic venues where 3 million
people visit 1,000 events each year.

Warwick Road, Kensington,
London SW5 9TA
☎ 020 7385 1200
@ info@eco.co.uk
🏠 www.eco.co.uk
📍 Page 119-K5

ExCeL London

ExCeL London, the international
exhibition and conference
centre, hosts a range of events
throughout the year, from
internationally acclaimed travel
trade exhibitions to high octane
sporting events for all the family,
as well as product launches,
conferences and corporate
hospitality functions.

One Western Gateway, Royal
Victoria Dock, Canning Town,
London E16 1XL
☎ 020 7069 5000
@ info@excel-london.co.uk
🏠 www.excel-london.co.uk
📍 Page 107-F6

Guildhall

Gresham Street, London EC2P 2EJ
☎ 020 7606 3030
🕒 020 7332 1313
@ guildhall.events@cityoflondon.
gov.uk
📍 Page 12-D3

Horse Guards Parade

Horse Guards Parade, Whitehall,
Westminster, London SW1A 2AX
☎ 020 7414 2357
🕒 020 7414 2479
📍 Page 16-D1

The Inner Temple and Gardens

Middle Temple Lane, London
EC4Y 7HL
☎ 020 7797 8250
@ enquiries@innertemple.org.uk
🖰 www.innertemple.org.uk
🕮 Page 11-J4

Kempton Park Racecourse

Sunbury TW16 5AQ
☎ 01932 782292
@ kempton@jockeyclub
racecourses.com
🖰 www.kempton.co.uk
🖨 01932 782044
🕮 Page 172-A3

Leicester Square

West End, London WC2H 7NA
🕮 Page 10-D6

Lord's Cricket Ground

St John's Wood, MCC Lord's
Cricket Ground, London NW8 8QN
☎ 020 7616 8500
🖰 www.lords.org
🕮 Page 2-B4

The O2

The O2 is one of London's largest
entertainment venues, centred
around its indoor music and sports
arena, which attracts global stars
and events, including the 2012
Olympic events.

Millennium Way, Greenwich,
London SE10 0BB
© 0871 984 0002
🖰 www.theo2.co.uk
🕮 Page 125-H2

Olympia National Hall

Hammersmith Road, Kensington,
London W14 8UX
☎ 020 7385 1200
@ info@eco.co.uk
🖰 www.eco.co.uk
🕮 Page 119-H3

The Roundhouse

As the third largest performing
arts centre in London, The
Roundhouse presents a varied
programme of international
performing arts including music,
theatre, dance, circus and digital
media to reflect the excitement
and diversity of 21st-century
culture.

Chalk Farm Road, London
NW1 8EH
☎ 020 7424 9991
© 087 0389 1846
@ info@roundhouse.org.uk
🖰 www.roundhouse.org.uk
🖨 020 7424 9992
🕮 Page 84-A5

Royal Horticultural Halls and Conference Centre

The Royal Horticultural Halls
and Conference Centre is
centrally located in the heart of
Westminster and comprises two
exhibition and event halls and
a conference centre. The venue
hosts all kind of events from trade
and consumer fairs to corporate
events and conferences.

80 Vincent Square, Victoria
London SW1P 2PE
☎ 020 7828 4125
@ horthalls@rhs.org.uk
🖰 www.horticultural-halls.co.uk
🖨 020 7834 2072
🕮 Page 16-C6

Trafalgar Square

Trafalgar Square provides a
stage for cultural, educational,
artistic and sporting events,
demonstrations, rallies,
ceremonies and festivals. It is also
home to Nelson's Column.

Trafalgar Square, Charing Cross,
London WC2N 5DN
☎ 020 7983 4813
🖰 www.london.gov.uk/mayor/
trafalgar_square/index.jsp
🕮 Page 10-D7

Twickenham Stadium

Rugby Road, Isleworth, London
TW1 1DZ
🖰 www.rfu.com/microsites/
twickenham/index.cfm
🕮 Page 155-K1

Wembley Conference & Exhibition Centre

Elvin House, Stadium Way,
Wembley, London HA9 0DW
☎ 0208 585 3501, 0208 585 3760
@ contacts@wembley.co.uk
🖰 www.whatsonwembley.com
🕮 Page 00 C2

Wembley Stadium

Wembley Stadium has been a
world stage for sporting and music
events ever since the 1880s. After
a period of renovation starting in
2002, the newly-designed stadium
now offers a range of facilities and
cutting-edge technologies.

Empire Way, Wembley, London
London HA9 0WS
☎ 020 8795 9000
@ info@wembleystadium.com
🖰 www.wembleystadium.com
🖨 020 8795 5050
🕮 Page 80-C2

Street by Street

LONDON

Key to map pages	ii-iii
Key to map symbols	iv-1
Enlarged map pages	2-19
Main map pages	20-217
Index – towns & villages	218-219
Index – streets	220-307
Index – featured places	308-329
Acknowledgements	330

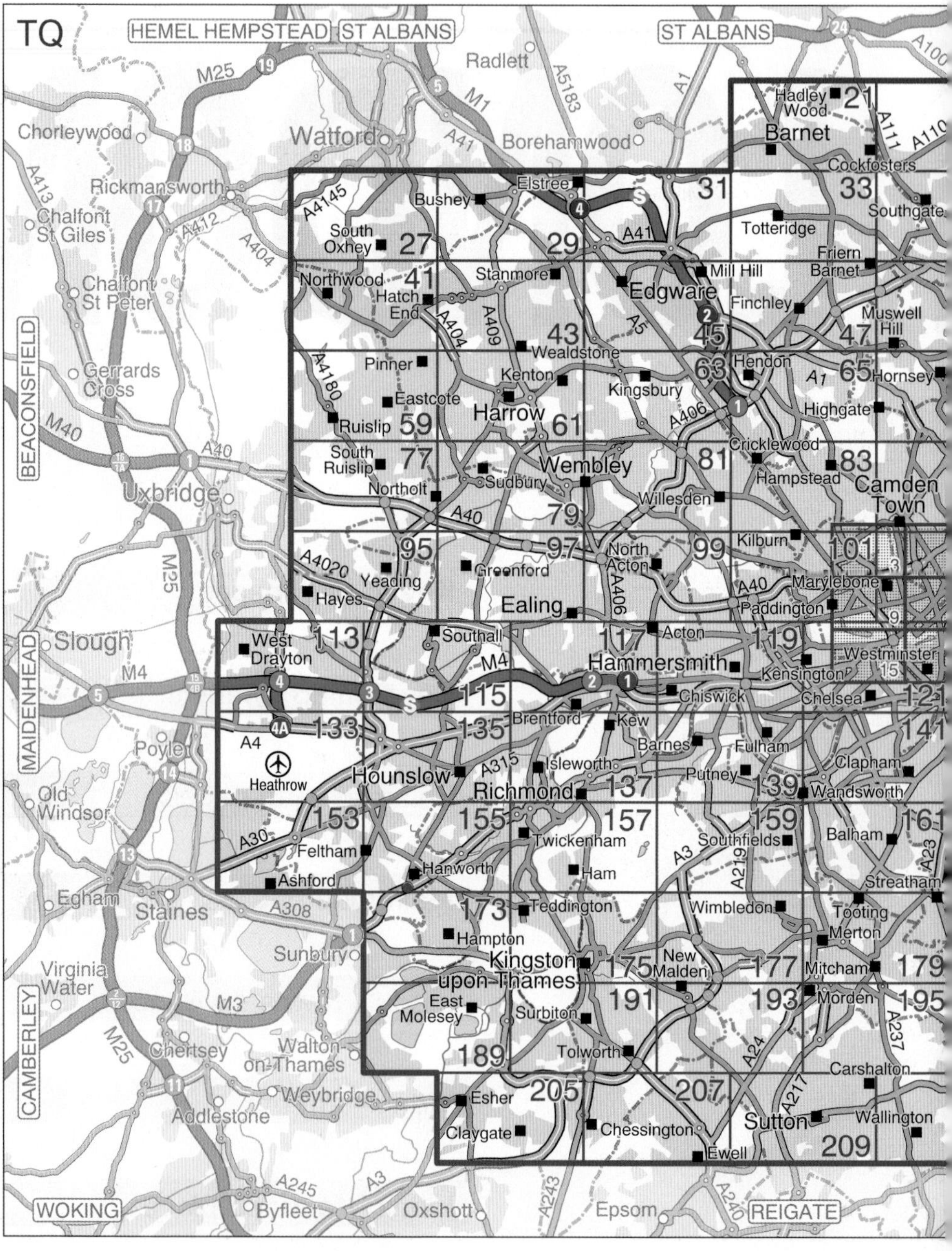

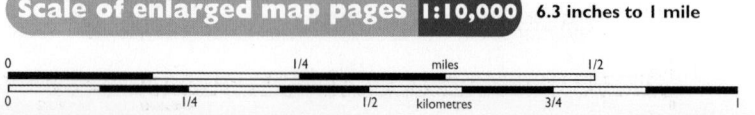

Scale of enlarged map pages 1:10,000 6.3 inches to 1 mile

0 — 1/4 — miles — 1/2

0 — 1/4 — 1/2 — kilometres — 3/4 — 1

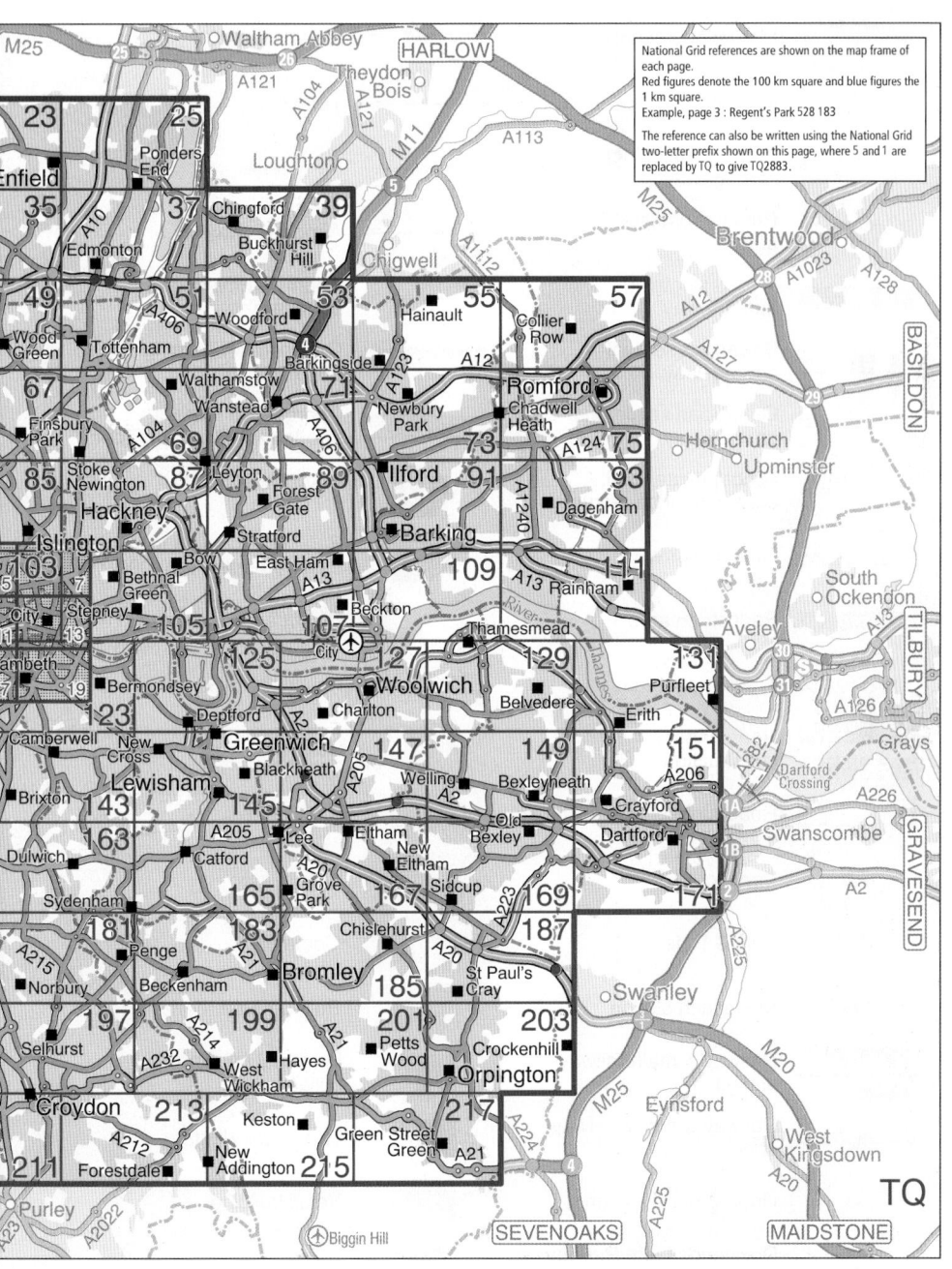

National Grid references are shown on the map frame of each page.
Red figures denote the 100 km square and blue figures the 1 km square.
Example, page 3 : Regent's Park 528 183

The reference can also be written using the National Grid two-letter prefix shown on this page, where 5 and 1 are replaced by TQ to give TQ2883.

3.6 inches to I mile **Scale of main map pages** **1:17,500**

| 0 | | 1/2 | | miles | | I |

| 0 | | 1/2 | | I | | kilometres | | I 1/2 |

Junction 9	Motorway & junction
Services	Motorway service area
	Primary road single/dual carriageway
Services	Primary road service area
	A road single/dual carriageway
	B road single/dual carriageway
	Other road single/dual carriageway
	Minor/private road, access may be restricted
← ←	One-way street
	Pedestrian area
	Track or footpath
	Road under construction
	Road tunnel
P	Parking
P+	Park & Ride
	Bus/coach station
	Railway & main railway station
	Railway & minor railway station
⊖	Underground station
⊖	Docklands Light Railway (DLR) station
⊖	Light railway & station

LC	Level crossing
	Tramway
	Ferry route
	Airport runway
	County, administrative boundary
	Congestion Charging Zone *
	Charge-free routes through the Charging Zone
17	Page continuation 1:17,500
3	Page continuation to enlarged scale 1:10,000
	River/canal, lake, pier
	Aqueduct, lock, weir
	Beach
	Woodland
	Park
	Cemetery
	Built-up area
	Industrial / business building
	Leisure building
	Retail building
	Other building
IKEA	IKEA store

* The AA central London Congestion Charging map is also available

City wall		Castle		

City wall

Hospital with 24-hour A&E department

Post Office

Public library

Tourist Information Centre

Seasonal Tourist Information Centre

Petrol station, 24 hour
Major suppliers only

Church/chapel

Public toilets

Toilet with disabled facilities

Public house
AA recommended

Restaurant
AA inspected

Hotel
AA inspected

Theatre or performing arts centre

Cinema

Golf course

Camping
AA inspected

Caravan site
AA inspected

Camping & caravan site
AA inspected

Theme park

Abbey, cathedral or priory

Castle

Historic house or building

National Trust property

Museum or art gallery

Roman antiquity

Ancient site, battlefield or monument

Industrial interest

Garden

Garden Centre
Garden Centre Association Member

Garden Centre
Wyevale Garden Centre

Arboretum

Farm or animal centre

Zoological or wildlife collection

Bird collection

Nature reserve

Aquarium

Visitor or heritage centre

Country park

Cave

Windmill

Distillery, brewery or vineyard

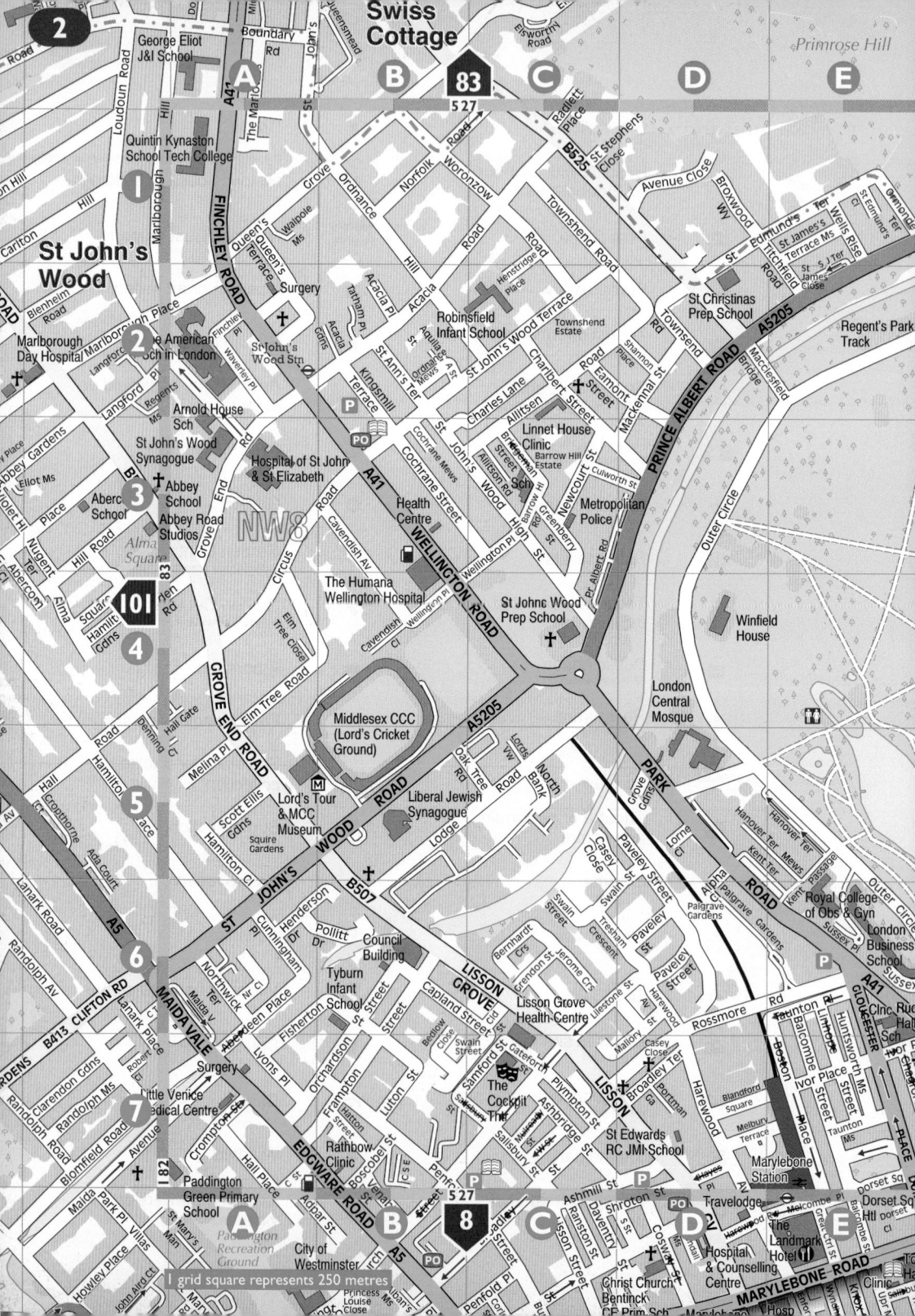

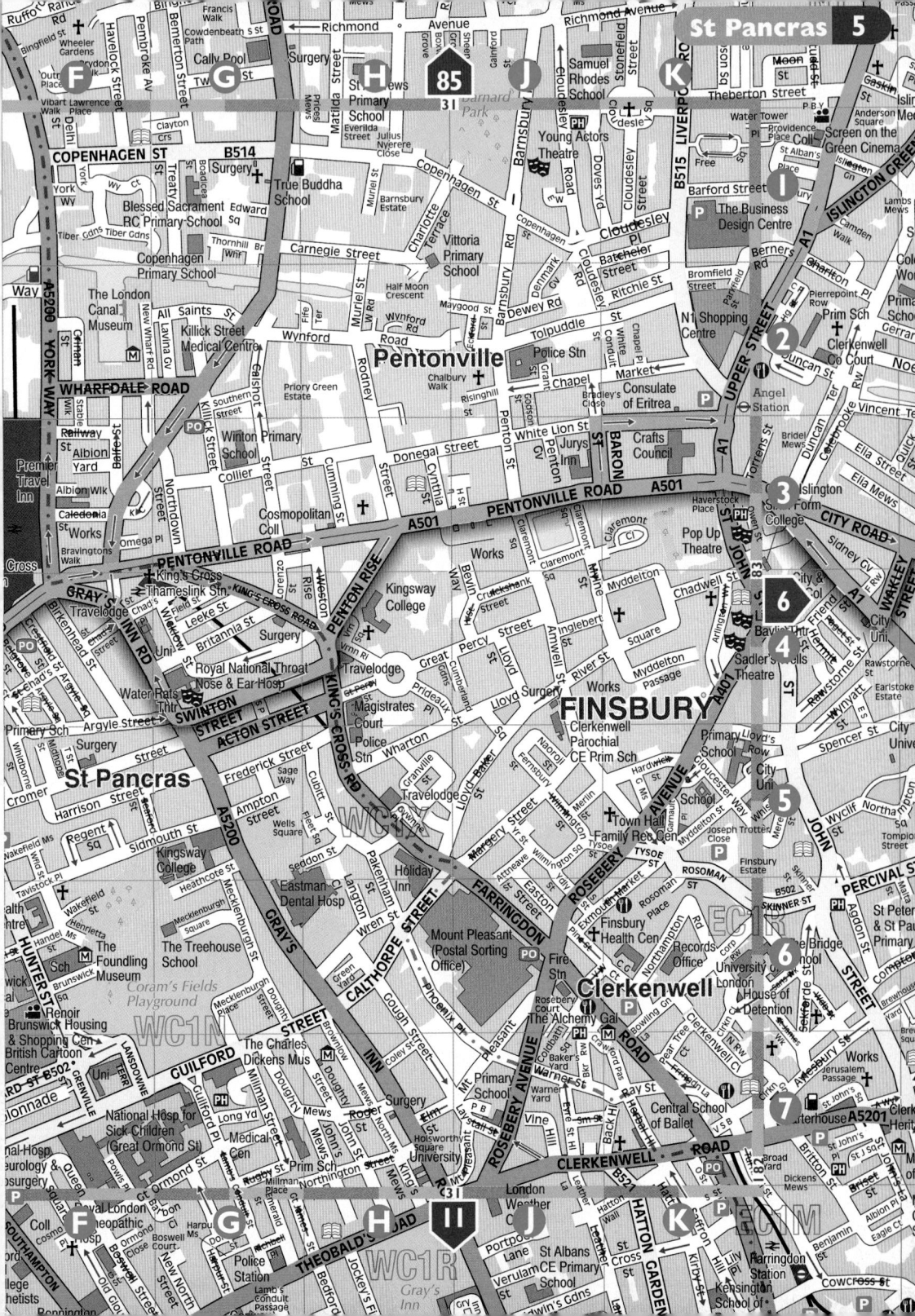

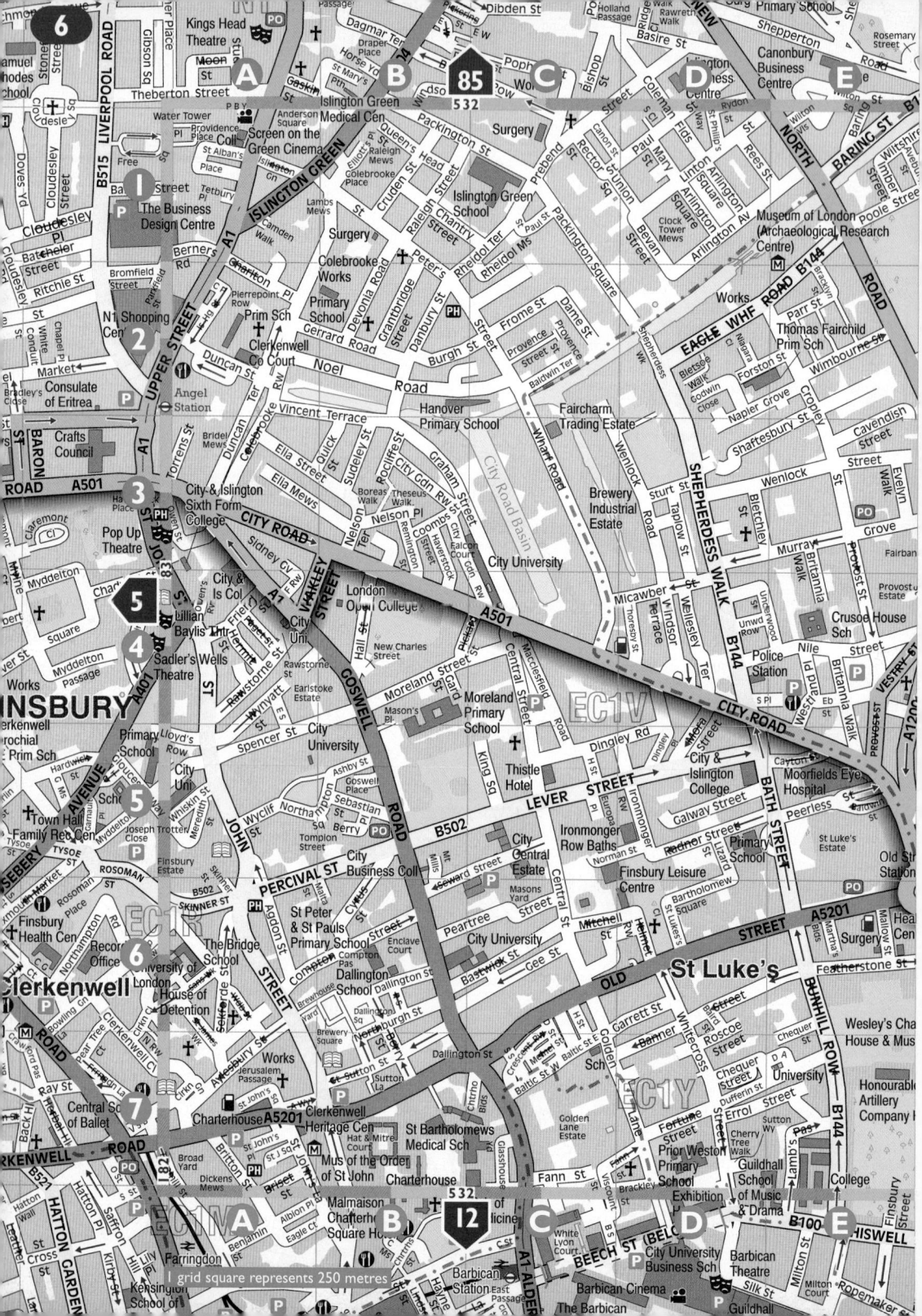

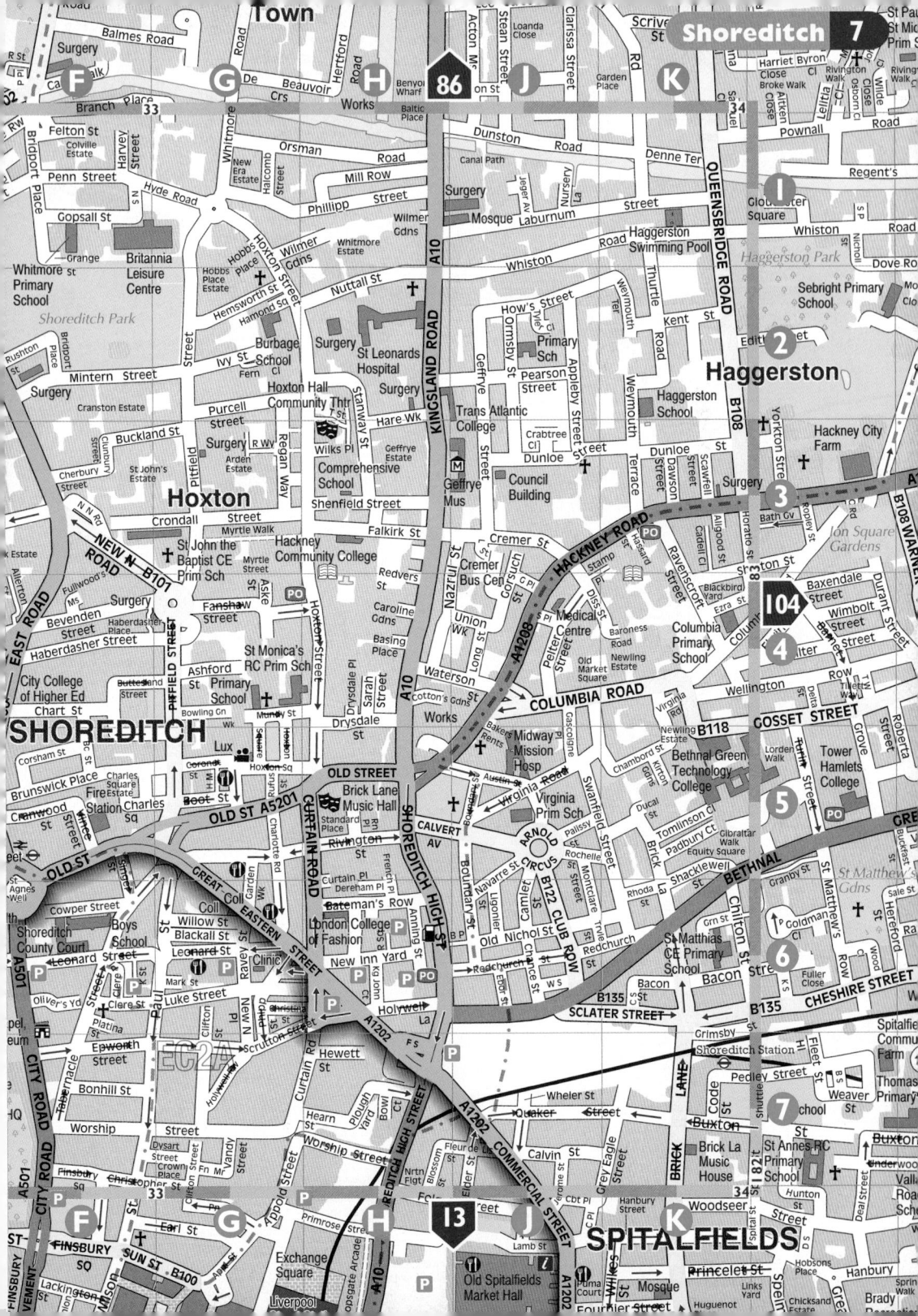

This is a map of the Shoreditch area.

86 **J** **K** **I** **2** **3** **104** **4** **5** **6** **7**

F **G** **H** **13** **J** **K**

Balmes Road
Surgery
Branch Place
Felton St
Colville Estate
Penn Street
Bridport Place
Gopsall St
Grange
Whitmore st Primary School
Shoreditch Park
Britannia Leisure Centre
Mintern Street
Surgery
Cranston Estate
Buckland St
St John's Estate
Cherbury St
Rushton St
Bridport Place

De Beauvoir Crs
Whitmore Road
Orsman Road
New Era Estate
Mill Row
Halcomb Street
Phillipp Street
Wilmer Gdns
Whitmore Estate
Hoxton Gdns
Hobbs Place Estate
Hemsworth Street
Nuttall St
Hamond Sq
Fern St
Ivy St
Burbage School
Surgery
St Leonards Hospital
Surgery
Hoxton Hall Community Thtr
Purcell Street
Surgery
Arden Estate
Regan Way
Comprehensive School
Shenfield Street
Falkirk St

Hyde Road
Hobbs Place
Hoxton Street
Wilmer Street

Hertford Road
Works
Baltic Place

Loanda Close
Stean Street
Acton Ms
Benyon Wharf
Canal Path
Dunston Road
Surgery
Mosque
Laburnum Street
Whiston Road

Clarissa Street
Garden Place

Scrive...
Harriet Byron Close
Broke Walk
Aitken Close
Pownall Road
Regent's
Gloucester Square
Whiston Rd
Haggerston Swimming Pool
Haggerston Park
Sebright Primary School
Hackney City Farm

Haggerston
Haggerston School
Surgery
Yorkton Street
Horatio St
Bath Gv
Ropley St

Hoxton
Crondall Street
Myrtle Walk
St John the Baptist CE Prim Sch
Myrtle Street
Hackney Community College
Aske St
PO

SHOREDITCH
New North Road
East Road
Fullwood's
Surgery
Bevenden Street
Haberdasher Place
Haberdasher Street
City College of Higher Ed Chart St
Buttesland St
Bowling Gn
St Monica's RC Prim Sch
Ashford St Primary School
Drysdale Pl
Sarah Swift Ct
Drysdale St

Pitfield Street
Fanshaw Street
Caroline Gdns
Basing Place
Waterson St
Cotton's Gdns
Works

Kingsland Road
Geffrye Mus
Council Building
Trans Atlantic College
Crabtree Cl
Dunloe Street
Dunloe Ct
Geffrye Estate
Wilks Pl
Hare Wk

How's Street
Primary Sch
Ormsby St
Pearson Street
Geffrye St
Weymouth Terrace
Appleby Street
Nazrul St
Cremer St
Cremer St
Redvers St
Union Wk

Thurlte Road
Kent Street
Dawson Street
Scawfell St
Allgood St
Cadell Ct
Ezra St
Columbia Road
Columbia Primary School
Newling Estate
Baroness Road
Old Market Square

Queensbridge Road
A10
Hackney Road
A4200
Medical Centre
Pelter St
Diss St
Stamp Pl
Hassard St
Ravenscourt Street
Blackbird Yard

Haggerston

Baxendale Street
Wimbolt Street
Durant Street
Ravenscroft Street
Baxter St
Wellington Row
Tilleys Wk
COSSET STREET
Roberta St
Grove St

Bethnal Green Technology College
Newling Estate
B118
Virginia Road
Gascoigne Pl
Chambord St
Kirton Gdns
Ducal St
Tomlinson Ct
Padbury Ct
Gibraltar Walk
Equity Square
Brick St
Rhoda St
Shacklewell St
B135
SCLATER STREET

SHOREDITCH
City College of Higher Ed
City Road
A501
Corsham St
Brunswick Place
Cranwood Street
Shoreditch County Court
Cowper Street
Boys School
Willow St
Blackall St
Leonard Street
Mark St
Clere St
Luke Street
Oliver's Yd
Epworth Street
Bonhill Street
Worship Street
Tabernacle St
Finsbury Sq
Christopher St
EC2A
Clifton Street
Scrutton St
Paul St
Ravey St
New North Pl
Christina St
Coll
Clinic

Great Eastern Street
Old St A5201
Old St
A501
St Agnes Well
Coronet
Lux
Boot St
Hoxton Sq
Phipp St

Curtain Road
Charlotte Rd
Rivington St
Curtain Pl
Garden Walk
Hewett St
Plough Yard
Bowl Ct
Hearn St
Worship Street
Appold St
Primrose St

Brick Lane Music Hall
Standard Place
Dereham Pl
Bateman's Row
London College of Fashion
New Inn Yard
Holywell La
New Inn Yard
Anning St

Shoreditch High St
Calvert Av
CALVERT AV
Boundary St
Navarre St
Camlet St
Old Nichol St
Rochelle St
Ligonier St
Redchurch Street
Chance St
Grey Eagle Street
Corbet Pl
Buxton Street

Arnold Circus
Virginia Prim Sch
Austin St
Swanfield Street
Montclare St
St Matthias CE Primary School
Bacon Street
B135
Sclater Street

Bethnal Green Rd
Granby St
Goldman's Cl
Fuller Close
Fuller St
CHESHIRE STREET
St Matthew's Gdns
Hereford St
Grn St
Roberta St
Tower Hamlets College

Shoreditch Station
Pedley Street
Fleet St
Weaver Street
Shuttle St
Grimsby St
Cobb St
Thomas Passmore Primary School
Spitalfields Community Farm
Buxton St
Underwood St
St Annes RC Primary School

SPITALFIELDS
Exchange Square
Liverpool
Appold St
A10
Commercial Street
A1202
Fleur de Lis St
Blossom St
Elder Street
Folgate St
Norton Folgate
Lamb St
Old Spitalfields Market Hall
Brushfield Street
Fort St
Crispin St
Artillery La
Gun St
Steward St
White's Row
Calvin St
Quaker Street
Wheler St
Hanbury Street
Puma Ct
Princelet Street
Hunton St
Woodseer Street
Deal St
Chicksand Street
Brady St
Hopkins St
Hanbury
Huguenot
Spelman St
Fournier Street
Mosque
Brick Lane Music House
St Annes RC Primary School
Brick Lane
B135
Valla... Road
Links Yard
Hobsons Place
FINSBURY SQ
SUN ST
B100
Earl St
Lackington St
Primrose St

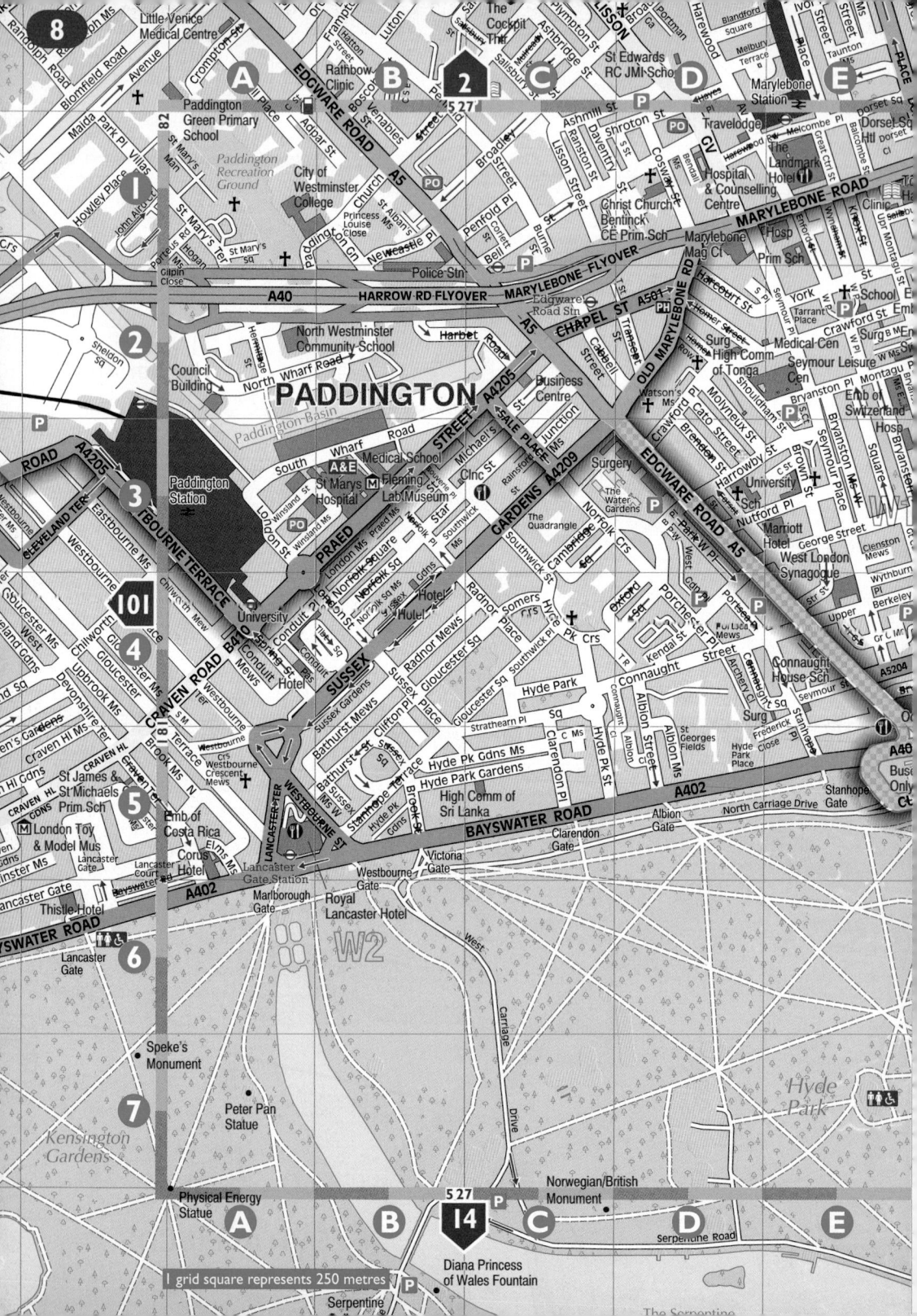

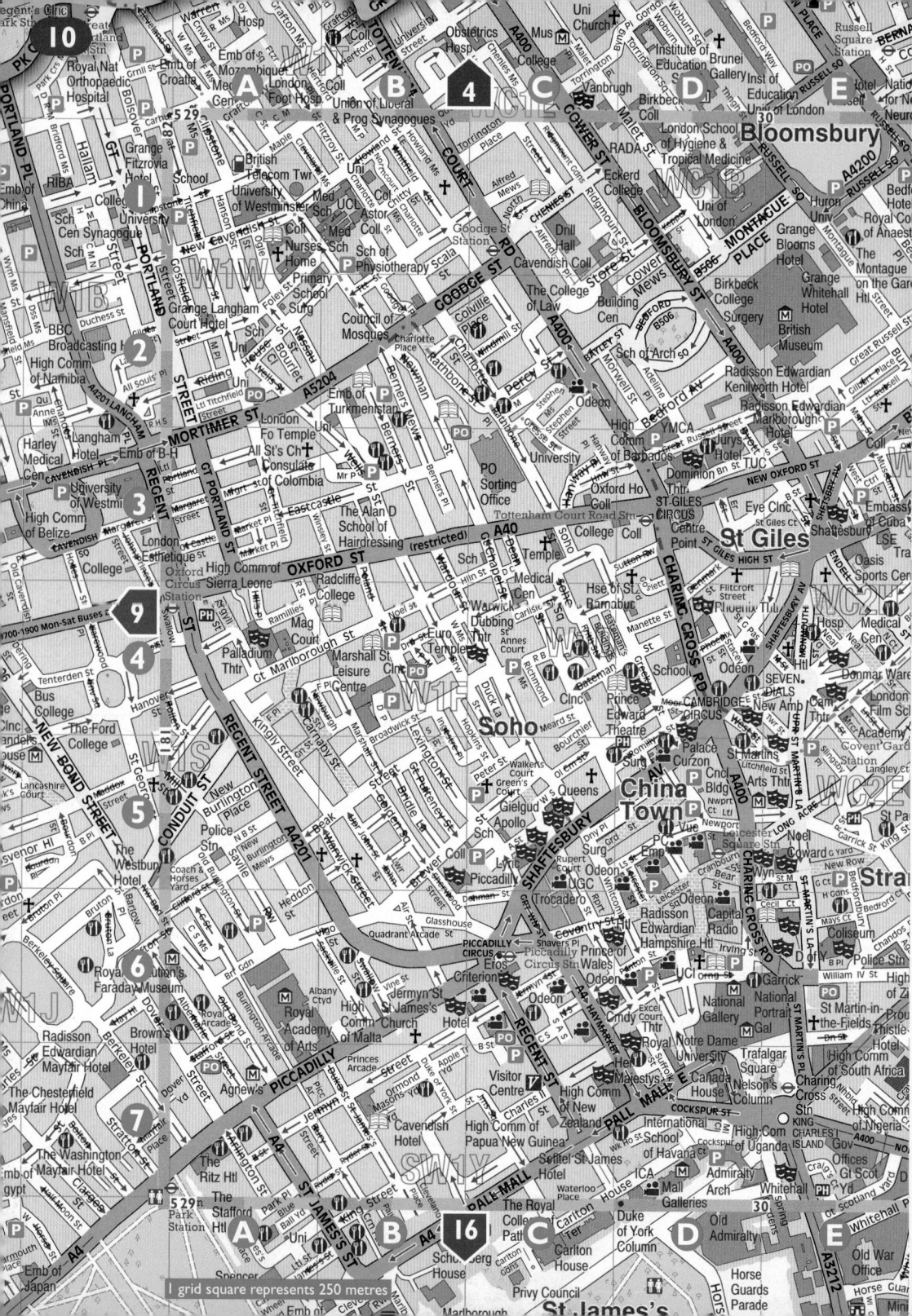

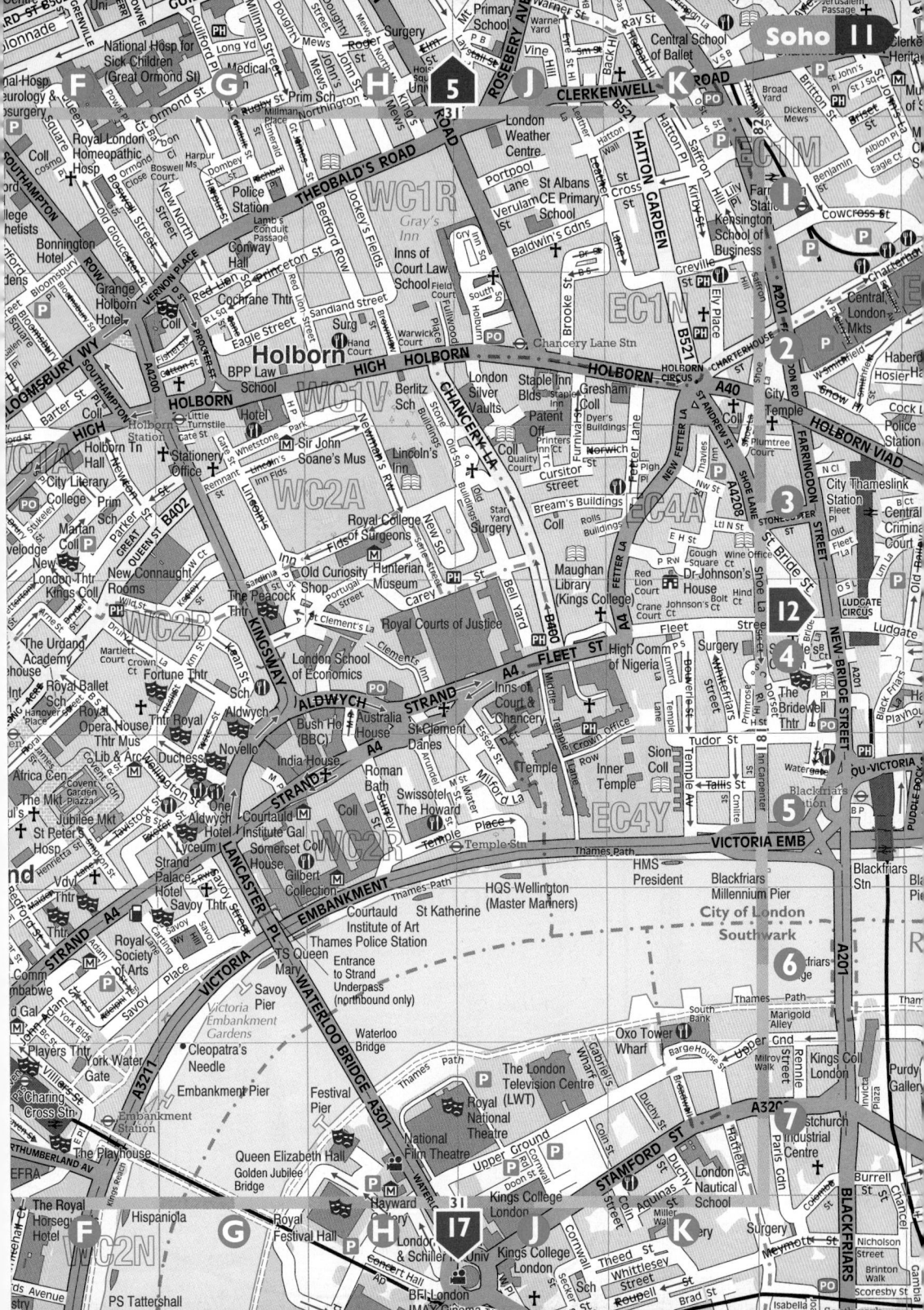

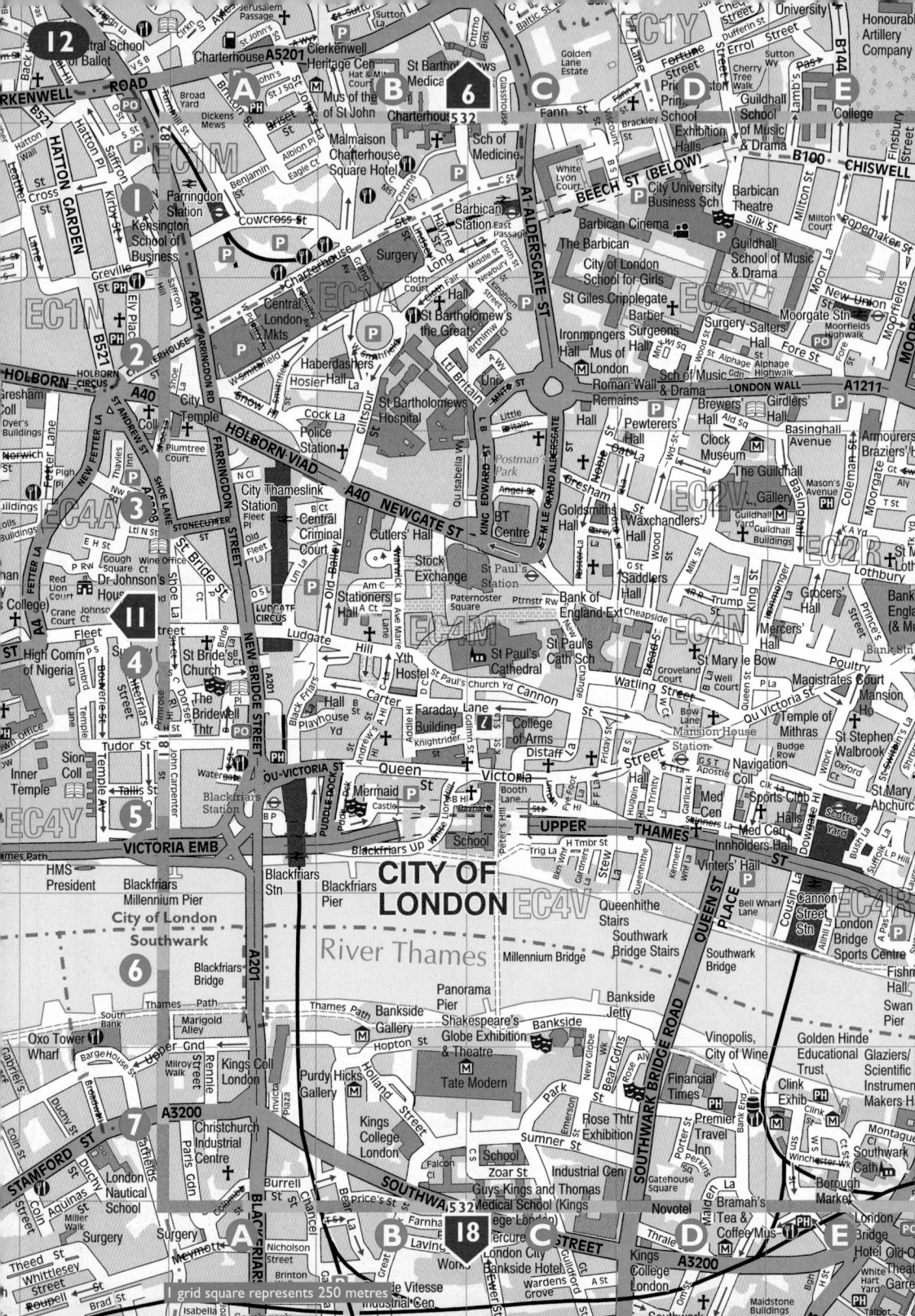

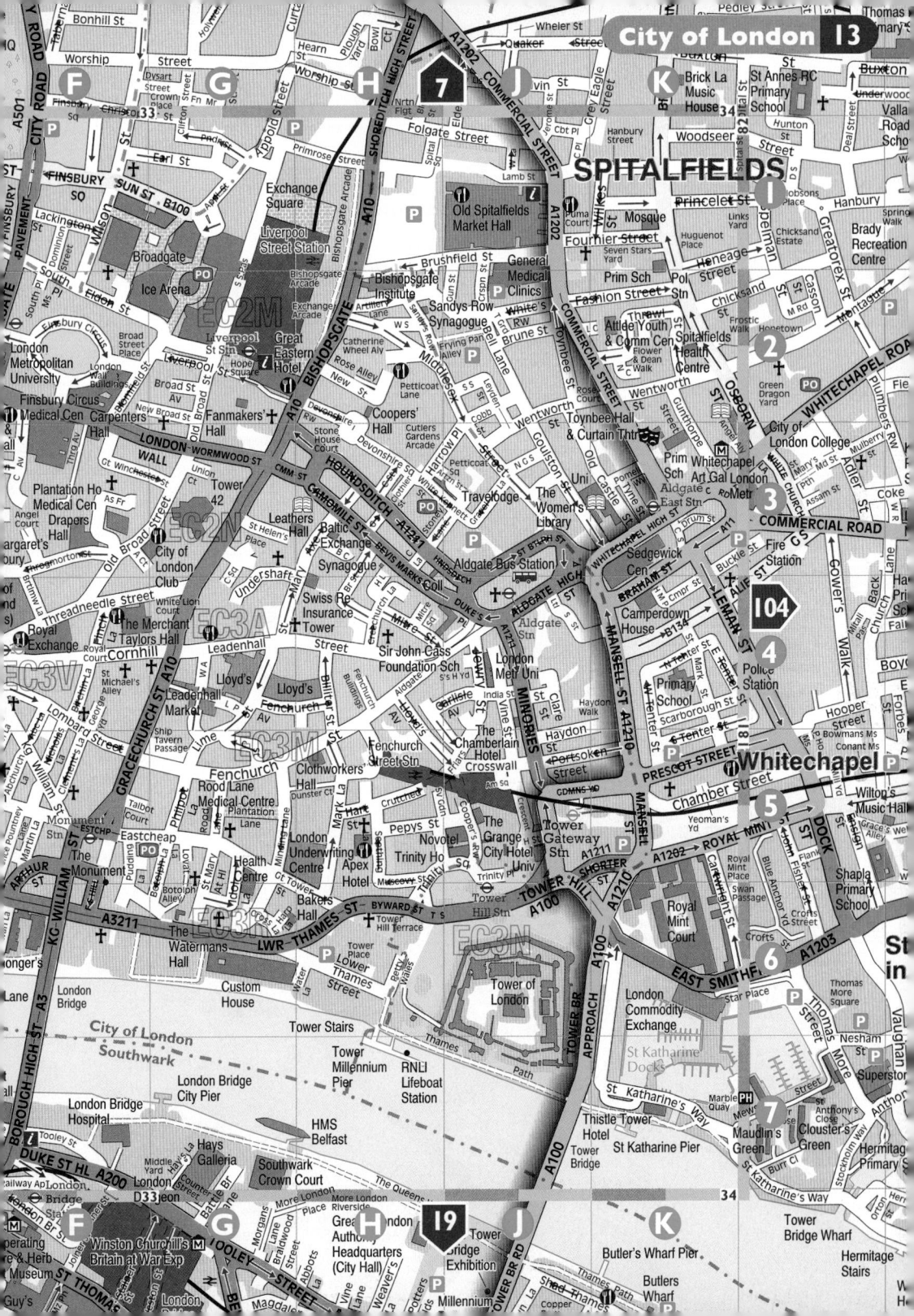

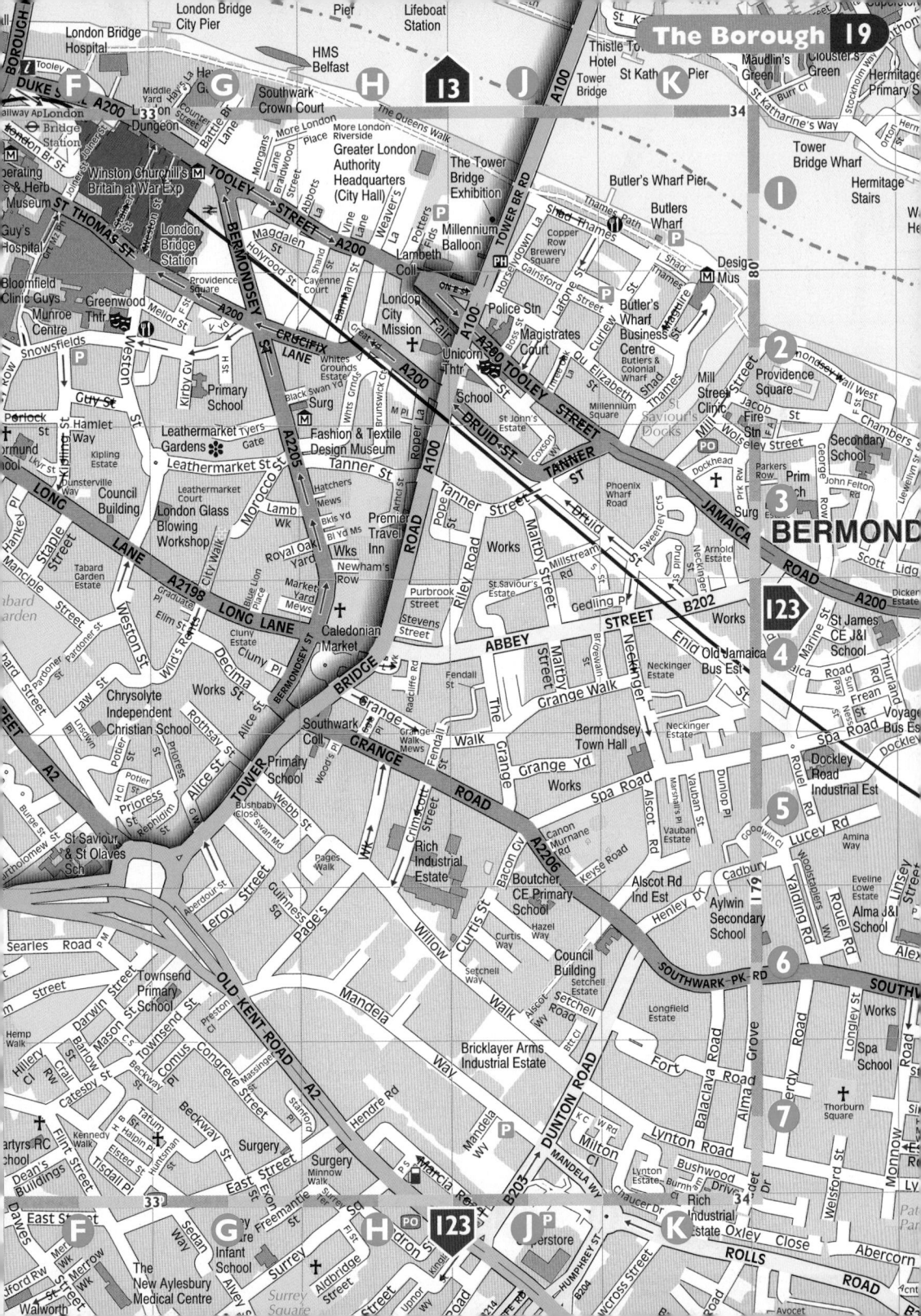

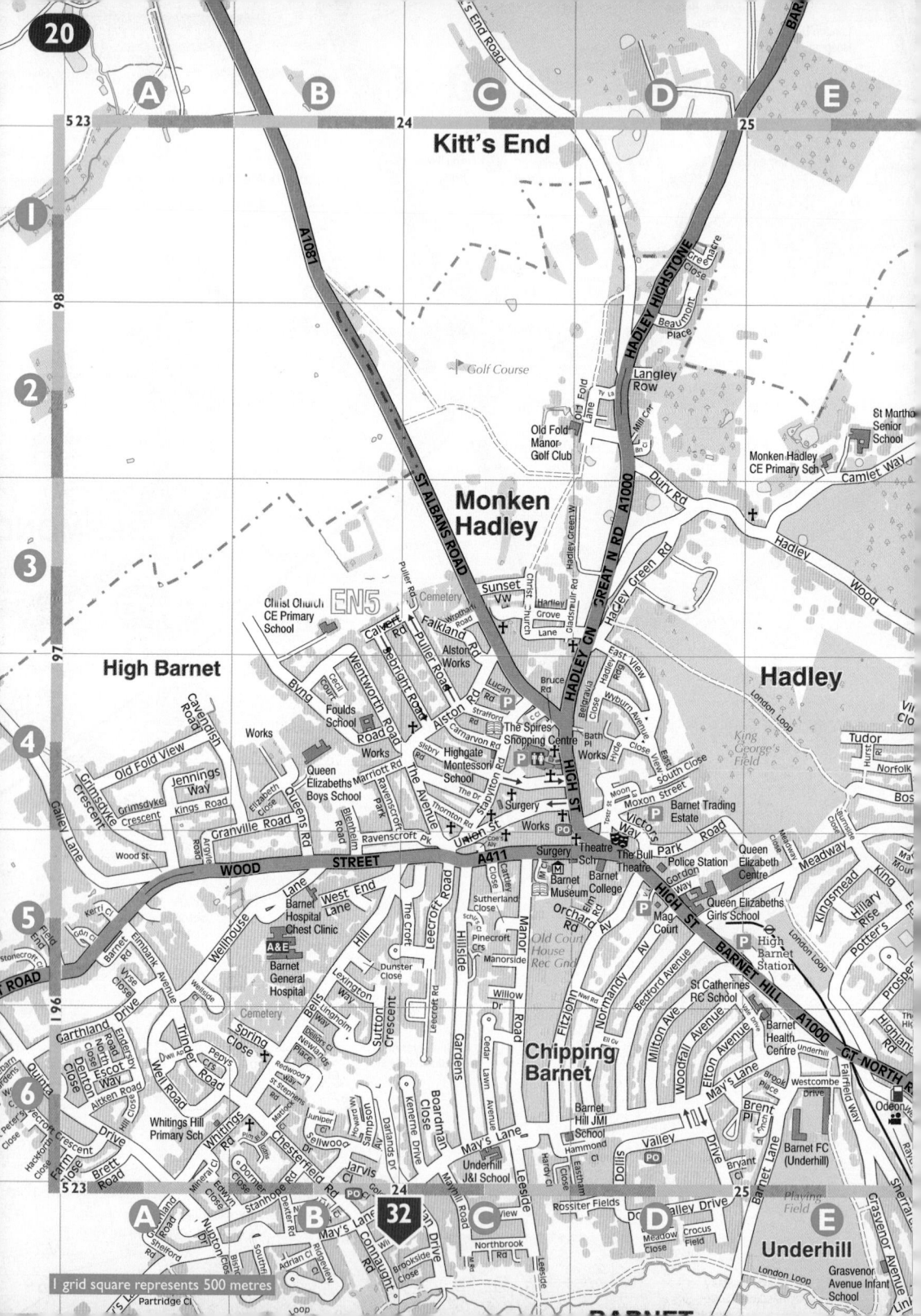

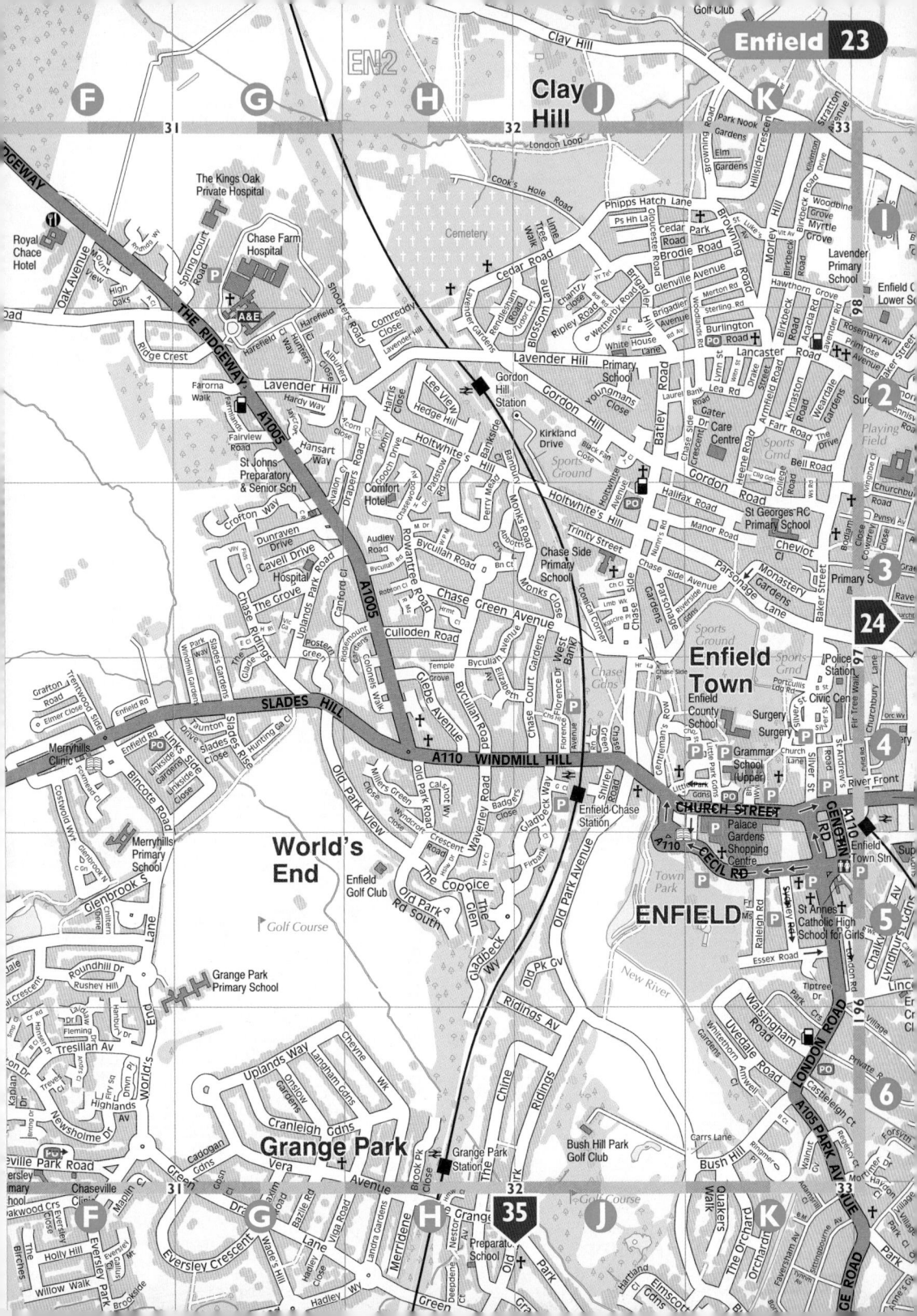

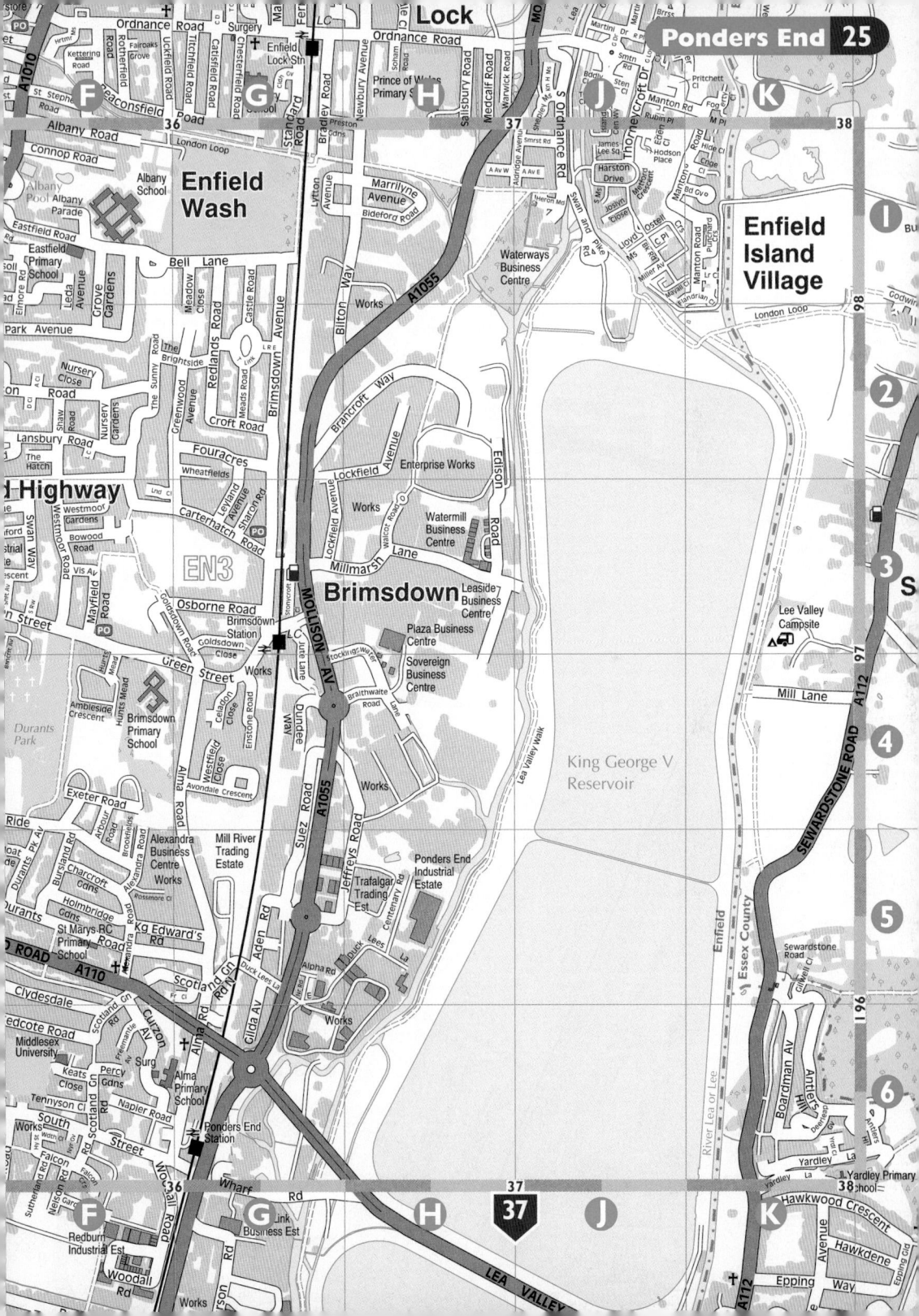

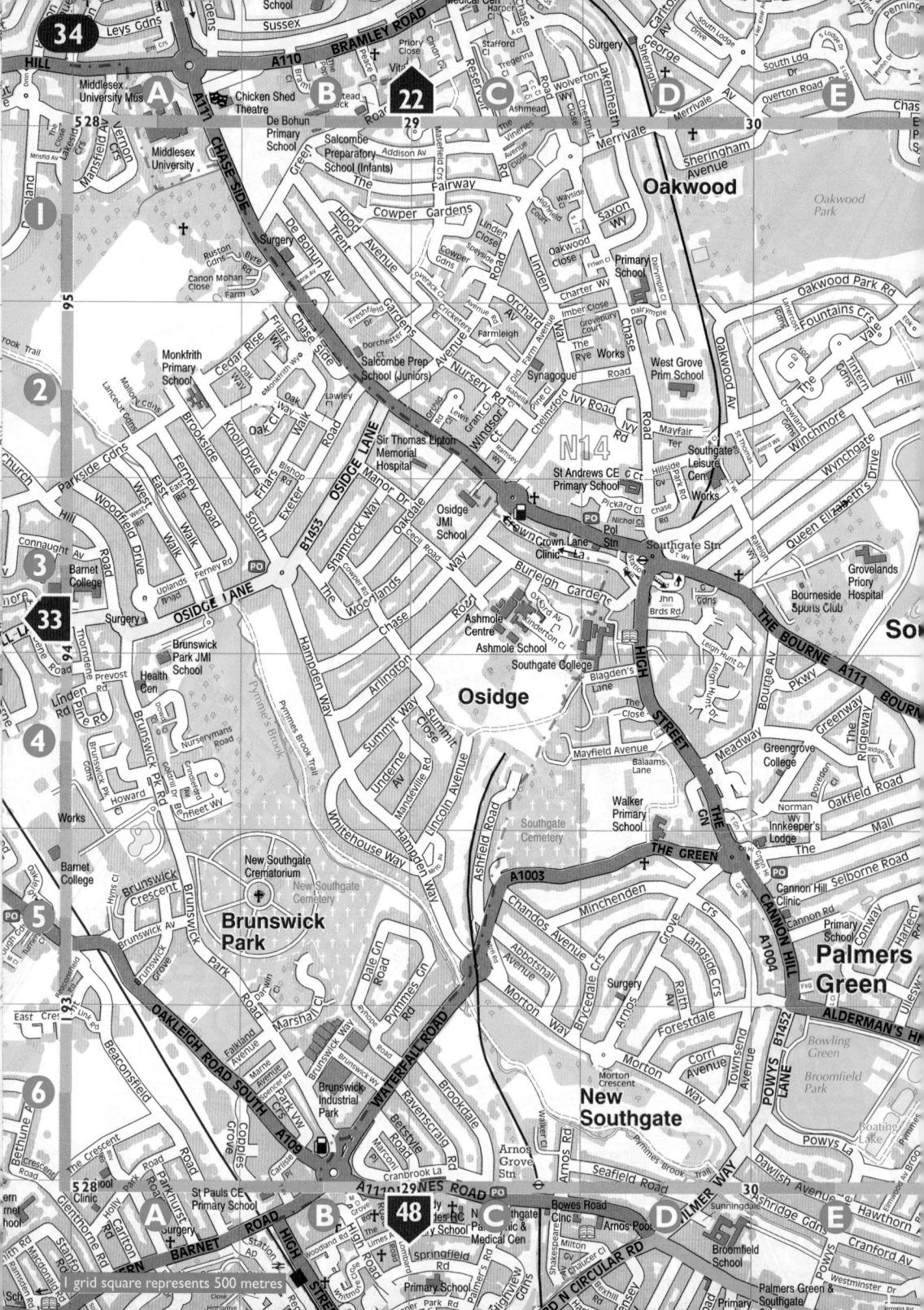

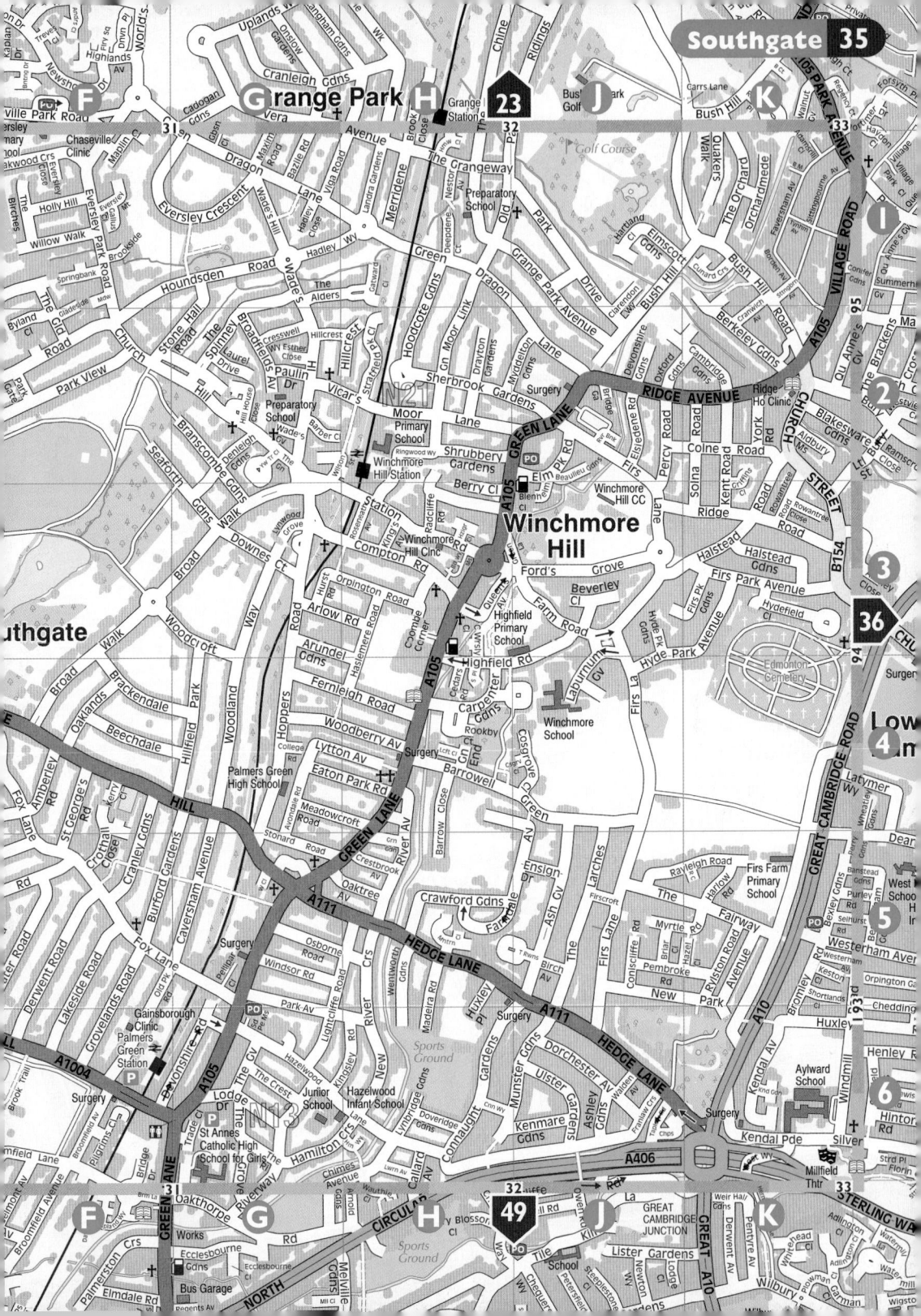

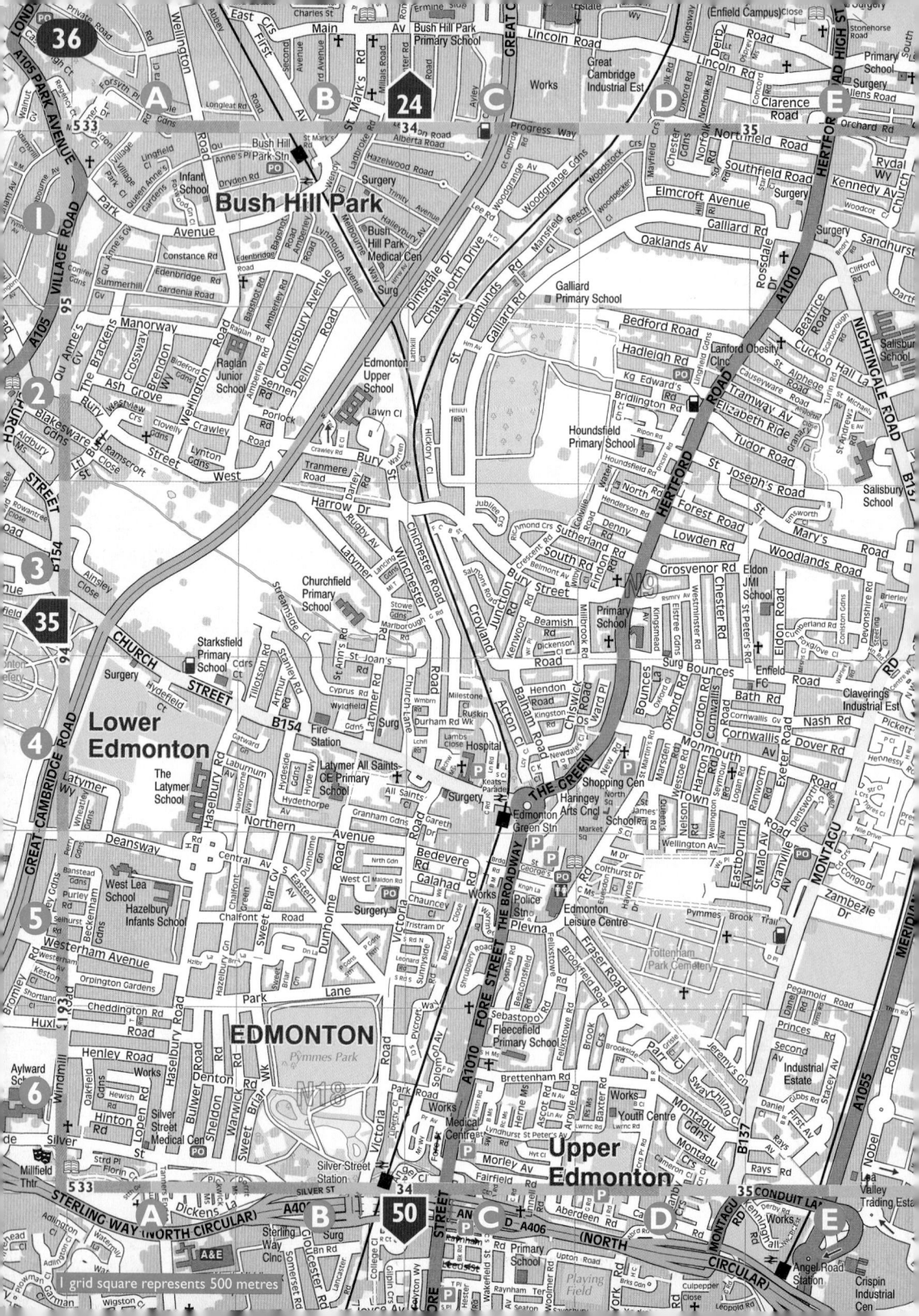

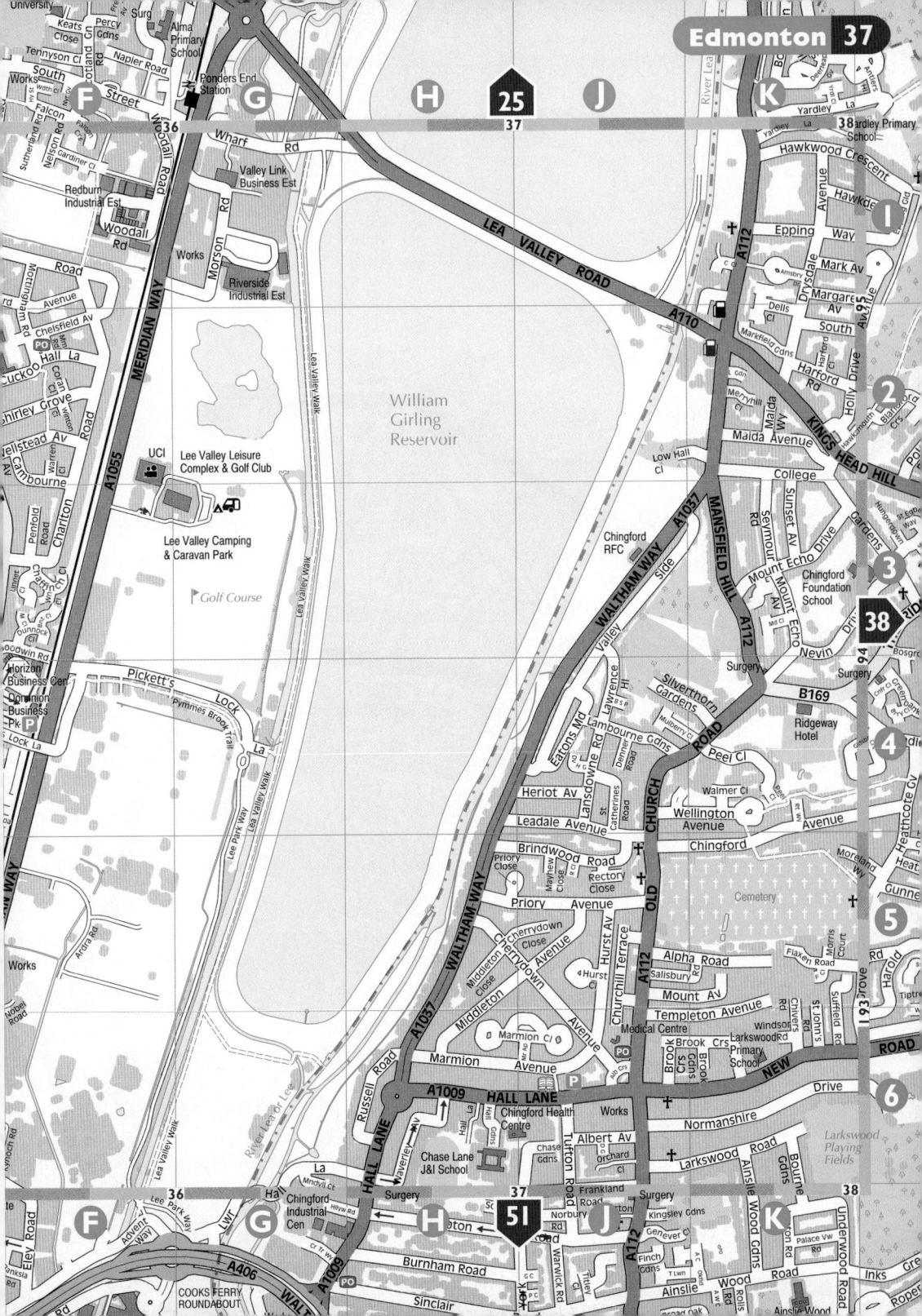

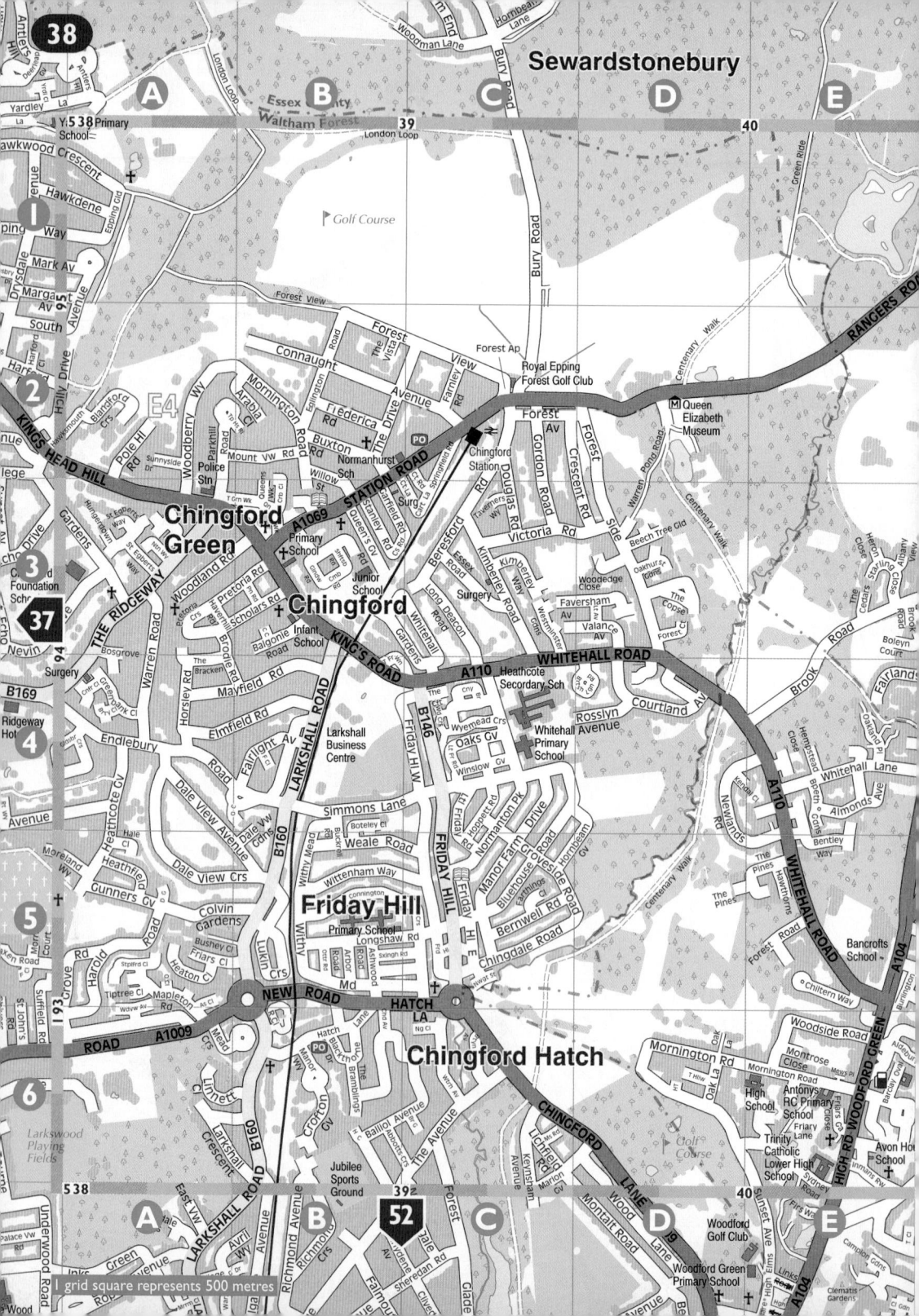

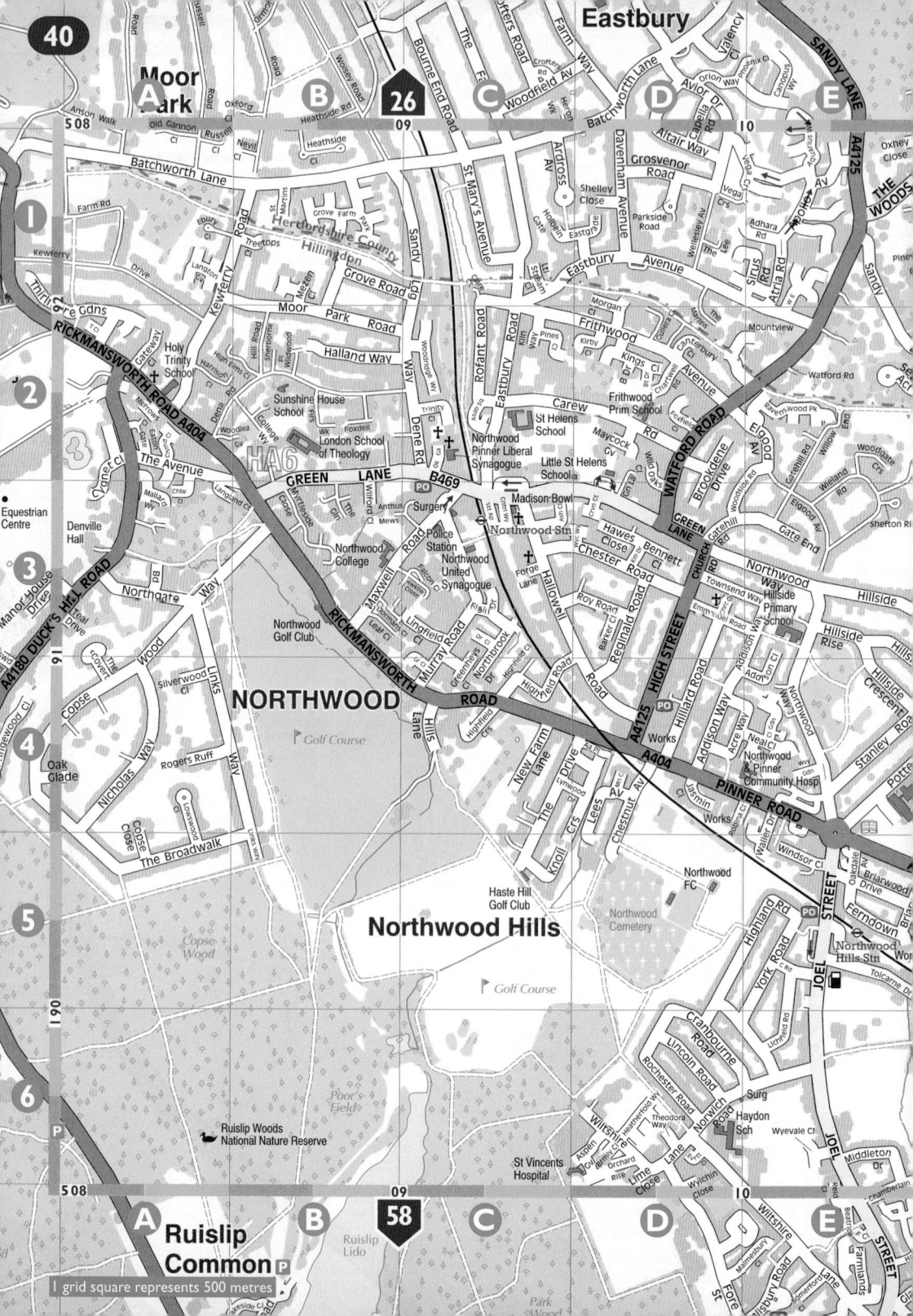

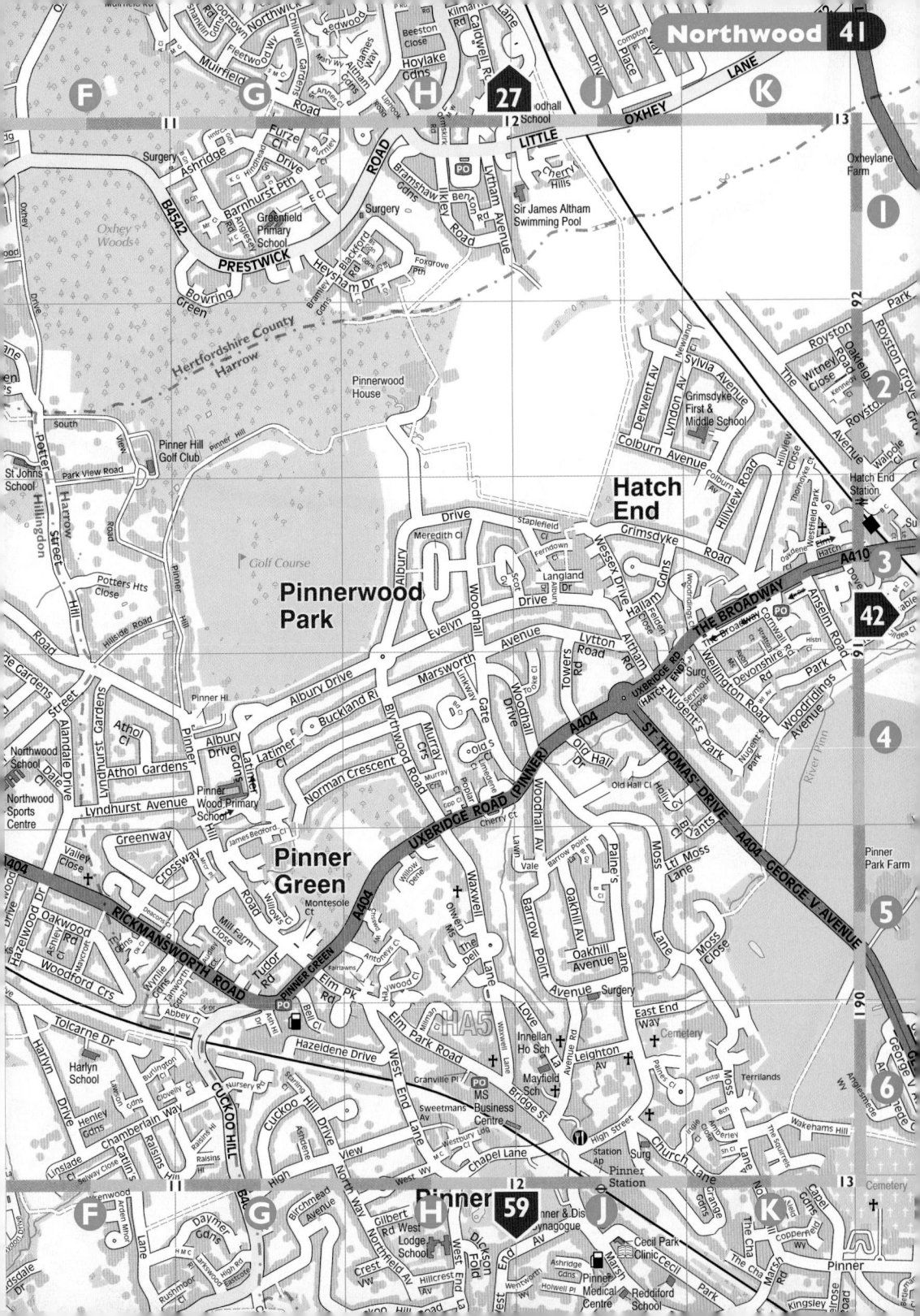

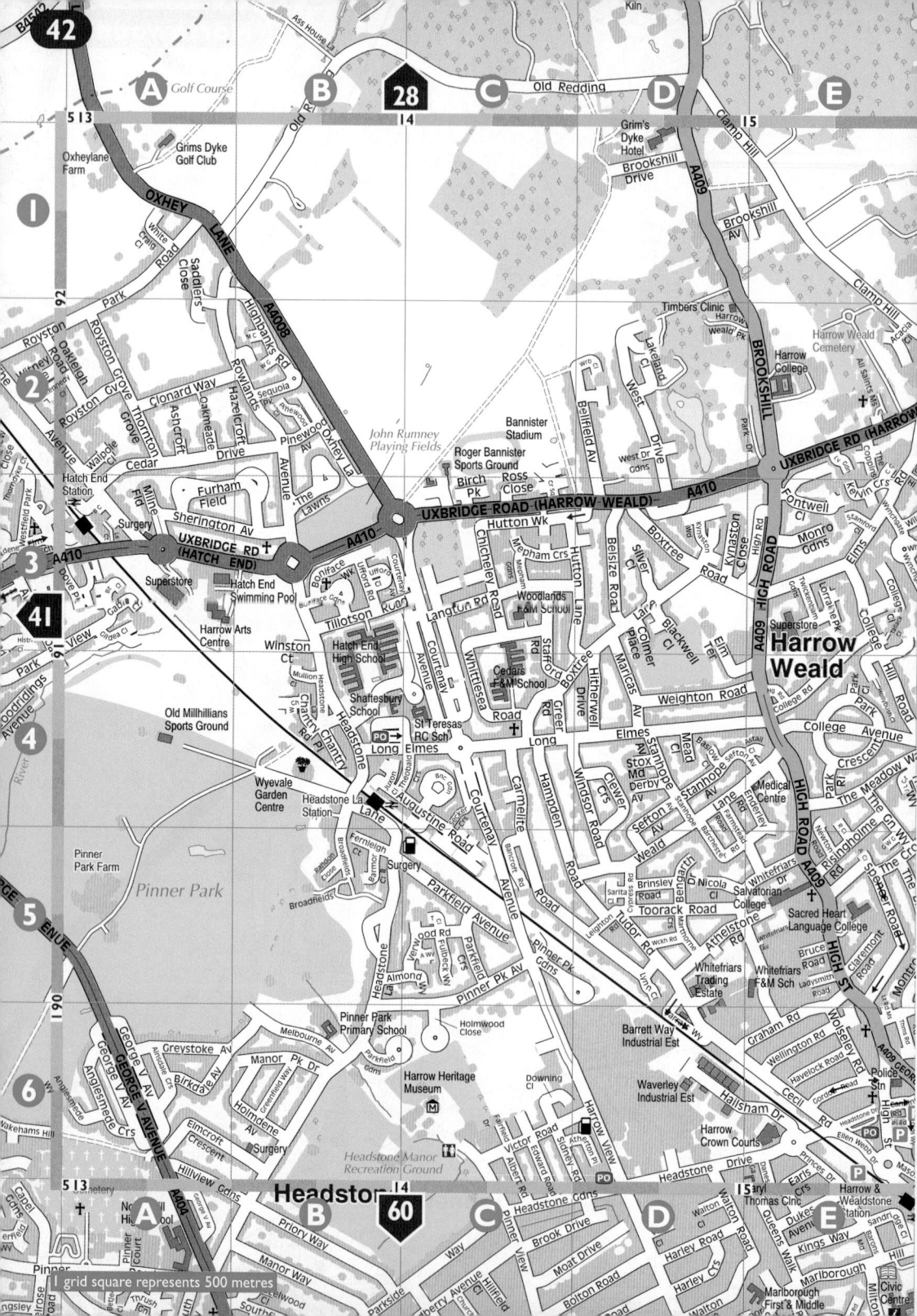

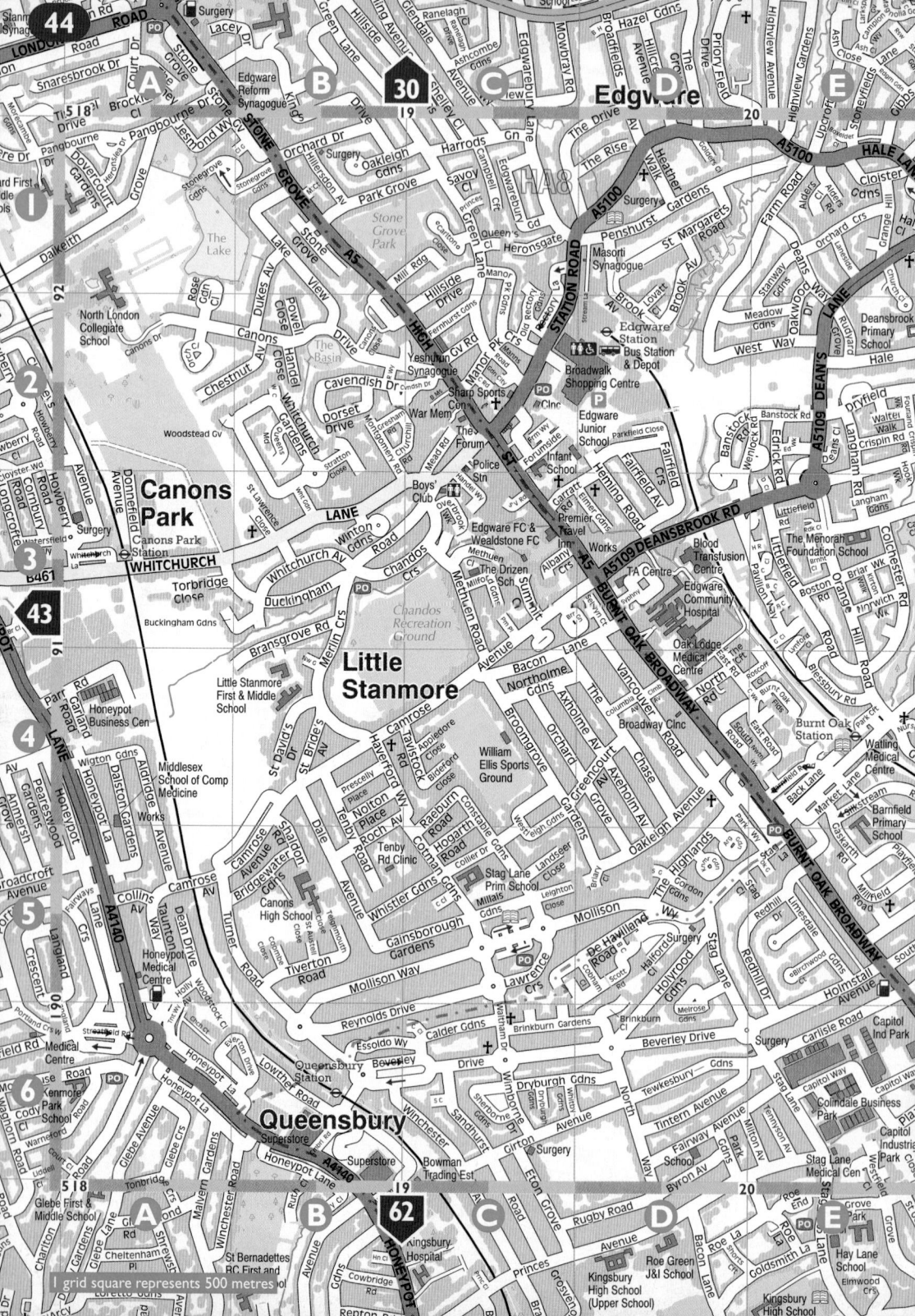

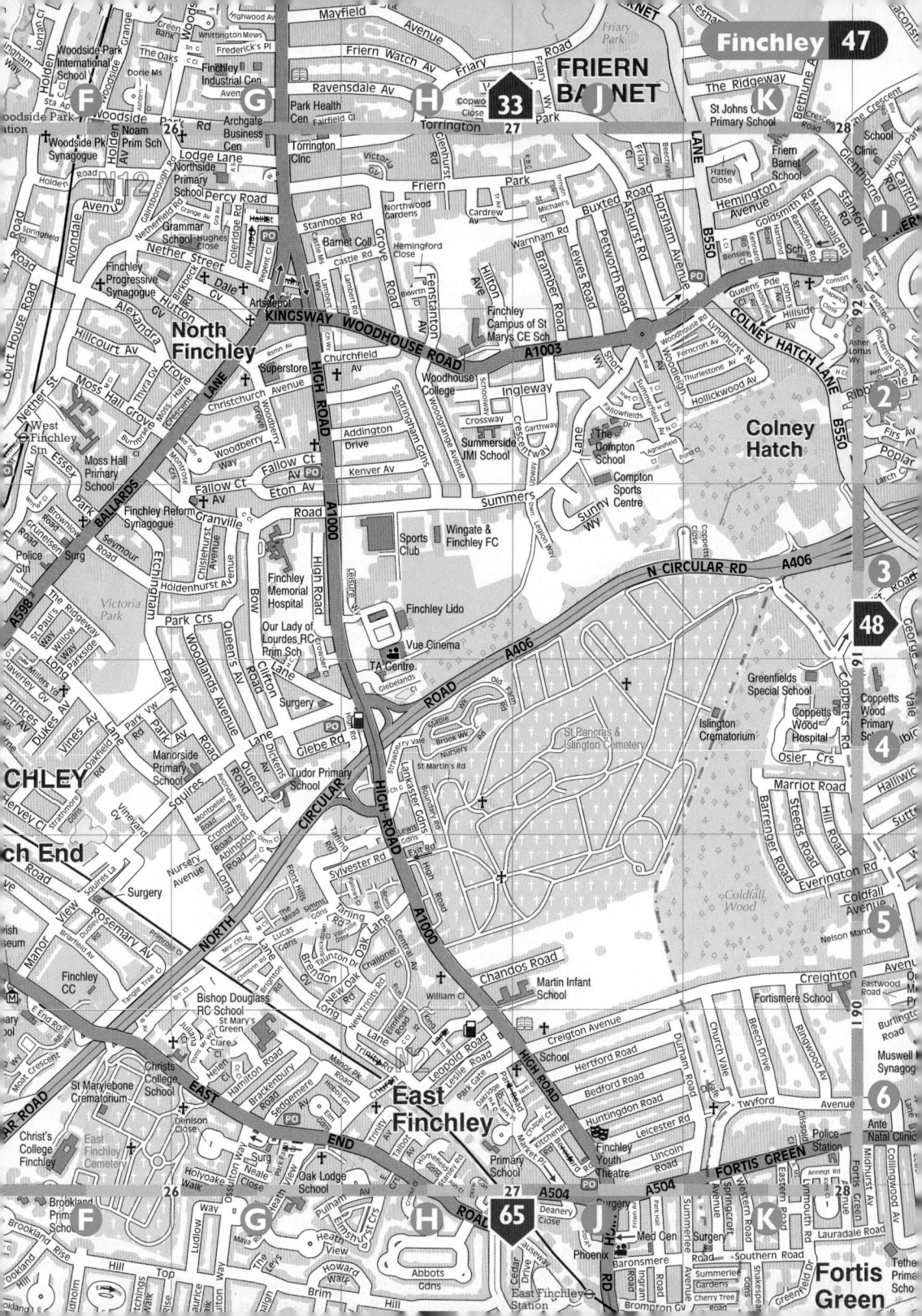

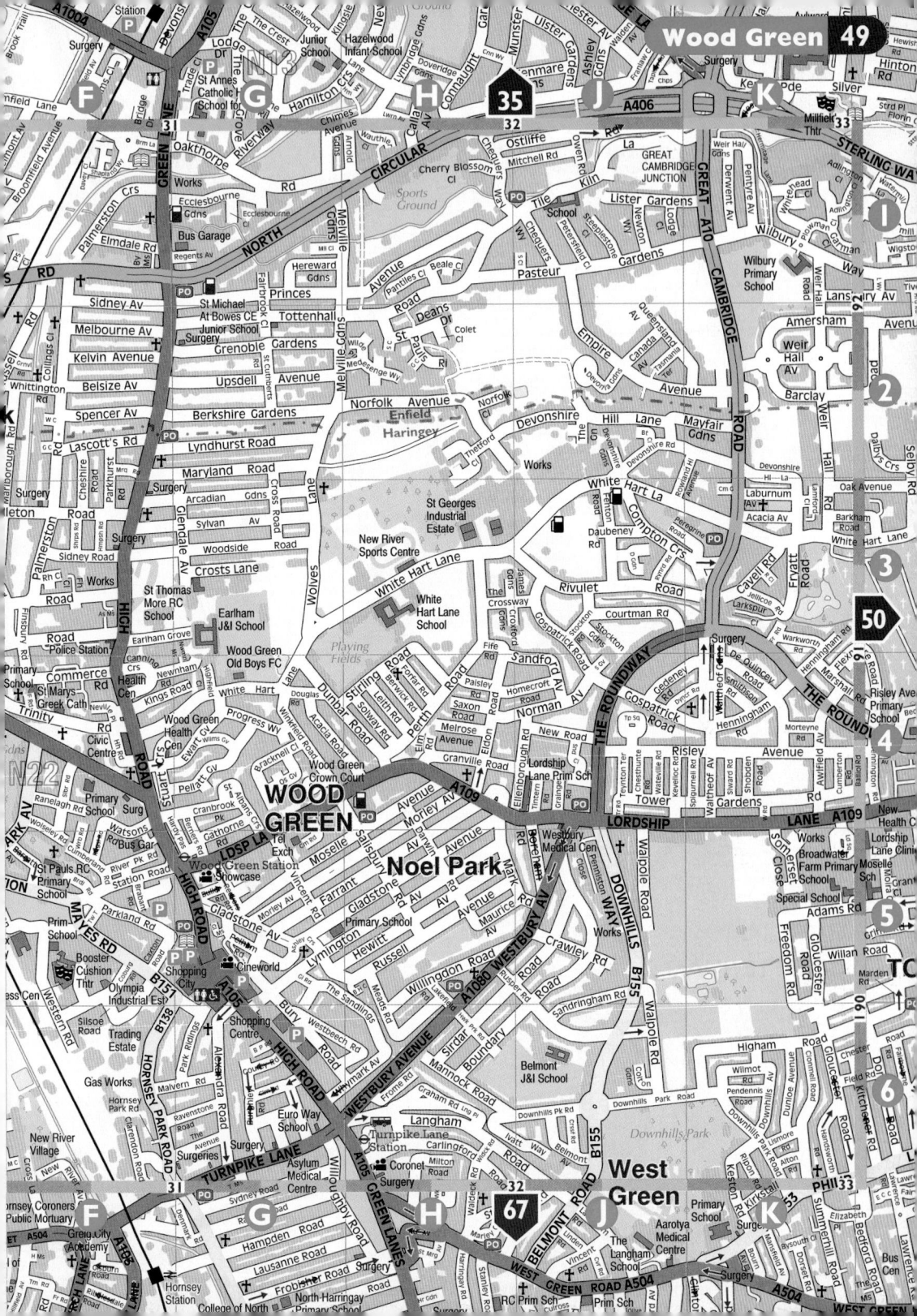

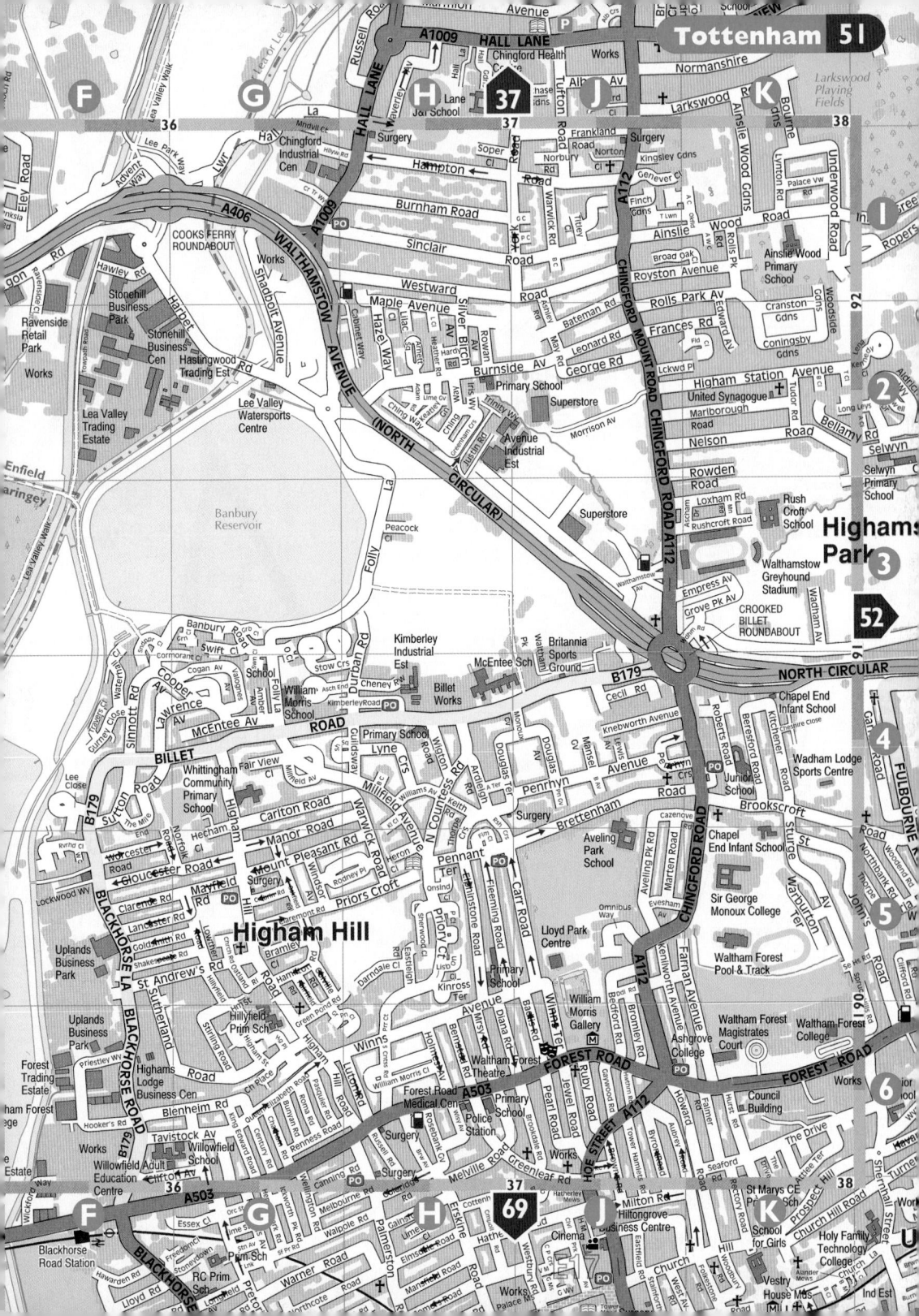

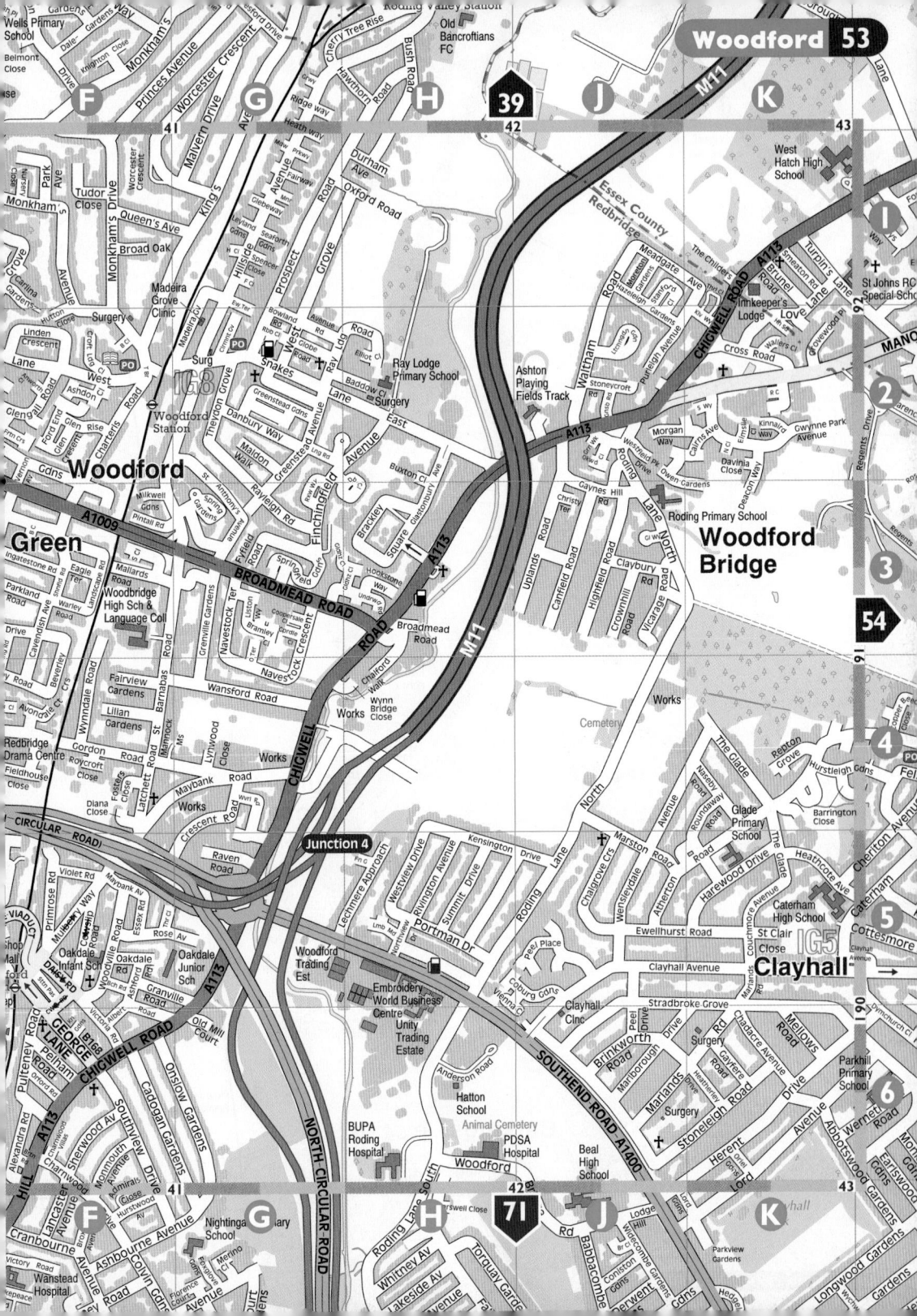

Park School

School Lane

Brocket Way

Bearing Way

Bearing Cl

ROMFORD

Greenway Rd

Baywood Close

Shuttle

Yellowgate Way

Lakeland Close

Manford

Copford

Richards Way

ROAD

Fox

F
G
H
J
K

46
47
48

I

Holt Way

Crossbow Rd

Burrow Close

The Burrow

North Adjister Road

Manford

Coppice Primary School

Fox Burrow Rd

Hainault Business Park

A1112

Arrowsmith

Fawn

Fletcher Road

Lowe

Pollard Road

Manford

New North Road

Branch Road

Falconer Road

Peregrine

Brewer Road

Fowler Road

Forest Park Cemetery & Crematorium

Hog Hill

Hainault Forest Golf Club

Hart Crescent

Hind Cl

Hursley Road

Manford Way

Manford Cross

PO

Surgery

Huntsman

Harbourer Rd

ROMFORD ROAD A1112

92

Lime Grove

Manford Wayn Health Cen

Kielder

Kesteven

New North

Bursiem

Tunstall Avenue

Stoke Avenue

Hainault Forest High School & the Learning Centre

Burnside Industrial Estate

Roebuck Road

Works

2

Penrith Road

Trentbridge Close

Wickets Way

Grace Close

Newcastle Avenue

John Bramston Primary School

Elmbridge Road

Roebuck Road Trading Estate

Forest Road

56

Rover Ave

Dryden Close

Hainault

Kennylands Road

Forest Road

3

Bracken Industrial Estate

LPR Sports Club

Hainault Road

56

16

4

Fairlop Waters

Hainault Works

Hainault Farm

Seven Kings Water

Redbridge

Barking and Dagenham

5

Painters Road

190

Hainault Road

Red House Farm

6

Rosehatch Av

Newhouse Av

Marks Junior Hlth Se Cli

Billet Road

Uplands Road

Arneways Av

Crabtree Avenue

Longhayes Av

Roles Gv

Roles Grove

Lawn Farm

F
G
H
73
J
K

46
47
48

rough

St James Gardens

Little Heath School

Little Heath

Gregory Rd

Dalrush Cl

Cavalier Cl

Surge

Sheepcotes Rd

Applegarth Drive

ters Close

Avenue

A12

EASTERN AVENUE

RM6

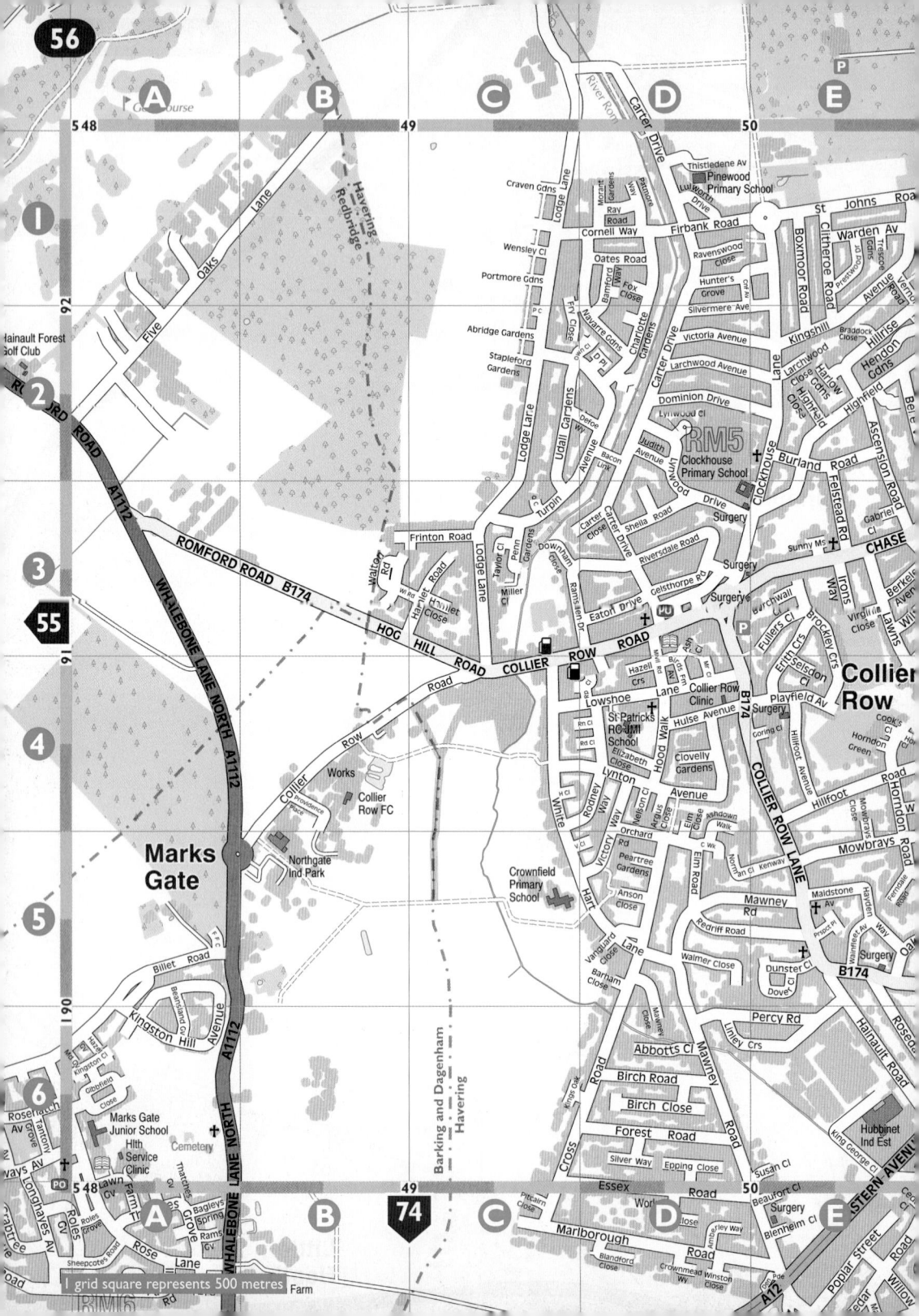

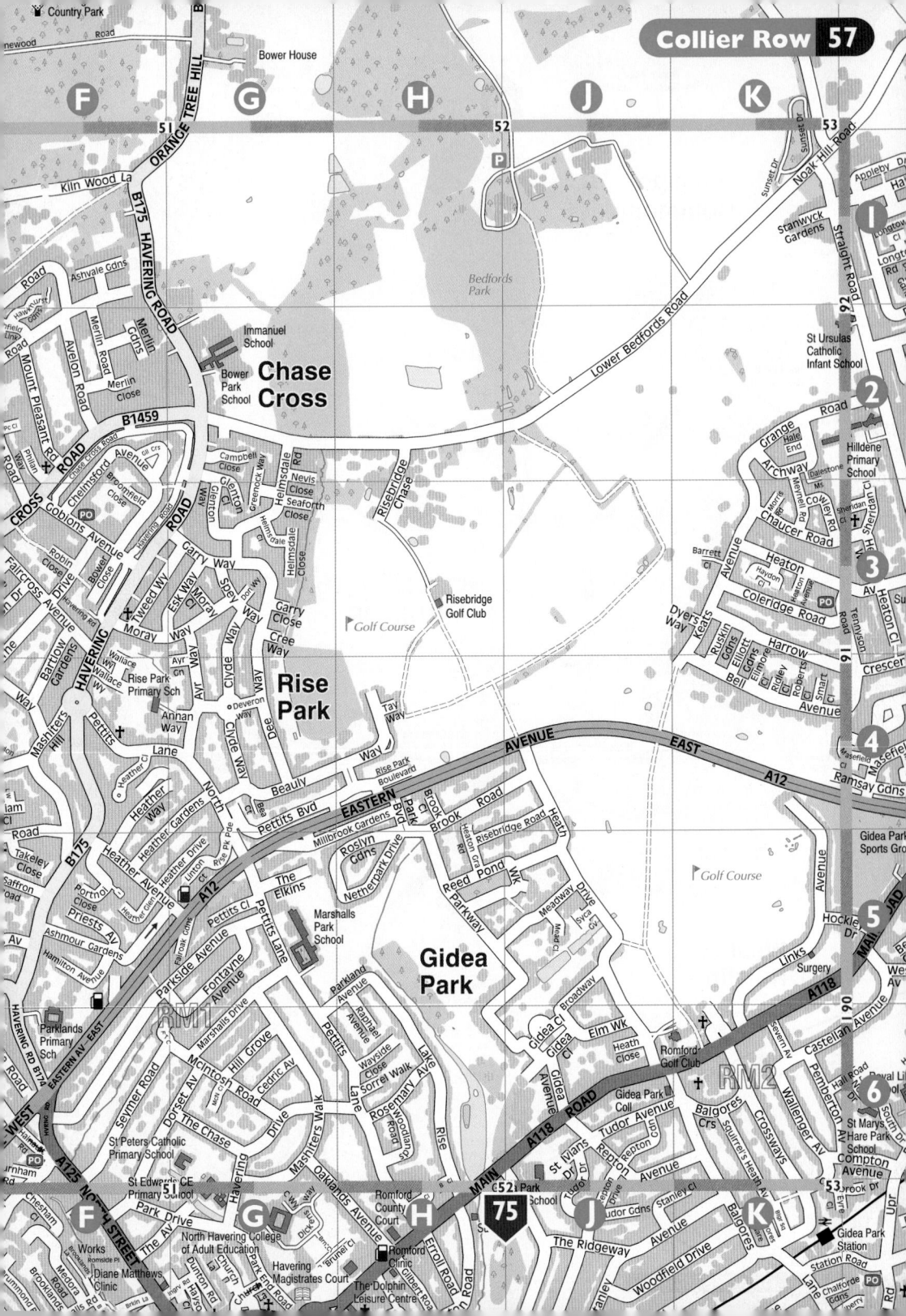

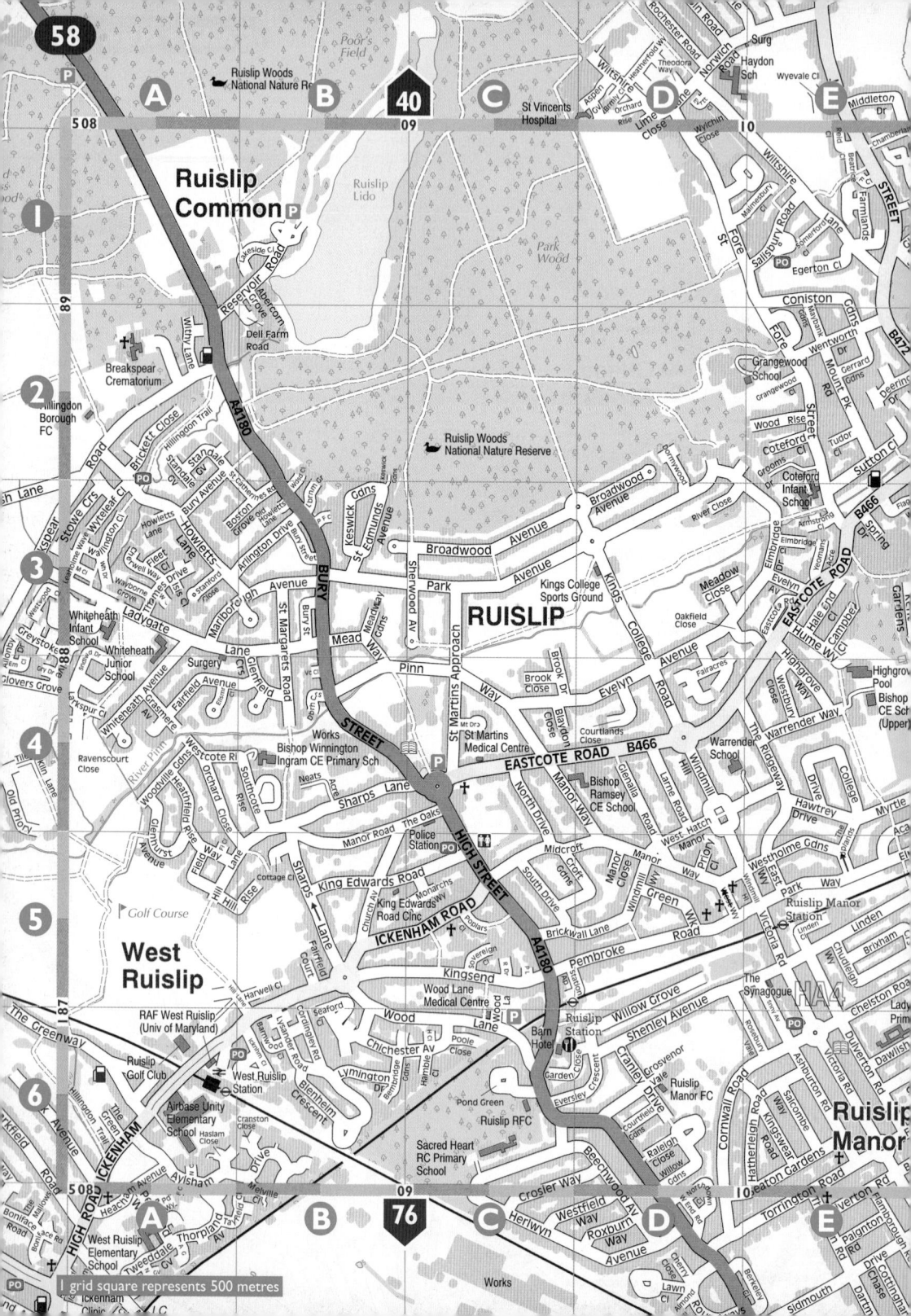

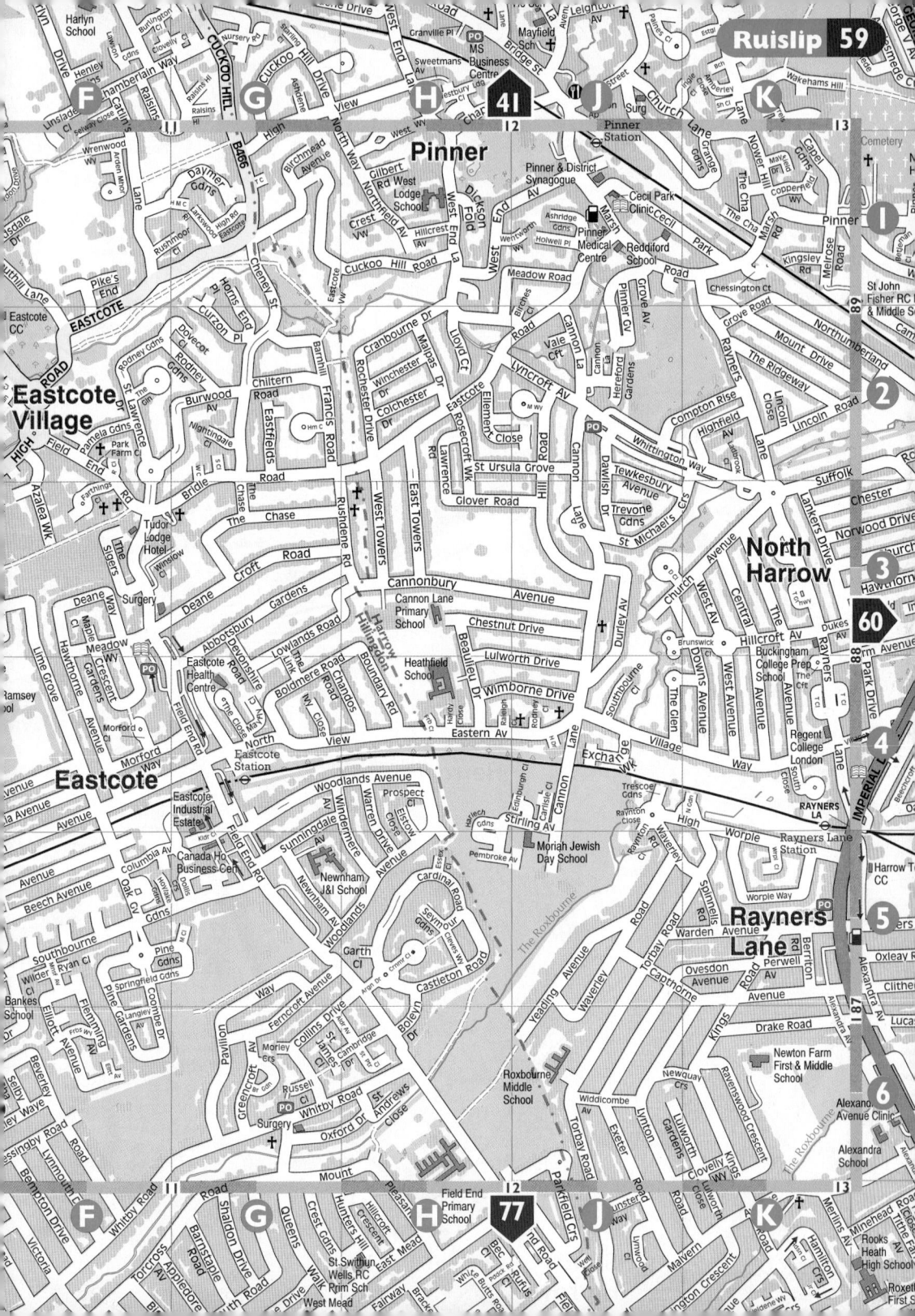

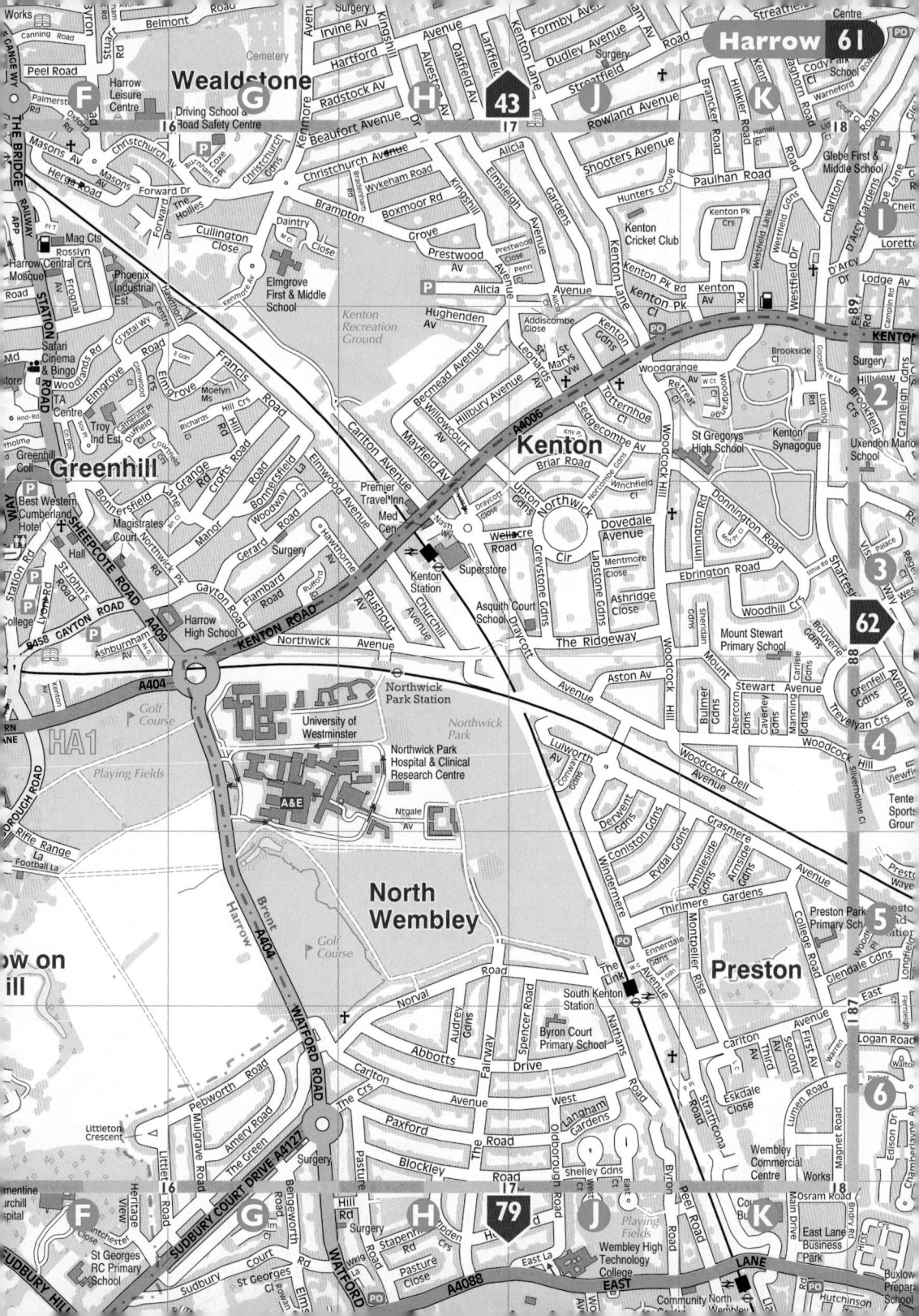

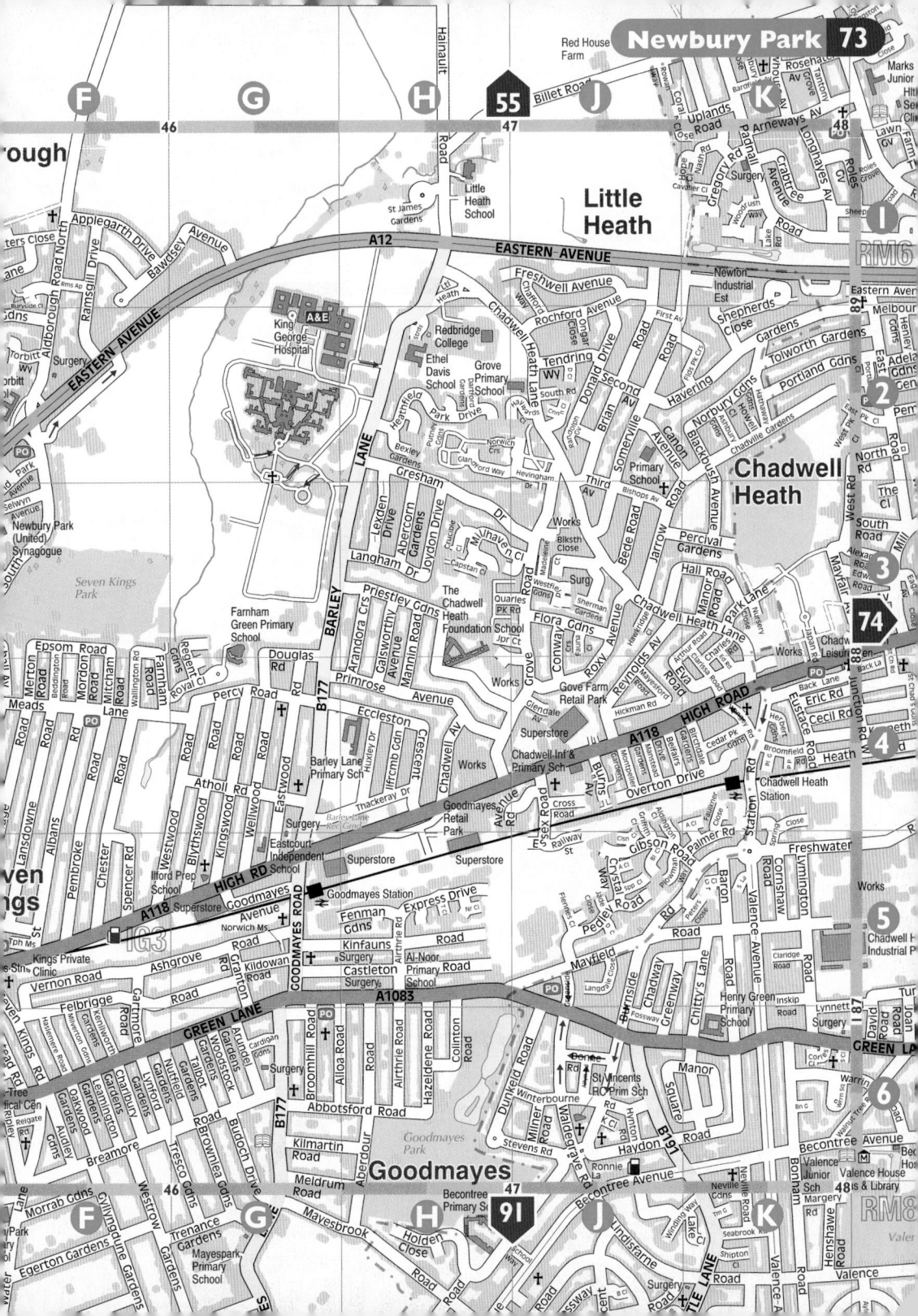

I grid square represents 500 metres

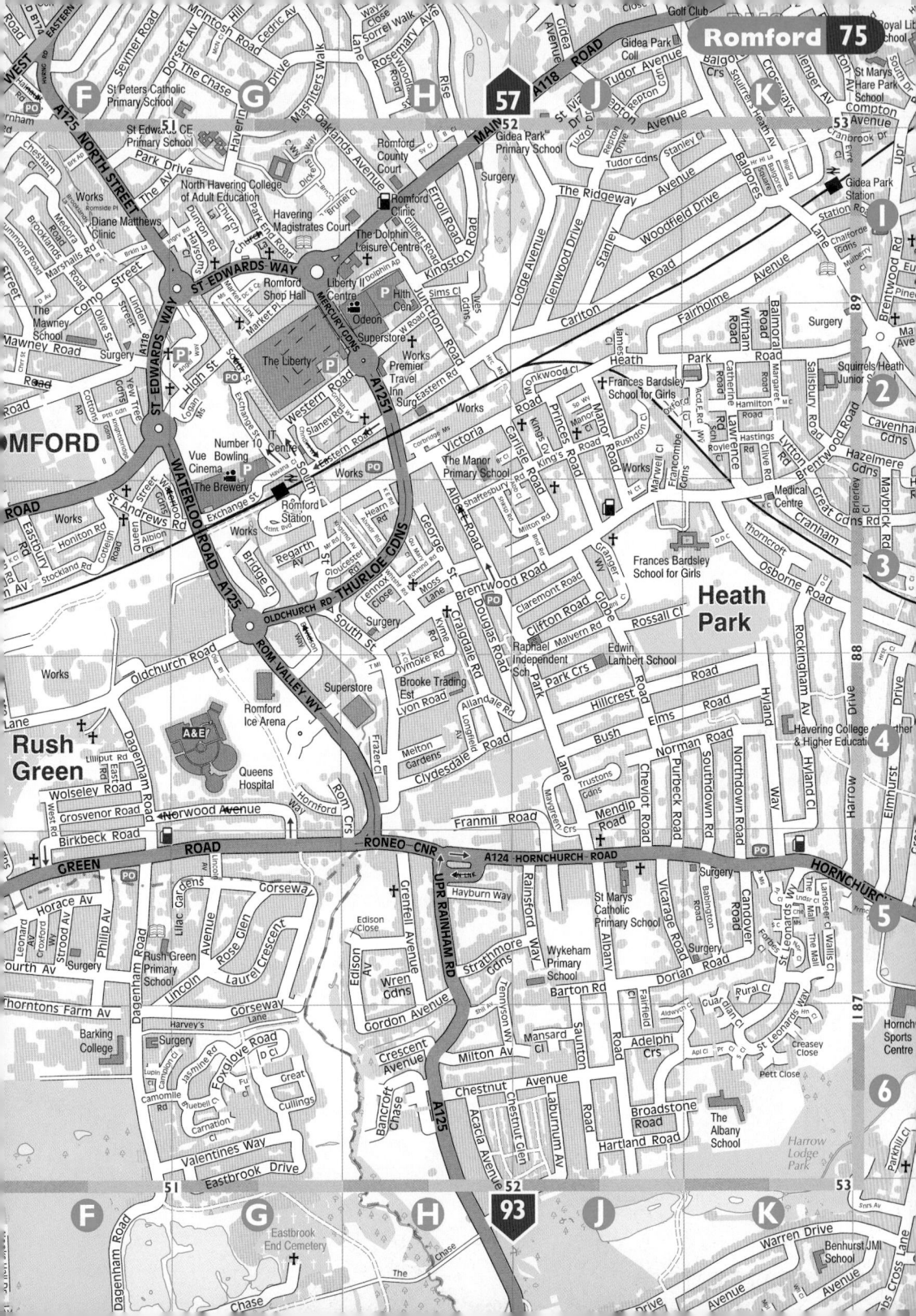

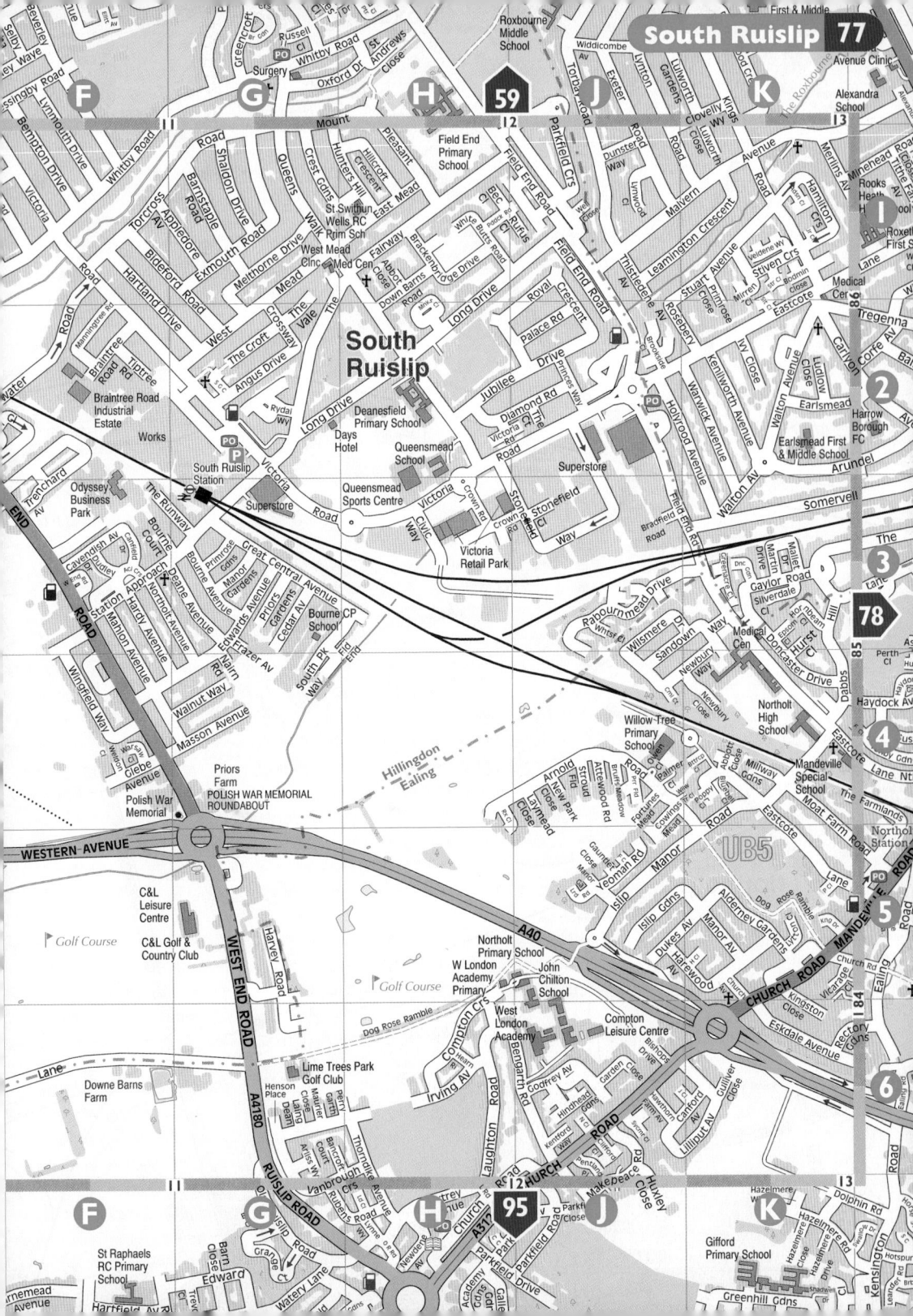

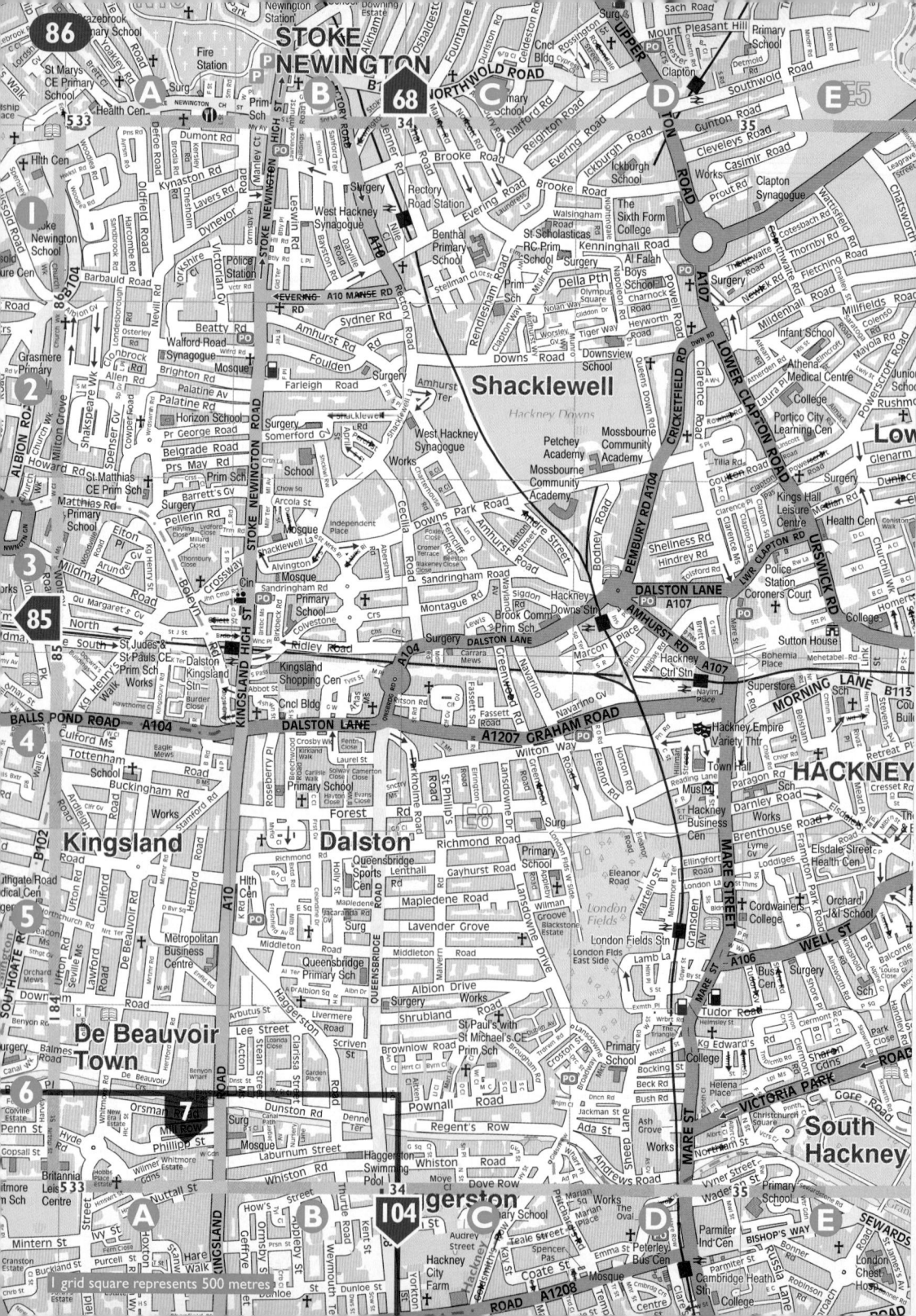

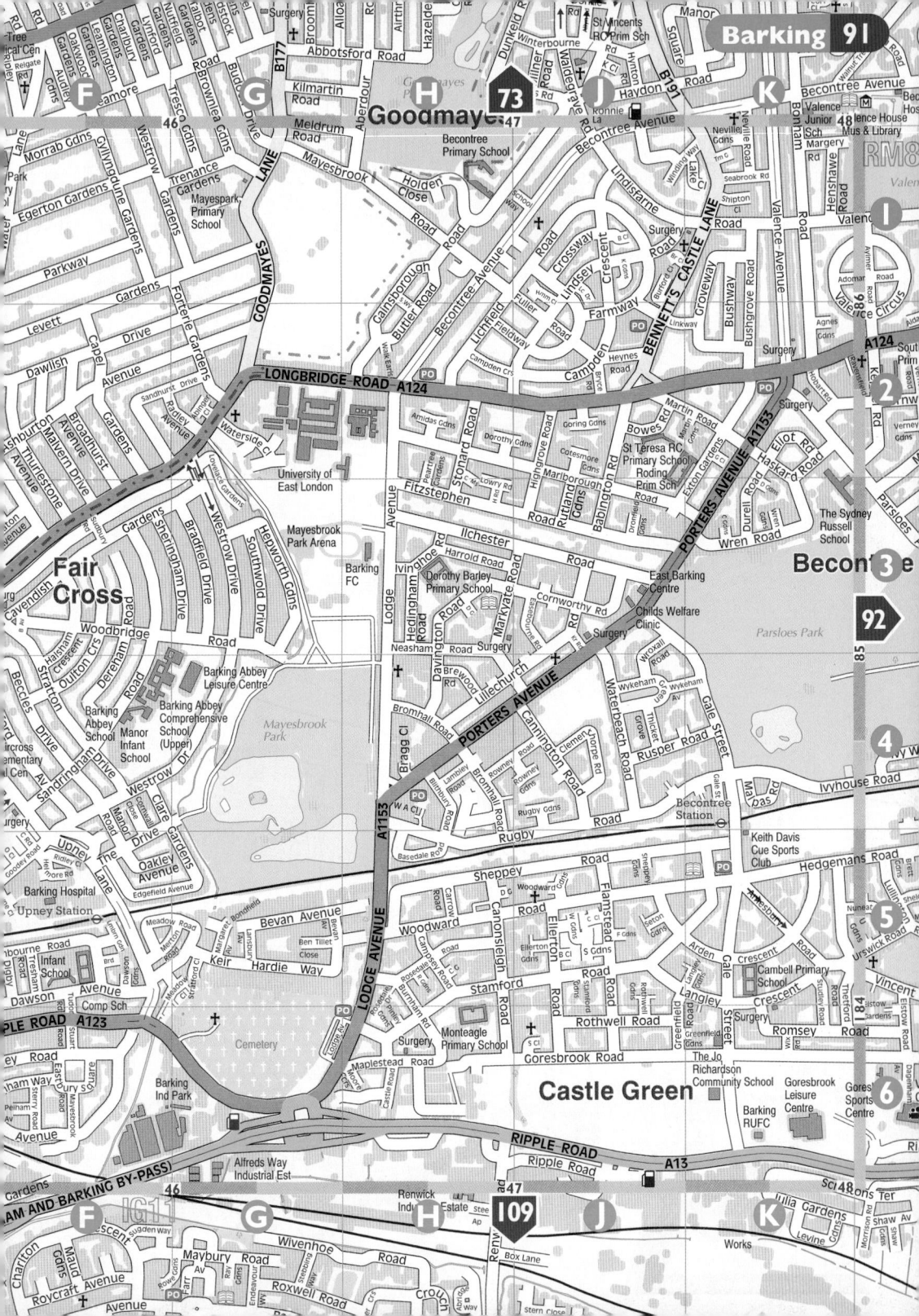

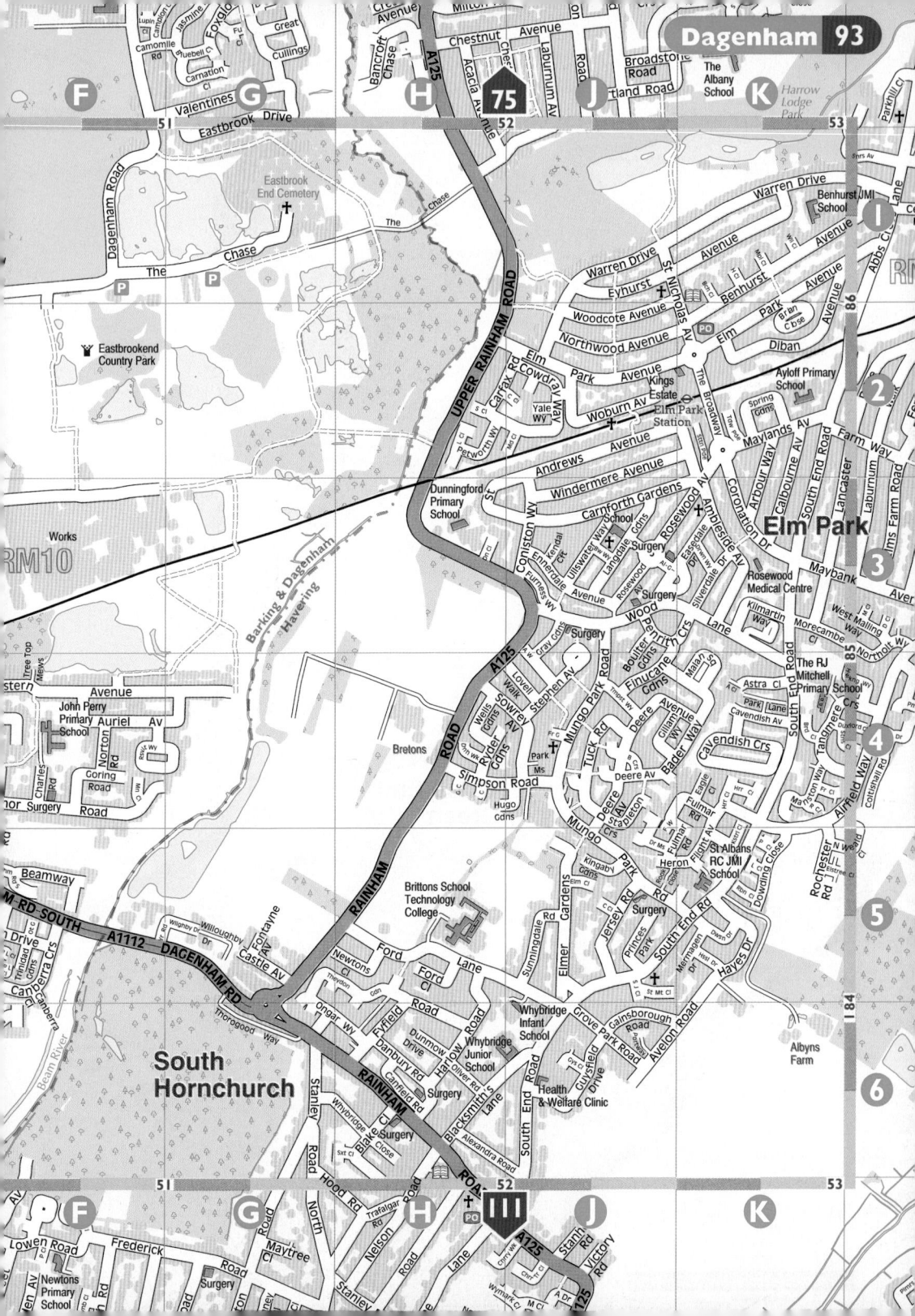

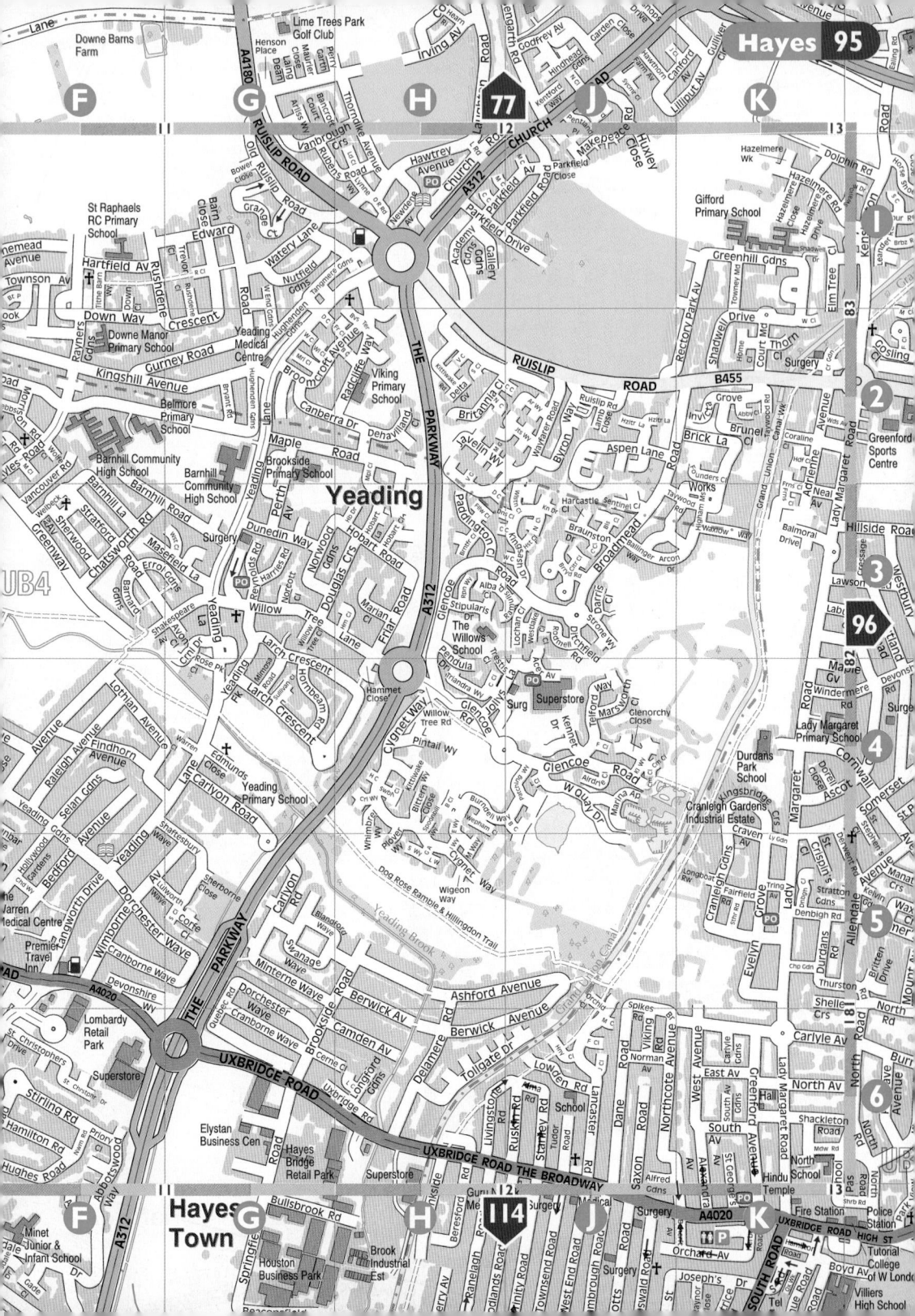

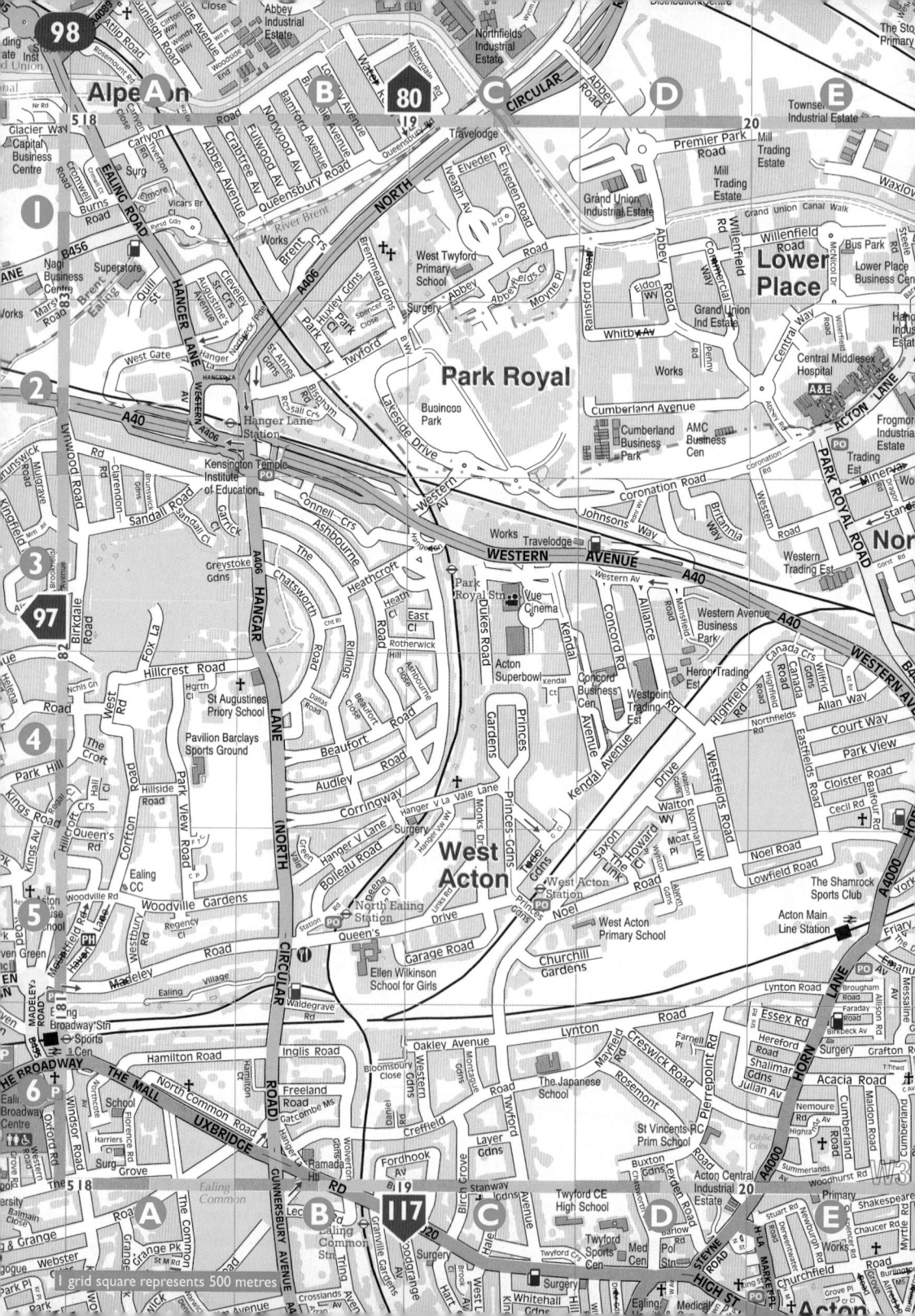

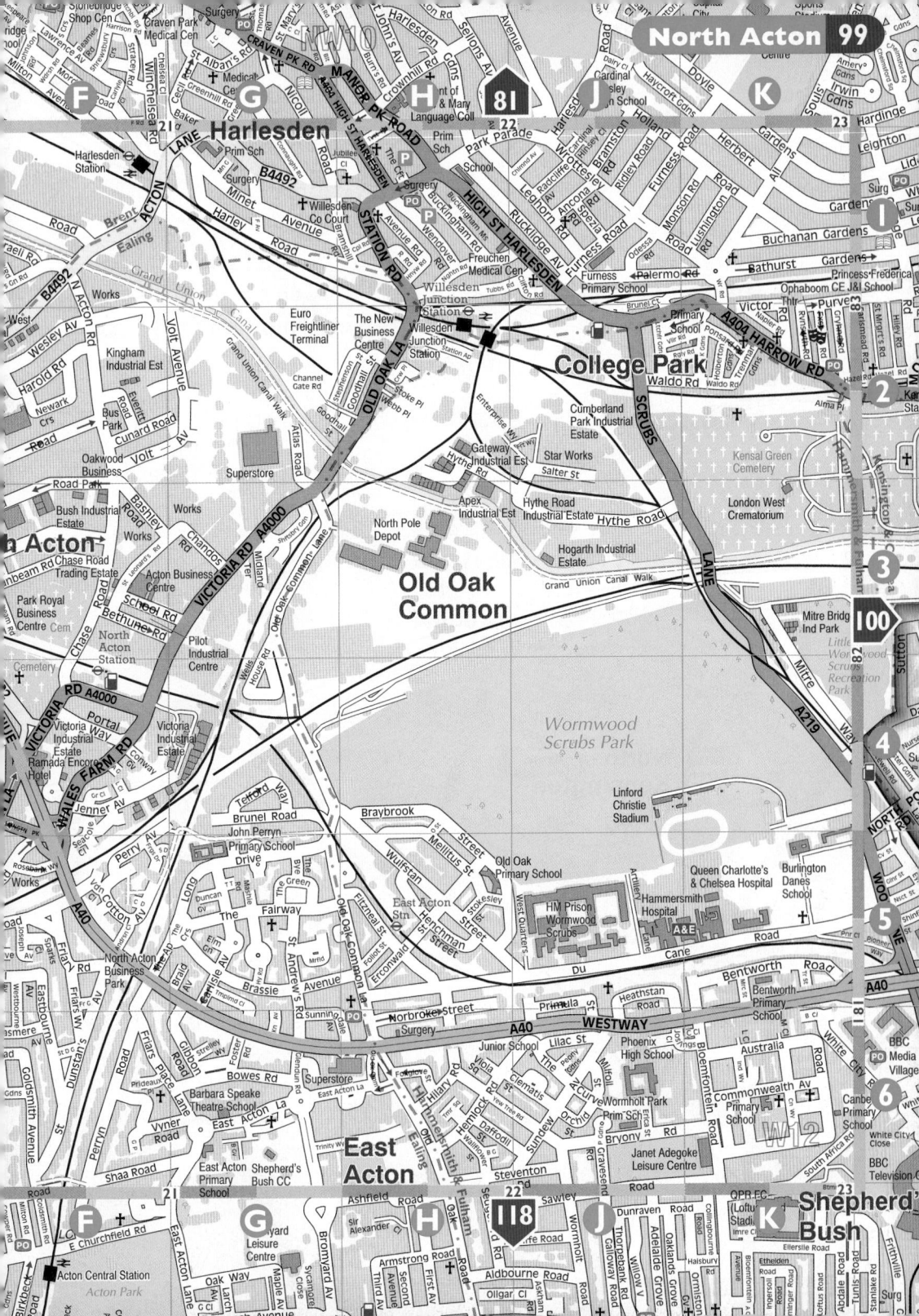

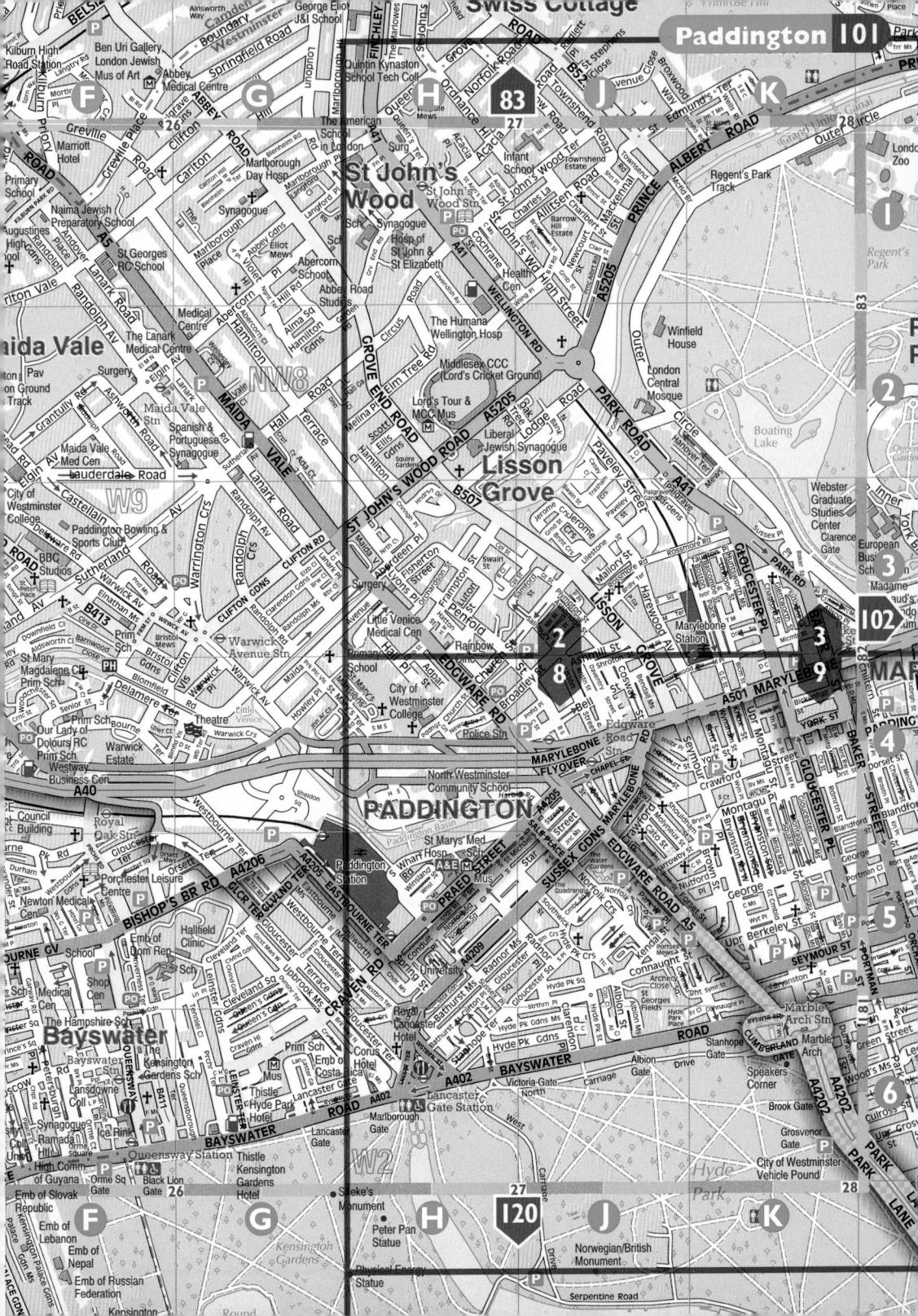

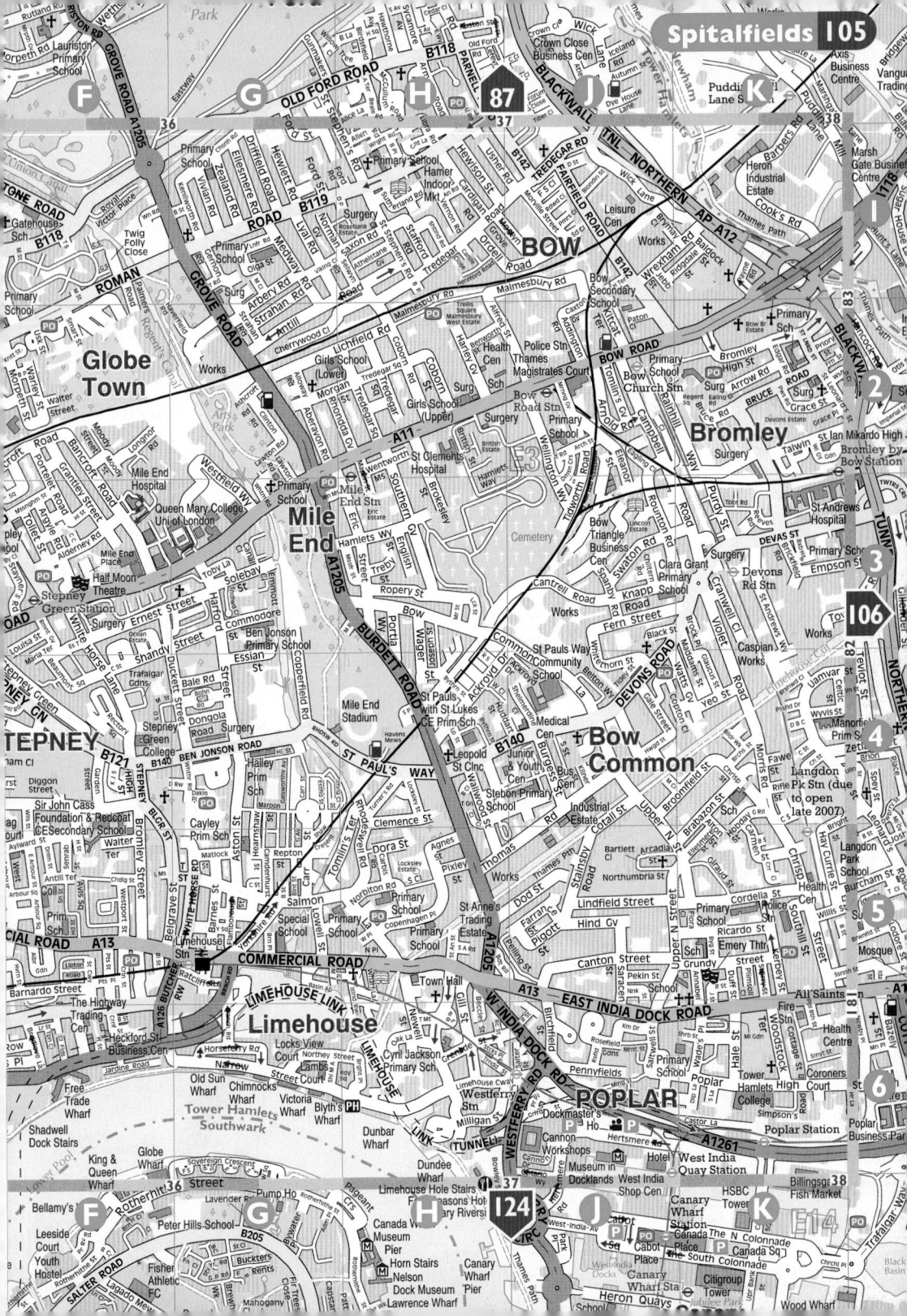

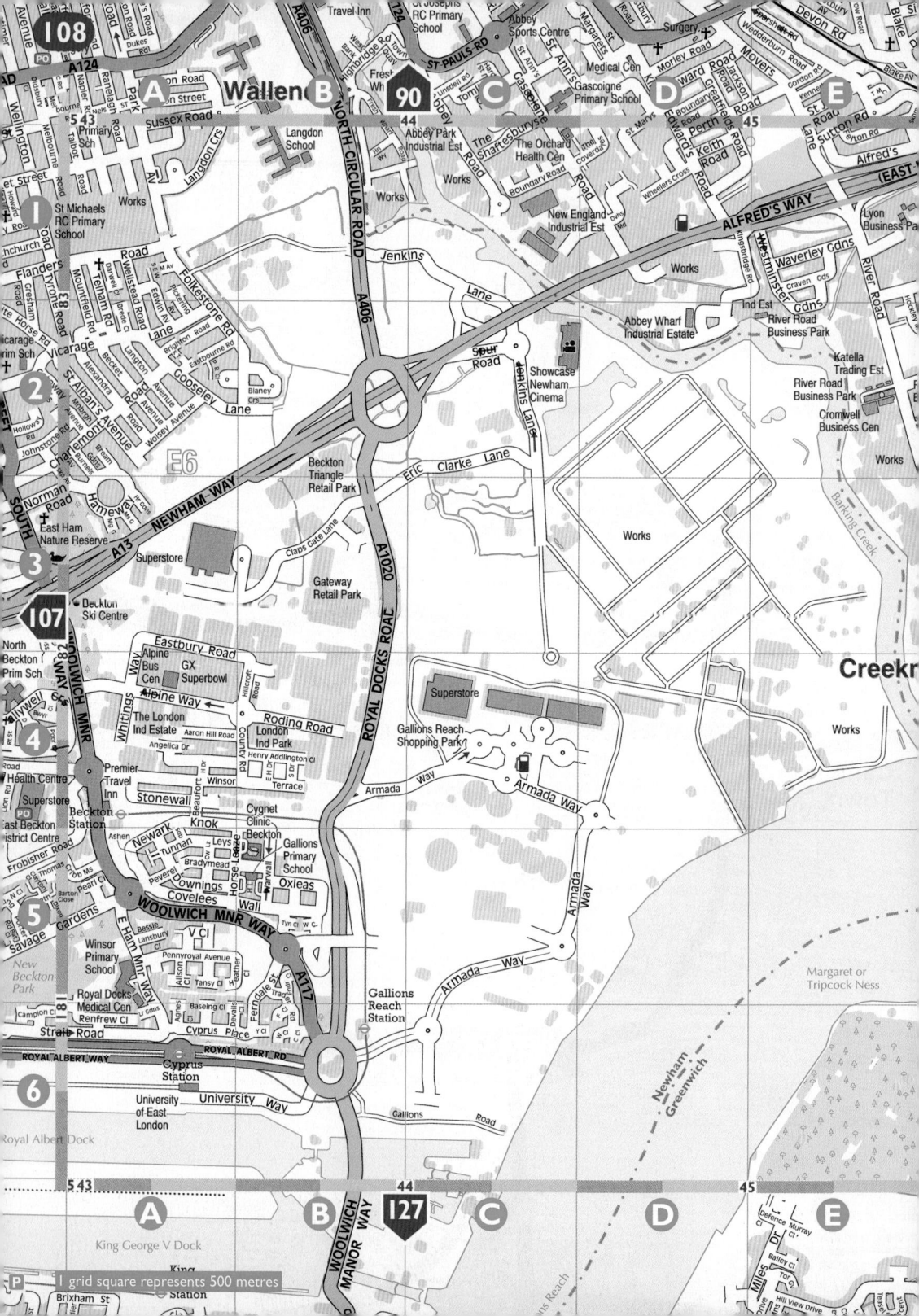

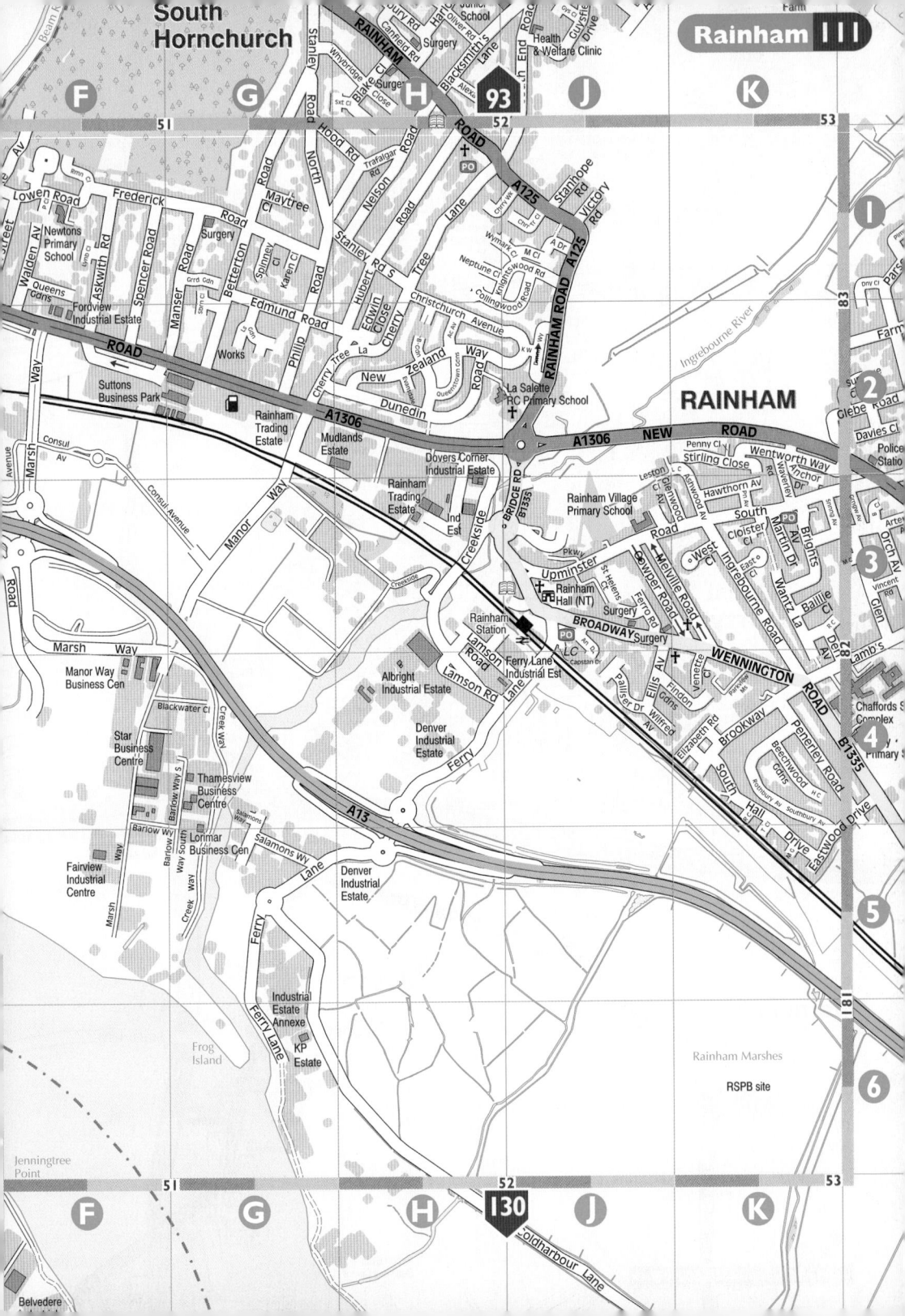

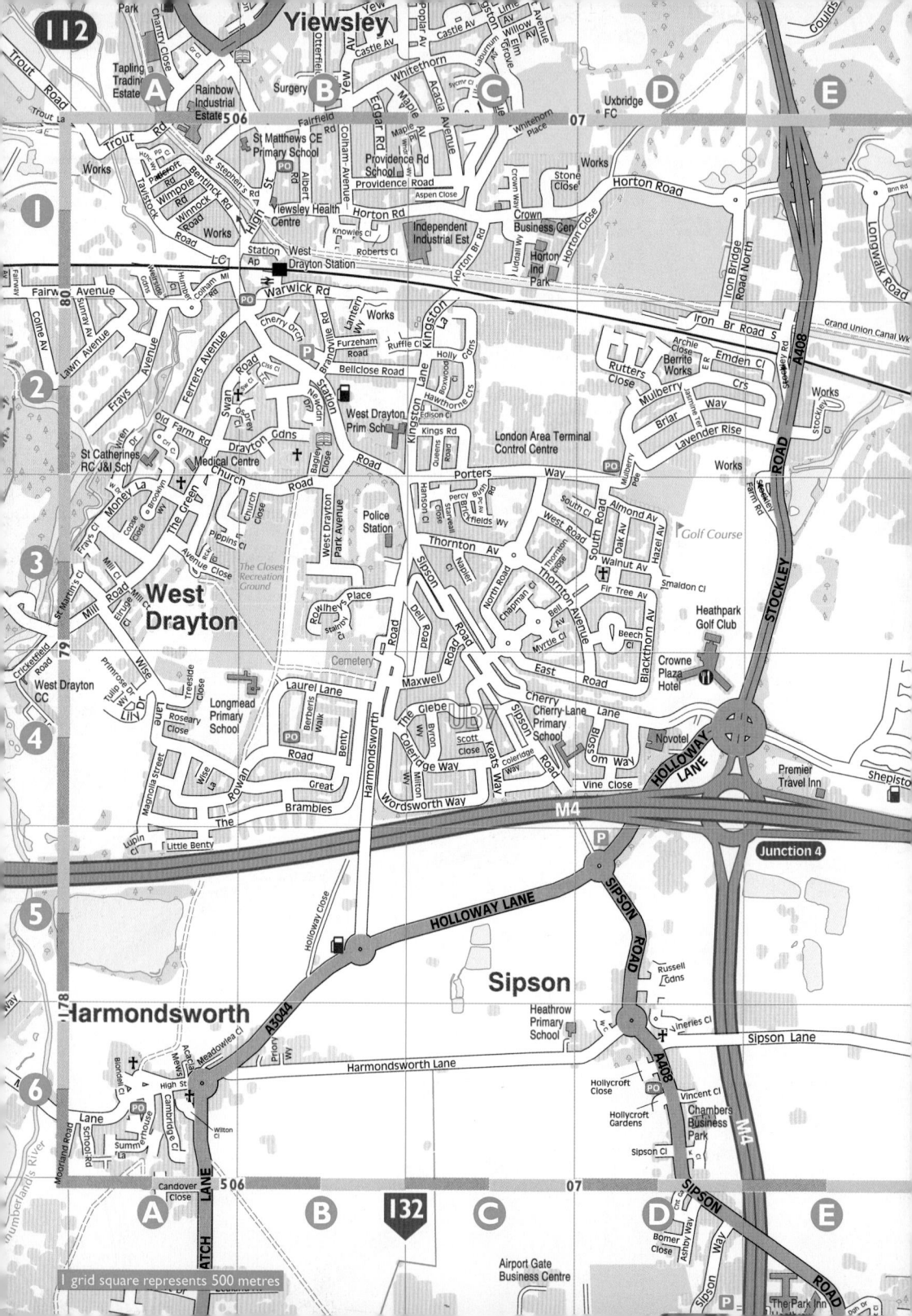

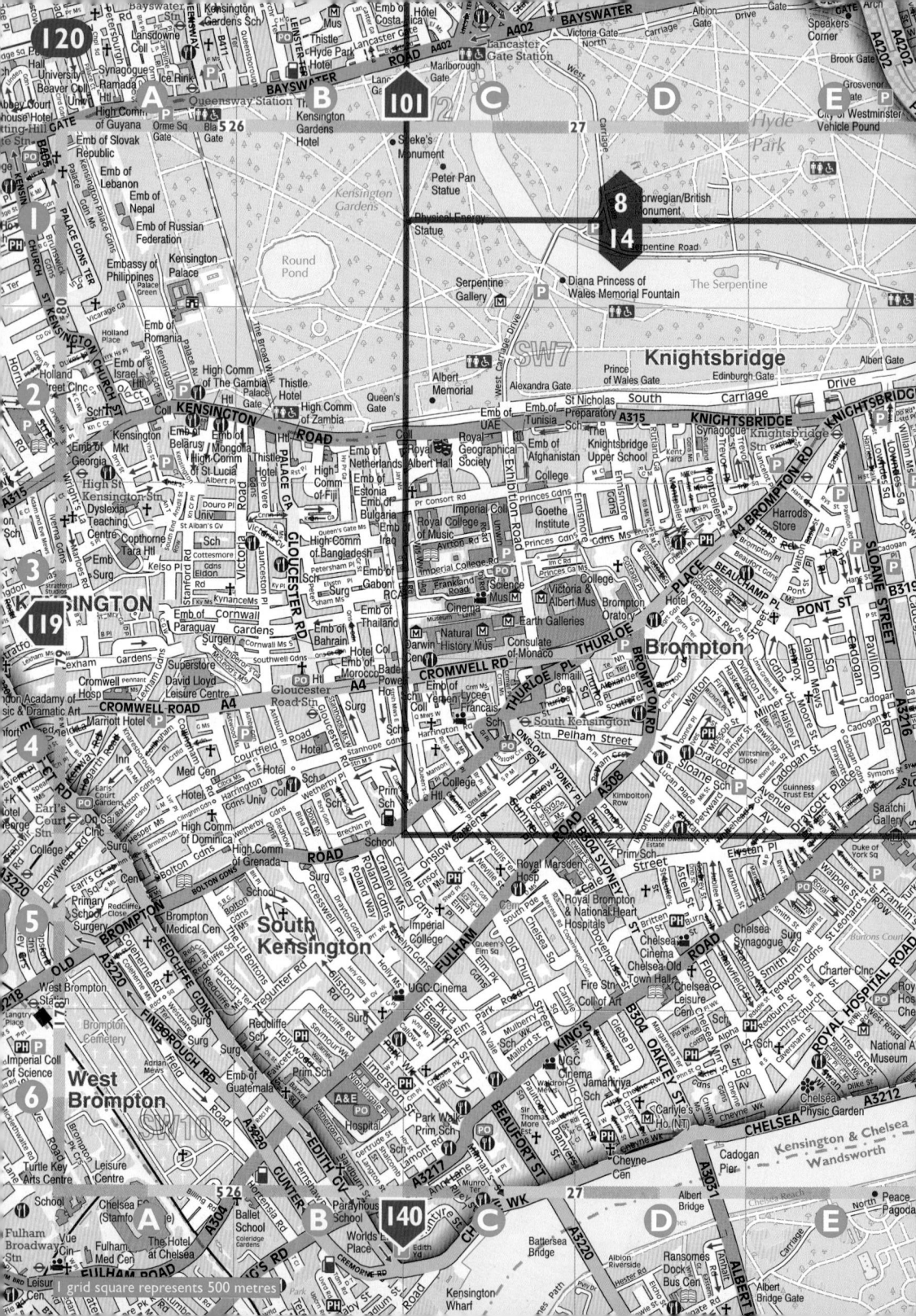

108

F G H J K

Newham
Greenwich

I

WESTERN WAY

2

3

128

4

5

6

Cyprus Station

University of East London

University Way

Gallions Road

King George V Dock

King George V Station

Woodman St

ALBERT ROAD

WOOLWICH MANOR WAY

Rymill St

A112 A117

PO

PIER ROAD

Old Station Museum

Woolwich Foot Tunnel

WOOLWICH FERRY

Gallions Reach

Waterfront Leisure Centre

Bell Water Gate

Firepower (Museum of Artillery)

WOOLWICH HIGH ST

Royal Arsenal

The Duke of Wellington Av

PO

Bingo

County Court

Mary St

BERESFORD STREET

Powis

JOHN WILSON ST

Mag Ct

Beresford Square

Indoor Market

Outdoor Market

Spray St

Vincent

Theatre

Woolwich Arsenal Station

Town Hall

University

St Thomas

Cncl Bldg

SEHA Hindu Temple

WELLINGTON ST

WOOLWICH NEW RD

GRAND DEPOT RD

Arthur

Crescent Road

Mulgrave Primary School

Military Barracks

WOOLWICH NEW ROAD

GRAND DEPOT ROAD

A205

St Peters RC Primary School

Frederick Place

Burrage Place

Brookhill Road

Boyard Road

Connaught Rd

Nightingale Vale

WOOLWICH

Nightingale Road

Kempt St

Ritter St

Eglinton Junior School

Eglinton Prim Sch

Nithd44 Road

Dallin Road

Erebus Drive

Pier Way

Canelot

Temple

Marlborough Road

Cadogan Road

Hastings

Hardinge Crs

Allenby Road

Tuppy St

Livesey Av

Argyl Rd

Armstrong Rd

Skeffington St

Seymour St

Tom Cribb Road

PLUMSTEAD ROAD

Gateway Bus Cen

A206

Greenwich Community College

Greenwich Community College

Naxey

Villas Rd

Polthorne Gv

Walmer

Terrace

Plumstead Station

WESTERN WAY A2016

Whinchat Road

Goldthorpe

Heronsgate Primary School

PETTMAN CRESCENT

A206

Hadden Road

Works

North Rd

Works

Boughton Road

Magistrates Court

Woolwich Crown Court

HM Prison Belmarsh

Battery Road

Defence Murray Cl

Miles Dr

Hill View Drive

New Acres Rd

Warepoint Dr

Ridge Close

Nuthatch Gardens

PLUMSTEAD HIGH STREET

Primary School

Police Sta

Leisure Cen

Richmond Place

Invermore Place

Dawson Close

Sandbach Place

Raglan Road

Hudson Rd

Surgery

Durham Road

Waverley Road

Vicarage

Congleton Grove

Cambridge Rd

Vica

Blenkeon

St Margarets Grove

Shree KS Swaminarayan Temple

Heavitree Road

Plumstead

PLUMSTEAD COMMON ROAD

St Margarets CE Prim Sch

Wernbrook St

St John's Ter

Plumstead Common

Warwick

Old Mill Rd

Waverley Ter

Ross

Macoma Road

Tuam Road

Chelsworth Drive

Alabama Street

Vambery Rd

Isla Rd

Plumcroft Road Primary School

Wrottesley Rd

Genesta Road

Vernham Rd

Kirk Lane

Ennis Rd

Rowton Road

Brinklow Crs

Plum

Ashridge Crs

Clothworkers Rd

Community College

Negus Sixth Form Centre

Greenslade Primary School

King's

The Slade

Kirkham St

Surgery

Mountbatten Cl

Melling Street

Timbercroft Primary School

Rockliffe Manor Primary School

Eastview Av

Thornhill

Landstead Road

Warland

Camdale Rd

147

WOOLWICH

Plumstead Common Rd

Primary School

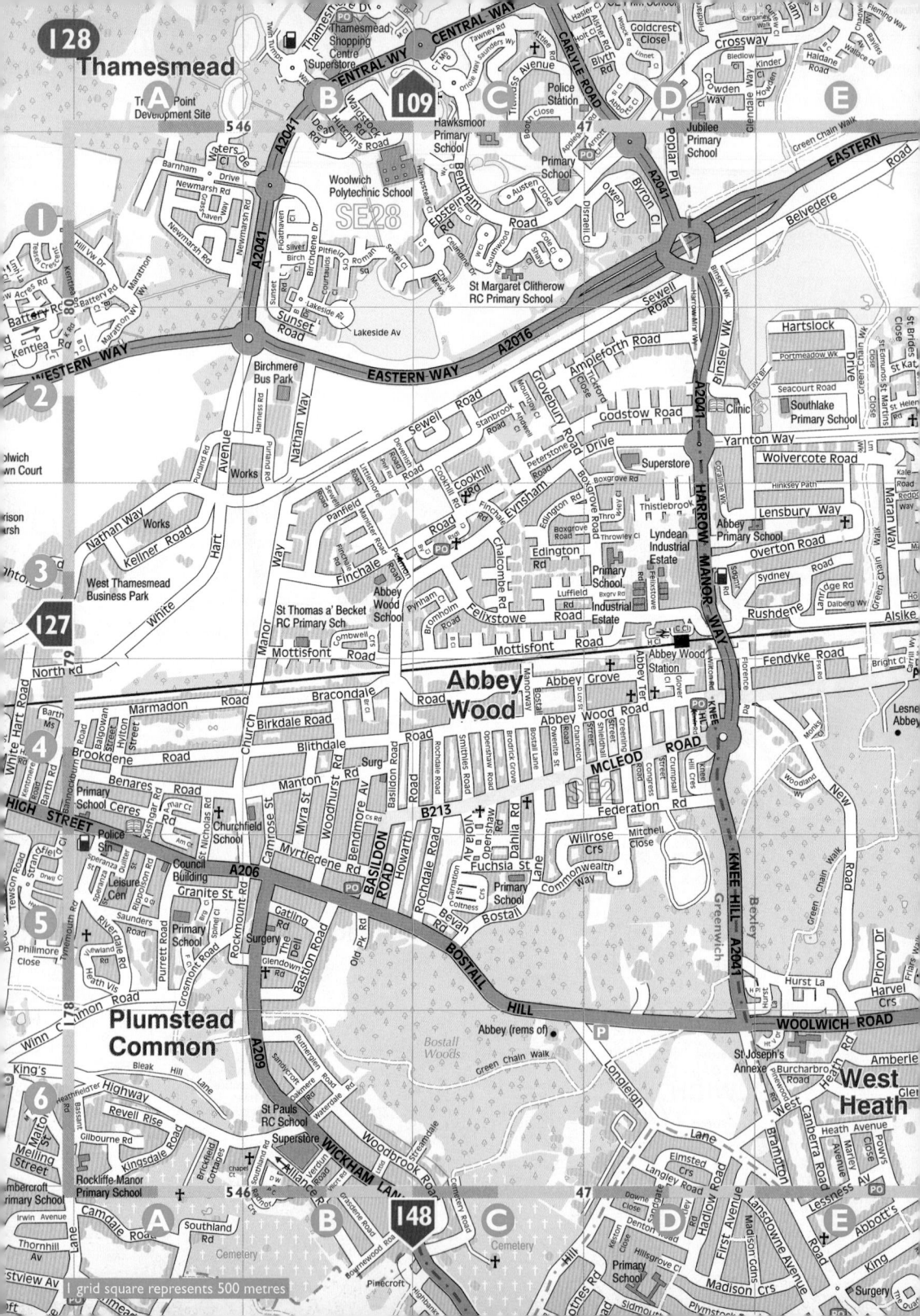

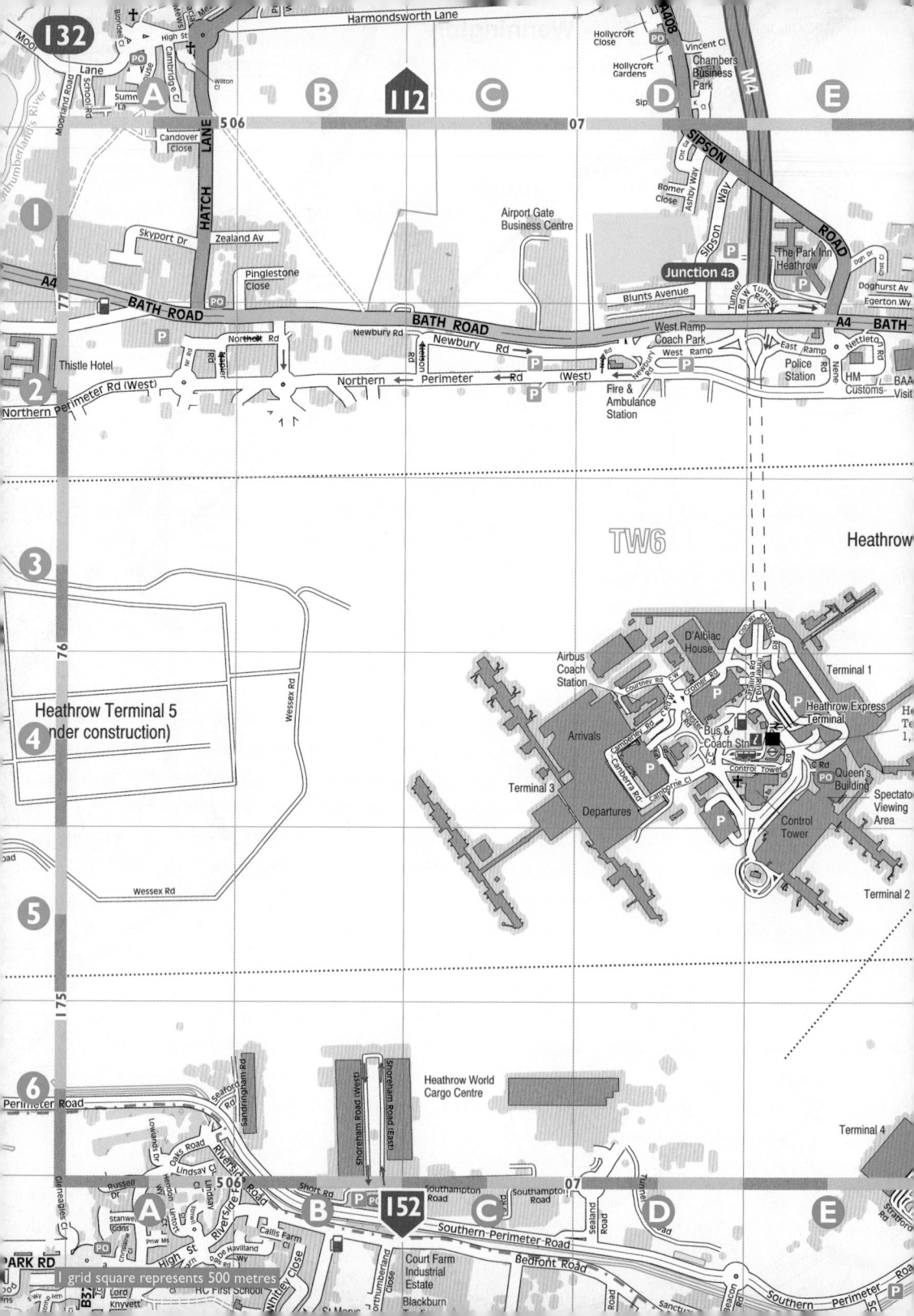

Harmondsworth Lane

Hollycroft Close

Vincent Cl

Chambers Business Park

Hollycroft Gardens

A **B** **112** **C** **D** **E**

Sip

SIPSON

Candover Close

5 06

HATCH LANE

Bomer Close

Ashby Way

Sipson Way

ROAD

I

Northumberland's River

Skyport Dr

Zealand Av

Airport Gate Business Centre

Tunnel Rd

The Park Inn Heathrow

Don Dr

Doghurst Av

Junction 4a

A4

77

Moorland Road

BATH ROAD

Pinglestone Close

PO

Blunts Avenue

A4

BATH

Egerton Wy

P

Nettleto Rd

Nene

HM Customs

BAA Visit

2

Thistle Hotel

P

Northolt Rd

Newbury Rd

Newbury Rd

West Ramp Coach Park

West Ramp

East Ramp

Police Station

Northern Perimeter Rd (West)

Linden

P

Northern ← Perimeter ← Rd (West)

Newbury

Fire & Ambulance Station

West Ramp

East Ramp

P

TW6

Heathrow

3

76

Wessex Rd

Airbus Coach Station

D'Albiac House

Terminal 1

Heathrow Terminal 5 (under construction)

Courtney Rd

Comer Rd

Heathrow Express Terminal

He Te 1,

4

P

Arrivals

Camberley Rd

Canberra Rd

Bus & Coach Stn

P

Control Tower

Cd Rd

P

Queen's Building

Terminal 3

Camborne Cl

Spectator Viewing Area

Departures

P

Control Tower

Wessex Rd

Terminal 2

5

I 75

Perimeter Road

6

Heathrow World Cargo Centre

Terminal 4

Lowlands Cr

Seaton Cl

Sandringham Dr

Shoreham Road (West)

Shoreham Road (East)

Oaks Road

Lindsay Cl

Short Rd

Southampton Road

Southampton Road

Sealand Road

07

Tunnel

A **B** **152** **C** **D** **E**

Glenagles Dr

Russell Wy

Lindsay

5 06

Riverside Road

Short Rd

Southern Perimeter Road

Sealand Road

Southern

Stanwell Gdns

PO

De Havilland Dr

Callis Farm Cl

Whitley Close

Court Farm Industrial Estate Blackburn

Bedfont Road

Beacon Rd

Seaford Rd

PARK RD

Pnw Ms

Lord Knyvett

RC First School

St Marys

Northumberland Close

Southern Perimeter Road

P

B3

I grid square represents 500 metres

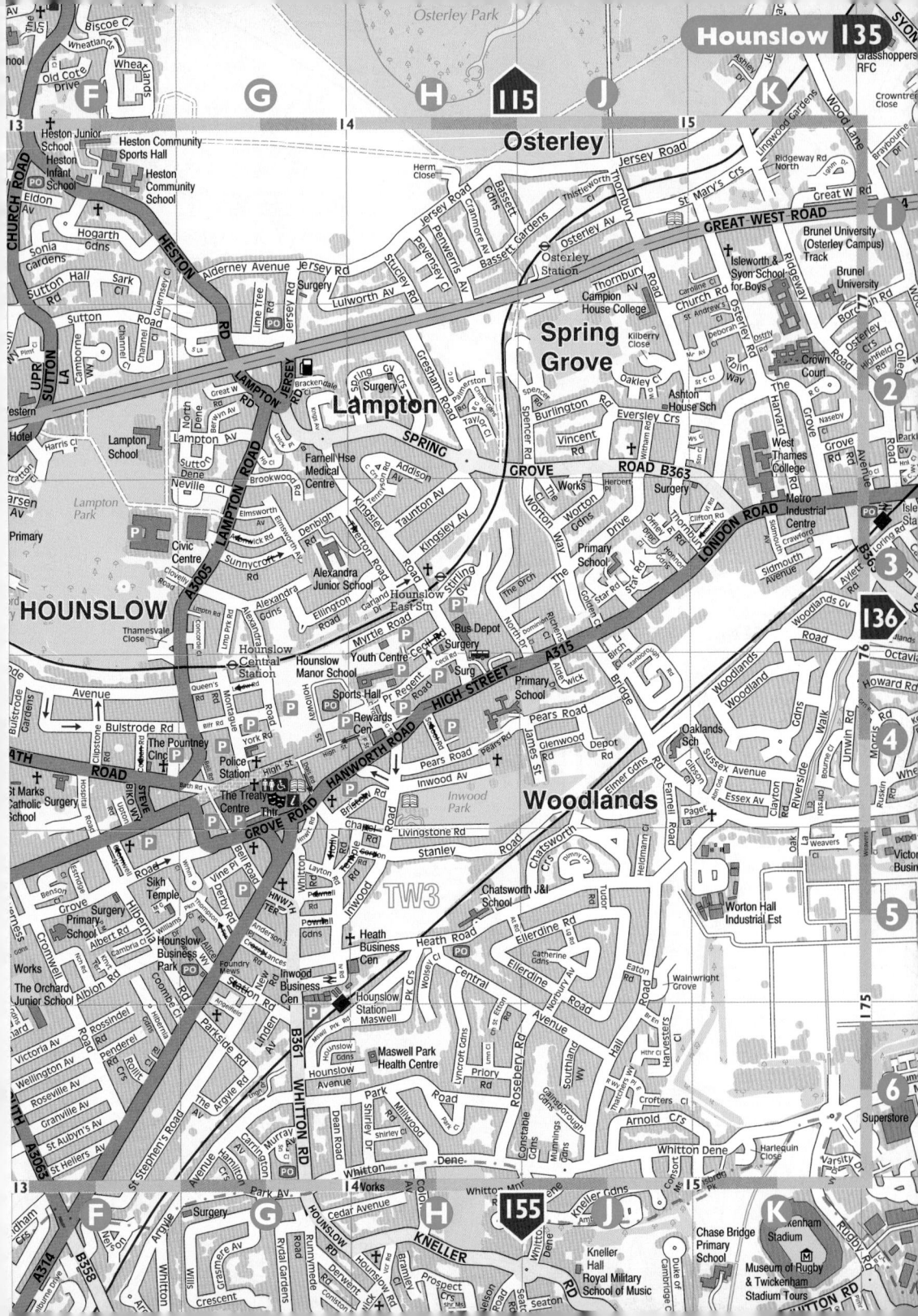

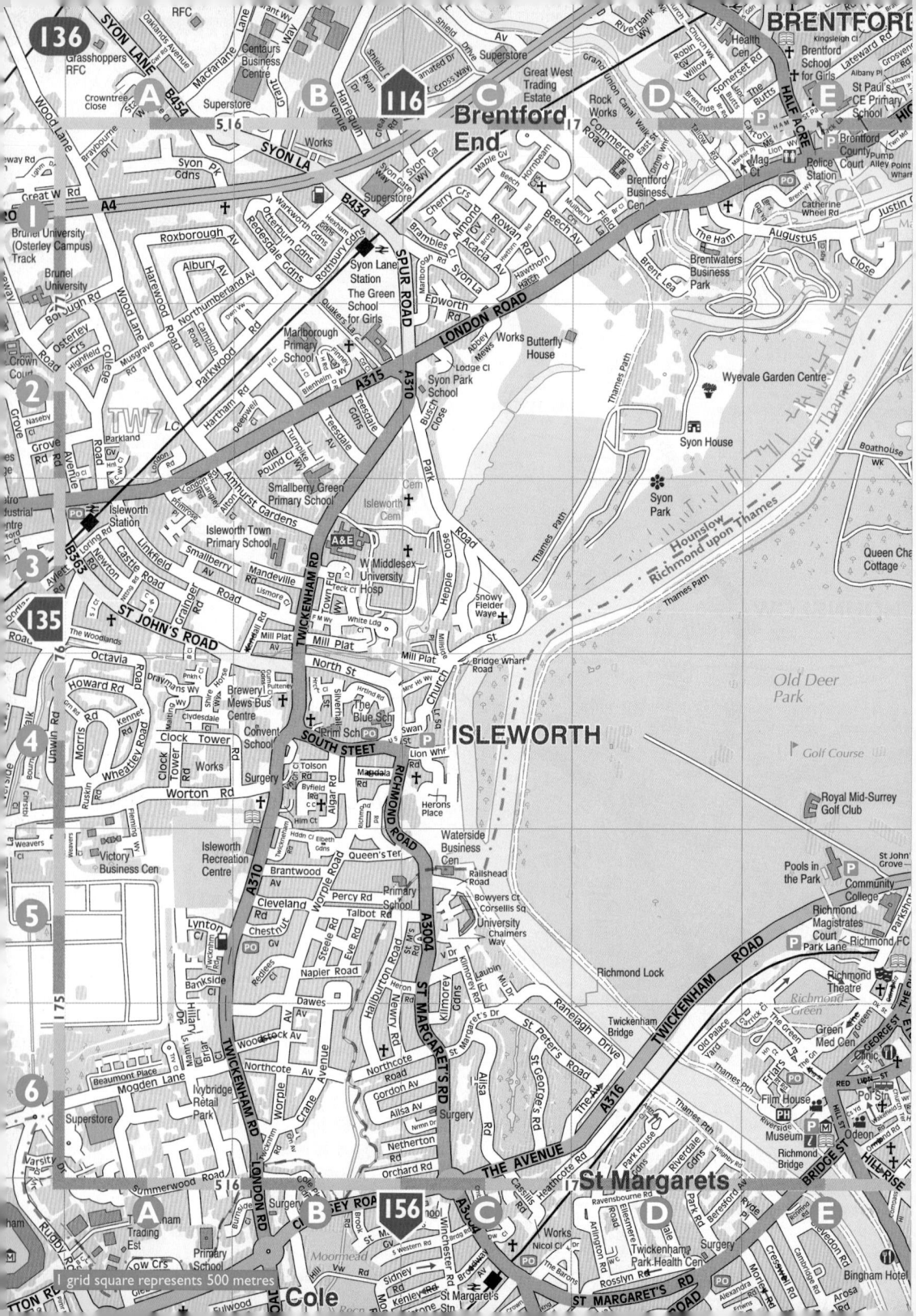

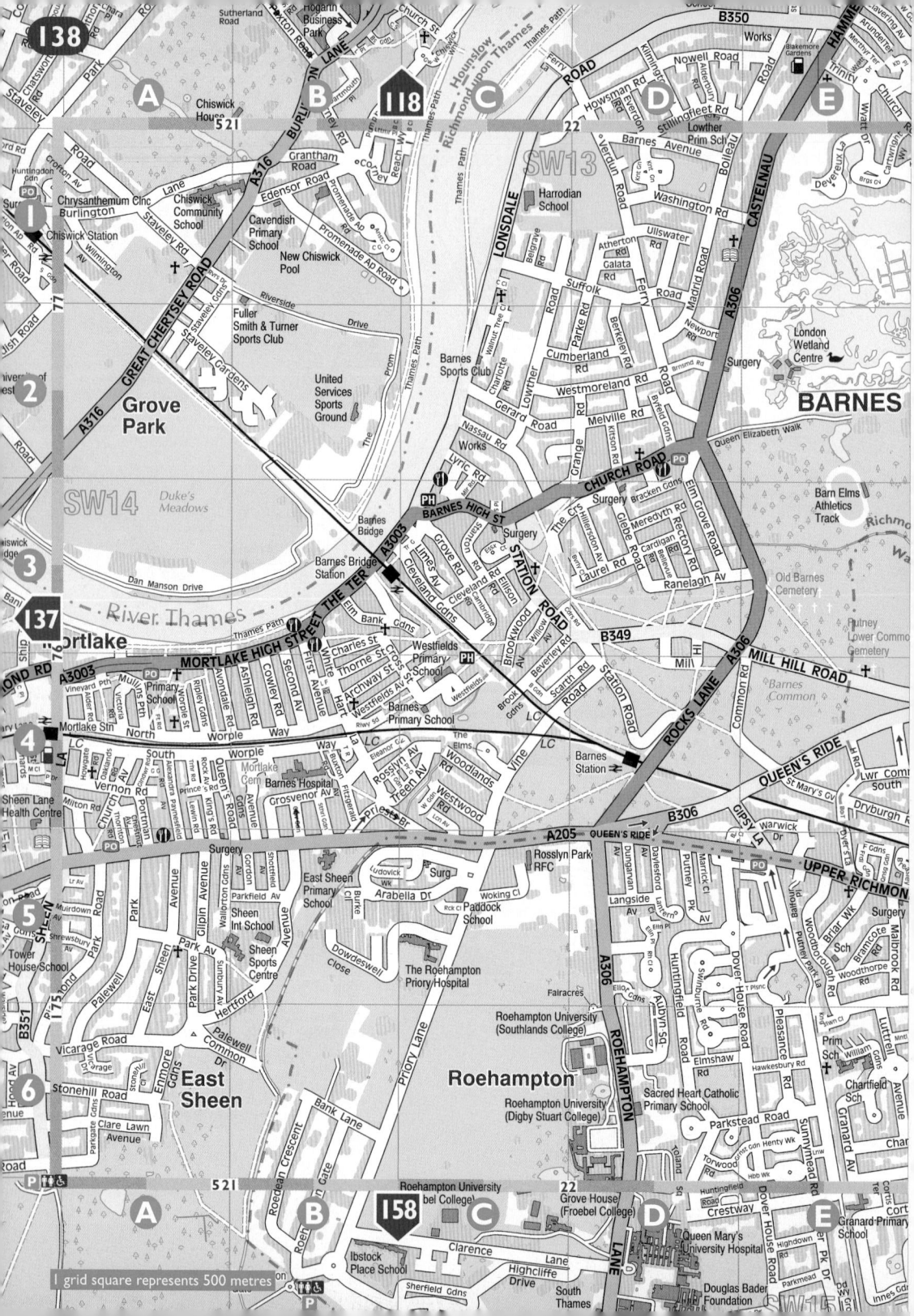

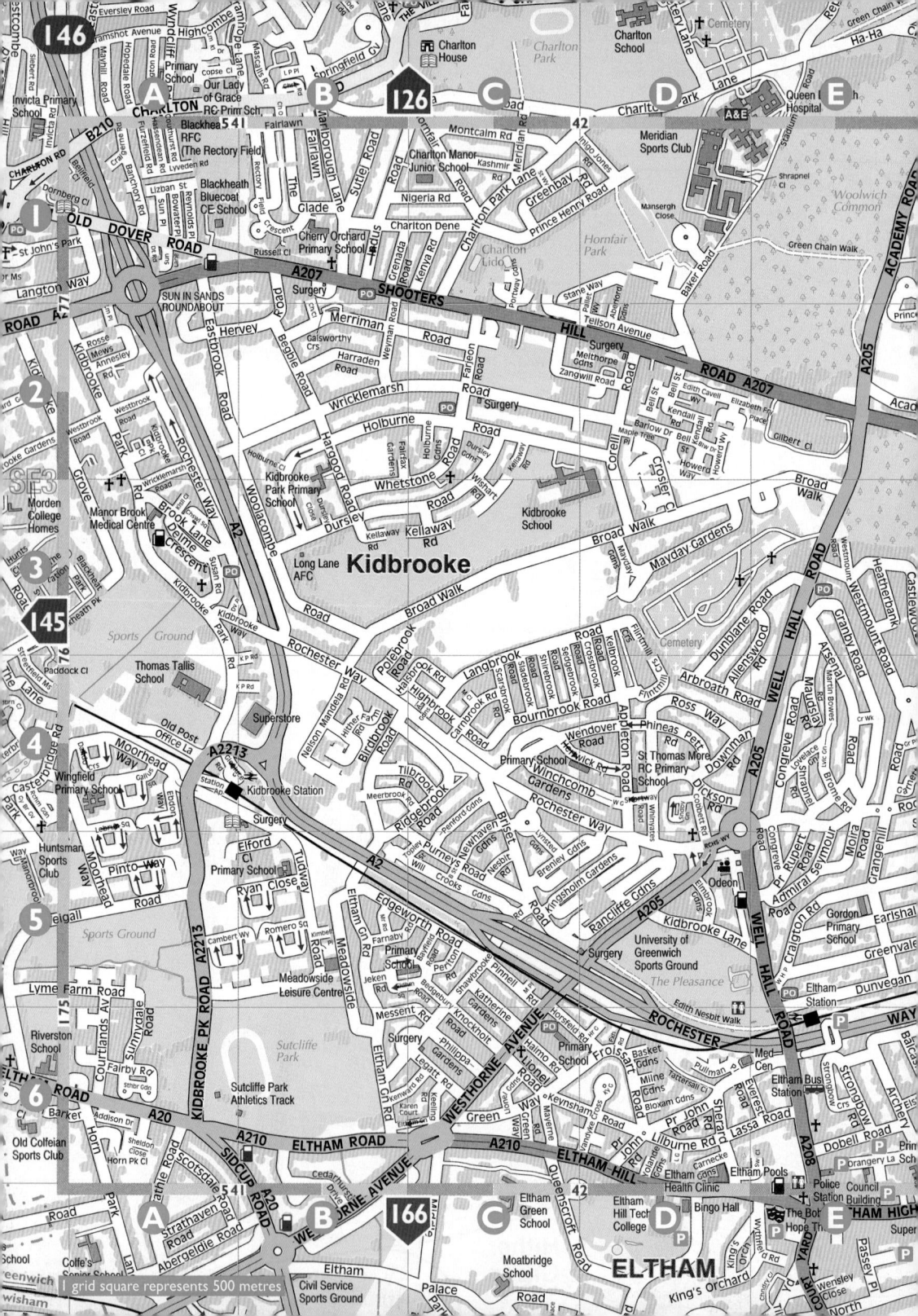

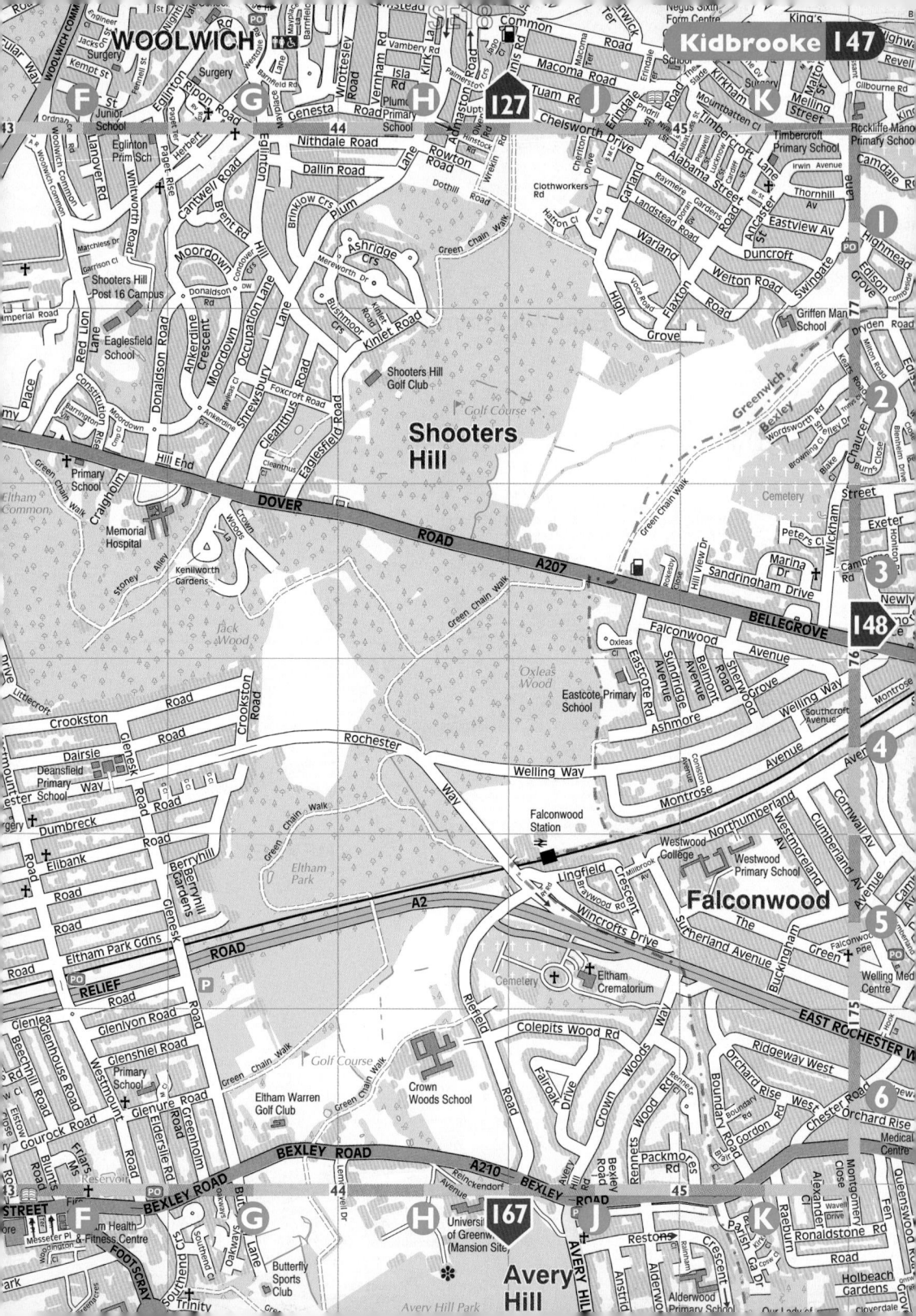

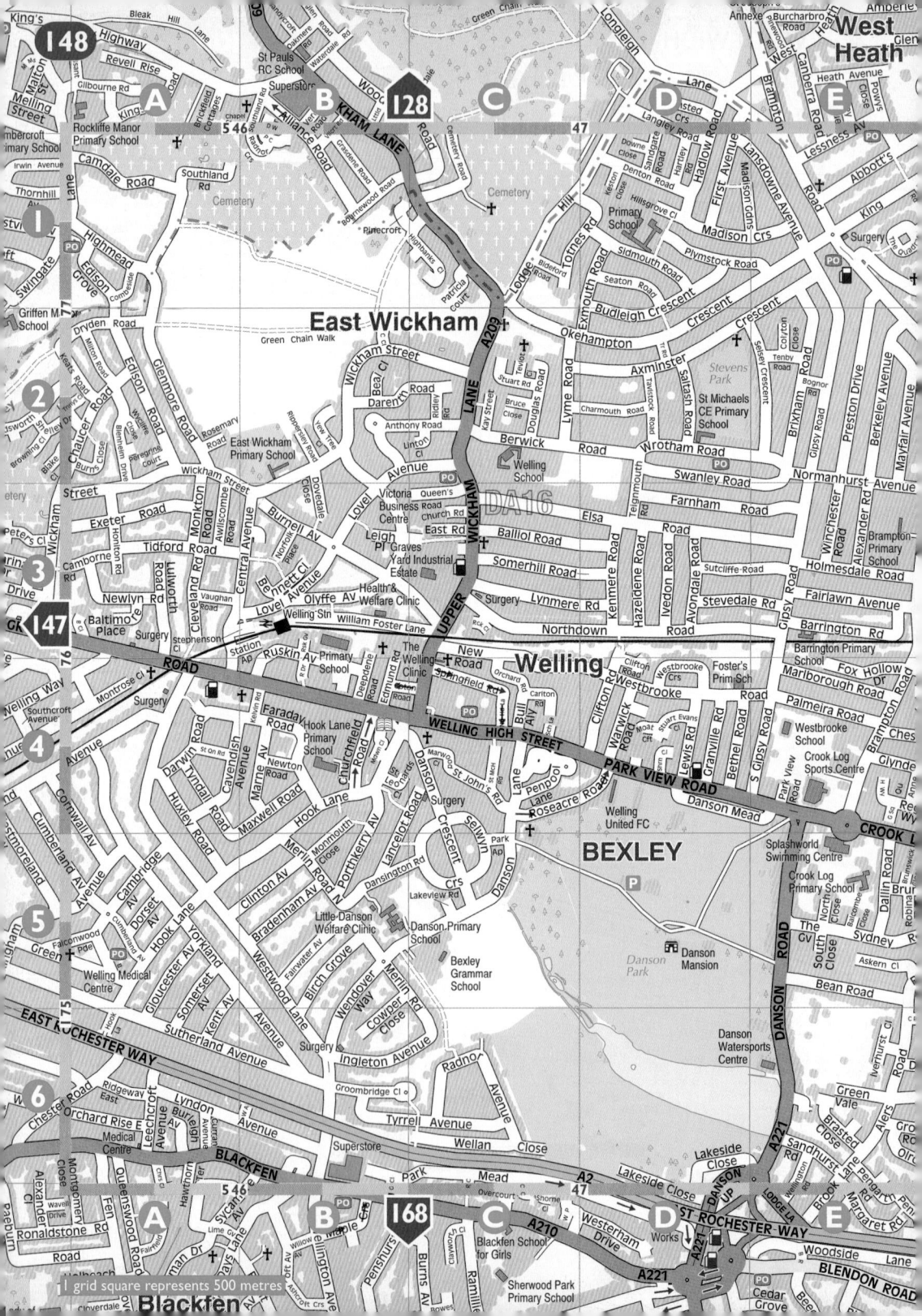

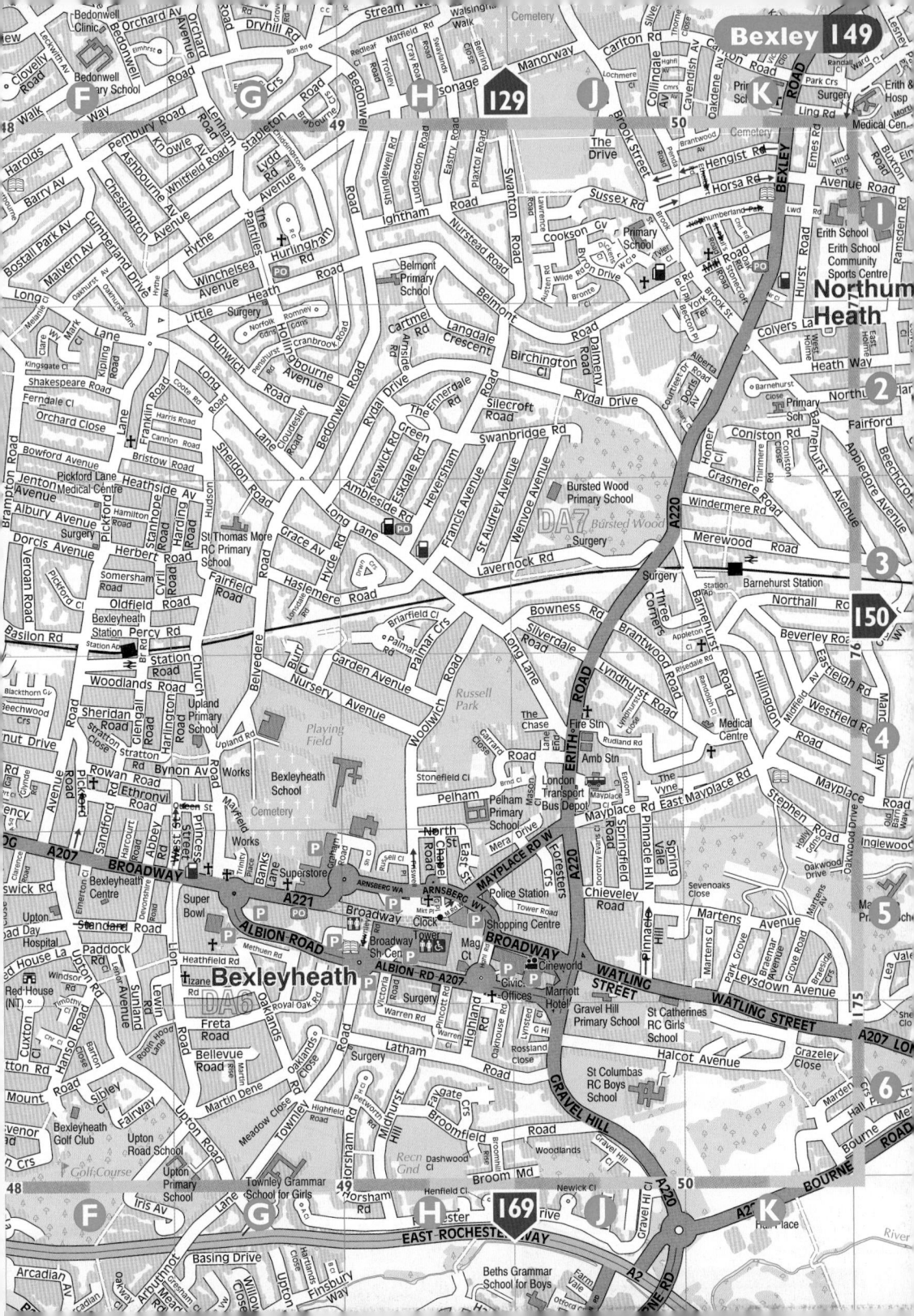

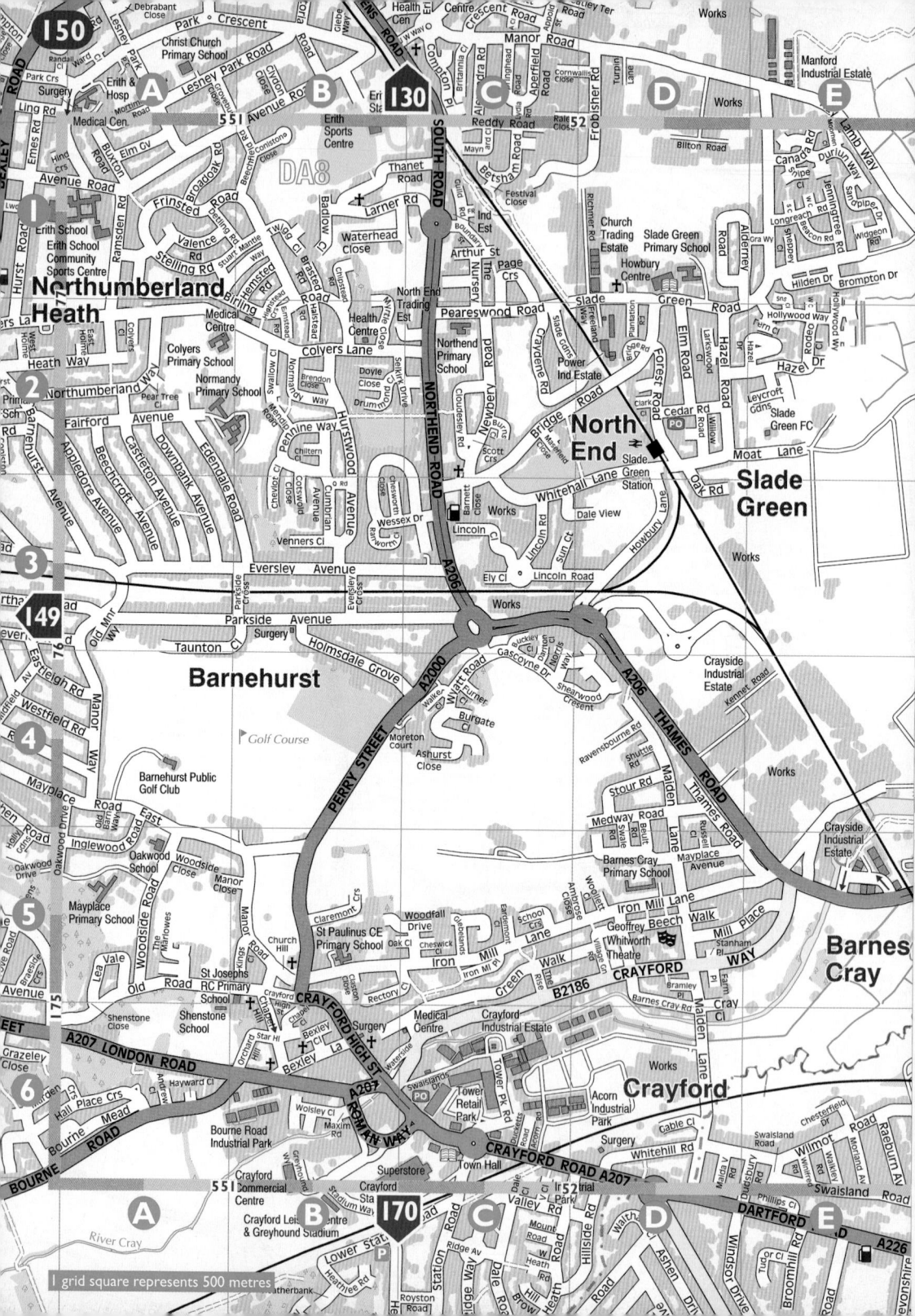

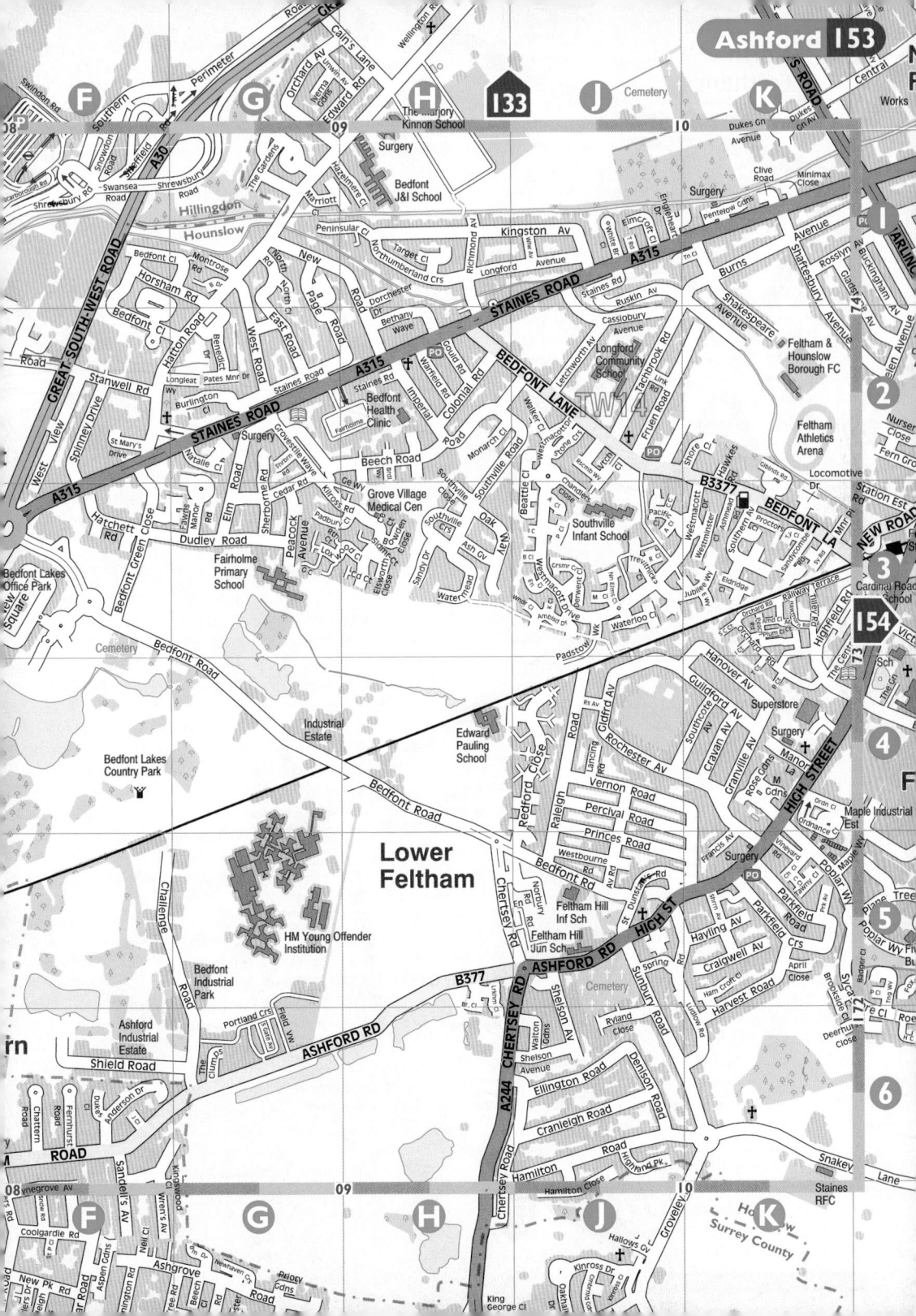

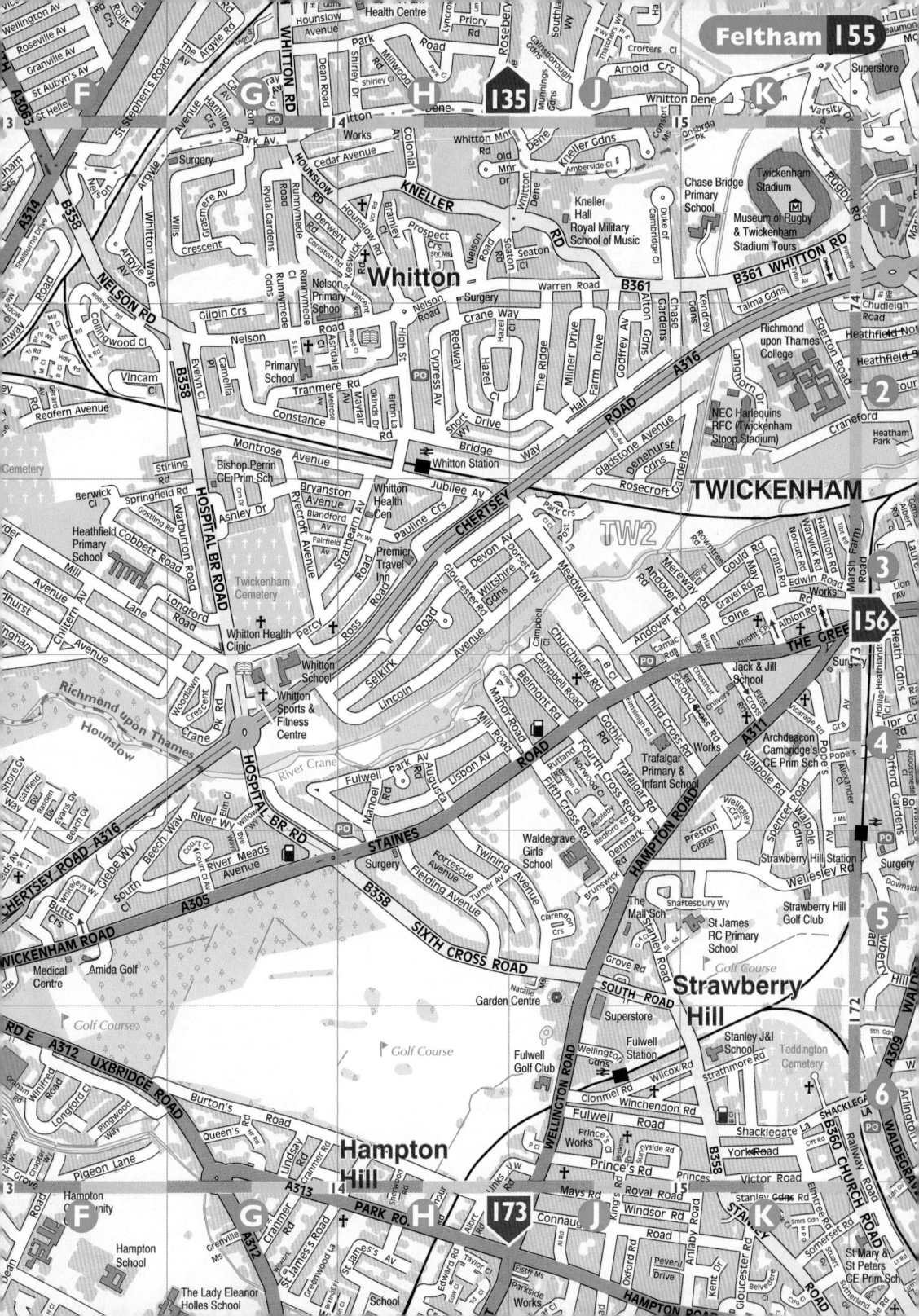

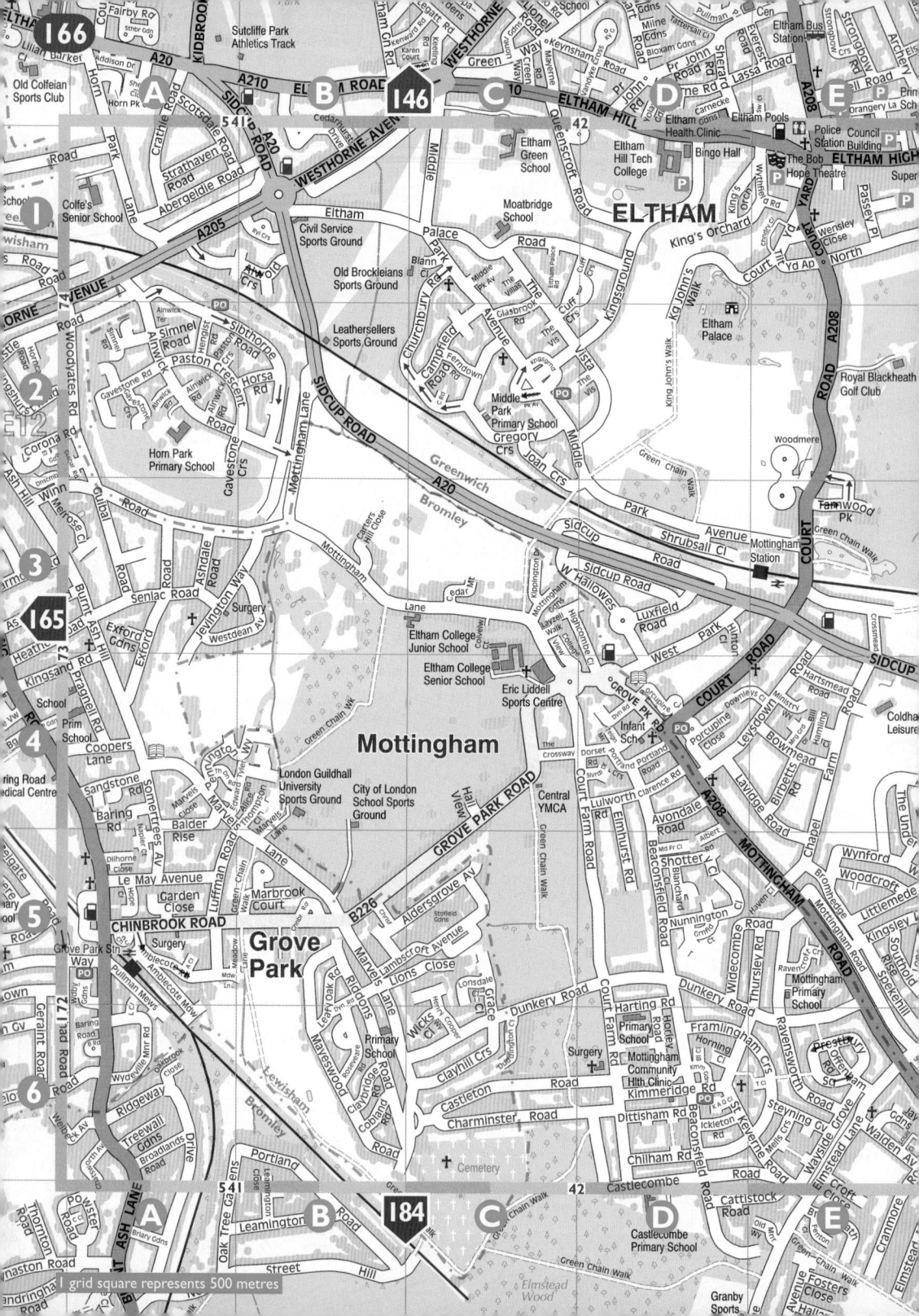

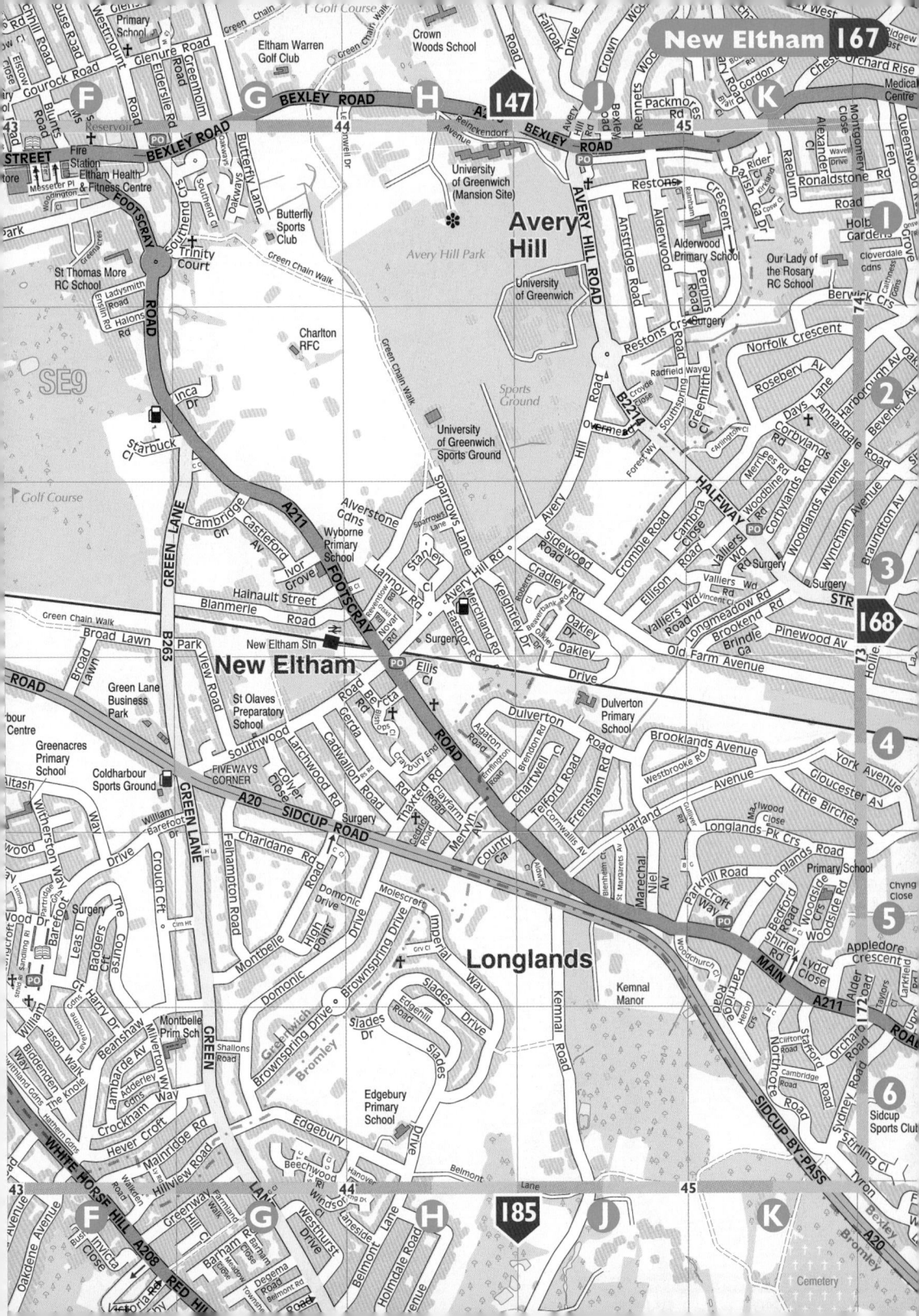

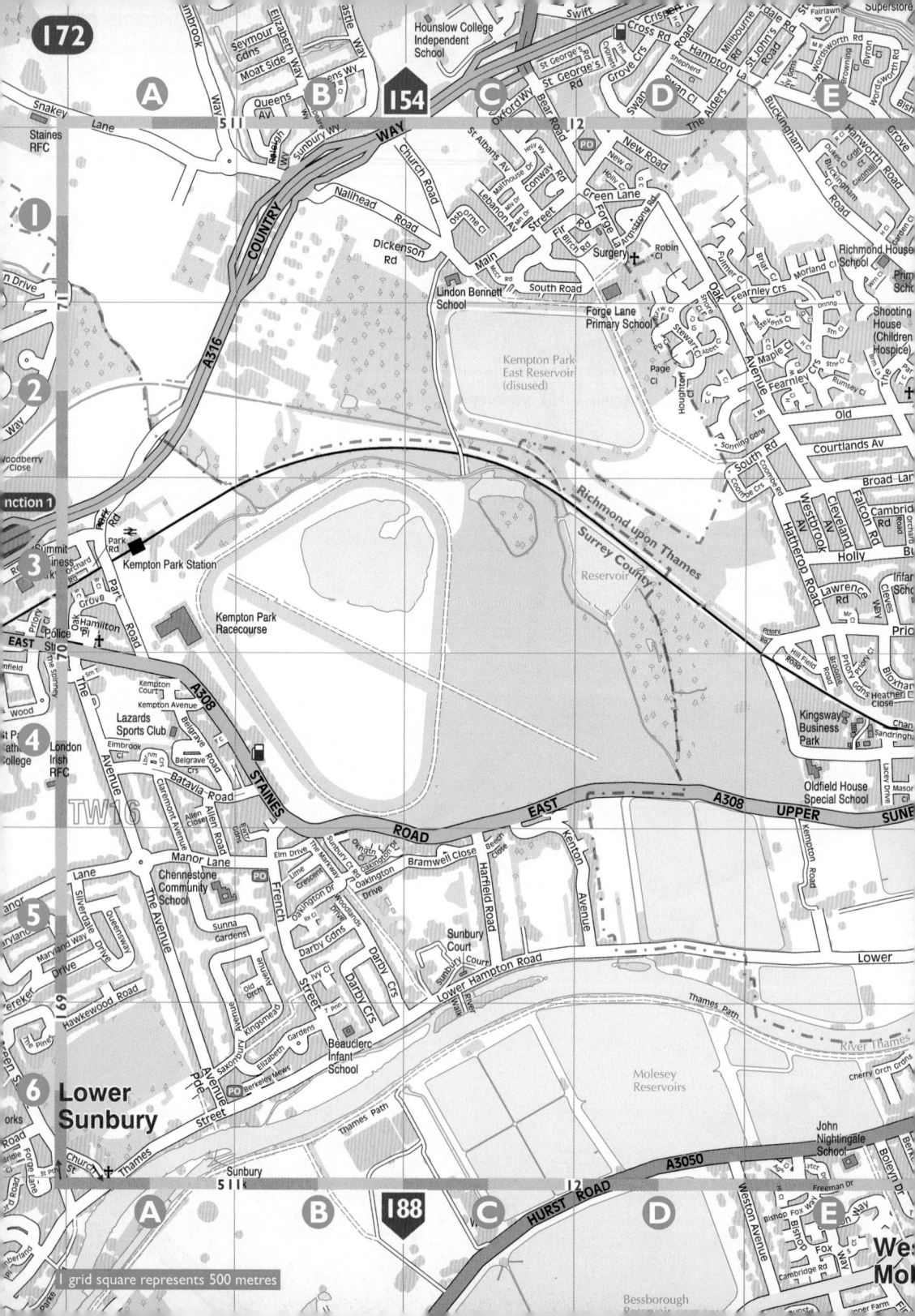

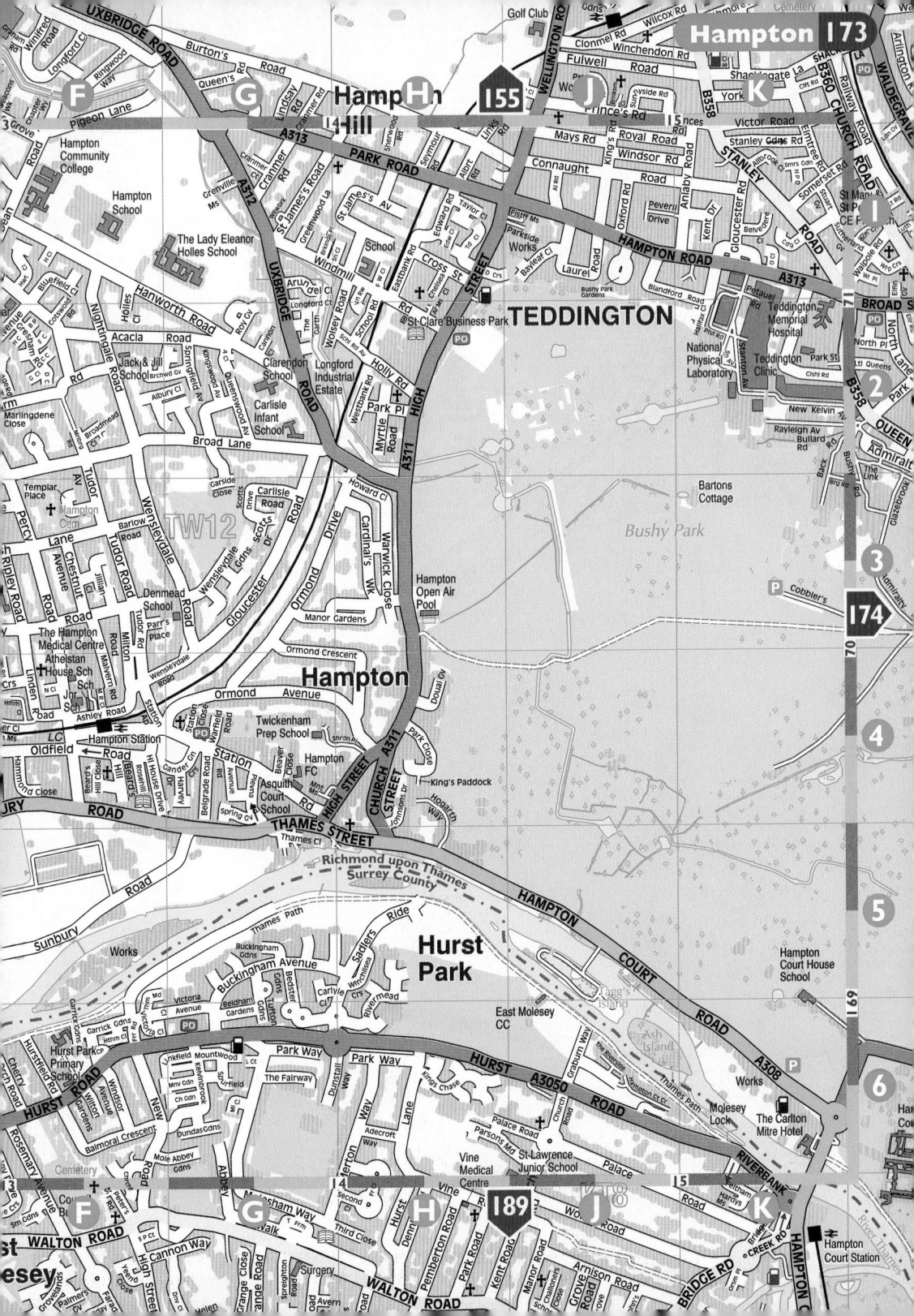

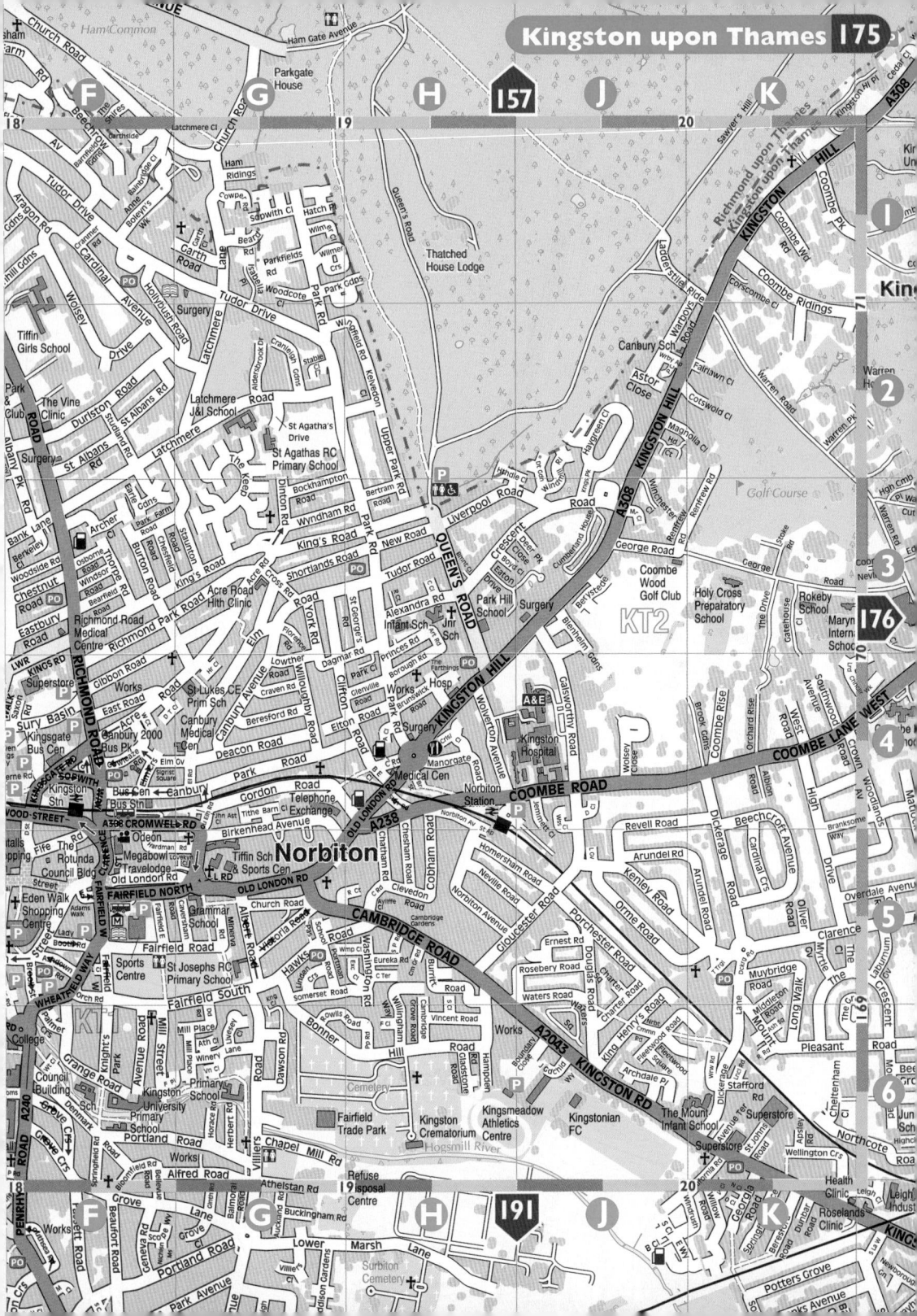

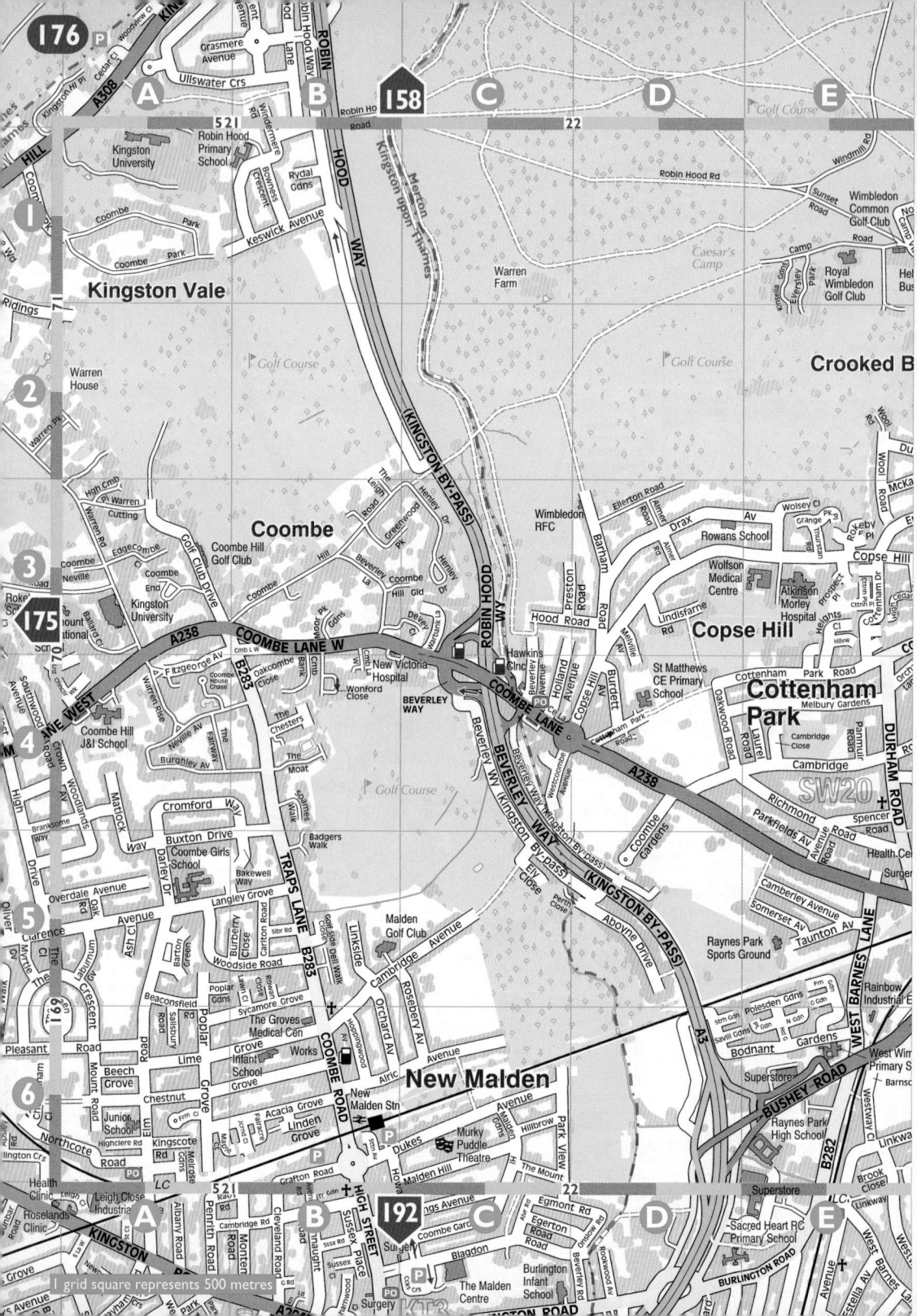

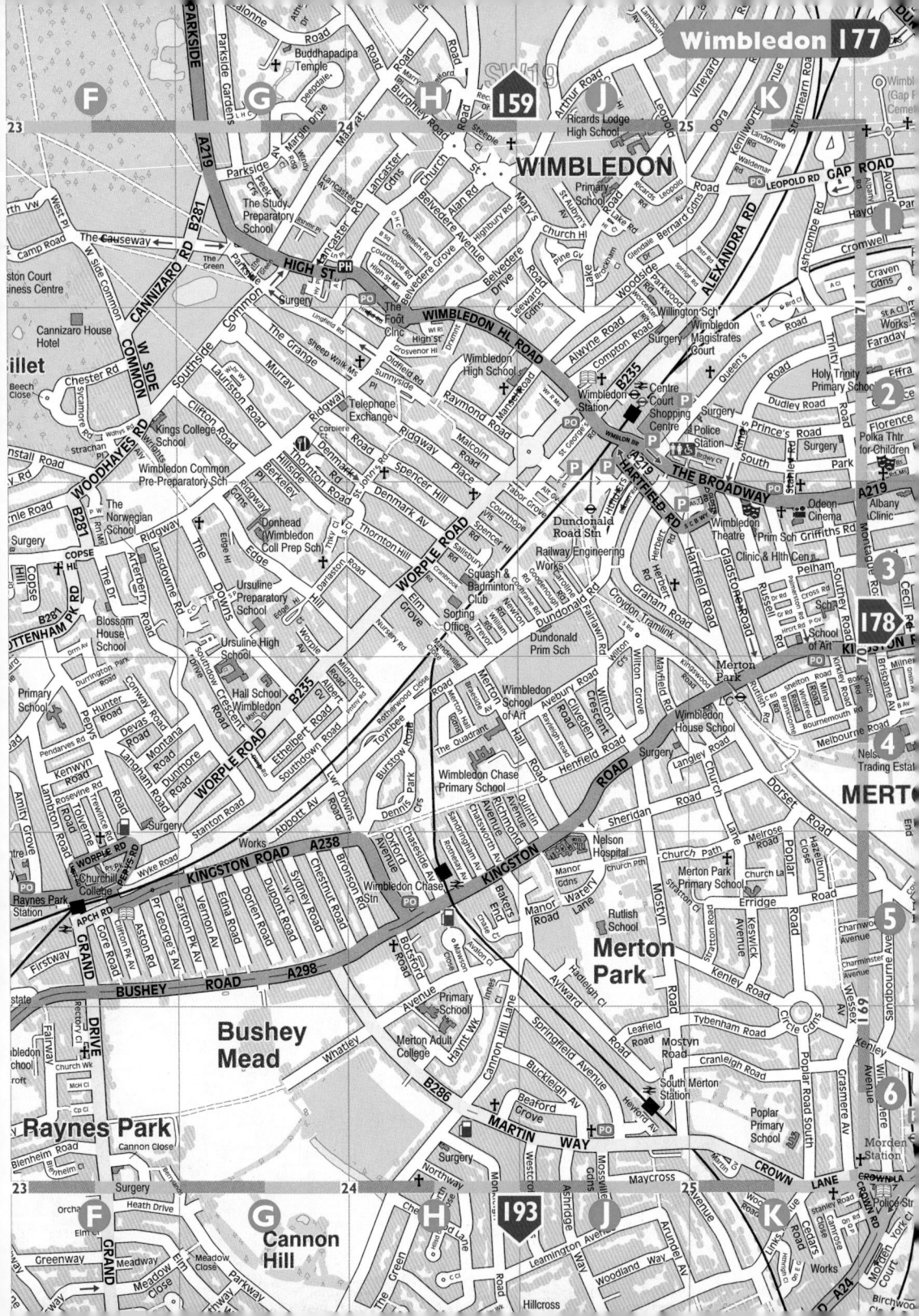

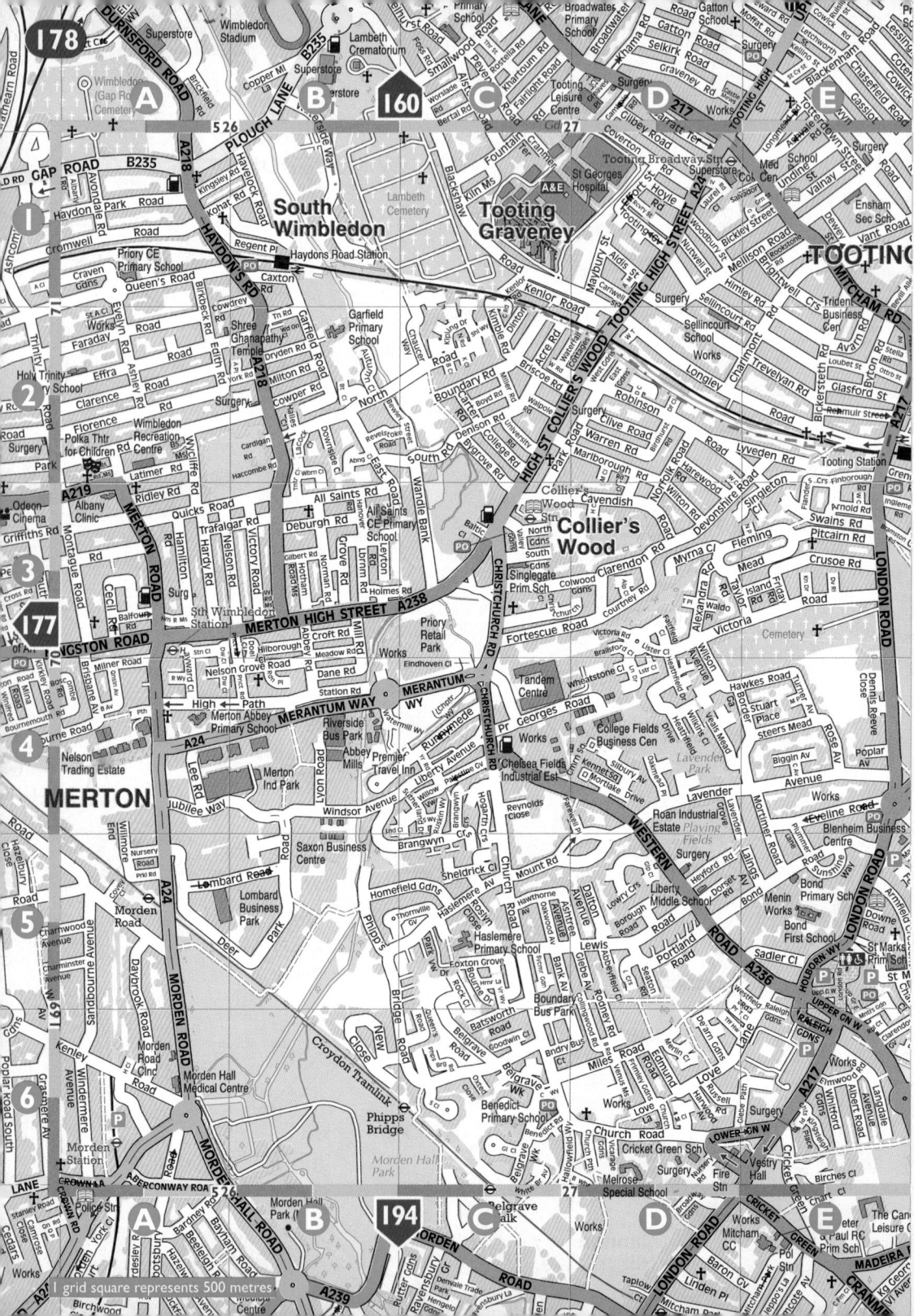

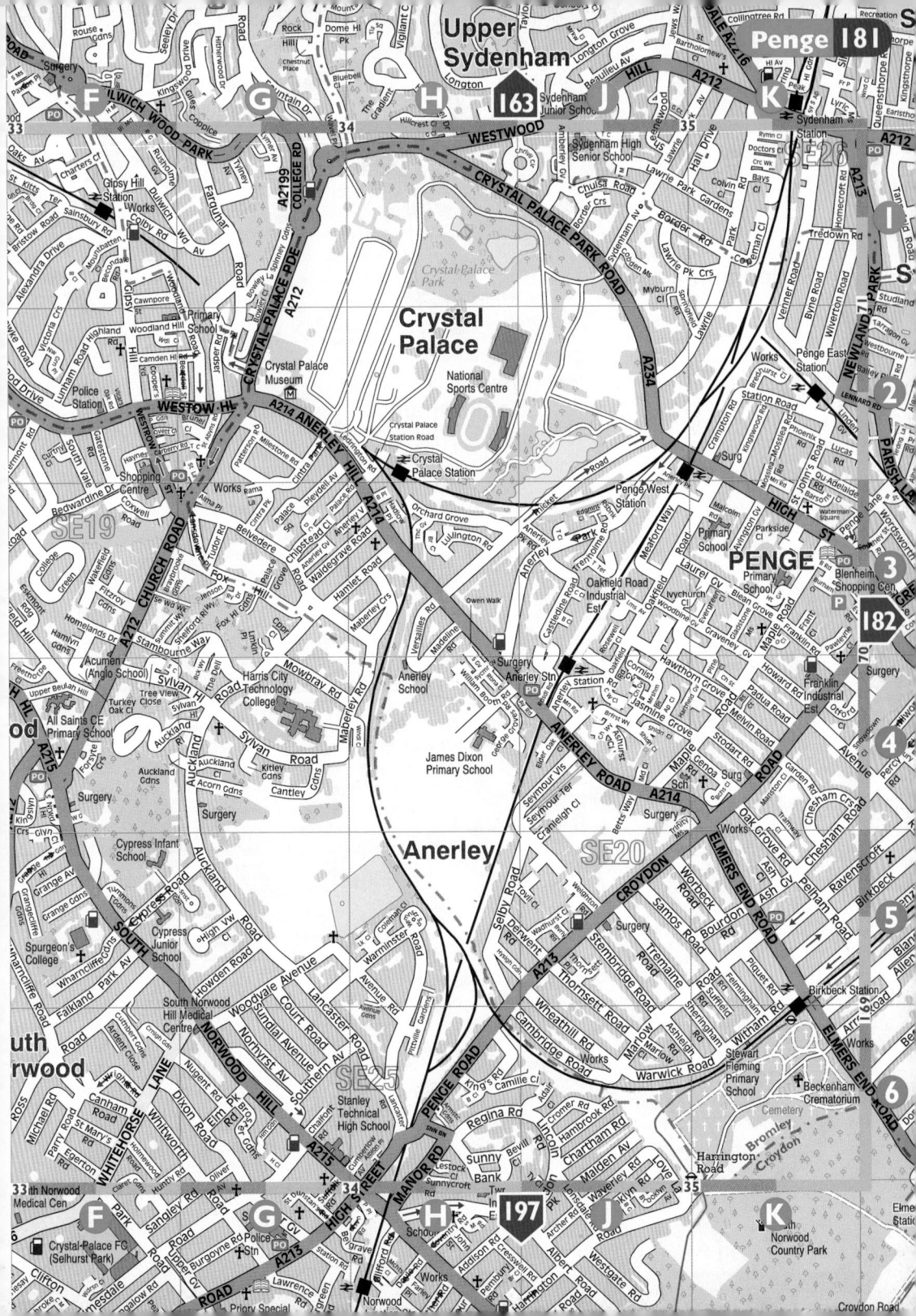

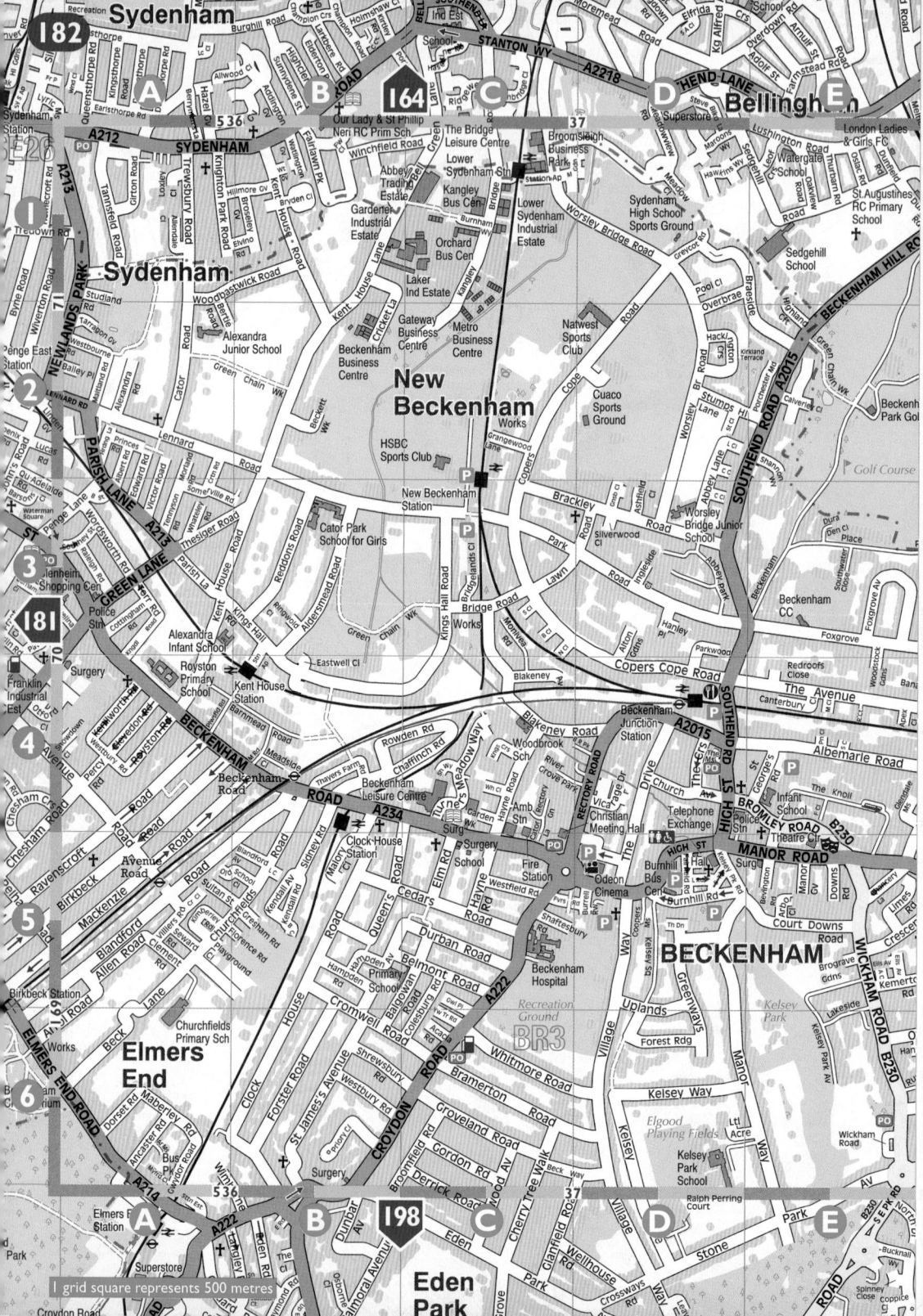

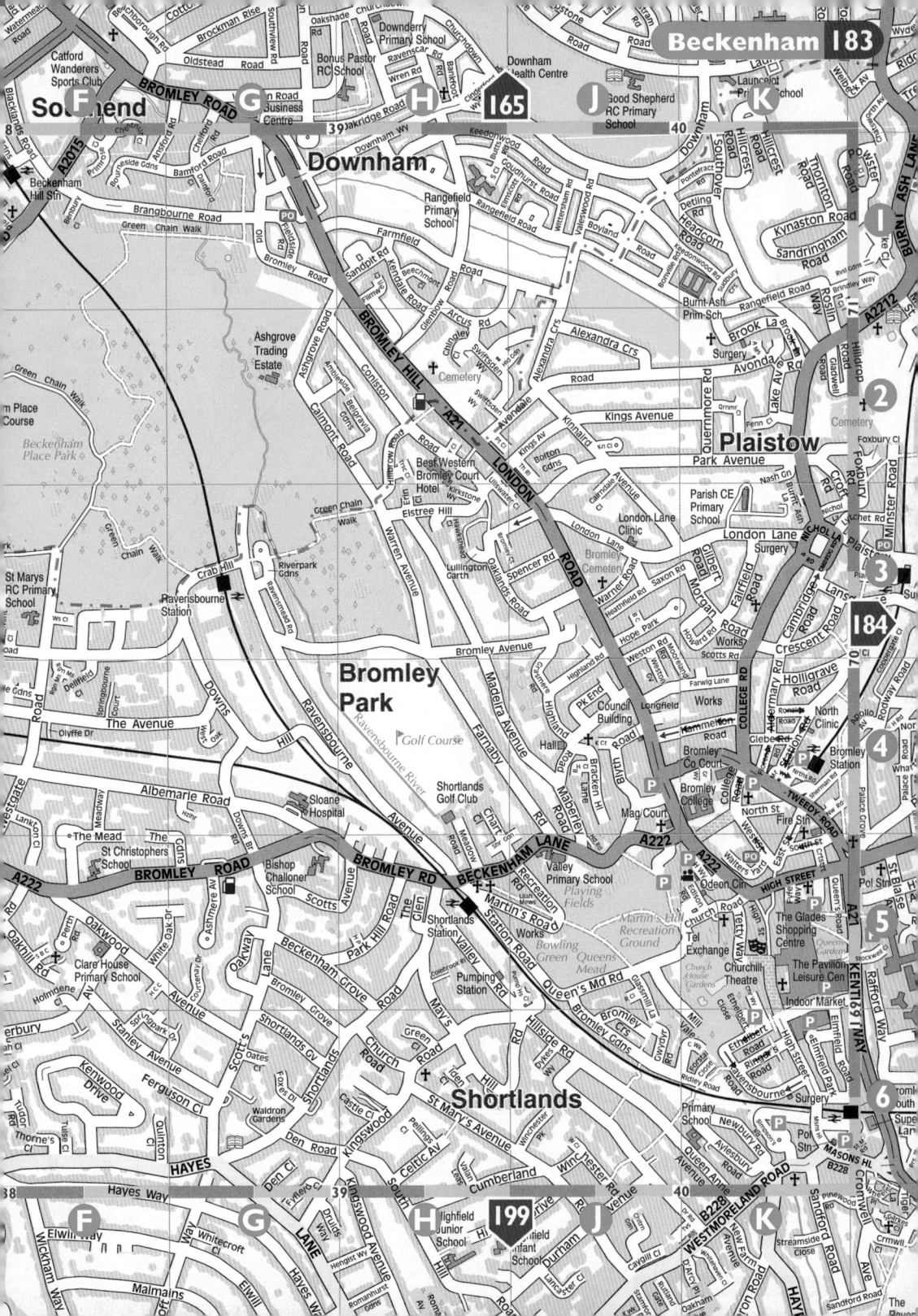

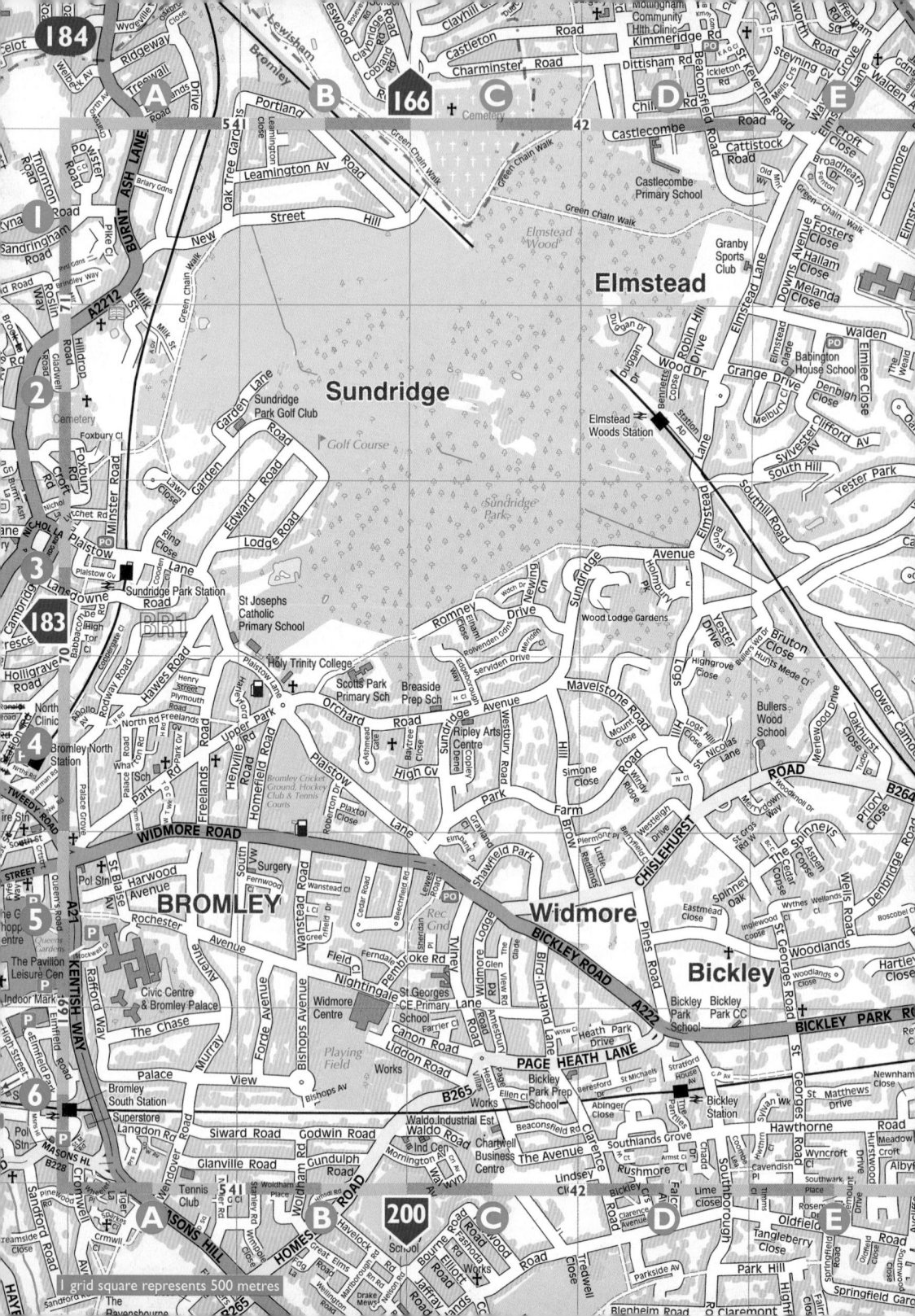

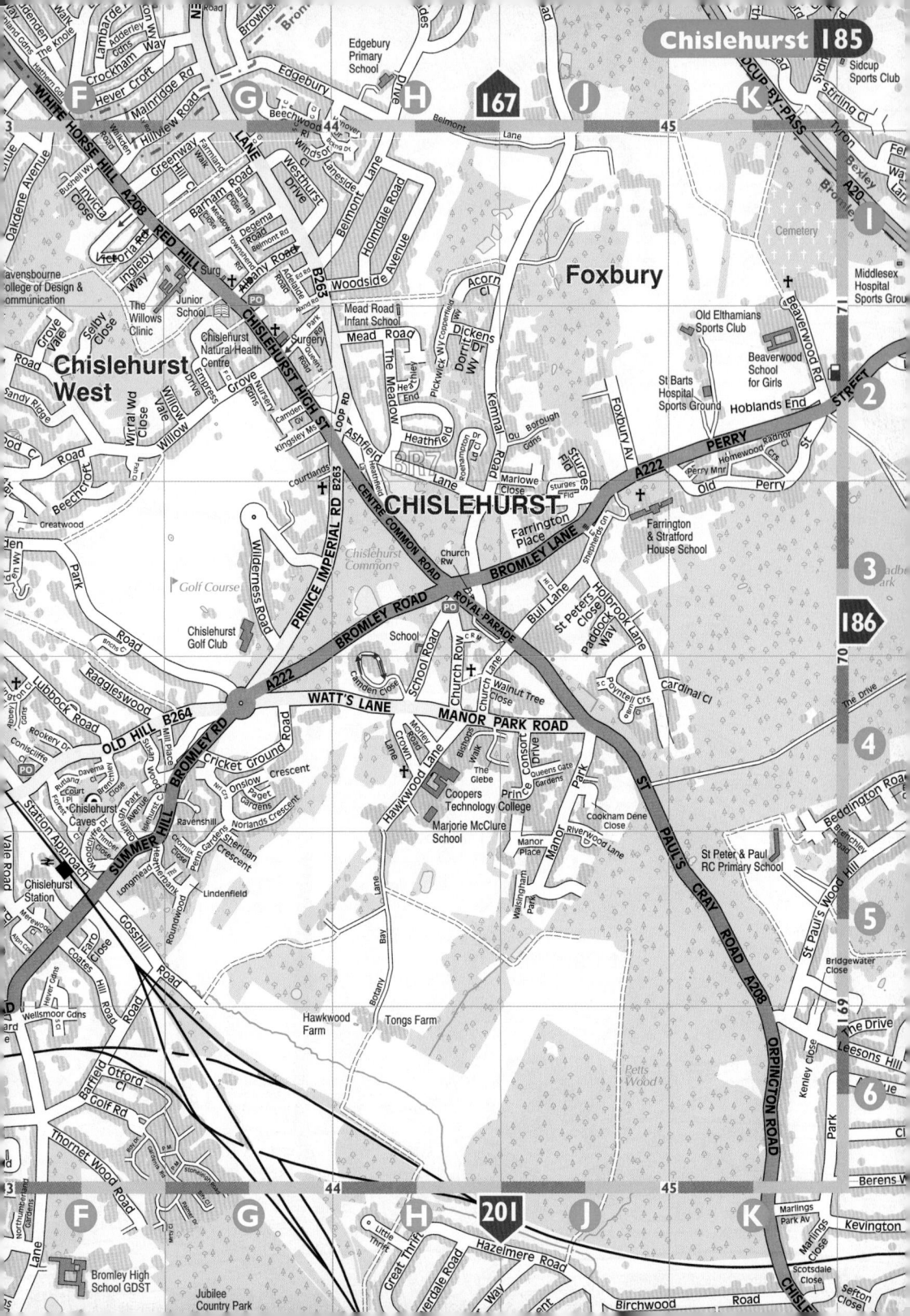

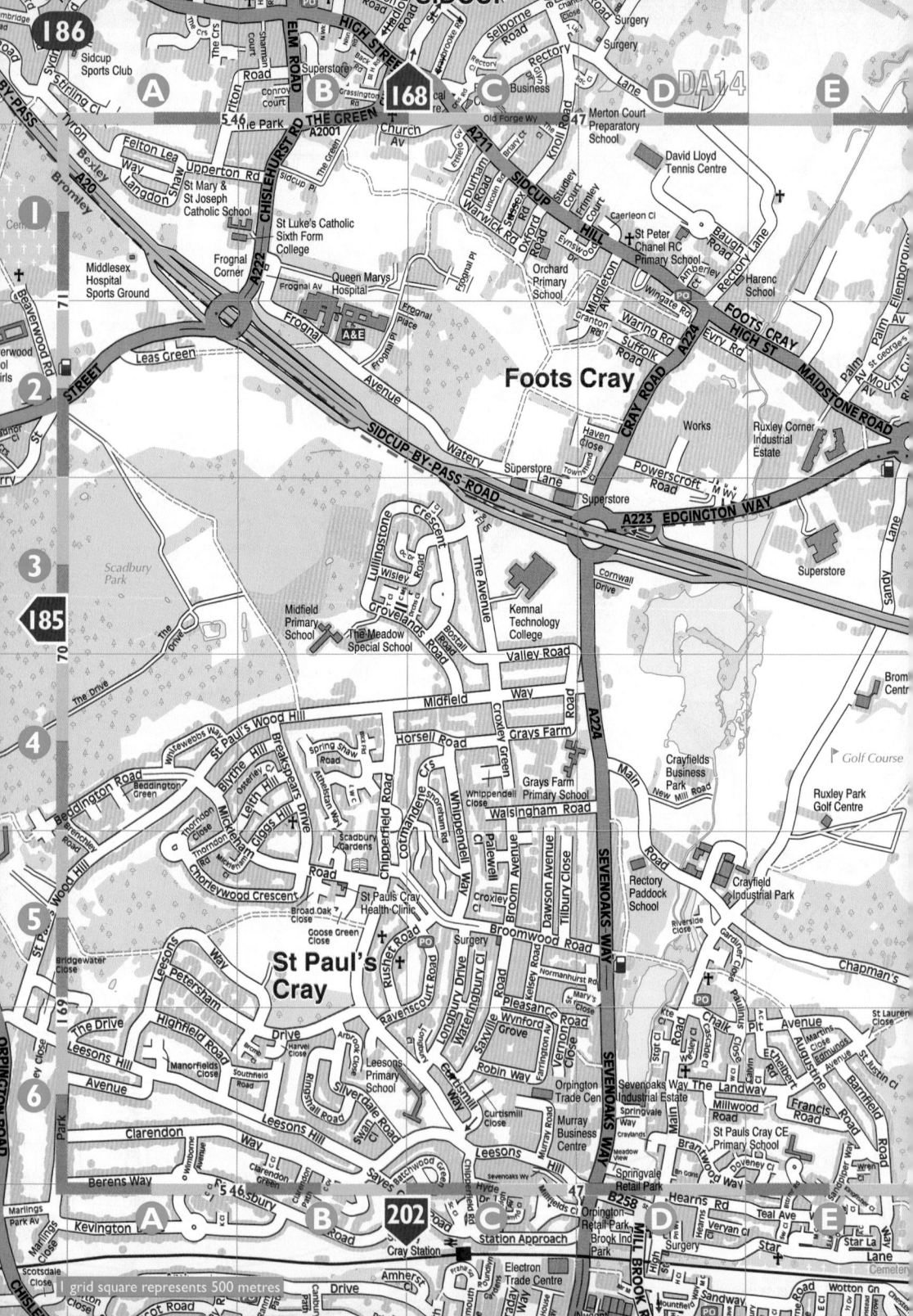

169

203

F G H J K

48 49 50

I
2
3
4
5
6

Ruxley

Stonehill Green

Hockenden

River Cray

The Grove

The Grove

The Spinney

cattons Wy

Cemetery

Parsonage Lane

James St Way

Manor Farm

Bexley Kent County

Norfield Road

Norfield Park

High Beeches

Bedensfield Clinic

PO

Burdett Close

Tower Cl

Thurstand Cl

Butlers Close

arvill Rd

Paddocks Close

Bercta Road

NORTH CRAY ROAD A223

Cray Rd

Honeyden Road

Cornell Close

Barton Rd

Whitney Walk

Golf Course

Birchwood Park Golf Club

Birchwood

Chalk Wood

Bexley

Bromley

MAIDSTONE ROAD

Old Maidstone Road

B2173

A20

A20

B2173

B2173

MAIDSTONE ROAD

Works

Pucknells Close

Upper Hockenden

Cookham Road

Garden Centre

Golf Course

Cray Valley Golf Club

y Ski

Kent County

Bromley

A20

Chapman's Lane

Hockenden Lane

Lane

Star Lane

Sheepcote Lane

Harst Way

Selah Dr

Leydenh

Conifer Way

Russett Way

Wisteri

Walnut

LONDON

Lawn Cl

Woodbine Rd

Crescent Gdns

Ash Cl

Heathwood Gdns

Cedar Close

The Croft

Sermon Drive

Farm Avenue

Laburnam Av

Lyburne Way

Dale Rd

Brook Road

Laven der Hill

Lynden

Mo Cl

Ro Road Way

Cherry Aven

Wd

LONDON A20

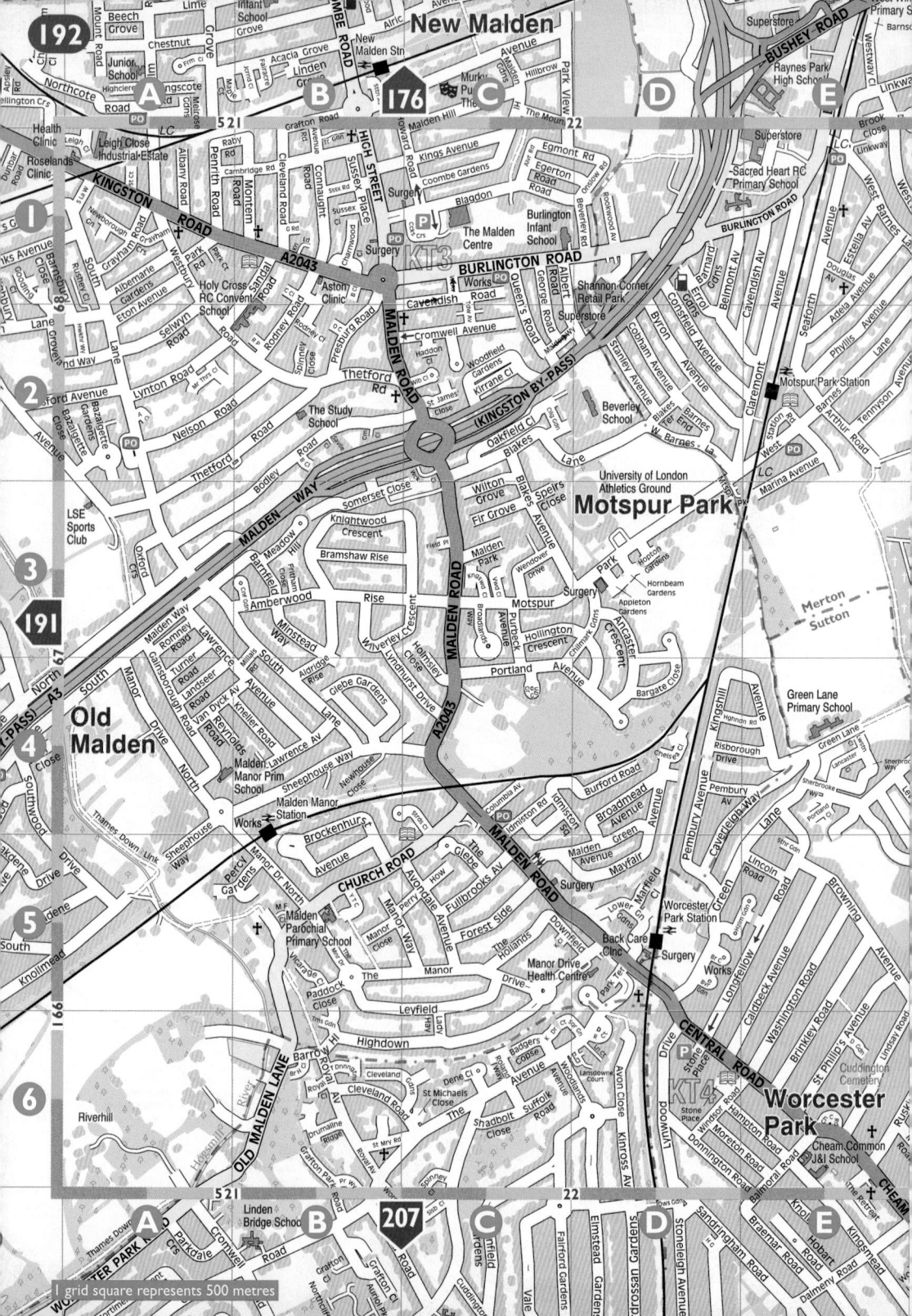

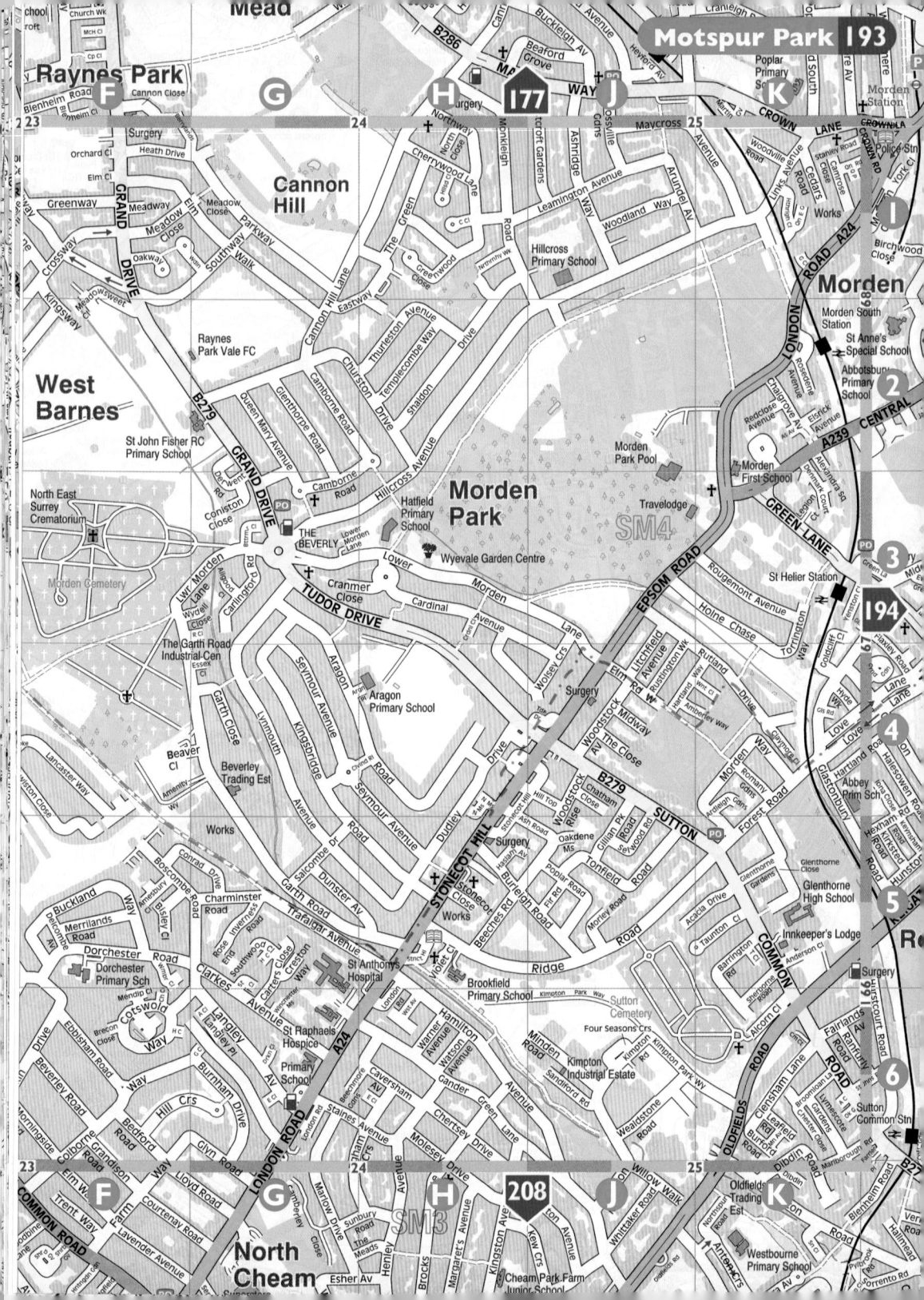

A B Lower Green 189 14 C D A307 E

513 65 15

I

Mill Road Douglas Lower Green Road PO ION ROAD PORTSMOUTH RO

Works
Esher
Station
Thames Ditton &
Esher Golf Club

Couchmo
Montgomery Avenue
Westmont
Summrot Road Hill

KINGSTO

Golf Course

Esher Gn
Drive
Surgery

Sandown Golf
Centre

Esher CE
High School

Sandown Park
Racecourse

PORTSMOUTH ROAD

Littleworth
Common

Littleworth
Close

Heathside

Medina Av

Hasefield

Heathside

Greer

Wayneflete Tower Avenue
Vincent Close
Winchester Av
Lane
More Lane

Sandown Grandstand &
Exhibition Centre

Sandown Sports Club
& Dry Ski Slope

Littleworth Common
Road

Penates

2

Electrical
Trades
Union College

Pelhams
Riverside Dr
Pelhams Walk
The Mall
D'Abernon
Esher Pl
Lytton Close
Esher Gn
Esher Pl Av
Esher Pl Av
Church St
Fennsford
Warren
Cl
Odeon
High St
High St
Hillbrow
Rd
Ashburnham
Park
Littleworth Pl
Littleworth La

New Road
Littleworth Road

Littlemead

Oaken Lane

Manor

ESHER

Civic
Centre

PO
Sandown Road
Martineau Close
Willowmere

3

Drake's
Moore Place
Golf Club
Golf Course

Lammas Lane
Hunting Cl
Clive Rd
Wolsey Road
Clive Rd
Belvedere Close
Broom Cl
Dawes
Grantley Pl
Simmons Ca
Cranford Ri
Esher
Park

Sandown
Av

Broomfields

Acorns
Wy
Rosebriar

Raleigh Dr
Loseberry Rd
Station Rd
Simmil Rd

The Avenue

West End
64
Gdns
Land

Esher Cl

Clare Hl (No2)
Clare Hill
Charlotte
Ct
Fir Tree
Cl
Lynne
Wk
Milbourne
Surgery
Milbourne Junior
School
Esher Church
Prim Sch
PH
Arbrook La
Hare

Judge
Walk
Meadow
Cavendish
Drive
Gdn

The Avenue

KT10

4

Park Close
Neville
Spt Club
Courtlands Avenue
Claremont Av
Hawkshill Way
Hawkshill Rd
The Mount
Old Chestnut Av
Claremont Pk Rd
Pk Road
Claremont Drive
Milbourne La
Orchard Way
Esher Church
Brendon Dr
High Garth
Milbrook

Milbourne
Lodge School

Claygate
Station
The Pde
PO
Athlone
Albans Crs
Torrington Cl
Foley Md

Gordon Road

5

STONY HILL
A307

Claremont
Park

PORTSMOUTH ROAD

Claremont
Fan Court
School

Haymeads
Dr
Home Farm
Cl
Cmbrn
Cl
Copsem
Dr
Lakeside
Dr
Copsem
Wy
Copsem LA
COPSEM LANE

Loseberry
Farm

Claremont Rd
Beaconsfield Cl
Beaconsfield
Qu Anne
Dr

Foley

Beaconsfield

163

Claremont Landscape
Garden (NT)

Arbrook
Common

6

Blackhills
Albany Cl
Meadway

A244

Arbrook
Farm

Birchmeod

513 14 15

A B C D E

Black
Pond

Esher Common

1 grid square represents 500 metres

The gle

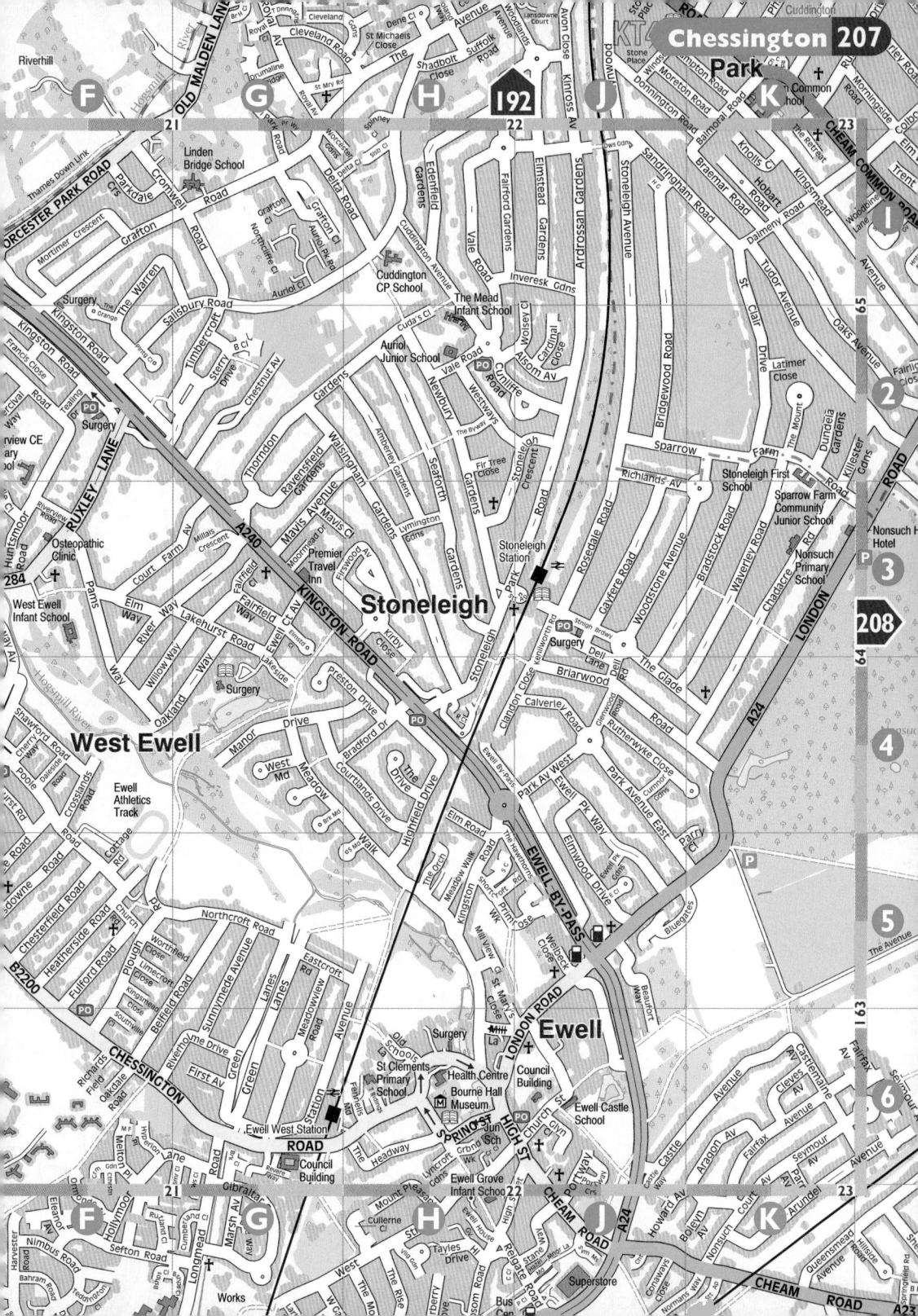

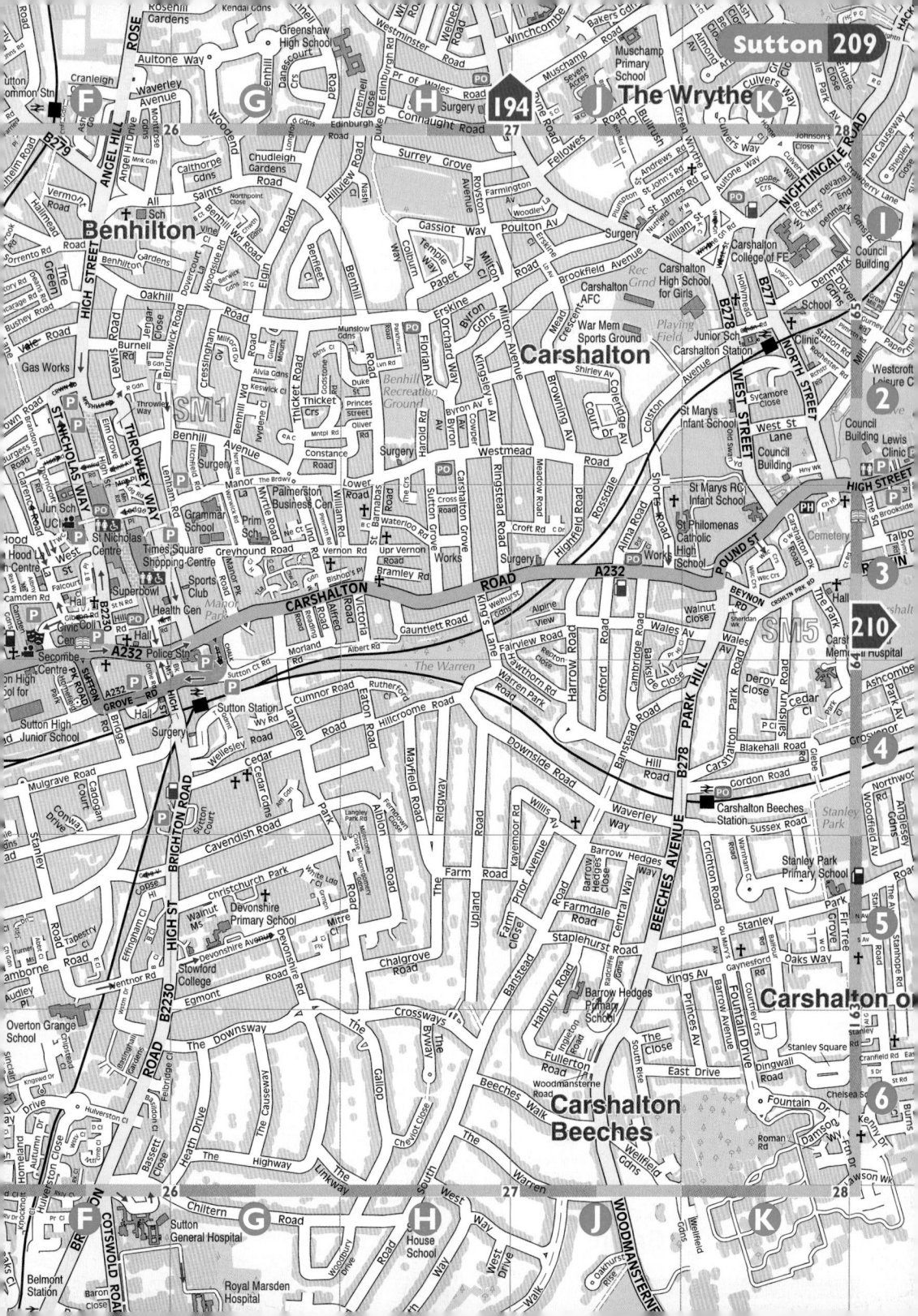

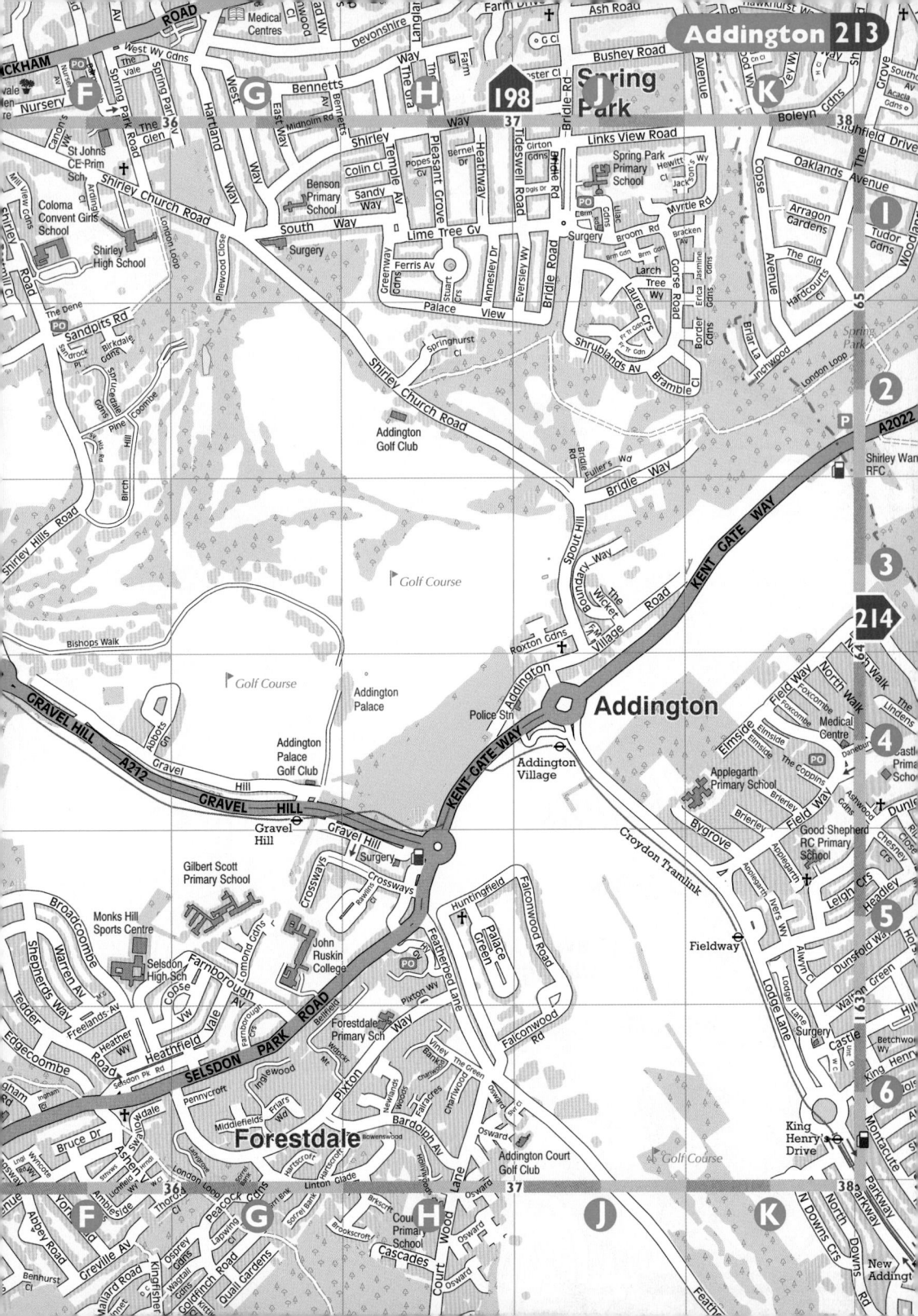

ORPINGTON

Goddington

Pratt's Bottom

Abbey Wood ...128 C4
Acton ...117 K1
Acton Green ...118 A4
Addington ...213 J4
Addiscombe ...197 G4
Aldborough Hatch ...72 E1
Aldersbrook ...71 C5
Alperton ...80 A6
Anerley ...181 H5
Ashford ...152 D6
Avery Hill ...167 H1
Balham ...160 E2
Bandonhill ...210 D3
Barking ...90 D5
Barkingside ...54 B6
Barnehurst ...150 A4
Barnes ...138 E2
Barnes Cray ...150 E5
Barnet ...32 D1
Barnet Gate ...31 G1
Barnsbury ...84 E5
Barwell ...205 J5
Battersea ...140 E1
Bayswater ...101 F6
Beckenham ...182 D5
Beckton ...107 K5
Becontree ...91 K3
Beddington ...195 K6
Beddington Corner ...195 F4
Bedford Park ...118 C3
Belgravia ...15 G6
Bell Green ...164 C5
Bellingham ...164 D6
Belmont ...43 C5
Belmont ...208 E6
Belvedere ...129 J5
Benhilton ...209 F1
Bermondsey ...123 G2
Berrylands ...191 G3
Bethnal Green ...104 D2
Bexley ...148 D5
Bexleyheath ...149 G5
Bickley ...184 D5
Blackfen ...168 A1
Blackheath ...145 J3
Blackheath Park ...145 K5
Blackwall ...106 B6
Bloomsbury ...10 D1
Bow ...105 J1
Bow Common ...105 J4
Bowes Park ...68 E2
Bowmans ...170 C2
Brentford ...116 E6
Brentford End ...116 C6
Brimsdown ...25 G3
Brixton ...142 D3
Broad Green ...196 C4
Brockley ...144 C6
Bromley ...105 K2
Bromley ...184 A5
Bromley Common ...200 C3
Bromley Park ...183 H4
Brompton ...14 C5
Brondesbury ...82 C4
Brondesbury Park ...82 B6
Brook Green ...119 F3
Broom Hill ...202 A4
Brunswick Park ...34 A5
Buckhurst Hill ...39 G5
Burnt Oak ...45 F3
Bushey ...28 C2
Bushey Heath ...28 E2
Bushey Mead ...177 G6
Bush Hill Park ...36 A1
Caldecote Hill ...29 F2
Camberwell ...143 G2
Camden Town ...84 A5
Canary Wharf ...124 D1
Canning Town ...107 F4
Canham Hill ...193 C1
Canonbury ...85 J4
Canons Park ...44 A3
Carpenders Park ...27 K4
Carshalton ...209 J2
Carshalton Beeches ...209 K5
Carshalton on the Hill ...209 G5
Castle Green ...91 J6
Catford ...165 F3
Chadwell Heath ...73 K2
Charlton ...126 C5
Chase Cross ...57 J1
Chattern Hill ...152 E6
Cheam ...208 C3
Chelsea ...121 F5
Chessington ...206 A4
Child's Hill ...64 C6
China Town ...10 C5
Chingford ...38 B3
Chingford Green ...38 A3
Chingford Hatch ...38 C6
Chipping Barnet ...20 B4
Chislehurst ...185 H3
Chislehurst West ...185 F2
Chiswick ...118 C4
Church End ...46 E5
Church End ...81 H5
City of London ...12 B5
Clapham ...141 G3
Clapham Park ...161 J1
Clapton Park ...87 H2
Claremont Park ...204 A5
Claygate ...205 F4
Clayhall ...53 K5
Clerkenwell ...5 J6
Cockfosters ...21 J6
Coldblow ...169 K4
Coldharbour ...150 D4
Cole Park ...156 B1
Colindale ...45 G6
College Park ...99 J2
Collier Row ...56 E4
Collier's Wood ...178 C3
Colney Hatch ...47 K2
Coney Hall ...214 C2
Coombe ...176 B3
Copse Hill ...176 D3
Cottenham Park ...176 E4

Cranbrook ...72 A4
Cranford ...133 K1
Cranley Gardens ...66 A1
Crayford ...150 D6
Creekmouth ...108 E4
Cricklewood ...82 B2
Crockenhill ...205 K3
Crofton ...201 J6
Crooked Billet ...176 E2
Crouch End ...66 C5
Croydon ...211 K1
Crystal Palace ...181 H2
Cubitt Town ...125 F4
Custom House ...107 J6
Dagenham ...92 D5
Dalston ...86 B5
Dartford ...171 F2
Dartmouth Park ...66 A6
Deacons Hill ...30 C1
De Beauvoir Town ...86 A6
Deptford ...124 C6
Derry Downs ...202 E3
Dollis Hill ...81 K1
Dormer's Wells ...96 B6
Downham ...183 G1
Ducks Island ...32 B2
Dudden Hill ...81 J2
Dulwich ...163 G4
Dulwich Village ...163 F2
Ealing ...97 J6
Earl's Court ...119 K5
Earlsfield ...160 B3
East Acton ...99 H6
East Barnet ...33 H2
East Bedfont ...152 E2
Eastbury ...26 D6
Eastcote ...59 F4
Eastcote Village ...59 F2
East Dulwich ...143 H6
East Finchley ...47 H6
East Ham ...107 J1
East Molesey ...189 H2
East Sheen ...138 A6
East Wickham ...148 B2
Eden Park ...198 C1
Edgware ...44 D2
Edmonton ...36 A6
Elmers End ...182 A6
Elm Park ...93 K3
Elmstead ...184 D1
Elstree ...30 A1
Eltham ...166 D1
Enfield ...23 J5
Enfield Highway ...24 E3
Enfield Island Village ...25 K1
Enfield Town ...23 K4
Enfield Wash ...25 G1
Erith ...130 C5
Esher ...204 C2
Ewell ...207 J6
Fair Cross ...91 F5
Fairlop ...54 E4
Falconwood ...147 K5
Farnborough ...216 A3
Feltham ...154 A4
Field Common ...188 E4
Finchley ...46 E4
Finsbury ...5 J4
Finsbury Park ...66 E6
Foots Cray ...186 C2
Forestdale ...213 G6
Forest Gate ...88 E3
Forest Hill ...164 A5
Fortis Green ...65 K1
Forty Hill ...24 B2
Foxbury ...185 J1
Friday Hill ...38 B5
Friern Barnet ...33 J6
Fulham ...139 G1
Fullwell Cross ...54 D4
Furzedown ...161 G6
Gants Hill ...71 K3
Gidea Park ...57 H5
Giggshill ...190 B4
Globe Town ...105 F2
Goddington ...217 J1
Golders Green ...64 C3
Goodmayes ...73 H6
Gospel Oak ...84 B2
Grange Hill ...54 D2
Grange Park ...23 G6
Greenford ...96 D3
Greenhill ...61 F2
Green Street Green ...216 E5
Greenwich ...125 G5
Grove Park ...138 A2
Grove Park ...166 B5
Hackbridge ...195 G6
Hackney ...86 E5
Hackney Wick ...87 J4
Hadley ...20 E4
Hadley Wood ...21 H1
Haggerston ...7 K2
Hainault ...55 F3
Hale End ...52 B2
Ham ...156 E5
Hammersmith ...118 E4
Hampstead ...83 H2
Hampstead Garden Suburb ...65 F2
Hampton ...173 G4
Hampton Hill ...155 H6
Hampton Wick ...174 C4
Hanwell ...115 J1
Hanworth ...154 C5
Harlesden ...99 G1
Harlington ...113 F6
Harringay ...67 G2
Harrow ...60 E5
Harrow on the Hill ...60 E5
Harrow Weald ...42 E3
Hatch End ...41 J3
Hatton ...133 H5
Hayes ...94 A4
Hayes ...200 A4
Hayes End ...94 B3
Hayes Town ...114 B1
Headstone ...60 B1

Heath Park ...75 K3
Heath Side ...170 C4
Hendon ...63 K2
Herne Hill ...162 D1
Heston ...134 E1
Higham Hill ...51 G5
Highams Park ...51 K3
High Barnet ...20 A4
Highbury ...85 H5
Highgate ...66 B3
Highwood Hill ...31 H4
Hinchley Wood ...205 F1
Hither Green ...165 H1
Hockenden ...187 J6
Holborn ...11 G2
Holders Hill ...46 B4
Holwell ...26 C1
Homerton ...87 F4
Honor Oak ...164 A1
Honor Oak Park ...164 B1
Hook ...206 A3
Hook Green ...170 C6
Hornsey ...66 E1
Hornsey Vale ...67 F2
Hounslow ...135 F3
Hounslow West ...134 C4
Hoxton ...7 J2
Hurst Park ...173 H5
Ilford ...90 B1
Isle of Dogs ...125 F4
Isleworth ...136 C4
Islington ...85 G6
Joydens Wood ...170 C6
Kennington ...121 K6
Kensal Green ...100 A1
Kensal Rise ...100 B1
Kensal Town ...100 C3
Kensington ...119 K3
Kentish Town ...84 B4
Kenton ...61 J2
Keston ...215 H2
Keston Mark ...215 H1
Kevingtown ...203 G3
Kew ...137 G1
Kidbrooke ...146 B3
Kilburn ...82 C6
Kingsbury ...62 D3
Kingsland ...86 A5
Kingston upon Thames ...174 D6
Kingston Vale ...176 A1
Kitt's End ...20 C1
Knightsbridge ...14 D2
Knight's Hill ...162 D5
Ladywell ...144 D5
Lambeth ...17 J4
Lampton ...135 G2
Lea Bridge ...87 F1
Lee ...165 J1
Lessness Heath ...129 J6
Lewisham ...145 F5
Leyton ...88 B1
Leytonstone ...70 D5
Limehouse ...105 G6
Lisson Grove ...8 B5
Little Heath ...73 J1
Little Ilford ...90 A3
Little Stanmore ...44 B4
Locksbottom ...216 B1
Long Ditton ...190 D5
Longlands ...167 H5
Lower Clapton ...86 E2
Lower Edmonton ...36 A4
Lower Feltham ...153 H5
Lower Green ...189 G6
Lower Holloway ...85 F3
Lower Place ...98 E1
Lower Sydenham ...164 A6
Loxford ...90 C3
Maida Vale ...100 E2
Maitland Park ...83 K4
Manor Park ...89 J2
Marks Gate ...56 A5
Marylebone ...9 G2
Mayfair ...9 J6
Maypole ...170 B3
Merry Hill ...28 B3
Merton ...177 K4
Merton Park ...177 J5
Mile End ...105 G3
Mill Hill ...45 J1
Mill Meads ...106 B1
Millwall ...124 D3
Mitcham ...179 F6
Monken Hadley ...20 C3
Monks Orchard ...197 K4
Moor Park ...26 A6
Morden ...193 K1
Morden Park ...193 H3
Mortlake ...137 K3
Motspur Park ...192 D3
Mottingham ...166 B4
Muswell Hill ...48 A5
Nash ...215 F4
Neasden ...81 F2
New Addington ...214 B5
New Barnet ...21 F6
New Beckenham ...182 B2
Newbury Park ...72 D5
New Charlton ...126 C4
New Cross ...144 B3
New Cross Gate ...144 B2
New Eltham ...167 G4
Newington ...17 K5
New Malden ...176 A4
New Town ...171 J1
Noel Park ...49 H5
Norbiton ...175 G5
Norbury ...180 C5
North Acton ...98 E3
North Cheam ...208 B1
North Cray ...169 H5
North End ...64 D6
North End ...150 C2
North Feltham ...134 A6
North Finchley ...47 G2
North Harrow ...59 K3

North Hyde ...114 D4
North Kensington ...100 B4
Northolt ...78 A5
North Sheen ...137 H4
Northumberland Heath ...149 K1
North Wembley ...61 H5
Northwood ...40 A4
Northwood Hills ...40 B5
North Woolwich ...126 D2
Norwood Green ...115 F4
Norwood New Town ...181 F5
Notting Hill ...100 C6
Nunhead ...143 K5
Oakleigh Park ...33 H4
Oakwood ...34 D1
Old Bexley ...169 H2
Old Ford ...87 G6
Old Malden ...192 A4
Old Oak Common ...99 H3
Orpington ...202 B6
Osidge ...34 C4
Osterley ...135 H1
Oxhey ...27 H1
Paddington ...8 A2
Palmers Green ...34 E5
Park Langley ...199 F3
Park Royal ...98 C2
Parsons Green ...139 K3
Peckham ...143 J3
Penge ...181 K3
Pentonville ...5 H2
Perivale ...79 J6
Petersham ...157 F3
Petts Wood ...201 J1
Pimlico ...121 H5
Pinner ...59 H1
Pinner Green ...41 G5
Pinnerwood Park ...41 G3
Plaistow ...106 D2
Plaistow ...183 K2
Plashet ...89 H4
Plumstead ...127 H5
Plumstead Common ...128 A6
Ponders End ...24 E6
Poplar ...105 J6
Poverest ...202 B1
Preston ...61 K5
Primrose Hill ...68 C5
Purfleet ...131 K5
Putney ...159 G2
Putney Heath ...159 F5
Putney Vale ...158 D5
Queensbury ...44 B6
Queen's Park ...100 C1
Rainham ...111 K2
Ramsden ...202 D5
Rayners Lane ...59 K5
Raynes Park ...177 F6
Redbridge ...71 G2
Regent's Park ...3 K3
Richmond ...137 F6
Richmond Hill ...157 F1
Rise Park ...57 G4
Roehampton ...158 B3
Romford ...74 E2
Rosehill ...194 A5
Rotherhithe ...124 A3
Roundshaw ...211 F4
Ruislip ...58 C3
Ruislip Common ...58 A1
Ruislip Gardens ...76 C1
Ruislip Manor ...58 E6
Rush Green ...75 F4
Rydens ...188 B6
St Paul's Cray ...186 B5
St George in the East ...104 C6
St Giles ...10 D3
St Helier ...194 B5
St James's ...16 C1
St Johns ...144 D3
St John's Wood ...2 A2
St Luke's ...6 D6
St Margarets ...156 D1
St Mary Cray ...202 D2
St Pancras ...5 F5
Sands End ...140 B2
Seething Wells ...190 C3
Selhurst ...196 E2
Seven Kings ...72 E5
Shacklewell ...86 C2
Shadwell ...104 E6
Shepherd's Bush ...118 E1
Shirley ...197 K6
Shooters Hill ...147 H2
Shoreditch ...7 F5
Shortlands ...183 H6
Sidcup ...168 C6
Silvertown ...126 B2
Sipson ...112 C5
Slade Green ...150 D3
Soho ...10 C4
Somers Town ...4 C3
Southall ...114 C2
South Beddington ...210 D4
Southborough ...200 E3
South Bromley ...106 B5
South Croydon ...211 H4
Southend ...165 F6
Southfields ...159 K3
Southgate ...34 E3
South Hackney ...86 E6
South Harrow ...78 B1
South Hornchurch ...93 F6
South Kensington ...120 B5
South Lambeth ...141 K1
South Norwood ...180 E6
South Oxhey ...27 K1
South Ruislip ...77 H2
South Tottenham ...68 A3
South Wimbledon ...178 B1
South Woodford ...52 E5
Spitalfields ...13 J1
Spring Grove ...135 J2
Spring Park ...198 D6

Stamford Hill ...68 B4
Stanmore ...43 H1
Stanwell ...152 A1
Stepney ...104 E4
Stockwell ...141 K4
Stoke Newington ...68 B6
Stonehill Green ...187 K2
Stoneleigh ...207 H3
Strand ...10 E5
Stratford ...88 A5
Stratford Marsh ...88 A4
Stratford New Town ...88 A4
Strawberry Hill ...155 J5
Streatham ...179 K1
Streatham Hill ...161 K3
Streatham Park ...161 H6
Streatham Vale ...179 G3
Stroud Green ...67 G3
Sudbury ...79 F3
Summerstown ...160 C4
Sundridge ...184 B2
Surbiton ...190 E5
Sutton ...208 E3
Swiss Cottage ...83 H6
Sydenham ...182 A1
Teddington ...173 J2
Temple Hill ...151 G5
Temple Mills ...87 K3
Thames Ditton ...190 B4
Thamesmead ...109 F6
The Borough ...18 D3
The Hyde ...63 H2
The Rookery ...26 E2
The Wrythe ...194 D6
Thornton Heath ...180 C6
Tokyngton ...80 D4
Tolworth ...191 H5
Tooting ...178 E1
Tooting Graveney ...178 C1
Tottenham ...50 A5
Tottenham Hale ...50 B6
Totteridge ...32 E3
Totteridge Green ...32 A3
Tufnell Park ...84 C2
Tulse Hill ...162 C3
Twickenham ...156 D3
Underhill ...32 E1
Upper Clapton ...68 C5
Upper Edmonton ...36 C6
Upper Elmers End ...198 C2
Upper Holloway ...66 C5
Upper Norwood ...180 E4
Upper Shirley ...212 A1
Upper Sydenham ...163 H6
Upper Tooting ...160 D5
Upper Walthamstow ...70 A1
Upton ...88 C3
Upton Park ...89 F3
Vale of Health ...83 H1
Vauxhall ...121 K5
Waddon ...195 K6
Walham Green ...139 K2
Wallend ...90 A6
Wallington ...210 A3
Walthamstow ...69 K2
Walworth ...122 D6
Wandle Park ...196 B6
Wandsworth ...139 K5
Wanstead ...71 F4
Wapping ...123 J1
Watford Heath ...27 J2
Wealdstone ...43 G6
Welling ...148 C4
Welsh Harp ...63 F5
Wembley ...80 A2
Wembley Park ...80 C1
West Acton ...98 C5
West Barnes ...193 F2
West Bedfont ...152 C2
Westbourne Green ...100 E3
West Brompton ...120 A6
West Drayton ...112 A3
West Dulwich ...162 E4
West Ealing ...116 B1
West Ewell ...207 F4
West Green ...49 J6
West Hampstead ...82 E3
West Harrow ...60 C4
West Heath ...65 F6
West Heath ...128 E6
West Hendon ...63 J4
West Hill ...159 H2
West Kensington ...119 G5
West Kilburn ...100 C3
Westminster ...16 B5
West Molesey ...188 E1
West Norwood ...162 D6
Weston Green ...189 K5
West Ruislip ...58 A5
West Wickham ...199 G5
Whetstone ...33 F4
Whitechapel ...13 K5
Whitton ...155 H1
Widmore ...184 C5
Willesden ...81 K5
Willesden Green ...81 K6
Wilmington ...170 E6
Wimbledon ...177 H1
Winchmore Hill ...35 H5
Wood End ...94 C5
Wood End Green ...94 C4
Woodford ...52 F2
Woodford Bridge ...53 K3
Woodford Green ...52 E3
Woodford Wells ...39 F5
Wood Green ...49 G4
Woodlands ...135 J3
Woodside ...197 H3
Woodside Park ...32 E6
Woolwich ...127 F6
Worcester Park ...192 E6
World's End ...23 G5
Yeading ...95 G3

USING THE STREET INDEX

Street names are listed alphabetically. Each street name is followed by its postal town or area locality, the Postcode District, the page number, and the reference to the square in which the name is found.

Standard index entries are shown as follows:

Aaron Hill Rd *EHAM* E6 ....**108** A4

Street names and selected addresses not shown on the map due to scale restrictions are shown in the index with an asterisk:

Abbeville Ms *CLAP* SW4 * **141** J6

GENERAL ABBREVIATIONS

ACC	ACCESS	CUTT	CUTTINGS	HOL	HOLLOW	NW	NORTH WEST
ALY	ALLEY	CV	COVE	HOSP	HOSPITAL	O/P	OVERPASS
AP	APPROACH	CYN	CANYON	HRB	HARBOUR	OFF	OFFICE
AR	ARCADE	DEPT	DEPARTMENT	HTH	HEATH	ORCH	ORCHARD
ASS	ASSOCIATION	DL	DALE	HTS	HEIGHTS	OV	OVAL
AV	AVENUE	DM	DAM	HVN	HAVEN	PAL	PALACE
BCH	BEACH	DR	DRIVE	HWY	HIGHWAY	PAS	PASSAGE
BLDS	BUILDINGS	DRO	DROVE	IMP	IMPERIAL	PAV	PAVILION
BND	BEND	DRY	DRIVEWAY	IN	INLET	PDE	PARADE
BNK	BANK	DWGS	DWELLINGS	IND EST	INDUSTRIAL ESTATE	PH	PUBLIC HOUSE
BR	BRIDGE	E	EAST	INF	INFIRMARY	PK	PARK
BRK	BROOK	EMB	EMBANKMENT	INFO	INFORMATION	PKWY	PARKWAY
BTM	BOTTOM	EMBY	EMBASSY	INT	INTERCHANGE	PL	PLACE
BUS	BUSINESS	ESP	ESPLANADE	IS	ISLAND	PLN	PLAIN
BVD	BOULEVARD	EST	ESTATE	JCT	JUNCTION	PLNS	PLAINS
BY	BYPASS	EX	EXCHANGE	JTY	JETTY	PLZ	PLAZA
CATH	CATHEDRAL	EXPY	EXPRESSWAY	KG	KING	POL	POLICE STATION
CEM	CEMETERY	EXT	EXTENSION	KNL	KNOLL	PR	PRINCE
CEN	CENTRE	F/O	FLYOVER	L	LAKE	PREC	PRECINCT
CFT	CROFT	FC	FOOTBALL CLUB	LA	LANE	PREP	PREPARATORY
CH	CHURCH	FK	FORK	LDG	LODGE	PRIM	PRIMARY
CHA	CHASE	FLD	FIELD	LGT	LIGHT	PROM	PROMENADE
CHYD	CHURCHYARD	FLDS	FIELDS	LK	LOCK	PRS	PRINCESS
CIR	CIRCLE	FLS	FALLS	LKS	LAKES	PRT	PORT
CIRC	CIRCUS	FM	FARM	LNDG	LANDING	PT	POINT
CL	CLOSE	FT	FORT	LTL	LITTLE	PTH	PATH
CLFS	CLIFFS	FTS	FLATS	LWR	LOWER	PZ	PIAZZA
CMP	CAMP	FWY	FREEWAY	MAG	MAGISTRATE	QD	QUADRANT
CNR	CORNER	FY	FERRY	MAN	MANSIONS	QU	QUEEN
CO	COUNTY	GA	GATE	MD	MEAD	QY	QUAY
COLL	COLLEGE	GAL	GALLERY	MDW	MEADOWS	R	RIVER
COM	COMMON	GDN	GARDEN	MEM	MEMORIAL	RBT	ROUNDABOUT
COMM	COMMISSION	GDNS	GARDENS	MI	MILL	RD	ROAD
CON	CONVENT	GLD	GLADE	MKT	MARKET	RDG	RIDGE
COT	COTTAGE	GLN	GLEN	MKTS	MARKETS	REP	REPUBLIC
COTS	COTTAGES	GN	GREEN	ML	MALL	RES	RESERVOIR
CP	CAPE	GND	GROUND	MNR	MANOR	RFC	RUGBY FOOTBALL CLUB
CPS	COPSE	GRA	GRANGE	MS	MEWS	RI	RISE
CR	CREEK	GRG	GARAGE	MSN	MISSION	RP	RAMP
CREM	CREMATORIUM	GT	GREAT	MT	MOUNT	RW	ROW
CRS	CRESCENT	GTWY	GATEWAY	MTN	MOUNTAIN	S	SOUTH
CSWY	CAUSEWAY	GV	GROVE	MTS	MOUNTAINS	SCH	SCHOOL
CT	COURT	HGR	HIGHER	MUS	MUSEUM	SE	SOUTH EAST
CTRL	CENTRAL	HL	HILL	MWY	MOTORWAY	SER	SERVICE AREA
CTS	COURTS	HLS	HILLS	N	NORTH	SH	SHORE
CTYD	COURTYARD	HO	HOUSE	NE	NORTH EAST	SHOP	SHOPPING

SKWY	SKYWAY
SMT	SUMMIT
SOC	SOCIETY
SP	SPUR
SPR	SPRING
SQ	SQUARE
ST	STREET
STN	STATION
STR	STREAM
STRD	STRAND
SW	SOUTH WEST
TDG	TRADING
TER	TERRACE
THWY	THROUGHWAY
TNL	TUNNEL
TOLL	TOLLWAY
TPK	TURNPIKE
TR	TRACK
TRL	TRAIL
TWR	TOWER
U/P	UNDERPASS
UNI	UNIVERSITY
UPR	UPPER
VA	VALE
VIAD	VIADUCT
VIL	VILLA
VIS	VISTA
VLG	VILLAGE
VLS	VILLAS
VW	VIEW
W	WEST
WD	WOOD
WHF	WHARF
WK	WALK
WKS	WALKS
WLS	WELLS
WY	WAY
YD	YARD
YHA	YOUTH HOSTEL

POSTCODE TOWNS AND AREA ABBREVIATIONS

ABR/ST	Abridge/Stapleford Abbotts	CEND/HSY/T	Crouch End/Hornsey/Turnpike Lane	FELT	Feltham
ABYW	Abbey Wood	CHARL	Charlton	FENCHST	Fenchurch Street
ACT	Acton	CHCR	Charing Cross	FITZ	Fitzrovia
ALP/SUD	Alperton/Sudbury	CHDH	Chadwell Heath	FLST/FETLN	Fleet Street/Fetter Lane
ARCH	Archway	CHEAM	Cheam	FNCH	Finchley
ASHF	Ashford (Surrey)	CHEL	Chelsea	FSBYE	Finsbury east
BAL	Balham	CHIG	Chigwell	FSBYPK	Finsbury Park
BANK	Bank	CHING	Chingford	FSBYW	Finsbury west
BAR	Barnet	CHSGTN	Chessington	FSTGT	Forest Gate
BARB	Barbican	CHST	Chislehurst	FSTH	Forest Hill
BARK	Barking	CHSWK	Chiswick	FUL/PGN	Fulham/Parsons Green
BARK/HLT	Barkingside/Hainault	CITYW	City of London west	GDMY/SEVK	Goodmayes/Seven Kings
BARN	Barnes	CLAP	Clapham	GFD/PVL	Greenford/Perivale
BAY/PAD	Bayswater/Paddington	CLAY	Clayhall	GINN	Gray's Inn
BCTR	Becontree	CLKNW	Clerkenwell	GLDGN	Golders Green
BECK	Beckenham	CLPT	Clapton	GNTH/NBYPK	Gants Hill/Newbury Park
BELMT	Belmont	CMBW	Camberwell	GNWCH	Greenwich
BELV	Belvedere	CONDST	Conduit Street	GPK	Gidea Park
BERM/RHTH	Bermondsey/Rotherhithe	COVGDN	Covent Garden	GTPST	Great Portland Street
BETH	Bethnal Green	CRICK	Cricklewood	GWRST	Gower Street
BFN/LL	Blackfen/Longlands	CROY/NA	Croydon/New Addington	HACK	Hackney
BGVA	Belgravia	CRW	Collier Row	HAMP	Hampstead
BKHH	Buckhurst Hill	DAGE	Dagenham east	HARH	Harold Hill
BKHTH/KID	Blackheath/Kidbrooke	DAGW	Dagenham west	HAYES	Hayes
BLKFR	Blackfriars	DART	Dartford	HBRY	Highbury
BMLY	Bromley	DEN/HRF	Denham/Harefield	HCH	Hornchurch
BMSBY	Bloomsbury	DEPT	Deptford	HCIRC	Holborn Circus
BORE	Borehamwood	DUL	Dulwich	HDN	Hendon
BOW	Bow	E/WMO/HCT	East & West Molesey/Hampton Court	HDTCH	Houndsditch
BROCKY	Brockley	EA	Ealing	HEST	Heston
BRXN/ST	Brixton north/Stockwell	EBAR	East Barnet	HGDN/ICK	Hillingdon/Ickenham
BRXS/STRHM	Brixton south/Streatham Hill	EBED/NFELT	East Bedfont/North Feltham	HGT	Highgate
BRYLDS	Berrylands	ECT	Earl's Court	HHOL	High Holborn
BTFD	Brentford	ED	Edmonton	HMSMTH	Hammersmith
BTSEA	Battersea	EDGW	Edgware	HNHL	Herne Hill
BUSH	Bushey	EDUL	East Dulwich	HNWL	Hanwell
BXLY	Bexley	EFNCH	East Finchley	HOL/ALD	Holborn/Aldwych
BXLYHN	Bexleyheath north	EHAM	East Ham	HOLWY	Holloway
BXLYHS	Bexleyheath south	ELTH/MOT	Eltham/Mottingham	HOM	Homerton
CAMTN	Camden Town	EMB	Embankment	HOR/WEW	Horton/West Ewell
CAN/RD	Canning Town/Royal Docks	EMPK	Emerson Park	HPTN	Hampton
CANST	Cannon Street station	EN	Enfield	HRW	Harrow
CAR	Carshalton	ENC/FH	Enfield Chase/Forty Hill	HSLW	Hounslow
CAT	Catford	ERITH	Erith	HSLWW	Hounslow west
CAVSQ/HST	Cavendish Square/Harley Street	ERITHM	Erith Marshes	HTHAIR	Heathrow Airport
CDALE/KGS	Colindale/Kingsbury	ESH/CLAY	Esher/Claygate	HYS/HAR	Hayes/Harlington
		EW	Ewell	IL	Ilford
		FARR	Farringdon	IS	Islington
		FBAR/BDGN	Friern Barnet/Bounds Green	ISLW	Isleworth

KENS	Kensington	PEND	Ponders End		
KIL/WHAMP	Kilburn/West Hampstead	PGE/AN	Penge/Anerley		
KTBR	Knightsbridge	PIM	Pimlico		
KTN/HRWW/WS	Kenton/Harrow Weald/Wealdstone	PIN	Pinner		
		PLMGR	Palmers Green		
KTTN	Kentish Town	PLSTW	Plaistow		
KUT/HW	Kingston upon Thames/Hampton Wick	POP/IOD	Poplar/Isle of Dogs		
KUTN/CMB	Kingston upon Thames north/Coombe	PUR	Purfleet		
		PUR/KEN	Purley/Kenley		
LBTH	Lambeth	PUT/ROE	Putney/Roehampton		
LEE/GVPK	Lee/Grove Park	RAIN	Rainham (Gt Lon)		
LEW	Lewisham	RCH/KEW	Richmond/Kew		
LEY	Leyton	RCHPK/HAM	Richmond Park/Ham		
LINN	Lincoln's Inn	RDART	Rural Dartford		
LOTH	Lothbury	REDBR	Redbridge		
LOU	Loughton	REGST	Regent Street		
LSQ/SEVD	Leicester Square/Seven Dials	RKW/CH/CXG	Rickmansworth/Chorleywood/Croxley Green		
LVPST	Liverpool Street	ROM	Romford		
MANHO	Mansion House	ROMW/RG	Romford west/Rush Green		
MBLAR	Marble Arch	RSEV	Rural Sevenoaks		
MHST	Marylebone High Street	RSLP	Ruislip		
MLHL	Mill Hill	RSQ	Russell Square		
MNPK	Manor Park	RYLN/HDSTN	Rayners Lane/Headstone		
MON	Monument	RYNPK	Raynes Park		
MORT/ESHN	Mortlake/East Sheen	SAND/SEL	Sanderstead/Selsdon		
MRDN	Morden	SCUP	Sidcup		
MTCM	Mitcham	SDTCH	Shoreditch		
MUSWH	Muswell Hill	SEVS/STOTM	Seven Sisters/South Tottenham		
MV/WKIL	Maida Vale/West Kilburn	SHB	Shepherd's Bush		
MYFR/PICC	Mayfair/Piccadilly	SKENS	South Kensington		
MYFR/PKLN	Mayfair/Park Lane	SNWD	South Norwood		
NFNCH/WDSPK	North Finchley/Woodside Park	SOCK/AV	South Ockendon/Aveley		
NKENS	North Kensington	SOHO/CST	Soho/Carnaby Street		
NOXST/BSQ	New Oxford Street/Bloomsbury Square	SOHO/SHAV	Soho/Shaftesbury Avenue		
NRWD	Norwood	SRTFD	Stratford		
NTGHL	Notting Hill	STAN	Stanmore		
NTHLT	Northolt	STBT	St Bart's		
NTHWD	Northwood	STHGT/OAK	Southgate/Oakwood		
NWCR	New Cross	STHL	Southall		
NWDGN	Norwood Green	STHWK	Southwark		
NWMAL	New Malden	STJS	St James's		
OBST	Old Broad Street	STJSPK	St James's Park		
ORP	Orpington	STJWD	St John's Wood		
OXHEY	Oxhey	STKPK	Stockley Park		
OXSTW	Oxford Street west	STLK	St Luke's		
PECK	Peckham	STMC/STPC	St Mary Cray/St Paul's Cray		

STNW/STAM ...... Stoke Newington/Stamford Hill
STP ...... St Paul's
STPAN ...... St Pancras
STRHM/NOR ...... Streatham/Norbury
STWL/WRAY ...... Stanwell/Wraysbury
SUN ...... Sunbury
SURB ...... Surbiton
SUT ...... Sutton
SWFD ...... South Woodford
SWLY ...... Swanley

SYD ...... Sydenham
TEDD ...... Teddington
THDIT ...... Thames Ditton
THHTH ...... Thornton Heath
THMD ...... Thamesmead
TOOT ...... Tooting
TOTM ...... Tottenham
TPL/STR ...... Temple/Strand
TRDG/WHET ...... Totteridge/Whetstone
TWK ...... Twickenham
TWRH ...... Tower Hill
UED ...... Upper Edmonton

UX/CGN ...... Uxbridge/Colham Green
VX/NE ...... Vauxhall/Nine Elms
WALTH ...... Walthamstow
WALW ...... Walworth
WAN ...... Wanstead
WAND/EARL ...... Wandsworth/Earlsfield
WAP ...... Wapping
WAT ...... Watford
WATW ...... Watford west
WBLY ...... Wembley
WBPTN ...... West Brompton

WCHMH ...... Winchmore Hill
WCHPL ...... Whitechapel
WDGN ...... Wood Green
WDR/YW ...... West Drayton/Yiewsley
WEA ...... West Ealing
WELL ...... Welling
WEST ...... Westminster
WESTW ...... Westminster west
WFD ...... Woodford
WHALL ...... Whitehall
WHTN ...... Whitton
WIM/MER ...... Wimbledon/Merton

WKENS ...... West Kensington
WLGTN ...... Wallington
WLSDN ...... Willesden
WNWD ...... West Norwood
WOOL/PLUM ...... Woolwich/Plumstead
WOT/HER ...... Walton-on-Thames/Hersham
WPK ...... Worcester Park
WWKM ...... West Wickham
YEAD ...... Yeading

Index – streets

1 Av – Ais

1

1 Av WOOL/PLUM SE18 ...... 127 G3

A

Aaron Hill Rd EHAM E6 ...... 108 A4
Abberley Ms BTSEA SW11 ...... 141 C4
Abbess Cl BRXS/STRHM SW2 ...... 162 C3
Abbeville Ms CLAP SW4 * 141 J6
Abbeville Rd CEND/HSY/T N8 ...... 66 D1
　CLAP SW4 ...... 161 H1
Abbey Av ALP/SUD HA0 ...... 98 A1
Abbey Cl HYS/HAR UB3 ...... 114 A1
　NTHLT UB5 ...... 95 K2
　PIN HA5 ...... 41 G6
　ROM RM7 ...... 75 H3
Abbey Crs BELV DA17 ...... 129 H4
Abbeydale Rd ALP/SUD HA0 ...... 80 B6
Abbey Dr DART DA2 ...... 170 B4
　TOOT SW17 ...... 179 H1
Abbeyfield Cl MTCM CR4 ...... 178 D5
Abbeyfield Est
　BERM/RHTH SE16 ...... 123 K4
Abbeyfield Rd
　BERM/RHTH SE16 ...... 123 K4
Abbeyfields Cl WLSDN NW10 ...... 98 L2
　HMSMTH W6 ...... 119 H6
　STHWK SE1 ...... 123 H4
　STJWD NW8 ...... 101 G1
Abbey Gv ABYW SE2 ...... 128 C4
Abbeyhill Rd BFN/LL DA15 ...... 168 D4
Abbey La BECK BR3 ...... 182 D3
　SRTFD E15 ...... 106 A1
Abbey Ms ISLW TW7 ...... 136 C2
　WALTH E17 ...... 69 J2
Abbey Mt BELV DA17 ...... 129 G5
Abbey Orchard St WEST SW1P 16 D4
Abbey Pde BECK BR3 ...... 182 D3
Abbey Pl DART DA1 * 151 G6
Abbey Rd BARK IG11 ...... 90 C6
　BELV DA17 ...... 128 E4
　BXLYHN DA7 ...... 149 F5
　CROY/NA CR0 ...... 211 H1
　EN EN1 ...... 24 A6
　GNTH/NBYPK IG2 ...... 72 D3
　KIL/WHAMP NW6 ...... 83 F6
　SRTFD E15 ...... 106 B1
　WIM/MER SW19 ...... 178 B4
　WLSDN NW10 ...... 80 D6
Abbey St PLSTW E13 ...... 106 E3
　STHWK SE1 ...... 19 J4
Abbey Ter ABYW SE2 ...... 128 D3
Abbey Vw MLHL NW7 ...... 31 H5
Abbey Wk E/WMO/HCT KT8 ...... 173 G6
Abbey Wood Rd ABYW SE2 ...... 128 C4
Abbot Cl RSLP HA4 ...... 77 H1
Abbotsbury Cl SRTFD E15 ...... 106 A1
　WKENS W14 ...... 119 J2
Abbotsbury Gdns PIN HA5 ...... 59 G3
Abbotsbury Ms PECK SE15 ...... 143 K4
Abbotsbury Rd MRDN SM4 ...... 193 K2
　WKENS W14 ...... 119 H2
　WWKM BR4 ...... 199 J6
Abbots Cl STMC/STPC BR5 ...... 201 H5
Abbots Dr RYLN/HDSTN HA2 ...... 60 A6
Abbotsford Av
　SEVS/STOTM N15 ...... 67 J1
Abbotsford Gdns WFD IG8 ...... 52 E3
Abbotsford Rd GDMY/SEVK IG3 ...... 73 G6
Abbots Gdns EFNCH N2 ...... 65 H3
Abbots Gn CROY/NA CR0 ...... 213 F4
Abbotshade Rd
　BERM/RHTH SE16 * 124 A1
Abbotshall Av STHGT/OAK N14 ...... 34 C5
Abbotshall Rd CAT SE6 ...... 165 G3
Abbots La STHWK SE1 ...... 19 H1
Abbotsleigh Rd
　STRHM/NOR SW16 ...... 161 H6
Abbots Mnr PIM SW1V * 121 G5
Abbotsmede Cl TWK TW1 ...... 156 A4
Abbots Pk BRXS/STRHM SW2 ...... 162 B3
Abbot's Pl KIL/WHAMP NW6 ...... 83 F6
Abbots Rd EDGW HA8 ...... 44 E3
　EHAM E6 ...... 89 H6
Abbots Ter CEND/HSY/T N8 ...... 66 E3
Abbotstone Rd
　PUT/ROE SW15 ...... 139 G4
Abbots Wk KENS W8 * 86 B4
Abbotswell Rd BROCKY SE4 ...... 144 C6
Abbots Wy BECK BR3 ...... 198 B3
Abbotswood Cl BELV DA17 ...... 129 F3
Abbotswood Gdns CLAY IG5 ...... 53 K6
Abbotswood Rd EDUL SE22 ...... 143 F5
　STRHM/NOR SW16 ...... 161 J5

Abbotswood Wy
　HYS/HAR UB3 ...... 114 A1
Abbott Av RYNPK SW20 ...... 177 G5
Abbott Cl HPTN TW12 ...... 172 D2
　NTHLT UB5 ...... 77 K4
Abbott Rd POP/IOD E14 ...... 106 B5
Abbotts Cl IS N1 * 85 J5
　ROMW/RG RM7 ...... 56 D6
　THMD SE28 ...... 109 J6
Abbotts Crs CHING E4 ...... 38 B6
　ENC/FH EN2 ...... 23 H3
Abbotts Dr ALP/SUD HA0 ...... 61 H6
Abbotts Md
　RCHPK/HAM TW10 * 156 D6
Abbotts Park Rd LEY E10 ...... 70 A4
Abbotts Rd BAR EN5 ...... 21 F5
　CHEAM SM3 ...... 208 C2
　MTCM CR4 ...... 195 H1
　STHL UB1 ...... 114 D1
Abbott's Wk BXLYHN DA7 ...... 148 E1
Abchurch La MANHO EC4N 13 F5
Abdale Rd SHB W12 ...... 118 E1
Abdale Rd SHB W12 ...... 118 E1
Aberavon Rd BOW E3 ...... 105 G2
Abercairn Rd
　STRHM/NOR SW16 ...... 179 H3
Aberconway Rd MRDN SM4 ...... 178 A6
Abercorn Cl MLHL NW7 ...... 46 C3
　STJWD NW8 ...... 101 G2
Abercorn Crs RYLN/HDSTN HA2 ...... 60 B5
Abercorn Gdns CHDH RM6 ...... 73 H5
　KTN/HRWW/WS HA3 ...... 61 K4
Abercorn Gv RSLP HA4 ...... 58 D1
Abercorn Ms
　RCHPK/HAM TW10 ...... 137 G6
Abercorn Pl STJWD NW8 ...... 101 G2
Abercorn Rd MLHL NW7 ...... 46 C3
　STAN HA7 ...... 43 J3
Abercorn Wy STHWK SE1 ...... 123 H5
Abercrombie Dr EN EN1 ...... 24 C2
Abercrombie St BTSEA SW11 ...... 140 D3
Aberdare Cl WWKM BR4 ...... 199 F6
Aberdare Gdns
　KIL/WHAMP NW6 ...... 83 F5
　MLHL NW7 ...... 46 B3
Aberdare Rd PEND EN3 ...... 24 E5
Aberdeen Cottages STAN HA7 * 43 J3
Aberdeen La HBRY N5 ...... 85 H3
Aberdeen Pde UED N18 * 50 D1
Aberdeen Pl HBRY N5 ...... 85 J3
Aberdeen Pl BAY/PAD W2 * 2 A7
Aberdeen Rd CROY/NA CR0 ...... 211 K2
　HBRY N5 ...... 85 J2
　KTN/HRWW/WS HA3 ...... 43 F6
　UED N18 ...... 50 D1
　WLSDN NW10 ...... 81 G3
Aberdeen Ter BKHTH/KID SE3 ...... 145 G3
Aberdour Rd GDMY/SEVK IG3 ...... 91 H1
Aberdour St STHWK SE1 ...... 19 G6
Aberfeldy St POP/IOD E14 ...... 106 A5
Aberford Gdns
　WOOL/PLUM SE18 ...... 146 D2
Aberfoyle Rd
　STRHM/NOR SW16 ...... 179 J3
Abergeldie Rd LEE/GVPK SE12 ...... 166 A1
Abernethy Rd LEW SE13 ...... 145 H5
Abersham Rd HACK E8 ...... 86 B3
Abery St WOOL/PLUM SE18 ...... 127 K4
Abingdon Cl STHWK SE1 * 19 K7
　WIM/MER SW19 ...... 178 B2
Abingdon Rd FNCH N3 ...... 47 G5
　KENS W8 ...... 119 K3
　STRHM/NOR SW16 ...... 179 K4
Abingdon St WEST SW1P 16 E4
Abingdon Vls KENS W8 ...... 119 K3
Abingdon Wy ORP BR6 ...... 217 H2
Abinger Av BELMT SM2 ...... 208 A6
Abinger Cl BMLY BR1 ...... 184 D6
　CROY/NA CR0 ...... 214 A4
　GDMY/SEVK IG3 ...... 72 E3
　WLGTN SM6 ...... 210 E3
Abinger Dr NRWD SE19 ...... 180 D3
Abinger Gdns ISLW TW7 ...... 135 K4
Abinger Gv DEPT SE8 ...... 124 C6
Abinger Ms MV/WKIL W9 ...... 100 E3
Abinger Rd CHSWK W4 ...... 118 C3
Ablett St BERM/RHTH SE16 ...... 123 K5
Abney Park Ter
　STNW/STAM N16 * 68 B6
Aboyne Dr RYNPK SW20 ...... 176 D5
Aboyne Rd TOOT SW17 ...... 160 C5
　WLSDN NW10 ...... 81 F3
Abraham Cl OXHEY WD19 ...... 27 F6
Abridge Gdns CRW RM5 ...... 56 C2
Abridge Wy BARK IG11 ...... 109 H1
Abyssinia Cl BTSEA SW11 ...... 140 D5
Abyssinia Rd BTSEA SW11 * 140 D5
Acacia Av BTFD TW8 ...... 136 C1
　HCH RM12 ...... 93 J4
　HYS/HAR UB3 ...... 94 D5
　RSLP HA4 ...... 58 E5
　TOTM N17 ...... 49 K3
　WBLY HA9 ...... 80 A3
Acacia Cl DEPT SE8 ...... 124 B4

　STAN HA7 ...... 42 E2
　STMC/STPC BR5 ...... 201 J2
Acacia Dr CHEAM SM3 ...... 193 J5
Acacia Gdns STJWD NW8 ...... 2 B2
　WWKM BR4 ...... 199 F6
Acacia Gv DUL SE21 ...... 162 E4
　NWMAL KT3 ...... 176 B6
Acacia Ms WDR/YW UB7 ...... 112 A6
Acacia Pl STJWD NW8 ...... 2 B2
Acacia Rd ACT W3 ...... 98 E6
　BECK BR3 ...... 182 C6
　DART DA1 ...... 171 F3
　ENC/FH EN2 ...... 23 K2
　HPTN TW12 ...... 173 F2
　MTCM CR4 ...... 179 F5
　STJWD NW8 ...... 2 B1
　STRHM/NOR SW16 ...... 179 K4
　WALTH E17 ...... 69 G3
　WAN E11 ...... 70 C6
　WDGN N22 ...... 49 G4
The Acacias EBAR EN4 * 21 H6
Acacia Wy BFN/LL DA15 ...... 168 A2
Academy Fields Rd GPK RM2 ...... 75 K2
Academy Gdns CROY/NA CR0 ...... 197 G5
　NTHLT UB5 ...... 95 H1
Academy Rd
　WOOL/PLUM SE18 ...... 146 E6
Acanthus Dr STHWK SE1 ...... 123 H5
Acanthus Rd BTSEA SW11 ...... 141 F4
Accommodation Rd
　GLDGN NW11 ...... 64 D4
Ace Pde CHSGTN KT9 ...... 206 A1
Acer Av YEAD UB4 ...... 95 J3
Acfold Rd FUL/PGN SW6 ...... 140 A2
Achilles Cl STHWK SE1 ...... 123 H5
Achilles Rd KIL/WHAMP NW6 ...... 82 E3
Achilles St NWCR SE14 ...... 144 B1
Acklam Rd NKENS W10 ...... 100 D4
Acklington Dr CDALE/KGS NW9 ...... 45 G4
Ackmar Rd FUL/PGN SW6 ...... 139 K2
Ackroyd Dr BOW E3 ...... 105 H4
Ackroyd Rd FSTH SE23 ...... 164 B2
Acland Cl WOOL/PLUM SE18 ...... 147 J1
Acland Crs CMBW SE5 ...... 142 E5
Acland Rd CRICK NW2 ...... 81 K4
Acle Cl BARK/HLT IG6 ...... 54 B4
Acock Gv NTHLT UB5 ...... 78 B2
Acol Crs RSLP HA4 ...... 77 F3
Acol Rd KIL/WHAMP NW6 ...... 83 F5
Aconbury Rd DAGW RM9 ...... 91 H6
Acorn Cl CHING E4 ...... 51 K1
　CHST BR7 ...... 185 H1
　EN EN1 ...... 23 G2
　HPTN TW12 ...... 173 G2
　STAN HA7 ...... 43 H3
Acorn Gdns ACT W3 ...... 99 F4
　NRWD SE19 ...... 181 F4
Acorn Gv HYS/HAR UB3 ...... 133 J1
　RSLP HA4 ...... 76 D2
Acorn Pde PECK SE15 ...... 143 J1
Acorn Wy BECK BR3 ...... 199 F2
　FSTH SE23 ...... 164 A5
　ORP BR6 ...... 216 B2
Acre Dr EDUL SE22 ...... 143 H5
Acre La BRXS/STRHM SW2 ...... 142 A5
　CAR SM5 ...... 210 A2
Acre Rd DAGE RM10 ...... 92 D5
　KUTN/CMB KT2 ...... 175 G3
　WIM/MER SW19 ...... 178 C2
Acre Wy NTHWD HA6 ...... 40 D4
Acris St WAND/EARL SW18 ...... 140 B6
Acton Cl ED N9 ...... 36 C4
Acton Hill Ms ACT W3 * 117 J1
Acton La ACT W3 ...... 117 K1
　WLSDN NW10 ...... 98 E2
Acton Ms HACK E8 ...... 86 B6
Acton St FSBYW WC1X 5 G6
Acuba Rd WAND/EARL SW18 ...... 160 A4
Acworth Cl ED N9 ...... 36 E2
Acworth Pl DART DA1 * 171 F1
Ada Ct MV/WKIL W9 ...... 101 G2
Ada Gdns POP/IOD E14 ...... 106 B5
　SRTFD E15 ...... 88 D6
Adair Cl SNWD SE25 ...... 181 J6
Adair Rd NKENS W10 ...... 100 C3
Adam & Eve Ms KENS W8 ...... 119 K3
Adam Cl CAT SE6 ...... 164 C6
　FSTH SE23 ...... 163 K4
Adam Ct SKENS SW7 * 120 B4
Adams Cl BRYLDS KT5 ...... 191 G3
　FNCH N3 ...... 46 E5
　WBLY HA9 ...... 62 D6
Adams Ct OBST EC2N 13 F3
Adams Ms TOOT SW17 ...... 160 E4
　WDGN N22 ...... 49 F5
Adamson Rd CAN/RD E16 ...... 106 E5
　HAMP NW3 ...... 83 H5
Adamson Wy BECK BR3 ...... 199 F2
Adams Pl HOLWY N7 ...... 85 F3
Adamsrill Cl EN EN1 ...... 35 K1
Adamsrill Rd SYD SE26 ...... 164 A6

Adams Rd BECK BR3 ...... 198 B2
　TOTM N17 ...... 49 K5
Adams Rw MYFR/PKLN W1K 9 H6
Adams Sq BXLYHS DA6 ...... 149 F4
Adam St CHCR WC2N 11 F6
Adams Wk KUT/HW KT1 ...... 175 F5
Adams Wy CROY/NA CR0 ...... 197 G3
Adam Wk FUL/PGN SW6 * 139 F1
Ada Pl BETH E2 ...... 86 C6
Adare Wk STRHM/NOR SW16 ...... 161 K4
Ada Rd ALP/SUD HA0 * 79 J1
　CMBW SE5 ...... 143 F1
Ada St HACK E8 ...... 86 D6
Adderley Gdns ELTH/MOT SE9 ...... 167 F6
Adderley Gv BTSEA SW11 ...... 141 F6
Adderley Rd
　KTN/HRWW/WS HA3 ...... 43 F4
Adderley St POP/IOD E14 ...... 106 A5
Addey Ms DEPT SE8 ...... 144 C1
Addington Dr
　NFNCH/WDSPK N12 ...... 47 H2
Addington Gv SYD SE26 ...... 164 B6
Addington Rd BOW E3 ...... 105 J2
　CAN/RD E16 ...... 106 C3
　CROY/NA CR0 ...... 196 C5
　FSBYPK N4 ...... 67 G4
　WWKM BR4 ...... 214 B1
Addington Sq CMBW SE5 ...... 142 D1
Addington St STHWK SE1 * 17 H3
Addington Village Rd
　CROY/NA CR0 ...... 213 J4
Addis Cl PEND EN3 ...... 25 F2
Addiscombe Av CROY/NA CR0 ...... 197 H4
Addiscombe Cl
　KTN/HRWW/WS HA3 ...... 61 J2
Addiscombe Court Rd
　CROY/NA CR0 ...... 197 F6
Addiscombe Gv CROY/NA CR0 ...... 196 E6
Addiscombe Rd CROY/NA CR0 ...... 197 F6
Addison Av HSLW TW3 ...... 135 H2
　NTCHL W11 ...... 119 H1
　STHGT/OAK N14 ...... 34 B1
Addison Bridge Pl
　WKENS W14 ...... 119 J4
Addison Cl NTHWD HA6 ...... 40 E4
　STMC/STPC BR5 ...... 201 H3
Addison Crs WKENS W14 ...... 119 H3
Addison Dr LEE/GVPK SE12 ...... 146 A6
Addison Gdns BRYLDS KT5 ...... 191 G1
　WKENS W14 ...... 119 G3
Addison Pl NTCHL W11 ...... 119 H1
　STHL UB1 * 96 A6
Addison Rd BARK/HLT IG6 ...... 54 C4
　HAYES BR2 ...... 200 C2
　PEND EN3 ...... 24 E2
　SNWD SE25 ...... 197 H1
　TEDD TW11 ...... 174 C2
　WALTH E17 ...... 69 K2
　WAN E11 ...... 71 F4
　WKENS W14 ...... 119 J3
Addison's Cl CROY/NA CR0 ...... 198 C6
Addison Ter CHSWK W4 * 117 K4
Addison Wy ESH/CLAY KT10 ...... 204 C5
　GLDGN NW11 ...... 64 E1
　HYS/HAR UB3 ...... 94 E5
　NTHWD HA6 ...... 40 D4
Addle Hill BLKFR EC4V 12 B5
Addle St CITYW EC2V * 12 D3
Adecroft Wy E/WMO/HCT KT8 ...... 173 H6
Adela Av NWMAL KT3 ...... 192 E2
Adelaide Cl EN EN1 ...... 24 A1
　STAN HA7 ...... 29 G6
Adelaide Gdns CHDH RM6 ...... 74 A2
Adelaide Gv SHB W12 ...... 118 D1
Adelaide Rd CHST BR7 ...... 185 G1
　HAMP NW3 ...... 83 H5
　HEST TW5 ...... 134 D1
　IL IG1 ...... 72 B6
　LEY E10 ...... 88 A1
　NWDGN UB2 ...... 114 C3
　PUT/ROE SW15 ...... 139 K6
　RCH/KEW TW9 ...... 137 G4
　SURB KT6 ...... 191 F2
　TEDD TW11 ...... 174 A1
　WEA W13 ...... 116 B2
Adelaide St CHCR WC2N 10 E6
Adelaide Ter BTFD TW8 ...... 116 E5
Adela St NKENS W10 ...... 100 C3
Adeline Pl RSQ WC1B 10 D2
Adeliza Cl BARK IG11 ...... 90 C5
Adelphi Crs HCH RM12 ...... 75 J6
　YEAD UB4 ...... 94 E2
Adelphi Ter CHCR WC2N 11 F6
Adelphi Wy YEAD UB4 ...... 94 E2
Adeney Cl HMSMTH W6 ...... 119 G6
Adenmore Rd CAT SE6 ...... 164 D2
Aden Rd IL IG1 ...... 72 B4
　PEND EN3 ...... 25 H4
Adhara Rd NTHWD HA6 ...... 40 E1
Adie Rd HMSMTH W6 ...... 119 F3

Adine Rd PLSTW E13 ...... 106 E3
Adler St WCHPL E1 ...... 104 C5
Adley St CLPT E5 ...... 87 G3
Addlington Cl UED N18 ...... 49 K1
Admaston Rd
　WOOL/PLUM SE18 ...... 147 H1
Admiral Cl STMC/STPC BR5 ...... 202 E1
Admiral Ms NKENS W10 ...... 100 B3
Admiral Pl BERM/RHTH SE16 ...... 124 B1
Admiral Pl SWFD E18 * 71 F1
Admiral Seymour Rd
　ELTH/MOT SE9 ...... 146 E5
Admiral's Ga GNWCH SE10 ...... 144 E3
Admiral Sq WBPTN SW10 * 140 C1
Admirals St DEPT SE8 ...... 144 D2
Admiral's Wk HAMP NW3 ...... 83 G1
Admirals Wy POP/IOD E14 ...... 124 E2
Admiralty Cl DEPT SE8 * 144 C2
Admiralty Rd TEDD TW11 ...... 174 A3
Admiral Wk MV/WKIL W9 ...... 100 E4
Adnams Wk RAIN RM13 ...... 93 J5
Adolf St CAT SE6 ...... 164 D6
Adolphus Rd FSBYPK N4 ...... 67 H6
Adolphus St DEPT SE8 ...... 144 C1
Adomar Rd BCTR RM8 ...... 91 K1
Adpar St BAY/PAD W2 ...... 8 A1
Adrian Cl BAR EN5 ...... 32 B1
Adrian Ms WBPTN SW10 ...... 120 A6
Adrienne Av STHL UB1 ...... 95 K3
Advance Rd WNWD SE27 ...... 162 D6
Advent Wy UED N18 ...... 51 F1
Adys Lawn CRICK NW2 ...... 81 K4
Adys Rd PECK SE15 ...... 143 G4
Aerodrome Rd CDALE/KGS NW9 ...... 45 H6
Aerodrome Wy HEST TW5 ...... 114 D6
Affleck St IS N1 * 5 H3
Afghan Rd BTSEA SW11 ...... 140 D4
Aftab Ter WCHPL E1 * 104 D3
Agamemnon Rd
　KIL/WHAMP NW6 ...... 82 D3
Agar Cl SURB KT6 ...... 191 G6
Agar Gv CAMTN NW1 ...... 84 D5
Agar Pl CAMTN NW1 ...... 84 C5
Agate Cl WAN E11 ...... 71 H5 (?)
Agate Rd HMSMTH W6 ...... 119 F3
Agatha Cl WAP E1W 123 J1
Agaton Rd ELTH/MOT SE9 ...... 167 H4
Agave Rd CRICK NW2 ...... 82 A2
Agdon St FSBYE EC1V 6 A6
Agincourt Rd HAMP NW3 ...... 83 K2
Agister Rd CHIG IG7 ...... 55 J1
Agnes Av IL IG1 ...... 90 A2
Agnes Cl EHAM E6 ...... 108 A6
Agnesfield Cl
　NFNCH/WDSPK N12 ...... 47 J2
Agnes Gdns BCTR RM8 ...... 91 K2
Agnes Riley Gdns CLAP SW4 * 161 H2
Agnes Rd ACT W3 ...... 118 C2
Agnes St POP/IOD E14 ...... 105 H5
Agnew Rd FSTH SE23 ...... 164 B2
Agricola Pl EN EN1 ...... 24 B6
Aidan Cl BCTR RM8 ...... 92 A2
Ailsa Av TWK TW1 ...... 136 B6
Ailsa Rd TWK TW1 ...... 136 C6
Ailsa St POP/IOD E14 ...... 106 A4
Ainger Rd HAMP NW3 ...... 83 K5
Ainsdale Cl ORP BR6 ...... 201 J5
Ainsdale Crs PIN HA5 ...... 42 A6
Ainsdale Dr STHWK SE1 ...... 123 H5
Ainsdale Rd EA W5 ...... 97 K3
　OXHEY WD19 ...... 27 G5
Ainsley Av ROMW/RG RM7 ...... 74 E3
Ainsley Cl ED N9 ...... 36 A3
Ainsley St BETH E2 ...... 104 D2
Ainslie Wood Crs CHING E4 ...... 51 K1
Ainslie Wood Gdns CHING E4 ...... 37 K6
Ainslie Wood Rd CHING E4 ...... 51 J1
Ainsty St BERM/RHTH SE16 ...... 123 K2
Ainsworth Cl CMBW SE5 * 143 F3
　CRICK NW2 ...... 81 J1
Ainsworth Rd CROY/NA CR0 ...... 196 C6
　HOM E9 ...... 86 E5
Ainsworth Wy STJWD NW8 ...... 83 G6
Aintree Av EHAM E6 ...... 89 J6
Aintree Crs BARK/HLT IG6 ...... 54 C5
Aintree Est FUL/PGN SW6 * 139 H1
Aintree Rd GFD/PVL UB6 ...... 97 H1
Aintree St FUL/PGN SW6 ...... 139 H1
Airco Cl CDALE/KGS NW9 ...... 44 E6
Airdrie Cl IS N1 ...... 85 F5
　YEAD UB4 ...... 95 J4
Airedale Av CHSWK W4 ...... 118 C5
Airedale Av South
　CHSWK W4 * 118 C5
Airedale Rd BAL SW12 ...... 160 E2
　EA W5 ...... 116 D3
Airlie Gdns IL IG1 ...... 72 B6
　KENS W8 ...... 119 K2
Air St REGST W1B 10 B6
Airthrie Rd GDMY/SEVK IG3 ...... 73 H1
Aisgill Av WKENS W14 ...... 119 J5

Aisher Rd THMD SE28 109 J6
Aislibie Rd LEE/GVPK SE12 145 H5
Aiten Pl HMSMTH W6 118 D4
Aitken Cl HACK E8 86 C6
MTCM CR4 194 E4
Aitken Rd BAR EN5 20 A6
CAT SE6 164 E4
Aitman Dr BTFD TW8 * 117 H5
Ajax Av CDALE/KGS NW9 45 G6
Ajax Rd KIL/WHAMP NW6 82 D2
Akabusi Cl CROY/NA CR0 197 H3
Akehurst St PUT/ROE SW15 158 D1
Akenside Rd HAMP NW3 83 H3
Akerman Rd BRXN/ST SW9 142 C2
SURB KT6 190 D3
Alabama St WOOL/PLUM SE18 147 J1
Alacross Rd EA W5 116 D2
Alan Cl DART DA1 151 F5
Alandale Dr PIN HA5 41 F4
Alander Ms WALTH E17 69 K1
Alan Dr BAR EN5 32 C1
Alan Gdns ROMW/RG RM7 74 C4
Alan Hocken Wy SRTFD E15 106 C1
Alan Rd WIM/MER SW19 177 H1
Alanthus Cl LEE/GVPK SE12 165 J1
Alaska St STHWK SE1 17 J2
Alba Cl YEAD UB4 95 H3
Albacore Crs LEW SE13 164 E1
Alba Gdns GLDGN NW11 64 C3
Albain Crs ASHF TW15 152 B4
Albany Cl BUSH WD23 28 D1
BXLY DA5 168 D2
ESH/CLAY KT10 204 A6
MORT/ESHN SW14 137 J5
SEVS/STOTM N15 67 H1
Albany Cottages HNWL W7 * 115 K1
Albany Ctyd MYFR/PICC W1J 10 B6
Albany Crs EDGW HA8 44 C3
ESH/CLAY KT10 204 E4
Albany Ms BMLY BR1 183 K2
CMBW SE5 122 D6
IS N1 85 G5
KUTN/CMB KT2 * 174 E2
SUT SM1 209 F3
Albany Pde BTFD TW8 * 117 F6
PEND EN3 25 F1
Albany Pk PEND EN3 * 25 F1
Albany Park Av PEND EN3 24 E2
Albany Park Rd
KUTN/CMB KT2 174 E2
Albany Pl BTFD TW8 116 E6
Albany Rd BELV DA17 129 G6
BTFD TW8 116 E6
BXLY DA5 168 D2
CHDH RM6 74 B3
CHST BR7 185 G1
FSBYPK N4 67 F3
HCH RM12 75 J5
MNPK E12 89 H2
NWMAL KT3 192 A1
RCHPK/HAM TW10 * 137 G6
UED N18 50 D1
WALTH E17 69 G3
WALW SE17 122 E6
WEA W13 97 H6
WIM/MER SW19 178 A1
Albany Rw EFNCH N2 * 65 J1
Albany St CAMTN NW1 3 K4
Albany Ter
RCHPK/HAM TW10 * 137 G6
The Albany KUTN/CMB KT2 174 E2
Albany Vw BKHH IG9 38 E3
Alba Pl NTGHL W11 100 D5
Albatross Cl EHAM E6 107 K3
Albatross St
WOOL/PLUM SE18 147 K1
Albemarle Ap GNTH/NBYPK IG2 72 B3
Albemarle Av WHTN TW2 154 E3
Albemarle Gdns
GNTH/NBYPK IG2 72 B3
NWMAL KT3 192 A1
Albemarle Pk BECK BR3 * 182 E4
STAN HA7 43 J1
Albemarle Rd BECK BR3 182 E4
EBAR EN4 33 J2
Albemarle St CONDST W1S 10 A6
Albemarle Wy FSBYE EC1V 6 A7
Alberon Gdns GLDGN NW11 64 D1
Alberta Av SUT SM1 208 C2
Alberta Est WALW SE17 122 C5
Alberta Rd EN EN1 36 B1
ERITH DA8 149 K2
Alberta St WALW SE17 122 C5
Albert Av CHING E4 37 J6
VX/NE SW8 142 A1
Albert Br BTSEA SW11 140 D1
Albert Bridge Ga BTSEA SW11 140 E1
Albert Bridge Rd BTSEA SW11 140 E2
Albert Carr Gdns
STRHM/NOR SW16 179 K1
Albert Cl HOM E9 86 D6
WDGN N22 48 D4
Albert Cottages WCHPL E1 * 104 C4
Albert Crs CHING E4 37 J6
Albert Dr WIM/MER SW19 159 H4
Albert Emb STHWK SE1 121 K5
Albert Gdns WCHPL E1 105 F5
Albert Ga KTBR SW1X 15 F2
Albert Gv RYNPK SW20 177 G4
Albert Ms BROCKY SE4 * 144 C5
FSBYPK N4 * 67 F5
KENS W8 120 B3
POP/IOD E14 * 105 G6
Albert Pl FNCH N3 46 E4
KENS W8 120 A2
Albert Rd BCTR RM8 74 B5
BELV DA17 129 G5
BKHH IG9 39 H4
BXLY DA5 169 H1
CAN/RD E16 126 D1
EA W5 97 H3
EBAR EN4 21 H5
ELTH/MOT SE9 166 D5
FSBYPK N4 67 F5
HAYES BR2 200 C2
HDN NW4 64 B1
HPTN TW12 173 H1
HSLW TW3 135 F5
HYS/HAR UB3 113 J3
IL IG1 90 C1
KIL/WHAMP NW6 100 D1
KUT/HW KT1 175 G5
LEY E10 70 A6
MLHL NW7 45 H1
MTCM CR4 178 E6
NWDGN UB2 114 C3
NWMAL KT3 192 C1
ORP BR6 217 G3
PGE/AN SE20 182 A3
RCHPK/HAM TW10 137 F6
RDART DA2 171 F5
ROM RM1 75 H3
RYLN/HDSTN HA2 42 C6
SEVS/STOTM N15 68 A3
SNWD SE25 197 J1
STMC/STPC BR5 202 C3
SUT SM1 209 H3
SWFD E18 53 F6
TEDD TW11 174 A2
TWK TW1 156 A3
WALTH E17 69 J2
WDGN N22 48 D4
WDR/YW UB7 112 B1
Albert Sq SRTFD E15 88 C3
VX/NE SW8 142 A1
Albert St CAMTN NW1 3 K1
NFNCH/WDSPK N12 47 G1
Albert Ter CAMTN NW1 84 A6
EA W5 * 97 H3
WLSDN NW10 * 81 F6
Albert Terrace Ms CAMTN NW1 3 G1
Albert Wy PECK SE15 143 J1
Albion Av MUSWH N10 48 A4
VX/NE SW8 141 J3
Albion Cl BAY/PAD W2 8 D5
ROMW/RG RM7 75 F3
Albion Dr HACK E8 86 B5
Albion Est BERM/RHTH SE16 * 123 K2
Albion Gdns HMSMTH W6 118 E4
Albion Ga BAY/PAD W2 8 D5
Albion Gv STNW/STAM N16 86 A2
Albion Ms BAY/PAD W2 8 D4
IS N1 85 G6
Albion Pl FARR EC1M 12 A1
HMSMTH W6 118 E4
SNWD SE25 181 H6
Albion Riverside BTSEA SW11 140 D1
Albion Rd BELMT SM2 209 H4
BXLYHS DA6 149 G5
HSLW TW3 135 F5
HYS/HAR UB3 94 C5
KUTN/CMB KT2 175 K4
STNW/STAM N16 85 K3
TOTM N17 50 B5
WALTH E17 52 A6
WHTN TW2 155 K3
Albion Sq HACK E8 86 B5
Albion St BAY/PAD W2 8 D4
BERM/RHTH SE16 123 K2
CROY/NA CR0 196 C5
Albion Ter CHING E4 * 25 K5
HACK E8 86 B5
Albion Villas Rd SYD SE26 163 K5
Albion Wk IS N1 5 F3
Albion Wy LEW SE13 145 F5
STBT EC1A 12 C2
WBLY HA9 80 C1
Albion Yd IS N1 5 F3
Albrighton Rd EDUL SE22 143 F4
Albuhera Cl ENC/FH EN2 23 G2
Albury Av BELMT SM2 208 A6
BXLYHN DA7 149 F3
ISLW TW7 136 A1
Albury Cl HOR/WEW KT19 206 D6
HPTN TW12 173 F2
Albury Dr PIN HA5 41 G4
Albury Ms MNPK E12 71 G5
Albury Rd CHSGTN KT9 206 A3
Albury St DEPT SE8 124 D6
Albyfield BMLY BR1 184 E6
Albyn Rd DEPT SE8 144 E3
Alcester Crs CLPT E5 68 D6
Alcester Rd WLGTN SM6 210 B2
Alcock Cl WLGTN SM6 210 D5
Alcock Rd HEST TW5 134 C1
Alconbury Rd CLPT E5 68 C6
Alcorn Cl CHEAM SM3 193 K6
Alcott Cl HNWL W7 97 F4
Aldborough Rd DAGE RM10 92 E4
Aldborough Rd North
GNTH/NBYPK IG2 73 F2
Aldborough Rd South
GDMY/SEVK IG3 72 E3
Aldbourne Rd SHB W12 118 C1
Aldbridge St WALW SE17 123 F5
Aldburgh Ms MHST W1U 9 H3
Aldbury Av WBLY HA9 80 D5
Aldbury Ms ED N9 35 K2
Aldebert Ter VX/NE SW8 142 A1
Aldeburgh Pl WFD IG8 38 E6
Aldeburgh St GNWCH SE10 125 K5
Alden Av SRTFD E15 106 D2
Aldenham Rd OXHEY WD19 27 J1
Aldenham St CAMTN NW1 4 B3
Alden Md PIN HA5 * 42 A3
Aldensley Rd HMSMTH W6 118 E3
Alderbrook Rd BAL SW12 161 G1
Alderbury Rd BARN SW13 118 D6
Alder Cl PECK SE15 123 G6
Alder Gv CRICK NW2 63 J6
Alderholt Wy PECK SE15 * 143 F1
Alderman Av BARK IG11 109 G2
Aldermanbury CITYW EC2V * 12 D3
Aldermanbury Sq CITYW EC2V 12 D2
Alderman Cl DART DA1 170 B2
Alderman Judge Ml
KUT/HW KT1 * 175 F5
Alderman's Hl PLMGR N13 34 E6
Aldermary Rd BMLY BR1 183 K4
Alder Ms ARCH N19 66 C6
Aldermoor Rd CAT SE6 164 C5
Alderney Av HEST TW5 135 G1
Alderney Gdns NTHLT UB5 77 K5
Alderney Ms STHWK SE1 18 E4
Alderney Rd ERITH DA8 150 D1
WCHPL E1 105 F3
Alderney St PIM SW1V 15 J7
Alder Rd MORT/ESHN SW14 138 A4
SCUP DA14 167 K5
Alders Av WFD IG8 52 C2
Aldersbrook Av EN EN1 24 A3
Aldersbrook Dr
KUTN/CMB KT2 175 G2
Aldersbrook La MNPK E12 89 K1
Aldersbrook Rd MNPK E12 71 G6
Alders Cl EA W5 116 E3
EDGW HA8 44 E1
WAN E11 71 F6
Aldersey Gdns BARK IG11 90 D4
Aldersford Cl BROCKY SE4 144 A5
Aldersgate St STBT EC1A 12 C1
Aldersgrove E/WMO/HCT KT8 189 J2
Aldersgrove Av ELTH/MOT SE9 166 B5
Aldershot Rd KIL/WHAMP NW6 82 D6
Aldershot Ter
WOOL/PLUM SE18 * 147 F1
Aldersmead Av CROY/NA CR0 198 A3
Aldersmead Rd BECK BR3 182 B3
Alderson Pl NWDGN UB2 115 H1
Alderson St NKENS W10 100 C3
Alders Rd EDGW HA8 44 E1
The Alders FELT TW13 172 D1
HEST TW5 114 E6
STRHM/NOR SW16 * 161 H6
WCHMH N21 35 G1
WWKM BR4 198 E5
Alderton Cl WLSDN NW10 63 F6
Alderton Crs HDN NW4 63 K2
Alderton Rd CROY/NA CR0 197 G4
HNHL SE24 142 D4
Alderton Wy HDN NW4 63 K2
Alderville Rd FUL/PGN SW6 139 J3
Alderwick Dr HSLW TW3 135 J4
Alderwood Ms EBAR EN4 21 G1
Alderwood Rd ELTH/MOT SE9 167 J1
Aldford St MYFR/PKLN W1K 9 G7
Aldgate FENCHST EC3M 13 H4
Aldgate Barrs WCHPL E1 * 13 K3
Aldgate High St TWRH EC3N 13 J4
Aldine St SHB W12 119 F2
Aldingham Gdns HCH RM12 93 J3
Aldington Cl BCTR RM8 73 J4
Aldington Rd CHARL SE7 126 C3
Aldis Ms TOOT SW17 178 D1
Aldis St TOOT SW17 178 D1
Aldred Rd KIL/WHAMP NW6 82 E3
Aldren Rd TOOT SW17 160 B5
Aldrich Crs CROY/NA CR0 214 A6
Aldriche Wy CHING E4 52 A2
Aldrich Gdns CHEAM SM3 208 D1
Aldrich Ter WAND/EARL SW18 160 B4
Aldridge Av EDGW HA8 30 D5
PEND EN3 25 J1
RSLP HA4 59 G6
STAN HA7 44 A5
Aldridge Ri NWMAL KT3 192 B4
Aldridge Road Vls NTGHL W11 100 D4
Aldridge Wk STHGT/OAK N14 34 E2
Aldrington Rd
STRHM/NOR SW16 179 H1
Aldsworth Cl MV/WKIL W9 101 F3
Aldwick Cl ELTH/MOT SE9 167 J5
Aldwick Rd CROY/NA CR0 211 F1
Aldworth Gv LEW SE13 165 F1
Aldworth Rd SRTFD E15 88 C5
Aldwych HOL/ALD WC2B 11 G4
Aldwych Av BARK/HLT IG6 72 C2
Aldwych Cl HCH RM12 75 J6
Alers Rd BXLYHS DA6 148 E6
Alesia Cl WDGN N22 48 E3
Alestan Beck Rd CAN/RD E16 107 H5
Alexander Av WLSDN NW10 81 K5
Alexander Cl BFN/LL DA15 147 K6
EBAR EN4 21 H5
HAYES BR2 199 K5
NWDGN UB2 115 H1
WHTN TW2 155 K4
Alexander Evans Ms
FSTH SE23 164 A4
Alexander Ms BAY/PAD W2 101 F5
Alexander Pl SKENS SW7 14 C6
Alexander Rd ARCH N19 84 E1
BXLYHN DA7 148 E3
CHST BR7 185 G2
Alexander Sq CHEL SW3 14 C6
Alexander St BAY/PAD W2 100 E5
Alexander Ter ABYW SE2 * 128 C5
Alexandra Av BTSEA SW11 * 141 F2
RYLN/HDSTN HA2 59 K5
RYLN/HDSTN HA2 60 A6
STHL UB1 95 K6
SUT SM1 208 E1
WDGN N22 48 D4
Alexandra Cl
RYLN/HDSTN HA2 78 A1
Alexandra Cottages
NWCR SE14 144 C2
Alexandra Ct STHGT/OAK N14 22 C6
Alexandra Crs BMLY BR1 183 J2
Alexandra Dr BRYLDS KT5 191 H4
NRWD SE19 181 F1
Alexandra Gdns CAR SM5 210 A6
HSLW TW3 135 G3
MUSWH N10 66 B1
Alexandra Ga SKENS SW7 14 A2
Alexandra Gv FSBYPK N4 67 H5
NFNCH/WDSPK N12 47 F1
Alexandra Ms EFNCH N2 47 K6
Alexandra Palace Wy
CEND/HSY/T N8 66 C1
MUSWH N10 48 C6
Alexandra Pde
RYLN/HDSTN HA2 * 78 B2
Alexandra Park Rd
MUSWH N10 48 B5
Alexandra Pl CROY/NA CR0 197 F5
SNWD SE25 196 E2
STJWD NW8 83 G6
Alexandra Rd BTFD TW8 * 116 E6
CEND/HSY/T N8 49 G6
CHDH RM6 73 K3
CHSWK W4 118 A2
CROY/NA CR0 197 F5
ED N9 * 36 D2
EHAM E6 108 A2
ERITH DA8 130 C6
HDN NW4 64 B1
HSLW TW3 135 G3
KUTN/CMB KT2 175 H3
LEY E10 88 A1
MORT/ESHN SW14 138 A4
MTCM CR4 178 D3
MUSWH N10 48 B4
PEND EN3 25 F5
RAIN RM13 93 H6
RCH/KEW TW9 137 G3
ROM RM1 75 H3
SEVS/STOTM N15 67 K2
STJWD NW8 83 G6
SWFD E18 53 F6
SYD SE26 182 A2
THDIT KT7 190 A2
TWK TW1 156 E1
WALTH E17 69 H3
WIM/MER SW19 177 K1
Alexandra Sq MRDN SM4 193 K2
Alexandra St CAN/RD E16 106 E4
NWCR SE14 144 B1
Alexandria Rd WEA W13 97 H6
Alexis St BERM/RHTH SE16 123 H4
Alfearn Rd CLPT E5 86 E2
Alford Gn CROY/NA CR0 214 B4
Alford Pl IS N1 * 6 D3
Alford Rd ERITH DA8 129 K5
Alfoxton Av SEVS/STOTM N15 67 H1
Alfreda St BTSEA SW11 141 G2
Alfred Cl CHSWK W4 118 A4
Alfred Gdns STHL UB1 114 D1
Alfred Ms GWRST WC1E 10 C1
Alfred Pl GWRST WC1E 10 C1
Alfred Rd ACT W3 117 K1
BAY/PAD W2 100 E4
BELV DA17 129 G5
BKHH IG9 39 H4
FELT TW13 154 B4
KUT/HW KT1 175 F6
RDART DA2 171 J6
SNWD SE25 197 H2
SRTFD E15 88 D3
SUT SM1 209 G3
Alfred's Gdns BARK IG11 108 E1
Alfred St BOW E3 105 H2
Alfred's Wy (East Ham &
Barking By-Pass)
BARK IG11 108 E1
Alfred Vls WALTH E17 * 70 A1
Alfreton Cl WIM/MER SW19 159 G5
Alfriston BRYLDS KT5 191 G3
Alfriston Av CROY/NA CR0 195 K4
RYLN/HDSTN HA2 60 A3
Alfriston Cl BRYLDS KT5 191 G3
DART DA1 170 B1
Alfriston Rd BTSEA SW11 140 E6
Algar Cl STAN HA7 43 F1
Algar Rd ISLW TW7 136 B4
Algarve Rd WAND/EARL SW18 160 A3
Algernon Rd HDN NW4 63 J3
KIL/WHAMP NW6 82 E6
LEW SE13 144 E5
Algiers Rd LEW SE13 144 D5
Alguin Ct STAN HA7 * 43 J2
Alibon Gdns DAGE RM10 92 C3
Alibon Rd DAGE RM10 92 C3
Alice La BOW E3 87 H6
Alice St STHWK SE1 19 G5
Alice Thompson Cl
LEE/GVPK SE12 166 B4
Alice Walker Cl HNHL SE24 * 142 C5
Alice Wy HSLW TW3 135 G5
Alicia Av KTN/HRWW/WS HA3 61 H1
Alicia Cl KTN/HRWW/WS HA3 61 J1
Alicia Gdns KTN/HRWW/WS HA3 61 H1
Alie St WCHPL E1 13 K4
Alington Crs CDALE/KGS NW9 62 E5
Alington Gv WLGTN SM6 210 D6
Alison Cl CROY/NA CR0 198 A5
EHAM E6 108 A5
Aliwal Ms BTSEA SW11 * 140 D5
Aliwal Rd BTSEA SW11 140 D5
Alkerden Rd CHSWK W4 118 B5
Alkham Rd STNW/STAM N16 68 B6
Allan Barclay Cl
SEVS/STOTM N15 68 B3
Allan Cl NWMAL KT3 192 A2
Allandale Av FNCH N3 46 C6
Allandale Pl ORP BR6 217 K1
Allandale Rd EMPK RM11 75 H4
Allan Wy ACT W3 98 E4
Allard Cl STMC/STPC BR5 202 D4
Allard Crs BUSH WD23 28 C4
Allardyce St CLAP SW4 142 A5
Allbrook Cl TEDD TW11 173 K1
Allcot Cl EBED/NFELT TW14 153 J3
Allcroft Rd KTTN NW5 84 A4
Allder Wy SAND/SEL CR2 211 H5
Allenby Av SAND/SEL CR2 211 J6
Allenby Cl GFD/PVL UB6 96 A2
Allenby Rd FSTH SE23 164 B5
STHL UB1 96 A3
WOOL/PLUM SE18 127 H3
Allen Cl MTCM CR4 179 G4
SUN TW16 172 A4
Allendale Av STHL UB1 96 A5
Allendale Cl CMBW SE5 142 E3
SYD SE26 182 A1
Allendale Rd GFD/PVL UB6 79 H4
Allen Edwards Dr VX/NE SW8 141 K2
Allen Rd BECK BR3 182 A5
BOW E3 105 H1
CROY/NA CR0 196 A4
STNW/STAM N16 86 A2
SUN TW16 172 A4
Allensbury Pl CAMTN NW1 84 D5
Allens Rd PEND EN3 24 E6
Allen St KENS W8 119 K3
Allenswood Rd ELTH/MOT SE9 146 E4
Allerford Ct HRW HA1 60 B4
Allerford Rd CAT SE6 164 E6
Allerton Rd STNW/STAM N16 67 J6
Allerton St IS N1 6 E4
Allestree Rd FUL/PGN SW6 139 H1
Alleyn Crs DUL SE21 162 E5
Alleyndale Rd BCTR RM8 73 J6
Alleyn Pk DUL SE21 162 E4
NWDGN UB2 114 E5
Alleyn Rd DUL SE21 162 E5
Allfarthing La
WAND/EARL SW18 160 B1
Allgood Cl MRDN SM4 193 G3
Allgood St BETH E2 7 K3
Allhallows La CANST EC4R 12 E6
Allhallows Rd EHAM E6 107 J5
All Hallows Rd TOTM N17 50 A4
Alliance Cl ALP/SUD HA0 79 K2
HSLWW TW4 134 E6
Alliance Rd ACT W3 98 D3
PLSTW E13 107 G4
WOOL/PLUM SE18 128 B6
Allied Wy ACT W3 * 118 B2
Allingham Cl HNWL W7 97 F6
Allington Av TOTM N17 50 A2
Allington Cl GFD/PVL UB6 78 C5
WIM/MER SW19 177 G1
Allington Rd HDN NW4 63 K2
NKENS W10 100 C2
ORP BR6 201 K6
RYLN/HDSTN HA2 60 B2
Allington St BGVA SW1W 15 K5
WESTW SW1E 16 A5
Allison Cl GNWCH SE10 145 F2
Allison Gv DUL SE21 163 F3
Allison Rd ACT W3 98 E5
CEND/HSY/T N8 67 G2
Allitsen Rd STJWD NW8 2 C3
Allitson Rd STJWD NW8 2 C3
Allnutt Wy CLAP SW4 141 J6
Alloa Rd DEPT SE8 124 A5
GDMY/SEVK IG3 73 H6
Allonby Gdns WBLY HA9 61 J5
Alloway Rd BOW E3 105 G2
Allport Ms WCHPL E1 * 104 E4
All Saints' Cl ED N9 36 B4
All Saints Dr BKHTH/KID SE3 145 J3
All Saints Ms STAN HA7 42 E2
All Saints Pas
WAND/EARL SW18 * 139 K6
All Saints' Rd ACT W3 117 K3
NTGHL W11 100 D4
SUT SM1 209 G1
WIM/MER SW19 178 B3
All Saints St IS N1 5 G2
Allsop Pl CAMTN NW1 3 F7
All Souls' Av WLSDN NW10 99 K1
All Souls' Pl REGST W1B 9 K2
Allum Wy TRDG/WHET N20 33 G3
Allwood Cl SYD SE26 164 A6
Alma Av CHING E4 52 A3
Almack Rd CLPT E5 86 E2
Alma Cl MUSWH N10 * 48 B4
Alma Ct RYLN/HDSTN HA2 * 60 D6
Alma Crs SUT SM1 208 C3
Alma Gv STHWK SE1 19 K7
Alma Pl NRWD SE19 181 G3
THHTH CR7 196 B2
WLSDN NW10 99 K2
Alma Rd BFN/LL DA15 168 B5
CAR SM5 209 J3
ESH/CLAY KT10 189 K5
MUSWH N10 48 A3
PEND EN3 25 G6
STHL UB1 95 J6
STMC/STPC BR5 202 E6
WAND/EARL SW18 140 B6
Alma Rw KTN/HRWW/WS HA3 * 42 D4
Alma Sq STJWD NW8 101 G2
Alma St KTTN NW5 84 B4
SRTFD E15 88 B4
Alma Ter BOW E3 87 H6
KENS W8 * 119 K3
WAND/EARL SW18 160 C2
Almeida St IS N1 85 H6
Almeric Rd BTSEA SW11 140 E5
Almer Rd RYNPK SW20 176 D3
Almington St FSBYPK N4 * 66 E5
Almond Av CAR SM5 194 E6
EA W5 117 F3
WDR/YW UB7 112 D3
Almond Cl FELT TW13 153 K3
HAYES BR2 201 F4
HYS/HAR UB3 94 C6
PECK SE15 143 H3
RSLP HA4 76 D1
Almond Gv BTFD TW8 136 C1
Almond Rd BERM/RHTH SE16 123 J4
TOTM N17 50 C3
Almonds Av BKHH IG9 38 E4
Almond Wy HAYES BR2 201 F4
MTCM CR4 195 J2
RYLN/HDSTN HA2 42 C5
Almorah Rd HEST TW5 134 C2
IS N1 85 K5
Almshouse La CHSGTN KT9 205 K6
Alnwick Gv MRDN SM4 194 A1
Alnwick Rd CAN/RD E16 107 G5
LEE/GVPK SE12 166 A2
Alnwick Ter LEE/GVPK SE12 166 A2
Alperton La ALP/SUD HA0 97 K2
Alperton St NKENS W10 100 C3
Alphabet Gdns CAR SM5 194 C3
Alpha Cl CAMTN NW1 2 D6
Alpha Est HYS/HAR UB3 * 113 H2
Alpha Gv POP/IOD E14 124 D2
Alpha Pl CHEL SW3 120 D6
KIL/WHAMP NW6 100 E1
MRDN SM4 * 193 G4
Alpha Rd BRYLDS KT5 191 G3
CHING E4 37 J5
CROY/NA CR0 197 F5
NWCR SE14 144 C2
PEND EN3 25 G5
TEDD TW11 173 J1
UED N18 50 C2
Alpha St PECK SE15 143 H3
Alphea Cl WIM/MER SW19 178 D3
Alpine Av BRYLDS KT5 191 K6

Alpine Cl *CROY/NA* CR0 ....212 A1
Alpine Copse *BMLY* BR1 ....185 F5
Alpine Gv *HOM* E9 ....86 E5
Alpine Rd *BERM/RHTH* SE16 ....123 K4
LEY E10 ....69 K6
Alpine Vw *CAR* SM5 ....209 J3
Alpine Wk *BUSH* WD23 ....28 E4
Alpine Wy *EHAM* E6 ....108 A4
Alric Av *NWMAL* KT3 ....176 B6
WLSDN NW10 ....81 F5
Alroy Rd *FSBYPK* N4 ....67 G4
Alsace Rd *WALW* SE17 ....123 F5
Alscot Rd *STHWK* SE1 ....19 K5
Alscot Wy *STHWK* SE1 ....19 J6
Alsike Rd *ERITHM* DA18 ....128 E3
Alsom Av *WPK* KT4 ....207 H2
Alston Cl *SURB* KT6 ....190 C4
Alston Rd *BAR* EN5 ....20 C4
TOOT SW17 ....160 C6
UED N18 ....50 D1
Altair Cl *TOTM* N17 ....50 C2
Altair Wy *NTHWD* HA6 ....40 D1
Altash Wy *ELTH/MOT* SE9 ....166 E4
Altenburg Av *WEA* W13 ....116 C3
Altenburg Gdns *BTSEA* SW11 ....140 E5
Alt Gv *WIM/MER* SW19 ....177 J3
Altham Ct *RYLN/HDSTN* HA2 * 42 B4
Altham Gdns *OXHEY* WD19 ....27 H6
Altham Rd *PIN* HA5 ....41 J4
Althea St *FUL/PGN* SW6 ....140 A3
Althorne Gdns *SWFD* E18 ....70 D1
Althorne Wy *DAGE* RM10 ....74 C6
Althorp Cl *BAR* EN5 ....31 J2
Althorpe Rd *HRW* HA1 * 60 C2
Althorp Rd *TOOT* SW17 ....160 E3
Altmore Av *EHAM* E6 ....89 K5
Alton Av *STAN* HA7 ....43 F3
Alton Cl *BXLY* DA5 ....169 F3
ISLW TW7 ....136 A3
Alton Gdns *BECK* BR3 ....182 D3
WHTN TW2 ....155 J1
Alton Rd *CROY/NA* CR0 ....211 G2
PUT/ROE SW15 ....158 D3
RCH/KEW TW9 ....137 F5
TOTM N17 ....49 K6
Alton St *POP/IOD* E14 ....105 K5
Altyre Cl *BECK* BR3 ....198 C2
Altyre Rd *CROY/NA* CR0 ....196 E6
Altyre Wy *BECK* BR3 ....198 C2
Alvanley Gdns
KIL/WHAMP NW6 ....83 F3
Alva Wy *OXHEY* WD19 ....27 H4
Alverstone Av *EBAR* EN4 ....33 H2
WAND/EARL SW18 ....159 K4
Alverstone Gdns
ELTH/MOT SE9 ....167 G3
Alverstone Rd *CRICK* NW2 ....82 A5
MNPK E12 ....90 A2
NWMAL KT3 ....192 C1
WBLY HA9 ....62 B5
Alverston Gdns *SNWD* SE25 ....197 F2
Alverton St *DEPT* SE8 ....124 C5
Alveston Av
KTN/HRWW/WS HA3 ....43 H6
Alveston Sq *SWFD* E18 * 52 E5
Alvey St *WALW* SE17 ....123 F5
Alvia Gdns *SUT* SM1 ....209 G2
Alvington Crs *HACK* E8 ....86 B3
Alway Av *HOR/WEW* KT19 ....206 E3
Alwold Crs *LEE/GVPK* SE12 ....166 B1
Alwyn Av *CHSWK* W4 ....118 A5
Alwyn Cl *BORE* WD6 ....30 B1
CROY/NA CR0 ....213 H5
Alwyne La *IS* N1 * 85 H5
Alwyne Pl *IS* N1 ....85 J4
Alwyne Rd *HNWL* W7 ....96 E6
IS N1 ....85 J5
WIM/MER SW19 ....177 J2
Alwyne Sq *IS* N1 ....85 J4
Alwyne Vls *IS* N1 ....85 H5
Alwyn Gdns *ACT* W3 ....98 D5
HDN NW4 ....63 J1
Alyn Bank *CEND/HSY/T* N8 * 66 D3
Alyth Gdns *GLDGN* NW11 ....64 D3
Amalgamated Dr *BTFD* TW8 ....116 B6
Amanda Cl *CHIG* IG7 ....54 D2
Amanda Ms *ROMW/RG* RM7 ....74 E2
Amar Ct *WOOL/PLUM* SE18 ....128 A4
Amardeep Ct
WOOL/PLUM SE18 ....128 A5
Amazon St *WCHPL* E1 ....104 D5
Ambassador Cl *HSLW* TW3 ....134 D3
Ambassador Gdns *EHAM* E6 ....107 K4
Ambassador Sq *POP/IOD* E14 ....124 E4
Amber Av *WALTH* E17 ....51 G4
Amberden Av *FNCH* N3 ....46 E6
Ambergate St *WALW* SE17 ....122 C5
Amber Gv *CRICK* NW2 ....64 B5
Amberley Cl *ORP* BR6 ....217 F3
PIN HA5 ....41 K6
Amberley Ct *SCUP* DA14 ....186 D1
Amberley Gdns
HOR/WEW KT19 ....207 H2
Amberley Gv *CROY/NA* CR0 ....197 G4
SYD SE26 ....163 J6
Amberley Rd *ABYW* SE2 ....128 E6
BKHH IG9 ....39 G3
EN EN1 ....36 B2
LEY E10 ....69 J4
MV/WKIL W9 ....100 E4
PLMGR N13 ....35 F4
Amberley Wy *HSLWW* TW4 ....134 B6
MRDN SM4 ....193 K4
ROMW/RG RM7 ....74 D1
Amberside Cl *ISLW* TW7 ....155 J1
Amber St *SRTFD* E15 * 88 B4
Amberwood Cl *WLGTN* SM6 ....210 E3
Amberwood Ri *NWMAL* KT3 ....192 B3
Amblecote Cl *LEE/GVPK* SE12 ....166 A5
Amblecote Meadow
LEE/GVPK SE12 ....166 A5
Amblecote Mdw
LEE/GVPK SE12 * 166 A5
Amblecote Rd *LEE/GVPK* SE12 ....166 A5
Ambler Rd *FSBYPK* N4 ....85 H1
Ambleside *BMLY* BR1 ....183 G2
Ambleside Av *BECK* BR3 ....198 B2
HCH RM12 ....93 K3
STRHM/NOR SW16 ....161 J6
WOT/HER KT12 ....188 B5
Ambleside Cl *HOM* E9 ....86 E3
LEY E10 ....69 K4
SEVS/STOTM N15 ....50 B6
Ambleside Crs *PEND* EN3 ....25 F4
Ambleside Dr
EBED/NFELT TW14 ....153 J3
Ambleside Gdns *BELMT* SM2 ....209 G4
REDBR IG4 ....71 J1
WBLY HA9 ....61 K5
Ambleside Rd *BXLYHN* DA7 ....149 H3
WLSDN NW10 ....81 H5
Ambrey Wy *WLGTN* SM6 ....210 D6
Ambrook Rd *BELV* DA17 ....129 H3
Ambrosden Av *WEST* SW1P 16 B5
Ambrose Av *GLDGN* NW11 ....64 D3
Ambrose Cl *DART* DA1 ....150 C5
ORP BR6 ....217 F1
Ambrose St *BERM/RHTH* SE16 ....123 J4
Amelia Cl *ACT* W3 ....117 J1
Amelia St *WALW* SE17 ....122 C5
Amen Cnr *STP* EC4M 12 B4
TOOT SW17 ....179 F2
Amen Ct *STP* EC4M 12 B4
Amenity Wy *MRDN* SM4 ....193 F4
America Sq *TWRH* EC3N 13 J5
America St *STHWK* SE1 ....18 C1
Amerland Rd *PUT/ROE* SW15 ....159 J1
Amersham Av *UED* N18 ....49 K2
Amersham Gv *NWCR* SE14 ....144 C1
Amersham Rd *CROY/NA* CR0 ....196 D3
NWCR SE14 ....144 C2
Amersham V *NWCR* SE14 ....144 C1
Amery Gdns *WLSDN* NW10 ....81 K6
Amery Rd *HRW* HA1 ....61 G6
Amesbury Av
BRXS/STRHM SW2 ....161 K4
Amesbury Cl *WPK* KT4 ....193 F5
Amesbury Dr *CHING* E4 ....37 K1
Amesbury Rd *BMLY* BR1 ....184 C6
DAGW RM9 ....91 K5
FELT TW13 ....154 C4
Ames Cottages *POP/IOD* E14 * 105 G4
Amethyst Ct *ORP* BR6 ....216 E4
Amethyst Rd *SRTFD* E15 ....88 B2
Amherst Av *WEA* W13 ....97 J5
Amherst Cl *STMC/STPC* BR5 ....202 B1
Amherst Dr *STMC/STPC* BR5 ....202 A1
Amherst Gdns *WEA* W13 * 97 J5
Amherst Rd *WEA* W13 ....97 J5
Amhurst Gdns *ISLW* TW7 ....136 A2
Amhurst Pde
STNW/STAM N16 * 68 B4
Amhurst Pk *STNW/STAM* N16 ....68 A4
Amhurst Rd *STNW/STAM* N16 ....86 B2
Amhurst Ter *HACK* E8 ....86 C2
Amidas Gdns *BCTR* RM8 ....91 H2
Amiel St *WCHPL* E1 ....104 E3
Amies St *BTSEA* SW11 ....140 E4
Amina Wy *BERM/RHTH* SE16 ....123 H3
Amis Av *HOR/WEW* KT19 ....206 C4
Amity Gv *RYNPK* SW20 ....177 F4
Amity Rd *SRTFD* E15 ....88 D5
Ammanford Gn
CDALE/KGS NW9 * 63 G3
Amner Rd *BTSEA* SW11 ....161 F1
Amor Rd *HMSMTH* W6 ....119 F3
Amott Rd *PECK* SE15 ....143 H4
Ampere Wy *CROY/NA* CR0 ....195 K4
Ampleforth Cl *ORP* BR6 ....217 J2
Ampleforth Rd *ABYW* SE2 ....128 C2
Ampthill Est *CAMTN* NW1 ....4 A3
Ampthill Sq *CAMTN* NW1 ....4 B3
Ampton St *FSBYW* WC1X 5 G5
Amroth Cl *FSTH* SE23 ....163 J3
Amroth Gn *CDALE/KGS* NW9 * 63 G3
Amsterdam Rd *POP/IOD* E14 ....125 F3
Amwell Cl *ENC/FH* EN2 ....23 K6
Amwell St *CLKNW* EC1R 5 J4
Amyand Cottages *TWK* TW1 ....156 C1
Amyand Park Gdns *TWK* TW1 ....156 C2
Amyand Park Rd *TWK* TW1 ....156 C2
Amy Cl *WLGTN* SM6 ....210 E5
Amyruth Rd *BROCKY* SE4 ....144 D6
Amy Warne Cl *EHAM* E6 ....107 J4
Anatola Rd *ARCH* N19 ....66 C6
Ancaster Crs *NWMAL* KT3 ....192 D3
Ancaster Ms *BECK* BR3 ....182 A6
Ancaster Rd *BECK* BR3 ....182 A6
Ancaster St *WOOL/PLUM* SE18 ....147 K1
Anchorage Cl *WIM/MER* SW19 ....177 K1
Anchor & Hope La *CHARL* SE7 ....126 B4
Anchor Cl *BARK* IG11 ....109 H2
Anchor Dr *RAIN* RM13 ....111 K3
Anchor St *BERM/RHTH* SE16 ....123 J4
Anchor Ter *WCHPL* E1 * 104 E3
Anchor Yd *FSBYE* EC1V * 6 D6
Ancill Cl *HMSMTH* W6 ....119 H6
Ancona Rd *WLSDN* NW10 ....99 J1
WOOL/PLUM SE18 ....127 J5
Andace Park Gdns *BMLY* BR1 * 184 B4
Andalus Rd *BRXN/ST* SW9 ....141 K4
Ander Cl *ALP/SUD* HA0 ....79 K2
Anderson Cl *ACT* W3 ....99 F5
CHEAM SM3 ....193 K5
WCHMH N21 ....23 F6
Anderson Dr *ASHF* TW15 ....153 F6
Anderson Rd *HOM* E9 ....87 F4
WFD IG8 ....53 H6
Anderson's Pl *HSLW* TW3 ....135 G5
Anderson Sq *IS* N1 ....6 A1
Anderson St *CHEL* SW3 ....120 E5
Anderson Wy *BELV* DA17 ....129 J2
Andover Av *CAN/RD* E16 ....107 H5
Andover Cl *EBED/NFELT* TW14 ....153 J3
GFD/PVL UB6 ....96 B3
Andover Pl *KIL/WHAMP* NW6 ....101 F1
Andover Rd *HOLWY* N7 ....67 F6
ORP BR6 ....201 K5
WHTN TW2 ....155 J3
Andover Ter *HMSMTH* W6 * 118 E4
Andre St *HACK* E8 ....86 C3
Andrew Borde St
LSQ/SEVD WC2H * 10 D3
Andrew Cl *BARK/HLT* IG6 ....54 D3
DART DA1 ....150 A6
Andrewes Gdns *EHAM* E6 ....107 J5
Andrew Pl *VX/NE* SW8 ....141 J2
Andrews Cl *BKHH* IG9 ....39 G4
HRW HA1 ....60 D4
STMC/STPC BR5 ....186 E6
WPK KT4 ....193 G6
Andrews Pl *RDART* DA2 ....170 B4
RDART DA2 ....170 D6
Andrews Rd *BETH* E2 ....86 D6
Andrew St *POP/IOD* E14 ....106 A5
Andrews Wk *WALW* SE17 ....122 C6
Andwell Cl *ABYW* SE2 ....128 C2
Anerley Gv *NRWD* SE19 ....181 G3
Anerley Hl *NRWD* SE19 ....181 G2
Anerley Pk *PGE/AN* SE20 ....181 J3
Anerley Park Rd *PGE/AN* SE20 ....181 J3
Anerley Rd *PGE/AN* SE20 ....181 J4
Anerley Station Rd
PGE/AN SE20 ....181 J4
Anerley V *NRWD* SE19 ....181 G3
Anfield Cl *BAL* SW12 ....161 H2
Angel Aly *WCHPL* E1 ....13 K2
Angel Cl *UED* N18 ....50 B1
Angel Corner Pde *UED* N18 * 50 C1
Angel Ct *LOTH* EC2R 13 F3
Angelfield *HSLW* TW3 ....135 G5
Angel Hl *SUT* SM1 ....209 F1
Angel Hill Dr *SUT* SM1 ....209 F1
Angelica Dr *EHAM* E6 ....108 A4
Angelica Gdns *CROY/NA* CR0 ....198 A5
Angel La *HYS/HAR* UB3 ....94 B4
SRTFD E15 ....88 B4
Angell Park Gdns
BRXN/ST SW9 ....142 B4
Angell Rd *BRXN/ST* SW9 ....142 C4
Angell Town Est
BRXN/ST SW9 * 142 B3
Angel Ms *PUT/ROE* SW15 ....158 D2
WCHPL E1 ....104 D6
Angel Pas *CANST* EC4R 12 E6
Angel Rd *HRW* HA1 ....60 E3
THDIT KT7 ....190 B5
Angel Rd (North Circular)
UED N18 ....50 D1
Angel Sq *FSBYE* EC1V * 6 A3
Angel St *STBT* EC1A 12 C3
Angel Wk *HMSMTH* W6 ....119 F4
Angel Wy *ROM* RM1 ....75 G2
Angerstein La *BKHTH/KID* SE3 ....145 J1
Anglers La *KTTN* NW5 ....84 B4
Anglers Reach *SURB* KT6 * 190 E2
Anglesea Ms
WOOL/PLUM SE18 ....127 G4
Anglesea Rd *KUT/HW* KT1 ....190 E1
STMC/STPC BR5 ....202 D3
WOOL/PLUM SE18 ....127 G4
Anglesey Cl *ASHF* TW15 ....152 D6
Anglesey Court Rd *CAR* SM5 ....210 A4
Anglesey Dr *RAIN* RM13 ....111 J3
Anglesey Gdns *CAR* SM5 ....210 A4
Anglesey Rd *OXHEY* WD19 ....41 G1
PEND EN3 ....24 D5
Anglesmede Crs *PIN* HA5 ....42 A6
Anglesmede Wy *PIN* HA5 ....41 K6
Angles Rd *STRHM/NOR* SW16 ....161 K6
Anglia Cl *TOTM* N17 ....50 D3
Anglian Rd *WAN* E11 ....88 B1
Anglo Rd *BOW* E3 ....105 H1
Angus Cl *CHSGTN* KT9 ....206 C3
Angus Dr *RSLP* HA4 ....77 G2
Angus Gdns *CDALE/KGS* NW9 ....45 F4
Angus Rd *PLSTW* E13 ....107 G2
Angus St *NWCR* SE14 ....144 B1
Anhalt Rd *BTSEA* SW11 ....140 D1
Ankerdine Crs
WOOL/PLUM SE18 ....147 G2
Anlaby Rd *TEDD* TW11 ....173 K1
Anley Rd *HMSMTH* W6 ....119 G2
Anmersh Gv *STAN* HA7 ....43 K4
Annabel Cl *POP/IOD* E14 ....105 K5
Anna Cl *HACK* E8 ....86 B6
Annandale Gv *HGDN/ICK* UB10 ....76 A1
Annandale Rd *BFN/LL* DA15 ....167 K2
CHSWK W4 ....118 B4
CROY/NA CR0 ....197 H6
GNWCH SE10 ....125 J6
Anna Neagle Cl *FSTGT* E7 ....88 E2
Annan Wy *ROM* RM1 ....57 F4
Anne Boleyn's Wk
CHEAM SM3 ....208 B5
KUTN/CMB KT2 ....175 F1
Anne Case Ms *NWMAL* KT3 * 176 A6
Anne Compton Ms
LEE/GVPK SE12 ....165 J2
Anne of Cleves Rd *DART* DA1 ....171 G1
Annesley Av *CDALE/KGS* NW9 ....45 F6
Annesley Cl *WLSDN* NW10 ....81 G1
Annesley Dr *CROY/NA* CR0 ....213 H2
Annesley Rd *BKHTH/KID* SE3 ....146 A2
Annesmere Gdns
BKHTH/KID SE3 ....146 C4
Anne St *PLSTW* E13 ....106 E3
Annette Cl *KTN/HRWW/WS* HA3 ....42 E5
Annette Rd *HOLWY* N7 ....85 F2
Anne Wy *BARK/HLT* IG6 ....54 C2
Annie Besant Cl *BOW* E3 * 87 H6
Anning St *WCHPL* E1 ....7 H6
Annington Rd *EFNCH* N2 ....47 K6
Annis Rd *HOM* E9 ....87 G4
Ann La *WBPTN* SW10 ....140 C1
Ann Moss Wy
BERM/RHTH SE16 ....123 K3
Ann's Cl *KTBR* SW1X 15 F3
Ann St *WOOL/PLUM* SE18 ....127 J4
Annsworthy Av *THHTH* CR7 ....180 E6
Annsworthy Crs *SNWD* SE25 ....180 E6
Ansar Gdns *WALTH* E17 ....69 G2
Ansdell Rd *PECK* SE15 ....143 K3
Ansdell St *KENS* W8 ....120 A3
Ansdell Ter *KENS* W8 ....120 A3
Ansell Gv *CAR* SM5 ....194 E5
Ansell Rd *TOOT* SW17 ....160 D5
Anselm Cl *CROY/NA* CR0 ....212 B1
Anselm Rd *FUL/PGN* SW6 ....119 K6
PIN HA5 ....41 K3
Ansford Rd *BMLY* BR1 ....183 F1
Ansleigh Pl *NTGHL* W11 ....100 B6
Anson Cl *ROMW/RG* RM7 ....56 D5
Anson Rd *ARCH* N19 ....84 C2
CRICK NW2 ....81 K3
Anson Wk *NTHWD* HA6 ....26 A6
Anstead Dr *RAIN* RM13 ....111 J1
Anstey Rd *PECK* SE15 ....143 H4
Anstice Cl *CHSWK* W4 ....138 B1
Anstridge Rd *ELTH/MOT* SE9 ....167 J1
Antelope Rd
WOOL/PLUM SE18 ....126 E3
Anthony Cl *MLHL* NW7 ....31 G6
OXHEY WD19 ....27 H3
Anthony Rd *GFD/PVL* UB6 ....96 E1
SNWD SE25 ....197 H3
WELL DA16 ....148 B2
Anthony's Cl *WAP* E1W 123 H1
Anthony St *WCHPL* E1 ....104 D5
Anthus Ms *NTHWD* HA6 ....40 B3
Antill Rd *BOW* E3 ....105 G2
SEVS/STOTM N15 ....68 C1
Antill Ter *WCHPL* E1 ....105 F5
Antlers Hl *CHING* E4 ....25 K6
Anton Crs *SUT* SM1 ....208 E1
Antoneys Cl *PIN* HA5 ....41 H5
Anton Pl *WBLY* HA9 ....80 D1
Anton St *HACK* E8 ....86 C3
Antrim Rd *HAMP* NW3 ....83 K4
Antrobus Cl *SUT* SM1 ....208 D3
Antrobus Rd *CHSWK* W4 ....117 K4
Anvil Cl *STRHM/NOR* SW16 ....179 H3
Anvil Ter *RDART* DA2 ....170 B4
Anworth Cl *WFD* IG8 ....53 F2
Aostle Wy *THHTH* CR7 ....180 C5
Apeldoorn Dr *WLGTN* SM6 ....210 E6
Aperfield Rd *ERITH* DA8 ....130 C6
Apex Cl *BECK* BR3 ....182 E4
Apex Pde *MLHL* NW7 * 31 F6
Aplin Wy *ISLW* TW7 ....135 K2
Apollo Av *BMLY* BR1 ....184 A4
NTHWD HA6 ....40 E1
Apollo Cl *HCH* RM12 ....75 K6
Apollo Pl *WAN* E11 ....88 C1
WBPTN SW10 * 140 C1
Apollo Wy *ERITH* DA8 ....130 A4
THMD SE28 ....127 J3
Apothecary St *BLKFR* EC4V * 12 A4
Appach Rd *BRXS/STRHM* SW2 ....142 B6
Apple Blossom Ct *VX/NE* SW8 ....141 J1
Appleby Cl *CHING* E4 ....52 A2
SEVS/STOTM N15 ....67 K2
STMC/STPC BR5 ....201 K4
UX/CGN UB8 ....94 A5
WHTN TW2 ....155 J4
Appleby Gdns
EBED/NFELT TW14 * 153 J3
Appleby Rd *CAN/RD* E16 ....106 E5
HACK E8 ....86 C5
Appleby St *BETH* E2 ....7 J2
Appledore Av *BXLYHN* DA7 ....149 K2
RSLP HA4 ....77 F1
Appledore Cl *EDGW* HA8 ....44 C4
HAYES BR2 ....199 J2
TOOT SW17 ....160 E4
Appledore Crs *SCUP* DA14 ....167 K5
Appledore Wy *MLHL* NW7 ....46 B3
Appleford Rd *NKENS* W10 ....100 C3
Apple Garth *BTFD* TW8 ....116 E4
Applegarth *CROY/NA* CR0 ....213 K5
ESH/CLAY KT10 ....205 F3
Applegarth Dr *DART* DA1 ....171 H4
GNTH/NBYPK IG2 ....73 F1
Applegarth Rd *THMD* SE28 ....128 C1
WKENS W14 * 119 G3
Apple Gv *CHSGTN* KT9 ....206 A2
EN EN1 ....24 A4
Apple Ldg *ALP/SUD* HA0 * 79 J1
Apple Market *KUT/HW* KT1 ....174 E5
Apple Rd *WAN* E11 ....88 C1
Appleton Cl *BXLYHN* DA7 ....149 K3
Appleton Dr *RDART* DA2 ....170 E5
Appleton Gdns *NWMAL* KT3 ....192 D3
Appleton Rd *ELTH/MOT* SE9 ....146 D4
Appletree Cl *PGE/AN* SE20 ....181 J4
Appletree Gdns *EBAR* EN4 ....21 J5
Apple Tree Yd *STJS* SW1Y 10 B7
Applewood Cl *CRICK* NW2 ....81 K1
TRDG/WHET N20 ....33 J3
Applewood Dr *PLSTW* E13 ....107 F3
Appold St *ERITH* DA8 ....130 C6
SDTCH EC2A 13 G1
Apprentice Wy *CLPT* E5 ....86 D2
Approach La *MLHL* NW7 ....46 C1
Approach Rd *BETH* E2 ....104 E1
E/WMO/HCT KT8 ....189 F2
EBAR EN4 ....21 G5
RYNPK SW20 ....177 F5
The Approach *ACT* W3 ....99 F5
EN EN1 ....24 D3
HDN NW4 ....64 B2
ORP BR6 ....202 A6
Aprey Gdns *HDN* NW4 ....64 A1
April Cl *FELT* TW13 ....153 K5
HNWL W7 ....96 E6
ORP BR6 ....217 F3
April Gln *FSTH* SE23 ....164 A5
April St *HACK* E8 ....86 B2
Apsley Cl *HRW* HA1 ....60 C2
Apsley Rd *NWMAL* KT3 ....175 K6
SNWD SE25 ....197 J1
Apsley Wy *CRICK* NW2 ....63 J6
MYFR/PICC W1J * 15 J1
Aquarius *TWK* TW1 * 156 C3
Aquarius Wy *NTHWD* HA6 ....40 E1
Aquila St *STJWD* NW8 ....2 B2
Aquinas St *STHWK* SE1 ....17 K1
Arabella Dr *PUT/ROE* SW15 ....138 B5
Arabia Cl *CHING* E4 ....38 B2
Arabin Rd *BROCKY* SE4 ....144 B5
Aragon Av *EW* KT17 ....207 K6
THDIT KT7 ....190 A2
Aragon Cl *ENC/FH* EN2 ....23 F1
HAYES BR2 ....200 E5
LOU IG10 ....39 J1
Aragon Dr *BARK/HLT* IG6 ....54 C3
RSLP HA4 ....59 H5
Aragon Pl *MRDN* SM4 ....193 H4
Aragon Rd *KUTN/CMB* KT2 ....175 F1
MRDN SM4 ....193 G4
Arandora Crs *CHDH* RM6 ....73 H4
Arbery Rd *BOW* E3 ....105 G2
Arbor Cl *BECK* BR3 ....182 E5
Arborfield Cl
BRXS/STRHM SW2 ....162 A3
Arbor Rd *CHING* E4 ....38 B5
Arbour Rd *PEND* EN3 ....25 F5
Arbour Sq *WCHPL* E1 ....105 F5
Arbour Wy *HCH* RM12 ....93 K3
Arbroath Gn *OXHEY* WD19 ....26 E5
Arbroath Rd *ELTH/MOT* SE9 ....146 D4
Arbrook Cl *STMC/STPC* BR5 ....186 B6
Arbrook La *ESH/CLAY* KT10 ....204 D4
Arbuthnot La *BXLY* DA5 ....169 F1
Arbuthnot Rd *NWCR* SE14 ....144 A3
Arbutus St *HACK* E8 ....86 B6
Arcade Chambers
ELTH/MOT SE9 * 167 F1
Arcade Pde *CHSGTN* KT9 * 206 A2
The Arcade *ELTH/MOT* SE9 * 167 F1
LVPST EC2M * 13 G2
WALTH E17 * 69 J1
Arcadia Av *FNCH* N3 ....46 E4
Arcadia Cl *CAR* SM5 ....210 A2
Arcadian Av *BXLY* DA5 ....169 F1
Arcadian Cl *BXLY* DA5 ....169 F1
Arcadian Gdns *WDGN* N22 ....49 G3
Arcadian Pl *WAND/EARL* SW18 ....159 H2
Arcadian Rd *BXLY* DA5 ....169 F2
Arcadia St *POP/IOD* E14 ....105 J5
Archangel St
BERM/RHTH SE16 ....124 A2
Archbishop's Pl
BRXS/STRHM SW2 ....162 A2
Archdale Ct *SHB* W12 ....118 E1
Archdale Pl *NWMAL* KT3 ....175 J6
Archdale Rd *EDUL* SE22 ....143 G6
Archel Rd *WKENS* W14 ....119 J6
Archer Cl *KUTN/CMB* KT2 ....175 F3
Archer Ct *FELT* TW13 ....153 K3
Archer Ms *HPTN* TW12 ....173 H2
Archer Rd *SNWD* SE25 ....197 J1
STMC/STPC BR5 ....202 B3
Archers Dr *PEND* EN3 ....24 E3
Archer Sq *NWCR* SE14 ....124 B6
Archer St *SOHO/SHAV* W1D 10 C5
Archery Cl *BAY/PAD* W2 ....8 D4
KTN/HRWW/WS HA3 ....43 F6
Archery Rd *ELTH/MOT* SE9 ....146 E6
The Arches *CHCR* WC2N * 11 F7
RYLN/HDSTN HA2 ....60 B6
Archibald Ms *MYFR/PKLN* W1K 9 H6
Archibald Rd *HOLWY* N7 ....84 D2
Archibold St *BOW* E3 ....105 J2
Archie Cl *WDR/YW* UB7 ....112 D2
Arch St *STHWK* SE1 ....18 C5
Archway *HARH* RM3 ....57 K2
Archway Cl *ARCH* N19 * 66 C6
NKENS W10 ....100 B4
WIM/MER SW19 ....160 A6
WLGTN SM6 * 210 E1
Archway Rd *HGT* N6 ....65 K2
Archway St *BARN* SW13 ....138 B4
Arcola St *HACK* E8 ....86 B3
Arcon Dr *NTHLT* UB5 ....95 J3
Arctic St *KTTN* NW5 ....84 B3
Arcus Rd *BMLY* BR1 ....183 H2
Ardbeg Rd *HNHL* SE24 ....162 E1
Arden Cl *BUSH* WD23 ....29 F2
HRW HA1 ....78 D1
THMD SE28 ....109 K5
Arden Court Gdns *EFNCH* N2 ....65 H4
Arden Crs *DAGW* RM9 ....91 K5
POP/IOD E14 ....124 D4
Arden Est *IS* N1 ....7 G3
Arden Gv *ORP* BR6 ....216 B2
Arden Mhor *PIN* HA5 ....59 F1
Arden Rd *FNCH* N3 ....46 D6
WEA W13 ....97 J6
Ardent Cl *SNWD* SE25 ....181 F6
Ardfern Av *STRHM/NOR* SW16 ....180 B6
Ardfillan Rd *CAT* SE6 ....165 G3
Ardgowan Rd *CAT* SE6 ....165 H2
Ardilaun Rd *HBRY* N5 ....85 J2
Ardingly Cl *CROY/NA* CR0 ....213 F1
Ardleigh Gdns *CHEAM* SM3 ....193 K5
Ardleigh Rd *IS* N1 ....86 A4
WALTH E17 ....51 H4
Ardleigh Ter *WALTH* E17 ....51 H4
Ardley Cl *CAT* SE6 ....164 B5
WLSDN NW10 ....81 G1
Ardlui Rd *WNWD* SE27 ....162 D4
Ardmay Gdns *SURB* KT6 * 191 F2
Ardmere Rd *LEW* SE13 ....165 G1
Ardmore La *BKHH* IG9 ....39 F3
Ardmore Pl *BKHH* IG9 * 39 F2
Ardoch Rd *CAT* SE6 ....165 G4
Ardra Rd *ED* N9 ....37 F5
Ardrossan Gdns *WPK* KT4 ....207 J1
Ardross Av *NTHWD* HA6 ....40 C1
Ardshiel Cl *PUT/ROE* SW15 ....139 G4
Ardwell Av *BARK/HLT* IG6 ....72 C2
Ardwell Rd *BRXS/STRHM* SW2 ....161 K4
Ardwick Rd *CRICK* NW2 ....82 E2
Arena Est *FSBYPK* N4 * 67 H3
The Arena *STKPK* UB11 * 113 F1
Argall Av *LEY* E10 ....69 G4
Argall Wy *LEY* E10 ....69 G5
Argenta Wy *WLSDN* NW10 ....80 D5
Argent Ct *SURB* KT6 * 191 H6
Argon Ms *FUL/PGN* SW6 ....139 K1
Argon Rd *UED* N18 ....50 E1
Argosy La *STWL/WRAY* TW19 ....152 A2
Argus Cl *ROMW/RG* RM7 ....56 D4
Argus Wy *NTHLT* UB5 ....95 J2
Argyle Av *HSLW* TW3 ....155 F1
Argyle Cl *WEA* W13 ....97 F3
Argyle Cnr *WEA* W13 * 97 H6
Argyle Pl *HMSMTH* W6 ....118 E4
Argyle Rd *BAR* EN5 ....20 A5
CAN/RD E16 ....107 F5
GFD/PVL UB6 ....97 F2
HSLW TW3 ....135 G6
IL IG1 ....72 A6
NFNCH/WDSPK N12 ....46 E1

RYLN/HDSTN HA2 ....60 B3
SRTFD E15 ....88 C2
TOTM N17 ....50 C4
UED N18 ....36 D6
WCHPL E1 ....105 F5
Argyle Sq STPAN WC1H *................5 F4
Argyle Rd STPAN WC1H *...............4 E5
Argyle Wk STPAN WC1H *..............4 E5
Argyle Av STHL UB1 ....115 C0
Argyll Cl BRXN/ST SW9 ....142 A4
Argyll Gdns EDGW HA8 ....44 D5
Argyll Rd KENS W8 ....119 K2
WOOL/PLUM SE18 ....127 H3
Argyll St REGST W1B 10 A4
Archie St STHWK SE1 ....19 H5
Arica Rd BROCKY SE4 ....144 B5
Ariel Rd KIL/WHAMP NW6 ....82 E4
Ariel Wy HSLWW TW4 ....134 A4
SHB W12 ....119 F1
Aristotle Rd CLAP SW4 ....141 J5
Arkell Gv NRWD SE19 ....180 C3
Arkindale Rd CAT SE6 ....165 F5
Arkley Crs WALTH E17 ....69 H2
Arkley Rd WALTH E17 ....124 C6
Arklow Rd NWCR SE14 ....123 H5
Arkwright Rd HAMP NW3 ....83 G3
Arlesford Rd BRXN/ST SW9 ....141 K4
Arlingford Rd
BRXS/STRHM SW2 ....162 B1
Arlington Av IS N1 ....6 D1
Arlington Cl BFN/LL DA15 ....167 K2
LEW SE13 ....145 C6
SUT SM1 ....193 K6
TWK TW1 * 156 C1
Arlington Ct HYS/HAR UB3 ....113 C5
Arlington Dr CAR SM5 ....194 E6
RSLP HA4 ....58 B3
Arlington Gdns CHSWK W4 ....117 K5
IL IG1 ....71 K4
Arlington Pde
BRXS/STRHM SW2 * 142 A5
Arlington Rd CAMTN NW1 ....3 K1
RCHPK/HAM TW10 ....156 E4
STHGT/OAK N14 ....34 B4
SURB KT6 ....190 F5
TEDD TW11 ....156 D6
TWK TW1 * 156 D1
WEA W13 ....97 H5
WFD IG8 ....52 E4
Arlington Sq IS N1 ....6 D1
Arlington St MYFR/PICC W1J 10 A7
Arlington Wy CLKNW EC1R 5 K4
Arliss Wy NTHLT UB5 ....77 G6
Arlow Rd WCHMH N21 ....35 G3
Armadale Cl TOTM N17 ....68 D1
Armadale Rd
EBED/NFELT TW14 ....133 K6
FUL/PGN SW6 ....139 K1
Armada St DEPT SE8 ....124 D6
Armada Wy EHAM E6 ....108 C5
Armagh Rd BOW E3 ....87 H6
Armfield Cl E/WMO/HCT KT8 ....188 E2
Armfield Rd ENC/FH EN2 ....23 K2
Arminger Rd SHB W12 ....118 E1
Armistice Gdns SNWD SE25 ....181 H6
Armitage Rd GLDGN NW11 ....64 C5
GNWCH SE10 ....125 J4
Armour Cl HOLWY N7 ....85 F4
Armour Rd DEPT SE8 ....144 D1
Armoury Wy
WAND/EARL SW18 ....139 K6
Armstead Wk DAGE RM10 ....92 C5
Armstrong Av WFD IG8 ....52 C2
Armstrong Cl BCTR RM8 ....73 K4
BMLY BR1 ....184 D6
EHAM E6 ....107 K5
RSLP HA4 ....58 B4
Armstrong Crs EBAR EN4 ....21 H4
Armstrong Rd ACT W3 ....118 C1
FELT TW13 ....172 E1
WOOL/PLUM SE18 ....127 H3
Armstrong Wy NWDGN UB2 ....115 H2
Armytage Rd HEST TW5 ....134 C1
Arnal Crs WAND/EARL SW18 ....159 H2
Arncliffe Cl FBAR/BDGN N11 ....48 A2
Arne Gv ORP BR6 ....217 F1
Arne St COVGDN WC2E 11 H4
Arnett Sq CHIG E4 ....51 H2
Arne Wk LEW SE13 ....145 J5
Arneways Av CHDH RM6 ....73 K1
Arneway St WEST SW1P 16 D5
Arney's La MTCM CR4 ....195 F3
Arngask Rd CAT SE6 ....165 C2
Arnheim Pl POP/IOD E14 ....124 D3
Arnison Rd E/WMO/HCT KT8 ....189 J1
Arnold Av East PEND EN3 ....25 J1
Arnold Av West PEND EN3 ....25 J1
Arnold Circ BETH E2 ....7 J5
Arnold Cl KTN/HRWW/WS HA3 .....62 B4
Arnewood Cl PUT/ROE SW15 ....158 D3
Arnold Dr CHSGTN KT9 ....205 K4
Arnold Est STHWK SE1 ....19 K3
Arnold Gdns PLMGR N13 ....49 H1
Arnold Rd BOW E3 ....105 J2
DAGW RM9 ....92 B5
NTHLT UB5 ....77 J4
SEVS/STOTM N15 ....50 B6
TOOT SW17 ....178 E3
Arnott Cl ter STAN HA7 * 43 F1
Arnos Gv STHGT/OAK N14 ....34 C6
Arnos Rd FBAR/BDGN N11 ....48 C1
Arnott Cl CHSWK W4 ....118 A4
THMD SE28 ....128 D1
Arnould Av CMBW SE5 ....142 E5
Arnsberg Wy BXLYHN DA7 ....149 H6
Arnside Gdns WBLY HA9 ....61 K5
Arnside Rd BXLYHN DA7 ....149 H2
Arnside St WALW SE17 ....122 D6
Arnulf St CAT SE6 ....164 E6
Arnull's Rd STRHM/NOR SW16 ...180 C2
Arodene Rd
BRXS/STRHM SW2 ....162 A1
Arosa Rd TWK TW1 ....156 E1

Arragon Gdns
STRHM/NOR SW16 ....179 K3
WWKM BR4 ....213 K1
Arragon Rd EHAM E6 ....89 H6
TWK TW1 ....156 B3
WAND/EARL SW18 ....159 K3
Arran Cl ERITH DA8 ....130 A6
WLGTN SM6 ....210 C2
Arran Dr MNPK E12 ....71 H5
STAN HA7 ....29 J6
Arran Gn OXHEY WD19 * 27 H6
Arran Ms EA W5 ....117 C1
Arran Rd CAT SE6 ....164 E4
Arran Wk IS N1 ....85 J5
Arran Wy ESH/CLAY KT10 ....189 G6
Arras Av MRDN SM4 ....194 B2
Arrol Rd BECK BR3 ....181 K6
Arrow Rd BOW E3 ....105 K2
Arrowsmith Rd CHIG IG7 ....55 F1
Arsenal Rd ELTH/MOT SE9 ....146 E3
Arsenal Wy WOOL/PLUM SE18 ...127 H4
Artemis Pl WAND/EARL SW18 .....159 J2
Arterberry Rd RYNPK SW20 ....177 F3
Arterial Purfleet
SOCK/AV RM15 ....131 K3
Artesian Cl ROM RM1 ....75 H3
WLSDN NW10 ....81 F5
Artesian Gv BAR EN5 ....21 C5
Artesian Houses
BAY/PAD W2 * 100 E5
Artesian Rd BAY/PAD W2 ....100 E5
Arthingworth St SRTFD E15 ....88 C6
Arthurdon Rd BROCKY SE4 ....144 D6
Arthur Gv WOOL/PLUM SE18 ......127 H4
Arthur Rd CHDH RM6 ....73 J4
ED N9 ....36 B4
EHAM E6 ....107 K1
HOLWY N7 ....85 F2
KUTN/CMB KT2 ....175 H3
NWMAL KT3 ....192 E2
WIM/MER SW19 ....159 J6
St CANST EC4R 13 F6
ERITH DA8 ....150 C1
Artichoke Hl WAP E1W 104 D6
Artichoke Pl CMBW SE5 * 142 E2
Artillery Cl GNTH/NBYPK IG2 ....72 C3
Artillery La SHB W12 ....13 H2
WCHPL E1 * 13 H2
Artillery Pas WCHPL E1 * 13 H2
Artillery Rw WOOL/PLUM SE18 ...126 E5
Artillery Rw WEST SW1P 16 C5
Artington Cl ORP BR6 ....216 C2
Artizan St WCHPL E1 ....13 H3
Artwell Cl LEY E10 ....69 K3
Arundel Av E/W KT17 ....207 K6
MRDN SM4 ....193 J1
Arundel Cl BTSEA SW11 ....140 D6
BXLY DA5 ....169 C1
HPTN TW12 ....173 G6
SRTFD E15 ....88 C2
Arundel Dr ORP BR6 ....217 H5
RYLN/HDSTN HA2 ....77 K2
WFD IG8 ....52 E3
Arundel Gdns EDGW HA8 ....45 G3
GDMY/SEVK IG3 ....73 C6
NTGHL W11 ....100 D6
WCHMH N21 ....35 G3
Arundel Gv IS N1 ....86 A3
Arundel Pl HOLWY N7 ....85 G4
Arundel Rd BELMT SM2 ....208 D5
CROY/NA CRO 196 E3
DART DA1 ....151 F5
EBAR EN4 ....21 J4
HSLWW TW4 ....134 B4
KUTN/CMB KT2 ....175 K5
Arundel Sq HOLWY N7 ....85 G4
Arundel St TPL/STR WC2R 11 H5
Arundel Ter BARN SW13 ....118 E6
Arvon Rd HBRY N5 ....85 G3
Asbaston Ter IL IG1 * 90 C4
Ascalon St VX/NE SW8 ....141 H1
Ascension Rd CRW RM5 ....56 C2
Ascham Dr CHING E4 ....51 K3
Ascham End WALTH E17 * 51 C4
Ascham St KTTN NW5 ....84 C3
Aschurch Rd CROY/NA CR0 ....197 G4
Ascot Cl BARK/HLT IG6 ....54 C2
NTHLT UB5 ....78 A3
Ascot Gdns STHL UB1 ....95 K4
Ascot Ms WLGTN SM6 ....210 C6
Ascot Pde CLAP SW4 * 141 K5
Ascot Rd EBED/NFELT TW14 ......152 D3
EHAM E6 ....107 K2
SEVS/STOTM N15 ....67 J3
STMC/STPC BR5 ....202 A1
TOOT SW17 ....179 F2
UED N18 ....50 B1
Ascott Av W5 ....117 F2
Ascott Ct PIN HA5 * 58 E1
Ashanti Ms HACK E8 * 86 D4
Ashbourne Sq NTHWD HA6 ....40 C2
Ashbourne Av BXLYHN DA7 ....149 F1
GLDGN NW11 ....64 D2
RYLN/HDSTN HA2 * 60 D6
SWFD E18 ....71 F1
TRDG/WHET N20 ....33 K4
Ashbourne Cl EA W5 ....98 B4
NFNCH/WDSPK N12 ....33 F6
EDUL SE22 ....143 G6
MLHL NW7 * 31 F6
Ashbourne Pde EA W5 * 98 B3
GLDGN NW11 * 64 D1
Ashbourne Ri ORP BR6 ....216 E2
Ashbourne Rd EA W5 ....98 B3
MTCM CR4 ....179 F2
Ashbourne Ter
WIM/MER SW19 ....177 K3
Ashbourne Wy GLDGN NW11 ....64 D1
Ashbridge Rd WAN E11 ....70 C4
Ashbridge St STJWD NW8 ....2 C2
Ashbrook EDGW HA8 * 44 B2
Ashbrook Rd ARCH N19 ....66 D6
DAGE RM10 ....92 D1
Ashburn Gdns SKENS SW7 ....120 B4
Ashburnham Av HRW HA1 ....61 F4

Ashburnham Cl EFNCH N2 ....47 H6
OXHEY WD19 * 26 E5
Ashburnham Dr OXHEY WD19 ......26 E5
Ashburnham Gdns HRW HA1 ....61 F3
Ashburnham Gv GNWCH SE10 ....144 D1
Ashburnham Pk
ESH/CLAY KT10 ....204 C2
Ashburnham Pl GNWCH SE10 .....144 E1
Ashburnham Retreat
GNWCH SE10 ....144 D1
Ashburnham Rd BELV DA17 ....129 K4
RCHPK/HAM TW10 ....156 C5
WBPTN SW10 * 140 B1
WLSDN NW10 ....100 A3
Ashburton Av CROY/NA CR0 ....197 J5
GDMY/SEVK IG3 ....91 F2
Ashburton Cl CROY/NA CR0 ....197 H5
Ashburton Gdns CROY/NA CR0 ...197 H6
Ashburton Rd CAN/RD E16 ....106 E5
CROY/NA CR0 ....197 H6
RSLP HA4 ....58 D6
Ashbury Gdns CHDH RM6 ....73 K2
Ashbury Pl WIM/MER SW19 ....178 B2
Ashbury Rd BTSEA SW11 ....140 E4
Ashby Av CHSGTN KT9 ....206 C4
Ashby Gv IS N1 ....85 J5
Ashby Ms BROCKY SE4 ....144 C4
Ashby Rd BROCKY SE4 ....144 C3
SEVS/STOTM N15 ....68 C2
Ashby St FSBYE EC1V 6 B5
Ashby Wk CROY/NA CR0 ....196 D5
Ashby Wy WDR/YW UB7 ....132 D1
Ashchurch Gv SHB W12 ....118 D3
Ashchurch Park Vls SHB W12 ......118 D3
Ashchurch Ter SHB W12 ....118 C3
Ash Cl CAR SM5 ....194 E6
CRW RM5 ....56 D3
EDGW HA8 ....30 E6
NWMAL KT3 ....176 A5
PGE/AN SE20 ....181 K5
RYNPK SW20 ....177 F6
STMC/STPC BR5 ....201 J3
STAN HA7 ....43 G2
SWLY BR8 ....187 K5
Ash Ms KTTN NW5 * 84 C3
Ashmill St STJWD NW8 ....8 C1
Ashmole St VX/NE SW8 ....122 A6
Ashmore Cl PECK SE15 ....143 H1
Ashmore Gv WELL DA16 ....147 J4
Ashmore Rd MV/WKIL W9 ....100 D2
Ashmount Est ARCH N19 ....66 C4
SEVS/STOTM N15 ....68 B2
Ashmount Ter EA W5 * 116 E4
Ashmour Gdns ROM RM1 ....57 F5
Ashneal Gdns HRW HA1 ....78 D1
Ashness Gdns GFD/PVL UB6 ....79 H4
Ashness Rd BTSEA SW11 ....140 E6
Ashridge Cl
KTN/HRWW/WS HA3 ....61 J3
Ashridge Crs
WOOL/PLUM SE18 ....147 H1
Ashridge Dr OXHEY WD19 * 26 E5
Ashridge Gdns PIN HA5 ....59 J1
PLMGR N13 ....48 E1
Ash Rd CHEAM SM3 ....193 H5
CROY/NA CR0 ....198 B2
DART DA1 ....171 G3
ORP BR6 ....217 G5
RDART DA2 ....171 J6
SRTFD E15 ....88 C3
Ash Rw HAYES BR2 ....201 F3
Ashstead Rd CLPT E5 ....68 C4
Ashton Cl SUT SM1 ....208 E2
Ashton Gdns CHDH RM6 ....74 A3
HSLWW TW4 ....134 E5
Ashton Rd SRTFD E15 ....88 B3
Ashton St POP/IOD E14 ....106 A6
Ashtree Av MTCM CR4 ....178 C5
Ash Tree Cl SURB KT6 ....191 F5
Ashtree Cl ORP BR6 ....216 B2
Ash Tree Dell CDALE/KGS NW9 ....62 E2
Ash Tree Wy CROY/NA CR0 ....198 B2
Ashurst Cl DART DA1 ....150 C4
NTHWD HA6 ....40 C3
PGE/AN SE20 ....181 J4
Ashurst Dr BARK/HLT IG6 ....72 C2
Ashurst Gdns
BRXS/STRHM SW2 * 162 B3
Ashurst Rd EBAR EN4 ....21 K6
NFNCH/WDSPK N12 ....47 J1
Ashurst Wk CROY/NA CR0 ....197 J6
Ashvale Gdns CRW RM5 ....57 F1
Ashville Rd WAN E11 ....70 B6
Ash Wk ALP/SUD HA0 ....79 J1
Ashwater Rd LEE/GVPK SE12 .....165 K3
Ashwell Cl EHAM E6 ....107 K5
Ashwin St HACK E8 ....86 B4
Ashwood Av RAIN RM13 ....111 K2
Ashwood Gdns CROY/NA CR0 .....213 K4
HYS/HAR UB3 ....113 J4
Ashwood Rd CHING E4 ....38 B5
Ashworth Cl CMBW SE5 ....142 E3
Ashworth Rd MV/WKIL W9 ....101 F1
Askern Cl BXLYHS DA6 ....148 E5
Aske St IS N1 ....7 G4
Askew Crs SHB W12 ....118 C2
Askew Rd NTHWD HA6 ....26 B4
SHB W12 ....118 C2
Askew Vls PLMGR N13 * 49 J5
Askham Rd SHB W12 ....118 D1
Askill Dr PUT/ROE SW15 ....139 H6
Askwith Rd RAIN RM13 ....111 F1
Asland Rd SRTFD E15 ....88 B6
Aslett St WAND/EARL SW18 ....160 A2
Asmara Rd CRICK NW2 ....82 C3
Asmuns Hl GLDGN NW11 ....64 E2
Asmuns Pl GLDGN NW11 ....64 D2
Aspen Cl EA W5 ....117 G2
ORP BR6 ....217 G6
WDR/YW UB7 ....112 C1
Aspen Copse BMLY BR1 ....184 E5
Aspen Dr ALP/SUD HA0 ....79 G2
Aspen Gdns MTCM CR4 ....195 F2

Ashland Pl MHST W1U 9 G1
Aspen Gv PIN HA5 ....40 D6
Aspen La NTHLT UB5 ....95 J2
Aspenlea Rd HMSMTH W6 ....119 G6
Aspen Wy FELT TW13 ....154 A5
POP/IOD E14 ....106 A6
Aspern Gv HAMP NW3 ....83 J3
Aspinall Rd BROCKY SE4 ....144 A4
Aspinden Rd
BERM/RHTH SE16 ....123 J4
Aspley Rd WAND/EARL SW18 ......140 A6
Asplins Rd TOTM N17 ....50 C4
Asplins Vis TOTM N17 ....50 C4
Asprey Ms BECK BR3 ....198 C2
Asquith Cl BCTR RM8 ....73 J5
Assam St WCHPL E1 ....104 C5
Assata Ms IS N1 ....85 H4
Assembly Pas WCHPL E1 ....104 E4
Assembly Wk CAR SM5 ....194 D4
Ass House La
KTN/HRWW/WS HA3 ....28 B6
Astall Cl KTN/HRWW/WS HA3 ....42 E4
Astbury Rd PECK SE15 ....143 K2
Astell St CHEL SW3 ....120 D5
Asteys Rw IS N1 ....85 H5
Astle St BTSEA SW11 ....141 F3
Astley Av CRICK NW2 ....82 A3
Aston Av KTN/HRWW/WS HA3 ......61 J4
Aston Cl BUSH WD23 ....28 C1
SCUP DA14 ....168 C5
Aston Gn HSLWW TW4 ....134 B3
Astonplace STRHM/NOR SW16 ...180 C3
Aston Rd EA W5 ....97 K5
ESH/CLAY KT10 ....204 E3
RYNPK SW20 ....177 F5
Astons Rd NTHWD HA6 ....26 A2
Aston St POP/IOD E14 ....105 C5
Aston Ter BAL SW12 * 161 G1
Astonville St
WAND/EARL SW18 ....159 K3
Astor Av ROMW/RG RM7 ....74 D3
Astor Cl KUTN/CMB KT2 ....175 J2
Astoria Pde ASHF TW15 * 152 D6
STRHM/NOR SW16 * 161 K5
Astra Cl HCH RM12 ....93 K4
Astrop Ms HMSMTH W6 ....119 F3
Astrop Ter HMSMTH W6 ....119 F3
Astwood Ms SKENS SW7 ....120 A4
Asylum Rd PECK SE15 ....143 J1
Atalanta St FUL/PGN SW6 ....139 G2
Atbara Rd TEDD TW11 ....174 C2
Atcham Rd HSLW TW3 ....135 H5
Atcost Rd BARK IG11 ....108 A3
Atheldene Rd
WAND/EARL SW18 ....160 B3
Athelney St CAT SE6 ....164 E5
Athelstane Gv BOW E3 ....105 H1
Athelstane Ms FSBYPK N4 ....67 G5
Athelstan Gdns
KIL/WHAMP NW6 ....82 C5
Athelstan Rd KUT/HW KT1 ....175 G6
RYLN/HDSTN HA2 ....78 A1
Athelstone Rd
KTN/HRWW/WS HA3 ....42 D5
Athena Cl KUT/HW KT1 ....175 G6
RYLN/HDSTN HA2 ....78 A1
Athenaeum Pl MUSWH N10 ....48 B5
Athenaeum Rd
TRDG/WHET N20 ....33 G3
Athenlay Rd PECK SE15 ....144 A6
Athenlay Rd PECK SE15 ....144 A6
Athenry Rd PECK SE15 ....144 A6
Athens Gdns MV/WKIL W9 * 100 E3
Atherden Rd CLPT E5 ....68 C4
Atherfold Rd BRXN/ST SW9 ....141 K4
Atherley Wy HSLWW TW4 ....154 C2
Atherstone Ms SKENS SW7 * 120 B4
Atherton Dr WIM/MER SW19 ....159 H1
Atherton Hts ALP/SUD HA0 ....79 J4
Atherton Ms FSTGT E7 ....88 D4
Atherton Pl RYLN/HDSTN HA2 ......42 D3
STHL UB1 ....96 B6
Atherton Rd BARN SW13 ....138 D1
CLAY IG5 ....53 J5
FSTGT E7 ....88 D4
Atherton St BTSEA SW11 ....140 D3
Athlone ESH/CLAY KT10 ....204 E4
Athlone Cl CLPT E5 ....86 D3
Athlone Cl WALTH E17 ....52 B6
Athlone Rd BRXS/STRHM SW2 ...162 A2
Athlone St KTTN NW5 ....84 A4
Athlon Rd ALP/SUD HA0 ....97 K1
Athol Cl PIN HA5 ....41 F4
Athole Gdns EN EN1 ....24 A6
Athol Gdns PIN HA5 ....41 F4
Athol Sq POP/IOD E14 ....106 A5
Athol Rd GDMY/SEVK IG3 ....73 C4
Athol Rd ERITH DA8 ....129 J5
Athol Sq POP/IOD E14 ....106 A5
Atkins Dr WWKM BR4 ....214 B1
Atkinson Cl ORP BR6 ....217 J6
Atkinson Rd CAN/RD E16 ....107 C4
LEY E10 ....69 J3
Atlanta Bvd ROM RM1 ....75 G2
Atlantic Cl SWLY BR8 ....187 J4
Atlantic Rd BRXN/ST SW9 ....142 B5
Atlantis Cl BARK IG11 ....109 G3
Atlas Gdns CHARL SE7 ....126 B4
Atlas Ms HACK E8 ....86 B4
Atlas Rd DART DA1 ....151 J4
FBAR/BDGN N11 ....48 A2
PLSTW E15 ....106 E1
WBLY HA9 ....81 F2
WLSDN NW10 ....99 G2
Atley Rd BOW E3 ....87 K6
Atlip Rd ALP/SUD HA0 ....80 A6
Atney Rd PUT/ROE SW15 ....139 H5
Atria Rd NTHWD HA6 ....26 D3
Attenborough Cl OXHEY WD19 ....27 J2
Atterbury Rd FSBYPK N4 ....67 H3
Atterbury St WEST SW1P 16 E7
Attewood Av WLSDN NW10 ....81 J1
Attewood Rd NTHLT UB5 ....77 J4
Attfield Cl TRDG/WHET N20 ....33 H4
Attlee Cl THHTH CR7 ....196 D3
YEAD UB4 * 95 F2
Attlee Dr DART DA1 ....151 K6

Attlee Rd *THMD* SE28	...109	H6
YEAD UB4	...94	E2
Attlee Ter *WALTH* E17	...69	K1
Attneave St *CLKNW* EC1R	...5	J6
Atwell Pl *THDIT* KT7	...190	B5
Atwell Rd *PECK* SE15 *	...143	H3
Atwick Av *RCH/KEW* TW9	...137	H5
Atwood Av *RCH/KEW* TW9	...137	H5
Atwood Rd *HMSMTH* W6	...118	E4
Aubert Pk *HBRY* N5	...85	H2
Aubert Rd *HBRY* N5	...85	H2
Aubrey Pl *STJWD* NW8	...101	G1
Aubrey Rd *CEND/HSY/T* N8	...66	E2
NTGHL W11	...119	J1
WALTH E17	...69	K1
Aubrey Wk *KENS* W8	...119	K1
Auburn Cl *NWCR* SE14	...144	B1
Aubyn Hl *WNWD* SE27	...162	D6
Aubyn Sq *PUT/ROE* SW15	...138	D6
Auckland Av *RAIN* RM13	...111	H2
Auckland Cl *NRWD* SE19	...181	G4
Auckland Gdns *NRWD* SE19	181	F4
Auckland Hl *WNWD* SE27	...162	D6
Auckland Ri *NRWD* SE19	...181	F4
Auckland Rd *BTSEA* SW11	...140	D5
IL IG1	...90	B1
KUT/HW KT1	...191	G1
LEY E10	...87	K1
NRWD SE19	...181	G4
Auckland St *LBTH* SE11	...122	A5
Aucuba Vls *WELL* DA16 *	...148	C4
Audax *CDALE/KGS* NW9 *	...45	J5
Auden Pl *CAMTN* NW1	...84	A6
CHEAM SM3 *	...208	A2
Audleigh Pl *CHIG* IG7	...54	A2
Audley Cl *BTSEA* SW11	...141	F4
MUSWH N10	...48	B3
Audley Ct *PIN* HA5	...41	G5
WAN E11	...70	D1
Audley Dr *CAN/RD* E16	...126	A1
Audley Gdns *GDMY/SEVK* IG3	...73	F6
Audley Pl *BELMT* SM2	...209	F5
Audley Rd *EA* W5	...98	B4
ENC/FH EN2	...23	H5
HDN NW4	...63	J5
RCHPK/HAM TW10	...137	G6
Audley Sq *MYFR/PKLN* W1K *	...9	H7
Audley St *MYFR/PKLN* W1K	...9	H7
Audley Gdns *BTSEA* SW11	...198	E3
Audrey Rd *IL* IG1	...90	B1
Audrey St *BETH* E2	...104	C1
Audric Cl *KUTN/CMB* KT2	...175	H4
Augurs La *PLSTW* E13	...107	F2
Augusta Cl *E/WMO/HCT* KT8	172	E6
Augusta Rd *WHTN* TW2	...155	H4
Augustine Rd *HMSMTH* W6	119	C3
KTN/HRWW/WS HA3	...42	B4
Augustus Cl *BTFD* TW8	...136	E1
SHB W12	...118	E2
STAN HA7	...29	K5
Augustus Rd *WIM/MER* SW19	159	H3
CAMTN NW1	...4	C1
Aultone Wy *CAR* SM5	...209	K1
SUT SM1	...208	E1
Auriton Pl *LBTH* SE11	...122	B5
Aurelia Gdns *CROY/NA* CRO	196	A2
Aurelia Rd *CROY/NA* CRO	...195	K3
Auriel Av *DAGE* RM10	...93	F4
Auriga Ms *IS* N1	...85	K5
Auriol Cl *WPK* KT4	...207	C1
Auriol Dr *CFD/PVL* UB6	...78	D5
Auriol Park Rd *WPK* KT4	...207	C1
Auriol Rd *WKENS* W14	...119	H4
Austell Gdns *MLHL* NW7	...31	C5
Austen Cl *THMD* SE28	...128	C1
Austen Rd *ERITH* DA8	...149	J1
RYLN/HDSTN HA2	...60	A6
Austin Av *HAYES* BR2	...200	D3
TWK TW1	...136	D6
Austin Cl *FSTH* SE23	...164	B2
Austin Friars *OBST* EC2N *	...13	F3
Austin Friars Sq *OBST* EC2N *	13	F3
Austin Rd *BTSEA* SW11	...141	F2
HYS/HAR UB3	...113	J2
STMC/STPC BR5	...202	B3
Austins La *HGDN/ICK* UB10	...76	A1
Austin St *BETH* E2	...7	J5
Austral Cl *BFN/LL* DA15	...168	A5
Australia Rd *SHB* W12	...99	K6
Austral St *LBTH* SE11	...18	A6
Austyn Gdns *BRYLDS* KT5 *	191	J5
Autumn Cl *EN* EN1	...24	D3
WIM/MER SW19	...178	B2
Autumn Dr *BELMT* SM2	...209	F6
Autumn Gv *BMLY* BR1	...184	A2
Autumn St *BOW* E3	...87	J6
Avalon Cl *ENC/FH* EN2	...23	G3
ORP BR6	...202	E6
RYNPK SW20	...177	H5
WEA W13	...97	G4
Avalon Rd *FUL/PGN* SW6	...140	A2
ORP BR6	...202	D6
WEA W13	...97	G3
Avard Gdns *ORP* BR6	...216	C2
Avarn Rd *TOOT* SW17	...178	E2
Avebury Rd *SURB* KT6	...190	D5
Avebury Rd *ORP* BR6	...216	D1
WAN E11	...70	B5
WIM/MER SW19	...177	J4
Avebury St *IS* N1	...6	E1
Aveley Cl *ERITH* DA8	...130	C6
Aveline St *LBTH* SE11	...122	A5
Aveling Park Rd *WALTH* E17	...57	J2
Avelon Rd *CRW* RM5	...57	F2
RAIN RM13	...93	J3
Ave Marie La *STP* EC4M	...12	B4
Avenell Rd *HBRY* N5	...85	H1
Avening Rd *WAND/EARL* SW18	159	K1
Avening Ter *WAND/EARL* SW18	...159	K1
Avenons Rd *PLSTW* E13	...106	E4
Avenue Cl *HEST* TW5	...134	A2
STHGT/OAK N14	...34	C1
STJWD NW8	...2	E2
WDR/YW UB7	...112	A3
Avenue Crs *ACT* W3	...117	H1
HEST TW5	...134	A2

Avenue Elmers *SURB* KT6	...191	F2
Avenue Gdns *ACT* W3	...117	J2
HEST TW5 *	...133	K1
MORT/ESHN SW14	...138	A2
SNWD SE25	...181	H6
TEDD TW11	...174	A3
Avenue Ms *MUSWH* N10	...48	B6
Avenue Pde *SUN* TW16	...172	A6
WCHMH N21 *	...35	K2
Avenue Park Rd *WNWD* SE27	162	C4
Avenue Rd *ACT* W3	...138	D1
BTFD TW8	...116	D5
BXLYHN DA7	...149	F4
CHDH RM6	...73	J4
ERITH DA8	...150	B1
FELT TW13	...153	J5
FSTGT E7	...89	F5
HGT N6	...66	C4
HPTN TW12	...173	G4
ISLW TW7	...136	A2
KUT/HW KT1	...175	F6
NFNCH/WDSPK N12	...33	G6
NWMAL KT3	...176	B6
PGE/AN SE20	...181	K4
PIN HA5	...41	J6
RYNPK SW20	...176	E5
SEVS/STOTM N15	...67	K2
SNWD SE25	...181	H6
STHGT/OAK N14	...34	C4
STHL UB1	...114	L1
STJWD NW8	...83	H6
STRHM/NOR SW16	...179	K6
TEDD TW11	...174	B3
WFD IG8	...53	G2
WLGTN SM6	...210	C5
WLSDN NW10	...99	H1
Avenue South *BRYLDS* KT5	...191	J4
Avenue Ter *NWMAL* KT3	...175	K6
OXHEY WD19 *	...27	J1
The Avenue *BAR* EN5	...20	C1
BECK BR3	...182	E4
BELMT SM2	...208	D6
BMLY BR1	...184	C6
BRYLDS KT5	...191	G3
BXLY DA5	...168	E3
CAR SM5	...210	A5
CEND/HSY/T N8	...66	F3
CHING E4	...52	B2
CHSWK W4	...118	B3
CLAP SW4	...141	F6
CROY/NA CRO	...212	A1
ESH/CLAY KT10	...204	E4
EW KT17	...208	A5
FBAR/BDGN N11	...34	B1
GNWCH SE10	...145	G1
HEST TW5	...133	K2
HPTN TW12	...172	E2
ISLW TW7	...135	G6
KIL/WHAMP NW6	...82	C6
KTN/HRWW/WS HA3	...43	F4
LOU IG10	...39	J1
MUSWH N10	...48	B6
NTHWD HA6	...40	A2
ORP BR6	...202	A6
PIN HA5	...41	K6
PIN HA5	...59	K3
RCH/KEW TW9	...137	G3
ROM RM1	...75	F1
STMC/STPC BR5	...186	C3
SUN TW16	...172	A5
TOTM N17	...50	B4
TWK TW1	...156	C1
WAN E11	...70	E3
WBLY HA9	...62	B6
WEA W13	...97	H6
WPK KT4	...192	D5
WDGN N22 *	...49	F5
WLSDN NW10	...99	F1
Averil Gv *STRHM/NOR* SW16	180	C2
Averill St *HMSMTH* W6	...119	G6
Avern Gdns *E/WMO/HCT* KT8	189	G1
Avern Rd *E/WMO/HCT* KT8	...189	G1
Avery Farm Rw *BCVA* SW1W *	...15	J7
Avery Gdns *CHDH/NBYPK* IG2	...71	K2
Avery Hill Rd *ELTH/MOT* SE9	167	H3
Avery Rw *MYFR/PKLN* W1K	...9	J5
Avery Wy *DART* DA1	...171	J4
Aviary Cl *CAN/RD* E16	...106	D5
Aviemore Cl *BECK* BR3	...198	C2
Aviemore Wy *BECK* BR3	...198	B2
Avignon Rd *BROCKY* SE4	...144	A4
Avington Gv *PGE/AN* SE20	...181	K3
Avington Wy *PECK* SE15 *	...143	G1
Avion Cl *CDALE/KGS* NW9	...45	J5
Avior Dr *NTHWD* HA6	...26	D2
Avis Sq *WCHPL* E1	...105	F5
Avoca Rd *TOOT* SW17	...161	F6
Avocet Cl *STHWK* SE1	...123	G5
Avocet Ms *THMD* SE28	...127	J3
Avon Cl *SUT* SM1	...209	G2
WPK KT4	...192	D6
YEAD UB4	...95	C3
Avon Ct *PIN* HA5 *	...42	A3
Avondale Av *CRICK* NW2	...81	C1
EBAR EN4	...33	K3
ESH/CLAY KT10	...205	G1
NFNCH/WDSPK N12	...47	F1
WPK KT4	...192	C5
Avondale Cl *LOU* IG10	...39	K2
Avondale Ct *SWFD* E18	...53	F4
Avondale Crs *PEND* EN3	...25	G4
REDBR IG4	...71	H2
Avondale Dr *HYS/HAR* UB3	...113	K1
LOU IG10	...39	K2
Avondale Gdns *HSLWW* TW4	134	D6
Avondale Park Gdns		
NTGHL W11 *	...100	C6
Avondale Park Rd *NTGHL* W11	100	C6
Avondale Pavement		
STHWK SE1 *	...123	H5
Avondale Ri *PECK* SE15	...143	G4
Avondale Rd *ASHF* TW15	...152	A5
BMLY BR1	...183	H1
CAN/RD E16	...106	C4
ELTH/MOT SE9	...166	D3
FNCH N3	...47	F4
KTN/HRWW/WS HA3	...43	F6

MORT/ESHN SW14	...138	A4
PLMGR N13	...35	G4
SAND/SEL CR2	...211	J4
SEVS/STOTM N15	...67	H2
WALTH E17	...69	J4
WELL DA16	...148	D1
WIM/MER SW19	...178	A1
Avondale Sq *STHWK* SE1	...123	H5
Avonley Rd *NWCR* SE14	...143	K1
Avon Ms *PIN* HA5	...41	K4
Avonmore Gdns *WKENS* W14 *	119	J4
Avonmore Pl *WKENS* W14	...119	H4
Avonmore Rd *WKENS* W14	...119	J4
Avonmouth Rd *DART* DA1	...151	G6
Avonmouth St *STHWK* SE1	...18	C4
Avon Rd *BROCKY* SE4	...144	D4
GFD/PVL UB6	...96	A3
WALTH E17	...52	B6
Avonstowe Cl *ORP* BR6	...216	C1
Avon Wy *SWFD* E18	...70	E1
Avonwick Rd *HSLW* TW3	...135	G3
Avril Wy *CHING* E4	...52	B1
Avro Wy *WLGTN* SM6	...210	E5
Awberry Ct *WATW* WD18 *	...26	B1
Awlfield Av *TOTM* N17	...49	K4
Awliscombe Rd *WELL* DA16	148	A3
Axeholm Av *EDGW* HA8	...44	D4
Axe St *BARK* IG11	...90	C6
Axholme Av *EDGW* HA8	...44	C4
Axis Ct *GNWCH* SE10	...125	H6
Axminster Crs *WELL* DA16	...148	D2
Axminster Rd *HOLWY* N7	...84	E1
Axon Pl *IL* IG1	...72	B6
Axtaine Rd *STMC/STPC* BR5	202	E4
Aybrook St *MHST* W1U	...9	G2
Aycliff Ct *KUT/HW* KT1 *	...175	H5
Aycliffe Cl *BMLY* BR1	...200	E1
Aycliffe Rd *SHB* W12	...118	C1
Aylands Cl *WBLY* HA9	...62	A6
Aylesbury Cl *FSTGT* E7 *	...88	D4
Aylesbury Rd *HAYES* BR2	...183	K6
WALW SE17	...122	E5
Aylesbury St *CLKNW* EC1R	...6	A7
WLSDN NW10	...81	F1
Aylesford Av *BECK* BR3	...198	B2
Aylesford St *PIM* SW1V	...121	J5
Aylesham Cl *MLHL* NW7	...45	J3
Aylesham Rd *ORP* BR6	...201	K4
Aylestone Av *KIL/WHAMP* NW6	...82	B5
Aylett Rd *ISLW* TW7	...135	K3
SNWD SE25	...197	J1
Ayley Cft *EN* EN1	...24	C6
Ayliffe Cl *KUT/HW* KT1	...175	H5
Aylmer Cl *STAN* HA7	...29	G6
Aylmer Dr *STAN* HA7	...29	G6
Aylmer Pde *EFNCH* N2 *	...65	J3
Aylmer Rd *BCTR* RM8	...92	A1
EFNCH N2	...65	J2
SHB W12	...118	B2
WAN E11	...70	D5
Ayloffe Rd *ELTH/MOT* SE9	...146	E6
Aylsham Dr *HGDN/ICK* UB10	...58	C3
Aylton Est *BERM/RHTH* SE16 *	...123	K2
Aylward Rd *FSTH* SE23	...164	A4
RYNPK SW20	...177	J5
Aylwards Ri *STAN* HA7	...29	G6
Aylward St *WCHPL* E1 *	...104	E5
Aynhoe Rd *WKENS* W14	...119	G4
Ayres Cl *PLSTW* E13	...106	E2
Ayres Crs *WLSDN* NW10	...81	F5
Ayres St *STHWK* SE1	...18	D2
Ayr Gn *ROM* RM1	...57	G4
Ayrsome Rd *STNW/STAM* N16	...86	A1
Ayrton Rd *SKENS* SW7 *	...14	A4
Ayr Wy *ROM* RM1	...57	G4
Aysgarth Rd *DUL* SE21	...162	E1
Aytoun Pl *BRXN/ST* SW9	...142	A3
Aytoun Rd *BRXN/ST* SW9	...142	A3
Azalea Cl *HNWL* W7	...116	A1
IL IG1	...90	B3
Azalea Ct *WFD* IG8 *	...52	C5
Azalea Wk *PIN* HA5	...59	F2
Azania Ms *KTTN* NW5 *	...84	B4
Azenby Rd *PECK* SE15	...143	G3
Azof St *GNWCH* SE10	...125	H4

B		
Baalbec Rd *HBRY* N5	...85	H3
Babbacombe Cl *CHSGTN* KT9	...205	K3
Babbacombe Gdns *REDBR* IG4	...71	J1
Babbacombe Rd *BMLY* BR1	...184	A4
Baber Bridge Pde		
EBED/NFELT TW14 *	...154	B1
Baber Dr *EBED/NFELT* TW14	...154	B1
Babington Ri *WBLY* HA9	...80	D4
Babington Rd *BCTR* RM8	...91	J3
HCH RM12	...75	K1
HDN NW4	...63	K1
STRHM/NOR SW16	...179	J1
Babmaes St *STJS* SW1Y	...10	C7
Bache's St *IS* N1	...7	F5
Back Church La *WCHPL* E1	...104	C5
Back Hl *CLKNW* EC1R	...5	K7
Back La *BTFD* TW8	...136	E1
BXLY DA5	...169	H2
CEND/HSY/T N8	...66	E2
CHDH RM6	...73	K4
EDGW HA8	...44	E4
HAMP NW3	...83	G2
RCHPK/HAM TW10	...156	D5
Backley Gdns *CROY/NA* CRO	...197	H4
Back Rd *SCUP* DA14	...168	B6
TEDD TW11	...173	K3
Bacon Gv *STHWK* SE1	...19	H5
Bacon La *CDALE/KGS* NW9	...62	E2
EDGW HA8	...44	C4
Bacon Link *CRW* RM5	...56	D2
Bacon's La *HGT* N6	...66	A6
Bacon St *BETH* E2	...7	K6
Bacton St *BETH* E2	...104	E2
Baddow Cl *DAGE* RM10	...92	C6

WFD IG8	...53	H2
Baden Rd *STHWK* SE1 *	...18	E2
Baden Powell Cl *DAGW* RM9	92	A6
SURB KT6	...191	G6
Baden Rd *CEND/HSY/T* N8	...66	D1
IL IG1	...90	B3
Bader Wy *RAIN* RM13	...93	K6
Badger Cl *FELT* TW13	...154	A5
HSLWW TW4	...134	B4
Badgers Cl *ENC/FH* EN2	...23	H4
HRW HA1	...60	D3
HYS/HAR UB3	...113	H1
Badgers Copse *ORP* BR6	...216	A1
WPK KT4	...192	C6
Badgers Ct *WPK* KT4 *	...192	C6
Badgers Cft *ELTH/MOT* SE9	167	F5
TRDG/WHET N20	...32	C3
Badgers Wk *NWMAL* KT3	...176	B5
Badlis Rd *WALTH* E17	...51	J5
Badlow Cl *ERITH* DA8	...150	B1
Badminton Cl *HRW* HA1 *	...60	E1
NTHLT UB5	...78	A4
Badminton Ms *CAN/RD* E16	125	K1
Badminton Rd *BAL* SW12	...161	F1
Badsworth Rd *CMBW* SE5	...142	D1
Bafton Ga *HAYES* BR2	...200	A5
Bagley Cl *WDR/YW* UB7	...112	B2
Bagley House		
WOOL/PLUM SE18 *	...146	D1
Bagley's La *FUL/PGN* SW6	...140	B2
Bagleys Spring *CHDH* RM6	...74	A1
Bagshot Ct		
WOOL/PLUM SE18 *	...147	F2
Bagshot Rd *EN* EN1	...36	B2
Bagshot St *WALW* SE17	...123	F5
Baildon St *DEPT* SE8	...144	C1
Bailey Cl *FBAR/BDGN* N11	...48	E3
THMD SE28	...127	K1
Bailey Cottages		
POP/IOD E14 *	...105	C4
Bailey Crs *CHSGTN* KT9	...205	K5
Bailey House		
WOOL/PLUM SE18 *	...146	D1
Bailey Ms *BRXS/STRHM* SW2	142	B6
CHSWK W4	...117	J6
Bailey Pl *SYD* SE26	...181	K2
Baillie Cl *RAIN* RM13	...111	K3
Bainbridge Cl		
RCHPK/HAM TW10	...175	F1
Bainbridge Rd *DAGW* RM9	...92	B2
Bainbridge St		
NOXST/BSQ WC1A	...10	D3
Baines Cl *SAND/SEL* CR2	...211	K3
Baird Av *STHL* UB1	...96	B6
Baird Cl *BUSH* WD23	...28	B3
CDALE/KGS NW9	...62	E3
LEY E10	...69	J5
Baird Gdns *NRWD* SE19	...163	F6
Baird Memorial Cottages		
STHGT/OAK N14 *	...34	D4
Baird Rd *EN* EN1	...24	D5
Baird St *STLK* EC1Y	...6	E6
Baizdon Rd *BKHTH/KID* SE3	145	H3
Baker Crs *DART* DA1	...171	G2
Baker La *MTCM* CR4	...179	F5
Baker Rd *WLSDN* NW10	...81	G6
WOOL/PLUM SE18	...146	D1
Bakers Av *WALTH* E17	...69	K3
Bakers Cl *DART* DA1	...171	G2
Bakers Fld *HOLWY* N7	...84	D2
Bakers Gdns *CAR* SM5	...194	D6
Bakers Hill *BAR* EN5	...21	F3
CLPT E5	...68	D5
Baker's Ms *MHST* W1U	...9	G3
Bakers Rents *BETH* E2	...7	J4
Bakers Rw *CLKNW* EC1R *	...5	K6
SRTFD E15	...106	C1
Baker St *CAMTN* NW1	...3	F7
EN EN1	...23	K3
MHST W1U	...2	F1
Bakery Cl *CLKNW* EC1R	...6	C7
Bakery Ct *BXSY/STRM* SW9 *	142	A1
Bakery Pl *BTSEA* SW11	...140	E5
Bakewell Wy *NWMAL* KT3	...176	B5
Balaams La *STHGT/OAK* N14	34	D4
Balaam St *PLSTW* E13	...106	E2
Balaclava Rd *STHWK* SE1	...19	K6
SURB KT6	...190	D4
Baldwin Crs *CMBW* SE5	...142	D2
Baldwin Gdns *HSLW* TW3	...135	H2
Baldwin's Gdns *FSBYW* WC1X	...11	J1
Baldwin's Pk *BXLY* DA5	...170	A4
Baldwyn's Rd *BXLY* DA5	...170	A4
Bale Rd *WCHPL* E1	...105	G4
Bales Ter *ED* N9 *	...36	B5
Balfern Gv *CHSWK* W4	...118	B5
Balfern St *BTSEA* SW11	...140	D3
Balfe St *IS* N1	...5	F3
Balfour Av *HNWL* W7	...116	A1
Balfour Gv *TRDG/WHET* N20	33	K5
Balfour Ms *ED* N9	...36	C5
MYFR/PKLN W1K	...9	H6
Balfour Pl *MYFR/PKLN* W1K	...9	H6
PUT/ROE SW15	...138	E5
Balfour Rd *ACT* W3	...98	E4
CAR SM5	...209	K5
HAYES BR2	...200	C2
HNWL W7	...115	K1
HSLW TW3	...135	G4

IL IG1	...72	B6
NWDGN UB2	...114	C3
SNWD SE25	...197	H1
WEA W13	...116	B1
WIM/MER SW19	...178	A3
Balfour St *STHWK* SE1	...18	E6
Balgonie Rd *CHING* E4	...38	B4
Balgores Crs *GPK* RM2	...57	K6
Balgores La *GPK* RM2	...75	K1
Balgores Sq *GPK* RM2	...75	K1
Balgowan Cl *NWMAL* KT3	...192	B2
Balgowan Rd *BECK* BR3	...182	C6
Balgowan St		
WOOL/PLUM SE18	...128	A4
Balham Gv *BAL* SW12	...161	F2
Balham High Rd *BAL* SW12	...161	G3
Balham Hl *BAL* SW12	...161	G3
Balham New Rd *BAL* SW12	...161	G2
Balham Park Rd *BAL* SW12	...161	F3
Balham Rd *ED* N9	...36	C4
Balham Station Rd *BAL* SW12	161	F3
Balkan Wk *WAP* E1W *	...104	D6
Balladier Wk *POP/IOD* E14	...105	K4
Ballamore Rd *BMLY* BR1	...165	K5
Ballance Rd *HOM* E9	...87	F4
Ballantine St		
WAND/EARL SW18	...140	B5
Ballard Cl *KUTN/CMB* KT2	...176	A3
Ballards Cl *DAGE* RM10	...92	D6
Ballards Farm Rd		
CROY/NA CRO	...212	D4
Ballards La *FNCH* N3	...47	F3
Ballards Ms *EDGW* HA8	...44	C3
Ballards Ri *SAND/SEL* CR2	...212	C4
Ballards Rd *CRICK* NW2 *	...63	J1
DAGE RM10	...92	E5
Ballards Wy *SAND/SEL* CR2	212	C4
Ballast Quay *GNWCH* SE10	...125	G5
Ballater Cl *OXHEY* WD19	...27	G6
Ballater Rd *BRXS/STRHM* SW2	141	K5
SAND/SEL CR2	...212	B3
Ballina St *FSTH* SE23	...164	A2
Ballingdon Rd *BTSEA* SW11	161	F1
Ballinger Wy *NTHLT* UB5	...95	J3
Balliol Av *CHING* E4	...38	B6
Balliol Rd *NKENS* W10	...100	A5
TOTM N17	...50	A4
WELL DA16	...148	C3
Balloch Rd *CAT* SE6	...165	G3
Ballogie Av *WLSDN* NW10	...81	G2
Ballow Cl *CMBW* SE5 *	...142	F1
Ball's Pond Pl *IS* N1 *	...85	K4
Bails Pond Rd *IS* N1	...85	K4
Balmain Cl *EA* W5	...97	K1
Balmer Rd *BOW* E3	...105	H1
Balmes Rd *IS* N1	...85	K6
Balmoral Av *BECK* BR3	...198	B1
FBAR/BDGN N11	...48	A2
Balmoral Cl *PUT/ROE* SW15 *	...159	G1
Balmoral Crs *E/WMO/HCT* KT8	173	F6
Balmoral Dr *STHL* UB1	...95	K4
YEAD UB4	...94	C3
Balmoral Gdns *BXLY* DA5	...169	G2
WEA W13	...116	B3
Balmoral Gv *HOLWY* N7	...85	F4
Balmoral Ms *SHB* W12	...118	C3
Balmoral Rd *CRICK* NW2	...81	K4
FSTGT E7	...89	G2
GPK RM2	...57	K1
KUT/HW KT1	...191	G1
RYLN/HDSTN HA2	...59	K2
WPK KT4	...207	K1
Balmore Crs *EBAR* EN4	...22	A6
Balmore St *ARCH* N19	...66	B6
Balmuir Gdns *PUT/ROE* SW15	139	F5
Balnacraig Av *WLSDN* NW10	...81	G2
Balniel Ga *PIM* SW1V	...121	J5
Baltic Cl *WIM/MER* SW19	...178	C5
Baltic St East *STLK* EC1Y	...6	C7
Baltic St West *FARR* EC1M	...6	C7
Baltimore Pl *WELL* DA16	...148	A3
Balvaird Pl *PIM* SW1V	...121	K5
Balvernie Gv		
WAND/EARL SW18	...159	J2
Bamber Rd *PECK* SE15 *	...143	F2
Bamborough Gdns *SHB* W12	119	F2
Bamford Av *ALP/SUD* HA0	...80	B6
Bamford Rd *BARK* IG11	...90	C4
BMLY BR1	...183	F5
Bamford Wy *CRW* RM5	...56	C1
Bampfylde Cl *WLGTN* SM6	...210	C1
Bampton Dr *MLHL* NW7	...45	J3
Bampton Rd *FSTH* SE23	...164	A5
Banavie Gdns *BECK* BR3	...183	F4
Banbury Cl *ENC/FH* EN2	...23	H1
Banbury Ct *BELMT* SM2	...208	E5
COVGDN WC2E *	...10	E5
Banbury Rd *HOM* E9	...87	F5
WALTH E17	...51	G3
Banbury St *BTSEA* SW11	...140	D3
Banchory Rd *BKHTH/KID* SE3	146	A1
Bancroft Av *EFNCH* N2	...65	J3
Bancroft Cha *FNCH* N12	...75	H6
Bancroft Gdns		
KTN/HRWW/WS HA3	...42	C4
ORP BR6	...202	A5
Bancroft Rd		
KTN/HRWW/WS HA3	...42	C5
WCHPL E1	...105	F2
Bandon Ri *WLGTN* SM6	...210	D4
Banfield Rd *PECK* SE15	...143	J5
Bangalore St *PUT/ROE* SW15	139	F3
Bangor Cl *NTHLT* UB5	...78	B3
Banim St *HMSMTH* W6	...118	E4
Banister Rd *NKENS* W10	...100	B2
Bank Av *MTCM* CR4	...178	D5
Bank Buildings *CHING* E4 *	...52	B2
Bankfoot Rd *BMLY* BR1	...165	H6
Bankhurst Rd *CAT* SE6	...164	C2
Bank La *KUTN/CMB* KT2	...174	E4
PUT/ROE SW15	...138	B6
Bank Ms *SUT* SM1	...209	G4
Banksia Rd *UED* N18	...50	E1
Bankside *ENC/FH* EN2	...23	G1
SAND/SEL CR2	...212	B4

STHL UB1 114 C1
STHWK SE1 12 C6
Bankside Av LEW SE13 145 F4
NTHLT UB5 94 E1
Bankside Cl BXLY DA5 170 A6
CAR SM5 209 J3
ISLW TW7 136 A5
Bankside Dr THDIT KT7 190 C6
Bankside Rd IL IG1 90 C3
Banks La BXLYHS DA6 149 G5
Banks Wy MNPK E12 90 A2
The Bank HGT N6 66 B5
Bankton Rd BRXS/STRHM SW2 142 B5
Bankwell Rd LEW SE13 145 H5
Banner St STLK EC1Y 6 D7
Banning St GNWCH SE10 125 H5
Bannister Cl
BRXS/STRHM SW2 162 B3
GFD/PVL UB6 78 D3
Bannister Gdns
STMC/STPC BR5 186 D6
Bannockburn Rd
WOOL/PLUM SE18 127 K4
Bannow Cl HOR/WEW KT19 207 G2
Banstead Gdns ED N9 35 K5
Banstead Rd CAR SM5 209 J4
Banstead St PECK SE15 143 K4
Banstead Wy WLGTN SM6 210 E3
Banstock Rd EDGW HA8 44 E2
Banting Dr WCHMH N21 23 F6
Banton Cl EN EN1 24 D3
Bantry St CMBW SE5 142 E1
Banwell Rd BXLY DA5 168 E1
Banyard Rd BERM/RHTH SE16 123 J3
Bapchild Pl STMC/STPC BR5 202 D1
Baptist Gdns KTTN NW5 84 A4
Barandon Wk NTGHL W11 * 100 B6
Barbara Castle Cl
FUL/PGN SW6 119 J6
Barbara Hucklesbury Cl
WDGN N22 49 H5
Barbauld Rd STNW/STAM N16 86 A1
Barber Cl WCHMH N21 35 G2
Barbers Rd SRTFD E15 105 K1
Barbican Rd GFD/PVL UB6 96 B5
Barb Ms HMSMTH W6 119 F3
Barbon Cl BMSBY WC1N 11 G1
Barbot Cl ED N9 36 C5
Barchard St WAND/EARL SW18 140 A6
Barchester Cl HNWL W7 116 A1
Barchester Rd
KTN/HRWW/WS HA3 42 D4
Barchester St POP/IOD E14 105 K4
Barclay Cl FUL/PGN SW6 * 139 K1
WATW WD18 26 E1
Barclay Ov WFD IG8 38 E6
Barclay Rd CROY/NA CR0 211 K1
FUL/PGN SW6 139 K1
PLSTW E13 107 G3
UED N18 49 K2
WALTH E17 70 A2
WAN E11 70 D5
Barcombe Av
BRXS/STRHM SW2 161 K4
Barcombe Cl STMC/STPC BR5 186 B6
Barden St WOOL/PLUM SE18 147 K1
Bardfield Av CHDH RM6 55 K6
Bardney Rd MRDN SM4 194 A1
Bardolph Av CROY/NA CR0 213 H6
Bardolph Rd HOLWY N7 84 E2
RCH/KEW TW9 137 G5
Bard Rd NKENS W10 100 B6
Bardsey Pl WCHPL E1 104 E4
Bardsey Wk IS N1 * 85 J4
Bardsley Cl CROY/NA CR0 212 B1
Bardsley La GNWCH SE10 125 F6
Barfett St NKENS W10 100 D3
Barfield Av TRDG/WHET N20 33 K4
Barfield Rd BMLY BR1 185 F6
WAN E11 * 70 D5
Barford Cl HDN NW4 45 J5
Barford St IS N1 5 K1
Barforth Rd PECK SE15 143 J4
Barfreston Wy PGE/AN SE20 181 J4
Bargate Cl NWMAL KT3 192 D4
WOOL/PLUM SE18 128 A5
Barge House Rd CAN/RD E16 127 G2
Barge House St STHWK SE1 11 K7
Barge La BOW E3 87 H6
Bargery Rd CAT SE6 164 E3
Barge Wk KUT/HW KT1 174 E5
Bargrove Cl PGE/AN SE20 181 H3
Bargrove Crs CAT SE6 164 C4
Barham Cl ALP/SUD HA0 79 H4
CHST BR7 185 G1
HAYES BR2 200 D5
ROMW/RG RM7 56 D5
Barham Ct ALP/SUD HA0 79 J4
Barham Rd CHST BR7 185 G1
DART DA1 171 K2
RYNPK SW20 176 D3
SAND/SEL CR2 211 J2
Baring Cl LEE/GVPK SE12 165 K4
Baring Rd CROY/NA CR0 197 H5
EBAR EN4 21 H4
LEE/GVPK SE12 166 A4
Baring St IS N1 6 E1
Barker Cl NTHWD HA6 40 D3
NWMAL KT3 191 J1
RCH/KEW TW9 137 J3
Barker Dr CAMTN NW1 84 D5
Barker St WBPTN SW10 120 B6
Barker Wk STRHM/NOR SW16 161 J5
Barkham Rd TOTM N17 49 K3
Bark Hart Rd ORP BR6 202 C5
Barking Rd EHAM E6 89 K6
PLSTW E13 107 F3
POP/IOD E14 106 C5
Bark Pl BAY/PAD W2 101 F6
Barkston Gdns ECT SW5 120 A4
Barkway Dr ORP BR6 216 A2
Barkwood Cl ROMW/RG RM7 74 E2
Barkworth Rd
BERM/RHTH SE16 123 J5
Barlborough St NWCR SE14 144 A1
Barlby Gdns NKENS W10 100 B3
Barlby Rd NKENS W10 100 A4
Barley Cl ALP/SUD HA0 79 K2
Barley La GDMY/SEVK IG3 73 G3
Barley Mow Pas CHSWK W4 118 A5
Barlow Cl WLGTN SM6 210 E4
Barlow Dr BKHTH/KID SE3 146 D2
Barlow Pl MYFR/PICC W1J 9 K6
Barlow Rd ACT W3 117 J1
CRICK NW2 82 D4
HPTN TW12 173 F3
Barlow St WALW SE17 19 F7
Barlow Wy RAIN RM13 111 F5
Barlow Wy South RAIN RM13 111 G5
Barmeston Rd CAT SE6 164 E4
Barmor Cl RYLN/HDSTN HA2 42 B5
Barmouth Av GFD/PVL UB6 97 F1
Barmouth Rd CROY/NA CR0 198 A6
WAND/EARL SW18 160 B1
Barnabas Rd HOM E9 87 F4
Barnaby Cl RYLN/HDSTN HA2 60 C6
Barnaby Pl SKENS SW7 14 A7
Barnard Cl CHST BR7 185 J4
SUN TW16 172 A3
WLGTN SM6 210 D5
WOOL/PLUM SE18 127 F4
Barnard Gdns NWMAL KT3 192 D1
YEAD UB4 95 F3
Barnard Hl MUSWH N10 48 B5
Barnard Ms BTSEA SW11 140 D5
Barnardo Dr BARK/HLT IG6 72 C1
Barnardo Gdns WCHPL E1 * 105 F5
Barnardo St WCHPL E1 105 F5
Barnard Rd BTSEA SW11 140 D5
EN EN1 24 D3
MTCM CR4 179 F6
Barnards Pl SAND/SEL CR2 211 H6
Barnby St CAMTN NW1 4 B3
SRTFD E15 88 C6
Barn Cl KTTN NW5 * 84 D3
NTHLT UB5 95 G1
Barn Crs STAN HA7 43 J2
Barneby Cl WHTN TW2 155 K3
Barnehurst Av BXLYHN DA7 149 K2
ERITH DA8 149 K2
Barnehurst Cl ERITH DA8 149 K2
Barnehurst Rd BXLYHN DA7 149 K3
Barn End Dr RDART DA2 171 F6
Barnes Av BARN SW13 138 D1
NWDGN UB2 114 E4
Barnes Br CHSWK W4 138 B3
Barnes Cl MNPK E12 89 H2
Barnes Cray Rd DART DA1 150 D5
Barnesdale Crs
STMC/STPC BR5 202 B3
Barnes End NWMAL KT3 192 D2
Barnes High St BARN SW13 138 C3
Barnes Rd IL IG1 90 C3
UED N18 36 E6
Barnes St POP/IOD E14 105 G5
Barnes Ter DEPT SE8 124 C5
Barnet Dr HAYES BR2 200 D6
Barnet Gate La BAR EN5 31 J2
Barnet Gv BETH E2 104 C2
Barnet Hl BAR EN5 20 D5
Barnet La BORE WD6 30 B1
TRDG/WHET N20 32 D3
Barnet Rd BAR EN5 31 H1
Barnett Cl ERITH DA8 150 C3
Barnetts Ct RYLN/HDSTN HA2 * 78 B1
Barnett St WCHPL E1 104 D5
Barnet Wy (Barnet By-Pass)
MLHL NW7 31 F2
Barnet Wood Rd HAYES BR2 200 C6
Barney Cl CHARL SE7 126 B5
Barn Fld HAMP NW3 * 83 K3
Barnfield NWMAL KT3 192 B3
Barnfield Av CROY/NA CR0 197 K6
KUTN/CMB KT2 156 E6
MTCM CR4 195 G1
Barnfield Cl FSBYPK N4 66 E4
SWLY BR8 203 K4
TOOT SW17 160 B5
Barnfield Gdns KUTN/CMB KT2 175 F1
WOOL/PLUM SE18 * 127 G6
Barnfield Pl POP/IOD E14 124 E4
Barnfield Rd BELV DA17 129 G6
EA W5 97 J3
EDGW HA8 44 E4
SAND/SEL CR2 212 A6
STMC/STPC BR5 186 E6
WOOL/PLUM SE18 127 G6
Barnfield Wood Cl BECK BR3 199 G3
Barnfield Wood Rd BECK BR3 199 H2
Barnham Dr THMD SE28 128 A1
Barnham Rd GFD/PVL UB6 96 C2
Barnham St STHWK SE1 19 H2
Barnhill PIN HA5 59 G2
Barn Hl WBLY HA9 62 D6
Barnhill Av HAYES BR2 199 K2
Barnhill La YEAD UB4 95 F2
Barnhill Rd WBLY HA9 80 E1
YEAD UB4 95 F3
Barnhurst Pth OXHEY WD19 41 G1
Barningham Wy
CDALE/KGS NW9 62 E3
Barnlea Cl FELT TW13 154 D4
Barnmead Gdns DAGW RM9 92 B3
Barnmead Rd BECK BR3 182 A4
DAGW RM9 92 B3
Barnock Cl DART DA1 170 B2
Barn Ri WBLY HA9 62 C5
Barnsbury Cl NWMAL KT3 191 K1
Barnsbury Crs BRYLDS KT5 191 K5
Barnsbury Est IS N1 5 H1
Barnsbury Gv HOLWY N7 85 F5
Barnsbury La BRYLDS KT5 191 K5
Barnsbury Pk IS N1 85 G5
Barnsbury Rd IS N1 5 J2
Barnsbury Sq IS N1 85 G5
Barnsbury St IS N1 85 G5
Barnsbury Ter IS N1 85 F5
Barnscroft RYNPK SW20 176 E6
Barnsdale Av POP/IOD E14 124 E4
Barnsdale Rd MV/WKIL W9 100 D3
Barnsley St WCHPL E1 104 D3
Barnstaple La LEW SE13 145 F5
Barnstaple Rd RSLP HA4 77 G1
Barnston Wk IS N1 * 85 J6
Barn St STNW/STAM N16 68 A6
Barn Wy WBLY HA9 62 C5
Barnwell Rd
BRXS/STRHM SW2 142 B6
DART DA1 151 J4
Barnwood Cl MV/WKIL W9 101 F3
RSLP HA4 58 B6
Baron Cl FBAR/BDGN N11 48 A1
Baroness Rd BETH E2 7 K4
Baronet Gv TOTM N17 50 C4
Baronet Rd TOTM N17 50 C4
Baron Gdns BARK/HLT IG6 54 D6
Baron Gv MTCM CR4 194 D1
Baron Rd BCTR RM8 73 K5
Barons Cl IS N1 * 5 J2
Baron's Court Rd WKENS W14 119 H5
Baronsfield Rd TWK TW1 * 156 C1
Barons Ga EBAR EN4 33 J1
Barons Keep WKENS W14 * 119 H5
Barons Md HRW HA1 60 E1
Baronsmead Rd BARN SW13 138 D2
Baronsmede EA W5 117 G2
Baronsmere Ct BAR EN5 * 20 C5
Baronsmere Rd EFNCH N2 65 J1
Baron's Pl STHWK SE1 17 K3
The Barons TWK TW1 156 C1
Baron St IS N1 5 K3
Baron's Wk CROY/NA CR0 198 B3
Barque Ms DEPT SE8 124 D6
Barrack Rd HSLWW TW4 134 C5
Barra Hall Rd HYS/HAR UB3 94 C6
Barratt Av WDGN N22 49 F5
Barratt Wy
KTN/HRWW/WS HA3 42 D6
Barrenger Rd MUSWH N10 47 K4
Barrett Cl HARH RM3 57 K3
Barrett Rd WALTH E17 70 A1
Barrett's Green Rd
WLSDN NW10 98 E1
Barrett's Gv STNW/STAM N16 86 A3
Barrett St MHST W1U 9 H4
Barrhill Rd BRXS/STRHM SW2 161 K4
Barriedale NWCR SE14 144 B2
Barrier Point Rd CAN/RD E16 126 B2
Barringer Sq TOOT SW17 161 F6
Barrington Cl CLAY IG5 53 K4
KTTN NW5 84 A3
Barrington Rd BRXN/ST SW9 142 C4
BXLYHN DA7 148 E3
CEND/HSY/T N8 66 D2
CHEAM SM3 193 K5
MNPK E12 90 A4
Barrington Vls
WOOL/PLUM SE18 147 F2
Barrington Wk NRWD SE19 * 181 F2
Barrow Av CAR SM5 209 K5
Barrow Cl WCHMH N21 35 H5
Barrowdene Cl PIN HA5 41 J5
Barrowell Gn WCHMH N21 35 H4
Barrowgate Rd CHSWK W4 117 K5
Barrow Hedges Cl CAR SM5 209 J5
Barrow Hedges Wy CAR SM5 209 J5
Barrow Hl WPK KT4 192 B6
Barrow Hill Cl WPK KT4 192 B6
Barrow Hill Est STJWD NW8 2 C3
Barrow Hill Rd STJWD NW8 2 C3
Barrow Point Av PIN HA5 41 J5
Barrow Point La PIN HA5 41 J5
Barrow Rd CROY/NA CR0 211 G3
STRHM/NOR SW16 179 J2
Barrs Rd WLSDN NW10 81 F5
Barry Av BXLYHN DA7 149 F1
SEVS/STOTM N15 68 B3
Barry Cl ORP BR6 216 E1
Barry Pde EDUL SE22 * 143 H5
Barry Rd EDUL SE22 163 H1
EHAM E6 107 J5
WLSDN NW10 80 E5
Barry Ter ASHF TW15 * 152 C4
Barset Rd PECK SE15 143 K4
Barsons Cl PGE/AN SE20 181 K3
Barston Rd WNWD SE27 162 D4
Barstow Crs
BRXS/STRHM SW2 162 A3
Barter St NOXST/BSQ WC1A 11 F2
Barth Ms WOOL/PLUM SE18 127 K4
Bartholomew Cl STBT EC1A 12 C2
WAND/EARL SW18 140 B5
Bartholomew La OBST EC2N 13 F3
Bartholomew Pl STBT EC1A 12 C2
Bartholomew Rd KTTN NW5 84 C4
Bartholomew Sq FSBYE EC1V 6 D6
Bartholomew St STHWK SE1 18 E5
Bartholomew Vls KTTN NW5 84 C4
Barth Rd WOOL/PLUM SE18 127 K4
Bartle Av EHAM E6 107 J1
Bartle Rd NTGHL W11 100 B5
Bartlett Cl POP/IOD E14 105 J5
Bartlett Ct FLST/FETLN EC4A * 11 K3
Bartlett St SAND/SEL CR2 211 K3
Bartlow Gdns CRW RM5 57 F4
Barton Av ROMW/RG RM7 74 E5
Barton Cl BXLYHS DA6 149 F6
EHAM E6 107 K5
HDN NW4 63 J2
HOM E9 86 E3
PECK SE15 143 J4
Barton Gn NWMAL KT3 176 A5
Barton Mdw BARK/HLT IG6 72 C1
Barton Rd HCH RM12 75 J5
SCUP DA14 187 F2
WKENS W14 119 H5
The Bartons BORE WD6 29 K1
Barton St WEST SW1P 16 E5
Bartram Rd BROCKY SE4 144 B6
FSTH SE23 164 B1
Bartrams La EBAR EN4 21 G1
Bartrip St HOM E9 87 G4
Barts Cl BECK BR3 198 D2
Barwell Ct CHSGTN KT9 * 205 J5
Barwell La CHSGTN KT9 205 J5
Barwick Rd FSTGT E7 89 F2
Barwood Av WWKM BR4 198 E5
Bascombe Gv DART DA1 170 B2
Bascombe St BRXS/STRHM SW2 162 B2
Basden Gv FELT TW13 155 F4
Basedale Rd DAGW RM9 91 H5
Baseing Cl EHAM E6 108 A6
Basevi Wy DEPT SE8 124 D6
Bashley Rd WLSDN NW10 99 F3
Basil Av EHAM E6 107 J2
Basildene Rd HSLWW TW4 134 C4
Basildon Av CLAY IG5 54 A4
Basildon Cl BELMT SM2 209 F6
WATW WD18 26 A1
Basildon Rd ABYW SE2 128 B5
Basil Gdns CROY/NA CR0 198 A5
WNWD SE27 180 D1
Basilon Rd BXLYHN DA7 149 F3
Basil St CHEL SW3 14 E4
Basin Ap POP/IOD E14 105 G5
Basing Cl THDIT KT7 190 A4
Basing Ct PECK SE15 143 G2
Basingdon Wy CMBW SE5 142 E5
Basing Dr BXLY DA5 169 G1
Basingfield Rd THDIT KT7 190 A4
Basinghall Av CITYW EC2V 12 E3
Basinghall Gdns BELMT SM2 209 F6
Basinghall St CITYW EC2V 12 E3
Basing Hl GLDGN NW11 64 D5
WBLY HA9 62 B6
Basing Pl BETH E2 7 H4
Basing St NTGHL W11 100 D5
Basing Wy FNCH N3 46 E6
THDIT KT7 190 A4
Basire St IS N1 85 J6
Baskerville Gdns WLSDN NW10 81 G2
Baskerville Rd
WAND/EARL SW18 160 D2
Basket Gdns ELTH/MOT SE9 146 D6
Baslow Cl KTN/HRWW/WS HA3 42 D4
Baslow Wk CLPT E5 87 F2
Basnett Rd BTSEA SW11 * 141 F4
Bassano St EDUL SE22 143 G6
Bassant Rd WOOL/PLUM SE18 128 A6
Bassein Park Rd SHB W12 118 C2
Bassett Cl BELMT SM2 209 F6
Bassett Gdns ISLW TW7 135 H1
Bassett Rd NKENS W10 100 B5
Bassetts Cl ORP BR6 216 B2
Bassett St KTTN NW5 84 A4
Bassetts Wy ORP BR6 216 B2
Bassett Wy GFD/PVL UB6 96 B5
Bassingham Rd ALP/SUD HA0 79 K4
WAND/EARL SW18 160 B2
Basswood Cl PECK SE15 143 J4
Bastable Av BARK IG11 109 G1
Bastion Rd ABYW SE2 128 B5
Baston Manor Rd WWKM BR4 215 F1
Baston Rd HAYES BR2 200 A6
Bastwick St FSBYE EC1V 6 B6
Basuto Rd FUL/PGN SW6 139 K2
Batavia Rd NWCR SE14 144 B1
SUN TW16 172 A4
Batchelor St IS N1 5 J2
Batchwood Gn
STMC/STPC BR5 202 B1
Batchworth La NTHWD HA6 40 A1
Bateman Cl BARK IG11 90 C4
Bateman Rd CHING E4 51 J2
Bateman's Buildings
SOHO/SHAV W1D 10 C4
Batemans Cnr CHSWK W4 * 118 A5
Bateman's Rw SDTCH EC2A 7 H6
Bateman St SOHO/SHAV W1D 10 D4
Bates Crs CROY/NA CR0 211 G4
STRHM/NOR SW16 179 H3
Bate St POP/IOD E14 105 H6
Bath Cl PECK SE15 143 K2
Bathgate Rd WIM/MER SW19 159 G5
Bath Gv BETH E2 104 C1
Bath House Rd CROY/NA CR0 195 K5
Bath Pas KUT/HW KT1 174 E5
Bath Pl BAR EN5 20 D4
SDTCH EC2A * 7 G5
Bath Rd CHSWK W4 118 B4
DART DA1 170 E2
ED N9 36 D4
FSTGT E7 89 H4
HSLW TW3 135 G4
HSLWW TW4 133 K2
HSLWW TW4 134 C3
WDR/YW UB7 132 A2
Baths Ap FUL/PGN SW6 * 139 J1
Bath St FSBYE EC1V 6 D5
Bath Ter STHWK SE1 18 C5
Bathurst Av WIM/MER SW19 178 A4
Bathurst Gdns WLSDN NW10 99 K1
Bathurst Ms BAY/PAD W2 8 B5
Bathurst Rd IL IG1 72 B5
Bathurst St BAY/PAD W2 8 B5
Bathway WOOL/PLUM SE18 127 F4
Batley Cl CAR SM5 194 E4
Batley Pl STNW/STAM N16 86 B1
Batley Rd ENC/FH EN2 23 J2
STNW/STAM N16 86 B1
Batman Cl SHB W12 118 E1
Batoum Gdns HMSMTH W6 119 F3
Batson St SHB W12 118 D2
Batsworth Rd MTCM CR4 178 C6
Batten Cl EHAM E6 107 K5
Batten Cottages
POP/IOD E14 * 105 G4
Batten St BTSEA SW11 140 D4
Battersby Rd CAT SE6 165 G4
Battersea Br WBPTN SW10 140 C1
Battersea Bridge Rd
BTSEA SW11 140 D1
Battersea Church Rd
BTSEA SW11 140 C2
Battersea High St BTSEA SW11 140 C3
Battersea Park Rd
BTSEA SW11 141 F2
Battersea Ri BTSEA SW11 140 D6
Battersea Sq BTSEA SW11 * 140 D1
Battery Rd THMD SE28 127 K2
Battishill St IS N1 85 H5
Battle Bridge La STHWK SE1 19 G1
Battle Bridge Rd CAMTN NW1 4 E3
Battle Cl WIM/MER SW19 178 B2
Battledean Rd HBRY N5 85 H3
Battle Rd ERITH DA8 129 K4
Batty St WCHPL E1 104 C5
Baudwin Rd CAT SE6 165 H4
Baugh Rd SCUP DA14 186 D1
The Baulk WAND/EARL SW18 159 K2
Bavant Rd STRHM/NOR SW16 179 K5
Bavaria Rd ARCH N19 66 E6
Bavdene Ms HDN NW4 63 K1
Bavent Rd CMBW SE5 142 D3
Bawdale Rd EDUL SE22 143 G6
Bawdsey Av GNTH/NBYPK IG2 73 F1
Bawtree Rd NWCR SE14 144 B1
Bawtry Rd TRDG/WHET N20 33 K5
Baxendale TRDG/WHET N20 33 G4
Baxendale St BETH E2 104 C2
Baxter Cl NWDGN UB2 115 G3
Baxter Rd CAN/RD E16 107 G5
IL IG1 90 B3
IS N1 85 K4
UED N18 36 D6
Bay Ct EA W5 * 117 F3
Baycroft Cl PIN HA5 * 41 G6
Bayfield Rd ELTH/MOT SE9 146 C5
Bayford Ms HACK E8 * 86 D5
Bayford Rd WLSDN NW10 100 B2
Bayford St HACK E8 86 D5
Bayham Pl CAMTN NW1 4 A1
Bayham Rd CHSWK W4 118 A3
MRDN SM4 194 A1
WEA W13 97 H6
Bayham St CAMTN NW1 4 A1
Bayhurst Dr NTHWD HA6 40 D2
Bayleaf Cl HPTN TW12 173 J1
Bayley St FITZ W1T 10 C2
Baylis Ms TWK TW1 156 B2
Baylis Rd STHWK SE1 17 J4
Bayliss Av THMD SE28 109 K6
Bayliss Cl ENC/FH EN2 22 E6
Bayly Rd DART DA1 171 K1
Bayne Cl EHAM E6 107 K5
Baynes Cl EN EN1 24 C2
Baynes Ms HAMP NW3 83 H4
Baynes St CAMTN NW1 84 C5
Baynham Cl BXLY DA5 169 G1
Bayonne Rd HMSMTH W6 119 H6
Bays Cl SYD SE26 181 K1
Bayshill Ri NTHLT UB5 78 B4
Bayston Rd STNW/STAM N16 86 B1
Bayswater Rd BAY/PAD W2 101 G6
Baythorne St BOW E3 105 H4
Baytree Cl BFN/LL DA15 168 A3
BMLY BR1 184 C4
Baytree Rd BRXS/STRHM SW2 142 A5
Bazalgette Cl NWMAL KT3 191 K2
Bazalgette Gdns NWMAL KT3 192 A2
Bazely St POP/IOD E14 106 A6
Bazile Rd WCHMH N21 35 G1
Beacham Cl CHARL SE7 126 C6
Beachborough Rd BMLY BR1 165 F6
Beachcroft Rd WAN E11 88 C1
Beach Gv FELT TW13 155 F5
Beachy Rd BOW E3 87 J5
Beacon Ga NWCR SE14 144 A4
Beacon Hl HOLWY N7 84 E3
Beacon Pl CROY/NA CR0 210 E1
Beacon Rd ERITH DA8 150 E1
HTHAIR TW6 152 D1
LEW SE13 165 G1
Beaconsfield Cl
BKHTH/KID SE3 125 K6
CHSWK W4 117 K5
Beaconsfield Cottages
TRDG/WHET N20 * 32 E5
Beaconsfield Gdns
ESH/CLAY KT10 204 E5
Beaconsfield Rd
BKHTH/KID SE3 125 K6
BMLY BR1 184 C6
BXLY DA5 170 B4
CAN/RD E16 106 D3
CHSWK W4 118 A3
CROY/NA CR0 196 E3
EA W5 116 D2
ED N9 36 C5
ELTH/MOT SE9 166 D5
ESH/CLAY KT10 204 E5
FBAR/BDGN N11 33 K5
LEY E10 * 88 A1
NWMAL KT3 176 A6
SEVS/STOTM N15 68 A1
SURB KT6 191 G4
TWK TW1 156 C2
WALTH E17 69 H4
WALW SE17 122 E6
WLSDN NW10 81 H4
YEAD UB4 114 B1
Beaconsfield Terrace Rd
WKENS W14 119 H3
Beaconsfield Wk
FUL/PGN SW6 139 J2
Beacontree Av WALTH E17 52 B4
Beacontree Rd WAN E11 70 D5
Beadlow Cl CAR SM5 194 C3
Beadman Pl WNWD SE27 * 162 C6
Beadman St WNWD SE27 162 C6
Beadnell Rd FSTH SE23 164 A3
Beadon Rd HAYES BR2 199 K1
HMSMTH W6 119 F4
Beaford Gv RYNPK SW20 177 H6
Beagle Cl FELT TW13 154 A6
Beagles Cl STMC/STPC BR5 202 E6
Beak St REGST W1B 10 A5
Beal Cl WELL DA16 148 B2
Beale Cl PLMGR N13 49 H1
Beale Pl BOW E3 105 H1
Beale Rd BOW E3 87 H6
Beal Rd IL IG1 72 A6
Beam Av DAGE RM10 92 D6
Beames Rd WLSDN NW10 81 F6
Beaminster Gdns BARK/HLT IG6 54 B6
Beamish Dr BUSH WD23 28 C3
Beamish Rd ED N9 36 C3
STMC/STPC BR5 202 D4
Beamway DAGE RM10 93 F5
Beanacre Cl HOM E9 87 H4
Bean Rd BXLYHS DA6 148 E5
Beanshaw ELTH/MOT SE9 167 F6
Beansland Gv CHDH RM6 56 A5
Bear Cl ROMW/RG RM7 74 D3
Beardell St NRWD SE19 181 G2
Beardow Gv STHGT/OAK N14 * 34 C1
Beard Rd KUT/CMB KT2 175 G1

Beardsfield PLSTW E13 88 E6
Beard's Hl HPTN TW12 173 F4
Beard's Hill Cl HPTN TW12 173 F4
Beardsley Wy ACT W3 118 A2
Bearfield Rd KUTN/CMB KT2 175 F3
Bear Gdns STHWK SE1 12 C7
Bear La STHWK SE1 12 B7
Bear Rd FELT TW13 154 C6
Bearstead Ri BROCKY SE4 164 C1
Bearstead Ter BECK BR3 * 182 D4
Bear St LSQ/SEVD WC2H 10 D5
Beatrice Av STRHM/NOR SW16 180 A6
WBLY HA9 80 A3
Beatrice Cl PIN HA5 58 E1
PLSTW E13 106 E3
Beatrice Pl KENS W8 120 A3
Beatrice Rd ED N9 36 E2
FSBYPK N4 67 G4
RCHPK/HAM TW10 137 G6
STHL UB1 114 E1
STHWK SE1 123 H4
WALTH E17 69 J2
Beattie Cl EBED/NFELT TW14 153 J3
Beattock Ri MUSWH N10 66 B1
Beatty Rd STAN HA7 43 J2
STNW/STAM N16 86 A2
Beatty St CAMTN NW1 * 4 A2
Beattyville Gdns CLAY IG5 54 A6
Beauchamp Pl CHEL SW3 14 D5
Beauchamp Rd BTSEA SW11 140 D5
E/WMO/HCT KT8 189 G2
FSTGT E7 89 F5
NRWD SE19 180 E4
SUT SM1 208 E3
TWK TW1 156 B2
Beauchamp St HCIRC EC1N 11 J2
Beauchamp Ter BARN SW13 138 E4
Beauclerc Rd HMSMTH W6 118 E3
Beauclerk Cl FELT TW13 154 A3
Beaufort EHAM E6 108 A4
Beaufort Av
KTN/HRWW/WS HA3 61 G1
Beaufort Cl CHING E4 51 K2
EA W5 98 B4
PUT/ROE SW15 159 F3
ROMW/RG RM7 74 E1
Beaufort Ct
RCHPK/HAM TW10 156 D6
Beaufort Dr GLDGN NW11 64 E1
Beaufort Gdns CHEL SW3 14 D4
HDN NW4 64 A3
HEST TW5 134 D2
IL IG1 72 A5
STRHM/NOR SW16 180 A3
Beaufort Rd EA W5 98 B4
KUT/HW KT1 191 F1
RCHPK/HAM TW10 156 D6
RSLP HA4 * 58 B6
TWK TW1 156 D2
Beaufort St CHEL SW3 120 C6
Beaufort Wy EW KT17 207 J5
Beaufoy Rd TOTM N17 50 B3
Beaufoy Wk LBTH SE11 17 H7
Beaulieu Av CAN/RD E16 126 A1
SYD SE26 163 J6
Beaulieu Cl CDALE/KGS NW9 63 G1
CMBW SE5 142 E4
HSLWW TW4 134 E6
MTCM CR4 179 F4
OXHEY WD19 27 G3
TWK TW1 156 E1
Beaulieu Dr PIN HA5 59 H3
Beaulieu Gdns WCHMH N21 35 J2
Beaulieu Pl CHSWK W4 117 K3
Beauly Ct ROM RM1 57 G4
Beauly Wy ROM RM1 57 G4
Beaumaris Gn
CDALE/KGS NW9 * 63 G3
Beaumont Av ALP/SUD HA0 79 J3
RCH/KEW TW9 137 G4
RYLN/HDSTN HA2 60 B3
WKENS W14 119 J5
Beaumont Cl KUTN/CMB KT2 175 H3
Beaumont Ct ALP/SUD HA0 79 J3
Beaumont Crs RAIN RM13 93 J4
WKENS W14 119 J5
Beaumont Gdns HAMP NW3 64 E6
Beaumont Gv WCHPL E1 105 F3
Beaumont Ms MHST W1U * 9 H1
PIN HA5 * 41 J6
Beaumont Pl BAR EN5 20 D2
FITZ W1T 4 B6
ISLW TW7 136 A6
Beaumont Ri ARCH N19 66 E5
Beaumont Rd CHSWK W4 117 K3
LEY E10 70 A4
NRWD SE19 180 D2
PLSTW E13 107 G2
STMC/STPC BR5 201 J3
WIM/MER SW19 159 H2
Beaumont Sq WCHPL E1 105 F4
Beaumont St CAVSQ/HST W1G 9 H1
Beaumont Ter LEW SE13 * 165 H2
Beaumont Wk HAMP NW3 83 K5
Beauvais Ter NTHLT UB5 95 H2
Beauval Rd EDUL SE22 163 G1
Beaverbank Rd
ELTH/MOT SE9 167 J3
Beaver Cl HPTN TW12 173 G4
MRDN SM4 193 F4
PGE/AN SE20 * 181 H3
Beaver Rd BARK/HLT IG6 55 J1
Beavers Crs HSLWW TW4 134 C5
Beavers La HSLWW TW4 134 B4
Beaverwood Rd CHST BR7 185 K1
Beavor La HMSMTH W6 118 D5
Bebbington Rd
WOOL/PLUM SE18 * 127 K4
Beblets Cl ORP BR6 217 F3
Beccles Dr BARK IG11 91 F4
Beccles St POP/IOD E14 105 H5
Bec Cl RSLP HA4 77 H1
Beck Cl LEW SE13 144 E2
Beckenham Gdns ED N9 36 A5
Beckenham Gv HAYES BR2 183 G5
Beckenham Hill Rd BECK BR3 182 E2
Beckenham La HAYES BR2 183 H5
Beckenham Place Pk
BECK BR3 182 E3
Beckenham Rd BECK BR3 182 A4
BECK BR3 198 E4
Becket Av EHAM E6 108 A2
Becket Cl SNWD SE25 197 H3
WIM/MER SW19 * 178 A4
Becket Fold HRW HA1 * 61 F2
Becket Rd UED N18 36 E6
Becket St STHWK SE1 18 E4
Beckett Cl BELV DA17 129 F3
STRHM/NOR SW16 161 J4
WLSDN NW10 81 F4
Becketts Cl EBED/NFELT TW14 154 A1
ORP BR6 217 F1
Becketts Pl KUT/HW KT1 174 E4
Beckett Wk BECK BR3 182 B2
Beckford Cl WKENS W14 119 J4
Beckford Dr STMC/STPC BR5 201 J4
Beckford Pl WALW SE17 * 122 D5
Beckford Rd CROY/NA CR0 197 G3
Beck La BECK BR3 182 A6
Becklow Rd SHB W12 118 D2
Beck River Pk BECK BR3 182 C4
Beck Rd HACK E8 86 D6
Becks Rd SCUP DA14 168 B5
Beckton Rd CAN/RD E16 106 D4
Beck Wy BECK BR3 182 C6
Beckway Rd
STRHM/NOR SW16 179 J5
Beckway St WALW SE17 19 G7
Beckwith Rd HNHL SE24 162 E1
Beclands Rd TOOT SW17 179 F2
Becmead Av
KTN/HRWW/WS HA3 61 H2
STRHM/NOR SW16 161 J6
Becondale Rd NRWD SE19 181 F1
Becontree Av BCTR RM8 91 H2
Bective Rd FSTGT E7 88 E2
PUT/ROE SW15 139 J5
Becton Pl ERITH DA8 149 J2
Bedale Rd ENC/FH EN2 23 J1
Bedale St STHWK SE1 * 18 E1
Beddington Cross
CROY/NA CR0 195 K4
Beddington Farm Rd
CROY/NA CR0 195 K6
Beddington Gdns CAR SM5 210 A4
Beddington Gn
STMC/STPC BR5 186 A4
Beddington Gv WLGTN SM6 210 D3
Beddington La CROY/NA CR0 195 J4
Beddington Rd GDMY/SEVK IG3 73 F4
STMC/STPC BR5 185 K4
Beddington Ter
CROY/NA CR0 * 196 A4
Bede Cl PIN HA5 41 H4
Bedens Rd SCUP DA14 187 F2
Bede Rd CHDH RM6 73 J3
Bedevere Rd ED N9 36 C5
Bedfont Cl EBED/NFELT TW14 153 F2
MTCM CR4 179 F5
Bedfont Green Cl
EBED/NFELT TW14 153 F3
Bedfont La EBED/NFELT TW14 153 H2
Bedfont Rd EBED/NFELT TW14 153 F3
STWL/WRAY TW19 152 C1
Bedford Av BAR EN5 20 D6
RSQ WC1B 10 D2
YEAD UB4 95 F5
Bedfordbury CHCR WC2N 10 E5
Bedford Cl CHSWK W4 138 C1
MUSWH N10 48 A3
Bedford Cnr CHSWK W4 * 118 B4
Bedford Ct CHCR WC2N 10 E6
Bedford Gdns KENS W8 119 K1
Bedford Hl BAL SW12 161 G4
Bedford Pk CROY/NA CR0 196 D5
Bedford Pl CROY/NA CR0 196 E5
RSQ WC1B 10 E1
Bedford Rd BFN/LL DA15 167 K5
CEND/HSY/T N8 66 D3
CHSWK W4 118 A3
CLAP SW4 141 K5
DART DA1 171 K2
ED N9 36 D2
EFNCH N2 47 J6
EHAM E6 90 A6
HRW HA1 60 C3
IL IG1 90 B1
MLHL NW7 31 G4
NTHWD HA6 26 B6
ORP BR6 202 C6
RSLP HA4 76 D2
SEVS/STOTM N15 67 K1
SWFD E18 52 E5
WALTH E17 51 J5
WDGN N22 48 E4
WEA W13 116 C1
WHTN TW2 155 J5
WPK KT4 193 F6
Bedford Rw GINN WC1R 11 H1
Bedford Sq RSQ WC1B 10 D2
Bedford St COVGDN WC2E 10 E5
Bedford Vls KUT/HW KT1 * 175 G5
Bedford Wy STPAN WC1H 4 D7
Bedgebury Gdns
WIM/MER SW19 159 H4
Bedgebury Rd ELTH/MOT SE9 146 C5
Bedivere Rd BMLY BR1 165 K5
Bedlow Cl STJWD NW8 2 B7
Bedlow Wy CROY/NA CR0 211 F2
Bedonwell Rd BELV DA17 129 G6
BXLYHN DA7 149 G2
Bedser Cl LBTH SE11 * 122 A6
THHTH CR7 180 D6
Bedser Dr GFD/PVL UB6 78 D3
Bedster Gdns
E/WMO/HCT KT8 173 G5
Bedwardine Rd NRWD SE19 181 F3
Bedwell Gdns HYS/HAR UB3 113 H5
Bedwell Rd BELV DA17 129 H5
TOTM N17 50 A4
Beeby Rd CAN/RD E16 107 F4
Beech Av ACT W3 118 B1
BFN/LL DA15 168 B2
BKHH IG9 39 F4
BTFD TW8 136 C1
RSLP HA4 59 F5
TRDG/WHET N20 33 J3
Beech Cl CAR SM5 194 E6
DEPT SE8 124 C6
ED N9 36 C1
HCH RM12 93 K1
PUT/ROE SW15 158 D2
SUN TW16 172 C5
WDR/YW UB7 112 D3
WIM/MER SW19 177 F2
Beech Copse BMLY BR1 184 E5
SAND/SEL CR2 212 A3
Beech Ct ELTH/MOT SE9 * 166 D1
Beechcroft CHST BR7 185 F3
Beechcroft Av BXLYHN DA7 150 A3
GLDGN NW11 64 D4
NWMAL KT3 175 K4
RKW/CH/CXG WD3 26 A1
RYLN/HDSTN HA2 60 A4
STHL UB1 114 E1
Beechcroft Cl HEST TW5 134 D1
ORP BR6 216 D2
STRHM/NOR SW16 180 A1
Beechcroft Gdns WBLY HA9 80 B1
Beechcroft Rd CHSGTN KT9 206 B2
MORT/ESHN SW14 * 137 K4
ORP BR6 216 D2
SWFD E18 53 F5
TOOT SW17 160 E5
Beechdale WCHMH N21 35 F4
Beechdale Rd
BRXS/STRHM SW2 162 A1
Beech Dell HAYES BR2 215 K2
Beech Dr EFNCH N2 47 K6
Beechen Cliff Wy ISLW TW7 136 A3
Beechengrove PIN HA5 41 K6
Beechen Pl FSTH SE23 163 K4
Beeches Av CAR SM5 209 J5
Beeches Cl PGE/AN SE20 181 K4
Beeches Rd CHEAM SM3 193 H5
TOOT SW17 160 E5
The Beeches CHING E4 * 38 B3
HNWL W7 * 116 A2
Beeches Wk BELMT SM2 209 H6
Beechfield Gdns
ROMW/RG RM7 74 E4
Beechfield Rd BMLY BR1 184 B5
CAT SE6 164 C3
ERITH DA8 150 B1
FSBYPK N4 67 J3
Beech Gdns DAGE RM10 92 D5
EA W5 117 F2
Beech Gv BARK/HLT IG6 54 E2
MTCM CR4 195 J2
NWMAL KT3 176 A6
Beech Hall Crs CHING E4 52 B3
Beech Hall Rd CHING E4 52 A3
Beech Hl EBAR EN4 21 H1
Beech Hill Av EBAR EN4 21 H2
Beechhill Rd ELTH/MOT SE9 147 F6
Beech House Rd
CROY/NA CR0 211 K1
Beech Lawns
NFNCH/WDSPK N12 * 47 H1
Beechmont Cl BMLY BR1 183 H1
Beechmore Gdns CHEAM SM3 193 G6
Beechmore Rd BTSEA SW11 140 E2
Beechmount Av HNWL W7 96 D4
Beecholme Av MTCM CR4 179 G4
Beecholme Est CLPT E5 * 86 E1
Beech Rd DART DA1 171 G3
EBED/NFELT TW14 153 H2
FBAR/BDGN N11 48 E2
ORP BR6 217 G5
STRHM/NOR SW16 179 K5
Beechrow KUTN/CMB KT2 157 F6
Beech St ROMW/RG RM7 74 E1
Beech St (Below) BARB EC2Y 12 C1
Beech Tree Cl IS N1 85 G5
STAN HA7 43 J1
Beech Tree Gld CHING E4 38 D3
Beech Tree Pl SUT SM1 209 F3
Beechvale Cl
NFNCH/WDSPK N12 47 J1
Beech Wk DART DA1 150 D5
MLHL NW7 45 F2
Beechway BXLY DA5 168 E1
Beech Wy WHTN TW2 155 F5
WLSDN NW10 81 F5
Beechwood Av FNCH N3 46 D6
GFD/PVL UB6 96 B2
HYS/HAR UB3 94 B6
ORP BR6 216 E4
RCH/KEW TW9 137 H2
RSLP HA4 58 D6
RYLN/HDSTN HA2 78 B1
THHTH CR7 196 C1
Beechwood Cl EFNCH N2 * 65 K1
MLHL NW7 45 G1
SURB KT6 190 D4
Beechwood Crs BXLYHN DA7 148 E4
Beechwood Dr HAYES BR2 215 H2
WFD IG8 52 D1
Beechwood Gdns CLAY IG5 71 K2
RAIN RM13 111 K4
RYLN/HDSTN HA2 78 B1
Beechwood Gv ACT W3 99 G6
Beechwood Ms ED N9 36 C4
Beechwood Pk SWFD E18 52 E6
Beechwood Ri CHST BR7 167 G6
Beechwood Rd
CEND/HSY/T N8 66 D1
HACK E8 86 B4
SAND/SEL CR2 212 A6
Beechworth Cl HAMP NW3 65 F6
Beecot La WOT/HER KT12 188 B6
Beecroft La BROCKY SE4 144 B6
Beecroft Ms BROCKY SE4 144 B6
Beecroft Rd BROCKY SE4 144 B6
Beehive Cl BORE WD6 29 K1
HACK E8 86 B5
Beehive La REDBR IG4 71 K2
Beehive Pl BRXN/ST SW9 142 B4
Beeken Dene ORP BR6 216 C2
Beeleigh Rd MRDN SM4 194 A1
Beeston Cl HACK E8 86 C3
OXHEY WD19 27 H6
Beeston Pl BGVA SW1W 15 K5
Beeston Rd EBAR EN4 33 H1
Beeston Wy
EBED/NFELT TW14 154 B1
Beethoven Rd BORE WD6 29 J2
Beethoven St NKENS W10 100 C2
Beeton Cl PIN HA5 42 A3
Begbie Rd BKHTH/KID SE3 146 B2
Beggar's Roost La SUT SM1 208 E4
Begonia Cl EHAM E6 107 J4
Begonia Pl HPTN TW12 173 F2
Beira St BAL SW12 161 G2
Bekesbourne St
POP/IOD E14 * 105 G5
Belcroft Cl BMLY BR1 183 J3
Beldham Gdns
E/WMO/HCT KT8 173 G6
Belfairs Dr CHDH RM6 73 J4
Belfairs Gdn OXHEY WD19 41 H1
Belfairs Gn OXHEY WD19 41 H1
Belfast Rd SNWD SE25 197 J1
STNW/STAM N16 68 B6
Belfield Rd HOR/WEW KT19 207 F6
Belford Gv WOOL/PLUM SE18 127 F4
Belfort Rd PECK SE15 143 K3
Belfry Cl BERM/RHTH SE16 123 J5
BMLY BR1 201 G1
Belgrade Rd HPTN TW12 173 G4
STNW/STAM N16 86 A2
Belgrave Cl ACT W3 117 K2
MLHL NW7 45 F1
STHGT/OAK N14 22 C6
STMC/STPC BR5 202 D1
Belgrave Crs SUN TW16 172 A4
Belgrave Gdns STAN HA7 43 J1
STHGT/OAK N14 22 D6
STJWD NW8 83 G6
Belgrave Ms South KTBR SW1X 15 H4
Belgrave Ms West KTBR SW1X 15 G4
Belgrave Pl KTBR SW1X 15 H5
Belgrave Rd BARN SW13 138 C1
HSLWW TW4 134 E4
IL IG1 71 K5
MTCM CR4 178 C6
PIM SW1V 16 B7
PLSTW E13 107 G3
SNWD SE25 197 G1
SUN TW16 172 A4
WALTH E17 69 J3
WAN E11 70 E5
Belgrave Sq KTBR SW1X 15 G4
Belgrave St WCHPL E1 105 F5
Belgrave Wk MTCM CR4 178 C6
Belgravia Cl BAR EN5 20 D4
Belgravia Gdns BMLY BR1 183 H2
Belgravia Ms KUT/HW KT1 190 E1
Belgrove St CAMTN NW1 4 E4
Belinda Rd BRXN/ST SW9 142 C4
Belitha Vls IS N1 85 G5
Bellamaine Cl THMD SE28 128 A2
Bellamy Cl EDGW HA8 30 E5
POP/IOD E14 124 D2
WKENS W14 119 J5
Bellamy Dr STAN HA7 43 H4
Bellamy Rd CHING E4 51 K2
ENC/FH EN2 * 23 K3
Bellamy St BAL SW12 161 G2
Bel La FELT TW13 154 D5
Bellarmine Cl THMD SE28 128 A1
Bellasis Av BRXS/STRHM SW2 161 K3
Bell Av HARH RM3 57 K4
WDR/YW UB7 112 C3
Bell Cl PIN HA5 41 G6
Bellclose Rd WDR/YW UB7 112 B2
Bell Dr WAND/EARL SW18 159 H2
Bellefield Rd STMC/STPC BR5 202 C2
Bellefields Rd BRXN/ST SW9 142 A4
Bellegrove Cl WELL DA16 148 A3
Bellegrove Rd WELL DA16 147 K3
Bellenden Rd PECK SE15 143 G3
Belle Staines Pleasaunce
CHING E4 37 J4
Belleville Rd BTSEA SW11 140 E6
Belle Vue GFD/PVL UB6 78 D6
Belle Vue La BUSH WD23 28 D3
Bellevue Pk THHTH CR7 180 D6
Bellevue Pl WCHPL E1 * 104 E3
Belle Vue Rd CRW RM5 56 E2
HDN NW4 64 B1
WALTH E17 52 B5
Bellevue Rd BARN SW13 138 D3
BXLYHS DA6 149 G6
FBAR/BDGN N11 34 A6
KUT/HW KT1 175 F6
TOOT SW17 160 E2
WEA W13 97 H3
Bellew St TOOT SW17 160 B5
Bell Farm Av DAGE RM10 92 E1
Bellfield CROY/NA CR0 213 G6
Bellfield Av
KTN/HRWW/WS HA3 42 D2
Bellfield Cl BKHTH/KID SE3 146 A1
Bell Gdns LEY E10 * 69 J5
STMC/STPC BR5 202 D2
Bellgate Ms KTTN NW5 84 B2
Bell Gn SYD SE26 164 C6
Bell Green La SYD SE26 182 C1
Bell House Rd ROMW/RG RM7 74 E5
Bellina Ms KTTN NW5 84 B2
Bellingham Gn CAT SE6 164 D5
Bellingham Rd CAT SE6 165 F5
Bell La CAN/RD E16 125 J1
HDN NW4 64 B1
PEND EN3 25 F1
TWK TW1 156 B3
WBLY HA9 * 61 K6
WCHPL E1 13 J2
Bell Meadow NRWD SE19 163 F6
Bello Cl HNHL SE24 162 C3
Bellot St GNWCH SE10 125 H5
Bell Pde HSLW TW3 * 135 G5
WWKM BR4 * 199 F6
Bellring Cl BELV DA17 129 H6
Bell Rd E/WMO/HCT KT8 189 J2
EN EN1 23 K2
HSLW TW3 135 G5
Bells Hl BAR EN5 20 B6
Bell St BAY/PAD W2 8 C1
WOOL/PLUM SE18 146 D2
Belltrees Gv
STRHM/NOR SW16 180 A1
Bell Water Ga
WOOL/PLUM SE18 127 F3
Bell Wharf La CANST EC4R 12 D6
Bellwood Rd PECK SE15 144 A5
Bell Yd LINN WC2A 11 J4
Bell Yard Ms STHWK SE1 19 H3
Belmont Av ALP/SUD HA0 80 B6
EBAR EN4 21 K6
ED N9 36 C3
NWDGN UB2 114 D3
NWMAL KT3 192 D2
PLMGR N13 48 E1
TOTM N17 49 J6
WELL DA16 147 K3
Belmont Cir
KTN/HRWW/WS HA3 * 43 H4
Belmont Cl CHING E4 52 B1
CLAP SW4 141 H4
EBAR EN4 21 K5
TRDG/WHET N20 33 F3
WFD IG8 39 F6
Belmont Gv CHSWK W4 118 A4
LEW SE13 145 G4
Belmont Hl LEW SE13 145 G4
Belmont La CHST BR7 185 H1
STAN HA7 43 J3
Belmont Pde CHST BR7 * 185 G1
GLDGN NW11 * 64 D2
Belmont Pk LEW SE13 145 G5
Belmont Park Cl LEW SE13 145 H5
Belmont Park Rd LEY E10 69 K3
Belmont Ri BELMT SM2 208 D6
Belmont Rd BECK BR3 182 B6
CHST BR7 185 G1
CLAP SW4 141 H4
ERITH DA8 149 J1
IL IG1 90 C1
KTN/HRWW/WS HA3 43 F6
SEVS/STOTM N15 67 J1
SNWD SE25 197 J2
WHTN TW2 155 J4
WLGTN SM6 210 C3
Belmont St CAMTN NW1 84 A5
Belmont Ter CHSWK W4 118 A4
Belmore Av YEAD UB4 94 E5
Belmore La HOLWY N7 84 D3
Belmore St VX/NE SW8 141 J2
Beloe Cl PUT/ROE SW15 138 D5
Belsham St HOM E9 86 E4
Belsize Av HAMP NW3 83 J3
PLMGR N13 49 F2
WEA W13 116 C3
Belsize Court Gdns HAMP NW3 83 H3
Belsize Crs HAMP NW3 83 H3
Belsize Gdns SUT SM1 209 F2
Belsize Gv HAMP NW3 83 J4
Belsize La HAMP NW3 83 H4
Belsize Ms HAMP NW3 * 83 H4
Belsize Pk HAMP NW3 83 H4
Belsize Park Gdns HAMP NW3 83 H4
Belsize Park Ms HAMP NW3 83 H4
Belsize Pl HAMP NW3 83 H3
Belsize Rd KIL/WHAMP NW6 83 G6
KTN/HRWW/WS HA3 42 D3
Belsize Sq HAMP NW3 83 H4
Belsize Ter HAMP NW3 83 H4
Belson Rd WOOL/PLUM SE18 126 E4
Beltane Dr WIM/MER SW19 159 G5
Belthorn Crs BAL SW12 161 H2
Belton Rd FSTGT E7 89 F5
SCUP DA14 168 B6
TOTM N17 50 A6
WAN E11 88 C2
WLSDN NW10 81 J4
Belton Wy BOW E3 105 J4
Beltran Rd FUL/PGN SW6 140 A3
Beltwood Rd BELV DA17 129 K4
Belvedere Av BARK/HLT IG6 54 B5
WIM/MER SW19 177 H1
Belvedere Buildings
STHWK SE1 18 B3
Belvedere Cl ESH/CLAY KT10 204 B3
TEDD TW11 173 K1
Belvedere Ct BELV DA17 129 G3
OXHEY WD19 27 J1
Belvedere Dr WIM/MER SW19 177 H1
Belvedere Gdns
E/WMO/HCT KT8 188 E2
Belvedere Gv WIM/MER SW19 177 H1
Belvedere Ms PECK SE15 143 K4
Belvedere Pl
BRXS/STRHM SW2 142 A5
Belvedere Rd ABYW SE2 128 E1
BXLYHN DA7 149 G4
HNWL W7 115 K3
LEY E10 69 G5
NRWD SE19 181 G3
STHWK SE1 17 G2
Belvedere Sq WIM/MER SW19 177 H1
Belvedere Strd
CDALE/KGS NW9 45 H5
The Belvedere WBPTN SW10 * 140 B2
Belvedere Wy
KTN/HRWW/WS HA3 62 A3
Belvoir Rd EDUL SE22 163 H2
Belvue Cl NTHLT UB5 78 A5
Belvue Rd NTHLT UB5 78 A5
Bembridge Cl KIL/WHAMP NW6 82 C5
Bembridge Gdns RSLP HA4 58 C6
Bemerton St IS N1 85 F6
Bemish Rd PUT/ROE SW15 139 G4
Bempton Dr RSLP HA4 59 F6
Bemsted Rd WALTH E17 51 H6
Benares Rd WOOL/PLUM SE18 128 A4
Benbow Rd HMSMTH W6 118 E3
Benbow St DEPT SE8 124 D6
Benbury Cl BMLY BR1 183 F1
Bench Fld SAND/SEL CR2 212 B4
The Bench
RCHPK/HAM TW10 * 156 D5
Bencroft Rd
STRHM/NOR SW16 179 H3

Bencurtis Pk WWKM BR4 214 B1
Bendall Ms CAMTN NW1 8 D1
Bendemeer Rd
PUT/ROE SW15 139 G4
Bendish Rd EHAM E6 89 J5
Bendmore Av ABYW SE2 128 B5
Bendon Va WAND/EARL SW18 160 A2
Benedict Cl ORP BR6 216 E1
Benedict Dr
EBED/NFELT TW14 153 G2
Benedict Rd BRXN/ST SW9 142 A4
MTCM CR4 178 C6
Benedict Wy EFNCH N2 * 47 G6
Benedict Whf MTCM CR4 178 D6
Benenden Gn HAYES BR2 199 K2
Benett Gdns
STRHM/NOR SW16 179 K5
Benfleet Cl SUT SM1 209 G1
Benfleet Wy FBAR/BDGN N11 34 A4
Bengal Rd IL IG1 90 B2
Bengarth Dr
KTN/HRWW/WS HA3 42 D5
Bengarth Rd NTHLT UB5 77 H6
Bengeworth Rd CMBW SE5 142 D4
HRW HA1 61 G6
Ben Hale Cl STAN HA7 43 G1
Benham Cl CHSGTN KT9 205 J4
Benham Gdns HSLWW TW4 134 E6
Benham Rd HNWL W7 96 E4
Benhill Av SUT SM1 209 G2
Benhill Rd CMBW SE5 142 E1
SUT SM1 209 H1
Benhill Wood Rd SUT SM1 209 G2
Benhilton Gdns SUT SM1 209 F1
Benhurst Av HCH RM12 93 K2
Benhurst La
STRHM/NOR SW16 180 B1
Benin St LEW SE13 165 G2
Benjafield Cl UED N18 36 D6
Benjamin Cl EMPK RM11 75 J3
HACK E8 86 C6
Benjamin Ms BAL SW12 161 H2
Benjamin St FARR EC1M 12 A1
Ben Jonson Rd WCHPL E1 105 G4
Benledi St POP/IOD E14 106 B5
Bennelong Cl SHB W12 99 K6
Bennerley Rd BTSEA SW11 140 E6
Bennet Cl KUT/HW KT1 174 D4
Bennetsfield Rd STKPK UB11 112 E1
Bennet's Hl BLKFR EC4V 12 B5
Bennett Cl HSLWW TW4 134 D6
NTHWD HA6 40 D3
WELL DA16 148 B3
Bennett Gv LEW SE13 144 E2
Bennett Pk BKHTH/KID SE3 145 J4
Bennett Rd BRXN/ST SW9 142 B3
CHDH RM6 74 A3
PLSTW E13 107 G3
Bennetts Av CROY/NA CR0 198 B6
GFD/PVL UB6 78 E6
Bennett's Castle La BCTR RM8 91 J2
Bennetts Cl MTCM CR4 179 G4
TOTM N17 50 B2
Bennetts Copse CHST BR7 184 D2
Bennett St CHSWK W4 118 B6
WHALL SW1A 10 A7
Bennetts Wy CROY/NA CR0 198 B6
Benningholme Rd EDGW HA8 45 G2
Bennington Rd TOTM N17 50 A4
WFD IG8 * 52 C3
Benn St HOM E9 87 G4
Benrek Cl BARK/HLT IG6 54 C3
Bensbury Cl PUT/ROE SW15 158 E2
Bensham Cl THHTH CR7 196 D1
Bensham Gv THHTH CR7 180 D5
Bensham La THHTH CR7 196 C1
Bensham Manor Rd
THHTH CR7 196 E2
Bensley Cl FBAR/BDGN N11 47 K1
Ben Smith Wy
BERM/RHTH SE16 123 H3
Benson Av PLSTW E13 107 G1
Benson Cl HSLW TW3 135 F5
Benson Quay WAP E1W 104 E6
Benson Rd CROY/NA CR0 211 G1
FSTH SE23 163 K3
Benthal Rd STNW/STAM N16 68 B6
Bentham Rd HOM E9 87 F4
THMD SE28 128 C1
Ben Tillet Cl BARK IG11 91 G5
CAN/RD E16 * 126 E1
Bentinck Ms MHST W1U 9 H3
Bentinck Rd WDR/YW UB7 112 A1
Bentinck St MHST W1U 9 H3
Bentley Cl WIM/MER SW19 159 K6
Bentley Dr CRICK NW2 82 D1
GNTH/NBYPK IG2 72 C3
Bentley Ms EN EN1 35 K1
Bentley Rd IS N1 86 A4
Bentley Wy STAN HA7 43 G1
WFD IG8 38 E5
Benton Rd IL IG1 72 D5
OXHEY WD19 41 H1
Benton's La WNWD SE27 162 D6
Benton's Ri WNWD SE27 180 E1
Bentry Cl BCTR RM8 74 A6
Bentry Rd BCTR RM8 74 A6
Bentworth Rd SHB W12 99 K5
Benwell Rd HOLWY N7 85 G2
Benwick Cl BERM/RHTH SE16 123 J4
Benwood Ct SUT SM1 209 G1
Benworth St BOW E3 105 H2
Benyon Rd IS N1 85 K6
Benyon Whf IS N1 86 A6
Berberis Wk WDR/YW UB7 112 B4
Berber Pde
WOOL/PLUM SE18 * 146 D1
Berber Rd BTSEA SW11 * 140 E6
Bercta Rd ELTH/MOT SE9 167 H4
Berenger Wk WBPTN SW10 * 140 C1
Berens Rd STMC/STPC BR5 202 D2
WLSDN NW10 100 B2
Berens Wy CHST BR7 202 A1
Beresford Av ALP/SUD HA0 80 C6
BRYLDS KT5 191 J5
HNWL W7 96 D4
TRDG/WHET N20 33 K4
TWK TW1 156 D1
Beresford Dr BMLY BR1 184 D6
WFD IG8 39 G6
Beresford Gdns CHDH RM6 74 A2
EN EN1 24 A5
HSLWW TW4 134 E6
Beresford Rd BELMT SM2 208 D5
CEND/HSY/T N8 67 G2
CHING E4 38 C3
EFNCH N2 47 J6
HBRY N5 85 K3
HRW HA1 60 D2
KUTN/CMB KT2 175 G4
NWMAL KT3 191 K1
STHL UB1 114 C1
WALTH E17 51 K4
Beresford Sq
WOOL/PLUM SE18 127 G4
Beresford St
WOOL/PLUM SE18 127 H3
Beresford Ter HBRY N5 85 J3
Berestede Rd HMSMTH W6 118 C5
Bere St WAP E1W 105 F6
Berger Cl STMC/STPC BR5 201 J3
Berger Rd HOM E9 87 F4
Berghem Ms WKENS W14 119 G3
Bergholt Av REDBR IG4 71 J2
Bergholt Crs STNW/STAM N16 68 A4
Bergholt Ms CAMTN NW1 84 C5
Bering Sq POP/IOD E14 124 D5
Bering Wk CAN/RD E16 107 H5
Berisford Ms
WAND/EARL SW18 160 B1
Berkeley Av BXLYHN DA7 148 E2
CLAY IG5 54 A5
CRW RM5 56 E3
GFD/PVL UB6 78 E4
HSLWW TW4 133 K2
Berkeley Cl KUTN/CMB KT2 175 F3
RSLP HA4 76 E1
STMC/STPC BR5 201 K4
Berkeley Ct WLGTN SM6 210 C1
Berkeley Crs DART DA1 171 J3
EBAR EN4 21 H6
Berkeley Dr E/WMO/HCT KT8 172 E6
Berkeley Gdns ESH/CLAY KT10 205 G5
KENS W8 119 K1
WCHMH N21 35 K2
Berkeley Ms MBLAR W1H 9 F3
SUN TW16 172 B6
Berkeley Pl WIM/MER SW19 177 G2
Berkeley Rd BARN SW13 138 D2
CDALE/KGS NW9 62 C1
CEND/HSY/T N8 66 D2
HGDN/ICK UB10 76 A5
MNPK E12 89 J3
SEVS/STOTM N15 67 K3
Berkeley Sq MYFR/PICC W1J 9 K6
The Berkeleys SNWD SE25 * 197 H1
Berkeley St MYFR/PICC W1J 9 K6
Berkeley Waye HEST TW5 134 D1
Berkhampstead Rd
BELV DA17 129 H5
Berkhamsted Av WBLY HA9 80 B4
Berkley Cl WHTN TW2 * 155 K5
Berkley Rd CAMTN NW1 83 K5
Berkshire Gdns PLMGR N13 49 G2
UED N18 50 D1
Berkshire Rd HOM E9 87 H4
Berkshire Wy MTCM CR4 195 K1
Bermans Wy WLSDN NW10 81 H2
Bermondsey St STHWK SE1 19 G1
Bermondsey Wall East
BERM/RHTH SE16 123 J2
Bermondsey Wall West
STHWK SE1 123 H2
Bernal Cl THMD SE28 109 K6
Bernard Ashley Dr CHARL SE7 126 A5
Bernard Av WEA W13 116 C3
Bernard Cassidy St
CAN/RD E16 106 D4
Bernard Gdns WIM/MER SW19 177 J1
Bernard Rd ROMW/RG RM7 74 E4
SEVS/STOTM N15 68 B2
WLGTN SM6 210 B3
Bernards Cl BARK/HLT IG6 54 C3
Bernard St BMSBY WC1N 4 E7
Bernays Cl STAN HA7 43 J2
Bernay's Gv BRXN/ST SW9 142 A5
Bernel Dr CROY/NA CR0 213 H1
Berne Rd THHTH CR7 196 C2
Berners Dr WEA W13 97 G6
Berners Ms FITZ W1T 10 B2
Berners Pl FITZ W1T 10 B3
Berners Rd IS N1 6 A2
WDGN N22 49 G4
Berners St FITZ W1T 10 B2
Berner Ter WCHPL E1 * 104 C5
Berney Rd CROY/NA CR0 196 E4
Bernhardt Crs STJWD NW8 2 C6
Bernhart Cl EDGW HA8 44 E3
Bernwell Rd CHING E4 38 C5
Berridge Gn EDGW HA8 44 C3
Berridge Ms KIL/WHAMP NW6 82 E3
Berridge Rd NRWD SE19 180 E1
Berriman Rd HOLWY N7 85 F1
Berriton Rd RYLN/HDSTN HA2 59 K5
Berrybank Cl CHING E4 38 A4
Berry Cl DAGE RM10 92 C3
WCHMH N21 35 H3
Berry Cottages POP/IOD E14 * 105 G5
Berry Ct HSLWW TW4 134 E6
Berrydale Rd YEAD UB4 95 J3
Berryfield Cl BMLY BR1 184 D4
Berry Field Cl WALTH E17 69 K1
Berryfield Rd WALW SE17 122 C5
Berryhill ELTH/MOT SE9 147 G5
Berry Hl STAN HA7 29 K6
Berryhill Gdns ELTH/MOT SE9 147 G5
Berrylands BRYLDS KT5 191 H2
ORP BR6 217 J1
RYNPK SW20 177 F6
Berrylands Rd BRYLDS KT5 191 G3
Berry La DUL SE21 162 E6
Berryman Cl BCTR RM8 91 J1
Berryman's La SYD SE26 164 A6
Berrymead Gdns ACT W3 117 K1
Berrymede Rd CHSWK W4 118 A3
Berry Pl FSBYE EC1V 6 B5
Berry St FSBYE EC1V 6 B7
Berry Wy EA W5 117 F3
Bertal Rd TOOT SW17 160 C6
Berthons Gdns WALTH E17 * 70 B2
Berthon St DEPT SE8 144 D1
Bertie Rd SYD SE26 182 A2
WLSDN NW10 81 J4
Bertram Rd EN EN1 24 C5
HDN NW4 63 J3
KUTN/CMB KT2 175 H3
Bertram St KTTN NW5 84 B1
Bertrand St LEW SE13 144 E4
Bertrand Wy THMD SE28 109 H6
Bert Rd THHTH CR7 196 D2
Bert Wy EN EN1 24 B5
Berwick Av YEAD UB4 95 H6
Berwick Cl STAN HA7 43 F2
WHTN TW2 155 F3
Berwick Crs BFN/LL DA15 167 K1
Berwick Gdns SUT SM1 209 G1
Berwick Rd CAN/RD E16 107 F5
WDGN N22 49 H4
WELL DA16 148 C2
Berwick St SOHO/CST W1F 10 B4
Berwyn Av HSLW TW3 135 G2
Berwyn Rd HNHL SE24 162 C3
RCHPK/HAM TW10 137 J5
Beryl Av EHAM E6 107 J4
Beryl Rd HMSMTH W6 119 G5
Berystede KUTN/CMB KT2 175 J3
Besant Cl CRICK NW2 * 82 C1
Besant Pl EDUL SE22 143 G5
Besant Placee EDUL SE22 143 G4
Besant Rd CRICK NW2 82 C2
Besant Wy WLSDN NW10 80 E3
Besley St STRHM/NOR SW16 179 H2
Bessant Dr RCH/KEW TW9 137 J2
Bessborough Pl PIM SW1V 121 J5
Bessborough Rd HRW HA1 60 D5
PUT/ROE SW15 158 D3
Bessborough St PIM SW1V 121 J5
Bessemer Rd CMBW SE5 142 E3
Bessie Lansbury Cl EHAM E6 108 A5
Bessingby Rd RSLP HA4 58 E6
Besson St NWCR SE14 143 K2
Bessy St BETH E2 * 104 E2
Best Ter SWLY BR8 * 203 K2
Bestwood St DEPT SE8 124 A4
Beswick Ms KIL/WHAMP NW6 83 F3
Betam Rd HYS/HAR UB3 113 G2
Betchworth Cl SUT SM1 209 H3
Betchworth Rd
GDMY/SEVK IG3 90 E1
Betchworth Wy CROY/NA CR0 214 A6
Betham Rd GFD/PVL UB6 96 D2
Bethany Waye
EBED/NFELT TW14 153 H2
Bethecar Rd HRW HA1 60 E2
Bethel Cl HDN NW4 64 B2
Bethell Av CAN/RD E16 106 D3
IL IG1 72 A4
Bethel Rd WELL DA16 148 D4
Bethersden Cl BECK BR3 182 C3
Bethnal Green Rd BETH E2 7 K6
Bethune Av FBAR/BDGN N11 33 K6
Bethune Rd STNW/STAM N16 67 K4
WLSDN NW10 99 F3
Bethwin Rd CMBW SE5 142 C1
Betjeman Cl RYLN/HDSTN HA2 60 A1
Betjeman Ct WDR/YW UB7 * 112 A1
Betony Cl CROY/NA CR0 198 A5
Betoyne Av CHING E4 38 C6
Betsham Rd ERITH DA8 150 C1
Betstyle Rd FBAR/BDGN N11 34 B6
Betterton Dr SCUP DA14 169 F4
Betterton Rd RAIN RM13 111 G1
Betterton St LSQ/SEVD WC2H 10 E4
Bettons Pk SRTFD E15 88 C6
Bettridge Rd FUL/PGN SW6 139 J3
Betts Cl BECK BR3 182 B5
Betts Ms WALTH E17 69 H3
Betts Rd CAN/RD E16 107 F5
Betts St WAP E1W 104 D6
Betts Wy PGE/AN SE20 181 J5
SURB KT6 190 C5
Beulah Av THHTH CR7 * 180 D5
Beulah Cl EDGW HA8 30 D5
Beulah Crs THHTH CR7 180 D5
Beulah Gv CROY/NA CR0 196 D3
Beulah Hl NRWD SE19 180 D2
Beulah Rd SUT SM1 208 E2
THHTH CR7 180 D6
WALTH E17 69 K2
WIM/MER SW19 177 J3
Beult Rd DART DA1 150 D4
Bevan Av BARK IG11 91 G5
Bevan Ct CROY/NA CR0 211 G3
Bevan Rd ABYW SE2 128 C5
EBAR EN4 21 K5
Bevan St IS N1 6 D1
Bev Callender Cl VX/NE SW8 141 G4
Bevenden St IS N1 7 F4
Beveridge Rd WLSDN NW10 81 G5
Beverley Av BFN/LL DA15 168 A2
HSLWW TW4 134 E5
RYNPK SW20 176 C4
Beverley Cl BARN SW13 138 D3
BTSEA SW11 140 C5
CHSGTN KT9 205 J2
WCHMH N21 35 J3
Beverley Ct BROCKY SE4 144 C4
Beverley Crs WFD IG8 53 F4
Beverley Dr EDGW HA8 44 B6
Beverley Gdns BARN SW13 138 C4
GLDGN NW11 64 C4
STAN HA7 43 G4
WBLY HA9 62 C5
WPK KT4 192 D5
Beverley La KUTN/CMB KT2 176 B3
Beverley Rd BARN SW13 138 C4
BXLYHN DA7 149 K3
CHING E4 52 B2
CHSWK W4 118 C5
DAGW RM9 92 A2
EHAM E6 107 H2
HAYES BR2 200 D6
KUT/HW KT1 174 D4
MTCM CR4 195 J1
NWDGN UB2 114 D4
NWMAL KT3 192 D1
PGE/AN SE20 181 J5
RSLP HA4 59 F6
WPK KT4 193 F6
Beverley Wy KUTN/CMB KT2 176 C4
Beverley Wy (Kingston
By-Pass) RYNPK SW20 176 C4
Beversbrook Rd ARCH N19 84 D1
Beverstone Rd
BRXS/STRHM SW2 142 A6
THHTH CR7 196 B1
Beverston Ms MBLAR W1H 8 E2
Bevill Allen Cl TOOT SW17 178 E2
Bevill Cl SNWD SE25 181 H6
Bevin Cl BERM/RHTH SE16 124 B1
Bevington Rd BECK BR3 182 E5
NKENS W10 * 100 C4
Bevington St
BERM/RHTH SE16 123 H2
Bevin Rd YEAD UB4 94 E2
Bevin Sq TOOT SW17 160 E5
Bevin Wy FSBYW WC1X 5 J3
Bevis Marks HDTCH EC3A 13 H3
Bewcastle Gdns ENC/FH EN2 22 E5
Bewdley St IS N1 85 G5
Bewick Ms PECK SE15 143 J1
Bewick St VX/NE SW8 141 G3
Bewley St WCHPL E1 104 D6
WIM/MER SW19 178 C2
Bewlys Rd WNWD SE27 180 C1
Bexhill Cl FELT TW13 154 D4
Bexhill Rd BROCKY SE4 164 C1
FBAR/BDGN N11 48 D1
MORT/ESHN SW14 137 K4
Bexley Cl DART DA1 150 B6
Bexley Gdns CHDH RM6 73 H2
ED N9 35 K5
Bexley High St BXLY DA5 169 H2
Bexley La DART DA1 150 B6
SCUP DA14 168 D4
Bexley Rd ELTH/MOT SE9 147 J6
ELTH/MOT SE9 167 F1
ERITH DA8 149 K1
Beynon Rd CAR SM5 209 K3
Bianca Rd PECK SE15 123 G6
Bibsworth Rd FNCH N3 46 D5
Bibury Cl PECK SE15 123 F6
Bicester Rd RCH/KEW TW9 137 H4
Bickenhall St MHST W1U 9 F1
Bickersteth Rd TOOT SW17 178 E2
Bickerton Rd ARCH N19 84 C1
Bickles Yd STHWK SE1 19 H3
Bickley Crs BMLY BR1 200 D1
Bickley Park Rd BMLY BR1 184 E6
Bickley Rd BMLY BR1 184 C5
LEY E10 69 K4
Bickley St TOOT SW17 178 E1
Bicknell Rd CMBW SE5 142 D4
Bicknoller Rd EN EN1 24 B2
Bicknor Rd ORP BR6 201 K4
Bidborough Cl HAYES BR2 199 J2
Bidborough St STPAN WC1H 4 E5
Biddenden Wy ELTH/MOT SE9 167 F6
Bidder St CAN/RD E16 106 C4
Biddestone Rd HOLWY N7 85 F2
Biddulph Rd MV/WKIL W9 101 F2
SAND/SEL CR2 211 J6
Bideford Av GFD/PVL UB6 97 H2
Bideford Cl EDGW HA8 44 C4
FELT TW13 154 E5
Bideford Gdns EN EN1 36 A2
Bideford Rd BMLY BR1 165 J5
PEND EN3 25 H1
RSLP HA4 77 F1
WELL DA16 148 C1
Bidwell Gdns FBAR/BDGN N11 48 C4
Bidwell St PECK SE15 * 143 J2
Biggerstaff Rd SRTFD E15 88 A6
Biggerstaff St FSBYPK N4 67 G6
Biggin Av MTCM CR4 178 E4
Biggin Hl NRWD SE19 180 C3
Biggin Wy NRWD SE19 180 C3
Bigginwood Rd
STRHM/NOR SW16 180 C3
Bigg's Rw PUT/ROE SW15 139 G4
Bigland St WCHPL E1 104 D5
Bignell Rd WOOL/PLUM SE18 127 G5
Bignold Rd FSTGT E7 88 E2
Big St CLPT E5 68 D5
Bigwood Rd GLDGN NW11 65 F3
Billet Rd CHDH RM6 55 J6
WALTH E17 51 F4
Billets Hart Cl HNWL W7 115 K2
Bill Hamling Cl ELTH/MOT SE9 166 E4
Billingford Cl BROCKY SE4 144 A5
Billing Pl WBPTN SW10 * 140 A1
Billing Rd WBPTN SW10 140 A1
Billings Cl DAGW RM9 91 J5
Billing St WBPTN SW10 * 140 A1
Billington Hl CROY/NA CR0 196 E6
Billington Rd NWCR SE14 144 A1
Billiter Sq FENCHST EC3M * 13 H4
Billiter St FENCHST EC3M 13 H4
Bill Nicholson Wy TOTM N17 50 B3
Billockby Cl CHSGTN KT9 206 B4
Billson St POP/IOD E14 125 F4
Bilton Rd ERITH DA8 150 D1
GFD/PVL UB6 79 H6
Bilton Wy HYS/HAR UB3 114 A2
PEND EN3 25 H2
Bina Gdns ECT SW5 120 B4
Bincote Rd ENC/FH EN2 23 F4
Binden Rd SHB W12 118 C3
Binfield Rd CLAP SW4 141 K2
SAND/SEL CR2 212 B3
Bingfield St IS N1 84 E6
Bingham Ct IS N1 * 85 H5
Bingham Pl CAMTN NW1 3 G7
MHST W1U 9 G1
Bingham Rd CROY/NA CR0 197 H5
Bingham St IS N1 85 J5
Bingley Rd CAN/RD E16 107 G5
GFD/PVL UB6 96 C3
Binney St MYFR/PKLN W1K 9 H5
Binns Rd CHSWK W4 118 B5
Binsey Wk ABYW SE2 128 D2
Binstead Cl YEAD UB4 95 J4
Binyon Crs STAN HA7 43 F1
Birbetts Rd ELTH/MOT SE9 166 E4
Birchanger Rd SNWD SE25 197 H2
Birch Av PLMGR N13 35 J5
Birch Cl BKHH IG9 39 H5
BTFD TW8 136 C1
CAN/RD E16 106 C4
HSLW TW3 135 J4
ROMW/RG RM7 56 D6
TEDD TW11 174 B1
Birch Ct WLGTN SM6 210 B2
Birchdale Gdns CHDH RM6 73 K4
Birchdale Rd FSTGT E7 89 G3
Birchdene Dr THMD SE28 128 B2
Birchen Cl CDALE/KGS NW9 63 F6
Birchend Cl SAND/SEL CR2 211 K4
Birchen Gv CDALE/KGS NW9 63 F6
Birches Cl MTCM CR4 178 E6
PIN HA5 59 J2
The Birches CHARL SE7 126 A6
CMBW SE5 * 143 F4
HSLWW TW4 * 154 E2
ORP BR6 216 A2
WCHMH N21 35 F1
Birchfield St POP/IOD E14 105 J6
Birch Gdns DAGE RM10 92 E1
Birch Gv ACT W3 117 H1
LEE/GVPK SE12 165 J2
WAN E11 88 C1
WELL DA16 148 B5
Birch Hl CROY/NA CR0 213 F3
Birchington Cl BXLYHN DA7 149 J2
Birchington Rd BRYLDS KT5 191 G4
CEND/HSY/T N8 66 D3
KIL/WHAMP NW6 82 E6
Birchin La BANK EC3V 13 F4
Birchlands Av BAL SW12 160 E2
Birch Md ORP BR6 201 F6
Birchmead Av PIN HA5 59 G1
Birchmere Rw BKHTH/KID SE3 145 J3
Birchmore Wk HBRY N5 85 J1
Birch Pk KTN/HRWW/WS HA3 42 C3
Birch Rd FELT TW13 172 C1
ROMW/RG RM7 56 D6
Birch Rw HAYES BR2 201 F4
Birch Tree Av WWKM BR4 214 D3
Birch Tree Wy CROY/NA CR0 197 J6
Birch Wk MTCM CR4 179 G4
Birchway HYS/HAR UB3 113 K1
Birchwood Av BECK BR3 198 C1
MUSWH N10 48 A6
SCUP DA14 168 C5
WLGTN SM6 210 A1
Birchwood Cl MRDN SM4 194 A1
Birchwood Ct EDGW HA8 44 E5
Birchwood Dr HAMP NW3 83 F1
RDART DA2 170 B6
Birchwood Gv HPTN TW12 173 F2
Birchwood La ESH/CLAY KT10 204 D6
Birchwood Rd RDART DA2 170 B6
STMC/STPC BR5 201 J1
SWLY BR8 187 K3
TOOT SW17 179 G1
Birchwood Ter SWLY BR8 * 187 K4
Birdbrook Cl DAGE RM10 92 E5
Birdbrook Rd BKHTH/KID SE3 146 B4
Birdcage Wk WESTW SW1E 16 B3
Birdham Cl BMLY BR1 200 D2
Birdhurst Av SAND/SEL CR2 211 K2
Birdhurst Gdns SAND/SEL CR2 211 K2
Birdhurst Ri SAND/SEL CR2 212 A3
Birdhurst Rd SAND/SEL CR2 212 A3
WAND/EARL SW18 140 B6
WIM/MER SW19 178 D2
Bird in Bush Rd PECK SE15 143 H1
Bird-in-Hand La BMLY BR1 184 C5
Bird-in-Hand Ms FSTH SE23 163 K4
Bird-in-Hand Pas FSTH SE23 163 K4
Birds Farm Av CRW RM5 56 D4
Birdsfield La BOW E3 87 H6
Bird St MHST W1U 9 H4
Bird Wk WHTN TW2 154 E3
Birdwood Cl TEDD TW11 155 K6
Birkbeck Av ACT W3 98 E6
GFD/PVL UB6 78 C6
Birkbeck Gv ACT W3 118 A2
Birkbeck Hl DUL SE21 162 C4
Birkbeck Ms ACT W3 * 99 F6
HACK E8 86 B3
Birkbeck Pl DUL SE21 162 C3
Birkbeck Rd ACT W3 118 A1
BECK BR3 182 A5
CEND/HSY/T N8 66 E1
EA W5 116 D4
ENC/FH EN2 23 K2
GNTH/NBYPK IG2 72 D2
HACK E8 86 B3
MLHL NW7 45 H1
NFNCH/WDSPK N12 47 G1
ROMW/RG RM7 75 F5
SCUP DA14 168 B5
TOTM N17 50 B4
WIM/MER SW19 178 A2
Birkbeck St BETH E2 104 D2
Birkbeck Wy GFD/PVL UB6 78 D6
Birkdale Av PIN HA5 42 A6
Birkdale Cl BERM/RHTH SE16 123 J5
ORP BR6 201 J5
THMD SE28 109 J5
Birkdale Gdns CROY/NA CR0 213 F2
OXHEY WD19 27 H5
Birkdale Rd ABYW SE2 128 B4
EA W5 98 A3
Birkenhead Av KUTN/CMB KT2 175 G5
Birkenhead St CAMTN NW1 5 F4
Birkhall Rd CAT SE6 165 G3
Birkwood Cl BAL SW12 161 J2
Birley Rd TRDG/WHET N20 33 G4
Birley St BTSEA SW11 141 F3
Birling Rd ERITH DA8 150 A1
Birnam Rd FSBYPK N4 67 F6
Birse Crs WLSDN NW10 81 G2
Birstal Gn OXHEY WD19 27 H6

Birstall Rd SEVS/STOTM N15 ....68 A2
Biscay Rd HMSMTH W6..........119 C5
Bisenden Rd CROY/NA CR0 ....197 F6
Bishop Butt Cl ORP BR6..........217 F1
Bishop Fox Wy
  E/WMO/HCT KT8................188 E1
Bishop Ken Rd
  KTN/HRWW/WS HA3............43 F5
Bishop King's Rd WKENS W14.119 H4
Bishop Rd STHGT/OAK N14.....34 B3
Bishopon Av BMLY BR1............184 B6
  CHDH RM6..........................73 J5
  FUL/PGN SW6......................139 G3
  NTHWD HA6.........................26 C6
  PLSTW E13...........................89 F6
The Bishops Av EFNCH N2......65 H3
Bishop's Bridge Rd
  BAY/PAD W2.......................101 F5
Bishop's Cl ARCH N19.............84 C1
  BAR EN5..............................32 B1
  CHSWK W4..........................117 K5
  ELTH/MOT SE9.....................167 H4
  EN EN1...............................24 D3
  RCHPK/HAM TW10..............156 E5
  SUT SM1.............................208 E1
  WALTH E17..........................69 K1
Bishop's Ct STP EC4M.............12 A3
Bishops Dr EBED/NFELT TW14.153 C1
  NTHLT UB5............................77 J6
Bishopsford Rd MRDN SM4....194 B4
Bishopsgate LVPST EC2M........13 H2
Bishopsgate Ar LVPST EC2M..13 G2
Bishops Gn EFNCH N2.............65 J3
  HPTN TW12.........................154 E6
Bishop's Hall KUT/HW KT1......174 E5
Bishops Md CMBW SE5 *.......142 D1
Bishop's Park Rd
  FUL/PGN SW6......................139 G5
  STRHM/NOR SW16................179 K4
Bishop's Pl SUT SM1..............209 G3
Bishop's Rd CROY/NA CR0......196 C4
  FUL/PGN SW6......................139 J2
  HGT N6................................65 K2
  HNWL W7............................115 K2
  HYS/HAR UB3........................94 A6
Bishop's Ter LBTH SE11...........17 K6
Bishopsthorpe Rd SYD SE26..163 K6
Bishop St IS N1.......................6 J6
Bishops Wk CHST BR7............185 H4
  CROY/NA CR0......................215 F5
Bishop's Wy BETH E2.............104 E1
Bishopswood Rd HGT N6.........65 K4
Bishop Wy WLSDN NW10.........81 C5
Bisley Cl WPK KT4...................193 F5
Bispham Rd WLSDN NW10.......98 B2
Bisson Rd SRTFD E15..............106 A1
Bisterne Av WALTH E17............52 B6
Bittacy Cl MLHL NW7...............46 B2
Bittacy Hl MLHL NW7..............46 B2
Bittacy Park Av MLHL NW7......46 B2
Bittacy Rd MLHL NW7..............46 B2
Bittern Cl HYS/HAR UB4............95 H4
Bittern Pl WDGN N22 *............49 F5
Bittern St STHWK SE1..............18 C2
Bittoms Ct KUT/HW KT1 *......174 E6
The Bittoms KUT/HW KT1.......174 E6
Bixley Cl NWDGN UB2............114 E4
Blackall St SDTCH EC2A............7 G6
Blackberry Farm Cl HEST TW5.134 D1
Blackberry Fld
  STMC/STPC BR5....................186 B4
Blackbird Hl WBLY HA9............62 E6
Blackbird Yd BETH E2................7 K4
Blackborne Rd DAGE RM10......92 C4
Black Boy La SEVS/STOTM N15..67 J2
Blackbrook La HAYES BR2......201 F2
Blackburne's Ms
  MYFR/PKLN W1K....................9 G5
Blackburn Rd KIL/WHAMP NW6.83 F4
Blackbush Av CHDH RM6..........73 K2
Blackbush Cl BELMT SM2.......209 F5
Blackdown Ter
  WOOL/PLUM SE18 *.............146 E2
Blackenham Rd TOOT SW17...160 C6
Blackett St PUT/ROE SW15....139 G4
Black Fan Cl ENC/FH EN2..........23 J2
Blackfen Pde BFN/LL DA15 *..168 B1
Blackfen Rd BFN/LL DA15......148 A6
Blackford Cl SAND/SEL CR2...211 H6
Blackford Rd OXHEY WD19......41 H1
Blackfriars Br STHWK SE1.........12 A6
Black Friars La BLKFR EC4V......12 A4
Blackfriars Pas BLKFR EC4V.....12 A5
Blackfriars Rd STHWK SE1.......12 A7
Blackfriars U/P BLKFR EC4V.....12 B5
Blackheath Av GNWCH SE10...145 H1
Blackheath Gv BKHTH/KID SE3.145 J3
Blackheath Hl GNWCH SE10...145 F2
Blackheath Pk BKHTH/KID SE3.145 K3
Blackheath Ri LEW SE13..........145 F2
Blackheath Rd GNWCH SE10...144 D6
Blackheath V BKHTH/KID SE3.145 H5
Black Horse Ct STHWK SE1 *...19 F5
Blackhorse La CROY/NA CR0...197 H4
  WALTH E17............................51 F6
Black Horse Pde PIN HA5 *......59 F2
Blackhorse Rd SCUP DA14......168 B6
Blackhorse Rd DEPT SE8.........124 B5
  WALTH E17............................51 F6
Blacklands Dr YEAD UB4............94 A3
Blacklands Rd CAT SE6...........165 F6
Blacklands Ter CHEL SW3..........14 E7
Black Lion La BAY/PAD W2......100 D5
Black Lion La HMSMTH W6......118 D4
Blackmans Cl DART DA1..........171 F3
Blackmans Yd WCHPL E1 *........7 K6
Blackmore Av STHL UB1..........115 J1
Blackmore Dr WLSDN NW10.....80 D5
Blackmore Rd BKHH IG9...........39 J2
Blackmore's Gv TEDD TW11...174 B2

Blackness Cottages
  HAYES BR2 *.........................215 H6
Blackness La HAYES BR2.........215 H6
Blackpool Gdns YEAD UB4.........94 C3
Blackpool Rd PECK SE15.........143 J3
Black Prince Rd LBTH SE11.......17 H7
Black Rod Cl HYS/HAR UB3.....113 J3
Blackrurn Wy HSLWW TW4.....134 D6
Blackshaw Rd TOOT SW17......178 C1
Blacksmith Cl CHDH RM6..........73 J5
Blacksmith's La RAIN RM13......93 H6
  STMC/STPC BR5....................202 D2
Black's Rd HMSMTH W6..........119 F5
Blackstock Rd FSBYPK N4..........67 H6
Blackstone Est HACK E8............86 C5
Blackstone Rd CRICK NW2.........82 B2
Black Swan Yd STHWK SE1.......19 H2
Blackthorn Av WDR/YW UB7...112 D4
Blackthorn Ct HEST TW5.........134 D1
Blackthorne Av CROY/NA CR0.197 K5
Blackthorne Dr CHING E4..........38 B6
Blackthorn Gv BXLYHN DA7....149 F4
Blackthorn Rd IL IG1..................90 D3
Blackthorn St BOW E3.............105 J3
Blackthorn Ter BRXN/ST SW9 *.142 B4
Blackwall La GNWCH SE10......125 H5
Blackwall Tunnel Ap
  POP/IOD E14.......................106 A4
Blackwall Tunnel Northern Ap
  BOW E3................................87 J6
  POP/IOD E14.........................106 A3
Blackwall Wy POP/IOD E14.....106 A6
Blackwater Cl FSTGT E7............88 C2
  RAIN RM13...........................111 F4
Blackwater St EDUL SE22........143 G6
Blackwell Cl CLPT E5.................87 G3
  KTN/HRWW/WS HA3..............42 D3
Blackwell Dr OXHEY WD19.......27 G1
Blackwell Gdns EDGW HA8.......30 C6
Blackwood St WALW SE17......122 E5
Bladindon Dr BXLY DA5..........168 D2
Bladon Gdns RYLN/HDSTN HA2..60 B3
Blagden's La STHGT/OAK N14..34 D4
Blagdon Gv CAT SE6................164 E1
  NWMAL KT3.........................192 C1
Blagdon Wk TEDD TW11........174 D2
Blagrove Rd NKENS W10.........100 C4
Blair Av CDALE/KGS NW9..........63 G4
  ESH/CLAY KT10....................189 H6
Blair Cl BFN/LL DA15..............147 K6
  HYS/HAR UB3........................85 J4
  IS N1....................................85 J4
Blairderry Rd
  BRXS/STRHM SW2................161 K4
Blairhead Dr OXHEY WD19.......27 F5
Blair St POP/IOD E14..............106 A5
Blake Av BARK IG11...................90 E6
Blake Cl CAR SM5...................194 D5
  NKENS W10.........................100 A4
  RAIN RM13............................93 H6
  WELL DA16..........................147 K2
Blakeden Dr ESH/CLAY KT10..205 F5
Blake Gdns DART DA1.............151 J5
  FUL/PGN SW6......................139 K2
Blakehall Rd CAR SM5.............209 K4
Blake Hall Rd WAN E11.............70 E5
Blake Ms RCH/KEW TW9.........137 J2
Blakemore Gdns BARN SW13..118 E6
Blakemore Rd
  STRHM/NOR SW16................161 K5
  THHTH CR7..........................196 A2
Blakemore Wy BELV DA17......129 F3
Blakeney Av BECK BR3............182 C4
Blakeney Cl CAMTN NW1 *........4 C2
  HACK E8...............................86 C6
  TRDG/WHET N20..................33 G5
Blakeney Rd BECK BR3............182 C4
Blaker Ct CHARL SE7 *...........146 B1
Blake Rd CAN/RD E16.............106 D3
  CROY/NA CR0......................197 F6
  FBAR/BDGN N11....................48 C3
  MTCM CR4............................178 E6
Blaker Rd SRTFD E15.............106 A1
Blakes Av NWMAL KT3...........192 C2
Blakes Cl WLSDN NW10............80 E6
Blake's Gn WWKM BR4...........199 F5
Blakes La NWMAL KT3............192 C2
Blakesley Av EA W5...................97 J5
Blake's Rd PECK SE15.............143 F1
Blakes Ter NWMAL KT3............192 D2
Blakesware Gdns ED N9............35 K2
Blakewood Cl FELT TW13........154 B6
Blanchard Cl ELTH/MOT SE9...166 D5
Blanchard Gv PEND EN3...........25 J1
Blanchard Wy HACK E8 *...........86 C4
Blanch Cl PECK SE15...............143 K1
Blanchedowne CMBW SE5......142 E6
Blanche St CAN/RD E16...........106 D3
Blanchland Rd MRDN SM4......194 A2
Blandfield Rd BAL SW12..........161 F2
Blandford Av BECK BR3............182 B5
  WHTN TW2..........................155 G3
Blandford Cl CROY/NA CR0.....210 E1
  EFNCH N2.............................65 G3
  ROMW/RG RM7.....................74 D1
Blandford Crs CHING E4............38 A2
Blandford Rd BECK BR3...........182 A5
  CHSWK W4..........................118 B3
  EA W5..................................116 D2
  NWDGN UB2........................114 D4
  TEDD TW11..........................173 K1
Blandford Sq CAMTN NW1.........2 D7
Blandford St MHST W1U...........9 H2
Blandford Waye YEAD UB4........95 G5
Blaney Crs EHAM E6...............108 B2
Blanmerle Rd ELTH/MOT SE9..167 G3
Blann Cl ELTH/MOT SE9..........146 C6
Blantyre St WBPTN SW10........140 C1
Blantyre Wk WBPTN SW10 *...140 C1
Blashford St LEW SE13............165 G1
Blawith Rd HRW HA1.................60 E1
Blaydon Cl RSLP HA4................58 A5
  TOTM N17............................50 D3
Blaydon Wk TOTM N17.............50 D3
Bleak Hill La
  WOOL/PLUM SE18................128 A6

Blean Gv PGE/AN SE20...........181 K3
Bleasdale Av GFD/PVL UB6......97 G1
Blechynden Gdns NKENS W10.100 B6
Blechynden St NKENS W10......100 C6
Bledlow Cl THMD SE28...........109 J6
Bledlow Ri GFD/PVL UB6..........96 C1
Bleeding Heart Yd
  HCIRC EC1N *........................11 K2
Blegborough Rd
  STRHM/NOR SW16................179 H2
Blendon Dr BXLY DA5.............168 E1
Blendon Rd BXLY DA5.............168 E1
Blendon Ter
  WOOL/PLUM SE18................127 H6
Blenheim Av GNTH/NBYPK IG2..72 A3
Blenheim CDALE/KGS NW9 *.....45 H5
Blenheim Av GNTH/NBYPK IG2..72 A3
Blenheim Cl DART DA1............171 F1
  GFD/PVL UB6 *......................96 D1
  ROMW/RG RM7......................75 F2
  RYNPK SW20.......................177 F6
  WCHMH N21.........................35 J3
  WLGTN SM6.........................210 C5
Blenheim Crs NTGHL W11.......100 C5
  RSLP HA4..............................58 B6
  SAND/SEL CR2.....................211 J5
  WFD IG8................................38 E4
Blenheim Gdns
  BRXS/STRHM SW2................162 A1
  CRICK NW2............................82 A3
  KUTN/CMB KT2....................175 J4
  WBLY HA9.............................80 A1
  WLGTN SM6.........................210 C4
Blenheim Gv PECK SE15.........143 H3
Blenheim Park Rd
  SAND/SEL CR2.....................211 J6
Blenheim Pas STJWD NW8 *......2 A1
Blenheim Pl TEDD TW11.........174 A1
Blenheim Ri SEVS/STOTM N15 *.68 B1
Blenheim Rd BAR EN5 *...........20 A5
  BFN/LL DA15........................168 D3
  BMLY BR1............................200 D1
  CHSWK W4..........................118 B3
  DART DA1............................171 F1
  EHAM E6.............................107 H2
  HRW HA2..............................60 B5
  ORP BR6..............................202 D6
  PGE/AN SE20.......................181 K3
  RYLN/HDSTN HA2.................60 B3
  RYNPK SW20.......................177 F6
  STJWD NW8.............................2 A1
  SUT SM1..............................208 E1
  WALTH E17............................51 F6
  WAN E11................................88 C2
Blenheim St CONDST W1S........9 J4
Blenheim Ter STJWD NW8 *.......2 A1
Blenheim Wy ISLW TW7.........136 B2
Blenkarne Rd BTSEA SW11....160 E1
Bleriot Rd HEST TW5..............134 B1
Blessbury Rd EDGW HA8..........44 E4
Blessington Rd LEW SE13.......145 G5
Blessing Wy BARK IG11..........109 J1
Bletchingley Cl THHTH CR7....196 C1
Bletchley St IS N1.....................6 E3
Bletchmore Cl HYS/HAR UB3.113 G6
Bletsoe Wk IS N1.......................6 E2
Blincoe Cl WIM/MER SW19....159 G4
Blissett St GNWCH SE10........145 F2
Bliss Ms NKENS W10...............100 C2
Blisworth Cl YEAD UB4.............95 J3
Blithbury Rd DAGW RM9...........91 H4
Blithdale Rd ABYW SE2..........128 B4
Blithfield St KENS W8..............120 A3
Blockley Rd ALP/SUD HA0........61 H6
Bloemfontein Av SHB W12.....118 E1
Bloemfontein Rd SHB W12.......99 K6
Blomfield Rd MV/WKIL W9.......101 F4
Blomfield St LVPST EC2M.........13 F2
Blomfield Vls BAY/PAD W2.....101 F4
Blomville Rd BCTR RM8............92 A1
Blondell Cl WDR/YW UB7.......112 A6
Blondel St BTSEA SW11..........141 F3
Blondin Av EA W5....................116 D4
Blondin St BOW E3..................105 J1
Bloomfield Crs
  GNTH/NBYPK IG2..................72 B3
Bloomfield Pl MYFR/PKLN W1K..9 K5
Bloomfield Rd HAYES BR2......200 C2
  HGT N6.................................66 A3
  KUT/HW KT1.......................191 F1
  WOOL/PLUM SE18................127 G5
Bloomfield Ter BGVA SW1W...121 F5
Bloomhall Rd NRWD SE19......180 E1
Bloom Park Rd FUL/PGN SW6.139 J1
Bloomsbury Cl EA W5...............98 B6
Bloomsbury Pl
  NOXST/BSQ WC1A..................11 F2
Bloomsbury Sq
  NOXST/BSQ WC1A..................11 F2
Bloomsbury St GWRST WC1E..10 D1
Bloomsbury Wy
  NOXST/BSQ WC1A..................11 F2
Blore Cl VX/NE SW8................141 J2
Blossom Cl DAGW RM9...........110 A1
  EA W5..................................117 F2
  SAND/SEL CR2.....................212 B3
Blossom La ENC/FH EN2...........23 J1
Blossom St WCHPL E1...............7 H7
Blossom Wy WDR/YW UB7.....112 D4
Blossom Waye HEST TW5.......114 D6
Blount St POP/IOD E14............105 G5
Bloxam Gdns ELTH/MOT SE9.146 D6
Bloxhall Rd LEY E10...................69 H5
Bloxham Crs HPTN TW12........172 E4
Bloxworth Cl WLGTN SM6......210 C1
Blucher Rd CMBW SE5............142 D1
Blue Anchor La
  BERM/RHTH SE16.................123 H4
Blue Anchor Yd WCHPL E1......104 C6
Blue Ball Yd WHALL SW1A.......16 A1
Bluebell Av MNPK E12...............89 J3
Bluebell Cl HOM E9....................86 E6

NTHLT UB5............................77 K4
  ORP BR6..............................75 G6
  ROMW/RG RM7.....................75 C6
  SYD SE26............................165 G6
  WLGTN SM6.........................195 G5
Bluebell Wy IL IG1.....................90 B4
Blueberry Cl WFD IG8................52 E2
Bluebird La DAGE RM10............92 C5
Bluebird Wy THMD SE28.........127 J2
Bluefield Cl HPTN TW12.........173 F1
Bluegates EW KT17.................207 J5
Bluehouse Rd CHING E4............38 C5
Blue Lion Pl STHWK SE1...........19 G4
Blue Riband Est
  CROY/NA CR0 *....................196 C6
Blundell Cl HACK E8..................86 C2
Blundell Rd EDGW HA8.............45 G3
Blundell St HOLWY N7...............84 E5
Blunden Cl BCTR RM8...............73 J5
Blunts Rd SAND/SEL CR2 *.....211 K5
Blunts Av WDR/YW UB7.........132 D1
Blunts Rd ELTH/MOT SE9.......147 F6
Blurton Rd CLPT E5...................87 F2
Blyth Cl TWK TW1...................156 A1
Blyth Cl POP/IOD E14.............125 G4
  STMC/STPC BR5...................186 A4
Blythe Hill La CAT SE6............164 C2
Blythe Hill Pl FSTH SE23 *......164 B2
Blythe Ms WKENS W14 *.........119 G3
Blythe Rd WKENS W14............119 G3
Blythe St BETH E2....................104 D2
Blytheswood Pl
  STRHM/NOR SW16................162 A6
Blythe V CAT SE6....................164 B3
Blyth Rd BMLY BR1.................183 J4
  HYS/HAR UB3......................113 H2
  THMD SE28.........................109 K6
  WALTH E17............................69 H4
Blyth's Whf POP/IOD E14 *.....105 G6
Blythswood Rd GDMY/SEVK IG3.73 G5
Blythwood Rd FSBYPK N4........66 E4
  PIN HA5................................41 H4
Boadicea St IS N1.......................5 J1
Boakes Cl CDALE/KGS NW9.......62 E1
Boardman Av CHING E4.............25 K6
Boardman Cl BAR EN5...............20 C6
Boardwalk Pl POP/IOD E14.....125 F1
Boar's Head Yd BTFD TW8.......136 E1
Boathouse Wk PECK SE15......143 G1
  RCH/KEW TW9......................136 E2
Boat Lifter Wy
  BERM/RHTH SE16.................124 B4
Boat Quay CAN/RD E16..........107 G6
Bob Anker Cl PLSTW E13........106 E2
Bobbin Cl CLAP SW4...............141 H4
Bob Marley Wy HNHL SE24....142 B5
Bockhampton Rd
  KUTN/CMB KT2....................175 G3
Bocking St HACK E8...................86 D6
Boddicott Cl WIM/MER SW19..159 H4
Boddington Gdns ACT W3.......117 H2
Bodell Cl BETH E2.....................23 K3
Bodiam Rd STRHM/NOR SW16..179 J3
Bodian Wy WLSDN NW10.........98 B2
Bodicea Ms HSLWW TW4........154 A1
Bodley Cl NWMAL KT3............192 B2
Bodley Rd NWMAL KT3...........192 B3
Bodmin Cl RYLN/HDSTN HA2...77 K1
  STMC/STPC BR5...................202 D5
Bodmin Gv MRDN SM4...........194 A1
Bodmin St WAND/EARL SW18.159 K3
Bodnant Gdns RYNPK SW20...176 D6
Bodney Rd CLPT E5...................68 D6
Boeing Wy NWDGN UB2.........114 A3
Bofors House CHARL SE7 *.....146 D1
Bognor Gdns OXHEY WD19 *....41 C1
Bognor Rd WELL DA16...........148 E2
Bohemia Pl HACK E8..................86 E4
Bohn Rd WCHPL E1.................105 G4
Bohun Gv EBAR EN4.................33 J1
Boileau Rd BARN SW13...........138 D1
  EA W5..................................98 B5
Bolden St DEPT SE8................144 E3
Boldero Pl STJWD NW8 *...........2 C7
Bolderwood Wy WWKM BR4...198 E6
Boldmere Rd PIN HA5................59 G4
Boleyn Av EN EN1.....................24 D2
Boleyn Cl LOU IG10...................39 J1
  WALTH E17............................69 J1
Boleyn Ct BKHH IG9..................38 E3
Boleyn Dr E/WMO/HCT KT8....172 E6
  RSLP HA4..............................58 H6
Boleyn Gdns DAGE RM10.........92 D5
  WWKM BR4.........................198 E6
Boleyn Rd EHAM E6...................89 H1
  FSTGT E7.............................88 E5
  STNW/STAM N16...................86 A5
Boleyn Wy BAR EN5..................21 G4
  BARK/HLT IG6........................54 C2
Bolina Rd BERM/RHTH SE16..123 K5
Bolingbroke Gv BTSEA SW11..140 D6
Bolingbroke Rd WKENS W14...119 G3
Bolingbroke Wk BTSEA SW11 *.140 C1
Bolingbroke Wy
  HYS/HAR UB3......................113 G1
Bollo Bridge Rd ACT W3.........117 K2
Bollo La ACT W3......................117 J3
Bolney Ga SKENS SW7..............14 C3
Bolney St VX/NE SW8.............142 A1
Bolsover St GTPST W1W............3 K7
Bolstead Rd MTCM CR4..........179 G4
Bolster Gv WDGN N22 *...........48 D4
Bolt Ct FLST/FETLN EC4A.........11 K4
Bolton Cl CHSGTN KT9............205 K4
  SYD SE26............................181 H1
Bolton Crs CMBW SE5.............142 B1
Bolton Dr MRDN SM4..............194 B4
Bolton Gdns BMLY BR1...........183 J2
  ECT SW5..............................120 A5
  TEDD TW11..........................174 B2
  WLSDN NW10......................100 A1
Bolton Gardens Ms
  WBPTN SW10......................120 B5
Bolton Pl IS N1 *.......................85 H5
Bolton Rd CHSGTN KT9..........205 K4
  CHSWK W4..........................137 K1

HRW HA1................................60 C1
  SRTFD E15............................88 D4
  STJWD NW8...........................83 F6
  UED N18................................50 C4
  WLSDN NW10........................81 G6
Boltons La HYS/HAR UB3.......133 F1
Boltons Pl ECT SW5................120 B5
The Boltons ALP/SUD HA0........79 F2
  WBPTN SW10 *....................120 B5
  WFD IG8................................38 E6
Bolton St MYFR/PICC W1J........9 K7
Bombay St BERM/RHTH SE16.123 J4
Bomer Cl WDR/YW UB7..........132 D1
Bomore Rd NTGHL W11..........100 B6
Bonar Pl CHST BR7..................184 D3
Bonar Rd PECK SE15...............143 H1
Bonchester Cl CHST BR7.........185 F3
Bonchurch Rd NKENS W10.....100 C4
  WEA W13..............................116 C1
Bondfield Av YEAD UB4.............94 C2
Bond Gdns WLGTN SM6.........210 C2
Bond Rd MTCM CR4................178 E5
  SURB KT6............................191 G6
Bond St EA W5...........................97 K6
  SRTFD E15............................88 C3
Bondway VX/NE SW8...............121 K6
Boneta Rd WOOL/PLUM SE18.126 E3
Bonfield Rd LEW SE13............145 F5
Bonham Gdns BCTR RM8..........73 K6
Bonham Rd BCTR RM8.............73 K6
  BRXS/STRHM SW2................142 A6
Bonheur Rd CHSWK W4..........118 A2
Bonhill St SDTCH EC2A..............7 F7
Boniface Gdns
  KTN/HRWW/WS HA3..............42 B3
Boniface Wk
  KTN/HRWW/WS HA3..............42 B3
Bonita Ms BROCKY SE4..........144 A4
Bonner Hill Rd KUT/HW KT1...175 H6
Bonner Rd BETH E2..................104 E1
Bonnersfield Cl HRW HA1.........61 G3
Bonnersfield La HRW HA1.........61 F3
Bonner St BETH E2..................104 E1
Bonneville Gdns CLAP SW4....161 H1
Bonnington Sq VX/NE SW8.....122 A6
Bonny St CAMTN NW1...............84 C5
Bonser Rd TWK TW1................156 A4
Bonsor St CMBW SE5..............143 F1
Bonville Gdns HDN NW4............63 J1
Bonville Rd BMLY BR1.............183 J1
Booker Rd UED N18...................50 C1
Boones Rd LEW SE13..............145 H5
Boone St LEW SE13.................145 H5
Boord St GNWCH SE10...........125 H3
Boothby Rd ARCH N19..............66 D6
Booth Cl HOM E9.......................86 D6
  THMD SE28.........................128 C1
Booth La BLKFR EC4V...............12 C5
Booth Rd CDALE/KGS NW9.......45 G5
  CROY/NA CR0 *....................196 C6
Boot St FSBYE EC1V..................7 G5
Bordars Rd HNWL W7................96 E4
Bordars Wk HNWL W7...............96 E4
Borden Av EN EN1......................35 K1
Border Crs SYD SE26...............181 J1
Border Gdns CROY/NA CR0.....213 K2
Border Ga MTCM CR4.............178 D4
Border Rd SYD SE26...............181 J1
Bordesley Rd MRDN SM4.......194 A1
Bordon Wk PUT/ROE SW15....158 D2
Boreas Wk IS N1.........................6 B3
Boreham Av CAN/RD E16........106 E5
Boreham Cl WAN E11................70 A5
Boreham Rd WDGN N22...........49 J4
Borgard Road CHARL SE7 *.....146 C6
Borgard Rd
  WOOL/PLUM SE18................126 E4
Borkwood Pk ORP BR6............216 E2
Borkwood Wy ORP BR6...........216 D2
Borland Rd PECK SE15............143 K5
  TEDD TW11..........................174 C2
Borneo St PUT/ROE SW15......139 F4
Borough High St STHWK SE1...18 D3
Borough Hl CROY/NA CR0.......211 H1
Borough Rd ISLW TW7.............135 K2
  KUTN/CMB KT2....................175 H4
  MTCM CR4...........................178 D6
  STHWK SE1............................18 A4
Borough Sq STHWK SE1..........18 C3
Borrett Cl WALW SE17............122 D5
Borrodaile Rd
  WAND/EARL SW18...............160 A1
Borrowdale Av
  KTN/HRWW/WS HA3..............43 G5
Borrowdale Cl REDBR IG4..........71 J1
Borthwick Ms WAN E11.............71 F1
Borthwick Rd CDALE/KGS NW9..63 H3
  SRTFD E15............................88 C2
Borthwick St DEPT SE8...........124 D5
Borwick Av WALTH E17..............51 H6
Bosbury Rd CAT SE6................165 F5
Boscastle Rd KTTN NW5............84 B1
Boscobel Cl BMLY BR1............184 E5
Boscobel Pl BGVA SW1W..........15 H6
Boscobel St BAY/PAD W2............2 B7
Boscombe Av LEY E10................70 B4
Boscombe Cl CLPT E5...............87 G3
Boscombe Gdns STRHM/NOR SW16..179 K2
Boscombe Rd SHB W12...........118 D2
  TOOT SW17..........................179 F2
  WIM/MER SW19...................177 K4
  WPK KT4..............................193 F5
Bose Cl FNCH N3......................46 C4
Bosgrove CHING E4...................38 A3
Boss St STHWK SE1..................19 J2
Bostall Heath ABYW SE2.........128 D5
Bostall Hl ABYW SE2...............128 C5
Bostall La ABYW SE2...............128 C5
Bostall Manorway ABYW SE2..128 C4
Bostall Park Av BXLYHN DA7...149 G1
Bostall Rd STMC/STPC BR5.....169 G5
Boston Gdns BTFD TW8...........116 E4
  CHSWK W4..........................118 B6
Boston Gv RSLP HA4.................58 A3
Boston Manor Rd BTFD TW8...116 C5
Boston Pde HNWL W7 *...........116 B4

Boston Park Rd BTFD TW8 * 116 D6
Boston Pl CAMTN NW1 2 E7
Boston Rd CROY/NA CR0 196 A3
EDGW HA8 44 E3
EHAM E6 107 J2
HNWL W7 115 K1
Bostonthorpe Rd HNWL W7 * 115 K2
Boston V HNWL W7 116 B4
Boswell Cl STMC/STPC BR5 202 D3
Boswell Ct BMSBY WC1N 11 F1
Boswell Rd THHTH CR7 196 D1
Boswell St BMSBY WC1N 11 F1
Bosworth Cl WALTH E17 51 H4
Bosworth Rd BAR EN5 20 E4
DAGE RM10 92 C2
FBAR/BDGN N11 48 D2
NKENS W10 100 C3
Botany Bay La CHST BR7 185 H5
Botany Cl EBAR EN4 21 J5
Botany Ter PUR RM19 * 131 K5
Boteley Cl CHING E4 38 B4
Botham Cl EDGW HA8 44 E3
Botha Rd PLSTW E13 107 F4
Bothwell Cl CAN/RD E16 106 E4
Bothwell St HMSMTH W6 119 G6
Botolph Aly MON EC3R 13 G6
Botolph La MON EC3R 13 G6
Botsford Rd RYNPK SW20 177 H5
Bott Rd RDART DA2 171 J6
Bott's Ms BAY/PAD W2 100 E5
Botwell Common Rd
HYS/HAR UB3 94 C6
Botwell Crs HYS/HAR UB3 94 C5
Botwell La HYS/HAR UB3 94 C6
Boucher Cl TEDD TW11 174 A1
Boughton Av HAYES BR2 199 J4
Boughton Rd THMD SE28 127 K3
Boulcott St WCHPL E1 105 F5
The Boulevard FUL/PGN SW6 140 B3
WFD IG8 54 A3
Boulogne Rd CROY/NA CR0 196 E3
Boulter Gdns RAIN RM13 93 J4
Boulton Rd BCTR RM8 92 A1
Boultwood Rd EHAM E6 107 K5
Bounces La ED N9 36 D4
Bounces Rd ED N9 36 D4
Boundaries Rd BAL SW12 160 E4
FELT TW13 154 B3
Boundary Av WALTH E17 69 H4
Boundary Business Ct
MTCM CR4 178 C6
Boundary Cl BAR EN5 20 D2
GDMY/SEVK IG3 90 E2
KUT/HW KT1 175 H6
NWDGN UB2 115 F5
Boundary La CMBW SE5 122 D6
PLSTW E13 107 H3
Boundary Ms STJWD NW8 83 G6
Boundary Pass WCHPL E1 7 H6
Boundary Rd BARK IG11 108 C1
BFN/LL DA15 147 K6
CAR SM5 210 A6
ED N9 36 E1
EFNCH N2 47 H4
PIN HA5 59 H3
PLSTW E13 107 G1
ROM RM1 75 J3
STJWD NW8 83 G6
WALTH E17 69 H4
WBLY HA9 80 A1
WDGN N22 49 J5
WIM/MER SW19 178 C2
Boundary Rw STHWK SE1 18 A2
Boundary St BETH E2 7 J5
ERITH DA8 150 C1
Boundary Wy CROY/NA CR0 213 J3
Boundfield Rd CAT SE6 165 J4
Bounds Green Rd
FBAR/BDGN N11 48 E3
Bourchier St SOHO/SHAV W1D 10 C5
Bourdon Pl MYFR/PKLN W1K 9 K5
Bourdon Rd PGE/AN SE20 181 K5
Bourdon St MYFR/PKLN W1K 9 K5
Bourke Cl CLAP SW4 161 K1
WLSDN NW10 81 G4
Bourlet Cl FITZ W1T 10 A2
Bourn Av EBAR EN4 21 H6
SEVS/STOTM N15 67 K1
Bournbrook Rd
BKHTH/KID SE3 146 C4
Bourne Av HYS/HAR UB3 113 F3
RSLP HA4 77 G3
STHGT/OAK N14 34 E4
Bourne Cl ISLW TW7 135 K4
THDIT KT7 190 A6
Bourne Ct RSLP HA4 77 F3
Bourne Dr MTCM CR4 178 C5
Bourne End Rd NTHWD HA6 26 C6
Bourne Est HCIRC EC1N * 11 J1
Bourne Gdns CHING E4 37 K6
Bournehall BUSH WD23 28 A1
Bournehall La BUSH WD23 28 A1
Bournehall Rd BUSH WD23 28 A1
Bourne Hl PLMGR N13 34 E4
Bourne Hill Cl PLMGR N13 * 35 F4
Bourne Md BXLY DA5 149 K6
Bournemead Av NTHLT UB5 94 E1
Bournemead Cl NTHLT UB5 94 E2
Bournemouth Cl PECK SE15 143 H3
Bournemouth Rd PECK SE15 143 H3
WIM/MER SW19 177 K4
Bourne Pde BXLY DA5 * 169 J2
Bourne Rd BXLY DA5 169 K1
CEND/HSY/T N8 66 E3
HAYES BR2 200 C1
WAN E11 88 D1
Bourneside Crs STHGT/OAK N14 34 D3
Bourneside Gdns CAT SE6 183 F1
Bourne St BGVA SW1W 15 G7
CROY/NA CR0 196 C6
Bourne Ter BAY/PAD W2 101 F4
The Bourne STHGT/OAK N14 34 E3
Bourne V HAYES BR2 199 K5
Bournevale Rd
STRHM/NOR SW16 161 K6
Bourne Vw GFD/PVL UB6 79 F4
Bourne Wy HAYES BR2 199 K6
HOR/WEW KT19 206 E2
SUT SM1 208 D3
SWLY BR8 187 K6
Bournewood Rd
STMC/STPC BR5 202 C4
WOOL/PLUM SE18 148 B1
Bournville Rd CAT SE6 164 D2
Bournwell Cl EBAR EN4 21 K4
Bourton Cl HYS/HAR UB3 113 K1
Bousfield Rd NWCR SE14 144 A3
Boutflower Rd BTSEA SW11 140 D5
Boutique Hall LEW SE13 * 145 F5
Bouverie Gdns
KTN/HRWW/WS HA3 61 K3
Bouverie Ms STNW/STAM N16 68 A6
Bouverie Pl BAY/PAD W2 8 B3
Bouverie Rd HRW HA1 60 C3
STNW/STAM N16 68 A6
Bouverie St EMB EC4Y 11 K4
Bouvier Rd PEND EN3 24 E1
Boveney Rd FSTH SE23 164 A2
Bovill Rd FSTH SE23 164 A2
Bovingdon Av WBLY HA9 80 C4
Bovingdon La CDALE/KGS NW9 45 G4
Bovingdon Rd FUL/PGN SW6 140 A2
Bovington Dr ARCH N19 66 C6
Bow Arrow La DART DA1 171 K1
Bowater Cl BRXS/STRHM SW2 161 K1
CDALE/KGS NW9 63 F2
Bowater Gdns SUN TW16 172 B4
Bowater Pl BKHTH/KID SE3 146 A1
Bowater Rd WBLY HA9 80 D1
WOOL/PLUM SE18 126 C3
Bow Bridge Est BOW E3 105 K2
Bow Churchyard STP EC4M * 12 D4
Bow Common La BOW E3 105 H3
Bowden Cl EBED/NFELT TW14 153 H3
Bowden St LBTH SE11 122 B5
Bowditch DEPT SE8 124 C5
Bowdon Rd WALTH E17 69 J4
Bowen Dr DUL SE21 163 F5
Bowen Rd HRW HA1 60 C4
Bowen St POP/IOD E14 105 K5
Bowens Wd CROY/NA CR0 * 213 H6
Bowenswood CROY/NA CR0 213 H6
Bower Av GNWCH SE10 145 H2
Bower Cl CRW RM5 57 F3
NTHLT UB5 95 G1
Bowerdean St FUL/PGN SW6 140 A3
Bowerman Av NWCR SE14 124 B6
Bower St WCHPL E1 * 105 F5
Bowes Cl BFN/LL DA15 168 C1
Bowes Rd ACT W3 99 G6
BCTR RM8 91 J2
FBAR/BDGN N11 48 B1
WOT/HER KT12 188 A6
Bowes Rd (North Circular)
PLMGR N13 48 E1
Bowfell Rd HMSMTH W6 119 F6
Bowford Av BXLYHN DA7 149 F2
Bowhill Cl BRXN/ST SW9 142 B1
Bowie Cl CLAP SW4 161 J2
Bowland Rd CLAP SW4 141 J5
WFD IG8 53 G2
Bowland Yd KTBR SW1X * 15 F3
Bow La NFNCH/WDSPK N12 47 G3
STP EC4M 12 D4
Bowl Ct WCHPL E1 7 H7
Bowley Cl NRWD SE19 181 G2
Bowley La NRWD SE19 181 G1
Bowley St POP/IOD E14 105 H6
Bowling Green Cl
PUT/ROE SW15 158 E2
Bowling Green Ct WBLY HA9 62 B6
Bowling Green La CLKNW EC1R 5 K7
Bowling Green Pl STHWK SE1 * 18 E2
Bowling Green Rw
WOOL/PLUM SE18 * 126 E4
Bowling Green St LBTH SE11 122 B6
Bowling Green Wk IS N1 7 G5
Bowls Cl STAN HA7 43 H1
Bowman Av CAN/RD E16 106 E5
Bowman Ms
WAND/EARL SW18 159 J3
Bowmans Cl WEA W13 116 C1
Bowmans Lea FSTH SE23 163 K2
Bowman's Meadow
WLGTN SM6 210 B1
Bowman's Ms HOLWY N7 84 E1
WCHPL E1 104 C6
Bowman's Pl HOLWY N7 84 E1
Bowmans Rd DART DA1 170 C2
Bowmead ELTH/MOT SE9 166 E4
Bowmore Wk CAMTN NW1 84 D5
Bowness Cl HACK E8 * 86 B4
Bowness Crs PUT/ROE SW15 176 B1
Bowness Dr HSLWW TW4 134 D5
Bowness Rd BXLYHN DA7 149 J3
CAT SE6 164 E2
Bowness Wy HCH RM12 93 J3
Bowood Rd CLAP SW4 141 F5
PEND EN3 25 F3
Bowring Gn OXHEY WD19 41 G1
Bow Rd BOW E3 105 J2
Bowrons Av ALP/SUD HA0 79 K5
Bowsley Ct FELT TW13 153 K4
Bow St COVGDN WC2E 11 F4
SRTFD E15 88 C3
Bowyer Cl EHAM E6 107 K4
Bowyer Pl CMBW SE5 142 D1
Bowyers Ct TWK TW1 136 C5
Bowyer St CMBW SE5 142 D1
Boxall Rd DUL SE21 163 F1
Boxelder Cl EDGW HA8 44 E1
Boxgrove Rd ABYW SE2 128 D3
Box La BARK IG11 109 J1
Boxley Rd MRDN SM4 194 B1
Boxley St CAN/RD E16 126 A1
Boxmoor Rd CRW RM5 56 E1
KTN/HRWW/WS HA3 61 H1
Boxoll Rd DAGW RM9 92 B2
Boxted Cl BKHH IG9 39 J3
Boxtree La
KTN/HRWW/WS HA3 42 C4
Boxtree Rd
KTN/HRWW/WS HA3 42 D3
Boxwood Cl WDR/YW UB7 112 C2
Boxworth Cl
NFNCH/WDSPK N12 47 H1
Boxworth Gv IS N1 85 F6
Boyard Rd WOOL/PLUM SE18 127 G5
Boyce Wy PLSTW E13 106 E3
Boycroft Av CDALE/KGS NW9 62 E3
Boyd Av STHL UB1 114 E1
Boyd Cl KUTN/CMB KT2 175 H3
Boydell Ct STJWD NW8 83 H6
Boyd Rd WIM/MER SW19 178 C2
Boyd St WCHPL E1 104 C5
Boyfield St STHWK SE1 18 B3
Boyland Rd BMLY BR1 183 J1
Boyle Av STAN HA7 43 G2
Boyle Farm Rd THDIT KT7 190 B3
Boyne Av HDN NW4 64 B1
Boyne Rd DAGE RM10 92 C1
LEW SE13 145 G4
Boyne Terrace Ms NTGHL W11 119 J1
Boyson Rd WALW SE17 122 D6
Boyton Cl CEND/HSY/T N8 48 E6
WCHPL E1 105 F3
Boyton Rd CEND/HSY/T N8 48 E6
Brabant Rd WDGN N22 49 F5
Brabazon Av WLGTN SM6 210 E5
Brabazon Rd HEST TW5 134 B1
NTHLT UB5 96 A1
Brabazon St POP/IOD E14 105 K5
Brabourne Cl NRWD SE19 181 F1
Brabourne Crs BXLYHN DA7 129 G6
Brabourne Ri BECK BR3 199 G2
Brabourn Gv PECK SE15 143 K3
Bracewell Av GFD/PVL UB6 79 F3
Bracewell Rd NKENS W10 100 A4
Bracewood Gdns
CROY/NA CR0 212 B1
Bracey St FSBYPK N4 * 66 E6
Bracken Av BAL SW12 161 F1
CROY/NA CR0 213 J1
Brackenbridge Dr RSLP HA4 77 H1
Brackenbury Gdns
HMSMTH W6 118 E3
Brackenbury Rd EFNCH N2 47 G6
HMSMTH W6 118 E3
Bracken Cl EHAM E6 107 K4
WHTN TW2 155 F2
Brackendale WCHMH N21 35 F4
Brackendale Cl HSLW TW3 135 G2
Brackendene RDART DA2 170 B6
Bracken Dr CHIG IG7 54 B2
Bracken End ISLW TW7 135 J6
Bracken Gdns BARN SW13 138 D3
Brackenhill RSLP HA4 * 77 J2
Bracken Hill Cl BMLY BR1 183 J4
Bracken Hill La BMLY BR1 183 J4
Bracken Ms ROMW/RG RM7 74 D3
The Brackens EN EN1 36 A2
ORP BR6 217 G3
The Bracken CHING E4 38 A4
Brackley Av PECK SE15 143 K4
Brackley Cl WLGTN SM6 210 E5
Brackley Rd BECK BR3 182 C3
CHSWK W4 118 B5
Brackley Sq WFD IG8 53 H3
Brackley St BARB EC2Y 12 D1
Brackley Ter CHSWK W4 118 B5
Bracklyn St IS N1 6 E2
Bracknell Cl WDGN N22 49 G4
Bracknell Gdns HAMP NW3 83 F3
Bracknell Wy HAMP NW3 83 F2
Bracondale ESH/CLAY KT10 204 C3
Bracondale Rd ABYW SE2 128 B4
Bracton La RDART DA2 170 C5
Bradbourne Rd BXLY DA5 169 H2
Bradbourne St FUL/PGN SW6 139 K3
Bradbury Cl NWDGN UB2 114 E4
Bradbury St STNW/STAM N16 86 A3
Braddock Cl CRW RM5 56 E2
ISLW TW7 136 A4
Braddon Ct BAR EN5 * 20 C4
Braddon Rd RCH/KEW TW9 137 G4
Braddyll St GNWCH SE10 125 H5
Bradenham Av WELL DA16 148 B5
Bradenham Cl WALW SE17 122 E6
Bradenham Rd
KTN/HRWW/WS HA3 61 H1
YEAD UB4 94 C2
Braden St MV/WKIL W9 101 F3
Bradfield Dr BARK IG11 91 G3
Bradfield Rd CAN/RD E16 125 K2
RSLP HA4 77 J3
Bradford Cl HAYES BR2 200 E5
SYD SE26 163 J6
TOTM N17 50 B2
Bradford Dr HOR/WEW KT19 207 H4
Bradford Rd ACT W3 118 B2
IL IG1 72 D5
Bradgate Rd CAT SE6 164 E1
Brading Crs WAN E11 71 F6
Brading Rd BRXS/STRHM SW2 162 A2
CROY/NA CR0 196 A3
Brading Ter SHB W12 118 D3
Bradiston Rd MV/WKIL W9 100 D2
Bradley Cl HOLWY N7 84 E5
Bradley Gdns WEA W13 97 H5
Bradley Rd NRWD SE19 180 D2
PEND EN3 25 G1
WDGN N22 49 F5
Bradley's Cl IS N1 5 J2
Bradley Stone Rd EHAM E6 107 K5
Bradman Rw EDGW HA8 * 44 E3
Bradmead VX/NE SW8 * 141 G2
Bradmore Park Rd
HMSMTH W6 118 E3
Bradshaw Cl WIM/MER SW19 177 K2
Bradshaw Cottages
POP/IOD E14 * 105 G5
Bradshaw Dr MLHL NW7 46 B3
Bradshaws Cl SNWD SE25 181 H6
Bradstock Rd EW KT17 207 K3
HOM E9 87 F4
Brad St STHWK SE1 17 K1
Bradwell Av DAGE RM10 74 C6
Bradwell Cl HCH RM12 93 K4
SWFD E18 70 D1
Bradwell Ms UED N18 36 C6
Bradwell Rd BKHH IG9 39 J3
Brady Dr BMLY BR1 185 F6
Bradymead EHAM E6 108 A5
Brady St WCHPL E1 104 D3
Braemar Av ALP/SUD HA0 79 K5
BXLYHN DA7 149 K5
THHTH CR7 180 C6
WDGN N22 48 E4
WIM/MER SW19 159 K4
WLSDN NW10 81 F1
Braemar Gdns BFN/LL DA15 167 J5
CDALE/KGS NW9 45 F4
WWKM BR4 199 F5
Braemar Rd BTFD TW8 116 E6
PLSTW E13 106 D3
SEVS/STOTM N15 68 A2
WPK KT4 207 K1
Braeside BECK BR3 182 D1
Braeside Av RYNPK SW20 177 H4
Braeside Cl PIN HA5 42 A3
Braeside Crs BXLYHN DA7 149 K5
Braeside Rd
STRHM/NOR SW16 179 H3
Braes St IS N1 85 H5
Braesyde Cl BELV DA17 129 G4
Brafferton Rd CROY/NA CR0 211 J2
Braganza St WALW SE17 122 C5
Bragg Cl BCTR RM8 91 H4
Bragg Rd TEDD TW11 173 K3
Braham St WCHPL E1 13 K4
Braid Av ACT W3 99 G5
Braid Cl FELT TW13 154 E4
Braidwood Rd CAT SE6 165 G3
Braidwood St STHWK SE1 19 G1
Brailsford Cl WIM/MER SW19 178 D3
Brailsford Rd
BRXS/STRHM SW2 162 B1
Brainton Av
EBED/NFELT TW14 154 A2
Braintree Av REDBR IG4 71 J2
Braintree Rd DAGE RM10 92 C1
RSLP HA4 77 F2
Braintree St BETH E2 * 104 E2
Braithwaite Av ROMW/RG RM7 74 C4
Braithwaite Gdns STAN HA7 43 J4
Braithwaite Rd PEND EN3 25 H4
Bramalea Cl HGT N6 66 A3
Bramall Cl SRTFD E15 88 D3
Bramber Ct BTFD TW8 117 F4
Bramber Rd
NFNCH/WDSPK N12 47 J1
WKENS W14 119 J6
Bramble Acres Cl BELMT SM2 208 E5
Bramble Banks CAR SM5 210 A6
Bramblebury Rd
WOOL/PLUM SE18 127 J5
Bramble Cl BECK BR3 199 F2
CROY/NA CR0 213 J2
SEVS/STOTM N15 68 C1
STAN HA7 43 K3
Bramble Cft ERITH DA8 129 K4
Brambledown Cl WWKM BR4 199 H3
Brambledown Rd CAR SM5 210 A5
SAND/SEL CR2 212 A6
Bramble Gdns SHB W12 99 H6
Bramble La HPTN TW12 172 E2
Brambles Cl ISLW TW7 136 C1
The Brambles CHIG IG7 54 C2
SUT SM1 * 194 C6
WDR/YW UB7 112 A5
WIM/MER SW19 * 177 J1
Bramblewood Cl CAR SM5 194 D5
The Bramblings CHING E4 38 B6
Bramcote Av MTCM CR4 194 E1
Bramcote Gv
BERM/RHTH SE16 123 K5
Bramcote Rd PUT/ROE SW15 138 E5
Bramdean Crs LEE/GVPK SE12 165 K3
Bramdean Gdns
LEE/GVPK SE12 165 K3
Bramerton Rd BECK BR3 182 C6
Bramerton St CHEL SW3 120 D6
Bramfield Rd BTSEA SW11 160 D1
Bramford Rd
WAND/EARL SW18 140 B5
Bramham Ct NTHWD HA6 * 40 C1
Bramham Gdns CHSGTN KT9 * 205 K3
ECT SW5 120 A5
Bramhope La CHARL SE7 126 A6
Bramlands Cl BTSEA SW11 140 D4
Bramley Cl HYS/HAR UB3 94 E6
ORP BR6 201 G5
PIN HA5 40 D6
SAND/SEL CR2 211 J3
STHGT/OAK N14 22 B6
WALTH E17 51 G5
WFD IG8 53 G3
WHTN TW2 155 H1
Bramley Crs GNTH/NBYPK IG2 72 A3
VX/NE SW8 141 J1
Bramley Gdns OXHEY WD19 41 G2
Bramley Hl SAND/SEL CR2 211 J2
Bramley Hyrst
SAND/SEL CR2 * 211 J3
Bramley Ldg ALP/SUD HA0 79 K3
Bramley Pde STHGT/OAK N14 22 C5
Bramley Pl DART DA1 150 D5
Bramley Rd BELMT SM2 208 B6
EA W5 116 D3
NKENS W10 100 B6
STHGT/OAK N14 22 B6
SUT SM1 209 H3
Bramley Wy HSLWW TW4 134 E6
WWKM BR4 198 E6
Brampton Cl CLPT E5 68 D6
Brampton Gv HDN NW4 63 K1
KTN/HRWW/WS HA3 61 G1
WBLY HA9 62 C5
Brampton La HDN NW4 64 A1
Brampton Park Rd WDGN N22 49 G6
Brampton Rd BXLYHN DA7 148 E4
CDALE/KGS NW9 62 C1
CROY/NA CR0 197 G4
EHAM E6 107 H3
OXHEY WD19 26 E5
SEVS/STOTM N15 67 J2
Bramshaw Gdns OXHEY WD19 41 H1
Bramshaw Ri NWMAL KT3 192 B3
Bramshaw Rd HOM E9 87 F4
Bramshill Gdns KTTN NW5 84 B1
Bramshill Rd WLSDN NW10 99 G1
Bramshot Av CHARL SE7 126 A6
Bramshot Wy OXHEY WD19 26 E4
Bramston Cl BARK/HLT IG6 55 F2
Bramston Rd MTCM CR4 178 E3
WLSDN NW10 99 J1
Bramwell Cl SUN TW16 172 C5
Bramwell Ms IS N1 85 F6
Brancaster Dr MLHL NW7 45 J3
Brancaster Rd
GNTH/NBYPK IG2 72 E3
STRHM/NOR SW16 161 K5
Brancepeth Gdns BKHH IG9 38 E4
Branch Hl HAMP NW3 83 G1
Branch Rd BARK/HLT IG6 55 H1
POP/IOD E14 105 G5
Branch St CMBW SE5 143 F1
Brancker Rd
KTN/HRWW/WS HA3 43 K6
Brancroft Wy PEND EN3 25 G2
Brand Cl FSBYPK N4 67 H5
Brandesbury Sq WFD IG8 54 A3
Brandlehow Rd
PUT/ROE SW15 139 J5
Brandon Est WALW SE17 122 C6
Brandon Ms BARB EC2Y * 12 E1
Brandon Rd DART DA1 171 K2
HOLWY N7 84 E5
NWDGN UB2 114 E5
SUT SM1 209 F2
WALTH E17 70 A1
Brandon St WALW SE17 18 D7
Brandram Ms LEW SE13 * 145 H5
Brandram Rd LEW SE13 145 H4
Brandreth Ct HRW HA1 * 61 F3
Brandreth Rd EHAM E6 107 K5
TOOT SW17 161 G4
The Brandries WLGTN SM6 210 D1
Brand St GNWCH SE10 145 F1
Brandville Gdns BARK/HLT IG6 72 B1
Brandville Rd WDR/YW UB7 112 B2
Brandy Wy BELMT SM2 208 E5
Brangbourne Rd BMLY BR1 183 F1
Brangton Rd LBTH SE11 122 A5
Brangwyn Crs
WIM/MER SW19 178 C5
Branksea St FUL/PGN SW6 139 H1
Branksome Av UED N18 50 B2
Branksome Cl TEDD TW11 155 J6
WOT/HER KT12 188 C6
Branksome Rd
BRXS/STRHM SW2 141 K6
WIM/MER SW19 177 K4
Branksome Wy
KTN/HRWW/WS HA3 62 B3
NWMAL KT3 175 K5
Bransby Rd CHSGTN KT9 206 A5
Branscombe Gdns WCHMH N21 35 G2
Branscombe St LEW SE13 144 E4
Bransdale Cl KIL/WHAMP NW6 82 E6
Bransell Cl SWLY BR8 203 K3
Bransgrove Rd EDGW HA8 44 B4
Branston Crs STMC/STPC BR5 201 J5
Branstone Rd RCH/KEW TW9 137 G2
Brants Wk HNWL W7 96 E3
Brantwood Av ERITH DA8 149 K1
ISLW TW7 136 B5
Brantwood Cl WALTH E17 * 51 K6
Brantwood Gdns ENC/FH EN2 22 E6
REDBR IG4 71 J2
Brantwood Rd BXLYHN DA7 149 J3
HNHL SE24 142 D6
SAND/SEL CR2 211 J6
TOTM N17 50 C2
Brantwood Wy
STMC/STPC BR5 186 D6
Brasenose Dr BARN SW13 119 F6
Brasher Cl GFD/PVL UB6 78 D3
Brassey Cl EBED/NFELT TW14 * 153 K3
Brassey Rd KIL/WHAMP NW6 82 D4
Brassey Sq BTSEA SW11 141 F4
Brassie Av ACT W3 99 G5
Brasted Cl BXLYHS DA6 148 E6
SYD SE26 163 K6
Brasted Rd ERITH DA8 150 B1
Brathway Rd
WAND/EARL SW18 159 K2
Bratley St WCHPL E1 104 C3
Braund Av GFD/PVL UB6 96 B3
Braundton Av BFN/LL DA15 168 A3
Braunston Dr YEAD UB4 95 J3
Bravington Pl MV/WKIL W9 100 D3
Bravington Rd MV/WKIL W9 100 D3
Bravingtons Wk IS N1 5 F3
Braxfield Rd BROCKY SE4 144 B5
Braxted Pk
STRHM/NOR SW16 180 A2
Brayard's Rd PECK SE15 143 J3
Braybourne Dr ISLW TW7 136 A1
Braybrooke Gdns NRWD SE19 181 F3
Braybrook St SHB W12 99 H4
Brayburne Av VX/NE SW8 141 H3
Braycourt Av WOT/HER KT12 188 B4
Bray Crs BERM/RHTH SE16 124 A2
Braydon Rd STNW/STAM N16 68 C5
Bray Dr CAN/RD E16 106 D6
Brayfield Ter IS N1 85 G5
Brayford Sq WCHPL E1 * 104 E5
Bray Pl CHEL SW3 120 E5
Bray Rd MLHL NW7 46 B2
Brayton Gdns ENC/FH EN2 22 D5
Braywood Rd ELTH/MOT SE9 147 J5
Brazil Cl CROY/NA CR0 195 K4
Breach La DAGW RM9 110 C2
Bread St STP EC4M 12 D5
Breakspears Dr
STMC/STPC BR5 186 B4
Breakspears Ms BROCKY SE4 144 D3
Breakspears Rd BROCKY SE4 144 C4
Bream Cl TOTM N17 68 D1
Bream Gdns EHAM E6 108 A2
Breamore Cl PUT/ROE SW15 158 D3
Breamore Rd GDMY/SEVK IG3 73 F6
Bream's Buildings LINN WC2A 11 J3
Bream St BOW E3 87 J5

Breamwater Gdns
RCHPK/HAM TW10 156 C5
Brearley Cl EDGW HA8 44 E3
Breasley Cl PUT/ROE SW15 138 E5
Breasy Pl HDN NW4 * 63 K1
Brechin Pl SKENS SW7 120 B5
Brecknock Rd ARCH N19 84 C2
Brecknock Road Est
ARCH N19 * 84 D3
Brecon Cl MTCM CR4 195 K1
WPK KT4 193 F6
Brecon Gn CDALE/KGS NW9 * 63 G3
Brecon Ms HOLWY N7 84 D3
Brecon Rd HMSMTH W6 119 H6
PEND EN3 24 E5
Brede Cl EHAM E6 108 A2
Bredgar Rd ARCH N19 66 C6
Bredhurst Cl PGE/AN SE20 181 K2
Bredon Rd CROY/NA CR0 197 G4
Breer St FUL/PGN SW6 140 A4
Breezer's Hl WAP E1W * 104 C6
Bremans Rw
WAND/EARL SW18 160 B4
Brember Rd RYLN/HDSTN HA2 60 C6
Bremer Ms WALTH E17 69 K1
Bremner Rd SKENS SW7 * 120 B3
Brenchley Cl CHST BR7 185 F4
HAYES BR2 199 J2
Brenchley Gdns EDUL SE22 163 K1
Brenchley Rd STMC/STPC BR5 185 K5
Brenda Rd TOOT SW17 160 E4
Brende Gdns E/WMO/HCT KT8 189 G2
Brendon SCUP DA14 * 168 B6
Brendon Av WLSDN NW10 81 G2
Brendon Cl ERITH DA8 150 B2
ESH/CLAY KT10 204 C4
HYS/HAR UB3 133 F1
Brendon Dr ESH/CLAY KT10 204 C4
Brendon Gdns
RYLN/HDSTN HA2 78 B2
Brendon Gv EFNCH N2 47 G5
Brendon Rd BCTR RM8 74 B5
ELTH/MOT SE9 167 J4
Brendon St MBLAR W1H 8 D3
Brendon Vls WCHMH N21 * 35 J3
Brendon Wy EN EN1 36 A2
Brenley Cl MTCM CR4 179 F6
Brenley Gdns ELTH/MOT SE9 146 C5
Brent Cl BXLY DA5 169 F3
Brentcot Cl WEA W13 97 H3
Brent Crs WLSDN NW10 98 B1
Brent Cross F/O HDN NW4 64 A3
Brentfield WLSDN NW10 80 D5
Brentfield Cl WLSDN NW10 81 F4
Brentfield Gdns CRICK NW2 * 64 B4
Brentfield Rd DART DA1 171 K1
WLSDN NW10 81 F4
Brentford Cl YEAD UB4 95 H3
Brent Gn HDN NW4 64 B2
Brentham Wy EA W5 97 K3
Brenthouse Rd HACK E8 86 D5
Brenthurst Rd WLSDN NW10 81 H4
Brentlands Dr DART DA1 171 K3
Brent La DART DA1 171 J2
Brent Lea BTFD TW8 136 D1
Brentmead Cl HNWL W7 96 E6
Brentmead Gdns WLSDN NW10 98 B1
Brenton St POP/IOD E14 105 G5
Brent Park Rd CDALE/KGS NW9 63 J5
Brent Pl BAR EN5 20 E6
Brent River Park Wk
GFD/PVL UB6 97 H2
Brent Rd BTFD TW8 116 D6
CAN/RD E16 106 E5
NWDGN UB2 114 B3
SAND/SEL CR2 212 D6
WOOL/PLUM SE18 147 G1
Brentside BTFD TW8 116 D6
Brentside Cl WEA W13 97 F3
Brent St HDN NW4 64 B2
Brent Ter CRICK NW2 64 A6
The Brent DART DA1 171 K2
Brentvale Av ALP/SUD HA0 80 B6
STHL UB1 115 J1
Brent View Rd CDALE/KGS NW9 63 J3
Brent Wy BTFD TW8 136 E1
FNCH N3 46 E2
WBLY HA9 80 D4
Brentwick Gdns BTFD TW8 117 F4
Brentwood Cl ELTH/MOT SE9 167 H3
Brentwood Rd ROM RM1 75 H3
Brereton Rd TOTM N17 50 B3
Bressenden Pl WESTW SW1E 15 K4
Bressey Av EN EN1 24 C2
Bressey Gv SWFD E18 52 D5
Brett Cl NTHLT UB5 95 H2
STNW/STAM N16 68 A6
Brett Crs WLSDN NW10 81 F6
Brettell St WALW SE17 122 E5
Brettenham Av WALTH E17 51 J4
Brettenham Rd UED N18 36 C6
WALTH E17 51 J5
Brett Gdns DAGW RM9 92 A5
Brett Pas HACK E8 86 D3
Brett Rd BAR EN5 32 A1
HACK E8 86 D3
Brett Vls ACT W3 * 99 F4
Brewers Fld RDART DA2 171 F6
Brewer St REGST W1B 10 B5
Brewery Cl ALP/SUD HA0 79 G3
Brewery Rd HAYES BR2 200 D5
HOLWY N7 84 E5
WOOL/PLUM SE18 127 J5
Brewery Sq FSBYE EC1V 6 B7
STHWK SE1 19 J1
Brewhouse La WAP E1W 123 J1
Brewhouse Rd
WOOL/PLUM SE18 126 E4
Brewhouse St PUT/ROE SW15 139 H5
Brewhouse Wk
BERM/RHTH SE16 124 B1
Brewhouse Yd FSBYE EC1V 6 A6
Brewood Rd BCTR RM8 91 H4
Brewster Gdns NKENS W10 100 A4
Brewster Rd LEY E10 69 K5
Brian Cl HCH RM12 93 K2
Brian Rd CHDH RM6 73 J2
Briants Cl PIN HA5 41 J5
Briant St NWCR SE14 144 A2
Briar Av STRHM/NOR SW16 180 A3
Briar Bank CAR SM5 210 A6
Briarbank Rd WEA W13 97 G5
Briar Cl BKHH IG9 39 H4
EFNCH N2 47 G5
HPTN TW12 172 E1
ISLW TW7 136 A6
PLMGR N13 35 J5
Briar Crs NTHLT UB5 78 B4
Briardale Gdns HAMP NW3 82 E1
Briarfield Av EFNCH N2 47 F6
Briarfield Cl BXLYHN DA7 149 H3
Briar Gdns HAYES BR2 199 J5
Briar La CAR SM5 210 A6
CROY/NA CR0 213 K2
Briar Rd BXLY DA5 170 A5
CRICK NW2 82 A2
KTN/HRWW/WS HA3 61 J2
STRHM/NOR SW16 179 K6
WHTN TW2 155 K3
Briarswood Wy ORP BR6 217 F3
Briar Wk EDGW HA8 44 E3
NKENS W10 * 100 C3
PUT/ROE SW15 138 E5
Briar Wy WDR/YW UB7 112 D2
Briarwood Cl
CDALE/KGS NW9 * 62 E3
FELT TW13 153 H5
Briarwood Ct WPK KT4 * 192 D5
Briarwood Dr NTHWD HA6 40 E5
Briarwood Rd CLAP SW4 141 J6
EW KT17 207 J4
Briary Cl EDGW HA8 44 D5
HAMP NW3 * 83 J5
Briary Ct SCUP DA14 186 C1
Briary Gdns BMLY BR1 184 A1
Briary La ED N9 36 A5
Brickbarn Cl WBPTN SW10 * 140 B1
Brick Ct EMB EC4Y * 11 J4
Brickett Cl RSLP HA4 58 A2
Brick Farm Cl RCH/KEW TW9 137 J2
Brickfield Cl BTFD TW8 136 D1
Brickfield Cottages
WOOL/PLUM SE18 128 A6
Brickfield Farm Gdns
ORP BR6 216 C2
Brickfield La BAR EN5 31 H1
HYS/HAR UB3 113 G6
Brickfield Rd BOW E3 105 K3
THHTH CR7 180 C4
WIM/MER SW19 160 A6
Brickfields RYLN/HDSTN HA2 60 D6
Brickfields Wy WDR/YW UB7 112 C3
Brickfield Vls CAR SM5 * 209 J1
Brick Kiln Cl OXHEY WD19 27 J1
Brick La BETH E2 7 K5
EN EN1 24 D3
NTHLT UB5 95 K2
STAN HA7 43 K3
Brick St MYFR/PKLN W1K 15 J1
Brickwall La RSLP HA4 58 C5
Brickwood Cl SYD SE26 163 J5
Brickwood Rd CROY/NA CR0 197 F6
Brideale Cl PECK SE15 123 G6
Bride Ct EMB EC4Y 12 A4
Bride La EMB EC4Y 12 A4
Bridel Ms FSBYE EC1V 6 A3
Bridewain St STHWK SE1 19 J4
Bridewell Pl BLKFR EC4V 12 A4
WAP E1W 123 J1
Bridford Ms GTPST W1W 9 K1
Bridge Av HMSMTH W6 119 F5
HNWL W7 96 D4
Bridge Cl EN EN1 24 D3
NKENS W10 100 B5
ROMW/RG RM7 75 G3
Bridge Dr PLMGR N13 35 F6
Bridge End WALTH E17 52 A4
Bridge End Cl KUTN/CMB KT2 175 H4
Bridgefield Rd SUT SM1 208 E4
Bridge Gdns E/WMO/HCT KT8 189 J1
Bridge Ga WCHMH N21 35 J2
Bridge House Quay
POP/IOD E14 125 F1
Bridgeland Rd CAN/RD E16 106 E6
Bridgelands Cl BECK BR3 182 C3
Bridge La BTSEA SW11 140 D2
GLDGN NW11 64 C2
Bridgeman Rd IS N1 85 F5
TEDD TW11 174 B2
Bridgeman St STJWD NW8 2 C3
Bridge Mdw NWCR SE14 124 A6
Bridgenhall Rd EN EN1 24 B2
Bridgen Rd BXLY DA5 169 F2
Bridge Pde
STRHM/NOR SW16 * 179 K1
WCHMH N21 * 35 J2
Bridge Pk WAND/EARL SW18 139 K6
Bridge Pl CROY/NA CR0 196 E5
PIM SW1V 15 K6
Bridgepoint Pl HGT N6 66 B5
Bridgeport Pl WAP E1W * 123 H1
Bridge Rd BECK BR3 182 C3
BXLYHN DA7 149 F4
CHSGTN KT9 206 A3
E/WMO/HCT KT8 189 K1
ED N9 36 C5
EHAM E6 89 K5
ERITH DA8 150 D2
HSLW TW3 135 J4
NWDGN UB2 114 E2
RAIN RM13 111 J3
SRTFD E15 88 B6
STMC/STPC BR5 202 C3
SUT SM1 209 F4
TWK TW1 156 C1
WALTH E17 69 H4
WBLY HA9 80 C1
WDGN N22 48 E4
WLGTN SM6 210 B3
WLSDN NW10 81 G4
Bridge Rw CROY/NA CR0 * 196 E5
Bridges Ct BTSEA SW11 140 C4
Bridges La CROY/NA CR0 210 E2
Bridges Rd STAN HA7 43 F1
Bridges Road Ms
WIM/MER SW19 178 A2
Bridge St CHSWK W4 118 A4
PIN HA5 41 H6
TWK TW1 156 E1
WHALL SW1A 16 E3
Bridge Ter LEW SE13 * 145 G5
SRTFD E15 88 B5
The Bridge EA W5 * 117 G1
KTN/HRWW/WS HA3 61 F1
Bridgetown Cl NRWD SE19 181 F1
Bridgeview HMSMTH W6 119 F5
Bridge Vls WIM/MER SW19 * 177 K1
Bridgewater Cl
STMC/STPC BR5 185 K5
Bridgewater Gdns EDGW HA8 44 B5
Bridgewater Rd ALP/SUD HA0 79 J5
SRTFD E15 88 A6
Bridgewater Sq BARB EC2Y * 12 C1
Bridgewater St BARB EC2Y 12 C1
Bridgewater Wy BUSH WD23 28 B1
Bridgeway ALP/SUD HA0 80 A5
BARK IG11 91 F5
Bridge Wy GLDGN NW11 64 D2
WHTN TW2 155 H2
Bridgeway St CAMTN NW1 4 B3
Bridge Wharf Rd ISLW TW7 136 C4
Bridgewood Cl PGE/AN SE20 181 J3
Bridgewood Rd
STRHM/NOR SW16 179 J3
WPK KT4 207 J2
Bridgford St
WAND/EARL SW18 160 B5
Bridgman Rd CHSWK W4 117 K3
Bridgwater Rd RSLP HA4 76 E2
Bridle Cl HOR/WEW KT19 206 E2
KUT/HW KT1 190 E1
Bridle La SOHO/CST W1F 10 B5
TWK TW1 156 C1
Bridle Pth CROY/NA CR0 210 E1
The Bridle Pth WFD IG8 52 C3
Bridlepath Wy
EBED/NFELT TW14 153 H2
Bridle Rd CROY/NA CR0 213 J2
ESH/CLAY KT10 205 H4
PIN HA5 59 G3
Bridle Wy CROY/NA CR0 213 J3
ORP BR6 216 C2
The Bridle Wy WLGTN SM6 210 C3
Bridlington Rd ED N9 36 D2
OXHEY WD19 27 H5
Bridport Av ROMW/RG RM7 74 D3
Bridport Pl IS N1 7 F2
Bridport Rd GFD/PVL UB6 78 B6
THHTH CR7 180 B6
UED N18 50 A1
Bridstow Pl BAY/PAD W2 100 E5
Brief St BRXN/ST SW9 142 C2
Brierley CROY/NA CR0 213 K4
Brierley Av ED N9 36 E3
Brierley Cl SNWD SE25 197 H1
Brierley Rd BAL SW12 161 H4
WAN E11 88 B2
Brierly Gdns BETH E2 * 104 E1
Brigade Cl RYLN/HDSTN HA2 60 D6
Brigade St BKHTH/KID SE3 * 145 J3
Brigadier Av ENC/FH EN2 23 J2
Brigadier Hl ENC/FH EN2 23 J1
Briggeford Cl CLPT E5 68 C6
Briggs Cl MTCM CR4 179 G4
Bright Cl BELV DA17 128 E4
Brightfield Rd LEE/GVPK SE12 145 H6
Brightling Rd BROCKY SE4 164 C1
Brightlingsea Pl POP/IOD E14 105 H6
Brightman Rd
WAND/EARL SW18 160 C3
Brighton Av WALTH E17 69 H2
Brighton Dr NTHLT UB5 * 78 A4
Brighton Rd BELMT SM2 209 G5
EFNCH N2 47 G5
EHAM E6 108 A2
SAND/SEL CR2 211 J6
STNW/STAM N16 86 A2
SURB KT6 190 D3
Brighton Ter BRXN/ST SW9 142 A5
Brights Av RAIN RM13 111 K3
Brightside Rd LEW SE13 165 G1
The Brightside PEND EN3 25 F2
Bright St POP/IOD E14 105 K5
Brightwell Cl CROY/NA CR0 196 B5
Brightwell Crs TOOT SW17 178 E1
Brig Ms DEPT SE8 124 D6
Brigstock Rd BELV DA17 129 J4
THHTH CR7 196 C2
Brill Pl CAMTN NW1 4 D3
Brim Hl EFNCH N2 65 G1
Brimpsfield Cl ABYW SE2 128 C3
Brimsdown Av PEND EN3 25 G2
Brimstone Cl ORP BR6 217 J5
Brindle Ga BFN/LL DA15 167 K4
Brindley Cl ALP/SUD HA0 79 J6
BXLYHN DA7 149 H4
Brindley St BROCKY SE4 144 C2
Brindley Wy BMLY BR1 183 K1
STHL UB1 96 B6
Brindwood Rd CHING E4 37 J5
Brinkburn Cl ABYW SE2 128 B4
EDGW HA8 44 D6
Brinkburn Gdns EDGW HA8 44 C6
Brinkley Rd WPK KT4 192 E6
Brinklow Crs
WOOL/PLUM SE18 147 G1
Brinkworth Rd CLAY IG5 53 J6
Brinkworth Wy HOM E9 87 H4
Brinsdale Rd HDN NW4 46 B6
Brinsley Rd
KTN/HRWW/WS HA3 42 D5
Brinsley St WCHPL E1 * 104 D5
Brinsworth Cl WHTN TW2 155 J4
Brinton Wk STHWK SE1 18 A1
Brion Pl POP/IOD E14 106 A4
Brisbane Av WIM/MER SW19 178 A4
Brisbane Rd IL IG1 72 C4
LEY E10 69 K6
Brisbane St CMBW SE5 142 E1
Briscoe Cl WAN E11 70 D6
Briscoe Rd WIM/MER SW19 178 C2
Briset Rd ELTH/MOT SE9 146 C4
Briset St FARR EC1M 12 A1
Briset Wy HOLWY N7 67 F6
Bristol Cl STWL/WRAY TW19 152 B1
WLGTN SM6 210 E6
Bristol Gdns MV/WKIL W9 101 F3
Bristol Ms MV/WKIL W9 101 F3
Bristol Park Rd WALTH E17 * 69 G1
Bristol Rd FSTGT E7 89 G4
GFD/PVL UB6 78 B6
MRDN SM4 194 B2
Briston Gv CEND/HSY/T N8 66 E3
Bristowe Cl BRXS/STRHM SW2 162 B1
Bristow Rd BXLYHN DA7 149 F2
CROY/NA CR0 210 E2
HSLW TW3 135 G4
NRWD SE19 181 F1
Britannia Cl CLAP SW4 141 J5
ERITH DA8 130 C6
NTHLT UB5 95 H2
Britannia Ga CAN/RD E16 125 K1
Britannia La WHTN TW2 155 H2
Britannia Rd BRYLDS KT5 191 G4
FUL/PGN SW6 140 A1
IL IG1 90 B1
NFNCH/WDSPK N12 33 G6
POP/IOD E14 124 D4
Britannia Rw IS N1 85 J6
Britannia St FSBYW WC1X 5 G4
Britannia Wk IS N1 6 E4
Britannia Wy FUL/PGN SW6 140 A1
STWL/WRAY TW19 152 A2
WLSDN NW10 98 D3
British Est BOW E3 105 H2
British Gv HMSMTH W6 118 C5
British Grove Pas CHSWK W4 * 118 C5
British Legion Rd CHING E4 38 D4
British St BOW E3 105 H2
Brittain Rd BCTR RM8 92 A1
Britten Cl BORE WD6 29 K1
GLDGN NW11 65 F5
Brittenden Pde ORP BR6 * 217 F4
Britten Dr STHL UB1 96 A5
Britten St CHEL SW3 120 D5
Brittidge Rd WLSDN NW10 * 81 G5
Britton Cl CAT SE6 165 G2
Britton St FARR EC1M 6 A7
Brixham Crs RSLP HA4 58 E5
Brixham Gdns GDMY/SEVK IG3 90 E3
Brixham Rd WELL DA16 148 E2
Brixham St CAN/RD E16 127 F1
Brixton Hl BRXS/STRHM SW2 162 A1
Brixton Hill Pl
BRXS/STRHM SW2 161 K2
Brixton Ov BRXS/STRHM SW2 142 B5
Brixton Rd BRXN/ST SW9 142 B5
Brixton Station Rd
BRXN/ST SW9 142 B4
Brixton Water La
BRXS/STRHM SW2 142 A6
Broadbent Cl HGT N6 66 B5
Broadbent St
MYFR/PKLN W1K * 9 J5
Broadberry Ct UED N18 50 D1
Broad Bridge Cl
BKHTH/KID SE3 145 K1
Broad Common Est
STNW/STAM N16 * 68 C5
Broadcoombe SAND/SEL CR2 213 F5
Broad Ct COVGDN WC2E * 11 F4
Broadcroft Av STAN HA7 43 K5
Broadcroft Rd
STMC/STPC BR5 201 J4
Broadeaves Cl SAND/SEL CR2 212 A3
Broadfield Cl CRICK NW2 82 A1
ROM RM1 75 H2
Broadfield Ct BUSH WD23 28 E4
Broadfield La CAMTN NW1 84 E5
Broadfield Pde EDGW HA8 * 30 D5
Broadfield Rd CAT SE6 165 H3
Broadfields E/WMO/HCT KT8 189 J3
RYLN/HDSTN HA2 42 B5
Broadfields Av EDGW HA8 30 D6
WCHMH N21 35 G2
Broadfields Hts EDGW HA8 30 D6
Broadfields La OXHEY WD19 27 F3
Broadfield Sq EN EN1 24 D4
Broadfields Wy WLSDN NW10 81 H3
Broadfield Wy BKHH IG9 39 G5
Broadgates Av EBAR EN4 21 F2
Broadgates Rd
WAND/EARL SW18 160 C3
Broad Green Av CROY/NA CR0 196 C4
Broadhead Strd
CDALE/KGS NW9 45 H5
Broadheath Dr CHST BR7 184 E1
Broadhinton Rd CLAP SW4 141 G4
Broadhurst Av EDGW HA8 30 D6
GDMY/SEVK IG3 91 F2
Broadhurst Cl KIL/WHAMP NW6 83 G4
Broadhurst Gdns
KIL/WHAMP NW6 83 G4
RSLP HA4 59 G6
Broadhusrt Cl
RCHPK/HAM TW10 137 G6
Broadlands FELT TW13 154 E5
Broadlands Av PEND EN3 24 D4
STRHM/NOR SW16 161 K4
Broadlands Cl HGT N6 66 A4
PEND EN3 24 D4
STRHM/NOR SW16 161 K4
Broadlands Rd BMLY BR1 166 A6
HGT N6 65 K4
Broadlands Wy NWMAL KT3 192 C3
Broad La CEND/HSY/T N8 67 F2
HPTN TW12 172 E3
RDART DA2 170 E6
SEVS/STOTM N15 68 C1
Broad Lawn ELTH/MOT SE9 167 F4
Broadlawns Ct
KTN/HRWW/WS HA3 43 F4
Broadley St STJWD NW8 8 C1
Broadley Ter CAMTN NW1 2 D7
Broadmead CAT SE6 164 D5
Broadmead Av WPK KT4 192 D4
Broadmead Cl HPTN TW12 173 F2
PIN HA5 * 41 J3
Broadmead Rd WFD IG8 52 E2
YEAD UB4 95 J3
Broad Oak WFD IG8 53 F1
Broad Oak Cl CHING E4 51 K1
STMC/STPC BR5 186 B5
Broadoak Rd ERITH DA8 150 A1
Broad Oaks SURB KT6 191 J5
Broad Oaks Wy HAYES BR2 199 J2
Broadstone Pl MHST W1U 9 G2
Broadstone Rd HCH RM12 75 J6
Broad St DAGE RM10 92 C5
TEDD TW11 174 A2
Broad Street Av LVPST EC2M 13 G2
Broad Street Pl LVPST EC2M 13 F2
Broadview CDALE/KGS NW9 62 C3
Broadview Rd
STRHM/NOR SW16 179 J3
Broad Wk BKHTH/KID SE3 146 B3
HEST TW5 134 C2
ORP BR6 217 K1
RCH/KEW TW9 137 G1
WCHMH N21 35 G3
Broadwalk RYLN/HDSTN HA2 * 60 B2
SWFD E18 52 E6
Broadwalk La GLDGN NW11 64 D4
The Broad Wk KENS W8 120 B2
The Broadwalk NTHWD HA6 40 A5
Broadwall STHWK SE1 11 K7
Broadwater Gdns ORP BR6 216 B2
Broadwater Rd THMD SE28 127 J3
TOOT SW17 160 D6
TOTM N17 50 A5
Broadway BARK IG11 90 C6
BXLYHS DA6 149 F5
GPK RM2 57 J6
HNWL W7 115 K1
RAIN RM13 111 J3
SRTFD E15 88 B5
STJSPK SW1H 16 C4
SURB KT6 191 J5
SWLY BR8 203 K3
WEA W13 116 B1
Broadway Av CROY/NA CR0 196 E2
TWK TW1 156 C1
Broadway Cl WFD IG8 53 F2
Broadway Ct WIM/MER SW19 177 K2
Broadway Gdns MTCM CR4 194 D1
Broadway Market HACK E8 86 D6
Broadway Market Ms
HACK E8 * 86 C6
Broadway Ms PLMGR N13 49 F1
STNW/STAM N16 68 B4
WCHMH N21 35 H3
Broadway Pde CHING E4 * 52 A2
HYS/HAR UB3 * 113 J2
RYLN/HDSTN HA2 * 60 B2
WDR/YW UB7 * 112 B2
The Broadway ACT W3 * 117 H2
BCTR RM8 74 B6
CDALE/KGS NW9 63 H3
CEND/HSY/T N8 66 E3
CHEAM SM3 208 C4
EA W5 97 K6
ED N9 36 C5
FBAR/BDGN N11 * 47 K1
HCH RM12 93 K2
KTN/HRWW/WS HA3 42 E5
MLHL NW7 45 G1
PIN HA5 41 K3
PLSTW E13 106 E1
RYLN/HDSTN HA2 * 60 D6
STAN HA7 43 J1
SUT SM1 209 G2
THDIT KT7 189 K5
WFD IG8 53 F2
WIM/MER SW19 177 J2
Broadwell Pde
KIL/WHAMP NW6 * 83 G4
Broadwick St SOHO/CST W1F 10 B5
Broadwood Av RSLP HA4 58 D3
Broadwood Ter WKENS W14 * 119 J4
Broad Yd FARR EC1M 6 A7
Brocas Cl HAMP NW3 83 J5
Brockdene Dr HAYES BR2 215 H2
Brockdish Av BARK IG11 91 F3
Brockenhurst
E/WMO/HCT KT8 188 E2
Brockenhurst Av WPK KT4 192 B5
Brockenhurst Gdns IL IG1 90 C3
MLHL NW7 45 G2
Brockenhurst Ms UED N18 36 C6
Brockenhurst Rd
CROY/NA CR0 197 J4
Brockenhurst Wy
STRHM/NOR SW16 179 J5
Brocket Wy CHIG IG7 54 E1
Brockham Cl WIM/MER SW19 177 J1
Brockham Crs CROY/NA CR0 214 B5
Brockham Dr
BRXS/STRHM SW2 162 A2
GNTH/NBYPK IG2 72 C3
Brockham St STHWK SE1 18 D4
Brockhurst Cl STAN HA7 43 F2
Brockill Crs BROCKY SE4 144 B5
Brocklebank Rd CHARL SE7 126 A4
WAND/EARL SW18 160 B2
Brocklehurst St NWCR SE14 144 A1
Brocklesby Rd SNWD SE25 197 J1
Brockley Av STAN HA7 30 A5
Brockley Cl STAN HA7 44 A1
Brockley Crs CRW RM5 56 E3
Brockley Cross BROCKY SE4 144 C4
Brockley Gv BROCKY SE4 144 C6
Brockley Hall Rd BROCKY SE4 164 B1
Brockley Hl STAN HA7 29 J4
Brockley Ms BROCKY SE4 144 B6
Brockley Pk FSTH SE23 164 B2
Brockley Ri FSTH SE23 164 B2
Brockley Rd BROCKY SE4 144 C6
FSTH SE23 164 B1
Brockleyside STAN HA7 29 K6
Brockley Vw FSTH SE23 164 B2
Brockley Wy FSTH SE23 144 A6
Brockman Ri BMLY BR1 165 G6
Brock Pl BOW E3 105 K3
Brock Rd PLSTW E13 107 F4
Brocks Dr CHEAM SM3 208 C1

Brockshot CI BTFD TW8 ....116 E6
Brock St PECK SE15 ....143 K4
Brockton CI ROM RM1.............75 H1
Brockway CI WAN E11.............70 C6
Brockwell Av BECK BR3.............198 E2
Brockwell CI STMC/STPC BR5....202 A2
Brockwell Park Gdns
  HNHL SE24.............162 C2
Brockwell Park Rw
  BRXS/STRHM SW2.............162 B2
Brodia Rd STNW/STAM N16.............86 A1
Brodie Rd CHING E4.............38 A3
  ENC/FH EN2.............23 J1
Brodie St STHWK SE1.............123 C5
Brodlove La WAP E1W.............105 F6
Brodrick Gv ABYW SE2.............128 C4
Brodrick Rd TOOT SW17.............160 E3
Brograve Gdns BECK BR3.............182 E5
Broke Farm Dr ORP BR6.............217 J6
Broken Whf BLKFR EC4V.............12 C5
Brokesley St BOW E3.............105 H3
Broke Wk HACK E8 *.............86 C6
Bromar Rd CMBW SE5.............143 F4
Bromborough Gn
  OXHEY WD19.............41 G1
Bromefield STAN HA7.............43 K3
Bromehead St WCHPL E1.............104 E5
Brome House CHARL SE7 *.............146 D1
Bromell's Rd CLAP SW4.............141 H4
Brome Rd ELTH/MOT SE9.............146 E4
Bromfelde Rd CLAP SW4.............141 J4
Bromfield St IS N1.............5 K2
Bromhall Rd BCTR RM8.............91 H4
Bromhedge ELTH/MOT SE9.............166 E5
Bromholm Rd ABYW SE2.............128 C3
Bromley Av BMLY BR1.............183 H1
Bromley Common HAYES BR2....200 D4
Bromley Crs HAYES BR2.............183 H6
  RSLP HA4.............76 D2
Bromley Gdns HAYES BR2.............183 J5
Bromley Gv HAYES BR2.............183 G5
Bromley Hall Rd POP/IOD E14...106 A4
Bromley High St BOW E3.............105 K2
Bromley HI BMLY BR1.............183 H2
Bromley La CHST BR7.............185 H3
Bromley Rd BECK BR3.............182 D4
  CAT SE6.............164 E5
  CHST BR7.............185 H3
  LEY E10.............69 K3
  TOTM N17.............50 B4
  UED N18.............35 K6
  WALTH E17.............51 J6
Bromley St WCHPL E1.............105 F4
Brompton Ar CHEL SW3 *.............14 E6
Brompton Dr HSLWW TW4.............134 E6
Brompton Cottages
  WBPTN SW10 *.............120 B6
Brompton Dr ERITH DA8.............150 E1
Brompton Gv EFNCH N2.............65 J1
Brompton Park Crs
  FUL/PGN SW6.............120 A6
Brompton PI CHEL SW3.............14 E4
Brompton Rd CHEL SW3.............14 D6
Brompton Sq CHEL SW3.............14 D5
Brompton Ter
  WOOL/PLUM SE18 *.............147 F2
Bromwich Av HGT N6.............84 A1
Bromyard Av ACT W3.............118 B1
Brondesbury Ms
  KIL/WHAMP NW6 *.............82 E5
Brondesbury Pk
  KIL/WHAMP NW6.............82 A5
Brondesbury Rd
  KIL/WHAMP NW6.............100 D1
Brondesbury Vls
  KIL/WHAMP NW6.............82 E5
Bronhill Ter TOTM N17 *.............50 C4
Bronsart Rd FUL/PGN SW6...139 H1
Bronson Rd RYNPK SW20.............177 G5
Bronte CI ERITH DA8.............149 J2
  FSTGT E7.............88 E2
  GNTH/NBYPK IG2.............72 A2
Bronte Gv DART DA1.............151 J5
Bronti CI WALW SE17.............122 E3
Bronze Age Wy BELV DA17...129 K3
Bronze St DEPT SE8.............144 D1
Brook Av EDGW HA8.............92 D5
  EDGW HA8.............44 D2
  WBLY HA9.............80 B1
Brookbank Av HNWL W7.............96 D4
Brookbank Rd LEW SE13.............144 E4
Brook CI ACT W3.............117 H1
  GPK RM2.............57 H4
  HOR/WEW KT19.............207 G6
  RSLP HA4.............58 C4
  RYNPK SW20.............177 F6
  STWL/WRAY TW19.............152 C2
  TOOT SW17.............161 F4
Brook Ct BECK BR3 *.............182 C4
Brook Crs CHING E4.............37 J6
  ED N9.............36 D6
Brookdale FBAR/BDGN N11....34 C6
Brookdale Rd BXLY DA5.............169 F1
  CAT SE6.............164 E2
  WALTH E17.............51 J2
Brookdene Av
  WOOL/PLUM SE18.............127 K4
Brook Dr HRW HA1.............61 F1
  LBTH SE11.............17 K5
  RSLP HA4.............58 C4
Brooke Av RYLN/HDSTN HA2...78 C1
Brooke CI BUSH WD23.............28 C2
Brookehowse Rd CAT SE6.............164 E5
Brookend Rd BFN/LL DA15...167 K3
Brooker CI POP/IOD E14.....105 H4
Brooke Rd STNW/STAM N16....86 A1
  WALTH E17.............70 A1
Brooke St HCIRC EC1N.............11 J2
Brooke Wy BUSH WD23.............28 D1
Brookfield Av EA W5.............97 K3
  MLHL NW7.............45 K2
Brookfield CI MLHL NW7.............45 K2

Brookfield Crs
  KTN/HRWW/WS HA3.............61 K2
  MLHL NW7.............45 K2
Brookfield Gdns
  ESH/CLAY KT10.............205 F4
Brookfield Pk KTTN NW5.............84 B1
Brookfield Rd CHSWK W4.............118 B2
  ED N9.............36 C5
  HOM E9.............87 G4
Brookfields PEND EN3.............25 F5
Brookfields Av MTCM CR4.....194 D2
Brook Gdns BARN SW13.............138 C4
  CHING E4.............37 K6
  KUTN/CMB KT2.............176 A3
Brook Ga MYFR/PKLN W1K.............9 F6
Brook Gn HMSMTH W6.............119 F3
Brookhill CI EBAR EN4.............21 H1
Brook Hill CI
  WOOL/PLUM SE18.............127 G5
Brookhill Rd EBAR EN4.............21 H6
  WOOL/PLUM SE18.............127 G5
Brookhouse Gdns CHING E4...38 C6
Brooking CI BCTR RM8.............91 J1
Brooking Rd FSTGT E7.............88 E3
Brookland CI GLDGN NW11....64 E1
Brookland Garth GLDGN NW11...64 E1
Brookland HI GLDGN NW11....64 E1
Brookland Ri GLDGN NW11....64 E1
Brooklands Ap ROM RM1.............75 F1
Brooklands Av BFN/LL DA15...167 J4
  WIM/MER SW19.............160 A4
Brooklands CI ROMW/RG RM7...75 F1
Brooklands Ct
  KIL/WHAMP NW6 *.............82 D5
  WCHMH N21.............23 K6
Brooklands Dr GFD/PVL UB6....79 J6
Brooklands La ROMW/RG RM7...75 F1
Brooklands Pk BKHTH/KID SE3...145 K4
Brooklands PI HPTN TW12.....173 G1
Brooklands Rd ROMW/RG RM7...75 F1
  THDIT KT7.............190 A5
The Brooklands ISLW TW7 *...135 J2
Brook La BKHTH/KID SE3.............146 B3
  BMLY BR1.............183 K2
  BXLY DA5.............168 E1
Brooklea CI CDALE/KGS NW9....45 G4
Brooklyn Av WDGN N22.............49 J4
Brooklyn CI CAR SM5.............194 D6
Brooklyn Gv SNWD SE25.............197 J1
Brooklyn Rd HAYES BR2.............200 C2
  SNWD SE25.............197 J1
Brooklyn Wy WDR/YW UB7...112 A3
Brookmead CROY/NA CR0.....195 H5
Brookmead Av BMLY BR1.....200 E2
Brookmead CI
  STMC/STPC BR5.............202 C4
Brook Meadow
  NFNCH/WDSPK N12.............33 G6
Brook Meadow CI WFD IG8....52 C6
Brookmead Rd CROY/NA CR0...195 H3
Brook Ms North BAY/PAD W2...101 G6
Brookmill Rd DEPT SE8.............144 D2
Brook Pk DART DA1.............171 J5
Brook Park CI WCHMH N21.....35 H1
Brook PI BAR EN5.............20 E6
Brook Ri BKHH IG9.............38 E4
  CEND/HSY/T N8.............66 E1
  CRICK NW2.............63 J6
  GNTH/NBYPK IG2.............72 H5
  SURB KT6.............191 F6
  THHTH CR7.............196 D1
  TWK TW1.............156 B1
  WDGN N22.............49 F4
Brook Rd South BTFD TW8.....116 E6
Brooks Av EHAM E6.............107 K3
Brooksbank St HOM E9 *.....87 F4
Brooksby Ms IS N1.............85 G5
Brooksby St IS N1.............85 G5
Brooksby's Wk HOM E9.............87 F3
Brookscroft CROY/NA CR0 *...213 H6
Brookscroft Rd WALTH E17...51 K4
Brookshill KTN/HRWW/WS HA3...42 E2
Brookshill Av
  KTN/HRWW/WS HA3.............42 D1
Brookshill Dr
  KTN/HRWW/WS HA3.............42 D1
Brookside BARK/HLT IG6.............54 C2
  CAR SM5.............210 A3
  EBAR EN4.............33 J1
  ORP BR6.............202 A4
  RYNPK SW20.............35 F1
Brookside CI BAR EN5.............20 C6
  FELT TW13.............153 K5
  KTN/HRWW/WS HA3.............61 K2
  RSLP HA4.............77 J2
Brookside Crs WPK KT4.............192 D5
Brookside Rd ARCH N19.............66 D6
  ED N9.............36 D6
  GLDGN NW11.............64 C3
  OXHEY WD19.............27 F2
  YEAD UB4.............95 G6
Brookside South EBAR EN4...33 J3
Brookside Wy CROY/NA CR0...198 A3
Brooks La CHSWK W4.............117 H6
Brook's Ms MYFR/PKLN W1K.....9 J5
Brooks Rd CHSWK W4.............117 H5
  PLSTW E13.............88 E6
Brook St BAY/PAD W2.............8 D5
  BELV DA17.............129 K5
  ERITH DA8.............149 K1
  KUT/HW KT1.............175 F5
  MYFR/PKLN W1K.............9 H6
  TOTM N17.............50 B5
Brooksville Av
  KIL/WHAMP NW6.............82 C6
Brookview Rd
  STRHM/NOR SW16.............179 H1
Brookville Rd FUL/PGN SW6...139 J1
Brook Wk EDGW HA8.............45 F1
  EFNCH N2.............47 H4
Brook Water La HDN NW4 *....64 B2

Brookway BKHTH/KID SE3.....145 K4
  RAIN RM13.............111 K4
Brookwood Av BARN SW13.....138 C4
Brookwood CI HAYES BR2.....199 J1
Brookwood Rd HSLW TW3.....135 G3
  WAND/EARL SW18.............159 J3
Broom Av STMC/STPC BR5.....186 C5
Broom CI ESH/CLAY KT10.............200 B3
  HAYES BR2.............200 D3
  TEDD TW11.............174 E2
Broomcroft Av NTHLT UB5...95 G2
Broome Rd HPTN TW12.............172 E3
Broome Wy CMBW SE5.............142 E1
Broomfield WALTH E17.............69 H4
Broomfield Av LOU IG10.............39 K1
  PLMGR N13.............35 F6
  PLMGR N13.............48 E1
Broomfield CI CRW RM5.............57 F3
Broomfield Cottages
  WEA W13.............116 C1
Broomfield La PLMGR N13.....34 E6
Broomfield PI WEA W13.............116 C1
Broomfield Rd BECK BR3.....198 B1
  BXLYHS DA6.............149 H6
  CHDH RM6.............73 K4
  RCH/KEW TW9.............137 G2
  SURB KT6.............191 G5
  TEDD TW11.............174 D2
  WEA W13.............116 C1
Broomfields ESH/CLAY KT10...204 C5
Broomfield St POP/IOD E14...105 J4
Broom Gdns CROY/NA CR0.....213 J1
Broomgrove Gdns EDGW HA8...44 C4
Broomhall Rd SAND/SEL CR2...211 K6
Broomhill Ri BXLYHS DA6.....149 H6
Broomhill Rd DART DA1.............170 E1
  GDMY/SEVK IG3.............73 G6
  ORP BR6.............202 B4
  WAND/EARL SW18.............159 K6
  WFD IG8.............52 E2
Broomhouse La
  FUL/PGN SW6.............139 K3
Broomhouse Rd
  FUL/PGN SW6.............139 K3
Broomloan La SUT SM1.............193 K6
Broom Md BXLYHS DA6.............169 H1
Broom Pk TEDD TW11.............174 E3
Broom Rd CROY/NA CR0.............213 J1
  TEDD TW11.............174 D1
Broomsleigh St
  KIL/WHAMP NW6 *.............82 E3
Broom Water TEDD TW11.....174 D1
Broom Water West
  TEDD TW11.............174 D1
Broomwood CI BXLY DA5.....170 A4
  CROY/NA CR0.............198 A2
Broomwood Rd BTSEA SW11...160 E1
  STMC/STPC BR5.............186 C5
Broseley Gv SYD SE26.............182 B1
Broster Gdns SNWD SE25.....181 G6
Brougham Rd ACT W3.............98 E5
  HACK E8.............86 C6
Brougham St BTSEA SW11.....140 E3
Brough CI KUTN/CMB KT2 *...156 E4
  VX/NE SW8.............141 K1
Broughinn Av FNCH N3.............46 D6
  RCHPK/HAM TW10.............156 D6
Broughton Dr BRXN/ST SW9...142 B5
Broughton Gdns HGT N6.............66 C3
Broughton Rd FUL/PGN SW6...140 A3
  ORP BR6.............201 J6
  STMC/STPC BR5.............186 C5
  THHTH CR7.............196 B3
  WEA W13.............97 H6
Broughton Road Ap
  FUL/PGN SW6.............140 A3
Broughton St VX/NE SW8.....141 G3
Brouncker Rd ACT W3.............117 K2
Brow Crs STMC/STPC BR5.....202 D5
Browell's La FELT TW13.............154 B4
Brown CI WLGTN SM6.............210 E5
Brownfield St POP/IOD E14...106 A5
Browngraves Rd
  HYS/HAR UB3.............133 F1
Brown Hart Gdns
  MYFR/PKLN W1K.............9 H5
Brownhill Rd CAT SE6.............165 F2
Browning Av HNWL W7.............97 F5
  SUT SM1.............209 J2
  WPK KT4.............192 E5
Browning CI HPTN TW12.....154 E6
  MV/WKIL W9.............101 G3
  WALTH E17.............51 K4
  WELL DA16.............147 K2
Browning Ms CAVSQ/HST W1G *...9 H7
Browning Rd DART DA1.............151 J5
  ENC/FH EN2.............23 K1
  MNPK E12.............89 K4
  WAN E11.............70 D4
Browning St WALW SE17.............122 C5
Browning Wy HEST TW5.............134 C2
Brownlea Gdns GDMY/SEVK IG3...73 G1
Brownlow CI EBAR EN4.............21 H6
Brownlow Ms BMSBY WC1N.....5 H7
Brownlow Rd CROY/NA CR0...212 A2
  FBAR/BDGN N11.............48 E2
  FNCH N3.............47 F1
  FSTGT E7.............88 E2
  HACK E8.............86 C6
  WALTH E17 *.............116 B1
  WLSDN NW10.............81 G5
Brownlow St GINN WC1R.............11 H2
Brownrigg Rd ASHF TW15.....152 D6
Brownspring Dr
  ELTH/MOT SE9.............167 G6
Brown's Rd BRYLDS KT5.............191 G4
  WALTH E17.............51 J6
Brown St MBLAR W1H.............8 E3
Brownswood Rd FSBYPK N4...67 J2
Broxash Rd BTSEA SW11.............161 F1
Broxbourne Av SWFD E18.....71 F1
Broxbourne House BOW E3...105 K3
Broxbourne Rd FSTGT E7.....88 E2
  ORP BR6.............202 A5
Broxholm Rd WNWD SE27...162 B5

Broxted Rd CAT SE6.............164 C4
Broxwood Wy STJWD NW8.....2 D1
Bruce Castle Rd TOTM N17...50 B4
Bruce CI NKENS W10.............100 B4
  WELL DA16.............148 C2
Bruce Dr SAND/SEL CR2.............213 G6
Bruce Gdns TRDG/WHET N20...33 K5
Bruce Gv ORP BR6.............202 B5
  TOTM N17.............50 B4
Bruce Rd BAR EN5.............20 C4
  BOW E3.............105 K2
  KTN/HRWW/WS HA3.............42 E5
  MTCM CR4.............179 F3
  SNWD SE25.............196 F1
  WLSDN NW10.............81 F5
Bruckner St NKENS W10.............100 C2
Brudenell Rd TOOT SW17.....160 E5
Bruffs Meadow NTHLT UB5...77 J4
Bruford Ct DEPT SE8.............124 D6
Bruges PI CAMTN NW1.............84 C5
Brumfield Rd HOR/WEW KT19...206 E3
Brunel CI HEST TW5.............134 A1
  NRWD SE19.............181 G2
  NTHLT UB5.............95 J2
  ROM RM1.............75 G1
Brunel Est BAY/PAD W2 *.....100 E4
Brunel House
  WOOL/PLUM SE18 *.............146 D1
Brunel Ms NKENS W10.............100 B2
Brunel Rd ACT W3.............99 G4
  BERM/RHTH SE16.............123 K2
  WALTH E17.............69 F3
  WFD IG8.............53 K1
Brunel St CAN/RD E16.............106 C5
Brunel Wk WHTN TW2.............155 F2
  TOTM N17.............50 C3
Brune St WCHPL E1.............13 J2
Brunner CI CLDGN NW11.............65 F4
Brunner Rd EA W5.............97 K2
  WALTH E17.............69 H2
Bruno PI CDALE/KGS NW9.....63 F2
Brunswick Av FBAR/BDGN N11...34 A5
Brunswick CI BXLYHS DA6.....148 E5
  PIN HA5.............59 J3
  THDIT KT7.............190 A5
  WHTN TW2.............155 J5
  WOT/HER KT12.............188 B6
Brunswick Crs STHWK SE1.....19 H5
Brunswick Crs FBAR/BDGN N11...34 A5
Brunswick Gdns BARK/HLT IG6...54 C5
  EA W5.............98 A2
  KENS W8.............119 K1
Brunswick Ms MBLAR W1H.....8 F3
  STRHM/NOR SW16.............179 J5
Brunswick Pk CMBW SE5.....142 E2
Brunswick Park Rd
  FBAR/BDGN N11.............34 A4
Brunswick PI CAMTN NW1.....7 F4
  IS N1.............7 F4
  NRWD SE19.............181 H3
Brunswick Quay
  BERM/RHTH SE16.............124 B3
Brunswick Rd BXLYHS DA6...148 E5
  EA W5.............97 K3
  KUTN/CMB KT2.............175 H4
  LEY E10.............70 A5
  PEND EN3.............25 F2
  SEVS/STOTM N15.............68 A2
  SUT SM1.............209 F2
Brunswick Sq BMSBY WC1N.....5 H6
  STHWK SE1.............18 C1
Brunswick St WALTH E17.............70 B2
Brunswick Vls CMBW SE5.....143 F2
Brunswick Wy FBAR/BDGN N11...34 B6
Brunton PI POP/IOD E14.............105 G5
Brushfield St WCHPL E1.............13 H1
Brushwood CI POP/IOD E14...106 A4
Brussels Rd BTSEA SW11.............140 C5
Bruton CI CHST BR7.............184 E3
Bruton La MYFR/PICC W1J.....9 K6
Bruton PI MYFR/PICC W1J.....9 K6
Bruton Rd MRDN SM4.............194 B1
Bruton St MYFR/PICC W1J.....9 K6
Bruton Wy WEA W13.............97 G4
Bryan Av WLSDN NW10.............81 K5
Bryan Rd BERM/RHTH SE16...124 C2
Bryanston Av WHTN TW2.....155 G3
Bryanston CI NWDGN UB2.....114 E4
Bryanston Ms East MBLAR W1H...8 E2
Bryanston Ms West MBLAR W1H...8 E2
Bryanston PI MBLAR W1H.....8 E2
Bryanston Sq MBLAR W1H.....8 E3
Bryanston St MBLAR W1H.....8 E4
Bryant CI BAR EN5.............20 D6
Bryant Rd NTHLT UB5.............95 F2
Bryant St SRTFD E15.............88 B5
Bryantwood Rd HOLWY N7...85 G3
Brycedale Crs STHGT/OAK N14...34 D6
Bryce Rd BCTR RM8.............91 J2
Bryden CI SYD SE26.............182 B1
Brydges PI CHCR WC2N.............10 E6
Brydges Rd SRTFD E15.............88 B3
Brydon Wk IS N1.............84 E1
Bryett Rd HOLWY N7.............84 E1
Brymay CI BOW E3.............105 J1
Brynmaer Rd BTSEA SW11.....140 E2
Bryn-Y-Mawr Rd EN EN1.....24 B5
Bryony Rd SHB W12.............99 J6
Buchanan CI WCHMH N21...23 F5
Buchanan Gdns WLSDN NW10...99 K1
Buchan Rd PECK SE15.............143 K4
Bucharest Rd
  WAND/EARL SW18.............160 B2
Buckden CI LEE/GVPK SE12...165 J1
Buckfast Rd MRDN SM4.............194 A1
Buckfast St BETH E2.............104 C2
Buckhold Rd
  WAND/EARL SW18.............159 K1
Buckhurst Av CAR SM5.............194 D5
Buckhurst St WCHPL E1.............104 D3
Buckhurst Wy BKHH IG9.............39 H5
Buckingham Av
  E/WMO/HCT KT8.............173 G5

EBED/NFELT TW14.............154 A1
  CFD/PVL UB6.............79 G6
  THHTH CR7.............180 B4
  TRDG/WHET N20.............33 G2
  WELL DA16.............147 K5
Buckingham CI EA W5.............97 J4
  EN EN1.............24 A3
  HPTN TW12.............172 E1
  STMC/STPC BR5.............201 K4
Buckingham Dr CHST BR7...185 G1
Buckingham Gdns
  E/WMO/HCT KT8.............173 G5
  STAN HA7.............44 A3
  THHTH CR7.............180 B5
Buckingham Ga WESTW SW1E...16 A4
Buckingham Ms IS N1.............86 A4
  STJWD NW8 *.............83 J1
  WESTW SW1E *.............16 A4
  WLSDN NW10.............99 H1
Buckingham Palace Rd
  BGVA SW1W.............15 K5
Buckingham Pde STAN HA7 *...43 J1
Buckingham PI WESTW SW1E...16 A4
Buckingham Rd EDGW HA8...44 B3
  HPTN TW12.............154 E6
  HRW HA1.............60 D2
  IL IG1.............72 D6
  IS N1.............86 A4
  KUT/HW KT1.............191 G1
  LEY E10.............70 A3
  MTCM CR4.............195 K2
  RCHPK/HAM TW10.............156 E4
  SRTFD E15.............88 D3
  WALTH E17.............51 H5
  WFD IG8.............52 E3
Buckingham St CHCR WC2N...10 F6
Buckland Crs HAMP NW3.............83 H5
Buckland Ri PIN HA5.............41 G4
Buckland Rd CHSGTN KT9...206 B3
  LEY E10.............70 A6
  ORP BR6.............216 E2
Bucklands OXHEY WD19 *.....27 H5
Bucklands Rd TEDD TW11.....174 D2
Buckland St IS N1 *.............7 F2
Bucklands Whf KUT/HW KT1 *...174 E5
Buckland Wk MRDN SM4.............194 B1
  ACT W3.............117 K2
Buckland Wy WPK KT4.............193 F5
Buck La CDALE/KGS NW9.............63 F2
Buckleigh Av RYNPK SW20...177 H6
Buckleigh Rd
  STRHM/NOR SW16.............179 K3
Buckleigh Wy NRWD SE19...181 G4
Bucklersbury MANHO EC4N...12 E4
Bucklers' Wy CAR SM5.............209 K1
Buckle St WCHPL E1.............13 K3
Buckley CI DART DA1.............150 E4
  FSTH SE23 *.............163 J2
Buckley Rd KIL/WHAMP NW6...82 D5
Buckmaster CI BRXN/ST SW9...142 B4
Buckmaster Rd BTSEA SW11...140 D5
Bucknall St NOXST/BSQ WC1A...10 D3
Bucknall Wy BECK BR3.............198 E1
Bucknell CI BRXS/STRHM SW2...142 A4
Buckner Rd BRXS/STRHM SW2...142 A5
Buckrell Rd CHING E4.............38 B4
Bucks Av OXHEY WD19.............27 J2
Buckstone CI FSTH SE23.............163 K1
Buckstone Rd UED N18.............50 C2
  IS N1 *.............84 B6
Buckters Rents
  BERM/RHTH SE16.............124 B1
Buckthorne Rd BROCKY SE4...164 B1
Budd CI NFNCH/WDSPK N12...33 F6
Buddings Cir WBLY HA9.............80 E1
Budge La MTCM CR4.............194 E4
Budge Rw MANHO EC4N.............12 E5
Budleigh Crs WELL DA16.....148 D2
Budoch Dr GDMY/SEVK IG3...73 G6
Buer Rd FUL/PGN SW6.............139 H3
Bugsby's Wy GNWCH SE10...125 J4
Bulganak Rd THHTH CR7.....196 D1
Bulinca St WEST SW1P *.............16 E7
Bullace Rw CMBW SE5.............142 E2
Bull All WELL DA16.............148 C4
Bullard Rd TEDD TW11.............173 K2
Bullards PI BETH E2.............105 F2
Bullbanks Rd BELV DA17.....129 K4
Bulleid Wy BGVA SW1W.............15 K7
Bullen St BTSEA SW11.............140 D3
Buller CI PECK SE15.............143 H1
Buller Rd BARK IG11.............90 E5
  THHTH CR7.............180 E6
  TOTM N17.............50 C5
  WDGN N22.............49 G5
  WLSDN NW10.............100 B2
Bullers CI SCUP DA14.............187 F1
Bullers Wood Dr CHST BR7...184 D4
Bullescroft Rd EDGW HA8...30 D5
Bullivant St POP/IOD E14...106 A6
Bull La CHST BR7.............185 J3
  DAGE RM10.............92 D1
  UED N18.............50 A1
Bullrush CI CAR SM5.............194 D6
  CROY/NA CR0.............197 F3
Bulls Aly MORT/ESHN SW14...138 A4
Bull's Br HYS/HAR UB3.............113 F4
Bulls Bridge Rd NWDGN UB2...114 B3
Bull's Gdns CHEL SW3.............14 D6
Bull's Gdns BAR EN5.............21 G5
Bull Yd PECK SE15.............143 H2
Bulmer Gdns
  KTN/HRWW/WS HA3.............61 K4
Bulstrode Av HSLW TW3.....134 E4
Bulstrode Gdns HSLW TW3...135 F4
Bulstrode PI MHST W1U.............9 H2
Bulstrode Rd HSLW TW3.....135 F4
Bulstrode St MHST W1U.............9 H3
Bulwer Court Rd WAN E11...70 B5
Bulwer Gdns BAR EN5.............21 G5
Bulwer Rd BAR EN5.............21 F5
  UED N18.............36 A6

WAN E11 ....70 B5
Bulwer St SHB W12......................119 F1
Bunces La WFD G8.......................52 D3
Bungalow Rd SNWD SE25.............197 F1
The Bungalows
  RYLN/HDSTN HA2 *....................77 K1
  STRHM/NOR SW16.......................119 G3
Bunhill Rw STLK EC1Y...................6 E6
Bunhouse Pl BGVA SW1W.............121 F5
Bunker's HI BELV DA17................129 H4
  GLDGN NW11............................65 G4
  SCUP SA14............................169 G5
Bunning Wy HOLWY N7..................84 E5
Bunn's La MLHL NW7....................45 G3
Bunsen St BOW E3.......................105 G1
Buntingbridge Rd
  BARK/HLT IG6.........................72 D2
Bunting Cl ED N9........................37 F3
  MTCM CR4.............................194 E2
Bunton St WOOL/PLUM SE18........127 F3
Bunyan Rd WALTH E17....................51 G6
Buonaparte Ms PIM SW1V.............121 J5
Burbage Cl HYS/HAR UB3..............84 B5
  STHWK SE1............................18 E5
Burbage Rd HNHL SE24...............162 E1
Burberry Cl NWMAL KT3...............176 B5
Burbridge Wy TOTM N17................50 C5
Burcham St POP/IOD E14.............105 K5
Burcharbro Rd ABYW SE2.............128 E6
Burchell Ct BUSH WD23.................28 C2
Burchell Rd LEY E10......................69 K5
  PECK SE15............................143 J2
Burchett Rd BOW E3....................105 H3
  CROY/NA CR0.........................196 E3
Burcote Rd WAND/EARL SW18......160 C3
Burden Cl BTFD TW8...................116 D5
Burdenshott Av
  RCHPK/HAM TW10....................137 J5
Burden Wy WAN E11......................71 H6
Burder Cl IS N1..........................86 A4
Burder Rd IS N1..........................86 A4
Burdett Av RYNPK SW20..............176 D4
Burdett Cl HNWL W7 *.................116 A1
  SCUP DA14...........................187 F1
Burdett Rd BOW E3....................105 H3
  CROY/NA CR0.........................196 E3
  RCH/KEW TW9.........................137 G2
Burdetts Rd DAGW RM9..................92 B6
Burdock Cl CROY/NA CR0.............198 A5
Burdock Rd TOTM N17....................50 C6
Burdon Cl TOOT SW17..................160 E6
Burdon La BELMT SM2.................208 D6
Burdon Pk BELMT SM2.................208 D6
Burfield Cl TOOT SW17................160 C6
Burford Cl BARK/HLT IG6...............72 C1
  BCTR RM8.............................91 J1
Burford Gdns PLMGR N13.............35 F5
Burford Rd BMLY BR1.................200 D1
  BTFD TW8............................117 F5
  CAT SE6.............................164 C4
  EHAM E6.............................107 J2
  SRTFD E15............................88 B5
  SUT SM1............................193 K6
  WPK KT4.............................192 D4
Burford Wk FUL/PGN SW6 *..........140 A1
Burford Wy CROY/NA CR0............214 A5
Burgate Cl DART DA1..................150 C4
Burges Gv BARN SW13.................118 E1
Burges Rd EHAM E6.....................90 A5
Burgess Av CDALE/KGS NW9............63 F3
Burgess Cl FELT TW13.................154 D6
Burgess Hl CRICK NW2...................82 E2
Burgess Ms WIM/MER SW19.........178 A2
Burgess Rd SRTFD E15..................88 C2
  SUT SM1............................209 F2
Burgess St POP/IOD E14.............105 J4
Burghill Rd SYD SE26..................164 B6
Burghley Av NWMAL KT3...............176 A4
Burghley Hall Cl
  WIM/MER SW19 *.....................159 H3
Burghley Pl MTCM CR4.................194 E1
Burghley Rd CEND/HSY/T N8...........49 G6
  KTTN NW5............................84 B2
  WAN E11.............................70 C5
  WIM/MER SW19........................159 H6
Burgh St IS N1...........................6 A2
Burgon St BLKFR EC4V...................12 B4
Burgos Cl CROY/NA CR0...............211 G4
Burgos Gv GNWCH SE10...............144 E2
Burgoyne Rd BRXN/ST SW9...........142 A4
  FSBYPK N4............................67 H3
  SNWD SE25...........................197 G1
Burham Cl PGE/AN SE20...............181 K3
Burhill Gv PIN HA5......................41 J6
Burke Cl PUT/ROE SW15...............138 B5
Burke St CAN/RD E16...................106 D4
Burket Cl NWDGN UB2.................114 D4
Burland Rd BTSEA SW11...............140 E6
  CRW RM5.............................56 E2
Burleigh Cl BFN/LL DA15...............148 A6
  WLGTN SM6..........................210 A1
Burleigh Gdns STHGT/OAK N14.......34 C3
Burleigh Pde STHGT/OAK N14 *......34 C3
Burleigh Pl PUT/ROE SW15.............139 G6
Burleigh Rd CHEAM SM3...............193 H5
  EN EN1..............................24 B5
Burleigh St COVGDN WC2E.............11 F5
Burleigh Wk CAT SE6..................165 F3
Burleigh Wy ENC/FH EN2................23 K4
Burley Cl CHING E4.......................51 J1
  STRHM/NOR SW16....................179 H4
Burley Rd CAN/RD E16.................107 G5
Burlington Ar CONDST W1S.............10 A6
Burlington Av RCH/KEW TW9.........137 H2
  ROMW/RG RM7........................74 D3
Burlington Cl
  EBED/NFELT TW14...................153 G2
  EHAM E6.............................107 J1
  MV/WKIL W9..........................100 E3
  ORP BR6.............................201 J6
  PIN HA5.............................58 E1
Burlington Gdns ACT W3...............118 A1
  CHDH RM6............................73 J4
  CHSWK W4............................117 K5
  CONDST W1S...........................10 A6
Burlington La CHSWK W4...............137 K1
Burlington Ms ACT W3.................117 K1

Burlington Pde CRICK NW2 *............82 B1
Burlington Pl FUL/PGN SW6............139 H1
  WFD IG8..............................38 E5
Burlington Ri EBAR EN4.................33 J3
  ENC/FH EN2...........................23 K2
  FUL/PGN SW6..........................159 H1
  MLSWH N10...........................48 A6
  NWMAL KT3..........................192 C1
  THHTH CR7..........................180 D5
Burma Rd STNW/STAM N16..............85 K2
Burmester Rd TOOT SW17..............160 B5
Burnaby Crs CHSWK W4................117 K6
Burnaby Gdns CHSWK W4..............117 J6
Burnaby St WBPTN SW10..............140 B1
Burnbrae Cl
  NFNCH/WDSPK N12...................47 F2
Burnbury Rd BAL SW12................161 H3
Burncroft Av PEND EN3.................24 E3
Burndell Wy YEAD UB4...................95 H4
Burnell Av RCHPK/HAM TW10.......174 C1
  WELL DA16..........................148 B3
Burnell Rd SUT SM1...................209 F2
Burnell Wk STHWK SE1..................123 G5
Burnels Av EHAM E6....................108 A2
Burness Cl HOLWY N7...................85 F4
Burne St CAMTN NW1......................8 C1
Burnet Cl HOM E9..........................86 E3
Burnett La BARK/HLT IG6................54 B5
Burnett Rd ERITH DA8.................131 G6
Burney Av BRYLDS KT5.................191 G2
Burney St GNWCH SE10................145 F1
Burnfoot Av FUL/PGN SW6.............139 H2
Burnham Av HGDN/ICK UB10..........76 A2
Burnham Cl EN EN1......................24 C1
  KTN/HRWW/WS HA3....................61 G1
  MLHL NW7.............................45 J3
  STHWK SE1............................19 K7
Burnham Crs DART DA1................151 F5
  WAN E11.............................71 G1
Burnham Dr WPK KT4...................193 G6
Burnham Gdns CROY/NA CR0.......197 G4
  HSLWW TW4..........................134 A2
  HYS/HAR UB3.........................113 G3
Burnham Rd CHING E4...................51 H1
  DAGW RM9............................91 H5
  DART DA1.............................151 G6
  MRDN SM4...........................194 A2
  ROMW/RG RM7........................74 E1
  SCUP DA14..........................169 F5
Burnham St KUTN/CMB KT2...........175 G4
Burnham Ter DART DA1 *..............151 G6
Burnham Wy SYD SE26................182 C1
  WEA W13.............................116 C4
Burnhill Rd BECK BR3..................182 D5
Burnley Cl OXHEY WD19................41 G1
Burnley Rd BRXN/ST SW9.............142 A3
  WLSDN NW10...........................81 H3
Burnsall St CHEL SW3.................120 D5
Burns Av BFN/LL DA15.................168 C1
  CHDH RM6............................73 J4
  EBED/NFELT TW14...................153 K1
  STHL UB1............................96 A6
Burns Cl CAR SM5......................210 A6
  ERITH DA8...........................150 C2
  WALTH E17............................70 A1
  WELL DA16...........................148 A2
  WIM/MER SW19........................178 C2
  YEAD UB4.............................94 E1
Burnside Av CHING E4...................51 H2
Burnside Cl BAR EN5.....................20 E4
  BERM/RHTH SE16.....................124 A1
  TWK TW1.............................156 B1
Burnside Crs ALP/SUD HA0.............79 J6
Burnside Rd BCTR RM8...................73 J5
Burns Rd ALP/SUD HA0...................98 A1
  BTSEA SW11.........................140 E3
  WEA W13.............................116 C2
  WLSDN NW10...........................81 H6
Burns Wy HEST TW5.....................134 C2
Burnt Ash Hl LEE/GVPK SE12..........165 J1
Burnt Ash La BMLY BR1................183 K2
Burnt Ash Rd LEE/GVPK SE12.......165 J1
Burnthwaite Rd FUL/PGN SW6......139 J1
Burnt Oak Broadway
  EDGW HA8.............................44 D3
Burnt Oak Flds EDGW HA8.............44 E4
Burnt Oak La BFN/LL DA15............168 C2
Burntwood Cl
  WAND/EARL SW18...................160 C3
Burntwood Grange Rd
  WAND/EARL SW18...................160 C3
Burntwood La TOOT SW17.............160 C4
Burntwood Vw NRWD SE19 *..........181 G1
Buross St WCHPL E1....................104 D5
Burpham Cl YEAD UB4...................95 H5
Burrage Gv WOOL/PLUM SE18......127 H4
Burrage Pl WOOL/PLUM SE18.......127 G5
Burrage Rd WOOL/PLUM SE18......127 H5
Burrard Rd CAN/RD E16...............106 E5
  KIL/WHAMP NW6.......................82 E3
Burr Bank Ter RDART DA2..............171 H6
Burr Cl BXLYHN DA7....................149 F4
  WAP E1W..............................123 H1
Burrell Cl CROY/NA CR0................198 B3
  EDGW HA8..............................30 D4
Burrell Rw BECK BR3....................182 D5
Burrell St STHWK SE1....................12 A7
Burrells Whf POP/IOD E14.............124 E5
Burrfield Dr STMC/STPC BR5.........202 E2
Burritt Rd KUT/HW KT1...............175 H5

Bursar St STHWK SE1 *..................19 G1
Burston Cl BFN/LL DA15..............168 A4
Burston Rd PEND EN3....................25 F5
Burslem Av BARK/HLT IG6..............55 G2
Burslem St WCHPL E1 *................104 D5
Burstock Rd PUT/ROE SW15.........139 H5
Burston Rd PUT/ROE SW15...........139 G6
Burtenshaw Rd THDIT KT7............190 B4
Burtley Cl FSBYPK N4....................67 J5
Burton Bank IS N1 *......................85 K5
Burton Cl CHSGTN KT9..................205 K5
  THHTH CR7...........................180 E6
Burton Gdns HEST TW5.................134 E2
Burton Gv WALW SE17..................122 E5
Burtonhole Cl MLHL NW7................32 B6
Burtonhole La MLHL NW7................32 C6
  MLHL NW7.............................46 B1
Burton La BRXN/ST SW9...............142 B3
Burton Ms BGVA SW1W..................15 H7
Burton Pl STPAN WC1H...................4 D1
Burton Rd BRXN/ST SW9...............142 C3
  KIL/WHAMP NW6.......................82 D5
  KUTN/CMB KT2.......................175 F3
  SWFD E18..............................53 F6
Burt Rd CAN/RD E16.....................126 B1
Burtwell La DUL SE21...................162 E6
Burwash Cl BXLY DA5....................169 H3
Burwash Rd
  WOOL/PLUM SE18...................127 J5
Burwell Av GFD/PVL UB6................78 E4
Burwell Cl WCHPL E1...................104 D5
Burwell Rd LEY E10......................69 G5
Burwood Av HAYES BR2................200 A6
  PIN HA5.............................59 G2
Burwood Cl SURB KT6..................191 H5
Burwood Gdns RAIN RM13.............111 H2
Burwood Pl BAY/PAD W2..................8 D3
  EBAR EN4............................21 G2
Bury Cl BERM/RHTH SE16..............124 A1
Bury Ct HDTCH EC3A......................13 H3
Bury Gv MRDN SM4.....................194 A2
Bury Pl NOXST/BSQ WC1A..............10 E2
Bury Rd DAGE RM10.......................92 D5
  EFNCH N2............................49 G6
Buryside Cl GNTH/NBYPK IG2..........73 F2
Bury St ED N9...........................36 C3
  HDTCH EC3A..........................13 H4
  RSLP HA4.............................58 B3
  STJS SW1Y............................10 A7
Bury St West ED N9.....................36 C2
Bury Wk CHEL SW3......................14 C7
Busby Pl KTTN NW5......................84 C4
Busch Cl ISLW TW7......................136 C2
Bushbaby Cl STHWK SE1 *..............19 G5
Bushberry Rd HOM E9....................87 G4
Bush Cl GNTH/NBYPK IG2.................72 C3
Bush Cottages
  WAND/EARL SW18...................139 K6
Bushell Cl BRXS/STRHM SW2.........162 A4
Bushell Gn BUSH WD23..................28 D4
Bushell St WAP E1W *..................123 H1
Bushell Wy CHST BR7..................185 F1
Bush Elms Rd EMPK RM11................75 J4
Bushey Av STMC/STPC BR5............201 J4
  SWFD E18..............................52 D6
Bushey Hill Rd CMBW SE5.............143 G2
Bushey La SUT SM1.....................208 E2
Bushey Lees BFN/LL DA15 *...........168 A1
Bushey Rd CROY/NA CR0...............198 D6
  HYS/HAR UB3........................113 H4
  PLSTW E13..............................89 J1
  RYNPK SW20.........................177 F5
Bushey Wy BECK BR3..................199 G3
Bushfield Cl EDGW HA8...................30 D4
Bushfield Crs EDGW HA8................30 D4
Bush Gv CDALE/KGS NW9................62 E4
  STAN HA7............................43 K3
Bushgrove Rd BCTR RM8.................91 K2
Bush Hl WCHMH N21......................35 J2
Bush Hill Pde ED N9 *...................35 K2
Bush Hl
  KTN/HRWW/WS HA3..................62 B3
Bushwood WAN E11........................70 D4
Bushwood Dr STHWK SE1...............19 K7
Bushwood Rd RCH/KEW TW9........137 H1
Bushy Parks Gdns HPTN TW12......173 J1
Bushy Park Rd TEDD TW11............174 D3
Bushy Rd TEDD TW11...................174 A3
Butcher Rw WAP E1W...................105 F5
Butchers Rd CAN/RD E16...............106 E5
Bute Av RCHPK/HAM TW10............157 F4
Bute Gdns HMSMTH W6................119 G4
  RCHPK/HAM TW10 *..................157 F5
  WLGTN SM6..........................210 C3
Bute Gdns West WLGTN SM6.........210 C3
Bute Ms GLDGN NW11....................65 F2
Bute Rd BARK/HLT IG6...................54 B6
  CROY/NA CR0........................196 B5
  WLGTN SM6..........................210 C2
Bute St SKENS SW7......................14 A6
Bute Wk IS N1 *..........................85 K4
Butler Av HRW HA1.......................60 D5
Butler Cl EDGW HA8......................44 D5
Butler Rd BCTR RM8......................91 H2

  HRW HA1.............................60 C4
  WLSDN NW10...........................81 H5
Butlers Cl HSLWW TW4.................134 E6
Butlers & Colonial Whf
  STHWK SE1...........................19 K2
Butler St BETH E2 *....................105 F2
Buttercup Cl NTHLT UB5..................78 A4
Buttercup Sq
  STWL/WRAY TW19 *...................152 A3
Butterfield Cl
  BERM/RHTH SE16 *...................123 H2
  TOTM N17.............................49 J2
  TWK TW1.............................156 A1
Butterfield House
  CHARL SE7 *...........................1
Butterfields WALTH E17...................70 A2
Butterfield Sq EHAM E6................107 K5
Butterfly La ELTH/MOT SE9............167 G1
Buttermere Cl CMBW SE5 *............142 E2
Butter Hl CAR SM5.....................210 A1
Butteridges Cl DAGW RM9...............92 B6
Butterly Av DART DA1..................171 J4
Buttermere Cl
  EBED/NFELT TW14...................153 J2
  MRDN SM4...........................195 G3
  SRTFD E15.............................88 C3
  STHWK SE1............................19 J7
Buttermere Dr PUT/ROE SW15.....139 H6
Buttermere Rd
  STMC/STPC BR5.....................202 E1
Buttermere Wk HACK E8..................86 B4
Butterwick HMSMTH W6.................119 F4
Butterworth Gdns WFD IG8.............52 E2
Buttesland St IS N1 *......................7 F4
Buttfield Cl DAGE RM10...................92 D4
Buttmarsh Cl
  WOOL/PLUM SE18...................127 G5
Buttsbury Rd IL IG1.....................90 C3
Butts Crs FELT TW13...................155 F5
Buttsmead NTHWD HA6...................40 A3
Butts Pce BMLY BR1 *...................95 F1
Butts Rd BMLY BR1......................183 H1
The Butts BTFD TW8.....................116 E6
Buxhall Crs HOM E9.......................87 H4
Buxted Rd EDUL SE22..................143 F5
  HACK E8..............................86 B5
  NFNCH/WDSPK N12....................47 J1
Buxton Cl WFD IG8.......................53 H2
Buxton Crs CHEAM SM3...............208 C2
Buxton Dr NWMAL KT3..................176 A5
  WAN E11.............................53 J4
Buxton Gdns ACT W3.....................98 D6
Buxton Ms CLAP SW4...................141 J3
Buxton Pth OXHEY WD19 *.............27 G5
Buxton Rd ARCH N19......................66 D5
  CHING E4.............................38 A2
  CRICK NW2............................81 K4
  EHAM E6.............................107 J2
  GNTH/NBYPK IG2......................72 E3
  MORT/ESHN SW14...................138 A4
  SRTFD E15.............................88 C3
  THHTH CR7...........................196 C2
  WALTH E17............................69 G1
Byam St FUL/PGN SW6..................140 B3
Byards Cft STRHM/NOR SW16......179 J4
Bychurch End TEDD TW11 *...........174 A1
Bycroft Rd STHL UB1......................96 A4
Bycroft St PGE/AN SE20 *.............182 A3
Bycullah Av ENC/FH EN2..................23 H4
Bycullah Rd ENC/FH EN2..................23 H3
Byelands Cl BERM/RHTH SE16......124 A1
The Bye ACT W3...........................99 G5
Byewaters WATW WD18.................26 A1
Bye Ways WHTN TW2..................155 G5
The Byeways BRYLDS KT5.............191 H2
The Bye Wy
  KTN/HRWW/WS HA3..................42 E4
The Byeway BELMT SM2................209 H6
  MORT/ESHN SW14...................137 K4
Byfeld Gdns BARN SW13...............138 D2
Byfield Cl BERM/RHTH SE16..........124 B2
Byfield Rd ISLW TW7...................136 B4
Byford Cl SRTFD E15.....................88 C5
Bygrove CROY/NA CR0.................213 K4
Bygrove St POP/IOD E14..............105 K5
Byland Cl ABYW SE2....................128 C3
Byne Rd CAR SM5.......................194 D6
  SYD SE26............................181 K2
Bynes Rd SAND/SEL CR2..............211 K5
Byng Pl GWRST WC1E......................4 D7
Byng Rd BAR EN5.........................20 B3
Byng St POP/IOD E14..................124 D2
Bynon Av BXLYHN DA7.................149 F4
Byre Rd STHGT/OAK N14................34 A1
Byrne Rd BAL SW12....................161 G4
Byron Av CDALE/KGS NW9...............62 E4
  HSLWW TW4..........................134 A2
  MNPK E12...........................89 J4
  NWMAL KT3..........................192 D2
  SUT SM1............................209 H2
Byron Av East SUT SM1...............209 H2
Byron Cl HACK E8..........................86 C6
  HPTN TW12.............................154 E5
  PGE/AN SE20.........................181 J6
  STRHM/NOR SW16.....................179 K6
  THMD SE28...........................109 J6
  WOT/HER KT12 *......................188 A5
Byron Ct ENC/FH EN2.....................23 H1
  ERITH DA8...........................149 J1
  DUL SE21............................162 E5
  HRW HA1.............................60 D3
  STAN HA7 *...........................43 H5
Byron Dr EFNCH N2.......................65 H4
Byron Gdns SUT SM1...................209 H2
Byron Hill Rd RYLN/HDSTN HA2......60 D6
Byron Ms HAMP NW3......................83 J2
  MV/WKIL W9.........................100 E3
Byron Rd ALP/SUD HA0...................79 J1
  CRICK NW2............................63 K6
  EA W5...............................117 G1
  HRW HA1.............................60 E3

  KTN/HRWW/WS HA3......................43 F6
  LEY E10.............................69 K5
  MLHL NW7.............................45 J1
  WALTH E17............................51 J6
Byron St ED N9 *.........................36 E4
Byron Wy NTHLT UB5......................95 J2
  WDR/YW UB7.........................112 C4
  YEAD UB4............................94 D4
Bysouth Cl CLAY IG5......................54 B4
  SEVS/STOTM N15......................67 K1
By The Wd OXHEY WD19.................27 J4
Bythorn St BRXN/ST SW9...............142 A4
Byton Rd TOOT SW17...................178 E2
Byward Av EBED/NFELT TW14.......154 B1
Byward St MON EC3R.....................13 H6
Bywater Pl BERM/RHTH SE16........124 B1
Bywater St CHEL SW3...................120 E5
The Byway BELMT SM2.................209 H6
  HOR/WEW KT19 *.....................207 H2
Bywell Pl GTPST W1W *..................10 A2
Bywood Av CROY/NA CR0.............197 K3

C

Cabbell St BAY/PAD W2....................8 C3
Cabinet Wy CHING E4......................51 H2
Cable Pl GNWCH SE10...................145 F2
Cables Cl ERITH DA8....................129 K3
Cable St WCHPL E1......................104 C6
Cable Trade Pk CHARL SE7 *..........125 K5
Cabot Sq POP/IOD E14.................124 D1
Cabot Wy EHAM E6........................89 H6
Cabul Rd BTSEA SW11.................140 D3
Cactus Cl CMBW SE5 *.................143 F3
Cadbury Cl ISLW TW7...................136 B2
Cadbury Rd BERM/RHTH SE16.........19 K6
Caddington Cl EBAR EN4.................21 J6
Caddington Rd CRICK NW2..............82 C1
Caddis Cl STAN HA7 *....................43 F5
Cadell Cl BETH E2..........................7 J3
Cade Rd GNWCH SE10..................145 G2
Cader Rd WAND/EARL SW18.........160 B1
Cadet Dr STHWK SE1...................123 G5
Cadet Pl GNWCH SE10.................125 H5
Cadiz Rd DAGE RM10.....................92 E5
Cadiz St WALW SE17....................122 D5
Cadmus Cl BRXN/ST SW9 *...........142 C1
Cadmer Cl NWMAL KT3................192 B1
Cadmus Cl CLAP SW4..................141 J3
Cadogan Cl HOM E9........................87 H5
  RYLN/HDSTN HA2......................78 B2
  TEDD TW11...........................173 K1
Cadogan Gdns BELMT SM2..............15 F7
Cadogan Gdns CHEL SW3...............15 F7
  FNCH N3................................47 F4
  SWFD E18..............................53 F6
  WCHMH N21............................23 G6
Cadogan Ga KTBR SW1X.................15 F6
Cadogan La KTBR SW1X...............15 G5
Cadogan Pl SURB KT6..................190 E2
Cadogan Pl KTBR SW1X..................15 F5
Cadogan Sq CHEL SW3..................15 F6
  KTBR SW1X...........................15 F6
Cadogan Ter HOM E9......................87 J5
Cadoxton Av SEVS/STOTM N15......68 B3
Cadwallon Rd ELTH/MOT SE9........167 G4
Caedmon Rd HOLWY N7...................85 F2
Caenwood Cl ESH/CLAY KT10.......204 B3
  SCUP DA14..........................186 D1
Caernarvon Cl MTCM CR4.............179 K6
Caernarvon Dr CLAY IG5.................54 A4
Caesars Wk MTCM CR4................194 E2
Cahill St STLK EC1Y *.....................6 E7
Cahir St POP/IOD E14..................124 E4
Cain's La EBED/NFELT TW14...........133 G6
Caird St NKENS W10....................100 D2
Cairn Av EA W5..........................116 E1
Cairndale Cl BMLY BR1................183 J3
Cairnfield Av CRICK NW2................81 G1
Cairngorm Cl TEDD TW11 *...........174 A1
Cairns Av WFD IG8........................53 K2
Cairns Cl DART DA1.....................151 G6
Cairns Rd BTSEA SW11................140 D6
Cairn Wy STAN HA7.......................43 F2
Cairo New Rd CROY/NA CR0.........196 C6
Cairo Rd WALTH E17......................51 J5
Caister Ms BAL SW12..................161 G2
Caister Park Rd SRTFD E15............88 D6
Caistor Rd BAL SW12..................161 G2
Caithness Gdns BFN/LL DA15........168 A1
Caithness Rd MTCM CR4..............179 G3
  WKENS W14..........................119 G3
Calabria Rd HBRY N5......................85 H4
Calais St CMBW SE5....................142 C2
Calbourne Av HCH RM12...............93 K3
Calbourne Rd BAL SW12...............160 E2
Caldecote Gdns BUSH WD23............29 F2
Caldecote La BUSH WD23................29 F1
Caldecot Rd CMBW SE5..................142 D3
Caldecott Wy CLPT E5...................87 F1
Calder Av GFD/PVL UB6.................97 F1
Calder Gdns EDGW HA8.................44 C6
Calder Rd MRDN SM4..................194 B2
Caldervale Rd CLAP SW4..............141 J6
Calderwood St
  WOOL/PLUM SE18...................127 F4
Caldew St CMBW SE5 *................142 E1
Caldicote Gn CDALE/KGS NW9 *......63 G3
Caldwell Rd OXHEY WD19................27 H6
Caldwell St BRXN/ST SW9.............142 A1
Caldy Rd BELV DA17....................129 J3
Caldy Wk IS N1 *..........................85 J4
Caledonian Rd
  GDMY/SEVK IG3......................73 H5
Caledonian Rd HOLWY N7................85 F3
  IS N1................................85 F6
Caledonian Sq CAMTN NW1 *...........84 D4
Caledonian Wharf Rd
  POP/IOD E14.........................125 G4

Caledonia Rd
  STWL/WRAY TW19 .....152 B3
Caledonia St IS N1 * 5 F3
Caledon Rd EHAM E6 .....89 K6
  WLGTN SM6 .....210 A2
Cale St CHEL SW3 .....120 D5
Calidore Cl
  BRXS/STRHM SW2 * 162 A1
California La BUSH WD23 .....28 D3
California Rd NWMAL KT3 .....191 H1
Callaby Ter IS N1 * 85 K4
Callaghan Cottages
  WCHPL E1 * 104 E4
Callander Rd CAT SE6 .....164 E4
The Callanders BUSH WD23 * 28 E3
Callard Av PLMGR N13 .....49 H1
Callcott Av KIL/WHAMP NW6 .....82 D5
Callcott St KENS W8 .....119 K1
Calendar Rd SKENS SW7 .....14 B4
Callingham Cl POP/IOD E14 .....105 H4
Callis Farm Cl
  STWL/WRAY TW19 .....152 B3
Callisons Pl GNWCH SE10 .....125 H5
Callis Rd WALTH E17 .....69 H3
Callow St WBPTN SW10 .....120 B6
Calmington Rd CMBW SE5 .....123 F6
Calmont Rd BMLY BR1 .....183 G2
Calne Av CLAY IG5 .....54 B4
Calonne Rd WIM/MER SW19 .....159 G6
Calshot Rd HTHAIR TW6 .....132 E3
Calshot St IS N1 * 5 L4
Calshot Wy ENC/FH EN2 .....23 H4
  HTHAIR TW6 .....132 E3
Calthorpe Gdns EDGW HA8 .....44 B1
  SUT SM1 .....209 G1
Calthorpe St FSBYW WC1X 5 M8
Calton Av DUL SE21 .....163 F1
Calton Rd BAR EN5 .....33 G1
Calverley Cl BECK BR3 .....182 E2
Calverley Crs DAGE RM10 .....74 C6
Calverley Gv ARCH N19 .....66 D5
Calverley Rd EW KT17 .....207 J4
Calvert Av WCHPL E1 * 7 K9
Calvert Cl BELV DA17 .....129 H4
  SCUP DA14 .....187 F2
Calvert Dr RDART DA2 .....170 B4
Calverton Rd EHAM E6 .....90 A6
Calvert Rd BAR EN5 .....20 C3
  GNWCH SE10 .....125 J5
Calvin Cl STMC/STPC BR5 .....186 E6
Calvin St WCHPL E1 .....7 L1
Calydon Rd CHARL SE7 .....126 A5
Calypso Crs PECK SE15 * 123 G6
Calypso Wy BERM/RHTH SE16 .....124 C3
Camac Rd WHTN TW2 .....155 J4
Camarthen Gn
  CDALE/KGS NW9 .....63 G3
Cambalt Rd PUT/ROE SW15 .....139 G6
Camberley Av EN EN1 .....24 A5
  RYNPK SW20 .....176 E5
Camberley Cl CHEAM SM3 .....208 B1
Camberley Rd HTHAIR TW6 .....132 D4
Cambert Wy BKHTH/KID SE3 .....146 A5
Camberwell Church St
  CMBW SE5 .....142 E2
Camberwell Glebe CMBW SE5 .....142 E2
Camberwell Gn CMBW SE5 .....142 E2
Camberwell Gv CMBW SE5 .....142 E2
Camberwell New Rd
  CMBW SE5 .....142 C1
Camberwell Station Rd
  CMBW SE5 .....142 D2
Cambeys Rd DAGE RM10 .....92 E5
Camborne Av WEA W13 .....116 D2
Camborne Cl HTHAIR TW6 .....132 D4
Camborne Crs HTHAIR TW6 .....132 D4
Camborne Ms
  WAND/EARL SW18 .....159 K2
Camborne Rd BELMT SM2 .....208 E5
  CROY/NA CR0 .....197 H4
  MRDN SM4 .....193 G2
  SCUP DA14 .....168 D5
  WAND/EARL SW18 .....159 K2
  WELL DA16 .....147 K3
Camborne Wy HEST TW5 .....135 F2
Cambourne Av ED N9 .....37 F2
Cambray Rd BAL SW12 .....161 H3
  ORP BR6 .....202 A4
Cambria Cl BFN/LL DA15 .....167 K3
  HSLW TW3 .....135 F5
Cambria Ct EBED/NFELT TW14 .....154 A2
Cambria Gdns
  STWL/WRAY TW19 .....152 B2
Cambrian Av GNTH/NBYPK IG2 .....72 C2
Cambrian Cl WNWD SE27 .....162 C5
Cambrian Gn CDALE/KGS NW9 .....63 G2
Cambrian Rd LEY E10 .....69 J3
  RCHPK/HAM TW10 .....157 G1
Cambria Rd CMBW SE5 .....142 D4
Cambria St FUL/PGN SW6 .....140 A1
Cambridge Av GFD/PVL UB6 .....79 F4
  KIL/WHAMP NW6 .....100 E1
  NWMAL KT3 .....176 C5
  WELL DA16 .....148 A5
Cambridge Barracks Rd
  WOOL/PLUM SE18 .....126 E4
Cambridge Circ
  SOHO/SHAV W1D 10 G4
Cambridge Cl HSLWW TW4 .....134 D5
  RYNPK SW20 .....176 E4
  WALTH E17 .....69 J3
  WDGN N22 .....49 G4
  WDR/YW UB7 .....112 A6
  WLSDN NW10 .....80 E1
Cambridge Crs BETH E2 .....104 D1
  TEDD TW11 * 174 B1
Cambridge Dr LEE/GVPK SE12 .....145 K6
  RSLP HA4 .....77 F2
Cambridge Gdns EN EN1 .....24 C3
  KIL/WHAMP NW6 .....100 E1
  KUT/HW KT1 .....175 H5
  MUSWH N10 .....48 B4
  NKENS W10 .....100 C5

TOTM N17 .....49 K3
WALTH E17 * 35 K2
Cambridge Ga CAMTN NW1 * 3 J6
Cambridge Gate Ms CAMTN NW1 * 3 K6
Cambridge Gn ELTH/MOT SE9 .....167 G3
Cambridge Gv HMSMTH W6 .....118 E4
  PGE/AN SE20 * 181 J4
Cambridge Grove Rd
  KUT/HW KT1 .....175 H6
Cambridge Heath Rd BETH E2 .....104 D2
Cambridge Pde EN EN1 * 24 C1
Cambridge Pk TWK TW1 .....156 E2
Cambridge Park Rd WAN E11 .....70 E4
Cambridge Pas HOM E9 .....86 E5
Cambridge Pl KENS W8 .....120 A2
Cambridge Rd BARK IG11 .....90 C5
  BARN SW13 .....138 C3
  BMLY BR1 .....183 K5
  BTSEA SW11 .....140 E2
  CAR SM5 .....209 J4
  CHING E4 .....38 B3
  E/WMO/HCT KT8 .....188 E1
  GDMY/SEVK IG3 .....72 E5
  HNWL W7 .....116 A3
  HPTN TW12 .....172 E5
  HSLWW TW4 .....134 D5
  KIL/WHAMP NW6 .....100 E1
  KUT/HW KT1 .....175 H5
  MTCM CR4 .....179 G1
  NWMAL KT3 .....176 B1
  PGE/AN SE20 .....181 H6
  RCH/KEW TW9 .....137 H1
  RYLN/HDSTN HA2 .....60 A2
  RYNPK SW20 .....176 E4
  SCUP DA14 .....167 K6
  STHL UB1 .....114 E1
  TEDD TW11 .....156 B4
  TWK TW1 .....156 E1
  WAN E11 .....70 E4
  WOT/HER KT12 .....188 A3
Cambridge Rd North
  CHSWK W4 .....117 J5
Cambridge Rd South
  CHSWK W4 .....117 J5
Cambridge Rw
  WOOL/PLUM SE18 .....127 G5
Cambridge Sq BAY/PAD W2 .....9 J3
Cambridge St PIM SW1V 121 G5
Cambridge Ter CAMTN NW1 * 3 J6
  ED N9 * 36 B2
Cambridge Terrace Ms
  CAMTN NW1 * 3 K5
Cambstone Rd LEE/GVPK SE12 * 116 A2
Cambus Rd CAN/RD E16 .....106 E4
Camdale Rd WOOL/PLUM SE18 .....148 A1
Camden Av FELT TW13 .....154 B4
  YEAD UB4 .....95 G6
Camden Cl CHST BR7 .....185 G3
Camden Gdns CAMTN NW1 * 84 B5
  SUT SM1 .....209 F3
  THHTH CR7 .....180 C6
Camden Gv CHST BR7 .....185 G2
Camden High St CAMTN NW1 .....4 A1
Camden Hill Rd NRWD SE19 .....181 F2
Camdenhurst St POP/IOD E14 .....105 G5
Camden Lock Pl CAMTN NW1 .....84 B5
Camden Ms CAMTN NW1 .....84 D4
Camden Park Rd CAMTN NW1 .....84 D4
  CHST BR7 .....184 E3
Camden Pas IS N1 .....6 C4
Camden Rd BXLY DA5 .....169 G3
  CAMTN NW1 .....84 B6
  CAR SM5 .....209 K3
  SUT SM1 .....209 F3
  WALTH E17 .....69 H3
  WAN E11 .....71 F1
Camden Rd Permanent Wy
  CAMTN NW1 * 4 C1
Camden Rw BKHTH/KID SE3 .....145 H3
  PIN HA5 * 41 G6
Camden Sq CAMTN NW1 .....84 D5
Camden St CAMTN NW1 .....84 D5
Camden Ter CAMTN NW1 * 84 D4
Camden Wk IS N1 .....6 A1
Camden Wy CHST BR7 .....184 E3
  THHTH CR7 .....180 C6
Camelford Wk NTGHL W11 * 100 C5
Camel Gv KUTN/CMB KT2 .....174 E1
Camellia Pl WHTN TW2 .....155 G2
Camellia St VX/NE SW8 .....141 K1
Camelot Cl THMD SE28 .....127 J3
  WIM/MER SW19 .....159 J6
Camel Rd CAN/RD E16 .....107 H6
Camera Pl WBPTN SW10 .....120 C6
Cameron Cl BXLY DA5 .....170 B5
  TRDG/WHET N20 .....33 J4
  UED N18 .....50 D1
Cameron Pl STRHM/NOR SW16 .....162 B5
Cameron Rd CAT SE6 * 164 C4
  CROY/NA CR0 .....196 C3
  GDMY/SEVK IG3 .....72 E5
  HAYES BR2 .....199 K2
Cameron Sq MTCM CR4 .....178 D4
Cameron Ter LEE/GVPK SE12 * 166 A5
Camerton Cl HACK E8 .....86 C6
Camilla Rd BERM/RHTH SE16 .....123 J4
Camille Cl SNWD SE25 .....181 H6
Camlan Rd BMLY BR1 .....165 J6
Camlet St BETH E2 .....7 L9
Camlet Wy EBAR EN4 .....20 E5
Camm Gdns KUT/HW KT1 .....175 G5
  THDIT KT7 .....189 K4
Camomile Av MTCM CR4 .....178 E4
Camomile St HDTCH EC3A 13 H4
Camomile Rd ROMW/RG RM7 .....75 F6
Campana Rd FUL/PGN SW6 .....139 K2
Campbell Av BARK/HLT IG6 .....72 C1
Campbell Cl ROM RM1 .....57 G2
  RSLP HA4 * 58 E3
  STRHM/NOR SW16 .....179 J1
  WHTN TW2 .....155 H4
  WOOL/PLUM SE18 .....147 F2

Campbell Cft EDGW HA8 .....44 C1
Campbell Gordon Wy
  CRICK NW2 .....81 K2
Campbell Rd BOW E3 .....105 J2
  CROY/NA CR0 .....196 C4
  EHAM E6 .....89 J6
  HNWL W7 .....96 E6
  SRTFD E15 .....88 C2
  TOTM N17 .....50 B4
  WALTH E17 .....69 G1
  WHTN TW2 .....155 J4
Campbell Wk IS N1 * 84 E6
Campden Gv KENS W8 .....119 K2
Campden Hill Gdns KENS W8 .....119 K1
Campden Hill Ga KENS W8 * 119 K2
Campden Hill Pl NTGHL W11 * 119 J1
Campden Hill Rd KENS W8 .....119 K2
Campden Hill Sq KENS W8 .....119 J1
Campden House Cl KENS W8 .....119 K2
Campden House Ter
  KENS W8 * 119 K1
Campden Rd SAND/SEL CR2 .....212 A3
Campden St KENS W8 .....119 K1
Campden Ter CHSWK W4 * 118 B5
Campen Cl WIM/MER SW19 .....159 H4
Camperdown St WCHPL E1 .....13 M4
Campfield Rd ELTH/MOT SE9 .....166 C2
Campion Cl CROY/NA CR0 .....212 A2
  EHAM E6 .....107 K6
  KTN/HRWW/WS HA3 .....43 K6
  ROMW/RG RM7 .....75 F6
Campion Ct ALP/SUD HA0 .....98 A1
Campion Gdns WFD IG8 .....52 E1
Campion Pl THMD SE28 .....128 C1
Campion Rd ISLW TW7 .....136 A2
  PUT/ROE SW15 .....139 F5
Campion Ter CRICK NW2 .....82 B1
Camplin Rd KTN/HRWW/WS HA3 .....62 A2
Camplin St NWCR SE14 .....144 A1
Camp Rd WIM/MER SW19 .....176 C1
Campsbourne Pde
  CEND/HSY/T N8 * 66 E1
The Campsbourne
  CEND/HSY/T N8 .....66 E1
Campsey Gdns DAGW RM9 .....91 H5
Campsey Rd DAGW RM9 .....91 H5
Campsfield Rd CEND/HSY/T N8 .....48 E6
Campshill Pl LEW SE13 .....145 F6
Campshill Rd LEW SE13 .....145 F6
Campus Rd WALTH E17 .....69 H3
Camp Vw WIM/MER SW19 .....176 E1
Camrose Av ERITH DA8 .....129 K6
  FELT TW13 .....154 A6
  STAN HA7 .....43 F4
Camrose Cl CROY/NA CR0 .....198 B4
  MRDN SM4 .....193 K1
Camrose St WOOL/PLUM SE18 .....128 B5
Canada Av UED N18 .....49 J2
Canada Crs ACT W3 .....98 E4
Canada Park Pde EDGW HA8 * 44 D4
  ERITH DA8 .....150 C1
Canada Sqaure POP/IOD E14 .....124 E1
Canada St BERM/RHTH SE16 .....124 A2
Canada Wy SHB W12 .....99 K6
Canadian Av CAT SE6 .....164 E3
Canal Ap DEPT SE8 .....124 B5
Canal Cl NKENS W10 .....100 B3
  WCHPL E1 .....105 H3
Canal Gv PECK SE15 .....123 H6
Canal Pth BETH E2 .....7 J1
Canal St CMBW SE5 .....122 E6
Canal Wk CROY/NA CR0 .....197 G3
  IS N1 .....85 K6
  WLSDN NW10 * 99 H3
Canal Wy NKENS W10 .....100 B3
Canal Whf GFD/PVL UB6 * 79 G6
Canal Yd NWDGN UB2 * 114 A4
Canberra Cl DAGE RM10 .....93 F5
  HDN NW4 .....45 J2
Canberra Crs DAGE RM10 .....93 G5
Canberra Dr NTHLT UB5 .....95 C2
Canberra Rd HTHAIR TW6 .....132 D4
  ABYW SE2 .....128 E6
  CHARL SE7 .....126 B6
  EHAM E6 .....89 K6
  WEA W13 .....116 B1
Canbury Av KUTN/CMB KT2 .....175 G4
Canbury Ms SYD SE26 .....163 H5
Canbury Park Rd
  KUTN/CMB KT2 .....175 F4
Canbury Pth STMC/STPC BR5 .....202 B1
Candahar Rd BTSEA SW11 .....140 D3
Candle Gv PECK SE15 .....143 J4
Candlelight Ct SRTFD E15 .....88 D4
Candler Ms TWK TW1 .....156 B2
Candler St SEVS/STOTM N15 * 67 K3
Candover Cl WDR/YW UB7 .....132 A1
Candover Rd HCH RM12 .....93 K4
Candover St GTPST W1W * 10 E3
Candy St BOW E3 .....87 H6
Caney Ms CRICK NW2 .....64 B6
Canfield Dr RSLP HA4 .....77 F3
Canfield Gdns KIL/WHAMP NW6 .....83 F5
Canfield Pl KIL/WHAMP NW6 .....83 G5
Canfield Rd RAIN RM13 .....93 H6
  WFD IG8 .....53 J3
Canford Av NTHLT UB5 .....95 J1
Canford Cl ENC/FH EN2 .....23 G3
Canford Gdns NWMAL KT3 .....192 B3
Canford Pl TEDD TW11 .....174 C2
Canford Rd CLAP SW4 .....141 F5
Canham Rd CHSWK W4 .....118 B3
  SNWD SE25 .....181 F6
Canmore Gdns
  STRHM/NOR SW16 .....179 H3
Cann Hall Rd WAN E11 .....88 D1
Canning Crs WDGN N22 .....49 F4

Canning Cross CMBW SE5 .....143 F3
Canning Rd CROY/NA CR0 .....197 G6
Canning Place Ms KENS W8 * 120 B3
Canning Rd CROY/NA CR0 .....197 G6
  HBRY N5 .....85 J1
  KTN/HRWW/WS HA3 .....61 G1
  SRTFD E15 .....106 C1
  WALTH E17 .....69 G1
Cannington Rd DAGW RM9 .....91 J4
Cannizaro Rd WIM/MER SW19 .....177 F2
Cannonbury Av PIN HA5 .....59 H5
Cannon Cl HPTN TW12 .....173 F2
  RYNPK SW20 .....177 F6
Cannon Dr POP/IOD E14 .....105 J6
Cannon Hill KIL/WHAMP NW6 .....83 F3
  STHGT/OAK N14 .....34 E5
Cannon Hill La RYNPK SW20 .....193 G2
Cannon La HAMP NW3 .....83 H1
  PIN HA5 .....59 J2
Cannon Pl CHARL SE7 .....126 D5
  HAMP NW3 .....83 H1
  STHGT/OAK N14 .....34 E5
Cannon St BLKFR EC4V 12 C4
Cannon Street Rd WCHPL E1 .....104 D5
Cannon St E/WMO/HCT KT8 .....189 F1
Canon Av CHDH RM6 .....73 J2
Canon Beck Rd
  BERM/RHTH SE16 .....123 K2
Canonbie Rd FSTH SE23 .....163 K2
Canonbury Crs IS N1 .....85 J5
Canonbury Gv IS N1 .....85 J5
Canonbury La IS N1 .....85 H5
Canonbury Pk North IS N1 .....85 J4
Canonbury Pk South IS N1 .....85 J4
Canonbury Pl IS N1 .....85 H4
Canonbury Rd EN EN1 .....24 A2
  IS N1 .....85 H4
Canonbury Sq IS N1 .....85 H5
Canonbury St IS N1 .....85 J5
Canonbury Vis IS N1 .....85 H5
Canonbury Yd East IS N1 * 85 H4
Canon Mohan Cl
  STHGT/OAK N14 .....34 A1
Canon Murnane Rd STHWK SE1 .....19 L3
Canon Rd BMLY BR1 .....184 B6
Canon Rw WHALL SW1A 17 J1
Canons Cl EDGW HA8 .....44 B2
  EFNCH N2 .....65 H4
Canons Cottages EDGW HA8 * 44 B2
Canons Cnr EDGW HA8 .....44 A1
Canonsleigh Rd DAGW RM9 .....91 H5
Canon St IS N1 .....6 C1
Canon's Wk CROY/NA CR0 .....213 F1
Canopus Wy NTHWD HA6 .....26 B6
  STWL/WRAY TW19 .....152 B2
Canrobert St BETH E2 .....104 D2
Cantelowes Av BFN/LL DA15 .....168 D4
  IL IG1 .....71 J4
Canterbury Cl BECK BR3 .....182 D5
  CMBW SE5 .....142 D3
  DART DA1 .....171 K2
  EHAM E6 .....107 K5
  GFD/PVL UB6 .....96 B4
  NTHWD HA6 .....40 D1
Canterbury Crs BRXN/ST SW9 .....142 B4
Canterbury Gv WNWD SE27 .....162 C5
Canterbury Pl WALW SE17 .....18 E7
Canterbury Rd CROY/NA CR0 .....196 A4
  FELT TW13 .....154 D4
  HRW HA1 .....60 B2
  KIL/WHAMP NW6 .....100 E1
  LEY E10 .....70 A4
  MRDN SM4 .....194 B3
Canterbury Ter
  KIL/WHAMP NW6 .....100 E1
Cantley Gdns GNTH/NBYPK IG2 .....72 D3
  NRWD SE19 .....181 G4
Cantley Rd HNWL W7 .....116 B3
Canton St POP/IOD E14 .....105 J5
Cantrell Rd BOW E3 .....105 J3
Cantwell Rd
  WOOL/PLUM SE18 .....147 G1
Canute Gdns
  BERM/RHTH SE16 .....124 A4
Canvey St STHWK SE1 .....12 C7
Cape Cl BARK IG11 .....90 B5
Capel Av WLGTN SM6 .....211 F4
  KTN/HRWW/WS HA3 .....61 K4
Capel Cl HAYES BR2 .....200 D5
  TRDG/WHET N20 .....33 G5
Capel Gdns GDMY/SEVK IG3 .....91 F2
  PIN HA5 .....59 K1
Capella Rd NTHWD HA6 .....40 D1
Capel Pl RDART DA2 .....170 D5
Capel Rd EBAR EN4 .....33 J1
  FSTGT E7 .....89 G2
  OXHEY WD19 .....27 J1
Capener's Cl KTBR SW1X 15 G3
Capern Rd WAND/EARL SW18 .....160 B3
Capital Interchange Wy
  BTFD TW8 .....117 H5
Capitol Wy CDALE/KGS NW9 .....44 E6
Capland St STJWD NW8 .....2 E9
Caple Pde WLSDN NW10 * 99 H1
Caple Rd WLSDN NW10 .....99 H1
Capra Cl YEAD UB4 .....94 E1
Capri Rd CROY/NA CR0 .....197 G4
Capstan Cl CHDH RM6 .....73 H3
Capstan Ride ENC/FH EN2 .....23 G3
Capstan Rd DEPT SE8 .....124 C4
Capstan Sq POP/IOD E14 .....125 F2
Capstan Wy BERM/RHTH SE16 .....124 B1
Capstone Rd BMLY BR1 .....165 J6
Capthorne Av
  RYLN/HDSTN HA2 .....59 J5
Capuchin Cl STAN HA7 .....43 H2
Capulet Ms CAN/RD E16 .....125 J1
Capworth St LEY E10 .....69 K4
Caractacus Cottage Vw
  WATW WD18 .....26 E2
Caractacus Gn WATW WD18 * 26 D2
Caradoc Cl BAY/PAD W2 .....100 D5
Caradoc Evans Cl
  FBAR/BDGN N11 * 48 B1

Caradoc St GNWCH SE10 .....125 H5
Caradon Cl WAN E11 .....70 C5
Caradon Wy SEVS/STOTM N15 .....67 K1
Caravel Cl MAN DEPT SE8 * 124 D6
Caraway Cl PLSTW E13 .....107 F4
Caraway Pl HMSMTH W6 .....210 B1
Carberry Rd NRWD SE19 .....181 F2
Carbery Av ACT W3 .....117 G2
Carbis Cl CHING E4 .....38 B3
Carbis Rd POP/IOD E14 .....105 H5
Cardale St POP/IOD E14 .....125 F3
Carden Rd PECK SE15 .....143 J4
Cardiff Rd HNWL W7 .....116 B3
  PEND 24 D5
  WATW WD18 .....27 F1
Cardiff St WOOL/PLUM SE18 .....147 K1
Cardigan Gdns GDMY/SEVK IG3 .....73 G6
Cardigan Pl LEW SE13 * 145 G3
Cardigan Rd BARN SW13 .....138 D3
  BOW E3 .....105 H1
  RCHPK/HAM TW10 .....157 F1
Cardigan St LBTH SE11 .....122 B5
Cardigan Wk IS N1 * 85 J5
Cardinal Av KUTN/CMB KT2 .....175 F1
  MRDN SM4 .....193 H3
Cardinal Bourne St
  STHWK SE1 .....19 F5
Cardinal Cl CHST BR7 .....185 J4
  EDGW HA8 .....44 E3
  MRDN SM4 .....193 H3
  WPK KT4 .....207 J2
Cardinal Crs NWMAL KT3 .....175 K5
Cardinal Dr BARK/HLT IG6 .....54 C2
  WOT/HER KT12 .....188 C3
Cardinal Hinsey Cl
  WLSDN NW10 .....99 J1
Cardinal Pl PUT/ROE SW15 .....139 G5
Cardinal Rd FELT TW13 .....154 A3
  RSLP HA4 .....59 H1
Cardinal's Wk HPTN TW12 .....173 H3
Cardinals Wy ARCH N19 .....66 D5
Cardinal Wy
  KTN/HRWW/WS HA3 .....42 E6
Cardine Ms PECK SE15 .....143 J1
Cardington Sq HSLWW TW4 .....134 C4
Cardington St CAMTN NW1 .....4 F7
Cardozo Rd HOLWY N7 .....84 E3
Cardrew Av
  NFNCH/WDSPK N12 .....47 H1
Cardross St HMSMTH W6 .....118 E3
Cardwell Rd HOLWY N7 * 84 E2
Cardwell Ter HOLWY N7 * 84 E2
Carew Cl HOLWY N7 .....67 F6
Carew Rd MTCM CR4 .....179 F5
  NTHWD HA6 .....40 C2
  THHTH CR7 .....180 C6
  TOTM N17 .....50 D4
  WEA W13 .....116 D2
  WLGTN SM6 .....210 C4
Carew St CMBW SE5 .....142 D3
Carew Wy OXHEY WD19 .....27 K5
  STMC/STPC BR5 .....202 D5
Carey Gdns VX/NE SW8 .....141 H2
Carey La CITYW EC2V 12 C3
Carey Pl PIM SW1V 16 F6
Carey Rd DAGW RM9 .....92 A2
Carey St LINN WC2A 11 M4
Carfax Pl CLAP SW4 .....141 J5
Carfax Rd HCH RM12 .....93 K5
  HYS/HAR UB3 .....113 K5
The Carfax SYD SE26 * 163 K5
Carfree Cl IS N1 .....85 G5
Cargill Rd WAND/EARL SW18 .....160 A3
Cargreen Rd SNWD SE25 .....197 G1
Carholme Rd FSTH SE23 .....164 C3
Carisbrook Cl EN EN1 .....24 B2
Carisbrooke Av BXLY DA5 .....168 E3
Carisbrooke Cl HSLWW TW4 .....154 E6
  STAN HA7 .....43 K5
  STNW/STAM N16 .....86 A2
Carisbrooke Gdns
  PECK SE15 .....143 G1
Carisbrooke Rd HAYES BR2 .....200 B1
  MTCM CR4 .....195 K1
  WALTH E17 .....69 G1
Carker's La KTTN NW5 .....84 B3
Carleton Cl ESH/CLAY KT10 .....189 J5
Carleton Gdns ARCH N19 * 84 C3
Carleton Rd DART DA1 .....171 K2
  HOLWY N7 .....84 D3
Carleton Vis KTTN NW5 * 84 C3
Carlile Cl BOW E3 .....105 H1
Carlina Gdns WFD IG8 .....53 F1
Carlingford Rd HAMP NW3 .....83 H2
  MRDN SM4 .....193 G3
  SEVS/STOTM N15 .....49 J6
Carlisle Av ACT W3 .....99 G5
  TWRH EC3N 13 J4
Carlisle Cl KUTN/CMB KT2 .....175 G4
  PIN HA5 .....59 J4
Carlisle Gdns IL IG1 .....71 J4
  KTN/HRWW/WS HA3 .....61 K4
Carlisle La STHWK SE1 .....17 M3
  WEST SW1P 16 A5
Carlisle Rd CDALE/KGS NW9 .....44 E6
  DART DA1 .....171 K1
  FSBYPK N4 .....67 G5
  HPTN TW12 .....173 G3
  KIL/WHAMP NW6 .....82 C6
  LEY E10 .....69 J5
  ROM RM1 .....75 H2
Carlisle St SOHO/SHAV W1D 10 F4
Carlisle Wk HACK E8 .....86 B4
Carlisle Wy TOOT SW17 .....179 F1
Carlos Pl MYFR/PKLN W1K 9 H6
Carlton Av EBED/NFELT TW14 .....134 B1
  HYS/HAR UB3 .....113 J3
  KTN/HRWW/WS HA3 .....43 K6
  SAND/SEL CR2 .....211 K5
  STHGT/OAK N14 .....22 D6

Carlton Av East WBLY HA9 ....61 K6
Carlton Av West ALP/SUD HA0 ......27 J4
Carlton Cl CHSGTN KT9 ....205 K4
 EDGW HA8 ....44 C1
 HAMP NW3 ....64 E6
Carlton Crs CHEAM SM3 ....208 C2
Carlton Dene EW KT17 * 207 K3
Carlton Dr BARK/HLT IG6 ....54 D6
 PUT/ROE SW15 ....139 G6
Carlton Gdns EA W5 ....97 J5
 STJS SW1Y 16
Carlton Ga MV/WKIL W9 ....100 E4
Carlton Gn SCUP DA14 * 168 A6
Carlton Gv PECK SE15 ....143 J2
Carlton HI STJWD NW8 ....101 G1
Carlton House Ter STJS SW1Y 16 C1
Carlton Ms KIL/WHAMP NW6 * 82 A5
Carlton Pde WBLY HA9 * 62 A5
Carlton Park Av RYNPK SW20 ....177 F5
Carlton Rd CHSWK W4 ....118 A2
 EA W5 ....97 J6
 ERITH DA8 ....129 K6
 FBAR/BDGN N11 ....48 A1
 FSBYPK N4 ....67 G4
 GPK RM2 ....75 J2
 MNPK E12 ....89 H2
 MORT/ESHN SW14 ....137 K4
 NWMAL KT3 ....176 B5
 SAND/SEL CR2 ....211 K5
 SCUP DA14 ....186 A1
 WALTH E17 ....51 G4
 WAN E11 ....70 D5
 WELL DA16 ....148 C4
 WOT/HER KT12 ....188 A4
Carlton Sq WCHPL E1 * 105 F3
Carlton St STJS SW1Y 10 C6
 UED UB4 ....35 K6
 WAN E11 ....71 F2
Carlton Tower PI KTBR SW1X 15 F4
Carlton V KIL/WHAMP NW6 ....100 E2
Cartwell St TOOT SW17 ....178 D1
Carlyle Av BMLY BR1 ....184 C6
 STHL UB1 ....95 K6
Carlyle Cl E/WMO/HCT KT8 ......173 G6
 EFNCH N2 ....65 G3
 WLSDN NW10 ....81 F6
Carlyle Ct WBPTN SW10 * 140 B2
Carlyle Gdns STHL UB1 ....95 K6
Carlyle Rd CROY/NA CR0 ....197 H6
 EA W5 ....116 D4
 MNPK E12 ....89 J2
 THMD SE28 ....109 H6
Carlyle Sq CHEL SW3 ....120 C5
Carlyon CI RYLN/HDSTN HA2 .....77 K2
Carlyon CI ALP/SUD HA0 ....80 A6
 YEAD UB4 ....95 G5
Carlyon Rd ALP/SUD HA0 ....98 A1
Carmalt Gdns PUT/ROE SW15 ....139 F6
Carmel Ct KENS W8 * 120 A2
Carmelite Rd
 KTN/HRWW/WS HA3 ....42 C4
Carmelite St EMB EC4Y 11 K6
Carmen Wy RCH/KEW TW9 ....137 H5
Carmen St POP/IOD E14 ....105 K5
Carmichael CI BTSEA SW11 * ...140 C4
 RSLP HA4 ....76 E2
Carmichael Ms
 WAND/EARL SW18 ....160 C2
Carminia Rd TOOT SW17 ....161 G4
Carnaby St SOHO/CST W1F 10 A4
Carnac St WNWD SE27 ....162 E6
Carnanton Rd WALTH E17 ....52 B4
Carnarvon Av EN EN1 ....24 B3
Carnarvon Dr HYS/HAR UB3 .....113 F5
Carnarvon Rd BAR EN5 ....20 C4
 LEY E10 ....69 J4
 SRTFD E15 ....88 D4
 SWFD E18 ....52 D4
Carnation St ROMW/RG RM7 .....75 G6
Carnation St ABYW SE2 ....128 C5
Carnbrook Rd BKHTH/KID SE3 ...146 C4
Carnecke Gdns ELTH/MOT SE9 ...146 D6
Carnegie CI PEND EN3 ....25 K1
 SURB KT6 ....191 G6
Carnegie PI WIM/MER SW19 .....159 G5
Carnegie St IS N1 ....5 H2
Carnet CI DART DA1 ....170 A2
Carnforth CI HOR/WEW KT19 ....206 D4
Carnforth Gdns HCH RM12 ....93 J3
Carnforth Rd
 STRHM/NOR SW16 ....179 J3
Carnoustie Dr IS N1 ....85 F5
Carnoustie CI THMD SE28 ....109 K5
Carnwath Rd FUL/PGN SW6 .....139 K4
Carol CI HDN NW4 ....64 B1
Carolina CI SRTFD E15 ....88 C3
Carolina Rd THHTH CR7 ....180 C5
Caroline CI CROY/NA CR0 ....212 A2
 ISLW TW7 ....135 K1
 MUSWH N10 ....48 B5
 STRHM/NOR SW16 ....162 A3
 WDR/YW UB7 * 112 A2
Caroline Ct STAN HA7 * 43 G2
Caroline Gdns BETH E2 ....7 H4
 PECK SE15 ....143 J1
Caroline PI BAY/PAD W2 ....101 F6
 BTSEA SW11 ....141 F3
 HYS/HAR UB3 ....133 H1
 OXHEY WD19 * 21 J1
Caroline PI WIM/MER SW19 .....177 J3
Caroline St WCHPL E1 ....105 F5
Caroline Ter BGVA SW1W 15 G7
Caroline Wk HMSMTH W6 ....119 H6
Carol St CAMTN NW1 ....84 C6
Carolyn Dr ORP BR6 ....217 G1
Carpenders Av OXHEY WD19 .....27 J5
Carpenter CI EW KT17 * 207 H6
Carpenter Gdns WCHMH N21 .....35 H4
Carpenters CI BAR EN5 ....33 F1
Carpenters Ms HOLWY N7 * 84 E3
Carpenters Rd SRTFD E15 ....87 K5
Carpenters St MYFR/PKLN W1K ...9 J3
Carrara Ms HACK E8 ....86 C3

Carrara Whf FUL/PGN SW6 ......139 H4
Carr CI STAN HA7 ....43 G2
Carre Ms CMBW SE5 ....142 C2
Carr Gv WOOL/PLUM SE18 ......126 D4
Carriage Dr East CHEL SW3 ....121 F6
Carriage Dr North
 BTSEA SW11 ....140 E1
Carriage Dr South
 BTSEA SW11 ....140 E2
Carriage Dr West BTSEA SW11 .140 E2
Carrick CI ISLW TW7 ....136 B4
Carrick Dr BARK/HLT IG6 ....54 C4
Carrick Ga ESH/CLAY KT10 .....204 C5
Carrick Ms DEPT SE8 ....124 D6
Carrill Wy BELV DA17 ....128 E4
Carrington Av HSLW TW3 ....135 G6
Carrington CI CROY/NA CR0 ....198 B4
Carrington Gdns FSTGT E7 ....88 E2
Carrington PI ESH/CLAY KT10 * 204 B2
 RCH/HAM TW10 ....137 H5
Carrington Sq
 KTN/HRWW/WS HA3 ....42 C3
Carrington St MYFR/PICC W1J ...15 J1
Carroll CI KTTN NW5 ....84 B2
Carroll CI SRTFD E15 ....88 D3
Carronade PI THMD SE28 ....127 H3
Carron CI POP/IOD E14 ....105 K5
Carroun Rd VX/NE SW8 ....142 A1
Carroway La GFD/PVL UB6 ....96 D2
Carr Rd DAGW RM9 ....91 H5
 NTHLT UB5 ....78 B5
 WALTH E17 ....51 H5
Carrs La WCHMH N21 ....23 K6
Carr St POP/IOD E14 ....105 G5
Carshalton Gv SUT SM1 ....209 H2
Carshalton Park Rd CAR SM5 ...209 K4
Carshalton PI CAR SM5 ....210 A3
Carshalton Rd MTCM CR4 ......195 F2
 SUT SM1 ....209 H2
Carsington Gdns DART DA1 .....171 G4
Carslake Rd PUT/ROE SW15 ....159 F1
Carson Rd CAN/RD E16 ....106 E4
 DUL SE21 ....162 E4
 EBAR EN4 ....21 K5
Carstairs Rd CAT SE6 ....165 F5
Carston CI LEE/GVPK SE12 .....145 J6
Carswell CI REDBR IG4 ....71 H1
Carswell Rd CAT SE6 ....165 F2
Carter CI CDALE/KGS NW9 ....63 F3
 CRW RM5 ....56 D3
 WLGTN SM6 ....210 D5
Carteret St STJSPK SW1H 16 C3
Carteret Wy DEPT SE8 ....124 B4
Carterhatch La EN EN1 ....24 C3
Carterhatch Rd PEND EN3 ......25 G3
Carter La BLKFR EC4V 12 B4
Carter PI WALW SE17 ....122 D5
Carter Rd PLSTW E13 ....89 F6
 WIM/MER SW19 ....178 C2
Carters CI KTTN NW5 * 84 D4
 WPK KT4 ....193 G6
Carters Hill CI ELTH/MOT SE9 ..166 A3
Carter's La STRHM/NOR SW16 ..180 A2
Carter's Yd WAND/EARL SW18 ..139 K6
Carthew Rd HMSMTH W6 ....118 E3
Carthew VIs HMSMTH W6 ....118 E3
Carthusian St FARR EC1M 12 C1
Carting La TPL/STR WC2R 11 F6
Cart La CHING E4 ....38 C5
Cartmel CI TOTM N17 ....50 D3
Cartmel Ct NTHLT UB5 ....77 J4
Cartmel Gdns MRDN SM4 ......194 B2
Cartmel Rd BXLYHN DA7 ....149 H2
Cartwright Gdns STPAN WC1H ...4 E5
Cartwright St WCHPL E1 ....13 K5
Cartwright Wy BARN SW13 .....138 E1
Carver CI CHSWK W4 ....117 K3
Carver Rd HNHL SE24 ....162 D1
Carville Crs BTFD TW8 ....117 F4
Cary Rd WAN E11 ....88 C2
Carysfort Rd CEND/HSY/T N8 ...66 D2
 STNW/STAM N16 ....85 K1
Cascade Av MUSWH N10 ....66 C1
Cascade CI STMC/STPC BR5 ...186 D6
Cascade Rd BKHH IG9 ....39 H5
Casella Rd NWCR SE14 ....144 A1
Casewick Rd WNWD SE27 .....180 C1
Casey CI STJWD NW8 ....2 C5
 STJWD NW8 ....2 D7
Casimir Rd CLPT E5 ....86 D1
Caspian CI HNWL SE24 ....142 E1
Caspian St CMBW SE5 ....142 E1
Caspian Wk CAN/RD E16 ....107 H5
Caspian Wy PUR RM19 ....131 K5
Cassandra CI NTHLT UB5 ....78 E2
Casselden Rd WLSDN NW10 ....81 F5
Cassidy Rd FUL/PGN SW6 .....139 K1
Cassilda Rd ABYW SE2 ....128 B4
Cassilis Rd POP/IOD E14 ......124 D2
 TWK TW1 ....156 C1
Cassiobury Av
 EBED/NFELT TW14 ....153 J2
Cassiobury Rd WALTH E17 ......69 F2
Cassland Rd HOM E9 ....87 F4
 THHTH CR7 ....196 E1
Casslee Rd CAT SE6 ....164 C2
Casson St WCHPL E1 ....104 C4
Castellain Rd MV/WKIL W9 .....101 F3
Castellane CI STAN HA7 * 57 K6
Castello Av PUT/ROE SW15 ....139 F6
Castelnau BARN SW13 ....138 E1
Casterbridge Rd
 BKHTH/KID SE3 ....145 K4
Casterton St HACK E8 ....86 D4
Castile Rd WOOL/PLUM SE18 ..127 F4
Castillon Rd CAT SE6 ....165 H4
Castlands Rd CAT SE6 ....164 C4
Castle Av CHING E4 ....52 B1
 EW KT17 ....207 J6
Castlebar HI EA W5 ....97 J4
Castlebar Ms EA W5 ....97 J4
Castlebar Pk EA W5 ....97 H4

Castlebar Rd WEA W13 ....97 J5
Castle Baynard St BLKFR EC4V ..12 C5
Castlebrook CI LBTH SE11 ....18 A6
Castle CI ACT W3 ....117 J2
 BUSH WD23 ....28 B1
 HAYES BR2 ....183 H6
 WIM/MER SW19 ....159 G5
Castlecombe Dr
 WIM/MER SW19 ....159 G5
Castlecombe Rd
 ELTH/MOT SE9 ....166 D6
Castle Ct BANK EC3V * 13 F4
 SYD SE26 ....164 B6
Castledine Rd PGE/AN SE20 ....181 J3
Castleford Av ELTH/MOT SE9 ..167 G3
Castleford CI TOTM N17 ....50 B2
Castlegate RCH/KEW TW9 .....137 G3
Castlehaven Rd CAMTN NW1 ....84 B5
Castle Hill Av CROY/NA CR0 ....213 K6
Castle Hill Pde WEA W13 * 97 H6
Castle La WESTW SW1E 16 A4
Castleleigh Ct ENC/FH EN2 ......23 J5
Castlemaine Av EW KT17 ......207 K6
 SAND/SEL CR2 ....212 B5
Castlemaine St WCHPL E1 .....104 D4
Castle Md CMBW SE5 * 142 D1
Castle Ms CAMTN NW1 ....84 A4
 NFNCH/WDSPK N12 ....47 G1
 TOOT SW17 ....160 D6
Castle Pde EW KT17 * 207 J5
Castlereagh St MBLAR W1H 8 E3
Castle Rd CAMTN NW1 ....84 B4
 DAGW RM9 ....91 H6
 ISLW TW7 ....136 A3
 NFNCH/WDSPK N12 ....47 G1
 NTHLT UB5 ....78 B4
 NWDGN UB2 ....114 E3
 PEND EN3 ....25 G2
Castle Rw CHSWK W4 * 118 A5
Castle St EHAM E6 ....107 G1
 KUT/HW KT1 * 175 F5
 WBLY HA9 ....80 A2
Castleton Av BXLYHN DA7 ......150 A2
 WBLY HA9 ....80 A1
Castleton CI CROY/NA CR0 .....198 B3
Castleton Gdns WBLY HA9 ....80 A1
Castleton Rd ELTH/MOT SE9 ...166 C6
 GDMY/SEVK IG3 ....73 H5
 MTCM CR4 ....195 J1
 RSLP HA4 ....59 H5
 WALTH E17 ....52 B5
Castletown Rd WKENS W14 ....119 H5
Castleview CI FSBYPK N4 ....67 J6
Castleview Gdns IL IG1 ....71 J5
Castle VIs CRICK NW2 * 81 J4
Castle Wk SUN TW16 * 172 B6
Castle Wy FELT TW13 ....154 B6
 WIM/MER SW19 ....159 G3
Castlewood Dr ELTH/MOT SE9 .146 E3
Castlewood Rd EBAR EN4 ....21 H4
 STNW/STAM N16 ....68 C3
Castle Yd HGT N6 ....66 A4
 RCH/KEW TW9 ....136 E6
 STHWK SE1 * 12 B7
Castor La POP/IOD E14 ....105 K6
Catalina Rd HTHAIR TW6 ......132 E4
Catalpa Ct LEW SE13 ....165 G1
Caterham Av CLAY IG5 ....53 K6
Caterham Rd LEW SE13 ....145 G4
Catesby St WALW SE17 * 19 F7
Catford Broadway CAT SE6 ....164 E2
Catford HI CAT SE6 ....164 C3
Catford Island CAT SE6 ....164 D3
Catford Rd CAT SE6 ....164 D2
Cathall Rd WAN E11 ....88 B1
Cathay St BERM/RHTH SE16 ...123 J2
Cathcart Dr ORP BR6 ....201 K6
Cathcart HI ARCH N19 ....84 C1
Cathcart Rd WBPTN SW10 ....120 A6
Cathcart St KTTN NW5 ....84 B4
Cathedral St STHWK SE1 * 12 E7
Catherall Rd HBRY N5 ....85 J1
Catherine CI LBU IG10 ....39 K1
Catherine Ct STHGT/OAK N14 ..22 C6
Catherine Dr RCH/KEW TW9 ...137 F5
Catherine Griffiths Ct
 CLKNW EC1R 5 K6
Catherine Gv GNWCH SE10 ....144 E2
Catherine PI HRW HA1 ....61 F2
 WESTW SW1E 16 A4
Catherine Rd GPK RM2 ....75 K2
 SURB KT6 ....190 E2
Catherine VIs RYNPK SW20 * ..176 E2
Catherine Wheel Aly
 LVPST EC2M 13 H2
Catherine Wheel Rd
 BTFD TW8 ....136 E1
Catherine Wheel Yd
 WHALL SW1A 16 A1
Cat HI EBAR EN4 ....21 J3
Cathles Rd BAL SW12 ....161 G1
Cathnor Rd SHB W12 ....118 E2
Catling CI FSTH SE23 ....163 K5
Catlin's La PIN HA5 ....40 E6
Catlin St BERM/RHTH SE16 ....123 J5
Cator La BECK BR3 ....182 C5
Cato Rd CLAP SW4 ....141 J4
Cator Rd CAR SM5 ....209 K4
 SYD SE26 ....182 A2
Cator St PECK SE15 ....123 G6
Cato St MBLAR W1H 8 D3
Catsey La BUSH WD23 ....28 C2
Catsey Wd BUSH WD23 ....28 C2
Catterick CI FBAR/BDGN N11 ...48 A2
Cattistock Rd ELTH/MOT SE9 ...184 D1
Cattley CI BAR EN5 ....20 C5
Catton St RSQ WC1B 11 G2
Caudwell Ter
 WAND/EARL SW18 * 160 C1
Caulfield Rd EHAM E6 ....89 K6
 PECK SE15 ....143 J3
Causeway EBED/NFELT TW14 ..134 A5
The Causeway BELMT SM2 ....209 G6

CAR SM5 ....210 A1
CHSGTN KT9 ....206 A2
EFNCH N2 ....65 H1
ESH/CLAY KT10 ....205 F5
TEDD TW11 ....174 A2
WAND/EARL SW18 ....140 A6
WIM/MER SW19 ....177 F1
Causeyware Rd ED N9 ....36 D2
Causton Cottages
 POP/IOD E14 * 105 G4
Causton Rd HGT N6 * 66 B4
Causton Sq DAGE RM10 ....92 C5
Causton St WEST SW1P 16 D7
Cautley Av CLAP SW4 ....141 H6
Cavalier CI CHDH RM6 ....73 J1
Cavalier Gdns HYS/HAR UB3 ....94 B6
Cavalry Crs HSLWW TW4 ......134 C5
Cavalry Gdns PUT/ROE SW15 ..139 J6
Cavan PI PIN HA5 ....41 K4
Cavaye PI WBPTN SW10 * 120 B5
Cavell Crs DART DA1 ....151 K5
Cavell Dr ENC/FH EN2 ....23 G3
Cavell Rd TOTM N17 ....49 K3
Cavell St WCHPL E1 ....104 D4
Cavendish Av BFN/LL DA15 ....168 B2
 ERITH DA8 ....129 K6
 FNCH N3 ....46 E6
 HCH RM12 ....93 K4
 HRW HA1 ....78 D2
 NWMAL KT3 ....192 E2
 RSLP HA4 ....77 G3
 STJWD NW8 ....2 B3
 WEA W13 ....97 G4
 WELL DA16 ....148 B4
Cavendish CI KIL/WHAMP NW6 ..82 D4
 STJWD NW8 ....2 B3
 UED UB4 ....94 C4
 YEAD UB4 ....94 C4
Cavendish Crs HCH RM12 ....93 K4
Cavendish Dr EDGW HA8 ....44 B3
 ESH/CLAY KT10 ....204 E3
 WAN E11 ....70 B5
Cavendish Gdns BARK IG11 .....91 F3
 CHDH RM6 ....73 K2
 CLAP SW4 * 161 H1
 IL IG1 ....71 J5
Cavendish Ms North
 GTPST W1W * 9 K1
Cavendish Ms South
 GTPST W1W 9 K1
Cavendish Pde CLAP SW4 * 141 H5
 HSLWW TW4 * 134 D3
Cavendish PI BMLY BR1 ....184 E6
 CAVSQ/HST W1G 9 K3
 KIL/WHAMP NW6 ....82 B5
Cavendish Rd BAR EN5 ....20 A4
 BELMT SM2 ....209 G6
 CHING E4 ....52 A2
 CHSWK W4 ....137 K2
 CLAP SW4 ....161 H1
 CROY/NA CR0 ....196 C5
 FSBYPK N4 ....67 H4
 KIL/WHAMP NW6 ....82 B5
 NWMAL KT3 ....192 C2
 UED N18 ....36 C3
 WIM/MER SW19 ....178 D3
Cavendish Sq CAVSQ/HST W1G ..9 K3
Cavendish St IS N1 ....6 E3
Cavendish Ter BOW E3 * 105 H2
 FELT TW13 * 153 K4
Cavendish Wy WWKM BR4 ....198 E5
Cavenham Gdns IL IG1 ....90 D1
Caverleigh Wy WPK KT4 ......192 D5
Caverley Gdns
 KTN/HRWW/WS HA3 ....61 K3
Cave Rd PLSTW E13 ....107 F1
 RCH/HAM TW10 ....156 D6
Caversham Av CHEAM SM3 ....193 H6
 PLMGR N13 ....35 H6
Caversham Flats CHEL SW3 * ..120 E6
Caversham Rd KTTN NW5 * 84 C4
 KUT/HW KT1 ....175 G5
 SEVS/STOTM N15 ....67 J3
Caversham St CHEL SW3 ......120 E6
Caverswall St SHB W12 ....100 A5
Cawdor Crs HNWL W7 ....116 B4
Cawnpore St NRWD SE19 .....181 F1
Caxton Gv BOW E3 ....105 J2
Caxton Ms BTFD TW8 ....116 E6
Caxton Rd NWDGN UB2 ....114 C3
 SHB W12 ....119 G1
 WDGN N22 ....49 F5
 WIM/MER SW19 ....178 B1
The Caxtons BRXN/ST SW9 * ..142 C1
Caxton St North CAN/RD E16 ..106 D5
Caxton St ROM SM1 ....75 G1
 WATW WD18 * 21 G5
Cayenne Ct STHWK SE1 ....19 H2
Caygill CI HAYES BR2 ....199 J1
Cayton PI GFD/PVL UB6 ....96 E1
Cayton Rd GFD/PVL UB6 ....96 E1
Cayton St FSBYE EC1V 6 D5
Cazenove Rd STNW/STAM N16 ..68 B3
 WALTH E17 ....51 H4
Cecil Av BARK IG11 ....90 D5
 EN EN1 ....24 C5
 WBLY HA9 ....80 B3
Cecil CI CHSGTN KT9 ....205 K2
 EA W5 ....97 K4
Cecil Ct BAR EN5 ....20 A4
 CHCR WC2N * 10 E6
Cecile Pk CEND/HSY/T N8 ......66 E3
Cecilia CI EFNCH N2 ....47 G6
Cecilia Rd HACK E8 ....86 B3
Cecil Pk PIN HA5 ....59 J1
Cecil PI MTCM CR4 ....194 E2
Cecil Rd ACT W3 ....98 E4
 CDALE/KGS NW9 ....45 F6
 CHDH RM6 ....73 K4
 CROY/NA CR0 ....195 K3
 ENC/FH EN2 ....23 J6
 HSLW TW3 ....135 H3
 HYS/HAR UB3 ....113 J2
 PIN HA5 ....41 H6
 ROM RM1 ....75 F4
 WALTH E17 ....69 J3

STHGT/OAK N14 ....34 B3
SUT SM1 ....208 D4
WALTH E17 ....51 J4
WAN E11 ....70 C6
WIM/MER SW19 ....178 A3
WLSDN NW10 ....81 G6
Cecil Wy HAYES BR2 ....199 K5
Cedar Av BFN/LL DA15 ....168 B2
 CHDH RM6 ....74 A2
 EBAR EN4 ....33 J2
 HYS/HAR UB3 ....94 E5
 PEND EN3 ....24 E6
 RSLP HA4 ....77 G3
 WDR/YW UB7 * 112 C1
 WHTN TW2 ....155 C1
Cedar CI BKHH IG9 ....39 H4
 BOW E3 ....87 H6
 CAR SM5 ....209 K4
 DUL SE21 ....162 D3
 HAYES BR2 ....215 J1
 IL IG1 ....90 D3
 KUTN/CMB KT2 ....158 A6
 ROMW/RG RM7 ....74 E5
 SWLY BR8 ....187 K5
Cedar Copse BMLY BR1 ....184 E5
Cedar Ct CHARL SE7 * 126 B6
 ELTH/MOT SE9 ....166 D1
 WIM/MER SW19 ....159 G5
Cedar Crs HAYES BR2 ....215 J1
Cedar Dr EFNCH N2 ....65 J1
 PIN HA5 ....42 A2
Cedar Gdns BELMT SM2 ....209 G4
Cedar Gv BXLY DA5 ....168 E1
 EA W5 ....116 E3
 STHL UB1 ....96 A4
Cedar Hts RCHPK/HAM TW10 ..157 F1
Cedarhurst BMLY BR1 * 183 H5
Cedar Lawn Av BAR EN5 ....20 C6
Cedar Mt ELTH/MOT SE9 ......166 C5
Cedarne Rd FUL/PGN SW6 ....140 A1
Cedar Park Gdns CHDH RM6 ...73 K4
Cedar Park Rd ENC/FH EN2 ....23 K1
Cedar PI CHARL SE7 * 126 B5
Cedar Ri STHGT/OAK N14 ......34 A2
Cedar Rd BELMT SM2 ....209 G4
 BMLY BR1 ....184 B5
 CRICK NW2 ....82 A2
 CROY/NA CR0 ....197 F6
 DART DA1 ....171 G4
 E/WMO/HCT KT8 ....189 K1
 EBED/NFELT TW14 ....153 J3
 ENC/FH EN2 ....23 H1
 ERITH DA8 ....150 D2
 HSLWW TW4 ....134 B3
 OXHEY WD19 ....27 G1
 ROMW/RG RM7 ....74 E1
 TOTM N17 ....50 B4
 WALTH E17 ....69 J2
Cedars Av MTCM CR4 ....195 F1
 WALTH E17 ....69 J2
Cedars CI HDN NW4 ....46 B6
 LEW SE13 ....145 G4
Cedars Cottages
 PUT/ROE SW15 * 158 D1
Cedars Ct ED N9 ....36 A4
Cedars Ms CLAP SW4 * 141 G5
Cedars Rd BARN SW13 ....138 D3
 BECK BR3 ....182 B5
 CHSWK W4 ....117 K6
 CLAP SW4 ....141 G4
 CROY/NA CR0 ....210 E1
 ED N9 ....36 C4
 KUT/HW KT1 ....174 D4
 MRDN SM4 ....193 K1
 SRTFD E15 ....88 C4
 WCHMH N21 ....35 H4
The Cedars BKHH IG9 ....38 E3
 HOM E9 * 87 F5
 SRTFD E15 * 174 A2
 TEDD TW11 * 174 A2
Cedar Tree Gv WNWD SE27 ...180 C1
Cedarville Gdns
 STRHM/NOR SW16 ....180 A2
Cedar Wk ESH/CLAY KT10 ....205 F4
Cedar Wy CAMTN NW1 ....84 D5
Cedric Av ROM RM1 ....75 G1
Cedric Rd ELTH/MOT SE9 .....167 H5
Celadon CI PEND EN3 ....25 G4
Celandine CI POP/IOD E14 ....105 J4
Celandine Dr HACK E8 ....86 B5
 THMD SE28 ....128 C2
Celandine Gv STHGT/OAK N14 ..22 C6
Celandine Wy SRTFD E15 .....106 C2
Celbridge Ms BAY/PAD W2 * ..101 F5
Celestial Gdns LEW SE13 .....145 G5
Celia Rd ARCH N19 ....84 C2
Celtic Av HAYES BR2 ....183 H6
Celtic St POP/IOD E14 ....105 K4
Cemetery La CHARL SE7 ......126 D6
Cemetery Rd ABYW SE2 ......148 C1
 FSTGT E7 ....88 D3
 TOTM N17 ....50 A3
Cenacle CI HAMP NW3 * 82 E1
Centaur Ct BTFD TW8 * 117 F5
Centaur St STHWK SE1 ....17 H4
Centenary Rd PEND EN3 ....25 J5
Centenary Wk CHING E4 ....38 D5
 LOU IG10 ....39 F1
 WAN E11 ....70 E6
 WFD IG8 ....52 C2
Centennial Av BORE WD6 ....29 J2
Centennial Pk BORE WD6 ....29 J2
Central Ar ASHF TW15 * 152 C6
Central Av E/WMO/HCT KT8 ..188 E2
 ED N9 ....36 A5
 EFNCH N2 ....47 H5
 EN EN1 ....24 E3
 HSLW TW3 ....135 H5
 HYS/HAR UB3 ....113 J2
 PIN HA5 ....59 K3
 WAN E11 ....70 B6
 WELL DA16 ....148 A3
 WLGTN SM6 ....210 E3
Central Buildings EA W5 * 97 K6

Central Circ HDN NW4 ....63 K2
Central Ct CHIG IG7 ....54 E1
Central Hall Buildings
  ARCH N19 * 66 C6
Central Pde ACT W3 * 117 H2
  BFN/LL DA15 * 168 B5
  E/WMO/HCT KT8 * 188 E1
  GFD/PVL UB6 * 97 G2
  HRW HA1 * 61 F2
  PEND EN3 * 24 E3
  PGE/AN SE20 * 182 A3
  STRHM/NOR SW16 * 161 K6
  SURB KT6 * 191 F3
  WALTH E17 * 69 J1
Central Park Av DAGE RM10 ....92 E2
Central Park Est
  HSLWW TW4 * 134 C5
Central Park Rd EHAM E6 ....107 J1
Central Pl SNWD SE25 * 197 H1
Central Rd ALP/SUD HA0 ....79 H3
  DART DA1 ....151 H6
  MRDN SM4 ....193 K4
  WPK KT4 ....192 D6
Central Sq E/WMO/HCT KT8 ....188 E1
  GLDGN NW11 * 64 E3
Central Ter BECK BR3 * 182 A6
Central Wy CAR SM5 ....29 J5
  EBED/NFELT TW14 ....134 A6
  NTHWD HA6 ....40 C3
  THMD SE28 ....109 H6
  WLSDN NW10 ....98 E2
Centre Av ACT W3 ....118 A1
Centre Common Rd CHST BR7 ......156 A5
Centre Dr DAGE RM10 ....110 D1
  WAN E11 ....70 B2
Centre St BETH E2 ....104 D1
Centre Wy ED N9 ....36 E4
Centric Ct CAMTN NW1 * 84 B6
Centurian Wy ERITHM DA18 ....129 C5
Centurion Cl HOLWY N7 ....85 F5
Centurion La BOW E3 ....105 H1
Centurion Sq CHARL SE7 * 146 C1
Centurion Wy PUR RM19 ....131 J4
Century Cl WATW WD18 * 26 A2
Century Ms CLPT E5 * 86 E2
Century Rd WALTH E17 ....51 G6
Cephas Av WCHPL E1 ....104 E3
Cephas St WCHPL E1 ....104 E3
Ceres Rd WOOL/PLUM SE18 ....128 A4
Cerise Rd PECK SE15 ....143 H2
Cerne Cl YEAD UB4 ....95 G6
Cerne Rd MRDN SM4 ....194 B3
Cervantes Ct BAY/PAD W2 * 101 F5
  NTHWD HA6 ....40 D4
Ceylon Rd WKENS W14 ....119 H3
Chabot Dr PECK SE15 ....143 J4
Chadacre Av CLAY IG5 ....53 K6
Chadacre Rd EW KT17 ....207 K3
Chadbourn St POP/IOD E14 ....105 K4
Chad Crs ED N9 ....36 E5
Chadd Dr BMLY BR1 ....184 D6
Chadville Gdns CHDH RM6 ....73 K2
Chadway DAGE RM9 ....73 J6
Chadwell Av CHDH RM6 ....73 H3
Chadwell Heath La CHDH RM6 ....73 H1
Chadwell St CLKNW EC1R 5 K4
Chadwick Av CHING E4 ....38 B6
  WCHMH N21 * 23 H6
  WIM/MER SW19 ....177 K2
Chadwick Cl PUT/ROE SW15 ....158 C2
  TEDD TW11 ....174 B2
Chadwick Pl SURB KT6 ....190 D3
Chadwick Rd IL IG1 ....90 B1
  PECK SE15 ....143 G3
  WAN E11 ....70 C4
  WLSDN NW10 ....81 H6
Chadwick St WEST SW1P 16 C6
Chadwick Wy THMD SE28 ....109 K6
Chadwin Rd PLSTW E13 ....107 F4
Chadworth Wy
  ESH/CLAY KT10 ....204 D3
Chaffinch Av CROY/NA CRO 198 A3
Chaffinch Cl CROY/NA CRO 198 A2
  ED N9 ....37 F5
  SURB KT6 ....206 C1
Chaffinch Cl ORP BR6 ....202 B4
Chaffinch La WATW WD18 ....26 D2
Chaffinch Rd BECK BR3 ....182 B4
Chagford St CAMTN NW1 * 2 E7
Chailey Av EN EN1 ....24 B3
Chailey Cl HEST TW5 ....134 C2
Chailey St CLPT E5 * 86 E1
Chalbury Wk IS N1 ....5 J2
Chalcombe Rd ABYW SE2 ....128 C3
Chalcot Cl BELMT SM2 ....208 E5
Chalcot Crs CAMTN NW1 ....83 K6
Chalcot Gdns HAMP NW3 ....83 K4
Chalcot Ms STRHM/NOR SW16 ....161 K5
Chalcot Rd CAMTN NW1 ....84 A6
Chalcot Sq CAMTN NW1 ....84 A5
Chalcott Gdns SURB KT6 * 190 D5
Chalcroft Rd LEW SE13 ....145 H6
Chaldon Rd FUL/PGN SW6 ....139 H1
Chale Rd BRXS/STRHM SW2 ....161 K1
Chalet Cl BXLY DA5 ....170 A6
Chalet Est MLHL NW7 * 31 J4
Chalfont Av WBLY HA9 ....80 D4
Chalfont Gn ED N9 ....36 A5
Chalfont Ms
  WAND/EARL SW18 ....159 J3
Chalfont Rd ED N9 ....36 A5
  HYS/HAR UB3 ....113 K2
  SNWD SE25 ....181 G6
Chalfont Wk PIN HA5 * 41 G5
Chalfont Wy WEA W13 ....116 C3
Chalford Cl E/WMO/HCT KT8 ....189 F1
Chalforde Gdns GPK RM2 ....75 K1
Chalford Rd DUL SE21 ....162 D6
Chalford Wlk WFD IG8 ....53 H4
Chalgrove Av MRDN SM4 ....193 K2
Chalgrove Crs CLAY IG5 ....53 J5

Chalgrove Gdns FNCH N3 ....46 C6
Chalgrove Rd BELMT SM2 ....209 H5
  HACK E8 ....86 E4
  TOTM N17 ....50 D4
Chalice Cl WLGTN SM6 ....210 D4
Chalkenden Cl PGE/AN SE20 ....181 J3
Chalk Farm Pde HAMP NW3 * 84 A5
Chalk Farm Rd CAMTN NW1 ....84 A5
Chalk Hill OXHEY WD19 ....27 J1
Chalk Hill Rd HMSMTH W6 ....119 G4
Chalkhill Rd WBLY HA9 ....80 C1
Chalklands WBLY HA9 ....80 E1
Chalk La EBAR EN4 ....21 K4
Chalkley Cl MTCM CR4 ....178 E5
Chalkmill Dr EN EN1 ....24 D4
Chalk Pit Av STMC/STPC BR5 ....186 E6
Chalk Pit Rd SUT SM1 ....209 G5
Chalk Rd PLSTW E15 ....107 F4
Chalkstone Cl WELL DA16 ....148 B2
Chalkwell Park Av EN EN1 ....24 A5
Chalky La CHSGTN KT9 ....205 K6
Challenge Cl WLSDN NW10 ....81 G6
Challice Wy BRXS/STRHM SW2 ......162 A3
Challin St PGE/AN SE20 ....181 K4
Challis Rd BTFD TW8 ....116 E5
Challoner Cl EFNCH N2 ....47 H5
Challoner Crs WKENS W14 ....119 J5
Challoners Ct E/WMO/HCT KT8 ......189 J1
Challoner St WKENS W14 ....119 J5
Chalmers Rd ASHF TW15 ....152 E6
Chalmers Rd East ASHF TW15 ....152 E6
Chalmers Wk WALW SE17 * 122 C6
Chalsey Rd
  EBED/NFELT TW14 ....134 A6
  TWK TW1 ....136 C5
Chalsey Rd BROCKY SE4 ....144 C5
Chalton Dr EFNCH N2 ....65 G3
Chalton St CAMTN NW1 ....4 C2
Chalton St PLSTW E15 ....107 F1
Chamberlain Cottages
  CMBW SE5 * 142 E2
Chamberlain Crs WWKM BR4 ....198 E5
Chamberlain Gdns HSLW TW3 ....135 H2
Chamberlain La PIN HA5 ....58 E1
Chamberlain Pl WALTH E17 ....51 G6
Chamberlain Rd EFNCH N2 ....47 G5
  WEA W13 ....116 B2
Chamberlain St CAMTN NW1 * 83 K5
Chamberlain Wy PIN HA5 ....41 F6
  SURB KT6 ....191 F4
Chamberlayne Av WBLY HA9 ....80 A1
Chamberlayne Rd
  WLSDN NW10 ....82 A6
Chamberlens Garages
  HMSMTH W6 * 118 E4
Chambers Gdns EFNCH N2 ....47 H4
Chambers La WLSDN NW10 ....81 K5
Chambers Rd HOLWY N7 ....84 E2
Chambers St
  BERM/RHTH SE16 ....123 H2
Chamber St WCHPL E1 ....13 K5
Chambon Pl HMSMTH W6 ....118 D4
Chambord St BETH E2 ....7 K5
Champa Cl TOTM N17 ....50 B5
Champion Crs SYD SE26 ....164 B6
Champion Gv CMBW SE5 ....142 E4
Champion Hl CMBW SE5 ....142 E4
Champion Park CMBW SE5 ....142 E3
Champion Rd SYD SE26 ....164 B6
Champness Cl WNWD SE27 ....162 E6
Champness Rd BARK IG11 ....91 F5
Champneys OXHEY WD19 * 27 J4
Champneys Cl BELMT SM2 ....208 D5
Chancellor Gdns
  SAND/SEL CR2 ....211 H6
Chancellor Gv DUL SE21 ....162 D4
Chancellor Pl CDALE/KGS NW9 ....45 H5
Chancellor's Rd HMSMTH W6 ....119 F5
Chancellors St HMSMTH W6 ....119 F5
Chancelot Rd ABYW SE2 ....128 C4
Chancel St STHWK SE1 ....12 A7
Chancery La BECK BR3 ....182 E5
  LINN WC2A 11 H2
Chancery Ms TOOT SW17 ....160 D4
Chance St BETH E2 ....7 J6
Chanctonbury Cl
  ELTH/MOT SE9 ....167 G5
Chanctonbury Gdns
  BELMT SM2 ....209 F5
Chanctonbury Wy
  NFNCH/WDSPK N12 ....32 E6
Chandler Av CAN/RD E16 ....106 E4
Chandler Cl HPTN TW12 ....172 E4
Chandlers Cl
  EBED/NFELT TW14 ....153 J3
Chandlers Ct LEE/GVPK SE12 * 166 A4
Chandlers Dr ERITH DA8 ....130 A3
Chandlers Ms POP/IOD E14 ....124 D2
Chandler St WAP E1W 123 J1
Chandlers Wy ROM RM1 ....75 G2
Chandler Wy PECK SE15 ....143 G1
Chandos Av EA W5 ....116 D4
  STHGT/OAK N14 ....34 C5
  TRDG/WHET N20 ....33 H3
  WALTH E17 * 51 J3
Chandos Cl BKHH IG9 ....39 F4
Chandos Crs EDGW HA8 ....44 C3
Chandos Pl CHCR WC2N 10 E6
Chandos Rd CRICK NW2 ....82 A3
  EFNCH N2 ....47 H5
  HRW HA1 ....60 C2
  PIN HA5 ....59 G4
  SRTFD E15 ....88 B3
  TOTM N17 ....50 B5
  WLSDN NW10 ....99 G3
Chandos St CAVSQ/HST W1G 9 K3
Chandos Wy GLDGN NW11 ....65 F5
Channel Cl HEST TW5 ....135 F2
Channel Gate Rd NKENS W10 ....100 H4
  WLSDN NW10 ....81 J4
Channel Islands Est IS N1 * 85 J4
Channelsea Rd SRTFD E15 ....88 B3

Chantress Cl DAGE RM10 ....92 E6
Chantrey Cl SCUP DA14 ....187 F1
Chantrey Rd BRXN/ST SW9 ....142 A4
Chantry Cl ABYW SE2 ....128 D3
  BAR EN5 ....31 H1
  ENC/FH EN2 ....23 J2
  KTN/HRWW/WS HA3 ....62 B2
  MV/WKIL W9 ....100 D3
Chantry Crs WLSDN NW10 ....81 G3
Chantry La HAYES BR2 ....200 C2
Chantry Rd CHSGTN KT9 ....206 B3
  KTN/HRWW/WS HA3 ....42 B4
Chantry Sq KENS W8 * 120 A3
Chantry St IS N1 ....6 B1
The Chantry CHING E4 * 38 A3
Chant Sq SRTFD E15 * 88 B5
Chant St SRTFD E15 ....88 B5
Chapel Cl DART DA1 ....150 B6
  WLSDN NW10 ....81 H3
Chapel Ct ENC/FH EN2 ....23 J2
  STHWK SE1 ....18 E2
  WOOL/PLUM SE18 ....128 A6
Chapel Farm Rd
  ELTH/MOT SE9 ....166 E5
Chapel Hl DART DA1 ....150 B6
Chapel House St POP/IOD E14 ....124 E5
Chapel La PIN HA5 ....41 H6
Chapel Market IS N1 ....5 J2
Chapel Mill Rd KUT/HW KT1 ....175 G6
Chapel Pl CAVSQ/HST W1G 9 J4
  IS N1 ....5 K3
  TOTM N17 ....50 C3
Chapel Rd BXLYHN DA7 ....149 H5
  HSLW TW3 ....135 H5
  IL IG1 ....90 B1
  TWK TW1 ....156 C2
  WEA W13 ....116 C1
  WNWD SE27 ....162 C6
Chapel Side BAY/PAD W2 * 101 F6
  ENC/FH EN2 ....23 J4
  KTBR SW1X 15 H4
Chapel Vw SAND/SEL CR2 ....212 D5
Chaplemount Rd WFD IG8 ....53 K2
Chaplin Cl ALP/SUD HA0 * 79 J4
  STHWK SE1 ....17 K2
Chaplin Ms LBTH SE11 ....122 B5
Chaplin Rd ALP/SUD HA0 ....79 J4
  CRICK NW2 ....81 J4
  SRTFD E15 ....106 C1
  TOTM N17 ....50 B6
Chapman Av GNTH/NBYPK IG2 ....72 D5
Chapman Rd BELV DA17 ....129 H5
  CROY/NA CRO 196 B5
  HOM E9 ....87 J4
Chapmans Gn WDGN N22 * 49 G4
Chapman's La STMC/STPC BR5 ......186 E5
  SWLY BR8 ....187 J4
Chapman Sq WIM/MER SW19 ....159 G4
Chapman St WCHPL E1 ....104 D6
Chapman Ter WDGN N22 * 49 H4
Chapter Rd CRICK NW2 ....81 K3
  WALW SE17 ....122 C5
Chapter Wy HPTN TW12 ....155 F6
Chara Pl CHSWK W4 ....118 A6
Charcroft Gdns PEND EN3 * 25 F4
Chardin Rd CHSWK W4 * 118 B4
Chardmore Rd
  STNW/STAM N16 ....68 C5
Chardwell Cl EHAM E6 ....107 J5
Charcecroft Wy WKENS W14 * 119 G2
Charford St CAN/RD E16 ....106 C3
Chargeable La PLSTW E15 ....106 D2
Chargeable St CAN/RD E16 ....106 D1
Chargrove Cl
  BERM/RHTH SE16 ....124 A2
Charing Cl ORP BR6 ....217 F2
Charing Cross Rd
  LSQ/SEVD WC2H 10 D5
Charlot Ct STJWD NW8 ....2 E7
Charlbury Av STAN HA7 ....43 K1
Charlbury Gdns
  GDMY/SEVK IG3 ....73 F6
Charlbury Gv EA W5 ....97 J5
Charlecote Gv SYD SE26 ....163 J5
Charlecote Rd BCTR RM8 ....92 A1
Charlemont Rd EHAM E6 ....107 K2
Charles Babbage Cl
  CHSGTN KT9 ....205 J5
Charles Barry Cl CLAP SW4 ....141 H4
Charles Cl SCUP DA14 ....168 C6
Charles Cobb Gdns
  CROY/NA CRO 211 G3
Charles Coveney Rd
  PECK SE15 ....143 G2
Charles Dickens Ter
  PGE/AN SE20 * 181 K3
Charlesfield ELTH/MOT SE9 ....166 B5
Charles Flemwell Ms
  CAN/RD E16 * 125 K1
Charles Grinling Wk
  WOOL/PLUM SE18 ....127 F4
Charles Haller St
  BRXS/STRHM SW2 ....162 B2
Charles La STJWD NW8 ....2 E1
Charles Pl CAMTN NW1 ....4 B5
Charles Rd CHDH RM6 ....73 K4
  DAGE RM10 ....93 H6
  FSTGT E7 ....89 G5
  WEA W13 ....97 G5
  WIM/MER SW19 ....177 K4
Charles II Pl CHEL SW3 * 120 E5
Charles II St STJS SW1Y 10 C7
Charles Sevright Dr MLHL NW7 ....46 B1
Charles Sq IS N1 ....7 F5
Charles Square Est IS N1 ....7 F5
Charles St BARN SW13 ....138 B4

  CAN/RD E16 ....126 B1
  CROY/NA CRO 211 J1
  EN EN1 ....24 B6
  HSLW TW3 ....134 C3
  MYFR/PICC W1J 9 K7
Charleston Cl FELT TW13 ....153 K5
Charleston St WALW SE17 ....18 D7
Charles St
  ENC/FH EN2 ....126 A1
Charleville Circ SYD SE26 ....163 H1
Charleville Rd WKENS W14 ....119 J5
Charleville Rd ERITH DA8 ....149 K1
Charlmont Rd TOOT SW17 ....178 D2
Charlock Wy WATW WD18 ....26 D1
Charlotte Cl BXLYHS DA6 ....149 F6
Charlotte Ct ESH/CLAY KT10 ....204 C3
Charlotte Despard Av
  BTSEA SW11 ....141 G2
Charlotte Gdns CRW RM5 ....56 D2
Charlotte Ms ESH/CLAY * 204 B2
  FITZ W1T 10 B1
  NKENS W10 ....100 B5
Charlotte Pde FSTH SE23 * 92 H3
Charlotte Park Av BMLY BR1 ....184 D6
Charlotte Pl FITZ W1T 10 B2
  PIM SW1V 16 A7
Charlotte Rd BARN SW13 ....138 C2
  IS N1 ....7 G5
  WLGTN SM6 ....210 C4
Charlotte Row CLAP SW4 ....141 H4
Charlotte St FITZ W1T 10 B1
Charlotte Ter IS N1 ....5 H1
Charlow Cl FUL/PGN SW6 ....140 B3
Charlton Church La
  CHARL SE7 ....126 B5
Charlton Crs BARK IG11 ....109 F1
Charlton Dene CHARL SE7 ....146 B1
Charlton King's Rd KTTN NW5 ....84 D3
Charlton La CHARL SE7 ....126 C5
Charlton Park La CHARL SE7 ....126 C6
Charlton Park Rd CHARL SE7 ....126 C6
Charlton Pl IS N1 ....6 A2
Charlton Rd BKHTH/KID SE3 ....145 K1
  ED N9 ....37 F5
  KTN/HRWW/WS HA3 ....61 K1
  WBLY HA9 ....62 B6
  WLSDN NW10 ....81 G6
Charlton Wy BKHTH/KID SE3 ....145 J1
Charlwood CROY/NA CRO 213 H6
Charlwood Cl
  KTN/HRWW/WS HA3 ....42 E2
Charlwood Pl PIM SW1V 16 B7
Charlwood Rd PUT/ROE SW15 ....139 G5
Charlwood St PIM SW1V 16 B7
Charlwood Ter PUT/ROE SW15 ....139 G5
Charminster Av
  WIM/MER SW19 ....177 K5
Charminster Rd
  ELTH/MOT SE9 ....166 C6
  WPK KT4 ....193 G5
Charmouth Rd WELL DA16 ....148 D2
Charnock Rd CLPT E5 ....86 D1
Charnwood Av
  WIM/MER SW19 ....177 K5
Charnwood Cl NWMAL KT3 ....192 B1
Charnwood Dr SWFD E18 ....53 F6
Charnwood Gdns
  POP/IOD E14 ....124 D4
Charnwood Pl TRDG/WHET N20 ....33 G5
Charnwood Rd SNWD SE25 ....196 E2
Charnwood St CLPT E5 * 68 C6
Charnwood Vis SWFD E18 ....53 F6
Charrington Rd CROY/NA CRO 196 C6
Charrington St CAMTN NW1 ....4 C2
Charsley Rd CAT SE6 ....164 E4
Chart Cl CROY/NA CRO 197 K3
  HAYES BR2 ....183 H4
  MTCM CR4 ....194 E1
Charter Av GNTH/NBYPK IG2 ....72 D5
Charter Cl BAR EN5 * 20 D5
Charter Ct NWMAL KT3 ....176 B6
Charter Dr BXLY DA5 ....169 F2
Charterhouse Av ALP/SUD HA0 ....79 J3
Charterhouse Buildings
  FARR EC1M 6 C7
Charterhouse Ms FARR EC1M 12 B1
Charterhouse Rd HACK E8 ....86 C3
  ORP BR6 ....217 G1
Charterhouse Sq FARR EC1M 12 A2
The Charterhouse FARR EC1M * 11 K2
  HCIRC EC1N 11 K2
Charteris Rd FSBYPK N4 ....67 F5
Charteris Rd KIL/WHAMP NW6 ....82 D6
  WFD IG8 ....53 F2
Charters Cl NRWD SE19 ....181 F1
Charter Sq KUT/HW KT1 ....175 J5
Charter Wy FNCH N3 ....46 D3
  STHGT/OAK N14 ....34 C1
Chartfield Av PUT/ROE SW15 ....138 E6
Chartfield Sq PUT/ROE SW15 * 139 G6
Chartham Gv WNWD SE27 ....162 B5
Chartham Rd SNWD SE25 ....181 J6
Chart Hills Cl THMD SE28 ....110 A5
Chartley Av CRICK NW2 ....81 G1
  STAN HA7 ....43 F2
Chartley Pde CRICK NW2 * 81 G1
Charlton Cl BELV DA17 ....129 G6
Chartridge OXHEY WD19 * 27 H4
Chartridge Cl BUSH WD23 ....28 C1
Chart St IS N1 ....7 F4
Chartwell Cl CROY/NA CRO 196 E5
  ELTH/MOT SE9 ....167 J4
  GFD/PVL UB6 ....78 C6
Chartwell Dr ORP BR6 ....216 D3
Chartwell Gdns CHEAM SM3 ....208 C4
Chartwell Pl CHEAM SM3 ....208 C2
  RYLN/HDSTN HA2 ....60 D6
Chartwell Wy PGE/AN SE20 ....181 J4
Charville La HGDN/ICK UB10 ....94 A1
Charwood STRHM/NOR SW16 ....162 B6
Chase Ct RYNPK SW20 ....177 H5
Chase Court Gdns ENC/FH EN2 ....23 J4
Chase Cross Rd CRW RM5 ....56 E1
Chasefield Rd TOOT SW17 ....160 E6

Chase Gdns CHING E4 ....37 J6
  WHTN TW2 ....155 J1
Chase Gn ENC/FH EN2 ....23 J4
Chase Green Av ENC/FH EN2 ....23 J3
Chase Hl ENC/FH EN2 ....23 J4
Chase La BARK/HLT IG6 ....72 D2
Chaseley Ct CHSWK W4 * 117 J4
Chasemore Ct MTCM CR4 * 194 E4
Chasemore Gdns
  CROY/NA CRO 211 G3
Chase Ridings ENC/FH EN2 ....23 G3
Chase Rd ACT W3 ....99 F3
  STHGT/OAK N14 ....34 D3
Chase Side ENC/FH EN2 ....23 J3
  STHGT/OAK N14 ....34 B2
Chase Side Av ENC/FH EN2 ....23 J3
Chaseside Av RYNPK SW20 ....177 H4
Chaseside Cl ROM RM1 * 57 G2
Chase Side Crs ENC/FH EN2 * 23 K2
Chase Side Pl ENC/FH EN2 * 23 J3
The Chase BMLY BR1 ....184 A6
  CLAP SW4 ....141 G4
  EDGW HA8 ....44 D4
  FSTGT E7 ....89 H2
  LOU IG10 ....39 H2
  PIN HA5 ....59 J2
  PIN HA5 ....60 A1
  ROM RM1 ....57 G6
  ROMW/RG RM7 ....93 F1
  STAN HA7 ....43 G2
  STRHM/NOR SW16 ....180 A3
  SUN TW16 ....172 A4
  WLGTN SM6 ....210 E3
Chaseville Pde WCHMH N21 * 23 F5
Chaseville Park Rd
  STHGT/OAK N14 ....22 E5
Chase Wy STHGT/OAK N14 ....34 B3
Chasewood Av ENC/FH EN2 ....23 H4
Chasewood Pk HRW HA1 * 78 E1
Chastilian Rd DART DA1 ....170 D2
Chatfield Rd BTSEA SW11 ....140 B4
  CROY/NA CRO 196 C5
Chatham Av HAYES BR2 ....199 K4
Chatham Cl CHEAM SM3 ....193 J4
  GLDGN NW11 ....64 E2
Chatham Pl HOM E9 ....86 E4
Chatham Rd BTSEA SW11 ....160 E1
  KUT/HW KT1 ....175 H5
  SWFD E18 ....52 D5
  WALTH E17 ....51 G6
Chatham St WALW SE17 ....18 E6
  WOOL/PLUM SE18 ....127 G3
Chatsworth Av BFN/LL DA15 ....168 B3
  BMLY BR1 ....184 A1
  HDN NW4 ....46 A5
  RYNPK SW20 ....177 H4
  WBLY HA9 ....80 B3
Chatsworth Cl CHSWK W4 * 117 K6
  HDN NW4 ....46 A5
  WWKM BR4 ....199 J6
Chatsworth Crs HSLW TW3 ....135 J5
Chatsworth Dr EN EN1 ....36 C6
Chatsworth Est CLPT E5 * 87 F2
Chatsworth Gdns ACT W3 ....116 C1
  NWMAL KT3 ....192 C2
  RYLN/HDSTN HA2 ....60 A3
Chatsworth Pl MTCM CR4 ....178 E6
  TEDD TW11 ....156 C5
Chatsworth Ri EA W5 ....98 B3
Chatsworth Rd CHEAM SM3 ....208 B2
  CHSWK W4 ....117 K6
  CLPT E5 ....86 E1
  CRICK NW2 ....82 B4
  CROY/NA CRO 211 K2
  DART DA1 ....151 F6
  EA W5 ....98 B3
  SRTFD E15 ....88 D3
  YEAD UB4 ....94 D3
Chatsworth Wy WNWD SE27 ....162 D4
Chattern Hl ASHF TW15 ....152 E6
Chattern Rd ASHF TW15 ....153 F6
Chatterton Ms FSBYPK N4 * 85 H1
Chatterton Rd FSBYPK N4 ....85 H1
  HAYES BR2 ....200 C2
Chatto Rd BTSEA SW11 ....140 E6
Chaucer Av HSLWW TW4 ....134 A3
  RCH/KEW TW9 ....137 H4
  YEAD UB4 ....94 E5
Chaucer Cl FBAR/BDGN N11 ....48 C1
Chaucer Dr STHWK SE1 * 19 K7
Chaucer Gdns SUT SM1 ....208 D2
Chaucer Gn CROY/NA CRO 197 K4
Chaucer Pk DART DA1 ....171 J2
Chaucer Rd ACT W3 ....117 K1
  ASHF TW15 ....152 B6
  BFN/LL DA15 ....168 D3
  FSTGT E7 ....88 E4
  HARH RM3 ....57 K3
  HNHL SE24 ....142 B6
  SUT SM1 ....208 E2
  WALTH E17 ....52 A4
  WAN E11 ....70 E3
  WELL DA16 ....147 K2
Chaucer Wy DART DA1 ....151 K5
  WIM/MER SW19 ....178 C2
Chauncey Cl ED N9 ....36 C5
Chaundrye Cl ELTH/MOT SE9 ....166 E6
Chaunter Rd CAN/RD E16 ....107 F5
Chave Rd RDART DA2 ....171 H5
Cheam Common Rd WPK KT4 ....192 E6
Cheam Man CHEAM SM3 * 208 C4
Cheam Park Wy CHEAM SM3 ....208 C4
Cheam Rd BELMT SM2 ....208 B6
Cheam St PECK SE15 * 143 J4
Cheapside CITYW EC2V 12 C4
  EFNCH N2 * 47 K6
  PLMGR N13 ....35 G6
  WDGN N22 * 49 G6
Cheddar Cl FBAR/BDGN N11 ....47 K2
Cheddar Wy YEAD UB4 ....95 H5
Cheddington Rd UED N18 ....36 A6
Cheesemans Ter WKENS W14 * 119 J5

Chelford Rd BMLY BR1 .... 183 G1
Chelmer Crs BARK IG11 .... 109 H1
Chelmer Rd HOM E9 .... 87 F3
Chelmsford Av RTM RM5 .... 57 F3
Chelmsford Cl BELMT SM2 .... 208 E6
EHAM E6 .... 96 A6
HMSMTH W6 .... 119 G6
Chelmsford Gdns IL IG1 .... 71 J4
Chelmsford Rd STHGT/OAK N14 ..... 34 C2
SWFD E18 .... 52 D4
WALTH E17 .... 51 H1
WAN E11 .... 70 B5
Chelmsford Sq WLSDN NW10 .... 82 A6
Chelsea Br VX/NE SW8 .... 121 G6
Chelsea Bridge Rd VX/NE SW8 .... 121 F6
Chelsea Bridge Rd
Chelsea Cl EDGW HA8 .... 44 C5
HPTN TW12 .... 173 H1
WLSDN NW10 .... 81 F6
WPK KT4 .... 192 D4
Chelsea Cts CRICK NW2 * 82 D4
WBPTN SW10 .... 140 A1
Chelsea Emb CHEL SW3 .... 120 E6
Chelsea Gdns BCVA SW1W * 121 F5
CHEAM SM3 .... 208 C2
WEA W13 .... 97 F4
Chelsea Harbour Dr
WBPTN SW10 .... 140 B2
Chelsea Manor Gdns
CHEL SW3 .... 120 D6
Chelsea Manor St CHEL SW3 ...... 120 D5
Chelsea Ms EMPK RM11 .... 75 K5
Chelsea Park Gdns CHEL SW3 ..... 120 C6
Chelsea Sq CAM SW3 .... 209 A6
CHEL SW3 .... 120 C5
Chelsea Towers CHEL SW3 * 120 D6
Chelsea Village
FUL/PGN SW6 * 140 A1
Chelsfield Av ED N9 .... 37 F2
Chelsfield Gdns SYD SE26 .... 163 K5
Chelsfield HI ORP BR6 .... 217 J6
Chelsfield La ORP BR6 .... 217 K2
STMC/STPC BR5 .... 202 E4
Chelsfield Rd STMC/STPC BR5 .... 202 D3
Chesham Rd CLAP SW4 .... 141 J4
SAND/SEL CR2 .... 211 K5
Chelston Rd RSLP HA4 .... 58 E6
Chelsworth Dr
WOOL/PLUM SE18 .... 127 J6
Cheltenham Av TWK TW1 .... 156 B2
Cheltenham Cl NTHLT UB5 .... 78 B4
NWMAL KT3 .... 175 K6
Cheltenham Gdns EHAM E6 .... 107 J1
LOU IG10 .... 39 J1
Cheltenham PI ACT W3 .... 117 K2
KTN/HRWW/WS HA3 .... 62 A1
Cheltenham Rd LEY E10 .... 70 A3
ORP BR6 .... 217 G6
PECK SE15 .... 143 K5
Cheltenham Ter CHEL SW3 .... 120 E5
Chelton Av MLHL NW7 .... 45 H2
Chelverton Rd PUT/ROE SW15 .... 139 G5
Chelwood Cl CHING E4 .... 37 K1
NTHWD HA6 .... 40 A3
Chelwood Gdns
RCH/KEW TW9 .... 137 H3
Chenappa Cl PLSTW E13 .... 106 E2
Chenduit Wy STAN HA7 .... 43 F1
Cheney Rw WALTH E17 .... 51 J4
Cheneys Rd WAN E11 .... 88 C1
Chenies St CAMTN NW1 .... 59 G1
Chenies PI CAMTN NW1 .... 4 C2
Chenies St GWRST WC1E 10 C1
The Chenies ORP BR6 .... 201 K5
RDART DA2 .... 170 B6
Chenies Wy WATW WD18 .... 26 C2
Cheniston Gdns KENS W8 .... 120 A3
Chepstow Cnr BAY/PAD W2 * 100 E5
Chepstow Crs GDMY/SEVK IG3 ..... 73 F3
NTCHL W11 .... 100 E6
Chepstow Gdns STHL UB1 .... 95 K5
Chepstow PI BAY/PAD W2 .... 100 E6
Chepstow Ri CROY/NA CRO 212 B1
Chepstow Rd BAY/PAD W2 .... 100 E5
CROY/NA CRO 212 A1
HNWL W7 .... 116 B3
Chepstow Vls NTGHL W11 .... 100 D6
Chequers BKHH IG9 .... 39 F3
Chequers Cl CDALE/KGS NW9 ...... 45 G2
STMC/STPC BR5 .... 202 A1
Chequers La DAGW RM9 .... 110 D5
Chequers Pde PLMGR N13 * 49 J1
The Chequers PIN HA5 * 41 H6
Chequer St STLK EC1Y 6 D7
Chequers Wy PLMGR N13 .... 49 J1
Cherbury Ct IS N1 .... 7 F3
Cherbury St IS N1 .... 7 F3
Cherimoya Gdns
E/WMO/HCT KT8 .... 173 G6
Cherington Rd HNWL W7 .... 116 A1
Cheriton Av CLAY IG5 .... 54 A5
HAYES BR2 .... 199 K2
Cheriton Cl EA W5 .... 98 A4
EBAR EN4 .... 21 K4
Cheriton Ct WOT/HER KT12 .... 188 B5
Cheriton Dr WOOL/PLUM SE18 .... 147 J1
Cheriton Sq TOOT SW17 .... 161 F4
Cherry Av STHL UB1 .... 114 C1
Cherry Blossom Cl PLMGR N13 .... 49 H4
Cherry Cl BRXS/STRHM SW2 * 162 B2
CAR SM5 .... 194 E6
CDALE/KGS NW9 .... 45 H5
EA W5 .... 116 E3
MRDN SM4 .... 193 H1
RSLP HA4 .... 58 B6
Cherrycot Ri ORP BR6 .... 216 C2
Cherry Ct PIN HA5 .... 41 H5
Cherry Crs BTFD TW8 .... 136 C1
Cherry Croft Gdns PIN HA5 * 41 K3
Cherrydown Av CHING E4 .... 37 H5
Cherrydown Cl CHING E4 .... 37 H5
Cherrydown Rd SCUP DA14 .... 168 E4
Cherrydown Wk
ROMW/RG RM7 .... 56 D5

Cherry Gdns DAGW RM9 .... 92 B3
NTHLT UB5 .... 78 B5
Cherry Garden St
BERM/RHTH SE16 .... 123 J2
Cherry Garth BTFD TW8 .... 116 E4
Cherry Gv HYS/HAR UB3 .... 114 A1
UX/CGN UB8 .... 94 A4
Cherry HI BAR EN5 .... 33 F1
KTN/HRWW/WS HA3 .... 42 E5
Cherry Hill Gdns CROY/NA CRO ... 211 F2
Cherry Hills OXHEY WD19 .... 41 J1
Cherrylands Cl
CDALE/KGS NW9 .... 62 G3
Cherry La WDR/YW UB7 .... 112 C4
Cherry Orch CHARL SE7 .... 126 B6
WDR/YW UB7 .... 112 B2
Cherry Orchard Cl
STMC/STPC BR5 .... 202 D2
Cherry Orchard Gdns
CROY/NA CRO 196 E5
E/WMO/HCT KT8 .... 172 E6
Cherry Orchard Rd
CROY/NA CRO 196 E5
E/WMO/HCT KT8 .... 173 F6
HAYES BR2 .... 200 D6
Cherry Rd PEND EN3 .... 24 E1
Cherry St ROMW/RG RM7 .... 75 F2
Cherry Tree Cl ALP/SUD HA0 ..... 79 G6
RAIN RM13 .... 86 E6
Cherry Tree Ct CHARL SE7 * 126 B6
RAIN RM13 .... 111 J1
Cherry Tree Dr
STRHM/NOR SW16 .... 161 K5
Cherry Tree HI EFNCH N2 .... 65 J2
Cherry Tree La RAIN RM13 .... 111 H2
RDART DA2 .... 170 C5
Cherry Tree Ri BKHH IG9 .... 39 G6
Cherry Tree Rd EFNCH N2 .... 65 K1
SRTFD E15 .... 88 C3
Cherry Tree Wk BECK BR3 .... 198 C1
STLK EC1Y 6 D7
WWKM BR4 .... 214 D2
Cherry Tree Wy STAN HA7 .... 43 H2
Cherry Wk HAYES BR2 .... 199 K5
RAIN RM13 .... 111 H1
Cherry Wy HOR/WEW KT19 .... 207 F5
Cherrywood Cl BOW E3 .... 105 G2
KUTN/CMB KT2 .... 175 H3
Cherrywood Dr
PUT/ROE SW15 .... 139 G6
Cherrywood La RYNPK SW20 .... 193 H1
Chertsey Dr CHEAM SM3 .... 193 H6
Chertsey Rd FELT TW13 .... 153 J5
IL IG1 .... 90 D2
TWK TW1 .... 155 J3
WAN E11 .... 70 B6
Chertsey St TOOT SW17 179
Chervil Cl FELT TW13 .... 153 K5
Chervil Ms THMD SE28 .... 128 C1
Cherwell Ct HOR/WEW KT19 .... 206 E2
Cherwell Wy RSLP HA4 .... 58 A3
Cheryls Cl FUL/PGN SW6 .... 140 A2
Cheseman St SYD SE26 .... 163 J5
Chesfield Rd KUTN/CMB KT2 ...... 175 F3
Chesham Av STMC/STPC BR5 .... 201 G3
Chesham Cl KTBR SW1X * 15 J5
ROMW/RG RM7 .... 75 F1
Chesham Crs PGE/AN SE20 .... 181 K4
Chesham Ms KTBR SW1X 15 G4
Chesham PI KTBR SW1X 15 G5
Chesham Rd KUT/HW KT1 .... 175 H5
PGE/AN SE20 .... 181 K4
WIM/MER SW19 .... 178 C2
Chesham St KTBR SW1X 15 G5
WLSDN NW10 .... 81 F1
Cheshire Cl MTCM CR4 .... 179 K6
WALTH E17 .... 51 K4
Cheshire Gdns CHSGTN KT9 .... 205 K4
Cheshire Rd WDGN N22 .... 49 F3
Cheshire St BETH E2 .... 104 C5
Chesholm Rd STNW/STAM N16 ...... 86 A1
Cheshunt Rd BELV DA17 .... 129 H5
FSTGT E7 .... 89 F4
Chesilton Rd FUL/PGN SW6 .... 139 J2
Chesil Wy YEAD UB4 .... 95 G2
Chesley Gdns EHAM E6 .... 107 J2
Chesney Crs CROY/NA CRO 214 A5
Chesney St BTSEA SW11 .... 141 F2
Chesnut Av North WALTH E17 ..... 70 B1
Chesnut Gv TOTM N17 .... 50 C6
Chesnut Rd TOTM N17 .... 50 C6
Chesnut Av FNCH N3 * 46 E5
Chessell Cl THHTH CR7 .... 196 C1
Chessington Av BXLYHN DA7 ...... 149 F1
FNCH N3 .... 46 D6
Chessington Cl
HOR/WEW KT19 .... 206 E4
Chessington Ct PIN HA5 * 59 K1
Chessington Hall Gdns
CHSGTN KT9 .... 205 K5
Chessington Hill Pk
CHSGTN KT9 .... 205 K3
Chessington Pde
CHSGTN KT9 * 205 K3
Chessington Rd CHSCTN KT9 ...... 206 D4
Chessington Wy WWKM BR4 .... 198 E6
Chesson Rd WKENS W14 .... 119 J6
Chesswood Wy PIN HA5 .... 41 H5
Chester Av RCHPK/HAM TW10 ..... 157 G1
WHTN TW2 .... 155 F3
Chester Cl BARN SW13 .... 138 E4
KTBR SW1X 15 H2
SUT SM1 .... 193 K6
Chester Cl North CAMTN NW1 ...... 3 K4
Chester Cl South CAMTN NW1 ...... 3 K5
Chester Crs HACK E8 .... 86 B3
Chester Dr RYLN/HDSTN HA2 ...... 60 A3

Chesterfield Gv EDUL SE22 ...... 143 G6
Chesterfield Ms FSBYPK N4 ...... 67 H2
Chesterfield Rd BAR EN5 .... 20 B6
CHSWK W4 .... 117 K6
FNCH N3 .... 46 E2
HOR/WEW KT19 .... 207 F5
LEY E10 .... 70 A4
Chesterfield St MYFR/PICC W1J ... 9 J7
Chesterfield Wy
HYS/HAR UB3 .... 113 K2
PECK SE15 .... 143 K1
Chesterford Gdns HAMP NW3 ...... 83 F2
Chesterford Rd MNPK E12 .... 90 A4
Chester Gdns MRDN SM4 .... 194 B2
PEND EN3 .... 36 D1
WEA W13 .... 97 H5
Chester Ga CAMTN NW1 .... 3 J4
Chester Ms KTBR SW1X 15 J4
Chester PI CAMTN NW1 .... 3 J3
Chester Rd ARCH N19 .... 66 B6
BFN/LL DA15 .... 147 K6
CAMTN NW1 .... 3 H3
CAN/RD E16 .... 106 C3
ED N9 .... 36 D3
FSTGT E7 .... 89 H5
GDMY/SEVK IG3 .... 73 F5
HSLWW TW4 .... 134 A4
HTHAIR TW6 .... 132 D4
NTHWD HA6 .... 40 C3
TOTM N17 .... 49 H6
WALTH E17 .... 69 F2
WAN E11 .... 71 F3
WIM/MER SW19 .... 177 F2
Chester Rw BCVA SW1W 15 G7
Chester Sq BCVA SW1W 15 J5
Chester Square Ms
BCVA SW1W * 15 J5
Chester St BETH E2 .... 86 C6
KTBR SW1X 15 H4
Chester Ter CAMTN NW1 .... 3 J3
Chester Wy LBTH SE11 .... 122 A5
Chesterton Cl GFD/PVL UB6 ...... 96 B1
WAND/EARL SW18 .... 139 K6
Chesterton Ct EA W5 * 97 K5
Chesterton Dr
STWL/WRAY TW19 .... 152 C3
Chesterton Rd NKENS W10 .... 100 C4
PLSTW E13 .... 106 E2
Chesterton Sq KENS W8 .... 119 J4
Chesterton Ter KUT/HW KT1 ...... 175 H5
PLSTW E13 .... 106 E2
Chester Wy LBTH SE11 .... 122 A5
Chestfield Cl HCH RM12 .... 93 K4
Chesthunte Rd TOTM N17 .... 49 J4
Chestnut Aly FUL/PGN SW6 * 119 J6
Chestnut Av ALP/SUD HA0 .... 79 H3
BKHH IG9 .... 39 H5
BTFD TW8 .... 116 E4
CEND/HSY/T N8 .... 66 E2
E/WMO/HCT KT8 .... 174 A6
EDGW HA8 .... 44 A2
ESH/CLAY KT10 .... 189 J4
FSTGT E7 .... 89 F2
HCH RM12 .... 75 J5
HOR/WEW KT19 .... 207 G2
HPTN TW12 .... 173 F3
MORT/ESHN SW14 .... 138 A4
NTHWD HA6 .... 40 D5
WWKM BR4 .... 214 C3
Chestnut Av North WALTH E17 .... 70 B1
Chestnut Cl ASHF TW15 .... 152 E6
BFN/LL DA15 .... 168 B4
BKHH IG9 .... 39 H5
CAR SM5 .... 194 E5
CAT SE6 .... 165 F6
HYS/HAR UB3 .... 133 J1
HYS/HAR UB3 .... 132 E1
NWCR SE14 .... 144 C2
ORP BR6 .... 217 G3
STHGT/OAK N14 .... 22 C6
STNW/STAM N16 .... 67 K6
STRHM/NOR SW16 .... 162 B6
Chestnut Cottages
TRDG/WHET N20 * 32 C3
Chestnut Dr BXLYHN DA7 .... 148 E4
KTN/HRWW/WS HA3 .... 43 F3
PIN HA5 .... 59 H3
WAN E11 .... 70 E1
Chestnut Gln HCH RM12 .... 75 J4
Chestnut Gv ALP/SUD HA0 .... 79 H3
BAL SW12 .... 161 F2
BARK/HLT IG6 .... 54 E2
EA W5 .... 116 E3
EBAR EN4 .... 33 J1
ISLW TW7 .... 136 B5
MTCM CR4 .... 195 J2
NWMAL KT3 .... 176 A6
SAND/SEL CR2 .... 212 D5

KIL/WHAMP NW6 .... 100 B1
NRWD SE19 .... 180 E3
The Chevenings SCUP DA14 .... 168 D5
Cheverton Rd ARCH N19 .... 66 D5
Chevington CRICK NW2 * 82 D4
Chevet St HOM E9 .... 87 G3
Cheviot Cl BELMT SM2 .... 209 H6
BUSH WD23 .... 28 C1
BXLYHN DA7 .... 150 B3
ENC/FH EN2 .... 23 K3
HYS/HAR UB3 .... 133 G1
Cheviot Gdns CRICK NW2 .... 64 A6
Cheviot Rd EMPK RM11 .... 75 J4
WNWD SE27 .... 180 C1
Cheviot Wy GNTH/NBYPK IG2 ...... 72 E2
Chevron Cl CAN/RD E16 .... 106 E5
Chevy Rd NWDGN UB2 .... 115 H2
Chewton Rd WALTH E17 .... 69 G1
Cheyne Av SWFD E18 .... 52 D6
WHTN TW2 .... 154 E3
Cheyne Cl HAYES BR2 .... 215 J1
Cheyne Gdns CHEL SW3 .... 120 D6
Cheyne HI BRYLDS KT5 .... 191 G3
Cheyne Ms CHEL SW3 .... 120 D6
Cheyne Park Dr WWKM BR4 .... 214 A1
Cheyne Pth HNWL W7 .... 97 F4
Cheyne Rw CHEL SW3 .... 120 D6
Cheyne Wk CHEL SW3 .... 120 D6
CROY/NA CRO 197 H6
HDN NW4 .... 64 A3
WBPTN SW10 .... 140 C1
WCHMH N21 .... 23 G6
Cheyneys Av EDGW HA8 .... 43 K2
Chichele Gdns CROY/NA CRO 212 A2
Chichele Rd CRICK NW2 .... 82 B3
Chicheley Rd
KTN/HRWW/WS HA3 .... 42 C3
Chicheley St STHWK SE1 .... 17 H2
Chichester Av RSLP HA4 .... 58 C6
Chichester Cl BKHTH/KID SE3 ... 146 B1
EHAM E6 .... 107 J5
HPTN TW12 .... 172 E2
STAN HA7 .... 44 A6
Chichester Gdns IL IG1 .... 71 K4
Chichester Rd BAY/PAD W2 * 101 F4
CROY/NA CRO 212 A1
ED N9 .... 36 B3
KIL/WHAMP NW6 .... 100 E1
WAN E11 .... 88 C1
Chichester St PIM SW1V 121 H5
Chichester Wy
EBED/NFELT TW14 .... 154 B2
POP/IOD E14 .... 125 G4
Chicksand St WCHPL E1 .... 13 K2
Chiddingfold
NFNCH/WDSPK N12 .... 32 E5
Chiddingstone Av
BXLYHN DA7 .... 149 G1
Chiddingstone St
FUL/PGN SW6 .... 139 K3
Chieftan Dr PUR RM19 .... 131 K4
Chievely Rd BXLYHN DA7 * 149 J4
Chieveley Rd BXLYHN DA7 .... 149 J5
Chignell PI WEA W13 .... 116 B1
Chigwell HI WAP E1W 104 D6
Chigwell Rd SWFD E18 .... 53 G5
Chilcott Cl ALP/SUD HA0 .... 79 J2
Childebert Rd TOOT SW17 .... 161 F4
Childeric Rd NWCR SE14 .... 144 B1
Childerley St FUL/PGN SW6 ...... 139 H2
Childers St DEPT SE8 .... 124 B6
The Childers WFD IG8 .... 53 K1
Child La GNWCH SE10 .... 125 J3
Child's Ms ECT SW5 * 119 K4
Child's PI ECT SW5 .... 119 K4
Child's St ECT SW5 .... 119 K4
Child's Wk ECT SW5 * 119 K4
Childs Wy GLDGN NW11 .... 64 D2
Chilham Cl BXLY DA5 .... 169 G2
GFD/PVL UB6 .... 97 G1
Chilham Rd ELTH/MOT SE9 .... 166 D6
Chilham Wy HAYES BR2 .... 199 K4
Chillerton Rd TOOT SW17 .... 179 F1
Chillingford Cl BTSEA SW11 * ... 140 B5
Chillingworth Gdns
TWK TW1 * 156 A4
Chillingworth Rd HOLWY N7 ...... 85 F3
Chilmark Gdns NWMAL KT3 .... 192 C3
Chilmark Rd
STRHM/NOR SW16 .... 179 J4
Chiltern Av BUSH WD23 .... 28 C1
WHTN TW2 .... 155 F3
Chiltern Cl BUSH WD23 .... 28 B1
BXLYHN DA7 .... 150 B2
CROY/NA CRO 212 A1
WPK KT4 .... 193 F6
Chiltern Ct BARK * 90 E3
Chiltern Dr BRYLDS KT5 .... 191 J3
Chiltern Gdns CRICK NW2 .... 82 B1
HAYES BR2 .... 199 J1
Chiltern Rd BOW E3 .... 105 J3
GNTH/NBYPK IG2 .... 72 D2
PIN HA5 .... 59 G2
The Chilterns BELMT SM2 * 209 F6
Chiltern St MHST W1U 9 G2
Chiltern Wy WFD IG8 .... 39 F3
Chilthorne Cl CAT SE6 .... 164 C2
Chilton Av EA W5 .... 116 E4
Chilton Gv DEPT SE8 .... 124 A4
Chilton Rd EDGW HA8 .... 44 C2
RCH/KEW TW9 .... 137 H4
Chilton St BETH E2 .... 7 K6
Chiltonian Ms LEW SE13 * 145 G5
Chilver St GNWCH SE10 .... 125 J5
Chilwell Gdns OXHEY WD19 .... 27 G6
Chilworth Ct WIM/MER SW19 ..... 159 G3
Chilworth Gdns SUT SM1 .... 209 G1
Chilworth Ms BAY/PAD W2 .... 101 G5
Chilworth St BAY/PAD W2 .... 101 G5
China Hall Ms
BERM/RHTH SE16 .... 123 K4
China Ms BRXS/STRHM SW2 .... 162 A2

Chinbrook Crs LEE/GVPK SE12 ... 166 A5
Chinbrook Rd LEE/GVPK SE12 ... 166 B5
Chinchilla Dr HSLWW TW4 .... 134 B3
The Chine ALP/SUD HA0 .... 80 H3
MUSWH N10 .... 66 C1
MUSWH N10 .... 35 H1
Chingdale Rd CHING E4 .... 38 C2
Chingford Av CHING E4 .... 37 K5
Chingford La WFD IG8 .... 38 C5
Chingford Mount Rd CHING E4 .... 51 J1
Chingford Rd CHING E4 .... 51 J3
Ching Wy CHING E4 .... 51 H2
Chinnery Cl EN EN1 .... 24 B1
Chinnor Crs GFD/PVL UB6 .... 96 C1
Chipka St POP/IOD E14 .... 125 F2
Chipley St NWCR SE14 .... 124 B6
Chippendale St CLPT E5 .... 87 F1
Chippenham Cl PIN HA5 .... 58 D1
Chippenham Gdns
KIL/WHAMP NW6 .... 100 E2
Chippenham Ms
MV/WKIL W9 .... 100 E3
Chippenham Rd MV/WKIL W9 ...... 100 E3
Chipperfield Rd
STMC/STPC BR5 .... 186 C6
Chipping Cl BAR EN5 .... 20 C4
Chipstead Av THHTH CR7 .... 196 C1
Chipstead Cl BELMT SM2 .... 209 F6
NRWD SE19 * 181 G1
Chipstead Gdns CRICK NW2 .... 63 K6
Chipstead Rd ERITH DA8 .... 150 B1
HTHAIR TW6 .... 132 E4
Chipstead St FUL/PGN SW6 ...... 139 K3
Chirk Cl YEAD UB4 .... 95 J3
Chisenhale Rd BOW E3 .... 105 G1
Chisholm Rd CROY/NA CRO 197 F6
RCHPK/HAM TW10 .... 157 G1
Chislehurst Av
NFNCH/WDSPK N12 .... 47 G3
Chislehurst High St CHST BR7 .. 185 G2
Chislehurst Rd BMLY BR1 .... 184 A4
ORP BR6 .... 202 A4
RCHPK/HAM TW10 .... 157 F1
SCUP DA14 .... 186 C1
STMC/STPC BR5 .... 201 K1
Chislet Cl BECK BR3 .... 182 D2
Chisley Rd SEVS/STOTM N15 ...... 68 A3
Chiswell Sq BKHTH/KID SE3 ..... 146 A3
STLK EC1Y 12 E1
Chiswick Br CHSWK W4 .... 137 K3
Chiswick Cl CROY/NA CRO 211 F1
Chiswick Common Rd
CHSWK W4 .... 118 A4
Chiswick High Rd CHSWK W4 ..... 117 H5
Chiswick House Grounds
CHSWK W4 .... 118 A6
Chiswick La CHSWK W4 .... 118 C6
Chiswick La South CHSWK W4 .... 118 C6
Chiswick Mi CHSWK W4 * 117 K3
Chiswick Pk CHSWK W4 * 117 K5
Chiswick Pier CHSWK W4 .... 138 C1
Chiswick Quay CHSWK W4 .... 137 K4
Chiswick Rd CHSWK W4 .... 117 K4
ED N9 .... 36 D4
Chiswick Sq CHSWK W4 * 118 C6
Chiswick Staithe CHSWK W4 ..... 137 K2
Chiswick Village CHSWK W4 ...... 117 J6
Chiswick Whf CHSWK W4 * 118 D6
Chittenden Cl WFD IG8 * 39 J4
Chitterfield Ga WDR/YW UB7 .... 112 D5
Chitty's La BCTR RM8 .... 73 J6
Chitty St FITZ W1T 10 B1
Chivalry Rd BTSEA SW11 .... 140 D6
Chivenor Gv KUTN/CMB KT2 ...... 174 E1
Chivers Rd CHING E4 .... 37 K6
Choats Manor Wy DAGW RM9 ...... 110 B2
Choats Rd BARK IG11 .... 109 H1
Chobham Gdns
WIM/MER SW19 .... 159 G4
Chobham Rd SRTFD E15 .... 88 B3
Cholmeley Cls HGT N6 * 66 B4
Cholmeley Pk HGT N6 .... 66 B5
Cholmley Gdns
KIL/WHAMP NW6 .... 82 E3
Cholmley Rd THDIT KT7 .... 190 C3
Cholmley Ter THDIT KT7 * 190 C4
Cholmley Vis THDIT KT7 * 190 C4
Cholmondeley Av
WLSDN NW10 .... 99 J1
Chopwell Cl SRTFD E15 * 88 B5
Chorleywood Crs
STMC/STPC BR5 .... 186 A5
Choumert Gv PECK SE15 .... 143 H3
Choumert Ms PECK SE15 .... 143 H3
Choumert Rd PECK SE15 .... 143 G4
Chow Sq HACK E8 .... 86 B3
Chrisaline Ct
STWL/WRAY TW19 .... 152 A1
Chrisp St POP/IOD E14 .... 105 K5
Christabel Cl ISLW TW7 .... 135 K4
Christchurch Av ERITH DA8 ..... 130 A4
KIL/WHAMP NW6 .... 82 B6
KTN/HRWW/WS HA3 .... 61 G3
NFNCH/WDSPK N12 .... 47 H3
RAIN RM13 .... 111 H2
TEDD TW11 .... 174 B1
Christchurch Cl ENC/FH EN2 ..... 23 J3
NFNCH/WDSPK N12 .... 47 J3
WIM/MER SW19 .... 178 C3
Christchurch Gdns
KTN/HRWW/WS HA3 .... 61 G1
Christchurch Hi HAMP NW3 .... 83 H1
Christ Church La BAR EN5 .... 20 C4
Christchurch Lea BAR * 20 C4
Christchurch Pk BELMT SM2 ..... 209 G5
Christ Church Rd BECK BR3 ..... 182 D5
BRYLDS KT5 .... 191 G3
CEND/HSY/T N8 .... 66 E3
Christchurch Rd BFN/LL DA15 ... 168 A6
BRXS/STRHM SW2 .... 162 A3
DART DA1 .... 171 J2
IL IG1 .... 72 A6
MORT/ESHN SW14 .... 137 J6
WIM/MER SW19 .... 178 A3

Christchurch Sq HOM E9..............86 E6
Christchurch St CHEL SW3.........120 E6
Christchurch Ter CHEL SW3 *....120 E6
Christchurch Wy GNWCH SE10..125 H5
Christian Flds
  STRHM/NOR SW16.................180 D3
Christian St WCHPL E1............104 C5
Christie Dr CROY/NA CR0.........197 N2
Christie Rd HOM E9..................87 G4
Christina Sq FSBYPK N4..............67 H5
Christina St SDTCH EC2A...............7 G2
Christine Worsley Cl
  WCHMH N21...........................35 H3
Christopher Av HNWL W7.........116 B3
Christopher Cl
  BFN/LL DA15........................124 A2
Christopher Gdns DAGW RM9.....91 K3
Christopher Pl CAMTN NW1 *........4 D4
Christopher Rd NWDGN UB2.....114 A4
Christophers Ms NTGHL W11 *..119 H1
Christopher St SDTCH EC2A...........7 F2
Christy Ter WFD IG8....................53 J5
Chryssell Rd BRXN/ST SW9.......142 B1
Chubworthy St NWCR SE14.......124 B6
Chudleigh Crs GDMY/SEVK IG3...90 E2
Chudleigh Gdns SUT SM1..........209 G1
Chudleigh Rd BROCKY SE4.........144 C6
  KIL/WHAMP NW6....................82 B5
  WHTN TW2...........................155 K1
Chudleigh St WCHPL E1............105 F5
Chudleigh Wy RSLP HA4.............58 E5
Chulsa Rd SYD SE26..................181 J1
Chumleigh Gdns CMBW SE5 *...123 F6
Chumleigh St CMBW SE5...........123 F6
Chumleigh Wk BRYLDS KT5.......191 G1
Church Ap DUL SE21.................162 E5
Church Av BECK BR3.................182 D4
  CAMTN NW1............................84 B4
  CHING E4................................52 B2
  MORT/ESHN SW14.................138 A5
  NTHLT UB5.............................77 K5
  NWDGN UB2.........................114 D3
  PIN HA5...................................59 J3
  RSLP HA4................................58 A3
  SCUP DA14...........................186 B1
Churchbury Cl EN EN1...............24 A3
Churchbury La EN EN1...............24 A4
Churchbury Rd ELTH/MOT SE9..166 C2
  EN EN1...................................24 A3
Church Cl EDGW HA8.................44 E1
  HSLW TW3............................134 E5
  HYS/HAR UB3........................94 A3
  KENS W8...............................120 A2
  NTHWD HA6...........................40 D3
  TRDG/WHET N20....................33 J5
  WKENS W14 *.......................119 J3
Church Crs FNCH N3..................53 F2
  HOM E9..................................87 F5
  MUSWH N10...........................66 B1
  TRDG/WHET N20....................33 J5
Churchcroft Cl BAL SW12 *.......161 F2
Churchdown BMLY BR1.............165 H6
Church Dr CDALE/KGS NW9.........63 H3
  RYLN/HDSTN HA2....................60 A3
  WWKM BR4...........................214 C1
Church Elm La DAGE RM10.........92 D4
  WALTH E17 *............................69 K1
Church Farm Cl EBAR EN4 *.......33 F1
Church Farm La CHEAM SM3....208 C4
Church Fld RDART DA2..............171 G4
Churchfield Av
  NFNCH/WDSPK N12................47 H2
  RYLN/HDSTN HA2....................94 D6
Churchfield Cl ACT W3..............117 K1
  HNWL W7.............................115 K2
  WEA W13.............................116 C1
  WELL DA16...........................148 B4
Churchfields E/WMO/HCT KT8..173 F5
  GNWCH SE10........................125 F6
  SWFD E18...............................52 E4
Churchfields Av FELT TW13......154 E5
Churchfields Rd BECK BR3.......182 A5
Church Fld Wd
  NFNCH/WDSPK N12................47 G2
  EA W5...................................116 E2
Church Garth ARCH N19 *..........66 D6
Church Ga FUL/PGN SW6..........139 H4
Church Gn BRXN/ST SW9 *........94 D5
  HYS/HAR UB3.........................94 B5
Church Gv KUT/HW KT1...........174 D5
  LEW SE13.............................144 K5
Church Hl CAR SM5.................209 K3
  DART DA1.............................150 B5
  HRW HA1................................60 E2
  ORP BR6...............................202 C5
  RDART DA2...........................171 G5
  WALTH E17.............................69 J1
  WCHMH N21...........................35 F2
  WIM/MER SW19....................177 J1
  WOOL/PLUM SE18................126 E3
Church Hill Rd CHEAM SM3......208 C2
  EBAR EN4................................33 J1
  SURB KT6..............................191 F2
  WALTH E17..............................69 K1
Church Hill Wd
  STMC/STPC BR5....................202 B2
Church Hollow PUR RM19.........131 K5
Church Hyde
  WOOL/PLUM SE18................127 K6
Churchill Av
  KTN/HRWW/WS HA3................61 H3
Churchill Cl EBED/NFELT TW14..153 J3
Churchill Gdns ACT W3...............98 C5
  PIM SW1V............................121 H6
Churchill Gdns Rd
  PIM SW1V............................121 H6
Churchill Pl POP/IOD E14.........124 E1
Churchill Rd CAN/RD E16.........107 G5
  CRICK NW2.............................82 A3
  EDGW HA8.............................44 B2
  KTTN NW5..............................84 B2
  SAND/SEL CR2......................211 K6
Churchill Ter CHING E4................37 J5

Churchill Wk HOM E9.................86 E3
Churchill Wy BMLY BR1...........183 K5
Church La CDALE/KGS NW9 *......62 E5
  CDALE/KGS NW9....................63 F5
  CEND/HSY/T N8.......................67 F1
  CHSGTN KT9.........................206 B4
  CHST BR7.............................185 H4
  DAGE RM10............................92 E5
  EA W5...................................116 D2
  ED N9....................................36 C4
  EFNCH N2...............................47 H6
  EN EN1...................................23 K4
  HAYES BR2...........................200 D5
  KTN/HRWW/WS HA3................41 K5
  PIN HA5..................................41 J6
  PUR RM19............................131 K5
  ROM RM1...............................75 G1
  TEDD TW11............................174 A1
  THDIT KT7.............................190 B3
  TOOT SW17...........................161 G6
  TOTM N17..............................50 A4
  TWK TW1..............................156 B3
  WALTH E17..............................69 K1
  WAN E11.................................70 C5
  WIM/MER SW19....................177 K5
  WLSDN NW10..........................81 J4
Churchley Rd SYD SE26...........163 J6
Church Manor Wy ABYW SE2....128 B4
Church Manorway ERITH DA8...130 A4
Church Meadow SURB KT6......190 D6
Churchmead Cl EBAR EN4...........33 J1
Churchmead Rd WLSDN NW10...81 J4
Church Md
  STRHM/NOR SW16................179 H4
Church Mt EFNCH N2..................65 H2
Church Paddock Ct
  WLGTN SM6..........................210 D1
Church Pas ASHF TW15 *.........152 C6
Church Pas BAR EN5................20 D4
Church Pth CHSWK W4.............117 K3
  MTCM CR4............................178 D6
  NFNCH/WDSPK N12................47 C1
  WAN E11.................................70 A3
  WIM/MER SW19....................177 J5
Church Pl EA W5........................116 E2
  MTCM CR4............................178 D6
Church Ri CHSGTN KT9.............206 B4
  FSTH SE23............................164 A3
Church Rd ACT W3...................117 K2
  ASHF TW15............................152 C6
  BARK IG11...............................90 C4
  BARN SW13..........................138 D3
  BKHH IG9................................39 F3
  BXLYHN DA7.........................149 G3
  CHEAM SM3..........................208 C4
  CROY/NA CR0........................211 J2
  E/WMO/HCT KT8...................189 K1
  ERITH DA8............................129 K5
  ESH/CLAY KT10.....................205 F4
  FELT TW13............................172 B1
  GNTH/NBYPK IG2.....................72 E5
  HAYES BR2...........................183 H6
  HAYES BR2...........................183 K5
  HAYES BR2...........................215 H5
  HDN NW4................................63 K1
  HEST TW5.............................114 A5
  HEST TW5...............................134 B1
  HNWL W7...............................96 A3
  HOR/WEW KT19....................207 F5
  HYS/HAR UB3........................113 J1
  IS N1......................................85 J4
  ISLW TW7..............................135 J2
  KUT/HW KT1.........................175 C5
  LEY E10..................................69 J5
  MNPK E12................................89 K3
  NRWD SE19...........................181 F3
  NTHLT UB5..............................95 J1
  NTHWD HA6...........................40 D3
  NWDGN UB2.........................114 C3
  ORP BR6...............................216 C3
  PEND EN3...............................25 G1
  RCHPK/HAM TW10................137 F6
  RCHPK/HAM TW10................156 A2
  SCUP DA14...........................168 B6
  STAN HA7................................43 H1
  SURB KT6..............................190 D6
  TEDD TW11............................155 K6
  TOTM N17..............................50 B3
  WDR/YW UB7........................112 A2
  WELL DA16...........................148 B3
  WIM/MER SW19....................177 H1
  WLGTN SM6..........................210 B3
  WLSDN NW10..........................81 G5
Church Rw CHST BR7...............185 H4
  FUL/PGN SW6........................140 A1
  HAMP NW3..............................83 G2
  WAND/EARL SW18 *...............139 K6
Church Row Ms CHST BR7........185 H5
Church St BAY/PAD W2................2 B1
  CHSWK W4............................118 C6
  CROY/NA CR0........................211 H1
  DAGE RM10............................92 D5
  ED N9....................................36 B2
  ENC/FH EN2.............................23 K4
  ESH/CLAY KT10.....................204 B2
  EW KT17...............................207 J6
  HPTN TW12...........................173 H4
  ISLW TW7..............................136 C4
  KUT/HW KT1.........................175 C5
  SRTFD E15...............................88 C6
  SUN TW16.............................172 A6
  TOTM N17..............................50 B4

Churchview Rd WHTN TW2.......155 J3
Church Wk BTFD TW8...............116 D6
  BUSH WD23............................28 A1
  CDALE/KGS NW9 *..................63 H5
  CRICK NW2..............................82 D1
  HYS/HAR UB3..........................94 C5
  RDART DA2............................171 G5
  RYNPK SW20.........................177 F6
  STNW/STAM N16.....................85 K2
  STRHM/NOR SW16................179 H4
  THDIT KT7.............................190 A5
Churchway CAMTN NW1..............4 D4
Church Wy TRDG/WHET N20.......33 J5
Churchyard Rw LBTH SE11.........18 B6
Churston Av PLSTW E13..............89 F6
Churston Cl
  BRXS/STRHM SW2 *..............162 C3
Churston Dr MRDN SM4............193 G2
Churston Gdns
  FBAR/BDGN N11......................48 C2
Churton Pl CHSWK W4 *............117 J6
Chyngton Cl BFN/LL DA15.......168 A5
Cibber Rd FSTH SE23...............164 A4
Cicada Rd WAND/EARL SW18...160 B1
Cicely Rd PECK SE15................143 H2
Cinderella Pth GLDGN NW11......65 F5
Cinderford Wy BMLY BR1..........165 H6
Cinema Pde EDGW HA8 *...........44 C2
Cinnamon Cl CROY/NA CR0 *....195 K4
  PECK SE15............................143 G1
Cinnamon St WAP E1W.............123 J1
Cintra Pk NRWD SE19..............181 G3
Circle Gdns WIM/MER SW19.....177 K6
The Circle CRICK NW2.................45 F2
  MLHL NW7..............................45 F2
The Circuits PIN HA5...................59 H1
Circular Rd TOTM N17................50 B6
Circular Wy WOOL/PLUM SE18..126 E6
Circus Ms MBLAR W1H *................8 C2
Circus Pl LVPST EC2M *...............13 F2
Circus Rd STJWD NW8..................2 A1
Circus St GNWCH SE10............145 F1
Cirencester St BAY/PAD W2 *....101 F4
Cissbury Ring North
  NFNCH/WDSPK N12................46 E1
Cissbury Ring South
  NFNCH/WDSPK N12................46 E1
Cissbury Rd SEVS/STOTM N15....67 K2
Citadel Pl LBTH SE11 *.............122 A5
Citizen Rd HOLWY N7.................85 G1
Citron Ter PECK SE15 *............143 J4
City Barracks SHB W12 *..........119 F1
City Garden Rw FSBYE EC1V........6 A3
  SDTCH EC2A.............................7 G6
  STLK EC1Y...............................6 D7
City Wk STHWK SE1....................19 G4
Civic Wy BARK/HLT IG6...............72 C1
  RSLP HA4................................77 H3
Clabon Ms KTBR SW1X.............14 E5
Clack St BERM/RHTH SE16......123 K2
Clacton Rd TOTM N17 *..............50 C5
  WALTH E17...............................69 J3
Claire Ct NFNCH/WDSPK N12....33 C6
Claire Gdns STAN HA7................43 J1
Claire Pl POP/IOD E14..............124 D3
Clairvale Rd HEST TW5.............134 C2
Clairview Rd
  STRHM/NOR SW16................179 G1
Clairville Gdns HNWL W7..........115 K1
Clamp Hl STAN HA7...................28 D6
Clancarty Rd FUL/PGN SW6......139 K3
Clandon Cl ACT W3...................117 J2
  EW KT17...............................207 H4
Clandon Gdns FNCH N3..............64 E1
Clandon Rd GDMY/SEVK IG3......72 E5
Clandon St DEPT SE8...............144 D3
Clandon Ter RYNPK SW20 *.......177 G5
Clanricarde Gdns BAY/PAD W2..100 E6
Clapgate Rd BUSH WD23............28 B1
Clapham Common North Side
  CLAP SW4.............................141 H5
Clapham Common South Side
  CLAP SW4.............................161 G1
Clapham Common West Side
  CLAP SW4.............................140 E5
Clapham Court Ter
  CLAP SW4 *..........................141 K6
Clapham High St CLAP SW4......141 J5
Clapham Manor St CLAP SW4...141 H4
Clapham Park Est CLAP SW4....141 J6
Clapham Park Rd CLAP SW4.....141 J5
Clapham Park Ter
  BRXS/STRHM SW2 *..............141 K5
Clapham Rd BRXN/ST SW9........141 K5
Clapham Rd South IS N1...........85 K4
Claps Gate La EHAM E6...........108 B3
Clapton Common CLPT E5...........68 C5
Clapton Pas CLPT E5..................86 E3
Clapton Sq CLPT E5....................86 E2
Clapton Ter CLPT E5....................68 D5
Clapton Wy CLPT E5...................86 C2
Clara Pl WOOL/PLUM SE18......127 F4
Clare Cl BORE WD6.....................30 B1
  EFNCH N2...............................47 G6
Clare Cnr ELTH/MOT SE9.........167 G2
Clare Ct NTHWD HA6.................40 C1
Claredale St BETH E2................104 C1
Clare Gdns BARK IG11.................91 F4
  FSTGT E7................................88 E2
  NTGHL W11 *.........................100 C5
Clare La IS N1.............................85 J5
Clare Lawn Av
  MORT/ESHN SW14.................138 A6
Clare Ms FUL/PGN SW6............140 A1
Claremont Av
  KTN/HRWW/WS HA3................62 A3
  NWMAL KT3..........................192 D2
  SUN TW16.............................172 A4
Claremont Cl
  BRXS/STRHM SW2 *..............162 A3
  CAN/RD E16..........................127 F1
  IS N1.......................................5 K3

ORP BR6...............................216 A2
Claremont Crs DART DA1.........150 B5
Claremont Dr ESH/CLAY KT10..204 B5
Claremont End
  ESH/CLAY KT10.....................204 B4
Claremont Gdns
  GDMY/SEVK IG3......................72 E6
  SURB KT6..............................191 F2
Claremont Gv CHSWK W4..........138 B1
  WFD IG8..................................53 G2
Claremont House
  WATW WD18 *..........................26 B1
Claremont La ESH/CLAY KT10..204 B3
Claremont Pk FNCH N3...............46 C4
Claremont Park Rd
  ESH/CLAY KT10.....................204 B4
Claremont Rd BMLY BR1...........200 D1
  CROY/NA CR0........................197 H5
  EBAR EN4................................21 C1
  EMPK RM11.............................75 J3
  ESH/CLAY KT10.....................204 E5
  FSTGT E7................................89 F3
  HGT N6....................................65 K4
  KTN/HRWW/WS HA3................42 E5
  MV/WKIL W9..........................100 C1
  SURB KT6..............................191 F3
  TEDD TW11............................174 A1
  TWK TW1..............................156 C2
  WALTH E17..............................51 G5
  WAN E11.................................88 B1
  WEA W13.................................97 G4
Claremont Sq IS N1.......................5 K3
Claremont St GNWCH SE10......124 E6
  UED N18..................................50 C2
Claremont Ter THDIT KT7 *.......190 C4
Claremont Vls CMBW SE5 *......142 E1
  KUT/HW KT1 *.......................175 G5
Claremont Wy CRICK NW2..........64 A4
Claremount Cl BMLY BR1 *.......200 D1
  CLAP SW4.............................161 J2
  IL IG1.....................................71 K3
  NWMAL KT3..........................175 K5
Clarence Cl BUSH WD23.............29 F2
  EBAR EN4................................33 J1
Clarence Crs CLAP SW4............161 J1
  SCUP DA14...........................168 C5
Clarence Gdns CAMTN NW1 *......3 K5
Clarence Gv CAMTN NW1 *..........3 K5
  CHIG IG7..................................54 A2
Clarence La PUT/ROE SW15.....158 C1
Clarence Ms BERM/RHTH SE16..124 A1
  CLPT E5..................................86 D3
  TOOT SW17...........................160 B5
Clarence Pas CAMTN NW1 *........5 F3
Clarence Pl CLPT E5...................86 E3
Clarence Rd BMLY BR1.............184 D6
  BXLYHS DA6.........................149 F5
  CAN/RD E16..........................106 C3
  CHSWK W4...........................117 H5
  CLPT E5..................................86 D3
  CROY/NA CR0........................196 E4
  DEPT SE8..............................124 E6
  ELTH/MOT SE9......................166 D4
  KIL/WHAMP NW6....................82 D5
  MNPK E12................................89 G2
  PEND EN3...............................25 G1
  RCH/KEW TW9......................137 G2
  SCUP DA14...........................168 C5
  SEVS/STOTM N15....................67 J2
  SUT SM1...............................209 F2
  TEDD TW11............................174 A2
  WDGN N22...............................48 E3
  WIM/MER SW19....................178 A2
  WLGTN SM6..........................210 B4
Clarence St KUT/HW KT1.........174 E5
  KUT/HW KT1.........................175 F5
  KUTN/CMB KT2.....................174 E5
  NWDGN UB2.........................114 C3
  RCH/KEW TW9......................137 F5
Clarence Ter CAMTN NW1 *..........3 H6
  HSLW TW3............................135 G5
Clarence Vls KUT/HW KT1 *.......175 G5
Clarence Wy CAMTN NW1 *.........84 B5
Clarenden Cl BAY/PAD W2 *........8 B6
Clarendon Cl BAY/PAD W2...........8 C6
  HOM E9...................................86 E5
  STMC/STPC BR5....................186 B6
Clarendon Crs WHTN TW2........155 J5
Clarendon Cross NTGHL W11....119 H1
Clarendon Dr PUT/ROE SW15...139 F5
Clarendon Gdns HDN NW4..........45 J6
  IL IG1.....................................71 K4
  MV/WKIL W9..........................101 G3
  WBLY HA9................................79 K2
Clarendon Gn
  STMC/STPC BR5....................201 K6
Clarendon Gv CAMTN NW1 *........4 D4
  MTCM CR4............................178 D6
  STMC/STPC BR5....................201 K6
Clarendon Ms BAY/PAD W2...........8 C5
  BORE WD6...............................30 B1
Clarendon Pl BAY/PAD W2...........8 C6
Clarendon Ri LEW SE13............145 F4
Clarendon Rd ASHF TW15.........152 C6
  CROY/NA CR0........................196 C6
  EA W5.....................................98 A2
  HRW HA1................................61 F3
  HYS/HAR UB3........................113 J2
  NTGHL W11...........................100 C6
  SEVS/STOTM N15....................67 J1
  SWFD E18................................52 E6
  WALTH E17..............................69 K3
  WAN E11.................................70 B3
  WDGN N22...............................49 F5
  WIM/MER SW19....................178 D2
  WLGTN SM6..........................210 C4
Clarendon St PIM SW1V............121 G5
Clarendon Ter MV/WKIL W9......101 G3
Clarendon Wy CHST BR7..........186 A6
  WCHMH N21...........................35 J1
Clarens St CAT SE6..................164 C4
Clare Pde GFD/PVL UB6 *..........78 D4
Clare Rd GFD/PVL UB6..............78 D4

HSLWW TW4.........................134 E4
NWCR SE14...........................144 C3
STWL/WRAY TW19................152 A3
WAN E11...................................70 B3
WLSDN NW10..........................81 J5
Clare St BETH E2......................104 D1
Claret Gdns SNWD SE25...........197 F1
Clareville Gv SKENS SW7 *.......120 B4
Clareville Grove Ms
  SKENS SW7 *.........................14 A7
Clareville Rd STMC/STPC BR5...201 H6
Clareville St SKENS SW7...........120 B4
Clare Wy BXLYHN DA7.............149 F2
Clarges Ms MYFR/PICC W1J.......9 J7
Clarges St MYFR/PICC W1J........9 K7
Claribel Rd BRXN/ST SW9.........142 C3
Clarice Wy WLGTN SM6............210 E6
Claridge Rd BCTR RM8...............73 K5
Clarissa Rd CHDH RM6..............73 K4
Clarissa St HACK E8....................7 K1
Clark Cl ERITH DA8...................150 D2
Clarke Ms ED N9.........................36 D5
Clarkers La KTTN NW5................84 B3
Clarkes Av WPK KT4..................193 G5
Clarkes Ms CAVSQ/HST W1G......9 H1
Clarks Md BUSH WD23...............28 C2
Clarkson Rd CAN/RD E16.........106 D5
Clarkson Rw CAMTN NW1 *..........4 A3
Clarkson St BETH E2..................104 D2
Clark's Rd IL IG1.........................72 D6
Clark St WCHPL E1....................104 C1
Clark Wy HEST TW5..................134 C1
Classon Cl WDR/YW UB7.........112 B2
Claston Cl DART DA1.................150 B5
Claude Monet Cl EDUL SE22 *...143 H6
Claude Rd LEY E10......................70 A3
  PECK SE15............................143 J3
  PLSTW E13..............................89 F6
Claude St POP/IOD E14.............124 D4
Claudia Pl WIM/MER SW19.......159 H3
Claudius Cl STAN HA7................29 K5
Claughton Rd PLSTW E13...........107 G1
Clauson Av NTHLT UB5...............78 B3
Clavell St GNWCH SE10............125 F6
Claverdale Rd
  BRXS/STRHM SW2..................162 A2
Clavering Cl TWK TW1..............156 B5
Clavering Rd MNPK E12..............71 H5
Claverings Ind Est
  ED N9......................................37 F4
Clavering Av BARN SW13.........118 E5
Claverley Gv FNCH N3................47 F5
Claverley Vls FNCH N3...............47 F5
Claverton St PIM SW1V.............121 H5
Clave St WAP E1W....................123 K1
Claxton Gv HMSMTH W6...........119 G5
Clay Av MTCM CR4...................179 G5
Claybank Gv LEW SE13............144 E4
Claybridge Rd LEE/GVPK SE12..166 B6
Claybrook Cl EFNCH N2...............47 H6
Claybrook Rd HMSMTH W6.......119 G6
Claybury BUSH WD23..................28 B2
Claybury Rd WFD IG8...................53 J3
Claydon SYD SE26 *.................163 J5
Claydown Ms
  WOOL/PLUM SE18................127 F5
Clayfarm Rd ELTH/MOT SE9.....167 H4
Claygate Cl HCH RM12................93 J2
Claygate Crs CROY/NA CR0......214 A5
Claygate La ESH/CLAY KT10....190 B6
Claygate Lodge Cl
  ESH/CLAY KT10.....................204 E5
Claygate Rd WEA W13..............116 C3
Clayhall Av CLAY IG5...................53 K5
Clayhill Crs ELTH/MOT SE9......166 C6
Claylands Pl VX/NE SW8...........142 B1
Claylands Rd VX/NE SW8..........122 A6
Clay La BUSH WD23...................28 E2
  STWL/WRAY TW19................152 B2
Claymore Cl MRDN SM4...........193 K4
Claypole Dr HEST TW5..............134 D1
Claypole Rd SRTFD E15............106 A1
Clayponds Av BTFD TW8...........116 E4
Clayponds Gdns EA W5.............116 E4
Clayponds La BTFD TW8...........117 F5
Clayside CHIG IG7.......................54 D2
Clays La SRTFD E15....................87 J3
Clays Lane Cl SRTFD E15............87 K3
Clay St MHST W1U.......................9 F2
Clayton Av ALP/SUD HA0............80 A5
Clayton Cl EHAM E6..................108 A5
Clayton Crs BTFD TW8..............116 E5
  IS N1.......................................5 G1
Clayton Croft Rd RDART DA2....170 D4
Clayton Dr DEPT SE8................124 B5
Clayton Fld CDALE/KGS NW9.....45 G4
Clayton Gn GNWCH SE10.........145 G2
Clayton Rd CHSGTN KT9..........205 J2
  HYS/HAR UB3........................113 J2
  ISLW TW7..............................135 K4
  PECK SE15............................143 H2
  ROMW/RG RM7.......................74 E5
Clayton St LBTH SE11...............122 B6
Clayton Ter YEAD UB4 *..............95 H4
Claytonville Ter BELV DA17 *....129 J2
Clay Wood Cl ORP BR6.............201 K4
Clayworth Cl BFN/LL DA15.......168 C1
Cleanthus Cl
  WOOL/PLUM SE18................147 G2
Cleanthus Rd
  WOOL/PLUM SE18................147 G2
Clearbrook Wy WCHPL E1.........104 E5
Clearwater Pl SURB KT6...........190 D3
Clearwater Ter NTGHL W11......119 G2
Clearwell Dr MV/WKIL W9.........101 F3
Cleave Av HYS/HAR UB3...........113 H4
  ORP BR6...............................217 F3
Cleaveland Rd SURB KT6..........190 E2
Cleaverholme Cl SNWD SE25...197 J3
Cleaver Sq LBTH SE11..............122 B5
Cleaver St LBTH SE11...............122 B5
Cleeve Ct EBED/NFELT TW14...153 H3
Cleeve Hl FSTH SE23................163 J3
Cleeve Park Gdns SCUP DA14...168 C5
  SUT SM1...............................194 A3
Clegg St PLSTW E13.................106 E1
  WAP E1W..............................123 J1
Clematis Cottages SHB W12 *....99 J5

Clematis Gdns *WFD* IG8 ....52 E1
Clematis St *SHB* W12 ....99 H6
Clem Attlee Ct *FUL/PGN* SW6 *..119 J3
Clem Attlee Pde
  FUL/PGN SW6 * 119 J6
Clemence St *DAGE* RM10 ....92 E6
Clemence St *POP/IOD* E14 ....105 H4
Clement Av *CLAP* SW4 ....141 J5
Clement Cl *CHSWK* W4 ....118 A4
  KIL/WHAMP NW6 ....82 B5
Clement Gdns *HYS/HAR* UB3 ....113 H4
Clementhorpe Rd *DAGW* RM9 ....91 J4
Clementina Rd *LEY* E10 ....69 H5
Clementine Cl *WEA* W13 ....116 C2
Clement Rd *BECK* BR3 ....182 A5
  WIM/MER SW19 ....177 H1
Clements Av *CAN/RD* E16 ....106 E6
Clements Cl
  NFNCH/WDSPK N12 ....33 F6
Clements Inn *LINN* WC2A 11 J4
Clements La *IL* IG1 ....80 A6
  MANHO EC4N 13 F5
Clements Pl *BTFD* TW8 ....116 E5
Clement's Rd
  BERM/RHTH SE16 ....123 H3
  EHAM E6 ....89 K5
  IL IG1 ....90 B1
  WOT/HER KT12 ....188 A6
Clendon Wy
  WOOL/PLUM SE18 ....128 J4
Clennam St *STHWK* SE1 * 18 D2
Clensham Ct *SUT* SM1 ....193 K6
Clensham La *SUT* SM1 ....193 K6
Clenston Ms *MBLAR* W1H 8 E3
Cleopatra Cl *STAN* HA7 ....29 K5
Clephane Rd *IS* N1 ....85 J4
Clere Pl *SDTCH* EC2A 7 F6
Clere St *SDTCH* EC2A 7 F6
Clerkenwell Cl *CLKNW* EC1R 5 K7
Clerkenwell Gn *CLKNW* EC1R 6 A7
Clerkenwell Rd *CLKNW* EC1R 5 J7
Clermont Rd *HOM* E9 ....86 E6
Clevedon Gdns *HEST* TW5 ......134 A3
  HYS/HAR UB3 ....113 G3
Clevedon Rd *KUT/HW* KT1 ......175 H5
  PGE/AN SE20 ....182 A4
  TWK TW1 ....156 E1
Cleveland Av *CHSWK* W4 ....118 C4
  HPTN TW12 ....172 E3
Cleveland Gdns *BARN* SW13 ....138 C3
  BAY/PAD W2 ....101 G5
  CRICK NW2 ....64 B6
  SEVS/STOTM N15 ....67 J2
  WPK KT4 ....192 B6
Cleveland Gv *WCHPL* E1 ....104 E3
Cleveland Ms *FITZ* W1T 10 A1
Cleveland Park Av *WALTH* E17 ..69 J1
Cleveland Park Crs *WALTH* E17 ..69 J1
Cleveland Pl *STJS* SW1Y 10 C7
Cleveland Ri *MRDN* SM4 ....193 G4
Cleveland Rd *BARN* SW13 ....138 C3
  CHSWK W4 ....118 A2
  ED N9 * 36 D2
  IL IG1 ....90 B1
  IS N1 ....85 K5
  ISLW TW7 ....136 B5
  NWMAL KT3 ....192 B1
  SWFD E18 ....52 E6
  WEA W13 ....97 G4
  WELL DA16 ....148 A3
  WPK KT4 ....192 B6
Cleveland Rw *WHALL* SW1A 16 B1
Cleveland Sq *BAY/PAD* W2 ......101 G5
Cleveland St *CAMTN* NW1 ....3 K7
Cleveland Ter *BAY/PAD* W2 ......101 G5
Cleveley Crs *EA* W5 ....98 A1
Cleveleys Rd *CLPT* E5 ....86 D1
Cleverly Cl *CHARL* SE7 ....126 A4
Cleverly Est *SHB* W12 ....118 D1
Cleve Rd *KIL/WHAMP* NW6 ....82 E5
  SCUP DA14 ....168 C5
Cleves Av *EW* KT17 ....207 K6
Cleves Cl *LOU* IG10 ....39 J1
Cleves Rd *EHAM* E6 ....89 H6
  RCHPK/HAM TW10 ....156 C5
Cleves Wk *BARK/HLT* IG6 ....54 C3
Cleves Wy *HPTN* TW12 ....172 E3
  RSLP HA4 ....59 H5
Clewer Crs *KTN/HRWW/WS* HA3 ..42 D4
Clichen Ms *CLPT* E5 ....87 F2
Clifden Rd *BTFD* TW8 ....116 E6
  CLPT E5 ....86 E5
  TWK TW1 ....156 A3
Cliffe Rd *SAND/SEL* CR2 ....211 K3
Clifford Av *CHST* BR7 ....184 E2
  CLAY IG5 ....71 J1
  MORT/ESHN SW14 ....137 K3
  WLGTN SM6 ....210 C2
Clifford Cl *NTHLT* UB5 ....77 J6
  PLSTW E13 * 107 F2
Clifford Dr *BRXN/ST* SW9 ......142 C5
Clifford Gdns *HYS/HAR* UB3 ....113 G4
  WLSDN NW10 ....100 A1
Clifford Gv *ASHF* TW15 ....152 D6
Clifford Rd *ALP/SUD* HA0 ....79 K6
  BAR EN5 ....21 F4
  CAN/RD E16 ....106 D3
  ED N9 ....24 E6
  HSLWW TW4 ....134 C4
  RCHPK/HAM TW10 ....156 B3
  SNWD SE25 ....197 H1
  WALTH E17 ....52 A5
Clifford St *CONDST* W1S 10 A6
Clifford Wy *WLSDN* NW10 ....81 H2
Cliff End *CAMTN* NW1 ....84 D4
Cliff Ter *DEPT* SE8 ....144 D3
Cliffview Rd *LEW* SE13 ....144 D4
Cliff Vls *CAMTN* NW1 ....84 D4
Cliff Wk *CAN/RD* E16 ....106 D4
Clifton Av *FELT* TW13 ....154 B6
  FNCH N3 ....46 D4
  KTN/HRWW/WS HA3 ....43 H5
  SHB W12 ....118 C2
  WALTH E17 ....69 F1
  WBLY HA9 ....80 B3
Clifton Cl *ORP* BR6 ....216 C3

Clifton Ct *BECK* BR3 * 182 E4
Clifton Crs *PECK* SE15 ....143 J1
Clifton Gdns *CHSWK* W4 ....118 A4
  ENC/FH EN2 ....22 E6
  GLDGN NW11 ....64 D5
  MV/WKIL W9 ....101 G3
  SEVS/STOTM N15 ....68 B3
Clifton Ga *WBPTN* SW10 * 120 B6
Clifton Gv *HACK* E8 ....86 C4
Clifton Hl *STJWD* NW8 ....101 G1
Clifton Ms *SNWD* SE25 ....197 F1
Clifton Pde *FELT* TW13 * 154 B6
Clifton Park Av *RYNPK* SW20 ..177 F5
Clifton Pl *BAY/PAD* W2 ....8 B5
  BERM/RHTH SE16 ....123 K2
  KUTN/CMB KT2 * 175 H4
  WBPTN SW10 * 120 B6
Clifton Ri *NWCR* SE14 ....144 B1
Clifton Rd *CAN/RD* E16 ....106 C4
  CEND/HSY/T N8 ....66 D3
  EMPK RM11 ....75 J3
  FNCH N3 ....47 F1
  FSTGT E7 ....89 H4
  GFD/PVL UB6 ....96 C5
  GNTH/NBYPK IG2 ....72 D3
  HTHAIR TW6 ....132 E5
  ISLW TW7 ....135 K3
  KTN/HRWW/WS HA3 ....62 D2
  KUTN/CMB KT2 ....175 H4
  MV/WKIL W9 ....101 G3
  NWDGN UB2 ....114 D4
  SCUP DA14 ....167 K6
  SNWD SE25 ....197 F1
  TEDD TW11 ....155 K6
  WDGN N22 ....48 C4
  WELL DA16 ....148 D4
  WIM/MER SW19 ....177 G2
  WLSDN NW10 ....100 B1
  WLSDN NW10 ....?? ??
Clifton St *SDTCH* EC2A 13 G1
Clifton Ter *FSBYPK* N4 ....65 G1
Clifton Vis *MV/WKIL* W9 ....101 F4
Clifton Wy *ALP/SUD* HA0 ....80 A6
  PECK SE15 ....143 K1
Cline Rd *FBAR/BDGN* N11 ....48 C2
Clinger Ct *IS* N1 ....7 H1
Clink St *STHWK* SE1 ....12 F7
Clinton Av *E/WMO/HCT* KT8 ....189 H1
  WELL DA16 ....148 B5
Clinton Crs *BARK/HLT* IG6 ....54 E2
Clinton Rd *BOW* E3 ....105 G2
  FSTGT E7 ....88 E2
  SEVS/STOTM N15 ....67 K1
Clinton Ter *DEPT* SE8 * 124 D6
  SUT SM1 * 209 G2
Clipper Cl *BERM/RHTH* SE16 * ..124 A1
Clipper Wy *LEW* SE13 ....145 F5
Clippesby Cl *CHSGTN* KT9 * 206 B4
Clipstone Ms *FITZ* W1T 10 A1
  GTPST W1W 10 A1
Clipstone Rd *HSLW* TW3 ....135 F4
Clipstone St *GTPST* W1W 9 K1
Clissold Cl *EFNCH* N2 ....47 K6
Clissold Crs *STNW/STAM* N16 ..85 K2
Clissold Rd *STNW/STAM* N16 ....85 J2
Clitheroe Av *RYLN/HDSTN* HA2 ..59 K5
Clitheroe Gdns *OXHEY* WD19 ....27 H5
Clitheroe Rd *BRXN/ST* SW9 ....141 K3
  CRW RM5 ....56 E1
Clitherow Av *HNWL* W7 ....116 B3
Clitherow Rd *BTFD* TW8 ....116 C5
Clitterhouse Crs *CRICK* NW2 ....64 A5
Clitterhouse Rd *CRICK* NW2 ....64 A5
  WK DA1 ....170 C1
Clive Av *WAND/EARL* SW18 ....160 B3
  UED N18 ....50 C2
Clive Ct *WLSDN* NW10 ....81 H5
Cliveden Cl *NFNCH/WDSPK* N12 ..33 G6
Cliveden Pl *BGVA* SW1W 15 G6
Cliveden Rd *WIM/MER* SW19 ..177 J4
Clivedon Ct *WEA* W13 ....97 H4
Clivedon Rd *CHING* E4 ....52 C1
Clive Rd *BELV* DA17 ....129 H4
  DUL SE21 ....162 E5
  EBED/NFELT TW14 ....153 K1
  EN EN1 ....24 C5
  ESH/CLAY KT10 ....204 B2
  GPK RM2 ....75 K2
  TWK TW1 ....156 A6
  WIM/MER SW19 ....178 D2
Clivesdale Dr *HYS/HAR* UB3 ....113 K1
Clive Wy *EN* EN1 ....24 C5
Cloak La *CANST* EC4R 12 E5
Clockhouse Av *BARK* IG11 ....90 C6
Clockhouse Cl *WIM/MER* SW19 ..159 F5
Clockhouse La *ASHF* TW15 ......152 D5
  CRW RM5 ....56 E3
Clock House Pde *PLMGR* N13 * ..49 G1
Clockhouse Pl *PUT/ROE* SW15 ..139 H6
Clock House Rd *BECK* BR3 ......182 B6
Clock Pde *ENC/FH* EN2 * 23 K6
Clock Tower Ms *IS* N1 * 109 H2
  THMD SE28 ....128 C1
Clock Tower Pl *HOLWY* N7 ......84 E4
Clock Tower Rd *ISLW* TW7 ......136 A4
Cloister Cl *RAIN* RM13 ....111 K1
  TEDD TW11 ....174 C1
Cloister Gdns *EDGW* HA8 ....44 E1
  SNWD SE25 ....197 J3
Cloister Rd *ACT* W3 ....98 E4
  CRICK NW2 ....82 D1
Cloisters Av *HAYES* BR2 ....200 E2
Clonard Wy *PIN* HA5 ....42 A6
Clonbrock Rd *STNW/STAM* N16 ..86 A2
Cloncurry St *FUL/PGN* SW6 ....139 F3
Clonmel Cl *RYLN/HDSTN* HA2 ..60 D5
Clonmel Rd *TOTM* N17 ....50 A6
  FUL/PGN SW6 ....139 J2
  TEDD TW11 ....155 H4
Clonmore St
  WAND/EARL SW18 ....159 J3
Clonmore Av *ORP* BR6 ....217 F3
Cloonmore Av *ORP* BR6 ....217 F3
Clorane Gdns *HAMP* NW3 ....82 E1
Closemead Cl *NTHWD* HA6 ......40 A2
The Close *ALP/SUD* HA0 ....80 A6
  BECK BR3 ....198 A1
  BUSH WD23 * 28 A1
  BXLY DA5 ....169 H1
  CAR SM5 ....209 J6

CHDH RM6 ....74 A3
CHEAM SM3 ....193 J4
CHING E4 ....52 A3
EBAR EN4 ....21 H1
GNTH/NBYPK IG2 ....72 E5
ISLW TW7 ....135 J3
MTCM CR4 ....194 E1
NWMAL KT3 ....175 K5
PIN HA5 ....59 J4
PIN HA5 ....59 K4
RCH/KEW TW9 ....137 J4
RDART DA2 ....171 F5
SCUP DA14 ....186 C1
SNWD SE25 * 197 H3
STHGT/OAK N14 ....34 D4
STMC/STPC BR5 ....201 J5
SURB KT6 ....191 F4
TRDG/WHET N20 ....32 D4
WBLY HA9 ....80 C1
WAN E11 ....88 C1
Cobham Av NWMAL KT3 ....192 D2
Cobham Ct MTCM CR4 ....178 C6
  BTSEA SW11 ....160 D2
  BRDF DA6 ....44 D5
  EN EN1 ....24 C4
  HAYES BR2 ....200 D4
  WLGTN SM6 ....210 E4
Cobham Ms CAMTN NW1 ....84 D5
Cobham Pl BXLYHS DA6 ....148 E5
  HEST TW5 ....134 B1
  KUT/HW KT1 ....175 H5
  WALTH E17 ....52 A4
Cobland Rd LEE/GVPK SE12 ......166 B6
Coborn Rd BOW E3 ....105 H2
Coborn St BOW E3 ....105 H2
Cobourg Rd CMBW SE5 ....123 G6
Cobourg St CAMTN NW1 ....4 B5
Cobden Ms SYD SE26 * 181 J1
Coburg Crs BRXS/STRHM SW2 ..162 A3
Coburg Dwellings WCHPL E1 * ..104 E6
Coburg Gdns CLAY IG5 ....53 H5
Cochran Rd WDGN N22 ....49 F5
Cochrane Ms STJWD NW8 ....2 B3
Cochrane Rd WIM/MER SW19 ....177 H3
Cochrane St STJWD NW8 ....2 B3
Cockcrow HI SURB KT6 * 190 E5
Cockerell Rd HLT IG7 ....69 G4
Cockfosters Pde EBAR EN4 * 22 A5
Cockfosters Rd EBAR EN4 ....22 A1
Cock La STBT EC1A 12 A2
Cockmannings La
  STMC/STPC BR5 ....202 E5
Cockmannings Rd
  STMC/STPC BR5 ....202 E5
Cocks Crs NWMAL KT3 ....192 C1
Cocksett Av ORP BR6 ....216 E4
Cockspur Ct WHALL SW1A 10 D7
Cockspur St STJS SW1Y 10 D7
Cocksure La SCUP DA14 ....169 H6
Coda Centre
  FUL/PGN SW6 * 139 H2
Code St WCHPL E1 ....7 K7
Codling Cl WAP E1W 123 H1
Codling Wy ALP/SUD HA0 ....79 K2
Codrington HI FSTH SE23 ....164 B2
Codrington Ms NTGHL W11 ......100 C5
Cody Cl KTN/HRWW/WS HA3 ......43 K6
  WLGTN SM6 ....210 D5
Cody Rd CAN/RD E16 ....106 B3
Coe Av SNWD SE25 ....197 H3
Coe's Aly BAR EN5 ....20 C5
Coffey St DEPT SE8 ....144 D1
Cogan Av WALTH E17 ....51 G4
Coin St STHWK SE1 ....17 K1
Coity Rd KTTN NW5 ....84 A4
Cokers La DUL SE21 ....162 D5
Coke St WCHPL E1 ....104 C5
Colbeck Ms SKENS SW7 ....120 A4
Colbeck Rd HRW HA1 ....60 C4
Colberg Pl STNW/STAM N16 * 68 A4
Colborne Wy WPK KT4 ....208 A1
Colbrook Av HYS/HAR UB3 ......113 G3
Colbrook Cl HYS/HAR UB3 ....113 G3
Colburn Wy SUT SM1 ....209 H1
Colby Rd NRWD SE19 ....181 F1
Colchester Dr PIN HA5 ....59 H2
Colchester Rd EDGW HA8 ....44 E3
  LEY E10 ....70 A4
  NTHWD HA6 ....40 E5
  WALTH E17 ....69 J3
Colchester St WCHPL E1 ....13 K3
Coldbath Sq CLKNW EC1R 5 J7
Coldbath St LEW SE13 ....144 E2
Cold Blow Crs BXLY DA5 ....170 A3
Cold Blow La NWCR SE14 ....144 A1
Coldershaw Rd WEA W13 ....116 B2
Coldfall Av MUSWH N10 ....47 K5
Coldharbour POP/IOD E14 ....125 F1
Coldharbour Crest
  ELTH/MOT SE9 * 167 F5
Coldharbour La BRXN/ST SW9 ..142 B5
  BUSH WD23 ....28 B1
  HYS/HAR UB3 ....113 J1
  RAIN RM13 ....130 D1
Coldharbour Pl CMBW SE5 ....142 D3
Coldharbour Rd CROY/NA CRO ..211 G3
Coldharbour Wy
  CROY/NA CRO 211 G3
Coldstream Gdns
  WAND/EARL SW18 ....159 J1
Colebeck Ms IS N1 ....85 H4
Colebert Av WCHPL E1 ....104 E3
Colebrook Cl MLHL NW7 ....46 A3
Colebrooke Av WEA W13 ....97 H5
Colebrooke Dr WAN E11 ....71 G4
Colebrooke Pl IS N1 ....6 B1
Colebrooke Rw IS N1 ....6 B2
Colebrook Rd STRHM/NOR SW16 ..179 K4
Colebrook St ERITH DA8 ....150 C5
Colebrook Wy FBAR/BDGN N11 ..48 B1
Coleby Pth CMBW SE5 * 142 E1
Cole Cl THMD SE28 ....128 C1
Coledale Dr STAN HA7 ....43 J3
Coleford Rd WAND/EARL SW18 ..140 B6
Cole Gdns HEST TW5 ....133 K6
Colegrave Rd SRTFD E15 ....88 B3
Colegrove Rd PECK SE15 ....123 G6
Coleherne Ms WBPTN SW10 ....120 A5
Coleherne Rd ECT SW5 ....120 A5
Colehill Gdns FUL/PGN SW6 * ..139 H2
Colehill La FUL/PGN SW6 ....139 H2
Coleman Cl SNWD SE25 ....181 H5
Coleman Flds IS N1 ....6 E1
Coleman Rd BELV DA17 ....129 H3
  CMBW SE5 ....143 F1

WAN E11 ....88 C1
EDGW HA8 ....44 D2
ENFH N21 ....24 C4
EN EN1 ....24 C4
HAYES BR2 ....200 D4
WLGTN SM6 ....210 E4
Cole Park Rd TWK TW1 ....156 B2
Colepits Wood Rd
  ELTH/MOT SE9 ....147 J6
Coleraine Rd BKHTH/KID SE3 ....125 J6
  CEND/HSY/T N8 ....49 G6
  SUT SM1 ....209 J2
Coleridge Av MNPK E12 ....89 J4
Coleridge Cl VX/NE SW8 ....141 G3
Coleridge Gdns
  KIL/WHAMP NW6 ....140 E1
  WBPTN SW10 ....140 B3
Coleridge Rd ASHF TW15 ....152 B6
  CEND/HSY/T N8 ....66 D3
  CROY/NA CRO 197 K4
  DART DA1 ....151 K5
  FSBYPK N4 ....67 G1
  HARH RM3 ....57 J3
  NFNCH/WDSPK N12 ....47 G1
  WALTH E17 ....69 H1
Coleridge Sq WEA W13 ....97 G5
Coleridge Wy GLDGN NW11 ....64 E1
Coleridge Wy ORP BR6 ....202 B3
  WDR/YW UB7 ....112 C4
  YEAD UB4 ....95 G3
Cole Rd TWK TW1 ....156 B1
Colesburg Rd BECK BR3 ....182 C6
Coles Crs RYLN/HDSTN HA2 ......60 C6
Coles Green Rd CRICK NW2 ......63 K6
Coleshill Rd TEDD TW11 ....173 K2
Colestown St BTSEA SW11 ......140 D3
Cole St STHWK SE1 ....18 D3
Colet Cl PLMGR N13 ....49 H2
Colet Gdns WKENS W14 ....119 G5
Coley St FSBYW WC1X 5 H7
Colfe & Hatcliffe Glebe
  LEW SE13 ....144 E5
Colfe Rd FSTH SE23 ....164 B3
Colham Av WDR/YW UB7 ....112 B1
Colham Mill Rd WDR/YW UB7 ....112 A2
Colina Ms CEND/HSY/T N8 ....66 D3
Colin Cl CDALE/KGS NW9 ....45 G3
  CROY/NA CRO 213 H1
  WWKM BR4 ....214 D1
Colin Crs CDALE/KGS NW9 ....45 H3
Colindale Av CDALE/KGS NW9 ....45 F6
Colindeep Gdns HDN NW4 ....63 J2
Colindeep La CDALE/KGS NW9 ....63 J2
Colin Dr CDALE/KGS NW9 ....63 J3
Colinette Rd PUT/ROE SW15 ....139 F5
Colin Gdns CDALE/KGS NW9 ......45 H4
Colin Park Rd CDALE/KGS NW9 ..45 G3
Colinton Rd GDMY/SEVK IG3 ......73 H1
Coliston Rd WAND/EARL SW18 ..159 K2
Collamore Av
  WAND/EARL SW18 ....160 D3
Collapit Cl HRW HA1 ....60 B3
Collard Pl CAMTN NW1 ....84 B5
College Ap GNWCH SE10 ....125 F6
Collerne Rd BKHTH/KID SE3 ......42 E4
College Cl KTN/HRWW/WS HA3 ..42 E3
  UED N18 ....50 B1
College Ct EA W5 * 98 A1
College Crs HAMP NW3 ....83 G4
College Cross IS N1 ....85 G5
College Dr RSLP HA4 ....58 E4
  THDIT KT7 ....189 K5
College East WCHPL E1 * 13 K2
College Gdns CHING E4 ....37 K2
  ENC/FH EN2 ....23 H2
  NWMAL KT3 ....192 C2
  REDBR IG4 ....71 J2
  TOOT SW17 ....160 D4
  UED N18 * 50 B1
College Gn NRWD SE19 ....181 F3
College Gv CAMTN NW1 ....4 C1
College HI CANST EC4R * 12 D5
College La KTTN NW5 ....84 B2
College Ms KTN/HRWW/WS HA3 ..42 E3
  WEST SW1P 16 E5
College Pde KIL/WHAMP NW6 *..82 C6
College Park Cl LEW SE13 ....145 G5
College Pl CAMTN NW1 ....84 C6
  WALTH E17 ....70 C1
  WBPTN SW10 * 140 B1
College Rd BMLY BR1 ....183 K4
  CROY/NA CRO 196 E6
  DUL SE21 ....163 F2
  ENC/FH EN2 ....23 J3
  HRW HA1 ....61 G1
  ISLW TW7 ....136 A2
  KTN/HRWW/WS HA3 ....42 E3
  TOTM N17 ....50 B2
  WALTH E17 ....70 A2
  WBLY HA9 ....61 K5
  WCHMH N21 ....35 G3
  WEA W13 ....97 H3
  WIM/MER SW19 ....178 C2
  WLSDN NW10 ....100 A1
Colesale Wd CDALE/KGS NW9 ....12 D5
College Ter FNCH N3 ....46 D5
College Vw ELTH/MOT SE9 ......166 C3
  HYS/HAR UB3 ....94 D4
  NTHWD HA6 ....40 D2
College Yd KIL/WHAMP NW6 * 82 C6
  KTTN NW5 ....84 B2
Collent St HOM E9 ....86 E4
Colless Rd SEVS/STOTM N15 ......68 B2
Collett Rd BERM/RHTH SE16 ....123 H3
Collett Wy NWDGN UB2 ....115 G2
Collier Cl EHAM E6 ....108 B6
  HOR/WEW KT19 ....206 C4
Collier Dr EDGW HA8 ....44 C5
Collier Row La CRW RM5 ....56 D1
Collier Row Rd CRW RM5 ....56 B1
Colliers Shaw HAYES BR2 ....215 J3
Collier St IS N1 ....5 G3
Colliers Water La THHTH CR7 ....196 B2
Collindale Av BFN/LL DA15 ......168 B3
  CDALE/KGS NW9 ....63 J1
  ERITH DA8 ....129 J6
Collingbourne Rd SHB W12 ......118 E1

Collingham Gdns ECT SW5 ......120 A4
Collingham Pl ECT SW5 ....120 A4
Collingham Rd ECT SW5 ....120 A4
Collings Cl WDGN N22 ....49 F2
Collington St GNWCH SE10 * ...125 C5
Collingtree Rd SYD SE26 ....163 K6
Collingwood Av BRYLDS KT5 ...191 K5
　MUSWH N10 ....48 A6
Collingwood Cl PGE/AN SE20 ...181 J4
Collingwood Rd WHTN TW2 ....155 F2
Collingwood Rd MTCM CR4 ......178 D5
　RAIN RM13 ....111 H1
　SEVS/STOTM N15 ....68 A1
　SUT SM1 ....208 E2
Collingwood St WCHPL E1 ....104 D3
Collins Av STAN HA7 ....44 A5
Collins Dr RSLP HA4 ....59 G6
Collinson St STHWK SE1 ....18 C3
Collinson Wk STHWK SE1 ....18 C3
Collins Rd HBRY N5 ....85 J2
Collins Sq BKHTH/KID SE3 ......145 J4
Collins St BKHTH/KID SE3 ....145 H3
Collinwood Av PEND EN3 ....24 E4
Collinwood Gdns
　GNTH/NBYPK IG2 ....71 K2
Collyer Av CROY/NA CR0 ....210 E2
Collyer Pl PECK SE15 ....143 H2
Collyer Rd CROY/NA CR0 ....210 E2
Colman Pde EN EN1 * 24 A4
Colman Rd CAN/RD E16 ....107 G4
Colmar Cl WCHPL E1 ....105 F3
Colmer Pl KTN/HRWW/WS HA3 ..42 D3
Colmer Rd STRHM/NOR SW16 ...179 E3
Colmore Ms PECK SE15 ....143 J2
Colmore Rd PEND EN3 ....24 E5
Colnbrook St STHWK SE1 ....18 A4
Colne Av OXHEY WD19 ....27 F1
Colne Ct HOR/WEW KT19 ....206 E2
Colne Rd CLPT E5 ....87 C2
　WCHMN N21 ....35 K2
　WHTN TW2 ....155 K3
Colne St PLSTW E13 ....106 E2
Colney Hatch La
　FBAR/BDGN N11 ....47 K2
　MUSWH N10 ....48 A3
Colne Rd DART DA1 ....171 J1
Cologne Rd BTSEA SW11 ....140 C5
Colombo Rd IL IG1 ....72 C6
Colombo St STHWK SE1 ....18 A1
Colomb St GNWCH SE10 ....125 H5
Colonial Av WHTN TW2 ....155 H1
Colonial Dr CHSWK W4 ....117 K4
Colonial Rd EBED/NFELT TW14 ..153 H2
Colonnade BMSBY WC1N 5 K6
The Colonnade DEPT SE8 * 124 C4
Colosseum Ter CAMTN NW1 * 3 K6
Colson Rd CROY/NA CR0 ....196 E6
Colson Wy STRHM/NOR SW16 ...161 H6
Colsterworth Rd
　SEVS/STOTM N15 ....68 B1
Colston Av CAR SM5 ....209 J2
Colston Rd FSTGT E7 ....89 H4
　MORT/ESHN SW14 ....137 K5
Colthurst Crs FSBYPK N4 ....67 J6
Colthurst Dr ED N9 ....36 D5
Coltness Crs ABYW SE2 ....128 C5
Colton Gdns TOTM N17 ....49 J6
Colton Rd HRW HA1 ....60 E2
Colts Yd WAN E11 * 70 D5
Columbas Dr HAMP NW3 ....65 H6
Columbia Av EDGW HA8 ....44 D5
　RSLP HA4 ....59 F5
　WPK KT4 ....192 C4
Columbia Rd BETH E2 ....7 K4
　PLSTW E13 ....106 D3
Columbine Whf PEND EN3 * 25 G6
Columbine Av EHAM E6 ....107 J4
　SAND/SEL CR2 ....211 H5
Columbus Gdns NTHWD HA6 ...40 A4
Colveley Ct LEW SE13 * 145 F3
Colveston Crs HACK E8 ....86 B3
Colville Est IS N1 ....7 G1
Colville Gdns NTGHL W11 ....100 D5
Colville Houses NTGHL W11 ....100 D5
Colville Ms NTGHL W11 ....100 D5
Colville Pl FITZ W1T 10 B2
Colville Rd ACT W3 ....117 J3
　ED N9 ....36 D3
　NTGHL W11 ....100 D5
　WALTH E17 ....51 G5
　WAN E11 ....88 A1
Colville Sq NTGHL W11 ....100 D5
Colville Square Ms
　NTGHL W11 * 100 D5
Colville Ter NTGHL W11 ....100 D5
Colvin Cl SYD SE26 ....181 K1
Colvin Gdns BARK/HLT IG6 ....54 C3
　CHING E4 ....38 A5
　SWFD E18 ....71 F1
Colvin Rd EHAM E6 ....89 J5
　THHTH CR7 ....196 B2
Colwall Gdns WFD IG8 ....52 E1
Colwell Rd EDUL SE22 ....143 G6
Colwick Cl HGT N6 ....66 D4
Colwith Rd HMSMTH W6 ....119 F6
Colwood Gdns
　WIM/MER SW19 ....178 D3
Colworth Gv WALW SE17 ....18 D7
Colworth Rd CROY/NA CR0 ....197 H5
　WAN E11 ....70 C3
Colwyn Av GFD/PVL UB6 ....97 F1
Colwyn Cl STRHM/NOR SW16 ...179 H1
Colwyn Crs HSLW TW3 ....135 H2
Colwyn Gn CDALE/KGS NW9 * 63 G3
Colwyn Rd CRICK NW2 ....81 K1
Colyer Cl ELTH/MOT SE9 ....167 G4
　WELL DA16 ....148 E2
Colyers La ERITH DA8 ....149 K2
Colyton Cl ALP/SUD HA0 ....79 J3
　WELL DA16 ....148 E2
Colyton La STRHM/NOR SW16 ...180 B1
Colyton Rd EDUL SE22 ....143 J6
Combe Av BKHTH/KID SE3 ....145 J1
Combedale Rd GNWCH SE10 ...125 K5

Combemartin Rd
　WAND/EARL SW18 ....159 H2
Comber Cl CRICK NW2 ....63 K6
Comber Gv CMBW SE5 ....142 D1
Combermere Rd
　BRXN/ST SW9 ....142 A4
　MRDN SM4 ....194 A3
Combe Rd WATW WD18 ....26 D1
Comberton Rd CLPT E5 ....68 D6
Combeside WOOL/PLUM SE18 ..148 A1
Combes Rd DAGW RM9 ....92 B6
Combwell Crs ABYW SE2 ....128 B3
Comely Bank Rd WALTH E17 ......70 A2
Comeragh Ms WKENS W14 ....119 H5
Comeragh Rd WKENS W14 ....119 H5
Comerford Rd BROCKY SE4 ......144 B5
Comet Cl MNPK E12 ....89 H2
Comet Pl DEPT SE8 ....144 D1
Comet Rd STWL/WRAY TW19 ...152 A2
Comet St DEPT SE8 ....144 D1
Commerce Rd BTFD TW8 ....116 D6
　WDGN N22 ....49 E4
Commerce Wy CROY/NA CR0 ...211 F1
Commercial Rd POP/IOD E14 ...105 G5
　UED N18 ....50 E1
　WCHPL E1 ....104 C5
Commercial St WCHPL E1 ....13 J2
Commercial Wy PECK SE15 ......143 H1
　WLSDN NW10 ....98 D1
Commerell Pl GNWCH SE10 .....125 J5
Commerell St GNWCH SE10 .....125 H5
Commodore Pde
　STRHM/NOR SW16 * 180 A3
Commodore St WCHPL E1 ....105 G3
Commondale PUT/ROE SW15 ...139 F3
Common La ESH/CLAY KT10 .....205 G5
　RDART DA2 ....170 D4
Common Rd BARN SW13 ....138 D4
　ESH/CLAY KT10 ....205 G5
　STAN HA7 ....28 D5
Commonside HAYES BR2 ....215 G2
Commonside East MTCM CR4 ...179 F6
Commonside West MTCM CR4 ...179 E6
The Common EA W5 ....117 F1
　NWDGN UB2 ....114 C4
　SRTFD E15 ....88 B1
　STAN HA7 ....29 F4
Commonwealth Av
　HYS/HAR UB3 ....94 D6
　SHB W12 ....99 K6
Commonwealth Rd TOTM N17 ...50 C3
Commonwealth Wy
　ABYW SE2 ....128 C5
Community Cl HEST TW5 ....134 A2
Community La HOLWY N7 ....84 D3
Community Rd GFD/PVL UB6 .....78 C6
　SRTFD E15 ....88 B3
Como Rd FSTH SE23 ....164 B4
Como St ROMW/RG RM7 ....75 F2
Compass Cl EDGW HA8 ....30 B6
Compass Hl RCHPK/HAM TW10 ..156 E1
Compayne Gdns
　KIL/WHAMP NW6 ....83 F5
Compton Av ALP/SUD HA0 ....79 H2
　EHAM E6 ....107 H1
　GPK RM2 ....57 K6
　HGT N6 ....65 J4
　IS N1 ....85 H4
Compton Cl CAMTN NW1 ....3 K5
　EA W5 ....98 A4
　ESH/CLAY KT10 ....204 D4
　GLDGN NW11 ....64 D3
　PECK SE15 ....143 H1
　WEA W13 ....97 G5
Compton Crs CHSGTN KT9 ....206 A4
　CHSWK W4 ....117 K6
　NTHLT UB5 ....77 H6
　TOTM N17 ....49 J3
Compton Pas FSBYE EC1V 6 B6
Compton Pl ERITH DA8 ....130 C6
　OXHEY WD19 ....27 J6
　STAN WC1H 4 E6
Compton Ri PIN HA5 ....59 J3
Compton Rd CROY/NA CR0 ....197 J5
　HYS/HAR UB3 ....94 C6
　IS N1 ....85 H4
　WCHMN N21 ....35 H3
　WIM/MER SW19 ....177 J2
　WLSDN NW10 ....100 B2
Compton St FSBYE EC1V 6 A6
Compton Ter IS N1 ....85 H4
　WCHMN N21 ....35 H3
Comreddy Cl ENC/FH EN2 ....23 H2
Comus Pl WALW SE17 ....19 F7
Comyn Rd BTSEA SW11 ....140 D5
Comyns Cl CAN/RD E16 ....106 D4
Comyns Rd DAGW RM9 ....92 C5
The Comyns BUSH WD23 ....28 C3
Conant Ms WCHPL E1 ....104 C6
Concanon Rd
　BRXS/STRHM SW2 ....142 A5
Concert Hall Ap STHWK SE1 * 17 H1
Concord Cl NTHLT UB5 ....95 H2
Concorde Cl HSLW TW3 ....135 G3
Concorde Dr EHAM E6 ....107 K4
Concord Rd ACT W3 ....98 D3
　PEND EN3 ....24 E6
Condell Rd VX/NE SW8 ....141 H2
Conder St POP/IOD E14 ....105 G5
Condover Crs
　WOOL/PLUM SE18 ....147 G1
Condray Pl BTSEA SW11 ....140 D1
Conduit Ct COVGDN WC2E * 10 E5
Conduit La SAND/SEL CR2 ....212 C3
　UED N18 ....50 E1
Conduit Ms BAY/PAD W2 ....8 A4
Conduit Pas BAY/PAD W2 * 8 A4
Conduit Pl BAY/PAD W2 ....8 A4
Conduit Rd WOOL/PLUM SE18 ...127 G5
Conduit St CONDST W1S 9 K5
Conduit Wy WLSDN NW10 ....80 E5
Conewood St HBRY N5 ....85 H1
Coney Burrows CHING E4 ....38 C4
Coney Hall Pde WWKM BR4 * ...214 C1
Coney Hill Rd WWKM BR4 ....199 H6

Coney Wy VX/NE SW8 ....122 A6
Conference Cl CHING E4 * 38 A4
Conference Rd ABYW SE2 ....128 D4
Congleton Gv
　WOOL/PLUM SE18 ....127 H5
Congo Dr ED N9 ....36 E5
Congo Rd WOOL/PLUM SE18 ...127 J5
Congress Rd ABYW SE2 ....128 D4
Congreve Rd ELTH/MOT SE9 ....146 E4
Congreve St WALW SE17 ....19 G7
Conical Cnr ENC/FH EN2 ....23 J3
Conifer Av CRW RM5 ....56 D1
Conifer Cl ORP BR6 ....216 D2
　EN EN1 ....35 J1
Conifer Gdns EN EN1 ....36 A1
　STRHM/NOR SW16 ....162 A5
　SUT SM1 ....194 A6
Conifers Cl TEDD TW11 ....174 D3
Conifer Wy ALP/SUD HA0 ....79 J1
　HYS/HAR UB3 ....94 B6
　SWLY BR8 ....187 K4
Coniger Rd FUL/PGN SW6 ....139 K3
Coningham Ms SHB W12 ....118 D1
Coningham Rd SHB W12 ....118 E2
Coningsby Av CDALE/KGS NW9 ..45 G5
Coningsby Cottages EA W5 * 116 E2
Coningsby Gdns CHING E4 ....51 K2
Coningsby Rd EA W5 ....116 D2
　FSBYPK N4 ....67 H4
　SAND/SEL CR2 ....211 J6
Conington Rd LEW SE13 ....144 E3
Conisbee Ct STHGT/OAK N14 ....22 C6
Conisborough Crs CAT SE6 ......165 F5
Coniscliffe Cl CHST BR7 ....185 F4
Coniscliffe Rd PLMGR N13 ......35 J5
Coniston Av BARK IG11 ....90 E5
　GFD/PVL UB6 ....97 H2
　WELL DA16 ....147 K3
Coniston Cl BARN SW13 ....138 C1
　BXLYHN DA7 ....149 K2
　CHSWK W4 ....137 K2
　DART DA1 ....170 C3
　ERITH DA8 ....150 B1
　MRDN SM4 ....193 K3
Coniston Ct BAY/PAD W2 * 8 C4
Coniston Gdns BELMT SM2 ......209 H4
　CDALE/KGS NW9 ....63 F2
　ED N9 ....36 E3
　PIN HA5 ....58 E1
　REDBR IG4 ....71 J1
　WBLY HA9 ....61 J3
Coniston Rd BMLY BR1 ....183 H2
　BXLYHN DA7 ....149 K2
　CROY/NA CR0 ....197 H4
　MUSWH N10 ....48 B5
　TOTM N17 ....50 D2
　WHTN TW2 ....155 G1
Coniston Wk HOM E9 ....86 E5
Conistone Wy HOLWY N7 ....84 E5
Conlan St NKENS W10 ....100 C3
Conley Rd WLSDN NW10 ....81 G4
Conley St GNWCH SE10 ....125 H5
Connaught Av ASHF TW15 ......152 B6
　EBAR EN4 ....33 K3
　EN EN1 ....24 B3
　HSLWW TW4 ....134 D6
　MORT/ESHN SW14 ....137 K4
Connaught Br CAN/RD E16 .....126 C1
Connaught Cl BAY/PAD W2 ....8 C4
　EN EN1 ....24 B3
　LEY E10 ....69 G6
　SUT SM1 ....209 H1
　UX/CGN UB8 * 94 A4
Connaught Dr GLDGN NW11 .....64 E1
Connaught Gdns MRDN SM4 ...194 B1
　MUSWH N10 ....48 B5
　PLMGR N13 ....35 H6
Connaught La IL IG1 ....72 C1
Connaught Ms FUL/PGN SW6 * ..139 J2
　HAMP NW3 * 83 H2
　WOOL/PLUM SE18 ....127 F5
Connaught Rd BAR EN5 ....32 B1
　CAN/RD E16 ....126 C1
　CHING E4 ....38 C2
　FSBYPK N4 ....67 G4
　IL IG1 ....72 D6
　KTN/HRWW/WS HA3 ....42 D3
　NWMAL KT3 ....192 B1
　RCHPK/HAM TW10 ....137 G6
　SUT SM1 ....194 D5
　TEDD TW11 ....173 J1
　WALTH E17 ....69 J2
　WEA W13 ....116 B1
　WLSDN NW10 ....99 G1
　WOOL/PLUM SE18 ....127 F5
Connaught Sq BAY/PAD W2 ....8 D4
Connaught St BAY/PAD W2 ....8 C4
Connaught Wy PLMGR N13 ......35 H6
Connell Crs EA W5 ....98 B3
Connemara Cl BORE WD6 * 30 E1
Connington Crs CHING E4 ....38 B5
Connop Rd PEND EN3 ....25 F1
Connor Cl BARK/HLT IG6 ....54 C6
　WAN E11 ....70 C5
Connor Rd DAGW RM9 ....92 B3
Connor St HOM E9 * 87 F6
Conolly Rd HNWL W7 ....115 K1
Conrad Dr WPK KT4 ....193 F5
Conroy Ct SCUP DA14 ....168 B6
Consfield Av NWMAL KT3 ....192 E1
Consort Cl FBAR/BDGN N11 ....47 K1
Consort Ms ISLW TW7 ....135 K6
Consort Rd PECK SE15 ....143 J3
Cons St STHWK SE1 ....17 K2
Constable Av CAN/RD E16 ......126 A1
Constable Cl GLDGN NW11 ....65 F3
　YEAD UB4 ....95 G3
Constable Crs SEVS/STOTM N15 ..68 C2
Constable Gdns EDGW HA8 ....44 C4
　ISLW TW7 ....135 K6
Constable Ms BCTR RM8 ....91 H2
Constable Wk DUL SE21 ....163 G5
Constance Crs HAYES BR2 .....199 J5
Constance Rd CROY/NA CR0 ...196 C4

EN EN1 ....36 A1
　SUT SM1 ....209 G2
　WHTN TW2 ....155 H2
Constance St CAN/RD E16 .....126 D1
Constantine Rd HAMP NW3 ......83 K2
Constitution HI MYFR/PICC W1J ..15 J2
Constitution Rd
　WOOL/PLUM SE18 ....147 F2
Consul Av DAGW RM9 ....110 E3
　RAIN RM13 ....111 F3
Content St WALW SE17 ....18 D7
Contessa Cl ORP BR6 ....216 E5
Control Tower Rd HTHAIR TW6 ..132 E4
Convent Cl BECK BR3 ....183 F1
Convent Gdns EA W5 ....116 D4
　NTGHL W11 ....100 D5
Convent HI NRWD SE19 ....180 D2
Convent Wy NWDGN UB2 ....114 B4
Conway Cl STAN HA7 ....43 G2
Conway Crs CHDH RM6 ....73 J4
　GFD/PVL UB6 ....96 E1
Conway Dr BELMT SM2 ....209 F4
　HYS/HAR UB3 ....113 G2
Conway Gdns ENC/FH EN2 ....24 A1
　MTCM CR4 ....195 J1
　WBLY HA9 ....61 J4
Conway Gv ACT W3 ....99 F4
Conway Ms FITZ W1T 10 A1
Conway Rd CRICK NW2 ....82 A1
　FELT TW13 ....172 C1
　HSLWW TW4 ....154 E2
　RYNPK SW20 ....177 F4
　SEVS/STOTM N15 ....67 J2
　STHGT/OAK N14 ....34 D4
　WOOL/PLUM SE18 ....127 J4
Conway St FITZ W1T 4 A7
Conybeare HAMP NW3 * 83 J5
Conyers Rd STRHM/NOR SW16 ...179 J1
Conyer St BOW E3 ....105 G1
Cooden Cl BMLY BR1 ....184 A3
Cookes Cl WAN E11 ....70 D6
Cookes La CHEAM SM3 ....208 C4
Cookham Cl NWDGN UB2 ....115 G3
Cookham Dene Cl CHST BR7 ....185 J4
Cookham Rd SCUP DA14 ....187 H4
Cookhill Rd ABYW SE2 ....128 C2
Cook's Cl CRW RM5 ....56 E2
Cooks Ferry Rbt UED N18 ....51 G1
Cook's Hole Rd ENC/FH EN2 ......23 J1
Cookson Gv ERITH DA8 ....38 B1
Cooks Rd SRTFD E15 ....105 K1
　WALW SE17 ....122 B1
Coolfin Rd CAN/RD E16 ....106 E5
Coolgardie Av CHING E4 ....52 B1
Coolhurst Rd HGT N6 ....66 D5
Cool Oak La CDALE/KGS NW9 ....63 H4
Coomassie Rd MV/WKIL W9 ....100 D3
Coombe Av CROY/NA CR0 ....212 A2
Coombe Bank NWMAL KT3 ....176 B4
Coombe Cl EDGW HA8 ....44 B5
　HSLW TW3 ....135 F5
Coombe Cnr WCHMN N21 ....35 H3
Coombe Crs HPTN TW12 ....172 D3
Coombe Dr KUTN/CMB KT2 ......176 D5
　RSLP HA4 ....59 F5
Coombefield Cl NWMAL KT3 ....192 B2
Coombe Gdns NWMAL KT3 ....192 C1
Coombe Hill Gld
　KUTN/CMB KT2 ....176 B3
Coombe Hill Rd
　KUTN/CMB KT2 ....176 B3
Coombe House Cha
　NWMAL KT3 ....176 A4
Coombehurst Cl EBAR EN4 ....21 K3
Coombe La CROY/NA CR0 ....212 D3
　RYNPK SW20 ....176 C4
Coombe La West
　KUTN/CMB KT2 ....175 K4
Coombe Ldg CHARL SE7 ....126 B6
Coombe Neville
　KUTN/CMB KT2 ....175 K3
Coombe Pk KUTN/CMB KT2 .....175 K1
Coombe Ridings
　KUTN/CMB KT2 ....175 K1
Coombe Rd BUSH WD23 ....28 D2
　CHSWK W4 ....118 B5
　HPTN TW12 ....172 E3
　KUTN/CMB KT2 ....175 K4
　NWMAL KT3 ....176 A4
　SAND/SEL CR2 ....212 B2
　SYD SE26 ....163 J6
　WDGN N22 ....49 G5
　WEA W13 ....116 C2
Coombe Wy CROY/NA CR0 ....195 K4
Coombe Vis
　WAND/EARL SW18 ....159 K2
Coombewood Dr CHDH RM6 ......74 B3
Coombe Wood Rd
　KUTN/CMB KT2 ....175 K1
Coombs St IS N1 ....6 B3
Coomer Ms FUL/PGN SW6 * 119 J6
Coomer Pl FUL/PGN SW6 ....119 J6
Cooms Wk EDGW HA8 ....44 D4
Cooperage Cl TOTM N17 ....50 B2
Cooper Av WALTH E17 ....51 F4
Cooper Cl STHWK SE1 ....17 J3
Cooper Crs CAR SM5 ....209 K1
Cooperdale Cl WFD IG8 ....53 G3
Cooper Rd CROY/NA CR0 ....211 G3
　HDN NW4 ....64 B3
　WLSDN NW10 ....81 J5
Coopersale Cl WFD IG8 ....53 G3
Coopersale Rd HOM E9 ....87 F3
Coopers Cl DAGE RM10 ....92 D4
　WCHPL E1 ....104 E3
Coopers Dr RDART DA2 ....170 B4
Coopers La CAMTN NW1 ....5 C4
　LEE/GVBK SE12 ....166 A4
　LEY E10 ....69 K5
Coopers Ms BECK BR3 ....182 D5

Cooper's Rd STHWK SE1 ....123 G5
Cooper's Rw TWRH EC3N 13 J3
Cooper St CAN/RD E16 ....106 D4
Coopers Yd IS N1 * 85 H6
　NRWD SE19 ....181 F2
Coote Rd BCTR RM8 ....92 B1
　BXLYHN DA7 ....149 G2
Copeland Rd PECK SE15 ....143 H3
　WALTH E17 ....69 J3
Copeman Cl SYD SE26 ....181 K1
Copenhagen Gdns CHSWK W4 * ..118 A2
Copenhagen Pl POP/IOD E14 ...105 H5
Copenhagen St IS N1 ....5 F1
Cope Pl KENS W8 ....119 K3
Copers Cope Rd BECK BR3 ....182 D2
Cope St BERM/RHTH SE16 ....124 A4
Copford Wk IS N1 * 85 J6
Copgate Pth
　STRHM/NOR SW16 ....180 A2
Copland Av ALP/SUD HA0 ....79 J3
Copland Cl ALP/SUD HA0 ....79 J3
Copland Ms ALP/SUD HA0 ....80 A5
Copland Rd ALP/SUD HA0 ....80 A5
Copleston Rd PECK SE15 ....143 G4
Copley Cl HNWL W7 * 96 E3
　WALW SE17 ....122 C6
Copley Dene BMLY BR1 ....184 C4
Copley Pk STRHM/NOR SW16 ...180 A2
Copley Rd STAN HA7 ....43 J1
Copley St WCHPL E1 ....105 F4
Coppard Gdns CHSGTN KT9 ...205 J4
Coppelia Rd BKHTH/KID SE3 ...145 J5
Coppen Rd BCTR RM8 ....74 B4
Copperas St DEPT SE8 ....124 E6
Copper Beech Cl CLAY IG5 ....54 A4
Copper Cl NRWD SE19 ....181 G3
　TOTM N17 ....50 C3
Copperdale Rd HYS/HAR UB3 ...113 K2
Copperfield BARK/HLT IG6 ....54 D2
Copperfield Dr
　SEVS/STOTM N15 ....68 B1
Copperfield Rd BOW E3 ....105 G3
　THMD SE28 ....109 J3
Copperfield St STHWK SE1 ....18 B2
Copperfield Wy CHST BR7 ....185 H2
　PIN HA5 ....59 K1
Coppergate Cl BMLY BR1 ....184 A4
Coppermead Cl CRICK NW2 ....82 A1
Copper Mill Dr ISLW TW7 ....136 A3
Copper Mill La TOOT SW17 ....160 B6
Coppermill La WALTH E17 ....68 E3
Copper Rw STHWK SE1 ....19 J1
Coppetts Cl NFNCH/WDSPK N12 ..33 H6
Coppetts Rd MUSWH N10 ....47 K4
Coppice Cl BECK BR3 ....198 E1
　RSLP HA4 ....58 A3
　RYNPK SW20 ....177 F6
Coppice Dr PUT/ROE SW15 ......158 D1
The Coppice BAR EN5 * 33 F1
　BXLY DA5 ....170 A5
　ENC/FH EN2 ....23 H5
　OXHEY WD19 ....27 G1
Coppice Wk TRDG/WHET N20 ...32 E3
Coppies Gv FBAR/BDGN N11 ....34 B6
Copping Cl CROY/NA CR0 ....212 A2
The Coppins CROY/NA CR0 ....213 K4
　KTN/HRWW/WS HA3 ....42 E2
Copse Cl BTSEA SW11 ....140 D5
Coppsfield E/WMO/HCT KT8 .....173 F6
Copse Av WWKM BR4 ....213 K1
Copse Cl CHARL SE7 ....146 A6
　NTHWD HA6 ....40 A4
　WDR/YW UB7 ....112 A3
Copse Gld SURB KT6 ....190 E4
Copse HI BELMT SM2 ....209 F5
　RYNPK SW20 ....176 E5
Copsem Dr ESH/CLAY KT10 .....204 B4
Copsem La ESH/CLAY KT10 .....204 B4
Copsem Wy ESH/CLAY KT10 .....204 D3
Copse Vw SAND/SEL CR2 ....213 G6
Copsewood Cl BFN/LL DA15 .....167 K1
Copse Wood Wy NTHWD HA6 ...40 A4
Coptefield Dr BELV DA17 ....128 E3
Copthall Av LOTH EC2R 13 F3
Copthall Dr MLHL NW7 ....45 J3
Copthall Gdns MLHL NW7 ....45 J3
　TWK TW1 ....156 B3
Copthorne Av BAL SW12 ....161 J2
　BARK/HLT IG6 ....54 B2
　HAYES BR2 ....200 E6
Copthorne Ms HYS/HAR UB3 ...113 H4
Coptic St NOXST/BSQ WC1A ...10 E3
Copton Cl BOW E3 ....105 K4
Copwood Cl
　NFNCH/WDSPK N12 ....33 H6
Coral Cl CHDH RM6 ....55 J5
Coraline Cl STHL UB1 ....95 K2
Coralline Wk ABYW SE2 ....128 D2
Coral Rw BTSEA SW11 ....140 B4
Coral St STHWK SE1 ....17 K3
Coram St BMSBY WC1N 4 E7
Coran Cl ED N9 ....37 F2
Corban Rd HSLW TW3 ....135 F4
Corbar Cl EBAR EN4 ....21 H1
Corbet Cl WLGTN SM6 ....195 F6
Corbet Ct BANK EC3V 13 F4
Corbet Gv FBAR/BDGN N11 ....48 E3
Corbett Rd WALTH E17 ....52 B5
　WAN E11 ....71 G3
Corbett's La BERM/RHTH SE16 ...123 K4
Corbicum WAN E11 ....70 C4
Corbiere Ct WIM/MER SW19 ....177 G2
Corbin's La RYLN/HDSTN HA2 ..78 D1
Corbridge Crs BETH E2 ....104 D1
Corbridge Ms ROM RM1 ....75 H2
Corbylands Rd BFN/LL DA15 .....167 K3
Corbyn St FSBYPK N4 ....66 E5
Corby Rd WLSDN NW10 ....99 F1
Cordelia Cl HNHL SE24 ....142 C5
Cordelia Gdns
　STWL/WRAY TW19 ....152 B2

Cordelia Rd STWL/WRAY TW19 ...152 B2
Cordelia St POP/IOD E14 ...105 K5
Cordingley Rd RSLP HA4 ...58 B6
Cording St POP/IOD E14 ...105 K4
Cordwell Rd LEW SE13 ...145 G6
Corelli Rd BKHTH/KID SE3 ...146 C3
Corfe Av RYLN/HDSTN HA2 ...78 A2
Corfe Cl HSLWW TW4 ...154 D3
  YEAD UB4 ...95 G5
Corfield Rd WCHMH N21 ...23 F6
Corfield St BETH E2 ...104 D3
Corfton Rd EA W5 ...98 A5
Coriander Av POP/IOD E14 ...106 B5
Cories Cl BCTR RM8 ...73 K6
Corinium Cl WBLY HA9 ...80 B2
Corinne Rd ARCH N19 ...84 C2
Corinthian Manorway
  ERITH DA8 ...130 A4
Corinthian Rd ERITH DA8 ...130 A4
Corkran Rd SURB KT6 ...190 E4
Cork St Ms CONDST W1S ...10 A6
Corkscrew HI WWKM BR4 ...199 F6
Cork Sq WAP E1W * ...104 C1
Cork St CONDST W1S ...10 A6
Cork Tree Wy CHING E4 ...51 G1
Corlett St CAMTN NW1 ...8 C1
Cormont Rd CMBW SE5 ...142 C2
Cormorant Cl WALTH E17 ...51 F4
Cormorant Rd FSTGT E7 ...88 D4
Cornbury Rd EDGW HA8 ...43 K3
Cornelia Dr YEAD UB4 ...95 G4
Cornelia St HOLWY N7 ...85 F4
Cornell Cl SCUP DA14 ...187 F2
Cornell Wy CRW RM5 ...56 D1
Corner Fielde
  BRXS/STRHM SW2 * ...162 A3
Corner Gn BKHTH/KID SE3 ...145 K4
Corner Rd CDALE/KGS NW9 ...45 H3
The Corner EA W5 * ...117 F1
Corney Reach Wy CHSWK W4 ...138 C1
Corney Rd CHSWK W4 ...118 B6
Cornflower La CROY/NA CRO ...198 A5
Cornflower Ter EDUL SE22 ...163 J1
Comford Cl HAYES BR2 ...199 K2
Comford Gv BAL SW12 ...161 G4
Cornhill BANK EC3V ...13 F4
Cornish Ct ED N9 ...36 D2
Cornish Gv PGE/AN SE20 ...181 J4
Corn Mill Dr ORP BR6 ...202 A4
Cornmill La LEW SE13 ...144 E4
Commow Dr WLSDN NW10 ...81 H3
Cornshaw Rd BCTR RM8 ...73 K5
Cornthwaite Rd CLPT E5 ...86 E1
Cornwall Av BETH E2 ...104 E2
  ESH/CLAY KT10 ...205 F5
  FNCH N3 ...46 E3
  STHL UB1 ...95 K4
  WDGN N22 ...48 E4
  WELL DA16 ...147 K4
Cornwall Cl BARK IG11 ...91 F4
Cornwall Crs NTGHL W11 ...100 C6
Cornwall Dr STMC/STPC BR5 ...186 D3
Cornwall Gdns SKENS SW7 ...120 A3
  SNWD SE25 ...197 G1
  WLSDN NW10 ...81 K4
Cornwall Gardens Wk
  KENS ...120 A3
Cornwall Gv CHSWK W4 ...118 B5
Cornwallis Av ED N9 ...36 A4
  ELTH/MOT SE9 ...167 J4
Cornwallis Cl ERITH DA8 ...130 C6
Cornwallis Gv ED N9 ...36 D4
Cornwallis Rd ARCH N19 ...66 E6
  DAGW RM9 ...92 A2
  ED N9 ...36 D4
  WALTH E17 ...51 F1
  WOOL/PLUM SE18 ...127 H4
Cornwallis Sq ARCH N19 ...66 E6
Cornwallis Wk ELTH/MOT SE9 ...146 E4
Cornwall Ms South
  SKENS SW7 ...120 B3
Cornwall Ms West
  SKENS SW7 * ...120 A3
Cornwall Rd BELMT SM2 ...208 D5
  CROY/NA CRO ...196 C6
  DART DA1 ...151 J4
  FSBYPK N4 ...67 G4
  HRW HA1 ...60 C3
  PIN HA5 ...41 K3
  RSLP HA4 ...58 D6
  SEVS/STOTM N15 ...67 K2
  STHWK SE1 ...17 J1
  TWK TW1 ...156 B3
Cornwall Sq LBTH SE11 * ...122 B5
Cornwall St WCHPL E1 ...104 D6
Cornwall Ter CAMTN NW1 ...3 F7
Cornwall Terrace Ms
  CAMTN NW1 ...3 F7
Corn Wy WAN E11 ...88 B1
Cornwood Cl EFNCH N2 ...65 H2
Cornwood Dr WCHPL E1 ...104 E5
Cornworthy Rd BCTR RM8 ...91 J3
Corona Rd LEE/GVPK SE12 ...165 K2
Coronation Cl BARK/HLT IG6 ...72 C1
  BXLY DA5 ...168 E1
Coronation Dr HCH RM12 ...93 K3
Coronation Rd HYS/HAR UB3 ...113 J4
  PLSTW E13 ...107 H2
  WLSDN NW10 ...98 D3
Coronation Vls WLSDN NW10 * ...98 D3
Coronet Rd ALP/SUD HA0 ...80 AJ
Coronet St IS N1 ...7 G5
Corporation Av HSLWW TW4 ...134 D5
Corporation Rw CLERKENWC1R ...5 K6
Corporation St HOLWY N7 ...84 E3
  SRTFD E15 ...88 C1
Corrance Rd
  BRXS/STRHM SW2 ...141 K5
Corri Av STHGT/OAK N14 ...34 D6
Corrib Dr SUT SM1 ...209 J3
Corrigan Cl HDN NW4 ...46 A6
Corringham Rd GLDGN NW11 ...64 E4
  WBLY HA9 ...62 C5
Corringway EA W5 ...98 B4
  GLDGN NW11 ...65 F4
Corris Gn CDALE/KGS NW9 ...63 G3

Corry Dr BRXN/ST SW9 ...142 C5
Corsair Cl STWL/WRAY TW19 ...152 A2
Corsair Rd STWL/WRAY TW19 ...152 B2
Corscombe Cl KUTN/CMB KT2 ...175 K1
Corsehill St STRHM/NOR SW16 ...179 H2
Corsellis Sq TWK TW1 ...136 C5
Corsham St IS N1 ...7 F5
Corsica St HBRY N5 ...85 H4
Cortayne Rd FUL/PGN SW6 * ...139 J3
Cortina Dr DAGW RM9 ...110 E2
Cortis Rd PUT/ROE SW15 ...158 E1
Cortis Ter PUT/ROE SW15 ...158 E6
Cortland Cl DART DA1 ...170 E1
Corunna Rd VX/NE SW8 ...141 H2
Corunna Ter VX/NE SW8 ...141 H2
Corwell Gdns UX/CGN UB8 ...94 A5
Corwell La UX/CGN UB8 ...94 A5
Coryton Pth MV/WKIL W9 ...100 D3
Cosbycote Av HNHL SE24 ...142 D6
Cosdach Av WLGTN SM6 ...210 D5
Cosedge Crs CROY/NA CRO ...211 G3
Cosgrove Cl WCHMH N21 ...35 J4
  YEAD UB4 ...95 H5
Cosmo Pl BMSBY WC1N ...11 F1
Cosmur St SHB W12 ...118 C3
Cossall Wk PECK SE15 ...143 J2
Cossar Ms BRXS/STRHM SW2 ...162 B1
Cosser St STHWK SE1 ...17 J4
Costa St PECK SE15 ...143 H3
Costons Av GFD/PVL UB6 ...96 D2
Costons La GFD/PVL UB6 ...96 D2
Cosway St CAMTN NW1 ...8 D1
Cotall St POP/IOD E14 ...105 J5
Coteford Cl PIN HA5 ...58 E2
Coteford St TOOT SW17 ...160 E6
Cotelands CROY/NA CRO ...212 A1
Cotesbach Rd CLPT E5 ...86 E1
Cotesmore Gdns BCTR RM8 ...91 J2
Cotford Rd THHTH CR7 ...196 D1
Cotham St WALW SE17 ...18 E7
Cotherstone Rd
  BRXS/STRHM SW2 ...162 A3
Cotleigh Av BXLY DA5 ...168 E4
Cotleigh Rd KIL/WHAMP NW6 ...82 E5
  ROMW/RG RM7 ...75 F3
Cotman Cl GLDGN NW11 ...65 F3
Cotmandene Crs
  STMC/STPC BR5 ...186 C5
Cotmans Cl HYS/HAR UB3 ...113 K1
Coton Rd WELL DA16 ...148 B4
Cotsford Av NWMAL KT3 ...191 K2
Cotswold Av BUSH WD23 ...28 C1
Cotswold Cl BXLYHN DA7 ...150 B3
  ESH/CLAY KT10 ...190 A6
  KUTN/CMB KT2 ...175 K2
Cotswold Gdns CRICK NW2 ...64 A5
  EHAM E6 ...107 J1
  GNTH/NBYPK IG2 ...72 C3
Cotswold Ga CRICK NW2 ...64 C5
Cotswold Gn ENC/FH EN2 ...23 F5
Cotswold Ms BTSEA SW11 ...140 C2
Cotswold Ri ORP BR6 ...202 A3
Cotswold Rd HPTN TW12 ...173 F2
  SUT SM2 ...209 F6
Cotswold St WNWD SE27 ...162 C6
Cotswold Wy ENC/FH EN2 ...23 F4
  WPK KT4 ...193 F6
Cottage Av HAYES BR2 ...200 D5
Cottage Gv RSLP HA4 ...58 B5
  RYLN/HDSTN HA2 ...60 B4
Cottage Field Cl SCUP DA14 ...168 D3
Cottage Gn CMBW SE5 ...142 E1
Cottage Gv BRXN/ST SW9 ...141 K4
  SURB KT6 ...190 E3
Cottage Pl CHEL SW3 ...14 C4
Cottage Rd HOLWY N7 ...85 F3
  HOR/WEW KT19 ...207 F5
The Cottages EDGW HA8 * ...44 D3
Cottage St POP/IOD E14 ...105 K6
Cottenham Dr CDALE/KGS NW9 ...45 H6
  RYNPK SW20 ...176 E3
Cottenham Park Rd
  RYNPK SW20 ...176 A4
Cottenham Pl RYNPK SW20 ...176 A3
Cotterill Rd SURB KT6 ...191 G6
Cottesbrook St NWCR SE14 ...144 B1
Cottesloe Ms STHWK SE1 * ...17 K4
Cottesmore Av CLAY IG5 ...53 K5
Cottesmore Gdns KENS W8 ...120 A3
Cottimore Av WOT/HER KT12 ...188 A5
Cottimore Crs WOT/HER KT12 ...188 A4
Cottimore La WOT/HER KT12 ...188 A5
Cottimore Ter WOT/HER KT12 ...188 A4
Cottingham Cha RSLP HA4 ...76 E1
Cottingham Rd PGE/AN SE20 ...182 A3
  VX/NE SW8 ...142 A1
Cottington Rd FELT TW13 ...154 C6
Cottington St LBTH SE11 ...122 B5
Cotton Av ACT W3 ...99 F5
Cotton Cl DAGW RM9 ...91 J5
  WAN E11 ...70 C6
Cotton Gardens Est LBTH SE11 ...18 A7
Cottongrass Cl CROY/NA CRO ...198 A5
Cotton Hl BMLY BR1 ...165 G6
Cotton La RTSEA SW11 ...140 C4
Cottons Ap ROMW/RG RM7 ...75 F2
Cottons Centre STHWK SE1 ...13 G7
Cotton's Gdns BETH E2 ...7 H4
Cotton St POP/IOD E14 ...106 A6
Couchmore Av CLAY IG5 ...53 K5
  ESH/CLAY KT10 ...189 K6
Coulgate St BROCKY SE4 ...144 B4
Coulson Cl BCTR RM8 ...73 J5
Coulson St CHEL SW3 ...120 E5
Coulter Cl YEAD UB4 ...95 J3
Coulter Rd HMSMTH W6 ...118 E3
Councillor St CMBW SE5 ...142 D1
Counter St STHWK SE1 ...13 G7
Countess Rd KTTN NW5 ...84 C3
Countisbury Av EN EN1 ...36 B2
Country Wy FELT TW13 ...172 B1
County Ga BAR EN5 ...33 F1
  ELTH/MOT SE9 ...167 H5
County Gv CMBW SE5 ...142 D2
County Pde BTFD TW8 * ...136 E1
County Rd EHAM E6 ...108 B4

THHTH CR7 ...180 C5
County St STHWK SE1 ...18 D5
Coupland Pl
  WOOL/PLUM SE18 ...127 H5
Courcy Rd CEND/HSY/T N8 ...49 G6
Courier Rd DAGW RM9 ...110 E3
Courland Gv VX/NE SW8 ...141 J3
Courland St VX/NE SW8 ...141 J3
The Course ELTH/MOT SE9 ...167 F5
Courtauld Rd ARCH N19 ...66 D5
Courtaulds Cl THMD SE28 ...128 B1
Court Av BELV DA17 ...129 G5
Court Cl KTN/HRWW/WS HA3 ...43 K5
  STJWD NW8 * ...83 H5
  WHTN TW2 ...155 G5
  WLGTN SM6 ...210 D5
Court Close Av WHTN TW2 ...155 G5
Court Crs CHSGTN KT9 ...205 K4
Court Downs Rd BECK BR3 ...182 E5
Court Dr CROY/NA CRO ...211 F2
  STAN HA7 ...30 A6
  SUT SM1 ...209 J2
Courtenay Av BELMT SM2 ...208 E6
  HGT N6 ...65 J4
  KTN/HRWW/WS HA3 ...42 C4
Courtenay Dr BECK BR3 ...183 G5
Courtenay Ms WALTH E17 ...69 G2
Courtenay Pl WALTH E17 ...69 G2
Courtenay Rd PGE/AN SE20 ...182 A3
  WALTH E17 ...51 F6
  WAN E11 * ...88 D1
  WBLY HA9 * ...79 K1
  WPK KT4 ...193 G1
Courtenay Sq LBTH SE11 * ...122 B5
Courtenay St LBTH SE11 ...122 A5
Courten Ms STAN HA7 * ...43 J3
Court Farm Av
  HOR/WEW KT19 ...207 G3
Court Farm Rd ELTH/MOT SE9 ...166 C4
  NTHLT UB5 ...78 A5
Courtfield Av HRW HA1 ...61 F2
Courtfield Crs HRW HA1 ...61 F2
Courtfield Gdns ECT SW5 ...120 A4
  RSLP HA4 ...58 D6
  WEA W13 ...97 G5
Courtfield Ms SKENS SW7 ...120 B4
Courtfield Ri WWKM BR4 ...214 B1
Courtfield Rd ECT SW5 ...120 B4
Court Gdns HOLWY N7 ...85 G4
Courtgate Cl MLHL NW7 ...45 H2
Courthill Rd LEW SE13 ...145 F6
Courthope Rd GFD/PVL UB6 ...96 D1
  HAMP NW3 ...83 K2
  WIM/MER SW19 ...177 H1
Courthope Vls
  WIM/MER SW19 ...177 H3
Courthouse La
  STNW/STAM N16 ...86 B2
Court House Rd FNCH N3 ...46 E6
Courtland Av CHING E4 ...38 D4
  IL IG1 ...71 K6
  MLHL NW7 ...31 F5
  STRHM/NOR SW16 ...180 A3
Courtland Gv THMD SE28 ...109 K6
Courtland Rd EHAM E6 ...89 J6
Courtlands CHST BR7 ...185 G5
  RCHPK/HAM TW10 ...137 H6
Courtlands Av HAYES BR2 ...199 H5
  HPTN TW12 ...172 E2
  LEE/GVPK SE12 ...146 A6
  RCH/KEW TW9 ...137 J3
  STHGT/OAK N14 ...34 B3
  STNW/STAM N16 ...86 A2
  UED N18 ...50 C1
  WIM/MER SW19 ...178 B2
Courtlands Dr HOR/WEW KT19 ...207 G4
Courtlands Rd BRYLDS KT5 ...191 H4
Court La DUL SE21 ...163 G2
Court Lane Gdns DUL SE21 ...163 F2
Court Lodge Dr BXLYHN DA7 ...149 J2
Courtleigh GLDGN NW11 * ...64 C1
Courtleigh Gdns GLDGN NW11 ...64 C1
Court Md NTHLT UB5 ...95 K2
Courtmead Cl HNHL SE24 ...162 D1
Courtnell St BAY/PAD W2 ...100 E5
Courtney Cl NRWD SE19 ...181 F2
Courtney Crs CAR SM5 ...209 K5
Courtney Pl CROY/NA CRO ...211 G1
Courtney Rd CROY/NA CRO ...211 G1
  HOLWY N7 ...85 G4
  WIM/MER SW19 ...178 D3
Courtney Wy HTHAIR TW6 ...132 D4
Courtrai Rd FSTH SE23 ...164 B1
Court Rd ELTH/MOT SE9 ...166 E3
  NWDGN UB2 ...114 E4
  SNWD SE25 ...181 G5
Court Rd (Orpington By-Pass)
  ORP BR6 ...217 J2
Courtside HGT N6 ...66 D6
  SYD SE26 ...163 K5
The Courts STRHM/NOR SW16 ...179 K3
Courtstreet BMLY BR1 ...183 K5
Court St WCHPL E1 ...104 D4
The Court MUSWH N10 * ...66 B4
Court Vw HGT N6 ...66 B4
Court Wy ACT W3 ...98 E4
  BARK/HLT IG6 ...54 C6
  CDALE/KGS NW9 ...63 G1
  WHTN TW2 ...156 A2
The Courtway OXHEY WD19 ...27 J4
Court Yd ELTH/MOT SE9 ...166 E1
Courtyard Ms STMC/STPC BR5 ...186 B1
The Courtyards WATW WD18 * ...26 B2
The Courtyard IS N1 ...85 F5
Cousin La CANST EC4R ...12 E6
Couthurst Rd BKHTH/KID SE3 ...146 A1
Coutts Av CHSGTN KT9 ...206 A3
Coval Gdns MORT/ESHN SW14 ...137 J5
Coval La MORT/ESHN SW14 ...137 J5
Coval Rd MORT/ESHN SW14 ...137 K5
Covelees Wall EHAM E6 ...108 B5
Covent Gdn COVGDN WC2E ...11 F5
Covent Garden Piazza
  COVGDN WC2E ...11 F5
Coventry Cl EHAM E6 ...107 K5
  KIL/WHAMP NW6 ...100 E1

Coventry Cross Est BOW E3 ...106 A3
Coventry Rd IL IG1 ...72 B5
  SNWD SE25 ...197 H1
  WCHPL E1 ...104 D3
Coventry St SOHO/SHAV W1D ...10 C6
Coverack Cl CROY/NA CRO ...198 B5
  STHGT/OAK N14 ...34 C1
Coverdale Gdns CROY/NA CRO ...212 B1
Coverdale Rd CRICK NW2 ...82 C5
  FBAR/BDGN N11 ...48 A2
  SHB W12 ...118 E1
The Coverdales BARK IG11 ...108 D1
Coverley Cl WCHPL E1 * ...104 C4
Coverton Rd TOOT SW17 ...160 D6
Covert Rd BARK/HLT IG6 ...55 F2
Coverts Rd ESH/CLAY KT10 ...205 F5
The Covert NRWD SE19 ...181 G3
  ORP BR6 ...201 K3
Covert Wy EBAR EN4 ...21 G3
Covet Wood Cl
  STMC/STPC BR5 ...202 A3
Covey Cl WIM/MER SW19 ...178 A5
Covington Gdns
  STRHM/NOR SW16 ...180 C3
Covington Wy
  STRHM/NOR SW16 ...180 C3
Cowbridge La BARK IG11 ...90 B5
Cowbridge Rd
  KTN/HRWW/WS HA3 ...62 B1
Cowcross St FARR EC1M ...12 A1
Cowdenbeath Pth IS N1 ...84 E6
Cowden Rd ORP BR6 ...202 A4
Cowden St CAT SE6 ...164 D6
Cowdray Rd HGDN/ICK UB10 ...76 A6
Cowdray Wy HCH RM12 ...93 J2
Cowdrey Cl EN EN1 ...24 A3
Cowdrey Ct DART DA1 ...170 E2
Cowdrey Rd WIM/MER SW19 ...178 A2
Cowen Av HRW HA1 ...60 D5
Cowgate Rd GFD/PVL UB6 ...96 D2
Cowick Rd TOOT SW17 ...160 E6
Cowings Md NTHLT UB5 ...77 J5
Cowland Av PEND EN3 ...24 E5
Cow La BUSH WD23 * ...28 A1
Cow Leaze EHAM E6 ...108 A5
Cowley Cl WAN E11 * ...88 C1
Cowley La WAN E11 * ...88 C1
Cowley Pl HDN NW4 ...64 A2
Cowley Rd ACT W3 ...118 C1
  BRXN/ST SW9 ...142 B2
  HARH RM3 ...57 K3
  IL IG1 ...71 K4
  MORT/ESHN SW14 ...138 B4
  WAN E11 ...71 F2
Cowley St WEST SW1P ...16 E4
Cowling Cl NTGHL W11 ...100 C6
Cowper Av EHAM E6 ...89 J5
  SUT SM1 ...209 H2
Cowper Cl HAYES BR2 ...200 C1
  WELL DA16 ...148 B6
Cowper Gdns STHGT/OAK N14 ...22 C6
  WLGTN SM6 ...210 C4
Cowper Rd ACT W3 ...118 A1
  BELV DA17 ...129 H4
  HAYES BR2 ...200 C1
  HNWL W7 ...97 F6
  KUTN/CMB KT2 ...175 G1
  RAIN RM13 ...111 J2
  STHGT/OAK N14 ...34 B3
  STNW/STAM N16 ...86 A3
  UED N18 ...50 C1
  WIM/MER SW19 ...178 B2
Cowper St STLK EC1Y * ...7 F6
Cowper Ter NKENS W10 * ...100 B4
Cowslip Rd SWFD E18 ...53 F6
Cowthorpe Rd VX/NE SW8 ...141 J2
Coxe Pl KTN/HRWW/WS HA3 ...61 G1
Cox La HOR/WEW KT19 ...206 E3
Coxmount Rd CHARL SE7 ...126 C5
Coxson Wy STHWK SE1 ...19 J3
Coxwell Rd NRWD SE19 ...181 F3
  WOOL/PLUM SE18 ...127 J5
Crabbs Croft Cl ORP BR6 * ...216 C3
Crab Hl BECK BR3 ...183 G3
Crabtree Av ALP/SUD HA0 ...98 A1
  CHDH RM6 ...73 K2
Crabtree Cl BETH E2 ...7 J3
Crabtree La FUL/PGN SW6 ...139 G1
Crabtree Manorway North
  BELV DA17 ...129 K2
Crabtree Manorway South
  BELV DA17 ...129 K3
Craddock Rd EN EN1 ...24 B4
Craddock St KTTN NW5 ...84 A4
Cradley Rd ELTH/MOT SE9 ...167 J3
Cragie Lea MUSWH N10 ...48 B5
Craigdale Rd EMPK RM11 ...75 H5
Craigen Av CROY/NA CRO ...197 J5
Craigerne Rd BKHTH/KID SE3 ...146 A1
Craig Gdns SWFD E18 ...52 D5
Craigholm WOOL/PLUM SE18 ...147 F3
Craigmuir Pk ALP/SUD HA0 ...80 B6
Craignair Rd
  BRXS/STRHM SW2 ...162 B2
Craignish Av
  STRHM/NOR SW16 ...180 A5
Craig Park Rd UED N18 ...36 D6
Craig Rd RCHPK/HAM TW10 ...156 D6
Craigton Rd ELTH/MOT SE9 ...146 E5
Craigweil Cl STAN HA7 ...43 K1
Craigweil Dr STAN HA7 ...43 K1
Craigwell Av FELT TW13 ...153 K5
Craik Ct KIL/WHAMP NW6 * ...100 D1
Crail Rw WALW SE17 ...19 F7
Cramer St MHST W1U ...9 H2
Crammond Cl HMSMTH W6 ...119 H6
Cramond Ct
  EBED/NFELT TW14 ...153 H3
Crampton Rd PGE/AN SE20 ...181 K2
Cranberry Cl NTHLT UB5 ...95 H1
Cranberry La CAN/RD E16 ...106 C3
Cranborne Av NWDGN UB2 ...115 F4
  SURB KT6 ...206 C1
Cranborne Rd BARK IG11 ...90 D6

Cranborne Waye YEAD UB4 ...95 G6
Cranbourne Av WAN E11 ...71 F1
Cranbourne Cl ESH/CLAY KT10 ...204 B6
  STRHM/NOR SW16 ...179 K6
Cranbourne Dr PIN HA5 ...59 H2
Cranbourne Gdns
  BARK/HLT IG6 ...54 C2
  GLDGN NW11 ...64 D2
Cranbourne Rd MNPK E12 ...89 J3
  MUSWH N10 ...48 B5
  NTHWD HA6 ...40 D6
  SRTFD E15 ...88 A2
Cranbourn St LSQ/SEVD WC2H ...10 D5
Cranbrook Cl HAYES BR2 ...199 K3
Cranbrook Dr ESH/CLAY KT10 ...189 H5
  GPK RM2 ...75 J3
  WHTN TW2 ...155 G3
Cranbrook La FBAR/BDGN N11 ...34 B6
Cranbrook Ms WALTH E17 ...69 G2
Cranbrook Pk WDGN N22 ...49 G4
Cranbrook Ri IL IG1 ...71 K3
Cranbrook Rd BARK/HLT IG6 ...54 C6
  BXLYHN DA7 ...149 G2
  CHSWK W4 ...118 B5
  DEPT SE8 ...144 D3
  EBAR EN4 ...33 J1
  HSLWW TW4 ...134 E5
  IL IG1 ...72 A4
  THHTH CR7 ...180 E5
  WIM/MER SW19 ...177 H3
Cranbrook St BETH E2 ...105 F1
Cranbury Rd FUL/PGN SW6 ...140 A3
Crane Av ACT W3 ...98 E6
  ISLW TW7 ...136 B6
Crane Cl DAGE RM10 ...92 C4
Crane Ct FLST/FETLN EC4A ...11 K4
  MORT/ESHN SW14 * ...137 K5
Cranford Cl WHTN TW2 ...155 G2
Cranford Wy WHTN TW2 ...155 J3
Crane Gdns HYS/HAR UB3 ...113 J4
Crane Gv HOLWY N7 ...85 G4
Crane Lodge Rd HEST TW5 ...114 A6
Crane Md BERM/RHTH SE16 ...124 A5
Crane Park Rd WHTN TW2 ...155 F4
Crane Rd STWL/WRAY TW19 ...152 C3
  WHTN TW2 ...155 J3
Cranesbill Cl CDALE/KGS NW9 ...45 G4
Cranes Dr BRYLDS KT5 ...191 F1
Cranes Pk BRYLDS KT5 ...191 F1
Cranes Park Av BRYLDS KT5 ...191 F1
Cranes St PECK SE15 ...143 G2
Craneswater HYS/HAR UB3 ...133 J1
Craneswater Pk NWDGN UB2 ...114 E5
Crane Wy WHTN TW2 ...155 G2
Cranfield Dr CDALE/KGS NW9 ...45 G4
Cranfield Rd BROCKY SE4 ...144 C4
Cranfield Rd East CAR SM5 * ...209 K6
Cranfield Rd West CAR SM5 ...209 K6
Cranford Av PLMGR N13 ...48 E1
  STWL/WRAY TW19 ...152 B2
Cranford Cl RYNPK SW20 ...176 E3
  STWL/WRAY TW19 ...152 B2
Cranford Cottages WAP E1W * ...105 F6
Cranford Dr HYS/HAR UB3 ...113 J4
Cranford La HEST TW5 ...134 C1
  HYS/HAR UB3 ...133 J2
Cranford Ms HAYES BR2 ...200 D3
Cranford Ri ESH/CLAY KT10 ...204 C3
Cranford Rd DART DA1 ...171 H3
Cranford St WAP E1W ...105 F6
Cranford Wy CEND/HSY/T N8 ...67 F2
Cranham Rd EMPK RM11 ...75 K3
Cranhurst Rd CRICK NW2 ...82 A3
Cranleigh Cl BXLY DA5 ...169 J1
  ORP BR6 ...217 G1
  PGE/AN SE20 ...181 J5
Cranleigh Gdns BARK IG11 ...90 D5
  KTN/HRWW/WS HA3 ...62 B3
  KUTN/CMB KT2 ...175 G2
  LOU IG10 ...39 K1
  SNWD SE25 ...181 F6
  STHL UB1 ...95 K5
  SUT SM1 ...194 A6
  WLGTN SM6 ...210 C5
Cranley Ms SKENS SW7 ...120 B5
Cranley Pl SKENS SW7 ...14 A7
Cranley Rd GNTH/NBYPK IG2 ...72 C4
  PLSTW E13 ...107 F4
Cranley Ter HDN NW4 * ...46 B5
Cranmer Av WEA W13 ...116 C3
Cranmer Cl MRDN SM4 ...193 G3
  RSLP HA4 ...59 H5
  STAN HA7 ...43 J3
Cranmer Ct HPTN TW12 ...173 G1
Cranmer Farm Cl MTCM CR4 ...194 E1
Cranmer Rd BRXN/ST SW9 ...142 B1
  CROY/NA CRO ...211 J1
  EDGW HA8 ...30 D4
  FSTGT E7 ...89 F2
  HPTN TW12 ...173 G1
  HYS/HAR UB3 ...94 C5
  KUTN/CMB KT2 ...175 F1
  MTCM CR4 ...194 E1
Cranmer Ter TOOT SW17 ...178 C1
Cranmore Av ISLW TW7 ...135 J1
Cranmore Rd BMLY BR1 ...165 H6
  CHST BR7 ...184 E1
Cranmore Wy MUSWH N10 ...66 C1

Cranston Cl HGDN/ICK UB10 ...58 B6
  HSLW TW3 ...134 D3
Cranston Est IS N1 ...7 F2
Cranston Gdns CHING E4 ...51 K2
Cranston Rd FSTH SE23 ...164 B3
Cranswick Rd
  BERM/RHTH SE16 ...123 J5
Crantock Rd CAT SE6 ...165 F4
Cranwell Cl BOW E3 ...105 K3
Cranwich Av WCHMH N21 ...35 K2
Cranwich Rd STNW/STAM N16 ...68 A4
Cranwood St FSBYE EC1V ...7 F3
Cranworth Crs CHING E4 ...38 D3
Cranworth Gdns
  BRXN/ST SW9 ...142 B2
Craster Rd BRXS/STRHM SW2 ...162 A2
Crathie Rd LEE/GVPK SE12 ...166 A1
Cravan Av FELT TW13 ...153 K4
Craven Av EA W5 ...97 J6
  STHL UB1 ...95 K5
Craven Cl STNW/STAM N16 * ...68 C4
  YEAD UB4 ...95 J4
Craven Gdns BARK IG11 ...108 E1
  BARK/HLT IG6 ...54 D5
  CRW RM5 ...56 C1
  WIM/MER SW19 ...178 A1
Craven Hill Gdns BAY/PAD W2 ...101 G6
Craven Ms BTSEA SW11 ...141 G4
Craven Pk WLSDN NW10 ...81 G6
Craven Park Ms WLSDN NW10 ...81 G6
Craven Park Rd
  SEVS/STOTM N15 ...68 B3
  WLSDN NW10 ...81 G6
Craven Pas CHCR WC2N ...10 E7
Craven Rd BAY/PAD W2 ...101 G6
  CROY/NA CR0 ...197 J5
  KUTN/CMB KT2 ...175 G4
  ORP BR6 ...217 K1
  WEA W13 ...97 J6
  WLSDN NW10 ...81 F6
Craven St CHCR WC2N ...10 E7
Craven Ter BAY/PAD W2 ...101 G6
Craven Wk CLPT E5 ...68 C4
Crawford Av ALP/SUD HA0 ...79 K3
Crawford Cl ISLW TW7 ...135 K3
Crawford Gdns NTHLT UB5 ...95 K2
  PLMGR N13 ...35 H5
Crawford Pas CLKNW EC1R ...5 J7
Crawford Pl MBLAR W1H ...8 D3
Crawford Rd CMBW SE5 ...142 D3
Crawford St MBLAR W1H ...8 E2
  MHST W1U ...9 F2
  WLSDN NW10 ...81 F5
Crawley Rd ED N9 ...36 B2
  LEY E10 ...69 K5
  WDGN N22 ...49 J4
Crawshaw Gv EDUL SE22 ...143 G5
Cray Av STMC/STPC BR5 ...202 C2
Craybrooke Rd SCUP DA14 ...168 C6
Craybury End ELTH/MOT SE9 ...167 H4
Cray Cl DART DA1 ...150 D4
Craydene Rd ERITH DA8 ...150 D2
Crayford High St DART DA1 ...150 D6
Crayford Rd DART DA1 ...150 C6
  HOLWY N7 ...84 D2
Crayford Wy DART DA1 ...150 D5
Crayke Hl CHSGTN KT9 ...206 A5
Craylands STMC/STPC BR5 ...186 D2
Crayleigh Ter SCUP DA14 * ...186 D2
Cray Rd BELV DA17 ...129 H6
  SCUP DA14 ...186 D2
  SWLY BR8 ...203 K3
Crays Pde STMC/STPC BR5 * ...186 D5
Cray Valley Rd
  STMC/STPC BR5 ...202 B2
Crealock Gv WFD IG8 ...52 D1
Crealock St WAND/EARL SW18 ...160 A1
Creasey Cl EMPK RM11 ...75 K6
Crebor St EDUL SE22 ...163 H1
Credenhall Dr HAYES BR2 ...200 E5
Credenhill St
  STRHM/NOR SW16 ...179 H2
Crediton Hl KIL/WHAMP NW6 ...83 F3
Crediton Rd WLSDN NW10 ...82 C5
Crediton Wy ESH/CLAY KT10 ...205 G3
Credon Rd BERM/RHTH SE16 ...123 J5
  PLSTW E13 ...107 G1
Creechurch La HDTCH EC3A ...13 H4
Creechurch Pl HDTCH EC3A * ...13 H4
Creed La BLKFR EC4V ...12 B4
Creek Cottages
  E/WMO/HCT KT8 * ...189 K1
Creek Rd BARK IG11 ...109 F2
  DEPT SE8 ...124 D6
  E/WMO/HCT KT8 ...189 K1
Creekside DEPT SE8 ...144 E1
  RAIN RM13 ...111 H3
Creek Wy RAIN RM13 ...111 G4
Creeland Gv CAT SE6 ...164 C3
Cree Wy ROM RM1 ...57 G3
Crefeld Cl HMSMTH W6 ...119 H6
Creffield Rd EA W5 ...98 C6
Creighton Av EFNCH N2 ...47 K5
  EHAM E6 ...107 H1
Creighton Cl SHB W12 ...99 K6
Creighton Rd EA W5 ...116 A2
  KIL/WHAMP NW6 ...100 B1
  TOTM N17 ...50 A3
Creigton Av EFNCH N2 ...47 J6
Cremer St BETH E2 ...7 J2
Cremorne Est WBPTN SW10 * ...120 C6
Cremorne Gdns
  HOR/WEW KT19 ...207 F6
Cremorne Rd WBPTN SW10 ...140 B1
Crescent TWRH EC3N ...13 J5
Crescent Ar GNWCH SE10 ...125 F6
Crescent Av HCH RM12 ...75 H6
Crescent Dr STMC/STPC BR5 ...201 G3
Crescent East EBAR EN4 ...21 G1
Crescent Gdns RSLP HA4 ...59 F4
  WIM/MER SW19 ...159 K5
Crescent Gv CLAP SW4 ...141 H5
  MTCM CR4 ...194 D1
Crescent La CLAP SW4 ...141 J6
Crescent Pl CHEL SW3 ...14 D6
Crescent Ri EBAR EN4 ...21 J6
  FNCH N3 * ...46 D4
Crescent Rd BECK BR3 ...182 E5
  BFN/LL DA15 ...168 A5
  BMLY BR1 ...183 K3
  CEND/HSY/T N8 ...66 D3
  CHING E4 ...38 C2
  DAGE RM10 ...92 D2
  EBAR EN4 ...33 J1
  ED N9 ...36 C3
  ENC/FH EN2 ...23 H5
  ERITH DA8 ...130 C6
  FBAR/BDGN N11 ...33 K6
  KUTN/CMB KT2 ...175 H3
  LEY E10 ...88 E6
  PLSTW E13 ...88 E6
  RYNPK SW20 ...177 G4
  SEVS/STOTM N15 * ...49 H6
  SWFD E18 ...53 G5
  WDGN N22 ...48 D4
  WOOL/PLUM SE18 ...127 G5
Crescent Rw STLK EC1Y ...6 C7
Crescent St IS N1 ...85 F5
The Crescent ACT W3 ...99 G5
  ALP/SUD HA0 ...61 H6
  BAR EN5 ...21 F4
  BARN SW13 ...138 C3
  BECK BR3 ...182 D4
  BXLY DA5 ...168 D2
  CRICK NW2 ...81 K1
  CROY/NA CR0 ...196 E3
  E/WMO/HCT KT8 ...188 E1
  FBAR/BDGN N11 ...72 A3
  HYS/HAR UB3 ...133 F1
  LOU IG10 ...39 H1
  NWMAL KT3 ...175 K5
  RYLN/HDSTN HA2 ...60 A6
  SCUP DA14 ...168 A6
  STHL UB1 ...114 D2
  SURB KT6 ...191 F2
  SUT SM1 ...209 H3
  WALTH E17 ...69 G2
  WIM/MER SW19 ...159 H5
  WWKM BR4 ...199 H5
Crescent Vw LOU IG10 ...39 H1
Crescent Wy BROCKY SE4 ...144 D4
  ORP BR6 ...216 E3
  STRHM/NOR SW16 ...180 A3
Crescentway
  NFNCH/WDSPK N12 ...47 J2
Crescent West EBAR EN4 ...21 G1
Crescent Wood Rd SYD SE26 ...163 H5
Cresford Rd FUL/PGN SW6 ...140 A2
Crespigny Rd HDN NW4 ...63 K3
Cressage Cl STHL UB1 ...96 A4
Cresset Rd HOM E9 ...86 E4
Cresset St CLAP SW4 ...141 J4
Cressfield Cl KTTN NW5 ...84 A3
Cressida Rd ARCH N19 ...66 C5
Cressingham Gv SUT SM1 ...209 G2
Cressingham Rd EDGW HA8 ...45 F1
  LEW SE13 ...145 F4
Cressington Cl
  STNW/STAM N16 * ...86 A3
Cresswell Pk BKHTH/KID SE3 ...145 J4
Cresswell Rd FELT TW13 ...154 D6
  SNWD SE25 ...197 J1
  TWK TW1 ...156 E1
Cresswell Wy WCHMH N21 ...35 G2
Cressy Houses WCHPL E1 * ...104 E4
Cressy Pl WCHPL E1 ...104 E4
Cressy Rd HAMP NW3 ...83 K2
Cressys Cnr HSLW TW3 * ...135 G4
Crestbrook Av PLMGR N13 ...35 H5
Crestbrook Pl PLMGR N13 * ...35 G5
Crest Dr PEND EN3 ...25 F1
Crestfield St CAMTN NW1 ...5 F4
Crest Gdns RSLP HA4 ...77 G1
Creston Wy WPK KT4 ...193 G5
Crest Rd CRICK NW2 ...63 J6
  HAYES BR2 ...199 J2
  SAND/SEL CR2 ...212 D5
The Crest BRYLDS KT5 ...191 H2
  HDN NW4 ...64 A2
  HOLWY N7 * ...84 D3
  PLMGR N13 ...35 G6
Crest Vw PIN HA5 ...59 H1
Crest View Dr STMC/STPC BR5 ...201 G2
Crestway PUT/ROE SW15 ...158 D1
Crestwood Wy HSLWW TW4 ...134 E6
Creswell Dr BECK BR3 ...198 E2
Creswick Rd ACT W3 ...98 D6
Creswick Wk GLDGN NW11 ...64 E1
Creukhorne Rd WLSDN NW10 * ...81 G5
Crewdson Rd BRXN/ST SW9 ...142 B1
Crewe Pl WLSDN NW10 ...99 H2
Crews St POP/IOD E14 ...124 D4
Crews Rd CRICK NW2 ...64 C6
  PECK SE15 * ...143 J3
Crichton Av WLGTN SM6 ...210 D3
Crichton Rd CAR SM5 ...209 K5
Crichton St VX/NE SW8 * ...141 H3
Cricketers Arms Rd
  ENC/FH EN2 * ...23 J3
Cricketers Cl CHSGTN KT9 ...205 K3
  ERITH DA8 ...130 B5
  STHGT/OAK N14 ...34 C2
Cricketers Ms BAL SW12 * ...161 G2
Cricketfield Rd CLPT E5 ...86 D2
Cricket Gn MTCM CR4 ...194 E1
Cricket Ground Rd CHST BR7 ...185 G4
Cricket La BECK BR3 ...182 B2
Cricket Rw EFNCH N2 * ...47 H6
Crickdale Av
  BRXS/STRHM SW2 ...161 K4
Cricklewood Broadway
  CRICK NW2 ...82 A1
Cricklewood La CRICK NW2 ...82 C2
Cridland St SRTFD E15 ...88 D1
Crieff Ct TEDD TW11 ...174 D3
Crieff Rd WAND/EARL SW18 ...160 B1
Criffel Av BRXS/STRHM SW2 ...161 J4
Crimscott St STHWK SE1 ...19 H5
Crimsworth Rd VX/NE SW8 ...141 J2
Crinan St IS N1 ...5 F2
Cringle St VX/NE SW8 ...141 H1
Cripplegate St BARB EC2Y * ...12 C1
Crispen Rd FELT TW13 ...154 D6
Crispian Cl WLSDN NW10 ...81 G2
Crispin Crs CROY/NA CR0 ...210 D1
Crispin Rd EDGW HA8 ...44 E2
Crispin St WCHPL E1 ...13 J2
Crisp Rd HMSMTH W6 ...119 F5
Cristowe Rd FUL/PGN SW6 * ...139 J3
Criterion Ms ARCH N19 ...66 D6
Crockenhill Rd STMC/STPC BR5 ...202 E3
Crockerton Rd TOOT SW17 ...160 E4
Crockham Wy ELTH/MOT SE9 ...167 F6
Crocus Cl CROY/NA CR0 ...198 A5
Crocus Fld BAR EN5 ...32 D1
Croft Av WWKM BR4 ...199 F5
Croft Cl ABYW SE2 ...129 C5
  CHST BR7 ...184 E1
  HDN NW4 ...45 K3
  MLHL NW7 ...31 G5
Croft Ct RSLP HA4 * ...58 D5
  SUT SM1 * ...194 C6
Croftdown Rd KTTN NW5 ...84 A1
Crofters Cl ISLW TW7 ...135 J6
Crofters Ct DEPT SE8 * ...124 A4
Crofters Md CROY/NA CR0 * ...213 H6
Crofters Rd NTHWD HA6 ...26 C6
Crofters Wy CAMTN NW1 ...84 D6
Croft Gdns HNWL W7 ...116 C2
  RSLP HA4 ...58 C5
Croft Lodge Cl WFD IG8 ...53 F2
Croft Ms NFNCH/WDSPK N12 ...33 G5
Crofton Av BXLY DA5 ...168 E2
  CHSWK W4 ...138 A1
  ORP BR6 ...201 H6
Crofton Gate Wy BROCKY SE4 ...144 B6
Crofton Gv CHING E4 ...38 B6
Crofton La STMC/STPC BR5 ...201 J5
Crofton Park Rd BROCKY SE4 ...164 C1
Crofton Rd CMBW SE5 ...143 F2
  ORP BR6 ...216 A2
  PLSTW E13 ...107 F3
Crofton Ter RCH/KEW TW9 ...137 G5
Crofton Wy BAR EN5 * ...33 F1
  ENC/FH EN2 ...23 G5
Croft Rd BMLY BR1 ...183 K2
  PEND EN3 ...25 G2
  STRHM/NOR SW16 ...180 B3
  SUT SM1 ...209 H3
  WIM/MER SW19 ...178 B3
Crofts La EN EN1 ...24 D1
Crofts Rd HRW HA1 ...61 G3
Croft St DEPT SE8 ...124 B4
  WCHPL E1 ...104 C6
The Croft ALP/SUD HA0 ...79 J3
  BAR EN5 ...20 C5
  CHING E4 ...38 C4
  EA W5 ...98 A4
  EDGW HA8 ...30 D4
  HEST TW5 ...134 D1
  PIN HA5 ...59 K3
  RSLP HA4 ...77 G2
  SWLY BR8 ...187 K6
  WLSDN NW10 ...81 H6
Croft Wy BFN/LL DA15 ...167 K5
  RCHPK/HAM TW10 ...156 C5
Crogsland Rd CAMTN NW1 ...84 A5
Croham Manor Rd
  SAND/SEL CR2 ...212 A5
Croham Mt SAND/SEL CR2 ...212 A6
Croham Park Av
  SAND/SEL CR2 ...212 B3
Croham Rd SAND/SEL CR2 ...211 K3
Croham Valley Rd
  SAND/SEL CR2 ...212 C4
Croindene Rd
  STRHM/NOR SW16 ...179 K4
Cromartie Rd ARCH N19 ...66 D4
Cromarty Rd EDGW HA8 ...30 D4
Cromarty Vis BAY/PAD W2 * ...101 G6
Crombie Cl REDBR IG4 ...71 K2
Crombie Ms BTSEA SW11 * ...140 D3
Crombie Rd BFN/LL DA15 ...167 J3
Cromer Hyde MRDN SM4 * ...194 A2
Crome Rd WLSDN NW10 ...81 G4
Cromer Rd BAR EN5 ...21 G5
  CHDH RM6 ...74 A3
  HTHAIR TW6 ...132 D4
  LEY E10 ...70 B4
  ROMW/RG RM7 ...74 E3
  SNWD SE25 ...181 J6
  TOOT SW17 ...179 F2
  TOTM N17 ...50 C5
Cromer Rd West HTHAIR TW6 ...132 D4
Cromer St STPAN WC1H ...5 F5
Cromer Ter HACK E8 * ...86 C3
Cromer Villas Rd
  WAND/EARL SW18 ...159 J1
Cromford Cl ORP BR6 ...216 E1
Cromford Rd PUT/ROE SW15 ...139 F5
Cromford Wy NWMAL KT3 ...176 A4
Cromlix Cl CHST BR7 ...185 G5
Crompton Pl PEND EN3 * ...25 J1
Crompton St BAY/PAD W2 ...2 A7
Cromwell Av HAYES BR2 ...200 A1
  HGT N6 ...66 B5
  HMSMTH W6 ...118 E5
  NWMAL KT3 ...192 C2
Cromwell Cl ACT W3 ...117 K1
  EFNCH N2 ...65 H2
  HAYES BR2 ...200 A1
  WOT/HER KT12 ...188 A4
Cromwell Crs ECT SW5 ...119 K4
Cromwell Gdns SKENS SW7 ...14 B6
Cromwell Gv HMSMTH W6 ...119 F3
Cromwell Ms SKENS SW7 * ...14 B6
Cromwell Pde ALP/SUD HA0 * ...98 A1
Cromwell Pl ACT W3 ...117 K1
  HGT N6 * ...66 B5
  MORT/ESHN SW14 ...137 K4
  SKENS SW7 ...14 B6
The Cross Wy
  KTN/HRWW/WS HA3 ...42 E5
The Crossway ELTH/MOT SE9 ...166 C4
  WDGN N22 ...49 H3
Croston St HACK E8 ...86 C6
Crosts La WDGN N22 ...49 H4
Crothall Cl PLMGR N13 ...35 F5
Crouch Av BARK IG11 ...109 J1
Crouch Cl BECK BR3 ...182 D2
Crouch Cft ELTH/MOT SE9 ...167 F6
Crouch End HI CEND/HSY/T N8 ...66 D4
Crouch Hall Rd CEND/HSY/T N8 ...66 D4
Crouch Hill CEND/HSY/T N8 ...66 E4
Crouchman's Cl SYD SE26 ...163 G5
Crouch Rd WLSDN NW10 ...81 F5
Crowborough Pth
  OXHEY WD19 ...27 H6
Crowborough Rd TOOT SW17 ...179 F1
Crowden Wy THMD SE28 ...109 J6
Crowder Cl NFNCH/WDSPK N12 ...47 G3
Crowder St WCHPL E1 ...104 D6
Crowfoot Cl HOM E9 ...87 H3
  THMD SE28 ...127 K1
Crowhurst Cl BRXN/ST SW9 ...142 B3
Crowhurst Wy
  STMC/STPC BR5 ...202 D2
Crowland Av HYS/HAR UB3 ...113 H4
Crowland Gdns
  STHGT/OAK N14 ...34 E2
Crowland Rd SEVS/STOTM N15 ...68 B2
  THHTH CR7 ...196 E1
Crowlands Av ROMW/RG RM7 ...74 D3
Crowland Ter IS N1 ...85 K5
Crowland Wk MRDN SM4 ...194 A3
Crow La ROMW/RG RM7 ...74 A4
Crowline Wk IS N1 * ...85 J4
Crowmarsh Gdns FSTH SE23 ...163 K2
Crown Ar KUT/HW KT1 * ...174 E5
Crownbourne Ct SUT SM1 * ...209 F2
Crown Buildings CHING E4 * ...38 B3
Crown Cl BOW E3 ...87 J6
  HYS/HAR UB3 ...113 J2
  KIL/WHAMP NW6 ...83 F4
  MLHL NW7 ...31 H4
  ORP BR6 ...217 G2
  WOT/HER KT12 ...188 B4
Crown Ct HOL/ALD WC2B ...11 F4
Crown Dale NRWD SE19 ...180 D2
Crownfield Av
  CNTH/NBYPK IG2 ...72 E2
Crownfield Rd SRTFD E15 ...88 B2
Crown HI CROY/NA CR0 ...196 D6
Crownhill Rd WFD IG8 ...53 J3
  WLSDN NW10 ...81 H6
Crown La CHST BR7 ...185 H4
  HAYES BR2 ...200 C2
  MRDN SM4 ...193 K1
  STHGT/OAK N14 ...34 C3
  STRHM/NOR SW16 ...180 B1
Crown Lane Gdns
  STRHM/NOR SW16 ...180 B1
Crown Lane Sp HAYES BR2 ...200 C3
Crownmead Wy
  ROMW/RG RM7 ...74 D1
Crown Office Rw EMB EC4Y ...11 J5
Crown Pde MRDN SM4 * ...194 A1
  STHGT/OAK N14 ...34 C3
Crown Pas STJS SW1Y ...16 B1
Crown Pl KTTN NW5 ...84 B4
  SDTCH EC2A ...7 G7
Crown Rd BARK/HLT IG6 ...72 D1
  EN EN1 ...24 D5
  KUTN/CMB KT2 ...175 F3
  MRDN SM4 ...193 K1
  MUSWH N10 ...48 A3
  ORP BR6 ...217 G3
  RSLP HA4 ...77 H3
  SUT SM1 ...209 F2
  TWK TW1 ...156 C1
Crownstone Rd
  BRXS/STRHM SW2 ...142 B6
Crown St ACT W3 ...117 J1
  CMBW SE5 ...142 D1
  DAGE RM10 ...92 E4
  RYLN/HDSTN HA2 ...60 D5
Crown Ter CRICK NW2 * ...82 B2
  RCH/KEW TW9 ...137 G5
  STHGT/OAK N14 * ...34 C3
Crowntree Cl ISLW TW7 ...116 A6
Crown Vis ACT W3 * ...117 K2
Crown Wy WDR/YW UB7 ...112 C1
Crown Woods La
  WOOL/PLUM SE18 ...127 G3
Crown Woods Wy
  ELTH/MOT SE9 ...147 J6
Crown Yd HSLW TW3 ...135 H4
Crowshott Av STAN HA7 ...43 J5
Crows Rd BARK IG11 ...90 B4
  BOW E3 ...106 B2
Crowther Av BTFD TW8 ...117 F5
Crowther Cl FUL/PGN SW6 * ...119 K5
Crowther Rd SNWD SE25 ...197 H1
Crowthorne Cl
  WAND/EARL SW18 ...159 J2
Crowthorne Rd NKENS W10 ...100 B5
Croxden Cl EDGW HA8 ...44 C6
Croxden Wk MRDN SM4 ...194 B3
Croxford Gdns WDGN N22 ...49 H3
Croxford Wy ROMW/RG RM7 ...75 F6
Croxley Cl STMC/STPC BR5 ...186 C5
Croxley Gn STMC/STPC BR5 ...186 C4
Croxley Rd MV/WKIL W9 ...100 D2
Croxley Vw WATW WD18 ...26 C1
Croxted Cl DUL SE21 ...162 D2
Croxted Ms EDUL SE22 ...163 G1
Croxted Rd DUL SE21 ...162 E4
Croyde Av GFD/PVL UB6 ...96 C2
  HYS/HAR UB3 ...113 H4
Croyde Cl BFN/LL DA15 ...167 J2
The Croydon F/O
  CROY/NA CR0 ...211 H2
Croydon Gv CROY/NA CR0 ...196 C5

Croydon Rd BECK BR3 198 A2
MTCM CR4 195 G2
PGE/AN SE20 181 J5
PLSTW E13 106 D3
WLGTN SM6 210 B2
WWKM BR4 214 C1
WWKM BR4 215 F1
Croyland Rd ED N9 36 C3
Croylands Dr SURB KT6 191 F4
Crozier Ter HOM E9 87 G3
Crucible Cl CHDH RM6 73 H3
Crucifix La STHWK SE1 19 G2
Cruden St IS N1 6 B1
Cruickshank St FSBYW WC1X 5 J4
Cruikshank Rd SRTFD E15 88 C2
Crummock Gdns
CDALE/KGS NW9 63 G2
Crumpsall St ABYW SE2 128 D4
Crundale Av CDALE/KGS NW9 62 C2
Crunden Rd SAND/SEL CR2 211 K5
Crusader Cl PUR RM19 131 K4
Crusader Gdns CROY/NA CR0 212 A1
Crusader Wy WATW WD18 26 D1
Crusoe Ms STNW/STAM N16 67 K6
Crusoe Rd ERITH DA8 130 A5
MTCM CR4 178 E3
Crutched Friars TWRH EC3N 13 H5
Crutchfield La WOT/HER KT12 188 A6
Crutchley Rd CAT SE6 165 J4
Crystal Palace NRWD SE19 * 181 H3
Crystal Palace Pde
NRWD SE19 181 G2
Crystal Palace Park Rd
SYD SE26 181 J1
Crystal Palace Rd EDUL SE22 163 H1
Crystal Palace Station Rd
NRWD SE19 181 H2
Crystal Ter NRWD SE19 180 E2
Crystal Wy BCTR RM8 73 J5
HRW HA1 61 F2
Cuba Dr PEND EN3 24 E3
Cuba St POP/IOD E14 124 D2
Cubitt Sq NWDGN UB2 * 115 H1
Cubitt St FSBYW WC1X 5 H5
Cubitt Ter CLAP SW4 141 H4
Cuckmere Wy STMC/STPC BR5 202 E5
Cuckoo Av HNWL W7 96 E3
Cuckoo Dene HNWL W7 96 D4
Cuckoo Hall La ED N9 36 E2
Cuckoo Hl PIN HA5 59 G1
Cuckoo Hill Dr PIN HA5 41 G6
Cuckoo Hill Rd PIN HA5 59 H1
Cuckoo La HNWL W7 96 E6
Cuda's Cl HOR/WEW KT19 207 H2
Cuddington Av WPK KT4 207 H1
Cudham La North ORP BR6 216 E6
Cudham St CAT SE6 164 E2
Cudworth St WCHPL E1 104 D3
Cuff Crs ELTH/MOT SE9 166 D1
Culford Gdns CHEL SW3 15 F7
Culford Gv IS N1 86 A4
Culford Ms IS N1 85 K4
Culford Rd IS N1 86 A6
Culgaith Gdns ENC/FH EN2 22 E5
Cullera Cl NTHWD HA6 40 D2
Culling Rd BERM/RHTH SE16 123 K3
Cullington Cl
KTN/HRWW/WS HA3 61 G1
Cullingworth Rd WLSDN NW10 81 K3
Culloden Cl BERM/RHTH SE16 123 H5
Culloden Rd ENC/FH EN2 23 H3
Culloden St POP/IOD E14 106 A5
Cullum St FENCHST EC3M 13 G5
Culmington Pde WEA W13 * 97 J6
Culmington Rd SAND/SEL CR2 211 J6
WEA W13 116 D1
Culmore Rd PECK SE15 143 J1
Culmstock Rd BTSEA SW11 141 F6
Culpepper Cl CHIG IG7 54 B2
UED N18 50 D1
Culross Cl SEVS/STOTM N15 67 J1
Culross St MYFR/PKLN W1K 9 G6
Culsac Rd SURB KT6 191 F6
Culverden Rd BAL SW12 161 H5
OXHEY WD19 27 F5
Culver Gv STAN HA7 43 J5
Culverhouse Gdns
STRHM/NOR SW16 162 A6
Culverlands Cl STAN HA7 29 H6
Culverley Rd CAT SE6 164 E3
Culvers Av CAR SM5 194 E6
Culvers Retreat CAR SM5 194 E5
Culverstone Cl HAYES BR2 199 J3
Culvers Wy CAR SM5 209 K1
Culvert Pl BTSEA SW11 141 F3
Culvert Rd BTSEA SW11 140 E3
SEVS/STOTM N15 68 A2
Culworth St STJWD NW8 2 C3
Cumberland Av WELL DA16 147 K4
WLSDN NW10 98 D2
Cumberland Cl BARK/HLT IG6 54 C4
HACK E8 86 B4
RYNPK SW20 177 G3
TWK TW1 156 C1
Cumberland Crs WKENS W14 119 H4
Cumberland Cresent
WKENS W14 * 119 H4
Cumberland Dr BXLYHN DA7 149 F1
CHSGTN KT9 206 A1
DART DA1 171 J2
ESH/CLAY KT10 190 B6
Cumberland Gdns FSBYW WC1X 5 H4
HDN NW4 * 46 B5
Cumberland Ga BAY/PAD W2 8 E5
CAMTN NW1 3 J4
Cumberland House
KUTN/CMB KT2 175 J3
Cumberland Market
CAMTN NW1 3 K4
Cumberland Ms LBTH SE11 122 B5
Cumberland Pk ACT W3 98 E6
Cumberland Pl CAMTN NW1 3 J4
CAT SE6 165 J3
Cumberland Rd ACT W3 98 E6
ASHF TW15 152 A5
BARN SW13 138 D2
ED N9 36 E3
HAYES BR2 199 H1
HNWL W7 116 A2
HRW HA1 60 B2
MNPK E12 89 H2
PLSTW E13 107 F4
RCH/KEW TW9 137 H2
SNWD SE25 197 J3
STAN HA7 44 B6
WALTH E17 51 G5
WDGN N22 49 F5
Cumberland St PIM SW1V 121 G5
Cumberland Ter CAMTN NW1 3 J3
PGE/AN SE20 * 181 J3
Cumberland Terrace Ms
CAMTN NW1 3 J3
Cumberlow Av SNWD SE25 181 H6
Cumberton Rd TOTM N17 49 K4
Cumbrae Gdns SURB KT6 190 E6
Cumbrian Av BXLYHN DA7 150 B3
Cumbrian Gdns CRICK NW2 64 B6
Cumming St IS N1 5 H3
Cumnor Cl BRXN/ST SW9 * 142 A3
Cumnor Gdns EW KT17 207 J4
Cumnor Rd BELMT SM2 209 G4
Cunard Crs WCHMH N21 35 K1
Cunard Rd WLSDN NW10 99 F2
Cundy Rd CAN/RD E16 107 G5
Cundy St BGVA SW1W 15 H7
Cunliffe Rd HOR/WEW KT19 207 H2
Cunliffe St STRHM/NOR SW16 179 H2
Cunningham Cl CHDH RM6 73 J2
WWKM BR4 198 E6
Cunningham Pk HRW HA1 60 D2
Cunningham Pl STJWD NW8 2 A6
Cunningham Rd
SEVS/STOTM N15 * 68 C1
Cunnington St CHSWK W4 117 K4
Cupar Rd BTSEA SW11 141 F2
Cupola Cl BMLY BR1 184 A1
Curates Wk RDART DA2 171 G5
Cureton St WEST SW1P * 121 J5
Curlew Cl THMD SE28 109 K6
Curlew St STHWK SE1 19 J2
Curlew Wy YEAD UB4 95 H4
Curnick's La WNWD SE27 162 D6
Curran Av BFN/LL DA15 148 A6
WLGTN SM6 210 A1
Currey Rd NTHLT UB5 78 C4
Curricle St ACT W3 118 B1
Currie Hill Cl WIM/MER SW19 159 J6
Curry Ri MLHL NW7 46 B2
Cursitor St FLST/FETLN EC4A 11 J3
Curtain Pl SDTCH EC2A 7 H6
Curtain Rd SDTCH EC2A 7 G7
Curthwaite Gdns ENC/FH EN2 22 D5
Curtis Dr ACT W3 99 F5
Curtis Field Rd
STRHM/NOR SW16 162 A6
Curtis La ALP/SUD HA0 80 A4
Curtismill Cl STMC/STPC BR5 186 C6
Curtismill Wy
STMC/STPC BR5 186 C6
Curtis Rd HOR/WEW KT19 206 E2
HSLWW TW4 154 E2
Curtis St STHWK SE1 19 J6
Curtis Wy STHWK SE1 19 J6
The Curve SHB W12 99 J6
Curwen Av FSTGT E7 89 F2
Curwen Rd SHB W12 118 D2
Curzon Av PEND EN3 25 F6
STAN HA7 43 G4
Curzon Cl ORP BR6 216 D2
Curzon Crs BARK IG11 109 F2
WLSDN NW10 81 G5
Curzon Pl PIN HA5 59 G2
Curzon Rd EA W5 97 H3
MUSWH N10 48 B5
THHTH CR7 196 B3
Curzon Sq MYFR/PICC W1J 15 H1
Curzon St MYFR/PICC W1J 9 K7
MYFR/PKLN W1K 15 H1
Cusack Cl TWK TW1 * 156 A6
Custom House Reach
BERM/RHTH SE16 * 124 C3
Cutcombe Rd CMBW SE5 142 D3
Cuthberga Cl BARK IG11 90 C5
Cuthbert Gdns SNWD SE25 181 F6
Cuthbert Rd CROY/NA CR0 196 C6
UED N18 50 C1
WALTH E17 52 A6
Cuthbert St BAY/PAD W2 2 A7
Cutlers Gardens Ar
LVPST EC2M 13 H3
Cutler St HDTCH EC3A 13 H3
The Cut STHWK SE1 17 K2
Cuxton Cl BXLYHS DA6 149 F6
Cyclamen Cl HPTN TW12 173 F2
Cyclamen Wy HOR/WEW KT19 206 E3
Cygnet Av EBED/NFELT TW14 154 C2
Cygnet Cl NTHWD HA6 40 A3
WLSDN NW10 81 F3
The Cygnets FELT TW13 154 D6
Cygnet St WCHPL E1 7 K6
Cygnet Wy YEAD UB4 95 H5
Cymbeline Ct HRW HA1 * 61 F3
Cynthia St IS N1 5 H3
Cypress Av WHTN TW2 155 H2
Cypress Cl CLPT E5 68 C6
Cypress Gdns BROCKY SE4 144 B6
Cypress Gv BARK/HLT IG6 54 E2
Cypress Rd
KTN/HRWW/WS HA3 42 D5
SNWD SE25 181 F5
Cypress Tree Cl BFN/LL DA15 168 A3
Cyprus Av FNCH N3 46 C5
Cyprus Cl FSBYPK N4 67 G3
Cyprus Gdns FNCH N3 46 C5
Cyprus Pl BETH E2 104 E1
EHAM E6 108 A6
Cyprus Rd ED N9 36 B4
FNCH N3 46 D5
Cyprus St BETH E2 104 E1
Cyrena Rd EDUL SE22 163 G1
Cyril Rd BXLYHN DA7 149 F3
ORP BR6 202 B4
Cyrus St FSBYE EC1V 6 B6
Czar St DEPT SE8 124 D6

D

Dabbling Cl ERITH DA8 * 150 E1
Dabbs Hill La NTHLT UB5 77 K4
D'Abernon Cl ESH/CLAY KT10 204 A2
Dabin Crs GNWCH SE10 145 F2
Dacca St DEPT SE8 124 C6
Dace Rd BOW E3 87 J6
Dacre Av CLAY IG5 54 A5
Dacre Cl GFD/PVL UB6 96 B1
Dacre Gdns LEW SE13 * 145 H5
Dacre Pk LEW SE13 145 H4
Dacre Pl LEW SE13 145 H4
Dacre Rd CROY/NA CR0 195 K4
PLSTW E13 89 F6
WAN E11 70 D5
Dacres Est FSTH SE23 * 164 A5
Dacres Rd FSTH SE23 164 A5
Dacre St STJSPK SW1H 16 C4
Dade Wy NWDGN UB2 114 E5
Daerwood Cl HAYES BR2 200 E5
Daffodil Cl CROY/NA CR0 198 A5
HPTN TW12 173 F2
Daffodil Gdns IL IG1 90 B3
Daffodil St SHB W12 99 H6
Dafforne Rd TOOT SW17 160 E5
Dagenham Av DAGW RM9 92 A6
Dagenham Rd DAGE RM10 92 E2
LEY E10 69 H5
RAIN RM13 93 F5
ROMW/RG RM7 75 F4
Dagger La BORE WD6 29 G1
Dagmar Av WBLY HA9 80 B2
Dagmar Gdns WLSDN NW10 100 B1
Dagmar Ms NWDGN UB2 114 D3
Dagmar Pas IS N1 85 H6
Dagmar Rd CMBW SE5 143 F2
DAGE RM10 92 E5
FSBYPK N4 67 G4
KUTN/CMB KT2 175 G4
NWDGN UB2 114 D3
SEVS/STOTM N15 67 K1
SNWD SE25 197 F1
WDGN N22 48 D4
Dagmar Ter IS N1 85 H6
Dagnall Pk SNWD SE25 197 F2
Dagnall Rd SNWD SE25 197 F2
Dagnall St BTSEA SW11 140 E3
Dagnan Rd BAL SW12 161 G2
Dagonet Rd BMLY BR1 165 K5
Dahlia Gdns IL IG1 90 B4
MTCM CR4 195 J1
Dahlia Rd ABYW SE2 128 C5
Dahomey Rd
STRHM/NOR SW16 179 H2
Daimler Wy WLGTN SM6 210 E5
Daines Cl MNPK E12 89 K1
Dainford Cl BMLY BR1 183 G1
Daintry Cl KTN/HRWW/WS HA3 61 G1
Dairsie Rd ELTH/MOT SE9 147 F4
Dairy Cl BMLY BR1 * 184 A3
THHTH CR7 180 D5
WLSDN NW10 81 J6
Dairy La WOOL/PLUM SE18 126 E4
Dairyman Cl CRICK NW2 * 82 B2
Daisy Cl CROY/NA CR0 198 A5
Daisy La FUL/PGN SW6 139 K4
Daisy Rd SWFD E18 53 F5
Dakin Pl WCHPL E1 105 G4
Dakota Cl WLGTN SM6 211 F5
Dalberg Rd BRXS/STRHM SW2 142 B6
Dalberg Wy ABYW SE2 128 E3
Dalby Rd WAND/EARL SW18 140 B5
Dalbys Crs TOTM N17 50 A2
Dalby St KTTN NW5 84 B4
Dalcross Rd HSLWW TW4 134 D3
Dale Av EDGW HA8 44 B4
HSLWW TW4 134 D4
Dalebury Rd TOOT SW17 160 E4
Dale Cl BAR EN5 33 F1
BKHTH/KID SE3 145 K4
DART DA1 170 C1
PIN HA5 41 F4
Dale Dr YEAD UB4 94 D3
Dale Gdns WFD IG8 39 F6
Dale Green Rd FBAR/BDGN N11 34 B5
Dale Gv NFNCH/WDSPK N12 47 G1
Daleham Gdns HAMP NW3 83 H3
Daleham Ms HAMP NW3 * 83 H4
Dalemain Ms CAN/RD E16 125 K1
Dale Park Av CAR SM5 194 E6
Dale Park Rd NRWD SE19 180 D4
Dale Rd DART DA1 170 C1
KTTN NW5 84 A3
STHL UB1 96 B4
SUT SM1 208 D2
SWLY BR8 187 K6
WALW SE17 122 C6
Dale Rw NTGHL W11 100 C5
Daleside ORP BR6 217 G3
Daleside Cl ORP BR6 217 G4
Daleside Rd HOR/WEW KT19 207 F4
STRHM/NOR SW16 179 G1
Dalestone Ms HARH RM3 57 K3
Dale St CHSWK W4 118 B5
The Dale HAYES BR2 215 H2
Dale Vw BAR EN5 * 20 D4
ERITH DA8 150 D3
Dale View Av CHING E4 38 A4
Dale View Crs CHING E4 38 A5
Dale View Gdns CHING E4 38 B5
Daleview Rd SEVS/STOTM N15 68 A3
Dalewood Gdns WPK KT4 192 E6
Dale Wood Rd ORP BR6 201 K5
Daley St HOM E9 87 F4
Daley Thompson Wy
VX/NE SW8 141 G4
Dalgarno Gdns NKENS W10 100 A4
Dalgarno Wy NKENS W10 100 A3
Dalkeith Gv STAN HA7 43 K1
Dalkeith Rd DUL SE21 162 D3
IL IG1 90 C1
Dallas Rd CHEAM SM3 208 C4
EA W5 98 B4
HDN NW4 63 J4
SYD SE26 163 J6
Dallas Ter HYS/HAR UB3 113 J3
Dallega Cl HYS/HAR UB3 94 B6
Dallinger Rd LEE/GVPK SE12 165 J1
Dalling Rd HMSMTH W6 118 E4
Dallington Sq FSBYE EC1V 6 B6
Dallington St FARR EC1M 6 B7
Dallin Rd BXLYHS DA6 148 E5
WOOL/PLUM SE18 147 G1
Dalmain Rd FSTH SE23 164 A3
Dalmally Rd CROY/NA CR0 197 G4
Dalmeny Av HOLWY N7 84 D2
STRHM/NOR SW16 180 B5
Dalmeny Cl ALP/SUD HA0 79 J4
Dalmeny Crs HSLW TW3 135 J5
Dalmeny Rd BAR EN5 33 G1
CAR SM5 210 A5
ERITH DA8 149 J2
HOLWY N7 84 D2
WPK KT4 207 K1
Dalmeyer Rd WLSDN NW10 81 H4
Dalmore Av ESH/CLAY KT10 205 F4
Dalmore Rd DUL SE21 162 D4
Dalrymple Cl STHGT/OAK N14 34 D2
Dalrymple Rd BROCKY SE4 144 C6
Dalston Gdns STAN HA7 44 A4
Dalston La HACK E8 86 B4
Dalton Av MTCM CR4 178 D5
Dalton Cl ORP BR6 216 E1
YEAD UB4 94 B3
Daltons Rd SWLY BR8 203 K6
Dalton St WNWD SE27 162 C4
Dalton Wy WAT WD17 27 H1
Dalwood St CMBW SE5 143 F2
Dalyell Rd BRXN/ST SW9 142 A4
Damask Crs CAN/RD E16 106 C3
Damer Ter WBPTN SW10 140 B1
Dames Rd FSTGT E7 88 E2
Dame St IS N1 6 C2
Damien St WCHPL E1 104 D4
Damon Cl SCUP DA14 168 C5
Damsel Ct BERM/RHTH SE16 * 123 H2
Damson Dr HYS/HAR UB3 94 E6
Damson Wy CAR SM5 209 K6
Damsonwood Rd NWDGN UB2 115 F3
Danbrook Rd
STRHM/NOR SW16 179 K4
Danbury Cl CHDH RM6 55 K6
Danbury Ms WLGTN SM6 210 B2
Danbury Rd LOU IG10 39 J1
RAIN RM13 93 H6
Danbury St IS N1 6 B2
Danbury Wy WFD IG8 53 G2
Danby St PECK SE15 143 G4
Dancer Rd FUL/PGN SW6 139 J2
RCH/KEW TW9 137 H4
Dandelion Cl ROMW/RG RM7 75 G6
Dando Crs BKHTH/KID SE3 146 A4
Dandridge Cl GNWCH SE10 125 J5
Danebury CROY/NA CR0 213 K4
Danebury Av PUT/ROE SW15 158 C2
Daneby Rd CAT SE6 165 F5
Dane Cl BXLY DA5 169 H2
ORP BR6 216 D3
Danecourt Gdns CROY/NA CR0 212 B1
Danecroft Rd HNHL SE24 142 D6
Danehurst Gdns REDBR IG4 71 J2
Danehurst St FUL/PGN SW6 139 H2
Daneland EBAR EN4 33 K1
Danemead Gv NTHLT UB5 78 B3
Danemere St PUT/ROE SW15 139 F4
Dane Pl BOW E3 105 G1
Dane Rd IL IG1 90 C3
STHL UB1 95 J6
UED N18 36 E6
WEA W13 97 J6
WIM/MER SW19 178 B4
Danesbury Rd FELT TW13 154 B4
Danescombe LEE/GVPK SE12 165 K3
Danescourt Crs SUT SM1 194 B6
Danescroft Av HDN NW4 * 64 B2
Danescroft Gdns HDN NW4 64 B2
Danesdale Rd HOM E9 87 G4
Danes Ga HRW HA1 42 E6
Danes Rd ROMW/RG RM7 74 E4
Dane St GINN WC1R 11 G2
Daneswood Av CAT SE6 165 F5
Danethorpe Rd ALP/SUD HA0 79 K4
Danetree Cl HOR/WEW KT19 206 E5
Danetree Rd HOR/WEW KT19 206 E5
Danette Gdns DAGE RM10 74 B6
Daneville Rd CMBW SE5 142 E2
Dangan Rd WAN E11 70 E3
Daniel Bolt Cl POP/IOD E14 105 K4
Daniel Cl HSLWW TW4 154 E2
TOOT SW17 178 D2
UED N18 36 E6
Daniel Gdns PECK SE15 143 G1
Daniell Wy CROY/NA CR0 195 K5
Daniel Pl HDN NW4 63 K3
Daniel Rd EA W5 98 B6
Daniel's Rd PECK SE15 143 K4
Dan Leno Wk FUL/PGN SW6 * 140 A1
Dan Mason Dr CHSWK W4 138 A3
Dansey Pl SOHO/SHAV W1D 10 C5
Dansington Rd WELL DA16 148 B5
Danson Crs WELL DA16 148 C4
Danson La WELL DA16 148 C5
Danson Md WELL DA16 148 D4
Danson Rd BXLYHS DA6 148 E6
Danson U/P BFN/LL DA15 168 D1
Dante Rd LBTH SE11 18 A6
Danube St CHEL SW3 120 D5
Danvers Rd CEND/HSY/T N8 66 D1
Danvers St CHEL SW3 120 C6
Daphne Gdns CHING E4 38 A5
Daphne St WAND/EARL SW18 160 B1
Daplyn St WCHPL E1 104 C4
D'Arblay St SOHO/CST W1F 10 B4
Darby Crs SUN TW16 172 B5
Darby Gdns SUN TW16 172 B5
Darcy Av WLGTN SM6 210 C2
Darcy Cl TRDG/WHET N20 33 H4
D'Arcy Dr KTN/HRWW/WS HA3 61 K1
D'Arcy Gdns DAGW RM9 92 B6
KTN/HRWW/WS HA3 62 A1
D'Arcy Pl HAYES BR2 199 K1
D'Arcy Rd CHEAM SM3 208 B2
Darcy Rd ISLW TW7 136 B2
STRHM/NOR SW16 179 K5
Darell Rd RCH/KEW TW9 137 H4
Darenth Rd DART DA1 171 K4
STNW/STAM N16 68 B4
WELL DA16 148 B2
Darent Valley Pth ERITH DA8 151 G2
Darfield Rd BROCKY SE4 144 C6
Darfield Wy NKENS W10 100 B6
Darfur St PUT/ROE SW15 139 G4
Dargate Cl NRWD SE19 181 G3
Darien Rd BTSEA SW11 140 C4
Darlands Dr BAR EN5 20 B6
Darlan Rd FUL/PGN SW6 139 J1
Darlaston Rd WIM/MER SW19 177 G3
Darley Cl CROY/NA CR0 198 A3
Darley Dr NWMAL KT3 176 A5
Darley Gdns MRDN SM4 194 A3
Darley Rd BTSEA SW11 160 E1
ED N9 36 B3
Darling Rd BROCKY SE4 144 D4
Darling Rw WCHPL E1 104 D3
Darlington Rd WNWD SE27 180 C1
Darlton Cl DART DA1 150 C4
Darmaine Cl SAND/SEL CR2 211 J5
Darndale Cl WALTH E17 51 H5
Darnley Rd HACK E8 86 D4
WFD IG8 52 E4
Darnley Ter NTGHL W11 119 G1
Darns Hl SWLY BR8 203 K4
Darrell Rd EDUL SE22 143 H6
Darren Cl FSBYPK N4 67 F4
Darrick Wood Rd ORP BR6 201 J6
Darris Cl YEAD UB4 95 J3
Darsley Dr VX/NE SW8 141 J2
Dartford Av ED N9 36 E1
Dartford Gdns CHDH RM6 73 H2
Dartford Rd BXLY DA5 169 K3
DART DA1 170 D1
Dartford St WALW SE17 122 D6
Dartmoor Wk POP/IOD E14 * 124 D4
Dartmouth Cl NTGHL W11 100 D5
Dartmouth Gv GNWCH SE10 145 F2
Dartmouth Hl GNWCH SE10 145 F2
Dartmouth Park Av KTTN NW5 84 B1
Dartmouth Park Hl ARCH N19 66 B6
KTTN NW5 84 C1
Dartmouth Park Rd KTTN NW5 84 B1
Dartmouth Pl CHSWK W4 118 B6
FSTH SE23 163 K4
Dartmouth Rd CRICK NW2 82 B4
HAYES BR2 199 K4
HDN NW4 63 J3
RSLP HA4 76 E1
SYD SE26 163 J5
Dartmouth Rw GNWCH SE10 145 F3
Dartmouth St STJSPK SW1H 16 C3
Dartmouth Ter GNWCH SE10 145 G2
Dartnell Rd CROY/NA CR0 197 G4
Dartrey Wk WBPTN SW10 * 140 B1
Dart St NKENS W10 100 D2
Darville Rd STNW/STAM N16 86 B1
Darwell Cl EHAM E6 108 A1
Darwin Cl FBAR/BDGN N11 34 B5
ORP BR6 216 D3
Darwin Dr STHL UB1 96 B5
Darwin Gdns OXHEY WD19 41 G1
Darwin Rd EA W5 116 D5
WDGN N22 49 H4
WELL DA16 148 A4
Darwin St WALW SE17 19 F6
Darynton Dr GFD/PVL UB6 96 D1
Dashwood Cl BXLYHS DA6 149 H6
Dashwood Rd CEND/HSY/T N8 67 F3
Dassett Rd WNWD SE27 180 C1
Datchelor Pl CMBW SE5 * 142 E2
Datchet Rd CAT SE6 164 C5
Date St WALW SE17 122 D5
Daubeney Gdns TOTM N17 49 J3
Daubeney Rd CLPT E5 87 G3
TOTM N17 49 J3
Dault Rd WAND/EARL SW18 160 B1
Davema Cl CHST BR7 185 F4
Davenant Rd ARCH N19 66 D6
Davenant St WCHPL E1 104 C4
Davenham Av NTHWD HA6 26 D6
Davenport Cl TEDD TW11 * 174 B2
Davenport Rd CAT SE6 164 E1
SCUP DA14 168 E4
Daventer Dr STAN HA7 43 F3
Daventry Av WALTH E17 69 J3
Daventry St CAMTN NW1 8 D1
Davern Cl GNWCH SE10 125 J4
Davey Cl HOLWY N7 85 F4
PLMGR N13 49 F1
Davey Rd HOM E9 87 J5
Davey St PECK SE15 123 G6
David Av GFD/PVL UB6 96 E2
David Cl HYS/HAR UB3 133 G1
Davidge St STHWK SE1 18 A3
David Ms MHST W1U 9 F1
David Rd BCTR RM8 74 A6
Davidson Gdns VX/NE SW8 141 K1
Davidson Rd CROY/NA CR0 197 F5
Davidson Wy ROMW/RG RM7 75 G3
David's Rd FSTH SE23 163 K3
David St SRTFD E15 88 B4
Davids Wy BARK/HLT IG6 54 E3
David Twigg Cl KUTN/CMB KT2 175 F4
Davies Cl CROY/NA CR0 197 G3
Davies La WAN E11 70 C6
Davies Ms MYFR/PKLN W1K 9 J5
Davies St MYFR/PKLN W1K 9 J5
Davies Wk ISLW TW7 135 J2
Davington Gdns BCTR RM8 91 H3
Davington Rd BCTR RM8 91 H4
Davinia Cl WFD IG8 53 K2
Davis Rd ACT W3 118 C1
CHSGTN KT9 206 C2
Davis St PLSTW E13 107 F1
Davisville Rd SHB W12 118 D2
Dawes Av ISLW TW7 136 B6
Dawes Ct ESH/CLAY KT10 204 B3
Dawes Rd FUL/PGN SW6 139 J1
Dawes St WALW SE17 122 E5
Dawley Pde HYS/HAR UB3 94 B6

Dawley Rd HYS/HAR UB3........94 B6
Dawlish Av GFD/PVL UB6........97 G1
  PLMGR N13........34 E6
  WAND/EARL SW18........160 A4
Dawlish Dr GDMY/SEVK IG3........91 F2
  PIN HA5........58 ..
  RSLP HA4........58 E6
Dawlish Rd CRICK NW2........82 B4
  LEY E10........70 A6
  TOTM N17........50 C6
Dawnay Gdns
  WAND/EARL SW18........160 A4
Dawnay Rd WAND/EARL SW18..160 A4
Dawn Cl HSLWW TW4........134 D4
Dawn Crs SRTFD E15........88 B6
Dawpool Rd CRICK NW2........63 H6
Daws La MLHL NW7........45 H1
Dawson Av BARK IG11........91 F5
  STMC/STPC BR5........186 C5
Dawson Cl HYS/HAR UB3........94 B6
  WOOL/PLUM SE18........127 H4
Dawson Dr RAIN RM13........93 K5
Dawson Gdns BARK IG11........91 F5
Dawson Pl BAY/PAD W2........100 E6
Dawson Rd CRICK NW2........82 A3
  KUT/HW KT1........175 G6
Dawson St BETH E2........7 K3
Dawson Ter ED N9 *........36 E3
Daybrook Rd WIM/MER SW19..178 A5
Daylesford Av PUT/ROE SW15..138 D5
Daymer Gdns PIN HA5........59 C1
Daysbrook Rd
  BRXS/STRHM SW2........162 A3
Dayton Dr ERITH DA8........131 C6
Dayton Gv PECK SE15........143 K2
Deacon Cl PUR/KEN CR8........210 E6
The Deacon Est CHING E4 *....51 H2
Deacon Ms IS N1........85 K5
Deacon Rd CRICK NW2........81 J4
  KUTN/CMB KT2........175 G4
Deacons Cl PIN HA5........41 F3
Deacons Hts BORE WD6........30 C1
Deacons Hl OXHEY WD19........27 G1
Deacons Leas ORP BR6........216 D2
Deacons Ri EFNCH N2........65 H2
Deacons Ter IS N1 *........85 K4
Deacons Wy HPTN TW12........155 F6
Deacon Wy WALW SE17........18 D6
  WFD IG8........53 K3
Deakin Cl WATW WD18........26 C2
Deakins Ter ORP BR6........202 B4
Deal Porters Wy
  BERM/RHTH SE16........123 K3
Deal Rd TOOT SW17........179 F2
Deals Gtwy LEW SE13........144 E2
Deal St WCHPL E1........104 C4
Dealtry Rd PUT/ROE SW15..139 F5
Deal Wk BRXN/ST SW9........
Dean Bradley St WEST SW1P..16 E6
  HOM E9........86 E3
Dean Ct ALP/SUD HA0........79 H1
Deancross St WCHPL E1........104 E5
Dean Dr STAN HA7........44 A5
Deane Av RSLP HA4........77 F3
Deane Ct NTHWD HA6 *........40 C4
Deane Croft Rd PIN HA5........59 G3
Deanery Cl EFNCH N2........65 J3
Deanery Ms MYFR/PKLN W1K *..9 H7
Deanery Rd SRTFD E15........88 C4
Deanery St MYFR/PKLN W1K......9 H7
Deane Wy RSLP HA4........59 F3
Dean Farrar St ST/JSPK SW1H..16 E4
Deanfield Gdns
  CROY/NA CRO *........211 K3
Dean Gdns WALTH E17........70 B1
Deanhill Ct
  MORT/ESHN SW14 *........137 J5
Deanhill Rd MORT/ESHN SW14..137 J5
Dean Rd CRICK NW2........82 A4
  CROY/NA CRO........211 K2
  HPTN TW12........173 F1
  HSLW TW3........135 C6
  THMD SE28........109 G6
Dean Ryle St WEST SW1P........16 E6
Deansbrook Cl EDGW HA8........44 D4
Deansbrook Rd EDGW HA8........44 D3
Deans Buildings WALW SE17..19 F7
Deans Cl CHSWK W4........117 J6
  CROY/NA CRO........212 B1
  EDGW HA8........44 E2
Dean's Ct STP EC4M........12 B4
Deanscroft Av CDALE/KGS NW9..62 E6
Deans Dr EDGW HA8........44 E1
  PLMGR N13........49 H2
Deans Gate Cl FSTH SE23........164 A5
Dean's La EDGW HA8........44 E1
Dean's Ms CAVSQ/HST W1G *..9 K3
Dean's Rd HNWL W7........116 A2
  SUT SM1........209 F1
Dean Stanley St WEST SW1P..16 E5
Dean St FSTGT E7........88 E3
  SOHO/SHAV W1D........10 C3
Deansway ED N9........36 A5
Deans Wy EDCW HA8........44 E1
Deansway EFNCH N2........65 H1
Deans Yd WEST SW1P........16 E4
Dean Trench St WEST SW1P..16 E5
Dean Wy NWDGN UB2........115 G2
De Arn Gdns MTCM CR4........178 D6
Dearsley Rd EN1........24 C4
Deason St SRTFD E15 *........88 A6
De Barowe Ms HBRY N5........
Debden Cl CDALE/KGS NW9..45 G4
  KUTN/CMB KT2........174 E1
  WFD IG8........53 G3
De Beauvoir Crs IS N1........7 H1
De Beauvoir Est IS N1 *........86 A5
De Beauvoir Rd IS N1........86 A5
De Beauvoir Sq IS N1........86 A5
Debnams Rd
  BERM/RHTH SE16........123 K4
De Bohun Av STHGT/OAK N14..34 B1
Deborah Cl ISLW TW7........135 K2
Deborah Crs RSLP HA4........58 B4

Debrabant Cl ERITH DA8........130 A6
De Broome Rd FELT TW13..154 B3
Deburgh Rd WIM/MER SW19..178 B3
Decima St STHWK SE1........19 G4
Decimus Ct THHTH CR7........196 E1
Deck Cl BERM/RHTH SE16....124 A1
Decoy Av GLDGN NW11........64 C2
De Crespigny Pk CMBW SE5..142 E3
Deeley Rd VX/NE SW8........141 J2
Deena Cl ACT W3........98 B5
Deepdale WIM/MER SW19......159 G6
Deepdale Av HAYES BR2........199 J1
Deepdale Cl FBAR/BDGN N11..48 A2
Deepdene Av CROY/NA CR0..212 B1
Deepdene Cl WAN E11........70 E1
Deepdene Ct WCHMH N21....35 H1
Deepdene Gdns
  BRXS/STRHM SW2........162 A2
Deepdene Rd HNHL SE24....142 D5
  WELL DA16........148 B4
Deepwell Cl ISLW TW7........136 B2
Deepwood La GFD/PVL UB6....96 D2
Deerbrook Rd HNHL SE24....162 C3
Deerdale Rd HNHL SE24......142 D5
Deere Av RAIN RM13........93 J4
Deerfield Cl CDALE/KGS NW9..63 H2
Deerhurst Cl FELT TW13......153 K6
Deerhurst Crs HPTN TW12....173 H1
Deerhurst Rd KIL/WHAMP NW6..82 E5
  STRHM/NOR SW16........180 A1
Deerings Dr PIN HA5........58 E2
Deerleap Gv CHING E4........25 K6
Dee Rd RCH/KEW TW9........137 G5
Deer Park Cl KUTN/CMB KT2..175 J4
Deer Park Gdns MTCM CR4 *..194 C1
Deer Park Rd WIM/MER SW19..178 B5
Deeside Rd TOOT SW17........160 C5
Dee St POP/IOD E14........106 A5
Dee Wy ROM RM1........57 G4
Defence Cl THMD SE28........127 K1
Defiant Wy WLGTN SM6........210 E5
Defoe Av RCH/KEW TW9......137 H1
Defoe Cl TOOT SW17........179 H2
Defoe Pl TOOT SW17........160 D4
Defoe Rd BERM/RHTH SE16..124 A2
  STNW/STAM N16........68 A6
Defoe Wy CRW RM5........56 C2
De Frene Rd SYD SE26........164 B6
Degema Rd CHST BR7........185 G1
Dehar Crs CDALE/KGS NW9..63 H4
De Havilland Dr
  WOOL/PLUM SE18........127 C6
De Havilland Ct IL IG1........72 D5
De Havilland Rd EDGW HA8..44 D5
  HEST TW5........134 B1
De Havilland Wy
  STWL/WRAY TW19........152 A1
Dekker Rd DUL SE21........163 F1
Delacourt Rd BKHTH/KID SE3..146 A1
Delafield Rd CHARL SE7........126 A5
Delaford Rd BERM/RHTH SE16..123 J5
Delaford St FUL/PGN SW6....139 H1
Delamare Crs CROY/NA CR0..197 K3
Delamere Av W5........117 F2
Delamere Rd EA W5........117 F2
  YEAD UB4........95 H6
Delamere St BAY/PAD W2....101 C4
Delamere Ter BAY/PAD W2..101 C4
Delancey Pas CAMTN NW1 *..3 K1
Delancey St CAMTN NW1........3 K1
De Lapre Ct STMC/STPC BR5..202 E4
De Laune St LBTH SE11........122 C6
Delaware Rd MV/WKIL W9....101 F3
Delawyk Crs HNHL SE24......162 E1
Delcombe Av WPK KT4........193 F5
Delhi Rd EN EN1........36 B2
Delhi St IS N1........5 F1
Delia St WAND/EARL SW18..160 A2
Delisle Rd THMD SE28........127 K2
Delius Ct BORE WD6........29 J1
Delius Gv SRTFD E15........106 A1
Delia Pth CLPT E5........86 C1
Dellbow Rd EBED/NFELT TW14..134 A6
  WFD IG8........53 K6
  WLGTN SM6........210 C2
Dell Farm Rd RSLP HA4........58 B2
Dellfield Cl BECK BR3........183 F4
Dell La EW KT17........207 J3
Dellors Cl BAR EN5........20 B6
Dellow Cl GNTH/NBYPK IG2..72 D4
Dellow St WCHPL E1........104 D6
Dell Rd EW KT17........207 J4
  PEND EN3........24 E1
  WDR/YW UB7........112 C3
Dells Cl CHING E4........25 K1
  TEDD TW11........174 A2
Dell's Ms PIM SW1V *........16 B7
The Dell ABYW SE2........128 B5
  ALP/SUD HA0........79 H3
  BECK BR3........182 D3
  BTFD TW8........116 D6
  BXLY DA5........170 B3
  EBED/NFELT TW14........154 A2
  NRWD SE19........181 G4
  NTHWD HA6........26 C4
  PIN HA5........41 H5
  WFD IG8........39 G3
Dell Wk NWMAL KT3........176 B5
Dell Wy WEA W13........97 J5
Dellwood Gdns CLAY IG5........54 A6
Delme Crs BKHTH/KID SE3..146 A3
Delmey Cl CROY/NA CR0......212 B1
Deloraine St DEPT SE8........144 D2
Delorme St HMSMTH W6......119 G6
Delta Centre ALP/SUD HA0 *..80 B6
Delta Cl WPK KT4........207 G1
Delta Est BETH E2 *........104 C2
Delta Gain OXHEY WD19........27 H4
Delta Gv NTHLT UB5........95 H2
Delta Rd WPK KT4........207 G1
Delta St BETH E2 *........104 C2
De Luci Rd ERITH DA8........129 K5
De Lucy St ABYW SE2........128 C4

Delvers Md DAGE RM10........92 E2
Delverton Rd WALW SE17....122 C5
Delvino Rd FUL/PGN SW6....139 K2
De Mandeville Ga EN EN1....24 C5
Demesne Rd WLGTN SM6....210 D2
De Montfort Pde
  STRHM/NOR SW16 *........161 K5
De Montfort Rd
  STRHM/NOR SW16........161 K5
De Morgan Rd FUL/PGN SW6..140 A4
Dempster Cl SURB KT6........190 D5
Dempster Rd
  WAND/EARL SW18........160 B1
Denbar Pde ROMW/RG RM7..74 E1
Denberry Dr SCUP DA14......168 C5
Denbigh Cl CHST BR7........185 F2
  NTGHL W11........100 D6
  STHL UB1........95 K5
  SUT SM1........208 D3
  WLSDN NW10........81 G5
Denbigh Gdns
  RCHPK/HAM TW10........137 G6
Denbigh Pl PIM SW1V........121 H5
Denbigh Rd EHAM E6........107 H2
  HSLW TW3........135 G3
  NTGHL W11........100 D6
  STHL UB1........95 K5
  WEA W13........97 H6
Denbigh St PIM SW1V........16 A7
Denbigh Ter NTGHL W11......100 D6
Denbridge Rd BMLY BR1......184 E5
Dene Av BFN/LL DA15........168 B1
  HSLW TW3........134 E4
Dene Cl BROCKY SE4........144 B4
  HAYES BR2........199 J4
  RDART DA2........170 B6
  WPK KT4........192 C6
Dene Dr ORP BR6........217 H1
Dene Gdns STAN HA7........43 J1
  THDIT KT7........190 B6
Denehurst Gdns ACT W3........117 J1
  HDN NW4........64 A3
  RCHPK/HAM TW10........137 H5
  WFD IG8........39 F6
  WHTN TW2........155 J2
The Dene CROY/NA CR0......213 F2
  E/WMO/HCT KT8........188 E2
  WBLY HA9........80 A2
  WEA W13........97 H4
Denewood Cl WATW WD18....26 C1
Denewood Rd HGT N6........65 K3
Dengie Wk IS N1 *........85 J6
Denham Cl WELL DA16........148 D4
Denham Dr GNTH/NBYPK IG2..72 D3
Denham Rd EBED/NFELT TW14..134 B2
  TRDG/WHET N20........33 K5
Denham Wy BARK IG11........90 E1
Denholme Rd MV/WKIL W9..100 D2
Denison Cl EFNCH N2........47 G6
Denison Rd EA W5........97 J3
  FELT TW13........153 J6
  WIM/MER SW19........178 C2
Deniston Av BXLY DA5........168 E4
Denleigh Gdns THDIT KT7 *..189 K3
  WCHMH N21........35 G3
Denman Dr ESH/CLAY KT10..205 G4
  GLDGN NW11........64 E2
Denman Dr North
  GLDGN NW11........64 E2
Denman Dr South
  GLDGN NW11........64 E2
Denman Rd PECK SE15........143 G2
Denman St SOHO/SHAV W1D..10 C6
Denmark Av WIM/MER SW19..177 H3
Denmark Ct MRDN SM4......193 K2
Denmark Gdns CAR SM5......209 K1
Denmark Gv IS N1........5 J2
Denmark Hill HNHL SE24....142 E5
Denmark Hill Dr
  CDALE/KGS NW9........45 J6
Denmark Rd BMLY BR1......184 A4
  CAR SM5........209 K1
  CEND/HSY/T N8........67 F1
  CMBW SE5........142 D2
  KIL/WHAMP NW6........100 D2
  KUT/HW KT1........175 F6
  SNWD SE25........197 H2
  WEA W13........97 H6
  WHTN TW2........155 J4
  WIM/MER SW19........177 G2
Denmark St LSO/SEVD WC2H..10 D4
  PLSTW E13........107 F4
  TOTM N17........50 D4
  WAN E11........71 F1
Denmark Ter EFNCH N2 *......47 K6
Denmead Rd CROY/NA CR0..196 C5
Denmead Rd SURB KT6........191 H6
Denner Rd CHING E4........37 J4
Denne Ter HACK E8........7 K1
Dennett Rd CROY/NA CR0..196 A4
Dennett's Gv NWCR SE14....144 A3
Dennett's Rd NWCR SE14....143 K2
Denning Av CROY/NA CR0..211 G3
Denning Cl HPTN TW12........172 E1
  STJWD NW8........101 G2
Dennington Park Rd
  KIL/WHAMP NW6........82 E4
The Denningtons WPK KT4..192 B6
Dennis Av WBLY HA9........80 B3
Dennis Gdns STAN HA7........43 J1
Dennis La STAN HA7........29 H6
Dennis Pde STHGT/OAK N14..34 D3
Dennis Park Crs WIM/MER SW19..177 H4
Dennis Reeve Cl MTCM CR4..178 E4
Dennis Rd E/WMO/HCT KT8..189 H1
Dennis Wy CLAP SW4........141 J4
Denny Crs LBTH SE11........122 B5

Denny Gdns DAGW RM9........91 H5
Denny Rd ED N9........36 D3
Denny St LBTH SE11........122 B5
Denny Rd HAYES BR2........
Denham Rd BTFD E15........88 C6
Densole Cl BECK BR3........182 B4
Densworth Gv ED N9........36 E4
Denton Cl BAR EN5........20 A6
Denton Gv WOT/HER KT12..188 D6
Denton Rd CEND/HSY/T N8..67 F2
  DART DA1........170 B2
  TWK TW1........156 E1
  UED N18........36 B6
  WELL DA16........148 D1
Denton St WAND/EARL SW18..160 A1
Denton Ter BXLY DA5 *........169 K4
Dents Rd BTSEA SW11........160 E1
Denvale Trade Pk MTCM CR4..194 C4
Denver Cl ORP BR6........201 K3
Denver Rd DART DA1........170 D2
  STNW/STAM N16........68 A4
Denyer St CHEL SW3........14 D6
Denzil Rd WLSDN NW10........81 H3
Deodar Rd PUT/ROE SW15..139 H5
Deodora Cl TRDG/WHET N20..33 K5
Depot Ap CRICK NW2........82 B2
Depot Rd HSLW TW3........135 H4
Depot St CMBW SE5........122 E6
Deptford Br DEPT SE8........144 D2
Deptford Broadway
  NWCR SE14........144 D1
Deptford Church St DEPT SE8..144 D1
Deptford Gn DEPT SE8........124 D6
Deptford High St DEPT SE8..144 D1
Deptford Strd DEPT SE8......124 D4
De Quincey Ms CAN/RD E16..125 K1
De Quincey Rd TOTM N17..49 K4
Derby Av KTN/HRWW/WS HA3..42 D4
  NFNCH/WDSPK N12........47 G2
  ROMW/RG RM7........74 E4
Derby Ga WHALL SW1A........16 E2
Derby Hl FSTH SE23........163 K4
Derby Hill Crs FSTH SE23..163 K4
Derby Rd BRYLDS KT5........191 H5
  CROY/NA CR0........196 C6
  FSTGT E7........89 H5
  GFD/PVL UB6........96 B6
  HOM E9........87 F6
  HSLW TW3........135 G5
  MORT/ESHN SW14........137 J5
  PEND EN3........24 E6
  SUT SM1........208 D4
  SWFD E18........52 D4
  UED N18........50 E1
  WIM/MER SW19........177 K3
Derby Rd Br MYFR/PICC W1J..9 H1
Dereham Pl SDTCH EC2A......7 H6
  SDTCH EC2A........7 H6
Dereham Rd BARK IG11........91 F4
Derek Av HOR/WEW KT19....206 C4
  WBLY HA9........80 D5
  WLGTN SM6........210 B1
Derek Cl HOR/WEW KT19....206 C4
Derek Walcott Cl HNHL SE24 *..142 C6
Deri Av RAIN RM13........111 K3
Dericote St HACK E8........86 C6
Deri Dene Cl
  STWL/WRAY TW19 *........152 B1
Derifall Cl EHAM E6........107 K4
Dering Pl CROY/NA CR0......211 J2
Dering Rd CROY/NA CR0......211 J2
Dering St OXSTW W1C........9 J4
Derinton Rd TOOT SW17......161 H6
Derley Rd NWDGN UB2........114 B3
Dermody Gdns LEW SE13 *..145 G6
Dermody Rd LEW SE13........145 G6
Deronda Rd HNHL SE24......162 C3
Deroy Cl CAR SM5........209 K4
Derrick Gdns CHARL SE7 *..126 B3
Derrick Rd BECK BR3........182 C6
Derry Downs STMC/STPC BR5..202 D3
Derry Rd CROY/NA CR0......210 E1
Derry St KENS W8........120 A2
Dersingham Av MNPK E12..89 K2
Dersingham Rd CRICK NW2..82 C2
Derwent Av CDALE/KGS NW9..63 G4
  EBAR EN4........33 K2
  MLHL NW7........45 F1
  PIN HA5........41 J2
  PUT/ROE SW15........158 B6
Derwent Cl EBED/NFELT TW14..153 J3
  ESH/CLAY KT10........204 E4
Derwent Crs BXLYHN DA7..149 H3
  NFNCH/WDSPK N12........47 G2
  STAN HA7........43 J5
Derwent Dr STMC/STPC BR5..202 A1
  YEAD UB4........94 C4
Derwent Gdns REDBR IG4..71 J1
  WBLY HA9........61 K5
Derwent Gv EDUL SE22......143 G5
Derwent Ri CDALE/KGS NW9..63 G3
Derwent Rd EA W5........116 D3
  PGE/AN SE20........181 H5
  PLMGR N13........35 G6
  RYNPK SW20........193 G3
  STHL UB1........95 K5
  WHTN TW2........155 F1
Derwent St GNWCH SE10....125 H5
Derwentwater Rd ACT W3..117 K1
Derwent Wy HCH RM12........93 K3
Deryng St WEA W13........116 B1
De Salis Rd HGDN/ICK UB10..94 A3
Desenfans Rd DUL SE21......163 F1
Desford Rd CAN/RD E16......106 C3
Desford Wy ASHF TW15........152 C4
Desmond St NWCR SE14....144 B6
Desmond Tutu Dr FSTH SE23..164 B3
Despard Rd ARCH N19........66 C5
Detling Rd BMLY BR1........183 K1
  ERITH DA8........150 A1
  NTHLT UB5........
Detmold Rd CLPT E5........68 E6
Devalls Cl EHAM E6........108 B6
Devana End CAR SM5........209 K1

Devas Rd RYNPK SW20........177 F4
Devas St BOW E3........105 K3
Devenay Rd SRTFD E15........88 D5
Devenish Rd ABYW SE2........128 B2
Deveraux Cl BECK BR3........199 F2
De Vere Cl WLGTN SM6........210 E5
  KENS W8........120 B2
Deverell St STHWK SE1........19 F4
De Vere Ms KENS W8 *........120 B3
Devereux Ct TPL/STR WC2R *..11 J5
Devereux La BARN SW13......138 E1
Devereux Rd BTSEA SW11....160 E1
Deveron Wy ROM RM1........57 G4
Devey Cl KUTN/CMB KT2........
Devizes St IS N1 *........7 F1
Devoke Wy WOT/HER KT12..188 C6
Devon Cl BKHH IG9........39 H4
  GFD/PVL UB6........79 J6
  TOTM N17........50 C6
Devoncroft Gdns TWK TW1..156 B2
Devon Gdns FSBYPK N4........67 H3
Devonhurst Pl CHSWK W4 *..118 A5
Devonia Gdns UED N18........49 J2
Devonia Rd IS N1........
Devon Man
  KTN/HRWW/WS HA3 *........61 J2
Devonport Gdns IL IG1........71 K3
Devonport Ms SHB W12 *....118 E1
Devonport Rd SHB W12......118 E1
Devonport St WCHPL E1......104 E5
Devon Ri EFNCH N2........
Devon Rd BARK IG11........90 E6
  BELMT SM2........208 C6
Devons Est BOW E3........105 K2
Devonshire Av BELMT SM2..209 G5
  DART DA1........170 E1
Devonshire Cl CAVSQ/HST W1G *..3 J8
  SRTFD E15........88 C2
Devonshire Ct FELT TW13 *..154 A4
Devonshire Crs MLHL NW7..46 B3
Devonshire Dr GNWCH SE10..144 E7
  SURB KT6........190 E5
Devonshire Gdns CHSWK W4..117 J7
  TOTM N17 *........49 J3
  WCHMH N21........35 J2
Devonshire Gv PECK SE15..123 J6
Devonshire Hill La TOTM N17..49 K3
Devonshire Ms South
  CAVSQ/HST W1G........9 J1
Devonshire Ms West
  CAVSQ/HST W1G........3 H7
  CRICK NW2........
  KENS W8........120 A3
Devonshire Pl CAVSQ/HST W1G *..3 H7
  CRICK NW2........
  KENS W8........120 A3
Devonshire Place Ms
  CAVSQ/HST W1G........9 H1
Devonshire Rd BELMT SM2..209 G5
  BXLYHS DA6........149 F5
  CAN/RD E16........107 G5
  CAR SM5........210 A3
  CHSWK W4........118 B5
  CROY/NA CR0........196 E4
  EA W5........116 D3
  ED N9........36 E3
  ELTH/MOT SE9........166 D4
  FELT TW13........154 D5
  FSTH SE23........164 A2
  GNTH/NBYPK IG2........72 D4
  HRW HA1........60 D3
  MLHL NW7........46 B3
  ORP BR6........202 B4
  PIN HA5........41 K5
  PIN HA5........59 G4
  PLMGR N13........35 F6
  STHL UB1........96 A4
  TOTM N17........49 J2
  WALTH E17........69 J3
  WIM/MER SW19........178 D3
Devonshire Rw BPT/STR EC2M..13 H2
Devonshire Row Ms
  GTPST W1W........3 K7
Devonshire Sq HAYES BR2..200 A1
  LVPST EC2M........13 H3
Devonshire St CAVSQ/HST W1G..3 H1
  CHSWK W4........118 B6
Devonshire Ter BAY/PAD W2..101 C5
  EDUL SE22 *........
Devonshire Wy CROY/NA CR0..198 C6
  YEAD UB4........
Devons Rd BOW E3........105 J3
Devon St PECK SE15........123 J6
Devon Wy CHSGTN KT9........205 H3
  HOR/WEW KT19........206 D3
Devon Waye HEST TW5........134 E1
De Walden St CAVSQ/HST W1G..9 H2
Dewar St PECK SE15........143 H4
Dewberry Gdns EHAM E6......107 J4
Dewberry St POP/IOD E14..106 A5
Dewey La BRXS/STRHM SW2..162 B1
Dewey Rd DAGE RM10........92 E4
  IS N1........5 J1
Dewey St TOOT SW17........178 E1
Dewhurst Rd HMSMTH W6..119 G3
Dewsbury Cl PIN HA5........59 J3
Dewsbury Gdns WPK KT4....207 J1
Dewsbury Rd WLSDN NW10..81 H3
Dexter Rd BAR EN5........32 B1
Deyncourt Rd TOTM N17......49 J4
Deynecourt Gdns WAN E11....71 G1
D'Eynsford Rd CMBW SE5..142 E1
Diadem Ct SOHO/CST W1F....10 C3
Diamedes Av
  STWL/WRAY TW19........152 A1
Diameter Rd STMC/STPC BR5..201 G4
Diamond Cl BCTR RM8........73 J5
Diamond Rd RSLP HA4........77 H2
Diamond St PECK SE15......143 F1
  WLSDN NW10........81 F5
Diamond Ter GNWCH SE10..145 F3
Diamond Wy DEPT SE8........124 D6
  SCUP DA14........169 ..
  SWFD E18........53 F4
Diana Cl CHING E4........38 A4
Diana Gdns SURB KT6........191 G6
Diana Pl CAMTN NW1........3 K6
Diana Rd WALTH E17........51 H2

Dianne Wy EBAR EN4 .....21 J5
Dianthus Cl ABYW SE2 * 128 C5
Diban Av HCH RM12 .....93 K2
Dibden St IS N1 .....75 J1
Dibdin Cl SUT SM1 .....208 E1
Dibdin Rd SUT SM1 .....208 E1
Dicey Av CRICK NW2 .....82 A3
Dickens Av DART DA1 .....151 K5
  FNCH N3 .....47 G4
Dickens Cl ERITH DA8 .....149 J1
  HYS/HAR UB3 .....113 H4
  RCHPK/HAM TW10 .....157 F4
Dickens Dr CHST BR7 .....185 H2
Dickens Est
  BERM/RHTH SE16 * 123 H3
Dickens La NLD N18 .....50 A1
Dickens Ms FARR EC1M 6 A7
Dickenson Cl ED N9 .....36 C3
Dickenson Rd CEND/HSY/T N8.....66 E4
  FELT TW13 .....172 B1
Dickenson's La SNWD SE25 .....197 H3
Dickenson's H SNWD SE25 .....197 H3
Dickens Rd EHAM E6 .....107 H1
Dickens Sq STHWK SE1 * 18 D4
Dickens Wy VX/NE SW8 .....141 G3
Dickens Wood Cl NRWD SE19 .....180 B6
Dickerage La NWMAL KT3 .....175 K6
Dickerage Rd KUT/HW KT1 .....175 K4
Dickson Fold PIN HA5 .....59 H1
Dickson House CHARL SE7 * 146 D1
Dickson Rd ELTH/MOT SE9 .....146 D4
Dick Turpin Wy
  EBED/NFELT TW14 .....133 J5
Didsbury Cl EHAM E6 .....89 K6
Digby Crs FSBYPK N4 .....67 J6
Digby Gdns DAGE RM10 .....92 C6
Digby Pl CROY/NA CRO 212 B1
Digby Rd BARK IG11 .....91 F5
  HOM E9 .....75 F5
Digby St BETH E2 .....104 E2
Diggon St WCHPL E1 .....105 F4
Dighton Rd WAND/EARL SW18.....140 B6
Dignum St IS N1 * 5 J2
Digswell St HOLWY N7 * 85 G4
Dilhorne Cl LEE/GVPK SE12 .....166 A5
Dilke St CHEL SW3 .....120 E6
Dillwyn Cl SYD SE26 .....164 B6
Dilston Cl NTHLT UB5 .....95 C2
Dilton Gdns PUT/ROE SW15 .....158 D3
Dimes Pl HMSMTH W6 .....118 E4
Dimmock Dr GFD/PVL UB6 .....78 D3
Dimond Cl FSTGT E7 .....88 E3
Dimsdale Dr BAR EN5 .....62 E5
  EN EN1 .....36 C3
Dimson Crs BOW E3 .....105 J3
Dingle Cl BAR EN5 .....25 K1
Dingle Gdns POP/IOD E14 *.....105 J6
Dingley La STRHM/NOR SW16.....161 J4
Dingley Pl FSBYE EC1V 6 D5
Dingley Rd FSBYE EC1V 6 C5
Dingwall Av CROY/NA CRO 196 D6
Dingwall Gdns CDALE/KGS NW11..44 E3
Dingwall Rd CAR SM5 .....209 K6
  CROY/NA CRO 196 E6
  WAND/EARL SW18 .....160 B2
Dinmont St BETH E2 * 104 D1
Dinsdale Gdns BAR EN5 .....21 F6
  SNWD SE25 .....197 F2
Dinsdale Rd BKHTH/KID SE3 .....125 J6
Dinsmore Rd BAL SW12 .....161 G2
Dinton Rd KUTN/CMB KT2 .....175 G3
  WIM/MER SW19 .....178 C2
Diploma Av EFNCH N2 .....65 J1
Dirleton Rd SRTFD E15 .....88 D6
Disbrowe Rd HMSMTH W6 .....119 H6
Discovery Wk WAP E1W 104 D6
Dishforth La CDALE/KGS NW9 .....45 G4
Disney Pl STHWK SE1 .....18 D2
Disney St STHWK SE1 .....18 D2
Dison Cl PEND EN3 .....25 F2
Disraeli Cl THMD SE28 .....128 C1
Disraeli Rd EA W5 .....116 E1
  FSTGT E7 .....88 E4
  PUT/ROE SW15 .....139 H5
  WLSDN NW10 .....98 E1
Diss St BETH E2 .....7 J4
Distaff La BLKFR EC4V 12 C5
Distillery La HMSMTH W6 .....119 F5
Distillery Rd HMSMTH W6 .....119 F5
Distin St LBTH SE11 .....17 J7
District Rd ALP/SUD HA0 .....79 H3
Ditchburn St POP/IOD E14 .....106 A6
Ditchfield Rd YEAD UB4 .....95 J3
Dittisham Rd ELTH/MOT SE9 .....166 D6
Ditton Cl THDIT KT7 * 190 B4
Ditton Grange Cl SURB KT6 .....190 E5
Ditton Grange Dr SURB KT6 .....190 E5
Ditton Hl SURB KT6 .....190 E5
Ditton Hill Rd SURB KT6 .....190 D5
Ditton Lawn THDIT KT7 .....190 B5
Ditton Pl PGE/AN SE20 .....181 J4
Ditton Reach THDIT KT7 .....190 C3
Ditton Rd BXLYHS DA6 .....148 E6
  NWDGN UB2 .....114 E5
  SURB KT6 .....191 F5
Dixey Cottages EFNCH N2 *.....65 J2
Dixon Cl EHAM E6 .....107 K5
Dixon Pl WKHM BR4 .....198 E5
Dixon Rd NWCR SE14 .....144 B2
  SNWD SE25 .....181 F6
Dobbin Cl KTN/HRWW/WS HA3..43 G5
Dobell Rd ELTH/MOT SE9 .....146 E4
Dobree Av WLSDN NW10 .....81 K5
Dobson Cl KIL/WHAMP NW6.....83 H5
Dockers Tanner Rd
  POP/IOD E14 .....124 D4
Dockhead STHWK SE1 .....19 K3
Dock Hill Av BERM/RHTH SE16..124 A2
Dockland St CAN/RD E16 .....127 F2
Dockley Rd BERM/RHTH SE16..123 H4
Dock Rd BTFD TW8 .....136 E1
  CAN/RD E16 .....106 D6
Dockside Rd CAN/RD E16 .....107 H6
Dock St WCHPL E1 .....104 C6
Dockwell Cl EBED/NFELT TW14..133 K5

Doctors Cl SYD SE26 .....181 K1
Docwra's Buildings IS N1 .....86 A4
Dodbrooke Rd WNWD SE27 .....162 B5
Doddington Av WBLW SE17 .....122 C6
Doddington Pl LBTH SE11 .....122 C6
Dodsley Pl ED N9 .....36 E5
Dodson St STHWK SE1 .....17 K3
Dod St POP/IOD E14 .....105 J5
Doebury Wk
  WOOL/PLUM SE18 .....128 B6
Doel Cl WIM/MER SW19 .....178 B3
Doggett Rd CAT SE6 .....164 D2
Doggetts Ct EBAR EN4 .....21 J5
Doghurst Av WDR/YW UB7 .....132 E1
Doghurst Dr WDR/YW UB7 .....132 E1
Dog Kennel Hl EDUL SE22 .....143 F4
Dog La WLSDN NW10 .....81 G2
Dog Rose Ramble YEAD UB4 .....76 E6
Dog Rose Ramble & Hillingdon
  Trail YEAD UB4 .....76 D6
  YEAD UB4 .....95 H5
Doherty Rd PLSTW E13 .....106 E3
Dolben Cl DEPT SE8 * 124 C4
Dolben St STHWK SE1 * 18 B1
Dolby Rd FUL/PGN SW6 .....139 J3
Doiland St LBTH SE11 .....122 A5
Dollary Pde KUT/HW KT1 * 175 J6
Dollis Av FNCH N3 .....46 D4
Dollis Crs RSLP HA4 .....59 G5
Dollis Hill Av CRICK NW2 .....81 K1
Dollis Hill Est CRICK NW2 * 81 K1
Dollis Hill La CRICK NW2 .....81 H3
Dollis Ms FNCH N3 * 46 D4
Dollis Pk FNCH N3 .....46 C4
Dollis Rd MLHL NW7 .....46 C4
Dollis Valley Dr BAR EN5 .....32 D1
Dollis Valley Green Wk
  BAR EN5 .....33 F2
  FNCH N3 .....46 C5
  HDN NW4 .....46 C5
Dollis Valley Wy EBAR EN4 .....21 H5
Dolman Cl FNCH N3 .....47 G5
Dolman Rd CHSWK W4 .....118 A4
Dolman St CLAP SW4 .....142 A5
Dolphin Ap ROM RM1 .....75 H1
Dolphin Cl BERM/RHTH SE16 .....124 A2
  SURB KT6 .....190 E3
  THMD SE28 .....109 K5
Dolphin La POP/IOD E14 .....105 K6
Dolphin Rd NTHLT UB5 .....95 K1
Dolphin Sq CHSWK W4 * 138 B1
  PIM SW1V 121 H5
Dolphin St KUT/HW KT1 .....175 F5
Dombey St BMSBY WC1N 11 G1
Dome Buildings
  RCH/KEW TW9 * 136 E6
Dome Hill Pk SYD SE26 .....163 H6
Domett Cl CMBW SE5 .....142 E5
Domingo St FSBYE EC1V 6 C6
Dominica Cl PLSTW E13 .....107 H2
Dominion Cl HSLW TW3 .....135 J3
Dominion Dr CRW RM5 .....56 D2
Dominion Pde HRW HA1 * 61 F2
Dominion Rd CROY/NA CRO 197 G4
  NWDGN UB2 .....114 D5
Dominion St LVPST EC2M 13 F1
Domonic Dr ELTH/MOT SE9 .....167 G5
Domville Cl TRDG/WHET N20 .....33 H4
Donald Dr CHDH RM6 .....73 J2
Donald Rd CROY/NA CRO 196 A3
  PLSTW E13 .....89 F1
Donaldson Rd
  KIL/WHAMP NW6 .....82 D6
  WOOL/PLUM SE18 .....147 F2
Donald Woods Gdns
  BRYLDS KT5 .....191 K5
Doncaster Dr NTHLT UB5 .....77 K3
Doncaster Gdns FSBYPK N4 * 67 J3
  NTHLT UB5 .....77 K3
Doncaster Gn OXHEY WD19 .....41 G1
Doncaster Rd ED N9 .....36 D2
Donegal St IS N1 .....5 H3
Doneraile St FUL/PGN SW6 .....139 G3
Dongola Rd PLSTW E13 .....107 F2
  TOTM N17 .....50 A6
  WCHPL E1 .....105 G4
Dongola Rd West PLSTW E13..107 F2
Donington Av BARK/HLT IG6 .....72 C3
Donkey Aly EDUL SE22 .....163 H2
Donkey La EN EN1 .....24 C3
Donnefield Av EDGW HA8 .....44 A2
Donne Pl CHEL SW3 .....14 D6
  MTCM CR4 .....195 C1
Donne Rd BCTR RM8 .....73 J6
Donnington Rd
  KTN/HRWW/WS HA3 .....61 K3
  WLSDN NW10 .....81 K6
  WPK KT4 .....192 D6
Donnybrook Rd
  STRHM/NOR SW16 .....179 J3
Donoghue Cottages
  POP/IOD E14 * 105 G4
Donovan Av MUSWH N10 .....48 B5
Donovan Pl WINCHMR N21 .....23 F6
Don Phelan Cl CMBW SE5 .....142 E2
Don Wy ROM RM1 .....57 G5
Doone Cl TEDD TW11 .....174 B2
Doon St STHWK SE1 .....11 J7
Dorado Gdns ORP BR6 .....217 K1
Doral Wy CAR SM5 .....209 K3
Dorando Cl SHB W12 * 99 K6
Doran Gv WOOL/PLUM SE18 .....147 K1
Doran Wk SRTFD E15 .....88 A6
Dora Rd WIM/MER SW19 .....177 K1
Dora St POP/IOD E14 .....105 H5
Dora Wy BRXN/ST SW9 .....142 B3
Dorchester Av BXLY DA5 .....168 E3
  PLMGR N13 .....35 J6
  RYLN/HDSTN HA2 .....60 A6
Dorchester Cl DART DA1 .....171 J3
  NTHLT UB5 .....78 B3
  STMC/STPC BR5 .....186 C5
Dorchester Ct CRICK NW2 .....82 A1
  HNHL SE24 .....142 D6
  STHGT/OAK N14 .....34 B1
Dorchester Dr
  EBED/NFELT TW14 .....153 H1
  HNHL SE24 .....142 D6

Dorchester Gdns CHING E4 .....37 J6
  GLDGN NW11 * 64 E1
Dorchester Gv CHSWK W4 .....118 C5
Dorchester Ms TWK TW1 .....156 D1
Dorchester Pde
  STRHM/NOR SW16 * 161 K4
Dorchester Rd MRDN SM4 .....194 B4
  NTHLT UB5 .....78 B3
  WPK KT4 .....193 F5
Dorchester Ter HDN NW4 * 46 B5
Dorchester Wy
  KTN/HRWW/WS HA3 .....62 B3
Dorchester Waye YEAD UB4 .....95 G5
Dorcis Av BXLYHN DA7 .....149 F3
Dordrecht Rd ACT W3 .....118 B1
Dore Av MNPK E12 .....90 A3
Doreen Av CDALE/KGS NW9 .....63 F5
Dore Gdns MRDN SM4 .....194 A4
Dorell Cl STHL UB1 .....95 K4
Dorian Rd HCH RM12 .....75 J5
Doria Rd FUL/PGN SW6 .....139 J3
Doric Wy CAMTN NW1 .....4 C4
Dorie Ms NFNCH/WDSPK N12.....33 F6
Dorien Rd RYNPK SW20 .....177 G5
Doris Av ERITH DA8 .....149 K2
Doris Rd FSTGT E7 .....88 E5
Dorking Cl DEPT SE8 .....124 C6
  WPK KT4 .....193 H6
Dorlcote Rd WAND/EARL SW18..160 C2
Dorman Pl ED N9 .....36 C4
Dormans Cl NTHWD HA6 .....40 B3
Dorman Wy STJWD NW8 .....83 H6
Dormer Cl BAR EN5 .....20 B6
  SRTFD E15 .....88 D4
Dormers Av STHL UB1 .....96 A5
Dormers Ri STHL UB1 .....96 B6
Dormer's Wells La STHL UB1 .....96 A6
Dormywood RSLP HA4 .....58 D2
Dornberg Cl BKHTH/KID SE3 ...145 K1
Dornberg Rd BKHTH/KID SE3 *..146 A1
Dorncliffe Rd FUL/PGN SW6 ...139 H3
Dorney Ri STMC/STPC BR5 .....202 A1
Dorney Wy HSLWW TW4 .....134 D6
Dornfell St KIL/WHAMP NW6 .....82 D3
Dornton Rd BAL SW12 .....161 G4
  SAND/SEL CR2 .....212 A3
Dorothy Av ALP/SUD HA0 .....80 A6
Dorothy Evans Cl BXLYHN DA7..149 J5
Dorothy Gdns BCTR RM8 .....91 H2
Dorothy Rd BTSEA SW11 .....140 E4
Dorrell Pl BRXN/ST SW9 .....142 B5
Dorrington St HCIRC EC1N 11 J1
Dorrington Wy BECK BR3 .....199 F2
Dorrit Ms ED N18 .....36 B6
Dorrit St STHWK SE1 * 18 D2
Dors Cl CDALE/KGS NW9 .....63 F4
Dorset Av NWDGN UB2 .....114 E4
  ROM RM1 .....57 F6
  WELL DA16 .....148 A5
  YEAD UB4 .....94 C3
Dorset Buildings EMB EC4Y * 12 A4
Dorset Cl CAMTN NW1 * 8 E1
  YEAD UB4 .....94 C2
Dorset Dr EDGW HA8 .....44 B2
  KTBR SW1X 15 H4
Dorset Est BETH E2 .....7 K3
Dorset Ms FNCH N3 .....46 E4
  MAYF/PICC W1J 15 J4
Dorset Pl SRTFD E15 .....88 B4
Dorset Ri EMB EC4Y 11 K4
Dorset Rd ASHF TW15 .....152 A5
  BECK BR3 .....182 A6
  EA W5 .....116 E3
  ELTH/MOT SE9 .....166 D4
  FSTGT E7 .....89 G5
  HRW HA1 .....60 C3
  MTCM CR4 .....178 D5
  SEVS/STOTM N15 .....67 K1
  VX/NE SW8 .....142 A1
  WALTH E17 .....69 J3
  WIM/MER SW19 .....177 K4
Dorset Sq CAMTN NW1 .....8 E1
  HOR/WEW KT19 .....206 E4
Dorset St MHST W1U 9 G2
Dorset Wy WHTN TW2 .....155 H3
Dorset Waye HEST TW5 .....134 E1
Dorton Cl PECK SE15 .....143 F1
Dorville Crs HMSMTH W6 .....118 E3
Dorville Rd LEE/GVPK SE12 ...145 K6
Dothill Rd WOOL/PLUM SE18 ...147 H1
Douai Gv HPTN TW12 .....173 H4
Doughty Ms BMSBY WC1N 5 G7
Doughty St BMSBY WC1N 5 G6
Douglas Av ALP/SUD HA0 .....80 A5
  NWMAL KT3 .....192 E1
  WALTH E17 .....51 J4
Douglas Cl BARK/HLT IG6 .....54 B3
  STAN HA7 .....43 G1
  WLGTN SM6 .....195 K5
Douglas Crs YEAD UB4 .....95 G3
Douglas Dr CROY/NA CRO 213 J1
Douglas Est IS N1 * 85 J4
Douglas Ms CRICK NW2 .....82 C1
Douglas Pth POP/IOD E14 .....125 F5
Douglas Pl POP/IOD E14 * 125 F5
Douglas Rd CAN/RD E16 .....106 E4
  CHING E4 .....38 C2
  ESH/CLAY KT10 .....189 G6
  GDMY/SEVK IG3 .....73 G4
  HSLW TW3 .....135 G4
  IS N1 .....85 J5
  KIL/WHAMP NW6 .....82 D6
  KUT/HW KT1 .....175 J5
  ROM RM1 .....75 H1
  STWL/WRAY TW19 .....152 A1
  SURB KT6 .....191 G6
  WELL DA16 .....148 C2
Douglas Rd North IS N1 .....85 J4
Douglas Rd South IS N1 .....85 J3
  MYFR/PICC W1J 15 J1
Douglas St WEST SW1P 16 C7
Douglas Ter WALTH E17 * 51 H4
Douglas Vis KUT/HW KT1 * 175 J5
Douglas Wy DEPT SE8 .....144 D1
Doulton Ms KIL/WHAMP NW6 .....83 F4
Dounesforth Gdns
  WAND/EARL SW18 .....160 A3

Douro Pl KENS W8 .....120 A3
Douro St BOW E3 .....105 J1
Douthwaite Sq WAP E1W 123 H1
Dove Ap EHAM E6 .....107 J4
Dove Cl MLHL NW7 .....45 J3
  NTHLT UB5 .....95 H3
  WLGTN SM6 .....211 F5
Dovecot Cl PIN HA5 .....59 G2
Dove Ct LOTH EC2R * 12 E4
Dovedale Av CLAY IG5 .....54 A4
  KTN/HRWW/WS HA3 .....62 B3
Dovedale Cl WELL DA16 .....148 B2
Dovedale Ri MTCM CR4 .....178 E3
Dovedale Rd EDUL SE22 .....143 J6
Dovedon Cl STHGT/OAK N14 .....34 E4
Dovehouse Md BARK IG11 .....108 D1
Dovehouse St CHEL SW3 .....120 D5
Dove Ms ECT SW5 .....120 B4
Doveney Cl STMC/STPC BR5 ...186 D6
Dove Pk PIN HA5 .....41 K3
Dove Rd IS N1 .....85 K4
Dover Cl CRICK NW2 .....64 B6
  CRW RM5 .....56 D2
Dovercourt Av THHTH CR7 ...196 B1
Dovercourt Est IS N1 * 85 K4
Dovercourt Gdns STAN HA7 .....44 A1
Dovercourt La SUT SM1 .....209 G1
Dovercourt Rd DUL SE21 .....163 F1
Doverfield Rd
  BRXS/STRHM SW2 * 161 K2
Dover Gdns CAR SM5 .....209 K1
Dover House Rd
  PUT/ROE SW15 .....138 D5
Doveridge Gdns PLMGR N13 ...35 H5
Dove Rw BETH E2 .....104 C1
Dover Park Dr PUT/ROE SW15..158 E1
Dover Patrol BKHTH/KID SE3 *..146 A3
Dover Rd ED N9 .....36 E4
  MNPK E12 .....71 G6
  NRWD SE19 .....180 E2
  WOOL/PLUM SE18 .....147 G3
Dover St CONDST W1S 9 K6
Dover Ter RCH/KEW TW9 * ...137 H5
Dover Yd MYFR/PICC W1J 9 K7
Doves Yd IS N1 .....5 J1
Doveton Rd SAND/SEL CR2 ...211 K3
Doveton St WCHPL E1 .....104 E3
Dowanhill Rd CAT SE6 .....165 G3
Dowd Cl FBAR/BDGN N11 .....34 A4
Dowdeswell Cl
  PUT/ROE SW15 .....138 D5
Dowding Cl HCH RM12 .....93 K5
Dowding Pl STAN HA7 .....43 G2
Dowdney Cl KTTN NW5 .....84 C3
Dower Av WLGTN SM6 .....210 B6
Dowgate Hl CANST EC4R 12 E5
Dowland St NKENS W10 .....100 C2
Dowlas St CMBW SE5 .....143 F1
Dowlerville Rd ORP BR6 .....217 F4
Dowman Cl WIM/MER SW19 ...178 A4
Downage HDN NW4 .....46 A5
Downalong BUSH WD23 .....28 D3
Downbank Av BXLYHN DA7 .....150 A3
Down Barns Rd RSLP HA4 .....77 H2
Down Cl NTHLT UB5 .....95 F1
Downderry Rd BMLY BR1 .....165 G5
Downe Cl WELL DA16 .....148 C6
Downend
  MTCM CR4 * 185 H6
Downe Rd HAYES BR2 .....215 J6
Downers Cottages CLAP SW4..141 H5
Downes Cl TWK TW1 .....156 C1
Downes Ct WCHMH N21 .....35 G3
Downfield WPK KT4 .....192 C5
Downfield Cl MV/WKIL W9 ...101 F3
Down Hall Rd KUT/HW KT1 ...174 E4
Downham Cl CRW RM5 .....56 C3
Downham Rd IS N1 .....85 K5
Downham Wy BMLY BR1 .....165 F1
Downhills Av TOTM N17 .....49 K6
Downhills Park Rd TOTM N17 ...49 J6
Downhills Wy TOTM N17 .....49 J5
Downhurst Av MLHL NW7 .....45 F1
Downing Cl RYLN/HDSTN HA2..42 C6
Downing Dr GFD/PVL UB6 .....78 D1
Downing Rd DAGW SW9 .....92 B6
Downing St WHALL SW1A 16 E2
Downland Cl TRDG/WHET N20..33 G3
Downleys Cl ELTH/MOT SE9 ...166 D4
Downman Rd ELTH/MOT SE9 ...146 D4
Down Pl HMSMTH W6 .....118 E5
Down Rd TEDD TW11 .....174 C2
Downs Av CHST BR7 .....167 K3
  DART DA1 .....171 K2
  PIN HA5 .....59 K3
Downs Bridge Rd BECK BR3 ...183 G4
Downs Court Pde HACK E8 * 86 D3
Downsell Rd SRTFD E15 .....88 B2
Downsfield Rd WALTH E17 .....69 G3
Downshall Av IL IG1 .....72 D5
Downshire Hl HAMP NW3 .....83 H2
Downside BECK BR3 .....182 D4
  TWK TW1 .....156 A5
Downside Cl WIM/MER SW19..178 B2
Downside Crs HAMP NW3 .....83 J3
  WEA W13 .....97 G3
Downside Rd BELMT SM2 .....209 J4
Downs La CLPT E5 * 86 D2
Downs Park Rd HACK E8 .....86 B3
  CLPT E5 .....86 C3
Downs Rd BECK BR3 .....182 E5
  CLPT E5 .....86 B3
  EN EN1 .....24 B5
  THHTH CR7 .....180 D4
Downs Side BELMT SM2 .....208 D6
The Downs RYNPK SW20 .....177 G3
Down St E/WMO/HCT KT8 .....189 F2
  MYFR/PICC W1J 15 J1
Downs Vw ISLW TW7 .....136 A2
Downsview Gdns NRWD SE19..180 D3
Downsview Rd NRWD SE19 ...180 C3
Downsway ORP BR6 .....216 E3
The Downsway BELMT SM2 ...209 G6
Downton Av
  BRXS/STRHM SW2 .....162 A4

Downtown Rd
  BERM/RHTH SE16 .....124 B2
Downway NFNCH/WDSPK N12....47 J3
Down Wy NTHLT UB5 .....95 F2
Dowrey St IS N1 .....85 G6
Dowsett Rd TOTM N17 .....50 C5
Dowson Cl CMBW SE5 .....142 E5
Doyce St STHWK SE1 * 18 C2
Doyle Cl ERITH DA8 .....150 B2
Doyle Gdns WLSDN NW10 .....81 K6
Doyle Rd SNWD SE25 .....197 H1
D'Oyley St BGVA SW1W 15 G6
Doynton St ARCH N19 * 66 B6
Draco Ga PUT/ROE SW15 * 139 F4
Draco St WALW SE17 .....122 D6
Dragonfly Cl PLSTW E13 .....107 F2
Dragon Rd LBTH SE11 .....17 H7
Dragoon Rd DEPT SE8 .....124 C5
Dragor Rd WLSDN NW10 .....98 E3
Drake Cl BERM/RHTH SE16 .....124 A2
Drake Crs THMD SE28 .....109 J5
Drakefell Rd NWCR SE14 .....144 A3
Drakefield Rd TOOT SW17 .....161 F5
Drake Ms HAYES BR2 .....200 B1
  HCH RM12 .....93 J4
Drake Rd BROCKY SE4 .....144 D4
  CHSGTN KT9 .....206 C3
  CROY/NA CRO 196 A4
  MTCM CR4 .....195 F3
  RYLN/HDSTN HA2 .....59 K6
Drake's Cl ESH/CLAY KT10 .....204 A3
Drakes Ctyd KIL/WHAMP NW6..82 D5
Drakes Dr NTHWD HA6 .....39 K2
  FSBYW WC1X 11 C2
Drakewood Rd
  STRHM/NOR SW16 .....179 J3
Draper Cl BELV DA17 .....129 G4
  ISLW TW7 .....135 J3
Draper Est STHWK SE1 * 18 B6
Draper Pl IS N1 .....6 B1
Drapers Rd ENC/FH EN2 .....23 H3
  SRTFD E15 .....88 B2
  TOTM N17 .....50 B6
Drappers Wy
  BERM/RHTH SE16 * 123 H4
Drawell Cl HAYES BR2 .....199 J4
Drawell Cl WOOL/PLUM SE18..127 K5
Drax Av RYNPK SW20 .....176 D3
Draxmont WIM/MER SW19 .....177 H2
Draycot Rd SURB KT6 .....191 H5
  WAN E11 .....71 F3
Draycott Av CHEL SW3 .....14 D6
  KTN/HRWW/WS HA3 .....61 H3
Draycott Cl CMBW SE5 .....142 E1
  CRICK NW2 .....82 B1
  KTN/HRWW/WS HA3 .....61 H3
Draycott Pl CHEL SW3 .....14 E7
Draycott Ter CHEL SW3 .....15 F6
Dray Ct ALP/SUD HA0 * 79 K1
Drayford Cl MV/WKIL W9 * 100 D3
Dray Gdns BRXS/STRHM SW2..142 A6
Draymans Ms PECK SE15 .....143 G3
Draymans Wy ISLW TW7 .....136 A4
Drayson Cl WALTH E17 .....51 H6
Drayson Ms KENS W8 .....119 K2
Drayton Av LOU IG10 .....39 K2
  ORP BR6 .....201 G5
  WEA W13 .....97 G6
Drayton Bridge Rd HNWL W7..97 F6
Drayton Cl HSLWW TW4 .....134 E6
  IL IG1 .....72 D6
Drayton Ct WDR/YW UB7 * 112 C4
Drayton Court Chambers
  WEA W13 * 97 H6
Drayton Gdns WBPTN SW10..120 B5
  WCHMH N21 .....35 H2
  WDR/YW UB7 .....112 A2
  WEA W13 .....97 G6
Drayton Gn WEA W13 .....97 G6
Drayton Green Rd WEA W13.....97 H6
Drayton Gv WEA W13 .....97 G6
Drayton Park HBRY N5 .....85 G3
Drayton Park Ms HOLWY N7 * 85 G3
Drayton Pk HOLWY N7 .....85 F3
Drayton Rd CROY/NA CRO 196 C6
  TOTM N17 .....50 A5
  WAN E11 .....70 B6
  WLSDN NW10 .....81 H6
  WEA W13 .....97 G6
Dreadnought St GNWCH SE10..125 H3
Drenon Sq HYS/HAR UB3 .....94 D1
Dresden Cl KIL/WHAMP NW6 .....83 F4
Dresden Rd ARCH N19 .....66 D4
Drew Av MLHL NW7 .....46 D2
Drewery Ct BKHTH/KID SE3 * 145 H4
Drew Gdns GFD/PVL UB6 .....79 F4
Drew Rd CAN/RD E16 .....126 D1
Drews Cottages
  STRHM/NOR SW16 * 161 J4
Drewstead Rd
  STRHM/NOR SW16 .....161 J4
Driffield Rd BOW E3 .....105 G1
The Drift HAYES BR2 .....215 H1
The Driftway MTCM CR4 .....179 F4
Drinkwater Rd
  RYLN/HDSTN HA2 .....60 B6
Drive Ct EDGW HA8 * 44 C1
The Drive ACT W3 * 98 E5
  BAR EN5 .....20 C4
  BAR EN5 .....33 G1
  BARK IG11 .....91 F5
  BECK BR3 .....182 D5
  BKHH IG9 .....38 E3
  BXLY DA5 .....168 E2
  CHING E4 .....38 C4
  CHST BR7 .....186 A4
  CRICK NW2 .....81 K3
  CRW RM5 .....57 F1
  EBED/NFELT TW14 .....154 B2
  EDGW HA8 .....44 C1
  ENC/FH EN2 .....23 K2
  ERITH DA8 .....149 J1
  FBAR/BDGN N11 .....48 B2
  FNCH N3 .....47 F2
  GLDGN NW11 .....64 C4
  HGT N6 .....47 K6

HOLWY N7 ......85 F3
HOR/WEW KT19 ......207 H4
HSLW TW3 ......135 J3
IL IG1 ......71 J3
KUTN/CMB KT2 ......175 K5
MRDN SM4 ......40 C4
NTHWD HA6 ......40 C4
ORP BR6 ......202 A6
RYLN/HDSTN HA2 ......60 A4
SCUP DA14 ......168 D3
SURB KT6 ......191 F4
SWFD E18 ......52 E6
THHTH CR7 ......196 E1
WALTH E17 ......51 K6
WKM BR4 ......199 C4
Dr Johnson Av TOOT SW17 ......160 C4
Droitwich CI SYD SE26 ......163 H5
Dromey Gdns
    KTN/HRWW/WS HA3 ......43 F3
Dromore Rd PUT/ROE SW15 ......159 H1
Dronfield Gdns BCTR RM8 ......91 J3
Droop St NKENS W10 ......100 C3
Drovers PI PECK SE15 ......143 J1
Drovers Rd SAND/SEL CR2 ......211 K3
Druce Rd DUL SE21 ......163 F1
Druid St STHWK SE1 ......19 J2
Druids Wy HAYES BR2 ......199 G1
Drumaline Rdg WPK KT4 ......192 B6
Drummond Av ROMW/RG RM7 ......75 F1
Drummond CI ERITH DA8 ......150 B2
Drummond Crs CAMTN NW1 ......4 C4
Drummond Dr STAN HA7 ......43 F3
Drummond Ga PIM SW1V 121 J5
Drummond Rd
    BERM/RHTH SE16 ......123 J3
    CROY/NA CRO 196 D6
    ROMW/RG RM7 ......74 E1
    WAN E11 ......71 F4
Drummonds PI RCH/KEW TW9 ......137 F5
Drummond St CAMTN NW1 ......4 A6
Drum St WCHPL E1 ......13 K3
Drury Crs CROY/NA CRO 196 B6
Drury La COVGDN WC2E 11 F4
    HOL/ALD WC2B 10 E3
Drury Rd HRW HA1 ......60 C4
Drury Wy WLSDN NW10 ......81 F3
Dryad St PUT/ROE SW15 ......139 G4
Dryburgh Gdns
    CDALE/KGS NW9 ......44 C6
Dryburgh Rd PUT/ROE SW15 ......138 E4
Dryden Av HNWL W7 ......97 F5
Dryden CI BARK/HLT IG6 ......55 F2
Dryden Rd EN EN1 ......36 A1
    KTN/HRWW/WS HA3 ......43 F4
    WELL DA16 ......148 A2
    WIM/MER SW19 ......178 B2
Dryden Wy ORP BR6 ......202 B5
Dryfield CI WLSDN NW10 ......80 E4
Dryfield Rd EDGW HA8 ......44 E2
Dryhill Rd BELV DA17 ......129 G6
Dryland Av ORP BR6 ......217 F2
Drylands Rd CEND/HSY/T N8 ......66 E3
Drysdale Av CHING E4 ......37 K1
Drysdale CI NTHWD HA6 ......40 D3
Drysdale PI IS N1 ......7 H4
Drysdale St IS N1 ......7 H5
Dublin Av HACK E8 ......86 C6
Du Burstow Ter HNWL W7 ......115 K2
Ducal St BETH E2 ......7 K5
Du Cane CI SHB W12 ......100 A5
Du Cane Rd SHB W12 ......99 K5
Duchess CI FBAR/BDGN N11 ......48 B1
    SUT SM1 ......209 G2
Duchess Gv BKHH IG9 ......39 F4
Duchess Ms CAVSQ/HST W1G 9 J2
Duchess of Bedfords Wk
    KENS W8 ......119 K2
Duchess St REGST W1B 9 K2
Duchy Rd EBAR EN4 ......21 H1
Duchy St STHWK SE1 ......11 K7
Ducie St CLAP SW4 ......141 K5
Duckett Rd FSBYPK N4 ......67 H3
Duckett St WCHPL E1 ......105 F4
Ducking Stool Ct ROM RM1 ......75 G1
Duck La SOHO/CST W1F 10 C4
Duck Lees La PEND EN3 ......25 G5
Du Cros Dr STAN HA7 ......43 K2
Du Cros Rd ACT W3 ......118 B1
Dudden Hill La WLSDN NW10 ......81 H3
Dudden Hill Pde
    WLSDN NW10 ......81 H2
Duddington CI ELTH/MOT SE9 ......166 D1
Dudley Av KTN/HRWW/WS HA3 ......43 J6
Dudley Dr MRDN SM4 ......193 H5
    RSLP HA4 ......77 F4
Dudley PI HYS/HAR UB3 ......113 G3
    WEA W13 ......116 C2
Dudley Rd EBED/NFELT TW14 ......153 G3
    FNCH N3 ......47 F5
    IL IG1 ......90 B2
    KIL/WHAMP NW6 ......100 C1
    KUT/HW KT1 ......175 G6
    NWDGN UB2 ......114 C2
    RCH/KEW TW9 ......137 G3
    RYLN/HDSTN HA2 ......60 C6
    WALTH E17 ......51 J5
    WIM/MER SW19 ......177 J2
Dudley St BAY/PAD W2 ......8 A2
Dudlington Rd CLPT E5 ......68 E6
Dudmaston Ms CHEL SW3 ......120 C5
Dudrich Ms EDUL SE22 ......143 G6
Dudsbury Rd DART DA1 ......170 E1
Dudset La HEST TW5 ......133 K2
Dufferin Av STLK EC1Y 6 D7
Dufferin Ct STLK EC1Y 6 D7
Duffield CI HRW HA1 ......61 F2
Duffield Dr SEVS/STOTM N15 ......68 B1
Duff St POP/IOD E14 ......105 K5
Dufour's PI SOHO/CST W1F 10 B4
Dugard Wy LBTH SE11 ......18 A7

Duggan Dr CHST BR7 ......184 D2
Dugolly Av WBLY HA9 ......80 D1
Duke Humphrey Rd
    BKHTH/KID SE3 ......145 H3
Duke of Cambridge CI
    WHTN TW2 ......155 J1
Duke of Edinburgh Rd
    SUT SM1 ......209 H1
The Duke of Wellington Av
    WOOL/PLUM SE18 ......127 H3
Duke of Wellington PI
    KTBR SW1X 16 A2
Duke of York Sq CHEL SW3 ......120 E5
Duke of York St STJS SW1Y 10 B7
Duke Rd BARK/HLT IG6 ......72 D1
    CHSWK W4 ......118 A5
Duke's Av CHSWK W4 ......118 A5
    EDGW HA8 ......44 B2
    FNCH N3 ......47 F4
    HRW HA1 ......60 E1
    HSLWW TW4 ......134 D5
    MUSWH N10 ......48 C6
    NTHLT UB5 ......77 J5
    NWMAL KT3 ......176 B5
    PIN HA5 ......59 K3
    RCHPK/HAM TW10 ......156 D6
Dukes CI ASHF TW15 ......153 F6
    HPTN TW12 ......172 E1
Dukes Ga CHSWK W4 * 117 K4
Dukes Green Av
    EBED/NFELT TW14 ......133 K6
    EBED/NFELT TW14 ......153 K1
Dukes La KENS W8 ......119 K2
Dukes Lane Chambers
    KENS W8 * 120 A2
Dukes Lane Man KENS W8 * 120 A2
Dukes Ms MHST W1U 9 H3
    MUSWH N10 ......48 B6
Dukes Orch BXLY DA5 ......169 K3
Dukes Pas WALTH E17 ......52 A3
Dukes Point HOT N6 ......66 B5
Dukes Rd ACT W3 ......98 C3
    CAMTN NW1 ......4 C5
    EHAM E6 ......90 A6
Dukesthorpe Rd SYD SE26 ......164 A6
Duke St MHST W1U 9 H3
    RCH/KEW TW9 ......136 E5
    SUT SM1 ......209 H2
Duke Street HI STHWK SE1 ......13 G1
Duke Street St James's
    MYFR/PICC W1J 10 B7
Duke's Wy MYFR/PKLN W1K 9 H5
Dulas St FSBYPK N4 ......67 F5
Dulford St NTGHL W11 ......100 C6
Dulka Rd BTSEA SW11 ......140 E6
Dulverton Rd ELTH/MOT SE9 ......167 H4
    RSLP HA4 ......58 E6
Dulwich Common DUL SE21 ......162 E3
The Dulwich Oaks DUL SE21 * 163 G3
Dulwich Rd HNHL SE24 ......142 B6
Dulwich Village DUL SE21 ......162 E1
Dulwich Wood Av NRWD SE19 ......181 G1
Dulwich Wood Pk NRWD SE19 ......163 H6
Dumbarton Rd
    BRXS/STRHM SW2 ......161 K1
Dumbleton CI KUT/HW KT1 ......175 J4
Dumbreck Rd ELTH/MOT SE9 ......147 F5
Dumfries CI OXHEY WD19 ......26 D5
Dumont Rd STNW/STAM N16 ......86 A1
Dumpton PI CAMTN NW1 ......84 A5
Dunbar Av BECK BR3 ......198 B1
    DAGE RM10 ......92 C2
    STRHM/NOR SW16 ......180 A5
Dunbar CI YEAD UB4 ......94 E4
Dunbar Ct WOT/HER KT12 ......188 B6
Dunbar Gdns DAGE RM10 ......92 C3
Dunbar Rd FSTGT E7 ......88 E4
    NWMAL KT3 ......191 K1
    WDGN N22 ......49 G4
Dunbar St WNWD SE27 ......162 D5
Dunblane Rd ELTH/MOT SE9 ......146 D4
Dunboyne Rd HAMP NW3 ......83 K3
Dunbridge St BETH E2 ......104 C3
Duncan CI BAR EN5 ......21 G5
Duncan Gv ACT W3 ......99 G5
Duncannon St CHCR WC2N 10 E6
Duncan Rd HACK E8 ......86 D6
    RCH/KEW TW9 ......137 F5
Duncan St IS N1 ......6 A2
Duncan Ter IS N1 ......6 A2
Dunch St WCHPL E1 ......104 D5
Duncombe HI FSTH SE23 ......164 B2
Duncombe Rd ARCH N19 ......66 D5
Duncrievie Rd LEW SE13 ......165 H1
Duncroft WOOL/PLUM SE18 ......128 A6
Dundalk Rd BROCKY SE4 ......144 B4
Dundas Gdns
    E/WMO/HCT KT8 ......173 G6
Dundas Rd PECK SE15 ......143 K3
Dundee Rd PLSTW E13 ......107 F1
    SNWD SE25 ......197 J2
Dundee St WAP E1W 123 J1
Dundee Wy PEND EN3 ......25 G4
Dundela Gdns WPK KT4 ......207 K2
Dundonald CI EHAM E6 ......107 J5
Dundonald Rd
    WIM/MER SW19 ......177 J3
    WLSDN NW10 ......82 B6
Dunedin Rd IL IG1 ......72 C2
    LEY E10 ......87 K1
    RAIN RM13 ......111 H2
Dunedin Wy YEAD UB4 ......95 G3
Dunelm St WCHPL E1 ......105 F5
Dunfield Rd CAT SE6 ......182 E1
Dunford Rd HOLWY N7 ......85 F2
Dungarvan Av PUT/ROE SW15 ......138 D5
Dunheved CI THHTH CR7 ......196 B3
Dunheved Rd North
    THHTH CR7 ......196 B3
Dunheved Rd South
    THHTH CR7 ......196 B3
Dunheved Rd West
    THHTH CR7 ......196 B3
Dunholme Gn ED N9 ......36 B5
Dunholme La ED N9 ......36 B5
Dunholme Rd ED N9 ......36 B5

Dunkeld Rd BCTR RM8 ......73 H6
    SNWD SE25 ......196 E1
Dunkery Rd ELTH/MOT SE9 ......166 C6
Dunkin Rd DART DA1 ......151 K5
Dunkirk St WNWD SE27 * 162 D6
Dunlace Rd CLPT E5 ......86 E2
Dunleary CI HSLWW TW4 ......154 E2
Dunley Dr CROY/NA CRO 214 A4
Dunloe Av TOTM N17 ......49 K6
Dunloe St BETH E2 ......7 J3
Dunlop PI BERM/RHTH SE16 ......19 K5
Dunmore Rd KIL/WHAMP NW6 ......82 C6
    RYNPK SW20 ......177 F4
Dunmow CI CHDH RM6 ......73 J2
    FELT TW13 * 154 D6
Dunmow Dr RAIN RM13 ......93 H1
Dunmow Rd SRTFD E15 ......88 B2
Dunmow Wk IS N1 * 85 J6
Dunnage Crs
    BERM/RHTH SE16 ......124 B4
Dunningford CI HCH RM12 ......93 H3
Dunn Mead CDALE/KGS NW9 ......45 H4
Dunnock CI ED N9 ......37 F3
Dunnock Rd EHAM E6 ......107 J5
Dunn St HACK E8 ......86 B3
Dunollie PI KTTN NW5 ......84 C3
Dunollie Rd KTTN NW5 ......84 C3
Dunoon Gdns FSTH SE23 * 164 A2
Dunoon Rd FSTH SE23 ......163 K2
Dunraven Dr ENC/FH EN2 ......23 G3
Dunraven Rd SHB W12 ......118 D1
Dunraven St MYFR/PKLN W1K 9 F5
Dunsany Rd HMSMTH W6 ......118 D3
Dunsbury CI BELMT SM2 ......209 F6
Dunsfold Wy CROY/NA CRO 213 K6
Dunsford Wy PUT/ROE SW15 ......158 E2
Dunsmore CI BUSH WD23 ......28 D1
    YEAD UB4 ......95 J3
Dunsmore Rd WOT/HER KT12 ......188 A3
Dunsmore Wy BUSH WD23 ......28 D1
Dunsmure Rd STNW/STAM N16 ......68 A5
Dunspring La CLAY IG5 ......54 B5
Dunstable Ms
    CAVSQ/HST W1G 9 H1
Dunstable Rd
    E/WMO/HCT KT8 ......188 D1
    RCH/KEW TW9 ......137 F5
Dunstall Rd RYNPK SW20 ......176 E2
Dunstall Wy E/WMO/HCT KT8 ......173 H6
Dunstan's Gv EDUL SE22 ......163 J1
Dunstan's Rd EDUL SE22 ......163 H2
Dunster Av MRDN SM4 ......193 G5
Dunster CI BAR EN5 ......20 B4
    CRW RM5 ......56 E5
Dunster Ct MON EC3R 13 G5
    CRW RM5 ......56 E5
Dunster Gdns KIL/WHAMP NW6 ......82 D5
    STNW/STAM N16 * 62 E5
Dunsterville Wy STHWK SE1 ......19 F3
Dunston Rd BTSEA SW11 ......141 F3
    HACK E8 ......7 J1
Dunston St HACK E8 ......86 B6
Dunton CI SURB KT6 ......191 F5
Dunton Rd LEY E10 ......69 K4
    ROM RM1 ......75 G1
    STHWK SE1 ......19 J7
Duntshill Rd
    WAND/EARL SW18 ......160 A3
Dunvegan CI E/WMO/HCT KT8 ......189 G1
Dunvegan Rd ELTH/MOT SE9 ......146 E5
Dunwich Rd BXLYHN DA7 ......149 G2
Dunworth Ms NTGHL W11 ......100 D5
Duplex Ride KTBR SW1X 15 F3
Dupont Rd RYNPK SW20 ......177 G2
Duppas Av CROY/NA CRO 211 H2
Duppas CI SHPTN TW17 ......188 A4
Duppas Hill La CROY/NA CRO 211 H2
Duppas Hill Ter CROY/NA CRO 211 H1
Duppas Rd CROY/NA CRO 211 G1
Dupree Rd CHARL SE7 ......126 A5
Dura Den CI BECK BR3 ......182 E3
Durand Gdns BRXN/ST SW9 ......142 A2
Durand Wy WLSDN NW10 ......80 E5
Durants Park Av PEND EN3 ......25 F5
Durants Rd PEND EN3 ......24 E5
Durant St BETH E2 ......104 C2
Durban Gdns DAGE RM10 ......92 D5
Durban Rd BECK BR3 ......182 C5
    GNTH/NBYPK IG2 ......72 E5
    SRTFD E15 ......106 C2
    TOTM N17 ......50 B2
    WALTH E17 ......51 H4
    WNWD SE27 ......162 D6
Durbin Rd CHSGTN KT9 ......206 A2
Durdans Rd STHL UB1 ......95 K5
Durell Gdns DAGW RM9 ......91 K3
Durell Rd DAGW RM9 ......91 K3
Durfey PI WALW SE17 ......122 E4
Durford Crs PUT/ROE SW15 ......158 E3
Durham Av HAYES BR2 ......199 J1
    HEST TW5 ......114 E6
    WFD IG8 ......53 H1
Durham HI BMLY BR1 ......165 J6
Durham House St
    CHCR WC2N 11 F6
Durham PI CHEL SW3 * 120 E5
Durham RI WOOL/PLUM SE18 ......127 H5
Durham Rd CAN/RD E16 ......106 C3
    DAGE RM10 ......92 D4
    EA W5 ......116 E3
    EBED/NFELT TW14 ......154 B2
    ED N9 ......36 C5
    EFNCH N2 ......47 J6
    HAYES BR2 ......199 K1
    HOLWY N7 ......67 F2
    MNPK E12 ......89 H2
    RYNPK SW20 ......176 E4
    SCUP DA14 ......186 C1
Durham Rw WCHPL E1 ......105 F4
Durham St LBTH SE11 ......122 A5

Earlsmead RYLN/HDSTN HA2 ......77 K2
Earlsmead Rd
    SEVS/STOTM N15 ......68 B2
    WLSDN NW10 ......100 A3
Earls Ms WAND/EARL SW18 ......160 B2
Earls Ter KENS W8 * 119 K3
Earlsthorpe Ms BAL SW12 ......161 F1
Earlsthorpe Rd SYD SE26 ......164 A6
Earlston Gv HOM E9 ......86 D6
Earls Wk BCTR RM8 ......91 H1
    KENS W8 ......119 K3
Earlswood Av THHTH CR7 ......196 B2
Earlswood Gdns CLAY IG5 ......54 A6
Earlswood St GNWCH SE10 ......125 H5
Early Ms CAMTN NW1 ......84 B6
Earnshaw St NOXST/BSQ WC1A 10 D3
Earsby St WKENS W14 ......119 H4
Easby Crs MRDN SM4 ......194 A3
Easebourne Rd BCTR RM8 ......91 J3
Easedale Dr HCH RM12 ......93 K3
Easleys Ms MHST W1U 9 H3
East Acton La ACT W3 ......99 G6
East Acton La ACT W3 ......99 G6
East Arbour St WCHPL E1 ......105 F5
Eastbank Rd HPTN TW12 ......173 H1
East Barnet Rd BAR EN5 ......21 G5
Eastbourne Av ACT W3 ......99 F5
Eastbourne Gdns
    MORT/ESHN SW14 ......137 K4
Eastbourne Ms BAY/PAD W2 ......101 G5
Eastbourne Rd BTFD TW8 ......116 E5
    CHSWK W4 ......117 K6
    EHAM E6 ......108 A2
    FELT TW13 ......154 C4
    SEVS/STOTM N15 ......68 A3
    TOOT SW17 ......179 F2
Eastbourne Ter BAY/PAD W2 ......101 G5
Eastbournia Av ED N9 ......36 E5
Eastbrook Av DAGE RM10 ......92 E2
    ED N9 ......36 E3
Eastbrook Rd DORMW/RG RM7 ......
Eastbrook Rd BKHTH/KID SE3 ......146 A2
Eastbury Av BARK IG11 ......90 E6
    EN EN1 ......24 A2
    NTHWD HA6 ......26 A6
Eastbury Ct OXHEY WD19 ......27 G2
Eastbury Gv CHSWK W4 ......118 B5
Eastbury Rd EHAM E6 ......108 A3
    KUTN/CMB KT2 ......175 F3
    NTHWD HA6 ......27 G2
    OXHEY WD19 ......27 G2
    ROMW/RG RM7 ......75 F2
    STMC/STPC BR5 ......201 J3
Eastbury Sq BARK IG11 ......91 F6
Eastbury Ter WCHPL E1 ......105 F3
Eastcastle St GTPST W1W 10 A3
Eastcheap FENCHST EC3M 13 G5
East Churchfield Rd ACT W3 ......118 A1
East CI EA W5 ......98 C3
    EBAR EN4 ......22 A5
    GFD/PVL UB6 ......96 A1
    RAIN RM13 ......111 K3
Eastcombe Av CHARL SE7 ......126 A6
Eastcote ORP BR6 ......217 G1
Eastcote Av E/WMO/HCT KT8 ......188 D2
    GFD/PVL UB6 ......79 G5
    RYLN/HDSTN HA2 ......60 B6
Eastcote La NTHLT UB5 ......77 K4
    RYLN/HDSTN HA2 ......78 C1
Eastcote La North NTHLT UB5 ......78 A4
Eastcote PI PIN HA5 ......58 C2
Eastcote Rd PIN HA5 ......59 G2
    RYLN/HDSTN HA2 ......78 B1
    WELL DA16 ......147 J3
Eastcote St BRXN/ST SW9 ......141 K3
Eastcote Vw PIN HA5 ......59 G1
East Ct ALP/SUD HA0 ......61 J6
East Crs EN EN1 ......24 B6
    FBAR/BDGN N11 ......33 K6
Eastcroft Rd HOR/WEW KT19 ......207 G5
East Cross Route HOM E9 ......87 H5
Eastdown Pk LEW SE13 ......145 G5
East Dr CAR SM5 ......209 J6
    NTHWD HA6 ......26 C4
    STMC/STPC BR5 ......202 C2
East Duck Lees La PEND EN3 ......25 H5
East Dulwich Gv EDUL SE22 ......143 F6
East Dulwich Rd EDUL SE22 ......143 G5
East End Rd EFNCH N2 ......47 G6
    FNCH N3 ......46 E4
East End Wy PIN HA5 ......41 J6
East Entrance DAGE RM10 ......110 D1
Eastern Av GNTH/NBYPK IG2 ......72 C3
    PIN HA5 ......59 H4
    REDBR IG4 ......71 J4
Eastern Av East ROM RM1 ......57 G5
Eastern Av West CHDH RM6 ......74 A1
Eastern Gtwy CAN/RD E16 ......107 G6
Eastern Perimeter Rd
    HTHAIR TW6 ......133 H3
Eastern Rd BROCKY SE4 ......144 D5
    EFNCH N2 ......47 K6
    PLSTW E13 ......107 F1
    ROM RM1 ......75 G2
    WALTH E17 ......70 A2
    WDGN N22 ......48 E4
Easternville Gdns
    GNTH/NBYPK IG2 ......72 C5
Eastern Wy THMD SE28 ......128 B2
East Ferry Rd POP/IOD E14 ......124 E4
Eastfield Gdns DAGE RM10 ......92 C2
Eastfield Rd CEND/HSY/T N8 ......48 E2
    DAGE RM10 ......92 C2
    EN EN3 ......25 G1
    PEND EN3 ......24 ...
    WALTH E17 ......69 F1
Eastfields PIN HA5 ......59 G2

Eastfields Av
WAND/EARL SW18 ....139 K5
Eastfields Rd ACT W3 ....98 E4
MTCM CR4 ....179 F5
Eastfield St POP/IOD E14 ....105 G4
East Gdns TOOT SW17 ....178 D2
Eastgate Cl THMD SE28 ....109 K5
Eastglade NTHWD HA6 ....40 C1
PIN HA5 ....41 K6
East Hall Rd STMC/STPC BR5 ....203 F4
Eastham Cl BAR EN5 ....20 D6
East Ham Manor Wy EHAM E6 ..108 A5
East Harding St
FLST/FETLN EC4A 11 K3
East Heath Rd HAMP NW3 ....83 H1
East Hl DART DA1 ....171 J2
WAND/EARL SW18 ....140 B6
WBLY HA9 ....62 C6
East Hill Dr DART DA1 ....171 J2
Eastholm GLDGN NW11 ....65 F1
East Holme ERITH DA8 ....150 A2
Eastholme HYS/HAR UB3 ....113 K1
East India Dock Rd
POP/IOD E14 ....105 J6
East India Wy CROY/NA CR0 ....197 G5
Eastlake Rd CMBW SE5 ....142 C3
Eastlands Crs EDUL SE22 ....163 G1
East La ALP/SUD HA0 ....79 J1
BERM/RHTH SE16 ....123 H2
KUT/HW KT1 ....174 E6
Eastlea Ms CAN/RD E16 ....106 C3
Eastleigh Av RYLN/HDSTN HA2 ....60 B6
Eastleigh Cl BELMT SM2 ....209 F5
CRICK NW2 ....81 G1
Eastleigh Rd BXLYHN DA7 ....149 K3
WALTH E17 ....51 H5
Eastleigh Wy
EBED/NFELT TW14 ....153 K3
Eastman Rd ACT W3 ....118 A2
East Md RSLP HA4 ....77 H1
Eastmead Av GFD/PVL UB6 ....96 B2
Eastmead Cl BMLY BR1 ....184 D5
Eastmearn Rd DUL SE21 ....162 D4
Eastmont Rd ESH/CLAY KT10 ....189 K6
Eastmoor Pl CHARL SE7 ....126 C3
Eastmoor St CHARL SE7 ....126 C3
East Mount St WCHPL E1 ....104 D4
Eastney Rd CROY/NA CR0 ....196 C5
Eastney St GNWCH SE10 ....125 G5
Eastnor Rd ELTH/MOT SE9 ....167 H3
Easton St FSBYW WC1X 5 J6
East Park Cl CHDH RM6 ....73 K2
East Parkside GNWCH SE10 ....125 H2
East Pas STBT EC1A 12 C1
East Pl WNWD SE27 ....162 D6
East Pole Cottages
STHGT/OAK N14 * 22 D5
East Poultry Av FARR EC1M 12 A2
East Rp HTHAIR TW6 ....132 E2
East Rd CHDH RM6 ....74 A2
CHEL SW3 ....121 F5
EBAR EN4 ....34 A3
EBED/NFELT TW14 ....153 G2
EDGW HA8 ....44 E4
IS N1 ....7 F4
KUTN/CMB KT2 ....175 F4
PEND EN3 ....24 E1
ROMW/RG RM7 ....75 F4
SRTFD E15 ....88 E6
WDR/YW UB7 ....112 C4
WELL DA16 ....148 C3
WIM/MER SW19 ....178 B2
East Rochester Wy
BFN/LL DA15 ....147 K6
DART DA1 ....170 A2
East Rw NKENS W10 ....100 C3
WAN E11 ....70 E3
Eastry Av HAYES BR2 ....199 J3
Eastry Rd ERITH DA8 ....149 H1
East Sheen Av
MORT/ESHN SW14 ....138 A6
East Side SHB W12 * 119 F2
Eastside Rd GLDGN NW11 ....64 D1
East Smithfield WAP E1W 13 K6
East St BARK IG11 ....90 C5
BMLY BR1 ....183 K5
BTFD TW8 ....136 D1
BXLYHN DA7 ....149 H5
WALW SE17 ....19 G7
East Surrey Gv PECK SE15 ....143 G1
East Tenter St WCHPL E1 ....13 K4
East Ter BFN/LL DA15 * 167 K3
East Towers PIN HA5 ....59 H3
East V ACT W3 * 118 C1
East Vw BAR EN5 ....20 D4
CHING E4 ....52 A1
Eastview Av
WOOL/PLUM SE18 ....147 K1
Eastville Av GLDGN NW11 ....64 D3
East Wk EBAR EN4 ....34 A3
HYS/HAR UB3 ....113 K2
East Wy CROY/NA CR0 ....198 B6
Eastway HAYES BR2 ....199 K4
HOM E9 ....87 G6
East Wy HYS/HAR UB3 ....113 K1
Eastway LEY E10 ....87 J2
MRDN SM4 ....193 G2
East Wy RSLP HA4 ....58 E5
Eastway WAN E11 ....71 F2
WLGTN SM6 ....210 C2
Eastway Crs RYLN/HDSTN HA2 ....60 B6
Eastwell Cl BECK BR3 ....182 B4
Eastwood Cl HOLWY N7 ....85 G3
SWFD E18 ....52 E5
TOTM N17 * 50 D3
Eastwood Dr RAIN RM13 ....111 K5
Eastwood Rd GDMY/SEVK IG3 ....73 G4
MUSWH N10 ....48 A5
SWFD E18 ....52 E5
WDR/YW UB7 ....112 D2
Eastwood St
STRHM/NOR SW16 ....179 H2
Eatington Rd LEY E10 ....70 B2
Eaton Cl BGVA SW1W 15 G6
STAN HA7 ....29 H6
Eaton Dr BRXN/ST SW9 ....142 C5
CRW RM5 ....56 D3
KUTN/CMB KT2 ....175 H3
Eaton Gdns DAGW RM9 ....92 A5
Eaton Ga BGVA SW1W 15 G6
NTHWD HA6 ....40 A2
Eaton La BGVA SW1W 15 K5
Eaton Ms North KTBR SW1X 15 H5
Eaton Ms South BGVA SW1W 15 H6
Eaton Ms West BGVA SW1W 15 H6
Eaton Park Rd PLMGR N13 ....35 G4
Eaton Pl KTBR SW1X 15 G6
Eaton Ri EA W5 ....97 K5
WAN E11 ....71 G2
Eaton Rd BELMT SM2 ....209 H4
EN EN1 ....24 A4
HDN NW4 ....64 A2
HSLW TW3 ....135 J5
SCUP DA14 ....168 E4
Eaton Rw BGVA SW1W 15 J4
Eatons Md CHING E4 ....37 J4
Eaton Sq BGVA SW1W 15 J5
Eaton Ter BGVA SW1W 15 G6
BOW E3 * 105 G2
Eaton Terrace Ms BGVA SW1W 15 G6
Eatonville Rd TOOT SW17 ....160 E4
Eatonville Vls TOOT SW17 ....160 E4
Ebbisham Dr VX/NE SW8 ....122 A6
Ebbisham Rd WPK KT4 ....193 F6
Ebbsfleet Rd CRICK NW2 ....82 C3
Ebdon Wy BKHTH/KID SE3 ....146 A4
Ebenezer St FSBYE EC1V 6 E4
Ebenezer Wk
STRHM/NOR SW16 ....179 H4
Ebley Cl PECK SE15 ....123 G6
Ebner St WAND/EARL SW18 ....140 A6
Ebor St WCHPL E1 ....7 J6
Ebrington Rd
KTN/HRWW/WS HA3 ....61 J3
Ebsworth St FSTH SE23 ....164 A2
Eburne Rd HOLWY N7 ....84 E1
Ebury Br BGVA SW1W 121 G5
Ebury Bridge Rd BGVA SW1W 121 G5
Ebury Cl HAYES BR2 ....215 J1
NTHWD HA6 ....40 A1
Ebury Ms BGVA SW1W 15 H6
Ebury Ms East BGVA SW1W 15 J6
Ebury Sq BGVA SW1W 15 J7
Ebury St BGVA SW1W 15 H7
Ecclesbourne Cl PLMGR N13 ....49 G1
Ecclesbourne Gdns PLMGR N13 ..49 G1
Ecclesbourne Rd IS N1 ....85 J5
THHTH CR7 ....196 D2
Eccles Rd BTSEA SW11 ....140 E5
Eccleston Cl EBAR EN4 ....21 K6
ORP BR6 * 201 J5
Eccleston Crs CHDH RM6 ....73 H4
Ecclestone Ct WBLY HA9 ....80 A3
Ecclestone Ms WBLY HA9 ....80 A3
Ecclestone Pl WBLY HA9 ....80 B3
Eccleston Ms KTBR SW1X 15 H5
Eccleston Pl BGVA SW1W 15 J6
Eccleston Rd WEA W13 ....97 G6
Eccleston Sq PIM SW1V 15 K7
Eccleston Square Ms PIM SW1V ..15 K7
Eccleston St BGVA SW1W 15 H5
Echelforde Dr ASHF TW15 ....152 D6
Echo Hts CHING E4 * 37 K3
Eckford St IS N1 ....5 J2
Eckstein Rd BTSEA SW11 ....140 D5
Eclipse Rd PLSTW E13 ....107 F4
Ector Rd CAT SE6 ....165 H4
Edans Ct SHB W12 ....118 C2
Edbrooke Rd MV/WKIL W9 ....100 E3
Eddiscombe Rd FUL/PGN SW6 ....139 J3
Eddy Cl ROMW/RG RM7 ....74 D3
Eddystone Rd BROCKY SE4 ....144 B6
Ede Cl HSLW TW3 ....134 E4
Edenbridge Cl
BERM/RHTH SE16 ....123 J5
STMC/STPC BR5 ....202 E1
Edenbridge Rd EN EN1 ....36 A1
HOM E9 * 87 F5
Eden Cl ALP/SUD HA0 ....79 K6
BXLY DA5 ....170 A6
HAMP NW3 ....64 E6
KENS W8 ....119 K3
PEND EN3 ....25 J1
Edencourt Rd
STRHM/NOR SW16 ....179 G2
Edendale Rd BXLYHN DA7 ....150 A2
Edenfield Gdns WPK KT4 ....207 H1
Eden Gv HOLWY N7 ....85 F3
WLSDN NW10 ....81 K4
Edenham Wy NKENS W10 ....100 D3
Edenhurst Av FUL/PGN SW6 ....139 J4
Eden Pde BECK BR3 * 198 B1
Eden Park Av BECK BR3 ....198 D1
Eden Rd BECK BR3 ....198 B1
BXLY DA5 ....169 K6
CROY/NA CR0 ....211 K2
WALTH E17 ....69 K2
WNWD SE27 ....180 C1
Edensor Rd CHSWK W4 ....138 B1
Eden St KUT/HW KT1 ....174 E5
Edenvale Rd MTCM CR4 ....179 F3
Edenvale St FUL/PGN SW6 ....140 A3
Eden Wk KUT/HW KT1 * 175 F5
Eden Wy BECK BR3 ....198 D2
BOW E3 ....87 H6
Ederline Av STRHM/NOR SW16 ..180 A6
Edgar Kail Wy CMBW SE5 ....143 F4
Edgarley Ter FUL/PGN SW6 * 139 H2
Edgar Rd BOW E3 ....105 K2
HSLWW TW4 ....154 E2
Edgar Wallace Cl PECK SE15 ....143 F1
Edgeborough Wy BMLY BR1 ....184 C4
Edgebury CHST BR7 ....167 G6
Edgecombe Cl KUTN/CMB KT2 ..176 A3
Edgecoombe SAND/SEL CR2 ....213 F6
Edgecote Cl ACT W3 ....117 K1
Edgefield Av BARK IG11 ....91 F5
Edge Hl WIM/MER SW19 ....177 G3
WOOL/PLUM SE18 ....127 G6
Edge Hill Av FNCH N3 ....64 E1
Edge Hill Ct WIM/MER SW19 ....177 G3
Edgehill Ct WOT/HER KT12 * 188 B5
Edgehill Gdns DAGE RM10 ....92 C2
Edgehill Rd CHST BR7 ....167 H5
MTCM CR4 ....179 G4
WEA W13 ....97 J5
Edgeley La CLAP SW4 ....141 J4
Edgeley Rd CLAP SW4 ....141 H4
Edgel St WAND/EARL SW18 ....140 A6
Edge Point Cl
STRHM/NOR SW16 ....180 C1
Edgepoint Cl WNWD SE27 * 180 C1
Edge St KENS W8 ....119 K1
Edgewood Dr ORP BR6 ....217 F3
Edgewood Gn CROY/NA CR0 ....198 A5
Edgeworth Av HDN NW4 ....63 J2
Edgeworth Cl HDN NW4 ....63 J2
Edgeworth Crs HDN NW4 ....63 J2
Edgeworth Rd EBAR EN4 ....21 J5
ELTH/MOT SE9 ....146 B5
Edgington Rd
STRHM/NOR SW16 ....179 J2
Edgington Wy SCUP DA14 ....186 D3
Edgwarebury Gdns EDGW HA8 ....44 C1
Edgwarebury La BORE WD6 ....30 B2
Edgware Rd BAY/PAD W2 ....2 A7
CDALE/KGS NW9 ....45 F6
CRICK NW2 ....82 A1
Edgware Road Burnt Oak
Broadway EDGW HA8 ....44 D3
Edgware Road High St
EDGW HA8 ....44 C2
Edgware Road The Hyde
CDALE/KGS NW9 ....63 G1
Edgware Road Wy CRICK NW2 ....63 H6
Edgware Wy (Watford
By-Pass) EDGW HA8 ....30 A4
Edinburgh Cl BETH E2 ....104 E1
PIN HA5 ....59 J4
Edinburgh Ct KUT/HW KT1 * 175 F6
Edinburgh Ga KTBR SW1X 14 E2
Edinburgh Rd HNWL W7 ....116 A2
PLSTW E13 ....107 F1
SUT SM1 ....194 B6
UED N18 * 50 C1
WALTH E17 ....69 J2
Edington Rd ABYW SE2 ....128 C3
PEND EN3 ....24 E3
Edison Av HCH RM12 ....75 H5
Edison Cl HCH RM12 ....75 H5
WDR/YW UB7 ....112 C2
Edison Dr STHL UB1 ....96 B5
WBLY HA9 ....62 A6
Edison Gv WOOL/PLUM SE18 ....148 A1
Edison Rd CEND/HSY/T N8 ....66 D3
HAYES BR2 ....183 K5
PEND EN3 ....25 H3
WELL DA16 ....148 A2
Edis St CAMTN NW1 ....84 A6
Edith Cavell Wy
WOOL/PLUM SE18 ....146 D2
Edith Gdns BRYLDS KT5 ....191 J4
Edith Gv WBPTN SW10 ....120 B6
Edithna St BRXN/ST SW9 ....141 K4
Edith Nesbit Wk
ELTH/MOT SE9 ....146 D5
Edith Neville Cottages
CAMTN NW1 ....4 C4
Edith Rd CHDH RM6 ....73 K4
EHAM E6 ....89 H5
FBAR/BDGN N11 ....48 D3
ORP BR6 ....217 G3
SNWD SE25 ....196 E2
SRTFD E15 ....88 B3
WIM/MER SW19 ....178 A2
WKENS W14 ....119 H4
Edith Rw FUL/PGN SW6 ....140 A2
Edith St BETH E2 ....7 K2
Edith Ter WBPTN SW10 * 140 B1
Edith Vls WKENS W14 ....119 J4
Edith Yd WBPTN SW10 ....140 C1
Edison Cl WALTH E17 ....69 J2
Edmansons Cl TOTM N17 ....50 B5
Edmeston Cl HOM E9 ....87 G4
Edmund Gv FELT TW13 ....154 E4
Edmund Halley Wy
GNWCH SE10 ....125 H2
Edmund Hurst Dr EHAM E6 ....108 B4
Edmund Rd MTCM CR4 ....178 D6
RAIN RM13 ....111 G2
STMC/STPC BR5 ....202 D3
WELL DA16 ....148 B4
Edmunds Av STMC/STPC BR5 ....186 E6
Edmunds Cl YEAD UB4 ....95 G4
Edmund St CMBW SE5 ....142 E1
Edmunds Wk EFNCH N2 ....65 J1
Edna Rd RYNPK SW20 ....177 G5
Edna St BTSEA SW11 ....140 D2
Edrick Rd EDGW HA8 ....44 E2
Edrick Wk EDGW HA8 ....44 E2
Edric Rd NWCR SE14 ....144 A1
Edridge Rd CROY/NA CR0 ....211 J1
Edward Av CHING E4 ....51 K1
MRDN SM4 ....194 C2
Edward Cl ED N9 ....36 B2
HPTN TW12 ....173 H1
Edward Ct CAN/RD E16 ....106 E4
Edwardes Pl WKENS W14 ....119 J3
Edward Gv EBAR EN4 ....21 H6
Edward Mann Cl East
WCHPL E1 * 105 F5
Edward Mann Cl West
WCHPL E1 * 105 F5
Edward Ms CAMTN NW1 * 3 K4
Edward Pl DEPT SE8 ....124 C6
Edward Rd BMLY BR1 ....184 A3
CHDH RM6 ....74 A3
CHST BR7 ....185 G1
CROY/NA CR0 ....197 F4
EBAR EN4 ....21 H6
EBED/NFELT TW14 ....133 G6
HPTN TW12 ....173 H1
NTHLT UB5 ....95 G1
PGE/AN SE20 ....182 A3
RYLN/HDSTN HA2 ....42 C6
WALTH E17 ....69 F1
Edwards Av RSLP HA4 ....77 G3
Edwards Cl WPK KT4 ....193 G6
Edward's Cottages IS N1 * 85 H5
Edwards Dr FBAR/BDGN N11 ....48 D3
Edward's La STNW/STAM N16 ....67 K6
Edwards Ms IS N1 ....85 H5
MHST W1U 9 G4
Edward Sq IS N1 ....5 G1
Edwards Rd BELV DA17 ....129 H4
Edward St CAN/RD E16 ....106 E3
DEPT SE8 ....124 C6
NWCR SE14 ....144 C1
Edward's Wy BROCKY SE4 ....144 D6
Edward Temme Av SRTFD E15 ....88 D5
Edward Tyler Rd
LEE/GVPK SE12 ....166 A4
Edward Wy ASHF TW15 ....152 C4
Edwina Gdns REDBR IG4 ....71 J2
Edwin Av EHAM E6 ....108 A2
Edwin Cl BXLYHN DA7 ....129 G6
RAIN RM13 ....111 H2
Edwin Hall Pl LEW SE13 ....165 G1
Edwin Pl CROY/NA CR0 ....196 E5
Edwin Rd EDGW HA8 ....45 F2
RDART DA2 ....170 E5
WHTN TW2 ....155 K3
Edwin's Md HOM E9 ....87 G2
Edwin St CAN/RD E16 ....106 E4
WCHPL E1 ....104 E3
Edwin Ware Ct PIN HA5 * 41 G5
Edwyn Cl BAR EN5 ....32 A1
Effie Pl FUL/PGN SW6 ....139 K1
Effie Rd FUL/PGN SW6 ....139 K1
Effingham Cl BELMT SM2 ....209 F5
Effingham Rd CEND/HSY/T N8 ....67 G2
CROY/NA CR0 ....196 A4
LEE/GVPK SE12 ....145 H6
SURB KT6 ....190 C4
Effort St TOOT SW17 ....178 D1
Effra Pde BRXS/STRHM SW2 ....142 B6
Effra Rd BRXS/STRHM SW2 ....142 B5
WIM/MER SW19 ....178 A2
Egan Wy HYS/HAR UB3 ....94 C6
Egbert St CAMTN NW1 ....84 A6
Egerton Cl DART DA1 ....170 E3
PIN HA5 ....58 E1
Egerton Crs CHEL SW3 ....14 D6
Egerton Dr GNWCH SE10 ....144 E2
Egerton Gdns CHEL SW3 ....14 D5
GDMY/SEVK IG3 ....91 F1
HDN NW4 ....63 K1
WEA W13 ....97 H5
WLSDN NW10 * 82 A6
Egerton Gardens Ms CHEL SW3 ..14 D5
Egerton Pl CHEL SW3 * 14 D5
Egerton Rd ALP/SUD HA0 ....80 B5
NWMAL KT3 ....192 C1
SNWD SE25 ....181 F6
STNW/STAM N16 ....68 B4
WHTN TW2 ....155 K2
Egerton Ter CHEL SW3 ....14 D5
Egerton Wy HYS/HAR UB3 ....132 E1
Egham Cl CHEAM SM3 ....193 H6
Egham Crs CHEAM SM3 ....208 C1
Egham Rd PLSTW E13 ....107 F4
Eglantine Rd
WAND/EARL SW18 ....140 B6
Egleston Rd MRDN SM4 ....194 A3
Eglington Rd CHING E4 ....38 B2
Eglinton Hl WOOL/PLUM SE18 ....127 G6
Eglinton Rd WOOL/PLUM SE18 ..127 F6
Egliston Ms PUT/ROE SW15 ....139 F4
Egliston Rd PUT/ROE SW15 ....139 F4
Eglon Ms CAMTN NW1 ....83 K5
Egmont Av SURB KT6 ....191 H5
Egmont Rd BELMT SM2 ....209 G5
NWMAL KT3 ....192 C1
SURB KT6 ....191 G5
WOT/HER KT12 ....188 A4
Egmont St NWCR SE14 ....144 A1
Egremont Rd WNWD SE27 ....162 B5
Egret Wy YEAD UB4 ....95 H4
Eider Cl SRTFD E15 ....88 D3
Eighteenth Rd MTCM CR4 ....195 K1
Eighth Av HYS/HAR UB3 ....113 K1
MNPK E12 ....89 K2
Eileen Rd SNWD SE25 ....196 E2
Eindhoven Cl CAR SM5 ....195 F5
WIM/MER SW19 ....178 C4
Eisenhower Dr EHAM E6 ....107 J4
Elaine Gv KTTN NW5 ....84 A3
Elam Cl CMBW SE5 ....142 C3
Elam St CMBW SE5 ....142 C3
Eland Rd BTSEA SW11 ....140 E4
CROY/NA CR0 ....211 H1
Elba Pl WALW SE17 * 18 D6
Elberon Av CROY/NA CR0 ....195 H3
Elbe St FUL/PGN SW6 ....140 B3
Elborough Rd SNWD SE25 ....197 H2
Elborough St
WAND/EARL SW18 ....159 K3
Elbury Dr CAN/RD E16 ....106 E5
Elcho St BTSEA SW11 ....140 D1
Elcot Av PECK SE15 ....143 J1
Elder Av CEND/HSY/T N8 ....66 E2
Elderberry Cl BARK/HLT IG6 ....54 B3
Elderberry Rd EA W5 ....117 F2
Elder Cl BFN/LL DA15 ....168 A3
TRDG/WHET N20 ....33 F4
Elder Ct BUSH WD23 ....28 E4
Elderfield Rd CLPT E5 ....87 F2
Elderfield Wk WAN E11 ....71 F2
Elderflower Wy SRTFD E15 ....88 C5
Elder Oak Cl PGE/AN SE20 ....181 J4
Elder Rd WNWD SE27 ....180 D1
Elderslie Cl BECK BR3 ....198 E3
Elderslie Rd ELTH/MOT SE9 ....147 F6
Elder St WCHPL E1 ....13 J1
Elderton Rd SYD SE26 ....164 B6
Eldertree Wy MTCM CR4 ....179 G4
Elder Wk IS N1 ....85 H6
Eldon Av CROY/NA CR0 ....197 K6
HEST TW5 ....135 F1
Eldon Gv HAMP NW3 ....83 H3
Eldon Pde WDGN N22 * 49 H4
Eldon Pk SNWD SE25 ....197 J1
Eldon Rd ED N9 ....36 E3
KENS W8 ....120 A3
WALTH E17 ....69 H1
WDGN N22 ....49 H4
Eldon St LVPST EC2M 13 F2
Eldon Wy WLSDN NW10 ....98 D1
Eldred Dr STMC/STPC BR5 ....202 E6
Eldridge Cl EBED/NFELT TW14 ..153 K3
Eleanora Ter SUT SM1 * 209 G3
Eleanor Cl BERM/RHTH SE16 ....124 A2
SEVS/STOTM N15 ....50 B6
Eleanor Crs MLHL NW7 ....46 B1
Eleanor Gdns BAR EN5 ....20 B6
BCTR RM8 ....92 B1
Eleanor Gv BARN SW13 ....138 B4
Eleanor Rd FBAR/BDGN N11 ....48 E2
HACK E8 ....86 D5
SRTFD E15 ....88 D4
Eleanor St BOW E3 ....105 J2
Electra Av HTHAIR TW6 ....133 J4
Electric Av BRXN/ST SW9 ....142 B5
Electric La BRXN/ST SW9 * 142 B5
Electric Pde SURB KT6 ....190 E3
Elephant & Castle STHWK SE1 ....18 B6
Elephant La BERM/RHTH SE16 ..123 K2
Elephant Rd WALW SE17 ....18 C6
Elers Rd HYS/HAR UB3 ....113 F4
WEA W13 ....116 D2
Eley Rd UED N18 ....51 F1
Elfindale Rd HNHL SE24 ....142 D6
Elfin Gv TEDD TW11 ....174 A1
Elford Cl BKHTH/KID SE3 ....146 B5
Elfort Rd HBRY N5 ....85 G2
Elfrida Crs CAT SE6 ....164 D6
Elf Rw WAP E1W 104 E6
Elfwine Rd HNWL W7 ....96 E4
Elgal Cl ORP BR6 ....216 B3
Elgar Av BRYLDS KT5 ....191 J5
EA W5 ....117 F2
STRHM/NOR SW16 ....179 K6
WLSDN NW10 ....81 F4
Elgar Cl BKHH IG9 ....39 H4
BORE WD6 ....29 J2
DEPT SE8 ....144 D1
PLSTW E13 ....107 G1
Elgar St BERM/RHTH SE16 ....124 B2
Elgin Av KTN/HRWW/WS HA3 ....43 H5
MV/WKIL W9 ....100 E3
SHB W12 ....118 E3
Elgin Cl SHB W12 ....118 E2
Elgin Crs HTHAIR TW6 ....133 H3
NTGHL W11 * 100 D5
Elgin Dr NTHWD HA6 ....40 C3
Elginmeads South
MV/WKIL W9 ....101 F2
Elgin Ms NTGHL W11 ....100 C5
Elgin Ms North MV/WKIL W9 ....101 F2
Elgin Rd CROY/NA CR0 ....197 G6
GDMY/SEVK IG3 ....72 E5
SUT SM1 ....209 G1
WDGN N22 ....48 C5
WLGTN SM6 ....210 C4
Elgood Av NTHWD HA6 ....40 E3
Elgood Cl NTGHL W11 ....100 C6
Elham Cl BMLY BR1 ....184 C3
Elia Ms IS N1 ....6 A3
Elias Pl VX/NE SW8 ....122 B6
Elia St IS N1 ....6 A3
Elibank Rd ELTH/MOT SE9 ....147 F5
Elim St STHWK SE1 ....19 G4
Elim Wy PLSTW E13 ....106 D2
Eliot Bank FSTH SE23 ....163 J4
Eliot Dr RYLN/HDSTN HA2 ....60 B6
Eliot Gdns PUT/ROE SW15 ....138 D5
Eliot Hl LEW SE13 ....145 F3
Eliot Ms STJWD NW8 ....101 G1
Eliot Pk LEW SE13 ....145 F3
Eliot Pl BKHTH/KID SE3 ....145 H3
Eliot Rd DAGW RM9 ....91 K2
Eliot V BKHTH/KID SE3 ....145 G3
Elizabethan Wy
STWL/WRAY TW19 ....152 A2
Elizabeth Av ENC/FH EN2 ....23 H4
IL IG1 ....72 D6
IS N1 ....85 J5
Elizabeth Barnes Ct
FUL/PGN SW6 * 140 A3
Elizabeth Br BGVA SW1W 15 J7
Elizabeth Cl BAR EN5 ....20 B4
MV/WKIL W9 ....101 G3
ROMW/RG RM7 ....56 D4
SUT SM1 ....208 D2
Elizabeth Clyde Cl
SEVS/STOTM N15 ....68 A1
Elizabeth Cottages
RCH/KEW TW9 ....137 G2
Elizabeth Fry Pl
WOOL/PLUM SE18 ....146 D2
Elizabeth Gdns ACT W3 ....118 C1
ISLW TW7 ....136 B5
STAN HA7 ....43 J2
SUN TW16 ....172 B6
Elizabeth Ms HAMP NW3 ....83 J4
Elizabeth Pl SEVS/STOTM N15 ....67 K1
Elizabeth Ride ED N9 ....36 D2
Elizabeth Rd EHAM E6 ....89 H6
RAIN RM13 ....111 K4
SEVS/STOTM N15 ....68 A2
Elizabeth Sq
BERM/RHTH SE16 ....105 G6
Elizabeth St BGVA SW1W 15 H6
Elizabeth Wy FELT TW13 ....154 B6
NRWD SE19 ....180 E3
STMC/STPC BR5 ....202 D2
Elkanette Ms TRDG/WHET N20 ....33 G4
Elkington Rd PLSTW E13 ....107 F3
The Elkins ROM RM1 ....57 G5
Elkstone Rd NKENS W10 ....100 D4
Ellaline Rd HMSMTH W6 ....119 G6
Ella Ms HAMP NW3 ....83 K2
Ellanby Crs UED N18 ....50 D1
Elland Rd PECK SE15 ....143 K5
WOT/HER KT12 ....188 C6
Ella Rd CEND/HSY/T N8 ....66 E4
Ellement Cl PIN HA5 ....59 H2
Ellenborough Pl
PUT/ROE SW15 ....138 D5
Ellenborough Rd SCUP DA14 ....186 E2
WDGN N22 ....49 J4
Ellenbridge Wy SAND/SEL CR2 ..212 A6
Ellen Cl BMLY BR1 ....184 C6
Ellen Ct ED N9 ....36 E4

Ell - Eri 247

Ellen St WCHPL E1 104 C5
Ellen Webb Dr
KTN/HRWW/WS HA3 42 E6
Elleray Rd TEDD TW11 174 A2
Ellerby St FUL/PGN SW6 139 G2
Ellerdale Cl HAMP NW3 83 G3
Ellerdale Rd HAMP NW3 83 G3
Ellerdale St LEW SE13 144 E5
Ellerdine Rd HSLW TW3 135 H5
Ellerker Gdns
RCHPK/HAM TW10 157 F1
Ellerman Av WHTN TW2 154 E3
Ellerslie Rd SHB W12 118 E1
Ellerton Gdns DAGW RM9 91 J5
Ellerton Rd BARN SW13 * 138 D2
DAGW RM9 91 J5
RYNPK SW20 176 D3
SURB KT6 191 G6
WAND/EARL SW18 160 C3
Ellery Rd NRWD SE19 180 E3
Ellery St PECK SE15 143 J3
Ellesborough Cl OXHEY WD19 41 G1
Ellesmere Av BECK BR3 182 E5
MLHL NW7 31 F5
Ellesmere Cl RSLP HA4 58 A4
WAN E11 70 D2
Ellesmere Gdns REDBR IG4 71 J3
Ellesmere Gv BAR EN5 20 D6
Ellesmere Rd BOW E3 105 G1
GFD/PVL UB6 96 C3
TWK TW1 156 D1
WLSDN NW10 81 J3
Ellesmere St POP/IOD E14 105 K5
Ellies Ms ASHF TW15 152 B4
Ellingfort Rd HACK E8 86 D5
Ellingham Rd CHSGTN KT9 205 K4
SHB W12 118 D2
SRTFD E15 88 B2
Ellington Rd FELT TW13 153 J6
HSLW TW3 135 G3
MUSWH N10 66 B1
Ellington St HOLWY N7 85 G4
Elliot Cl SRTFD E15 88 C5
WBLY HA9 80 B1
WFD IG8 53 H2
Elliot Rd HDN NW4 63 K3
Elliott Av RSLP HA4 59 F6
Elliott Gdns HARH RM3 57 K4
Elliott Rd BRXN/ST SW9 142 C1
CHSWK W4 118 B4
HAYES BR2 200 C1
STAN HA7 43 G2
THHTH CR7 196 C1
Elliott's Pl IS N1 6 B1
Elliott Sq HAMP NW3 83 J5
Elliott's Rw LBTH SE11 18 B6
Ellis Av RAIN RM13 111 J4
Ellis Cl EDGW HA8 45 G2
ELTH/MOT SE9 167 H4
WLSDN NW10 82 A4
Elliscombe Mt CHARL SE7 * 126 B6
Elliscombe Rd CHARL SE7 126 B6
Ellisfield Dr PUT/ROE SW15 158 C2
Ellison Gdns NWDGN UB2 114 E4
Ellison Rd BARN SW13 138 C3
BFN/LL DA15 167 J3
STRHM/NOR SW16 179 J3
Ellis Rd MTCM CR4 194 E3
NWDGN UB2 115 H1
Ellis St KTBR SW1X 15 F6
Ellis Wy DART DA1 * 171 J4
Ellmore Cl HARH RM3 57 K4
Ellora Rd STRHM/NOR SW16 179 J1
Ellsworth St BETH E2 * 104 D2
Elmar Rd SEVS/STOTM N15 67 K1
Elm Av EA W5 117 F1
OXHEY WD19 27 J2
RSLP HA4 58 E5
Elmbank STHGT/OAK N14 34 E2
Elmbank Av BAR EN5 20 A5
Elmbank Dr BMLY BR1 184 C5
Elm Bank Gdns BARN SW13 138 B3
Elmbank Wy HNWL W7 96 D4
Elmbourne Dr BELV DA17 129 J4
Elmbourne Rd TOOT SW17 161 G5
Elmbridge Av BRYLDS KT5 191 K3
Elmbridge Cl RSLP HA4 58 E3
Elmbridge Dr RSLP HA4 58 E3
Elmbridge Rd BARK/HLT IG6 55 G2
Elmbridge Wk HACK E8 * 86 C5
Elmbrook Cl SUN TW16 172 A4
Elmbrook Gdns ELTH/MOT SE9 146 D5
Elmbrook Rd SUT SM1 208 D2
Elm Cl BKHH IG9 39 H4
BRYLDS KT5 191 K4
CAR SM5 194 E5
DART DA1 171 F3
HDN NW4 64 B2
HYS/HAR UB3 94 E5
ROMW/RG RM7 56 D4
RYLN/HDSTN HA2 60 B3
RYNPK SW20 193 F1
SAND/SEL CR2 211 K4
STWL/WRAY TW19 152 A3
WAN E11 71 F3
WHTN TW2 155 G4
Elm Cottages MTCM CR4 * 178 E5
Elmcourt Rd WNWD SE27 162 C4
Elm Crs EA W5 117 F2
KUTN/CMB KT2 175 F4
Elmcroft CEND/HSY/T N8 67 F2
Elmcroft Av BFN/LL DA15 168 A2
ED N9 36 D1
GLDGN NW11 64 D4
WAN E11 71 F2
Elmcroft Cl CHSGTN KT9 * 206 A1
EA W5 97 K5
EBED/NFELT TW14 153 J1
Elmcroft Crs GLDGN NW11 64 C4
RYLN/HDSTN HA2 42 A6
Elmcroft Dr CHSGTN KT9 206 A1
Elmcroft Gdns CDALE/KGS NW9 62 C2
Elmcroft Rd ORP BR6 202 B4
Elmcroft St CLPT E5 86 E2
Elmdale Rd PLMGR N13 49 F1
Elmdene BRYLDS KT5 191 K5
Elmdene Cl BECK BR3 198 C2
Elmdene Rd
WOOL/PLUM SE18 127 G5
Elmdon Rd HSLWW TW4 134 C3
HTHAIR TW6 133 J4
Elm Dr RYLN/HDSTN HA2 60 B3
SUN TW16 172 B5
Elmer Cl ENC/FH EN2 23 F4
RAIN RM13 93 J5
Elmer Gdns EDGW HA8 44 D3
ISLW TW7 135 J4
RAIN RM13 93 J5
Elmer Rd CAT SE6 165 F2
Elmer's Dr TEDD TW11 174 C2
Elmers End Rd BECK BR3 181 K6
Elmerside Rd BECK BR3 198 B1
Elmers Rd SNWD SE25 197 H4
Elmfield Av CEND/HSY/T N8 66 E2
MTCM CR4 179 F4
TEDD TW11 174 A1
Elmfield Cl HRW HA1 60 E6
Elmfield Pk BMLY BR1 183 K6
Elmfield Rd BMLY BR1 183 K6
CHING E4 38 A4
EFNCH N2 47 H6
NWDGN UB2 114 D3
TOOT SW17 161 G4
WALTH E17 69 F3
Elmfield Wy MV/WKIL W9 100 E4
SAND/SEL CR2 212 B6
Elm Friars Wk CAMTN NW1 84 D5
Elm Gdns EFNCH N2 47 G6
ENC/FH EN2 23 K1
ESH/CLAY KT10 205 F4
MTCM CR4 195 J1
Elmgate Av FELT TW13 154 A5
Elmgate Gdns EDGW HA8 44 E1
Elm Gn ACT W3 99 G5
Elmgreen Cl SRTFD E15 88 C6
Elm Gv CEND/HSY/T N8 66 E3
CRICK NW2 82 B2
ERITH DA8 150 A1
KUTN/CMB KT2 175 F4
ORP BR6 202 A5
PECK SE15 143 H3
RYLN/HDSTN HA2 60 A4
SUT SM1 209 F2
WIM/MER SW19 177 H3
Elmgrove Crs HRW HA1 61 F2
Elmgrove Gdns HRW HA1 61 G2
Elm Grove Pde CAR SM5 * 210 A1
Elm Grove Rd BARN SW13 138 D3
Elmgrove Rd CROY/NA CR0 197 J5
Elm Grove Rd EA W5 117 F2
Elmgrove Rd HRW HA1 61 F2
Elm Hall Gdns WAN E11 71 F3
Elm Hatch PIN HA5 41 K3
Elmhurst BELV DA17 129 F6
Elmhurst Av EFNCH N2 * 47 H6
MTCM CR4 179 F3
Elmhurst Crs EFNCH N2 65 H1
Elmhurst Dr SWFD E18 52 E5
Elmhurst Rd ELTH/MOT SE9 166 D4
FSTGT E7 89 F5
TOTM N17 50 A5
Elmhurst St CLAP SW4 141 J4
Elmhurst Wy LOU IG10 39 K2
Elmington Cl BXLY DA5 169 J2
Elmington Est CMBW SE5 142 E1
Elmington Rd CMBW SE5 142 E2
Elmira St LEW SE13 144 E4
Elm La CAT SE6 164 C4
Elmlee Cl CHST BR7 184 E2
Elmley St WOOL/PLUM SE18 127 J4
Elmore Cl ALP/SUD HA0 98 A1
Elmore Rd PEND EN3 25 F2
WAN E11 88 A1
Elmore St IS N1 85 K5
Elm Pde SCUP DA14 * 168 B6
Elm Pk BRXS/STRHM SW2 162 A1
STAN HA7 43 H1
Elm Park Av HCH RM12 93 K2
SEVS/STOTM N15 68 B2
Elm Park Gdns HDN NW4 64 B2
WBPTN SW10 120 C5
Elm Park La CHEL SW3 120 C5
Elm Park Rd CHEL SW3 120 C6
FNCH N3 46 D3
LEY E10 69 G6
PIN HA5 41 H6
SNWD SE25 181 G6
WCHMH N21 35 J2
Elm Pl SKENS SW7 120 C5
Elm Rd BAR EN5 20 D5
BECK BR3 182 C5
CHSGTN KT9 206 A2
DART DA1 171 G3
EBED/NFELT TW14 153 G3
ERITH DA8 150 D2
ESH/CLAY KT10 205 F4
EW KT17 207 H4
FSTGT E7 88 D4
KUTN/CMB KT2 175 G4
MORT/ESHN SW14 137 K4
NWMAL KT3 176 A6
ORP BR6 217 G5
ROMW/RG RM7 56 D5
SCUP DA14 168 B6
THHTH CR7 196 D1
WALTH E17 70 A2
WAN E11 70 B6
WBLY HA9 80 A3
WDGN N22 49 H4
WLGTN SM6 195 F5
Elm Rd West CHEAM SM3 193 J4
Elm Rw HAMP NW3 83 G1
Elms Av HDN NW4 64 A2
MUSWH N10 48 B6
Elmscott Gdns WCHMH N21 35 J1
Elmscott Rd BMLY BR1 183 J1
Elms Ct ALP/SUD HA0 79 F2
Elms Crs CLAP SW4 161 H1
Elmsdale Rd WALTH E17 69 H1
Elms Gdns ALP/SUD HA0 79 G2
DAGW RM9 92 B2
Elmshaw Rd PUT/ROE SW15 138 D6
Elmshurst Crs EFNCH N2 65 G1
Elmside CROY/NA CR0 213 K4
Elmside Rd WBLY HA9 80 C1
Elms La ALP/SUD HA0 79 G2
Elmsleigh Av
KTN/HRWW/WS HA3 61 H1
Elmsleigh Rd WHTN TW2 155 J4
Elmslie Cl WFD IG8 53 K2
Elms Ms BAY/PAD W2 8 A5
Elms Park Av ALP/SUD HA0 79 G2
Elms Rd CLAP SW4 141 H6
KTN/HRWW/WS HA3 42 E3
Elmstead Av CHST BR7 184 E1
WBLY HA9 62 A5
Elmstead Cl HOR/WEW KT19 207 G3
TRDG/WHET N20 32 E4
Elmstead Gdns WPK KT4 207 J1
Elmstead Gld CHST BR7 184 E2
Elmstead La CHST BR7 184 D3
Elmstead Rd ERITH DA8 150 B2
GDMY/SEVK IG3 72 E6
Elmsted Crs WELL DA16 128 D6
The Elms BARN SW13 138 C4
ESH/CLAY KT10 * 205 F5
NFNCH/WDSPK N12 * 47 J1
TOOT SW17 * 161 F5
WLGTN SM6 * 210 C2
Elmstone Rd FUL/PGN SW6 139 K2
Elmstone Ter
STMC/STPC BR5 * 202 D1
Elm St FSBYW WC1X 5 H7
Elmsworth Av HSLW TW3 135 G3
Elm Ter CRICK NW2 82 E1
ELTH/MOT SE9 167 F1
KTN/HRWW/WS HA3 42 D3
Elmton Wy CLPT E5 86 C1
Elm Tree Av ESH/CLAY KT10 189 J4
Elm Tree Cl NTHLT UB5 95 K2
STJWD NW8 2 A4
Elm Tree Ct CHARL SE7 * 126 B6
Elm Tree Rd STJWD NW8 2 A5
Elmtree Rd TEDD TW11 173 K1
Elm Vis HNWL W7 * 96 E6
Elm Wk GPK RM2 57 J6
HAMP NW3 64 E6
ORP BR6 215 K1
RYNPK SW20 193 F1
Elm Wy FBAR/BDGN N11 48 A2
HOR/WEW KT19 207 F3
WLSDN NW10 81 G2
WPK KT4 208 A1
Elmwood CHIG IG7 54 D2
Elmwood Av FELT TW13 154 A5
KTN/HRWW/WS HA3 61 G2
PLMGR N13 48 E1
Elmwood Cl EW KT17 207 J5
WLGTN SM6 195 G6
Elmwood Crs CDALE/KGS NW9 62 E1
Elmwood Dr BXLY DA5 169 F2
EW KT17 207 J5
Elmwood Gdns HNWL W7 96 E5
Elmwood Rd CHSWK W4 117 K6
CROY/NA CR0 196 C4
HNHL SE24 142 E6
MTCM CR4 178 E6
Elmworth Gv DUL SE21 162 E4
Elnathan Ms MV/WKIL W9 101 F3
Elphinstone Rd WALTH E17 51 H5
Elphinstone St HBRY N5 85 H2
Elrick Cl ERITH DA8 130 B6
Elrington Rd HACK E8 86 C4
WFD IG8 52 E1
Elruge Cl WDR/YW UB7 112 A3
Elsa Cottages POP/IOD E14 * 105 G4
Elsa Rd WELL DA16 148 D3
Elsa St WCHPL E1 * 105 G4
Elsdale St HOM E9 86 E4
Elsden Ms BETH E2 * 104 E1
Elsden Rd TOTM N17 50 B4
Elsenham Rd MNPK E12 89 K3
Elsenham St
WAND/EARL SW18 159 J3
Elsham Rd WAN E11 88 C2
WKENS W14 119 H2
Elsham Ter WKENS W14 * 119 H2
Elsiedene Rd WCHMH N21 35 J2
Elsie Lane Ct BAY/PAD W2 100 E4
Elsiemaud Rd BROCKY SE4 144 C6
Elsie Rd EDUL SE22 143 G5
Elsinore Av
STWL/WRAY TW19 * 152 B2
Elsinore Gdns CRICK NW2 * 82 C1
Elsinore Rd FSTH SE23 164 B3
Elsinore Wy RCH/KEW TW9 137 J4
Elsley Rd BTSEA SW11 140 E4
Elspeth Rd ALP/SUD HA0 80 A3
BTSEA SW11 140 E5
Elsrick Av MRDN SM4 193 K2
Elstan Wy CROY/NA CR0 198 B4
Elsted St WALW SE17 19 F7
Elstow Cl ELTH/MOT SE9 146 E6
RSLP HA4 59 H4
Elstow Gdns DAGW RM9 92 A6
Elstow Rd DAGW RM9 92 A6
Elstree Cl HCH RM12 93 K5
Elstree Gdns BELV DA17 129 F4
ED N9 36 D3
IL IG1 90 C3
Elstree Hl BMLY BR1 183 H3
Elstree Hl South BORE WD6 29 K2
Elstree Pk BORE WD6 * 31 F1
Elstree Rd BORE WD6 29 G1
BUSH WD23 28 D3
Elswick Rd LEW SE13 144 E4
Elswick St FUL/PGN SW6 140 B3
Elsworth Cl
EBED/NFELT TW14 153 H3
Elsworthy THDIT KT7 189 K3
Elsworthy Ri HAMP NW3 83 J5
Elsworthy Rd HAMP NW3 83 J6
Elsworthy Ter HAMP NW3 83 J5
Elsynge Rd WAND/EARL SW18 140 C6
Eltham Gn ELTH/MOT SE9 146 B6
Eltham Green Rd
ELTH/MOT SE9 146 B6
Eltham High St ELTH/MOT SE9 166 E1
Eltham Hl ELTH/MOT SE9 146 C6
Eltham Palace Rd
ELTH/MOT SE9 166 C1
Eltham Park Gdns
ELTH/MOT SE9 147 F5
Eltham Rd ELTH/MOT SE9 146 B6
Elthiron Rd FUL/PGN SW6 139 K2
Elthorne Av HNWL W7 116 A2
Elthorne Ct FELT TW13 154 B3
Elthorne Park Rd HNWL W7 116 A3
Elthorne Rd ARCH N19 66 D6
CDALE/KGS NW9 63 F4
Elthorne Wy CDALE/KGS NW9 63 F3
Elthruda Rd LEW SE13 165 G1
Eltisley Rd IL IG1 90 B2
Elton Av ALP/SUD HA0 79 H3
BAR EN5 20 D6
GFD/PVL UB6 79 F4
Elton Cl KUT/HW KT1 174 D3
Elton Pl STNW/STAM N16 86 A3
Elton Rd KUTN/CMB KT2 175 G4
Eltringham St
WAND/EARL SW18 140 B5
Elvaston Ms SKENS SW7 * 120 B3
Elvaston Pl SKENS SW7 120 B3
Elveden Pl WLSDN NW10 98 C1
Elveden Rd WLSDN NW10 98 C1
Elvedon Rd FELT TW13 153 J5
Elvendon Rd FBAR/BDGN N11 48 E2
Elver Gdns BETH E2 104 C2
Elverson Ms DEPT SE8 * 144 C1
Elverson Rd DEPT SE8 144 E3
Elverton St WEST SW1P 16 C6
Elvington Gn HAYES BR2 199 J2
Elvington La CDALE/KGS NW9 45 G4
Elvino Rd SYD SE26 182 A1
Elvis Rd CRICK NW2 82 A4
Elwill Wy BECK BR3 199 G1
Elwin St BETH E2 104 C2
Elwood St HBRY N5 85 H1
Elwyn Gdns LEE/GVPK SE12 165 K2
Ely Cl ERITH DA8 150 C3
NWMAL KT3 176 C5
Ely Cottages VX/NE SW8 * 142 A1
Ely Gdns DAGE RM10 92 E1
Elyne Rd FSBYPK N4 67 G3
Ely Pl HCIRC EC1N 11 K2
WFD IG8 54 A1
Ely Rd CROY/NA CR0 196 E2
HSLWW TW4 134 B4
HTHAIR TW6 133 J3
LEY E10 70 A3
Elysian Av STMC/STPC BR5 201 K3
Elysium Pl FUL/PGN SW6 139 J3
Elysium St FUL/PGN SW6 139 J3
Elystan Cl WLGTN SM6 210 C6
Elystan Pl CHEL SW3 120 D5
Elystan St CHEL SW3 14 C7
Elystan Wk IS N1 5 J1
Emanuel Av ACT W3 98 E5
Embankment PUT/ROE SW15 139 G4
Embankment Gdns CHEL SW3 120 E6
Embankment Pl CHCR WC2N 11 F7
The Embankment TWK TW1 156 B3
Embassy Ct SCUP DA14 168 C5
WLGTN SM6 * 210 B4
Emba St BERM/RHTH SE16 123 H2
Ember Cl STMC/STPC BR5 201 H4
Embercourt Rd THDIT KT7 189 K3
Ember Farm Av
E/WMO/HCT KT8 189 J3
Ember Farm Wy
E/WMO/HCT KT8 189 J2
Ember Gdns THDIT KT7 189 K4
Ember La ESH/CLAY KT10 189 J5
Emblem Ct EDUL SE22 143 H6
Embleton Rd LEW SE13 144 E5
OXHEY WD19 26 E5
Embry Cl STAN HA7 29 G6
Embry Dr STAN HA7 43 G2
Embry Wy STAN HA7 43 G1
Emden Cl WDR/YW UB7 112 D2
Emden St FUL/PGN SW6 140 A2
Emerald Cl CAN/RD E16 107 J5
Emerald Gdns BCTR RM8 74 C5
Emerald Sq NWDGN UB2 114 C3
Emerald St BMSBY WC1N 11 G1
Emerson Gdns
KTN/HRWW/WS HA3 62 B3
Emerson Rd IL IG1 72 A4
Emerson St STHWK SE1 12 C7
Emerton Cl BXLYHS DA6 149 F5
Emery Hill St WEST SW1P 16 B5
Emery St STHWK SE1 17 K4
Emes Rd ERITH DA8 149 K1
Emilia Cl PEND EN3 24 D6
Emily St CAN/RD E16 106 D5
Emlyn Rd SHB W12 118 B2
Emmanuel Rd BAL SW12 161 H3
NTHWD HA6 40 D3
Emma Rd PLSTW E13 106 D1
Emma St BETH E2 104 D1
Emma Ter RYNPK SW20 * 177 F3
Emmaus Wy CHIG IG7 54 A1
Emmott Av BARK/HLT IG6 72 C2
Emmott Cl GLDGN NW11 65 G3
WCHPL E1 105 G3
Emperor's Ga SKENS SW7 120 A3
Empire Av UED N18 49 J2
Empire Pde UED N18 * 49 K2
WBLY HA9 * 80 C1
Empire Rd GFD/PVL UB6 79 J6
Empire Sq STHWK SE1 18 E3
Empire Wy WBLY HA9 80 B2
Empire Wharf Rd
POP/IOD E14 125 G4
Empress Av CHING E4 51 K3
IL IG1 72 A6
MNPK E12 71 G6
WFD IG8 52 D3
Empress Dr CHST BR7 185 G2
Empress Pde CHING E4 * 51 J3
Empress Pl FUL/PGN SW6 119 K5
Empress St WALW SE17 122 D6
Empson St BOW E3 105 K3
Emsworth Cl ED N9 36 E3
Emsworth Rd BARK/HLT IG6 54 B5
Emsworth St
BRXS/STRHM SW2 162 A4
Emu Rd VX/NE SW8 141 G3
Ena Rd STRHM/NOR SW16 179 K6
Enbrook St NKENS W10 100 C2
Enclave Ct FSBYE EC1V 6 B6
Endale Cl CAR SM5 194 E6
Endeavour Wy BARK IG11 109 G1
CROY/NA CR0 195 K4
WIM/MER SW19 160 A6
Endell St LSQ/SEVD WC2H 10 E3
Enderby St GNWCH SE10 125 H5
Enderley Rd
KTN/HRWW/WS HA3 42 D4
Endersby Rd BAR EN5 20 A6
Endersleigh Gdns HDN NW4 63 J1
Endlebury Rd CHING E4 38 A4
Endlesham Rd BAL SW12 161 F2
Endsleigh Gdns IL IG1 71 K5
STPAN WC1H 4 C6
SURB KT6 190 D3
Endsleigh Pl STPAN WC1H 4 D6
Endsleigh Rd NWDGN UB2 114 E4
WEA W13 97 G6
Endsleigh St STPAN WC1H 4 D6
Endway BRYLDS KT5 191 H4
Endwell Rd BROCKY SE4 144 B3
Endymion Rd
BRXS/STRHM SW2 162 A2
FSBYPK N4 67 H4
Energen Cl WLSDN NW10 81 G4
Enfield Rd ACT W3 117 J2
BTFD TW8 116 E5
ENC/FH EN2 22 E4
HTHAIR TW6 133 H3
IS N1 86 A5
Enford St CAMTN NW1 8 E1
Engadine Cl CROY/NA CR0 212 B1
Engadine St
WAND/EARL SW18 159 J3
Engate St LEW SE13 145 F5
Engel Pk MLHL NW7 46 A2
Engineer Cl WOOL/PLUM SE18 127 F6
Engineers Wy WBLY HA9 80 C2
England's La HAMP NW3 83 K4
England Wy NWMAL KT3 191 J1
Englefield Cl CROY/NA CR0 196 D3
ENC/FH EN2 23 G3
STMC/STPC BR5 202 A1
Englefield Crs STMC/STPC BR5 202 B2
Englefield Pth
STMC/STPC BR5 202 B1
Englefield Rd IS N1 85 K5
Engleheart Dr
EBED/NFELT TW14 153 J1
Engleheart Rd CAT SE6 164 E2
Englewood Rd BAL SW12 161 G1
English St BOW E3 105 H3
Enid St BERM/RHTH SE16 19 K4
Enmore Av SNWD SE25 197 H2
Enmore Gdns
MORT/ESHN SW14 138 A6
Enmore Rd PUT/ROE SW15 139 F5
SNWD SE25 197 H2
STHL UB1 96 A3
Ennerdale Av HCH RM12 93 J3
STAN HA7 43 J6
Ennerdale Cl
EBED/NFELT TW14 153 J3
SUT SM1 208 D2
Ennerdale Dr CDALE/KGS NW9 63 G2
Ennerdale Gdns WBLY HA9 61 J5
Ennerdale Rd BXLYHN DA7 149 H2
RCH/KEW TW9 137 G3
Ennersdale Rd LEW SE13 145 G6
Ennismore Av CHSWK W4 118 B4
GFD/PVL UB6 78 E4
Ennismore Gdns SKENS SW7 14 C4
THDIT KT7 189 K3
Ennismore Gardens Ms
SKENS SW7 14 C4
Ennismore Ms SKENS SW7 14 C4
Ennismore St SKENS SW7 14 C4
Ennis Rd FSBYPK N4 67 G5
WOOL/PLUM SE18 127 J6
Ensign Cl STWL/WRAY TW19 152 A3
Ensign Dr PLMGR N13 35 J5
Ensign St WCHPL E1 104 C6
Ensign Wy STWL/WRAY TW19 152 A3
WLGTN SM6 210 E5
Enslin Rd ELTH/MOT SE9 167 F1
Ensor Ms SKENS SW7 120 C5
Enstone Rd PEND EN3 25 G4
Enterprise Cl CROY/NA CR0 196 B6
Enterprise Rw
SEVS/STOTM N15 68 B2
Enterprise Wy TEDD TW11 174 A1
WAND/EARL SW18 139 K5
WLSDN NW10 99 H2
Enterprize Wy DEPT SE8 * 124 C4
Epcot Ms WLSDN NW10 * 100 B2
Epirus Ms FUL/PGN SW6 139 K1
Epirus Rd FUL/PGN SW6 139 K1
Epping Cl POP/IOD E14 124 D4
ROMW/RG RM7 56 D6
Epping Gld CHING E4 38 A1
Epping New Rd BKHH IG9 39 F2
Epping Pl IS N1 85 G4
Epping Wy CHING E4 37 K1
Epple Rd FUL/PGN SW6 139 J2
Epsom Cl BXLYHN DA7 149 J4
NTHLT UB5 77 K3
Epsom Rd CROY/NA CR0 211 G2
GDMY/SEVK IG3 73 F3
LEY E10 70 A3
MRDN SM4 193 J3
Epstein Rd THMD SE28 128 C1
Epworth Rd ISLW TW7 136 C2
Epworth St SDTCH EC2A 7 F7
Equity Sq BETH E2 7 K5
Erasmus St WEST SW1P 16 D7
Erconwald St SHB W12 99 H5
Erebus Dr THMD SE28 127 H3
Eresby Dr BECK BR3 198 D5
Eresby Pl KIL/WHAMP NW6 82 E5
Erica Gdns CROY/NA CR0 213 K2
Erica St SHB W12 99 J6
Eric Clarke La BARK IG11 108 C2
Ericcson Cl WAND/EARL SW18 139 K6
Eric Est BOW E3 105 H3

Eric Rd CHDH RM6...73 K4
FSTGT E7...88 E2
WLSDN NW10...81 H4
Eric St BOW E3...105 H3
Eridge Green Cl
STMC/STPC BR5...202 D5
Eridge Rd CHSWK W4...118 A3
Erin Cl BMLY BR1...183 H5
Erindale WOOL/PLUM SE18...127 J6
Erindale Ter WOOL/PLUM SE18..127 J6
Erin Ms WDGN N22...49 H4
Erith Cl PUR RM19...131 K4
Erith Crs CRW RM5...56 E4
Erith High St ERITH DA8...130 C6
Erith Rd BELV DA17...129 J5
RYNPK SW20...
Erlanger Rd NWCR SE14...144 A2
Erlesmere Gdns HNWL W7...116 B3
Erlich Cottages WCHPL E1 *...104 E4
Ermine Rd LEW SE13...144 E5
SEVS/STOTM N15...68 B2
Ermine Side EN EN1...24 C6
Ermington Rd ELTH/MOT SE9..167 H4
Ernald Av EHAM E6...107 J1
Erncroft Wy TWK TW1...156 A1
Ernest Av WNWD SE27...162 C6
Ernest Cl BECK BR3...198 C2
Ernest Gdns CHSWK W4...117 J6
Ernest Gv BECK BR3...198 C2
Ernest Rd KUT/HW KT1...175 J5
Ernest St WCHPL E1...105 F3
Ernle Rd RYNPK SW20...176 E3
Ernshaw Pl PUT/ROE SW15...139 H6
Erpingham Rd PUT/ROE SW15..139 F4
Erridge Rd WIM/MER SW19...177 K5
Errington Rd MV/WKIL W9...100 D3
Errol Gdns NWMAL KT3...192 D1
YEAD UB4...95 F3
Errol St ROM RM1...75 H1
Errol St STLK EC1Y...6 E5
Escreet Gv WOOL/PLUM SE18..127 F4
Esher Av CHEAM SM3...208 B1
ROMW/RG RM7...74 E3
WOT/HER KT12...188 A5
Esher Cl BXLY DA5...169 F3
Esher Crs HTHAIR TW6...133 J3
Esher Gn ESH/CLAY KT10...204 B2
Esher Green Dr
ESH/CLAY KT10...204 A1
Esher Ms ESH/CLAY KT10...204 A4
Esher Park Av ESH/CLAY KT10..204 D3
Esher Place Av ESH/CLAY KT10.204 A3
Esher Rd E/WMO/HCT KT8....189 J2
GDMY/SEVK IG3...90 E1
Eskdale Av NTHLT UB5...77 K6
Eskdale Cl WBLY HA9...61 K6
Eskdale Rd BXLYHN DA7...149 H3
Eskmont Rdg NRWD SE19...181 F3
Esk Rd PLSTW E13...107 F3
Esk Wy ROM RM1...57 G3
Esmar Crs CDALE/KGS NW9...63 J3
Esmeralda Rd STHWK SE1...123 H4
Esmond Cl RAIN RM13 *...111 K2
Esmond Gdns CHSWK W4 *...118 A4
Esmond Rd CHSWK W4...118 A3
KIL/WHAMP NW6...82 D6
Esmond St PUT/ROE SW15...139 H5
Esparto St WAND/EARL SW18..160 A2
Essenden Rd BELV DA17...129 H5
SAND/SEL CR2...212 A5
Essendine Rd MV/WKIL W9...100 E2
Essex Av ISLW TW7...135 K4
ROMW/RG RM7...74 D1
RSLP HA4...45 G7
WALTH E17...69 G1
Essex Ct BARN SW13...138 C3
EMB EC4Y *...11 J4
Essex Gdns FSBYPK N4...67 H3
Essex Pk FNCH N3...46 E1
Essex Park Ms ACT W3...118 B1
Essex Pl CHSWK W4...117 K4
Essex Place Sq CHSWK W4 *..118 A4
Essex Rd ACT W3...98 E6
BARK IG11...90 D5
CHDH RM6...73 J5
CHING E4...38 C3
CHSWK W4...118 A4
DAGE RM10...92 E3
DART DA1 *...171 G1
ENC/FH EN2...23 K5
IS N1...85 J5
LEY E10...70 A3
MNPK E12...89 J3
ROMW/RG RM7...74 D1
SWFD E18...53 F5
WALTH E17...69 G3
Essex Rd South WAN E11...70 B4
Essex St FSTGT E7...88 E3
TPL/STR WC2R...11 J4
Essex Vls KENS W8...119 K2
Essex Whf CLPT E5 *...69 F6
Essian St WCHPL E1...105 G4
Essoldo Wy EDGW HA8...44 B6
Estate Wy LEY E10...69 H5
Estcourt Rd FUL/PGN SW6...139 J1
SNWD SE25...197 J3
Estella Av NWMAL KT3...192 E1
Estelle Rd HAMP NW3...83 K2
Esterbrooke St WEST SW1P...16 C7
Este Rd BTSEA SW11...140 D4
Esther Cl WCHMH N21...35 G2
Esther Rd WAN E11...70 C4

Estoria Cl BRXS/STRHM SW2..162 B2
Estreham Rd
STRHM/NOR SW16...179 J2
Estridge Cl HSLW TW3...135 F5
Estuary Cl BARK IG11...109 H2
Eswyn Rd TOOT SW17...160 E6
Etchingham Park Rd FNCH N3..47 G4
Etchingham Rd SRTFD E15...88 A2
Eternit Wk FUL/PGN SW6...139 F2
Etfield Gv SCUP DA14...186 C1
Ethelbert Cl BMLY BR1...183 K5
Ethelbert Gdns REDBR IG4...71 J1
Ethelbert Rd BMLY BR1...183 K6
ERITH DA8...149 K1
RDART DA2...171 H6
RYNPK SW20...177 G4
STMC/STPC BR5...186 E6
Ethelbert St BAL SW12...161 G3
Ethelburga St BTSEA SW11...140 D2
Etheldene Av MUSWH N10...66 C1
Ethelden Rd SHB W12...118 E1
Etheldred Est LBTH SE11...17 J7
Ethel Rd CAN/RD E16...107 F6
Ethel St WALW SE17 *...18 D7
Ethel Ter ORP BR6...217 J3
Etheridge Rd CRICK NW2...64 A4
Etherley Rd SEVS/STOTM N15..67 J2
Etherow St EDUL SE22...163 H2
Etherstone Rd
STRHM/NOR SW16...162 B6
Ethnard Rd PECK SE15...123 J6
Ethronvi Rd BXLYHN DA7...149 F4
Etloe Rd LEY E10...69 J6
Eton Av ALP/SUD HA0...79 K2
EBAR EN4...33 J1
HAMP NW3...83 J5
HEST TW5...114 E6
NFNCH/WDSPK N12...47 G3
NWMAL KT3...192 A2
Eton Cl WAND/EARL SW18...160 A2
Eton College Rd HAMP NW3...83 K4
Eton Garages HAMP NW3 *...83 J4
Eton Gv CDALE/KGS NW9...44 C6
LEW SE13...145 H4
Eton Pl HAMP NW3 *...84 A5
Eton Ri HAMP NW3 *...83 K4
Eton Rd HAMP NW3...83 K5
HYS/HAR UB3...133 J1
IL IG1...90 C2
ORP BR6...217 H2
Eton St RCH/KEW TW9...136 E6
Eton Vs HAMP NW3...83 K4
Etta St DEPT SE8...124 B6
Etton Rd HSLW TW3...135 H6
Ettrick St POP/IOD E14...106 A5
Etwell Pl BRYLDS KT5...191 G3
Euesdon Cl ED N9...36 D5
Eugenia Rd BERM/RHTH SE16..123 K5
Eureka Rd KUT/HW KT1 *...175 H5
Europa Pl FSBYE EC1V...6 C5
Europe Rd WOOL/PLUM SE18..126 E3
Eustace Pl WOOL/PLUM SE18..126 E4
Eustace Rd CHDH RM6...73 K4
EHAM E6...107 J2
FUL/PGN SW6...139 K1
Euston Centre CAMTN NW1 *...4 A6
Euston Rd CAMTN NW1...4 A6
CROY/NA CRO...196 B5
Euston Sq CAMTN NW1...4 C5
Euston St CAMTN NW1...4 C6
Evandale Rd BRXN/ST SW9...142 C3
Evangelist Rd KTTN NW5...84 B2
Evans Cl HACK E8...86 B4
Evansdale RAIN RM13...111 H2
Evans Gv FELT TW13...155 F4
Evans Rd CAT SE6...165 H4
Evanston Av CHING E4...52 A3
Evanston Gdns REDBR IG4...71 J3
Eva Rd CHDH RM6...73 J4
RYNPK SW20...181 K3
PGE/AN SE20...
Eveline Lowe Est
BERM/RHTH SE16...123 H3
Eveline Rd MTCM CR4...178 E4
Evelyn Av CDALE/KGS NW9...63 F1
RSLP HA4...58 E3
Evelyn Ct WHTN TW2...155 G2
Evelyn Denington Rd
EHAM E6...107 J3
Evelyn Dr PIN HA5...41 H3
Evelyn Est DEPT SE8...124 B6
Evelyn Gdns RCH/KEW TW9...137 F4
Evelyn Gv EA W5...117 G1
STHL UB1...95 K5
Evelyn Rd CAN/RD E16...125 K1
EBAR EN4...21 K5
RCH/KEW TW9...137 F4
RCHPK/HAM TW10...156 D5
WALTH E17...70 A1
WIM/MER SW19...178 A1
Evelyn St DEPT SE8...124 B4
GNWCH SE10...125 G6
Evelyn Ter RCH/KEW TW9...137 F4
Evelyn Wk IS N1...6 E3
Evelyn Wy WLGTN SM6...210 D2
Evensyde WATW WD18...26 A1
Evenwood Cl PUT/ROE SW15 *.139 H6
Everard Av HAYES BR2...199 K5
Everard Wy WBLY HA9...61 K3
Everatt Cl WAND/EARL SW18 *.159 J1
Everdon Rd BARN SW13...118 D6
Everest Pl POP/IOD E14...106 A4
Everest Rd ELTH/MOT SE9...166 E6
STWL/WRAY TW19...152 B6
Everett Cl BUSH WD23...28 E3
PIN HA5...
Everett Cl PECK SE15...
The Everglades HSLW TW3 *..135 H4
Everglade Strd
CDALE/KGS NW9...45 H4
Evergreen Cl PGE/AN SE20...181 K3
Evergreen Ct
STWL/WRAY TW19 *...152 A2
Evergreen Sq HACK E8...86 B5
Evergreen Wy HYS/HAR UB3...94 D6
STWL/WRAY TW19...152 A2

Everilda St IS N1...5 H1
Evering Rd STNW/STAM N16....86 C1
Everington Rd MUSWH N10....47 K5
Everington St HMSMTH W6...119 G6
Everitt Rd WLSDN NW10...99 F2
Everleigh St FSBYPK N4...67 F5
Eve Rd ISLW TW7...136 B5
SRTFD E15...106 C1
TOTM N17...50 A6
WAN E11...88 C2
Eversfield Gdns EDGW HA8...44 C3
Eversfield Rd RCH/KEW TW9..137 G3
Evershed Wk CHSWK W4...117 K3
Eversholt St CAMTN NW1...4 B3
Evershot Rd FSBYPK N4...67 F5
Eversleigh Rd BAR EN5...21 G6
BTSEA SW11...140 E4
EHAM E6...89 H6
FNCH N3...46 D3
Eversley Av BXLYHN DA7...150 B3
WBLY HA9...62 C6
Eversley Cl WCHMH N21...35 F1
Eversley Crs ISLW TW7...135 J2
RSLP HA4...58 C6
WCHMH N21...35 F1
Eversley Cross BXLYHN DA7..150 B3
Eversley Mt WCHMH N21...35 F1
Eversley Park Rd WCHMH N21..35 F1
Eversley Pk WCHMH N21...35 F1
Eversley Rd BRYLDS KT5...191 G5
CHARL SE7...126 A6
NRWD SE19...180 D3
Eversley Wy CROY/NA CRO....213 J2
Everthorpe Rd PECK SE15...143 G4
Everton Buildings CAMTN NW1..4 A5
Everton Dr STAN HA7...44 B6
Everton Rd CROY/NA CRO...197 H5
Evesham Av WALTH E17...51 J5
Evesham Cl BELMT SM2...208 E5
GFD/PVL UB6...96 B1
Evesham Gn MRDN SM4...194 A3
Evesham Rd FBAR/BDGN N11..48 C1
MRDN SM4...194 A3
SRTFD E15...88 D5
Evesham St NTGHL W11...100 B6
Evesham Ter SURB KT6 *...190 D3
Evesham Wk BRXN/ST SW9...142 B3
CMBW SE5...142 E3
Evesham Wy BTSEA SW11...141 F4
CLAY IG5...54 A6
Evry Rd SCUP DA14...186 D2
Ewald Rd FUL/PGN SW6...139 J3
Ewanrigg Ter WFD IG8...53 G1
Ewart Gv WDGN N22...49 G4
Ewart Pl BOW E3 *...105 H1
Ewart Rd FSTH SE23...164 A2
Ewe Cl HOLWY N7...84 E4
Ewell By-Pass EW KT17...207 J5
Ewell Court Av
HOR/WEW KT19...207 G3
Ewellhurst Rd CLAY IG5...53 J5
Ewell Park Gdns EW KT17...207 K5
Ewell Park Wy EW KT17...207 K4
Ewell Rd CHEAM SM3...208 B2
SURB KT6...190 C4
SURB KT6...191 G3
Ewen Crs BRXS/STRHM SW2..162 B2
Ewer St STHWK SE1...
Ewhurst Av SAND/SEL CR2...212 B6
Ewhurst Cl BELMT SM2...208 A6
WCHPL E1...104 E4
Ewhurst Rd BROCKY SE4...164 C1
Exbury Rd CAT SE6...164 D4
Excel Ct LGSVD WC2E *...
Excel Marina CAN/RD E16...106 E6
Excelsior Cl KUT/HW KT1...175 H5
Excel Waterfront
CAN/RD E16...107 F6
Exchange Ar LVPST EC2M...13 G2
Exchange Ct COVGDN WC2E *..11 F6
Exchange Sq SDTCH EC2A *...13 G1
Exchange St ROM RM1...75 G2
Exchange Wk PIN HA5...59 J4
Exeforde Av ASHF TW15...152 D6
Exeter Cl EHAM E6...107 K5
Exeter Gdns IL IG1...71 J5
Exeter Ms FUL/PGN SW6...139 K1
Exeter Pde CRICK NW2 *...82 C4
Exeter Rd CAN/RD E16...106 E4
CRICK NW2...82 C3
CROY/NA CRO...197 F4
DAGE RM10...92 D4
ED N9...36 E4
FELT TW13...154 E5
HTHAIR TW6...133 H4
PEND EN3...25 F1
RYLN/HDSTN HA2...59 J6
STHGT/OAK N14...34 A4
WALTH E17...69 J2
WELL DA16...148 A3
Exeter St COVGDN WC2E...11 G5
Exeter Wy HTHAIR TW6...133 H3
NWCR SE14...144 C1
Exford Gdns LEE/GVPK SE12..166 A3
Exford Rd LEE/GVPK SE12...166 A4
Exhibition Grounds
WBLY HA9 *...80 D2
Exhibition Rd SKENS SW7...14 B5
Exit Rd EFNCH N2...47 H5
Exmoor Cl BARK/HLT IG6...54 C4
Exmoor St NKENS W10...100 B4
Exmouth Market CLKNW EC1R..5 K6
Exmouth Ms CAMTN NW1...4 B5
Exmouth Pl HACK E8...86 D5
Exmouth Rd RSLP HA4...77 G1
WALTH E17...69 H2
WELL DA16...148 D2
YEAD UB4...94 C2
Exmouth St WCHPL E1...104 E5
Exning Rd CAN/RD E16...106 D3
Exon St WALW SE17...19 G7
Explorer Av STWL/WRAY TW19.152 B3
Explorer Dr WATW WD18...26 D1
Express Dr GDMY/SEVK IG3...73 H5
Exton Gdns BCTR RM8...91 J3
Exton Rd WLSDN NW10...80 E5

Exton St STHWK SE1...17 J1
Eyhurst Av HCH RM12...93 J1
Eyhurst Cl CRICK NW2...63 K6
Eylewood Rd WNWD SE27...180 D1
Eynella Rd DUL SE21...163 G2
Eynham Rd SHB W12...100 A5
Eynsford Cl STMC/STPC BR5..201 H4
Eynsford Crs SCUP DA14...168 D3
Eynsford Rd GDMY/SEVK IG3..72 E6
Eynsham Dr ABYW SE2...128 C3
Eynswood Dr SCUP DA14...186 C2
Eyot Gdns HMSMTH W6...118 C5
Eyre Cl GPK RM2...75 K1
Eyre Street HI CLKNW EC1R...5 J7
Eythorne Rd BRXN/ST SW9...142 B2
Ezra St BETH E2...7 K4

F

Faber Gdns HDN NW4...63 J2
Fabian Rd FUL/PGN SW6...139 J1
Fabian St EHAM E6...107 K3
The Facade FSTH SE23 *...163 K4
Factory La CROY/NA CRO...196 B6
TOTM N17...50 B5
Factory Pl POP/IOD E14...125 F5
Factory Rd CAN/RD E16...126 C1
Factory Yd HNWL W7 *...115 K1
Faesten Wy BXLY DA5...170 B5
Fagg's Rd EBED/NFELT TW14..133 K6
Fairacre ISLW TW7 *...136 B6
NWMAL KT3...176 B1
Fairacres CROY/NA CRO...213 H6
PUT/ROE SW15...138 C5
Fairbairn Gn BRXN/ST SW9...142 C2
Fairbank Av ORP BR6...216 C1
Fairbank Est IS N1 *...6 E3
Fairbanks Rd TOTM N17...50 B6
Fairbourne Rd TOTM N17...50 A6
Fairbridge Rd ARCH N19...66 D6
Fairbrook Cl PLMGR N13...49 G1
Fairby Rd LEE/GVPK SE12...146 B5
Fairchild Cl BTSEA SW11 *...140 C3
Fairchild Pl SDTCH EC2A *...7 H7
Fairchild St SDTCH EC2A...7 H7
Fair Cl BUSH WD23...28 B2
Fairclough St WCHPL E1...104 C5
Faircross Av BARK IG11...90 C5
CRW RM5...57 F3
Fairdale Gdns HYS/HAR UB3..113 K2
PUT/ROE SW15...138 E5
Fairey Av HYS/HAR UB3...113 H3
Fairfax Av EW KT17...207 K6
Fairfax Cl WOT/HER KT12...188 A5
Fairfax Gdns BKHTH/KID SE3..146 B2
Fairfax Ms CAN/RD E16...126 A1
CEND/HSY/T N8 *...67 H1
PUT/ROE SW15...139 F5
Fairfax Pl KIL/WHAMP NW6...83 G5
WKENS W14...119 H3
Fairfax Rd CEND/HSY/T N8...67 G1
CHSWK W4...118 B3
KIL/WHAMP NW6...83 G5
TEDD TW11...174 B3
Fairfield Av EDGW HA8...44 D2
HDN NW4...63 K3
OXHEY WD19...27 G5
RSLP HA4...58 A4
WHTN TW2...155 G3
Fairfield Cl BFN/LL DA15...168 A1
HCH RM12...75 J5
HOR/WEW KT19...207 G3
MTCM CR4...178 D3
NFNCH/WDSPK N12...33 G6
Fairfield Cnr KUT/HW KT1 *...175 G5
Fairfield Ct RSLP HA4 *...58 B5
Fairfield Dr GFD/PVL UB6...79 K6
RYLN/HDSTN HA2...42 C6
WAND/EARL SW18...140 A6
Fairfield East KUT/HW KT1...175 F5
Fairfield Gdns CEND/HSY/T N8.66 E2
Fairfield Gv CHARL SE7...126 C6
Fairfield North
KUT/HW KT1...175 F5
Fairfield Pth CROY/NA CRO....211 K1
Fairfield Pl KUT/HW KT1...175 F6
Fairfield Rd BECK BR3...182 D5
BMLY BR1...183 K3
BOW E3...105 J1
BXLYHN DA7...149 G3
CEND/HSY/T N8...66 E2
CROY/NA CRO...211 K1
IL IG1...90 B4
KUT/HW KT1...175 F5
STHL UB1...95 K4
STMC/STPC BR5...201 J1
UED N18...36 C6
WALTH E17...51 G4
WDR/YW UB7...112 B1
WFD IG8...53 F2

Fairhazel Gdns
KIL/WHAMP NW6...83 F4
Fairholme EBED/NFELT TW14..153 G2
Fairholme Av GPK RM2...75 J2
Fairholme Cl FNCH N3...64 C1
Fairholme Ct PIN HA5 *...42 A2
Fairholme Crs YEAD UB4...94 D3
Fairholme Gdns FNCH N3...46 C6
Fairholme Rd CROY/NA CRO...196 B4
HRW HA1...60 E2
IL IG1...72 A4
SUT SM1...208 D4
WKENS W14...119 H5
Fairholt Cl STNW/STAM N16 *...68 A5
Fairholt Rd SKENS SW7...14 D4
Fairholt St SKENS SW7...14 D4
Fairland Rd SRTFD E15...88 D4
Fairlands Av BKHH IG9...38 E4
SUT SM1...193 K6
THHTH CR7...196 A1
Fairlawn CHARL SE7...146 B1
Fairlawn Av BXLYHN DA7...148 E3
CHSWK W4...117 K4
EFNCH N2...65 J1
Fairlawn Cl ESH/CLAY KT10...205 F4
FELT TW13...154 E6
KUTN/CMB KT2...175 K2
STHGT/OAK N14...34 D1
Fairlawn Ct CHARL SE7 *...146 B1
Fairlawn Dr WFD IG8...52 E3
Fairlawn Gdns STHL UB1 *...95 K6
Fairlawn Gv CHSWK W4...117 K4
Fairlawn Pk SYD SE26...182 B1
Fairlawn Rd WIM/MER SW19...177 J3
Fairlawns PIN HA5...41 G5
TWK TW1...156 D1
Fairlea Pl EA W5...97 J4
Fairlie Gdns FSTH SE23...163 K2
Fairlight Av CHING E4...38 B4
WFD IG8...52 E2
WLSDN NW10...99 G1
Fairlight Cl CHING E4...38 B4
WPK KT4...208 A2
Fairlight Rd TOOT SW17...160 C6
Fairlop Cl HCH RM12...93 K4
Fairlop Gdns BARK/HLT IG6...54 C5
Fairlop Rd BARK/HLT IG6...54 C5
WAN E11...70 B4
Fairmead BMLY BR1...200 E1
BRYLDS KT5...191 J5
Fairmead Cl BMLY BR1...200 E1
HEST TW5...134 C1
NWMAL KT3...176 A6
Fairmead Crs EDGW HA8...30 E6
Fairmead Gdns REDBR IG4...71 J2
Fairmead Rd ARCH N19...84 E1
CROY/NA CRO...196 B4
Fairmile Av STRHM/NOR SW16.179 J1
Fairmont Cl BELV DA17 *...129 G5
Fairmount Rd
BRXS/STRHM SW2...162 A1
Fairoak Cl STMC/STPC BR5...201 G4
Fairoak Dr ELTH/MOT SE9...147 H5
Fairoak Gdns ROM RM1...57 G5
Fair Oak Pl BARK/HLT IG6...54 C5
Fairseat Cl BUSH WD23...28 E4
Fairstead Wk IS N1 *...85 J6
Fair St HSLW TW3...135 H4
STHWK SE1...19 J2
Fairthorn Rd CHARL SE7...125 K5
Fairview ERITH DA8...150 C1
Fairview Av ALP/SUD HA0...79 K4
Fairview Cl SYD SE26...182 B1
Fair View Cl WALTH E17...51 G4
Fairview Ct HDN NW4 *...46 B5
Fairview Crs RYLN/HDSTN HA2..60 A5
Fairview Dr CHIG IG7...54 E1
ORP BR6...216 D2
STWL/WRAY TW19...152 A1
Fairview Gdns WFD IG8...53 F4
Fairview Pl BRXS/STRHM SW2.162 A2
Fairview Rd ENC/FH EN2...23 G2
SEVS/STOTM N15...68 B2
STRHM/NOR SW16...179 K3
SUT SM1...209 H3
Fairview Vls CHING E4 *...51 J3
Fairview Wy EDGW HA8...30 C6
Fairwater Av WELL DA16...148 B5
Fairway BXLYHS DA6...149 F6
RYNPK SW20...193 F1
STMC/STPC BR5...201 J2
WFD IG8...53 G1
Fairway Cl CROY/NA CRO...198 B2
GLDGN NW11...65 G4
HOR/WEW KT19...206 E2
HSLWW TW4...134 C6
Fairway Ct MLHL NW7 *...31 F5
Fairway Dr GFD/PVL UB6...78 B5
THMD SE28...109 K5
Fairway Gdns BECK BR3...199 G3
IL IG1...90 C3
Fairways ISLW TW7...135 K1
STAN HA7...44 A5
TEDD TW11...174 E3
WALTH E17...70 A1
The Fairway ACT W3...99 G5
ALP/SUD HA0...61 H1
BAR EN5...33 F1
E/WMO/HCT KT8...173 G6
HAYES BR2...200 E3
HNWL W7...96 B5
MLHL NW7...31 F5
NTHLT UB5...78 C4
NTHWD HA6...26 C5
NWMAL KT3...176 A4
RSLP HA4...77 G2
STHGT/OAK N14...22 B6
Fairweather Cl
SEVS/STOTM N15...68 A1
Fairweather Rd
STNW/STAM N16...68 C3
Fairwyn Rd SYD SE26...164 B6
Faithfield BUSH WD23...27 J1
Fakenham Cl MLHL NW7...45 J3
NTHLT UB5...78 C4
Fakruddin St WCHPL E1...104 C3
Falaize Av IL IG1...90 B3

Falcon Av BMLY BR1 200 D1
Falconberg Ct
SOHO/SHAV W1D * 10 C3
Falcon Cl CHSWK W4 117 J6
DART DA1 151 J6
NTHWD HA6 40 C3
STHWK SE1 12 B7
Falcon Ct IS N1 6 B3
Falcon Crs PEND EN3 25 F6
Falcon Dr STWL/WRAY TW19 152 A1
Falconer Rd BARK/HLT IG6 55 J1
BUSH WD23 28 A1
Falcon Gv BTSEA SW11 140 D4
Falcon La BTSEA SW11 140 D4
Falcon Rd BTSEA SW11 140 D4
HPTN TW12 172 E3
PEND EN3 25 F6
Falcon St PLSTW E13 106 E3
Falcon Ter BTSEA SW11 * 140 D4
Falcon Wy CDALE/KGS NW9 45 G5
KTN/HRWW/WS HA3 62 A2
POP/IOD E14 124 E4
WAN E11 70 E1
Falconwood Av WELL DA16 147 J3
Falconwood Pde WELL DA16 147 K5
Falconwood Rd CROY/NA CR0 213 J6
Falcourt Cl SUT SM1 209 F3
Falkirk Gdns OXHEY WD19 41 H1
Falkirk St IS N1 7 H3
Falkland Av FBAR/BDGN N11 34 A6
FNCH N3 46 E3
Falkland Park Av SNWD SE25 181 F6
Falkland Pl KTTN NW5 84 C3
Falkland Rd BAR EN5 20 C3
CEND/HSY/T N8 67 H1
KTTN NW5 84 C3
Falloden Wy GLDGN NW11 64 E1
Fallow Cl CHIG IG7 55 F1
Fallow Ct BERM/RHTH SE16 * 123 H5
Fallow Court Av
NFNCH/WDSPK N12 47 G3
Fallowfield STAN HA7 29 G5
Fallowfield Ct STAN HA7 29 G5
Fallow Flds LOU IG10 39 H2
Fallowfields Dr
NFNCH/WDSPK N12 47 J2
Fallows Cl EFNCH N2 47 H5
Fallsbrook Rd
STRHM/NOR SW16 179 G2
Falman Cl ED N9 36 C3
Falmer Rd EN EN1 24 A5
SEVS/STOTM N15 67 J2
WALTH E17 51 K6
Falmouth Av CHING E4 52 B1
Falmouth Cl LEE/GVPK SE12 145 J6
WDGN N22 49 F3
Falmouth Gdns REDBR IG4 71 H1
Falmouth Rd STHWK SE1 18 D5
Falmouth St SRTFD E15 88 B3
Falstaff Cl DART DA1 170 B2
Falstaff Ms HPTN TW12 173 J1
Fambridge Cl SYD SE26 164 C6
Fambridge Rd BCTR RM8 74 C5
Fane St WKENS W14 119 J6
Fanns Ri PUR RM19 131 K4
Fann St FARR EC1M 6 C7
Fanshawe Av BARK IG11 90 C4
Fanshawe Crs DAGW RM9 92 A3
Fanshawe Rd
RCHPK/HAM TW10 156 D6
Fanshaw St IS N1 7 G4
Fantail Cl THMD SE28 109 J5
Fanthorpe St PUT/ROE SW15 139 F4
Faraday Av SCUP DA14 168 C4
Faraday Cl HOLWY N7 85 F4
WATW WD18 26 B1
Faraday Pl E/WMO/HCT KT8 189 F1
Faraday Rd ACT W3 98 E6
E/WMO/HCT KT8 189 F1
NKENS W10 100 C4
SRTFD E15 88 D4
STHL UB1 96 B6
WELL DA16 148 B4
WIM/MER SW19 178 A2
Faraday Wy STMC/STPC BR5 202 C1
WOOL/PLUM SE18 126 C3
Fareham Rd
EBED/NFELT TW14 154 B2
Fareham St SOHO/CST W1F * 10 C3
Farewell Pl MTCM CR4 178 C4
Faringdon Av HAYES BR2 201 G3
Faringford Rd SRTFD E15 88 C5
Farjeon Rd BKHTH/KID SE3 146 C2
Farleigh Av HAYES BR2 199 K4
Farleigh Court Rd
CROY/NA CR0 196 A6
Farleigh Pl STNW/STAM N16 86 B2
Farleigh Rd STNW/STAM N16 86 B2
Farley Dr GDMY/SEVK IG3 72 E5
Farley Pl SNWD SE25 197 H1
Farley Rd CAT SE6 165 F2
SAND/SEL CR2 212 D5
Farlington Pl PUT/ROE SW15 158 E2
Farlow Rd PUT/ROE SW15 139 G4
Farlton Rd WAND/EARL SW18 160 A2
Farman Ter
KTN/HRWW/WS HA3 * 61 K1
Farm Av ALP/SUD HA0 79 J4
CRICK NW2 82 C1
RYLN/HDSTN HA2 60 A4
STRHM/NOR SW16 161 K6
SWLY BR8 187 K6
Farmborough Cl HRW HA1 60 D4
Farm Cl BELMT SM2 209 H5
BKHH IG9 39 G5
DAGE RM10 92 E5
FUL/PGN SW6 * 139 K1
STHL UB1 96 B6
WWKM BR4 214 D1
Farmcote Rd LEE/GVPK SE12 165 K3
Farm Cottages
E/WMO/HCT KT8 * 190 B1
Farmdale Rd CAR SM5 209 J5
CHARL SE7 125 K5
Farm Dr CROY/NA CR0 198 C6
Farmer Rd LEY E10 69 K5
Farmers Rd CMBW SE5 142 C1
Farmer St KENS W8 * 119 K1
Farmfield Rd BMLY BR1 183 H1
Farmhouse Rd
STRHM/NOR SW16 179 H3
Farmilo Rd WALTH E17 69 J4
Farmington Av SUT SM1 209 H1
Farmlands ENC/FH EN2 23 G2
PIN HA5 58 E1
The Farmlands NTHLT UB5 77 K4
Farmland Wk CHST BR7 185 G1
Farm La CROY/NA CR0 198 C6
FUL/PGN SW6 119 K6
STHGT/OAK N14 34 B1
Farmleigh STHGT/OAK N14 34 C2
Farm Pl DART DA1 150 D5
KENS W8 119 K1
Farm Rd BELMT SM2 209 H5
EDGW HA8 44 E1
ESH/CLAY KT10 189 F5
HSLWW TW4 154 D3
MRDN SM4 194 A2
NTHWD HA6 40 A1
WCHMH N21 35 J3
WLSDN NW10 81 F6
Farmstead Rd CAT SE6 164 E6
KTN/HRWW/WS HA3 42 D4
Farm St MYFR/PICC W1J 9 J6
The Farm WIM/MER SW19 * 159 G2
Farm V BXLY DA5 169 J1
Farm Wk GLDGN NW11 64 D3
Farmway BCTR RM8 91 J2
Farm Wy BKHH IG9 39 G6
HCH RM12 93 K2
NTHWD HA6 26 C6
WPK KT4 208 A1
Farnaby Rd BMLY BR1 183 H4
ELTH/MOT SE9 146 B5
Farnan Av WALTH E17 51 J5
Farnan Rd STRHM/NOR SW16 179 K1
Farnborough Av
SAND/SEL CR2 213 G5
WALTH E17 * 51 G6
Farnborough Cl WBLY HA9 62 D6
Farnborough Common
ORP BR6 216 A2
Farnborough Crs HAYES BR2 199 J5
SAND/SEL CR2 213 G6
Farnborough Hl ORP BR6 216 E3
Farnborough Wy ORP BR6 216 B3
PECK SE15 * 143 F1
Farncombe St
BERM/RHTH SE16 123 H2
Farndale Av PLMGR N13 35 H5
Farndale Crs GFD/PVL UB6 96 D2
Farnell Ms ECT SW5 120 A5
Farnell Pl ACT W3 98 D6
Farnell Rd ISLW TW7 135 J4
Farnham Cl TRDG/WHET N20 33 G2
Farnham Gdns RYNPK SW20 176 E5
Farnham Pl STHWK SE1 18 B1
Farnham Rd GDMY/SEVK IG3 73 F4
WELL DA16 148 D3
Farnham Royal LBTH SE11 122 A5
Farningham Rd TOTM N17 50 C3
Farnley Rd CHING E4 38 C2
SNWD SE25 196 E1
Farnol Rd DART DA1 151 K6
Faro Cl BMLY BR1 185 F5
Faroe Rd WKENS W14 119 G3
Farorna Wk ENC/FH EN2 23 G2
Farquhar Rd NRWD SE19 181 G1
WIM/MER SW19 159 K5
Farquharson Rd CROY/NA CR0 196 D4
Farrance Rd CHDH RM6 74 A3
Farrance St POP/IOD E14 105 J5
Farrant Av WDGN N22 49 G5
Farrant Cl ORP BR6 217 G5
Farr Av BARK IG11 109 G1
Farren Rd FSTH SE23 164 B4
Farrer Ms CEND/HSY/T N8 66 C1
Farrer Rd CEND/HSY/T N8 66 C1
KTN/HRWW/WS HA3 62 A2
Farrier Cl BMLY BR1 184 C6
Farrier Pl SUT SM1 209 F1
Farrier Rd NTHLT UB5 96 A1
Farrier St CAMTN NW1 84 B5
Farriers Wy BORE WD6 31 F1
Farrier Wk WBPTN SW10 120 B6
Farringdon La CLKNW EC1R 5 K7
Farringdon Rd CLKNW EC1R 5 J6
HCIRC EC1N 12 A2
Farringdon St
FLST/FETLN EC4A 12 A3
Farrington Av STMC/STPC BR5 186 C6
Farrington Pl CHST BR7 185 J3
Farrins Rents
BERM/RHTH SE16 124 B1
Farrow La NWCR SE14 143 K1
Farrow Pl BERM/RHTH SE16 124 B3
Farr Rd ENC/FH EN2 23 K2
Farthingale Wk SRTFD E15 88 B5
Farthing Aly STHWK SE1 * 123 H2
Farthing Flds WAP E1W 123 J1
Farthings Cl CHING E4 38 C5
PIN HA5 59 F3
The Farthings KUTN/CMB KT2 175 H4
Farthing St HAYES BR2 215 K5
Farwell Rd SCUP DA14 168 C6
Farwig La BMLY BR1 183 K4
Fashion St WCHPL E1 13 J2
Fashoda Rd HAYES BR2 200 C1
Fassett Rd HACK E8 86 C4
KUT/HW KT1 191 F1
Fassett Sq HACK E8 86 C4
Fauconberg Rd CHSWK W4 117 K6
Faulkner Cl BCTR RM8 73 K4
Faulkner St NWCR SE14 143 K2
Fauna Cl CHDH RM6 73 J3
STAN HA7 29 K6
Faunce St WALW SE17 122 C6
Favart Rd FUL/PGN SW6 139 K2
Faversham Av CHING E4 38 C3
EN EN1 35 K1
Faversham Rd BECK BR3 182 C5
CAT SE6 164 C3
MRDN SM4 194 A3
Fawcett Cl BTSEA SW11 140 C3
STRHM/NOR SW16 162 B6
Fawcett Est CLPT E5 * 68 C5
Fawcett Rd CROY/NA CR0 211 H1
WLSDN NW10 81 H5
Fawcett St WBPTN SW10 120 B6
Fawcus Cl ESH/CLAY KT10 204 E4
Fawe Park Rd PUT/ROE SW15 139 J5
Fawe St POP/IOD E14 105 K4
Fawkes Av DART DA1 171 J4
Fawley Rd KIL/WHAMP NW6 83 F3
Fawnbrake Av HNHL SE24 142 C6
Fawn Rd CHIG IG7 55 F1
PLSTW E13 107 G1
Fawns Manor Rd
EBED/NFELT TW14 153 G3
Fawood Av WLSDN NW10 81 F5
Faygate Crs BXLYHS DA6 149 H6
Faygate Rd BRXS/STRHM SW2 162 A4
Fayland Av STRHM/NOR SW16 179 H1
Fearnley Crs HPTN TW12 172 E2
Fearon St GNWCH SE10 125 K5
Featherbed La SAND/SEL CR2 213 H5
Feathers Pl GNWCH SE10 125 G6
Featherstone Av FSTH SE23 163 J4
Featherstone Rd MLHL NW7 45 K2
NWDGN UB2 114 D3
Featherstone St STLK EC1Y 6 E6
Featherstone Ter NWDGN UB2 114 D3
Featley Rd BRXN/ST SW9 142 C4
Federal Rd GFD/PVL UB6 97 J1
Federation Rd ABYW SE2 128 D4
Fee Farm Rd ESH/CLAY KT10 205 F5
Feeny Cl WLSDN NW10 81 H2
Felbridge Av STAN HA7 43 G4
Felbridge Cl BELMT SM2 209 F6
STRHM/NOR SW16 162 B6
Felbrigge Rd GDMY/SEVK IG3 73 F6
Felday Rd LEW SE13 164 E1
Felden Cl PIN HA5 41 J3
Felden St FUL/PGN SW6 139 J2
Feldman Cl STNW/STAM N16 68 C5
Felgate Ms HMSMTH W6 118 E4
Felhampton Rd
ELTH/MOT SE9 167 G5
Felix Av CEND/HSY/T N8 66 E3
Felix Pl BRXS/STRHM SW2 142 B6
Felix Rd WEA W13 97 G6
Felixstowe Rd ABYW SE2 128 D3
ED N9 36 C6
SEVS/STOTM N15 50 B6
WLSDN NW10 99 K2
Felix St BETH E2 * 104 D1
Fellbrigg Rd EDUL SE22 143 G6
Fellbrigg St WCHPL E1 104 D3
Fellbrook RCHPK/HAM TW10 156 C5
Fellmongers Yd CROY/NA CR0 211 J1
Fellowes Cl YEAD UB4 95 H3
Fellowes Rd CAR SM5 209 J1
Fellows Rd HAMP NW3 83 H5
Fell Rd CROY/NA CR0 211 J1
Felltram Wy CHARL SE7 125 K5
Felmersham Cl CLAP SW4 141 K5
Felmingham Rd PGE/AN SE20 181 K5
Felsberg Rd BRXS/STRHM SW2 161 K2
Fels Cl DAGE RM10 92 D1
Fels Farm Av DAGE RM10 92 E1
Felsham Ms PUT/ROE SW15 139 G4
Felsham Rd PUT/ROE SW15 139 F4
Felspar Cl WOOL/PLUM SE18 128 A5
Felstead Av CLAY IG5 54 A4
Felstead Rd CRW RM5 56 E2
HOM E9 87 J4
LOU IG10 39 J2
ORP BR6 202 C6
WAN E11 70 E4
Felstead St HOM E9 87 H4
Felsted Rd CAN/RD E16 107 H5
Feltham Av E/WMO/HCT KT8 189 K1
Felthambrook Wy FELT TW13 154 A6
Feltham Rd ASHF TW15 152 E6
MTCM CR4 178 E5
Felton Cl STMC/STPC BR5 201 G3
Felton Lea SCUP DA14 186 A1
Felton Rd BARK IG11 108 E1
WEA W13 116 D2
Felton St IS N1 7 F1
Fencepiece Rd BARK/HLT IG6 54 C2
Fenchurch Av FENCHST EC3M 13 G4
Fenchurch Buildings
FENCHST EC3M 13 H4
Fenchurch Pl FENCHST EC3M * 13 H5
Fenchurch St FENCHST EC3M 13 G5
Fendall Rd HOR/WEW KT19 206 E3
Fendall St STHWK SE1 19 H5
Fendt Cl CAN/RD E16 106 D5
Fendyke Rd BELV DA17 128 E3
Fenelon Pl WKENS W14 119 J4
Fen Gv BFN/LL DA15 168 A1
Fenham Rd PECK SE15 143 H1
Fenman Ct TOTM N17 50 D4
Fenman Gdns GDMY/SEVK IG3 73 H5
Fenn Cl BMLY BR1 183 K2
Fennel Cl CAN/RD E16 106 C3
CROY/NA CR0 198 A5
Fennells Md EW KT17 207 G6
Fennel St WOOL/PLUM SE18 127 F6
Fenner Cl BERM/RHTH SE16 123 J4
Fenner Sq BTSEA SW11 * 140 C4
Fenning St STHWK SE1 19 G2
Fenn St HOM E9 87 F3
Fenstanton Av
NFNCH/WDSPK N12 47 H2
Fen St CAN/RD E16 106 D6
Fentiman Rd VX/NE SW8 122 A6
Fentiman Wy RYLN/HDSTN HA2 60 B6
Fenton Cl BRXN/ST SW9 * 142 A3
CHST BR7 184 E1
HACK E8 86 B4
Fenton Rd TOTM N17 49 J3
Fenton's Av PLSTW E13 107 F2
Fenton St WCHPL E1 104 D5
Fenwick Gv PECK SE15 143 H4
Fenwick Pl BRXN/ST SW9 141 K4
SAND/SEL CR2 211 H5
Fenwick Rd PECK SE15 143 H4
Ferdinand Pl CAMTN NW1 84 A5
Ferdinand St CAMTN NW1 84 A5
Ferguson Av BRYLDS KT5 191 G2
Ferguson Cl BECK BR3 183 F6
Ferguson Dr ACT W3 99 F5
Ferguson's Cl POP/IOD E14 124 D4
Fergus Rd HBRY N5 85 H3
Ferme Park Rd CEND/HSY/T N8 66 E2
Fermor Rd FSTH SE23 164 B3
Fermoy Rd GFD/PVL UB6 96 B4
MV/WKIL W9 100 D3
Fern Av MTCM CR4 195 J1
Fernbank BKHH IG9 39 F3
Fernbank Av ALP/SUD HA0 79 F2
WOT/HER KT12 188 D4
Fernbank Ms BAL SW12 161 G1
Fernbrook Dr RYLN/HDSTN HA2 60 B4
Fernbrook Rd LEW SE13 165 H1
Ferncliff Rd HACK E8 86 C3
Fern Cl ERITH DA8 150 E2
IS N1 7 G2
Fern Ct NWCR SE14 144 A4
Ferncroft Av HAMP NW3 82 E1
NFNCH/WDSPK N12 47 J2
RSLP HA4 59 G6
Ferndale BMLY BR1 184 B5
Ferndale Av HSLWW TW4 134 D4
WALTH E17 70 B2
Ferndale Cl BXLYHN DA7 149 F2
Ferndale Rd CLAP SW4 141 K5
CRW RM5 56 E5
FSTGT E7 89 F5
SEVS/STOTM N15 68 B3
SNWD SE25 197 J2
WAN E11 70 D6
Ferndale St EHAM E6 108 B6
Ferndale Ter HRW HA1 61 F1
Ferndale Wy ORP BR6 216 D3
Ferndell Av BXLY DA5 170 A5
Fern Dene WEA W13 97 H4
Ferndene Rd HNHL SE24 142 D5
Fernden Wy ROMW/RG RM7 74 D3
Ferndown NTHWD HA6 40 E5
Ferndown Av ORP BR6 201 J5
Ferndown Cl BELMT SM2 209 H4
PIN HA5 41 J3
Ferndown Rd ELTH/MOT SE9 166 C2
OXHEY WD19 27 G6
Ferney Meade Wy ISLW TW7 136 B3
Ferney Rd EBAR EN4 34 A3
Fern Gv EBED/NFELT TW14 154 A2
Fernhall Dr REDBR IG4 71 H2
Fernham Rd THHTH CR7 196 D1
Fernhead Rd MV/WKIL W9 100 D3
Fernhill Ct WALTH E17 52 B5
Fernhill Gdns KUTN/CMB KT2 174 E1
Fernhill St CAN/RD E16 126 E1
Fernholme Rd PECK SE15 144 A6
Fernhurst Gdns EDGW HA8 44 C2
Fernhurst Rd ASHF TW15 153 F6
CROY/NA CR0 197 H4
FUL/PGN SW6 139 H2
Fern La HEST TW5 114 E5
Fernlea Rd BAL SW12 161 G3
MTCM CR4 179 F5
Fernleigh Cl CROY/NA CR0 211 G2
MV/WKIL W9 100 D2
Fernleigh Ct RYLN/HDSTN HA2 42 B5
WBLY HA9 62 A5
Fernleigh Rd WCHMH N21 35 G4
Fernley Cl PIN HA5 58 E1
Fernsbury St FSBYW WC1X 5 J5
Fernshaw Cl WBPTN SW10 * 120 B6
Fernshaw Rd WBPTN SW10 120 B6
Fernside BKHH IG9 39 F3
GLDGN NW11 64 E6
Fernside Av FELT TW13 154 A6
MLHL NW7 31 F5
Fernside Rd BAL SW12 160 E3
Ferns Rd SRTFD E15 88 C4
Fern St BOW E3 105 J3
Fernthorpe Rd
STRHM/NOR SW16 179 H2
Ferntower Rd HBRY N5 85 K3
Fern Wk BERM/RHTH SE16 123 H5
Fernways IL IG1 90 B1
Fernwood Av ALP/SUD HA0 79 J4
STRHM/NOR SW16 161 J6
Fernwood Cl BMLY BR1 184 B5
Fernwood Crs TRDG/WHET N20 33 K5
Ferny Hl EBAR EN4 21 K1
Ferranti Cl WOOL/PLUM SE18 126 C3
Ferraro Cl HEST TW5 115 F6
Ferrers Av WDR/YW UB7 112 A2
WLGTN SM6 210 D2
Ferrers Rd STRHM/NOR SW16 179 J1
Ferrestone Rd CEND/HSY/T N8 67 F2
Ferrey Ms BRXN/ST SW9 142 B3
Ferriby Cl IS N1 85 G5
Ferrier St WAND/EARL SW18 140 A5
Ferring Cl RYLN/HDSTN HA2 60 C5
Ferrings DUL SE21 163 F4
Ferris Av CROY/NA CR0 213 H1
Ferris Rd EDUL SE22 143 H5
Ferron Rd CLPT E5 * 86 D1
Ferro Rd RAIN RM13 111 J3
Ferryhills Cl OXHEY WD19 27 G5
Ferry La BARN SW13 118 C6
BTFD TW8 117 F6
RAIN RM13 111 H4
TOTM N17 68 D1
Ferrymead Av GFD/PVL UB6 96 A1
Ferrymead Dr GFD/PVL UB6 96 A2
Ferrymead Gdns GFD/PVL UB6 96 C1
Ferrymoor RCHPK/HAM TW10 156 C5
Ferry Rd BARN SW13 138 D1
E/WMO/HCT KT8 173 F6
TEDD TW11 174 C1
THDIT KT7 190 C3
TWK TW1 156 C3
Ferry Sq BTFD TW8 117 F6
Ferry St POP/IOD E14 125 F5
Festing Rd PUT/ROE SW15 139 G4
Festival Cl BXLY DA5 168 E3
ERITH DA8 150 C1
Festoon Wy CAN/RD E16 107 H6
Fetter La FLST/FETLN EC4A 11 K4
Ffinch St DEPT SE8 144 D1
Fidler Pl BUSH WD23 28 B1
Field Cl BKHH IG9 39 G5
BMLY BR1 184 B5
CHING E4 51 K2
CHSGTN KT9 205 J3
CRICK NW2 63 J6
E/WMO/HCT KT8 189 G2
HSLWW TW4 134 A2
HYS/HAR UB3 133 F1
RSLP HA4 58 A5
Fieldcommon La
WOT/HER KT12 188 D5
Field Cottages EFNCH N2 * 47 K6
FUL/PGN SW6 * 139 J3
Field Ct GINN WC1R 11 H2
Field End RSLP HA4 77 H4
Fieldend TEDD TW11 156 A6
Field End Cl OXHEY WD19 27 J2
Field End Rd PIN HA5 59 F2
RSLP HA4 77 J1
Fieldend Rd
STRHM/NOR SW16 179 H4
Fielders Cl EN EN1 24 A5
RYLN/HDSTN HA2 60 D5
Fieldfare Rd THMD SE28 109 J6
Fieldgate St WCHPL E1 104 C4
Fieldhouse Cl SWFD E18 53 F4
Fieldhouse Rd BAL SW12 161 H3
Fielding Av WHTN TW2 155 H5
Fielding La HAYES BR2 200 B1
Fielding Rd CHSWK W4 118 B3
WKENS W14 119 G3
The Fieldings FSTH SE23 163 K3
Fielding Ter EA W5 * 98 B6
Field La BTFD TW8 136 D1
TEDD TW11 174 B1
Field Md CDALE/KGS NW9 45 G3
Fieldpark Gdns CROY/NA CR0 198 B5
Field Pl NWMAL KT3 192 C3
Field Rd EBED/NFELT TW14 154 A1
FSTGT E7 88 E2
HMSMTH W6 119 H6
OXHEY WD19 27 J1
TOTM N17 49 K6
Fieldsend Rd CHEAM SM3 208 C3
Fields Est HACK E8 * 86 C5
Fieldside Cl ORP BR6 216 C2
Fieldside Cottages
TRDG/WHET N20 * 32 D2
Fieldside Rd BMLY BR1 183 G1
Fields Park Crs CHDH RM6 73 K2
Field St FSBYW WC1X 5 G4
Field Vw FELT TW13 153 G6
Fieldview WAND/EARL SW18 160 C3
Fieldview Cottages
STHGT/OAK N14 * 34 D4
Fieldway BCTR RM8 91 H2
Field Wy CROY/NA CR0 213 K5
GFD/PVL UB6 78 B6
RSLP HA4 58 A5
Fieldway STMC/STPC BR5 201 J3
Field Wy WLSDN NW10 80 E5
Fieldway Crs HBRY N5 85 G3
Fiennes Cl BCTR RM8 73 J5
Fiesta Dr RAIN RM13 110 E3
Fife Rd CAN/RD E16 106 E4
KUT/HW KT1 175 F5
MORT/ESHN SW14 137 K6
WDGN N22 49 H4
Fife Ter IS N1 5 H2
Fifield Pth FSTH SE23 164 A5
Fifth Av HYS/HAR UB3 113 J1
MNPK E12 89 K2
NKENS W10 100 C3
Fifth Cross Rd WHTN TW2 155 J4
Fifth Wy WBLY HA9 80 D2
Figge's Rd MTCM CR4 179 F3
Fig Tree Cl WLSDN NW10 81 G6
Filby Rd CHSGTN KT9 206 B4
Filey Av STNW/STAM N16 68 C5
Filey Cl BELMT SM2 209 G5
Filey Waye RSLP HA4 58 E6
Fillebrook Av EN EN1 24 A3
Fillebrook Rd WAN E11 70 B5
Filmer Chambers
FUL/PGN SW6 * 139 J2
Filmer Rd FUL/PGN SW6 139 J2
Filton Cl CDALE/KGS NW9 45 G5
Finborough Rd TOOT SW17 178 E3
WBPTN SW10 120 A6
Finchale Rd ABYW SE2 128 C3
Fincham Cl HGDN/ICK UB10 76 A1
Finch Av WNWD SE27 162 E6
Finch Cl BAR EN5 20 E6
Finch Dr EBED/NFELT TW14 154 C2
Finch Gdns CHING E4 51 J1
Finchingfield Av WFD IG8 53 G3
Finch La BANK EC3V 13 F4
Finchley Cl DART DA1 171 K1
Finchley La HDN NW4 64 B1
Finchley Pk
NFNCH/WDSPK N12 33 G6
Finchley Pl STJWD NW8 2 A2
Finchley Rd GLDGN NW11 64 D2
HAMP NW3 82 E2
STJWD NW8 2 A1
Finchley Vls
NFNCH/WDSPK N12 * 33 H6
Finchley Wy FNCH N3 46 E2
Finch Ms PECK SE15 * 143 G2
Finden Rd FSTGT E7 89 G3
Findhorn Av YEAD UB4 95 F4
Findhorn St POP/IOD E14 106 A5
Findon Cl RYLN/HDSTN HA2 * 78 B1
WAND/EARL SW18 159 K1
Findon Gdns RAIN RM13 111 J4
Findon Rd ED N9 36 D3
SHB W12 118 D2
Fingal St GNWCH SE10 125 J5
Finglesham Cl STMC/STPC BR5 202 E5
Finland Rd BROCKY SE4 144 B4
Finland St BERM/RHTH SE16 124 B3
Finlays Cl CHSGTN KT9 206 C3
Finlay St FUL/PGN SW6 139 G2
Finney La ISLW TW7 136 B2
Finnis St BETH E2 104 D2
Finnymore Rd DAGW RM9 92 A5
Finsbury Av LVPST EC2M * 13 F2

Finsbury Circ LVPST EC2M 13 F2
Finsbury Cottages WDGN N22 48 E3
Finsbury Est CLKNW EC1R 5 K5
FSBYE EC1V * 6 A5
Finsbury Market SDTCH EC2A 7 G7
Finsbury Park Av FSBYPK N4 67 J3
Finsbury Park Rd FSBYPK N4 85 H1
Finsbury Pavement
LVPST EC2M 13 F1
Finsbury Rd WDGN N22 49 F4
Finsbury Sq SDTCH EC2A 13 F1
Finsbury St STLK EC1Y 12 E1
Finsbury Wy BXLY DA5 169 G1
Finsen Rd CMBW SE5 142 D5
Finstock Rd NKENS W10 100 B5
Finucane Dr STMC/STPC BR5 202 D4
Finucane Gdns RAIN RM13 93 J4
Finucane Ri BUSH WD23 28 C4
Fiona Ct ENC/FH EN2 * 23 H4
Firbank Cl CAN/RD E16 107 H4
ENC/FH EN2 23 J5
Firbank Dr OXHEY WD19 27 J2
Firbank Rd CRW RM5 56 D1
PECK SE15 143 J3
Fircroft Gdns HRW HA1 78 E1
Fircroft Rd CHSGTN KT9 206 B2
TOOT SW17 160 E5
Firdene BRYLDS KT5 191 K5
Fir Dene ORP BR6 215 K1
Fire Bell Aly SURB KT6 191 F3
Firebell Ms SURB KT6 191 F3
Firecrest Dr HAMP NW3 83 F1
Firefly Cl WLGTN SM6 * 210 E5
Firefly Gdns EHAM E6 107 J3
Firethorn Cl EDGW HA8 30 E6
Fir Gv NWMAL KT3 192 C3
Fir Grove Rd BRXN/ST SW9 * 142 B3
Firhill Rd CAT SE6 164 D5
Firle Pl WAND/EARL SW18 160 B2
Firmin Rd DART DA1 171 F1
Fir Rd CHEAM SM3 193 J5
FELT TW13 172 C1
Firs Av FBAR/BDGN N11 48 A2
MORT/ESHN SW14 137 K5
MUSWH N10 48 A6
Firsby Av CROY/NA CR0 198 A5
Firsby Rd STNW/STAM N16 68 C5
Firs Cl ESH/CLAY KT10 204 E4
FSTH SE23 164 A2
MTCM CR4 179 G5
MUSWH N10 48 A6
Firscroft PLMGR N13 35 J5
Firs Dr HEST TW5 134 A2
Firside Gv BFN/LL DA15 168 A3
Firs La PLMGR N13 35 J5
Firs Park Av WCHMH N21 35 K3
Firs Park Gdns WCHMH N21 35 K3
First Av ACT W3 118 C1
BXLYHN DA7 148 D1
CHDH RM6 73 J2
DAGE RM10 110 D1
E/WMO/HCT KT8 188 E1
EN EN1 24 B6
HDN NW4 64 A1
HOR/WEW KT19 207 G6
HYS/HAR UB3 113 J1
MNPK E12 89 J2
MORT/ESHN SW14 138 B3
NKENS W10 100 D3
PLSTW E13 106 E2
UED N18 36 E6
WALTH E17 52 B6
WBLY HA9 61 K6
WOT/HER KT12 188 A3
First Cl E/WMO/HCT KT8 189 H1
First Cross Rd WHTN TW2 155 K4
First Dr WLSDN NW10 80 E5
The Firs BXLY DA5 170 A3
EA W5 97 K4
EBED/NFELT TW14 * 153 H1
EDGW HA8 * 31 F6
TRDG/WHET N20 33 H3
First St CHEL SW3 14 D6
Firstway RYNPK SW20 177 F5
First Wy WBLY HA9 80 D2
Firs Wk NTHWD HA6 40 B2
WFD IG8 52 E1
Firswood Av HOR/WEW KT19 207 G3
Firth Gdns FUL/PGN SW6 139 H2
Firtree Av MTCM CR4 179 F5
Fir Tree Av WDR/YW UB7 112 D3
Fir Tree Cl EA W5 98 A5
ESH/CLAY KT10 204 C3
HOR/WEW KT19 207 H2
ORP BR6 217 F3
ROM RM1 57 F6
STRHM/NOR SW16 179 H1
Fir Tree Gdns CROY/NA CR0 213 J2
Fir Tree Gv CAR SM5 209 K5
Fir Tree Pl ASHF TW15 * 152 D6
Fir Tree Rd HSLWW TW4 134 D5
Fir Trees Cl BERM/RHTH SE16 124 B1
Fir Tree Wk EN EN1 24 A4
Fir Wk CHEAM SM3 208 B4
Fisher Cl CROY/NA CR0 197 G5
GFD/PVL UB6 96 A2
Fisherdene ESH/CLAY KT10 205 G5
Fisherman Cl
RCHPK/HAM TW10 156 D6
Fishermans Dr
BERM/RHTH SE16 124 A2
Fisher Rd KTN/HRWW/WS HA3 43 F5
Fishers Cl STRHM/NOR SW16 161 J5
Fishers Ct NWCR SE14 144 A2
Fisher's La CHSWK W4 118 A4
Fisher St CAN/RD E16 106 E4
HHOL WC1V 11 G2
Fisher's Wy BELV DA17 129 K1
Fisherton St STJWD NW8 2 A7
Fishguard Wy CAN/RD E16 127 H1
Fishponds Rd HAYES BR2 215 H3
TOOT SW17 160 D6
Fish Street Hl MON EC3R 13 F6
Fisons Rd CAN/RD E16 125 K1
Fitzalan Rd ESH/CLAY KT10 204 E5
FNCH N3 46 C6
Fitzalan St LBTH SE11 17 J6
Fitzgeorge Av NWMAL KT3 176 A4
WKENS W14 119 H4
Fitzgerald Av
MORT/ESHN SW14 138 B4
Fitzgerald Rd
MORT/ESHN SW14 138 A4
THDIT KT7 190 B3
WAN E11 70 E2
Fitzhardinge St MBLAR W1H 9 G3
Fitzhugh Gv
WAND/EARL SW18 160 C1
Fitzjames Av CROY/NA CR0 197 H6
WKENS W14 119 H4
Fitzjohn Av BAR EN5 20 C6
Fitzjohn's Av HAMP NW3 83 H3
Fitzmaurice Pl MYFR/PICC W1J * 9 K7
Fitzneal St SHB W12 99 H5
Fitzroy Cl HGT N6 65 K5
Fitzroy Crs CHSWK W4 * 138 A1
Fitzroy Gdns NRWD SE19 181 F3
Fitzroy Ms FITZ W1T 4 A7
Fitzroy Pk HGT N6 65 K5
Fitzroy Rd CAMTN NW1 84 A6
Fitzroy Sq FITZ W1T 4 A7
Fitzroy St FITZ W1T 4 A7
Fitzstephen Rd BCTR RM8 91 H3
Fitzwarren Gdns HGT N6 66 C5
Fitzwilliam Av RCH/KEW TW9 137 G3
Fitzwilliam Ms CAN/RD E16 106 E6
CAN/RD E16 125 K1
Fitzwilliam Rd CLAP SW4 141 H4
Fitz Wygram Cl HPTN TW12 173 H1
Five Acre CDALE/KGS NW9 45 H5
Fiveacre Cl CROY/NA CR0 196 B3
Five Elms Rd DAGW RM9 92 B1
HAYES BR2 215 G1
Five Fields Cl OXHEY WD19 27 K5
Five Oak Ms BMLY BR1 165 K5
Five Oaks La CHIG IG7 56 A2
Fiveways Cnr ELTH/MOT SE9 167 G4
Five Ways Jct HDN NW4 45 J4
Fiveways Rd BRXN/ST SW9 142 B3
Fladbury Rd SEVS/STOTM N15 67 K3
Fladgate Rd WAN E11 70 C3
Flag Cl CROY/NA CR0 198 A5
Flag Wk PIN HA5 58 E3
Flambard Rd HRW HA1 61 G3
Flamborough Rd RSLP HA4 76 E1
Flamborough St POP/IOD E14 105 G5
Flamborough Wk
POP/IOD E14 * 105 G5
Flamingo Wk HCH RM12 93 J5
Flamstead Gdns DAGW RM9 91 J5
Flamstead Rd DAGW RM9 91 J5
Flamsted Av WBLY HA9 80 C4
Flamsteed Rd CHARL SE7 126 D5
Flanchford Rd SHB W12 118 C3
Flanders Crs TOOT SW17 178 E3
Flanders Rd CHSWK W4 118 B4
EHAM E6 107 K1
Flanders Wy HOM E9 87 F4
Flandrian Cl PEND EN3 25 J2
Flank St WCHPL E1 104 C6
Flask Wk HAMP NW3 83 G2
Flather Cl STRHM/NOR SW16 179 H2
Flavell Ms GNWCH SE10 125 H5
Flaxen Cl CHING E4 37 K5
Flaxen Rd CHING E4 37 K5
Flaxley Rd MRDN SM4 194 A3
Flaxman Rd CMBW SE5 142 C3
Flaxman Ter STPAN WC1H 4 D5
Flaxton Rd WOOL/PLUM SE18 147 J2
Flecker Cl STAN HA7 43 F1
Fleece Dr ED N9 36 C6
Fleece Rd SURB KT6 190 D5
Fleece Wk HOLWY N7 * 84 E4
Fleeming Cl WALTH E17 51 H5
Fleeming Rd WALTH E17 51 H5
Fleet Cl E/WMO/HCT KT8 188 E2
RSLP HA4 58 A3
Fleet Pl FLST/FETLN EC4A 12 A3
Fleet Rd HAMP NW3 83 J3
Fleetside E/WMO/HCT KT8 188 E3
Fleet Sq FSBYW WC1X 5 G5
Fleet St EMB EC4Y 11 K4
Fleet Street Hl WCHPL E1 * 104 C3
Fleet Ter CAT SE6 * 165 F2
Fleetwood Cl CAN/RD E16 107 H4
CHSGTN KT9 205 K5
CROY/NA CR0 212 B1
Fleetwood Rd KUT/HW KT1 175 J6
WLSDN NW10 81 J3
Fleetwood Sq KUT/HW KT1 175 J6
Fleetwood St STNW/STAM N16 68 A6
Fleetwood Wy OXHEY WD19 27 G6
Fleming Cl MV/WKIL W9 100 E3
WBPTN SW10 * 120 B6
Fleming Ct CROY/NA CR0 211 G3
Fleming Dr WCHMH N21 23 F6
Fleming Md MTCM CR4 178 D3
Fleming Rd STHL UB1 96 B5
WALW SE17 122 C6
Fleming Wk CDALE/KGS NW9 * 45 G5
Fleming Wy ISLW TW7 136 A4
THMD SE28 109 K6
Flemming Av RSLP HA4 59 F6
Flempton Rd LEY E10 69 G5
Fletcher Cl EHAM E6 108 B6
Fletcher La LEY E10 70 A4
Fletcher Rd CHIG IG7 55 F1
CHSWK W4 117 K3
Fletchers Cl HAYES BR2 200 A1
Fletcher St WCHPL E1 104 C6
Fletching Rd CHARL SE7 126 C6
CLPT E5 86 E1
Fletton Rd FBAR/BDGN N11 48 E3
Fleur De Lis St WCHPL E1 7 J7
Fleur Gates WIM/MER SW19 159 G2
Flexmere Rd TOTM N17 49 K4
Flight Ap CDALE/KGS NW9 * 45 H4
Flimwell Cl BMLY BR1 183 H1
Flint Cl ORP BR6 * 217 F4
SRTFD E15 88 D4
Flint Down Cl
STMC/STPC BR5 * 186 B4
Flintmill Crs ELTH/MOT SE9 146 D4
Flinton St WALW SE17 123 F5
Flint St WALW SE17 19 F7
Flitcroft St LSQ/SEVD WC2H 10 D4
Floathaven Cl THMD SE28 128 B1
Flock Mill Pl WAND/EARL SW18 160 A3
Flockton St BERM/RHTH SE16 123 H2
Flodden Rd CMBW SE5 142 D2
Flood La TWK TW1 * 156 B3
Flood St CHEL SW3 120 D5
Flood Wk CHEL SW3 120 D6
Flora Cl POP/IOD E14 105 K5
STAN HA7 29 K5
Flora Gdns CHDH RM6 73 J3
Floral Pl IS N1 85 K3
Floral St COVGDN WC2E 11 F5
Flora St BELV DA17 129 G5
Florence Av ENC/FH EN2 23 J4
MRDN SM4 194 B2
Florence Cl WOT/HER KT12 188 A4
Florence Ct WAN E11 71 F1
Florence Dr ENC/FH EN2 23 J4
Florence Elson Cl MNPK E12 90 A2
Florence Gdns CHSWK W4 117 K6
Florence Rd ABYW SE2 128 D4
BECK BR3 182 A5
BMLY BR1 183 K4
CHSWK W4 118 A3
EA W5 98 A6
EHAM E6 89 G6
FELT TW13 154 A3
FSBYPK N4 67 F4
KUTN/CMB KT2 175 G3
NWCR SE14 144 C2
NWDGN UB2 114 C4
PLSTW E13 106 E1
SAND/SEL CR2 211 K6
WIM/MER SW19 178 A2
WOT/HER KT12 188 A4
Florence St CAN/RD E16 106 D3
HDN NW4 64 A1
IS N1 85 H5
Florence Ter NWCR SE14 144 C2
Florence Vls HGT N6 * 66 B4
Florence Wy BAL SW12 160 E3
Florey Sq WCHMH N21 23 F6
Florfield Rd HACK E8 86 D4
Florian Av SUT SM1 209 H2
Florian Rd PUT/ROE SW15 139 H5
Florida Cl BUSH WD23 28 D4
Florida Rd THHTH CR7 180 C4
Florida St BETH E2 104 D2
Florin Ct UED N18 36 A6
Floris Pl CLAP SW4 141 H4
Floriston Av HGDN/ICK UB10 76 A5
Floriston Cl STAN HA7 43 H4
Floriston Gdns STAN HA7 43 H4
Floss St PUT/ROE SW15 139 F3
Flower & Dean Wk WCHPL E1 13 K2
Flower La MLHL NW7 45 H1
Flower Ms GLDGN NW11 64 C3
Flowerpot Cl SEVS/STOTM N15 68 B3
Flowers Cl CRICK NW2 81 J1
Flowers Ms ARCH N19 66 C6
Floyd Rd CHARL SE7 126 B5
Floyer Cl RCHPK/HAM TW10 137 G6
Fludyer St LEW SE13 145 H5
Foley Ms ESH/CLAY KT10 204 E4
Foley Rd ESH/CLAY KT10 204 E5
Foley St GTPST W1W 10 A2
Folgate St WCHPL E1 13 H1
Foliot St SHB W12 99 H5
Folkestone Rd EHAM E6 108 A1
UED N18 36 C6
WALTH E17 69 K1
Folkingham La
CDALE/KGS NW9 45 F4
Folkington Cnr
NFNCH/WDSPK N12 46 D1
Follett St POP/IOD E14 106 A5
Folly La CHING E4 51 H3
Folly Wall POP/IOD E14 125 F2
Fontaine Rd
STRHM/NOR SW16 180 A2
Fontarabia Rd BTSEA SW11 141 F5
Fontayne Av RAIN RM13 93 G5
ROM RM1 57 G5
Fontenoy Rd BAL SW12 161 G4
Fonteyne Gdns WFD IG8 53 H5
Fonthill Ms FSBYPK N4 67 F6
Fonthill Rd FSBYPK N4 67 F6
Font Hills EFNCH N2 47 G5
Fontley Wy PUT/ROE SW15 158 D2
Fontwell Cl
KTN/HRWW/WS HA3 42 E3
NTHLT UB5 78 A4
Fontwell Dr HAYES BR2 201 F2
Football La HRW HA1 61 F5
Footbury Hill Rd ORP BR6 202 B4
The Footpath
PUT/ROE SW15 * 138 D6
Foots Cray High St SCUP DA14 186 D2
Foots Cray La SCUP DA14 168 D3
Footscray Rd ELTH/MOT SE9 167 F1
Forbes Cl CRICK NW2 81 J1
HCH RM12 75 K5
Forbes St WCHPL E1 104 C5
Forbes Wy RSLP HA4 59 F6
Forburg Rd STNW/STAM N16 68 C5
Ford Cl HRW HA1 60 D4
RAIN RM13 93 H5
THHTH CR7 196 C3
Fordcroft Rd STMC/STPC BR5 202 C2
Forde Av BMLY BR1 184 B6
Fordel Rd CAT SE6 165 G3
Ford End WFD IG8 53 F2
Fordham Rd EBAR EN4 21 H4
Fordham St WCHPL E1 104 C5
Fordhook Av EA W5 98 B6
Fordingley Rd MV/WKIL W9 100 D2
Fordington Rd HGT N6 65 K1
Ford La RAIN RM13 93 H5
Fordmill Rd CAT SE6 164 D4
Ford Rd ASHF TW15 152 C6
BOW E3 105 G1
DAGE RM10 92 C5
Ford's Gv WCHMH N21 35 J3
Fords Park Rd CAN/RD E16 106 E5
Ford Sq WCHPL E1 104 D4
Ford St BOW E3 87 G6
CAN/RD E16 106 D5
Fordwich Cl ORP BR6 202 A4
Fordwych Rd CRICK NW2 82 C3
Fordyce Rd LEW SE13 165 F1
Fordyke Rd BCTR RM8 74 A6
Foreland Ct HDN NW4 46 C4
Foreland St WOOL/PLUM SE18 127 J4
Foremark Cl BARK/HLT IG6 55 F2
Foreshore DEPT SE8 124 C5
Forest Ap CHING E4 38 C2
WFD IG8 52 E3
Forest Av CHIG IG7 54 A1
CHING E4 38 C2
Forest Cl CHST BR7 185 F5
WAN E11 70 D2
WFD IG8 39 F6
Forest Ct CHING E4 38 D3
WAN E11 70 C1
Forestdale STHGT/OAK N14 34 D6
Forest Dr HAYES BR2 215 J2
MNPK E12 89 H1
WFD IG8 52 B3
Forest Dr East WAN E11 70 B4
Forest Dr West WAN E11 70 A4
Forest Edge BKHH IG9 39 G5
Forester Rd PECK SE15 143 J5
Foresters Cl WLGTN SM6 210 D5
Foresters Crs BXLYHN DA7 149 J5
Foresters Dr WALTH E17 70 B1
WLGTN SM6 210 D6
Forest Gdns TOTM N17 50 B5
Forest Ga CDALE/KGS NW9 63 G1
Forest Gld CHING E4 52 C1
WAN E11 70 C3
Forest Gv HACK E8 86 B4
Forest Hill Rd EDUL SE22 163 J1
Forestholme Cl FSTH SE23 163 K4
SYD SE26 * 181 K1
Forest La CHIG IG7 54 A1
FSTGT E7 88 E3
Forest Mount Rd WFD IG8 52 B3
Fore St BARB EC2Y 12 E2
ED N9 36 C6
PIN HA5 58 E2
Forest Rdg BECK BR3 182 D6
HAYES BR2 215 J2
Forest Ri WALTH E17 70 B1
Forest Rd BARK/HLT IG6 54 E4
CHEAM SM3 193 K5
ED N9 36 D3
ERITH DA8 150 D2
FELT TW13 154 B5
FSTGT E7 88 E2
HACK E8 86 B4
RCH/KEW TW9 137 H1
ROMW/RG RM7 56 D6
TOTM N17 68 E1
WALTH E17 51 J6
WAN E11 70 B4
WFD IG8 38 E5
Forest Side BKHH IG9 39 G3
CHING E4 38 D2
FSTGT E7 89 F2
WPK KT4 192 C5
Forest St FSTGT E7 88 E3
The Forest WAN E11 70 C1
Forest Vw CHING E4 38 B2
WAN E11 70 D4
Forest View Av LEY E10 70 B2
Forest View Rd MNPK E12 89 J2
WALTH E17 52 A4
Forest Wy BFN/LL DA15 167 J2
STMC/STPC BR5 202 B2
WFD IG8 39 F6
Forfar Rd BTSEA SW11 141 F2
WDGN N22 49 H4
Forge Cl HAYES BR2 199 K5
Forge Cottages EA W5 * 116 E1
Forge Dr ESH/CLAY KT10 205 G5
Forge La CHEAM SM3 208 C5
FELT TW13 172 D1
NTHWD HA6 40 C3
RCHPK/HAM TW10 157 F3
Forge Ms CROY/NA CR0 213 J3
Forge Pl CAMTN NW1 84 A4
Forman Pl STNW/STAM N16 86 B2
Formby Av
KTN/HRWW/WS HA3 43 J6
Formosa St MV/WKIL W9 101 F3
Formunt Cl CAN/RD E16 106 D4
Forres Gdns GLDGN NW11 64 E3
Forrester Pth SYD SE26 * 163 K6
Forrest Gdns
STRHM/NOR SW16 180 A6
Forris Av HYS/HAR UB3 113 J1
Forset St MBLAR W1H 8 D3
Forstal Cl HAYES BR2 183 K6
Forster Cl CHING E4 52 B3
Forster Rd BECK BR3 182 B6
BRXS/STRHM SW2 161 K2
TOTM N17 50 B6
WALTH E17 69 G3
Forsters Cl CHDH RM6 74 B3
Forston St IS N1 6 E2
Forsyte Crs NRWD SE19 181 F4
Forsyth Gdns WALW SE17 122 C6
Forsythia Cl IL IG1 90 B3
Forsyth Pl EN EN1 24 A6
Forterie Gdns GDMY/SEVK IG3 91 G1
Fortescue Av WHTN TW2 155 H5
Fortescue Rd EDGW HA8 45 F4
WIM/MER SW19 178 C3
Fortess Gv KTTN NW5 84 C3
Fortess Rd KTTN NW5 84 C2
Fortess Wk KTTN NW5 84 B3
Forthbridge Rd BTSEA SW11 141 F5
Fortis Cl CAN/RD E16 107 G5
Fortis Gn EFNCH N2 47 K6
Fortis Green Av EFNCH N2 48 A6
Fortis Green Rd MUSWH N10 48 A6
Fortismere Av MUSWH N10 48 A6
Fortnam Rd ARCH N19 66 D6
Fortnums Acre STAN HA7 43 F2
Fort Rd NTHLT UB5 78 A5
STHWK SE1 19 K7
Fortrose Cl POP/IOD E14 106 B5
Fortrose Gdns
BRXS/STRHM SW2 161 K3
Fort St CAN/RD E16 126 A1
WCHPL E1 * 13 H2
Fortuna Cl HOLWY N7 * 85 F4
Fortunegate Rd WLSDN NW10 81 H5
Fortune Green Rd
KIL/WHAMP NW6 82 E3
Fortune La BORE WD6 29 K1
Fortune Pl STHWK SE1 123 G5
Fortunes Md NTHLT UB5 77 J4
Fortune St STLK EC1Y 6 D7
Fortune Wy WLSDN NW10 99 J2
Forty Acre La CAN/RD E16 106 E4
Forty Av WBLY HA9 80 B1
Forty Cl WBLY HA9 80 B1
Forty La WBLY HA9 62 E6
Forum Cl BOW E3 87 J6
Forum Magnum Sq STHWK SE1 17 G2
Forumside EDGW HA8 44 C2
The Forum E/WMO/HCT KT8 189 G1
Forum Wy EDGW HA8 44 C2
Forval Cl MTCM CR4 194 E2
Forward Dr
KTN/HRWW/WS HA3 61 G1
Fosbury Ms BAY/PAD W2 101 F6
Foscote Ms MV/WKIL W9 100 E3
Foscote Rd HDN NW4 63 K3
Foskett Rd FUL/PGN SW6 139 J3
Foss Av CROY/NA CR0 211 G3
Fossdene Rd CHARL SE7 126 A5
Fossdyke Cl YEAD UB4 95 J4
Fosse Wy WEA W13 97 G4
Fossil Rd LEW SE13 144 D4
Fossington Rd BELV DA17 128 E4
Foss Rd TOOT SW17 160 C6
Fossway BCTR RM8 73 J6
Foster La CITYW EC2V 12 C3
Foster Rd ACT W3 99 G6
CHSWK W4 118 A5
PLSTW E13 106 E3
Fosters Cl CHST BR7 184 E1
SWFD E18 53 F4
Foster St HDN NW4 64 A1
Foster Wk HDN NW4 64 A1
Fothergill Cl PLSTW E13 88 E6
Fothergill Dr WCHMH N21 22 E6
Fotheringham Rd EN EN1 24 B5
Foubert's Pl SOHO/CST W1F 10 A4
Foulden Rd STNW/STAM N16 86 B2
Foulden Ter STNW/STAM N16 86 B2
Foulis Ter SKENS SW7 14 A7
Foulser Rd TOOT SW17 160 E5
Foulsham Rd THHTH CR7 180 D6
Foundation Pl
ELTH/MOT SE9 * 147 F6
Founder Cl EHAM E6 108 B5
Founders Cl NTHLT UB5 95 K2
Founders Gdns NRWD SE19 180 D3
Foundry Cl BERM/RHTH SE16 124 B1
Foundry Ms CAMTN NW1 4 B6
HSLW TW3 135 G5
Foundry Pl
WAND/EARL SW18 * 160 A2
Fountain Cl UX/CGN UB8 94 A4
Fountain Dr CAR SM5 209 K6
NRWD SE19 163 G6
Fountain Green Sq
BERM/RHTH SE16 123 H2
Fountain Ms HAMP NW3 83 K4
Fountain Pl BRXN/ST SW9 142 B2
Fountain Rd THHTH CR7 180 D5
TOOT SW17 178 C1
Fountains Av FELT TW13 154 E5
Fountains Cl FELT TW13 154 E4
Fountains Crs STHGT/OAK N14 34 E2
Fountayne Rd
SEVS/STOTM N15 68 C1
STNW/STAM N16 68 C6
Fount St VX/NE SW8 141 J1
Fouracres PEND EN3 25 G2
Fourland Wk EDGW HA8 44 E2
Fournier St WCHPL E1 13 J1
Four Seasons Cl BOW E3 105 J1
Four Seasons Crs CHEAM SM3 193 J6
Fourth Av HYS/HAR UB3 113 J1
MNPK E12 89 K2
NKENS W10 100 C3
ROMW/RG RM7 74 E5
Fourth Cross Rd WHTN TW2 155 J4
Fourth Wy WBLY HA9 80 E2
The Four Tubs BUSH WD23 28 D2
The Four Wents CHING E4 38 B4
Fowey Av REDBR IG4 71 H2
Fowey Cl WAP E1W 123 J1
Fowler Cl BTSEA SW11 140 C4
SCUP DA14 187 F1
Fowler Rd BARK/HLT IG6 55 J1
FSTGT E7 88 E2
IS N1 85 H6
Fowler's Wk EA W5 97 K3
Fownes St BTSEA SW11 140 D4
Fox & Knot St FARR EC1M * 12 B1
Foxberry Rd BROCKY SE4 144 B5
Foxborough Gdns
BROCKY SE4 164 D1
Foxbourne Rd TOOT SW17 161 F4
Fox Burrow Rd BARK/HLT IG6 55 J1
Foxbury Av CHST BR7 185 J2
Foxbury Cl BMLY BR1 184 A2
ORP BR6 217 G3
Foxbury Dr ORP BR6 217 G4
Foxbury Rd BMLY BR1 183 K2
Fox Cl BORE WD6 29 K1
CAN/RD E16 106 E4
CRW RM5 56 D1
ORP BR6 217 G3
WCHPL E1 104 E3
Foxcombe CROY/NA CR0 213 K4
Foxcroft Rd
WOOL/PLUM SE18 147 G2
Foxdell NTHWD HA6 40 B2
Foxearth Sp SAND/SEL CR2 212 E6
Foxes Dl BKHTH/KID SE3 145 K4
HAYES BR2 183 G6
Foxfield Cl NTHWD HA6 40 D2
Foxfield Rd ORP BR6 201 J6

Foxglove Cl BFN/LL DA15 ...168 B1
ED N9 ...36 E3
STHL UB1 ...95 J6
STWL/WRAY TW19 ...152 A3
Foxglove Gdns MAR...1 ...71 G1
Foxglove La CHSGTN KT9 ...206 C2
Foxglove Pth THMD SE28 ...127 K2
Foxglove St ACT W3 ...99 H6
Foxglove Wy WLGTN SM6 ...195 F5
Foxgrove STHGT/OAK N14 ...34 E5
Fox Gv WOT/HER KT12 ...188 A4
Foxgrove Av BECK BR3 ...182 E5
Foxgrove Pth OXHEY WD19 ...41 H1
Foxgrove Rd BECK BR3 ...182 E5
Foxham Rd ARCH N19 ...84 D1
Fox HI HAYES BR2 ...215 G3
NRWD SE19 ...181 G3
Fox Hill Cl
NRWD SE19 ...181 G3
Foxhole Rd ELTH/MOT SE9 ...146 D6
Fox Hollow Cl
WOOL/PLUM SE18 ...127 K5
Fox Hollow Dr BXLYHN DA7 ...148 E4
Foxholt Gdns WLSDN NW10 ...80 E5
Foxhome Cl CHST BR7 ...185 F2
Fox House Rd BELV DA17 ...129 J4
Foxlands Crs DAGE RM10 ...92 E3
Foxlands Rd DAGE RM10 ...92 E3
Fox La EA W5 ...98 A4
HAYES BR2 ...215 F3
PLMGR N13 ...35 F4
Foxlees ALP/SUD HA0 ...79 G2
Foxley Cl HACK E8 ...86 C3
Foxley Rd CMBW SE5 ...142 E6
THHTH CR7 ...196 C1
Foxleys OXHEY WD19 ...27 J5
Foxley Sq BRXN/ST SW9 *...142 C1
Foxmead Cl ENC/FH EN2 ...23 F4
Foxmore St BTSEA SW11 ...140 E2
Fox Rd CAN/RD E16 ...106 D4
Foxton Gv MTCM CR4 ...178 C5
Foxwarren ESH/CLAY KT10 ...205 F6
Foxwell St BROCKY SE4 ...144 B4
Foxwood Cl FELT TW13 ...154 A5
MLHL NW7 ...31 G6
Foxwood Green Cl EN EN1 ...36 A4
Foxwood Rd BKHTH/KID SE3 ...145 J5
Foyle Rd BKHTH/KID SE3 ...125 J6
TOTM N17 ...50 C4

Framfield Cl
NFNCH/WDSPK N12 ...32 E6
Framfield Rd HBRY N5 ...85 H3
HNWL W7 ...97 F5
MTCM CR4 ...179 F3
Framlingham Crs
ELTH/MOT SE9 ...166 D6
Frampton Cl BELMT SM2 ...208 E5
Frampton Park Rd HOM E9 ...86 E4
Frampton Rd HSLWW TW4 ...134 D6
Frampton St STJWD NW8 ...2 B7
Francemary Rd LEW SE13 ...144 D6
Frances Rd CHING E4 ...51 J2
Frances St WOOL/PLUM SE18 ...126 E4
Franche Court Rd TOOT SW17 ...160 B5
Francis Av BXLYHN DA7 ...149 H3
FELT TW13 ...153 K5
IL IG1 ...72 D6
Francis Barber Cl
STRHM/NOR SW16 *...162 A6
Franciscan Rd TOOT SW17 ...161 F6
Francis Chichester Wy
BTSEA SW11 ...141 F2
Francis Cl HOR/WEW KT19 ...207 F2
Francis Gv WIM/MER SW19 ...177 J3
Francis Ms LEE/GVPK SE12 *...165 J1
Francis Rd CROY/NA CR0 ...196 C4
DART DA1 ...151 G6
EFNCH N2 *...65 K1
GFD/PVL UB6 ...97 J1
HRW HA1 ...61 G2
HSLWW TW4 ...134 C3
LEY E10 ...70 A6
PIN HA5 ...59 G2
STMC/STPC BR5 ...186 E6
WLGTN SM6 ...210 C4
Francis St SRTFD E15 ...88 C3
WEST SW1P ...16 A6
Francis Ter ARCH N19 ...84 C1
Francis Wk IS N1 ...85 F6
Francklyn Gdns EDGW HA8 ...30 C5
Francombe Gdns ROM RM1 ...75 J3
Franconia Rd CLAP SW4 ...141 H6
Frank Burton Cl CHARL SE7 ...126 A5
Frank Dixon Cl DUL SE21 ...163 F2
Frank Dixon Wy DUL SE21 ...163 F3
Frankfurt Rd HNHL SE24 ...142 D6
Frankham St DEPT SE8 ...144 D1
Frankland Cl
BERM/RHTH SE16 ...123 J3
WFD IG8 ...53 G1
Frankland Rd CHING E4 ...51 J1
SKENS SW7 ...14 A5
Franklin Cl KUT/HW KT1 ...175 H6
LEW SE13 ...144 E2
TRDG/WHET N20 ...33 G2
WNWD SE27 ...162 C5
Franklin Crs MTCM CR4 ...195 H1
Franklin Rd BXLYHN DA7 ...149 F2
PGE/AN SE20 ...181 K3
Franklins Ms RYLN/HDSTN HA2 ...60 C6
Franklin Sq WKENS W14 ...119 J5
Franklin's Rw CHEL SW3 ...120 E5
Franklin St BOW E3 ...105 K2
SEVS/STOTM N15 ...68 A3
Franklyn Rd WLSDN NW10 ...81 H5
WOT/HER KT12 ...188 A3
Franks Av NWMAL KT3 ...191 K1
Franks Wood Av
STMC/STPC BR5 ...201 H2
Franlaw Crs PLMGR N13 ...35 J6
Franml Rd HCH RM12 ...75 H4
Fransfield Gv SYD SE26 ...163 J5
Franshams BUSH WD23 ...28 A4
Frant Cl PGE/AN SE20 ...181 K3

Frant Rd THHTH CR7 ...196 C2
Fraser Cl BXLY DA5 ...169 K3
Fraser Rd ED N9 ...36 D5
EHAM E6 ...129 K5
GFD/PVL UB6 ...79 F1
WALTH E17 ...69 K2
Fraser St CHSWK W4 ...118 B5
Frating Crs WFD IG8 ...52 E2
Frays Av WDR/YW UB7 ...112 A2
Frays Wy WDR/YW UB7 ...112 A3
Frazer Av RSLP HA4 ...77 G3
Frazer Cl ROM RM1 ...75 H4
Frazier St STHWK SE1 ...17 H3
Frean St BERM/RHTH SE16 ...123 H3
Freda Corbett Cl PECK SE15 ...143 H1
Frederica Rd CHING E4 ...38 B2
Frederica St HOLWY N7 *...85 F5
Frederick Cl BAY/PAD W2 ...8 D5
SUT SM1 ...208 D2
Frederick Crs BRXN/ST SW9 ...142 C1
PEND EN3 ...24 E5
Frederick Gdns CROY/NA CR0 ...196 C3
SUT SM1 ...208 D2
Frederick Pl
WOOL/PLUM SE18 ...127 G5
Frederick Rd RAIN RM13 ...111 F1
SUT SM1 ...208 D2
WALTH E17 ...122 C6
Frederick's Pl LOTH EC2R *...12 E4
NFNCH/WDSPK N12 ...33 G6
Frederick Sq
BERM/RHTH SE16 ...105 G6
Frederick's Rw FSBYE EC1V *...6 A3
Frederick St FSBYW WC1X ...5 G5
Frederick Ter HACK E8 *...86 B5
Frederic Ms KTBR SW1X *...15 G3
Fredora Av HYS/HAR UB4 ...94 D3
Freeborne Gdns RAIN RM13 ...93 J4
Freedom Cl WALTH E17 ...69 F1
Freedom Rd TOTM N17 ...49 K6
Freedom St BTSEA SW11 ...140 E3
Freegrove Rd HOLWY N7 ...84 E3
Freeland Pk HDN NW4 ...46 C5
Freeland Rd EA W5 ...98 B6
Freelands Av SAND/SEL CR2 ...213 F6
Freelands Gv BMLY BR1 ...184 A4
Freelands Rd BMLY BR1 ...184 A4
Freeland Wy ERITH DA8 ...150 D2
Freeling St IS N1 *...85 F6
Freeman Cl NTHLT UB5 ...77 J5
Freeman Dr E/WMO/HCT KT8 ...188 E1
Freeman Rd MRDN SM4 ...194 C2
Freemans La HYS/HAR UB3 ...94 C6
Freemantle Av PEND EN3 ...25 F6
Freemantle St WALW SE17 ...123 F5
Freemasons Rd CAN/RD E16 ...107 F5
CROY/NA CR0 ...197 F5
Freesia Cl ORP BR6 ...217 F3
Freethorpe Cl NRWD SE19 ...181 F4
Freightmaster Est
RAIN RM13 *...130 D4
Freke Rd BTSEA SW11 ...141 F4
Fremantle Rd BARK/HLT IG6 ...54 B5
BELV DA17 ...129 H4
Fremont St HOM E9 ...86 E6
French Pl SDTCH EC2A *...7 H5
French St SUN TW16 ...172 B5
Frendsbury Rd BROCKY SE4 ...144 B5
Frensham Cl STHL UB1 ...95 K3
Frensham Dr CROY/NA CR0 ...214 A5
PUT/ROE SW15 ...158 D3
Frensham Rd ELTH/MOT SE9 ...167 J4
Frensham St PECK SE15 ...123 H6
Frere St BTSEA SW11 ...140 D3
Freshfield Av HACK E8 ...86 B5
Freshfield Cl LEW SE13 ...145 G5
Freshfield Dr STHGT/OAK N14 ...34 B2
Freshfields CROY/NA CR0 ...198 B5
Freshford St TOOT SW17 ...160 B5
Freshwater Cl TOOT SW17 ...179 F2
Freshwater Rd BCTR RM8 ...73 K5
TOOT SW17 ...179 F2
Freshwell Av CHDH RM6 ...73 J1
Fresh Wharf Rd BARK IG11 ...108 B1
Freshwood Cl BECK BR3 ...182 E4
Freshwood Wy WLGTN SM6 ...210 C6
Freston Gdns EBAR EN4 ...22 A6
Freston Pk FNCH N3 ...46 D5
Freston Rd NKENS W10 ...100 B6
Freta Rd BXLYHS DA6 ...149 G6
Frewin Rd WAND/EARL SW18 ...160 C3
Friar Ms WNWD SE27 ...162 C5
Friar Rd STMC/STPC BR5 ...202 B2
YEAD UB4 ...95 H3
Friars Av PUT/ROE SW15 ...158 C3
TRDG/WHET N20 ...33 J5
Friars Cl CHING E4 ...38 A5
IL IG1 ...72 C5
NTHLT UB5 *...95 H2
STHWK SE1 *...12 B7
Friars Gdns ACT W3 ...99 F5
Friars Gate Cl WFD IG8 ...38 E6
Friars La RCH/KEW TW9 ...136 E6
Friars Md POP/IOD E14 ...125 F3
Friars Ms ELTH/MOT SE9 ...147 F6
Friars Place La ACT W3 ...99 F5
Friars Rd EHAM E6 ...89 H6
Friars Stile Rd
RCHPK/HAM TW10 ...157 F1
Friars Wk ABYW SE2 ...128 E5
STHGT/OAK N14 ...34 B3
Friars Wy ACT W3 ...99 F5
Friary Est PECK SE15 *...143 H1
Friary La WFD IG8 ...38 E6
Friary Pk NFNCH/WDSPK N12 *...33 J6
Friary Park Ct ACT W3 *...98 E5
Friary Rd ACT W3 ...99 F5
NFNCH/WDSPK N12 ...33 G6
PECK SE15 ...143 H1
Friary Wy NFNCH/WDSPK N12...33 J6
Friday HI CHING E4 ...38 C3
Friday HI East CHING E4 ...38 D3
Friday HI West CHING E4 ...38 C4

Friday Rd ERITH DA8 ...130 A5
MTCM CR4 ...178 E3
Friday St STP EC4M ...12 C5
Frideswide Pl KTTN NW5 ...84 C3
Friendly Pl LEW SE13 ...144 E2
Friendly St DEPT SE8 ...144 D2
Friendly Street Ms DEPT SE8 ...144 D3
Friendship Wy SRTFD E15 *...88 A6
Friends' Rd CROY/NA CR0 ...211 K1
Friend St FSBYE EC1V ...6 A4
Friern Barnet La
TRDG/WHET N20 ...33 H4
Friern Barnet Rd
FBAR/BDGN N11 ...48 A1
Friern Mount Dr
TRDG/WHET N20 ...33 G2
Friern Pk NFNCH/WDSPK N12...47 H1
Friern Rd EDUL SE22 ...163 H1
Friern Watch Av
NFNCH/WDSPK N12 ...33 H6
Frigate Ms DEPT SE8 ...124 D6
Frimley Av WLGTN SM6 ...210 E3
Frimley Cl CROY/NA CR0 ...214 A5
WIM/MER SW19 ...159 H4
Frimley Ct SCUP DA14 ...186 D1
Frimley Crs CROY/NA CR0 ...214 A5
Frimley Gdns MTCM CR4 ...178 D6
Frimley Rd CHSGTN KT9 ...205 K3
GDMY/SEVK IG3 ...91 F1
Frimley Wy WCHPL E1 *...105 F3
Frinstead Gv STMC/STPC BR5 ...202 E1
Frinsted Rd ERITH DA8 ...150 A1
Frinton Cl OXHEY WD19 ...27 F2
Frinton Dr WFD IG8 ...52 B3
Frinton Ms GNTH/NBYPK IG2 ...72 A3
Frinton Rd CRW RM5 ...56 E3
EHAM E6 ...107 H2
SCUP DA14 ...169 F4
SEVS/STOTM N15 ...68 A3
TOOT SW17 ...179 F2
Friston St FUL/PGN SW6 ...140 A3
Friswell Pl BXLYHN DA7 ...149 H5
Fritham Cl NWMAL KT3 ...192 B3
Frith Ct MLHL NW7 ...46 C3
Frith La MLHL NW7 ...46 C3
Frith Manor Farm Cotts
MLHL NW7 *...46 C1
Frith Rd CROY/NA CR0 ...196 D6
WAN E11 ...88 A2
Frith St SOHO/SHAV W1D ...10 C4
Frithville Gdns SHB W12 ...119 F1
Frithwood Av NTHWD HA6 ...40 D2
Frizlands La DAGE RM10 ...92 D1
Frobisher Cl BUSH WD23 ...28 A1
PIN HA5 ...59 H4
Frobisher Crs BARB EC2Y *...12 D1
STWL/WRAY TW19 ...152 B2
Frobisher Gdns LEY E10 *...69 K3
Frobisher Ms ENC/FH EN2 ...23 K5
Frobisher Rd CEND/HSY/T N8 ...67 G1
EHAM E6 ...107 K5
ERITH DA8 ...150 D1
Froghall La CHIG IG7 ...54 D1
Frogley Rd EDUL SE22 ...143 G5
Frogmore WAND/EARL SW18 ...159 K1
Frogmore Av YEAD UB4 ...94 C3
Frogmore Cl CHEAM SM3 ...208 B1
YEAD UB4 ...94 C3
Frogmore Gdns CHEAM SM3...208 C2
YEAD UB4 ...94 C3
Frognal HAMP NW3 ...83 G3
Frognal Av HRW HA1 ...61 F1
SCUP DA14 ...186 B2
Frognal Cl HAMP NW3 ...83 G3
Frognal Gdns HAMP NW3 ...83 G2
Frognal La HAMP NW3 ...82 E3
Frognal Pde HAMP NW3 *...83 G3
Frognal Pl SCUP DA14 ...186 C1
Frognal Ri HAMP NW3 ...83 G2
Frognal Wy HAMP NW3 ...83 F2
Froissart Rd ELTH/MOT SE9 ...146 C5
Frome Rd SEVS/STOTM N15 ...68 A3
Frome St IS N1 ...6 C2
Fromondes Rd CHEAM SM3 ...208 C3
Fromows Cnr CHSWK W4 *...117 K5
Frostic Wk WCHPL E1 *...13 K2
Froude St VX/NE SW8 ...141 G3
Fryatt Rd TOTM N17 ...49 K3
Fry Cl CRW RM5 ...56 C1
Fryday Grove Ms BAL SW12 *...161 H2
Fryent Cl CDALE/KGS NW9 ...62 C3
Fryent Crs CDALE/KGS NW9 ...63 G3
Fryent Flds CDALE/KGS NW9 ...63 G3
Fryent Gv CDALE/KGS NW9 ...63 G3
Fryent Wy CDALE/KGS NW9 ...62 B3
Frying Pan Aly WCHPL E1 ...13 H2
Fry Rd EHAM E6 ...89 H5
WLSDN NW10 ...81 H6
Fryston Av CROY/NA CR0 ...197 H6
Fuchsia Cl ROMW/RG RM7 ...75 G1
Fuchsia St ABYW SE2 ...128 C5
Fulbeck Dr CDALE/KGS NW9 ...45 G4
Fulbeck Wy RYLN/HDSTN HA2 ...42 C3
Fulbourne Rd WALTH E17 ...52 A5
Fulbourne St WCHPL E1 ...104 D4
Fulbrook Ms ARCH N19 ...84 C2
Fulbrook Rd HOLWY N7 *...84 E4
Fulford Gv OXHEY WD19 ...27 F4
Fulford Rd HOR/WEW KT19 ...207 F6
Fulford St BERM/RHTH SE16 ...123 J2
Fulham Broadway
FUL/PGN SW6 ...139 K1
Fulham Cl HGDN/ICK UB10 ...94 A3
Fulham Est FUL/PGN SW6 ...119 K6
Fulham High St FUL/PGN SW6...139 H3
Fulham Palace Rd
FUL/PGN SW6 ...139 G4
Fulham Park Gdns
FUL/PGN SW6 ...139 J3
Fulham Park Rd FUL/PGN SW6...139 J3
Fulham Rd FUL/PGN SW6 ...139 H3
WBPTN SW10 ...120 B6
Fullbrooks Av WPK KT4 ...192 C5
Fuller Cl BETH E2 *...104 C3
BUSH WD23 ...28 D2
ORP BR6 ...217 F3

Fuller Rd BCTR RM8 ...91 J1
Fullers Av SURB KT6 ...191 G6
SWFD E18 ...52 D5
Fullers Cl CRW RM5 ...56 C1
Fullers Rd SWFD E18 ...52 D4
Fuller St HDN NW4 ...64 A1
Fullers Wy North SURB KT6 ...206 B1
Fullers Wy South CHSGTN KT9 ...206 A2
Fullerton Rd CAR SM5 ...209 J6
CROY/NA CR0 ...197 G4
WAND/EARL SW18 ...140 B6
Fuller Wy HYS/HAR UB3 ...113 J5
Fullwell Av CLAY IG5 ...54 A4
Fullwood Pl GINN WC1R *...11 H2
Fulmar Ct BRYLDS KT5 *...191 G3
Fulmar Rd HCH RM12 ...93 K5
Fulmead St FUL/PGN SW6 ...140 A2
Fulmer Cl HPTN TW12 ...172 D1
Fulmer Rd CAN/RD E16 ...107 H4
Fulmer Wy WEA W13 ...116 C3
Fulready Rd LEY E10 ...70 B2
Fulstone Cl HSLWW TW4 ...134 E5
Fulthorp Rd BKHTH/KID SE3 ...145 J3
Fulton Ms BAY/PAD W2 *...101 G6
Fulton Rd WBLY HA9 ...62 D6
Fulwell Park Av WHTN TW2 ...155 H4
Fulwell Rd TEDD TW11 ...155 J6
Fulwich Rd DART DA1 ...171 J1
Fulwood Av ALP/SUD HA0 ...98 B1
Fulwood Gdns TWK TW1 ...156 A1
Fulwood Wk WIM/MER SW19...159 H3
Furber St HMSMTH W6 ...118 E3
Furham Fld PIN HA5 ...42 A3
Furley Rd PECK SE15 ...143 H1
Furlong Cl WLGTN SM6 ...195 G5
Furlong Rd HOLWY N7 ...85 G4
Furmage St WAND/EARL SW18...160 A2
Furneaux Av WNWD SE27 ...180 C1
Furner Cl DART DA1 ...150 C4
Furness Rd FUL/PGN SW6 ...140 A3
MRDN SM4 ...194 A3
RYLN/HDSTN HA2 ...60 B5
WLSDN NW10 ...99 J1
Furness Wy HCH RM12 ...93 J3
Furnival St FLST/FETLN EC4A ...11 J3
Furrow La HOM E9 ...86 E3
The Furrows WOT/HER KT12 ...188 B6
Fursby Av FNCH N3 ...46 E2
Further Acre CDALE/KGS NW9...45 H5
Furtherfield Cl CROY/NA CR0 ...196 B3
Further Green Rd CAT SE6 ...165 H3
Furze Cl OXHEY WD19 ...41 G1
Furzedown Dr TOOT SW17 ...179 G2
Furzedown Rd
STRHM/NOR SW16 ...161 G6
TOOT SW17 ...179 G1
Furze Farm Cl CHDH RM6 ...56 A5
Furzefield CHST BR7 ...185 G2
Furzefield Rd BKHTH/KID SE3 ...126 A6
Furzeground Wy STKPW UB11 ...113 J2
Furzeham Rd WDR/YW UB7 ...112 B2
Furzehill Sq STMC/STPC BR5 ...202 E1
Furze Rd THHTH CR7 ...180 D6
Furze St BOW E3 ...105 J4
Fyfe Foot La BLKFR EC4V *...12 C5
Fyfe Wy BMLY BR1 *...183 K5
Fyfield Cl BRXN/ST SW9 ...142 A4
HAYES BR2 ...199 H2
Fyfield Rd BRXN/ST SW9 ...142 A4
EN EN1 ...24 A4
RAIN RM13 ...93 H1
WALTH E17 ...52 B6
WFD IG8 ...53 G3
Fynes St WEST SW1P ...16 C6

G

Gable Cl DART DA1 ...150 D6
PIN HA5 ...42 A3
Gable Ct SYD SE26 ...163 J6
Gable Ms HAYES BR2 ...200 D6
Gables Cl CMBW SE5 ...143 F2
LEE/GVPK SE12 ...165 K3
The Gables NRWD SE19 *...181 F4
WBLY HA9 *...80 B1
Gabriel Cl CRW RM5 ...57 H1
FELT TW13 ...154 D6
Gabrielle Cl WBLY HA9 ...80 B1
Gabriel St FSTH SE23 ...164 A2
Gabriel's Whf STHWK SE1 *...11 J7
Gad Cl PLSTW E13 ...107 F2
Gaddesden Av WBLY HA9 ...80 B4
Gade Cl HYS/HAR UB3 ...114 A1
Gadesden Rd HOR/WEW KT19...206 E5
Gadsbury Cl CDALE/KGS NW9 ...63 H3
Gadwall Cl CAN/RD E16 ...107 F5
Gage Rd CAN/RD E16 ...106 C4
Gage St BMSBY WC1N ...11 F1
Gainford St IS N1 ...85 G6
Gainsborough Av DART DA1 ...151 F6
MNPK E12 ...90 A3
Gainsborough Cl BECK BR3 ...182 D3
ESH/CLAY KT10 ...189 K5
Gainsborough Ct SHB W12 ...119 F2
Gainsborough Gdns EDGW HA8...44 B5
GLDGN NW11 ...64 D4
HAMP NW3 ...83 H1
ISLW TW7 ...135 J6
Gainsborough Ms DUL SE21 ...162 D3
SYD SE26 ...163 J5
Gainsborough Rd BCTR RM8 ...91 H1
CHSWK W4 ...118 C4
NFNCH/WDSPK N12 ...47 F1
NWMAL KT3 ...192 A5
RAIN RM13 ...111 J1
RCH/KEW TW9 ...137 G3
SRTFD E15 ...106 C2
WAN E11 ...70 D4
WFD IG8 ...53 J2
Gainsborough Sq BXLYHS DA6...148 E4
Gainsborough St HOM E9 *...87 H4

Gainsborough Ter
BELMT SM2 *...208 D5
Gainsford Rd WALTH E17 ...69 H1
Gainsford St STHWK SE1 ...19 J2
Gairloch Rd CMBW SE5 ...143 F3
Gaisford St KTTN NW5 ...84 C4
Gaitskell Rd ELTH/MOT SE9 ...167 H3
Gaitskell Wy STHWK SE1 *...18 C2
Galahad Rd BMLY BR1 ...165 K5
ED N9 ...36 C5
Galata Rd BARN SW13 ...138 D1
Galatea Sq PECK SE15 ...143 J4
Galbraith St POP/IOD E14 ...125 F3
Galdana Av BAR EN5 ...21 G4
Galeborough Av WFD IG8 ...52 B3
Gale Cl HPTN TW12 ...172 D2
MTCM CR4 ...178 C1
Galena Rd HMSMTH W6 ...118 E4
Galen Pl NOXST/BSQ WC1A ...11 F2
Galesbury Rd
WAND/EARL SW18 ...160 B1
Gales Gdns BETH E2 ...104 D2
Gale St BOW E3 ...105 J4
DAGW RM9 ...91 K6
Gales Wy WFD IG8 ...53 J3
Galgate Cl WIM/MER SW19 ...159 H3
Gallants Farm Rd EBAR EN4 ...33 K3
Galleon Cl BERM/RHTH SE16 ...124 A2
ERITH DA8 ...130 B3
Galleons Dr BARK IG11 ...109 G2
The Galleries IS N1 *...6 A1
Gallery Gdns NTHLT UB5 ...95 H1
Gallery Rd DUL SE21 ...162 E3
Galleywall Rd
BERM/RHTH SE16 ...123 J4
Galleywood Crs CRW RM5 ...57 F2
Galliard Rd ED N9 ...36 C2
Gallia Rd HBRY N5 ...85 H3
Gallions Cl BARK IG11 ...109 G2
Gallions Rd CAN/RD E16 ...108 C6
CHARL SE7 ...125 J4
Gallions View Rd THMD SE28 ...127 K2
Gallon Cl CHARL SE7 ...126 B4
The Gallop BELMT SM2 ...209 H6
SAND/SEL CR2 ...212 D5
Galloway Path CROY/NA CR0 ...211 K2
Galloway Rd SHB W12 ...118 D1
Gallus Cl WCHMH N21 ...35 F1
Gallus Sq BKHTH/KID SE3 ...146 A4
Galpin's Rd THHTH CR7 ...195 K1
Galsworthy Av CHDH RM6 ...73 H4
POP/IOD E14 ...105 G4
Galsworthy Cl THMD SE28 ...128 C1
Galsworthy Crs
BKHTH/KID SE3 ...146 B2
Galsworthy Rd CRICK NW2 ...82 C2
KUTN/CMB KT2 ...175 J4
Galton St NKENS W10 ...100 C3
Galva Cl EBAR EN4 ...22 A5
Galveston Rd PUT/ROE SW15...139 J6
Galway Cl BERM/RHTH SE16 ...123 J5
Galway St FSBYE EC1V ...6 D5
Gambetta St VX/NE SW8 ...141 G3
Gambia St STHWK SE1 ...18 B1
Gambole Rd TOOT SW17 ...160 D6
Games Rd EBAR EN4 ...21 K4
Gamlen Rd PUT/ROE SW15 ...139 G5
Gamuel Cl WALTH E17 ...69 J3
Gander Green Crs HPTN TW12...173 A4
Gander Green La CHEAM SM3 ...193 H6
SUT SM1 ...208 D2
Gandhi Cl WALTH E17 ...69 J3
Gandolfi St PECK SE15 ...123 F6
Ganton St REGST W1B ...10 A4
Ganton Wk OXHEY WD19 *...27 J6
Gantshill Crs GNTH/NBYPK IG2...72 A2
Garage Rd ACT W3 ...98 C5
Garbrand Wk EW KT17 ...207 H6
Garbutt Pl MHST W1U *...9 H1
Garden Av BXLYHN DA7 ...149 G4
MTCM CR4 ...179 G3
Garden City EDGW HA8 ...44 C2
Garden Cl BAR EN5 ...20 B4
CHING E4 ...51 J1
HPTN TW12 ...172 E1
LEE/GVPK SE12 ...166 A5
NTHLT UB5 ...77 J6
PUT/ROE SW15 ...158 E2
RSLP HA4 ...58 B6
WLGTN SM6 ...210 E3
Garden Ct CHSWK W4 *...117 K3
EMB EC4Y *...11 J4
HPTN TW12 ...172 E1
Gardeners Rd CROY/NA CR0 ...196 C5
Garden Flats HMSMTH W6 *...119 F3
Gardenia Rd BMLY BR1 ...185 F6
EN EN1 ...36 A1
Gardenia Wy WFD IG8 ...52 E2
Garden La BMLY BR1 ...184 A2
BRXS/STRHM SW2 ...162 A3
Garden Lodge Ct EFNCH N2 *...47 H6
Garden Pl HACK E8 ...7 K1
RDART DA2 ...171 G5
Garden Rd BMLY BR1 ...184 A2
PGE/AN SE20 ...181 K4
RCH/KEW TW9 ...137 H3
STJWD NW8 ...2 A4
WOT/HER KT12 ...188 A3
Garden Rw STHWK SE1 ...18 A4
The Gardens BECK BR3 ...183 F5
CEND/HSY/T N8 ...49 F6
EBED/NFELT TW14 ...153 G1
EDUL SE22 ...143 H5
ESH/CLAY KT10 ...204 A3
HRW HA1 ...60 C3
PIN HA5 ...59 K3
Garden St WCHPL E1 ...105 G4
Garden Studios BAY/PAD W2 *...101 G4
Garden Ter PIM SW1V *...121 J5
Garden Vis ALP/SUD HA0 *...79 K5
Garden Wk BECK BR3 ...182 C4
SDTCH EC2A ...7 G5

Garden Wy WLSDN NW10 ....80 E4
Gardiner Av CRICK NW2 * 82 A3
Gardiner Cl BCTR RM8 ....91 K2
Gardiner Dr
STMC/STPC BR5 ....186 D5
Gardiner House CHARL SE7 * .146 D1
Gardner Cl WAN E11 ....71 F3
Gardners Cl FBAR/BDGN N11..34 A4
Gardners La BLKFR EC4V 12 C5
Gardnor Rd HAMP NW3 ....83 H2
Gard St FSBYE EC1V 6 B4
Garendon Gdns MRDN SM4..194 A4
Garendon Rd MRDN SM4 ....194 A4
Gareth Cl WPK KT4 ....193 G6
Gareth Dr ED N9 ....36 C5
Gareth Gv BMLY BR1 ....165 K6
Garfield Ms BTSEA SW11 ....141 G4
Garfield Rd BTSEA SW11 ....141 F4
CHING E4 ....38 B3
PEND EN3 ....25 F1
PLSTW E13 ....106 D3
TWK TW1 ....156 B3
WIM/MER SW19 ....178 B2
Garford St POP/IOD E14 ....105 J6
Garganey Wk THMD SE28 ....109 K6
Garibaldi St WOOL/PLUM SE18 123 K6
Garland Dr HSLW TW3 ....135 H3
Garland Rd STAN HA7 ....43 K4
WOOL/PLUM SE18 ....147 J1
Garlick HI BLKFR EC4V 12 D5
Garlies Rd FSTH SE23 ....164 B5
Garlinge Rd CRICK NW2 ....82 D4
Garman Cl UED N18 ....49 K1
Garman Rd TOTM N17 ....50 E3
Garnault Ms CLKNW EC1R 5 K5
Garnault Pl CLKNW EC1R 5 K5
Garnault Rd EN EN1 ....24 B1
Garner Cl BCTR RM8 ....73 K5
Garner St BETH E2 ....104 C1
Garnet Rd THHTH CR7 ....196 D1
WLSDN NW10 ....81 G4
Garnet St WAP E1W 104 E6
Garnett Cl ELTH/MOT SE9 ....147 F4
Garnett Rd HAMP NW3 ....83 K3
Garnham St STNW/STAM N16 ..68 B6
Garnies Cl PECK SE15 ....143 G1
Garrad's Rd
STRHM/NOR SW16 ....161 J3
Garrard Cl BXLYHN DA7 ....149 H4
CHST BR7 ....185 G1
Garratt La WAND/EARL SW18 ..140 A6
Garratt Rd EDGW HA8 ....44 C5
Garratts Rd BUSH WD23 ....28 C2
Garratt Ter TOOT SW17 ....160 D6
Garrett Cl ACT W3 ....99 F4
Garrett St STLK EC1Y 6 C6
Garrick Av GLDGN NW11 ....64 D3
Garrick Cl EA W5 ....98 A3
RCH/KEW TW9 ....136 D6
WAND/EARL SW18 ....140 B5
Garrick Crs CROY/NA CRO 197 F6
Garrick Dr HDN NW4 ....46 A5
WOOL/PLUM SE18 ....147 F1
Garrick Gdns E/WMO/HCT KT8..173 F6
Garrick Pk HDN NW4 ....46 B5
Garrick Rd CDALE/KGS NW9 ....63 H3
GFD/PVL UB6 ....96 B3
RCH/KEW TW9 ....137 H3
Garrick St COVGDN WC2E 10 E5
Garrick Wy HDN NW4 ....46 B3
Garrick Yd CHCR WC2N 10 E5
Garrison Cl HSLWW TW4 ....134 E6
WOOL/PLUM SE18 ....147 F1
Garrison La CHSGTN KT9 ....206 A5
Garrison Rd BOW E3 ....87 J6
Garry Cl ROM RM1 ....57 G3
Garry Wy ROM RM1 ....57 G3
Garsdale Ter WKENS W14 * 119 J5
Garside Cl HPTN TW12 ....173 G3
THMD SE28 ....127 J3
Garsington Ms BROCKY SE4 ....144 C4
Garter Wy BERM/RHTH SE16 ..124 A2
Garth Cl KUTN/CMB KT2 ....175 G1
MRDN SM4 ....193 G4
RSLP HA4 ....59 H5
Garth Ms EA W5 * 98 A3
Garthorne Rd FSTH SE23 ....164 A2
Garth Rd CHSWK W4 ....118 A6
CRICK NW2 ....64 D6
KUTN/CMB KT2 ....175 G1
MRDN SM4 ....193 G3
Garthside KUTN/CMB KT2 ....175 F1
The Garth HPTN TW12 ....173 G2
KTN/HRWW/WS HA3 ....61 G1
NFNCH/WDSPK N12 * 47 J2
Garthway NFNCH/WDSPK N12 ..47 J2
Gartmoor Gdns
WIM/MER SW19 ....159 J3
Gartmore Rd GDMY/SEVK IG3..73 F5
Garton Pl WAND/EARL SW18..160 B1
Gartons Cl PEND EN3 ....24 E6
Gartons Wy BTSEA SW11 ....140 B4
Garvary Rd CAN/RD E16 ....107 F5
Garway Rd BAY/PAD W2 ....101 F5
Gascoigne Gdns WFD IG8 ....52 C3
Gascoigne Pl BETH E2 ....7 J4
Gascoigne Rd BARK IG11 ....90 C6
Gascony Av KIL/WHAMP NW6..82 E5
Gascoyne Dr DART DA1 ....150 C4
Gascoyne Rd HOM E9 ....87 F5
Gaselee St POP/IOD E14 ....106 A6
Gasholder Pl LBTH SE11 ....122 A5
Gaskarth Rd BAL SW12 ....161 G1
EDGW HA8 ....44 E5
Gaskell Rd HGT N6 ....65 K3
Gaskell St CLAP SW4 ....141 K3
Gaskin St IS N1 ....5 J1
Gaspar Ms ECT SW5 * 120 A4
Gassiot Rd TOOT SW17 ....160 E6
Gassiot Wy SUT SM1 ....209 H1
Gastein Rd HMSMTH W6 ....119 G6
Gaston Bell Cl RCH/KEW TW9..137 G4
Gaston Rd MTCM CR4 ....179 F6
Gataker St BERM/RHTH SE16...123 J3
Gatcombe Ms EA W5 ....98 B6
Gatcombe Rd ARCH N19 ....84 D1
Gatcombe Wy EBAR EN4 ....21 K4
Gate Cottages EDGW HA8 * 30 C4
Gate End NTHWD HA6 ....40 E3
Gateforth St STJWD NW8 ....2 C7
Gatehill Rd NTHWD HA6 ....40 E3
Gatehouse Cl KUTN/CMB KT2..175 K3
Gatehouse Sq STHWK SE1 * 12 D7
Gateley Rd BRXN/ST SW9 ....142 A4
Gate Ms SKENS SW7 ....14 D3
Gater Dr ENC/FH EN2 ....23 K2
Gates Ct WALW SE17 * 122 D5
Gates Green Rd WWKM BR4..214 E2
Gateside Rd TOOT SW17 ....160 E5
Gatestone Rd NRWD SE19 ....181 F2
Gate St HOL/ALD WC2B 11 G3
Gateway WALW SE17 ....122 D6
Gateway Ar IS N1 * 6 A2
Gateway Cl NTHWD HA6 ....40 A2
Gateway Gdns EHAM E6 ....107 K2
Gateway Ms HACK E8 * 86 B3
The Gateways
RCH/KEW TW9 * 136 E5
Gatfield Gv FELT TW13 ....154 E5
Gathorne Rd WDGN N22 ....49 G5
Gathorne St BETH E2 * 105 F1
Gatley Av HOR/WEW KT19..206 D3
Gatliff Cl BGVA SW1W * 121 G5
Gatliff Rd BGVA SW1W 121 G6
Gatling Rd ABYW SE2 ....128 B5
Gatonby St PECK SE15 ....143 G2
Gatton Cl BELMT SM2 * 209 F6
Gatton Rd TOOT SW17 ....160 D6
Gattons Wy SCUP DA14 ....169 G6
Gatward Cl WCHMH N21 ....35 H1
Gatward Gn ED N9 ....36 B4
Gatwick Rd WAND/EARL SW18..159 J2
Gauden Cl CLAP SW4 ....141 J4
Gauden Rd CLAP SW4 ....141 J4
Gaumont Ter SHB W12 * 119 F2
Gauntlet Cl NTHLT UB5 ....77 J5
Gauntlet Ct ALP/SUD HA0 ....79 H3
Gauntlett Rd SUT SM1 ....209 H5
Gaunt St STHWK SE1 ....18 B4
Gautrey Rd PECK SE15 ....143 K3
Gavel St WALW SE17 * 19 F6
Gaverick Ms POP/IOD E14 ....124 D4
Gavestone Crs LEE/GVPK SE12..166 A2
Gavestone Rd LEE/GVPK SE12..166 A2
Gavina Cl MRDN SM4 ....194 D2
Gawain Wk ED N9 ....36 C5
Gawber St BETH E2 ....104 E2
Gawsworth Cl SRTFD E15 ....88 D3
Gawthorne Av MLHL NW7 * 46 C1
Gay Cl CRICK NW2 ....81 K3
Gaydon La CDALE/KGS NW9..45 G4
Gayfere Rd CLAY IG5 ....53 K6
EW KT17 ....207 J3
Gayfere St WEST SW1P 16 E5
Gay Gdns DAGE RM10 ....92 E2
Gayhurst Rd HACK E8 ....86 C5
Gaylor Rd NTHLT UB5 ....77 K3
Gaynesford Rd CAR SM5 ....209 K5
FSTH SE23 ....164 A4
Gaynes Hill Rd WFD IG8 ....53 J3
Gay Rd SRTFD E15 ....106 B1
Gaysham Av GNTH/NBYPK IG2..72 A2
Gayton Crs HAMP NW3 ....83 H2
Gayton Rd HAMP NW3 ....83 H2
HRW HA1 ....61 G3
Gayville Rd BTSEA SW11 ....160 E1
Gaywood Cl BRXS/STRHM SW2..162 A3
Gaywood Rd WALTH E17 ....51 J6
Gaywood St STHWK SE1 ....18 B5
Gaza St WALW SE17 ....122 B5
Geariesville Gdns BARK/HLT IG6..72 B1
Gearing Cl TOOT SW17 ....161 G6
Geary Rd WLSDN NW10 ....81 J3
Geary St HOLWY N7 ....85 F3
Geddes Pl BXLYHS DA6 * 149 G4
Gedeney Rd TOTM N17 ....49 J4
Gedling Pl STHWK SE1 * 19 J4
Geere Rd SRTFD E15 ....88 D6
Gees Ct MHST W1U 9 H4
Gee St FSBYE EC1V 6 C6
Geffrye Est IS N1 * 7 H3
Geffrye St BETH E2 ....7 J1
Geldart Rd PECK SE15 ....143 J1
Gelderston Rd CLPT E5 ....68 D6
Gellatly Rd NWCR SE14 ....143 K5
Gelsthorpe Rd CRW RM5 ....56 D3
General Gordon Pl
WOOL/PLUM SE18 ....127 G3
General Wolfe Rd
GNWCH SE10 ....145 G2
Genesis Cl STWL/WRAY TW19..152 C5
Genesta Rd WOOL/PLUM SE18..127 G6
Geneva Dr BRXN/ST SW9 ....142 B5
Geneva Gdns CHDH RM6 ....74 A2
Geneva Rd KUT/HW KT1 ....191 F1
THHTH CR7 ....196 D2
Genever Cl CHING E4 ....51 J1
Genista Rd UED N18 ....50 D1
Genoa Av PUT/ROE SW15 ....139 F6
Genoa Rd PGE/AN SE20 ....181 K4
Genotin Rd EN EN1 ....23 K4
Gentleman's Rw ENC/FH EN2..23 J4
Geoffrey Cl CMBW SE5 ....142 D3
Geoffrey Gdns EHAM E6 ....107 J1
Geoffrey Rd BROCKY SE4 ....144 C4
George Beard Rd DEPT SE8 ..124 C4
George Crs MUSWH N10 ....48 A3
George Downing Est
STNW/STAM N16 * 68 B6
George Gange Wy
KTN/HRWW/WS HA3 ....43 G6
George Groves Rd
CROY/NA CRO 181 H4
George La HAYES BR2 ....200 A5
LEW SE13 ....165 F1
SWFD E18 ....52 E5
George Lowe Ct
BAY/PAD W2 * 101 F4
George Mathers Rd
LBTH SE11 * 18 A6
Gilda Crs STNW/STAM N16 ..68 C5
Gildea Cl PIN HA5 ....42 A3
Gildea St GTPST W1W 9 K2
Gilden Crs KTTN NW5 ....84 A3
Gildersome St
WOOL/PLUM SE18 ....127 F6
Gilders Rd CHSGTN KT9 ....206 B5
Giles Coppice NRWD SE19 ....163 G6
Giles Crs DUL SE21 ....163 F1
Gilkes Pl DUL SE21 ....163 F1
Gillam Wy RAIN RM13 ....93 J4
Gillan Gn BUSH WD23 ....28 C4
Gillards Ms WALTH E17 * 69 J1
Gillards Wy WALTH E17 ....69 J1
Gill Av CAN/RD E16 ....106 E5
Gill Cl WATW WD18 ....26 A1
Gillender St BOW E3 ....106 A3
Gillespie Rd HBRY N5 ....85 G1
Gillett Av EHAM E6 ....107 J1
Gillett Pl HACK E8 * 86 B3
Gillett Rd THHTH CR7 ....196 E1
Gillett St STNW/STAM N16 ..86 A3
Gillfoot CAMTN NW1 * 4 A4
Gillham Ter TOTM N17 * 50 C2
Gillian Park Rd CHEAM SM3..193 J4
Gillian St LEW SE13 ....144 E6
Gillies St KTTN NW5 ....84 A3
Gillingham Ms PIM SW1V 15 K6
Gillingham Rd CRICK NW2 ....82 C1
Gillingham Row PIM SW1V 16 A6
Gillingham St PIM SW1V 15 K7
Gillison Wk
BERM/RHTH SE16 * 123 H3
Gilman Dr SRTFD E15 ....88 C6
Gilmans Rd STMC/STPC BR5..202 C5
Gill St POP/IOD E14 ....105 H5
Gillum Cl EBAR EN4 ....33 K3
Gilmore Rd LEW SE13 ....145 G5
Gilpin Av MORT/ESHN SW14..138 A5
Gilpin Cl MTCM CR4 ....178 D5
Gilpin Crs UED N18 ....50 B1
WHTN TW2 ....155 G2
Gilpin Rd CLPT E5 ....87 G2
Gilpin Wy HYS/HAR UB3 ....133 G1
Gilroy Cl RAIN RM13 ....93 J4
Gilroy Wy STMC/STPC BR5..202 C4
Gilsland Rd THHTH CR7 ....196 E1
Gilstead Rd FUL/PGN SW6 ..140 A3
Gilston Rd WBPTN SW10 ....120 B5
Gilton Rd CAT SE6 ....165 H5
Giltspur St STBT EC1A 12 B3
Gilwell Cl CHING E4 ....25 K5
Gippeswyck Cl PIN HA5 ....41 H4
Gipsy Hill NRWD SE19 ....181 F1
Gipsy La BARN SW13 ....118 C6
PUT/ROE SW15 ....138 D4
Gipsy Road Gdns WNWD SE27..162 D6
Giralda Cl CAN/RD E16 ....107 H4
Giraud St POP/IOD E14 ....105 K5
Girdlers Rd HMSMTH W6 ....119 G4
Girdwood Rd
WAND/EARL SW18 ....159 H2
Girling Wy EBED/NFELT TW14..133 K4
Gironde Rd FUL/PGN SW6 ....139 J1
Girton Av CDALE/KGS NW9 ..44 C6
Girton Cl NTHLT UB5 ....78 C4
Girton Gdns CROY/NA CRO..213 J1
Girton Rd NTHLT UB5 ....78 C4
SYD SE26 ....182 A1
Gisbourne Cl WLGTN SM6 ....210 D1
Gisburn Rd CEND/HSY/T N8..67 F1
Gissing Wk IS N1 * 85 G5
Gittens Cl BMLY BR1 ....165 J6
Glacier Wy ALP/SUD HA0 ....97 K1
Gladbeck Wy ENC/FH EN2 ....23 J5
Gladding Rd MNPK E12 ....89 H2
Glade Cl SURB KT6 * 190 E6
Glade Gdns CROY/NA CRO..198 B4
Glade La NWDGN UB2 ....115 G2
Gladeside CROY/NA CRO 198 A4
WCHMH N21 ....35 F2
Gladiator St FSTH SE23 ....164 B1
Glading Ter STNW/STAM N16..68 B1
Gladioli Cl HPTN TW12 ....173 F2
Gladsdale Dr PIN HA5 ....58 E1
Gladsmuir Cl WOT/HER KT12..188 B6
Gladsmuir Rd ARCH N19 ....66 C5
BAR EN5 ....20 C3
Gladstone Av
EBED/NFELT TW14 ....153 K1
MNPK E12 ....89 J5
WDGN N22 ....49 H5
Gladstone Gdns HSLW TW3..135 H2
Gladstone Ms KIL/WHAMP NW6..82 D4
PGE/AN SE20 ....181 K3
WDGN N22 ....49 G5
Gladstone Pde CRICK NW2 * ..82 A1
Gladstone Park Gdns
CRICK NW2 ....81 K1
Gladstone Pl BAR EN5 ....20 B5
E/WMO/HCT KT8 * 189 G2
Gladstone Rd BKHH IG9 ....39 G3
CHSWK W4 * 118 A3
CROY/NA CRO 196 E4
DART DA1 ....171 J1
KUT/HW KT1 ....175 H6
NWDGN UB2 ....114 D2
ORP BR6 ....216 C3
SURB KT6 ....190 E6
Gladstone St STHWK SE1 ....18 A4
Gladstone Ter VX/NE SW8 ..141 G2
WNWD SE27 * 162 D6
Gladstone Wy
KTN/HRWW/WS HA3 ....42 E6
Gladwell Rd BMLY BR1 ....183 K2
CEND/HSY/T N8 ....67 F3
Gladwyn Rd PUT/ROE SW15..139 G4
Gladys Rd KIL/WHAMP NW6..82 E5
Glaisher St DEPT SE8 ....124 E6
Glamis Crs HYS/HAR UB3 ....113 F3
Glamis Pl WAP E1W 104 E6
Glamis Rd WAP E1W 104 E6
Glamis Wy NTHLT UB5 ....78 C4
Glamorgan Cl MTCM CR4 ....179 K6
Glamorgan Rd KUT/HW KT1..174 D5
Glandford Wy CHDH RM6 ....73 H2
Glanfield Rd BECK BR3 ....198 C1
Glanleam Rd STAN HA7 ....29 K6
Glanville Ms STAN HA7 ....43 G1
Glanville Rd BRXS/STRHM SW2..141 K6
HAYES BR2 ....184 A6
Glasbrook Av WHTN TW2 ....154 E3
Glasbrook Rd ELTH/MOT SE9..166 C2
Glaserton Rd STNW/STAM N16..68 A4
Glasford St TOOT SW17 ....178 E2
Glasgow Rd PLSTW E13 ....107 F1
UED N18 ....50 D1
Glasgow Ter PIM SW1V 121 H5
Glaskin Ms HOM E9 ....87 G4
Glasse Cl WEA W13 ....97 G6
Glasshill St STHWK SE1 ....18 B2
Glasshouse Flds WAP E1W..105 F6
Glasshouse St REGST W1B ..10 B6
Glasshouse Wk LBTH SE11..121 K5
Glasshouse Yd FARR EC1M ..6 C7
Glasslyn Rd CEND/HSY/T N8..66 D2
Glassmill La HAYES BR2 ....183 J6
Glass St BETH E2 * 104 D3
Glass Yd WOOL/PLUM SE18..127 F3
Glastonbury Av WFD IG8 ....53 H3
Glastonbury Rd
STMC/STPC BR5 ....202 E5
Glastonbury Pl WCHPL E1 ..104 E5
Glastonbury Rd ED N9 ....36 C3
MRDN SM4 ....193 K4
Glastonbury St
KIL/WHAMP NW6 ....82 D3
Glaston Ct EA W5 * 116 E1
Glaucus St BOW E3 ....106 A4
Glazbury Rd WKENS W14 ....119 H4
Glazebrook Cl DUL SE21 ....162 E4
Glazebrook Rd TEDD TW11..174 A3
Glebe Av ENC/FH EN2 ....23 H5
HCDN/ICK UB10 ....76 A2
KTN/HRWW/WS HA3 ....44 A6
MTCM CR4 ....178 D5
RSLP HA4 ....77 F4
WFD IG8 ....52 E2
Glebe Cl CHSWK W4 * 118 B5
HCDN/ICK UB10 ....76 A2
Glebe Cr BKHTH/KID SE3 * ..145 J1
EA W5 * 116 E1
STAN HA7 ....43 J1
Glebe Cottages
NFNCH/WDSPK N12 * 47 H1
Glebe Ct BKHTH/KID SE3 ..145 J3
EA W5 ....116 E1
KTN/HRWW/WS HA3 ....62 A1
MTCM CR4 ....178 E6
Glebe Pl CHEL SW3 ....120 D6
Glebe Rd BARN SW13 ....138 D3
BELMT SM2 ....208 C5
BMLY BR1 ....183 K4
CAR SM5 ....209 K4
CEND/HSY/T N8 ....67 F1
DAGE RM10 ....92 D4
FNCH N3 ....47 F5
HACK E8 ....86 B6
RAIN RM13 ....111 K2
STAN HA7 ....43 J1
WLSDN NW10 * 81 H4
Glebe Side TWK TW1 ....156 A1
Glebe Sq MTCM CR4 * 178 E6
Glebe St CHSWK W4 ....118 B5
The Glebe BKHTH/KID SE3 ..145 H4
CHST BR7 ....185 H4
STRHM/NOR SW16 * 161 J6
WDR/YW UB7 ....112 D4
WPK KT4 ....192 C6
Glebe Wy ERITH DA8 ....130 B6
FELT TW13 ....155 F5
WWKM BR4 ....199 G6
Gledhow Gdns ECT SW5 ....120 B4
Gledstanes Rd WKENS W14..119 H5
Gledwood Av YEAD UB4 ....94 D4
Gledwood Crs YEAD UB4 ....94 D4
Gledwood Dr YEAD UB4 ....94 D4
Gledwood Gdns YEAD UB4..94 D4
Gleed Av BUSH WD23 ....28 D4
Gleeson Dr ORP BR6 ....217 F3
Glegg Pl PUT/ROE SW15 * ..139 G5
Glenaffric Av POP/IOD E14..125 H4
Glen Albyn Rd
WIM/MER SW19 ....159 G4
Glenalla Rd RSLP HA4 ....58 D4
Glenalmond Rd
KTN/HRWW/WS HA3 ....62 A1
Glenalvon Wy
WOOL/PLUM SE18 ....126 D4
Glena Mt SUT SM1 ....209 G2
Glenarm Rd CLPT E5 ....86 E2
Glen Av ASHF TW15 ....152 C6
Glenavon Cl ESH/CLAY KT10..205 G4
Glenavon Rd SRTFD E15 ....88 C5

George Groves Rd continues...

George Ms BRXN/ST SW9 ....142 B3
George Rd CHING E4 ....51 J5
KUTN/CMB KT2 ....175 K3
NWMAL KT3 ....192 C2
George Rw BERM/RHTH SE16..123 H2
Georges Md BORE WD6 ....30 A1
George Sq HOLWY N7 * 85 F4
George St BARK IG11 ....90 C5
CAN/RD E16 ....106 D5
CROY/NA CRO 196 E6
HNWL W7 ....115 K1
HSLW TW3 ....134 E3
MBLAR W1H 8 E3
NWDGN UB2 ....114 D4
RCH/KEW TW9 ....136 E6
ROM RM1 ....75 H3
Georgetown Cl NRWD SE19..181 F1
Georgette Pl GNWCH SE10 ..145 C1
Georgeville Gdns BARK/HLT IG6..72 B1
George V Wy GFD/PVL UB6..79 H5
George Wyver Cl
WIM/MER SW19 ....159 H2
George Yd BANK EC3V 13 H4
Georgiana St CAMTN NW1 * ..84 C6
Georgian Cl HAYES BR2 ....200 A5
STAN HA7 ....43 G3
Georgian Ct WBLY HA9 ....80 C4
Georgian Wy HRW HA1 ....60 D6
Georgia Rd NWMAL KT3 ....191 K1
THHTH CR7 ....180 C4
Georgina Gdns BETH E2 * 7 K4
Geraint Rd BMLY BR1 ....165 K5
Geraldine Rd CHSWK W4 ....117 H6
WAND/EARL SW18 ....140 B6
Geraldine St LBTH SE11 ....18 A5
Gerald Rd BCTR RM8 ....74 B6
BGVA SW1W 15 H6
CAN/RD E16 ....106 D3
Gerard Av HSLWW TW4 ....155 F1
Gerard Gdns RAIN RM13 ....111 G1
Gerard Rd BARN SW13 ....138 C2
HRW HA1 ....61 G3
Gerards Cl BERM/RHTH SE16..123 K5
Gerda Rd ELTH/MOT SE9 ....167 G4
Gerdview Dr RDART DA2 ....171 F6
Germander Wy SRTFD E15 ..106 C2
Geron Wy CRICK NW2 ....81 K5
Gerrard Gdns PIN HA5 ....58 E2
Gerrard Pl SOHO/SHAV W1D * ..10 D5
Gerrard St SOHO/SHAV W1D..10 D5
Gerridge St STHWK SE1 ....17 K3
Gertrude Rd BELV DA17 ....129 H4
Gertrude St WBPTN SW10 ..120 B6
Gervase Cl WBLY HA9 ....80 E1
Gervase Rd EDGW HA8 ....44 E4
Gervase St PECK SE15 ....143 J1
Ghent St CAT SE6 ....164 D4
Ghent Wy HACK E8 * 86 B4
Giant Arches Rd HNHL SE24..162 D2
Giant Tree HI BUSH WD23 ....28 D4
Gibbfield Cl CHDH RM6 ....56 A6
Gibbins Rd SRTFD E15 ....88 A5
Gibbon Rd ACT W3 ....99 G6
KUTN/CMB KT2 ....175 F4
PECK SE15 ....143 K4
Gibbons Ms GLDGN NW11 ....64 D2
Gibbons Rd WLSDN NW10 ....81 F5
Gibbs Av NRWD SE19 ....180 E2
Gibbs Cl NRWD SE19 ....180 E2
Gibbs Couch OXHEY WD19..27 H5
Gibbs Gn EDGW HA8 ....30 E6
Gibbs Green Cl WKENS W14..119 J5
Gibbs Rd UED N18 ....36 E6
Gibbs Sq NRWD SE19 * 180 E1
Gibraltar Wk BETH E2 ....7 K5
Gibson Cl CHSGTN KT9 ....205 J3
ISLW TW7 ....135 J4
WCHMH N21 ....23 G6
Gibson Gdns STNW/STAM N16 *..68 B6
Gibson Rd BCTR RM8 ....73 J5
LBTH SE11 ....17 H7
SUT SM1 ....209 F3
Gibson's HI STRHM/NOR SW16..180 B1
Gibson Sq IS N1 ....85 G6
Gibson St GNWCH SE10 ....125 H5
Gideon Cl BELV DA17 ....129 J4
Gideon Ms EA W5 ....116 E2
Gideon Rd BTSEA SW11 ....141 F4
Giesbach Rd ARCH N19 ....66 C6
Giffard Rd UED N18 ....50 A1
Giffin St DEPT SE8 ....144 D1
Gifford Gdns HNWL W7 ....96 D4
Gifford St IS N1 ....84 E6
Gift La SRTFD E15 ....88 C6
Giggs Hill STMC/STPC BR5..186 B5
Giggs Hill Gdns THDIT KT7..190 B5
Giggs Hill Rd THDIT KT7 ....190 B5
Gilbert Cl WIM/MER SW19 * ..178 A4
WOOL/PLUM SE18 ....146 E2
Gilbert Gv EDGW HA8 ....45 F4
Gilbert Pl NOXST/BSQ WC1A..10 E2
Gilbert Rd BELV DA17 ....129 H3
BMLY BR1 ....183 K3
LBTH SE11 ....17 K7
PIN HA5 ....59 H1
ROM RM1 ....75 H1
WIM/MER SW19 ....178 B3
Gilbert St HSLW TW3 ....135 H4
MYFR/PKLN W1K 9 H4
SRTFD E15 ....88 C2
SUT SM1 * 208 E4
Gilbey Rd TOOT SW17 ....160 D6
Gilbeys Yd CAMTN NW1 ....84 A6
Gilbourne Rd
WOOL/PLUM SE18 ....128 A6
Gilda Av PEND EN3 ....25 G6

Glenbarr Cl ELTH/MOT SE9 .....147 G4
Glenbow Rd BMLY BR1 ....183 H2
Glenbrook North ENC/FH EN2...23 F5
Glenbrook Rd KIL/WHAMP NW6...82 E3
Glenbrook South ENC/FH EN2...23 F5
Glenbuck Rd SURB KT6 ....190 E3
Glenburnie Rd TOOT SW17 .....160 E5
Glencairn Dr EA W5 ....97 J4
Glencairne Cl CAN/RD E16 .....107 H4
Glencairn Rd
  STRHM/NOR SW16............179 K3
Glencoe Av GNTH/NBYPK IG2...72 E4
Glencoe Rd BUSH WD23.........28 A1
  DAGE RM10..................92 C2
  YEAD UB4...................95 J4
Glencorse Gn OXHEY WD19 *...53 F2
Glen Crs WFD IG8.............53 F2
Glendale Av CHDH RM6.........73 J4
  EDGW HA8...................30 B6
  WDGN N22...................49 G3
Glendale Cl ELTH/MOT SE9 ....147 F4
Glendale Dr WIM/MER SW19....177 J1
Glendale Gdns WBLY HA9.......61 K5
Glendale Ms BECK BR3.........182 E4
Glendale Rd ERITH DA8........129 K4
Glendale Wy THMD SE28.......128 D1
Glendall St BRXN/ST SW9.....142 A4
Glendarvon St PUT/ROE SW15..139 G4
Glendevon Cl EDGW HA8.......30 D3
Glendish Rd TOTM N17.........50 C4
Glendor Gdns MLHL NW7........31 F6
Glendower Crs ORP BR6........202 B3
Glendower Gdns
  MORT/ESHN SW14............138 A4
Glendower Pl SKENS SW7.......14 A6
Glendower Rd CHING E4........38 B3
  MORT/ESHN SW14............138 A4
Glendown Rd ABYW SE2........128 B5
Glendun Rd ACT W3............99 G6
Gleneagle Ms
  STRHM/NOR SW16............179 J1
Gleneagle Rd
  STRHM/NOR SW16............179 J1
Gleneagles STAN HA7..........43 H2
Gleneagles Cl
  BERM/RHTH SE16............123 J5
  ORP BR6....................201 J5
  OXHEY WD19 *...............41 H1
Gleneldon Ms
  STRHM/NOR SW16............179 K1
Gleneldon Rd
  STRHM/NOR SW16............161 K6
Glenelg Rd BRXS/STRHM SW2...141 K6
Glenesk Rd ELTH/MOT SE9.....147 F5
Glenfarg Rd CAT SE6..........165 G3
Glenfield Crs RSLP HA4.......58 B4
Glenfield Rd BAL SW12........161 G3
  WEA W13....................116 C2
Glenfinlas Wy CMBW SE5......142 C1
Glenforth St GNWCH SE10.....125 J4
Glengall Br POP/IOD E14.....124 E3
Glengall Gv POP/IOD E14.....124 E3
Glengall Rd BXLYHN DA7......149 F4
  EDGW HA8...................30 D5
  KIL/WHAMP NW6..............82 D6
  PECK SE15..................123 G6
  WFD IG8....................52 E2
Glengall Ter PECK SE15......123 G6
Glen Gdns CROY/NA CRO.......211 G1
Glengarnock Av POP/IOD E14..125 F4
Glengarry Rd EDUL SE22......143 F5
Glenham Dr GNTH/NBYPK IG2...72 B2
Glenhead Cl ELTH/MOT SE9....147 G4
Glenhill Cl FNCH N3..........46 E5
Glenhouse Rd ELTH/MOT SE9...147 F6
Glenhurst Av BXLY DA5.......169 G3
  KTTN NW5...................84 A2
  RSLP HA4...................58 A5
Glenhurst Ri NRWD SE19......180 D3
Glenhurst Rd BTFD TW8.......116 D6
  NFNCH/WDSPK N12...........47 H1
Glenilla Rd HAMP NW3........83 J4
Glenister Park Rd
  STRHM/NOR SW16............179 H3
Glenister Rd GNWCH SE10.....125 J5
Glenlea Rd ELTH/MOT SE9.....147 F6
Glenloch Rd HAMP NW3........24 E3
  PEND EN3...................24 E3
Glenluce Rd BKHTH/KID SE3...146 A1
Glenluge Rd BKHTH/KID SE3...125 K6
Glenlyon Rd ELTH/MOT SE9....147 F6
Glenmill HPTN TW12..........172 E1
Glenmore Lawns WEA W13 *....97 G5
Glenmore Pde ALP/SUD HA0 *..80 A6
Glenmore Rd HAMP NW3........83 J4
  WELL DA16..................148 A1
Glenmore Wy BARK IG11.......109 G2
Glenmore Rd WNWD SE27.......162 B5
Glenny Rd BARK IG11.........90 C4
Glenorchy Cl YEAD UB4.......95 J4
Glenparke Rd FSTGT E7.......89 F4
Glen Ri WFD IG8.............53 F2
Glen Rd CHSGTN KT9..........206 A1
  PLSTW E15..................107 G3
  WALTH E17..................69 H2
Glen Road End WLGTN SM6.....210 B7
Glenrosa St FUL/PGN SW6.....140 B3
Glenroy St SHB W12..........100 A5
Glensdale Rd BROCKY SE4.....144 C4
Glenshiel Rd ELTH/MOT SE9...147 F6
Glenside CHIG IG7...........54 B2
Glentanner Wy TOOT SW17.....160 C5

Glenthorne Av CROY/NA CRO...197 K5
Glenthorne Cl CHEAM SM3.....193 K5
Glenthorne Gdns BARK/HLT IG6..54 A6
  CHEAM SM3..................193 K5
Glenthorne Rd FBAR/BDGN N11..47 K1
  HMSMTH W6..................118 E4
  KUT/HW KT1.................191 G1
  WALTH E17..................69 G2
Glenthorpe Rd MRDN SM4......193 G2
Glenton Cl ROM RM1..........57 J3
Glenton Rd LEW SE13.........145 H5
Glenton Wy ROM RM1..........57 J3
Glentrammon Av ORP BR6......217 F4
Glentrammon Cl ORP BR6......217 F4
Glentrammon Gdns ORP BR6....217 F4
Glentrammon Rd ORP BR6......217 F4
Glentworth St CAMTN NW1......3 F7
Glenure Rd ELTH/MOT SE9.....147 F6
Glenview ABYW SE2...........128 E6
Glen View Rd BMLY BR1.......184 C5
Glenville Av ENC/FH EN2.....23 J1
Glenville Gv DEPT SE8.......144 C1
Glenville Ms WAND/EARL SW18..160 A2
Glenville Rd KUTN/CMB KT2...175 H4
Glenwood Av CDALE/KGS NW9...63 G5
  RAIN RM13..................111 J3
Glenwood Cl HRW HA1.........61 F2
Glenwood Dr GPK RM2.........75 J2
Glenwood Gdns
  GNTH/NBYPK IG2.............72 A2
Glenwood Gv CDALE/KGS NW9...62 E5
Glenwood Rd CAT SE6.........164 C5
  EW KT17....................207 J4
  HSLW TW3...................135 H3
  MLHL NW7...................31 G5
  SEVS/STOTM N15.............67 H2
Glenwood Rw NRWD SE19 *.....181 G4
Glenworth Av POP/IOD E14....125 G4
Gliddon Dr CLPT E5..........86 D2
Gliddon Rd WKENS W14........119 H4
Glimpsing Gn ERITH DA18.....129 F3
Gload Crs STMC/STPC BR5.....202 E6
Globe Pond Rd
  BERM/RHTH SE16............124 B1
Globe Rd EMPK RM11..........75 J3
  SRTFD E15..................88 D3
  WCHPL E1...................104 E2
  WFD IG8....................53 G3
Globe St STHWK SE1..........18 E3
Globe Ter BETH E2...........104 E2
Glossop Rd SAND/SEL CR2.....211 K6
Gloster Rd NWMAL KT3........192 B1
Gloucester Av BFN/LL DA15...167 K4
  CAMTN NW1..................84 A5
  WELL DA16..................148 A4
Gloucester Circ GNWCH SE10..145 F1
Gloucester Cl THDIT KT7......190 B5
  WLSDN NW10.................81 F5
Gloucester Ct MTCM CR4 *.....195 K2
  RCH/KEW TW9 *..............137 H1
Gloucester Crs CAMTN NW1....84 B6
Gloucester Dr FSBYPK N4.....67 H6
  GLDGN NW11.................64 E1
Gloucester Gdns
  BAY/PAD W2.................101 G5
  EBAR EN4...................21 J6
  GLDGN NW11.................64 D4
  IL IG1.....................71 J4
  SUT SM1....................194 A6
Gloucester Ga CAMTN NW1......3 J2
Gloucester Gate Ms CAMTN NW1..3 J2
Gloucester Gv EDGW HA8......45 F4
Gloucester Ms BAY/PAD W2....101 G5
  LEY E10....................69 J4
Gloucester Ms West
  BAY/PAD W2.................101 G5
Gloucester Pde BFN/LL DA15 *..148 B6
  HYS/HAR UB3 *..............113 F5
Gloucester Pl CAMTN NW1......9 F7
  MHST W1U...................9 F2
Gloucester Place Ms
  MBLAR W1H..................9 F2
Gloucester Rd ACT W3........117 K2
  BAR EN5....................20 E6
  BELV DA17..................129 G5
  CROY/NA CR0................196 E4
  DART DA1...................171 E1
  EA W5......................116 D2
  ENC/FH EN2.................23 J1
  FELT TW13..................154 B3
  HPTN TW12..................173 G3
  HRW HA1....................60 B2
  KUT/HW KT1.................175 H5
  LEY E10....................69 J4
  MNPK E12...................89 K3
  RCH/KEW TW9................137 H1
  ROM RM1....................75 H3
  SKENS SW7..................14 B3
  TOTM N17...................49 K6
  WALTH E17..................51 F5
  WAN E11....................71 G2
  WLSDN NW2..................155 H3
Gloucester Sq BAY/PAD W2.....8 B5
  HACK E8 *..................86 C6
Gloucester St PIM SW1V......121 H5
Gloucester Ter BAY/PAD W2...101 F5
  STHGT/OAK N14 *............34 D3
Gloucester Wk KENS W8 *.....119 K2
Gloucester Wy CLKNW EC1R.....5 K5
Glover Cl ABYW SE2..........128 D4
Glover Dr UED N18...........51 F2
Glover Rd PIN HA5...........59 H3
Glycena Rd BTSEA SW11.......140 E4
Glyn Av EBAR EN4............21 H5
Glyn Cl EW KT17.............207 J6
  SNWD SE25..................197 F3
Glyn Ct STAN HA7............43 H2
Glyndebourne Pk ORP BR6.....216 B1
Glynde Ms CHEL SW3..........14 D5
Glynde Rd BXLYHN DA7........148 E4
Glynde St BROCKY SE4........164 C6
Glyndon Rd WOOL/PLUM SE18...127 H4
Glyn Dr SCUP DA14...........168 C6

Glynfield Rd WLSDN NW10.....81 G5
Glyn Rd CLPT E5.............87 F2
  PEND EN3...................24 E5
  WPK KT4....................193 G6
Glyn St LBTH SE11...........122 A5
Goat La EN EN1..............24 A1
Goat Rd MTCM CR4............195 F4
Goat Wharf BTFD TW8.........117 F6
Gobions Av CRW RM5..........57 F3
Godalming Av WLGTN SM6......210 E3
Godalming Rd POP/IOD E14....105 K4
Godbold Rd SRTFD E15........106 C2
Goddard Pl ARCH N19.........84 C1
Goddard Rd BECK BR3.........198 B1
Goddards Wy IL IG1..........72 D5
Coddington Crs DAD TW5......217 H2
Goddington La ORP BR6.......217 G1
Godfrey Av NTHLT UB5........77 J6
  WHTN TW2...................155 J2
Godfrey Rd WOOL/PLUM SE18...126 D4
Godfrey St CHEL SW3.........120 D5
  SRTFD E15..................106 A1
Godfrey Wy HSLW TW4.........154 D6
Goding St LBTH SE11.........121 K5
Godley Rd WAND/EARL SW18....160 C3
Godliman St BLKFR EC4V......12 B4
Godman Rd PECK SE15.........143 J3
Godolphin Cl PLMGR N13......49 H2
Godolphin Pl ACT W3.........99 F6
Godolphin Rd SHB W12........118 E2
Godric Crs CROY/NA CRO......214 B6
Godson Rd CROY/NA CRO.......211 G1
Godson St IS N1.............5 J2
Godstone Rd SUT SM1.........209 G2
  TWK TW1....................156 C1
Godstow Rd ABYW SE2.........128 D2
Godwin Cl HOR/WEW KT19......206 E4
  IS N1......................6 E2
Godwin Rd FSTGT E7..........89 F2
  HAYES BR2..................184 B6
Goffers Rd BKHTH/KID SE3....145 H3
Goidel Cl WLGTN SM6.........210 D2
Golborne Gdns NKENS W10 *...100 C3
Golborne Ms NKENS W10.......100 C4
Golborne Rd NKENS W10.......100 C4
Golda Cl BAR EN5............32 B1
Goldbeaters Gv EDGW HA8.....45 G3
Goldcliff Cl MRDN SM4.......193 K4
Goldcrest Cl CAN/RD E16.....107 H4
  THMD SE28..................109 H3
Goldcrest Ms EA W5..........97 K4
Goldcrest Wy BUSH WD23......28 C1
Golden Cl HSLW TW5..........135 J3
Golden Crs HYS/HAR UB3......113 J1
Golden Cross Ms NTGHL W11 *..100 D5
Golden Hind Pl DEPT SE8 *...124 C4
Golden Jubilee Br STHWK SE1..11 H7
Golden La STLK EC1Y..........6 C7
Golden Lane Est STLK EC1Y....6 C7
Golden Mnr HNWL W7..........96 E6
Golden Pde WALTH E17 *......52 A6
Golden Plover Cl CAN/RD E16..106 E5
Golden Sq SOHO/CST W1F......10 B5
Golden Yd HAMP NW3 *........83 G2
Golders Cl EDGW HA8.........44 D1
Golders Gdns GLDGN NW11.....64 C4
Golders Green Crs
  GLDGN NW11.................64 D4
Golders Green Rd GLDGN NW11..64 C4
Golders Manor Dr GLDGN NW11..63 F6
Golderslea GLDGN NW11 *......64 E5
Golders Park Cl GLDGN NW11...64 E5
Golders Ri HDN NW4..........46 B4
Golders Wy GLDGN NW11.......64 C4
Goldfinch Cl ORP BR6........217 C3
Goldfinch Rd THMD SE28......127 J3
Goldhawk Ms SHB W12.........118 E2
Goldhawk Rd HMSMTH W6.......118 C4
Goldhaze Cl WFD IG8.........53 H3
Gold Hill EDGW HA8..........45 F2
Goldhurst Ter KIL/WHAMP NW6..83 F5
Golding St WCHPL E1.........104 C5
Goldingham Av LOU IG10......39 K1
Goldington Crs CAMTN NW1.....4 C2
Goldington St CAMTN NW1......4 C2
Gold La EDGW HA8............45 G2
Goldney Rd MV/WKIL W9.......100 E3
Goldrill Dr FBAR/BDGN N11...34 A4
Goldsboro Rd VX/NE SW8......141 J2
Goldsborough Crs CHING E4...37 K4
Goldsdown Cl PEND EN3.......25 G3
Goldsdown Rd PEND EN3.......24 E2
Goldsmid St WOOL/PLUM SE18 *..127 K5
Goldsmith Av ACT W3.........99 F6
  CDALE/KGS NW9..............63 G2
  MNPK E12...................89 J4
  ROMW/RG RM7................74 D4
Goldsmith Cl RYLN/HDSTN HA2..60 A5
Goldsmith La CDALE/KGS NW9 *..62 D1
Goldsmith Rd
  KIL/WHAMP NW6..............83 F6

Comm Rd BERM/RHTH SE16......123 H3
Gomshall Av WLGTN SM6.......210 E3
Gondar Gdns CRICK NW2.......82 D3
Gonson St DEPT SE8..........124 E6
Gonston Cl WIM/MER SW19.....159 H4
Gonville Crs NTHLT UB5......78 B4
Gonville Rd THHTH CR7.......196 A2
Gonville St FUL/PGN SW6.....139 H4
Goodall Rd WAN E11..........88 A1
Gooden Ct HRW HA1...........78 E1
Goodenough Rd
  WIM/MER SW19...............177 J3
Gooderly Rd BARK IG11.......91 F5
Goodge Pl FITZ W1T..........10 B2
Goodge St FITZ W1T..........10 B2
Goodhall Cl STAN HA7........43 H2
Goodhall St WLSDN NW10......99 H2
Goodhart Wy WWKM BR4........199 H3
Goodhew Rd CROY/NA CRO......197 H3
Goodhall Cl NWMAL KT3.......191 K1
Gooding Cl NWMAL KT3........191 K1
Goodinge Cl HOLWY N7........84 E4
Goodman Crs
  BRXS/STRHM SW2.............161 K4
Goodman Rd LEY E10..........70 A4
Goodmans Ct ALP/SUD HA0.....79 K2
Goodman's Yd TWRH EC3N......13 J5
Goodmayes Av GDMY/SEVK IG3..73 G5
Goodmayes La GDMY/SEVK IG3..91 C2
Goodmayes Rd GDMY/SEVK IG3..73 G5
Goodmead Rd ORP BR6.........202 C5
Goodrich Rd EDUL SE22.......163 G1
Goodson Rd WLSDN NW10.......81 G5
Goods Wy CAMTN NW1..........4 E2
Goodway Gdns POP/IOD E14....106 B5
Goodwin Cl BERM/RHTH SE16....19 K5
  MTCM CR4...................178 C6
Goodwin Dr SCUP DA14........168 E4
Goodwin Gdns CROY/NA CRO....211 H4
Goodwin Rd CROY/NA CRO......211 H3
  SHB W12....................118 D2
Goodwins Ct CHCR WC2N.......10 E5
Goodwin St FSBYPK N4........67 G6
Goodwood Dr NTHLT UB5.......78 A4
Goodwood Pde BECK BR3.......198 B2
Goodwood Rd NWCR SE14.......144 B1
Goodwyn Av MLHL NW7.........45 G1
Goodwyn's V MUSWH N10.......48 A4
Goodyers Gdns HDN NW4.......64 B2
Goosander Wy THMD SE28......127 J3
Goose Green Cl
  STMC/STPC BR5..............186 B5
Gooseley La EHAM E6.........108 A2
Goossens Cl SUT SM1.........209 C3
Gophir La CANST EC4R........12 E5
Gopsall St IS N1............7 F1
Gordon Av CHING E4..........52 C2
  HCH RM12...................75 H6
  MORT/ESHN SW14.............138 B5
  STAN HA7...................42 E5
  TWK TW1....................156 B6
Gordonbrock Rd BROCKY SE4...144 D6
Gordon Cl WALTH E17.........69 J3
Gordon Cottages KENS W8 *...119 K2
Gordon Crs CROY/NA CRO......197 F5
  HYS/HAR UB3................113 K4
Gordondale Rd
  WIM/MER SW19...............159 K4
Gordon Gdns EDGW HA8........44 D5
Gordon Gv CMBW SE5..........142 C3
Gordon Hl ENC/FH EN2........23 J2
Gordon House Rd KTTN NW5....84 A2
Gordon Pl KENS W8...........119 K2
Gordon Rd ASHF TW15.........152 B5
  BARK IG11..................90 E6
  BECK BR3...................182 C6
  BELV DA17..................129 K4
  BFN/LL DA15................167 K1
  BRYLDS KT5.................191 G4
  CAR SM5....................209 K4
  CHDH RM6...................74 A3
  CHING E4...................38 C2
  CHSWK W4...................117 J6
  DART DA1...................171 H2
  ED N9......................36 D4
  ENC/FH EN2.................23 J1
  ESH/CLAY KT10..............204 E5
  FBAR/BDGN N11..............48 D2
  FINCH N3...................46 D3
  FSTGT E7...................89 F2
  HACK E8....................86 B4
  HRW HA1....................60 E1
  HSLWW TW4..................134 D5
  IL IG1.....................90 D1
  KTN/HRWW/WS HA3............42 E6
  KUTN/CMB KT2...............175 H4
  NWDGN UB2..................114 D4
  PECK SE15..................143 J2
  RCH/KEW TW9................137 G3
  SRTFD E15..................88 B2
  SWFD E18...................53 F5
  WAN E11....................70 E4
Gordon Sq STPAN WC1H.........4 C6
Gordon St PLSTW E13.........106 E2
  STPAN WC1H.................4 B6
Gordon Wy BAR EN5...........20 D5
  BMLY BR1...................183 K4
Gorefield Pl KIL/WHAMP NW6...100 E1
Gore Rd HOM E9..............86 E6
  RYNPK SW20.................177 F5
Goresbrook Rd DAGW RM9......91 J5
Gore St SKENS SW7...........14 A4
Gorham Pl NTGHL W11.........100 C6
Goring Cl CRW RM5...........56 E4
Goring Gdns DAGW RM9........91 J2
Goring Rd DAGE RM10.........93 F5
  FBAR/BDGN N11 *............48 E2
Goring St HDTCH EC3A........13 H3
Goring Wy GFD/PVL UB6.......96 C1
Gorleston Rd SEVS/STOTM N15..67 K2
Gorleston St WKENS W14......119 H4
Gorman Rd WOOL/PLUM SE18....126 E4
Gorringe Park Av MTCM CR4...178 E3
Gorse Cl CAN/RD E16.........106 E5

Gorse Rd TOOT SW17..........179 F1
Gorse Rd CROY/NA CRO........213 J1
  STMC/STPC BR5..............203 H6
Gorseway ROMW/RG RM7........75 C6
Gorst Rd BTSEA SW11.........160 E1
  WLSDN NW10.................98 E3
Gorsuch Pl BETH E2..........7 J4
Gorsuch St BETH E2..........7 J4
Gosberton Rd BAL SW12.......160 E3
Gosbury Hl CHSGTN KT9.......206 A2
Gosfield Rd BCTR RM8........74 C5
  EW KT19....................9 K1
Gosford Gdns REDBR IG4......71 K2
Gosforth La OXHEY WD19......26 E5
Gosforth Pth OXHEY WD19.....26 E5
Goshawk Gdns YEAD UB4.......94 C2
Goslett Yd SOHO/SHAV W1D....10 D4
Gosling Cl GFD/PVL UB6......96 A2
Gosling Wy BRXN/ST SW9......142 B2
Gospatrick Rd TOTM N17......49 H4
Gosport Rd WALTH E17........69 H2
Gosport Wy PECK SE15........143 G1
Cossage Rd WOOL/PLUM SE18...127 J5
Gosset St BETH E2...........7 J4
Gosshill Rd CHST BR7........185 F5
Gossington Cl CHST BR7......167 G6
Gosterwood St DEPT SE8......124 B6
Gostling Rd WHTN TW2........155 F3
Goston Gdns THHTH CR7.......180 B6
Goswell Rd FSBYE EC1V.......6 B4
Gothic Cl DART DA1..........171 K6
Gothic Ct HYS/HAR UB3 *.....113 C6
Gothic Rd WHTN TW2..........155 J4
Gottfried Ms KTTN NW5.......84 C2
Goudhurst Rd BMLY BR1.......183 H1
Gough Rd EN EN1.............24 E2
  SRTFD E15..................88 D2
Gough Sq FLST/FETLN EC4A....11 K3
Gough St FSBYW WC1X.........5 H6
Goulding Gdns THHTH CR7.....180 D5
Gould Rd EBED/NFELT TW14....153 G3
  WHTN TW2...................155 K3
Goulton Rd CLPT E5..........86 D2
Goulton Rd HACK E8..........13 J3
Gourley Pl SEVS/STOTM N15...68 A2
Gourley St SEVS/STOTM N15...68 A2
Gourock Rd ELTH/MOT SE9.....147 F6
Govan St BETH E2............7 H6
Govier Cl SRTFD E15.........88 C5
Gowan Av FUL/PGN SW6........139 H2
Gowan Rd WLSDN NW10.........81 K4
Gower Cl CLAP SW4...........161 H1
Gower Ms GWRST WC1E.........10 D2
Gower Pl GWRST WC1E.........4 B6
Gower Rd FSTGT E7...........88 E4
  ISLW TW7...................116 A6
Gower St GWRST WC1E.........4 B6
Gower's Wk WCHPL E1.........104 C5
Gowland Pl BECK BR3.........182 C5
Gowlett Rd PECK SE15........143 H4
Gowrie Rd BTSEA SW11........141 F4
Graburn Wy E/WMO/HCT KT8....173 H6
Grace Av BXLYHN DA7.........149 G3
Gracechurch St BANK EC3V....13 F5
Grace Cl BARK/HLT IG6.......55 F2
  EDGW HA8...................44 E3
  ELTH/MOT SE9...............166 C4
Gracedale Rd
  STRHM/NOR SW16............179 C1
Gracefield Gdns
  STRHM/NOR SW16............161 K5
Grace Jones Cl HACK E8......86 C4
Grace Pl BOW E3.............105 K2
Grace Rd CROY/NA CRO........196 D5
Graces Aly WCHPL E1.........104 C6
Graces Ms CMBW SE5..........142 E3
  STJWD NW8 *................2 A1
Grace's Rd CMBW SE5.........143 F3
Grace St BOW E3.............105 K2
The Gradient SYD SE26.......163 H6
Graduate Pl STHWK SE1.......19 G4
Graeme Rd EN EN1............24 A3
Graemesdyke Av
  MORT/ESHN SW14.............137 J4
Grafton Cl HSLWW TW4........154 D3
  WEA W13....................97 G5
  WPK KT4....................192 C6
Grafton Crs CAMTN NW1.......84 B4
Grafton Gdns BCTR RM8.......74 A6
  FSBYPK N4..................67 J3
Grafton Ms FITZ W1T.........4 A7
Grafton Park Rd WPK KT4.....192 B6
Grafton Pl CAMTN NW1........4 C5
Grafton Rd ACT W3...........98 E6
  BCTR RM8...................74 A6
  CROY/NA CR0................196 C5
  ENC/FH EN2.................23 F4
  HRW HA1....................60 C2
  KTTN NW5...................84 A3
  NWMAL KT3..................192 B1
  WPK KT4....................207 H1
Grafton Sq CLAP SW4.........141 H4
Grafton St CONDST W1S.......9 K6
Grafton Ter KTTN NW5........83 K3
  FITZ W1T...................10 A1
Grafton Yd KTTN NW5 *.......84 B4
Graham Av MTCM CR4..........179 F4
  WEA W13....................116 C2
Graham Cl CROY/NA CRO.......198 D6
Grahame Park Wy MLHL NW7....45 H3
Graham Gdns SURB KT6........191 F5
Graham Rd BXLYHN DA7........149 H5
  CHSWK W4...................118 A3
  HACK E8....................86 C4
  HDN NW4....................63 K3
  HPTN TW12..................155 F6
  KTN/HRWW/WS HA3............42 E6
  MTCM CR4...................179 F4
  PLSTW E13..................106 E2
  SEVS/STOTM N15.............49 H6
  WIM/MER SW19...............177 J3
Graham St IS N1.............6 B3

Graham Ter BFN/LL DA15 *....168 C1
BCVA SW1W....15 H7
Grainger Cl NTHLT UB5....78 C3
Grainger Rd ISLW TW7....136 A3
WDGN N22....49 J4
Gramer Cl WAN E11....70 B6
Grampian Gdns CRICK NW2....64 C5
HYS/HAR UB3....133 C1
ORP BR6....202 A3
Grampian Rd BELMT SM2....209 G5
Gramsci Wy CAT SE6....164 E5
Granada St TOOT SW17....178 E1
Granard Av PUT/ROE SW15....138 E6
Granard Rd BTSEA SW11....160 E2
Granary Cl ED N9....36 E2
Granary Rd WCHPL E1....104 D5
Granary Sq IS N1....85 G4
Granary St CAMTN NW1 *....
Granby Rd ELTH/MOT SE9....146 C3
WOOL/PLUM SE18....127 G3
Granby St BETH E2....7 K6
Granby Ter CAMTN NW1....
Grand Av BRYLDS KT5....191 J5
FARR EC1M....12 B1
MUSWH N10....66 A1
WBLY HA9....80 C3
Grand Av East WBLY HA9....80 D3
Grand Depot Rd
WOOL/PLUM SE18....127 G4
Grand Dr NWDGN UB2....115 H2
RYNPK SW20....177 F6
Granden Rd
STRHM/NOR SW16....179 K5
Grandison Rd BTSEA SW11....140 E6
WPK KT4....193 F6
Grand Junction Whf IS N1 *....6 C3
Grand Pde FSBYPK N4 *....67 H3
MORT/ESHN SW14 *....137 K5
SURB KT6 *....191 H5
WBLY HA9 *....62 D6
Grand Union Canal Wk
BTFD TW8....116 D6
HNWL W7....115 K3
HYS/HAR UB3....113 K3
MV/WKIL W9 *....100 E4
NWDCN UB2....114 B3
NWDGN UB2....114 D4
RKW/CH/CXG WD3....26 A1
STHL UB1....95 K3
WDR/YW UB7....112 E2
WLSDN NW10....99 G2
Grand Union Cl MV/WKIL W9....100 D4
Grand Union Crs HACK E8 *....86 C6
Grand Union Wk CAMTN NW1 *....84 B5
Grand Wk WCHPL E1 *....105 G3
Granfield St BTSEA SW11 *....140 C2
Grange Av EBAR EN4....33 J3
KTN/HRWW/WS HA3....43 K5
NFNCH/WDSPK N12....47 G1
SNWD SE25....181 F5
TRDG/WHET N20....32 C2
WFD IG8....52 E2
WHTN TW2....155 K4
Grangecliffe Gdns SNWD SE25 *....
Grange Cl BFN/LL DA15....168 B5
E/WMO/HCT KT8....189 G1
NFNCH/WDSPK N12....
WHTN TW2....
HYS/HAR UB3....94 C4
WFD IG8....52 E3
Grange Ct ALP/SUD HA0 *....
BELMT SM2 *....209 F5
HRW HA1 *....79 F1
NTHLT UB5 *....95 G1
PIN HA5 *....41 J6
WLGTN SM6 *....210 B1
Grangecourt Rd
STNW/STAM N16....68 A5
Grangedale Cl NTHWD HA6....40 C4
Grange Dr CHST BR7....184 D2
ORP BR6....217 J6
Grange Farm Cl
RYLN/HDSTN HA2....60 C6
Grange Gdns HAMP NW3....83 F1
PIN HA5....59 K1
SNWD SE25....181 F5
STHGT/OAK N14....34 D5
Grange Gv IS N1....85 J4
SNWD SE25....181 F5
Grangehill Pl ELTH/MOT SE9....146 E4
Grangehill Rd ELTH/MOT SE9....146 E5
Grange Houses HBRY N5 *....85 J2
Grange La DUL SE21....163 G4
Grange Ms FELT TW13 *....153 G5
Grangemill Rd CAT SE6....164 D5
Grange Pk WEA W5....116 E1
Grange Pk Av WCHMH N21....35 J2
Grange Park Pl RYNPK SW20....176 E3
Grange Park Rd LEY E10....69 K6
THHTH CR7....180 E6
Grange Pl KIL/WHAMP NW6....82 E5
Grange Rd BARN SW13....138 D2
BELMT SM2....208 E5
CHSGTN KT9....206 A2
CHSWK W4....117 J5
E/WMO/HCT KT8....189 G1
EA W5....
EDGW HA8....45 F2
HARH RM3....57 K2
HGT N6....
HRW HA1....61 G3
HYS/HAR UB3....94 C5
IL IG1....90 C2
KUT/HW KT1....175 F6
LEY E10....
ORP BR6....201 H6
PLSTW E13....106 D2
RYLN/HDSTN HA2....60 D6
SEVS/STOTM N15....
STHL UB1....114 D2
STHWK SE1....19 H5
TOTM N17....50 C2
WALTH E17....69 G2

WLSDN NW10....81 K4
Granger Wy EMPK RM11....75 J3
Grange St IS N1....7 F1
The Grange ALP/SUD HA0....80 C2
CROY/NA CRO....198 C6
NWMAL KT3 *....192 D2
STHWK SE1 *....19 J4
WIM/MER SW19....177 G2
WKENS W14 *....119 J4
WOT/HER KT12....188 A6
WPK KT4....207 F2
Grange V BELMT SM2....209 F5
Grangeview Rd
TRDG/WHET N20....33 G3
Grange Wk STHWK SE1....19 H5
Grange Walk Ms STHWK SE1....19 H5
Grange Wy ERITH DA8....150 E1
Grangeway KIL/WHAMP NW6....82 E5
NFNCH/WDSPK N12....33 F6
WFD IG8....39 G6
Grangeway Gdns REDBR IG4....71 J2
The Grangeway BXLY DA5....169 G3
Grangewood BXLY DA5....169 G3
Grangewood Cl PIN HA5....58 E3
Grangewood La BECK BR3....182 C2
Grangewood St EHAM E6....89 H6
Grangewood St STHWK SE1....19 J3
Granham Gdns ED N9....36 B4
Granite St WOOL/PLUM SE18....128 A5
Granleigh Rd WAN E11....70 C6
Gransden Av HACK E8....86 D5
Gransden Rd SHB W12....118 C2
Grantbridge St IS N1....6 B2
Grantchester KUT/HW KT1 *....175 H5
Grantchester Cl HRW HA1....79 F1
Grant Cl STHGT/OAK N14....34 C2
TOTM N17....50 A5
Grantham Cl EDGW HA8....30 A5
Grantham Gdns CHDH RM6....74 A3
Grantham Pl MYFR/PKLN W1K...15 J1
Grantham Rd BRXN/ST SW9....141 K4
CHSWK W4....138 B1
MNPK E12....90 A1
Grantley Pl ESH/CLAY KT10....204 B3
Grantley Rd HSLWW TW4....134 B3
Grantley St WCHPL E1....105 F2
Grantock Rd WALTH E17....52 B4
Granton Rd GDMY/SEVK IG3....73 G5
SCUP DA14....168 A6
STRHM/NOR SW16....179 H4
Grant Pl CROY/NA CRO....197 G5
Grant Rd BTSEA SW11....140 D4
CROY/NA CRO....197 G5
KTN/HRWW/WS HA3....42 E6
Grants Cl MLHL NW7....46 A3
Grant St IS N1....5 K3
PLSTW E13....106 E2
Grant Ter STNW/STAM N16 *....68 C4
Grantully Rd MV/WKIL W9....101 F2
Grant Wy ISLW TW7....116 B6
Granville Av BRXN/ST SW9 *....142 B5
FELT TW13....153 K4
HSLW TW3....135 F6
Granville Cl CROY/NA CRO....197 F6
Granville Gdns EA W5....117 C1
STRHM/NOR SW16....180 A4
Granville Gv LEW SE13....145 F4
Granville Ms SCUP DA14....168 B6
Granville Pk LEW SE13....145 F4
Granville Pl FUL/PGN SW6....140 A1
MBLAR W1H....9 G4
NFNCH/WDSPK N12 *....47 G3
PIN HA5....41 H6
Granville Rd BAR EN5....20 E4
CEND/HSY/T N8....67 F3
CRICK NW2....64 D6
HYS/HAR UB3....113 J4
IL IG1....72 B5
KIL/WHAMP NW6....100 E1
NFNCH/WDSPK N12....47 G3
PLMGR N13....49 F2
SCUP DA14....168 B6
SWFD E18....53 F1
WALTH E17....52 A5
WAND/EARL SW18....159 J2
WDGN N22....49 H4
WELL DA16....148 D4
WIM/MER SW19....177 K3
Granville Sq PECK SE15 *....143 F1
Granville St FSBYW WC1X....5 H5
Grape St LSQ/SEVD WC2H....10 E3
Graphite Sq LBTH SE11 *....122 A5
Grasdene Rd
WOOL/PLUM SE18....148 B1
Grasmere Av ACT W3....99 F6
HSLW TW3....155 G1
ORP BR6....216 B1
PUT/ROE SW15....158 A6
RSLP HA4....58 B3
WBLY HA9....61 H3
WIM/MER SW19....177 K6
Grasmere Cl
EBED/NFELT TW14....153 J3
Grasmere Ct WDGN N22....49 F2
Grasmere Gdns
KTN/HRWW/WS HA3....43 G5
ORP BR6....216 B1
REDBR IG4....71 J2
Grasmere Rd BMLY BR1....183 J4
BXLYHN DA7....149 K2
MUSWH N10....48 B4
ORP BR6....216 B1
PLSTW E13....106 E1
SNWD SE25....197 J3
STRHM/NOR SW16....180 A1
Grasshaven Wy THMD SE28....128 A1
Grassington Cl FBAR/BDGN N11..48 A2
Grassington Rd SCUP DA14....168 B6
Grassmount FSTH SE23....163 H4
Grass Pk FNCH N3....46 D4
Grassway WLGTN SM6....210 C2
Grasvenor Av BAR EN5....32 E1
Grately Wy PECK SE15 *....143 F1
Gratton Rd WKENS W14....119 H3

Gratton Ter CRICK NW2....82 B1
Gravel Hl BXLYHS DA6....149 K6
CROY/NA CRO....213 G4
FNCH N3....46 D5
Gravel Hill Cl BXLYHS DA6....169 J1
Gravel La WCHPL E1....13 J5
Gravelly Hill COUL/CHIP CR5....
Gravel Rd HAYES BR2....200 D6
WHTN TW2....155 K5
Gravelwood Cl CHST BR7....167 H5
Gravenel Gdns TOOT SW17....178 D1
Graveney Gv PGE/AN SE20....181 K3
Graveney Rd TOOT SW17....160 D6
Gravesend Rd SHB W12....99 J6
Gray Av BCTR RM8....74 B5
Gray Gdns RAIN RM13....93 J4
Grayham Crs NWMAL KT3....192 A1
Grayham Rd NWMAL KT3....192 A1
Grayland Cl BMLY BR1....184 C1
Grayling Cl CAN/RD E16....106 C3
Grayling Ct EA W5 *....116 E1
Grayling Rd STNW/STAM N16....67 K1
Grayling Sq BETH E2 *....104 C2
Grays Cottages
STMC/STPC BR5 *....186 D4
Grays Farm Rd
STMC/STPC BR5....186 C4
Grayscroft Rd
STRHM/NOR SW16....179 J3
Grays Farm Rd
STMC/STPC BR5....186 C4
Grayshott Rd BTSEA SW11....141 F4
Gray's Inn Rd FSBYW WC1X....5 H4
Gray's Inn Sq GINN WC1R....11 J1
Grays La ASHF TW15....152 E6
Grayswood Gdns RYNPK SW20..176 E5
Gray's Yd MHST W1U *....9 H4
Graywood Ct
NFNCH/WDSPK N12....47 G3
Grazebrook Rd
STNW/STAM N16....67 K6
Grazeley Cl BXLYHS DA6....149 K6
Great Benty WDR/YW UB7....112 B4
Great Brownings DUL SE21....163 G6
Great Bushey Dr
TRDG/WHET N20....33 F3
Great Cambridge Jct
PLMGR N13....49 J1
Great Cambridge Rd EN EN1....24 C2
UED N18....49 K1
Great Castle St REGST W1B....10 A3
Great Central Av RSLP HA4....77 G3
Great Central St CAMTN NW1....2 E7
Great Central Wy WBLY HA9....80 E3
WLSDN NW10....81 G3
Great Chapel St
SOHO/SHAV W1D....10 C3
Great Chart St BTSEA SW11....140 B4
Great Chertsey Rd CHSWK W4..138 A2
FELT TW13....154 C6
Great Church La HMSMTH W6..119 G5
Great College St WEST SW1P..16 E4
Great Cross Av GNWCH SE10...145 H1
Great Cullings ROMW/RG RM7..75 G6
Great Cumberland Ms
MBLAR W1H....8 E3
Great Cumberland Pl
MBLAR W1H....8 E4
Great Dover St STHWK SE1....18 E4
Greatdown Rd HNWL W7....97 F3
Great Eastern Rd SRTFD E15....88 B5
Great Eastern St SDTCH EC2A....7 G6
Great Eastern Whf
BTSEA SW11....140 D1
Great Elms Rd HAYES BR2....200 B1
Great Fld CDALE/KGS NW9....45 G4
Greatfield Av EHAM E6....107 K3
Greatfield Cl ARCH N19....84 C2
BROCKY SE4....144 D5
Greatfields Rd BARK IG11....90 D6
Great Galley Cl BARK IG11....109 H2
Great Gardens Rd EMPK RM11..75 J3
Great Gatton Cl CROY/NA CRO..198 B4
Great George St STJSPK SW1H..16 D3
Great Guildford St STHWK SE1..18 C1
Great Harry Dr ELTH/MOT SE9..167 F6
Great James St BMSBY WC1N....11 H1
Great Marlborough St
REGST W1B....10 A4
Great Maze Pond STHWK SE1....19 F1
Great New St
FLST/FETLN EC4A *....11 K3
Great North Leisure Pk
NFNCH/WDSPK N12 *....47 H3
Great North Rd BAR EN5....20 D3
BAR EN5....33 F1
Great North Wy (Barnet
By-Pass) HDN NW4....45 K4
Greatorex St WCHPL E1....104 C4
Great Ormond St BMSBY WC1N..11 F1
Great Percy St FSBYW WC1X....5 J4
Great Portland St REGST W1B....9 K1
Great Pulteney St
SOHO/CST W1F....10 B5
Great Queen St DART DA1....171 J1
HOL/ALD WC2B....11 F4
Great Russell St
NOXST/BSQ WC1A....10 E2
Great St Thomas Apostle
BLKFR EC4V....12 D5
Great Scotland Yd
WHALL SW1A....16 E1
Great Smith St WEST SW1P....16 D4
Great South-west Rd
EBED/NFELT TW14....133 K4
HSLWW TW4....134 A3
Great Spilmans EDUL SE22....143 F6
Great Strd CDALE/KGS NW9....45 H5
Great Suffolk St STHWK SE1....18 B2
Great Sutton St FSBYE EC1V....6 B7
Great Swan Aly LOTH EC2R....12 E3
Great Thrift STMC/STPC BR5...201 H1
Great Titchfield St GTPST W1W....9 K1
Great Tower St MON EC3R....13 G6
Great Trinity La BLKFR EC4V....12 D5
Great Turnstile HHOL WC1V....11 H2
Great Western Rd NTGHL W11..100 D4

Great West Rd BTFD TW8....116 D5
HEST TW5....134 E1
HEST TW5....135 G2
HMSMTH W6....118 E5
ISLW TW7....135 K1
Great West Road Chiswick
CHSWK W4....118 C6
Great West Road Ellesmere Rd
CHSWK W4....117 K6
Great West Road Hogarth La
CHSWK W4....118 A6
Great Winchester St
OBST EC2N....13 F3
Great Windmill St
SOHO/SHAV W1D....10 C6
Greatwood CHST BR7....185 F3
Great Yd STHWK SE1 *....19 H2
Greaves Cl BARK IG11....90 E5
Greaves Cottages
POP/IOD E14 *....105 G4
Greaves Pl TOOT SW17....160 D6
Grebe Av YEAD UB4....95 H5
Grebe Cl BARK IG11....109 G3
FSTGT E7....88 D3
WALTH E17....51 C3
Grebe Ct SUT SM1....208 C2
Grebe Ter KUT/HW KT1 *....175 F6
Grecian Crs NRWD SE19....180 C2
Greek St SOHO/SHAV W1D....10 D4
Greenacre Cl BAR EN5....20 D1
NTHLT UB5....77 K3
Greenacre Pl WLGTN SM6....195 G6
Green Acres CROY/NA CRO....212 B1
SCUP DA14 *....168 A6
Greenacres ELTH/MOT SE9....167 F1
ELTH/MOT SE9....167 F1
Greenacres Cl ORP BR6....216 C2
Greenacres Dr STAN HA7....43 H5
Greenacre Sq
BERM/RHTH SE16 *....124 A2
Greenacre Wk STHGT/OAK N14..34 D5
Greenall Cl CHES/WCR EN8....25 F1
Green Arbour Ct STBT EC1A *....12 A3
Green Av MLHL NW7....31 F6
WEA W13....116 C3
Greenaway Av UED N18 *....51 F1
Greenaway Gdns HAMP NW3....82 E2
Green Bank
NFNCH/WDSPK N12....33 F6
WAP E1W....123 J1
Greenbank Av ALP/SUD HA0....79 G3
Greenbank Cl CHING E4....38 A4
Greenbanks Crs HDN NW4....64 C1
Greenbanks DART DA1....171 H4
Greenbay Rd CHARL SE7....146 C1
Greenberry St STJWD NW8....2 C3
Greenbrook Av EBAR EN4....21 G2
Green Chain Wk BMLY BR1....183 H3
BMLY BR1....183 H5
CHARL SE7....146 A4
CHST BR7....185 G3
ELTH/MOT SE9....147 G6
HAYES BR2....184 C5
SYD SE26....182 A2
THMD SE28....128 E1
WOOL/PLUM SE18....128 E6
Green Cl CAR SM5....194 E6
CDALE/KGS NW9....62 E5
FELT TW13....172 D1
GLDGN NW11....65 G4
HAYES BR2....183 H6
HAYES BR2....199 J5
Greencoat Pl WEST SW1P....16 B5
Greencoat Rw WEST SW1P....16 B5
Green Court Av CROY/NA CRO..197 J6
Greencourt Av EDGW HA8....44 D4
Green Court Gdns
CROY/NA CRO....197 J6
Greencourt Rd
STMC/STPC BR5....201 K2
Greencroft EDGW HA8....44 E1
Greencroft Av RSLP HA4....59 G6
Greencroft Gdns EN EN1....24 A4
KIL/WHAMP NW6....83 F5
Green Dragon La BTFD TW8....117 F5
WCHMH N21....35 H1
Green Dragon Yd WCHPL E1....104 C4
Green Dr STHL UB1....115 F1
Green End CHSGTN KT9....205 K2
WCHMH N21....35 H4
Greenend Rd CHSWK W4....118 B2
Green Farm Cl ORP BR6....217 F3
Greenfell Man DEPT SE8....124 C5
Greenfield Av BRYLDS KT5....191 K3
Greenfield Dr BMLY BR1....184 B5
EFNCH N2....65 K1
Greenfield Gdns CRICK NW2....64 C1
DAGW RM9....91 K6
STMC/STPC BR5....201 H6
Greenfield Rd DAGW RM9....91 K6
SEVS/STOTM N15....68 A2
WCHPL E1....104 C5
Greenfields STHL UB1....96 A6
Greenfield Wy
RYLN/HDSTN HA2....42 B6
Greenford Av HNWL W7....96 E4
STHL UB1....95 K6
Greenford Gdns GFD/PVL UB6..96 B2
Greenford Rd GFD/PVL UB6....78 E5
STHL UB1....96 A4
SUT SM1....209 F2
Green Gdns ORP BR6....216 C3
Greengate GFD/PVL UB6....79 H4
Greengate St PLSTW E13....107 F1
Greenhalgh Wk EFNCH N2....65 G1
Greenham Cl STHWK SE1....17 J3
Greenham Crs CHING E4....51 H2
Greenham Rd MUSWH N10....48 A5
Greenhaven Dr THMD SE28....109 J5
Greenheys Cl NTHWD HA6....40 C4
Greenheys Dr SWFD E18....52 D6
Greenhill BKHH IG9....39 G5
HAMP NW3....83 H2
SUT SM1....194 B6

WBLY HA9....62 D6
Green Hl WOOL/PLUM SE18....126 E5
Greenhill Ct BAR EN5 *....21 F3
Greenhill Crs WATW WD18....26 C1
Greenhill Gdns NTHLT UB5....95 K1
Greenhill Gv MNPK E12....89 J3
Greenhill Pde BAR EN5 *....21 G6
WLSDN NW10....
Greenhill Rd HRW HA1....60 E3
WLSDN NW10....81 G6
Greenhill's Rents FARR EC1M *..12 A1
Greenhill Ter NTHLT UB5....95 K1
Greenhill Wy HRW HA1....60 E3
WBLY HA9....62 D6
Greenhithe Cl BFN/LL DA15....167 K2
Greenholm Rd ELTH/MOT SE9..147 G6
Green Hundred Rd PECK SE15..123 H6
Greenhurst Rd WNWD SE27....180 B1
Greening St ABYW SE2....128 D4
Greenland Crs NWDGN UB2....114 B3
Greenland Ms DEPT SE8....124 A5
Greenland Pl CAMTN NW1 *....84 B6
Greenland Quay
BERM/RHTH SE16....124 B4
Greenland Rd BAR EN5....32 A1
CAMTN NW1....84 B6
Greenlands HOR/WEW KT19..206 D3
Greenland St CAMTN NW1 *....84 B6
Greenland Wy CROY/NA CRO..195 J4
Green La BCTR RM8....
CHSGTN KT9....206 A6
E/WMO/HCT KT8....189 G2
EDGW HA8....30 C5
ELTH/MOT SE9....167 G4
FELT TW15....172 D1
HDN NW4....64 B2
HNWL W7....115 K2
HSLWW TW4....134 A3
IL IG1....72 D6
MRDN SM4....194 A4
NTHWD HA6....40 B3
NWMAL KT3....191 K2
OXHEY WD19....27 J3
PGE/AN SE20....182 A3
STAN HA7....29 H6
THHTH CR7....180 C4
UX/CGN UB8....94 A4
WPK KT4....192 E6
Green Lane Cottages
STAN HA7 *....29 H5
Green Lanes HOR/WEW KT19..207 G6
PLMGR N13....49 F1
SEVS/STOTM N15....
WCHMH N21....35 H4
Greenlaw Ct EA W5 *....97 K5
Greenlaw Gdns NWMAL KT3....192 C4
Greenlawn La BTFD TW8....116 E5
Green Lawns
NFNCH/WDSPK N12 *....47 F2
RSLP HA4 *....59 G5
Greenlaw St
WOOL/PLUM SE18....127 F3
Greenleaf Cl
BRXS/STRHM SW2 *....162 B2
Greenleafe Dr BARK/HLT IG6....54 B6
Greenleaf Rd EHAM E6....89 G6
WALTH E17....
Greenlea Pk WIM/MER SW19 *..178 D4
Greenleigh Av STMC/STPC BR5..202 C1
Greenlink Wk RCH/KEW TW9..137 J2
Green Man La
EBED/NFELT TW14....133 K3
WEA W13....97 G6
Greenman St IS N1....85 J5
Greenmead Cl SNWD SE25....197 H2
Green Moor Link WCHMH N21...35 H2
Greenmoor Rd PEND EN3....24 E3
Greenoak Pl EBAR EN4....21 K3
Green Oaks NWDGN UB2 *....159 C6
Greenoak Wy WIM/MER SW19..159 G5
Greenock Rd ACT W3....117 J3
STRHM/NOR SW16....179 J4
Greenock Wy ROM RM1....57 G3
Green Pde WHLY W7 *....155 C1
Greenpark Wy GFD/PVL UB6....78 E3
Green Pond Cl WALTH E17....51 H1
Green Pond Rd WALTH E17....51 G6
Green Ride CHING E4....38 B1
TRDG/WHET N20....33 G5
Greenroof Wy GNWCH SE10....125 J5
Greens Cl LOU IG10....39 K1
Greenstone Ms WAN E11....70 E3
Green St BOW E3 *....
FSTGT E7....89 F3
MYFR/PKLN W1K....9 G6
PEND EN3....25 H4
Greenstreet Hl NWCR SE14 *..144 K4
Greenswards BUSH WD23....28 B1
Green Ter CLKNW EC1R....5 K5
The Green ACT W3....99 G5
BKHH IG9....39 F3
BXLYHN DA7....149 H2
CAR SM5 *....210 A2
CROY/NA CRO....213 H6
ED N9....36 C4
FELT TW13....154 A4
HAYES BR2....199 K4

HEST TW5 ....115 F6
HGDN/ICK UB10 ....58 A6
HRW HA1 ....61 G6
MRDN SM4 ....193 H1
NWDGN UB2 ....114 E2
NWMAL KT3 ....175 K6
RCH/KEW TW9 ....136 E6
SCUP DA14 ....168 B6
SRTFD E15 ....88 D4
STHGT/OAK N14 ....34 C5
STMC/STPC BR5 ....209 F1
SUT SM1 ....209 F1
TOTM N17 ....49 J2
WAN E11 ....71 F3
WCHMH N21 ....35 G2
WDR/YW UB7 ....112 A3
WELL DA16 ....147 K5
WHTN TW2 ....155 K3
WIM/MER SW19 ....177 G1
WLGTN SM6 ....195 F6
Green V BXLYHS DA6 ....148 E6
EA W5 ....98 D5
Greenvale Rd ELTH/MOT SE9 ..146 E5
Green Verges STAN HA7 ....43 K3
Green Vw CHSGTN KT9 ....206 B3
Greenview Av BECK BR3 ....198 B3
Greenview CI ARCH N19 ....118 B1
Green Wk DART DA1 ....150 C5
HDN NW4 ....46 A2
NWDGN UB2 ....115 F5
RSLP HA4 ....58 D5
STHWK SE1 ....19 G5
WFD IG8 ....53 J2
The Green Wk CHING E4 ....38 A5
Greenway BCTR RM8 ....67 J7
Green Wy ELTH/MOT SE9 ....146 C6
HAYES BR2 ....200 D3
Greenway KTN/HRWW/WS HA3 ..62 A2
PIN HA5 ....41 H5
RYNPK SW20 ....193 F1
STHGT/OAK N14 ....34 E4
TRDG/WHET N20 ....32 E4
WLGTN SM6 ....210 C2
YEAD UB4 ....95 F3
Greenway Av WALTH E17 ....70 E1
Greenway CI SEVS/STOTM N15 ..68 B1
CDALE/KGS NW9 ....44 E5
FBAR/BDGN N11 ....48 A2
FSBYPK N4 ....67 J6
TRDG/WHET N20 ....32 E4
Greenway Ct IL IG1 ....72 A5
Greenway Gdns
CDALE/KGS NW9 ....44 E5
CROY/NA CRO 213 H1
GFD/PVL UB6 ....96 B2
Green Way Gdns
KTN/HRWW/WS HA3 ....42 E5
Greenways BECK BR3 ....182 D5
ESH/CLAY KT10 ....204 E2
NFNCH/WDSPK N12 * 47 G2
The Greenways TWK TW1 ....156 B1
The Greenway CDALE/KGS NW9 ..45 F5
HSLWW TW4 ....134 E5
The Green Wy
KTN/HRWW/WS HA3 ....42 E4
The Greenway PIN HA5 ....59 K5
Greenwell St GTPST W1W 3 K7
Greenwich Church St
GNWCH SE10 * 125 F6
Greenwich Foot Tnl
GNWCH SE10 ....125 F5
Greenwich High Rd
GNWCH SE10 ....144 E1
Greenwich Hts CHARL SE7 * ..146 D1
Greenwich Park St
GNWCH SE10 ....125 G6
Greenwich Quay DEPT SE8 ....124 E6
Greenwich South St
GNWCH SE10 ....125 G6
Greenwich Vw POP/IOD E14 ..124 E4
PEND EN3 ....25 C2
Greenwood Cl BFN/LL DA15 ...168 B4
MRDN SM4 ....193 H1
STMC/STPC BR5 ....201 K2
THDIT KT7 ....190 B5
Greenwood Dr CHING E4 ....52 A1
Greenwood Gdns BARK/HLT IG6 ..54 C3
PLMGR N13 ....35 H5
Greenwood La HPTN TW12 ....173 G1
Greenwood Pk
KUTN/CMB KT2 ....176 B3
Greenwood PI KTTN NW5 ....84 B3
CROY/NA CRO 196 D4
HACK E8 ....86 B6
MTCM CR4 ....179 J6
PLSTW E13 ....106 D1
THDIT KT7 ....190 B5
Greenwood Ter WLSDN NW10 ..81 F6
Green Wrythe Crs CAR SM5 ...194 D5
Green Wrythe La CAR SM5 .....194 C5
Green Yd FSBYW WC1X 5 H6
Greer Rd KTN/HRWW/WS HA3 ..42 C4
Greet St STHWK SE1 ....17 K2
Greg CI LEY E10 ....70 A3
Gregor Ms BKHTH/KID SE3 ....145 K1
Gregory Crs ELTH/MOT SE9 ...166 C2
Gregory PI KENS W8 ....120 A2
Gregory Rd CHDH RM6 ....73 K1
NWDGN UB2 ....115 G3
Greig CI CEND/HSY/T N8 ....66 E2
Greig Ter WALW SE17 ....122 C6
Grena Gdns RCH/KEW TW9 ...137 G5
Grenaby Av CROY/NA CRO 196 E4
Grenaby Rd CROY/NA CRO 196 E4
Grenada Rd CHARL SE7 ....146 B1
Grenade St POP/IOD E14 ....105 H6
Grenadier St CAN/RD E16 ......127 F1
Grena Rd RCH/KEW TW9 ....137 G5
Grenard CI PECK SE15 ....143 H1
Grena Rd RCH/KEW TW9 ....137 G5
Grendon Gdns WBLY HA9 ....62 C6
Grendon St STJWD NW8 ....2 C6

Grenfell Av HCH RM12 ....75 H5
Grenfell Cl MLHL NW7 * 45 K2
Grenfell Gdns
KTN/HRWW/WS HA3 ....62 A4
Grenfell Rd WTGHL W11 ....100 B6
TOOT SW17 ....178 E2
Grenoble Gdns PLMGR N13 ....49 G2
Grenville Cl BRYLDS KT5 ....191 K5
FNCH N3 ....46 D4
Grenville Gdns WFD IG8 ....53 G4
Grenville Ms ARCH N19 ....66 E5
HPTN TW12 ....173 G1
Grenville PI MLHL NW7 * 45 F1
SKENS SW7 * 120 B3
Grenville Rd ARCH N19 ....66 E5
Grenville St BMSBY WC1N * 5 F7
Gresham Av TRDG/WHET N20 ..33 K6
Gresham CI BXLY DA5 ....169 F1
ENC/FH EN2 ....23 J4
Gresham Dr CHDH RM6 ....73 H2
Gresham Gdns GLDGN NW11 ....64 C5
Gresham Rd BECK BR3 ....182 B5
BRXN/ST SW9 ....142 B4
CAN/RD E16 ....107 F5
EDGW HA8 ....44 B2
EHAM E6 ....107 K1
HPTN TW12 ....173 F2
HSLW TW3 ....135 H2
SNWD SE25 * 197 H1
WLSDN NW10 ....81 F3
Gresham St CITYW EC2V 12 C3
Gresham Wy WIM/MER SW19 ..159 K5
Gresley CI SEVS/STOTM N15 * ..67 K1
WALTH E17 ....69 G1
Gresley Rd ARCH N19 ....66 C5
Gressenhall Rd
WAND/EARL SW18 ....159 J1
Greswell St FUL/PGN SW6 ......139 G3
Gretton Rd TOTM N17 ....50 A3
Greville CI TWK TW1 ....156 C2
Greville Ms KIL/WHAMP NW6 ....83 F6
Greville PI KIL/WHAMP NW6 ...101 F1
Greville Rd KIL/WHAMP NW6 ...101 F1
RCHPK/HAM TW10 ....157 G1
WALTH E17 ....70 A1
Greville St HCIRC EC1N 11 K2
Grey CI GLDGN NW11 ....65 G3
Greycoat PI WEST SW1P 16 C5
Greycoat St WEST SW1P 16 C5
Greycot Rd BECK BR3 ....182 D1
Grey Eagle St WCHPL E1 ....13 K1
Greyfell CI STAN HA7 * 43 H1
Greyhound Hl HDN NW4 ....45 J6
Greyhound La
STRHM/NOR SW16 ....179 K2
Greyhound Rd HMSMTH W6 ...119 G6
SUT SM1 ....209 G3
TOTM N17 ....50 A6
WLSDN NW10 ....99 K2
Greyhound Ter
STRHM/NOR SW16 ....179 K2
Greyhound Wy DART DA1 ....150 B6
Greyladies Gdns
GNWCH SE10 * 145 F3
Greys Park CI HAYES BR2 ....215 G3
Greystead Rd FSTH SE23 ....163 K2
Greystoke Av PIN HA5 ....42 A6
Greystoke Cottages EA W5 * 98 A3
Greystoke Gdns BARK/HLT IG6 ..54 C3
KTN/HRWW/WS HA3 ....61 J5
Greyswood Av UED N18 * 51 F1
Greyswood St
STRHM/NOR SW16 ....179 G2
Grierson Rd FSTH SE23 ....164 B1
Griffin Centre
EBED/NFELT TW14 * 154 A1
Griffin Cl WLSDN NW10 ....81 K3
Griffin Manor Wy THMD SE28 ...127 J3
Griffin Rd TOTM N17 ....50 B5
WOOL/PLUM SE18 ....127 K5
Griffin's Cl WCHMH N21 ....35 K3
Griffin Wy THMD SE28 ....127 K3
Griffith Cl BCTR RM8 ....73 J4
Griffiths Rd WIM/MER SW19 ....177 K3
Griggs Ap IL IG1 ....72 C6
Griggs Rd LEY E10 ....70 A3
Grigg's PI STHWK SE1 ....19 H5
Grimsby Gv CAN/RD E16 ....127 G2
Grimsby St BETH E2 ....7 K6
Grimsdyke Crs BAR EN5 ....20 A4
Grimsdyke Rd PIN HA5 ....41 J3
Grimsel Pth CMBW SE5 ....142 C1
Grimshaw Cl HGT N6 * 66 A4
Grimshaw Wy ROM RM1 ....75 G2
Grimston Rd FUL/PGN SW6 .....139 J3
Grimwade Av CROY/NA CRO ...212 C1
Grimwade CI PECK SE15 ....143 K4
Grimwood Rd TWK TW1 ....156 A1
Grindall CI CROY/NA CRO 211 H2
Grindal St STHWK SE1 ....17 J3
Grindleford Av
FBAR/BDGN N11 ....34 A4
Grindley Gdns CROY/NA CRO * ..197 G3
Grinling PI DEPT SE8 ....124 C6
Grinstead Rd DEPT SE8 ....124 B5
Grisle Ct ED N9 ....36 D6
Grittleton Av WBLY HA9 ....80 D4
Grittleton Rd MV/WKIL W9 ....100 E3
Grocers' Hall Ct LOTH EC2R * 12 E4
Groombridge Cl WELL DA16 .....148 B5
Groombridge Rd HOM E9 ....87 F5
Groom Cl HAYES BR2 ....200 A1
Groom Crs WAND/EARL SW18 ..160 C2
Groomfield Cl TOOT SW17 ....161 F6
Grooms Dr PIN HA5 ....58 E1
Grosmont Rd
WOOL/PLUM SE18 ....128 A5
Grosse Wy PUT/ROE SW15 .....158 E1
Grosvenor Av CAR SM5 ....209 K4
HBRY N5 ....85 K3

MORT/ESHN SW14 ....138 B4
RYLN/HDSTN HA2 ....60 B4
YEAD UB4 ....94 D1
Grosvenor Cottages
KTBR SW1X 15 G6
Grosvenor Crs CDALE/KGS NW9 ..62 C1
DART DA1 ....151 G6
Grosvenor Crescent Ms
KTBR SW1X 15 H3
Grosvenor Gdns BCVA SW1W ...15 H5
CRICK NW2 ....82 A4
GLDGN NW11 ....64 D3
KUTN/CMB KT2 ....174 E2
MORT/ESHN SW14 ....138 B4
MUSWH N10 ....48 A4
STHGT/OAK N14 ....22 D6
WFD IG8 ....52 E2
WLGTN SM6 ....210 C5
Grosvenor Gardens Ms East
BCVA SW1W * 15 K4
Grosvenor Gardens Ms North
BCVA SW1W 15 J5
Grosvenor Ga MYFR/PKLN W1K ..9 J5
Grosvenor Hl MYFR/PKLN W1K ..9 J5
WIM/MER SW19 ....177 H2
Grosvenor Pde EA W5 * 117 F2
Grosvenor Pk CMBW SE5 ....142 D1
Grosvenor Park Rd WALTH E17 ..69 K2
Grosvenor Pl KTBR SW1X 15 H3
Grosvenor Ri East WALTH E17 ....69 K2
Grosvenor Rd BCTR RM8 ....74 B5
BELV DA17 ....129 H6
BTFD TW8 ....116 E6
BXLYHS DA6 ....148 E6
CHSWK W4 ....117 K5
ED N9 ....36 D3
FNCH N3 ....46 D3
FSTGT E7 ....89 F4
HNWL W7 ....116 B1
HSLWW TW4 ....134 E4
IL IG1 ....90 C1
LEY E10 ....70 A5
MUSWH N10 ....48 B4
NTHWD HA6 ....40 D1
NWDGN UB2 ....114 E3
PIM SW1V 121 H6
RCHPK/HAM TW10 ....137 F6
ROMW/RG RM7 ....75 F4
SNWD SE25 * 197 H1
STMC/STPC BR5 ....201 K5
TWK TW1 ....156 B2
WAN E11 ....71 F2
WLGTN SM6 ....210 B5
WWKM BR4 ....198 E6
Grosvenor Sq MYFR/PKLN W1K ..9 H5
Grosvenor St MYFR/PKLN W1K ..9 J6
Grosvenor V RSLP HA4 ....58 D6
Grosvenor Vs CLPT E5 ....68 C6
Grosvenor Wharf Rd
POP/IOD E14 ....125 G4
Grote's Buildings
BKHTH/KID SE3 ....145 H3
Grote's PI BKHTH/KID SE3 ......145 H3
Groton Rd WAND/EARL SW18 ..160 A4
Grotto Ct STHWK SE1 * 18 C2
Grotto Pas MHST W1U 9 H1
Grotto Rd TWK TW1 ....156 A4
Grove Av CHING E4 ....96 E5
MUSWH N10 ....48 C5
PIN HA5 ....59 J1
SUT SM1 ....208 E4
TWK TW1 ....156 A3
Grove Bank OXHEY WD19 ....27 H1
Grovebury Cl ERITH DA8 ....130 A6
Grovebury Ct STHGT/OAK N14 ..34 C2
Grovebury Rd ABYW SE2 ....128 C2
Grove Cl FSTH SE23 ....164 A3
HAYES BR2 ....199 K6
KUT/HW KT1 ....191 G1
STHGT/OAK N14 * 34 B2
Grove Cottages CHEL SW3 ......120 D6
CHSWK W4 ....118 B6
Grove Ct E/WMO/HCT KT8 ......189 J2
EA W5 * 117 F1
Grove Crs CDALE/KGS NW9 ......62 E1
FELT TW13 ....154 D6
KUT/HW KT1 ....175 F6
SWFD E18 ....53 F1
WOT/HER KT12 ....188 A4
Grove Crescent Rd SRTFD E15 ..88 B4
Grovedale Rd ARCH N19 ....66 D6
Grove Dwellings WCHPL E1 * ...104 E4
Grove End KTTN NW5 ....84 B2
SWFD E18 ....53 F1
Grove End La ESH/CLAY KT10 ..189 J5
Grove End Rd STJWD NW8 ....2 B3
Grove Farm Pk NTHWD HA6 ......40 B1
Grove Footpath BRYLDS KT5 ...191 F1
Grove Gdns HDN NW4 ....63 J2
PEND EN3 ....25 G2
STJWD NW8 ....2 C5
TEDD TW11 ....156 B6
Grove Green Rd WAN E11 ....88 A1
Groveherst Rd DART DA1 ....151 J4
Grove Hl HRW HA1 ....61 F2
SWFD E18 ....52 D5
Grove Hill Rd CMBW SE5 ....143 F4
HRW HA1 ....61 F2
Grove House Rd
CEND/HSY/T N8 * 66 E1
Groveland Av
STRHM/NOR SW16 ....180 A3
Groveland Ct STP EC4M 12 D4
Groveland Rd BECK BR3 ....182 C6
Grovelands E/WMO/HCT KT8 ...189 F1
Grovelands Cl CMBW SE5 ....143 F3
RYLN/HDSTN HA2 ....77 K1
Grovelands Rd STHGT/OAK N14 ..35 G4
SEVS/STOTM N15 ....68 D3
Grovelands Rd STMC/STPC BR5 ..186 A5
Groveland Wy NWMAL KT3 ......191 K2
Grove La CMBW SE5 ....142 E2
KUT/HW KT1 ....191 F1

Grove Market Pl
ELTH/MOT SE9 * 166 E1
Grove Ms HMSMTH W6 ....119 F3
Grove Mill Pl CAR SM5 ....210 A1
Grove Pk CDALE/KGS NW9 ....62 E1
CMBW SE5 ....143 F3
WAN E11 ....71 F2
Grove Park Av CHING E4 ....51 K5
Grove Park Br CHSWK W4 ....137 K1
Grove Park Gdns CHSWK W4 ...137 K1
Grove Park Ms CHSWK W4 ....137 K1
Grove Park Rd CHSWK W4 ....137 K1
ELTH/MOT SE9 ....166 D4
RAIN RM13 ....93 J6
SEVS/STOTM N15 ....68 A1
Grove Park Ter CHSWK W4 ......137 K1
Grove Pl ACT W3 ....117 K1
BAL SW12 * 161 G1
HAMP NW3 ....83 H1
Grove Rd ACT W3 ....117 K1
BARN SW13 ....138 C5
BELV DA17 ....129 G4
BMLY BR1 ....184 A4
BORE WD6 ....24 C1
BOW E3 ....87 G6
BTFD TW8 ....116 D5
BXLYHN DA7 ....149 K5
CHDH RM6 ....73 J4
CHING E4 ....38 C5
CRICK NW2 ....82 A4
E/WMO/HCT KT8 ....189 J1
EBAR EN4 ....21 J4
EDGW HA8 ....44 C2
FBAR/BDGN N11 * 48 D1
HOM E9 ....87 F5
ISLW TW7 ....135 K2
MTCM CR4 ....179 G5
NFNCH/WDSPK N12 ....47 H1
PIN HA5 ....59 J2
RCHPK/HAM TW10 ....157 G1
SEVS/STOTM N15 ....155 K6
SURB KT6 ....190 E2
SUT SM1 ....208 E4
SWFD E18 ....52 E5
THHTH CR7 ....196 B1
WALTH E17 ....69 K2
WAN E11 ....70 D5
WHTN TW2 ....155 J5
WIM/MER SW19 ....178 B3
Grover Rd OXHEY WD19 ....27 H1
Groveside Cl ACT W3 ....98 C5
CAR SM5 ....194 D6
Groveside Rd CHING E4 ....38 C5
Grovestile Waye
EBED/NFELT TW14 ....153 H3
Grove St BERM/RHTH SE16 ......124 B2
Grove Ter KTTN NW5 ....84 B2
STHL UB1 * 96 A6
TEDD TW11 ....156 B6
Grove Terrace Ms KTTN NW5 * ...84 B1
The Grove BXLYHS DA6 ....148 E5
CDALE/KGS NW9 ....62 D2
CEND/HSY/T N8 ....66 D2
EA W5 ....116 E1
EDGW HA8 ....30 D6
ENC/FH EN2 ....23 G3
FELT TW13 ....154 D6
FSBYPK N4 ....67 F6
GLDGN NW11 ....64 C5
HGT N6 ....66 A6
ISLW TW7 ....135 K2
PLMGR N13 ....35 G5
SCUP DA14 ....187 F1
TEDD TW11 ....156 B6
WOT/HER KT12 ....188 A4
Groveway BCTR RM8 ....91 K2
BRXN/ST SW9 ....142 A2
DUL SE22 * 143 F5
Groveway EDUL SE22 ....143 F5
Groveway ISLW TW7 * 136 A3
Grove Wk EA W5 * 117 F1
WLY HA9 ....80 E3
Grove Wy E/WMO/HCT KT8 ......189 J2
EA W5 * 117 F1
Grove Yd CDALE/KGS NW9 ....62 D1
Grovewood Pl WFD IG8 ....53 K2
Grummant Rd PECK SE15 ....143 G2
Grundy St POP/IOD E14 ....105 K5
Gruneisen Rd FNCH N3 ....47 F3
Guardian Cl EMPK RM11 ....75 K6
Gubyon Av HNHL SE24 ....142 D6
Guernsey Cl HEST TW5 ....135 F1
Guernsey Gv HNHL SE24 ....162 D2
Guernsey Rd WAN E11 ....85 J0
LEY E10 ....70 B5
Guibal Rd LEE/GVPK SE12 ......166 A3
Guildersfield Rd
STRHM/NOR SW16 ....179 K3
Guildford Av FELT TW13 ....153 K4
Guildford Gv GNWCH SE10 ......144 E2
EHAM E6 ....107 J5
Guildford Rd CROY/NA CRO 196 E3
CITYW EC2V 12 D3
Guildhall Yd CITYW EC2V 12 D3
Guildhouse St PIM SW1V 16 A7
Guildown Av
NFNCH/WDSPK N12 ....33 G6
Guild Rd CHARL SE7 ....126 C5
ERITH DA8 ....150 C1
Guildford Rd WALTH E17 ....51 K5
Guilford Av BRYLDS KT5 ....191 G2
Guilford Pl BMSBY WC1N 5 G7
Guilford St BMSBY WC1N 5 F7
Guillemot Pl WDGN N22 * 49 F5
Guinness Cl HAYES UB3 ....113 G3
Guinness Ct CROY/NA CRO * ...197 G6
Guinness Sq STHWK SE1 ....19 G5
Guinness Trust
STNW/STAM N16 * 68 B3
Guinness Trust Est CHEL SW3 ...14 E7

SRTFD E15 * 88 D6
Guion Rd FUL/PGN SW6 ....139 J3
Guiland Wk IS N1 * 85 J4
Gulliver Cl NTHLT UB5 ....77 K6
Gulliver Rd BFN/LL DA15 ....167 K3
Gulliver St BERM/RHTH SE16 ...124 C3
Gumleigh Rd EA W5 ....116 D4
Gumley Gdns ISLW TW7 ....136 B4
Gunating Rd STMC/STPC BR5 ..201 H6
Gumbulph Rd HAYES BR2 ....184 B6
Gunmakers La BOW E3 ....87 G6
Gunnell Cl CROY/NA CRO 197 H3
SYD SE26 * 163 H6
Gunner La WOOL/PLUM SE18 ..127 F5
Gunnersbury Av ACT W3 ....117 H4
Gunnersbury Av (North
Circular Rd) EA W5 ....98 B6
Gunnersbury Cl CHSWK W4 * ...117 J5
Gunnersbury Crs ACT W3 ....117 H2
Gunnersbury Dr EA W5 ....117 G2
Gunnersbury Gdns ACT W3 .....117 G2
Gunnersbury La ACT W3 ....117 G1
Gunnersbury Ms CHSWK W4 ...117 J5
Gunners Gv CHING E4 ....38 A5
Gunners Rd TOOT SW17 ....160 C4
Gunning St
WOOL/PLUM SE18 ....127 K4
Gunstor Rd STNW/STAM N16 * ..86 A2
Gun St WCHPL E1 ....13 J2
Gunter Gv EDGW HA8 ....45 F4
WBPTN SW10 ....120 B6
Gunterstone Rd WKENS W14 ...119 H5
Gunthorpe St WCHPL E1 ....13 K2
Gunton Rd CLPT E5 ....68 E5
TOOT SW17 ....179 F2
Gunwhale Cl
BERM/RHTH SE16 ....124 A1
Gunyard Ms
WOOL/PLUM SE18 ....146 D1
Gurdon Rd CHARL SE7 ....125 K5
Gurnell Gv WEA W13 ....97 F3
Gurney Cl BARK IG11 ....90 B4
SRTFD E15 ....88 C3
Gurney Crs CROY/NA CRO 196 A5
Gurney Dr EFNCH N2 ....65 F3
FUL/PGN SW6 ....140 B4
NTHLT UB5 ....95 F2
SRTFD E15 ....88 C3
Guthrie St CHEL SW3 ....120 D5
Gutter La CITYW EC2V 12 C3
Guyatt Gdns MTCM CR4 ....179 F5
Guy Barnett Gv
BKHTH/KID SE3 ....145 K4
Guy Rd WLGTN SM6 ....210 E1
Guyscliff Rd LEW SE13 ....145 F6
Guysfield Cl RAIN RM13 ....93 J6
Guysfield Dr RAIN RM13 ....93 J6
Guy St STHWK SE1 ....19 F3
Gwalior Rd PUT/ROE SW15 ......139 G5
Gwendolen Av
PUT/ROE SW15 ....139 G6
Gwendoline Av PLSTW E13 ....89 F1
Gwendwr Rd WKENS W14 ....119 H5
Gweneth Cottages
EDGW HA8 * 44 C2
Gwillim Cl BFN/LL DA15 ....168 B1
Gwydor Rd BECK BR3 ....198 A1
Gwydyr Rd HAYES BR2 ....183 J6
Gwyn Cl FUL/PGN SW6 ....140 B1
Gwynne Av CROY/NA CRO 198 A4
Gwynne Park Av WFD IG8 ....53 K2
Gwynne Rd BTSEA SW11 ....140 C3
Gwynne Whf CHSWK W4 ....118 E6
Gylcote Cl CMBW SE5 ....142 E5
Gyles Pk STAN HA7 ....43 J4
Gyllyngdune Gdns
GDMY/SEVK IG3 ....91 F1
Gywnne Pl FSBYW WC1X 5 H5

H

Haarlem Rd WKENS W14 ....119 G3
Haberdasher Pl IS N1 * 7 F4
Haberdasher St IS N1 ....7 F4
Habington Cl CMBW SE5 * 142 E1
Hackbridge Gn CAR SM5 ....209 K4
Haccombe Rd WIM/MER SW19 ..178 B2
Hackbridge Park Gdns
CAR SM5 ....194 E6
Hackbridge Rd CAR SM5 ....195 F6
Hackford Rd BRXN/ST SW9 ......142 A2
Hackford Wk BRXN/ST SW9 .....142 B2
Hackington Crs BECK BR3 ....182 D2
Hackney Gv HACK E8 * 86 D4
Hackney Rd BETH E2 ....7 J4
Hackney Wick HOM E9 ....87 H4
Hadar Cl TRDG/WHET N20 ....32 E3
Hadden Rd THMD SE28 ....128 A3
Hadden Wy GFD/PVL UB6 ....78 D4
Haddington Rd BMLY BR1 ....165 G5
Haddo Cl EN EN1 ....36 C1
NWMAL KT3 ....192 C2
Haddon Gv BFN/LL DA15 ....168 B2
Haddon Rd STMC/STPC BR5 ....202 B4
SUT SM1 ....209 F2
Haddo St GNWCH SE10 ....124 E6
Hadfield Cl STHL UB1 ....95 K3
Hadfield Rd STWL/WRAY TW19 ..152 A1
Hadleigh Cl RYNPK SW20 ....177 J5
WCHPL E1 ....104 E3
Hadleigh Dr BELMT SM2 ....208 E6
Hadleigh Rd ED N9 ....36 D2
Hadleigh St BETH E2 ....104 E3
Hadley Cl WCHMH N21 ....23 G6
Hadley Common BAR EN5 ....21 J1
Hadley Gdns CHSWK W4 ....118 A5
NWDGN UB2 ....114 E6
Hadley Gn BAR EN5 ....20 D3
Hadley Green Rd BAR EN5 ....20 D3
Hadley Gn West BAR EN5 ....20 C3
Hadley Gv BAR EN5 ....20 C3

Hadley Highstone BAR EN5 20 D2
Hadley Pde BAR EN5 * 20 C4
Hadley Rdg BAR EN5 20 D4
Hadley Rd BAR EN5 21 F5
BELV DA17 129 G4
EBAR EN4 22 A1
MTCM CR4 195 J1
Hadley St KTTN NW5 84 B4
Hadley Wy WCHMH N21 35 G1
Hadley Wood Rd BAR EN5 20 E3
Hadlow Pl NRWD SE19 181 H3
Hadlow Rd SCUP DA14 168 B6
WELL DA16 148 D1
Hadrian Cl BOW E3 87 J6
STWL/WRAY TW19 152 B2
Hadrian Est BETH E2 * 104 C1
Hadrian's Ride EN EN1 24 B6
Hadrian St GNWCH SE10 125 H5
Hadrian Wy STWL/WRAY TW19 152 B2
Hadyn Park Rd SHB W12 118 D2
Hafer Rd BTSEA SW11 140 E5
Hafton Rd CAT SE6 165 H3
Haggard Rd TWK TW1 156 C2
Hagger Ct WALTH E17 * 52 B6
Haggerston Rd HACK E8 86 B5
Hague St BETH E2 104 C2
Ha-ha Rd WOOL/PLUM SE18 126 E6
Haig Rd STAN HA7 43 J1
Haig Rd East PLSTW E13 107 G2
Haig Rd West PLSTW E13 107 G2
Haigville Gdns BARK/HLT IG6 72 B1
Hailes Cl WIM/MER SW19 178 B2
Haileybury Av EN EN1 36 C1
Haileybury Rd ORP BR6 217 G2
Hailey Rd ERITHM DA18 129 H2
Hailsham Av
BRXS/STRHM SW2 162 A4
Hailsham Cl SURB KT6 190 E4
Hailsham Dr HRW HA1 42 D6
Hailsham Rd TOOT SW17 179 F2
Hailsham Ter UED N18 * 49 K1
Haimo Rd ELTH/MOT SE9 146 C6
Hainault Buildings LEY E10 * 70 A5
Hainault Gore CHDH RM6 74 A2
Hainault Rd BARK/HLT IG6 55 H3
CHDH RM6 55 H6
CHDH RM6 74 B3
CRW RM5 56 E6
WAN E11 70 A5
Hainault St ELTH/MOT SE9 167 G3
IL IG1 72 B6
Haines Wk MRDN SM4 194 A4
Hainford Cl PECK SE15 144 A5
Haining Cl CHSWK W4 117 H5
Hainthorpe Rd WNWD SE27 162 C5
Hainton Cl WCHPL E1 104 D5
Halberd Ms CLPT E5 68 D6
Halbutt St DAGW RM9 92 B2
Halcomb St IS N1 7 G1
Halcot Av BXLYHS DA6 149 J6
Halcrow St WCHPL E1 104 E4
Haldane Cl MUSWH N10 48 B3
PEND EN3 25 K1
Haldane Pl WAND/EARL SW18 160 A3
Haldane Rd EHAM E6 107 H2
FUL/PGN SW6 139 J1
STHL UB1 96 C6
THMD SE28 109 K6
Haldan Rd CHING E4 52 A2
Haldon Rd WAND/EARL SW18 159 J1
Hale Cl CHING E4 38 A5
EDGW HA8 44 E1
ORP BR6 216 C2
Hale Dr MLHL NW7 44 E2
Hale End HARH RM3 57 K2
Hale End Cl RSLP HA4 58 E3
Hale End Rd CHING E4 52 B2
Halefield Rd TOTM N17 50 C4
Hale Gdns ACT W3 117 H1
SEVS/STOTM N15 68 C1
TOTM N17 50 C6
Hale Grove Gdns MLHL NW7 45 F1
Hale House
WOOL/PLUM SE18 * 146 D1
Hale La EDGW HA8 44 E1
MLHL NW7 45 F1
Hale Rd EHAM E6 107 J3
TOTM N17 50 C6
Halesowen Rd MRDN SM4 194 A4
Hales St DEPT SE8 144 D1
Hale St POP/IOD E14 105 K6
Halesworth Rd LEW SE13 144 E4
The Hale CHING E4 52 B3
TOTM N17 50 C6
Haley Rd HDN NW4 64 A3
Half Acre BTFD TW8 116 E6
Half Acre Ms BTFD TW8 136 E1
Half Acre Rd HNWL W7 115 K1
Half Moon Crs IS N1 5 H2
Half Moon La DUL SE21 142 E6
HNHL SE24 162 E1
Half Moon Pas WCHPL E1 13 K4
Halfmoon Pas WCHPL E1 * 13 K4
Half Moon St MYFR/PICC W1J 9 K7
Halford Cl EDGW HA8 44 D5
Halford Rd FUL/PGN SW6 119 K6
LEY E10 70 B2
RCHPK/HAM TW10 137 F6
Halfway Ct PUR RM19 131 K4
Halfway St BFN/LL DA15 167 K3
Haliburton Rd TWK TW1 136 B6
Haliday Wk IS N1 85 K4
Halifax Cl TEDD TW11 173 K2
Halifax Rd ENC/FH EN2 23 J3
GFD/PVL UB6 78 B6
Halifax St SYD SE26 163 J5
Halifield Dr BELV DA17 129 F3
Haling Gv SAND/SEL CR2 211 J5
Haling Park Gdns
SAND/SEL CR2 211 H4
Haling Park Rd SAND/SEL CR2 211 J4
Haling Rd SAND/SEL CR2 211 K4
Halkin Ar KTBR SW1X 15 G4
Halkin Ms KTBR SW1X * 15 G4
Halkin Pl KTBR SW1X 15 G4
Halkin St KTBR SW1X 15 H3
Hallam Cl CHST BR7 184 E1
Hallam Gdns PIN HA5 41 J3
Hallam Ms GTPST W1W 9 K1
Hallam Rd BARN SW13 138 E4
SEVS/STOTM N15 67 H1
Hallam St GTPST W1W 9 K1
Halland Wy NTHWD HA6 40 B2
Hall Cl EA W5 98 A4
Hall Ct TEDD TW11 174 A1
Hall Dr SYD SE26 181 K1
Halley Gdns LEW SE13 145 G5
Halley Rd FSTGT E7 89 G4
Halley St POP/IOD E14 105 G4
Hall Farm Cl STAN HA7 29 H6
Hall Farm Dr WHTN TW2 155 J2
Hallfield Est BAY/PAD W2 * 101 G5
Hallford Wy DART DA1 171 F1
Hall Gdns CHING E4 37 H6
Halliday Sq NWDGN UB2 115 J1
Halliford St IS N1 85 J5
Halliwell Rd BRXS/STRHM SW2 162 A1
Halliwick Court Pde
NFNCH/WDSPK N12 * 47 K1
Halliwick Rd MUSWH N10 48 A4
Hall La CHING E4 51 H1
HDN NW4 45 J5
HYS/HAR UB3 133 G1
Hallmead Rd SUT SM1 209 F1
Hall Oak Wk KIL/WHAMP NW6 82 D4
Hallowell Av CROY/NA CR0 210 E2
Hallowell Cl MTCM CR4 179 F6
Hallowell Rd NTHWD HA6 40 C3
Hallowes Crs OXHEY WD19 26 E5
Hallowfield Wy MTCM CR4 178 C6
Hall Pl BAY/PAD W2 2 A7
Hall Place Crs BXLY DA5 149 K6
Hall Rd CHDH RM6 73 J3
DART DA1 151 J5
EHAM E6 89 K6
GPK RM2 57 K6
ISLW TW7 135 J6
MV/WKIL W9 101 G2
SRTFD E15 88 B2
WLGTN SM6 210 B6
Hallside Rd EN EN1 24 B1
Hall St FSBYE EC1V 6 B4
NFNCH/WDSPK N12 47 G1
Hallsville Rd CAN/RD E16 106 D5
Hallswelle Pde GLDGN NW11 * 64 D2
Hallswelle Rd GLDGN NW11 64 D2
The Hall BKHTH/KID SE3 145 K4
Hall Vw ELTH/MOT SE9 166 C4
Hallywell Crs EHAM E6 107 K4
Halons Rd ELTH/MOT SE9 167 F2
Halpin Pl WALW SE17 19 F7
Halsbrook Rd BKHTH/KID SE3 146 B4
Halsbury Cl STAN HA7 43 H1
Halsbury Rd SHB W12 118 E1
Halsbury Rd East NTHLT UB5 78 C2
Halsbury Rd West NTHLT UB5 78 B3
Halsend HYS/HAR UB3 * 114 A1
Halsey St CHEL SW3 14 E6
Halsham Crs BARK IG11 91 F4
Halsmere Rd CMBW SE5 142 C2
Halstead Cl CROY/NA CR0 211 J1
Halstead Gdns WCHMH N21 35 K3
Halstead Rd EN EN1 24 A5
ERITH DA8 150 B2
WAN E11 71 F2
WCHMH N21 35 K3
Halston Cl BTSEA SW11 160 E1
Halstow Rd GNWCH SE10 125 K5
WLSDN NW10 100 B2
Halsway HYS/HAR UB3 113 K1
Halton Cl FBAR/BDGN N11 47 K2
Halton Cross St IS N1 * 85 H6
Halton Rd IS N1 85 H5
Halt Pde CDALE/KGS NW9 * 63 F1
Halt Robin Rd BELV DA17 129 J4
Hambalt Rd CLAP SW4 141 H6
Hamble Cl RSLP HA4 58 C6
Hambledon WALW SE17 * 122 E6
Hambledon Ct EA W5 * 98 A6
Hambledon Gdns SNWD SE25 181 G6
Hambledon Pl DUL SE21 163 G3
Hambledon Rd
WAND/EARL SW18 159 J2
Hambledown Rd
BFN/LL DA15 * 167 J2
Hamble St FUL/PGN SW6 140 A4
Hambleton Cl WPK KT4 193 F6
Hambro Av HAYES BR2 199 K5
Hambrook Rd SNWD SE25 181 J6
Hambro Rd STRHM/NOR SW16 179 J2
Hambrough Rd STHL UB1 114 D1
Ham Common
RCHPK/HAM TW10 156 E5
Ham Croft Cl FELT TW13 153 K5
Hamden Crs DAGE RM10 92 D1
Hamel Cl KTN/HRWW/WS HA3 61 K1
Hameway EHAM E6 108 A3
Ham Farm Rd
RCHPK/HAM TW10 156 E6
Hamfrith Rd SRTFD E15 88 D4
Ham Gate Av
RCHPK/HAM TW10 157 G6
Hamilton Av BARK/HLT IG6 72 B1
CHEAM SM3 193 H6
ED N9 36 C2
ROM RM1 57 F5
SURB KT6 191 H6
Hamilton Cl BERM/RHTH SE16 124 B2
EBAR EN4 21 J5
STJWD NW8 2 A5
TEDD TW11 174 C2
TOTM N17 50 B6
Hamilton Ct EA W5 98 B6
Hamilton Crs HSLW TW3 135 G6
PLMGR N13 35 G6
RYLN/HDSTN HA2 77 K1
Hamilton Gdns STJWD NW8 101 G2
Hamilton La HBRY N5 85 H2
Hamilton Ms MYFR/PICC W1J 15 J2
Hamilton Pde FELT TW13 * 153 K6
Hamilton Pk HBRY N5 85 H2
Hamilton Pk West HBRY N5 85 H2
Hamilton Pl MYFR/PKLN W1K 15 H1
SUN TW16 172 A3
Hamilton Rd BTFD TW8 116 E6
BXLYHN DA7 149 F3
CHSWK W4 118 B3
EA W5 98 A6
EBAR EN4 21 J5
ED N9 36 C2
EFNCH N2 47 G6
GLDGN NW11 64 B4
GPK RM2 75 K2
HRW HA1 60 E2
HYS/HAR UB3 95 F6
IL IG1 90 B2
OXHEY WD19 27 F5
SCUP DA14 168 B6
SRTFD E15 106 C2
STHL UB1 114 E1
THHTH CR7 180 E6
WALTH E17 51 G5
WHTN TW2 155 K3
WIM/MER SW19 178 A3
WLSDN NW10 81 J3
WNWD SE27 162 E6
Hamilton Road Ms
WIM/MER SW19 178 A3
Hamilton Sq
NFNCH/WDSPK N12 * 47 G2
Hamilton St DEPT SE8 124 D6
Hamilton Ter STJWD NW8 101 G2
Hamilton Wy FNCH N3 46 E2
PLMGR N13 35 H6
WLGTN SM6 210 D6
Hamlea Cl LEE/GVPK SE12 145 K6
Hamlet Cl CRW RM5 56 C3
LEW SE13 145 H5
Hamlet Gdns HMSMTH W6 118 D4
Hamlet Rd CRW RM5 56 C3
NRWD SE19 181 G3
Hamlet Sq CRICK NW2 82 C1
Hamlets Wy BOW E3 105 H3
The Hamlet CMBW SE5 142 E4
Hamlet Wy STHWK SE1 19 F3
Hamlin Crs PIN HA5 59 G2
Hamlyn Cl EDGW HA8 30 A5
Hamlyn Gdns NRWD SE19 181 F3
Hammelton Rd BMLY BR1 183 K4
Hammers La MLHL NW7 31 J6
Hammersmith Br
HMSMTH W6 118 E5
Hammersmith Bridge Rd
BARN SW13 118 E6
HMSMTH W6 119 F5
Hammersmith Broadway
HMSMTH W6 119 F4
Hammersmith Emb
HMSMTH W6 * 119 F6
Hammersmith F/O
HMSMTH W6 119 F5
Hammersmith Gv
HMSMTH W6 119 F4
Hammersmith Rd
HMSMTH W6 119 G4
Hammersmith Ter
HMSMTH W6 * 118 D5
Hammerton Cl BXLY DA5 170 B5
Hammet Cl YEAD UB4 95 H4
Hammett St TWRH EC3N 13 J5
Hammond Av MTCM CR4 179 G5
Hammond Cl BAR EN5 20 D6
GFD/PVL UB6 78 D3
HPTN TW12 173 F4
Hammond Rd EN EN1 24 D4
NWDGN UB2 114 D3
Hammonds Cl BCTR RM8 91 J1
Hammond St KTTN NW5 84 C4
Hamond Cl SAND/SEL CR2 211 H6
Hamonde Cl EDGW HA8 30 D4
Hamond Sq IS N1 7 G2
Ham Park Rd FSTGT E7 88 E5
Hampden Av BECK BR3 182 B5
Hampden Cl CAMTN NW1 4 D3
Hampden Gurney St
MBLAR W1H 8 E4
Hampden La TOTM N17 50 C4
Hampden Rd ARCH N19 66 D6
BECK BR3 182 B5
CEND/HSY/T N8 67 G1
KTN/HRWW/WS HA3 42 C4
KUT/HW KT1 175 H6
MUSWH N10 48 A3
TOTM N17 50 C4
Hampden Wy STHGT/OAK N14 34 B3
Hampermill La OXHEY WD19 26 E3
Hampshire Cl UED N18 50 D1
Hampshire Hog La
HMSMTH W6 * 118 E4
Hampshire Rd WDGN N22 49 F3
Hampshire St KTTN NW5 * 84 D4
Hampson Wy VX/NE SW8 142 A2
Hampstead Av WFD IG8 54 A3
Hampstead Cl THMD SE28 128 C1
Hampstead Gdns GLDGN NW11 64 E3
Hampstead Ga HAMP NW3 83 G3
Hampstead Gn HAMP NW3 83 J3
Hampstead Gv HAMP NW3 83 G2
Hampstead Hill Gdns
HAMP NW3 83 J2
Hampstead La HGT N6 65 K4
Hampstead Rd CAMTN NW1 4 A5
Hampstead Sq HAMP NW3 83 G1
Hampstead Wy GLDGN NW11 64 E2
Hampton Cl FBAR/BDGN N11 48 A1
KIL/WHAMP NW6 100 E2
RYNPK SW20 * 177 F3
Hampton Ct IS N1 85 H4
Hampton Court Av
E/WMO/HCT KT8 189 J3
Hampton Court Crs
E/WMO/HCT KT8 * 173 J6
Hampton Court Cresent
E/WMO/HCT KT8 173 J6
Hampton Court Est
THDIT KT7 * 189 K2
Hampton Court Rd
E/WMO/HCT KT8 173 K6
E/WMO/HCT KT8 174 C6
Hampton Court Wy
E/WMO/HCT KT8 189 K1
Hampton La FELT TW13 154 D6
Hampton Ri
KTN/HRWW/WS HA3 62 A3
Hampton Rd CHING E4 51 H1
CROY/NA CR0 196 D3
FSTGT E7 89 F3
IL IG1 90 C2
TEDD TW11 173 J1
WAN E11 70 B5
WHTN TW2 155 J5
WPK KT4 192 D6
Hampton Rd East FELT TW13 154 E6
Hampton Rd West FELT TW13 154 D4
Hampton St WALW SE17 18 B7
Ham Ridings
RCHPK/HAM TW10 175 G1
Ham Shades Cl BFN/LL DA15 168 A5
Ham St RCHPK/HAM TW10 156 D4
The Ham BTFD TW8 136 D1
Ham Vw CROY/NA CR0 198 B3
Ham Yd SOHO/SHAV W1D * 10 C5
Hanameel St CAN/RD E16 125 K1
Hanbury Cl HDN NW4 46 A6
Hanbury Ct HRW HA1 * 61 F3
Hanbury Dr WCHMH N21 23 F5
Hanbury Rd ACT W3 117 J2
TOTM N17 50 D5
Hanbury St WCHPL E1 13 K1
Hancock Rd BOW E3 106 A2
NRWD SE19 180 E2
Handa Wk IS N1 85 J4
Hand Ct HHOL WC1V 11 H2
Handcroft Rd CROY/NA CR0 196 C5
Handel Cl EDGW HA8 44 B2
Handel Pde EDGW HA8 * 44 C2
Handel Pl WLSDN NW10 81 F4
Handel St BMSBY WC1N 5 F6
Handel Wy EDGW HA8 44 C3
Handen Rd LEE/GVPK SE12 145 H6
Handforth Rd BRXN/ST SW9 142 B1
IL IG1 90 B1
Handley Gv CRICK NW2 82 B1
Handley Page Rd WLGTN SM6 211 F5
Handley Rd HOM E9 86 E5
Handowe Cl HDN NW4 63 J1
Handside Cl WPK KT4 193 G5
Handsworth Av CHING E4 52 B2
Handsworth Cl OXHEY WD19 26 E5
Handsworth Rd TOTM N17 49 K6
Handtrough Wy BARK IG11 108 B1
Hanford Cl WAND/EARL SW18 159 K3
Hangar La (North Circular Rd)
EA W5 98 B3
Hangar Ruding OXHEY WD19 27 K5
Hanger Gn EA W5 98 C3
Hanger La EA W5 98 A2
EA W5 98 B6
Hanger La (North Circular
Road) EA W5 98 A2
Hanger Vale La EA W5 98 B5
Hanger View Wy ACT W3 98 C5
Hankey Pl STHWK SE1 19 F3
Hankins La MLHL NW7 31 G4
Hanley Gdns FSBYPK N4 67 F5
Hanley Pl BECK BR3 182 D3
Hanley Rd FSBYPK N4 66 E5
Hanmer Wk HOLWY N7 67 F6
Hannah Cl BECK BR3 182 E6
WLSDN NW10 80 E2
Hannah Mary Wy
STHWK SE1 * 123 H4
Hannards Wy BARK/HLT IG6 55 H1
Hannay La ARCH N19 66 D4
Hannell Rd FUL/PGN SW6 139 H1
Hannen Rd WNWD SE27 * 162 C5
Hannibal Rd STWL/WRAY TW19 152 B2
WCHPL E1 104 E4
Hannibal Wy CROY/NA CR0 211 F3
Hannington Rd CLAP SW4 141 G4
Hanover Av CAN/RD E16 125 K1
FELT TW13 153 K3
Hanover Cir HYS/HAR UB3 94 A5
Hanover Cl CHEAM SM3 208 C2
RCH/KEW TW9 137 H1
Hanover Dr CHST BR7 185 H1
Hanover Gdns BARK/HLT IG6 54 C3
LBTH SE11 122 B6
Hanover Pk PECK SE15 143 H2
Hanover Pl COVGDN WC2E 11 F4
Hanover Rd SEVS/STOTM N15 68 B1
WIM/MER SW19 178 B3
WLSDN NW10 82 A5
Hanover Sq CONDST W1S 9 K4
Hanover Steps BAY/PAD W2 * 8 D4
Hanover St CONDST W1S 9 K4
CROY/NA CR0 211 H1
Hanover Ter CAMTN NW1 2 E5
Hanover Terrace Ms
CAMTN NW1 2 E5
Hanover Wy BXLYHS DA6 148 E4
Hanover Yd IS N1 * 6 B2
Hansard Ms WKENS W14 119 G2
Hansart Wy ENC/FH EN2 23 G2
Hans Crs KTBR SW1X 14 E4
Hanselin Cl STAN HA7 43 F1
Hansen Dr WCHMH N21 23 F6
Hanshaw Dr EDGW HA8 45 F4
Hansler Gv E/WMO/HCT KT8 189 J2
Hansler Rd EDUL SE22 143 G6
Hansol Rd BXLYHS DA6 149 F6
Hansom Ter BMLY BR1 * 184 A4
Hanson Cl BAL SW12 161 G2
BECK BR3 * 182 E2
MORT/ESHN SW14 137 K4
WDR/YW UB7 112 C3
Hanson Gdns STHL UB1 114 D2
Hanson St GTPST W1W 10 A1
Hans Pl KTBR SW1X 14 E4
Hans Rd CHEL SW3 14 E4
Hans St KTBR SW1X 15 F5
Hanway Pl FITZ W1T 10 C3
Hanway Rd HNWL W7 96 D5
Hanway St FITZ W1T 10 C3
Hanworth Rd HPTN TW12 154 E6
HSLW TW3 135 G5
HSLWW TW4 154 E2
Hanworth Ter HSLW TW3 135 G5
Hapgood Cl GFD/PVL UB6 78 D3
Harben Pde HAMP NW3 * 83 H5
Harben Rd KIL/WHAMP NW6 83 G5
Harberson Rd BAL SW12 161 G3
SRTFD E15 88 D6
Harberton Rd ARCH N19 66 C5
Harbet Rd BAY/PAD W2 8 B2
UED N18 51 F1
Harbex Cl BXLY DA5 169 J2
Harbinger Rd POP/IOD E14 124 E4
Harbledown Pl
STMC/STPC BR5 202 D1
Harbledown Rd FUL/PGN SW6 139 K2
Harbord Cl CMBW SE5 142 E3
Harbord St FUL/PGN SW6 139 G2
Harborne Cl OXHEY WD19 41 G1
Harborough Av BFN/LL DA15 167 K2
Harborough Rd
STRHM/NOR SW16 162 A6
Harbour Av WBPTN SW10 140 B2
Harbourer Rd BARK/HLT IG6 55 H1
Harbour Exchange Sq
POP/IOD E14 124 E2
Harbour Rd CMBW SE5 142 D4
Harbour Yd WBPTN SW10 * 140 B2
Harbridge Av PUT/ROE SW15 158 C2
Harbury Rd CAR SM5 209 J6
Harbut Rd BTSEA SW11 140 C5
Harcastle Cl YEAD UB4 95 J3
Harcombe Rd STNW/STAM N16 86 A1
Harcourt Av BFN/LL DA15 168 D1
EDGW HA8 30 E5
MNPK E12 89 K2
WLGTN SM6 210 B2
Harcourt Buildings EMB EC4Y * 11 J5
Harcourt Cl ISLW TW7 136 B4
Harcourt Fld WLGTN SM6 210 B2
Harcourt Ms GPK RM2 75 H2
Harcourt Rd BROCKY SE4 144 C5
BXLYHS DA6 149 F5
SRTFD E15 106 D1
THHTH CR7 196 A3
WDGN N22 48 D4
WIM/MER SW19 177 K3
WLGTN SM6 210 B2
Harcourt St MBLAR W1H 8 D2
Harcourt Ter WBPTN SW10 120 A5
Hardcastle Cl CROY/NA CR0 197 H3
Hardcourts Cl WWKM BR4 213 K2
Hardel Wk BRXS/STRHM SW2 162 B2
Hardens Manorway
WOOL/PLUM SE18 126 C3
Harders Rd PECK SE15 143 J3
Hardess St HNHL SE24 142 D4
Hardie Cl WLSDN NW10 81 F3
Hardie Rd DAGE RM10 92 E1
Harding Cl CROY/NA CR0 212 B1
KUTN/CMB KT2 175 G4
WALW SE17 122 D6
Hardinge Rd UED N18 50 A1
WLSDN NW10 82 A6
Hardinge St WCHPL E1 104 E5
WOOL/PLUM SE18 127 G3
Harding Rd BXLYHN DA7 149 G3
Hardings La PGE/AN SE20 182 A2
Hardinge Crs
WOOL/PLUM SE18 127 H3
Hardman Rd CHARL SE7 126 A5
KUTN/CMB KT2 175 F5
Hardres Ter STMC/STPC BR5 * 202 E6
Hardwick Cl STAN HA7 43 J1
Hardwicke Av HEST TW5 * 135 F2
Hardwicke Ms FSBYW WC1X * 5 H5
Hardwicke Rd CHSWK W4 117 K4
PLMGR N13 48 E1
RCHPK/HAM TW10 156 D6
Hardwicke St BARK IG11 90 C6
Hardwick Gn WEA W13 97 H4
Hardwick Pl
STRHM/NOR SW16 179 H3
Hardwick St CLKNW EC1R 5 K5
Hardwick's Wy
WAND/EARL SW18 139 K6
Hardwidge St STHWK SE1 19 G2
Hardy Av CAN/RD E16 125 K1
RSLP HA4 77 F3
Hardy Cl BAR EN5 20 C6
BERM/RHTH SE16 124 A2
PIN HA5 59 H4
Hardy Cottages
GNWCH SE10 * 125 G6
Hardy Gv DART DA1 151 K5
Hardy Pas WDGN N22 49 F4
Hardy Rd BKHTH/KID SE3 125 J6
CHING E4 51 H2
WIM/MER SW19 178 A3
Hardys Ms E/WMO/HCT KT8 189 K1
Hardy Wy ENC/FH EN2 23 G2
Hare & Billet Rd
BKHTH/KID SE3 145 G2
Harebell Dr EHAM E6 108 A4
Hare Ct EMB EC4Y * 11 J4
Harecourt Rd IS N1 85 J4
Haredale Rd HNHL SE24 142 D5
Haredon Cl FSTH SE23 164 A2
Harefield ESH/CLAY KT10 204 E1
Harefield Av BELMT SM2 208 C6
Harefield Cl ENC/FH EN2 23 G2
Harefield Ms BROCKY SE4 144 C4
Harefield Rd BROCKY SE4 144 C4
CEND/HSY/T N8 66 D2
SCUP DA14 168 E5
STRHM/NOR SW16 180 A3
Hare Hall La GPK RM2 75 K1
Hare La ESH/CLAY KT10 204 E4
Hare Marsh BETH E2 104 C3
Hare Rw BETH E2 104 D1
Haresfield Rd DAGE RM10 92 C4
Hare St WOOL/PLUM SE18 127 F3
Hare Wk IS N1 7 H3
Harewood Av NTHLT UB5 77 J5
STJWD NW8 2 D6
Harewood Cl NTHLT UB5 77 K5
Harewood Dr CLAY IG5 53 K5
Harewood Pl CONDST W1S 9 K4
Harewood Rd ISLW TW7 136 A1
OXHEY WD19 27 F5

SAND/SEL CR2................212 A4
WIM/MER SW19.............178 D2
Harewood Rw CAMTN NW1 *......8 D1
Harewood Ter NWDGN UB2....114 E4
Harfield Gdns CMBW SE5 *...143 F4
Harfield Rd SUN TW16......172 C5
Harford Cl CHING E4.........37 K2
Harford St WCHPL E1.......105 G3
Harford Wk EFNCH N2........65 H1
Harglace Ter CDALE/KGS NW9 *..45 G6
Hargood Cl
  KTN/HRWW/WS HA3..........62 A3
Hargood Rd BKHTH/KID SE3..146 B2
Hargrave Pk ARCH N19........66 C6
Hargrave Pl KTTN NW5........84 A3
Hargrave Rd ARCH N19........66 C6
Hargwyne St BRXN/ST SW9....142 A4
Haringey Rd CEND/HSY/T N8....66 E1
Harington Ter UED N18 *......35 K6
Harkett Cl KTN/HRWW/WS HA3...43 F5
Harland Av CROY/NA
  CROY/NA CR0..............212 C1
Harland Cl WIM/MER SW19....178 A6
Harland Rd LEE/GVPK SE12...165 K3
Harlands Gv ORP BR6.........216 C6
Harlech Gdns HEST TW5......114 C6
  PIN HA5...................59 H4
Harlech Rd STHGT/OAK N14....34 E5
Harlequin Cl ISLW TW7 *....135 K6
  YEAD UB4..................95 H4
Harlequin Ct EA W5 *........97 J5
Harlequin Rd TEDD TW11 *...174 C5
Harlescott Rd PECK SE15....144 A5
Harlesden Gdns WLSDN NW10...81 H6
Harlesden Rd WLSDN NW10.....81 K6
Harley Crs HRW HA1..........60 D3
Harleyford BMLY BR1........184 B4
Harleyford Rd LBTH SE11....122 A6
Harleyford St LBTH SE11....122 A6
Harley Gdns ORP BR6........216 E2
  WBPTN SW10................120 B5
Harley Gv BOW E3...........105 H2
Harley Pl CAVSQ/HST W1G......9 J2
Harley Rd HAMP NW3..........83 H5
  HRW HA1...................60 D1
  WLSDN NW10................99 G1
Harley St CAVSQ/HST W1G......9 J1
Harley Vls WLSDN NW10 *......99 G1
Harlinger St WOOL/PLUM SE18.126 D3
Harlington Cl HYS/HAR UB3...133 F1
Harlington Rd BXLYHN DA7...149 G4
Harlington Rd East
  EBED/NFELT TW14...........154 A2
Harlington Rd West
  EBED/NFELT TW14...........154 A1
Harlow Gdns CRW RM5.........56 E2
Harlow Rd PLMGR N13.........35 K5
  RAIN RM13.................111 G4
Harlyn Dr PIN HA5...........41 F6
Harman Av WFD IG8...........52 D5
Harman Cl CHING E4..........38 B6
  CRICK NW2.................82 C1
  STHWK SE1 *...............123 H5
Harman Dr BFN/LL DA15......168 A1
  CRICK NW2.................82 C1
Harman Rd EN EN1............24 B6
Harmondsworth La
  WDR/YW UB7...............112 B6
Harmondsworth Rd
  WDR/YW UB7...............112 B4
Harmony Cl CLDGN NW11......64 C2
  WLGTN SM6................210 E6
Harmony Pl STHWK SE1......123 G5
Harmony Wy BMLY BR1.......183 K5
  HDN NW4...................64 A1
Harmood Gv CAMTN NW1........84 B5
Harmood St CAMTN NW1........84 B4
Harmsworth Ms STHWK SE1 *...17 K5
Harmsworth St LBTH SE11....122 C6
Harmsworth Wy
  TRDG/WHET N20.............32 D3
Harness Rd THMD SE28.......128 A2
Harold Av BELV DA17........129 G5
  HYS/HAR UB3...............113 J3
Harold Rd CEND/HSY/T N8.....67 F2
  CHING E4..................38 A5
  NRWD SE19................180 A3
  PLSTW E13................107 F1
  RDART DA2................171 J6
  SEVS/STOTM N15............68 B2
  SUT SM1..................209 H2
  WAN E11...................70 C5
  WFD IG8...................52 E3
  WLSDN NW10................99 F2
Haroldstone Rd WALTH E17....69 F2
Harpenden Rd MNPK E12.......71 G6
  WNWD SE27...............162 C4
Harper Cl STHGT/OAK N14.....22 C5
Harper Rd EHAM E6..........107 K5
  STHWK SE1 *...............18 D4
Harpers Yd ISLW TW7 *......136 A3
  TOTM N17 *................50 B4
Harp Island Cl WLSDN NW10..63 G6
Harpley Sq WCHPL E1.......104 E3
Harpour Rd BARK IG11........90 C4
Harp Rd HNWL W7.............97 F3
Harpsden St BTSEA SW11....141 F2
Harpur Ms BMSBY WC1N........11 G1
Harpur St BMSBY WC1N........11 G1
Harraden Rd BKHTH/KID SE3..146 B2
Harrier Cl HCH RM12........111 J5
Harrier Ms THMD SE28........127 J2
Harrier Rd CDALE/KGS NW9....45 G5
Harriers Cl EA W5...........98 A6
Harrier Wy EHAM E6.........107 K4
Harries Rd YEAD UB4.........95 J3
Harriet Cl HACK E8..........86 C6
Harriet Gdns CROY/NA CR0...197 H6
Harriet St KTBR SW1X........15 F3
Harriet Tubman Cl
  BRXS/STRHM SW2...........162 B2

Harriet Wk KTBR SW1X........15 F3
Harriet Wy BUSH WD23........28 D2
Harringay Gdns
  CEND/HSY/T N8.............67 H1
Harringay Rd SEVS/STOTM N15..67 H2
Harrington Cl CROY/NA CR0..195 K6
  WLSDN NW10................81 F1
Harrington Ct NKENS W10 *..100 D2
Harrington Gdns SKENS SW7..120 A4
Harrington Hl CLPT E5........68 D5
Harrington Rd SKENS SW7.....14 A6
  SNWD SE25................197 J1
  WAN E11...................70 C5
Harrington Sq CAMTN NW1......4 A2
Harrington St CAMTN NW1......4 A4
Harrington Wy
  WOOL/PLUM SE18...........126 C3
Harriott Cl GNWCH SE10.....125 J4
Harris Cl ENC/FH EN2........23 H1
  HSLW TW3.................135 F2
Harrison Cl NTHWD HA6.......40 A2
  TRDG/WHET N20.............33 J3
Harrison Rd DAGE RM10.......92 D4
  WLSDN NW10................81 F1
Harrison's Ri CROY/NA CR0..211 H1
Harrison St STPAN WC1H.......5 F5
Harrisons Whf PUR RM19.....131 K5
Harris Rd BXLYHN DA7.......149 F2
  DAGW RM9..................92 B3
Harris St CMBW SE5.........142 E1
  WALTH E17.................51 J4
Harrods Gn EDGW HA8.........44 C1
Harrogate Rd OXHEY WD19.....27 G5
Harrold Rd BCTR RM8.........91 H4
Harrow Av EN EN1............36 B1
Harroway Rd BTSEA SW11....140 C3
Harrowby St MBLAR W1H........8 E3
Harrow Cl CHSGTN KT9.......205 K5
Harrow Crs HARH RM3.........57 J3
Harrowdene Cl ALP/SUD HA0...79 K2
Harrowdene Gdns TEDD TW11..174 B3
Harrowdene Rd ALP/SUD HA0...79 K2
Harrow Dr ED N9.............36 B3
Harrowes Meade EDGW HA8.....30 C5
Harrow Fields Gdns HRW HA1..78 E1
Harrowgate Rd HOM E9........87 G5
Harrow Gn WAN E11...........88 C1
Harrow La POP/IOD E14......106 A6
Harrow Manor Wy ABYW SE2..128 D1
Harrow Pk HRW HA1...........60 E6
Harrow Pl WCHPL E1..........13 H5
Harrow Rd ALP/SUD HA0.......79 G2
  BARK IG11................108 E1
  CAR SM5..................209 J4
  EBED/NFELT TW14..........152 D4
  IL IG1...................90 C2
  MV/WKIL W9...............100 E3
  WAN E11...................88 D1
  WBLY HA9..................80 A3
  WLSDN NW10................99 K2
Harrow Road F/O BAY/PAD W2...8 B2
Harrowside CAMTN NW1 *.......8 D1
Harrow Vw HGDN/ICK UB10.....94 A2
  HYS/HAR UB3...............94 E6
  RYLN/HDSTN HA2............42 D6
Harrow View Rd EA W5........97 H3
Harrow Weald Pk
  KTN/HRWW/WS HA3...........42 D2
Harston Dr PEND EN3.........25 J1
Hartcliff Ct HNWL W7 *.....116 A2
Hart Crs CHIG IG7...........55 F1
Hart Dyke Rd
  STMC/STPC BR5............202 D6
Harte Rd HSLW TW3..........134 E3
Hartfield Av NTHLT UB5......95 F1
Hartfield Crs WIM/MER SW19.177 J3
  WWKM BR4.................214 E1
Hartfield Rd CHSGTN KT9....205 K3
  WIM/MER SW19.............177 J3
  WWKM BR4.................214 E2
Hartfield Ter BOW E3.......105 J1
Hartford Av
  KTN/HRWW/WS HA3...........43 G6
Hartford Rd BXLY DA5.......169 H1
  HOR/WEW KT19.............206 D4
Hart Gv EA W5..............117 H1
  STHL UB1..................96 A4
Hartham Cl HOLWY N7.........84 E3
  ISLW TW7.................136 B2
Hartham Rd HOLWY N7.........84 E3
  ISLW TW7.................136 A2
  TOTM N17..................50 B5
Hartington Cl HRW HA1.......78 E2
  ORP BR6..................216 C3
Hartington Rd CAN/RD E16...107 F5
  CHSWK W4................137 K2
  NWDGN UB2 *..............114 E3
  TWK TW1..................156 C2
  VX/NE SW8................141 K2
  WALTH E17 *...............69 G3
  WEA W13..................97 H6
Hartismere Rd FUL/PGN SW6..139 J1
Hartlake Rd HOM E9..........87 F4
Hartland Cl EDGW HA8........30 C4
  WCHMH N21.................35 J1
Hartland Dr EDGW HA8........30 C4
  RSLP HA4..................77 F1
Hartland Rd CAMTN NW1.......84 B5
  FBAR/BDGN N11.............47 K1
  HCH RM12..................75 J6
  HPTN TW12................155 J2
  ISLW TW7.................136 B3
  KIL/WHAMP NW6............100 D1
  MRDN SM4.................193 K4
  SRTFD E15.................88 D1
Hartland Road Arches
  CAMTN NW1 *...............84 A5
Hartlands Cl BXLY DA5......169 G1
The Hartlands HEST TW5.....114 A6
Hartland Wy CROY/NA CR0....198 B6
  MRDN SM4.................193 H4
Hartley Av EHAM E6..........89 J1
  MLHL NW7..................45 H1

Hartley Cl BMLY BR1........184 E5
  MLHL NW7..................45 H1
Hartley Rd CROY/NA CR0.....196 D6
  WELL DA16................148 D1
Hartley St BETH E2.........104 E2
Hartmann Rd CAN/RD E16....126 C1
Hartnoll St HOLWY N7........85 F3
Harton Cl BMLY BR1.........184 C4
Harton Rd ED N9.............36 D4
Harton St DEPT SE8.........144 D2
Hartsbourne Av BUSH WD23....28 C4
Hartsbourne Cl BUSH WD23....28 D4
Hartsbourne Rd BUSH WD23....28 D4
Harts Cv WFD IG8............52 E1
Hartshorn Gdns EHAM E6.....108 A3
Harts La BARK IG11..........90 B5
  NWCR SE14................144 B1
Hartslock Dr ABYW SE2......128 E2
Hartsmead Rd ELTH/MOT SE9..166 E4
Hart Sq MRDN SM4...........194 A2
Hart St MON EC3R............13 H5
Hartswood Gdns SHB W12 *...118 C3
Hartswood Gn BUSH WD23......28 D4
Hartswood Rd SHB W12.......118 C2
Hartsworth Cl PLSTW E13....106 D1
Hartville Rd WOOL/PLUM SE18.127 K4
Hartwell Dr CHING E4........52 A2
Hartwell St HACK E8.........86 B4
Harvard Hl CHSWK W4........117 J5
Harvard Rd CHSWK W4........117 J5
  ISLW TW7.................135 K2
  LEW SE13.................145 F6
Harvel Cl CHST BR7.........186 B6
Harvel Crs ABYW SE2........128 E5
Harvest Bank Rd WWKM BR4..214 E1
Harvest La THDIT KT7.......190 B3
Harvest Rd FELT TW13.......153 K6
Harvest Wy SWLY BR8........203 K4
Harvey Dr HPTN TW12........173 G4
Harvey Gdns CHARL SE7 *....126 B5
  WAN E11...................70 E5
Harvey Rd CMBW SE5.........142 E2
  HSLW TW4.................154 D5
  IL IG1....................90 B3
  NTHLT UB5.................77 G5
  WALTH E17.................51 J5
Harvey's La ROMW/RG RM7.....75 G6
Harvey St IS N1.............7 F1
Harvill Rd SCUP DA14.......186 E1
Harvington Wk HACK E8 *.....86 C5
Harvist Rd KIL/WHAMP NW6..100 C1
Harwell Cl RSLP HA4.........58 B5
Harwood Av BMLY BR1.......184 A5
  MTCM CR4.................178 D6
Harwood Cl ALP/SUD HA0 *....79 K2
  NFNCH/WDSPK N12...........47 J2
Harwood Ms FUL/PGN SW6....139 K1
Harwood Rd FUL/PGN SW6....140 A1
Harwood Ter FUL/PGN SW6...140 A2
Hascombe Ter CMBW SE5 *....142 E3
Haselbury Rd ED N9..........36 A5
Haseley End FSTH SE23 *....163 K2
Haselrigge Rd CLAP SW4.....141 J5
Haslam Av CHEAM SM3........193 H5
Haslam Cl HGDN/ICK UB10.....94 B5
  IS N1.....................85 G5
Haslam St PECK SE15.......143 G2
Haslemere Av EBAR EN4......33 K3
  HDN NW4...................64 B3
  HEST TW5.................134 B3
  HNWL W7..................116 B3
  MTCM CR4.................178 C5
  WAND/EARL SW18...........160 A4
Haslemere Cl HPTN TW12 *...172 E1
  WLGTN SM6................210 E3
Haslemere Gdns FNCH N3......46 D6
Haslemere Heathrow Est
  HSLWW TW4 *..............133 J6
Haslemere Rd BXLYHN DA7....149 H3
  CEND/HSY/T N8.............66 D3
  GDMY/SEVK IG3.............73 F6
  THHTH CR7................196 C2
  WCHMH N21.................35 H4
Hasler Cl THMD SE28........109 J6
Hasluck Gdns BAR EN5........33 G1
Hassard St BETH E2 *.........7 K3
Hassendean Rd
  BKHTH/KID SE3............126 A6
Hassocks Cl SYD SE26.......163 J5
Hassocks Rd
  STRHM/NOR SW16...........179 J4
Hassock Wd HAYES BR2.......215 H2
Hassop Rd CRICK NW2.........82 B2
Hassted St CHARL SE7.......126 C5
Hastings Av BARK/HLT IG6....72 C1
Hastings Cl ALP/SUD HA0 *...79 K2
  BAR EN5...................21 G5
  PECK SE15................143 H1
Hastings Dr SURB KT6.......190 D3
Hastings Rd CROY/NA CR0....197 G5
  FBAR/BDGN N11.............48 C1
  GPK RM2...................57 J6
  HAYES BR2................200 D5
  TOTM N17..................49 K4
  WEA W13..................97 H6
Hastings St STPAN WC1H.......5 F5
Hastings Ter
  SEVS/STOTM N15 *..........67 J2
Hastings Wd WOOL/PLUM SE18.127 H3
Hastoe Cl YEAD UB4..........95 J3
Hatcham Park Ms NWCR SE14..144 A1
Hatcham Park Rd NWCR SE14..144 A1
Hatcham Rd PECK SE15.......123 K6
Hatchard Rd ARCH N19........66 D1
Hatchcroft HDN NW4..........45 K6
Hatchers Ms STHWK SE1......19 H3

Hatchett Rd
  EBED/NFELT TW14..........153 F3
Hatch Gv CHDH RM6...........74 A1
Hatch La CHING E4...........38 C6
  WDR/YW UB7...............132 A1
Hatch Pl KUTN/CMB KT2......175 G1
Hatch Rd STRHM/NOR SW16....179 K5
The Hatch PEND EN3..........25 H2
Hatchwoods WFD IG8..........38 D6
Hatcliffe Cl BKHTH/KID SE3.145 J4
Hatcliffe St GNWCH SE10....125 J5
Hatfield Cl BARK/HLT IG6....54 B6
  BELMT SM2................208 E6
  MTCM CR4.................194 C1
Hatfield Ct BKHTH/KID SE3..145 K1
Hatfield Rd CHSWK W4.......118 A2
  HNWL W7..................116 B1
  SRTFD E15.................88 C3
Hatfields STHWK SE1.........11 K7
Hathaway Cl BARK/HLT IG6....54 B6
  HAYES BR2................200 E5
  RSLP HA4..................76 D2
  STAN HA7..................43 G1
Hathaway Crs MNPK E12.......90 A4
Hathaway Gdns CHDH RM6......73 J2
  WEA W13...................97 G4
Hathaway Rd CROY/NA CR0....196 C4
Hatherleigh Cl CHSGTN KT9..205 K3
  MRDN SM4.................193 K1
Hatherleigh Rd RSLP HA4.....58 E6
Hatherley Crs BFN/LL DA15..168 B4
Hatherley Gdns
  CEND/HSY/T N8.............66 E3
  EHAM E6..................107 H2
Hatherley Gv BAY/PAD W2....101 F5
Hatherley Ms WALTH E17......69 J1
Hatherley Rd RCH/KEW TW9..137 G2
  SCUP DA14................168 B5
  WALTH E17.................69 H1
Hatherley St WEST SW1P......16 B7
Hathern Gdns ELTH/MOT SE9..167 H6
Hatherop Rd HPTN TW12......172 E3
Hathorne Cl PECK SE15.....143 J3
Hathorne Ter ARCH N19 *.....66 D5
Hathway St PECK SE15.......143 K3
Hatley Av BARK/HLT IG6......72 C1
Hatley Cl FBAR/BDGN N11.....47 K1
Hatley Rd FSBYPK N4.........67 F6
Hat & Mitre Ct FARR EC1M.....6 B7
Hatteraick St
  BERM/RHTH SE16...........123 K2
Hattersfield Cl BELV DA17..129 G4
Hatters La WATW WD18........26 B1
Hatton Cl WOOL/PLUM SE18...147 J1
Hatton Cross Est
  HTHAIR TW6...............133 J5
Hatton Gdn HCIRC EC1N.......11 K1
Hatton Gdns MTCM CR4......194 E2
Hatton Rd CROY/NA CR0.....196 B5
  EBED/NFELT TW14..........153 K5
  HTHAIR TW6...............133 J5
Hatton Rw STJWD NW8 *........2 B7
Hatton St STJWD NW8..........2 B7
Hatton Wall HCIRC EC1N......11 J1
Haunch of Venison Yd
  OXSTW W1C.................9 J4
Havana Cl ROM RM1...........75 G2
Havana Rd WIM/MER SW19....159 K4
Hannah St POP/IOD E14......124 E2
Havelock Cl SHB W12 *........99 K6
Havelock Pl HRW HA1.........60 E3
Havelock Rd BELV DA17......129 G4
  CROY/NA CR0..............197 G6
  DART DA1.................170 E2
  HAYES BR2................200 B1
  KTN/HRWW/WS HA3...........42 E6
  NWDGN UB2................114 D3
  TOTM N17..................50 C5
  WIM/MER SW19.............178 B1
Havelock St IS N1...........84 E6
  IL IG1....................90 B1
Havelock Ter VX/NE SW8 *...141 G1
Havelock Wk FSTH SE23 *....163 K3
Haven Cl ELTH/MOT SE9......166 E5
  SCUP DA14................186 D2
  SWLY BR8.................203 K6
  WIM/MER SW19.............159 G5
  YEAD UB4..................95 F2
Haven Gn EA W5..............97 K6
Havenhurst Ri ENC/FH EN2....23 G3
Havens Ms BOW E3...........105 H4
Haven La EA W5..............98 A5
Haven Rd ASHF TW15.........152 E5
Haven St CAMTN NW1 *........84 B5
Havenswood Ct
  KUTN/CMB KT2.............175 J2
The Haven RCH/KEW TW9......137 H4
Havenwood WBLY HA9..........80 D1
Haverfield Est BTFD TW8....117 F6
Haverfield Gdns
  RCH/KEW TW9..............137 H1
Haverfield Rd BOW E3.......105 F2
Haverford Wy EDGW HA8.......44 B4
Havergal Vls
  SEVS/STOTM N15 *..........67 H1
Haverhill Rd BAL SW12......161 H3
  CHING E4..................38 A3
Havering Gdns CHDH RM6......73 J2
Havering Rd ROM RM1.........75 G1
Havering St WCHPL E1.......105 F5
Havering Wy BARK IG11......109 H2
Haversham Cl HCT N6........173 G1
Haversham Pl HGT N6.........65 K6
Haverstock Hl HAMP NW3......83 K3
Haverstock Pl FSBYE EC1V *...6 C4
Haverstock Rd KTTN NW5......84 A3
Haverstock St IS N1..........6 C3
Haverthwaite Rd ORP BR6....216 D1
Havil St CMBW SE5..........143 F2
Havisham Pl NRWD SE19......180 C2
Hawarden Gv HNHL SE24......162 D2

Hawarden Hl CRICK NW2.......81 J1
Hawarden Rd WALTH E17.......69 F1
Hawbridge Rd WAN E11........70 B5
Hawes Cl NTHWD HA6..........40 D5
Hawes La WWKM BR4..........199 G6
Hawes Rd BMLY BR1..........184 A4
  UED N18...................51 H1
Hawes St IS N1..............85 H5
Haweswater Ho ISLW TW7 *...136 A6
Hawgood St BOW E3..........105 J4
Hawkdene CHING E4...........37 K1
Hawke Park Rd WDGN N22......49 H2
Hawke Pl BERM/RHTH SE16 *..124 A2
Hawke Rd NRWD SE19.........180 E2
Hawker Rd CROY/NA CR0......211 G4
Hawkesbury Rd
  PUT/ROE SW15.............138 E6
Hawkesfield Rd FSTH SE23..164 C4
Hawkesley Cl TWK TW1.......156 B5
Hawkes Rd EBED/NFELT TW14..153 K2
  MTCM CR4.................178 D4
Hawkewood Rd SUN TW16.....172 B6
Hawkhurst Gdns CRW RM5......57 F2
Hawkhurst Rd
  STRHM/NOR SW16...........179 J4
Hawkhurst Wy NWMAL KT3....192 A2
  WWKM BR4.................214 A1
Hawkins Cl EDGW HA8.........45 F1
  HRW HA1...................61 F4
Hawkins Rd TEDD TW11.......174 C2
Hawkins Ter CHARL SE7......126 D5
Hawkins Wy CAT SE6.........182 D1
Hawkley Gdns WNWD SE27....162 C5
Hawkridge Cl CHDH RM6.......73 J3
Hawksbrook La BECK BR3.....198 E3
Hawkshaw Cl
  BRXS/STRHM SW2...........161 K2
Hawkshead Cl BMLY BR1......183 H3
Hawkshead Rd CHSWK W4......118 B3
  WLSDN NW10................81 H5
Hawkshill Cl ESH/CLAY KT10.204 A4
Hawkshill Pl ESH/CLAY KT10.204 A4
Hawkslade Rd PECK SE15.....144 A6
Hawksley Rd STNW/STAM N16...85 K1
Hawks Ms GNWCH SE10 *......145 F1
Hawksmoor Cl EHAM E6......107 J5
  WOOL/PLUM SE18...........128 A5
Hawksmoor Ms WCHPL E1.....104 D6
Hawksmoor St HMSMTH W6....119 G6
Hawksmouth CHING E4.........37 K2
Hawks Rd KUT/HW KT1........175 G5
Hawkstone Est
  BERM/RHTH SE16...........123 K4
Hawkstone Rd
  BERM/RHTH SE16...........123 K4
Hawkwell Wk IS N1 *.........85 J6
Hawkwood Crs CHING E4.......37 K1
Hawkwood La CHST BR7.......185 H4
Hawkwood Mt CLPT E5.........68 D5
Hawlands Dr PIN HA5.........59 J4
Hawley Cl HPTN TW12........172 E2
Hawley Crs CAMTN NW1........84 B5
Hawley Ms CAMTN NW1 *.......84 B5
  DART DA1.................171 H4
Hawley Rd CAMTN NW1.........84 B5
  DART DA1.................171 H4
  UED N18...................51 J1
Hawley St CAMTN NW1.........84 B5
Hawstead La ORP BR6........217 K6
Hawstead Rd CAT SE6........164 E1
Hawsted BKHH IG9 *..........39 F2
Hawthorn Av PLMGR N13.......48 E1
  RAIN RM13................111 J3
  THHTH CR7................180 C4
Hawthorn Centre HRW HA1 *...61 F1
Hawthorn Cl HEST TW5.......134 A1
  HPTN TW12................173 F1
  STMC/STPC BR5............201 J5
  TOOT SW17................179 F1
Hawthornden Cl
  NFNCH/WDSPK N12...........47 J2
Hawthorndene Cl HAYES BR2..199 J6
Hawthorndene Rd HAYES BR2..199 J6
Hawthorn Dr RYLN/HDSTN HA2..60 A4
  WWKM BR4.................214 C2
Hawthorne Av BOW E3.........87 H6
  CAR SM5..................210 A5
  HRW HA1...................61 G5
  MTCM CR4.................178 C5
  RSLP HA4..................59 F3
Hawthorne Cl BMLY BR1......184 E6
  IS N1.....................86 A4
Hawthorne Ct NTHWD HA6 *....40 E4
Hawthorne Crs WDR/YW UB7...112 C2
Hawthorne Gdns CDALE/KGS NW9.45 G6
Hawthorne Rd BMLY BR1......184 E6
  UED N18...................50 B2
  WALTH E17.................51 J6
Hawthorne Wy ED N9..........36 B4
  STWL/WRAY TW19...........152 A2
Hawthorn Farm Av NTHLT UB5..77 J5
Hawthorn Gdns EA W5........116 E3
Hawthorn Gv ENC/FH EN2......23 J1
  PGE/AN SE20..............181 J4
Hawthorn Hatch BTFD TW8....136 C1
Hawthorn Ms MLHL NW7........46 C6
  HYS/HAR UB3 *.............94 D6
Hawthorn Rd BTFD TW8.......136 C1
  BXLYHS DA6...............149 G5
  CEND/HSY/T N8.............48 D6
  DART DA1.................171 G4
  FELT TW13................153 K5
  SUT SM1..................209 H3
  WFD IG8..................52 D4
  WLGTN SM6................210 B5
  WLSDN NW10................81 J5
Hawthorns WFD IG8...........38 E5
Hawthorn Ter BFN/LL DA15..168 A1
Hawthorn Wk NKENS W10......100 C3
Hawtrey Av NTHLT UB5........95 H1
Hawtrey Dr RSLP HA4.........58 E4
Hawtrey Rd HAMP NW3.........83 J5
Haxted Rd BMLY BR1.........184 A4
Hayburn Wy HCH RM12.........75 H5

Hay Cl *SRTFD* E15 ....88 C5
Haycroft Gdns *WLSDN* NW10.....81 J6
Haycroft Rd
  BRXS/STRHM SW2............141 K6
  SURB KT6......................190 E6
Hay Currie St *POP/IOD* E14...105 K5
Hayday Rd *CAN/RD* E16.......106 E4
Hayden Dell *BUSH* WD23..........27 K1
Haydens Ct *STMC/STPC* BR5...202 D2
Hayden's Pl *NTGHL* W11..........100 D5
Haydock Av *NTHLT* UB5.............78 A4
Haydock Gn *NTHLT* UB5.............78 A4
Haydon Cl *CDALE/KGS* NW9.......62 C1
  EN EN1...........................36 A1
  HARH RM3.........................57 K3
Haydon Dell Farm
  BUSH WD23........................27 K2
Haydon Dr *PIN* HA5.................58 E1
Haydon Park Rd
  WIM/MER SW19...................177 K1
Haydon's Rd *WIM/MER* SW19...178 A1
  OXHEY WD19.......................27 J1
Haydon St *TWRH* EC3N.............13 J5
Haydon Wk *WCHPL* E1.............13 K4
Haydon Wy *WAND/EARL* SW18...140 D5
Hayes Cha *WWKM* BR4...........199 C5
Hayes Cl *HAYS* BR2...............199 K6
Hayes Dr *RAIN* RM13.............93 K5
Hayes End Dr *YEAD* UB4...........94 B4
Hayes End Rd *YEAD* UB4...........94 B4
Hayesford Park Dr *HAYES* BR2..199 J2
Hayes Gdn *HAYES* BR2.............199 K6
Hayes Gv *EDUL* SE22.............143 C5
Hayes Hl *HAYES* BR2.............199 J5
Hayes Hill Rd *HAYES* BR2.......199 J5
Hayes La *BECK* BR3.............183 C6
  HAYES BR2.......................200 A1
Hayes Mead Rd *HAYES* BR2.....199 H5
Hayes Pl *CAMTN* NW1.............2 C7
Hayes Rd *HAYES* BR2.............199 K1
  NWDGN UB2......................114 B4
Hayes St *HAYES* BR2.............200 A5
Hayes Wd Av *HAYES* BR2.......200 A5
Hayes Wy *BECK* BR3.............199 F1
Hayfield Pas *WCHPL* E1..........104 E3
Hayfield Rd *STMC/STPC* BR5...202 D2
Haygarth Pl *WIM/MER* SW19...177 G1
Haygreen Cl *KUTN/CMB* KT2...175 J2
Hay Hl *MYFR/PICC* W1J.............9 K6
Hayland Cl *CDALE/KGS* NW9......63 F1
Hay La *CDALE/KGS* NW9............63 F1
Haylett Gdns *KUT/HW* KT1 *....190 E1
Hayling Av *FELT* TW13...........153 K5
Hayling Cl *STNW/STAM* N16......86 A3
Hayling Rd *OXHEY* WD19..........26 D5
Hayman Crs *YEAD* UB4.............94 B1
Haymarket *STJS* SW1Y.............10 C6
Haymeads Dr *ESH/CLAY* KT10...204 C4
Haymer Gdns *WPK* KT4...........207 J1
Haymerle Rd *PECK* SE15.........123 H6
Haymill Cl *GFD/PVL* UB6..........97 F2
Hayne Rd *BECK* BR3.............182 C5
Haynes Cl *BKHTH/KID* SE3.......145 H4
  FBAR/BDGN N11....................34 A5
  TOTM N17.........................50 D3
Haynes Dr *ED* N9...................36 D5
Haynes La *NRWD* SE19...........181 F2
Haynes Rd *ALP/SUD* HA0...........80 A5
Hayne St *STBT* EC1A..............12 B1
Haynt Wk *RYNPK* SW20...........177 H6
Hay Pl *SWLY* BR8 *................203 K3
Hay's La *STHWK* SE1...............13 G1
Haysleigh Gdns *PGE/AN* SE20...181 H5
Hay's Ms *MYFR/PICC* W1J............9 J7
Haysoms Cl *ROM* RM1..............63 G4
Haystall Cl *YEAD* UB4.............94 C1
Hay St *BETH* E2.....................86 C6
Hayter Rd *BRXS/STRHM* SW2...141 K6
Hayton Cl *HACK* E8..................86 B4
Hayward Cl *DART* DA1...........150 A6
  WIM/MER SW19...................178 A3
Hayward Dr *DART* DA1...........171 J5
Hayward Gdns *PUT/ROE* SW15...159 F1
Hayward Rd *THDIT* KT7...........190 A5
  TRDG/WHET N20....................33 G4
Haywards Cl *CHDH* RM6.............73 J2
Hayward's Pl *CLKNW* EC1R *......6 A7
Haywood Cl *PIN* HA5...............41 H5
Haywood Ri *ORP* BR6.............216 E3
Haywood Rd *HAYES* BR2.........200 C1
Hazel Av *WDR/YW* UB7...........112 D3
Hazelbank *BRYLDS* KT5.........191 K5
Hazelbank Rd *CAT* SE6...........165 G4
Hazelbourne Rd *BAL* SW12.....161 G1
Hazelbrook Gdns
  BARK/HLT IG6......................54 D2
Hazelbury Cl *WIM/MER* SW19...177 K5
Hazelbury Gn *ED* N9................36 A5
Hazelbury La *ED* N9.................36 A5
Hazel Cl *BTFD* TW8 *.............136 C1
  CDALE/KGS NW9..................45 H5
  CROY/NA CR0......................198 A4
  HCH RM12.........................93 K1
  MTCM CR4.........................195 H1
  PLMGR N13.........................35 K5
  WHTN TW2........................155 J2
Hazelcroft *PIN* HA5................42 A2
Hazeldean Rd *WLSDN* NW10......81 F5
Hazeldene Dr *PIN* HA5.............41 G6
Hazeldene Gdns
  HGDN/ICK UB10...................76 A6
Hazeldene Rd *GDMY/SEVK* IG3..73 H6
  WELL DA16........................148 D3
Hazeldon Rd *BROCKY* SE4.......144 B6
Hazel Dr *ERITH* DA8.............150 E2
Hazeleigh Gdns *WFD* IG8..........53 J1
Hazel Gdns *EDGW* HA8.............30 D6
Hazel Gv *ALP/SUD* HA0.............80 A6
  CHDH RM6........................56 A6
  EN EN1............................36 C1
  ORP BR6..........................201 G6

SYD SE26 ....164 A6
Hazelhurst *BECK* BR3.............183 G4
Hazelhurst Rd *TOOT* SW17.....160 C6
Hazel La *BARK/HLT* IG6............54 E3
Hazell Crs *CRW* RM5................56 D1
Hazellville Rd *ARCH* N19...........66 D4
Hazelmere Cl
  EBED/NFELT TW14................153 G1
  NTHLT UB5..........................95 K1
Hazelmere Dr *NTHLT* UB5 *.......95 K1
Hazelmere Gdns *EMPK* RM11...75 K2
Hazelmere Rd
  KIL/WHAMP NW6...................82 D6
  NTHLT UB5.........................95 K1
  STMC/STPC BR5...................201 H1
Hazelmere Wk *NTHLT* UB5........95 K1
Hazelmere Wy *HAYES* BR2.......199 K3
Hazel Rd *DART* DA1...............171 C4
  ERITH DA8........................150 D2
  SRTFD E15 *........................88 C3
Hazel Rw *NFNCH/WDSPK* N12 *...47 H1
Hazeltree La *NTHLT* UB5...........95 J2
Hazel Wk *HAYES* BR2.............201 F3
Hazel Wy *CHING* E4.................51 H2
  STHWK SE1........................19 J4
Hazelwood Av *MRDN* SM4.......194 A1
Hazelwood Cl *CLPT* E5.............87 C1
  EA W5..............................117 F2
  RYLN/HDSTN HA2..................60 B1
Hazelwood Ct *SURB* KT6.........191 F5
Hazelwood Dr *PIN* HA5.............41 F5
Hazelwood La *PLMGR* N13........35 G6
Hazelwood Park Cl *CHIG* IG7.....54 E1
Hazelwood Rd *EN* EN1..............36 B1
  RKW/CH/CXG WD3...................26 A1
  WALTH E17..........................69 G2
Hazlebury Rd *FUL/PGN* SW6....140 A3
Hazledean Rd *CROY/NA* CR0.....196 E6
Hazledene Rd *CHSWK* W4.......117 K6
Hazlemere Gdns *WPK* KT4.......192 D5
Hazlewell Rd *PUT/ROE* SW15...139 F6
Hazlewood Crs *NKENS* W10.....100 C3
Hazlitt Cl *FELT* TW13.............154 D6
Hazlitt Ms *WKENS* W14 *.........119 H3
Hazlitt Rd *WKENS* W14...........119 H3
Heacham Av *HGDN/ICK* UB10....76 A1
Headcorn Rd *BMLY* BR1.........183 J1
  THHTH CR7........................196 A1
  TOTM N17...........................50 B3
Headfort Pl *KTBR* SW1X..........15 H3
Headington Rd
  WAND/EARL SW18................160 B3
Headlam Cl *CLAP* SW4...........161 J2
Headlam St *WCHPL* E1...........104 D3
Headley Ap *GNTH/NBYPK* IG2....72 B3
Headley Av *WLGTN* SM6.........211 F3
Headley Cl *CHSGTN* KT9.........206 C4
Headley Dr *CROY/NA* CR0.......214 A5
  GNTH/NBYPK IG2...................72 B3
Heads Ms *NTGHL* W11..........100 E5
Headstone Dr *HRW* HA1 *........42 E6
Headstone Gdns
  RYLN/HDSTN HA2...................60 C1
Headstone La
  KTN/HRWW/WS HA3.............42 B4
Headstone Pde *HRW* HA1 *......60 D1
Headstone Rd *HRW* HA1...........60 D3
Heads Wk *WCHPL* E1.............105 F5
Headway Cl
  RCHPK/HAM TW10..............156 D6
The Headway *EW* KT17...........207 H6
Heald St *NWCR* SE14.............144 C2
Healey Rd *WATW* WD18............26 D1
Healey St *CAMTN* NW1 *..........84 B4
Healy Dr *ORP* BR6.................217 F2
Hearne Rd *CHSWK* W4...........117 H5
Hearn Ri *NTHLT* UB5................77 H6
Hearn Rd *ROM* RM1.................75 H4
Hearn's Buildings *WALW* SE17...19 F7
Hearns Cl *STMC/STPC* BR5.....202 D1
Hearnshaw St *POP/IOD* E14 *...105 G5
Hearns Rd *STMC/STPC* BR5.....202 D1
Hearn St *SDTCH* EC2A...............7 H7
Hearnville Rd *BAL* SW12........161 F3
Heatham Pk *WHTN* TW2.........156 A2
Hearn Av *BXLYHN* DA7...........149 J1
Heathbourne Rd *BUSH* WD23....28 E4
Heath Brow *HAMP* NW3............83 G1
Heath Cl *EA* W5.....................98 B3
  GLDGN NW11........................65 F4
  HYS/HAR UB3......................133 C2
  SAND/SEL CR2.....................211 H4
  STMC/STPC BR5..................202 D3
Heathclose Av *DART* DA1.......170 E2
Heathclose Rd *DART* DA1.......170 D3
Heathcote Av *CLAY* IG5...........53 K5
Heathcote Gv *CHING* E4...........38 A5
Heathcote Rd *TWK* TW1..........156 C1
Heathcote St *BMSBY* WC1N........5 G6
Heathcote Wy *WDR/YW* UB7....112 A1
Heathcroft *EA* W5 *..................98 B3
Heathcroft Gdns *WALTH* E17....52 B4
Heathdale Av *HSLWW* TW4.....134 D4
Heathdene Dr *BELV* DA17.......129 J4
Heathdene Rd
  STRHM/NOR SW16................180 A3
  WLGTN SM6......................210 B5
Heath Dr *BELMT* SM2.............209 G6
  GPK RM2...........................57 J3
  HAMP NW3...........................83 G2
  RYNPK SW20......................193 F1
Heathedge *SYD* SE26 *............163 J4
Heathend Rd *BXLY* DA5...........170 B3
Heather Av *ROM* RM1...............57 F4
Heatherbank *CHST* BR7...........185 F5
  ELTH/MOT SE9....................146 E3
Heatherbank Cl *DART* DA1......170 B1
Heather Cl *EHAM* E6..............108 B5
  HPTN TW12.......................172 E4
  ISLW TW7..........................135 J6
  LEW SE13.........................165 C1
  ROM RM1............................57 F4
  VX/NE SW8........................141 G4
Heatherdale Cl *KUTN/CMB* KT2...175 H2
Heatherdene Cl *MTCM* CR4.....194 C1

NFNCH/WDSPK N12 ....47 G4
Heather Dr *DART* DA1...........170 D2
  ENC/FH EN2........................23 H3
  RM1 RM1............................57 F4
Heatherfold Wy *PIN* HA5..........40 D6
Heather Gdns *BELMT* SM2.......208 E4
  GLDGN NW11.......................64 C3
  ROM RM1............................57 F5
Heather Gln *ROM* RM1.............57 F5
Heatherley Dr *CLAY* IG5...........53 K6
Heather Park Dr *ALP/SUD* HA0...80 D6
Heather Pde
  ALP/SUD HA0 *.....................80 B5
Heather Pl *ESH/CLAY* KT10.....204 B2
Heather Rd *CHING* E4..............51 H2
  CRICK NW2.........................63 K5
  LEE/GVPK SE12...................165 K4
Heatherset Cl *ESH/CLAY* KT10...204 B2
Heatherset Gdns
  STRHM/NOR SW16................180 A3
Heatherside Rd
  HOR/WEW KT19...................207 F5
  SCUP DA14........................168 D5
The Heathers
  STWL/WRAY TW19................152 C2
Heather Wk *EDGW* HA8............44 D1
  NKENS W10........................100 C3
Heather Wy *ROM* RM1.............57 F4
  SAND/SEL CR2....................213 F6
  STAN HA7...........................43 F2
Heatherwood Cl *MNPK* E12.......71 F6
Heatherwood Dr *YEAD* UB4......94 B1
Heathfield *CHING* E4................38 A5
  CHST BR7.........................185 H2
  HRW HA1 *.........................61 F4
Heathfield Av
  WAND/EARL SW18................160 C2
Heathfield Cl *CAN/RD* E16.......107 H4
  HAYES BR2........................215 G3
  OXHEY WD19......................27 G1
Heathfield Dr *MTCM* CR4.......178 D4
Heathfield Gdns *CHSWK* W4....117 K5
  CROY/NA CR0 *...................211 J2
  GLDGN NW11........................64 B3
  WAND/EARL SW18................160 C1
Heathfield La *CHST* BR7.........185 H2
Heathfield North *WHTN* TW2...155 K2
Heathfield Pk *CRICK* NW2.........82 A4
Heathfield Park Dr *CHDH* RM6...73 H2
Heathfield Ri *RSLP* HA4............58 A4
Heathfield Rd *ACT* W3.............117 J2
  BMLY BR1.........................183 H4
  BXLYHS DA6.......................149 G5
  CROY/NA CR0....................211 K2
  KUTN/CMB KT2...................175 G4
  SAND/SEL CR2....................211 K4
  WAND/EARL SW18................160 C1
Heathfield South *WHTN* TW2...156 A2
Heathfield Sq
  WAND/EARL SW18................160 C2
Heathfield St *CHSWK* W4.........117 K5
  WOOL/PLUM SE18................127 K6
Heathfield V *SAND/SEL* CR2....213 F6
Heath Gdns *DART* DA1...........171 F3
  TWK TW1...........................156 A4
Heathgate *GLDGN* NW11...........65 F3
Heathgate Pl *HAMP* NW3.........83 K2
Heath Gv *PGE/AN* SE20...........181 K3
Heath Hurst Rd *HAMP* NW3......83 J2
Heathland Rd *STNW/STAM* N16...68 A5
Heathlands Cl *TWK* TW1.........156 A4
Heathlands Ct *HSLWW* TW4.....134 D6
Heathlands Ri *DART* DA1.........170 E2
Heathlands Wy *HSLWW* TW4...134 D6
Heath La *BKHTH/KID* SE3........145 J3
  DART DA1.........................170 E5
Heathlee Rd *BKHTH/KID* SE3...145 J3
  DART DA1..........................170 B1
Heath Ldg *BUSH* WD23...........28 D3
Heathman's Rd *FUL/PGN* SW6...139 J2
Heath Md *WIM/MER* SW19......159 G5
Heath Park Dr *BMLY* BR1.......184 D6
Heath Park Rd *GPK* RM2..........75 J2
Heath Ri *BXLY* DA5...............169 K3
  PUT/ROE SW15...................159 G1
Heath Rd *BXLY* DA5..............169 K3
  CHDH RM6..........................73 K4
  DART DA1..........................170 C1
  HGDN/ICK UB10....................94 A3
  HRW HA1...........................60 C4
  HSLW TW3.........................135 H5
  OXHEY WD19.......................27 H1
  THHTH CR7........................180 C6
  TWK TW1...........................156 A3
  VX/NE SW8........................141 J3
Heath's Cl *EN* EN1.................23 K3
Heathside *ESH/CLAY* KT10......204 E1
  HAMP NW3..........................83 J2
  HSLWW TW4......................154 E2
Heath Side *STMC/STPC* BR5....201 J3
Heathside Cl *ESH/CLAY* KT10...204 E1
  GNTH/NBYPK IG2...................72 D2
Heathside Rd *HSLWW* TW4.....154 E2
Heathstan Rd *SHB* W12...........99 J6
Heath St *DART* DA1...............171 G2
  HAMP NW3..........................83 G1
The Heath *HNWL* W7 *...........115 J2
Heath Vw *EFNCH* N2................65 G1
Heathview Av *DART* DA1.........170 B1
Heathview Crs *DART* DA1.......170 D2
Heath View Dr *ABYW* SE2.......128 E6
Heathview Gdns
  PUT/ROE SW15...................159 F2
Heathview Rd *THHTH* CR7.......196 B1
Heath Vls *WAND/EARL* SW18 *...160 B3
  WOOL/PLUM SE18................128 A5
Heathville Rd *ARCH* N19..........66 E4
Heathwall St *BTSEA* SW11......140 E4
Heathway *BKHTH/KID* SE3......145 K1
  CROY/NA CR0....................213 H1
  DAGW RM9..........................92 B3
Heath Wy *ERITH* DA8.............149 K2
Heathway *NWDGN* UB2 *........114 C4

WFD IG8 ....39 G6
Heathwood Gdns *CHARL* SE7...126 D4
  SWLY BR8.........................187 K5
Heathwood Pde *SWLY* BR8 *...187 K5
Heathwood Wk *BXLY* DA5.......170 E3
Heaton Av *HARH* RM3...............57 K3
Heaton Cl *CHING* E4................38 A5
Heaton Grange Rd *GPK* RM2.....57 H4
Heaton Rd *MTCM* CR4...........179 F3
  PECK SE15........................143 J4
Heaven Tree Cl *IS* N1..............85 K3
Heaver Rd *BTSEA* SW11 *........140 C4
Heavitree Cl
  WOOL/PLUM SE18................127 J5
Heavitree Rd
  WOOL/PLUM SE18................127 J5
Hebden Ter *TOTM* N17..............50 A2
Hebdon Rd *TOOT* SW17.........160 D5
Heber Rd *CRICK* NW2..............82 B3
  EDUL SE22........................163 G1
Hebron Rd *HMSMTH* W6........118 E3
Hecham Cl *WALTH* E17.............51 C5
Heckfield Pl *FUL/PGN* SW6.....139 K1
Heckford Cl *WATW* WD18..........26 A1
Heckford St *WAP* E1W.............105 F6
Hector St *WOOL/PLUM* SE18 *..127 K4
Heddington Gv *HOLWY* N7.........85 F3
Heddon Cl *ISLW* TW7.............136 B5
Heddon Court Av *EBAR* EN4.....21 K6
Heddon Court Rd *EBAR* EN4 *...22 A6
Heddon Rd *EBAR* EN4...............21 K6
Heddon St *CONDST* W1S...........10 A6
Hedge Hl *ENC/FH* EN2.............23 H2
Hedge La *PLMGR* N13...............35 J6
Hedgeley *REDBR* IG4................71 J1
Hedgemans Rd *DAGW* RM9......91 K5
Hedgemans Wy *DAGW* RM9.......92 A4
Hedgerley Gdns *GFD/PVL* UB6...96 C1
Hedger's Gv *HOM* E9 *.............87 G4
Hedger St *LBTH* SE11.............18 A6
Hedgewood Gdns *CLAY* IG5......72 A2
Hedgley St *LEE/GVPK* SE12....145 J6
Hedingham Cl *IS* N1.................85 J5
Hedingham Rd *BCTR* RM8.........91 H3
Hedley Rd *WHTN* TW2...........155 F2
Hedley Rw *HBRY* N5................85 K3
Heenan Cl *BARK* IG11...............90 C4
Heene Rd *ENC/FH* EN2.............23 K3
Heidegger Crs *BARN* SW13.....138 E1
Heigham Rd *EHAM* E6..............89 J5
Heighton Gdns *CROY/NA* CR0...211 H3
Heights Cl *RYNPK* SW20.........176 E5
The Heights *BECK* BR3...........183 F5
  CHARL SE7.........................126 B5
  NTHLT UB5..........................78 A3
Heiron St *WALW* SE17...........122 C6
Helby Rd *CLAP* SW4..............161 J1
Helder Gv *LEE/GVPK* SE12.....165 J2
Helder St *SAND/SEL* CR2.......211 K4
Heldmann Cl *HSLW* TW3.........135 J5
Helegan Cl *ORP* BR6..............217 F2
Helena Pl *HACK* E8..................86 D6
Helena Rd *EA* W5.....................97 K4
  PLSTW E15.........................106 D1
  WALTH E17..........................69 J2
  WLSDN NW10.......................81 K3
Helena Sq *BERM/RHTH* SE16...105 G6
Helen Av *EBED/NFELT* TW14...154 A2
Helen Cl *DART* DA1...............170 E2
  E/WMO/HCT KT8.................189 C1
  EFNCH N2..........................47 G6
Helenslea Av *GLDGN* NW11......64 D5
Helen St *WOOL/PLUM* SE18 *..127 G4
Helford Cl *RSLP* HA4................58 C6
Helios Rd *WLGTN* SM6...........195 F5
Helix Gdns *BRXS/STRHM* SW2..162 A1
Helix Rd *BRXS/STRHM* SW2....162 A1
Hellings St *WAP* E1W..............123 H1
Helme Cl *WIM/MER* SW19.......177 J1
Helmet Rw *FSBYE* EC1V............6 D6
Helmore Rd *BARK* IG11............91 F5
Helmsdale Cl *HYS/HAR* UB3....95 H6
  ROM RM1............................57 G3
Helmsdale Rd *ROM* RM1..........57 G3
  STRHM/NOR SW16...............179 H4
Helmsley Pl *HACK* E8................86 D5
Helmsley St *HACK* E8................86 D5
Helperby Rd *WLSDN* NW10......81 G5
Helsinki Sq *BERM/RHTH* SE16...124 C3
Helston Cl *PIN* HA5.................41 K3
Helvetia St *CAT* SE6..............164 C4
Hemans St *VX/NE* SW8...........141 J1
Hemery Rd *GFD/PVL* UB6.........78 D3
Hemingford Cl
  NFNCH/WDSPK N12...............47 H1
Hemingford Rd *CHEAM* SM3...208 A2
  IS N1.................................85 F6
Heming Rd *EDGW* HA8.............44 D3
Hemington Av *FBAR/BDGN* N11..47 K1
Hemlock Rd *SHB* W12..............99 H6
Hemmen La *HYS/HAR* UB3........94 D6
Hemming Cl *HPTN* TW12........173 F4
Hemmings Cl *SCUP* DA14......168 C2
Hemmingswood
  HOR/WEW KT19...................206 E4
Hemming St *WCHPL* E1...........104 C3
Hemmingway Cl *KTTN* NW5......84 A2
Hempstead Cl *BKHH* IG9.........38 E4
Hempstead Rd *WALTH* E17.......52 B6
Hemstal Rd *KIL/WHAMP* NW6....82 E5
Hemsted Rd *ERITH* DA8.........150 B2
Hemswell Dr *CDALE/KGS* NW9...45 G4
Hemsworth Ct *IS* N1..................7 G2
Hemsworth St *IS* N1.................7 G2
Henchman St *SHB* W12............99 H5
Hendale Av *HDN* NW4.............45 J6
Henderson Cl *EMPK* RM11.......75 K6
  WLSDN NW10......................80 D4
Henderson Dr *DART* DA1.......151 K5
  STJWD NW8.........................2 A4
Henderson Rd *CROY/NA* CR0...196 E3
  ED N9................................36 D3
  FSTGT E7...........................89 G4
  WAND/EARL SW18................160 D2

YEAD UB4 ....94 E2
Hendham Rd *TOOT* SW17......160 D4
Hendon Av *FNCH* N3................46 C5
Hendon Gdns *CRW* RM5...........56 C2
Hendon Gv *HOR/WEW* KT19...206 C6
Hendon Hall Ct *HDN* NW4 *......46 B5
Hendon La *FNCH* N3................46 C6
Hendon Park Rw
  GLDGN NW11 *.....................64 D3
Hendon Rd *ED* N9....................36 C4
Hendon Wy *CRICK* NW2 *.........64 D4
  HDN NW4............................45 K5
  STWL/WRAY TW19...............152 A1
Hendon Wood La *MLHL* NW7...31 J3
Hendren Cl *GFD/PVL* UB6........78 D3
Hendre Rd *STHWK* SE1............19 H7
Hendrick Av *BAL* SW12..........160 E1
Heneage La *HDTCH* EC3A.........13 H4
Heneage St *WCHPL* E1............13 K1
Henfield Cl *ARCH* N19..............66 C5
  BXLY DA5..........................169 H1
Henfield Rd *WIM/MER* SW19...177 J4
Hengelo Gdns *MTCM* CR4......194 C1
Hengist Rd *ELTH/MOT* SE9.....167 F1
  ERITH DA8.........................149 K1
Hengist Wy *HAYES* BR2.........199 G1
Hengrave Rd *FSTH* SE23.......163 K2
Hengrove Ct *BXLY* DA5.........169 F3
Hengrove Crs *ASHF* TW15......152 A5
Henley Av *CHEAM* SM3.........208 C1
Henley Cl *BERM/RHTH* SE16 *..123 K2
  GFD/PVL UB6 *.....................96 C1
  ISLW TW7..........................136 A2
Henley Dr *KUTN/CMB* KT2......176 C3
  STHWK SE1..........................19 K6
Henley Rd *CAN/RD* E16.........126 E2
  IL IG1................................90 B2
  UED N18.............................36 A6
  WLSDN NW10.......................82 A6
Henley St *BTSEA* SW11..........141 F3
Henley Wy *FELT* TW13...........172 C1
Hennel Cl *FSTH* SE23.............163 K5
Hennessy Rd *ED* N9.................36 E4
Henniker Gdns *EHAM* E6........107 H2
Henniker Ms *CHEL* SW3.........120 C6
Henniker Rd *SRTFD* E15...........88 B3
Henningham Rd *TOTM* N17......49 K4
Henning St *BTSEA* SW11.......140 D2
Henrietta Cl *DEPT* SE8.........124 D6
Henrietta Ms *BMSBY* WC1N.......5 F6
Henrietta Pl *CAVSQ/HST* W1Q....9 J4
Henrietta St *COVGDN* WC2E.....11 F5
  SRTFD E15..........................88 A3
Henriques St *WCHPL* E1.........104 C5
Henry Addlington Cl *EHAM* E6..108 B4
Henry Cl *ENC/FH* EN2..............24 A1
Henry Cooper Wy
  ELTH/MOT SE9...................166 C5
Henry Darlot Dr *MLHL* NW7......46 C1
Henry Dent Cl *CMBW* SE5......142 E4
Henry Dickens Ct *NTGHL* W11..100 B6
Henry Doulton Dr *TOOT* SW17..161 F6
Henry Jackson Rd
  PUT/ROE SW15...................139 G2
Henry Macaulay Av
  KUTN/CMB KT2...................174 E4
Henry Peters Dr *TEDD* TW11...173 K1
Henry Rd *EBAR* EN4.................21 H6
  EHAM E6.............................107 J1
  FSBYPK N4..........................67 J5
Henry's Av *WFD* IG8.................52 D1
Henryson Rd *BROCKY* SE4.....144 D6
Henry St *BMLY* BR1...............184 A4
Henry Tate Ms
  STRHM/NOR SW16................180 B1
Hensford Gdns *SYD* SE26.......163 J6
Henshall St *IS* N1....................85 K4
Henshawe Rd *BCTR* RM8.........91 K1
Henshaw St *WALW* SE17..........18 E6
Henslowe Rd *EDUL* SE22......143 H6
Henson Av *CRICK* NW2.............82 A3
Henson Cl *ORP* BR6...............201 C6
Henson Pl *NTHLT* UB5..............77 G6
Henstridge Pl *STJWD* NW8........2 C2
Henty Cl *BTSEA* SW11...........140 D1
Henty Wk *PUT/ROE* SW15.......138 E6
Henville Rd *BMLY* BR1.............84 B4
Henwick Rd *ELTH/MOT* SE9....146 C4
Henwood Side *WFD* IG8............54 A2
Hepburn Gdns *HAYES* BR2.....199 J5
Hepple Cl *ISLW* TW7...............136 C3
Hepscott Rd *HOM* E9 *.............88 A4
Hepworth Gdns *BARK* IG11.......91 G3
Hepworth Rd
  STRHM/NOR SW16................179 K3
Herald Gdns *WLGTN* SM6.......210 B1
Heralds Pl *LBTH* SE11..............18 A6
Herald St *BETH* E2.................104 D3
Herald Wk *CLKNW* EC1R *.........5 K7
Herbert Crs *KTBR* SW1X.........15 F4
Herbert Gdns *CHDH* RM6.........73 K4
  CHSWK W4..........................117 J6
  WLSDN NW10.......................99 K1
Herbert Ms *BRXS/STRHM* SW2...162 B1
  WOOL/PLUM SE18................135 J3
Herbert Rd *BXLYHN* DA7.......149 F3
  CDALE/KGS NW9...................63 J3
  FBAR/BDGN N11....................48 A1
  GDMY/SEVK IG3....................72 E6
  IL IG1.................................90 B2
  KUT/HW KT1........................175 H6
  MNPK E12............................89 J2
  SEVS/STOTM N15...................68 B2
  STHL UB1...........................114 E1
  WALTH E17..........................69 H4
  WIM/MER SW19...................177 J3
  WOOL/PLUM SE18................147 F1
Herbert St *KTTN* NW5...............84 A3
  PLSTW E13.........................106 E1
Herbrand St *BMSBY* WC1N........4 E6
Hercules Pl *HOLWY* N7.............84 E1
Hercules Rd *STHWK* SE1..........17 J5
Hercules St *HOLWY* N7.............84 E1
Hereford Av *EBAR* EN4.............33 K3
Hereford Gdns *IL* IG1................71 J4

PIN HA5 ....59 J2
WHTN TW2 * 155 H3
Hereford Ms BAY/PAD W2 * ...100 E5
Hereford Pl NWCR SE14 * 144 C1
Hereford Retreat PECK SE15 ...143 H1
Hereford Rd ACT W3 ....95 J6
BAY/PAD W2 ....100 E5
BOW E3 ....105 H1
EA W5 ....116 D3
FELT TW13 ....154 B5
WAN E11 ....71 F2
Hereford Sq SKENS SW7 ....128 E5
Hereford St CLAP SW4 * 104 C3
Hereford Wy CHSGTN KT9 ......205 J3
Herent Dr CLAY IG5 ....53 K6
Heretage Cl BRXN/ST SW9 ......142 C4
Hereward Gdns PLMGR N13 ......49 C1
Hereward Rd TOOT SW17 ....161 E6
Herga Rd HRW/HRWW/WS HA3 ...61 F1
Heriot Av CHING E4 ....37 J4
Heriot Rd HDN NW4 ....64 A2
Heriots Cl STAN HA7 ....29 C6
Heritage HI HAYES BR2 ....215 G3
Heritage Pl
WAND/EARL SW18 * 160 C1
Heritage Vw HRW HA1 ....79 F1
Herkomer Cl BUSH WD23 ....28 B1
Herlwyn Av RSLP HA4 ....76 C1
Herlwyn Gdns TOOT SW17 ......160 E6
Herm Cl ISLW TW7 ....135 H1
Hermes Cl MV/WKIL W9 ....100 E3
Hermes St IS N1 ....5 J3
Hermes Wy WLGTN SM6 ....210 D5
Hermiston Av CEND/HSY/T N8 ...66 E2
Hermitage Cl ABYW SE2 ....128 D3
ENC/FH EN2 ....23 H5
ESH/CLAY KT10 ....205 G4
RCHPK/HAM TW10 * 136 E6
SWFD E18 ....70 D1
Hermitage Cottages
STAN HA7 * 42 E1
Hermitage Gdns CRICK NW2 ......82 E1
NRWD SE19 ....180 D3
Hermitage La CRICK NW2 ....82 E1
CROY/NA CR0 ....197 G4
STRHM/NOR SW16 ....180 A3
UED N18 ....49 K1
Hermitage Rd FSBYPK N4 ....67 J3
NRWD SE19 ....180 D2
Hermitage Rw HACK E8 * 86 C3
The Hermitage BARN SW13 * 138 C2
FELT TW13 ....153 J5
FSTH SE23 ....163 K3
KUT/HW KT1 * 190 E1
LEW SE13 ....145 F3
RCHPK/HAM TW10 ....136 E6
Hermitage Wk SWFD E18 ....70 D1
Hermitage Wall WAP E1W 123 H1
Hermitage Wy STAN HA7 * 43 G4
Hermit Pl KIL/WHAMP NW6 ....82 E6
Hermit Rd CAN/RD E16 ....106 D4
Hermit St FSBYE EC1V 6 A4
Hermon Gv HYS/HAR UB3 ....113 K1
Hermon HI WAN E11 ....70 E1
Herndon Rd
WAND/EARL SW18 ....140 B6
Herne Cl HYS/HAR UB3 * 94 B6
WLSDN NW10 ....81 F3
Herne Ct BUSH WD23 * 28 C3
Herne HI HNHL SE24 ....142 D5
Herne Hill Rd HNHL SE24 ....142 D5
Herne Ms UED N18 ....36 C6
Herne Rd BUSH WD23 ....28 B1
SURB KT6 ....190 E6
WLSDN NW10 ....81 G4
Heron Cl BKHH IG9 ....39 F3
WALTH E17 ....51 H5
WLSDN NW10 ....81 G4
Heron Crs SCUP DA14 ....167 K6
Herondale SAND/SEL CR2 ....213 F6
Herondale Av
WAND/EARL SW18 ....160 C3
Heron Dr FSBYPK N4 ....67 J6
Heron Flight Av HCH RM12 ....93 J5
Herongate Rd MNPK E12 ....71 G6
Heron HI BELV DA17 ....129 G4
Heron Md PEND EN3 ....25 J1
Heron Ms IL IG1 ....72 B6
Heron Quays POP/IOD E14 ....124 D1
Heron Rd CROY/NA CR0 * 197 F5
TWK TW1 ....136 C5
Heronsforde WEA W13 ....97 J5
Heronsgate EDGW HA8 ....44 C1
Herons Lea HGT N6 ....65 K3
Heronslea Dr STAN HA7 ....44 A1
Herons PI ISLW TW7 ....136 C4
Herons Ri EBAR EN4 ....21 J5
Heron Wk NTHWD HA6 ....26 C6
Heron Wy EBED/NFELT TW14 ....133 K5
Herrick Rd HBRY N5 ....85 J1
Herrick St WEST SW1P 16 D7
Herries St NKENS W10 ....100 C1
Herringham Rd CHARL SE7 ....126 B3
Herrongate Cl EN EN1 ....24 B3
Hersant Cl WLSDN NW10 ....81 J6
Herschell Rd FSTH SE23 ....164 A2
Hersham Cl PUT/ROE SW15 ......158 D2
Hersham Rd WOT/HER KT12 ....188 A4
Hershell Ct
MORT/ESHN SW14 * 137 J5
Hertford Av
MORT/ESHN SW14 ....138 A4
Hertford Cl EBAR EN4 ....21 H4
Hertford Ct STAN HA7 * 43 F2
Hertford End Ct NTHWD HA6 * 40 C1
Hertford PI FITZ W1T 4 B7
Hertford Rd BARK IG11 ....90 A5
EBAR EN4 ....21 G4
ED N9 ....36 D3
ENC/FH EN2 ....24 A1
GNTH/NBYPK IG2 ....72 E5
IS N1 ....86 A6
PEND EN3 ....24 E2

Hertford Road High St
PEND EN3 ....24 D2
Hertford Sq MYFR/PICC W1J 15 J1
Hertford Wy MTCM CR4 ....195 K1
Hertslet Rd HOLWY N7 ....85 F1
Hertsmere Rd POP/IOD E14 ......124 D1
Hertswood Ct BAR EN5 * 20 C5
Hervey Cl FNCH N3 ....46 E4
Hervey Park Rd WALTH E17 ....69 G1
Hesa Rd HYS/HAR UB3 ....94 E5
Hesewall Cl CLAP SW4 ....141 H3
Hesketh Pl NTGHL W11 ....100 C6
Hesketh Rd FSTGT E7 ....88 E1
Heslop Rd BAL SW12 ....160 E3
Hesper Ms ECT SW5 ....120 A5
Hesperus Crs POP/IOD E14 ....124 E4
Hessel Rd WEA W13 ....116 B2
Hessel St WCHPL E1 ....104 D5
Hesselyn Dr RAIN RM13 ....93 K5
Hestercombe Av
FUL/PGN SW6 ....139 H3
Hesterman Wy CROY/NA CR0 ....195 H5
Hester Rd BTSEA SW11 ....140 D1
Hester Ter RCH/KEW TW9 ....137 H4
Heston Av HEST TW5 ....114 D6
Heston Grange La HEST TW5 ....114 E6
Heston Rd HEST TW5 ....115 F1
Heston St DEPT SE8 ....144 D2
Heswell Gn OXHEY WD19 * 26 E5
Hetherington Rd CLAP SW4 ......141 K5
Hetley Rd SHB W12 ....118 E1
Heton Gdns HDN NW4 ....63 J1
Hevelius Cl GNWCH SE10 ....125 J5
Hever Cft ELTH/MOT SE9 ....167 F6
Hever Gdns BMLY BR1 ....185 F5
Heverham Rd
WOOL/PLUM SE18 ....127 K4
Heversham Rd BXLYHN DA7 .....149 H3
Hevingham Dr CHDH RM6 ....73 J5
Hewens Rd HGDN/ICK UB10 ....94 A2
Hewer St NKENS W10 ....100 B4
Hewett Cl STAN HA7 ....29 H6
Hewetts Quay BARK IG11 ....90 B6
Hewett St SDTCH EC2A 7 H7
Hewish Rd UED N18 ....36 A6
Hewison St BOW E3 ....105 H1
Hewitt Av WDGN N22 ....49 H5
Hewitt Cl CROY/NA CR0 ....213 J1
Hewitt Rd CEND/HSY/T N8 ....67 G2
Hewlett Rd BOW E3 ....105 G1
The Hexagon HGT N6 ....65 K5
Hexal Rd CAT SE6 ....165 H5
Hexham Gdns ISLW TW7 ....136 B1
Hexham Rd BAR EN5 ....21 F5
MRDN SM4 ....194 A5
WNWD SE27 ....162 D4
Heybourne Rd TOTM N17 ....50 D3
Heybridge Av
STRHM/NOR SW16 ....180 A2
Heybridge Dr BARK/HLT IG6 ....54 D6
Heybridge Wy LEY E10 ....69 F4
Heyford Av RYNPK SW20 ....177 J6
VX/NE SW8 ....141 K1
Heyford Rd MTCM CR4 ....178 D5
Heyford Ter VX/NE SW8 * 141 K1
Heygate Est WALW SE17 ....18 D6
Heygate St WALW SE17 ....18 C7
Heynes Rd BCTR RM8 ....91 J2
Heysham Dr OXHEY WD19 ....41 G1
Heysham La HAMP NW3 ....83 G1
Heysham Rd SEVS/STOTM N15 ...67 K3
Heythorp St
WAND/EARL SW18 ....159 J4
Heywood Av CDALE/KGS NW9 ....45 G4
Heyworth Rd CLPT E5 ....86 D2
SRTFD E15 ....88 D3

Hibbert Rd
KTN/HRWW/WS HA3 ....43 F5
WALTH E17 ....69 H4
Hibbert St BTSEA SW11 ....140 B4
Hibernia Gdns HSLW TW3 ....135 F6
Hibernia Rd HSLW TW3 ....135 F5
Hichisson Rd PECK SE15 ....144 A6
Hickin Cl CHARL SE7 ....126 C4
Hickin St POP/IOD E14 ....125 F3
Hickling Rd IL IG1 ....90 B3
Hickman Av CHING E4 ....52 B1
Hickman Cl CAN/RD E16 ....107 H4
Hickman Rd CHDH RM6 ....73 J4
Hickory Cl ED N9 ....36 C2
Hicks Av GFD/PVL UB6 ....96 D2
Hicks Cl BTSEA SW11 ....140 C4
Hicks St DEPT SE8 ....124 B5
Hidcote Gdns RYNPK SW20 ......176 E6
Hide PI WEST SW1P 16 C7
Hide Rd HRW HA1 ....60 D1
Higham Hill Rd WALTH E17 ....51 G4
Higham Ms NTHLT UB5 ....95 K3
Higham Pl WALTH E17 * 51 G4
Higham Rd TOTM N17 ....49 K6
WFD IG8 ....52 E2
Higham Station Av CHING E4 ....51 K2
The Highams WALTH E17 * 52 A4
Higham St WALTH E17 * 51 G4
Highbank PI
WAND/EARL SW18 * 160 A3
Highbanks Cl WELL DA16 ....148 B1
Highbanks Rd PIN HA5 ....42 B2
Highbank Wy CEND/HSY/T N8 .....67 G3
Highbarrow Rd CROY/NA CR0 ....197 G5
High Beech SAND/SEL CR2 ....212 A5
High Beeches ORP BR6 ....217 G4
SCUP DA14 ....187 F1
Highbridge Rd BARK IG11 ....90 B6
Highbrook Rd BKHTH/KID SE3 ...146 C4
High Broom Crs WWKM BR4 .....198 E4
Highbury Av THHTH CR7 ....180 B5
Highbury Cnr HBRY N5 ....85 H1
Highbury Crs HBRY N5 ....85 G2
Highbury Est HBRY N5 ....85 J2
Highbury Gra HBRY N5 ....85 H1
Highbury Gv HBRY N5 ....85 H2
Highbury HI HBRY N5 ....85 H2

Highbury New Pk HBRY N5 ....85 J4
Highbury Pk HBRY N5 ....85 H1
Highbury Pl HBRY N5 ....85 H2
Highbury Qd HBRY N5 ....85 J1
Highbury Rd WIM/MER SW19 ....177 H1
Highbury Station Pde
HBRY N5 * 85 G1
Highbury Station Rd IS N1 * 85 G4
Highbury Ter HBRY N5 ....85 H2
Highbury Terrace Ms HBRY N5 ...85 H3
High Cedar Dr RYNPK SW20 .....176 E5
Highclere Av HNWL W7 * 116 D6
Highclere Rd NWMAL KT3 ....176 A6
Highclere St SYD SE26 ....164 B6
Highcliffe Dr PUT/ROE SW15 ....158 C1
Highcliffe Gdns REDBR IG4 ....71 J2
Highcombe CHARL SE7 ....126 A6
Highcombe Cl ELTH/MOT SE9 ...166 C4
High Coombe Pl
KUTN/CMB KT2 ....176 A3
Highcroft CDALE/KGS NW9 ....63 G2
Highcroft Av ALP/SUD HA0 ....80 B5
Highcroft Gdns GLDGN NW11 .....64 D3
Highcroft Rd ARCH N19 ....66 E4
High Cross Rd TOTM N17 ....50 C2
Highcross Wy PUT/ROE SW15 ...158 D3
Highdaun Dr
STRHM/NOR SW16 ....196 A1
Highdown WPK KT4 ....192 B6
Highdown Rd PUT/ROE SW15 ....158 E2
High Dr NWMAL KT3 ....175 K4
High Elms WFD IG8 ....52 E1
High Elms Cl NTHWD HA6 ....40 A2
High Elms Rd ORP BR6 ....216 C6
Highfield Av CDALE/KGS NW9 .....62 E2
ERITH DA8 ....129 K6
GFD/PVL UB6 ....78 E3
GLDGN NW11 ....64 B4
ORP BR6 ....217 F4
PIN HA5 ....59 K2
WBLY HA9 ....62 B5
Highfield Cl CDALE/KGS NW9 .....62 E2
CRW RM5 ....56 E2
LEW SE13 ....165 G2
NTHWD HA6 ....40 C4
SURB KT6 ....190 D5
WDGN N22 ....49 G4
Highfield Crs STHGT/OAK N14 ....34 C1
NTHWD HA6 ....40 C4
Highfield Dr HAYES BR2 ....199 H1
HOR/WEW KT19 ....207 H5
PIN HA5 ....59 H2
WWKM BR4 ....213 K1
Highfield Gdns GLDGN NW11 .....64 C3
Highfield HI NRWD SE19 ....180 E3
Highfield Link CRW RM5 ....56 E2
Highfield Rd ACT W3 ....98 E4
BMLY BR1 ....200 E1
BXLYHS DA6 ....149 G6
BXLYHS DA6 ....149 G6
CHST BR7 ....186 A6
CRW RM5 ....56 E2
DART DA1 ....171 G2
FELT TW13 ....153 K3
GLDGN NW11 * 64 C3
ISLW TW7 ....136 A1
NTHWD HA6 ....40 C4
SUT SM1 ....209 J3
WCHMH N21 ....35 H4
WFD IG8 ....53 J3
Highfield Rd North DART DA1 ....171 G2
Highfield Rd South DART DA1 ....171 G3
Highfields Gv HGT N6 ....65 K5
High Foleys ESH/CLAY KT10 .....205 H5
High Garth ESH/CLAY KT10 ....204 C4
Highgate Av HGT N6 ....66 A4
Highgate Cl HGT N6 ....66 A4
Highgate Edge EFNCH N2 * 65 J2
Highgate High St HGT N6 ....66 A5
Highgate HI ARCH N19 ....66 B6
Highgate Rd KTTN NW5 ....84 A1
Highgate Spinney
CEND/HSY/T N8 * 66 D3
Highgate West HI HGT N6 ....66 A6
High Gv BMLY BR1 ....184 B4
WOOL/PLUM SE18 ....147 J1
Highgrove Ms CAR SM5 ....209 K1
Highgrove Rd BCTR RM8 ....91 J3
Highgrove Wy RSLP HA4 ....58 E3
High Hill Ferry CLPT E5 ....68 D5
High Holborn HHOL WC1V 11 F3
Highland Av DAGE RM10 ....92 E1
HNWL W7 ....96 E5
LOU IG10 ....39 K1
Highland Cottages
WLGTN SM6 * 210 B2
Highland Cft BECK BR3 ....182 E2
Highland Dr BUSH WD23 ....28 B2
Highland Pk FELT TW13 ....153 H6
Highland Rd BMLY BR1 ....183 J4
BXLYHS DA6 ....149 H6
NRWD SE19 ....181 F2
Highlands OXHEY WD19 ....27 J5
Highlands Av ACT W3 ....98 E6
WCHMH N21 ....35 H4
Highlands Cl HSLW TW3 ....135 G2
Highlands La WOT/HER KT12 ....188 C4
Highlands Rd BAR EN5 ....20 E6
STMC/STPC BR5 ....202 C4
The Highlands BAR EN5 * 21 F6
EDGW HA8 ....44 D5
Highland Ter LEW SE13 * 144 E4
High La HNWL W7 ....96 D5
Highlea Cl CDALE/KGS NW9 ....45 G4
High Level Dr SYD SE26 ....163 H6
Highlever Rd NKENS W10 ....100 A4
High Limes NRWD SE19 * 181 F2
High Md HRW HA1 ....61 F2
Highmead WOOL/PLUM SE18 .....148 A1
High Md WWKM BR4 ....198 D6
Highmead Crs ALP/SUD HA0 ......80 B5
High Meadow Cl PIN HA5 ....59 F1
High Meadow Crs
CDALE/KGS NW9 ....63 G2

High Mdw CHIG IG7 ....54 D1
High Meads Rd CAN/RD E16 .....107 H5
Highmore Rd BKHTH/KID SE3 ...145 H1
High Mt HDN NW4 ....63 J5
High Oaks Cl ERITH DA8 * 23 F1
The High Pde
STRHM/NOR SW16 * 161 K5
High Park Rd RCH/KEW TW9 ....137 H2
High Pth WIM/MER SW19 ....178 A4
High Point ELTH/MOT SE9 ....167 G5
High Rdg MUSWH N10 * 48 B4
Highridge Pl ENC/FH EN2 * 23 F1
High Rd BKHH IG9 ....39 F4
BUSH WD23 ....28 D3
CHDH RM6 ....74 B3
FBAR/BDGN N11 ....48 B2
GDMY/SEVK IG3 ....73 G5
KTN/HRWW/WS HA3 ....42 E4
LEY E10 ....69 K3
NFNCH/WDSPK N12 ....47 C3
RDART DA2 ....170 E5
SRVS/STOTM N15 ....50 B6
TOTM N17 ....50 B6
TRDG/WHET N20 ....33 G2
WBLY HA9 ....80 A3
WDGN N22 ....49 F4
WLSDN NW10 ....81 J4
High Rd Eastcote PIN HA5 ....59 G1
High Rd Ickenham
HGDN/ICK UB10 ....76 A1
High Rd Leyton LEY E10 ....69 K6
High Rd Leytonstone WAN E11 ....88 A1
High Rd Woodford Gn WFD IG8 ...52 E1
Highshore Rd PECK SE15 ....143 G3
Highstead Crs ERITH DA8 ....150 B2
Highstone Av WAN E11 ....70 E3
High St ACT W3 ....117 K1
BAR EN5 ....20 C4
BARK/HLT IG6 ....54 C6
BECK BR3 ....182 D5
BMLY BR1 ....183 K6
BORE WD6 ....29 K1
BTFD TW8 ....116 E6
BUSH WD23 ....28 A3
CAR SM5 ....209 K3
CEND/HSY/T N8 ....66 E1
CHEAM SM3 ....208 C4
CROY/NA CR0 ....211 J1
DART DA1 ....171 J2
EA W5 ....97 K6
ESH/CLAY KT10 ....204 B3
ESH/CLAY KT10 ....205 F4
EW KT17 ....207 J6
FBAR/BDGN N11 ....48 B1
FELT TW13 ....153 K4
HEST TW5 ....114 D6
HPTN TW12 ....173 G4
HRW HA1 ....60 E3
HSLW TW3 ....135 F4
HYS/HAR UB3 ....113 C6
KTN/HRWW/WS HA3 ....42 E6
KUT/HW KT1 ....174 D4
KUT/HW KT1 ....174 D5
MLHL NW7 ....45 K1
NTHWD HA6 ....40 C3
NWMAL KT3 ....192 B1
ORP BR6 ....202 C4
ORP BR6 ....216 C3
PGE/AN SE20 ....181 K3
PIN HA5 ....41 J6
PLSTW E13 ....106 E1
PUR RM19 ....131 K4
ROM RM1 ....75 C2
RSLP HA4 ....58 C5
SCUP DA14 ....168 B6
SNWD SE25 ....197 G1
SRTFD E15 ....88 B6
STHGT/OAK N14 ....34 D3
STMC/STPC BR5 ....202 D1
STWL/WRAY TW19 ....152 A1
SUT SM1 ....209 F2
SUT SM1 ....209 F2
TEDD TW11 ....174 B1
THDIT KT7 ....190 B4
THHTH CR7 ....196 D1
WALTH E17 ....51 J4
WAN E11 ....71 F3
WBLY HA9 ....80 B2
WDR/YW UB7 ....112 B2
WDR/YW UB7 ....112 B1
WHTN TW2 ....155 H2
WIM/MER SW19 ....177 H2
WWKM BR4 ....198 E5
High St Collier's Wd
WIM/MER SW19 * 178 C3
High St Harlesden
WLSDN NW10 ....99 H1
High St Harlington
HTHAIR 133 G2
HYS/HAR UB3 ....113 C6
High Street Ms
WIM/MER SW19 ....177 H1
High St North MNPK E12 ....89 J4
High St South EHAM E6 ....107 K2
High Timber St BLKFR EC4V 12 C5
High Tor Cl BMLY BR1 ....184 A3
High Trees BRXS/STRHM SW2 ...162 B3
CROY/NA CR0 ....198 B5
EBAR EN4 ....21 J6
High Vw PIN HA5 ....59 H1
WATW WD18 ....26 D1
Highview Av EDGW HA8 ....44 E1
WLGTN SM6 ....211 F3
High View Cl NRWD SE19 ....181 G3
Highview Gdns EDGW HA8 ....44 E1
FBAR/BDGN N11 ....48 C1
FNCH N3 ....46 C6
High View Rd NRWD SE19 ....180 E2
SWFD E18 ....52 D6
High View Rd WEA W13 ....97 G5
Highview Ter DART DA1 * 151 G6
The Highway BELMT SM2 ....209 G6
ORP BR6 ....217 H3

STAN HA7 ....43 F4
WCHPL E1 ....104 C6
Highwood Av
NFNCH/WDSPK N12 ....33 G6
Highwood Cl FSTH SE23 ....163 H3
ORP BR6 ....201 H6
Highwood Dr ORP BR6 ....201 H6
Highwood Gdns CLAY IG5 ....53 K5
Highwood Gv MLHL NW7 ....45 F1
Highwood HI MLHL NW7 ....31 H5
Highwood Rd ARCH N19 ....84 E1
High Worple RYLN/HDSTN HA2 ...59 J2
Highworth Rd FBAR/BDGN N11 ...48 D2
Hilary Av MTCM CR4 ....179 F6
Hilary Cl ERITH DA8 ....149 J2
FUL/PGN SW6 ....140 A1
Hilary Rd SHB W12 ....99 H6
Hilberry Ct BUSH WD23 * 28 C3
Hilbert Rd CHEAM SM3 ....208 B2
Hilborough Cl WIM/MER SW19 ...178 B3
Hilborough Rd HACK E8 * 86 B5
Hilborough Wy ORP BR6 ....216 C3
Hilda Lockert Wk
BRXN/ST SW9 * 142 C3
Hilda Rd CAN/RD E16 ....106 C3
EHAM E6 ....89 J5
Hilda Ter BRXN/ST SW9 * 142 B3
Hilda Vale Rd ORP BR6 ....216 C4
Hildenborough Gdns
BMLY BR1 ....183 H2
Hilden Dr ERITH DA8 ....150 C1
Hildenlea Pl HAYES BR2 ....183 H5
Hildreth St BAL SW12 ....161 G3
Hildyard Rd FUL/PGN SW6 * 119 K6
Hiley Rd WLSDN NW10 ....100 A3
Hilgrove Rd KIL/WHAMP NW6 ......83 F5
Hillary Gdns STAN HA7 * 43 J5
Hillary Crs WOT/HER KT12 ....188 B5
Hillary Dr ISLW TW7 ....136 A5
Hillary Ri BAR EN5 ....20 E5
Hillary Rd NWDGN UB2 ....115 F3
Hillbeck Cl PECK SE15 ....143 K1
Hillbeck Wy GFD/PVL UB6 ....78 D1
Hillborne Cl HYS/HAR UB3 ....113 K5
Hillborough Cl
WIM/MER SW19 * 178 B3
Hillbrook Rd TOOT SW17 ....161 F5
Hill Brow BMLY BR1 ....184 C4
DART DA1 ....170 C1
Hillbrow NWMAL KT3 ....176 C4
Hillbrow Rd BXLY DA5 ....170 A6
Hillbrow Rd BMLY BR1 ....183 H5
ESH/CLAY KT10 ....204 C2
Hillbury Av
KTN/HRWW/WS HA3 ....43 H2
Hillbury Rd TOOT SW17 ....161 G5
Hill Cl BAR EN5 ....20 B6
CHST BR7 ....185 G1
CRICK NW2 ....81 K1
GLDGN NW11 ....64 E3
HAMP NW3 ....82 E1
STAN HA7 ....29 H5
Hillcote Av STRHM/NOR SW16 ...180 B3
Hillcourt Av
NFNCH/WDSPK N12 ....47 F2
Hillcourt Rd EDUL SE22 ....163 J1
Hill Crs BRYLDS KT5 ....191 G2
BXLY DA5 ....169 K3
HRW HA1 ....61 G2
TRDG/WHET N20 ....33 F4
WPK KT4 ....193 F6
Hill Crest BFN/LL DA15 ....168 B2
Hillcrest HGT N6 ....66 A4
HNHL SE24 ....142 E5
Hill Crest SURB KT6 * 191 F4
Hillcrest WCHMH N21 ....35 H2
Hillcrest Av EDGW HA8 ....30 D6
GLDGN NW11 ....64 C3
PIN HA5 ....59 H1
Hillcrest Cl BECK BR3 ....198 C5
SYD SE26 ....163 H6
Hillcrest Gdns CRICK NW2 ....81 J1
ESH/CLAY KT10 ....205 F2
FNCH N3 ....46 D6
Hillcrest Rd ACT W3 ....117 H1
BMLY BR1 ....184 A3
DART DA1 ....170 C2
EA W5 ....98 A4
EMPK RM11 ....75 J4
HGT N6 ....66 B4
ORP BR6 ....202 B6
WALTH E17 ....52 B5
Hillcrest Vw BECK BR3 ....198 C3
Hillcroft Crs EA W5 * 97 K5
EA W5 ....98 A4
OXHEY WD19 ....27 H1
RSLP HA4 ....77 H1
WBLY HA9 ....80 B2
Hillcroft Rd EHAM E6 ....108 B4
Hillcroome Rd BELMT SM2 ....209 H4
Hillcross Av MRDN SM4 ....193 H5
Hillcroft Rd SUT SM1 * 208 D2
Hilldown Rd HAYES BR2 ....199 H5
STRHM/NOR SW16 ....179 K3
WBLY HA9 ....62 D5
Hilldrop Crs HOLWY N7 ....84 D3
Hilldrop Est HOLWY N7 * 84 D3
Hilldrop La HOLWY N7 ....84 D3
Hilldrop Rd BMLY BR1 ....184 A2
HOLWY N7 ....84 D3
Hill End ORP BR6 ....202 A6
WOOL/PLUM SE18 ....127 G6
Hillendale Av BARN SW13 ....138 D3
EDGW HA8 ....44 B1
Hillery Cl WALW SE17 ....19 F7
Hill Farm Rd NKENS W10 ....100 A4
Hillfield Av ALP/SUD HA0 ....80 A5
CDALE/KGS NW9 ....63 G2
CEND/HSY/T N8 ....67 F1
MRDN SM4 ....194 D3
Hillfield Cl RYLN/HDSTN HA2 .....60 C3
Hillfield La South BUSH WD23 ...28 E1
Hillfield Pde MUSWH N10 ....48 C4
Hillfield Pk MUSWH N10 ....66 B1

WCHMH N21.....................................35 G4
Hillfield Park Ms MUSWH N10....66 B1
Hill Field Rd HPTN TW12.............172 E3
Hillfield Rd KIL/WHAMP NW6.......82 D5
Hillfoot Av CRW RM5.....................56 E4
Hillfoot Rd CRW RM5.....................56 E4
Hillgate Pl BAL SW12...................161 G1
KENS W8
Hillgate St KENS W8....................119 K1
Hill Gv FELT TW13........................154 E4
ROM RM1...57 G6
Hill House Av STAN HA7..............43 F3
Hill House Cl WCHMH N21..........35 G2
Hill House Dr HPTN TW12..........173 F4
Hill House Rd
  STRHM/NOR SW16...................180 A1
Hilliard Rd NTHWD HA6...............40 D4
Hilliard's Ct WAP E1W *.............123 K1
Hillier Cl BAR EN5.........................33 F1
Hillier Gdns CROY/NA CR0........211 G3
Hillier Pl CHSGTN KT9................205 K4
Hillier Rd BTSEA SW11...............160 E1
Hillier's La CROY/NA CR0..........210 C1
Hillingdon Av
  STWL/WRAY TW19......................152 B3
Hillingdon Rd BXLYHN DA7.......149 K4
Hillingdon St WALW SE17..........122 C6
Hillington Trail HYS/HAR UB3....113 K5
Hill La RSLP HA4...........................58 A5
Hillrise Av ALP/SUD HA0.............79 H1
  CAR SM5......................................209 J4
  HRW HA1..61 D2
  MTCM CR4...................................179 G4
  MUSWH N10...................................47 K4
  NTHWD HA6...................................40 B2
  PIN HA5..41 K3
  RDART DA2..................................171 H4
  STJWD NW8..................................101 G1
  SUT SM1......................................209 F3
Hillsboro Rd EDUL SE22............143 F6
Hillsborough Gn OXHEY WD19 *..26 E5
Hillsgrove Cl WELL DA16...........148 D1
Hill Side BAR EN5.........................21 G6
  CDALE/KGS NW9...........................63 H1
  ESH/CLAY KT10 *.......................204 B3
  WIM/MER SW19..........................177 G2
  WLSDN NW10..................................81 F6
Hillside Av FBAR/BDGN N11......47 K2
  WBLY HA9......................................80 B2
  WFD IG8...53 G1
Hillside Cl MRDN SM4................193 H1
  STJWD NW8.................................101 F1
  WFD IG8...53 G1
Hillside Crs ENC/FH EN2..............23 K1
  NTHWD HA6...................................40 E4
  OXHEY WD19..................................27 H1
  RYLN/HDSTN HA2........................60 C6
Hillside Dr EDGW HA8.................44 C2
Hillside Gdns BAR EN5...............20 C6
  BRXS/STRHM SW2 *...................162 B4
  EDGW HA8.....................................30 B6
  FBAR/BDGN N11 *.........................48 C2
  HGT N6..66 A3
  KTN/HRWW/WS HA3....................62 A4
  NTHWD HA6...................................40 E3
  WALTH E17.....................................52 B6
  WLGTN SM6.................................210 C5
Hillside Gv MLHL NW7..................45 J1
  STHGT/OAK N14............................34 D2
Hillside La HAYES BR2...............199 K6
Hillside Ri NTHWD HA6.................40 E3
Hillside Rd BELMT SM2...............208 D5
  BRXS/STRHM SW2.......................162 A4
  CROY/NA CR0.............................211 H5
  DART DA1.....................................170 D1
  EA W5..98 A4
  HAYES BR2..................................183 J6
  NTHWD HA6...................................40 E3
  PIN HA5...42 A4
  SEVS/STOTM N15..........................68 A4
  STHL UB1..96 A3
The Hillside ORP BR6..................217 H6
Hills La NTHWD HA6......................40 C4
Hillsleigh Rd KENS W8...............119 J1
Hills Ms EA W5 *............................98 A6
Hills Pl SOHO/SHAV W1D............10 N4
Hill's Rd BKHH IG9.........................39 F3
Hillstowe St CLPT E5......................86 E6
Hill St MYFR/PICC W1J...................9 J7
  RCH/KEW TW9............................136 E6
Hill Top CHEAM SM3....................193 J4
  GLDGN NW11...................................65 F1
Hilltop WALTH E17 *.......................51 K6
Hilltop Av WLSDN NW10...............80 E5
Hilltop Gdns DART DA1...............151 J6
  HDN NW4...45 K5
  ORP BR6..201 K6
Hilltop Rd KIL/WHAMP NW6.........82 E5
Hill Top Vw WFD IG8 *...................53 K2
Hilltop Wy STAN HA7....................29 G5
Hillview RYNPK SW20..................176 B3
Hillview Av
  KTN/HRWW/WS HA3....................62 A2
Hillview Cl PIN HA5........................41 K2
  WBLY HA9..80 B1
Hillview Crs IL IG1..........................71 K3
  ORP BR6..202 A5
Hill View Dr THMD SE28.............127 K1
  WELL DA16..................................147 K3

Hill View Gdns CDALE/KGS NW9..63 F2
Hillview Gdns HDN NW4...............64 B1
  RYLN/HDSTN HA2..........................42 A6
Hill View Rd ESH/CLAY KT10.....205 G5
  ORP BR6..202 A5
  TWK TW1......................................156 B1
Hillview Rd CHST BR7.................185 F1
  MLHL NW7.......................................32 B6
  PIN HA5...41 K3
  SUT SM1.......................................209 G1
Hillway CDALE/KGS NW9..............63 G5
  HGT N6...66 A6
Hillworth BECK BR3 *..................182 E5
Hillworth Rd
  BRXS/STRHM SW2......................162 B2
Hillyard Rd HNWL W7....................96 E4
Hillyard St BRXN/ST SW9..........142 B2
Hillyfield WALTH E17......................51 G5
Hillyfield Cl HOM E9.......................87 G3
Hilly Fids BROCKY SE4..................144 C2
Hilly Fields Crs BROCKY SE4.....144 D5
Hilsea St CLPT E5............................86 E2
Hilton Av NFNCH/WDSPK N12....47 H1
Himalayan Wy WATW WD18..........26 D1
Himley Rd TOOT SW17.................178 D1
Hinchley Cl ESH/CLAY KT10......205 F1
Hinchley Dr ESH/CLAY KT10.....205 F1
Hinchley Wy ESH/CLAY KT10.....205 G1
Hinckley Rd EDUL SE22.............143 H5
Hind Cl CHIG IG7.............................55 F1
Hind Ct FLST/FETLN EC4A..........11 K4
Hind Crs ERITH DA8.....................149 K1
Hinde Ms MHST W1U *.....................9 H3
Hindes Rd HRW HA1......................60 D2
Hinde St MHST W1U.........................9 H3
Hind Gv POP/IOD E14...................105 J5
Hindhead Gdns NTHLT UB5...........77 J6
Hindhead Gn OXHEY WD19...........41 G1
Hindhead Wy WLGTN SM6..........210 E3
Hindmans Rd EDUL SE22............143 H6
Hindmans Wy DAGW RM9............110 B3
Hindmarsh Cl WCHPL E1 *...........104 C6
Hindrey Rd CLPT E5........................86 D3
Hindsley's Pl FSTH SE23.............163 K4
Hinkler Rd KTN/HRWW/WS HA3...43 K6
Hinksey Pth ABYW SE2.................128 E3
Hinstock Rd
  WOOL/PLUM SE18.......................147 H1
Hinton Av HSLWW TW4...............134 C5
Hinton Cl ELTH/MOT SE9...........166 D3
Hinton Rd BRXN/ST SW9............142 C4
  UED N18..36 A6
  WLGTN SM6.................................210 C4
Hippodrome Pl NTGHL W11.........100 C6
Hirst Crs WBLY HA9.......................80 A1
Hitcham Rd WALTH E17..................69 H4
Hitherbroom Rd
  HYS/HAR UB3.............................113 K1
Hither Farm Rd
  BKHTH/KID SE3............................146 B4
Hitherfield Rd BCTR RM8...............74 A6
  STRHM/NOR SW16.....................162 A4
Hither Green La LEW SE13.........165 C1
Hitherwell Rd
  KTN/HRWW/WS HA3....................42 D4
Hitherwood Dr NRWD SE19.........163 G6
Hive La IS N1 *.................................28 D4
Hoadly Rd STRHM/NOR SW16....161 J5
Hobart Cl YEAD UB4.......................95 H3
Hobart Gdns THHTH CR7.............180 E6
Hobart La YEAD UB4.......................95 H3
Hobart Pl BCVA SW1W...................15 J5
  RCHPK/HAM TW10.....................157 G2
Hobart Rd BARK/HLT IG6................54 C5
  DAGW RM9.......................................91 K2
  WPK KT4.......................................207 K1
  YEAD UB4..95 H4
Hobbayne Rd HNWL W7................96 D5
Hobbes Wk PUT/ROE SW15.......158 E2
Hobbs Gn EFNCH N2......................47 G6
Hobbs Pl IS N1 *................................7 G1
Hobbs Place Est IS N1....................7 G2
Hobbs Rd WNWD SE27................162 D6
Hobby St PEND EN3.........................25 F6
Hobday St POP/IOD E14..............105 K5
Hoblands End CHST BR7..............185 K2
Hobsons Pl WCHPL E1 *..............104 C4
Hobury St WBPTN SW10..............120 B6
Hockenden La SWLY BR8............187 H6
Hocker St BETH E2 *.........................7 J5
Hockley Av EHAM E6....................107 J1
Hockley Dr GPK RM2......................57 K5
Hockley Ms BARK IG11.................108 E1
Hockliffe Rd CRICK NW2.................82 D1
Hocroft Av CRICK NW2...................82 D1
Hocroft Rd CRICK NW2...................82 D1
Hocroft Wk CRICK NW2 *...............82 D1
Hodder Dr GFD/PVL UB6................97 F1
Hoddesdon Rd BELV DA17..........129 H5
Hodes Rw HAMP NW3.....................83 K2
Hodford Rd GLDGN NW11...............64 D5
Hodges Wy WATW WD18.................26 E1
Hodgkins Cl THMD SE28..............128 C6
Hodgkins Ms STAN HA7.................43 H1
Hodister Cl CMBW SE5.................142 D1
Hodnet Gv BERM/RHTH SE16.....124 A4
Hodson Crs STMC/STPC BR5.....202 E5
Hodson Pl PEND EN3......................25 J1
Hoe La EN EN1..................................24 D1
Hoe St WALTH E17...........................69 J2
The Hoe OXHEY WD19....................27 H4
Hoffmann Gdns
  SAND/SEL CR2............................212 C4
Hoffman Sq IS N1 *............................7 F4
Hofland Rd WKENS W14...............119 H3
Hogan Ms BAY/PAD W2...................8 A1
Hogarth Av ASHF TW15.................153 G4
  EW5...98 A4
Hogarth Crs CROY/NA CR0.........196 D4
  WIM/MER SW19............................178 C4
Hogarth Gdns HEST TW5..............135 F1
Hogarth Hl GLDGN NW11...............64 D1
Hogarth Pl ECT SW5 *..................120 A4
Hogarth Rd BCTR RM8....................91 H5
  ECT SW5..120 A4

EDGW HA8..44 C5
Hogarth Ter CHSWK W4 *.............118 B6
Hogarth Wy HPTN TW12...............173 H4
Hog Hill Rd CRW RM5.....................56 B2
Hogshead Pas WAP E1W *............104 D6
Hogsmill Wy HOR/WEW KT19.....206 D3
Holbeach Gdns BFN/LL DA15.....167 K1
Holbeach Rd CAT SE6...................164 E2
Holbeck Row PECK SE15...............143 H1
Holbein Ga NTHWD HA6.................40 C1
Holbein Ms BCVA SW1W..............121 F5
Holbein Pl BGVA SW1W...................15 G7
Holborn HCIRC EC1N........................11 J2
Holborn Cir HCIRC EC1N...............11 K2
Holborn Pl HHOL WC1V...................11 K2
Holborn Viad STBT EC1A................12 A3
Holbrook Cl EN EN1...........................24 C1
Holbrook La CHST BR7.................185 J3
Holbrook Rd SRTFD E15................106 D1
Holbrook Wy HAYES BR2.............200 E3
Holburne Cl BKHTH/KID SE3......146 B2
Holburne Gdns
  BKHTH/KID SE3...........................146 B2
Holburne Rd BKHTH/KID SE3.....146 B2
Holcombe Hl MLHL NW7.................31 J5
Holcombe Rd IL IG1..........................72 A4
  TOTM N17..50 B6
Holcombe St HMSMTH W6...........118 E5
Holcote Cl BELV DA17 *................129 F3
Holden Av CDALE/KGS NW9..........62 E5
  NFNCH/WDSPK N12......................47 F1
Holdenby Rd BROCKY SE4...........144 B6
Holden Cl BCTR RM8........................91 H2
Holdenhurst Av FNCH N3................47 F3
Holden Rd NFNCH/WDSPK N12....33 F6
Holden St BTSEA SW11................141 F3
Holdernesse Rd ISLW TW7..........136 B2
  TOOT SW17...................................160 E5
Holderness Wy WNWD SE27......180 D1
Holders Hill Av HDN NW4................46 B5
Holders Hill Crs HDN NW4..............46 B5
Holders Hill Dr HDN NW4................46 B6
Holders Hill Gdns HDN NW4..........46 C5
Holders Hill Pde MLHL NW7 *.......46 C4
Holders Hill Rd HDN NW4...............46 B5
Holford Ms FSBYW WC1X *..............5 C4
Holford Rd HAMP NW3....................83 G1
Holford St FSBYW WC1X..................5 K4
Holford Wy FSBYW WC1X *.............5 J5
Holgate Av BTSEA SW11..............140 C4
Holgate Gdns DAGE RM10.............92 C5
Holgate St CHARL SE7..................126 C3
Holland Av BELMT SM2.................208 E5
  RYNPK SW20................................176 C4
Holland Cl HAYES BR2.................199 J6
  ROMW/RG RM7................................74 E1
  STAN HA7..43 H1
  TRDG/WHET N20..............................33 H2
Holland Dr FSTH SE23...................164 B5
Holland Gdns BTFD TW8...............117 C5
  WKENS W14....................................119 H3
Holland Gv BRXN/ST SW9...........142 B1
Holland Pk NTGHL W11.................119 H1
Holland Park Av
  NTGHL W11.....................................119 H1
Holland Park Gdns
  NTGHL W11.....................................119 H1
Holland Park Ms NTGHL W11.......119 J1
Holland Park Rd WKENS W14......119 J3
Holland Park Ter NTGHL W11.......119 H1
Holland Pas IS N1 *..........................85 J6
Holland Rd EHAM E6......................89 J1
  KENS W8...12 B7
Holland St KENS W8......................119 K2
  STHWK SE1.......................................12 B7
Holland Villas Rd WKENS W14....119 H1
Holland Wk KENS W8.....................43 G1
Holland Wy HAYES BR2...............199 J6
Hollar Rd STNW/STAM N16............86 B1
Hollen St SOHO/CST W1F...............10 B4
Holles Cl HPTN TW12....................173 F2
Holles St CAVSQ/HST W1G.............9 K3
Holley Rd ACT W3...........................118 B2
Hollickwood Av
  NFNCH/WDSPK N12.......................47 K2
Holliday Sq BTSEA SW11 *...........140 C4
Hollidge Wy DAGE RM10................92 D5
Hollies Av BFN/LL DA15................167 K3
Hollies Cl STRHM/NOR SW16.....180 B2
  TWK TW1...156 A4
Hollies End MLHL NW7....................45 K1
Hollies Rd EA W5.............................116 D4
The Hollies
  KTN/HRWW/WS HA3......................61 G1
Hollies Wy BAL SW12 *.................161 F2
Holligrave Rd BMLY BR1...............183 K4
Hollingbourne Av
  BXLYHN DA7...................................149 G2
Hollingbourne Gdns WEA W13......97 H4
Hollingbourne Rd HNHL SE24.....162 D1
Hollingsworth Rd
  CROY/NA CR0.............................212 D4
Hollington Crs NWMAL KT3........192 C3
Hollington Rd EHAM E6................107 K2
  TOTM N17..50 C5
Hollingworth Cl
  E/WMO/HCT KT8...........................188 E1
Hollingworth Rd
  STMC/STPC BR5.........................201 G4
Hollman Gdns
  STRHM/NOR SW16.....................180 C2

Holloway Cl WDR/YW UB7...........112 D5
Holloway La WDR/YW UB7...........112 D4
Holloway Rd ARCH N19...................66 D6
  EHAM E6...107 K2
  HOLWY N7..85 F1
  WAN E11...88 B1
Holloway St HSLW TW3................135 G4
The Hollow WFD IG8........................38 D6
Holly Av STAN HA7...........................44 A5
  WOT/HER KT12.............................188 C5
Holly Bank MUSWH N10 *..............48 A3
Hollybank Cl HPTN TW12..............173 F1
Hollybrake Cl CHST BR7...............185 J3
Hollybush Cl
  KTN/HRWW/WS HA3......................42 E4
  OXHEY WD19...................................27 C2
  WAN E11..70 E2
Hollybush Gdns BETH E2.............104 D2
Hollybush Hl WAN E11.....................70 D4
Hollybush Pl BETH E2....................104 D2
Hollybush Rd KUTN/CMB KT2....175 F1
Holly Bush Steps HAMP NW3 *....83 F3
Hollybush St PLSTW E13..............107 F2
Hollybush Ter NRWD SE19 *.........181 F2
Hollybush V HAMP NW3..................83 G2
Holly Cl BECK BR3..........................199 F1
  BKHH IG9...39 H5
  FELT TW13......................................172 D1
  WLGTN SM6....................................210 B5
  WLSDN NW10...................................81 G5
Holly Crs BECK BR3.......................198 C2
  WFD IG8..52 B5
Hollycroft Av HAMP NW3...............82 E1
  WBLY HA9...62 B6
Hollycroft Cl SAND/SEL CR2......212 A5
  WDR/YW UB7..................................112 D6
Hollydale Cl NTHLT UB5..................78 B3
Hollydale Dr HAYES BR2..............215 K1
Hollydale Rd PECK SE15...............143 K2
Hollydown Wy WAN E11..................88 B1
Holly Dr CHING E4............................37 K2
Holly Farm Rd NWDGN UB2.........114 D5
Hollyfield Av FBAR/BDGN N11......47 K1
Hollyfield Rd BRYLDS KT5...........191 G5
Holly Gdns BXLYHN DA7..............149 G6
  WDR/YW UB7................................112 C2
Hollygrove BUSH WD23 *................28 D2
Holly Gv CDALE/KGS NW9.............62 E4
  PECK SE15.....................................143 G3
  PIN HA5...41 J4
Hollygrove Cl HSLW TW3..............134 E5
Holly Hedge Ter LEW SE13...........145 G6
Holly Hl HAMP NW3..........................83 G2
  WCHMH N21......................................35 F1
Holly Hill Rd BELV DA17................129 J5
Holly Lodge Gdns HGT N6.............66 A6
Hollymead CAR SM5......................209 K1
Holly Ms WBPTN SW10..................120 B5
Holly Mt HAMP NW3 *......................83 G2
Holly Park Gdns FNCH N3...............46 E6
Holly Park Rd FBAR/BDGN N11....47 K1
  HNWL W7...116 A1
Holly Pk FNCH N3.............................46 D6
  FSBYPK N4..67 F4
Holly Rd CHSWK W4 *....................118 A4
  DART DA1...171 G3
  HPTN TW12....................................173 H2
  HSLW TW3.......................................135 G5
  ORP BR6...217 G5
  TWK TW1...156 B3
  WAN E11...70 D4
Holly St HACK E8..............................86 B5
Hollytree Cl WIM/MER SW19........159 G3
Hollytree Pde SCUP DA14 *..........186 D1
Hollyview Cl HDN NW4....................63 J3
Holly Vls HMSMTH W6...................118 E3
Holly Wk HAMP NW3........................83 G2
Holly Wy MTCM CR4......................195 J1
Hollywood Gdns YEAD UB4............95 H5
Hollywood Ms WBPTN SW10 *.....120 B6
Hollywood Rd CHING E4..................51 G1
  WBPTN SW10................................120 B6
Hollywoods CROY/NA CR0...........213 H6
Holman Ct EW KT17 *....................207 J6
Holman Rd BTSEA SW11...............140 C3
  HOR/WEW KT19............................206 D3
Holmbridge Gdns PEND EN3.........25 F5
Holmbrook Dr HDN NW4..................64 B2
Holmbury Ct BUSH WD23...............28 E6
Holmbury Ct WIM/MER SW19.......178 A2
Holmbury Gdns HYS/HAR UB3....113 J1
Holmbury Gv CROY/NA CR0.........214 A6
Holmbury Mnr SCUP DA14 *.........168 B6
Holmbury Pk BMLY BR1................184 C1
Holmbury Vw CLPT E5.....................68 D5
Holmbush Rd PUT/ROE SW15.....159 H1
Holmcote Gdns HBRY N5................85 J3
Holmcroft Wy HAYES BR2............200 E2
Holmdale Gdns HDN NW4..............64 B2
Holmdale Rd CHST BR7.................185 H1
  KIL/WHAMP NW6...........................82 E3
Holmdale Ter SEVS/STOTM N15....68 A4
Holmdene Av HNHL SE24.............142 D6
  MLHL NW7..31 J6
  RYLN/HDSTN HA2..........................42 B6
Holmdene Cl BECK BR3................183 F5
Holmebury Cl BUSH WD23.............28 E4
Holmead Rd FUL/PGN SW6.........140 A1
Holmebury Ct ISLW TW7...............136 B4
Holme Lacey Rd
  LEE/GVPK SE12............................165 J1
Holmes Av MLHL NW7......................46 B1
  WALTH E17..51 H6
Holmes Cl EDUL SE22...................143 H5
Holmesdale Av
  MORT/ESHN SW14.......................137 J4
Holmesdale Cl SNWD SE25.........181 G6
Holmesdale Rd BXLYHN DA7......148 E3
  HGT N6...66 B5
  RCH/KEW TW9...............................137 G2
  SNWD SE25.....................................196 E2

TEDD TW11......................................174 D3
Holmesley Rd FSTH SE23...........164 B1
Holmes Rd KTTN NW5.....................84 B4
  TWK TW1...156 A4
  WIM/MER SW19............................178 B3
Holmes Ter STHWK SE1..................17 J2
Holme Wy STAN HA7........................43 F2
Holmewood Gdns
  BRXS/STRHM SW2......................162 A2
Holmewood Rd
  BRXS/STRHM SW2......................161 K2
  SNWD SE25.....................................181 F6
Holmfield Av HDN NW4....................64 B2
Holmhurst Rd BELV DA17.............129 J5
Holmleigh Av DART DA1................151 F5
Holm Oak Cl PUT/ROE SW15......159 J1
Holmsdale Gv BXLYHN DA7........150 B3
Holmshaw Cl SYD SE26................164 B6
Holmside Ri OXHEY WD19..............27 F5
Holmside Rd BAL SW12................161 F1
Holmsley Cl NWMAL KT3.............192 C3
Holmstall Av CDALE/KGS NW9......44 E6
Holmstall Pde EDGW HA8 *............44 E6
Holmwood Cl BELMT SM2...........208 B6
  NTHLT UB5..78 B4
  RYLN/HDSTN HA2..........................42 C6
Holmwood Gdns FNCH N3.............46 E5
  WLGTN SM6...................................210 B4
Holmwood Gv MLHL NW7..............45 F1
Holmwood Rd BELMT SM2..........208 A6
  CHSGTN KT9..................................206 A3
  GDMY/SEVK IG3...............................72 E6
Holne Cha EFNCH N2.......................65 G3
  MRDN SM4......................................193 K3
Holness Rd SRTFD E15.................88 D4
Holroyd Rd ESH/CLAY KT10........205 G6
  PUT/ROE SW15.............................139 F5
Holstein Wy ERITH DA18...............128 E3
Holstock Rd IL IG1............................72 C1
Holsworth Cl RYLN/HDSTN HA2...60 C2
Holsworthy Sq FSBYW WC1X..........5 H7
Holsworthy Wy CHSGTN KT9.......205 J4
Holt Cl CHIG IG7................................55 F1
  MUSWH N10......................................66 A1
  THMD SE28.....................................109 H6
Holton St WCHPL E1......................105 F3
Holt Rd ALP/SUD HA0......................79 G1
  CAN/RD E16....................................126 D1
The Holt BARK/HLT IG6...................54 C2
  MRDN SM4 *...................................193 K1
  WLGTN SM6...................................210 C2
Holt Wy CHIG IG7.............................55 F1
Holtwhite Av ENC/FH EN2...............23 J3
Holtwhite's Hl ENC/FH EN2............23 H2
Holwell Pl PIN HA5............................59 J1
Holwood Cl WOT/HER KT12..........188 B5
Holwood Park Av ORP BR6...........215 K2
Holwood Pl CLAP SW4 *.................141 J5
Holybourne Av
  PUT/ROE SW15.............................158 D2
Holyhead Cl BOW E3.......................105 J2
Holyoake Ct BERM/RHTH SE16...124 B2
Holyoake Wk EA W5.........................97 J3
  EFNCH N2..47 G6
Holyoak Rd LBTH SE11...................18 A6
Holyport Rd FUL/PGN SW6..........139 F1
Holyrood Gdns EDGW HA8.............44 D5
Holyrood Ms CAN/RD E16............125 K1
Holyrood Rd BAR EN5......................33 G1
Holyrood St STHWK SE1................19 G2
Holywell Cl BERM/RHTH SE16...123 J5
  BKHTH/KID SE3.............................125 K6
  EBED/NFELT TW14........................153 H2
  ORP BR6..217 G2
Holywell La SDTCH EC2A................7 H6
Holywell Rw SDTCH EC2A................7 G5
Holywell Wy
  STWL/WRAY TW19......................152 B3
Home Cl CAR SM5..........................194 E6
  NTHLT UB5..95 K2
Home Ct FELT TW13 *....................153 K5
  SURB KT6 *....................................190 E2
Homecroft Rd SYD SE26..............181 K1
  WDGN N22..49 H4
Home Farm Cl ESH/CLAY KT10...204 B4
  THDT KT7..190 A4
Home Farm Gdns
  WOT/HER KT12.............................188 B6
Homefarm Rd HNWL W7................96 E6
Homefield Av GNTH/NBYPK IG2...72 E2
Homefield Cl STMC/STPC BR5.....202 C1
  WLSDN NW10...................................80 E4
  YEAD UB4..95 H3
Homefield Gdns EFNCH N2............47 H6
  MTCM CR4......................................178 B5
Homefield Ms BECK BR3...............182 D4
Homefield Pk SUT SM1................209 F4
Homefield Rd BMLY BR1...............184 B4
  CHSWK W4..118 C4
  EDGW HA8..45 F2
  WALTH E17..177 H2
  WBLY HA9...79 G5
  WIM/MER SW19............................177 C2
  WOT/HER KT12.............................188 C4
Homefield St IS N1 *..........................7 G3
The Homefield MRDN SM4 *.........193 K1
Home Gdns DAGE RM10...................92 E1
  DART DA1..171 H1
Homeland Dr BELMT SM2............208 F6
Homelands Dr NRWD SE19...........181 F3
Home Lea ORP BR6.......................217 F3
Homeleigh Rd PECK SE15.............144 A6
Homemead Rd MDN SM4 *...............1 H1
Homemead Rd CROY/NA CR0......195 H5
  HAYES BR2....................................200 C2
Home Park Rd
  WIM/MER SW19............................159 K5
Home Park Ter KUT/HW KT1........174 E5
Home Park Wk KUT/HW KT1........190 E1
Home Rd BTSEA SW11..................140 D3
Homer Dr POP/IOD E14..................124 D4
Homer Rd CROY/NA CR0...............198 A3
  HOM E9...87 G4

Homer Rw CAMTN NW1 ....8 D2
Homersham Rd KUT/HW KT1 ....175 H5
Homer St MBLAR W1H 8 D2
Homerton Gv HOM E9 ....87 F3
Homerton High St HOM E9 ....87 F3
Homerton Rd HOM E9 ....87 F3
Homerton Row HOM E9 ....86 E3
Homerton Ter HOM E9 ....86 E4
Homesdale Cl WAN E11 ....70 E2
Homesdale Rd HAYES BR2 ......200 B6
                ORP B6 ....201 K4
Homestead GLDGN NW11 ....64 C2
Homestall Rd EDUL SE22 ....143 K6
Homestead Gdns
            ESH/CLAY KT10 ....204 E3
Homestead Paddock
            STHGT/OAK N14 ....22 B6
Homestead Pk CRICK NW2 ....81 H1
Homestead Rd BCTR RM8 ....74 B6
            FUL/PGN SW6 ....139 J1
            ORP BR6 ....217 H5
The Homestead DART DA1 ....171 F1
Homewillow Cl WCHMH N21 ....35 H1
Homewood Cl HPTN TW12 ....172 E2
Homewood Crs CHST BR7 ....185 K2
Homewood Gdns
            SNWD SE25 * 197 F2
Honduras St FSBYE EC1V 6 B7
Honeybourne Rd
            KIL/WHAMP NW6 ....83 F3
Honeybourne Wy
            STMC/STPC BR5 ....201 H5
Honeybrook Rd BAL SW12 ....161 H2
Honey Cl DAGE RM10 ....92 E4
Honeyden Rd SCUP DA14 ....187 F2
Honeyman Cl CRICK NW2 ....82 A1
Honeypot Cl CDALE/KGS NW9 ....62 B1
Honeypot La CDALE/KGS NW9 ....62 B1
            KTN/HRWW/WS HA3 ....44 B6
            STAN HA7 ....44 A4
Honeysett Rd TOTM N17 ....50 B5
Honeysuckle Cl STHL UB1 ....95 J6
Honeysuckle Gdns
            CROY/NA CR0 ....198 A4
Honeywell Rd BTSEA SW11 .....160 D1
Honeywood Rd ISLW TW7 * 136 B5
            WLSDN NW10 ....81 H1
Honeywood Wk CAR SM5 ....209 K2
Honister Cl STAN HA7 ....43 H4
Honister Gdns STAN HA7 ....43 H4
Honister Pl STAN HA7 ....43 H4
Honiton Gdns MLHL NW7 * 46 C2
            PECK SE15 * 143 K3
Honiton Rd KIL/WHAMP NW6 ......100 D1
            ROMW/RG RM7 ....75 F3
            WELL DA16 ....148 A3
Honley Rd CAT SE6 ....164 E2
Honnor Gdns ISLW TW7 ....135 J5
Honor Oak Pk FSTH SE23 ....163 E3
Honor Oak Ri FSTH SE23 ....163 K1
Honor Oak Rd FSTH SE23 ....163 K3
Hood Av MORT/ESHN SW14 .....137 K6
            STHGT/OAK N14 ....34 B1
            STMC/STPC BR5 ....202 C2
Hood Cl CROY/NA CR0 ....196 C5
Hoodcote Gdns WCHMH N21 .....35 H2
Hood Rd RAIN RM13 ....93 G6
            RYNPK SW20 ....176 C3
Hood Wk ROMW/RG RM7 ....56 D4
Hooker's Rd WALTH E17 ....51 F5
Hook Farm Rd HAYES BR2 ....200 C2
Hook Green La RDART DA2 ......170 C6
Hooking Gn RYLN/HDSTN HA2 ....60 B2
Hook La WELL DA16 ....148 A6
Hook Ri North SURB KT6 ....206 B1
Hook Ri South CHSGTN KT9 .....206 B1
Hook Rd CHSGTN KT9 ....205 K5
            HOR/WEW KT19 ....206 E5
            SURB KT6 ....191 F6
Hooks Hall Dr DAGE RM10 ....92 E1
Hookstone Wy WFD IG8 ....53 H3
The Hook BAR EN5 ....33 H1
Hook (U/P (Kingston By-Pass)
            CHSGTN KT9 ....205 K1
Hook Wk EDGW HA8 ....44 E2
Hooper Rd CAN/RD E16 ....106 E5
Hooper's Ms ACT W3 * 117 K1
Hoop La GLDGN NW11 ....64 D4
Hope Cl BTFD TW8 ....117 F5
            BKHH IG9 ....38 H4
            IS N1 ....85 J4
            LEE/GVPK SE12 ....166 A5
            SUT SM1 ....209 G3
Hopedale Rd CHARL SE7 ....126 A6
Hopefield Av
            KIL/WHAMP NW6 ....100 C1
Hope Gdns ACT W3 * 117 J2
Hope La ELTH/MOT SE9 ....167 G5
Hope Pk BMLY BR1 ....183 J3
Hopes Cl HEST TW5 ....115 F6
Hope Sq LVPST EC2M 13 G2
Hope St BTSEA SW11 ....140 C5
Hopetown St WCHPL E1 * 13 K2
Hopewell St CMBW SE5 ....142 E1
Hopewell Yd CMBW SE5 ....142 E1
Hopgood St SHB W12 ....119 F1
Hopkins Cl MUSWH N10 ....48 A3
Hopkins Ms SRTFD E15 ....88 D6
Hopkinsons Pl CAMTN NW1 * 84 B1
Hopkins Rd LEY E10 ....69 K4
Hopkins St SOHO/CST W1F 10 B4
Hoppett Rd CHING E4 ....38 C5
Hoppety Rd YEAD UB4 ....94 B3
Hoppingwood Av NWMAL KT3 ..176 B6
Hop Pk BMLY YEAD UB4 ....94 B3
Hopton Gdns NWMAL KT3 ....192 D3
Hopton Pde
            STRHM/NOR SW16 * 179 K1
Hopton Rd
            STRHM/NOR SW16 ....179 K1
            WOOL/PLUM SE18 ....127 G3

Hoptons Gdns STHWK SE1 * 12 B7
Hopton St STHWK SE1 ....12 B7
Hoptree Cl
            NFNCH/WDSPK N12 ....33 F6
Hopwood Cl TOOT SW17 ....160 B5
Hopwood Rd WALW SE17 ....122 E6
Hopwood Wk HACK E8 * 86 C5
Horace Av ROMW/RG RM7 ....75 F5
Horace Rd BARK/HLT IG6 ....54 C6
            FSTGT E7 ....89 F2
            KUT/HW KT1 ....175 F5
Horatio Pl POP/IOD E14 ....125 F2
Horatio St BETH E2 ....7 K3
Horatius Wy CROY/NA CR0 ......211 F4
Horbury Crs NTGHL W11 ....100 E6
Horbury Ms NTGHL W11 ....100 D6
Horder Rd FUL/PGN SW6 ....139 H2
Hordle Prom East PECK SE15 ...143 G1
Hordle Prom North PECK SE15 ..143 G1
Hordle Prom West PECK SE15 ...143 F1
Horley Cl BXLYHS DA6 ....149 H6
Horley Rd ELTH/MOT SE9 ....166 D6
Hormead Rd MV/WKIL W9 ....100 D3
Hornbeam Cl IL IG1 ....90 D5
            LBTH SE11 ....17 J6
            MLHL NW7 ....31 H5
            NTHLT UB5 ....77 K3
Hornbeam Gdns BTFD TW8 ......136 C1
Hornbeam Gdns NWMAL KT3 ..192 D3
Hornbeam Gv CHING E4 ....38 D5
Hornbeam Rd BKHH IG9 ....39 H5
            YEAD UB4 ....95 C4
Hornbeams Ri BOW E3 ....87 H6
Hornbeams Ri FBAR/BDGN N11 ..48 A2
Hornbeam Wy HAYES BR2 ....201 F3
Hornbuckle Cl
            RYLN/HDSTN HA2 ....60 D6
Hornby Cl HAMP NW3 ....83 H5
Horncastle Cl LEE/GVPK SE12 .165 K2
Horncastle Rd LEE/GVPK SE12 .165 K2
Hornchurch Cl KUTN/CMB KT2 ..174 E1
Hornchurch Rd HCH RM12 ....75 H5
Horndean Cl PUT/ROE SW15 ....158 D3
Horndon Cl CRW RM5 ....56 E4
Horndon Gn CRW RM5 ....56 E4
Horndon Rd CRW RM5 ....56 E4
Horne House CHARL SE7 * 146 C1
Horner La MTCM CR4 ....178 C5
Horne Wy PUT/ROE SW15 ....139 F3
Hornfair Rd CHARL SE7 ....146 C1
Hornford Wy ROMW/RG RM7 .....75 G4
Horniman Dr FSTH SE23 ....163 J3
Horning Cl ELTH/SE23 * 163 J3
Horning Cl ELTH/MOT SE9 ....166 D6
Horn La ACT W3 ....117 K1
            GNWCH SE10 ....125 K4
            WFD IG8 ....52 E2
Horn Link Wy GNWCH SE10 .....125 K3
Horn Park Cl LEE/GVPK SE12 ...146 A6
Horn Park La LEE/GVPK SE12 ...146 A6
Horns Cft BARK IG11 ....90 E5
Horns End Pl PIN HA5 ....59 G2
Hornsey Chambers CLPT E5 * 68 D6
Hornsey La HGT N6 ....66 C6
Hornsey Lane Est ARCH N19 ......66 D4
Hornsey Lane Gdns HGT N6 ....66 C5
Hornsey Park Rd
            CEND/HSY/T N8 ....49 F6
Hornsey Ri ARCH N19 ....66 C4
Hornsey Rise Gdns ARCH N19 ....66 D4
Hornsey Rd ARCH N19 ....66 C4
Hornsey St HOLWY N7 ....85 F3
Hornshay St PECK SE15 ....123 K6
Horns Rd BARK/HLT IG6 ....72 C2
Hornton Pl KENS W8 ....119 K2
Hornton St KENS W8 ....119 K2
Horsa Rd ERITH DA8 ....149 K1
            LEE/GVPK SE12 ....166 B2
Horsebridges Cl DAGW RM9 ....92 A6
Horsecroft Cl ORP BR6 ....202 C5
Horsecroft Rd EDGW HA8 ....45 F3
Horse Fair KUT/HW KT1 ....174 E5
Horseferry Pl GNWCH SE10 .....125 F6
Horseferry Rd POP/IOD E14 .....105 G6
            WEST SW1P 16 C5
Horse Guards Av WHALL SW1A ..16 D1
Horse Guards Rd WHALL SW1A ..16 D1
Horse La EHAM E6 ....108 B6
Horsell Rd HBRY N5 ....85 G3
            STMC/STPC BR5 ....186 B4
Horselydown La STHWK SE1 .....19 J2
Horsenden Av GFD/PVL UB6 ......78 E3
Horsenden Crs GFD/PVL UB6 .....79 F3
Horsenden La North
            GFD/PVL UB6 ....78 E4
Horsenden La South
            GFD/PVL UB6 ....79 G6
Horseshoe Cl CRICK NW2 ....63 K6
            POP/IOD E14 ....125 F5
Horse Shoe Crs NTHLT UB5 ....96 A1
Horseshoe La ENF/FH EN2 ....23 J4
            TRDG/WHET N20 ....32 B3
Horseshoe Ms
            BRXS/STRHM SW2 ....141 K5
Horse Yd IS N1 * 85 H6
Horsfeld Gdns ELTH/MOT SE9 .146 D6
Horsfeld Rd ELTH/MOT SE9 .....146 C6
Horsford Rd
            BRXS/STRHM SW2 ....142 A6
Horsham Av
            NFNCH/WDSPK N12 ....47 J1
Horsham Rd BXLYHS DA6 ....169 H1
            EBED/NFELT TW14 ....153 F1
Horsley Dr CROY/NA CR0 ....214 A5
            KUTN/CMB KT2 ....174 E1
Horsley Rd BMLY BR1 ....184 A4
            CHING E4 ....38 A1
Horsley St WALW SE17 ....122 E6
Horsmans Pl DART DA1 * 171 H2
Horsman St CMBW SE5 ....122 D6
Horsmonden Cl ORP BR6 ....201 K4
Horsmonden Rd BROCKY SE4 ..144 C6
Hortensia Rd WBPTN SW10 ......140 B1
Horticultural Pl CHSWK W4 ....118 A5
Horton Av CRICK NW2 ....82 C2
Horton Bridge Rd
            WDR/YW UB7 ....112 C1

Horton Cl WDR/YW UB7 ....112 C1
Horton Pde WDR/YW UB7 * 112 C1
Horton Rd HACK E8 ....86 D4
            WDR/YW UB7 ....112 B1
Horton St LEW SE13 ....144 E4
Horton Wy CROY/NA CR0 ....198 A2
Hortus Rd NWDGN UB2 ....114 D2
Hosack Rd TOOT SW17 ....161 F4
Hoser Av LEE/GVPK SE12 ....165 K4
Hosier La STBT EC1A 12 B2
Hoskins Cl CAN/RD E16 ....107 C5
            HYS/HAR UB3 ....113 J5
Hoskins St GNWCH SE10 ....125 C5
Hospital Bridge Rd WHTN TW2 .155 F3
Hospital Rd HSLW TW3 ....135 F4
Hospital Wy LEW SE13 ....165 G1
Hotham Cl E/WMO/HCT KT8 .....173 F6
Hotham Rd PUT/ROE SW15 ......139 F4
Hotham Road Ms
            WIM/MER SW19 ....178 B3
Hotham St SRTFD E15 ....88 C6
Hothfield Pl BERM/RHTH SE16 .123 K3
Hotspur Rd NTHLT UB5 ....96 A1
Hotspur St LBTH SE11 ....122 B5
Houblon Rd
            RCHPK/HAM TW10 ....137 F6
Houghton Cl HACK E8 ....86 B4
            HPTN TW12 ....172 E2
Houghton Rd SEVS/STOTM N15 .68 B1
Houghton St LINN WC2A * 11 H4
Houlder Crs CROY/NA CR0 ....211 H4
Houndsden Rd WCHMH N21 ....35 F1
Houndsditch HDTCH EC3A 13 H3
Houndsfield Rd ED N9 ....36 D2
Hounslow Gdns HSLW TW3 ......135 G5
Hounslow Rd
            EBED/NFELT TW14 ....154 A2
            FELT TW13 ....154 C6
            WHTN TW2 ....155 H1
Houseman Wy CMBW SE5 ....142 E1
Houston Rd FSTH SE23 ....164 B4
            SURB KT6 ....190 C3
Hove Av WALTH E17 ....69 H2
Hoveden Rd CRICK NW2 ....82 B3
Hove Gdns SUT SM1 ....194 A5
Hoveton Rd THMD SE28 ....109 J5
Howard Av BXLY DA5 ....168 E3
Howard Cl ACT W3 ....98 D5
            BUSH WD23 ....28 E2
            CRICK NW2 ....82 C2
            FBAR/BDGN N11 ....34 B6
            HPTN TW12 ....173 H5
            LOU IG10 ....39 J1
Howard Rd BARK IG11 ....90 D6
            BMLY BR1 ....183 K3
            CRICK NW2 ....82 B2
            DART DA1 ....171 K1
            EHAM E6 ....107 K1
            IL IG1 ....90 B2
            ISLW TW7 ....136 A4
            NWMAL KT3 ....176 B6
            PGE/AN SE20 ....181 K4
            SEVS/STOTM N15 ....68 A3
            SNWD SE25 ....197 H2
            STHL UB1 ....96 B5
            STNW/STAM N16 ....86 A2
            SURB KT6 ....191 G3
            WALTH E17 ....51 J4
            WLGTN SM6 * 88 C1
Howards Cl PIN HA5 * 41 F5
Howards Crest Cl BECK BR3 ....183 F5
Howard's La PUT/ROE SW15 ....139 F5
Howard's Rd PLSTW E13 ....106 E2
Howard St THDIT KT7 ....190 C4
Howards Wy
            WAND/EARL SW18 ....160 A2
Howard Wk EFNCH N2 ....65 G1
Howard Wy BAR EN5 ....20 B6
Howarth Rd ABYW SE2 ....128 B5
Howberry Cl EDGW HA8 ....43 K2
Howberry Rd EDGW HA8 ....43 K5
            THHTH CR7 ....180 E4
Howbury La ERITH DA8 ....150 E2
Howbury Rd PECK SE15 ....143 K4
Howcroft Crs FNCH N3 ....46 E2
Howcroft La GFD/PVL UB6 ....96 D2
Howden Cl THMD SE28 ....109 K6
Howden Rd SNWD SE25 ....181 G5
Howden St PECK SE15 ....143 H4
Howe Cl ROMW/RG RM7 ....56 C1
Howell Cl CHDH RM6 ....73 K2
Howell Wk STHWK SE1 ....18 B7
Howerd Wy BKHTH/KID SE3 .....146 D2
Howes Cl FNCH N3 ....46 E6
Howfield Pl TOTM N17 * 50 B6
Howgate Rd
            MORT/ESHN SW14 ....138 A4
Howick Pl WESTW SW1E 16 B5
Howie St BTSEA SW11 ....140 D1
Howitt Cl HAMP NW3 ....83 J4
Howitt Rd HAMP NW3 ....83 J4
Howitts Cl ESH/CLAY KT10 ....204 A4
Howland Ct PIN HA5 ....42 A2
Howland Est BERM/RHTH SE16 .123 K3
Howland Ms East FITZ W1T 10 B1
Howland St FITZ W1T 10 B1
Howland Wy
            BERM/RHTH SE16 ....124 B2
Howletts La RSLP HA4 ....58 A3
Howletts Rd HNHL SE24 ....162 D1
Howley Pl BAY/PAD W2 ....101 G4
Howley Rd CROY/NA CR0 ....211 H1
Howsman Rd BARN SW13 ....118 D6
Howson Rd BROCKY SE4 ....144 B5
Howson Ter
            RCHPK/HAM TW10 * 157 F1
Hows St BETH E2 ....7 K1
Howton Pl BUSH WD23 ....28 D3
Hoxton Market IS N1 ....7 G5
Hoxton Sq IS N1 ....7 G5
Hoxton St IS N1 ....7 H5
Hoylake Gdns MTCM CR4 ....179 H6
            OXHEY WD19 ....27 H6
            RSLP HA4 ....59 G5
Hoylake Rd ACT W3 ....99 G5
Hoyland Cl PECK SE15 * 143 J1
Hoyle Rd TOOT SW17 ....178 D1

Hoy St CAN/RD E16 ....106 D5
Hubbard Dr CHSGTN KT9 ....205 J4
Hubbard Rd WNWD SE27 ....162 D6
Hubbard St SRTFD E15 ....88 C6
Hubbard St SRTFD E15 * 88 C6
Hubert Gv BRXN/ST SW9 ....141 K4
Hubert Rd EHAM E6 ....107 H2
            RAIN RM13 ....111 H1
Huddart St BOW E3 ....105 H4
Huddleston Cl BETH E2 * 104 E1
Huddlestone Rd CRICK NW2 ....81 K4
            FSTGT E7 ....88 E2
Huddleston Rd HOLWY N7 ....84 C1
Hudson Cl SHB W12 * 99 K6
Hudson Pl WOOL/PLUM SE18 ...127 H5
Hudson Rd BXLYHN DA7 ....149 G3
            HYS/HAR UB3 ....133 H5
Huggin Hl BLKFR EC4V 12 D5
Huggin Pl BRXS/STRHM SW2 ...162 A3
Hughan Rd SRTFD E15 ....88 B3
Hugh Dalton Av FUL/PGN SW6 .119 J6
Hughenden Av
            KTN/HRWW/WS HA3 ....61 H2
Hughenden Gdns NTHLT UB5 .....95 G3
Hughenden Rd WPK KT4 ....192 D4
Hughes Cl NFNCH/WDSPK N12 ..47 G1
Hughes Rd HYS/HAR UB3 ....95 F6
Hughes Ter CAN/RD E16 * 106 D4
Hugh Gaisford St
            FUL/PGN SW6 * 119 J6
Hugh Ms PIM SW1V 15 K7
Hugh Pl WEST SW1P 16 C6
Hugh St PIM SW1V 15 K7
Hugo Gdns RAIN RM13 ....93 H4
Hugo Rd ARCH N19 ....84 C2
Huguenot Pl
            WAND/EARL SW18 ....140 B6
Huitt Sq BTSEA SW11 ....140 C4
Hullbridge Ms IS N1 ....85 K5
Hull Cl BERM/RHTH SE16 ....124 A1
Hull St FSBYE EC1V 6 C5
Hulme Pl STHWK SE1 ....18 D3
Hulse Av BARK IG11 ....90 D4
            ROMW/RG RM7 ....56 E2
Hulsewood Cl RDART DA2 ....170 E5
Hulverston Cl BELMT SM2 ....209 F6
Humber Cl WDR/YW UB7 ....112 A1
Humber Dr NKENS W10 ....100 B3
Humber Rd BKHTH/KID SE3 .....125 K6
            CRICK NW2 ....81 J6
            DART DA1 ....151 G6
Humberstone Rd PLSTW E13 ...107 G2
Humbolt Rd HMSMTH W6 ....119 H6
Humes Av HNWL W7 ....116 A3
Humphrey Cl CLAY IG5 * 53 K3
Humphrey St STHWK SE1 * 19 J7
Humphries Cl DAGW RM9 ....92 B3
Hundred Acre
            CDALE/KGS NW9 ....45 H5
Hungerford Bridge CHCR WC2N ..11 F6
Hungerford Rd HOLWY N7 ....84 E3
Hungerford St WCHPL E1 * 104 D5
Hunsdon Cl DAGW RM9 ....92 A4
Hunsdon Rd NWCR SE14 ....144 A1
Hunslett St BETH E2 * 104 E1
Hunston Rd MRDN SM4 ....193 K5
Hunt Cl BKHTH/KID SE3 * 145 K3
            NTGHL W11 ....119 G1
Hunter Cl STHWK SE1 ....19 F5
            TOOT SW17 ....161 F3
            WLGTN SM6 ....210 E6
Hunter Ct CMBW SE5 * 142 E5
Huntercombe Gdns
            OXHEY WD19 ....41 G1
Hunter Rd RYNPK SW20 ....177 F4
            THHTH CR7 ....180 E6
Hunters Cl BXLY DA5 ....170 B5
Hunters Ct RCH/KEW TW9 ....136 E6
Hunter's Gv CRW RM5 ....56 D1
            HYS/HAR UB3 ....113 K1
            KTN/HRWW/WS HA3 ....61 J1
            ORP BR6 ....216 C2
Hunters Hall Rd DAGE RM10 ....92 C1
Hunters La WATW WD18 ....26 A1
Hunters Meadow NRWD SE19 ..163 F6
Hunters Rd CHSGTN KT9 ....206 A1
Hunters Sq DAGE RM10 ....92 C2
Hunter St BMSBY WC1N 5 G5
Hunters Wy CROY/NA CR0 ....212 A2
            ENC/FH EN2 ....23 G2
Huntingdon Cl MTCM CR4 ....195 K1
            NTHLT UB5 ....78 C5
Huntingdon Gdns CHSWK W4 ...137 K1
            WPK KT4 ....193 F6
Huntingdon Rd ED N9 ....36 E3
            EFNCH N2 ....47 J6
Huntingdon St CAN/RD E16 ......106 D5
            IS N1 ....85 F5
Huntingfield CROY/NA CR0 ....213 H5
Huntingfield Rd
            PUT/ROE SW15 ....138 D5
Hunting Gate Cl ENC/FH EN2 .....23 G4
Hunting Gate Dr CHSGTN KT9 ..206 A5
Hunting Gate Ms WHTN TW2 * .155 K3
Huntland Cl RAIN RM13 ....111 K4
Huntley St GWRST WC1E 10 C1
Huntley Wy RYNPK SW20 * 176 D5
Huntly Dr FNCH N3 ....46 E2
Huntly Rd SNWD SE25 ....197 E1
Hunton St WCHPL E1 ....104 C4
Hunt Rd NWDGN UB2 ....115 F3
Hunt's Cl BKHTH/KID SE3 ....145 K3
Hunt's La SRTFD E15 ....106 A1
Huntsman St WALW SE17 ....19 F6
Huntsman Cl FELT TW13 ....154 A6
Huntsman St WALW SE17 ....19 F6
Hunts Medde Cl CHST BR7 ....184 D3
Hunts Medde Cl CHST BR7 ....184 E3

Huntsmoor Rd
            HOR/WEW KT19 ....207 F3
Huntspill St TOOT SW17 ....160 B5
Hunts Slip Rd DUL SE21 ....163 F5
Huntsworth Ms CAMTN NW1 ....3 H3
Hurdwick Pl CAMTN NW1 * 4 A2
Hurley Cl WOT/HER KT12 ....188 A1
Hurley Crs BERM/RHTH SE16 ...124 A1
Hurley Rd GFD/PVL UB6 ....96 B6
Hurlfield RDART DA2 ....171 F5
Hurlingham Gdns
            FUL/PGN SW6 ....139 J4
Hurlingham Pk
            FUL/PGN SW6 * 139 J3
Hurlingham Rd BXLYHN DA7 .....149 G1
            FUL/PGN SW6 ....139 J3
Hurlingham Sq
            FUL/PGN SW6 * 139 K4
Hurlock St HBRY N5 ....85 H1
Hurlstone Rd SNWD SE25 ....196 E2
Hurn Court Rd HSLWW TW4 .....134 C3
Huron Cl ORP BR6 ....216 E4
Huron Rd TOOT SW17 ....161 F4
Hurren Cl BKHTH/KID SE3 ....145 H4
Hurricane House
            WOOL/PLUM SE18 * 126 D3
Hurricane Rd WLGTN SM6 ....210 E5
Hurry Cl SRTFD E15 ....88 C5
Hurst Av CHING E4 ....37 J5
            HGT N6 ....66 C4
Hurstbourne ESH/CLAY KT10 ...205 F4
Hurstbourne Gdns BARK IG11 ....90 D4
Hurstbourne Rd FSTH SE23 .....164 B3
Hurst Cl CHING E4 ....37 J5
            CHSGTN KT9 ....206 C3
            GLDGN NW11 ....65 F4
            HAYES BR2 ....199 J1
            NTHLT UB5 ....77 K4
Hurstcourt Rd SUT SM1 ....194 A5
Hurstdene Av HAYES BR2 ....199 J5
Hurstdene Gdns
            SEVS/STOTM N15 ....68 A4
Hurstfield HAYES BR2 ....199 K2
Hurstfield Crs YEAD UB4 ....94 C4
Hurstfield Rd E/WMO/HCT KT8 .173 F6
Hurst La ABYW SE2 ....128 E5
            E/WMO/HCT KT8 ....189 H1
Hurstleigh Gdns CLAY IG5 ....53 K4
Hurst Pl ABYW SE2 ....128 D5
            DART DA1 * 171 F1
Hurst Ri BAR EN5 ....20 E4
Hurst Rd BFN/LL DA15 ....168 C4
            BKHH IG9 ....39 H3
            BXLY DA5 ....169 F3
            CROY/NA CR0 ....211 K3
            E/WMO/HCT KT8 ....173 H6
            ERITH DA8 ....150 B2
            WALTH E17 ....51 K6
            WCHMH N21 ....35 G3
            WOT/HER KT12 ....188 C1
Hurst St HNHL SE24 ....162 C1
Hurst View Rd SAND/SEL CR2 ..212 A4
Hurst Wy SAND/SEL CR2 ....212 A4
Hurstway Rd NTGHL W11 * 100 B6
Hurstway Wk NTGHL W11 * 100 B6
Hurstwood Av BXLY DA5 ....169 F3
            ERITH DA8 ....150 B2
Hurstwood Dr BMLY BR1 ....184 E6
Hurstwood Rd GLDGN NW11 ......64 C1
Hurtwood Rd WOT/HER KT12 ...188 E4
Huson Cl HAMP NW3 * 83 J5
Hussain Cl HRW HA1 ....78 E4
Hussars Cl HSLWW TW4 ....134 C3
Husseywell Crs HAYES BR2 .....199 K5
Hutchings St POP/IOD E14 ....124 D2
Hutchings Wk GLDGN NW11 ....65 F1
Hutchins Cl SRTFD E15 ....88 A5
Hutchinson Ter WBLY HA9 ....79 K1
Hutton Cl GFD/PVL UB6 ....78 D3
            WFD IG8 ....53 F3
Hutton Gv NFNCH/WDSPK N12 ..47 F2
Hutton La KTN/HRWW/WS HA3 ..42 C3
Hutton Rw EDGW HA8 ....44 E3
Hutton St EMB EC4Y 11 K4
Hutton Wk
            KTN/HRWW/WS HA3 ....42 C3
Huxbear St BROCKY SE4 ....144 C6
Huxley Cl NTHLT UB5 ....77 J5
Huxley Dr CHDH RM6 ....73 H4
Huxley Gdns WLSDN NW10 ....98 B2
Huxley Pde UED N18 * 49 K1
Huxley Pl PLMGR N13 ....35 H3
Huxley Rd LEY E10 ....70 A6
            UED N18 ....35 K6
            WELL DA16 ....148 A4
Huxley Sayze UED N18 * 49 K1
Huxley St NKENS W10 ....100 C2
Hyacinth Cl HPTN TW12 ....173 F2
            IL IG1 ....90 B4
Hyacinth Rd PUT/ROE SW15 ....158 D3
Hyde Cl BAR EN5 ....20 D4
            PLSTW E13 ....106 E1
Hyde Crs CDALE/KGS NW9 ....63 G2
Hyde Dr STMC/STPC BR5 ....202 C1
Hyde Estate Rd
            CDALE/KGS NW9 ....63 H2
Hyde Farm Ms BAL SW12 ....161 J3
Hydefield Cl WCHMH N21 ....35 K3
Hydefield Ct ED N9 ....36 A4
Hyde La BTSEA SW11 ....140 D2
Hyde Park Av WCHMH N21 ....35 J4
Hyde Park Cnr MYFR/PICC W1J ..15 H2
Hyde Park Crs BAY/PAD W2 ....8 D4
Hyde Park Gdns BAY/PAD W2 ....8 D5
            WCHMH N21 ....35 J4
Hyde Park Gardens Ms
            BAY/PAD W2 ....8 B5
Hyde Park Gate SKENS SW7 .....120 B3
Hyde Park Gate Ms
            SKENS SW7 * 120 B2
Hyde Park Pl BAY/PAD W2 ....8 D5
Hyde Park Sq BAY/PAD W2 ....8 C4

Hyde Park St BAY/PAD W2 ...8 C3
Hyderabad Wy SRTFD E15 ...88 C5
Hyde Rd BXLYHN DA7 ...149 G3
　IS N1 ...7 F1
　RCHPK/HAM TW10 ...137 G6
Hydeside Gdns ED N9 ...36 B4
Hyde's Pl IS N1 ...85 H5
Hyde St DEPT SE8 ...124 D6
The Hyde CDALE/KGS NW9 ...45 F6
　CDALE/KGS NW9 ...63 G2
Hydethorpe Av ED N9 ...36 B4
Hydethorpe Rd BAL SW12 ...161 H3
Hyde V GNWCH SE10 ...145 F1
Hyde Wk MRDN SM4 ...193 K4
Hyde Wy ED N9 ...36 B4
　HYS/HAR UB3 ...113 J4
Hyland Cl EMPK RM11 ...75 K3
Hylands Rd WALTH E17 ...52 D5
Hyland Wy EMPK RM11 ...75 K4
Hylton St WOOL/PLUM SE18 ...128 A4
Hynton Rd BCTR RM8 ...73 J6
Hyperion Pl HOR/WEW KT19 ...207 F6
Hyrstdene SAND/SEL CR2 ...211 H2
Hyson Rd BERM/RHTH SE16 ...123 J5
Hythe Av BXLYHN DA7 ...129 G1
Hythe Cl STMC/STPC BR5 ...202 D1
　UED N18 ...36 C6
Hythe Rd THHTH CR7 ...196 D1
　WLSDN NW10 ...99 H2
Hythe St DART DA1 ...171 H1
Hyver HI BAR EN5 ...31 F1

I

Ibbotson Av CAN/RD E16 ...106 D5
Ibbott St WCHPL E1 ...104 E3
Iberian Av WLGTN SM6 ...210 D2
Ibis La CHSWK W4 ...137 K2
Ibis Wy YEAD UB4 ...95 H5
Ibscott Cl DAGE RM10 ...92 E4
Ibsley Gdns PUT/ROE SW15 ...158 D3
Ibsley Wy EBAR EN4 ...21 J6
Iceland Rd BOW E3 ...87 J6
Ickburgh Est CLPT E5 * ...68 D6
Ickburgh Rd CLPT E5 ...86 D1
Ickenham Cl RSLP HA4 ...58 B6
Ickenham Rd RSLP HA4 ...43 J4
Ickleton Rd ELTH/MOT SE9 ...166 D6
Icknield Dr GNTH/NBYPK IG2 ...72 B2
Ickworth Park Rd WALTH E17 ...69 C1
Ida Cl SEVS/STOTM N15 ...67 K2
Ida St POP/IOD E14 ...106 A5
Iden Cl HAYES BR2 ...183 H6
Idlecombe Rd TOOT SW17 ...179 F2
Idmiston Rd SRTFD E15 ...88 D3
　WPK KT4 ...192 C4
Idmiston Sq WPK KT4 ...192 C4
Idol La MON EC3R ...13 G6
Idonia St DEPT SE8 ...144 C1
Iffley Rd HMSMTH W6 ...118 E3
Ifield Rd WBPTN SW10 ...120 A6
Ightham Rd ERITH DA8 ...149 H1
Ilbert St NKENS W10 ...100 C2
Ilchester PI WKENS W14 ...119 J3
Ilchester Rd BCTR RM8 ...91 H3
Ildersly Gv DUL SE21 ...162 E4
Ilderton Rd BERM/RHTH SE16 ...123 K5
Ilex Cl SUN TW16 ...172 B5
Ilex Rd WLSDN NW10 ...81 H4
Ilex Wy STRHM/NOR SW16 ...180 B1
Ilford HI IL IG1 ...90 A1
　MNPK E12 ...89 K2
Ilford La IL IG1 ...90 B2
Ilfracombe Gdns CHDH RM6 ...73 H4
Ilfracombe Rd BMLY BR1 ...165 J5
Iliffe St WALW SE17 ...122 C5
Iliffe Yd WALW SE17 ...122 C5
Ilkley Cl NRWD SE19 * ...180 E2
Ilkley Rd FBAR/BDGN N11 ...48 A2
Ilkley Rd CAN/RD E16 ...107 G4
　OXHEY WD19 ...41 H1
Illingworth Wy EN EN1 ...24 A6
Ilmington Rd
　KTN/HRWW/WS HA3 ...61 K3
Ilminster Gdns BTSEA SW11 ...140 D5
Imber Cl STHGT/OAK N14 ...34 C2
Imber Cross THDIT KT7 ...190 A4
Imber Gv ESH/CLAY KT10 ...189 J4
Imber Park Rd ESH/CLAY KT10 ...189 J5
Imber St IS N1 ...7 F4
Imperial Av STNW/STAM N16 * ...86 A2
Imperial Cl RYLN/HDSTN HA2 ...60 A3
Imperial College Rd
　SKENS SW7 * ...14 B4
Imperial Crs FUL/PGN SW6 ...140 B3
Imperial Dr RYLN/HDSTN HA2 ...60 B3
Imperial Gdns MTCM CR4 ...179 G6
Imperial Ms EHAM E6 ...107 H1
Imperial PI CHST BR7 ...202 D2
Imperial Rd EBED/NFELT TW14 ...153 H2
　FUL/PGN SW6 ...140 A2
　WDGN N22 ...48 E5
Imperial Sq FUL/PGN SW6 ...140 A2
Imperial St BOW E3 ...106 A2
Imperial Wy CHST BR7 ...167 H5
　CROY/NA CR0 ...211 F5
　KTN/HRWW/WS HA3 ...62 A3
Imre Cl SHB W12 ...118 E1
Inca Dr ELTH/MOT SE9 ...167 G2
Inchmery Rd CAT SE6 ...164 E4
Inchwood CROY/NA CR0 ...213 K2
Independent PI HACK E8 ...86 B5
Independents Rd
　BKHTH/KID SE3 ...145 J4
Inderwick Rd CEND/HSY/T N8 ...67 F3
Indescon Ct POP/IOD E14 ...124 E2
India St TWRH EC3N ...13 J4
India Wy SHB W12 ...99 K6
Indigo Ms POP/IOD E14 * ...106 A6
　STNW/STAM N16 ...85 K1
Indus Rd CHARL SE7 ...146 B1

Infant House
　WOOL/PLUM SE18 * ...146 D1
Ingal Rd PLSTW E13 ...106 E3
Ingate PI VX/NE SW8 ...141 G2
Ingatestone Rd MNPK E12 ...71 C5
　SNWD SE25 ...197 J2
　WFD IG8 ...53 F3
Ingelow Rd VX/NE SW8 ...141 G3
Ingersoll Rd PEND EN3 ...24 E1
　SHB W12 ...118 E1
Ingestre PI SOHO/CST W1F ...10 B4
Ingestre Rd FSTGT E7 ...88 E2
　KTTN NW5 ...84 B2
Ingham Cl SAND/SEL CR2 ...213 F6
Ingham Rd KIL/WHAMP NW6 ...82 E2
　SAND/SEL CR2 ...212 E6
Ingleborough St
　BRXN/ST SW9 ...142 B3
Ingleby Dr HRW HA1 ...78 D1
Ingleby Rd DAGE RM10 ...92 D4
　HOLWY N7 ...84 E1
　IL IG1 ...72 B5
Ingleby Wy CHST BR7 ...185 F1
　WLGTN SM6 ...210 D6
Ingle Cl PIN HA5 ...41 K6
Ingledew Rd
　WOOL/PLUM SE18 ...127 J5
Inglefield Sq WAP E1W * ...123 J1
Inglehurst Gdns REDBR IG4 ...71 K2
Inglemere Rd FSTH SE23 ...164 A5
　MTCM CR4 ...178 E3
Ingleside Cl BECK BR3 ...182 D3
Ingleside Gv BKHTH/KID SE3 ...125 J6
Inglewood Cl BARK/HLT IG6 ...55 F2
　POP/IOD E14 ...124 D4
Inglewood Copse BMLY BR1 ...184 D5
Inglewood Rd BXLYHN DA7 ...150 A5
　KIL/WHAMP NW6 ...82 E3
Inglis Rd CROY/NA CR0 ...197 G5
　EA W5 ...98 B6
Inglis St CMBW SE5 ...142 C2
Ingram Av GLDGN NW11 ...65 G4
Ingram Cl LBTH SE11 ...17 H6
　STAN HA7 ...43 J1
Ingram Rd DART DA1 ...171 H3
　EFNCH N2 ...65 J2
　THHTH CR7 ...180 E4
Ingrave Rd ROM RM1 ...75 F1
Ingrave St BTSEA SW11 ...140 D4
Ingrebourne Rd RAIN RM13 ...111 K3
Ingress St CHSWK W4 ...118 B5
Inigo Jones Rd CHARL SE7 ...146 D1
Inks Gn CHING E4 ...52 A1
Inkwell Cl NFNCH/WDSPK N12 ...47 H2
Inman Rd WAND/EARL SW18 ...160 B2
　WLSDN NW10 ...81 G6
Inmans Rw WFD IG8 ...38 E6
Inner Cir CAMTN NW1 ...3 G5
Inner Park Rd
　WIM/MER SW19 ...159 G3
Inner Ring East HTHAIR TW6 ...132 E4
Innes Cl RYNPK SW20 ...177 H5
Innes Gdns PUT/ROE SW15 ...158 E1
Innes St PECK SE15 ...143 F1
Innes Yd CROY/NA CR0 ...211 J1
Inniskilling Rd PLSTW E13 ...107 G1
Innovation Cl ALP/SUD HA0 ...80 A6
Inskip Cl LEY E10 ...69 K6
Inskip Rd BCTR RM8 ...73 K5
Institute PI HACK E8 ...86 D3
Instone Rd DART DA1 ...171 H2
Integer Gdns WAN E11 ...70 B4
International Av HEST TW5 ...114 D5
Inver Ct BAY/PAD W2 * ...101 F5
Inveresk Gdns WPK KT4 ...207 J1
Inverforth Cl HAMP NW3 ...65 G6
Inverforth Rd FBAR/BDGN N11 ...48 B1
Inverine Rd CHARL SE7 ...126 A5
Invermore PI
　WOOL/PLUM SE18 ...127 H4
Inverness Av EN EN1 ...24 A2
Inverness Dr BARK/HLT IG6 ...54 E2
Inverness Gdns KENS W8 ...120 A1
Inverness Ms BAY/PAD W2 ...101 F6
Inverness Rd HSLW TW3 ...134 E5
　NWDGN UB2 ...114 D4
　UED N18 ...50 D1
　WPK KT4 ...193 G5
Inverness St CAMTN NW1 ...84 B6
Inverness Ter BAY/PAD W2 ...101 F6
　WDGN N22 * ...48 C4
Inverton Rd PECK SE15 ...144 A5
Invicta Cl CHST BR7 ...185 F1
　EBED/NFELT TW14 ...153 J3
Invicta Gv NTHLT UB5 ...95 K2
Invicta Pde SCUP DA14 * ...168 C6
Invicta Plaza STHWK SE1 ...12 A7
Invicta Rd BKHTH/KID SE3 ...145 K1
Inville Rd WALW SE17 ...122 E5
Inwood Av HSLW TW3 ...135 G4
Inwood Cl CROY/NA CR0 ...198 B6
Inwood Rd HSLW TW3 ...135 H5
Inworth St BTSEA SW11 ...140 D3
Inworth Wk IS N1 * ...85 J6
Iona Cl CAT SE6 ...164 D2
　MRDN SM4 ...194 A4
Ion Sq BETH E2 * ...104 C1
Ipswich Rd TOOT SW17 ...179 G2
Ireland Cl EHAM E6 ...107 K4
Ireland PI WDGN N22 ...48 E5
Irene Ms HNWL W7 * ...116 A1
Irene Rd FUL/PGN SW6 ...139 K2
　ORP BR6 ...202 A4
Ireton Cl MUSWH N10 ...48 A3
Ireton St BOW E3 ...105 J3
Iris Av BXLY DA5 ...169 F1
Iris Cl CROY/NA CR0 ...198 A5

　EHAM E6 ...107 J4
　SURB KT6 * ...191 G4
Iris Crs BXLYHN DA7 ...129 G6
Iris Rd HOR/WEW KT19 ...206 D3
Iris Wy CHING E4 ...51 H2
Irkdale Av EN EN1 ...24 C1
Iron Bridge Cl NWDGN UB2 ...115 H1
　WLSDN NW10 ...81 G3
Ironbridge Rd STKPK UB11 * ...112 D1
Iron Bridge Rd STKPK UB11 * ...112 E1
Iron Bridge Rd North
　WDR/YW UB7 ...112 D1
Iron Bridge Rd South
　WDR/YW UB7 ...112 D2
Iron Mill Pl DART DA1 ...150 C5
Iron Mill Rd WAND/EARL SW18 ...160 A1
Ironmonger La CITYW EC2V ...12 E4
Ironmonger Pl POP/IOD E14 ...124 E4
Ironmonger Rw FSBYE EC1V ...6 C5
Ironmongers Pl POP/IOD E14 ...124 D4
Ironside Cl BERM/RHTH SE16 ...124 A2
Iron Wy CRW RM5 ...56 E3
Irvine Av KTN/HRWW/WS HA3 ...45 G6
Irvine Cl TRDG/WHET N20 ...33 J4
Irving Av NTHLT UB5 ...77 H6
Irving Gv BRXN/ST SW9 ...142 A3
Irving Ms IS N1 ...85 J4
Irving Rd WKENS W14 ...119 G3
Irving Wy LSQ/SEVD WC2H ...10 D6
　CDALE/KGS NW9 ...63 H2
Irwell Est BERM/RHTH SE16 * ...123 K2
Irwin Av WOOL/PLUM SE18 ...147 K1
Irwin Gdns WLSDN NW10 ...81 K6
Isaac Wy STHWK SE1 ...18 D2
Isabella Cl STHGT/OAK N14 ...34 C2
Isabella Ct RCHPK/HAM TW10 ...157 C1
Isabella Dr ORP BR6 ...216 C2
Isabella Ms IS N1 * ...86 A4
Isabella PI KUTN/CMB KT2 ...175 G1
Isabella Rd HOM E9 * ...86 E3
Isabella St STHWK SE1 ...18 A1
Isabel St BRXN/ST SW9 ...142 A2
Isambard Ms POP/IOD E14 ...124 E3
Isambard PI BERM/RHTH SE16 ...123 K1
Isis Cl PUT/ROE SW15 ...139 F5
　RSLP HA4 ...58 A3
Isis St WAND/EARL SW18 ...160 B4
Island Centre Wy PEND EN3 ...25 J1
Island Farm Av
　E/WMO/HCT KT8 ...188 E2
Island Farm Rd
　E/WMO/HCT KT8 ...188 E2
Island Rd BERM/RHTH SE16 ...124 A4
　MTCM CR4 ...178 E3
Island Rw POP/IOD E14 ...105 H5
Isla Rd WOOL/PLUM SE18 ...127 G6
Islay Gdns HSLWW TW4 ...134 C6
Islay Wk IS N1 * ...85 J4
Islay Whf POP/IOD E14 * ...106 A4
Isledon Rd HOLWY N7 ...85 G1
Islehurst Cl CHST BR7 ...185 F4
Islington Gn IS N1 ...6 A2
Islington High St IS N1 ...6 B2
Islington Park Ms IS N1 ...85 H5
Islington Park St IS N1 ...85 H5
Islington Town Hall IS N1 ...85 H5
Islip Gdns EDGW HA8 ...45 F2
　NTHLT UB5 ...77 J5
Islip Manor Rd NTHLT UB5 ...77 J5
Islip St KTTN NW5 ...84 C3
Ismailia Rd FSTGT E7 ...89 F5
Isom Cl PLSTW E13 ...107 F2
　EN EN1 ...24 B6
　HSLW TW3 ...135 J4
　MHST W1U ...9 H4
Ivanhoe Rd CMBW SE5 ...143 G4
　HSLWW TW4 ...134 C4
Ivatt PI WKENS W14 ...119 J5
Ivatt Wy SEVS/STOTM N15 ...49 H6
Iveagh Av WLSDN NW10 ...98 C1
Iveagh Cl HOM E9 ...87 F6
　WLSDN NW10 ...98 C1
Ivedon Rd WELL DA16 ...148 D3
Ive Farm Cl LEY E10 ...69 J6
Ive Farm La LEY E10 ...69 J6
Iveley Rd CLAP SW4 ...141 H2
Ivere Dr BAR EN5 ...33 F1
Iverhurst Cl BXLYHS DA6 ...148 E6
Iverna Ct KENS W8 ...119 K3
Iverna Gdns
　EBED/NFELT TW14 ...133 C6
　KENS W8 ...119 K3
Iverson Rd KIL/WHAMP NW6 ...82 D4
Ivers Wy CROY/NA CR0 ...213 K5
Ives Gdns ROM RM1 * ...75 H1
Ives Rd CAN/RD E16 ...106 C4
Ives St CHEL SW3 ...14 D6
Ivimey St BETH E2 * ...104 C2
Ivinghoe Cl EN EN1 ...24 A3
Ivinghoe Rd BCTR RM8 ...91 H3
　BUSH WD23 ...28 D2
Ivor Gv ELTH/MOT SE9 ...167 G3
Ivor PI CAMTN NW1 ...2 E7
Ivor St CAMTN NW1 ...84 C5
Ivory Ct FELT TW13 ...153 K5
Ivorydown BMLY BR1 ...165 K6
Ivychurch Cl PGE/AN SE20 ...181 J3
Ivy Church La WALW SE17 * ...123 C5
Ivy Cl DART DA1 ...171 H4
　PIN HA5 ...59 G4
　RYLN/HDSTN HA2 ...77 K2
　SUN TW16 ...172 B5
Ivy Ct BERM/RHTH SE16 * ...123 H5
Ivy Crs CHSWK W4 ...117 K4
Ivydale Rd CAR SM5 ...194 E6
　PECK SE15 ...144 A4
Ivyday Gv STRHM/NOR SW16 ...162 A5
Ivydene E/WMO/HCT KT8 ...188 E2
Ivydene Cl SUT SM1 ...209 G2
Ivy Gdns CEND/HSY/T N8 ...66 E3
　MTCM CR4 ...179 H6
Ivyhouse Rd DAGW RM9 ...91 K4
Ivy La HSLWW TW4 ...134 E5
Ivymount Rd WNWD SE27 ...162 B5

Ivy Rd BROCKY SE4 ...144 C5
　CAN/RD E16 ...106 E5
　CRICK NW2 ...82 A2
　HSLW TW3 ...135 G5
　STHGT/OAK N14 ...34 D2
　SURB KT6 ...191 H6
　TOOT SW17 ...178 D1
　WALTH E17 ...69 J3
Ivy St IS N1 ...7 H3
Ivy Wk DACW RM9 ...92 A4
　NTHWD HA6 * ...40 C6
Ixworth Pl CHEL SW3 ...14 C7
Izane Rd BXLYHS DA6 ...149 G5

J

Jacaranda Cl NWMAL KT3 ...176 B6
Jacaranda Gv HACK E8 ...86 B5
Jackass La HAYES BR2 ...215 F4
Jack Clow Rd SRTFD E15 ...106 C1
Jack Cornwell St MNPK E12 ...90 A2
Jack Dash Wy EHAM E6 ...107 J3
Jackman Ms WLSDN NW10 ...81 G1
Jackman St HACK E8 ...86 D6
Jackson Cl HOM E9 ...87 F5
Jackson Rd BARK IG11 ...90 D6
　EBAR EN4 ...33 J1
　HAYES BR2 ...200 E5
　HOLWY N7 ...85 F2
Jackson's La HGT N6 ...66 A4
Jackson's Pl CROY/NA CR0 ...196 E5
Jackson St WOOL/PLUM SE18 ...127 F6
Jackson's Wy CROY/NA CR0 ...213 J1
Jackson Wy HOR/WEW KT19 ...206 C6
　NWDGN UB2 ...115 G2
Jack Walker Ct HBRY N5 ...85 H2
Jacobs Cl DAGE RM10 ...92 D2
Jacob St STHWK SE1 ...19 K3
Jacob's Well Ms MHST W1U ...9 H3
Jacqueline Cl NTHLT UB5 ...77 J6
Jacqueline Creft Ter HGT N6 * ...66 A3
Jacqueline Vls WALTH E17 * ...70 A2
Jade Cl BCTR RM8 ...73 J5
　CAN/RD E16 ...107 H5
　CRICK NW2 ...64 B4
Jade Ter KIL/WHAMP NW6 * ...83 C5
Jaffe Rd IL IG1 ...72 C5
Jaffray Rd HAYES BR2 ...200 C1
Jaggard Wy BAL SW12 ...160 E2
Jago Cl WOOL/PLUM SE18 ...127 H6
Jago Wk CMBW SE5 ...142 E1
Jamaica Rd BERM/RHTH SE16 ...123 J3
　THHTH CR7 ...196 C3
Jamaica St WCHPL E1 ...104 E4
James Av BCTR RM8 ...74 B5
James Bedford Cl PIN HA5 ...41 G5
James Cl GLDGN NW11 * ...64 C3
　GPK RM2 ...57 J5
　PLSTW E13 ...106 E1
James Collins Cl MV/WKIL W9 ...100 D3
James Gdns TOTM N17 ...49 J3
James Joyce Wk
　BRXN/ST SW9 ...142 C5
James Joyes Wk HNHL SE24 * ...142 C5
James La WAN E11 ...71 F2
James Lee Sq PEND EN3 ...25 J1
Jameson St KENS W8 ...119 K1
James PI TOTM N17 ...50 B4
James St BARK IG11 ...90 C5
　COVGDN WC2E ...11 F5
　EN EN1 ...24 B6
　HSLW TW3 ...135 J4
　MHST W1U ...9 H4
Jamestown Rd CAMTN NW1 ...84 A6
Jamestown Wy POP/IOD E14 ...106 B6
James Watt Wy ERITH DA8 ...130 C6
James Yd CHING E4 * ...52 B2
Jamuna Cl POP/IOD E14 ...105 G4
Jane St WCHPL E1 ...104 D5
Janet St POP/IOD E14 ...124 D3
Janeway Pl BERM/RHTH SE16 ...123 J2
Janeway St BERM/RHTH SE16 ...123 J2
Janson Cl SRTFD E15 ...88 C3
　WLSDN NW10 ...81 F1
Janson Rd SRTFD E15 ...88 C3
Jansons Rd SEVS/STOTM N15 ...50 A6
Japan Crs FSBYPK N4 ...67 F5
Japan Rd CHDH RM6 ...73 K3
Jardine Rd WAP E1W ...105 F6
Jarrett Cl BRXS/STRHM SW2 ...162 C3
Jarrow Cl MRDN SM4 ...194 A2
Jarrow Rd BERM/RHTH SE16 ...123 K4
　CHDH RM6 ...73 J3
　TOTM N17 ...68 D1
Jarrow Wy HOM E9 ...87 H2
Jarvis Cl BAR EN5 ...20 B6
Jarvis Rd EDUL SE22 ...143 G5
　SAND/SEL CR2 ...211 K4
Jasmin Cl NTHWD HA6 ...40 D4
Jasmine Cl IL IG1 ...90 B3
　ORP BR6 ...201 G6
　STHL UB1 ...95 J6
Jasmine Ct LEE/GVPK SE12 ...165 K1
Jasmine Gdns CROY/NA CR0 ...213 K1
　RYLN/HDSTN HA2 ...60 A6
Jasmine Gv PGE/AN SE20 ...181 J4
Jasmine Ter WDR/YW UB7 ...112 D2
Jasmin Rd HOR/WEW KT19 ...206 D4
Jason Wk ELTH/MOT SE9 ...167 F6
Jasper Cl PEND EN3 ...24 E1
Jasper Rd CAN/RD E16 ...107 H5
　NRWD SE19 ...181 G2
Javelin Wy NTHLT UB5 ...95 H2
Jaycroft ENC/FH EN2 ...23 G2
Jay Gdns CHST BR7 ...166 E6
Jay Ms SKENS SW7 ...14 A3
Jean Batten Cl WLGTN SM6 ...211 F5
Jebb Av BRXS/STRHM SW2 ...161 K1
Jebb St BOW E3 ...105 J1

Jedburgh Rd PLSTW E13 ...107 G2
Jedburgh St BTSEA SW11 ...141 F5
Jeddo Ms SHB W12 ...118 C2
Jeddo Rd SHB W12 ...118 C2
Jefferson Cl GNTH/NBYPK IG2 ...72 B2
　WEA W13 ...116 C4
Jeffrey's Pl CAMTN NW1 ...84 C5
Jeffreys Rd CLAP SW4 ...141 K3
　PEND EN3 ...25 H5
Jeffrey's St CAMTN NW1 ...84 B5
Jeffs Cl HPTN TW12 * ...173 G2
Jeffs Rd SUT SM1 ...208 D2
Jeger Av BETH E2 ...7 J1
Jeken Rd ELTH/MOT SE9 ...146 B5
Jelf Rd BRXS/STRHM SW2 ...142 B6
Jellicoe Gdns STAN HA7 ...43 G2
Jellicoe Rd TOTM N17 ...49 K3
　WATW WD18 ...26 E1
Jemmett Cl KUTN/CMB KT2 ...175 J4
Jem Paterson Ct HRW HA1 * ...78 E2
Jengar Cl SUT SM1 ...209 F2
Jenkins La BARK IG11 ...108 C2
Jenkins Rd PLSTW E13 ...107 F3
Jenner Av ACT W3 ...99 F4
Jenner Cl SCUP DA14 ...168 B6
Jenner Rd STNW/STAM N16 ...68 B1
Jenner Wy HOR/WEW KT19 ...206 C6
Jennett Rd CROY/NA CR0 ...211 G1
Jennifer Rd BMLY BR1 ...165 J5
Jennings Cl SURB KT6 ...190 D4
Jennings Rd EDUL SE22 ...163 G1
Jennings Wy BAR EN5 ...20 A4
Jenningtree Rd ERITH DA8 ...150 E1
Jenningtree Wy BELV DA17 ...129 K2
Jenny Hammond Cl WAN E11 ...88 D1
Jenson Wy NRWD SE19 ...181 G3
Jenton Av BXLYHN DA7 ...149 F3
Jephson Rd FSTGT E7 ...89 G5
Jephson St CMBW SE5 ...142 E2
Jephtha Rd
　WAND/EARL SW18 ...159 K1
Jeppo's La MTCM CR4 ...194 E1
Jerdan Pl FUL/PGN SW6 ...139 K1
Jeremiah St POP/IOD E14 ...105 K5
Jeremy's Gn UED N18 ...36 D6
Jermyn St STJS SW1Y ...10 A7
Jerningham Av CLAY IG5 ...54 B5
Jerningham Rd NWCR SE14 ...144 B3
Jerome Crs STJWD NW8 ...2 C6
Jerome St WCHPL E1 ...13 J1
Jerrard St LEW SE13 ...144 E4
Jerrold St IS N1 * ...7 H3
Jersey Av KTN/HRWW/WS HA3 ...43 H5
Jersey Dr STMC/STPC BR5 ...201 J3
Jersey Rd CAN/RD E16 ...107 G4
　HNWL W7 ...116 B2
　HSLW TW3 ...135 G2
　IL IG1 ...90 B2
　IS N1 ...85 J4
　ISLW TW7 ...135 J1
　LEY E10 ...70 B5
　RAIN RM13 ...93 J5
　TOOT SW17 ...179 G3
Jersey St BETH E2 ...104 D2
Jerusalem Pas CLKNW EC1R ...6 A7
Jervis Ct MYFR/PICC W1J ...9 K5
　WOOL/PLUM SE18 ...147 G1
Jerviston Gdns
　STRHM/NOR SW16 ...180 B2
Jervois House
　WOOL/PLUM SE18 * ...146 D1
Jesmond Av WBLY HA9 ...80 B4
Jesmond Cl MTCM CR4 ...179 G6
Jesmond Dene HAMP NW3 * ...83 G4
Jesmond Rd CROY/NA CR0 ...197 G4
Jesmond Wy STAN HA7 ...44 A1
Jessam Av CLPT E5 ...68 D5
Jessamine Rd HNWL W7 ...115 K1
Jessamine Ter SWLY BR8 * ...187 K4
Jesse Rd LEY E10 ...70 B5
Jessett Cl ERITH DA8 ...130 A4
Jessica Rd WAND/EARL SW18 ...160 B1
Jessop Av NWDGN UB2 ...114 E4
Jessops Wy CROY/NA CR0 ...195 H3
Jessup Cl WOOL/PLUM SE18 ...127 H4
Jetstar Wy NTHLT UB5 ...95 J2
Jevington Wy LEE/GVPK SE12 ...166 A3
Jewel Rd WALTH E17 ...51 J6
Jewry St TWRH EC3N ...13 J4
Jews Rw WAND/EARL SW18 ...140 A4
Jews Wk SYD SE26 ...163 J6
Jeymer Av WLSDN NW2 ...81 K3
Jeymer Dr GFD/PVL UB6 ...78 C6
Jeypore Rd WAND/EARL SW18 ...160 B2
Jillian Cl HPTN TW12 ...173 F3
Jim Bradley Cl
　WOOL/PLUM SE18 ...127 F4
Joan Crs ELTH/MOT SE9 ...166 C2
Joan Gdns BCTR RM8 ...74 A6
Joan Rd BCTR RM8 ...74 A6
Joan St STHWK SE1 ...18 A1
Jocelyn Rd RCH/KEW TW9 ...137 F4
Jocelyn St PECK SE15 ...143 H2
Jockey's Flds FSBYW WC1X ...11 H1
Jodane St DEPT SE8 ...124 C4
Jodrell Cl ISLW TW7 ...136 B2
Jodrell Rd BOW E3 ...87 H6
Joel St NTHWD HA6 ...40 D5
Johanna St STHWK SE1 * ...17 J3
John Adam St CHCR WC2N ...11 F7
John Aird Ct BAY/PAD W2 ...101 G4
John Archer Wy
　WAND/EARL SW18 ...160 C1
John Ashby Cl
　BRXS/STRHM SW2 ...161 K1
John Austin Cl KUTN/CMB KT2 ...175 G4
John Bradshaw Rd
　STHGT/OAK N14 ...34 D3
John Burns Dr BARK IG11 ...90 E6
John Campbell Rd
　STNW/STAM N16 ...86 A3
John Carpenter St EMB EC4Y ...11 K5
John Felton Rd
　BERM/RHTH SE16 ...123 H2
John Gooch Dr ENC/FH EN2 ...23 H5
John Goodchild Wy
　KUT/HW KT1 ...175 J6

John Harrison Wy
  BERM/RHTH SE16................124 B3
  GNWCH SE10................125 J3
John Islip St WEST SW1P................16 E7
John Lamb Ct
  KTN/HRWW/WS HA3................42 E4
John Maurice Cl WALW SE17................18 E6
John McKenna Wk
  BERM/RHTH SE16 *................123 H3
John Parker Sq BTSEA SW11 *...140 C4
John Penn St LEW SE13................144 E2
John Perrin Pl
  KTN/HRWW/WS HA3................62 A4
John Prince's St
  CAVSQ/HST W1G................9 K3
John Rennie Wk WAP E1W...104 D6
John Roll Wy
  BERM/RHTH SE16................123 H3
John Ruskin St CMBW SE5...142 C1
John's Cl ASHF TW15................153 F6
John's Cv HDN NW4................64 A1
John Silkin La DEPT SE8................124 A3
Johns La MRDN SM4................194 B2
John's Ms BMSBY WC1N *................5 H7
John Smith Av FUL/PGN SW6...139 J1
John Smith Ms POP/IOD E14...106 B6
Johnson Cl HACK E8................86 C6
Johnson Rd CROY/NA CRO...196 E4
  HAYES BR2................200 C2
  HEST TW5................134 B1
  WLSDN NW10................81 G4
Johnson's Cl CAR SM5................209 K1
Johnson's Ct FLST/FETLN EC4A...11 K4
Johnsons Dr HPTN TW12................173 H4
Johnson's Pl PIM SW1V................121 H5
Johnson St NWDGN UB2................114 D3
  WCHPL E1................104 E5
Johnsons Wy WLSDN NW10...98 D3
John Spencer Sq IS N1 *................85 H4
John's Pl WCHPL E1................104 D5
John's Ter CROY/NA CRO................197 F5
Johnston Cl BRXN/ST SW9...142 A2
Johnstone Rd EHAM E6................107 K2
Johnstone Ter CRICK NW2................82 B1
Johnston Rd WFD IG8................52 E1
John St BMSBY WC1N................5 H7
  EN EN1................24 B6
  HSLW TW3................135 H4
  SNWD SE25................197 H1
  SRTFD E15................88 D6
John Trundle Highwalk
  BARB EC2Y *................12 C1
John Watkin Cl
  HOR/WEW KT19................206 D6
John Williams Cl NWCR SE14...124 H4
John Wilson St
  WOOL/PLUM SE18................127 F4
John Woolley Cl LEW SE13...145 H5
Joiners Arms Yd CMBW SE5 *...142 D2
Joiner St STHWK SE1................19 F1
Jollys La HYS/HAR UB4................96 A4
Jonathan St LBTH SE11................122 A5
Jonson Cl MTCM CR4................195 G1
  YEAD UB4................94 C4
Jordan Cl RYLN/HDSTN HA2...77 K1
Jordan Rd GFD/PVL UB6................79 H6
Jordans Cl DAGE RM10................92 D2
Jordans Ms WHTN TW2................155 K4
Joseph Av ACT W3................99 F5
Joseph Hardcastle Cl
  NWCR SE14................144 A1
Josephine Av
  BRXS/STRHM SW2................142 A6
Joseph Locke Wy
  ESH/CLAY KT10................
Joseph Powell Cl BAL SW12...161 H1
Joseph Ray Rd WAN E11................70 C6
Joseph St BOW E3................105 H4
Joseph Trotter Cl CLKNW EC1R...5 K5
Joshua Cl MUSWH N10................48 B3
  SAND/SEL CR2................211 H5
Joshua St POP/IOD E14................106 A5
Joubert St BTSEA SW11................140 E3
Jowett St PECK SE15................143 G1
Joyce Av UED N18................50 B1
Joyce Green La DART DA1...151 H2
  ERITH DA8................151 H2
Joyden's Wood Rd BXLY DA5...170 B5
Joydon Dr CHDH RM6................73 H3
Joyners Cl DAGW RM9................92 B2
Jubilee Av CHING E4................52 A2
  ROMW/RG RM7................74 D2
  WHTN TW2................155 H3
Jubilee Cl CDALE/KGS NW9...63 F3
  KUT/HW KT1................174 D4
  ROMW/RG RM7................74 D2
  WLSDN NW10................99 G1
Jubilee Crs ED N9................36 E4
Jubilee Dr RSLP HA4................77 G3
Jubilee Gdns STHL UB1................96 A4
Jubilee Market COVGDN WC2E *...11 F5
Jubilee Pl CHEL SW3................120 D5
Jubilee Rd CHEAM SM3................208 B5
  GFD/PVL UB6................79 J6
Jubilee St WCHPL E1................104 E5
Jubilee Ter FUL/PGN SW6................139 H3
The Jubilee GNWCH SE10 *...144 E1
Jubilee Wy ESH/CLAY KT10 *...189 K5
Jubilee Wy CHSGTN KT9................174 E4
  EBED/NFELT TW14................153 K3
  SCUP DA14................168 B4
  WIM/MER SW19................178 A4
Judd St STPAN WC1H................4 E5
Jude Hearn La HYS/HAR UB3...94 A5
Judges' Wk HAMP NW3................83 C1
Judge Wk ESH/CLAY KT10................204 E4
Judith Av CRW RM5................56 D2
Juer St BTSEA SW11................140 D1
Jugglers Ap ORP BR6................202 B5
Jules Thorn Av EN EN1................24 B5
Julia Gdns BARK IG11................109 K1
Juliana Cl EFNCH N2................47 G6

Julian Av ACT W3................98 D6
Julian Cl BAR EN5................21 F4
Julian Hl HRW HA1................60 E6
Julian Pl POP/IOD E14................124 E5
Julian Rd ORP BR6................217 G4
Julian Tayler Pth FSTH SE23 *...163 J4
Julia St KTTN NW5................116 D5
Juliette Rd PLSTW E13................106 E1
Julius Wy SOCK/AV RM15................131 J2
Julius Caesar Wy STAN HA7...29 K6
Julius Nyerere Cl IS N1................5 H1
Junction Av BTSEA SW11................140 D4
Junction Ms BAY/PAD W2................8 C3
Junction Pl BAY/PAD W2 *................8 B3
Junction Rd ARCH N19................84 C1
  DART DA1................171 G1
  EA W5................116 D4
  ED N9................36 C3
  HRW HA1................60 E3
  PLSTW E13................89 F6
  ROM RM1................75 H1
  SAND/SEL CR2................211 K4
  TOTM N17................50 C6
Junction Rd East CHDH RM6...74 A4
Junction Rd West CHDH RM6...73 K4
Juniper Cl BAR EN5................20 B6
  CHSGTN KT9................206 B3
  WBLY HA9................80 B3
Juniper Ct CHDH RM6................73 H3
  KTN/HRWW/WS HA3................43 F4
  NTHWD HA6 *................40 E4
Juniper Crs CAMTN NW1................84 A5
Juniper Gdns WAND/EARL SW18...140 B5
Juniper Gdns MTCM CR4................179 H4
Juniper La EHAM E6................107 J4
Juniper Rd IL IG1................90 A2
Juniper St WCHPL E1 *................104 E6
Juno Wy NWCR SE14................124 A6
Jupiter Wy HOLWY N7................85 F4
Jupp Rd SRTFD E15................88 B5
Jupp Rd West SRTFD E15................88 B6
Justice Wk CHEL SW3 *................120 D6
Justin Cl BTFD TW8................136 E1
Justin Rd CHING E4................51 H2
Jute La PEND EN3................25 G3
Jutland Rd CAT SE6................164 E1
  PLSTW E13................106 E3
Jutsums Av ROMW/RG RM7...74 D5
Jutsums La ROMW/RG RM7...74 D3
Juxon Cl KTN/HRWW/WS HA3...42 B4
Juxon St LBTH SE11................17 H6

K

Kaduna Cl PIN HA5................58 E2
Kale Rd ERITH DA18................128 E2
Kambala Rd BTSEA SW11................140 C3
Kangley Bridge Rd SYD SE26...182 C1
Kaplan Dr WCHMN N21................23 F6
Kara Wy CRICK NW2................82 B2
Karen Cl RAIN RM13................111 G1
Karen Ct BMLY BR1................183 J4
  ELTH/MOT SE9................146 B6
Karenza Ct WBLY HA9................61 J4
Karina Cl CHIG IG7................54 E1
Karma Wy RYLN/HDSTN HA2...60 A5
Kashgar Rd WOOL/PLUM SE18...128 A5
Kashmir Rd CHARL SE7................146 C1
Kassala Rd BTSEA SW11................140 E2
Katharine St CROY/NA CRO...211 J1
Katharine Gdns BARK/HLT IG6...54 C3
  ELTH/MOT SE9................146 E6
Katherine Rd EHAM E6................89 H5
  ALP/SUD HA0................
Kathleen Av ACT W3................98 E4
  ALP/SUD HA0................
Kathleen Rd BTSEA SW11................140 E4
Kayemoor Rd BELMT SM2...209 J5
Kay Rd BRXN/ST SW9................141 K3
Kays Ter SWFD E18 *................52 D5
Kay St BETH E2................104 C1
  SRTFD E15................88 B5
  WELL DA16................148 C2
Kean St HOL/ALD WC2B................11 G4
Keatley Gn CHING E4................51 H2
Keats Av CAN/RD E16................126 A1
  HARH RM3................57 K3
Keats Cl CHIG IG7................54 C2
  PEND EN3................25 H1
  WAN E11................71 F2
  WIM/MER SW19................178 C2
  YEAD UB4................94 B4
Keats Est STNW/STAM N16 *...68 B6
Keats Gv HAMP NW3................83 J2
Keats Pde ED N9................36 C4
Keats Rd BELV DA17................129 K3
  WELL DA16................147 K2
Keats Wy CROY/NA CRO................197 K3
  GFD/PVL UB6................96 B4
  WDR/YW UB7................112 A4
Keble Cl NTHLT UB5................78 C3
  WPK KT4................192 C5
Keble Pl BARN SW13................118 E6
Keble St TOOT SW17................160 B6
Kechill Gdns HAYES BR2................199 K4
Kedleston Dr STMC/STPC BR5...186 D6
Kedleston Wk BETH E2 *................104 D2
Keeble Cl WOOL/PLUM SE18 *...127 G6
Keedonwood Rd BMLY BR1...183 J1
Keel Cl BARK IG11................109 J1
Keele Cl WATW WD18 *................26 E1
Keeley Rd CROY/NA CRO................196 D6
Keeley St HOL/ALD WC2B................11 G4
Keeling Rd ELTH/MOT SE9...146 C6
Keely Cl EBAR EN4................21 J6
Keemor Cl WOOL/PLUM SE18 *...147 F1
Keens Cl STRHM/NOR SW16...179 J1
Keen's Yd IS N1................85 H4
Keepers Ms TEDD TW11................174 D2
The Keep BKHTH/KID SE3................145 K3

KUTN/CMB KT2................175 G2
Keesey St WALW SE17................19 (?)
Keeley Rd BERM/RHTH SE16...123 J3
Keeton's Rd BERM/RHTH SE16...123 J3
Keevil Dr WIM/MER SW19...159 G2
Keighley Cl HOLWY N7................84 E2
Keightley Dr ELTH/MOT SE9...167 H3
Keildon Rd BTSEA SW11................140 E5
Keir Hardie Est CLPT E5 *...68 D5
Keir Hardie Wy BARK IG11...91 G1
  YEAD UB4 *................94 E2
Keith Connor Cl VX/NE SW8...141 G4
Keith Gv SHB W12................118 D2
Keith Rd BARK IG11................108 D1
  HYS/HAR UB3................113 H3
  WALTH E17................51 H4
Kelbrook Rd BKHTH/KID SE3...146 D3
Kelburn Wy RAIN RM13................111 J2
Kelceda Cl CRICK NW2................63 J6
Kelf Gv HYS/HAR UB3................94 D6
Kelfield Gdns NKENS W10................100 B5
Kelfield Ms NKENS W10................100 B5
Kelland Cl CEND/HSY/T N8 *...66 D2
Kelland Rd PLSTW E13................106 E3
Kellaway Rd BKHTH/KID SE3...146 C3
Keller Crescent MNPK E12...89 K2
Kellerton Rd LEW SE13................145 H6
Kellett Rd BRXS/STRHM SW2...142 B5
Kelling Gdns CROY/NA CRO...196 C4
Kellino St TOOT SW17................160 E6
Kellner Rd THMD SE28................128 A3
Kell St STHWK SE1................18 B4
Kelly Av PECK SE15................143 G2
Kelly Cl WLSDN NW10................81 F1
Kelly Ms MV/WKIL W9 *................100 D4
Kelly Rd MLHL NW7................46 C2
Kelly St CAMTN NW1................84 B4
Kelly Wy CHDH RM6................74 A2
Kelman Cl CLAP SW4................141 J3
Kelmore Gv EDUL SE22................143 H5
Kelmscott Cl WALTH E17................51 H4
  WATW WD18................26 E1
Kelmscott Gdns SHB W12...118 D3
Kelmscott Rd BTSEA SW11...160 E4
Kelross Rd HBRY N5................85 H2
Kelsall Cl BKHTH/KID SE3...146 A3
Kelsall Ms RCH/KEW TW9...137 J2
Kelsey La BECK BR3................182 D6
Kelsey Park Av BECK BR3...182 E6
Kelsey Park Rd BECK BR3...182 D5
Kelsey Rd STMC/STPC BR5...186 D5
Kelsey Sq BECK BR3................182 D5
Kelsey St BETH E2................104 C3
Kelsey Wy BECK BR3................182 D6
Kelsie Wy BARK/HLT IG6................54 E2
Kelso Pl KENS W8................120 A3
Kelso Rd CAR SM5................194 B4
Kelston Rd BARK/HLT IG6................54 B5
Kelton Vls KUT/HW KT1 *................175 G5
Kelvedon Cl KUTN/CMB KT2...175 H2
Kelvedon Ho BRXN/ST SW9...142 B3
Kelvedon Rd FUL/PGN SW6...139 J1
Kelvin Av WDGN N22................49 F2
Kelvinbrook E/WMO/HCT KT8...173 G6
Kelvin Cl HOR/WEW KT19................206 C4
Kelvin Crs KTN/HRWW/WS HA3...42 E3
Kelvin Dr TWK TW1................156 C1
Kelvin Gdns CROY/NA CRO...196 A4
  STHL UB1................96 A5
Kelvin Gv CHSGTN KT9................205 K1
  SYD SE26................163 J5
Kelvington Cl CROY/NA CRO...198 B4
Kelvington Rd PECK SE15................164 A5
Kelvin Pde ORP BR6................201 K5
Kelvin Rd HBRY N5................85 H2
  WELL DA16................148 B4
Kember St IS N1................85 F5
Kemble Dr HAYES BR2................215 J1
Kemble Rd CROY/NA CRO................211 H1
  FSTH SE23................164 A3
  TOTM N17................50 C4
Kemble St HOL/ALD WC2B................11 G4
Kembleton Rd BECK BR3................182 E5
  CMBW SE5................142 D4
  CROY/NA CRO................197 G4
Kemey's St HOM E9................87 G3
Kemnal Rd CHST BR7................186 A1
Kempe Rd KIL/WHAMP NW6...100 B1
Kemp Gdns CROY/NA CRO................196 D3
Kempley Rd HAMP NW3................83 H2
Kemp Pl BUSH WD23................28 A1
Kemps Dr NTHWD HA6................40 E6
  POP/IOD E14................105 J6
Kempsford Gdns ECT SW5...119 K5
Kempsford Rd LBTH SE11................17 K7
Kempshott Rd
  STRHM/NOR SW16................179 K3
Kempson Rd FUL/PGN SW6...139 K2
Kempthorne Rd DEPT SE8................124 B4
Kempton Av NTHLT UB5................78 A4
  SUN TW16................172 B4
Kempton Cl ERITH DA8................129 K6
  HGDN/ICK UB10................76 A2
Kempton Ct SUN TW16................172 B4
Kempton Pk SUN TW16 *................172 B4
Kempton Rd EHAM E6................89 K6
  HPTN TW12................172 E5
Kempton Wk CROY/NA CRO...198 B3
Kempt St WOOL/PLUM SE18...127 F6
Kemsing Cl BXLY DA5................169 F2
  THHTH CR7................196 D1
Kemsing Rd GNWCH SE10...125 K5
Kemsley SE3................145 J3
Kenbury Gdns CMBW SE5................142 D3
Kenbury St CMBW SE5................142 D3
Kenchester Cl VX/NE SW8...141 K1
Kendal Av ACT W3................98 C4
  BARK IG11................90 E5
  UED N18................35 K6
Kendal Cl BRXN/ST SW9................142 C1
  EBED/NFELT TW14................153 J3
  YEAD UB4................94 C2
Kendale Rd BMLY BR1................183 H1
Kendal Gdns SUT SM1................194 A6
  UED N18................35 K6
Kendall Av BECK BR3................182 B5
  SAND/SEL CR2................211 K6

Kendall Pl MHST W1U................9 G2
Kendall Rd BECK BR3................182 B5
  ISLW TW7................136 B3
  WOOL/PLUM SE18................146 D2
Kendalmere Cl MUSWH N10...48 B4
Kendal Pde UED N18................35 K6
Kendal Pl PUT/ROE SW15................139 J6
Kendal Rd WLSDN NW10................81 J2
Kendal Steps BAY/PAD W2 *...8 C4
Kender St NWCR SE14................143 K1
Kendoa Rd CLAP SW4................141 J5
Kendon Cl WAN E11................71 F2
Kendra Hall Rd SAND/SEL CR2...211 H5
Kendrey Gdns WHTN TW2................155 K1
Kendrick Ms SKENS SW7 *................14 A6
Kendrick Pl SKENS SW7................14 A6
Kenelm Cl HRW HA1................79 G1
Kenerne Dr BAR EN5................20 C6
Kenilford Rd BAL SW12................161 G2
Kenilworth Av
  RYLN/HDSTN HA2................77 K2
  WALTH E17................51 J5
  WIM/MER SW19................177 K1
Kenilworth Crs EN EN1................24 A2
Kenilworth Gdns
  GDMY/SEVK IG3................73 F6
  LOU IG10................39 K1
  OXHEY WD19................41 C1
  STHL UB1................95 K4
  WOOL/PLUM SE18................147 G5
  YEAD UB4................94 D4
Kenilworth Rd ASHF TW15................152 A5
  BOW E3................105 G1
  EA W5................117 F1
  EDGW HA8................30 E7
  EW KT17................207 J4
  KIL/WHAMP NW6................82 D6
  PGE/AN SE20................182 A4
  STMC/STPC BR5................201 H3
Kenilworth Ter BELMT SM2...208 E5
Kenley Av CDALE/KGS NW9...45 G1
Kenley Cl BXLY DA5................169 H2
  CHST BR7................185 K6
  EBAR EN4................21 J5
Kenley Gdns THHTH CR7................196 C1
Kenley Rd KUT/HW KT1................175 J5
  TWK TW1................156 C1
  WIM/MER SW19................177 K6
Kenley Wk CHEAM SM3................208 B2
  NTGHL W11 *................119 H1
Kenlor Rd TOOT SW17................178 C1
Kenmare Dr MTCM CR4................178 E3
Kenmare Gdns PLMGR N13...35 J6
Kenmare Rd THHTH CR7................196 B3
Kenmere Gdns ALP/SUD HA0...80 D6
Kenmere Rd WELL DA16................148 D3
Kenmont Gdns WLSDN NW10...99 K2
Kenmore Av
  KTN/HRWW/WS HA3................61 G2
Kenmore Crs YEAD UB4................94 D2
Kenmore Gdns EDGW HA8...44 D5
Kenmore Rd
  KTN/HRWW/WS HA3................61 J1
  HACK E8................86 D4
Kenmure Rd HACK E8 *................86 D4
Kenmure Yd HACK E8 *................86 D4
Kennacraig Cl CAN/RD E16...126 A1
Kennard Rd FBAR/BDGN N11...47 K1
  SRTFD E15................88 B5
Kennard St BTSEA SW11................141 F2
  CAN/RD E16................126 A3
Kennedy Av PEND EN3................36 E1
Kennedy Cl MTCM CR4................179 F5
  PIN HA5................41 K2
  PLSTW E13................106 E1
  STMC/STPC BR5................201 J5
Kennedy Rd BARK IG11................90 E6
  HNWL W7................96 E4
Kennedy Wk WALW SE17................19 F7
Kennet Cl BTSEA SW11................140 C5
Kennet Dr YEAD UB4................95 J4
Kenneth Av IL IG1................90 B3
Kenneth Crs CRICK NW2................81 K3
Kenneth Gdns STAN HA7................43 C2
Kenneth More Rd IL IG1...90 B1
Kenneth Rd CHDH RM6................74 A4
Kennet Rd DART DA1................150 D4
  ISLW TW7................136 A4
  MV/WKIL W9................100 D5
Kennet Sq MTCM CR4................178 D4
Kennet St WAP E1W................123 H1
Kennett Wharf La BLKFR EC4V...12 D5
Kenninghall Rd CLPT E5................86 C1
  UED N18................50 E1
Kenning St BERM/RHTH SE16...123 K2
Kenning Ter IS N1................7 H1
Kennings Wy LBTH SE11................122 B5
Kennington Gdns
  KUT/HW KT1................174 E6
Kennington La LBTH SE11................122 A5
Kennington Ov LBTH SE11................122 A6
Kennington Park Gdns
  LBTH SE11................122 C6
Kennington Park Pl
  LBTH SE11................122 B6
Kennington Park Rd
  LBTH SE11................122 B6
Kennington Rd LBTH SE11................17 J7
Kenny Dr CAR SM5................210 A6
Kennylands Rd BARK/HLT IG6...55 G1
Kenny Rd MLHL NW7................46 C2
Kenrick Pl MHST W1U................9 G1
Kensal Rd NKENS W10................100 C3
Kensal Wharf NKENS W10 *...100 C3
Kensington Av MNPK E12................89 K4
  THHTH CR7................180 B4
Kensington Church Ct
  KENS W8................120 A2
Kensington Church St
  KENS W8................119 K1
Kensington Church Wk
  KENS W8................120 A2
Kensington Cl
  FBAR/BDGN N11 *................48 A1
Kensington Ct KENS W8 *................120 A2
Kensington Court Gdns
  KENS W8 *................120 A3

Kensington Court Ms
  KENS W8 *................120 A3
Kensington Court Pl KENS W8...120 A3
Kensington Dr WFD IG8................53 H3
Kensington Gdns IL IG1................71 K5
Kensington Gardens Sq
  BAY/PAD W2 *................101 F5
Kensington Ga KENS W8................120 B3
Kensington Hall Gdns
  WKENS W14 *................119 J5
Kensington High St
  KENS W8 *................119 H4
  WKENS W14................119 H4
Kensington Ml KENS W8................119 K1
Kensington Palace KENS W8 *...120 A1
Kensington Palace Gdns
  KENS W8................120 A1
Kensington Park Gdns
  NTGHL W11................100 D6
Kensington Park Ms
  NTGHL W11................100 D5
Kensington Park Rd
  NTGHL W11................100 E6
Kensington Pl KENS W8................119 K1
Kensington Rd KENS W8................120 B2
  NTHLT UB5................96 A1
  ROMW/RG RM7................74 E3
Kensington Sq KENS W8................120 A2
Kensington Ter SAND/SEL CR2...211 K5
Kent Av DAGW RM9................110 C1
  WEA W13................97 H4
  WELL DA16................148 A6
Kent Cl MTCM CR4................195 K1
  ORP BR6................216 E4
Kent Ct CDALE/KGS NW9 *................45 G5
Kent Dr EBAR EN4................21 K5
  TEDD TW11 *................173 K1
Kentford Wy NTHLT UB5................77 J6
Kent Gdns RSLP HA4................58 E3
  WEA W13................97 H4
Kent Gate Wy CROY/NA CRO...213 H4
Kent House La BECK BR3................182 B2
Kent House Rd BECK BR3................182 A3
Kentish Rd BELV DA17................129 H4
Kentish Town Rd CAMTN NW1...84 B4
Kentish Wy BMLY BR1................184 A5
Kentlea Rd THMD SE28................127 K2
Kentmere Rd
  WOOL/PLUM SE18................127 K4
Kenton Av HRW HA1................61 F6
  STHL UB1................96 A6
  SUN TW16................172 C5
Kenton Gdns
  KTN/HRWW/WS HA3................61 J2
Kenton La KTN/HRWW/WS HA3...43 G4
  KTN/HRWW/WS HA3................61 K1
Kenton Park Av
  KTN/HRWW/WS HA3................61 K1
Kenton Park Cl
  KTN/HRWW/WS HA3................61 J1
Kenton Park Crs
  KTN/HRWW/WS HA3................61 K1
Kenton Park Pde
  KTN/HRWW/WS HA3................61 J1
Kenton Park Rd
  KTN/HRWW/WS HA3................61 J1
Kenton Rd HOM E9................87 F4
  HRW HA1................61 H4
  KTN/HRWW/WS HA3................61 A2
Kenton St STPAN WC1H................4 E7
Kenton Wy YEAD UB4................94 C2
Kent Pas CAMTN NW1................2 E5
Kent Rd CHSWK W4................117 K3
  DAGE RM10................92 D3
  DART DA1................171 F3
  E/WMO/HCT KT8................189 H1
  KUT/HW KT1................174 E6
  RCH/KEW TW9................137 H1
  STMC/STPC BR5................202 C3
  WCHMN N21................35 K3
  WWKM BR4................198 E5
Kent St BETH E2................7 F2
  PLSTW E13................107 F2
Kent View Gdns
  GDMY/SEVK IG3................72 E6
Kent Wy SURB KT6................206 A1
Kentwell Cl BROCKY SE4 *................144 B5
Kentwode Gn BARN SW13................138 D1
Kent Yd SKENS SW7 *................14 C3
Kenver Av NFNCH/WDSPK N12...47 H2
Kenward Rd ELTH/MOT SE9...146 B6
Ken Wy WBLY HA9................62 E6
Kenway Rd ECT SW5................120 A4
Kenwood Av BECK BR3................183 F6
Kenwood Cl CLAY IG5................72 A1
Kenwood Cl HAMP NW3................83 H5
  SWFD E18................53 F6
Kenwood Rd ED N9................36 A6
  HGT N6................65 K3
Kenworthy Rd HOM E9................87 G4
Kenwyn Dr CRICK NW2................81 C1
Kenwyn Rd CLAP SW4................141 J5
  DART DA1................171 H4
  RYNPK SW20................177 F4
Kenya Rd CHARL SE7................146 C1
Kenyngton Pl
  KTN/HRWW/WS HA3................61 J2
Kenyon St FUL/PGN SW6................139 G2
Keogh Rd SRTFD E15................88 C4
Kepler Rd CLAP SW4................141 K4
Keppel Rd DAGW RM9................92 A2
  EHAM E6................89 K5
Keppel St GWRST WC1E................10 D1
Kerbela St BETH E2................104 C3
Kerbey St POP/IOD E14................105 K5
Kerfield Crs CMBW SE5................142 E2
Kerfield Pl CMBW SE5................142 E2
Kerri Cl BAR EN5................20 A5
Kerrison Pl EA W5................116 E1
Kerrison Rd BTSEA SW11................140 D4
  EA W5................116 E1
  SRTFD E15................88 B6
Kerry Av SOCK/AV RM15................131 J2
  STAN HA7................29 K6
Kerry Cl CAN/RD E16................107 F5

PLMGR N13 .....35 F4
Kerry Ct STAN N14 .....24 C6
Kerry Pth NWCR SE14 .....129 G6
Kerry Rd NWCR SE14 .....124 C6
Kersfield Rd PUT/ROE SW15 .159 C1
Kershaw Cl WAND/EARL SW18 .160 C1
Kershaw Rd DAGE RM10 .....92 C1
Kersley Ms BTSEA SW11 * 140 E2
Kersley Rd STNW/STAM N16 .....86 A1
Kersley St BTSEA SW11 .....140 E3
Kerswell Cl SEVS/STOTM N15 .....68 A2
Kerwick Cl HOLWY N7 .....85 F5
Keslake Rd KIL/WHAMP NW6 .....100 B1
Kessock Cl TOTM N17 .....68 D2
Kesteven Cl BARK/HLT IG6 .....55 F2
Keston Av HAYES BR2 .....215 C3
Keston Cl UED N18 .....35 K5
WELL DA16 .....148 D1
Keston Gdns HAYES BR2 .....215 C3
Keston Park Cl HAYES BR2 .....215 K2
Keston Rd PECK SE15 .....143 H4
THHTH CR7 .....196 B2
TOTM N17 .....49 K6
Kestrel Av EHAM E6 .....107 J4
HNHL SE24 .....142 C6
Kestrel Cl CDALE/KGS NW9 .....45 C5
HCH RM12 .....93 K5
KUTN/CMB KT2 .....156 H6
WLSDN NW10 .....81 F3
Kestrel Pl NWCR SE14 * 124 B6
Kestrel Wy CROY/NA CRO 214 B6
HYS/HAR UB3 .....113 C2
Keswick Av PUT/ROE SW15 .....176 B1
WIM/MER SW19 .....177 K5
Keswick Cl SUT SM1 .....209 G2
Keswick Gdns REDBR IG4 .....71 J2
RSLP HA4 .....58 B3
WBLY HA9 .....80 A3
Keswick Ms EA W5 .....97 F3
Keswick Rd BXLYHN DA7 .....149 H3
ORP BR6 .....202 A5
PUT/ROE SW15 .....159 H6
WHTN TW2 .....155 H1
WWKM BR4 .....199 H6
Kettering St
STRHM/NOR SW16 .....179 G2
Kett Gdns BRXS/STRHM SW2 .....142 A6
Kettlebaston Rd LEY E10 .....69 H5
Kettlewell Cl FBAR/BDGN N11 .....48 A2
Kevelioc Rd TOTM N17 .....49 J4
Kevin Cl HSLWW TW4 .....134 C3
Kevington Cl STMC/STPC BR5 .....202 A1
Kevington Dr CHST SE7 .....202 A1
Kew Br RCH/KEW TW9 .....117 H6
Kew Br Arches CHSWK W4 * 117 H6
Kew Bridge Ct BTFD TW8 .....117 H5
Kew Bridge Rd BTFD TW8 .....117 H6
Kew Crs CHEAM SM3 .....208 D1
Kewferry Dr NTHWD HA6 .....40 A1
Kewferry Rd NTHWD HA6 .....40 A2
Kew Foot Rd RCH/KEW TW9 .....137 F5
Kew Gardens Rd
RCH/KEW TW9 .....137 C1
Kew Gn RCH/KEW TW9 .....117 H6
Kew Meadow Pth
RCH/KEW TW9 .....137 H2
Kew Riverside Pk
ELTH/MOT SE9 .....167 J2
Kew Rd RCH/KEW TW9 .....117 G6
RCH/KEW TW9 .....137 F5
Key Cl WCHPL E1 .....104 D3
Keyes Rd CRICK NW2 .....82 B3
DART DA1 .....151 K5
Keymer Rd BRXS/STRHM SW2 .....162 A4
Keynes Cl EFNCH N2 .....47 K6
Keynsham Av WFD IG8 .....38 C6
Keynsham Gdns
ELTH/MOT SE9 .....146 D6
Keynsham Rd ELTH/MOT SE9 .....146 D6
MRDN SM4 .....194 A5
Keyse Rd STHWK SE1 .....19 J5
Keysham Av HEST TW5 .....133 K2
Keystone Crs IS N1 .....5 F3
Keyworth Cl CLPT E5 .....87 G2
Keyworth St STHWK SE1 .....18 B4
Kezia St DEPT SE8 .....124 B5
Khama Rd TOOT SW17 .....160 E1
Khartoum Rd IL IG1 .....90 B3
PLSTW E13 .....107 F2
TOOT SW17 .....160 D1
Khyber Rd BTSEA SW11 .....140 D3
Kibworth St VX/NE SW8 .....142 A1
Kidbrooke Gdns
BKHTH/KID SE3 .....145 K3
Kidbrooke Gv BKHTH/KID SE3 .....145 J2
Kidbrooke La ELTH/MOT SE9 .....146 D5
Kidbrooke Park Cl
BKHTH/KID SE3 .....146 A2
Kidbrooke Park Rd
LEE/GVPK SE12 .....146 A2
Kidbrooke Wy BKHTH/KID SE3 .....146 A3
Kidderminster Pl
CROY/NA CRO 196 C5
Kidderminster Rd
CROY/NA CRO 196 D4
Kidderpore Av HAMP NW3 .....82 E2
Kidderpore Gdns HAMP NW3 .....82 E2
Kidd Pl CHARL SE7 .....126 D5
Kielder Cl BARK/HLT IG6 .....55 F2
Kiffen St SDTCH EC2A 7 F6
Kilberry Cl ISLW TW7 .....135 J2
Kilburn Br KIL/WHAMP NW6 .....82 E6
Kilburn High Rd
KIL/WHAMP NW6 .....83 H4
Kilburn La NKENS W10 .....100 B2
Kilburn Park Rd
KIL/WHAMP NW6 .....100 E2
KIL/WHAMP NW6 .....101 F1
Kilburn Priory ST/WD NW8 .....83 H1
Kilburn Sq KIL/WHAMP NW6 .....82 E6
Kilburn V KIL/WHAMP NW6 .....82 E6
Kildare Cl RSLP HA4 .....59 G5
Kildare Rd CAN/RD E16 .....106 E4
Kildare Ter BAY/PAD W2 .....100 E5
Kildoran Rd CLAP SW4 .....141 K6

Kildowan Rd GDMY/SEVK IG3 .....73 G5
Kilgour Rd FSTH SE23 .....164 B1
Kilkie St FUL/PGN SW6 .....140 B3
Killarney Rd
WAND/EARL SW18 .....160 B1
Kilburns Mill Cl WLGTN SM6 .....195 G6
Kilearn Rd CAT SE6 .....165 H3
Killester Gdns WPK KT4 .....207 K2
Killick St IS N1 .....5 G2
Killieser Av BRXS/STRHM SW2 .....161 K4
Killip Cl CAN/RD E16 .....106 D5
Killowen Av NTHLT UB5 .....78 C3
Killowen Rd HOM E9 * 87 F4
Killyon Rd VX/NE SW8 .....141 H3
Kilmaine Rd FUL/PGN SW6 .....139 H1
Kilmarnock Gdns BCTR RM8 .....91 J1
Kilmarnock Rd OXHEY WD19 .....27 H6
Kilmarsh Rd HMSMTH W6 .....119 F4
Kilmartin Av
STRHM/NOR SW16 .....180 B6
Kilmartin Rd GDMY/SEVK IG3 .....73 G6
Kilmartin Wy HCH RM12 .....93 K3
Kilmington Rd BARN SW13 .....118 D6
Kilmorey Gdns TWK TW1 .....136 C5
Kilmorey Rd TWK TW1 .....136 C5
Kilmorie Rd FSTH SE23 .....164 B3
Kiln Cl HYS/HAR UB3 .....113 G6
Kilner St POP/IOD E14 .....105 J4
Kiln Ms TOOT SW17 .....178 C1
Kiln Pl KTTN NW5 .....84 A2
Kilnside ESH/CLAY KT10 .....205 G5
Kiln Wy NTHWD HA6 .....40 C1
Kiln Wood La ABR/ST RM4 .....57 F1
Kilpatrick Wy YEAD UB4 .....95 J4
Kilravock St NKENS W10 .....100 C3
Kilross Rd EBED/NFELT TW14 .....153 G3
Kilsha Rd WOT/HER KT12 * 188 A3
Kilsby Wk DAGW RM9 .....91 H5
Kimberley Av EHAM E6 .....107 J1
GNTH/NBYPK IG2 .....72 E4
PECK SE15 .....143 K4
ROMW/RG RM7 .....74 E3
Kimberley Ct KIL/WHAMP NW6 .....82 C5
Kimberley Dr SCUP DA14 .....168 E4
Kimberley Gdns EN EN1 .....24 C4
FSBYPK N4 .....67 H2
Kimberley Rd BECK BR3 .....182 A5
BRXN/ST SW9 .....141 K3
CAN/RD E16 .....106 C5
CHING E4 .....38 C3
CROY/NA CRO 196 C5
KIL/WHAMP NW6 .....82 C6
TOTM N17 .....50 C5
UED N18 .....50 D2
WALTH E17 .....51 G4
WAN E11 .....70 B6
Kimberley Wy CHING E4 .....38 C3
Kimber Rd WAND/EARL SW18 .....159 K2
Kimble Cl WATW WD18 * 26 C1
Kimble Crs STHL UB1 .....95 J3
Kimble Rd WIM/MER SW19 .....178 C2
Kimbolton Cl LEE/GVPK SE12 .....165 J4
Kimmeridge Gdns
ELTH/MOT SE9 .....166 D6
Kimmeridge Rd
ELTH/MOT SE9 .....166 D6
Kimpton Park Wy CHEAM SM3 .....193 J6
Kimpton Rd CHEAM SM3 .....208 D1
CMBW SE5 .....142 E2
Kinburn St BERM/RHTH SE16 * 124 A2
Kincaid Rd PECK SE15 .....143 J1
Kincardine Gdns
MV/WKIL W9 * 100 E3
Kinch Gv WBLY HA9 .....62 B4
Kinder Cl THMD SE28 .....109 K6
Kinder St WCHPL E1 .....104 D5
Kinderton Cl STHGT/OAK N14 .....34 C3
Kinfauns Rd
BRXS/STRHM SW2 .....162 B4
GDMY/SEVK IG3 .....73 J4
Kingaby Gdns RAIN RM13 .....93 J5
King Alfred Av CAT SE6 .....164 D5
King & Queen Cl
ELTH/MOT SE9 .....166 D6
King & Queen St WALW SE17 .....122 D5
King Arthur Cl PECK SE15 .....143 K1
King Charles Cl BRYLDS KT5 .....191 G4
King Charles I Island
WHALL SW1A 10 E7
King Charles Rd BRYLDS KT5 .....191 G3
King Charles St WHALL SW1A 16 D2
King Charles Ter WAP E1W * 104 D7
King Charles Wk
WIM/MER SW19 .....159 H3
Kingcup Cl CROY/NA CRO 198 A5
King David La WCHPL E1 .....104 E6
Kingdon Rd KIL/WHAMP NW6 .....82 E4
King Edward Av DART DA1 .....171 G1
King Edward Dr CHSGTN KT9 .....206 A1
King Edward Rd BAR EN5 .....20 E5
LEY E10 .....70 A5
OXHEY WD19 .....27 F1
ROM RM1 .....75 H5
WALTH E17 .....51 H4
King Edward's Gdns ACT W3 .....117 H1
King Edward's Gv TEDD TW11 .....174 C2
King Edward's Rd BARK IG11 .....90 D6
ED N9 .....36 D3
HACK E8 .....86 B6
PEND EN3 .....25 F5
RSLP HA4 .....58 B6
King Edward St STBT EC1A 12 C3
King Edward Wk STHWK SE1 .....17 K4
Kingfield Rd EA W5 .....97 K3
Kingfield St POP/IOD E14 .....125 F4
Kingfisher Cl
KTN/HRWW/WS HA3 .....43 H5
STMC/STPC BR5 .....202 E1
THMD SE28 .....109 J6
Kingfisher Dr
RCHPK/HAM TW10 .....156 D6

Kingfisher Ms LEW SE13 .....144 E6
Kingfisher Pl WDGN N22 * 49 F5
Kingfisher St EHAM E6 .....107 J4
Kingfisher Wy BECK BR3 .....198 A2
WLSDN NW10 * 81 F4
King Gdns CROY/NA CRO 211 H5
King Garth Ms FSTH SE23 .....163 K4
King George Av BUSH WD23 .....28 B1
CAN/RD E16 .....107 H5
GNTH/NBYPK IG2 .....72 D3
WOT/HER KT12 .....188 C5
King George Ct ROMW/RG RM7 .....56 E6
King George Sq
RCHPK/HAM TW10 .....157 G1
King George St GNWCH SE10 .....145 F1
King George VI Av MTCM CR4 .....194 E1
Kingham Cl NTGHL W11 .....119 H2
WAND/EARL SW18 .....160 B2
King Harolds Wy BXLYHN DA7 .....148 E1
King Henry Ms HRW HA1 .....60 E5
ORP BR6 .....217 F2
King Henry's Dr CROY/NA CRO 214 A6
King Henry's Reach
HMSMTH W6 .....119 F6
King Henry's Rd HAMP NW3 .....83 K5
KUT/HW KT1 .....175 J6
King Henry's Wk IS N1 .....86 A4
King Henry Ter WAP E1W * 104 D6
Kinghorn St STBT EC1A * 12 C2
King James Ct STHWK SE1 .....18 B3
King James St STHWK SE1 .....18 B3
King John Ct SDTCH EC2A 7 H6
King John Ct WFD IG8 * 53 F4
King John's Wk ELTH/MOT SE9 .....146 D6
Kinglake St WALW SE17 * 123 F5
Kinglet Cl FSTGT E7 .....88 E4
Kingly Ct REGST W1B * 10 B5
Kingly St REGST W1B 10 A4
King & Queen Cl
ELTH/MOT SE9 * 166 D6
King & Queen St WALW SE17 .....122 D5
King & Queen Whf
BERM/RHTH SE16 * 124 A1
Kingsand Rd LEE/GVPK SE12 .....165 K4
King's Arms Yd LOTH EC2R 12 E3
King's Av BAL SW12 .....161 J3
BMLY BR1 .....183 J2
CAR SM5 .....209 J5
CHDH RM6 .....73 K3
EA W5 .....97 K5
GFD/PVL UB6 .....96 B5
HSLW TW3 .....135 G2
MUSWH N10 .....48 A6
NWMAL KT3 .....192 C1
NWDGN N21 .....35 H5
WFD IG8 .....53 F2
Kings Av BAL SW12 .....161 J3
King's Bench St STHWK SE1 .....18 B2
King's Bench Wk EMB EC4Y * 11 K5
Kingsbridge Av ACT W3 .....116 D2
Kingsbridge Ct POP/IOD E14 .....124 D4
Kingsbridge Crs STHL UB1 .....95 K3
Kingsbridge Dr MLHL NW7 .....46 B5
Kingsbridge Rd BARK IG11 .....108 D1
MRDN SM4 .....193 G4
NKENS W10 .....100 A6
NWDGN UB2 .....114 E4
WOT/HER KT12 .....188 A4
Kingsbury Gn
CDALE/KGS NW9 .....62 E2
Kingsbury Rd CDALE/KGS NW9 .....62 D2
IS N1 .....86 A4
Kingsbury Ter IS N1 .....86 A4
King Chs Av E/WMO/HCT KT8 .....173 H6
Kingsclere Cl PUT/ROE SW15 .....158 D2
Kingsclere Pl ENC/FH EN2 .....23 J3
Kingscliffe Gdns
WIM/MER SW19 .....159 J4
Kings Cl DART DA1 .....150 B5
HDN NW4 .....64 B1
LEY E10 .....69 K4
NTHWD HA6 .....40 D2
THDIT KT7 .....190 B3
WOT/HER KT12 .....188 B4
King's College Rd HAMP NW3 * 83 H5
RSLP HA4 .....58 D4
Kingscote Rd CHSWK W4 .....118 A3
CROY/NA CRO 197 J4
NWMAL KT3 .....176 A6
Kingscote St BLKFR EC4V 12 A5
Kingscourt Rd
STRHM/NOR SW16 .....161 K5
King's Crs FSBYPK N4 .....85 J1
Kingscroft Rd CRICK NW2 .....82 D4
King's Cross Br IS N1 * 5 F4
King's Cross Rd FSBYW WC1X 5 H5
Kingsdale Gdns NTGHL W11 .....119 G1
Kingsdale Rd PGE/AN SE20 .....182 A4
WOOL/PLUM SE18 .....128 A6
Kingsdown Wy HAYES BR2 .....199 K3
Kings Dr BRYLDS KT5 .....191 H4
Kings Pde CAR SM5 * 209 J3
THDIT KT7 .....190 C5
WBLY HA9 .....62 D6
Kingsend RSLP HA4 .....58 B5
Kingsend Ct RSLP HA4 * 58 C5
Kings Farm WALTH E17 * 51 K4
Kings Farm Av
RCHPK/HAM TW10 .....137 H5
Kingsfield Av RYLN/HDSTN HA2 .....60 B2
Kingsfield Ct OXHEY WD19 .....27 H2
Kingsfield Rd HRW HA1 * 60 D4

OXHEY WD19 .....27 H2
Kingsfield Ter DART DA1 * 171 G1
Kingsford St KTTN NW5 .....83 K3
Kingsford Wy EHAM E6 .....107 K4
Kingsgate WBLY HA3 .....80 B1
Kingsgate Av FNCH N3 .....46 E6
Kingsgate Cl BXLYHN DA7 .....149 F2
STMC/STPC BR5 .....186 D6
Kingsgate Pl KIL/WHAMP NW6 .....82 E5
Kingsgate Rd KIL/WHAMP NW6 .....82 E5
KUT/HW KT1 .....175 F4
Kingsground ELTH/MOT SE9 .....166 D2
King's Gv PECK SE15 .....143 J2
ROM RM1 .....75 J2
Kings Hall Ms LEW SE13 * 145 F4
Kings Hall Rd BECK BR3 .....182 A3
Kings Head HI CHING E4 .....37 K2
King's Hwy WOOL/PLUM SE18 .....128 A5
Kingshill Av CRW RM5 .....56 E2
KTN/HRWW/WS HA3 .....61 H1
NTHLT UB5 .....77 K6
WPK KT4 .....192 D4
YEAD UB4 .....94 E2
Kingshill Cl YEAD UB4 * 94 E2
Kingshill Ct BAR EN5 * 20 C5
Kingsholm Gdns
ELTH/MOT SE9 .....146 C5
Kingshurst Rd LEE/GVPK SE12 .....165 K2
Kings Keep HAYES BR2 * 183 H6
KUT/HW KT1 * 191 F1
Kingsland Gn STNW/STAM N16 .....86 A4
Kingsland High St HACK E8 .....86 B4
Kingsland Pas HACK E8 * 86 A4
Kingsland Rd BETH E2 .....7 H2
HACK E8 .....86 B5
PLSTW E13 .....107 C2
Kingsland Shopping Centre
HACK E8 .....86 B4
King's La SUT SM1 .....209 H4
Kingslawn Cl PUT/ROE SW15 .....138 E6
Kingsleigh Cl BTFD TW8 .....116 E6
Kingsleigh Pl MTCM CR4 .....194 E1
Kingsleigh Wk HAYES BR2 .....199 J1
Kingsley Av DART DA1 .....135 H3
HSLW TW3 .....135 H3
STHL UB1 .....96 A6
SUT SM1 .....209 H2
Kingsley Cl DAGE RM10 .....92 D2
EFNCH N2 .....65 C2
Kingsley Ct EDGW HA8 * 30 D4
CROY/NA CRO 196 B5
WPK KT4 .....192 E6
Kingsley Dr WPK KT4 .....192 D4
Kingsley Gdns CHING E4 .....51 J1
Kingsley Ms CHST BR7 .....185 G2
IL IG1 .....72 A6
KENS W8 .....120 A3
WAP E1W * 104 D6
Kingsley Pl HGT N6 .....66 A4
Kingsley Rd BARK/HLT IG6 .....54 C4
CROY/NA CRO 196 B5
FSTGT E7 .....88 E4
HSLW TW3 .....135 H3
KIL/WHAMP NW6 .....82 D6
ORP BR6 .....217 H3
PIN HA5 .....59 K3
PLMCR N13 .....35 H6
RYLN/HDSTN HA2 .....78 C2
WALTH E17 .....52 A5
WIM/MER SW19 .....178 A1
Kingslyn Crs NRWD SE19 .....181 F5
Kings MI HMSMTH W6 * 119 F4
Kingsman St
WOOL/PLUM SE18 .....126 E4
Kingsmead BAR EN5 .....20 E5
RCHPK/HAM TW10 .....157 G1
Kingsmead Av CDALE/KGS NW9 .....63 F4
ED N9 .....36 D3
MTCM CR4 .....179 H6
ROM RM1 .....75 G3
SUN TW16 .....172 B6
SURB KT6 .....191 H6
WPK KT4 .....207 K1
Kingsmead Cl BFN/LL DA15 .....168 B4
HOR/WEW KT19 .....207 F6
TEDD TW11 .....174 B2
Kingsmead Dr NTHLT UB5 .....77 K5
Kingsmead Pde NTHLT UB5 * 77 K5
Kingsmead Ter NTHLT UB5 * 77 K5
Kingsmead Rd
BRXS/STRHM SW2 .....162 B4
Kingsmead Wy CLPT E5 .....87 G2
Kingsmere Cl PUT/ROE SW15 .....139 G4
Kingsmere Pk CDALE/KGS NW9 .....62 E5
Kingsmere Pl
STNW/STAM N16 * 67 K5
Kingsmere Rd
WIM/MER SW19 .....159 G4
King's Ms BMSBY WC1N 5 H7
CLAP SW4 .....141 K6
Kingsmill Gdns DAGW RM9 .....92 B3
Kingsmill Rd DAGW RM9 .....92 B3
Kingsmill Ter STJWD NW8 .....2 C2
Kingsnympton Pk
KUTN/CMB KT2 .....175 J3
Kings Oak ROMW/RG RM7 .....56 C6
King's Orch ELTH/MOT SE9 .....166 D1
King's Paddock HPTN TW12 .....173 H4
Kings Pde CAR SM5 * 209 J3
THMD SE28 * 110 D1
TOTM N17 * 50 B6
WLSDN NW10 * 99 J1
Kingspark Ct SWFD E18 .....52 E6
Kings Pas WAN E11 * 70 C4
Kings Pl BARK IG11 .....90 C5
BKHH IG9 .....39 G4
CHSWK W4 .....117 K5
STHWK SE1 .....18 C2
Kings Quay WBPTN SW10 * 140 B2

Kings Reach EMB EC4Y * 11 K5
WHALL SW1A 17 F1
Kings Ride Ga
RCHPK/HAM TW10 .....137 H5
Kingsridge Gdns DART DA1 .....171 C1
Kings Rd BAR EN5 .....20 A4
BARK IG11 .....90 C5
CHEL SW3 .....120 C6
CHING E4 .....38 B3
EA W5 .....97 K4
FELT TW13 .....154 A2
FUL/PGN SW6 .....140 B1
KUTN/CMB KT2 .....175 G3
MORT/ESHN SW14 .....138 A4
MTCM CR4 .....179 F6
ORP BR6 .....217 F2
PLSTW E13 .....89 F6
RCHPK/HAM TW10 .....137 G6
ROM RM1 .....75 J2
RYLN/HDSTN HA2 .....59 H3
SNWD SE25 .....181 H6
SURB KT6 .....190 D5
TEDD TW11 .....156 C1
TOTM N17 * 50 B4
TWK TW1 .....156 C1
UED N18 .....50 C1
WAN E11 .....70 C4
WDGN N22 .....49 F4
WIM/MER SW19 .....177 K2
WLSDN NW10 .....81 K5
WOT/HER KT12 .....188 A6
King's Scholars' Pas PIM SW1V 16 A4
King Stairs Cl
BERM/RHTH SE16 .....123 J2
King's Ter CAMTN NW1 * 4 A1
Kingsthorpe Rd SYD SE26 .....164 A6
Kingston Av CHEAM SM3 .....208 C3
EBED/NFELT TW14 .....153 H1
Kingston By-Pass
ESH/CLAY KT10 .....204 E1
RYNPK SW20 .....176 C2
Kingston Cl CHDH RM6 .....56 A6
NTHLT UB5 .....77 K5
TEDD TW11 .....174 C2
Kingston Crs BECK BR3 .....182 C4
CROY/NA CRO 210 D1
Kingston Hall Rd KUT/HW KT1 .....174 E6
Kingston HI KUTN/CMB KT2 .....174 E4
Kingston Hill Av CHDH RM6 .....56 A6
Kingston Hill Pl
KUTN/CMB KT2 .....158 A6
Kingston House Est
SURB KT6 * 190 C3
Kingston La TEDD TW11 .....174 C2
WDR/YW UB7 .....112 C2
Kingston Ldg NWMAL KT3 .....192 B1
Kingston Rd
KTN/HRWW/WS HA3 .....43 H3
EBAR EN4 .....21 H6
ED N9 .....36 C4
HOR/WEW KT19 .....207 G3
IL IG1 .....90 C2
KUT/HW KT1 .....175 F6
NWDGN UB2 .....114 E2
NWMAL KT3 .....192 A1
PUT/ROE SW15 .....158 E3
ROM RM1 .....75 H1
RYNPK SW20 .....177 H3
TEDD TW11 .....174 C2
WIM/MER SW19 .....177 K3
Kingston Sq NRWD SE19 .....180 E1
Kingston V PUT/ROE SW15 .....158 A4
Kingstown St CAMTN NW1 .....83 K6
Kings St ACT W3 .....117 K1
CTYW EC2V 12 D4
COVGDN WC2E 10 E5
EFNCH N2 .....65 J1
HMSMTH W6 .....118 D4
NWDGN UB2 .....114 D3
PLSTW E15 .....106 C1
RCH/KEW TW9 .....136 E6
TOTM N17 .....50 B4
TWK TW1 .....156 B3
WHALL SW1A 16 B1
King Street Cloisters
HMSMTH W6 * 118 E4
King Street Pde TWK TW1 * 156 B3
Kingswater Pl BTSEA SW11 * 140 D1
Kings Wy CROY/NA CRO 211 F3
Kingsway HOL/ALD WC2B 11 G4
Kings Wy HRW HA1 .....60 E1
Kingsway HYS/HAR UB3 .....94 A1
MORT/ESHN SW14 .....137 J4
NFNCH/WDSPK N12 .....47 G1
NWMAL KT3 .....193 F1
PEND EN3 .....24 D6
STMC/STPC BR5 .....201 J2
STNW/WRAY TW19 .....152 A3
WBLY HA9 .....80 A3
WWKM BR4 .....214 D1
Kingsway Av SAN/SEL CR2 .....212 E6
Kingsway Crs RYLN/HDSTN HA2 .....60 C1
Kingsway Pde
STNW/STAM N16 * 85 K1
Kingsway Pl CLKNW EC1R * 5 K5
Kingsway Rd CHEAM SM3 .....208 C5
Kingswear Rd KTTN NW5 .....84 B1
RSLP HA4 .....58 E6
Kingswood Av BELV DA17 .....129 G4
HAYES BR2 .....215 H1
HPTN TW12 .....173 G2
HSLW TW3 .....134 E3
KIL/WHAMP NW6 .....82 C6
THHTH CR7 .....196 B2
Kingswood Cl ASHF TW15 .....153 F6
BAR EN5 .....20 A4
DART DA1 .....171 F1
EN EN1 .....24 A5
NWMAL KT3 .....192 C3
STMC/STPC BR5 .....201 J4
SURB KT6 .....191 F4
VX/NE SW8 .....141 K1
Kingswood Ct LEW SE13 .....165 G1
Kingswood Dr BELMT SM2 .....209 F6
CAR SM5 .....194 E4

DUL SE21.............................163 F6
Kingswood Pk FNCH N3...............46 D5
Kingswood Pl LEW SE13............145 H5
Kingswood Rd
  BRXS/STRHM SW2...............161 K1
  CHSWK W4..........................117 K3
  GDMY/SEVK IG3.....................73 C5
  HAYES BR2...........................183 H6
  PGE/AN SE20.........................181 K2
  WAN E11................................70 C4
  WBLY HA9..............................67 J1
  WIM/MER SW19.....................177 J4
Kingswood Ter CHSWK W4........117 K3
Kingswood Wy WLGTN SM6......210 E3
Kingsworth Cl BECK BR3...........198 B2
Kingsworthy Cl KUT/HW KT1.....175 G6
Kings Yd PUT/ROE SW15 *.........139 G5
  SRTFD E15 *...........................76 C7
Kingthorpe Rd WLSDN NW10.....81 F5
Kingthorpe Ter WLSDN NW10 *...81 F5
Kingwell Rd EBAR EN4.................21 H1
Kingweston Cl CRICK NW2..........82 C1
King William La GNWCH SE10....125 H5
King William St CANST EC4R......13 G6
King William Wk GNWCH SE10...125 F6
Kingwood Rd FUL/PGN SW6.......139 H1
Kiniet Rd WOOL/PLUM SE18......147 H2
Kinloch Dr CDALE/KGS NW9.......63 G4
Kinloch St HOLWY N7 *................85 F1
Kinloss Gdns FNCH N5................46 D6
Kinloss Rd CAR SM5.................194 B4
Kinnaird Av BMLY BR1...............183 J2
  CHSWK W4...........................137 K1
Kinnaird Cl BMLY BR1...............183 J2
Kinnaird Wy WFD IG8..................53 K2
kinnéar Rd SHB W12.................118 C2
Kinnerton Pl North
  KTBR SW1X *...........................15 F3
Kinnerton Pl South
  KTBR SW1X *...........................15 F3
Kinnoul Rd HMSMTH W6...........119 H6
Kinross Av WPK KT4..................192 D6
Kinross Cl KTN/HRWW/WS HA3...62 B3
Kinross Ter WALTH E17................51 H5
Kinsale Rd PECK SE15................143 H4
Kinsella Gdns WIM/MER SW19...176 E2
Kintyre Cl STRHM/NOR SW16.....180 A5
Kinveachy Gdns CHARL SE7........126 D5
Kinver Rd SYD SE26...................163 K6
Kipling Dr WIM/MER SW19.........178 C2
Kipling Est STHWK SE1 *.............19 F3
Kipling St STHWK SE1.................19 F3
Kipling Ter ED N9 *......................35 K5
Kippington Dr ELTH/MOT SE9....166 C3
Kirby Cl BARK/HLT IG6.................54 D2
  HOR/WEW KT19....................207 H3
  LOU IG10.................................39 J2
  NTHWD HA6.............................40 D2
Kirby Est BERM/RHTH SE16 *.....123 J3
Kirby St HCIRC EC1N...................11 K1
Kirchen Rd WEA W13....................97 H6
Kirkdale SYD SE26....................163 J4
Kirkdale Cnr SYD SE26 *............163 K6
Kirkdale Rd WAN E11..................70 C5
Kirkfield Cl WEA W13.................116 C1
Kirkham Rd EHAM E6.................107 J5
Kirkham St WOOL/PLUM SE18...127 K6
Kirkland Av CLAY IG5...................54 A5
Kirkland Cl BFN/LL DA15...........167 K1
Kirkland Dr ENC/FH EN2..............23 J2
Kirkland Ter BECK BR3...............182 D2
Kirkland Wk HACK E8...................86 B4
Kirk La WOOL/PLUM SE18.........127 H6
Kirkleas Rd SURB KT6................191 F5
Kirklees Rd BCTR RM8..................91 J3
  THHTH CR7............................196 B2
Kirkley Rd WIM/MER SW19.........177 K4
Kirkly Cl SAND/SEL CR2.............212 A6
Kirkmichael Rd POP/IOD E14....106 A5
Kirkside Rd BKHTH/KID SE3......125 K6
Kirkstall Av SEVS/STOTM N15.....67 K1
Kirkstall Gdns
  BRXS/STRHM SW2.................161 J3
Kirksted Rd MRDN SM4..............194 A5
Kirkstone Wy BMLY BR1............183 H3
Kirkton Rd SEVS/STOTM N15......68 A1
Kirkwall Pl BETH E2 *.................104 E2
Kirkwood Rd PECK SE15............143 J3
Kirn Rd WEA W13..........................97 H6
Kirrane Cl NWMAL KT3..............192 C2
Kirtley Rd SYD SE26..................164 B6
Kirtling St VX/NE SW8................141 H1
Kirton Cl CHSWK W4..................118 A4
Kirton Gdns BETH E2 *...................7 K5
Kirton Ldg WAND/EARL SW18 *..160 A1
Kirton Rd PLSTW E13................107 G1
Kirton Wk EDGW HA8..................44 E3
Kirwyn Wy CMBW SE5...............142 D1
Kitcat Ter BOW E3......................105 J2
Kitchener Rd EFNCH N2 *.............47 J6
  FSTGT E7................................89 F4
  THHTH CR7............................180 E6
  TOTM N17................................50 A6
  WALTH E17...............................51 J4
Kite Pl BETH E2 *.......................104 C2
Kite Yd BTSEA SW11 *...............140 E2
Kitley Gdns NRWD SE19............181 G4
Kitson Rd BARN SW13................138 D2
  CMBW SE5............................142 D1
Kittiwake Rd NTHLT UB5..............95 H2
Kittiwake Wy YEAD UB4...............95 H4
Kitto Rd NWCR SE14..................144 A3
Kiver Rd ARCH N19......................66 E6
Kiwi Ter EHAM E6......................108 A2
Klea Av CLAP SW4.....................161 H1
Knapmill Rd CAT SE6.................164 D4
Knapmill Wy CAT SE6................164 D4
Knapp Cl WLSDN NW10...............81 G4
Knapp Rd ASHF TW15.................152 C6

BOW E3.................................105 J3
Knapton Ms TOOT SW17............179 F2
Knaresborough Dr
  WAND/EARL SW18.................160 A3
Knaresborough Pl IECT SW5......120 A4
Knatchbull Rd CMBW SE5.........142 C2
  WLSDN NW10.........................99 F1
Knebworth Av WALTH E17............51 J4
Knebworth Rd
  STNW/STAM N16 *...................86 A2
Knee Hill ABYW SE2...................128 D5
Knee Hill Crs ABYW SE2............128 D4
Kneller Gdns ISLW TW7.............155 J1
Kneller Rd BROCKY SE4............144 B5
  NWMAL KT3...........................192 B4
  WHTN TW2.............................155 H1
Knevett Ter HNWL TW3...............135 J5
Knight Cl BCTR RM8.....................73 J6
Knighten St WAP E1W *..............123 J1
Knighthead Point
  POP/IOD E14 *.......................124 D2
Knightland Rd CLPT E5................68 D6
Knighton Cl ROMW/RG RM7........75 F3
  SAND/SEL CR2.......................211 H6
  WFD IG8..................................39 F6
Knighton Dr WFD IG8...................39 F4
Knighton La BKHH IG9.................39 F4
Knighton Park Rd SYD SE26......182 A1
Knighton Rd FSTGT E7.................88 E1
  ROMW/RG RM7........................75 F4
Knightrider Ct BLKFR EC4V *.......12 D5
Knightrider St BLKFR EC4V.........12 C5
Knight's Av EA W5.....................117 F2
Knightsbridge SKENS SW7.........14 D3
Knightsbridge Gdns
  ROMW/RG RM7........................75 F3
Knightsbridge Gn KTBR SW1X *...14 E3
Knights Chambers ED N9 *..........36 E5
Knights Cl E/WMO/HCT KT8......188 E2
Knights Hl WNWD SE27..............180 C1
Knight's Hill Sq WNWD SE27.....162 C6
Knight's La ED N9........................36 C5
Knights Manor Wy DART DA1 *...171 J1
Knights Pk KUT/HW KT1.............175 F6
Knight's Pl WHTN TW2...............155 K3
Knights Rd CAN/RD E16.............217 H3
  STAN HA7................................29 H5
Knights Wk LBTH SE11.................18 A7
Knights Wy BARK/HLT IG6............54 C2
Knightswood Cl EDGW HA8..........30 E4
Knightswood Rd RAIN RM13......111 H1
Knightwood Crs NWMAL KT3.....192 B3
Knivet Rd FUL/PGN SW6............119 K6
Knobs Hill Rd SRTFD E15.............87 K6
Knockholt Rd ELTH/MOT SE9....146 C6
Knole Cl CROY/NA CRO *...........197 K3
Knole Rd DART DA1...................170 D3
The Knole ELTH/MOT SE9..........167 F6
Knoll Crs NTHWD HA6..................40 D5
Knoll Dr STHGT/OAK N14............34 A1
Knollmead BRYLDS KT5.............191 H5
Knoll Ri ORP BR6.......................202 A5
Knoll Rd BXLY DA5....................169 H2
  SCUP DA14............................186 C1
  WAND/EARL SW18.................140 A6
Knolls Cl WPK KT4.....................207 K1
The Knoll BECK BR3..................182 E4
  EA W5.....................................97 J4
  HAYES BR2............................199 K6
  PIN HA5 *................................41 H5
Knollys Cl STRHM/NOR SW16....162 C5
Knolly's Rd STRHM/NOR SW16...162 B5
Knottisford St BETH E2...............105 F2
Knotts Green Ms LEY E10.............69 K3
Knotts Green Rd LEY E10.............69 K3
Knowle Av BXLYHN DA7.............149 F1
Knowle Cl BRXN/ST SW9............142 B4
Knowle Rd HAYES BR2...............200 E7
  WHTN TW2.............................155 K3
Knowles Cl WDR/YW UB7...........112 B1
Knowles Hill Crs LEW SE13........145 G6
Knowlton Gn HAYES BR2............199 J2
Knowsley Av STHL UB1...............115 C1
Knowsley Rd BTSEA SW11..........140 E3
Knox Rd FSTGT E7........................88 D4
Knox St CAMTN NW1 *....................8 E1
Knoyle St NWCR SE14................124 B6
Kohat Rd WIM/MER SW19...........178 A1
Koh-i-noor Av BUSH WD23...........28 A1
Kossuth St GNWCH SE10..........125 H5
Kramer Ms ECT SW5 *................119 K5
Kreedman Wk HACK E8 *..............86 C5
Kuala Gdns STRHM/NOR SW16..180 A4
Kydbrook Cl STMC/STPC BR5....201 H4
Kylemore Cl EHAM E6.................107 H1
Kylemore Rd KIL/WHAMP NW6...82 E5
Kymberley Rd HRW HA1 *............60 E3
Kyme Rd ROM RM1.......................75 H3
Kynance Gdns STAN HA7.............43 J4
Kynance Ms SKENS SW7............120 A3
Kynance Pl KENS W8.................120 B3
Kynaston Av THHTH CR7............196 D2
Kynaston Cl
  KTN/HRWW/WS HA3................42 D1
Kynaston Crs THHTH CR7..........196 D2
Kynaston Rd BMLY BR1..............183 K1
  ENC/FH EN2.............................23 K2
  STMC/STPC BR5...................202 C4
  STNW/STAM N16......................86 A1
  THHTH CR7............................196 D2
Kynaston Wd
  KTN/HRWW/WS HA3................42 D1
Kynersley Cl CAR SM5..............209 K1
Kynoch Rd UED N18.....................37 F6
Kyrle Rd BTSEA SW11................161 F1
Kyverdale Rd STNW/STAM N16...68 B4

![L]

Laburnum Av DART DA1.............171 F3
  ED N9......................................36 A4
  HCH RM12................................75 J4
  SUT SM1.................................209 J1

TOTM N17.................................49 K3
Laburnum Cl ALP/SUD HA0..........80 C6
  CHING E4................................51 H2
  PECK SE15............................143 K1
Laburnum Ct STAN HA7................29 J6
Laburnum Crs SUN TW16...........172 A4
Laburnum Gdns CROY/NA CRO..198 A4
  HSLW TW3.............................134 C5
Laburnum Gv CDALE/KGS NW9...62 E4
  HSLW TW3.............................134 C5
  NWMAL KT3...........................176 A5
  RSLP HA4.................................58 B3
  STHL UB1................................95 K3
  WCHMN N21...........................35 J4
Laburnum Rd HYS/HAR UB3.....113 J4
  MTCM CR4.............................179 F5
  WIM/MER SW19.....................178 B3
Laburnum St BETH E2...................7 J2
  STWL/WRAY TW19................152 C3
Lacebark Cl BFN/LL DA15.........168 A2
Lacewing Cl PLSTW E13............106 E2
Lacey Cl ED N9...........................36 C4
Lacey Dr BCTR RM8.....................91 H1
  EDGW HA8..............................30 A4
  HPTN TW12............................172 E4
Lackington St SDTCH EC2A.........13 F1
Lacock Cl WIM/MER SW19.........178 B2
Lacon Rd EDUL SE22.................143 H5
Lacrosse Wy
  STRHM/NOR SW16...............179 J4
Lacy Rd PUT/ROE SW15...........139 G5
Ladas Rd WNWD SE27...............180 D1
Ladbroke Crs NTGHL W11..........100 C5
Ladbroke Gdns NTGHL W11.......100 D6
Ladbroke Gv NKENS W10...........100 B3
  NTGHL W11............................119 H1
Ladbroke Ms NTGHL W11 *........119 H1
  NTGHL W11............................119 J1
Ladbroke Rd EN EN1...................36 B1
  NTGHL W11............................119 H1
Ladbroke Sq NTGHL W11...........100 D6
Ladbroke Ter NTGHL W11...........119 H1
Ladbroke Wk NTGHL W11...........119 J1
Ladbrook Cl PIN HA5....................59 K2
Ladbrooke Crs SCUP DA14........168 E5
Ladbrook Rd SNWD SE25..........196 E1
Ladderstile Ride
  KUTN/CMB KT2.....................175 J1
Ladderswood Wy
  FBAR/BDGN N11.....................48 C1
Lady Alesford Av STAN HA7.........43 H1
Lady Booth Rd KUT/HW KT1......175 F5
Ladycroft Gdns ORP BR6...........216 C3
Ladycroft Rd LEW SE13.............144 E4
Ladycroft Wk STAN HA7...............43 K4
Ladycroft Wy ORP BR6...............216 C3
Lady Forsdyke Wy
  HOR/WEW KT19....................206 C6
Ladygate La RSLP HA4.................58 A3
Ladygrove CROY/NA CRO...........213 G6
Lady Harewood Wy
  HOR/WEW KT19....................206 C6
Lady Hay WPK KT4....................192 C6
Lady Margaret Rd ARCH N19.......84 C2
  KTTN NW5...............................84 C3
  STHL UB1................................95 K5
Ladymount WLGTN SM6............210 D2
Ladyship Ter EDUL SE22 *..........163 J2
Ladysmith Av EHAM E6..............107 J1
  GNTH/NBYPK IG2.....................72 D4
Ladysmith Rd CAN/RD E16.........106 D2
  ELTH/MOT SE9......................167 F1
  EN EN1.....................................24 B3
  KTN/HRWW/WS HA3................42 E3
  TOTM N17................................50 D1
  UED N18...................................50 C1
Lady Somerset Rd KTTN NW5......84 B2
Ladywell Cl BROCKY SE4...........144 D6
Ladywell Rd LEW SE13..............144 D6
Ladywell St SRTFD E15................88 D1
Ladywell Water Tower
  BROCKY SE4 *.......................144 D6
Lafone Av FELT TW13.................154 B3
Lafone St STHWK SE1..................19 J2
Lagado Ms BERM/RHTH SE16....124 A1
Lagonda Av BARK/HLT IG6...........55 F7
Lagonda Wy DART DA1...............151 F5
Lagoon Rd STMC/STPC BR5......202 C2
Laidlaw Dr WCHMN N21...............22 E7
Laing Cl BARK/HLT IG6.................54 D2
Laing Dean NTHLT UB5.................95 F1
Lainlock Pl HSLW TW3...............135 G2
Lainson St WAND/EARL SW18...159 K2
Lairdale Cl DUL SE21.................162 D3
Lairs Cl HOLWY N7 *....................84 E4
Laitwood Rd BAL SW12..............161 G3
Lake Av BMLY BR1.....................183 K2
Lake Cl BCTR RM8 *.....................91 K1
Lakedale Rd
  WOOL/PLUM SE18.................127 K5
Lake Dr BUSH WD23....................28 C4
Lakefield Rd WDGN N22...............49 H5
Lakehall Gdns THHTH CR7.........196 C2
Lakehall Rd THHTH CR7.............196 C2
Lake House Rd WAN E11..............88 E1
Lakehurst Rd HOR/WEW KT19...207 G3
Lakeland Cl
  KTN/HRWW/WS HA3................42 D2
Lakenheath STHGT/OAK N14......34 D1
Lake Ri ROM RM1........................57 H6
Lake Rd CHDH RM6......................73 J2
  CROY/NA CRO.......................198 C6
  DAGW RM9............................110 D2
  LEY E10....................................69 K4
  WIM/MER SW19.....................177 J1
Lakeside BECK BR3...................182 E6
  ENC/FH EN2.............................23 G6
  HOR/WEW KT19....................207 H3
  WEA W13.................................97 G3
  WLGTN SM6..........................210 B2
Lakeside Av REDBR IG4................71 H1

THMD SE28.............................128 B2
Lakeside Cl BFN/LL DA15..........168 A2
  RSLP HA4.................................58 B1
  SNWD SE25............................181 H5
Lakeside Crs EBAR EN4................33 K1
Lakeside Dr ESH/CLAY KT10......204 A4
  HAYES BR2............................215 J1
  WLSDN NW10..........................98 B2
Lakeside Rd PLMGR N13.............35 F6
  WKENS W14...........................119 G3
Lakeside Wy WBLY HA9................80 B2
Lake Vw BAR HAYES BR2...........215 G3
Lakeswood Rd
  STMC/STPC BR5...................201 G3
The Lake BUSH WD23.................28 D3
Lake Vw EDGW HA8....................44 B1
Lake View Est PGN E3 *..............105 F1
Lakeview Rd WELL DA16.............148 C5
  WNWD SE27...........................180 C1
Lake View Ter UED N18 *..............36 B6
Lakis Cl HAMP NW3 *...................83 G2
Laleham Av MLHL NW7................31 F4
Laleham Ct SUT SM1 *...............209 G3
Laleham Rd CAT SE6..................165 F1
Lalor St FUL/PGN SW6...............139 H3
Lambarde Av ELTH/MOT SE9.....167 F6
Lamb Cl NTHLT UB5......................95 J2
Lamberhurst Cl
  STMC/STPC BR5...................202 E5
Lamberhurst Rd BCTR RM8.........74 B5
  WNWD SE27...........................162 B6
Lambert Av RCH/KEW TW9........137 H4
Lambert Jones Ms BARB EC2Y *..12 C1
Lambert Rd BRXS/STRHM SW2...141 K1
  CAN/RD E16............................107 F5
  NFNCH/WDSPK N12................47 H1
Lambert's Pl CROY/NA CRO.......196 E5
Lambert's Rd BRYLDS KT5.........191 G2
Lambert St IS N1..........................85 G5
Lambeth Br LBTH SE11.................17 G6
Lambeth High St LBTH SE11........17 G6
Lambeth Hill BLKFR EC4V............12 C5
Lambeth Palace Rd STHWK SE1...17 G5
Lambeth Rd CROY/NA CRO.........196 B4
  LBTH SE11...............................17 G5
Lambeth Wk LBTH SE11...............17 H6
  PECK SE15 *..........................143 G1
Lambkins Ms WALTH E17.............70 A1
Lamb La HACK E8..........................86 D5
Lamble St KTTN NW5...................84 A2
Lambley Rd DAGW RM9..............91 H4
Lambolle Pl HAMP NW3................83 J4
Lambolle Rd HAMP NW3...............83 J4
Lambourn Cl HNWL W7...............116 A2
  KTTN NW5 *.............................84 C2
  SAND/SEL CR2......................211 H6
Lambourne Av
  WIM/MER SW19.....................159 J6
Lambourne Gdns BARK IG11.......91 F5
  CHING E4..................................37 K5
  EN EN1.....................................24 B3
Lambourne Gv
  BERM/RHTH SE16.................124 A5
  KUT/HW KT1..........................175 J5
Lambourne Pl BKHTH/KID SE3...146 A2
Lambourne Rd BARK IG11............91 G6
  GDMY/SEVK IG3.....................73 G6
  CHIG IG7...................................54 E1
Lambourn Rd CLAP SW4............141 G4
Lambrook Ter FUL/PGN SW6......139 H2
Lamb's Conduit Pas
  FSBYW WC1X............................11 G1
Lambscroft Av ELTH/MOT SE9...166 B5
Lambs Gv BARK IG11 *.................90 E5
Lambs Meadow WFD IG8..............53 H5
Lambs Ms IS N1............................5 K1
Lamb's Pas STLK EC1Y.................6 E7
Lamb St WCHPL E1.......................13 J1
Lambs Wk ENC/FH EN2................23 J3
Lambton Pl NTGHL W11 *..........100 D6
Lambton Rd ARCH N19.................66 E5
  RYNPK SW20...........................177 F5
Lamb Wk STHWK SE1...................19 G3
Lamerock Rd BMLY BR1.............165 J6
Lamerton Rd BARK/HLT IG6.........54 B5
Lamerton St DEPT SE8...............124 D6
Lamford Cl TOTM N17...................49 K3
Lamington St HMSMTH W6........118 E4
Lamlash St LBTH SE11..................18 B6
Lammas Av MTCM CR4...............179 F5
Lammas Gn SYD SE26 *.............163 J5
Lammas Park Gdns EA W5.........116 D2
Lammas Rd HOM E9.....................87 F5
  LEY E10....................................69 G5
  RCHPK/HAM TW10................156 D6
Lammermoor Rd BAL SW12 *.....161 G2
Lamont Rd WBPTN SW10............120 C6
Lamont Road Pas
  WBPTN SW10 *......................120 C6
Lamorbey Cl BFN/LL DA15.........168 A4
Lamorbey Pk BFN/LL DA15 *......168 C3
Lamorna Cl ORP BR6..................202 B4
  WALTH E17...............................52 B5
Lamorna Gv STAN HA7.................43 K4
Lampard Gv STNW/STAM N16.....68 B5
Lampern Sq BETH E2 *...................7 K4
Lampeter Sq HMSMTH W6.........119 H6
Lamplighter Cl WCHPL E1...........104 E3
Lamp's Rd DART DA1..................171 J1
Lampmead Rd LEE/GVPK SE12..145 H6
Lamport Cl WOOL/PLUM SE18...126 E4
Lampton Av HEST TW5...............135 G2
Lampton House Cl
  WIM/MER SW19.....................159 G6
Lampton Park Rd HSLW TW3......135 G3
Lampton Rd HEST TW5...............135 G2
Lamson Rd RAIN RM13...............111 H4
Lanacre Av CDALE/KGS NW9.......45 G4
Lanadron Cl ISLW TW7 *.............136 A3
Lanark Cl EA W5...........................97 J4
Lanark Pl MV/WKIL W9.................101 G3
Lanark Rd KIL/WHAMP NW6.......101 F1
Lanbury Rd PECK SE15..............144 A5

Lancashire Ct MYFR/PKLN W1K...9 J5
Lancaster Av BARK IG11...............90 E5
  EBAR EN4.................................21 H1
  MTCM CR4.............................195 K2
  WAN E11...................................71 F1
  WIM/MER SW19.....................177 F1
  WNWD SE27...........................162 C4
Lancaster Cl ASHF TW15............152 B6
  CDALE/KGS NW9.....................45 H3
  HAYES BR2............................199 J1
  KTN/HRWW/WS HA3 *.............42 D1
  STNW/STAM N16 *...................86 A2
  TOTM N17 *..............................50 D6
  WPK KT4................................192 E6
Lancaster Ct WOT/HER KT12.....188 A4
Lancaster Dr HAMP NW3..............83 J4
  HCH RM12................................75 J5
  POP/IOD E14..........................125 F1
Lancaster Garde BMLY BR1........200 D2
Lancaster Gdns
  KUTN/CMB KT2.....................174 E1
  WIM/MER SW19.....................177 F1
Lancaster House
  WOOL/PLUM SE18.................146 D1
Lancaster Ms BAY/PAD W2........101 G6
  RCHPK/HAM TW10................157 F1
  WIM/MER SW19.....................140 A6
Lancaster Pk
  RCHPK/HAM TW10................137 F6
Lancaster Pl COVGDN WC2E.......11 G6
  TWK TW1...............................156 B2
  WIM/MER SW19.....................177 G1
Lancaster Rd EBAR EN4...............21 K2
  ENC/FH EN2.............................23 K2
  FBAR/BDGN N11......................48 B2
  FSBYPK N4................................67 F5
  FSTGT E7..................................88 E5
  NKENS W10............................100 B5
  NTHLT UB5...............................78 B5
  NTHLT UB5................................78 B4
  RYLN/HDSTN HA2.....................60 A2
  SNWD SE25............................181 H6
  STHL UB1.................................95 J6
  UED N18...................................50 B1
  WALTH E17...............................51 F5
  WAN E11...................................70 C5
  WIM/MER SW19.....................177 G1
  WLSDN NW10...........................81 H3
Lancaster Stables HAMP NW3 *...83 J4
Lancaster St STHWK SE1.............18 B3
Lancaster Ter BAY/PAD W2..........8 A5
Lancaster Wk HYS/HAR UB3.......94 A5
Lancaster Wy WPK KT4..............193 F4
Lancaster West NTGHL W11 *.....100 C5
Lancastrian Rd WLGTN SM6......210 E5
Lancefield St NKENS W10...........100 D2
Lancell St STNW/STAM N16 *.......68 A6
Lancelot Crs ALP/SUD HA0.........79 K2
Lancelot Gdns EBAR EN4.............34 A2
Lancelot Pde ALP/SUD HA0 *......79 K2
Lancelot Pl SKENS SW7...............14 E4
Lancelot Rd ALP/SUD HA0...........79 K3
  BARK/HLT IG6..........................54 E2
  WELL DA16...........................148 B5
Lance Rd HRW HA1......................60 C4
Lancer Sq KENS W8 *................120 A2
Lancey Cl CHARL SE7................126 C4
Lanchester Rd HGT N6.................65 K2
Lancing Gdns ED N9....................36 B3
Lancing Rd CROY/NA CRO.........196 A3
  FELT TW13.............................153 J4
  GNTH/NBYPK IG2.....................72 D3
  ORP BR6................................202 C6
Lancing St CAMTN NW1................4 C5
Landale Gdns DART DA1.............171 F3
Landau Ter HAYES BR2..............215 J2
Landau Wy ERITH DA8................131 G5
Landcroft Rd EDUL SE22............163 G1
Landells Rd EDUL SE22.............163 G1
Landford Rd PUT/ROE SW15......139 F4
Landgrove Rd
  WIM/MER SW19.....................177 K1
Landleys Plo HOLWY N7 *............84 D3
Landmann Wy NWCR SE14........124 A5
Landon Pl KTBR SW1X..................14 E4
Landons Cl POP/IOD E14............125 F1
Landor Rd BRXN/ST SW9...........141 K4
Landor Wk SHB W12...................118 D2
Landra Gdns WCHMN N21............35 H1
Landridge Rd FUL/PGN SW6.......139 H3
Landrock Rd CEND/HSY/T N8.......66 E3
Landscape Rd WFD IG8................52 E3
Landseer Av MNPK E12................90 A3
Landseer Cl EDGW HA8................44 D5
  EMPK RM11.............................75 K4
  WIM/MER SW19.....................178 B4
Landseer Rd ARCH N19................84 C1
  EN EN1.....................................24 C6
  NWMAL KT3...........................192 A4
  SUT SM1................................208 E4
Land's End BORE WD6..................29 K1
Landstead Rd
  WOOL/PLUM SE18.................147 J1
The Landway STMC/STPC BR5...186 D6
Lane Cl CRICK NW2......................81 K1
Lane End BXLYHN DA7...............149 J4
Lane Gdns BUSH WD23................28 E2
  ESH/CLAY KT10......................205 F5
Lane Ms MNPK E12......................89 K1
Lanercost Gdns
  STHGT/OAK N14.......................34 E2
Lanercost Rd
  BRXS/STRHM SW2.................162 B4
Laneside CHST BR7....................185 G1
  EDGW HA8...............................44 E1
Laneside Av BCTR RM8................74 B4
The Lane BKHTH/KID SE3...........145 K4
  STJWD NW8...........................101 G2
Laneway PUT/ROE SW15...........138 E6
Lanfranc Rd BOW E3...................105 G1
Lanfrey Pl WKENS W14...............119 J5
Langbourne Av HGT N6................66 A6

Langbourne Wy
ESH/CLAY KT10 205 G4
Langbrook Rd BKHTH/KID SE3 146 C4
Langcroft Cl CAR SM5 209 K1
Langdale Av MTCM CR4 178 E6
Langdale Cl BCTR RM8 73 J5
MORT/ESHN SW14 137 J5
ORP BR6 216 B1
Langdale Crs BXLYHN DA7 149 H2
Langdale Dr YEAD UB4 94 C1
Langdale Gdns HCH RM12 93 J3
Langdale Pde MTCM CR4 * 178 E5
Langdale Rd GNWCH SE10 145 F1
THHTH CR7 196 B1
Langdale St WCHPL E1 * 104 D5
Langdon Ct WLSDN NW10 81 G6
Langdon Crs EHAM E6 108 A1
Langdon Dr CDALE/KGS NW9 62 E5
Langdon House
WOOL/PLUM SE18 * 146 D1
Langdon Pk TEDD TW11 174 D3
Langdon Park Rd HGT N6 66 B4
Langdon Pl MORT/ESHN SW14 137 K4
Langdon Rd EHAM E6 90 A6
HAYES BR2 184 A6
MRDN SM4 194 B2
Langdon Shaw SCUP DA14 186 A1
Langdon Wk MRDN SM4 194 B2
Langdon Wy STHWK SE1 123 H4
Langford Cl HACK E8 86 C3
SEVS/STOTM N15 68 A3
STJWD NW8 101 G1
Langford Crs EBAR EN4 21 K5
Langford Gn CMBW SE5 143 F4
Langford Pl SCUP DA14 168 B5
STJWD NW8 101 G1
Langford Rd EBAR EN4 21 K5
FUL/PGN SW6 140 A3
WFD IG8 53 G2
Langfords BKHH IG9 39 H4
Langham Ct RSLP HA4 * 77 F3
Langham Dr GDMY/SEVK IG3 73 H3
Langham Gdns ALP/SUD HA0 61 J6
EDGW HA8 44 E3
RCHPK/HAM TW10 156 D6
WCHMH N21 23 G6
WEA W13 97 H6
Langham House Cl
RCHPK/HAM TW10 156 E6
Langham Pde
SEVS/STOTM N15 * 49 H6
Langham Park Pl HAYES BR2 199 J1
Langham Pl CHSWK W4 118 B6
REGST W1B 9 K3
SEVS/STOTM N15 49 H6
Langham Rd EDGW HA8 44 E2
RYNPK SW20 177 F4
SEVS/STOTM N15 67 J1
TEDD TW11 174 C1
Langham St GTPST W1W 10 A2
REGST W1B 9 K2
Langhedge Cl UED N18 50 B2
Langhedge La UED N18 50 B2
Langholm Cl BAL SW12 161 J2
Langholme BUSH WD23 28 C3
Langhorn Dr WHTN TW2 155 K2
Langhorne Rd DAGE RM10 92 C5
Langland Ct NTHWD HA6 40 A3
Langland Crs STAN HA7 43 K5
Langland Dr PIN HA5 41 J3
Langland Gdns CROY/NA CR0 198 C6
HAMP NW3 83 F3
Langler Rd WLSDN NW10 100 A2
Langley Av RSLP HA4 59 F6
SURB KT6 190 E5
WPK KT4 193 G6
Langley Ct BECK BR3 * 198 E1
COVGDN WC2E 10 E5
Langley Crs DAGW RM9 91 J5
EDGW HA8 30 E5
HYS/HAR UB3 133 J1
WAN E11 71 G4
Langley Dr ACT W3 117 J2
WAN E11 71 F4
Langley Gdns DAGW RM9 91 K5
STMC/STPC BR5 201 G3
Langley Gv NWMAL KT3 176 A5
Langley La VX/NE SW8 121 K6
Langley Pk MLHL NW7 45 G2
Langley Park Rd BELMT SM2 209 H5
Langley Pl WPK KT4 193 G6
Langley Rd BECK BR3 198 A1
ISLW TW7 136 A3
SAND/SEL CR2 213 F6
SURB KT6 191 F4
WELL DA16 128 D6
WIM/MER SW19 177 J4
Langley Rw BAR EN5 20 D2
Langley St LSQ/SEVD WC2H 10 E4
Langley Wy WWKM BR4 199 G5
Langley Wd BECK BR3 * 199 H2
Langmead Dr BUSH WD23 28 D3
Langmead St WNWD SE27 162 C6
Langport Ct WOT/HER KT12 188 B5
Langridge Ms HPTN TW12 172 E2
Langroyd Rd TOOT SW17 160 E4
Langside Av PUT/ROE SW15 138 D5
Langside Crs STHGT/OAK N14 34 D5
Langston Hughes Cl
HNHL SE24 * 142 C5
Lang St WCHPL E1 104 E3
Langthorn Ct LOTH EC2R * 13 F3
Langthorne Rd WAN E11 88 B1
Langthorne St FUL/PGN SW6 139 G2
Langton Av EHAM E6 108 A2
TRDG/WHET N20 33 G2
Langton Cl FSBYW WC1X 5 H5
Langton Gv NTHWD HA6 40 A1
Langton Ri EDUL SE22 163 J2
Langton Rd BRXN/ST SW9 142 C2
CRICK NW2 82 A1
E/WMO/HCT KT8 189 H2
KTN/HRWW/WS HA3 42 C3
Langton St WBPTN SW10 120 B6
Langton Vls TOTM N17 * 50 C4
Langton Wy BKHTH/KID SE3 145 K2
CROY/NA CR0 212 B2
Langtry Pl FUL/PGN SW6 119 K6
Langtry Rd NTHLT UB5 95 H1
STJWD NW8 83 F6
Langtry Wk STJWD NW8 83 G6
Langwood Cha TEDD TW11 174 D2
Langworth Cl RDART DA2 171 G5
Langworth Dr YEAD UB4 95 F5
Lanhill Rd MV/WKIL W9 100 E3
Lanier Rd LEW SE13 165 G1
Lanigan Dr HSLW TW3 135 G6
Lankaster Gdns EFNCH N2 47 H4
Lankers Dr RYLN/HDSTN HA2 59 K3
Lankton Cl BECK BR3 183 F4
Lannock Rd HYS/HAR UB3 113 J1
Lannoy Rd ELTH/MOT SE9 167 H3
Lanrick Rd POP/IOD E14 106 B5
Lanridge Rd ABYW SE2 128 E3
Lansbury Av BARK IG11 91 G5
CHDH RM6 74 A2
EBED/NFELT TW14 154 A1
UED N18 49 K1
Lansbury Cl WLSDN NW10 80 E3
Lansbury Crs DART DA1 151 K6
Lansbury Dr YEAD UB4 94 E3
Lansbury Gdns POP/IOD E14 * 106 B5
Lansbury Rd PEND EN3 25 F2
Lansbury Wy UED N18 50 A1
Lanscombe Wk VX/NE SW8 * 141 K1
Lansdell Rd MTCM CR4 179 F5
Lansdown Cl WOT/HER KT12 188 B5
Lansdowne Av BXLYHN DA7 148 D1
ORP BR6 201 G5
Lansdowne Cl BRYLDS KT5 191 J6
TWK TW1 156 A3
Lansdowne Copse WPK KT4 * 192 D6
Lansdowne Ct WPK KT4 192 D6
Lansdowne Crs NTGHL W11 100 C6
Lansdowne Dr HACK E8 86 D6
Lansdowne Gdns VX/NE SW8 141 K2
Lansdowne Gn VX/NE SW8 141 K1
Lansdowne Gv WLSDN NW10 81 G2
Lansdowne Hl WNWD SE27 162 C5
Lansdowne La CHARL SE7 126 C5
Lansdowne Ms CHARL SE7 126 C5
NTGHL W11 119 J1
Lansdowne Pl NRWD SE19 181 G3
STHWK SE1 19 F4
Lansdowne Ri NTGHL W11 100 C6
Lansdowne Rd BMLY BR1 183 K3
CHING E4 37 J4
CROY/NA CR0 196 E6
FNCH N3 46 D3
GDMY/SEVK IG3 73 F5
HACK E8 86 C4
HOR/WEW KT19 206 E5
HSLW TW3 135 G4
MUSWH N10 48 C5
NTGHL W11 100 C6
RYNPK SW20 177 F3
STAN HA7 43 J2
SWFD E18 52 E6
TOTM N17 50 C4
WALTH E17 69 J3
WAN E11 70 D6
Lansdowne Ter BMSBY WC1N 5 F7
Lansdowne Wk NTGHL W11 119 H1
Lansdowne Wy VX/NE SW8 141 K2
Lansdowne Wood Cl
WNWD SE27 162 C5
Lansdown Rd FSTGT E7 89 G5
SCUP DA14 168 C5
Lansfield Av UED N18 36 C6
Lantern Cl ALP/SUD HA0 79 K3
ORP BR6 216 B2
PUT/ROE SW15 138 D5
Lanterns Ct POP/IOD E14 124 E3
Lantern Wy WDR/YW UB7 112 B2
Lant St STHWK SE1 18 C2
Lanvanor Rd PECK SE15 143 K3
Lapford Cl MV/WKIL W9 * 100 D3
Lapse Wood Wk FSTH SE23 163 J3
Lapstone Gdns
KTN/HRWW/WS HA3 61 J3
Lapwing Cl ERITH DA8 * 150 E1
Lapwing Ter FSTGT E7 89 H3
Lapwing Wy YEAD UB4 95 H5
Lapworth Cl ORP BR6 202 D6
Lapworth Ct BAY/PAD W2 101 F4
Lara Cl CHSGTN KT9 206 A5
LEW SE13 165 F1
Larbert Rd STRHM/NOR SW16 179 H4
Larch Av ACT W3 118 B1
Larch Cl BAL SW12 161 G4
DEPT SE8 124 C6
FBAR/BDGN N11 48 A3
Larch Crs HOR/WEW KT19 206 D4
YEAD UB4 95 G4
Larch Dene ORP BR6 201 F6
Larch Dr CHSWK W4 * 117 H5
Larches Av MORT/ESHN SW14 138 A5
The Larches PLMGR N13 35 J5
Larch Gv BFN/LL DA15 168 A3
Larch Rd CRICK NW2 82 A2
DART DA1 171 G3
LEY E10 69 J6
Larch Tree Wy CROY/NA CR0 213 J1
Larch Wy HAYES BR2 201 F4
Larchwood Av CRW RM5 56 D2
Larchwood Cl CRW RM5 56 E2
Larchwood Rd ELTH/MOT SE9 167 G4
Larcombe Cl CROY/NA CR0 212 B2
Larcom St WALW SE17 18 D7
Larden Rd ACT W3 118 B2
Largewood Av SURB KT6 191 H6
Larissa St WALW SE17 * 19 F7
Larkbere Rd SYD SE26 164 B6
Larken Cl BUSH WD23 28 C3
Larken Dr BUSH WD23 28 C3
Larkfield Av
KTN/HRWW/WS HA3 43 H6
Larkfield Rd RCH/KEW TW9 137 F5
SCUP DA14 168 A5
Larkhall La CLAP SW4 141 K3
Larkhall Ri CLAP SW4 141 H4
Larkham Cl FELT TW13 153 H5
Larkhill Ter
WOOL/PLUM SE18 * 147 F1
Lark Rw BETH E2 86 E6
Larksfield Gv EN EN1 24 D2
Larkshall Crs CHING E4 38 A6
Larkshall Rd CHING E4 52 B2
Larkspur Cl CDALE/KGS NW9 62 D2
ORP BR6 202 D6
TOTM N17 49 K3
Larkspur Gv EDGW HA8 30 E6
Larkspur Wy HOR/WEW KT19 206 E3
Larkswood Cl ERITH DA8 150 D2
Larkswood Ri PIN HA5 59 G1
Larkswood Rd CHING E4 37 J6
Lark Wy CAR SM5 194 D4
Larkway Cl CDALE/KGS NW9 63 F1
Larnach Rd HMSMTH W6 119 G6
Larne Rd RSLP HA4 58 D4
Larner Rd ERITH DA8 150 B1
Larpent Av PUT/ROE SW15 139 F6
Larwood Cl GFD/PVL UB6 78 D3
Lascelles Av HRW HA1 60 D4
Lascelles Cl WAN E11 70 B6
Lascott's Rd WDGN N22 49 F2
Lassa Rd ELTH/MOT SE9 146 D6
Lassell St GNWCH SE10 125 G5
Lasseter Pl BKHTH/KID SE3 125 H6
Latchett Rd SWFD E18 53 F4
Latchingdon Gdns WFD IG8 53 J2
Latchmere Cl
RCHPK/HAM TW10 175 F1
Latchmere La KUTN/CMB KT2 175 G2
Latchmere Rd BTSEA SW11 140 E3
KUTN/CMB KT2 175 F2
Latchmere St BTSEA SW11 140 E3
Lateward Rd BTFD TW8 116 E6
Latham Cl EHAM E6 107 J5
Latham Rd BXLYHS DA6 149 H6
TWK TW1 156 A2
Latham's Wy CROY/NA CR0 196 A6
Lathkill Cl EN EN1 36 C2
Lathom Rd EHAM E6 89 K5
Latimer Av EHAM E6 89 K6
Latimer Cl PIN HA5 41 G4
WATW WD18 26 C2
WPK KT4 207 K2
Latimer Gdns PIN HA5 41 G4
Latimer Pl NKENS W10 100 A5
Latimer Rd BAR EN5 21 F4
CROY/NA CR0 * 211 H1
FSTGT E7 89 F2
NKENS W10 100 A4
SEVS/STOTM N15 68 A3
TEDD TW11 174 A1
WIM/MER SW19 178 A2
Latona Rd PECK SE15 123 H6
La Tourne Gdns ORP BR6 216 C1
Lattimer Pl CHSWK W4 138 B1
Latton Cl ESH/CLAY KT10 204 B2
WOT/HER KT12 188 E4
Latymer Gdns FNCH N3 * 46 C5
Latymer Rd ED N9 36 B4
Latymer Wy ED N9 35 K4
Laubin Cl TWK TW1 136 C5
Lauder Cl NTHLT UB5 95 H1
Lauderdale Dr
RCHPK/HAM TW10 156 E5
Lauderdale Pde
MV/WKIL W9 * 101 F2
Lauderdale Pl BARB EC2Y * 12 D2
Lauderdale Rd MV/WKIL W9 101 F2
Laud St CROY/NA CR0 211 J1
LBTH SE11 122 A5
Laughton Rd NTHLT UB5 95 H1
Launcelot Rd BMLY BR1 165 K6
Launcelot St STHWK SE1 17 J3
Launceston Gdns GFD/PVL UB6 79 J6
Launceston Pl KENS W8 120 B3
Launceston Rd GFD/PVL UB6 79 J6
Launch St POP/IOD E14 125 F3
Launders Ga ACT W3 * 117 J2
Laundress La STNW/STAM N16 86 C1
Laundry Rd HMSMTH W6 119 H6
Laura Cl EN EN1 24 A6
WAN E11 71 G2
Lauradale Rd EFNCH N2 65 K1
Laura Pl CLPT E5 86 E2
Laura Ter FSBYPK N4 * 67 H6
Laurel Av TWK TW1 156 A3
Laurel Bank
NFNCH/WDSPK N12 * 33 G6
Laurel Bank Gdns
FUL/PGN SW6 139 J3
Laurel Bank Rd ENC/FH EN2 23 J2
Laurel Cl BARK/HLT IG6 54 C2
BFN/LL DA15 168 B5
DART DA1 171 F3
OXHEY WD19 27 H2
TOOT SW17 178 D1
Laurel Crs CROY/NA CR0 213 J1
ROMW/RG RM7 75 G5
Laurel Dr WCHMH N21 35 G2
Laurel Gdns CHING E4 37 K2
HNWL W7 115 K1
HSLWW TW4 134 D5
MLHL NW7 31 F5
Laurel Gv PGE/AN SE20 181 K3
SYD SE26 182 A1
Laurel La WDR/YW UB7 112 B4
Laurel Pk KTN/HRWW/WS HA3 43 F3
Laurel Rd BARN SW13 138 D3
HPTN TW12 173 J1
RYNPK SW20 176 E4
The Laurels BRXN/ST SW9 * 142 C1
BUSH WD23 * 28 E4
RDART DA2 * 171 F5
Laurel St HACK E8 86 B4
Laurel Vw NFNCH/WDSPK N12 33 F5
Laurel Vls HNWL W7 * 115 K2
Laurel Wy SWFD E18 70 D1
TRDG/WHET N20 32 E5
Laurence Ms SHB W12 118 D2
Laurence Pountney Hl
CANST EC4R 12 E5
Laurence Pountney La
CANST EC4R 12 E5
MANHO EC4N 13 F5
Laurie Gv NWCR SE14 144 B2
Laurie Rd HNWL W7 96 E4
Laurier Rd CROY/NA CR0 197 G4
KTTN NW5 84 B1
Laurimel Cl STAN HA7 43 H2
Laurino Pl BUSH WD23 28 C4
Lauriston Rd HOM E9 87 F6
WIM/MER SW19 177 G2
Lausanne Rd CEND/HSY/T N8 67 G1
PECK SE15 143 K3
Lavender Av CDALE/KGS NW9 62 E5
MTCM CR4 178 D4
WPK KT4 208 A1
Lavender Cl CAR SM5 210 A2
CHEL SW3 120 C6
HAYES BR2 200 D3
Lavender Ct E/WMO/HCT KT8 173 G6
Lavender Gdns BTSEA SW11 140 E4
ENC/FH EN2 23 H1
KTN/HRWW/WS HA3 42 E2
Lavender Gv HACK E8 86 C5
MTCM CR4 178 D4
Lavender Hl BTSEA SW11 140 E4
ENC/FH EN2 23 H2
Lavender Pl IL IG1 90 B3
Lavender Ri WDR/YW UB7 112 D2
Lavender Rd
BERM/RHTH SE16 124 B1
BTSEA SW11 140 C4
CROY/NA CR0 196 A3
ENC/FH EN2 23 K2
HOR/WEW KT19 206 D4
SUT SM1 209 H2
WLGTN SM6 210 A3
Lavender St SRTFD E15 88 C4
Lavender Sweep BTSEA SW11 140 E5
Lavender Ter BTSEA SW11 * 140 D4
Lavender V WLGTN SM6 210 D4
Lavender Wk BTSEA SW11 140 E5
Lavender Wy CROY/NA CR0 198 A3
Lavengro Rd WNWD SE27 162 D4
Lavenham Rd
WAND/EARL SW18 159 J4
Lavernock Rd BXLYHN DA7 149 H3
Lavers Rd STNW/STAM N16 86 A1
Laverstoke Gdns
PUT/ROE SW15 158 C2
Laverton Ms ECT SW5 120 A4
Laverton Pl ECT SW5 120 A4
Lavidge Rd ELTH/MOT SE9 166 D4
Lavina Gv IS N1 5 G2
Lavington Cl HOM E9 87 H4
Lavington Rd CROY/NA CR0 211 F1
WEA W13 116 C1
Lavington St STHWK SE1 18 B1
Lavinia Rd DART DA1 171 J1
Lawdon Gdns CROY/NA CR0 211 H2
Lawford Gdns DART DA1 151 F6
Lawford Rd CHSWK W4 137 K1
IS N1 86 A5
KTTN NW5 84 C4
Lawless St POP/IOD E14 * 105 K6
Lawley Rd STHGT/OAK N14 34 B2
Lawley St CLPT E5 86 E2
Lawn Cl BMLY BR1 184 A3
EN EN1 36 B2
NWMAL KT3 176 B5
RSLP HA4 76 D1
SWLY BR8 187 K5
Lawn Crs RCH/KEW TW9 137 H3
Lawn Farm Gv CHDH RM6 74 A1
Lawn Gdns HNWL W7 115 K1
Lawn House Cl POP/IOD E14 125 F2
Lawn La VX/NE SW8 121 K6
Lawn Rd BECK BR3 182 D3
HAMP NW3 83 K3
Lawns Ct WBLY HA9 * 62 C6
The Lawns BELMT SM2 208 C5
BKHTH/KID SE3 * 145 J4
CHING E4 51 J1
NRWD SE19 180 E4
PIN HA5 42 B3
SCUP DA14 168 C6
Lawns Wy CRW RM5 56 E3
Lawnswood BAR EN5 * 20 C6
Lawn Ter BKHTH/KID SE3 145 J4
The Lawn NWDGN UB2 115 F5
Lawn V PIN HA5 41 J5
Lawrence Av MLHL NW7 31 G6
MNPK E12 90 A2
NWMAL KT3 192 B4
PLMGR N13 35 H6
WALTH E17 51 G4
WLSDN NW10 81 F6
Lawrence Buildings
STNW/STAM N16 86 B1
Lawrence Campe Cl
TRDG/WHET N20 33 H5
Lawrence Cl SEVS/STOTM N15 68 A1
SHB W12 99 K6
Lawrence Ct MLHL NW7 45 G1
OXHEY WD19 * 27 H5
Lawrence Crs DAGE RM10 92 D1
EDGW HA8 44 C5
Lawrence Dr HGDN/ICK UB10 76 A2
Lawrence Gdns MLHL NW7 31 H5
Lawrence Hl CHING E4 37 J4
Lawrence Hill Gdns DART DA1 171 F1
Lawrence Hill Rd DART DA1 171 F1
Lawrence La CITYW EC2V 12 D4
Lawrence Pde ISLW TW7 * 136 C4
Lawrence Pl IS N1 * 84 E6
Lawrence Rd EA W5 116 D4
EHAM E6 89 J6
ERITH DA8 149 J1
GPK RM2 75 K2
HPTN TW12 172 E3
HSLWW TW4 134 B5
PIN HA5 59 H2
PLSTW E13 89 F6
RCHPK/HAM TW10 156 D6
SEVS/STOTM N15 68 A1
SNWD SE25 197 G1
UED N18 36 D6
WWKM BR4 214 E2
YEAD UB4 94 A1
Lawrence St CAN/RD E16 106 D4
CHEL SW3 120 D6
MLHL NW7 31 H6
Lawrence Wy WLSDN NW10 80 E1
Lawrence Yd
SEVS/STOTM N15 68 A1
Lawrie Park Av SYD SE26 181 J1
Lawrie Park Crs SYD SE26 181 K1
Lawrie Park Gdns SYD SE26 181 J1
Lawrie Park Rd SYD SE26 181 K2
Laws Cl SNWD SE25 196 E1
Lawson Cl CAN/RD E16 107 G5
IL IG1 90 D3
WIM/MER SW19 159 G5
Lawson Gdns DART DA1 151 G6
PIN HA5 41 F6
Lawson Rd DART DA1 151 G5
PEND EN3 24 E2
STHL UB1 95 K3
Law St STHWK SE1 19 F4
Lawton Rd BOW E3 105 G2
EBAR EN4 21 H4
LEY E10 70 A5
Laxcon Cl WLSDN NW10 81 F3
Laxey Rd ORP BR6 217 F4
Laxley Cl CMBW SE5 142 C1
Laxton Pl CAMTN NW1 3 K6
Layard Rd BERM/RHTH SE16 123 J4
EN EN1 24 B2
THHTH CR7 180 E5
Layard Sq BERM/RHTH SE16 123 J4
Laycock St IS N1 85 G4
Layer Gdns ACT W3 98 C6
Layfield Cl HDN NW4 63 K4
Layfield Crs HDN NW4 63 K4
Layfield Rd HDN NW4 63 K4
Layhams Rd WWKM BR4 214 C2
Laymarsh Cl BELV DA17 129 G3
Laymead Cl NTHLT UB5 77 J4
Laystall St FSBYW WC1X 5 J7
Layton Crs CROY/NA CR0 211 G3
Layton Pl RCH/KEW TW9 137 H2
Layton Rd BTFD TW8 116 E5
HSLW TW3 135 G5
Layzell Wk ELTH/MOT SE9 166 C3
Lazenby Ct COVGDN WC2E * 10 E5
Leabank Cl HRW HA1 78 E1
Leabank Sq HOM E9 87 J4
Leabank Vw SEVS/STOTM N15 68 C3
Leabourne Rd STNW/STAM N16 68 C3
Lea Bridge Rd LEY E10 69 F6
WALTH E17 70 A2
Lea Cl WHTN TW2 154 E2
Lea Cottages MTCM CR4 * 179 F5
Lea Crs RSLP HA4 76 D2
Leacroft Av BAL SW12 160 E2
Leacroft Cl WCHMH N21 35 H4
Leadale Av CHING E4 37 J4
Leadale Rd STNW/STAM N16 68 C3
Leadbeaters Cl
FBAR/BDGN N11 47 K1
Leadenhall Pl BANK EC3V 13 G4
Leadenhall St BANK EC3V 13 G4
Leader Av MNPK E12 90 A3
The Leadings WBLY HA9 80 E1
Leaf Cl NTHWD HA6 40 B3
THDIT KT7 189 K2
Leaf Gv WNWD SE27 180 B1
Leafield Cl STRHM/NOR SW16 180 C2
Leafield La SCUP DA14 169 G6
Leafield Rd RYNPK SW20 177 J6
SUT SM1 193 K6
Leafy Gv HAYES BR2 215 G3
Leafy Oak Rd LEE/GVPK SE12 166 B6
Leafy Wy CROY/NA CR0 197 G6
Lea Gdns WBLY HA9 80 B3
Leagrave St CLPT E5 86 E1
Lea Hall Gdns LEY E10 * 69 J5
Lea Hall Rd LEY E10 69 J5
Leahurst Rd LEW SE13 * 165 H1
Leake St STHWK SE1 17 H2
Lealand Rd SEVS/STOTM N15 68 B3
Leaming Cl MNPK E12 89 J3
Leamington Av BMLY BR1 184 B1
MRDN SM4 193 J1
ORP BR6 216 E2
WALTH E17 69 J2
Leamington Cl BMLY BR1 166 B6
HSLW TW3 135 H6
Leamington Crs
RYLN/HDSTN HA2 77 J1
Leamington Gdns
GDMY/SEVK IG3 73 F6
Leamington Pk ACT W3 99 F4
Leamington Pl YEAD UB4 94 D3
Leamington Rd NWDGN UB2 114 C4
Leamington Road Vls
NTGHL W11 100 D4
Leamore St HMSMTH W6 118 E4
Leamouth Rd EHAM E6 107 J5
POP/IOD E14 106 B5
Leander Rd BRXS/STRHM SW2 162 A1
NTHLT UB5 96 A1
THHTH CR7 196 A1
Learner Dr RYLN/HDSTN HA2 60 A6
Lea Rd BECK BR3 182 D5
ENC/FH EN2 23 K2
NWDGN UB2 114 D4
Learoyd Gdns EHAM E6 108 A6
Leas Cl CHSGTN KT9 206 B5
Leas Dl ELTH/MOT SE9 167 F5
Leas Gn CHST BR7 186 A2
Leaside Av MUSWH N10 48 A6
Leaside Rd CLPT E5 68 E5
Leasowes Rd LEY E10 69 J5
Leathart Cl HCH RM12 93 K5
Leatherbottle Gn
ERITHM DA18 129 G3
Leather Cl MTCM CR4 179 F5
Leatherdale St WCHPL E1 * 105 F2
Leather Gdns SRTFD E15 88 C6
Leatherhead Cl
STNW/STAM N16 68 A5
Leatherhead Rd CHSGTN KT9 205 K5
Leather La CLKNW EC1R 5 J7
HCIRC EC1N 11 J1
Leathermarket Ct STHWK SE1 19 G3
Leathermarket St STHWK SE1 19 G3
Leather Rd BERM/RHTH SE16 124 A4
Leathersellers Cl BAR EN5 * 20 C4

Leather St WAP E1W................105 F6
Leathsale Rd RYLN/HDSTN HA2...78 B1
Leathwaite Rd BTSEA SW11....140 C5
Leathwell Rd DEPT SE8.............144 E3
Lea V DART DA1...........................150 A5
Lea Valley Rd CHING E4................37 J2
Lea Valley Wk CLPT E5.................68 D4
TOTM N17...............................50 D5
Leaveland Cl BECK BR3...............198 D1
Leaver Gdns GFD/PVL UB6..........96 D1
Leavesden Rd STAN N13.................7 J2
Leaway CLPT E5 *..........................68 C5
Lebanon Av FELT TW13...............172 C1
Lebanon Gdns
    WAND/EARL SW18.............159 K1
Lebanon Pk TWK TW1.................156 C3
Lebanon Rd CROY/NA CR0.........197 F5
    WAND/EARL SW18.............139 K6
Lebrun Sq BKHTH/KID SE3.........146 A5
Lechmere Ap WFD IG8...................53 G5
Lechmere Rd CRICK NW2.............81 K4
Leckford Rd
    WAND/EARL SW18.............160 B4
Leckhampton Pl
    BRXS/STRHM SW2.............162 B2
Leckwith Av ABYW SE2...............129 F6
Lecky St SKENS SW7..................120 C5
Leconfield Av BARN SW13...........138 C4
Leconfield Rd HBRY N5.................85 K3
Leda Av PEND EN3.........................25 F2
Leda Rd WOOL/PLUM SE18.........126 E3
Ledbury Ms North
    NTGHL W11........................100 E6
Ledbury Ms West NTGHL W11.....100 E6
Ledbury Rd CROY/NA CR0...........211 K2
    NTGHL W11........................100 D5
Ledbury St PECK SE15................143 H1
Ledrington Rd NRWD SE19..........181 G2
Ledway Dr WBLY HA9....................62 B4
Lee Av CHDH RM6..........................74 A5
Leechcroft Av BFN/LL DA15........148 A6
Leechcroft Rd WLGTN SM6..........210 A1
Lee Church St LEW SE13.............145 H5
Lee Cl WALTH E17...........................51 F4
Lee Conservancy Rd HOM E9........87 H3
Leecroft Rd BAR EN5.....................20 C6
Leeds Cl ORP BR6.......................202 E6
Leeds Rd IL IG1.............................72 D5
Lee Gn STMC/STPC BR5..............202 B2
Lee High Rd LEW SE13................145 H5
Leeke St FSBYW WC1X....................4 M6
Leeland Rd WEA W13...................116 B1
Leeland Ter WEA W13..................116 B1
Leeland Wy WLSDN NW10.............81 G2
Leemount Cl HDN NW4 *................64 B1
Lee Pk BKHTH/KID SE3................145 J5
    UED N18...............................51 F1
Lee Rd BKHTH/KID SE3................145 J4
    EN EN1...................................36 C1
    GFD/PVL UB6.........................79 J6
    MLHL NW7..............................46 A3
    WIM/MER SW19....................178 A4
Lees Av NTHWD HA6......................40 D4
Leeside BAR EN5............................32 C1
Leeside Crs GLDGN NW11.............64 D4
Leeside Rd TOTM N17.....................50 E3
Leeson Rd HNHL SE24 *..............142 B6
Leesons Hi CHST BR7..................186 A5
Leesons Wy STMC/STPC BR5......186 A5
Lees Pl MYFR/PKLN W1K..................9 G5
The Lees CROY/NA CR0...............198 C6
Lee St HACK E8...............................86 B6
Lee Ter BKHTH/KID SE3...............145 H4
The Lee NTHWD HA6.....................40 D1
Lee Vw ENC/FH EN2.......................23 H2
Leeward Gdns
    WIM/MER SW19....................177 J2
Leeway DEPT SE8..........................124 C5
The Leeways CHEAM SM3 *........208 C4
Leewood Cl LEE/GVPK SE12 *.....165 J1
Lefevre Wk BOW E3........................87 H6
Leffern Rd SHB W12.....................118 D2
Lefroy Rd SHB W12......................118 C2
Left Side STHGT/OAK N14 *...........34 D3
Legard Rd HBRY N5.........................85 H1
Legatt Rd ELTH/MOT SE9.............146 C6
Leggatt Rd SRTFD E15.................106 A1
Legge St LEW SE13......................145 F6
Leghorn Rd WLSDN NW10.............99 J1
    WOOL/PLUM SE18.............127 J5
Legion Cl IS N1............................85 G4
Legion Rd GFD/PVL UB6................96 C1
Legion Ter BOW E3.........................87 H6
Legion Wy NFNCH/WDSPK N12...47 J3
Legon Av ROMW/RG RM7...............74 E5
Legrace Av HSLWW TW4..............134 C3
Leicester Av MTCM CR4...............195 K1
Leicester Cl WPK KT4...................208 A2
Leicester Gdns GDMY/SEVK IG3...72 E4
Leicester Pl LSQ/SEVD WC2H *.....10 D5
Leicester Rd BAR EN5....................21 F6
    CROY/NA CR0......................197 F4
    EFNCH N2..............................47 J6
    WAN E11...................................71 F2
    WLSDN NW10.........................81 F5
Leicester Sq LSQ/SEVD WC2H.....10 D5
Leicester St LSQ/SEVD WC2H......10 D5
Leigham Av
    STRHM/NOR SW16...............161 K5
Leigham Cl
    STRHM/NOR SW16...............162 B5
Leigham Court Rd
    STRHM/NOR SW16...............162 A5
Leigham Dr ISLW TW7..................135 K1
Leigham Hall Pde
    STRHM/NOR SW16...............161 K5
Leigham V STRHM/NOR SW16....162 B5
Leigh Av REDBR IG4........................71 H1
Leigh Cl NWMAL KT3....................192 A1
Leigh Ct RYLN/HDSTN HA2 *.........78 D1
Leigh Crs CROY/NA CR0..............213 K6
Leigh Gdns WLSDN NW10............100 A1
Leigh Hunt Dr STHGT/OAK N14.....34 D4
Leigh Orchard Cl
    STRHM/NOR SW16...............162 A5

Leigh Pl FELT TW13.....................154 B3
    WELL DA16............................148 B3
Leigh Rd EHAM E6..........................90 A5
    HBRY N5.................................85 H2
    HSLW TW3............................135 J5
    LEY E10....................................70 A4
Leigh Rodd OXHEY WD19..............27 J5
Leigh St STPAN WC1H.....................4 E7
Leigh Ter STMC/STPC BR5 *........186 C6
The Leigh KUTN/CMB KT2............176 B2
Leighton Av MNPK E12...................90 A3
    PIN HA5...................................41 J5
Leighton Cl EDGW HA8..................44 C5
Leighton Crs KTTN NW5.................84 C5
Leighton Gdns WLSDN NW10......100 A1
Leighton Gv KTTN NW5...................84 C5
Leighton Rd EN EN1........................36 C1
    KTN/HRWW/WS HA3.............42 D5
    KTTN NW5.............................84 C5
    WEA W13...............................116 B2
Leighton St CROY/NA CR0...........196 C5
Leila Parnell Pl CHARL SE7.........126 B6
Leinster Av MORT/ESHN SW14...137 K4
Leinster Gdns BAY/PAD W2.........101 G5
Leinster Ms BAY/PAD W2.............101 G5
Leinster Rd MUSWH N10................66 B1
Leinster Sq BAY/PAD W2..............100 D6
Leinster Ter BAY/PAD W2.............101 G6
Leisure Wy NFNCH/WDSPK N12...47 H3
Leith Cl CDALE/KGS NW9...............63 F5
Leithcote Gdns
    STRHM/NOR SW16...............162 A6
Leithcote Pth
    STRHM/NOR SW16...............162 A5
Leith Hl STMC/STPC BR5...............186 B4
Leith Rd WDGN N22........................49 H4
Leith Towers BELMT SM2 *..........209 F5
Lela Av HSLWW TW4.....................134 B3
Lelitia Cl HACK E8...........................86 C6
Leman St WCHPL E1........................13 K4
Le May Av LEE/GVPK SE12...........166 A5
Lemark Cl STAN HA7.......................43 J2
Lemmon Rd GNWCH SE10............125 H6
Lemna Rd WAN E11..........................70 C4
Lemonwell Dr ELTH/MOT SE9......147 G6
Lemsford Cl SEVS/STOTM N15......68 C2
Lena Crs ED N9................................36 E4
Lena Gdns HMSMTH W6...............119 F3
Lena Kennedy Cl CHING E4............52 A2
Lendal Ter CLAP SW4....................141 J4
Lenelby Rd SURB KT6...................191 H5
Len Freeman Pl FUL/PGN SW6....119 J6
Lenham Rd BXLYHN DA7...............129 G6
    LEE/GVPK SE12.....................145 J3
    SUT SM1................................209 F2
    THHTH CR7...........................180 E5
Lennard Av WWKM BR4................199 H6
Lennard Cl WWKM BR4.................199 H6
Lennard Rd CROY/NA CR0...........196 D5
    PGE/AN SE20........................182 A2
    SYD SE26..............................181 K2
Lennard Ter PGE/AN SE20 *.........182 A2
Lennon Rd CRICK NW2....................82 A4
Lennox Cl ROM RM1.........................75 H3
Lennox Gdns CROY/NA CR0..........211 H2
    IL IG1......................................71 K5
    KTBR SW1X.............................14 E6
    WLSDN NW10..........................81 H2
Lennox Gardens Ms CHEL SW3....14 E6
Lennox Rd FSBYPK N4....................67 F6
    WALTH E17...............................69 H3
Lenor Cl BXLYHS DA6..................149 F5
Lensbury Wy ABYW SE2...............128 E3
Lens Rd FSTGT E7............................89 G5
Lenthall Rd HACK E8........................86 B5
Lenthorp Rd GNWCH SE10..........125 J4
Lentmead Rd BMLY BR1...............165 J5
Lenton Ri RCH/KEW TW9..............137 F4
Lenton St WOOL/PLUM SE18.......127 J4
Leof Crs CAT SE6...........................182 E1
Leominster Rd MRDN SM4............194 B3
Leominster Wk MRDN SM4...........194 B3
Leonard Av MRDN SM4.................194 B2
    ROMW/RG RM7........................75 F5
Leonard Ct KENS W8.....................119 K3
Leonard Pl HAYES BR2 *..............215 J1
    STNW/STAM N16....................86 A2
Leonard Rd CHING E4.....................51 H6
    ED N9......................................36 B5
    FSTGT E7..................................88 E4
    NWDGN UB2..........................114 C4
    STRHM/NOR SW16...............179 H1
Leonard St CAN/RD E16................126 D1
    SDTCH EC2A.............................7 H9
Leontine Cl PECK SE15..................143 H1
Leopold Av WIM/MER SW19.........177 J1
Leopold Ms HOM E9........................86 E6
Leopold Rd EA W5........................117 G1
    EFNCH N2..............................47 J5
    UED N18..................................50 D1
    WALTH E17................................69 J2
    WIM/MER SW19....................159 J6
    WLSDN NW10..........................81 G5
Leopold St BOW E3........................105 H4
Leo St PECK SE15.........................143 K1
Leppoc Rd CLAP SW4...................141 J6
Leroy St STHWK SE1......................19 H6
Lerry Cl WKENS W14......................119 J6
Lescombe Cl FSTH SE23...............164 B5
Lescombe Rd FSTH SE23..............164 B5
Lesley Cl BXLY DA5.......................169 J2
Leslie Gdns BELMT SM2...............208 E5
Leslie Grove Pl CROY/NA CR0......196 F5
Leslie Park Rd CROY/NA CR0.......197 F5
Leslie Rd CAN/RD E16..................107 F5
    EFNCH N2................................47 J6
    WAN E11...................................88 B2
Lesney Pk ERITH DA8....................150 A6
Lesney Park Rd ERITH DA8...........130 A6
Lessar Av CLAP SW4.....................141 H6
Lessingham Av TOOT SW17.........160 E6
Lessing St FSTH SE23...................164 B2

Lessington Av ROMW/RG RM7.....74 E3
Lessness Av BXLYHN DA7...........148 E1
Lessness Pk BELV DA17...............129 G5
Lessness Rd MRDN SM4..............194 B3
Lester Av CAN/RD E16..................106 C5
Lestock Cl SNWD SE25................181 H6
Leston Cl RAIN RM13....................111 K2
Leswin Pl STNW/STAM N16...........86 B1
Leswin Rd STNW/STAM N16..........86 B1
Letchford Gdns WLSDN NW10......99 J2
Letchford Ms WLSDN NW10 *.......99 J2
Letchford Ter
    KTN/HRWW/WS HA3...............42 B4
Letchworth Av
    EBED/NFELT TW14...............153 J2
Letchworth Cl HAYES BR2...........199 K2
    OXHEY WD19..........................21 H1
Letchworth Dr HAYES BR2...........199 K2
Letchworth St TOOT SW17..........160 E6
Letterstone Rd FUL/PGN SW6.....139 J1
Lettice St FUL/PGN SW6..............139 J3
Lett Rd SRTFD E15..........................88 B5
Leucha Rd WALTH E17....................69 G2
Levana Cl WIM/MER SW19...........159 H3
Levehurst Wy CLAP SW4..............141 K3
Leven Cl OXHEY WD19...................41 H1
Levendale Rd FSTH SE23.............164 B4
Leven Rd POP/IOD E14..................106 A4
Leven Wy HYS/HAR UB3................94 C6
Leverett St CHEL SW3.....................14 D6
Leverholme Gdns
    ELTH/MOT SE9.....................167 F6
Leverson St
    STRHM/NOR SW16...............179 H2
Lever St FSBYE EC1V.......................6 D8
Leverton Pl KTTN NW5...................84 C3
Leverton St KTTN NW5....................84 C3
Levett Gdns GDMY/SEVK IG3........91 F2
Levett Rd BARK IG11.....................109 K1
Levine Gdns BARK IG11................110 A1
Levison Wy ARCH N19.....................66 E6
Lewes Cl NTHLT UB5.......................78 A4
Lewesdon Cl WIM/MER SW19.....159 G3
Lewes Rd BMLY BR1.....................184 C5
    NFNCH/WDSPK N12...............47 J1
Leweston Pl STNW/STAM N16......68 B4
Lewgars Av CDALE/KGS NW9........62 E3
Lewing Cl ORP BR6........................201 K5
Lewin Rd BXLYHS DA6..................149 F5
    MORT/ESHN SW14...............138 A4
    STRHM/NOR SW16...............179 J2
Lewis Av WALTH E17.......................51 J4
Lewis Crs WLSDN NW10................80 E3
Lewis Gdns EFNCH N2....................47 H5
    SEVS/STOTM N15...................68 C3
Lewis Gv LEW SE13......................145 F5
Lewisham High St LEW SE13........145 F4
Lewisham Hl LEW SE13................145 F3
Lewisham Pk LEW SE13................164 E1
Lewisham Rd LEW SE13...............144 E2
Lewisham Wy BROCKY SE4..........144 C3
Lewis Rd BCTR RM8........................74 A6
    MTCM CR4............................178 C5
    RCH/KEW TW9 *...................136 E6
    SCUP DA14............................168 E5
    STHL UB1..............................114 D2
    SUT SM1................................209 F2
    WELL DA16...........................148 D4
Lexden Cl CAMTN NW1...................84 B5
Lexington St WPK KT4..................192 E6
Lewis Wy DAGE RM10....................92 D4
Lexden Rd ACT W3..........................98 D6
    MTCM CR4............................195 J1
Lexham Gdns ECT SW5.................119 K4
    KENS W8...............................119 K4
Lexham Ms KENS W8.....................119 J4
Lexington St SOHO/CST W1F.........10 B4
Lexington Wy BAR EN5...................20 A5
Lexton Gdns BAL SW12.................161 J3
Leyborne Av WEA W13..................116 D2
Leyborne Pk RCH/KEW TW9.........137 H2
Leybourne Cl HAYES BR2.............199 K3
Leybourne Rd CAMTN NW1 *.........84 B5
    CDALE/KGS NW9....................63 G4
    HDN/ICK UB10..........................76 A6
    WAN E11...................................88 D1
Leybourne St CAMTN NW1.............84 B5
Leyburn Cl WALTH E17....................70 A1
Leyburn Gdns CROY/NA CR0........197 F6
Leyburn Gv UED N18........................50 C2
Leyburn House CHARL SE7 *.........146 D1
Leyburn Rd UED N18.......................50 C2
Leycroft Gdns ERITH DA8.............150 E2
Leyden St WCHPL E1.......................13 J2
Leydon Cl BERM/RHTH SE16.......124 A1
Leyes Rd CAN/RD E16...................107 G6
Leyfield WPK KT4...........................192 B5
Leyland Av PEND EN3......................25 G5
Leyland Gdns WFD IG8.....................53 G1
Leyland Rd LEE/GVPK SE12.........165 K1
Leylang Rd NWCR SE14................144 A1
Leys Av DAGE RM10........................92 E6
Leys Cl DAGE RM10.........................92 E5
    HRW HA1..................................60 D2
Leysdown Av BXLYHN DA7...........149 K5
Leysdown Rd ELTH/MOT SE9.......166 D4
Leysfield Rd SHB W12...................118 D2
Leys Gdns EBAR EN4.......................22 A6
Leyspring Rd WAN E11....................70 D5
Leys Rd East PEND EN3...................25 G2
The Leys EFNCH N2..........................65 G1
    KTN/HRWW/WS HA3..............43 G5
Ley St IL IG1......................................72 C6
Leyswood Dr GNTH/NBYPK IG2....72 E2
Leythe Rd ACT W3.........................117 K2
Leyton Cross Rd RDART DA2.......170 D5
Leyton Gra LEY E10.........................69 J6
Leyton Green Rd LEY E10...............70 A3
Leyton Park Rd LEY E10..................70 A6
Leyton Rd SRTFD E15......................88 C3
    WIM/MER SW19....................178 B3
Leytonstone Rd SRTFD E15...........88 C4
Leywick St SRTFD E15....................88 C6
Lezayre Rd ORP BR6.....................217 F4
Liardet St NWCR SE14..................124 B6
Liberia Rd HBRY N5.........................85 H4

The Limes Av FBAR/BDGN N11.....48 B1
Limes Cl CAR SM5.........................194 D6
    FBAR/BDGN N11....................48 C1
Limesdale Gdns EDGW HA8..........44 E5
Limes Field Rd
    MORT/ESHN SW14...............138 B4
Limesford Rd PECK SE15.............144 A5
Limes Gdns WAND/EARL SW18..159 K1
Limes Gv LEW SE13.....................145 F5
Limes Rd BECK BR3.....................182 E5
    CROY/NA CR0........................196 E5
Limes Rw ORP BR6.......................216 B3
The Limes CMBW SE5..................143 F4
    PUR RM19.............................131 K5
    WAND/EARL SW18...............159 K1
Limestone Wk ERITH DA18...........128 E2
Lime St FENCHST EC3M.................13 G5
    WALTH E17...............................69 G1
Lime Street Pas BANK EC3V *.......13 G4
Lime St Pas.....................................13 G4
Lime Tree Av ESH/CLAY KT10......189 J5
Limetree Cl BRXS/STRHM SW2..162 A3
Lime Tree Ct PIN HA5......................42 A3
Limetree Ct PIN HA5........................42 A3
Lime Tree Gv CROY/NA CR0.........213 H1
Lime Tree Pl MTCM CR4...............179 G4
Lime Tree Rd HEST TW5...............135 G2
Lime Tree Ter CAT SE6.................164 C3
Lime Tree Wk BUSH WD23...........28 E3
    ENC/FH EN2............................23 J1
    WWKM BR4............................214 D2
Lime Wk SRTFD E15 *.....................88 C6
Limewood Cl BECK BR3................199 F2
    WALTH E17...............................69 H1
    WEA W13................................97 H5
Limewood Rd ERITH DA8..............149 K1
Limpsfield Av THHTH CR7.............196 A2
Linacre Cl PECK SE15...................143 J4
Linacre Rd CRICK NW2...................81 H4
Linchmere Rd LEE/GVPK SE12....165 J2
Lincoln Av ROMW/RG RM7............75 G5
    STHGT/OAK N14......................34 B4
    WHTN TW2............................155 H4
    WIM/MER SW19....................159 G3
Lincoln Cl ERITH DA8....................150 C3
    GFD/PVL UB6...........................78 C6
    RYLN/HDSTN HA2...................59 K2
Lincoln Crs EN EN1...........................24 A5
Lincoln Dr OXHEY WD19.................27 G5
Lincoln Est BOW E3.......................105 J3
Lincoln Gdns IL IG1..........................71 J4
Lincoln Green Rd
    STMC/STPC BR5...................202 A2
Lincoln Ms KIL/WHAMP NW6.........82 D5
Lincoln Pde EFNCH N2 *.................47 J6
Lincoln Rd ALP/SUD HA0................79 K4
    EFNCH N2................................47 A6
    EN EN1.....................................24 A5
    HSLW TW5.............................135 G6
    MTCM CR4.............................195 K2
    NTHWD HA6............................40 D6
    NWMAL KT3...........................175 J6
    PLSTW E13.............................107 F3
    RYLN/HDSTN HA2...................59 K2
    SCUP DA14............................186 D1
    SNWD SE25............................181 J6
    SWFD E18................................52 D4
    WPK KT4................................192 E5
Lincoln's Inn Flds LINN WC2A.........11 H3
The Lincolns MLHL NW7..................31 H5
Lincoln St CHEL SW3......................14 F7
    WAN E11...................................88 C1
Lincoln Ter BELMT SM2 *..............208 E5
Lincoln Wy EN EN1..........................24 A6
Lincombe Rd BMLY BR1................165 J5
Lindal Crs ENC/FH EN2...................22 E6
The Lindales TOTM N17...................50 C2
Lindal Rd BROCKY SE4.................144 C6
Linden Av DART DA1.......................171 F3
    EN EN1.....................................24 C2
    HSLW TW3.............................135 G6
    RSLP HA4.................................58 E5
    THHTH CR7............................196 C1
    WBLY HA9................................80 A4
    WLSDN NW10........................100 B1
Linden Cl ORP BR6........................217 G3
    RSLP HA4.................................58 E5
    STAN HA7.................................43 H1
    STHGT/OAK N14......................22 B6
    THDIT KT7..............................190 B4
Linden Cottages
    WIM/MER SW19 *..................177 H2
Linden Crs GFD/PVL UB6................79 F4
    KUT/HW KT1..........................175 G5
    WFD IG8...................................53 F2
Lindenfield CHST BR7.....................185 G2
Linden Gdns BAY/PAD W2.............100 D6
    CHSWK W4..............................118 A5
    EN EN1.....................................24 C2
Linden Gv NWMAL KT3.................176 B6
    PECK SE15..............................143 J4
    PGE/AN SE20.........................181 K4
    TEDD TW11............................174 A1
Linden Lea EFNCH N2......................65 G2
    PIN HA5....................................41 K3
Linden Leas WWKM BR4...............199 G6
Linden Ms ABYW DA2 *....IS N1......85 J6
Linden Pl MTCM CR4.....................194 D1
Linden Rd FBAR/BDGN N11...........33 K4
    HPTN TW12............................173 F4
    MUSWH N10..............................48 A5
    SEVS/STOTM N15....................67 H3
The Lindens CHSWK W4...............137 K2
    CROY/NA CR0........................214 A4
    NFNCH/WDSPK N12 *..............47 H1
Linden Wy STHGT/OAK N14..........34 C3
Lindfield Gdns HAMP NW3..............83 F3
Lindfield Rd CROY/NA CR0...........197 G3
    EA W5.......................................97 J3

Lindfield St POP/IOD E14 105 J5
Lindhill Cl PEND EN3 25 F3
Lindisfarne Md HOM E9 87 G2
Lindisfarne Rd BCTR RM8 91 J1
RYNPK SW20 176 D3
Lindley Est PECK SE15 143 H1
Lindley Pl RCH/KEW TW9 137 H2
Lindley Rd LEY E10 70 A6
Lindley St WCHPL E1 104 E4
Lindore Rd BTSEA SW11 140 E5
Lindores Rd CAR SM5 194 B5
Lindo St PECK SE15 143 K3
Lind Rd SUT SM1 209 G3
Lindrop St FUL/PGN SW6 140 B3
Lindsay Cl CHSGTN KT9 206 A5
STWL/WRAY TW19 152 A1
Lindsay Dr KTN/HRWW/WS HA3 62 A3
Lindsay Rd HPTN TW12 155 G6
WPK KT4 192 E6
Lindsay Sq PIM SW1V 121 J5
Lindsell St GNWCH SE10 145 F2
Lindsey Cl BMLY BR1 184 C6
MTCM CR4 195 K1
Lindsey Gdns
EBED/NFELT TW14 * 153 G2
Lindsey Ms IS N1 85 J5
Lindsey Rd BCTR RM8 91 J1
Lindsey St FARR EC1M 12 B1
Lind St DEPT SE8 144 E3
Lindum Rd TEDD TW11 174 D3
Lindway WNWD SE27 180 C1
Linfield Cl HDN NW4 46 A6
Linford Rd WALTH E17 52 A6
Linford St VX/NE SW8 141 H2
Lingards Rd LEW SE13 145 F5
Lingey Cl BFN/LL DA15 168 A4
Lingfield Cl EN EN1 36 A1
NTHWD HA6 40 C3
Lingfield Ct NTHLT UB5 * 96 A1
Lingfield Crs ELTH/MOT SE9 147 J5
Lingfield Gdns ED N9 36 D2
Lingfield Rd WIM/MER SW19 177 G2
WPK KT4 208 A1
Lingham St BRXN/ST SW9 141 K3
Lingholm Wy BAR EN5 20 B6
Ling Rd CAN/RD E16 106 E4
ERITH DA8 129 K6
Lingwell Rd TOOT SW17 160 D5
Lingwood Gdns ISLW TW7 135 K1
Lingwood Rd CLPT E5 68 C4
Linhope St CAMTN NW1 2 E6
Linkfield E/WMO/HCT KT8 173 F6
Link Fld HAYES BR2 199 K3
Linkfield Rd ISLW TW7 136 A3
Link La WLGTN SM6 210 D4
Linklea Cl CDALE/KGS NW9 45 G3
Link Rd DAGW RM9 110 D1
EBED/NFELT TW14 153 J2
FBAR/BDGN N11 34 A6
WLGTN SM6 195 F5
Links Av GPK RM2 57 K5
MRDN SM4 193 K1
Links Dr TRDG/WHET N20 32 E3
Links Gdns STRHM/NOR SW16 180 B3
Linkside CHIG IG7 54 C1
NFNCH/WDSPK N12 46 D2
NWMAL KT3 176 B5
Linkside Cl ENC/FH EN2 23 F4
Linkside Gdns ENC/FH EN2 23 F4
Links Rd ACT W3 98 C5
CRICK NW2 63 H6
TOOT SW17 179 F2
WFD IG8 52 E1
WWKM BR4 199 F5
Links Side ENC/FH EN2 23 F4
The Links WALTH E17 69 G1
Link St HOM E9 86 E4
Links Vw DART DA1 171 F3
FNCH N3 46 D3
Links View Cl STAN HA7 43 G2
Linksview Ct HPTN TW12 * 155 J6
Links View Rd CROY/NA CR0 213 J1
HPTN TW12 173 H1
Links Wy BECK BR3 198 D3
NTHWD HA6 40 A4
TOOT SW17 178 E2
Linksway HDN NW4 46 B5
NTHWD HA6 40 B4
Links Yd WCHPL E1 13 K1
The Link ACT W3 98 D5
ALP/SUD HA0 61 J5
CRICK NW2 63 J5
NTHLT UB5 * 77 K3
PEND EN3 25 G2
PIN HA5 59 G3
TEDD TW11 174 A3
Link Wy HAYES BR2 200 D4
RCHPK/HAM TW10 156 C4
Linkway BCTR RM8 91 J2
FSBYPK N4 67 J4
NWMAL KT3 192 E1
PIN HA5 41 H4
RYNPK SW20 176 E6
The Linkway BAR EN5 32 E1
BELMT SM2 209 G6
Linkwood Wk CAMTN NW1 84 D5
Linley Crs ROMW/RG RM7 56 D6
Linley Rd TOTM N17 50 A5
Linnell Cl GLDGN NW11 65 F3
Linnell Dr GLDGN NW11 65 F3
Linnell Rd CMBW SE5 143 F3
UED N18 50 C1
Linnet Cl BUSH WD23 28 C3
ED N9 37 F3
THMD SE28 109 J6
Linnet Ms BAL SW12 161 F2
Linnett Cl CHING E4 38 A6
Linom Rd CLAP SW4 141 K5
Linscott Rd CLPT E5 86 E2
Linsdell Rd BARK IG11 90 C6
Linsey St BERM/RHTH SE16 123 H4
Linslade Cl HSLWW TW4 134 D6
PIN HA5 59 F1
Linslade Rd ORP BR6 217 G4
Linstead St KIL/WHAMP NW6 82 E5
Linstead Wy
WAND/EARL SW18 159 H2
Lintaine Cl HMSMTH W6 * 119 H6
Linthorpe Av ALP/SUD HA0 79 J4
Linthorpe Rd EBAR EN4 21 J4
STNW/STAM N16 68 A4
Linton Cl CAR SM5 194 E4
CHARL SE7 126 B5
WELL DA16 148 C2
Linton Ct ROM RM1 57 G5
Linton Gdns EHAM E6 107 J5
Linton Gv WNWD SE27 180 C1
Linton Rd BARK IG11 90 C5
Linton St IS N1 6 D1
Lintott Ct STWL/WRAY TW19 152 A1
Linver Rd FUL/PGN SW6 139 J3
Linwood Cl CMBW SE5 143 G3
Linwood Crs EN EN1 24 C2
Linzee Rd CEND/HSY/T N8 66 E1
Lion Av TWK TW1 156 A3
Lion Cl BROCKY SE4 164 D1
Lionel Gdns ELTH/MOT SE9 146 C6
Lionel Ms NKENS W10 * 100 C4
Lionel Rd ELTH/MOT SE9 146 C6
Lionel Rd North BTFD TW8 117 F3
Lionel Rd South BTFD TW8 117 G5
Lion Gate Gdns RCH/KEW TW9 137 G4
Lion Gate Ms
WAND/EARL SW18 159 K2
Lion Mills BETH E2 * 104 C1
Lion Park Av CHSGTN KT9 206 C2
Lion Rd BXLYHS DA6 149 F5
CROY/NA CR0 196 D2
ED N9 36 C4
EHAM E6 107 K4
TWK TW1 156 A3
Lions Cl LEE/GVPK SE12 166 B5
Lion Wy BTFD TW8 136 E1
Lion Wharf Rd ISLW TW7 136 C4
Liphook Cl HCH RM12 93 H2
Liphook Crs FSTH SE23 163 K2
Liphook Rd OXHEY WD19 27 H6
Lipton Rd WCHPL E1 105 F5
Lisbon Av WHTN TW2 155 H4
Lisbon Cl WALTH E17 51 H5
Lisburne Rd HAMP NW3 83 K2
Lisford St PECK SE15 143 H2
Lisgar Ter WKENS W14 119 J4
Liskeard Cl CHST BR7 185 H2
Liskeard Gdns BKHTH/KID SE3 145 K2
Lisle Cl TOOT SW17 161 G6
Lisle St LSQ/SEVD WC2H 10 D5
Lismore WIM/MER SW19 * 177 J1
Lismore Circ KTTN NW5 83 K3
Lismore Cl ISLW TW7 136 B3
Lismore Rd SAND/SEL CR2 212 A4
TOTM N17 49 K6
Lismore Wk IS N1 85 J4
Lissant Cl SURB KT6 190 D4
Lissenden Gdns KTTN NW5 84 A2
Lisson Gv CAMTN NW1 2 C7
Lisson St CAMTN NW1 8 C1
Lister Cl ACT W3 99 F4
MTCM CR4 178 D4
Lister Gdns UED N18 49 J1
Lister Rd WAN E11 70 C5
Liston Rd CLAP SW4 141 H4
TOTM N17 50 C4
Liston Wy WFD IG8 53 G3
Listowel Cl BRXN/ST SW9 142 B1
Listowel Rd DAGE RM10 92 C1
Listria Pk STNW/STAM N16 68 A6
Litchfield Av MRDN SM4 193 J4
SRTFD E15 * 88 C4
Litchfield Gdns WLSDN NW10 81 J4
Litchfield Rd SUT SM1 209 G2
Litchfield St LSQ/SEVD WC2H 10 D5
Litchfield Wy GLDGN NW11 65 G2
Lithgow's Rd HTHAIR TW6 133 H5
Lithos Rd HAMP NW3 83 F4
Little Acre BECK BR3 182 D6
Little Albany St CAMTN NW1 3 K6
Little Argyll St REGST W1B * 10 A4
Little Benty WDR/YW UB7 112 A5
Little Birches BFN/LL DA15 167 K4
The Little Boltons
WBPTN SW10 120 A5
Little Bornes DUL SE21 163 F6
Little Britain STBT EC1A 12 C3
Littlebrook Cl CROY/NA CR0 198 A3
Littlebrook Manor Wy
DART DA1 151 K6
Little Brownings FSTH SE23 163 J4
Littlebury Rd CLAP SW4 * 141 J4
Little Bury St ED N9 36 A2
Little Bushey La BUSH WD23 28 D1
Little Cedars
NFNCH/WDSPK N12 33 G6
Little Chester St KTBR SW1X 15 J4
Little Cloisters WEST SW1P 16 E4
Littlecombe Cl
PUT/ROE SW15 * 159 G1
Little Common STAN HA7 29 G5
Littlecote Cl WIM/MER SW19 159 G2
Littlecote Pl PIN HA5 41 J4
Little Cottage Pl
GNWCH SE10 * 144 E1
Little Ct WWKM BR4 199 H6
Littlecroft ELTH/MOT SE9 147 F4
Littledale ABYW SE2 128 B6
Little Deans Yd WEST SW1P 16 E4
Little Dimocks BAL SW12 161 G4
Little Dorrit Ct STHWK SE1 18 D2
Little Ealing La EA W5 116 D4
Little Edward St CAMTN NW1 * 3 K4
Little Elms HYS/HAR UB3 133 G1
Little Essex St TPL/STR WC2R * 11 J5
Little Ferry Rd TWK TW1 * 156 C3
Littlefield Cl ARCH N19 84 C2
KUT/HW KT1 175 F5
Littlefield Rd EDGW HA8 44 E3
Little Friday Rd CHING E4 38 C4
Little Gearies BARK/HLT IG6 72 B1
Little George St WEST SW1P 16 E3
Little Green St KTTN NW5 * 84 B2
Littlegrove EBAR EN4 33 J1
Little Heath CHARL SE7 126 D6
CHDH RM6 73 H1
Little Heath Rd BXLYHN DA7 149 G2
Littleheath Rd SAND/SEL CR2 212 D6
Little Ilford La MNPK E12 89 K2
Littlejohn Rd HNWL W7 97 F5
STMC/STPC BR5 202 B3
Little Marlborough St
REGST W1B * 10 A4
Littlemead ESH/CLAY KT10 204 D2
Littlemede ELTH/MOT SE9 166 E5
Littlemoor Rd IL IG1 90 D1
Littlemore Rd ABYW SE2 128 B2
Little Moss La PIN HA5 41 J5
Little Newport St
LSQ/SEVD WC2H 10 D5
Little New St FLST/FETLN EC4A 11 K3
Little Orchard Cl PIN HA5 * 41 J5
Little Oxhey La OXHEY WD19 41 J1
Little Park Dr FELT TW13 154 C4
Little Park Gdns ENC/FH EN2 23 K4
Little Pluckett's Wy BKHH IG9 39 H3
Little Portland St REGST W1B 9 K3
Little Potters BUSH WD23 28 D2
Little Queens Rd TEDD TW11 174 A2
Little Queen St DART DA1 171 J2
Little Redlands BMLY BR1 184 D5
Little Rd HYS/HAR UB3 113 J2
Littlers Cl WIM/MER SW19 178 C4
Little Russell St
NOXST/BSQ WC1A 10 E2
Little St James's St
WHALL SW1A 16 A1
Little St Leonards
MORT/ESHN SW14 137 K4
Little Smith St WEST SW1P 16 D4
Little Somerset St TWRH EC3N 13 J4
Littlestone Cl BECK BR3 182 D2
Little Strd CDALE/KGS NW9 45 H5
Little Stream Cl NTHWD HA6 40 C1
Little Thrift STMC/STPC BR5 201 H1
Little Titchfield St GTPST W1W 10 A2
Littleton Av CHING E4 38 D3
Littleton Crs HRW HA1 61 F6
Littleton Rd HRW HA1 61 F6
Littleton St WAND/EARL SW18 160 B4
Little Trinity La BLKFR EC4V 12 D5
Little Turnstile HHOL WC1V 11 G2
Littlewood LEW SE13 145 F6
Little Wood Cl STMC/STPC BR5 186 B4
Littlewood Cl WEA W13 116 C3
Littleworth Av ESH/CLAY KT10 204 D3
Littleworth Common Rd
ESH/CLAY KT10 204 D2
Littleworth La ESH/CLAY KT10 204 D2
Littleworth Pl ESH/CLAY KT10 204 D2
Littleworth Rd ESH/CLAY KT10 204 D3
Livermere Rd HACK E8 86 B6
Liverpool Gv WALW SE17 122 E5
Liverpool Rd CAN/RD E16 106 C4
EA W5 116 E2
HOLWY N7 85 G4
KUTN/CMB KT2 175 H3
LEY E10 70 A3
THHTH CR7 180 D6
Liverpool St LVPST EC2M 13 G2
Livesey Cl KUT/HW KT1 175 G6
THMD SE28 127 H3
Livesey Pl STHWK SE1 123 H6
Livingstone Rd BTSEA SW11 140 C4
HSLW TW3 135 H5
PLMGR N13 48 E2
SRTFD E15 88 A6
STHL UB1 95 H6
THHTH CR7 180 E5
WALTH E17 69 K3
Lizard St FSBYE EC1V 6 D5
Lizban St BKHTH/KID SE3 146 A1
Llanelly Rd CRICK NW2 82 D1
Llanover Rd WBLY HA9 79 K1
WOOL/PLUM SE18 147 F1
Llanthony Rd MRDN SM4 194 C3
Llanvanor Rd CRICK NW2 64 D6
Llewellyn St BERM/RHTH SE16 123 H2
Lloyd Av STRHM/NOR SW16 179 K4
Lloyd Baker St FSBYW WC1X 5 J5
Lloyd Ct PIN HA5 59 H2
Lloyd Ms PEND EN3 25 J1
Lloyd Park Av CROY/NA CR0 212 B2
Lloyd Rd DAGW RM9 92 B4
EHAM E6 89 K6
WALTH E17 69 F1
WPK KT4 208 A1
Lloyd's Av FENCHST EC3M 13 H4
Lloyd's Pl BKHTH/KID SE3 * 145 H3
Lloyd Sq FSBYW WC1X 5 J5
Lloyd's Rw CLKNW EC1R 5 K5
Lloyd St FSBYW WC1X 5 J4
Lloyds Wy BECK BR3 198 B2
Lloyd Thomas Ct WDGN N22 * 49 F3
Lloyd Vls BROCKY SE4 144 D3
Loampit Hl LEW SE13 144 D3
Loampit V LEW SE13 144 E4
Loanda Cl HACK E8 86 B6
Loats Rd BRXS/STRHM SW2 161 K1
Locarno Rd ACT W3 117 K1
GFD/PVL UB6 96 C3
Lochaber Rd LEW SE13 145 H5
Lochaline St HMSMTH W6 119 F6
Lochan Cl YEAD UB4 95 J3
Lochinvar St BAL SW12 161 G2
Lochmere Cl ERITH DA8 129 J6
Lochnagar St POP/IOD E14 106 A4
Lock Cha BKHTH/KID SE3 145 H4
Lock Cl NWDGN UB2 115 H2
Locke Cl RAIN RM13 93 H4
Lockesley Dr STMC/STPC BR5 202 A3
Lockesley Sq SURB KT6 * 190 E3
Locket Rd KTN/HRWW/WS HA3 43 F5
Locket Road Ms
KTN/HRWW/WS HA3 42 E5
Lockfield Av PEND EN3 25 G3
Lockgate Cl HOM E9 87 H3
Lockhart Cl HOLWY N7 85 F4
PEND EN3 24 D6
Lockhart St BOW E3 105 H3
Lockhurst St CLPT E5 87 F2
Lockington Rd VX/NE SW8 141 G2
Lock Keepers Cottages
TOTM N17 * 68 D1
Lockmead Rd LEW SE13 145 F4
SEVS/STOTM N15 68 C3
Lock Rd RCHPK/HAM TW10 156 D6
Lock's La MTCM CR4 179 F4
Locksley Est POP/IOD E14 105 H5
Locksley St POP/IOD E14 105 H4
Locksmeade Rd
RCHPK/HAM TW10 156 C6
Lockton St NTGHL W11 * 100 B6
Lockwell Rd DAGE RM10 92 C1
Lockwood Cl SYD SE26 164 A6
Lockwood Pl CHING E4 51 J2
Lockwood Sq
BERM/RHTH SE16 123 J3
Lockwood Wy CHSGTN KT9 206 C3
WALTH E17 51 F5
Lockyer Cl PEND EN3 25 K1
Lockyer St STHWK SE1 19 F3
Locomotive Dr
EBED/NFELT TW14 153 K2
Locton Gn BOW E3 * 87 H6
Loddiges Rd HOM E9 86 E5
Loder St PECK SE15 143 K1
Lodge Av CROY/NA CR0 211 G1
DAGW RM9 91 H6
DART DA1 171 F1
GPK RM2 75 J2
KTN/HRWW/WS HA3 62 A1
Lodge Cl EDGW HA8 * 44 B2
ISLW TW7 136 C2
ORP BR6 202 C5
UED N18 49 J1
WLGTN SM6 195 F5
Lodge Ct ALP/SUD HA0 * 80 A3
Lodge Crs ORP BR6 202 C5
Lodge Dr PLMGR N13 35 G6
Lodge Gdns BECK BR3 198 C2
Lodge Hl REDBR IG4 71 J1
WELL DA16 148 C1
Lodgehill Park Cl
RYLN/HDSTN HA2 60 B6
Lodge La BXLY DA5 168 E1
CROY/NA CR0 213 K5
CRW RM5 56 C1
NFNCH/WDSPK N12 47 G1
Lodge Mansions Pde
PLMGR N13 * 35 G6
Lodge Ms HBRY N5 * 85 J2
Lodge Pl SUT SM1 209 F3
Lodge Rd BMLY BR1 184 B3
CROY/NA CR0 196 C3
HDN NW4 64 A1
STJWD NW8 2 B5
SUT SM1 209 F3
WLGTN SM6 210 B3
The Lodge SHB W12 * 119 G2
Lodge Vls WFD IG8 52 D3
Lodge Wy ASHF TW15 152 B4
Lodore Gdns CDALE/KGS NW9 63 G2
Lodore St POP/IOD E14 106 A5
Lofthouse Pl CHSGTN KT9 205 J4
Loftie St BERM/RHTH SE16 123 H2
Lofting Rd IS N1 85 G5
Loftus Rd BARK IG11 90 C4
SHB W12 118 E1
Loftus Vls SHB W12 * 118 E1
Logan Cl HSLWW TW4 134 E4
PEND EN3 25 F2
Logan Ms ECT SW5 119 K4
ROM RM1 75 G2
Logan Pl ECT SW5 119 K4
Logan Rd ED N9 36 D4
WBLY HA9 62 A6
The Logans BAR EN5 * 20 B4
Logs Hl CHST BR7 184 D4
Logs Hill Cl CHST BR7 184 D4
Lolesworth Cl WCHPL E1 13 K2
Lollard St LBTH SE11 17 H6
Loman St STHWK SE1 18 B2
Lomas Cl CROY/NA CR0 214 A5
Lombard Av GDMY/SEVK IG3 72 E5
PEND EN3 24 E2
Lombard La EMB EC4Y 11 K4
Lombard Rd BTSEA SW11 140 C3
FBAR/BDGN N11 48 B1
WIM/MER SW19 178 A5
Lombard St BANK EC3V 13 F4
Lombard Vls FBAR/BDGN N11 * 48 B1
Lombard Wall CHARL SE7 126 A3
Lombardy Cl WFD IG8 54 B3
Lombardy Pl BAY/PAD W2 101 F6
Lomond Cl ALP/SUD HA0 80 B5
SEVS/STOTM N15 68 A1
Lomond Gdns SAND/SEL CR2 213 G5
Lomond Gv CMBW SE5 142 E1
Loncroft Rd CMBW SE5 123 F6
Londesborough Rd
STNW/STAM N16 86 A2
London Br CANST EC4R 13 F6
London Bridge St STHWK SE1 19 F1
London Bridge Wk
STHWK SE1 * 13 F7
London City Airport Link
CAN/RD E16 106 D6
Londonderry Pde ERITH DA8 * 150 A1
London Flds HACK E8 * 86 D5
London Fields East Side
HACK E8 86 D5
London Fields West Side
HACK E8 86 C5
London La BMLY BR1 183 K3
HACK E8 86 D5
London Loop BORE WD6 30 E2
CROY/NA CR0 213 F1
ENC/FH EN2 23 J1
ORP BR6 201 G5
SAND/SEL CR2 213 F6
WWKM BR4 214 B2
WWKM BR4 214 E1
London Ms BAY/PAD W2 8 B4
London Rd SOCK/AV RM15 131 K2
ASHF TW15 152 D4
BARK IG11 90 C5
BMLY BR1 183 J3
BUSH WD23 27 J1
CHEAM SM3 208 B1
CROY/NA CR0 196 C5
DART DA1 150 A6
ENC/FH EN2 23 K6
EW KT17 207 K3
FSTH SE23 163 K3
HRW HA1 60 E6
ISLW TW7 135 K3
ISLW TW7 136 B6
KUTN/CMB KT2 175 G5
MRDN SM4 193 K2
MTCM CR4 194 D1
MTCM CR4 195 F4
PLSTW E13 106 E1
ROMW/RG RM7 74 C3
SOCK/AV RM15 131 J1
STAN HA7 29 K6
STAN HA7 43 J1
STHWK SE1 18 B4
STRHM/NOR SW16 180 A5
SWLY BR8 187 K5
THHTH CR7 196 B1
TWK TW1 156 B2
WBLY HA9 80 A3
WLGTN SM6 210 B2
London Stile CHSWK W4 117 H5
London St BAY/PAD W2 8 B4
FENCHST EC3M * 13 H5
London Ter BETH E2 * 104 C1
London Wall CITYW EC2V 12 D2
LVPST EC2M 13 F3
London Wall Buildings
LVPST EC2M 13 F2
Lonesome Wy MTCM CR4 179 G4
Long Acre COVGDN WC2E 10 E4
ORP BR6 202 E6
Long Acre Ct WEA W13 * 97 G4
Longacre Pl CAR SM5 * 210 A4
Longacre Rd WALTH E17 52 B4
Longbeach Rd BTSEA SW11 140 E4
Longboat Rw STHL UB1 95 K5
Longbridge Rd BARK IG11 90 D4
BCTR RM8 91 G2
Longbridge Wy LEW SE13 145 F6
Longbury Cl STMC/STPC BR5 186 C6
Longbury Dr STMC/STPC BR5 186 C6
Longcliffe Pth OXHEY WD19 26 E5
Long Ct PUR RM19 131 K4
Longcroft ELTH/MOT SE9 167 F5
Long Cft OXHEY WD19 27 F2
Longcrofte Rd EDGW HA8 43 K3
Long Deacon Rd CHING E4 38 C3
Longdon Wd HAYES BR2 215 J2
Longdown Rd CAT SE6 164 D6
Long Dr ACT W3 99 G5
GFD/PVL UB6 78 B6
RSLP HA4 77 H2
WDR/YW UB7 * 112 B2
Long Elmes
KTN/HRWW/WS HA3 42 C4
Longfellow Rd WALTH E17 69 H3
WCHPL E1 * 105 G2
WPK KT4 192 D5
Longfellow Wy STHWK SE1 * 19 K7
Longfield BMLY BR1 183 J4
Long Fld CDALE/KGS NW9 45 G4
Longfield Av EA W5 97 J6
EMPK RM11 75 H4
MLHL NW7 45 J3
WALTH E17 69 G1
WBLY HA9 62 A5
WLGTN SM6 195 F5
Longfield Crs SYD SE26 163 K5
Longfield Dr
MORT/ESHN SW14 137 J6
MTCM CR4 178 D4
Longfield Est STHWK SE1 19 K6
Longfield Rd EA W5 97 J5
Longfield St
WAND/EARL SW18 159 K2
Longford Av
EBED/NFELT TW14 153 J1
STHL UB1 96 A6
STWL/WRAY TW19 152 B3
Longford Cl FELT TW13 154 D5
HPTN TW12 155 F6
YEAD UB4 95 H6
Longford Ct HOR/WEW KT19 206 E2
HPTN TW12 173 G2
Longford Gdns SUT SM1 209 G1
YEAD UB4 95 H6
Longford Rd WHTN TW2 155 G3
Longford St CAMTN NW1 3 K6
Longford Wy
STWL/WRAY TW19 152 B3
Longhayes Av CHDH RM6 55 K6
Longheath Gdns
CROY/NA CR0 197 K2
Longhedge St BTSEA SW11 141 F3
Longhill Rd CAT SE6 165 G4
Longhook Gdns NTHLT UB5 94 E2
Longhurst Rd CROY/NA CR0 197 J3
LEW SE13 145 H6
Longland Dr TRDG/WHET N20 33 F5
Longlands Park Crs
BFN/LL DA15 167 K5
Longlands Rd BFN/LL DA15 167 K5
Long La BXLYHN DA7 149 F1
CROY/NA CR0 197 K3
FNCH N3 47 F4
STBT EC1A 12 B1
STHWK SE1 19 F3
STWL/WRAY TW19 152 C3
Longleat Rd EN EN1 24 A6
Longleat Wy
EBED/NFELT TW14 153 F2
Longleigh La ABYW SE2 128 D6
Longley Av ALP/SUD HA0 80 B6
Longley Rd CROY/NA CR0 196 C4
HRW HA1 60 D2
TOOT SW17 178 D2
Long Leys CHING E4 51 K2
Longley St STHWK SE1 123 H4
Longley Wy CRICK NW2 82 A1
Longmans Cl WATW WD18 26 A1
Long Mark Rd CAN/RD E16 107 H5
Longmarsh La THMD SE28 127 K1
Long Md CDALE/KGS NW9 45 H4
Longmead CHST BR7 185 F5

Longmead Dr SCUP DA14..........168 E4
Long Meadow KTTN NW5 *........84 D4
Long Meadow Cl WWKM BR4....199 F4
Longmeadow Rd
  BFN/LL DA15...............167 K3
Longmead Rd HYS/HAR UB3....94 B6
  THDIT KT7....................189 K4
  TOOT SW17...................178 E1
Longmoore St PIM SW1V..........16 A7
Longmoor Av BAR EN5..............33 C1
Longnor Rd WCHPL E1............105 F2
Long Pond Rd BKHTH/KID SE3..145 G2
Longport Cl BARK/HLT IG6........55 C2
Long Reach Rd BARK IG11......109 F5
Longreach Rd ERITH DA8........150 E1
Longridge La STHL UB1............96 B6
Longridge Rd ECT SW5............119 K4
Long Rd CLAP SW4..................141 H5
Longshaw Rd CHING E4.............38 B5
Longshore DEPT SE8..............124 C4
Longstaff Crs
  WAND/EARL SW18.........159 K2
Longstaff Rd
  WAND/EARL SW18.........159 K1
Longstone Av WLSDN NW10......81 H5
Longstone Rd TOOT SW17......179 G1
Long St BETH E2........................7 J4
Longthornton Rd
  STRHM/NOR SW16........179 H5
Longton Av SYD SE26.............163 H6
Longton Gv SYD SE26.............163 J6
Longville Rd LBTH SE11.............18 A6
Long Wk NWMAL KT3..............175 K6
  STHWK SE1....................19 J4
Longwalk Rd STKPK UB11......112 C2
Longwood Dr PUT/ROE SW15..158 D2
Longwood Gdns CLAY IG5........71 K1
Longworth Cl THMD SE28........109 K5
Long Yd BMSBY WC1N................5 G7
The Loning CDALE/KGS NW9....63 H1
  PEND EN3......................24 E1
Lonsdale Av EHAM E6.............107 J3
  ELTH/MOT SE9...............166 C5
  UX/CGN UB8...................94 A5
Lonsdale Crs GNTH/NBYPK IG2..72 B3
Lonsdale Dr ENC/FH EN2..........22 E6
Lonsdale Dr North ENC/FH EN2..22 E6
Lonsdale Gdns THHTH CR7.....196 A1
Lonsdale Ms NTGHL W11.........100 D5
  RCH/KEW TW9 *............137 H2
Lonsdale Pl IS N1......................85 G5
Lonsdale Rd BARN SW13........138 C1
  BXLYHN DA7.................149 G5
  CHSWK W4....................118 C4
  KIL/WHAMP NW6...........100 D1
  NTGHL W11...................100 D5
  NWDGN UB2..................114 C3
  SNWD SE25...................197 J1
  WAN E11..........................70 C5
Lonsdale Sq IS N1....................85 G5
Loobert Rd SEVS/STOTM N15..50 A6
Looe Gdns BARK/HLT IG6.........54 B6
Loop Rd CHST BR7..................185 H2
Lopen Rd UED N18.....................42 A3
Loraine Cl PEND EN3.................24 E6
Loraine Cottages HOLWY N7 *..85 F2
  HOLWY N7......................85 F2
Lord Av CLAY IG5......................71 K1
Lord Chancellor Wk
  KUTN/CMB KT2.............175 K4
Lord Gdns CLAY IG5..................71 J1
Lord Hills Rd BAY/PAD W2......101 F4
Lord Holland La
  BRXN/ST SW9 *............142 B3
Lord Knyvett Cl
  STWL/WRAY TW19.......152 A1
Lord Knyvetts Ct
  STWL/WRAY TW19 *....152 B1
Lord Napier Pl HMSMTH W6....118 D5
Lord North St WEST SW1P........16 E5
Lord Roberts Ms
  FUL/PGN SW6..............140 A1
Lords Cl DUL SE21..................162 D4
  FELT TW13....................154 D4
Lordship Gv STNW/STAM N16..67 K6
Lordship La EDUL SE22...........163 G1
  WDGN N22......................49 H4
Lordship Park Ms
  STNW/STAM N16............67 J6
Lordship Pl CHEL SW3.............120 D6
Lordship Rd NTHLT UB5............77 J5
  STNW/STAM N16............67 K6
Lordship Ter STNW/STAM N16 *..67 J6
Lordsmead Rd TOTM N17.........50 A4
Lord St CAN/RD E16.................126 D1
Lords Vw STJWD NW8.................2 C5
Lord Warwick St
  WOOL/PLUM SE18.........126 E3
Lorenzo St FSBYW WC1X...........5 G4
Loretto Gdns
  KTN/HRWW/WS HA3.......62 A1
Lorian Cl NFNCH/WDSPK N12..33 F6
Loring Rd ISLW TW7................136 A3
  TRDG/WHET N20............33 J3
Loris Rd HMSMTH W6..............119 F3
Lorn Ct BRXN/ST SW9.............142 B3
Lorne Av CROY/NA CR0...........198 A4
Lorne Cl STJWD NW8..................2 D5
Lorne Gdns CROY/NA CR0.......198 B4
  NTGHL W11...................119 G1
Lorne Rd FSBYPK N4.................67 F5
  FSTGT E7.......................89 F2
  KTN/HRWW/WS HA3......43 F5
  RCHPK/HAM TW10........137 G6
  WALTH E17....................51 J4
Lorne Ter FNCH N3 *.................46 D5
Lorraine Pk
  KTN/HRWW/WS HA3.......42 E3

Lorrimore Rd WALW SE17........122 C6
Lorrimore Sq WALW SE17........122 C6
Loseberry Rd ESH/CLAY KT10..204 D3
Lothair Rd EA W5....................116 E2
Lothair Rd North FSBYPK N4....67 H3
Lothair Rd South FSBYPK N4....67 G4
Lothbury LOTH EC2R..................12 E3
Lothian Av YEAD UB4................95 F4
Lothian Cl ALP/SUD HA0............79 G2
Lothian Rd BRXN/ST SW9........142 C1
Lothrop St NKENS W10............100 C2
Lots Rd WBPTN SW10..............140 B1
Loubet St TOOT SW17.............178 E2
Loudoun Av BARK/HLT IG6........72 C1
Loudoun Rd STJWD NW8..........83 G6
Loughborough Pk
  BRXN/ST SW9...............142 C5
Loughborough Rd
  BRXN/ST SW9...............142 C5
Loughborough St LBTH SE11...122 A5
Lough Rd HOLWY N7.................85 F4
Loughton Wy BKHH IG9.............39 H4
Louisa Cl HOM E9......................86 E5
Louisa St WCHPL E1................105 F4
Louis Cl CHST BR7..................166 E6
Louise Bennett Cl HNHL SE24 *..142 C5
Louise Gdns RAIN RM13..........111 G2
Louise Rd SRTFD E15................88 C4
Louisville Rd TOOT SW17........161 F5
Louvaine Rd BTSEA SW11.......140 C5
Lovage Ap EHAM E6.................107 J4
Lovat Cl CRICK NW2...................81 H1
Lovat La FENCHST EC3M...........13 G5
Lovatt Cl EDGW HA8..................44 D2
Loveday Rd WEA W13...............116 C1
Lovegrove St STHWK SE1........123 H5
Lovegrove Wk POP/IOD E14....125 F1
Lovekyn Cl KUTN/CMB KT2.....175 G5
Lovelace Av HAYES BR2..........201 F3
Lovelace Gdns BARK IG11.........91 G3
  SURB KT6......................190 E4
Lovelace Gn ELTH/MOT SE9....146 E4
Lovelace Rd DUL SE21.............162 D4
  EBAR EN4.......................33 J2
Lovelace Vls THDIT KT7 *.........190 C4
Love La BXLY DA5....................169 H1
  CHEAM SM3..................208 C4
  CITYW EC2V....................12 D3
  MRDN SM4....................193 K4
  MTCM CR4.....................178 E6
  PIN HA5...........................41 J6
  SNWD SE25...................181 J6
  SURB KT6......................190 E6
  TOTM N17........................50 B3
  WFD IG8...........................53 K2
  WOOL/PLUM SE18.........127 F4
Lovel Av WELL DA16.................148 B3
Lovelinch Cl PECK SE15..........123 K6
Lovell Pl BERM/RHTH SE16.....124 B3
Lovell Rd RCHPK/HAM TW10..156 D5
  STHL UB1.........................96 B5
Lovell Wk RAIN RM13................93 J4
Loveridge Ms KIL/WHAMP NW6..82 D4
Loveridge Rd KIL/WHAMP NW6..82 D4
Lovett Dr CAR SM5..................194 B4
Lovetts Pl WAND/EARL SW18 *..140 B6
Lovett Wy WLSDN NW10...........80 E3
Love Wk CMBW SE5................142 E3
Lovibonds Av ORP BR6............216 B1
Lowbrook Rd IL IG1....................90 B2
Lowden Rd ED N9......................36 D3
  HNHL SE24....................142 C5
  STHL UB1.........................95 J6
Lowe Av CAN/RD E16...............106 E4
Lowe Cl CHIG IG7......................55 C1
Lowell St POP/IOD E14.............105 G5
Lowen Rd RAIN RM13...............111 F1
Lower Addiscombe Rd
  CROY/NA CR0...............196 E5
Lower Addison Gdns
  WKENS W14..................119 H2
Lower Bedfords Rd ROM RM1..57 J2
Lower Belgrave St BGVA SW1W..15 J5
Lower Boston Rd HNWL W7.....115 K1
Lower Broad St DAGE RM10.....92 C6
Lower Camden CHST BR7........184 E4
Lower Church St
  CROY/NA CR0...............196 C6
Lower Clapton Rd CLPT E5........86 D2
Lower Clarendon Wk
  NTGHL W11...................100 C5
Lower Common South
  PUT/ROE SW15.............138 E4
Lower Coombe St
  CROY/NA CR0...............211 J2
Lower Downs Rd RYNPK SW20..177 G4
Lower Gravel Rd HAYES BR2...200 D5
Lower Green Gdns WPK KT4...192 D5
Lower Green Rd
  ESH/CLAY KT10.............189 H6
Lower Gn West MTCM CR4......178 E6
Lower Grosvenor Pl
  BGVA SW1W....................15 J4
Lower Grove Rd
  RCHPK/HAM TW10........157 G1
Lower Hall La CHING E4.............51 C1
Lower Hampton Rd SUN TW16..172 C5
Lower Ham Rd
  KUTN/CMB KT2.............174 E2
Lower James St
  SOHO/CST W1F *............10 B5
Lower John St
  SOHO/CST W1F *............10 B5
Lower Kenwood Av
  ENC/FH EN2....................22 E6
Lower Kings Rd
  KUTN/CMB KT2.............175 F4
Lower Lea Crossing
  POP/IOD E14.................106 C6
Lower Maidstone Rd
  FBAR/BDGN N11.............48 C2
Lower Mardyke Av RAIN RM13..110 E1
Lower Marsh STHWK SE1..........17 J3
Lower Marsh La BRXLDS KT5..191 G1
Lower Merton Ri HAMP NW3.....83 J5
Lower Morden La MRDN SM4..193 F3

Lower Mortlake Rd
  RCH/KEW TW9...............137 F5
Lower Paddock Rd
  WATW WD19...................27 J1
Lower Park Rd BELV DA17......129 H4
  FBAR/BDGN N11.............48 C1
Lower Queen's Rd BKHH IG9....39 J4
Lower Richmond Rd
  PUT/ROE SW15.............139 F4
  RCH/KEW TW9...............137 J4
Lower Rd BELV DA17...............129 J3
  BERM/RHTH SE16.........123 J3
  ERITH DA8....................130 A4
  RYLN/HDSTN HA2..........60 D6
  STMC/STPC BR5...........202 C4
  SUT SM1........................209 H3
Lower Sand Hills SURB KT6....190 D4
Lower Sloane St BGVA SW1W..15 F7
Lower Sq ISLW TW7................136 C4
Lower Station Rd DART DA1....170 B1
Lower Strd CDALE/KGS NW9....45 H5
Lower Sunbury Rd
  E/WMO/HCT KT8............172 E5
  HPTN TW12....................173 F5
Lower Tail OXHEY WD19...........27 J5
Lower Teddington Rd
  KUT/HW KT1.................174 E4
Lower Ter HAMP NW3.................83 G1
Lower Thames St MON EC3R....13 G6
Lower Tub BUSH WD23.............28 D2
Lower Wood Rd
  ESH/CLAY KT10.............205 H4
Lowestoft Cl WILLY HA9...........61 K6
The Lowe CHIG IG7...................55 C1
Lowfield Rd ACT W5...................98 E5
  KIL/WHAMP NW6...........82 E6
Lowfield St DART DA1..............171 H2
Low Hall Cl CHING E4.................37 J2
Low Hall La WALTH E17.............69 G3
Lowick Rd HRW HA1..................60 E1
Lowland Gdns ROMW/RG RM7..74 D3
Lowlands Dr
  STWL/WRAY TW19.......132 A6
Lowlands Rd HRW HA1..............60 E4
  PIN HA5...........................59 H4
Lowman Rd HOLWY N7.............85 F2
Lowndes Cl KTBR SW1X...........15 H5
Lowndes Pl SOHO/CST W1F *..10 A4
Lowndes Pl KTBR SW1X............15 H5
Lowndes Sq KTBR SW1X...........15 G4
Lowndes St KTBR SW1X............15 G4
Lowood St WCHPL E1..............104 D6
Lowry Cl ERITH DA8.................130 A4
Lowry Crs MTCM CR4..............178 D5
Lowry Rd BCTR RM8..................91 H3
Lowshoe La CRW RM5...............56 D1
Lowson Gv OXHEY WD19...........27 J2
Lowswood Cl NTHWD HA6.........40 A4
Lowther Dr ENC/FH EN2.............22 E5
Lowther Hl FSTH SE23..............164 B2
Lowther Man BARN SW13 *......138 D2
Lowther Rd BARN SW13...........138 C2
  HOLWY N7 *....................85 G3
  KUTN/CMB KT2.............175 G4
  STAN HA7........................44 B5
  WALTH E17....................51 G5
Lowth Rd CMBW SE5...............142 D3
Loxford Av EHAM E6.................107 H1
Loxford La IL IG1........................90 C4
Loxford Rd BARK IG11................90 B4
Loxham Rd CHING E4..................51 K3
Loxham St STPAN WC1H *...........5 F5
Loxley Cl SYD SE26.................182 A1
Loxley Rd HPTN TW12.............154 E6
  WAND/EARL SW18........160 B3
Loxton Rd FSTH SE23..............164 A3
Loxwood Cl EBED/NFELT TW14..153 F3
  STMC/STPC BR5...........202 E6
Loxwood Rd SEVS/STOTM N15..50 A6
Lubbock Rd CHST BR7.............184 E4
Lubbock St NWCR SE14...........143 K1
Lucan Pl CHEL SW3...................14 C6
Lucan Rd BAR EN5.....................20 C4
Lucas Av EHAM E6.....................89 K6
  RYLN/HDSTN HA2..........60 A6
Lucas Cl WLSDN NW10 *...........81 J5
Lucas Gdns EFNCH N2...............47 G5
Lucas Rd PGE/AN SE20............181 K2
Lucas Sq GLDGN NW11.............64 E3
Lucas St BROCKY SE4..............144 C5
Lucerne Cl PLMGR N13.............34 E5
Lucerne Gv WALTH E17.............70 B1
Lucerne Ms HBRY N5.................85 H2
  ORP BR6.......................202 A5
  THHTH CR7...................196 C1
Lucey Rd BERM/RHTH SE16....123 H3
Lucey Wy BERM/RHTH SE16...123 H3
Lucien Rd TOOT SW17.............161 G6
  WIM/MER SW19............160 A4
Lucknow St WOOL/PLUM SE18..147 K1
Lucorn Cl LEE/GVPK SE12.......165 J1
Luctons Av BKHH IG9.................39 G3
Luddesdon Rd ERITH DA8........149 H1
Ludford Cl CROY/NA CR0..........211 H2
Ludgate Broadway
  BLKFR EC4V *.................12 B4
Ludgate Cir STP EC4M...............12 A4
Ludgate Hl STP EC4M................12 A4
Ludgate Sq STP EC4M................12 B4
Ludham Cl BARK/HLT IG6..........54 C4
  THMD SE28...................109 J5
Ludlow Cl HAYES BR2..............183 K6
  RYLN/HDSTN HA2..........77 K2
Ludlow Md OXHEY WD19...........27 F2
Ludlow Rd EA W5.......................97 J3
  FELT TW13....................153 K5
Ludlow St FSBYE EC1V *.............6 C6
Ludlow Wy EFNCH N2................65 G1
Ludovick Wk PUT/ROE SW15...138 B5
Luffield Rd ABYW SE2..............128 C3
Luffman Rd LEE/GVPK SE12....166 A6
Lugard Rd PECK SE15..............143 J3
Lugg Ap MNPK E12....................90 A2
Luke St SDTCH EC2A...................7 C6
Lukin Crs CHING E4....................38 B5
Lukin St WCHPL E1..................104 E6
Lullingstone Cl
  STMC/STPC BR5...........186 D4

Lullingstone Crs
  STMC/STPC BR5...........186 B5
Lullingstone La LEW SE13........165 G1
Lullingstone Rd BELV DA17.....129 G6
Lullington Garth BMLY BR1......183 H5
  NFNCH/WDSPK N12........46 D1
Lullington Rd DAGW RM9.........92 A5
  PGE/AN SE20.................181 H3
Lulot Gdns ARCH N19................66 B6
Lulworth Av HEST TW5..............135 H1
  WBLY HA9.......................61 J4
Lulworth Cl RYLN/HDSTN HA2..77 K4
Lulworth Crs MTCM CR4..........178 D5
Lulworth Dr CRW RM5...............56 D1
  PIN HA5...........................59 H4
Lulworth Gdns
  RYLN/HDSTN HA2..........59 J6
Lulworth Rd ELTH/MOT SE9....166 D4
  PECK SE15....................143 J3
  WELL DA16....................148 A3
Lulworth Waye YEAD UB4..........95 F5
Lumen Rd WBLY HA9.................61 K6
Lumley Cl BELV DA17...............129 H6
Lumley Flats BGVA SW1W *......121 F5
Lumley Gdns CHEAM SM3.......208 C4
Lumley Rd CHEAM SM3............208 C4
Lumley St OXSTW W1C................9 H4
Luna Rd THHTH CR7................180 D6
Lundin Wk OXHEY WD19 *.........27 H6
Lundy Dr HYS/HAR UB3............113 J4
Lundy Wk IS N1 *.......................85 J4
Lunham Rd NRWD SE19...........181 F2
Lupin Cl BRXS/STRHM SW2.....162 C4
  CROY/NA CR0...............198 A5
  ROMW/RG RM7..............75 F6
  WDR/YW UB7................112 A5
Lupton Cl LEE/GVPK SE12.......166 A6
Lupton St KTTN NW5..................84 C2
Lupus St PIM SW1V..................121 G6
Lurgan Av HMSMTH W6............119 G6
Lurline Gdns BTSEA SW11.......141 F2
Luscombe Wy VX/NE SW8........141 K1
Lushington Rd CAT SE6............182 E1
  WLSDN NW10.................99 K1
Lushington Ter HACK E8 *..........86 C3
Luther Cl EDGW HA8.................30 E4
Luther King Cl WALTH E17.........69 H3
Luther Ms TEDD TW11..............174 A1
Luther Rd TEDD TW11..............174 A1
Luton Pl GNWCH SE10.............145 F1
Luton Rd PLSTW E13................107 G3
  SCUP DA14....................168 D5
  WALTH E17....................51 H1
Luton St STJWD NW8..................2 B7
Luttrell Av PUT/ROE SW15......138 E6
Lutwyche Rd FSTH SE23..........164 C4
Luxborough La CHIG IG7............39 H6
Luxborough St CAMTN NW1........9 G1
  MHST W1U.......................9 G1
Luxemburg Ms SRTFD E15.......88 C3
Luxemburg Gdns
  HMSMTH W6..................119 G4
Luxfield Rd ELTH/MOT SE9......166 D3
Luxford St BERM/RHTH SE16...124 A4
Luxmore St BROCKY SE4.........144 C2
Luxor St CMBW SE5.................142 D4
Lyall Av DUL SE21....................163 F6
Lyall Ms KTBR SW1X.................15 C5
Lyall Ms West KTBR SW1X.........15 C5
Lyall St KTBR SW1X..................15 C5
Lyal Rd BOW E3.......................105 C1
Lycett Pl SHB W12...................118 D2
Lych Gate Rd ORP BR6............202 B5
Lych Gate Wk HYS/HAR UB3....94 D5
Lyconby Gdns CROY/NA CR0..198 B4
Lydd Cl BFN/LL DA15...............167 K5
Lydden Gv WAND/EARL SW18..160 A2
Lydden Rd WAND/EARL SW18..160 A2
Lydd Rd BXLYHN DA7...............149 G1
Lydeard Rd EHAM E6.................89 K5
Lydford Cl STNW/STAM N16 *....86 B2
Lydford Rd CRICK NW2..............82 A4
  MV/WKIL W9.................100 D3
  SEVS/STOTM N15..........67 K3
Lydhurst Av BRXS/STRHM SW2..162 A4
Lydon Rd CLAP SW4.................141 H4
Lydstep Rd CHST BR7..............167 F6
Lyford Rd WAND/EARL SW18...160 C2
Lyford St WOOL/PLUM SE18....126 D4
Lygon Pl BGVA SW1W *.............15 J5
Lyham Cl BRXS/STRHM SW2...161 K1
Lyham Rd BRXS/STRHM SW2..141 K6
Lyle Cl MTCM CR4....................195 F4
Lyme Farm Rd LEE/GVPK SE12..145 K5
Lyme Gv HOM E9........................86 E5
Lyme Rd WELL DA16.................148 C2
Lymescote Gdns SUT SM1.......193 K6
Lyme St CAMTN NW1.................84 C5
Lyme Ter CAMTN NW1...............84 C5
Lyminge Cl SCUP DA14............168 A6
Lyminge Gdns
  WAND/EARL SW18........160 D3
Lymington Av WDGN N22.........49 G5
Lymington Cl
  STRHM/NOR SW16........179 J5
  EHAM E6.........................89 K5
Lymington Gdns
  HOR/WEW KT19............207 H3
Lymington Rd BCTR RM8...........73 K5
  KIL/WHAMP NW6............83 F4
Lyminster Cl YEAD UB4.............95 J3
Lympstone Gdns PECK SE15...123 H6
Lynbridge Gdns PLMGR N13....35 H6
Lynbrook Cl RAIN RM13............111 F1
  PECK SE15....................123 F6
Lynch Cl UX/CGN UB8................46 A3

Lyndale Av CRICK NW2..............82 D1
Lyndale Cl BKHTH/KID SE3.....125 J6
Lyndale Hampton Court Wy
  ESH/CLAY KT10.............189 K4
Lynden Wy SWLY BR8..............203 J4
Lyndhurst Av BRYLDS KT5......191 J5
  MLHL NW7......................45 C2
  NFNCH/WDSPK N12........47 C2
  STHL UB1......................115 G1
  STRHM/NOR SW16........179 J5
  WHTN TW2.....................155 G3
Lyndhurst Cl BXLYHN DA7.......149 J4
  CROY/NA CR0...............212 B1
  ORP BR6........................216 B2
  WLSDN NW10.................81 F1
Lyndhurst Ct BELMT SM2 *......208 E5
Lyndhurst Dr LEY E10................70 A4
  NWMAL KT3...................192 B3
Lyndhurst Gdns BARK IG11.......90 E4
  EN EN1............................24 A4
  FNCH N3.........................46 C4
  GNTH/NBYPK IG2............72 D3
  HAMP NW3......................83 H3
  PIN HA5...........................41 F4
Lyndhurst Gv CMBW SE5.........143 F3
Lyndhurst Leys HAYES BR2 *...183 H6
Lyndhurst Prior SNWD SE25 *..181 F6
Lyndhurst Rd BXLYHN DA7......149 J4
  CHING E4.........................52 A3
  GFD/PVL UB6..................96 B3
  HAMP NW3......................83 H3
  THHTH CR7...................196 B1
  UED N18..........................42 B3
  WDGN N22......................49 C2
Lyndhurst Sq PECK SE15.........143 G2
Lyndhurst Ter HAMP NW3.........83 H3
Lyndhurst Wy BELMT SM2.......208 E6
  PECK SE15....................143 G2
Lyndon Av BFN/LL DA15...........148 A6
  PIN HA5...........................41 J3
  WLGTN SM6..................210 A1
Lyndon Rd BELV DA17.............129 H4
Lyndon Yd TOOT SW17............160 A6
Lyne Crs WALTH E17..................51 H4
Lyneham Wk CLPT E5 *.............87 H3
Lynette Av CLAP SW4...............161 G1
Lynford Cl EDGW HA8................44 E4
  GDMY/SEVK IG3..............73 F1
Lynford Ter ED N9......................36 B3
Lynhurst Rd HGDN/ICK UB10..76 A5
Lynmere Rd WELL DA16...........148 C3
Lyn Ms STNW/STAM N16 *........86 B1
  BOW E3.........................105 H3
Lynmouth Av EN EN1.................24 B6
  MRDN SM4....................193 G4
Lynmouth Dr RSLP HA4.............59 F6
Lynmouth Gdns GFD/PVL UB6..79 H6
  HEST TW5......................134 C1
Lynmouth Ri STMC/STPC BR5..202 C1
Lynmouth Rd EFNCH N2............47 J5
  GNTH/NBYPK IG2............73 C2
  SEVS/STOTM N15..........68 C1
  STNW/STAM N16............68 B5
  WALTH E17....................69 G3
Lynn Cl KTN/HRWW/WS HA3....42 D5
Lynne Cl ORP BR6....................217 F4
Lynne Wk ESH/CLAY KT10.......204 C3
Lynn Ms WAN E11 *...................70 C6
Lynn Rd BAL SW12...................161 G2
  GNTH/NBYPK IG2............72 D4
  WAN E11..........................70 C6
Lynn St ENC/FH EN2..................23 K2
Lynscott Wy SAND/SEL CR2....211 H6
Lynstead Cl BMLY BR1..............184 B5
Lynsted Cl BXLYHS DA6...........149 B5
Lynsted Ct BECK BR3 *.............182 B5
Lynsted Gdns ELTH/MOT SE9..146 C3
Lynton Av CDALE/KGS NW9......63 H1
  NFNCH/WDSPK N12........47 C1
  ROMW/RG RM7..............56 D4
  STMC/STPC BR5...........202 C1
  WEA W13.........................97 G5
Lynton Cl CHSGTN KT9............206 A2
  ISLW TW7.....................136 A5
  WLSDN NW10.................81 G4
Lynton Crs GNTH/NBYPK IG2...72 B3
Lynton Est STHWK SE1............123 H5
Lynton Gdns EN EN1..................36 A1
  FBAR/BDGN N11.............48 D3
Lynton Md TRDG/WHET N20.....32 E5
Lynton Rd ACT W3......................98 D7
  CEND/HSY/T N8...............66 D2
  CHING E4.........................51 K1
  KIL/WHAMP NW6...........100 D1
  NWMAL KT3...................192 A2
  RYLN/HDSTN HA2..........59 J6
  STHWK SE1.....................19 L7
Lynton Ter ACT W3 *..................98 E5
Lynwood Cl CRW RM5................56 D2
  RYLN/HDSTN HA2..........77 J1
  SWFD E18.......................53 G1
Lynwood Dr CRW RM5...............56 D2
  NTHWD HA6....................40 C4
  WPK KT4........................192 D6
Lynwood Gdns CROY/NA CR0..211 F2
  STHL UB1.........................95 K5
Lynwood Gv ORP BR6..............201 K4
  WCHMH N21...................35 C3
Lynwood Rd EA W5....................98 A2
  THDIT KT7....................190 A6
  TOOT SW17...................160 E4
Lynwood Ter
  WIM/MER SW19 *...........177 J4
Lyon Meade STAN HA7..............43 J4
Lyon Park Av ALP/SUD HA0......80 B5
Lyon Rd HRW HA1......................61 F3
  ROM RM1........................75 H4
  WIM/MER SW19............178 B4
  WOT/HER KT12.............188 D6
Lyonsdown Av BAR EN5............33 G1
Lyonsdown Rd BAR EN5............33 G1
Lyons Pl STJWD NW8...................2 A7
Lyon St IS N1............................85 F5

Lyons Wk *WKENS* W14..............119 H4
Lyon Wy *GFD/PVL* UB6..............78 E6
Lyoth Rd *STMC/STPC* BR5..........201 H6
Lyric Dr *GFD/PVL* UB6..............96 B5
Lyric Ms *SYD* SE26..................163 K6
Lyric Rd *BARN* SW13................138 C2
Lysander *CDALE/KGS* NW9 *......45 H4
Lysander Gdns *SURB* KT6..........116 D5
Lysander Gv *ARCH* N19.............66 D5
Lysander Ms *ARCH* N19.............66 E5
Lysander Rd *CROY/NA* CR0.......211 H4
RSLP HA4................................58 B6
Lysander Wy *ORP* BR6..............216 C1
Lysia St *FUL/PGN* SW6.............139 G1
Lytchet Rd *BMLY* BR1...............183 K3
Lytchet Wy *PEND* EN3................24 E2
Lytchgate Cl *SAND/SEL* CR2 ....212 A5
Lytcott Dr *E/WMO/HCT* KT8 ......172 E6
Lytcott Gv *EDUL* SE22..............143 G6
Lytham Av *OXHEY* WD19...........41 H1
Lytham St *WALW* SE17.............122 E6
Lyttelton Rd *EFNCH* N2..............65 G2
LEY E10....................................87 K1
Lyttleton Cl *HAMP* NW3..............83 J5
Lyttleton Rd *CEND/HSY/T* N8 *...49 G6
Lytton Av *PEND* EN3...................25 C1
PLMGR N13................................35 G4
Lytton Cl *EFNCH* N2...................65 H2
LNTHLT UB5................................47 F5
Lytton Gdns *WLGTN* SM6..........210 D2
Lytton Gv *PUT/ROE* SW15.........139 G6
Lytton Rd *BAR* EN5....................21 G5
GPK RM2...................................75 K2
PIN HA5....................................41 J5
WAN E11....................................70 C4
Lyveden Rd *BKHTH/KID* SE3 ....146 A1
TOOT SW17...............................178 D2

Madras Pl *HOLWY* N7.................85 G4
Madras Rd *IL* IG1......................90 B2
Madrid Rd *BARN* SW13.............138 D2
Madron St *WALW* SE17.............123 F5
Mafeking Av *BTFD* TW8............117 F6
EHAM E6..................................107 H1
GNTH/NBYPK IG2........................72 D4
Mafeking Rd *CAN/RD* E16.........106 D3
EN EN1....................................24 B1
TOTM N17..................................50 C5
Magazine Ga *BAY/PAD* W2 *........8 D7
Magdala Av *ARCH* N19...............66 C6
Magdala Rd *ISLW* TW7.............136 B4
SAND/SEL CR2............................211 K5
Magdalene Gdns *EHAM* E6........108 A3
Magdalen Rd
WAND/EARL SW18.....................160 B3
Magdalen Gv *ORP* BR6............217 H2
Magee St *LBTH* SE11...............122 B6
Magellan Pl *POP/IOD* E14.........124 D5
Magnaville Rd *BUSH* WD23.........28 E2
Magnet Rd *WBLY* HA9................61 K6
Magnin Cl *HACK* E8....................86 C6
Magnolia Cl *KUTN/CMB* KT2.....175 J2
LEY E10.....................................69 J6
Magnolia Ct
KTN/HRWW/WS HA3...................62 B4
Magnolia Gdns *EDGW* HA8.........30 E6
Magnolia Pl *CLAP* SW4.............141 K6
EA W5 *....................................97 K4
Magnolia Rd *CHSWK* W4..........117 H6
Magnolia St *WDR/YW* UB7........112 A4
Magnolia Wy *NFNWEW* KT19......206 D3
Magnolia Whf *CHSWK* W4 *........117 H6
Magpie Cl *CDALE/KGS* NW9.......45 G5
EN EN1.....................................23 E2
FSTGT E7...................................88 D3
Magpie Hall Cl *HAYES* BR2.......200 D15
Magpie Hall La *HAYES* BR2.......200 D3
Magpie Hall Rd *STAN* HA7.........28 A4
Magri Wk *WCHPL* E1.................124 B6
Maguire Dr *RCHPK/HAM* TW10.156 D6
Maguire St *STHWK* SE1 *...........19 K2
Mahlon Av *RSLP* HA4.................77 F3
Mahogany Cl
BERM/RHTH SE16.....................124 B1
Mahon Cl *EN* EN1......................24 B2
Maida Av *BAY/PAD* W2..............101 G4
CHING E4...................................37 K2
Maida Rd *BELV* DA17................129 H3
Maida V *MV/WKIL* W9...............101 G2
STJWD NW8...............................2 B1
Maida Vale Rd *DART* DA1..........170 D1
Maida Wy *CHING* E4...................37 K2
Maiden Erlegh Av *BXLY* DA5.....169 F3
Maiden La *CAMTN* NW1...............84 D5
COVGDN WC2E...........................11 F6
DART DA1.................................150 D5
STHWK SE1................................18 D1
Maidenstone Hl *GNWCH* SE10...145 F2
Maidstone Av *CRW* RM5...........56 E5
Maidstone Buildings Ms
STHWK SE1.................................18 D1
Maidstone Rd *FBAR/BDGN* N11...48 D2
SCUP DA14................................186 A2
Main Av *EN* EN1........................24 B6
NTHWD HA6...............................40 B6
Main Barracks
WOOL/PLUM SE18 *....................126 E5
Main Dr *GFD/PVL* UB6 *............97 G2
WBLY HA9...................................79 K1
Mainridge Rd *CHST* BR7..........167 F6
Main Rd *ORP* BR6......................217 J6
ROM RM1....................................75 H1
SCUP DA14...............................167 K5
STMC/STPC BR5.........................186 D4
SWLY BR8.................................205 K3
Main St *FELT* TW13..................172 C1
Maise Webster Cl
STWL/WRAY TW19 *...................152 A2
Maismore St *PECK* SE15..........123 H6
The Maisonettes *SUT* SM1........208 D3
Maitland Cl *GNWCH* SE10.........144 E1
HSLWW TW4..............................134 E4
WOT/HER KT12.........................188 D6
Maitland Park Rd *HAMP* NW3.....83 K4
Maitland Park Vls *HAMP* NW3.....83 K4
Maitland Rd *PGE/AN* SE20........181 J4
CHING E4....................................52 B5
RYLN/HDSTN HA2.......................60 C4
SRTFD E15.................................88 D4
Majendie Rd
WOOL/PLUM SE18......................127 J5
Major Cl *BRXN/ST* SW9.............142 C4
Major Rd *BERM/RHTH* SE16 *...123 H3
SRTFD E15..................................88 B4
Makepeace Av *HGT* N6...............66 A6
Makepeace Rd *NTHLT* UB5.........95 J1
WAN E11.....................................70 E1
Makins St *CHEL* SW3.................14 D7
Malabar St *POP/IOD* E14..........124 D2
Malam Gdns *POP/IOD* E14........106 A6
Malam Sq *RAIN* RM13.................93 J2
Malbrook Rd *PUT/ROE* SW15...138 E5
Malcolm Cl *PGE/AN* SE20 *.......181 K3
Malcolm Ct *STAN* HA7................43 J1
Malcolm Dr *SURB* KT6..............190 E5
Malcolm Pl *BETH* E2.................104 E5
Malcolm Rd *PGE/AN* SE20........181 K3
SNWD SE25..............................197 H3
WCHPL E1.................................104 E3
WIM/MER SW19.........................177 H2
Malcolms Wy *STHGT/OAK* N14 *..22 C6
Malcolm Wy *WAN* E11................70 E1
Maiden Av *GFD/PVL* UB6............78 E4
SNWD SE25...............................197 J1
Malden Green Av *WPK* KT4.......192 C5
Malden Hl *NWMAL* KT3.............176 C3
Malden Hill Gdns *NWMAL* KT3...176 C3
Malden Pk *NWMAL* KT3.............192 C3
Malden Pl *KTTN* NW5..................84 A3
Malden Rd *CHEAM* SM3............208 B2
KTTN NW5..................................83 K3
NWMAL KT3..............................192 C4
Malden Wy *NWMAL* KT3...........192 A3

Maldon Cl *CMBW* SE5 *............143 F4
IS N1...85 J6
Maldon Rd *ACT* W3....................98 E6
ED N9.......................................36 B5
ROMW/RG RM7...........................74 E4
WLGTN SM6..............................210 B3
Maldon Wk *WFD* IG8..................53 G2
Malet Rd *GWRST* WC1E................4 C7
Malet Av *WNWD* SE27..............162 C4
Malford Gv *SWFD* E18................52 D6
Malfort Rd *CMBW* SE5...............143 F4
Malham Cl *FBAR/BDGN* N11......48 A2
Malham Rd *FSTH* SE23.............164 A3
Malham Ter *UED* N18 *................50 D2
Mallams Ms *BRXN/ST* SW9.......142 B4
Mallard Cl *BAR* EN5...................33 H1
DART DA1.................................151 J6
HNWL W7..................................115 K2
KIL/WHAMP NW6.......................100 E1
WHTN TW2................................155 F2
Mallard Ct *WALTH* E17 *.............69 J3
Mallard Pl *TWK* TW1................156 B5
WDGN N22..................................49 F5
Mallards Ct *OXHEY* WD19..........27 K5
Mallards Rd *BARK* IG11............109 G3
Mallard St *CHEL* SW3.................15 G8
Mallard Wk *BECK* BR3...............198 A2
Mallard Wy *CDALE/KGS* NW9....62 E4
NTHWD HA6................................40 A3
WLGTN SM6..............................210 C6
Mail Chambers *KENS* W8 *.......119 K1
Mallet Dr *NTHLT* UB5..................77 K3
Mallet Rd *LEW* SE13.................165 G1
Malling Cl *CROY/NA* CR0...........197 K3
Malling Gdns *MRDN* SM4..........194 B3
Malling Wy *HAYES* BR2............199 J4
Mallinson Rd *BTSEA* SW11.......140 D6
CROY/NA CR0............................210 E1
Mallord St *CHEL* SW3...............120 C6
Mallory Cl *BROCKY* SE4............144 B5
Mallory Gdns *EBAR* EN4.............34 A2
Mallory St *STJWD* NW8.................2 C7
Mallow Cl *CROY/NA* CR0...........198 A5
Mallow Md *MLHL* NW7................46 C3
Mallow St *FSBYE* EC1V................6 E6
Mall Rd *HMSMTH* W6................118 E5
The Mall *BRXN/ST* SW9..............98 A6
EMPK RM11.................................75 K5
KTN/HRWW/WS HA3.....................62 B3
MORT/ESHN SW14.....................137 K6
STHGT/OAK N14..........................34 E5
SURB KT6.................................190 E2
WHALL SW1A...............................16 C2
Mall Vis *HMSMTH* W6...............118 E5
Malmains Cl *BECK* BR3.............199 G2
Malmains Wy *BECK* BR3...........199 F1
Malmesbury Cl *PIN* HA5..............58 E1
Malmesbury Rd *BOW* E3...........105 H2
CAN/RD E16..............................106 D4
MRDN SM4................................194 B4
SWFD E18...................................52 D4
Malmesbury Ter *CAN/RD* E16...106 D4
Malmesbury West Est *BOW* E3..105 H2
Malory Cl *BECK* BR3.................182 B5
Malpas Dr *PIN* HA5....................59 H2
Malpas Rd *BROCKY* SE4...........144 C3
BROW E8....................................91 K4
DAGE RM9..................................91 K6
HACK E8.....................................86 C4
Malta Rd *LEY* E10.......................69 J5
Malta St *FSBYE* EC1V...................6 A6
Maltby Cl *ORP* BR6...................202 B5
Maltby Dr *EN* EN1.......................24 D1
Maltby Rd *CHSGTN* KT9............206 C4
Maltby St *STHWK* SE1................19 K4
Malthouse Dr *CHSWK* W4.........118 C6
FELT TW13................................172 C1
Maltings Pl *FUL/PGN* SW6.........140 A2
STHWK SE1.................................19 H2
The Maltings *ORP* BR6..............202 A5
ROM RM1....................................75 H1
SNWD SE25 *.............................181 F6
Malting Wy *ISLW* TW7..............136 A4
Malton Ms *NKENS* W10 *...........100 C5
WOOL/PLUM SE18......................127 K6
Malton Rd *WOOL/PLUM* SE18...127 K6
Malton St *WOOL/PLUM* SE18...127 K6
Maltravers St *TPL/STR* WC2R....11 H5
Malt St *STHWK* SE1..................123 H6
Malva Cl *WAND/EARL* SW18.....140 A6
Malvern Av *BXLYHN* DA7...........149 F1
CHING E4....................................52 B5
RYLN/HDSTN HA2.......................77 J2
Malvern Cl *BUSH* WD23.............28 C1
MTCM CR4................................179 H6
NKENS W10..............................100 D4
SURB KT6.................................191 F5
Malvern Ct *FELT* TW13.............172 C1
SKENS SW7................................14 B6
Malvern Dr *FELT* TW13............172 C1
WFD IG8.....................................53 G2
Malvern Gdns *CRICK* NW2.........64 C6
KTN/HRWW/WS HA3...................62 A1
LOU IG10.....................................39 K1
Malvern Ms *KIL/WHAMP* NW6...100 E2
Malvern Pl *KIL/WHAMP* NW6...100 D2
EHAM E6.....................................89 J6
EMPK RM11.................................75 J3
HACK E8......................................86 C5
HPTN TW12...............................173 H2
HYS/HAR UB3.............................133 H1
KIL/WHAMP NW6.......................100 E2
ORP BR6...................................217 H2
SURB KT6.................................191 F6
TNTH CR7..................................196 B1
TOTM N17...................................50 A4
WAN E11.....................................70 C6
Malvern Ter *ED N9........................36 B3
IS N1...85 G6
Malvern Wy *WEA* W13................97 H4
Malwood Rd *BAL* SW12.............161 G1
Malyons Rd *LEW* SE13.............144 E6
Malyons Ter *LEW* SE13.............144 E6
Managers St *POP/IOD* E14 *.....125 F1
Manaton Cl *PECK* SE15.............143 J4
Manaton Crs *STHL* UB1...............96 A5
Manbey Gv *SRTFD* E15...............88 C4
Manbey Park Rd *SRTFD* E15......88 C4
Manbey Rd *SRTFD* E15..............88 C4

Manbey St *SRTFD* E15................88 C4
Manbre Rd *HMSMTH* W6..........119 F6
Manbrough Av *EHAM* E6...........108 A2
Manchester Dr *NKENS* W10 *....100 C3
Manchester Gv *POP/IOD* E14...125 F5
Manchester Ms *MHST* W1U..........9 G2
Manchester Rd *POP/IOD* E14...125 F5
SEVS/STOTM N15........................67 K4
THHTH CR7................................180 D6
Manchester Sq *MBLAR* W1U........9 G3
Manchester St *MHST* W1U...........9 G2
Manchester Wy *DAGE* RM10 *....92 D2
Manchuria Rd *BTSEA* SW11......161 F1
Manciple St *STHWK* SE1............19 F3
Mandalay Rd *CLAP* SW4...........141 H6
Mandarin Wy *YEAD* UB4.............95 H5
Mandela Cl *WLSDN* NW10..........80 E5
Mandela Rd *CAN/RD* E16..........106 E5
Mandela St *BRXN/ST* SW9.......142 B1
CAMTN NW1................................84 C1
Mandela Wy *STHWK* SE1............19 J7
Mandeville Cl *WIM/MER* SW19..177 F4
Mandeville Ct *CHING* E4..............37 G6
Mandeville Dr *SURB* KT6..........190 E5
Mandeville Pl *MHST* W1U............9 H3
Mandeville Rd *ISLW* TW7...........136 B3
NTHLT UB5..................................78 A4
STHGT/OAK N14..........................34 B4
Mandeville St *CLPT* E5...............87 G1
Mandrake Rd *TOOT* SW17.........160 E5
Mandrake Wy *SRTFD* E15 *.........88 C5
Mandrell Rd
BRXS/STRHM SW2....................141 K6
Manette St *LSQ/SEVD* WC2H....10 D4
Manford Cross *CHIG* IG7.............55 G1
Manford Wy *CHIG* IG7.................55 J2
CHIG IG7....................................55 F1
Manfred Rd *PUT/ROE* SW15....139 J6
Manger Rd *HOLWY* N7................84 E4
Mangold Wy *ERITHM* DA18......128 E3
Manilla St *POP/IOD* E14............124 D2
Manister Rd *ABYW* SE2............128 B3
Manley Ct *STNW/STAM* N16......86 B1
Manley St *CAMTN* NW1...............84 A1
Mann Cl *CROY/NA* CR0..............211 J1
Manningford Cl *FSBYE* EC1V *.....6 A4
Manning Gdns
KTN/HRWW/WS HA3...................61 K4
Manning Pl *RCHPK/HAM* TW10.157 G1
Manning Rd *DAGE* RM10............92 C5
STMC/STPC BR5........................202 E2
WALTH E17..................................69 G1
Manningtree Cl
WIM/MER SW19..........................159 H3
Manningtree Rd *RSLP* HA4..........77 F2
Manningtree St *WCHPL* E1........104 C5
Mannin Rd *CHDH* RM6................73 H4
Mannock Ms *SWFD* E18..............53 G4
Mannock Rd *DART* DA1..............151 J4
WDGN N22..................................49 H6
Mann's Cl *ISLW* TW7.................136 A6
Manns Rd *EDGW* HA8.................44 C2
Manoel Rd *WHTN* TW2.............155 H3
Manor Av *BROCKY* SE4............144 C3
HSLWW TW4..............................134 C4
NTHLT UB5..................................78 A5
Manorbrook *BKHTH/KID* SE3....145 K5
Manor Cl *BAR* EN5......................20 C5
CDALE/KGS NW9.........................62 D2
DAGE RM10.................................92 E5
DART DA1.................................150 A5
MLHL NW7 *...............................45 F1
RDART DA2................................170 D5
ROM RM1....................................75 J2
RSLP HA4....................................58 D5
THMD SE28...............................109 J5
WPK KT4....................................192 A5
Manor Cottages *NTHWD* HA6.....40 D4
Manor Cottages Ap *EFNCH* N2...47 G5
Manor Ct *ACT* W3 *...................117 H4
E/WMO/HCT KT8 *.....................189 F1
HRW HA1 *..................................61 F3
KUTN/CMB KT2 *........................175 G4
WBLY HA9...................................80 B2
Manor Court Rd *HNWL* W7..........96 D6
Manor Crs *BRYLDS* KT5............191 H3
Manor Cft *EDGW* HA8 *..............44 E5
Manordene Cl *THDIT* KT7...........190 B5
Manordene Rd *THMD* SE28.......109 J5
Manor Dr *BRYLDS* KT5..............191 H3
ESH/CLAY KT10..........................205 F1
FELT TW13................................172 C1
HOR/WEW KT19..........................207 G4
MLHL NW7 *................................45 F1
STHGT/OAK N14...........................34 B2
TRDG/WHET N20..........................33 J5
WBLY HA9...................................80 B3
Manor Dr North *NWMAL* KT3.....192 A4
The Manor Dr *WPK* KT4............192 B5
Manor Est *BERM/RHTH* SE16...123 J4
Manor Farm *BERM/RHTH* SE16..123 F5
Manor Farm Dr *CHING* E4...........38 C5
Manor Farm Rd *ALP/SUD* HA0...97 K1
STRHM/NOR SW16....................180 B5
Manorfield Cl *ARCH* N19.............84 C1
Manorfields Cl *CHST* BR7..........186 A6
Manor Gdns *ACT* W3.................117 H4
CLAP SW4 *...............................141 J6
HOLWY N7...................................85 F2
HPTN TW12...............................173 G3
RSLP HA4....................................77 G3
RYNPK SW20.............................177 J5
SAND/SEL CR2..........................212 A4
STMC/STPC BR5........................185 J1
Manor Ga *NTHLT* UB5................77 J5
Manorgate Rd *KUTN/CMB* KT2..175 H4
Manor Gv *BECK* BR3.................182 E5
PGE/AN SE20............................182 A1
RCH/KEW TW9............................137 H5
Manor Hall Av *HDN* NW4............46 B5
Manor Hall Dr *HDN* NW4.............46 B5
Manor Hall Gdns *LEY* E10............69 J5
Manor House Dr
KIL/WHAMP NW6.........................82 B5
Manor House Wy *ISLW* TW7.....136 C4

Manor La *FELT* TW13................153 K4
HYS/HAR UB3.............................113 G6
LEW SE13...................................145 J4
SUN TW16.................................172 A5
SUT SM1...................................209 G3
Manor Lane Ter *LEW* SE13.......145 H4
Manor Ms *KIL/WHAMP* NW6......82 A1
Manor Mt *FSTH* SE23...............163 K3
Manor Pde *HRW* HA1 *...............61 F3
STNW/STAM N16 *......................68 B6
Manor Pk *CHST* BR7.................185 J5
LEW SE13...................................145 H5
RCH/KEW TW9..........................137 G5
Manor Park Crs *EDGW* HA8........44 C2
Manor Park Dr
RYLN/HDSTN HA2.......................42 D6
Manor Park Gdns *EDGW* HA8.....44 C1
Manor Park Rd *CHST* BR7.........185 H4
EFNCH N2....................................47 G1
MNPK E12...................................89 H2
SUT SM1...................................209 G3
WLSDN NW10..............................81 H6
WWKM BR4................................198 E5
Manor Pl *CHST* BR7..................185 J5
EBED/NFELT TW14.....................153 K3
MTCM CR4................................179 G1
SUT SM1...................................209 F3
WALW SE17...............................122 D5
Manor Rd *BAR* EN5.....................20 C5
BARK IG11...................................91 F4
BECK BR3.................................182 D5
BELMT SM2...............................208 D5
BFN/LL DA15.............................168 A5
BXLY DA5.................................169 J3
CAN/RD E16..............................106 C4
CHDH RM6...................................73 K3
CHIG IG7....................................54 C2
DAGE RM10.................................92 E4
DART DA1.................................150 B3
E/WMO/HCT KT8......................189 J1
ENC/FH EN2................................23 K3
ERITH DA8................................130 C6
HAYES BR2...............................183 J6
HRW HA1.....................................61 G3
HYS/HAR UB3............................133 G5
LEY E10.......................................69 J4
LOU IG10.....................................39 F1
MTCM CR4................................179 H6
RCH/KEW TW9...........................137 G4
RCHPK/HAM TW10....................156 E3
RSLP HA4....................................58 B5
RYNPK SW20.............................177 J5
SNWD SE25..............................197 H1
STNW/STAM N16.........................68 A4
TEDD TW11...............................174 B1
TOTM N17...................................50 C4
WALTH E17.................................51 G5
WDGN N22...................................48 E2
WEA W13....................................97 G6
WHTN TW2................................155 H4
WLGTN SM6..............................210 B2
Manor Rd North
ESH/CLAY KT10.........................190 A6
ESH/CLAY KT10.........................205 F1
WLGTN SM6..............................210 B2
Manor Rd South
ESH/CLAY KT10.........................204 E3
Manor Road Pl *BAR* EN5 *..........20 C5
Manorside *BAR* EN5....................20 C5
Manor Sq *BCTR* RM8..................73 J6
Manor V *BTFD* TW8..................116 E5
Manor Vw *FNCH* N3....................47 F5
Manor Wy *BECK* BR3................182 D6
BKHTH/KID SE3.........................145 K5
BXLY DA5.................................169 H5
BXLYHN DA7.............................150 A4
CDALE/KGS NW9........................63 G1
CHING E4....................................38 B6
Manorway *EN* EN1......................36 A2
Manor Wy *HAYES* BR2..............199 J6
MTCM CR4................................179 H6
NWDGN UB2..............................114 C4
RAIN RM13................................111 G3
RSLP HA4....................................58 B5
SAND/SEL CR2..........................212 A4
STMC/STPC BR5........................186 D4
Manorway *WFD* IG8....................53 G1
The Manor Wy *WLGTN* SM6......210 B2
Mansard Beeches *TOOT* SW17..179 F1
Mansard Cl *HCH* RM12...............75 J5
PIN HA5......................................41 H6
Manse Cl *HYS/HAR* UB3...........113 G6
Mansel Gv *WALTH* E17................51 J4
Mansell Rd *ACT* W3..................118 A1
GFD/PVL UB6.............................96 B4
Mansell St *WCHPL* E1................13 K4
Mansel Rd *WIM/MER* SW19......177 H2
Mansergh Cl *CHARL* SE7..........126 B6
Manser Rd *STNW/STAM* N16......86 B1
Mansfield Av *EBAR* EN4............21 G2
RSLP HA4....................................59 F5
SEVS/STOTM N15........................67 K1
Mansfield Cl *ED* N9....................36 C1
STMC/STPC BR5........................202 E4
Mansfield Hl *CHING* E4................38 A3
Mansfield Ms *CAVSQ/HST* W1G..9 J2
HAMP NW3.................................83 K3
IL IG1..71 J4
SAND/SEL CR2..........................211 K4
WALTH E17..................................69 H1
WAN E11.....................................71 F3
Mansfield St *CAVSQ/HST* W1G...9 J2
Mansford St *BETH* E2................104 D2
Manship Rd *MTCM* CR4............179 F4
Mansion Cl *BRXN/ST* SW9........142 B2
Mansion Gdns *HAMP* NW3.........83 F1
Mansion House Pl
MANHO EC4N *............................12 E4
The Mansions *ECT* SW5............120 A5
Manson Ms *SKENS* SW7 *.........120 B4

Manson Pl SKENS SW7..............14 A7
Manstead Gdns CHDH RM6..........73 J4
RAIN RM13.............................111 K5
Manston Av NWDGN UB2.........115 F4
Manston Cl PGE/AN SE20.........181 K4
Manstone Rd CRICK NW2............82 C5
Manston Gv KUTN/CMB KT2....174 E1
Manston Wy HCH RM12.............93 K4
Manthorpe Rd
WOOL/PLUM SE18..................127 H5
Mantilla Rd TOOT SW17...........161 F6
Mantle Rd BROCKY SE4...........144 B4
Mantlet Cl STRHM/NOR SW16...179 H3
Mantle Wy SRTFD E15................88 C5
Manton Av HNWL W7................116 A2
Manton Cl HYS/HAR UB3.............94 A6
Manton Rd ABYW SE2................128 B4
PEND EN3.................................25 K1
Mantua St BTSEA SW11...........140 C4
Mantus Cl WCHPL E1...............104 E3
Mantus Rd WCHPL E1...............104 E3
Manus Wy TRDG/WHET N20......33 G4
Manville Gdns TOOT SW17.......161 H5
Manville Rd TOOT SW17...........161 F4
Manwood Rd BROCKY SE4.......164 C1
Manwood St CAN/RD E16.........126 E1
Many Gates BAL SW12..............161 G4
Mapesbury Ms CDALE/KGS NW9..63 J3
Mapesbury Rd CRICK NW2..........82 C4
Mapeshill Pl CRICK NW2.............82 A4
Mape St BETH E2.....................104 D3
Maple Av ACT W3....................118 B3
CHING E4.................................51 H2
RYLN/HDSTN HA2.....................60 B6
Maple Cl BARK/HLT IG6.............39 H5
BKHH IG9..................................39 H5
CLAP SW4................................161 J1
FNCH N3....................................46 E2
HCH RM12.................................93 K1
HPTN TW12..............................154 D2
MTCM CR4..............................179 G4
RSLP HA4..................................59 F3
STMC/STPC BR5.....................201 J2
STNW/STAM N16.......................68 C3
YEAD UB4.................................95 H2
Maple Crs BFN/LL DA15...........168 B1
Maplecroft Cl EHAM E6............107 H5
Mapledale Av CROY/NA CR0....212 D1
Mapledene Est HACK E8.............86 C5
Mapledene Rd HACK E8..............86 C5
Maple Gdns ASHF TW15..........152 B4
EDGW HA8...............................45 G3
Maple Gv BTFD TW8.................136 C1
CDALE/KGS NW9........................62 E4
EA W5....................................116 E3
NWDGN UB2.............................95 G4
Maple Leaf Cl
BARK/RAIN SE16 *...................124 A2
STRHM/NOR SW16...................180 A1
Maple Leaf Dr BFN/LL DA15.....168 A1
Maple Leaf Sq
BERM/RHTH SE16 *...................124 A2
TOTM N17.................................50 C3
WDR/YW UB7..........................112 C1
Maple Rd DART DA1.................171 K5
PGE/AN SE20..........................181 J3
SURB KT6................................190 E2
WAN E11...................................70 C3
YEAD UB4.................................95 G2
Maples Pl WCHPL E1 *.............104 D4
Maplestead Rd
BRXS/STRHM SW2..................162 A2
DAGW RM9................................91 H6
The Maples ESH/CLAY KT10 *....205 G5
KUT/HW KT1 *..........................174 D3
Maple St BETH E2....................104 C1
FITZ W1T...................................10 E1
ROMW/RG RM7..........................74 E1
Maplethorpe Rd THHTH CR7....196 B1
Mapleton Cl HAYES BR2...........199 K2
Mapleton Rd CHING E4................38 A6
EN EN1....................................24 E3
WAND/EARL SW18...................160 A1
Mapleton Rd CHING E4................38 A6
EN EN1....................................24 E3
WAND/EARL SW18...................159 K1
Maple Tree Pl BKHTH/KID SE3..146 D2
Maple Wk NKENS W10 *...........100 B3
Maple Wy FELT TW13...............153 K5
Maplin Cl WCHMH N21...............23 F6
Maplin Rd CAN/RD E16.............106 E5
Maplin St BOW E3....................105 H2
Mapperley Dr WFD IG8................52 C3
Marabou Cl MNPK E12................89 J3
Maran Wy ERITHM DA18...........128 E3
Marathon Wy THMD SE28..........128 A2
Marban Rd MV/WKIL W9............100 D2
Marble Cl ACT W3.....................117 J1
Marble Dr CRICK NW2.................64 B5
Marble Hill Cl TWK TW1............156 C2
Marble Hill Gdns TWK TW1......156 C2
Marble Quay WAP E1W *...........13 J7
Marbrook Ct LEE/GVPK SE12...166 B5
Marcella Rd BRXN/ST SW9.......142 B3
Marcellina Wy ORP BR6...........216 E1
Marcet Rd DART DA1................151 F6
Marchant Rd WAN E11................70 B6
Marchant St NWCR SE14.........124 B6
Marchbank Rd WKENS W14......119 J6
Marchmont Rd
RCHPK/HAM TW10...................137 G6
WLGTN SM6.............................210 C6
Marchmont St BMSBY WC1N......4 E6
Marchside Cl HEST TW5...........134 C2
Marchwood Cl CMBW SE5........143 F1
Marchwood Crs EA W5................97 K5
Marcia Rd STHWK SE1................19 H7
Marcilly Rd WAND/EARL SW18..140 C6
Marconi Pl FBAR/BDGN N11.......34 B6
Marconi Rd LEY E10....................69 J5
Marconi Wy STHL UB1................96 B5
Marcon Pl HACK E8.....................86 D4
Marco Rd HMSMTH W6.............118 E3

Marcus Garvey Ms EDUL SE22..163 J1
Marcus Garvey Wy HNHL SE24..142 B5
Marcus Rd DART DA1................170 D2
Marcus St SRTFD E15.................88 C6
WAND/EARL SW18...................160 A1
Marcus Ter WAND/EARL SW18..160 A1
Mardale Dr CDALE/KGS NW9......63 F2
Mardell Rd CROY/NA CR0.........198 A2
Marden Av HAYES BR2.............199 K3
Marden Crs BXLY DA5..............149 K6
CROY/NA CR0.........................196 A3
Marden Rd CROY/NA CR0.........196 A4
ROM RM1...................................75 G3
TOTM N17.................................50 A5
Marden Sq BERM/RHTH SE16...123 J3
Marder Rd WEA W13..................116 B2
Mardyke Cl RAIN RM13.............110 E1
Marechal Niel Av BFN/LL DA15..167 J5
Marechal Niel Pde
SCUP DA14 *...........................167 J5
Maresfield CROY/NA CR0.........212 A1
Maresfield Gdns HAMP NW3.......83 G3
Mare St HACK E8.......................86 D4
Marfield Cl WPK KT4.................192 D5
Marfleet Cl CAR SM5................194 D6
Margaret Av CHING E4................37 K2
Margaret Bondfield Av
BARK IG11..................................91 G5
Margaret Ct FITZ W1T *..............10 B3
Margaret Gardner Dr
ELTH/MOT SE9.........................166 E4
Margaret Ingram Cl
FUL/PGN SW6 *........................119 J6
Margaret Lockwood Cl
KUT/HW KT1 *..........................191 G1
Margaret Rd BXLY DA5.............168 E1
EBAR EN4..................................21 H6
GPK RM2...................................75 K4
STNW/STAM N16.......................68 B5
Margaret St CAVSQ/HST W1G.....9 K3
GTPST W1W.............................10 A3
Margaretta Ter CHEL SW3........120 D6
Margaretting Rd MNPK E12.......71 G6
Margaret Wy REDBR IG4.............71 J3
Margate Rd BRXS/STRHM SW2..141 K6
Margery Park Rd FSTGT E7........88 E4
Margery Rd BCTR RM8................91 K1
Margery St CLKNW EC1R.............5 J5
Margin Dr WIM/MER SW19.......177 F1
Margravine Gdns
HMSMTH W6............................119 G5
Margravine Rd HMSMTH W6.....119 G6
Marguerite Vls RYNPK SW20 *..176 E3
Marham Gdns MRDN SM4........194 B3
WAND/EARL SW18...................160 D3
Maria Cl STHWK SE1................123 H4
Marian Cl YEAD UB4.................95 H3
Marian Pl BETH E2...................104 D1
Marian Rd STRHM/NOR SW16..179 H4
Marian Sq BETH E2 *.................104 D1
Marian St BETH E2 *..................104 D1
Marian Wy WLSDN NW10...........81 H5
Maria Ter WCHPL E1.................105 F4
Maria Theresa Cl NWMAL KT3..192 A2
Maricas Av KTN/HRWW/WS HA3..42 D4
Marie Curie CMBW SE5 *...........143 F2
Marie Lloyd Wk HACK E8 *..........86 C4
Marigold Aly STHWK SE1.............12 A6
Marigold Cl STHL UB1.................95 J6
Marigold Rd TOTM N17................50 E3
Marigold St BERM/RHTH SE16...123 J2
Marigold Wy CROY/NA CR0......198 A5
Marina Ap YEAD UB4..................95 J4
Marina Av NWMAL KT3.............192 E2
Marina Cl HAYES BR2...............199 J1
Marina Dr DART DA1.................171 K1
WELL DA16...............................147 K3
Marina Gdns ROMW/RG RM7....74 D2
Marina Wy TEDD TW11.............174 E3
Marine Ct PUR/KEN CR8...........131 H4
Marine Dr BARK IG11................109 H2
WOOL/PLUM SE18...................126 E4
Marinefield Rd FUL/PGN SW6..140 A3
Mariner Gdns
RCHPK/HAM TW10...................156 C5
Mariner Rd MNPK E12................90 A2
Mariners Ms POP/IOD E14.........125 G4
Mariners St BERM/RHTH SE16..123 F3
Marion Cl BARK/HLT IG6............54 D3
Marion Crs STMC/STPC BR5.....202 C2
Marion Gv WFD IG8.....................38 C5
Marion Ms DUL SE21.................163 F5
Marion Rd MLHL NW7.................45 J1
THHTH CR7..............................196 D2
Marischal Rd LEW SE13............145 G4
Maritime Quay POP/IOD E14....124 D5
Maritime St BOW E3.................105 H3
Marius Rd TOOT SW17..............161 F4
Marjorie Gv BTSEA SW11.........140 E5
Mark Av CHING E4......................37 K1
Mark Cl BXLYHN DA7................149 F2
HAYES BR2..............................215 J2
STHL UB1................................115 F1
Markeston Gn OXHEY WD19 *....27 H6
Market Chambers
ENC/FH EN2 *............................23 K4
Market Est HOLWY N7.................84 E4
Market La EDGW HA8..................44 E4
Market Link ROM RM1...............75 G2
Market Meadow
STMC/STPC BR5.....................202 D1
Market Ms MYFR/PICC W1J.......9 J7
Market Pde BMLY BR1 *............183 K4
ED N9 *.....................................36 C4
EWKT17 *................................207 H6
FELT TW13 *.............................154 D4
LEY E10 *...................................69 K3
SCUP DA14 *...........................168 B6
SNWD SE25 *...........................197 H2
STNW/STAM N16 *....................68 C1
Market Pl ACT W3.....................117 K1
BERM/RHTH SE16 *.................123 H4
BTFD TW8.................................136 D1
BXLYHS DA6............................149 H5
DART DA1................................171 J5

EFNCH N2...................................47 J6
GTPST W1W...............................10 A3
KUT/HW KT1 *..........................174 E5
MRDN SM4...............................194 A3
RAIN RM13...............................111 H1
Market Rd HOLWY N7.................84 D5
RCH/KEW TW9.........................137 H4
Market Sq ED N9.........................36 C4
WOOL/PLUM SE18...................127 F4
Market Ter BTFD TW8 *.............117 F6
The Market CAR SM5 *..............194 B5
COVGDN WC2E...........................11 F5
Market Yard Ms STHWK SE1......19 G4
Markfield Gdns CHING E4............37 K3
Markfield Rd SEVS/STOTM N15...68 C1
Markham Pl CHEL SW3..............120 E5
Markham Sq CHEL SW3.............120 E5
Markham St CHEL SW3..............120 D5
Markhole Cl HPTN TW12...........172 E3
Markhouse Av WALTH E17..........69 F3
Markhouse Rd WALTH E17.........69 H3
Mark La MON EC3R......................13 H5
Markmanor Av WALTH E17..........69 H4
Mark Sq SDTCH EC2A..................7 G6
Mark St SDTCH EC2A...................7 G6
SRTFD E15.................................88 C5
Mark Ter RYNPK SW20 *...........177 F3
Markwade Cl MNPK E12 *...........71 H5
The Markway SUN TW16............172 B5
Markwell Cl SYD SE26..............163 J6
Markyate Rd BCTR RM8..............91 H3
Marlands Rd CLAY IG5................53 K6
Marlborough Av EDGW HA8........30 D5
HACK E8....................................86 C6
RSLP HA4...................................34 C5
STHGT/OAK N14........................34 C5
Marlborough Cl ORP BR6...........202 A4
TRDG/WHET N20........................33 K5
WALW SE17...............................18 B7
WIM/MER SW19........................178 D2
Marlborough Ct REGST W1B *......10 A5
Marlborough Crs CHSWK W4....118 B3
HYS/HAR UB3............................133 G1
Marlborough Dr CLAY IG5............53 J6
Marlborough Gdns
TRDG/WHET N20........................33 K5
Marlborough Ga BAY/PAD W2 *....8 A6
Marlborough Gv STHWK SE1.....123 H5
Marlborough Hl HRW HA1............60 E1
STJWD NW8...............................83 G1
Marlborough La CHARL SE7......126 B6
Marlborough Ms
BRXS/STRHM SW2...................142 A4
Marlborough Pde FSBYPK N4 *...67 J7
Marlborough Park Av
BFN/LL DA15.............................168 B3
Marlborough Pl STJWD NW8.....101 G1
Marlborough Rd ARCH N19.........66 E6
BCTR RM8..................................91 J2
CHING E4...................................52 A1
CHSWK W4..............................117 K5
DART DA1................................171 F1
EA W5....................................116 E2
ED N9..36 B3
FELT TW13..............................154 C5
FSTGT E7..................................89 G5
HAYES BR2..............................200 B1
HPTN TW12.............................173 F2
NWDGN UB2.............................114 B3
RCHPK/HAM TW10...................157 G1
ROMW/RG RM7.........................74 E1
SAND/SEL CR2.........................211 J5
SRTFD E15.................................88 C2
SUT SM1..................................208 E1
Marlborough St CHEL SW3..........14 C7
Marlborough Yd ARCH N19.........66 D6
Marler Rd FSTH SE23................164 B3
Marley Av BXLYHN DA7............128 E6
Marley Cl GFD/PVL UB6..............96 A2
SEVS/STOTM N15.....................67 H1
Marley Rd BERM/RHTH SE16 *..124 A4
Marlingdene Cl HPTN TW12......173 F2
Marlings Cl CHST BR7...............201 K1
Marlings Park Av CHST BR7......201 K1
Marlins Cl SUT SM1..................209 G3
Marlins Meadow WATW WD18...26 B1
Marloes Cl ALP/SUD HA0............79 K3
Marloes Rd KENS W8................120 A3
Marlow Av PUR/KEN CR8.........131 K4
Marlow Cl PGE/AN SE20...........181 J6
Marlow Ct CDALE/KGS NW9.......45 H6
Marlow Crs TWK TW1...............156 A1
Marlow Dr CHEAM SM3............208 A1
Marlowe Cl BARK/HLT IG6..........54 C4
CHST BR7................................185 J3
Marlowe Gdns ELTH/MOT SE9..147 F6
Marlowe Rd WALTH E17.............70 A1
Marlowes NFNLT UB5.................95 F5
The Marlowes DART DA1...........150 A5
STJWD NW8...............................83 G1
Marlowe Wy CROY/NA CR0.....195 K6
Marlow Gdns HYS/HAR UB3.....113 G3
Marlow Rd EHAM E6.................107 K2
NWDGN UB2.............................114 E3
PGE/AN SE20..........................181 J5
Marlow Wy BERM/RHTH SE16..124 A2
Marl Rd WAND/EARL SW18......140 A5
Marlton St GNWCH SE10...........125 J5
Marlwood Cl BFN/LL DA15........167 K4
Marlyon Rd BARK/HLT IG6..........55 H1
Marmadon Rd
WOOL/PLUM SE18...................128 A4
Marmion Ap CHING E4.................37 J6
Marmion Av CHING E4.................37 H6
Marmion Cl CHING E4..................37 H6
Marmion Ms BTSEA SW11........141 F4
Marmion Rd BTSEA SW11.........141 F5

Marmont Rd PECK SE15............143 H2
Marmora Rd EDUL SE22...........164 A1
Marmot Rd HSLWW TW4..........134 C4
Marne Av FBAR/BDGN N11........36 B6
WELL DA16...............................148 B4
Marnell Wy HSLWW TW4..........134 C4
Marne St NKENS W10................100 C2
Marney Rd BTSEA SW11...........141 F5
Marnfield Crs
BRXS/STRHM SW2...................162 A3
Marnham Av CRICK NW2............82 C2
Marnham Crs GFD/PVL UB6.......96 B1
Marnham Cresent
GFD/PVL UB6.............................96 A1
Marnock Rd BROCKY SE4.........144 C6
Maroon St POP/IOD E14............105 G4
Maroons Wy CAT SE6................182 D1
Marquess Rd IS N1.....................85 K4
Marquess Rd North IS N1 *.........85 J4
Marquis Cl ALP/SUD HA0............80 B5
Marquis Rd CAMTN NW1.............84 C5
FSBYPK N4................................67 H5
WDGN N22..................................49 F3
Marrabon Cl BFN/LL DA15........168 B3
Marrick Cl PUT/ROE SW15.......138 D5
Married Quarters EDGW HA8 *....45 H1
Marriner Ct HYS/HAR UB3 *.......94 C6
Marriot Rd MUSWH N10 *...........47 K4
Marriott Cl EBED/NFELT TW14..153 G1
Marriott Rd BAR EN5...................20 B4
DART DA1................................171 H5
FSBYPK N4................................67 F5
SRTFD E15.................................88 C6
Marriotts Cl CDALE/KGS NW9....63 H3
Marriotts Yd BAR EN5 *...............20 C4
Marryat Cl HSLWW TW4...........134 E5
Marryat Pl WIM/MER SW19......159 H6
Marryat Rd WIM/MER SW19.....177 G1
Marsala Rd LEW SE13...............144 E5
Marsden Rd ED N9.......................36 D4
PECK SE15..............................143 G4
Marsden Wy ORP BR6...............216 E1
Marsh Av HOR/WEW KT19.......207 H6
Marsh Cl MLHL NW7...................31 G5
Marsh Dr CDALE/KGS NW9........63 H3
Marsh Farm Rd WHTN TW2......156 A3
Marshfield St POP/IOD E14.......125 F3
Marshgate La SRTFD E15...........87 K6
Marsh Green Rd DAGE RM10......92 C6
Marsh Hl HOM E9.......................87 G3
Marsh La LEY E10........................69 H6
MLHL NW7.................................31 G5
STAN HA7...................................43 K2
TOTM N17...................................50 D3
Marsh Rd ALP/SUD HA0..............79 K1
PIN HA5.....................................59 K1
Marshside Cl ED N9.....................36 E4
Marsh St DART DA1...................151 K3
POP/IOD E14 *........................124 E4
Marsh Wall POP/IOD E14.........124 D2
Marsh Wy RAIN RM13...............111 F5
Marsland Cl WALW SE17..............18 C8
Marston Av CHSGTN KT9.........206 A4
DAGE RM10...............................92 C1
KIL/WHAMP NW6......................83 G5
Marston Ct WOT/HER KT12 *....188 B5
Marston Rd CLAY IG5..................53 J5
TEDD TW11.............................174 C1
Marston Wy NRWD SE19...........180 C3
Marsworth Av PIN HA5................41 H4
Marsworth Cl WATW WD18 *......26 C1
YEAD UB4.................................96 A3
Martaban Rd STNW/STAM N16...68 A1
Martara Ms WALW SE17...........122 D5
Martello St HACK E8....................86 D5
Martell Rd DUL SE21.................162 E5
Martel Pl HACK E8 *....................86 B4
Marten Rd WALTH E17................51 J5
Martens Av BXLYHN DA7..........149 K5
Martens Cl BXLYHN DA7..........149 K5
Martham Cl BARK/HLT IG6.........55 G4
THMD SE28.............................109 K6
Martha Rd SRTFD E15................88 C4
Martha's Buildings FSBYE EC1V...6 E6
Martha St WCHPL E1.................104 E5
Marthorne Crs
KTN/HRWW/WS HA3..................42 D5
Martin Bowes Rd
ELTH/MOT SE9.........................146 E4
Martin Ct POP/IOD E14 *...........125 F2
Martin Crs CROY/NA CR0.........196 B5
Martindale MORT/ESHN SW14..137 K6
Martindale Av CAN/RD E16.......106 E6
ORP BR6...................................217 G3
Martindale Rd BAL SW12..........161 G2
HSLWW TW4............................134 D4
Martin Dene BXLYHS DA6.........149 G6
Martin Dr NTHLT UB5..................77 K4
RAIN RM13...............................111 K3
Martineau Cl ESH/CLAY KT10...204 E3
Martineau Dr TWK TW1............156 C5
Martineau Rd HBRY N5...............85 H2

Martineau St WCHPL E1............104 E6
Martingales Cl
RCHPK/HAM TW10...................156 E5
Martin Gv MRDN SM4...............177 K6
Martin La CANST EC4R...............13 F5
Martin Ri BXLYHS DA6..............149 G6
Martin Rd BCTR RM8..................91 J2
RDART DA2..............................171 F5
Martins CL STMC/STPC BR5.....186 D4
WWKM BR4..............................199 G6
Martins Mt BAR EN5...................20 E5
Martins Pl THMD SE28..............127 K1
Martin's Rd HAYES BR2............183 H5
The Martins SYD SE26..............181 J1
WBLY HA9 *................................62 B2
Martin St THMD SE28...............127 K1
Martin Wy MRDN SM4..............177 H6
Martlet Gv NTHLT UB5................95 H2
Martlett Ct HOL/ALD WC2B........11 F4
Martock Cl KTN/HRWW/WS HA3..61 J1
Martock Gdns FBAR/BDGN N11..47 K1
Marton Cl CAT SE6....................164 D5
Marton Rd STNW/STAM N16 *....68 A6
Marvell Av YEAD UB4.................94 E4
Marvels La LEE/GVPK SE12......166 A4
Marvels La East LEE/GVPK SE12..166 B5
Marville Rd FUL/PGN SW6........139 J1
Marvin St HACK E8 *...................86 D4
Marwell Cl ROM RM1..................75 J1
WWKM BR4..............................199 J6
Marwood Cl WEA W13...............148 C4
Marwood Dr MLHL NW7...............46 B5
Mary Adelaide Cl
PUT/ROE SW15........................158 B6
Maryat Sq FUL/PGN SW6 *.......139 H2
Maryatt Av RYLN/HDSTN HA2....60 B6
Marybank WOOL/PLUM SE18...126 E4
Mary Cl KTN/HRWW/WS HA3......62 B1
Mary Datchelor Cl CMBW SE5...142 E2
Maryfield Cl BXLY DA5................170 B5
Maryland Pk SRTFD E15..............88 C3
MV/WKIL W9............................100 E3
SRTFD E15.................................88 C3
THHTH CR7 *............................180 C4
WDGN N22..................................49 G2
Maryland Sq SRTFD E15.............88 C3
Marylands Rd MV/WKIL W9......100 E3
Maryland St SRTFD E15..............88 C3
Maryland Wk IS N1 *...................85 J6
Mary Lawrenson Pl
BKHTH/KID SE3........................145 J1
Marylebone F/O BAY/PAD W2 *....8 C2
Marylebone High St
CAVSQ/HST W1G........................9 H2
Marylebone La MHST W1U............9 H3
Marylebone Ms CAVSQ/HST W1G..9 J2
Marylebone Pas GTPST W1W.....10 B3
Marylebone Rd CAMTN NW1.......8 D1
Marylee Wy LBTH SE11...............17 H7
Maryon Gv CHARL SE7.............126 D4
Maryon Ms HAMP NW3...............83 J2
Maryon Rd CHARL SE7.............126 D4
Mary Peters Dr GFD/PVL UB6.....78 D3
Mary Pl NTGHL W11.................100 C6
Mary Rose Cl HPTN TW12........173 F4
Maryrose Wy TRDG/WHET N20..33 H3
Mary Seacole Cl HACK E8 *.......86 B6
Mary's Ter TWK TW1................156 B2
Mary St CAN/RD E16.................106 D4
IS N1...6 D1
Mary Ter CAMTN NW1 *...............4 A1
Mary Wy OXHEY WD19................27 G6
Masbro' Rd WKENS W14...........119 G3
Mascalls Ct CHARL SE7 *..........126 B6
Mascalls Rd CHARL SE7...........126 B6
Mascotts Cl CRICK NW2..............81 K1
Masefield Av STAN HA7...............43 F1
STHL UB1..................................96 A6
Masefield Cl ERITH DA8............150 C2
HARH RM3.................................58 A3
Masefield Crs STHGT/OAK N14...22 C6
Masefield Gdns EHAM E6..........108 A3
Masefield La YEAD UB4..............95 F3
Masefield Rd HPTN TW12 *........154 E4
Masefield Vw ORP BR6.............216 C1
Masefield Wy
STWL/WRAY TW19...................152 C3
Mashie Rd ACT W3......................99 G5
Mashiters Hill ROM RM1.............57 G6
Mashiters Wk ROM RM1.............57 G6
Maskall Cl BRXS/STRHM SW2..162 B3
Maskell Rd TOOT SW17............160 B5
Maskelyne Cl BTSEA SW11......140 D2
Mason Cl BERM/RHTH SE16.....123 H5
BXLYHN DA7............................149 J4
CAN/RD E16.............................106 E6
HPTN TW12.............................172 E4
RYNPK SW20............................177 G4
Mason Ct WBLY HA9 *...............62 B1
Mason Rd SUT SM1..................209 F3
Mason's Arms Ms CONDST W1S...9 J4
Mason's Av CITYW EC2V............12 E3
CROY/NA CR0...........................211 J2
KTN/HRWW/WS HA3..................42 E6
Masons Ct EW KT17 *...............207 J6
Masons Hill HAYES BR2............183 K6
WOOL/PLUM SE18...................127 G4
Mason's PI FSBYE EC1V...............6 B4
MTCM CR4..............................178 E4
Masons Yd FSBYE EC1V..............6 A4
STJS SW1Y................................10 B7
Massey Cl FBAR/BDGN N11........48 B1
Massie Rd HACK E8.....................86 C4
Massingberd Wy TOOT SW17...161 G6
Massinger St WALW SE17..........19 G6
Massingham St WCHPL E1.........105 F3
Masson Av RSLP HA4..................77 G4
Masterman Rd EHAM E6...........107 J2

Masters Cl STRHM/NOR SW16 179 H2
Masters Dr BERM/RHTH SE16 123 J5
Master's St WCHPL E1 105 F4
Mast House Ter
POP/IOD E14 * 124 D4
Masthouse Ter POP/IOD E14 124 D4
Mastmaker Rd POP/IOD E14 124 D2
Mast Quay WOOL/PLUM SE18 126 E3
Maswell Park Crs HSLW TW3 135 H6
Maswell Park Rd HSLW TW3 135 G6
Matcham Rd WAN E11 88 C1
Matchless Dr
WOOL/PLUM SE18 147 F1
Matfield Cl HAYES BR2 199 K2
Matfield Rd BELV DA17 129 H6
Matham Gv EDUL SE22 143 G5
Matham Rd E/WMO/HCT KT8 189 J2
Matheson Rd WKENS W14 119 J4
Mathews Av EHAM E6 108 A1
Mathews Park Av SRTFD E15 88 D4
Mathews Yd LSQ/SEVD WC2H * 10 E4
Mathieson Ct STHWK SE1 18 B3
Matilda Cl NRWD SE19 180 E3
Matilda St IS N1 5 H1
Matlock Cl BAR EN5 20 B6
HNHL SE24 142 D5
Matlock Crs CHEAM SM3 208 C2
OXHEY WD19 27 G5
Matlock Gdns CHEAM SM3 208 C2
Matlock Pl CHEAM SM3 208 C2
Matlock Rd LEY E10 70 A3
Matlock St POP/IOD E14 105 G5
Matlock Wy NWMAL KT3 176 A4
Matthew Cl NKENS W10 * 100 B3
Matthew Ct MTCM CR4 195 J2
Matthews Rd GFD/PVL UB6 78 D3
Matthews St BTSEA SW11 * 140 E3
Matthias Rd STNW/STAM N16 85 K3
Mattingly Wy PECK SE15 143 G1
Mattison Rd FSBYPK N4 67 G3
Mattock La WEA W13 116 D1
Maud Cashmore Wy
WOOL/PLUM SE18 126 E3
Maude Rd CMBW SE5 143 F3
WALTH E17 69 G2
Maudesville Cottages
HNWL W7 115 K1
Maude Ter WALTH E17 69 G2
Maud Gdns BARK IG11 109 F1
PLSTW E13 106 D1
Maudlins Gn WAP E1W * 123 H1
Maud Rd LEY E10 88 A1
PLSTW E13 106 D1
Maudslay Rd ELTH/MOT SE9 146 E4
Maud St CAN/RD E16 106 D4
Maud Wilkes Cl KTTN NW5 84 C3
Mauleverer Rd
BRXS/STRHM SW2 141 K6
Maundeby Wk WLSDN NW10 * 81 G3
Maunder Rd HNWL W7 115 K1
Maunsel St WEST SW1P 16 C6
Maurice Av WDGN N22 49 H5
Maurice Brown Cl MLHL NW7 * 46 B1
Maurice Browne Cl MLHL NW7 46 B1
Maurice St SHB W12 99 K5
Maurice Wk GLDGN NW11 65 G1
Maurier Cl NTHLT UB5 77 G6
Mauritius Rd GNWCH SE10 125 H4
Maury Rd STNW/STAM N16 68 C6
Mauveine Gdns HSLW TW3 135 F5
Mavelstone Rd BMLY BR1 184 C4
Maverton Rd BOW E3 * 87 J6
Mavis Av HOR/WEW KT19 207 G3
Mavis Cl HOR/WEW KT19 207 G3
Mawbey Pl STHWK SE1 123 G5
Mawbey Rd STHWK SE1 123 G5
Mawbey St VX/NE SW8 141 K1
Mawney Cl ROMW/RG RM7 56 D6
Mawney Rd ROMW/RG RM7 56 D6
Mawson Cl RYNPK SW20 177 H5
Mawson La CHSWK W4 118 C6
Maxey Gdns DAGW RM9 92 A2
Maxey Rd DAGW RM9 92 A2
WOOL/PLUM SE18 127 H4
Maxfield Cl TRDG/WHET N20 33 G2
Maxilla Wk NKENS W10 100 B5
Maximfeldt Rd ERITH DA8 130 B5
Maxim Rd DART DA1 150 B6
ERITH DA8 130 B5
WCHMH N21 35 G1
Maxted Pk HRW HA1 60 E4
Maxted Rd PECK SE15 143 H4
Maxwell Cl CROY/NA CR0 195 K5
HYS/HAR UB3 94 E6
Maxwell Gdns ORP BR6 217 F1
Maxwell Ri OXHEY WD19 27 J2
Maxwell Rd FUL/PGN SW6 140 A1
NTHWD HA6 40 B3
WDR/YW UB7 112 B4
WELL DA16 148 B5
Maxwelton Av MLHL NW7 45 F1
Maxwelton Cl MLHL NW7 45 F1
Maya Cl PECK SE15 143 J3
Mayall Cl PEND EN3 25 J1
STHWK SE1 18 D1
Mayall Rd HNHL SE24 142 C6
Maya Pl FBAR/BDGN N11 48 D3
Maya Rd EFNCH N2 65 G1
May Av STMC/STPC BR5 202 C2
Maybank Av ALP/SUD HA0 79 G3
HCH RM12 93 K3
SWFD E18 53 F5
Maybank Gdns PIN HA5 58 E1
Maybank Rd SWFD E18 53 G4
May Bate Av KUTN/CMB KT2 174 E4
Mayberry Pl BRYLDS KT5 191 G4
Maybourne Cl SYD SE26 181 J2
Maybury Cl EN EN1 24 D1
STMC/STPC BR5 201 G2
Maybury Gdns WLSDN NW10 81 J5
Maybury Ms HGT N6 66 C4
Maybury Rd BARK IG11 109 G1
PLSTW E13 107 G3
Maybury St TOOT SW17 178 D1
Maychurch Cl STAN HA7 43 K4
May Cl CHSGTN KT9 206 B4
Maycock Gv NTHWD HA6 40 D2
Maycroft PIN HA5 41 F5
Maycross Av MRDN SM4 193 J1
Mayday Gdns BKHTH/KID SE3 146 D3
Mayday Rd THHTH CR7 196 C3
Mayefield Rd THHTH CR7 196 A1
Mayerne Rd ELTH/MOT SE9 146 C6
Mayesbrook Rd BARK IG11 91 F6
GDMY/SEVK IG3 91 G1
Mayesford Rd CHDH RM6 73 J4
Mayes Rd WDGN N22 49 F5
Mayeswood Rd
LEE/GVPK SE12 166 B6
Mayfair Av BXLYHN DA7 148 E2
CHDH RM6 73 K3
IL IG1 71 K6
WHTN TW2 155 H2
WPK KT4 192 D5
Mayfair Cl BECK BR3 182 E4
SURB KT6 191 F5
Mayfair Ct EDGW HA8 44 B1
Mayfair Gdns TOTM N17 49 K2
WFD IG8 52 E3
Mayfair Ms CAMTN NW1 * 83 K5
Mayfair Pl MYFR/PICC W1J 9 K7
Mayfair Rd DART DA1 151 G6
Mayfair Ter STHGT/OAK N14 34 D2
Mayfield BXLYHN DA7 149 G4
Mayfield Av CHSWK W4 118 B4
KTN/HRWW/WS HA3 61 H2
NFNCH/WDSPK N12 33 G6
ORP BR6 202 A5
STHGT/OAK N14 34 C4
WEA W13 116 C3
WFD IG8 52 E2
Mayfield Cl CLAP SW4 141 J6
HACK E8 86 B5
PGE/AN SE20 181 J4
THDIT KT7 190 C5
Mayfield Crs ED N9 36 D1
THHTH CR7 196 A1
Mayfield Dr PIN HA5 59 K1
Mayfield Gdns HDN NW4 64 B3
HNWL W7 96 D5
Mayfield Rd ACT W3 98 D6
BCTR RM8 73 J5
BELMT SM2 209 H4
BELV DA17 129 K4
BMLY BR1 200 D2
CEND/HSY/T N8 67 F3
CHING E4 38 A4
HACK E8 * 86 B5
PEND EN3 25 F3
PLSTW E13 106 D3
SAND/SEL CR2 211 K6
SHB W12 118 B2
WALTH E17 51 G5
WIM/MER SW19 177 J4
Mayfields WBLY HA9 62 C6
Mayfields Cl WBLY HA9 62 C6
Mayfield Vls SCUP DA14 * 186 D2
Mayflower Cl
BERM/RHTH SE16 124 A4
RSLP HA4 58 A3
Mayflower Rd BRXN/ST SW9 141 K4
Mayflower St
BERM/RHTH SE16 123 K2
Mayfly Cl PIN HA5 59 G4
STMC/STPC BR5 202 E1
Mayford Cl BAL SW12 160 E2
BECK BR3 182 A6
Mayford Rd BAL SW12 160 E2
May Gdns ALP/SUD HA0 97 J2
BORE WD6 29 K1
Maygood St IS N1 5 J2
Maygreen Crs EMPK RM11 75 J4
Maygrove Rd KIL/WHAMP NW6 82 D4
Mayhew Cl CHING E4 37 J5
Mayhill Rd BAR EN5 32 C1
CHARL SE7 126 A6
Maylands Av HCH RM12 93 K2
Maylands Dr SCUP DA14 168 E5
Maylands Rd OXHEY WD19 27 G6
Maynard Cl ERITH DA8 150 C1
FUL/PGN SW6 140 B1
SEVS/STOTM N15 68 A2
Maynard Rd WALTH E17 70 A2
Maynards Quay WAP E1W * 104 E6
Maynooth Gdns CAR SM5 194 E4
Mayola Rd CLPT E5 86 E2
Mayo Rd CROY/NA CR0 196 E2
WLSDN NW10 81 G4
Mayow Rd SYD SE26 164 A6
Mayplace Av DART DA1 150 D5
Mayplace Cl BXLYHN DA7 149 J4
Mayplace La
WOOL/PLUM SE18 127 G6
Mayplace Rd BXLYHN DA7 149 K4
Mayplace Rd East
BXLYHN DA7 149 K4
Mayplace Rd West
BXLYHN DA7 149 H5
Maypole Crs BARK/HLT IG6 54 D3
ERITH DA8 131 G6
May Rd CHING E4 51 J2
PLSTW E13 106 E1
RDART DA2 171 J6
WHTN TW2 155 K3
Mayroyd Av SURB KT6 191 H6
May's Buildings Ms
GNWCH SE10 145 G1
Mays Ct CHCR WC2N 10 E6
May's Hill Rd HAYES BR2 183 J6
May's La BAR EN5 31 K2
Maysoule Rd BTSEA SW11 140 C5
Mays Rd TEDD TW11 173 J1
May St WKENS W14 119 J5
Mayswood Gdns DAGE RM10 92 E4
Maythorne Cottages
LEW SE13 165 G1
Mayton St HOLWY N7 85 F1
Maytree Cl EDGW HA8 30 E5
RAIN RM13 111 G1
Maytree Ct MTCM CR4 179 F6
Maytree La STAN HA7 43 F3
Maytree Wk
BRXS/STRHM SW2 * 162 B4
Mayville Est STNW/STAM N16 * 86 A3
Mayville Rd IL IG1 90 B3
WAN E11 88 C1
Maywood Cl BECK BR3 * 182 E3
Maze Hl BKHTH/KID SE3 145 J1
GNWCH SE10 125 H6
Mazenod Av KIL/WHAMP NW6 82 E5
Maze Rd RCH/KEW TW9 137 H1
McAdam Dr ENC/FH EN2 23 H3
McAuley Cl ELTH/MOT SE9 147 F6
STHWK SE1 17 J4
McCall Cl CLAP SW4 141 K3
McCall Crs CHARL SE7 126 D5
McCarthy Rd FELT TW13 172 C1
McCoid Wy STHWK SE1 18 C3
McCrone Ms HAMP NW3 83 J3
McCudden Rd DART DA1 151 J4
McCullum Rd BOW E3 87 H6
McDermott Cl BTSEA SW11 140 D3
McDermott Rd PECK SE15 143 H4
McDonough Cl CHSGTN KT9 206 A2
McDougall Ct RCH/KEW TW9 137 H3
McDowall Cl CAN/RD E16 106 E4
McDowall Rd CMBW SE5 142 D2
McEntee Av WALTH E17 51 G4
McEwan Wy SRTFD E15 * 88 B6
McGrath Rd SRTFD E15 88 D4
McGregor Rd NTGHL W11 100 D5
McIntosh Cl ROM RM1 57 G6
WLGTN SM6 210 E5
McIntosh Rd ROM RM1 57 G6
McKay Rd RYNPK SW20 176 E3
Mc Kellar Cl BUSH WD23 28 C4
McKerrell Rd PECK SE15 143 H2
McKillop Wy SCUP DA14 186 D3
McLeod Rd ABYW SE2 128 D4
McLeod's Ms SKENS SW7 120 A3
McMillan St DEPT SE8 * 124 D6
McNair Rd NWDGN UB2 115 F3
McNeil Rd CMBW SE5 143 F3
McNicol Dr WLSDN NW10 98 E1
McRae La MTCM CR4 194 E4
Mead Cl CAMTN NW1 84 A5
GPK RM2 57 J5
KTN/HRWW/WS HA3 42 D4
Mead Ct CDALE/KGS NW9 62 E2
Mead Crs CHING E4 38 A6
DART DA1 171 G3
SUT SM1 209 J2
Meadcroft Rd LBTH SE11 122 B6
Meade Cl CHSWK W4 117 H6
Meadfield EDGW HA8 30 D4
Mead Fld RYLN/HDSTN HA2 * 77 K1
Meadfoot Rd
STRHM/NOR SW16 179 H4
Meadgate Av WFD IG8 53 J1
Mead Gv CHDH RM6 55 K6
Mead House La YEAD UB4 94 B3
Meadlands Dr
RCHPK/HAM TW10 156 E4
Meadow Av CROY/NA CR0 198 A3
Meadowbank BKHTH/KID SE3 145 J4
BRYLDS KT5 191 G3
HAMP NW3 83 K5
OXHEY WD19 27 G2
WCHMH N21 35 F1
Meadowbank Cl FUL/PGN SW6 139 F1
Meadowbank Gdns HEST TW5 133 K2
Meadowbank Rd
CDALE/KGS NW9 63 F4
Meadow Cl BAR EN5 32 D1
BARK IG11 91 G5
BXLYHS DA6 149 G6
CAT SE6 182 D1
CHING E4 37 K3
CHST BR7 185 G1
ESH/CLAY KT10 205 F1
HOM E9 87 H4
HSLWW TW4 155 F2
NTHLT UB5 96 A1
PEND EN3 25 G2
RCHPK/HAM TW10 157 F3
RSLP HA4 58 D3
RYNPK SW20 193 G1
Meadowcourt Rd
BKHTH/KID SE3 145 J5
Meadow Cft BMLY BR1 184 E6
Meadowcroft BUSH WD23 * 28 B1
Meadowcroft Cl PLMGR N13 * 35 H4
Meadowcroft Rd PLMGR N13 35 G4
Meadow Dr HDN NW4 46 A5
MUSWH N10 48 B6
Meadowford Cl THMD SE28 109 G6
Meadow Gdns EDGW HA8 44 E2
Meadow Garth WLSDN NW10 80 E4
Meadow Hl NWMAL KT3 192 B3
Meadow La LEE/GVPK SE12 166 B5
Meadowlea Cl WDR/YW UB7 112 A6
Meadow Ms VX/NE SW8 142 A1
Meadow Pl CHSWK W4 * 138 B1
VX/NE SW8 141 K1
Meadow Rd BARK IG11 91 G5
DAGW RM9 92 B4
ESH/CLAY KT10 204 E4
FELT TW13 154 D4
HAYES BR2 183 H4
PIN HA5 59 H1
ROMW/RG RM7 74 E5
STHL UB1 95 K6
SUT SM1 209 J2
VX/NE SW8 142 A1
WIM/MER SW19 178 B3
Meadow Rw STHWK SE1 18 C5
Meadows Cl LEY E10 69 J6
Meadowside BKHTH/KID SE3 146 B5
DART DA1 171 H3
TWK TW1 156 E2
WOT/HER KT12 188 B6
Meadowside Rd BELMT SM2 208 C6
The Meadows ORP BR6 217 J4
Meadow Stile CROY/NA CR0 211 J1
Meadowsweet Cl
CAN/RD E16 107 H4
NWMAL KT3 193 F2
The Meadow CHST BR7 185 H2
Meadow Vw BFN/LL DA15 168 C1
HRW HA1 60 E5
STMC/STPC BR5 186 D6
Meadowview Rd BXLY DA5 169 F1
CAT SE6 164 D6
HOR/WEW KT19 207 G6
Meadow View Rd THHTH CR7 196 C2
YEAD UB4 94 B3
Meadow Wk DAGW RM9 92 B4
EW KT17 207 H5
RDART DA2 171 F6
SWFD E18 70 E1
WLGTN SM6 210 B1
Meadow Wy CDALE/KGS NW9 63 F2
CHSGTN KT9 206 A3
ORP BR6 216 A1
RSLP HA4 59 F4
WBLY HA9 79 K2
Meadow Waye HEST TW5 134 D1
The Meadow Wy
KTN/HRWW/WS HA3 42 E4
Mead Pl CROY/NA CR0 196 C5
HOM E9 86 E4
Mead Plat WLSDN NW10 80 E4
Mead Rd CHST BR7 185 H2
DART DA1 171 G3
EDGW HA8 44 C2
RCHPK/HAM TW10 156 D5
Mead Rw STHWK SE1 17 J4
Meadside Cl BECK BR3 182 B4
Meads La GDMY/SEVK IG3 73 F4
Meads Rd PEND EN3 25 G2
WDGN N22 49 H5
The Meads CHEAM SM3 208 B1
EDGW HA8 45 F2
MRDN SM4 * 194 D2
The Mead BECK BR3 183 F5
EFNCH N2 47 G5
OXHEY WD19 27 J5
WEA W13 97 H4
WLGTN SM6 210 D4
WWKM BR4 199 G5
Meadvale Rd CROY/NA CR0 197 G4
EA W5 97 H3
Mead Wy CROY/NA CR0 198 B6
HAYES BR2 199 K3
RSLP HA4 58 B3
Meadway ASHF TW15 152 D6
BAR EN5 20 E5
BECK BR3 183 F4
BRYLDS KT5 191 K5
ESH/CLAY KT10 204 B6
GDMY/SEVK IG3 90 E2
GLDGN NW11 65 F3
GPK RM2 57 J5
RYNPK SW20 193 F1
STHGT/OAK N14 34 D4
WFD IG8 53 G1
WHTN TW2 155 J3
Meadway Cl BAR EN5 20 E4
GLDGN NW11 65 F3
PIN HA5 42 B2
Meadway Ct EA W5 * 98 B4
Meadway Gdns RSLP HA4 58 B3
The Meadway BKHH IG9 39 H3
BKHTH/KID SE3 145 G3
ORP BR6 217 H3
Meaford Wy PGE/AN SE20 181 J3
Meanley Rd MNPK E12 89 J3
Meard St SOHO/CST W1F 10 C4
Meath Cl STMC/STPC BR5 202 C2
Meath Rd IL IG1 90 C1
SRTFD E15 106 D1
Meath St BTSEA SW11 141 G2
Mecklenburgh Pl BMSBY WC1N 5 G6
Mecklenburgh Sq BMSBY WC1N 5 G6
Mecklenburgh St BMSBY WC1N 5 G6
Medburn St CAMTN NW1 4 C2
Medcroft Gdns
MORT/ESHN SW14 137 K5
Medebourne Cl
BKHTH/KID SE3 145 K4
Medesenge Wy PLMGR N13 49 H2
Medfield St PUT/ROE SW15 158 D2
Medhurst Cl BOW E3 105 G1
Median Rd CLPT E5 86 E3
Medina Av ESH/CLAY KT10 204 E1
Medina Rd HOLWY N7 85 G1
Medland Cl WLGTN SM6 195 F5
Medlar Cl NTHLT UB5 95 H1
Medlar St CMBW SE5 142 D2
Medley Rd KIL/WHAMP NW6 82 E4
Medora Rd BRXS/STRHM SW2 162 A1
ROMW/RG RM7 75 F1
Medusa Rd CAT SE6 164 E1
Medway Cl CROY/NA CR0 197 K3
IL IG1 90 C3
Medway Dr GFD/PVL UB6 97 F1
Medway Gdns ALP/SUD HA0 79 G2
Medway Pde GFD/PVL UB6 * 97 F1
Medway Rd BOW E3 105 G1
DART DA1 150 D4
Medway St WEST SW1P 16 C5
Medwin St CLAP SW4 142 A5
Meerbrook Rd BKHTH/KID SE3 146 B4
Meeson Rd SRTFD E15 88 D5
Meeson St CLPT E5 87 G2
Meesons Whf SRTFD E15 * 106 A1
Meeting Field Pth HOM E9 * 86 E4
Meeting House Aly
WAP E1W * 123 J1
Meeting House La PECK SE15 143 J2
Mehetabel Rd HOM E9 86 E4
Meister Cl IL IG1 72 D5
Melanda Cl CHST BR7 184 E1
Melanie Cl BXLYHN DA7 149 F2
Melbourne Av PIN HA5 42 B6
WDGN N22 49 F2
WEA W13 116 B1
Melbourne Cl ORP BR6 201 K4
WLGTN SM6 210 C3
Melbourne Gdns CHDH RM6 74 A2
Melbourne Gv EDUL SE22 143 G5
Melbourne Ms BRXN/ST SW9 142 B2
CAT SE6 165 F1
Melbourne Pl HOL/ALD WC2B 11 H4
Melbourne Rd BUSH WD23 28 B1
EHAM E6 107 K1
IL IG1 72 B5
LEY E10 69 K4
TEDD TW11 174 D2
WALTH E17 69 H1
WIM/MER SW19 177 K4
WLGTN SM6 210 B3
Melbourne Sq BRXN/ST SW9 142 B2
Melbourne Ter EDUL SE22 * 143 F5
FUL/PGN SW6 * 140 A1
Melbourne Wy EN EN1 36 B1
Melbury Av NWDGN UB2 115 G3
Melbury Cl CHST BR7 184 E2
ESH/CLAY KT10 205 H4
Melbury Ct KENS W8 119 K3
Melbury Dr CMBW SE5 143 F1
Melbury Gdns RYNPK SW20 176 E4
Melbury Rd
KTN/HRWW/WS HA3 62 B2
WKENS W14 119 J3
Melbury Ter CAMTN NW1 2 D7
Melcombe Gdns
KTN/HRWW/WS HA3 62 B3
Melcombe Pl CAMTN NW1 8 E1
Melcombe St CAMTN NW1 3 F7
Meldex Cl MLHL NW7 46 A2
Meldon Cl FUL/PGN SW6 * 140 A2
Meldone Cl BRYLDS KT5 191 J3
Meldrum Cl STMC/STPC BR5 202 D3
Meldrum Rd GDMY/SEVK IG3 73 G6
Melfield Gdns CAT SE6 164 E6
Melford Av BARK IG11 90 E4
Melford Cl CHSGTN KT9 206 B3
Melford Rd EDUL SE22 163 H3
EHAM E6 107 K3
IL IG1 72 D6
WALTH E17 69 H1
WAN E11 70 C6
Melfort Av THHTH CR7 180 C6
Melfort Rd THHTH CR7 180 C6
Melgund Rd HBRY N5 85 G3
Melina Cl HYS/HAR UB3 94 B4
Melina Pl STJWD NW8 2 A5
Melina Rd SHB W12 118 E2
Melior Pl STHWK SE1 * 19 G2
Melior St STHWK SE1 19 F2
Meliot Rd CAT SE6 165 G4
Meller Cl CROY/NA CR0 210 E1
Melling Dr EN EN1 24 C2
Melling St WOOL/PLUM SE18 127 K6
Mellish Gdns WFD IG8 52 E1
Mellish St POP/IOD E14 124 D3
Mellison Rd TOOT SW17 178 D1
Melliss Av RCH/KEW TW9 137 J2
Mellitus St SHB W12 99 H5
Mellor Cl WOT/HER KT12 188 E4
Mellow La East HGDN/ICK UB10 94 A3
Mellows Rd CLAY IG5 53 K6
WLGTN SM6 210 D3
Mells Crs ELTH/MOT SE9 166 E6
Mell St GNWCH SE10 125 H5
Melody La HBRY N5 85 H3
Melody Rd WAND/EARL SW18 160 B1
Melon Pl KENS W8 119 K2
Melon Rd PECK SE15 143 H2
WAN E11 88 C1
Melrose Av CRICK NW2 82 A3
DART DA1 170 B2
GFD/PVL UB6 96 B1
MTCM CR4 179 G3
STRHM/NOR SW16 180 A6
WDGN N22 49 H4
WHTN TW2 155 G2
WIM/MER SW19 159 J4
Melrose Cl GFD/PVL UB6 96 B1
LEE/GVPK SE12 165 K3
YEAD UB4 94 E4
Melrose Crs ORP BR6 216 D2
Melrose Dr STHL UB1 115 F1
Melrose Gdns EDGW HA8 44 D6
HMSMTH W6 119 F3
NWMAL KT3 176 A6
Melrose Rd BARN SW13 138 C3
PIN HA5 59 K1
WAND/EARL SW18 159 J1
WIM/MER SW19 177 K5
Melrose Ter HMSMTH W6 119 F2
Melrose Vls BECK BR3 * 182 D5
Melsa Rd MRDN SM4 194 B3
Melthorne Dr RSLP HA4 77 G1
Melthorpe Gdns
BKHTH/KID SE3 146 C2
Melton Cl RSLP HA4 59 G5
Melton Flds HOR/WEW KT19 207 F6
Melton Gdns ROM RM1 75 H4
Melton Pl HOR/WEW KT19 207 F6
Melton St CAMTN NW1 4 B5
Melville Av GFD/PVL UB6 79 F3
RYNPK SW20 176 D3
SAND/SEL CR2 212 B3
Melville Cl HGDN/ICK UB10 76 B1
Melville Ct DEPT SE8 124 A4
Melville Gdns PLMGR N13 49 H2
Melville Pl IS N1 85 J5
Melville Rd BARN SW13 138 D2
CRW RM5 56 D3
RAIN RM13 111 J3
SCUP DA14 168 D4
WALTH E17 69 H1
WLSDN NW10 81 F5
Melville Villas Rd ACT W3 * 118 A1
Melvin Rd PGE/AN SE20 181 K4
Memel St STLK EC1Y 6 C7
Memorial Av SRTFD E15 106 C2
Memorial Cl HEST TW5 114 E6
Memorial Sq KUT/HW KT1 174 E5
Mendip Cl HYS/HAR UB3 133 G1
SYD SE26 163 K6
WPK KT4 193 F6
Mendip Dr CRICK NW2 64 C6
Mendip Houses BETH E2 * 104 E2
Mendip Rd BTSEA SW11 140 B4
BUSH WD23 28 C1
EMPK RM11 75 J4
ERITH DA8 150 B2
GNTH/NBYPK IG2 72 E2
Mendora Rd FUL/PGN SW6 139 H1
Menelik Rd CRICK NW2 82 C2
Menlo Gdns NRWD SE19 180 E3
Menon Dr ED N9 36 D5

Menotti St BETH E2 * 104 C3
Mentmore Cl
KTN/HRWW/WS HA3 ....61 J3
Mentmore Ter HACK E8 ....86 D5
Meon Rd ACT W3 ....117 K2
Meopham Rd MTCM CR4 ....179 H4
Mepham Crs
KTN/HRWW/WS HA3 ....42 C3
Mepham Gdns
KTN/HRWW/WS HA3 ....42 C3
Mepham St STHWK SE1 ....17 J1
Mera Dr BXLYHN DA7 ....149 J5
Merantum Wy
WIM/MER SW19 ....178 B4
Merbury Cl LEW SE13 ....145 F6
THMD SE28 ....127 J1
Merbury Rd THMD SE28 ....127 J1
Merbury St WOOL/PLUM SE18 ....127 G3
Mercator Pl POP/IOD E14 ....124 D5
Mercator Rd LEW SE13 ....145 G5
Mercer Cl THDIT KT7 ....190 A4
Merceron Houses BETH E2 * 104 E2
Merceron St WCHPL E1 ....104 D3
Mercer Pl PIN HA5 ....41 G5
Mercers Cl GNWCH SE10 ....125 J4
Mercers Cottages WCHPL E1 * 105 G5
Mercers Ms ARCH N19 ....84 D2
Mercers Pl HMSMTH W6 ....119 F4
Mercers Rd ARCH N19 ....84 D1
Mercer St LSQ/SEVD WC2H 10 E4
Merchants Cl SNWD SE25 ....197 H1
Merchant St BOW E3 * 105 H2
Merchiston Rd CAT SE6 ....165 G4
Merchland Rd ELTH/MOT SE9 ....167 H3
Mercia Gv LEW SE13 ....145 F5
Mercier Rd PUT/ROE SW15 ....139 H6
Mercury Gdns ROM RM1 ....75 H2
Mercury House
HYS/HAR UB3 * 113 J2
Mercury Rd BTFD TW8 ....116 D5
Mercury Wy NWCR SE14 ....124 A6
Mercy Ter LEW SE13 ....144 E6
Merebank La WLGTN SM6 ....211 F3
Mere Cl ORP BR6 ....201 G6
PUT/ROE SW15 ....159 G2
Meredith Av CRICK NW2 ....82 A3
Meredith Cl PIN HA5 ....41 H3
Meredith Ms BROCKY SE4 * 144 C5
Meredith St CLKNW EC1R 6 A5
PLSTW E13 ....106 E2
Meredyth Rd BARN SW13 ....138 D3
Mere End CROY/NA CR0 ....198 A4
Mereside ORP BR6 ....201 F6
Mereside Pk ASHF TW15 * 153 F6
Meretone Cl BROCKY SE4 ....144 B5
Merevale Crs MRDN SM4 ....194 B3
Mereway Rd WHTN TW2 ....155 J3
Merewood Cl BMLY BR1 ....185 F5
Merewood Gdns
CROY/NA CR0 ....198 A4
Merewood Rd BXLYHN DA7 ....149 K3
Mereworth Cl HAYES BR2 ....199 J2
Mereworth Dr
WOOL/PLUM SE18 ....147 G1
Meriden Cl BARK/HLT IG6 ....54 C4
BMLY BR1 ....184 C3
Meridian Rd CHARL SE7 ....146 C1
Meridian Sq SRTFD E15 ....88 B5
Meridian Wy ED N9 ....37 F2
UED N18 ....50 E2
Merifield Rd ELTH/MOT SE9 ....146 B5
Merino Cl WAN E11 ....71 G1
Merivale Rd HRW HA1 ....60 D4
PUT/ROE SW15 ....139 H5
Merlewood Dr CHST BR7 ....184 E4
Merley Ct CDALE/KGS NW9 ....62 E5
Merlin Cl CROY/NA CR0 ....212 A2
CRW RM5 ....57 F2
MTCM CR4 ....178 D6
NTHLT UB5 ....95 G2
WLGTN SM6 ....211 F4
Merlin Crs EDGW HA8 ....44 B4
Merlin Gdns CRW RM5 ....57 F2
Merling Cl CHSGTN KT9 ....205 K3
Merlin Gv BARK/HLT IG6 ....54 B3
BECK BR3 ....198 C1
Merlin Rd CRW RM5 ....57 F2
MNPK E12 ....71 H6
WELL DA16 ....148 B5
Merlin Rd North WELL DA16 ....148 B5
Merlins Av RYLN/HDSTN HA2 ....77 K1
Merlin St FSBYW WC1X 5 J5
Mermagen Dr RAIN RM13 ....93 K5
Mermaid Ct STHWK SE1 ....18 E2
Merredene St
BRXS/STRHM SW2 ....162 A1
Merriam Av HOM E9 ....87 H4
Merriam Cl CHING E4 ....52 A1
Merrick Rd NWDGN UB2 ....114 E4
Merrick Sq STHWK SE1 ....18 E4
Merridene WCHMH N21 ....35 H1
Merrielands Crs DAGW RM9 ....110 C1
Merrilands Rd WPK KT4 ....193 F5
Merrilees Rd BFN/LL DA15 ....167 K2
Merrilyn Cl ESH/CLAY KT10 ....205 G4
Merriman Rd BKHTH/KID SE3 ....146 B2
Merrington Rd FUL/PGN SW6 ....119 K6
Merrion Av STAN HA7 ....43 K1
Merritt Gdns CHSGTN KT9 ....205 K4
Merritt Rd BROCKY SE4 ....144 C6
Merrivale STHGT/OAK N14 ....34 D1
Merrivale Av REDBR IG4 ....71 H1
Merrivale Ms WDR/YW UB7 * 112 A1
Merrow Rd BELMT SM2 ....208 B6
Merrows Cl NTHWD HA6 ....40 A2
Merrow St WALW SE17 ....122 E5
Merrow Wk WALW SE17 ....122 E5
Merrow Wy CROY/NA CR0 ....214 A4
Merrydown Wy CHST BR7 ....184 E4
Merryfield BKHTH/KID SE3 ....145 J3
Merryfield Gdns STAN HA7 ....43 J1
Merryfield Wy CAT SE6 ....164 E2
Merryhill Cl CHING E4 ....37 K2
Merry Hill Mt BUSH WD23 ....28 B3
Merry Hill Rd BUSH WD23 ....28 A2
Merryhills Dr ENC/FH EN2 ....22 E5
Merryweather Cl DART DA1 ....171 J1
Merryweather Ct NWMAL KT3 ....192 B2
Mersey Rd WALTH E17 ....51 H6
Mersham Dr CDALE/KGS NW9 ....62 D2
Mersham Pl PGE/AN SE20 ....181 J4
THHTH CR7 ....180 E5
Mersham Rd THHTH CR7 ....180 E6
Merten Rd CHDH RM6 ....74 A4
Merthyr Ter BARN SW13 ....118 E6
Merton Av CHSWK W4 ....118 C4
NTHLT UB5 ....78 C3
Merton Gdns STMC/STPC BR5 ....201 G2
Merton Hall Gdns
RYNPK SW20 ....177 H4
Merton Hall Rd
WIM/MER SW19 ....177 J4
Merton High St
WIM/MER SW19 ....178 B3
Merton La HGT N6 ....65 K6
Merton Pl WIM/MER SW19 * 178 B4
Merton Ri HAMP NW3 ....83 J5
Merton Rd BARK IG11 ....91 F5
ENC/FH EN2 ....23 K1
GDMY/SEVK IG3 ....73 F4
RYLN/HDSTN HA2 ....60 C5
SNWD SE25 ....197 G2
WALTH E17 ....70 A2
WAND/EARL SW18 ....159 K2
WIM/MER SW19 ....178 A3
Merton Wy E/WMO/HCT KT8 ....189 H1
Mertoun Ter MBLAR W1H * 8 E3
Merttins Rd PECK SE15 ....144 A5
Meru Cl KTTN NW5 ....84 A3
Mervan Rd BRXS/STRHM SW2 ....142 B5
Mervyn Av ELTH/MOT SE9 ....167 H5
Mervyn Rd WEA W13 ....116 B3
Messaline Av ACT W3 ....98 E5
Messent Rd ELTH/MOT SE9 ....146 B6
Messeter Pl ELTH/MOT SE9 ....167 F1
Messina Av KIL/WHAMP NW6 ....82 E5
Meteor St BTSEA SW11 ....141 F5
Meteor Wy WLGTN SM6 ....210 E5
Metford Crs PEND EN3 ....25 J1
Methley St LBTH SE11 ....122 B5
Methuen Cl EDGW HA8 ....44 C3
Methuen Pk MUSWH N10 ....48 B5
Methuen Rd BELV DA17 ....129 J4
BXLYHS DA6 ....149 G5
EDGW HA8 ....44 C3
Methwold Rd NKENS W10 ....100 B4
Metro Centre
STMC/STPC BR5 * 202 C3
Metropolitan Cl POP/IOD E14 ....105 J4
Metropolitan Whf WAP E1W * 123 K1
Mews North BGVA SW1W 15 J5
Mews Pl WFD IG8 ....38 E6
Mews South PIM SW1V 121 H5
Mews St WAP E1W 13 K7
The Mews BECK BR3 ....182 D4
CEND/HSY/T N8 ....67 G1
NFNCH/WDSPK N12 * 47 F1
REDBR IG4 ....71 H2
ROM RM1 ....75 G1
SEVS/STOTM N15 ....68 A1
STRHM/NOR SW16 * 180 A4
TWK TW1 * 156 C1
Mexfield Rd PUT/ROE SW15 ....139 J6
Meyer Gn EN EN1 ....24 C1
Meyer Rd ERITH DA8 ....129 K6
Meymott St STHWK SE1 ....18 A1
Meynell Crs HOM E9 ....87 F5
Meynell Gdns HOM E9 ....87 F5
Meynell Rd HARH RM3 ....57 K3
HOM E9 ....87 F5
Meyrick Rd BTSEA SW11 ....140 C4
WLSDN NW10 ....81 J4
Mezen Cl NTHWD HA6 ....40 B1
Miah Ter WAP E1W * 123 H1
Micawber St IS N1 ....6 D4
Michael Gaynor Cl HNWL W7 ....116 A1
Michaelmas Cl RYNPK SW20 ....177 F6
Michael Rd FUL/PGN SW6 ....140 A2
SNWD SE25 ....181 F6
WAN E11 ....70 C5
Michaels Cl LEW SE13 ....145 H4
Micheldever Rd
LEE/GVPK SE12 ....165 H1
Michelham Gdns TWK TW1 ....156 A5
Michelsdale Dr RCH/KEW TW9 ....137 F5
Michel Wk WOOL/PLUM SE18 ....127 G5
Michigan Av MNPK E12 ....89 J2
Michleham Down
NFNCH/WDSPK N12 ....32 D6
Mickleham Cl STMC/STPC BR5 ....186 A5
Mickleham Gdns CHEAM SM3 ....208 C4
Mickleham Rd
STMC/STPC BR5 ....186 A4
Mickleham Wy CROY/NA CR0 ....214 B5
Micklethwaite Rd
FUL/PGN SW6 ....119 K6
Midcroft RSLP HA4 ....58 C5
Middle Dartrey Wk
WBPTN SW10 * 140 B1
Middle Dene MLHL NW7 ....31 F5
Middlefield STJWD NW8 ....83 H6
Middlefielde WEA W13 ....97 H4
Middlefields CROY/NA CR0 ....213 G6
WEA W13 ....97 H4
Middle Green Cl BRYLDS KT5 ....191 G3
Middleham Gdns UED N18 ....50 C2
Middleham Rd UED N18 ....50 C2
Middle La CEND/HSY/T N8 ....66 E2
TEDD TW11 ....174 A2
Middle Lane Ms
CEND/HSY/T N8 ....66 E2
Middle Park Av ELTH/MOT SE9 ....166 C1
Middle Rd EBAR EN4 ....33 J1
PLSTW E13 ....106 E2
RYLN/HDSTN HA2 ....60 D6
STRHM/NOR SW16 ....179 H5
Middle Rw NKENS W10 ....100 C3
Middlesborough Rd UED N18 ....50 C2
Middlesex Cl STHL UB1 ....96 B3
Middlesex Pl HOM E9 ....86 E4
Middlesex Rd MTCM CR4 ....195 K2
Middlesex St WCHPL E1 ....13 H2
Middle St CROY/NA CR0 ....196 D6
STBT EC1A 12 C1
Middle Temple La EMB EC4Y 11 J4
Middleton Av CHING E4 ....37 H6
GFD/PVL UB6 ....96 D1
SCUP DA14 ....186 D2
Middleton Cl CHING E4 ....37 H5
Middleton Dr
BERM/RHTH SE16 ....124 A2
PIN HA5 ....40 E6
Middleton Gdns
GNTH/NBYPK IG2 ....72 B3
Middleton Gv HOLWY N7 ....84 E3
Middleton Ms HOLWY N7 ....84 E3
Middleton Pl GTPST W1W 10 A2
Middleton Rd GLDGN NW11 ....64 E4
HACK E8 ....86 B5
HYS/HAR UB3 ....94 B4
MRDN SM4 ....194 B3
NWMAL KT3 ....175 K6
Middleton St BETH E2 ....104 D2
Middleton Wy LEW SE13 ....145 G5
Middleway GLDGN NW11 ....65 F2
Middle Wy STRHM/NOR SW16 ....179 J5
The Middle Wy
KTN/HRWW/WS HA3 ....43 F5
Middle Yd STHWK SE1 ....13 F7
Midfield Av BXLYHN DA7 ....149 K4
Midfield Wy STMC/STPC BR5 ....186 C4
Midford Pl FITZ W1T * 4 B7
Midholm GLDGN NW11 ....65 F1
WBLY HA9 ....62 C5
Midholm Cl GLDGN NW11 * 65 F1
Midholm Rd CROY/NA CR0 ....213 G1
Midhope St STPAN WC1H 5 F5
Midhurst Av CROY/NA CR0 ....196 B4
MUSWH N10 ....48 A6
Midhurst Cl HCH RM12 ....93 J2
Midhurst Gdns HGDN/ICK UB10 ....76 A5
Midhurst Hl BXLYHS DA6 ....149 H6
Midhurst Pde MUSWH N10 * 48 A6
Midhurst Rd WEA W13 ....116 B2
Midhurst Wy CLPT E5 ....86 C2
Midland Arches CRICK NW2 * 63 K6
Midland Crs HAMP NW3 ....83 G4
Midland Rd CAMTN NW1 ....4 E4
LEY E10 ....70 A5
Midland Ter CRICK NW2 ....82 B1
WLSDN NW10 ....99 G3
Midlothian Rd BOW E3 ....105 H3
Midmoor Rd BAL SW12 ....161 H3
WIM/MER SW19 ....177 G4
Midship Cl BERM/RHTH SE16 * 124 A1
Midship Point POP/IOD E14 * 124 D2
Midstrath Rd WLSDN NW10 ....81 G2
Midsummer Av HSLWW TW4 ....134 E5
Midway CHEAM SM3 ....193 J4
WOT/HER KT12 ....188 A6
Midwinter Cl WELL DA16 ....148 B4
Midwood Cl CRICK NW2 ....81 J1
Mighell Av REDBR IG4 ....71 H2
Milan Rd STHL UB1 ....114 E2
Milborne Gv WBPTN SW10 ....120 B5
Milborne St HOM E9 ....86 E4
Milborough Crs
LEE/GVPK SE12 ....165 H2
Milbourne La ESH/CLAY KT10 ....204 C4
Milbrook ESH/CLAY KT10 ....204 C4
Milcote St STHWK SE1 ....18 A3
Mildenhall Rd CLPT E5 ....86 E2
Mildmay Av IS N1 ....85 K4
Mildmay Gv North IS N1 ....85 K3
Mildmay Gv South IS N1 ....85 K3
Mildmay Pk IS N1 ....85 K3
Mildmay Pl STNW/STAM N16 * 86 A3
Mildmay Rd IL IG1 ....90 B1
IS N1 ....85 K3
ROMW/RG RM7 ....74 E2
Mildmay St IS N1 ....85 K4
Mildred Av HYS/HAR UB3 ....113 G4
NTHLT UB5 ....78 B3
Mildred Cl DART DA1 ....171 K1
Mildred Rd ERITH DA8 ....130 B5
Mile End Pl WCHPL E1 ....105 F3
Mile End Rd BOW E3 ....105 H2
WCHPL E1 ....104 E4
The Mile End WALTH E17 ....51 F4
Mile Rd WLGTN SM6 ....195 F5
Miles Dr THMD SE28 ....127 K1
Milespit Hl MLHL NW7 ....45 K1
Miles Pl BRYLDS KT5 * 191 G1
Miles Rd CEND/HSY/T N8 ....48 E6
MTCM CR4 ....178 D6
Miles St VX/NE SW8 ....121 K6
Milestone Cl BELMT SM2 ....209 H4
ED N9 ....36 C4
Milestone Rd NRWD SE19 ....181 G2
Miles Wy TRDG/WHET N20 ....33 J4
Milfoil St SHB W12 ....99 J6
Milford Cl ABYW SE2 ....129 F6
Milford Gdns ALP/SUD HA0 ....79 K3
CROY/NA CR0 ....197 K2
EDGW HA8 ....44 C3
Milford Gv SUT SM1 ....209 G2
Milford La TPL/STR WC2R 11 J5
Milford Ms STRHM/NOR SW16 ....162 A6
Milford Rd STHL UB1 ....96 A6
WEA W13 ....116 C1
Milk St BMLY BR1 ....184 A2
CAN/RD E16 ....127 G1
CITYW EC2V 12 D3
Milkwell Gdns WFD IG8 ....53 F3
Milkwell Yd CMBW SE5 ....142 D2
Milkwood Rd HNHL SE24 ....142 C6
Milk Yd WAP E1W 104 E6
Millais Av MNPK E12 ....90 A3
Millais Crs HOR/WEW KT19 ....207 G3
Millais Gdns EDGW HA8 ....44 C5
Millais Rd EN EN1 ....24 B6
NWMAL KT3 ....192 B4
WAN E11 ....88 A2
Millais Wy HOR/WEW KT19 ....206 E2
Millard Cl STNW/STAM N16 ....86 A3
Millars Meadow
BKHTH/KID SE3 ....145 J6
Millbank WEST SW1P 16 E6
Millbank Est WEST SW1P 16 D7
Millbank Wy LEE/GVPK SE12 ....145 K6
Millbourne Rd FELT TW13 ....154 D6
Mill Br BAR EN5 * 20 D6
Millbrook Av ELTH/MOT SE9 ....147 J5
Millbrook Gdns CHDH RM6 ....74 A3
GPK RM2 ....57 G5
Millbrook Rd BRXN/ST SW9 ....142 C4
ED N9 ....36 D3
Mill Brook Rd STMC/STPC BR5 ....202 D1
Mill Cl CAR SM5 * 195 F6
WDR/YW UB7 ....112 A3
Mill Cnr BAR EN5 ....20 D2
Mill Ct WDR/YW UB7 ....112 A3
Millennium Br STHWK SE1 ....12 C6
Millennium Cl CAN/RD E16 ....106 E5
Millennium Dr POP/IOD E14 ....125 G3
Millennium Pl BETH E2 * 104 D1
Millennium Sq STHWK SE1 ....19 J2
Millennium Wy GNWCH SE10 ....125 H2
Millennium Whf POP/IOD E14 ....125 G4
Miller Av PEND EN3 ....25 J1
Miller Cl BMLY BR1 ....183 K1
CRW RM5 ....56 C3
MTCM CR4 ....194 E4
Miller Rd CROY/NA CR0 ....196 A5
WIM/MER SW19 ....178 C2
Miller's Av HACK E8 ....86 B3
Millers Cl MLHL NW7 ....31 J6
Miller's Ct CHSWK W4 ....118 C5
Millers Green Cl ENC/FH EN2 ....23 H4
Miller's Ter HACK E8 ....86 B3
Miller St CAMTN NW1 ....4 A2
Miller's Wy HMSMTH W6 ....119 G2
Millers Yd FNCH N3 ....47 F4
Miller Wk STHWK SE1 ....17 K1
Millet Rd GFD/PVL UB6 ....96 B2
Mill Farm Cl PIN HA5 ....41 G5
Mill Farm Crs HSLWW TW4 ....154 D3
Millfield Av WALTH E17 ....51 H4
Millfield La HGT N6 ....66 A6
Millfield Pl HGT N6 ....66 A6
Millfield Rd EDGW HA8 ....44 E5
HSLWW TW4 ....154 D3
Millfields Cl STMC/STPC BR5 ....202 C1
Millfields Rd CLPT E5 ....86 E2
Mill Gdns SYD SE26 ....163 J6
Mill Gn MTCM CR4 * 195 F4
Mill Green Rd MTCM CR4 ....195 F4
Millgrove St BTSEA SW11 ....141 F2
Millharbour POP/IOD E14 ....124 E3
Millhaven Cl CHDH RM6 ....73 H3
Mill Hl BARN SW13 ....138 D4
Mill Hill Gv ACT W3 * 117 J1
Mill Hill Rd ACT W3 ....117 J2
BARN SW13 ....138 E4
Mill Hill Ter ACT W3 ....117 J1
Millhouse Pl WNWD SE27 ....162 C6
Millicent Rd LEY E10 * 69 H5
Milligan St POP/IOD E14 ....105 H6
Milling Rd EDGW HA8 ....45 F3
Millington Rd HYS/HAR UB3 ....113 H3
Mill La CAR SM5 ....210 A2
CHDH RM6 ....74 A3
CHING E4 ....25 K4
CRICK NW2 ....82 C3
CROY/NA CR0 ....211 G1
EW KT17 ....207 H6
WFD IG8 ....52 D1
WOOL/PLUM SE18 ....127 F5
Millman Ms BMSBY WC1N * 5 G7
Millman Pl BMSBY WC1N * 5 G7
Millman St BMSBY WC1N 5 G7
Millmark Gv NWCR SE14 ....144 B3
Millmarsh La PEND EN3 ....25 G3
Mill Mead Rd TOTM N17 ....50 D6
Mill Pl CHST BR7 ....185 F4
DART DA1 ....150 D5
KUT/HW KT1 ....175 G6
POP/IOD E14 ....105 G5
Mill Plat ISLW TW7 ....136 B4
Mill Plat Av ISLW TW7 ....136 B3
Mill Pond Cl VX/NE SW8 ....141 J1
Millpond Est
BERM/RHTH SE16 * 123 J2
Mill Pond Rd DART DA1 ....171 H1
Mill Rdg EDGW HA8 ....44 B1
Mill Rd CAN/RD E16 ....126 A1
ERITH DA8 ....149 K1
ESH/CLAY KT10 ....189 F6
IL IG1 ....90 A1
RDART DA2 ....171 J6
WDR/YW UB7 ....112 A3
WHTN TW2 ....155 H4
WIM/MER SW19 ....178 B3
Mill Rw BXLY DA5 * 169 J2
IS N1 ....7 H1
Mills Gv HDN NW4 ....64 B1
POP/IOD E14 ....106 A4
Millshot Cl FUL/PGN SW6 ....139 F2
Millshott Cl WHALL SW1A 10 D7
Millside CAR SM5 ....194 E6
Millside Pl ISLW TW7 ....136 C3
Millson Cl TRDG/WHET N20 ....33 H4
Mills Rw CHSWK W4 ....118 A4
Millstream Cl PLMGR N13 ....49 G1
Millstream Rd STHWK SE1 ....19 J4
Mill St CONDST W1S 9 K5
KUT/HW KT1 ....175 F6
STHWK SE1 ....19 K3
Mill V HAYES BR2 ....183 K6
Mill View Cl EW KT17 ....207 H5
Mill View Gdns CROY/NA CR0 ....213 F1
Millwall Dock Rd POP/IOD E14 ....124 D3
Mill Wy EBED/NFELT TW14 ....134 A6
MLHL NW7 ....45 G1
Millway Gdns NTHLT UB5 ....77 K4
Millwell Crs CHIG IG7 ....54 D1
Millwood Rd HSLW TW3 ....135 H6
STMC/STPC BR5 ....186 D6
Millwood St NKENS W10 ....100 C4
Mill Yd WCHPL E1 ....104 C6
Milman Cl PIN HA5 ....41 H6
Milman Rd KIL/WHAMP NW6 ....100 B1
Milman's St WBPTN SW10 ....140 C1
Milne Fld PIN HA5 ....42 A3
Milne Gdns ELTH/MOT SE9 ....146 D6
Milner Ct BUSH WD23 ....28 B1
Milner Dr WHTN TW2 ....155 J2
Milner Pl IS N1 ....85 H5
Milner Rd BCTR RM8 ....73 J6
KUT/HW KT1 ....174 E6
MRDN SM4 ....194 C2
SRTFD E15 ....106 C2
THHTH CR7 ....180 D6
WIM/MER SW19 ....178 A4
Milner Sq IS N1 * 85 G5
Milner St CHEL SW3 ....14 E6
Milnthorpe Rd CHSWK W4 ....118 A6
Milo Rd EDUL SE22 ....163 G1
Milroy Wk STHWK SE1 ....11 K7
Milson Rd WKENS W14 ....119 H3
Milton Av BAR EN5 ....20 D6
CDALE/KGS NW9 ....44 D6
CROY/NA CR0 ....196 E4
EHAM E6 ....89 H5
HCH RM12 ....75 H6
HGT N6 ....66 C4
SUT SM1 ....209 H1
WLSDN NW10 ....81 F6
Milton Cl EFNCH N2 ....65 G3
STHWK SE1 ....19 J7
SUT SM1 ....209 H1
YEAD UB4 ....94 E5
Milton Ct BARB EC2Y 12 E1
Milton Court Rd NWCR SE14 ....144 B1
Milton Crs GNTH/NBYPK IG2 ....72 C4
Milton Gdns STWL/WRAY TW19 ....152 C3
Milton Gv FBAR/BDGN N11 ....48 C1
STNW/STAM N16 ....85 K2
Milton Pk HGT N6 ....66 C4
Milton Rd ACT W3 ....118 A1
BELV DA17 ....129 H4
CDALE/KGS NW9 * 63 J4
CROY/NA CR0 ....196 E4
HGT N6 ....66 C4
HNHL SE24 ....142 C6
HNWL W7 ....97 F6
HPTN TW12 ....173 F3
HRW HA1 ....60 E1
MLHL NW7 ....45 J1
MORT/ESHN SW14 ....138 A4
MTCM CR4 ....179 F3
ROM RM1 ....75 J3
SEVS/STOTM N15 ....49 H6
SUT SM1 ....208 E2
WALTH E17 ....69 J1
WELL DA16 ....148 A2
WIM/MER SW19 ....178 B2
WLGTN SM6 ....210 C4
Milton St BARB EC2Y 12 E1
Milton Wy WDR/YW UB7 ....112 C4
Milverton Dr HGDN/ICK UB10 ....76 A2
Milverton Gdns GDMY/SEVK IG3 ....73 F6
Milverton Rd KIL/WHAMP NW6 ....82 A5
Milverton St LBTH SE11 ....122 B5
Milverton Wy ELTH/MOT SE9 ....167 F6
Milward St WCHPL E1 ....104 D4
Mimosa Cl ORP BR6 ....202 D6
Mimosa Rd YEAD UB4 ....95 G4
Mimosa St FUL/PGN SW6 ....139 J2
Minard Rd CAT SE6 ....165 H2
Mina Rd STHWK SE1 ....123 F5
WIM/MER SW19 ....177 K4
Minchenden Crs
STHGT/OAK N14 ....34 D5
Mincing La MON EC3R 13 G5
Minden Rd CHEAM SM3 ....193 H6
PGE/AN SE20 ....181 J4
Minehead Rd RYLN/HDSTN HA2 ....78 A1
STRHM/NOR SW16 ....180 A1
Mineral Cl BAR EN5 ....32 A1
Mineral St WOOL/PLUM SE18 ....127 K4
Minera Ms BGVA SW1W 15 H6
Minerva Cl BRXN/ST SW9 ....142 B1
SCUP DA14 ....167 K6
Minerva Rd CHING E4 ....51 K3
KUT/HW KT1 ....175 G5
WLSDN NW10 ....98 E3
Minerva St BETH E2 ....104 D1
Minet Av WLSDN NW10 ....99 G1
Minet Dr HYS/HAR UB3 ....113 K1
Minet Gdns HYS/HAR UB3 ....114 A1
WLSDN NW10 ....99 G1
Minet Rd BRXN/ST SW9 ....142 C3
Minford Gdns WKENS W14 ....119 G2
Ming St POP/IOD E14 ....105 J6
Minimax Cl EBED/NFELT TW14 ....153 K1
Ministry Wy ELTH/MOT SE9 ....166 E4
Mink Ct HSLWW TW4 ....134 B3
Minniedale BRYLDS KT5 ....191 G2
Minnow Wk WALW SE17 ....19 H7
Minories TWRH EC3N 13 J4
Minshull Pl BECK BR3 * 182 D3
Minshull St VX/NE SW8 * 141 J2
Minson Rd HOM E9 ....87 F6
Minstead Gdns PUT/ROE SW15 ....158 C2
Minstead Wy NWMAL KT3 ....192 B3
Minster Av SUT SM1 ....193 K6
Minster Ct MON EC3R * 13 G5
Minster Dr CROY/NA CR0 ....212 A2
Minster Gdns E/WMO/HCT KT8 ....188 E1
Minster Rd BMLY BR1 ....184 A3
CRICK NW2 ....82 C3
Minster Wk CEND/HSY/T N8 ....66 E1
Minstrel Gdns BRYLDS KT5 ....191 G1
Mintern Cl PLMGR N13 ....35 H5
Minterne Av NWDGN UB2 ....115 F4
Minterne Rd
KTN/HRWW/WS HA3 ....62 B2
Minterne Waye YEAD UB4 ....95 G5
Mintern St IS N1 ....7 F2
Minton Ms KIL/WHAMP NW6 ....83 F4
Mint Rd WLGTN SM6 ....210 B3
Mint St STHWK SE1 ....18 C2
Mint Wk CROY/NA CR0 ....211 J1
Mirabel Rd FUL/PGN SW6 ....139 J1
Miranda Cl WCHPL E1 ....104 E4
Miranda Rd ARCH N19 ....66 C5
Mirfield St CHARL SE7 ....126 C3
Miriam Rd WOOL/PLUM SE18 ....127 K5
Mirren Cl RYLN/HDSTN HA2 ....77 K2
Miskin Rd DART DA1 ....171 F2
Missenden Cl
EBED/NFELT TW14 ....153 J3
Missenden Gdns MRDN SM4 ....194 B3
Mission Gv WALTH E17 ....69 H2

Mission Pl *PECK* SE15............143 H2
Mistletoe Cl *CROY/NA* CR0........198 A5
Misty's Fld *WOT/HER* KT12........188 B5
Mitali Pas *WCHPL* E1...............104 C5
Mitcham La *STRHM/NOR* SW16...179 H4
Mitcham Pk *MTCM* CR4..............194 E1
Mitcham Rd *CROY/NA* CR0..........195 K3
  EHAM E6....................107 J2
  GDMY/SEVK IG3..............73 F4
  TOOT SW17...................178 E1
Mitchellbrook Wy
  NWMAL KT3...................81 F4
Mitchell Cl *ABYW* SE2............128 D5
  BELV DA17...................129 K3
  DART DA1....................171 H4
Mitchell Rd *ORP* BR6.............217 F2
  PLMGR N13...................49 H1
Mitchell St *FSBYE* EC1V............6 C1
Mitchley Rd *TOTM* N17............50 C6
Mitford Rd *ARCH* N19.............66 E6
Mitre Cl *BELMT* SM2..............209 G5
Mitre Rd *SRTFD* E15.............106 C1
  STHWK SE1....................17 K2
Mitre Sq *HDTCH* EC3A.............13 H4
Mitre St *HDTCH* EC3A.............13 H4
The Mitre *POP/IOD* E14...........105 H6
Mitre Wy *NKENS* W10..............99 K4
Moat Cl *ORP* BR6................217 F4
Moat Crs *FNCH* N3.................47 F6
Moat Cft *WELL* DA16.............148 D3
Moat Dr *HRW* HA1................60 C1
  RSLP HA4....................58 C4
Moat Farm Rd *NTHLT* UB5.........77 K4
Moat La *ERITH* DA8..............150 D2
Moat Pl *ACT* W3..................98 D5
  BRXN/ST SW9................142 A4
Moat Side *FELT* TW13............154 B6
  PEND EN3....................24 E5
The Moat *NWMAL* KT3.............176 B4
Moberly Rd *CLAP* SW4............161 J2
Modbury Gdns *KTTN* NW5............4 A1
Model Cottages *WEA* W13*........116 C2
Model Farm Cl *ELTH/MOT* SE9....166 D5
Moelyn Ms *HRW* HA1...............61 G2
Moffat Rd *PLMGR* N13............48 C3
  THHTH CR7..................180 D6
  TOOT SW17..................160 D6
Mogden La *ISLW* TW7.............156 A6
Mohmmad Khan Rd *WAN* E11 *....70 D5
Moiety Rd *POP/IOD* E14..........124 D3
Moira Cl *TOTM* N17...............50 A5
Moira Rd *ELTH/MOT* SE9.........146 E5
Moir Cl *SAND/SEL* CR2...........212 C6
Molash Rd *STMC/STPC* BR5.......202 E1
Mole Abbey Gdns
  E/WMO/HCT KT8.............173 G6
Mole Ct *E/WMO/HCT* KT8..........189 F2
Molember Ct *E/WMO/HCT* KT8....189 G2
Molember Rd
  E/WMO/HCT KT8.............189 G2
Molescroft *ELTH/MOT* SE9........167 H5
Molesey Av *E/WMO/HCT* KT8......188 D2
Molesey Dr *CHEAM* SM3..........193 H6
Molesey Park Av
  E/WMO/HCT KT8.............189 G2
Molesey Park Cl
  E/WMO/HCT KT8.............189 H2
Molesey Park Rd
  E/WMO/HCT KT8.............189 G2
Molesford Rd *FUL/PGN* SW6......139 K2
Molesham Ct *E/WMO/HCT* KT8....173 G6
Molesham Wy
  E/WMO/HCT KT8.............189 G1
Molesworth St *LEW* SE13........145 F5
Mollison Av *PEND* EN3............24 E6
Mollison Dr *WLGTN* SM6.........210 E5
Mollison Wy *EDGW* HA8............44 C5
Molly Huggins Cl *BAL* SW12.....161 H2
Molyneux Dr *TOOT* SW17.........161 G6
Molyneux St *MBLAR* W1H............9 J2
Monarch Cl *EBED/NFELT* TW14...153 H2
  RAIN RM13....................111 J1
  WWKM BR4...................214 D2
Monarch Dr *CAN/RD* E16........107 H4
Monarch Ms
  STRHM/NOR SW16...........180 B1
Monarch Pde *MTCM* CR4*.........178 E5
Monarch Pl *BKHH* IG9.............39 G4
Monarch Rd *BELV* DA17..........129 H3
Monarchs Wy *RSLP* HA4............58 B5
Monarch Wy *GNTH/NBYPK* IG2....72 D3
Mona Pk *PECK* SE15..............143 K3
Monastery Gdns *ENC/FH* EN2......23 K3
Mona St *CAN/RD* E16............106 D4
Monaveen Gdns
  E/WMO/HCT KT8.............173 G6
Monck's Rw
  WAND/EARL SW18*...........159 J1
Monck St *WEST* SW1P.............16 D5
Monclar Rd *CMBW* SE5...........142 E5
Moncorvo Cl *SKENS* SW7..........14 C3
Moncrieff Cl *EHAM* E6...........107 J5
Moncrieff St *PECK* SE15.........143 H3
Monday Aly *STNW/STAM* N16......86 B1
Mondial Wy *HYS/HAR* UB3........133 F1
Monega Rd *FSTGT* E7..............89 G4
Money La *WDR/YW* UB7...........112 A3
Monier Rd *BOW* E3.................87 J5
Monivea Rd *BECK* BR3............182 C3
Monk Dr *CAN/RD* E16.............106 E6
Monkchester Cl *SWTH* IG7.........37 J1
Monkfrith Wy *STHGT/OAK* N14....34 B2
Monkham's Av *WFD* IG8............53 F1
Monkham's Dr *WFD* IG8............53 F1
Monkham's La *WFD* IG8............39 F6
Monkleigh Rd *MRDN* SM4........177 H6
Monks Av *BAR* EN5................33 G1
  E/WMO/HCT KT8.............188 E2
Monks Cl *ENC/FH* EN2..............23 J3
  RSLP HA4....................77 H2

Ryln/HDSTN HA2 *..................60 A6
Monks Crs *WOT/HER* KT12........188 A5
Monksdene Gdns *SUT* SM1.......209 F1
Monks Orch *DART* DA1...........171 F4
Monks Orchard Rd *BECK* BR3....198 D5
Monks Pk *WBLY* HA9...............80 E4
Monks Park Gdns *WBLY* HA9.......80 D5
Monks Rd *ENC/FH* EN2.............23 J3
Monk St *WOOL/PLUM* SE18.......115 F4
Monks Wy *BECK* BR3.............198 D3
  GLDGN NW11..................64 D4
  STMC/STPC BR5..............201 H5
Monkswood Gdns *CLAY* IG5........54 A6
Monk Ter *FSTH* SE23............164 C4
Monkton Rd *WELL* DA16.........148 A3
Monkton St *LBTH* SE11...........17 K6
Monkville Av *GLDGN* NW11........64 D1
Monkville Pde *GLDGN* NW11 *.....64 D1
Monkwell Sq *BARB* EC2Y..........12 D2
Monkwood Cl *ROM* RM1............75 J2
Monmouth Av *KUT/HW* KT1......174 D3
  SWFD E18.....................71 F1
Monmouth Cl *CHSWK* W4.........118 A3
  MTCM CR4...................195 K1
  WELL DA16..................148 B5
Monmouth Gv *BTFD* TW8.........117 F4
Monmouth Rd *BAY/PAD* W2......100 E5
Monmouth Rd *BAY/PAD* W2......100 E5
  DACW RM9....................92 B3
  ED N9........................36 C3
  EHAM E6....................107 K2
  HYS/HAR UB3................113 H1
Monmouth St *LSQ/SEVD* WC2H...10 E4
Monnery Rd *ARCH* N19............84 C1
Monnow Rd *STHWK* SE1..........123 H5
Mono La *FELT* TW13.............154 A4
Monoux Gv *WALTH* E17............51 J4
Monroe Crs *EN* EN1................24 D2
Monroe Dr *MORT/ESHN* SW14....137 J6
Monro Gdns
  KTN/HRWW/WS HA3............42 E3
Monro Pl *HOR/WEW* KT19........206 C6
Monsell Rd *FSBYPK* N4............85 H1
Monson Rd *NWCR* SE14.........144 A1
  WLSDN NW10.................99 J1
Mons Wy *HAYES* BR2.............200 D3
Montacute Rd *BUSH* WD23........28 E2
  CAT SE6....................164 C2
  CROY/NA CR0................214 A6
  MRDN SM4...................194 C2
Montagu Crs *UED* N18.............36 D6
Montague Av *BROCKY* SE4........144 C5
  HNWL W7....................116 A1
Montague Cl *STHWK* SE1...........12 F7
  WOT/HER KT12...............188 A4
Montague Hall Pl *BUSH* WD23.....28 A1
Montague Pl *GWRST* WC1E.........10 C1
Montague Rd *CEND/HSY/T* N8....67 F2
  CROY/NA CR0...............196 C5
  HACK E8.....................86 C3
  HNWL W7...................116 A1
  HSLW TW3...................135 G4
  NWDGN UB2.................114 D4
  RCHPK/HAM TW10............157 F1
  SEVS/STOTM N15 *............68 A2
  WAN E11.....................70 D6
  WEA W13.....................97 H5
  WIM/MER SW19...............178 A3
Montague Sq *PECK* SE15.........143 K1
Montague St *RSQ* WC1B...........10 E2
  STBT EC1A....................12 C2
Montague Ter *HAYES* BR2........199 K1
Montague Waye *NWDGN* UB2.....114 D3
Montagu Gdns *UED* N18...........36 D6
  WLGTN SM6.................210 C2
Montagu Man *MHST* W1U............9 F2
Montagu Ms North *MBLAR* W1H....9 F2
Montagu Ms South *MBLAR* W1H....8 E3
Montagu Ms West *MBLAR* W1H.....8 E3
Montagu Pl *MBLAR* W1H............8 E2
Montagu Rw *HDN* NW4.............63 J3
  UED N18.....................50 D1
Montagu Rw *MHST* W1U.............9 F2
Montagu Sq *MBLAR* W1H............9 F2
Montagu St *MBLAR* W1H............9 F3
Montait Rd *WFD* IG8..............52 D1
Montana Gdns *SUT* SM1..........209 G3
  SYD SE26...................182 C1
Montana Rd *RYNPK* SW20.........177 F1
  TOOT SW17..................161 F5
Montbretia Cl
  STMC/STPC BR5..............202 D1
Montcalm Cl *HAYES* BR2..........199 K3
  YEAD UB4....................95 F2
Montcalm Rd *CHARL* SE7........146 C1
Montclare St *BETH* E2..............7 J5
Monteagle Av *BARK* IG11.........90 C4
Monteagle Wy *PECK* SE15........143 J4
Montefiore St *VX/NE* SW8........141 G3
Montem Rd *FSTH* SE23...........164 C2
  NWMAL KT3..................192 B1
Montem St *FSBYPK* N4..............67 F5
Montenotte Rd
  CEND/HSY/T N8...............66 C2
Monterey Cl *BXLY* DA5...........169 K4
Montesole Ct *PIN* HA5.............41 G5
Montesquieu Ter
  CAN/RD E16 *..................106 C5
Montford Pl *LBTH* SE11..........122 B6
Montford Rd *BARK/HLT* IG6......54 C2
Montfort Pl *WIM/MER* SW19......159 G3
Montgomerie Ms *FSTH* SE23......163 K2
Montgomery Av
  ESH/CLAY KT10..............189 K6
Montgomery Cl *BFN/LL* DA15....147 K6
  MTCM CR4 *..................195 K1
Montgomery Gdns
  BELMT SM2..................209 H5
Montgomery Rd *CHSWK* W4......117 K4
  EDGW HA8....................44 A2
Monthope Rd *BTSEA* SW11......160 E1
Monthorpe Rd *WCHPL* E1........104 C4
Montolieu Gdns
  PUT/ROE SW15...............138 E6

Montpelier Av *BXLY* DA5........168 A2
  EA W5........................97 J4
Montpelier Gdns *CHDH* RM6......73 J4
  EHAM E6....................107 H2
Montpelier Gv *KTTN* NW5.........84 C3
Montpelier Ms *CHEL* SW3.........14 D4
Montpelier Pl *SKENS* SW7.........14 D4
  WCHPL E1....................104 E5
Montpelier Ri *GLDGN* NW11......64 C4
  FNCH N3.....................47 C4
  PECK SE15..................143 J2
  SUT SM1....................209 G2
Montpelier Rw
  BKHTH/KID SE3..............145 J3
  TWK TW1....................156 D2
Montpelier Sq *SKENS* SW7........14 D3
Montpelier St *SKENS* SW7.........14 D3
Montpelier Ter *SKENS* SW7.......14 D3
Montpelier V *BKHTH/KID* SE3 *..145 J3
Montpelier Wk *SKENS* SW7........14 D4
Montpelier Wy *GLDGN* NW11.....64 C4
Montrave Rd *PGE/AN* SE20......181 K2
Montreal Pl *HOL/ALD* WC2B.......11 G5
Montreal Rd *IL* IG1...............72 C4
Montrell Rd *BRXS/STRHM* SW2...161 K3
Montrose Av *EDGW* HA8..........45 F5
  KIL/WHAMP NW6..............100 C1
  WELL DA16..................147 J4
  WHTN TW2...................155 G2
Montrose Cl *WELL* DA16.........148 A4
  WFD IG8.....................52 E1
Montrose Crs *ALP/SUD* HA0.......80 A4
  NFNCH/WDSPK N12............47 F2
Montrose Gdns *MTCM* CR4.......178 E6
  SUT SM1....................194 A6
Montrose Pl *KTBR* SW1X..........15 H3
Montrose Rd
  EBED/NFELT TW14............153 C1
  KTN/HRWW/WS HA3............42 E5
Montrose Vls *HMSMTH* W6 *.....118 D5
Montserrat Av *WFD* IG8...........52 B3
Montserrat Cl *NRWD* SE19......180 E1
Montserrat Rd *PUT/ROE* SW15...139 H5
Monument Wy *TOTM* N17..........68 B1
Monza St *WAP* E1W...............104 E6
Moodkee St *BERM/RHTH* SE16...123 K3
Moody St *WCHPL* E1..............105 F2
Moon Ct *LEE/GVPK* SE12 *.......145 K5
Moon La *BAR* EN5.................20 C4
Moon St *IS* N1....................85 H6
Moorcroft Gdns *HAYES* BR2......200 D2
Moorcroft Rd
  STRHM/NOR SW16...........161 K5
Moorcroft Wy *PIN* HA5.............59 J2
Moordown *WOOL/PLUM* SE18.....147 G2
Moore Cl *MORT/ESHN* SW14......137 K4
  MTCM CR4...................179 G5
Moore Crs *DACW* RM9..............91 H6
Moorefield Rd *TOTM* N17...........50 B6
Mooreland Rd *BMLY* BR1........183 J2
Moore Park Rd *FUL/PGN* SW6....140 A1
Moore Rd *NRWD* SE19...........180 D2
Moore St *CHEL* SW3................14 E6
  WBLY HA9...................208 E6
Moorey Cl *SRTFD* E15..............88 D1
Moorfield Av *EA* W5...............97 K3
Moorfield Rd *CHSGTN* KT9......206 A3
  ORP BR6....................202 B4
  PEND EN3....................24 E2
Moorfields *LVPST* EC2M...........12 E2
Moorfields Highwalk
  BARB EC2Y...................12 E2
Moorgate *LOTH* EC2R.............12 E3
Moorgate Pl *LOTH* EC2R *........12 E3
Moorhead Wy *BKHTH/KID* SE3...146 A3
Moorhouse Rd *BAY/PAD* W2......100 E5
  KTN/HRWW/WS HA3............43 K4
The Moorings *CHSWK* W4 *......117 H6
Moorland Cl *CRW* RM5.............56 D4
Moorland Rd *BRXN/ST* SW9......142 C5
Moorlands Av *MLHL* NW7..........45 K2
Moor La *BARB* EC2Y..............12 E2
  CHSGTN KT9.................206 B3
Moor Lane Crossing
  WATW WD18...................26 A2
Moor Mead Rd *TWK* TW1.........156 B1
Moor Park Gdns
  KUTN/CMB KT2...............176 B3
Moor Park Rd *NTHWD* HA6........26 A4
Moorside Rd *BMLY* BR1..........165 H6
Moor St *SOHO/SHAV* W1D.........10 D4
Moorville Rd *OXHEY* WD19........27 F3
Moor Vw *WATW* WD18..............26 E2
Morant Gdns *CRW* RM5.............56 D1
Morant St *POP/IOD* E14..........105 J6
Morat St *BRXN/ST* SW9..........142 A1
Moravian Pl *WBPTN* SW10........120 C6
Moravian St *BETH* E2.............104 E1
Moray Av *HYS/HAR* UB3..........113 J1
Moray Cl *EDGW* HA8................30 D4
  ROM RM1....................57 J2
Moray Ms *HOLWY* N7...............67 F1
Moray Rd *HOLWY* N7................67 F1
Moray Wy *ROM* RM1................57 J3
Morcambe Cl *WALW* SE17..........18 D7
Mordaunt Gdns *DACW* RM9........92 A5
Mordaunt Rd *WLSDN* NW10.......99 F1
Mordaunt St *BRXN/ST* SW9......142 A4
Morden Ct *MRDN* SM4...........194 A1
Morden Court Pde
  MRDN SM4 *..................178 A6
Morden Gdns *GFD/PVL* UB6........79 H3
  MTCM CR4...................194 C1
Morden Hall Rd *MRDN* SM4......178 A4
Morden Hl *LEW* SE13.............145 F3
Morden La *LEW* SE13.............145 F2

Morden Rd *BKHTH/KID* SE3......145 K3
  CHDH RM6....................74 A2
  MTCM CR4...................194 C1
  WIM/MER SW19...............178 A5
Morden Road Ms
  BKHTH/KID SE3..............145 K3
Morden St *LEW* SE13.............145 K3
Morden Wharf Rd
  CNWCH SE10.................125 H3
Mordon Rd *GDMY/SEVK* IG3.......73 F4
Mordred Rd *CAT* SE6.............165 H4
Morecambe Cl *HCH* RM12..........93 K3
  WCHPL E1....................105 F4
Morecambe Gdns *STAN* HA7......29 K6
Morecambe St *POP/IOD* E14.....124 E5
Morecambe Ter *UED* N18 *........35 K6
Moree Cl *CAN/RD* E16...........106 D5
  WKENS W14..................119 G4
Morecoombe Cl
  KUTN/CMB KT2...............175 J3
Moree Wy *UED* N18................36 C6
Moreland Cottages *BOW* E3 *....105 J1
Moreland St *FSBYE* EC1V...........6 B4
Moreland Wy *CHING* E4.............37 K5
More La *ESH/CLAY* KT10..........204 B1
Morella Rd *BAL* SW12............160 E2
More London Pl *STHWK* SE1.......19 H1
More London Riverside
  STHWK SE1...................19 H1
Moremead Rd *CAT* SE6..........164 E6
Morena St *CAT* SE6..............164 E2
Moresby Av *BRYLDS* KT5.........191 J4
Moresby Rd *CLPT* E5...............68 D5
Mores Gdn *CHEL* SW3 *..........120 C6
Moretaine Rd *ASHF* TW15.......152 A5
Moreton Av *ISLW* TW7...........135 J2
Moreton Cl *CLPT* E5...............68 E6
  MLHL NW7....................46 A2
  SEVS/STOTM N15..............67 K3
Moreton Ct *DART* DA1...........150 B4
Moreton Gdns *WFD* IG8............53 J1
Moreton Pl *PIM* SW1V.............16 B7
  SEVS/STOTM N15..............67 K3
Moreton St *PIM* SW1V............121 J5
Moreton Ter *PIM* SW1V..........121 H5
Moreton Terrace Ms North
  PIM SW1V....................121 H5
Moreton Terrace Ms South
  PIM SW1V....................121 H5
Morford Cl *RSLP* HA4..............59 F4
Morford Wy *RSLP* HA4.............59 F4
Morgan Av *WALTH* E17.............70 B1
Morgan Cl *DAGE* RM10............92 C5
Morgan Rd *BMLY* BR1............183 K3
  HOLWY N7....................85 G3
  NKENS W10..................100 D4
Morgan's La *HYS/HAR* UB3........94 B4
  STHWK SE1...................19 G1
Morgan St *BOW* E3................105 G2
  CAN/RD E16..................106 D4
Morgan Wy *WFD* IG8..............53 K2
Moriarty Cl *BMLY* BR1...........201 G1
Moriarty Cl *HOLWY* N7............84 D2
Morie St *WAND/EARL* SW18......140 A5
Morieux Rd *LEY* E10................69 H5
Moring Rd *TOOT* SW17...........161 F6
Morkyns Wk *DUL* SE21 *.........163 F5
Morland Av *CROY/NA* CR0........197 F5
  DART DA1....................150 D6
Morland Cl *GLDGN* NW11..........65 F5
  HPTN TW12..................172 E1
  MTCM CR4...................178 D6
Morland Gdns *STHL* UB1.........115 G1
  WLSDN NW10.................81 F5
Morland Ms *IS* N1................85 G5
Morland Rd *CROY/NA* CR0........197 F5
  DAGE RM10..................92 C5
  IL IG1......................72 B6
  KTN/HRWW/WS HA3............62 B1
  PGE/AN SE20................182 A3
  SUT SM1....................209 G4
  WALTH E17...................69 F3
Morley Av *CHING* E4...............52 B3
  UED N18.....................50 C2
  WDGN N22....................49 H4
Morley Cl *ORP* BR6..............201 H6
Morley Crs *EDGW* HA8.............30 E4
  RSLP HA4....................59 G1
Morley Crs East *STAN* HA7.......43 J6
Morley Crs West *STAN* HA7......43 J6
Morley Hl *ENC/FH* EN2............23 K1
Morley Rd *BARK* IG11.............90 D6
  CHDH RM6....................74 A2
  CHST BR7...................185 H4
  LEW SE13...................145 F5
  LEY E10......................70 B4
  SRTFD E15..................106 D1
  TWK TW1....................156 E1
Morley St *STHWK* SE1.............17 K3
Morna Rd *CMBW* SE5.............142 D3
Morning La *HOM* E9...............86 E4
Morningside Rd *WPK* KT4........192 E6
Mornington Av *HAYES* BR2......200 C2
  IL IG1......................72 A4
  WKENS W14..................119 J4
Mornington Cl *BXLY* DA5.........170 A3
  WFD IG8.....................39 F6
Mornington Crs *CAMTN* NW1....4 A2
  HEST TW5...................134 A2
Mornington Gv *BOW* E3.........105 J2
Mornington Ms *CMBW* SE5......142 D2
Mornington Pl *CAMTN* NW1........4 A1
  NWCR SE14..................144 A1
  WAN E11.....................70 D1
  WFD IG8.....................38 E6
Mornington Rd *CHING* E4..........38 B2
  GFD/PVL UB6..................96 B4
  NWCR SE14..................144 A1
  WAN E11.....................70 D1
  WFD IG8.....................38 E6
Mornington St *CAMTN* NW1......3 K2
Mornington Ter *CAMTN* NW1....3 K1
Mornington Wk
  RCHPK/HAM TW10............156 D6
Morocco St *STHWK* SE1............19 G3

Morpeth Gv *HOM* E9...............87 F6
Morpeth Rd *HOM* E9...............87 F6
Morpeth St *BETH* E2.............105 F2
Morpeth Ter *WEST* SW1P..........16 A5
Morpeth Wk *TOTM* N17 *..........50 D3
Morrab Gdns *GDMY/SEVK* IG3.....73 F3
Morrel Cl *BAR* EN5................21 G4
Morrells Yd *LBTH* SE11..........122 B5
Morris Av *MNPK* E12...............89 K3
Morris Bishop Ter *HGT* N6 *......66 A3
Morris Cl *CROY/NA* CR0..........198 B3
  ORP BR6....................216 E1
Morris Ct *CHING* E4...............37 K5
Morris Gdns *DART* DA1..........151 K6
  WAND/EARL SW18............159 K2
Morrison Av *CHING* E4.............51 J1
  TOTM N17....................50 A6
Morrison Rd *BARK* IG11.........110 A1
  YEAD UB4....................95 F2
Morrison St *BTSEA* SW11........141 F4
Morris Pl *FSBYPK* N4...............67 G6
Morris Rd *BCTR* RM8...............74 B6
  HARH RM3....................57 J3
  ISLW TW7...................136 A4
  POP/IOD E14................105 K4
  SRTFD E15...................88 C2
Morris St *WCHPL* E1.............104 D5
Morriston Cl *OXHEY* WD19.........41 G1
Morse Cl *PLSTW* E13.............106 E2
Morshead Rd *MV/WKIL* W9.......100 E2
Morson Rd *PEND* EN3.............37 C1
Morteyne Rd *TOTM* N17...........49 K4
Mortham St *SRTFD* E15............88 B6
Mortimer Cl *BUSH* WD23..........28 B1
  CRICK NW2....................82 D1
  STRHM/NOR SW16...........161 J4
Mortimer Crs *KIL/WHAMP* NW6....83 F1
  WPK KT4....................207 F1
Mortimer Dr *EN* EN1...............23 K6
Mortimer Pl *KIL/WHAMP* NW6.....83 F1
Mortimer Rd *EHAM* E6...........107 K2
  ERITH DA8..................130 A6
  IS N1........................86 A5
  MTCM CR4...................178 E4
  ORP BR6....................202 B6
  WEA W13.....................97 J3
  WLSDN NW10.................100 A2
Mortimer Sq *NTGHL* W11.........100 B6
Mortimer St *GTPST* W1W...........9 K3
Mortimer Ter *KTTN* NW5 *........84 B2
Mortlake Cl *CROY/NA* CR0........210 E1
Mortlake Dr *MTCM* CR4..........178 D4
Mortlake High St
  MORT/ESHN SW14............138 A4
Mortlake Rd *CAN/RD* E16........107 F5
  IL IG1......................90 C2
  RCH/KEW TW9................137 H1
Morton Cl *CLAP* SW4.............141 H1
  WLGTN SM6.................211 F5
Morton Crs *STHGT/OAK* N14......34 D6
Morton Gdns *WLGTN* SM6.......210 C3
Morton Ms *ECT* SW5..............120 A4
Morton Pl *STHWK* SE1.............17 J5
Morton Rd *IS* N1..................85 J5
  MRDN SM4...................194 C2
  SRTFD E15...................88 D5
Morton Wy *STHGT/OAK* N14.......34 C6
Morvale Cl *BELV* DA17...........129 G4
Morval Rd *BRXS/STRHM* SW2....142 A6
Morven Rd *TOOT* SW17...........160 E5
Morville St *BOW* E3...............105 J1
Morwell St *RSQ* WC1B.............10 C2
Moscow Pl *BAY/PAD* W2..........101 F6
Moscow Rd *BAY/PAD* W2.........100 E6
Moselle Av *WDGN* N22.............49 G5
Moselle Cl *CEND/HSY/T* N8 *.....49 F6
Moselle Pl *TOTM* N17 *............50 B3
Moselle St *TOTM* N17..............50 B3
Mossborough Cl
  NFNCH/WDSPK N12............47 F2
Mossbury Rd *BTSEA* SW11......140 D4
Moss Cl *PIN* HA5..................41 K5
  WCHPL E1...................104 C4
Mossdown Cl *BELV* DA17........129 H4
Mossford Gn *BARK/HLT* IG6.......54 B6
Mossford La *BARK/HLT* IG6........54 B5
Mossford St *BOW* E3..............105 H3
Moss Gdns *FELT* TW13...........153 K4
  SAND/SEL CR2...............213 F5
Moss Hall Crs
  NFNCH/WDSPK N12............47 F2
Moss Hall Gv
  NFNCH/WDSPK N12............47 F2
Mossla Rd *PIN* HA5...............41 K6
Mosslea Rd *HAYES* BR2..........200 C2
  ORP BR6....................216 C1
  PGE/AN SE20................181 K4
Mossop St *CHEL* SW3..............14 D6
Moss Rd *DAGE* RM10...............92 C5
Mossville Gdns *MRDN* SM4......177 J6
Moston Cl *HYS/HAR* UB3.........113 J5
Mostyn Av *WBLY* HA9.............80 B3
Mostyn Gdns *WLSDN* NW10......100 B2
Mostyn Gv *BOW* E3.................87 J1
Mostyn Rd *BRXN/ST* SW9.......142 B2
  EDGW HA8....................45 G3
  WIM/MER SW19...............177 J6
Mosul Wy *HAYES* BR2............200 D3
Mosyer Dr *STMC/STPC* BR5......202 E6
Motcomb St *KTBR* SW1X...........15 G4
Moth Cl *WLGTN* SM6.............210 E5
The Mothers Sq *CLPT* E5 *......86 D2
Moth House
  WOOL/PLUM SE18.............146 D1
Motley Av *EAST* E1 *.............104 C2
Motspur Pk *NWMAL* KT3.........192 D3
Mottingham Gdns
  ELTH/MOT SE9...............166 C3
Mottingham La
  LEE/GVPK SE12..............166 B3
  ELTH/MOT SE9...............166 E5
Mottisfont Rd *ABYW* SE2.........128 C3
Moulins Rd *HOM* E9...............86 E5
Moulton Av *HSLW* TW3..........134 D3

Moundfield Rd
STNW/STAM N16.............................68 C3
Mountacre CI SYD SE26...............163 H6
Mount Adon Pk EDUL SE22.........163 H2
Mountague PI POP/IOD E14...106 A6
Mount Angelus Rd
PUT/ROE SW15.............................158 C2
Mount Ararat Rd
RCHPK/HAM TW10...................137 F6
Mount Ash Rd SYD SE26...........163 E6
Mount Av CHING E4.......................37 J5
EA W5..97 K4
STHL UB1..86 A5
Mountbatten CI NRWD SE19.......181 F1
Mountbatten Ct BKHH IG9..........39 H4
Mountbel Rd STAN HA7................43 C5
Mount CI BMLY BR1..................184 D4
SAND/SEL CR2...............................210 A6
EA W5..97 J4
EBAR EN4.......................................22 A5
Mountcombe CI SURB KT6.........191 F4
Mount Cottages BXLYHS DA6 *...149 F5
Mount Culver Av SCUP DA14...168 E2
Mount Dr RYLN/HDSTN HA2......59 K2
WBLY HA9......................................62 E6
Mountearl Gdns
STRHM/NOR SW16......................162 A5
Mount Echo Av CHING E4............37 K3
Mount Echo Dr CHING E4.............37 K3
Mount Ephraim La
STRHM/NOR SW16......................161 J5
Mount Ephraim Rd
STRHM/NOR SW16......................161 J5
Mountfield CI CAT SE6...............165 G2
Mountfield Rd EA W5..................97 K5
EHAM E6.......................................108 A1
FNCH N3...46 E6
Mountfield Ter CAT SE6.............165 G2
Mountfield Wy
STMC/STPC BR5.........................202 D1
Mountfort Crs IS N1.....................85 G5
Mountfort Ter IS N1.....................85 G5
Mount Gdns SYD SE26...............163 J5
Mount Gv EDGW HA8...................30 E5
Mount Mws HPTN TW12.............173 G4
Mount Mills FSBYE EC1V................6 B5
Mount Nod Rd
STRHM/NOR SW16......................162 A5
Mount Pde EBAR EN4 *...............21 J3
Mount Pk CAR SM5......................210 A6
SAND/SEL CR2...............................211 H6
Mount Park Av HRW HA1.............60 E6
SAND/SEL CR2...............................211 H6
Mount Park Crs EA W5................97 K5
HRW HA1..78 D1
PIN HA5...58 E2
Mount PI ACT W3.........................117 J1
Mount Pleasant ALP/SUD HA0...80 A6
EBAR EN4...21 J3
FSBYW WC1X....................................5 H7
HRW HA1..60 E6
RSLP HA4..59 G6
WNWD SE27.................................162 D6
Mount Pleasant Crs
FSBYPK N4 *....................................67 F4
Mount Pleasant HI CLPT E5.......68 D5
Mount Pleasant La CLPT E5.......68 D5
Mount Pleasant PI
WOOL/PLUM SE18......................127 K4
Mount Pleasant Rd CRW RM5...57 F2
DART DA1......................................171 J1
EA W5..97 J3
LEW SE13......................................165 F1
NWMAL KT3..................................175 K6
TOTM N17..50 A6
WALTH E17......................................51 G5
WLSDN NW10.................................69 J5
Mount Pleasant VIs FSBYPK N4...67 F4
Mount Ri FSTH SE23...................163 K4
Mount Rd BCTR RM8....................74 B5
BXLYHS DA6.................................149 F6
CHSGTN KT9..................................206 B3
CRICK NW2.......................................64 B1
DART DA1......................................170 C1
EBAR EN4...21 J6
FELT TW13....................................154 D5
HDN NW4..63 J3
HYS/HAR UB3................................113 K2
IL IG1..90 B3
MTCM CR4.....................................178 C5
NRWD SE19 *................................180 E2
NWMAL KT3..................................176 A6
RYNPK SW20...................................177 F4
WBLY HA9..62 D6
Mount Vw ENC/FH EN2.................23 F1
NTHWD HA6....................................26 A6
Mountview CI NWDGN UB2 *....114 C4
Mountview Rd
CDALE/KGS NW9............................63 F1
CHING E4...38 B2

ESH/CLAY KT10............................205 H5
FSBYPK N4......................................67 H3
Mountview Rd ORP BR6.............202 B4
Mountview Wd WALTH SE27.....162 C5
Mount Wy CAR SM5...................210 A6
Mountwood E/WMO/HCT KT8...173 G6
Movers La BARK IG11.................90 D6
Mowatt CI ARCH N19...................66 D5
Mowbray Gdns NTHLT UB5 *.....78 A6
Mowbray Rd BAR EN5 ....21 G6
EDGW HA8..30 C5
KIL/WHAMP NW6............................82 C5
NRWD SE19...................................181 G4
RCHPK/HAM TW10.......................156 D5
Mowbrays CI CRW RM5..............56 E4
Mowbrays Rd CRW RM5.............56 E5
Mowlem St BETH E2...................104 D1
Mowll St BRXN/ST SW9............142 B1
Moxon CI PLSTW E13.................106 D1
Moxon St BAR EN5.......................20 D4
MHST W1U..9 G2
Moye CI BETH E2 *.....................104 C1
Moyers Rd LEY E10......................70 A4
Moylan Rd HMSMTH W6...........119 H6
Moyne PI WLSDN NW10...............98 C2
Moynihan Dr WCHMH N21...........22 E6
Moys CI CROY/NA CRO..............195 K3
Moyser Rd STRHM/NOR SW16...179 G1
Mozart St NKENS W10................100 D2
Mucheney Rd MRDN SM4..........194 B3
Muggeridge CI SAND/SEL CR2...211 K3
Muggeridge Rd DAGE RM10.......92 D2
Muirdown Av
MORT/ESHN SW14.......................137 K5
Muir Dr WAND/EARL SW18......140 E6
Muirfield ACT W3.........................99 G5
Muirfield CI BERM/RHTH SE16...123 J5
OXHEY WD19....................................41 G1
Muirfield Crs POP/IOD E14.......124 E3
Muirfield Gn OXHEY WD19...........27 G6
Muirfield Rd OXHEY WD19..........27 G6
Muirkirk Rd CAT SE6.................165 F3
Muir Rd CLPT E5...........................86 C1
Muir St CAN/RD E16...................126 E1
Mulberry Av STWL/WRAY TW19...152 B3
Mulberry Business Pk
WDR/YW UB7................................112 D2
Mulberry CI CEND/HSY/T N8.......66 E2
CHEL SW3 *...................................120 C6
EBAR EN4...37 J4
GPK RM2...75 K1
HDN NW4..45 J4
NTHLT UB5..95 J1
STRHM/NOR SW16......................161 H6
Mulberry Dr PUR RM19..............131 J4
Mulberry La CROY/NA CRO......197 G5
Mulberry Ms NWCR SE14..........144 C2
Mulberry Pde WDR/YW UB7......112 D3
Mulberry Rd ELTH/MOT SE9.....146 C5
HMSMTH W6.................................118 D5
Mulberry Rd HACK E8..................86 B5
Mulberry St WCHPL E1..............104 C5
Mulberry Wk CHEL SW3............120 C6
Mulberry Wy BARK IG11.............72 C1
BELV DA17....................................129 K2
SWFD E18...53 F5
Mulgrave Rd BELMT SM2..........208 D5
CROY/NA CRO..............................211 J1
EA W5..97 K2
HRW HA1..61 G6
WKENS W14...................................119 J6
WLSDN NW10..................................81 H2
WOOL/PLUM SE18......................126 E4
Mulholland CI MTCM CR4.........179 G5
Mullards CI MTCM CR4..............194 E5
Mullet Gdns BETH E2.................104 C2
Mullins Pth MORT/ESHN SW14...138 A4
Mullion CI KTN/HRWW/WS HA3...42 B4
Mullion Wk OXHEY WD19............27 H6
Mull Wk IS N1 *............................85 J4
Mulready St STJWD NW8...............2 C7
Multi Wy ACT W3........................118 B2
Multon Rd WAND/EARL SW18...160 C2
Mumford Mills GNWCH SE10 *...144 D1
Mumford Rd HNHL SE24............142 C6
Muncaster CI ASHF TW15.........152 D6
Muncaster Rd CLAP SW4...........140 E5
ASHF TW15...................................152 D6
Muncies Ms CAT SE6.................165 F4
Mundania Rd EDUL SE22...........163 J1
Munday Rd CAN/RD E16.............106 E5
Munden St WKENS W14.............119 H3
Mundesly CI OXHEY WD19..........27 G6
Mundford Rd CLPT E5..................68 E6
Mundon Gdns IL IG1.....................72 D5
Mund St WKENS W14.................119 J5
Mundy St IS N1 ....7 G4
Mungo-pk CI BUSH WD23 *.......28 C4
Mungo Park Rd RAIN RM13........93 J5
Mungo Park Wy
STMC/STPC BR5.........................202 E4
Munnery Wy ORP BR6...............216 B1
Munnings Gdns ISLW TW7........135 J6
Munnium Dr FBAR/BDGN N11 *...48 C2
Munroe Ter WBPTN SW10.........140 C1
Munro Rd BUSH WD23...............28 B1
Munro Ms NKENS W10...............100 C4
Munro Ter WBPTN SW10............120 C6
Munro Wy CLPT E5......................87 G3
Munster Av HSLWW TW4...........134 D5
Munster Ct FUL/PGN SW6.........139 J3
Munster Gdns PLMGR N13..........35 J6
Munster Ms FUL/PGN SW6 *.....139 J1
Munster Rd FUL/PGN SW6.........139 J2
TEDD TW11...................................174 C2
Munster Sq CAMTN NW1..............3 K6
Munton Rd WALW SE17...............18 D6
Murchison Av BXLY DA5............168 E3
Murchison Rd LEY E10.................70 A6
Murdock CI CAN/RD E16.............106 D5
Murdock St PECK SE15..............123 J6
Murfett CI WIM/MER SW19........159 H4
Muriel St IS N1 ....5 H2
Murillo Rd LEW SE13.................145 G5
Murphy St STHWK SE1.................17 J3

Murray Av BMLY BR1.................184 A6
HSLW TW3....................................135 G6
Murray CI THMD SE28...............127 K1
Murray Crs PIN HA5.....................41 H4
Murray Gv IS N1 ....6 E3
Murray House
WOOL/PLUM SE18 *...................146 D1
Murray Ms CAMTN NW1.............84 D5
Murray Rd EA W5.......................116 D4
NTHWD HA6....................................40 C4
RCHPK/HAM TW10.......................156 C6
STMC/STPC BR5...........................188 E6
WIM/MER SW19............................177 G2
Murray Sq CAN/RD E16..............106 E6
Murray St CAMTN NW1................84 D5
Murray Ter HAMP NW3 *.............83 G2
Murray Ter CHIG IG7......................54 C2
Musard Rd HMSMTH W6............119 H6
Musbury St WCHPL E1...............104 E5
Muscatel PI CMBW SE5..............143 F2
Muschamp Rd CAR SM5............194 D6
PECK SE15....................................143 G4
Muscovy St MON EC3R................13 H6
Museum St NOXST/BSQ WC1A...10 E3
Musgrave CI EBAR EN4................21 G2
Musgrave Crs FUL/PGN SW6.....139 K2
Musgrave Rd ISLW TW7.............136 A2
Musgrove Rd NWCR SE14..........144 A2
Musjid Rd BTSEA SW11..............140 C3
Musquash Wy HSLWW TW4.......134 B3
Muston Rd CLPT E5.......................68 D6
Muswell Av MUSWH N10.............48 B5
Muswell HI MUSWH N10..............66 B1
Muswell Hill Broadway
MUSWH N10....................................66 B1
Muswell Hill PI MUSWH N10......66 A1
Muswell Hill Rd MUSWH N10......66 A1
Muswell Ms MUSWH N10.............48 B5
Muswell Rd MUSWH N10..............48 B5
Mutrix Rd KIL/WHAMP NW6.........82 E6
Mutter Rd CLAP SW4.................141 J1
Mutton PI CAMTN NW1................84 A4
Muybridge Rd NWMAL KT3........175 J5
Myatt Rd BRXN/ST SW9.............142 C2
Mycenae Rd BKHTH/KID SE3...145 K1
Myddelton Av EN EN1...................24 A1
Myddelton Gdns WCHMH N21.....35 J2
Myddelton Pas CLKNW EC1R......5 K4
Myddelton Pk TRDG/WHET N20...33 H5
Myddelton Rd CEND/HSY/T N8....48 E6
Myddelton Sq CLKNW EC1R..........5 K4
Myddelton St CLKNW EC1R...........6 A5
Myddleton Av FSBYPK N4...........67 J6
Myddleton Rd WDGN N22............48 E3
Myers La NWCR SE14.................124 A6
Mylis CI SYD SE26.......................163 J6
Myline CI HMSMTH W6 *............118 D5
Myline St CLKNW EC1R.................5 J4
Myrna CI WIM/MER SW19..........178 D3
Myron PI LEW SE13.....................145 F3
Myrtle Aly WOOL/PLUM SE18...127 F3
Myrtle Av EBED/NFELT TW14.....133 H6
RSLP HA4..58 E4
Myrtleberry CI HACK E8 *...........86 C4
Myrtle CI EBAR EN4......................33 J3
ERITH DA8.....................................150 B1
UX/CGN UB8.................................112 C4
Myrtledene Rd ABYW SE2.........128 B5
Myrtle Gdns HNWL W7...............115 K1
Myrtle Gv ENC/FH EN2..................23 K1
NWMAL KT3..................................175 K5
Myrtle Rd ACT W3......................117 K1
CROY/NA CRO..............................213 J1
DART DA1......................................171 G4
EHAM E6..89 J6
HPTN TW12....................................173 H2
HSLW TW3.....................................135 H3
IL IG1...72 B6
SUT SM1..209 G3
WALTH E17 *....................................51 G5
Myrtleside CI NTHWD HA6...........40 B3
Myrtle St IS N1 ....7 G3
Myrtle Wk IS N1..............................7 G3
Mysore Rd BTSEA SW11............140 E5
Myton Rd DUL SE21....................162 E5

N

Nadine St CHARL SE7................126 B5
Nagle CI WALTH E17.....................52 B5
Nag's Head La WELL DA16.........148 C4
Nags Head Rd PEND EN3.............24 E5
Nairne Gv HNHL SE24.................142 E6
Nairn Gn OXHEY WD19.................26 E5
Nairn Rd RSLP HA4.......................77 G4
Nairn St POP/IOD E14.................106 A4
Nallhead Rd FELT TW13.............172 B1
Namba Roy CI
STRHM/NOR SW16......................162 A6
Namton Dr THHTH CR7..............196 A1
Nan Clark's La MLHL NW7...........31 H4
Nancy Downs OXHEY WD19.......27 G2
Nankin St POP/IOD E14..............105 J5
Nansen Rd BTSEA SW11............141 F5
Nansen Village
NFNCH/WDSPK N12 *....................33 F6
Nantes CI WAND/EARL SW18....140 B3
Nant Rd CRICK NW2......................64 D6
Nant St BETH E2..........................104 D2
Naoroji St FSBYW WC1X................5 J5
Napier Av FUL/PGN SW6............139 J4
POP/IOD E14.................................124 E5
Napier CI DEPT SE8.....................144 C1
EMPK RM11.....................................75 K6
WDR/YW UB7................................112 C3
Napier CI LEE/GVPK SE12.........166 A4
WKENS W14...................................119 J3
Napier Gv IS N1..............................6 D3
Napier PI WKENS W14................119 J3
Napier Rd ALP/SUD HA0...............79 K6
BELV DA17....................................129 G4

HAYES BR2..................................184 A6
ISLW TW7....................................136 B5
PEND EN3......................................25 F6
SAND/SEL CR2............................211 K5
SRTFD E15....................................88 C1
TOTM N17......................................49 H1
WAN E11.......................................88 C1
WDR/YW UB7..............................132 A2
WKENS W14................................119 J3
WLSDN NW10...............................99 K2
Napier Ter IS N1.............................85 H5
Napoleon Rd CLPT E5...................86 D1
TWK TW1..156 C2
Napton CI YEAD UB4.....................95 J3
Narbonne Av CLAP SW4............161 H1
Narboro Ct ROM RM1....................75 J5
Narborough CI HGDN/ICK UB10...58 A6
Narborough St FUL/PGN SW6...140 A3
Narcissus Rd KIL/WHAMP NW6...82 E3
Narford Rd CLPT E5......................86 C1
Narrow Boat CI THMD SE28......127 J2
Narrow St ACT W3.......................117 H1
POP/IOD E14.................................105 G6
Narrow Wy HAYES BR2...............200 D3
Nascot St SHB W12.....................100 A5
Naseby CI ISLW TW7..................135 K2
KIL/WHAMP NW6 *.........................83 G5
Naseby Rd CLAY IG5......................53 K6
DAGE RM10......................................92 C1
NRWD SE19...................................180 E2
Nash CI SUT SM1........................209 H1
Nash Gn BMLY BR1.....................183 K3
Nash La HAYES BR2....................215 G4
Nash Rd BROCKY SE4.................164 B5
CHDH RM6..73 K1
ED N9...36 E4
Nash St CAMTN NW1......................3 K6
Nash Wy KTN/HRWW/WS HA3...61 J3
Nasmyth St HMSMTH W6..........118 E3
Nassau Rd BARN SW13..............138 C2
Nassau St GTPST W1W.................10 A2
Nassington Rd HAMP NW3...........83 J2
Natalie CI EBED/NFELT TW14....153 G2
Natalie Ms WHTN TW2...............155 J5
Natal Rd FBAR/BDGN N11.............48 C2
IL IG1..90 A2
STRHM/NOR SW16......................179 J2
THHTH CR7....................................180 E6
Nathaniel CI WCHPL E1................13 K2
Nathans Rd ALP/SUD HA0............61 J6
Nathan Wy ABYW SE2................128 B2

National Ter
BERM/RHTH SE16 *......................123 J2
Nation Wy CHING E4.....................38 A3
Naval Rw POP/IOD E14...............106 A6
Navarino Gv HACK E8...................86 C4
Navarino Rd HACK E8...................86 C4
Navarre Gdns CRW RM5..............56 C4
Navarre Rd EHAM E6..................107 J1
Navarre St BETH E2.........................7 J7
Navenby CI CHING E4.....................38 A5
Navestock CI CHING E4 *.............38 A5
Navestock Crs WFD IG8...............53 G3
Navigator Dr NWDGN UB2.........115 H2
Navy St CLAP SW4......................141 J4
Nayim PI HACK E8.........................86 D4
Naylor Gv PEND EN3......................25 F5
Naylor Rd PECK SE15..................143 J1
TRDG/WHET N20.............................33 G4
Nazareth CI PECK SE15..............143 J3
Nazrul St BETH E2...........................7 J4
Neal Av STHL UB1..........................96 A3
Neal CI NTHWD HA6......................40 E4
Nealden St BRXN/ST SW9..........142 A4
Neale CI EFNCH N2........................47 G6
Neal St LSQ/SEVD WC2H.............10 E4
Neal Ter FSTH SE23 *..................164 A3
Near Acre CDALE/KGS NW9..........45 H4
Neasden CI WLSDN NW10.............81 G3
Neasden La WLSDN NW10............81 G2
Neasden La North
WLSDN NW10..................................81 G1
Neasham Rd BCTR RM8................91 H5
Neate St CMBW SE5....................123 G6
Neath Gdns MRDN SM4.............194 B3
Neathouse PI PIM SW1V 16 A6
Neats Acre RSLP HA4...................58 B4
Neatscourt Rd EHAM E6..............107 J4
Neckinger BERM/RHTH SE16........19 K4
Neckinger Est
BERM/RHTH SE16.........................124 A2
Neckinger St STHWK SE1.............19 K3
Nectarine Wy LEW SE13............144 E3
Needham Rd BAY/PAD W2.........100 D5
Needleman St
BERM/RHTH SE16.........................124 A2
Neeld Crs HDN NW4......................63 K2
WBLY HA9..80 D3
Nelgarde Rd CAT SE6.................164 D2
Nella Rd HMSMTH W6.................119 G6
Neldale Rd BERM/RHTH SE16....123 K4
Nello James Gdns
WNWD SE27...................................162 E6
Nelson CI CROY/NA CRO............196 C5
EBED/NFELT TW14 *....................153 J2
KIL/WHAMP NW6..........................100 D2
ROMW/RG RM7...............................56 E6
WOT/HER KT12..............................188 A5
Nelson Gdns BETH E2.................104 C2
HSLW TW3....................................155 F1
Nelson Grove Rd
WIM/MER SW19............................178 A4
Nelson Mandela CI
MUSWH N10....................................47 K5
Nelson Mandela Rd
BKHTH/KID SE3.............................146 B4
Nelson PI IS N1.................................6 B3
Nelson Rd BELV DA17................129 G5
CEND/HSY/T N8...............................67 F2
CHING E4...51 K1
DART DA1......................................171 K4
ED N9...36 D5
GNWCH SE10................................125 F6

HAYES BR2..................................200 B1
HRW HA1......................................132 C2
HTHAIR TW6................................132 C2
NWMAL KT3................................192 A2
PEND EN3.......................................37 F1
RAIN RM13..................................111 H1
SCUP DA14....................................168 C5
SEVS/STOTM N15..........................68 A1
STAN HA7......................................43 J2
WAN E11.......................................70 E1
WHTN TW2...................................155 F1
WIM/MER SW19..........................178 A3
Nelson Sq STHWK SE1.................18 A2
Nelsons Rw CLAP SW4...............141 J5
Nelson St CAN/RD E16................106 D6
EHAM E6...89 J1
WCHPL E1.......................................104 D5
Nelsons Yd CAMTN NW1 *.............4 A2
Nelson Ter FSBYE EC1V.................6 B3
Nelson Wk HOR/WEW KT19.......206 D1
Nemoure Rd ACT W3....................98 E6
Nene Gdns FELT TW13...............154 E4
Nene Rd HTHAIR TW6.................132 C2
Nepaul Rd BTSEA SW11.............140 D3
Nepean St PUT/ROE SW15.........158 D2
Neptune CI RAIN RM13...............111 H1
Neptune Rd HRW HA1..................60 D3
HTHAIR TW6 *...............................133 F1
Neptune St BERM/RHTH SE16...123 K3
Nesbit CI BKHTH/KID SE3..........145 H4
Nesbit Rd ELTH/MOT SE9...........146 C5
Nesbitts Aly BAR EN5 *................20 D4
Nesbitt Sq NRWD SE19 *............181 F3
Nesham St WAP E1W...................13 H1
Ness Rd ERITH DA8.....................131 G6
Ness St BERM/RHTH SE16.........123 H5
Nesta Rd WFD IG8........................52 D2
Nestle's Av HYS/HAR UB3...........113 J3
Nestor Av WCHMH N21.................35 H1
Netheravon Rd CHSWK W4........116 C4
HNWL W7.......................................116 A1
Netheravon Rd South
CHSWK W4....................................118 C6
Netherby Rd EA W5.....................116 D3
Netherby Rd ENC/FH EN2............22 E5
Netherbury Rd EA W5.................116 D3
Netherby Gdns ENC/FH EN2........22 E5
Nethercourt Av FNCH N3.............46 E2
Netherfield Gdns BARK IG11.......90 D5
Netherfield Rd
NFNCH/WDSPK N12 *......................47 F1
TOOT SW17...................................161 F5
Netherford Rd CLAP SW4..........141 H3
Netherhall Gdns HAMP NW3.......83 G3
Netherhall Wy HAMP NW3...........83 G3
Netherlands Rd BAR EN5..............33 H1
Netherleigh CI HGT N6...................66 B6
Netherpark Dr GPK RM2...............57 H5
Nether St FNCH N3........................46 E4
FNCH N3...47 F2
Netherton Gv WBPTN SW10......120 B6
Netherton Rd SEVS/STOTM N15...67 K3
TWK TW1..136 B6
Netherwood Rd WKENS W14......119 G3
Netherwood St
KIL/WHAMP NW6............................82 D5
Netley CI CHEAM SM3.................208 B3
CROY/NA CRO..............................214 A5
Netley Dr WOT/HER KT12...........188 D4
Netley Gdns MRDN SM4.............194 B4
Netley Rd BTFD TW8...................117 F6
GNTH/NBYPK IG2............................72 D2
MRDN SM4.....................................194 B4
WALTH E17.......................................69 H2
Netley St CAMTN NW1....................4 A5
Nettlecombe CI BELMT SM2.......209 F6
Nettleden Av WBLY HA9...............80 C4
Nettlefold PI WNWD SE27..........162 C5
Nettlestead CI BECK BR3............182 C3
Nettleton Rd HTHAIR TW6..........132 E2
NWCR SE14....................................144 A1
Nettlewood Rd
STRHM/NOR SW16......................179 J3
Neuchatel Rd CAT SE6................164 C4
Nevada CI NWMAL KT3...............191 K1
Nevada St GNWCH SE10............145 F1
Nevern PI ECT SW5.....................119 K4
Nevern Rd ECT SW5....................119 K4
Nevern Sq ECT SW5...................119 K5
Nevil CI NTHWD HA6.....................40 B1
Nevill Av NWMAL KT3.................176 A4
Neville CI ACT W3........................117 K2
HSLW TW3....................................135 G3
KIL/WHAMP NW6.............................2 A1
PECK SE15....................................143 H1
SCUP DA14....................................168 A5
WAN E11...88 C1
Neville Dr EFNCH N2.....................65 G3
Neville Gdns BCTR RM8...............91 K1
Neville Gill CI
WAND/EARL SW18.......................159 K1
Neville PI WDGN N22....................49 F4
Neville Rd BARK/HLT IG6.............54 C2
BCTR RM8..73 K6
CROY/NA CRO..............................196 E4
EA W5..97 K2
FSTGT E7..88 E5
KUT/HW KT1..................................175 H5
RCHPK/HAM TW10.......................156 C5
Neville St SKENS SW7................120 C5
Neville Ter SKENS SW7 *...........120 C5
Neville Wk CAR SM5...................194 D4
Nevill Rd STNW/STAM N16...........86 A1
Nevill Wy LOU IG10........................39 J1
Nevin Dr CHING E4.........................37 K3
Nevinson CI WAND/EARL SW18...160 C1
Nevis CI ROM RM1........................57 G2
Nevis Rd TOOT SW17..................161 F4
New Acres Rd THMD SE28.........127 K2
Newall Rd HTHAIR TW6...............133 G1
Newark Crs WLSDN NW10............99 F2
Newark Knok EHAM E6................108 A5

Newark Rd *SAND/SEL* CR2 ....211 K4
Newark St *WCHPL* E1 ....104 D4
New Ash Cl *EFNCH* N2 ....47 H6
New Barn Rd *WLGTN* SM6 ....211 T4
New Barns Av *MTCM* CR4 ....195 J1
New Barn St *CAN/RD* E16 ....107 F4
PLSTW E13 ....106 E5
Newbery Rd *ERITH* DA8 ....150 C2
Newbold Cottages
WCHPL E1 * 104 E5
Newbolt Av *CHEAM* SM5 ....208 A3
Newbolt Rd *STAN* HA7 ....43 F2
New Bond St *CONDST* W1S 9 K4
Newborough Gn *NWMAL* KT3 ......192 A1
New Brent St *HDN* NW4 ....64 A3
New Bridge St *EMB* EC4Y 12 A4
New Broad St *LVPST* EC2M 13 F2
New Broadway *EA* W5 ....97 J6
Newburgh Rd *ACT* W3 ....117 K1
Newburgh St *SOHO/CST* W1F 10 A4
New Burlington Ms
CONDST W1S * 10 A5
New Burlington Pl
CONDST W1S 10 A5
New Burlington St
CONDST W1S 10 A5
Newburn St *LBTH* SE11 ....122 A5
Newbury Cl *NTHLT* UB5 ....66 A4
Newbury Gdns
HOR/WEW KT19 ....207 H2
Newbury Ms *KTTN* NW5 ....84 A4
Newbury Rd *CHING* E4 ....52 A3
EDGW/NBYPK IG2 ....72 E3
HAYES BR2 ....183 K6
HTHAIR TW6 ....132 B2
Newbury St *STBT* EC1A 12 C2
Newbury V *VX/NE* SW8 ....141 G4
New Butt La *DEPT* SE8 * 78 H4
Newby Cl *EN* EN1 ....24 A3
Newby Pl *POP/IOD* E14 ....106 A6
Newby St *VX/NE* SW8 ....141 G4
Newcastle Av *BARK/HLT* IG6 ....55 C2
Newcastle Cl *FLST/FETLN* EC4A 12 A3
Newcastle Pl *BAY/PAD* W2 ....8 C2
Newcastle Rw *CLKNW* EC1R 5 K7
New Cavendish St
CAVSO/HST W1G * 9 H2
New Change *STP* EC4M 12 C4
New Charles St *FSBYE* EC1V 6 B4
New Church Rd *CMBW* SE5 ....142 D1
New City Rd *PLSTW* E13 ....107 C2
New Cl *FELT* TW13 ....172 D1
WIM/MER SW19 ....178 B6
New College Ms *IS* N1 * 85 G5
New College Pde *HAMP* NW3 * 83 J5
Newcombe Gdns *HSLWW* TW4 ..134 E5
STRHM/NOR SW16 * 45 C1
MLHL NW7 ....45 C1
Newcombe St *KENS* W8 * 119 K1
Newcome Gdns
STRHM/NOR SW16 ....161 K6
Newcomen Rd *BTSEA* SW11 ......140 C4
WAN E11 * 88 D1
Newcomen St *STHWK* SE1 ....18 E2
New Compton St
LSO/SEVD WC2H * 10 D4
New Ct *EMB* EC4Y * 11 J5
NTHLT UB5 ....78 B5
Newcourt St *STJWD* NW8 ....2 C3
New Crane Ph *WAP* E1W * 123 K1
New Crescent Yd
WLSDN NW10 * 99 H1
New Cross Rd *NWCR* SE14 ....144 C1
Newdales Cl *ED* N9 ....36 C4
Newdene Av *NTHLT* UB5 ....95 H1
Newdigate
STRHM/NOR SW16 * 162 B6
Newell St *POP/IOD* E14 ....105 H6
New End *HAMP* NW3 ....83 G1
New End Sq *HAMP* NW3 ....83 H2
Newent Cl *CAR* SM5 ....194 E5
PECK SE15 ....143 F1
New Era Est *IS* N1 * 7 G1
New Farm Av *HAYES* BR2 ....199 K1
New Farm La *NTHWD* HA6 ....40 C4
New Ferry Ap
WOOL/PLUM SE18 ....127 F3
New Fetter La
FLST/FETLN EC4A 11 K3
Newfield Cl *HPTN* TW12 ....173 F4
Newfield Ri *CRICK* NW2 ....81 J1
New Forest La *CHIG* IG7 ....54 A2
Newgate *CROY/NA* CR0 ....196 D5
New Garden Dr *WDR/YW* UB7 ....112 B2
Newgate Cl *FELT* TW15 ....154 D4
Newgate St *CHING* E4 ....38 C5
STBT EC1A * 12 B3
New Globe Wk *STHWK* SE1 ....12 C7
New Goulston St *WCHPL* E1 ....13 J3
New Green Pl
BRXS/STRHM SW2 ....162 B2
NRWD SE19 * 180 E1
Newhall Gdns *WOT/HER* KT12 ...188 B6
Newham's Rw *STHWK* SE1 ....19 H5
Newham Wy *CAN/RD* E16 ....106 D4
EHAM E6 ....107 K3
Newhaven Cl *HYS/HAR* UB3 ......113 J4
Newhaven Gdns
ELTH/MOT SE9 ....146 C5
Newhaven La *CAN/RD* E16 ....106 E4
New Heston Rd *HEST* TW5 ....134 E1
Newhouse Av *CHDH* RM6 ....55 K6
Newhouse Cl *NWMAL* KT3 ....192 B4
Newhouse Wk *MRDN* SM4 ....194 B4
Newick Cl *BXLY* DA5 ....169 J1
Newick Rd *CLPT* E5 ....86 E1
Newing Gn *BMLY* BR1 ....184 C3
Newington Barrow Wy
HOLWY N7 * 85 F1
Newington Butts *WALW* SE17 ......18 B7
Newington Cswy *STHWK* SE1 ......18 C4
Newington Gn *IS* N1 ....85 K3
Newington Green Rd *IS* N1 ....85 K3

New Inn Broadway
SDTCH EC2A * 7 H6
New Inn Sq *SDTCH* EC2A * 7 H6
New Inn St *SDTCH* EC2A * 7 H6
New Inn Yd *SDTCH* EC2A * 7 H6
New Kelvin Av *TEDD* TW11 ....173 K2
New Kent Rd *WALW* SE17 ....18 D6
New King's Rd *FUL/PGN* SW6 ....139 K2
New King St *DEPT* SE8 ....124 D6
Newland Cl *PIN* HA5 ....41 K2
Newland Ct *WBLY* HA9 ....62 C6
Newland Dr *EN* EN1 ....24 D2
Newland Gdns *WEA* W13 ....116 B2
Newland Rd *CEND/HSY/T* N8 ....48 E6
Newlands Av *THDIT* KT7 ....189 K5
Newlands Cl *ALP/SUD* HA0 ....79 J4
EDGW HA8 ....30 A5
NWDGN UB2 ....114 D5
Newlands Pk *SYD* SE26 ....181 K2
Newlands Pl *BAR* EN5 ....20 B6
Newlands Quay *WAP* E1W 104 E6
Newlands Rd
STRHM/NOR SW16 ....179 K5
WFD IG8 ....52 E4
The Newlands *WLGTN* SM6 ......210 C5
Newland St *CAN/RD* E16 ....126 D1
Newlands Wy *CHSGTN* KT9 ......205 J3
Newlands Woods
CROY/NA CR0 ....213 H6
Newling Cl *EHAM* E6 ....107 K5
Newling Est *BETH* E2 *................7 K5
New London St *MON* EC3R * 13 H5
New Lydenburg St *CHARL* SE7 ...126 B3
Newlyn Cl *ORP* BR6 ....217 G2
Newlyn Gdns *RYLN/HDSTN* HA2 ...59 K4
Newlyn Rd *BAR* EN5 ....20 D5
TOTM N17 ....50 B4
WELL DA16 ....148 A3
Newman Ms *WDGN* N22 ....49 G3
Newman Rd *BMLY* BR1 ....183 K4
CROY/NA CR0 ....196 A4
HYS/HAR UB3 ....95 H6
PLSTW E13 ....107 F2
WALTH E17 ....69 G2
Newmans La *SURB* KT6 ....190 E3
Newman's Rw *LINN* WC2A 11 H2
Newman St *FITZ* W1T 10 B2
Newman's Wy *EBAR* EN4 ....21 G3
Newmarket Av *NTHLT* UB5 ....78 A3
Newmarsh Rd *THMD* SE28 ......128 A1
New Mill Rd *STMC/STPC* BR5 .....186 D4
Newminster Ct *ENC/FH* EN2 * 23 H5
Newminster Rd *MRDN* SM4 ....194 B4
New Mount St *SRTFD* E15 ....88 B5
Newnham Av *RSLP* HA4 ....59 G5
Newnham Cl *LOU* IG10 ....39 H1
NTHLT UB5 ....78 C3
THHTH CR7 ....180 D6
Newnham Gdns *NTHLT* UB5 ......78 C4
Newnham Gn *WDGN* N22 * 49 G4
Newnham Rd *WDGN* N22 ....49 F4
Newnhams Cl *BMLY* BR1 ....184 E6
Newnham Ter *STHWK* SE1 ....17 J4
Newnham Wy
KTN/HRWW/WS HA3 ....62 A2
New North Pl *SDTCH* EC2A * 7 G6
New North Rd *BARK/HLT* IG6 ......54 D3
IS N1 ....7 F3
New North St *BMSBY* WC1N 11 G1
Newnton Cl *FSBYPK* N4 ....67 K4
New Oak Rd *EFNCH* N2 ....47 G5
New Oxford St
NOXST/BSQ WC1A * 10 E3
New Pde *ASHF* TW15 * 152 C6
WDR/YW UB7 * 112 B1
New Park Av *PLMGR* N13 ....35 K5
New Park Cl *NTHLT* UB5 ....77 J5
New Park Est *UED* N18 ....50 E1
New Park Rd
BRXS/STRHM SW2 ....161 K2
New Place Sq
BERM/RHTH SE16 * 123 J3
New Plaistow Rd *SRTFD* E15 ....88 C6
New Pond Pde *RSLP* HA4 * 76 E2
Newport Av *PLSTW* E13 ....107 F3
POP/IOD E14 ....106 C1
Newport Ct *LSO/SEVD* WC2H 10 D5
Newport Pl *SOHO/SHAV* W1D *...10 D5
Newport Rd *BARN* SW13 ....138 D2
HTHAIR TW6 ....132 D4
LEY E10 ....70 B6
WALTH E17 ....69 G1
YEAD UB4 ....94 B4
Newport St *LBTH* SE11 ....17 G7
Newquay Crs *RYLN/HDSTN* HA2 ...59 H6
Newquay Gdns *OXHEY* WD19 .....27 F4
Newquay Rd *CAT* SE6 ....164 E4
New Quebec St *MBLAR* W1H 9 F4
New River Av *CEND/HSY/T* N8 ......49 F3
New River Crs *PLMGR* N13 ....35 H4
New River Wy *FSBYPK* N4 ....67 K4
New Rd *ABYW* SE2 ....128 E4
BORE WD6 ....29 K1
CHING E4 ....116 E6
CEND/HSY/T N8 ....66 E1
CHING E4 ....37 K6
DAGE RM10 ....110 C1
DAGW RM9 ....92 C6
E/WMO/HCT KT8 ....173 F6
EBED/NFELT TW14 ....153 C1
EBED/NFELT TW14 ....154 A3
ED N9 ....36 C4
ESH/CLAY KT10 ....204 C2
FELT TW13 ....172 D1
GDMY/SEVK IG3 ....72 E6
HRW HA1 ....79 J1
HSLW TW3 ....135 G5
HYS/HAR UB3 ....133 F1
KUTN/CMB KT2 ....175 H3
MLHL NW7 ....46 D2
MTCM CR4 ....195 F5
ORP BR6 ....202 E6
RAIN RM13 ....111 J2
RCHPK/HAM TW10 ....156 E5
SOCK/AV RM15 ....131 J1
TOTM N17 ....50 B4

UX/CGN UB8 ....94 A3
WCHPL E1 ....104 C4
WDGN N22 ....49 J4
WELL DA16 ....148 C4
New Road Hl *HAYES* BR2 ....215 J6
New Row *CHCR* WC2N 10 E5
Newry Rd *TWK* TW1 ....136 B5
Newsam Av *SEVS/STOTM* N15 ...67 K2
Newsholme Dr *WCHMH* N21 ....22 F6
New Spring Gardens Wk
STHWK SE1 * 121 K5
New Sq *EBED/NFELT* TW14 ....153 F3
LINN WC2A 11 H3
Newstead Av *ORP* BR6 ....216 D1
New Street Sq
FLST/FETLN EC4A 11 K3
New Tank Hill Rd *PUR* RM19 ......131 K3
Newton Av *ACT* W3 ....117 K2
MUSWH N10 ....48 A4
Newton Cl *RYLN/HDSTN* HA2 ......60 A6
WALTH E17 ....69 G3
Newton Gv *CHSWK* W4 ....118 B4
Newton Rd *POP/IOD* E14 ....124 D4
Newton Rd *ACT* W3 ....117 K2
ALP/SUD HA0 ....80 B5
BAY/PAD W2 ....101 F5
CRICK NW2 ....82 A1
ISLW TW7 ....136 A3
KTN/HRWW/WS HA3 ....42 E5
SEVS/STOTM N15 ....68 B2
SRTFD E15 ....88 B3
WELL DA16 ....148 B4
WIM/MER SW19 ....177 H5
Newtons Cl *RAIN* RM13 ....93 G5
Newton St *HOL/ALD* WC2B 11 F3
Newton's Yd
WAND/EARL SW18 ....139 K6
Newton Ter *HAYES* BR2 ....200 C5
Newton Wk *EDGW* HA8 ....44 D4
Newton Wy *UED* N18 ....49 J1
New Tower Buildings
WAP E1W * 123 J1
Newtown St *BTSEA* SW11 ....141 G2
New Trinity Rd *EFNCH* N2 ....47 H6
New Union Cl *POP/IOD* E14 ......125 F3
New Union St *BARB* EC2Y 12 D2
New Vls *TOTM* N17 * 50 C4
New Wanstead *WAN* E11 ....70 E3
New Way Rd *CDALE/KGS* NW9 ....63 H1
New Wharf Rd *IS* N1 ....5 G2
New Zealand Wy *RAIN* RM13 .....111 H2
Niagara Av *EA* W5 ....116 D4
Niagara Cl *IS* N1 ....6 D2
Nibthwaite Rd *HRW* HA1 ....60 E2
Nicholas Cl *GFD/PVL* UB6 ....96 B1
Nicholas Gdns *EA* W5 ....116 E1
Nicholas La *MANHO* EC4N 13 F5
Nicholas Rd *BCTR* RM8 ....74 B6
BORE WD6 ....30 B1
CROY/NA CR0 ....210 E2
WCHPL E1 ....104 E3
Nicholas Wy *NTHWD* HA6 ....40 A4
Nicholay Rd *ARCH* N19 ....66 D5
Nicholes Rd *HSLW* TW3 ....135 F5
Nichol La *BMLY* BR1 ....183 K3
Nichollsfield Wk *HOLWY* N7 ....84 E3
Nicholl St *BETH* E2 ....86 C6
Nicholls Cl *FSBYPK* N4 * 67 G5
Nichols Gn *EA* W5 ....98 A4
Nicholson Dr *BUSH* WD23 ....28 C3
Nicholson House *CHARL* SE7 * ...146 D1
Nicholson Ms *KUT/HW* KT1 ......191 F1
Nicholson Rd *STNW/STAM* N16 ....68 C4
Nicholson St *STHWK* SE1 ....18 A1
Nickelby Cl *THMD* SE28 ....109 J5
Nickols Wk *WAND/EARL* SW18 ...140 A5
Nicola Cl *KTN/HRWW/WS* HA3 ....42 D5
SAND/SEL CR2 ....211 J4
Nicola Ms *BARK/HLT* IG6 ....54 B3
Nicoll Pl *HDN* NW4 ....63 K3
Nicoll Rd *WLSDN* NW10 ....81 G6
Nicolson Rd *STMC/STPC* BR5 ....202 E4
Niederwald Rd *SYD* SE26 ....164 B6
Nield Rd *HYS/HAR* UB3 ....113 J2
Nigel Cl *NTHLT* UB5 ....95 J1
Nigel Fisher Wy *CHSGTN* KT9 ....205 K5
Nigel Ms *IL* IG1 ....90 B2
Nigel Playfair Av *HMSMTH* W6 ..118 E5
Nigel Rd *FSTGT* E7 ....89 G3
PECK SE15 ....143 H4
Nigeria Rd *CHARL* SE7 ....146 B1
Nightingale Av *CHING* E4 ....52 C1
Nightingale Cl *CAR* SM5 ....195 F6
CHING E4 ....38 C6
CHSWK W4 ....117 K6
PIN HA5 ....59 G3
Nightingale Cnr
STMC/STPC BR5 * 202 E1
Nightingale Ct *SUT* SM1 ....209 G3
Nightingale Dr
HOR/WEW KT19 ....206 D4
Nightingale Gv *LEW* SE13 ....145 G6
Nightingale La *BAL* SW12 ....161 F2
BMLY BR1 ....184 A5
CEND/HSY/T N8 ....66 E1
RCHPK/HAM TW10 ....157 F1
WAN E11 ....71 G2
Nightingale Ms *KUT/HW* KT1 * ...174 E6
LBTH SE11 ....17 K6
Nightingale Pl *WBPTN* SW10 ....120 B6
WOOL/PLUM SE18 ....127 F6
Nightingale Rd *CAR* SM5 ....209 K1
CLPT E5 ....86 D1
E/WMO/HCT KT8 ....189 G2
EN EN1 ....36 C1
HNWL W7 ....116 A1

HPTN TW12 ....173 F2
STMC/STPC BR5 ....201 H3
WDGN N22 ....48 E4
WLSDN NW10 ....99 H2
WOT/HER KT12 ....188 B4
Nightingale Sq *BAL* SW12 ....161 F2
The Nightingales
STWL/WRAY TW19 ....152 C3
Nightingale V
WOOL/PLUM SE18 ....127 G6
Nightingale Wk *BAL* SW12 ....161 G1
Nightingale Wy *EHAM* E6 ....107 J4
Nile Cl *STNW/STAM* N16 ....86 B3
Nile Dr *ED* N9 ....36 E4
Nile Rd *PLSTW* E13 ....107 G1
Nile St *IS* N1 ....6 D4
Nile Ter *PECK* SE15 ....123 G5
Nimmo Dr *BUSH* WD23 ....28 D2
Nimrod Cl *NTHLT* UB5 ....95 H2
Nimrod Pas *IS* N1 ....86 A4
Nimrod Rd *STRHM/NOR* SW16 ...179 G2
Nina Mackay Cl *SRTFD* E15 * 88 B6
Nine Acres Cl *MNPK* E12 ....89 J3
Nine Elms Cl
EBED/NFELT TW14 ....153 J3
Nine Elms La *VX/NE* SW8 ....141 H1
Nineteenth Rd *MTCM* CR4 ....195 K1
Ninhams Wd *ORP* BR6 ....216 A2
Ninth Av *HYS/HAR* UB3 ....94 E6
Nisbett Wk *SCUP* DA14 ....168 B6
Nithdale Rd *WOOL/PLUM* SE18 ..147 G1
Nithsdale Gv *HGDN/ICK* UB10 .....76 A1
Niton Cl *BAR* EN5 ....32 B1
Niton Rd *RCH/KEW* TW9 ....137 H4
Niton St *FUL/PGN* SW6 ....139 G1
No1 St *WOOL/PLUM* SE18 ....127 G3
No2 St *WOOL/PLUM* SE18 ....127 G3
Noak Hill Rd *ABR/ST* RM4 ....57 K1
Nobel Dr *HYS/HAR* UB3 ....133 G1
Nobel Rd *UED* N18 ....36 E6
Noble Cnr *HEST* TW5 * 135 F2
Noble St *CITYW* EC2V 12 C3
Noel Rd *ACT* W3 ....98 C5
EHAM E6 ....107 J3
IS N1 ....6 B2
Noel St *SOHO/CST* W1F 10 B4
Nolan Wy *CLPT* E5 ....86 C2
Nolton Pl *EDGW* HA8 ....44 B4
Nonsuch Cl *CHIG* IG7 ....54 B2
Nonsuch Pl *CHEAM* SM5 * 208 B5
Nora Gdns *HDN* NW4 ....64 B1
Norbiton Av *KUT/HW* KT1 ....175 H5
Norbiton Common Rd
KUT/HW KT1 ....175 J6
Norbiton Rd *POP/IOD* E14 ....105 H5
Norbreck Pde *EA* W5 ....98 A2
Norbroke St *SHB* W12 ....99 H6
Norburn St *NKENS* W10 ....100 C4
Norbury Av *HSLW* TW3 ....135 K5
STRHM/NOR SW16 ....180 A4
Norbury Cl *STRHM/NOR* SW16 ..180 B4
Norbury Court Rd
STRHM/NOR SW16 ....179 K5
Norbury Crs
STRHM/NOR SW16 ....180 B5
Norbury Cross
STRHM/NOR SW16 ....179 K6
Norbury Gdns *CHDH* RM6 ....73 K2
Norbury Hl *STRHM/NOR* SW16 ..180 B3
Norbury Ri *STRHM/NOR* SW16 ...179 K6
Norbury Rd *CHING* E4 ....51 J1
FELT TW13 ....153 K5
THHTH CR7 ....180 D5
Norbury V *KUT/HW* KT1 * 175 G5
Norcombe Gdns
KTN/HRWW/WS HA3 ....61 J3
Norcott Cl *YEAD* UB4 ....95 G3
Norcott Rd *STNW/STAM* N16 ......68 C6
Norcroft Gdns *EDUL* SE22 ....163 H2
Norcutt Rd *WHTN* TW2 ....155 K3
Norderfeldt Rd *ERITH* DA8 ....130 A5
Norfield Rd *RDART* DA2 ....169 K6
Norfolk Av *PLMGR* N13 ....49 J2
SEVS/STOTM N15 ....68 B3
Norfolk Cl *DART* DA1 ....171 K4
EBAR EN4 ....22 A5
EFNCH N2 ....47 J6
PLMGR N13 ....49 H2
TWK TW1 * 56 C2
Norfolk Crs *BAY/PAD* W2 ....8 D2
BFN/LL DA15 ....167 K2
Norfolk Gdns *BXLYHN* DA7 ......149 G2
Norfolk House Rd
STRHM/NOR SW16 ....161 K5
Norfolk Ms *NKENS* W10 ....100 C4
Norfolk Rd *BAR* EN5 ....20 E4
BARK IG11 ....90 E5
DAGE RM10 ....92 D3
EHAM E6 ....89 K6
ESH/CLAY KT10 ....204 E3
FELT TW13 ....154 B3
GDMY/SEVK IG3 ....72 E5
HRW HA1 ....60 B2
PEND EN3 ....36 D1
ROMW/RG RM7 ....74 D2
STJWD NW8 ....2 B1
THHTH CR7 ....180 D6
WALTH E17 ....51 F4
WIM/MER SW19 ....178 D3
WLSDN NW10 ....81 G5
Norfolk Rw *STHWK* SE1 ....17 H5
Norfolk Sq *BAY/PAD* W2 ....8 B4
Norfolk Square Ms *BAY/PAD* W2 ...8 B4
Norfolk St *FSTGT* E7 ....88 E3
Norgrove St *BAL* SW12 ....161 F2
Norhyrst Av *SNWD* SE25 ....181 G3
Norland Pl *NTGHL* W11 ....119 H1
Norlands Crs *CHST* BR7 ....185 G4
Norlands Ga *CHST* BR7 * 185 G4
Norland Sq *NTGHL* W11 ....119 H1
Norley V *PUT/ROE* SW15 ....158 D3

Norlington Rd *LEY* E10 ....70 A5
Norman Av *FELT* TW15 ....154 D4
STHL UB1 ....95 J6
TWK TW1 ....156 C2
WDGN N22 ....49 J4
Normanby Cl *PUT/ROE* SW15 ....139 K6
Normanby Rd *WLSDN* NW10 ......81 H3
Norman Cl *ORP* BR6 ....216 C1
ROMW/RG RM7 ....56 D5
Norman Crs *HEST* TW5 ....134 C1
PIN HA5 ....41 G4
Normand Gdns *WKENS* W14 * ...119 H6
Normand Ms *WKENS* W14 ....119 H6
Normand Rd *WKENS* W14 ....119 J6
Normandy Av *BAR* EN5 ....20 D6
Normandy Cl *SYD* SE26 ....164 B5
Normandy Rd *HYS/HAR* UB3 .....113 J1
Normandy Rd *BRXN/ST* SW9 ....142 B2
Normandy Ter *CAN/RD* E16 ......107 F5
Normandy Wy *ERITH* DA8 ....150 B2
Norman Gv *BOW* E3 ....105 G1
Normanhurst Av *WELL* DA16 ....148 C2
Normanhurst Dr *TWK* TW1 ......156 C4
Normanhurst Rd
BRXS/STRHM SW2 ....162 A4
STMC/STPC BR5 ....186 C5
WOT/HER KT12 ....188 C6
Norman Pde *SCUP* DA14 * 169 F5
Norman Rd *BELV* DA17 ....129 J3
DART DA1 ....171 H5
EHAM E6 ....107 K3
EMPK RM11 ....75 K4
GNWCH SE10 ....144 E1
IL IG1 ....90 B3
SEVS/STOTM N15 ....68 C1
SUT SM1 ....208 E3
THHTH CR7 ....196 C2
WAN E11 ....70 B1
WIM/MER SW19 ....178 B3
Norman's Bldgs *FSBYE* EC1V * 6 D5
WLSDN NW10 ....81 J4
Normanshield Av *KUT/HW* KT1 ...174 D3
Normanshield Cl *BUSH* WD23 .....28 B2
Normanshire Dr *CHING* E4 ....37 J6
Normans Md *WLSDN* NW10 ......81 F4
Normans St *FSBYE* EC1V 6 D5
Norman Ter *KIL/WHAMP* NW6 * ...82 D3
Normanton Av
WAND/EARL SW18 ....159 K4
Normanton Pk *CHING* E4 ....38 C5
Normanton Rd *SAND/SEL* CR2 ...212 A4
Normanton St *STRHM/NOR* SW16 ...180 A1
Norman Wy *ACT* W3 ....98 D4
STHGT/OAK N14 ....34 D5
Normington Cl
STRHM/NOR SW16 ....180 B1
Norrice Lea *EFNCH* N2 ....65 H2
Norris St *STJS* SW1Y 10 C6
Norris Wy *DART* DA1 ....150 C4
Norroy Rd *PUT/ROE* SW15 ....139 G5
Norrys Cl *EBAR* EN4 ....21 K5
Norrys Rd *EBAR* EN4 ....21 K5
Norseman Cl *GDMY/SEVK* IG3 ....73 H5
Norseman Wy *GFD/PVL* UB6 ......96 B6
Norstead Pl *PUT/ROE* SW15 .....158 D4
North Access Rd *WALTH* E17 ......69 F3
North Acre *CDALE/KGS* NW9 ......45 G4
North Acton Rd *WLSDN* NW10 ....99 F1
Northall Rd *BXLYHN* DA7 ....149 K3
Northampton Gv *IS* N1 ....85 K3
Northampton Pk *IS* N1 ....85 J4
Northampton Rd *CLKNW* EC1R 5 K6
CROY/NA CR0 ....197 H6
PEND EN3 ....25 G4
Northampton Rw *CLKNW* EC1R * ...5 K6
Northampton Sq *FSBYE* EC1V 6 A5
Northampton St *IS* N1 ....85 J5
Northanger Rd
STRHM/NOR SW16 ....179 K2
North Ap *NTHWD* HA6 ....26 A4
North Audley St
MYFR/PKLN W1K 9 G5
North Av *CAR* SM5 ....210 A5
HYS/HAR UB3 ....94 E6
RCH/KEW TW9 ....137 H2
RYLN/HDSTN HA2 ....60 B6
STHL UB1 ....96 A6
UED N18 ....36 C6
WEA W13 ....97 G5
North Bank *STJWD* NW8 ....2 C5
Northbank Rd *WALTH* E17 ....52 A4
North Birkbeck Rd *WAN* E11 ......88 B1
Northborough Rd
STRHM/NOR SW16 ....179 K5
Northbourne *HAYES* BR2 ....199 K6
Northbourne Rd *CLAP* SW4 ......141 J5
Northbrook Dr *NTHWD* HA6 ......40 C4
Northbrook Rd *BAR* EN5 ....32 C1
CROY/NA CR0 ....196 E3
IL IG1 ....72 A6
LEW SE13 ....165 G1
WDGN N22 ....48 E3
Northburgh St *FSBYE* EC1V 6 B6
BXLYHN DA6 ....149 K5
CHIG IG7 ....55 G5
DAGE RM10 ....74 D6
EBED/NFELT TW14 ....153 G2
MRDN SM4 ....193 J4
North Carriage Dr *BAY/PAD* W2 ....8 D5
Northchurch *WALW* SE17 * 19 G7
Northchurch Rd *IS* N1 ....86 A5
WBLY HA9 ....80 C3
Northchurch Ter *IS* N1 ....86 A5
North Circular *PLMGR* N13 ....49 K1
WALTH E17 ....51 K4
North Circular Rd *BARK* IG11 ......90 A5
CHDH E4 ....38 C6
CRICK NW2 ....63 J4
FNCH N3 ....46 E3
GLDGN NW11 ....64 C3
REDBR IG4 ....71 F4
WLSDN NW10 ....80 C3
Northcliffe Cl *WPK* KT4 ....207 G1
Northcliffe Dr *TRDG/WHET* N20 ...32 D3
North Cl *BAR* EN5 ....20 A6
BXLYHN DA6 ....149 G5
CHIG IG7 ....55 G5
DAGE RM10 ....92 C7
EBED/NFELT TW14 ....153 G1
MRDN SM4 ....193 H1
North Colonnade
POP/IOD E14 ....124 E1
North Common Rd *EA* W5 ....98 A6

Northcote Av BRYLDS KT5.....191 H4
EA W5.....98 A6
ISLW TW7.....136 B6
STHL UB1.....95 J6
Northcote Rd BTSEA SW11.....140 D5
CROY/NA CR0.....195 J4
NWMAL KT3.....175 K6
SCUP DA14.....167 K6
TWK TW1.....136 B6
WLSDN NW10.....81 G5
Northcott Av WDGN N22.....48 E4
North Countess Rd WALTH E17.....51 H5
Northcourt FITZ W1T.....10 B1
North Cray Rd SCUP DA14.....187 F2
North Crs CAN/RD E16.....106 B3
FNCH N3.....45 H3
GWRST WC1E.....10 C1
Northcroft Rd HOR/WEW KT19.207 G5
WEA W13.....116 C2
North Cross Rd BARK/HLT IG6.....72 C1
EDUL SE22.....143 G6
Northdene CHIG IG7.....54 D1
North Dene HSLW TW5.....135 G2
MLHL NW7.....31 F5
Northdene Gdns
SEVS/STOTM N15.....68 B3
Northdown Cl RSLP HA4.....76 D1
Northdown Gdns
GNTH/NBYPK IG2.....72 E2
Northdown Rd EMPK RM11.....75 K4
WELL DA16.....148 C3
Northdown St IS N1.....5 G3
North Dr BECK BR3.....198 E1
HSLW TW3.....135 H3
ORP BR6.....216 E2
RSLP HA4.....58 C4
STRHM/NOR SW16.....161 H6
North End BKHH IG9.....39 G2
CROY/NA CR0.....196 D6
HAMP NW5.....65 G5
North End Av HAMP NW3.....65 G6
North End Crs WKENS W14.....119 J4
North End La ORP BR6.....216 B6
Northend Rd ERITH DA8.....150 C2
North End Rd FUL/PGN SW6.....139 K1
GLDGN NW11.....64 D1
WBLY HA9.....80 D1
WKENS W14.....119 J4
North End Wy HAMP NW3.....65 G6
Northern Av ED N9.....36 B4
Northern Rd MRDN SM4.....193 H1
Northern Perimeter Rd
HTHAIR TW6.....133 F2
Northern Perimeter Rd (West)
HTHAIR TW6.....132 B2
Northern Relief Rd BARK IG11.....90 C5
North Eyot Gdns
HMSMTH W6.....118 C5
Northey St POP/IOD E14.....105 G6
North Farm LOU IG10.....39 C1
Northfield Av PIN HA5.....59 H1
STMC/STPC BR5.....202 D3
WEA W13.....116 C2
Northfield Cl BMLY BR1.....184 B4
HYS/HAR UB3.....113 J3
Northfield Crs CHEAM SM3.....208 C2
Northfield Pde
HYS/HAR UB3 *.....113 J3
Northfield Rd DACW RM9.....92 B2
EBAR EN4.....21 J4
ED N9 *.....24 D6
EHAM E6.....89 K4
HEST TW5.....134 C1
PEND EN3.....36 D1
STNW/STAM N16.....68 A1
WEA W13.....116 C2
Northfields WAND/EARL SW18..139 K5
North Gdns WIM/MER SW19.....178 C3
Northgate Dr CDALE/KGS NW9.....63 G3
North Gower St CAMTN NW1.....4 A5
North Gv HGT N6.....66 A4
SEVS/STOTM N15.....67 K2
North HI HGT N6.....65 K3
North Hill Av HGT N6.....65 K4
North Hyde Gdns
HYS/HAR UB3.....113 K3
NWDGN UB2.....114 D3
North Hyde La NWDGN UB2.....114 D5
North Hyde Rd HYS/HAR UB3.....115 H3
North Hyde Whf
NWDGN UB2 *.....114 B4
Northiam NFNCH/WDSPK N12..32 E6
Northiam St HACK E8.....86 D6
Northington St BMSBY WC1N..11 G1
Northlands Av ORP BR6.....216 E2
Northlands St CMBW SE5.....142 D5
North La TEDD TW11.....174 A2
North Lodge Cl
PUT/ROE SW15 *.....139 G6
North Ms BMSBY WC1N.....5 H7
North Mt TRDG/WHET N20 *..33 J3
Northolme Av EDGW HA8.....31 F6
Northolme Gdns EDGW HA8.....44 C4
Northolme Ri ORP BR6.....201 K6
Northolt Av RSLP HA4.....77 F3
Northolt Gdns GFD/PVL UB6...78 E2
Northolt Rd RYLN/HDSTN HA2...78 A2
WDR/YW UB7.....132 A2
Northover BMLY BR1.....165 J6
North Pde EDGW HA8.....44 C4
STHL UB1 *.....96 A5
North Pk ELTH/MOT SE9.....166 E1
North Pas WAND/EARL SW18...139 K6
North Peckham Est
PECK SE15.....143 G1
TEDD TW11.....174 A2
Northpoint Cl SUT SM1.....209 G1
North Pole La HAYES BR2.....214 D4
North Pole Rd SHB W12.....100 A5
Northport St IS N1.....7 F1

North Ri BAY/PAD W2 *.....8 D4
North Rd BELV DA17.....129 J3
BMLY BR1.....184 A4
BTFD TW8.....117 F6
CHDH RM6.....74 A2
DART DA1.....170 C1
EA W5.....116 E3
EBED/NFELT TW14.....153 G1
ED N9.....36 D3
EDGW HA8.....44 D4
GDMY/SEVK IG3.....73 F2
HEST TW5.....114 B6
HGT N6.....66 A4
HOLWY N7.....84 E4
HYS/HAR UB3.....94 B4
RCH/KEW TW9.....137 H5
STHL UB1.....96 A6
SURB KT6.....190 E5
WDR/YW UB7.....112 C3
WIM/MER SW19.....178 C2
WOOL/PLUM SE18.....127 K4
WWKM BR4.....198 E5
Northrop Rd HTHAIR TW6.....133 H2
North Rw MYFR/PKLN W1K.....9 F5
North Several
BKHTH/KID SE3 *.....145 J3
Northside BMLY BR1.....183 K4
North Side Wandsworth
Common WAND/EARL SW18..140 B6
North Sq HENDON NW11.....64 E3
North St BARK IG11.....90 C5
BMLY BR1.....183 K4
BXLYHN DA7.....149 H5
CAR SM5.....209 K1
CLAP SW4.....141 G4
DART DA1.....171 G2
HDN NW4.....64 A2
ISLW TW7.....136 B4
PLSTW E13.....107 F1
ROM RM1.....75 F1
North Tenter St WCHPL E1.....13 K4
North Ter CHEL SW3.....14 C5
Northumberland Aly
FENCHST EC3M *.....13 H4
Northumberland Av
CHCR WC2N.....10 E7
EN EN1.....24 D1
ISLW TW7.....136 A2
MNPK E12.....71 G5
WELL DA16.....147 K5
Northumberland Cl ERITH DA8.149 K1
STWL/WRAY TW19.....152 B1
Northumberland Crs
EBED/NFELT TW14.....153 H1
Northumberland Gdns
BMLY BR1.....201 F1
ED N9.....36 B5
MTCM CR4.....195 H1
Northumberland Gv TOTM N17..50 D3
Northumberland Pk
ERITH DA8.....149 K1
TOTM N17.....50 C3
Northumberland Pl
BAY/PAD W2.....100 E5
Northumberland Rd BAR EN5...33 C1
EHAM E6.....107 J5
RYLN/HDSTN HA2.....60 A4
WALTH E17.....69 J2
Northumberland St
CHCR WC2N.....10 E7
Northumberland Wy
HMSMTH W6 *.....118 D5
North Verbena Gdns
HMSMTH W6 *.....118 D5
North Vw CL EA W5.....97 J3
PIN HA5.....59 G4
WIM/MER SW19.....176 E1
Northview Dr WFD IG8.....53 H5
Northview Pde HOLWY N7 *..84 E1
North View Rd
CEND/HSY/T N8.....48 D6
North Vis CAMTN NW1.....84 D4
North Wk CROY/NA CR0.....213 K4
North Wy CDALE/KGS NW9.....44 D6
ED N9.....36 E4
FBAR/BDGN N11.....48 C2
Northway GLDGN NW11.....65 F2
MRDN SM4.....177 H6
North Wy PIN HA5.....41 G6
Northway Crs MLHL NW7.....31 G6
Northway Rd CMBW SE5.....142 D4
CROY/NA CR0.....197 C3
Northways Pde HAMP NW3 *..83 H5
North Weald Cl HCH RM12.....93 K5
North Weald La
KUTN/CMB KT2.....174 E1
North Wharf Rd BAY/PAD W2..8 A2
Northwick Av
KTN/HRWW/WS HA3.....61 G3
Northwick Cir
KTN/HRWW/WS HA3.....61 J3
Northwick Cl STJWD NW8.....2 A6
Northwick Park Rd HRW HA1..61 F3
Northwick Rd ALP/SUD HA0...79 K6
OXHEY WD19.....27 G1
Northwick Ter STJWD NW8.....2 A6
Northwold Dr PIN HA5.....41 G6
Northwold Rd
STNW/STAM N16.....68 B6
Northwood Av HCH RM12.....93 J2
Northwood Gdns CLAY IG5.....72 A1
GFD/PVL UB6.....79 F3
NFNCH/WDSPK N12.....47 H1
Northwood PI ERITHM DA18..129 C3
Northwood Rd CAR SM5.....210 A4
FSTH SE23.....164 A3
HGT N6.....66 C4
HTHAIR TW6.....132 A2
THHTH CR7.....180 D5
Northwood Wy NTHWD HA6....40 D4

North Woolwich Rd
CAN/RD E16.....125 K1
North Worple Wy
MORT/ESHN SW14.....138 A4
Norton Av BRYLDS KT5.....191 J4
Norton CL CHING E4.....51 J1
Norton Folgate WCHPL E1.....7 H7
Norton Gdns
STRHM/NOR SW16.....179 K5
Norton Rd ALP/SUD HA0.....79 K4
DAGE RM10 *.....93 G5
LEY E10.....69 H4
Norval Gn BRXN/ST SW9 *.....142 B3
Norval Rd ALP/SUD HA0.....61 H6
Norway Ga BERM/RHTH SE16..124 B3
Norway PI POP/IOD E14.....105 H5
Norway St GNWCH SE10.....124 E6
Norwich Crs CHDH RM6.....73 H2
Norwich Ms GDMY/SEVK IG3...73 G2
Norwich Rd FSTGT E7.....88 E3
GFD/PVL UB6.....78 B6
THHTH CR7.....180 D6
Norwich St FLST/FETLN EC4A..11 J3
Norwich Wk EDGW HA8.....44 E3
Norwood Av ALP/SUD HA0.....80 B6
ROMW/RG RM7.....75 F4
Norwood Cl CRICK NW2.....82 C1
NWDGN UB2.....115 F4
WHTN TW2.....155 J4
Norwood Dr RYLN/HDSTN HA2.59 K3
Norwood Gdns NWDGN UB2..114 E4
YEAD UB4.....95 G3
Norwood Green Rd
NWDGN UB2.....115 F4
Norwood High St WNWD SE27.162 D6
Norwood Park Rd
WNWD SE27.....180 D1
Norwood Rd HNHL SE24.....162 C3
NWDGN UB2.....114 D3
Notley St CMBW SE5.....142 E1
Notson Rd SNWD SE25.....197 J1
Notting Barn Rd NKENS W10..100 B3
Nottingdale Sq NTGHL W11 *..119 H1
Nottingham Av CAN/RD E16..107 G4
Nottingham Ct
LSO/SEVD WC2H.....10 E4
Nottingham PI CAMTN NW1.....3 G6
Nottingham Rd ISLW TW7.....136 A3
LEY E10.....70 A3
SAND/SEL CR2.....211 J3
TOOT SW17.....160 E5
Nottingham St MHST W1U.....9 G1
Nottingham Ter CAMTN NW1...3 G7
Notting Hill Ga KENS W8.....119 K1
Nova Ms CHEAM SM3.....193 H4
Novar Cl ORP BR6.....202 A4
Novar Rd ELTH/MOT SE9.....167 H3
Novello St FUL/PGN SW6.....139 K2
Nowell Rd BARN SW13.....118 D6
Nower HI PIN HA5.....59 K1
Noyna Rd TOOT SW17.....160 E5
Nubia Wy BMLY BR1.....165 H6
Nuding Cl LEW SE13.....144 D4
Nugent Rd ARCH N19.....66 E5
SNWD SE25.....181 G6
Nugents Ct PIN HA5 *.....41 J4
Nugent Ter STJWD NW8.....101 C1
Nuneaton Rd DACW RM9.....91 K5
Nunhead Crs PECK SE15.....143 J4
Nunhead La PECK SE15.....143 J4
Nunnington Cl ELTH/MOT SE9.166 D5
Nunn's Rd ENC/FH EN2.....23 J3
Nupton Dr BAR EN5.....32 A1
Nurse Cl EDGW HA8.....44 E4
Nursery Av BXLYHN DA7.....149 G4
CROY/NA CR0.....198 A6
FNCH N3.....47 F5
Nursery Cl BROCKY SE4.....144 C3
CHDH RM6.....73 K3
CROY/NA CR0.....198 A6
EBED/NFELT TW14.....154 A2
ORP BR6.....202 A4
OXHEY WD19.....27 F3
PEND EN3.....25 F2
PUT/ROE SW15.....139 G6
SWLY BR8.....187 K5
WFD IG8.....53 F1
Nursery Gdns CHST BR7.....185 F3
HPTN TW12.....154 E6
HSLWW TW4.....134 E5
PEND EN3.....25 F2
Nursery La BETH E2.....7 J1
FSTGT E7.....88 E4
NKENS W10.....100 A4
Nurserymans Rd
FBAR/BDGN N11.....34 A4
Nursery Rd BRXN/ST SW9.....142 A4
EFNCH N2.....47 H4
HACK E8.....86 C4
MTCM CR4.....194 D1
PIN HA5.....41 G6
STHGT/OAK N14.....34 C4
SUT SM1.....209 G2
THHTH CR7.....196 E1
WIM/MER SW19.....177 H5
WIM/MER SW19.....178 A5
Nursery Rw BAR EN5 *.....20 C4
WALW SE17.....18 E7
Nursery St TOTM N17.....50 B3
The Nursery ERITH DA8.....150 C1
Nursery Wk HDN NW4.....45 K6
Nurstead Rd ERITH DA8.....149 H1
Nutborn St NKENS W10.....100 C2
Nutbrook St PECK SE15.....143 H4
Nutbrowne Rd DACW RM9.....92 B6
Nutcroft Rd PECK SE15.....143 J1
Nutfield Cl CAR SM5.....209 J1
FBAR/BDGN N11.....48 B2
Nutfield Gdns GDMY/SEVK IG3.73 H6
NTHLT UB5.....95 G1
Nutfield Rd CRICK NW2.....81 H1
EDUL SE22.....143 G6
SRTFD E15.....88 A2

THHTH CR7.....196 C1
Nutfield Wy ORP BR6.....201 F6
Nutford PI MBLAR W1H.....8 D3
Nuthatch Cl STWL/WRAY TW19.152 C3
Nuthatch Gdns THMD SE28...127 J2
Nuthurst Av
BRXS/STRHM SW2.....162 A4
Nutley Ter HAMP NW3.....83 H4
Nutmead Cl BXLY DA5.....169 K3
Nutmeg Cl CAN/RD E16.....106 B3
Nutmeg La POP/IOD E14.....106 B5
Nuttall St IS N1.....7 H2
Nutter La WAN E11.....71 G2
Nutt Gv EDGW HA8.....29 K4
Nut Tree Cl ORP BR6.....217 K1
Nutt St PECK SE15.....143 G1
Nutwell St TOOT SW17.....178 D1
Nuxley Rd BELV DA17.....129 G6
Nyanza St WOOL/PLUM SE18..147 J1
Nylands Av RCH/KEW TW9.....137 H5
Nymans Gdns RYNPK SW20..176 E6
Nynehead St NWCR SE14.....144 B1
Nyon Gv CAT SE6.....164 C4
Nyssa Cl WFD IG8.....53 K2
Nyton Cl ARCH N19.....66 E5

O

Oak Av CEND/HSY/T N8.....66 E1
CROY/NA CR0.....198 D6
ENC/FH EN2.....23 F2
HEST TW5.....134 C1
HPTN TW12.....172 D1
MUSWH N10.....48 B3
TOTM N17.....49 K3
WDR/YW UB7.....112 A1
Oakbank CROY/NA CR0.....214 A4
Oakbank Av WOT/HER KT12..188 E4
Oakbank Gv HNHL SE24.....142 D5
Oakbrook Cl BMLY BR1.....166 A6
Oakbury Rd FUL/PGN SW6.....140 A3
Oak Cl DART DA1.....150 D4
STHGT/OAK N14.....34 B2
Oakcombe Cl NWMAL KT3.....176 B4
Oak Cottage Cl CAT SE6.....165 H3
Oak Cottages HNWL W7 *.....115 K2
Oak Crs CAN/RD E16.....106 C4
Oakcroft Cl PIN HA5.....41 F5
Oakcroft Rd CHSGTN KT9.....206 B2
LEW SE13.....145 G3
Oakcroft Vls CHSGTN KT9.....206 B2
Oakdale STHGT/OAK N14.....34 B3
Oakdale Av
KTN/HRWW/WS HA3.....62 A3
NTHWD HA6.....40 E5
Oakdale Cl OXHEY WD19.....27 G2
Oakdale Gdns CHING E4.....52 A1
Oakdale Rd FSBYPK N4.....67 J3
FSTGT E7.....89 F5
OXHEY WD19.....27 G5
PECK SE15.....144 A4
STRHM/NOR SW16.....179 K1
SWFD E18.....53 F5
WAN E11.....70 B6
Oakdene Av MTCM CR4.....195 F4
Oakdene Av CHST BR7.....185 F1
ERITH DA8.....129 K6
THDIT KT7.....190 B5
Oak Dene Cl EMPK RM11.....75 K3
Oakdene Cl PIN HA5.....41 K3
Oakdene Dr BRYLDS KT5.....191 K5
Oakdene Ms CHEAM SM3.....193 J5
Oakdene Pk FNCH N3.....46 D3
Oakdene Rd STMC/STPC BR5..202 B3
Oakden St LBTH SE11.....17 K6
Oak Dr ESH/CLAY KT10.....205 F4
Oaken La ESH/CLAY KT10.....204 E2
Oakenshaw Cl SURB KT6.....191 F4
Oakeshott Av HGT N6.....66 A6
Oakey La STHWK SE1.....17 J4
Oakfield CHING E4.....51 K1
Oakfield Av
KTN/HRWW/WS HA3.....43 H6
Oakfield Cl NWMAL KT3.....192 C2
RSLP HA4.....58 E3
Oakfield Gdns BECK BR3.....198 E2
CAR SM5.....194 D5
GFD/PVL UB6.....96 C2
UED N18.....36 A6
Oakfield La DART DA1.....171 G4
HAYES BR2.....215 G2
RDART DA2.....170 D4
Oakfield Park Rd DART DA1..171 G4
Oakfield Rd ASHF TW15.....152 E6
CROY/NA CR0.....196 D6
EFNCH N2.....47 H4
EHAM E6.....89 J7
FNCH N3.....47 F4
FSBYPK N4.....67 G3
IL IG1.....90 B1
PGE/AN SE20.....181 J4
STHGT/OAK N14.....34 E4
WALTH E17.....51 G1
WIM/MER SW19.....159 G5
Oakfields Rd GLDGN NW11.....64 C3
Oakfield St WBPTN SW10.....120 B6
Oakford Rd KTTN NW5.....84 C2
Oak Gdns CROY/NA CR0.....198 D6
EDGW HA8.....44 E5
Oak Gv CRICK NW2.....82 C2
RSLP HA4.....58 E4
WWKM BR4.....199 F5
Oak Grove Rd PGE/AN SE20..181 K4
Oak Hall Rd WAN E11.....71 F3
Oakham Cl CAT SE6.....164 B4
Oakham Dr HAYES BR2.....199 J2
Oakhampton Rd MLHL NW7...46 A3
Oakhill ESH/CLAY KT10.....205 G4
Oak HI WFD IG8.....52 B5
Oakhill Av HAMP NW3.....83 F2

PIN HA5.....41 J5
Oak Hill Crs SURB KT6.....191 F4
WFD IG8.....52 C5
Oak Hill Gdns WFD IG8.....52 C4
Oak Hill Gv SURB KT6.....191 F4
Oak Hill Pk HAMP NW3.....83 F2
Oak Hill Park Ms HAMP NW3...83 G2
Oakhill Rd BECK BR3.....183 F5
ORP BR6.....202 A6
PUT/ROE SW15.....139 J6
STRHM/NOR SW16.....179 K4
Oakhill Rd SURB KT6.....191 F3
Oakhill Rd SUT SM1.....209 F1
Oak Hill Wy HAMP NW3.....83 G2
Oakhouse Rd BXLYHS DA6....149 H6
Oakhurst Av BXLYHN DA7.....149 F1
EBAR EN4.....33 J2
Oakhurst Cl BARK/HLT IG6.....54 B2
CHST BR7.....184 E4
TEDD TW11.....173 K1
WALTH E17 *.....70 C1
Oakhurst Gdns BXLYHN DA7..149 F1
CHING E4.....38 C3
WALTH E17.....70 C1
Oakhurst Gv EDUL SE22.....143 H5
Oakhurst Rd HOR/WEW KT19..206 E4
Oakington Av HYS/HAR UB3..113 G4
RYLN/HDSTN HA2.....60 A4
WBLY HA9.....80 B1
Oakington Cl SUN TW16.....172 B5
Oakington Dr SUN TW16.....172 B5
Oakington Manor Dr WBLY HA9..80 C3
Oakington Rd MV/WKIL W9...100 E3
Oakington Wy CEND/HSY/T N8..66 E3
Oakland Pl BKHH IG9.....38 E4
Oakland Rd SRTFD E15.....88 C2
Oaklands WCHMH N21.....35 F4
Oaklands Av BFN/LL DA15.....168 A2
ED N9.....36 D1
ESH/CLAY KT10.....189 J5
ISLW TW7.....116 A6
OXHEY WD19.....27 F3
ROM RM1.....57 F6
THHTH CR7.....196 B1
WWKM BR4.....213 K1
Oaklands Cl ALP/SUD HA0.....79 K3
BXLYHS DA6.....149 G6
CHSGTN KT9.....205 J2
STMC/STPC BR5.....201 J4
Oaklands Dr WHTN TW2.....155 H2
Oaklands Ga NTHWD HA6.....40 C2
Oaklands Gv SHB W12.....118 D1
Oaklands La BARN SW13.....138 B2
BAR EN5.....32 D2
Oaklands Ms CRICK NW2 *.....82 B2
Oaklands Pk ALP/SUD HA0 *..79 K4
Oaklands Pl BCTR RM8.....92 B2
BRXN/ST SW9 *.....142 B3
Oaklands Rd BMLY BR1.....183 H3
BXLYHS DA6.....149 G5
CEND/HSY/T N8.....67 F3
CRICK NW2.....82 B2
MORT/ESHN SW14.....138 A4
TRDG/WHET N20.....32 D2
Oaklands Wy WLGTN SM6.....210 D5
Oakland Wy HOR/WEW KT19..207 G4
Oak La EFNCH N2.....47 H5
FBAR/BDGN N11.....48 C2
ISLW TW7.....135 J4
POP/IOD E14.....105 H6
TWK TW1.....156 B2
WFD IG8.....38 D4
Oakleafe Gdns BARK/HLT IG6..54 B6
Oakleigh Av EDGW HA8.....44 D5
SURB KT6.....191 H5
TRDG/WHET N20.....33 H3
Oakleigh Cl TRDG/WHET N20..33 K5
Oakleigh Ct EDGW HA8.....44 E5
Oakleigh Crs TRDG/WHET N20..33 J5
Oakleigh Dr RKW/CH/CXG WD3..26 A1
Oakleigh Gdns EDGW HA8.....44 C1
ORP BR6.....216 E2
TRDG/WHET N20.....33 G3
Oakleigh Ms TRDG/WHET N20..33 H4
Oakleigh Park Av CHST BR7..185 F5
Oakleigh Pk North
TRDG/WHET N20.....33 H3
Oakleigh Pk South
TRDG/WHET N20.....33 H3
Oakleigh Rd HGDN/ICK UB10..76 A5
PIN HA5.....41 K2
Oakleigh Rd North
TRDG/WHET N20.....33 H3
Oakleigh Rd South
FBAR/BDGN N11.....34 A6
Oakleigh Wy MTCM CR4.....179 G4
SURB KT6.....191 H5
Oakley Av BARK IG11.....91 F5
CROY/NA CR0.....210 E2
EA W5.....98 C6
Oakley Cl CHING E4.....38 A5
EHAM E6.....107 J5
HNWL W7.....96 E6
ISLW TW7.....135 J2
Oakley Ct MTCM CR4 *.....195 F6
Oakley Crs FSBYE EC1V *.....6 B3
Oakley Dr CAT SE6.....165 G1
ELTH/MOT SE9.....167 J4
HAYES BR2.....215 J1
Oakley Gdns CEND/HSY/T N8..67 F2
CHEL SW3.....120 D6
Oakley Pk BXLY DA5.....168 D2
Oakley PI STHWK SE1.....123 G5
Oakley Rd BAR EN5.....21 H1
HRW HA1.....60 E3
IS N1.....85 K5
SAND/SEL CR2.....212 B6
SNWD SE25.....197 J2
Oakley Sq CAMTN NW1.....4 B2
Oakley St CHEL SW3.....120 D6
Oakley Yd BETH E2 *.....7 K6
Oak Lodge Av CHIG IG7.....54 D1
Oak Lodge Cl STAN HA7.....43 J1
Oak Lodge Dr WWKM BR4.....198 E4
Oaklodge Wy MLHL NW7.....45 H2
Oakmead Av HAYES BR2.....199 K3
Oakmeade PIN HA5.....42 A2
Oakmead Gdns EDGW HA8....31 F6
Oakmead PI MTCM CR4.....178 D4
Oakmead Rd BAL SW12.....161 G3

CROY/NA CR0 .....195 J5
Oakmere Rd ABYW SE2 .....128 B6
Oakmoor Wy CHIG IG7 .....54 E1
Oakmore Gdns
STMC/STPC BR5 .....202 E1
Oak Park Gdns
WIM/MER SW19 .....159 G3
Oakridge Dr EFNCH N2 .....47 H6
Oakridge Rd BMLY BR1 .....165 H6
Oak Ri BKHH IG9 .....39 H5
Oak Rd EA W5 .....97 K6
ERITH DA8 .....149 K1
ERITH DA8 .....150 D2
NWMAL KT3 .....176 A5
Oak Rw MTCM CR4 .....179 H5
Oaks Av CRW RM5 .....56 E5
FELT TW13 .....154 D4
NRWD SE19 .....181 F1
WPK KT4 .....207 K2
Oaksford Av SYD SE26 .....165 J5
Oaks Gv CHING E4 .....38 C4
Oakshade Rd BMLY BR1 .....165 G6
Oakshaw Rd
WAND/EARL SW18 .....160 A2
Oaks La CROY/NA CR0 .....212 E1
GNTH/NBYPK IG2 .....72 E2
Oaks Rd CROY/NA CR0 .....212 D3
STWL/WRAY TW19 .....132 A6
The Oaks CHSGTN KT9 .....205 J1
FELT TW13 * 154 D4
HAYES BR2 * 201 F3
MRDN SM4 * 193 H1
NFNCH/WDSPK N12 .....33 F6
OXHEY WD19 .....27 G3
RSLP HA4 .....58 B4
WFD IG8 .....52 C3
WOOL/PLUM SE18 .....127 H5
YEAD UB4 .....94 D4
Oak St ROMW/RG RM7 .....74 E2
Oaks Wy CAR SM5 .....209 K5
SURB KT6 .....190 E6
Oakthorpe Rd PLMGR N13 .....49 G1
Oaktree Av PLMGR N13 .....35 C5
Oak Tree Cl EA W5 * 97 K4
STAN HA7 .....43 J5
Oak Tree Ct BORE WD6 * 29 K1
Oak Tree Dl CDALE/KGS NW9 .....62 E2
Oak Tree Dr TRDG/WHET N20 .....33 F5
Oak Tree Gdns BMLY BR1 .....184 A1
Oaktree Gv IL IG1 .....90 D3
Oak Tree Rd STJWD NW8 .....2 B3
Oakview Cl OXHEY WD19 .....27 G1
Oakview Gdns EFNCH N2 .....65 H1
Oakview Gv CROY/NA CR0 .....198 B5
Oakview Rd CAT SE6 .....182 E1
Oak Village HAMP NW3 * 84 A3
Oak Vis GLDGN NW11 * 64 D3
Oak Wy ACT W3 .....118 B1
CROY/NA CR0 .....198 A3
EBED/NFELT TW14 .....153 H3
RYNPK SW20 .....193 F1
Oak Wy STHGT/OAK N14 .....34 B2
Oakway Cl BXLY DA5 .....169 F1
Oakways ELTH/MOT SE9 .....167 G1
Oakwood WLGTN SM6 .....210 B6
Oakwood Av BECK BR3 .....183 F5
CHSGTN KT9 .....206 B5
HAYES BR2 .....184 A6
MTCM CR4 .....178 C5
STHGT/OAK N14 .....34 D2
STHL UB1 .....96 A6
Oakwood Cl CHST BR7 .....184 C2
LEW SE13 .....165 G1
STHGT/OAK N14 .....34 C1
WFD IG8 .....53 J2
Oakwood Ct WKENS W14 .....119 J3
Oakwood Crs GFD/PVL UB6 .....79 G4
WCHMN N21 .....35 F1
Oakwood Dr BXLYHN DA7 .....149 K5
EDGW HA8 .....44 E2
NRWD SE19 .....180 E2
Oakwood Gdns GDMY/SEVK IG3 .....73 F6
ORP BR6 .....216 B1
SUT SM1 .....193 K6
Oakwood La WKENS W14 .....119 J3
Oakwood Pde
STHGT/OAK N14 * 22 C6
Oakwood Park
Cottages WCHMH N21 * 35 F1
Oakwood Park Rd
STHGT/OAK N14 .....34 C1
Oakwood Pl CROY/NA CR0 .....196 B3
GLDGN NW11 * 64 D3
PIN HA5 .....201 H6
PIN HA5 .....41 F5
RYNPK SW20 .....176 D4
Oakworth Rd NKENS W10 .....100 A4
Oarsman Pl E/WMO/HCT KT8 .....189 K1
Oast House Wy
STMC/STPC BR5 .....202 C1
Oates Cl HAYES BR2 .....183 G6
Oates Rd CRW RM5 .....56 D1
Oatfield Rd ORP BR6 .....202 A5
Oatland Ri WALTH E17 .....51 C5
Oatlands Rd PEND EN3 .....24 E2
Oat La CITYW EC2V 12 C3
Oban Cl PLSTW E13 .....107 G3
Oban Rd PLSTW E13 .....107 G2
THHTH CR7 .....196 E1
Oban St POP/IOD E14 .....106 B5
Oberstein Rd BTSEA SW11 .....140 C5
Oborne Cl HNHL SE24 .....142 C6
Observatory Gdns KENS W8 .....119 K2
Observatory Rd
MORT/ESHN SW14 .....137 K5
SKENS SW7 .....14 B5
Occupation La EA W5 .....116 E4
WOOL/PLUM SE18 .....147 G2
Occupation Rd WALW SE17 .....122 D5
WEA W13 .....116 C2
Ocean Est WCHPL E1 .....105 F3
Ocean St WCHPL E1 .....105 F4
Ockendon Ms IS N1 * 85 K4
Ockendon Rd IS N1 .....85 K3

Ockham Dr STMC/STPC BR5 .....186 B3
Ockley Rd CROY/NA CR0 .....196 A4
STRHM/NOR SW16 .....161 K6
Octagon Ar LVPST EC2M * 13 G2
Octavia Cl MTCM CR4 .....194 D2
Octavia Ms CRICK NW2 * 81 K4
Octavia Rd ISLW TW7 .....136 A4
Octavia St BTSEA SW11 .....140 D2
Octavius St DEPT SE8 .....144 D1
October Pl HDN NW4 * 46 B6
Odard Rd E/WMO/HCT KT8 .....189 F1
Odell Cl BARK IG11 .....91 F5
Odell Wk LEW SE13 .....144 E4
Odeon Pde ELTH/MOT SE9 * 146 D5
GFD/PVL UB6 * 79 H4
HOLWY N7 * 84 E1
ISLW TW7 * 135 K3
Odessa Rd FSTGT E7 .....88 D2
WLSDN NW10 .....99 J1
Odessa St BERM/RHTH SE16 .....124 C3
Odger St BTSEA SW11 .....140 E3
Odhams Wk LSQ/SEVD WC2H * 10 E4
Odsey Vis FSBYPK N4 * 67 G3
Offa's Md HOM E9 .....87 G2
Offenham Rd ELTH/MOT SE9 .....166 E6
Offerton Rd CLAP SW4 .....141 H4
Offham Slope
NFNCH/WDSPK N12 .....46 D1
The Office Village SRTFD E15 * 88 C5
Offley Pl ISLW TW7 .....135 J3
Offley Rd BRXN/ST SW9 .....142 B1
Offord Cl TOTM N17 .....50 C3
Offord Rd IS N1 .....84 E5
Offord St HOLWY N7 .....85 F5
Ogilby St WOOL/PLUM SE18 .....126 E4
Oglander Rd PECK SE15 .....143 G5
Ogle St GTPST W1W 10 A1
Oglethorpe Rd DAGE RM10 .....92 B1
Ohio Rd PLSTW E13 .....106 D3
Oil Mill La HMSMTH W6 .....118 D5
Okeburn Rd TOOT SW17 .....179 F1
Okehampton Crs WELL DA16 .....148 C2
Okehampton Rd WLSDN NW10 .....82 A6
Olaf St NTGHL W11 .....100 B6
Old Bailey STP EC4M 12 B4
Old Barn Cl BELMT SM2 .....208 C5
Old Barn Wy BXLYHN DA7 .....150 A5
Old Barrack Yd KTBR SW1X * 15 G3
Old Bellgate Whf
POP/IOD E14 .....124 D3
Oldberry Rd EDGW HA8 .....45 F2
Old Bethnal Green Rd
BETH E2 .....104 D2
Old Bexley La BXLY DA5 .....170 A4
Old Bond St CONDST W1S 10 A6
Oldborough Rd ALP/SUD HA0 .....61 J6
Old Brewers Ms HAMP NW3 .....83 H2
Old Bridge Cl NTHLT UB5 .....96 A1
Old Bridge St KUT/HW KT1 .....174 E1
Old Broad St LVPST EC2M 13 G3
Old Bromley Rd BMLY BR1 .....183 G1
Old Brompton Rd ECT SW5 .....119 K5
Old Buildings LINN WC2A 11 J3
Old Burlington St CONDST W1S 10 A5
Oldbury Cl STMC/STPC BR5 .....202 E1
Oldbury Pl MHST W1U 9 H1
Oldbury Rd EN EN1 .....24 C3
Old Castle St WCHPL E1 .....13 K3
Old Cavendish St
CAVSQ/HST W1G 9 J5
Old Chapel Rd SWLY BR8 .....203 K4
Old Chestnut Av
ESH/CLAY KT10 .....204 A4
Old Church La CDALE/KGS NW9 .....62 E4
GFD/PVL UB6 .....97 G2
STAN HA7 .....43 J1
Old Church Pth
ESH/CLAY KT10 .....204 B2
Oldchurch Ri ROMW/RG RM7 .....75 G3
Old Church Rd CHING E4 .....37 J6
Oldchurch Rd ROMW/RG RM7 .....75 G3
Old Church Rd WCHPL E1 * 105 F5
Old Church St CHEL SW3 .....120 C6
Old Claygate La
ESH/CLAY KT10 .....205 G4
Old Compton St
SOHO/SHAV W1D 10 C5
Old Cote Rd HEST TW5 .....115 F6
Old Court Pl KENS W8 .....120 A2
Old Ctyd BMLY BR1 .....184 A4
Old Dairy Ms BAL SW12 .....161 F3
KTTN NW5 * 84 B4
Old Deer Pk HCH/KEW TW9 * 137 F4
Old Deer Park Gdns
RCH/KEW TW9 .....137 F4
Old Devonshire Rd BAL SW12 .....161 F2
Old Dock Cl RCH/KEW TW9 .....117 H6
Old Dover Rd BKHTH/KID SE3 .....145 K1
Old Farm Av BFN/LL DA15 .....167 J3
STHGT/OAK N14 .....34 B2
Old Farm Cl HSLWW TW4 .....134 E5
Old Farm Rd EFNCH N2 .....47 H4
HPTN TW12 .....172 E2
WDR/YW UB7 .....112 A2
Old Farm Rd East
BFN/LL DA15 .....168 A4
Old Farm Rd West
BFN/LL DA15 .....167 K4
KTTN NW5 * 84 B4
Oldfield Cl BMLY BR1 .....200 E1
GFD/PVL UB6 .....78 E3
STAN HA7 .....43 G1
Oldfield Farm Gdns
GFD/PVL UB6 .....78 D6
Oldfield Gv BERM/RHTH SE16 .....124 A4
Oldfield La North GFD/PVL UB6 .....78 C5
Oldfield La South GFD/PVL UB6 .....96 C4
Oldfield Ms HGT N6 .....66 C5
Oldfield Rd ACT W3 .....118 C2
BMLY BR1 .....200 E1
BXLYHN DA7 .....149 F3
HMP N6 .....66 C5
STNW/STAM N16 .....86 A1
WIM/MER SW19 .....177 H2
WLSDN NW10 .....81 H5
Oldfields Circ NTHLT UB5 .....78 C4
Oldfields Rd SUT SM1 .....208 D1
Old Fish Street HI BLKFR EC4V * 12 C5

Old Fleet La FLST/FETLN EC4A 12 A3
Old Fold Cl BAR EN5 * 20 D2
Old Fold La BAR EN5 .....20 D2
Old Fold Vw BAR EN5 .....20 A4
Old Ford Rd BETH E2 .....104 E1
BOW E3 .....87 H6
EN EN1 .....24 B1
Old Forge Cl STAN HA7 .....29 G6
Old Forge Rd ARCH N19 .....66 D6
EN EN1 .....24 B1
Old Forge Wy SCUP DA14 .....168 C6
Old Gannon Cl NTHWD HA6 .....26 A6
Old Gloucester St BMSBY WC1N 11 F1
Old Hall Cl PIN HA5 .....41 J4
Old Hall Dr PIN HA5 .....41 J4
Oldham Ter ACT W3 .....117 K2
Old HI CHST BR7 .....185 F4
ORP BR6 .....216 E4
Oldhill St STNW/STAM N16 .....68 C5
Old Homesdale Rd HAYES BR2 .....200 B1
Old Hospital Cl BAL SW12 * 160 E3
Old House Cl WIM/MER SW19 .....177 H1
Old House Gdns TWK TW1 * 156 D1
Old Howletts La RSLP HA4 .....58 B3
Old Jamaica Rd
BERM/RHTH SE16 .....123 H3
Old James St PECK SE15 .....143 J4
Old Jewry LOTH EC2R * 12 E4
Old Kenton La CDALE/KGS NW9 .....62 D2
Old Kent Rd PECK SE15 .....123 J6
Old Kingston Rd WPK KT4 .....206 D1
Old Lodge Wy STAN HA7 .....43 G1
Old London Rd KUTN/CMB KT2 .....175 F5
Old Maidstone Rd SCUP DA14 .....187 G3
Old Maiden La WORK KT4 * 192 D6
Old Manor Dr ISLW TW7 .....155 H1
Old Manor Rd NWDGN UB2 .....114 C4
Old Manor Wy BXLYHN DA7 .....150 A3
CHST BR7 .....184 E1
Old Manor Yd ECT SW5 * 120 A4
Old Market Sq BETH E2 * 7 J4
Old Marylebone Rd CAMTN NW1 .....8 D2
Old Mill Ct SWFD E18 .....53 G6
Old Mill Rd WOOL/PLUM SE18 .....127 J6
Old Mitre Ct EMB EC4Y * 11 K4
Old Montague St WCHPL E1 .....104 C4
Old Nichol St BETH E2 .....7 J6
Old North St FSBYW WC1X * 11 G1
Old Oak Common La
WLSDN NW10 .....99 G3
Old Oak La WLSDN NW10 .....99 H2
Old Oak Rd ACT W3 .....118 C1
Old Orch SUN TW16 .....172 B5
Old Orchard Cl EBAR EN4 .....21 H1
The Old Orch HAMP NW3 * 83 K2
Old Palace Rd CROY/NA CR0 .....211 J1
Old Palace Yd RCH/KEW TW9 .....136 D6
Old Paradise St LBTH SE11 .....17 G6
Old Park Av BAL SW12 .....161 F1
ENC/FH EN2 .....23 J5
Old Park Gv ENC/FH EN2 .....23 J5
Old Park La MYFR/PKLN W1K 15 J1
Old Park Ms HEST TW5 .....134 E1
Old Park Ridings WCHMH N21 .....35 J1
Old Park Rd ABYW SE2 .....128 B5
ENC/FH EN2 .....23 H4
PLMGR N13 .....35 F5
Old Park Rd South ENC/FH EN2 .....23 H5
Old Park Vw ENC/FH EN2 .....23 G4
Old Pearson St GNWCH SE10 * 144 E1
Old Perry St CHST BR7 .....185 K5
Old Post Office La
BKHTH/KID SE3 .....146 A4
Old Pound Cl ISLW TW7 .....136 B2
Old Pye St WEST SW1P 16 C4
Old Quebec St MBLAR W1H 9 F4
Old Queen St STJSPK SW1H 16 D3
Old Rectory Gdns EDGW HA8 .....44 C2
Old Redding
KTN/HRWW/WS HA3 .....42 B1
Oldridge Rd BAL SW12 .....161 F2
Old Rd DART DA1 .....150 B4
LEW SE13 .....145 H5
PEND EN3 .....24 E2
Old Royal Free Sq IS N1 * 5 K1
Old Ruislip Rd NTHLT UB5 .....95 H1
Old's Ap WATW WD18 .....26 A3
Old School Cl BECK BR3 .....182 B5
Old School Crs FSTGT E7 .....88 E4
Old School Pl CROY/NA CR0 .....211 G2
Old Schools La EW KT17 .....207 H6
Old School Ter CHEAM SM3 * 208 B5
Old Seacoal La STP EC4M 12 A4
Old South Cl PIN HA5 .....41 H4
Old South Lambeth Rd
VX/NE SW8 * 141 K1
Old Sq LINN WC2A 11 H3
Old Stable Ms HBRY N5 * 85 J1
Old Station Gdns TEDD TW11 * 174 B2
Old Station Rd HYS/HAR UB3 .....113 J3
The Old Station Yd WALTH E17 * 70 A1
Oldstead Rd BMLY BR1 .....165 G6
Old St FSBYE EC1V 6 C6
PLSTW E13 .....107 F1
SDTCH EC2A 7 G5
Old Studio Cl CROY/NA CR0 .....196 E4
Old Swan Yd CAR SM5 .....209 K2
Old Town CLAP SW4 .....141 H4
CROY/NA CR0 .....211 H1
Old Tramyard
WOOL/PLUM SE18 .....127 K4
Old Woolwich Rd
GNWCH SE10 .....125 G5
Old York Rd WAND/EARL SW18 .....140 A5
Oleander Cl ORP BR6 .....216 D3
O'Leary Sq WCHPL E1 .....104 E4
Olga St BOW E3 .....105 G1
Olinda Rd STNW/STAM N16 .....68 B3
Oliphant St NKENS W10 .....100 C2
Olive Gv SEVS/STOTM N15 .....67 J1
Oliver Av SNWD SE25 .....197 G1
Oliver Cl CHSWK W4 .....117 J6
Oliver Gdns EHAM E6 .....107 J4
Oliver Gv SNWD SE25 .....197 G1
Oliver Ms PECK SE15 .....143 H3
Olive Rd CRICK NW2 .....82 A2
DART DA1 .....171 G3

EA W5 .....116 E3
PLSTW E13 .....107 G2
WIM/MER SW19 .....178 D3
Oliver Rd LEY E10 .....87 K1
NWMAL KT3 .....175 K5
RAIN RM13 .....93 H6
SUT SM1 .....209 H2
WALTH E17 .....70 A2
Oliver's Yd STLK EC1Y 7 F6
Olive St ROMW/RG RM7 .....75 F3
Ollerton Av BOW E3 .....87 H6
Ollerton Rd FBAR/BDGN N11 .....48 D1
Olley Cl WLGTN SM6 .....210 E5
Ollgar Cl SHB W12 .....118 C1
Olliffe St POP/IOD E14 .....125 F3
Olmar St STHWK SE1 .....123 H6
Olney Rd WALW SE17 .....122 D6
Olron Crs BXLYHS DA6 .....148 E6
Olven Rd WOOL/PLUM SE18 .....147 H1
Olveston Wk CAR SM5 .....194 C3
Olwen Ms PIN HA5 .....41 H5
Olyffe Av WELL DA16 .....148 B5
Olyffe Dr BECK BR3 .....183 F4
Olympia Wy WKENS W14 .....119 H3
Olympic Wy GFD/PVL UB6 .....78 B6
WBLY HA9 .....80 C2
Olympus Gv WDGN N22 .....49 G4
Olympus Sq CLPT E5 .....86 D1
Oman Av CRICK NW2 .....82 A3
O'Meara St STHWK SE1 .....18 D1
Omega PI IS N1 .....5 F3
Omega St NWCR SE14 .....144 C2
Ommaney Rd NWCR SE14 .....144 A2
Omnibus Wy WALTH E17 .....51 J5
Ondine Rd PECK SE15 .....143 G5
Onega Ga BERM/RHTH SE16 .....124 B3
One Tree Cl FSTH SE23 .....163 K1
Ongar Cl CHDH RM6 .....73 J2
Ongar Rd FUL/PGN SW6 .....119 K6
Ongar Wy RAIN RM13 .....93 H6
Onra Rd WALTH E17 .....69 J4
Onslow Av RCHPK/HAM TW10 .....137 F6
Onslow Cl CHING E4 .....38 B4
NKENS W10 .....100 D3
Onslow Crs CHST BR7 .....185 G4
SKENS SW7 * 14 B7
Onslow Dr SCUP DA14 .....168 E5
Onslow Gdns MUSWH N10 .....66 B2
SKENS SW7 .....14 A7
SWFD E18 .....53 G6
THDIT KT7 .....189 K5
WCHMH N21 .....23 G6
WLGTN SM6 .....210 C5
Onslow Ms East SKENS SW7 .....14 A7
Onslow Ms West SKENS SW7 .....14 A7
Onslow Pde STHGT/OAK N14 * 34 B3
Onslow Rd CROY/NA CR0 .....196 B4
NWMAL KT3 .....176 D1
RCHPK/HAM TW10 .....157 F1
Onslow Sq SKENS SW7 .....14 B7
Onslow St CLKNW EC1R 5 K7
Onslow Wy THDIT KT7 .....189 K5
Ontario St STHWK SE1 .....18 B5
Ontario Wy POP/IOD E14 .....124 D1
On The HI OXHEY WD19 .....27 J4
Onyx Ms SRTFD E15 .....88 C4
Opal Cl CAN/RD E16 .....107 H5
Opal Ms IL IG1 .....72 B6
Opal St LBTH SE11 .....18 A7
Openshaw Rd ABYW SE2 .....128 C5
Openview WAND/EARL SW18 .....160 B3
Ophir Ter PECK SE15 .....143 H2
Opossum Wy HSLWW TW4 .....134 B4
Oppenheim Rd LEW SE13 .....145 F3
Oppidans Rd HAMP NW3 .....83 K5
Optima Pk DART DA1 * 150 D4
Orange Court La ORP BR6 .....216 A6
Orange Gv CHIG IG7 .....54 C2
WAN E11 .....88 C1
Orange Hill Rd EDGW HA8 .....44 E3
Orange PI BERM/RHTH SE16 .....123 K3
Orangery La ELTH/MOT SE9 .....146 E6
The Orangery
RCHPK/HAM TW10 .....156 D4
Orange St LSQ/SEVD WC2H 10 D6
WAP E1W 123 H1
Orange Tree HI ABR/ST RM4 .....57 F1
Oransay Rd IS N1 .....85 J4
Oratory La CHEL SW3 .....120 C5
Orbain Rd FUL/PGN SW6 .....139 H1
Orbel St BTSEA SW11 .....140 D2
Orb St WALW SE17 .....18 E7
Orchard Av BELV DA17 .....129 G6
CROY/NA CR0 .....198 B6
DART DA1 .....170 C2
EBED/NFELT TW14 .....133 G6
FBAR/BDGN N11 .....48 C1
HEST TW5 .....114 E6
MTCM CR4 .....195 F5
NWMAL KT3 .....176 B3
STHGT/OAK N14 .....34 C2
STHL UB1 .....114 E1
THDIT KT7 .....190 B5
TRDG/WHET N20 .....33 H4
Orchard Cl ASHF TW15 .....152 E6
BUSH WD23 .....28 D3
BXLYHN DA7 .....149 F2
CHING E4 * 37 J6
EDGW HA8 .....44 A2
FSTH SE23 .....163 K1
HOR/WEW KT19 .....206 D4
IS N1 .....85 J5
NKENS W10 .....100 C4
RSLP HA4 .....58 E4
RYNPK SW20 .....193 F1
THDIT KT7 .....190 B5
WOT/HER KT12 .....188 A4

EDGW HA8 .....44 B1
Orchard Gdns CHSGTN KT9 .....206 A2
CHSGTN KT9 .....63 G1
ESH/CLAY KT10 .....189 J5
GFD/PVL UB6 .....79 H5
Orchard Gn ORP BR6 .....201 K6
Orchard Gv CROY/NA CR0 .....198 B4
EDGW HA8 .....44 C4
KTN/HRWW/WS HA3 .....62 B2
PGE/AN SE20 .....181 H5
Orchard HI DART DA1 .....150 B6
LEW SE13 .....144 E3
Orchard La E/WMO/HCT KT8 .....189 J3
RYNPK SW20 .....176 E4
WFD IG8 .....39 G6
Orchardleigh Av PEND EN3 .....25 F3
Orchardmede WCHMH N21 .....35 K1
Orchard Ms IS N1 .....85 K5
TOOT SW17 .....160 B5
Orchard PI POP/IOD E14 .....106 C6
STMC/STPC BR5 * 186 D6
TOTM N17 .....50 B3
Orchard Ri CROY/NA CR0 .....198 B5
KUTN/CMB KT2 .....175 K4
PIN HA5 .....40 D6
RCHPK/HAM TW10 .....137 J5
Orchard Ri East BFN/LL DA15 .....147 K6
Orchard Ri West BFN/LL DA15 .....147 K6
Orchard Rd BAR EN5 .....20 D5
BELV DA17 .....129 H4
BMLY BR1 .....184 B4
BTFD TW8 .....116 D6
CHSGTN KT9 .....206 A2
DAGE RM10 .....92 C6
FELT TW13 .....153 K4
HGT N6 .....66 B4
HSLWW TW12 .....134 E6
HSLWW TW4 .....134 E6
HYS/HAR UB3 .....113 J4
KUT/HW KT1 .....175 F5
ORP BR6 .....216 B3
ORP BR6 .....217 J6
PEND EN3 .....24 E6
RCH/KEW TW9 .....137 H4
ROMW/RG RM7 .....56 E5
SCUP DA14 .....167 K6
SUN TW16 .....172 A6
SUT SM1 .....208 D3
TWK TW1 .....156 A4
WELL DA16 .....148 C3
Orchardson St STJWD NW8 .....2 A7
Orchard St DART DA1 * 171 H1
MBLAR W1H 9 G4
WALTH E17 .....69 G1
Orchard Ter EN EN1 * 36 C1
Orchardville BKHTH/KID SE3 * 145 J3
CHSWK W4 .....117 K4
EW KT17 .....207 H5
GLDGN NW11 .....64 D3
NWMAL KT3 .....176 B3
TRDG/WHET N20 .....33 F3
WCHMH N21 .....35 J3
The Orchard Vls SCUP DA14 * 186 D2
Orchard Wy ASHF TW15 .....152 C4
CROY/NA CR0 .....198 B4
EN EN1 .....24 A4
ESH/CLAY KT10 .....204 C4
RDART DA2 .....171 J7
SUT SM1 .....209 H2
Orchid Cl CHSGTN KT9 .....205 J5
EHAM E6 .....107 J4
STHL UB1 .....95 J5
Orchid Gdns HSLWW TW4 .....134 E5
Orchid Rd STHGT/OAK N14 .....34 C2
Orchid St SHB W12 .....99 J6
Orde Hall St BMSBY WC1N * 5 G7
Ordell Rd BOW E3 .....105 H1
Ordnance Cl FELT TW13 .....153 K4
Ordnance Crs GNWCH SE10 .....125 H2
Ordnance HI STJWD NW8 .....2 B1
Ordnance Ms STJWD NW8 .....2 B2
Ordnance Rd CAN/RD E16 .....106 D4
WOOL/PLUM SE18 .....127 F6
Oregon Av MNPK E12 .....72 C6
Oregon Cl NWMAL KT3 .....191 K1
Oregon Sq ORP BR6 .....201 J5
Orestes Ms KIL/WHAMP NW6 .....82 E3
Orford Gdns TWK TW1 .....156 A4
Orford Rd CAT SE6 .....164 E5
SWFD E18 .....53 F6
WALTH E17 .....69 K2
Oriel Ct HAMP NW3 * 83 G2
Oriel Dr BARN SW13 .....119 F6
Oriel Gdns CLAY IG5 .....53 K6
Oriel Rd HOM E9 .....87 F4
Oriel Wy NTHLT UB5 .....78 B5
Oriental Rd CAN/RD E16 .....126 C1
Orient St LBTH SE11 .....18 A6
Orient Wy CLPT E5 .....87 F1
LEY E10 .....69 F5
Oriole Wy THMD SE28 .....109 H6
Orion Rd MUSWH N10 .....48 A2
Orion Wy NTHWD HA6 .....26 D3
Orissa Rd WOOL/PLUM SE18 .....127 K5
Orkney St BTSEA SW11 .....141 F3
Orlando Rd CLAP SW4 .....141 H3
Orleans Rd NRWD SE19 .....180 E2
TWK TW1 .....156 C3
Orleston Ms HOLWY N7 .....85 G4
Orleston Rd HOLWY N7 .....85 G4
Orley Farm Rd HRW HA1 .....78 E1
Orme Ct BAY/PAD W2 .....101 F6
Ormeley Rd BAL SW12 .....161 G2
Orme La BAY/PAD W2 .....101 F6
Orme Rd KUT/HW KT1 .....175 J5
SUT SM1 .....209 F4
Ormerod Gdns MTCM CR4 .....179 F5
Ormesby Cl THMD SE28 .....109 K6
Ormesby Wy
KTN/HRWW/WS HA3 .....62 B3
Orme Sq BAY/PAD W2 .....101 F6
Orme Square Ga BAY/PAD W2 .....101 F6

Ormiston Gv SHB W12 ...118 E1
Ormiston Rd GNWCH SE10 ...125 K5
Ormond Av HPTN TW12 ...173 G4
Ormond Cl BMSBY WC1N ...11 F1
Ormond Crs HPTN TW12 ...173 G5
Ormonde Av HOR/WEW KT19 ...207 F6
ORP BR6 ...201 K4
Ormonde Ct EA W5 * ...2 E1
Ormonde Ga CHEL SW3 * ...120 E5
Ormonde Pl BGVA SW1W ...15 H7
Ormonde Rd BKHH IG9 ...39 G3
Ormonde Rd
MORT/ESHN SW14 ...137 J4
NTHWD HA6 ...26 B6
Ormonde Ter STJWD NW8 ...2 E1
Ormond Rd ARCH N19 ...66 C6
RCHPK/HAM TW10 ...156 E6
Ormond Yd STJS SW1Y ...10 B7
Ormsby BELMT SM2 * ...209 F5
Ormsby Gdns GFD/PVL UB6 ...96 C1
Ormsby Pl STNW/STAM N16 ...86 B1
Ormsby St BETH E2 * ...7 J1
Ormside St PECK SE15 ...123 K6
Ormskirk Rd OXHEY WD19 ...27 H6
Ornan Rd HAMP NW3 ...83 J3
Oronsay Wk IS N1 * ...85 J4
Orpheus St CMBW SE5 ...142 E2
Orpington By-Pass ORP BR6 ...217 K3
Orpington Gdns UED N18 ...36 A5
Orpington Rd CHST BR7 ...185 K6
WCHMH N21 ...35 G5
Orpwood Cl HPTN TW12 ...172 E2
Orsett Ms BAY/PAD W2 ...101 G5
Orsett St LBTH SE11 ...122 A5
Orsett Ter BAY/PAD W2 ...101 G5
WFD IG8 ...53 C4
Orsman Rd IS N1 ...7 G1
Orton Gv EN EN1 ...24 B2
Orton St WAP E1W ...216 K2
Orville Rd BTSEA SW11 ...140 C3
Orwell Cl HYS/HAR UB3 ...94 C6
Orwell Ct PLSTW E13 ...107 C1
Osbaldeston Rd
STNW/STAM N16 ...68 C6
Osberton Rd LEE/GVPK SE12 ...145 K6
Osbert St WEST SW1P ...16 C7
Osborn Cl HACK E8 ...86 C6
Osborne Av STWL/WRAY TW19 ...152 C3
Osborne Cl BECK BR3 ...198 B1
EBAR EN4 ...21 K4
BKHH IG9 ...39 F3
CRICK NW2 ...81 K4
EMPK RM11 ...75 K3
FSBYPK N4 ...67 G5
FSTGT E7 ...89 H4
HOM E9 ...87 H4
HSLW TW3 ...134 E4
KUTN/CMB KT2 ...175 F5
LEY E10 ...87 K1
PEND EN3 ...25 G3
PLMGR N13 ...35 J6
STHL UB1 ...96 C5
THHTH CR7 ...180 D5
Osborne Sq DAGW RM9 ...92 B2
Osborne Ter TOOT SW17 * ...179 F1
Osborn Gdns MLHL NW7 ...46 A3
Osborn La FSTH SE23 ...164 B2
Osborn St WCHPL E1 ...13 K2
Osborn Ter BKHTH/KID SE3 ...145 J5
Osbourne Ct
RYLN/HDSTN HA2 * ...60 B1
Oscar Faber Pl IS N1 * ...7 G3
Oscar St BROCKY SE4 ...144 D5
Oseney Crs KTTN NW5 ...84 C4
Osgood Av ORP BR6 ...217 F5
Osgood Gdns ORP BR6 ...217 F3
Osier Crs MUSWH N10 ...34 A3
Osiers Rd WAND/EARL SW18 ...139 K5
The Osiers WATW WD18 ...26 A1
Osier St WCHPL E1 ...104 E3
Osier Wy LEY E10 ...87 K1
MTCM CR4 ...194 E2
Oslac Rd CAT SE6 ...183 K1
Osman Rd ED N9 ...36 C5
HMSMTH W6 * ...119 F3
Osmond Cl RYLN/HDSTN HA2 ...60 C6
Osmond Gdns WLGTN SM6 ...210 C3
Osmund St SHB W12 * ...99 H5
Osnaburgh St CAMTN NW1 ...3 K6
Osnaburgh Ter CAMTN NW1 ...3 K6
Osney Wk MRDN SM4 ...194 C3
Osprey Cl EHAM E6 ...107 J4
HAYES BR2 ...200 D5
SUT SM1 ...208 D3
WALTH E17 ...51 G4
WAN E11 ...70 E1
WDR/YW UB7 ...112 A2
Osprey Est BERM/RHTH SE16 ...124 A4
Osprey Ms PEND EN3 ...24 E6
Ospringe Cl PGE/AN SE20 ...181 K3
Ospringe Rd KTTN NW5 ...84 C2
Osram Rd WBLY HA9 ...79 K1
Ossian Rd FSBYPK N4 ...67 F4
Ossian Ms FSBYPK N4 ...67 F4
Ossington Buildings
MHST W1U * ...9 G1
Ossington Cl BAY/PAD W2 * ...100 E6
Ossington St BAY/PAD W2 ...101 F6
Ossory Rd STHWK SE1 ...123 H5
Ossulston St CAMTN NW1 ...4 D3
Ostade Rd BRXS/STRHM SW2 ...162 A2
Osten Ms SKENS SW7 * ...120 A3
Osterberg Rd DART DA1 ...151 J5

Osterley Av ISLW TW7 ...135 J1
Osterley Cl STMC/STPC BR5 ...186 B4
Osterley Crs ISLW TW7 ...135 K2
Osterley Gdns THHTH CR7 ...180 C5
Osterley La ISLW TW7 ...115 H4
Osterley Park Rd NWDGN UB2 ...114 E3
HNWL W7 ...115 K2
Osterley Rd ISLW TW7 ...135 K2
STNW/STAM N16 ...86 A2
Ostliffe Rd PLMGR N13 ...49 H1
Oswald Rd STHL UB1 ...114 D1
Oswald's Md HOM E9 ...87 C2
Oswald St CLPT E5 ...87 F1
Oswald Ter CRICK NW2 * ...82 A1
Osward CROY/NA CRO ...213 H6
Osward Pl ED N9 ...36 C4
Osward Rd BAL SW12 ...160 E4
Oswin St LBTH SE11 ...18 B6
Oswyth Rd CMBW SE5 ...143 F3
Otford Cl BMLY BR1 ...185 F6
BXLY DA5 ...169 J1
PGE/AN SE20 ...181 K4
Otford Crs BROCKY SE4 ...164 C1
Othello Cl LBTH SE11 ...122 C5
Otis St BOW E3 ...106 B2
Otley Ct FBAR/BDGN N11 ...48 A2
Otley Dr GNTH/NBYPK IG2 ...72 B5
Otley Rd CAN/RD E16 ...107 C5
Otley Ter CLPT E5 ...69 F6
Otley Wy OXHEY WD19 ...27 G3
Otlinge Rd STMC/STPC BR5 ...202 E1
Ottawa Gdns DAGE RM10 ...93 F5
Ottaway St CLPT E5 ...86 C1
Otterbourne Rd CHING E4 ...38 B5
CROY/NA CRO ...196 D6
Otterburn Gdns ISLW TW7 ...136 B1
Otterburn St TOOT SW17 ...179 F2
Otter Cl SRTFD E15 ...88 A6
Otterden St ORP BR6 ...216 B3
Otterden St CAT SE6 ...164 D4
Otter Rd GFD/PVL UB6 ...96 C3
Otters Cl STMC/STPC BR5 ...202 E1
Otto Cl SYD SE26 * ...164 C5
Otto St WALW SE17 ...122 C6
Otway Gdns BUSH WD23 ...28 E2
Oulton Cl THMD SE28 ...109 J5
Oulton Crs BARK IG11 ...91 F4
Oulton Rd SEVS/STOTM N15 ...67 K2
Oulton Wy OXHEY WD19 ...27 K6
Oundle Av BUSH WD23 ...28 C1
Ouseley Rd BAL SW12 ...160 E3
Outer Cir CAMTN NW1 ...3 F2
Outgate Rd WLSDN NW10 ...81 H5
Outram Pl IS N1 * ...84 E6
Outram Rd CROY/NA CRO ...197 H5
EHAM E6 ...89 J6
WDGN N22 ...48 D4
Outwich St HDTCH EC3A * ...13 H3
Oval Ct EDGW HA8 * ...44 E3
Oval Pl VX/NE SW8 ...142 A1
Oval Rd CAMTN NW1 ...84 B6
CROY/NA CRO ...196 E6
Oval Rd North DAGE RM10 ...110 D1
Oval Rd South DAGE RM10 ...110 E1
The Oval BETH E2 ...104 D1
BFN/LL DA15 ...168 B2
Oval Wy LBTH SE11 ...122 A5
Overbrae BECK BR3 ...182 D2
Overbrook Wk EDGW HA8 ...44 C3
Overbury Av BECK BR3 ...182 E1
Overbury Rd FSBYPK N4 ...67 K3
Overbury St CLPT E5 ...87 F2
Overcliff Rd BROCKY SE4 ...144 D4
Overcourt Cl BFN/LL DA15 ...168 C1
Overdale Av NWMAL KT3 ...175 K5
Overdale Rd EA W5 ...116 D3
Overdown Rd CAT SE6 ...164 D5
Overhill Cottages MTCM CR4 * ...179 F5
Overhill Rd EDUL SE22 ...163 H2
PUR/KEN CR8 ...210 E7
Overhill Wy BECK BR3 ...199 G2
Overlea Rd CLPT E5 ...68 C4
Overmead BFN/LL DA15 ...167 G2
Overstand Cl BECK BR3 ...198 D2
Overstone Gdns CROY/NA CRO ...198 C4
Overstone Rd HMSMTH W6 ...119 F4
Overton Cl ISLW TW7 ...136 A2
WLSDN NW10 ...80 E4
Overton Dr CHDH RM6 ...71 F4
WAN E11 ...71 F4
Overton Rd ABYW SE2 ...128 D3
BELMT SM2 ...208 E5
BRXN/ST SW9 ...142 B3
LEY E10 ...69 H4
STHGT/OAK N14 ...22 E6
Overton's Yd CROY/NA CRO ...211 J1
Overy Liberty DART DA1 ...171 H2
Overy St DART DA1 ...171 J1
Ovesdon Av RYLN/HDSTN HA2 ...59 K5
Ovett Cl NRWD SE19 ...181 F2
Ovex Cl POP/IOD E14 ...125 F3
Ovington Gdns CHEL SW3 ...14 D5
Ovington Ms CHEL SW3 ...14 D5
Ovington Sq CHEL SW3 ...14 D5
Ovington St CHEL SW3 ...14 D5
Owen Cl CROY/NA CRO ...196 E3
CRW RM5 ...56 C2
NTHLT UB5 ...77 J4
THMD SE28 ...109 K3
YEAD UB4 ...95 F2
Owen Gdns WFD IG8 ...53 J2
Owenite St ABYW SE2 ...128 C4
Owens Rd PLMGR N13 ...49 H1
Owens Ms WAN E11 ...70 C6
Owen St FSBYE EC1V ...6 A4
Owen's Rw FSBYE EC1V ...6 K3
Owen Wk PGE/AN SE20 ...181 H3
Owen Wy WLSDN NW10 ...80 H3
Owgan Cl CMBW SE5 ...142 E1
Oxberry Av FUL/PGN SW6 ...139 H3
Oxenden Wood Rd ORP BR6 ...217 H4
Oxendon St SOHO/SHAV W1D * ...10 C6
Oxenford St PECK SE15 ...143 G4
Oxenholme CAMTN NW1 ...4 B3
Oxenpark Av WBLY HA9 ...62 A4

Oxestalls Rd DEPT SE8 ...124 B5
Oxford Rd HEST TW5 ...115 F5
HYS/HAR UB3 ...133 J1
RYNPK SW20 ...177 H5
STHGT/OAK N14 ...34 C5
Oxford Cl ED N9 ...36 C4
GPK RM2 ...75 K2
MTCM CR4 ...179 H6
NTHWD HA6 ...26 A6
Oxford Ct MANHO EC4N ...12 E5
Oxford Crs NWMAL KT3 ...192 A5
Oxford Dr RSLP HA4 ...59 C6
Oxford Gdns CHSWK W4 ...117 K5
NKENS W10 ...100 B5
TRDG/WHET N20 ...33 H5
Oxford Ga HMSMTH W6 ...119 G4
Oxford Ms BXLY DA5 ...169 H3
Oxford Rd CAR SM5 ...209 J4
EA W5 ...97 K6
ED N9 ...36 D4
FSBYPK N4 ...67 G5
HRW HA1 ...60 D2
IL IG1 ...90 C3
KIL/WHAMP NW6 ...100 E1
KTN/HRWW/WS HA3 ...43 F6
NRWD SE19 ...180 E2
PEND EN3 ...24 D6
PUT/ROE SW15 ...139 H5
SCUP DA14 ...186 C1
SRTFD E15 ...88 B4
TEDD TW11 ...173 J1
WDGN N22 ...48 E5
WFD IG8 ...53 H1
WLGTN SM6 ...210 C3
Oxford Rd North CHSWK W4 ...117 J5
Oxford Rd South CHSWK W4 ...117 J5
Oxford Rw SUN TW16 ...172 B6
Oxford Sq BAY/PAD W2 ...8 D4
Oxford St OXSTW W1C ...9 G5
Oxford Wk STHL UB1 ...114 E1
Oxford Wy FELT TW13 ...154 C6
Oxgate Centre CRICK NW2 * ...63 K5
Oxgate Court Pde CRICK NW2 * ...63 K6
Oxgate Gdns CRICK NW2 ...81 K1
Oxgate La CRICK NW2 ...63 K6
Oxhawth Crs HAYES BR2 ...201 F2
Oxhey Av OXHEY WD19 ...27 J3
Oxhey Dr NTHWD HA6 ...41 F1
Oxhey La OXHEY WD19 ...27 K5
OXHEY WD19 ...27 J3
PIN HA5 ...42 B2
Oxhey Ridge Cl NTHWD HA6 ...27 G2
Oxhey Rd OXHEY WD19 ...27 G2
Oxleas EHAM E6 ...108 B5
Oxleas Cl WELL DA16 ...147 J3
Oxleay Rd RYLN/HDSTN HA2 ...60 A5
Oxleigh Cl NWMAL KT3 ...192 B2
Oxley Cl STHWK SE1 ...123 J5
Oxleys Rd CRICK NW2 ...81 K1
Oxlow La DAGE RM10 ...92 C2
Oxonian St EDUL SE22 ...143 G5
Oxted Cl MTCM CR4 ...178 C6
Oxtoby Wy STRHM/NOR SW16 ...179 J4
Oyster Catchers Cl
CAN/RD E16 ...107 F5
Ozolins Wy WCHPL E1 ...104 E5
Ozolins Wy CAN/RD E16 ...106 D5

P

Pablo Neruda HNHL SE24 ...142 C1
Paceheath Cl CRW RM5 ...57 F2
Pace Pl WCHPL E1 ...104 D5
Pacific Cl EBED/NFELT TW14 ...153 J3
Pacific Rd CAN/RD E16 ...106 C5
Packham Cl ORP BR6 ...217 J1
Packington Sq IS N1 ...6 C1
Packington St IS N1 ...6 A1
Packmores Rd ELTH/MOT SE9 ...167 J3
Padbury Cl EBED/NFELT TW14 ...153 G3
Padbury Ct BETH E2 ...7 K5
Padcroft Rd WDR/YW UB7 ...112 A1
Paddenswick Rd HMSMTH W6 ...118 D3
Paddington Cl YEAD UB4 ...95 H3
Paddington Gn BAY/PAD W2 ...8 B2
Paddington St MHST W1U ...9 G1
Paddock Cl BKHTH/KID SE3 ...145 K4
NTHLT UB5 ...96 A1
ORP BR6 ...216 B2
OXHEY WD19 ...27 J1
SYD SE26 ...164 A6
WPK KT4 ...192 B5
Paddock Gdns NRWD SE19 ...181 F2
Paddock Rd BXLYHS DA6 ...149 F5
CRICK NW2 ...81 J1
Paddocks Cl RYLN/HDSTN HA2 ...78 B2
STMC/STPC BR5 ...202 E6
The Paddocks EA W5 ...116 B3
EBAR EN4 ...21 K4
MLHL NW7 * ...46 D2
WBLY HA9 ...62 D6
Paddock Wy CHST BR7 ...185 J3
PUT/ROE SW15 ...159 F2
Padfield Rd BRXN/ST SW9 ...142 D4
Padley Cl CHSGTN KT9 ...206 B3
Padnall Rd CHDH RM6 ...74 A1
Padstow Cl ORP BR6 ...217 F2
Padstow Rd ENC/FH EN2 ...23 H2
Padstow Wk
EBED/NFELT TW14 ...153 J3
Padua Rd PGE/AN SE20 ...181 K4
Pagden St VX/NE SW8 ...141 G2
Pagden St VX/NE SW8 ...141 G2
Pageant Crs
BERM/RHTH SE16 ...124 C1
Pageant Wk CROY/NA CRO ...212 A1
Page Av WBLY HA9 ...80 E1
Page Cl DAGW RM9 ...92 A3
HPTN TW12 ...172 D2
KTN/HRWW/WS HA3 ...62 B2
Page Crs CROY/NA CRO ...211 H3
ERITH DA8 ...150 C1
Page Green Rd
SEVS/STOTM N15 * ...68 C2

Page Green Ter
SEVS/STOTM N15 ...68 B2
Page Heath La BMLY BR1 ...184 C6
Page Heath Vls BMLY BR1 * ...184 C6
Pagehurst Rd CROY/NA CRO ...197 H4
Page Meadow MLHL NW7 ...45 J3
Page Rd EBED/NFELT TW14 ...153 C1
Page's HI MUSWH N10 ...48 A5
Page's La MUSWH N10 ...48 A5
Page's Wk STHWK SE1 ...19 H5
Page St MLHL NW7 ...46 A3
WEST SW1P ...16 D6
Paget Av SUT SM1 ...209 H1
Paget Cl HPTN TW12 ...155 J6
Paget Gdns CHST BR7 ...185 G4
Paget La ISLW TW7 ...135 J4
Paget Pl KUTN/CMB KT2 * ...175 K2
THDIT KT7 ...190 B5
Paget Ri WOOL/PLUM SE18 ...147 F1
Paget Rd HGDN/ICK UB10 ...94 A1
IL IG1 ...90 B2
STNW/STAM N16 ...67 K5
Paget St FSBYE EC1V ...6 A4
Paget Ter WOOL/PLUM SE18 ...127 G6
Pagitts Gra EBAR EN4 ...21 F2
Pagoda Av RCH/KEW TW9 ...137 G4
Pagoda Gdns BKHTH/KID SE3 ...145 G3
Pagoda Gv WNWD SE27 ...162 D4
Paignton Rd RSLP HA4 ...76 E1
SEVS/STOTM N15 ...68 A3
Paines Cl PIN HA5 ...41 J5
Paine's La PIN HA5 ...41 J4
Pain's Cl MTCM CR4 ...179 G5
Painsthorpe Rd
STNW/STAM N16 ...86 A1
Painters Ms BERM/RHTH SE16 ...123 H4
Painters Rd GNTH/NBYPK IG2 ...55 G6
Paisley Rd CAR SM5 ...194 C5
WDGN N22 ...49 H5
Paisley Ter CAR SM5 ...194 B4
Pakeman St HOLWY N7 ...85 F1
Pakenham Cl BAL SW12 ...161 F3
Pakenham St FSBYW WC1X ...5 H6
Palace Av KENS W8 ...120 A2
Palace Ct BAY/PAD W2 ...101 F6
KTN/HRWW/WS HA3 ...62 A3
Palace Court Gdns
MUSWH N10 ...48 C6
Palace Garden Ms KENS W8 ...120 A1
Palace Gdns BECK BR3 ...39 H5
Palace Gardens Ter KENS W8 ...119 K1
Palace Ga KENS W8 ...120 A2
Palace Gates Rd WDGN N22 ...48 E4
Palace Gn CROY/NA CRO ...213 H5
KENS W8 ...120 A1
Palace Gv BMLY BR1 ...184 A4
NRWD SE19 ...181 G3
Palace Ms FUL/PGN SW6 * ...139 J1
WALTH E17 ...69 H1
Palace Pde WALTH E17 * ...69 H1
Palace Rd BMLY BR1 ...184 A4
BRXS/STRHM SW2 ...162 A3
CEND/HSY/T N8 ...66 E2
E/WMO/HCT KT8 ...173 J6
FBAR/BDGN N11 ...48 B1
KUT/HW KT1 ...190 E1
NRWD SE19 ...181 G3
RSLP HA4 ...77 J2
Palace Sq NRWD SE19 ...181 G3
Palace St WESTW SW1E ...15 K4
Palace Vw BMLY BR1 ...184 A6
LEE/GVPK SE12 ...165 K4
Palace View Rd CHING E4 ...51 K1
Palamos Rd LEY E10 ...69 J5
Palatine Av STNW/STAM N16 ...86 A2
Palatine Rd STNW/STAM N16 ...86 A2
Palemead Cl FUL/PGN SW6 ...139 G2
Palermo Rd WLSDN NW10 ...99 J1
Palestine Gv WIM/MER SW19 ...178 C4
Palewell Cl STMC/STPC BR5 ...186 C5
Palewell Common Dr
MORT/ESHN SW14 ...138 A6
Palewell Pk MORT/ESHN SW14 ...138 A6
Palfrey Pl VX/NE SW8 ...142 A1
Palgrave Av STHL UB1 ...96 A6
Palgrave Gdns CAMTN NW1 ...2 D6
Palgrave Rd SHB W12 ...118 C3
Palissy St BETH E2 * ...7 J4
Pallant Wy ORP BR6 ...216 A1
Palliser Dr RAIN RM13 ...111 J4
Palliser Rd WKENS W14 ...119 H5
Pall Ml STJS SW1Y ...10 C7
Pall Mall East STJS SW1Y ...10 D7
Pall Mall Pl STJS SW1Y * ...10 B7
Palmar Crs BXLYHN DA7 ...149 H3
Palmar Rd BXLYHN DA7 ...149 H3
Palmarsh Rd STMC/STPC BR5 ...202 E1
Palm Av SCUP DA14 ...186 E2
Palm Cl LEY E10 ...87 K1
Palmeira Rd BXLYHN DA7 ...148 E4
CHEAM SM3 ...208 A2
Palmer Av BUSH WD23 ...28 A2
CHEAM SM3 ...208 A2
Palmer Cl HEST TW5 ...135 F2
NTHLT UB5 ...77 J4
WWKM BR4 ...199 G2
Palmer Crs KUT/HW KT1 ...175 F6
Palmer Dr BMLY BR1 ...201 G1
Palmer Gdns BAR EN5 ...20 B6
Palmer Pl HOLWY N7 ...85 G3
Palmer Rd BCTR RM8 ...73 K5
PLSTW E13 ...107 F3
Palmers Gv E/WMO/HCT KT8 ...189 F1
Palmers La EN EN1 ...24 E1
Palmers Rd BETH E2 ...105 F1
FBAR/BDGN N11 ...48 D1
MORT/ESHN SW14 ...137 K4
WIM/MER SW19 ...178 A5
Palmerston Crs PLMGR N13 ...49 F1
WOOL/PLUM SE18 ...127 H6
Palmerston Gv
WIM/MER SW19 ...177 K3
Palmerston Rd ACT W3 ...117 K3

BKHH IG9 ...39 G4
CAR SM5 ...209 K2
CROY/NA CRO ...196 E2
FSTGT E7 ...89 F3
HSLW TW3 ...135 H2
KIL/WHAMP NW6 ...82 D5
KTN/HRWW/WS HA3 * ...42 E6
MORT/ESHN SW14 ...137 K5
ORP BR6 ...216 C2
SUT SM1 ...209 G3
WALTH E17 ...69 G1
WDGN N22 ...49 F3
WHTN TW2 ...155 K1
WIM/MER SW19 ...177 K3
Palmerston Wy VX/NE SW8 * ...141 G1
Palmers St STJSPK SW1H ...16 C4
Palmers Whf KUT/HW KT1 * ...174 E5
Palm Gv EA W5 ...117 F3
Palm Rd ROMW/RG RM7 ...74 E2
Pamela Ct
CDALE/KGS NW9 * ...47 F2
Pams Wy HOR/WEW KT19 ...207 F3
Pancras La MANHO EC4N ...12 D4
Pancras Rd CAMTN NW1 ...4 D2
Pandian Wy KTTN NW5 ...84 D4
Pandora Rd KIL/WHAMP NW6 ...82 E4
Panfield Ms GNTH/NBYPK IG2 ...72 A3
Panfield Rd ABYW SE2 ...128 B3
Pangbourne Av NKENS W10 ...100 A4
Pangbourne Dr STAN HA7 ...43 K1
Panhard Pl STHL UB1 ...96 B6
Pank Av BAR EN5 ...21 G6
Pankhurst Av CAN/RD E16 ...126 A1
Pankhurst Cl ISLW TW7 ...136 A4
NWCR SE14 ...144 A1
Pankhurst Rd WOT/HER KT12 ...188 B4
Pankridge OXHEY WD19 ...27 H4
Panmure Cl HBRY N5 ...85 H2
Panmure Rd SYD SE26 ...163 J5
Pansy Gdns SHB W12 ...99 J6
Panther Dr WLSDN NW10 ...81 F3
Pantiles Cl PLMGR N13 ...49 H1
The Pantiles BMLY BR1 ...184 D6
BUSH WD23 ...28 C1
BXLYHN DA7 ...149 G1
Panton Cl CROY/NA CRO ...196 C5
Panton St STJS SW1Y ...10 D6
Paper Buildings EMB EC4Y * ...11 K5
Papermill Cl CAR SM5 ...210 A2
Papillons Wk BKHTH/KID SE3 ...145 K3
Papworth Gdns HOLWY N7 ...85 F3
Papworth Wy
BRXS/STRHM SW2 ...162 B2
Parade Ms BRXS/STRHM SW2 ...162 A4
Parade Ter CDALE/KGS NW9 * ...63 J3
The Parade BROCKY SE4 * ...144 C2
BTSEA SW11 ...140 E5
CAR SM5 ...209 K3
CROY/NA CRO ...195 K3
DART DA1 ...150 C6
EA W5 ...98 A6
EDUL SE22 ...143 F4
ESH/CLAY KT10 ...204 B3
FSBYPK N4 ...67 G6
GFD/PVL UB6 * ...96 C5
KUT/HW KT1 ...175 F5
OXHEY WD19 ...27 J1
PGE/AN SE20 * ...181 K4
RCH/KEW TW9 ...137 H4
SUT SM1 ...208 D3
SYD SE26 * ...163 J6
WLGTN SM6 ...210 C3
WLCTN SM6 * ...211 F3
Paradise Pas HOLWY N7 * ...85 F4
Paradise Rd CLAP SW4 ...141 K3
RCH/KEW TW9 ...137 F6
Paradise Rw BETH E2 * ...104 D2
Paradise St BERM/RHTH SE16 ...123 J2
Paragon Cl CAN/RD E16 ...106 E5
Paragon Gv BRYLDS KT5 ...191 G3
Paragon Ms STHWK SE1 ...19 F6
The Paragon BKHTH/KID SE3 ...145 K3
HACK E8 ...86 D4
Parbury Rd FSTH SE23 ...164 B1
Parchmore Rd THHTH CR7 ...180 C5
Parchmore Wy THHTH CR7 ...180 C5
Pardoe Rd LEY E10 ...70 A3
Pardon St FSBYE EC1V ...6 B7
Pardoner St STHWK SE1 ...19 K6
Parfett St WCHPL E1 ...13 K3
Parfitt Cl HAMP NW3 ...65 G2
Parfrey St HMSMTH W6 ...119 F6
Parham Dr GNTH/NBYPK IG2 ...72 B3
Parish Cl HCH RM12 ...75 J4
Parish Gate Dr BFN/LL DA15 ...167 K1
Parish La PGE/AN SE20 ...182 A3
Parish Whf WOOL/PLUM SE18 ...126 D4
Park Ap BERM/RHTH SE16 ...123 K3
WELL DA16 ...148 C5
Park Av BARK IG11 ...90 C4
BMLY BR1 ...183 K4
CAR SM5 ...210 A4
CRICK NW2 ...81 K4
EHAM E6 ...90 A6
EN EN1 ...24 B6
FNCH N3 ...47 F4
GLDGN NW11 ...65 F5
HSLW TW3 ...155 G5
IL IG1 ...72 B6
MORT/ESHN SW14 ...138 A5
ORP BR6 ...202 B6
PEND EN3 ...25 F1
PLMGR N13 ...35 H4
RSLP HA4 ...58 E4
SRTFD E15 ...88 C4
STHL UB1 ...114 E1
STHCT/OAK N14 ...34 C5
WDGN N22 ...48 E5
WFD IG8 ...53 G1
WLSDN NW10 ...99 F2
WWKM BR4 ...199 F6
Park Av East EW KT17 ...207 H4

Park Avenue Ms MTCM CR4......179 G3
Park Av North CEND/HSY/T N8......66 D1
WLSDN NW10......81 K3
Park Avenue Rd TOTM N17......50 D3
Park Av South CEND/HSY/T N8......66 D1
Park Av West EW KT17......207 J4
Park Bvd GPK RM2......57 H4
Park Cha WBLY HA9......80 B2
Park Cl CAR SM5......209 K4
CRICK NW2......81 J1
HOM E9......86 E6
HPTN TW12......173 H4
HSLW TW3......135 H6
KTN/HRWW/WS HA3......42 E4
KUTN/CMB KT2......175 H4
NFNCH/WDSPK N12 *......33 H6
SKENS SW7 *......14 E3
WKENS W14......119 J3
WLSDN NW10......98 B2
Park Cottages FNCH N3 *......46 D5
Park Ct DUL SE21 *......162 E5
NWMAL KT3......192 A1
SYD SE26 *......181 J2
WBLY HA9......80 A3
Park Crs EMPK RM11......75 J4
ENC/FH EN2......23 K5
ERITH DA8......129 K6
FNCH N3......47 F3
KTN/HRWW/WS HA3......42 E4
REGST W1B......3 J7
WHTN TW2......155 J3
Park Crescent Ms East
GTPST W1W......3 K7
Park Crescent Ms West
CAVSQ/HST W1G......3 J7
Park Cft EDGW HA8......44 E4
Parkcroft Rd LEE/GVPK SE12......165 J2
Parkdale Crs WPK KT4......207 F1
Parkdale Rd
WOOL/PLUM SE18......127 K5
Park Dr ACT W3......117 H3
CHARL SE7......126 D6
DAGE RM10......92 E1
GLDGN NW11......65 F5
KTN/HRWW/WS HA3......42 D2
MORT/ESHN SW14......138 A6
ROM RM1......75 F1
RYLN/HDSTN HA2......60 A4
WCHMH N21......35 J1
Park End BMLY BR1......183 J4
HAMP NW3......83 J2
Park End Rd ROM RM1......75 G1
Parker Cl CAN/RD E16......126 D1
CAR SM5......209 K4
Parker Ms HOL/ALD WC2B *......11 F3
Parke Rd BARN SW13......138 D2
Parker Rd CROY/NA CR0......211 J2
Parker's Rw STHWK SE1......19 K3
Parker St CAN/RD E16......126 D1
HOL/ALD WC2B......11 F3
Parker Ter FSTH SE23......164 C4
Parkes Rd CHIG IG7......55 F1
Park Farm Cl EFNCH N2......47 G6
PIN HA5......59 F2
Park Farm Rd BMLY BR1......184 D4
KUTN/CMB KT2......175 F3
Parkfield Av FELT TW13......153 K5
MORT/ESHN SW14......138 B5
NTHLT UB5......95 H1
RYLN/HDSTN HA2......42 C5
Parkfield Cl EDGW HA8......44 D2
NTHLT UB5......95 J1
Parkfield Crs FELT TW13......153 K5
RSLP HA4......59 J6
RYLN/HDSTN HA2......42 C5
Parkfield Dr NTHLT UB5......95 H1
Parkfield Gdns
RYLN/HDSTN HA2......42 B6
Parkfield Pde FELT TW13 *......153 K5
Parkfield Rd FELT TW13......153 K5
NTHLT UB5......95 J1
NWCR SE14......144 C2
RYLN/HDSTN HA2......78 C1
WLSDN NW10......81 J5
Parkfields CROY/NA CR0......198 C5
PUT/ROE SW15......139 F5
Parkfields Av CDALE/KGS NW9......63 F5
RYNPK SW20......176 E4
Parkfields Cl CAR SM5......210 A2
Parkfields Rd KUTN/CMB KT2......175 G1
Parkfield St IS N1......5 K2
Parkfield Wy HAYES BR2......200 E3
Park Gdns CDALE/KGS NW9......44 D6
ERITH DA8......130 A4
KUTN/CMB KT2......175 G1
Parkgate BKHTH/KID SE3......145 J4
Park Ga EA W5......97 K4
EFNCH N2......47 H6
WCHMH N21......35 F2
Parkgate Av EBAR EN4......21 G2
Parkgate Cl KUTN/CMB KT2......175 J2
Park Gate Ct HPTN TW12 *......173 H1
Parkgate Crs EBAR EN4......21 G2
Parkgate Gdns
MORT/ESHN SW14......138 A6
Parkgate Ms HGT N6......66 C4
Parkgate Rd BTSEA SW11......140 D1
WLGTN SM6......210 A3
Park Gates RYLN/HDSTN HA2 *......78 A2
Park Gv BMLY BR1......184 A4
BXLYHN DA7......149 K5
EDGW HA8......44 B1
FBAR/BDGN N11......48 D3
SRTFD E15......88 E6
Park Grove Rd WAN E11......70 C6
Park Hall Rd DUL SE21......162 E5
EFNCH N2......65 J1
Parkham St BTSEA SW11......140 D2
Park Hl BMLY BR1......200 D1
CAR SM5......209 K4
CLAP SW4......141 J6
EA W5......97 K4
FSTH SE23......163 K4
RCHPK/HAM TW10......157 G1
Park Hill Cl CAR SM5......209 K3
Park Hill Ri CROY/NA CR0......212 B1
Parkhill Rd BFN/LL DA15......167 K5
BXLY DA5......169 G2
CHING E4......38 A2
Park Hill Rd CROY/NA CR0......212 A2
Parkhill Rd HAMP NW3......83 K4
Park Hill Rd HAYES BR2......183 H5
WLGTN SM6......210 B5
Park Hill Wk HAMP NW3......83 K3
Parkholme Rd HACK E8......86 C4
Park House Gdns TWK TW1......136 D6
Parkhouse St CMBW SE5......142 E1
Parkhurst Gdns BXLY DA5......169 H2
Parkhurst Rd BXLY DA5......169 H2
FBAR/BDGN N11......34 A6
HOLWY N7......84 E2
MNPK E12......90 A2
SUT SM1......209 H2
TOTM N17......50 C5
WALTH E17 *......69 G1
WDGN N22......49 F3
Parkland Av ROM RM1......57 H5
Parkland Gv ASHF TW15......152 D6
ISLW TW7......136 A2
Parkland Md BMLY BR1......185 G6
Parkland Rd ASHF TW15......152 D6
WDGN N22......49 F5
WFD IG8......53 F3
Parklands BRYLDS KT5......191 G2
BUSH WD23 *......28 C1
HGT N6......66 B4
Parklands Cl EBAR EN4......21 H1
GNTH/NBYPK IG2......72 C4
MORT/ESHN SW14......137 K6
Parklands Dr FNCH N3......46 C6
Parklands Pde HEST TW5 *......134 C3
Parklands Rd
STRHM/NOR SW16......179 G1
Parklands Wy WPK KT4......192 B6
Park La CAR SM5......210 A3
CHDH RM6......73 K3
CHEAM SM3......208 C4
CROY/NA CR0......211 K1
EMPK RM11......75 J4
HCH RM12......93 K4
HEST TW5......133 K1
MYFR/PKLN W1K......9 G6
RCH/KEW TW9......136 E5
RYLN/HDSTN HA2......78 B1
SRTFD E15 *......88 A6
STAN HA7......29 G5
TEDD TW11......174 A2
TOTM N17......50 C3
UED N18......36 B5
WBLY HA9......80 B2
YEAD UB4......94 C4
Park Lane Cl TOTM N17......50 C3
Parklea Cl CDALE/KGS NW9......45 G4
Parkleigh Rd WIM/MER SW19......178 A5
Parkleys RCHPK/HAM TW10......156 E6
Parkleys Pde
RCHPK/HAM TW10 *......156 E6
Park Md BFN/LL DA15......148 B6
Parkmead PUT/ROE SW15......158 E1
Park Md RYLN/HDSTN HA2......78 B1
Parkmead Gdns MLHL NW7......45 H2
Park Ms GNWCH SE10......125 J5
NKENS W10......100 C1
RAIN RM13......93 J4
STWL/WRAY TW19......152 C2
Park Pde ACT W3 *......117 H3
HYS/HAR UB3 *......94 C5
WLSDN NW10......99 H1
Park Piazza LEW SE13......165 G1
Park Pl ACT W3......117 H4
BMLY BR1 *......184 A4
EA W5......116 E1
HPTN TW12......173 H2
IS N1......85 K6
POP/IOD E14......124 D1
WBLY HA9......80 B2
WHALL SW1A......16 A1
Park Place Vls BAY/PAD W2......101 G4
Park Ridings CEND/HSY/T N8......49 G6
Park Ri KTN/HRWW/WS HA3......42 E4
Park Rise Rd FSTH SE23......164 B3
Park Rd ALP/SUD HA0......80 A4
BAR EN5......20 D5
BECK BR3......182 C3
BMLY BR1......184 A4
BRYLDS KT5......191 G3
BUSH WD23......28 A1
CAMTN NW1......3 F7
CDALE/KGS NW9......63 F4
CDALE/KGS NW9......63 J4
CEND/HSY/T N8......66 E3
CEND/HSY/T N8......67 H1
CHEAM SM3......208 C4
CHST BR7......185 G2
CHSWK W4......118 A6
DART DA1......171 K2
E/WMO/HCT KT8......189 H1
EBAR EN4......21 H5
EFNCH N2......47 H6
ESH/CLAY KT10......204 B2
FBAR/BDGN N11......48 D3
FELT TW13......154 C6
HDN NW4......63 J4
HNWL W7......97 F6
HPTN TW12......173 H1
HSLW TW3......135 H6
IL IG1......90 D1
ISLW TW7......136 C2
KUT/HW KT1......174 D4
KUTN/CMB KT2......175 G1
LEY E10......69 J5
MNPK E12......71 F6
MNPK E12......89 H2
NWMAL KT3......192 A1
PLSTW E13......89 G6
RCHPK/HAM TW10......157 G1
SNWD SE25......197 F1
SRTFD E15......88 E6
STHGT/OAK N14......34 D2
STJWD NW8......2 D5
STMC/STPC BR5......202 D3
SUN TW16......172 A3
TEDD TW11......174 A3
TWK TW1......156 D1
UED N18......36 B6
WALTH E17......69 H2
WIM/MER SW19......178 C2
WLGTN SM6......195 G6
WLGTN SM6......210 B3
WLSDN NW10 *......81 G6
YEAD UB4......94 C4
Park Rd East ACT W3......117 K2
Park Rd North ACT W3......117 J2
CHSWK W4......118 A6
Park Rw GNWCH SE10......125 G6
Park Royal Rd WLSDN NW10......98 E2
Parkshot RCH/KEW TW9......136 E5
Parkside BECK BR3 *......182 E5
Park Side BKHH IG9......39 F4
Parkside BKHTH/KID SE3 *......145 J1
CHEAM SM3......208 C4
Park Side CRICK NW2......81 J1
Parkside FNCH N3......47 F4
HPTN TW12......173 J1
Park Side HYS/HAR UB3 *......94 C6
Parkside MLHL NW7......45 J2
OXHEY WD19 *......27 G1
SCUP DA14......168 C4
WIM/MER SW19......177 G1
Parkside Av BMLY BR1......200 D1
BXLYHN DA7......150 A3
ROM RM1......57 F5
WIM/MER SW19......177 G1
Parkside Cl PGE/AN SE20......181 K3
Parkside Crs BRYLDS KT5......191 K3
HOLWY N7......85 G1
Parkside Cross BXLYHN DA7......150 B3
Parkside Dr EDGW HA8......30 C5
Parkside Est HOM E9 *......87 F6
Parkside Gdns EBAR EN4......33 K3
WIM/MER SW19......159 G6
Parkside Pde DART DA1 *......150 C3
Parkside Rd BELV DA17......129 J4
HSLW TW3......135 G6
NTHWD HA6......40 D1
Parkside St BTSEA SW11......141 F2
Parkside Ter ORP BR6 *......202 B5
UED N18 *......35 K6
Parkside Wy RYLN/HDSTN HA2......60 B1
Park Sq East CAMTN NW1......3 J6
Park Square Ms CAMTN NW1......3 J7
Park Sq West CAMTN NW1......3 J6
Parkstead Rd PUT/ROE SW15......138 D6
Park Steps BAY/PAD W2 *......8 D5
Parkstone Av UED N18......50 B1
Parkstone Rd PECK SE15 *......143 H3
WALTH E17......52 A6
Park St CROY/NA CR0......196 D6
MYFR/PKLN W1K......9 G6
STHWK SE1......12 C7
TEDD TW11......173 K2
Park Ter CAR SM5 *......209 J1
PEND EN3 *......25 G1
WPK KT4......192 D5
The Park CAR SM5......209 K3
EA W5......116 E1
GLDGN NW11......65 F5
HGT N6......66 A4
SCUP DA14......186 A1
Parkthorne Cl
RYLN/HDSTN HA2 *......60 B3
Parkthorne Dr
RYLN/HDSTN HA2......60 A3
Parkthorne Rd BAL SW12......161 J2
Park Vw ACT W3......98 E4
NWMAL KT3......176 C6
PIN HA5......41 K4
WBLY HA9......80 D3
WCHMH N21......35 F2
Park View Ct
NFNCH/WDSPK N12 *......33 J6
Park View Crs
FBAR/BDGN N11......34 B6
Park View Dr MTCM CR4......178 C5
Park View Est HBRY N5 *......85 J2
Parkview Gdns CLAY IG5......71 K1
Park View Gdns HDN NW4......64 A2
WDGN N22 *......49 G4
Parkview Ms RAIN RM13......111 K4
Park View Rd CRICK NW2......81 H2
Parkview Rd CROY/NA CR0......197 H5
Park View Rd EA W5......98 A4
ELTH/MOT SE9......167 G4
FNCH N3......47 F4
PIN HA5......41 F1
STHL UB1......115 F1
TOTM N17......50 D5
WELL DA16......148 C4
Park Village East CAMTN NW1......3 K2
Park Village West CAMTN NW1......3 J2
Park Vls TOOT SW17 *......178 D1
Parkville Rd FUL/PGN SW6......139 J1
Park Vis GNWCH SE10......125 G6
Park Vista Apartments
CAN/RD E16......106 D2
Park Wk WBPTN SW10......120 B6
Park Wy BXLY DA5......170 C5
Parkway CROY/NA CR0......214 A6
Park Wy E/WMO/HCT KT8......173 H6
EBED/NFELT TW14......154 A2
EDGW HA8......44 D4
ENC/FH EN2......23 G3
Parkway ERITHM DA18......129 F3
GDMY/SEVK IG3......91 F1
Park Wy GLDGN NW11......64 C2
Parkway GPK RM2......57 H5
RAIN RM13......111 J3
Park Wy RSLP HA4......58 E5
Parkway RYNPK SW20......193 G1
STHGT/OAK N14......34 E4
Park Wy TRDG/WHET N20......33 K6
Parkway WFD IG8......53 G1
The Parkway HEST TW5......113 K6
NTHLT UB5......95 H2
NWDGN UB2......114 A3
Park West BAY/PAD W2......8 D3
Park West Pl BAY/PAD W2......8 D3
Parkwood BECK BR3......182 D3
Parkwood Av ESH/CLAY KT10......189 H5
Parkwood Ms HGT N6......66 B3
Parkwood Rd BXLY DA5......169 G2
ISLW TW7......136 A2
WIM/MER SW19......177 J1
Parliament Ct WCHPL E1 *......13 H2
Parliament Hl HAMP NW3......83 J2
Parliament Hill Flds
KTTN NW5 *......84 A1
Parliament Sq WEST SW1P......16 E3
Parliament St WHALL SW1A......16 E2
Parma Crs BTSEA SW11......140 E5
Parmiter St BETH E2......104 D1
Parnell Cl EDGW HA8......30 D6
SHB W12......118 E3
Parnell Rd BOW E3......87 H6
Parnham St POP/IOD E14 *......105 G5
Parolles Rd ARCH N19......66 C5
Paroma Rd BELV DA17......129 H3
Parr Av EW KT17......207 K6
Parr Cl ED N9......36 D6
Parr Rd EHAM E6......89 H6
STAN HA7......43 K4
Parrs Cl SAND/SEL CR2......211 K6
Parr's Pl HPTN TW12......173 F3
Parr St IS N1......6 E2
Parry Av EHAM E6......107 K5
Parry Cl EW KT17......207 K5
Parry Pl WOOL/PLUM SE18......127 G4
Parry Rd NKENS W10......100 C2
SNWD SE25......181 F6
Parry St VX/NE SW8......121 K6
Parsifal Rd KIL/WHAMP NW6......82 E3
Parsloes Av DAGW RM9......92 A3
Parsonage Cl HYS/HAR UB3......94 D5
Parsonage Gdns ENC/FH EN2......23 J3
Parsonage La ENC/FH EN2......23 K3
SCUP DA14......169 G6
Parsonage Manorway
BELV DA17......129 H6
Parsonage St POP/IOD E14......125 F4
Parsons Crs EDGW HA8......30 C5
Parsons Gn FUL/PGN SW6......139 K2
Parsons Green La
FUL/PGN SW6......139 K2
Parsons Gv EDGW HA8......30 C5
Parsons La RDART DA2......170 E5
Parson's Md CROY/NA CR0......196 C5
E/WMO/HCT KT8......173 H6
Parsons Rd PLSTW E13......107 G1
Parson St HDN NW4......46 A6
Parthenia Rd FUL/PGN SW6......139 K2
Partingdale La MLHL NW7......46 B1
Partington Cl ARCH N19......66 D5
Partridge Cl BAR EN5......32 A1
BUSH WD23 *......28 C3
CAN/RD E16......107 H4
STAN HA7......30 A6
Partridge Dr ORP BR6......216 C1
Partridge Gn ELTH/MOT SE9......167 F5
Partridge Rd HPTN TW12......172 E2
SCUP DA14......167 K5
Partridge Sq EHAM E6......107 J4
Partridge Wy WDGN N22......48 E4
Pasadena Cl HYS/HAR UB3......113 K2
Pascal St VX/NE SW8......141 J1
Pascoe Rd LEW SE13......145 G6
Pasley Cl WALW SE17......122 D5
Pasquier Rd WALTH E17......51 G6
Passey Pl ELTH/MOT SE9......166 E1
Passfield Dr POP/IOD E14......105 K4
Passmore Gdns
FBAR/BDGN N11......48 D2
Passmore St BGVA SW1W......15 G7
Pasteur Cl CDALE/KGS NW9......45 G5
Pasteur Gdns UED N18......49 J1
Paston Cl WLGTN SM6......210 C1
Paston Crs LEE/GVPK SE12......166 A2
Pastor St LBTH SE11......18 B6
Pasture Cl ALP/SUD HA0......79 H1
BUSH WD23......28 C2
Pasture Rd ALP/SUD HA0......61 H6
CAT SE6......165 J3
DAGW RM9......92 B3
The Pastures OXHEY WD19......27 F2
TRDG/WHET N20......32 D3
Patcham Ter VX/NE SW8......141 G2
Patching Wy YEAD UB4......95 J4
Paternoster Rw STP EC4M......12 C4
Paternoster Sq STP EC4M......12 B4
Pater St KENS W8......119 K3
Pates Manor Dr
EBED/NFELT TW14......153 G2
Pathfield Rd
STRHM/NOR SW16......179 J2
The Path WIM/MER SW19......178 A4
The Pathway OXHEY WD19......27 H3
Patience Rd BTSEA SW11......140 D3
Patio Cl CLAP SW4......161 J1
Patmore St VX/NE SW8......141 H2
Patmore Wy CRW RM5......56 D1
Patmos Rd BRXN/ST SW9......142 C1
Paton Cl BOW E3......105 J2
Patricia Ct WELL DA16......148 C1
Patricia Vls TOTM N17 *......50 D4
Patrick Rd PLSTW E13......107 G2
Patriot Sq BETH E2......104 D1
Patrol Pl CAT SE6......164 E1
Patshull Pl KTTN NW5......84 C4
Patshull Rd KTTN NW5......84 C4
Pattenden Rd CAT SE6......164 C3
Patten Rd WAND/EARL SW18......160 D2
Patterdale Cl BMLY BR1......183 H2
Patterdale Rd PECK SE15......143 K1
Patterson Rd NRWD SE19......181 G2
Pattina Wk BERM/RHTH SE16......124 B1
Pattison Rd CRICK NW2......82 E1
Paul Cl SRTFD E15......88 C5
Paulet Rd CMBW SE5......142 C3
Paulet Wy WLSDN NW10 *......81 G5
Paul Gdns CROY/NA CR0......197 G6
Paulhan Rd
KTN/HRWW/WS HA3......61 K1
Paulin Dr WCHMH N21......35 G2
Pauline Crs WHTN TW2......155 H3
Paulinus Cl STMC/STPC BR5......186 D6
Paul Julius Cl POP/IOD E14......106 B6
Paul Robeson Cl EHAM E6......108 A2
Paul St SDTCH EC2A......7 G6
SRTFD E15......88 C6
Paultons Sq CHEL SW3......120 C6
Paultons St CHEL SW3......120 C6
Pauntley St ARCH N19......66 C5
Paveley Dr BTSEA SW11......140 D1
Paveley St STJWD NW8......2 D6
Pavement Sq CROY/NA CR0......197 H5
The Pavement CLAP SW4......141 H5
EA W5 *......117 F3
TEDD TW11 *......174 C3
WAN E11 *......70 A5
WIM/MER SW19 *......177 J2
WNWD SE27 *......162 D6
Pavet Cl DAGE RM10......92 D4
Pavilion Ldg
RYLN/HDSTN HA2 *......60 D5
Pavilion Ms FNCH N3......46 E6
Pavilion Pde SHB W12 *......100 A5
Pavilion Rd IL IG1......71 K4
KTBR SW1X......15 F5
Pavilion St KTBR SW1X......15 F5
The Pavilion VX/NE SW8 *......141 J1
Pavilion Wy EDGW HA8......44 E3
RSLP HA4......59 G6
Pavillion Sq TOOT SW17......160 D5
Pavillion Ter SHB W12 *......100 A5
Pawleyne Cl PGE/AN SE20......181 K3
Pawsey Cl PLSTW E13......88 E6
Pawson's Rd THHTH CR7......196 D3
Paxford Rd ALP/SUD HA0......61 H6
Paxton Cl RCH/KEW TW9......137 G3
WOT/HER KT12......188 B4
Paxton Pl WNWD SE27......163 F6
Paxton Rd BMLY BR1......183 K3
CHSWK W4......118 B6
FSTH SE23......164 B5
TOTM N17......50 C3
Paxton Ter PIM SW1V......121 G6
Payne Cl BARK IG11......90 E5
Paynell Ct BKHTH/KID SE3......145 H4
Payne Rd BOW E3......105 K1
Paynesfield Av
MORT/ESHN SW14......138 A4
Paynesfield Rd BUSH WD23......29 F2
Payne St DEPT SE8......144 C1
Paynes Wk HMSMTH W6......119 H6
Payzes Gdns WFD IG8 *......52 D2
Peabody Av PIM SW1V *......121 G5
Peabody Cl CROY/NA CR0......197 K5
GNWCH SE10 *......144 E2
PIM SW1V......121 G5
Peabody Cottages
HNHL SE24 *......162 D2
Peabody Est BTSEA SW11 *......140 D5
CHEL SW3......120 D6
CLKNW EC1R *......5 K7
CMBW SE5 *......142 E2
FUL/PGN SW6 *......119 K6
HMSMTH W6 *......119 F5
HNHL SE24......162 D2
NKENS W10 *......100 A4
STHWK SE1 *......11 K7
STHWK SE1 *......12 C7
STLK EC1Y *......6 D7
TOTM N17 *......50 A4
Peabody Hl DUL SE21......162 C3
Peabody Sq IS N1 *......85 J6
Peabody Ter CLKNW EC1R *......5 K7
Peace Cl GFD/PVL UB6......78 D6
SNWD SE25......197 F1
STHGT/OAK N14......22 B6
Peace Gv WBLY HA9......80 D1
Peace St WOOL/PLUM SE18......127 F6
Peaches Cl BELMT SM2......208 C5
Peach Gv WAN E11......88 B1
Peach Rd FELT TW13......153 K3
NKENS W10......100 B2
Peachum Rd BKHTH/KID SE3......125 J6
Peacock Av
EBED/NFELT TW14......153 G3
Peacock Cl CHING E4......51 H3
Peacock St WALW SE17......18 B7
Peacock Yd WALW SE17......18 B7
Peaketon Av REDBR IG4......71 H2
Peak Hl SYD SE26......163 K6
Peak Hill Av SYD SE26......163 K6
Peak Hill Gdns SYD SE26......163 K6
The Peak SYD SE26......163 K5
Peal Gdns WEA W13......97 G2
Peall Rd CROY/NA CR0......196 A3
Pearce Cl MTCM CR4......179 F5
Pearcefield Av FSTH SE23......163 K3
Pear Cl CDALE/KGS NW9......63 F1
NWCR SE14......144 B1
Pearcroft Rd WAN E11......70 B6
Peardon St VX/NE SW8......141 G4
Peareswood Gdns STAN HA7......43 K4
Peareswood Rd ERITH DA8......150 C2
Pearfield Rd FSTH SE23......164 B5
Pearl Cl CRICK NW2......64 B4
EHAM E6......108 A5
Pearl Rd WALTH E17......51 J6
Pearl St WAP E1W......123 J1
Pearman St STHWK SE1......17 K4
Pear Pl STHWK SE1......17 J2
Pear Rd WAN E11......88 B1
Pearscroft Ct FUL/PGN SW6......140 A2
Pearscroft Rd FUL/PGN SW6......140 A3
Pearse St PECK SE15......123 F6
Pearson Cl BAR EN5......21 F4
Pearson's NWCR SE14......144 D2
Pearson's Rd NWCR SE14 *......144 D2
Pearson St BETH E2......7 J2
Pearson Wy DART DA1......171 J4
MTCM CR4......179 F4
Pears Rd HSLW TW3......135 J4
Peartree Av TOOT SW17......178 E2
Pear Tree Cl CHSGTN KT9......206 C3
ERITH DA8......150 A2
Peartree Cl HAYES BR2......200 C2
Pear Tree Cl MTCM CR4......178 E6
Pear Tree Ct CLKNW EC1R......5 K7
Peartree Gdns BCTR RM8......91 H3
ROMW/RG RM7......56 D5
Peartree La WAP E1W *......104 E6
Peartree Rd EN EN1......24 A4
Peartree St FSBYE EC1V......6 B6
Peartree Wy GNWCH SE10......125 K4

Pearwood Cottages
STAN HA7 * 29 J4
Peary Pl BETH E2.................104 E2
Pease Cl HCH RM12................93 K5
Peasmead Ter CHING E4 *..........38 A6
Peatfield Cl BFN/LL DA15.........167 K5
Pebworth Rd HRW HA1..............61 G6
Peckarmans Wd SYD SE26..........163 H5
Peckett Sq HBRY N5 *.............85 J2
Peckford Pl BRXN/ST SW9.........142 B4
Peckham Gv PECK SE15............143 F7
Peckham High St PECK SE15.......143 H2
Peckham Hill St PECK SE15.......143 H1
Peckham Park Rd PECK SE15.......143 H1
Peckham Rd CMBW SE5............143 F2
Peckham Rye EDUL SE22...........143 H5
Pecks Yd WCHPL E1 *..............13 J1
Peckwater St KTTN NW5............84 C3
Pedlars Wk HOLWY N7 *............84 E3
Pedley Rd BCTR RM8...............73 J5
Pedley St WCHPL E1................7 K7
Pedro St CLPT E5.................87 F1
Peek Crs WIM/MER SW19..........177 C1
Peel Cl CHING E4.................38 A3
ED N9...........................36 C5
Peel Dr CDALE/KGS NW9............45 H6
CLAY IG5........................53 J6
Peel Gv BETH E2.................104 E1
Peel Pas KENS W8................119 J1
Peel Pl CLAY IG5.................53 J5
Peel Prec KIL/WHAMP NW6.........100 D1
KIL/WHAMP NW6..................100 E2
KTN/HRWW/WS HA3.................42 E6
Peel Rd SWFD E18.................53 D4
SWFD E18........................52 D4
Peel St KENS W8.................119 K1
Peerglow Est PEND EN3 *...........24 E6
Peerless St FSBYE EC1V.............6 E5
Pegamoid Rd UED N18...............36 E5
Pegasus Cl STNW/STAM N16 *.......85 K2
Pegasus Ct RTFD TW8.............117 C5
Pegasus Pl FUL/PGN SW6 *........139 K2
LBTH SE11......................122 B6
Pegasus Rd CROY/NA CRO...........211 C4
Pegley Gdns LEE/GVPK SE12.......165 K4
Pegwell St WOOL/PLUM SE18.......147 K1
Pekin St POP/IOD E14............105 J5
Peldon Wk IS N1 *................85 H6
Pelham Av BARK IG11...............91 F6
Pelham Cottages BXLY DA5 *......169 H4
Pelham Crs SKENS SW7.............14 C7
Pelham Pl SKENS SW7..............14 C6
Pelham Rd BXLYHN DA7............149 H4
IL IG1...........................72 A6
PGE/AN SE20....................181 K5
SEVS/STOTM N15..................68 B1
SWFD E18........................53 F6
WDGN N22........................49 G5
WIM/MER SW19...................177 K3
Pelhams Cl ESH/CLAY KT10.........204 A2
Pelhams St SKENS SW7..............14 C6
Pelhams Wk ESH/CLAY KT10.........204 A3
Pelier St WALW SE17.............122 D6
Pelinore Rd CAT SE6.............165 H4
Pellant Rd FUL/PGN SW6.........139 H1
Pellatt Gv WDGN N22..............49 G4
Pellatt Rd EDUL SE22............143 G6
WBLY HA9........................62 A6
Pellerin Rd STNW/STAM N16.......86 A3
Pellings Cl HAYES BR2...........183 H6
Pelling St POP/IOD E14..........105 H5
Pellipar Cl PLMGR N13............35 G5
Pellipar Rd WOOL/PLUM SE18.....126 E5
Pelly Rd PLSTW E13...............106 E1
SRTFD E15........................88 E6
Pelter St BETH E2.................7 J4
Pelton Rd GNWCH SE10............125 H5
Pembar Av WALTH E17 *.............51 G6
Pemberley Cha
HOR/WEW KT19...................206 D3
Pemberley Cl HOR/WEW KT19......206 D3
Pember Rd WLSDN NW10...........100 B2
Pemberton Av GPK RM2.............57 K6
Pemberton Gdns ARCH N19..........84 C1
CHDH RM6........................73 K3
Pemberton Pl ESH/CLAY KT10 *...204 C1
HACK E8.........................86 D5
Pemberton Rd
E/WMO/HCT KT8..................189 H1
HRN N4..........................67 H2
Pemberton Rw
FLST/FETLN EC4A.................11 K3
Pemberton Ter ARCH N19...........84 C1
Pembridge Av WHTN TW2...........154 E3
Pembridge Crs NTGHL W11.........100 D6
Pembridge Gdns
BAY/PAD W2.....................100 E6
Pembridge Ms NTGHL W11.........100 E6
Pembridge Pl BAY/PAD W2.........100 E6
Pembridge Rd NTGHL W11.........119 K1
Pembridge Sq BAY/PAD W2........100 E6
Pembridge Vls BAY/PAD W2.......100 E6
Pembroke Av BRYLDS KT5.........191 J2
EN N1...........................24 D2
IS N1............................84 E6
KTN/HRWW/WS HA3.................43 H6
PIN HA5.........................59 K6
Pembroke Cl ERITH DA8...........129 K4
KTBR SW1X.......................15 H3
KENS W8........................119 J4
Pembroke Ms KENS W8.............119 K3
MUSWH N10.......................48 A4
Pembroke Pde ERITH DA8 *.......129 K5
ISLW TW7.......................135 K3
KENS W8........................119 J4
Pembroke Rd BMLY BR1............184 B5
CEND/HSY/T N8...................66 E2
EHAM E6........................107 K4
ERITH DA8......................129 K5
GDMY/SEVK IG3...................73 F5
KENS W8........................119 J4
MTCM CR4.......................179 F5
MUSWH N10.......................48 A4
NTHWD HA6.......................26 A5
PLMGR N13........................35 J5
RSLP HA4.........................58 C5
SEVS/STOTM N15..................68 B2
WALTH E17.......................69 K2
WBLY HA9........................61 K4
Pembroke Sq KENS W8.............119 K3
Pembroke Ter STJWD NW8 *..........2 A1
Pembroke Vls KENS W8............119 K4
Pembroke Wk KENS W8.............119 K4
Pembrook Ms BTSEA SW11 *........140 C5
Pembury Cl BRXN/ST SW9.........142 B2
Pembury Av WORPK KT4............192 D5
Pembury Cl CLPT E5 *.............86 D3
HAYES BR2......................199 J4
Pembury Ct HYS/HAR UB3.........113 G6
Pembury Crs SCUP DA14...........169 H5
Pembury Rd BXLYHN DA7..........149 F1
CLPT E5........................86 D3
SNWD SE25......................197 H1
TOTM N17........................50 B5
Pemdevon Rd CROY/NA CR0........196 B4
Pemell Cl WCHPL E1.............104 E3
Pemerich Cl HYS/HAR UB3 *......113 J5
Pempath Pl WBLY HA9.............61 K1
Penally Pl IS N1 *...............85 K6
Penang St WAP E1W..............123 J1
Penard Rd NWDGN UB2.............115 F3
Penarth St PECK SE15...........123 K6
Penates ESH/CLAY KT10...........204 D2
Penberth Rd CAT SE6............165 F4
Penbury Rd NWDGN UB2...........114 E4
Pencombe Ms NTGHL W11..........100 D6
Pencraig Wy PECK SE15..........123 J6
Pencroft Dr DART DA1...........171 F2
Pendall Cl EBAR EN4..............21 J5
Penda Rd ERITH DA8.............149 J1
Pendarves Rd RYNPK SW20........177 F4
Penda's Md HOM E9................87 G2
Pendell Av HYS/HAR UB3.........133 J1
Pendennis Rd ORP BR6...........202 D6
STRHM/NOR SW16.................161 K6
TOTM N17........................49 K6
Penderel Rd HSLW TW3...........135 F6
Penderry Ri CAT SE6............165 G4
Penderyn Wy HOLWY N7............84 D2
Pendlebury House
CHARL SE7 *....................146 D1
Pendle Rd STRHM/NOR SW16.......161 J6
Pendlestone Rd WALTH E17........69 K3
Pendragon Rd BMLY BR1..........165 K5
Pendrell Rd NWCR SE14..........144 A6
Pendrell St WOOL/PLUM SE18.....127 J6
Pendula Dr YEAD UB4..............95 H4
Pendulum Ms HACK E8.............86 B3
Penerley Rd CAT SE6............164 E3
RAIN RM13......................111 K4
Penfold Cl CROY/NA CR0.........211 G1
Penfold La BXLY DA5............168 E5
Penfold Rd BAY/PAD W2............8 C1
Penfold Rd ED N9.................37 F3
Penfold St STJWD NW8.............2 B6
Penford Gdns ELTH/MOT SE9......146 C5
Penford St CMBW SE5............142 C3
Pengarth Rd BXLY DA5...........168 E1
Penge La PGE/AN SE20...........181 K3
Penge Rd PLSTW E13............89 G5
SNWD SE25......................181 H6
Penhale Cl ORP BR6.............217 G2
Penhall Rd CHARL SE7...........126 C4
Penhill Rd BXLY DA5............168 D2
Penhurst Rd BARK/HLT IG6........54 B3
Penifather La GFD/PVL UB6.......96 D2
Peninsular Cl
HOR/WEW KT19...................206 D3
Peninsular Park Rd CHARL SE7...125 K5
Penistone Rd
STRHM/NOR SW16.................179 K3
Penketh Dr HRW HA1...............78 D1
Penmon Rd ABYW SE2.............128 B3
Pennack Rd PECK SE15...........123 G6
Pennant Ms ECT SW5.............120 A4
Pennant Ter WALTH E17 *.........51 H5
Pennard Rd SHB W12.............119 F2
The Pennards SUN TW16..........172 B5
Penn Cl GFD/PVL UB6...........96 B1
KTN/HRWW/WS HA3.................43 J3
Penner Cl WIM/MER SW19.........159 H4
Penners Gdns SURB KT6..........191 F4
Pennethorne Cl HOM E9...........86 E6
Pennethorne Rd PECK SE15.......143 J1
Penney Cl DART DA1.............171 G2
Penn Gdns CHST BR7.............185 F2
CRW RM5.........................56 C3
Pennine Dr CRICK NW2............64 C6
Pennine La CRICK NW2 *...........64 C6
Pennine Pde CRICK NW2 *.........64 C6
Pennine Wy BXLYHN DA7..........150 B2
HYS/HAR UB3....................133 F6
Pennington Cl CRW RM5...........56 C2
Pennington Dr WCHMH N21.........22 E6
Pennington St WAP E1W..........104 D6
Pennington Wy
LEE/GVPK SE12..................166 A4
Penniston Cl TOTM N17...........49 J5
Penn La BXLY DA5...............168 E1
Penn Rd HOLWY N7................84 E3
Penn St IS N1....................7 F1
Penny Cl RAIN RM13.............111 K2
Pennycroft CROY/NA CR0.........213 G6
Pennyfields POP/IOD E14........105 J6
Pennymead Pl ESH/CLAY KT10.....204 A5
Penny Ms WAND/EARL SW18........139 K6
Pennymoor Wk MV/WKIL W9........100 D2
Pennyroyal Av EHAM E6..........108 A5
Penpool La WELL DA16...........148 C4
Penrhyn Av WALTH E17............51 J4
Penrhyn Crs
MORT/ESHN SW14.................137 K5

WALTH E17.......................51 J4
Penrhyn Gdns KUT/HW KT1.........190 E1
Penrhyn Gv WALTH E17............51 J4
Penrhyn Rd KUT/HW KT1..........191 F1
Penrith Cl BECK BR3............182 E4
PUT/ROE SW15...................139 H6
Penrith Crs RCH RM12............93 J3
Penrith Pl WNWD SE27...........162 C4
Penrith Rd BARK/HLT IG6.........55 F2
NWMAL KT3......................192 A1
Perpins Rd ELTH/MOT SE9........147 J6
Penrith St STRHM/NOR SW16......179 H2
Penrose Av OXHEY WD19...........27 J4
Penrose Gv WALW SE17...........122 D5
Penrose St WALW SE17...........122 D5
Penryn St CAMTN NW1..............4 C2
Perry St STHWK SE1..............19 H7
Pensbury Pl VX/NE SW8..........141 H3
Pensbury St VX/NE SW8..........141 H3
Penscroft Av RCH/KEW TW9.......137 H3
Pensford Av RCH/KEW TW9........137 H3
Penshurst Av BFN/LL DA15.......168 B1
Penshurst Gdns EDGW HA8.........44 D2
Penshurst Gn HAYES BR2.........199 J2
Penshurst Rd BXLYHN DA7........149 G2
HOM E9..........................87 F5
THHTH CR7......................196 C2
TOTM N17........................50 B3
Penshurst Wy BELMT SM2......208 E5
STMC/STPC BR5..................202 A5
Pensilver Cl EBAR EN4............21 J5
Penstemon Cl FNCH N3............46 E2
Pentelow Gdns
EBED/NFELT TW14................153 K1
Pentire Rd WALTH E17............52 B4
Pentland Av EDGW HA8............30 D4
Pentland Cl ED N9...............36 E4
GLDGN NW11......................64 C6
Pentland Gdns WAND/EARL SW18...160 B1
Pentland Pl NTHLT UB5.........77 J6
KIL/WHAMP NW6..................100 E2
Pentlands Cl MTCM CR4..........179 G6
Pentland St WAND/EARL SW18.....160 B1
Pentlow St PUT/ROE SW15........139 F3
Pentlow Wy BKHH IG9.............39 J2
Pentney Rd BAL SW12............161 H3
CHING E4........................38 B3
RYNPK SW20.....................177 H4
Penton Gv IS N1..................5 J3
Penton Pl WALW SE17.............18 B7
Penton Ri FSBYW WC1X............5 H4
Penton St IS N1..................5 J2
Pentonville Rd IS N1.............5 F3
Pentrich Av EN EN1...............24 C1
Pentridge St PECK SE15.........143 G1
Pentyre Av UED N18..............49 K1
Penwerris Av ISLW TW7..........135 H1
Penwith Rd WAND/EARL SW18......160 A5
Penwortham Rd
STRHM/NOR SW16.................179 G2
Penylan Pl EDGW HA8.............44 C4
Penywern Rd ECT SW5............119 K5
Penzance Pl NTGHL W11..........119 H1
Penzance St NTGHL W11..........119 H1
Peony Gdns SHB W12..............99 J6
Pepler Ms CMBW SE5.............123 G5
Peploe Rd KIL/WHAMP NW6........100 B1
Peplow Cl WDR/YW UB7...........112 A1
Pepper Cl EHAM E6..............107 K4
Peppercorn Cl THHTH CR7........180 E5
Peppermead Sq LEW SE13.........144 D6
Peppermint Cl CROY/NA CR0......195 K4
Peppermint Pl WAN E11...........88 C1
Pepper St POP/IOD E14..........124 E3
STHWK SE1......................18 C2
Pepys Crs BAR EN5...............20 A6
CAN/RD E16.....................125 K1
Pepys Est DEPT SE8.............124 A4
Pepys Park Est DEPT SE8........124 C4
Pepys Rd NWCR SE14.............144 A2
RYNPK SW20.....................177 F5
Perceval Av HAMP NW3............83 J3
Percheron Rd BORE WD6...........31 F1
Perch St HACK E8................86 B2
Percival Ct TOTM N17............50 B3
Percival Rd EN EN1..............24 B5
FELT TW13......................153 J4
MORT/ESHN SW14.................137 K6
ORP BR6........................201 G6
Percival St FSBYE EC1V...........6 A6
Percy Av ASHF TW15.............152 C6
Percy Bush Rd WDR/YW UB7.......112 C3
Percy Gdns PEND EN3.............25 F6
WPK KT4.........................192 B5
WHTN TW2.......................155 G3
Percy Ms FITZ W1T...............10 C2
Percy Rd BXLYHN DA7............149 F5
CAN/RD E16.....................106 C4
GDMY/SEVK IG3...................73 G4
HPTN TW12......................173 F3
ISLW TW7.......................136 B5
MTCM CR4.......................195 F4
NFNCH/WDSPK N12.................47 G1
PGE/AN SE20....................182 A4
ROMW/RG RM7.....................56 E6
SNWD SE25......................197 G2
WAN E11.........................70 C4
WCHMH N21........................35 J2
WHTN TW2.......................155 G3
Peregrine Cl WLSDN NW10.........81 F2
Peregrine Ct WELL DA16.........148 A2
Peregrine Gdns CROY/NA CR0.....198 B1
Peregrine Rd BARK/HLT IG6.......55 H1
TOTM N17........................50 E4
Peregrine Wy WIM/MER SW19......159 H1
Perham Rd WKENS W14............119 H5
Peridot St EHAM E6.............107 J4
Perifield DUL SE21.............162 D3
Perimeade Rd ALP/SUD HA0........97 J1

Periton Rd ELTH/MOT SE9........146 C5
Perivale Gdns WEA W13...........97 H3
Perivale La GFD/PVL UB6.........97 G3
Perivale Village GFD/PVL UB6 *..97 H2
Perkin Cl ALP/SUD HA0...........79 H3
HSLW TW3.......................135 G5
Perkin's Rents WEST SW1P........16 C4
Perkins Rd BARK/HLT IG6.........72 D2
Perkins Sq STHWK SE1............12 D7
Perks Cl BKHTH/KID SE3..........45 H5
Perpins Rd ELTH/MOT SE9........147 J6
Perran Rd BRXS/STRHM SW2.......162 C4
Perrers Rd HMSMTH W6...........118 E3
Perrin Rd ALP/SUD HA0...........79 F2
Perrins Ct HAMP NW3 *...........83 G2
Perrins Wk HAMP NW3.............83 G2
Perry Av ACT W3.................99 F5
Perry Cl RAIN RM13.............111 F1
Perry Ct SEVS/STOTM N15 *.......68 A3
Perryfield Wy CDALE/KGS NW9.....63 H3
RCHPK/HAM TW10.................156 C4
Perry Gdns ED N9................36 A5
Perry Garth NTHLT UB5...........77 G6
Perry Gv DART DA1..............151 K5
Perry Hall Cl ORP BR6..........202 B4
Perry Hall Rd ORP BR6..........202 A4
Perry Hl CAT SE6...............164 C4
Perry How WPK KT4..............192 C5
Perry Ri FSTH SE23.............164 B5
Perry St CHST BR7..............185 K2
Perrymans Farm Rd
GNTH/NBYPK IG2..................72 C3
Perry Md BUSH WD23..............28 C2
ENC/FH EN2......................23 H3
Perrymead St FUL/PGN SW6.......140 A2
Perry Rd BARK/HLT IG6 *.........72 C2
BERM/RHTH SE16..................123 K2
Perry Ri FSTH SE23.............164 B5
Perry Rd DAGW RM9..............110 C3
Perrys Pl FITZ W1T..............10 C3
Perry St CHST BR7..............185 K2
DART DA1.......................150 B4
Perry v FSTH SE23..............163 K4
Persant Rd CAT SE6.............165 H5
Perseverance Pl BRXN/ST SW9....142 B1
Pershore Cl GNTH/NBYPK IG2......72 B2
Pershore Gv CAR SM5............194 C4
Pert Cl MUSWH N10...............48 B3
Perth Av CDALE/KGS NW9..........63 F4
YEAD UB4........................95 H3
Perth Cl NTHLT UB5..............78 A4
NWMAL KT3......................191 K2
Perth Rd BARK IG11.............108 D1
BECK BR3.......................183 F5
FSBYPK N4.......................67 G5
GNTH/NBYPK IG2..................72 B2
LEY E10.........................69 G6
PLSTW E13......................107 F1
WDGN N22........................49 H4
Perth Ter GNTH/NBYPK IG2........72 C4
Perwell Av RYLN/HDSTN HA2.......59 K5
Petauel Rd TEDD TW11...........173 K1
Petavel Rd TEDD TW11...........173 K2
Peter Av WLSDN NW10.............81 K5
Peterboat Cl GNWCH SE10........125 H4
Peterborough Ms
FUL/PGN SW6....................139 K3
Peterborough Rd CAR SM5........194 D3
FUL/PGN SW6....................139 K3
HRW HA1.........................60 E5
LEY E10.........................70 A3
Peterborough Vls
FUL/PGN SW6....................140 A2
Petergate BTSEA SW11...........140 B5
Peters Cl DAGE RM10.............73 K5
STAN HA7........................43 K2
WELL DA16......................147 K3
Petersham Cl
RCHPK/HAM TW10.................156 E4
SUT SM1........................208 E3
Petersham Dr
STMC/STPC BR5..................186 A5
Petersham La SKENS SW7.........120 B3
Petersham Ms SKENS SW7.........120 B3
Petersham Pl SKENS SW7.........120 B3
Petersham Rd
RCHPK/HAM TW10.................156 E4
Peter's HI BLKFR EC4V............12 C5
Peterstone Rd ABYW SE2.........128 C3
Peterstow Cl WIM/MER SW19......159 H4
Peter St SOHO/CST W1F...........10 C5
Peterwood Wy CROY/NA CR0.......196 A6
Petherton Rd HBRY N5............85 J3
Petiver Cl HOM E9...............86 E5
Petley Rd HMSMTH W6............119 F6
Peto Pl CAMTN NW1................3 K5
Peto St North CAN/RD E16.......106 D5
Petrie Cl CRICK NW2.............82 C4
Petros Gdns KIL/WHAMP NW6 *.....83 F3
Petro St South CAN/RD E16......106 D5
Pettacre Cl THMD SE28..........127 H3
Pett Cl EMPK RM11...............75 K5
Petten Cl STMC/STPC BR5........202 E5
Petten Gv STMC/STPC BR5........202 D5
Petticoat La WCHPL E1...........13 H2
Petticoat Sq WCHPL E1...........13 J3
Petticoat Twr WCHPL E1 *........13 J3
Pettits Bvd ROM RM1.............57 G5
Pettits Cl ROM RM1..............57 G5
Pettits La ROM RM1..............57 G5
Pettits La North ROM RM1........57 G4
Pettit's Pl DAGE RM10...........92 C3
Pettiward Cl PUT/ROE SW15......139 F5
Pettley Gdns ROMW/RG RM7........75 F2
Pettman Crs THMD SE28..........127 J3
Pettsgrove Av ALP/SUD HA0.......79 J3
Pett's HI NTHLT UB5.............78 B3
Pett St WOOL/PLUM SE18.........126 D4
Petts Wood Rd
STMC/STPC BR5..................201 K2
Petty France WESTW SW1E.........16 B4
Petty Wales MON EC3R............13 H6
Petworth Cl NTHLT UB5...........77 K6
Petworth Gdns HGDN/ICK UB10....76 A6

RYNPK SW20.....................176 E6
Petworth Rd BXLYHS DA6.........149 H6
NFNCH/WDSPK N12.................47 H1
Petworth St BTSEA SW11.........140 D2
Petworth Wy HCH KM12...........93 J3
Petyt Pl CHEL SW3 *............120 D6
Petyward CHEL SW3...............14 D7
Pevensey Av EN EN1..............24 A3
FBAR/BDGN N11...................48 D1
Pevensey Cl ISLW TW7...........135 H1
Pevensey Rd FELT TW13..........154 E3
FSTGT E7........................88 E2
TOOT SW17......................160 C6
Peveret Cl FBAR/BDGN N11 *......48 B1
Peveril Dr TEDD TW11...........173 J1
Pewsey Cl CHING E4..............51 J1
Peyton Pl GNWCH SE10...........125 F6
Pharaoh Cl MTCM CR4...........194 E4
Pheasant Cl CAN/RD E16.........107 F5
Phelp St WALW SE17.............122 E6
Phelps Wy HYS/HAR UB3..........133 J4
Phene St CHEL SW3..............120 D6
Philan Wy CRW RM5...............57 F2
Philbeach Gdns ECT SW5.........119 K5
Philchurch Pl WCHPL E1.........104 C5
Philimore Cl
WOOL/PLUM SE18.................127 K5
Philip Gdns CROY/NA CR0........198 C6
Philip La SEVS/STOTM N15........67 K1
Philippa Gdns ELTH/MOT SE9.....146 C5
Philip Rd RAIN RM13............111 G2
Philips Cl CAR SM5.............195 F5
Philip St PLSTW E13............106 E3
Philip Wk PECK SE15............143 H4
Phillimore Gdns Cl
KENS W8........................119 K3
Phillimore Gardens
WLSDN NW10......................82 A6
Phillimore PI KENS W8..........119 K3
Phillimore Wk KENS W8..........119 K3
Phillip St IS N1................7 H1
Phillips Cl DART DA1...........170 E1
Philpot La FENCHST EC3M.........13 G5
Philpot St WCHPL E1 *..........104 D5
Phineas Pett Rd
ELTH/MOT SE9...................146 D2
Phipp's Bridge Rd MTCM CR4.....178 D3
Phipps Hatch La ENC/FH EN2......23 J1
Phipp's Ms BSVD SW1W *..........15 K5
Phipp St SDTCH EC2A..............7 G6
Phoebeth Rd LEW SE13...........144 D6
Phoenix Cl HACK E8 *..........7 K6
NTHWD HA6.......................26 D6
WALTH E17.......................51 H5
WWKM BR4.......................199 H5
Phoenix Dr HAYES BR2...........215 H1
Phoenix Pk BTFD TW8............116 E5
Phoenix Pl DART DA1............171 G2
FSBYW WC1X.......................5 J6
Phoenix Rd CAMTN NW1.............4 C4
PGE/AN SE20....................181 K2
Phoenix St LSQ/SEVD WC2H........10 D4
Phoenix Wy HEST TW5............114 C6
Phoenix Wharf Rd STHWK SE1......19 K3
Phyllis Av NWMAL KT3...........193 F2
Physic Pl CHEL SW3.............120 E6
Picardy Manorway BELV DA17.....129 J3
Picardy Rd BELV DA17...........129 H5
Picardy St BELV DA17...........129 H3
Piccadilly MYFR/PICC W1J........10 A7
Piccadilly Ar MYFR/PICC W1J....10 A7
Piccadilly Circ REGST W1B.......10 C6
Pickard Cl STHGT/OAK N14........34 D3
Pickard St FSBYE EC1V............6 B4
Pickering Av EHAM E6...........108 A2
Pickering Gdns CROY/NA CR0.....197 G3
FBAR/BDGN N11...................48 A2
Pickering Ms BAY/PAD W2........101 F5
Pickering Pl WHALL SW1A *.......16 B1
Pickets Cl BUSH WD23............28 D3
Pickets St BAL SW12............161 F2
Pickett Cft STAN HA7 *..........43 K4
Pickett's Lock La ED N9.........37 F3
Pickford Cl BXLYHN DA7.........149 F3
Pickford La BXLYHN DA7.........149 F3
Pickford Rd BXLYHN DA7.........149 F4
Pickhurst Gn HAYES BR2.......199 J4
Pickhurst La WWKM BR4..........199 J3
Pickhurst Md HAYES BR2.........199 J4
Pickhurst Pk HAYES BR2.........199 G2
Pickhurst Ri WWKM BR4..........199 G5
Pickwick Ms UED N18.............50 A1
Pickwick Pl HRW HA1.............60 E4
Pickwick Rd DUL SE21...........162 E2
Pickwick St STHWK SE1...........18 C3
Pickwick Wy CHST BR7...........185 H2
Pickworth Cl VX/NE SW8 *.......141 K1
Picton Pl MHST W1U..............9 H4
Picton St CMBW SE5.............142 E1
Pied Bull Yd IS N1...............6 A1
Piedmont Rd
WOOL/PLUM SE18.................127 J5
Pier Head WAP E1W *............123 J1
Piermont Rd EDUL SE22..........143 J6
Pierpoint Ar B1 N1 *............6 A2
Pierrepoint Rd ACT W3...........98 D6
Pierrepoint Rw IS N1 *...........6 A2
Pier Rd CAN/RD E16.............126 C1
EBED/NFELT TW14................134 A6
ERITH DA8......................130 B6
Pier St POP/IOD E14............125 F4
Pier Ter WAND/EARL SW18........140 B5
Pier Wy THMD SE28..............127 J3
Pigeon La HPTN TW12............155 G5
Pigott St POP/IOD E14..........105 J5
Pike Cl BMLY BR1...............184 A1
Pike Rd MLHL NW7................31 F6
Pike's End PIN HA5..............59 F1

Pikestone Cl YEAD UB4 * 95 J3
Pilgrimage St STHWK SE1 ....18 E3
Pilgrim Cl MRDN SM4 ....34 A4
Pilgrim Hl WNWD SE27 ....162 D6
Pilgrims Cl NTHLT UB5 ....78 C5
  PLMGR N13 ....35 F6
Pilgrims Ct DART DA1 ....151 K6
Pilgrims Ms ASHF TW15 * 152 C6
Pilgrims Pl HAMP NW3 ....83 H2
Pilgrims Ri EBAR EN4 ....21 J6
Pilgrim St BLKFR EC4V * 12 A4
Pilgrims Wy ARCH N19 ....66 D5
  SAND/SEL CR2 ....212 B4
  WBLY HA9 ....62 D5
Pilkington Rd ORP BR6 ....216 C1
  PECK SE15 ....143 J3
Pilot Cl DEPT SE8 ....124 C6
Pilsden Cl WIM/MER SW19 ....159 G3
Piltdown Rd OXHEY WD19 ....27 H6
Pilton Pl WALW SE17 ....122 D5
Pimlico Rd BGVA SW1W 121 F5
Pinchbeck Rd ORP BR6 ....217 H4
Pinchin & Johnsons Yd
  WCHPL E1 * 104 C6
Pinchin St WCHPL E1 ....104 C6
Pincott Pl BROCKY SE4 ....144 A4
Pincott Rd BXLYHN DA6 ....149 H6
  WIM/MER SW19 ....178 B4
Pindar St SDTCH EC2A 13 G1
Pindock Ms MV/WKIL W9 ....101 F3
Pine Apple Cl WESTW SW1E * 16 A4
Pine Av SRTFD E15 ....88 B3
  WWKM BR4 ....199 G6
Pine Cl LEY E10 ....69 J6
  PGE/AN SE20 ....181 K4
  STAN HA7 ....29 H6
  STHGT/OAK N14 ....34 C2
Pine Coombe CROY/NA CRO.....213 F2
Pinecrest Gdns ORP BR6 ....216 C1
Pinecroft KTN/HRWW/WS HA3...62 B2
  WOOL/PLUM SE18 ....148 B1
Pinecroft Crs BAR EN5 ....20 C5
Pinefield Cl POP/IOD E14 * 105 J6
Pine Gdns BRYLDS KT5 ....191 H5
  RSLP HA4 ....59 G1
Pine Gld ORP BR6 ....215 K2
Pine Gv FSBYPK N4 ....66 E6
  TRDG/WHET N20 ....32 D3
  WIM/MER SW19 ....177 J1
Pinelands Cl BKHTH/KID SE3 * ..145 J1
Pineleees Ct
  MORT/ESHN SW14 * 137 K5
Pine Rdg CAR SM5 ....210 A6
Pine Rd CRICK NW2 ....82 A2
  FBAR/BDGN N11 ....34 A4
Pines Cl NTHWD HA6 ....40 C2
Pines Rd BMLY BR1 ....184 B1
The Pines NRWD SE19 * 180 C2
  STHGT/OAK N14 ....22 C6
  WFD IG8 ....38 E5
Pine St CLKNW EC1R 5 J6
Pine Tree Cl HEST TW5 ....134 A2
Pine Wk BRYLDS KT5 ....191 H3
Pinewood Av BFN/LL DA15 ....167 K3
  PIN HA5 ....42 B2
  RAIN RM13 ....111 K3
Pinewood Cl CROY/NA CRO 213 G1
  NTHWD HA6 ....40 E1
  ORP BR6 ....201 H5
  PIN HA5 ....42 B2
Pinewood Dr ORP BR6 ....216 E3
Pinewood Gv EA W5 ....97 J5
Pinewood Ldg BUSH WD23 * 28 D3
Pinewood Ms
  STWL/WRAY TW19 ....152 A1
Pinewood Pl RDART DA2 ....170 B4
Pinewood Rd ABYW SE2 ....128 E6
  FELT TW13 ....154 A5
Pinfold Rd STRHM/NOR SW16..161 K6
Pinglestone Cl WDR/YW UB7 ....132 B1
Pinkcoat Cl FELT TW13 ....154 A5
Pinkham Way North Circular
  Rd NFNCH/WDSPK N12 ....47 K3
Pinkwell Av HYS/HAR UB3 ....113 G4
Pinkwell La HYS/HAR UB3 ....113 G4
Pinley Gdns DAGW RM9 ....91 H6
Pinnacle Hl BXLYHN DA7 ....149 J5
Pinnacle Hl North
  BXLYHN DA7 ....149 J4
Pinn Cl RTH/LL/MOT SE9 ....146 C5
Pinner Ct PIN HA5 ....60 A1
Pinner Gn PIN HA5 ....41 G5
Pinner Gv PIN HA5 ....59 J1
Pinner Hl PIN HA5 ....41 F5
Pinner Hill Rd PIN HA5 ....41 G5
Pinner Park Av
  RYLN/HDSTN HA2 ....42 C5
Pinner Park Gdns
  RYLN/HDSTN HA2 ....42 C5
Pinner Rd HRW HA1 ....60 B2
  NTHWD HA6 ....40 B2
  OXHEY WD19 ....27 J1
  PIN HA5 ....59 K1
Pinn Wy RSLP HA4 ....58 B6
Pintail Cl EHAM E6 ....107 J4
Pintail Rd WFD IG8 ....52 E5
Pintail Wy YEAD UB4 ....95 H5
Pinto Cl BORE WD6 * 31 F1
Pinto Wy BKHTH/KID SE3.........146 A5
Pioneer Cl SHB W12 ....99 K5
Pioneer St PECK SE15 ....143 H2
Pioneer Wy SHB W12 ....100 A5
  WATW WD18 ....26 D1
Piper Cl HOLWY N7 ....85 F4
Piper Rd KUT/HW KT1 ....175 H6
Pipers Gdns CROY/NA CRO......198 B4
Pipers Green La EDGW HA8 ....30 A5
Pipewell Rd CAR SM5 ....194 D4
Pippin Cl CRICK NW2 ....81 J1
  CROY/NA CRO 198 C1
Pippins Cl WDR/YW UB7 ....112 A3

Piquet Rd PGE/AN SE20 ....181 K5
Pirbright Crs CROY/NA CRO......214 A4
Pirbright Rd
  WOOL/PLUM SE18 ....127 H4
Pirie Cl CAR/RD E16 ....159 J3
Pitcairn Cl ROMW/RG RM7 ....74 C1
Pitcairn Rd MTCM CR4 ....178 E3
Pitchford St SRTFD E15 ....88 B5
Pitfield Crs THMD SE28 ....128 B1
Pitfield St IS N1 ....7 G4
Pitfield Wy PEND EN3 ....24 E2
  WLSDN NW10 ....81 F4
Pitfold Rd LEE/GVPK SE12 ......165 K2
Pitlake CROY/NA CRO 196 C6
Pitman St CMBW SE5 ....142 D1
Pitsea Pl WCHPL E1 ....105 F5
Pitsea St WCHPL E1 ....105 F5
Pitshanger La EA W5 ....97 H3
Pitt Crs WIM/MER SW19 ....160 A6
Pittman Gdns IL IG1 ....90 C3
Pitt Rd ORP BR6 ....216 C2
  KUT/HDSTN HA2 ....60 A6
  THHTH CR7 ....196 D2
Pitts Head Ms MYFR/PICC W1J..15 J2
Pittsmead Av HAYES BR2.........199 K4
Pitt St KENS W8 ....119 K2
Pittville Gdns SNWD SE25 ....181 H6
Pixley St POP/IOD E14 ....105 H5
Pixton Wy CROY/NA CRO 213 H5
Place Farm Av ORP BR6...........201 K5
Plaistow Gv BMLY BR1 ....184 A3
Plaistow La BMLY BR1..............183 K3
Plaistow Park Rd PLSTW E13....107 F1
Plaistow Rd PLSTW E13 ....106 E1
  SRTFD E15 ....88 D6
Plane St SYD SE26 ....163 J5
Plane Tree Crs FELT TW13.......154 A5
Plantagenet Cl WPK KT4 ....207 F2
Plantagenet Gdns CHDH RM6....73 K4
Plantagenet Pl CHDH RM6 ....73 K4
Plantagenet Rd BAR EN5 ....21 G5
Plantain Gdns WAN E11 * 88 B1
Plantain Pl STHWK SE1 ....18 E2
Plantation Dr STMC/STPC RM5..202 E5
Plantation La FENCHST EC3M...13 G5
Plantation Rd ERITH DA8 ....150 D2
The Plantation
  BKHTH/KID SE3 ....145 K3
Plashet Gv EHAM E6 ....89 G6
Plashet Rd PLSTW E13 ....88 E6
Plassy Rd CAT SE6 ....164 E2
Platina St SDTCH EC2A 7 F7
Plato Rd BRXS/STRHM SW2......141 K5
Platt's La HAMP NW3 ....82 E1
Platt St CAMTN NW1 ....4 C2
Plawsfield Rd BECK BR3 ....182 A4
Plaxtol Cl BMLY BR1 ....184 B4
Plaxtol Rd ERITH DA8 ....149 H1
Playfair Cl HMSMTH W6 ....119 F5
Playfield Crs CRW RM5 ....56 E4
Playfield Rd EDGW HA8 ....44 E5
Playford Rd FSBYPK N4 ....67 F6
Playgreen Wy CAT SE6 ....164 D6
Playground Cl BECK BR3 ....182 A5
Playhouse Ct STHWK SE1 * 18 C2
Playhouse Yd BLKFR EC4V * 12 B4
Plaza Pde ALP/SUD HA0 * 80 A1
Plaza Wk CDALE/KGS NW9 ....44 E6
Pleasance Rd PUT/ROE SW15...138 E5
  STMC/STPC RM5 ....186 C5
The Pleasance PUT/ROE SW15..138 E5
Pleasant Gv CROY/NA CRO......213 H1
Pleasant Pl IS N1 ....85 H5
Pleasant Vw ERITH DA8 ....130 B5
  ORP BR6 ....216 C3
Pleasant Wy ALP/SUD HA0 * 97 J1
Plender St CAMTN NW1 ....4 B1
Pleshey Rd ARCH N19 ....64 D1
Plesman Wy WLGTN SM6 * 210 E6
Plevna Crs SEVS/STOTM N15...68 A3
Plevna Rd ED N9 ....36 C5
  HPTN TW12 ....173 G4
Plevna St POP/IOD E14 ....125 F3
Pleydell Av HMSMTH W6 ....118 C4
  NRWD SE19 ....181 G3
Pleydell Est FSBYE EC1V 6 D5
Pleydell Gdns NRWD SE19 * 181 G2
Pleydell St EMB EC4Y 11 K4
Plimsoll Cl POP/IOD E14 ....105 K5
Plimsoll Rd FSBYPK N4 ....85 H1
Plough Farm Cl RSLP HA4 ....58 B3
Plough La CROY/NA CRO 210 E2
  EDUL SE22 ....143 G6
  PUR/KEN CR8 ....210 E6
  TEDD TW11 ....173 K2
  WIM/MER SW19 ....159 J6
Plough Lane Cl WLGTN SM6 ....210 E3
Ploughmans Cl CAMTN NW1 ......84 D6
Ploughmans End ISLW TW7 .....135 J6
Plough Pl FLST/FETLN EC4A 11 K3
Plough Rd BTSEA SW11 ....140 C4
  HOR/WEW KT19 ....207 F5
Plough Ter BTSEA SW11 ....140 C5
Plough Wy BERM/RHTH SE16..124 A4
Plough Yd SDTCH EC2A 7 H7
Plover Wy BERM/RHTH SE16...124 B3
  YEAD UB4 ....95 H5
Plowden Buildings
  EMB EC4Y * 11 J5
Plowman Cl UED N18 ....49 K1
Plowman Wy BCTR RM8 ....73 K5
Plumbers Rw WCHPL E1 ....104 C5
Plumbridge St GNWCH SE10 *..145 F2
Plum Cl FELT TW13 ....153 K4
Plum Garth BTFD TW8 ....116 E4
Plum La WOOL/PLUM SE18 ......147 G1
Plummer La MTCM CR4 ....178 E5
Plumpton Wy CAR SM5 ....209 J1
Plumstead Common Rd
  WOOL/PLUM SE18 ....127 H6
Plumstead High St
  WOOL/PLUM SE18 ....127 K4

Plumstead Rd
  WOOL/PLUM SE18 ....127 H4
  WLGTN SM6 ....210 D5
Plumtree Cl DAGE RM10 ....92 E4
Plumtree Ct FLST/FETLN EC4A..11 K3
Plymouth Rd BMLY BR1.............184 A4
  CAN/RD E16 ....106 E5
Plymouth Whf POP/IOD E14......125 G4
Plympton Av KIL/WHAMP NW6..82 D5
Plympton Cl BELV DA17 ....129 F3
Plympton Pl STJWD NW8 * 2 C7
Plympton Rd KIL/WHAMP NW6..82 D5
Plympton St STJWD NW8 ....2 C7
Plymstock Rd WELL DA16 ....148 D1
Pocklington Cl CDALE/KGS NW9..45 G5
Pocock Av WDR/YW UB7 ....112 C3
Pocock St STHWK SE1 ....18 A2
Podmore Rd
  WAND/EARL SW18 ....140 B5
Poet's Rd HBRY N5 ....85 K3
Poets Wy HRW HA1 ....60 E1
Pointalls Cl FNCH N3 ....47 G5
Point Cl GNWCH SE10 ....145 F2
Pointer Cl THMD SE28 ....109 K5
Pointers Cl POP/IOD E14..........124 E5
Point Hl GNWCH SE10 ....145 F2
Point Pl WBLY HA9 ....80 D5
Point Pleasant
  WAND/EARL SW18 ....139 K5
Point Wharf La BTFD TW8.........136 E1
Poland St SOHO/SHAV W1F 10 B4
Polebrook Rd BKHTH/KID SE3...146 B4
Polecroft La CAT SE6 ....164 C4
Pole Hill Rd CHING E4 ....38 A2
  HGDN/ICK UB10 ....94 A2
Polesden Gdns RYNPK SW20....176 E6
Polesworth Rd DAGW RM9 ....110 B1
Polish War Memorial Rbt
  RSLP HA4 ....77 G4
Pollard Cl CAN/RD E16 ....106 E6
  CHIG IG7 ....55 G1
  HOLWY N7 ....85 F3
Pollard Rd MRDN SM4 ....194 C2
  TRDG/WHET N20 ....33 J4
Pollard Rw BETH E2 * 104 C2
Pollards Crs
  STRHM/NOR SW16 ....179 K6
Pollards Hl East
  STRHM/NOR SW16 ....180 A6
Pollards Hl North
  STRHM/NOR SW16 ....180 A6
Pollards Hl South
  STRHM/NOR SW16 ....179 K6
Pollards Hl West
  STRHM/NOR SW16 ....179 K6
Pollard St BETH E2 * 104 C2
Pollards Wood Rd
  STRHM/NOR SW16 ....179 K5
Pollen St CONDST W1S 9 K4
Pollitt Dr STJWD NW8 ....2 B6
Polperro Cl ORP BR6 ....202 A3
Polperro Ms LBTH SE11 ....17 K6
Polsted Rd CAT SE6 ....164 C2
Polthorne Gv
  WOOL/PLUM SE18 ....127 J4
Polworth Rd
  STRHM/NOR SW16 ....179 K1
Polygon Rd CAMTN NW1 ....4 C3
The Polygon CLAP SW4 * 141 H5
Polytechnic St
  WOOL/PLUM SE18 ....127 F4
Pomell Wy WCHPL E1 ....13 K3
Pomeroy St PECK SE15 ....143 K1
Pomfret Rd CMBW SE5 ....142 C4
Pomoja La ARCH N19 ....66 E1
Pond Cl BKHTH/KID SE3 ....145 K3
  NFNCH/WDSPK N12 ....47 J2
Pond Cottage La BECK BR3......198 D4
Ponder St HOLWY N7 ....85 F5
Pond Farm Est CLPT E5 * 86 E1
Pondfield Rd DAGE RM10 ....92 D5
  HAYES BR2 ....199 H5
  ORP BR6 ....216 B1
Pond Gn RSLP HA4 ....58 C6
Pond Hill Gdns CHEAM SM3 ....208 C4
Pond Lees Cl DAGE RM10 ....93 F5
Pond Md DUL SE21 ....5 G4
Pond Pl CHEL SW3 ....14 C7
Pond Rd BKHTH/KID SE3..........145 J4
  SRTFD E15 ....106 C1
Pondside Cl HYS/HAR UB3.......133 G1
Pond Sq HGT N6 * 65 J5
Pond St HAMP NW3 ....83 J3
Pondwood Rd SRTFD E15 ....88 C4
Ponler St WCHPL E1 ....104 D5
Ponsard Rd WLSDN NW10 ....99 K2
Ponsford St HOM E9 ....86 E4
Ponsonby Pl WEST SW1P 121 J5
Ponsonby Rd PUT/ROE SW15...158 D2
Ponsonby Ter WEST SW1P 121 J5
Ponteract Rd BMLY BR1............183 K1
Ponton Rd VX/NE SW8 ....141 J1
Pont St KTBR SW1X 14 E5
Pont Street Ms KTBR SW1X 14 E5
Pool Cl BECK BR3 ....182 D2
  E/WMO/HCT KT8 ....188 E2
Pool Ct CAT SE6 ....164 D4
Poole Cl RSLP HA4 ....58 C6
Poole Court Rd HSLW TW3 ....134 D3
Poole Rd HOM E9 ....87 F4
  HOR/WEW KT19 ....207 F4
Pooles Buildings FSBYW WC1X..5 J7
Pooles La WBPTN SW10 * 140 B6
Pooles Pk FSBYPK N4 ....67 G6
Poole St IS N1 ....7 F1
Poole Wy YEAD UB4 ....94 C2
Pooley Dr MORT/ESHN SW14...137 K4
Poolmans St
  BERM/RHTH SE16 ....124 A2
Pool Rd E/WMO/HCT KT8 ....188 E2
  HRW HA1 ....60 D4
Poolsford Rd CDALE/KGS NW9..45 G1
Poonah St WCHPL E1 ....104 E5
Pope Cl EBED/NFELT TW14......153 J3
  WIM/MER SW19 ....178 C2
Pope's Av WHTN TW2 ....155 K4

Popes Dr FNCH N3 ....46 E4
Popes Gv CROY/NA CRO 213 H1
  WHTN TW2 ....155 K4
Pope's La EA W5 ....116 D4
Pope's Rd BRXN/ST SW9 ....142 B5
Pope St STHWK SE1 ....19 H3
Popham Cl FELT TW13 ....154 D5
Popham Gdns
  RCH/KEW TW9 * 137 J4
Popham Rd IS N1 ....85 J6
Popham St IS N1 ....85 J6
Popinjays Rw CHEAM SM3 * 208 B3
Poplar Av MTCM CR4 ....178 E4
  LEW SE13 ....145 F6
  ORP BR6 ....201 G3
Poplar Bath St POP/IOD E14.....105 K6
Poplar Cl HOM E9 ....87 H3
  PIN HA5 ....41 H4
Poplar Court Pde TWK TW1 * 156 D1
Poplar Crs HOR/WEW KT19 .....206 E4
Poplar Farm Cl
  HOR/WEW KT19 ....206 E4
Poplar Gdns NWMAL KT3..........176 A5
Poplar Gv FBAR/BDGN N11 ....48 A2
  HMSMTH W6 ....119 F2
  NWMAL KT3 ....176 A5
  WBLY HA9 ....80 E1
Poplar High St POP/IOD E14.....105 K6
Poplar La BECK BR3 ....198 E2
Poplar Ms SHB W12 * 100 A1
Poplar Pl BAY/PAD W2 ....101 F6
  HYS/HAR UB3 ....113 J4
  THMD SE28 ....109 J6
Poplar Rd CHEAM SM3 ....193 J5
  HNHL SE24 ....142 D5
  WIM/MER SW19 ....177 K5
Poplar Rd South
  WIM/MER SW19 ....177 K6
Poplars Av CRICK NW2 ....58 C5
Poplars Rd WALTH E17 ....69 K3
The Poplars STHGT/OAK N14 * ..22 B6
Poplar St ROMW/RG RM7 ....74 E1
Poplar Vw WBLY HA9 * 61 K6
Poplar Wk CROY/NA CRO 196 D6
  HNHL SE24 ....142 D5
Poplar Wy BARK/HLT IG6 ....72 C1
  FELT TW13 ....153 K5
Poppins Ct FLST/FETLN EC4A....12 A4
Poppleton Rd WAN E11 ....70 C3
Poppy Cl BELV DA17 ....129 J3
  NTHLT UB5 ....77 K4
  WLGTN SM6 ....195 F5
Poppy La CROY/NA CRO 197 K4
Porchester Garden Ms
  BAY/PAD W2 * 101 F5
Porchester Gdns BAY/PAD W2..101 F6
Porchester Ga BAY/PAD W2 * ...120 E1
Porchester Md BECK BR3...........182 E2
Porchester Ms BAY/PAD W2.....101 F5
  KUT/HW KT1 ....175 J5
Porchester Sq BAY/PAD W2.....101 F5
Porchester Square Ms
  BAY/PAD W2 * 101 F5
Porchester Ter BAY/PAD W2.....101 G6
Porch Wy TRDG/WHET N20........33 K5
Porcupine Cl ELTH/MOT SE9....166 D4
Porlock Av RYLN/HDSTN HA2.....60 C5
Porlock Rd EN EN1 ....36 B2
Porlock St STHWK SE1 ....19 F2
Porrington Cl CHST BR7 ....184 E4
Portal Cl RSLP HA4 ....76 E2
  WNWD SE27 ....162 B5
Portobury Gv BTFD TW8 ....116 D5
Portbury Cl PECK SE15 * 143 H2
Portcullis Lodge Rd EN EN1 ....23 K4
Portelet Rd WCHPL E1 ....105 F2
Porten Houses WKENS W14 * 119 H3
Porten Rd WKENS W14 ....119 H3
Porter Rd EHAM E6 ....107 K5
Porters Av DAGW RM9 ....91 G5
Porter Sq ARCH N19 ....66 E5
Porter St MHST W1U 9 F1
  STHWK SE1 ....12 D7
Porters Wk WAP E1W * 104 D6
Porters Wy WDR/YW UB7 ....112 C3
Porteus Rd BAY/PAD W2 ....8 A1
Portgate Cl MV/WKIL W9 ....100 D3
Porthallow Cl ORP BR6 ....217 F2
Porthcawe Rd SYD SE26 ....164 B6
Porthkerry Av WELL DA16.........148 B5
Portia Wy BOW E3 ....105 H3
The Porticos CHEL SW3 * 120 B5
Portinscale Rd PUT/ROE SW15..139 H6
Portland Av BFN/LL DA15 ....168 B1
  NWMAL KT3 ....192 C4
  STNW/STAM N16 ....68 B5
Portland Cl CHDH RM6 ....74 A1
  WPK KT4 ....192 D4
Portland Cottages
  CROY/NA CRO * 195 J4
Portland Crs ELTH/MOT SE9....166 D1
  FELT TW13 ....153 G6
  GFD/PVL UB6 ....96 B4
  STAN HA7 ....43 K6
Portland Crs West STAN HA7.....43 K6
Portland Dr ENC/FH EN2 ....24 A1
Portland Gdns CHDH RM6 ....73 K2
  FSBYPK N4 ....67 H3
Portland Gv VX/NE SW8 ....142 A2
Portland Ms SOHO/CST W1F 10 B4
Portland Pl REGST W1B * 9 J2
  SNWD SE25 ....197 H1
Portland Ri FSBYPK N4 ....67 H5
Portland Rd ASHF TW15 ....152 B5
  BMLY BR1 ....166 B6
  ELTH/MOT SE9 ....166 D1
  KUT/HW KT1 ....175 F6
  MTCM CR4 ....178 D6
  NTGHL W11 ....100 C6
  NTGHL W11 ....119 H1
  NWDGN UB2 ....115 F4
  SEVS/STOTM N15 ....68 A1
  SNWD SE25 ....197 J1

YEAD UB4 ....94 C2
Portland Sq WAP E1W 123 J1
Portland St WALW SE17 ....122 E5
Portland Ter RCH/KEW TW9 * ...136 E5
Portman Av
  MORT/ESHN SW14 ....138 A4
Portman Cl BXLY DA5 ....170 B3
  BXLYHS DA6 ....148 E4
  MBLAR W1H 9 F3
Portman Dr WFD IG8 ....53 H5
Portman Gdns CDALE/KGS NW9..45 F6
Portman Ga CAMTN NW1 ....2 D7
Portman Ms South MBLAR W1H ..9 F3
Portman Pl BETH E2 ....104 E2
Portman Rd KUT/HW KT1 ....175 G5
Portman Sq MBLAR W1H 9 F3
Portman St MBLAR W1H 9 F4
Portman Towers MBLAR W1H * ...9 F3
Portmeadow Wk ABYW SE2 ....128 E2
Portmeers Cl WALTH E17 * 69 H3
Portmore Gdns CRW RM5 ....56 C1
Portnall Rd MV/WKIL W9 ....100 D2
Portnoi Cl ROM RM1 ....57 F5
Portobello Ct NTHL W11 * 100 D6
Portobello Ms NTGHL W11 ....100 E6
Portobello Rd NKENS W10 ....100 C4
  NTGHL W11 ....100 E6
Portpool La FSBYW WC1X 11 J1
Portree Cl ED N9 * 36 C1
Portree St POP/IOD E14 ....106 B5
Portsdown EDGW HA8 * 44 C1
Portsdown Av GLDGN NW11 ....64 D3
Portsea Ms BAY/PAD W2 ....8 D4
Portsea Pl BAY/PAD W2 ....8 D4
Portslade Rd VX/NE SW8 ....141 H3
Portsmouth Av THDIT KT7 ....190 B4
Portsmouth Ms CAN/RD E16 ......107 F6
Portsmouth Rd
  ESH/CLAY KT10 ....204 A4
  KUT/HW KT1 ....174 E6
  PUT/ROE SW15 ....158 E3
  SURB KT6 ....190 E5
Portsmouth St LINN WC2A * 11 H4
Portsoken St TWRH EC3N 13 J5
Portugal Gdns WHTN TW2 * 155 H4
Portugal St LINN WC2A 11 H4
Portway RAIN RM13 ....93 J6
  SRTFD E15 ....88 D6
Portway Crs EW KT17 ....207 J6
Portway Gdns
  WOOL/PLUM SE18 ....146 C2
Postern Gn ENC/FH EN2 ....23 G3
The Postern BARB EC2Y * 12 D2
Post La WHTN TW2 ....155 J4
Posthill Cl CROY/NA CRO 212 E1
Post Office Ap FSTGT E7 ....89 F3
Post Office Wy VX/NE SW8 ....141 J1
Postway Ms IL IG1 * 90 B1
Potier St STHWK SE1 ....19 F4
Potter Cl MTCM CR4 ....179 G5
Potteries La ENC/FH EN2 * 23 J5
The Potteries BAR EN5 * 20 E6
Potterne Cl WIM/MER SW19 ....159 G2
Potters Cl CROY/NA CRO 198 B5
  PECK SE15 * 143 F1
Potters Flds STHWK SE1 * 19 H1
Potters Gv NWMAL KT3 ....191 K1
Potters Heights Cl PIN HA5 ....41 F3
Potter's La BAR EN5 ....20 E5
  STRHM/NOR SW16 ....179 J2
Potters Ms BORE WD6 * 29 J1
Potter's Rd BAR EN5 ....21 F5
  FUL/PGN SW6 ....140 B3
Potter St NTHWD HA6 ....40 E4
Potter Street Hl PIN HA5 ....41 F3
Pottery La NTGHL W11 ....119 H1
Pottery Rd BTFD TW8 ....117 G5
  BXLY DA5 ....169 K4
Pottery St BERM/RHTH SE16 * ...123 J2
Pott St BETH E2 ....104 D2
Poulett Gdns TWK TW1 ....156 A4
Poulett Rd EHAM E6 ....107 K1
Poulter Pk MRDN SM4 * 194 C2
Poulters Wd HAYES BR2 ....215 H5
Poulton Av SUT SM1 ....209 H1
Poulton Cl HACK E8 * 86 D4
Poultry LOTH EC2R 12 E4
Pound Cl ORP BR6 ....201 J6
  SURB KT6 ....190 D5
Pound Court Dr ORP BR6 ....201 J6
Pound Farm Cl
  ESH/CLAY KT10 ....189 J5
Pound La WLSDN NW10 ....81 J4
Pound Park Rd CHARL SE7 ....126 C5
Pound Pl ELTH/MOT SE9 ....167 F5
Pound St CAR SM5 ....209 K3
Pountney Rd BTSEA SW11 ....141 F4
Poverest Rd STMC/STPC BR5....202 A2
Powder Mill La DART DA1 ....171 J4
  WHTN TW2 ....154 E3
Powell Cl EDGW HA8 ....44 B2
Powell Gdns DAGE RM10 ....92 C2
Powell Rd BKHH IG9 ....39 G2
  CLPT E5 ....86 D1
Power Rd CHSWK W4 ....117 H4
Powerscroft Rd CLPT E5 ....86 D2
  SCUP DA14 ....186 D3
Powis Ct BUSH WD23 * 28 D3
Powis Gdns GLDGN NW11 ....64 D4
  NTGHL W11 ....100 D5
Powis Ms NTGHL W11 ....100 D5
Powis Pl BMSBY WC1N 5 F7
Powis Rd BOW E3 ....105 K2
Powis Sq NTGHL W11 ....100 D5
Powis St WOOL/PLUM SE18......127 F3
Powlett Pl CAMTN NW1 * 84 B5
Pownall Gdns HSLW TW3...........135 G5
Pownall Rd HACK E8 ....86 C6
  HSLW TW3 ....135 G5
Powster Rd BMLY BR1 ....165 K1
Powys Cl BXLYHN DA7 ....128 E6
Powys La PLMGR N13 ....48 E1
  STHGT/OAK N14 ....34 E6
Poynders Rd CLAP SW4..............161 J2
Poynings Cl ORP BR6 ....202 D6
Poynings Rd ARCH N19 ....84 C1

Poynings Wy
 NFNCH/WDSPK N12 ....46 E1
Poyntell Crs CHST BR7.......185 J4
Poynter Rd EN EN1............24 B6
Poynton Rd TOTM N17.........50 C5
Poyntz Rd BTSEA SW11......140 E3
Poyser St BETH E2 ....104 D1
Praed Ms BAY/PAD W2..........8 B3
Praed St BAY/PAD W2...........8 A3
Pragel St PLSTW E13.........107 C1
Pragnell Rd LEE/GVPK SE12..166 A4
Prague Pl BRXS/STRHM SW2...141 K6
Prah Rd FSBYPK N4............67 G6
Prairie St VX/NE SW8........141 F3
Pratt Ms CAMTN NW1 ....4 A1
Pratt St CAMTN NW1 ....4 A1
Pratt Wk LBTH SE11..........17 H6
Prayle Gv CRICK NW2..........64 B5
Prebend Gdns HMSMTH W6....118 C4
Prebend St IS N1..............6 C1
Prescot St WCHPL E1..........13 K5
Prescott Av STMC/STPC BR5..201 G3
Prescott Cl EMPK RM11........75 K5
Prescott Pl CLAP SW4........141 J4
Presentation Ms
 BRXS/STRHM SW2............162 A4
Presidents Dr WAP E1W.......123 J1
President St FSBYE EC1V *.....6 C4
Prespa Cl ED N9.............36 E4
Press Rd WLSDN NW10..........81 F1
Prestage Wy POP/IOD E14....106 A6
Prestbury Rd FSTGT E7........89 G3
Prestbury Sq ELTH/MOT SE9..166 E6
Prested Rd BTSEA SW11......140 D5
Preston Av CHING E4..........52 B2
Preston Cl STHWK SE1.........19 G6
 WHTN TW2.................155 K5
Preston Ct BAR EN5...........21 G5
 WOT/HER KT12..............188 B5
Preston Dr BXLYHN DA7........137 H1
 HOR/WEW KT19.............207 G4
 WAN E11...................71 G2
Preston Gdns IL IG1..........71 J3
 WLSDN NW10................81 G4
Preston Hill KTN/HRWW/WS HA3..62 A4
Preston Pl CRICK NW2.........81 J4
Preston Rd
 KTN/HRWW/WS HA3...........62 A4
 NRWD SE19................180 C2
 RYNPK SW20...............176 D3
 WAN E11...................70 C5
Preston's Rd POP/IOD E14....125 F1
 WWKM BR4.................214 E1
Preston Waye
 KTN/HRWW/WS HA3...........62 A5
Prestwich Ter CLAP SW4 *....141 J6
Prestwick Cl NWDGN UB2.....114 C5
Prestwick Rd OXHEY WD19......27 H5
Prestwood OXHEY WD19 *........27 J4
Prestwood Av
 KTN/HRWW/WS HA3...........61 H1
Prestwood Cl
 WOOL/PLUM SE18...........148 B1
Prestwood Dr CRW RM5.........56 E1
Prestwood Gdns
 CROY/NA CRO..............196 D4
Prestwood St IS N1 *...........6 D3
Pretoria Av WALTH E17........69 G1
Pretoria Crs CHING E4........38 A3
Pretoria Pde BROCKY SE4 *...144 D3
Pretoria Rd CAN/RD E16.....106 D2
 CHING E4..................38 A3
 IL IG1....................90 B2
 LEY E10...................69 F6
 ROMW/RG RM7...............74 E1
 STRHM/NOR SW16...........179 G2
 TOTM N17..................50 B2
Pretoria Rd North UED N18....50 B1
Prevost Rd FBAR/BDGN N11.....34 A4
Price Cl MLHL NW7............31 G5
 TOOT SW17................160 E5
Price Rd CROY/NA CRO.......211 H3
Price's St STHWK SE1.........18 B1
Pricklers Hl BAR EN5.........21 F6
Prickley Rd HAYES BR2.......199 J5
Priddy's Yd CROY/NA CRO.....196 D6
Prideaux Pl ACT W3...........99 F6
 FSBYW WC1X................5 H4
Prideaux Rd BRXN/ST SW9....141 K4
Pridham Rd THHTH CR7........196 E1
Priestfield Rd FSTH SE23....164 B5
Priestlands Park Rd
 BFN/LL DA15..............168 A5
Priestley Cl STNW/STAM N16...68 B4
Priestley Gdns CHDH RM6.....73 H3
Priestley Rd MTCM CR4.......179 F5
Priestley Wy CRICK NW2.......63 J5
 WALTH E17.................51 F6
Priest Park Av
 RYLN/HDSTN HA2............60 A6
Priests Av ROM RM1...........57 F5
Priests Br MORT/ESHN SW14..138 B4
Prima Rd BRXN/ST SW9.......142 B1
Primrose Av ENC/FH EN2.......23 K2
 GDMY/SEVK IG3............73 G4
Primrose Cl BOW E3 *........105 J1
 CAT SE6..................183 F1
 FNCH N3...................47 F1
 RYLN/HDSTN HA2............77 K1
 WLGTN SM6................195 G5
Primrose Dr WDR/YW UB7......112 A4
Primrose Gdns BUSH WD23......28 B2
 HAMP NW3..................83 J4
 RSLP HA4..................77 G3
Primrose Hl EMB EC4Y........11 K4

Primrose Hill Rd HAMP NW3....83 K5
Primrose Hill Studios
 CAMTN NW1 *...............84 A6
Primrose La CROY/NA CRO.....197 K5
Primrose Ms CAMTN NW1 *......83 K5
Primrose Pl ISLW TW7........136 A3
Primrose Rd LEY E10..........69 K5
 SWFD E18..................53 F5
Primrose Sq HOM E9...........86 E5
Primrose St SDTCH EC2A.......13 G1
Primrose Wk EW KT17.........207 H5
 NWCR SE14................144 B1
Primula St SHB W12...........99 J6
Prince Albert Rd CAMTN NW1 ...3 J2
 STJWD NW8..................2 D3
Prince Arthur Ms HAMP NW3....83 G2
Prince Arthur Rd HAMP NW3....83 H2
Prince Charles Dr HDN NW4....64 A4
Prince Charles Rd
 BKHTH/KID SE3............145 J2
Prince Charles Wy
 WLGTN SM6................210 B1
Prince Consort Dr CHST BR7..185 J4
Prince Consort Rd SKENS SW7..14 A4
Princedale Rd NTGHL W11.....119 H1
Prince Edward Rd HOM E9......87 J4
Prince George Av
 STHGT/OAK N14.............22 D6
Prince George Rd
 STNW/STAM N16.............86 A1
Prince Georges Av
 WIM/MER SW19.............178 C4
Prince Henry Rd CHARL SE7..126 B5
Prince Imperial Rd CHST BR7..185 G3
 WOOL/PLUM SE18...........146 D6
Prince John Rd ELTH/MOT SE9..146 D6
Princelet St WCHPL E1........13 K1
Prince of Orange La
 GNWCH SE10...............145 F1
Prince of Wales Cl HDN NW4...63 K1
Prince of Wales Dr
 BTSEA SW11...............140 E2
 VX/NE SW8................141 G1
Prince of Wales Ga SKENS SW7..14 C2
Prince of Wales Pas
 CAMTN NW1 *...............4 A5
Prince of Wales Rd
 BKHTH/KID SE3............145 J2
 CAN/RD E16...............107 G5
 KTTN NW5..................84 B4
 SUT SM1..................194 C6
Prince of Wales Ter
 CHSWK W4.................118 B5
 KENS W8 *................120 A2
Prince Regent La PLSTW E13..107 C3
Prince Regent Ms CAMTN NW1 *..4 A5
Prince Regent Rd HSLW TW3..135 H4
Prince Rupert Rd
 ELTH/MOT SE9.............146 D5
Princes Av ACT W3...........117 H3
 CAR SM5..................209 K5
 CDALE/KGS NW9.............62 C1
 FNCH N3...................47 F1
 GFD/PVL UB6...............96 B5
 MUSWH N10.................48 C1
 PLMGR N13.................49 G1
 STMC/STPC BR5............201 K2
 SURB KT6.................191 H6
 WDGN N22..................48 D4
 WFD IG8...................53 F2
Princes Cl CDALE/KGS NW9....62 C1
 EDGW HA8..................44 C1
 FSBYPK N4.................67 H5
 HPTN TW12................155 J6
 SCUP DA14................168 E5
Princes Ct WBLY HA9..........80 A3
Princes Dr HRW HA1...........42 E6
Princes Gdns ACT W3..........98 C5
 EA W5.....................97 J3
 SKENS SW7 *...............14 A4
Prince's Ga SKENS SW7........14 A3
Princes Gate Ct SKENS SW7....14 A3
Princes Gate Ms SKENS SW7....14 A4
Princes La MUSWH N10.........48 A6
Prince's Ms BAY/PAD W2 *....100 E6
 HMSMTH W6 *..............119 F5
 HSLW TW3.................135 F5
 IS N1.....................85 K5
Princes Pde GLDGN NW11 *.....64 C3
Princes Pk RAIN RM13.........93 J6
Princes Park Av GLDGN NW11...64 C3
 HYS/HAR UB3...............94 B6
Princes Park Cir HYS/HAR UB3..94 B6
Princes Park La HYS/HAR UB3..94 B6
Princes Park Pde
 HYS/HAR UB3...............94 B6
Princes Pl NTCHL W11........119 H1
Prince's Pln HAYES BR2......200 D4
Princes Ri LEW SE13.........145 F2
Princes Riverside Rd
 BERM/RHTH SE16...........124 A1
Princes Rd BARK/HLT IG6......72 D1
 BKHH IG9..................39 G4
 DART DA1.................170 E3
 FELT TW13................153 J5
 KUTN/CMB KT2..............175 H3
 MORT/ESHN SW14...........138 A4
 NWDGN UB2................114 E3
 RCH/KEW TW9..............137 G6
 ROM RM1...................75 H2
 TEDD TW11................155 J6
 UED N18...................36 E6
 WEA W13..................116 C1
 WIM/MER SW19.............177 K2
Princess Alice Wy THMD SE28..127 J2
Princess Av WBLY HA9.........62 A6
Princess Crs FSBYPK N4.......67 H6
Princesses Pde DART DA1 *...150 C6
Princess La RSLP HA4.........58 C5

Princess Louise Cl BAY/PAD W2..8 B1
Princess May Rd
 STNW/STAM N16.............86 A2
Princess Ms HAMP NW3 *.......83 H4
Princess Pde ORP BR6 *......216 A1
Prince's Sq BAY/PAD W2.......100 E6
 CROY/NA CRO..............196 D3
 KIL/WHAMP NW6............100 E1
Princess St BXLYHN DA7......149 G4
 STHWK SE1.................18 B5
 CROY/NA CRO..............196 D3
Prince's St RCH/KEW TW9......137 F5
 REGST W1B..................9 K4
 SUT SM1..................209 H2
 TOTM N17..................50 D5
Prince's Ter PLSTW E13.......89 F6
Prince St DEPT SE8...........124 C6
Princes Wy BKHH IG9..........39 G4
 CROY/NA CRO..............211 K3
 RSLP HA4..................77 J2
 WIM/MER SW19.............159 G2
 WWKM BR4.................214 D2
Prince's Yd NTGHL W11.......119 H1
Princethorpe Rd SYD SE26....164 A6
Princeton St GINN WC1R.......11 H1
Pringle Gdns
 STRHM/NOR SW16...........161 H6
Printers Inn Ct
 FLST/FETLN EC4A...........11 J3
Printinghouse La
 HYS/HAR UB3..............113 H2
Printing House Yd BETH E2 *...7 H5
Priolo Rd CHARL SE7.........126 B5
Prior Av BELMT SM2..........209 J5
Prior Bolton St IS N1........85 H4
Prioress Rd WNWD SE27......162 C5
Prioress St STHWK SE1........19 G5
Prior Rd IL IG1..............90 A1
Priors Cft WALTH E17.........51 G5
Priorsford Av BECK BR3......182 B5
Priors Gdns RSLP HA4.........77 G3
Priors Md EN EN1.............24 C1
Prior St GNWCH SE10.........145 F1
Priory Av ALP/SUD HA0........79 F2
 CEND/HSY/T N8.............66 D1
 CHEAM SM3................208 B2
 CHING E4..................37 H5
 HNWL W7.................116 A1
 STMC/STPC BR5............201 J3
 WALTH E17.................69 J2
Priory Cl ALP/SUD HA0........79 F2
 BECK BR3.................182 B6
 CHING E4..................37 H5
 DART DA1.................151 F6
 FNCH N3...................46 D4
 HPTN TW12................172 E4
 HYS/HAR UB3...............95 F6
 RSLP HA4..................59 F5
 STAN HA7..................29 F6
 STHGT/OAK N14.............22 B6
 SWFD E18..................52 E4
 TRDG/WHET N20.............32 D2
 WIM/MER SW19 *...........178 A4
Priory Cottages EA W5 *......98 B4
Priory Ct BLKFR EC4V *.......12 A4
 VX/NE SW8................141 J2
 WALTH E17.................51 H6
Priory Crs ALP/SUD HA0.......79 G1
 CHEAM SM3................208 B2
 NRWD SE19................180 D2
Priory Dr ABYW SE2..........128 E5
 STAN HA7..................29 F5
Priory Field Dr EDGW HA8.....30 D6
Priory Gdns ALP/SUD HA0......79 G2
 BARN SW13................138 C4
 CEND/HSY/T N8.............66 E2
 CHSWK W4.................118 B4
 DART DA1.................151 G6
 HGT N6....................66 B3
 HPTN TW12................172 E4
 SNWD SE25................197 G1
Priory Green Est IS N1........5 G2
Priory Gv VX/NE SW8.........141 K2
Priory Hl ALP/SUD HA0........79 G2
 DART DA1.................171 G1
Priory La E/WMO/HCT KT8.....189 F1
 PUT/ROE SW15.............138 C6
Priory Leas ELTH/MOT SE9 *..166 D3
Priory Market Pl DART DA1 *..171 F1
Priory Ms HNWL W7............95 K5
Priory Pk BKHTH/KID SE3.....145 J4
Priory Park Rd ALP/SUD HA0...79 G2
 KIL/WHAMP NW6.............82 D6
Priory Pl DART DA1..........171 G1
Priory Rd BARK IG11..........90 D5
 CEND/HSY/T N8.............67 F1
 CHEAM SM3................208 B2
 CHSGTN KT9...............206 A1
 CHSWK W4.................118 A3
 CROY/NA CRO..............196 B4
 DART DA1.................171 G1
 EHAM E6...................89 H6
 HPTN TW12................172 E3
 HSLW TW3.................135 H6
 KIL/WHAMP NW6.............83 F5
 MUSWH N10.................48 B4
 RCH/KEW TW9..............117 H6
Priory St BOW E3 *..........105 K2
Priory Ter KIL/WHAMP NW6.....83 F6
The Priory BKHTH/KID SE3....145 J5
 CROY/NA CRO *............211 G1
 ORP BR6 *................202 C4
Priory Vw BUSH WD23..........28 E2
Priory Vs FBAR/BDGN N11 *....47 K2
Priory Wk WBPTN SW10........120 B5
Priory Wy NWDGN UB2.........114 C3
 RYLN/HDSTN HA2............60 B1
 WDR/YW UB7..............112 B6
Pritchard's Rd BETH E2......104 C1
Pritter Rd BERM/RHTH SE16 *..123 H3
Private Rd EN EN1............23 K6
Probert Rd BRXS/STRHM SW2..142 B6
Probyn Rd BRXS/STRHM SW2...162 C4
Procter St GINN WC1R.........11 G2
Proctor Cl MTCM CR4.........179 F4

Proctors Cl EBED/NFELT TW14..153 K3
Progress Wy CROY/NA CRO.....196 A6
 EN EN1....................36 C1
 WDGN N22..................49 G4
Promenade Approach Rd
 CHSWK W4.................138 B2
The Promenade CHSWK W4......138 B2
 EDGW HA8 *................44 C1
Prospect Cl BELV DA17.......129 H4
 HSLW TW5.................134 C2
 RSLP HA4..................59 H4
 SYD SE26.................163 J6
Prospect Cottages
 WAND/EARL SW18...........139 K5
Prospect Crs WHTN TW2.......155 H1
Prospect Hl WALTH E17........69 K1
Prospect Pl CHSWK W4 *......118 A5
 CRICK NW2.................82 D1
 CRW RM5...................56 E1
 EFNCH N2..................65 H1
 HAYES BR2................184 A6
 RYNPK SW20...............176 D5
 WAP E1W..................123 K1
Prospect Rd BAR EN5..........20 D5
 CRICK NW2.................82 D1
 SURB KT6.................190 D5
 WFD IG8...................39 G6
Prospect St BERM/RHTH SE16..123 J2
Prospect V WOOL/PLUM SE18...126 D4
Prospero Rd ARCH N19.........66 D5
Protea Cl CAN/RD E16.........106 D3
Prothero Gdns HDN NW4........63 K2
Prothero Rd FUL/PGN SW6.....139 H1
Prout Gv WLSDN NW10..........81 G1
Prout Rd CLPT E5.............86 D1
Provence St IS N1.............6 D2
Providence Av
 RYLN/HDSTN HA2............60 A5
Providence Cl HOM E9 *.......87 F7
Providence Ct MYFR/PKLN W1K...9 H5
Providence La HYS/HAR UB3...133 G1
Providence Pl CRW RM5........56 B4
 IS N1......................6 B2
Providence Rd WDR/YW UB7...112 B1
Providence Row G BOW E3.....104 D2
Providence Sq STHWK SE1 *....19 J1
Providence Yd BETH E2 *.....104 C2
Provincial Ter PGE/AN SE20 *..182 A3
Provost Est IS N1............7 E4
Provost Rd HAMP NW3..........83 K5
Provost St IS N1..............7 E6
Prowse Av BUSH WD23..........28 C4
Prowse Pl CAMTN NW1 *........84 B5
Pruden Cl STHGT/OAK N14 *....34 C4
Prusom St WAP E1W............123 J1
Pucknells Cl SWLY BR8.......187 K4
Pudding La MON EC3R..........13 F6
Pudding Mill La SRTFD E15....105 K1
Puddle Dock BLKFR EC4V.......12 B5
Puffin Cl BARK IG11.........109 H2
 BECK BR3.................198 A2
Pulborough Rd
 WAND/EARL SW18...........159 J2
Pulborough Wy HSLWW TW4....134 B5
Pulford Rd SEVS/STOTM N15....67 K3
Pulham Av EFNCH N2...........65 H1
Puller Rd BAR EN5............20 C3
Pulleyns Av EHAM E6.........107 J2
Pullman Gdns PUT/ROE SW15..159 F1
Pullman Ms LEE/GVPK SE12...166 A6
Pullman Pl ELTH/MOT SE9....146 D6
Pulross Rd BRXN/ST SW9.....142 A4
Pulteney Cl BOW E3 *.........87 H6
Pulteney Rd SWFD E18.........53 F2
 ISLW TW7 *...............136 B4
Pulteney Rd SWFD E18.........53 F2
Pulton Pl FUL/PGN SW6.......139 K1
Puma Ct WCHPL E1.............13 J1
Pump Aly BTFD TW8...........136 E1
Pump Cl NTHLT UB5.............96 A1
Pump House Cl HAYES BR2.....183 J5
 CHSWK W4.................138 B1
Pump La HYS/HAR UB3.........113 K2
 NWCR SE14................143 H1
Punchard Crs PEND EN3 *......25 J3
Punderson's Gdns BETH E2....104 D2
Purbeck Av NWMAL KT3........192 C3
Purbeck Dr CRICK NW2.........64 B6
Purbeck Rd EMPK RM11.........75 J2
Purbrook St STHWK SE1........19 H4
Purcell Crs FUL/PGN SW6.....119 G6
Purcell Crescent FUL/PGN SW6..139 H1
Purcell Ms WLSDN NW10........81 G5
Purcell Rd GFD/PVL UB6.......96 B4
Purcers Cross Rd
 FUL/PGN SW6..............139 J2
Purchese St CAMTN NW1 *......4 C2
Purdy St BOW E3.............105 K3
Purelake Ms LEW SE13 *......145 G4
Purfleet Industrial Access Rd
 SOCK/AV RM15.............131 J6
Purkis Cl UX/CGN UB8.........94 A6
Purland Cl BCTR RM8..........74 B5
Purland Rd THMD SE28.......128 B2
Purleigh Av WFD IG8..........53 J2
Purley Av CRICK NW2..........64 C6
Purley Cl CLAY IG5...........54 A5
Purley Pl IS N1..............85 H5
Purley Rd ED N9..............35 K5
 SAND/SEL CR2.............211 K6
Purley Wy CROY/NA CRO.......196 A5
Purneys Rd ELTH/MOT SE9....146 C5
Purrett Rd WOOL/PLUM SE18..128 A5
Pursers Cross Rd
 FUL/PGN SW6..............139 J2
Pursewardens Cl WEA W13.....116 D1
Pursley Rd MLHL NW7..........45 K3
Purves Rd WLSDN NW10.........99 K2
Putney Br PUT/ROE SW15......139 H4
Putney Bridge Ap
 FUL/PGN SW6..............139 H4
Putney Bridge Rd
 PUT/ROE SW15.............139 J5

Putney Common
 PUT/ROE SW15.............139 F4
Putney Ex PUT/ROE SW15 *....139 G5
Putney Gdns CHDH RM6.........73 H2
Putney Heath PUT/ROE SW15..158 E1
Putney Heath La
 PUT/ROE SW15.............159 G1
Putney High St
 PUT/ROE SW15.............139 H5
Putney Hl PUT/ROE SW15.....159 G2
Putney Park Av
 PUT/ROE SW15.............138 D5
Putney Park La
 PUT/ROE SW15.............138 E5
Puttenham Cl OXHEY WD19......27 G5
Pycombe Cnr
 NFNCH/WDSPK N12..........32 D6
Pycroft Wy ED N9............36 C6
Pylbrook Rd SUT SM1.........208 E1
Pylon Wy CROY/NA CRO.......195 K5
Pym Cl EBAR EN4..............21 H6
Pymers Md DUL SE21..........162 D5
Pymmes Brook Trail EBAR EN4..21 J8
 EBAR EN4..................33 K2
 ED N9.....................36 D5
 STHGT/OAK N14.............34 E6
Pymmes Cl PLMGR N13.........49 F1
 TOTM N17..................50 A4
Pymmes Gdns North ED N9.....36 B5
Pymmes Gdns South ED N9.....36 B5
Pymmes Green Rd
 BAR/BDGN N11..............34 B6
Pymmes Rd PLMGR N13..........48 E2
Pymms Brook Dr EBAR EN4......21 J5
Pyne Rd SURB KT6............191 H5
Pynham Cl ABYW SE2..........128 B3
Pynnacles Cl STAN HA7.........43 H1
Pyrland Rd HBRY N5............86 A1
 RCHPK/HAM TW10...........157 G1
Pyrmont Gv WNWD SE27.......162 C5
Pyrmont Rd CHSWK W4.........117 H6
Pytchley Crs NRWD SE19.....180 D2
Pytchley Rd EDUL SE22.......143 F4

The Quadrangle BAY/PAD W2......8 C3
 HNHL SE24 *..............142 D6
 WBPTN SW10 *.............140 B2
Quadrant Ar REGST W1B.......10 B6
Quadrant Cl HDN NW4..........63 K2
Quadrant Gv KTTN NW5.........83 K3
Quadrant Rd RCH/KEW TW9....136 E5
 THHTH CR7................196 C1
The Quadrant BELMT SM2.....209 G4
 BXLYHN DA7...............148 E1
 EDGW HA8 *................44 C2
 NKENS W10 *..............100 B2
 RCH/KEW TW9..............136 E6
 RYLN/HDSTN HA2 *..........42 D6
 RYNPK SW20...............177 H4
Quad Rd WBLY HA9.............79 K1
Quaggy Wk BKHTH/KID SE3....145 K5
Quainton St WLSDN NW10.......81 F1
Quaker La NWDGN UB2.........115 F3
Quakers Course
 CDALE/KGS NW9.............45 H4
Quakers La ISLW TW7.........136 B1
Quakers Pl FSTGT E7..........89 H3
Quaker St WCHPL E1...........13 J1
Quality Ct LINN WC2A.........11 J3
Quantock Cl HYS/HAR UB3 *....133 G1
Quantock Gdns CRICK NW2......64 B6
Quantock Ms PECK SE15......143 H3
Quantock Rd BXLYHN DA7.....150 B5
Quarles Cl CRW RM5...........56 C3
Quarles Park Rd CHDH RM6....73 H3
Quarrendon St FUL/PGN SW6..139 K3
Quarr Rd CAR SM5............194 C3
Quarry Ms PUR RM19..........131 K4
Quarry Park Rd SUT SM1......208 D4
Quarry Ri SUT SM1...........208 D4
Quarry Rd WAND/EARL SW18...160 B1
Quartermile La LEY E10.......87 K2
Quatre Ports CHING E4........52 B1
Quay House POP/IOD E14 *....124 D2
Quebec Ms MBLAR W1H..........9 F4
Quebec Rd GNTH/NBYPK IG2....72 C4
 YEAD UB4..................95 G6
Quebec Wy
 BERM/RHTH SE16...........124 A2
Queen Adelaide Rd
 PGE/AN SE20..............181 K3
Queen Anne Av HAYES BR2....183 K6
Queen Anne Dr
 ESH/CLAY KT10............204 E5
Queen Anne Ga BXLYHN DA7...148 E4
Queen Anne Ms
 CAVSQ/HST W1G..............9 K2
Queen Anne Rd HOM E9.........87 F4
Queen Anne's Cl WHTN TW2...155 J5
Queen Anne's Gdns
 CHSWK W4.................118 B3
 EA W5....................117 F2
 EN EN1....................36 A1
 MTCM CR4 *...............179 F5
Queen Anne's Gv CHSWK W4...118 B3
 EA W5....................117 F2
 EN EN1....................36 A1
Queen Anne's Pl EN EN1.......36 A1
Queen Anne St
 CAVSQ/HST W1G..............9 K3
Queen Anne Ter WAP E1W *....104 D6
Queen Borough Gdns
 CHST BR7 *...............185 J2
Queenborough Gdns
 GNTH/NBYPK IG2............72 A1
Queen Caroline Est
 HMSMTH W6...............119 F5
Queen Caroline St
 HMSMTH W6...............119 F5

Queen Elizabeth Buildings
EMB EC4Y *...........11 J5
Queen Elizabeth College
GNWCH SE10 *...........145 F1
Queen Elizabeth Gdns
MRDN SM4...........193 K1
Queen Elizabeth Rd
KUTN/CMB KT2...........175 G5
WALTH E17...........51 G6
Queen Elizabeth's Cl
STNW/STAM N16...........67 K6
Queen Elizabeth's Dr
STHGT/OAK N14...........34 E3
Queen Elizabeth St STHWK SE1...19 J2
Queen Elizabeth's Wk
STNW/STAM N16...........67 K6
WLGTN SM6...........210 D2
Queen Elizabeth Wk
BARN SW13...........138 E2
Queenhithe BLKFR EC4V...........12 D6
Queen Isabella Wy STBT EC1A...12 B3
Queen Margaret's Gv IS N1...........86 A3
Queen Mary Av RYNPK SW20...193 C2
Queen Mary Rd ROM RM1...........75 H3
SURB KT6...........206 C1
Queen Mary Rd NRWD SE19...180 C2
Queen Mary's Av CAR SM5...........209 K5
Queen Mother Ga
MYFR/PICC W1J...........15 H1
Queens Acre CHEAM SM3...........208 B5
Queens Av FELT TW13...........154 B6
FNCH N3...........47 C3
GFD/PVL UB6...........96 B5
KTN/HRWW/WS HA3...........48 A6
MUSWH N10...........48 A6
TRDG/WHET N20...........33 H4
WCHMH N21...........35 H3
WFD IG8...........53 F1

Queensberry Ms West
SKENS SW7 *...........14 A6
Queensberry Pl MNPK E12...........89 H3
SKENS SW7...........14 A6
Queensberry Wy SKENS SW7 *...14 A6
Queensborough Ms
BAY/PAD W2 *...........101 C6
Queensborough Studios
BAY/PAD W2 *...........101 F6
Queensborough Ter
BAY/PAD W2...........101 C6
Queensbridge Pk ISLW TW7...155 K1
Queensbridge Rd HACK E8...........7 K1
Queensbury Rd ALP/SUD HA0...80 A6
CDALE/KGS NW9...........63 F4
Queens Circ VX/NE SW8...........141 G1
Queen's Cl EDGW HA8...........44 C1
ESH/CLAY KT10 *...........204 B2
WLGTN SM6...........210 B3
Queen's Club Gdns
WKENS W14...........119 H6
Queens Club Ter
WKENS W14 *...........119 J6
Queenscourt WBLY HA9...........80 A2
Queen's Crs KTTN NW5...........84 A4
RCHPK/HAM TW10...........137 G6
Queenscroft Rd
ELTH/MOT SE9...........146 C6
Queensdale Crs NTGHL W11...119 C1
Queensdale Pl NTGHL W11...119 H1
Queensdale Rd NTGHL W11...119 H1
Queensdale Wk NTGHL W11...119 H1
Queens Down Rd CLPT E5...........86 D2
Queens Dr BRYLDS KT5...........191 H4
EA W5...........98 B5
FSBYPK N4...........67 H6
LEY E10...........69 J4
THDIT KT7...........190 B3
Queen's Elm Sq CHEL SW3...........120 C5
Queen's Gdns BAY/PAD W2...101 C6
EA W5...........97 J4
HEST TW5...........134 A5
RAIN RM13...........111 F1
Queens Garth FSTH SE23 *...163 K4
Queens Ga SKENS SW7...........120 B2
Queensgate Gdns CHST BR7...185 J4
Queensgate Gdns
PUT/ROE SW15...........138 E6
Queen's Gate Gdns
SKENS SW7...........120 B3
Queen's Gate Ms SKENS SW7...120 B3
Queensgate Pl
KIL/WHAMP NW6...........82 E5
Queen's Gate Pl SKENS SW7...120 B3
Queen's Gate Place Ms
SKENS SW7...........120 B4
Queen's Gate Ter SKENS SW7...120 B3
Queen's Gv STJWD NW8...........2 A1
Queen's Grove Rd CHING E4...38 B3
Queen's Head St IS N1...........6 B1
Queens Keep TWK TW1 *...........156 D1
WIM/MER SW19...........178 A4
Queensland Cl WALTH E17...51 H5
Queensland Rd HOLWY N7...........85 G2
Queens La MUSWH N10...........48 B6
Queens Md EDGW HA8...........44 B2
Queensmead STJWD NW8...........83 H6
Queen's Mead Rd HAYES BR2...183 J5
Queensmere Cl
WIM/MER SW19...........159 G4
Queensmere Rd
WIM/MER SW19...........159 G4
Queensmill Rd FUL/PGN SW6...139 C1
Queens Pde
CEND/HSY/T N8 *...........67 H1
CRICK NW2 *...........82 A4
EA W5 *...........98 B5
FBAR/BDGN N11 *...........47 K1
FBAR/BDGN N11 *...........48 E3
HDN NW4 *...........63 K2
Queens Parade Cl
FBAR/BDGN N11 *...........47 K1
Queens Park Gdns FELT TW13...153 J5
Queen's Pl MRDN SM4...........193 K1
Queens Prom KUT/HW KT1...190 E1
Queen Sq BMSBY WC1N...........5 F7

Queen's Ride BARN SW13...........138 E4
Queen's Ri RCHPK/HAM TW10...157 G1
Queens Rd BAR EN5...........20 B4
BARK IG11...........90 C5
BECK BR3...........182 B5
BKHH IG9...........39 F4
BMLY BR1...........183 K5
CHST BR7...........185 G2
CROY/NA CRO...........196 C3
EA W5...........98 A5
ED N9...........36 D4
EN EN1...........24 A5
ERITH DA8...........130 B6
FBAR/BDGN N11...........48 E3
FELT TW13...........154 A3
FNCH N3...........47 C4
HDN NW4...........64 A2
HPTN TW12...........155 C6
HSLW TW3...........135 C4
HYS/HAR UB3...........94 C5
KUTN/CMB KT2...........175 H3
MORT/ESHN SW14...........138 A4
MRDN SM4...........193 K1
MTCM CR4...........178 C6
NWDGN UB2...........114 C2
NWMAL KT3...........192 C1
PECK SE15...........143 K2
PLSTW E13...........89 F6
RCHPK/HAM TW10...........157 C1
TEDD TW11...........174 A2
THDIT KT7...........190 A2
TWK TW1...........156 A3
WALTH E17...........69 H3
WAN E11...........70 C4
WDR/YW UB7...........112 C2
WELL DA16...........148 C3
WIM/MER SW19...........177 K2
WLSDN NW10...........81 J5
Queen's Rd West PLSTW E13...........106 E1
Queen's Rw WALW SE17...........122 E6
Queens Ter ISLW TW7...........136 B5
PLSTW E13...........89 F6
STJWD NW8...........2 A4
THDIT KT7...........190 B3
WCHPL E1 *...........104 E3
Queen Terrace Cottages
HNWL W7 *...........115 K2
Queensthorpe Ms SYD SE26 *...164 A6
Queensthorpe Rd SYD SE26...164 A6
Queenstown Gdns RAIN RM13...111 H2
Queenstown Rd VX/NE SW8...121 C6
Queen St BXLYHN DA7...........149 G4
CROY/NA CRO...........211 J2
ERITH DA8 *...........130 B6
MYFR/PICC W1J...........9 J7
ROMW/RG RM7...........75 F3
TOTM N17...........50 A2
Queen Street Pl CANST EC4R...12 D6
Queensville Rd BAL SW12...........161 J2
Queens Wk ASHF TW15...........152 A6
CDALE/KGS NW9...........62 E6
CHING E4...........38 B3
EA W5...........97 J3
HRW HA1...........60 E2
RSLP HA4...........77 C1
Queens Walk Ter RSLP HA4 *...77 C1
The Queens Wk STHWK SE1...........13 H7
Queensway BAY/PAD W2...........101 F6
CROY/NA CRO...........211 F4
Queens Wy FELT TW13...........154 B6
HDN NW4...........64 A2
Queensway PEND EN3...........24 E5
STMC/STPC BR5...........201 H2
SUN TW16...........172 A5
WWKM BR4...........214 E2
Queens Well Av
TRDG/WHET N20...........33 J6
Queen's Whf HMSMTH W6...........119 F5
Queenswood Av HPTN TW12...173 C2
HSLW TW3...........134 E3
THHTH CR7...........196 B2
WALTH E17...........52 A4
WLGTN SM6...........210 D3
Queenswood Gdns WAN E11...........70 E5
Queenswood Pk FNCH N3...........46 C5
Queenswood Rd
BFN/LL DA15...........168 A1
FSTH SE23...........164 A5
Queen's Wood Rd HGT N6...........66 B3
Queen's Yd FITZ W1T...........4 A7
Queen Victoria Av
ALP/SUD HA0...........79 K5
Queen Victoria St BLKFR EC4V...12 A5
Queen Victoria Ter
WAP E1W *...........104 D6

R

Rabbit Rw KENS W8 *...........119 K1
Rabbits Rd MNPK E12...........89 J2
Rabournmead Dr NTHLT UB5...77 J5
Raby Rd NWMAL KT3...........192 A1
Raby St POP/IOD E14 *...........105 C5
Raccoon Wy HSLWW TW4...134 B3
Rachel Cl BARK/HLT IG6...........72 D1
Rackham Cl WELL DA16...........148 C3
Rackham Ms
STRHM/NOR SW16...........179 H2
Racton Rd FUL/PGN SW6...........119 K6
Radbourne Av EA W5...........116 D4
Radbourne Cl CLPT E5...........87 F2
Radbourne Ct
KTN/HRWW/WS HA3 *...........61 H3
Radbourne Crs WALTH E17...52 B6
Radbourne Rd BAL SW12...........161 H2
Radbourne Av ENC/FH EN2...........99 J1
Radcliffe Gdns CAR SM5...........209 J5
Radcliffe Rd CROY/NA CRO...197 C6
KTN/HRWW/WS HA3...........43 C5
STHWK SE1 *...........19 H4
WDGN N21...........35 J4
Radcliffe Sq PUT/ROE SW15...159 C1
Radcliffe Wy NTHLT UB5...........95 H2
Radcot St LBTH SE11...........122 B5
Raddington Rd NKENS W10...100 C4
Radfield Wy BFN/LL DA15...167 J2
Radford Rd LEW SE13...........165 F1
Radford Rd WLSDN NW10 *...90 C2
Radford Wy BARK IG11...........109 F2
Radipole Rd FUL/PGN SW6...........139 J2
Radius Pk EBED/NFELT TW14 *.133 J5
Radland Rd CAN/RD E16...........106 E5
Radlet Av SYD SE26...........163 J5
Radlett Cl FSTGT E7...........88 D4
Radlett Pl STJWD NW8...........2 C1
Radley Av GDMY/SEVK IG3...91 F2
Radley Cl EBED/NFELT TW14...153 J3
Radley Ct BERM/RHTH SE16...124 A2
Radley Gdns
KTN/HRWW/WS HA3...........62 A1
Radley Ms KENS W8...........119 K3
Radley Rd TOTM N17...........50 B5
Radley's La SWFD E18...........52 E5
Radleys Md DAGE RM10...........92 D4
Radley Sq CLPT E5 *...........68 E6
Radley Ter CAN/RD E16...........106 D4
Radlix Rd LEY E10...........69 J5
Radnor Av HRW HA1...........60 E2
WELL DA16...........148 C6
Radnor Cl CHST BR7...........185 K2
MTCM CR4...........195 K2
Radnor Crs REDBR IG4...........71 K2
WOOL/PLUM SE18...........148 B1
Radnor Gdns EN EN1...........24 A2
TWK TW1...........156 A4
Radnor Ms BAY/PAD W2...........8 B4
Radnor Rd HRW HA1...........60 D2
KIL/WHAMP NW6...........82 C6
PECK SE15...........143 H1
TWK TW1...........156 A4
Radnor St FSBYE EC1V...........6 E6
Radnor Ter WKENS W14...........119 J4
Radnor Wk CHEL SW3...........120 D5
CROY/NA CRO...........198 B4
Radnor Wy WLSDN NW10...........98 D3
Radstock Av
KTN/HRWW/WS HA3...........43 C6
Radstock Cl FBAR/BDGN N11...48 A1
Radstock St BTSEA SW11...........140 D1
DART DA1...........150 E6
Raeburn Av BRYLDS KT5...........191 J3
SURB KT6...........191 J3
Raeburn Cl GLDGN NW11...........65 C3
KUT/HW KT1...........174 D5
Raeburn Rd BFN/LL DA15...167 K1
EDGW HA8...........44 C5
YEAD UB4...........94 B1
Raeburn St BRXS/STRHM SW2...141 K5
Rafford Wy BMLY BR1...........184 A5
Raggleswood CHST BR7...........185 F4
Raglan Cl HSLWW TW4...........134 E6
Raglan Ct SAND/SEL CR2...........211 H3
Raglan Gdns OXHEY WD19...........27 C3
Raglan Rd BELV DA17...........129 C4
EN EN1...........36 B2
HAYES BR2...........200 B1
WALTH E17...........70 A2
WOOL/PLUM SE18...........127 H5
Raglan Ter RYLN/HDSTN HA2 *...78 B2
Raglan Vis WALTH E17 *...........70 A2
Raglan Wy NTHLT UB5...........78 E4
Ragley Cl ACT W3...........117 K2
Raider Cl ROMW/RG RM7...........56 D4
Railey Ms KTTN NW5...........84 C3
Railshead Rd ISLW TW7...........136 C5
Railton Rd HNHL SE24...........142 B6
Railway Ap FSBYPK N4...........67 H6
HRW HA1...........61 F1
STHWK SE1...........12 E7
TWK TW1...........156 B2
WLGTN SM6...........210 B4
Railway Av BRXN/ST SW9 *...142 B5
Railway Cottages
HMSMTH W6 *...........119 F2
SRTFD E15 *...........106 C1
WIM/MER SW19 *...........160 A6
Railway Gv NWCR SE14...........144 C1
Railway Pl BELV DA17...........129 H3
Railway Rd EDUL SE22...........143 F5
Railway Rd TEDD TW11...........155 K6
Railway Side BARN SW13...........138 B4
Railway Station Whf LEY E10 *...69 G5
Railway St BCTR RM8...........73 J5
IS N1...........5 F4
Railway Ter FELT TW13...........153 K3
LEW SE13...........144 E6
WALTH E17...........52 A4
Rainborough Cl WBLY HA9...........80 A4

Rainbow Av POP/IOD E14...........124 E5
Rainbow Ct OXHEY WD19...........27 G1
Rainbow Quay
BERM/RHTH SE16...........124 B3
Rainbow St CMBW SE5...........143 F1
Raine St WAP E1W...........123 J1
Rainham Cl BTSEA SW11...........160 E1
ELTH/MOT SE9...........167 K1
Rainham Rd RAIN RM13...........111 J2
WLSDN NW10...........100 A2
Rainham Rd North DAGE RM10...92 D1
Rainham Rd South DAGE RM10...92 E1
Rainhill Wy BOW E3...........105 J2
Rainsborough Av DEPT SE8...........124 B5
Rainsford Cl STAN HA7...........43 J1
Rainsford Rd WLSDN NW10...........98 D2
Rainsford St BAY/PAD W2...........8 C3
Rainsford Wy HCH RM12...........75 J5
Rainton Rd CHARL SE7...........125 K5
Rainville Rd HMSMTH W6...........119 F6
Raisins Hl PIN HA5...........41 G6
Raith Av STHGT/OAK N14...........34 D5
Raleigh Av WLGTN SM6...........210 D2
YEAD UB4...........95 F4
Raleigh Cl ERITH DA8...........130 C6
HDN NW4...........64 A2
PIN HA5...........59 H4
Raleigh Dr BRYLDS KT5...........191 K5
ESH/CLAY KT10...........204 D3
TRDG/WHET N20...........33 J4
Raleigh Gdns
BRXS/STRHM SW2...........162 A1
MTCM CR4...........178 E6
Raleigh Ms IS N1...........6 B1
ORP BR6...........217 F3
Raleigh Rd CEND/HSY/T N8...67 G1
ENC/FH EN2...........24 C3
FELT TW13...........153 J4
NWDGN UB2...........114 D5
PGE/AN SE20...........182 A3
RCH/KEW TW9...........137 G4
Raleigh St IS N1...........6 B1
Raleigh Wy FELT TW13...........172 B1
STHGT/OAK N14...........34 D3
Ralph Perring Ct BECK BR3...........198 D1
Ralston St CHEL SW3...........120 E5
Ralston Wy OXHEY WD19...........27 H4
Rama Cl STRHM/NOR SW16...179 K3
Ramac Wy CHARL SE7...........126 A4
Rama La NRWD SE19...........181 G3
Rambler Cl STRHM/NOR SW16...161 H6
Rame Cl TOOT SW17...........179 F1
Ramillies Cl BRXS/STRHM SW2...161 K1
Ramillies Pl SOHO/CST W1F...10 A4
Ramillies Rd BFN/LL DA15...168 C1
CHSWK W4...........118 A4
MLHL NW7...........31 G4
Ramillies St SOHO/SHAV W1D...10 A4
Ramones Ter MTCM CR4 *...195 H1
Rampart St WCHPL E1...........104 D5
Ram Pas KUT/HW KT1...........174 E5
Rampayne St PIM SW1V...........121 J5
Rampton Cl CHING E4...........37 J5
Ramsay Gdns HARH RM3...........57 K3
Ramsay Ms CHEL SW3...........120 D6
Ramsay Pl HRW HA1 *...........60 E3
Ramsay Rd ACT W3...........117 K3
FSTGT E7...........88 C1
Ramsdale Rd TOOT SW17...........179 F1
Ramsden Cl STMC/STPC BR5...202 D5
Ramsden Dr CRW RM5...........56 C5
Ramsden Ga BAL SW12 *...........161 C2
Ramsden Rd BAL SW12...........161 F2
ERITH DA8...........150 A1
FBAR/BDGN N11...........47 K1
ORP BR6...........202 C4
Ramsey Cl CDALE/KGS NW9...63 H3
GFD/PVL UB6...........78 D3
Ramsey Dr THHTH CR7...........196 B3
Ramsey Rd THHTH CR7...........196 C3
Ramsey Wk IS N1...........85 K4
Ramsey Wy STHGT/OAK N14...34 C2
Ramsgate Cl CAN/RD E16...........126 A1
Ramsgate St HACK E8 *...........86 B4
Ramsgill Ap GNTH/NBYPK IG2...73 F1
Ramsgill Dr GNTH/NBYPK IG2...73 F2
Rams Gv CHDH RM6...........74 A1
Ramulis Dr YEAD UB4...........95 J3
Ramus Wood Av ORP BR6...........216 E3
Rancliffe Gdns ELTH/MOT SE9...146 D5
Rancliffe Rd EHAM E6...........107 J1
Randall Av CRICK NW2...........81 G1
Randall Cl BTSEA SW11...........140 D2
ERITH DA8...........129 K6
Randall Pl GNWCH SE10...........145 F1
Randall Rd LBTH SE11...........122 K5
Randall Rw LBTH SE11...........17 H7
Randalls Rd BELV DA17...........84 E6
Randisbourne Gdns CAT SE6 *...164 E5
Randle Rd RCHPK/HAM TW10...156 D6
Randlesdown Rd CAT SE6...........164 D5
Randolf Rd HAYES BR2...........200 E5
Randolph Av MV/WKIL W9...........101 G5
Randolph Cl BXLYHN DA7...........150 A4
KUTN/CMB KT2...........175 K1
Randolph Crs MV/WKIL W9...........101 G3
Randolph Gdns
KIL/WHAMP NW6...........101 F1
Randolph Ms MV/WKIL W9...101 G3
Randolph Rd MV/WKIL W9...........101 G3
STHL UB1...........114 E2
Randolph St CAMTN NW1...........84 C5
Ranelagh Av BARN SW13...........138 D3
FUL/PGN SW6...........139 J4
Ranelagh Br BAY/PAD W2 *...101 F4
Ranelagh Dr EDGW HA8...........30 C3
TWK TW1...........156 C5
Ranelagh Gdns BXLYHN DA7...........43 J6
CHSWK W4...........138 A1
FUL/PGN SW6...........139 H4
IL IG1...........72 A5
WAN E11...........71 H2
Ranelagh Gv BCVA SW1W...........121 F5

Ranelagh Rd ALP/SUD HA0...........79 K4
EA W5...........116 E2
EHAM E6...........90 A6
PIM SW1V...........121 H5
SRTFD E15...........106 C1
STHL UB1...........114 C1
TOTM N17...........50 A2
WAN E11...........88 C2
WDGN N22...........49 F4
WLSDN NW10...........99 H1
Ranfurly Rd SUT SM1...........193 K6
Rangefield Rd BMLY BR1...........183 H1
Rangemoor Rd
SEVS/STOTM N15...........68 B2
Rangers Rd BKHH IG9...........38 E2
Rangeworth Pl BFN/LL DA15...168 A5
Rangoon St TWRH EC3N *...........13 J4
Rankin Cl CDALE/KGS NW9...........45 G6
Ranleigh Gdns BXLYHN DA7...150 G1
Ranmere St BAL SW12...........161 G3
Ranmoor Cl HRW HA1...........60 D1
Ranmoor Gdns HRW HA1...........60 D1
Ranmore Av CROY/NA CRO...212 B1
Ranmore Pth
STMC/STPC BR5...........202 B1
Ranmore Rd BELMT SM2...........208 B6
Rannoch Cl EDGW HA8...........30 D4
Rannoch Rd HMSMTH W6...........119 F6
Rannock Av CDALE/KGS NW9...63 G4
Ransom Cl OXHEY WD19...........27 G2
Ransom Rd CHARL SE7 *...........126 B5
Ranston St CAMTN NW1...........8 C1
Ranulf Rd CRICK NW2...........82 D2
Ranwell Cl BOW E3 *...........87 H6
Ranworth Cl ERITH DA8...........150 B3
Ranworth Rd ED N9...........36 E4
Ranyard Cl CHSGTN KT9...........206 B1
Raphael Dr THDIT KT7...........190 A5
Raphael St SKENS SW7...........14 E3
Rapier Cl PUR RM19...........131 J4
Rasper Rd TRDG/WHET N20...33 G4
Rastell Av BRXS/STRHM SW2...161 J4
Ratcliffe Cl LEE/GVPK SE12...165 K2
Ratcliffe Cross St WCHPL E1 *...105 F5
Ratcliffe La POP/IOD E14...........105 G5
Ratcliff Rd FSTGT E7...........89 G3
Rathbone Market
CAN/RD E16 *...........106 D4
Rathbone Pl FITZ W1T...........10 C2
Rathbone Sq CROY/NA CRO *...211 J2
Rathbone St CAN/RD E16...........106 D4
FITZ W1T...........10 B2
Rathcoole Av CEND/HSY/T N8...67 F2
Rathcoole Gdns
CEND/HSY/T N8...........67 F2
Rathfern Rd CAT SE6...........164 C3
Rathgar Av WEA W13...........116 D1
Rathgar Cl FNCH N3...........46 D5
Rathgar Rd BRXN/ST SW9...........142 C4
Rathmell Dr CLAP SW4...........161 J1
Rattray Rd BRXS/STRHM SW2...142 B5
Raul Rd PECK SE15...........143 H2
Raveley St KTTN NW5...........84 C2
Ravencroft Crs ELTH/MOT SE9.166 E5
Ravenet St BTSEA SW11...........141 G2
Ravenfield Rd TOOT SW17...........160 E5
Ravenhill Rd PLSTW E13...........89 G1
Ravenna Rd PUT/ROE SW15...139 G6
Ravenoak Wy CHIG IG7...........54 E1
Raven Park Rd GFD/PVL UB6...96 C2
Raven Rd SWFD E18...........53 G5
Raven Rw WCHPL E1...........104 D4
Ravensbourne Av HAYES BR2...183 G4
STWL/WRAY TW19...........152 C3
Ravensbourne Gdns CLAY IG5...54 A4
WEA W13...........97 H4
Ravensbourne Pk CAT SE6...........164 D2
Ravensbourne Park Crs
CAT SE6...........164 C2
Ravensbourne Pl LEW SE13...144 E3
Ravensbourne Rd BMLY BR1...183 K5
CAT SE6...........164 C2
DART DA1...........150 D4
Ravenscar Rd BMLY BR1...........165 H6
SURB KT6...........191 G6
Ravenscourt Av HMSMTH W6...118 D4
Ravenscourt Cl DEN/HRF UB9...58 A4
Ravenscourt Gdns
HMSMTH W6...........118 C4
Ravenscourt Pk HMSMTH W6...118 C4
Ravenscourt Pl HMSMTH W6...118 E4
Ravenscourt Rd HMSMTH W6...118 E4
STMC/STPC BR5...........186 B6
Ravenscourt Sq HMSMTH W6...118 C4
Ravenscraig Rd
FBAR/BDGN N11...........34 B6
Ravenscroft Av GLDGN NW11...64 D4
WBLY HA9...........62 A5
Ravenscroft Cl CAN/RD E16...106 E4
Ravenscroft Cottages
BAR EN5 *...........32 E1
Ravenscroft Pk BAR EN5...........20 B5
Ravenscroft Rd BECK BR3...........181 K5
CAN/RD E16...........106 E4
CHSWK W4...........117 K4
Ravenscroft St BETH E2...........7 K3
Ravensdale Av
NFNCH/WDSPK N12...........33 G6
Ravensdale Gdns NRWD SE19...180 E3
Ravensdale Rd HSLWW TW4...134 D4
STNW/STAM N16...........68 B3

Ravensdon St LBTH SE11 ......122 B5
Ravensfield DAGW RM9 ......91 K2
Ravensfield Gdns
HOR/WEW KT19 ......207 G3
Ravenshaw St
KIL/WHAMP NW6 ......82 D3
Ravenshill CHST BR7 ......185 G4
Ravenshurst Av HDN NW4 ......64 A1
Ravenside CI UED N18 ......51 J3
Ravenslea Rd BAL SW12 ......160 E2
Ravensleigh Gdns BMLY BR1 ......183 K1
Ravensmead Rd HAYES BR2 ......183 G3
Ravensmede Wy CHSWK W4 ......118 C4
Ravens Ms LEE/GVPK SE12 * 145 K6
Ravenstone Rd
CDALE/KGS NW9 * 63 H3
CEND/HSY/T N8 ......49 F6
Ravenstone St BAL SW12 ......161 F3
Ravens Wy LEE/GVPK SE12 ......145 K6
Ravenswood BXLY DA5 ......169 F3
Ravenswood Av SURB KT6 ......191 H6
WWKM BR4 ......199 F5
Ravenswood Ct
KUTN/CMB KT2 ......175 K2
Ravenswood Crs
RYLN/HDSTN HA2 ......59 K6
WWKM BR4 ......199 F5
Ravenswood Gdns ISLW TW7 ......135 K2
Ravenswood Pk NTHWD HA6 ......40 E2
Ravenswood Rd BAL SW12 ......161 G2
CROY/NA CRO 211 H1
WALTH E17 ......70 A1
Ravensworth Rd
ELTH/MOT SE9 ......166 E6
WLSDN NW10 ......99 K2
Ravey St SDTCH EC2A ......
Ravine Gv WOOL/PLUM SE18 ......127 K6
Rav Pinter CI STNW/STAM N16 ......68 B4
Rawlings CI BECK BR3 ......199 F2
ORP BR6 ......217 F3
Rawlings Crs WBLY HA9 ......80 E1
Rawlings St CHEL SW3 ......14 E6
Rawlins CI FNCH N3 ......46 C6
SAND/SEL CR2 ......213 H5
Rawnsley Av MTCM CR4 ......194 C2
Rawreth Wk IS N1 * 85 J6
Rawson St BTSEA SW11 ......141 G2
Rawsthorne CI CAN/RD E16 ......126 E1
Rawstone PI FSBYE EC1V * 6 A4
Rawstorne St FSBYE EC1V 6 A4
Ray Bell Ct BROCKY SE4 ......144 C3
Raydean Rd BAR EN5 ......20 E6
Raydons Gdns DAGW RM9 ......92 A2
Raydons Rd DAGW RM9 ......92 A3
Raydon St ARCH N19 ......66 B6
Rayfield CI HAYES BR2 ......200 D5
Rayford Av LEE/GVPK SE12 ......165 J2
Rayford CI DART DA1 ......151 F6
Ray Gdns BARK IG11 ......109 G1
STAN HA7 ......43 J1
Ray Lamb Wy ERITH DA8 ......150 E1
Rayleas CI WOOL/PLUM SE18 ......147 G2
Rayleigh Av TEDD TW11 ......173 K2
Rayleigh CI PLMGR N13 ......35 K5
Rayleigh Ct KUT/HW KT1 ......175 H5
Rayleigh Ri SAND/SEL CR2 ......212 A4
Rayleigh Rd CAN/RD E16 ......126 A1
PLMGR N13 ......35 J5
WFD IG8 ......53 G3
WIM/MER SW19 ......177 J4
Ray Lodge Rd WFD IG8 ......53 H2
Raymead Av THHTH CR7 ......196 B2
Raymere Gdns
WOOL/PLUM SE18 ......147 K1
WEA W13 ......116 B3
Raymond Buildings
GINN WC1R * 11 H1
Raymond Av SYD SE26 ......181 K1
Raymond Rd BECK BR3 ......198 B1
GNTH/NBYPK IG2 ......72 D4
PLSTW E13 ......89 C5
WIM/MER SW19 ......177 H2
Raymouth Rd
BERM/RHTH SE16 ......123 K4
Rayne Ct SWFD E18 ......70 D1
Rayners CI ALP/SUD HA0 ......79 K3
Rayners Gdns NTHLT UB5 ......95 F2
Rayners La PIN HA5 ......59 F1
RYLN/HDSTN HA2 ......60 A5
Rayner's Rd PUT/ROE SW15 ......139 H6
Raynes Av WAN E11 ......71 G4
Raynes Pk RYNPK SW20 ......177 F5
Raynham Av UED N18 ......50 C1
Raynham Rd HMSMTH W6 ......118 E4
UED N18 ......50 C1
Raynham Ter UED N18 ......50 C1
Raynor CI STHL UB1 ......114 E1
Raynor PI IS N1 ......6 E2
Raynton CI RYLN/HDSTN HA2 ......59 J5
YEAD UB4 ......94 C3
Raynton Dr YEAD UB4 ......94 C3
YEAD UB4 ......94 D3
Ray Rd CRW RM5 ......56 D1
E/WMO/HCT KT8 ......189 G2
Rays Av UED N18 ......36 E6
Rays Rd UED N18 ......36 E6
WWKM BR4 ......199 F4
Ray St CLKNW EC1R 5 K7
Ray Street Br CLKNW EC1R * 5 K7
Raywood CI HYS/HAR UB3 ......133 F1
Reachview CI CAMTN NW1 ......84 C5
Read CI THDIT KT7 ......190 B4
Reading La HACK E8 ......86 D4
Reading Rd NTHLT UB5 ......78 B3
SUT SM1 ......209 G3
Reading Wy MLHL NW7 ......46 C1
Reads CI IL IG1 ......90 B1
Reapers CI CAMTN NW1 ......84 D6
Reapers Wy ISLW TW7 ......135 K6
Reardon Pth WAP E1W * 123 J1
Reardon St WAP E1W 123 J1
Reardon St NWCR SE14 ......143 K1
Reckitt Rd CHSWK W4 ......118 B5
Record St PECK SE15 ......123 K6

Recovery St TOOT SW17 ......178 D1
Recreation Av ROMW/RG RM7 ......74 E2
Recreation Rd HAYES BR2 ......183 J5
NWDGN UB2 ......114 C4
SYD SE26 ......164 A6
Recreation Wy MTCM CR4 ......179 K6
Rectar PI ARCH N19 ......66 B6
Rectory CI CHING E4 ......37 J5
DART DA1 ......171 G1
FNCH N3 ......46 D4
RYNPK SW20 ......177 F5
SCUP DA14 ......168 C6
STAN HA7 ......43 H2
SURB KT6 ......190 D6
Rectory Field Crs CHARL SE7 ......146 B1
Rectory Gdns BECK BR3 * 182 D4
CEND/HSY/T N8 ......66 E1
CHST BR7 * 185 H4
NTHLT UB5 ......77 K6
Rectory Gn BECK BR3 ......182 C4
Rectory Gv CLAP SW4 ......141 H4
CROY/NA CRO 196 C6
HPTN TW12 ......154 C6
Rectory La BUSH WD23 ......28 A1
EDGW HA8 ......44 C2
SCUP DA14 ......168 C6
STAN HA7 ......43 H1
SURB KT6 ......190 D5
TOOT SW17 ......179 F1
WLGTN SM6 ......210 C2
Rectory Orch WIM/MER SW19 ......159 H6
Rectory Park Av NTHLT UB5 ......95 K2
Rectory PI CHST BR7 * 185 H4
WOOL/PLUM SE18 ......127 F4
Rectory Rd BARN SW13 ......138 D3
BECK BR3 ......182 D4
DAGE RM10 ......92 C5
HAYES BR2 ......215 H5
HSLWW TW4 ......134 A3
HYS/HAR UB3 ......94 E5
MNPK E12 ......89 K3
STNW/STAM N16 ......68 B1
SUT SM1 ......208 E1
WALTH E17 ......51 K5
Rectory Sq WCHPL E1 ......105 F4
Reculver Ms UED N18 ......36 C6
Reculver Rd BERM/RHTH SE16 ......124 A5
Red Anchor CI CHEL SW3 ......120 C6
Redan PI BAY/PAD W2 * 101 F5
Redan St WKENS W14 ......119 G3
Redan Ter CMBW SE5 ......142 C3
Red Barracks Rd
WOOL/PLUM SE18 ......126 E4
Redberry Gv SYD SE26 ......163 K5
Redbourne Av FNCH N3 ......46 E4
Redbourne Dr THMD SE28 ......109 K5
Redbridge Gdns CMBW SE5 ......143 F1
Redbridge La East REDBR IG4 ......71 J2
Redbridge La West WAN E11 ......71 G3
Redburn St CHEL SW3 ......120 E6
Redbury CI RAIN RM13 ......111 K3
Redcar CI NTHLT UB5 ......78 B4
Redcar St CMBW SE5 ......142 D1
Redcastle CI WAP E1W 104 E6
Red Cedars Rd ORP BR6 ......201 K4
Redchurch St BETH E2 ......7 J6
Redcliffe CI ECT SW5 * 120 A5
Redcliffe Gdns IL IG1 ......72 A5
WBPTN SW10 ......120 A5
Redcliffe Ms WBPTN SW10 ......120 A5
Redcliffe PI WBPTN SW10 ......120 B6
Redcliffe Rd WBPTN SW10 ......120 B5
Redcliffe Sq WBPTN SW10 ......120 A5
Redcliffe St WBPTN SW10 * 120 A6
Redclose Av MRDN SM4 ......193 K2
Redclyffe Rd PLSTW E13 ......89 G6
Redcroft Rd STHL UB1 ......96 B6
Redcross Wy STHWK SE1 ......18 D2
Reddings CI MLHL NW7 ......31 H6
The Reddings MLHL NW7 ......31 H5
Reddington CI SAND/SEL CR2 ......211 K6
Reddins Rd PECK SE15 ......143 H1
Reddons Rd BECK BR3 ......182 B3
Reddy Rd ERITH DA8 ......130 C6
Rede PI BAY/PAD W2 ......100 E5
Redesdale Gdns ISLW TW7 ......136 B1
Redesdale St CHEL SW3 ......120 E6
Redfern Av HSLWW TW4 ......155 F2
Redfern Rd CAT SE6 ......165 F2
WLSDN NW10 ......81 G5
Redfield La ECT SW5 ......119 K4
Redfield Ms ECT SW5 * 119 K4
Redford Av THHTH CR7 ......196 A1
WLGTN SM6 ......210 E4
Redford CI FELT TW13 ......153 J4
Redford Wk IS N1 * 85 H6
Redgate Dr HAYES BR2 ......200 A6
Redgate Ter PUT/ROE SW15 ......159 G1
Redgrave CI CROY/NA CRO 197 G3
Redgrave Rd PUT/ROE SW15 ......139 G5
Redgrave Ter BETH E2 * 104 C2
Redhall Ter EA W5 * 98 C6
Red HI CHST BR7 ......185 F1
Redhill Dr EDGW HA8 ......44 E5
Redhill St CAMTN NW1 ......3 K4
Red House La BXLYHS DA6 ......148 E5
Red House Rd CROY/NA CRO 195 J3
Red House Sq IS N1 * 85 J5
Redington Gdns HAMP NW3 ......83 F2
Redington Rd HAMP NW3 ......83 F1
Redland Gdns
E/WMO/HCT KT8 * 188 E1
Redlands Rd PEND EN3 ......25 G2
Redlands Wy
BRXS/STRHM SW2 ......161 K2
Red La ESH/CLAY KT10 ......205 G4
Redleaf CI BXLYHN DA7 ......129 H6
Redlees CI ISLW TW7 ......136 B5
Red Lion CI STMC/STPC BR5 * 202 D7
WALW SE17 ......122 E6
Redlion Ct FLST/FETLN EC4A * 11 K3
HSLW TW3 * 135 G4
Red Lion HI EFNCH N2 ......47 H5
Red Lion La WOOL/PLUM SE18 ......147 F2
Red Lion Pde PIN HA5 * 41 J6

Red Lion PI
WOOL/PLUM SE18 * 147 F2
Red Lion Rd SURB KT6 ......191 H6
Red Lion Rw CMBW SE5 ......122 D6
Red Lion Sq GINN WC1R 11 G2
WAND/EARL SW18 * 139 K6
Red Lion St GINN WC1R 11 G2
RCH/KEW TW9 ......136 E6
Red Lion Yd MYFR/PKLN W1K * 9 H7
Red Lodge Crs BXLY DA5 ......170 B5
Red Lodge Rd BXLY DA5 ......170 A5
WWKM BR4 ......199 F5
Redman CI NTHLT UB5 ......95 G1
Redman's Rd WCHPL E1 ......104 E4
Redmead La WAP E1W * 123 H1
Redmead Rd HYS/HAR UB3 ......113 H4
Redmore Rd HMSMTH W6 ......118 E4
Red Oak CI ORP BR6 ......216 B1
Red PI MYFR/PKLN W1K 9 G5
Redpoll Wy ERITH DA18 ......128 E3
Red Post HI HNHL SE24 ......142 E6
Redriffe Rd PLSTW E13 ......106 D6
Redriff Rd BERM/RHTH SE16 ......124 B3
ROMW/RG RM7 ......56 D5
Redroofs CI BECK BR3 ......182 E4
Redruth CI WDGN N22 ......49 F3
Redruth Rd HOM E9 ......86 E6
Redstart CI EHAM E6 ......107 J4
NWCR SE14 * 144 B1
Redston Rd CEND/HSY/T N8 ......66 D1
Redvers Rd WDGN N22 ......49 G5
Redvers St IS N1 ......7 H4
Redwald Rd CLPT E5 ......87 F2
Redway Dr WHTN TW2 ......155 H2
Redwing Ms CMBW SE5 ......142 D3
Redwing Rd WLGTN SM6 ......210 E5
Redwood CI BERM/RHTH SE16 ......124 B1
BFN/LL DA15 ......168 B3
BOW E3 ......105 J1
OXHEY WD19 ......27 G6
STHGT/OAK N14 ......34 D2
Redwood Ct CRICK NW2 * 82 C2
Redwood Gdns CHIG IG7 ......55 G1
CHING E4 * 25 K4
Redwood Gv EA W5 ......116 C3
Redwood Ms VX/NE SW8 ......141 G4
Redwood Wy BAR EN5 ......20 B6
Reece Ms SKENS SW7 ......14 A6
Reed Av ORP BR6 ......216 E1
Reed CI CAN/RD E16 ......106 E4
LEE/GVPK SE12 ......145 K6
Reede Rd DAGE RM10 ......92 C4
Reede Wy DAGE RM10 ......92 D4
Reedham CI TOTM N17 ......68 D4
Reedham Rd BECK SE15 * 143 H3
Reedholm Vis STNW/STAM N16 ......85 K2
Reed PI CLAP SW4 ......141 J5
Reed Pond Wk GPK RM2 ......57 H1
Reed Rd TOTM N17 ......50 B6
Reedsfield CI ASHF TW15 ......152 E5
Reedsfield Rd ASHF TW15 ......152 E6
Reedworth St LBTH SE11 ......17 K7
Reenglass Rd STAN HA7 ......29 K6
Rees Dr STAN HA7 ......30 A6
Rees Gdns CROY/NA CRO 197 G3
Rees St IS N1 ......6 E1
Reets Farm CI CDALE/KGS NW9 ......63 G3
Reeves Av CDALE/KGS NW9 ......63 F4
Reeves Cnr CROY/NA CRO 196 C6
Reeves Ms MYFR/PKLN W1K 9 G6
Reeves Rd BOW E3 ......105 K3
WOOL/PLUM SE18 ......127 G6
Reform Rw TOTM N17 ......50 B5
Reform St BTSEA SW11 ......140 E3
Regal CI EA W5 ......97 K4
WCHPL E1 ......104 C4
Regal Ct MTCM CR4 ......178 E6
UED N18 ......50 B1
Regal Crs WLGTN SM6 ......210 B1
Regal Dr FBAR/BDGN N11 ......48 B1
Regal La CAMTN NW1 ......3 H1
Regal PI WCHEL SW3 ......120 E6
Regal Rw PECK SE15 ......143 K2
Regal Wy KTN/HRWW/WS HA3 ......62 A3
Regal Wy IS N1 ......5 G6
Regarder Rd CHIG IG7 ......55 H1
Regarth Av ROM RM1 ......75 G3
Regency CI CHIG IG7 ......54 C1
EA W5 ......98 A5
HPTN TW12 ......172 E1
Regency Crs HDN NW4 ......46 B5
Regency Dr RSLP HA4 ......58 C6
Regency Gdns WOT/HER KT12 ......188 C5
Regency Lawn KTTN NW5 * 84 B1
Regency Ms BECK BR3 ......183 F4
WLSDN NW10 ......81 J4
Regency Pde HAMP NW3 * 83 H5
Regency St WEST SW1P 16 D6
Regency St WEST SW1P 16 D7
Regency Ter HGT N6 * 65 K5
SEVS/STOTM N15 ......67 K3
Regency Wk CROY/NA CRO 198 B3
Regency Wy BXLYHS DA6 ......148 E4
Regeneration Rd
BERM/RHTH SE16 ......124 A4
Regent CI HSLWW TW4 ......134 A2
KTN/HRWW/WS HA3 ......62 A3
NFNCH/WDSPK N12 ......47 H1
Regent Ct GDMY/SEVK IG3 ......73 G3
Regent Pde BELMT SM2 * 209 G4
Regent PI CROY/NA CRO 197 G5
WIM/MER SW19 ......178 A1
Regent Rd BRYLDS KT5 ......191 G3
HNHL SE24 ......142 C1
Regents Bridge Gdns
VX/NE SW8 ......121 K6
Regents CI SAND/SEL CR2 ......212 A4
YEAD UB4 ......94 C4
Regents Dr HAYES BR2 ......215 H3
Regents Ms STJWD NW8 ......101 G1
Regent's Park Rd CAMTN NW1 ......84 A6

FNCH N3 ......64 D1
Regent's Park Ter CAMTN NW1 ......84 B6
Regents PI LOU IG10 ......39 H2
Regents Plaza
KIL/WHAMP NW6 * 101 F1
Regent Sq BELV DA17 ......129 J4
BOW E3 ......105 K2
STPAN WC1H 5 F5
Regent's Rw BETH E2 ......86 C6
Regent St CHSWK W4 ......117 H5
REGST W1B 10 A4
WLSDN NW10 ......100 B2
Regent Whf IS N1 * 5 G2
Regina Rd DEPT SE8 ......144 D1
FSBYPK N4 ......67 F5
NWDGN UB2 ......114 D4
SNWD SE25 ......181 H6
WEA W13 ......116 B1
Regina Ter WEA W13 ......116 B1
Regis Rd KTTN NW5 ......84 B3
Regnart Buildings CAMTN NW1 * 4 B5
Reid CI HYS/HAR UB3 ......94 C5
PIN HA5 ......40 E6
Reidhaven Rd
WOOL/PLUM SE18 ......127 K4
Reigate Av SUT SM1 ......194 A5
Reigate Rd BMLY BR1 ......165 J5
GDMY/SEVK IG3 ......73 F6
Reigate Wy WLGTN SM6 ......210 E3
Reighton Rd CLPT E5 ......68 C6
Reinckendorf Av
ELTH/MOT SE9 ......147 H6
Reizel CI STNW/STAM N16 ......68 B5
Relay Rd SHB W12 ......100 A6
Relf Rd PECK SE15 ......143 H4
Reliance Sq BETH E2 * 7 H6
Reliance Sq SDTCH EC2A 7 H6
Relton Ms SKENS SW7 ......14 C4
Rembrandt CI BGVA SW1W * 121 F5
POP/IOD E14 ......125 G3
Rembrandt Ct HOR/WEW KT19 ......207 H4
Rembrandt Rd EDGW HA8 ......44 C5
LEW SE13 ......145 H5
Rembrandt Wy
WOT/HER KT12 ......188 A6
Remington Rd EHAM E6 ......107 J5
SEVS/STOTM N15 ......67 K3
Remington St FSBYE EC1V 6 B3
Remnant St HOL/ALD WC2B 11 G3
Remus Rd BOW E3 ......87 J5
Rendle CI CROY/NA CRO 197 G2
Rendlesham Rd CLPT E5 ......86 C2
ENC/FH EN2 ......23 H2
Renforth St BERM/RHTH SE16 ......123 K3
Renfrew CI EHAM E6 ......108 A6
Renfrew Rd HSLWW TW4 ......134 C3
KUTN/CMB KT2 ......175 K3
LBTH SE11 ......18 A6
Renmuir St TOOT SW17 ......178 E2
Rennell St LEW SE13 ......145 F4
Renness Rd WALTH E17 ......51 G6
Rennets CI ELTH/MOT SE9 ......147 K6
Rennets Wood Rd
ELTH/MOT SE9 ......147 J6
Rennie Est BERM/RHTH SE16 ......123 J4
Rennie Est BERM/RHTH SE16 ......123 J4
Rennie St STHWK SE1 ......12 A7
Renown CI CROY/NA CRO 196 C4
ROMW/RG RM7 ......56 C4
Rensburg Rd WALTH E17 ......69 F2
Rensburg Vis WALTH E17 ......69 F2
Renshaw CI BELV DA17 ......129 G6
Renters Av HDN NW4 ......64 A3
Renton CI BRXS/STRHM SW2 * 162 A1
Renton Dr STMC/STPC BR5 ......202 E4
Renwick Rd BARK IG11 ......109 H3
Repens Wy YEAD UB4 ......95 H3
Rephidim St STHWK SE1 ......19 G5
Replingham Rd
WAND/EARL SW18 ......159 J3
Reporton Rd FUL/PGN SW6 ......139 H2
Repository Rd
WOOL/PLUM SE18 ......126 E6
Repton Av ALP/SUD HA0 ......79 J2
GPK RM2 ......57 J6
HYS/HAR UB3 ......113 H4
Repton CI CAR SM5 ......209 J3
Repton Ct BECK BR3 ......182 E4
Repton Dr GPK RM2 ......75 J1
Repton Gdns GPK RM2 ......57 J6
Repton Gv CLAY IG5 ......53 K4
Repton Rd KTN/HRWW/WS HA3 ......62 A1
ORP BR6 ......217 G2
Repton St POP/IOD E14 ......105 G5
Repulse CI CRW RM5 ......56 D4
Reservoir CI THHTH CR7 ......180 E6
Reservoir Rd BROCKY SE4 ......144 B3
RSLP HA4 ......58 A2
STHGT/OAK N14 ......22 C6
Resham CI NWDGN UB2 ......114 B3
Resolution Wy DEPT SE8 ......144 D1
Restell CI BKHTH/KID SE3 ......125 H6
Restmor Wy CAR SM5 ......195 H6
Reston PI KENS W8 ......120 A2
Restons Crs ELTH/MOT SE9 ......167 J1
Restormel CI HSLW TW3 ......135 F6
Retford St BETH E2 ......7 H3
Retingham Wy CHING E4 ......37 K4
Retreat CI KTN/HRWW/WS HA3 ......61 J2
Retreat PI HOM E9 ......86 E4
Retreat Rd RCHPK/HAM TW10 ......136 E6
The Retreat BRYLDS KT5 ......191 G3
CDALE/KGS NW9 ......63 F2
MORT/ESHN SW14 ......138 B4
ORP BR6 ......217 H4
RYLN/HDSTN HA2 ......60 B1
THHTH CR7 ......196 E1
WPK KT4 ......192 E6

SUT SM1 ......208 D4
Revelon Rd BROCKY SE4 ......144 B5
Revelstoke Rd
WAND/EARL SW18 ......159 K4
WIM/MER SW19 ......159 H6
WIM/MER SW19 ......178 D2
Reventlow Rd ELTH/MOT SE9 ......167 H5
Reverdy Rd STHWK SE1 ......123 H4
Reverend CI RYLN/HDSTN HA2 ......78 B1
Revere Wy HOR/WEW KT19 ......207 G6
Revesby Rd CAR SM5 ......194 D3
Review Rd CRICK NW2 ......63 H6
DAGE RM10 ......110 D1
Rex PI MYFR/PKLN W1K 9 G6
Rex Rd DAGW RM9 * 46 E5
Reydon Av WAN E11 ......71 G3
Reynard CI BMLY BR1 ......185 G3
Reynard Dr NRWD SE19 ......181 G3
Reynard PI NWCR SE14 * 124 B6
Reynardson Rd TOTM N17 ......49 J3
Reynolds Av CHDH RM6 ......73 J4
CHSGTN KT9 ......206 A5
MNPK E12 ......90 A3
Reynolds CI CAR SM5 ......194 E5
GLDGN NW11 ......65 F4
WIM/MER SW19 ......178 C4
Reynolds Dr EDGW HA8 ......44 B6
Reynolds PI BKHTH/KID SE3 ......146 A1
RCHPK/HAM TW10 ......157 G1
Reynolds Rd CHSWK W4 ......117 K3
NWMAL KT3 ......192 A4
PECK SE15 ......143 K6
YEAD UB4 ......95 G3
Reynolds Wy CROY/NA CRO 212 A2
Rheidol Ms IS N1 ......6 B2
Rheidol Ter IS N1 ......6 B2
Rheingold Wy WLGTN SM6 ......210 E6
Rheola CI TOTM N17 ......50 B4
Rhoda St BETH E2 ......7 K6
Rhodes Av WDGN N22 ......48 B4
Rhodesia Rd BRXN/ST SW9 ......141 K3
WAN E11 ......70 B6
Rhodes St HOLWY N7 ......85 F3
Rhodeswell Rd POP/IOD E14 ......105 H4
Rhodrons Av CHSGTN KT9 ......206 A3
Rhyl Rd GFD/PVL UB6 ......97 F1
Rhyl St KTTN NW5 ......84 A4
Rhys Av FBAR/BDGN N11 ......48 D3
Rialto Rd MTCM CR4 ......179 F5
Ribble CI WFD IG8 ......53 G2
Ribblesdale Av
FBAR/BDGN N11 ......47 K2
NTHLT UB5 ......78 B3
Ribblesdale Rd CEND/HSY/T N8 ......67 F1
STRHM/NOR SW16 ......179 F2
Ribbon Dance Ms CMBW SE5 ......142 E2
Ribchester Av GFD/PVL UB6 ......97 F2
Ribston CI HAYES BR2 ......200 E6
Ricardo St POP/IOD E14 ......105 K5
Ricards Rd WIM/MER SW19 ......177 J1
Rice Pde STMC/STPC BR5 ......201 J3
Richard CI WOOL/PLUM SE18 ......126 D4
Richard House Dr CAN/RD E16 ......107 H5
Richards Av ROMW/RG RM7 ......74 E3
Richards CI BUSH WD23 ......28 D2
HRW HA1 ......61 G2
HYS/HAR UB3 ......133 H4
Richards Cottages CAR SM5 * 209 K3
Richards Fld HOR/WEW KT19 ......207 F6
Richardson CI HACK E8 * 86 B6
Richardson Rd SRTFD E15 ......106 C1
Richardson's Ms FITZ W1T * 4 A7
Richard's PI CHEL SW3 ......14 D6
WALTH E17 ......51 J6
Richard St WCHPL E1 ......104 D5
Richbell PI BMSBY WC1N 11 G1
Richborne Ter VX/NE SW8 ......142 A1
Richborough Rd
STMC/STPC BR5 ......202 E1
Richborough Rd CRICK NW2 ......82 C2
Richens CI HSLW TW3 ......135 J3
Riches Rd IL IG1 ......72 C6
Richfield Rd BUSH WD23 ......28 D3
Richford Rd SRTFD E15 ......88 D6
Richford St HMSMTH W6 ......119 F2
Richlands Av EW KT17 ......207 J3
Richmer Rd ERITH DA8 ......150 D1
Richmond Av CHING E4 ......52 B1
EBED/NFELT TW14 ......153 H1
IS N1 ......5 J1
RYNPK SW20 ......177 H4
Richmond Br TWK TW1 ......156 D3
Richmond Buildings
SOHO/SHAV W1D 10 C4
Richmond CI WALTH E17 ......69 H3
Richmond Crs CHING E4 ......52 B1
IS N1 ......5 J1
ED N9 ......36 C3
Richmond Dr WFD IG8 ......53 K2
Richmond Gdns HDN NW4 ......63 J2
KTN/HRWW/WS HA3 ......43 F3
Richmond Gv CROY/NA CRO 210 D1
Richmond Gv IS N1 ......85 H5
Richmond HI
RCHPK/HAM TW10 ......157 F1
Richmond Ms SOHO/CST W1F 10 C4
Richmond Pde TWK TW1 * 156 D1
Richmond PI
WOOL/PLUM SE18 ......127 H4
Richmond Rd BAR EN5 ......21 G6
CHING E4 ......38 B3
CROY/NA CRO 210 D1
EA W5 ......117 F2
EFNCH N2 ......47 G5
FBAR/BDGN N11 ......48 D2
FSTGT E7 ......89 F3
HACK E8 ......86 B5
IL IG1 ......90 C1
ISLW TW7 ......136 B5

CRICK NW2.....82 A1
EHAM E6.....107 J3
IL IG1.....90 B4
MUSWH N10.....85 B5
Roman Sq THMD SE28.....128 B1
Roman Wy CROY/NA CRO.....196 C6
DART DA1.....150 B6
EN EN1.....24 B6
HOLWY N7.....85 F4
Romany Gdns CHEAM SM3.....193 K4
Romany Ri STMC/STPC BR5.....201 H5
Roma Rd WALTH E17.....51 C6
Romberg Rd TOOT SW17.....161 F5
Romborough Gdns LEW SE13.....145 F6
Romborough Wy LEW SE13.....145 F6
Rom Crs ROMW/RG RM7.....75 J2
Romeland BORE WD6.....29 K1
Romero Cl BRXN/ST SW9.....142 A4
Romero Sq BKHTH/KID SE3.....146 B5
Romeyn Rd STRHM/NOR SW16.....162 A4
Romford Rd CHIG IG7.....55 K2
CRW RM5.....56 E6
MNPK E12.....90 A1
SRTFD E15.....88 D4
Romford St WCHPL E1.....104 C4
Romilly Dr OXHEY WD19.....27 J1
Romilly Rd FSBYPK N4.....85 H1
Romilly St SOHO/SHAV W1D.....10 D5
Rommany Rd WNWD SE27.....162 E6
Romney Cl CHSGTN KT9.....206 A3
GLDGN NW11.....65 C5
NWCR SE14.....143 K1
RYLN/HDSTN HA2.....59 H5
TOTM N17.....50 D4
Romney Dr BMLY BR1.....184 C3
RYLN/HDSTN HA2.....59 H5
Romney Gdns BXLYHN DA7.....149 G2
Romney Rd GNWCH SE10.....125 F6
NWMAL KT3.....192 A3
WOOL/PLUM SE18.....127 H3
YEAD UB4.....94 B1
Romney Rw CRICK NW2 *.....64 B6
Romney St WEST SW1P.....16 D5
Romola Rd HNHL SE24.....162 C3
Romsey Cl ORP BR6.....216 C2
Romsey Rd DAGW RM9.....91 J4
WEA W13.....97 G6
Romside Pl ROMW/RG RM7 *.....75 J1
Rom Valley Wy ROMW/RG RM7.....75 J3
Ronald Av SRTFD E15.....106 C2
Ronald Cl BECK BR3.....198 C2
Ronalds Rd BMLY BR1.....183 K4
HBRY N5.....85 G3
Ronaldstone Rd BFN/LL DA15.....167 K1
Rona Rd HAMP NW3.....84 C2
Ronart St KTN/HRWW/WS HA3.....43 F6
Rona Wk IS N1.....85 K4
Rondu Rd CRICK NW2.....82 C5
Ronelean Rd SURB KT6.....206 B1
Roneo Cnr HCH RM12.....75 H5
Roneo Link HCH RM12.....75 H5
Ronfearn Av STMC/STPC BR5.....202 E2
Ron Green Ct ERITH DA8.....130 A5
Ron Leighton Wy EHAM E6.....89 J6
Ronnie La BCTR RM8.....73 J1
Ronver Rd LEE/GVPK SE12.....165 K3
Rood La FENCHST EC3M.....13 G5
Rookby Ct WCHMH N21.....35 H4
Rook Cl RAIN RM13.....93 J5
WBLY HA9.....80 D1
Rookeries Cl FELT TW13.....154 A5
Rookery Dr CHST BR7.....185 F1
Rookery Gdns STMC/STPC BR5.....202 D2
Rookery La HAYES BR2.....200 C3
Rookery Rd CLAP SW4.....141 H5
The Rookery
STRHM/NOR SW16 *.....179 K1
Rookery Wy CDALE/KGS NW9.....63 H2
Rookesley Rd STMC/STPC BR5.....202 E4
Rookfield Av MUSWH N10.....66 C1
Rookfield Cl MUSWH N10.....66 C1
Rookley Cl BELMT SM2.....209 F6
Rooks Ter WDR/YW UB7 *.....112 B2
Rookstone Rd TOOT SW17.....178 E1
Rookwood Av NWMAL KT3.....192 D1
WLGTN SM6.....210 D3
Rookwood Gdns CHING E4 *.....38 D4
Rookwood Rd STNW/STAM N16.....68 B3
Roosevelt Wy DAGE RM10.....93 F4
Rootes Dr NKENS W10.....100 B3
Ropemaker Rd BERM/RHTH SE16.....124 B2
Ropemaker's Flds
POP/IOD E14 *.....105 H6
Ropemaker St BARB EC2Y.....12 E1
Roper La STHWK SE1.....19 H5
Ropers Av CHING E4.....52 A1
Ropers Orch CHEL SW3 *.....120 D6
Roper St ELTH/MOT SE9.....146 E6
Roper Wy MTCM CR4.....179 F5
Ropery St BOW E3.....105 H3
Rope St BERM/RHTH SE16.....124 B3
Ropewalk Gdns WCHPL E1.....104 C5
Ropewalk Ms HACK E8 *.....86 B5
Rope Yard Rails
WOOL/PLUM SE18.....127 G3
Ropley St BETH E2.....104 C1
Rosa Alba Ms HBRY N5.....85 J3
Rosa Av ASHF TW15.....152 D6
Rosaline Rd FUL/PGN SW6.....139 H1
Rosaline Ter FUL/PGN SW6 *.....139 H1
Rosamond St SYD SE26.....163 J5
Rosamond Vls
MORT/ESHN SW14 *.....138 A5
Rosamund Cl SAND/SEL CR2.....211 K2
Rosamun Rd NWDGN UB2.....114 D4
Rosary Cl HSLW TW3.....134 D3
Rosary Gdns ASHF TW15.....152 E6
BUSH WD23.....28 E2
SKENS SW7.....120 B4
Rosary Ga BTSEA SW11.....141 G1
Roscoe St STLK EC1Y.....12 D1
Roscoff Cl EDGW HA8.....44 E4
Roseacre Cl WAN W13.....97 H4
Roseacre Rd WELL DA16.....148 C4
Rose Aly LVPST EC2M.....13 H2

STHWK SE1.....12 D7
Rose & Crown Yd STJS SW1Y *.....16 B6
Rosebank Cl WDR/YW UB7.....112 A4
Rose Av MRDN SM4.....194 B2
MTCM CR4.....178 E4
SWFD E18.....53 F5
Rosebank PGE/AN SE20.....181 J3
Rosebank Av ALP/SUD HA0.....79 F2
Rose Bank Cl
NFNCH/WDSPK N12.....47 J1
Rosebank Cl TEDD TW11.....174 B2
Rosebank Est BOW E3.....105 H1
Rosebank Gdns ACT W3 *.....99 F5
BOW E3.....105 H1
Rosebank Gv WALTH E17.....51 H6
Rosebank Rd HNWL W7.....115 K2
WALTH E17.....69 J3
Rosebank Wk CAMTN NW1 *.....84 D5
Rosebank Wy ACT W3.....99 F5
Roseberry Gdns DART DA1.....171 F2
FSBYPK N4.....67 H4
ORP BR6.....216 E1
Roseberry Pl HACK E8.....86 B4
Roseberry St
BERM/RHTH SE16.....123 J4
Rosebery Av BFN/LL DA15.....167 K2
CLKNW EC1R.....5 J6
MNPK E12.....89 J4
NWMAL KT3.....176 C5
RYLN/HDSTN HA2.....77 J2
THHTH CR7.....180 D5
TOTM N17.....50 C5
Rosebery Ct CLKNW EC1R.....5 J6
Rosebery Gdns
CEND/HSY/T N8 *.....66 E2
SUT SM1.....209 F2
WEA W13.....97 G5
Rosebery Ms MUSWH N10.....48 C5
Rosebery Pde WEY KT17 *.....207 H5
Rosebery Rd BUSH WD23.....28 B3
CLAP SW4.....161 K1
HSLW TW3.....135 H6
KUT/HW KT1.....175 J4
MUSWH N10.....48 C5
SUT SM1.....208 D4
Rosebine Av WHTN TW2.....155 J2
Rosebriars ESH/CLAY KT10.....204 C3
Rosebury Rd FUL/PGN SW6.....140 A3
Rosebury Gv WFD IG8.....54 A3
Rosebury V RSLP HA4.....58 E6
Rose Ct WCHPL E1.....13 J2
Rosecourt Rd CROY/NA CRO.....196 A3
Rosecroft Av HAMP NW3.....82 E1
Rosecroft Cl STMC/STPC BR5.....202 D3
Rosecroft Ct NTHWD HA6 *.....40 A2
Rose Croft Gdns ALP/SUD HA0.....81 J1
Rosecroft Gdns WHTN TW2.....155 J3
Rosecroft Rd STHL UB1.....96 A3
Rosecroft Wk ALP/SUD HA0.....79 K3
PIN HA5.....59 H2
Rose Di ORP BR6.....216 D2
Rosedale Av HYS/HAR UB3.....94 B4
Rosedale Cl ABYW SE2.....128 C3
HNWL W7.....116 A2
STAN HA7.....43 H2
Rosedale Dr DAGW RM9.....91 H6
Rosedale Gdns DAGW RM9.....91 H6
Rosedale Pl CROY/NA CRO.....198 A4
Rosedale Rd DAGW RM9.....91 H5
EW KT17.....207 J3
FSTGT E7.....89 G3
RCH/KEW TW9.....137 G2
Rosedene AV CROY/NA CRO.....195 K4
GFD/PVL UB6.....96 A2
MRDN SM4.....193 K2
STRHM/NOR SW16.....162 A5
Rosedene Cl DART DA1.....171 F2
Rosedene Gdns
GNTH/NBYPK IG2.....72 A1
Rosedene Rd TER LEY.....69 K6
Rosedew Rd HMSMTH W6.....119 G6
Rose End WPK KT4.....193 G5
Rosefield Cl CAR SM5.....209 J3
Rosefield Gdns POP/IOD E14.....105 J6
Rose Garden Cl EDGW HA8.....44 A2
Rose Gdns EA W5.....116 E3
FELT TW13.....153 K4
STHL UB1.....96 A3
STWL/WRAY TW19.....152 A2
Rose Gln CDALE/KGS NW9.....63 F1
Rosehart Ms NTGHL W11.....100 E5
Rosehatch Av CHDH RM6.....55 K6
Roseheath Rd HSLWW TW4.....134 E6
Rosehill ESH/CLAY KT10.....205 F5
HPTN TW12.....173 F4
Rose HI SUT SM1.....194 A6
Rosehill Av SUT SM1.....194 B5
Rosehill Court Pde
MRDN SM4 *.....194 B4
Rosehill Gdns GFD/PVL UB6.....79 F3
SUT SM1.....194 A6
Rose Hill Pk West SUT SM1.....194 B5
Rosehill Rd WAND/EARL SW18.....160 B1
Roseland Cl TOTM N17.....49 K3
Rose La CHDH RM6.....74 A1
Rose Lawn BUSH WD23.....28 C3
Roseleigh Av HBRY N5.....85 H2
Roseleigh Cl TWK TW1.....156 E1
Rosemary Av E/WMO/HCT KT8.....173 F6
ED N9.....36 D3
EN EN1.....23 K2
FNCH N3.....47 F4
HSLWW TW4.....134 C3
ROM RM1.....57 H6
Rosemary Cl CROY/NA CRO.....195 K4
Rosemary Dr POP/IOD E14.....106 B5
REDBR IG4.....71 H2
Rosemary Gdns BCTR RM8.....73 K5
CHSGTN KT9.....206 A2
Rosemary La
MORT/ESHN SW14 *.....137 K4
Rosemary Rd PECK SE15.....143 G1
TOOT SW17.....160 A5

WELL DA16.....148 A2
Rosemary St IS N1.....85 K6
Rosemead CDALE/KGS NW9.....63 H4
Rosemead Av FELT TW13.....153 J4
MTCM CR4.....179 H6
WBLY HA9.....80 A3
Rose Ms UED N18.....36 D6
Rosemont Av
NFNCH/WDSPK N12.....47 G2
Rosemont Rd ACT W3.....98 D6
HAMP NW3.....83 G4
NWMAL KT3.....175 K6
RCHPK/HAM TW10.....157 F1
Rosemoor St CHEL SW3.....14 E7
Rosemount Cl WFD IG8.....53 K2
Rosemount Dr BMLY BR1.....200 E1
Rosemount Rd ALP/SUD HA0.....80 A3
WEA W13.....97 G5
Rosenau Crs BTSEA SW11.....140 E2
Rosenau Rd BTSEA SW11.....140 E2
Rosendale Rd HNHL SE24.....162 D2
Rosendale Rd HNHL SE24.....162 D2
Roseneath Pl
STRHM/NOR SW16.....162 B6
Roseneath Rd BTSEA SW11.....161 F1
Rosen's Wk EDGW HA8.....30 D5
Rosenthal Rd CAT SE6.....164 E1
Rosenthorpe Rd PECK SE15.....144 A6
Rose Park Cl YEAD UB4.....95 H3
The Rosery CROY/NA CRO.....198 A3
Rose Sq CHEL SW3 *.....120 C5
The Roses WFD IG8 *.....52 D3
Rose St COVGDN WC2E.....10 E5
Rosethorn Cl BAL SW12.....161 H2
Rosetta Cl VX/NE SW8.....141 K1
Roseveare Rd LEE/GVPK SE12.....166 B6
Roseville Av HSLW TW3.....135 F6
Roseville Rd HYS/HAR UB3.....113 K5
Rosevine Rd RYNPK SW20.....177 F4
Rose Wk BRYLDS KT5.....191 J2
WWKM BR4.....199 G6
Roseway DUL SE21.....162 E1
Rose Wy LEE/GVPK SE12.....145 K6
Rosewell Cl PGE/AN SE20.....181 J3
Rosewood Cl SCUP DA14.....168 D5
Rosewood Ct BARK/HLT IG6.....54 C5
Rosewood Ct KUTN/CMB KT2.....175 H3
Rosewood Dr ENC/FH EN2.....23 F1
Rosewood Gv SUT SM1.....194 B6
Rosewood Ter PGE/AN SE20 *.....181 K3
Rosher Cl SRTFD E15.....88 B5
Rosina St HOM E9.....87 F4
Roskell Rd PUT/ROE SW15.....139 G4
Roslin Rd ACT W3.....117 J3
Roslin Wy BMLY BR1.....183 K1
Roslyn Cl MTCM CR4.....178 C5
Roslyn Rd SEVS/STOTM N15.....67 K2
Roslyn Ms SEVS/STOTM N15 *.....68 A2
Rosmead Rd NTGHL W11.....100 C6
Rosoman Pl CLKNW EC1R.....5 K6
Rosoman St CLKNW EC1R.....5 K5
Ross Av BCTR RM8.....74 B2
MLHL NW7.....46 C1
Ross Cl HYS/HAR UB3.....113 G4
KTN/HRWW/WS HA3.....42 B3
NTHLT UB5.....78 D2
Rossdale SUT SM1.....209 J3
Rossdale Dr CDALE/KGS NW9.....62 E5
ED N9.....36 E1
Rosse Ms BKHTH/KID SE3.....146 A2
Rossendale St CLPT E5.....68 D6
Rossendale Wy CAMTN NW1.....84 C5
Rossetti Rd BERM/RHTH SE16.....123 J5
Rossindel Rd HSLW TW3.....135 F6
Rossington Cl EN EN1.....24 D1
Rossington St CLPT E5.....68 C6
Rossiter Flds BAR EN5.....32 D1
Rossiter Rd BAL SW12.....161 G3
Rossland Cl BXLYHS DA6.....149 H6
Rosslyn Av BARN SW13.....138 B4
BCTR RM8.....74 B4
CHING E4.....53 G1
EBAR EN4.....33 J1
EBED/NFELT TW14.....153 K1
Rosslyn Cl HYS/HAR UB3.....94 B4
WWKM BR4.....214 D1
Rosslyn Crs HRW HA1.....61 F1
WBLY HA9.....80 A1
Rosslyn Hl HAMP NW3.....83 H3
Rosslyn Ms HAMP NW3 *.....83 H2
Rosslyn Park Ms HAMP NW3.....83 H3
Rosslyn Rd BARK IG11.....90 D5
TWK TW1.....156 D1
WALTH E17.....70 A1
Rossmore Cl CAMTN NW1 *.....2 D7
PEND EN3.....25 F5
Rossmore Rd CAMTN NW1.....2 D6
Ross Pde WLGTN SM6.....210 B4
Ross Rd DART DA1.....170 D1
SNWD SE25.....181 H6
WHTN TW2.....155 H4
WLGTN SM6.....210 C4
Ross Wy ELTH/MOT SE9.....146 D4
NTHWD HA6.....40 D1
Rossway Dr BUSH WD23.....28 C1
Rostella Rd TOOT SW17.....160 C6
Rostrevor Av SEVS/STOTM N15.....68 B3
Rostrevor Gdns HYS/HAR UB3.....113 H1
Rostrevor Ms FUL/PGN SW6.....139 J2
Rostrevor Rd FUL/PGN SW6.....139 J2
WIM/MER SW19.....177 K1
Rotary St STHWK SE1 *.....18 A4
Rothbury Av RAIN RM13.....111 K4
Rothbury Cottages
GNWCH SE10.....125 H4
Rothbury Gdns ISLW TW7.....136 B1
Rothbury Rd HOM E9.....87 H5

Rotherfield Rd CAR SM5.....210 A2
Rotherfield St IS N1.....85 J5
Rotherham Wy STHWK SE1 *.....18 E1
Rotherhill Av
STRHM/NOR SW16.....179 J2
Rotherhithe New Rd
BERM/RHTH SE16.....123 J5
Rotherhithe Old Rd
BERM/RHTH SE16.....124 A4
Rotherhithe St
BERM/RHTH SE16.....123 K2
BERM/RHTH SE16.....124 A1
Rotherhithe Tnl
BERM/RHTH SE16.....123 K2
Rotherwick Hl EA W5.....98 B3
Rotherwick Rd GLDGN NW11.....64 E4
Rotherwood Cl RYNPK SW20.....177 H4
Rotherwood Rd
PUT/ROE SW15.....139 G4
Rothery St IS N1 *.....85 H5
Rothery Ter BRXN/ST SW9 *.....142 C1
Rothesay Av GFD/PVL UB6.....78 D4
RCHPK/HAM TW10.....137 J5
RYNPK SW20.....177 H5
Rothesay Rd SNWD SE25.....196 E1
Rothsay Rd FSTGT E7.....89 G5
Rothsay St STHWK SE1.....19 G4
Rothschild Rd CHSWK W4.....117 K4
Rothschild St WNWD SE27.....162 D6
Rothwell Gdns DAGW RM9.....91 J5
Rothwell Rd DAGW RM9.....91 J6
Rothwell St CAMTN NW1.....83 K6
Rotterdam Dr POP/IOD E14.....125 F3
Rouel Rd BERM/RHTH SE16.....123 H4
Rougemont Av MRDN SM4.....193 K3
The Roughs NTHWD HA6.....26 C5
Roundacre WIM/MER SW19.....159 G5
Roundaway Rd CLAY IG5.....53 K5
Roundel Cl BROCKY SE4.....144 C5
Round Gv CROY/NA CRO.....198 B4
Roundhay Cl FSTH SE23.....164 A4
Roundhedge Wy ENC/FH EN2.....23 F1
Round Hl SYD SE26.....163 J4
Roundhill Dr ENC/FH EN2.....23 F5
Roundlyn Gdns
STMC/STPC BR5.....202 C1
Roundtable Rd BMLY BR1.....165 K5
Roundtree Rd ALP/SUD HA0.....79 H4
Roundways RSLP HA4.....76 D1
The Roundway
ESH/CLAY KT10.....205 H5
TOTM N17.....49 K4
WATW WD18.....26 D2
Roundwood CHST BR7.....185 G5
Roundwood Av STKPK UB11.....113 F2
Roundwood Cl RSLP HA4.....58 B4
Roundwood Pk
WLSDN NW10 *.....81 J6
Roundwood Rd WLSDN NW10.....81 G4
Roundwood Ter
STNW/STAM N16.....68 A4
Rounton Rd BOW E3.....105 J3
Roupell Rd BRXS/STRHM SW2.....162 A3
Roupell St STHWK SE1.....17 K1
Rousden St CAMTN NW1.....84 C5
Rouse Gdns DUL SE21.....163 F6
Rous Rd BKHH IG9.....39 K3
Routemaster Cl PLSTW E13.....107 F2
Routh Ct EBED/NFELT TW14.....153 F2
Routh Rd WAND/EARL SW18.....160 E2
Rover Av BARK/HLT IG6.....55 F2
Rowallan Rd FUL/PGN SW6.....139 H1
Rowan Av CHING E4.....51 H2
Rowan Cl ALP/SUD HA0.....79 G1
EA W5.....117 F2
IL IG1.....90 D3
NWMAL KT3.....176 B5
STRHM/NOR SW16.....179 H4
Rowan Crs DART DA1.....171 F3
STRHM/NOR SW16.....179 H4
Rowan Dr CDALE/KGS NW9.....45 J6
Rowan Gdns CROY/NA CRO.....212 B1
Rowan Rd BTFD TW8.....136 C1
BXLYHN DA7.....149 F4
HMSMTH W6.....119 G4
STRHM/NOR SW16.....179 H5
WDR/YW UB7.....112 A4
The Rowans PLMGR N13.....35 F5
Rowan Ter PGE/AN SE20 *.....181 H4
WIM/MER SW19 *.....177 H1
Rowantree Ms ENC/FH EN2.....23 H1
Rowantree Rd ENC/FH EN2.....23 H1
WCHMH N21.....35 K3
Rowan Wk EFNCH N2.....65 G2
HAYES BR2.....200 E5
NKENS W10.....100 C3
Rowanwood Av BFN/LL DA15.....168 B3
Rowben Cl TRDG/WHET N20.....33 F3
Rowberry Cl FUL/PGN SW6.....139 F1
Rowcross St STHWK SE1.....123 G5
Rowdell Rd NTHLT UB5.....78 A1
Rowden Pde CHING E4 *.....51 J2
Rowden Rd BECK BR3.....182 B4
CHING E4.....51 J2
HOR/WEW KT19.....206 E2
Rowditch La BTSEA SW11.....141 F3
Rowdon Av WLSDN NW10.....81 K5
Rowdown Crs CROY/NA CRO.....214 B6
Rowdowns Rd DAGW RM9.....92 B6
Rowe Gdns BARK IG11.....109 F1
Rowe La HOM E9.....86 E3
Rowena Crs BTSEA SW11.....140 D3
Rowfant Rd TOOT SW17.....161 F3
Rowhill Rd CLPT E5.....86 D2
Rowington Cl BAY/PAD W2.....101 F4
Rowland Av
KTN/HRWW/WS HA3.....43 J6
Rowland Gv SYD SE26.....163 J5
Rowland Hill Av TOTM N17.....49 J3
Rowland Hill St HAMP NW3.....83 J3
Rowland Pl NTHWD HA6 *.....40 C3

Rowlands Av PIN HA5.....42 A2
Rowlands Cl HGT N6 *.....66 A6
MLHL NW7.....45 J5
Rowlands Rd BCTR RM8.....74 B6
Rowland Wy WIM/MER SW19.....178 A4
Rowlatt Cl RDART DA2.....171 F6
Rowley Av BFN/LL DA15.....168 C2
Rowley Cl ALP/SUD HA0.....80 B5
OXHEY WD19.....27 H2
Rowley Cottages
WKENS W14 *.....119 J4
Rowley Gdns FSBYPK N4.....67 J4
Rowley Rd SEVS/STOTM N15.....67 J2
Rowley Wy STJWD NW8.....101 G6
Rowlheys Pl WDR/YW UB7.....112 B3
Rowlls Rd KUT/HW KT1.....175 G6
Rowney Gdns DAGW RM9.....91 J4
Rowney Rd DAGW RM9.....91 J4
Rowntree Clifford Cl
PLSTW E13.....107 F3
Rowntree Cl KIL/WHAMP NW6 *.....82 E4
Rowntree Rd WHTN TW2.....155 K3
Rowse Cl SRTFD E15.....88 A6
Rowsley Av HDN NW4.....46 A6
Rowstock Gdns HOLWY N7.....84 D4
Roxborough Av HRW HA1.....60 D4
ISLW TW7.....136 A1
Roxborough Pk HRW HA1.....60 E4
Roxborough Rd HRW HA1.....60 D2
Roxbourne Cl NTHLT UB5.....77 H4
Roxburgh Rd WNWD SE27.....180 C1
Roxburn Wy RSLP HA4.....76 C1
Roxby Pl FUL/PGN SW6.....119 K6
Roxeth Green Av
RYLN/HDSTN HA2.....60 C6
RYLN/HDSTN HA2.....78 B1
Roxeth Gv RYLN/HDSTN HA2.....78 B2
Roxeth Hl RYLN/HDSTN HA2.....60 D6
Roxley Rd LEW SE13.....164 E1
Roxton Gdns CROY/NA CRO.....213 H4
Roxwell Rd BARK IG11.....109 G1
SHB W12.....118 D2
Roxwell Wy WFD IG8.....53 G3
Roxy Av CHDH RM6.....73 J4
Royal Albert Rd EHAM E6.....108 A6
Royal Albert Wy CAN/RD E16.....107 J6
Royal Ar CANST V.....10 A6
Royal Arsenal West
WOOL/PLUM SE18 *.....127 K5
Royal Av CHEL SW3.....120 E5
WPK KT4.....192 B6
Royal Botanic Gdns
RCH/KEW TW9.....137 F1
Royal Circ WNWD SE27.....162 B5
Royal Cl DEPT SE8.....124 C6
CDMY/SEVK IG3.....73 F5
ORP BR6.....216 B2
STNW/STAM N16.....68 C4
WIM/MER SW19.....159 G4
WPK KT4.....192 B6
Royal College St CAMTN NW1.....84 C5
Royal Ct BANK EC3V.....13 F4
ELTH/MOT SE9.....166 E3
EN EN1 *.....36 A1
Royal Crs GNTH/NBYPK IG2.....72 D3
RSLP HA4.....77 J2
Royal Crescent Ms
NTGHL W11.....119 G2
Royal Docks Rd EHAM E6.....108 B4
Royal Dr FBAR/BDGN N11.....48 A2
Royal Herbert Pavilions
WOOL/PLUM SE18 *.....146 E2
Royal Hl GNWCH SE10.....145 F1
Royal Hospital Rd CHEL SW3.....120 E6
Royal Ms BELMT SM2.....161 G2
Royal Mint Pl WCHPL E1.....13 K5
Royal Mint St WCHPL E1.....13 K5
Royal Naval Pl NWCR SE14.....144 C1
Royal Oak Ms TEDD TW11.....174 B1
Royal Oak Pl EDUL SE22.....163 J4
Royal Oak Rd BXLYHS DA6.....149 G6
HACK E8.....86 D4
Royal Oak Yd STHWK SE1.....19 G3
Royal Opera Ar STJS SW1Y *.....10 C7
Royal Orchard Cl
WAND/EARL SW18.....159 H2
Royal Pde BKHTH/KID SE3.....145 H3
CHST BR7.....185 H3
FUL/PGN SW6 *.....119 J6
RCH/KEW TW9 *.....137 H1
Royal Pde Ms CHST BR7 *.....185 H3
Royal Rd CAN/RD E16.....107 G5
LBTH SE11.....122 C6
SCUP DA14.....168 E5
TEDD TW11.....173 J1
Royal Route WBLY HA9.....80 B2
Royal St STHWK SE1.....17 H4
Royal Victor Pl BETH E2.....105 H1
Roycraft Av BARK IG11.....109 F1
Roycroft Cl
BRXS/STRHM SW2 *.....162 B3
SWFD E18.....53 F4
Roydene Rd
WOOL/PLUM SE18.....127 K6
Roydon Cl LOU IG10.....39 J2
Roy Gdns GNTH/NBYPK IG2.....72 E1
Roy Gv HPTN TW12.....173 G2
Royle Cl GPK RM2.....75 K2
Royle Crs WEA W13.....97 G3
Roy Rd NTHWD HA6.....40 D3
Roy Sq POP/IOD E14.....105 G6
Royston Av CHING E4.....51 H4
SUT SM1.....209 H1
WLGTN SM6.....210 D2
Royston Cl HEST TW5.....134 A2
Royston Gdns IL IG1.....71 H3
Royston Gv PIN HA5.....41 K2
Royston Park Rd PIN HA5.....41 K2
Royston Rd DART DA1.....170 D6
PGE/AN SE20.....182 A4
RCHPK/HAM TW10.....137 F6
The Roystons BRYLDS KT5.....191 J2
Royston St BETH E2.....104 E1
Rozel Rd VX/NE SW8.....141 H3
Rubastic Rd NWDGN UB2.....114 B3
Rubens Pl CLAP SW4.....141 K5

Rubens Rd NTHLT UB5.....................95 G1
Rubens St CAT SE6..........................164 C4
Ruby Ms WALTH E17 *........................51 J6
Ruby Rd WALTH E17..........................51 J6
Ruby St PECK SE15.........................123 J6
  WLSDN NW10...............................80 E5
Ruby Triangle PECK SE15 *...............123 J6
Ruckholt Cl LEY E10.........................87 K1
Rucklidge Av WLSDN NW10..................99 H1
Rudall Crs HAMP NW3........................83 H2
Ruddington Cl CLPT E5......................87 G2
Ruddock Cl EDGW HA8.......................44 E3
Ruddstreet Cl
  WOOL/PLUM SE18........................127 G4
Rudgwick Ter STJWD NW8 *..................2 D1
Rudland Rd BXLYHN DA7....................149 J4
Rudloe Rd BAL SW12........................161 H2
Rudolf Pl VX/NE SW8.......................121 K6
Rudolph Rd BUSH WD23....................28 D1
  KIL/WHAMP NW6..........................100 E1
  PLSTW E13................................106 D1
Rudyard Gv EDGW HA8......................44 E2
Ruffetts Cl SAND/SEL CR2.................212 D5
The Ruffetts SAND/SEL CR2................212 D5
Ruffle Cl WDR/YW UB7......................112 B2
Rufford Cl KTN/HRWW/WS HA3.............61 G3
Rufford St IS N1.............................84 E2
Rufford Street Ms IS N1 *..................84 E1
Rufus Cl RSLP HA4...........................77 H1
Rufus St FSBYE EC1V..........................7 G5
Rugby Av ALP/SUD HA0......................79 J2
  ED N9.....................................36 B3
  GFD/PVL UB6..............................96 D1
Rugby Cl HRW HA1...........................60 E1
Rugby Gdns DAGW RM9.......................91 J4
Rugby La CDALE/KGS NW9....................62 C1
  CHSWK W4.................................118 B2
  DAGW RM9................................91 H5
  TWK TW1..................................155 K1
Rugby St BMSBY WC1N..........................5 G7
Rugg St POP/IOD E14......................105 J6
Ruislip Cl GFD/PVL UB6.....................96 B5
Ruislip Ct RSLP HA4 *......................58 D6
Ruislip Rd GFD/PVL UB6......................96 B3
  NTHLT UB5.................................77 G6
  WEA W13..................................97 G3
Ruislip Rd East GFD/PVL UB6...............96 D3
Ruislip St TOOT SW17......................160 E6
Rumbold Rd FUL/PGN SW6...................140 A1
Rum Cl WAP E1W.............................104 D6
Rumsey Cl HPTN TW12.......................172 E2
Rumsey Rd BRXN/ST SW9...................142 A4
Runbury Cir CDALE/KGS NW9................63 C1
Runcorn Cl TOTM N17........................68 D1
Runcorn Pl NTGHL W11......................100 C6
Rundell Crs HDN NW4.........................63 K2
Runes Cl MTCM CR4........................194 C1
Runnelfield HRW HA1........................78 E1
Runnymede WIM/MER SW19...................178 C4
Runnymede Cl WHTN TW2....................155 C1
Runnymede Crs
  STRHM/NOR SW16.........................179 J4
Runnymede Gdns
  GFD/PVL UB6..............................96 D1
  HSLW TW3.................................155 C1
Runnymede Rd WHTN TW2...................155 C1
The Runway RSLP HA4.........................77 F3
Rupack St BERM/RHTH SE16 *..............123 K2
Rupert Av WBLY HA9..........................80 A3
Rupert Ct E/WMO/HCT KT8 *...............189 F1
  SOHO/SHAV W1D............................10 C5
Rupert Gdns BRXN/ST SW9.................142 C3
Rupert Rd ARCH N19..........................84 D1
  CHSWK W4.................................118 B3
  KIL/WHAMP NW6..........................100 D1
Rupert St SOHO/SHAV W1D...................10 C6
Rural Cl EMPK RM11.........................75 K5
Rural Wy STRHM/NOR SW16.................179 C3
Rusbridge Cl HACK E8.......................86 C3
Ruscoe Rd CAN/RD E16......................106 D5
Ruscombe Wy
  EBED/NFELT TW14........................153 J2
Rusham Rd BAL SW12........................160 E1
Rushbrook Crs WALTH E17...................51 H4
Rushbrook Rd ELTH/MOT SE9...............167 H4
Rush Common Ms
  BRXS/STRHM SW2.........................162 A2
Rushcroft Rd
  BRXS/STRHM SW2.........................142 B5
  CHING E4..................................51 K3
Rushden Cl NRWD SE19.....................180 E3
Rushdene BERM/RHTH SE16 *...............123 D3
Rushdene Av EBAR EN4.......................33 J2
Rushdene Cl NTHLT UB5......................95 C1
Rushdene Crs NTHLT UB5....................95 F1
Rushdene Rd PIN HA5.........................59 G3
Rushden Gdns CLAY IG5......................54 A2
  MLHL NW7.................................46 A2
Rushdon Cl ROM RM1.........................75 F3
Rushet Rd STMC/STPC BR5.................186 B5
Rushett Cl THDIT KT7.......................190 C5
Rushett Rd THDIT KT7......................190 C4
Rushey Cl NWMAL KT3.......................192 A1
Rushey Gn CAT SE6.........................164 E3
Rushey Hl ENC/FH EN2.......................23 F5
Rushey Md BROCKY SE4......................164 C5
Rush Green Gdns
  ROMW/RG RM7..............................74 E5
Rush Green Rd ROMW/RG RM7...............74 E5
Rushgrove Av CDALE/KGS NW9................63 H1
Rushgrove Pde
  CDALE/KGS NW9............................63 G2
Rushgrove St
  WOOL/PLUM SE18.........................126 E4
Rush Hill Ms BTSEA SW11..................141 F4
Rush Hill Rd BTSEA SW11..................141 F4
Rushley Cl HAYES BR2......................215 H2
Rushmead BETH E2..........................104 D2
  RCHPK/HAM TW10.........................156 C5
Rushmead Cl CROY/NA CRO..................212 B2
Rushmere Ct WPK KT4......................192 D6
Rushmere Pl WIM/MER SW19................177 C1
Rushmon Pl CHEAM SM3 *..................208 C4
Rushmon Vls NWMAL KT3 *.................192 C1

Rushmoor Cl PIN HA5........................59 G1
Rushmore Cl BMLY BR1.....................184 D6
Rushmore Ct WATW WD18 *..................26 B1
Rushmore Rd CLPT E5........................86 E2
Rusholme Av DAGE RM10.....................92 C1
Rusholme Gv NRWD SE19....................181 F1
Rusholme Rd PUT/ROE SW15...............159 G1
Rushout Av
  KTN/HRWW/WS HA3.........................61 H3
Rushton St IS N1.............................7 F2
Rushworth St STHWK SE1.....................18 B2
Rushy Meadow La CAR SM5.................194 D6
Ruskin Av EBED/NFELT TW14...............153 J2
  MNPK E12..................................89 K4
  RCH/KEW TW9.............................137 H1
  WELL DA16...............................148 B4
Ruskin Cl GLDGN NW11.......................65 F3
Ruskin Dr ORP BR6.........................216 E1
  WELL DA16...............................148 B4
  WPK KT4..................................192 E6
Ruskin Gdns EA W5..........................97 K3
  HARH IG43.................................57 K4
  KTN/HRWW/WS HA3..........................62 B2
Ruskin Gv DART DA1........................151 K6
  WELL DA16...............................148 B3
Ruskin Rd BELV DA17.......................129 H4
  CAR SM5..................................210 A3
  CROY/NA CRO.............................196 C6
  ISLW TW7.................................136 A4
  STHL UB1..................................95 J6
  TOTM N17..................................50 B4
Ruskin Wk ED N9 *..........................36 C3
  HNHL SE24................................162 D4
Ruskin Wy WIM/MER SW19..................178 C5
Rusland Av ORP BR6........................216 D1
Rusland Park Rd HRW HA1...................60 E1
Rusper Cl CRICK NW2.........................82 A1
  STAN HA7..................................29 J6
Rusper Rd DAGW RM9.........................91 J4
  WDGN N22.................................49 H5
Russell Cl BECK BR3.......................182 E6
Russell Av WDGN N22.......................49 H5
Russell Cl BKHTH/KID SE3.................146 B1
  BXLYHN DA7..............................149 H5
  CHSWK W4................................118 C6
  DART DA1.................................150 D4
  NTHWD HA6.................................40 A1
  RSLP HA4..................................59 G6
  WLSDN NW10...............................80 E5
Russell Cl BAR EN5 *.......................21 C5
  WHALL SW1A................................16 B1
Russell Gdns GLDGN NW11...................64 C3
  RCHPK/HAM TW10.........................156 D4
  WDR/YW UB7...............................112 B3
  WIM/MER SW20.............................33 J4
  WKENS W14...............................119 H3
Russell Gardens Ms
  WKENS W14...............................119 H2
Russell Gv BRXN/ST SW9...................142 B2
  MLHL NW7..................................45 G1
Russell Kerr Cl CHSWK W4 *...............137 K1
Russell La TRDG/WHET N20...................33 K4
Russell Pl HAMP NW3........................83 J3
Russell Rd BKHH IG9.........................39 G3
  CAN/RD E16..............................106 E5
  CDALE/KGS NW9............................63 C4
  CEND/HSY/T N8............................66 D3
  CHING E4..................................37 H6
  EN EN1....................................24 B1
  MTCM CR4.................................178 D6
  NTHLT UB5.................................78 C3
  NTHWD HA6.................................26 A5
  SEVS/STOTM N15............................68 A2
  TRDG/WHET N20............................33 J4
  WALTH E17.................................51 H6
  WALTH E17.................................69 K3
  WDGN N22..................................49 F2
  WHTN TW2................................156 A1
  WIM/MER SW19............................177 K3
  WKENS W14...............................119 H3
Russell Sq RSQ WC1B........................10 E1
Russell St HOL/ALD WC2B....................11 G4
Russell Wy OXHEY WD19.....................27 H1
  SUT SM1.................................209 F3
Russet Cl HGDN/ICK UB10....................94 A3
Russet Crs HOLWY N7 *......................85 F3
Russet Dr CROY/NA CRO....................198 B5
Russets Cl CHING E4.........................38 B6
Russett Cl ORP BR6........................217 H3
Russia Dock Rd
  BERM/RHTH SE16 *.......................124 B1
Russia La BETH E2..........................104 E1
Russia Rw CITYW EC2V.......................12 D4
Rusthall Av CHSWK W4......................118 A3
Rusthall Cl CROY/NA CRO..................197 K3
Rustic Av STRHM/NOR SW16................179 G5
Rustic Pl ALP/SUD HA0......................79 K2
Rustington Wk CHEAM SM3.................193 J4
Ruston Av BRYLDS KT5......................191 J4
Ruston Gdns STHGT/OAK N14................34 A5
Ruston Ms NTGHL W11......................100 C5
Ruston Rd WOOL/PLUM SE18...............126 D3
Ruston St BOW E3............................87 H6
Rust Sq CMBW SE5..........................142 E1
Rutford Rd STRHM/NOR SW16..............179 K1
Ruth Cl STAN HA7............................62 B1
Rutherford Cl BELMT SM2...................209 H4
Rutherford St WEST SW1P....................16 C6
Rutherford Wy BUSH WD23...................28 E1
  WBLY HA9..................................80 C1
Rutherglen Rd ABYW SE2....................128 B6
Rutherwyke Rd EW KT17....................207 J4
Ruthin Cl CDALE/KGS NW9...................63 G3
Ruthin Rd BKHTH/KID SE3...................125 K6
Ruthven St HOM E9...........................87 F6
Rutland Av BFN/LL DA15...................168 A3
Rutland Cl BXLY DA5.......................168 E3
  CHST BR7.................................206 B4
  DART DA1.................................171 G5
  MORT/ESHN SW14.........................137 J4
  WIM/MER SW19............................178 D3
Rutland Ct CHST BR7......................185 F4
  SKENS SW7................................14 D1
Rutland Dr MRDN SM4.......................193 K4

RCHPK/HAM TW10...........................156 E3
Rutland Gdns BCTR RM8......................91 J3
  CROY/NA CRO.............................212 A1
  FSBYPK N4.................................67 H3
  SKENS SW7.................................14 D3
  WEA W13 *.................................97 G4
Rutland Gardens Ms
  SKENS SW7.................................14 D3
Rutland Ga BELV DA17......................129 J5
  HAYES BR2................................215 J2
  SKENS SW7.................................14 C4
Rutland Ga South SKENS SW7 *............14 C4
Rutland Gv HMSMTH W6.....................118 E5
Rutland Ms STJWD NW8 *.....................83 H6
Rutland Ms South SKENS SW7..............14 C4
Rutland Pk CAT SE6........................164 C4
  CRICK NW2.................................82 A4
Rutland Pl BUSH WD23.......................28 D3
  FARR EC1M.................................12 B1
Rutland Rd FSTGT E7........................89 H5
  HOM E9....................................87 F6
  HRW HA1...................................60 C5
  HYS/HAR UB3.............................113 G4
  IL IG1.....................................90 B2
  STHL UB1..................................96 A3
  WALTH E17.................................69 J3
  WAN E11...................................71 G2
  WHTN TW2................................155 J4
Rutland St SKENS SW7.......................14 D4
Rutland Wk CAT SE6.......................164 C4
Rutland Wy STMC/STPC BR5................202 E3
Rutley Cl WALW SE17......................122 C6
Rutter Gdns MTCM CR4.....................194 C1
Rutters Cl WDR/YW UB7....................112 D2
Rutt's Ter NWCR SE14......................144 A2
The Rutts BUSH WD23.........................28 D3
Ruvigny Gdns PUT/ROE SW15..............139 G4
Ruxley Cl HOR/WEW KT19...................206 D4
  SCUP DA14................................186 E2
Ruxley Crs ESH/CLAY KT10.................205 H5
Ruxley La HOR/WEW KT19...................206 E4
Ruxley Ms HOR/WEW KT19..................206 D3
Ruxley Rdg ESH/CLAY KT10................205 G5
Ruxley Towers
  ESH/CLAY KT10 *.........................205 G5
Ryan Cl BKHTH/KID SE3....................146 A5
  RSLP HA4..................................59 F5
Ryan Ct OXHEY WD19 *.......................27 J2
Ryan Dr BTFD TW8..........................116 A6
Ryarsh Crs ORP BR6........................216 E2
Rycroft Wy TOTM N17 *......................50 B6
Rycullf Sq BKHTH/KID SE3.................145 J3
Rydal Cl HDN NW4...........................46 C4
Rydal Crs GFD/PVL UB6......................97 H2
Rydal Dr BXLYHN DA7......................149 H2
  WWKM BR4................................199 G6
Rydal Gdns CDALE/KGS NW9.................63 G2
  HSLW TW3................................155 G1
  PUT/ROE SW15............................176 B1
  WBLY HA9..................................61 J5
Rydal Mt HAYES BR2 *......................199 J1
Rydal Rd STRHM/NOR SW16................179 J1
Rydal Wy PEND EN3..........................36 E1
  RSLP HA4..................................77 G2
Rydens Av WOT/HER KT12...................188 B4
Rydens Cl WOT/HER KT12...................188 B4
Rydens Gv WOT/HER KT12...................188 C6
Ryde Pl TWK TW1...........................156 D1
Ryder Cl BUSH WD23..........................28 B1
Ryder Dr BERM/RHTH SE16.................123 J5
Ryder Gdns RAIN RM13.......................93 H4
Ryder St STJS SW1Y.........................10 B7
Ryde Vale Rd BAL SW12....................161 G4
Rydon Ms WIM/MER SW19....................177 F3
Rydston Cl HOLWY N7........................85 F5
Rye Cl BXLY DA5............................169 J1
Ryecotes Md DUL SE21......................163 F3
Rye Crs STMC/STPC BR5....................202 E5
Ryecroft Av CLAY IG5.......................53 K6
  WHTN TW2................................155 G3
Ryecroft Rd LEW SE13......................145 F6
  STMC/STPC BR5...........................201 J3
  STRHM/NOR SW16.........................180 A2
Ryecroft Rd FUL/PGN SW6..................140 A2
Ryecroft St FUL/PGN SW6..................140 A2
Ryefield Av HGDN/ICK UB10.................76 A6
Ryefield Crs PIN HA5 *.....................40 E5
Ryefield Pde NTHWD HA6 *...................40 E5
Ryefield Rd NRWD SE19....................180 D2
Rye Hill Pk PECK SE15....................143 K5
Ryelands Crs LEE/GVPK SE12..............166 B1
Rye La PECK SE15..........................143 H3
Rye Pk PECK SE15..........................144 A5
The Rye STHGT/OAK N14......................34 C2
Rye Wk PUT/ROE SW15......................139 G6
Rye Wy EDGW HA8............................44 B2
Ryfold Rd WIM/MER SW19..................159 K5
Ryhope Rd FBAR/BDGN N11...................34 B6
Ryland Cl FELT TW13......................153 J6
Rylandes Rd CRICK NW2......................81 J1
  SAND/SEL CR2............................212 D6
Ryland Rd KTTN NW5 *.......................84 B4
Rylett Crs SHB W12........................118 C2
Rylett Rd SHB W12.........................118 C2
Rylston Rd FUL/PGN SW6...................119 J6
  PLMGR N13.................................35 K5
Rymer Rd CROY/NA CRO....................197 F4
Rymer St HNHL SE24.......................162 C1
Rymill St CAN/RD E16......................127 F1
Rysbrack St CHEL SW3.......................14 E4
Rythe Cl CHSGTN KT9......................205 J5
Rythe Ct THDIT KT7........................190 B4
Rythe Rd ESH/CLAY KT10...................204 D3
Ryves Cottages MTCM CR4 *...............179 F5

Sabbarton St CAN/RD E16.................106 D5
Sabine Rd BTSEA SW11.....................140 E4
Sable Cl HSLWW TW4.......................134 B4
Sable St IS N1..............................85 H5
Sach Rd CLPT E5.............................68 D6
Sackville Av HAYES BR2...................199 K5

Sackville Cl RYLN/HDSTN HA2..............78 D1
Sackville Est
  STRHM/NOR SW16.........................161 K5
Sackville Gdns IL IG1.......................71 K5
Sackville Rd BELMT SM2...................208 E5
  RDART DA2................................171 H5
Saddlers Cl PIN HA5........................42 A1
Saddlers Ms KUT/HW KT1...................174 D4
Saddlescombe Wy
  NFNCH/WDSPK N12..........................46 E1
Sadler Cl MTCM CR4........................178 E5
Sadlers Gate Ms
  PUT/ROE SW15............................139 F4
Sadlers Ride E/WMO/HCT KT8..............173 H5
Saffron Av POP/IOD E14...................106 B6
Saffron Cl CROY/NA CRO...................195 K5
  GLDGN NW11................................64 D2
Saffron Hl HCIRC EC1N......................11 K1
Saffron Rd CRW RM5.........................57 F5
Saffron St HCIRC EC1N......................11 K1
Saffron Wy SURB KT6......................190 E5
Sage Cl EHAM E6...........................107 K4
Sage Ms EDUL SE22........................143 G6
Sage St WCHPL E1..........................104 E6
Sage Wy FSBYW WC1X..........................5 G5
Saigasso Cl CAN/RD E16...................107 H5
Sail St LBTH SE11..........................17 H6
Sainfoin Rd TOOT SW17....................161 F4
Sainsbury Rd NRWD SE19...................181 F1
St Agatha's Dr KUTN/CMB KT2.............175 G2
St Agatha's Gv CAR SM5..................194 E5
St Agnes Cl HOM E9.........................86 E6
St Agnes Pl LBTH SE11....................122 C6
St Agnes Well STLK EC1Y......................7 F6
St Aidan's Rd EDUL SE22..................163 J1
  WEA W13.................................116 C2
St Albans Av CHSWK W4....................118 A3
  EHAM E6.................................107 K2
  FELT TW13...............................172 C1
St Albans Crs WDGN N22....................49 G4
St Albans Farm
  EBED/NFELT TW14........................134 B6
St Albans Gdns TEDD TW11................174 B1
St Alban's Gv CAR SM5....................194 D4
  KENS W8..................................120 A3
St Albans La GLDGN NW11...................64 E5
St Alban's Ms BAY/PAD W2...................8 B1
St Alban's Pl IS N1..........................6 A1
St Albans Rd BAR EN5.......................20 C2
  DART DA1................................171 J1
  GDMY/SEVK IG3.............................73 F5
  KTTN NW5..................................84 A1
  KUTN/CMB KT2............................175 F2
  SUT SM1.................................208 D2
  WFD IG8...................................52 E3
  WLSDN NW10...............................81 G6
St Alban's St STJS SW1Y...................10 C6
St Albans Ter HMSMTH W6..................119 H6
St Alfege Pas GNWCH SE10.................125 F6
St Alfege Rd CHARL SE7....................126 C6
St Alphage Gdns BARB EC2Y................12 D2
St Alphage Highwalk
  BARB EC2Y.................................12 D2
St Alphage Wk EDGW HA8 *..................44 E5
St Alphege Rd ED N9........................36 E2
St Alphonsus Rd CLAP SW4................141 H5
St Amunds Cl CAT SE6.....................164 D6
St Andrews Av ALP/SUD HA0.................79 G3
  HCH RM12..................................93 J2
St Andrews Cl
  BERM/RHTH SE16 *.......................123 J5
  CRICK NW2 *...............................81 K1
  ISLW TW7................................135 K2
  NFNCH/WDSPK N12 *........................33 G6
  RSLP HA4..................................59 H6
  STAN HA7..................................43 J5
  THDIT KT7................................190 D4
  THMD SE28...............................109 K5
  WIM/MER SW19............................178 A2
St Andrew's Dr
  STMC/STPC BR5...........................202 C3
St Andrew's Gv
  STNW/STAM N16.............................67 K5
St Andrew's Hl BLKFR EC4V...................12 B5
St Andrews Ms BAL SW12...................161 J3
  BKHTH/KID SE3...........................145 K1
  STNW/STAM N16.............................67 K4
St Andrew's Pl CAMTN NW1....................3 J5
St Andrew's Rd ACT W3......................99 G5
  CAR SM5.................................209 J1
  CDALE/KGS NW9.............................63 F5
  CROY/NA CRO..............................211 J2
  ED N9.....................................36 E2
  EN EN1....................................24 A5
  GLDGN NW11................................64 D3
  HNWL W7.................................115 K2
  IL IG1.....................................71 J5
  PLSTW E13................................107 F2
  ROMW/RG RM7...............................75 F3
  SCUP DA14................................168 E5
  SURB KT6................................190 E3
  WALTH E17.................................51 G5
  WAN E11...................................70 C3
  WKENS W14...............................119 H6
  WLSDN NW10................................81 K4
St Andrew's Sq NTGHL W11.................100 C5
St Andrew St HCIRC EC1N....................11 K2
St Andrews Ter OXHEY WD19 *...............41 G1
St Andrew St TWRH EC3N.....................13 J4
St Andrews Wy BOW E3.....................105 K3
St Anna Rd BAR EN5 *.......................20 B6
St Anne's Av
  STWL/WRAY TW19..........................152 A2
St Anne's Cl HGT N6........................84 A4
  OXHEY WD19................................27 G4
St Annes Cl SHO/CST W1F...................10 C4
St Annes Gdns WLSDN NW10...................98 B2
St Anne's Pas POP/IOD E14 *..............105 H5
St Anne's Rd ALP/SUD HA0...................79 K5
  LEY E10...................................69 K6
St Anne's Rw POP/IOD E14................105 H5
St Ann's BARK IG11.........................90 C6

St Anns Rd HDN NW4 *.......................45 K6
St Ann's Crs WAND/EARL SW18..............160 B1
St Ann's Gdns KTTN NW5 *..................84 A4
St Ann's Hl WAND/EARL SW18..............160 A5
St Ann's Park Rd
  WAND/EARL SW18.........................160 B1
St Ann's Rd BARK IG11......................90 C6
  BARN SW13................................138 C3
  ED N9.....................................36 B4
  HRW HA1...................................60 E3
  NTGHL W11................................100 B6
  SEVS/STOTM N15............................67 K2
St Ann's St WEST SW1P......................16 D4
St Ann's Ter STJWD NW8......................2 B2
St Ann's Vls NTGHL W11....................119 G1
St Anselms Rd HYS/HAR UB3...............113 J2
St Anthony's Av WFD IG8....................53 G3
St Anthonys Cl TOOT SW17.................160 D4
  WAP E1W *................................123 H1
St Anthony's Wy
  EBED/NFELT TW14........................133 J5
St Antony's Rd FSTGT E7....................89 F5
St Arvans Cl CROY/NA CRO.................212 A1
St Asaph Rd BROCKY SE4...................144 A4
St Aubyn's Av HSLW TW3...................135 F6
  WIM/MER SW19............................177 H1
St Aubyns Cl ORP BR6.....................217 F1
St Aubyns Gdns ORP BR6...................202 A6
St Aubyn's Rd NRWD SE19..................181 G2
St Audrey Av BXLYHN DA7..................149 H3
St Augustine's Av ALP/SUD HA0.............98 A1
  SAND/SEL CR2.............................211 J5
  WBLY HA9..................................80 A1
St Augustine's Rd BELV DA17.............129 G4
  CAMTN NW1.................................84 D5
St Austell Cl EDGW HA8.....................44 B5
St Austell Rd LEW SE13....................145 F1
St Awdry's Rd BARK IG11....................90 D6
St Barnabas Cl BECK BR3..................183 F5
  EDUL SE22...............................143 F6
St Barnabas' Gdns
  E/WMO/HCT KT8...........................189 F2
St Barnabas Rd MTCM CR4.................179 F3
  SUT SM1.................................209 H3
  WALTH E17.................................69 J3
  WFD IG8...................................53 F4
St Barnabas St BCVA SW1V.................121 F5
St Barnabas Ter HOM E9......................87 F3
St Barnabas Vls VX/NE SW8................141 K2
St Bartholomew's Cl
  SYD SE26................................163 K6
St Bartholomew's Rd
  EHAM E6.................................107 J1
St Benets Cl TOOT SW17...................160 D4
St Benet's Gv CAR SM5....................194 B4
St Benjamins Dr ORP BR6..................217 J6
St Bernards CROY/NA CRO..................212 A1
St Bernards Cl WNWD SE27.................162 E6
St Bernard's Rd EHAM E6...................89 J6
St Blaise Av BMLY BR1....................184 A5
St Botolph St TWRH EC3N...................13 J3
St Bride's Av EDGW HA8.....................44 B4
St Brides Cl ERITHM DA18.................128 E2
St Bride St FLST/FETLN EC4A...............12 A3
St Catherines Cl FELT TW13...............153 K3
St Catherine's Dr NWCR SE14.............144 A3
St Catherines Ms CHEL SW3.................14 E6
St Catherines Rd CHING E4..................37 J4
  RSLP HA4..................................58 A2
St Chads Cl SURB KT6.....................190 D4
St Chad's Gdns CHDH RM6...................74 A4
St Chad's Pl FSBYW WC1X.....................5 F4
St Chad's Rd CHDH RM6......................74 A4
St Chad's St STPAN WC1H.....................5 F4
St Charles Pl NKENS W10..................100 C4
St Charles Sq NKENS W10..................100 C4
St Christopher's Cl ISLW TW7 *...........135 K2
St Christophers Dr
  HYS/HAR UB3...............................95 F6
St Christopher's Ms
  WLGTN SM6................................210 C3
St Christopher's Pl MHST W1U...............9 H4
St Clair Cl CLAY IG5.......................53 K5
St Clair Dr WPK KT4......................207 K1
St Clair Pl PLSTW E13....................107 F1
St Clair Rd CROY/NA CRO..................197 K6
St Clare St TWRH EC3N......................13 J4
St Clements Cl PUR RM19..................131 K4
St Clements Ct HOLWY N7 *.................85 C5
St Clements St HOLWY N7....................85 C5
St Clements Yd EDUL SE22 *...............143 C6
St Cloud Rd WNWD SE27...................162 D6
St Crispins Cl HAMP NW3....................83 J2
  STHL UB1..................................95 K5
St Cross St HCIRC EC1N.....................11 K1
St Cuthberts Gdns PIN HA5 *...............41 K3
St Cuthbert's Rd CRICK NW2................82 D4
  PLMGR N13.................................49 G2
St Cyprian's St TOOT SW17...............160 E6
St David's Cl
  BERM/RHTH SE16 *.......................123 J5
  WBLY HA9..................................80 E1
  WWKM BR4................................198 E4
St David's Dr EDGW HA8.....................44 A4
St David's Pl HDN NW4......................63 K4
St Davids Cl WBLY HA9......................80 E1
St David's Pl HDN NW4 *....................63 K4
St Denis Rd WNWD SE27....................162 E6
St Dionis Rd FUL/PGN SW6.................139 J3
St Donatt's Rd NWCR SE14.................144 C3
St Dunstan's Av ACT W3.....................99 F6
St Dunstans Cl HYS/HAR UB3..............113 J4
St Dunstan's Gdns ACT W3 *................99 F6
St Dunstan's Hl MON EC3R...................13 G6
  SUT SM1.................................208 C2
St Dunstan's La MON EC3R...................13 G6
St Dunstan's Rd FELT TW13...............153 J5
  FSTGT E7..................................89 G4
  HMSMTH W6...............................119 G5
  HNWL W7.................................115 K2
  HSLWW TW4...............................134 B3
  SNWD SE25...............................197 G1
St Edmunds Av RSLP HA4.....................58 B3

St Edmunds Cl ERITHM DA18 128 E2
STJWD NW8 2 E1
TOOT SW17 160 D4
St Edmunds Dr STAN HA7 43 G4
St Edmund's La WHTN TW2 155 G2
St Edmunds Rd DART DA1 151 K5
ED N9 36 C2
IL IG1 71 K3
St Edmunds Sq BARN SW13 119 F6
St Edmund's Ter STJWD NW8 2 D1
St Edward's Cl GLDGN NW11 64 E3
St Edwards Wy ROM RM1 75 G1
St Egberts Wy CHING E4 38 A3
St Elmo Rd SHB W12 118 C2
St Elmos Rd BERM/RHTH SE16 124 B2
St Erkenwald Ms BARK IG11 90 D6
St Erkenwald Rd BARK IG11 90 D6
St Ervans Rd NKENS W10 100 C4
St Faith's Cl ENC/FH EN2 23 J2
St Faith's Rd DUL SE21 162 C3
St Fidelis' Rd ERITH DA8 130 A4
St Fillans Rd CAT SE6 165 F3
St Francis Cl ORP BR6 201 K3
OXHEY WD19 27 F3
St Francis Rd EDUL SE22 143 F5
St Francis Wy IL IG1 90 D2
St Gabriel's Cl WAN E11 71 F5
St Gabriel's Rd CRICK NW2 82 B3
St George's ED N9 36 C5
St George's Av CDALE/KGS NW9 62 E1
EA W5 116 E2
FSTGT E7 89 F5
HOLWY N7 84 D2
STHL UB1 95 K6
St George's Circ STHWK SE1 18 A3
St Georges Cl ALP/SUD HA0 79 G1
GLDGN NW11 64 D3
THMD SE28 109 K5
VX/NE SW8 141 H2
St George's Ct STP EC4M * 12 A3
St George's Dr OXHEY WD19 27 G2
PIM SW1V 121 G5
St Georges Flds BAY/PAD W2 8 D5
St George's Gdns SURB KT6 191 J6
St George's Gv TOOT SW17 160 C5
St George's Industrial Est
KUTN/CMB KT2 174 E1
St George's La MON EC3R * 13 F5
St George's Ms CAMTN NW1 83 K5
CHSWK W4 * 117 K6
DEPT SE8 124 C4
St Georges Pde CAT SE6 * 164 C4
St George's Rd BECK BR3 182 E4
BMLY BR1 184 E5
CHSWK W4 118 A2
DAGW RM9 92 B2
EN EN1 24 B1
FELT TW13 154 D6
FSTGT E7 89 F5
GLDGN NW11 64 D3
HNWL W7 116 A1
IL IG1 71 K4
KUTN/CMB KT2 175 H3
LEY E10 88 A1
MTCM CR4 179 G6
PLMGR N13 35 F5
RCH/KEW TW9 137 G4
SCUP DA14 186 E2
STHWK SE1 18 A5
STMC/STPC BR5 201 J3
TWK TW1 136 C6
WIM/MER SW19 177 J2
WLGTN SM6 210 B3
St Georges Rd West BMLY BR1 184 D5
St George's Sq FSTGT E7 89 F5
NWMAL KT3 * 176 B6
PIM SW1V 121 J5
St George's Square Ms
PIM SW1V 121 J5
St George's Ter CAMTN NW1 83 K5
PECK SE15 * 143 H1
St George St CONDST W1S 9 K5
St George's Wk CROY/NA CR0 211 J1
St George's Wy PECK SE15 123 F6
St Gerards Cl CLAP SW4 141 H6
St German's Pl BKHTH/KID SE3 145 K3
St German's Rd FSTH SE23 164 B3
St Giles Av DAGE RM10 92 D5
HGDN/ICK UB10 76 A2
St Giles Churchyard
BARB EC2Y * 12 D2
St Giles Circ SOHO/SHAV W1D 10 D3
St Giles Cl DAGE RM10 92 D5
HEST TW5 134 D1
ORP BR6 216 D3
St Giles Ct LSQ/SEVD WC2H 10 D3
St Giles High St
LSQ/SEVD WC2H 10 D3
St Giles Pas LSQ/SEVD WC2H 10 D4
St Giles Rd CMBW SE5 143 F2
St Gothard Rd WNWD SE27 162 E6
St Gregory Cl RSLP HA4 77 G2
St Helena Rd
BERM/RHTH SE16 124 A4
St Helena St FSBYW WC1X * 5 J5
St Helena Ter RCH/KEW TW9 * 136 E6
St Helens THDIT KT7 * 189 K4
St Helens Ct RAIN RM13 111 J3
St Helen's Crs
STRHM/NOR SW16 180 A4
St Helen's Gdns NKENS W10 100 B5
St Helen's Pl HDTCH EC3A 13 G3
St Helens Rd ERITHM DA18 128 E2
IL IG1 71 K3
STRHM/NOR SW16 180 A5
WEA W13 116 C1
St Helier Av MRDN SM4 194 B4
St Heliers Av HSLWW TW4 135 F6
St Helier's Rd LEY E10 69 K3
St Hildas Cl KIL/WHAMP NW6 * 82 B6
TOOT SW17 160 D4
St Hilda's Rd BARN SW13 118 E6
St Hughes Cl TOOT SW17 * 160 D4
St Hugh's Rd PGE/AN SE20 181 J4
St Ivians Dr GPK RM2 57 J6
St James Av SUT SM1 208 E3
TRDG/WHET N20 33 J5
WEA W13 116 B1
St James Cl EBAR EN4 21 H4
NWMAL KT3 192 C2
RSLP HA4 59 G6
STJWD NW8 2 E2
TRDG/WHET N20 33 J5
St James' Ct WESTW SW1E * 16 B4
St James' Gdns ALP/SUD HA0 79 K5
CHDH RM6 73 H1
St James Ms POP/IOD E14 * 125 F3
St James Pl DART DA1 171 G1
St James Rd CAR SM5 209 J1
ED N9 36 D4
MTCM CR4 179 F3
SRTFD E15 88 D3
SURB KT6 190 E3
SUT SM1 208 E4
St James's NWCR SE14 144 B2
St James's Av BECK BR3 182 B6
BETH E2 104 E1
HPTN TW12 173 H1
St James's Chambers
STJS SW1Y * 10 B7
St James's Cl TOOT SW17 * 160 E4
TOOT SW17 * 179 F1
WOOL/PLUM SE18 127 H5
St James's Cottages
RCH/KEW TW9 * 136 E6
St James's Ct KUT/HW KT1 * 175 F6
WESTW SW1E 16 B4
St James's Crs BRXN/ST SW9 142 B4
St James's Dr BAL SW12 160 E3
St James's Gdns CAMTN NW1 * 4 A5
NTGHL W11 119 H1
St James's Gv BTSEA SW11 140 E3
St James's La MUSWH N10 66 B1
St James's Market STJS SW1Y * 10 C6
St James's Ms WALTH E17 69 G2
St James's Pk CROY/NA CR0 196 D4
St James's Pl WHALL SW1A 16 A1
St James Sq SURB KT6 190 D4
St James's Rd
BERM/RHTH SE16 123 H3
CROY/NA CR0 196 D4
HPTN TW12 173 G1
KUT/HW KT1 174 E5
St James's Rw CHSGTN KT9 * 205 K4
St James's Sq STJS SW1Y 10 C7
St James's St WALTH E17 69 G2
WHALL SW1A 10 A7
St James's Ter STJWD NW8 2 E2
St James's Terrace Ms
STJWD NW8 2 E1
St James St HMSMTH W6 119 F5
St James Ter BAL SW12 * 161 F3
ORP BR6 * 217 J6
St James Wk CLKNW EC1R 6 A7
St James Wy BXLY DA5 169 H2
SCUP DA14 187 F1
St Jerome's Gv HYS/HAR UB3 94 A5
St Joan's Rd ED N9 36 B4
St John Cl FUL/PGN SW6 * 139 K1
St John's Av FBAR/BDGN N11 47 K1
PUT/ROE SW15 139 G6
WLSDN NW10 81 H6
St John's Church Rd HOM E9 * 86 E3
St John's Cl FUL/PGN SW6 * 139 K1
RAIN RM13 93 J5
STHGT/OAK N14 34 C1
TRDG/WHET N20 * 33 G4
WBLY HA9 80 A3
St Johns Cottages
PGE/AN SE20 * 181 K3
St John's Ct BKHH IG9 39 F3
ISLW TW7 136 A3
St John's Crs BRXN/ST SW9 142 B4
St John's Dr
WAND/EARL SW18 160 A3
WOT/HER KT12 188 B5
St John's Gdns NTGHL W11 100 D6
St John's Gv ARCH N19 66 D6
BARN SW13 * 138 C3
RCH/KEW TW9 136 E5
St John's Hl BTSEA SW11 140 D5
St John's Hill Gv BTSEA SW11 140 C5
St John's La FARR EC1M 6 A7
St Johns Pde SCUP DA14 * 168 C6
WEA W13 * 116 C1
St John's Pk BKHTH/KID SE3 145 K1
St John's Pl FARR EC1M 6 A7
St John's Rd BARK IG11 90 E6
BTSEA SW11 140 D5
CAN/RD E16 106 E5
CAR SM5 209 J1
CHING E4 37 K6
CROY/NA CR0 211 H1
CRW RM5 56 E1
E/WMO/HCT KT8 189 J1
EHAM E6 89 J6
ERITH DA8 130 A5
FELT TW13 154 E6
GLDGN NW11 64 D4
GNTH/NBYPK IG2 72 E4
HRW HA1 61 F3
ISLW TW7 136 A3
KUT/HW KT1 174 D5
NWDGN UB2 114 D3
NWMAL KT3 175 K6
PGE/AN SE20 181 K3
RCH/KEW TW9 137 F5
SCUP DA14 168 C6
SEVS/STOTM N15 68 A3
STMC/STPC BR5 201 J3
SUT SM1 193 K6
WALTH E17 51 K5
WBLY HA9 79 K2
WELL DA16 148 C4
WIM/MER SW19 177 H3
St John's Sq FARR EC1M 6 A7
St John's Ter FSTGT E7 89 F4
NKENS W10 100 B3
WOOL/PLUM SE18 127 H6
St John St FSBYE EC1V 5 K3
St John's V BROCKY SE4 144 D3
St John's Vls ARCH N19 66 D6
KENS W8 120 A3
St John's Wy ARCH N19 66 D5
St John's Wood High St
STJWD NW8 2 B3
St John's Wood Pk STJWD NW8 2 A1
St John's Wood Rd STJWD NW8 2 A6
St John's Wood Ter STJWD NW8 2 C2
St Josephs Cl NKENS W10 100 C4
ORP BR6 217 F2
St Joseph's Dr STHL UB1 114 E1
St Josephs Gv HDN NW4 63 K1
St Joseph's Rd ED N9 36 D2
St Joseph's St VX/NE SW8 * 141 G2
St Joseph's V LEW SE13 145 H4
St Jude's Rd BETH E2 104 D1
St Jude St STNW/STAM N16 86 A3
St Julian's Cl
STRHM/NOR SW16 * 162 B6
St Julian's Farm Rd
WNWD SE27 162 B6
St Julian's Rd KIL/WHAMP NW6 82 D5
St Justin Cl STMC/STPC BR5 186 E6
St Katharine's Prec
CAMTN NW1 * 3 J2
St Katharine's Wy WAP E1W 13 K7
St Katherines Rd
ERITHM DA18 128 E2
St Katherines Wk
NTGHL W11 * 100 B6
St Keverne Rd ELTH/MOT SE9 166 D6
St Kilda Rd ORP BR6 202 A5
WEA W13 116 B2
St Kilda's Rd HRW HA1 60 E3
STNW/STAM N16 67 K5
St Kitts Ter NRWD SE19 181 F1
St Laurence Cl
STMC/STPC BR5 186 E6
St Laurence's Cl
KIL/WHAMP NW6 82 B6
St Lawrence Cl EDGW HA8 44 B3
St Lawrence Cottages
POP/IOD E14 * 125 F1
St Lawrence Dr PIN HA5 59 F2
St Lawrence St POP/IOD E14 125 F1
St Lawrence Ter NKENS W10 100 C4
St Lawrence Wy
BRXN/ST SW9 * 142 B3
St Leonard's Av CHING E4 52 C2
KTN/HRWW/WS HA3 61 J2
St Leonards Cl WELL DA16 148 B4
St Leonard's Gdns HEST TW5 134 D1
Saint Leonards Gdns IL IG1 90 C3
St Leonards Ri ORP BR6 216 E2
St Leonard's Rd CROY/NA CR0 211 H1
ESH/CLAY KT10 205 F4
MORT/ESHN SW14 137 K4
POP/IOD E14 106 A5
SURB KT6 190 E2
THDIT KT7 190 B3
WEA W13 97 J6
WLSDN NW10 99 F3
St Leonard's Sq KTTN NW5 84 A4
SURB KT6 190 E2
St Leonard's St BOW E3 105 K2
St Leonard's Ter CHEL SW3 120 E5
St Leonard's Wk
STRHM/NOR SW16 180 A3
St Leonards Wy EMPK RM11 75 K5
St Loo Av CHEL SW3 120 D6
St Louis Rd WNWD SE27 162 E6
St Loy's Rd TOTM N17 50 A5
St Lucia Dr SRTFD E15 88 D6
St Luke's Av CLAP SW4 141 J5
ENC/FH EN2 23 K1
IL IG1 90 B3
St Luke's Cl SNWD SE25 197 J3
St Luke's Est FSBYE EC1V 6 E6
St Luke's Ms NTGHL W11 100 D5
St Luke's Rd NTGHL W11 100 D4
St Lukes's Cl FSBYE EC1V 6 D6
St Luke's Sq CAN/RD E16 106 D5
St Luke's St CHEL SW3 120 D5
St Lukes Yd MV/WKIL W9 * 100 D1
St Malo Av ED N9 36 E5
St Margarets BARK IG11 90 D6
KUTN/CMB KT2 * 175 K1
St Margarets Av ASHF TW15 152 E6
BFN/LL DA15 167 J5
CHEAM SM3 208 C1
RYLN/HDSTN HA2 78 C1
SEVS/STOTM N15 67 H1
TRDG/WHET N20 33 G3
St Margarets Cl ORP BR6 217 H2
St Margarets Ct
PUT/ROE SW15 * 138 E5
St Margaret's Crs
PUT/ROE SW15 * 138 E6
St Margaret's Dr TWK TW1 136 C6
St Margaret's Gv TWK TW1 156 B1
WAN E11 88 D1
WOOL/PLUM SE18 127 H6
St Margarets La KENS W8 * 120 A3
St Margarets Ms
KUTN/CMB KT2 * 175 K1
St Margaret's Rd BROCKY SE4 144 C5
EDGW HA8 44 D1
HNWL W7 115 K2
MNPK E12 71 G6
RSLP HA4 58 B3
TOTM N17 50 A6
TWK TW1 136 C5
WLSDN NW10 100 A2
St Margaret's Ter
WOOL/PLUM SE18 127 H5
St Margaret St WEST SW1P 16 E3
St Mark's Cl BAR EN5 21 F4
FUL/PGN SW6 139 K2
St Mark's Crs CAMTN NW1 * 84 A6
St Marks Ga HOM E9 87 H5
St Mark's Gv WBPTN SW10 140 A1
St Mark's Hl SURB KT6 191 F3
St Mark's Pl NTGHL W11 100 C5
WIM/MER SW19 * 177 J2
St Mark's Ri HACK E8 86 B3
St Mark's Rd EA W5 117 F1
EN EN1 36 B1
HAYES BR2 184 A6
HNWL W7 115 K2
MTCM CR4 178 E5
NKENS W10 100 B5
SNWD SE25 197 H1
TEDD TW11 174 C3
St Mark's Sq CAMTN NW1 3 G1
St Mark St WCHPL E1 13 K4
St Marks Vls FSBYPK N4 * 67 F6
St Martins NTHWD HA6 40 B1
St Martins Ap RSLP HA4 58 C4
St Martin's Av EHAM E6 107 H1
St Martin's Cl CAMTN NW1 84 C6
EN EN1 24 D2
ERITHM DA18 128 E2
OXHEY WD19 27 G6
St Martins Ct CHCR WC2N 10 E5
St Martin's La BECK BR3 198 E2
CHCR WC2N 10 E5
St Martin's Le Grand STBT EC1A 12 C3
St Martin's Pl CHCR WC2N 10 E6
St Martin's Rd BRXN/ST SW9 142 A3
DART DA1 171 J1
ED N9 36 D4
EFNCH N2 47 H4
St Martin's St LSQ/SEVD WC2H * 10 D6
St Martin's Wy TOOT SW17 160 B5
St Mary Abbot's Pl KENS W8 119 J3
St Mary Abbots Ter
WKENS W14 * 119 J3
St Mary At Hl MON EC3R 13 G6
St Mary Av WLGTN SM6 210 A1
St Mary Axe HDTCH EC3A 13 H4
St Marychurch St
BERM/RHTH SE16 123 K2
St Mary Graces Ct WCHPL E1 * 13 K6
St Mary Newington Cl
WALW SE17 * 123 F5
St Mary Rd WALTH E17 69 K1
St Marys BARK IG11 108 D1
St Mary's Ap MNPK E12 89 K3
St Mary's Av FNCH N3 46 D5
HAYES BR2 183 H6
NTHWD HA6 40 C1
NWDGN UB2 115 G4
STWL/WRAY TW19 152 A2
TEDD TW11 * 174 A2
WAN E11 71 F3
St Mary's Cl CHSGTN KT9 206 B5
EW KT17 207 H5
STMC/STPC BR5 186 C5
TOTM N17 50 C4
St Marys Ct HMSMTH W6 * 118 C3
St Mary's Crs HDN NW4 45 K6
HYS/HAR UB3 94 D6
ISLW TW7 135 K1
STWL/WRAY TW19 152 A2
St Mary's Dr
EBED/NFELT TW14 153 F2
St Marys Est
BERM/RHTH SE16 * 123 K2
St Mary's Gdns LBTH SE11 17 K6
St Marys Ga KENS W8 120 A3
St Mary's Gn EFNCH N2 47 G6
St Mary's Gv BARN SW13 138 E4
CHSWK W4 117 J6
IS N1 85 H4
RCH/KEW TW9 137 G5
St Mary's Man BAY/PAD W2 101 G4
St Marys Ms KIL/WHAMP NW6 * 83 F5
St Mary's Pth IS N1 * 85 H6
WCHPL E1 * 104 C5
St Mary's Pl EA W5 116 E2
KENS W8 120 A3
St Mary's Rd BXLY DA5 169 K3
CEND/HSY/T N8 66 E1
E/WMO/HCT KT8 189 J2
EA W5 116 E2
EBAR EN4 33 K2
ED N9 36 E3
GLDGN NW11 64 C4
HYS/HAR UB3 94 D6
IL IG1 72 C6
LEY E10 88 A1
PECK SE15 143 K3
PLSTW E13 107 F1
SNWD SE25 181 F6
SURB KT6 190 E3
WIM/MER SW19 177 H1
WLSDN NW10 81 G6
WPK KT4 192 B6
St Mary's Sq BAY/PAD W2 8 A1
EA W5 * 116 E2
St Mary's Ter BAY/PAD W2 8 A1
BORE WD6 * 29 K1
St Mary St WOOL/PLUM SE18 127 F4
St Marys Vw
KTN/HRWW/WS HA3 61 J2
St Mary's Wk HYS/HAR UB3 94 D6
LBTH SE11 17 K6
St Marys Wy CHIG IG7 54 A1
St Matthew's Av SURB KT6 191 F5
St Matthews Cl OXHEY WD19 27 H1
RAIN RM13 93 J5
St Matthews Ct SRTFD E15 88 D5
St Matthews Dr BMLY BR1 184 E6
St Matthew's Rd
BRXS/STRHM SW2 142 A6
EA W5 117 F1
St Matthew's Rw BETH E2 104 C2
St Matthew St WEST SW1P 16 C4
St Matthias Cl CDALE/KGS NW9 63 H2
St Maur Rd FUL/PGN SW6 139 J2
St Meddens CHST BR7 * 185 J3
St Mellion Cl THMD SE28 109 K5
St Merryn Cl
WOOL/PLUM SE18 147 J1
St Michael's Aly BANK EC3V 13 F4
St Michaels Av ED N9 36 E2
WBLY HA9 80 C4
St Michaels Cl BMLY BR1 184 D6
CAN/RD E16 107 H4
ERITHM DA18 * 128 E2
FNCH N3 46 D5
NFNCH/WDSPK N12 47 J1
WOT/HER KT12 188 B6
WPK KT4 192 C6
St Michaels Ct GLDGN NW11 * 64 D4
St Michael's Crs PIN HA5 59 J3
St Michael's Gdns NKENS W10 100 C4
St Michael's Ms BGVA SW1W 15 G7
St Michaels Ri WELL DA16 * 148 C2
St Michael's Rd BRXN/ST SW9 142 A3
CRICK NW2 82 A2
CROY/NA CR0 196 D5
WELL DA16 148 C4
WLGTN SM6 210 C4
St Michael's St BAY/PAD W2 8 B3
St Michaels Ter HGT N6 * 66 A5
WDGN N22 48 E5
St Mildred's Ct LOTH EC2R * 12 E4
St Mildreds Rd CAT SE6 165 H2
St Nicholas Av HCH RM12 93 J1
St Nicholas Cl BORE WD6 29 K1
St Nicholas Glebe TOOT SW17 179 F2
St Nicholas Rd SUT SM1 209 F3
THDIT KT7 190 A3
WOOL/PLUM SE18 128 A5
St Nicholas St DEPT SE8 144 C2
St Nicholas Wy SUT SM1 209 F2
St Nicolas La CHST BR7 184 D4
St Ninian's Ct TRDG/WHET N20 33 K5
St Norbert Rd BROCKY SE4 144 B5
St Olaf's Rd FUL/PGN SW6 139 H1
St Olave's Rd EHAM E6 90 A6
St Olave's Wk
STRHM/NOR SW16 179 H5
St Onge Pde EN EN1 * 23 K4
St Oswald's Pl LBTH SE11 122 A5
St Oswald's Rd
STRHM/NOR SW16 180 C4
St Oswulf St WEST SW1P * 16 D7
St Pancras Gdns CAMTN NW1 4 D1
St Pancras Wy CAMTN NW1 84 C5
St Paul's Av
BERM/RHTH SE16 * 124 A1
CRICK NW2 81 K4
KTN/HRWW/WS HA3 62 B2
St Paul's Church Yd STP EC4M 12 B4
St Paul's Cl CAR SM5 194 D5
CHARL SE7 126 C5
CHSGTN KT9 205 K2
EA W5 117 G2
HSLW TW3 134 E3
HYS/HAR UB3 113 G5
St Paul's Cray Rd CHST BR7 185 J4
St Pauls Crs CAMTN NW1 84 D5
HDN NW4 * 64 A1
St Paul's Dr SRTFD E15 88 B3
St Pauls Ms CAMTN NW1 84 D5
St Paul's Pl IS N1 85 K4
St Pauls Ri PLMGR N13 49 H2
St Pauls Rd BARK IG11 90 C6
BTFD TW8 116 E6
ERITH DA8 149 K1
IS N1 85 J4
RCH/KEW TW9 137 G4
THHTH CR7 180 D6
TOTM N17 50 C3
St Pauls Ter WALW SE17 * 122 C6
St Paul St IS N1 6 C1
St Paul's Wy FNCH N3 47 F3
POP/IOD E14 105 H4
St Paul's Wood Hl
STMC/STPC BR5 185 K5
St Peter's Av BETH E2 104 C2
UED N18 36 C6
WALTH E17 70 C1
St Petersburgh Ms
BAY/PAD W2 * 101 F6
St Petersburgh Pl
BAY/PAD W2 101 F6
St Peter's Cl BETH E2 104 C1
BUSH WD23 28 D3
CHST BR7 185 J3
GNTH/NBYPK IG2 72 E1
RSLP HA4 59 H6
TOOT SW17 160 D4
St Peters Ct BKHTH/KID SE3 * 145 J6
E/WMO/HCT KT8 189 F1
HDN NW4 64 A2
St Peter's Gdns WNWD SE27 162 B5
St Peter's Gv HMSMTH W6 118 D4
St Peters Ms FSBYPK N4 * 67 H2
St Peters Pl MV/WKIL W9 101 F3
St Peter's Rd CROY/NA CR0 211 K2
E/WMO/HCT KT8 189 F1
ED N9 36 D3
HMSMTH W6 * 118 D5
KUT/HW KT1 175 H5
STHL UB1 96 A4
TWK TW1 136 C6
St Peter's Sq BETH E2 * 104 C1
HMSMTH W6 118 C5
St Peter's St IS N1 6 B1
SAND/SEL CR2 211 K3
St Peter's Ter FUL/PGN SW6 139 J1
St Peter's Vls HMSMTH W6 118 D4
St Peter's Wy EA W5 97 K4
HYS/HAR UB3 113 G5
IS N1 * 86 A5
St Philip's Av WPK KT4 192 E6
St Philip Sq VX/NE SW8 * 141 G3
St Philip's Rd HACK E8 86 C4
SURB KT6 190 E3
St Philip St VX/NE SW8 141 G3
St Philip's Wy IS N1 85 J6
St Quentin Rd WELL DA16 148 A4
St Quintin Av NKENS W10 100 A4
St Quintin Gdns NKENS W10 100 A4
St Quintin Rd PLSTW E13 107 F2
St Raphael's Wy WLSDN NW10 80 E3
St Regis Cl MUSWH N10 48 B5
St Ronans Cl EBAR EN4 21 H1
St Ronans Crs WFD IG8 52 E3
St Rule St VX/NE SW8 141 H3
St Saviours Ct WDGN N22 48 D5
St Saviour's Est STHWK SE1 19 J4
St Saviour's Rd
BRXS/STRHM SW2 142 A6
CROY/NA CR0 196 D3
Saints Cl WNWD SE27 162 C6
Saints Dr FSTGT E7 89 K4
St Silas Pl KTTN NW5 84 A4
St Simon's Av PUT/ROE SW15 139 F6
St Stephen's Av SHB W12 118 E2
WALTH E17 70 A2

WEA W13 97 H5
St Stephens Cl KTTN NW5 * 83 K3
STHL UB1 96 A4
STJWD NW8 2 C1
WALTH E17 69 K2
St Stephen's Crs BAY/PAD W2 100 E5
THHTH CR7 180 B6
St Stephen's Gdns
BAY/PAD W2 100 E5
TWK TW1 156 D1
St Stephen's Gv LEW SE13 145 F4
St Stephen's Ms BAY/PAD W2 100 E4
St Stephens Pde WHALL SW1A 16 E2
St Stephens Rd BAR EN5 20 B6
BOW E3 105 H1
EHAM E6 89 G5
HSLW TW3 155 F1
WALTH E17 69 K2
WDR/YW UB7 112 A1
WEA W13 97 H5
St Stephens Ter VX/NE SW8 * 141 K1
St Stephen's Wk SKENS SW7 * 120 B4
St Swithin's La MANHO EC4N 12 E5
St Swithun's Rd LEW SE13 * 145 G6
St Theresa's Rd
EBED/NFELT TW14 133 J5
St Thomas Cl SURB KT6 191 G5
St Thomas Ct BXLY DA5 169 H2
St Thomas' Dr PIN HA5 41 J4
STMC/STPC BR5 201 H5
St Thomas Gdns IL IG1 90 C4
St Thomas Rd BELV DA17 129 K2
CAN/RD E16 106 E5
CHSWK W4 137 K1
STHGT/OAK N14 34 D2
St Thomas's Gdns KTTN NW5 84 A4
St Thomas's Pl HOM E9 * 86 E5
St Thomas's Rd FSBYPK N4 67 G6
WLSDN NW10 81 G6
St Thomas's Sq HOM E9 86 D5
St Thomas St STHWK SE1 19 F1
St Thomas's Wy FUL/PGN SW6 139 J1
St Ursula Gv PIN HA5 59 H2
St Ursula Rd STHL UB1 96 A5
St Vincent Cl WNWD SE27 180 C1
St Vincent Rd WHTN TW2 155 H1
St Vincents Av DART DA1 151 K6
St Vincents La MLHL NW7 46 A1
St Vincents Rd DART DA1 171 K1
St Vincent St MHST W1U 9 H2
St Wilfrid's Cl EBAR EN4 * 21 J6
St Wilfrid's Rd EBAR EN4 21 H6
St Winefride's Av MNPK E12 89 K3
St Winifred's Cl CHIG IG7 54 C1
St Winifred's Rd TEDD TW11 174 C2
Sakura Dr FBAR/BDGN N11 48 D4
Saladin Dr PUR RM19 131 K4
Salamanca Pl STHWK SE1 17 G7
Salamanca St STHWK SE1 17 G7
Salamander Cl KUTN/CMB KT2 174 D1
Salamander Quay
KUT/HW KT1 * 174 E4
Salamons Wy RAIN RM13 111 G5
Salcombe Dr CHDH RM6 74 B3
MRDN SM4 193 G5
Salcombe Gdns MLHL NW7 46 A2
Salcombe Rd ASHF TW15 152 B6
STNW/STAM N16 86 B3
WALTH E17 69 H4
Salcombe Wy RSLP HA4 58 E6
Salcott Rd BTSEA SW11 140 E6
CROY/NA CR0 210 E1
Salehurst Cl
KTN/HRWW/WS HA3 62 A2
Salehurst Rd BROCKY SE4 164 C1
Salem Pl CROY/NA CR0 211 J1
Sale Pl BAY/PAD W2 8 C2
Sale St BETH E2 104 C3
Salford Rd BRXS/STRHM SW2 161 J3
Salhouse Cl THMD SE28 109 J5
Salisbury Av BARK IG11 90 E5
FNCH N3 46 D5
SUT SM1 208 D4
Salisbury Cl WALW SE17 18 E7
WPK KT4 207 H1
Salisbury Ct EMB EC4Y 11 K4
Salisbury Gdns
WIM/MER SW19 * 177 H3
Salisbury Pavement
FUL/PGN SW6 * 139 K1
Salisbury Pl BRXN/ST SW9 142 C1
MBLAR W1H 8 E1
MHST W1U 9 F1
Salisbury Prom
CEND/HSY/T N8 * 67 H2
Salisbury Rd BAR EN5 20 C4
BXLY DA5 169 H3
CAR SM5 209 K4
CHING E4 37 J5
DAGE RM10 92 D4
FELT TW13 154 B3
FSBYPK N4 67 H2
FSTGT E7 88 E4
GDMY/SEVK IG3 72 E6
GPK RM2 75 K2
HAYES BR2 200 D2
HRW HA1 60 D2
HSLWW TW4 134 B4
LEY E10 70 A6
MNPK E12 89 J3
NWDGN UB2 * 114 D4
NWMAL KT3 176 A6
PIN HA5 58 E1
RCH/KEW TW9 137 F5
SNWD SE25 197 H3
WALTH E17 70 A2
WDGN N22 49 H5
WEA W13 116 C2
WIM/MER SW19 177 H3
WPK KT4 207 F2
Salisbury Sq EMB EC4Y * 11 K4
Salisbury St ACT W3 117 K2
STJWD NW8 2 C7
Salisbury Ter PECK SE15 143 K4
Salisbury Wk ARCH N19 66 C6
Salix Cl SUN TW16 172 A3
Sally Murray Cl MNPK E12 90 A2
Salmen Rd PLSTW E13 106 E1
Salmond Cl STAN HA7 43 G2
Salmon La POP/IOD E14 105 G5
Salmon Ms KIL/WHAMP NW6 * 82 E3
Salmon Rd BELV DA17 129 H5
DART DA1 151 J4
Salmons Rd CHSGTN KT9 206 A4
ED N9 36 C3
Salmon St CDALE/KGS NW9 62 E4
POP/IOD E14 * 105 H5
Salomons Rd PLSTW E13 107 G4
Salop Rd WALTH E17 69 F3
Saltash Cl SUT SM1 208 D2
Saltash Rd BARK/HLT IG6 54 D3
WELL DA16 148 D2
Saltcoats Rd CHSWK W4 118 B2
Saltcote Cl DART DA1 170 B1
Saltcroft Cl WBLY HA9 62 D5
Salter Cl RYLN/HDSTN HA2 77 K1
Salterford Rd TOOT SW17 179 F2
Salter Rd BERM/RHTH SE16 124 B2
Salters' Hall Ct MANHO EC4N * 12 E5
Salter's Hl NRWD SE19 180 E1
Salters Rd NKENS W10 100 B3
WALTH E17 70 B1
Salters Rw IS N1 * 85 K4
Salter St POP/IOD E14 105 J6
WLSDN NW10 99 J2
Salterton Rd HOLWY N7 84 E1
Saltford Cl ERITH DA8 130 B5
Saltley Cl EHAM E6 107 J5
Saltoun Rd BRXS/STRHM SW2 142 B5
Saltram Cl SEVS/STOTM N15 68 B1
Saltram Crs MV/WKIL W9 100 D2
Saltwell St POP/IOD E14 105 J6
Saltwood Cl ORP BR6 217 J2
Saltwood Gv WALW SE17 * 122 E5
Salusbury Rd KIL/WHAMP NW6 82 C6
Salvador TOOT SW17 178 D1
Salvia Gdns GFD/PVL UB6 97 G1
Salvin Rd PUT/ROE SW15 139 G4
Salway Cl WFD IG8 52 E3
Salway Rd SRTFD E15 88 B4
Samantha Cl WALTH E17 69 H4
Sam Bartram Cl CHARL SE7 126 B5
Samels Ct HMSMTH W6 118 D5
Samford St STJWD NW8 2 C7
Samira Cl WALTH E17 69 H3
Samos Rd PGE/AN SE20 181 J5
Sampson Av BAR EN5 20 B6
Sampson Cl BELV DA17 128 E3
Sampson St WAP E1W * 123 H1
Samson St PLSTW E13 107 G1
Samuel Cl HACK E8 86 B6
NWCR SE14 124 A6
WOOL/PLUM SE18 126 D4
Samuel Gray Gdns
KUTN/CMB KT2 174 E4
Samuel Lewis Trust Dwellings
CHEL SW3 * 120 D5
CMBW SE5 * 142 D2
HACK E8 * 86 C2
WKENS W14 * 119 H4
Samuel St WOOL/PLUM SE18 126 E4
Sancroft Cl CRICK NW2 81 K1
Sancroft Rd
KTN/HRWW/WS HA3 43 F5
Sancroft St LBTH SE11 122 B5
Sanctuary Cl DART DA1 171 G1
Sanctuary Ms HACK E8 86 B4
Sanctuary Rd HTHAIR TW6 152 D1
Sanctuary St STHWK SE1 18 D3
The Sanctuary BXLY DA5 168 E1
WEST SW1P 16 D4
Sandall Cl EA W5 98 A3
Sandall Rd EA W5 98 A3
KTTN NW5 84 C4
Sandal Rd NWMAL KT3 192 B1
UED N18 50 C1
Sandal St SRTFD E15 88 C6
Sandalwood Cl WCHPL E1 105 G3
Sandalwood Dr RSLP HA4 58 A4
Sandalwood Rd FELT TW13 154 A5
Sandbach Pl
WOOL/PLUM SE18 127 H5
Sandbourne Av
WIM/MER SW19 178 A6
Sandbourne Rd NWCR SE14 144 B3
Sandbrook Cl MLHL NW7 45 F2
Sandbrook Rd STNW/STAM N16 86 A1
Sandby Gn ELTH/MOT SE9 146 D4
Sandcliff Rd ERITH DA8 130 A4
Sandcroft Cl PLMGR N13 49 H2
Sandell's Av ASHF TW15 153 F6
Sandell St STHWK SE1 17 J2
Sanders Cl HPTN TW12 173 H1
Sanders La MLHL NW7 46 B3
Sanderson Cl KTTN NW5 * 84 B2
Sanders Pde
STRHM/NOR SW16 * 179 K2
Sanderstead Av GLDGN NW11 64 C6
Sanderstead Cl BAL SW12 161 H2
Sanderstead Rd LEY E10 69 G5
SAND/SEL CR2 211 K5
STMC/STPC BR5 202 C3
Sandfield Gdns THHTH CR7 180 C6
Sandfield Pl THHTH CR7 180 D6
Sandfield Rd THHTH CR7 180 C6
Sandford Av WDGN N22 49 H4
Sandford Rd BXLYHS DA6 149 F5
EHAM E6 107 K2
HAYES BR2 199 K1
Sandford Rw WALW SE17 122 E5
Sandford St FUL/PGN SW6 140 A1
Sandgate Cl ROMW/RG RM7 74 E4
Sandgate La
WAND/EARL SW18 160 D3
Sandgate Rd WELL DA16 148 D1
Sandgate St PECK SE15 123 J6
Sandhills WLGTN SM6 210 D2
The Sandhills WBPTN SW10 * 120 B6
Sandhurst Av BRYLDS KT5 191 J4
RYLN/HDSTN HA2 60 B5
Sandhurst Cl CDALE/KGS NW9 44 C6
SAND/SEL CR2 212 A6
Sandhurst Dr GDMY/SEVK IG3 91 G2
Sandhurst Pde CAT SE6 * 165 F3
Sandhurst Rd BFN/LL DA15 168 A5
BXLY DA5 148 E6
CAT SE6 165 G3
CDALE/KGS NW9 44 C6
ED N9 36 E1
ORP BR6 217 K1
Sandhurst Wy SAND/SEL CR2 212 A5
Sandifer Dr CRICK NW2 82 B1
Sandiford Rd CHEAM SM3 193 J6
Sandiland Crs HAYES BR2 199 J6
Sandilands CROY/NA CR0 212 C1
Sandilands Rd FUL/PGN SW6 140 A2
Sandison St PECK SE15 143 G4
Sandland St GINN WC1R 11 H2
Sandling Ri ELTH/MOT SE9 167 F5
Sandlings Cl PECK SE15 143 J3
The Sandlings WDGN N22 49 H6
Sandmartin Wy WLGTN SM6 195 F5
Sandmere Rd CLAP SW4 141 K5
Sandon Cl ESH/CLAY KT10 189 J5
Sandow Crs HYS/HAR UB3 113 J3
Sandown Av DAGE RM10 92 E4
ESH/CLAY KT10 204 C3
Sandown Cl HEST TW5 133 K2
Sandown Ct BELMT SM2 * 209 F5
DAGE RM10 92 E4
SYD SE26 * 163 J5
Sandown Dr CAR SM5 210 A6
Sandown Ga ESH/CLAY KT10 189 J6
Sandown Rd ESH/CLAY KT10 204 C2
SNWD SE25 197 J2
Sandown Wy NTHLT UB5 77 J4
Sandpiper Cl
BERM/RHTH SE16 124 C2
WALTH E17 51 F3
Sandpiper Dr ERITH DA8 150 E1
Sandpiper Rd SUT SM1 208 D3
Sandpiper Ter CLAY IG5 * 54 B6
Sandpiper Wy STMC/STPC BR5 202 E1
Sandpit Pl CHARL SE7 126 D5
Sandpit Rd BMLY BR1 183 H1
DART DA1 151 F5
Sandpits Rd CROY/NA CR0 213 F2
RCHPK/HAM TW10 156 E4
Sandra Cl HSLW TW3 135 G6
WDGN N22 49 J4
Sandridge Cl HRW HA1 60 E1
Sandridge St ARCH N19 66 C6
Sandringham Av RYNPK SW20 177 H4
Sandringham Cl EN EN1 24 A3
WIM/MER SW19 159 G3
Sandringham Crs
RYLN/HDSTN HA2 78 A1
Sandringham Dr ASHF TW15 152 A6
RDART DA2 170 B4
WELL DA16 147 K3
Sandringham Gdns
BARK/HLT IG6 54 C6
CEND/HSY/T N8 66 E3
E/WMO/HCT KT8 189 F1
HEST TW5 133 K2
NFNCH/WDSPK N12 47 H2
Sandringham Ms EA W5 97 K6
HPTN TW12 172 E4
Sandringham Rd BARK IG11 91 F4
BMLY BR1 183 K1
CRICK NW2 81 K3
CROY/NA CR0 196 D2
FSTGT E7 89 G3
GLDGN NW11 64 C4
HACK E8 86 B3
HTHAIR TW6 132 B6
LEY E10 70 B4
NTHLT UB5 78 A5
WDGN N22 49 J6
WPK KT4 207 J1
Sandrock Pl CROY/NA CR0 213 F2
Sandrock Rd LEW SE13 144 D4
Sands End La FUL/PGN SW6 140 A2
Sandstone La CAN/RD E16 107 G6
Sandstone Pl ARCH N19 66 B6
Sandstone Rd LEE/GVPK SE12 166 A4
Sands Wy WFD IG8 53 K2
Sandtoft Rd CHARL SE7 126 A6
Sandway Rd STMC/STPC BR5 202 D1
Sandwell Crs KIL/WHAMP NW6 82 E4
Sandwich St STPAN WC1H 4 E5
Sandwick Cl MLHL NW7 45 J3
Sandy Bury ORP BR6 216 D1
Sandycombe Rd
EBED/NFELT TW14 153 K3
RCH/KEW TW9 137 H3
Sandycoombe Rd TWK TW1 156 D1
Sandycroft ABYW SE2 128 B6
Sandy Dr EBED/NFELT TW14 153 H3
Sandy Hill Av
WOOL/PLUM SE18 127 G5
Sandy Hill La
WOOL/PLUM SE18 127 G4
Sandyhill Rd IL IG1 90 B2
Sandy Hill Rd WLGTN SM6 210 C6
WOOL/PLUM SE18 127 G5
Sandy La BELMT SM2 208 C6
KTN/HRWW/WS HA3 62 B3
MTCM CR4 179 F4
NTHWD HA6 26 D4
ORP BR6 202 B4
RCHPK/HAM TW10 156 D4
SCUP DA14 186 E3
TEDD TW11 174 C4
WOT/HER KT12 188 A3
Sandy La North WLGTN SM6 210 D3
Sandy La South WLGTN SM6 210 C6
Sandy Ldg PIN HA5 * 42 A2
Sandy Lodge Ct NTHWD HA6 * 40 C1
Sandy Lodge La NTHWD HA6 26 C4
Sandy Lodge Wy NTHWD HA6 40 C2
Sandy Md HOR/WEW KT19 206 C6
Sandymount Av STAN HA7 43 J1
Sandy Rdg CHST BR7 185 F2
Sandy Rd HAMP NW3 65 F6
Sandy's Rw WCHPL E1 13 H2
Sandy Wy CROY/NA CR0 213 H1
Sanford La STNW/STAM N16 68 B6
Sanford St NWCR SE14 124 B6
Sanford Ter STNW/STAM N16 86 B1
Sanger Av CHSGTN KT9 206 B3
Sangley Rd CAT SE6 164 E2
SNWD SE25 197 F1
Sangora Rd BTSEA SW11 140 C5
Sankara Ct WAND/EARL SW18 160 A4
Sansom Rd WAN E11 * 70 D6
Sansom St CMBW SE5 142 E1
Sans Wk CLKNW EC1R 6 A6
Santley St CLAP SW4 141 K5
Santos Rd WAND/EARL SW18 139 K6
Saperton Wk LBTH SE11 17 H6
Saphora Cl ORP BR6 216 D3
Sapphire Cl BCTR RM8 73 J5
Sapphire Rd DEPT SE8 124 B4
WLSDN NW10 80 E5
Saracen Cl CROY/NA CR0 196 E3
Saracen's Head Yd
FENCHST EC3M 13 H4
Saracen St POP/IOD E14 105 J5
Sarah St IS N1 7 H4
Saratoga Rd CLPT E5 86 E2
Sardinia St HOL/ALD WC2B 11 G4
Sarita Cl KTN/HRWW/WS HA3 42 D5
Sark Cl HEST TW5 135 F1
Sarnesfield Rd ENC/FH EN2 * 23 K5
Sarre Rd CRICK NW2 82 D3
STMC/STPC BR5 202 D2
Sarsen Av HSLW TW3 134 E3
Sarsfeld Rd BAL SW12 160 E3
Sarsfield Rd GFD/PVL UB6 97 H1
Sartor Rd PECK SE15 144 A5
Sarum Ter BOW E3 * 105 H3
Satanita Cl CAN/RD E16 107 H5
Satchell Md CDALE/KGS NW9 45 H4
Satchwell Rd BETH E2 104 C2
Sattar Ms STNW/STAM N16 * 85 K1
Sauls Gn WAN E11 88 C1
Saunders Cl IL IG1 72 D5
POP/IOD E14 * 105 H6
Saunders Ness Rd
POP/IOD E14 125 G4
Saunders Rd
WOOL/PLUM SE18 128 A5
Saunders St LBTH SE11 17 J6
Saunders Wy DART DA1 171 J4
THMD SE28 109 H6
Saunderton Rd ALP/SUD HA0 79 H3
Saunton Av HYS/HAR UB3 133 J1
Saunton Rd HCH RM12 75 J6
Savage Gdns EHAM E6 107 K5
TWRH EC3N 13 H5
Savanah Cl PECK SE15 143 G1
Savernake Ct STAN HA7 43 J2
Savernake Rd ED N9 36 C1
HAMP NW3 83 K2
Savery Dr SURB KT6 190 D4
Savile Cl NWMAL KT3 192 B2
THDIT KT7 190 A5
Savile Gdns CROY/NA CR0 197 G6
Savile Rw CONDST W1S 10 A5
Saville Rd CAN/RD E16 126 D1
CHDH RM6 74 B3
CHSWK W4 118 A3
TWK TW1 156 A3
Saville Rw HAYES BR2 199 J5
PEND EN3 25 F3
Savill Gdns RYNPK SW20 176 D6
Savill Rw WFD IG8 52 D2
Savona Cl WIM/MER SW19 177 G3
Savona St VX/NE SW8 141 H1
Savoy Av HYS/HAR UB3 113 H5
Savoy Cl EDGW HA8 44 C1
SRTFD E15 88 C6
Savoy Ct TPL/STR WC2R * 11 F6
Savoy Hl TPL/STR WC2R 11 G6
Savoy Ms BRXN/ST SW9 141 K4
Savoy Pde EN EN1 * 24 A4
Savoy Pl CHCR WC2N 11 F6
Savoy Rd DART DA1 151 F6
Savoy Rw TPL/STR WC2R 11 G5
Savoy Steps TPL/STR WC2R * 11 G6
Savoy St TPL/STR WC2R 11 G5
Savoy Wy TPL/STR WC2R 11 G6
Sawbill Cl YEAD UB4 95 H4
Sawkins Cl WIM/MER SW19 159 G4
Sawley Rd SHB W12 118 D1
Sawtry Cl CAR SM5 194 D4
Sawyer Cl ED N9 36 C4
Sawyers Cl DAGE RM10 92 E4
Sawyer's Hl RCHPK/HAM TW10 157 G2
Sawyers Lawn WEA W13 97 G5
Sawyer St STHWK SE1 18 C2
Saxby Rd BRXS/STRHM SW2 161 K2
Saxham Rd BARK IG11 90 E6
Saxlingham Rd CHING E4 38 B5
Saxon Av FELT TW13 154 E4
Saxonbury Av SUN TW16 172 A6
Saxonbury Cl MTCM CR4 178 C6
Saxonbury Gdns SURB KT6 190 D5
Saxon Cl SURB KT6 190 E3
WALTH E17 69 J4
Saxon Dr ACT W3 98 D5
Saxonfield Cl
BRXS/STRHM SW2 162 A2
Saxon Rd BMLY BR1 183 J3
BOW E3 105 H1
EHAM E6 107 K3
IL IG1 90 B4
KUTN/CMB KT2 175 F4
RDART DA2 171 H6
SNWD SE25 196 E2
STHL UB1 114 D1
WBLY HA9 80 E1
WDGN N22 49 H4
Saxon Wy STHGT/OAK N14 34 D1
Saxony Pde HYS/HAR UB3 94 A4
Saxton Cl LEW SE13 145 G4
Saxville Rd STMC/STPC BR5 186 C6
Sayesbury La UED N18 50 C1
Sayes Court Rd
STMC/STPC BR5 186 B6
Sayes Court St DEPT SE8 124 C5
Scadbury Gdns
STMC/STPC BR5 186 B5
Scads Hill Cl ORP BR6 202 A3
Scala St FITZ W1T 10 B1
Scales Rd TOTM N17 50 B6
Scammell Wy WATW WD18 26 D1
Scampston Ms NKENS W10 100 B5
Scampton Rd
STWL/WRAY TW19 152 C1
Scandrett St WAP E1W * 123 J1
Scarba Wk IS N1 85 K4
Scarborough Rd ED N9 36 E2
FSBYPK N4 67 G5
HTHAIR TW6 153 F1
WAN E11 70 B5
Scarborough St WCHPL E1 13 K4
Scarbrook Rd CROY/NA CR0 211 J1
Scarle Rd ALP/SUD HA0 79 K4
Scarlet Cl STMC/STPC BR5 202 C1
Scarlet Rd CAT SE6 165 H5
Scarsbrook Rd BKHTH/KID SE3 146 C4
Scarsdale Pl KENS W8 120 A3
Scarsdale Rd RYLN/HDSTN HA2 78 C1
Scarsdale Vls KENS W8 119 K3
Scarth Rd BARN SW13 138 D4
Scawen Cl CAR SM5 210 A2
Scawen Rd DEPT SE8 124 B5
Scawfell St BETH E2 7 K3
Scaynes Link
NFNCH/WDSPK N12 32 E6
Sceptre Rd BETH E2 104 E2
Scholars Cl BAR EN5 20 C5
Scholars Rd BAL SW12 161 H3
CHING E4 38 A3
Scholars Wy GPK RM2 75 K2
Scholefield Rd ARCH N19 66 D6
Schonfeld Sq STNW/STAM N16 67 K6
Schoolbank Rd GNWCH SE10 125 J4
School Crs DART DA1 150 C5
School House La TEDD TW11 174 D3
Schoolhouse La WAP E1W * 105 F6
School La BUSH WD23 28 B3
KUT/HW KT1 174 D4
PIN HA5 * 59 J1
SURB KT6 191 H5
WELL DA16 148 C4
School Pas KUT/HW KT1 175 G5
STHL UB1 114 E1
School Rd CHST BR7 185 H4
DAGE RM10 92 C6
E/WMO/HCT KT8 189 J1
HPTN TW12 173 H2
HSLW TW3 135 H4
KUT/HW KT1 * 174 D4
MNPK E12 89 K2
WDR/YW UB7 112 A6
WLSDN NW10 99 F3
School Road Av HPTN TW12 173 H2
School Sq GNWCH SE10 125 J3
School Wy BCTR RM8 91 H1
Schoolway NFNCH/WDSPK N12 47 H2
Schooner Cl BARK IG11 109 H2
BERM/RHTH SE16 124 A2
POP/IOD E14 125 G3
Schubert Rd BORE WD6 29 K1
PUT/ROE SW15 139 J6
Sclater St WCHPL E1 7 J6
Scoble Pl STNW/STAM N16 86 B2
Scoles Crs BRXS/STRHM SW2 162 B3
Scope Wy KUT/HW KT1 191 F1
Scoresby St STHWK SE1 18 A1
Scorton Av GFD/PVL UB6 97 G1
Scotch Common WEA W13 97 H4
Scoter Cl WFD IG8 53 F3
Scot Gv PIN HA5 41 H3
Scotia Rd BRXS/STRHM SW2 162 B2
Scotland Gn TOTM N17 50 B5
Scotland Green Rd PEND EN3 25 F6
Scotland Green Rd North
PEND EN3 25 G5
Scotland Rd BKHH IG9 39 G3
Scotney Cl ORP BR6 216 A2
Scots Cl STWL/WRAY TW19 152 A3
Scotsdale Cl CHEAM SM3 208 C5
STMC/STPC BR5 201 K1
Scotsdale Rd LEE/GVPK SE12 146 A6
Scotswood St CLKNW EC1R * 5 K6
Scotswood Wk TOTM N17 * 50 D3
Scott Cl HOR/WEW KT19 206 E3
STRHM/NOR SW16 180 A4
WDR/YW UB7 112 C4
Scott Crs ERITH DA8 150 C2
RYLN/HDSTN HA2 60 B5
Scott Ellis Gdns STJWD NW8 2 A5
Scottes La BCTR RM8 73 K5
Scott Farm Cl THDIT KT7 190 C5
Scott Gdns HEST TW5 134 C1
Scott Lidgett Crs
BERM/RHTH SE16 123 H2
Scott Rd EDGW HA8 44 D5
Scotts Av HAYES BR2 183 G5
Scotts Dr HPTN TW12 173 G3
Scotts Farm Rd
HOR/WEW KT19 206 E4
Scott's La HAYES BR2 183 G6
Scotts Pas WOOL/PLUM SE18 * 127 G4
Scotts Rd BMLY BR1 183 K3
LEY E10 70 A5
NWDGN UB2 114 B3
SHB W12 118 E2
Scott St WCHPL E1 104 D3
Scott's Yd MANHO EC4N 12 E5
Scott Trimmer Wy HSLW TW3 134 D3
Scottwell Dr CDALE/KGS NW9 63 H2
Scoulding Rd CAN/RD E16 106 E5
Scouler St POP/IOD E14 106 B6
Scout Ap WLSDN NW10 81 G2
Scout La CLAP SW4 141 H4
Scout Wy MLHL NW7 31 F6
Scovell Crs STHWK SE1 * 18 C3
Scovell Rd STHWK SE1 18 C3
Scrattons Ter BARK IG11 109 K1
Scriven St HACK E8 86 B6
Scrooby St CAT SE6 164 E1
Scrubs La WLSDN NW10 99 J2
Scrutton Cl BAL SW12 161 J2
Scrutton St SDTCH EC2A 7 G7
Scutari Rd EDUL SE22 143 J6
Scylla Crs HTHAIR TW6 152 E2
Scylla Rd HTHAIR TW6 152 E1
PECK SE15 143 J4
Seabright St BETH E2 104 D2
Seabrook Dr WWKM BR4 199 H6

Seabrook Gdns ROMW/RG RM7 .74 C4
Seabrook Rd BCTR RM8.............91 K1
Seaburn Cl RAIN RM13.............111 G2
Seacole Cl ACT W3.....................99 F5
Seacourt Rd ABYW SE2...........128 C2
Seacroft Gdns OXHEY WD19 ...27 H5
Seafield Rd FBAR/BDGN N11 ...34 D6
Seaford Cl RSLP HA4................58 B6
Seaford Rd EN EN1....................24 A5
HTHAIR TW6.......................132 A6
SEVS/STOTM N15...................67 K2
WALTH E17.............................51 J3
WEA W13..............................116 C1
Seaford St STPAN WC1H...........5 F5
Seaforth Av NWMAL KT3..........192 D2
Seaforth Cl ROM RM1................57 G3
Seaforth Crs HBRY N5...............85 J3
Seaforth Gdns
HOR/WEW KT19...................207 H3
WCHMH N21...........................35 G3
WFD IG8..................................53 G1
Seaforth Pl WESTW SW1E.........16 B4
Seager Buildings DEPT SE8 * .144 D2
Seager Pl BOW E3...................105 H4
Seagrave Cl WCHPL E1 *..........105 F4
Seagrave Rd FUL/PGN SW6.....119 K6
Seagull La CAN/RD E16...........106 E6
Sealand Rd HTHAIR TW6.........152 D1
Seal St HACK E8........................86 B2
Searles Cl BTSEA SW11...........140 D1
Searles Dr EHAM E6.................108 B4
Searles Rd STHWK SE1..............19 F6
Seasprite Cl NTHLT UB5...........95 J2
Seaton Av GDN/SEVK IG3..........90 E3
Seaton Cl LBTH SE11................122 C5
PLSTW E13...........................106 E3
PUT/ROE SW15.....................158 E3
WHTN TW2............................155 J1
Seaton Dr ASHF TW15.............152 D4
Seaton Gdns RSLP HA4.............76 E1
Seaton Rd ALP/SUD HA0 *.......98 A1
DART DA1.............................170 D2
HYS/HAR UB3.......................113 G4
MTCM CR4...........................178 D5
WELL DA16............................128 C6
WHTN TW2............................155 H1
Seaton St UED N18....................50 C1
Sebastian St FSBYE EC1V...........6 A5
Sebastopol Rd ED N9.................36 C6
Sebbon St IS N1........................85 H5
Sebergham Gr MLHL NW7..........31 H1
Sebert Rd FSTGT E7...................89 G2
Sebright Rd BAR EN5.................20 B3
Secker Crs KTN/HRWW/WS HA3.42 C4
Secker St STHWK SE1................17 J1
Second Av ACT W3...................118 C1
CHDH RM6.............................62 A5
DAGE RM10..........................110 D1
EN EN1...................................24 B6
HDN NW4................................64 B1
HYS/HAR UB3.......................113 J1
MNPK E12...............................89 J2
MORT/ESHN SW14.................138 B4
NKENS W10...........................100 C3
PLSTW E13...........................106 E2
UED N18.................................36 E4
WALTH E17.............................69 J2
WBLY HA9...............................61 K5
WOT/HER KT12.....................188 A5
Second Cl E/WMO/HCT KT8...189 H1
Second Cross Rd WHTN TW2...155 K4
Second Wy WBLY HA9...............80 D2
Sedan Wy WALW SE17.............123 F5
Sedcombe Cl SCUP DA14.........168 C6
Sedcote Rd PEND EN3................24 E6
Sedding St KTBR SW1X..............15 G6
Seddon Rd MRDN SM4..............194 C2
Seddon St FSBYW WC1X............5 H5
Sedgebrook Rd
BKHTH/KID SE3....................146 C3
Sedgecombe Av
KTN/HRWW/WS HA3.............61 J2
Sedgefield Rd SHB W12...........118 C1
Sedgehill Rd CAT SE6...............182 D1
Sedgemere Av EFNCH N2...........47 G6
Sedgemere Rd ABYW SE2........128 D5
Sedgemoor Dr DAGE RM10......92 C2
Sedge Rd TOTM N17..................50 E3
Sedgeway CAT SE6...................165 J3
Sedgmoor Pl CMBW SE5..........143 F1
Sedgwick Rd LEY E10.................70 A6
Sedgwick St HOM E9.................87 F3
Sedleigh Rd
WAND/EARL SW18................159 J1
Sedlescombe Rd
FUL/PGN SW6......................119 J6
Sedley Cl EN EN1.......................24 D1
Sedley Pl OXSTW W1C................9 J4
Sednem Ct PECK SE15..............143 H3
Sedum Cl CDALE/KGS NW9........62 D2
Seeley Dr DUL SE21.................163 F6
Seelig Av CDALE/KGS NW9........63 J4
Seely Rd TOOT SW17................179 F2
Seething La TWRH EC3N............13 H5
Seething Wells La SURB KT6...190 D3
Sefton Av KTN/HRWW/WS HA3.45 F1
Sefton Cl STNW/STAM BR5.....202 A1
Sefton Ct ENC/FH EN2 *............23 H2
Sefton Rd CROY/NA CR0..........197 H5
STMC/STPC BR5...................202 A1
Sefton St PUT/ROE SW15.........139 F3
Sekforde St CLKNW EC1R...........6 A7
Sekhon Ter FELT TW13.............155 F5
Selah Dr SWLY BR8..................187 K6
Selan Gdns YEAD UB4................95 F4
Selbie Av WLSDN NW10.............81 H3
Selborne Gdns GFD/PVL UB6....97 J1
HDN NW4................................63 H2
Selborne Rd CMBW SE5...........142 E3
CROY/NA CR0.......................212 A1
IL IG1.....................................72 A6

NWMAL KT3...........................176 B5
SCUP DA14............................168 C6
STHGT/OAK N14......................34 C5
WALTH E17.............................69 H2
WDGN N22..............................49 F4
Selbourne Av SURB KT6...........191 G6
Selby Cha RSLP HA4..................59 F6
Selby Cl CHSGTN KT9..............206 A5
CHST BR7..............................185 F2
Selby Gdns STHL UB1................96 A3
Selby Gn CAR SM5...................194 D4
Selby Rd CAR SM5...................194 D4
EA W5......................................97 H3
PGE/AN SE20.........................181 H5
PLSTW E13............................107 F4
TOTM N17...............................50 A2
WAN E11.................................88 C1
Selby St WCHPL E1..................104 C3
Selden Rd PECK SE15...............143 K3
Selhurst Cl WIM/MER SW19....159 G3
Selhurst New Rd SNWD SE25...197 F3
Selhurst Pl SNWD SE25.............197 F3
Selhurst Rd ED N9......................36 A5
SNWD SE25...........................197 F2
Selinas La BCTR RM8.................74 A4
Selkirk Dr ERITH DA8...............150 B2
Selkirk Rd TOOT SW17.............160 D6
WHTN TW2............................155 H4
Sellers Hall Cl FNCH N3.............46 E3
Sellincourt Rd TOOT SW17......178 D1
Sellindge Cl BECK BR3.............182 C3
Sellons Av WLSDN NW10...........81 H6
Sellwood Dr BAR EN5................20 B6
Selsdon Av SAND/SEL CR2......211 K4
SURB KT6.............................191 F2
Selsdon Rd WDGN N22.............213 G6
Selsdon Rd CRICK NW2..............63 H6
PLSTW E13...........................107 G1
SAND/SEL CR2.....................211 K3
SAND/SEL CR2.....................212 A5
WAN E11.................................70 D6
WNWD SE27.........................162 C5
Selsdon Wy POP/IOD E14........124 E3
Selsea Pl STNW/STAM N16........86 A3
Selsey Crs WELL DA16.............148 E2
Selsey St BOW E3.....................105 J4
Selvage La MLHL NW7................45 F1
Selway Cl PIN HA5.....................58 E1
Selwood Pl SKENS SW7...........120 C5
Selwood Rd CHEAM SM3..........193 J5
CHSGTN KT9........................205 J3
CROY/NA CR0.......................197 J6
Selwood Ter SKENS SW7.........120 C5
Selworthy Cl WAN E11...............70 E2
Selworthy Rd CAT SE6.............164 C5
Selwyn Av CHING E4..................52 A2
GDMY/SEVK IG3.....................73 F3
RCH/KEW TW9......................137 G4
Selwyn Cl HSLWW TW4............134 D5
Selwyn Ct EDGW HA8................44 D3
Selwyn Crs WELL DA16............148 C5
Selwyn Rd BOW E3...................105 H1
NWMAL KT3..........................192 A2
PLSTW E13.............................89 F6
WLSDN NW10.........................81 F5
Semley Pl BCVA SW1W..............15 H7
STRHM/NOR SW16................180 A5
Semley Rd STRHM/NOR SW16.179 K5
Senate St PECK SE15................143 K3
Seneca Rd THHTH CR7..............196 D1
Senga Rd WLGTN SM6.............195 H5
Senhouse Rd CHEAM SM3.......208 B1
Senior St BAY/PAD W2.............101 F4
Senlac Rd LEE/GVPK SE12.......166 A3
Sennen Rd EN EN1.....................36 B2
Senrab St WCHPL E1................105 F5
Sentamu Cl HNHL SE24............162 C3
Sentinel Cl NTHLT UB5...............95 J3
September Wy STAN HA7...........43 H2
Sequoia Cl BUSH WD23.............28 D3
Sequoia Gdns ORP BR6............202 A4
Sequoia Pk PIN HA5...................42 B2
Serbin Cl LEY E10......................70 A4
Serenaders Rd BRXN/ST SW9...142 B3
Serjeant's Inn EMB EC4Y *........11 H3
Sermon La STP EC4M *.............11 H3
Sermon Dr SWLY BR8...............187 K6
Sermon La BLKFR EC4V.............12 C4
Serpentine Rd BAY/PAD W2......8 E7
Service Route No 1 SRTFD E15..88 B5
Service Route No 2 SRTFD E15..88 B5
Service Route No 3 SRTFD E15..88 B4
Serviden Dr BMLY BR1.............184 C4
Setchell Est STHWK SE1 *..........19 J6
Setchell Rd STHWK SE1..............19 J6
Setchell Wy STHWK SE1.............19 J6
Seth St BERM/RHTH SE16........123 K2
Seton Gdns DAGW RM9..............91 J5
Settles St WCHPL E1................104 C5
Settrington Rd FUL/PGN SW6..140 A3
Shafto Ms KTBR SW1X...............14 E5
Seven Acres CAR SM5..............194 D6
NTHWD HA6...........................40 E2
Seven Dials LSQ/SEVD WC2H...10 E4
Sevenex Pde WBLY HA9 *...........80 A3
Seven Kings Rd
GDMY/SEVK IG3.....................72 E5
Seven Kings Wy
KUTN/CMB KT2.....................174 E4
Sevenoaks Cl BXLYHN DA7......149 K5
Sevenoaks Rd BROCKY SE4.....164 C1
Sevenoaks Wy
STMC/STPC BR5...................186 D5
Seven Sisters Rd FSBYPK N4......67 H6
Seven Stars Yd WCHPL E1 *.......13 K1
Seventh Av HYS/HAR UB3.......113 K1
MNPK E12...............................89 K2
Severnake Cl POP/IOD E14......124 D4
Severn Av GPK RM2...................57 K6
NKENS W10...........................100 C2
Severn Dr EN EN1......................24 C1
ESH/CLAY KT10.....................190 B6
WOT/HER KT12.....................188 C6
Severn Wy WLSDN NW10...........81 H3

Severus Rd BTSEA SW11..........140 D5
Seville Ms IS N1..........................86 A5
Seville St KTBR SW1X.................15 F3
Sevington Rd HDN NW4..............63 K3
Sevington St MV/WKIL W9........101 F3
Seward Rd BECK BR3................182 A5
HNWL W7..............................116 B2
Sewardstone Rd BETH E2........104 E1
CHING E4..................................25 K5
Seward St FSBYE EC1V...............6 C6
Sewdley St CLPT E5....................87 F1
Sewell Rd ABYW SE2................128 B3
Sewell St PLSTW E13................106 E2
Sextant Av POP/IOD E14...........125 G4
Sexton Cl RAIN RM13.................93 H6
Seymour Av EW KT17...............207 K6
MRDN SM4............................193 G4
TOTM N17...............................50 E5
Seymour Cl E/WMO/HCT KT8...189 H2
LOU IG10................................39 J1
PIN HA5...................................41 K4
Seymour Dr HAYES BR2............200 E5
Seymour Gdns BROCKY SE4....144 A4
BRYLDS KT5...........................191 G2
FELT TW13............................154 A6
IL IG1.......................................71 K5
RSLP HA4................................59 K6
TWK TW1...............................156 C2
Seymour Ms MBLAR W1H............9 G3
Seymour Pl MBLAR W1H..............8 E2
SNWD SE25...........................197 J1
Seymour Rd CAR SM5..............210 A3
CEND/HSY/T N8......................67 H2
CHING E4..................................37 K5
CHSWK W4...........................117 K4
E/WMO/HCT KT8...................189 H2
ED N9.......................................36 D4
EHAM E6..................................89 H1
FNCH N3..................................47 F3
HPTN TW12...........................173 H1
KUT/HW KT1..........................174 E4
LEY E10....................................69 H5
MTCM CR4............................195 F4
WIM/MER SW19....................159 G5
Seymour St BAY/PAD W2.............8 E4
MBLAR W1H.............................8 E4
WOOL/PLUM SE18................127 H4
Seymour Ter PGE/AN SE20......181 J4
Seymour Vls PGE/AN SE20......181 J4
Seymour Wk WBPTN SW10.....120 B6
Seyssel St POP/IOD E14............125 F4
Shaa Rd ACT W3........................99 F6
Shacklegate La TEDD TW11......155 K6
Shackleton Cl FSTH SE23.........163 J4
Shackleton Rd STHL UB1............95 K6
Shacklewell La HACK E8.............86 B3
Shacklewell Rd HACK E8.............86 B2
Shacklewell St BETH E2...............7 K6
Shadbolt Av CHING E4................51 G1
Shadbolt Cl WPK KT4................192 C6
Shad Thames STHWK SE1............19 K1
Shadwell Dr NTHLT UB5..............95 K2
Shadwell Gdns WCHPL E1 *.....104 E6
Shadwell Pierhead WAP E1W...104 E6
Shady Bush Cl BUSH WD23.........28 C2
Shaef Wy TEDD TW11...............174 B3
Shafter Rd DAGE RM10..............93 F4
Shaftesbury Av BAR EN5............21 G5
EBED/NFELT TW14.................153 K1
KTN/HRWW/WS HA3...............61 K3
NWDGN UB2...........................115 F4
PEND EN3................................25 F2
RYLN/HDSTN HA2..................60 D1
SOHO/SHAV W1D..................10 C5
Shaftesbury Cir
YLN/HDSTN HA2....................60 C5
Shaftesbury Gdns
WLSDN NW10.........................99 G3
Shaftesbury Ms CLAP SW4......141 H6
KENS W8...............................119 K3
Shaftesbury Pde
RYLN/HDSTN HA2 *.................60 D2
Shaftesbury Pl BARB EC2Y *......12 C2
Shaftesbury Rd ARCH N19..........66 E5
BECK BR3.............................182 C5
CAR SM5...............................194 C4
CHING E4..................................38 C3
FSTGT E7.................................89 G5
LEY E10....................................88 A5
RCH/KEW TW9......................137 F4
ROM RM1................................75 J3
UED N18..................................49 K2
WALTH E17.............................69 K2
The Shaftesburys BARK IG11...108 C1
Shaftesbury St IS N1...................6 E4
Shaftesbury Ter
HMSMTH W6 *......................119 F5
Shaftesbury Wy WHTN TW2.....155 J5
Shaftesbury Waye YEAD UB4.....95 G4
Shafteswood Rd TOOT SW17...160 E6
Shafton Ms HOM E9 *.................87 F6
Shafton Rd HOM E9....................87 F6
Shakespeare Av
EBED/NFELT TW14.................153 K1
FBAR/BDGN N11.....................47 K2
WLSDN NW10.........................80 E6
YEAD UB4................................95 F5
Shakespeare Crs MNPK E12.......89 K3
WLSDN NW10.........................80 E6
Shakespeare Dr
KTN/HRWW/WS HA3...............62 B3
Shakespeare Gdns EFNCH N2....47 K3
Shakespeare Rd ACT W3...........117 K1
BXLYHN DA7..........................149 F2
DART DA1..............................151 K5
FNCH N3..................................46 E4
HNHL SE24............................142 C5
HNWL W7..............................116 A1
MLHL NW7...............................31 J6
WALTH E17.............................51 G4
WLSDN NW10 *.......................81 H6
Shakespeare Sq BARK/HLT IG6..54 C2

Shakespeare Ter
RCH/KEW TW9 *....................137 H4
Shakespeare Wy FELT TW13....154 B6
Shakspeare Ms
STNW/STAM N16....................86 A2
Shakspeare Wk
STNW/STAM N16....................86 A2
Shalbourne Sq HOM E9..............87 H4
Shalcomb St WBPTN SW10.....120 B6
Shaldon Dr MRDN SM4.............193 H2
RSLP HA4................................77 G1
Shaldon Rd EDGW HA8..............44 B5
Shalfleet Dr NKENS W10...........100 B6
Shalford Cl ORP BR6................216 C2
Shalford Ct IS N1 *.....................6 A2
Shalimar Gdns ACT W3..............98 E6
Shalimar Rd ACT W3 *................98 E6
Shallons Rd ELTH/MOT SE9.....167 G6
Shalstone Rd
MORT/ESHN SW14................137 J4
Shalston Vls SURB KT6.............191 G3
Shamrock Rd CROY/NA CR0.....196 A3
Shamrock St CLAP SW4............141 J4
Shamrock Wy STHGT/OAK N14..34 B3
Shandon Rd CLAP SW4.............161 H1
Shand St STHWK SE1.................19 H2
Shandy St WCHPL E1................105 F4
Shanklin Gdns OXHEY WD19.....27 G6
Shanklin Rd CEND/HSY/T N8......66 D2
SEVS/STOTM N15...................68 C1
Shannon Cl CRICK NW2.............82 B1
NWDGN UB2..........................114 C5
Shannon Gv BRXN/ST SW9......142 A5
Shannon Pl STJWD NW8..............2 D2
Shannon Wy BECK BR3............182 E2
Shap Crs CAR SM5...................194 E5
Shapland Wy PLMGR N13...........49 F1
Shapwick Cl FBAR/BDGN N11....47 K1
Shardcroft Av HNHL SE24........142 C6
Shardeloes Rd BROCKY SE4 *..144 C3
NWCR SE14...........................144 C3
Shard's Sq PECK SE15.............123 H6
Sharland Cl THHTH CR7............196 B3
Sharman Ct SCUP DA14...........168 B6
Sharnbrooke Cl WELL DA16.....148 D4
Sharon Cl SURB KT6.................190 D5
Sharon Gdns HOM E9.................86 E6
Sharon Rd CHSWK W4..............118 A5
PEND EN3................................25 J3
Sharples Hall St CAMTN NW1....83 K5
Sharpleshall St CAMTN NW1......83 J5
Sharpness Cl YEAD UB4............95 J4
Sharp Wy DART DA1.................151 J5
Sharratt St PECK SE15.............123 K6
Sharsted St WALW SE17............122 C5
Sharvel La YEAD UB4..................76 E6
Shavers Pl MYFR/PICC W1J......10 C6
Shaw Av BARK IG11..................110 A1
Shaw Cl BMLY BR1...................165 J5
EDUL SE22.............................143 F5
PEND EN3................................25 F2
Shaw's Cottages FSTH SE23....164 B5
Shaw Sq WALTH E17..................51 G4
The Shaw CHST BR7 *...............185 H5
Shaw Wy WLGTN SM6..............210 E6
Shaxton Crs CROY/NA CR0......214 A6
Sheaf Cottages THDIT KT7 *.....189 K5
Shearing Dr CAR SM5...............194 B4
Shears Cl DART DA1.................171 F4
Shearwater Cl BARK IG11.........109 G2
Shearwater Rd SUT SM1...........208 D3
Shearwater Wy YEAD UB4.........95 G5
Sheaves Cl SEVD WC2H...........190 ??
Sheepcote Cl HEST TW5.............133 K6
Sheaveshill Pde
CDALE/KGS NW9 *..................63 G1
Sheen Common Dr
RCHPK/HAM TW10................137 H5
Sheen Court Rd
RCHPK/HAM TW10................137 H5
Sheendale Rd RCH/KEW TW9...137 G5
Sheenewood SYD SE26............181 J1
Sheen Gate Gdns
MORT/ESHN SW14................137 K5
Sheen Gv IS N1...........................85 G6
Sheen La MORT/ESHN SW14....137 K5
Sheen Pk RCH/KEW TW9.........137 G5
Sheen Rd RCH/KEW TW9.........137 F5
STMC/STPC BR5...................202 A1
Sheen Wy WLGTN SM6............211 F3
Sheen Wd MORT/ESHN SW14..137 J6
Sheepcote Cl HEST TW5...........133 K6
Sheepcote La BTSEA SW11......140 E3
Sheepcote Rd
KTN/HRWW/WS HA3...............61 G3
Sheepcotes Rd CHDH RM6........73 K1
Sheephouse Wy NWMAL KT3..192 B4
Sheep La HACK E8......................86 D6
Sheep Walk Ms
WIM/MER SW19....................177 G2
Sheerwater Rd CAN/RD E16......107 H4
Sheffield Rd HTHAIR TW6.........153 F1
Sheffield St LINN WC2A *............11 G4
Sheffield Ter KENS W8..............119 K2
Shefton Ri NTHWD HA6.............40 E3
Sheila Cl CRAY DA5..................168 E2
Shelbourne Cl PIN HA5...............59 K1
Shelbourne Rd TOTM N17..........50 D4
Shelburne Dr HSLWW TW4.......155 F1
Shelbury Cl SCUP DA14............168 B5

Shelbury Rd EDUL SE22............163 J1
Sheldon Av CLAY IG5..................53 K5
HGT N6.....................................65 K4
Sheldon Cl LEE/GVPK SE12.....146 A6
PGE/AN SE20.........................181 J4
Sheldon Pl BETH E2..................104 C1
Sheldon Rd BXLYHN DA7.........149 G2
CRICK NW2..............................82 B2
DAGW RM9.............................91 K5
UED N18..................................50 A4
Sheldon Sq BAY/PAD W2..........101 G4
Sheldon St CROY/NA CR0........211 J1
Sheldrake Cl CAN/RD E16........126 E1
Sheldrake Pl KENS W8..............119 J2
Sheldrick Cl MTCM CR4............178 C5
Shelduck Cl SRTFD E15..............88 D3
Sheldwich Ter HAYES BR2 *......200 E3
Shelford Pl STNW/STAM N16......85 K1
Shelford Ri NRWD SE19............181 G3
Shelford Rd BAR EN5..................32 A1
Shelgate Rd BTSEA SW11.........160 D1
Shell Cl HAYES BR2..................200 E3
Shellduck Cl CDALE/KGS NW9...45 G5
Shelley Av GFD/PVL UB6............96 D2
HCH RM12...............................75 H6
MNPK E12...............................89 J4
Shelley Cl EDGW HA8................30 C6
GFD/PVL UB6..........................96 D2
NTHWD HA6...........................40 E1
ORP BR6...............................216 E1
PECK SE15............................143 J3
YEAD UB4................................94 E4
Shelley Crs HEST TW5.............134 C2
STHL UB1................................95 K5
Shelley Dr WELL DA16..............147 K2
Shelley Gdns ALP/SUD HA0.......61 J6
Shelley Rd WLSDN NW10...........81 F6
Shelley Wy WIM/MER SW19.....178 C2
Shellgrove Rd
STNW/STAM N16....................86 A3
Shellness Rd CLPT E5...............86 D4
Shell Rd LEW SE13..................144 E4
Shellwood Rd BTSEA SW11.....140 E3
Shelmerdine Cl BOW E3............105 J4
Shelson Av FELT TW13.............153 J6
Shelson Pde FELT TW13 *.........153 J6
Shelton Rd WIM/MER SW19.....177 K4
Shelton St LSQ/SEVD WC2H.....10 E4
Shenfield Rd WFD IG8.................53 F3
Shenfield St IS N1........................7 H3
Shenley Av RSLP HA4..................58 D6
Shenley Rd CMBW SE5.............143 F2
DART DA1.............................171 K1
HEST TW5.............................134 D2
Shenstone Cl DART DA1...........150 A6
Shepherd Cl FELT TW13...........154 D6
Shepherdess Pl FSBYE EC1V......6 D5
Shepherdess Wk IS N1................6 D3
Shepherd Market
MYFR/PICC W1J....................10 A7
Shepherd's Bush Gn SHB W12..119 F2
Shepherd's Bush Market
SHB W12..............................119 F2
Shepherd's Bush Pl SHB W12 *..119 G2
Shepherd's Bush Rd
HMSMTH W6.........................119 F4
Shepherds Cl CHDH RM6...........73 K2
HOM E9...................................86 E6
ORP BR6...............................217 F1
STAN HA7...............................43 G1
Shepherds Gn CHST BR7..........185 J3
Shepherd's Hi HGT N6................66 A4
Shepherds La DART DA1...........170 D3
HOM E9...................................87 F3
THMD SE28............................127 K1
Shepherd's Leas
ELTH/MOT SE9......................147 J5
Shepherds Pl MYFR/PKLN W1K..9 G5
Shepherds Wk BUSH WD23........28 D4
CRICK NW2..............................63 K6
HAMP NW3..............................83 H3
Shepherds Wy SAND/SEL CR2..213 F5
Shepiston La HYS/HAR UB3.....112 E4
Shepley Cl CAR SM5................210 A1
Sheppard Ms PEND EN3.............25 G1
Sheppard Cl EN EN1...................24 D1
KUT/HW KT1..........................191 F1
Sheppard Dr
BERM/RHTH SE16..................123 J5
Sheppard St CAN/RD E16.........106 D3
Shepperton Rd IS N1...................85 K6
STMC/STPC BR5...................186 C4
Sheppey Cl ERITH DA8.............150 E1
Sheppey Gdns DAGW RM9.........91 J6
Sheppey Rd DAGW RM9.............91 H5
Sheppey Wk IS N1 *....................85 J5
Shepton Houses BETH E2 *......104 E2
Sherard Rd ELTH/MOT SE9......146 D6
Sheraton St SOHO/CST W1F *....10 C4
Sherborne Av NWDGN UB2......115 F4
PEND EN3................................25 F3
Sherborne Cl YEAD UB4..............95 G5
Sherborne Ct CAR SM5.............194 D4
Sherborne Gdns
CDALE/KGS NW9....................44 C6
WEA W13................................97 H5
Sherborne La MANHO EC4N......12 E5
Sherborne Pl NTHWD HA6.........40 B2
Sherborne Rd CHEAM SM3.......193 K6
CHSGTN KT9........................206 A3
EBED/NFELT TW14................153 G3
STMC/STPC BR5...................202 A2
Sherborne St IS N1.....................85 K6
Sherborne Vls BAR EN5 *...........20 E5
Sherboro Rd SEVS/STOTM N15...68 B3
Sherbrooke Cl BXLYHN DA7.....149 H5
Sherbrooke Rd FUL/PGN SW6..139 J1
Sherbrooke Ter
FUL/PGN SW6 *.....................139 H1
Sherbrooke Gdns WCHMH N21..35 H2
Shere Cl CHSGTN KT9.............205 K3
Sheredan Rd CHING E4...............52 B1
Shere Rd GNTH/NBYPK IG2.......72 A3
Sherfield Cl NWMAL KT3..........191 J1
Sherfield Gdns PUT/ROE SW15.158 C2

Sheridan Cl *HARH* RM3 . . . . .57 K3
Sheridan Ct *DART* DA1 . . . . .151 K5
  HSLWW TW4 . . . . .134 D6
Sheridan Crs *CHST* BR7 . . . . .185 C5
Sheridan Gdns
  KTN/HRWW/WS HA3 . . . . .61 K3
Sheridan Rd *BMLY* BR1 . . . . .184 C5
  HPTN TW12 . . . . .173 H4
Sheridan Rd *BELV* DA17 . . . . . . .129 H4
  BXLYHN DA7 . . . .
  FSTGT E7 . . . . .88 D1
  MNPK E12 . . . . .89 J3
  OXHEY WD19 . . . . .27 H2
  RCHPK/HAM TW10 . . . . .156 D5
  WIM/MER SW19 . . . . .177 J4
Sheridan St *WCHPL* E1 . . . . .104 D5
Sheridan Ter *NTHLT* UB5 * 78 B3
Sheridan Wk *BECK* BR3 . . . . . . .209 K3
  GLDGN NW11 . . . . .64 E5
Sheringham Av *MNPK* E12 . . . . . .89 K3
  ROMW/RG RM7 . . . . .74 E4
  STHGT/OAK N14 . . . . .34 D1
  WHTN TW2 . . . . .154 E3
Sheringham Dr *BARK* IG11 . . . . . .91 F3
Sheringham Rd *HOLWY* N7 . . . . . .85 C4
  PGE/AN SE20 . . . . .181 K6
Sherington Av *PIN* HA5 . . . . .41 K3
Sherington Rd *BKHTH/KID* SE3 .126 A6
Sherland Rd *TWK* TW1 . . . . .156 A3
Sherlies Av *ORP* BR6 . . . . .201 K6
Sherlock Ms *MHST* W1U 9 G1
Sherman Gdns *CHDH* RM6 . . . .
Sherman Rd *BMLY* BR1 . . . . .183 K4
Shernhall St *WALTH* E17 . . . . .70 A2
Sherrard Rd *FSTGT* E7 . . . . .89 G4
Sherrards Wy *BAR* EN5 . . . . .20 E6
Sherrick Green Rd
  WLSDN NW10 . . . . .81 K3
Sherriff Cl *ESH/CLAY* KT10 . . . . .189 D6
Sherriff Rd *KIL/WHAMP* NW6 . . . .82 E4
Sherringham Av *FELT* TW13 . . . .153 K5
  TOTM N17 . . . . .50 C5
Sherrock Gdns *HDN* NW4 . . . . . . .63 J1
Sherry Ms *BARK* IG11 . . . . .90 D6
Sherwin Rd *NWCR* SE14 . . . . . . .144 A2
Sherwood *SURB* KT6 . . . . .190 B6
Sherwood Av *GFD/PVL* UB6 . . . . .78 E4
  RSLP HA4 . . . . .58 C3
  STRHM/NOR SW16 . . . . .179 K4
  SWFD E18 . . . . .53 F3
  YEAD UB4 . . . . .95 F5
Sherwood Cl *BXLY* DA5 . . . . . . .168 D1
  WALTH E17 . . . . .51 H5
  WEA W13 . . . . .116 C1
Sherwood Ct *MBLAR* W1H 8 E2
Sherwood Gdns *BARK* IG11 . . . . . .90 D5
  BERM/RHTH SE16 . . . . .123 H5
  POP/IOD E14 . . . . .124 D4
Sherwood House
  RYLN/HDSTN HA2 * 60 C6
Sherwood Park Av
  BFN/LL DA15 . . . . .168 B2
Sherwood Park Rd *MTCM* CR4 .195 J1
  SUT SM1 . . . . .208 E3
Sherwood Rd *BARK/HLT* IG6 . . . . .72 D1
  CROY/NA CR0 . . . . .197 J5
  HDN NW4 . . . . .46 A6
  HPTN TW12 . . . . .173 H1
  RYLN/HDSTN HA2 . . . . .60 C6
  WELL DA16 . . . . .147 K1
  WIM/MER SW19 . . . . .177 J3
Sherwoods Rd *OXHEY* WD19 . . . .27 J2
Sherwood St *REGST* W1B 10 B5
  TRDG/WHET N20 . . . . .33 H5
Sherwood Ter *TRDG/WHET* N20 .33 H5
Sherwood Wy *WWKM* BR4 . . . . .199 F6
Shetland Cl *BORE* WD6 . . . . .31 F1
Shetland Rd *BOW* E3 . . . . .105 H1
Shield Dr *BTFD* TW8 . . . . .116 A6
Shieldhall St *ABYW* SE2 . . . . . . .128 D4
Shield Rd *ASHF* TW15 . . . . .153 F6
Shifford Pth *FSTH* SE23 . . . . .164 A5
Shillibeer Pl *MBLAR* W1H 8 D2
Shillingford Cl *MLHL* NW7 . . . . . . .46 B3
Shillingford St *IS* N1 . . . . .85 H6
Shilling Pl *HNWL* W7 * 116 B1
Shinfield St *SHB* W12 . . . . .100 A5
Shinglewell Rd *ERITH* DA8 . . . . .149 H1
Shinners Cl *SNWD* SE25 . . . . . . .197 H2
Ship & Mermaid Rw
  STHWK SE1 * 19 F2
Shipka Rd *BAL* SW12 . . . . .161 G3
Ship La *MORT/ESHN* SW14 . . . .137 K4
Shipman Rd *CAN/RD* E16 . . . . . .107 F5
  FSTH SE23 . . . . .164 A4
Ship St *DEPT* SE8 . . . . .144 D2
Ship Tavern Pas *BANK* EC3V 13 G5
Shipton Cl *BCTR* RM8 . . . . .91 K1
Shipton St *BETH* E2 . . . . .7 K4
Shipwright Rd
  BERM/RHTH SE16 . . . . .124 B2
Shipwright Yd *STHWK* SE1 * 19 G1
Shirburn Cl *FSTH* SE23 . . . . .163 K2
Shirbutt St *POP/IOD* E14 . . . . . . .105 J6
Shirebrook Rd *BKHTH/KID* SE3 .146 C4
Shire Ct *EW* KT17 . . . . .207 H5
Shirehall Cl *HDN* NW4 . . . . .64 B3
Shirehall Gdns *HDN* NW4 . . . . . . .64 B3
Shirehall La *HDN* NW4 . . . . .64 B3
Shirehall Pk *HDN* NW4 . . . . .64 B3
Shire Horse Wy *ISLW* TW7 . . . .136 A4
Shire La *ORP* BR6 . . . . .217 F3
Shire Ms *WHTN* TW2 . . . . .155 H1
Shires Pl *WAND/EARL* SW18 . . .160 B2
The Shires *RCHPK/HAM* TW10 .157 F6
Shirland Ms *MV/WKIL* W9 . . . . . .100 D2
Shirland Rd *MV/WKIL* W9 . . . . . .100 E3
Shirley Av *BXLY* DA5 . . . . .168 E2
  CROY/NA CR0 . . . . .197 K5
  SUT SM1 . . . . .209 J2
Shirley Church Rd
  CROY/NA CR0 . . . . .213 F1
Shirley Cl *DART* DA1 . . . . .151 F5
  HSLW TW3 . . . . .135 H6
  WALTH E17 * 69 K2
Shirley Crs *BECK* BR3 . . . . .198 B1

Shirley Dr *HSLW* TW3 . . . . .135 H6
Shirley Gdns *BARK* IG11 . . . . .90 E4
  HNWL W7 . . . . .116 A1
Shirley Gv *BTSEA* SW11 . . . . . . .141 F4
  FBAR/BDGN N11 * . . . .
Shirley Hills Rd *CROY/NA* CR0 . .213 F5
Shirley Oaks Rd *CROY/NA* CR0 .198 A5
Shirley Park Rd *CROY/NA* CR0 . .197 J5
Shirley Rd *CHSWK* W4 . . . . .118 A2
  CROY/NA CR0 . . . . .197 K6
  ENC/FH EN2 . . . . .23 J4
  SCUP DA14 . . . . .167 K5
  SRTFD E15 . . . . .88 C5
  WLGTN SM6 . . . . .210 C6
Shirley Rw *SNWD* SE25 * 181 H5
Shirley St *CAN/RD* E16 . . . . .106 D5
Shirley Wy *CROY/NA* CR0 . . . . . .213 H1
Shirlock Rd *HAMP* NW3 . . . . .83 K2
Shirwell Cl *MLHL* NW7 . . . . .46 B3
Shobden Rd *TOTM* N17 . . . . .49 K4
Shobroke Cl *CRICK* NW2 . . . . .82 A2
Shoebury Rd *EHAM* E6 . . . . .89 K5
Shoe La *FLST/FETLN* EC4A 11 K3
  HCIRC EC1N 12 A2
Sholden Gdns *STMC/STPC* BR5 .202 D2
Shooters Av
  KTN/HRWW/WS HA3 * 61 J1
Shooters Hill Rd *GNWCH* SE10 . .145 H2
Shooters Rd *ENC/FH* EN2 . . . . . . .23 F1
Shoot-up Hl *CRICK* NW2 . . . . .82 C4
Shore Cl *EDED/NFELT* TW14 . . . .153 K2
  HPTN TW12 . . . . .172 D2
Shoreditch High St *WCHPL* E1 . . .13 H1
Shore Gv *FELT* TW13 . . . . .155 F4
Shoreham Cl *CROY/NA* CR0 . . . .197 K3
  WAND/EARL SW18 . . . . .140 A6
Shoreham Rd
  STMC/STPC BR5 . . . . .186 C4
Shoreham Rd (East)
  HTHAIR TW6 . . . . .132 B6
Shoreham Rd (West)
  HTHAIR TW6 . . . . .132 B6
Shoreham Wy *HAYES* BR2 . . . . .199 K3
Shore Pl *HOM* E9 . . . . .86 E5
Shore Rd *HOM* E9 . . . . .86 E5
Shore Wy *BRXN/ST* SW9 . . . . . .142 B3
Shorncliffe Rd *STHWK* SE1 . . . . .123 G5
Shorndean St *CAT* SE6 . . . . .165 F3
Shorne Cl *BFN/LL* DA15 . . . . .168 C1
  STMC/STPC BR5 . . . . .202 E1
Shornefield Cl *BMLY* BR1 . . . . . .185 F6
Shornolds Rd *FUL/PGN* SW6 . . .139 K1
Shortcroft Rd *EW* KT17 . . . . .207 H5
Shortcrofts Rd *DAGW* RM9 . . . . .92 B4
Shorter St *TWRH* EC3N 13 K6
Shortgate *NFNCH/WDSPK* N12 . .32 D6
Shortlands *HMSMTH* W6 . . . . . . .119 G4
  HYS/HAR UB3 . . . . .113 G6
Shortlands Cl *BELV* DA17 . . . . . .129 G3
  UED N18 . . . . .35 K6
Shortlands Gdns *HAYES* BR2 . . .183 H5
Shortlands Gv *HAYES* BR2 . . . . .183 G6
Shortlands Rd *HAYES* BR2 . . . . .183 G6
  KUTN/CMB KT2 . . . . .175 G3
  LEY E10 .69 K4
Short La *STWL/WRAY* TW19 . . . .152 C2
Short Rd *CHSWK* W4 . . . . .118 B6
  HTHAIR TW6 . . . . .152 B1
  WAN E11 . . . . .70 C6
Shorts Cft *CDALE/KGS* NW9 . . . .62 E1
Shorts Gdns *LSQ/SEVD* WC2H * .10 E4
Shorts Rd *CAR* SM5 . . . . .209 J2
Short St *HDN* NW4 . . . . .64 A1
  STHWK SE1 . . . . .17 K2
Shortway *ELTH/MOT* SE9 . . . . . .166 C5
Short Wy *NFNCH/WDSPK* N12 . . .47 J2
  WHTN TW2 . . . . .155 H1
Shotfield *WLGTN* SM6 . . . . .210 B4
Shott Cl *SUT* SM1 . . . . .209 G3
Shottendane Rd
  FUL/PGN SW6 . . . . .139 K2
Shottery Cl *ELTH/MOT* SE9 . . . . .166 D5
Shottfield Av
  MORT/ESHN SW14 . . . . .138 B5
Shoulder of Mutton Aly
  POP/IOD E14 * 105 G6
Shouldham St *MBLAR* W1H 8 D2
Showers Wy *HYS/HAR* UB3 . . . .113 K1
Shrapnel Cl *WOOL/PLUM* SE18 .146 D1
Shrapnel Rd *ELTH/MOT* SE9 . . . .146 E4
Shrewsbury Av
  KTN/HRWW/WS HA3 . . . . .62 A1
  MORT/ESHN SW14 . . . . .138 A5
Shrewsbury Cl *SURB* KT6 . . . . . .191 F6
Shrewsbury Crs *WLSDN* NW10 . .81 F6
Shrewsbury La
  WOOL/PLUM SE18 . . . . .147 G2
Shrewsbury Ms *BAY/PAD* W2 . . .100 E5
Shrewsbury Rd *BAY/PAD* W2 . . .100 E5
  BECK BR3 . . . . .194 D4
  CAR SM5 . . . . .194 D4
  FBAR/BDGN N11 . . . . .48 D2
  FSTGT E7 . . . . .89 H4
  HTHAIR TW6 . . . . .155 F1
Shrewsbury St *NKENS* W10 . . . .100 A3
Shrewton Rd *TOOT* SW17 . . . . . .178 E3
Shroffold Rd *BMLY* BR1 . . . . .165 H6
Shropshire Cl *MTCM* CR4 . . . . . .195 K1
Shropshire Rd *WDGN* N22 . . . . . .49 F3
Shroton St *CAMTN* NW1 . . . . .8 C1
The Shrubberies *CHIG* IG7 . . . . .54 C1
  SWFD E18 . . . . .52 E5
Shrubbery Gdns *WCHMH* N21 . . .35 H2
Shrubbery Rd *ED* N9 . . . . .36 C5
  STHL UB1 . . . . .114 E1
  STRHM/NOR SW16 . . . . .179 K1
The Shrubbery *SURB* KT6 * 191 F5
Shrubland Cl *TRDG/WHET* N20 * .33 H4
Shrubland Gv *WPK* KT4 . . . . .208 A1
Shrubland Rd *BARK* E8 . . . . .86 C6
  WALTH E17 . . . . .69 J2
Shrublands Av *CROY/NA* CR0 . . .213 J2
Shrublands Cl *CHIG* IG7 . . . . .54 C2
  SYD SE26 . . . . .163 K5
  TRDG/WHET N20 . . . . .33 H3
Shrubsall Cl *ELTH/MOT* SE9 . . . .166 D3
Shubbery Cl *IS* N1 . . . . .6 E1

Shuna Wk *IS* N1 * 85 K4
Shurland Av *EBAR* EN4 . . . . .33 H1
Shurland Gdns *PECK* SE15 * 143 G1
Shurlock Dr *ORP* BR6 . . . . .216 C2
Shuters Sq *WKENS* W14 * 119 J5
Shuttle Cl *BFN/LL* DA15 . . . . .168 A2
Shuttlemead *BXLY* DA5 . . . . .169 G2
Shuttle Rd *DART* DA1 . . . . .150 D4
Shuttle St *WCHPL* E1 . . . . .104 C3
Shuttleworth Rd *BTSEA* SW11 . .140 C3
Sibella Rd *CLAP* SW4 . . . . .141 J3
Sibley Cl *BMLY* BR1 . . . . .200 D2
  BXLYHS DA6 . . . . .149 F6
Sibley Gv *UX/CGN* UB8 . . . . .94 A4
Sibthorpe Rd *LEE/GVPK* SE12 . .166 B2
Sibthorp Rd *MTCM* CR4 * 178 E5
Sibton Rd *CAR* SM5 . . . . .194 D4
Sicilian Av *NOXST/BSQ* WC1A * . .11 F2
Sidbury St *FUL/PGN* SW6 . . . . . .139 H2
Sidcup By-Pass Rd *SCUP* DA14 .167 K6
Sidcup Hill *SCUP* DA14 . . . . .186 C1
Sidcup Hill Gdns *SCUP* DA14 * . .186 D1
Sidcup Pl *SCUP* DA14 . . . . .186 B1
Sidcup Rd *ELTH/MOT* SE9 . . . . .166 D3
  LEE/GVPK SE12 . . . . .146 A6
Siddeley Dr *HSLWW* TW4 . . . . . .134 D4
Siddons La *CAMTN* NW1 . . . . .3 F7
Siddons Rd *CROY/NA* CR0 . . . . .211 G1
  FSTH SE23 . . . . .164 B4
  TOTM N17 . . . . .50 C4
Side Rd *WALTH* E17 . . . . .69 H2
Sidewood Rd *ELTH/MOT* SE9 . . .167 J3
Sidford Pl *STHWK* SE1 . . . . .17 H5
Sidings Ms *HOLWY* N7 . . . . .85 G1
The Sidings *LOU* IG10 . . . . .39 J1
  WAN E11 . . . . .70 A5
Sidmouth Av *ISLW* TW7 . . . . .135 K3
Sidmouth Cl *OXHEY* WD19 . . . . . .27 F4
Sidmouth Dr *RSLP* HA4 . . . . .76 C1
Sidmouth Pde *CRICK* NW2 * 82 A5
Sidmouth Rd *CRICK* NW2 . . . . . . .82 A5
  LEY E10 .88 A1
  PECK SE15 . . . . .143 G2
  STMC/STPC BR5 . . . . .202 C2
  WELL DA16 . . . . .148 D1
Sidmouth St *STPAN* WC1H 5 F5
Sidney Av *PLMGR* N13 . . . . .49 F1
Sidney Elson Wy *EHAM* E6 . . . . .108 A1
Sidney Gdns *BTFD* TW8 . . . . . . .116 E6
Sidney Gv *FSBYE* EC1V 6 A3
Sidney Rd *BECK* BR3 . . . . .182 B5
  BRXN/ST SW9 . . . . .142 A3
  FSTGT E7 . . . . .88 E1
  RYLN/HDSTN HA2 . . . . .42 C6
  SNWD SE25 . . . . .197 H2
  TWK TW1 . . . . .156 B1
  WDGN N22 . . . . .49 F3
Sidney Sq *WCHPL* E1 . . . . .104 E4
Sidney St *WCHPL* E1 . . . . .104 E5
Sidworth St *HACK* E8 . . . . .86 D5
Siebert Rd *BKHTH/KID* SE3 . . . .125 K6
Siemens Rd *WOOL/PLUM* SE18 .126 C3
Sienna Ter *CRICK* NW2 * 63 J6
Sierra Dr *DAGE* RM10 . . . . .110 E1
Sigdon Rd *HACK* E8 . . . . .86 C4
The Sigers *PIN* HA5 . . . . .59 F3
Signmakers Yd *CAMTN* NW1 * 3 K1
Sigrist Sq *KUTN/CMB* KT2 . . . . . .175 F4
Silbury Av *MTCM* CR4 . . . . .178 D4
Silbury St *IS* N1 . . . . .6 E4
Silecroft Rd *BXLYHN* DA7 . . . . . .149 H2
Silesia Buildings *HACK* E8 . . . . . .86 D5
Silex St *STHWK* SE1 . . . . .18 B3
Silk Cl *LEE/GVPK* SE12 . . . . .145 K6
Silkfield Rd *CDALE/KGS* NW9 . . .63 G2
Silk Mill Rd *OXHEY* WD19 . . . . . . .27 F2
Silk Mills Pth *LEW* SE13 . . . . .145 F4
Silkstream Pde *EDGW* HA8 * 44 E4
Silkstream Rd *EDGW* HA8 . . . . . .44 E4
Silk St *BARB* EC2Y 12 D1
Silsoe Rd *WDGN* N22 . . . . .49 F5
Silver Birch Av *CHING* E4 . . . . . . .51 H1
Silver Birch Cl *CAT* SE6 . . . . .164 C5
  FBAR/BDGN N11 . . . . .48 A2
  RDART DA2 . . . . .170 B6
  TOTM N17 . . . . .49 G3
Silver Birch Ms *BARK/HLT* IG6 . . .54 E2
Silverbirch Wk *HAMP* NW3 * 83 K4
Silvercliffe Gdns *EBAR* EN4 . . . . .21 J5
Silver Cl *KTN/HRWW/WS* HA3 . . .42 D3
  NWCR SE14 . . . . .144 B1
Silver Crs *CHSWK* W4 . . . . .117 J4
Silverdale *CAMTN* NW1 * 4 E4
  ENC/FH EN2 . . . . .22 E5
  SYD SE26 . . . . .163 K6
Silverdale Centre
  ALP/SUD HA0 * 80 B6
Silverdale Cl *HNWL* W7 . . . . .115 K1
  NTHLT UB5 . . . . .77 K3
  SUT SM1 . . . . .208 D2
Silverdale Dr *ELTH/MOT* SE9 . . .166 D4
  HCH RM12 . . . . .93 K3
  SUN TW16 . . . . .172 A5
Silverdale Gdns *HYS/HAR* UB3 .113 J2
Silverdale Rd *BXLYHN* DA7 . . . .149 J3
  CHING E4 . . . . .52 B2
  HYS/HAR UB3 . . . . .113 J2
  STMC/STPC BR5 . . . . .186 B6
  WALTH E17 . . . . .201 H1
Silverdene
  NFNCH/WDSPK N12 * 47 F2
Silver Dene *PUT/ROE* SW15 * . . .139 F6
Silvergate *WPK* KT4 . . . . .206 E3
Silverhall St *ISLW* TW7 . . . . .136 B4
Silverholme Cl
  KTN/HRWW/WS HA3 . . . . .62 A4
Silver Jubilee Wy *HSLWW* TW4 .134 A3
Silver La *WWKM* BR4 . . . . .199 G6
Silverleigh Rd *THHTH* CR7 . . . . .196 A1
Silvermere Av *CRW* RM5 . . . . . . .56 D2
Silvermere Dr *UED* N18 . . . . .51 F1
Silvermere Rd *CAT* SE6 . . . . .164 E1
Silvermere Rw *SNWD* SE25 * . . .181 H5
Silver Rd *LEW* SE13 . . . . .144 E4
  NKENS W10 . . . . .100 B6

Silver Spring Cl *ERITH* DA8 . . . . .129 J6
Silverston Wy *STAN* HA7 . . . . .43 J2
Silver St *EN* EN1 . . . . .23 K4
  UED N18 . . . . .35 K6
Silverthorne Rd *VX/NE* SW8 . . . .141 G5
Silverthorn Gdns *CHING* E4 . . . . .37 J4
Silverton Rd *HMSMTH* W6 . . . . .139 G1
Silvertown Wy *CAN/RD* E16 . . . .106 D5
Silvertree La *GFD/PVL* UB6 . . . . .96 D2
Silver Wy *ROMW/RG* RM7 . . . . . .56 D6
Silverwood Cl *BECK* BR3 . . . . . . .182 D3
  CROY/NA CR0 . . . . .213 H6
  NTHWD HA6 . . . . .40 A4
Silvester Rd *EDUL* SE22 . . . . . . .143 G6
Silvester St *STHWK* SE1 . . . . .18 E3
Silwood Est Regeneration
  Area *BERM/RHTH* SE16 . . . . .124 A5
Silwood St *BERM/RHTH* SE16 . . .124 A5
Simmil Rd *ESH/CLAY* KT10 . . . . .204 E3
Simmons Cl *TRDG/WHET* N20 . . .33 J4
Simmons Dr *BCTR* RM8 . . . . .92 A1
Simmons Gdns *ESH/CLAY* KT10 .204 C3
Simmons La *CHING* E4 . . . . .38 B4
Simmons Rd
  WOOL/PLUM SE18 . . . . .127 G5
Simmons' Wy *TRDG/WHET* N20 .33 J4
Simms Cl *CAR* SM5 . . . . .194 D6
Simms Gdns *EFNCH* N2 . . . . .47 G5
Simms Rd *STHWK* SE1 . . . . .123 H4
Simnel Rd *LEE/GVPK* SE12 . . . . .166 A2
Simon Cl *NTGHL* W11 . . . . .100 D6
Simonds Rd *LEY* E10 . . . . .69 J6
Simone Cl *BMLY* BR1 . . . . .184 C4
Simons Wk *SRTFD* E15 . . . . .88 B3
Simpson Cl *WCHMH* N21 * 23 F6
Simpson Dr *ACT* W3 . . . . .99 F5
Simpson Rd *HSLWW* TW4 . . . . . .154 E2
  RAIN RM13 . . . . .93 H4
  RCHPK/HAM TW10 . . . . .156 D6
Simpson's Rd *HAYES* BR2 . . . . . .183 K6
  POP/IOD E14 . . . . .105 K6
Simpson St *BTSEA* SW11 . . . . . .140 C3
Simpson Wy *SURB* KT6 . . . . .190 D3
Simrose Ct *WAND/EARL* SW18 .139 K6
Sims Ct *ROM* RM1 * . . . .
Sinclair Dr *BELMT* SM2 . . . . .209 F6
Sinclair Gdns *WKENS* W14 . . . . .119 G2
Sinclair Gv *GLDGN* NW11 . . . . . . .64 B3
Sinclair Rd *CHING* E4 . . . . .51 H1
  WKENS W14 . . . . .119 H3
Sinclare Cl *EN* EN1 . . . . .24 B2
Singapore Rd *WEA* W13 . . . . . . .116 B1
Singer St *FSBYE* EC1V 7 F5
Singleton Cl *CROY/NA* CR0 . . . . .196 D4
  HCH RM12 . . . . .93 H2
  TOOT SW17 . . . . .178 E3
Singleton Rd *DAGW* RM9 . . . . . . .92 B3
Singleton Scarp
  NFNCH/WDSPK N12 . . . . .46 E1
Sinnott Rd *WALTH* E17 . . . . .51 F4
Sion Rd *TWK* TW1 . . . . .156 C3
Sipson Cl *WDR/YW* UB7 . . . . . . .112 D6
Sipson La *HYS/HAR* UB3 . . . . . . .112 E6
  WDR/YW UB7 . . . . .112 E6
Sipson Rd *WDR/YW* UB7 . . . . . . .112 C3
  WDR/YW UB7 . . . . .112 C3
Sipson Wy *WDR/YW* UB7 . . . . . .132 D1
Sir Abraham Dawes Cottages
  PUT/ROE SW15 * 139 H5
Sir Alexander Cl *ACT* W3 . . . . . .118 C1
Sir Cyril Black Wy
  WIM/MER SW19 . . . . .177 K3
Sirdar Rd *MTCM* CR4 . . . . .179 F2
  NTGHL W11 . . . . .100 B6
  WDGN N22 . . . . .49 J5
Sir John Kirk Cl *CMBW* SE5 . . . .142 D1
Sir Thomas More Est
  CHEL SW3 . . . . .120 C6
Sirus Rd *NTHWD* HA6 . . . . .40 E1
Sise La *MANHO* EC4N * 12 E4
Sisley Rd *BARK* IG11 . . . . .90 E6
Sispara Gdns
  WAND/EARL SW18 . . . . .159 J1
Sissinghurst Cl *BMLY* BR1 . . . . .183 H1
Sissinghurst Rd *CROY/NA* CR0 . .197 H4
Sister Mabels Wy *PECK* SE15 . . .143 H1
Sisters Av *BTSEA* SW11 . . . . . . .140 E5
Sistova Rd *BAL* SW12 . . . . .161 G3
Sisulu Pl *BRXN/ST* SW9 . . . . . . .142 B4
Sittingbourne Av *EN* EN1 . . . . .35 K1
Sitwell Gv *STAN* HA7 . . . . .43 F1
Siverst Cl *NTHLT* UB5 . . . . .78 B4
Siviter Wy *DAGE* RM10 . . . . .92 D5
Siward Rd *HAYES* BR2 . . . . .184 A1
  TOOT SW17 . . . . .160 B6
  TOTM N17 . . . . .49 K4
Sixth Av *HYS/HAR* UB3 . . . . .113 J1
  MNPK E12 . . . . .89 K2
  NKENS W10 . . . . .100 C3
Sixth Cross Rd *WHTN* TW2 . . . . .155 H5
Skardu Rd *CRICK* NW2 . . . . .82 C3
Skeena Hl *WAND/EARL* SW18 . .159 H2
Skeet Hill La *STMC/STPC* BR5 . .203 G6
Skeffington Rd *EHAM* E6 . . . . .89 K6
Skeffington St
  WOOL/PLUM SE18 . . . . .127 H3
Skelbrook St
  WAND/EARL SW18 . . . . .160 A4
Skelgill Rd *PUT/ROE* SW15 . . . . .139 J5
Skelley Rd *SRTFD* E15 . . . . .88 D6
Skelton Cl *HACK* E8 * 86 B4
Skelton Rd *FSTGT* E7 . . . . .88 E4
Skelton's La *LEY* E10 . . . . .69 K4
Skelwith Rd *HMSMTH* W6 . . . . .119 F6
Skerne Rd *KUTN/CMB* KT2 . . . . .174 E4
Skerne Wk *KUTN/CMB* KT2 . . . .174 E4
Sketchley Gdns
  BERM/RHTH SE16 . . . . .124 A5
Sketty Rd *EN* EN1 . . . . .24 B4
Skiers St *SRTFD* E15 . . . . .88 C6
Skiffington Cl
  BRXS/STRHM SW2 . . . . .162 B3
Skinner Pl *BGVA* SW1W * 15 G7
Skinners La *BLKFR* EC4V 12 D5
  HEST TW5 . . . . .135 G2
Skinner St *CLKNW* EC1R 6 A6

Skipsey Av *EHAM* E6 . . . . .107 K2
Skipton Cl *FBAR/BDGN* N11 . . . . .48 A2
Skipton Dr *HYS/HAR* UB3 . . . . . .113 F3
Skipworth Rd *HOM* E9 . . . . .86 E6
Skylines Village
  POP/IOD E14 * 125 F2
Sky Peals Rd *WFD* IG8 . . . . .52 B4
Skyport Dr *WDR/YW* UB7 . . . . . .132 A1
Sladebrook Rd *BKHTH/KID* SE3 .146 C4
Sladedale Rd
  WOOL/PLUM SE18 . . . . .127 K5
Slade Gdns *ERITH* DA8 . . . . .150 C2
Slade Green Rd *ERITH* DA8 . . . .150 D2
Sladen Pl *CLPT* E5 . . . .
Slades Cl *ENC/FH* EN2 . . . . .23 G4
Slades Dr *CHST* BR7 . . . . .167 H6
Slades Gdns *ENC/FH* EN2 . . . . . .23 G3
Slades Hill *ENC/FH* EN2 . . . . .23 G4
Slades Ri *ENC/FH* EN2 . . . . .23 G4
The Slade *WOOL/PLUM* SE18 . .127 K6
Slade Wk *WALW* SE17 . . . . .122 C6
Slade Wy *MTCM* CR4 . . . . .179 F4
Slagrove Pl *BROCKY* SE4 . . . . . .144 B5
Slaithburn St *WDPTN* SW10 . . . .
Slaithwaite Rd *LEW* SE13 . . . . . .145 F5
Slaney Pl *HOLWY* N7 . . . .
Slaney Rd *ROM* RM1 . . . . .75 G2
Slattery Rd *FELT* TW13 . . . . .154 C3
Sleaford Gn *OXHEY* WD19 . . . . . .27 H5
Sleaford St *VX/NE* SW8 . . . . .141 H1
Sledmere Ct
  EBED/NFELT TW14 . . . . .153 H3
Slievemore Ct *CLAP* SW4 . . . . . .141 J4
Slingsby Pl *LSQ/SEVD* WC2H 10 E5
Slippers Pl *BERM/RHTH* SE16 . . .123 J3
Sloane Av *CHEL* SW3 . . . . .14 D6
Sloane Ct East *CHEL* SW3 . . . . . .121 F5
Sloane Ct West *CHEL* SW3 . . . . .121 F5
Sloane Gdns *BGVA* SW1W 15 G7
  ORP BR6 . . . . .216 C1
Sloane Sq *BGVA* SW1W 15 G7
Sloane St *KTBR* SW1X 15 F3
Sloane Ter *KTBR* SW1X 15 F5
Sloane Wk *CROY/NA* CR0 . . . . . .198 C3
Slocum Cl *THMD* SE28 . . . . .109 J6
Slough La *CDALE/KGS* NW9 . . . . .62 E3
Sly St *WCHPL* E1 * 104 D5
Smaldon Cl *WDR/YW* UB7 * 112 D5
Smallberry Av *ISLW* TW7 . . . . . . .136 A3
Smallbrook Ms *BAY/PAD* W2 * . . . .
Smalley Cl *STNW/STAM* N16 . . . .86 B1
Smallwood Rd *TOOT* SW17 . . . .160 C6
Smarden Cl *BELV* DA17 . . . . .129 H5
Smart Cl *HARH* RM3 . . . . .57 K4
Smart's Pl *NOXST/BSQ* WC1A . . .11 F3
  UED N18 . . . . .50 C1
Smart St *BETH* E2 . . . . .105 F2
Smeaton Ct
  WAND/EARL SW18 . . . . .159 K2
  WFD IG8 . . . . .53 K1
Smeaton St *WAP* E1W 123 J1
Smedley St *VX/NE* SW8 . . . . .141 J3
Smeed Rd *BOW* E3 . . . . .87 J5
Smiles Pl *LEW* SE13 . . . . .145 F3
Smith Cl *BERM/RHTH* SE16 . . . .124 A1
Smithfield St *STBT* EC1A 12 A2
Smithies Rd *ABYW* SE2 . . . . .128 C4
Smith's Ct *SOHO/SHAV* W1D * . . .10 C5
Smithson Rd *TOTM* N17 . . . . .49 K5
Smith St *WEST* SW1P . . . .
Smith St *BRYLDS* KT5 . . . . .191 G5
  CHEL SW3 . . . . .120 E5
Smith Ter *CHEL* SW3 . . . . .120 E5
Smithwood Cl
  WIM/MER SW19 . . . . .159 H4
Smithy St *WCHPL* E1 . . . . .104 E4
Smugglers Wy
  WAND/EARL SW18 . . . . .140 A5
Smyrk's Rd *WALW* SE17 . . . . . . .123 F5
Smyrna Rd *KIL/WHAMP* NW6 . . . .82 E5
Smythe St *POP/IOD* E14 . . . . . . .105 K6
Snakes La *EBAR* EN4 . . . . .22 B4
Snakes La East *WFD* IG8 . . . . .53 G2
Snakes La West *WFD* IG8 . . . . . . .52 E2
Snakey La *FELT* TW13 . . . . .153 K6
Snaresbrook Dr *STAN* HA7 . . . . . .29 K6
Snaresbrook Rd *WALTH* E17 . . . . .70 C1
Snarsgate St *NKENS* W10 . . . . . .100 A4
Sneath Av *GLDGN* NW11 . . . . .64 D4
Snell's Pk *UED* N18 . . . . .50 B2
Sneyd Rd *CRICK* NW2 . . . . .82 A3
Snipe Cl *ERITH* DA8 . . . . .150 E1
Snowberry Cl *SRTFD* E15 . . . . . . .88 B2
Snowberry Cl *FBAR/BDGN* N11 . .48 A1
Snowbury Rd *FUL/PGN* SW6 . . .140 A3
Snowden Dr *CDALE/KGS* NW9 . . .63 G3
Snowden St *SDTCH* EC2A . . . .
Snowdon Crs *HYS/HAR* UB3 . . . .113 F1
Snowdon Dr *CDALE/KGS* NW9 . . .63 G3
Snowdown Cl *PGE/AN* SE20 . . . .181 K4
Snowdrop Cl *HPTN* TW12 . . . . . .173 F2
Snow Hl *STBT* EC1A 12 A2
Snowsfields *STHWK* SE1 . . . . .19 F2
Snowshill Rd *MNPK* E12 . . . . .89 J3
Snowy Fielder Waye
  ISLW TW7 . . . . .136 C3
Soames St *PECK* SE15 . . . . .143 G4
Soames Wk *NWMAL* KT3 . . . . . .176 B4
Soane Cl *EA* W5 . . . . .116 E2
Soaphouse La *BTFD* TW8 . . . . . .137 F1
Soho Sq *SOHO/SHAV* W1D 10 C3
Soho St *SOHO/SHAV* W1D * 10 C3
Sojourner-truth Cl *HACK* E8 . . . . .86 D4
Sojourner-truth Cl *HACK* E8 . . . . .86 D4
Solander Gdns *WCHPL* E1 . . . . .104 D6
Solebay St *WCHPL* E1 . . . . .105 G3
Solent Ri *PLSTW* E13 . . . . .106 E2
Solent Rd *KIL/WHAMP* NW6 . . . . .82 E3
Solna Av *PUT/ROE* SW15 . . . . . .139 F6
Solna Rd *WCHMH* N21 . . . . .35 K3
Solomon Av *UED* N18 . . . . .50 C6
Solomon's Pas *PECK* SE15 . . . . .143 J5
Solon New Rd *CLAP* SW4 . . . . . .141 K5
Solon Rd *BRXS/STRHM* SW2 . . .141 K5
Solway Cl *HACK* E8 * 86 B4
  HSLWW TW4 . . . . .134 D4
Solway Rd *EDUL* SE22 . . . . .143 H5
  WDGN N22 . . . . .49 H4
Somaford Gv *EBAR* EN4 . . . . .33 H1

Somali Rd CRICK NW2......................82 D2
Somerby Rd BARK IG11.....................90 D5
Somercoates Cl EBAR EN4..................21 J4
Somerden Rd STMC/STPC BR5..202 E4
Somerfield Rd FSBYPK N4.................67 H6
Somerfield St
  BERM/RHTH SE16.......................124 A5
Somerford Cl PIN HA5.....................58 E1
Somerford Gv STNW/STAM N16..86 B2
  TOTM N17...............................50 C3
Somerford St WCHPL E1 *..............104 D3
Somerford Wy
  BERM/RHTH SE16.......................124 B2
Somerhill Av BFN/LL DA15..............168 C2
Somerhill Rd WELL DA16.................148 C3
Somerleyton Rd BRXN/ST SW9..142 E5
Somers Cl CAMTN NW1 *.................4 C2
Somers Crs BAY/PAD W2....................8 C4
Somerset Av CHSGTN KT9...............205 K2
  RYNPK SW20...........................176 E5
  WELL DA16.............................148 A6
Somerset Cl NWMAL KT3.................192 B3
  TOTM N17...............................50 B1
  WFD IG8................................52 E4
Somerset Gdns HGT N6.....................66 B4
  LEW SE13..............................144 E3
  STRHM/NOR SW16.......................180 A6
  TEDD TW11.............................173 K1
  TOTM N17...............................50 B1
Somerset Sq WKENS W14 *...............119 H3
Somerset Wave HEST TW5................134 D5
Somersham Rd BXLYHN DA7...........149 F5
  WALTH E17..............................51 K4
Somers Wy BUSH WD23.....................28 C3
Somerton Av RCH/KEW TW9..........137 J4
Somerton Rd CRICK NW2..................82 B1
  PECK SE15.............................143 J5
Somertrees Av LEE/GVPK SE12..166 A5
Somervell Rd RYLN/HDSTN HA2..77 J4
Somerville Av BARN SW13...............119 F6
Somerville Rd CHDH RM6...............73 J2
  DART DA1..............................171 J1
  PGE/AN SE20..........................182 A3
Sonderburg Rd HOLWY N7.................67 F6
Sondes St WALW SE17....................122 E6
Songhurst Cl CROY/NA CR0..........196 A3
Sonia Cl OXHEY WD19......................27 G3
Sonia Gdns HEST TW5....................135 F1
  NFNCH/WDSPK N12.......................33 G6
  WLSDN NW10.............................81 H2
Sonning Gdns HPTN TW12.............172 D2
Sonning Rd SNWD SE25.................197 H5
Soper Cl CHING E4.........................51 H4
  FSTH SE23.............................164 A3
Soper Ms PEND EN3.........................25 J1
Sophia Cl HOLWY N7........................85 F4
Sophia Rd CAN/RD E16.................107 F5
  LEY E10................................69 K5
Sopwith Av CHSGTN KT9...............206 A3
Sopwith Cl KUTN/CMB KT2..........175 G1
Sopwith Rd HEST TW5..................134 A5
Sopwith Wy KUTN/CMB KT2..........175 F4
  VX/NE SW8..............................141 G1
Sorrel Bank CROY/NA CR0 *........213 G6
Sorrel Cl THMD SE28....................128 B1
Sorrel Gdns EHAM E6....................107 J4
Sorrell Cl BRXN/ST SW9 *.............142 B3
  NWCR SE14.............................144 A1
Sorrel Wk ROM RM1........................57 H6
Sorrento Rd SUT SM1...................209 F1
Sotheby Rd HBRY N5.......................85 J2
Sotheran Cl HACK E8......................86 C6
Soudan Rd BTSEA SW11.................140 E2
Souldern Rd WKENS W14 *............119 G3
Sounds Ldg SWLY BR8....................205 K5
South Access Rd LEY E10................69 G4
South Africa Rd SHB W12................99 K6
Southall Cl HEST TW5..................114 A6
Southall La HEST TW5...................114 A6
Southall Pl STHWK SE1....................18 E3
Southampton Buildings
  LINN WC2A *............................11 J2
Southampton Gdns
  MTCM CR4.............................195 K2
Southampton Ms CAN/RD E16...126 A1
Southampton Pl
  NOXST/BSQ WC1A.........................11 K3
Southampton Rd HAMP NW3...........83 K3
  HTHAIR TW6...........................152 C1
Southampton Rw
  NOXST/BSQ WC1A.........................11 G1
  RSQ WC1B...............................10 E1
Southampton St
  COVGDN WC2E...........................11 F5
Southampton Wy CMBW SE5..........142 E1
Southam St NKENS W10..................100 C3
South Ap NTHWD HA6.....................26 B5
South Audley St
  MYFR/PKLN W1K...........................9 K6
South Av CAR SM5.......................210 A5
  CHING E4...............................38 A5
  RCH/KEW TW9...........................137 H5
  STHL UB1..............................95 K6
South Avenue Gdns STHL UB1.....95 K6
  SURB KT6.............................191 F3

Southbank THDIT KT7.....................190 C4
South Bank Ter SURB KT6 *...........191 F3
South Birkbeck Rd WAN E11..........88 B1
South Black Lion La
  HMSMTH W6............................118 D5
South Bolton Gdns
  WBPTN SW10...........................120 A5
Southborough Cl SURB KT6...........190 E5
Southborough Rd BMLY BR2........200 D2
Southborough Rd BMLY BR1........184 D6
  HOM E9.................................86 E6
  SURB KT6.............................191 F5
Southborough Rd (The Lane)
  SURB KT6 *............................191 F5
Southbourne HAYES BR2...............199 K4
Southbourne Av EN EN1...................24 C5
Southbourne Cl PIN HA5..................59 H4
Southbourne Crs HDN NW4..............64 C1
Southbourne Gdns IL IG1.................90 C3
  LEE/GVPK SE12.......................146 A4
  RSLP HA4..............................59 F5
Southbridge Pl CROY/NA CR0....211 J2
Southbridge Rd CROY/NA CR0....211 J2
Southbridge Wy NWDGN UB2.....114 D2
Southbrook Rd
  LEE/GVPK SE12.......................165 H1
  STRHM/NOR SW16.....................179 K4
Southbury Av EN EN1.....................24 C5
Southbury Rd EN EN1....................24 B5
South Carriage Dr KTBR SW1X...15 F2
  SKENS SW7..............................14 C3
Southchurch Rd EHAM E6.............107 K1
South Cl BAR EN5..........................20 D4
  BXLYHS DA6............................148 E5
  DAGE RM10.............................92 C6
  MRDN SM4.............................193 J4
  PIN HA5................................59 K4
  WDR/YW UB7............................112 D3
  WHTN TW2.............................155 F5
The South Colonnade
  POP/IOD E14...........................124 D1
Southcombe St WKENS W14........119 H4
Southcote Av BRYLDS KT5..........191 J4
  FELT TW13.............................153 K4
Southcote Ri RSLP HA4....................58 B4
Southcote Rd ARCH N19..................84 C2
  SNWD SE25...........................197 J2
  WALTH E17..............................69 H1
South Countess Rd WALTH E17....51 H6
South Crs CAN/RD E16.................106 B4
Southcroft Av WELL DA16.............147 K4
  WWKM BR4.............................198 E1
Southcroft Rd ORP BR6.................216 E1
  STRHM/NOR SW16.....................179 G2
South Cross Rd BARK/HLT IG6....72 C2
South Croxted Rd DUL SE21........162 E6
Southdale CHIG IG7.......................54 D2
Southdean Gdns
  WIM/MER SW19.......................159 J4
South Dene MLHL NW7...................31 F5
Southdown Av HNWL W7...............116 B3
Southdown Crs
  GNTH/NBYPK IG2.........................72 C2
  RYLN/HDSTN HA2.......................60 C5
Southdown Rd CAR SM5...............210 A6
  EMPK RM11............................75 K4
  RYNPK SW20...........................177 G4
Southdown Vis
  SEVS/STOTM N15 *........................67 H2
South Dr ORP BR6........................216 E5
  RSLP HA4..............................58 C5
South Ealing Rd EA W5.................116 E2
South Eastern Av ED N9...................36 B5
South Eaton Pl BGVA SW1W..........15 H6
South Eden Park Rd BECK BR3...198 E2
South Edwardes Sq KENS W8......119 J3
South End CROY/NA CR0..............211 J2
  KENS W8...............................120 A3
Southend Cl ELTH/MOT SE9.........147 G6
Southend Crs ELTH/MOT SE9.......147 F7
South End La CAT SE6.................164 D6
Southend Rd BECK BR3...............182 D4
  CLAY IG5................................53 J6
  EHAM E6................................89 K5
South End Rd HAMP NW3................83 J2
  RAINHAM RM13.........................93 J6
Southend Rd (North Circular
  Rd) WALTH E17...........................52 B4
Southend Rd (North Circular
  Rd) SWFD E18............................52 D5
South End Rw KENS W8................120 A3
Southern Av
  EBED/NFELT TW14.....................153 K4
  SNWD SE25...........................181 G6
Southern Down FELT TW13 *......154 B3
Southern Dr LOU IG10.....................39 K1
Southerngate Wy NWCR SE14....144 B1
Southern Gv BOW E3....................105 H2
Southern Perimeter Rd
  HTHAIR TW6...........................152 E1
Southern Rd FNCH N3....................65 K1
  PLSTW E13.............................107 F1
Southern Rw NKENS W10.............100 B5
Southern St IS N1...........................5 G2
Southern Wy GNWCH SE10............125 J4
  ROMW/RG RM7..........................74 C3
Southerton Rd HMSMTH W6 *....119 F4
South Esk Rd FSTGT E7..................89 G4
Southey Rd BRXN/ST SW9...........142 B2
  SEVS/STOTM N15......................68 A2
  WIM/MER SW19.......................177 K3
Southey St PGE/AN SE20...............182 A3
Southfield BAR EN5.......................32 B1
Southfield Gdns TWK TW1............156 A6
Southfield Pk RYLN/HDSTN HA2...60 B1
Southfield Rd CHST BR7...............185 K5
  CHSWK W4.............................118 B3
  PEND EN3...............................36 D1
  WAN E11................................88 C3
Southfields HDN NW4....................45 K6
Southfields Ms
  WAND/EARL SW18 *..................159 K1
Southfields Rd
  WAND/EARL SW18....................159 K1

Southfleet Rd ORP BR6.................216 E1
South Gdns WBLY HA9 *.................62 C6
  WIM/MER SW19.......................178 C5
South Gate Av FELT TW13...........153 G6
Southgate Gv IS N1........................85 K5
Southgate Rd IS N1........................85 K6
South Gipsy Rd WELL DA16........149 F4
South Gv HGT N6............................66 A5
  SEVS/STOTM N15.......................67 K2
  WALTH E17..............................69 H2
South Hall Dr RAIN RM13............111 K5
South Hl CHST BR7........................184 E2
  HGT N6.................................40 C4
South Hill Av RYLN/HDSTN HA2...78 C1
South Hill Gv HRW HA1...................78 E3
South Hill Pk HAMP NW3................83 J2
South Hill Park Gdns
  HAMP NW3..............................83 J2
South Hill Rd HAYES BR2.............199 H1
Southholme Cl NRWD SE19.........181 F4
Southhill La PIN HA5.....................58 E1
Southill Rd CHST BR7.................184 D3
Southill St POP/IOD E14..............105 K5
South Island Pl BRXN/ST SW9...142 A1
South Kensington Station Ar
  SKENS SW7 *............................14 B6
South Lambeth Pl VX/NE SW8....122 A6
South Lambeth Rd
  VX/NE SW8............................141 K1
Southland Rd
  WOOL/PLUM SE18.....................128 B6
  WOOL/PLUM SE18.....................148 A1
Southlands Av ORP BR6................216 E2
Southlands Dr
  WIM/MER SW19.......................159 G4
Southlands Gv BMLY BR1............184 D6
Southlands Rd HAYES BR2.........200 C1
Southland Wy HSLW TW3............155 J6
South La KUT/HW KT1..................174 E6
  NWMAL KT3...........................192 A1
South La West NWMAL KT3.........192 A1
South Lodge Av MTCM CR4........195 K1
South Lodge Crs ENC/FH EN2.....22 D5
South Lodge Dr
  STHGT/OAK N14......................22 D5
South Md CDALE/KGS NW9..........45 H4
  HOR/WEW KT19.......................207 H5
Southmead Rd
  WIM/MER SW19.......................159 H3
South Molton La
  MYFR/PKLN W1K..........................9 J4
South Molton Rd CAN/RD E16...106 E5
South Molton St
  MYFR/PKLN W1K..........................9 J4
Southmont Rd ESH/CLAY KT10..189 K6
Southmoor Wy HOM E9...................87 H4
South Mt TRDG/WHET N20 *........33 G4
South Norwood HI
  SNWD SE25...........................181 F4
South Oak Rd
  STRHM/NOR SW16....................162 A6
Southold Ri ELTH/MOT SE9.........166 E5
Southolm St BTSEA SW11............141 G2
South Ordnance Rd PEND EN3....25 J1
Southover BMLY BR1...................183 K1
  NFNCH/WDSPK N12.....................32 E6
Southover Dr BARK IG11................91 G6
Southover Rd CMBW NW11............64 D5
  KTN/HRWW/WS HA3....................62 A2
Southwold Dr BARK IG11...............91 G3
Southwold Rd BXLY DA5...............169 J1
  CLPT E5.................................68 D6
Southwood Av HGT N6....................66 A4
  KUTN/CMB KT2........................175 K4
Southwood Cl BMLY BR1..............200 E1
  WPK KT4..............................193 G5
Southwood Dr BRYLDS KT5.........191 K4
Southwood Gdns ESH/CLAY KT10...189 K2
  GNTH/NBYPK IG2........................72 B3
Southwood Hall
  CROY/NA CR0 *.......................196 B3
Southwood La HGT N6....................66 A4
Southwood Lawn Rd HGT N6.......66 A4
Southwood Rd ELTH/MOT SE9....167 G4
  THMD SE28............................128 C1
South Worple Wy
  MORT/ESHN SW14....................138 A4
Southy Ms CAN/RD E16...............125 K1
Sovereign Cl EA W5.......................97 J4
  RSLP HA4..............................58 C5
  WAP E1W...............................104 D6
Sovereign Ct E/WMO/HCT KT8...188 E1
Sovereign Crs
  BERM/RHTH SE16.....................105 G6
Sovereign Gv ALP/SUD HA0.........79 K1
Sovereign Ms BETH E2 *..................7 J2
  EBAR EN4...............................34 A1
Sovereign Pk WLSDN NW10 *.......98 D3
Sovereign Pl HRW HA1...................61 F2
Sovereign Rd BARK IG11.............109 J2
Sowerby Cl ELTH/MOT SE9..........146 E5
Sowrey Av RAIN RM13....................93 H4
Space Waye
  EBED/NFELT TW14....................134 A6
Spafield St CLKNW EC1R.................5 J7
Spa Green Est CLKNW EC1R *........5 J4
Spa Hl NRWD SE19.......................180 E4
Spalding Cl EDGW HA8....................45 F3
Spalding Rd HDN NW4....................64 B3
  TOOT SW17............................179 H2
Spanby Rd BOW E3.......................105 J3
Spaniards Cl GLDGN NW11............65 G5
Spaniards End GLDGN NW11........65 G4
Spaniards Rd HAMP NW3...............65 G6
Spanish Pl MHST W1U *...................9 H3
Spanish Rd WAND/EARL SW18...140 B6
Sparkbridge Rd HRW HA1..............60 E1
Sparkes Cl BMLY BR2..................200 A1
Sparke Ter CAN/RD E16................106 D5
Sparkford Gdns
  FBAR/BDGN N11 *......................48 A1
Sparks Cl ACT W3...........................99 F5
  BCTR RM8..............................73 K6
  HPTN TW12............................172 D2
Spa Rd BERM/RHTH SE16...............19 J5
Sparrow Cl HPTN TW12................172 D2
Sparrow Dr STMC/STPC BR5......201 H5
Sparrow Farm Dr
  EBED/NFELT TW14....................154 C2
Sparrow Farm Rd EW KT17..........207 K3
Sparrow Gn DAGE RM10................92 D2
Sparrows Herne BUSH WD23.........28 B2
Sparrows La ELTH/MOT SE9........167 H3

Sparrows Wy BUSH WD23................28 C3
Sparrows Wick BUSH WD23 *.........28 C3
Sparsholt Rd ARCH N19..................67 F5
  BARK IG11...............................90 E6
Spartan Cl WLGTN SM6.................210 E5
Sparta St GNWCH SE10................145 F1
Speakers Ct CROY/NA CR0 *.......196 E5
Spearman St
  WOOL/PLUM SE18 *...................127 F6
Spear Ms ECT SW5......................119 K4
Spears Rd ARCH N19.....................66 E5
Speart La HEST TW5....................134 D1
Spectrum Pl WALW SE17..............122 E5
Spedan Cl HAMP NW3.....................83 F1
Speedwell St DEPT SE8................144 D1
Speedy Pl STPAN WC1H..................4 E5
Speer Rd THDIT KT7.....................190 A3
Speirs Cl NWMAL KT3..................192 C3
Spekehill ELTH/MOT SE9..............166 E5
Speke Rd THHTH CR7..................180 E5
Speldhurst Cl HAYES BR2............199 J2
Speldhurst Rd CHSWK W4............118 A3
  HOM E9.................................87 F5
Spellbrook Wk IS N1 *....................85 J1
Spelman St WCHPL E1...................104 C4
Spence Cl BERM/RHTH SE16........124 C2
  YEAD UB4..............................94 A4
Spencer Av CT FNCH N3.................46 D5
  ORP BR6................................217 J6
  WFD IG8................................53 G1
  WLSDN NW10............................98 B2
Spencer Dr EFNCH N2...................65 G3
Spencer Gdns
  MORT/ESHN SW14....................137 K6
  WIM/MER SW19.......................177 H2
Spencer Hill Rd
  WIM/MER SW19.......................177 H3
Spencer House SURB KT6 *.........191 F2
Spencer Ms CLAP SW4..................141 K2
  HMSMTH W6...........................119 H6
Spencer Pk WAND/EARL SW18....140 C6
Spencer Pas BETH E2 *.................104 C1
Spencer Pl CROY/NA CR0.............196 E4
  IS N1...................................85 H5
  WEST SW1P...............................16 B5
Spencer Ri KTTN NW5....................84 B2
Spencer Rd ACT W3......................117 K1
  ALP/SUD HA0............................61 J6
  BMLY BR1.............................183 J3
  BTSEA SW11...........................140 C5
  CEND/HSY/T N8.........................49 F6
  CHSWK W4.............................137 K1
  E/WMO/HCT KT8......................189 F1
  EHAM E6................................89 H1
  FBAR/BDGN N11.........................34 B6
  GDMY/SEVK IG3..........................72 E3
  ISLW TW7..............................135 J2
  KTN/HRWW/WS HA3....................42 E5
  MTCM CR4.............................195 F1
  RAIN RM13............................111 F2
  RYNPK SW20...........................176 E5
  SAND/SEL CR2........................212 A3
  TOTM N17...............................50 C4
  WALTH E17..............................52 A1
  WIM/MER SW19.......................177 K3
  WLSDN NW10............................99 G1
Spencer St CLKNW EC1V..................5 J5
  NWDGN UB2...........................114 C3
Spencer Wk PUT/ROE SW15.........139 G5
Spenser Ms DUL SE21...................162 E3
Spenser Rd HNHL SE24.................142 C6
Spenser St WESTW SW1E...............16 B4
Spensley Wk STNW/STAM N16......85 K1
Speranza St WOOL/PLUM SE18...128 A4
Sperling Rd TOTM N17....................50 B5
Spert St POP/IOD E14..................105 G6
Speyside STHGT/OAK N14..............34 C1
Spey St POP/IOD E14...................106 A4
Spey Wy ROM RM1.........................57 G3
Spezia Rd WLSDN NW10.................99 J1
Spicer Cl BRXN/ST SW9...............142 C3
  WOT/HER KT12........................188 B3
Spices Yd CROY/NA CR0..............211 J2
Spielman Rd DART DA1..................151 J5
Spigurnell Rd TOTM N17.................49 K4
Spikes Bridge Rd STHL UB1...........95 J6
Spindle Cl WOOL/PLUM SE18.......126 D3
Spindlewood Gdns
  CROY/NA CR0.........................212 A2
Spindrift Av POP/IOD E14...........124 E4
Spinel Cl WOOL/PLUM SE18........128 A5
Spinnaker Cl BARK IG11...............109 J2
Spinnells Rd RYLN/HDSTN HA2...59 K5
Spinney Cl BECK BR3...................183 F1
  NWMAL KT3...........................192 B1
  RAIN RM13............................111 G1
  WPK KT4..............................192 D5
Spinney Dr EBED/NFELT TW14...153 F2
Spinney Gdns DAGW RM9................92 A3
  NRWD SE19...........................181 F1
Spinney Oak BMLY BR1.................184 D5
The Spinneys BMLY BR1...............184 E5
The Spinney ALP/SUD HA0.............61 J6
  BAR EN5................................20 D3
  BARN SW13.............................118 E6
  CHEAM SM3...........................208 A2
  NFNCH/WDSPK N12 *..................47 F1
  SCUP DA14............................187 F1
  STAN HA7..............................43 K1
  STRHM/NOR SW16....................161 H5
  WAN E11................................70 E3
The Spires DART DA1...................171 G4
Spirit Quay WAP E1W...................123 H1
Spital Sq WCHPL E1........................13 H1
Spital St DART DA1.....................171 G1
  WCHPL E1..............................104 C4
Spital Yd WCHPL E1 *....................13 H1
Spitfire Est HEST TW5 *...............114 A6
Spitfire House
  WOOL/PLUM SE18 *...................146 D1
Spitfire Ms WIM/MER SW19 *......171 F5
Spitfire Wy HEST TW5.................114 A5
Spode Wk KIL/WHAMP NW6............83 F4
Spondon Rd SEVS/STOTM N15.....68 C1
Spoonbill Wy YEAD UB4................95 H4
Spooner Wk WLGTN SM6.............210 D3

Sportsbank St CAT SE6 165 F2
Sportsman Pl BETH E2 86 C6
Spottons Gv TOTM N17 49 J4
Spout Hl CROY/NA CR0 213 J3
Spratt Hall Rd WAN E11 70 E3
Spray St WOOL/PLUM SE18 127 G4
Spreighton Rd
E/WMO/HCT KT8 189 G1
Sprimont Pl CHEL SW3 120 E5
Springall St PECK SE15 143 J1
Springbank WCHMH N21 35 F1
Springbank Rd LEW SE13 165 H1
Springbank Wk CAMTN NW1 84 D5
Springbourne Ct BECK BR3 183 F4
Spring Bridge Rd EA W5 97 K6
Spring Cl BAR EN5 20 B6
BCTR RM8 73 K5
Springclose La CHEAM SM3 208 C4
Spring Cnr FELT TW13 * 153 K5
Spring Cottages SURB KT6 * 190 E2
Spring Court Rd ENC/FH EN2 23 G1
Springcroft Av EFNCH N2 47 K6
Springdale Rd STNW/STAM N16 85 K2
Spring Dr PIN HA5 58 E3
Springfield BUSH WD23 28 D3
CLPT E5 68 D5
Springfield Av HPTN TW12 173 G2
MUSWH N10 48 C6
RYNPK SW20 177 J6
Springfield Cl
NFNCH/WDSPK N12 47 F1
STAN HA7 29 G5
Springfield Dr GNTH/NBYPK IG2 72 C2
Springfield Gdns BMLY BR1 200 E1
CDALE/KGS NW9 63 F2
CLPT E5 68 D5
RSLP HA4 59 F5
WFD IG8 53 G3
WWKM BR4 198 E6
Springfield Gv CHARL SE7 126 B6
Springfield La KIL/WHAMP NW6 83 F6
Springfield Mt CDALE/KGS NW9 63 G2
Springfield Parade Ms
PLMGR N13 35 G6
Springfield Pl NWMAL KT3 191 K1
Springfield Ri SYD SE26 163 J6
Springfield Rd BMLY BR1 200 E1
BXLYHN DA7 149 J4
CHING E4 38 C3
EHAM E6 89 K5
FBAR/BDGN N11 48 C1
HNWL W7 115 K1
HRW HA1 60 E3
KUT/HW KT1 191 F1
SEVS/STOTM N15 68 C1
SRTFD E15 * 106 C2
STJWD NW8 83 G6
SYD SE26 181 J2
TEDD TW11 174 B1
THHTH CR7 180 D4
WALTH E17 69 H3
WELL DA16 148 C4
WHTN TW2 155 F3
WIM/MER SW19 177 J1
WLGTN SM6 210 B3
YEAD UB4 114 B1
Springfield Wk
KIL/WHAMP NW6 83 F6
Spring Gdns
E/WMO/HCT KT8 189 H2
HBRY N5 85 J3
HCH RM12 93 K2
ORP BR6 217 H4
ROMW/RG RM7 74 E2
WFD IG8 53 G3
WHALL SW1A 10 E7
WLGTN SM6 210 C3
Spring Gv CHSWK W4 117 H6
HPTN TW12 173 G4
LOU IG10 39 H1
MTCM CR4 179 F4
Spring Grove Crs HSLW TW3 135 H2
Spring Grove Rd HSLW TW3 135 H2
RCHPK/HAM TW10 137 G6
Springhead Rd ERITH DA8 130 C6
Spring Hl CLPT E5 68 C4
SYD SE26 163 K6
Springhill Cl CMBW SE5 142 E4
Springhurst Cl CROY/NA CR0 213 H2
Spring Lake STAN HA7 29 H6
Spring La CLPT E5 68 D5
EFNCH N2 48 A6
SNWD SE25 197 J3
Spring Ms MHST W1U * 9 F1
Spring Park Av CROY/NA CR0 198 A6
Springpark Dr BECK BR3 183 F6
FSBYPK N4 67 J5
Spring Park Rd CROY/NA CR0 198 A6
Spring Pl KTTN NW5 84 A3
Springpond Rd DAGW RM9 92 A3
Springrice Rd LEW SE13 165 G1
Spring Rd FELT TW13 153 J5
Spring Shaw Rd
STMC/STPC BR5 186 B4
Spring St BAY/PAD W2 8 A4
EW KT17 207 H6
Spring Tide Cl PECK SE15 * 143 H2
Spring V BXLYHN DA7 149 J5
Springvale Av BTFD TW8 116 E5
Spring V North DART DA1 171 G2
Spring V South DART DA1 * 171 G2
Springvale Ter WKENS W14 119 G3
Springvale Wy
STMC/STPC BR5 186 D6
Spring Villa Rd EDGW HA8 44 C3
Spring Vls WEA W13 * 116 C1
Spring Wk WCHPL E1 104 C4
Springwater Cl
WOOL/PLUM SE18 * 147 F2
Springwell Av WLSDN NW10 81 H6
Springwell Rd HEST TW5 134 C2
STRHM/NOR SW16 162 B6
Springwood Cl BOW E3 105 J1
Springwood Crs EDGW HA8 30 E4
Springwood Wy ROM RM1 75 J2
Sprowston Ms FSTGT E7 88 E4
Sprowston Rd FSTGT E7 88 E3
Sprucedale Gdns
CROY/NA CR0 213 F2
WLGTN SM6 210 E6
Spruce Hills Rd WALTH E17 51 K5
Sprules Rd BROCKY SE4 144 B3
Spurfield E/WMO/HCT KT8 173 G6
Spurgeon Av NRWD SE19 180 E4
Spurgeon Rd NRWD SE19 180 E3
Spurgeon St STHWK SE1 18 E5
Spurling Rd DAGW RM9 92 B4
EDUL SE22 * 143 G5
Spurrell Av BXLY DA5 170 A6
Spur Rd BARK IG11 108 C2
EBED/NFELT TW14 134 A6
EDGW HA8 30 B6
ISLW TW7 136 B1
ORP BR6 202 B6
SEVS/STOTM N15 * 67 K1
STHWK SE1 17 J2
WHALL SW1A 16 A3
Spurstowe Rd HACK E8 86 D4
Spurstowe Ter HACK E8 86 C3
The Square CAR SM5 210 A3
HMSMTH W6 119 F5
IL IG1 72 A4
RCH/KEW TW9 137 F6
STKPK UB11 113 G1
WFD IG8 52 E1
Squarey St TOOT SW17 160 B5
Squire Gdns STJWD NW8 2 A5
Squires Ct WIM/MER SW19 159 K6
Squires La FNCH N3 47 G4
Squire's Mt HAMP NW3 83 H1
Squires Wy RDART DA2 170 A6
Squires Wood Dr CHST BR7 * 184 E3
Squirrel Cl HSLWW TW4 134 B4
Squirrel Ms WEA W13 * 97 G6
Squirrels Cl NFNCH/WDSPK N12 33 G6
Squirrels Gn WPK KT4 192 C6
Squirrel's Heath Av GPK RM2 57 K6
The Squirrels BUSH WD23 28 D1
LEW SE13 145 G4
PIN HA5 41 K6
Squirries St BETH E2 104 C2
Stable Cl KUTN/CMB KT2 175 G2
NTHLT UB5 96 A1
Stable Ms TWK TW1 * 156 A3
WNWD SE27 180 D1
Stables End ORP BR6 216 C1
The Stables Market
CAMTN NW1 * 84 B5
Stables Wy LBTH SE11 122 B5
Stable Wk EFNCH N2 47 H4
IS N1 5 F2
Stable Wy NKENS W10 100 A5
Stable Yard Rd WHALL SW1A 16 B2
Stacey Av UED N18 36 E6
Stacey Cl LEY E10 70 B2
Stacey St HOLWY N7 85 G1
LSQ/SEVD WC2H 10 D4
Stackhouse St KTBR SW1X 14 E4
Stacy Pth CMBW SE5 * 143 F1
Staddon Cl BECK BR3 198 B1
Staddon Ct BECK BR3 198 B1
Stadium Rd HDN NW4 63 K4
WOOL/PLUM SE18 146 E1
Stadium St WBPTN SW10 140 B1
Stadium Wy DART DA1 170 B1
WBLY HA9 80 B2
Staffa Rd LEY E10 69 G5
Stafford Cl CHEAM SM3 208 C4
KIL/WHAMP NW6 100 E2
STHGT/OAK N14 22 C6
WALTH E17 69 H3
Stafford Cross CROY/NA CR0 211 F3
Stafford Gdns CROY/NA CR0 211 F3
Stafford Pl RCHPK/HAM TW10 157 G2
WESTW SW1E 16 A4
Stafford Rd BOW E3 105 H1
CROY/NA CR0 211 G2
FSTGT E7 89 G5
KIL/WHAMP NW6 100 E2
KTN/HRWW/WS HA3 42 C3
NWMAL KT3 175 K6
RSLP HA4 76 D2
SCUP DA14 167 K6
WLGTN SM6 210 C4
Staffordshire St PECK SE15 143 H2
Stafford St CONDST W1S 10 A7
Stafford Ter KENS W8 119 K3
Stag Cl EDGW HA8 44 D5
Staggart Gn CHIG IG7 55 F1
Stag La BKHH IG9 39 G4
CDALE/KGS NW9 44 E6
PUT/ROE SW15 158 C5
Stag Pl WESTW SW1E 16 A4
Stags Wy ISLW TW7 116 A6
Stainbank Rd MTCM CR4 179 G6
Stainby Cl WDR/YW UB7 112 B3
Stainby Rd TOTM N17 50 B6
Stainer St STHWK SE1 19 F1
Staines Av CHEAM SM3 193 G6
Staines Rd EBED/NFELT TW14 134 C6
EBED/NFELT TW14 152 E3
IL IG1 90 D2
WHTN TW2 155 H5
Staines Rd East SUN TW16 172 C4
Stainforth Rd GNTH/NBYPK IG2 72 D4
WALTH E17 69 J1
Staining La CITYW EC2V 12 D3
Stainmore Cl CHST BR7 185 J4
Stainsbury St BETH E2 104 E1
Stainsby Pl POP/IOD E14 * 105 J5
Stainsby Rd POP/IOD E14 105 J5
Stainton Rd CAT SE6 165 G2
PEND EN3 24 E2
Stalbridge St CAMTN NW1 8 D1
Stalham St BERM/RHTH SE16 123 J3
Stalham Wy BARK/HLT IG6 54 B4
Stambourne Wy NRWD SE19 181 F3
WWKM BR4 214 B1
Stambourne Woodland Wk
NRWD SE19 181 F3
Stamford Brook Av
HMSMTH W6 118 C3
Stamford Brook Gdns
HMSMTH W6 118 C3
Stamford Brook Rd
HMSMTH W6 118 C3
Stamford Cl HAMP NW3 * 83 G1
KTN/HRWW/WS HA3 42 E3
SEVS/STOTM N15 68 C1
STHL UB1 96 A6
Stamford Cottages
WBPTN SW10 * 140 A1
Stamford Dr HAYES BR2 199 J1
Stamford Gdns DAGW RM9 91 J5
Stamford Gv East
STNW/STAM N16 68 C5
Stamford Gv West
STNW/STAM N16 68 C5
Stamford Hl STNW/STAM N16 68 B5
Stamford Rd DAGW RM9 91 H5
EHAM E6 89 J6
IS N1 86 A5
SEVS/STOTM N15 68 C2
Stamford St STHWK SE1 11 J7
Stamp Pl BETH E2 7 J3
Stanborough Cl HPTN TW12 172 E2
Stanborough Pas HACK E8 86 B4
Stanborough Rd HSLW TW3 135 J4
Stanbridge Pl WCHMH N21 35 H4
Stanbridge Rd PUT/ROE SW15 139 F4
Stanbrook Rd ABYW SE2 128 C2
Stanbury Ct HAMP NW3 83 K4
Stanbury Rd PECK SE15 143 K3
Stancroft CDALE/KGS NW9 63 G1
Standale Gv RSLP HA4 58 A2
Standard Pl SDTCH EC2A 7 H5
Standard Rd BELV DA17 129 H5
BXLYHS DA6 149 F5
HSLWW TW4 134 D4
PEND EN3 25 G1
WLSDN NW10 98 E3
Standen Rd WAND/EARL SW18 159 K2
Standfield Rd DAGE RM10 92 C3
Standish Rd HMSMTH W6 118 D4
Stane Cl WIM/MER SW19 178 A3
Stane Gv VX/NE SW8 141 J3
Stane Wy WOOL/PLUM SE18 146 C1
Stanford Cl HPTN TW12 172 E2
ROMW/RG RM7 74 D3
RSLP HA4 58 A3
WFD IG8 53 J2
Stanford Pl WALW SE17 19 G7
Stanford Rd FBAR/BDGN N11 47 K1
SKENS SW7 120 A3
STRHM/NOR SW16 179 K5
Stanford St PIM SW1V 16 C7
Stanford Wy
STRHM/NOR SW16 179 J5
Stangate Gdns STAN HA7 29 H6
Stanger Rd SNWD SE25 197 H1
Stanham Pl DART DA1 150 D5
Stanham Rd DART DA1 151 F6
Stanhope Av FNCH N3 46 D6
HAYES BR2 199 K5
KTN/HRWW/WS HA3 42 D4
Stanhope Cl
BERM/RHTH SE16 * 124 A2
Stanhope Gdns BCTR RM8 92 B1
FSBYPK N4 67 H3
HGT N6 66 C3
IL IG1 71 K5
MLHL NW7 45 H1
SKENS SW7 120 B4
Stanhope Ga BAY/PAD W2 8 E5
MYFR/PKLN W1K 15 H1
Stanhope Gv BECK BR3 198 C2
Stanhope Ms East SKENS SW7 120 B4
Stanhope Ms South
SKENS SW7 120 B4
Stanhope Ms West SKENS SW7 120 B4
Stanhope Pde CAMTN NW1 3 K4
Stanhope Park Rd
GFD/PVL UB6 96 C3
Stanhope Pl BAY/PAD W2 8 E5
Stanhope Rd BAR EN5 32 B1
BCTR RM8 74 B6
BFN/LL DA15 168 B6
BXLYHN DA7 149 F3
CAR SM5 210 A5
CROY/NA CR0 212 A1
GFD/PVL UB6 96 C4
HGT N6 66 C3
NFNCH/WDSPK N12 47 G1
RAIN RM13 111 J1
WALTH E17 69 K2
Stanhope Rw MYFR/PICC W1J * 15 J1
Stanhope St CAMTN NW1 4 A4
Stanhope Ter BAY/PAD W2 8 B5
WHTN TW2 * 156 A2
Stanier Cl WKENS W14 119 J5
Stanlake Rd SHB W12 119 F1
Stanlake Vls SHB W12 119 F1
Stanley Av ALP/SUD HA0 80 A5
BARK IG11 109 F2
BCTR RM8 74 B5
BECK BR3 183 F6
GFD/PVL UB6 78 C6
GPK RM2 75 J1
NWMAL KT3 192 D2
Stanley Cl ALP/SUD HA0 80 A5
ELTH/MOT SE9 167 H3
GPK RM2 75 J1
VX/NE SW8 122 A6
Stanley Crs NTGHL W11 100 D6
Stanleycroft Cl ISLW TW7 135 K2
Stanley Gdns ACT W3 118 B2
CRICK NW2 82 A3
MTCM CR4 * 179 F2
NTGHL W11 100 D6
WLGTN SM6 210 C4
Stanley Gardens Rd
TEDD TW11 173 K1
Stanley Gv CROY/NA CR0 196 B3
VX/NE SW8 141 F3
Stanley Park Dr ALP/SUD HA0 80 B6
Stanley Park Rd CAR SM5 209 K5
WLGTN SM6 210 B5
Stanley Pas CAMTN NW1 4 E3
Stanley Rd ACT W3 117 J3
BELMT SM2 209 F4
CAR SM5 209 K6
CAR SM5 210 A5
CHING E4 38 B3
CROY/NA CR0 196 B4
ED N9 36 B3
EFNCH N2 65 H1
EN EN1 24 A4
FBAR/BDGN N11 48 D2
HAYES BR2 184 B6
HSLW TW3 135 H5
IL IG1 72 D6
MNPK E12 89 J4
MORT/ESHN SW14 137 J5
MRDN SM4 193 K1
MTCM CR4 179 F3
MUSWH N10 48 B3
NTHWD HA6 40 E4
ORP BR6 202 A5
RYLN/HDSTN HA2 60 C6
SCUP DA14 168 B5
SEVS/STOTM N15 67 H1
SRTFD E15 88 B6
STHL UB1 95 J6
SWFD E18 52 D4
TEDD TW11 173 K1
WALTH E17 69 K3
WBLY HA9 80 B4
WHTN TW2 155 J5
WIM/MER SW19 177 K3
Stanley Rd North RAIN RM13 111 G1
Stanley Rd South RAIN RM13 111 H1
Stanley Sq CAR SM5 209 K6
Stanley St DEPT SE8 144 C1
Stanley Ter ARCH N19 * 66 E6
BXLYHS DA6 * 149 H5
Stanley Wy STMC/STPC BR5 202 C2
Stanmer St BTSEA SW11 140 D3
Stanmore Gdns RCH/KEW TW9 137 G4
SUT SM1 209 G1
Stanmore Hl STAN HA7 43 H1
Stanmore Rd BELV DA17 129 K4
RCH/KEW TW9 137 G4
SEVS/STOTM N15 67 H1
WAN E11 70 D5
Stanmore St IS N1 85 F6
Stanmore Ter BECK BR3 182 D5
Stannard Ms HACK E8 * 86 C4
Stannard Rd HACK E8 86 C4
Stannary Pl LBTH SE11 122 B5
Stannary St LBTH SE11 122 B6
Stannet Wy WLGTN SM6 210 C2
Stansbury Sq NKENS W10 100 C2
Stansfeld Rd CAN/RD E16 107 H5
Stansfield Rd BRXN/ST SW9 142 A4
HSLWW TW4 134 A3
Stansgate Rd DAGE RM10 74 C6
Stanstead Cl HAYES BR2 199 J2
Stanstead Gv CAT SE6 164 C3
Stanstead Rd FSTH SE23 164 B3
WAN E11 71 F2
Stansted Cl HCH RM12 93 K4
Stansted Crs BXLY DA5 168 E3
Stansted Rd HTHAIR TW6 152 C1
Stanswood Gdns CMBW SE5 143 F1
Stanthorpe Cl
STRHM/NOR SW16 * 179 K1
Stanthorpe Rd
STRHM/NOR SW16 179 K1
Stanton Av TEDD TW11 173 K2
Stanton Cl HOR/WEW KT19 206 D3
STMC/STPC BR5 202 D4
WPK KT4 193 G5
Stanton Rd BARN SW13 138 C3
CROY/NA CR0 196 D4
RYNPK SW20 177 G5
Stanton St PECK SE15 * 143 H2
Stanton Wy SYD SE26 164 C6
Stanway Cl CHIG IG7 54 E1
Stanway Gdns ACT W3 117 H1
EDGW HA8 44 E2
Stanway St IS N1 7 H2
Stanwell Cl STWL/WRAY TW19 152 A1
Stanwell Gdns
STWL/WRAY TW19 152 A1
Stanwell Rd ASHF TW15 152 B6
EBED/NFELT TW14 153 F2
HTHAIR TW6 152 E2
Stanwick Rd WKENS W14 119 J4
Stanworth St STHWK SE1 19 J3
Stanwyck Gdns HARH RM3 57 K1
Stapenhill Rd ALP/SUD HA0 79 H1
Staple Cl BXLY DA5 170 A5
Staplefield Cl
BRXS/STRHM SW2 * 161 K3
PIN HA5 41 J3
Stapleford Av GNTH/NBYPK IG2 72 E2
Stapleford Cl CHING E4 38 A5
KUT/HW KT1 175 H5
WIM/MER SW19 159 H2
Stapleford Gdns CRW RM5 56 C2
Stapleford Rd ALP/SUD HA0 79 K5
Stapleford Wy BARK IG11 109 H2
Staplehurst Rd CAR SM5 209 J5
LEW SE13 145 G6
Staple Inn HHOL WC1V 11 J2
Staples Cl BERM/RHTH SE16 124 B1
Staple St STHWK SE1 19 F3
Stapleton Crs RAIN RM13 93 J5
Stapleton Gdns CROY/NA CR0 211 G3
Stapleton Hall Rd FSBYPK N4 67 G4
Stapleton Rd BXLYHN DA7 149 G1
ORP BR6 217 F1
TOOT SW17 161 F5
Stapleton Vls
STNW/STAM N16 * 86 A2
Stapley Rd BELV DA17 129 H5
Stapylton Rd BAR EN5 20 C4
Star & Garter Hl
RCHPK/HAM TW10 157 F3
Starboard Wy POP/IOD E14 124 D3
Starbuck Cl ELTH/MOT SE9 167 F2
Starch House La BARK/HLT IG6 54 D5
Star Cl PEND EN3 36 E1
Starcross St CAMTN NW1 4 B5
Starfield Rd SHB W12 118 D2
Star Hl DART DA1 150 B6
Star La CAN/RD E16 106 D3
STMC/STPC BR5 202 E1
Starling Cl BKHH IG9 38 E3
PIN HA5 41 G6
Starling Rd CROY/NA CR0 198 B3
Starmans Cl DAGW RM9 92 A6
Star Pl WAP E1W 13 K6
Star Rd HGDN/ICK UB10 94 A3
ISLW TW7 135 J3
WKENS W14 119 J6
Star St BAY/PAD W2 8 B3
Starts Cl ORP BR6 216 A1
Starts Hill Av ORP BR6 216 B3
Starts Hill Rd ORP BR6 216 B2
Starveall Cl WDR/YW UB7 112 C3
Star Yd LINN WC2A 11 J3
State Farm Av ORP BR6 216 B2
Staten Gdns TWK TW1 156 A3
Statham Gv STNW/STAM N16 85 K1
UED N18 50 A1
Station Ap ALP/SUD HA0 79 H4
BAR EN5 21 G5
BECK BR3 182 B4
BELMT SM2 208 C5
BKHH IG9 * 39 H6
BKHTH/KID SE3 146 A4
BXLYHN DA7 149 F3
BXLYHN DA7 149 K3
CAMTN NW1 * 3 G7
CHING E4 * 38 C2
CHING E4 * 52 B2
CHST BR7 184 D2
CHST BR7 185 F4
CROY/NA CR0 * 196 E6
DART DA1 171 H1
ESH/CLAY KT10 205 F1
FBAR/BDGN N11 48 B1
FSTGT E7 * 89 F2
FUL/PGN SW6 * 139 H4
GFD/PVL UB6 78 C5
GLDGN NW11 * 64 B4
HAYES BR2 199 K5
HOR/WEW KT19 207 H3
HPTN TW12 173 F4
HYS/HAR UB3 113 J3
KUT/HW KT1 175 H5
NFNCH/WDSPK N12 33 F6
NTHWD HA6 40 C3
ORP BR6 202 A6
ORP BR6 217 H3
OXHEY WD19 27 H5
PIN HA5 41 J6
RCH/KEW TW9 137 H2
RSLP HA4 58 C5
RSLP HA4 77 F3
SAND/SEL CR2 211 K6
STMC/STPC BR5 202 C1
STRHM/NOR SW16 179 J1
SURB KT6 190 E3
SWFD E18 * 53 F5
SYD SE26 182 C1
WALTH E17 69 J2
WAN E11 70 E2
WAN E11 * 88 C2
WDR/YW UB7 112 B1
WELL DA16 148 B4
WFD IG8 * 53 G2
WLSDN NW10 99 H2
Station Approach Rd
CHSWK W4 137 K1
Station Ar GTPST W1W * 3 K7
Station Av HOR/WEW KT19 207 G6
NWMAL KT3 176 B6
RCH/KEW TW9 137 H2
Station Buildings HAYES BR2 * 199 K5
Station Chambers EA W5 * 98 C3
Station Cl HPTN TW12 173 G4
Station Cottages WDGN N22 * 48 E5
Station Crs ALP/SUD HA0 79 H4
ASHF TW15 152 B6
BKHTH/KID SE3 125 K5
SEVS/STOTM N15 67 K1
Stationers Hall Ct STP EC4M * 12 B4
Station Est BECK BR3 198 A1
Station Estate Rd
EBED/NFELT TW14 154 A3
Station Garage Ms
STRHM/NOR SW16 * 179 J2
Station Gdns CHSWK W4 137 K1
Station Gv ALP/SUD HA0 80 A4
Station Hl HAYES BR2 199 K6
Station House Ms ED N9 36 C6
Station Pde ACT W3 * 98 C5
BAL SW12 * 161 F3
BARK IG11 90 C5
BECK BR3 * 198 A1
BELMT SM2 * 209 G4
BMLY BR1 * 183 K4
BXLYHN DA7 * 149 F3
CHSWK W4 * 117 K4
CHSWK W4 * 137 K1
CLPT E5 * 86 D1
CRICK NW2 82 A4
EA W5 * 117 G1
EBAR EN4 * 22 A5
EBED/NFELT TW14 * 154 A2
EDGW HA8 * 44 A3
EHAM E6 * 89 J5
HCH RM12 93 K2
KTN/HRWW/WS HA3 * 43 H5
NTHLT UB5 * 78 A5
NTHLT UB5 * 78 B3
PLSTW E13 * 89 G6
RCH/KEW TW9 137 H2
ROM RM1 75 G3
RSLP HA4 * 58 A6
RYLN/HDSTN HA2 * 78 B2
STHGT/OAK N14 34 D3
Station Pas PECK SE15 143 K2
SWFD E18 53 F5
Station Pl FSBYPK N4 67 G6
Station Ri WNWD SE27 162 C4
Station Rd ASHF TW15 152 C6
BAR EN5 21 F6
BARK/HLT IG6 54 D6
BARN SW13 138 C3
BCTR RM8 73 K5
BELV DA17 129 H3
BMLY BR1 183 K4

BXLYHN DA7 ....149 F4
CAR SM5 ....209 K2
CHDH RM6 ....73 K4
CHING E4 ....38 B3
CHSGTN KT9 ....206 A3
CROY/NA CR0 ....196 C5
DART DA1 ....170 C1
EA W5 ....98 B5
EDGW HA8 ....44 C2
ESH/CLAY KT10 ....189 J6
ESH/CLAY KT10 ....204 D3
FBAR/BDGN N11 ....48 B1
FNCH N5 ....46 E4
GPK RM2 ....75 K1
HAYES BR2 ....183 H5
HDN NW4 ....63 J3
HNWL W7 ....115 K1
HOLWY N7 ....84 C1
HPTN TW12 ....173 G4
HRW HA1 ....60 B2
HRW HA1 ....61 F1
HSLW TW3 ....135 G5
HYS/HAR UB3 ....123 H1
IL IG1 ....72 B6
IL IG1 ....90 B1
KUT/HW KT1 ....174 E4
KUTN/CMB KT2 ....175 H4
LEW SE13 ....145 F4
MLHL NW7 ....84 C1
MNPK E12 ....89 H2
NWMAL KT3 ....192 E2
ORP BR6 ....202 A6
PGE/AN SE20 ....181 K2
RYLN/HDSTN HA2 ....60 B2
SCUP DA14 ....168 B5
SNWD SE25 ....197 C1
STMC/STPC BR5 ....202 D1
TEDD TW11 ....174 B2
THDIT KT7 ....190 A4
TOTM N17 ....50 D2
TWK TW1 ....156 A3
WALTH E17 ....69 G3
WCHMH N21 ....35 H3
WDGN N22 ....48 E5
WDGN N22 ....49 F5
WIM/MER SW19 ....178 B4
WLSDN NW10 ....99 H1
WWKM BR4 ....199 F6
Station Rd North BELV DA17...129 J3
Station Sq STMC/STPC BR5 ....201 H2
Station St SRTFD E15...........88 C5
Station Ter CMBW SE5..........142 D2
WLSDN NW10 ....100 B1
Station Vw GFD/PVL UB6.........78 D6
Station Wy KBLRH IG9..........39 H6
CHEAM SM3 ....208 C4
ESH/CLAY KT10 ....204 E4
Station Yd ASHF TW15 * 152 C6
RSLP HA4 ....58 B6
STHL UB1 * 114 E2
TWK TW1 ....156 B2
Staunton Rd KUTN/CMB KT2....175 G3
Staunton St DEPT SE8..........124 C6
Staveley Cl HOLWY N7 * 84 E2
PECK SE15...............143 K2
Staveley Gdns CHSWK W4.......138 A2
Staveley Rd CHSWK W4..........117 K6
Stave Hill CRICK NW2..........82 A5
Stave Yard Rd
BERM/RHTH SE16..........124 B1
Stavordale Rd CAR SM5........194 B4
HBRY N5 ....85 H2
Stayner's Rd WCHPL E1........105 F3
Stayton Rd SUT SM1...........208 E1
Steadfast Rd KUT/HW KT1......174 E4
Stead St WALW SE17 ....18 C7
Steam Farm La
EBED/NFELT TW14.........133 J5
Stean St HACK E8.............86 B6
Stebbing Wy BARK IG11........109 G1
Stebondale St POP/IOD E14....124 E5
Stedly SCUP DA14 * 168 B6
Stedman Cl BXLY DA5..........170 B5
Steed Cl EMPK RM11............75 K6
Steedman St WALW SE17.........18 C7
Steel Ap BARK IG11...........109 H1
Steele Rd CHSWK W4...........117 K3
ISLW TW7 ....136 B5
TOTM N17 ....50 A6
WAN E11 ....88 E1
WLSDN NW10 ....98 E1
Steele's Ms North HAMP NW3 *..83 K4
Steele's Ms South HAMP NW3...83 K4
Steele's Rd HAMP NW3 * 83 K4
Steeles Studios HAMP NW3 *...104 C5
Steel's La WCHPL E1..........104 E5
Steep Cl ORP BR6 ....217 G4
Steep Hl CROY/NA CR0 ....212 A2
STRHM/NOR SW16 ....161 J5
Steeplands BUSH WD23.........28 B2
Steeple Cl FUL/PGN SW6.......139 H4
WIM/MER SW19 ....177 H1
Steeplestone Cl UED N18......49 J1
Steeple Wk IS N1 * 6 E2
Steerforth St
WAND/EARL SW18..........160 A4
Steering Cl ED N9 ....36 E3
Steers Md MTCM CR4...........178 E4
Steers Wy BERM/RHTH SE16....124 B2
Stella Rd TOOT SW17..........178 E2
Stelling Rd ERITH DA8........150 A1
Stellman Cl CLPT E5..........86 C1
Stembridge Rd PGE/AN SE20...181 J5
Stephan Cl HACK E8...........86 C6
Stephen Av RAIN RM13.........93 J4
Stephen Cl ORP BR6 ....217 F1
Stephendale Rd
FUL/PGN SW6.............140 A4
Stephen Ms FITZ W1T..........10 C2
Stephen Rd BXLYHN DA7........149 K4
Stephenson Rd WALTH E17......148 A3
Stephenson Rd HNWL W7........97 F5
WALTH E17 ....69 G2

WHTN TW2 ....155 F2
Stephenson St CAN/RD E16....106 C4
WLSDN NW10 ....99 G2
Stephenson Wy CAMTN NW1....4 B6
Stephen's Rd SRTFD E15.......88 C6
Stephen St FITZ W1T * 10 C5
Stepney Csw WCHPL E1.........105 F5
Stepney Gn WCHPL E1..........104 E4
Stepney High St WCHPL E1....105 F4
Stepney Wy MTCM CR4.........179 F4
WCHPL E1 ....104 E4
Sterling Av WLSDN NW10.......80 B6
Sterling Cl WLSDN NW10........81 J5
Sterling Gdns NWCR SE14.....124 B6
Sterling Pl EA W5............117 F4
Sterling Rd ENC/FH EN2.......23 K2
Sterling Wy (North Circular)
UED N18 ....49 K1
Stern Cl BARK IG11..........109 J1
Sterndale Rd DART DA1.......171 J2
WKENS W14 * 119 C3
Sterne St SHB W12...........119 G2
Sternhall La PECK SE15......143 H4
Sternhold Av
BRXS/STRHM SW2..........161 K4
Sterry Crs DAGE RM10.........92 C3
Sterry Dr HOR/WEW KT19.....207 G3
THDIT KT7 ....189 K3
Sterry Gdns DAGE RM10........92 C4
Sterry Rd BARK IG11..........91 F6
DAGE RM10 ....92 C2
Sterry St STHWK SE1 ....18 E3
Steucers La FSTH SE23.......164 B3
Steve Biko La CAT SE6.......164 B6
Steve Biko Rd HOLWY N7 ......85 G1
Steve Biko Wy HSLW TW3......135 F4
Stevedale Rd WELL DA16......148 D3
Stevedore St WAP E1W........123 J1
Stevenage Rd EHAM E6 ....90 A6
FUL/PGN SW6.............139 G2
Stevens Av HOM E9............86 E4
Stevens Cl BECK BR3.........182 D2
BXLY DA5 ....170 A6
HPTN TW12 ....172 E2
PIN HA5.................59 G2
Stevens Gn BUSH WD23.........28 B3
Stevens' La ESH/CLAY KT10...205 G5
Stevenson Cl BAR EN5.........33 H1
ERITH DA8...............150 E1
Stevenson Crs
BERM/RHTH SE16..........123 H5
Stevens Rd DAGE RM10.........73 H6
Stevens St STHWK SE1 * 19 H4
Steventon Rd SHB W12........118 D1
Stewart Cl CDALE/KGS NW9 *...62 E3
CHST BR7 ....185 G1
HPTN TW12 ....172 D2
Stewart Rd SRTFD E15.........88 B2
Stewartsby Cl UED N18........49 J1
Stewart's Gv CHEL SW3.......120 C5
Stewart's La VX/NE SW8......141 G1
Stewart St POP/IOD E14......125 F2
Stewart's La BLKFR EC4V......12 C5
Steyne Rd ACT W3............117 K1
Steyning Wy ELTH/MOT SE9....166 E6
Steynings Wy
NFNCH/WDSPK N12.........46 E1
Steyning Wy HSLWW TW4......134 B5
Steynton Av BXLY DA5........168 E4
Stickland Rd BELV DA17......129 H4
Stickleton Cl GFD/PVL UB6....96 B2
Stilecroft Gdns ALP/SUD HA0..79 H1
Stile Hall Gdns CHSWK W4....117 H5
Stiles Cl ERITH DA8..........130 E5
BMLY BR1 ....200 E3
Stillingfleet Rd BARN SW13...138 D1
Stillington St WEST SW1P.....16 B6
Stillness Rd FSTH SE23......164 B1
Stipularis Dr YEAD UB4.......95 H3
Stirling Av PIN HA5..........59 J4
WLGTN SM6 ....210 E5
Stirling Cl RAIN RM13.......111 K2
SCUP DA14 ....167 K6
STRHM/NOR SW16..........179 H2
Stirling Dr ORP BR6.........217 H3
Stirling Gv HSLW TW3........135 H3
Stirling Rd ACT W3..........117 J5
BRXN/ST SW9 ....141 K4
HYS/HAR UB3 ....94 E6
KTN/HRWW/WS HA3 ....42 E6
PLSTW E13 ....107 F1
TOTM N17 ....50 C4
WALTH E17 ....51 C6
WDGN N22 ....49 H4
WHTN TW2 ....155 F2
Stirling Wy BRYLDS KT5......191 J3
Stirling Wy BORE WD6.........31 F1
CROY/NA CR0 ....195 K4
Stiven Crs RYLN/HDSTN HA2...77 K1
St John's Est IS N1 ....7 F3
STHWK SE1 ....19 K1
St Martin-in-the-fields
CHCR WC2N * 10 C6
Stockbury Rd CROY/NA CR0....197 K3
Stockdale Rd BCTR RM8........74 B6
Stockdove Wy GFD/PVL UB6.....97 F2
Stocker Gdns DAGW RM9........91 J5
Stockfield Rd ESH/CLAY KT10..204 E3
STRHM/NOR SW16..........162 A5
Stockford Av MLHL NW7........46 C3
Stockholm Rd
BERM/RHTH SE16..........123 K5
Stockholm Wy WAP E1W........123 H1
Stockhurst Cl PUT/ROE SW15..139 F3
Stockingswater La PEND EN3...25 G3
Stockland Rd ROMW/RG RM7....75 F3
Stock La RDART DA2..........171 H6
Stockley Cl WDR/YW UB7......112 E2
Stockley Farm Rd
WDR/YW UB7.............112 E3
Stock Orchard Crs HOLWY N7...85 F3
Stock Orchard St HOLWY N7....85 F3
Stockport Rd
STRHM/NOR SW16.........179 J4

Stocksfield Rd WALTH E17 *...52 A6
Stocks Pl POP/IOD E14.......105 H6
Stock St PLSTW E13..........106 C1
Stockton Cl BAR EN5..........21 G5
Stockton Gdns MLHL NW7.......31 F5
UED N18 ....50 C2
Stockton Rd TOTM N17.........49 J5
UED N18 ....50 C2
Stockwell Av BRXN/ST SW9....142 A4
Stockwell Cl BMLY BR1.......184 A5
Stockwell Gdns BRXN/ST SW9..142 A3
Stockwell La BRXN/ST SW9....142 A3
Stockwell Park Crs
BRXN/ST SW9.............142 A3
Stockwell Park Rd
BRXN/ST SW9.............142 A3
Stockwell Park Wk
BRXN/ST SW9.............142 A4
Stockwell Rd BRXN/ST SW9....142 A3
Stockwell St GNWCH SE10.....125 F6
Stockwell Ter BRXN/ST SW9...142 A3
Stodart Rd PGE/AN SE20......181 K4
Stofield Gdns ELTH/MOT SE9..166 C5
Stofford Cl WIM/MER SW19....159 H5
Stoke Av BARK/HLT IG6........55 C2
Stokenchurch St
FUL/PGN SW6.............140 A2
Stoke Newington Church St
STNW/STAM N16............85 K1
Stoke Newington Common
STNW/STAM N16............86 B1
Stoke Newington High St
STNW/STAM N16............86 B1
Stoke Newington Rd
STNW/STAM N16............86 B3
Stoke Pl WLSDN NW10.........99 H2
Stoke Rd KUTN/CMB KT2......175 K3
Stokesby Rd CHSGTN KT9.....206 B4
Stokesley St SHB W12........99 H5
Stokes Rd CROY/NA CR0......198 A3
Stoll Cl CRICK NW2...........82 A1
Stonard Rd BCTR RM8..........91 H3
PLMGR N13 ....35 G5
Stonards Hl LOU IG10.........39 K1
Stondon Pk FSTH SE23.......164 B1
Stonebridge Pk WLSDN NW10...81 F5
Stonebridge Rd
SEVS/STOTM N15..........68 B2
Stonebridge Wy WBLY HA9......80 D4
Stone Buildings LINN WC2A....11 H2
Stonechat Sq EHAM E6........107 J4
Stone Cl BCTR RM8............74 A5
CLAP SW4 ....141 H3
WDR/YW UB7.............112 C1
Stonecot Cl CHEAM SM3......193 H5
Stonecot Hl CHEAM SM3......193 H6
Stone Crs EBED/NFELT TW14...153 J2
Stonecroft Rd ERITH DA8.....150 A1
Stonecroft Wy CROY/NA CR0...195 K4
Stonecrop Cl CDALE/KGS NW9..45 F6
Stonecutter St
FLST/FETLN EC4A...........12 A3
Stonecroft Cl BXLYHN DA7....149 H4
RSLP HA4 ....58 A6
Stonefield Cl BXLYHN DA7....149 H4
RSLP HA4 ....58 A6
Stonefield St IS N1 ....85 G6
Stonefield Wy CHARL SE7.....146 C1
Stonegate Cl STMC/STPC BR5..186 D6
Stone Gv EDGW HA8............30 A6
Stonegrove Gdns EDGW HA8....44 A1
Stonehall Av IL IG1..........71 J3
Stone Hall Gdns KENS W8 *...120 A3
Stone Hall Rd WCHMH N21......35 F2
Stoneham Rd FBAR/BDGN N11...48 C1
Stonehill Cl MORT/ESHN SW14.138 A6
Stonehill Rd CHSWK W4.......117 H5
MORT/ESHN SW14.........137 K6
Stonehills Ct DUL SE21......163 F5
Stonehills Wds Pk
SCUP DA14 * 187 J2
Stonehorse Rd PEND EN3.......24 E6
Stone House Ct LVPST EC2M....13 H1
Stonehouse La RSEV TN14.....217 K6
Stonehouse Rd RSEV TN14.....217 K6
Stoneleigh Av EN EN1.........24 D1
WPK KT4 ....207 J1
Stoneleigh Broadway
EW KT17 ....207 J3
Stoneleigh Crs
HOR/WEW KT19...........207 J3
Stoneleigh Park Av
CROY/NA CR0 ....198 A3
Stoneleigh Park Rd
HOR/WEW KT19...........207 J3
Stoneleigh Pl NTGHL W11....100 B6
Stoneleigh Rd BMLY BR1......185 G6
CAR SM5 ....194 D4
CLAY IG5 ....53 K6
TOTM N17 ....50 B5
Stoneleigh St NTGHL W11....100 B6
Stoneleigh Ter ARCH N19......66 B6
Stonell's Rd TOOT SW17......160 E5
Stonemasons Cl
SEVS/STOTM N15..........67 K1
Stonenest St FSBYPK N4.......67 F5
Stone Park Av BECK BR3......198 E1
Stone Pl WPK KT4............192 D6
Stone Rd HAYES BR2..........199 J3
Stones Cross Rd SWLY BR8....203 K2
Stones End St STHWK SE1......18 C3
Stonewall EHAM E6...........108 A4
Stonewood Rd ERITH DA8......130 B5
Stoney Aly WOOL/PLUM SE18..147 F2
Stoneyard La POP/IOD E14....105 K6
Stoneycroft Cl LEE/GVPK SE12.165 J2
Stoneycroft Rd WFD IG8.......53 J2
Stoneydown WALTH E17.........69 G1
Stoneydown Av WALTH E17......69 G1
Stoneyfields Gdns EDGW HA8...30 E4
Stoneyfields La EDGW HA8.....44 E1
Stoney La HDTCH EC3A.........13 H3
Stoney St STHWK SE1 ....12 E7
Stonhouse St CLAP SW4.......141 J4

Stonnell's Rd BTSEA SW11....140 E6
Stonor Rd WKENS W14........119 J4
Stonycroft Cl PEND EN3.......25 C3
Stopes St PECK SE15.........143 G1
Stopford Rd PLSTW E13........88 E6
WALW SE17 ....122 C5
Store Rd CAN/RD E16.........127 F2
Storers Quay POP/IOD E14....125 G4
Store St GWRST WC1E..........10 C2
SRTFD E15 ....88 B3
Storey Rd HGT N6.............65 K5
WALTH E17 ....51 G3
Storey's Ga STJSPK SW1H......16 D3
Stories Ms CMBW SE5..........143 F3
Stories Rd CMBW SE5.........143 F4
Stork Rd FSTGT E7............88 D4
Storksmead Rd EDGW HA8.......45 C3
Storks Rd BERM/RHTH SE16 *..123 H3
Stormont Rd BTSEA SW11......141 F5
HGT N6 ....65 K5
Stormont Wy CHSGTN KT9.....205 J3
Stornoway Rd CROY/NA CR0....197 C6
Storrington Rd
CROY/NA CR0 ....197 G5
Story St IS N1...............85 F5
Stothard St WCHPL E1 ....104 E3
Stott Cl WAND/EARL SW18.....160 C1
Stoughton Av CHEAM SM3.....208 B3
Stoughton Cl LBTH SE11.......17 H7
PUT/ROE SW15 ....158 D3
Stour Av NWDGN UB2..........115 F3
Stourcliffe St MBLAR W1H......8 E4
Stour Cl HAYES BR2..........215 C2
Stourhead Cl WIM/MER SW19...159 C2
Stourhead Gdns RYNPK SW20...176 D6
Stour Rd BOW E3..............87 J7
DAGE RM10 ....74 C6
DART DA1 ....150 D4
Stourton Av FELT TW13......154 E6
Stowage DEPT SE8............124 E6
The Stowage DEPT SE8........124 D6
Stowe Crs RSLP HA4..........58 A3
Stowe Gdns ED N9.............36 B3
Stow Rd SEVS/STOTM N15.......50 A6
Stowe Rd ORP BR6...........217 H2
SHB W12 ....118 E2
Stowting Rd ORP BR6.........216 E2
Stox Md KTN/HRWW/WS HA3......42 E4
Stracey Rd WLSDN NW10........81 F6
Strachan Pl RYNPK SW20......177 F2
Stradbroke Dr CHIG IG7.......54 B2
Stradbroke Gv BKHH IG9.......39 H5
Stradbroke Pk CHIG IG7.......54 B2
Stradbroke Rd HBRY N5........85 J2
Stradbrook Cl
RYLN/HDSTN HA2..........77 K1
Stradella Rd HNHL SE24......162 D1
Strafford Av CLAY IG5........54 A5
Strafford Rd ACT W3.........117 K1
BAR EN5 ....20 C4
HSLW TW3 ....134 E4
TWK TW1 ....156 B2
Strafford St POP/IOD E14....124 D2
Strahan Rd BOW E3...........105 C2
Straight Rd HARH RM3.........57 J4
Straightsmouth GNWCH SE10...145 F1
The Straight NWDGN UB2......114 C2
Strait Rd EHAM E6...........107 K6
Straker's Rd EDUL SE22......143 J5
Strand CHCR WC2N.............11 F6
Strand Dr RCH/KEW TW9......137 J1
Strandfield Cl
WOOL/PLUM SE18..........127 K5
Strand-on-the-Green
CHSWK W4...............117 H6
Strand Pl UED N18............49 K3
Strangways Ter WKENS W14...119 J3
Stranraer Wy IS N1 ....84 E5
Strasburg Rd BTSEA SW11.....141 G1
Stratfield Park Cl WCHMH N21.35 H2
Stratfield Rd BARK IG11.......91 C5
Stratford Ct NWMAL KT3......192 A1
Stratford Gv PUT/ROE SW15...139 C5
Stratford House Av BMLY BR1.184 D6
Stratford Pl OXSTW W1C........9 J4
Stratford Rd HTHAIR TW6.....152 E1
KENS W8 ....119 K3
NWDGN UB2 ....114 D4
PLSTW E13 ....88 E6
THHTH CR7 ....196 B1
YEAD UB4 ....95 F3
Stratford Studios KENS W8...119 K3
Stratford Vs CAMTN NW1.......84 C5
Strathan Cl WAND/EARL SW18..159 G1
Strathaven Rd
LEE/GVPK SE12..........166 A1
Strathbrook Rd
STRHM/NOR SW16.........162 A6
Strathcona Rd WBLY HA9.......61 K6
Strathdale STRHM/NOR SW16...180 A1
Strathdon Dr TOOT SW17......160 C5
Stratheam Av HYS/HAR UB3...133 J1
WHTN TW2 ....155 H3
Stratheam Cottages
TRDG/WHET N20 * 32 E5
Stratheam Pl BAY/PAD W2......8 C5
WIM/MER Rd SUT SM1......208 E3
Stratheam Rd BKHTH/KID SE3.145 K2
WIM/MER SW19 ....177 K4
Strathleven Rd
BRXS/STRHM SW2.........141 K6
Strathmore Gdns EDGW HA8....44 D5
FNCH N3 ....47 F4
KENS W8 ....119 K1
Strathmore Rd CROY/NA CR0...196 D4
TEDD TW11 ....155 K6
WIM/MER SW19 ....159 K5
Strathnairn St STHWK SE1 *..123 H4
Strathray Gdns HAMP NW3 *....83 J4
Strathville Rd
WAND/EARL SW18.........159 K4

Strathyre Av
STRHM/NOR SW16.........180 B6
Stratton Av WLGTN SM6......210 D6
Stratton Cl BXLYHN DA7......149 F4
EDGW HA8 ....44 B2
HSLW TW3 ....134 E2
WIM/MER SW19 ....177 J6
WOT/HER KT12 * 188 B5
Stratton Ct PIN HA5.........59 K1
Strattondale St POP/IOD E14.125 F3
Stratton Dr BARK IG11........90 E4
Stratton Gdns STHL UB1.......95 K5
Stratton Rd BXLYHN DA7......149 F4
WIM/MER SW19 ....177 K5
Stratton St MYFR/PICC W1J....9 K7
Strauss Rd CHSWK W4.........118 A2
Strawberry Flds ORP BR6.....216 C5
Strawberry Hill Cl TWK TW1.156 A5
Strawberry La CAR SM5......209 K1
Strawberry Ter MUSWH N10 *..47 K4
Strawberry V EFNCH N2........47 H3
TWK TW1 ....156 A5
Streakes Field Rd CRICK NW2..63 J4
Streamdale ABYW SE2.........128 C6
Stream La EDGW HA8...........44 D2
Streamline Ms EDUL SE22.....163 H1
Streamside Cl ED N9..........36 B5
HAYES BR2 ....199 K2
Stream Wy BELV DA17........129 H6
Streatfeild Av EHAM E6.......89 K6
Streatfield Rd
KTN/HRWW/WS HA3.........43 J6
Streatham Common
STRHM/NOR SW16 * 179 J3
Streatham Common North
STRHM/NOR SW16.........180 A1
Streatham Common South
STRHM/NOR SW16.........180 A2
Streatham Ct
STRHM/NOR SW16.........161 K5
Streatham Gn
STRHM/NOR SW16 * 161 K6
Streatham High Rd
STRHM/NOR SW16.........161 K6
Streatham Hl
BRXS/STRHM SW2.........161 K3
Streatham Pl
BRXS/STRHM SW2.........161 K3
Streatham Rd MTCM CR4......179 G3
Streatham St NOXST/BSQ WC1A.10 E3
Streatham Vale
STRHM/NOR SW16.........179 H3
Streathbourne Rd TOOT SW17.161 F4
Streatley Pde
STRHM/NOR SW16 * 161 K4
Streatley Pl HAMP NW3.......83 H2
Streatley Rd KIL/WHAMP NW6..82 D5
Streeters La WLGTN SM6.....210 D1
Streetfield Ms BKHTH/KID SE3.145 K3
Streimer Rd SRTFD E15......106 A1
Strelley Wy ACT W3...........99 G6
Stretton Rd CROY/NA CR0....197 F4
RCHPK/HAM TW10.........156 D4
Strickland Av DART DA1......151 J5
Strickland Rw
WAND/EARL SW18.........160 C2
Strickland St DEPT SE8......144 D3
Stride Rd PLSTW E13.........106 D1
Strimon Cl ED N9............36 E4
Stripling Wy WATW WD18......26 E1
Strode Cl MUSWH N10.........48 A3
Strode Rd FSTGT E7..........88 E2
FUL/PGN SW6 ....139 G1
TOTM N17 ....50 A5
WLSDN NW10 ....81 K4
Strone Rd FSTGT E7..........89 G4
Strone Wy YEAD UB4..........95 J3
Strongbow Crs ELTH/MOT SE9.146 E6
Strongbow Rd ELTH/MOT SE9..146 E6
Strongbridge Cl
RYLN/HDSTN HA2..........60 A5
Stronsa Rd SHB W12.........118 C3
Strood Av ROMW/RG RM7......75 F5
Stroud Crs PUT/ROE SW15....158 D4
Stroudes Cl WPK KT4.........192 C4
Stroud Fld NTHLT UB5........77 J5
Stroud Ga RYLN/HDSTN HA2...78 B2
Stroud Green Rd FSBYPK N4...67 G5
Stroud Green Wy
CROY/NA CR0 ....197 K3
Stroud Rd SNWD SE25........197 H3
WIM/MER SW19 ....159 K5
Strouds Cl BCTR RM8 * 73 H6
Stroud's Pl BETH E2 ....13 J2
Strutton Gnd STJSPK SW1H....16 C4
Strype St WCHPL E1...........13 K2
Stuart Av CDALE/KGS NW9.....63 J4
EA W5 ....117 G2
HAYES BR2 ....199 K5
RYLN/HDSTN HA2 ....77 J1
WOT/HER KT12 ....188 A5
Stuart Crs CROY/NA CR0.....213 H1
HYS/HAR UB3 ....94 A5
WDGN N22 ....48 E4
Stuart Evans Cl WELL DA16..148 D4
Stuart Gv TEDD TW11........173 K1
Stuart Mantle Wy ERITH DA8..150 A1
Stuart Rd ACT W3............99 F5
BARK IG11 ....91 G5
EBAR EN4 ....33 J2
KIL/WHAMP NW6..........100 E2
KTN/HRWW/WS HA3 ....43 F6
PECK SE15 ....143 K5
RCHPK/HAM TW10.........156 C4
THHTH CR7 ....196 D1
WELL DA16 ....148 C2
WIM/MER SW19 ....159 K5
Stubbs Cl CDALE/KGS NW9.....62 E2

Stubbs Dr *BERM/RHTH* SE16...123 J5
Stubbs Wy *WIM/MER* SW19...178 C4
Stucley Pl *CAMTN* NW1...84 B5
Stucley Rd *HEST* TW5...135 H1
Studdridge St *FUL/PGN* SW6...139 K3
Studd St *IS* N1...6 A1
Studholme Ct *HAMP* NW3 *...82 E2
Studholme St *PECK* SE15...143 J1
Studio Ms *HDN* NW4...64 A1
Studio Pl *KTBR* SW1X...15 F3
The Studios *BUSH* WD23...28 A1
Studland Cl *BFN/LL* DA15...168 A5
Studland Rd *HNWL* W7...96 D5
  KUTN/CMB KT2...175 F2
  SYD SE26...182 A1
Studland St *HMSMTH* W6...118 E4
Studley Av *CHING* E4...52 B5
Studley Cl *CLPT* E5...87 H1
Studley Ct *SCUP* DA14...186 C1
Studley Dr *REDBR* IG4...71 H3
Studley Grange Rd *HNWL* W7...115 K3
Studley Rd *CLAP* SW4...141 K2
  DAGW RM9...91 K6
  FSTGT E7...89 F4
Stukeley Rd *FSTGT* E7...89 F5
Stukeley St *HOL/ALD* WC2B...11 F3
Stumps Hill La *BECK* BR3...182 D2
Sturdy Rd *PECK* SE15...143 J5
Sturge Av *WALTH* E17...52 A4
Sturgeon Rd *WALW* SE17...122 D5
Sturges Fld *CHST* BR7...185 J3
Sturgess Av *HDN* NW4...63 K4
Sturge St *STHWK* SE1...18 C3
Sturmer Wy *HOLWY* N7...85 F3
Sturminster Cl *YEAD* UB4...95 H5
Sturrock Cl *SEVS/STOTM* N15...67 K1
Sturry St *POP/IOD* E14...105 K5
Sturt St *IS* N1...6 D3
Stutfield St *WCHPL* E1...104 C5
Styles Gdns *BRXN/ST* SW9...142 C4
Styles Wy *BECK* BR3...199 F1
Sudbourne Rd
  BRXS/STRHM SW2...141 K6
Sudbrooke Rd *BAL* SW12...160 E1
Sudbrook Gdns
  RCHPK/HAM TW10...157 F5
Sudbrook La
  RCHPK/HAM TW10...157 F3
Sudbury Av *ALP/SUD* HA0...79 J1
  WBLY HA9...79 K1
Sudbury Court Dr *HRW* HA1...79 G1
Sudbury Court Rd *HRW* HA1...79 G1
Sudbury Crs *ALP/SUD* HA0...79 F1
  BMLY BR1...183 K1
Sudbury Cft *ALP/SUD* HA0...79 F1
Sudbury Gdns *CROY/NA* CRO...212 A2
Sudbury Heights Av
  GFD/PVL UB6...79 G3
Sudbury HI *HRW* HA1...78 E1
Sudbury Hill Cl *ALP/SUD* HA0...79 F2
Sudbury Rd *BARK* IG11...91 F3
Sudeley St *IS* N1...6 B2
Sudlow Rd *WAND/EARL* SW18...139 K5
Suez Av *GFD/PVL* UB6...97 F1
Suez Rd *PEND* EN3...25 G5
Suffield Rd *CHING* E4...37 K6
  PGE/AN SE20...181 K5
  SEVS/STOTM N15 *...68 B2
Suffolk La *CANST* EC4R...12 E6
Suffolk Park Rd *WALTH* E17...69 G1
Suffolk Rd *BARK* IG11...90 D5
  DAGE RM10...92 D3
  DART DA1...171 H1
  GDMY/SEVK IG3...73 G2
  PEND EN3...24 D6
  PLSTW E13...106 D2
  RYLN/HDSTN HA2...59 K3
  SCUP DA14...186 D2
  SEVS/STOTM N15...67 K3
  SNWD SE25...197 H1
  WLSDN NW10...81 G5
  WPK KT4...192 C6
Suffolk St *FSTGT* E7...88 E3
  STJS SW1Y...10 D7
Suffolk Vlls
  WAND/EARL SW18 *...159 K2
Sugar House La *SRTFD* E15...106 A1
Sugar Loaf Wk *BETH* E2 *...104 E2
Sugden Rd *BTSEA* SW11...141 F4
  THDIT KT7...190 B5
Sugden Wy *BARK* IG11...109 G1
Sulgrave Gdns *HMSMTH* W6...119 F2
Sulgrave Rd *HMSMTH* W6...119 F2
Sulina Rd *BRXS/STRHM* SW2...161 K2
Sulivan Ct *FUL/PGN* SW6...139 K3
Sulivan Rd *FUL/PGN* SW6...139 K4
Sulivan Av *CAN/RD* E16...107 H4
Sullivan Cl *BTSEA* SW11...140 D4
  DART DA1...170 E1
  E/WMO/HCT KT8...173 F6
  YEAD UB4...95 G4
Sullivan Rd *LBTH* SE11...17 K6
Sullivan Wy *BORE* WD6...29 J1
Sultan Rd *WAN* E11...53 F4
Sultan St *BECK* BR3...182 A5
  CMBW SE5...18 C7
Sumatra Rd *KIL/WHAMP* NW6...82 E4
Sumburgh Rd *BAL* SW12...161 F1
Summer Av *E/WMO/HCT* KT8...189 K2
Summercourt Rd *WCHPL* E1...104 E5
Summer Crossing *THDIT* KT7...190 A2
Summerene Cl
  STRHM/NOR SW16...179 H3
Summerfield Av
  KIL/WHAMP NW6...100 C1
  NFNCH/WDSPK N12 *...47 J2
Summerfield La *SURB* KT6...190 E6
Summerfield Rd *EA* W5...97 H3
  LOU IG10...39 H1
Summerfield St
  LEE/GVPK SE12...165 J2
Summer Gdns
  E/WMO/HCT KT8...189 K2
Summer Gv *BORE* WD6...29 K1
Summer HI *CHST* BR7...185 F5
Summerhill Cl *ORP* BR6...216 E2
Summerhill Gv *EN* EN1...36 A1
Summerhill Rd *DART* DA1...171 G2
  SEVS/STOTM N15...67 K1
Summerhill Wy *MTCM* CR4...179 F4
Summerhouse Av *HEST* TW5...134 D2
Summerhouse La
  WDR/YW UB7...112 A6
Summerhouse Rd
  STNW/STAM N16...68 A6
Summerland Gdns
  MUSWH N10...48 B6
Summerlands Av *ACT* W3...98 E6
Summerlee Av *EFNCH* N2...65 K1
Summerlee Gdns *EFNCH* N2...65 K1
Summerley St
  WAND/EARL SW18...160 A4
Summer HI *WATW* WD18 *...26 D1
Summer Rd *E/WMO/HCT* KT8...189 G2
  THDIT KT7...190 A2
Summersby Rd *HGT* N6...66 B3
Summers Cl *BELMT* SM2...208 D6
  WBLY HA9...62 D5
Summerskille Cl *ED* N9...36 D4
Summers La
  NFNCH/WDSPK N12...47 H3
Summers Rw
  NFNCH/WDSPK N12...47 J2
Summers St *CLKNW* EC1R...5 J7
Summerstown *TOOT* SW17...160 B5
Summerton Wy *THMD* SE28...109 K6
Summer Trees *SUN* TW16...172 A4
Summerville Gdns *SUT* SM1...208 D4
Summerwood Rd *ISLW* TW7...156 A1
Summit Av *CDALE/KGS* NW9...63 F2
Summit Cl *CDALE/KGS* NW9...63 F2
  EDGW HA8...44 C3
  STHGT/OAK N14...34 C3
Summit Dr *WFD* IG8...53 H5
Summit Est *STNW/STAM* N16 *...68 C4
Summit Rd *NTHLT* UB5...78 A5
  WALTH E17...69 K1
Summit Wy *NRWD* SE19...181 F3
  STHGT/OAK N14...34 B4
Sumner Av *PECK* SE15...143 G2
Sumner Cl *ORP* BR6...216 C2
Sumner Gdns *CROY/NA* CRO...196 C5
Sumner Pl *CHEL* SW3...14 B7
  SKENS SW7 *...14 B7
Sumner Place Ms *SKENS* SW7 *...14 B7
Sumner Rd *CROY/NA* CRO...196 C5
  HRW HA1...60 C4
  PECK SE15...143 G1
Sumner Rd South
  CROY/NA CRO...196 B5
Sumner St *STHWK* SE1...12 C7
Sumpter Cl *HAMP* NW3...83 G4
Sunbeam Crs *NKENS* W10...100 A3
Sunbeam Rd *WLSDN* NW10...99 F3
Sunbury Av *MLHL* NW7...45 F1
  MORT/ESHN SW14...138 A5
Sunbury Ct *BAR* EN5 *...20 C5
  SUN TW16...172 C5
Sunbury Cdns *MLHL* NW7...45 F1
Sunbury La *BTSEA* SW11...140 C2
Sunbury Rd *CHEAM* SM3...208 B1
  FELT TW13...153 J5
Sunbury St *WOOL/PLUM* SE18...126 E3
Sunbury Wy *FELT* TW13...172 B1
Suncroft Pl *SYD* SE26...163 K5
Sunderland Mt *FSTH* SE23 *...164 A4
Sunderland Rd *EA* W5...116 E3
  FSTH SE23...164 A4
Sunderland Ter *BAY/PAD* W2 *...101 F5
Sunderland Wy *MNPK* E12...71 H6
Sundew Av *SHB* W12...99 J6
Sundew Ct *ALP/SUD* HA0 *...98 A1
Sundorne Rd *CHARL* SE7...126 A5
Sundra Wk *WCHPL* E1 *...105 F3
Sundridge Av *BMLY* BR1...184 C4
  WELL DA16...147 J4
Sundridge Cl *DART* DA1...171 K1
Sundridge Pde *BMLY* BR1 *...184 A1
Sundridge Pl *CROY/NA* CRO...197 H5
Sundridge Rd *CROY/NA* CRO...197 H5
Sunfields Pl *BKHTH/KID* SE3...146 A1
Sun in Sands Rbt
  BKHTH/KID SE3...146 A1
Sunken Rd *CROY/NA* CRO...212 E3
Sunkist Wy *WLGTN* SM6...210 E6
Sunland Av *BXLYHS* DA6...149 F5
Sun La *BKHTH/KID* SE3...146 A1
Sunleigh Rd *ALP/SUD* HA0...80 A6
Sunley Gdns *GFD/PVL* UB6...97 G1
Sunlight Cl *WIM/MER* SW19 *...178 B2
Sunlight Sq *BETH* E2...104 D2
Sunningdale *CS* *SUN* TW16...172 A5
Sunningdale Av *ACT* W3...99 G6
  BARK IG11...90 D6
  FELT TW13...154 D4
  RAIN RM13...111 K3
  RSLP HA4...59 G5
Sunningdale Cl
  BERM/RHTH SE16...123 J5
  STAN HA7...43 G3
  SURB KT6...191 F6
  THMD SE28...110 A5
Sunningdale Gdns
  CDALE/KGS NW9...62 E2
  KENS W8 *...119 K3
Sunningdale Ldg *EDGW* HA8 *...44 B1
Sunningdale Rd *BMLY* BR1...200 E1
  RAIN RM13...93 J5
  SUT SM1...208 D2
Sunninghill Rd *HDN* NW4...45 K6
Sunningfields Crs *HDN* NW4...45 K5
Sunninghill Ct *ACT* W3 *...117 J1
Sunninghill Rd *LEW* SE13...144 E3
Sunny Bank *SNWD* SE25...181 H6
Sunny Crs *WLSDN* NW10...80 E5
Sunnycroft Rd *HSLW* TW3...135 G3
  SNWD SE25...197 H1
  STHL UB1...96 A4
Sunnydale *ORP* BR6...201 F6
Sunnydale Gdns *MLHL* NW7...45 F2
Sunnydale Rd *LEE/GVPK* SE12...146 A4
Sunnydene Av *CHING* E4...52 B1
  RSLP HA4...58 E5
Sunnydene Gdns *ALP/SUD* HA0...79 J4
Sunnydene St *SYD* SE26...164 B6
Sunny Gardens Rd *HDN* NW4...46 A6
Sunny HI *HDN* NW4...45 K6
Sunnyhill Cl *CLPT* E5...87 G2
Sunnyhill Rd
  STRHM/NOR SW16...161 K6
Sunnyhurst Cl *SUT* SM1...208 E1
Sunnymead Av *MTCM* CR4...179 J6
Sunnymead Rd
  PUT/ROE SW15...138 D6
Sunnymede Av
  HOR/WEW KT19...207 G6
  CAR SM5...194 B1
Sunnymede Dr *BARK/HLT* IG6...72 B1
Sunny Nook Gdns
  SAND/SEL CR2...211 K4
Sunny PI *HDN* NW4...64 A1
The Sunny Rd *PEND* EN3...25 F2
Sunnyside *CAT* SE6 *...164 C2
  CRICK NW2...82 D1
  WOT/HER KT12...188 B2
Sunnyside Dr *CHING* E4...38 A4
Sunnyside Pl *WIM/MER* SW19...177 H2
Sunnyside Rd *ARCH* N19...116 E1
  EA W5...116 E1
  IL IG1...90 C1
  LEY E10...69 J5
  TEDD TW11...155 J6
Sunnyside Rd East *ED* N9...36 C5
Sunnyside Rd North *ED* N9...36 B5
Sunnyside Rd South *ED* N9...36 B5
Sunny Vw *CDALE/KGS* NW9...63 F2
Sunny Wy *NFNCH/WDSPK* N12...47 J3
Sun Pas *BERM/RHTH* SE16...123 H3
Sunray Av *BRYLDS* KT5...191 J6
  HAYES BR2...200 D3
  HNHL SE24...142 E6
  WDR/YW UB7...112 A2
Sunrise Cl *FELT* TW13...154 E5
Sun Rd *W KENS* W14...119 J5
Sunset Av *CHING* E4...37 K3
  WFD IG8...52 E1
Sunset Cl *ERITH* DA8...150 E1
Sunset Dr *ABR/ST* RM4...57 K1
Sunset Gdns *SNWD* SE25...181 G5
Sunset Rd *HNHL* SE24...142 D5
  THMD SE28...128 B2
  WIM/MER SW19...176 E1
Sunset Vw *BAR* EN5...20 C3
Sunshine Wy *MTCM* CR4...178 E5
Sun St *LYPST* EC2M...13 G1
Superior Dr *ORP* BR6...217 F4
Surbiton Ct *SURB* KT6...190 D3
Surbiton Court Ms *SURB* KT6...190 E3
Surbiton Crs *KUT/HW* KT1...191 F1
Surbiton Hall Cl *KUT/HW* KT1...191 F3
Surbiton Hill Pk *BRYLDS* KT5...191 G2
Surbiton Hill Rd *SURB* KT6...191 F1
Surbiton Rd *KUT/HW* KT1...190 E1
Surlingham Cl *THMD* SE28...109 K6
Surma Cl *WCHPL* E1...104 D3
Surmans Cl *DAGW* RM9...91 J6
Surrendale Pl *MV/WKIL* W9...100 E3
Surrey Canal Rd *PECK* SE15...123 K6
Surrey Cl *FNCH* N3...46 C6
Surrey Crs *CHSWK* W4...117 H5
Surrey Gdns *FSBYPK* N4...67 J3
Surrey Gv *SUT* SM1...209 H1
  WALW SE17 *...123 F5
Surrey La *BTSEA* SW11...140 D2
Surrey Ms *WNWD* SE27...163 F6
Surrey Mt *FSTH* SE23...163 J3
Surrey Quays Rd
  BERM/RHTH SE16...124 A3
Surrey Rd *BARK* IG11...90 E5
  DAGE RM10...92 D3
  HRW HA1...60 C2
  PECK SE15...144 A6
  WWKM BR4...198 E5
Surrey Rw *STHWK* SE1...18 A2
Surrey Sq *WALW* SE17 *...123 F5
Surrey St *CROY/NA* CRO...211 J1
  PLSTW E13...107 F2
  TPL/STR WC2R...11 H5
Surrey Ter *WALW* SE17...19 H7
Surrey Water Rd
  BERM/RHTH SE16...124 A1
Surridge Gdns *NRWD* SE19...180 E2
Surr St *HOLWY* N7...84 E3
Sury Basin *KUTN/CMB* KT2...175 F4
Susannah St *POP/IOD* E14...105 K5
Susan Rd *BKHTH/KID* SE3...146 A3
Susan Wd *CHST* BR7...185 F4
Sussex Av *ISLW* TW7...135 K4
Sussex Cl *ARCH* N19...66 E6
  NWMAL KT3...192 B1
  REDBR IG4...71 H4
  TWK TW1...156 C1
Sussex Crs *NTHLT* UB5...78 A4
Sussex Gdns *BAY/PAD* W2...8 B5
  CHSGTN KT9...205 K4
  FNCH N3...46 C1
  HGT N6...65 K2
Sussex Ga *HGT* N6...65 K2
Sussex Ms *CRW* RM5...56 E3
Sussex Ms East *BAY/PAD* W2...8 B5
Sussex Ms West *BAY/PAD* W2...8 B5
Sussex Pl *BAY/PAD* W2...8 B5
  CAMTN NW1...3 F5
  ERITH DA8...150 B2
  HMSMTH W6...119 F5
  NWMAL KT3...192 B1
Sussex Ring
  NFNCH/WDSPK N12...46 E1
Sussex Rd *CAR* SM5...209 K4
  DART DA1...171 J2
  EHAM E6...108 A1
  ERITH DA8...149 J1
  HGDN/ICK UB10...76 A2
  HRW HA1...60 C2
  MTCM CR4 *...195 K2
  NWDGN UB2...114 C3
  NWMAL KT3...192 B1
  SAND/SEL CR2...211 K4
  STMC/STPC BR5...202 D5
  WWKM BR4...198 E5
Sussex Sq *BAY/PAD* W2...8 B5
Sussex St *PIM* SW1V...121 G5
  PLSTW E13...107 F2
Sussex Ter *PGE/AN* SE20 *...181 K3
Sussex Wy *ARCH* N19...66 E6
  EBAR EN4...22 B6
Sutcliffe Cl *GLDGN* NW11...65 F2
Sutcliffe Rd *WELL* DA16...148 D3
  WOOL/PLUM SE18...127 K6
Sutherland Av *HYS/HAR* UB3...113 K4
  MV/WKIL W9...101 F3
  STMC/STPC BR5...202 A3
  WEA W13...97 H5
  WELL DA16...147 J5
Sutherland Cl *BAR* EN5...20 C5
Sutherland Ct *CDALE/KGS* NW9...62 C2
Sutherland Dr
  WIM/MER SW19...178 C4
Sutherland Gdns
  MORT/ESHN SW14...138 B4
  SUN TW16...172 A5
  WPK KT4...192 E5
Sutherland Gv *TEDD* TW11...173 K1
  WAND/EARL SW18...159 J2
Sutherland House *WALTH* E17 *...51 G6
Sutherland Pl *BAY/PAD* W2...100 E5
Sutherland Rd *BELV* DA17...129 H3
  BOW E3...105 H1
  CHSWK W4...118 A6
  CROY/NA CRO...196 B4
  ED N9...36 C3
  PEND EN3...37 F1
  STHL UB1...95 K5
  TOTM N17...50 C4
  WALTH E17...51 C6
  WEA W13...97 G5
Sutherland Rw *PIM* SW1V...121 G5
Sutherland Sq *WALW* SE17...122 D5
Sutherland St *PIM* SW1V...121 G5
Sutherland Vls *WEA* W13 *...97 G6
Sutherland Wk *WALW* SE17...122 D5
Sutlej Rd *CHARL* SE7...146 B1
Sutterton St *HOLWY* N7...85 F5
Sutton Cl *BECK* BR3...182 E4
  CHSWK W4 *...117 K6
  LOU IG10...39 J2
  PIN HA5...58 E2
Sutton Common Rd
  CHEAM SM3...193 K5
  SUT SM1...208 D6
Sutton Ct *BELMT* SM2...209 G5
  CHSWK W4 *...117 K6
Sutton Court Rd *CHSWK* W4...117 K6
  PLSTW E13...107 G2
  SUT SM1...209 G4
Sutton Crs *BAR* EN5...20 B6
Sutton Dene *HSLW* TW3...135 G2
Sutton Dwelling Est
  CHEL SW3 *...120 D5
Sutton Est *IS* N1 *...85 H5
The Sutton Est *IS* N1 *...85 H5
Sutton Gdns *CROY/NA* CRO...197 G2
Sutton Gv *SUT* SM1...209 H3
Sutton Hall Rd *HEST* TW5...135 F1
Sutton La *HSLW* TW3...134 E3
  SUT SM1...209 G5
Sutton La North *CHSWK* W4...117 K5
Sutton La South *CHSWK* W4...117 K6
Sutton Park Rd *SUT* SM1...209 F4
Sutton Pl *HOM* E9...86 E5
Sutton Rd *BARK* IG11...108 E2
  HEST TW5...135 F2
  MUSWH N10...48 A4
  PLSTW E13...106 D3
  WALTH E17...51 F4
Sutton Row *SOHO/SHAV* W1D...10 C5
Sutton Sq *HEST* TW5...135 F2
  HOM E9...86 E5
Sutton St *WCHPL* E1...104 E5
Sutton Wy *HEST* TW5...134 E2
  NKENS W10...100 A4
  STLK EC1Y...6 D7
Swaby Rd *WAND/EARL* SW18...160 B3
Swaffham Wy *SEVS/STOTM* N15 *...68 C1
Swaffield Rd
  WAND/EARL SW18...160 B2
Swain Cl *STRHM/NOR* SW16...179 G2
Swain Rd *THHTH* CR7...196 D2
Swains Cl *WDR/YW* UB7...112 C2
Swains La *HGT* N6...66 A5
Swainson Rd *ACT* W3...118 C2
Swains Rd *TOOT* SW17...178 E3
Swain St *STJWD* NW8...2 B7
Swaisland Dr *DART* DA1...170 E1
Swaislands Dr *DART* DA1...150 D6
Swaledale Cl *FBAR/BDGN* N11...48 A2
Swale Rd *DART* DA1...150 D4
Swallands Rd *CAT* SE6...164 D5
Swallow Cl *BUSH* WD23...28 B3
  ERITH DA8...150 B2
  NWCR SE14...143 K6
Swallowdale *SAND/SEL* CR2...213 F6
Swallow Dr *NTHLT* UB5...96 A1
  WLSDN NW10...81 F4
Swallowfield Rd *CHARL* SE7...126 A5
Swallowfield Wy
  HYS/HAR UB3...113 G2
Swallow Gdns
  STRHM/NOR SW16...179 J1
Swallow Pl *REGST* W1B...9 K4
Swallow St *EHAM* E6...107 J4
  REGST W1B...10 B6
Swanage Rd *CHING* E4...52 A3
  WAND/EARL SW18...160 B1
Swanage Waye *YEAD* UB4...95 G5
Swan & Pike Rd *PEND* EN3...25 J1
Swan Ap *EHAM* E6...107 J4
Swanbridge Rd *BXLYHN* DA7...149 H2
The Swan Centre *TOOT* SW17 *...160 D5
Swan Cl *CROY/NA* CRO...197 F4
  FELT TW13...154 D6
Swandon Wy
  WAND/EARL SW18...140 A5
Swan Dr *CDALE/KGS* NW9...45 G5
Swanfield St *BETH* E2...7 J5
Swan Island *TWK* TW1 *...156 B5
Swan La *CANST* EC4R...12 E6
  DART DA1...170 C2
  LOU IG10...33 G5
  TRDG/WHET N20...33 G5
Swanley Rd *WELL* DA16...148 D2
Swan Md *STHWK* SE1...19 G5
Swan Ms *BRXN/ST* SW9...142 A3
  FUL/PGN SW6...139 J2
Swan Pas *WCHPL* E1 *...13 K6
Swan Pl *BARN* SW13...138 C3
Swan Rd *BERM/RHTH* SE16...123 K2
  FELT TW13...154 D6
  STHL UB1...96 B5
  WDR/YW UB7...112 A2
  WOOL/PLUM SE18...126 C3
Swanscombe Rd *CHSWK* W4...118 B5
  NTGHL W11...119 G1
Swansea Rd
  EBED/NFELT TW14...153 F1
  PEND EN3...24 E5
Swanston Pth *OXHEY* WD19...27 G5
Swan St *ISLW* TW7...136 C4
  STHWK SE1...18 D4
Swanton Gdns
  WIM/MER SW19...159 G3
Swanton Rd *ERITH* DA8...149 H1
Swan Wk *CHEL* SW3...120 E6
Swan Wy *PEND* EN3...25 J3
Swanwick Cl *PUT/ROE* SW15...158 C2
Swan Yd *IS* N1...85 H4
Sward Rd *STMC/STPC* BR5...202 B3
Swaton Rd *BOW* E3...105 J3
Swaylands Rd *BELV* DA17...129 H6
Swaythling Cl *UED* N18...36 D6
Swedenborg Gdns
  WCHPL E1...104 C6
Sweden Ga *BERM/RHTH* SE16...124 B4
Sweeney Crs *STHWK* SE1...19 K3
Sweeps La *STMC/STPC* BR5...202 E2
Sweet Briar Gn *ED* N9...36 B5
Sweet Briar Gr *ED* N9...36 B5
Sweet Briar Wk *UED* N18...36 B6
Sweetmans Av *PIN* HA5...41 H6
Sweets Wy *TRDG/WHET* N20...33 H4
Swete St *PLSTW* E13...106 E1
Sweyn Pl *BKHTH/KID* SE3...145 K3
Swift Cl *HYS/HAR* UB3...94 D5
  RYLN/HDSTN HA2...60 A6
  THMD SE28...109 H6
  WALTH E17...51 G3
Swift Rd *FELT* TW13...154 D5
  NWDGN UB2...114 C3
Swiftsden Wy *BMLY* BR1...183 H2
Swift St *FUL/PGN* SW6...139 J2
Swinbrook Rd *NKENS* W10...100 C4
Swinburne Crs *CROY/NA* CRO...197 K4
Swinburne Rd *PUT/ROE* SW15...138 D6
Swinderby Rd *ALP/SUD* HA0...80 A4
Swindon Cl *GDMY/SEVK* IG3...72 E6
Swindon Rd *HTHAIR* TW6...153 F5
Swindon St *SHB* W12...118 E1
Swinfield Cl *FELT* TW13...154 D6
Swingate La *BRXN/ST* SW9 *...142 C4
Swingate La
  WOOL/PLUM SE18...147 K1
Swinnerton St *HOM* E9...87 G3
Swinton Cl *WBLY* HA9...62 D5
Swinton Pl *FSBYW* WC1X...5 G4
Swinton St *FSBYW* WC1X...5 G4
Swires Shaw *HAYES* BR2...215 H2
Swithland Gdns
  ELTH/MOT SE9...166 E6
Swyncombe Av *EA* W5...116 C4
Swynford Gdns *HDN* NW4...63 J1
Sybil Phoenix Cl *DEPT* SE8...124 B5
Sybil Ms *FSBYPK* N4...67 H3
Sybourn St *WALTH* E17...69 H4
Sycamore Av *BFN/LL* DA15...168 A1
  BOW E3 *...87 H6
  EA W5...116 E3
  HYS/HAR UB3...94 E6
Sycamore Cl *ACT* W3...118 B1
  CAN/RD E16...106 C3
  CAR SM5...209 K2
  EBAR EN4...33 H1
  EDGW HA8...30 E6
  FELT TW13...153 J5
  NTHLT UB5...77 J6
  SAND/SEL CR2...211 J4
Sycamore Gdns *MTCM* CR4...178 C5
  SHB W12...118 E2
Sycamore Gv *CAT* SE6...165 F1
  CDALE/KGS NW9...62 E4
  CPK RM2...57 J5
  NWMAL KT3...176 B6
  PGE/AN SE20...181 H4
Sycamore HI *FBAR/BDGN* N11...48 A2
Sycamore Ms *CLAP* SW4...141 H4
Sycamore Rd *DART* DA1...171 G2
  WIM/MER SW19...177 F2
Sycamore St *FSBYE* EC1V...6 C7
Sycamore Wk *NKENS* W10...100 C3
Sycamore Wy *TEDD* TW11...174 D2
Sydcote *DUL* SE21 *...162 D4
Sydenham Av *SED* SE26...181 J1
Sydenham Cl *ROM* RM1...75 H1
Sydenham Cottages
  LEE/GVPK SE12...166 B4
Sydenham HI *FSTH* SE23...163 K4
  SYD SE26...163 J3
Sydenham Pk *SYD* SE26...163 K5
Sydenham Park Rd *SYD* SE26...163 K5
Sydenham Ri *FSTH* SE23...163 H4
Sydenham Rd *CROY/NA* CRO...196 D5
  SYD SE26...163 K6
Sydenham Station Ap
  SYD SE26...163 K6
Sydmons Ct *FSTH* SE23 *...163 K2
Sydner Rd *STNW/STAM* N16...86 B2
Sydney Cl *SKENS* SW7...14 B7

Sydney Gv HDN NW4 64 A2
Sydney Ms CHEL SW3 14 B7
Sydney Pl SKENS SW7 14 B7
Sydney Rd ABYW SE2 128 E3
BARK/HLT IG6 54 C5
BXLYHS DA6 148 E5
CEND/HSY/T N8 67 G1
EBED/NFELT TW14 153 K3
ENC/FH EN2 23 K5
MUSWH N10 48 B4
RCH/KEW TW9 137 F5
RYNPK SW20 177 G5
SCUP DA14 167 K6
SUT SM1 208 E2
TEDD TW11 174 A1
WAN E11 71 F3
WEA W13 116 B1
WFD IG8 52 E1
Sydney St CHEL SW3 120 D5
Sydney Ter ESH/CLAY KT10 * 205 F4
Sylvan Av CHDH RM6 74 B3
MLHL NW7 45 G2
WDGN N22 49 G3
Sylvan Gdns SURB KT6 190 E4
Sylvan Gv CRICK NW2 82 B2
PECK SE15 123 J6
Sylvan Hl NRWD SE19 181 G4
Sylvan Rd FSTGT E7 88 E4
IL IG1 72 C6
NRWD SE19 181 G4
WALTH E17 * 69 J2
WAN E11 70 E2
Sylvan Ter PECK SE15 * 143 J1
Sylvan Wk BMLY BR1 184 E6
Sylvan Wy BCTR RM8 91 H1
WWKM BR4 214 C2
Sylverdale Rd CROY/NA CR0 211 H1
Sylvester Av CHST BR7 184 E2
Sylvester Pth HACK E8 * 86 D4
Sylvester Rd ALP/SUD HA0 79 J3
EFNCH N2 47 G5
HACK E8 * 86 D4
WALTH E17 * 69 H4
Sylvia Av PIN HA5 41 K2
Sylvia Gdns WBLY HA9 80 D5
Symes Ms CAMTN NW1 4 A2
Symington Ms HOM E9 87 F3
Symister Ms IS N1 * 7 G5
Symons Cl PECK SE15 143 K4
Symons St CHEL SW3 15 F7
Symphony Cl EDGW HA8 44 D3
Symphony Ms NKENS W10 100 C2
Syon Gate Wy BTFD TW8 136 C1
Syon La ISLW TW7 116 A6
ISLW TW7 136 C1
Syon Pk ISLW TW7 * 136 C4
Syon Park Gdns ISLW TW7 136 A1

T

Tabard Garden Est STHWK SE1 18 E2
Tabard St STHWK SE1 18 E4
Tabernacle Av PLSTW E13 106 E3
Tabernacle St SDTCH EC2A 7 F7
Tableer Av CLAP SW4 141 H6
Tabley Rd HOLWY N7 84 E2
Tabor Gdns CHEAM SM3 208 D4
Tabor Gv WIM/MER SW19 177 H3
Tabor Rd HMSMTH W6 118 E3
Tachbrook Rd
EBED/NFELT TW14 153 J2
NWDGN UB2 114 C4
Tachbrook St PIM SW1V 16 B7
Tack Ms BROCKY SE4 144 D4
Tadema Rd WBPTN SW10 140 B1
Tadmor St SHB W12 119 G1
Tadworth Av NWMAL KT3 192 C1
Tadworth Pde HCH RM12 93 K2
Tadworth Rd CRICK NW2 63 J6
Taeping St POP/IOD E14 124 E4
Taffy's How MTCM CR4 178 D6
Tait Rd CROY/NA CR0 197 F4
Takeley Cl CRW RM5 57 F5
Talacre Rd KTTN NW5 84 A4
Talbot Av EFNCH N2 47 H6
OXHEY WD19 27 J2
Talbot Cl SEVS/STOTM N15 68 B1
Talbot Ct BANK EC3V 13 F5
Talbot Crs HDN NW4 63 J2
Talbot Gdns GDMY/SEVK IG3 73 G6
Talbot Pl BKHTH/KID SE3 145 H3
Talbot Rd ALP/SUD HA0 79 K3
CAR SM5 210 A3
DAGW RM9 92 B5
EDUL SE22 143 F5
EHAM E6 108 A1
FSTGT E7 88 E2
HGT N6 66 A3
ISLW TW7 136 B5
KTN/HRWW/WS HA3 43 F5
NTGHL W11 100 D5
NWDGN UB2 114 D4
SEVS/STOTM N15 68 B1
THHTH CR7 196 E1
WDGN N22 48 C5
WEA W13 * 97 G6
WHTN TW2 155 K3
Talbot Sq BAY/PAD W2 8 A4
Talbot Wk NTGHL W11 100 C5
WLSDN NW10 * 81 G4
Talbot Yd STHWK SE1 18 E1
Talcott Pth
BRXS/STRHM SW2 * 162 B3
Talfourd Pl PECK SE15 143 G2
Talfourd Rd PECK SE15 143 G2
Talgarth Rd WKENS W14 119 H5
Talgarth Wk CDALE/KGS NW9 63 G2
Talisman Cl GDMY/SEVK IG3 73 H5
Talisman Sq SYD SE26 163 H6
Talisman Wy WBLY HA9 80 B1
Tallack Cl KTN/HRWW/WS HA3 42 E3
Tallack Rd LEY E10 69 H5
Tall Elms Cl HAYES BR2 199 J2
Tallis Cl CAN/RD E16 107 F5
Tallis Gv CHARL SE7 126 A6
Tallis St EMB EC4Y 11 K5
Tallis Vw WLSDN NW10 81 F4
Tallow Rd BTFD TW8 116 D6
Tall Trees STRHM/NOR SW16 180 A6
Talma Gdns WHTN TW2 155 K2
Talmage Cl FSTH SE23 163 K2
Talman Gv STAN HA7 43 K2
Talma Rd BRXS/STRHM SW2 142 B5
Talwin St BOW E3 105 K2
Tamar Cl BOW E3 * 87 H6
Tamarind Yd WAP E1W * 123 H1
Tamarisk Sq SHB W12 99 H6
Tamar St CHARL SE7 126 D4
Tamesis Gdns WPK KT4 192 B6
Tamian Wy HSLWW TW4 134 B5
Tamworth Av WFD IG8 52 C2
Tamworth La MTCM CR4 179 G6
Tamworth Pk MTCM CR4 195 G1
Tamworth Pl CROY/NA CR0 * 196 D6
Tamworth Rd CROY/NA CR0 196 D6
Tamworth St FUL/PGN SW6 119 K6
Tancred Rd FSBYPK N4 67 H3
Tandridge Dr ORP BR6 201 J5
Tanfield Av CRICK NW2 81 H2
Tanfield Rd CROY/NA CR0 211 J2
Tangier Rd RCHPK/HAM TW10 137 J4
Tangleberry Cl BMLY BR1 200 E1
Tangle Tree Cl FNCH N3 47 F5
Tanglewood Cl CROY/NA CR0 212 E1
STAN HA7 28 E5
Tanglewood Wy FELT TW13 154 A5
Tangley Gv PUT/ROE SW15 158 C2
Tangley Park Rd HPTN TW12 * 172 E1
Tangmere Crs HCH RM12 93 K4
Tangmere Gdns NTHLT UB5 95 G1
Tangmere Gv KUTN/CMB KT2 174 E1
Tangmere Wy CDALE/KGS NW9 45 G5
Tanhouse Fld KTTN NW5 * 84 D3
Tankerton Houses
STPAN WC1H * 5 F5
Tankerton Rd SURB KT6 191 G6
Tankerton St STPAN WC1H 5 F5
Tankerton Ter CROY/NA CR0 * 196 A4
Tankerville Rd
STRHM/NOR SW16 179 J3
Tank Hill Rd PUR RM19 131 K4
Tankridge Rd CRICK NW2 63 K6
The Tanneries WCHPL E1 * 104 E3
Tanners Cl WOT/HER KT12 188 A3
Tanners End La UED N18 36 A6
Tanner's Hl DEPT SE8 144 D2
Tanners La BARK/HLT IG6 54 C6
Tanners Ms DEPT SE8 144 C2
Tanner St BARK IG11 90 C4
STHWK SE1 19 J3
Tannery Cl CROY/NA CR0 198 A2
DAGE RM10 92 D1
Tannington Ter HBRY N5 85 G1
Tannsfeld Rd SYD SE26 182 A1
Tansley Cl HOLWY N7 84 D3
Tanswell St STHWK SE1 * 17 J3
Tansy Cl EHAM E6 108 A5
Tantallon Rd BAL SW12 161 F3
Tant Av CAN/RD E16 106 D5
Tanza Rd HAMP NW3 83 K2
Tanworth Cl NTHWD HA6 40 A2
Tanworth Gdns PIN HA5 41 F5
Tan Yard La BXLY DA5 * 169 H2
Tanza Rd HAMP NW3 83 K2
Tapestry Cl BELMT SM2 209 F5
Taplow Ct MTCM CR4 194 D1
Taplow Rd PLMGR N13 35 J6
Taplow St IS N1 6 D3
Tappesfield Rd PECK SE15 143 K4
Tapping Cl KUTN/CMB KT2 * 175 H3
Tapp St WCHPL E1 104 D3
Tapster St BAR EN5 20 D4
Taransay Wk IS N1 85 K4
Tara Ter BROCKY SE4 * 144 B4
Tarbert Rd EDUL SE22 143 F6
Tarbert Wk WCHPL E1 104 E6
Target Cl EBED/NFELT TW14 153 H1
Tariff Rd UED N18 50 D1
Tarleton Gdns FSTH SE23 163 J3
Tarling Cl SCUP DA14 168 C5
Tarling Rd CAN/RD E16 106 D5
EFNCH N2 47 G5
Tarling St WCHPL E1 104 D5
Tarnbank ENC/FH EN2 22 E6
Tarn St STHWK SE1 18 C5
Tarnwood Pk ELTH/MOT SE9 166 E3
Tarragon Cl NWCR SE14 * 144 B1
Tarragon Gv SYD SE26 182 A2
Tarrant Pl MBLAR W1H 8 E2
Tarriff Crs DEPT SE8 124 C4
Tarrington Cl
STRHM/NOR SW16 * 161 J6
Tarver Rd WALW SE17 122 C5
Tarves Wy GNWCH SE10 144 E1
Tash Pl FBAR/BDGN N11 * 48 B1
Tasker Cl HYS/HAR UB3 133 F1
Tasker Rd HAMP NW3 83 K3
Tasmania Ter UED N18 49 J2
Tasman Rd BRXN/ST SW9 141 K4
Tasso Rd HMSMTH W6 119 H6
Tate Gdns BUSH WD23 28 E2
Tate Rd CAN/RD E16 126 E1
SUT SM1 208 E3
Tatham Pl STJWD NW8 2 B2
Tatnell Rd FSTH SE23 164 B1
Tattersall Cl ELTH/MOT SE9 146 D6
Tatton Crs CLPT E5 68 B4
Tatum Rd WLSDN NW10 80 E5
Tatum St WALW SE17 19 F7
Tauheed Cl FSBYPK N4 67 J6
Taunton Av HSLW TW3 135 H3
RYNPK SW20 176 E5
Taunton Cl BARK/HLT IG6 55 F2
BXLYHN DA7 150 A4
CHEAM SM3 193 K5
Taunton Dr EFNCH N2 47 G5
ENC/FH EN2 23 G4
Taunton Ms CAMTN NW1 2 E7
Taunton Pl CAMTN NW1 2 E6
Taunton Rd GFD/PVL UB6 78 B5
LEE/GVPK SE12 145 H6
Taunton Wy STAN HA7 44 A6
Tavern Cl CAR SM5 194 D4
Taverners Cl NTGHL W11 119 H1
Taverner Sq HBRY N5 * 85 J2
Taverners Wy CHING E4 38 C3
Tavistock Av GFD/PVL UB6 97 G1
MLHL NW7 46 B3
WALTH E17 51 F6
Tavistock Cl STNW/STAM N16 * 86 A3
Tavistock Ct COVGDN WC2E * 11 F5
Tavistock Crs MTCM CR4 195 K1
NTGHL W11 100 D5
Tavistock Gdns GDMY/SEVK IG3 90 E2
Tavistock Gv CROY/NA CR0 196 E4
Tavistock Ms NTGHL W11 * 100 D5
Tavistock Pl STHGT/OAK N14 * 34 B1
STPAN WC1H 5 F6
Tavistock Rd CAR SM5 194 C5
CROY/NA CR0 196 E5
EDGW HA8 44 B4
FSBYPK N4 67 K3
HAYES BR2 199 K1
HGDN/ICK UB10 76 B3
NTGHL W11 100 D5
SWFD E18 52 E6
WAN E11 88 D2
WDR/YW UB7 112 A1
WELL DA16 148 D2
WLSDN NW10 99 H1
Tavistock Sq STPAN WC1H 4 D6
Tavistock St COVGDN WC2E 11 F5
Tavistock Ter ARCH N19 84 E1
Taviton St STPAN WC1H 4 C6
Tavy Br ABYW SE2 128 D2
Tavy Cl LBTH SE11 122 B5
Tawney Rd THMD SE28 109 H6
Tawny Cl FELT TW13 153 K5
WEA W13 116 C1
Tawny Wy BERM/RHTH SE16 124 A4
Tayben Av WHTN TW2 155 K1
Taybridge Rd BTSEA SW11 141 F4
Tayburn Cl POP/IOD E14 106 A5
Tayfield Cl HGDN/ICK UB10 76 B1
Taylor Av RCH/KEW TW9 137 J3
Taylor Cl CRW RM5 56 C3
DEPT SE8 124 C6
HPTN TW12 173 H1
HSLW TW3 135 H2
ORP BR6 217 F2
TOTM N17 50 C3
Taylor Rd MTCM CR4 178 D3
WLGTN SM6 210 B3
Taylor Rw RDART DA2 171 F5
Taylor's Buildings
WOOL/PLUM SE18 127 G4
Taylors Cl SCUP DA14 168 A6
Taylors Ct FELT TW13 153 K4
Taylor's Gn ACT W3 * 99 G5
Taylor's La BAR EN5 20 D2
SYD SE26 163 J6
WLSDN NW10 81 G5
Taylors Md MLHL NW7 * 45 J1
Taymount Ri FSTH SE23 163 K4
Tayport Cl IS N1 85 F5
Tayside Dr EDGW HA8 30 D5
Tay Wy ROM RM1 57 H4
Taywood Rd NTHLT UB5 95 J3
STHL UB1 95 K2
Teak Cl BERM/RHTH SE16 124 B1
Teal Av STMC/STPC BR5 202 E1
Teal Cl CAN/RD E16 107 H4
Teal Dr NTHWD HA6 40 A3
Teale St BETH E2 104 C1
Tealing Dr HOR/WEW KT19 207 F2
Teal Pl SUT SM1 208 D3
Teasel Cl CROY/NA CR0 198 A5
Teasel Crs THMD SE28 127 K1
Teasel Wy SRTFD E15 106 C2
Teather St CMBW SE5 143 F1
Tebworth Rd TOTM N17 50 B3
Technology Pk
CDALE/KGS NW9 * 45 F6
Teck Cl ISLW TW7 136 B3
Tedder Cl CHSGTN KT9 205 J3
RSLP HA4 76 E3
Tedder Rd SAND/SEL CR2 213 F5
Teddington Pk TEDD TW11 174 A1
Teddington Park Rd
TEDD TW11 156 B6
Tedworth Gdns CHEL SW3 120 E5
Tedworth Sq CHEL SW3 * 120 E5
Tees Av GFD/PVL UB6 96 E1
Teesdale Av ISLW TW7 136 B2
Teesdale Cl BETH E2 104 C1
Teesdale Gdns ISLW TW7 136 B2
SNWD SE25 181 F5
Teesdale Rd WAN E11 70 D3
Teesdale St BETH E2 104 D2
Teesdale Yd BETH E2 * 104 D1
The Tee ACT W3 99 G5
Teevan Cl CROY/NA CR0 197 H4
Teevan Rd CROY/NA CR0 197 H4
Teign Ms ELTH/MOT SE9 166 D4
Teignmouth Cl CLAP SW4 141 J5
EDGW HA8 44 B5
Teignmouth Gdns
GFD/PVL UB6 97 G1
Teignmouth Rd CRICK NW2 82 B3
WELL DA16 148 D3
Telcote Wy RSLP HA4 * 59 G4
Telegraph Hl HAMP NW3 83 F1
Telegraph La ESH/CLAY KT10 205 F2
Telegraph Ms GDMY/SEVK IG3 73 F5
Telegraph Pas
BRXS/STRHM SW2 161 K2
Telegraph Pl POP/IOD E14 124 E4
Telegraph Rd PUT/ROE SW15 158 E2
Telegraph St LOTH EC2R 12 E3
Telephone Pl WKENS W14 * 119 J6
Telferscot Rd BAL SW12 161 J3
Telford Av BRXS/STRHM SW2 161 K3
Telford Cl NRWD SE19 181 G2
WALTH E17 69 G4
Telford Dr WOT/HER KT12 188 B4
Telford Rd CDALE/KGS NW9 63 J4
ELTH/MOT SE9 167 J4
NKENS W10 100 C4
STHL UB1 96 B6
WHTN TW2 155 F2
Telford Rd North Circular Rd
FBAR/BDGN N11 48 C2
Telfords Yd WAP E1W * 104 C6
Telford Ter PIM SW1V * 121 H6
Telford Wy ACT W3 99 G4
YEAD UB4 95 J4
Telham Rd EHAM E6 108 A1
Tell Gv EDUL SE22 143 G5
Tellisford ESH/CLAY KT10 204 B2
Tellson Av WOOL/PLUM SE18 146 D2
Telscombe Cl ORP BR6 201 K6
Temeraire Pl BTFD TW8 117 G5
Temeraire St
BERM/RHTH SE16 123 K2
Tempelhof Av HDN NW4 64 A4
Temperley Rd BAL SW12 161 F2
Tempest Wy RAIN RM13 93 J4
Templar Dr THMD SE28 109 K5
Templar Pl HPTN TW12 173 F3
Templars Av GLDGN NW11 64 D3
Templars Ct DART DA1 * 151 K6
Templars Crs FNCH N3 46 E5
Templars Dr
KTN/HRWW/WS HA3 * 42 D2
Templar St CMBW SE5 142 C3
Temple Av BCTR RM8 74 C5
CROY/NA CR0 213 H1
EMB EC4Y 11 K5
TRDG/WHET N20 33 H2
Temple Cl FNCH N3 46 D5
THMD SE28 127 H3
WAN E11 70 C4
Templecombe Rd HOM E9 86 E6
Templecombe Wy MRDN SM4 193 H2
Temple Dwellings BETH E2 * 104 D1
Temple Fortune Hl
GLDGN NW11 64 E2
Temple Fortune La
GLDGN NW11 64 E3
Temple Gdns BCTR RM8 91 K1
EMB EC4Y * 11 J5
GLDGN NW11 64 D3
WCHMH N21 * 35 H4
Temple Gv ENC/FH EN2 23 H4
GLDGN NW11 64 E3
Temple Hl DART DA1 151 J6
Temple Hill Sq DART DA1 151 J6
Temple La EMB EC4Y 11 K4
Templeman Rd HNWL W7 97 F4
Templemead Cl ACT W3 99 G5
Temple Mead Cl STAN HA7 43 H2
Temple Mills La LEY E10 87 K2
SRTFD E15 88 A3
Temple Pde BAR EN5 * 33 H2
Temple Pl TPL/STR WC2R 11 H5
Temple Rd CEND/HSY/T N8 67 F1
CHSWK W4 117 K3
CRICK NW2 82 A2
CROY/NA CR0 211 K2
EA W5 116 E3
EHAM E6 89 J6
HSLW TW3 135 H5
RCH/KEW TW9 137 G3
Temple Sheen Rd
MORT/ESHN SW14 137 K5
Temple St BETH E2 104 D1
Temple Ter WDGN N22 * 49 G5
Templeton Av CHING E4 37 J6
Templeton Cl NRWD SE19 180 E4
STNW/STAM N16 * 86 A3
Templeton Pl ECT SW5 119 K4
Templeton Rd FSBYPK N4 67 K3
Temple Wy SUT SM1 209 H1
Templewood WEA W13 97 H4
Templewood Av HAMP NW3 83 F1
Templewood Gdns HAMP NW3 83 F1
Temple Yd BETH E2 104 C2
Tempsford Cl ENC/FH EN2 23 J4
Temsford Cl RYLN/HDSTN HA2 42 C5
Tenbury Cl FSTGT E7 89 H3
Tenbury Ct BAL SW12 161 J3
Tenby Av KTN/HRWW/WS HA3 43 H5
Tenby Cl CHDH RM6 74 A3
Tenby Gdns NTHLT UB5 78 A4
Tenby Rd CHDH RM6 74 A3
EDGW HA8 44 B4
PEND EN3 24 E4
WALTH E17 69 G2
WELL DA16 148 E2
Tench St WAP E1W * 123 J1
Tenda Rd STHWK SE1 123 J4
Tendring Wy CHDH RM6 73 J2
Tenham Av BRXS/STRHM SW2 161 J4
Tenison Wy STHWK SE1 17 J1
Tenniel Cl BAY/PAD W2 101 G5
Tennison Rd SNWD SE25 197 G1
Tennis St STHWK SE1 18 E2
Tenniswood Rd EN EN1 24 B2
Tennyson Av CDALE/KGS NW9 44 E6
MNPK E12 89 J5
NWMAL KT3 192 E2
TWK TW1 156 A3
WAN E11 70 E4
Tennyson Cl
EBED/NFELT TW14 153 K1
PEND EN3 25 F6
WELL DA16 147 K2
Tennyson Rd DART DA1 151 K6
HNWL W7 97 F6
HSLW TW3 135 H3
KIL/WHAMP NW6 82 D6
LEY E10 69 K5
MLHL NW7 45 J1
PGE/AN SE20 182 A3
SRTFD E15 88 C5
WALTH E17 69 H3
WIM/MER SW19 178 B2
Tennyson St VX/NE SW8 141 G3
Tennyson Wy HCH RM12 75 H5
Tensing Rd NWDGN UB2 115 F3
Tentelow La NWDGN UB2 115 G3
Tenterden Cl ELTH/MOT SE9 166 E6
HDN NW4 46 B6
Tenterden Dr HDN NW4 46 B6
Tenterden Gdns CROY/NA CR0 197 H4
HDN NW4 46 B6
Tenterden Gv HDN NW4 64 A1
Tenterden Rd BCTR RM8 74 B6
CROY/NA CR0 197 J4
TOTM N17 50 B3
Tenterden St CONDST W1S 9 K4
Tenter Gnd WCHPL E1 13 J2
Tent Peg La STMC/STPC BR5 201 H2
Tent St WCHPL E1 104 D3
Teredo St LEW SE13 144 E3
Terling Cl WAN E11 88 D1
Terling Rd BCTR RM8 74 C6
Terling Wk IS N1 * 85 J6
Terminus Pl BGVA SW1W 15 K5
Terrace Gdns BARN SW13 138 C3
Terrace La RCHPK/HAM TW10 157 F1
Terrace Rd HOM E9 87 F5
PLSTW E13 88 E6
WOT/HER KT12 188 A4
The Terrace BARN SW13 138 B3
BETH E2 * 104 E2
CHING E4 * 38 C5
DEPT SE8 * 124 C4
EFNCH N2 * 66 A1
FNCH N3 * 46 D5
FSTH SE23 * 164 B2
KIL/WHAMP NW6 82 E6
Terrace Vls HMSMTH W6 * 118 D5
Terrace Wk DAGW RM9 92 A3
Terrac St RCH/KEW TW9 137 G5
Terrapin Rd TOOT SW17 161 G5
Terretts Pl IS N1 85 H5
Terrick Rd WDGN N22 48 E4
Terrick St SHB W12 99 K5
Terrilands PIN HA5 41 K6
Terront Rd SEVS/STOTM N15 67 J2
Tessa Sanderson Wy
GFD/PVL UB6 78 D3
Testerton Rd NTGHL W11 * 100 B6
Testerton Wk NTGHL W11 * 100 B6
Tetbury Pl IS N1 6 A1
Tetcott Rd WBPTN SW10 140 B1
Tetherdown MUSWH N10 48 A6
Tetty Wy BMLY BR1 183 K5
Teversham La VX/NE SW8 141 K2
Teviot Cl WELL DA16 148 C2
Teviot St POP/IOD E14 106 A4
Tewkesbury Av FSTH SE23 163 J3
PIN HA5 59 J3
Tewkesbury Cl LOU IG10 39 J1
Tewkesbury Gdns
CDALE/KGS NW9 44 D6
Tewkesbury Rd CAR SM5 194 C5
SEVS/STOTM N15 67 K4
WEA W13 116 B1
Tewkesbury Ter
FBAR/BDGN N11 48 C2
Tewson Rd WOOL/PLUM SE18 127 K5
Teynham Av EN EN1 35 K1
Teynham Gn HAYES BR2 199 K2
Teynton Ter TOTM N17 49 J4
Thackeray Av TOTM N17 50 C5
Thackeray Cl ISLW TW7 136 B3
WIM/MER SW19 177 G3
Thackeray Dr CHDH RM6 73 H4
Thackeray Ms HACK E8 86 C4
Thackeray Rd EHAM E6 107 H1
VX/NE SW8 141 G3
Thackeray St KENS W8 120 A3
Thakeham Cl SYD SE26 181 J1
Thalia Cl GNWCH SE10 125 G6
Thame Rd BERM/RHTH SE16 124 A2
Thames Av DAGW RM9 110 E2
GFD/PVL UB6 97 F1
WBPTN SW10 140 B2
Thames Bank
MORT/ESHN SW14 137 K3
Thamesbank Pl THMD SE28 109 J5
Thames Cir POP/IOD E14 124 D4
Thames Cl HPTN TW12 173 G5
RAIN RM13 111 K5
Thames Down Link
BRYLDS KT5 191 K2
HOR/WEW KT19 206 E2
NWMAL KT3 192 A5
WPK KT4 207 F1
Thames Dr RSLP HA4 58 A3
Thames Eyot TWK TW1 * 156 B4
Thames Ga DART DA1 151 K6
Thamesgate Cl
RCHPK/HAM TW10 156 C6
Thameside TEDD TW11 174 E3
Thames Meadow
E/WMO/HCT KT8 173 F6
Thamesmere Dr THMD SE28 109 G6
Thames Pth BARN SW13 138 C2
BTFD TW8 137 F1
CLPT E5 87 F1
GNWCH SE10 125 F6
ISLW TW7 136 D3
POP/IOD E14 124 D3
SRTFD E15 106 A1
STHWK SE1 121 K5
SUN TW16 172 B6
TWRH EC3N 13 H7
WEST SW1P 17 F5
Thames Pl PUT/ROE SW15 139 G4
Thamespoint TEDD TW11 * 174 E3
Thames Quay WBPTN SW10 * 140 B2
Thames Reach KUT/HW KT1 * 174 E4
Thames Rd BARK IG11 109 G2
CAN/RD E16 126 C1
CHSWK W4 117 J6
DART DA1 150 D4
Thames Side KUT/HW KT1 174 E4
THDIT KT7 190 C3
Thames St GNWCH SE10 124 E6
HPTN TW12 173 G5
KUT/HW KT1 174 E5
SUN TW16 172 A6
Thamesvale Cl HSLW TW3 135 F3
Thames Village CHSWK W4 137 K2
Thamley PUR RM19 131 K4
Thanescroft Gdns
CROY/NA CR0 212 A1
Thanet Dr HAYES BR2 215 H1
Thanet Pl CROY/NA CR0 211 J2

Thanet Rd BXLY DA5 169 H2
ERITH DA8 150 B1
Thanet St STPAN WC1H 4 E5
Thane Vls HOLWY N7 85 F1
Thant Cl LEY E10 87 K2
Tharp Rd WLGTN SM6 210 D3
Thatcham Gdns
TRDG/WHET N20 33 G2
Thatcher Cl WDR/YW UB7 112 B2
Thatchers Wy ISLW TW7 135 J6
Thatches Gv CHDH RM6 74 A1
Thavies Inn FLST/FETLN EC4A 11 K3
Thaxted Pl RYNPK SW20 177 G3
Thaxted Rd BKHH IG9 39 J2
ELTH/MOT SE9 167 H4
Thaxton Rd FUL/PGN SW6 119 J6
Thayers Farm Rd BECK BR3 182 B4
Thayer St MHST W1U 9 H3
Theatre Sq SRTFD E15 88 B4
Theatre St BTSEA SW11 140 E4
Theberton St IS N1 85 G6
The Beverly MRDN SM4 193 G3
The Courtyard HAYES BR2 215 J4
Theed St STHWK SE1 17 J1
Thelma Gv TEDD TW11 174 B2
Theobald Crs
KTN/HRWW/WS HA3 42 C4
Theobald Rd CROY/NA CR0 196 C6
WALTH E17 69 H4
Theobald's Rd GINN WC1R 11 G1
Theobald St STHWK SE1 18 E5
Theodora Wy PIN HA5 40 D6
Theodore Rd LEW SE13 165 G1
Therapia La CROY/NA CR0 195 K4
Therapia Rd EDUL SE22 163 K1
Theresa Rd HMSMTH W6 118 D4
Theresa's Wk SAND/SEL CR2 211 K6
Thermopylae Ga POP/IOD E14 124 E4
Theseus Wk IS N1 6 B3
Thesiger Rd PGE/AN SE20 182 A3
Thessaly Rd VX/NE SW8 141 J2
Thetford Cl PLMGR N13 49 H2
Thetford Rd ASHF TW15 152 B6
DAGW RM9 91 K5
NWMAL KT3 192 B2
Theydon Gdns RAIN RM13 93 G5
Theydon Gv WFD IG8 53 G2
Theydon Rd CLPT E5 68 E6
Theydon St WALTH E17 69 H4
Thicket Crs SUT SM1 209 G2
Thicket Gv DAGW RM9 91 J4
PGE/AN SE20 181 H3
Thicket Rd PGE/AN SE20 181 J3
SUT SM1 209 G2
Thicket Ter PGE/AN SE20 * 181 H3
Third Av ACT W3 118 C1
CHDH RM6 73 J3
DAGE RM10 92 D6
EN EN1 24 B6
HYS/HAR UB3 113 J1
MNPK E12 89 J2
NKENS W10 100 C2
PLSTW E13 106 E2
WALTH E17 69 J2
WBLY HA9 61 K6
Third Cl E/WMO/HCT KT8 189 G1
Third Cross Rd WHTN TW2 155 J4
Third Wy WBLY HA9 80 D2
Thirleby Rd EDGW HA8 45 F4
WEST SW1P 16 B5
Thirlmere Av GFD/PVL UB6 97 J2
Thirlmere Gdns WBLY HA9 61 J5
Thirlmere Ri BMLY BR1 183 J2
Thirlmere Rd BXLYHN DA7 149 K3
MUSWH N10 48 B4
STRHM/NOR SW16 161 J6
Thirsk Cl NTHLT UB5 78 A4
Thirsk Rd BTSEA SW11 141 F4
MTCM CR4 179 F3
SNWD SE25 196 E1
Thirza Rd DART DA1 171 K1
Thislefield Cl BXLY DA5 168 E3
Thistlebrook ABYW SE2 128 D3
Thistlecroft Gdns STAN HA7 43 K5
Thistledene THDIT KT7 189 K3
Thistledene Av CRW RM5 56 D1
RSLP HA4 77 J1
Thistle Gv WBPTN SW10 * 120 B5
Thistlemead CHST BR7 185 G5
Thistlewaite Rd CLPT E5 86 D1
Thistlewood Cl HOLWY N7 67 F6
Thistleworth Cl ISLW TW7 135 J1
Thistley Cl NFNCH/WDSPK N12 47 J2
Thomas a Beckett Cl HRW HA1 79 F2
Thomas Baines Rd
BTSEA SW11 140 C4
Thomas Cribb Ms EHAM E6 107 K5
Thomas Dean Rd SYD SE26 * 164 C6
Thomas Dinwiddy Rd
LEE/GVPK SE12 166 A4
Thomas Doyle St STHWK SE1 18 A4
Thomas' La CAT SE6 164 E2
Thomas Moore St WAP E1W 104 C6
Thomas Moore Wy EFNCH N2 47 G6
Thomas More St WAP E1W * 104 C6
Thomas North Ter
CAN/RD E16 * 106 D4
Thomas Pl KENS W8 * 120 A3
Thomas Rd POP/IOD E14 105 H5
Thomas St WOOL/PLUM SE18 127 F4
Thomas Wall Cl SUT SM1 209 F3
Thompson Av CMBW SE5 142 D1
RCH/KEW TW9 137 J4
Thompson Cl CHEAM SM3 193 K5
IL IG1 72 C6
Thompson Rd DAGW RM9 92 B1
EDUL SE22 163 G1
HSLW TW3 135 G5
Thompson's Av CMBW SE5 * 142 D1
Thomson Crs CROY/NA CR0 196 B5
Thomson Rd
KTN/HRWW/WS HA3 42 E6
Thorburn Sq STHWK SE1 123 H4
Thorburn Wy
WIM/MER SW19 * 178 C4
Thoresby St IS N1 6 D4
Thorkhill Gdns THDIT KT7 190 B5
Thorkhill Rd THDIT KT7 190 C5
Thornaby Gdns UED N18 50 D2
Thorn Av BUSH WD23 28 C3
Thornbury Av ISLW TW7 135 J1
Thornbury Cl STNW/STAM N16 86 A3
Thornbury Rd CLAP SW4 161 K1
ISLW TW7 135 J1
Thornbury Sq HGT N6 66 C5
Thornby Rd CLPT E5 86 E1
Thorncliffe Rd CLAP SW4 161 K1
NWDGN UB2 114 E5
Thorn Cl HAYES BR2 201 F3
NTHLT UB5 95 K2
Thorncombe Rd EDUL SE22 143 F6
Thorn Ct BELMT SM2 * 209 F5
Thorncroft EMPK RM11 75 K3
Thorncroft Rd SUT SM1 209 F2
Thorncroft St VX/NE SW8 141 K1
Thorndean St
WAND/EARL SW18 160 B4
Thorndene Av TRDG/WHET N20 33 J3
Thorndike Av NTHLT UB5 77 H6
Thorndike Cl WBPTN SW10 140 B1
Thorndike Rd IS N1 85 K4
Thorndike St PIM SW1V * 16 C7
Thorndon Cl STMC/STPC BR5 186 A5
Thorndon Gdns
HOR/WEW KT19 207 G2
Thorndon Rd STMC/STPC BR5 186 A5
Thorndyke Ct PIN HA5 41 K3
Thorne Cl CAN/RD E16 106 E5
ERITH DA8 129 K6
ESH/CLAY KT10 205 G5
WAN E11 88 C2
Thorneloe Gdns CROY/NA CR0 211 H3
Thorne Rd VX/NE SW8 141 K1
Thorne's Cl BECK BR3 183 F6
Thorne St BARN SW13 138 B4
Thornet Wood Rd BMLY BR1 201 F1
Thorney Crs BTSEA SW11 140 D1
Thorneycroft Cl
WOT/HER KT12 188 B3
Thorneycroft Dr PEND EN3 25 J1
Thorney Hedge Rd CHSWK W4 117 J4
Thorney St WEST SW1P 16 E6
Thornfield Av MLHL NW7 46 C4
Thornfield Pde MLHL NW7 * 46 C3
Thornfield Rd SHB W12 118 E2
Thornford Rd LEW SE13 145 F6
Thorngate Rd MV/WKIL W9 100 E3
Thorngrove Rd PLSTW E13 89 F6
Thornham Gv SRTFD E15 88 B3
Thornham St GNWCH SE10 124 E6
Thornhaugh St STPAN WC1H 4 D7
Thornhill Av SURB KT6 191 G6
WOOL/PLUM SE18 147 K1
Thornhill Bridge Whf IS N1 5 G1
Thornhill Crs IS N1 85 F5
Thornhill Gdns BARK IG11 90 E5
LEY E10 69 K6
Thornhill Gv IS N1 85 F5
Thornhill Rd CROY/NA CR0 196 D4
IS N1 85 G5
LEY E10 69 K6
NTHWD HA6 26 A6
SURB KT6 191 F6
Thornhill Sq IS N1 85 F6
Thornlaw Rd WNWD SE27 162 B6
Thornley Cl TOTM N17 50 C3
Thornley Dr RYLN/HDSTN HA2 60 B6
Thornsbeach Rd CAT SE6 165 F3
Thornsett Pl PGE/AN SE20 181 J5
Thornsett Rd PGE/AN SE20 181 J5
WAND/EARL SW18 160 A4
Thornsett Ter PGE/AN SE20 * 181 J5
Thornton Av
BRXS/STRHM SW2 161 J4
CHSWK W4 118 B4
CROY/NA CR0 196 A3
WDR/YW UB7 112 C3
Thornton Cl WDR/YW UB7 112 C3
Thornton Dene BECK BR3 182 D5
Thornton Gdns BAL SW12 161 J3
Thornton Gv PIN HA5 42 A2
Thornton Hl WIM/MER SW19 177 H3
Thornton Pl MBLAR W1H 8 E1
Thornton Rd BAL SW12 161 J2
BAR EN5 20 C4
BELV DA17 * 129 J4
BMLY BR1 183 K1
CAR SM5 194 D4
IL IG1 90 B2
MORT/ESHN SW14 138 A5
THHTH CR7 196 B2
UED N18 36 E5
WAN E11 70 B6
WIM/MER SW19 177 G2
Thornton Rw THHTH CR7 196 B2
Thorntons Farm Av
ROMW/RG RM7 74 E6
Thornton St BRXN/ST SW9 142 B3
Thornton Wy GLDGN NW11 65 F2
Thorntree Rd CHARL SE7 126 C5
Thornville Gv MTCM CR4 178 C5
Thornville St DEPT SE8 144 D2
Thornwood Cl SWFD E18 53 F5
Thornwood Rd LEW SE13 145 H6
Thorogood Gdns SRTFD E15 88 C3
Thorogood Wy RAIN RM13 93 G6
Thorold Rd IL IG1 72 B6
WDGN N22 48 E3
Thoroughfare Names
STNW/STAM N16 * 86 A2
Thorparch Rd VX/NE SW8 141 J2
Thorpebank Rd SHB W12 118 D1
Thorpe Cl NKENS W10 100 C5
ORP BR6 201 K6
SYD SE26 * 164 A6
Thorpe Ct TOOT SW17 160 D6
Thorpe Crs OXHEY WD19 27 F2
WALTH E17 51 H5
Thorpedale Gdns
GNTH/NBYPK IG2 72 A1
Thorpedale Rd FSBYPK N4 66 E5
Thorpe Hall Rd WALTH E17 52 A4
Thorpe Rd BARK IG11 90 D5
EHAM E6 89 K6
FSTGT E7 88 E1
KUTN/CMB KT2 175 F3
SEVS/STOTM N15 68 A3
WALTH E17 52 A5
Thorpewood Av SYD SE26 163 J4
Thorpland Av HGDN/ICK UB10 76 A1
Thorsden Wy NRWD SE19 * 181 F1
Thorverton Rd CRICK NW2 82 C1
Thoydon Rd BOW E3 105 G1
Thrale Rd STRHM/NOR SW16 179 H1
Thrale St STHWK SE1 18 D1
Thrasher Cl HACK E8 * 86 B6
Thrawl St WCHPL E1 13 K2
Threadneedle St LOTH EC2R 13 F4
Three Colts La BETH E2 104 D3
Three Colt St POP/IOD E14 * 105 H6
Three Corners BXLYHN DA7 149 J3
Three Kings Yd MYFR/PKLN W1K 9 J5
Three Meadows Ms
KTN/HRWW/WS HA3 43 F4
Three Mill La BOW E3 106 A2
Three Oak La STHWK SE1 19 J2
Threshers Pl NTGHL W11 100 C6
Thriffwood SYD SE26 163 K5
Thrigby Rd CHSGTN KT9 206 B4
Throckmorten Rd
CAN/RD E16 107 F5
Throgmorton Av OBST EC2N 13 F3
Throgmorton St OBST EC2N 13 F3
Throwley Cl ABYW SE2 128 D3
Throwley Rd SUT SM1 209 F3
Throwley Wy SUT SM1 209 F2
Thrupp Cl MTCM CR4 179 G5
Thrush Gn RYLN/HDSTN HA2 60 A1
Thrush St WALW SE17 122 D5
Thunderer Rd DAGW RM9 110 B3
Thurbarn Rd CAT SE6 182 E1
Thurland Rd BERM/RHTH SE16 123 H3
Thurlby Cl WFD IG8 53 K1
Thurlby Rd ALP/SUD HA0 79 K4
WNWD SE27 162 B6
Thurleigh Av BAL SW12 161 F1
Thurleigh Rd BAL SW12 160 E1
Thurleston Av MRDN SM4 193 H2
Thurlestone Av GDMY/SEVK IG3 91 F2
NFNCH/WDSPK N12 47 K2
Thurlestone Rd WNWD SE27 162 B5
Thurloe Cl SKENS SW7 14 C6
Thurloe Gdns ROM RM1 75 G3
Thurloe Pl SKENS SW7 14 C5
Thurloe Place Ms SKENS SW7 * 14 B6
Thurloe Sq SKENS SW7 14 C6
Thurloe St SKENS SW7 14 B6
Thurlow Cl CHING E4 51 K2
Thurlow Gdns ALP/SUD HA0 * 79 K3
BARK/HLT IG6 54 D2
Thurlow Hl DUL SE21 162 D3
Thurlow Park Rd DUL SE21 162 D4
Thurlow Rd HAMP NW3 83 H3
HNWL W7 116 B2
Thurlow St WALW SE17 123 F5
Thurlow Ter KTTN NW5 83 K3
Thurlow Wk WALW SE17 123 F5
Thurlston Rd RSLP HA4 76 E1
Thursland Rd SCUP DA14 187 F2
Thursley Crs CROY/NA CR0 214 B5
Thursley Gdns
WIM/MER SW19 159 G4
Thursley Rd ELTH/MOT SE9 166 E5
Thurso St TOOT SW17 160 C6
Thurstan Rd RYNPK SW20 176 E3
Thurston Rd DEPT SE8 144 E3
STHL UB1 95 K5
Thurtle Rd BETH E2 7 K1
Thwaite Cl ERITH DA8 129 K6
Thyer Cl ORP BR6 216 C2
Thyra Gv NFNCH/WDSPK N12 47 F2
Tibbatt's Rd BOW E3 105 K3
Tibbenham Pl CAT SE6 164 E3
Tibberton Sq IS N1 * 85 J5
Tibbets Cl WIM/MER SW19 159 G3
Tibbet's Ride PUT/ROE SW15 159 G2
Tiber Cl BOW E3 87 J6
Tiber Gdns IS N1 5 F1
Ticehurst Cl STMC/STPC BR5 186 B3
Ticehurst Rd FSTH SE23 164 B4
Tickford Cl ABYW SE2 128 D2
Tidal Basin Rd CAN/RD E16 106 D6
Tidenham Gdns CROY/NA CR0 212 A1
Tideswell Rd CROY/NA CR0 213 J1
PUT/ROE SW15 139 F5
Tideway Cl RCHPK/HAM TW10 156 C6
Tideway Wk VX/NE SW8 * 121 H6
Tidey St BOW E3 105 J4
Tidford Rd WELL DA16 148 A3
Tidworth Rd BOW E3 105 J3
Tiepigs La WWKM BR4 199 H6
Tierney Rd BRXS/STRHM SW2 161 K3
Tierney Ter
BRXS/STRHM SW2 * 161 K3
Tiger La HAYES BR2 200 A1
Tiger Wy CLPT E5 86 D2
Tigres Cl ED N9 36 E4
Tilbrook Rd BKHTH/KID SE3 146 B4
Tilbury Cl PECK SE15 143 G1
STMC/STPC BR5 186 C5
Tilbury Rd EHAM E6 107 K1
LEY E10 70 A4
Tildesley Rd PUT/ROE SW15 159 F1
Tile Farm Rd ORP BR6 216 D1
Tilehurst Rd CHEAM SM3 208 C3
WAND/EARL SW18 160 C3
Tile Kiln La BXLY DA5 169 K4
HGT N6 66 C5
PLMGR N13 49 J1
Tileyard Rd HOLWY N7 84 E5
Tilford Av CROY/NA CR0 214 A5
Tilford Gdns WIM/MER SW19 159 G3
Tilia Cl SUT SM1 208 D3
Tilia Rd CLPT E5 86 D2
Tiller Rd POP/IOD E14 124 D3
Tillett Cl WLSDN NW10 80 E4
Tillet Wy BETH E2 104 C2
Tilley Rd FELT TW13 153 K3
Tillingbourne Gdns FNCH N3 46 D6
Tillingbourne Gn
STMC/STPC BR5 202 B2
Tillingbourne Wy FNCH N3 64 D1
Tillingham Wy
NFNCH/WDSPK N12 32 E6
Tilling Rd CRICK NW2 63 K5
Tilling Wy WBLY HA9 * 79 K1
Tillman St WCHPL E1 104 D5
Tilloch St IS N1 * 85 F5
Tillotson Rd ED N9 36 B4
IL IG1 72 A4
KTN/HRWW/WS HA3 42 B3
Tilney Gdns IS N1 85 K4
Tilney Rd DAGW RM9 92 B4
NWDGN UB2 114 B4
Tilney St MYFR/PKLN W1K 9 H7
Tilson Cl CMBW SE5 143 F1
Tilson Gdns BRXS/STRHM SW2 161 K2
Tilson Rd TOTM N17 50 C4
Tilston Cl WAN E11 88 D1
Tilton St FUL/PGN SW6 119 H6
The Tiltwood ACT W3 98 E6
Tilt Yard Ap ELTH/MOT SE9 166 E1
Timber Cl CHST BR7 185 F5
Timbercroft HOR/WEW KT19 207 G2
Timbercroft La
WOOL/PLUM SE18 127 K6
Timberdene Av BARK/HLT IG6 54 C4
Timberland Cl PECK SE15 * 143 H1
Timberland Rd WCHPL E1 * 104 D5
Timber Mill Wy CLAP SW4 141 J4
Timber Pond Rd
BERM/RHTH SE16 124 A2
Timberslip Dr WLGTN SM6 210 D6
The Timbers CHEAM SM3 * 208 C4
Timber St FSBYE EC1V * 6 C6
Timberwharf Rd
SEVS/STOTM N15 68 C3
Time Sq HACK E8 * 86 B3
Times Sq SUT SM1 * 209 F3
Timms Cl BMLY BR1 200 E1
Timothy Cl BXLYHS DA6 149 F6
Tindal St BRXN/ST SW9 142 C2
Tine Rd CHIG IG7 54 E1
Tinniswood Cl HBRY N5 85 G3
Tinsley Cl SNWD SE25 181 J6
Tinsley Rd WCHPL E1 104 E4
Tintagel Crs EDUL SE22 143 G5
Tintagel Dr STAN HA7 43 K1
Tintagel Rd ORP BR6 202 D6
Tintern Av CDALE/KGS NW9 44 A6
Tintern Cl PUT/ROE SW15 139 H6
WIM/MER SW19 178 B3
Tintern Gdns STHGT/OAK N14 34 E2
Tintern Rd CAR SM5 194 C5
WDGN N22 49 J4
Tintern St CLAP SW4 141 K5
Tintern Wy RYLN/HDSTN HA2 60 B5
Tinto Rd CAN/RD E16 106 E4
Tinworth St STHWK SE1 121 K5
Tippetts Cl ENC/FH EN2 23 J2
Tipthorpe Rd BTSEA SW11 141 F4
Tipton Dr CROY/NA CR0 212 A2
Tiptree Cl CHING E4 38 A5
Tiptree Crs CLAY IG5 54 A6
Tiptree Dr ENC/FH EN2 23 K5
Tiptree Rd RSLP HA4 77 F2
Tirlemont Rd SAND/SEL CR2 211 J5
Tirrell Rd CROY/NA CR0 196 D3
Tisbury Rd STRHM/NOR SW16 179 K5
Tisdall Pl WALW SE17 19 F7
Titan Ct BTFD TW8 117 G5
Titchborne Rw BAY/PAD W2 8 D4
Titchfield Rd CAR SM5 194 C5
STJWD NW8 2 D2
Titchfield Wk CAR SM5 194 C4
Titchwell Rd
WAND/EARL SW18 160 C3
Tite St CHEL SW3 120 E6
Tithe Barn Cl KUTN/CMB KT2 175 G4
Tithe Barn Wy NTHLT UB5 95 F1
Tithe Cl MLHL NW7 45 J4
WOT/HER KT12 188 A3
YEAD UB4 94 D4
Tithe Ct HDN NW4 * 45 J4
Tithe Farm Av
RYLN/HDSTN HA2 78 A1
Tithe Farm Cl RYLN/HDSTN HA2 78 A1
Tithe Wk MLHL NW7 45 J4
Titian Av BUSH WD23 28 E2
Titley Cl CHING E4 51 J1
Titmus Cl UX/CGN UB8 94 A5
Titmuss Av THMD SE28 109 H6
Titmuss St SHB W12 * 118 E2
Tiverton Av CLAY IG5 54 A6
Tiverton Cl CROY/NA CR0 197 G4
Tiverton Rd ALP/SUD HA0 98 A1
EDGW HA8 44 B5
HSLW TW3 135 G3
RSLP HA4 76 E1
SEVS/STOTM N15 67 K3
UED N18 50 A1
WLSDN NW10 82 B6
Tiverton St STHWK SE1 18 C4
Tiverton Wy CHSGTN KT9 205 J3
MLHL NW7 46 B3
Tivoli Gdns WOOL/PLUM SE18 126 D4
Tivoli Rd CEND/HSY/T N8 66 D2
HSLWW TW4 134 D5
WNWD SE27 180 D1
Toad La HSLWW TW4 134 E5
Tobago St POP/IOD E14 124 D2
Tobin Cl HAMP NW3 83 J5
Toby La WCHPL E1 105 G3
Toby Wy SURB KT6 191 J6
Tokenhouse Yd LOTH EC2R 12 E3
Tokyngton Av WBLY HA9 80 C4
Toland Sq PUT/ROE SW15 138 D6
Tolcarne Dr PIN HA5 40 E5
Toley Av KTN/HRWW/WS HA3 62 A4
Tollbridge Cl NKENS W10 100 C3
Tollesbury Gdns BARK/HLT IG6 54 D6
Tollet St WCHPL E1 105 F3
Tollgate Dr DUL SE21 163 F4
YEAD UB4 95 H6
Tollgate Gdns
KIL/WHAMP NW6 * 100 E1
Tollgate Rd EHAM E6 107 J4
Tollhouse La WLGTN SM6 210 C6
Tollhouse Wy ARCH N19 66 C6
Tollington Pk FSBYPK N4 67 F6
Tollington Pl FSBYPK N4 67 F6
Tollington Rd HOLWY N7 85 F2
Tollington Wy HOLWY N7 84 E1
Tolmer's Sq CAMTN NW1 4 B6
Tolpits La WATW WD18 26 B2
Tolpuddle Av PLSTW E13 89 G6
Tolpuddle St IS N1 5 J2
Tolsford Rd HACK E8 86 D3
Tolson Rd ISLW TW7 136 B4
Tolverne Rd RYNPK SW20 177 F4
Tolworth Broadway SURB KT6 191 H5
Tolworth Cl SURB KT6 191 J5
Tolworth Gdns CHDH RM6 73 K2
Tolworth Park Rd SURB KT6 191 G6
Tolworth Ri North
BRYLDS KT5 191 K4
Tolworth Ri North (Kingston
By-pass) BRYLDS KT5 191 K5
Tolworth Ri South
BRYLDS KT5 191 K5
NWMAL KT3 192 A4
Tolworth Rd SURB KT6 191 F6
Tolworth U/P (Kingston
By-Pass) SURB KT6 206 C1
Tom Cribb Rd THMD SE28 127 J3
Tom Groves Cl SRTFD E15 88 B3
Tom Hood Cl SRTFD E15 88 B3
Tom Jenkinson Rd
CAN/RD E16 125 K1
Tomlin's Gv BOW E3 105 J2
Tomlinson Cl BETH E2 7 K5
CHSWK W4 117 J5
Tomlins Orch BARK IG11 90 C6
Tomlin's Ter POP/IOD E14 105 G5
Tom Mann Cl BARK IG11 90 E6
Tom Nolan Cl SRTFD E15 106 C1
Tompion St FSBYE EC1V 6 A5
Tom Smith Cl GNWCH SE10 125 H6
Tomswood Hl BARK/HLT IG6 54 C4
Tomswood Rd CHIG IG7 54 A2
Tonbridge Crs
KTN/HRWW/WS HA3 62 A1
Tonbridge Rd
E/WMO/HCT KT8 188 D1
Tonbridge St STPAN WC1H 4 E5
Tonfield Rd CHEAM SM3 193 J5
Tonge Cl BECK BR3 198 D2
Tonsley Hl WAND/EARL SW18 140 A6
Tonsley Pl WAND/EARL SW18 140 A6
Tonsley Rd WAND/EARL SW18 140 A6
Tonsley St WAND/EARL SW18 140 A6
Tonstall Rd MTCM CR4 179 F5
Tooke Cl PIN HA5 41 J4
Tookey Cl KTN/HRWW/WS HA3 62 B4
Took's Ct FLST/FETLN EC4A 11 J3
Tooley St STHWK SE1 19 G1
Toorack Rd
KTN/HRWW/WS HA3 42 D5
Tooting Bec Gdns
STRHM/NOR SW16 161 J6
Tooting Bec Rd TOOT SW17 161 F5
Tooting Gv TOOT SW17 178 D1
Tooting High St TOOT SW17 178 D2
Tootswood Rd HAYES BR2 199 H2
Topcliffe Dr ORP BR6 216 D2
Topham Sq TOTM N17 49 J4
Topham St CLKNW EC1R * 5 J6
Top House Ri CHING E4 38 A2
Topiary Sq RCH/KEW TW9 137 G4
Topley St ELTH/MOT SE9 146 B5
Topmast Point POP/IOD E14 * 124 D2
Top Pk BECK BR3 199 H2
Topsfield Cl CEND/HSY/T N8 66 D2
Topsfield Pde
CEND/HSY/T N8 * 66 E2
Topsfield Rd CEND/HSY/T N8 66 E2
Topsham Rd TOOT SW17 160 E5
Torbay Rd KIL/WHAMP NW6 82 D5
RYLN/HDSTN HA2 59 J6
Torbay St CAMTN NW1 * 84 B5
Torbitt Wy GNTH/NBYPK IG2 73 F2
Torbridge Cl EDGW HA8 44 A3
Torcross Dr FSTH SE23 163 K4
Torcross Rd RSLP HA4 77 F1
Tor Gdns KENS W8 119 K2
Tor Gv THMD SE28 127 K1
Tormead Cl SUT SM1 208 E4
Tormount Rd
WOOL/PLUM SE18 127 K6
Toronto Av MNPK E12 89 K2
Toronto Rd IL IG1 72 B5
Torquay Gdns REDBR IG4 71 H1
Torquay St BAY/PAD W2 101 F4
Torrens Rd BRXS/STRHM SW2 142 A6
SRTFD E15 88 D4
Torrens Sq SRTFD E15 88 D4
Torrens St FSBYE EC1V 6 A3
Torres Sq POP/IOD E14 124 D5
Torrey Dr BRXN/ST SW9 142 B3
Torriano Av KTTN NW5 84 D3
Torriano Cottages KTTN NW5 84 D3
Torriano Ms KTTN NW5 84 C3
Torridge Gdns PECK SE15 143 K5
Torridge Rd THHTH CR7 196 C2
Torridon Rd CAT SE6 165 G3
Torrington Av
NFNCH/WDSPK N12 47 H1
Torrington Cl ESH/CLAY KT10 204 E4
Torrington Dr
RYLN/HDSTN HA2 78 B2
Torrington Gdns
FBAR/BDGN N11 48 C2
GFD/PVL UB6 79 J6
Torrington Gv
NFNCH/WDSPK N12 47 J1
Torrington Pk
NFNCH/WDSPK N12 33 H6
Torrington Pl FITZ W1T 10 B1
GWRST WC1E 4 C7
WAP E1W 123 H1
Torrington Rd BCTR RM8 74 B5
ESH/CLAY KT10 204 E4
GFD/PVL UB6 79 J6
RSLP HA4 76 E1
Torrington Sq CROY/NA CR0 * 196 E4

STPAN WC1H 4 D7
Torrington Sq MRDN SM4 ....193 K4
Tor Rd WELL DA16.......................148 D2
Torr Rd PGE/AN SE20...................182 A3
Torver Rd HRW HA1.......................60 E1
Torver Wy ORP BR6.....................216 C1
Torwood Rd PUT/ROE SW15.......138 D4
Tothill St STJSPK SW1H................16 C5
Totnes Rd WELL DA16.................148 C1
Totnes Wk FBAR/BDGN N11 *.......48 C1
Tottan Ter WCHPL E1 *................105 F5
Tottenhall Rd PLMGR N13.............49 G2
Tottenham Court Rd FITZ W1T........4 B7
Tottenham Gn East
  SEVS/STOTM N15......................68 B1
Tottenham Gn East South Side
  SEVS/STOTM N15......................68 B1
Tottenham Ms FITZ W1T *.............10 B1
Tottenham Rd IS N1.......................86 A4
Tottenham St FITZ W1T.................10 B2
Totterdown St TOOT SW17..........160 E6
Totteridge Common
  TRDG/WHET N20.......................31 K4
Totteridge La TRDG/WHET N20 ...32 A4
Totteridge Village
  TRDG/WHET N20.......................32 D3
Totternhoe Cl
  KTN/HRWW/WS HA3.................61 J2
Totton Rd THHTH CR7.................180 B6
Toulmin St STHWK SE1.................18 C5
Toulon St CMBW SE5..................142 D1
Tournay Rd FUL/PGN SW6..........139 K1
Toussaint Wk
  BERM/RHTH SE16....................123 H5
Tovil Cl PGE/AN SE20..................181 H5
Towcester Rd BOW E3.................105 K3
Tower Br WAP E1W *.....................13 J7
Tower Bridge App TWRH EC3N......13 J7
Tower Bridge Ms ALP/SUD HA0....79 F2
Tower Bridge Rd STHWK SE1........19 H4
Tower Buildings WAP E1W *........123 J1
Tower Cl BARK/HLT IG6.................54 B2
  HAMP NW3.................................83 H3
  ORP BR6..................................202 A6
  PGE/AN SE20...........................181 J3
Tower Ct LSQ/SEVD WC2H *.........10 E4
Tower Gdns ESH/CLAY KT10.......205 H5
Tower Gardens Rd TOTM N17........49 J4
Tower Hamlets Rd FSTGT E7.........88 D2
  WALTH E17.................................51 J4
Tower Hl TWRH EC3N....................13 J6
Tower Hill Ter MON EC3R *............13 H6
Tower La WBLY HA9 *....................79 K1
Tower Ms CLPT E5..........................87 G3
  WALTH E17.................................51 J4
Tower Mill Rd CMBW SE5 *..........143 F1
Tower Park Rd DART DA1.............150 C6
Tower Pl MON EC3R.......................13 H6
Tower Ri RCH/KEW TW9..............137 F4
Tower Rd BELV DA17...................129 K4
  BXLYHN DA7............................149 J5
  DART DA1................................149 J5
  ORP BR6..................................202 A6
  TWK TW1.................................156 A5
  WLSDN NW10............................81 J5
Tower Royal MANHO EC4N *.........12 D5
Towers Av HGDN/ICK UB10..........94 A2
Towers Ct HGDN/ICK UB10 *........94 A2
Towers Pl RCH/KEW TW9............137 F6
Towers Rd PIN HA5........................41 J4
  STHL UB1...................................96 A3
Tower St LSQ/SEVD WC2H...........10 E4
Tower Ter WGDN N22 *.................49 F5
Tower Vw CROY/NA CRO.............198 B5
Towfield Rd FELT TW13...............154 E4
Towncourt Crs
  STMC/STPC BR5.......................201 H2
Towncourt La STMC/STPC BR5....201 J3
Towncourt Pth FSBYPK N4 ....67 H4
Town End Pde KUT/HW KT1 *......174 E6
Towney Md NTHLT UB5..................95 K1
Town Farm Wy
  STWL/WRAY TW19 *.................152 A2
Townfield Rd HYS/HAR UB3.........113 K1
Townfield Sq HYS/HAR UB3.........113 J1
Town Field Wy ISLW TW7.............136 B3
Town Hall Approach Rd
  SEVS/STOTM N15......................68 B1
Townhall Av CHSWK W4..............118 A5
Town Hall Pde
  BRXS/STRHM SW2 *.................142 A5
Town Hall Rd BTSEA SW11.........140 E4
Townholm Crs HNWL W7.............116 A3
Town La STWL/WRAY TW19........152 A2
Townley Ct SRTFD E15...................88 D4
Townley Rd BXLYHS DA6............149 H5
  EDUL SE22...............................143 G4
Townley St WALW SE17................122 E5
Town Meadow BTFD TW8............136 E1
Townmead Rd FUL/PGN SW6......140 B3
  RCH/KEW TW9.........................137 J3
Town Quay BARK IG11...................90 C6
Town Rd ED N9..............................36 D4
Townsend Av STHGT/OAK N14......34 D6
Townsend La CDALE/KGS NW9.....63 F4
Townsend Ms
  WAND/EARL SW18....................160 B4
Townsend Rd SEVS/STOTM N15...68 C2
  STHL UB1.................................114 D1
  STJWD NW8.................................2 B2
  WOOL/PLUM SE18...................127 C3
Townsend St STHWK SE1.............19 G6
Townsend Wy NTHWD HA6..........40 D3
Townsend Yd HGT N6...................66 B5
Townshend Cl SCUP DA14...........186 D2
Townshend Est STJWD NW8 *........2 C2
Townshend Rd CHST BR7............185 G1
  RCH/KEW TW9.........................137 G5
  STJWD NW8.................................2 C1
Townshend Ter RCH/KEW TW9...137 G5
Townson Av NTHLT UB5................94 K1
Townson Wy NTHLT UB5...............94 K1
Town Whf ISLW TW7 *..................136 C4
Towpath WOT/HER KT12 *...........188 A1
Towpath Rd UED N18.....................51 F2

Towpath Wy CROY/NA CRO........197 G3
Towton Rd WNWD SE27..............162 D4
Toynbec Cl CHST BR7..................167 G6
Toynbee Rd RYNPK SW20...........177 H4
Toynbee St WCHPL E1...................13 J2
Toyne Wy HGT N6..........................65 K3
Tracey Av CRICK NW2 *.................82 A3
Trade Cl PLMGR N13.....................35 G6
Trader Rd EHAM E6......................108 B6
Tradescant Rd VX/NE SW8...........141 K1
Trading Estate Rd
  WLSDN NW10 *..........................98 E3
Trafalgar Av PECK SE15...............123 G6
  TOTM N17..................................50 A2
  WPK KT4...................................193 C5
Trafalgar Chambers
  CHEL SW3 *..............................120 C5
Trafalgar Gdns KENS W8 *...........120 A3
  WCHPL E1................................105 F4
Trafalgar Gv GNWCH SE10..........125 G6
Trafalgar Ms HOM E9 *..................87 H4
Trafalgar Pl UED N18.....................50 E1
  WAN E11....................................70 E1
Trafalgar Rd DART DA1................171 H4
  GNWCH SE10...........................125 H5
  RAIN RM13...............................111 H1
  WHTN TW2...............................155 J4
  WIM/MER SW19........................178 A3
Trafalgar Sq STJS SW1Y *.............10 D7
Trafalgar St WALW SE17...............122 E5
Trafalgar Wy CROY/NA CRO........196 B6
  POP/IOD E14............................125 F1
Trafford Cl BARK/HLT IG6..............55 F2
  SRTFD E15.................................88 A3
Trafford Rd THHTH CR7...............196 A2
Trahorn Cl WCHPL E1...................105 F3
Tramway Av ED N9........................36 D2
  SRTFD E15.................................88 B5
Tramway Ct PGE/AN SE20 *.........181 K4
Tramway Path MTCM CR4...........194 D1
Tranby Ms HOM E9 *......................87 F3
Tranley Ms HAMP NW3 *...............83 J2
Tranmere Rd ED N9........................36 B2
  WAND/EARL SW18....................160 B4
  WHTN TW2...............................155 G2
Tranquil Pas BKHTH/KID SE3 *....145 J3
Tranquil Ri ERITH DA8..................130 B5
Tranquil V BKHTH/KID SE3..........145 J3
Transept St CAMTN NW1.................8 C2
Transmere Rd STMC/STPC BR5...201 H3
Transom Ct BERM/RHTH SE16....124 B4
Transom Sq POP/IOD E14............124 E5
Transport Av BTFD TW8...............116 C6
Tranton Rd BERM/RHTH SE16....123 J3
Traps La NWMAL KT3...................176 B5
Travellers Site CHING E4 *.............51 H3
Travellers Wy HEST TW5.............134 B3
Travers Cl WALTH E17...................51 F4
Travers Rd HOLWY N7...................85 G1
Treacy Cl BUSH WD23...................28 C4
Treadgold St NTGHL W11.............100 B6
Treadway St BETH E2...................104 D1
Treaty Centre HSLW TW3 *..........135 G4
Treaty St IS N1..................................5 G1
Trebeck St MYFR/PICC W1J............9 J7
Trebovir Rd ECT SW5...................119 K5
Treby St BOW E3..........................105 H3
Trecastle Wy HOLWY N7................84 D2
Tredegar Rd BOW E3....................105 H1
  FBAR/BDGN N11........................48 D3
  RDART DA2..............................170 D5
Tredegar Sq BOW E3...................105 H2
Tredenwen Rd HACK E8.................86 C6
Tredown Rd SYD SE26..................181 K1
Tredwell Ct BRXS/STRHM SW2 *.162 A4
  HAYES BR2 *............................200 C1
Tredwell Rd WNWD SE27............162 C6
Tree Cl RCHPK/HAM TW10..........156 E3
Treen Av BARN SW13...................138 C4
Tree Rd CAN/RD E16....................107 G5
Treeside Cl WDGN UB7 *.............112 A4
Tree Top Ms DAGE RM10..............93 F4
Treetops Cl ABYW SE2.................129 F5
  NTHWD HA6.............................40 A3
Treetops Vw LOU IG10...................39 H1
Tree View Cl NRWD SE19............181 F4
Treewall Gdns BMLY BR1.............166 A6
Trefgarne Rd DAGE RM10.............74 C6
Trefoil Rd WAND/EARL SW18......140 B6
Tregaron Av CEND/HSY/T N8.........66 E4
Tregaron Gdns NWMAL KT3........192 B1
Tregarvon Rd BTSEA SW11.........141 F5
Tregenna Av RYLN/HDSTN HA2....78 A2
Tregenna Cl STHGT/OAK N14........22 C6
Tregony Rd ORP BR6...................217 F2
Trego Rd HOM E9..........................87 J5
Tregothnan Rd BRXN/ST SW9.....141 K4
Tregunter Rd WBPTN SW10........120 B6
Trehearn Rd BARK/HLT IG6...........54 D3
Treherne Ct BRXN/ST SW9 *.......142 C2
Trehern Rd MORT/ESHN SW14...138 A4
Trehurst St CLPT E5.......................87 G3
Trelawney Est HOM E9 *................86 E4
Trelawney Rd BARK/HLT IG6.........54 D3
Trelawn Rd BRXS/STRHM SW2...142 B4
  LEY E10.....................................69 K6
Trelawny Cl WALTH E17.................69 K1
Trellis Sq BOW E3........................105 H2
Treloar Gdns NRWD SE19............180 E2
Trelwney Est HOM E9 *..................86 E4
Tremadoc Rd CLAP SW4..............141 J5
Tremaine Cl BROCKY SE4............144 D3
Tremaine Rd PGE/AN SE20..........181 J5
Trematon Pl TEDD TW11..............174 D3
Tremlett Gv ARCH N19...................84 C1
Tremlett Ms ARCH N19...................84 C1
Trenance Gdns GDMY/SEVK IG3...91 G1
Trenchard Av RSLP HA4.................77 F3
Trenchard Cl CDALE/KGS NW9.....45 G4
  STAN HA7.................................43 G2
Trenchard St GNWCH SE10.........125 C5
Trenchold St VX/NE SW8 *...........141 K1
Trenear Cl ORP BR6.....................217 G2
Trenholme Cl PGE/AN SE20.........181 J3
Trenholme Rd PGE/AN SE20........181 J3
Trenmar Gdns WLSDN NW10........99 K2
Trent Av EA W5...........................116 D3

Trentbridge Cl BARK/HLT IG6........55 F2
Trent Ct WAN E11 *........................70 E2
Trent Gdns STHGT/OAK N14........34 B1
Trenton Dr STMC/STPC BR5........202 J3
Trentham St
  WAND/EARL SW18....................159 K3
Trent Pk EBAR EN4 *.....................22 C3
Trent Rd BKHH IG9........................39 F3
  BRXS/STRHM SW2...................142 A6
Trent Wy WPK KT4......................208 A1
  YEAD UB4..................................94 D2
Trentwood Side ENC/FH EN2........22 E5
Treport St WAND/EARL SW18......160 A2
Tresco Cl BMLY BR1....................183 H2
Trescoe Gdns CRW RM5................56 C1
Tresham Crs STJWD NW8...............2 C6
Tresco Gdns GDMY/SEVK IG3......73 F6
Tresco Rd PECK SE15..................143 J5
Tresham Rd BARK IG11..................91 F5
Tresilian Av WCHMH N21...............35 F1
Tressillian Crs BROCKY SE4........144 D4
Tressillian Rd BROCKY SE4.........144 D4
Trestis Cl YEAD UB4......................95 H3
Treswell Rd DAGE RM9................92 A6
Tretawn Gdns MLHL NW7..............31 G6
Tretawn Pk MLHL NW7.................31 G6
Trevanion Rd WKENS W14 *........119 H5
Treve Av HRW HA1........................60 C4
Trevelyan Av MNPK E12.................89 K2
Trevelyan Crs
  KTN/HRWW/WS HA3.................61 K4
Trevelyan Gdns WLSDN NW10 *....82 A6
Trevelyan Rd SRTFD E15...............88 D2
  TOOT SW17..............................178 E2
Treveris St STHWK SE1.................18 B1
Treverton St NKENS W10............100 B3
Treves Cl WCHMH N21..................23 F6
Treville St PUT/ROE SW15...........158 E2
Treviso Rd FSTH SE23.................164 A4
Trevithick Cl
  EBED/NFELT TW14...................153 J5
Trevithick St DEPT SE8................124 D6
Trevone Gdns PIN HA5...................59 J3
Trevor Cl EBAR EN4......................33 J1
  HAYES BR2...............................199 K4
  ISLW TW7.................................136 B5
  KTN/HRWW/WS HA3.................43 J1
  NTHLT UB5.................................95 C1
Trevor Crs RSLP HA4....................76 D2
Trevor Gdns EDGW HA8...............45 F4
  NTHLT UB5.................................95 C1
Trevor Pl SKENS SW7....................14 D3
Trevor Rd EDGW HA8...................45 F4
  HYS/HAR UB3...........................113 H2
  WFD IG8.....................................52 E3
  WIM/MER SW19........................177 H3
Trevor Sq SKENS SW7..................14 D3
Trevor St SKENS SW7...................14 D3
Trevose Rd WALTH E17.................52 B4
Trevose Wy OXHEY WD19.............27 G5
Trewenna Dr CHSGTN KT9..........205 K3
Trewince Rd RYNPK SW20..........177 F5
Trewint St WAND/EARL SW18.....160 B4
Trewsbury Rd SYD SE26..............182 A1
Triandra Wy YEAD UB4..................95 H4
Triangle Est LBTH SE11 *.............122 A5
Triangle Pas EBAR EN4 *...............21 G5
Triangle Pl CLAP SW4..................141 J5
Triangle Rd HACK E8......................86 D6
The Triangle BFN/LL DA15 *........168 B2
  HACK E8....................................86 D6
  KUT/HW KT1............................175 K5
Triangle Wy ACT W3....................117 H3
Trident Cl CHEL SW3 *..................14 D7
Trident St BERM/RHTH SE16......124 A4
Trident Wy NWDGN UB2.............114 A3
Trig La BLKFR EC4V *....................12 C5
Trigo Ct HOR/WEW KT19 *..........207 F6
Trigon Rd VX/NE SW8..................142 A1
Trilby Rd FSTH SE23....................164 A4
Trim St NWCR SE14.....................124 C6
Trinder Rd ARCH N19....................67 F5
  BAR EN5.....................................20 A6
Tring Av ACT W3..........................117 G2
  STHL UB1...................................96 A4
  WBLY HA9..................................80 C4
Tring Cl GNTH/NBYPK IG2............72 D2
Trinidad Gdns DAGE RM10............93 F5
Trinidad St POP/IOD E14.............105 H6
Trinity Av EN EN1.........................36 B1
  EFNCH N2..................................47 H1
Trinity Buoy Whf
  POP/IOD E14 *.........................106 B4
Trinity Church Rd BARN SW13.....118 E6
Trinity Church Sq STHWK SE1.......18 D4
Trinity Cl CLAP SW4 *..................141 H5
  HACK E8....................................86 B4
  HAYES BR2...............................200 D5
  HSLWW TW4............................134 D5
  LEW SE13.................................145 G5
  NTHWD HA6.............................40 B2
  WAN E11....................................70 C6
Trinity Ct ELTH/MOT SE9 *..........167 G3
Trinity Crs TOOT SW17................160 E4
Trinity Dr UX/CGN UB8..................94 A5
Trinity Est DEPT SE8...................124 C5
Trinity Gdns BRXN/ST SW9.........142 A5
  CAN/RD E16.............................106 D3
  DART DA1................................171 G1
Trinity Gv GNWCH SE10..............145 F2
Trinity Ms PGE/AN SE20..............181 K4
  WKENS W10 *..........................100 B4
Trinity Pde HSLW TW3 *..............135 G3
  WLGTN SM6 *..........................210 B4
Trinity Pk CHING E4 *...................51 G3
Trinity Pl BXLYHS DA6................149 F5
  TWRH EC3N...............................13 J6
Trinity Ri BRXS/STRHM SW2.......162 C2
Trinity Rd BARK/HLT IG6...............54 B2
  EFNCH N2..................................47 H1
  RCH/KEW TW9.........................137 G4
  STHL UB1.................................114 D1
  WAND/EARL SW18....................160 B4
  WDGN N22..................................48 D5
  WIM/MER SW19........................177 K2

Trinity Sq TWRH EC3N..................13 H6
Trinity St CAN/RD E16.................106 D4
  ENC/FH EN2...............................23 J3
  STHWK SE1................................18 D3
Trinity Wy ACT W3........................99 G6
  CHING E4....................................51 H2
Trio Pl STHWK SE1.......................18 D3
Tristan Sq BKHTH/KID SE3.........145 H4
Tristram Cl WALTH E17..................52 B6
Tristram Rd BMLY BR1.................165 J6
Triton Sq CAMTN NW1....................4 A6
Tritton Av CROY/NA CRO.............210 E2
Tritton Rd DUL SE21....................162 E5
Triumph Cl HYS/HAR UB3............133 F2
Triumph Rd EHAM E6...................107 K5
Trojan Wy CROY/NA CRO.............211 F1
Troon Cl BERM/RHTH SE16.........123 J5
  THMD SE28...............................109 K5
Troon St WCHPL E1......................105 G5
Trosley Rd BELV DA17.................129 H6
Trossachs Rd EDUL SE22.............143 H4
Trothy Rd STHWK SE1..................123 H4
Trott Rd MUSWH N10....................48 A3
Trott St BTSEA SW11...................140 D3
Trotwood CHIG IG7........................54 D2
Troughton Rd CHARL SE7............126 A5
Troutbeck Rd NWCR SE14...........144 B1
Trout Rd WDR/YW UB7................112 A1
Trouville Rd CLAP SW4................161 H1
Trowbridge Rd HOM E9..................87 H4
Trowlock Av TEDD TW11..............174 E2
Trowlock Wy TEDD TW11.............174 E2
Troy Ct KENS W8.........................119 K3
Troy Rd NRWD SE19....................180 E2
Troy Town PECK SE15.................143 H4
Trubshaw Rd NWDGN UB2..........115 G3
Trueman Cl EDGW HA8..................44 D3
Trulock Rd TOTM N17....................50 C3
Truman's Rd STNW/STAM N16.....86 A3
Trumpers Wy HNWL W7...............116 A3
Trumpington Rd FSTGT E7.............88 D2
Trundle St STHWK SE1..................18 C3
Trundlers End DEPT SE8 *............124 B6
Trundley's Ter DEPT SE8..............124 A4
Truro Gdns IL IG1..........................71 J4
Truro St KTTN NW5........................84 A4
Truro Rd WALTH E17......................69 H1
  WDGN N22.................................48 E3
Trusedale Rd EHAM E6................107 K5
Truslove Rd WNWD SE27............180 B1
Trussley Rd HMSMTH W6............119 F3
Trustons Gdns EMPK RM11...........75 J4
Tryfan Cl REDBR IG4......................71 H2
Tryon Cl REDBR IG4 *...................71 H2
Tryon Crs HOM E9.........................86 E6
Tryon St CHEL SW3.....................120 E5
Trystings Cl ESH/CLAY KT10.......205 G4
Tuam Rd WOOL/PLUM SE18.......127 J6
Tubbenden Cl ORP BR6...............216 E1
Tubbenden Dr ORP BR6...............216 D2
Tubbenden La ORP BR6...............216 E2
Tubbenden La South ORP BR6.....216 D3
Tubbs Rd WLSDN NW10................99 H1
Tuck Rd RAIN RM13......................93 J4
Tudor Av GPK RM2.......................57 J6
  HPTN TW12..............................173 F2
  WPK KT4...................................207 K1
Tudor Cl ASHF TW15....................152 B6
  BRXS/STRHM SW2 *.................162 A1
  CDALE/KGS NW9........................62 E5
  CHEAM SM3..............................208 B5
  CHSGTN KT9.............................206 A3
  CHST BR7..................................184 E4
  HAMP NW3................................83 J3
  HGT N6.....................................66 C4
  HPTN TW12..............................173 H1
  MLHL NW7..................................32 A6
  PIN HA5......................................58 E2
  WFD IG8.....................................53 F1
  WLGTN SM6..............................210 D5
Tudor Ct ELTH/MOT SE9 *...........146 D5
  SWFD E18..................................53 F3
  STHL UB1 *................................95 K6
  WALTH E17 *..............................52 A3
Tudor Ct North WBLY HA9............80 C3
Tudor Ct South WBLY HA9............80 C3
Tudor Crs BARK/HLT IG6...............54 C2
  ENC/FH EN2...............................23 K1
Tudor Dr GPK RM2.......................75 J1
  KUTN/CMB KT2.........................175 F1
  MRDN SM4...............................193 G3
  WOT/HER KT12........................188 D5
Tudor Enterprise Pk
  KTN/HRWW/WS HA3 *...............42 D6
Tudor Est WLSDN NW10...............98 C1
Tudor Gdns ACT W3.....................98 D4
  BARN SW13..............................138 B4
  CDALE/KGS NW9........................62 E5
  GPK RM2....................................75 J1
  TWK TW1.................................156 A3
  WWKM BR4..............................214 A1
Tudor Gv HOM E9..........................86 E5
  TRDG/WHET N20 *.....................33 J4
Tudor Pde ELTH/MOT SE9 *........146 D5
  NRWD SE19 *...........................181 G3
Tudor Pl MTCM CR4.....................178 D3
  SOHO/SHAV W1D *....................10 C4
Tudor Rd BAR EN5.......................20 E4
  BARK IG11.................................91 F1
  BECK BR3.................................183 F6
  ED N9..36 D2
  HACK E8.....................................86 B6
  HPTN TW12..............................173 F3
  HSLW TW3................................135 J5
  KTN/HRWW/WS HA3.................43 F5
  KUTN/CMB KT2.........................175 H3
  NWDGN UB2.............................114 C3
  PGE/AN SE20............................181 K5
  PIN HA5......................................41 G5
  SNWD SE25..............................197 J2
  STHL UB1...................................95 J5
Tudor Sq HYS/HAR UB3...............94 B4
Tudor St EMB EC4Y.......................11 K5

Tudor Wy ACT W3.........................117 H2
  STHGT/OAK N14........................34 D3
  STMC/STPC BR5.......................201 J5
Tudway Rd BKHTH/KID SE3.........146 B5
Tufnail Rd DART DA1...................171 J1
Tufnell Park Rd HOLWY N7...........85 F2
Tufter Rd CHIG IG7........................55 F1
Tufton Gdns E/WMO/HCT KT8.....173 G5
Tufton Rd CHING E4......................51 J2
Tufton St WEST SW1P...................16 E5
Tugboat St THMD SE28................128 A1
Tugela Rd CROY/NA CRO.............196 E3
Tugela St CAT SE6.......................164 C4
Tugmutton Cl ORP BR6................216 B2
Tuilerie St BETH E2.........................7 K1
Tulip Cl CROY/NA CRO.................198 A5
  EHAM E6...................................108 A4
  HPTN TW12..............................172 E2
  NWDGN UB2.............................115 H2
Tulip Gdns CHING E4.....................38 B5
  IL IG1..90 B4
Tulip Wy WDR/YW UB7................112 A4
Tull St MTCM CR4.......................194 E4
Tulse Cl BECK BR3.......................183 F6
Tulse Hill BRXS/STRHM SW2......162 B3
Tulsemere Rd WNWD SE27.........162 E4
Tummons Gdns SNWD SE25........197 F5
Tuncombe Rd UED N18.................36 A6
Tunis Rd SHB W12........................119 F1
Tunley Gn POP/IOD E14 *............105 H4
Tunley Rd TOOT SW17.................161 F4
  WLSDN NW10............................81 G6
Tunmarsh La PLSTW E13.............107 G2
Tunnan Leys EHAM E6.................108 A5
Tunnel Av GNWCH SE10..............125 H3
Tunnel Gdns FBAR/BDGN N11.....48 B3
Tunnel Link Rd HTHAIR TW6.......132 D6
Tunnel Rd BERM/RHTH SE16......123 K2
Tunnel Rd East WDR/YW UB7.....132 D2
Tunnel Rd West WDR/YW UB7.....132 D2
Tunstall Av BARK/HLT IG6............55 G2
Tunstall Rd BRXN/ST SW9...........142 A5
  CROY/NA CRO.........................197 F5
Tunstock Wy BELV DA17.............129 F3
Tunworth Cl CDALE/KGS NW9.....62 E3
Tunworth Crs PUT/ROE SW15.....158 C1
Tupelo Rd LEY E10........................69 K6
Tuppy St THMD SE28...................127 H3
Turene Cl WAND/EARL SW18......140 A5
Turin Rd ED N9.............................36 E2
Turin St BETH E2...........................7 K3
Turkey Oak Cl NRWD SE19.........181 F4
Turks Rw CHEL SW3....................121 F5
Turle Rd FSBYPK N4 *...................67 F6
  STRHM/NOR SW16...................179 K5
Turlewray Cl FSBYPK N4...............67 F5
Turley Cl SRTFD E15.....................88 C6
Turnagain La
  FLST/FETLN EC4A *...................12 A3
Turnage Rd BCTR RM8.................74 A4
Turnant Rd TOTM N17...................49 H3
Turnberry Cl
  BERM/RHTH SE16....................123 J5
  HDN NW4....................................46 B5
Turnberry Ct OXHEY WD19 *.........27 G5
Turnberry Wy ORP BR6...............201 J5
Turnbury Cl THMD SE28..............109 K5
Turner Av MTCM CR4..................178 E4
  SEVS/STOTM N15....................68 A1
  WHTN TW2...............................155 H5
Turner Cl ALP/SUD HA0................79 K4
  BRXN/ST SW9...........................142 C2
  GLDGN NW11 *..........................65 F3
Turner Ct CMBW SE5 *................142 E5
  DART DA1................................151 J5
Turner Dr GLDGN NW11...............65 F3
Turner Ms BELMT SM2................209 F5
Turner Rd EDGW HA8...................44 A5
  NWMAL KT3..............................192 A4
  WALTH E17.................................70 A1
Turners Cl TRDG/WHET N20.........33 K3
Turners Meadow Wy
  BECK BR3.................................182 C4
Turner St CAN/RD E16.................106 D5
  WCHPL E1................................104 D4
Turners Wy CROY/NA CRO..........196 B6
Turner's Wd GLDGN NW11...........65 G5
Turneville Rd WKENS W14...........119 J6
Turney Rd DUL SE21...................162 D2
Turnham Green Ter
  CHSWK W4................................118 B4
Turnham Rd BROCKY SE4............144 B6
Tunmmill St FARR EC1M.................5 K7
Turnpike Cl DEPT SE8..................144 C1
Turnpike Dr ORP BR6...................217 J6
Turnpike La CEND/HSY/T N8.........67 G1
  SUT SM1...................................209 G3
Turnpike Ms CEND/HSY/T N8 *.....49 G6
Turnpike Pde
  SEVS/STOTM N15 *....................49 H6
Turnpike Wy ISLW TW7................136 B2
Turnstone Cl CDALE/KGS NW9 *...45 G5
  PLSTW E13...............................106 E2
Turnstone Ter W13 *......................97 H7
Turpentine La PIM SW1V..............121 G5
Turpin Cl WAP E1W......................105 F6
Turpington Cl HAYES BR2............200 D3
Turpington La HAYES BR2...........200 D4
Turpin La ERITH DA8...................130 D6
Turpin Rd EBED/NFELT TW14.....153 K1
Turpin's La WFD IG8......................53 K1
Turpington Rd CRCK NW2 *...........63 K6
  GNWCH SE10...........................125 F1
Turpin Wy WLGTN SM6...............210 B6
Turquand St WALW SE17...............18 D7
Turret Gv CLAP SW4...................141 H4
Turville St BETH E2 *......................7 J5
Tuscan Rd WOOL/PLUM SE18....127 J5
Tuskar St GNWCH SE10..............125 H5
Tweeddale Gv HGDN/ICK UB10...76 A1
Tweeddale Rd CAR SM5...............194 C5

Tweedmouth Rd PLSTW E13 107 F1
Tweed Wy ROM RM1 57 F3
Tweedy Rd BMLY BR1 183 K4
Twelvetrees Crs BOW E3 106 B3
Twentyman Cl WFD IG8 52 E1
Twickenham Br TWK TW1 136 D6
Twickenham Cl CROY/NA CR0 211 F1
Twickenham Gdns
GFD/PVL UB6 79 G3
KTN/HRWW/WS HA3 42 E3
Twickenham Rd FELT TW13 154 E5
FELT TW13 155 F5
ISLW TW7 136 A6
RCH/KEW TW9 136 D6
TEDD TW11 174 B1
WAN E11 70 B6
Twig Folly Cl BETH E2 105 F1
Twig Folly Whf BETH E2 * 105 F1
Twigg Cl ERITH DA8 150 B1
Twilley St WAND/EARL SW18 160 A2
Twine Cl BARK IG11 109 H2
Twine Ct WCHPL E1 104 E6
Twineham Gn
NFNCH/WDSPK N12 32 E6
Twine Ter BOW E3 * 105 H3
Twining Av WHTN TW2 155 H5
Twinn Rd MLHL NW7 46 C2
Twin Tumps Wy THMD SE28 109 G6
Twisden Rd KTTN NW5 84 B2
Twisleton Ct DART DA1 171 G1
Twybridge Wy WLSDN NW10 80 E5
Twycross Ms GNWCH SE10 125 H5
Twyford Abbey Rd
WLSDN NW10 98 B2
Twyford Av ACT W3 98 C6
EFNCH N2 47 K6
Twyford Crs ACT W3 117 H1
Twyford Rd CAR SM5 194 C5
IL IG1 90 C3
RYLN/HDSTN HA2 60 B4
Twyford St IS N1 85 F6
Tyas Rd CAN/RD E16 106 D3
Tybenham Rd WIM/MER SW19 177 K6
Tyberry Rd PEND EN3 24 D4
Tyburn La HRW HA1 60 E4
Tyburn Wy MBLAR W1H 9 F5
Tye La ORP BR6 216 C3
Tyers Ga STHWK SE1 19 G3
Tyers St LBTH SE11 122 A5
Tyers Ter LBTH SE11 122 A5
Tyeshurst Cl ABYW SE2 129 F5
Tylecroft Rd
STRHM/NOR SW16 179 K5
Tylehurst Gdns IL IG1 90 C3
Tyler Cl BETH E2 7 J2
ERITH DA8 149 J1
Tylers Ga KTN/HRWW/WS HA3 62 A3
Tylers Green Rd SWLY BR8 203 K4
Tyler St GNWCH SE10 125 H5
Tylney Av NRWD SE19 181 G1
Tylney Rd BMLY BR1 184 C5
FSTGT E7 89 G2
Tynan Cl EBED/NFELT TW14 153 K3
Tyndale La IS N1 85 H5
Tyndale Ter IS N1 85 H5
Tyndall Rd LEY E10 70 A6
WELL DA16 148 A4
Tyneham Cl BTSEA SW11 * 141 F4
Tyneham Rd BTSEA SW11 141 F3
Tynemouth Cl EHAM E6 108 B5
Tynemouth Dr EN EN1 24 C1
Tynemouth Rd MTCM CR4 179 F3
SEVS/STOTM N15 68 B1
WOOL/PLUM SE18 127 K5
Tynemouth St FUL/PGN SW6 140 B3
Tynemouth Ter
SEVS/STOTM N15 * 68 B1
Tyne St WCHPL E1 13 K3
Tynsdale Rd WLSDN NW10 81 G5
Type St BETH E2 105 F1
Tyrawley Rd FUL/PGN SW6 140 A2
Tyre La CDALE/KGS NW9 * 63 G1
Tyrell Cl HRW HA1 78 E2
Tyrone Rd EHAM E6 107 K1
Tyron Wy SCUP DA14 167 K6
Tyrrell Av WELL DA16 148 B6
Tyrrell Rd EDUL SE22 143 H5
Tyrrel Wy CDALE/KGS NW9 63 H4
Tyrwhitt Rd BROCKY SE4 144 D4
Tysoe St CLKNW EC1R 5 K5
Tyson Gdns FSTH SE23 * 163 K2
Tyson Rd FSTH SE23 163 K2
Tyssen Rd STNW/STAM N16 * 86 B1
Tyssen St HACK E8 86 B4
IS N1 7 H2
Tytherton Rd ARCH N19 84 D1

U

Uamvar St POP/IOD E14 105 K4
Uckfield Gv MTCM CR4 179 F4
Udall Gdns CRW RM5 56 C2
Udall St WEST SW1P 16 B7
Udney Park Rd TEDD TW11 174 B2
Uffington Rd WLSDN NW10 81 J6
WNWD SE27 162 B6
Ufford Cl KTN/HRWW/WS HA3 42 B3
Ufford Rd KTN/HRWW/WS HA3 42 B3
Ufford St STHWK SE1 17 K2
Ufton Rd IS N1 86 A5
Uhura Sq STNW/STAM N16 * 86 A1
Ullathorne Rd
STRHM/NOR SW16 161 H6
Ulleswater Rd STHGT/OAK N14 34 E6
Ulleswater Vls
STHGT/OAK N14 * 34 E6
Ullin St POP/IOD E14 106 A4
Ullswater Cl BMLY BR1 183 H2
PUT/ROE SW15 * 158 A6
YEAD UB4 94 C1
Ullswater Ct
RYLN/HDSTN HA2 * 60 A4
Ullswater Crs PUT/ROE SW15 158 A6
Ullswater Rd BARN SW13 138 D1
WNWD SE27 162 C5
Ullswater Wy HCH RM12 93 J3
Ulster Gdns PLMGR N13 35 J6
Ulster Pl CAMTN NW1 3 J7
Ulundi Rd BKHTH/KID SE3 125 H6
Ulva Rd PUT/ROE SW15 139 G5
Ulverscroft Rd EDUL SE22 143 H6
Ulverston Rd WALTH E17 52 B5
Ulysses Rd KIL/WHAMP NW6 82 E3
Umberston St WCHPL E1 * 104 C5
Umbria St PUT/ROE SW15 158 D1
Umfreville Rd FSBYPK N4 67 H3
Undercliff Rd LEW SE13 144 E4
Underhill BAR EN5 20 E6
Underhill Ct BAR EN5 * 20 E6
Underhill Rd EDUL SE22 143 H6
Underhill St CAMTN NW1 3 K1
Underne Av STHGT/OAK N14 34 B4
Undershaft HDTCH EC3A 13 G4
Undershaw Rd BMLY BR1 165 H5
Underwood CROY/NA CR0 214 A4
Underwood Rd CHING E4 51 K1
WCHPL E1 104 C3
WFD IG8 53 H3
Underwood Rw IS N1 6 D4
Underwood St IS N1 6 D4
The Underwood
ELTH/MOT SE9 166 E4
Undine Rd POP/IOD E14 124 E4
Undine St TOOT SW17 178 E1
Uneeda Dr GFD/PVL UB6 78 D6
Union Cl WAN E11 88 B2
Union Ct CLAP SW4 141 K3
OBST EC2N 13 G3
Union Dr WCHPL E1 * 105 G3
Union Gv VX/NE SW8 141 J3
Union Ms BRXN/ST SW9 141 K3
Union Pk GNWCH SE10 125 J5
Union Rd ALP/SUD HA0 80 A4
CROY/NA CR0 196 D4
FBAR/BDGN N11 48 D2
HAYES BR2 200 C2
NTHLT UB5 96 A1
VX/NE SW8 141 J3
Union Sq IS N1 6 C1
Union St BAR EN5 20 C5
KUT/HW KT1 174 E5
SRTFD E15 88 B6
STHWK SE1 18 B1
Union Wk BETH E2 7 J4
Unity Cl CROY/NA CR0 213 K6
NRWD SE19 180 D1
WLSDN NW10 81 J4
Unity Ms CAMTN NW1 4 C2
Unity Wy WOOL/PLUM SE18 126 C3
University Cl MLHL NW7 45 H3
University Gdns BXLY DA5 169 G2
University Pl ERITH DA8 149 J1
University Rd WIM/MER SW19 178 C2
University St FITZ W1T 4 B7
University Wy CAN/RD E16 108 A6
DART DA1 151 K5
Unwin Av EBED/NFELT TW14 133 G6
Unwin Cl PECK SE15 123 H6
Unwin Rd ISLW TW7 135 K4
SKENS SW7 14 B4
Upbrook Ms BAY/PAD W2 101 G5
Upcerne Rd WBPTN SW10 140 B1
Upcroft Av EDGW HA8 44 E1
Updale Rd SCUP DA14 168 A6
Upfield CROY/NA CR0 212 D1
Upfield Rd HNWL W7 97 F3
Uphall Rd IL IG1 90 B3
Upham Park Rd CHSWK W4 118 B4
Uphill Dr CDALE/KGS NW9 62 E2
MLHL NW7 45 G1
Uphill Gv MLHL NW7 31 G6
Uphill Rd MLHL NW7 31 G6
Upland Rd BELMT SM2 209 H5
BXLYHN DA7 149 G4
EDUL SE22 143 H6
PLSTW E13 106 E3
SAND/SEL CR2 211 K3
Uplands BECK BR3 182 D5
Uplands Cl MORT/ESHN SW14 137 J6
Uplands Park Rd ENC/FH EN2 23 G3
Uplands Rd CEND/HSY/T N8 67 F2
CHDH RM6 73 K1
EBAR EN4 34 A3
ORP BR6 202 C5
WFD IG8 53 J3
The Uplands RSLP HA4 58 E5
Uplands Wy WCHMH N21 23 G6
Upminster Rd South
RAIN RM13 111 J3
Upney La BARK IG11 91 F5
Upnor Wy WALW SE17 123 F5
Uppark Dr GNTH/NBYPK IG2 72 C3
Upper Abbey Rd BELV DA17 129 G4
Upper Addison Gdns
WKENS W14 119 H2
Upper Bank St POP/IOD E14 124 E1
Upper Bardsey Wk IS N1 * 85 J4
Upper Belgrave St KTBR SW1X 15 H4
Upper Berenger Wk
WBPTN SW10 * 140 C1
Upper Berkeley St MBLAR W1H 8 E4
Upper Beulah Hl NRWD SE19 181 F4
Upper Blantyre Wk
WBPTN SW10 * 140 C1
Upper Brighton Rd SURB KT6 190 E4
Upper Brockley Rd
BROCKY SE4 144 C3
Upper Brook St
MYFR/PKLN W1K 9 G5
Upper Butts BTFD TW8 116 D6
Upper Caldy Wk IS N1 * 85 J4
Upper Camelford Wk
NTGHL W11 * 100 C5
Upper Cavendish Av FNCH N3 46 E6
Upper Cheyne Rw CHEL SW3 120 D6
Upper Clapton Rd CLPT E5 68 D6
Upper Clarendon Wk
NTGHL W11 * 100 C5
Upper Dartrey Wk
WBPTN SW10 * 140 B1
Upper Dengie Wk IS N1 * 85 J6
Upper Elmers End Rd
BECK BR3 198 B2
Upper Farm Rd
E/WMO/HCT KT8 188 E1
Upper Gn East MTCM CR4 178 E5
Upper Gn West MTCM CR4 178 E5
Upper Grosvenor St
MYFR/PKLN W1K 9 G6
Upper Grotto Rd TWK TW1 156 A4
Upper Gnd STHWK SE1 11 J7
Upper Gv SNWD SE25 197 F1
Upper Grove Rd BELV DA17 129 G6
Upper Gulland Wk IS N1 * 85 J4
Upper Ham Rd
RCHPK/HAM TW10 156 E6
Upper Handa Wk IS N1 * 85 K4
Upper Harley St CAMTN NW1 3 H6
Upper Hawkwell Wk IS N1 * 85 J6
Upper Hitch OXHEY WD19 27 J3
Upper Holly Hill Rd BELV DA17 129 J5
Upper John St SOHO/CST W1F 10 B5
Upper Lismore Wk IS N1 * 85 J4
Upper Ldg KENS W8 * 120 A1
Upper Ml HMSMTH W6 118 D5
Upper Marsh STHWK SE1 17 H4
Upper Montagu St MBLAR W1H 8 E1
Upper Mulgrave Rd
BELMT SM2 208 C5
Upper North St POP/IOD E14 105 K5
Upper Paddock Rd
OXHEY WD19 27 J1
Upper Park Rd BELV DA17 129 J4
BMLY BR1 184 A4
FBAR/BDGN N11 48 C1
HAMP NW3 83 K4
KUTN/CMB KT2 175 H2
Upper Phillimore Gdns
KENS W8 * 119 K2
Upper Rainham Rd HCH RM12 93 H2
Upper Ramsey Wk IS N1 85 K4
Upper Rawreth Wk IS N1 * 85 J6
Upper Richmond Rd
PUT/ROE SW15 138 E5
Upper Richmond Rd West
RCHPK/HAM TW10 137 H5
Upper Rd PLSTW E13 106 E2
WLGTN SM6 210 E3
Upper St Martin's La
LSQ/SEVD WC2H 10 E4
Upper Selsdon Rd
SAND/SEL CR2 212 C6
Upper Sheppey Wk IS N1 85 J4
Upper Sheridan Rd BELV DA17 129 H4
Upper Shirley Rd
CROY/NA CR0 212 E1
Upper Sq ISLW TW7 136 B4
Upper St IS N1 5 K2
Upper Sunbury Rd
HPTN TW12 172 E4
Upper Sutton La HEST TW5 135 F2
Upper Tachbrook St PIM SW1V 16 A6
Upper Tail OXHEY WD19 27 J5
Upper Talbot Wk NTGHL W11 * 100 C5
Upper Teddington Rd
KUT/HW KT1 174 D4
Upper Ter HAMP NW3 83 G1
Upper Thames St BLKFR EC4V 12 C5
Upper Tollington Pk
FSBYPK N4 67 G5
Upperton Rd SCUP DA14 186 A1
Upperton Rd East PLSTW E13 107 G2
Upperton Rd West PLSTW E13 107 G2
Upper Tooting Pk TOOT SW17 160 E4
Upper Tooting Rd TOOT SW17 160 E6
Upper Town Rd STHL UB1 96 B3
Upper Tulse Hl
BRXS/STRHM SW2 162 A2
Upper Vernon Rd SUT SM1 209 H3
Upper Walthamstow Rd
WALTH E17 70 B1
Upper Whistler Wk
WBPTN SW10 * 140 B1
Upper Wickham La
WELL DA16 148 C3
Upper Wimpole St
CAVSQ/HST W1G 9 H1
Upper Woburn Pl CAMTN NW1 4 D5
Uppingham Av STAN HA7 43 J6
Upsdell Av PLMGR N13 49 G2
Upstall St CMBW SE5 142 C2
Upton Av FSTGT E7 88 E5
Upton Cl BXLY DA5 169 G1
CRICK NW2 82 C1
Upton Dene BELMT SM2 209 F5
Upton Gdns
KTN/HRWW/WS HA3 61 J3
Upton La FSTGT E7 89 F4
Upton Lodge Cl BUSH WD23 28 C2
Upton Park Rd FSTGT E7 89 F5
Upton Rd BXLYHS DA6 149 F5
HSLW TW3 135 F4
THHTH CR7 180 E5
UED N18 50 C1
WOOL/PLUM SE18 127 H6
Upton Rd South BXLY DA5 169 G1
Upway NFNCH/WDSPK N12 47 J3
Upwood Rd LEE/GVPK SE12 165 K1
STRHM/NOR SW16 179 K4
Urban Ms FSBYPK N4 67 H4
Urlwin St CMBW SE5 122 D6
Urlwin Wk BRXN/ST SW9 142 B2
Urmston Dr WIM/MER SW19 159 H3
Ursula Ms FSBYPK N4 67 H5
Ursula St BTSEA SW11 140 D2
Urswick Gdns DAGW RM9 92 A5
Urswick Rd CLPT E5 86 E3
DAGW RM9 92 A5
Usborne Ms VX/NE SW8 142 A1
Usher Rd BOW E3 87 H6
Usk Rd BTSEA SW11 140 B5
Usk St BETH E2 105 F2
Uvedale Rd DAGE RM10 92 C1
ENC/FH EN2 23 K5
Uverdale Rd WBPTN SW10 140 B1
Uxbridge Rd EA W5 98 A6
FELT TW13 154 C4
HGDN/ICK UB10 94 A3
HPTN TW12 155 F6
HPTN TW12 173 G1
KUT/HW KT1 190 E1
SHB W12 118 D1
STHL UB1 115 F1
WEA W13 116 C1
Uxbridge Rd (Harrow Weald)
KTN/HRWW/WS HA3 42 C3
Uxbridge Rd (Hatch End)
PIN HA5 41 J4
Uxbridge Road High St
STHL UB1 114 E1
Uxbridge Rd (Pinner) PIN HA5 41 J4
Uxbridge Rd (Stanmore)
STAN HA7 43 F2
Uxbridge Rd The Broadway
YEAD UB4 95 H6
Uxbridge St KENS W8 119 K1
Uxendon Crs WBLY HA9 62 A5
Uxendon Hl WBLY HA9 62 B5

V

Valance Av CHING E4 38 D3
Valan Leas HAYES BR2 183 H6
Vale Cl EFNCH N2 47 K6
MV/WKIL W9 101 G2
ORP BR6 216 A2
TWK TW1 * 156 B5
Vale Cottages
PUT/ROE SW15 * 158 B5
Vale Ct ACT W3 * 118 C1
Vale Crs PUT/ROE SW15 158 B6
Vale Cft ESH/CLAY KT10 205 F5
PIN HA5 59 J2
Vale Dr BAR EN5 20 D5
Vale End EDUL SE22 143 G5
Vale Gv ACT W3 118 A1
FSBYPK N4 67 J4
Vale La ACT W3 98 C4
Valence Av BCTR RM8 73 K5
Valence Circ BCTR RM8 91 K1
Valence Rd ERITH DA8 150 A1
Valence Wood Rd BCTR RM8 91 K1
Valencia Rd STAN HA7 29 J6
Valency Cl NTHWD HA6 26 D6
Valentia Pl BRXN/ST SW9 142 B5
Valentine Av BXLY DA5 169 F4
Valentine Pl STHWK SE1 18 A2
Valentine Rd HOM E9 * 87 F4
RYLN/HDSTN HA2 78 B1
Valentines Rd IL IG1 72 B5
Valentines Wy ROMW/RG RM7 75 G6
Vale of Health HAMP NW3 83 G1
Valerian Wy SRTFD E15 106 C2
Vale Ri GLDGN NW11 64 D5
Vale Rd BMLY BR1 185 F5
DART DA1 170 E3
ESH/CLAY KT10 204 E6
FSBYPK N4 67 J4
FSTGT E7 89 F4
MTCM CR4 179 J6
SUT SM1 209 F2
WPK KT4 207 H1
Vale Rw HBRY N5 85 H1
Vale Royal HOLWY N7 84 E5
Vale St DUL SE21 162 E5
Valeswood Rd BMLY BR1 183 J1
Vale Ter FSBYPK N4 67 J3
The Vale ACT W3 118 A1
CHEL SW3 120 C6
CROY/NA CR0 198 A6
EBED/NFELT TW14 154 A1
GLDGN NW11 82 B1
HEST TW5 114 D6
MUSWH N10 48 A4
RSLP HA4 77 G2
STHGT/OAK N14 34 E2
WFD IG8 52 E3
Valetta Gv PLSTW E13 106 E1
Valetta Rd ACT W3 118 B2
Valette St HACK E8 * 86 D4
Valiant Cl NTHLT UB5 95 H2
ROMW/RG RM7 56 C5
Valiant Wy EHAM E6 107 K4
Vallance Rd MUSWH N10 48 C5
WCHPL E1 104 C3
Vallentin Rd WALTH E17 70 A1
Valley Av NFNCH/WDSPK N12 33 H6
Valley Cl DART DA1 170 C1
LOU IG10 39 K1
PIN HA5 41 F5
Valley Dr CDALE/KGS NW9 62 D2
Valleyfield Rd
STRHM/NOR SW16 180 A1
Valley Fields Crs ENC/FH EN2 23 G3
Valley Gdns ALP/SUD HA0 80 B5
WIM/MER SW19 178 C3
Valley Gv CHARL SE7 126 B5
Valley Hl LOU IG10 39 K1
Valley Pk WATW WD18 * 26 A2
Valley Rd DART DA1 170 C1
ERITH DA8 129 K4
HAYES BR2 183 H5
STMC/STPC BR5 186 C4
STRHM/NOR SW16 162 A6
Valley Side CHING E4 37 J3
Valley Vw BAR EN5 32 C1
Valley Wk CROY/NA CR0 197 K6
Valliere Rd WLSDN NW10 99 J2
Valliers Wood Rd BFN/LL DA15 167 K3
Vallis Wy CHSGTN KT9 205 K2
WEA W13 97 G4
Valmar Rd CMBW SE5 142 D2
Val McKenzie Av HOLWY N7 85 G1
Valnay St TOOT SW17 178 E1
Valognes Av WALTH E17 51 G4
Valonia Gdns
WAND/EARL SW18 159 J1
Vambery Rd
WOOL/PLUM SE18 127 H6
Vanbrough Crs NTHLT UB5 95 G1
Vanbrugh Dr WOT/HER KT12 188 B4
Vanbrugh Flds BKHTH/KID SE3 125 J6
Vanbrugh Hl GNWCH SE10 125 J5
Vanbrugh Pk BKHTH/KID SE3 145 J1
Vanbrugh Park Rd
BKHTH/KID SE3 145 J1
Vanbrugh Park Rd West
BKHTH/KID SE3 145 J1
Vanbrugh Rd CHSWK W4 118 A3
Vanbrugh Ter BKHTH/KID SE3 145 J2
Vanburgh Cl CAN/RD E16 107 H4
ORP BR6 201 K5
Vancouver Cl ORP BR6 217 G2
Vancouver Man EDGW HA8 * 44 D4
Vancouver Rd EDGW HA8 44 D4
FSTH SE23 164 B4
RCHPK/HAM TW10 156 D6
YEAD UB4 95 F3
Vanderbilt Rd
WAND/EARL SW18 160 B3
Vanderbilt Vls SHB W12 * 119 G2
Vanderville Gdns EFNCH N2 47 G5
Vandome Cl CAN/RD E16 107 F5
Vandon St STJSPK SW1H 16 B4
Van Dyck Av NWMAL KT3 192 A4
Vandyke Cl PUT/ROE SW15 159 G1
Vandyke Cross ELTH/MOT SE9 146 D6
Vandy St SDTCH EC2A 7 G7
Vane Cl HAMP NW3 83 H3
KTN/HRWW/WS HA3 62 B3
Vanessa Cl BELV DA17 129 H5
Vanessa Wy BXLY DA5 170 B5
Van Gogh Cl ISLW TW7 136 B4
Vanguard CDALE/KGS NW9 * 45 G3
Vanguard Cl CAN/RD E16 106 E4
CROY/NA CR0 196 C5
ROMW/RG RM7 56 D5
Vanguard St DEPT SE8 144 D2
Vanguard Wy CROY/NA CR0 212 B2
HTHAIR TW6 133 H3
WLGTN SM6 210 E5
Vanneck Sq PUT/ROE SW15 * 138 D6
Vanoc Gdns BMLY BR1 165 K6
Vansittart Rd FSTGT E7 88 E2
Vansittart St NWCR SE14 144 B1
Vanston Pl FUL/PGN SW6 139 K1
Vantage Pl KENS W8 119 K3
Vant Rd TOOT SW17 178 E1
Varcoe Rd BERM/RHTH SE16 123 J5
Vardens Rd BTSEA SW11 140 C6
Varden St WCHPL E1 104 D5
Vardon Cl ACT W3 99 F5
Varley Dr TWK TW1 136 C5
Varley Rd CAN/RD E16 107 F5
Varley Wy MTCM CR4 178 C5
Varna Rd FUL/PGN SW6 139 H1
HPTN TW12 * 173 G4
Varndell St CAMTN NW1 4 A4
Varsity Dr TWK TW1 135 K6
Varsity Rw MORT/ESHN SW14 137 K3
Vartry Rd SEVS/STOTM N15 68 A3
Vassall Rd BRXN/ST SW9 142 B1
Vauban Est BERM/RHTH SE16 19 K5
Vauban St BERM/RHTH SE16 19 K5
Vaughan Av HDN NW4 63 J2
HMSMTH W6 118 C4
Vaughan Est BETH E2 * 7 J4
Vaughan Gdns IL IG1 71 K4
Vaughan Rd CMBW SE5 142 D3
HRW HA1 60 C4
SRTFD E15 88 D4
THDIT KT7 190 C4
WELL DA16 148 A3
Vaughan St BERM/RHTH SE16 124 C2
Vaughan Wy WAP E1W 104 C6
Vaughan Williams Cl DEPT SE8 144 D1
Vauxhall Br VX/NE SW8 121 K5
Vauxhall Bridge Rd PIM SW1V 16 B7
Vauxhall Gdns SAND/SEL CR2 211 J4
Vauxhall Gv VX/NE SW8 122 A6
Vauxhall Pl DART DA1 171 H2
Vauxhall St LBTH SE11 122 A5
Vauxhall Wk LBTH SE11 122 A5
Vawdrey Cl WCHPL E1 104 E3
Veals Md MTCM CR4 178 D4
Vectis Gdns TOOT SW17 179 G2
Vectis Rd TOOT SW17 179 G2
Veda Rd LEW SE13 144 D5
Vega Crs NTHWD HA6 40 D1
Vega Rd BUSH WD23 28 C2
Veitch Cl EBED/NFELT TW14 153 J2
Veldene Wy RYLN/HDSTN HA2 77 K1
Vellum Dr CAR SM5 210 A1
Venables Cl DAGE RM10 92 D2
Venables St BAY/PAD W2 8 B1
STJWD NW8 2 B7
Vencourt Pl HMSMTH W6 118 D5
Venetian Rd CMBW SE5 142 D3
Venetia Rd EA W5 116 E2
FSBYPK N4 67 H3
Venette Cl RAIN RM13 111 K4
Venner Rd SYD SE26 181 K2
Venners Cl BXLYHN DA7 150 B3
Venn St CLAP SW4 141 H5
Ventnor Av STAN HA7 43 H4
Ventnor Dr TRDG/WHET N20 33 F5
Ventnor Gdns BARK IG11 90 E4
Ventnor Rd BELMT SM2 209 F5
NWCR SE14 144 A1
Ventnor Ter SEVS/STOTM N15 * 68 C1
Venture Cl BXLY DA5 169 F2
Venue St POP/IOD E14 105 K4
Venus Ms MTCM CR4 178 D6
Venus Rd WOOL/PLUM SE18 126 E3
Vera Av WCHMH N21 23 G6
Vera Ct OXHEY WD19 27 H2
Vera Lynn Cl FSTGT E7 88 E2
Vera Rd FUL/PGN SW6 139 H2
Verbena Cl CAN/RD E16 106 D3
Verbena Gdns HMSMTH W6 118 D5
Verdant La CAT SE6 165 H3
Verdayne Av CROY/NA CR0 198 A5
Verderers Rd CHIG IG7 55 G1
Verdun Rd BARN SW13 138 D1
WOOL/PLUM SE18 128 B6
Vereker Rd WKENS W14 * 119 H5
Vere St CAVSQ/HST W1G 9 J4
Vermont Cl ENC/FH EN2 23 H5
Vermont Rd NRWD SE19 180 E2

SUT SM1 .....209 F1
WAND/EARL SW18 .....160 A1
Verney Gdns DAGW RM9 .....92 A2
Verney Rd BERM/RHTH SE16 .....123 J5
DAGW RM9 .....92 A3
Verney St WLSDN NW10 .....69 J1
Verney Wy BERM/RHTH SE16 .....123 J5
Vernham Rd
WOOL/PLUM SE18 .....127 H6
Vernon Av MNPK E12 .....89 K2
RYNPK SW20 .....177 G5
WFD IG8 .....53 F5
Vernon Cl HOR/WEW KT19 .....206 H4
STMC/STPC BR5 .....186 C6
STWL/WRAY TW19 .....152 B3
Vernon Crs EBAR EN4 .....34 A1
Vernon Dr STAN HA7 .....43 G4
Vernon Pl FSBYW WC1X 5 H4
Vernon Ri FSBYW WC1X 5 H1
GFD/PVL UB6 .....78 D3
Vernon Rd BOW E3 .....105 H1
CEND/HSY/T N8 * 49 G6
CRW RM5 .....56 E1
FELT TW13 .....153 J4
GDMY/SEVK IG3 .....73 F5
MORT/ESHN SW14 .....138 A4
SRTFD E15 .....88 C5
SUT SM1 .....209 G3
WALTH E17 .....51 J1
WAN E11 .....70 C5
Vernon Sq FSBYW WC1X 5 H1
Vernon St WKENS W14 .....119 H4
Vernon Yd NTGHL W11 .....100 D6
Verona Ct BXLYHN DA7 * 149 F5
CHSWK W4 .....118 B5
Verona Dr SURB KT6 .....191 F6
Veronica Gdns
STRHM/NOR SW16 .....179 H4
Veronica Rd TOOT SW17 .....161 G5
Veronique Gdns BARK/HLT IG6 * 72 C2
Verran Rd BAL SW12 * 161 G2
Versailles Rd PGE/AN SE20 .....181 H3
Verulam Av WALTH E17 .....69 H4
Verulam Ct CDALE/KGS NW9 * 63 J4
Verulam Rd GFD/PVL UB6 .....96 A3
Verulam St FSBYW WC1X 11 J1
Verwood Dr EBAR EN4 .....21 K4
Verwood Rd RYLN/HDSTN HA2 .....42 C5
Veryan Cl STMC/STPC BR5 .....202 D1
Vespan Rd SHB W12 .....118 D2
Vesta Rd BROCKY SE4 .....144 B3
Vestris Rd FSTH SE23 .....164 A4
Vestry Ms CMBW SE5 .....143 F2
Vestry Rd CMBW SE5 .....143 F2
WALTH E17 * 69 K2
Vestry St IS N1 .....6 E4
Vevey St CAT SE6 .....164 C4
Viaduct Pl BETH E2 * 104 D2
Viaduct St BETH E2 .....104 D2
The Viaduct MUSWH N10 * 66 B1
SWFD E18 .....52 E5
Vian St LEW SE13 .....144 E4
Vibart Gdns BRXS/STRHM SW2 .....162 A2
Vibart Wk IS N1 * 5 K1
Vibia Cl STWL/WRAY TW19 .....152 A2
Vicarage Av CHARL SE7 .....126 B5
Vicarage Cl ERITH DA8 .....129 K6
NTHLT UB5 .....77 K6
RSLP HA4 .....58 B4
WPK KT4 .....192 B5
Vicarage Ct BECK BR3 * 182 B6
BTSEA SW11 .....140 C5
Vicarage Dr BARK IG11 .....90 C5
BECK BR3 .....182 D4
MORT/ESHN SW14 .....138 A6
Vicarage Farm Rd HEST TW5 .....134 D2
Vicarage Flds WOT/HER KT12 .....188 B3
Vicarage Gdns MTCM CR4 .....178 D6
Vicarage Ga KENS W8 .....120 A2
Vicarage Gv CMBW SE5 .....142 E2
Vicarage La EHAM E6 .....107 K2
IL IG1 .....72 D6
SRTFD E15 .....88 C4
Vicarage Ms CHSWK W4 * 118 B6
Vicarage Pde
SEVS/STOTM N15 * 67 J1
Vicarage Pk WOOL/PLUM SE18 .....127 H5
Vicarage Rd BXLY DA5 .....169 J3
CROY/NA CR0 .....211 G1
DAGE RM10 .....92 D5
HCH RM12 .....75 J5
HDN NW4 .....63 J3
KUT/HW KT1 .....174 E5
LEY E10 .....69 K4
MORT/ESHN SW14 .....137 K6
SRTFD E15 .....88 D5
SUT SM1 .....208 E2
TEDD TW11 .....174 B1
TOTM N17 .....50 C3
WATW WD18 .....26 A1
WFD IG8 .....53 J3
WHTN TW2 .....155 H1
WHTN TW2 .....155 K4
WOOL/PLUM SE18 .....127 H5
Vicarage Wk BTSEA SW11 * 140 C1
WLSDN NW10 .....81 G2
Vicars Bridge Cl ALP/SUD HA0 .....98 A1
Vicar's Cl IS EN EN1 .....24 A3
HOM E9 .....86 E6
SRTFD E15 .....88 C6
Vicars Hill LEW SE13 .....144 E5
Vicars Moor La WCHMH N21 .....35 G2
Vicars Oak Rd NRWD SE19 .....181 F2
Vicar's Rd KTTN NW5 .....84 A3
Viceroy Cl EFNCH N2 * 65 J1
Viceroy Pde EFNCH N2 * 65 J1
Viceroy Rd VX/NE SW8 .....141 K2
Vickers Cl WLGTN SM6 .....211 F5
Vickers Rd ERITH DA8 .....130 A5
Victor Gv ALP/SUD HA0 .....80 A5
Victoria Ar WESTW SW1E 15 K4
Victoria Av CRW RM5 .....56 E5
E/WMO/HCT KT8 .....173 G6
EHAM E6 .....89 H6
FNCH N3 .....46 D4
HSLW TW3 .....135 F6
SURB KT6 .....190 E5

WBLY HA9 .....80 D4
WLGTN SM6 .....210 A1
Victoria Cl E/WMO/HCT KT8 .....173 F6
BAR EN5 .....21 H6
HRW HA1 * 61 F3
HYS/HAR UB3 .....94 B5
Victoria Cottages
RCH/KEW TW9 .....137 G2
WCHPL E1 * 104 C4
Victoria Crs NRWD SE19 .....181 F2
SEVS/STOTM N15 .....67 K1
WIM/MER SW19 .....177 J3
Victoria Dock Rd CAN/RD E16 .....106 E6
Victoria Dr WIM/MER SW19 .....159 G2
Victoria Embankment
CHCR WC2N * 11 F6
Victoria Gdns HEST TW5 .....134 D2
NTGHL W11 .....119 K1
Victoria Gv BAY/PAD W2 .....8 B5
KENS W8 .....120 B3
Victoria Grove Ms
BAY/PAD W2 * 101 F6
Victoria La BAR EN5 .....20 D5
Victoria Ms KIL/WHAMP NW6 .....82 E1
WAND/EARL SW18 .....160 B3
Victorian Gv STNW/STAM N16 .....86 A1
Victorian Rd STNW/STAM N16 .....86 A1
Victoria Pde RCH/KEW TW9 * 137 H2
Victoria Park Rd HOM E9 .....86 E6
Victoria Park Sq BETH E2 .....104 E2
Victoria Pk Studios HOM E9 * 86 E4
Victoria Pl RCH/KEW TW9 .....136 E6
Victoria Ri CLAP SW4 .....141 G4
Victoria Rd ACT W3 .....99 F4
BARK IG11 .....90 B4
BFN/LL DA15 .....168 A5
BKHH IG9 .....39 H4
BMLY BR1 .....184 A5
CHING E4 .....38 B3
CHST BR7 .....185 F1
DAGE RM10 .....92 E3
DART DA1 .....151 G6
EA W5 .....97 H4
EBAR EN4 .....21 H5
EBED/NFELT TW14 .....153 K2
FELT TW13 .....154 A4
FSBYPK N4 .....67 F4
HAYES BR2 .....200 C1
HDN NW4 .....64 A1
KENS W8 .....120 B3
KIL/WHAMP NW6 .....100 D1
KUT/HW KT1 .....175 G5
MLHL NW7 .....45 H1
MORT/ESHN SW14 .....138 A4
MTCM CR4 .....178 D3
NWDGN UB2 .....114 E3
PLSTW E13 .....106 E1
ROM RM1 .....75 H2
RSLP HA4 .....58 E6
SURB KT6 .....190 E3
SUT SM1 .....209 H3
TEDD TW11 .....174 B2
TWK TW1 .....156 C2
UED N18 .....36 B6
WALTH E17 .....52 A5
WAN E11 .....88 B2
WDGN N22 .....48 B4
Victoria Sq BGVA SW1W 15 K4
Victoria St BELV DA17 .....129 G5
SRTFD E15 .....88 C5
WESTW SW1E 15 K5
Victoria Ter EA W5 * 116 E1
Victoria Vls RCH/KEW TW9 .....137 G4
Victoria Wy CHARL SE7 .....126 A5
Victoria Yd WCHPL E1 * 104 C5
Victor Rd PGE/AN SE20 .....182 A3
RYLN/HDSTN HA2 .....42 C6
TEDD TW11 .....173 K1
WLSDN NW10 .....99 K2
Victors Dr HPTN TW12 * 172 D2
Victors Wy BAR EN5 .....20 D4
Victory Av MRDN SM4 .....194 B2
Victory Cl STWL/WRAY TW19 .....152 B3
Victory Pk WBLY HA9 * 79 K1
Victory Pl WALW SE17 * 181 F2
WALW SE17 .....18 E6
Victory Rd RAIN RM13 .....111 J2
WAN E11 .....71 F1
WIM/MER SW19 .....178 B3
Victory Road Ms
WIM/MER SW19 .....178 B3
Victory Wy BERM/RHTH SE16 .....124 B2
HEST TW5 .....114 B5
ROMW/RG RM7 .....56 D5
Vienna Cl WFD IG8 .....53 H5
View Cl CHIG IG7 .....54 D1
HGT N6 .....65 K4
HRW HA1 .....60 D1
View Crs CEND/HSY/T N8 .....66 D2
Viewfield Cl
KTN/HRWW/WS HA3 .....62 A4
Viewfield Rd BFN/LL DA15 .....168 D3
WAND/EARL SW18 .....159 J1
Viewland Rd
WOOL/PLUM SE18 .....128 A5
View Rd HGT N6 .....65 K4
The View ABYW SE2 .....129 F5
Viga Rd WCHMH N21 .....35 G1
Vigilant Cl SYD SE26 .....163 H6
Vignoles Rd ROMW/RG RM7 .....74 C4
Vigo St CONDST W1S 10 A6
Viking Cl BOW E3 .....105 G1
Viking Gdns EHAM E6 .....107 J4
Viking Pl LEY E10 .....69 H5
Viking Rd STHL UB1 .....95 J6
Viking Wy ERITH DA8 .....129 K3

Villacourt Rd
WOOL/PLUM SE18 .....148 B1
Village Ar CHING E4 * 38 C1
Village Cl CHING E4 .....52 A1
HAMP NW3 * 83 H3
Village Green Rd DART DA1 .....150 D5
Village Ms CDALE/KGS NW9 * 63 F6
Village Mt HAMP NW3 * 83 G2
Village Park Cl EN EN1 .....36 A1
Village Rd EN EN1 .....35 K6
FNCH N3 .....46 C5
Village Rw BELMT SM2 .....208 E5
The Village CHARL SE7 .....126 C6
HAMP NW3 * 65 G6
Village Wy ASHF TW15 .....152 C6
BARK/HLT IG6 .....54 B4
BECK BR3 .....182 D5
DUL SE21 .....162 E1
PIN HA5 .....59 J4
WLSDN NW10 .....81 F2
Village Wy East PIN HA5 .....59 H4
Villa Rd BRXN/ST SW9 .....142 B4
Villas Rd WOOL/PLUM SE18 .....127 H4
Villa St WALW SE17 .....122 E5
Villiers Av BRYLDS KT5 .....191 G2
WHTN TW2 .....154 E3
Villiers Cl BRYLDS KT5 .....191 G1
LEY E10 .....69 J6
Villiers Gv BELMT SM2 .....208 B6
Villiers Rd BECK BR3 .....182 A5
CRICK NW2 .....81 J4
ISLW TW7 .....135 K3
KUT/HW KT1 .....175 G6
OXHEY WD19 .....27 J1
STHL UB1 .....114 E1
Villiers St CHCR WC2N 11 F7
Vincam Cl WHTN TW2 .....155 F2
Vincennes Est WNWD SE27 .....162 E6
Vincent Av BRYLDS KT5 .....191 K6
Vincent Cl BAR EN5 .....20 E4
BARK/HLT IG6 .....54 D2
BFN/LL DA15 .....167 K3
ESH/CLAY KT10 .....204 B1
HAYES BR2 .....200 A1
WDR/YW UB7 .....112 D6
Vincent Gdns CRICK NW2 .....81 H1
Vincent Pde FSBYPK N4 * 66 E5
Vincent Rd ACT W3 .....117 K3
ALP/SUD HA0 .....80 B5
CHING E4 .....52 A2
CROY/NA CR0 .....197 G4
DAGW RM9 .....92 A5
HSLWW TW4 .....134 C4
ISLW TW7 .....135 J2
KUT/HW KT1 .....175 H6
SEVS/STOTM N15 .....67 G2
WDGN N22 .....49 G5
WOOL/PLUM SE18 .....127 G4
Vincent Sq CAN/RD E16 .....106 B3
WEST SW1P 16 B6
Vincent St CAN/RD E16 .....106 D4
WEST SW1P 16 C6
Vincent Ter IS N1 .....6 A2
Vine Cl SEVS/STOTM N15 * 67 J1
SURB KT6 .....191 G3
SUT SM1 .....209 F1
WDR/YW UB7 .....112 D4
Vine Cottages HNWL W7 * 115 K1
WCHPL E1 * 104 C5
Vine Ct KTN/HRWW/WS HA3 .....62 A3
WCHPL E1 .....104 C4
Vine Gdns IL IG1 .....90 C3
Vinegar Aly WALTH E17 .....51 K6
Vinegar St WAP E1W 123 J1
Vine Hi CLKNW EC1R 5 J7
Vine La STHWK SE1 .....19 H1
Vine Pl HSLW TW3 .....135 G5
Vineries Cl WDR/YW UB7 .....112 D6
The Vineries CAT SE6 * 164 D3
EN EN1 .....24 A4
STHGT/OAK N14 .....34 C1
Vine Rd BARN SW13 .....138 C4
E/WMO/HCT KT8 .....189 H1
ORP BR6 .....217 F4
SRTFD E15 .....88 D5
Vine Rw RCHPK/HAM TW10 * 137 F6
Viners Cl WOT/HER KT12 .....188 B3
Vines Av FNCH N3 .....47 F4
Vine Sq WKENS W14 * 119 J5
Vine St MYFR/PICC W1J 10 B6
ROMW/RG RM7 .....74 E2
TWRH EC3N 13 J4
Vine Street Br FARR EC1M 5 K7
Vine Yd STHWK SE1 .....18 D2
Vineyard Av MLHL NW7 .....46 C3
Vineyard Cl CAT SE6 .....164 D3
KUT/HW KT1 .....175 G6
Vineyard Gv FNCH N3 .....47 F4
Vineyard Hill Rd
WIM/MER SW19 .....159 K6
Vineyard Ms CLKNW EC1R * 5 J6
Vineyard Pth
MORT/ESHN SW14 .....138 A4
Vineyard Rd FELT TW13 .....153 K5
Vineyard Rw KUT/HW KT1 .....174 D4
The Vineyard
RCHPK/HAM TW10 .....136 E6
Vineyard Wk CLKNW EC1R * 5 J6
Viney Bank CROY/NA CR0 .....213 H6
Viney Rd LEW SE13 .....144 E4
Vining St BRXS/STRHM SW2 .....142 A5
Vinlake Av UX/CGN UB10 .....76 A1
Vinson Cl ORP BR6 .....202 B5
Vintry Ms WALTH E17 .....69 J1
Viola Av ABYW SE2 .....128 C4
EBED/NFELT TW14 .....154 A1
STWL/WRAY TW19 .....152 A3
Viola Sq SHB W12 .....99 H6
Violet Av ENC/FH EN2 .....23 J1
Violet Cl CAN/RD E16 .....106 C3
CHEAM SM3 .....193 H5
DEPT SE8 .....124 C6
WLGTN SM6 .....195 F5

Violet Gdns CROY/NA CR0 .....211 H3
Violet Hi STJWD NW8 .....101 G1
Violet La SAND/SEL CR2 .....211 H5
Violet Rd BOW E3 .....105 K3
SWFD E18 .....53 F5
WALTH E17 .....69 J3
Violet St BETH E2 .....104 D3
Virgil Pl STHWK SE1 .....17 H4
Virgil St STHWK SE1 .....17 H4
Virginia Cl CRW RM5 .....56 E5
NWMAL KT3 .....175 K1
Virginia Gdns BARK/HLT IG6 .....54 D5
Virginia Rd BETH E2 .....7 K4
THHTH CR7 .....180 D4
Virginia St WCHPL E1 * 104 C6
Viscount Cl FBAR/BDGN N11 .....48 B1
Viscount Dr EHAM E6 .....107 K4
Viscount Gv NTHLT UB5 .....95 H2
Viscount Rd
STWL/WRAY TW19 .....152 A2
Viscount St BARB EC2Y 6 C7
Vista Av PEND EN3 .....25 F3
Vista Dr REDBR IG4 .....71 H2
The Vista CHING E4 * 38 B2
ELTH/MOT SE9 .....166 D2
Vista Wy KTN/HRWW/WS HA3 .....62 A3
Viveash Cl HYS/HAR UB3 .....113 J5
Vivian Av HDN NW4 .....64 A2
WBLY HA9 .....80 C4
Vivian Cl OXHEY WD19 .....26 E3
Vivian Gdns OXHEY WD19 .....26 E3
WBLY HA9 .....80 C3
Vivian Rd BOW E3 .....105 G1
Vivian Wy EFNCH N2 .....65 J2
Vivien Cl CHSGTN KT9 .....206 A5
Vivienne Cl TWK TW1 .....156 E1
Vixen Ms HACK E8 * 86 B6
Voce Rd WOOL/PLUM SE18 .....147 J1
Voewood Cl NWMAL KT3 .....192 C3
Voltaire Rd CLAP SW4 .....141 J4
Volt Av WLSDN NW10 .....99 G2
Volta Wy CROY/NA CR0 .....196 A5
Voluntary Pl WAN E11 .....70 E3
Vorley Rd ARCH N19 .....66 C6
Voss St BETH E2 .....104 C2
Voyagers Cl THMD SE28 .....109 J5
Vulcan Cl EHAM E6 .....108 A5
Vulcan Ga ENC/FH EN2 .....23 G3
Vulcan Rd BROCKY SE4 .....144 C3
Vulcan Ter BROCKY SE4 .....144 C3
Vulcan Wy HOLWY N7 .....85 F4
WLGTN SM6 .....210 E6
Vyner Rd ACT W3 .....99 F6
Vyner St BETH E2 .....104 D1
The Vyne BXLYHN DA7 .....149 J4
Vyse Cl BAR EN5 .....20 A5

W

Wadbrook St KUT/HW KT1 .....174 E5
Wadding St WALW SE17 .....18 E7
Waddington Cl EN EN1 .....24 A5
Waddington Rd SRTFD E15 .....88 B3
Waddington St SRTFD E15 .....88 B4
Waddington Wy NRWD SE19 .....180 D4
Waddon Cl CROY/NA CR0 .....211 G2
Waddon Court Rd
CROY/NA CR0 .....211 G2
Waddon Marsh Wy
CROY/NA CR0 .....196 A5
Waddon New Rd
CROY/NA CR0 .....211 H1
Waddon Park Av
CROY/NA CR0 .....211 G2
Waddon Rd CROY/NA CR0 .....211 G1
Waddon Wy CROY/NA CR0 .....211 G4
Wade House STHWK SE1 * 123 H2
Wade Rd CAN/RD E16 .....107 G5
Wade's Gv WCHMH N21 .....35 G2
Wade's Hi WCHMH N21 .....35 G1
Wade's La TEDD TW11 .....174 B1
Wadeson St BETH E2 .....104 D1
Wade's Pl POP/IOD E14 .....105 K6
Wadeville Av CHDH RM6 .....74 A3
Wadeville Cl BELV DA17 .....129 H6
Wadham Av WALTH E17 .....51 K3
Wadham Gdns GFD/PVL UB6 .....78 D3
HAMP NW3 .....83 J6
Wadham Rd CHING E4 .....51 J3
PUT/ROE SW15 .....139 H5
Wadhurst Cl PGE/AN SE20 .....181 J5
Wadhurst Rd CHSWK W4 .....118 A3
VX/NE SW8 .....141 H2
Wadsworth Cl GFD/PVL UB6 .....97 J1
PEND EN3 .....25 F6
Wadsworth Rd GFD/PVL UB6 .....97 H1
Wager St BOW E3 .....105 H3
Waghorn Rd
KTN/HRWW/WS HA3 .....43 K6
PLSTW E13 .....107 G1
Waghorn St PECK SE15 .....143 H4
Wagner St PECK SE15 .....143 K1
Wagstaff Gdns DAGW RM9 .....91 J5
Wagtail Cl CDALE/KGS NW9 .....45 G5
EN EN1 * 24 C1
Wagtail Wy BECK BR3 .....199 F2
Wagtail Wy STMC/STPC BR5 .....202 E1
Waid Cl DART DA1 .....171 J1
Waights Ct KUT/HW KT1 .....175 F4
Wainfleet Av CRW RM5 .....56 E5
Wainford Cl
WIM/MER SW19 .....159 G3
Wainwright Gv ISLW TW7 .....135 J5
Waite Davies Rd
LEE/GVE SE12 .....165 J2
Waite St CMBW SE5 .....123 G6
Wakefield Gdns IL IG1 .....71 J3
NRWD SE19 .....181 F3
Wakefield Ms STPAN WC1H 4 F6
Wakefield Rd FBAR/BDGN N11 .....48 D1
RCHPK/HAM TW10 .....136 E6

SEVS/STOTM N15 .....68 B2
Wakefield St EHAM E6 .....89 J6
STPAN WC1H 5 F5
UED N18 .....50 C1
Wakehams Hi PIN HA5 .....41 K6
Wakeham St IS N1 .....85 K4
Wakehurst Rd BTSEA SW11 .....140 E6
Wakeling La ALP/SUD HA0 .....79 H1
Wakeling Rd HNWL W7 .....97 F4
Wakeling St WCHPL E1 .....105 G5
Wakelin Rd SRTFD E15 .....106 C1
Wakeman Rd WLSDN NW10 .....100 A2
Wakemans Hill Av
CDALE/KGS NW9 .....63 F2
Wakering Rd BARK IG11 .....90 C5
Wakerley Cl EHAM E6 .....107 K5
Wakley St FSBYE EC1V 6 B4
Walberswick St VX/NE SW8 .....141 K1
Walbrook MANHO EC4N 12 E5
Walburgh St WCHPL E1 .....104 D5
Walcorde Av WALW SE17 .....18 D7
Walcot Rd PEND EN3 .....25 H3
Walcot Sq LBTH SE11 .....17 K6
Walcott St WEST SW1P * 16 A6
Waldeck Gv WNWD SE27 .....162 C5
Waldeck Rd CHSWK W4 .....117 H6
DART DA1 .....171 J2
MORT/ESHN SW14 .....137 K4
SEVS/STOTM N15 .....67 H1
WEA W13 .....97 H5
Waldegrave Gdns TWK TW1 .....156 A5
Waldegrave Pk TWK TW1 .....156 A6
Waldegrave Rd BCTR RM8 .....73 J6
BMLY BR1 .....200 D1
CEND/HSY/T N8 * 49 G6
EA W5 .....98 A6
NRWD SE19 .....181 G3
TWK TW1 .....156 A6
WALW SE17 .....18 C7
Waldegrove CROY/NA CR0 .....212 B1
Waldemar Av FUL/PGN SW6 .....139 H2
WEA W13 .....116 D1
Waldemar Rd WIM/MER SW19 .....177 K1
Walden Av CHST BR7 .....166 E6
PLMGR N13 .....35 J6
RAIN RM13 .....111 F1
Walden Cl BELV DA17 .....129 G5
Walden Gdns THHTH CR7 .....196 A1
Waldenhurst Rd
STMC/STPC BR5 .....202 E4
Walden Pde CHST BR7 * 184 E2
Walden Rd CHST BR7 .....184 E2
TOTM N17 .....49 K4
Waldens Cl STMC/STPC BR5 .....202 E4
Waldenshaw Rd FSTH SE23 .....163 K3
Waldens Rd STMC/STPC BR5 .....203 F3
Walden St WCHPL E1 .....104 D5
Walden Wy BARK/HLT IG6 .....54 E3
MLHL NW7 .....46 A2
Waldo Cl CLAP SW4 .....141 H6
Waldo Pl MTCM CR4 .....178 D3
Waldorf Cl SAND/SEL CR2 .....211 H6
Waldo Rd BMLY BR1 .....184 B1
WLSDN NW10 .....99 K2
Waldram Crs FSTH SE23 .....163 K3
Waldram Park Rd FSTH SE23 .....164 A3
Waldrist Wy ERITH DA18 .....129 G2
Waldron Gdns HAYES BR2 .....183 G6
Waldronhyrst CROY/NA CR0 .....211 H2
Waldron Ms CHEL SW3 .....120 C6
Waldron Rd RYLN/HDSTN HA2 .....60 E5
WAND/EARL SW18 .....160 B3
The Waldrons CROY/NA CR0 .....211 H2
Waldron's Yd RYLN/HDSTN HA2 .....60 D6
Waldstock Rd THMD SE28 .....109 G6
Waleran Cl STAN HA7 * 43 F2
Walerand Rd LEW SE13 .....145 F3
Wales Av CAR SM5 .....209 J3
Wales Cl PECK SE15 .....143 J1
Wales Farm Rd ACT W3 .....99 F4
Waleton Acres WLGTN SM6 * 210 C4
Waley St WCHPL E1 * 105 G4
Walfield Av TRDG/WHET N20 .....33 F2
Walford Rd STNW/STAM N16 .....86 A2
Walfrey Gdns DAGW RM9 .....92 A5
Walham Green Ct
FUL/PGN SW6 * 140 A1
Walham Gv FUL/PGN SW6 .....139 K1
Walham Ri WIM/MER SW19 .....177 H2
Walham Yd FUL/PGN SW6 .....139 K1
Walkden Rd CHST BR7 .....167 F6
Walker Cl DART DA1 .....151 J2
EBED/NFELT TW14 .....153 J2
FBAR/BDGN N11 .....34 C6
HNWL W7 .....115 K1
HPTN TW12 .....172 E2
WOOL/PLUM SE18 .....127 H4
Walker's Ct SOHO/CST W1F 10 C5
Walkerscroft Md CAT SE6 .....164 E4
DUL SE21 .....162 E3
The Walks EFNCH N2 .....47 H6
Wallace Cl THMD SE28 .....109 K6
Wallace Crs CAR SM5 .....209 K3
Wallace Rd IS N1 .....85 J4
Wallace Wy ROM RM1 * 57 F4
Wallbutton Rd BROCKY SE4 .....144 B3
Wallcote Av CRICK NW2 .....64 B5
Walled Garden Cl BECK BR3 .....198 E1
Wall End Rd EHAM E6 .....90 A5
Wallenger Av GPK RM2 .....57 K6
Waller Dr NTHWD HA6 .....40 E4
Waller Rd NWCR SE14 .....144 A3
Wallers Cl DAGW RM9 .....92 A6
WFD IG8 .....53 K2
Wallflower St SHB W12 .....99 H6
Wallgrave Rd ECT SW5 .....120 A4
Wallhouse Rd ERITH DA8 .....151 F1
Wallingford Av NKENS W10 .....100 B4
Wallington Cl RSLP HA4 .....58 A3
Wallington Rd GDMY/SEVK IG3 .....73 H4
Wallis Cl BTSEA SW11 .....140 C4
EMPK RM11 .....75 K5
RDART DA2 .....170 D3
Wallis Rd HOM E9 .....87 H4
STHL UB1 .....96 B5

Wallorton Gdns
  MORT/ESHN SW14............138 A5
Walkdale BARB EC2Y *............12 D2
Wall St IS N1............85 K4
Wallwood Rd WAN E11............70 B4
Wallwood St POP/IOD E14............105 H4
Walmar Cl EBAR EN4............21 H2
Walmar Cl CHING E4............37 K4
  ORP BR6............216 D2
  ROMW/RG RM7............56 D5
Walmer Gdns WEA W13............116 B2
Walmer Rd NTGHL W11............100 C6
Walmer Ter WOOL/PLUM SE18...127 H4
Walmgate Rd GFD/PVL UB6......79 H6
Walmington Fold
  NFNCH/WDSPK N12............46 E2
Walm La CRICK NW2............82 B4
Walney Wk IS N1 *............85 J4
Walnut Av WDR/YW UB7............112 D3
Walnut Cl BARK/HLT IG6............72 C1
  CAR SM5............209 K3
  DEPT SE8............124 C6
  HYS/HAR UB3............94 C6
Walnut Ct EA W5 *............117 F2
Walnut Gdns SRTFD E15............88 C3
Walnut Gv EN EN1............23 K6
Walnut Ms BELMT SM2............209 G5
Walnut Rd LEY E10............69 J6
Walnuts Rd ORP BR6............202 B5
Walnut Tree Av DART DA1............171 H4
  MTCM CR4 *............178 D6
Walnut Tree Cl BARN SW13......138 C2
  CHST BR7............185 H4
Walnut Tree Rd BCTR RM8......73 K6
  BTFD TW8............117 F6
  ERITH DA8............130 B5
  GNWCH SE10 *............125 H5
  HEST TW5............134 E1
Walnut Tree Wk LBTH SE11......17 J6
Walnut Wy BKHH IG9............39 H5
  RSLP HA4............77 G4
Walpole Av RCH/KEW TW9......137 G3
Walpole Cl PIN HA5............42 A2
  WEA W13............116 C2
Walpole Crs TEDD TW11............174 A1
Walpole Gdns CHSWK W4............117 K5
  WHTN TW2............155 K4
Walpole Ms STJWD NW8............2 A1
  HAYES BR2............200 C2
  SURB KT6............191 F4
  SWFD E18............52 D4
  TEDD TW11............174 A1
  WHTN TW2............155 K4
  TOTM N17............49 J5
  WALTH E17............69 C1
  WHTN TW2............155 K4
  WIM/MER SW19............178 C2
Walpole St CHEL SW3............120 E5
Walrond Av WBLY HA9............80 A3
Walsham Cl STNW/STAM N16....68 C5
  THMD SE28............109 H6
Walsham Rd
  EBED/NFELT TW14............154 A2
  NWCR SE14............144 A3
Walsingham Gdns
  HOR/WEW KT19............207 G2
Walsingham Pk CHST BR7......185 J5
Walsingham Rd CLAP SW4......161 F1
  CLPT E5............86 C1
  ENC/FH EN2............23 K6
  MTCM CR4............194 E2
  STMC/STPC BR5............186 C4
  WEA W13 *............116 B1
Walsingham Wk BELV DA17......129 H6
Walter Rodney Cl MNPK E12......89 K4
Walters Rd HYS/HAR UB3......113 J2
  PEND EN3............24 E6
  SNWD SE25............197 F1
Walter St BETH E2............105 F2
  KUTN/CMB KT2 *............175 F4
Walters Yd BMLY BR1............183 K5
Walter Ter WCHPL E1............105 F5
Walter Wk EDGW HA8............44 E2
Waltham Av CDALE/KGS NW9....62 C3
  HYS/HAR UB3............113 F3
Waltham Cl DART DA1............170 D4
  STMC/STPC BR5............202 E5
Waltham Dr EDGW HA8............44 C5
Waltham Pk WALTH E17 *......51 J3
Waltham Park Wy CHING E4......51 J3
Waltham Rd CAR SM5............194 C5
  NWDGN UB2............114 D3
  WFD IG8............53 J2
Walthamstow Av CHING E4......51 G1
Waltham Wy CHING E4............37 H5
Waltheof Av TOTM N17............49 K4
Waltheof Gdns TOTM N17......49 K4
Walton Av CHEAM SM3............208 D1
  NWMAL KT3............192 C1
  RYLN/HDSTN HA2............77 K2
  WBLY HA9............80 D1
Walton Cl CRICK NW2............63 K6
  HRW HA1............60 D1
  VX/NE SW8............141 K1
Walton Dr HRW HA1............60 D1
  WLSDN NW10............81 F4
Walton Gdns ACT W3............98 D4
  FELT TW13............153 J6
  WBLY HA9............62 A6
Walton Gn CROY/NA CRO......213 K6
Walton Gn WOT/HER KT12......188 C6
Walton Park La
  WOT/HER KT12............188 D6
Walton Pl CHEL SW3............14 E4
Walton Rd CRW RM5............56 B5
  HRW HA1............60 D1
  MNPK E12............90 A2
  PLSTW E13............107 G1
  SCUP DA14............168 C5
  SEVS/STOTM N15 *............68 B1
  WOT/HER KT12............188 C2

Walton St CHEL SW3............14 D6
  ENC/FH EN2............23 K2
Walton Vis IS N1 *............86 A5
Walton Wy ACT W3............98 D4
  MTCM CR4............195 H1
Walt Whitman Cl HNHL SE24 *..142 C5
Walverns Cl OXHEY WD19......27 G1
Walworth Pl WALW SE17......122 D5
Walworth Rd STHWK SE1......18 C6
Walwyn Av BMLY BR1............200 C1
Wanborough Dr
  PUT/ROE SW15............158 E3
Wanderer Dr BARK IG11......109 J2
Wandle Bank CROY/NA CRO....210 E1
  WIM/MER SW19............178 C2
Wandle Ct CROY/NA CRO *....210 E1
Wandle Court Gdns
  CROY/NA CRO............210 E1
Wandle Rd CROY/NA CRO......210 E1
  CROY/NA CRO *............210 E1
  MRDN SM4............194 C2
  TOOT SW17............160 D4
  WLGTN SM6............195 G6
Wandle Side CROY/NA CRO....211 F1
  WLGTN SM6............210 B1
Wandle Wy MTCM CR4............194 E2
  WAND/EARL SW18............160 A3
Wandsworth Br
  WAND/EARL SW18............140 A6
Wandsworth Bridge Rd
  FUL/PGN SW6............140 A6
Wandsworth Common West
  Side WAND/EARL SW18......140 B6
Wandsworth High St
  WAND/EARL SW18............139 K6
Wandsworth Rd VX/NE SW8....141 J4
Wangey Rd CHDH RM6............73 K4
Wanless Rd HNHL SE24......142 D4
Wanley Rd CMBW SE5............142 E5
Wanlip Rd PLSTW E13............107 F3
Wanlip Rd PLSTW E13............107 F3
Wannock Gdns BARK/HLT IG6..54 B3
Wansbeck Rd HOM E9............87 H5
Wansdown Pl FUL/PGN SW6....140 A1
Wansey St WALW SE17............18 D7
Wansford Rd WFD IG8............53 G4
Wanstead La IL IG1............71 J3
Wanstead Park Av MNPK E12..71 H4
Wanstead Park Rd IL IG1......71 J5
Wanstead Pl WAN E11............70 E3
Wanstead Rd BMLY BR1......184 B5
Wansunt Rd BXLY DA5............169 K3
Wantage Rd LEE/GVPK SE12..145 J6
Wantz La RAIN RM13............111 K3
Wantz Rd DAGE RM10............92 D2
Wapping Dock St WAP E1W *..123 J1
Wapping High St WAP E1W......123 H1
Wapping La WAP E1W............123 K1
Wapping Wall WAP E1W......123 K1
Warbank La KUTN/CMB KT2....176 E5
Warbeck Rd SHB W12............118 E1
Warberry Rd WDGN N22............49 F5
Warboys Ap KUTN/CMB KT2....175 J2
Warboys Crs CHING E4............52 A1
Warboys Rd KUTN/CMB KT2....175 J2
Warburton Cl IS N1............86 A4
  KTN/HRWW/WS HA3............42 D2
Warburton Rd HACK E8............86 D6
  WHTN TW2............155 C3
Warburton St HACK E8............86 D6
  SAND/SEL CR2............212 A5
Wardalls Gv NWCR SE14 *......143 K1
Ward Cl ERITH DA8............130 A6
  RYLN/HDSTN HA2............45 G3
Wardell Cl EDGW HA8............45 C3
Warden Av CRW RM5............56 E1
  RYLN/HDSTN HA2............59 J5
Warden Rd KTTN NW5............84 A4
Wardens Gv STHWK SE1......18 C1
Wardle St HOM E9............87 F5
Wardley St WAND/EARL SW18..160 A2
Wardo Av FUL/PGN SW6......139 H2
Wardour Ms SOHO/CST W1F...10 B3
Wardour St SOHO/CST W1F....10 C4
Ward Rd ARCH N19............84 C2
  SRTFD E15............88 B6
Wardrobe Pl BLKFR EC4V *......12 B4
The Wardrobe
  RCH/KEW TW9 *............136 E6
Wards Rd GNTH/NBYPK IG2....72 D4
Wards Wharf Ap CAN/RD E16..126 C2
Wareham Cl HSLW TW3............135 G5
Waremead Rd
  GNTH/NBYPK IG2............72 B2
Warepoint Dr THMD SE28......127 J2
Warfield Rd
  EBED/NFELT TW14............153 H2
  HPTN TW12............173 C4
  WLSDN NW10............100 B3
Warfield Yd WLSDN NW10 *....100 B3
Wargrave Av SEVS/STOTM N15..68 B3
Wargrave Rd RYLN/HDSTN HA2..78 A1
Warham Rd FSBYPK N4............67 G2
  KTN/HRWW/WS HA3............43 G5
  SAND/SEL CR2............211 J5
Warham St CMBW SE5............142 C1
Waring Cl ORP BR6............217 F4
Waring Dr ORP BR6............217 F4
Waring Rd SCUP DA14............186 D2
Waring St WNWD SE27......162 D6
Warkworth Gdns ISLW TW7....136 B1
Warkworth Rd TOTM N17......49 K3
Warland Rd WOOL/PLUM SE18..147 J1
Warley Av BCTR RM8............74 B4
  YEAD UB4............94 E4
Warley Rd CLAY IG5............54 A4
  ED N9............36 E4
  WFD IG8............53 F3
  YEAD UB4............94 E5
Warley St BETH E2............105 F2
Warlingham Rd THHTH CR7....196 C1
Warlock Rd MV/WKIL W9......100 D3
Warlters Cl HOLWY N7............84 E2
Warlters Rd HOLWY N7............84 E2
Warltersville Rd ARCH N19......66 E4
Warming Cl CLPT E5 *............87 F1
Warmington Rd HNHL SE24....162 D1

Warmington St PLSTW E13....106 E3
Warminster Rd SNWD SE25....181 H5
Warminster Sq SNWD SE25....181 H5
Warminster Wy MTCM CR4....179 G4
Warnwell Av CDALE/KGS NW9..63 H1
Warndon St BERM/RHTH SE16..123 K4
Wareford Pl OXHEY WD19......27 J1
Warneford Rd
  KTN/HRWW/WS HA3............43 K6
Warne Pl SCUP DA14 *............168 D6
Warner Av CHEAM SM3......193 H6
Warner Cl CDALE/KGS NW9....63 H4
  HPTN TW12............172 E1
  HYS/HAR UB3............133 G1
  SRTFD E15............88 C3
Warner Pl BETH E2............104 C1
Warner Rd BMLY BR1............183 J3
  CEND/HSY/T N8............66 D1
  CMBW SE5............142 D2
  WALTH E17............69 G1
Warner St CLKNW EC1R............5 J7
Warner Ter POP/IOD E14 *......105 J4
Warner Yd CLKNW EC1R............5 J7
Warnford Rd ORP BR6............217 F3
Warnham Court Rd CAR SM5..209 K5
Warnham Rd
  NFNCH/WDSPK N12............47 J1
Warple Ms ACT W3............118 B2
Warple Wy ACT W3............118 B2
Warren Av BMLY BR1............183 H3
  ORP BR6............217 F3
  RCHPK/HAM TW10............137 J5
  SAND/SEL CR2............213 F5
  WAN E11 *............88 B1
Warren Cl BXLYHS DA6......149 H6
  ED N9............37 F2
  ESH/CLAY KT10............204 C2
  WBLY HA9............61 K6
  YEAD UB4............95 G4
Warren Ct CHARL SE7............126 B5
  ED N9............36 B2
Warren Cutting
  KUTN/CMB KT2............176 A3
Warrender Rd ARCH N19......84 C1
Warrender Wy RSLP HA4......44 E6
Warren Dr GFD/PVL UB6......96 B3
  HCH RM12............93 J1
  ORP BR6............217 H3
  RSLP HA4............59 H5
Warren Dr North BRYLDS KT5..191 J5
Warren Dr South BRYLDS KT5..191 K5
The Warren Dr WAN E11............71 G4
Warren Flds STAN HA7 *......29 J6
Warren Gdns ORP BR6............217 G3
Warren La STAN HA7............29 G4
Warren Gdns SRTFD E15......88 C3
  LEY E10............88 A1
  ORP BR6............217 F3
Warren Ms FITZ W1T............10 A1
  WHTN TW2............155 J1
  WIM/MER SW19............155 H6
Warren Pk KUTN/CMB KT2....176 A4
Warren Park Rd SUT SM1......209 H4
Warren Pond Rd CHING E4......38 D3
Warren Ri NWMAL KT3............176 A6
Warren Rd BARK/HLT IG6......72 D2
  BUSH WD23............28 C3
  BXLYHS DA6............149 H6
  CHING E4............38 A4
  CRICK NW2............63 F6
  CROY/NA CRO............197 F5
  DART DA1............171 H5
  HAYES BR2............199 K6
  KUTN/CMB KT2............175 K2
  LEY E10............88 A1
  ORP BR6............217 F3
  SCUP DA14............168 D5
  WAN E11............71 G4
  WHTN TW2............155 J1
  WIM/MER SW19............178 D2
Warrens Shawe La EDGW HA8..30 D4
Warren St FITZ W1T............4 E7
The Warren BELMT SM2......209 H6
  HEST TW5............134 E1
  MNPK E12............89 J2
  WPK KT4............207 F2
  YEAD UB4............94 E5
Warren Wy MLHL NW7............46 C2
Warren Wood Cl HAYES BR2..199 H6
Warriner Dr ED N9............36 C5
Warriner Gdns BTSEA SW11..140 E2
Warrington Crs MV/WKIL W9..101 G3
Warrington Gdns
  MV/WKIL W9............101 G3
Warrington Pl POP/IOD E14 *..125 F1
Warrington Rd BCTR RM8......73 K6
  CROY/NA CRO............211 H1
  HRW HA1............60 E2
  RCHPK/HAM TW10............136 E6
Warrington Sq BCTR RM8......73 K6
Warsaw Cl RSLP HA4............77 F4
Warspite Rd
  WOOL/PLUM SE18............126 D3
Warton Rd SRTFD E15............88 A6
Warwall EHAM E6............108 B5
Warwick Av EDGW HA8............30 C5
  MV/WKIL W9............101 G4
  RYLN/HDSTN HA2............77 K2

Warwick La STP EC4M............12 B4
Warwick Pde
  KTN/HRWW/WS HA3 *............43 H5
Warwick Pl EA W5............116 E2
  MV/WKIL W9............101 G4
  THDIT KT7 *............190 B3
Warwick Pl North PIM SW1V *..16 A7
Warwick Rd BAR EN5............21 F5
  CHING E4............51 J1
  EA W5............117 F1
  FBAR/BDGN N11............48 D2
  HSLWW TW4............134 A3
  KUT/HW KT1............174 D4
  MNPK E12............89 J3
  NWDGN UB2............114 E3
  SCUP DA14............186 C1
  SRTFD E15............88 D4
  SUT SM1............209 G3
  THDIT KT7............190 A2
  THHTH CR7............180 B6
  UED N18............36 B6
  WALTH E17............71 F2
  WAN E11............71 F2
  WDR/YW UB7............112 B1
  WELL DA16............148 D4
  WHTN TW2............155 K3
  WKENS W14............119 J4
Warwick Rw WESTW SW1E....16 A4
Warwickshire Pth DEPT SE8..144 C1
Warwick Sq PIM SW1V............16 A7
  STP EC4M............12 B3
Warwick Square Ms PIM SW1V..16 A7
Warwick St RECST W1B............10 B5
Warwick Ter WALTH E17 *......70 B2
  WOOL/PLUM SE18............127 J6
Warwick Wy DART DA1............171 H4
  ERITH DA8............150 D2
Warwick Yd STLK EC1Y *............6 D7
Washington Av MNPK E12......89 J2
Washington Cl BOW E3............105 K2
Washington Rd BARN SW13....138 D1
  EHAM E6............89 G5
  KUT/HW KT1............175 H5
  SWFD E18............52 D5
  WPK KT4............192 E6
Wastdale Rd FSTH SE23......164 A3
Watchfield Ct CHSWK W4 *....117 K5
The Watch
  NFNCH/WDSPK N12............33 G6
Watcombe Rd SNWD SE25....197 J2
Waterbank Rd CAT SE6............164 E5
Waterbeach Rd DAGW RM9....91 J4
Water Brook La HDN NW4......64 A2
Watercress Pl IS N1............86 A5
Waterdale Rd ABYW SE2......128 B6
Waterden Crs SRTFD E15......87 J5
Waterden Rd SRTFD E15......87 J5
Waterer Ri WLGTN SM6............210 D4
Waterfall Cottages
  WIM/MER SW19............178 C2
Waterfall Rd FBAR/BDGN N11..34 B6
  WIM/MER SW19............178 C2
Waterfall Ter TOOT SW17......178 D2
Waterfield Cl BELV DA17......129 H3
  THMD SE28............128 C1
Waterfield Cottages
  MORT/ESHN SW14 *............137 J5
Waterfield Gdns SNWD SE25..197 F1
Waterford Rd FUL/PGN SW6..140 A2
Waterford Wy WLSDN NW10..81 K3
The Waterfront BORE WD6 *....29 H1
  DEPT SE8 *............124 B3
The Water Gdns BAY/PAD W2..8 C3
Watergate EMB EC4Y............12 A5
Watergate St DEPT SE8............124 D6
The Watergate OXHEY WD19..27 H4
Waterhall Av CHING E4............52 C1
Waterhall Cl WALTH E17......51 F4
Waterhead Cl ERITH DA8......150 B1
Waterhouse Cl HAMP NW3......83 H3
Wateridge Cl POP/IOD E14....124 D3
Wateringbury Cl
  STMC/STPC BR5............186 C6
Water La CAMTN NW1............84 B6
  ED N9............36 D3
  GDMY/SEVK IG3............91 F1
  KUT/HW KT1............174 E5
  MON EC3R............13 H6
  NWCR SE14............143 K1
  PUR RM19............131 K4
  SCUP DA14............169 G5
  SRTFD E15............88 B4
  TWK TW1............156 B3
Water Lily Cl NWDGN UB2....115 H2
Waterloo Br STHWK SE1............11 H6
Waterloo Cl EBED/NFELT TW14..153 J3
  HOM E9............86 E3
Waterloo Gdns BETH E2......104 E1
  ROMW/RG RM7............75 F3
  STHWK SE1............17 J1
  SUT SM1............209 H3
Waterloo Ter IS N1............85 H5
Waterlow Rd ARCH N19............66 C5
Waterman Cl OXHEY WD19....27 F1
Watermans
  KUTN/CMB KT2 *............175 F3
Watermans Ms EA W5 *......98 A6
Waterman Sq PGE/AN SE20..181 K5
Waterman St PUT/ROE SW15..139 G4
Waterman Wy WAP E1W......123 J1
Watermead
  EBED/NFELT TW14............153 H3
Watermead La CAR SM5......194 E4
Watermeadow Cl ERITH DA8..150 E1
Watermeadow La
  FUL/PGN SW6............140 B3

Watermead Rd CAT SE6............165 F6
Watermead Wy TOTM N17......50 E5
Watermens Sq PGE/AN SE20 *..181 K5
Water Ms PECK SE15............143 K5
Watermill Cl
  RCHPK/HAM TW10............156 D5
Watermill La UED N18............50 A1
Water Mill Wy FELT TW13......154 E4
Watermill Wy WIM/MER SW19..178 B4
Watermint Quay CLPT E5......68 C4
Watermint Quay CLPT E5......68 C4
Water Rd ALP/SUD HA0............80 B5
Water's Edge FUL/PGN SW6 *..139 G2
Watersedge HOR/WEW KT19..206 E3
Watersfield Wy EDGW HA8......43 K3
Waterside BECK BR3 *............182 C4
  WALTH E17............50 B6
Waterside Av BECK BR3............198 E2
Waterside Cl BARK IG11......91 G2
  BERM/RHTH SE16............123 H2
  BOW E3............87 H6
  NTHLT UB5............95 K3
  SURB KT6............191 F6
  THMD SE28............128 A1
Waterside Ct LEW SE13 *......145 G5
Waterside Dr WOT/HER KT12..188 A2
Waterside Rd NWDGN UB2....115 F3
Waterside Wy TOOT SW17....179 G1
Watersmeet Wy THMD SE28..109 K5
Waterson St BETH E2............7 H5
Watersplash Cl KUT/HW KT1..175 F6
Watersplash La HEST TW5....114 A5
  HYS/HAR UB3............113 K4
Waterside Rd CAT SE6............165 H5
  KUT/HW KT1............175 J6
Waters Sq KUT/HW KT1......175 J6
Water St TPL/STR WC2R............11 J5
Water Tower Hl CROY/NA CRO..211 K2
Water Tower Pl IS N1............5 K1
Waterworks La CLPT E5......69 F6
Waterworks Rd
  BRXS/STRHM SW2............161 K1
Watery La HYS/HAR UB3......113 G5
  NTHLT UB5............95 G1
  RYNPK SW20............177 J5
  STMC/STPC BR5............186 D1
Wates Wy MTCM CR4............194 E3
Wateville Rd TOTM N17............49 J4
Watford Cl BTSEA SW11......140 D2
Watford Heath OXHEY WD19..27 H1
Watford Heath Farm
  OXHEY WD19 *............27 H2
Watford Rd BORE WD6............26 E1
  CAN/RD E16............106 E4
  HRW HA1............60 E4
  NTHWD HA6............40 E2
Watford Rd WDN NW4............31 F6
Watford Wy (Barnet By-Pass)
  MLHL NW7............45 D1
Watkin Rd WBLY HA9............80 D1
Watkinson Rd HOLWY N7......85 F4
Watling Av EDGW HA8............44 E4
Watling Ct STP EC4M............12 D4
Watlings Cl CROY/NA CRO....198 B3
Watling St BXLYHS DA6......149 K6
  PECK SE15............123 F6
  STP EC4M............12 C4
Wat Tyler Rd GNWCH SE10..145 F3
Wauthier Cl PLMGR N13......49 H1
Wavell Dr BFN/LL DA15......167 K1
Wavel Ms KIL/WHAMP NW6....83 F5
Wavel Pl SYD SE26............165 G6
Wavendon Av CHSWK W4......118 A5
Waveney Av PECK SE15......143 J5
Waveney Cl WAP E1W............123 H1
Waverley Av BRYLDS KT5......191 J3
  CHING E4............51 G1
  SUT SM1............194 A6
  WALTH E17............70 B1
  WBLY HA9............80 B3
  WHTN TW2............154 B2
Waverley Cl E/WMO/HCT KT8..189 F2
  HAYES BR2............200 C2
  HYS/HAR UB3............113 G4
Waverley Crs
  WOOL/PLUM SE18............127 J6
Waverley Gdns BARK IG11....108 E1
  BARK/HLT IG6............54 C5
  EHAM E6............107 J4
  NTHWD HA6............40 E4
Waverley Gv FNCH N3............46 C2
Waverley Pl FSBYPK N4 *......67 H5
  STJWD NW8............2 B2
Waverley Rd CEND/HSY/T N8..66 D3
  ENC/FH EN2............23 F4
  EW KT17............207 K5
  RAIN RM13............111 K2
  RYLN/HDSTN HA2............59 J4
  SNWD SE25............197 J1
  STHL UB1............96 A6
  SWFD E18............53 G4
  TOTM N17............50 D5
  WALTH E17............52 A3
  WOOL/PLUM SE18............127 H5
Waverley Wy CAR SM5............209 J4

Waverton Rd
WAND/EARL SW18 ....160 B2
Waverton St *MYFR/PICC* W1J 9 J7
Wavertree Rd
BRXS/STRHM SW2 ....162 A3
SWFD E18 ....52 E5
Waxlow Crs *STHL* UB1 ....96 A5
Waxlow Rd *WLSDN* NW10 ....98 E1
Waxlow Wy *NTHLT* UB5 ....95 K3
Waxwell La *PIN* HA5 ....41 H6
Wayborne Gv *RSLP* HA4 ....58 A3
Waye Av *HEST* TW5 ....133 K2
Wayfarer Rd *NTHLT* UB5 ....95 J2
Wayford St *BTSEA* SW11 .....140 D3
Wayland Av *HACK* E8 ....86 C5
Waylands *HYS/HAR* UB3 ....94 B4
Waylett Pl *ALP/SUD* HA0 ....79 K2
WNWD SE27 ....162 C5
Wayne Cl *ORP* BR6 ....217 F1
Wayneflete Tower Av
ESH/CLAY KT10 ....204 A1
Waynflete Av *CROY/NA* CR0 ...211 H2
Waynflete Sq *NKENS* W10 ....100 B6
Waynflete St
WAND/EARL SW18 ....160 B2
Wayside *CROY/NA* CR0 *.......213 K4
GLDGN NW11 ....64 C5
MORT/ESHN SW14 ....137 K5
Wayside Av *BUSH* WD23 ....28 D1
Wayside Cl *ROM* RM1 ....57 H6
STHGT/OAK N14 ....34 C1
Wayside Ct *TWK* TW1 ....156 D1
Wayside Gdns *DAGE* RM10 ....92 C3
Wayside Gv *ELTH/MOT* SE9 ..166 E6
Wayside Ms *GNTH/NBYPK* IG2 ...72 A3
Weald Cl *BERM/RHTH* SE16 ..123 J5
HAYES BR2 ....200 D6
Weald La *KTN/HRWW/WS* HA3 ...42 D5
Weald Ri *KTN/HRWW/WS* HA3 ...43 F3
Weald Sq *CLPT* E5 *............68 C6
Wealdstone Rd *CHEAM* SM3 ..193 J6
The Weald *CHST* BR7 ....184 C2
Weald Wy *ROMW/RG* RM7 .....74 D3
YEAD UB4 ....94 C2
Wealdwood Gdns *PIN* HA5 ....42 A2
Weale Rd *CHING* E4 ....38 B4
Weardale Gdns *ENC/FH* EN2 ...23 K2
Weardale Rd *LEW* SE13 ......145 G6
Wear Pl *BETH* E2 ....104 D2
Wearside Rd *LEW* SE13 ......144 E5
Weatherley Cl *BOW* E3 ....105 H4
Weaver Cl *CROY/NA* CR0 ......212 B2
EHAM E6 ....108 B6
Weavers Cl *ISLW* TW7 ....135 K5
Weaver's La *STHWK* SE1 ....19 H2
Weavers Ter *FUL/PGN* SW6 * ..119 K6
Weaver St *WCHPL* E1 ....104 C3
Weavers Wy *CAMTN* NW1 .....84 D6
Weaver Wk *WNWD* SE27 ......162 C6
Webb Cl *NKENS* W10 ....100 A3
Webber Cl *BORE* WD6 ....29 K1
ERITH DA8 ....150 E1
Webber Rw *STHWK* SE1 ....17 K4
Webber St *STHWK* SE1 ....17 K2
Webb Est *CLPT* E5 * 68 C4
Webb Pl *WLSDN* NW10 ....99 H2
Webb Rd *BKHTH/KID* SE3 .....125 J6
Webbscroft Rd *DAGE* RM10 ...92 D2
Webb St *STHWK* SE1 ....19 G4
Webster Gdns *EA* W5 ....97 K1
Webster Rd *BERM/RHTH* SE16 ..123 H3
WAN E11 ....88 A1
Wedderburn Rd *BARK* IG11 ....90 E6
HAMP NW3 *....................40 A3
Wedgewood Ct *NTHWD* HA6 *..40 A3
Wedgwood Wk
KIL/WHAMP NW6 * 83 F3
Wedgwood Wy *NRWD* SE19 ..180 D3
Wedlake St *NKENS* W10 ......100 C3
Wedmore Av *CLAY* IG5 ....54 A4
Wedmore Gdns *ARCH* N19 .....66 E6
Wedmore Ms *ARCH* N19 ....84 D1
Wedmore St *ARCH* N19 ....84 D1
Weech Rd *KIL/WHAMP* NW6 ....82 E2
Weedington Rd *KTTN* NW5 .....84 A3
Weedley Sq *BTSEA* SW11 *.....140 C4
Weigall Rd *LEE/GVPK* SE12 ...145 K5
Weighhouse St *MYFR/PKLN* W1K ...9 H5
Weighton Rd
KTN/HRWW/WS HA3 ....42 D4
PGE/AN SE20 ....181 J5
Weihurst Gdns *SUT* SM1 ......209 H3
Weimar St *PUT/ROE* SW15 ...139 H4
Weirdale Av *TRDG/WHET* N20 ..33 K4
Weir Hall Av *UED* N18 ....49 K2
Weir Hall Gdns *UED* N18 ......49 K1
Weir Hall Rd *UED* N18 ....49 K2
Weir Rd *BAL* SW12 ....161 H3
BXLY DA5 ....169 J2
WIM/MER SW19 ....160 A1
Weirside Gdns *WDR/YW* UB7 ..112 A1
Weirs Pas *CAMTN* NW1 ....4 D4
Weiss Rd *PUT/ROE* SW15 .....139 G4
Welbeck Av *BFN/LL* DA15 .....168 B3
BMLY BR1 ....165 K6
YEAD UB4 ....95 F3
Welbeck Cl *EBAR* EN4 ....33 H1
EHAM E6 ....107 H2
**RYLN/HDSTN* HA2 ....60 B5
SUT SM1 ....209 H3
Welbeck St *CAVSO/HST* W1G 9 J3
Welbeck Vls *WCHMH* N21 * 35 J3
Welbeck Wy *CAVSO/HST* W1G 9 J4
Welby St *PLSTW* E15 ....107 C1
Welch Pl *PIN* HA5 ....41 G4
Welcome Ct *ISLW* TW7 *.........44 A3
Weldon Cl *RSLP* HA4 ....77 F5
Weldon Dr *E/WMO/HCT* KT8 ..188 E1
Weld Pl *FBAR/BDGN* N11 ....48 B1
Welfare Rd *SRTFD* E15 ....88 C5
Welford Cl *CLPT* E5 ....87 F1
Welford Pl *WIM/MER* SW19 ...159 H4

Welham Rd *TOOT* SW17 ....179 F1
Welhouse Rd *CAR* SM5 ....194 D6
Wellacre Rd
KTN/HRWW/WS HA3 ....61 H3
Welland Cl *BFN/LL* DA15 ......148 C6
Welland Gdns *GFD/PVL* UB6 ...97 F1
Wellands Cl *BMLY* BR1 ....184 E5
Welland St *GNWCH* SE10 .....125 F6
Well Ap *BAR* EN5 ....20 C6
Wellbrook Rd *ORP* BR6 ....216 A2
Welby Cl *ED* N9 ....36 D3
Well Cl *RSLP* HA4 ....77 J1
STRHM/NOR SW16 ....162 A6
Wellclose Sq *WCHPL* E1 ......104 C6
Wellclose St *WCHPL* E1 ....104 C6
Wellcome Av *DART* DA1 ....151 H5
Well Cottage Cl *WAN* E11 ......71 G4
Well Ct *STP* EC4M 12 D4
Welldon Crs *HRW* HA1 ....60 E3
Weller St *STHWK* SE1 ....18 C2
Wellesley Av *HMSMTH* W6 ....118 E3
NTHWD HA6 ....40 D1
Wellesley Ct *MV/WKIL* W9 .....101 G2
Wellesley Court Rd
CROY/NA CR0 ....196 E6
Wellesley Crs *WHTN* TW2 .....155 K4
Wellesley Gv *CROY/NA* CR0 ..196 E6
Wellesley Pde *WHTN* TW2 * ..155 K5
Wellesley Park Ms *ENC/FH* EN2 ...23 H1
Wellesley Rd *CAMTN* NW1 * 4 C1
KTTN NW5 ....84 A3
Wellesley Rd *BELMT* SM2 .....209 G4
CHSWK W4 ....117 H5
CROY/NA CR0 ....196 D5
HRW HA1 ....60 E2
IL IG1 ....72 B6
KTTN NW5 ....84 A3
WALTH E17 ....69 J3
WAN E11 ....70 E2
WHTN TW2 ....155 K5
Wellesley St *WCHPL* E1 ....105 F4
Wellesley Ter *IS* N1 ....6 D4
Wellfield Av *MUSWH* N10 ....48 B6
Wellfield Gdns *CAR* SM5 .....209 J6
Wellfield Rd
STRHM/NOR SW16 ....161 K6
Wellfit St *HNHL* SE24 ....142 C4
Wellgarth *GFD/PVL* UB6 ....79 H4
Wellgarth Rd *GLDGN* NW11 ...65 F5
Well Gv *TRDG/WHET* N20 ....33 G2
Well Hall Pde *ELTH/MOT* SE9 ...146 E5
Well Hall Rd *ELTH/MOT* SE9 ..146 E5
Wellhouse La *BAR* EN5 ....20 A5
Wellhouse Rd *BECK* BR3 ......198 C1
Wellhurst Cl *ORP* BR6 ....217 F5
Welling High St *WELL* DA16 ..148 C4
Wellington Av *BFN/LL* DA15 ..168 B1
CHING E4 ....37 J4
ED N9 ....36 D5
HSLW TW3 ....135 F6
PIN HA5 ....41 K4
SEVS/STOTM N15 ....68 A3
WPK KT4 ....208 A1
Wensley Av *WFD* IG8 ....52 D3
Wensley Cl *CRW* RM5 ....56 C1
ELTH/MOT SE9 ....166 E1
FBAR/BDGN N11 ....48 A2
Wensleydale Av *CLAY* IG5 .....53 J5
Wensleydale Gdns *HPTN* TW12 ..173 G3
Wensleydale Rd *HPTN* TW12 ..173 F4
Wensley Rd *UED* N18 ....50 D2
Wentland Cl *CAT* SE6 ....165 G4
Wentland Rd *CAT* SE6 ....165 G4
Wentworth Av *FNCH* N3 ....46 E3
Wentworth Cl *ASHF* TW15 ....152 E6
FNCH N3 ....47 F3
HAYES BR2 ....199 J4
MRDN SM4 ....193 K4
ORP BR6 ....216 E3
SURB KT6 ....190 E6
THMD SE28 ....109 K5
Wentworth Dr *DART* DA1 .....170 D2
PIN HA5 ....58 E2
Wentworth Gdns *PLMGR* N13 ...35 H5
Wentworth Hl *WBLY* HA9 ......62 B5
Wentworth Ms *BOW* E3 ....105 H3
Wentworth Pk *FNCH* N3 ....47 F3
Wentworth Pl *STAN* HA7 *......43 H2
Wentworth Rd *BAR* EN5 ....20 B3
CROY/NA CR0 ....196 B4
GLDGN NW11 ....64 D4
MNPK E12 ....89 H2
NWDGN UB2 ....114 B4
Wentworth St *WCHPL* E1 ....13 K2
Wentworth Wy *PIN* HA5 ....59 J1
RAIN RM13 ....111 K2
Wenvoe Av *BXLYHN* DA7 ......149 J3
Wepham Cl *YEAD* UB4 ....95 H5
Wernbrook St
WOOL/PLUM SE18 ....127 H6
Werndee Rd *SNWD* SE25 .....197 H1
Werneth Hall Rd *CLAY* IG5 ....53 K6
Werrington St *CAMTN* NW1 .....4 B3
Werter Rd *PUT/ROE* SW15 ...139 H5
Wesleyan Pl *KTTN* NW5 ....84 B2
Wesley Av *CAN/RD* E16 ....125 K1
HSLW TW3 ....134 D3
WLSDN NW10 ....99 F2
Wesley Cl *HOLWY* N7 ....67 F6
LBTH SE11 ....17 K6
RYLN/HDSTN HA2 ....60 C6
STMC/STPC BR5 ....186 D6
Wesley Rd *HYS/HAR* UB3 ......94 E6
LEY E10 ....70 A4
WLSDN NW10 ....80 E6
Wesley Sq *NTGHL* W11 ....100 C5
Wesley St *CAVSO/HST* W1G 9 H3
Wessex Av *WIM/MER* SW19 ..177 K5
Wessex Cl *GDMY/SEVK* IG3 * ..73 J4
KUT/HW KT1 ....175 J4
THDIT KT7 ....190 A5
Wessex Dr *ERITH* DA8 ....150 A3

RAIN RM13 ....93 H4
Wells House Rd *WLSDN* NW10 ..99 H4
Wellside Cl *BAR* EN5 ....20 A5
Wellside Gdns
MORT/ESHN SW14 ....137 K5
Wells Ms *FITZ* W1T *.............10 B2
Wellsmoor Gdns *BMLY* BR1 ..185 F6
Wells Park Rd *SYD* SE26 .....163 H5
Wells Pl *CMBW* SE5 ....143 F1
WAND/EARL SW18 ....160 B2
Wells Ri *STJWD* NW8 ....2 E1
Wells Rd *BMLY* BR1 ....184 E5
SHB W12 ....119 F2
Wells Sq *FSBYW* WC1X 5 G5
Wells St *GTPST* W1W 10 A2
Wellstead Av *ED* N9 ....36 E2
Wellstead Rd *EHAM* E6 ....108 A1
Wells Ter *FSBYPK* N4 ....67 G1
The Wells *STHGT/OAK* N14 ....34 D3
Well St *HOM* E9 ....86 E5
SRTFD E15 ....88 C4
Wells Wy *SKENS* SW7 ....14 A4
WALW SE17 ....122 E5
Well Wk *HAMP* NW3 ....83 H1
Wellwood Rd *GDMY/SEVK* IG3 ...73 G5
Welsford St *STHWK* SE1 ......123 H5
Welsh Cl *PLSTW* E13 ....106 E2
Welshpool St *HACK* E8 *........86 C6
Welshside Rd *CDALE/KGS* NW9 * ...63 G2
Welstead Wy *CHSWK* W4 .....118 C4
Weltje Rd *HMSMTH* W6 ....118 D5
Welton Rd *WOOL/PLUM* SE18 ..147 K1
Welwyn Av *EBED/NFELT* TW14 ..153 J1
Welwyn St *BETH* E2 ....105 F2
Welwyn Wy *YEAD* UB4 ....94 C3
Wembley Hill Rd *WBLY* HA9 ...80 B3
Wembley Park Dr *WBLY* HA9 ...80 B2
Wembley Rd *HPTN* TW12 .....173 F4
Wembley Wy *WBLY* HA9 ....80 D4
Wemborough Rd *STAN* HA7 ....43 J3
Wembury Ms *HGT* N6 ....66 C4
Wembury Rd *HGT* N6 ....66 B4
Wemyss Rd *BKHTH/KID* SE3 ..145 J3
Wendela Ct *HRW* HA1 ....78 E1
Wendell Rd *SHB* W12 ....118 C2
Wendling Rd *SUT* SM1 ....194 C5
Wendon St *BOW* E3 ....87 H6
Wendover Cl *YEAD* UB4 ....95 H3
Wendover Dr *NWMAL* KT3 ....192 C3
Wendover Rd *ELTH/MOT* SE9 ..146 C2
HAYES BR2 ....200 A1
WLSDN NW10 ....99 H1
Wendover Wy *BUSH* WD23 ....28 C1
ORP BR6 ....202 B3
WELL DA16 ....148 B6
Wenlock Gdns *HDN* NW4 * 63 J1
IS N1 ....6 C3
Wenlock Rd *EDGW* HA8 ....44 D4
IS N1 ....6 C3
Wenlock St *IS* N1 ....6 D3
Wennington Rd *BOW* E3 .....105 F1
RAIN RM13 ....111 K4

PIN HA5 ....41 J3
Wessex Gdns *GLDGN* NW11 ....64 C5
Wessex La *GFD/PVL* UB6 ....96 D1
Wessex Rd *HTHAIR* TW6 ....132 B4
Wessex St *BETH* E2 ....104 E2
Wessex Ter *MTCM* CR4 *.......194 D7
Wessex Wk *RDART* DA2 ....170 A4
Wessex Wy *GLDGN* NW11 ......64 C5
Messon Md *CMBW* SE5 ....142 D1
Westacott *YEAD* UB4 ....94 C4
Westacott Cl *ARCH* N19 ....66 D5
West Arbour St *WCHPL* E1 ....105 F5
West Av *FNCH* N3 ....46 E2
HDN NW4 ....64 B2
HYS/HAR UB3 ....59 K4
PIN HA5 ....59 K4
STHL UB1 ....95 K6
WALTH E17 ....69 K2
WLGTN SM6 ....210 E3
West Avenue Rd *WALTH* E17 ...69 J1
West Bank *BARK* IG11 ....90 B1
ENC/FH EN2 ....23 J4
STNW/STAM N16 ....68 A4
Westbank Rd *HPTN* TW12 ....173 H2
West Barnes La *NWMAL* KT3 ..192 C2
Westbeech Rd *WDGN* N22 ......49 G2
Westbere Dr *STAN* HA7 ....43 K1
Westbere Rd *CRICK* NW2 ......82 C2
Westbourne Av *ACT* W3 ....99 F5
CHEAM SM3 ....193 H6
Westbourne Crs *BAY/PAD* W2 ...8 A5
Westbourne Crescent Ms
BAY/PAD W2 ....8 A5
Westbourne Dr *FSTH* SE23 ...164 A4
Westbourne Gdns
BAY/PAD W2 ....101 F5
Westbourne Ga *BAY/PAD* W2 ...8 B5
Westbourne Gv *BAY/PAD* W2 ..100 E5
Westbourne Grove Ms
NTGHL W11 ....100 E5
Westbourne Grove Ter
BAY/PAD W2 ....101 F5
Westbourne Park Rd
BAY/PAD W2 ....100 D5
NTGHL W11 ....100 C5
Westbourne Pl *ED* N9 ....36 D6
Westbourne Rd *BXLYHN* DA7 ..148 E1
CROY/NA CR0 ....197 G3
FELT TW13 ....153 J5
HOLWY N7 ....85 F4
SYD SE26 ....182 A2
Westbourne St *BAY/PAD* W2 ....8 A5
Westbourne Ter *BAY/PAD* W2 ...8 A4
Westbourne Terrace Ms
BAY/PAD W2 ....101 G5
Westbourne Terrace Rd
BAY/PAD W2 ....101 G4
Westbridge Cl *SHB* W12 ....118 D1
Westbridge Rd *BTSEA* SW11 ..140 C2
Westbrook Av *HPTN* TW12 ....172 E5
Westbrook Cl *EBAR* EN4 ....21 H4
Westbrook Crs *EBAR* EN4 ......21 H4
Westbrooke Crs *WELL* DA16 ..148 D4
Westbrooke Rd *BFN/LL* DA15 ..167 J4
WELL DA16 ....148 C4
Westbrook Rd *BKHTH/KID* SE3 ..146 A1
HEST TW5 ....134 E1
THHTH CR7 ....180 E5
Westbury Av *WDGN* N22 * 49 H6
Westbury La *BKHH* IG9 ....39 G4
Westbury Lodge Cl *PIN* HA5 ..41 H6
Westbury Pl *BTFD* TW8 ....116 E6
Westbury Rd *ALP/SUD* HA0 ....80 A5
BARK IG11 ....90 D6
BECK BR3 ....182 B6
BMLY BR1 ....184 C4
CROY/NA CR0 ....196 E3
EA W5 ....98 A5
FBAR/BDGN N11 ....48 C2
FELT TW13 ....154 C3
FSTGT E7 ....89 F3
IL IG1 ....72 A6
NFNCH/WDSPK N12 ....46 E2
NTHWD HA6 ....26 D6
NWMAL KT3 ....192 A1
PGE/AN SE20 ....182 A4
WBLY HA9 ....62 B5
Westbury Ter *FSTGT* E7 ....89 F4
West Carriage Dr *BAY/PAD* W2 ..14 B2
West Central St
LSQ/SEVD WC2H 10 E3
West Chantry
KTN/HRWW/WS HA3 ....42 B4
Westchester Dr *HDN* NW4 .....46 B6
Westcliffe Vls *KUT/HW* KT1 * ..175 G5
West Cl *ASHF* TW15 ....152 B6
EBAR EN4 ....22 A6
ED N9 ....36 C1
GFD/PVL UB6 ....96 C1
RAIN RM13 ....111 K3
WBLY HA9 ....62 B5
Westcombe Av *CROY/NA* CR0 ..195 K3
Westcombe Dr *BAR* EN5 ....20 E6
Westcombe Hl *BKHTH/KID* SE3 ..125 K6
Westcombe Lodge Dr
YEAD UB4 ....94 B4
Westcombe Park Rd
BKHTH/KID SE3 ....145 K1
West Common Rd *HAYES* BR2 ..215 J3
Westcoombe Av *RYNPK* SW20 ..176 C4
Westcote Ri *RSLP* HA4 ....58 A4
Westcote Rd
STRHM/NOR SW16 ....179 H1
Westcott Cl *BMLY* BR1 ....200 D2
CROY/NA CR0 ....213 K6
SEVS/STOTM N15 ....68 B3

Westcott Crs *HNWL* W7 ....96 E4
Westcott House
POP/IOD E14 *...................105 J6
Westcott Rd *WALW* SE17 ......122 C6
West Ct *ALP/SUD* HA0 ....79 J1
Westcott Cl *CRICK* NW2 ....82 C2
PEND EN3 ....24 E1
West Cromwell Rd *ECT* SW5 ..119 K4
West Cross Route *SHB* W12 ..100 B6
West Cross Wy *BTFD* TW8 ....116 C6
Westdale Rd
WOOL/PLUM SE18 ....127 F6
Westdean Av *LEE/GVPK* SE12 ..166 A3
Westdean Cl
WAND/EARL SW18 ....160 A1
Westdown Rd *CAT* SE6 ....164 C2
SRTFD E15 ....88 A2
West Drayton Park Av
WDR/YW UB7 ....112 B5
West Drayton Rd *UX/CGN* UB8 ..94 A4
West Dr *BELMT* SM2 ....208 B6
KTN/HRWW/WS HA3 ....42 D2
STRHM/NOR SW16 ....161 G6
West Drive Gdns
KTN/HRWW/WS HA3 ....42 D2
West Eaton Pl *BGVA* SW1W 15 G6
West Eaton Place Ms
KTBR SW1X 15 G6
West Ella Rd *WLSDN* NW10 ....81 G5
West End Av *LEY* E10 ....70 A2
PIN HA5 ....59 J1
West End Cl *WLSDN* NW10 .....80 E5
West End Ct *PIN* HA5 ....59 J1
West End Gdns *NTHLT* UB5 .....95 G1
West End La *BAR* EN5 ....20 B5
ESH/CLAY KT10 ....204 A3
HYS/HAR UB3 ....133 G1
KIL/WHAMP NW6 ....83 F4
PIN HA5 ....41 H6
West End Rd *RSLP* HA4 ....76 E2
RSLP HA4 ....76 E2
STHL UB1 ....114 D1
Westerdale Rd *GNWCH* SE10 ..125 J5
Westerfield Rd
SEVS/STOTM N15 ....68 B2
Westergate Rd *ABYW* SE2 .....129 F6
Westerham Av *BFN/LL* DA15 ..167 H6
Westerham Rd *HAYES* BR2 ...215 H4
LEY E10 ....69 K4
Westerley Crs *SYD* SE26 .....182 C1
Western Av *DAGE* RM10 ....92 D4
EA W5 ....98 A2
GFD/PVL UB6 ....97 F2
GLDGN NW11 ....64 B3
RSLP HA4 ....77 F5
Western Ct *FNCH* N3 * 46 E2
Western Gdns *EA* W5 ....98 C6
Western Gtwy *CAN/RD* E16 ...106 E6
Western La *BAL* SW12 ....161 F2
Western Man *BAR* EN5 * 21 F6
Western Ms *MV/WKIL* W9 .....100 D3
Western Pde *BAR* EN5 ....20 D5
Western Pl *BERM/RHTH* SE16 ..123 K2
Western Rd *BRXN/ST* SW9 ....142 B4
EA W5 ....97 K6
EFNCH N2 ....47 K3
MTCM CR4 ....194 D6
NWDGN UB2 ....114 C3
PLSTW E13 ....89 F6
ROM RM1 ....208 E3
SUT SM1 ....70 A2
WALTH E17 ....70 A2
WDGN N22 ....48 E5
WLSDN NW10 ....98 E3
Western Ter *HMSMTH* W6 *....118 D5
Western Vw *HYS/HAR* UB3 ....113 J2
Westernville Gdns
CNTH/NBYPK IG2 ....72 C4
Western Wy *BAR* EN5 ....32 E1
THMD SE28 ....127 K3
Westferry Circ *POP/IOD* E14 ..124 D1
Westferry Rd *POP/IOD* E14 ...105 J6
Westfield Cl *CDALE/KGS* NW9 ..44 E6
FUL/PGN SW6 * 139 H2
PEND EN3 ....25 G4
SUT SM1 ....208 D2
WBPTN SW10 ....140 B1
Westfield Dr
KTN/HRWW/WS HA3 ....61 K1
Westfield Gdns *CHDH* RM6 ....73 J2
KTN/HRWW/WS HA3 ....61 K1
Westfield La
KTN/HRWW/WS HA3 ....61 K1
Westfield Pk *PIN* HA5 ....41 K3
Westfield Park Dr *WFD* IG8 ....53 K3
Westfield Rd *BECK* BR3 ....182 C5
BXLYHN DA7 ....149 K4
CROY/NA CR0 ....196 C6
DAGW RM9 ....92 A2
MLHL NW7 ....31 G3
MTCM CR4 ....178 D6
SURB KT6 ....190 E2
SUT SM1 ....208 D2
WEA W13 ....116 C1
WOT/HER KT12 ....188 D5
Westfields *BARN* SW13 ....138 C4
Westfields Av *BARN* SW13 ....138 B4
Westfields Rd *ACT* W3 ....98 D4
Westfield St
WOOL/PLUM SE18 ....126 C3
Westfield Wy *RSLP* HA4 ....76 D1
WCHPL E1 ....105 G2
West Garden Pl *BAY/PAD* W2 ....8 D4
West Gdns *TOOT* SW17 ....178 D2
WAP E1W 104 D6
West Ga *EA* W5 ....98 A2
Westgate Est
EBED/NFELT TW14 * 152 E3
Westgate Rd *BECK* BR3 ....183 F4
DART DA1 ....171 G1

SNWD SE25 ....197 J1
Westgate St HACK E8 ....86 C6
Westgate Ter WBPTN SW10 ...120 A5
Westglade ct
  KTN/HRWW/WS HA3 ....61 K2
West Green Pl GFD/PVL UB6 ...78 D6
West Green Rd
  SEVS/STOTM N15 ....67 K1
West Gv GNWCH SE10 ....55 C2
  WFD IG8 ....53 C2
Westgrove La GNWCH SE10 ...145 F2
West Halkin St KTBR SW1X ...15 G4
West Hallowes ELTH/MOT SE9 166 C3
West Ham La SRTFD E15 ....88 C6
West Hampstead Ms
  KIL/WHAMP NW6 ....83 F4
West Harding St
  FLST/FETLN EC4A * 11 K3
West Hatch Mnr RSLP HA4 ...58 D5
Westbury Gdns
  MORT/ESHN SW14 ....137 J6
West Heath Av GLDGN NW11 ...64 E5
West Heath Cl DART DA1 * ...170 C1
  HAMP NW3 ....82 E1
West Heath Dr GLDGN NW11 ...64 E5
West Heath Gdns HAMP NW3 ...82 E1
West Heath Rd ABYW SE2 .....128 E6
  DART DA1 ....170 C1
  HAMP NW3 ....64 E6
West Hl DART DA1 ....171 G1
  RYLN/HDSTN HA2 ....60 B6
  SAND/SEL CR2 ....212 A6
  WAND/EARL SW18 ....139 K6
  WBLY HA9 ....62 B5
  WIM/MER SW19 ....159 G2
West Hill Dr DART DA1 ....171 F1
West Hill Pk HGT N6 ....65 K6
West Hill Ri DART DA1 * 171 G1
West Hill Rd WAND/EARL SW18.159 K1
West Hill Wy TRDG/WHET N20..33 F3
Westholm GLDGN NW11 ....65 F1
West Holme ERITH DA8 ....149 K2
Westholme ORP BR6 ....201 K4
Westholme Gdns RSLP HA4 ....46 A6
Westhorne Av ELTH/MOT SE9 166 B1
Westhorpe Gdns HDN NW4 ....46 A6
Westhorpe Rd PUT/ROE SW15 .139 F2
West House Cl
  WIM/MER SW19 ....159 H3
Westhurst Dr CHST BR7 ....185 G1
West India Av POP/IOD E14 ..124 D1
West India Dock Rd
  POP/IOD E14 ....105 J6
  YEAD UB4 ....95 F5
Westlake Cl PLMGR N13 ....35 G5
  YEAD UB4 ....95 J3
Westland Cl
  STWL/WRAY TW19 * 152 B1
Westland Dr HAYES BR2 ....199 J6
Westland Pl FSBYE EC1V 6 E4
Westlands Cl HYS/HAR UB3 ..113 K4
Westlands Ter BAL SW12 .....161 H1
Westlea Rd HNWL W7 ....116 B3
Westleigh Av PUT/ROE SW15..139 F6
Westleigh Dr BMLY BR1 ....184 D5
Westleigh Gdns EDGW HA8 ...44 C4
West Links ALP/SUD HA0 ....97 K2
Westlinton Cl MLHL NW7 ......46 C2
West Lodge Av ACT W3 ....117 H1
West Lodge Ct ACT W3 * 117 H1
Westmacott Dr
  EBED/NFELT TW14 ....153 K3
West MI KENS W8 * 119 K1
West Malling Wy HCH RM12...93 K3
West Md HOR/WEW KT19 ......207 G4
Westmead PUT/ROE SW15 ....158 E2
West Md RSLP HA4 ....47 F2
Westmede BARK/HLT IG6 ....54 C2
Westmere Dr MLHL NW7 ....31 F3
West Mersea Cl CAN/RD E16 ..126 A1
West Ms PIM SW1V * 15 J7
  TOTM N17 * 50 D5
Westminster Av THHTH CR7 ..180 C5
Westminster Br WHALL SW1A...17 F3
Westminster Bridge Rd
  WHALL SW1A 17 F3
Westminster Cl
  EBED/NFELT TW14 ....153 K3
  TEDD TW11 ....174 B1
Westminster Dr PLMGR N13...48 E1
Westminster Gdns BARK IG11..108 E1
  BARK/HLT IG6 ....54 C2
  CHING E4 ....38 C3
Westminster Rd ED N9 ....36 D3
  HNWL W7 ....115 K1
  SUT SM1 ....194 C6
Westmoat Cl BECK BR3 ....183 F3
Westmont Rd ESH/CLAY KT10..189 K6
Westmoor Gdns PEND EN3 ....25 F3
Westmoor Rd PEND EN3 ....25 F3
Westmoor St CHARL SE7 .....126 C4
Westmoreland Av WELL DA16 147 K5
Westmoreland Dr BELMT SM2 209 F6
Westmoreland Rd BMLY BR1 ..183 K6
  EA W5 ....97 K4
  PIM SW1V * 121 G5
Westmoreland St
  CAVSQ/HST W1G 9 H2
Westmoreland Ter
  ASHF SE20 * 181 J3
  PIM SW1V * 121 G5
Westmorland Cl MNPK E12....71 H6
  TWK TW1 ....156 C1
Westmorland Rd HRW HA1 ....60 D3
  WALTH E17 ....69 J5
Westmount Rd ELTH/MOT SE9 146 E3
Westmount Ct EA W5 * 98 B4
West Oak BECK BR3 ....183 G4
Westoe Rd ED N9 ....36 D4
Weston Av E/WMO/HCT KT8 ..188 D1
  THDIT KT7 ....189 K4

Weston Dr STAN HA7 ....43 H4
Weston Gdns ISLW TW7 ....135 J2
Weston Gn DAGW RM9 ....92 A2
  THDIT KT7 ....189 K6
Weston Green Rd
  ESH/CLAY KT10 ....189 J5
Weston Gv BMLY BR1 ....183 J4
Weston Pk CEND/HSY/T N8 ....66 E3
  KUT/HW KT1 ....175 F5
  THDIT KT7 ....189 K6
Weston Park Cl THDIT KT7 *..189 K5
Weston Ri FSBYW WC1X 5 H4
Weston Rd BMLY BR1 ....183 J4
  CHSWK W4 ....117 K3
  DAGW RM9 ....92 A2
  ENC/FH EN2 ....23 K3
  THDIT KT7 ....189 K5
Weston St STHWK SE1 ....19 F2
Weston Wk HACK E8 ....86 D5
Westover Cl BELMT SM2 .....209 F6
Westover Hill HAMP NW3 .....64 E6
Westover Rd
  WAND/EARL SW18 ....160 B1
Westow Hl NRWD SE19 ....181 F2
Westow St NRWD SE19 ....181 F3
West Pk ELTH/MOT SE9 ....166 D4
West Park Av RCH/KEW TW9 ..137 J2
West Park Cl CHDH RM6 ....73 K2
  HEST TW5 ....114 E6
West Park Rd NWDGN UB2....115 J1
  RCH/KEW TW9 ....137 H2
West Parkside GNWCH SE10 ..125 H2
Westpole Av EBAR EN4 ....22 B5
Westport Rd PLSTW E13 ....107 F3
Westport St WCHPL E1 ....105 F5
West Poultry Av FARR EC1M...12 A2
West Quarters SHB W12 ....99 J5
West Quay Dr YEAD UB4 ....95 J4
West Ridge Gdns GFD/PVL UB6..96 C1
West Ri BAY/PAD W2 * 8 D5
West Rd CHDH RM6 ....74 A3
  CHEL SW3 ....120 E5
  CLAP SW4 ....141 J6
  EA W5 ....98 A4
  EBAR EN4 ....34 A3
  EBED/NFELT TW14 ....153 G2
  KUTN/CMB KT2 ....175 K4
  ROMW/RG RM7 ....75 F3
  SRTFD E15 ....88 D6
  TOTM N17 ....50 D2
  WDR/YW UB7 ....112 C3
West Rw NKENS W10 ....100 C3
Westrow Dr BARK IG11 ....91 G3
Westrow Gdns GDMY/SEVK IG3..73 F5
West Sheen V RCH/KEW TW9..137 G5
West Side Common
  WIM/MER SW19 ....177 F2
Westside HDN NW4 ....45 K5
West Smithfield STBT EC1A....12 A2
West Sq LBTH SE11 ....18 A5
West St BETH E2 ....104 D1
  BMLY BR1 ....183 K4
  BXLYHN DA7 ....149 G5
  CAR SM5 ....209 K2
  CROY/NA CR0 ....211 J2
  ERITH DA8 ....130 A4
  HRW HA1 ....60 D5
  LSQ/SEVD WC2H *........10 D4
  SUT SM1 ....209 F3
  WALTH E17 ....69 K2
  WAN E11 ....88 C1
West Street La CAR SM5 .....209 K2
West Street Pl CROY/NA CR0 *.211 J2
West Temple Sheen
  MORT/ESHN SW14 ....137 J6
West Tenter St WCHPL E1 .....13 K4
West Ter BFN/LL DA15 *.......167 K3
West Towers PIN HA5 ....59 H4
West Vw EBED/NFELT TW14 ..153 F3
Westview HNWL W7 * 96 E5
Westview Cl NKENS W10 .....100 A5
  WLSDN NW10 ....81 H3
Westview Ct BORE WD6 ....29 K1
Westview Crs ED N9 ....36 A2
Westview Dr WFD IG8 ....53 H5
West View Gdns BORE WD6 ...29 K1
West View Rd DART DA1 ......171 J1
  STRHM/NOR SW16...........
Westville Rd SHB W12 ....118 D2
  THDIT KT7 ....190 B4
  HYS/HAR UB3 ....113 K1
Westward Rd CHING E4 ....51 H1
Westward Wy
  KTN/HRWW/WS HA3 ....62 B3
West Warwick PI PIM SW1V *..16 A7
West Wy CROY/NA CR0 ....198 B6
  EDGW HA8 ....44 D2
  HEST TW5 ....134 D2
Westway NKENS W10 ....100 C4
  PIN HA5 ....59 H1
  RSLP HA4 ....58 A3
Westway RYNPK SW20 ....192 E1
  SHB W12 ....99 J6
West Wk EBAR EN4 ....34 B5
  HYS/HAR UB3 ....113 K1
West Wy Gdns CROY/NA CR0.198 A6
Westways HOR/WEW KT19 ...207 H2
Westwell Cl STMC/STPC BR5.202 E5
Westwell Rd
  STRHM/NOR SW16 ....179 K2
Westwell Road Ap
  STRHM/NOR SW16 ....179 K2
Westwick Gdns HMSMTH W6 .119 G2
  HSLWW TW4 ....134 A3
Westwood Av NRWD SE19 ...180 D4
  RYLN/HDSTN HA2 ....78 B2
Westwood Cl BMLY BR1 ....184 C4
  ESH/CLAY KT10 ....204 C1
Westwood Gdns BARN SW13..138 C4
Westwood HI SYD SE26 ....181 H1
Westwood La WELL DA16 ....148 B5

Westwood Pk FSTH SE23 ....163 K3
Westwood PI SYD SE26 * 181 H1
Westwood Rd BARN SW13 .....138 C4
  GDMY/SEVK IG3 ....73 F5
West Woodside BXLY DA5 ....169 F3
Wetheral Dr STAN HA7 ....43 H4
Wetherby Cl NTHLT UB5 ....78 B4
Wetherby Gdns ECT SW5 ....120 B5
Wetherby Ms ECT SW5 ....120 A5
Wetherby PI ECT SW5 ....120 A4
Wetherby Rd ENC/FH EN2 .....23 J2
Wetherden St WALTH E17 .....69 H4
Wetherell Rd HOM E9 ....87 F6
Wetherill Rd MUSWH N10 .....48 A4
Wexford Rd BAL SW12 ....160 E2
Weybourne St
  WAND/EARL SW18 ....160 B4
Weybridge Ct
  BERM/RHTH SE16 * 123 J5
Weybridge Rd THHTH CR7 ....196 B1
Weydown Cl WIM/MER SW19..159 H3
Weyhill Rd WCHPL E1 * 104 C5
Weyland Rd BCTR RM8 ....92 B1
Weyman Rd BKHTH/KID SE3 ..146 B2
Weymouth Av EA W5 ....116 D3
  MLHL NW7 ....45 G1
Weymouth Cl EHAM E6 ....108 B5
Weymouth Ct BELMT SM2 ....209 F6
Weymouth Ms CAVSQ/HST W1G..9 H1
Weymouth Rd YEAD UB4 ....94 C2
Weymouth St CAVSQ/HST W1G..9 H1
Weymouth Ter BETH E2 ....7 K2
Weymouth Vis FSBYPK N4 * ...67 G6
Weymouth Wk STAN HA7 .....43 G2
Whadcoat St FSBYPK N4 ....67 G6
Whalebone Av CHDH RM6 .....74 B3
Whalebone Gv CHDH RM6 .....74 B3
Whalebone La North
  CHDH RM6 ....74 A1
  CRW RM5 ....56 A3
Whalebone La South
  BCTR RM8 ....74 B5
Whales Yd SRTFD E15 * 88 C5
Wharfdale Cl FBAR/BDGN N11...48 A2
Wharfdale Rd IS N1 * 5 F2
Wharfedale Gdns THHTH CR7..196 A1
Wharfedale St ECT SW5 .....120 A5
Wharf La POP/IOD E14 ....105 H5
  TWK TW1 * 156 B2
Wharf PI BETH E2 ....86 D6
Wharf Rd IS N1 ....6 C3
  IS N1 ....6 C2
  PEND EN3 ....25 H1
  SRTFD E15 ....88 B6
Wharfside Cl ERITH DA8 ....130 C6
Wharfside Rd POP/IOD E14 ...106 C5
Wharf St CAN/RD E16 ....106 C4
Wharf Ter PUT/ROE SW15 * ..139 H5
Wharncliffe Dr STHL UB1 .....115 J1
Wharncliffe Gdns SNWD SE25.181 F5
Wharncliffe Rd SNWD SE25...180 E5
Wharton Cl WLSDN NW10 .....81 G4
Wharton Cottages
  FSBYW WC1X * 5 H5
Wharton Rd BMLY BR1 ....184 A4
Wharton St FSBYW WC1X 5 H5
Whateley Rd EDUL SE22 .....143 G6
  PGE/AN SE20 ....182 A3
Whatley Av RYNPK SW20 ....177 G6
Whatman Rd FSTH SE23 ....164 A2
Wheastone Av NKENS W10 *..100 C4
Wheatfields PEND EN3 ....25 G2
Wheathill Rd PGE/AN SE20 ...181 J5
Wheatlands HEST TW5 ....115 F6
Wheatlands Rd TOOT SW17 ..161 F5
Wheatley Cl HDN NW4 ....45 J5
  HYS/HAR UB3 ....94 E6
Wheatley Gdns ED N9 ....36 A4
Wheatley Rd ISLW TW7 ......136 A4
Wheatley St
  CAVSQ/HST W1G * 9 H1
Wheatley Terrace Rd
  ERITH DA8 ....130 C6
Wheat Sheaf Cl NTHLT UB5 ...77 J3
Wheatsheaf Cl POP/IOD E14.124 E4
Wheatsheaf La FUL/PGN SW6.139 F1
  VX/NE SW8 ....141 K1
Wheatsheaf Rd ROM RM1 .....75 H3
Wheatsheaf Ter
  FUL/PGN SW6 * 139 J1
Wheatstone Cl
  WIM/MER SW19 ....178 A4
Wheatstone Rd NKENS W10 ..100 C4
Wheeler Gdns IS N1 * 84 E6
Wheeler La WCHPL E1 ....13 J1
Wheelers Dr RSLP HA4 * 58 A3
Wheelers Cross BARK IG11...108 D1
Wheelock Cl ERITH DA8 ....149 J1
Wheelwright St HOLWY N7 ....85 F5
Whelan Wy WLGTN SM6 .....210 D1
Wheler St WCHPL E1 * 7 J7
Whellock Rd CHSWK W4 ....118 B3
Whenman Av BXLY DA5 ....169 K4
Whetstone Cl TRDG/WHET N20..33 H4
Whetstone Rk BKHTH/KID SE3.146 B3
Whewell Rd ARCH N19 ....66 E6
Whichcote St STHWK SE1 * ...17 J1
Whidborne Cl DEPT SE8 ....144 D3
Whidborne St STPAN WC1H 5 F5
Whimbrel Wy YEAD UB4 ....95 H5
Whinchat Rd THMD SE28 ......127 J3
Whinfell Cl STRHM/NOR SW16.179 J1
Whinyates Rd ELTH/MOT SE9 146 D4
Whippendell Cl
  STMC/STPC BR5 ....186 C4
Whippendell Wy
  STMC/STPC BR5 ....186 C4
Whipps Cross Rd WAN E11 ....70 C3
Whiskin St CLKNW EC1R 6 A5
Whistler Gdns EDGW HA8 .....44 B5
Whistlers Av BTSEA SW11 ...140 C1

Whistler St HBRY N5 ....85 H3
Whistler Wk WBPTN SW10 * ..140 B1
Whiston Rd BETH E2 ....7 J2
Whitakers Wy LOU IG10 ....39 H1
Whitbread Cl TOTM N17 ....50 C4
Whitbread Rd BROCKY SE4 ...144 B5
Whitburn Rd LEW SE13 ....144 E5
Whitby Av WLSDN NW10 ....98 D2
Whitby Gdns CDALE/KGS NW9..44 C6
  SUT SM1 ....194 C6
Whitby Pde RSLP HA4 * 59 G6
Whitby Rd RSLP HA4 ....77 F1
  RYLN/HDSTN HA2 ....78 C1
  SUT SM1 ....194 C6
  WOOL/PLUM SE18 ....126 E4
Whitby St WCHPL E1 * 7 J6
Whitcher Cl NWCR SE14 ....124 B6
Whitcher PI CAMTN NW1 ......84 C4
Whitchurch Av EDGW HA8 .....44 A3
Whitchurch Cl EDGW HA8 .....44 B2
Whitchurch Gdns EDGW HA8 ..44 B2
Whitchurch La EDGW HA8 .....43 K3
Whitchurch Pde EDGW HA8 ...44 C3
Whitchurch Rd NKENS W10 ..100 B6
Whitcomb St SOHO/SHAV W1D..10 C5
Whitcome Ms RCH/KEW TW9..137 J2
Whiteadder Wy POP/IOD E14..124 E4
Whitear Wk SRTFD E15 ....88 B4
Whitebarn La DAGE RM10 ....110 C1
Whitebeam Av HAYES BR2 ...201 H4
Whitebeam Cl VX/NE SW8 * ..142 A1
White Bear PI HAMP NW3 * ...83 H2
White Bear Yd CLKNW EC1R *..5 J7
White Bridge Cl
  EBED/NFELT TW14 ....153 J1
White Butts Rd RSLP HA4 .....77 H1
Whitechapel High St
  TWRH EC3N 13 K3
Whitechapel Rd WCHPL E1 ...104 C5
White Church La WCHPL E1 ...104 C5
White City Cl SHB W12 ....100 A6
White City Rd SHB W12 ....100 A6
White Conduit St IS N1 * 5 K2
Whitecote Rd STHL UB1 ....96 C5
White Craig Cl PIN HA5 ....42 A1
Whitecroft Cl BECK BR3 ....199 C1
Whitecroft Wy BECK BR3 ....199 F1
Whitefield Av CRICK NW2 .....82 A6
Whitefield Cl PUT/ROE SW15.159 H1
Whitefoot La BMLY BR1 ....165 G6
Whitefoot Ter BMLY BR1 .....165 J5
Whitefriars Av
  KTN/HRWW/WS HA3 ....42 E5
Whitefriars Dr
  KTN/HRWW/WS HA3 ....42 E5
Whitefriars St EMB EC4Y 11 K4
White Gate Gdns
  KTN/HRWW/WS HA3 * 42 E5
Whitehall Cl WHALL SW1A 16 E1
Whitehall Ct WHALL SW1A 16 E1
Whitehall Crs CHSGTN KT9 ..205 K3
Whitehall Gdns ACT W3 ....117 H1
  CHING E4 ....38 C3
  CHSWK W4 ....117 J6
  WHALL SW1A 16 E1
Whitehall La BKHH IG9 ....38 E4
  ERITH DA8 ....150 C3
Whitehall Pk ARCH N19 ....66 C5
Whitehall Park Rd CHSWK W4.117 H6
Whitehall PI WHALL SW1A 16 E1
  WLGTN SM6 ....210 B2
Whitehall Rd CHING E4 ....38 C4
  HAYES BR2 ....200 C2
  HNWL W7 ....116 B2
  HRW HA1 ....60 E4
  THHTH CR7 ....196 B2
Whitehall St TOTM N17 ....50 C3
White Hart Av THMD SE28....128 A3
White Hart La BARN SW13 .....138 B3
  ROMW/RG RM7 ....56 D4
  WDGN N22 ....49 H3
White Hart Rd ORP BR6 ....202 B4
  WOOL/PLUM SE18 ....127 K4
White Hart St LBTH SE11 ....122 B5
White Hart Ter TOTM N17 * ...50 B3
White Hart Yd STHWK SE1 ....18 E1
Whitehaven Cl HAYES BR2 ...199 K1
Whitehaven St STJWD NW8 .....2 C7
Whitehead Cl RDART DA2 * ...171 J5
  WAND/EARL SW18 ....160 B2
Whitehead's Gv CHEL SW3 ....15 L7
White Heart Av UX/CGN UB8 ..94 A4
White Heron Ms TEDD TW11 *.174 A2
Whitehill Rd DART DA1 ....150 D6
Whitehorse La SNWD SE25...197 F2
White Horse La WCHPL E1 ....105 F4
Whitehorse Rd CROY/NA CR0.196 D4
White Horse Rd EHAM E6 ....108 A2
  WCHPL E1 ....105 G5
Whitehorse Rd WCHPL E1 ....105 G5
White Horse St MYFR/PICC W1J.15 K1
White House Dr STAN HA7 ....29 J6
White House La ENC/FH EN2 ..23 J2
Whitehouse Wy
  STHGT/OAK N14 ....34 A4
Whitehurst Dr UED N18 * 51 F1
Whitekennett St HDTCH EC3A..13 H3
Whitelands Crs
  WAND/EARL SW18 ....159 H2
White Ledges WEA W13 ....97 J6
Whitelegg Rd PLSTW E13 ....106 D1
Whiteley Rd NRWD SE19 .....180 E1
Whiteleys Wy FELT TW13 ....155 F5
Whiteley Cl LOTH EC2R * 13 G4
  PECK SE15 * 143 J3
White Lion HI BLKFR EC4V 12 B5
White Lion St IS N1 ....5 K3
White Ldg NRWD SE19 ....180 C3
White Lodge Cl BELMT SM2 ..209 G5
  ISLW TW7 * 136 B3

EFNCH N2 ....65 J3
ISLW TW7 ....136 B3
The White Ldg BAR EN5 * 20 C3
White Lyon Ct STBT EC1A 12 C1
White Oak Dr BECK BR3 ......183 F5
White Oak Gdns BFN/LL DA15.168 A2
Whiteoaks La GFD/PVL UB6 ...96 D1
White Orchards STAN HA7 ....43 G6
  TRDG/WHET N20 ....32 D3
White Post La HOM E9 ....87 J4
White Post St NWCR SE14 ....143 K1
White Rd SRTFD E15 ....88 C5
White's Av GNTH/NBYPK IG2 ..72 E3
White's Grounds STHWK SE1...19 H2
White's Grounds Est STHWK SE1.19 H2
Whites Meadow BMLY BR1 *..201 F1
White's Rw WCHPL E1 ....13 J2
White's Sq CLAP SW4 ....141 J5
Whitestile Rd BTFD TW8 .....116 D5
Whitestone La HAMP NW3 .....83 G1
Whitestone Wk HAMP NW3 ....83 G1
White St STHL UB1 ....114 C2
Whitethorn Gdns
  CROY/NA CR0 ....197 G6
  ENC/FH EN2 ....23 K6
Whitethorn St BOW E3 ....105 J3
Whitewebbs Wy
  STMC/STPC BR5 ....186 A4
Whitfield Ct RYNPK SW20 ....177 G5
Whitfield PI FITZ W1T * 4 A7
Whitfield Rd BXLYHN DA7 ...149 G1
  EHAM E6 ....89 G5
  GNWCH SE10 ....145 G2
Whitford Gdns MTCM CR4 ...178 E6
Whitgift Av SAND/SEL CR2 ...211 J3
Whitgift Rd CROY/NA CR0 ....211 J1
  STHWK SE1 * 17 G6
Whitings Rd BAR EN5 ....20 A6
Whitings Wy EHAM E6 ....108 A4
Whitland Rd CAR SM5 ....194 C5
Whitley Cl STWL/WRAY TW19.152 B1
Whitley Rd TOTM N17 ....50 A5
Whitlock Dr WIM/MER SW19..159 H3
Whitman Rd WCHPL E1 ....105 G3
Whitmead Cl SAND/SEL CR2..211 K4
Whitmore Cl FBAR/BDGN N11..48 B1
Whitmore Est IS N1 ....7 H1
Whitmore Gdns WLSDN NW10.100 A1
Whitmore Rd BECK BR3 .....182 C6
  HRW HA1 ....60 D4
  IS N1 ....7 G1
Whitnell Wy PUT/ROE SW15 *.139 F6
Whitney Av REDBR IG4 ....71 H1
Whitney Rd LEY E10 ....69 J4
Whitney Wk SCUP DA14 ......187 J2
Whitstable Cl BECK BR3 .....182 C4
  RSLP HA4 ....58 B4
Whitstable PI CROY/NA CR0 ..211 J3
Whitstone La BECK BR3 .....198 E2
Whittaker Av RCH/KEW TW9 *.136 E6
Whittaker Rd CHEAM SM3 ....208 D1
  EHAM E6 ....89 G5
Whittaker St BCVA SW1W 15 G7
Whittaker Wy STHWK SE1 * ..123 H4
Whittell Gdns SYD SE26 .....163 K5
Whittingstall Rd
  FUL/PGN SW6 ....139 J2
  UED N18 ....36 D4
Whittington Av
  BANK EC3V * 13 G4
Whittington Ms
  NFNCH/WDSPK N12 ....33 G6
Whittington Rd WDGN N22 .....48 E3
Whittington Wy PIN HA5 ....59 J2
Whittlebury Cl CAR SM5 ....209 K5
Whittle Cl STHL UB1 ....96 B5
  WALTH E17 ....69 G3
Whittle Rd HEST TW5 ....134 B1
  NWDGN UB2 ....115 G2
Whittlesea Cl
  KTN/HRWW/WS HA3 ....42 C3
Whittlesea Pth
  KTN/HRWW/WS HA3 ....42 C4
Whittlesea Rd
  KTN/HRWW/WS HA3 ....42 C3
Whittlesey St STHWK SE1 .....17 K1
Whitton Av East GFD/PVL UB6.78 E3
Whitton Av West NTHLT UB5...78 B3
Whitton Cl GFD/PVL UB6 ....79 H4
Whitton Dene HSLW TW3 .....135 G6
  WHTN TW2 ....155 J1
Whitton Dr GFD/PVL UB6 ....79 G4
Whitton Manor Rd WHTN TW2.155 H1
Whitton Rd HSLW TW3 ....135 G5
  WHTN TW2 ....155 K1
Whitton Waye HSLW TW3 ....155 F1
Whitton Wk PLSTW E13 ......106 E2
Whitwell Rd PLSTW E13 .....106 E2
  WOOL/PLUM SE18 * 147 F1
Whitworth St GNWCH SE10 ..125 H5
Whoriton Rd PECK SE15 .....143 J4
Whybridge Cl RAIN RM13 .....93 H6
Whymark Av WDGN N22 ....49 G6
Whytecroft HEST TW5 ....134 C1
Whyteville Rd FSTGT E7 * 89 F4
Wichling Cl STMC/STPC BR5 ..202 E5
Wickersley Rd BTSEA SW11..141 F3
Wickers Oake NRWD SE19 ...163 G6
Wicket Rd GFD/PVL UB6 ....79 H3
Wickets, The ASHF TW15 * ...152 B6
Wicket, The CROY/NA CR0 ....213 J3
Wickford St WCHPL E1 ....104 E3
Wickford Wy WALTH E17 ....51 F7
Wickham Av CHEAM SM3 ....208 B3
  CROY/NA CR0 ....198 B6
Wickham Cha WWKM BR4 ....199 G4
Wickham Cl HNWL W7 * 116 A1
  NWMAL KT3 ....192 C3
  PEND EN3 ....24 D4
  WCHPL E1 ....104 E4
Wickham Court Rd
  WWKM BR4 ....199 F6
Wickham Crs WWKM BR4 ....199 F6
Wickham Gdns BROCKY SE4 ..144 C4
Wickham La ABYW SE2 ....128 B5
Wickham Ms BROCKY SE4 ...144 C3
Wickham Rd BECK BR3 ....182 E6
  BROCKY SE4 ....144 C3
  CHING E4 ....52 A5
  CROY/NA CR0 ....197 K6

KTN/HRWW/WS HA3 ....42 D5
Wickham St LBTH SE11 ......122 A5
WELL DA16..................147 K3
Wick La BOW E3.............87 J1
Wickliffe Av FNCH N3.......46 C5
Wickliffe Gdns WBLY HA9...62 D6
Wick Rd HOM E9.............87 G4
 TEDD TW11.................155 J6
Wicks CI ELTH/MOT SE9.....166 C6
Wicksteed CI BXLY DA5......170 A5
Wickwood St CMBW SE5......142 C3
Widdenham Rd HOLWY N7....85 F2
Widdicombe Av
 RYLN/HDSTN HA2............59 J6
Widdin St SRTFD E15........88 C5
Widecombe Gdns REDBR IG4..71 J1
Widecombe Rd ELTH/MOT SE9..166 D5
Widecombe Wy EFNCH N2....65 H2
Widegate St WCHPL E1......13 H2
Widenham CI PIN HA5.......59 G2
Wide Wy MTCM CR4..........179 J6
Widgeon CI CAN/RD E16.....107 F5
Widgeon Rd ERITH DA8......150 E1
Widley Rd MV/WKIL W9......100 E3
Widmore Lodge Rd BMLY BR1..184 C5
Widmore Rd BMLY BR1.......184 A5
Wieland Rd NTHWD HA6......40 E5
Wigeon Wy YEAD UB4........95 H5
Wiggins La RCHPK/HAM TW10..156 D5
Wiggins Md CDALE/KGS NW9..45 H3
Wigginton Av WBLY HA9.....80 C4
Wightman Rd CEND/HSY/T N8..67 J1
Wigley Rd FELT TW13........154 C4
Wigmore PI MHST W1U.......9 J3
Wigmore Rd CAR SM5........194 C6
Wigmore St MHST W1U.......9 G3
Wigram Rd WAN E11.........71 G3
Wigram Sq WALTH E17.......52 A6
Wigston CI UED N18.........50 A1
Wigston Rd PLSTW E13......107 F3
Wigton PI LBTH SE11........122 B5
Wigton Rd WALTH E17.......51 H4
Wilberforce Rd CLAP SW4 *..141 J5
Wilberforce Rd
 CDALE/KGS NW9.............63 J3
 FSBYPK N4.................85 H1
Wilberforce Wy
 WIM/MER SW19..............177 G2
Wilbury Wy UED N18........49 K1
Wilcot Av OXHEY WD19......27 J2
Wilcot CI OXHEY WD19......27 J2
Wilcox Ct VX/NE SW8........141 K1
Wilcox Rd SUT SM1 *........209 F2
 TEDD TW11.................155 J6
 VX/NE SW8.................141 K1
Wildacres NTHWD HA6.......26 D6
Wild Ct HOL/ALD WC2B......11 G3
Wildcroft Gdns STAN HA7...41 K4
Wildcroft Rd PUT/ROE SW15..159 F2
Wilde CI HACK E8...........86 C6
Wilde PI PLMGR N13.........49 H2
 WAND/EARL SW18...........160 C2
Wilder CI RSLP HA4.........59 F5
Wilderness Rd CHST BR7....185 G3
The Wilderness
 E/WMO/HCT KT8.............189 H2
 HPTN TW12.................155 G6
Wild Goose Dr NWCR SE14...143 E2
Wilde Rd ERITH DA8........149 J2
Wilderton Rd
 STNW/STAM N16.............68 A4
Wildfell Rd CAT SE6........164 E2
Wild Goose Dr NWCR SE14...143 E2
Wild Hatch GLDGN NW11.....64 E3
Wild Oaks CI NTHWD HA6....40 D2
Wild St HOL/ALD WC2B......11 F4
Wildwood CI LEE/GVPK SE12..165 J2
Wildwood NTHWD HA6........40 D6
Wildwood Gv NW3...........65 G5
Wildwood Rd GLDGN NW11...65 G5
Wildwood Ter GLDGN NW11..65 G5
Wilford CI ENC/FH EN2 *...23 K4
 NTHWD HA6................40 B3
Wilfred Av RAIN RM13.......111 J4
Wilfred Owen CI
 WIM/MER SW19..............178 B2
Wilfrid Gdns ACT W3........98 E4
Wilkes Rd BTFD TW8........117 F6
Wilkes St WCHPL E1.........13 K1
 MTCM CR4.................178 E6
Wilkins CI HYS/HAR UB3.....113 J5
 MTCM CR4.................178 E6
Wilkinson Gdns SNWD SE25..181 F4
Wilkinson Rd CAN/RD E16...107 G5
Wilkinson St VX/NE SW8....142 A1
Wilkinson Wy CHSWK W4....118 A2
Wilks Av DART DA1..........171 J4
Wilks Gdns CROY/NA CR0....198 B5
Wilks PI IS N1.............7 H3
Willan Rd TOTM N17........49 K5
Willan Wall CAN/RD E16....106 D6
Willcocks CI CHSGTN KT9...206 A1
Willcott Rd ACT W3.........117 J1
Will Crooks Gdns
 ELTH/MOT SE9..............146 C5
Willenfield Rd WLSDN NW10..98 E1
Willenhall Av BAR EN5......33 G1
Willenhall Rd HYS/HAR UB3..94 E6
Willenhall Rd
 WOOL/PLUM SE18...........127 G5
Willersley Av BFN/LL DA15..168 A3
Willersley CI BFN/LL DA15..168 A3
Willesden La KIL/WHAMP NW6..82 B5
Willesden La KTTN NW5.....84 A5
Willett CI NTHLT UB5.......95 G2
 STMC/STPC BR5............201 K3
Willett Rd THHTH CR7......196 B2
Willett Wy STMC/STPC BR5..201 J2
William Ash CI DAGW RM9...91 H4
William Barefoot Dr
 ELTH/MOT SE9.............167 F6
William Booth Rd
 PGE/AN SE20..............181 H4
William Carey Wy HRW HA1..60 E3
William CI CRW RM5.........56 E4
 ERITH DA8................147 H5
 LEW SE13.................145 G4
 NWDGN UB2................115 H2
William Covell CI ENC/FH EN2 *..23 F1
William Dr STAN HA7........43 G2
William Ellis Wy
 BERM/RHTH SE16 *.........123 H3
William Foster La WELL DA16..148 B3
William Gdns PUT/ROE SW15..138 E6
William Guy Gdns BOW E3...105 K2
William Iv St CHCR WC2N...10 E6
William Margrie CI
 PECK SE15................143 H3
William Ms KTBR SW1X......15 F3
William Morley CI EHAM E6..89 H6
William Morris CI WALTH E17..51 H6
William Morris Wy
 FUL/PGN SW6..............140 B4
William Petty Wy
 STMC/STPC BR5............202 D5
William Rd CAMTN NW1......4 A5
 SUT SM1..................209 G3
 WIM/MER SW19.............177 H5
Williams Av WALTH E17......51 H4
William's Buildings
 WCHPL E1 *...............104 E3
Williams CI CEND/HSY/T N8 *..66 D3
 FUL/PGN SW6..............139 H1
Williams Dr HSLW TW3......135 F5
Williams Gv SURB KT6......190 D5
 WDGN N22.................49 F5
Williams La MORT/ESHN SW14..137 K4
 MRDN SM4.................194 B3
Williamson CI GNWCH SE10..125 J5
Williamson Rd FSBYPK N4...67 H3
Williamson St HOLWY N7....84 E2
Williamson Wy MLHL NW7....46 C2
Williams Sq BERM/RHTH SE16..124 B1
Williams Rd NWDGN UB2....114 D4
 WEA W13..................116 B1
Williams Ter CROY/NA CR0..211 G4
William St BARK IG11.......90 C6
 CAR SM5..................209 J1
 KTBR SW1X................15 F3
 LEY E10..................69 K3
 TOTM N17.................50 B3

EA W5......................117 F2
EN EN1.....................24 B2
ERITH DA8..................150 D2
HAMP NW3...................83 H2
NWMAL KT3..................191 K1
WLGTN SM6..................210 B5
Willows Av MRDN SM4........194 A2
Willows CI PIN HA5.........41 G5
Willows Ter WLSDN NW10 *..99 H1
The Willows BECK BR3......182 D4
 EBAR EN4.................33 J1
 ESH/CLAY KT10............204 E4
 OXHEY WD19...............27 F2
Willow St CHING E4.........38 B3
 ROMW/RG RM7..............74 E1
 SDTCH EC2A...............7 G6
Willow Ter PGE/AN SE20 *..181 J4
Willow Tree CI BOW E3.....87 C6
Willowtree CI HGDN/ICK UB10..76 A1
Willow Tree CI NTHLT UB5..77 J4
 WAND/EARL SW18...........159 K1
 YEAD UB4.................95 G3
Willow Tree La YEAD UB4...95 H3
Willow Tree Rd BOW E3.....87 H3
Willow Tree Wk BMLY BR1...184 A4
Willowtree Wy THHTH CR7...180 B4
Willow Vw CHST BR7........186 E2
 SHB W12..................118 D1
Willow Wk WIM/MER SW19...178 C4
 ORP BR6..................216 B1
 SEVS/STOTM N15...........67 H1
 STHWK SE1................19 H6
 WALTH E17................51 H4
 WCHMH N21................35 F1
Willow Wy ALP/SUD HA0.....79 G1
 FNCH N3..................47 F3
 HOR/WEW KT19.............207 F4
 NTGHL W11................100 B6
 SYD SE26.................163 J5
 WHTN TW2.................155 G5
Willow Wood Crs SNWD SE25..197 F3
Willow Wren Whf
 POP/IOD E14 *............114 A4
Will Rd KTTN NW5 *.........84 B4
Willrose Crs ABYW SE2.....128 C5
Wills Crs HSLW TW3.........155 J1
Wills Gv MLHL NW7..........45 J1
Wilman Gv HACK E8..........86 C5
Wilmar CI YEAD UB4.........94 B3
Wilmar Gdns WWKM BR4......198 E5
Wilmer CI KUTN/CMB KT2....175 G1
Wilmer Crs KUTN/CMB KT2...175 G1
Wilmer Gdns IS N1..........7 H1
Wilmer Lea CI SRTFD E15...88 B5
Wilmer PI STNW/STAM N16...68 B6
Wilmer Wy FBAR/BDGN N11..48 B3
Wilmington Av CHSWK W4....138 A1
 ORP BR6..................202 D6
Wilmington Court Rd
 RDART DA2................170 D5
Wilmington Gdns BARK IG11..90 D5
Wilmington Sq FSBYW WC1X..5 J5
Wilmington St FSBYW WC1X..5 J5
Wilmot CI PECK SE15........143 H1
Wilmot PI CAMTN NW1.......84 C5
 HNWL W7..................115 K1
Wilmot Rd CAR SM5.........209 K3
 DART DA1.................151 H6
 LEY E10..................69 K6
 TOTM N17.................50 B6
Wilmot St BETH E2..........104 D3
Wilmount St
 WOOL/PLUM SE18...........127 G4
Wilna Rd WAND/EARL SW18...160 B2
Wilsham St NTGHL W11......100 B1
Wilshaw CI HDN NW4.........45 J6
Wilshaw St NWCR SE14......144 D2
Wilsmere Dr
 KTN/HRWW/WS HA3..........42 E3
 NTHLT UB5................77 J4
Wilson Av MTCM CR4........178 D4
Wilson CI SAND/SEL CR2....211 K3
 WBLY HA9.................62 A3
Wilson Dr WBLY HA9........62 A3
Wilson Gdns HRW HA1.......60 C4
Wilson Gv BERM/RHTH SE16..123 J3
Wilson Rd CHSGTN KT9......206 B4
 CMBW SE5.................142 E2
 IL IG1...................71 K4
 PLSTW E13................107 H2
Wilson's Av TOTM N17......50 B5
Wilson's PI POP/IOD E14...105 H5
Wilson's Rd HMSMTH W6.....119 G5
Wilson St LVPST EC2M......13 F1
 WALTH E17................70 A2
 WCHMH N21................35 H3
Wilson Wk CHSWK W4 *......118 C4
Wilstone CI YEAD UB4......95 J3
Wilthorne Gdns DAGE RM10..92 D5
Wilton Av CHSWK W4........118 B5
Wilton CI WDR/YW UB7......112 A6
Wilton Crs KTBR SW1X......15 G3
 WIM/MER SW19.............177 J4
Wilton Dr CRW RM5.........56 E3
Wilton Est HACK E8........86 C4
Wilton Gdns E/WMO/HCT KT8..173 F6
 EBED/NFELT TW14..........21 H5
Wilton Gv NWMAL KT3.......192 C3
 WIM/MER SW19.............177 J3
Wilton Ms HACK E8 *.......86 D4
 KTBR SW1X................15 H4
Wilton PI KTBR SW1X.......15 G3
Wilton Rd ABYW SE2........128 E3
 EBAR EN4.................21 K5
 HSLW TW4.................134 C4
 MUSWH N10................48 A5
 PIM SW1V.................16 K5
 WIM/MER SW19.............178 D2
Wilton Rw KTBR SW1X.......15 G3
Wilton Sq IS N1...........85 K6
Wilton Ter KTBR SW1X......15 G4
Wilton Vis IS N1 *........85 K6
Wilton Wk FELT TW13.......154 A4
Wilton Wy HACK E8.........86 C4

Wiltshire CI CHEL SW3.....14 D7
 MLHL NW7.................45 H1
Wiltshire Gdns FSBYPK N4..67 J3
 WHTN TW2.................155 H5
Wiltshire La PIN HA5......40 D1
 ORP BR6..................202 B4
Wiltshire Rd BRXN/ST SW9..142 B4
 THHTH CR7................180 B6
Wimbart Rd
 BRXS/STRHM SW2...........162 A2
Wimbledon Park Side
 PUT/ROE SW15............158 C2
Wimbledon Br
 WIM/MER SW19.............177 J2
Wimbledon Hill Rd
 WIM/MER SW19.............177 H2
Wimbledon Park Rd
 WIM/MER SW19.............159 H5
Wimbledon Park Side
 WIM/MER SW19.............159 G4
Wimbledon Rd TOOT SW17...160 B6
Wimbolt St BETH E2........104 C2
Wimborne Av NWDGN UB2....115 H3
 STMC/STPC BR5............186 A6
 YEAD UB4.................95 H4
Wimborne CI BKHH IG9......39 G4
 LEE/GVPK SE12............145 J6
 WPK KT4..................193 D5
Wimborne Dr CDALE/KGS NW9..44 A4
 PIN HA5..................59 H4
Wimborne Gdns WEA W13....97 H5
Wimborne Rd ED N9.........36 C4
 TOTM N17.................50 A5
Wimborne St IS N1.........6 E2
Wimbourne St IS N1........6 E2
Wimpole CI BMLY BR1.......200 B1
 KUT/HW KT1...............175 H6
Wimpole Ms CAVSQ/HST W1G..9 J3
Wimpole Rd WDR/YW UB7....112 A1
Wimpole St CAVSQ/HST W1G..9 J3
Wimshurst CI CROY/NA CR0..195 K5
Winans Wk BRXN/ST SW9.....142 B3
Wincanton Crs NTHLT UB5...78 A3
Wincanton Gdns BARK/HLT IG6..54 B6
Wincanton Rd
 WAND/EARL SW18...........159 J2
Winchcombe Rd CAR SM5....194 C4
Winchcomb Gdns
 ELTH/MOT SE9.............146 D4
Winchelsea Av BXLYHN DA7..149 G1
Winchelsea CI PUT/ROE SW15..139 G6
Winchelsea Rd FSTGT E7....88 E2
 TOTM N17.................50 A5
 WLSDN NW10...............99 F1
Winchelsey Ri SAND/SEL CR2..212 B4
Winchendon Rd FUL/PGN SW6..139 J1
 TEDD TW11................155 F5
Winchester Av CDALE/KGS NW9..44 A4
 HEST TW5.................114 D6
 KIL/WHAMP NW6............82 D6
Winchester CI ENC/FH EN1 *..36 A1
 ESH/CLAY KT10............204 A2
 HAYES BR2................183 J6
 KUTN/CMB KT2.............175 J3
 LBTH SE11................18 B7
Winchester Dr PIN HA5.....59 H2
Winchester Ms WPK KT4.....193 G6
Winchester Pk HAYES BR2...183 J6
Winchester PI HACK E8.....86 B3
 HGT N6...................66 B6
Winchester Rd BXLYHN DA7..148 E3
 CHING E4.................52 A3
 ED N9....................36 B3
 FELT TW13................154 E5
 HAMP NW3.................83 H5
 HAYES BR2................183 J6
 HGT N6...................66 B6
 HYS/HAR UB3..............133 H1
 IL IG1...................90 D1
 KTN/HRWW/WS HA3..........62 A1
 ORP BR6..................217 J2
 TWK TW1..................156 C1
Winchester Sq STHWK SE1..12 E7
Winchester St ACT W3......117 J1
 PIM SW1V.................16 D7
Winchester Wk STHWK SE1..12 E7
Winchfield CI
 KTN/HRWW/WS HA3.........61 J3
Winchfield Rd SYD SE26....182 B1
Winchilsea Crs
 E/WMO/HCT KT8............173 H5
Winchmore Hill Rd
 STHGT/OAK N14............34 C2
Winchmore Vls WCHMH N21 *..35 F2
Winckley CI
 KTN/HRWW/WS HA3.........62 A1
Wincott St LBTH SE11......17 K6
Wincrofts Dr ELTH/MOT SE9..147 J5
Windall CI NRWD SE19......181 H4
Windborough Rd CAR SM5....210 A5
Windermere Av FNCH N3.....46 E6
 HCH RM12.................93 J1
 KIL/WHAMP NW6............82 D6
 RSLP HA4.................59 G4
 WBLY HA9.................61 J3
 WIM/MER SW19.............178 A6
Windermere CI DART DA1....170 E3
 EBED/NFELT TW14..........153 J3
 ORP BR6..................216 B1
 STWL/WRAY TW19...........152 A4
Windermere Gdns REDBR IG4..71 J2
Windermere Gv WBLY HA9....61 J2
Windermere Rd ARCH N19....66 C6
 BXLYHN DA7...............149 K3
 CROY/NA CR0..............197 G5
 EA W5....................116 D3
 MUSWH N10................48 B4
 PUT/ROE SW15.............158 B6
 STHL UB1.................95 K4
 STRHM/NOR SW16...........179 H4
 WWKM BR4.................199 H6
Windermere Wy
 WDR/YW UB7...............112 B1

Windfield CI SYD SE26.....164 A6
Windham Rd RCH/KEW TW9...137 G4
Windlass PI DEPT SE8......124 B4
Windlesham Gv
 WIM/MER SW19.............159 G3
Windley CI FSTH SE23......163 K4
Windmill CI LEW SE13 *....145 F3
 STHWK SE1................123 H4
 SURB KT6.................190 C4
Windmill Dr CLAP SW4......141 G6
 CRICK NW2................82 C1
Windmill Gdns ENC/FH EN2..23 G3
Windmill Gv CROY/NA CR0...196 D4
Windmill HI ENC/FH EN2....23 H4
 HAMP NW3.................83 G1
 RSLP HA4.................58 D5
Windmill La BAR EN5.......31 H1
 BUSH WD23................28 E3
 GFD/PVL UB6..............96 B4
 HAYES BR2................215 G2
 NWDGN UB2................115 H2
 SRTFD E15................88 B4
 SURB KT6.................190 C4
Windmill Pas CHSWK W4 *...118 B4
Windmill Ri KUTN/CMB KT2..175 J3
Windmill Rd CHSWK W4......118 B4
 CROY/NA CR0..............196 D4
 EA W5....................116 D3
 HPTN TW12................173 G1
 MTCM CR4.................195 H2
 UED N18..................35 K5
 WAND/EARL SW18...........160 C1
 WIM/MER SW19.............178 B4
Windmill Rw LBTH SE11.....122 B5
Windmill St BUSH WD23.....28 E3
 FITZ W1T.................10 C2
Windmill St STHWK SE1 *...17 K1
Windmill Wy RSLP HA4......58 D5
Windrose CI BERM/RHTH SE16..124 A2
Windrush NWMAL KT3........191 J1
Windrush CI BTSEA SW11 *..140 C5
 CHSWK W4.................137 K1
Windrush La FSTH SE23.....164 A5
Windrush Rd WLSDN NW10...81 F6
Windsor Av CHEAM SM3......208 C1
 E/WMO/HCT KT8............173 F6
 EDGW HA8.................30 D6
 NWMAL KT3................191 K2
 WALTH E17................51 F5
 WIM/MER SW19.............178 B4
Windsor CI CHST BR7.......185 G1
 EFNCH N2.................65 K4
 NTHWD HA6................40 E5
 RYLN/HDSTN HA2...........60 A5
 WNWD SE27................162 D6
Windsor Ct PIN HA5 *......41 H6
 STHGT/OAK N14............34 C2
Windsor Crs RYLN/HDSTN HA2..78 A2
 WBLY HA9.................62 C1
Windsor Dr ASHF TW15.....152 A6
 DART DA1.................170 D1
 EBAR EN4.................33 K1
 ORP BR6..................217 G4
Windsor Gdns CROY/NA CR0..210 E1
 HYS/HAR UB3..............113 G3
 MV/WKIL W9...............100 E4
 WLGTN SM6................210 A3
Windsor Ms CAT SE6 *......165 G3
Windsor Park Rd
 HYS/HAR UB3..............133 J1
Windsor Rd BAR EN5........32 A1
 BCTR RM8.................73 K6
 BXLYHN DA6...............149 F5
 CHING E4.................37 K6
 CRICK NW2................81 K4
 EA W5....................98 A6
 FNCH N3..................46 C5
 FSTGT E7.................89 F3
 HOLWY N7.................84 E1
 HSLWW TW4................134 B3
 IL IG1...................90 C2
 KTN/HRWW/WS HA3.........42 C4
 KUTN/CMB KT2.............175 F3
 LEY E10..................70 A6
 NWDGN UB2................114 D3
 PLMGR N13................35 G5
 RCH/KEW TW9..............137 G3
 TEDD TW11................155 J1
 THHTH CR7................180 C5
 TOTM N17.................50 C5
 WAN E11..................71 F5
 WPK KT4..................192 D6
The Windsors BKHH IG9.....39 J4
Windsor St IS N1..........85 H6
Windsor Ter IS N1.........6 E4
Windsor Wy CMBW SE5 *.....142 E3
Windsor Wy WKENS W14......119 G4
Windsor Whf DEPT SE15.....123 J6
Windstock CI
 BERM/RHTH SE16...........124 C3
Windus Rd STNW/STAM N16...68 B5
Windy Ridge BMLY BR1......184 D4
Windy Ridge CI
 WIM/MER SW19.............177 G1
Wine CI WAP E1W...........104 E6
Wine Office Ct
 FLST/FETLN EC4A..........11 K3
Winey La KUT/HW KT1.......175 G6
Winey CI CHSGTN KT9......205 J5
Winforton St GNWCH SE10...145 F2
Winfrith Rd WAND/EARL SW18..160 B2
Wingate Crs CROY/NA CR0...195 K3
Wingate Rd IL IG1.........90 B3
 HMSMTH W6................118 E3
 SHB W12..................118 E3
Wingfield Ct WATW WD18 *..26 B1
Wingfield Ms PECK SE15....143 H4
Wingfield Rd KUTN/CMB KT2..175 G2
 SRTFD E15................88 C3
 WALTH E17................51 J6
Wingfield St PECK SE15....143 H4
Wingfield Wy RSLP HA4.....77 F4
Wingford Rd
 BRXS/STRHM SW2...........161 K1
Wingmore Rd HNHL SE24.....142 D4
Wingrave Rd HMSMTH W6.....119 F6

Wingrove Rd CAT SE6 .....165 H4
Wings CI SUT SM1 .....208 E2
Winifred St EBAR EN5 .....31 H1
Winifred PI KTN/HRWW/WDSPK N12 ..47 C1
Winifred Rd BCTR RM8 .....74 A6
DART DA1 .....150 E6
ERITH DA8 .....130 B5
HPTN TW12 .....155 F6
WIM/MER SW19 .....177 K4
Winifred St CAN/RD E16 .....126 E1
Winifred Ter EN EN1 .....36 B2
PLSTW E13 .....106 E1
Winkfield Rd WDGN N22 .....49 G4
Winkley St BETH E2 .....104 D1
Winkworth Cottages
WCHPL E1 * 104 E3
Winlaton Rd BMLY BR1 .....165 G6
Winmill Rd BCTR RM8 .....92 B1
Winn Common Rd
WOOL/PLUM SE18 .....127 K6
Winnett St SOHO/SHAV W1D ..10 C5
Winnington CI EFNCH N2 .....65 H5
Winnington Rd EFNCH N2 .....65 H4
PEND EN3 .....24 E1
Winnipeg Dr ORP BR6 .....217 G4
Winnock Rd WDR/YW UB7 ..112 A2
Winn Rd LEE/GVPK SE12 .....165 K3
Winns Av WALTH E17 .....51 H6
Winns Ms SEVS/STOTM N15 ..68 A1
Winns Ter WALTH E17 .....51 J5
Winsbeach WALTH E17 .....52 B6
Winscombe Crs EA W5 .....97 K3
Winscombe St ARCH N19 .....84 B1
Winscombe Wy STAN HA7 .....43 G1
Winsford Rd CAT SE6 .....164 C5
Winsford Ter UED N18 * 49 K1
Winsham Gv BTSEA SW11 .....141 E6
Winslade Rd
BRXS/STRHM SW2 .....141 K6
Winslade Ms BAY/PAD W2 ..8 A3
Winsland St BAY/PAD W2 .....8 A3
Winsley St GTPST W1W 10 A3
Winslow CI PIN HA5 .....59 F3
WLSDN NW10 .....81 G1
Winslow Gv CHING E4 .....38 C3
Winslow Rd HMSMTH W6 .....119 F6
Winslow Wy FELT TW13 .....154 D5
Winsor Ter EHAM E6 .....108 B4
Winstanley Rd BTSEA SW11 ..140 C4
Winston Av CDALE/KGS NW9 ..63 G4
Winston CI KTN/HRWW/WS HA3 ..43 F2
ROMW/RG RM7 .....74 D1
Winston Ct
KTN/HRWW/WS HA3 .....42 B4
Winston House SURB KT6 * ..191 F2
Winston Rd STNW/STAM N16 ..85 K2
Winston Wy IL IG1 .....90 B1
Winter Av EHAM E6 .....89 J6
Winterborne Av ORP BR6 .....216 D1
Winterbourne Rd BCTR RM8 ..73 J6
CAT SE6 .....164 C3
THHTH CR7 .....196 B1
Winter Box Wk
RCHPK/HAM TW10 .....137 G6
Winterbrook Rd HNHL SE24 ..162 D1
Winterburn CI FBAR/BDGN N11 ..48 A2
Winterfold CI WIM/MER SW19 ..159 H4
Winters Rd THDIT KT7 .....190 C4
Winterstoke Rd CAT SE6 .....164 C3
Winterton PI WBPTN SW10 ..120 B6
Winterwell Rd
BRXS/STRHM SW2 .....141 K6
Winthorpe Rd PUT/ROE SW15 ..139 H5
Winthorpe St WCHPL E1 * ..104 D4
Winthrop St WCHPL E1 * ..104 D4
Winton Av FBAR/BDGN N11 ..48 C3
Winton CI ED N9 .....37 F2
Winton Gdns EDGW HA8 .....44 B3
Winton Rd ORP BR6 .....216 B2
The Wintons BUSH WD23 * ..28 D3
Winton Wy STRHM/NOR SW16 ..180 B1
Wirral Wood CI CHST BR7 ..185 F2
Wisbeach Rd CROY/NA CRO ..196 D2
Wisborough Rd SAND/SEL CR2 ..212 B6
Wisdons CI DAGE RM10 .....74 D5
Wise La MLHL NW7 .....45 J2
WDR/YW UB7 .....112 A4
Wiseman Rd LEY E10 * 69 J6
Wise Rd SRTFD E15 .....88 A6
Wiseton Rd TOOT SW17 .....160 D3
Wishaw Wk FBAR/BDGN N11 ..48 C2
Wisley Rd BTSEA SW11 .....140 D5
STMC/STPC BR5 .....186 B3
Wistaria CI ORP BR6 .....201 G6
Wisteria CI IL IG1 .....90 B3
MLHL NW7 .....45 H2
Wisteria Rd LEW SE13 .....145 G5
Witanhurst La HGT N6 .....66 A5
Witan St BETH E2 .....104 D2
Witham CI LOU IG10 .....39 J1
Witham Rd DAGE RM10 .....92 C3
GPK RM2 .....75 K2
ISLW TW7 .....135 J2
PGE/AN SE20 .....181 K6
WEA W13 .....116 B1
Withens CI STMC/STPC BR5 * ..202 D1
Witheridge La IL IG1 .....90 B3
Witherington Rd HBRY N5 * ..85 G3
Withers Md CDALE/KGS NW9 ..45 H4
Witherston Wy ELTH/MOT SE9 ..167 F4
Withycombe Rd
WIM/MER SW19 .....159 G2
Withy La RSLP HA4 .....40 C3
Withy Md CHIG IG4 .....38 B5
Witley Crs CROY/NA CRO ..214 A4
Witley Gdns NWDGN UB2 ..114 E4
Witley Rd ARCH N19 .....66 D6
Witney CI PIN HA5 .....41 K2
Witney Pth FSTH SE23 .....164 A5
Wittenham Wy CHING E4 .....38 B5
Wittering CI KUTN/CMB KT2 ..174 E6
Wittersham Rd BMLY BR1 ..183 J1
Wivenhoe CI PECK SE15 .....143 J4
Wivenhoe Ct HSLW TW3 ..134 E5
Wivenhoe Rd BARK IG11 .....109 H1

Wiverton Rd SYD SE26 .....181 K2
Wix Rd DAGW RM9 .....91 K6
Wix's La CLAP SW4 .....141 G5
Woburn WEA W13 * 97 H4
Woburn Av HCH RM12 .....93 J2
BUSH WD23 .....28 C1
THMD SE28 .....109 K5
WIM/MER SW19 .....178 B2
Woburn PI STPAN WC1H 4 E6
Woburn Rd CAR SM5 .....194 D5
CROY/NA CRO 196 D5
Woburn Sq STPAN WC1H * ..4 D7
Woburn Wk STPAN WC1H * ..4 D7
Wodeham Gdns WCHPL E1 ..104 D4
Wodehouse Av CMBW SE5 ..143 G2
Wodehouse Rd DART DA1 ..151 K5
Woffington CI HOM/HW KT1 ..174 D4
Woking CI PUT/ROE SW15 ..138 C5
Woldham PI HAYES BR2 .....200 B1
Woldham Rd HAYES BR2 .....200 B1
Wolds Dr ORP BR6 .....216 A2
Wolfe CI HAYES BR2 .....199 K5
YEAD UB4 .....95 F2
Wolfe Crs CHARL SE7 .....126 C5
Wolferton Rd MNPK E12 .....89 K2
Wolfington Rd WNWD SE27 ..162 C6
Wolfram CI LEW SE13 .....145 H6
Wolftencroft CI BTSEA SW11 ..140 D3
Wollaston CI STHWK SE1 .....18 B6
Wolmer CI EDGW HA8 .....30 C6
Wolmer Gdns EDGW HA8 .....30 B4
Wolseley Av WAND/EARL SW18,159 K4
Wolseley Gdns CHSWK W4 ..117 J6
Wolseley Rd CEND/HSY/T N8 ..66 D3
CHSWK W4 .....117 K4
FSTGT E7 .....89 F5
KTN/HRWW/WS HA3 .....42 E6
MTCM CR4 .....195 F4
ROMW/RG RM7 .....75 F4
WDGN N22 .....49 F4
Wolseley St STHWK SE1 .....19 K3
Wolsey Av EHAM E6 .....108 A2
THDIT KT7 .....190 A2
WALTH E17 .....51 H6
Wolsey CI HSLW TW3 .....135 H5
KUTN/CMB KT2 .....175 J4
NWDGN UB2 .....115 H3
RYNPK SW20 .....176 E3
WPK KT4 .....207 J2
Wolsey Crs CROY/NA CRO ..214 A6
MRDN SM4 .....193 J4
Wolsey Dr KUTN/CMB KT2 ..175 F1
WOT/HER KT12 .....188 C5
Wolsey Gdns BARK/HLT IG6 ..54 B4
Wolsey Gv EDGW HA8 .....45 F3
ESH/CLAY KT10 .....204 B2
Wolsey Ms KTTN NW5 .....84 C4
ORP BR6 .....217 F3
Wolsey Rd ASHF TW15 .....152 B6
E/WMO/HCT KT8 .....189 J1
EN EN1 .....24 D3
ESH/CLAY KT10 .....204 B2
HPTN TW12 .....173 H2
IS N1 .....85 K3
NTHWD HA6 .....26 A4
Wolsey St WCHPL E1 .....104 E4
Wolsey Wy CHSGTN KT9 .....206 C3
Wolsley CI DART DA1 .....150 B6
Wolstonbury
NFNCH/WDSPK N12 * 46 E1
Wolvercote Rd ABYW SE2 ..128 E2
Wolverley St BETH E2 * 104 D2
Wolverton Av KUTN/CMB KT2 ..175 H4
Wolverton Gdns EA W5 .....98 B6
HMSMTH W6 .....119 G4
Wolverton Rd STAN HA7 .....43 H2
Wolverton Wy STHGT/OAK N14 ..22 C5
Wolves La WDGN N22 .....49 G2
Womersley Rd CEND/HSY/T N8 ..67 F3
Wonersh Wy BELMT SM2 .....208 B6
Wonford CI KUTN/CMB KT2 ..176 B4
Wontner CI IS N1 .....85 J5
Wontner Rd BAL SW12 .....160 E4
Woodall CI CHSGTN KT9 .....205 J5
Woodall Rd PEND EN3 .....37 F1
Woodbank Rd BMLY BR1 .....165 J5
Woodbastwick Rd SYD SE26 ..182 A2
Woodberry Av
RYLN/HDSTN HA2 .....60 C1
WCHMH N21 .....35 G4
Woodberry CI MLHL NW7 .....45 J3
Woodberry Crs MUSWH N10 ..48 B6
Woodberry Down FSBYPK N4 ..67 J5
Woodberry Gdns
NFNCH/WDSPK N12 .....47 G2
Woodberry Gv BXLY DA5 ..170 A3
FSBYPK N4 .....67 J4
NFNCH/WDSPK N12 .....47 G2
Woodberry Wy CHING E4 .....38 A2
NFNCH/WDSPK N12 .....47 G2
Woodbine CI WHTN TW2 .....155 J4
Woodbine Gv ENC/FH EN2 ..23 K1
PGE/AN SE20 .....181 J3
Woodbine La WPK KT4 .....207 K1
Woodbine PI WAN E11 .....70 E3
Woodbines Av KUT/HW KT1 ..174 E6
Woodbine Ter HOM E9 * 86 E4
Woodbourne Av
STRHM/NOR SW16 .....161 J5
Woodbourne Dr
ESH/CLAY KT10 .....205 F4
Woodbourne Gdns
WLGTN SM6 .....210 B5
Woodbridge CI HOLWY N7 ..67 F2
Woodbridge Rd BARK IG11 ..91 F3
Woodbridge St CLKNW EC1R ..6 A6
Woodbrook Rd ABYW SE2 ..128 B6
Woodburn CI HDN NW4 .....64 B2
Woodbury CI CROY/NA CRO ..197 G6
WAN E11 .....71 F1
Woodbury Gdns
LEE/GVPK SE12 .....166 A5
Woodbury Park Rd WEA W13 ..97 H3

Woodbury Rd WALTH E17 .....69 K1
Woodbury St TOOT SW17 ..178 D1
Woodchester Sq BAY/PAD W2 ..101 F4
Woodchurch CI SCUP DA14 ..167 J5
Woodchurch Dr BMLY BR1 ..184 C3
Woodchurch Rd
KIL/WHAMP NW6 .....82 E5
Wood CI BETH E2 .....104 C3
BXLY DA5 .....170 B5
CDALE/KGS NW9 .....63 F4
HRW HA1 .....60 E5
Woodclyffe Dr CHST BR7 ..185 F5
Woodcock Dell Av
KTN/HRWW/WS HA3 .....61 J4
Woodcock HI
KTN/HRWW/WS HA3 .....61 J3
Woodcocks CAN/RD E16 ..107 G4
Woodcombe Crs FSTH SE23 ..163 K3
Woodcot CI PEND EN3 .....36 E1
Woodcote Av HCH RM12 .....93 J2
MLHL NW7 .....46 B2
THHTH CR7 .....196 C1
WLGTN SM6 .....210 B6
Woodcote CI KUTN/CMB KT2 ..175 G2
PEND EN3 .....36 E1
Woodcote Dr ORP BR6 .....201 J4
Woodcote Gn WLGTN SM6 ..210 C6
Woodcote Ms LOU IG10 .....39 H2
WLGTN SM6 .....210 B4
Woodcote PI WNWD SE27 * ..180 C1
Woodcote Rd WAN E11 .....71 F4
WLGTN SM6 .....210 B4
Woodcroft ELTH/MOT SE9 ..166 E5
NFNCH/WDSPK N12 .....47 H3
WCHMH N21 .....35 F3
Woodcroft Av MLHL NW7 .....45 G3
STAN HA7 .....43 G4
Woodcroft Crs
BERM/RHTH SE16 .....124 A2
GNWCH SE10 .....125 H5
Woodcroft Rd THHTH CR7 ..196 C2
Wood Crest BELMT SM2 * ..209 G5
Wood Dene PECK SE15 * ..143 J2
Wood Dr CHST BR7 .....184 D2
Woodedge CI CHING E4 .....38 D3
Wooden Bridge Ter
WNWD SE27 * 162 C5
Wood End HYS/HAR UB3 ..113 J4
Wood End CI NTHLT UB5 ..78 D3
Woodend Gdns ENC/FH EN2 ..22 E5
Wood End Gdns NTHLT UB5 ..78 C3
Wood End Gn YEAD UB4 ..94 B4
Wood End Green Rd
HYS/HAR UB3 .....94 B4
Wood End La NTHLT UB5 ..78 B4
Wood End Rd HRW HA1 .....61 J4
Woodend Rd WALTH E17 .....52 A5
The Wood End WLGTN SM6 ..210 B6
Wooder Gdns FSTGT E7 .....88 E2
Woodfall Av BAR EN5 .....20 D6
Woodfall Dr DART DA1 .....150 C5
Woodfall Rd FSBYPK N4 .....67 G6
Woodfall St CHEL SW3 .....120 E5
Woodfarrs CMBW SE5 .....142 E5
Wood Fld HAMP NW3 * 83 K3
Woodfield ALP/SUD HA0 ..79 J1
Woodfield Av ALP/SUD HA0 ..79 J1
CAR SM5 .....210 A4
CDALE/KGS NW9 .....63 G1
EA W5 .....97 J3
STRHM/NOR SW16 .....161 J4
Woodfield CI ENC/FH EN2 ..24 A4
NRWD SE19 .....180 D3
Woodfield Crs EA W5 .....97 J3
Woodfield Dr EBAR EN4 .....34 A3
GPK RM2 .....75 J1
Woodfield Gdns
NWMAL KT3 .....192 C2
Woodfield Gv
STRHM/NOR SW16 .....161 J5
Woodfield La
STRHM/NOR SW16 .....161 J5
Woodfield PI MV/WKIL W9 ..100 D4
Woodfield Ri BUSH WD23 ..28 D2
Woodfield Rd EA W5 .....97 J3
HSLWW TW4 .....134 A3
MV/WKIL W9 .....100 D4
THDIT KT7 .....190 A6
Woodfields CI
STRHM/NOR SW16 * 161 J5
Woodford Av GNTH/NBYPK IG2 ..71 K2
Woodford Bridge Rd
REDBR IG4 .....71 J1
Woodford Crs PIN HA5 .....41 F5
Woodford New Rd WFD IG8 ..70 C1
Woodford PI WBLY HA9 .....62 A3
Woodford Rd FSTGT E7 .....89 F2
SWFD E18 .....70 E1
Woodgate Av CHSGTN KT9 ..205 K3
Woodgate Crs NTHWD HA6 ..40 E2
Woodgate Dr
STRHM/NOR SW16 .....179 J3
Woodger Rd SHB W12 .....119 F2
Woodget CI EHAM E6 .....107 J5
Woodgrange Av EA W5 .....117 G1
EN EN1 .....36 C1
KTN/HRWW/WS HA3 .....61 K2
NFNCH/WDSPK N12 .....47 H2
Woodgrange CI
KTN/HRWW/WS HA3 .....61 K2
Woodgrange Gdns EN EN1 ..36 C1
Woodgrange Rd FSTGT E7 ..88 E2
Woodgrange Ter EN EN1 * ..36 C1
Woodhall Av DUL SE21 .....163 G5
PIN HA5 .....41 H4
Woodhall Dr DUL SE21 .....163 G5
PIN HA5 .....41 H5
Woodhall Ga PIN HA5 .....41 H3
Woodhall La OXHEY WD19 ..27 H5
Woodham Ct SWFD E18 .....70 D1
Woodham Rd CAT SE6 .....165 F5
Woodhatch CI EHAM E6 .....107 J4
Woodhaven Gdns
BARK/HLT IG6 .....72 C1

Woodhayes Rd
WIM/MER SW19 .....177 F3
Woodhead Dr ORP BR6 .....216 E1
Woodheyes Rd WLSDN NW10 ..81 F3
Woodhill WOOL/PLUM SE18 ..126 D4
Woodhill Crs
KTN/HRWW/WS HA3 .....61 K3
Woodhouse Av GFD/PVL UB6 ..97 F1
Woodhouse CI EDUL SE22 ..143 H5
GFD/PVL UB6 .....97 F1
HYS/HAR UB3 .....113 H4
Woodhouse Eaves NTHWD HA6 ..40 E1
Woodhouse Gv FSTGT E7 ..89 J4
Woodhouse Rd
NFNCH/WDSPK N12 .....47 G2
WAN E11 .....70 D6
Woodhurst Av
STMC/STPC BR5 .....201 H3
Woodhurst Rd ABYW SE2 ..128 B5
ACT W3 .....117 K1
Woodington CI ELTH/MOT SE9 ..167 F1
Woodknoll Dr CHST BR7 ..184 E4
Woodland Ap GFD/PVL UB6 ..79 G4
Woodland CI CDALE/KGS NW9 ..62 E3
HOR/WEW KT19 * 207 G4
NRWD SE19 .....181 F2
WFD IG8 .....39 F5
Woodland Crs
BERM/RHTH SE16 .....124 A2
GNWCH SE10 .....125 H5
Woodland Gdns ISLW TW7 ..135 K4
MUSWH N10 .....66 B1
Woodland Gv CROY/NA CRO ..211 G5
GNWCH SE10 .....125 H5
Woodland HI NRWD SE19 ..181 F2
Woodland Ms
STRHM/NOR SW16 .....161 K5
Woodland Ri GFD/PVL UB6 ..79 G4
MUSWH N10 .....66 B1
Woodland Rd FBAR/BDGN N11 ..48 B1
NRWD SE19 .....181 F1
THHTH CR7 .....196 B1
Woodlands BXLYHS DA6 ..149 J5
GLDGN NW11 .....64 C3
RYLN/HDSTN HA2 .....60 C2
RYNPK SW20 .....193 F1
Woodlands Av ACT W3 .....117 J1
BFN/LL DA15 .....167 K3
CHDH RM6 .....73 K4
FNCH N3 .....47 G2
NWMAL KT3 .....175 K6
RSLP HA4 .....59 G5
WAN E11 .....71 F5
WPK KT4 .....192 C6
Woodlands CI BMLY BR1 ..184 E5
ESH/CLAY KT10 .....205 F5
GLDGN NW11 .....64 C2
SUN TW16 .....172 B5
Woodlands Dr STAN HA7 ..43 F3
SUN TW16 .....172 B5
Woodlands Gdns WALTH E17 * ..70 C1
Woodlands Gv ISLW TW7 ..135 K3
Woodlands Pk BXLY DA5 ..169 K6
Woodlands Park Rd
GNWCH SE10 .....125 J6
SEVS/STOTM N15 .....67 J2
Woodlands Rd BARN SW13 ..138 C4
BMLY BR1 .....184 C1
BXLYHN DA7 .....149 F4
ED N9 .....36 E3
ENC/FH EN2 .....23 K2
HRW HA1 .....61 F2
IL IG1 .....90 C1
ISLW TW7 .....135 K4
ORP BR6 .....217 G4
ROM RM1 .....57 H6
STHL UB1 .....114 C1
SURB KT6 .....190 E4
WALTH E17 .....52 A6
WAN E11 .....70 C6
Woodlands St LEW SE13 ..165 G2
Woodlands Ter SLW SE13 * ..203 K3
The Woodlands
BRXN/ST SW9 * 142 C1
ESH/CLAY KT10 .....189 H6
HRW HA1 .....60 E6
ISLW TW7 .....136 A3
LEW SE13 .....165 G2
NRWD SE19 .....180 D3
ORP BR6 .....217 H4
STAN HA7 * 43 H1
WLGTN SM6 .....210 B6
Woodland St HACK E8 * ..86 B4
Woodlands Wy
PUT/ROE SW15 .....139 J6
Woodland Ter CHARL SE7 ..126 D4
Woodland Wk HAMP NW3 ..83 J3
HOR/WEW KT19 .....206 D2
Woodland Wy ABYW SE2 ..128 E3
BRYLDS KT5 .....191 J6
CROY/NA CRO 198 B5
MLHL NW7 .....45 H2
MRDN SM4 .....193 J1
MTCM CR4 .....179 F3
STMC/STPC BR5 .....201 H1
WCHMH N21 .....35 G4
WFD IG8 .....39 F6
WWKM BR4 .....214 A1
Wood La CDALE/KGS NW9 ..63 F5
DAGE RM10 .....74 C6
HCH RM12 .....93 H3
HGT N6 .....66 B3
ISLW TW7 .....136 A1
RSLP HA4 .....58 B4
STAN HA7 .....29 G5
WFD IG8 .....52 D1
Woodlawn CI
PUT/ROE SW15 .....139 J6
Woodlawn Crs WHTN TW2 ..155 G4
Woodlawn Dr FELT TW13 ..154 C4
Woodlawn Rd FUL/PGN SW6 ..139 G1
Woodlea Dr HAYES BR2 .....199 H3
Woodlea Gv NTHWD HA6 ..40 A1
Woodlea Rd STNW/STAM N16 ..86 A1

Woodleigh Av
NFNCH/WDSPK N12 .....47 J2
Woodleigh Gdns
STRHM/NOR SW16 .....161 K5
Woodley CI TOOT SW17 ..178 E3
Woodley La CAR SM5 .....209 J1
Woodley Rd ORP BR6 .....202 E2
Wood Lodge Gdns BMLY BR1 ..184 D3
Wood Lodge La WWKM BR4 ..214 A1
Woodman Pth BARK/HLT IG6 ..54 C4
Woodman Rd BARK/HLT IG6 ..54 C4
CHIC IG7 .....55 F1
Woodmans Gv WLSDN NW10 ..81 H2
Woodmansterne Rd CAR SM5 ..209 J6
STRHM/NOR SW16 .....179 H3
Wood Md TOTM N17 .....50 C2
Woodmere ELTH/MOT SE9 ..166 E2
Woodmere Av CROY/NA CRO ..198 A4
Woodmere CI BTSEA SW11 ..141 F4
CROY/NA CRO 198 A4
Woodmere Gdns
CROY/NA CRO 198 A4
Woodnook Rd
STRHM/NOR SW16 .....179 G1
Woodpecker CI BUSH WD23 ..28 C3
ED N9 .....36 D1
KTN/HRWW/WS HA3 .....43 F4
Woodpecker Ms LEW SE13 ..145 G5
Woodpecker Mt CROY/NA CRO ..213 G6
Woodpecker Rd NWCR SE14 ..124 B6
THMD SE28 .....109 J6
Woodquest Av HNHL SE24 ..162 D1
Wood Ride EBAR EN4 .....21 H2
STMC/STPC BR5 .....201 J2
Woodridge CI ENC/FH EN2 ..23 H2
Woodridings Av PIN HA5 ..41 K5
Woodridings CI PIN HA5 ..41 K5
Woodriffe Rd WAN E11 .....70 B4
Wood Ri PIN HA5 .....58 E2
Woodrow WOOL/PLUM SE18 ..126 D4
Woodrow Av YEAD UB4 .....94 D4
Woodrow CI GFD/PVL UB6 ..79 H5
Woodrow Ct TOTM N17 .....50 D3
Woodrush CI NWCR SE14 ..144 B1
Woodrush Wy CHDH RM6 ..73 K1
Woodseer St WCHPL E1 .....13 K1
Woodsford Rd WAN E11 * ..119 H2
Woodshire Rd DAGE RM10 ..92 D1
Woodside BKHH IG9 .....39 G4
GLDGN NW11 .....64 E2
ORP BR6 .....217 G3
WIM/MER SW19 .....177 J1
Woodside Av ALP/SUD HA0 ..80 A5
CHST BR7 .....185 H1
ESH/CLAY KT10 .....189 K4
HGT N6 .....65 J2
NFNCH/WDSPK N12 .....33 G6
SNWD SE25 .....197 J3
Woodside CI ALP/SUD HA0 ..80 A5
BRYLDS KT5 .....191 K4
BXLYHN DA7 .....150 A5
RSLP HA4 .....58 B3
STAN HA7 .....43 H1
WFD IG8 .....117 F1
Woodside Court Rd
CROY/NA CRO 197 H4
Woodside Crs BFN/LL DA15 ..167 K5
Woodside Dr RDART DA2 ..170 B6
Woodside End ALP/SUD HA0 ..80 A5
Woodside Gdns CHING E4 ..51 K1
TOTM N17 .....50 D5
Woodside Grange Rd
NFNCH/WDSPK N12 .....33 F6
Woodside Gn SNWD SE25 ..197 J3
Woodside Gv
NFNCH/WDSPK N12 .....33 G5
Woodside La BXLY DA5 .....168 E1
TRDG/WHET N20 .....33 F5
Woodside Pde BFN/LL DA15 * ..167 K5
Woodside Park Av WALTH E17 ..70 B1
Woodside Park Rd
NFNCH/WDSPK N12 .....33 F6
Woodside PI ALP/SUD HA0 ..80 A6
Woodside Rd BFN/LL DA15 ..167 K5
BMLY BR1 .....200 D1
BXLYHN DA7 .....150 A5
KUTN/CMB KT2 .....175 F2
NTHWD HA6 .....40 D2
NWMAL KT3 .....176 A5
PLSTW E13 .....107 G3
SNWD SE25 .....197 J3
SUT SM1 .....209 G1
WFD IG8 .....38 E6
WGD? WDGN? 48 E6
WFD IG8 .....96 D1
Woodside Wy CROY/NA CRO ..197 H3
MTCM CR4 .....179 G4
Wood's Ms MYFR/PKLN W1K ..9 F5
Wood's PI STHWK SE1 .....19 H5
Woodspring Rd
WIM/MER SW19 .....159 H4
Wood's Rd PECK SE15 .....143 J2
Woodstead Gv EDGW HA8 ..44 A3
The Woods NTHWD HA6 ..40 E1
Woodstock Av CHEAM SM3 ..193 J4
GLDGN NW11 .....64 C4
ISLW TW7 .....136 B6
STHL UB1 .....95 K2
WEA W13 .....116 B3
Woodstock CI BXLY DA5 ..169 G3
STAN HA7 .....43 K4
Woodstock Crs ED N9 .....36 D1
Woodstock Gdns BECK BR3 ..182 E4
GDMY/SEVK IG3 .....73 G6
HYS/HAR UB3 .....94 D4
Woodstock Gra EA W5 * ..117 F1
Woodstock Gv SHB W12 ..119 G2
Woodstock La North
SURB KT6 .....190 D6
Woodstock La South
CHSGTN KT9 .....205 J2

Woodstock Ms CAVSQ/HST W1C...9 H2
Woodstock Ri CHEAM SM3...193 J3
Woodstock Rd ALP/SUD HA0...80 B5
  BUSH WD23...28 E2
  CAR SM5...210 A3
  CHSWK W4...118 B4
  CROY/NA CR0...211 K1
  FSBYPK N4...67 C5
  FSTCT E7...89 C5
  GLDGN NW11...45 J3
  WALTH E17...52 B5
Woodstock St CAN/RD E16...106 D5
  OXSTW W1C...9 J4
Woodstock Ter POP/IOD E14...105 K6
Woodstock Wy MTCM CR4...179 H5
Woodstone Av EW KT17...207 J3
Wood St BAR EN5...20 A5
  CAN/RD E16...107 F6
  CHSWK W4...118 B5
  CITYW EC2V...12 D5
  KUT/HW KT1...174 E5
  MTCM CR4...195 F4
  WALTH E17...52 A6
Woodsyre SYD SE26...163 G6
Woodthorpe Rd
  PUT/ROE SW15...138 E5
Woodtree CI HDN NW4...46 B5
Wood V FSTH SE23...163 J3
  MUSWH N10...66 C2
Woodvale Av SNWD SE25...181 G6
Woodvale Rd BAR EN5...21 F4
  EA W5...98 A6
  GLDGN NW11...64 C4
  KIL/WHAMP NW6...100 D1
  MRDN SM4...193 K1
  RCHPK/HAM TW10...156 C5
  STNW/STAM N16...86 A3
  SWFD E18...53 G1
  THHTH CR7...180 E6
  WALTH E17...69 C1
  WAN E11...70 D5
Woodville St
  WAND/EARL SW18...140 B6
Wood Whf GNWCH SE10...124 E6
Woodward Av HDN NW4...63 J2
Woodward CI ESH/CLAY KT10...205 F4
Woodwarde Rd EDUL SE22...163 F1
Woodward Gdns DAGW RM9...91 J5
  STAN HA7...43 F3
Woodward Rd DAGW RM9...91 F6
Wood Wy ORP BR6...201 F6
Woodway Crs HRW HA1...61 G3
Woodwaye OXHEY WD19...27 G2
Woodwell St
  WAND/EARL SW18...140 B6
Woodyard La DUL SE21...163 F2
Woodyates Rd LEE/GVPK SE12..165 K1
Woolacombe Wy
  BKHTH/KID SE3...146 B3
Woolacombe Wy
  HYS/HAR UB3...113 H4
Woolbrook Rd DART DA1...170 B1
Wooler St WALW SE17...122 E5
Woolf CI THMD SE28...128 C1
Woolf Ms STPAN WC1H...5 A4
Woollaston Rd FSBYPK N4...67 H3
Woollett CI DART DA1...150 D5
Woolmead Av CDALE/KGS NW9...63 J4
Woolmer Gdns UED N18...50 C2
Woolmer Rd UED N18...50 C1
Woolmore St POP/IOD E14...106 A6
Woolneigh St FUL/PGN SW6...140 A4
Woolridge Wy HOM E9 *...86 E5
Woo Rd RYNPK SW20...176 E3
Woolstaplers Wy
  BERM/RHTH SE16...123 H3
Woolston CI WALTH E17...51 F5
Woolstone Rd FSTH SE23...164 B4
Woolwich Church St
  CHARL SE7...126 D4
Woolwich Common
  WOOL/PLUM SE18...127 F6
Woolwich Foot Tnl
  CAN/RD E16...127 F2
Woolwich High St
  WOOL/PLUM SE18...127 F3
Woolwich Manor Wy
  CAN/RD E16...127 G1
Woolwich Manorway
  CAN/RD E16...127 G2
Woolwich Manor Wy
  EHAM E6...107 K3
Woolwich New Rd
  WOOL/PLUM SE18...127 G5
Woolwich Rd ABYW SE2...128 E6
  BXLYHN DA7...149 H4
  CHARL SE7...126 B4
  GNWCH SE10...125 K5
Wooster Gdns POP/IOD E14 ...106 B5
Wootton Gv FNCH N3...46 E4
Wootton St STHWK SE1 *...17 K2
Worcester Av TOTM N17...50 C5
Worcester CI CRICK NW2...81 J1
  CROY/NA CR0...198 C6
  MTCM CR4...179 F4
Worcester Crs WOT/HER KT12...188 B6
  MLHL NW7...31 C5
  WFD IG8...53 F1
Worcester Dr CHSWK W4...118 B3
Worcester Gdns GFD/PVL UB6...78 B4
  IL IG1...71 J4
  WPK KT4...207 G1

Worcester Ms
  KIL/WHAMP NW6...83 F4
Worcester Park Rd WPK KT4...206 E1
Worcester Rd BELMT SM2...208 E5
  MNPK E12...89 K1
  WALTH E17...51 F5
  WIM/MER SW19...177 J2
Worcesters Av EN EN1...24 C1
Wordsworth Av GFD/PVL UB6...96 D1
  MNPK E12...89 J5
  SWFD E18...52 D6
Wordsworth Dr CHEAM SM3...208 A2
Wordsworth Pde
  CEND/HSY/T N8 *...67 H1
Wordsworth PI HAMP NW3...83 K3
Wordsworth Rd HPTN TW12...154 E6
  PGE/AN SE20...182 A3
  STHWK SE1...19 J7
  STNW/STAM N16...86 A2
  WELL DA16...147 K2
  WLGTN SM6...210 C4
Wordsworth Wk GLDGN NW11...64 D3
Wordsworth Wy DART DA1...151 K5
  WDR/YW UB7...112 B4
Worfield St BTSEA SW11...140 D1
Worgan St BERM/RHTH SE16...124 A3
  LBTH SE11...122 A5
Worland Rd SRTFD E15...88 C5
Worlds End Est
  WBPTN SW10 *...140 C1
Worlds End La ORP BR6...217 G5
  WCHMH N21...23 F6
Worlds End Pas
  WBPTN SW10 *...140 C1
Worleys Dr ORP BR6...216 D2
Worlidge St HMSMTH W6...119 F5
Worlingham Rd EDUL SE22...143 G5
Wormholt Rd SHB W12...118 D1
Wormholt Ter SHB W12 *...118 D1
Wormwood St OBST EC2N...13 G3
Wornington Rd NKENS W10...100 C4
Woronzow Rd ST/JWD NW8...2 B1
Worple Av ISLW TW7...136 B6
  WIM/MER SW19...177 G3
Worple CI RYLN/HDSTN HA2...59 K5
Worple Rd ISLW TW7...136 B5
  RYNPK SW20...177 G4
Worple Road Ms
  WIM/MER SW19...177 J2
Worple St MORT/ESHN SW14...138 A4
Worple Wy RCHPK/HAM TW10..137 F6
  RYLN/HDSTN HA2...59 K5
Worship St SDTCH EC2A...7 G7
Worslade Rd TOOT SW17...160 C6
Worsley Bridge Rd SYD SE26...182 C1
Worsley Gv CLPT E5...86 C2
Worsley Rd WAN E11...88 B2
Worsopp Dr CLAP SW4...141 H6
Worth CI ORP BR6...216 E2
Worthfield CI HOR/WEW KT19...207 F5
Worth Gv WALW SE17 *...122 E5
Worthing CI SRTFD E15...88 C6
Worthing Rd HEST TW5...114 E6
Worthington CI MTCM CR4...195 G1
Worthington Rd SURB KT6...191 G5
Wortley Rd CROY/NA CR0...196 B4
  EHAM E6...89 H5
Worton Gdns ISLW TW7...135 J3
Worton Hall Est ISLW TW7...136 A4
Worton Rd ISLW TW7...135 J3
Wotton Gn STMC/STPC BR5...202 E1
Wotton Rd CRICK NW2...82 A2
  DEPT SE8...124 C6
Wouldham Rd CAN/RD E16...106 D5
Wouldham Ter
  STMC/STPC BR5 *...186 C6
Wragby Rd WAN E11 *...88 C1
Wrampling PI ED N9...36 C3
Wray Av CLAY IG5...54 A6
Wray Crs FSBYPK N4...66 E5
Wrayfield Rd CHEAM SM3...208 B1
Wray Rd BELMT SM2...208 D6
Wraysbury CI HSLWW TW4...134 D6
Wrays Wy YEAD UB4...94 C4
Wrekin Rd WOOL/PLUM SE18...147 H1
Wren Av CRICK NW2...82 A3
  NWDGN UB2...114 E4
Wren CI CAN/RD E16...106 D5
  ED N9...37 F3
  STMC/STPC BR5...186 E6
Wren Crs BUSH WD23...28 C3
Wren Dr WDR/YW UB7...112 A3
Wren Gdns DAGW RM9...91 K3
  HCH RM12...75 H5
Wren Ms LEW SE13 *...145 H5
Wren Rd CMBW SE5...142 E2
  DAGW RM9...91 K3
  SCUP DA14...168 C6
Wren St FSBYW WC1X...5 H5
Wrentham Av WLSDN NW10...100 B1
Wrenthorpe Rd BMLY BR1...165 H6
Wrenwood Wy PIN HA5...59 F1
Wrexham Rd BOW E3...105 J1
Wricklemarsh Rd
  BKHTH/KID SE3...146 B2
Wrigglesworth St NWCR SE14..144 A1
Wright CI LEW SE13...145 G5
Wright Rd HEST TW5...134 B1
Wrights Aly WIM/MER SW19...177 G2
Wrights CI DAGE RM10...92 D2
Wrights La KENS W8...119 K3
Wrights PI WLSDN NW10 *...80 E4
Wright's Rd BOW E3...105 H1
  SNWD SE25...181 F6
Wright's Wy WLGTN SM6...210 B2
Wrigley CI CHING E4 *...52 B1
Wrotham Rd BAR EN5...20 C3
  CAMTN NW1 *...84 C5
  WEA W13...116 D1
  WELL DA16...148 D2
Wrottesley Rd WLSDN NW10...99 J1
  WOOL/PLUM SE18...127 H6
Wroughton Rd BTSEA SW11...160 E1
Wroughton Ter HDN NW4 *...63 K1
Wroxall Rd DAGW RM9...91 J4
Wroxham Gdns
  FBAR/BDGN N11...48 C3

Wroxham Rd THMD SE28...109 K6
Wroxham Wy BARK/HLT IG6...54 B4
Wroxton Rd PECK SE15...143 K3
Wrythe La CAR SM5...209 K1
Wrythe Green Rd CAR SM5...209 K1
Wrythe The CAR SM5...194 C5
Wrythe The CAR SM5...194 C5
Wulfstan St SHB W12...99 H5
Wyatt CI BERM/RHTH SE16...124 C2
  BUSH WD23...28 E2
  FELT TW13...154 C3
  YEAD UB4...94 E4
Wyatt Dr BARN SW13...118 E6
Wyatt Park Rd
  BRXS/STRHM SW2...162 A4
Wyatt Rd DART DA1...150 C4
  FSTGT E7...88 E4
  HBRY N5...85 J1
Wyatt's La WALTH E17...52 A2
Wybert St CAMTN NW1...3 K6
Wyborne Wy WLSDN NW10...80 E5
Wyburn Av BAR EN5...20 D4
Wychcombe Studios
  HAMP NW3 *...83 K4
Wyche Gv SAND/SEL CR2...211 J6
Wycherley CI BKHTH/KID SE3...145 J1
Wycherley Crs BAR EN5...33 F1
Wychwood Av EDGW HA8...43 J2
  THHTH CR7...180 D6
Wychwood CI EDGW HA8...43 J2
Wychwood End HGT N6...66 C4
Wychwood Gdns CLAY IG5...71 K1
Wychwood Wy NTHWD HA6...40 D3
Wycliffe CI WELL DA16...148 A2
Wycliffe Rd BTSEA SW11...141 F3
  WIM/MER SW19...178 A1
Wyclif St FSBYE EC1V...6 A5
Wycombe Gdns GLDGN NW11...64 E6
Wycombe PI
  WAND/EARL SW18...160 B1
Wycombe Rd ALP/SUD HA0...80 C6
  GNTH/NBYPK IG2...71 K2
  TOTM N17...50 C4
Wydell CI MRDN SM4...193 F3
Wydehurst Rd CROY/NA CR0..197 H4
Wydeville Manor Rd
  LEE/GVPK SE12...166 A6
Wye CI ASHF TW15...152 E6
  ORP BR6...202 A4
  RSLP HA4...58 A3
Wyemead Crs CHING E4...38 C4
Wye St BTSEA SW11...140 C3
Wyevale CI NTHWD HA6...40 E6
Wyfields CLAY IG5...54 A5
Wyfold Rd FUL/PGN SW6...139 H2
Wyke CI ISLW TW7...116 A6
Wyke Gdns HNWL W7...116 A3
Wykeham Av DAGW RM9...91 J4
Wykeham CI WDR/YW UB7...112 D6
Wykeham Gn DAGW RM9...91 J4
Wykeham HI WBLY HA9...62 B5
Wykeham Ri TRDG/WHET N20...32 C3
Wykeham Rd HDN NW4...64 A2
  KTN/HRWW/WS HA3...61 H1
Wyke Rd BOW E3...87 J5
  RYNPK SW20...177 F5
Wylchin CI PIN HA5...58 D1
Wyldes CI GLDGN NW11...65 G5
Wyldfield Gdns ED N9...36 B4
Wyld Wy WBLY HA9...80 D4
Wyleu St FSTH SE23...164 B2
Wylie Rd NWDGN UB2...115 F3
Wyllen CI WCHPL E1...104 E3
Wylo Dr BAR EN5...31 J1
Wymering Rd MV/WKIL W9...100 E2
Wymond St PUT/ROE SW15...139 F4
Wynan Rd POP/IOD E14...124 E5
Wynaud Crs WDGN N22...49 F2
Wyncham Av BFN/LL DA15...167 K3
Wynchgate
  KTN/HRWW/WS HA3...42 E3
  STHGT/OAK N14...22 D6
Wyncote Wy SAND/SEL CR2...213 F6
Wyncroft CI BMLY BR1...184 E6
Wyndale Av CDALE/KGS NW9...62 C3
Wyndcliff Rd CHARL SE7...126 A6
Wyndcroft CI ENC/FH EN2...23 H4
Wyndham Av BELMT SM2...208 E5
  ORP BR6...201 H5
Wyndham Crs HSLWW TW4...154 E1
  KTTN NW5...84 A4
Wyndham Est CMBW SE5...142 D1
Wyndham Ms MBLAR W1H...8 E2
Wyndham PI MBLAR W1H...8 E2
Wyndham Rd CMBW SE5...142 D1
  EBAR EN4...33 K3
  EHAM E6...89 H5
  KUTN/CMB KT2...175 G3
  WEA W13...116 C3
Wyndham St CAMTN NW1...8 E1
Wyndhurst CI SAND/SEL CR2..211 H5
Wyneham Rd HNHL SE24...142 E6
Wynell Rd FSTH SE23...164 A5
Wynford Gv STMC/STPC BR5...186 C6
Wynford PI BELV DA17...129 H5
Wynford Rd IS N1...5 H2
Wynford Wy ELTH/MOT SE9...166 E5
Wynlie Gdns PIN HA5...41 F5
Wynn Bridge CI WFD IG8...53 H4
Wynndale Rd SWFD E18...53 F4
Wynne Rd BRXN/ST SW9...142 B3
Wynn's Av BFN/LL DA15...148 B6
Wynnstay Gdns KENS W8...119 K3
Wynter St BTSEA SW11...140 B5
Wynton Gdns SNWD SE25...197 G2
Wynton PI ACT W3...98 D5
Wynyard Ter LBTH SE11...122 A5
Wynyatt St FSBYE EC1V...6 A4
Wyre Gv EDGW HA8...30 D7
  HYS/HAR UB3...113 K4
Wyresdale Crs GFD/PVL UB6...97 F2
Wyteleaf CI RSLP HA4...58 A3
Wythburn PI MBLAR W1H...8 E4
Wythenshawe Rd DAGE RM10..92 C1
Wythes CI BMLY BR1...184 E5
Wythes Rd CAN/RD E16...126 D1
Wythfield Rd ELTH/MOT SE9...166 E6

Wyvenhoe Rd
  RYLN/HDSTN HA2...78 C1
Wyvern CI DART DA1...171 F2
  ORP BR6...217 H1
Wyvern Est NWMAL KT3 *...176 D6
Wyvil Rd VX/NE SW8...141 K1
Wyvis St POP/IOD E14...105 K4

Y

Yabsley St POP/IOD E14...125 F1
Yalding Gv STMC/STPC BR5...202 E1
Yalding Rd BERM/RHTH SE16...123 H3
Yale CI HSLWW TW4...134 E6
Yale Wy HCH RM12...93 J2
Yarborough Rd
  WIM/MER SW19...178 C4
Yardley CI CHING E4...25 K6
Yardley La CHING E4...25 K5
Yardley St FSBYW WC1X...5 J6
Yarmouth Crs TOTM N17...68 D2
Yarmouth PI MYFR/PICC W1J...15 J1
Yarnton Wy ABYW SE2...128 D2
  ERITH DA18...129 G3
Yarrow Crs EHAM E6...107 J4
Yateley St WOOL/PLUM SE18...126 C3
Yeading Av RYLN/HDSTN HA2...59 J6
Yeading Fk YEAD UB4...95 G4
Yeading Gdns YEAD UB4...95 F4
Yeading La NTHLT UB5...95 G3
  YEAD UB4...95 F5
Yeames CI WEA W13...97 G5
Yeate St IS N1...85 K5
Yeatman Rd HGT N6...65 K3
Yeats CI LEW SE13 *...145 G3
  WLSDN NW10...81 G4
Ye Cnr OXHEY WD19...27 H1
Yeend CI E/WMO/HCT KT8...189 F1
Yeldham Rd HMSMTH W6...119 G5
Yeldham Vis HMSMTH W6 *...119 G5
Yelverton Rd BTSEA SW11...140 C3
Yenston CI MRDN SM4...193 K3
Yeoman CI EHAM E6...108 B6
Yeoman Dr STWL/WRAY TW19..152 B3
Yeoman Rd NTHLT UB5...77 J5
Yeomans Acre RSLP HA4...58 E3
Yeoman's Rw CHEL SW3...14 D5
Yeoman St BERM/RHTH SE16..124 B4
Yeomans Wy PEND EN3 *...24 D3
Yeoman's Yd WCHPL E1...13 K5
Yeomen Wy BARK/HLT IG6...54 C2
Yeo St BOW E3...105 K4
Yeovil CI ORP BR6...201 K6
Yeovilton PI KUTN/CMB KT2..174 E1
Yerbury Rd ARCH N19...66 D1
Yester Dr CHST BR7...184 D3
Yester Pk CHST BR7...184 D3
Yester Rd CHST BR7...184 E3
Yew CI BKHH IG9...39 H4
Yewdale CI BMLY BR1...183 H2
Yewfield Rd WLSDN NW10...81 H5
Yew Gv CRICK NW2...82 B2
The Yews ASHF TW15 *...152 E6
Yewtree CI MUSWH N10...48 A4
  RYLN/HDSTN HA2...48 A4
Yew Tree Ct WCHMH N21...35 G2
  WELL DA16...148 B2
  WPK KT4...192 B5
Yew Tree Ct BORE WD6...29 K1
Yew Tree Gdns CHDH RM6...74 A2
  ROMW/RG RM7...75 F2
Yew Tree Rd BECK BR3...182 C6
  SHB W12...99 H6
Yew Tree Wk HSLWW TW4...134 E6
Yew Wk HRW HA1...60 E5
Yoakley Rd STNW/STAM N16...86 A1
Yoke CI HOLWY N7...84 E3
Yolande Gdns ELTH/MOT SE9..146 D6
York Av BFN/LL DA15...167 K4
  HNWL W7...115 K1
  HYS/HAR UB3...94 A3
  MORT/ESHN SW14...137 K6
  STAN HA7...43 H4
York Br CAMTN NW1...3 G6
York Buildings CHCR WC2N...11 F6
York CI CMBW SE5 *...142 D3
  EHAM E6...107 K5
  HNWL W7...115 K1
  MRDN SM4...194 A1
York Ga CAMTN NW1...3 H7
  STHGT/OAK N14...34 E2
York Gv PECK SE15...143 K2
York HI WNWD SE27...162 C5
York House PL KENS W8...120 A2
Yorkland Av WELL DA16...148 A5
York Ms IL IG1...90 A1
  KTTN NW5...84 B3
York Pde BTFD TW8 *...116 E5
  CDALE/KGS NW9...63 J5
York Ri BTSEA SW11...140 E6
  ORP BR6...201 K6
York Rd ACT W3...98 E5
  BAR EN5...21 G6
  BELMT SM2...208 E6
  BTFD TW8...116 E5
  BTSEA SW11...140 B5
  CHING E4...51 J1
  EA W5...116 D3
  FBAR/BDGN N11...48 D2
  FSTGT E7...88 E4
  FSTH SE23...164 B4
  IG1 IL...72 A6
  IL IG1...90 A1
  KUTN/CMB KT2...175 G3
  LEY E10...69 F1
  NTHWD HA6...40 E5
  RAIN RM13...93 F5
  RCHPK/HAM TW10...137 G5
  STHWK SE1...17 H2

  TEDD TW11...155 K6
  UED N18...51 G1
  WALTH E17...69 F2
  WCHMH N21...35 K2
  WIM/MER SW19...178 A3
Yorkshire CI STNW/STAM N16...86 A1
Yorkshire Gdns UED N18...50 D1
Yorkshire Grey YCI GINN WC1R *..11 G2
Yorkshire Rd MTCM CR4...195 K2
  POP/IOD E14...105 G5
York Sq POP/IOD E14...105 G5
York St MBLAR W1H...8 E2
  MTCM CR4...195 F4
York Street Chambers
  MHST W1U *...9 F1
York Ter ENC/FH EN2...23 J1
  ERITH DA8...149 K2
York Ter East CAMTN NW1...3 H7
York Ter West CAMTN NW1...3 H7
Yorkton St BETH E2...104 C1
York Wy CHSGTN KT9...205 K5
  FELT TW13...154 E5
  IS N1...5 F2
  TRDG/WHET N20...33 K5
York Way Est HOLWY N7...84 E4
Youngmans CI ENC/FH EN2...23 J2
Young Rd CAN/RD E16...107 G5
Youngs Rd GNTH/NBYPK IG2...72 D2
Young St KENS W8...120 A2
Yoxley Ap GNTH/NBYPK IG2...72 C3
Yoxley Dr GNTH/NBYPK IG2...72 C3
Yukon Rd BAL SW12...161 G2
Yunus Khan CI WALTH E17...69 J3

Z

Zambezie Dr ED N9...36 E5
Zampa Rd BERM/RHTH SE16..123 K5
Zander Ct BETH E2...104 C2
Zangwill Rd BKHTH/KID SE3...146 C2
Zealand Av WDR/YW UB7...132 A1
Zealand Rd BOW E3...105 G1
Zelah Rd STMC/STPC BR5...202 C4
Zennor Rd BAL SW12...161 H3
Zenoria St EDUL SE22...143 G5
Zermatt Rd THHTH CR7...196 D2
Zetland St POP/IOD E14...106 A4
Zion PI THHTH CR7...196 E1
Zion Rd THHTH CR7...196 E1
Zoar St STHWK SE1...12 C7
Zoffany St ARCH N19...66 D6

2 Willow Road
HAMP NW3 ....83 J2

22 Jermyn Street Hotel
STJS SW1Y 10 B6

51 Buckingham Gate Hotel
WESTW SW1E 16 B4

AAIS
DART DA1 ....171 H2

Aarotya Medical Centre
SEVS/STOTM N15 ....67 J1

The Abbey Clinic
VX/NE SW8 ....141 H2

The Abbey Clinic
BELV DA17 ....129 C5

Abbey Christian School for the English Language
STJWD NW8 ....101 G1

Abbey College London
BAY/PAD W2 ....100 E5

The Abbey Court Townhouse Hotel
BAY/PAD W2 ....100 E6

Abbey Industrial Estate
ALP/SUD HA0 ....80 E6
MTCM CR4 ....194 E2

Abbey Lane Commercial Estate
SRTFD E15 ....106 B1

Abbey Medical Centre
STJWD NW8 ....83 F6

Abbey Mills
WIM/MER SW19 ....178 B4

Abbey Park Industrial Estate
BARK IG11 ....108 B1

Abbey Primary School
ABYW SE2 ....128 D3
MRDN SM4 ....193 K4

Abbey Road Health Centre
SRTFD E15 ....88 C5

Abbey Road Studios
STJWD NW8 ....101 G1

Abbey Sports Centre
BARK IG11 ....90 C6

Abbey Trading Estate
SYD SE26 ....182 B1

Abbey Wharf Industrial Estate
BARK IG11 ....108 D2

Abbey Wood School
MRDN SM4 ....193 K2

Abbotsbury Primary School
MRDN SM4 ....193 K2

ABC Cinema
HAMP NW3 ....83 J5
PUT/ROE SW15 ....139 H4

Abercorn School
MBLAR W1H 8 E2
STJWD NW8 ....101 G1

Aberdeen Wharf
WAP E1W 123 J1

Aberglen Industrial Estate
HYS/HAR UB3 ....113 G2

Abingdon House School
KENS W8 ....119 K3

Abney Park Cemetery
STNW/STAM N16 ....68 A6

Acacia Business Centre
WAN E11 ....88 C1

The Academy at Peckham
PECK SE15 ....143 G2

The Academy School
HAMP NW3 ....83 H2

Acland Burghley School
KTTN NW5 ....84 B2

Acorn Industrial Park
DART DA1 ....150 D6

Acorn Medical Centre
TWK TW1 ....156 B3

Acre Road Health Clinic
KUTN/CMB KT2 ....175 G3

Acton Business Centre
WLSDN NW10 ....99 F3

Acton Central Industrial Estate
ACT W3 ....98 D6

Acton Health Centre
ACT W3 ....117 K1

Acton High School
ACT W3 ....117 H2

Acton Hospital
ACT W3 ....117 H2

Acton Lane Medical Centre
CHSWK W4 ....117 K2

Acton Park Industrial Estate
ACT W3 ....118 A2
ACT W3 ....118 C1

Acton Superbowl
ACT W3 ....98 C4

Acton Swimming Baths
ACT W3 ....117 K1

Acumen (Anglo School)
NRWD SE19 ....181 F4

Adams Bridge Business Centre
WBLY HA9 ....80 D3

Adamsrill Primary School
SYD SE26 ....164 B5

Adath Yisroel Cemetery
EN EN1 ....24 B2

Addey & Stanhope School
NWCR SE14 ....144 C2

Addington Court Golf Club
CROY/NA CR0 ....213 H6

Addington Golf Club
CROY/NA CR0 ....213 G2

Addington Palace Golf Club
CROY/NA CR0 ....213 G4

Addiscombe CC
CROY/NA CR0 ....212 C1

Addison Primary School
WKENS W14 ....119 G3

Adelphi Theatre
COVGDN WC2E 11 F6

Adler Industrial Estate
HYS/HAR UB3 ....113 G2

Admiral Hyson Industrial Estate
STHWK SE1 ....123 J4

Admiralty Arch
STJS SW1Y 10 D7

ADT College
PUT/ROE SW15 ....139 J6

The Adult College of Barking & Dagenham
BARK IG11 ....90 E4

Adult Education Centre
DART DA1 ....171 J2
POP/IOD E14 ....125 F3

Aerodrome Hotel
CROY/NA CR0 ....211 G4

Africa Centre
COVGDN WC2E 11 F5

Agency of Jewish Education
HDN NW4 ....51 K5

Agnew's
CONDST W1S 10 A7

Agora Shopping Centre
PECK SE15 ....143 H5

Ainslie Wood Primary School
CHING E4 ....51 K1

Airbase Unity Elementary School
RSLP HA4 ....58 A6

Airbus Coach Station
HTHAIR TW6 ....132 C4

Air Call Business Centre
CDALE/KGS NW9 ....45 F6

Airedale Physiotherapy Clinic
CHSWK W4 ....118 C5

Airlinks Golf Club
NWDGN UB2 ....114 B4

Air Links Industrial Estate
HEST TW5 ....114 B5

Airport Gate Business Centre
WDR/YW UB7 ....132 C1

Aksaray Sports Club
STNW/STAM N16 ....85 K2

The Alan D School of Hairdressing
GTPST W1W 10 B3

Albany Centre & Theatre
DEPT SE8 ....144 C1

Albany Clinic
BFN/LL DA15 ....168 B6
WIM/MER SW19 ....178 A3

The Albany College
HDN NW4 ....63 K2

Albany Park Canoe & Sailing Club
KUTN/CMB KT2 ....174 E2

Albany School (Grant Maintained)
PEND EN3 ....25 F1

Albany School
HCH RM12 ....75 K6

Albemarle Primary School
WIM/MER SW19 ....159 H4

Albert Memorial
SKENS SW7 ....14 A2

Albion Health Centre
WCHPL E1 ....104 D4

Albion J & I School
BERM/RHTH SE16 ....123 K2

Albion Street Health Centre
BERM/RHTH SE16 ....123 K2

Albright Industrial Estate
RAIN RM13 ....111 H4

The Alchemy Gallery
CLKNW EC1R 5 J6

Alderbrook Primary School
BAL SW12 ....161 G2

Aldersbrook County Secondary School
MNPK E12 ....71 G5

Aldersbrook Primary School
MNPK E12 ....71 F5

Alderwood Primary School
ELTH/MOT SE9 ....167 J1

Aldgate Bus Station
HDTCH EC3A 13 J3

Aldwych Theatre
HOL/ALD WC2B 11 G4

Alexander McLeod Primary School
ABYW SE2 ....128 C5

Alexandra Avenue Clinic
RYLN/HDSTN HA2 ....59 K6

Alexandra Business Centre
PEND EN3 ....25 F5

Alexandra Infant School
KUTN/CMB KT2 ....175 H3
PGE/AN SE20 ....182 A3

Alexandra Junior School
HSLW TW3 ....135 G3
SYD SE26 ....182 A2

Alexandra Palace (Historic House)
WDGN N22 ....48 D6

Alexandra Palace Ice Rink
WDGN N22 ....48 D5

Alexandra Park School
FBAR/BDGN N11 ....48 C3

Alexandra Primary School
WDGN N22 ....49 F5

Alexandra School
RYLN/HDSTN HA2 ....59 K6

Al Falah Boys School
CLPT E5 ....86 D1

Alfred Salter Primary School
BERM/RHTH SE16 ....124 A2

Alfreds Way Industrial Estate
BARK IG11 ....91 G6

Alibris Primary School
STHL UB1 ....96 A5

Allen Edwards Primary School
CLAP SW4 ....141 K2

The All England Lawn Tennis & Croquet Club
WIM/MER SW19 ....159 G5

Allergy Clinic
CAVSO/HST W1G 9 J2

Alleyns Junior School
EDUL SE22 ....143 F6

Allfarthing JMI School
WAND/EARL SW18 ....160 B1

All Saints Benhilton CE Primary School
SUT SM1 ....209 F1

All Saints Catholic School & Technology College
BCTR RM8 ....74 C5

All Saints CE Junior School
WIM/MER SW19 ....181 F4

All Saints CE Primary School
BKHTH/KID SE3 ....145 H3
CAR SM5 ....210 A3
CRICK NW2 ....82 D1
FUL/PGN SW6 ....139 H5
PUT/ROE SW15 ....139 F4
TRDG/WHET N20 ....33 H4
WIM/MER SW19 ....178 B3

All Souls CE Primary School
GTPST W1W 10 A2

Allum Medical Centre
WAN E11 ....70 B4

Alma Primary School
BERM/RHTH SE16 ....123 H4
PEND EN3 ....25 F6

Almeida Theatre
IS N1 ....85 H5

Al-Noor Primary School
GDMY/SEVK IG3 ....73 H5

Alperton Cemetery
ALP/SUD HA0 ....79 K6

Alperton Community School
ALP/SUD HA0 ....80 A5

Alperton High School
ALP/SUD HA0 ....79 K6

Alperton Sports Ground
WBLY HA0 ....97 K1

Alpha Business Centre
WALTH E17 ....69 H2

Alpha Preparatory School
HRW HA1 ....60 E2

Alpine Business Centre
EHAM E6 ....108 A4

Al Sadiq High School for Boys & Al-Zahra Girls School
KIL/WHAMP NW6 ....82 C5

Alscot Road Industrial Estate
STHWK SE1 ....19 K6

Altmore Infant School
EHAM E6 ....89 K5

The Alton School
PUT/ROE SW15 ....158 C2

Ambler Primary School
FSBYPK N4 ....85 H1

Ambleside Junior School
WOT/HER KT12 ....188 B5

AMC Business Centre
WLSDN NW10 ....98 D2

American Intercontinental University
MHST W1U 9 H2

The American School in London
STJWD NW8 ....83 G6

AMF Bowling
LEW SE13 ....145 F4

Amida Golf
FELT TW13 ....155 F5

Ampthill Square Medical Centre
CAMTN NW1 ....4 B3

Anchorage Point Industrial Estate
CHARL SE7 ....126 B3

Anchor Bay Industrial Estate
ERITH DA8 ....150 C1

Anchor Retail Park
WCHPL E1 ....104 E3

Andover Medical Centre
HOLWY N7 ....85 F1

The Andrew Ewing Primary School
HEST TW5 ....134 E1

Anerley School
NRWD SE19 ....181 H4

Angel Centre
DART DA1 ....171 H1

Angerstein Business Park
GNWCH SE10 ....125 K4

Anglian Industrial Estate
BARK IG11 ....109 F3

Animal Cemetery
REDBR IG4 ....53 H6

Annemount School
EFNCH N2 ....65 G3

Annunciation RC Infant School
EDGW HA8 ....45 F4

The Annunciation RC Junior School
MLHL NW7 ....45 F2

Anson Primary School
CRICK NW2 ....82 B3

Ante Natal Clinic
EFNCH N2 ....48 A6

Antonys RC Primary School
WFD IG8 ....38 E6

Apex Hotel
MON EC3R 13 H5

Apex Industrial Estate
WLSDN NW10 ....99 H3

Apex Retail Park
FELT TW15 ....154 E2

Apollo Theatre
SOHO/SHAV W1D 10 C5

Apollo Victoria Theatre
PIM SW1V 16 A5

Apostolic Nuncio
WIM/MER SW19 ....159 F5

Applegarth Primary School
CROY/NA CR0 ....213 K4

Apsley House, The Wellington Museum
KTBR SW1X 15 G2

Aquarius Business Park
CRICK NW2 ....63 J5

Aquarius Golf Club
EDUL SE22 ....143 K6

Aragon Primary School
MRDN SM4 ....193 H4

Arcadia Shopping Centre
EA W5 ....97 K6

Arcadia University
BAY/PAD W2 ....101 F6

The Archbishop Lanfranc School
CROY/NA CR0 ....195 K3

Archbishop Michael Ramsey Technology College
CMBW SE5 ....142 C1

Archbishop Sumners CE Primary School
LBTH SE11 ....17 K7

Archbishop Tenisons CE School
CROY/NA CR0 ....212 B1

Archbishop Tenison's School
VX/NE SW8 ....122 A6

Archdale Business Centre
RYLN/HDSTN HA2 ....60 C6

Archdeacon Cambridge's CE Primary School
WHTN TW2 ....155 K4

Arches Business Centre
NWDGN UB2 ....114 E2

Arches Leisure Centre
GNWCH SE10 ....125 G6

Archgate Business Centre
NFNCH/WDSPK N12 ....33 G6

Architecture Association School of Architecture
RSQ WC1B 10 C2

Archway Business Centre
ARCH N19 ....84 D1

Archway Leisure Centre
ARCH N19 ....66 C6

Arena Estate
FSBYPK N4 ....67 H3

Argyle Primary School
STPAN WC1H 5 F5

Arklow Trading Estate
NWCR SE14 ....124 B6

Armourers & Braziers' Hall
LOTH EC2R 12 E3

Arndale Health Centre
WAND/EARL SW18 ....159 K1

Arnhem Wharf Primary School
POP/IOD E14 ....124 C3

Arnold House School
STJWD NW8 ....2 A2

Arnos Pool
FBAR/BDGN N11 ....48 D1

Arsenal FC (Emirates Stadium)
HOLWY N7 ....85 G2

Art School
BECK BR3 ....198 B2

Artsdepot
NFNCH/WDSPK N12 ....47 G1

The Arts Educational School
CHSWK W4 ....118 A4

Arts Theatre
LSQ/SEVD WC2H 10 D5

Ashbourne College
WBPTN SW10 ....120 B6

Ashburnham Primary School
WBPTN SW10 ....140 C1

Ashburton Community School
CROY/NA CR0 ....197 J4

Ashburton Primary School
CROY/NA CR0 ....197 J3

Ashby Mill School
CLAP SW4 ....141 K6

Ashfield Junior School
BUSH WD23 ....28 B2

Ashford Clinic
ASHF TW15 ....152 B5

Ashford High School
ASHF TW15 ....152 B5

Ashford Industrial Estate
ASHF TW15 ....153 F6

The Ashford & St Peters Hospital
STWL/WRAY TW19 ....152 B4

Ashford Sports Club
ASHF TW15 ....152 C3
STWL/WRAY TW19 ....152 C3

Ashgrove College
WALTH E17 ....51 J6

Ashgrove Trading Estate
BMLY BR1 ....183 G2

Ashleigh Commercial Estate
CHARL SE7 ....126 B4

Ashmead Primary School
BROCKY SE4 ....144 D3

Ashmole Centre
STHGT/OAK N14 ....34 C3

Ashmole Primary School
VX/NE SW8 ....122 A6

Ashmole School
STHGT/OAK N14 ....34 C3

Ashmount Primary School
ARCH N19 ....66 D4

Ashton House School
ISLW TW7 ....135 J2

Ashton Playing Fields Track
WFD IG8 ....53 J2

Aspen House School
LBTH SE11 ....122 C6

Aspen House Secondary & Primary School
BRXS/STRHM SW2 ....161 K3

Asquith Court School
HPTN TW12 ....173 G2
KTN/HRWW/WS HA3 ....61 J1

Asquith School
PEND EN3 ....24 E1

Assembly Rooms
SURB KT6 ....191 F1

Associated Newspapers
BERM/RHTH SE16 ....124 A3

Aston Clinic
NWMAL KT3 ....192 B1

Aston House School
EA W5 ....97 K5

Asylum Medical Centre
CEND/HSY/T N8 ....49 G6

Athelney Primary School
CAT SE6 ....164 D5

Athelstan House School
HPTN TW12 ....173 F4

Athenaeum Hotel
MYFR/PICC W1J 15 J1

Athena Medical Centre
CLPT E5 ....86 E2

Atherton Leisure Centre
SRTFD E15 ....88 D4

Athlone House Hospital
HGT N6 ....65 K5

Athlon Industrial Estate
ALP/SUD HA0 ....97 K1

Atkinson Morley Hospital
RYNPK SW20 ....176 E3

Atlantic House (Richmond American International University)
KENS W8 ....120 A3

Atlas Business Centre
CRICK NW2 ....63 K6

Atlas Transport Estate
BTSEA SW11 ....140 B3

Attlee Youth & Community Centre
WCHPL E1 ....13 K2

Auriol Junior School
HOR/WEW KT19 ....207 H2

Australia House
HOL/ALD WC2B 11 H4

Aveling Park School
WALTH E17 ....51 J5

Avenue House Museum
FNCH N3 ....46 D5

Avenue House School
WEA W13 ....97 K5

Avenue Industrial Estate
CHING E4 ....51 H2

Avenue Primary School
KIL/WHAMP NW6 ....82 C5
MNPK E12 ....89 J2

Avondale Park Primary School
NTGHL W11 ....100 B6

Avon House School
WFD IG8 ....38 E6

Avon Trading Estate
WKENS W14 ....119 J4

Axis Business Centre
SRTFD E15 ....87 K6

The Aylesham Centre
PECK SE15 ....143 H2

Ayloff Primary School
HCH RM12 ....93 K2

Aylward First & Middle Schools
STAN HA7 ....43 K1

Aylward School
UED N18 ....35 K6

Aylwin Secondary School
STHWK SE1 ....19 K6

BAA Heathrow Visitor Centre
HTHAIR TW6 ....132 E2

Babington House School
CHST BR7 ....184 E2

Back Care Clinic
WPK KT4 ....192 D5

Bacon's College
BERM/RHTH SE16 ....124 B1

Baden Powell House
SKENS SW7 ....120 B4

Bagnigge Hotel
KENS W8 ....120 B2

Bakers Hall
MON EC3R 13 H6

Balaam Leisure Centre
PLSTW E13 ....106 E3

Bales College
NKENS W10 ....100 B2

Balfour Business Centre
NWDGN UB2 ....114 C3

Balgowan Primary School
BECK BR3 ....182 B5

Balham Boys Preparatory Secondary School
BAL SW12 ....161 G2

Balham Girls Preparatory Secondary School
TOOT SW17 ....160 E5

Balham Health Centre
BAL SW12 ....161 G4

Balham Leisure Centre
TOOT SW17 ....161 F4

Balmoral Trading Estate
BARK IG11 ....109 F3

Baltic Exchange
HDTCH EC3A 13 H3

Bancrofts School
WFD IG8 ....38 E5

Bandon Hill Cemetery
WLGTN SM6 ....210 D3

Bandon Hill Primary School
WLGTN SM6 ....210 D4

Bangabandhu Primary School
BETH E2 ....104 E2

Bank of England Extension
CITYW EC2V 12 C4

Bank of England (& Museum)
LOTH EC2R 12 E4

Bankside Gallery
STHWK SE1 ....12 B6

Bankside Jetty
STHWK SE1 ....12 C6

Bankside Park Industrial Estate
BARK IG11 ....109 G2

Bannister Stadium
KTN/HRWW/WS HA3 ....42 C2

Bannockburn Primary School
WOOL/PLUM SE18 ....**128** A4
Banqueting House Whitehall
WHALL SW1A **16** E1
Barbara Speake Theatre
School
ACT W3 ....**99** G6
Barber Surgeons' Hall
BARB EC2Y **12** D2
Barbican Cinema
BARB EC2Y **12** C1
The Barbican
BARB EC2Y **12** C1
Barbican Theatre
BARB EC2Y **12** D1
Barclay J & I School
LEY E10 ....**70** B3
Barham Primary School
ALP/SUD HA0 ....**79** J4
Baring Primary School
LEE/GVPK SE12 ....**165** K2
Baring Road Medical Centre
BMLY BR1 ....**165** K4
Barkantine Clinic
POP/IOD E14 ....**124** D2
Barking Abbey
Comprehensive School
(Lower) *IL* IG1 ....**90** D3
Barking Abbey
Comprehensive School
(Upper) *BARK* IG11 ....**91** F4
Barking Abbey Industrial
Estate
BARK IG11 ....**90** B6
Barking Abbey Leisure Centre
BARK IG11 ....**91** G4
Barking Abbey School
BARK IG11 ....**91** F4
Barking College
ROMW/RG RM7 ....**75** F6
Barking Football Club
BARK IG11 ....**91** H3
Barking Hospital
BARK IG11 ....**91** F5
Barking Industrial Park
BARK IG11 ....**91** F6
Barking RUFC
DAGW RM9 ....**91** K6
Barkingside Cemetery
BARK/HLT IG6 ....**54** B6
Barkingside FC
BARK/HLT IG6 ....**72** D1
Barlby Primary School
NKENS W10 ....**100** B3
Barley Lane Primary School
GDMY/SEVK IG3 ....**73** G4
Barnabas Medical Centre
NTHLT UB5 ....**78** C4
Barn Croft Primary School
WALTH E17 ....**69** G3
Barnehurst Primary School
ERITH DA8 ....**149** K2
Barnehurst Public Golf Club
BXLYHN DA7 ....**150** A4
Barn Elms Athletics Track
BARN SW13 ....**138** E3
Barn Elms Water Sports
Centre
PUT/ROE SW15 ....**139** F3
Barnes Cray Primary School
DART DA1 ....**150** D5
Barnes Hospital
MORT/ESHN SW14 ....**138** B4
Barnes Primary School
BARN SW13 ....**138** B4
Barnes Sports Club
BARN SW13 ....**138** C2
Barnet College
BAR EN5 ....**20** C5
CDALE/KGS NW9 ....**45** H4
EBAR EN4 ....**33** K3
FBAR/BDGN N11 ....**33** K5
HDN NW4 ....**63** J3
NFNCH/WDSPK N12 ....**47** C1
Barnet Copthall Pool
HDN NW4 ....**45** K3
Barnet Copthall Stadium
HDN NW4 ....**46** A4
Barnet County Court
BAR EN5 ....**21** G5
FNCH N3 ....**46** E4
Barnet FC (Underhill)
BAR EN5 ....**20** E6
Barnet General Hospital
BAR EN5 ....**20** B5
Barnet Health Centre
BAR EN5 ....**20** E6
Barnet JMI School
BAR EN5 ....**20** D6
Barnet Hospital Chest Clinic
BAR EN5 ....**20** B5
Barnet Magistrates Court
BAR EN5 ....**20** C5
Barnet Museum
BAR EN5 ....**20** C5
Barnet Trading Estate
BAR EN5 ....**20** D2
Barnfield Primary School
EDGW HA8 ....**44** E4
Barnhill Community High
School
YEAD UB4 ....**95** F2
Barn Hotel
RSLP HA4 ....**58** C6
Barnsbury Complex
HOLWY N7 ....**85** G5
Barnsbury School for Girls
IS N1 ....**85** G4
Barons Court Theatre
WKENS W14 ....**119** H5
Barrett Industrial Park
BOW E3 ....**106** A3
Barrett Industrial Park
STHL UB1 ....**115** F1
Barrett Way Industrial
Estate
KTN/HRWW/WS HA3 ....**42** D6

Barrington Primary School
WELL DA16 ....**148** E3
Barrow Hedges Primary
School
CAR SM5 ....**209** J5
Barrow Hill Junior School
STJWD NW8 ....**2** C3
Barton House Health Centre
STNW/STAM N16 ....**85** K1
Barwell Business Park
CHSGTN KT9 ....**205** K5
Bassett House School
NKENS W10 ....**100** B5
Baston School
HAYES BR2 ....**200** A6
Bath Factory Estate
HNHL SE24 ....**162** D1
Battersea Arts Centre (BAC)
BTSEA SW11 ....**140** E4
Battersea Business Centre
BTSEA SW11 ....**141** F4
Battersea Dogs' Home
VX/NE SW8 ....**141** G1
Battersea Sports Centre
BTSEA SW11 ....**140** C4
Battersea Technology College
BTSEA SW11 ....**140** E2
Battersea Tutorial College
TOOT SW17 ....**161** H4
BBC Broadcasting House
REGST W1B **9** K2
BBC Media Village
SHB W12 ....**100** A6
BBC Studios
MV/WKIL W9 ....**101** F3
BBC Television Centre
SHB W12 ....**100** A6
BBC Worldwide
SHB W12 ....**100** A5
Beal High School
REDBR IG4 ....**53** J6
Beam Primary School
DAGE RM10 ....**110** E1
Beatrice Tate School
BETH E2 ....**104** D2
Beatrix Potter Primary School
WAND/EARL SW18 ....**160** B3
Beauclerc Infant School
SUN TW16 ....**172** B6
The Beaufort Hotel
CHEL SW3 ....**14** E5
Beaumont Primary School
LEY E10 ....**69** K4
Beaver College
BAY/PAD W2 ....**100** E6
The Beavers Community
Primary School
HSLWW TW4 ....**134** B4
Beaverwood School for Girls
CHST BR7 ....**185** K2
Beckenham Business Centre
BECK BR3 ....**182** D2
Beckenham Crematorium
BECK BR3 ....**181** K6
Beckenham CC
BECK BR3 ....**182** E3
Beckenham Hospital
BECK BR3 ....**182** C5
Beckenham Leisure Centre
BECK BR3 ....**182** B4
Beckenham Place Park
Golf Course
BECK BR3 ....**182** E2
Beckenham RFC
BECK BR3 ....**198** B1
Beckenham Town FC
BECK BR3 ....**198** D5
Becket Sports Centre
DART DA1 ....**171** F1
Beckford Primary School
KIL/WHAMP NW6 ....**82** D3
Beckmead School
BECK BR3 ....**198** D5
The Beck Theatre
HYS/HAR UB3 ....**94** D5
Beckton Ski Centre
EHAM E6 ....**108** A3
Beckton Special School
CAN/RD E16 ....**107** H4
Beckton Triangle Retail
Park
EHAM E6 ....**108** B2
Becontree Day Hospital
BCTR RM8 ....**74** A6
Becontree Primary School
BCTR RM8 ....**191** J1
Bective House Clinic
PUT/ROE SW15 ....**139** J3
Beddington Infants School
WLGTN SM6 ....**210** C1
Beddington Medical Centre
CROY/NA CR0 ....**210** E2
Beddington Park Primary
School
CROY/NA CR0 ....**210** D1
Beddington Trading Estate
CROY/NA CR0 ....**195** K5
Bedelsford School
KUT/HW KT1 ....**175** F6
Bedensfield Clinic
SCUP DA14 ....**187** F1
Bedfont Health Clinic
EBED/NFELT TW14 ....**153** H2
Bedfont Industrial Park
ASHF TW15 ....**153** G5
Bedfont J & I School
EBED/NFELT TW14 ....**153** H1
Bedfont Lakes Country Park
EBED/NFELT TW14 ....**153** F4
Bedfont Lakes Office Park
EBED/NFELT TW14 ....**153** F3
Bedford Hotel
RSQ WC1B **11** F1
Bedington Infant School
WLGTN SM6 ....**210** C2
Bedonwell Clinic
ABYW SE2 ....**129** F6

Bedonwell Medical Centre
BELV DA17 ....**129** G5
Bedonwell Primary School
BXLYHN DA7 ....**129** F6
Beecholme Primary School
MTCM CR4 ....**179** G4
Beechwood School
STRHM/NOR SW16 ....**161** K5
Beehive Preparatory School
REDBR IG4 ....**71** K1
The Beehive School
ARCH N19 ....**66** D4
Beis Hamedrash Elyon
GLDGN NW11 ....**64** C4
Beis Malka Girls School
STNW/STAM N16 ....**68** B5
Beis Rochel D'Satmar Girls
School
STNW/STAM N16 ....**68** A4
Beis Trana Girls School
STNW/STAM N16 ....**68** A4
Beis Yaakov Primary School
CDALE/KGS NW9 ....**45** F6
Bellamy's Wharf
BERM/RHTH SE16 ....**124** A1
Bellenden Primary School
PECK SE15 ....**143** H4
Bellenden Road Business
Centre
PECK SE15 ....**143** G3
Bellenden Road Retail Park
PECK SE15 ....**143** G2
Bellerbys College
DEPT SE8 ....**124** E6
Belleville Primary School
BTSEA SW11 ....**140** E6
Belle Vue Cinema
WLSDN NW10 ....**81** K5
Bell Industrial Estate
CHSWK W4 ....**117** K4
Bellingham Trading Estate
CAT SE6 ....**164** E5
Bell Lane JMI School
HDN NW4 ....**64** B1
Belmont First & Middle School
KTN/HRWW/WS HA3 ....**43** F5
Belmont J & I School
WDGN N22 ....**49** J6
Belmont (Mill Hill Preparatory
School)
MLHL NW7 ....**31** J5
Belmont Park School
LEY E10 ....**70** A3
Belmont Primary School
CHSWK W4 ....**118** A4
ERITH DA8 ....**149** H1
Belmore Primary School
YEAD UB4 ....**95** F2
Belvedere Day Hospital
WLSDN NW10 ....**81** J6
Belvedere Industrial Estate
BELV DA17 ....**130** A1
Belvedere Link Business Park
ERITH DA8 ....**129** K3
Belvedere Primary School
BELV DA17 ....**129** J4
Belvue Business Centre
NTHLT UB5 ....**78** B5
Belvue School
NTHLT UB5 ....**78** A6
Benedict House Preparatory
School
BFN/LL DA15 ....**168** A6
Benedict Primary School
MTCM CR4 ....**178** C6
Benhurst JMI School
RCH RM12 ....**93** H1
Ben Jonson Primary School
WCHPL E1 ....**105** G3
Bensham Manor School
THHTH CR7 ....**196** D2
Benson Primary School
CROY/NA CR0 ....**213** G1
Bentalls Shopping Centre
KUT/HW KT1 ....**174** E5
Bermondsey Town Hall
STHWK SE1 ....**19** G3
Bermondsey Trading Estate
BERM/RHTH SE16 ....**123** K4
Berrymede Infant School
ACT W3 ....**117** J2
Berrymede Junior School
ACT W3 ....**117** J2
Bertram House School
TOOT SW17 ....**161** F4
Bessemer Grange J & I School
HNHL SE24 ....**142** E6
Bessemer Park Industrial
Estate
BRXN/ST SW9 ....**142** C5
Best Western Bromley Court
Hotel
BMLY BR1 ....**183** H2
Best Western Cumberland
Hotel
HRW HA1 ....**61** F2

Best Western Hotel
HAMP NW3 ....**83** H5
Best Western Lodge Hotel
PUT/ROE SW15 ....**139** J6
Best Western Master Robert
Hotel
HEST TW5 ....**134** E2
Best Western Mostyn Hotel
MBLAR W1H **9** F4
Beth Jacob Grammar School
HDN NW4 ....**64** A1
Bethlem Royal Hospital
BECK BR3 ....**198** D4
Bethnal Green Technology
College
BETH E2 ....**7** K5
Beths Grammar School
BXLY DA5 ....**169** H1
Beulah Infant School
THHTH CR7 ....**180** D5
Beverley School
NWMAL KT3 ....**192** D2
Beverley Trading Estate
MRDN SM4 ....**193** G4
Bevington Primary School
NKENS W10 ....**100** C4
Bexley CC
BXLY DA5 ....**169** H3
Bexley College
BELV DA17 ....**129** K4
Bexley Grammar School
WELL DA16 ....**148** C5
Bexleyheath Centre
BXLYHS DA6 ....**149** F5
Bexleyheath Golf Club
BXLYHS DA6 ....**149** F6
Bexleyheath Marriott Hotel
BXLYHS DA6 ....**149** J5
Bexleyheath School
BXLYHN DA7 ....**149** G4
Bexley RFC
BXLY DA5 ....**169** H2
BFI London IMAX Cinema
STHWK SE1 ....**17** H1
Bickley Park CC
BMLY BR1 ....**184** D5
Bickley Park Preparatory
School
BMLY BR1 ....**184** C6
Bickley Primary School
BMLY BR1 ....**184** D5
Big Ben
WHALL SW1A **17** F3
Bigland Green Primary School
WCHPL E1 ....**104** D5
Billingsgate Fish Market
POP/IOD E14 ....**124** E1
Bingham Hotel
TWK TW1 ....**156** E1
Birchmere Business Park
THMD SE28 ....**128** B2
Birchwood Park Golf Course
RDART DA2 ....**187** K3
Bird College
SCUP DA14 ....**168** B5
Birkbeck College
GWRST WC1E **4** D7
RSQ WC1B **10** D2
Birkbeck Primary School
SCUP DA14 ....**168** C5
Bishop Challoner Catholic
Collegiate School
WCHPL E1 ....**104** E6
Bishop Challoner Girls
School
WCHPL E1 ....**104** C6
Bishop Challoner School
HAYES BR2 ....**183** G5
Bishop Douglas RC School
EFNCH N2 ....**47** G5
Bishop Gilpin Primary School
WIM/MER SW19 ....**177** J1
Bishop John Robinson CE
Primary School
THMD SE28 ....**109** H6
Bishop Justus CE (Secondary)
School
HAYES BR2 ....**200** D4
Bishop Perrin CE Primary
School
WHTN TW2 ....**155** G2
Bishop Ramsey CE School
RSLP HA4 ....**58** D4
Bishop Ramsey CE School
(Upper)
RSLP HA4 ....**58** E4
Bishopsgate Institute
LVPST EC2M **13** H2
Bishop Stopfords School
EN EN1 ....**24** C3
Bishop Thomas Grant School
STRHM/NOR SW16 ....**180** A1
Bishop Winnington Ingram
CE Primary School
RSLP HA4 ....**58** B4
Bittacy Business Centre
MLHL NW7 ....**46** C2
Blackburn Trading Estate
STWL/WRAY TW19 ....**152** C1
Blackfen Medical Centre
BFN/LL DA15 ....**148** A6
Blackfen School for Girls
BFN/LL DA15 ....**168** C1
Blackfriars Millennium Pier
EMB EC4Y **11** K5
Blackfriars Pier
BLKFR EC4V **12** B5
Blackheath Bluecoat CE
School
BKHTH/KID SE3 ....**146** A1
Blackheath Business Estate
BKHTH/KID SE3 ....**145** F2
Blackheath High School GDST
BKHTH/KID SE3 ....**145** J5

Blackheath High Senior
School
BKHTH/KID SE3 ....**145** K1
Blackheath Hospital
BKHTH/KID SE3 ....**145** J4
Blackheath Preparatory
School
BKHTH/KID SE3 ....**145** K2
Blackheath RFC
(The Rectory Field)
BKHTH/KID SE3 ....**146** A1
Blackwall Trading Estate
POP/IOD E14 ....**106** B4
Blair Peach Primary School
STHL UB1 ....**114** C1
Blake College
GTPST W1W **10** A1
Blanche Nevile School
MUSWH N10 ....**48** A6
Blenheim Business Centre
MTCM CR4 ....**178** E4
Blenheim Primary School
ORP BR6 ....**202** E6
Blenheim Shopping Centre
PGE/AN SE20 ....**181** K3
Blessed Dominic RC Primary
School
CDALE/KGS NW9 ....**45** G3
Blessed Sacrament RC
Primary School
IS N1 ....**5** F1
Blood Transfusion Centre
EDGW HA8 ....**44** D3
Bloomfield Clinic Guys
STHWK SE1 ....**19** F2
Bloomsbury College
FUL/PGN SW6 ....**139** K1
Bloomsbury Theatre
GWRST WC1E **4** C6
Blossom House School
RYNPK SW20 ....**177** F3
Blossoms Inn Medical
Centre
BLKFR EC4V **12** D5
Blue Gate Fields Primary
School
WCHPL E1 ....**104** E6
The Blue School
ISLW TW7 ....**136** B4
Blyth's Wharf
POP/IOD E14 ....**105** G6
BMI Medical Centre
CAVSQ/HST W1G **9** H2
Bnois Jerusalem School
STNW/STAM N16 ....**67** K4
The Bob Hope Theatre
ELTH/MOT SE9 ....**166** E1
Bodywise Natural Health
Centre
BETH E2 ....**104** E2
Boleyn Cinema
EHAM E6 ....**107** H1
Bolingbroke Hospital
BTSEA SW11 ....**140** D6
Bolingbroke Primary School
BTSEA SW11 ....**140** C2
Bond First School
MTCM CR4 ....**178** E5
Bond Primary School
MTCM CR4 ....**178** E5
Bonner Primary School
BETH E2 ....**105** F1
Bonneville Primary School
CLAP SW4 ....**161** H1
Bonnington Hotel
RSQ WC1B **11** F1
Bonus Pastor Roman Catholic
School
BMLY BR1 ....**165** G6
Boomes Industrial Estate
RAIN RM13 ....**111** H3
Booster Cushion Theatre
WDGN N22 ....**49** F5
Borough Market
STHWK SE1 ....**12** E7
Boston Business Park
HNWL W7 ....**115** K3
Boston University
HYS/HAR UB3 ....**113** K5
Botwell RC Primary School
HYS/HAR UB3 ....**113** J2
Boundary Business Park
MTCM CR4 ....**178** C5
Bounds Green Health Centre
FBAR/BDGN N11 ....**48** D3
Bounds Green Industrial
Estate
FBAR/BDGN N11 ....**48** B2
Bounds Green Primary
School
FBAR/BDGN N11 ....**48** E3
Bourne CP School
RSLP HA4 ....**77** G3
Bourne Hall Health Centre
EW KT17 ....**207** H6
Bourne Hall Museum
EW KT17 ....**207** H6
Bourne Road Industrial Park
DART DA1 ....**150** A6
Bournemede Sports Club
STHGT/OAK N14 ....**34** E3
Bousfield Primary School
WBPTN SW10 ....**120** B6
Boutcher CE Primary School
STHWK SE1 ....**19** J5
Bowater House
SKENS SW7 ....**14** E3
Bow County Court
SRTFD E15 ....**88** C4
Bowden House Clinic
HRW HA1 ....**60** E6
Bower Park School
ROM RM1 ....**57** G2
Bowes Primary School
FBAR/BDGN N11 ....**48** D1
Bowes Road Clinic
FBAR/BDGN N11 ....**48** D1

Bow Industrial Park
SRTFD E15 ....87 J5
Bowling Club
EA W5 ....97 J6
Bowls Club
PUT/ROE SW15 ....139 F3
STRHM/NOR SW16 ....161 K4
Bowman Trading Estate
CDALE/KGS NW9 ....44 C6
Bow Secondary School
BOW E3 ....105 J1
Bow Triangle Business Centre
BOW E3 ....105 J3
Boxgrove Primary School
ABYW SE2 ....128 D3
Boys' Club
EDGW HA8 ....44 C3
BPP Law School
HHOL WC1V 11 G2
Brackenbury Health Centre
HMSMTH W6 ....118 E3
Brackenbury Primary School
HMSMTH W6 ....118 E3
Bracken Industrial Estate
BARK/HLT IG6 ....55 F3
Bracton Centre
RDART DA2 ....170 C4
Brady Recreation Centre
WCHPL E1 ....104 C4
Braeside Senior School
BKHH IG9 ....39 F3
Braincroft Primary School
CRICK NW2 ....81 H1
Braintree Road Industrial Estate
RSLP HA4 ....77 F2
Bramah's Tea & Coffee Museum
STHWK SE1 ....18 D1
Brampton College
HDN NW4 ....64 A1
Brampton Manor School
EHAM E6 ....107 H3
Brampton Primary School
BXLYHN DA7 ....148 E3
EHAM E6 ....107 J2
Brandlehow Primary School
PUT/ROE SW15 ....139 J5
Branollys Health Centre
PLSTW E13 ....106 E3
Breakspear Crematorium
RSLP HA4 ....58 A2
Breaside Preparatory School
BMLY BR1 ....184 B4
Brecknock Primary School
HOLWY N7 ....84 D4
Bredinghurst School
PECK SE15 ....143 K5
Brent Adult College
WLSDN NW10 ....81 F6
Brent Arts Council
CRICK NW2 ....81 J1
Brent Child & Family Clinic
WLSDN NW10 ....81 H3
Brent Cross Shopping Centre
HDN NW4 ....64 A4
Brentfield Medical Centre
WLSDN NW10 ....81 F4
Brentfield Primary School
WLSDN NW10 ....81 F4
Brentford Business Centre
BTFD TW8 ....136 D1
Brentford County Court
BTFD TW8 ....136 E1
Brentford FC London Broncos RLFC (Griffin Park)
BTFD TW8 ....116 E6
Brentford Fountain Leisure Centre
BTFD TW8 ....117 G5
Brentford Health Centre
BTFD TW8 ....116 D6
Brentford School for Girls
BTFD TW8 ....116 E6
Brent Knoll School
FSTH SE23 ....164 A5
Brent Magistrates Court House
WLSDN NW10 ....81 G4
Brent Park Industrial Estate
NWDGN UB2 ....114 A3
Brentside First School
HNWL W7 ....96 E4
Brentside High School
HNWL W7 ....96 E3
Brentside Primary School
HNWL W7 ....96 E3
Brent Trading Estate
WLSDN NW10 ....81 G3
Brent Valley Golf Club
HNWL W7 ....96 E6
Brentwaters Business Park
BTFD TW8 ....136 D1
Brewers' Hall
CITYW EC2V 12 D2
Brewery Industrial Estate
IS N1 ....6 C3
Brewery Mews Business Centre
ISLW TW7 ....136 A4
The Brewery
ROMW/RG RM7 ....75 G3
Brick Lane Music Hall
EMB E16 ....126 C1
FSBYE EC1V 7 H5
Brick Lane Music House
WCHPL E1 ....7 K7
Bricklayer Arms Industrial Estate
STHWK SE1 ....19 J7
The Bridewell Theatre
EMB EC4Y 12 A4
The Bridge Business Centre
NWDGN UB2 ....115 F2
Bridge Lane Theatre
BTSEA SW11 ....140 D2

The Bridge Leisure Centre
SYD SE26 ....182 C1
Bridge Park Business & Leisure Centre
WLSDN NW10 ....80 D5
The Bridge School
ARCH N19 ....66 C6
CLKNW EC1R 6 A6
HOLWY N7 ....84 D4
Brigham Young University
BAY/PAD W2 ....100 E6
Bright Sparks Montessori School
WKENS W14 ....119 G2
Brigstock Medical Centre
THHTH CR7 ....196 C2
Brimsdown Industrial Estate
PEND EN3 ....24 E3
Brimsdown Primary School
PEND EN3 ....25 F4
Brindishe Primary School
LEE/GVPK SE12 ....145 J6
Britain & London Visitor Centre
STJS SW1Y 10 C7
Britannia Business Centre
CRICK NW2 ....82 B2
Britannia Leisure Centre
IS N1 ....7 F1
Britannia Sports Ground
WALTH E17 ....51 J3
Britannia Village Primary School
CAN/RD E16 ....126 A1
British Cartoon Centre
BMSBY WC1N 5 F1
British College of Osteopathy
HAMP NW3 ....83 G4
British Dental Association
CAVSQ/HST W1G 9 J2
The British Hernia Centre
HDN NW4 ....63 K2
British Library
CAMTN NW1 ....4 D4
British Library Newspaper Library
CDALE/KGS NW9 ....45 G6
British Medical Association
STPAN WC1H 4 D6
British Museum
RSQ WC1B 10 E2
British Telecom Tower
GTPST W1W 10 A1
BRIT School for Performing Arts
CROY/NA CR0 ....196 E6
Brittons School Technology College
RAIN RM13 ....93 H5
Brixton Academy
BRXN/ST SW9 ....142 B4
Brixton Recreation Centre
BRXN/ST SW9 ....142 B4
Broadfields Primary School
EDGW HA8 ....30 C4
Broadgate
LVPST EC2M 13 F1
Broadgate Ice Arena
LVPST EC2M 13 F2
Broadhurst School
KIL/WHAMP NW6 ....83 G5
Broadmead J & I School
EDGW HA8 ....44 C2
Broadwalk Shopping Centre
EDGW HA8 ....44 C2
Broadwater Farm Primary School
TOTM N17 ....49 K5
Broadwater Primary School
TOOT SW17 ....160 C6
Broadway Clinic
EDGW HA8 ....44 D4
Broadway Retail Park
CRICK NW2 ....82 B2
Broadway Shopping Centre
BXLYHS DA6 ....149 H5
HMSMTH W6 ....119 F5
Broadway Square Shopping Centre
BXLYHS DA6 ....149 H5
Broadway Squash & Fitness Centre
HMSMTH W6 ....119 F4
Brocklebank Health Centre
WAND/EARL SW18 ....160 A2
Brocklebank Industrial Estate
GNWCH SE10 ....125 K4
Brockley Cross Business Centre
BROCKY SE4 ....144 B4
Brockley Primary School
BROCKY SE4 ....144 C6
Brockwell Lido
HNHL SE24 ....162 C1
Bromet Primary School
OXHEY WD19 ....27 H2
Bromley Cemetery
BMLY BR1 ....183 J3
Bromley College of Further & Higher Education
HAYES BR2 ....200 C3
BMLY BR1 ....183 J4
Bromley County Court
BMLY BR1 ....183 K4
Bromley FC
HAYES BR2 ....200 A2
Bromley Golf Club
HAYES BR2 ....200 D4
Bromley High School GDST
BMLY BR1 ....201 F1
Bromley Industrial Centre
BMLY BR1 ....184 C6
Bromley Mall Indoor Market
BMLY BR1 ....183 K5
Bromley Museum
ORP BR6 ....202 C4

Bromley Road Infant School
BECK BR3 ....182 E4
Bromley Road Retail Park
CAT SE6 ....164 E4
Bromley Ski Centre
STMC/STPC BR5 ....186 E4
Bromley Tennis Centre
ORP BR6 ....216 D1
Brompton Cemetery
WBPTN SW10 ....120 A6
Brompton Medical Centre
ECT SW5 ....120 A5
Brompton Oratory
SKENS SW7 ....14 C5
Bromyard Leisure Centre
ACT W3 ....118 B1
Brondesbury College for Boys
KIL/WHAMP NW6 ....82 B5
Brook Community Primary School
HACK E8 ....86 C3
Brooke Trading Estate
ROM RM1 ....75 H4
Brookfield Primary School
CHEAM SM3 ....193 H5
HGT N6 ....66 B6
Brook House FC
YEAD UB4 ....94 D2
Brook Industrial Estate
YEAD UB4 ....114 C1
Brook Industrial Park
STMC/STPC BR5 ....202 D1
Brooklands Primary School
GLDGN NW11 ....65 F1
Brooklands Primary School
BKHTH/KID SE3 ....145 K4
Brook Lane Business Centre
BTFD TW8 ....116 E5
Brookmarsh Trading Estate
DEPT SE8 ....144 E1
Brookmead Industrial Estate
CROY/NA CR0 ....195 H3
Brookside Primary School
YEAD UB4 ....95 G2
Broomfield House School
RCH/KEW TW9 ....137 G2
Broomfield School
FBAR/BDGN N11 ....48 D1
Broomsleigh Business Park
SYD SE26 ....182 C1
Broomwood Hall Lower School
BAL SW12 ....160 E1
STRHM/NOR SW16 ....161 J1
Brothwick Wharf
DEPT SE8 ....124 D5
Brownlow Medical Centre
FBAR/BDGN N11 ....48 E1
Brown's Hotel
MYFR/PICC W1J 9 K6
Bruce Castle Museum
TOTM N17 ....50 A4
Bruce Grove Primary School
TOTM N17 ....50 B5
Brunei Gallery
STPAN WC1H 4 D7
Brunel Engine House
BERM/RHTH SE16 ....123 K2
Brunel University
GLDGN NW11 ....64 B3
ISLW TW7 ....135 K1
TWK TW1 ....156 C5
Brunel University (Osterley Campus) Track
ISLW TW7 ....135 K1
Brunswick Health Centre
FBAR/BDGN N11 ....34 A4
Brunswick Housing & Shopping Centre
BMSBY WC1N 5 F6
Brunswick Industrial Park
FBAR/BDGN N11 ....34 B6
Brunswick Medical Centre
BMSBY WC1N 4 C6
Brunswick Park JMI School
STHGT/OAK N14 ....34 A3
Brunswick Park Primary School
CMBW SE5 ....142 E1
BT Centre
STBT EC1A 12 C3
Buckhurst Hill FC
BKHH IG9 ....39 J3
Buckhurst Hill Primary School
BKHH IG9 ....39 J4
Buckingham College Preparatory School
PIN HA5 ....59 K3
Buckingham College School
HRW HA1 ....60 E2
Buckingham Palace
WHALL SW1A 15 K3
Buckingham Primary School
HPTN TW12 ....172 E1
Buckingham Road Cemetery
IL IG1 ....72 D6
Buckland Infant School
CHSGTN KT9 ....206 B3
Building Centre
GWRST WC1E 10 C2
Building Crafts College
SRTFD E15 ....88 A5
Bullers Wood School
CHST BR7 ....184 E4
Bullsbridge Industrial Estate
NWDGN UB2 ....114 A4
The Bull Theatre
BAR EN5 ....20 D5
BUPA Roding Hospital
REDBR IG4 ....53 H6
Burbage School
IS N1 ....7 G2
Burdett Coutts CE Primary School
WEST SW1P 16 C5
Burgess Business Park
CMBW SE5 ....142 E1

Burgess Park Tennis Centre
CMBW SE5 ....122 D6
Burlington Danes School
SHB W12 ....99 K5
Burlington Infant School
NWMAL KT3 ....192 C1
Burnham Trading Estate
DART DA1 ....151 G5
Burnhill Business Centre
BECK BR3 ....182 D5
Burnley Road Clinic
WLSDN NW10 ....81 J3
Burnside Industrial Estate
BARK/HLT IG6 ....55 H1
Burnt Ash Primary School
BMLY BR1 ....183 K1
Burnt Oak Junior School
BFN/LL DA15 ....168 B3
Burntwood School
TOOT SW17 ....160 C4
Bursted Wood Primary School
BXLYHN DA7 ....149 J3
Burwell Industrial Estate
LEY E10 ....69 G5
Burwood School
BELMT SM2 ....202 E6
Bushey Golf & Country Club
BUSH WD23 ....28 A1
Bushey Hall School
BUSH WD23 ....27 K1
Bushey Health Centre
BUSH WD23 ....27 K1
Bushey Heath Primary School
BUSH WD23 ....28 D3
Bushey Museum & Art Gallery
BUSH WD23 ....28 A1
Bush Hill Park Golf Club
WCHMN N21 ....23 J6
Bush Hill Park Medical Centre
EN N1 ....36 B1
Bush Hill Park Primary School
EN N1 ....24 C6
Bush House (BBC)
HOL/ALD WC2D 11 G4
Bush Industrial Estate
ARCH N19 ....84 C1
WLSDN NW10 ....99 F3
The Business Academy Bexley
ERITHM DA18 ....129 F2
The Business Design Centre
IS N1 ....5 K1
Business Training & Solutions
CDALE/KGS NW9 ....45 H4
Bute House Preparatory School for Girls
HMSMTH W6 ....119 F4
Butlers Wharf
STHWK SE1 ....19 K1
Butler's Wharf Business Centre
STHWK SE1 ....19 K2
Butler's Wharf Pier
STHWK SE1 ....19 K1
Butterfly House
ISLW TW7 ....136 C2
Butterfly Sports Club
ELTH/MOT SE9 ....167 G1
Buxlow Preparatory School
WBLY HA9 ....80 A1
Buzzard Creek Industrial Estate
BARK IG11 ....109 F2
BARK IG11 ....109 F4
Byam Shaw School of Art
ARCH N19 ....66 C6
Byfleet Industrial Estate
WATW WD18 ....26 A3
Bygrove Primary School
POP/IOD E14 ....105 K5
Byron Court Primary School
ALP/SUD HA0 ....61 J6
Cabot Place
POP/IOD E14 ....124 D1
Cadogan Pier
CHEL SW3 ....120 D6
Caledonian Market
STHWK SE1 ....19 H4
Cally Pool
IS N1 ....85 F6
Calverton Primary School
CAN/RD E16 ....107 H5
Cambell Primary School
DAGW RM9 ....91 K5
Camberwell Business Centre
CMBW SE5 ....142 E1
Camberwell College of Arts
CMBW SE5 ....143 F2
Camberwell Leisure Centre
CMBW SE5 ....142 E2
Camberwell New Cemetery
PECK SE15 ....164 A1
Camberwell Trading Estate
CMBW SE5 ....142 C3
Cambridge Park Bowling & Sports Club
TWK TW1 ....156 D1
Cambridge School
HMSMTH W6 ....118 E4
Cambridge Theatre
LSQ/SEVD WC2H 10 E4
Camden Arts Centre
HAMP NW3 ....83 F3
Camden House Clinic
BKHTH/KID SE3 ....145 H3
Camden Junior School
CAR SM5 ....209 K2
Camden Market
CAMTN NW1 ....84 A5
Camden Mews Day Hospital
CAMTN NW1 ....84 C4
Camden People's Theatre
CAMTN NW1 ....4 A5
Camden School for Girls
KTTN NW5 ....84 C4
Camden Theatre
CAMTN NW1 ....4 A2

Camden Town Hall & St Pancras Library
CAMTN NW1 ....4 E4
Cameron Primary School
PECK SE15 ....143 J1
Cameron House School
CHEL SW3 ....120 C6
Camperdown House
WCHPL E1 ....13 K4
Campion House College
ISLW TW7 ....135 J1
Campsbourne J & I School
CEND/HSY/T N8 ....48 E6
Canada House
STJS SW1Y 10 D7
Canada House Business Centre
RSLP HA4 ....59 G5
Canada Place
POP/IOD E14 ....124 D1
Canada Square
POP/IOD E14 ....124 E1
Canada Water Retail Park
BERM/RHTH SE16 ....124 A3
Canada Wharf Museum
BERM/RHTH SE16 ....124 C1
Canal Cafe Theatre
BAY/PAD W2 ....101 G4
Canary Riverside
BERM/RHTH SE16 ....124 C1
Canary Wharf Pier
POP/IOD E14 ....124 C1
Canberra Primary School
SHB W12 ....99 K6
Canbury Business Centre
KUTN/CMB KT2 ....175 F4
Canbury 2000 Business Park
KUTN/CMB KT2 ....175 F4
Canbury Medical Centre
KUTN/CMB KT2 ....175 G4
Canbury School
KUTN/CMB KT2 ....175 J2
Cann Hall Primary School
WAN E11 ....88 D2
Cannizaro House Hotel
WIM/MER SW19 ....177 F2
Cannon Hill Clinic
STHGT/OAK N14 ....34 E5
Cannon Lane Primary School
PIN HA5 ....59 H3
Cannon Sports Club
CANST EC4R 12 D5
Cannon Trading Estate
WBLY HA9 ....80 D2
Cannon Wharf Business Centre
DEPT SE8 ....124 B4
Cannon Workshops
POP/IOD E14 ....105 J6
Canon Barnett Primary School
WCHPL E1 ....13 K3
Canonbury Business Centre
IS N1 ....85 J6
Canonbury Primary School
IS N1 ....85 H4
Canon Palmer RC High School
IL IG1 ....72 C6
Canons High School
EDGW HA8 ....44 B5
The Canons Leisure Centre
MTCM CR4 ....194 E1
Canterbury Industrial Estate
NWCR SE14 ....124 A6
Cantium Retail Park
STHWK SE1 ....123 H6
Capital Business Centre
ALP/SUD HA0 ....97 K1
MTCM CR4 ....194 E2
SAND/SEL CR2 ....211 K4
Capital City Academy
WLSDN NW10 ....81 K6
The Capital Hotel
CHEL SW3 ....14 E3
Capital Industrial Estate
BELV DA17 ....129 J4
BELV DA17 ....129 K1
Capital Radio
LSQ/SEVD WC2H 10 D4
Capital Wharf
WAP E1W 123 H1
Capitol Industrial Park
CDALE/KGS NW9 ....44 C6
Caplan Estate
MTCM CR4 ....179 F4
Cardiff Road Industrial Estate
WATW WD18 ....27 F1
Cardinal Hinsley High School
WLSDN NW10 ....81 J6
Cardinal Pole RC School
HOM E9 ....87 G4
Cardinal Pole RC Secondary Lower School
HOM E9 ....87 F5
Cardinal Road Infant School
FELT TW13 ....154 A3
The Cardinal Vaughan Memorial School
WKENS W14 ....119 H2
Cardinal Wiseman RC School Technology and Art College
GFD/PVL UB6 ....97 G1
Cardwell Primary School
WOOL/PLUM SE18 ....126 E4
Carew Manor School
WLGTN SM6 ....210 D1
Carlisle Infant School
HPTN TW12 ....173 G2
Carlton House
STJS SW1Y 16 C1
The Carlton Mitre Hotel
E/WMO/HCT KT8 ....173 K6
Carlton Primary School
KTTN NW5 ....84 A3
Carlton Vale Infant School
MV/WKIL W9 ....100 D2

Carlyle's House (NT)
CHEL SW3 ....120 D6
Carnwath Road Industrial
Estate
FUL/PGN SW6 ....140 A4
Carpenders Park Cemetery
OXHEY WD19 ....27 K6
Carpenters Business Park
SRTFD E15 ....87 J4
Carpenters' Hall
OBST EC2N 13 F2
Carpenters Primary School
SRTFD E15 ....88 A6
Carshalton AFC
SUT SM1 ....209 J1
Carshalton College of
Further Education
CAR SM5 ....209 K1
Carshalton High School
for Boys
CAR SM5 ....194 C6
Carshalton High School
for Girls
CAR SM5 ....209 J1
Carshalton War Memorial
Hospital
CAR SM5 ....209 K3
Carterhatch Primary School
EN EN1 ....24 D2
Caryl Thomas Clinic
HRW HA1 ....60 E1
The Cassel Hospital
RCHPK/HAM TW10 ....156 E6
Cassidy Medical Centre
FUL/PGN SW6 ....139 K1
Castilion Primary School
THMD SE28 ....109 J5
Castlebar Special School
WEA W13 ....97 G4
Castlecombe Primary School
ELTH/MOT SE9 ....184 D1
Castle Hill Primary School
CROY/NA CRO 214 A4
Castle Industrial Estate
WALW SE17 ....18 C6
Casualty Plus' Clinic
BTFD TW8 ....116 D5
Caterham High School
CLAY IG5 ....53 K5
Catford Cricket & Sports
Club
CAT SE6 ....164 E3
Catford Cyphers CC
CAT SE6 ....164 C4
Catford Girls School
CAT SE6 ....165 G5
Catford Trading Estate
CAT SE6 ....164 E4
Catford Wanderers Sports
Club
CAT SE6 ....165 F6
Cathall Leisure Centre
WAN E11 ....88 B1
Cathedral School of St Saviour
& St Mary Overie
STHWK SE1 ....18 D1
Cator Park School for Girls
BECK BR3 ....182 B3
Cavendish College
FITZ W1T 10 C1
Cavendish Hotel
STJS SW1Y 10 B7
Cavendish Primary School
CHSWK W4 ....138 B1
Cavendish School
BERM/RHTH SE16 ....123 K4
The Cavendish School
CAMTN NW1 ....84 B6
Cavendish Special School
HNWL W7 ....97 F5
Caxton Hall
STJSPK SW1H 16 C4
Caxton Trading Estate
HYS/HAR UB3 ....113 H2
Cayley Primary School
WCHPL E1 ....105 G4
Cecil Park Clinic
PIN HA5 ....59 J1
The Cedar School
FSTGT E7 ....89 G4
Cedars First & Middle School
KTN/HRWW/WS HA3 ....42 C4
The Cedars Primary School
HEST TW5 ....133 K1
Cedar Way Industrial Estate
CAMTN NW1 ....84 D5
Cenotaph
WHALL SW1A 16 E2
Centaurs Business Centre
ISLW TW7 ....116 B6
Centaurs RFC
ISLW TW7 ....116 A6
Central Business Centre
WLSDN NW10 ....81 G3
Central Criminal Court
STP EC4M 12 A3
Centrale Shopping Centre
CROY/NA CRO 196 D6
Central Foundation Boys
School
SDTCH EC2A 7 F6
Central Foundation Girls
School (Lower)
BOW E3 ....105 G2
Central Foundation Girls
School (Upper)
BOW E3 ....105 H2
Central Hall
STJSPK SW1H 16 D3
Central Hendon Clinic
HDN NW4 ....63 K1
Central London County Court
CAVSO/HST W1G J7
Central London Golf Club
TOOT SW17 ....160 C4
Central London Markets
STBT EC1A 12 A2

Central Medical Centre
MRDN SM4 ....194 A1
Central Middlesex Hospital
WLSDN NW10 ....98 E2
Central Park Arena
DART DA1 ....171 H3
Central Park Primary School
EHAM E6 ....107 H1
Central St Martins College of
Art & Design
RSQ WC1B 11 G2
Central School of Ballet
CLKNW EC1R 5 K7
Central School of Fashion
GTPST W1W 10 A7
Central School of Speech
& Drama
HAMP NW3 ....83 H5
Central Square Shopping
Centre
WBLY HA9 ....80 A4
Centre Court Shopping
Centre
WIM/MER SW19 ....177 J2
Centre Point
LSQ/SEVD WC2H 10 D3
Chace Community School
EN EN1 ....24 A2
The Chadwell Heath
Foundation School
CHDH RM6 ....73 H3
Chadwell Heath Industrial
Park
BCTR RM8 ....74 A5
Chadwell Heath Leisure
School
CHDH RM6 ....73 K3
Chadwell Infant & Primary
School
CHDH RM6 ....73 J4
Chaffinch Business Park
BECK BR3 ....182 A6
Chailey Industrial Estate
HYS/HAR UB3 ....113 K2
Chalcot School
CAMTN NW1 ....84 B4
Chalgrove Primary School
FNCH N3 ....46 C6
Chalkhill Primary School
WBLY HA9 ....80 D1
The Chamberlain Hotel
TWRH EC3N 13 J5
Chambers Business Park
WDR/YW UB7 ....112 D6
Chambers Wharf
BERM/RHTH SE16 ....123 H2
Chandlers Field Primary
School
E/WMO/HCT KT8 ....189 F2
Chandos Business Centre
WLGTN SM6 ....210 C4
Channelsea Business Centre
SRTFD E15 ....106 B1
Channing School
HGT N6 ....66 B5
Chapel End Infant School
WALTH E17 ....51 K4
Chapel End Junior School
WALTH E17 ....51 K4
Chapman Park Industrial
Estate
WLSDN NW10 ....81 H4
Charing Cross Hospital
HMSMTH W6 ....119 G6
The Charles Dickens Museum
BMSBY WC1N 5 G7
Charles Dickens Primary
School
STHWK SE1 ....18 C3
Charles Edward Brooke
School (Lower School)
CMBW SE5 ....142 C2
Charles Edward Brooke
School (Upper School)
BRXN/ST SW9 ....142 C2
Charlotte Sharman Primary
School
LBTH SE11 ....18 A5
Charlotte Turner Primary
School
DEPT SE8 ....124 D6
Charlton Athletic FC
(The Valley)
CHARL SE7 ....126 B5
Charlton Health & Fitness
Centre
CHARL SE7 ....126 B5
Charlton House
CHARL SE7 ....126 C6
Charlton Manor Junior
School
CHARL SE7 ....146 C2
Charlton RFC
ELTH/MOT SE9 ....167 G2
Charlton School
CHARL SE7 ....126 D6
Charrington Bowl
SURB KT6 ....191 J6
Charville Primary School
YEAD UB4 ....94 C1
Charter Clinic
CHEL SW3 ....120 E5
Charterhouse
CLKNW EC1R 6 A7
Charteris Road Sports Centre
KIL/WHAMP NW6 ....82 D6
Cherner Nightingale Hospital
& Counselling Centre
CAMTN NW1 ....8 D1
The Charter School
HNHL SE24 ....142 E6
Chartwell Business Centre
BMLY BR1 ....184 D6
Chase Bridge Primary School
WHTN TW2 ....155 K1

Chase Farm Hospital
ENC/FH EN2 ....23 G1
Chase Lane J & I School
CHING E4 ....37 H6
Chase Lane Primary School
CHING E4 ....37 K6
Chase Road Trading Estate
WLSDN NW10 ....99 F3
Chase Side Primary School
ENC/FH EN2 ....23 J3
Chaseville Clinic
WCHMH N21 ....35 F1
Chatsworth Infant School
BFN/LL DA15 ....168 B3
Chatsworth J & I School
HSLW TW3 ....135 H5
Chaucer Clinic
NWDGN UB2 ....115 J2
Cheam Common J & I School
WPK KT4 ....192 E6
Cheam Fields Primary School
CHEAM SM3 ....208 C3
Cheam High School
CHEAM SM3 ....208 C2
Cheam Leisure Centre
CHEAM SM3 ....208 B2
Cheam Park Farm Junior
School
CHEAM SM3 ....208 C1
Cheam Sports Club
CHEAM SM3 ....208 C5
Chelsea Barracks
BCVA SW1W 121 F5
Chelsea Bridge Business
Centre
VX/NE SW8 ....141 G1
Chelsea Centre & Theatre
WBPTN SW10 ....140 B1
Chelsea Cinema
CHEL SW3 ....120 D5
The Chelsea Club Leisure
Centre
FUL/PGN SW6 ....120 A6
Chelsea College of Art &
Design
CHEL SW3 ....120 D5
FUL/PGN SW6 ....140 A4
SHB W12 ....118 E2
WEST SW1P 121 K5
Chelsea FC
(Stamford Bridge)
FUL/PGN SW6 ....140 A1
Chelsea Fields Industrial
Estate
WIM/MER SW19 ....178 C4
Chelsea Leisure Centre
CHEL SW3 ....120 D5
Chelsea Old Town Hall
CHEL SW3 ....120 D5
Chelsea Physic Garden
CHEL SW3 ....120 E6
Chelsea & Westminster
Hospital
WBPTN SW10 ....120 B6
Chelsea Wharf
WBPTN SW10 ....140 C1
Chennestone Community
School
SUN TW16 ....172 A5
Cherington House Health
Centre
HNWL W7 ....116 A1
Cherry Garden Pier
BERM/RHTH SE16 ....123 J2
Cherry Garden School
BERM/RHTH SE16 ....123 H4
Cherry Lane Primary School
WDR/YW UB7 ....112 C4
Cherry Orchard Primary
School
CHARL SE7 ....146 B1
Chessington CC
CHSGTN KT9 ....205 J5
Chessington Community
College & Sports Centre
CHSGTN KT9 ....205 K5
Chessington Golf Club
CHSGTN KT9 ....205 K5
The Chesterfield Mayfair
Hotel
MYFR/PICC W1J 9 J7
Chesterton Primary School
BTSEA SW11 ....141 F2
Chestnut Grove School
BAL SW12 ....161 F3
Chestnuts Primary School
SEVS/STOTM N15 ....67 J2
Cheyne Centre
CHEL SW3 ....120 D6
Chicken Shed Theatre
STHGT/OAK N14 ....22 A6
Chigwell Golf Club
CHIG IG7 ....54 A1
Childeric Primary School
NWCR SE14 ....144 B1
Childs Hill Clinic
CRICK NW2 ....64 D6
Childs Hill Primary School
CRICK NW2 ....82 C1
Childs Welfare Clinic
BCTR RM8 ....91 J3
Chiltonian Industrial Estate
LEE/GVPK SE12 ....165 J1
Chimnocks Wharf
POP/IOD E14 ....105 G6
Chingford CE Infant School
CHING E4 ....38 B3
Chingford CE Junior School
CHING E4 ....38 B3
Chingford Foundation
School
CHING E4 ....37 K3
Chingford Hall Primary School
CHING E4 ....51 H2
Chingford Health Centre
CHING E4 ....37 H6
Chingford Industrial Centre
CHING E4 ....51 G1

Chingford RFC
CHING E4 ....37 J3
Chisenhale Primary School
BOW E3 ....105 G1
Chislehurst Caves
CHST BR7 ....185 F4
Chislehurst Cemetery
CHST BR7 ....185 K1
Chislehurst Golf Club
CHST BR7 ....185 G3
Chislehurst Natural Health
Centre
CHST BR7 ....185 G2
Chislehurst & Sidcup
Grammar School
BFN/LL DA15 ....168 C4
Chiswick & Bedford Park
Preparatory School
CHSWK W4 ....118 B4
Chiswick Business Park
CHSWK W4 ....117 J4
Chiswick Community School
CHSWK W4 ....138 A1
Chiswick House
CHSWK W4 ....118 A3
Chrisp Street Health Centre
POP/IOD E14 ....105 K5
Christ Church Bentinck CE
Primary School
CAMTN NW1 ....8 C1
Christ Church Brondesbury
CE J & I School
KIL/WHAMP NW6 ....82 D6
Christ Church CE Infant
School
NWMAL KT3 ....176 B6
Christ Church CE Junior
School
NWMAL KT3 ....176 A6
Christ Church CE Primary
School
BAR EN5 ....20 B3
BRXN/ST SW9 ....142 B2
BRXS/STRHM SW2 ....162 A3
BRYLDS KT5 ....175 H5
BTSEA SW11 ....140 D4
CHEL SW3 ....120 E6
FSTH SE23 ....164 A4
WOOL/PLUM SE18 ....147 F2
Christchurch CE Primary
School
HAMP NW3 ....83 H1
WCHPL E1 ....13 K2
Christ Church CE Middle School
EA W5 ....97 K6
Christchurch Industrial
Centre
STHWK SE1 ....12 A7
Christ Church Primary School
ERITH DA8 ....130 A6
Christchurch Primary School
IL IG1 ....72 B5
Christ Church School
CAMTN NW1 ....3 K3
Christian Meeting Hall
BECK BR3 ....182 D4
Christopher Hatton Primary
School
FSBYW WC1X 5 J7
Christ's College Finchley
FNCH N3 ....47 F6
Christs College School
EFNCH N2 ....47 F6
Christ the King RC First
School
STWL/WRAY TW19 ....152 A1
Christ the King RC Primary
School
FSBYPK N4 ....67 F5
Christ the King Sixth Form
College
LEW SE13 ....145 G4
Chrysalis Theatre
BAL SW12 ....161 F3
Chrysanthemum Clinic
CHSWK W4 ....137 K1
Chrysolyte Independent
Christian School
STHWK SE1 ....19 F4
Church Down Adult School
LEE/GVPK SE12 ....165 K4
Church End Medical Centre
WLSDN NW10 ....81 G4
Church Farm House Museum
HDN NW4 ....45 K6
Church Farm Swimming Pool
EBAR EN4 ....33 K2
Churchfield Primary School
ED N9 ....36 B3
Churchfield School
WOOL/PLUM SE18 ....128 A4
Churchfields J & I School
SWFD E18 ....52 E4
Churchfields Primary School
BECK BR3 ....182 A6
Church Hill Primary School
EBAR EN4 ....34 A3
Church House
WEST SW1P 16 D4
Churchill Clinic
STHWK SE1 ....17 K4
Churchill College
RYNPK SW20 ....177 F5
Churchill Gardens Primary
School
PIM SW1V 121 H5
Churchill Museum & Cabinet
War Rooms
STJSPK SW1H 16 D2
Churchill Theatre
BMLY BR1 ....183 K5
Church Mead Infant School
LEY E10 ....69 J5
Church Mead Junior School
LEY E10 ....69 J5

Church Stairs
BERM/RHTH SE16 ....123 J2
Church Trading Estate
ERITH DA8 ....150 D1
Cineworld Cinema
BXLYHS DA6 ....149 J5
FELT TW13 ....154 A4
WDGN N22 ....49 G5
Citigroup Tower
POP/IOD E14 ....124 E1
City Business Centre
BERM/RHTH SE16 ....123 K2
City Business College
FSBYE EC1V 6 B5
City Central Estate
FSBYE EC1V 6 C5
City College of Higher
Education
IS N1 ....7 F4
City & Guilds of London Art
School
LBTH SE11 ....122 B5
City Health Centre
FSBYE EC1V 6 E4
City & Islington College
FSBYE EC1V 6 A4
FSBYE EC1V 6 B6
FSBYPK N4 ....67 H6
HBRY N5 ....85 G4
HOLWY N7 ....84 E2
IS N1 ....85 J6
STLK EC1Y 6 C1
City & Islington Sixth Form
College
FSBYE EC1V 6 A3
City Literary College
HHOL WC1V 11 F3
City of East London College
WCHPL E1 ....104 C5
The City of London Academy
STHWK SE1 ....123 H5
The City of London Academy
EDUL SE22 ....143 H6
City of London Business
College
SEVS/STOTM N15 ....68 A2
SEVS/STOTM N15 ....68 C2
City of London Cemetery
MNPK E12 ....71 J6
City of London Club
OBST EC2N 13 G3
City of London Crematorium
WCHPL E1 ....104 C5
City of London Crematorium
MNPK E12 ....89 H1
City of London Magistrates
Court
LOTH EC2R 12 E4
City of London School
BLKFR EC4V 12 B5
City of London School for Girls
BARB EC2Y 6 C3
City of London School Sports
Ground
LEE/GVPK SE12 ....166 B4
City of Westminster Cemetery
HNWL W7 ....116 A1
City of Westminster College
BAY/PAD W2 ....8 A1
MV/WKIL W9 ....100 D2
MV/WKIL W9 ....101 F3
City of Westminster Vehicle
Pound
MYFR/PKLN W1K 9 F6
City University
FSBYE EC1V 6 A4
FSBYE EC1V 6 B3
IS N1 ....6 C5
STBT EC1A 12 C2
WCHPL E1 ....104 D4
City University Business
School
BARB EC2Y 12 D1
Civic Centre & Bromley
Palace
BMLY BR1 ....184 A5
Civic Medical Centre
HRW HA1 ....60 E1
Civil Service Recreation
Centre
WEST SW1P 16 D5
Civil Service Sports Ground
LEE/GVPK SE12 ....166 B1
Clapham Common Clinic
CLAP SW4 ....141 J5
Clapham Manor Primary
School
CLAP SW4 ....141 H4
Clapham Manor Street
Public Baths
CLAP SW4 ....141 J4
Clapham North Business
Centre
CLAP SW4 ....141 J4
Clapham Picture House
CLAP SW4 ....141 H5
Clapton Girls Technology
College
CLPT E5 ....86 E2
Clapton Jewish Boys
School
CLPT E5 ....68 B3
Ciara Grant Primary
School
BOW E3 ....105 J3
Clare House Primary School
BECK BR3 ....183 F5
Claremont Clinic
FSTGT E7 ....89 G3
Claremont Fan Court
School
ESH/CLAY KT10 ....204 B4
Claremont High School
KTN/HRWW/WS HA3 ....62 A2
Claremont Landscape
Garden (NT)
ESH/CLAY KT10 ....204 A5

Claremont Way Industrial
Estate
CRICK NW2 ....64 A5
Clarence House
WHALL SW1A 16 B2
Clarendon Primary School
ASHF TW15 ....152 C5
Clarendon Special School
HPTN TW12 ....173 G2
Claridge's Hotel
MYFR/PKLN W1K 9 J5
Claverings Industrial Estate
ED N9 ....36 E4
Claygate Primary School
ESH/CLAY KT10 ....204 E5
Clayhall Clinic
CLAY IG5 ....53 J6
Clayponds Hospital
BTFD TW8 ....117 F4
Cleeve Park School
SCUP DA14 ....168 D5
Clementine Churchill Hospital
HRW HA1 ....78 E1
Cleopatra's Needle
CHCR WC2N 11 G7
Clerkenwell County Court
IS N1 ....6 A2
Clerkenwell Heritage Centre
FARR EC1M 6 A7
Clerkenwell Parochial CE
Primary School
CLKNW EC1R 5 J5
Cleveland Primary School
IL IG1 ....90 B2
Cleves Primary School
EHAM E6 ....89 H6
C & L Golf & Country Club
NTHLT UB5 ....77 F5
Clifton Lodge School
EA W5 ....97 J6
Clifton Primary School
NWDGN UB2 ....114 D4
Clink Exhibition
STHWK SE1 ....12 E7
Clissold Leisure Centre
STNW/STAM N16 ....85 K1
Clissold Park Natural Health
Centre
STNW/STAM N16 ....68 A6
Clitterhouse Primary School
CRICK NW2 ....64 B6
C & L Leisure Centre
RSLP HA4 ....77 F5
Clockhouse Industrial Estate
EBED/NFELT TW14 ....152 E3
Clockhouse Primary School
CRW PR5 ....56 D2
Clock Museum
CITYW EC2V 12 D3
Cloisters Business Centre
VX/NE SW8 ....141 G1
Clore Gallery
WEST SW1P 16 E7
Clore Tikva School
BARK/HLT IG6 ....54 C5
Clothworkers' Hall
FENCHST EC3M 13 H5
Clouster's Green
WAP E1W 123 H1
Cobbold School
WLSDN NW10 ....81 H4
Cobourg Primary School
CMBW SE5 ....123 G6
Cochrane Theatre
GINN WC1R 11 G2
Cockfosters Sports Ground
EBAR EN4 ....21 K4
The Cockpit Theatre
STJWD NW8 ....2 C7
Coldharbour Industrial
Estate
CMBW SE5 ....142 D3
Coldharbour Leisure Centre
ELTH/MOT SE9 ....166 E4
Coldharbour Sports Ground
ELTH/MOT SE9 ....167 F4
Colebrooke Primary School
IS N1 ....6 A2
Colegrave School
SRTFD E15 ....88 B3
Coleraine Park Primary School
TOTM N17 ....50 D4
Coleridge Primary School
HGT N6 ....66 D4
Colet Court
BARN SW13 ....118 D5
Colfe's Preparatory School
LEE/GVPK SE12 ....165 K1
Colfe's Senior School
LEE/GVPK SE12 ....165 K1
Colindale Business Park
CDALE/KGS NW9 ....44 E6
Colindale Hospital
CDALE/KGS NW9 ....45 G6
Colindale Primary School
CDALE/KGS NW9 ....63 H1
Coliseum Theatre
CHCR WC2N 10 E6
College Fields Business Centre
WIM/MER SW19 ....178 D4
College of Arms
BLKFR EC4V 12 C4
College of Central London
SDTCH EC2A 7 G6
College of Fuel Technology
HGT N6 ....66 A3
The College of Law
FITZ W1T 10 C2
LINN WC2A 11 J3
College of North East London
CEND/HSY/T N8 ....67 G1
SEVS/STOTM N15 ....68 B1
WDGN N22 ....48 C4
College of North West London
KIL/WHAMP NW6 ....82 E6
WBLY HA9 ....80 C1
WLSDN NW10 ....81 H3

College of Organists
FLST/FETLN EC4A 11 K2
College Park School
BAY/PAD W2 ....101 F5
Collier Row Clinic
CRW RM5 ....56 D4
Collier Row FC
CRW RM5 ....56 B4
Collingwood Business Centre
ARCH N19 ....84 E1
Collingwood Preparatory
School
WLGTN SM6 ....210 B3
Collins Method School
CRICK NW2 ....82 A4
Collis Primary School
TEDD TW11 ....174 C2
Colnbrook School
OXHEY WD19 ....27 G4
Colonna Convent Girls School
CROY/NA CR0 ....213 F1
Colonnades Leisure Park
CROY/NA CR0 ....211 G4
The Colonnades Shopping
Centre
BCVA SW1W 15 J6
Colours Sports Club
SUT SM1 ....209 G3
Columbia Primary School
BETH E2 ....7 K4
Colvestone Primary School
HACK E8 ....86 B3
Colville Primary School
NTGHL W11 ....100 D5
Colyers Lane Medical Centre
ERITH DA8 ....150 A2
Colyers Primary School
ERITH DA8 ....150 A2
Comber Grove Primary
School
CMBW SE5 ....142 D1
Comedy Theatre
STJS SW1Y 10 C6
Comfort Hotel
ENC/FH EN2 ....23 H3
Comfort Inn
ECT SW5 ....119 K4
HYS/HAR UB3 ....113 H5
Commonwealth Institute
WKENS W14 ....119 J3
Community Arts Centre
GNWCH SE10 ....144 E1
Community Care Centre
ENC/FH EN2 ....23 K2
Community Centre
(Island History Trust)
POP/IOD E14 ....125 F4
Community College and
School
GNWCH SE10 ....145 H1
The Community College
HACK E8 ....86 D6
Compass Theatre
HGDN/ICK UB10 ....76 A1
Complementary Health
Centre
LEE/GVPK SE12 ....165 H1
Compton Leisure Centre
NTHLT UB5 ....77 J6
The Compton School
NFNCH/WDSPK N12 ....47 J2
Compton Sports Centre
NFNCH/WDSPK N12 ....47 J2
Concord Business Centre
ACT W3 ....98 D4
Conductive Education Centre
MUSWH N10 ....48 C6
Conduit House
GNWCH SE10 ....145 G1
Coney Hill School
HAYES BR2 ....199 J6
Connaught Business Centre
CDALE/KGS NW9 ....63 H2
CROY/NA CR0 ....211 F4
MTCM CR4 ....194 E2
The Connaught Hotel
MYFR/PKLN W1K 9 H6
Connaught House Group
BAY/PAD W2 ....8 E4
Connaught School for Girls
WAN E11 ....70 C5
Conrad Hotel
WBPTN SW10 ....140 B3
Consort Clinic
PECK SE15 ....143 J4
Consulate General of Monaco
SKENS SW7 ....14 A6
Consulate of Burkina Faso
BTSEA SW11 ....140 B4
Consulate of Chile
CAVSQ/HST W1G 3 J7
Consulate of Colombia
GTPST W1W 10 A3
Consulate of Eritrea
IS N1 ....5 K2
Consulate of Guinea
MYFR/PKLN W1K 9 G6
Consulate of Panama
MYFR/PICC W1J 15 J1
Convent of Jesus & Mary
Infant School
CRICK NW2 ....82 A4
Convent of Jesus & Mary
Language College
WLSDN NW10 ....81 H6
Conway Hall
FSBYW WC1X 11 G1
Conway Medical Centre
WOOL/PLUM SE18 ....127 J5
Conway Primary School
WOOL/PLUM SE18 ....127 K4
Coombe Girls School
NWMAL KT3 ....176 A5
Coombe Hill Golf Club
KUTN/CMB KT2 ....176 A3

Coombe Hill J & I School
NWMAL KT3 ....176 A4
Coombe Wood Golf Club
KUTN/CMB KT2 ....175 J3
Coopers' Hall
LVPST EC2M 13 H2
Coopers Lane Primary School
LEE/GVPK SE12 ....165 K4
Coopers Technology College
CHST BR7 ....185 H4
Copenhagen Primary School
IS N1 ....5 F1
Copland Specialist Science
College
WBLY HA9 ....80 D3
Coppermill Primary School
WALTH E17 ....69 F2
Coppetts Wood Hospital
MUSWH N10 ....47 K4
Coppetts Wood Primary
School
MUSWH N10 ....48 A4
Coppice Primary School
CLPT IG7 ....55 G1
Copthall School
MLHL NW7 ....45 K3
Copthorne Tara Hotel
KENS W8 ....120 A3
Cordwainers College
HACK E8 ....86 E5
Corinthian Casuals FC
SURB KT6 ....206 C1
Coroner Cinema
KENS W8 ....119 K1
SEVS/STOTM N15 ....49 H6
Corpus Christi RC Primary
School
BRXS/STRHM SW2 ....142 A6
Corus Hotel
BAY/PAD W2 ....8 A5
BORE WD6 ....30 A2
Cosmopolitan College
IS N1 ....5 G3
Coston Secondary Modern
Girls School
GFD/PVL UB6 ....96 C1
Coteford Infant School
PIN HA5 ....58 E2
Courtauld Institute Gallery
TPL/STR WC2R 11 G5
Courtauld Institute of Art
TPL/STR WC2R 11 H6
Court Farm Industrial Estate
STWL/WRAY TW19 ....152 C1
Courtfield Medical Centre
ECT SW5 ....120 A4
Courtland JMI School
MLHL NW7 ....31 G4
Covent Garden Flower
Market
VX/NE SW8 ....121 J6
Covent Garden Medical
Centre
LSO/SEVD WC2H 10 E4
CPFC Soccer & Sports Centre
BRXN/ST SW9 ....142 A4
Crafts Council
IS N1 ....5 K3
Crampton Primary School
WALW SE17 ....18 B7
Cranbrook College
IL IG1 ....72 A6
Cranford Community College
HEST TW5 ....114 A6
Cranford Infant School
HSLWW TW4 ....133 K3
Cranford Junior School
HSLWW TW4 ....134 A3
Cranford Park Junior School
HYS/HAR UB3 ....113 J4
Cranford Park Primary
School
HYS/HAR UB3 ....113 J2
Cranleigh Gardens Industrial
Estate
STHL UB1 ....95 K4
Cranmer Primary School
MTCM CR4 ....194 E1
The Craven Gallery
HMSMTH W6 ....118 E4
Craven Park Health Centre
WLSDN NW10 ....81 F6
Craven Park Medical Centre
WLSDN NW10 ....81 F6
Crawford Primary School
CMBW SE5 ....142 D2
Crayfield Industrial Park
STMC/STPC BR5 ....186 D5
Crayfields Business Park
STMC/STPC BR5 ....186 D4
Crayford Commercial Centre
DART DA1 ....150 B6
Crayford Industrial Estate
DART DA1 ....150 C6
Crayford Leisure Centre &
Greyhound Stadium
DART DA1 ....170 B1
Crayford Medical Centre
DART DA1 ....150 C6
Crayside Industrial Estate
DART DA1 ....150 D4
Cray Valley Golf Club
STMC/STPC BR5 ....187 F4
Creekmouth Industrial Estate
BARK IG11 ....109 F3
Creek Road Health Centre
DEPT SE8 ....124 D6
Creek Road Industrial Estate
DEPT SE8 ....124 E6
Cremer Business Centre
BETH E2 ....7 J3
Crewe House
MYFR/PICC W1J 9 J7
Cricket Green School
MTCM CR4 ....178 D6
Cricket Pavilion
WEST SW1P 16 C6

Cricklefield Stadium
IL IG1 ....72 E6
Cricklewood Trading Estate
CRICK NW2 ....82 C1
Crispin Industrial Centre
UED N18 ....50 E1
Criterion Theatre
MYFR/PICC W1J 10 B6
Crockenhill Primary School
SWLY BR8 ....203 K3
Crofton Leisure Centre
BROCKY SE4 ....164 D1
Crofton School
BROCKY SE4 ....164 D1
Croham Hurst Golf Club
SAND/SEL CR2 ....212 B4
Cromer Road Primary School
BAR EN5 ....21 F4
Cromwell Business Centre
BARK IG11 ....108 E2
Cromwell Hospital
KENS W8 ....120 A4
Crook Log Primary School
BXLYHS DA6 ....148 E5
Crook Log Sports Centre
WELL DA16 ....148 E4
Crossways Academy
BROCKY SE4 ....144 B3
Crouch End Art School
CEND/HSY/T N8 ....66 E2
Crouch End Health Centre
CEND/HSY/T N8 ....66 E2
Crouch Hill Recreation Centre
CEND/HSY/T N8 ....66 E1
Crowland Primary School
SEVS/STOTM N15 ....68 C2
Crowlands Primary School
ROMW/RG RM7 ....74 E3
Crown Business Centre
WDR/YW UB7 ....112 C1
Crown Close Business Centre
BOW E3 ....87 J6
Crown Court
ISLW TW7 ....135 K2
Crown Court at the Borough
STHWK SE1 ....18 B2
Crowndale Health Centre
CAMTN NW1 ....4 B2
Crowne Plaza Hotel
WDR/YW UB7 ....112 D4
Crownfield Primary School
ROMW/RG RM7 ....56 C5
Crown Lane Clinic
STHGT/OAK N14 ....34 C3
Crown Lane Primary School
WNWD SE27 ....162 D6
Crown Moran Hotel
CRICK NW2 ....82 B2
Crown Trading Centre
HYS/HAR UB3 ....113 H2
Crown Woods School
ELTH/MOT SE9 ....147 H6
Croydon Airport Industrial
Estate
CROY/NA CR0 ....211 G5
Croydon Bowling Club
SAND/SEL CR2 ....211 J3
Croydon Cemetery
CROY/NA CR0 ....196 A2
Croydon Clocktower Cinema
CROY/NA CR0 ....211 J1
Croydon College
CROY/NA CR0 ....211 K1
Croydon Crematorium
THHTH CR7 ....195 K2
Croydon Fairfield Halls
Cinema
CROY/NA CR0 ....211 K1
Croydon FC
SNWD SE25 ....197 K2
Croydon Road Industrial
Estate
BECK BR3 ....197 K3
Croydon Sports Arena
SNWD SE25 ....197 K2
Crusader Industrial Estate
FSBYPK N4 ....67 J3
Crusoe House School
IS N1 ....6 E4
Crystal Palace FC
(Selhurst Park)
SNWD SE25 ....197 F1
Crystal Palace Museum
NRWD SE19 ....181 G2
Cuaco Sports Ground
BECK BR3 ....182 D2
Cubitt Town Primary School
POP/IOD E14 ....125 F3
Cuddington Cemetery
WPK KT4 ....192 E6
Cuddington CP School
WPK KT4 ....207 H1
Cuddington Croft Primary
School
BELMT SM2 ....208 B6
Culloden Primary School
POP/IOD E14 ....106 B5
Culvers House Primary
School
MTCM CR4 ....195 F5
Cumberland Business Park
WLSDN NW10 ....98 D2
The Cumberland Hotel
OXSTW W1C 9 F4
Cumberland Park Industrial
Estate
WLSDN NW10 ....99 J2
The Cumming Museum
WALW SE17 ....18 C7
Cumnor House School
SAND/SEL CR2 ....211 H6
Curwen Primary School
PLSTW E13 ....106 E1
Curzon Mayfair Cinema
MYFR/PICC W1J 15 J1
Curzon Soho Cinema
SOHO/SHAV W1D 10 D5

Custom House
MON EC3R 13 G6
Cutlers' Hall
STP EC4M 12 B3
Cutty Sark Clipper Ship
GNWCH SE10 ....125 F6
Cygnet Clinic Beckton
EHAM E6 ....108 B4
Cygnus Business Centre
WLSDN NW10 ....81 H3
Cypress Infant School
SNWD SE25 ....181 F5
Cypress Junior School
SNWD SE25 ....181 F5
Cyprus College of Art
WNWD SE27 ....162 C6
Cyril Jackson Primary School
POP/IOD E14 ....105 H6
Dagenham Chest Clinic
BCTR RM8 ....92 B1
Dagenham Priory
Comprehensive School &
Performing Arts College
DAGE RM10 ....92 D5
Dagenham & Redbridge FC
DAGE RM10 ....92 D3
Dagenham Superbowl
DAGE RM10 ....110 D1
Dagenham Swimming Pool
DAGE RM10 ....74 C2
Daiglen School
BKHH IG9 ....39 G3
Daily Telegraph
POP/IOD E14 ....124 D3
Dairy Meadow Primary
School
NWDGN UB2 ....114 E3
D'Albiac House
HTHAIR TW6 ....132 D3
Dali Universe
STHWK SE1 ....17 G2
Dallington School
FSBYE EC1V 6 B6
Dalmain Primary School
FSTH SE23 ....164 B3
Damilola Taylor Centre
PECK SE15 ....143 G1
Danegrove Primary School
EBAR EN4 ....33 J1
Danesfield Manor School
WOT/HER KT12 ....188 A6
Danetree School
HOR/WEW KT19 ....206 D3
Danson Mansion
BXLYHS DA6 ....148 D5
Danson Primary School
WELL DA16 ....148 C5
Danson Watersports Centre
BXLYHS DA6 ....148 D6
Darell Primary School
RCH/KEW TW9 ....137 H4
Darent Industrial Park
ERITH DA8 ....131 G3
Darrick Wood Primary School
ORP BR6 ....216 B3
Darrick Wood School
ORP BR6 ....216 B1
Darrick Wood Sports Centre
ORP BR6 ....216 C1
Darrick Wood Swimming
Pool
ORP BR6 ....216 B1
Dartford Adult Education
Centre
DART DA1 ....171 F2
Dartford County Court
DART DA1 ....171 H1
Dartford Golf Club
DART DA1 ....170 E4
Dartford Grammar School
for Boys
DART DA1 ....171 F1
Dartford Grammar School
for Girls
DART DA1 ....171 F2
Dartford Magistrates Court
DART DA1 ....171 G1
Dartford Museum & Library
DART DA1 ....171 F2
Dartford Natural Health
Centre
DART DA1 ....171 F2
Dartford Technology
College
DART DA1 ....171 F2
Dartford West Health Centre
DART DA1 ....171 F1
Darwin Centre
SKENS SW7 ....14 A5
Dashmesh Darbar Sikh Temple
MNPK E12 ....89 K4
Datapoint Business Centre
BOW E3 ....106 B3
Daubeney Primary School
CLPT E5 ....87 G2
The David Beckham Academy
GNWCH SE10 ....125 J2
David Livingstone Primary
School
THHTH CR7 ....180 D4
David Lloyd Leisure Centre
KENS W8 ....120 A4
NFNCH/WDSPK N12 ....47 H3
David Lloyd Sports Centre
EN N1 ....24 C3
David Lloyd Tennis Centre
SCUP DA14 ....186 A1
Davidson Primary School
CROY/NA CR0 ....197 G4
Davies Lane Primary School
WAN E11 ....70 D6
Davies's College
STHWK SE1 ....18 E2
Dawlish Primary School
LEY E10 ....70 A6
Days Hotel
MLHL NW7 ....30 E4

Days Hotel London South
Ruislip
RSLP HA4 ....17 G2
Days Inn
PIM SW1V 121 H5
Days Lane Primary School
BFN/LL DA15 ....168 A1
Dean College of London
HOLWY N7 ....85 F1
Deansfield Primary School
RSLP HA4 ....77 H2
Deansbrook Primary School
MLHL NW7 ....44 E2
Deansfield Primary School
ELTH/MOT SE9 ....147 F4
De Bohun Primary School
STHGT/OAK N14 ....22 B6
Delta Wharf
GNWCH SE10 ....125 G2
Denmead School
HPTN TW12 ....173 F3
Denvale Trade Centre
STMC/STPC BR5 ....202 C2
Denver Industrial Estate
RAIN RM13 ....111 H4
Department for Environment,
Food and Rural Affairs
CHCR WC2N 10 E7
Department for Transport
WEST SW1P 16 D6
Department of Art & Design
(London Metropolitan
University) WCHPL E1 ....13 K3
Department of Economics
(London Metropolitan
University) TWRH EC3N 13 J4
Department of Education
STJSPK SW1H 16 D3
Department of Health
WHALL SW1A 16 E2
Department of Sociology &
Anthropology (Goldsmiths
University of London)
NWCR SE14 ....144 B2
Department of Trade &
Industry
STJSPK SW1H 16 C4
Deptford Business Centre
NWCR SE14 ....124 A5
Deptford Green School
NWCR SE14 ....144 C1
Deptford Park Business
Centre
DEPT SE8 ....124 B5
Deptford Park Primary School
DEPT SE8 ....124 B5
Deptford Trading Estate
DEPT SE8 ....124 B5
Dersingham Infant School
MNPK E12 ....89 K3
Derwentwater Primary
School
ACT W3 ....117 K1
Design Museum
STHWK SE1 ....19 K1
Deutsche Schule
RCHPK/HAM TW10 ....156 E3
Devonshire Hospital
MHST W1U 9 H1
Devonshire House
Preparatory School
HAMP NW3 ....83 H3
Devonshire House School
HAMP NW3 ....83 G3
Devonshire Primary School
BELMT SM2 ....209 G5
Diamond College
SOHO/SHAV W1D 10 D3
Diana Fountain
E/WMO/HCT KT8 ....174 A5
Diana Matthews Clinic
ROMW/RG RM7 ....75 F1
Dilloway Industrial Estate
NWDGN UB2 ....114 D2
Discovery Business Park
BERM/RHTH SE16 ....123 H3
Docklands Medical Centre
POP/IOD E14 ....124 D4
Docklands Sailing Centre
POP/IOD E14 ....124 D3
Docklands Sailing &
Watersports Centre
BERM/RHTH SE16 ....124 C3
Dockmaster's House
POP/IOD E14 ....105 J6
Dockwell's Industrial Estate
EBED/NFELT TW14 ....134 A6
Dockyard Industrial Estate
WOOL/PLUM SE18 ....126 D3
Dog Kennel Hill Primary
School
EDUL SE22 ....143 F4
Dokal Industrial Estate
NWDGN UB2 ....114 D2
Dollis Infant School
MLHL NW7 ....46 A3
Dollis Junior School
MLHL NW7 ....46 A3
The Dolphin Leisure Centre
ROM RM1 ....75 H1
The Dolphin School
BTSEA SW11 ....140 D6
The Dominie
BTSEA SW11 ....140 E6
Dominion Business Park
ED N9 ....37 F4
Dominion Theatre
RSQ WC1B 10 D3
Donhead (Wimbledon College
Preparatory School)
WIM/MER SW19 ....177 G3
Donmar Warehouse Theatre
LSQ/SEVD WC2H 10 E4

Donnington Primary School
WLSDN NW10 ....81 K5
The Dorchester Hotel
MYFR/PKLN W1K 9 H7
Dorchester Primary School
WPK KT4 ....193 H5
Dorma Trading Park
LEY E10 ....69 F5
Dormers Wells High School
STHL UB1 ....96 A5
Dormers Wells Leisure Centre
STHL UB1 ....96 B5
Dormers Wells Medical Centre
STHL UB1 ....96 A5
Dormers Wells Primary School
STHL UB1 ....96 B6
Dorothy Barley Primary
School
BCTR RM8 ....91 H3
Dorset Road Infant School
ELTH/MOT SE9 ....166 D4
Dorset Square Hotel
CAMTN NW1 ....8 E1
Douglas Bader Foundation
PUT/ROE SW15 ....158 D1
Dovers Corner Industrial
Estate
RAIN RM13 ....111 H2
Downderry Primary School
BMLY BR1 ....165 H6
Downe Manor Primary School
NTHLT UB5 ....95 F2
Downham Health Centre
BMLY BR1 ....165 H6
Downhills Primary School
TOTM N17 ....67 K1
Downsell Primary School
SRTFD E15 ....88 B2
Downshall Primary School
GNTH/NBYPK IG2 ....72 E4
Downsview Primary School
NRWD SE19 ....180 D3
Downsview School
CLPT E5 ....86 D2
Drapers Hall
LOTH EC2R 13 F3
Drapers Sports Ground
SRTFD E15 ....88 A2
The Draycott Hotel
CHEL SW3 ....15 F6
Drayton Green Primary School
WEA W13 ....97 G6
Drayton Manor High School
HNWL W7 ....97 F6
Drayton Park Primary School
HBRY N5 ....85 G3
DRCA Business Centre
BTSEA SW11 ....141 F2
Drew Primary School
CAN/RD E16 ....126 D1
Driving School & Road Safety
Centre
KTN/HRWW/WS HA3 ....43 G6
The Drizen School
EDGW HA8 ....44 C3
Dr Johnson's House
FLST/FETLN EC4A 11 K3
Dr Triplett's CE J & I School
HYS/HAR UB3 ....94 D5
Drury Way Industrial Estate
WLSDN NW10 ....81 F2
Duchess Theatre
COVGDN WC2E 11 G5
Ducks Infants School
DUL SE21 ....163 G5
Duff Miller College
SKENS SW7 ....120 B3
Duke of York Column
STJS SW1Y 16 D1
Duke of York Theatre
CHCR WC2N 10 E6
Dulverton Primary School
ELTH/MOT SE9 ....167 J4
Dulwich College
DUL SE21 ....163 F3
Dulwich College Preparatory
School
DUL SE21 ....163 F5
Dulwich College Track
DUL SE21 ....163 F4
Dulwich Hamlet FC
EDUL SE22 ....143 F5
Dulwich Hamlet Junior School
EDUL SE22 ....162 E1
Dulwich Hospital
EDUL SE22 ....143 H5
Dulwich Leisure Centre
EDUL SE22 ....143 H5
Dulwich Medical Centre
EDUL SE22 ....143 H6
Dulwich Picture Gallery
DUL SE21 ....162 E2
Dulwich & Sydenham Hill
Golf Club
DUL SE21 ....163 H4
Dulwich Village CE Infant
School
DUL SE21 ....163 F1
Dunbar Wharf
POP/IOD E14 ....105 H6
Duncombe Primary School
ARCH N19 ....66 E5
Dundee Wharf
POP/IOD E14 ....105 H6
Dundonald Primary School
WIM/MER SW19 ....177 J3
Dunningford Primary School
HCH RM12 ....93 H3
Dunraven School & Upper
School
STRHM/NOR SW16 ....162 A5
Duppas Junior School
CROY/NA CR0 ....211 H3
Durand Primary School
BRXN/ST SW9 ....142 A2
Durands Wharf
BERM/RHTH SE16 ....124 C2

Durants School
PEND EN3 ....24 E2
Durdans Park Primary School
STHL UB1 ....95 K4
Durston House School
EA W5 ....97 K5
Dysart School
KUTN/CMB KT2 ....156 E6
SURB KT6 ....191 F4
Dyslexia Teaching Centre
SKENS SW7 ....120 A5
Eaglesfield School
WOOL/PLUM SE18 ....147 F2
Eagle Trading Estate
MTCM CR4 ....194 E3
Ealdham Primary School
ELTH/MOT SE9 ....146 B5
Ealing Abbey
EA W5 ....97 J5
Ealing Abbey Scriptorium
WEA W13 ....97 J5
The Ealing Broadway Centre
EA W5 ....97 K6
Ealing Central Sports Ground
GFD/PVL UB6 ....97 G1
Ealing College Upper School
WEA W13 ....97 G5
Ealing CC
EA W5 ....98 A5
Ealing Film Studios
EA W5 ....116 D1
Ealing Golf Club
GFD/PVL UB6 ....97 H2
Ealing, Hammersmith & West
London College
ACT W3 ....117 J1
WKENS W14 ....119 G4
Ealing Hospital
NWDGN UB2 ....115 J2
Ealing Independent College
EA W5 ....97 J6
Ealing Northern Sports
Centre
GFD/PVL UB6 ....78 D2
Ealing Park Health Centre
EA W5 ....116 E4
Ealing Road Trading Estate
BTFD TW8 ....116 E5
Ealing Sports Centre
EA W5 ....98 A6
Ealing Tutorial College
EA W5 ....97 K6
Ealing & West London College
EA W5 ....116 D1
Eardley Primary School
STRHM/NOR SW16 ....179 H2
Earlham J & I School
WDGN N22 ....49 G3
Earlham Primary School
FSTGT E7 ....88 D3
Earl's Court Exhibition Centre
ECT/PGN SW6 ....119 K5
Earlsfield Primary School
WAND/EARL SW18 ....160 B4
Earlsmead First & Middle
School
RYLN/HDSTN HA2 ....77 K2
Earlsmead Primary School
SEVS/STOTM N15 ....68 B1
Earth Galleries
SKENS SW7 ....14 B5
East Acton Primary School
ACT W3 ....99 G6
East Barking Centre
BCTR RM8 ....91 J3
East Barnet Health Centre
EBAR EN4 ....21 H6
East Barnet School
EBAR EN4 ....21 H4
East Beckton District Centre
EHAM E6 ....107 K4
Eastbrook Comprehensive
School
DAGE RM10 ....92 E2
Eastbrook End Cemetery
ROMW/RG RM7 ....93 G1
Eastbrookend Country Park
ROMW/RG RM7 ....93 F2
Eastbury Comprehensive
School
BARK IG11 ....91 F6
Eastbury Farm JMI School
NTHWD HA6 ....26 D6
Eastbury Infant School
BARK IG11 ....91 F5
Eastcote CC
PIN HA5 ....59 F2
Eastcote Health Centre
PIN HA5 ....59 G4
Eastcote Industrial Estate
RSLP HA4 ....59 G4
Eastcote Lane Cemetery
RYLN/HDSTN HA2 ....78 B1
Eastcote Primary School
WELL DA16 ....147 J4
Eastcourt Independent
School
GDMY/SEVK IG3 ....73 G5
East End Computing &
Business College
WCHPL E1 ....104 D5
Eastern Business Park
HTHAIR TW6 ....133 J3
Eastfield Primary School
PEND EN3 ....24 E6
East Finchley Cemetery
EFNCH N2 ....47 F6
East Finchley Medical Centre
EFNCH N2 ....65 J1
East Finchley School of
English
EFNCH N2 ....47 J6
Eastgate Business Park
LEY E10 ....69 G5
East Greenwich Christ Church
CE Primary School
GNWCH SE10 ....125 H4

East Ham Industrial Estate
EHAM E6 ....107 H3
East Ham Jewish Cemetery
EHAM E6 ....107 J2
East Ham Leisure Centre
EHAM E6 ....89 K6
East Ham Memorial Hospital
EHAM E6 ....89 H5
East Ham Nature Reserve
EHAM E6 ....107 K3
East Lane Business Park
WBLY HA9 ....79 K1
Eastlea Community Centre
CAN/RD E16 ....106 D3
Eastlea Community School
CAN/RD E16 ....106 C3
East London Business
College
WAN E11 ....70 C2
East London Cemetery
PLSTW E13 ....106 D2
East London Crematorium
SRTFD E15 ....106 D2
East London RFC
EHAM E6 ....107 K4
East London RUFC
SRTFD E15 ....106 D1
Eastman Dental Hospital
FSBYW WC1X 5 G6
East Molesey CC
E/WMO/HCT KT8 ....173 H6
East Sheen Cemetery
RCHPK/HAM TW10 ....137 H6
East Sheen Primary School
MORT/ESHN SW14 ....138 B5
East Thamesmead Business
Park
ERITHM DA18 ....129 G2
East Wickham Primary School
WELL DA16 ....148 A2
Eaton Manor RFC
WAN E11 ....71 G2
Eaton Square Preparatory
School
BGVA SW1W 15 J6
Eaton Square School
PIM SW1V 16 A7
Ecclesbourne Primary School
THHTH CR7 ....196 D2
Eckerd College
GWRST WC1E 10 C1
Ecole de Mime Corporel
Dramatique & Theatre
FSBYW WC1X ARCH N19 ....66 E5
Eden College
STHWK SE1 ....18 B4
Edenham High School
CROY/NA CR0 ....198 B4
Eden High School
FUL/PGN SW6 ....139 J2
Eden Medical Centre
WKENS W14 ....119 J4
Edenvale Child Health Clinic
WAND/EARL SW18 ....179 F3
Eden Walk Shopping Centre
KUT/HW KT1 ....175 F5
Edes Business Park
WLGTN SM6 ....195 H6
Edgebury Primary School
CHST BR7 ....167 H6
Edge Business Centre
CRICK NW2 ....63 K6
Edgebury Cemetery
EDGW HA8 ....30 C4
Edgware Clinic
EDGW HA8 ....44 C2
Edgware College
KIL/WHAMP NW6 ....83 G4
Edgware Community Hospital
EDGW HA8 ....44 D3
Edgware FC & Wealdstone FC
EDGW HA8 ....44 C3
Edgware Infant School
EDGW HA8 ....44 C2
Edgware Junior School
EDGW HA8 ....44 D2
Edinburgh Primary School
WALTH E17 ....69 H2
Edith Neville Primary School
CAMTN NW1 ....4 C3
Edmonton Cemetery
WCHMH N21 ....35 K4
Edmonton County Court
UED N18 ....50 C1
Edmonton Green Shopping
Centre
ED N9 ....36 D4
Edmonton Leisure Centre
ED N9 ....36 C5
Edmonton Upper School
EN EN1 ....36 B2
Edmund Waller Primary
School
NWCR SE14 ....144 A3
Education Centre
WOOL/PLUM SE18 ....127 G5
Edward Betham CE Primary
School
GFD/PVL UB6 ....96 D2
Edward Pauling School
FELT TW13 ....153 H4
Edward Wilson Primary
School
BAY/PAD W2 ....101 F4
Edwin Lambert School
EMPK RM11 ....75 J3
Effra Road Retail Park
BRXS/STRHM SW2 ....142 B6
Effra Site (St George Wharf)
under development
VX/NE SW8 ....121 K5
The Egerton House Hotel
CHEL SW3 ....14 D5
Eglinton Junior School
WOOL/PLUM SE18 ....127 F6
Eglinton Primary School
WOOL/PLUM SE18 ....147 F1

Elbourne Trading Estate
BELV DA17 ....129 J3
Eldenwall Industrial Estate
BCTR RM8 ....74 A5
Eldon JMI School
ED N9 ....36 D3
Eleanor Palmer Primary
School
KTTN NW5 ....84 C2
Eleanor Smith Special School
PLSTW E13 ....106 E1
Electrical Trades Union
College
ESH/CLAY KT10 ....204 A3
Electric Cinema
NTGHL W11 ....100 D5
Electron Trade Centre
STMC/STPC BR5 ....202 C1
Elephant & Castle Leisure
Centre
LBTH SE11 ....18 B6
Elephant & Castle Shopping
Centre
LBTH SE11 ....18 B5
Elers Clinic
HYS/HAR UB3 ....113 G4
Elfrida Primary School
CAT SE6 ....164 E6
Eliot Bank Primary School
FSTH SE23 ....163 J4
Elizabeth Garrett Anderson
Hospital
CAMTN NW1 ....4 D5
Elizabeth Selby Infant School
BETH E2 ....104 C2
Elizabeth Trading Estate
NWCR SE14 ....124 A6
Ellen Wilkinson Primary
School
CAN/RD E16 ....107 H4
Ellen Wilkinson School
for Girls
ACT W3 ....98 B5
Ellerslie Square Industrial
Estate
BRXS/STRHM SW2 ....141 K5
Ellingham Primary School
CHSGTN KT9 ....205 K5
Elliott School
PUT/ROE SW15 ....159 F1
Elmbridge Leisure Centre
WOT/HER KT12 ....188 A2
Elm Court School
WNWD SE27 ....162 C4
Elmgrove First & Middle
School
KTN/HRWW/WS HA3 ....61 G1
Elmhurst Primary School
FSTGT E7 ....89 F5
Elmhurst School
SAND/SEL CR2 ....211 K3
Elm Lea Trading Estate
TOTM N17 ....50 C5
Elmwood Junior School
CROY/NA CR0 ....196 C4
Elm Wood Primary School
DUL SE21 ....162 E5
Elsdale Street Health Centre
HOM E9 ....86 E5
Elsley Primary School
WBLY HA9 ....80 B4
Elsley School
BTSEA SW11 ....141 E4
Eltham Bus Station
ELTH/MOT SE9 ....146 E6
Eltham CE Primary School
ELTH/MOT SE9 ....146 E6
Eltham College Junior School
ELTH/MOT SE9 ....166 C3
Eltham College Senior School
ELTH/MOT SE9 ....166 C3
Eltham Crematorium
ELTH/MOT SE9 ....147 J5
Eltham Green School
ELTH/MOT SE9 ....166 C1
Eltham Health Clinic
ELTH/MOT SE9 ....146 D6
Eltham Health & Fitness
Centre
ELTH/MOT SE9 ....167 F1
Eltham Hill Technology
College
ELTH/MOT SE9 ....166 D1
Eltham Palace
ELTH/MOT SE9 ....166 D2
Eltham Pools
ELTH/MOT SE9 ....146 D6
Eltham Warren Golf Club
ELTH/MOT SE9 ....147 G6
Elthorne Park High School
HNWL W7 ....116 A3
Elthorne Sports Centre
HNWL W7 ....116 A3
Elystan Business Centre
YEAD UB4 ....95 G6
Emanuel School
BTSEA SW11 ....140 C6
Embankment Pier
CHCR WC2N 11 G7
Embassy of Afghanistan
SKENS SW7 ....14 A3
Embassy of Albania
BGVA SW1W 15 K5
Embassy of Algeria
NTGHL W11 ....119 H1
Embassy of Angola
MYFR/PKLN W1K 9 G7
Embassy of Argentina
MYFR/PKLN W1K 9 J2
Embassy of Armenia
KENS W8 ....120 A3
Embassy of Austria
KTBR SW1X 15 G4
Embassy of Bahrain
SKENS SW7 ....120 B3
Embassy of Belarus
KENS W8 ....120 A2

Embassy of Belgium
KTBR SW1X 15 H5
Embassy of Bolivia
BGVA SW1W 15 H5
Embassy of Bosnia-Herzegovina
CAVSQ/HST W1G 9 K3
Embassy of Brazil
MYFR/PKLN W1K 9 G5
Embassy of Bulgaria
KTBR SW1X 120 B3
Embassy of Cameroon
NTCHL W11 ....119 H1
Embassy of China
CAVSQ/HST W1G 9 J1
Embassy of Costa Rica
BAY/PAD W2 ....101 G6
Embassy of Cote D'Ivoire
KTBR SW1X 15 H4
Embassy of Croatia
GTPST W1W 3 K7
Embassy of Cuba
CAVSQ/VD WC2H 10 E3
Embassy of Democratic Republic of The Congo
KTBR SW1X 15 F5
Embassy of Denmark
KTBR SW1X 14 E4
Embassy of Dominican Republic
BAY/PAD W2 ....101 F5
Embassy of Ecuador
KTBR SW1X 14 E4
Embassy of Egypt
MYFR/PKLN W1J 9 J7
Embassy of Estonia
SKENS SW7 ....120 B3
Embassy of Ethiopia
KTBR SW1X 14 B3
Embassy of Finland
KTBR SW1X 15 G4
Embassy of France
KTBR SW1X 15 F2
Embassy of Georgia
KENS W8 ....120 A2
Embassy of Germany
KTBR SW1X 15 G4
Embassy of Ghana
HGT N6 ....66 B5
Embassy of Greece
NTGHL W11 ....119 J1
Embassy of Guatemala
WBPTN SW10 ....120 A6
Embassy of Honduras
MBLAR W1H 9 F1
Embassy of Hungary
KTBR SW1X 15 H5
Embassy of Iceland
KTBR SW1X 15 G4
Embassy of Indonesia
MYFR/PKLN W1K 9 H6
Embassy of Iran
SKENS SW7 ....14 B5
Embassy of Iraq
SKENS SW7 ....120 B3
Embassy of Ireland
KTBR SW1X 15 J3
Embassy of Israel
KENS W8 ....120 A2
Embassy of Italy
MYFR/PKLN W1K 9 H5
Embassy of Japan
KENS W8 ....119 K2
Embassy of Jordan
KENS W8 ....119 K2
Embassy of Korea
WESTW SW1E 16 B4
Embassy of Krygyzstan
MBLAR W1H 8 E2
Embassy of Kuwait
KTBR SW1X 15 F2
Embassy of Latvia
CAMTN NW1 ....3 G7
Embassy of Lebanon
KENS W8 ....120 A1
Embassy of Liberia
BAY/PAD W2 ....100 E6
Embassy of Lithuania
MBLAR W1H 8 E2
Embassy of Luxembourg
KTBR SW1X 15 G3
Embassy of Mexico
MYFR/PICC W1J 15 J1
Embassy of Mongolia
KENS W8 ....120 A2
Embassy of Morocco
SKENS SW7 ....120 B3
Embassy of Mozambique
FITZ W1T 4 A7
Embassy of Myanmar
MYFR/PICC W1J 9 J7
Embassy of Nepal
KENS W8 ....120 A1
Embassy of Netherlands
SKENS SW7 ....120 B2
Embassy of Norway
KTBR SW1X 15 H4
Embassy of Paraguay
SKENS SW7 ....120 A3
Embassy of Peru
KTBR SW1X 15 F4
Embassy of Philippines
KENS W8 ....120 A1
Embassy of Poland
CAVSQ/HST W1G 9 H2
Embassy of Portugal
KTBR SW1X 15 G3
Embassy of Qatar
MYFR/PKLN W1K 15 H1
Embassy of Romania
KENS W8 ....120 A2
Embassy of Russian Federation
KENS W8 ....120 A1
Embassy of Saudi Arabia
MYFR/PICC W1J 9 J7

Embassy of Senegal
CRICK NW2 ....82 A5
Embassy of Slovak Republic
KENS W8 ....120 A1
Embassy of Slovenia
MHST W1U 9 J3
Embassy of Spain
KTBR SW1X 15 H4
Embassy of Sudan
WHALL SW1A 16 A1
Embassy of Sweden
MBLAR W1H 8 E2
Embassy of Switzerland
MBLAR W1H 8 E2
Embassy of Syria
KTBR SW1X 15 G3
Embassy of Thailand
SKENS SW7 ....120 B3
Embassy of the Holy See
WIM/MER SW19 ....159 F5
Embassy of the Republic of Gabon
SKENS SW7 ....120 B3
Embassy of Tunisia
SKENS SW7 ....14 B3
Embassy of Turkey
KTBR SW1X 15 H3
Embassy of Turkmenistan
FITZ W1T 10 B2
Embassy of Ukraine
NTCHL W11 ....119 H1
Embassy of United Arab Emirates
BAY/PAD W2 ....14 B2
Embassy of Uruguay
SKENS SW7 ....14 D4
Embassy of USA
MYFR/PKLN W1K 9 G5
Embassy of Uzbekistan
NTGHL W11 ....119 J1
Embassy of Venezuela
SKENS SW7 ....14 B5
Embassy of Yemen
SKENS SW7 ....14 A5
Emberhurst School
ESH/CLAY KT10 ....189 J4
Ember Sports Club
ESH/CLAY KT10 ....189 H5
Embroidery World Business Centre
WFD IG8 ....53 H5
EMD Walthamstow Cinema
WALTH E17 ....69 J1
Emery Theatre
POP/IOD E14 ....105 K5
Emmanuel CE Primary School
KIL/WHAMP NW6 ....82 E5
Empire Cinema
LSO/SEVD WC2H 10 D5
Enolsleigh Industrial Estate
NWDGN UB2 ....114 D4
Enfield Business Centre
PEND EN3 ....24 E3
Enfield Chace Lower School
ENC/FH EN2 ....24 A1
Enfield College
PEND EN3 ....24 E4
Enfield County School
ENC/FH EN2 ....23 K4
Enfield CC
EN EN1 ....24 E4
Enfield FC
ED N9 ....36 E4
Enfield Golf Club
ENC/FH EN2 ....23 H5
Enfield Grammar School (Upper)
ENC/FH EN2 ....23 K4
English Martyrs RC Primary School
WALW SE17 ....18 E7
WCHPL E1 ....13 K4
English National Ballet School
WBPTN SW10 ....140 A4
Ensham Secondary School
TOOT SW17 ....178 E1
Enterprise Business Park
POP/IOD E14 ....124 E2
Enterprise Industrial Estate
BERM/RHTH SE16 ....123 K5
Epsom & Ewell High School
HOR/WEW KT19 ....206 E4
Eric Liddell Sports Centre
ELTH/MOT SE9 ....166 C4
Eridge House Preparatory School
FUL/PGN SW6 ....139 J3
Erith & District Hospital
ERITH DA8 ....130 A6
Erith Health Centre
ERITH DA8 ....130 B6
Erith Library & Museum
ERITH DA8 ....130 B5
Erith Playhouse
ERITH DA8 ....130 C5
Erith School
ERITH DA8 ....149 K1
Erith School Community Sports Centre
ERITH DA8 ....149 K1
Erith Small Business Centre
ERITH DA8 ....130 C6
Erith Sports Centre
ERITH DA8 ....130 B6
Erith Stadium
ERITH DA8 ....130 B6
Ernest Bevin College
TOOT SW17 ....160 D5
Eros
MYFR/PICC W1J 10 C1
Esher CE High School
ESH/CLAY KT10 ....204 A1
Esher Church Primary School
ESH/CLAY KT10 ....204 A4
Esher College
THDIT KT7 ....189 K4

Esher RFC
WOT/HER KT12 ....188 D6
Essendine Primary School
KIL/WHAMP NW6 ....100 E2
Essex Primary School
MNPK E12 ....89 J4
Ethelburga GM School
BTSEA SW11 ....140 D2
Ethel Davis School
CHDH RM6 ....73 H2
Euro Business Centre
SRTFD E15 ....88 D6
Eurolink Business Centre
BRXS/STRHM SW2 ....142 B5
Europa Trading Estate
ERITH DA8 ....130 A5
European Business Centre
CDALE/KGS NW9 ....45 F6
European Business School London
CAMTN NW1 ....3 F6
European College of Business Management
SDTCH EC2A 7 G6
European School of Economics
KTBR SW1X 15 H3
European Vocational College
HDTCH EC3A 13 H4
Euro Way School
CEND/HSY/T N8 ....49 G6
Euro Way School London
FSBYPK N4 ....67 H4
Euston Centre University of Westminster
CAMTN NW1 ....4 A6
Euston Tower
CAMTN NW1 ....4 A6
Evans Business Centre
CRICK NW2 ....81 J1
Eveline Lowe Primary School
PECK SE15 ....123 G5
Evendine College
SOHO/SHAV W1D 10 C3
Eversley Medical Centre
CROY/NA CR0 ....196 B3
Eversley Primary School
WCHMH N21 ....22 E6
Everyman Cinema
HAMP NW3 ....83 G2
Evolution House
RCH/KEW TW9 ....137 F3
Ewell Athletics Track
HOR/WEW KT19 ....207 F4
Ewell Castle Junior School
EW KT17 ....207 H6
Ewell Castle School
EW KT17 ....207 J6
Ewell Grove Infant School
EW KT17 ....207 H6
ExCeL Exhibition Centre
CAN/RD E16 ....107 F6
Exchange Square
SDTCH EC2A 13 G1
The Exchange
IL IG1 ....72 B6
Exhibition Halls
BARB EC2Y 12 D1
WBLY HA9 ....80 C2
Eye Clinic
NOXST/BSQ WC1A 10 D3
Faculty of Engineering & Science (University of Westminster)
FITZ W1T 10 B1
Faircharm Trading Estate
DEPT SE8 ....144 E1
IS N1 ....6 C2
The Faircross Complementary Medical Centre
BARK IG11 ....90 E4
Fairfield Clinic
BKHH IG9 ....39 F3
Fairfield Pool & Leisure Centre
DART DA1 ....171 H2
Fairfield Trade Park
KUT/HW KT1 ....175 G6
Fairholme Primary School
EBED/NFELT TW14 ....153 G3
Fairlawn Primary School
FSTH SE23 ....163 K2
Fairley House School
PIM SW1V 16 C7
Fairlop Primary School
BARK/HLT IG6 ....54 C4
Fairview Industrial Centre
RAIN RM13 ....111 F5
Fairview Industrial Estate
HYS/HAR UB3 ....113 J2
Fairview Medical Centre
STRHM/NOR SW16 ....179 K4
Fairway Primary School
MLHL NW7 ....31 F4
Fairways Business Park
LEY E10 ....69 G6
Falconbrook Primary School
BTSEA SW11 ....140 C3
Falcon Business Centre
BTSEA SW11 ....140 D5
Falcon Park Industrial Estate
WLSDN NW10 ....81 G3
The Falcon School for Girls
EA W5 ....117 G1
Falkner House School
SKENS SW7 ....120 A3
Family Records Centre
FSBYW WC1X 5 J5
Fanmakers' Hall
LVPST EC2M 13 G2
Fan Museum
GNWCH SE10 ....145 F1
Faraday Building
BLKFR EC4V 12 B4
Farm Lane Trading Estate
FUL/PGN SW6 ....119 K6

Farnborough Primary School
ORP BR6 ....216 D3
Farnell House Medical Centre
HSLW TW3 ....135 G2
Farnham Green Primary School
GDMY/SEVK IG3 ....73 G3
Farrington & Stratford House School
CHST BR7 ....185 J5
Fashion & Textile Design Museum
STHWK SE1 ....19 H3
Featherstone High School
NWDGN UB2 ....114 C4
Featherstone Industrial Estate
NWDGN UB2 ....114 D2
Featherstone Road Health Clinic
NWDGN UB2 ....114 D3
Feinex Trading Estate
WLGTN SM6 ....195 F6
Feltham Airparcs Leisure Centre
FELT TW13 ....154 C4
Feltham Athletics Arena
EBED/NFELT TW14 ....153 K2
Felthambrook Industrial Estate
FELT TW13 ....154 A5
Feltham Community College
FELT TW13 ....154 B4
Feltham Hill Infant School
FELT TW13 ....153 J5
Feltham Hill Junior School
FELT TW13 ....153 J5
Feltham & Hounslow Borough FC
EBED/NFELT TW14 ....153 K2
Feltham Superbowl
FELT TW13 ....154 A4
Fenstanton J & I School
BRXS/STRHM SW2 ....162 B3
Fenton House
HAMP NW3 ....83 G1
Ferrier Industrial Estate
WAND/EARL SW18 ....140 A4
Ferry Island Retail Park
TOTM N17 ....50 B6
Ferry Lane Industrial Estate
RAIN RM13 ....111 J4
WALTH E17 ....50 E6
Ferry Lane Primary School
TOTM N17 ....68 D1
Festival Pier
STHWK SE1 ....11 H7
Field End Primary School
RSLP HA4 ....77 H1
Fielding Primary School
WEA W13 ....116 C2
Film House Cinema
RCH/KEW TW9 ....136 E6
Financial Times
POP/IOD E14 ....106 A5
STHWK SE1 ....12 D7
Finchley Campus of St Marys CE School
NFNCH/WDSPK N12 ....47 H2
Finchley Catholic High School
NFNCH/WDSPK N12 ....33 G5
Finchley CC
FNCH N3 ....47 F5
Finchley Golf Club
MLHL NW7 ....46 D2
Finchley Industrial Centre
NFNCH/WDSPK N12 ....33 G6
Finchley Lido
NFNCH/WDSPK N12 ....47 H3
Finchley Memorial Hospital
NFNCH/WDSPK N12 ....47 G3
Finchley Youth Theatre
FNCH N3 ....47 J6
Finsbury Circus Medical Centre
LVPST EC2M 13 F2
Finsbury Health Centre
CLKNW EC1R 5 J6
Finsbury Leisure Centre
FSBYE EC1V 6 D5
Finsbury Park Track
FSBYPK N4 ....67 H4
Finton House School
TOOT SW17 ....160 E4
Fircroft Primary School
TOOT SW17 ....160 E4
Fire Brigade Museum
STHWK SE1 ....18 C2
Firepower (Museum of Artillery)
WOOL/PLUM SE18 ....127 G3
Firs Farm Primary School
PLMGR N13 ....35 K5
Fisher Athletic FC
BERM/RHTH SE16 ....124 A1
Fishmonger's Hall
CANST EC4R 12 E6
Fitness Unlimited Leisure Centre
BOW E3 ....105 J1
Fitzjohns Primary School
HAMP NW3 ....83 H3
Fitzrovia Medical Centre
FITZ W1T 4 A7
Fitzroy Nuffield Hospital
MBLAR W1H 8 E3
Five Bridges
LBTH SE11 ....122 A5
Five Elms Primary School
DAGW RM9 ....92 B1
Five Ways Business Centre
FELT TW13 ....154 A5
Flamsteed House Museum
GNWCH SE10 ....145 G1
Flaxman Sports Centre
CMBW SE5 ....142 D3
Fleecefield Primary School
ED N9 ....36 C6

Fleet Primary School
HAMP NW3 ....83 K3
Fleetway Business Park
GFD/PVL UB6 ....97 H1
Fleming Lab Museum
BAY/PAD W2 ....8 B3
Flora Gardens Primary School
HMSMTH W6 ....118 E4
Florence Nightingale Museum
STHWK SE1 ....17 G3
Flutters Leisure Centre
FUL/PGN SW6 ....139 K1
FOB School
CLPT E5 ....68 C4
Follys End Christian High School
SNWD SE25 ....197 F3
The Foot Clinic
WIM/MER SW19 ....177 H2
Fordbridge Medical Centre
ASHF TW15 ....152 C6
The Ford Office
CONDST W1S 9 K4
Foregate Business Park
BELV DA17 ....129 K2
Ford Industrial Park
DAGW RM9 ....110 D2
Fordview Industrial Estate
RAIN RM13 ....111 F2
Foreign & Commonwealth Office
WHALL SW1A 16 D3
Foreland Medical Centre
NTCHL W11 ....100 C6
Forest Business Park
LEY E10 ....69 F4
Forestdale Primary School
CROY/NA CR0 ....213 G6
Foresters Primary School
WLGTN SM6 ....210 D4
Forest Gate Community School
FSTGT E7 ....88 E3
Forest Hill Business Centre
FSTH SE23 ....163 K4
Forest Hill Industrial Estate
FSTH SE23 ....163 K4
Forest Hill Pools
SYD SE26 ....163 K4
Forest Hill School
FSTH SE23 ....164 A5
Forest House Business Centre
WAN E11 ....70 D2
Forest Industrial Park
BARK/HLT IG6 ....54 C3
Forest Park Cemetery & Crematorium
BARK/HLT IG6 ....55 J1
Forest Road Medical Centre
WALTH E17 ....51 H6
Forest School
WALTH E17 ....51 F6
Forest Trading Estate
WALTH E17 ....70 C1
Forge Close Clinic
HAYES BR2 ....199 K5
Forge Lane Primary School
FELT TW13 ....172 D2
The Former Health Centre
CHARL SE7 ....126 C4
Forster Park Primary School
CAT SE6 ....165 H5
Fortismere School
EFNCH N2 ....47 K5
Fortune Theatre
HOL/ALD WC2B 11 F4
The Forum
EDGW HA8 ....44 C2
Fossdene Primary School
CHARL SE7 ....126 A5
Foster's Primary School
WELL DA16 ....148 D4
Foulds School
BAR EN5 ....20 B4
The Foundling Museum
BMSBY WC1N 5 F4
Fountayne Business Centre
SEVS/STOTM N15 ....68 C1
Fountayne Road Health Centre
STNW/STAM N16 ....68 C6
Four Seasons Hotel
BERM/RHTH SE16 ....124 C1
MYFR/PKLN W1K 15 J2
Foxfield Primary School
WOOL/PLUM SE18 ....127 H5
Fox Primary School
KENS W8 ....119 K1
Frances Bardsley School for Girls
ROM RM1 ....75 J2
Franciscan Primary School
TOOT SW17 ....161 F6
Francis Holland School
BGVA SW1W 15 H7
CAMTN NW1 ....2 E1
Frank Barnes Primary School
STJWD NW8 ....2 C1
Franklin Industrial Estate
PGE/AN SE20 ....181 K4
Freehold Industrial Centre
HSLWW TW4 ....134 B6
Free Trade Wharf
WAP E1W 105 F6
Freightliners City Farm
HOLWY N7 ....85 F4
Fresh Wharf Estate
BARK IG11 ....90 B6
Freuchen Medical Centre
WLSDN NW10 ....99 H1
Freud Museum
HAMP NW3 ....83 H4
Friars Primary Foundation School
STHWK SE1 ....18 A2
Friends House
CAMTN NW1 ....4 C5

Friern Barnet School
FBAR/BDGN N11 ....47 K1
Friern Bridge Retail Park
FBAR/BDGN N11 ....48 B2
Fritnwood Primary School
NTHWD HA6 ....40 D2
Frogmore Industrial Estate
HBRY N5 ....85 J2
HYS/HAR UB3 ....113 H2
WLSDN NW10 ....98 E2
Fryent Country Park
KTN/HRWW/WS HA3 ....62 C4
Fryent Medical Centre
CDALE/KGS NW9 ....62 K4
Fryent Primary School
CDALE/KGS NW9 ....62 K4
Fulham Cemetery
FUL/PGN SW6 ....139 G1
Fulham Clinic
FUL/PGN SW6 ....119 H6
Fulham Cross Secondary
School
FUL/PGN SW6 ....139 G1
Fulham FC (Craven Cottage)
PUT/ROE SW15 ....139 F2
Fulham Medical Centre
FUL/PGN SW6 ....140 A1
Fulham Palace
FUL/PGN SW6 ....139 G3
Fulham Pools
FUL/PGN SW6 ....119 H6
Fulham Preparatory School
WKENS W14 ....119 H6
Fulham Pre-Preparatory
School
FUL/PGN SW6 ....139 H3
Fulham Primary School
FUL/PGN SW6 ....119 K6
Fuller Smith & Turner
Sports Club
CHSWK W4 ....138 B2
Fullwell Cross Health Centre
BARK/HLT IG6 ....54 C5
Fullwell Cross Swimming Pool
& Recreation Centre
BARK/HLT IG6 ....54 C5
Fulwood Primary School
BARK/HLT IG6 ....72 C1
Fulwell Golf Club
HPTN TW12 ....155 J6
Furness Primary School
WLSDN NW10 ....99 J1
Furzedown Primary School
TOOT SW17 ....179 G2
Furze Infant School
CHDH RM6 ....74 A3
Future Business College
CONDST W1S 9 K4
Gainsborough Clinic
PLMGR N13 ....35 F6
Gainsborough Primary School
HOM E9 ....87 G7
SRTFD E15 ....106 C2
Galewyall Primary School
BERM/RHTH SE16 ....123 J4
Galliard Primary School
ED N9 ....36 C1
Gallions Mount Primary
School
WOOL/PLUM SE18 ....128 A5
Gallions Primary School
EHAM E6 ....108 B5
Gallions Reach Shopping Park
EHAM E6 ....108 B4
Gants Hill Medical Centre
GNTH/NBYPK IG2 ....72 A3
Gardener Industrial Estate
SYD SE26 ....182 B1
Garden House School
BCVA SW1W 121 F5
Garden Primary School
MTCM CR4 ....179 J6
Garden Suburb Primary
School
GLDGN NW11 ....64 D2
Garfield Primary School
FBAR/BDGN N11 ....48 B1
WIM/MER SW19 ....178 B2
Garratt Park Secondary
Special School
WAND/EARL SW18 ....160 A5
Garrick Industrial Centre
CDALE/KGS NW9 ....63 H2
Garrick Theatre
LSQ/SEVD WC2H 10 E6
Garth Primary School
MRDN SM4 ....194 C2
The Garth Road Industrial
Centre
MRDN SM4 ....193 F4
Gascoigne Primary School
BARK IG11 ....90 C6
Gate Cinema
KENS W8 ....119 K1
Gatehouse School
BETH E2 ....105 F1
The Gatehouse Theatre
HGT N6 ....66 A4
Gate Theatre
NTGHL W11 ....119 K1
Gateway Business Centre
SYD SE26 ....182 B2
WOOL/PLUM SE18 ....127 H3
Gateway Industrial Estate
WLSDN NW10 ....99 H2
Gatton School
TOOT SW17 ....160 D6
Gayhurst Primary School
HACK E8 ....86 C5
Gearies Infant School
GNTH/NBYPK IG2 ....72 A2
Gearies Junior School
GNTH/NBYPK IG2 ....72 B2
Geffrye Museum
BETH E2 ....7 H3
Gemini Business Estate
NWCR SE14 ....124 A5

General Medical Clinics
WCHPL E1 ....13 J1
Genesis Cinema
WCHPL E1 ....104 E3
Geoffrey Chaucer
Technology College
STHWK SE1 ....18 E5
The Geoffrey Lloyd Foulkes
Clinic
IL IG1 ....72 A6
Geoffrey Whitworth Theatre
DART DA1 ....150 D5
George Eliot J & I School
STJWD NW8 ....83 G6
George Greens School
POP/IOD E14 ....125 F5
George Mitchell School
LEY E10 ....69 K5
George Spicer Primary School
EN EN1 ....24 B4
George Tomlinson Primary
School
WAN E11 ....70 C5
Germal College
FSBYPK N4 ....67 G5
Gibbs Green Special School
WKENS W14 ....119 J5
Gibson Business Centre
TOTM N17 ....50 B2
The Gibson Business Centre
TOTM N17 ....50 B3
Gidea Park College
GPK RM2 ....57 J3
Gideon Primary School
CLAP SW4 ....129 G5
The Cielgud Theatre
SOHO/CST W1F 10 C5
Giffin Business Centre
DEPT SE8 ....144 D1
Gifford Primary School
NTHLT UB5 ....95 K1
Gilbert Collection
TPL/STR WC2R 11 G5
Gilbert Colvin Primary School
CLAY IG5 ....54 A4
Gilbert Scott Primary School
SAND/SEL CR2 ....213 G5
Gillespie Primary School
HBRY N5 ....85 H1
Girdlers' Hall
CITYW EC2V 12 D2
Glade Primary School
CLAY IG5 ....53 K4
The Glades Shopping Centre
BMLY BR1 ....183 K5
Gladstone Medical Centre
CRICK NW2 ....81 H2
Gladstone Park Primary School
WLSDN NW10 ....81 J3
Glaziers/Scientific Instrument
Makers Hall
STHWK SE1 ....12 C7
Glebe First & Middle School
KTN/HRWW/WS HA3 ....61 K1
Glebe Primary School
HGDN/ICK UB10 ....76 B2
Glebe School
WWKM BR4 ....199 G6
Gleen Lecky Health Centre
PUT/ROE SW15 ....139 G5
Glenbrook Primary School
CLAP SW4 ....161 J1
Glencairn Sports Club
FBAR/BDGN N11 ....48 C3
Grand Union Industrial
Estate
WLSDN NW10 ....98 D1
Glendower Preparatory
School
SKENS SW7 ....120 B4
Glenham College
IL IG1 ....72 B6
Glenlyn Medical Centre
E/WMO/HCT KT8 ....189 H2
Glenthorne High School
CHEAM SM3 ....193 K5
Globe Primary School
BETH E2 ....104 E2
Globe Wharf
BERM/RHTH SE16 ....105 F6
Gloucester Primary School
PECK SE15 ....143 F1
Godolphin & Latymer School
HMSMTH W6 ....118 E4
Godwin Junior School
FSTGT E7 ....89 F2
Godwin Primary School
DAGW RM9 ....92 A5
Goethe Institute
SKENS SW7 ....14 B4
Golborne Medical Centre
NKENS W10 ....100 D3
Goldbeaters Primary School
EDGW HA8 ....45 H4
Golden Hinde Educational
Trust
STHWK SE1 ....12 E6
Golders Green Crematorium
GLDGN NW11 ....64 D4
Golders Green Health Centre
GLDGN NW11 ....65 F5
Golders Hill Health Centre
GLDGN NW11 ....65 G3
Golders Hill School
GLDGN NW11 ....64 E4
Goldhawk Industrial Estate
SHB W12 ....118 E3
Goldsmiths College
BROCKY SE4 ....144 C4
LEW SE13 ....145 H5
Goldsmiths College Sports
Ground
SCUP DA14 ....169 G5
Goldsmiths Hall
STBT EC1A 12 C3
Gonville Primary School
THHTH CR7 ....196 A3
Gooding Health Centre
HOLWY N7 ....84 D4

Goodmayes Retail Park
GDMY/SEVK IG3 ....73 H4
Goodrich J & I School
EDUL SE22 ....163 H1
Good Shepherd RC Primary
School
BMLY BR1 ....165 J6
CROY/NA CR0 ....213 K5
The Good Shepherd RC
Primary School
SHB W12 ....118 C2
Goodwyn School
MLHL NW7 ....45 J1
Goose Green Primary School
EDUL SE22 ....143 G5
Goose Green Trading Estate
EDUL SE22 ....143 H5
Gordonbrock Primary School
BROCKY SE4 ....144 D6
Gordon Hospital
WEST SW1P 16 C7
Gordon House Health Centre
WEA W13 ....116 C1
Gordon Infant School
IL IG1 ....90 D1
Gordon Primary School
ELTH/MOT SE9 ....146 E5
Goresbrook Leisure Centre
DAGW RM9 ....91 K6
Goresbrook Sports Centre
DAGW RM9 ....91 K6
The Goring Hotel
BGVA SW1W 15 K4
Gorringe Park Primary School
MTCM CR4 ....179 F4
Gosai Cinema
WEA W13 ....116 C1
Gosbury Hill Health Centre
CHSGTN KT9 ....206 A2
Gosford Primary School
REDBR IG4 ....71 K2
Gospel Oak Primary School
HAMP NW3 ....84 A2
Gove Farm Retail Park
CHDH RM6 ....73 J4
Gower House School
CDALE/KGS NW9 ....62 K6
Grace Business Centre
MTCM CR4 ....194 E3
Grace Theatre at the
Latchmere
BTSEA SW11 ....140 E3
Graduate School of
Management
TOTM N17 ....50 B4
Grafton Primary School
BCTR RM8 ....74 A6
HOLWY N7 ....84 D1
Grahame Park Health Centre
CDALE/KGS NW9 ....45 G4
Grahame Park J & I School
CDALE/KGS NW9 ....45 G4
Granard Business Centre
MLHL NW7 ....45 G2
Granard Primary School
PUT/ROE SW15 ....158 E1
Granby Sports Club
CHST BR7 ....184 D1
Grand Avenue Primary School
BRYLDS KT5 ....191 K4
Grande Vitesse Industrial
Centre
STHWK SE1 ....18 B1
Grange Blooms Hotel
RSQ WC1B 10 E1
The Grange City Hotel
TWRH EC3N 13 J5
Grange First & Middle School
RYLN/HDSTN HA2 ....60 B5
Grange Fitzrovia Hotel
GTPST W1W 9 K1
Grange Holborn Hotel
NOXST/BSQ WC1A 11 F2
Grange Langham Court Hotel
GTPST W1W 9 K2
The Grange Museum
CRICK NW2 ....81 H2
Grange Park Clinic
YEAD UB4 ....94 D3
Grange Park Preparatory
School
WCHMH N21 ....35 H1
Grange Park Primary School
WCHMH N21 ....23 G5
YEAD UB4 ....94 D3
Grange Primary School
CAN/RD E16 ....106 D3
EA W5 ....116 E2
STHWK SE1 ....19 G5
Grange Rochester Hotel
WEST SW1P 16 C6
Grange Strathmore Hotel
SKENS SW7 ....120 B3
Grange Whitehall Hotel
RSQ WC1B 10 E2
Grangewood Independent
School
FSTGT E7 ....89 H5
Grangewood School
PIN HA5 ....58 E2
Granton Primary School
STRHM/NOR SW16 ....179 H5
Granville Road Industrial
Estate
CRICK NW2 ....64 D6
Grasmere Primary School
STNW/STAM N16 ....85 K2
Grasshoppers RFC
ISLW TW7 ....116 A6
Grassroots School
HPTN TW12 ....173 F4
Grasvenor Avenue Infant
School
BAR EN5 ....32 E1

Gravel Hill Primary School
BXLYHS DA6 ....149 J6
Graveney School
TOOT SW17 ....179 G2
Graves Yard Industrial Estate
WELL DA16 ....148 B3
Grays Farm Primary School
STMC/STPC BR5 ....186 C4
Grazebrook Primary School
STNW/STAM N16 ....68 A6
Great Cambridge Industrial
Estate
EN EN1 ....24 D6
Great Chapel Street Medical
Centre
SOHO/SHAV W1D 10 C3
Great Eastern Hotel
LVPST EC2M 13 G2
Greater London Authority
Headquarters (City Hall)
STHWK SE1 ....19 H1
Great Jubilee Wharf
WAP E1W 123 K1
Great Scotland Yard
WHALL SW1A 10 E7
Great Western Industrial Park
NWDGN UB2 ....115 G2
Great West Trading Estate
BTFD TW8 ....116 C6
Greenacres Primary School
ELTH/MOT SE9 ....167 F4
The Green CE Primary School
TOTM N17 ....50 B6
Green Dragon Primary School
BTFD TW8 ....117 F5
Greenfield Medical Centre
CRICK NW2 ....82 C1
Greenfield Primary School
OXHEY WD19 ....41 G1
Greenfields Junior School
SHB W12 ....99 H6
Greenfields Special School
MUSWH N10 ....47 K4
Greenford Avenue Medical
Centre
HNWL W7 ....96 E4
Greenford Green Clinic
GFD/PVL UB6 ....78 E3
Greenford High School
STHL UB1 ....96 A2
Greenford Industrial Estate
GFD/PVL UB6 ....78 B6
Greenford Park Cemetery
GFD/PVL UB6 ....96 B4
Greenford Road Medical
Centre
GFD/PVL UB6 ....96 D1
Greenford Sports Centre
STHL UB1 ....96 A2
Greengate Medical Centre
PLSTW E13 ....107 F2
Greengrove College
STHGT/OAK N14 ....34 E4
Greenheath Business Centre
BETH E2 ....104 D2
Greenhill College
HRW HA1 ....61 F2
Greenhill Park Medical Centre
WLSDN NW10 ....81 G6
Greenland Pier
BERM/RHTH SE16 ....124 C3
Green Lane Business Park
ELTH/MOT SE9 ....167 G4
Green Lane Primary School
WPK KT4 ....192 E4
Greenleaf Primary School
WALTH E17 ....51 H6
Greenmead Primary School
PUT/ROE SW15 ....138 E6
The Green School for Girls
ISLW TW7 ....136 B1
Greenshaw High School
SUT SM1 ....194 B6
Greenshields Industrial Estate
CAN/RD E16 ....125 K1
Greenside Primary School
SHB W12 ....118 D2
Greenslade Primary School
WOOL/PLUM SE18 ....127 J6
Green Street Green Primary
School
ORP BR6 ....217 F4
Greenvale School
FSTH SE23 ....164 B5
Greenwich Centre Business
Park
DEPT SE8 ....144 E1
Greenwich Cinema
GNWCH SE10 ....145 F1
Greenwich Community
College
WOOL/PLUM SE18 ....127 G4
WOOL/PLUM SE18 ....127 J6
Greenwich Industrial Estate
CHARL SE7 ....126 A4
GNWCH SE10 ....144 E1
Greenwich Natural Health
Centre
GNWCH SE10 ....145 F1
Greenwich Pier
GNWCH SE10 ....125 F5
Greenwich School of
Management
GNWCH SE10 ....145 F1
Greenwich Theatre &
Art Gallery
GNWCH SE10 ....145 G1
Greenwood Primary School
NTHLT UB5 ....78 D4
Greenwood Theatre
STHWK SE1 ....19 F2
Green Wrythe Primary School
CAR SM5 ....194 C5
Greig City Academy
CEND/HSY/T N8 ....67 F1
Gresham College
HCIRC EC1N 11 J2

Gresham Way Industrial
Estate
WIM/MER SW19 ....160 A5
Grey Coat Hospital CE School
For Girls
WEST SW1P 16 C5
The Greycoat Hospital
WEST SW1P 16 C5
Grey Court School
RCHPK/HAM TW10 ....156 E5
Griffen Manor School
WOOL/PLUM SE18 ....147 K2
Grimsdyke First & Middle
School
PIN HA5 ....41 K2
Grims Dyke Golf Club
PIN HA5 ....42 A1
Grim's Dyke Hotel
KTN/HRWW/WS HA3 ....42 D1
Grinling Gibbons Primary
School
DEPT SE8 ....124 C6
Grist Memorial Sports Club
E/WMO/HCT KT8 ....189 K2
Grocers' Hall
CITYW EC2V 12 F4
Grosvenor House Hotel
MYFR/PKLN W1K 9 G6
The Grove Health Centre
SHB W12 ....118 E3
Grove College (Froebel College)
PUT/ROE SW15 ....158 C1
Grove House Primary School
for Deaf Children
WNWD SE27 ....162 C4
Grovelands Priory Hospital
STHGT/OAK N14 ....34 E3
Grovelands School
WOT/HER KT12 ....188 A3
Grove Medical Centre
DEPT SE8 ....124 B4
The Grove Medical Centre
ARCH N19 ....66 D6
Grove Park Industrial Estate
CDALE/KGS NW9 ....63 F1
Grove Park Primary School
CHSWK W4 ....117 K6
Grove Park School
CDALE/KGS NW9 ....62 C1
Grove Primary School
CHDH RM6 ....73 H2
Grove Road Primary School
HSLW TW3 ....135 F5
The Groves Medical Centre
NWMAL KT3 ....176 B6
Grove Village Medical Centre
EBED/NFELT TW14 ....153 H3
Guardian Angels RC Primary
School
BOW E3 ....105 G3
Guardian Newspapers
POP/IOD E14 ....124 E2
Guards' Chapel and Museum
STJSPK SW1H 16 C3
Guildhall Annex
KUT/HW KT1 ....174 E6
Guildhall Art Gallery
CITYW EC2V 12 D3
Guildhall School of Music
and Drama
BARB EC2Y 12 D1
STLK EC1Y 6 D7
Gumley House Convent
School
ISLW TW7 ....136 B4
Gunnersbury Catholic
School
BTFD TW8 ....116 D5
Gunnersbury Park Museum
ACT W3 ....117 H3
Gurnell Leisure Centre
WEA W13 ....97 G2
Guru Gobind Singh Khalsa
College
CHIG IG7 ....39 K3
Guru Nanak Medical Centre
STHL UB1 ....114 C1
Guy's Hospital
STHWK SE1 ....19 F1
Guys Kings and Thomas
Medical School (Kings
College London)
STHWK SE1 ....12 C7
Gwyn Jones Primary School
WAN E11 ....70 B4
GX Superbowl
EHAM E6 ....108 A4
Gypsy Moth IV
GNWCH SE10 ....125 F5
Haberdashers Askes
Hatcham College
NWCR SE14 ....144 A3
Haberdashers' Hall
STLK EC1A 12 A2
Hackbridge Primary School
WLCTN SM6 ....195 H6
Hackney Business Centre
HACK E8 ....86 D4
Hackney City Farm
BETH E2 ....104 C1
Hackney Community College
IS N1 ....7 G3
Hackney Empire Variety
Theatre
HACK E8 ....86 D4
Hackney Free & Parochial CE
School
HOM E9 ....86 E4
The Hackney Museum
HACK E8 ....86 D4
Hackney Sports Centre
HOM E9 ....87 J2
Hadley Wood Golf Club
EBAR EN4 ....21 J2
Hadley Wood Primary
School
EBAR EN4 ....21 G1

The Haelan Clinic
CEND/HSY/T N8 ....66 E3
Haggerston School
BETH E2 ....7 K2
Haggerston Swimming Pool
BETH E2 ....7 K1
Hague Primary School
BETH E2 ....104 D3
Hailey Road Business Park
ERITHM DA18 ....129 H2
Haimo Primary School
ELTH/MOT SE9 ....146 C6
Hainault Business Park
BARK/HLT IG6 ....55 J1
Hainault Forest Golf Club
CHIG IG7 ....55 K2
Hainault Forest High School
& the Learning Centre
BARK/HLT IG6 ....55 C1
Hakim Qureshi Clinic
NWDGN UB2 ....114 D3
The Hale Clinic
CAMTN NW1 ....3 K7
Half Moon Theatre
WCHPL E1 ....105 F3
Haling Manor High School
SAND/SEL CR2 ....211 H5
The Halkin Hotel
KTBR SW1X 15 H3
Halley Primary School
POP/IOD E14 ....105 G4
Hallfield Clinic
BAY/PAD W2 ....101 G5
Hallfield Primary School
BAY/PAD W2 ....101 G5
The Hall Junior School
HAMP NW3 ....83 H4
Hallmark Trading Estate
WBLY HA9 ....80 E2
Hall Place
BXLY DA5 ....169 K1
Halls Business Centre
HYS/HAR UB3 ....113 K3
The Hall School
HAMP NW3 ....83 H4
Hall School Wimbledon
RYNPK SW20 ....177 G4
Hall School Wimbledon
Junior Dept
PUT/ROE SW15 ....158 D5
Hallsville Primary School
CAN/RD E16 ....106 E5
Halstow Primary School
GNWCH SE10 ....125 J5
Hambrough Primary School
STHL UB1 ....114 D1
Hamer Indoor Market
BOW E3 ....105 H1
Ham Health Clinic
RCHPK/HAM TW10 ....156 D5
Ham House (NT)
RCHPK/HAM TW10 ....156 D5
Hamilton Road Industrial
Estate
WNWD SE27 ....162 E6
Hamlet International
Industrial Estate
ERITH DA8 ....130 A5
Hammersmith Apollo
HMSMTH W6 ....119 F5
Hammersmith Cemetery
HMSMTH W6 ....119 G5
Hammersmith Hospital
SHB W12 ....99 J5
Hammersmith Industrial
Estate
HMSMTH W6 ....119 F6
Hammersmith New
Cemetery
RCH/KEW TW9 ....137 J3
Hammersmith Palais
HMSMTH W6 ....119 F4
Hammersmith Physio &
Sports Injury Clinic
HMSMTH W6 ....119 F4
Hammersmith & West
London College
WKENS W14 ....119 H4
Hampden Gurney School
MBLAR W1H 8 D3
Ham & Petersham CC
RCHPK/HAM TW10 ....156 E6
The Hampshire School
BAY/PAD W2 ....101 F6
SKENS SW7 ....14 C3
Hampstead College of
Fine Art
HAMP NW3 ....83 J4
Hampstead CC
KIL/WHAMP NW6 ....83 F3
Hampstead Golf Club
GLDGN NW11 ....65 G4
Hampstead Medical Centre
HAMP NW3 ....83 G2
Hampstead Parochial CE
School
HAMP NW3 ....83 G2
Hampstead School
CRICK NW2 ....82 C2
The Hampstead School of Art
HAMP NW3 ....82 E2
Hampstead School of English
KIL/WHAMP NW6 ....82 E2
Hampstead Theatre
HAMP NW3 ....83 H5
Hampton Cemetery
HPTN TW12 ....173 F3
Hampton Community
College
HPTN TW12 ....173 F1
Hampton Court House School
E/WMO/HCT KT8 ....173 K5
Hampton Court Palace
E/WMO/HCT KT8 ....174 A6
Hampton Court Palace
Golf Club
SURB KT6 ....190 D2

Hampton Farm Industrial
Estate
FELT TW13 ....154 D5
Hampton FC
HPTN TW12 ....173 G4
Hampton Hill Junior School
HPTN TW12 ....173 H1
Hampton Infant School
HPTN TW12 ....172 E3
Hampton Junior School
HPTN TW12 ....173 F4
The Hampton Medical Centre
HPTN TW12 ....173 F3
Hampton Open Air Pool
HPTN TW12 ....173 H3
Hampton Road Industrial
Park
CROY/NA CR0 ....196 D3
Hampton School
HPTN TW12 ....173 F1
Hampton Wick Infant School
TEDD TW11 ....174 D3
Handel's House
MYFR/PKLN W1K 9 J5
Handsworth Health Clinic
CHING E4 ....52 B2
Handsworth Primary School
CHING E4 ....52 B2
Hanover Primary School
IS N1 ....6 B2
Hanover Trading Estate
HOLWY N7 ....84 E3
Hanover West Industrial
Estate
WLSDN NW10 ....98 C2
Hanworth Trading Estate
FELT TW13 ....154 D5
Harbinger Primary School
POP/IOD E14 ....124 D4
Harborough School
ARCH N19 ....66 D6
Harenc School
SCUP DA14 ....186 D1
Hargrave Park Primary
School
ARCH N19 ....66 C6
Haringey Arts Council
ED N9 ....36 C3
Haringey Community Health
Clinic
SEVS/STOTM N15 ....68 B1
Haringey Magistrates Court
HGT N6 ....66 A3
Harlesden Primary School
WLSDN NW10 ....99 G1
Harley Medical Centre
CAVSQ/HST W1G 9 K3
The Harley Medical Centre
CANST EC4R 12 D5
Harley Street Clinic
CAVSQ/HST W1G 9 J2
The Harley Street Clinic
CAVSQ/HST W1G 9 J1
Harlington Community
School
HYS/HAR UB3 ....113 G4
Harlyn Primary School
PIN HA5 ....41 F3
The Harold Macmillan
Medical Centre
HRW HA1 ....60 D1
Harp Business Centre
CRICK NW2 ....63 J6
Harpley School
WCHPL E1 ....104 E3
Harrington Hill Primary
School
CLPT E5 ....68 D5
Harris City Technology College
NRWD SE19 ....181 G4
Harrodian School
BARN SW13 ....138 C1
Harrods Store
CHEL SW3 ....14 E4
Harrovian Business Village
HRW HA1 ....60 D4
Harrow Arts Centre
PIN HA5 ....42 A3
Harrow Borough FC
RYLN/HDSTN HA2 ....78 A2
Harrow College
HRW HA1 ....60 E4
KTN/HRWW/WS HA3 ....42 E2
Harrow CC
HRW HA1 ....78 E2
Harrow Crown Courts
HRW HA1 ....42 D6
Harrow Heritage Museum
RYLN/HDSTN HA2 ....42 C6
Harrow High School
HRW HA1 ....61 G3
Harrow Leisure Centre
KTN/HRWW/WS HA3 ....42 E3
Harrow Magistrates Court
HRW HA1 ....61 F1
Harrow RFC
STAN HA7 ....29 H5
Harrow Road Health Centre
MV/WKIL W9 ....100 E4
Harrow School
HRW HA1 ....60 E6
Harrow Town CC
RYLN/HDSTN HA2 ....60 E4
Harrow Weald Cemetery
KTN/HRWW/WS HA3 ....42 E2
Harry Gosling Primary School
WCHPL E1 ....104 C5
Hartley Primary School
EHAM E6 ....89 J4
Hartsbourne Golf &
Country Club
BUSH WD23 ....28 C4
Hartsbourne Primary School
BUSH WD23 ....28 C4
Harvington School
EA W5 ....97 J3

Haseltine Primary School
SYD SE26 ....164 C6
Haslemere Business Centre
EN EN1 ....24 D5
Haslemere Industrial Estate
EBED/NFELT TW14 ....133 K6
WAND/EARL SW18 ....160 A4
Haslemere Primary School
MTCM CR4 ....178 C5
Hasmonean High School
Boys Site
HDN NW4 ....46 B5
Hasmonean High School
Girls Site
MLHL NW7 ....45 J4
Hasmonean Primary School
HDN NW4 ....64 B2
Haste Hill Golf Club
NTHWD HA6 ....40 C5
Hastings Clinic
BRXS/STRHM SW2 ....142 A6
Hastingwood Trading Estate
UED N18 ....51 G2
Hatcham Mews Business
Centre
NWCR SE14 ....144 A1
Hatch End High School
KTN/HRWW/WS HA3 ....42 B3
Hatch End Swimming Pool
PIN HA5 ....42 A3
Hatfield Primary School
MRDN SM4 ....193 H3
Hathaway Primary School
HNWL W7 ....97 F4
Hatton School
WFD IG8 ....53 H6
Havelock Primary School
NWDGN UB2 ....114 E3
Haven Green Clinic
EA W5 ....97 K5
Havering College of Further
& Higher Education
EMPK RM11 ....75 K4
Havering Magistrates Court
ROM RM1 ....75 G2
Haverstock School
HAMP NW3 ....84 A4
Hawes Down Clinic
WWKM BR4 ....199 C6
Hawes Down Primary School
WWKM BR4 ....199 G5
The Hawker Centre
KUTN/CMB KT2 ....174 E1
Hawkesdown House School
KENS W8 ....119 K1
Hawkins Clinic
PUT/ROE SW15 ....139 G5
RYNPK SW20 ....176 C4
Hawksmoor Primary School
THMD SE28 ....109 H6
Hawley Infant School
CAMTN NW1 ....84 B5
Haydon School
PIN HA5 ....40 D6
Hayes Bridge Middle School
STHL UB1 ....114 D2
Hayes Bridge Retail Park
YEAD UB4 ....95 G6
Hayes CC
HYS/HAR UB3 ....94 D5
Hayes FC
HYS/HAR UB3 ....94 D6
Hayes Grove Priory Hospital
HAYES BR2 ....199 K6
The Hayes Manor School
HYS/HAR UB3 ....94 B5
Hayes Park J & I School
YEAD UB4 ....94 D3
Hayes Pool
HYS/HAR UB3 ....113 J1
Hayes Primary School
HAYES BR2 ....200 A5
Hayes School
HAYES BR2 ....200 A6
Hayes Social and Sports Club
HYS/HAR UB3 ....94 D4
Hayes Stadium Sports Centre
HYS/HAR UB3 ....94 B5
Hay Lane School
CDALE/KGS NW9 ....62 E1
Haymerle School
PECK SE15 ....123 H6
Hays Galleria
STHWK SE1 ....13 G7
Hayward Gallery
STHWK SE1 ....17 H1
Hazelbury Infants School
ED N9 ....36 A5
Hazeldene Medical Centre
WBLY HA9 ....80 D4
Hazelwood Infant School
PLMGR N13 ....35 H6
Hazelwood Junior School
PLMGR N13 ....35 G6
Headstart Montessori School
TOOT SW17 ....160 B5
The Health Clinic
SKENS SW7 ....14 B6
Healy Medical Centre
CLPT E5 ....68 D5
The Heart Hospital
CAVSQ/HST W1G 9 H2
Heathbrook Primary School
VX/NE SW8 ....141 H4
Heath Business Centre
HSLW TW3 ....135 H5
Heathcote Secondary School
CHING E4 ....38 C4
Heathfield College
HAYES BR2 ....215 G4
Heathfield Primary School
WHTN TW2 ....155 F3
Heathfield School
PIN HA5 ....59 H4
Heath House Preparatory
School
BKHTH/KID SE3 ....145 J3

The Heathland School
HSLWW TW4 ....154 E1
Heathmere Primary School
PUT/ROE SW15 ....158 D3
Heathpark Golf Club
WDR/YW UB7 ....112 D3
Heathrow Airport
HTHAIR TW6 ....132 E3
Heathrow Airport Central
Bus & Coach Station
HTHAIR TW6 ....132 D4
Heathrow International
Trading Estate
HSLWW TW4 ....134 A4
Heathrow Medical Centre
HYS/HAR UB3 ....113 C5
Heathrow Primary School
WDR/YW UB7 ....112 C6
Heathrow World Cargo
Centre
HTHAIR TW6 ....132 C4
Heathside Preparatory
School
HAMP NW3 ....83 G2
Heathway Industrial Estate
DAGE RM10 ....92 D2
Heathway Medical Centre
DAGW RM9 ....92 B2
Heavers Farm Primary School
SNWD SE25 ....197 G2
Heber Primary School
EDUL SE22 ....163 G1
Heckford Street Business
Centre
WAP E1W 105 F6
Hedges & Butler Estate
SRTFD E15 ....106 A1
Hedgewood School
YEAD UB4 ....94 C2
Helena Road Clinic
WLSDN NW10 ....81 K2
Heliport Industrial Estate
BTSEA SW11 ....140 C3
Hellenic College of London
KTBR SW1X 14 C1
Helston Court Business
Centre
WIM/MER SW19 ....176 E1
Henderson Hospital
BELMT SM2 ....208 E6
Hendon Cemetery
MLHL NW7 ....46 B4
Hendon Crematorium
MLHL NW7 ....46 B3
Hendon FC
CRICK NW2 ....64 D4
Hendon Golf Club
MLHL NW7 ....46 A3
Hendon Preparatory School
HDN NW4 ....46 B3
Hendon School
HDN NW4 ....46 B4
Hendon Secretarial College
HDN NW4 ....63 K2
Hendon Youth Sports
Centre
CRICK NW2 ....64 B4
Henrietta Barnett School
GLDGN NW11 ....65 F2
Henry Cavendish Primary
School
BAL SW12 ....161 H3
Henry Compton School
FUL/PGN SW6 ....139 G2
Henry Fawcett Primary
School
LBTH SE11 ....122 B6
Henry Green Primary School
BCTR RM8 ....73 K5
Henry Maynard J & I School
WALTH E17 ....70 A2
Henwick Primary School
ELTH/MOT SE9 ....146 C4
Herbert Morrison Primary
School
VX/NE SW8 ....141 K1
Hereward House School
HAMP NW3 ....83 J4
Her Majestys' Theatre
STJS SW1Y 10 D7
Hermitage Primary School
WAP E1W 123 H1
Herne Hill School
HNHL SE24 ....142 D6
Herne Hill Stadium
(Cycle Centre)
HNHL SE24 ....162 E1
Heron Industrial Estate
SRTFD E15 ....105 K1
Heronsgate Primary School
THMD SE28 ....127 J3
Heron Trading Estate
ACT W3 ....98 D4
Hersham Trading Estate
WOT/HER KT12 ....188 D2
Heston Community School
HEST TW5 ....135 F1
Heston Community Sports
Hall
HEST TW5 ....135 F1
Heston Industrial Mall
HEST TW5 ....134 E1
Heston Infant School
HEST TW5 ....135 F1
Heston Junior School
HEST TW5 ....135 F1
Heston Park CC
HEST TW5 ....114 E6
Heston Swimming Baths
HEST TW5 ....114 E6
Higgs Industrial Estate
HNHL SE24 ....142 C4
Highams Lodge Business
Centre
WALTH E17 ....51 F6
Highams Park School
CHING E4 ....52 B2

Highbury Corner Magistrates
Court
HOLWY N7 ....85 G4
Highbury Fields School
HBRY N5 ....85 H2
Highbury Grove School
HBRY N5 ....85 J3
Highbury Park Clinic
HBRY N5 ....85 H1
Highbury Pool
HBRY N5 ....85 H4
Highbury Quadrant Primary
School
HBRY N5 ....85 J1
Highbury Square
Development
HBRY N5 ....85 H1
High Commission of Angola
MHST W1U 9 F2
High Commission of Antigua &
Barbuda
MYFR/PICC W1J 9 G3
High Commission of Bahamas
SKENS SW7 ....120 B3
High Commission of
Bangladesh
SKENS SW7 ....120 B3
High Commission of
Barbados
FITZ W1T 10 C3
High Commission of Belize
CAVSQ/HST W1G 9 K3
High Commission of
Botswana
OXSTW W1C 9 J4
High Commission of Brunei
KTBR SW1X 15 G4
High Commission of Canada
MYFR/PKLN W1K 9 H5
High Commission of Cyprus
MYFR/PKLN W1K 9 H5
High Commission of
Dominica
ECT SW5 ....120 A4
High Commission of Fiji
SKENS SW7 ....120 B2
High Commission of Grenada
ECT SW5 ....120 A5
High Commission of Guyana
BAY/PAD W2 ....101 F6
High Commission of Jamaica
SKENS SW7 ....14 A3
High Commission of Kenya
CAVSQ/HST W1G 9 J1
High Commission of Lesotho
KTBR SW1X 15 G4
High Commission of Malawi
MYFR/PKLN W1K 9 J5
High Commission of Malaysia
KTBR SW1X 15 H3
High Commission of Maldives
MHST W1U 9 K2
High Commission of Malta
CONDST W1S 10 B6
High Commission of Namibia
CAVSQ/HST W1G 9 K2
High Commission of
New Zealand
STJS SW1Y 10 C7
High Commission of Nigeria
CHCR WC2N 10 E7
EMB EC4Y 11 K4
High Commission of Pakistan
KTBR SW1X 15 F4
High Commission of
Papua New Guinea
STJS SW1Y 10 B7
High Commission of St Lucia
KENS W8 ....120 A2
High Commission of
Seychelles
MHST W1U 9 F1
High Commission of
Sierra Leone
REGST W1B 10 A3
High Commission of Singapore
KTBR SW1X 15 F3
High Commission of
South Africa
CHCR WC2N 10 E6
High Commission of Sri Lanka
BAY/PAD W2 ....8 B5
High Commission of Swaziland
WESTW SW1E 16 A4
High Commission of
the Gambia
KENS W8 ....120 A2
High Commission of Tonga
MBLAR W1H 8 D2
High Commission of Trinidad
& Tobago
KTBR SW1X 15 G4
High Commission of Uganda
WHALL SW1A 10 D7
High Commission of Zambia
SKENS SW7 ....120 B2
High Commission
of Zimbabwe
CHCR WC2N 10 E6
High Cross Centre
SEVS/STOTM N15 ....68 C1
High Elms Country Park
ORP BR6 ....216 C5
High Elms Golf Club
ORP BR6 ....216 C5
Highfield Infant School
HAYES BR2 ....199 J1
Highfield Junior School
HAYES BR2 ....199 H1
Highfield Primary School
WCHMH N21 ....35 H3
Highfield School
WAND/EARL SW18 ....160 D2
Highgate Cemetery
HGT N6 ....66 A5
Highgate Golf Club
EFNCH N2 ....65 J3

Highgate Junior School
HGT N6 .....65 K4
Highgate Montessori School
BAR EN5 .....20 C4
Highgate Primary School
HGT N6 .....65 K3
Highgate Private Hospital
HGT N6 .....65 K3
Highgate School
HGT N6 .....65 K4
Highgate Wood School
MUSWH N10 .....66 C2
Highgrove Pool
RSLP HA4 .....58 E4
Highlands J & I School
IL IG1 .....71 K5
Highlands Primary School
IL IG1 .....71 K5
Highshore School
PECK SE15 .....143 G2
High View Primary School
BTSEA SW11 .....140 C5
Highview Primary School
WLGTN SM6 .....210 E3
The Highway Primary School
ORP BR6 .....217 J3
The Highway Trading Centre
WAP E1W 105 F6
Hillbrook Primary School
TOOT SW17 .....160 E6
Hillcroft College
SURB KT6 .....191 F3
Hillcross Primary School
MRDN SM4 .....193 J1
Hillgate Hill Murugan Temple
HGT N6 .....66 B4
Hill House Preparatory School
CHEL SW3 .....120 D6
Hill House School
KTBR SW1X 14 E5
Hill Mead Infant School
BRXS/STRHM SW9 .....142 C5
Hillmead Primary School
BRXS/ST SW9 .....142 C5
Hills Grove Primary School
WELL DA16 .....148 D1
Hillside Primary School
NTHWD HA6 .....40 E3
STMC/STPC BR5 .....202 D4
Hillyfield Primary School
WALTH E17 .....51 G6
Hilly Fields Medical Centre
BROCKY SE4 .....144 D6
Hilton Docklands Pier
BERM/RHTH SE16 .....124 C1
The Hiltongrove Business Centre
WALTH E17 .....69 J1
Hinchley Wood Primary School
ESH/CLAY KT10 .....190 B6
Hinchley Wood School & Sixth Form Centre
ESH/CLAY KT10 .....190 B6
Hinley Clinic
LBTH SE11 .....17 K7
Hispaniola
WHALL SW1A 17 F1
Hitherfield Primary School
STRHM/NOR SW16 .....162 B4
Hither Green Cemetery
CAT SE6 .....165 J4
Hither Green Primary School
LEW SE13 .....165 G1
HM Customs
HTHAIR TW6 .....132 E2
HM Prison
BRXS/STRHM SW2 .....161 K1
HOLWY N7 .....84 E2
HOLWY N1 .....84 F4
SHB W12 .....99 J5
THMD SE28 .....127 K3
WAND/EARL SW18 .....160 C2
HMS Belfast
STHWK SE1 .....13 H7
HMS President
EMB EC4Y 11 K5
HM Young Offender Institution
FELT TW13 .....153 G5
Hobbayne First & Middle School
HNWL W7 .....97 F5
Hobbayne Primary School
HNWL W7 .....96 E5
Hogarth Business Park
CHSWK W4 .....118 B6
Hogarth Industrial Estate
WLSDN NW10 .....99 J3
Hogarth's House
CHSWK W4 .....118 A6
Holbeach Primary School
CAT SE6 .....164 D2
Holborn College
WOOL/PLUM SE18 .....126 C4
Holborn College Independent School
HMSMTH W6 .....119 F5
Holborn Medical Centre
BMSBY WC1N 5 G7
Holborn Town Hall
HHOL WC1V 11 F3
Holiday Inn
CAMTN NW1 .....84 B5
FSBYW WC1X 5 H5
Holland House
WKENS W14 .....119 J2
Holland House School
EDGW HA8 .....30 C6
Holland Park Pre-Preparatory School
WKENS W14 .....119 J3
Holland Park School
KENS W8 .....119 J2
Holland Park Theatre
WKENS W14 .....119 J2

Holland Street Clinic
KENS W8 .....119 K2
Hollickwood JMI School
MUSWH N10 .....48 B3
Holloway School
HOLWY N7 .....84 D3
Hollydale Primary School
PECK SE15 .....143 K3
The Hollyfield School
SURB KT6 .....191 F2
Holly House Private Hospital
BKHH IG9 .....39 F4
Holly Park JMI School
FBAR/BDGN N11 .....48 A1
Hollywood Bowl
BERM/RHTH SE16 .....124 A3
The Holme
CAMTN NW1 .....3 F5
Holmleigh Primary School
STNW/STAM N16 .....68 B5
Holy Cross Preparatory School
KUTN/CMB KT2 .....175 K3
Holy Cross Primary School
FUL/PGN SW6 .....139 K2
Holy Cross RC Convent School
NWMAL KT3 .....192 A1
Holy Cross RC Primary School
CAT SE6 .....165 F3
Holy Family RC Primary School
BKHTH/KID SE3 .....146 A5
POP/IOD E14 .....105 J6
Holy Family Technology College
WALTH E17 .....69 K1
Holy Ghost RC Primary School
BAL SW12 .....160 E2
Holy Innocents Catholic Primary School
ORP BR6 .....217 F1
Holy Trinity CE Junior School
WLGTN SM6 .....210 C2
Holy Trinity CE Primary School
BRXS/STRHM SW2 .....162 A2
DART DA1 .....151 F6
EFNCH N2 .....47 H6
KIL/WHAMP NW6 .....83 G4
KTBR SW1X 15 G6
NTHWD HA6 .....40 A2
RCHPK/HAM TW10 .....137 H5
SYD SE26 .....163 K4
Holy Trinity College
BMLY BR1 .....184 B4
Holy Trinity in St Silas
CAMTN NW1 .....84 B5
Holy Trinity Primary School
HACK E8 .....86 B4
WIM/MER SW19 .....177 K2
Holy Trinity School
BFN/LL DA15 .....168 B3
CHEL SW3 .....15 F6
Holywell School
WATW WD18 .....26 D1
Homefield Preparatory School
SUT SM1 .....208 D2
Home Office
STJSPK SW1H 16 B3
Homerton College of Technology
HOM E9 .....86 E3
Homerton University Hospital
HOM E9 .....87 F3
Homoeopathic Health Centre
PLSTW E13 .....106 E3
The Homoeopathic Health Centre
MLHL NW7 .....45 H1
Honeypot Business Centre
STAN HA7 .....44 A4
Honeypot Lane Centre
STAN HA7 .....43 K4
Honeypot Medical Centre
STAN HA7 .....44 A5
Honeywell Primary School
BTSEA SW11 .....160 E1
Honor Oak Crematorium
FSTH SE23 .....144 A6
Honor Oak Gallery
FSTH SE23 .....164 A1
Honor Oak Health Centre
BROCKY SE4 .....144 B5
Honourable Artillery Company HQ
STLK EC1V 6 E7
Hook Lane Primary School
WELL DA16 .....148 B4
Hook Rise South Industrial Park
CHSGTN KT9 .....206 B1
Hope Primary School
CMBW SE5 .....143 F1
Horizon Business Centre
ED N9 .....37 F4
Horizon Industrial Estate
PECK SE15 .....123 H6
Horizon School
STNW/STAM N16 .....86 A2
The Horniman Museum & Gardens
FSTH SE23 .....163 J5
Horniman Primary School
FSTH SE23 .....163 J4
Horn Park Primary School
LEE/GVPK SE12 .....166 A2
Hornsby House School
BAL SW12 .....161 F3
Hornsey Central Hospital
CEND/HSY/T N8 .....66 C2
Hornsey Rise Health Centre
ARCH N19 .....66 D4
Hornsey Secondary School for Girls
CEND/HSY/T N8 .....67 F2

Horn Stairs
BERM/RHTH SE16 .....124 C1
Horseferry Road Magistrates Court
WEST SW1P 16 D5
Horse Guards Parade
WHALL SW1A 16 D1
Horsenden Hill Golf Club
GFD/PVL UB6 .....79 H4
Horsenden Primary School
GFD/PVL UB6 .....78 E4
Horton Country Park
HOR/WEW KT19 .....206 C6
Horton Industrial Park
WDR/YW UB7 .....112 C1
Horton Park Golf & Country Club
HOR/WEW KT19 .....206 E5
Hortus Cemetery
NWDGN UB2 .....114 E2
Hospital of St John & St Elizabeth
STJWD NW8 .....2 A3
The Hotel at Chelsea
FUL/PGN SW6 .....140 A1
Hotel Ibis
CAMTN NW1 .....4 B5
CAN/RD E16 .....107 F6
FUL/PGN SW6 .....119 K6
GNWCH SE10 .....125 F6
HYS/HAR UB3 .....133 H2
POP/IOD E14 .....106 A6
SRTFD E15 .....88 C4
WBLY HA9 .....80 C5
The Hotel Russell
RSQ WC1B 4 F7
Hotham Primary School
PUT/ROE SW15 .....139 G5
Hotspur Industrial Estate
TOTM N17 .....50 D2
Houndsfield Primary School
ED N9 .....36 C2
Hounslow Business Park
HSLW TW3 .....135 F5
Hounslow CC
HSLW TW3 .....134 E3
Hounslow Cemetery
HSLWW TW4 .....154 E2
Hounslow College Independent School
FELT TW13 .....154 C6
Hounslow Heath Golf Club
HSLWW TW4 .....134 C6
Hounslow Heath Infant School
HSLWW TW4 .....134 D4
Hounslow Heath Junior School
HSLWW TW4 .....134 D4
Hounslow Manor School
HSLW TW3 .....135 G4
Hounslow Manor Sports Hall
HSLW TW3 .....135 G4
Hounslow Town Primary School
HSLW TW3 .....135 H4
House of Detention
CLKNW EC1R 6 K6
House of St Barnabas
SOHO/SHAV W1D 10 C4
Houses of Parliament
WHALL SW1A 17 F3
Houston Business Park
YEAD UB4 .....114 B1
Howard Primary School
SAND/SEL CR2 .....211 J2
Howbury Centre
ERITH DA8 .....150 D1
Howland Quay
BERM/RHTH SE16 .....124 A3
Hoxton Hall Community Theatre
IS N1 .....7 G2
HQS Wellington (Master Mariners)
TPL/STR WC2R 11 J6
HSBC Sports Club
BECK BR3 .....182 B2
HSBC Tower
POP/IOD E14 .....124 E1
Hubbinet Industrial Estate
ROMW/RG RM7 .....56 E6
Huddleston Primary School
CLKNW EC1R 5 K5
The Humana Wellington Hospital
STJWD NW8 .....2 B4
Humber Trading Estate
CRICK NW2 .....63 K6
Hunterian Museum
LINN WC2A 11 H3
Hunters Hall Primary School
DAGE RM10 .....92 D3
Hunter Street Health Centre
STPAN WC1H 4 E6
Huntsman Sports Club
BKHTH/KID SE3 .....145 K5
Hurlingham Business Park
FUL/PGN SW6 .....139 K4
Hurlingham & Chelsea Secondary School
FUL/PGN SW6 .....139 J4
Hurlingham House
FUL/PGN SW6 .....139 J4
Hurlingham Private School
PUT/ROE SW15 .....139 J5
Huron University
RSQ WC1B 10 E1
Hurricane Trading Centre
CDALE/KGS NW9 .....45 H4
Hurstmere School
BFN/LL DA15 .....168 C3
Hurst Park Primary School
E/WMO/HCT KT8 .....173 F6
Hurst Primary School
BXLY DA5 .....169 F3

Hyatt Carlton Tower Hotel
KTBR SW1X 15 F5
Hyatt Regency-The Churchill
MBLAR W1H 9 F3
The Hyde Industrial Estate
CDALE/KGS NW9 .....63 H2
The Hyde School
CDALE/KGS NW9 .....63 H2
Hyland House School
WALTH E17 .....52 B5
Hyleford Leavers Unit School
BARK/HLT IG6 .....54 D5
Hyleford School
IL IG1 .....90 E3
Hythe Road Industrial Estate
WLSDN NW10 .....99 J3
Ian Mikardo High School
BOW E3 .....105 K2
Ibstock Place School
PUT/ROE SW15 .....158 B1
ICA Cinema
STJS SW1Y 10 D7
Ickburgh School
CLPT E5 .....86 D1
Ickenham Clinic
HGDN/ICK UB10 .....76 A1
Ihlara Sport FC
HBRY N5 .....85 J2
IKEA Store Brent Park
WLSDN NW10 .....81 F3
IKEA Store Croydon
CROY/NA CR0 .....196 A5
IKEA Store Edmonton
UED N18 .....50 E2
Ilderton Primary School
PECK SE15 .....123 K6
Ilford County High School
BARK/HLT IG6 .....54 C5
Ilford Golf Club
IL IG1 .....71 K5
Ilford Jewish Primary School
BARK/HLT IG6 .....54 D6
Ilford Medical Centre
IL IG1 .....90 B1
Ilford Preparatory School
GDMY/SEVK IG3 .....73 F5
Ilford Retail Park
IL IG1 .....72 C6
Ilford Swimming Pool
IL IG1 .....72 C6
Ilford Ursuline High School
IL IG1 .....72 B6
Iman Zakaria Academy
FSTGT E7 .....89 F3
Imber Court Trading Estate
E/WMO/HCT KT8 .....189 J3
Immaculate CE Primary School
STRHM/NOR SW16 .....179 K2
Immanuel College
BUSH WD23 .....28 E2
Immanuel School
ROM RM1 .....57 G2
Imperial College
PUT/ROE SW15 .....139 G3
SKENS SW7 .....14 A4
Imperial College Athletic Ground
HYS/HAR UB3 .....113 F6
Imperial College of Science
SKENS SW7 .....14 A3
Imperial College of Science & Technology
SKENS SW7 .....14 B3
Imperial College School of Medicine
PIM SW1V 16 C7
WDR/YW UB7 .....112 C1
Imperial War Museum
STHWK SE1 .....17 K5
Imperial War Museum Annexe
LBTH SE11 .....17 K5
Inchbald School of Design
BGVA SW1W 15 H6
Independent Industrial Estate
WDR/YW UB7 .....112 C1
Independent Jewish School
HDN NW4 .....64 B2
India House
HOL/ALD WC2B 11 G5
Infant College
IL IG1 .....72 A6
Innellan House School
PIN HA5 .....41 J6
Inner London Sessions House (Crown Court)
STHWK SE1 .....18 C4
Innholders Hall
CANST EC4R 12 D5
Innkeeper's Lodge
BECK BR3 .....198 D3
CHEAM SM3 .....193 K5
NTHLT UB5 .....78 A4
SAND/SEL CR2 .....211 J4
STHGT/OAK N14 .....34 E5
WAN E11 .....70 E1
WFD IG8 .....53 K2
Inns of Court & Chancery
TPL/STR WC2R 11 J4
Inns of Court Law School
GINN WC1R 11 H1
Institute of Education
GWRST WC1E 4 C7
Institute of Education University of London
RSQ WC1B 4 D7
Intercontinental Hotel
MYFR/PICC W1J 15 H2
International Community School
CAMTN NW1 .....3 G7
International School of Havana
STJS SW1Y 10 D7
International School of London
ACT W3 .....117 H4

International Trading Estate
NWDGN UB2 .....114 A3
Invicta Industrial Estate
SRTFD E15 .....106 A2
Invicta Primary School
BKHTH/KID SE3 .....125 K6
Invicta Sports Club
DART DA1 .....151 G6
Inwood Business Centre
HSLW TW3 .....135 G5
IQRA Independent School
BRXN/ST SW9 .....142 B4
Ironmonger Row Baths
FSBYE EC1V 6 C5
Ironmongers Hall
STBT EC1A 12 C2
Islamia Girls School
KIL/WHAMP NW6 .....82 C6
Islamic College for Advanced Study
WLSDN NW10 .....81 K5
The Islamic Grammar School
WAND/EARL SW18 .....159 J2
Island Clinic
POP/IOD E14 .....125 F2
Isleworth Cemetery
ISLW TW7 .....136 B3
Isleworth Recreation Centre
ISLW TW7 .....136 A5
Isleworth & Syon School for Boys
ISLW TW7 .....135 K1
Isleworth Town Primary School
ISLW TW7 .....136 A3
Islington Arts & Media School
FSBYPK N4 .....67 F5
Islington Business Centre
IS N1 .....85 J6
Islington Crematorium
MUSWH N10 .....47 K4
Islington Green Medical Centre
IS N1 .....85 H6
Islington Green School
IS N1 .....6 B1
Islington Tennis Centre
HOLWY N7 .....84 E4
Islington Town Hall
IS N1 .....85 H5
Ismaili Centre
SKENS SW7 .....14 B6
Italia Conti Academy of Theatre Arts
BRXN/ST SW9 .....141 K4
Italian Hospital
PIM SW1V 16 A6
Ithaca College
SKENS SW7 .....120 B4
Ivybridge Primary School
TWK TW1 .....156 A1
Ivybridge Retail Park
ISLW TW7 .....136 A6
Ivydale Primary School
PECK SE15 .....144 A5
Jack & Jill School
HPTN TW12 .....173 F2
WHTN TW2 .....155 K4
Jack Taylor School
STJWD NW8 .....83 G6
Jack Tizard School
FUL/PGN SW6 .....139 G2
SHB W12 .....100 A6
Jacques Prevert School
HMSMTH W6 .....119 G4
Jamahiriya School
CHEL SW3 .....120 D6
James Allens Preparatory Girls School
HNHL SE24 .....142 E6
James Dixon Primary School
PGE/AN SE20 .....181 H4
Jamestown Mental Health Centre
HAMP NW3 .....83 K5
James Wolfe Primary School
GNWCH SE10 .....144 E1
Jamiatul Ummah School
WCHPL E1 .....104 D5
Janet Adegoke Leisure Centre
SHB W12 .....99 J6
The Japanese School
ACT W3 .....98 C6
Japan Green Medical Centre
ACT W3 .....117 J1
Jenner Health Centre
FSTH SE23 .....164 B3
Jenny Hammond Primary School
WAN E11 .....88 C2
Jermyn Street Theatre
MYFR/PICC W1J 10 B6
Jessop Primary School
HNHL SE24 .....142 C5
Jewel Tower
WEST SW1P 16 E4
Jewish Cemetery
GLDGN NW11 .....64 E3
Jewish Community Theatre
HNHL SE24 .....142 E4
Jewish Free School
KTN/HRWW/WS HA3 .....62 B3
KTN NW5 .....84 D4
The Jewish Museum
CAMTN NW1 .....3 J1
FNCH N3 .....46 E5
Johanna Primary School
STHWK SE1 .....17 J3
John Ball Primary School
BKHTH/KID SE3 .....145 H3
John Betts Primary School
HMSMTH W6 .....118 D3
John Bramston Primary School
BARK/HLT IG6 .....55 G2
John Burns Primary School
BTSEA SW11 .....141 F3

John Chilton School
NTHLT UB5 ....**77** J5
John Dixon Clinic
BERM/RHTH SE16 ....**123** J3
John Donne Primary School
PECK SE15 ....**143** J2
John F Kennedy Special School
SRTFD E15 ....**88** B6
John Keble CE Primary School
WLSDN NW10 ....**99** H1
John Kelly Boys & Girls Technology College
CRICK NW2 ....**81** H1
The John Loughborough School
TOTM N17 ....**50** B5
John Lyon School
RYLN/HDSTN HA2 ....**60** D5
John Nightingale School
E/WMO/HCT KT8 ....**172** E6
John Orwell Sports Centre
WAP E1W **123** H1
John Paul II RC School
WIM/MER SW19 ....**159** G2
John Perryn Primary School
ACT W3 ....**99** G5
John Perry Primary School
DAGE RM10 ....**93** F4
John Roan Lower School
BKHTH/KID SE3 ....**145** J1
John Roan School
BKHTH/KID SE3 ....**145** H1
John Ruskin Special School
SAND/SEL CR2 ....**213** G5
John Ruskin Primary School
WALW SE17 ....**122** D6
John Scott Health Centre
FSBYPK N4 ....**67** J5
John Scurr Primary School
WCHPL E1 ....**104** E3
John Smith House
WALW SE17 ....**18** C7
Johnsons Industrial Estate
HYS/HAR UB3 ....**113** K3
John Stainer Primary School
BROCKY SE4 ....**144** B4
The Jo Richardson Community School
DAGW RM9 ....**91** K6
Joseph Clarke Special School
CHING E4 ....**52** B2
Joseph Hood Primary School
RYNPK SW20 ....**177** H5
Joseph Lancaster Primary School
STHWK SE1 ....**18** D5
Joydens Wood Infant School
RDART DA2 ....**170** B6
Joydens Wood Junior School
BXLY DA5 ....**170** B6
Jubilee Country Park
BMLY BR1 ....**201** G1
Jubilee Market
COVGDN WC2E **11** F5
Jubilee Primary School
BRXS/STRHM SW2 ....**162** B1
THMD SE28 ....**109** J6
Jubilee Sports Ground
CHING E4 ....**38** B6
Julians Primary School
STRHM/NOR SW16 ....**162** B6
Jumeirah Carlton Tower Hotel
KTBR SW1X **15** F4
Junior & Youth Centre
BOW E3 ....**105** H4
Juno Way Industrial Estate
NWCR SE14 ....**124** A6
Jurys Clifton-Ford Hotel
MHST W1U **9** H2
Jurys Great Russell Street
RSQ WC1B **10** D3
Jurys Inn
CROY/NA CR0 ....**196** D6
Jurys Inn Chelsea
FUL/PGN SW6 ....**140** B2
Jurys Inn Hotel
HTHAIR TW6 ....**33** J4
Jurys Inn Islington
IS N1 ....**5** J3
Jurys Kensington Hotel
SKENS SW7 ....**14** A7
JVC Business Park
CRICK NW2 ....**63** J5
Kaizen Primary School
PLSTW E13 ....**107** F3
Kangley Business Centre
SYD SE26 ....**182** C1
Katella Trading Estate
BARK IG11 ....**108** E2
Katherine Road Medical Centre
FSTGT E7 ....**89** G4
Keats House Museum
HAMP NW3 ....**83** H2
Keble Preparatory School
WCHMH N21 ....**35** G2
Keen Students Supplementary School
WCHPL E1 ....**104** C4
Keir Hardie Primary School
CAN/RD E16 ....**106** E4
Keith Davis Cue Sports Club
DAGW RM9 ....**91** K5
Kelmscott Community Centre
WALTH E17 ....**69** H3
Kelmscott Leisure Centre
WALTH E17 ....**69** H3
Kelmscott School
WALTH E17 ....**69** H3
Kelsey Park School
BECK BR3 ....**182** D6
Kelvin Industrial Estate
GFD/PVL UB6 ....**78** B6
GFD/PVL UB6 ....**96** D2
Kemnal Technology College
STMC/STPC BR5 ....**186** C3

Kempton Park Racecourse
SUN TW16 ....**172** A3
Ken Barrington Centre
LBTH SE11 ....**122** A6
Kender Primary School
NWCR SE14 ....**143** K2
Kenmont Primary School
WLSDN NW10 ....**99** J2
Kenmore Park Middle School
KTN/HRWW/WS HA3 ....**43** K6
Kenneth More Theatre
IL IG1 ....**90** C1
Kensal Green Cemetery
WLSDN NW10 ....**99** K2
Kensal Rise Primary School
KIL/WHAMP NW6 ....**100** B1
Kensington and Chelsea College
NKENS W10 ....**100** C3
Kensington Avenue Primary School
THHTH CR7 ....**180** B4
Kensington Business Centre
SKENS SW7 ....**14** D4
Kensington & Chelsea College
NKENS W10 ....**119** J2
Kensington & Chelsea Town Hall
KENS W8 ....**119** K2
The Kensington Dyslexia Teaching Centre
KENS W8 ....**120** A3
The Kensington Gardens School
BAY/PAD W2 ....**101** F6
Kensington Leisure Centre
NTGHL W11 ....**100** B6
Kensington Market
KENS W8 ....**120** A2
Kensington Palace
KENS W8 ....**120** A1
Kensington Park School
REGST W1B **9** K1
Kensington Preparatory School
FUL/PGN SW6 ....**139** J2
Kensington Primary School
MNPK E12 ....**89** K4
Kensington School of Business
HCIRC EC1N **11** K1
Kensington Temple Institute of Education
EA W5 ....**98** A2
Kensington Wharf
WBPTN SW10 ....**140** C1
Kentish Memorial College
FNCH N3 ....**46** C5
Kentish Town CE Primary School
KTTN NW5 ....**84** C3
Kentish Town Health Centre
KTTN NW5 ....**84** C4
Kentish Town Industrial Estate
KTTN NW5 ....**84** B3
Kentish Town Sports Centre
KTTN NW5 ....**84** A4
Kenton Clinic
KTN/HRWW/WS HA3 ....**62** A2
Kenton CC
KTN/HRWW/WS HA3 ....**61** J1
Kent Park Industrial Estate
PECK SE15 ....**123** J6
Kenwood House
HAMP NW3 ....**65** J5
The Kerem School
EFNCH N2 ....**47** H2
Keston CE Primary School
HAYES BR2 ....**215** H3
Kew Bridge Steam Museum
BTFD TW8 ....**117** G5
Kew College
RCH/KEW TW9 ....**137** H1
Kew Gardens (Royal Botanic Gardens)
BTFD TW8 ....**137** F2
Kew Palace
RCH/KEW TW9 ....**137** F1
Kew Retail Park
RCH/KEW TW9 ....**137** J2
Kew Riverside Primary School
RCH/KEW TW9 ....**137** J3
Keyplan & Roxburghe College
FITZ W1T **4** B7
Keyworth Primary School
WALW SE17 ....**122** C5
Khaisa College London
HRW HA1 ....**61** F3
Kidbrooke Park Primary School
BKHTH/KID SE3 ....**146** B3
Kidbrooke School
BKHTH/KID SE3 ....**146** C3
Kilburn Park Junior School
KIL/WHAMP NW6 ....**100** D1
Killick Street Medical Centre
IS N1 ....**5** G2
Kilmorie Primary School
FSTH SE23 ....**164** B4
Kimberley Industrial Estate
WALTH E17 ....**51** H3
Kimpton Industrial Estate
CHEAM SM3 ....**193** J6
King Alfred School
GLDGN NW11 ....**65** F5
King Athelstan Primary School
KUT/HW KT1 ....**175** G5
King Edwards Road Clinic
RSLP HA4 ....**58** B5
King Edward VII Hospital for Officers
MHST W1U **9** H1
King Fahad Academy (Girls Upper School)
EA W5 ....**116** D2

The Kingfisher Medical Centre
DEPT SE8 ....**124** C6
The Kingfisher Sports Centre
KUT/HW KT1 ....**175** F5
King George Hospital
GDMY/SEVK IG3 ....**73** G2
Kingham Industrial Estate
WLSDN NW10 ....**99** F2
King & Queen Wharf
BERM/RHTH SE16 ....**105** F6
Kings Avenue Medical Centre
STHL UB1 ....**96** C5
Kings Avenue School
CLAP SW4 ....**141** K6
Kingsbury Green Primary School
CDALE/KGS NW9 ....**62** D2
Kingsbury High School (Lower School)
CDALE/KGS NW9 ....**62** E1
Kingsbury High School (Upper School)
CDALE/KGS NW9 ....**62** E1
Kingsbury Hospital
CDALE/KGS NW9 ....**62** C1
Kingsbury Tamil School
CLAP SW4 ....**44** D6
Kingsbury Trading Estate
CDALE/KGS NW9 ....**62** E3
Kings College (Hampstead Campus)
HAMP NW3 ....**82** E2
King's College Hospital
CMBW SE5 ....**142** D4
Kings College London
CMBW SE5 ....**142** E3
HOL/ALD WC2B **11** H4
STHWK SE1 ....**12** A7
STHWK SE1 ....**18** D1
WEST SW1P **16** B6
Kings College London - Law
TPL/STR WC2R **11** H5
Kings College London (Waterloo Campus)
STHWK SE1 ....**17** J1
Kings College School
WIM/MER SW19 ....**177** F2
Kings College School of Medicine & Dentistry
CMBW SE5 ....**142** E3
DUL SE21 ....**162** E1
Kings College Sports Ground
RSLP HA4 ....**58** C3
Kings College London - Humanities
TPL/STR WC2R **11** G5
Kingsdale School
DUL SE21 ....**163** F5
Kings Estate
HCH RM12 ....**93** J2
Kingsford Community School
PLSTW E13 ....**107** G3
Kingsgate Business Centre
KUTN/CMB KT2 ....**175** F4
Kingsgate Primary School
KIL/WHAMP NW6 ....**82** E5
Kings Hall Leisure Centre
CLPT E5 ....**86** E3
Kings Head Theatre
IS N1 ....**85** G6
Kingsland College of Business Studies
SRTFD E15 ....**106** B1
Kingsland Health Centre
HACK E8 ....**86** B5
Kingsland Shopping Centre
HACK E8 ....**86** B4
Kingsley Primary School
CROY/NA CR0 ....**196** A5
Kings Mall Shopping Centre
HMSMTH W6 ....**119** F4
Kingsmeadow Athletics Centre
KUT/HW KT1 ....**175** H6
Kingsmead Primary School
CLPT E5 ....**87** G2
Kingsmead School
EN EN1 ....**24** C5
The Kings Oak Private Hospital
ENC/FH EN2 ....**23** G1
King Solomon High School
BARK/HLT IG6 ....**54** D5
Kings Private Clinic
GDMY/SEVK IG3 ....**73** F5
Kings School of English
BECK BR3 ....**182** C5
Kings Stairs
BERM/RHTH SE16 ....**123** J2
Kingston Business Centre
CHSGTN KT9 ....**206** A1
Kingston College of Further Education
KUT/HW KT1 ....**175** F6
Kingston College Theatre
KUT/HW KT1 ....**174** E6
Kingston Crematorium
KUT/HW KT1 ....**175** H6
Kingston Crown Court
KUT/HW KT1 ....**174** E6
Kingston Grammar School
KUT/HW KT1 ....**175** G5
Kingston Hospital
KUTN/CMB KT2 ....**175** H4
Kingstonian FC
NWMAL KT3 ....**175** H4
Kingston University
BRYLDS KT5 ....**191** H2
KUT/HW KT1 ....**175** F6
KUTN/CMB KT2 ....**176** A1
KUTN/CMB KT2 ....**176** A3
PUT/ROE SW15 ....**158** C4
King Street College
HMSMTH W6 ....**119** F4

Kingsway Business Park
HPTN TW12 ....**172** E4
Kingsway College
CAMTN NW1 ....**4** A6
FSBYW WC1X **5** H4
KTTN NW5 ....**84** B4
STPAN WC1H **5** C5
Kingswood Primary School
WNWD SE27 ....**162** E6
Kisharon School
GLDGN NW11 ....**64** D3
K+K Hotel George
ECT SW5 ....**119** K4
KLC School of Design
WBPTN SW10 ....**140** B2
Knightsbridge Barracks
SKENS SW7 ....**14** D3
Knightsbridge Medical Centre
KTBR SW1X **15** F4
The Knightsbridge Under School
SKENS SW7 ....**120** B4
Knollmead Primary School
BRYLDS KT5 ....**191** K6
Knowledge Point School
HOLWY N7 ....**85** F4
Kobi Nazrul Primary School
WCHPL E1 ....**104** C5
KP Estate
RAIN RM13 ....**111** G6
Kubrick Business Estate
FSTGT E7 ....**89** F2
Laban Centre for Movement & Dance
DEPT SE8 ....**144** E1
Laburnum Health Centre
DAGE RM10 ....**74** C6
Lady Bankes Primary School
RSLP HA4 ....**58** E5
The Lady Eleanor Holles School
HPTN TW12 ....**173** G1
Lady Margaret Primary School
STHL UB1 ....**95** K4
Lady Margaret School
FUL/PGN SW6 ....**139** K2
Ladywell Arena
LEW SE13 ....**164** E1
Ladywell Cemetery
BROCKY SE4 ....**144** C6
Ladywell Leisure Centre
LEW SE13 ....**145** F3
Lake Business Centre
TOTM N17 ....**50** C2
Laker Industrial Estate
BECK BR3 ....**182** C1
Lambeth Academy
CLAP SW4 ....**141** H6
Lambeth Cemetery
TOOT SW17 ....**160** B1
Lambeth College
BRXS/STRHM SW2 ....**142** A6
CLAP SW4 ....**141** H6
STHWK SE1 ....**18** H1
STRHM/NOR SW16 ....**161** K4
VX/NE SW8 ....**141** J2
Lambeth County Court
LBTH SE11 ....**122** B5
Lambeth Crematorium
TOOT SW17 ....**160** B6
Lambeth Hospital
BRXN/ST SW9 ....**141** K4
Lambeth Palace
STHWK SE1 ....**17** G5
Lambs Court
POP/IOD E14 ....**105** G6
Lamont Business Centre
CROY/NA CR0 ....**195** K4
Lamorbey Swimming Centre
BFN/LL DA15 ....**168** B4
Lampton School
HSLW TW3 ....**135** F2
The Lanark Medical Centre
MV/WKIL W9 ....**101** F2
Lancaster House
WHALL SW1A **16** A2
Lancasterian Primary School
TOTM N17 ....**50** A4
Lancaster Road Industrial Estate
EBAR EN4 ....**21** H6
Lancelot Medical Centre
ALP/SUD HA0 ....**79** K3
The Landmark Hotel
CAMTN NW1 ....**8** E1
The Lanesborough Hotel
KTBR SW1X **15** G2
Lanford Obesity Clinic
ED N9 ....**36** D2
Langbourne Primary School
DUL SE21 ....**163** F5
Langdon Down Centre
TEDD TW11 ....**174** D3
Langdon Park School
POP/IOD E14 ....**105** K5
Langdon School
EHAM E6 ....**108** B1
Langford Primary School
FUL/PGN SW6 ....**140** A3
Langham Hotel
CAVSQ/HST W1G **9** K3
The Langham School
SEVS/STOTM N15 ....**67** J1
Langhedge Lane Industrial Estate
UED N18 ....**50** B2
Langley Park Girls School & Sports Centre
BECK BR3 ....**198** E2
Langley Park Golf Club
BECK BR3 ....**199** G3
Langley Park School for Boys
BECK BR3 ....**198** E3
Langthorne Health Centre
WAN E11 ....**88** B1
Langthorne Hospital
WAN E11 ....**88** B2

Lansbury Lawrence Primary School
POP/IOD E14 ....**105** K5
Lansdowne College
BAY/PAD W2 ....**101** F6
Lansdowne School
BRXN/ST SW9 ....**142** A4
La Retraite RC Girls School
BAL SW12 ....**161** H2
Lark Hall Primary School
CLAP SW4 ....**141** J3
Larkshall Business Centre
CHING E4 ....**38** C4
Larmenier Infant School
HMSMTH W6 ....**119** G4
La Sainte Union Convent School
KTTN NW5 ....**84** A1
La Salette RC Primary School
RAIN RM13 ....**111** J2
Latchmere J & I School
KUTN/CMB KT2 ....**175** G2
Latchmere Leisure Centre
BTSEA SW11 ....**140** E3
Lathom Junior School
EHAM E6 ....**89** J5
Latymer All Saints CE Primary School
ED N9 ....**36** B3
The Latymer Preparatory School
HMSMTH W6 ....**118** D5
The Latymer School
ED N9 ....**36** A4
Latymer Upper School
HMSMTH W6 ....**118** D4
Launcelot Primary School
BMLY BR1 ....**165** K6
Laurance Haines School
WATW WD18 ....**26** E1
Laurel Clinic
EA W5 ....**98** B3
Lauriston Primary School
HOM E9 ....**87** F6
Lavender Primary School
ENC/FH EN2 ....**23** K1
Lawdale Junior School
BETH E2 ....**104** C2
Lawrence Trading Estate
GNWCH SE10 ....**125** H4
Lawrence Wharf
BERM/RHTH SE16 ....**124** C1
Laycock Primary School
IS N1 ....**85** G4
Lazards Sports Club
SUN TW16 ....**172** A3
Leadenhall Market
BANK EC3V **13** G4
Lea Park Trading Estate
LEY E10 ....**69** H4
Leaside Business Centre
PEND EN3 ....**25** H3
Leathermarket Gardens
STHWK SE1 ....**19** G3
Leathersellers Sports Ground
LEE/GVPK SE12 ....**166** B2
Leathers Hall
HDTCH EC3A **13** G3
Lea Valley Primary School
TOTM N17 ....**50** C3
Lea Valley Trading Estate
UED N18 ....**36** E6
UED N18 ....**51** F2
L'Ecoles Des Petits School
FUL/PGN SW6 ....**140** A3
Lee Manor Primary School
LEW SE13 ....**165** H1
Leeside Court
BERM/RHTH SE16 ....**124** A1
Leeside Trading Estate
TOTM N17 ....**50** E3
Leesons Primary School
STMC/STPC BR5 ....**186** B6
Lee Valley Campsite
CHING E4 ....**25** K3
Lee Valley Ice Centre
LEY E10 ....**69** F6
Lee Valley Leisure Complex & Golf Club
ED N9 ....**37** G2
Lee Valley Watersports Centre
CHING E4 ....**51** G2
The Leigh City Technology College
DART DA1 ....**171** K3
The Leigh City Technology College (West Campus)
DART DA1 ....**171** K3
Leigh Close Industrial Estate
NWMAL KT3 ....**192** A1
Leighton House Museum
WKENS W14 ....**119** J3
Lemuel Findlay Supplementary School
SEVS/STOTM N15 ....**68** B1
Lena Gardens Primary School
HMSMTH W6 ....**119** F3
Leo Baeck College Centre for Jewish Education
FNCH N3 ....**46** E5
Leopold Primary School
WLSDN NW10 ....**81** H5
Leopold Street Clinic
BOW E3 ....**105** H4
Lesnes Abbey
BELV DA17 ....**128** C4
Lesnes Abbey (remains of)
ABYW SE2 ....**128** C6
Lessness Heath Primary School
BELV DA17 ....**129** H5

Lewin Mead Community
Mental Health Centre
STRHM/NOR SW16 ....179 J2
Lewis Clinic
CAR SM5 ....210 A2
Lewisham Bridge Primary
School
LEW SE13 ....144 E4
Lewisham Business Centre
NWCR SE14 ....124 A6
Lewisham Centre
LEW SE13 ....145 F4
Lewisham College
DEPT SE8 ....144 D2
Lewisham Coroners Office
LEW SE13 ....144 E6
Lewisham Crematorium
CAT SE6 ....165 J4
Lewisham Lions Centre
BERM/RHTH SE16 ....123 K5
Lewisham Police Station
LEW SE13 ....145 F4
The Leys Primary School
DAGE RM10 ....92 C5
Leyton Business Centre
LEY E10 ....69 H6
Leyton Cross
RDART DA2 ....170 D4
Leyton FC
LEY E10 ....69 H5
Leyton Industrial Village
LEY E10 ....69 F4
Leyton Leisure Centre
LEY E10 ....69 K4
Leyton Orient FC
(Matchroom Stadium)
LEY E10 ....87 K1
Leytonstone School
WAN E11 ....70 C3
Leyton VI Form College
LEY E10 ....70 B3
Leyton Youth Sports Ground
LEY E10 ....69 K5
The Liberty City Clinic
SDTCH EC2A 7 G6
Liberty II Centre
ROM RM1 ....75 G1
Liberty Middle School
MTCM CR4 ....178 D5
The Liberty
ROM RM1 ....75 G2
Library & Community
Centre
BTSEA SW11 ....140 C4
Lilian Baylis Technology
School
LBTH SE11 ....122 A5
Lilian Baylis School
LBTH SE11 ....17 H7
VX/NE SW8 ....121 K6
Lilian Baylis Theatre
CLKNW EC1R 6 A4
Lilian Bishop School of
English
SKENS SW7 ....14 A6
Limehouse Hole Stairs
BERM/RHTH SE16 ....124 C1
Limes Farm Primary School
CHIG IG7 ....54 D2
Lime Trees Park Golf Club
NTHLT UB5 ....77 G6
Lincoln Road Clinic
EN EN1 ....24 C6
Lincoln's Inn
LINN WC2A 11 H3
Linden Bridge School
WPK KT4 ....207 G1
Linden Lodge School
WIM/MER SW19 ....159 H3
Lindon Bennett School
FELT TW13 ....172 C1
Linford Christie Stadium
SHB W12 ....99 J4
The Link Day Primary School
CROY/NA CR0 ....210 E2
The Link Secondary School
CROY/NA CR0 ....211 F2
Links Primary School
TOOT SW17 ....179 F2
Linley House School
BRYLDS KT5 ....191 G3
Linley Sambourne House
WKENS W14 ....119 J2
Linnet House Clinic
STJWD NW8 ....2 C3
Linton Mead Primary
School
THMD SE28 ....109 H6
Lionel Road Primary School
BTFD TW8 ....117 F4
Lion House School
PUT/ROE SW15 ....139 C5
Lismarrine Industrial Park
BORE WD6 ....29 H1
Lisson Grove Health Centre
STJWD NW8 ....2 C1
Lister Community School
PLSTW E13 ....107 F1
The Lister Hospital
BGVA SW1W 121 C5
Little Danson Welfare Clinic
WELL DA16 ....148 B5
Little Eden & Eden High
School
FELT TW13 ....154 C4
Little Hands Theatre
HDN NW4 ....64 A1
Little Heath School
CHDH RM6 ....73 H1
Little Ilford School
MNPK E12 ....89 K3
Little St Helens School
NTHWD HA6 ....40 C2

Little Stanmore First &
Middle School
EDGW HA8 ....44 A4
Little Wandsworth School
TOOT SW17 ....161 F4
Livesey Museum for Children
PECK SE15 ....123 J6
Livingstone Hospital
DART DA1 ....171 J2
Livingstone Primary School
EBAR EN4 ....21 H4
The Livity School
BRXS/STRHM SW2 ....141 K6
Lloyd Park Centre
WALTH E17 ....51 J5
Lloyd's
FENCHST EC3M 13 G4
Lloyds Register CC
DUL SE21 ....162 E3
Locks View Court
POP/IOD E14 ....105 C6
Lockwood Industrial Park
TOTM N17 ....50 D6
Lombard Business Centre
BTSEA SW11 ....140 C3
Lombards Business Park
CROY/NA CR0 ....196 A4
WAND/EARL SW18 ....160 C1
WIM/MER SW19 ....178 B5
Lombard Trading Estate
CHARL SE7 ....126 A4
Lombardy Retail Park
HYS/HAR UB3 ....95 F6
London Academy
EDGW HA8 ....30 B6
London Academy of Music
& Dramatic Art
KENS W8 ....119 K4
London Aquarium
WHALL SW1A 17 C3
London Area Terminal
Control Centre
WDR/YW UB7 ....112 C2
London Arena
POP/IOD E14 ....124 E3
London Bridge City Pier
STHWK SE1 ....13 C7
London Bridge Hospital
STHWK SE1 ....13 F7
London Bridge Hotel
STHWK SE1 ....18 E1
London Bridge Sports Centre
CANST EC4R 12 E6
London Business School
CAMTN NW1 ....2 E6
The London Canal Museum
IS N1 ....5 F2
London Capital College
CAMTN NW1 ....84 B6
London Chest Hospital
BETH E2 ....104 E1
London City Airport
CAN/RD E16 ....126 D1
London City College (English
Language Institute &
Schiller International
University STHWK SE1 ....17 H1
London City Mission
STHWK SE1 ....19 H2
The London Clinic
CAVSQ/HST W1G 3 H7
London College of Business
& Computer Services
CLAP SW4 ....141 J5
London College of Business
& Computing
BETH E2 ....104 D1
London College of
Communication
LBTH SE11 ....18 B5
London College of Fashion
CAVSQ/HST W1G 9 K3
MHST W1U 9 H3
SDTCH EC2A 7 H6
London College of Further
Education
LBTH SE11 ....18 A7
London College of Higher
Education
CLAP SW4 ....141 G4
London College of
International Business
Studies HHOL WC1V 11 F2
The London College
KENS W8 ....119 K1
London Commodity Exchange
WAP E1W 13 K6
London Cornish RFC
PUT/ROE SW15 ....158 C5
London Dungeon
STHWK SE1 ....13 F7
London Electronics College
ECT SW5 ....119 K5
London Esthetique
CAVSQ/HST W1G 9 K3
London Eye
STHWK SE1 ....17 G2
London Eye Clinic
CAVSQ/HST W1G 9 J2
London Fields Primary School
HACK E8 ....86 D6
London Foot Hospital
FITZ W1T 4 A7
London Gender Clinic
HDN NW4 ....63 K3
London Glass Blowing
Workshop
STHWK SE1 ....19 C5
London Group Business Park
CRICK NW2 ....63 H5
London Guildhall University
TWRH EC3N 13 J5
London Guildhall University
Sports Ground
LEE/GVPK SE12 ....166 B4
London Heart Clinic
CAVSQ/HST W1G 9 J2

The London Industrial Estate
EHAM E6 ....108 A4
London Industrial Park
EHAM E6 ....108 B4
London International Film
School
LSQ/SEVD WC2H 10 E4
The London Irish Youth
Theatre
HGT N6 ....66 B5
London Islamic School /
Madrasah
WCHPL E1 ....104 D5
London IT College
GNTH/NBYPK IG2 ....72 A3
London Jewish Girls High
School
HDN NW4 ....64 A2
London Ladies & Girls FC
CAT SE6 ....182 E1
London Lane Clinic
BMLY BR1 ....183 J3
London Lighthouse
NTGHL W11 ....100 C5
London Living Theatre
SYD SE26 ....164 A6
London Marriott Hotel
MBLAR W1H 83 J5
MYFR/PKLN W1K 9 H5
STHWK SE1 ....17 C2
London Marriott Hotel
Park Lane
OXSTW W1C 9 F5
London Marriott West India
Quay Hotel
POP/IOD E14 ....105 J6
London Metropolitan
University
HBRY N5 ....85 J3
HOLWY N7 ....85 F3
HOLWY N7 ....85 G1
LVPST EC2M 13 F2
WCHPL E1 ....13 J3
WCHPL E1 ....104 C5
London Nautical School
STHWK SE1 ....11 K7
London Open College
FSBYE EC1V 6 B4
London Oratory School
FUL/PGN SW6 ....139 K1
London Road Medical Centre
CROY/NA CR0 ....196 B3
London School of Economics
CLKNW EC1R 5 K5
HHOL WC1V 10 E3
HOL/ALD WC2B 11 C4
STHWK SE1 ....12 C7
London School of Hygiene &
Tropical Medicine
GWRST WC1E 10 D1
London School of Theology
NTHWD HA6 ....40 A5
London Scottish Golf Club
WIM/MER SW19 ....158 K5
London Silver Vaults
LINN WC2A 11 J2
The London Television Centre
(LWT)
STHWK SE1 ....11 J7
London Tourist Board &
Convention Centre
BGVA SW1W 15 J4
London Toy & Model Museum
BAY/PAD W2 ....101 C6
London Transport Bus Depot
BXLYHN DA7 ....149 J4
London Underwriting Centre
MON EC3R 13 C5
London Weather Centre
HCIRC EC1N 11 J1
The London Welbeck Hospital
CAVSQ/HST W1C 9 H2
London Welsh FC
RCH/KEW TW9 ....137 F4
London Welsh School
CRICK NW2 ....82 A4
London West Crematorium
WLSDN NW10 ....99 K3
London Wetland Centre
BARN SW13 ....138 E2
London Zoo
CAMTN NW1 ....3 G2
Lonesome Primary School
MTCM CR4 ....179 G5
Long Ditton County Infant
School
SURB KT6 ....190 D5
Longfield Primary School
RYLN/HDSTN HA2 ....60 A3
Longford Community School
EBED/NFELT TW14 ....153 J2
Longford Industrial Estate
HPTN TW12 ....173 C2
Longlands Primary School
BFN/LL DA15 ....167 K5
Long Lane AFC
BKHTH/KID SE3 ....146 B3
Longmead Primary School
WDR/YW UB7 ....112 A4
Longshaw Primary School
CHING E4 ....38 B5
Lord Chancellors Department
WEST SW1P 16 D5
Lord Lister Health Centre
FSTGT E7 ....88 E2
Lordship Lane Clinic
TOTM N17 ....50 A5
Lordship Lane Primary
School
WDGN N22 ....49 J4
Lord's Tour & MCC Museum
STJWD NW8 ....2 A5
Lorimer Business Centre
RAIN RM13 ....111 G5
Loughborough Primary
School
CMBW SE5 ....142 C3

Lovelace Primary School
CHSGTN KT9 ....205 J3
Lovell's Wharf
GNWCH SE10 ....125 G5
Lower Clapton Health
Centre
CLPT E5 ....86 E3
Lower Place Business Centre
WLSDN NW10 ....98 E1
Lower Sydenham Industrial
Estate
SYD SE26 ....182 C1
Lowfield Medical Centre
DART DA1 ....171 H2
Low Hall Sports Ground
LEY E10 ....69 F3
Lowther Primary School
BARN SW13 ....118 D6
Loxford School of Science &
Technology
IL IG1 ....90 D7
Loyola Preparatory School
BKHH IG9 ....39 C3
LPR Sports Club
BARK/HLT IG6 ....55 F4
LSE Sports Club
NWMAL KT3 ....192 A3
LT Lost Property Office
CAMTN NW1 ....3 F7
Lubavitch House School
(Senior Girls)
STNW/STAM N16 ....68 B4
Lucas Vale Primary School
DEPT SE8 ....144 D2
Lutomer House Business
Centre
POP/IOD E14 ....124 E1
Lux Cinema
IS N1 ....7 G5
Lycee Francais
SKENS SW7 ....14 A6
Lycee Francais
Charles De Gaulle
BTSEA SW11 ....141 C5
The Lyceum Theatre
COVGDN WC2E 11 G5
Lyndean Industrial Estate
ABYW SE2 ....128 D3
Lyndhurst House Preparatory
School
HAMP NW3 ....83 H3
Lyndhurst Primary School
CMBW SE5 ....142 E3
Lyon Business Park
BARK IG11 ....108 C1
Lyon Park J & I School
ALP/SUD HA0 ....80 B5
Lyonsdown School
BAR EN5 ....21 G6
Lyric Theatre
SOHO/SHAV W1D 10 C5
Lyric Theatre Hammersmith
HMSMTH W6 ....119 F4
Mabwin Supplementary
School
ED N9 ....36 D4
Macaulay CE Primary School
CLAP SW4 ....141 C5
Madame Tussauds & The
London Auditorium
CAMTN NW1 ....3 F7
Madeira Grove Clinic
WFD IG8 ....53 F1
Madison Bowl
NTHWD HA6 ....40 C3
Madni Girls School
WCHPL E1 ....104 D5
Madrasah-E-Darul Qirat
Majidiah School
WCHPL E1 ....104 D6
Mahatma Gandhi Industrial
Estate
BRXN/ST SW9 ....142 C4
Maida Vale Medical Centre
MV/WKIL W9 ....101 F2
Malcolm Primary School
PGE/AN SE20 ....181 K3
The Malden Centre
NWMAL KT3 ....192 C1
Malden Golf Club
NWMAL KT3 ....176 B5
Malden Manor Primary
School
NWMAL KT3 ....192 B4
Malden Parochial Primary
School
WPK KT4 ....192 B5
Malden Road Baths
CHEAM SM3 ....208 B2
Malham Road Industrial
Estate
FSTH SE23 ....164 A3
Mall Galleries
STJS SW1Y 10 D7
The Mall School
WHTN TW2 ....155 J5
Malmaison Charterhouse
Square Hotel
FARR EC1M 12 B1
Malmesbury Primary School
MRDN SM4 ....194 B4
Malorees J & I School
KIL/WHAMP NW6 ....82 B5
Malory School
BMLY BR1 ....165 K6
Mandarin Oriental Hotel
KTBR SW1X 15 F2
The Mandeville Hotel
MHST W1U 9 H3
Mandeville Primary School
CLPT E5 ....87 C1
Mandeville Special School
NTHLT UB5 ....77 K4
Manford Industrial Estate
ERITH DA8 ....130 E6
Manford Way Health Centre
BARK/HLT IG6 ....55 F2

Manor Brook Medical Centre
BKHTH/KID SE3 ....146 A3
Manor Drive Health Centre
WPK KT4 ....192 C5
Manorfield Primary School
POP/IOD E14 ....105 K4
Manor Infant School
BARK IG11 ....91 F4
Manor Oak Primary School
STMC/STPC BR5 ....202 E2
Manor Park Cemetery
FSTGT E7 ....89 H2
Manor Park Crematorium
FSTGT E7 ....89 G2
Manor Park Methodist School
MNPK E12 ....89 J2
Manor Park Primary School
SUT SM1 ....209 G3
Manor Primary School
SRTFD E15 ....106 C1
The Manor Primary School
ROM RM1 ....75 H2
Manorside Primary School
FNCH N3 ....47 F4
Manor Special School
WLSDN NW10 ....100 B1
Manor Way Business Centre
RAIN RM13 ....111 F4
Mansion House
MANHO EC4N 12 E4
Mapledown School
CRICK NW2 ....64 B4
Maple Grove Business Centre
HSLWW TW4 ....134 B5
Maple House School
THHTH CR7 ....180 D6
Maple Industrial Estate
FELT TW13 ....153 K4
Maple Infant School
SURB KT6 ....190 E2
Maples Business Centre
IS N1 ....85 G5
Marble Arch
MBLAR W1H 9 F5
Marble Hill House
TWK TW1 ....156 D2
Maria Fidelis Convent
Lower School
CAMTN NW1 ....4 B5
Maria Fidelis Convent
Upper School
CAMTN NW1 ....4 C4
Maria Montessori Childrens
House
HAMP NW3 ....83 H3
Mariner Business Centre
CROY/NA CR0 ....211 F3
Marian Richardson Primary
School
WCHPL E1 ....105 F5
Marion Vian Primary School
BECK BR3 ....198 A2
Maritime Greenwich College
DEPT SE8 ....144 D1
Maritime Industrial Estate
CHARL SE7 ....126 A4
Maritime Museum
GNWCH SE10 ....125 H4
Marjorie McClure School
CHST BR7 ....185 H4
The Marjory Kinnon School
EBED/NFELT TW14 ....133 H6
Market Trading Estate
NWDGN UB2 ....114 A4
Marks Gate Junior School
CHDH RM6 ....56 A6
Marlborough CC
DUL SE21 ....163 H3
Marlborough Day Hospital
STJWD NW8 ....101 C1
Marlborough First & Middle
School
HRW HA1 ....60 E1
Marlborough House
STJS SW1Y 16 B1
Marlborough Primary School
CHEL SW3 ....14 D7
ISLW TW7 ....136 B2
Marlborough School
BFN/LL DA15 ....168 B3
Marlborough Trading Estate
RCH/KEW TW9 ....137 J2
Marlowe Business Centre
NWCR SE14 ....144 B1
Marner Primary School
BOW E3 ....105 K3
Marriott Hotel
ECT SW5 ....120 A4
KIL/WHAMP NW6 ....107 F1
HYS/HAR UB3 ....133 G2
MBLAR W1H 8 D3
Marshalls Park School
ROM RM1 ....57 G5
Marshall Street Leisure Centre
SOHO/CST W1F 10 B4
Marsh Gate Business Centre
SRTFD E15 ....106 A1
Marshgate Primary School
RCHPK/HAM TW10 ....137 G6
Marshgate Trading Estate
SRTFD E15 ....87 K5
Marsh Green School
DAGW RM9 ....110 C1
Martan College
HOL/ALD WC2B 11 F3
Martinbridge Industrial Estate
EN EN1 ....24 C6
Martindale Industrial Estate
EN EN1 ....24 A6
Martin Infant School
EFNCH N2 ....47 J5
Marvels Lane Primary School
LEE/GVPK SE12 ....166 B6
Mary Boone School
WKENS W14 ....119 H4
Maryland Industrial Estate
SRTFD E15 ....88 C3

Maryland Primary School SRTFD E15 ...88 C3
Marylebone Health Centre CAMTN NW1 ...3 H7
Marylebone Magistrates Court CAMTN NW1 ...8 D1
Marymount International School KUTN/CMB KT2 ...175 K3
Mary Wallace Theatre TWT TW1 ...156 B3
Maswell Park Health Centre HSLW TW3 ...135 H6
Matilda Marks Kennedy Primary MLHL NW7 ...45 F1
Matrix Business Centre DART DA1 ...151 H6
Maudlin's Green WAP E1W ...13 K7
The Maudsley Hospital CMBW SE5 ...142 E3
Maughan Library Kings College LINN WC2A ...11 J3
Mawbrey Brough Health Centre VX/NE SW8 ...141 K1
The Mawney School ROMW/RG RM7 ...75 F2
Mayday University Hospital THHTH CR7 ...196 C3
Mayesbrook Park Arena BARK IG11 ...91 G3
Mayespark Primary School GDMY/SEVK IG3 ...91 G1
Mayfield Primary School HNWL W7 ...96 D5
Mayfield School PIN HA5 ...41 J6
Mayflower Primary School POP/IOD E14 ...105 J5
Mayplace Primary School BXLYHN DA7 ...150 A5
Maypole Primary School RDART DA2 ...170 B5
Maytime School IL IG1 ...90 A1
Mayville J & P School WAN E11 ...88 C1
McEntee School WALTH E17 ...51 H4
McKay Trading Estate NKENS W10 ...100 C3
McMillan Clinic HYS/HAR UB3 ...94 A6
The Mead Infant School WPK KT4 ...207 H1
Meadlands Primary School RCHPK/HAM TW10 ...156 D6
Meadowgate School BROCKY SE4 ...144 A4
Meadowside Leisure Centre BKHTH/KID SE3 ...146 B5
The Meadow Special School STMC/STPC BR5 ...186 B3
Mead Road Infant School CHST BR7 ...185 H2
The Medical Centre WAND/EARL SW18 ...160 A1
Medical Express Clinic CAVSQ/HST W1G ...9 J1
Mednurs Clinic SEVS/STOTM N15 ...67 K3
Megabowl KUTN/CMB KT2 ...175 F5
Melcombe Primary School HMSMTH W6 ...119 G6
Meli-white House Hotel CAMTN NW1 ...3 K6
Mellish Industrial Estate WOOL/PLUM SE18 ...126 C3
Mellow Lane School HGDN/ICK UB10 ...94 A3
Melrose Special School MTCM CR4 ...178 D6
Memorial Hospital WOOL/PLUM SE18 ...147 F3
The Menorah Foundation School EDGW HA8 ...44 E3
Menorah Grammar School GLDGN NW11 ...64 C4
Menorah Primary School GLDGN NW11 ...64 C4
Mercers' Hall CITYW EC2V ...12 D4
The Merchant Taylors Hall BANK EC3V ...13 F4
Merchant Taylors Centre NTHWD HA6 ...26 C3
Mercure London City Bankside Hotel STHWK SE1 ...18 C1
Meridian Clinic BRXN/ST SW9 ...142 A4
Meridian Locality Mental Health Centre CHARL SE7 ...126 B6
Meridian Primary School GNWCH SE10 ...125 C5
Meridian Sports Club CHARL SE7 ...146 D1
Meridian Trading Estate CHARL SE7 ...126 C6
Merlin Primary School BMLY BR1 ...165 K5
Merlin School PUT/ROE SW15 ...139 G6
Mermaid Theatre BLKFR EC4V ...12 B5
Merrielands Retail Park DAGW RM9 ...92 B6
Merry Hill Infant School BUSH WD23 ...28 B2

Merryhills Clinic ENC/FH EN2 ...23 F4
Merryhills Primary School ENC/FH EN2 ...23 F5
Merton Abbey Primary School WIM/MER SW19 ...178 A4
Merton Adult College RYNPK SW20 ...177 H6
Merton College MRDN SM4 ...193 J3
Merton Court Preparatory School SCUP DA14 ...168 D6
Merton Industrial Park WIM/MER SW19 ...178 B4
Merton Park Primary School WIM/MER SW19 ...177 J5
Merton Road Industrial Estate WAND/EARL SW18 ...159 K2
Metro Business Centre SYD SE26 ...182 C2
The Metro Golf Centre HDN NW4 ...46 A4
Metro Industrial Centre ISLW TW7 ...135 K3
Metropolitan Business Centre IS N1 ...86 A5
Metropolitan Hospital STHWK SE1 ...17 K4
The Metropolitan Hotel MYFR/PKLN W1K ...15 J1
Metropolitan Police Hayes Sports Club HAYES BR2 ...199 J6
Metropolitan Police Training School; Hendon CDALE/KGS NW9 ...45 H6
Metropolitan Tabernacle STHWK SE1 ...18 B6
Metro Trading Centre WBLY HA9 ...80 D2
Michael Faraday Primary School WALW SE17 ...122 E5
Michael Manley Industrial Estate VX/NE SW8 ...141 H2
Michael Sobell Sinai School KTN/HRWW/WS HA3 ...62 C3
The Michael Tippett School LBTH SE11 ...17 K7
Midas Business Centre DAGE RM10 ...92 C2
Midas Industrial Estate DAGE RM10 ...92 C2
Middle Park Primary School ELTH/MOT SE9 ...166 C2
Middle Row Primary School NKENS W10 ...100 C3
Middlesex Business Centre NWDGN UB2 ...115 F2
Middlesex CCC (Lord's Cricket Ground) STJWD NW8 ...2 B4
Middlesex Guildhall STJSPK SW1H ...16 D3
Middlesex Hospital Medical School FITZ W1T ...10 B1
Middlesex Hospital Nurses Home GTPST W1W ...10 A1
Middlesex Hospital School of Physiotherapy FITZ W1T ...10 B1
Middlesex Hospital Sports Ground CHST BR7 ...186 A1
Middlesex School of Complementary Medicine STAN HA7 ...44 A4
Middlesex University ARCH N19 ...66 C5
EBAR EN4 ...34 A1
GLDGN NW11 ...65 F5
HDN NW4 ...64 B1
PEND EN3 ...25 F6
STHGT/OAK N14 ...22 C5
WDGN N22 ...48 E5
Middlesex University (Enfield Campus) PEND EN3 ...24 D6
Middlesex University Museum EBAR EN4 ...22 A6
Middlesex University (Trent Park Campus) EBAR EN4 ...22 C3
Midfield Primary School STMC/STPC BR5 ...186 B3
Midway Mission Hospital BETH E2 ...7 J5
Milbourne Lodge Junior School ESH/CLAY KT10 ...204 C3
Milbourne Lodge School ESH/CLAY KT10 ...204 D4
Mile End & Bow Business WCHPL E1 ...104 D4
Mile End Hospital WCHPL E1 ...105 F2
Mile End Stadium POP/IOD E14 ...105 H4
Milehams Industrial Estate PUR RM19 ...131 K3
Miles Coverdale Primary School SHB W12 ...119 F2
Milestone Hotel KENS W8 ...120 A2
Millbank Millennium Pier WEST SW1P ...16 E7
Millbank Primary School WEST SW1P ...16 D7

Millbank Tower WEST SW1P ...16 E7
Millennium Arena BTSEA SW11 ...141 F1
Millennium Bailey's Hotel SKENS SW7 ...120 B4
Millennium Balloon STHWK SE1 ...19 H1
Millennium Gloucester Hotel ECT SW5 ...120 A4
Millennium Harbour POP/IOD E14 ...124 C2
Millennium Hotel KTBR SW1X ...15 F3
Millennium Hotel London Mayfair MYFR/PKLN W1K ...9 H6
The Millennium Primary School GNWCH SE10 ...125 J3
Millennium Quay DEPT SE8 ...124 E6
Millennium Wharf POP/IOD E14 ...125 G3
Mill Farm Business Park HSLWW TW4 ...154 D2
Millfields J & I School CLPT E5 ...86 E2
Millfield Theatre UED N18 ...35 K6
Mill Green Business Park MTCM CR4 ...194 E4
Mill Hill Cemetery MLHL NW7 ...46 A2
Mill Hill County High MLHL NW7 ...31 G4
The Mill Hill CC MLHL NW7 ...32 A5
Mill Hill Golf Club MLHL NW7 ...31 G4
Mill Hill Industrial Estate MLHL NW7 ...45 H2
Mill Hill School MLHL NW7 ...31 K6
Mill Lane Medical Centre KIL/WHAMP NW6 ...82 E3
Mill Lane Trading Estate CROY/NA CR0 ...211 F1
Mill River Trading Estate PEND EN3 ...25 G5
Millside Industrial Estate DART DA1 ...151 G5
Mill Street Clinic STHWK SE1 ...19 K2
Mill Trading Estate WLSDN NW10 ...98 D1
The Mill Trading Estate WLSDN NW10 ...98 E2
Millwall FC (The New Den) BERM/RHTH SE16 ...123 K5
Milmead Industrial Estate TOTM N17 ...50 D5
Milton Natural Health Centre HGT N6 ...66 C4
Minet Clinic HYS/HAR UB3 ...113 K1
Minet J & I School HYS/HAR UB3 ...114 A1
Ministry of Defence WHALL SW1A ...16 E1
Mint Business Park CAN/RD E16 ...106 C4
Mirravale Trading Estate CHDH RM6 ...74 A4
Mission Grove Primary School WALTH E17 ...69 H2
Mitcham CC MTCM CR4 ...194 D1
Mitcham Golf Club MTCM CR4 ...195 F2
Mitcham Industrial Estate MTCM CR4 ...179 F4
Mitcham Vale High School MTCM CR4 ...179 G5
Mitchell Brook Primary School WLSDN NW10 ...81 F4
Mitre Bridge Industrial Park NKENS W10 ...99 K3
Mitre House Hotel BAY/PAD W2 ...8 A4
Moatbridge School ELTH/MOT SE9 ...166 C1
The Moat School FUL/PGN SW6 ...139 H3
Moberly Sports & Education Centre WLSDN NW10 ...100 B2
Molesey Hospital E/WMO/HCT KT8 ...189 F2
Mollison Drive Health Centre WLGTN SM6 ...210 E5
Monega Primary School MNPK E12 ...89 H3
Monken Hadley CE Primary School BAR EN5 ...20 E2
Monkfrith Primary School EBAR EN4 ...34 A2
Monks Hill Sports Centre SAND/SEL CR2 ...213 F5
Monks Orchard Primary School CROY/NA CR0 ...198 A2
The Montague on the Gardens Hotel RSQ WC1B ...10 E1
Montbelle Primary School ELTH/MOT SE9 ...167 F6
Montcalm-Hotel Nikko MBLAR W1H ...9 F4
Monteagle Primary School DAGW RM9 ...91 H6

Montem Primary School HOLWY N7 ...85 F1
Montpelier Primary School EA W5 ...97 K4
The Monument CANST EC4R ...13 F5
Moore Place Golf Club ESH/CLAY KT10 ...204 A3
Moorfields Eye Hospital FSBYE EC1V ...6 E5
Moor Lane Junior School CHSGTN KT9 ...206 B3
Moor Park Industrial Estate WATW WD18 ...26 A2
Mora Primary School CRICK NW2 ...82 A2
Morden Cemetery MRDN SM4 ...193 F3
Morden College Homes BKHTH/KID SE3 ...145 K3
Morden First School MRDN SM4 ...193 K2
Morden Hall Medical Centre WIM/MER SW19 ...178 A6
Morden Hall Park (NT) MRDN SM4 ...194 B1
Morden Mount Primary School LEW SE13 ...144 E3
Morden Park Pool MRDN SM4 ...193 J2
Morden Road Clinic WIM/MER SW19 ...178 A6
More House School KTBR SW1X ...15 F5
Moreland Primary School FSBYE EC1V ...6 B4
Moriah Jewish Day School PIN HA5 ...59 J5
Morley College STHWK SE1 ...17 K4
Morningside Primary School HOM E9 ...86 E4
Mornington Sports & Fitness Centre BETH E2 ...84 B6
Morpeth School BETH E2 ...104 E2
Mortimer Road Clinic WLSDN NW10 ...100 A2
Mortimer School STRHM/NOR SW16 ...161 J4
Mortlake Cemetery MORT/ESHN SW14 ...138 B4
Mortlake Crematorium RCH/KEW TW9 ...137 J3
Moselle School TOTM N17 ...50 A5
Mosiah Foundation Supplementary School STNW/STAM N16 ...68 A5
Mossbourne Community Academy HACK E8 ...86 C2
Mossford Green Primary School BARK/HLT IG6 ...54 C5
Moss Hall Primary School FNCH N3 ...47 F2
The Mother & Baby Clinic HOM E9 ...86 E4
Mottingham Community Health Clinic ELTH/MOT SE9 ...166 D6
Mottingham Primary School ELTH/MOT SE9 ...166 E5
Mount Carmel RC Primary School EA W5 ...116 D3
Mount Carmel RC Technology College for Girls ARCH N19 ...66 D5
The Mount Infant School NWMAL KT3 ...175 K2
Mount Medical Centre FELT TW13 ...154 D4
Mount School MLHL NW7 ...45 K1
Mount Stewart Primary School KTN/HRWW/WS HA3 ...61 K3
Mowlem Primary School BETH E2 ...104 E1
Mowlem Trading Estate TOTM N17 ...50 E3
MPR Eurotots School KIL/WHAMP NW6 ...82 B5
MS Business Centre PIN HA5 ...41 H6
MSP Business Centre WBLY HA9 ...80 D2
Mudchute City Farm POP/IOD E14 ...125 F4
Mudlands Estate RAIN RM13 ...111 G2
Mulberry Business Centre BERM/RHTH SE16 ...124 A2
Mulberry House School CRICK NW2 ...82 C3
Mulberry Primary School TOTM N17 ...50 B5
Mulberry School for Girls WCHPL E1 ...104 D5
Mulgrave Primary School WOOL/PLUM SE18 ...127 F4
Munroe Centre STHWK SE1 ...19 F2
Murky Puddle Theatre NWMAL KT3 ...176 C6
Murray Business Centre STMC/STPC BR5 ...186 C6
Muschamp Primary School CAR SM5 ...194 D6
Museum in Docklands POP/IOD E14 ...105 J2
Museum of Fulham Palace FUL/PGN SW6 ...139 G3

Museum of Garden History STHWK SE1 ...17 F5
Museum of London BARB EC2Y ...12 C2
Museum of London (Archaeological Research Centre) IS N1 ...6 D1
Museum of Richmond TWK TW1 ...136 E6
Museum of Rugby & Twickenham Stadium Tours WHTN TW2 ...155 K1
Museum of the Artillery in the Rotunda CHARL SE7 ...126 D5
Museum of the Order of St John FARR EC1M ...6 B7
Musical Museum BTFD TW8 ...117 F6
Muswell Hill Bowling Club MUSWH N10 ...48 A6
Muswell Hill Golf Club MUSWH N10 ...48 B4
Muswell Hill Primary School MUSWH N10 ...48 B6
Myatt Garden Primary School BROCKY SE4 ...144 C3
Myatts Field Clinic BRXN/ST SW9 ...142 C2
N1 Shopping Centre IS N1 ...5 K2
Nagi Business Centre ALP/SUD HA0 ...97 K1
Nags Head Shopping Centre HOLWY N7 ...84 E1
Naima Jewish Preparatory School KIL/WHAMP NW6 ...101 F1
Nash College of Further Education WWKM BR4 ...214 D1
The National Archives RCH/KEW TW9 ...137 J1
National Army Museum CHEL SW3 ...120 E6
National Film Theatre STHWK SE1 ...11 H7
National Gallery LSQ/SEVD WC2H ...10 D6
National Hospital for Neurology & Neurosurgery RSQ WC1B ...4 E7
National Hospital for Sick Children (Great Ormond Street) BMSBY WC1N ...5 F7
National Maritime Museum GNWCH SE10 ...125 G6
National Physical Laboratory TEDD TW11 ...173 K2
National Portrait Gallery LSQ/SEVD WC2H ...10 D6
National Sports Centre NRWD SE19 ...181 H2
National Temperance Hospital CAMTN NW1 ...4 A4
National Youth Theatre of Great Britain HOLWY N7 ...84 E1
Natural History Museum SKENS SW7 ...14 A5
Natural Therapy Clinic TOOT SW17 ...179 G1
Natwest Sports Club BECK BR3 ...182 C2
Navigation College CANST EC4R ...12 D5
NEC Harlequins RFC (Twickenham Stoop Stadium) WHTN TW2 ...155 K2
Negus Sixth Form Centre WOOL/PLUM SE18 ...127 J6
Nelson Dock Museum BERM/RHTH SE16 ...124 C1
Nelson Hospital RYNPK SW20 ...177 J5
Nelson Primary School EHAM E6 ...108 A1
WHTN TW2 ...155 G1
Nelson's Column STJS SW1Y ...10 D7
Nelson Trading Estate WIM/MER SW19 ...178 A4
Neo Clinic PIM SW1V ...16 A6
The New Ambassadors Theatre LSQ/SEVD WC2H ...10 D4
New Atlas Wharf POP/IOD E14 ...124 C3
The New Aylesbury Medical Centre WALW SE17 ...122 E5
New Brentford Cemetery HSLW TW3 ...134 E3
Newbury Park Health Centre GNTH/NBYPK IG2 ...72 D3
The New Business Centre WLSDN NW10 ...99 H2
New Caledonian Wharf BERM/RHTH SE16 ...124 C3
New Chiswick Pool CHSWK W4 ...138 B1
New City Primary School PLSTW E13 ...107 G2
New Connaught Rooms HOL/ALD WC2B ...11 F3
New Covent Garden Market VX/NE SW8 ...141 J1
New Crane Wharf WAP E1W ...123 K1
New Cross Sports Arena NWCR SE14 ...144 B1

New End Primary School
HAMP NW3 ....**83** G2

New End Theatre
HAMP NW3 ....**83** G1

New England Industrial
Estate
BARK IG11 ....**108** C1

Newfield Primary School
WLSDN NW10 ....**81** H5

Newham College of Further
Education
EHAM E6 ....**107** K1
SRTFD E15 ....**88** C5

Newham General Hospital
PLSTW E13 ....**107** G3

Newham Leisure Centre
PLSTW E13 ....**107** G4

Newham Medical Centre
PLSTW E13 ....**107** G1

Newham Sixth Form College
PLSTW E13 ....**107** F3

Newham Training &
Education Centre
SRTFD E15 ....**88** C4

New Health Centre
TOTM N17 ....**50** A4

Newington Court Business
Centre
STHWK SE1 ....**18** C5

Newington Green Primary
School
STNW/STAM N16 ....**86** A3

Newington Industrial
Estate
WALW SE17 ....**18** B7

New Kings Primary School
FUL/PGN SW6 ....**139** J3

Newland House School
TWK TW1 ....**156** A6

New London Theatre
LSQ/SEVD WC2H **11** F3

Newnham J & I School
RSLP HA4 ....**59** C5

New North Community
School
IS N1 ....**85** J5

Newport J & I School
WDGN N22 ....**49** H3

New River Sports Centre
WDGN N22 ....**49** H3

New River Village
CEND/HSY/T N8 ....**49** F6

New Rush Hall School
IL IG1 ....**72** C6

New School
FUL/PGN SW6 ....**139** J2

New Scotland Yard
STJSPK SW1H **16** C4

News International
WAP E1W **104** D6

New Southgate Cemetery
FBAR/BDGN N11 ....**34** B5

New Southgate Crematorium
FBAR/BDGN N11 ....**34** B5

New Southgate Industrial
Estate
FBAR/BDGN N11 ....**48** C1

New Southgate Pain Clinic &
Medical Centre
FBAR/BDGN N11 ....**48** C1

New Spitalfields Market
LEY E10 ....**87** J2

Newstead Wood School
for Girls
ORP BR6 ....**216** D1

Newton Farm First & Middle
School
RYLN/HDSTN HA2 ....**59** K6

Newton Industrial Estate
CHDH RM6 ....**73** K1

Newton Medical Centre
BAY/PAD W2 ....**101** F5

Newton Preparatory School
VX/NE SW8 ....**141** G1

Newtons Primary School
RAIN RM13 ....**111** F1

New Victoria Hospital
KUTN/CMB KT2 ....**176** B4

New Woodlands School
BMLY BR1 ....**165** H6

Nightingale Clinic
PLSTW E13 ....**107** G1

Nightingale Primary School
CLPT E5 ....**86** C1
SWFD E18 ....**71** G1
WDGN N22 ....**48** B4
WOOL/PLUM SE18 ....**127** G6

Nightingale School
TOOT SW17 ....**160** D4

The Nightingale Centre
STHWK SE1 ....**17** G3

Noam Primary School
NFNCH/WDSPK N12 ....**47** F1

Noel Coward
CHCR WC2N **10** E5

Noel Park Primary School
WDGN N22 ....**49** H5

No 41 Hotel
WESTW SW1E **15** K4

Nonsuch High School for Girls
CHEAM SM3 ....**208** B5

Nonsuch House Hotel
EW KT17 ....**208** A3

Nonsuch Primary School
EW KT17 ....**207** K3

Noor Ul Islam School
LEY E10 ....**70** A6

Norbury Complementary
Therapy Clinic
STRHM/NOR SW16 ....**180** A4

Norbury First & Middle School
HRW HA1 ....**60** E2

Norbury Health Centre
STRHM/NOR SW16 ....**180** A5

Norbury Manor Primary
School
STRHM/NOR SW16 ....**179** K4

Norbury Manor Secondary
Girls School
STRHM/NOR SW16 ....**180** B4

Norbury Trading Estate
STRHM/NOR SW16 ....**180** A5

Norfolk House School
MUSWH N10 ....**48** B5

Norland Place School
NTGHL W11 ....**119** H1

Norlington School
LEY E10 ....**70** B5

Normand Croft Community
School
WKENS W14 ....**119** J6

Normandy Primary School
BXLYHN DA7 ....**150** A2

Normanhurst School
CHING E4 ....**38** B2

Norman Park Athletics Track
HAYES BR2 ....**200** A3

Norman Shaw Building
(MP's Offices)
WHALL SW1A **16** E2

North Acton Business Park
ACT W3 ....**99** F5

North Beckton Primary School
EHAM E6 ....**107** K3

North Bridge House
HAMP NW3 ....**83** G4

North Bridge House School
HAMP NW3 ....**83** H4

North Bridge House Senior
School
CAMTN NW1 ....**3** J1

Northbrook CE School
LEE/GVPK SE12 ....**145** H6

Northbury Primary School
BARK IG11 ....**90** B4

North Clinic
BMLY BR1 ....**183** K4

Northcote Lodge School
BTSEA SW11 ....**160** D1

North Croydon Medical
Centre
THHTH CR7 ....**196** C3

North Ealing Primary School
WEA W13 ....**97** H3

North East Surrey
Crematorium
NWMAL KT3 ....**193** F3

Northend Primary School
ERITH DA8 ....**150** C2

North End Trading Estate
ERITH DA8 ....**150** B1

North Feltham Trading Estate
EBED/NFELT TW14 ....**134** A5

Northfields Industrial Estate
ALP/SUD HA0 ....**80** C6

Northfields Prospect
Business Centre
PUT/ROE SW15 ....**139** J5

Northgate Business Centre
EN EN1 ....**24** D4

Northgate Clinic
CDALE/KGS NW9 ....**63** G3

Northgate Industrial Park
CRW RM5 ....**56** B5

North Harringay Primary
School
CEND/HSY/T N8 ....**67** G1

North Havering College of
Adult Education
ROM RM1 ....**75** G1

North Kensington
Video-Drama Project
NKENS W10 ....**100** C5

North London Collegiate
School
EDGW HA8 ....**44** A2

The North London Hospice
NFNCH/WDSPK N12 ....**33** F5

North London School of
Physiotherapy
ARCH N19 ....**66** C5

North London Tutorial College
HDN NW4 ....**64** A3

North Middlesex Golf Club
NFNCH/WDSPK N12 ....**33** H5

North Middlesex Hospital
UED N18 ....**50** A1

Northolt Aerodrome
RSLP HA4 ....**76** E4

Northolt High School
NTHLT UB5 ....**77** K4

Northolt Primary School
NTHLT UB5 ....**77** H5

Northolt Road Clinic
RYLN/HDSTN HA2 ....**78** C1

Northolt Swimarama
NTHLT UB5 ....**78** A4

North Pole Depot
WLSDN NW10 ....**99** H3

North Primary School
STHL UB1 ....**95** K6

Northside Primary School
NFNCH/WDSPK N12 ....**47** G1

The North Street Health
Centre
CLAP SW4 ....**141** H4

Northumberland Heath
Medical Centre
ERITH DA8 ....**150** A1

Northumberland Heath
Primary School
ERITH DA8 ....**149** J1

Northumberland Park
Community School
TOTM N17 ....**50** C3

Northumberland Park
Industrial Estate
TOTM N17 ....**50** D2

Northview Primary School
WLSDN NW10 ....**81** G2

Northway School
MLHL NW7 ....**30** D4

North West Kent College
RDART DA2 ....**170** E4

North West London Jewish
Primary School
CRICK NW2 ....**82** C5

North West London Medical
Centre
MV/WKIL W9 ....**101** C2

North Westminster
Community School
BAY/PAD W2 ....**8** A2

North Westminster
Community Secondary
School *MV/WKIL* W9 ....**100** E3

North Weylands Industrial
Estate
WOT/HER KT12 ....**188** D6

Northwick Park Hospital &
Clinical Research Centre
HRW HA1 ....**61** H4

Northwold Primary School
CLPT E5 ....**68** C6

Northwood Cemetery
NTHWD HA6 ....**40** D3

Northwood College
NTHWD HA6 ....**40** B3

Northwood Football Club
NTHWD HA6 ....**40** D5

Northwood Golf Club
NTHWD HA6 ....**40** D3

Northwood & Pinner
Community Hospital
NTHWD HA6 ....**40** D2

Northwood Preparatory
School
RKW/CH/CXG WD3 ....**26** A4

Northwood Primary School
ERITH DA18 ....**129** F3

Northwood School
NTHWD HA6 ....**41** F4

Northwood Sports
Centre
NTHWD HA6 ....**41** F4

Norwegian/British
Monument
BAY/PAD W2 ....**8** C7

The Norwegian School
WIM/MER SW19 ....**177** F3

Norwood Green Infant
School
NWDGN UB2 ....**114** D5

Norwood Green Junior
School
NWDGN UB2 ....**114** D5

Norwood Heights Shopping
Centre
NRWD SE19 ....**181** F2

Norwood School
NRWD SE19 ....**180** D1

Notre Dame RC Girls School
STHWK SE1 ....**18** A4

Notre Dame RC Primary
School
WOOL/PLUM SE18 ....**127** G6

Notre Dame University
LSQ/SEVD WC2H **10** D6

Notting Hill & Ealing High
School Senior Department
WEA W13 ....**97** H4

Novello Theatre
HOL/ALD WC2B **11** G5

Novotel
CAMTN NW1 ....**4** D4
CAN/RD E16 ....**107** F6
GNWCH SE10 ....**144** E1
STHWK SE1 ....**18** D1
TWRH EC3N **13** H5
WDR/YW UB7 ....**112** D4

Novotel London Waterloo
STHWK SE1 ....**17** G6

Novotel London West
HMSMTH W6 ....**119** G5

Nower Hill High School
PIN HA5 ....**60** A1

NTGB Sports Ground
EHAM E6 ....**90** A4

Nuffield Hospital
ENC/FH EN2 ....**23** J3

Nugent Shopping Park
STMC/STPC BR5 ....**202** C1

Number 10 Bowling
ROM RM1 ....**75** G2

Nutrition Clinic
MHST W1U **9** G1

The O2
POP/IOD E14 ....**125** G1

O2 Centre
HAMP NW3 ....**83** G4

Oakdale Infant School
SWFD E18 ....**53** F5

Oakdale Junior School
SWFD E18 ....**53** G5

Oakfield Preparatory School
DUL SE21 ....**162** E4

Oakfield Primary School
DART DA1 ....**171** G4

Oakfield Road Industrial
Estate
PGE/AN SE20 ....**181** J3

Oak Hill Health Centre
SURB KT6 ....**191** F3

Oakhill Primary School
WFD IG8 ....**52** C2

Oakington Manor School
WBLY HA9 ....**80** D3

Oakland CP School
EBAR EN4 ....**33** K1

Oaklands Primary School
HNWL W7 ....**116** A2

Oaklands School
ISLW TW7 ....**135** K4

Oaklands Secondary School
BETH E2 ....**104** C3

Oak Lane Cemetery
TWK TW1 ....**156** B2

Oak Lane Medical Centre
TWK TW1 ....**156** C2

Oakleigh School
TRDG/WHET N20 ....**33** J5

Oak Lodge JMI School
MBAR BR4 ....**198** E4

Oak Lodge Medical Centre
EDGW HA8 ....**44** D3

Oak Lodge School
BAL SW12 ....**160** E2
EFNCH N2 ....**47** G6

Oakthorpe Primary School
UED N18 ....**49** J1

Oak Tree Medical Centre
GDMY/SEVK IG3 ....**72** E6

Oakwood Business Park
WLSDN NW10 ....**99** F2

Oakwood Medical Centre
STHGT/OAK N14 ....**22** C6

Oakwood Sports Centre
BXLYHN DA7 ....**150** A5

Oasis Sports Centre
LSQ/SEVD WC2H **10** E3

Obstetrics Hospital
GWRST WC1E **4** B7

Occupational Health
Centre
CROY/NA CR0 ....**211** K1

Odeon Cinema
BAR EN5 ....**20** E6
BAY/PAD W2 ....**8** E4
BERM/RHTH SE16 ....**124** A3
CAMTN NW1 ....**3** K4
ELTH/MOT SE9 ....**146** D5
ESH/CLAY KT10 ....**204** B2
FITZ W1T **10** C2
HAMP NW3 ....**83** H5
HAYES BR2 ....**183** K5
HOLWY N7 ....**84** E3
KENS W8 ....**119** J3
KUT/HW KT1 ....**175** F5
MUSWH N10 ....**66** A1
RCH/KEW TW9 ....**136** E6
ROM RM1 ....**75** H2
STJS SW1Y **10** C6
STRHM/NOR SW16 ....**161** K5
SWFD E18 ....**52** E5
WIM/MER SW19 ....**177** K3

Odeon Covent Gardens
Cinema
LSQ/SEVD WC2H **10** D4

Odeon Wardour Street
Cinema
SOHO/SHAV W1D **10** C5

Odessa Infant School
FSTGT E7 ....**88** E3

Odyssey Business Park
RSLP HA4 ....**77** F3

Old Actonians Sports Club
EA W5 ....**117** G2

Old Admiralty
STJS SW1Y **16** D1

Old Bancroftians FC
BKHH IG9 ....**39** H6

Old Barnes Cemetery
BARN SW13 ....**138** C3

Old Beckenham RFC
WWKM BR4 ....**214** B1

Old Bellgate Wharf
POP/IOD E14 ....**124** C3

Old Bexley Business Park
BXLY DA5 ....**169** J2

Old Bexley CE Primary
School
BXLY DA5 ....**169** G3

Old Brocklehans Sports
Ground
LEE/GVPK SE12 ....**166** B1

Old Bromlians CC
HAYES BR2 ....**200** A2

Old Cemetery
EDUL SE22 ....**163** J1

Old Colfeian Sports Club
LEE/GVPK SE12 ....**145** J6

Old Curiosity Shop
LINN WC2A **11** G3

Old Elthamians Sports Club
CHST BR7 ....**185** K2

Oldfield House Special School
HPTN TW12 ....**172** E4

Oldfield Primary School
GFD/PVL UB6 ....**96** D1

Oldfields Trading Estate
SUT SM1 ....**208** E1

Old Fold Manor Golf Club
BAR EN5 ....**20** C2

Old Ford Primary School
BOW E3 ....**105** H1

Oldhill Medical Centre
STNW/STAM N16 ....**68** B5

Old Jamaica Business Estate
BERM/RHTH SE16 ....**19** K4

Old Lansun Sports Ground
RYLN/HDSTN HA2 ....**60** C2

Old Millhillians Sports Ground
RYLN/HDSTN HA2 ....**42** A4

Old Oak Primary School
SHB W12 ....**99** H5

Old Operating Theatre &
Herb Garret Museum
STHWK SE1 ....**18** E1

Old Owens Sports Ground
TRDG/WHET N20 ....**33** H5

Old Palace Primary School
BOW E3 ....**105** K2

Old Palace School
CROY/NA CR0 ....**211** H1

Old Royal Naval College
GNWCH SE10 ....**125** G5

Old Royal Observatory
Greenwich
GNWCH SE10 ....**145** G1

Old Spitalfields Market Hall
WCHPL E1 ....**13** J1

Old Station Museum
CAN/RD E16 ....**127** F2

Old Sun Wharf
POP/IOD E14 ....**105** G6

Old Tiffinians Sports Ground
E/WMO/HCT KT8 ....**189** K2

Old Treasury
WHALL SW1A **16** E2

Old Vicarage School
RCHPK/HAM TW10 ....**157** F1

Old Vic Theatre
STHWK SE1 ....**17** K2

Old War Office
WHALL SW1A **16** E1

Old Wilsonians Sports Club
WWKM BR4 ....**199** H5

Olga Primary School
BOW E3 ....**105** G1

Oliver Business Park
WLSDN NW10 ....**98** E1

Oliver Goldsmith Primary
School
CDALE/KGS NW9 ....**63** F2
CMBW SE5 ....**143** G2

Oliver House Preparatory
School
CLAP SW4 ....**161** G1

Olympia
WKENS W14 ....**119** H3

Olympia Industrial Estate
WDGN N22 ....**49** F5

Olympic Industrial Estate
WBLY HA9 ....**80** D2

Olympic Retail Park
WBLY HA9 ....**80** C2

Olympic Trading Estate
WBLY HA9 ....**80** D2

One Aldwych Hotel
COVGDN WC2E **11** G5

The One Stanley Medical
Centre
ALP/SUD HA0 ....**80** A5

On Sai Clinic
ECT SW5 ....**120** A4

Open Air Theatre
CAMTN NW1 ....**3** G5

The Open University
FSBYW WC1X **5** G4
HAMP NW3 ....**82** E2

Ophaboom Theatre
WLSDN NW10 ....**99** K1

Optimax Laser Eye Clinic
HAMP NW3 ....**83** G4

Orange Tree Theatre
RCH/KEW TW9 ....**137** F5

Orchard Business Centre
BECK BR3 ....**182** C1

The Orchard Health Centre
BARK IG11 ....**108** C1

Orchard Hill College
WLGTN SM6 ....**210** B4

Orchard House School
CHSWK W4 ....**118** A4

Orchard J & I School
HOM E9 ....**86** E5

The Orchard Junior School
HSLWW TW4 ....**135** F5

Orchard Primary School
SCUP DA14 ....**186** C1

The Orchard School
E/WMO/HCT KT8 ....**189** J2

Orchard Shopping Centre
DART DA1 ....**171** H1

The Orchard Theatre
DART DA1 ....**171** H1

Orchard Way Primary School
CROY/NA CR0 ....**198** B4

Oriel Primary School
FELT TW13 ....**154** D5

Orient Industrial Park
LEY E10 ....**69** J6

Orion Business Centre
NWCR SE14 ....**124** A5

Orleans House Gallery
TWK TW1 ....**156** C3

Orleans Infant School
TWK TW1 ....**156** C2

Orley Farm School
HRW HA1 ....**78** D1

Orpington College of Further
Education
ORP BR6 ....**202** B5

The Orpington Halls
ORP BR6 ....**202** B6

Orpington Hospital
ORP BR6 ....**217** F2

Orpington Mental Health
Centre
ORP BR6 ....**217** F1

Orpington Retail Park
STMC/STPC BR5 ....**202** D1

Orpington Superbowl
ORP BR6 ....**202** B5

Orpington Trade Centre
STMC/STPC BR5 ....**186** C6

Osidge JMI School
STHGT/OAK N14 ....**34** C3

Osier Industrial Estate
WAND/EARL SW18 ....**139** K5

Osmani Primary School
WCHPL E1 ....**104** C4

Osteopathic Clinic
HOR/WEW KT19 ....**207** F3

Osterley Park & House (NT)
ISLW TW7 ....**115** H6

Osterley RFC
NWDGN UB2 ....**115** G3

Our Lady Immaculate RC
Primary School
BRYLDS KT5 ....**191** J5

Our Lady of Dolours RC
Primary School
BAY/PAD W2 ....**101** F4

Our Lady of Grace RC Junior
School
CRICK NW2 ....**81** K1

Our Lady of Grace RC Primary
School
CHARL SE7 ....**126** A6

Our Lady of Lourdes RC
Primary School
BKHTH/KID SE3 ....**145** G4
FBAR/BDGN N11 ....**48** B1

WAN E11 ....70 D3
WLSDN NW10 ....80 E6
Our Lady of Muswell RC
Primary School
MUSWH N10 ....48 A5
Our Lady of the Rosary RC
School
ELTH/MOT SE9 ....167 K1
Our Lady of the Sacred Heart
School
HOLWY N7 ....85 F3
Our Lady of the Visitation RC
Combined Primary School
GFD/PVL UB6 ....96 C3
Our Lady of Victories RC
Primary School
SKENS SW7 ....120 B4
Our Lady of Victorys RC
Primary School
PUT/ROE SW15 ....139 C5
Our Lady Queen of Heaven
RC Primary School
WIM/MER SW19 ....159 G2
Our Lady RC Primary School
POP/IOD E14 ....105 K5
Our Lady & St Johns RC
Primary School
BTFD TW8 ....116 D5
Our Lady & St Joseph Primary
School
IS N1 ....86 A4
Our Lady & St Philip Neri RC
Infant School
FSTH SE23 ....164 A1
Our Lady & St Phillip Neri RC
Primary School
SYD SE26 ....164 B6
Our Ladys Catholic Primary
School
DART DA1 ....171 G1
Our Ladys RC Primary School
CAMTN NW1 ....84 C6
Oval Business Centre
LBTH SE11 ....122 A5
Oval House Theatre
LBTH SE11 ....122 B6
Oval Primary School
CROY/NA CR0 ....197 F5
Overton Grange School
BELMT SM2 ....209 F6
Oxford Gardens Primary
School
NKENS W10 ....100 B5
Oxford House College
SOHO/SHAV W1D 10 C3
Oxhey Infant School
OXHEY WD19 ....27 J1
Oxhey Park Golf Centre
OXHEY WD19 ....27 H3
Oxhey Wood Primary School
OXHEY WD19 ....27 G6
Oxo Tower Wharf
STHWK SE1 ....11 K6
Paddington Bowling &
Sports Club
MV/WKIL W9 ....101 F3
Paddington Green Primary
School
BAY/PAD W2 ....2 A7
Paddington Recreation
Ground Athletics Track
KIL/WHAMP NW6 ....100 E2
Paddock School
PUT/ROE SW15 ....138 C5
Pain Relief Clinic
HDN NW4 ....63 K3
Paint Pots Montessori School
WBPTN SW10 ....120 B6
Pakeman Primary School
HOLWY N7 ....85 F1
Palace Gardens Shopping
Centre
ENC/FH EN2 ....23 K4
Palace of Westminster
WHALL SW1A 17 F3
Palace Theatre
SOHO/SHAV W1D 10 D5
Palladium Theatre
SOHO/CST W1F 10 A4
Palmers Green High School
WCHMH N21 ....35 G4
Palmerston Business Centre
SUT SM1 ....209 G3
Palm House
RCH/KEW TW9 ....137 G2
Panorama Pier
STHWK SE1 ....12 B6
Paradise Swimming Pools
MLHL NW7 ....45 G1
Paray House School
FUL/PGN SW6 ....139 J3
Parayhouse School
WBPTN SW10 ....140 B1
Parchmore Medical Centre
THHTH CR7 ....180 D6
Pardes House & Beis Yaakov
School
FNCH N3 ....46 D5
Parent Infant Clinic
HAMP NW3 ....83 G3
Parish CE Primary School
BMLY BR1 ....183 K3
Parish Church CE Primary
School
CROY/NA CR0 ....211 H1
Park Business Centre
KIL/WHAMP NW6 ....100 C2
Parkes Townhouse Hotel
CHEL SW3 ....14 D4
Parkfield Industrial Estate
BTSEA SW11 ....141 F3
Parkfield JMI School
HDN NW4 ....63 K4
Parkgate House School
CLAP SW4 ....141 G3
Park Hall Trading Estate
WNWD SE27 ....162 D5

Park High School
STAN HA7 ....43 K5
Park Hill Junior School
CROY/NA CR0 ....211 K1
Parkhill Primary School
CLAY IG5 ....53 K6
Park Hill School
KUTN/CMB KT2 ....175 H3
Park House Medical Centre
KIL/WHAMP NW6 ....100 C1
Park House RFC
HAYES BR2 ....200 B6
The Park Inn Heathrow
WDR/YW UB7 ....132 E1
Parklands Primary School
ROM RM1 ....57 F6
Park Lane Primary School
WBLY HA9 ....80 A2
Park Medical Centre
BERM/RHTH SE16 ....124 A4
Park Mews Small Business
Centre
HNHL SE24 ....162 D1
Park Road Clinic
CEND/HSY/T N8 ....66 D2
Park Road Swimming
Centre
CEND/HSY/T N8 ....66 D2
Park Royal Business Centre
WLSDN NW10 ....99 F3
Park School for Girls
IL IG1 ....72 A6
Parkside Business Estate
DEPT SE8 ....124 C6
Parkside Clinic
NTGHL W11 ....100 C5
Parkside Health
NTGHL W11 ....100 C5
Parkside Hospital
WIM/MER SW19 ....159 C5
Park Walk Primary School
WBPTN SW10 ....120 C6
Parkway Primary School
ERITHM DA18 ....129 F3
Parkway Trading Estate
HEST TW5 ....114 B6
Parkwood Primary School
FSBYPK N4 ....67 H6
Parliament Hill Fields
Athletics Track
HAMP NW3 ....83 K2
Parliament Hill Lido
HAMP NW3 ....84 A2
Parliament Hill School
KTTN NW5 ....84 A2
Parmiter Industrial Centre
BETH E2 ....104 D1
Parnells Sports Ground
KTN/HRWW/WS HA3 ....62 B3
Parsloes Primary School
DAGW RM9 ....92 B4
Parsons Green Health Clinic
FUL/PGN SW6 ....139 K2
Passport Language Schools
BMLY BR1 ....184 A4
Patent Office
FLST/FETLN EC4A 11 J2
The Patrick Doody Clinic &
Health Centre
WIM/MER SW19 ....177 K3
Pattinson Clinic
RCH/KEW TW9 ....136 E6
The Paul Robeson Theatre
HSLW TW3 ....135 G4
Pavilion Barclays Sports
Ground
EA W5 ....98 A4
The Pavilion Leisure Centre
BMLY BR1 ....183 K5
Pavilion Restaurant
RCH/KEW TW9 ....137 F3
Paxton Primary School
NRWD SE19 ....181 G2
PDSA Hospital
REDBR IG4 ....53 H6
Peace Pagoda
CHEL SW3 ....140 E1
Peacock Estate
TOTM N17 ....50 B2
Peacock Industrial Estate
TOTM N17 ....50 B2
The Peacock Theatre
HOL/ALD WC2B 11 G4
Peall Road Industrial Estate
CROY/NA CR0 ....196 A3
Peckham Park Primary
School
PECK SE15 ....143 H1
The Peckham Pulse Health
& Leisure Centre
PECK SE15 ....143 H2
Pelham Primary School
BXLYHN DA7 ....149 H4
WIM/MER SW19 ....177 K3
Pembridge Hall
BAY/PAD W2 ....100 E6
Pendragon Secondary School
BMLY BR1 ....165 K5
Pentavia Retail Park
MLHL NW7 ....45 H5
Penwortham Primary School
STRHM/NOR SW16 ....179 G2
Percival David Foundation of
Chinese Art
STPAN WC1H 4 D6
Perivale Industrial Park
GFD/PVL UB6 ....97 G1
Perivale New Business Centre
GFD/PVL UB6 ....97 J1
Perivale Park Athletics Track
GFD/PVL UB6 ....96 E2
Perivale Park Golf Course
GFD/PVL UB6 ....96 E2
Perivale Primary School
GFD/PVL UB6 ....97 J1
Perrin Road Clinic
ALP/SUD HA0 ....79 H2

Perry Hall Primary School
ORP BR6 ....202 A3
Perrymount Primary School
FSTH SE23 ....164 A4
Petchy Academy
CLPT E5 ....86 C2
Peterborough Primary
School
FUL/PGN SW6 ....139 K3
Peterborough & St Margarets
High School
STAN HA7 ....28 E5
Peter Hills School
BERM/RHTH SE16 ....124 A1
Peter James Business
Centre
HYS/HAR UB3 ....113 K2
Peterley Business Centre
BETH E2 ....104 D1
Peter Pan Statue
BAY/PAD W2 ....8 A7
The Petersham Hotel
RCHPK/HAM TW10 ....157 F2
Petric Museum of Egyptian
Archaeology
GWRST WC1E 4 C7
Petts Hill Primary School
NTHLT UB5 ....78 B3
Pewterers' Hall
CITYW EC2V 12 D2
Phoenix Business Centre
POP/IOD E14 ....105 J4
Phoenix Cinema
EFNCH N2 ....65 J1
Phoenix College
MRDN SM4 ....194 A2
Phoenix High School
SHB W12 ....99 J6
Phoenix Industrial Estate
HRW HA1 ....61 F1
Phoenix Leisure Centre
CAT SE6 ....164 E2
Phoenix School
HAMP NW3 ....83 H4
Phoenix Secondary &
Primary School
BOW E3 ....105 H2
Phoenix Theatre
LSQ/SEVD WC2H 10 D4
Phoenix Trading Estate
GFD/PVL UB6 ....79 J6
Physical Energy Statue
BAY/PAD W2 ....14 A1
Piccadilly Theatre
SOHO/SHAV W1D 10 C5
Pickford Lane Medical Centre
BXLYHN DA7 ....149 F2
Pickhurst Infant School
WWKM BR4 ....199 H3
Pickhurst Junior School
WWKM BR4 ....199 J3
Picture House Cinema
SRTFD E15 ....88 B4
Pilgrims Way J & I School
PECK SE15 ....123 K6
Pilot Industrial Centre
WLSDN NW10 ....99 G3
Pilton Estate
CROY/NA CR0 ....196 C6
Pimlico School
PIM SW1V 121 H5
Pinewood Primary School
CRW RM5 ....56 D1
Pinkwell Primary School
HYS/HAR UB3 ....113 F4
Pinnacles Cricket & Squash
Club
SUT SM1 ....208 E4
Pinner Hill Golf Club
PIN HA5 ....41 F2
Pinner Medical Centre
PIN HA5 ....59 J1
Pinner Park Primary School
PIN HA5 ....42 B6
Pinner View Medical Centre
HRW HA1 ....60 C2
Pinner Wood Primary School
PIN HA5 ....41 G4
Pioneers Industrial Park
CROY/NA CR0 ....195 K5
Pippins School
ASHF TW15 ....152 C6
Pitshanger Manor Museum
EA W5 ....116 D1
Plaisterers Hall
STBT EC1A 12 C2
Plaistow Hospital
PLSTW E13 ....107 F1
Plaistow Primary School
PLSTW E13 ....89 G6
Plantation House Medical
Centre
LOTH EC2R 13 F3
Plashet Jewish Cemetery
MNPK E12 ....89 H4
Plashet Road Medical Centre
FSTGT E7 ....89 G4
Plashet School
EHAM E6 ....89 J5
Players Theatre
CHCR WC2N 11 F7
The Playhouse
CHCR WC2N 11 F7
Plaza Business Centre
PEND EN3 ....25 H3
Pleasance Theatre
HOLWY N7 ....84 E4
Plumcroft Primary School
WOOL/PLUM SE18 ....127 H6
Plumstead Leisure Centre
WOOL/PLUM SE18 ....128 A5
Plumstead Manor School
WOOL/PLUM SE18 ....127 J5
The Pointer School
BKHTH/KID SE3 ....145 K2
Police Cadet School
WAN E11 ....70 E5

The Polish Institute & Sikorski
Museum
SKENS SW7 ....14 B3
Polish War Memorial
RSLP HA4 ....77 F4
Polka Theatre for Children
WIM/MER SW19 ....178 A2
Ponders End Industrial
Estate
PEND EN3 ....25 H5
Pooles Park Primary School
FSBYPK N4 ....67 F6
Pools in the Park
RCH/KEW TW9 ....136 E5
Pope John Primary School
SHB W12 ....99 K6
Pop In Business Centre
WBLY HA9 ....80 D3
Poplar Business Park
POP/IOD E14 ....106 A6
Poplar Primary School
WIM/MER SW19 ....177 K6
Pop Up Theatre
CLKNW EC1R 5 K3
Porchester Leisure Centre
BAY/PAD W2 ....101 F5
Portcullis House
WHALL SW1A 17 F3
Portico City Learning
Centre
CLPT E5 ....86 C2
The Portland Hospital
REGST W1B 3 K7
Portland House Medical
Centre
GFD/PVL UB6 ....96 B3
Portland Medical Centre
SNWD SE25 ....197 J2
Portland Place School
REGST W1B 9 K1
The Portman Clinic
HAMP NW3 ....83 H4
Portobello Market
NKENS W10 ....100 C4
Portobello Medical Centre
NTGHL W11 ....100 C5
Pound Park Nursery School
CHARL SE7 ....126 A5
The Pountney Clinic
HSLW TW5 ....135 F4
Poverest Primary School
STMC/STPC BR5 ....202 B2
Powergate Business Park
WLSDN NW10 ....99 F2
Power Industrial Estate
ERITH DA8 ....150 C2
The Power Station London
(under re-development)
VX/NE SW8 ....141 G1
Premier Cinema
PECK SE15 ....143 H3
Premier Travel Inn
BARK IG11 ....90 B6
BTFD TW8 ....117 F6
CAN/RD E16 ....107 H6
CHDH RM6 ....74 A2
CROY/NA CR0 ....211 G4
CROY/NA CR0 ....212 C3
ECT SW5 ....120 A4
EDGW HA8 ....44 C5
EHAM E6 ....108 A4
FUL/PGN SW6 ....139 H4
GFD/PVL UB6 ....97 G2
HOR/WEW KT19 ....207 G5
HTHAIR TW6 ....133 H2
HYS/HAR UB3 ....112 E4
IS N1 ....5 F3
KTN/HRWW/WS HA3 ....61 H3
PUR RM19 ....131 J5
REDBR IG4 ....71 H2
STHWK SE1 ....12 C7
STHWK SE1 ....17 G2
STHWK SE1 ....19 H5
STPAN WC1H 4 D5
WBLY HA9 ....80 C1
WHTN TW2 ....155 H5
WIM/MER SW19 ....178 B4
YEAD UB4 ....95 F4
Prendergast School
BROCKY SE4 ....144 D5
Preston Manor School
WBLY HA9 ....62 B6
Preston Medical Centre
WBLY HA9 ....80 A1
Preston Park Primary School
WBLY HA9 ....61 K5
Priestmead First & Middle
Schools
KTN/HRWW/WS HA3 ....43 H6
Primary School
CHEL SW3 ....120 D5
Primrose Hill School
CAMTN NW1 ....84 A4
Primrose Montessori School
HBRY N5 ....85 J1
Prince Charles Cinema
LSQ/SEVD WC2H 10 D5
Prince Edward Theatre
SOHO/SHAV W1D 10 C4
Prince of Wales Theatre
STJS SW1Y 10 C6
Princes College
NOXST/BSQ WC1A 10 E3
Princes Court Business
Centre
WAP E1W 104 D6
Princes Park Stadium
DART DA1 ....171 K3
Princes Plain Primary School
HAYES BR2 ....200 D4
Princess Avenue School
CDALE/KGS NW9 ....48 B6
Princess Frederica CE J & I
School
WLSDN NW10 ....99 K1

Princess Grace Hospital
MHST W1U 3 G7
Princess Louise Hospital
NKENS W10 ....100 A4
Princess May Primary School
STNW/STAM N16 ....86 A3
Princess of Wales
Conservatory
RCH/KEW TW9 ....137 G1
The Princess Royal
Distribution Centre
WLSDN NW10 ....80 D6
The Princess Royal
University Hospital
ORP BR6 ....216 A1
Prior Weston Primary School
STLK EC1Y 6 D7
Priory CE Primary School
WIM/MER SW19 ....178 A1
The Priory Leisure Centre
STMC/STPC BR5 ....202 D5
Priory Retail Park
WIM/MER SW19 ....178 C3
Priory School
STMC/STPC BR5 ....202 D5
Priory Shopping Centre
DART DA1 ....171 G1
Priory Special School
SNWD SE25 ....197 G1
The Priory
ORP BR6 ....202 C4
Privy Council
STJS SW1Y 16 C1
Privy Council Office
WHALL SW1A 16 E1
Progress Business Park
CROY/NA CR0 ....196 A6
Pronto Trading Estate
YEAD UB4 ....94 C4
Prospect House School
PUT/ROE SW15 ....159 G2
Proteus School
KIL/WHAMP NW6 ....83 F5
Proud Gallery
CHCR WC2N 10 E6
Providence Road School
WDR/YW UB7 ....112 B1
Provident Industrial Estate
HYS/HAR UB3 ....113 K2
PS Tattershall Castle
WHALL SW1A 17 F1
Pump House
BERM/RHTH SE16 ....124 B1
Pump Lane Industrial Estate
HYS/HAR UB3 ....114 A2
The Purcell School
HRW HA1 ....78 D1
Purdy Hicks Gallery
STHWK SE1 ....12 A7
Purfleet Industrial Park
SOCK/AV RM15 ....131 J1
Purfleet Primary School
PUR RM19 ....131 K4
Purley Oaks Primary School
SAND/SEL CR2 ....211 K5
Pursuit Centre
WAP E1W 104 E6
Putney Animal Hospital
PUT/ROE SW15 ....139 C5
Putney Arts Theatre
PUT/ROE SW15 ....139 G5
Putney Exchange Shopping
Centre
PUT/ROE SW15 ....139 G5
Putney High School
PUT/ROE SW15 ....139 G6
Putney Leisure Centre
PUT/ROE SW15 ....139 F5
Putney Lower Common
Cemetery
BARN SW13 ....138 E3
Putneymead Medical Centre
PUT/ROE SW15 ....139 F5
Putney Park School
PUT/ROE SW15 ....138 E5
Putney School of Art
PUT/ROE SW15 ....139 H5
Putney Vale Cemetery
PUT/ROE SW15 ....158 C4
Putney Vale Crematorium
PUT/ROE SW15 ....158 D4
Pylon Trading Estate
CAN/RD E16 ....106 B3
Quadrant Business Park
KIL/WHAMP NW6 ....82 C6
Quality Hotel
HRW HA1 ....60 D3
PIM SW1V 15 K7
WBLY HA9 ....80 C2
Quebec Industrial Estate
BERM/RHTH SE16 ....124 B2
Queen Charlotte's & Chelsea
Hospital
SHB W12 ....99 K5
Queen Charlotte's Cottage
RCH/KEW TW9 ....136 E3
Queen Elizabeth Centre
BAR EN5 ....20 C5
Queen Elizabeth Conference
Centre
WEST SW1P 16 D3
Queen Elizabeth Hall
STHWK SE1 ....11 G7
Queen Elizabeth Hospital
WOOL/PLUM SE18 ....126 E6
Queen Elizabeth II School
WV/WKIL W9 ....100 D3
Queen Elizabeth Museum
CHING E4 ....38 C2
Queen Elizabeths Boys School
BAR EN5 ....20 B4
Queen Elizabeths Girls School
BAR EN5 ....20 C5
Queen Elizabeth Stadium
EN EN1 ....24 B3
Queenhithe Stairs
BLKFR EC4V 12 C6

Queen Mary College University of London
WCHPL E1 ....105 F3
Queen Mary's Hospital
HAMP NW3 ....83 G1
Queen Mary's Hospital
SCLP DA14 ....186 B1
Queen Mary's Hospital for Children
SUT SM1 ....194 B5
Queen Mary's University Hospital
PUT/ROE SW15 ....158 D1
Queen Mary & Westfield College
SWFD E18 ....52 E4
Queen Mother Sports Centre
PIM SW1V 16 A6
Queensbridge Primary School
HACK E8 ....86 B5
Queensbridge Sports Centre
HACK E8 ....86 B5
Queen's Building
HTHAIR TW6 ....132 E4
The Queens CE Primary School
RCH/KEW TW9 ....137 C1
Queen's Club
WKENS W14 ....119 H5
Queens College London
CAVSQ/HST W1G 9 J2
Queen's Gallery
BCVA SW1W 15 K3
Queens Gate School
SKENS SW7 ....120 B4
Queens Hospital
ROMW/RG RM7 ....75 G4
The Queens House
GNWCH SE10 ....125 G6
Queens Manor Primary School
FUL/PGN SW6 ....139 F1
Queensmead School
RSLP HA4 ....77 H2
Queensmead Sports Centre
RSLP HA4 ....77 H3
Queens Medical Centre
RCHPK/HAM TW10 ....137 G6
Queensmill School
FUL/PGN SW6 ....139 K3
Queens Park Community School
WLSDN NW10 ....82 A6
Queens Park Health Centre
NKENS W10 ....100 C2
Queens Park Primary School
NKENS W10 ....100 C2
Queens Park Rangers FC (Loftus Road Stadium)
SHB W12 ....118 E1
Queen's Road Cemetery
CROY/NA CR0 ....196 D3
Queens Theatre
SOHO/SHAV W1D 10 C5
Queensway Business Centre
PEND EN3 ....24 E5
Queenswell Infant School
TRDG/WHET N20 ....33 H4
Queen Victoria Memorial
WHALL SW1A 16 A3
The Questors Theatre
EA W5 ....97 J6
Quwwat Ul Islam Girl's School
FSTGT E7 ....88 E4
Radcliffe College
SOHO/SHAV W1D 10 A4
Radisson Edwardian Berkshire Hotel
OXSTW W1C 9 J4
Radisson Edwardian Grafton Hotel
CAMTN NW1 ....4 A6
Radisson Edwardian Hampshire Hotel
LSQ/SEVD WC2H 10 D6
Radisson Edwardian Hotel
HYS/HAR UB3 ....133 F1
Radisson Edwardian Kenilworth Hotel
RSQ WC1B 10 D2
Radisson Edwardian Marlborough Hotel
RSQ WC1B 10 D2
Radisson Edwardian Mayfair Hotel
MYFR/PICC W1J 9 K6
Radisson Edwardian Mountbatten Hotel
LSQ/SEVD WC2H 10 E4
Radisson Edwardian Vanderbilt Hotel
SKENS SW7 ....120 B4
Radisson SAS Portman Hotel
MBLAR W1H 9 F3
Raglan Infant School
EN EN1 ....36 A1
Raglan Junior School
EN EN1 ....36 A1
Raglan Primary School
HAYES BR2 ....200 B1
Railton Road Clinic
HNHL SE24 ....142 C6
Rainbow Industrial Estate
RYNPK SW20 ....176 E5
Rainbow Montessori School
KIL/WHAMP NW6 ....83 F5
Rainbow Quay
BERM/RHTH SE16 ....124 B3
Raines Foundation School
BETH E2 ....104 D2
Rainham Hall (NT)
RAIN RM13 ....111 J3
Rainham Trading Estate
RAIN RM13 ....111 G2
Rainham Village Primary School
RAIN RM13 ....111 J3

Ramac Industrial Estate
CHARL SE7 ....125 K5
Ramada Encore Hotel
ACT W3 ....99 F4
Ramada Hotel
BAY/PAD W2 ....101 F6
EA W5 ....98 B6
Randal Cremer Primary School
BETH E2 ....7 J2
Ranelagh Gardens (Site of Chelsea Flower Show)
CHEL SW3 ....121 F5
Ranelagh Primary School
SRTFD E15 ....106 C1
Rangefield Primary School
BMLY BR1 ....183 H1
Ransomes Dock Business Centre
BTSEA SW11 ....140 D1
Raphael Independent School
CAN/RD E16 ....75 J3
The Rathbone Education Centre
CAN/RD E16 ....106 D4
Rathbow Clinic
BAY/PAD W2 ....2 B7
Rathfern Primary School
FSTH SE23 ....164 C3
Ravenor Primary School
GFD/PVL UB6 ....96 A2
Ravensbourne College of Design & Communication
CHST BR7 ....185 F1
The Ravensbourne School
HAYES BR2 ....200 A1
Ravenscourt Park Preparatory School
HMSMTH W6 ....118 D4
Ravenscroft Medical Centre
GLDGN NW11 ....64 D4
Ravenscroft Primary School
CAN/RD E16 ....106 E3
Ravenscroft School
TRDG/WHET N20 ....32 D2
Ravenside Retail Park
UED N18 ....51 F2
Ravensquay Business Centre
STMC/STPC BR5 ....202 C2
Ravenstone Primary School
BAL SW12 ....161 F3
Ravenswood Industrial Estate
WALTH E17 ....70 A1
Ravens Wood School
HAYES BR2 ....215 H1
Ray Cochrane Beauty School
CAMTN NW1 ....9 F1
Ray Lodge Primary School
WFD IG8 ....53 H2
Raynes Park High School
RYNPK SW20 ....176 E6
Raynes Park Sports Ground
RYNPK SW20 ....176 D5
Raynes Park Vale FC
RYNPK SW20 ....193 G2
Raynham Primary School
UED N18 ....50 C1
RCA
SKENS SW7 ....120 B3
RCA Sculpture School
BTSEA SW11 ....140 C1
Reay Primary School
BRXN/ST SW9 ....142 B1
Records Office
CLKNW EC1R 5 K6
Rectory Business Centre
SCUP DA14 ....168 C6
Rectory Paddock School
STMC/STPC BR5 ....186 D5
Redbridge College
CHDH RM6 ....73 H2
Redbridge Drama Centre
SWFD E18 ....52 E4
Redbridge Museum
IL IG1 ....90 B1
Redbridge Primary School
REDBR IG4 ....72 B2
Redbridge Sports Centre
BARK/HLT IG6 ....54 D4
Redbridge Tuition Service
GNTH/NBYPK IG2 ....72 D3
Redburn Industrial Estate
PEND EN3 ....37 F1
Redcliffe School
WBPTN SW10 ....120 B6
Reddiford School
PIN HA5 ....59 J1
Redford Lodge Psychiatric Hospital
ED N9 ....36 C4
Red Gates School
CROY/NA CR0 ....211 G3
Redhill Junior School
CHST BR7 ....185 G1
Red House (NT)
BXLYHS DA6 ....149 F5
Redlands Primary School
WCHPL E1 ....104 E4
Red Lion Business Park
SURB KT6 ....191 G6
Redriff Primary School
BERM/RHTH SE16 ....124 B2
Red Rose Trading Estate
EBAR EN4 ....21 H6
Regal International College
ALP/SUD HA0 ....80 A3
Regent Business Centre
HYS/HAR UB3 ....114 A2
Regent College London
PIN HA5 ....59 K4
Regent's Park Barracks
CAMTN NW1 ....3 J3
Regents Park Clinic
CAMTN NW1 ....2 E6

Regents Park Medical Centre
CAMTN NW1 ....3 K4
Regent's Park Track
STJWD NW8 ....2 E2
Regina Coeli RC Primary School
SAND/SEL CR2 ....211 H5
Renaissance Chancery Court Hotel
HHOL WC1V 11 G2
The Renaissance Hotel
HTHAIR TW6 ....133 F2
Renoir Cinema
BMSBY WC1N 5 F6
Renwick Industrial Estate
BARK IG11 ....109 H1
Rewards Centre
HSLW TW3 ....135 H4
Reynard Mills Trading Estate
BTFD TW8 ....116 D5
Reynolds Performing Arts
BARAT DA2 ....170 B4
Reynolds Sports Centre
ACT W3 ....117 H2
Rhodes Avenue Primary School
WDGN N22 ....48 C4
Rhodes Farm Clinic
MLHL NW7 ....32 A6
Rhyl Primary School
KTTN NW5 ....84 A4
RIBA Library Drawings & Manuscript Collection
MBLAR W1H 9 F3
Ricards Lodge High School
WIM/MER SW19 ....159 J6
Richard Alibon Primary School
DAGE RM10 ....92 C3
Richard Atkins Primary School
BRXS/STRHM SW2 ....161 K2
Richard Cloudesley School
STLK EC1Y 6 C7
Richard Cobden Primary School
CAMTN NW1 ....4 B1
Richdales Istitute
ALP/SUD HA0 ....79 K6
Rich Industrial Estate
PECK SE15 ....123 J6
STHWK SE1 ....19 H5
Richmond Adult & Community College
RCH/KEW TW9 ....136 E5
Richmond American International University
RCHPK/HAM TW10 ....157 F1
The Richmond Clinic
RCH/KEW TW9 ....137 G5
Richmond Community College
TWK TW1 ....156 A3
Richmond FC
RCH/KEW TW9 ....136 E5
Richmond Gate Hotel
RCHPK/HAM TW10 ....157 F2
The Richmond Golf Club
RCHPK/HAM TW10 ....157 F4
The Richmond Green Medical Centre
RCH/KEW TW9 ....136 E6
Richmond Hill Hotel
RCHPK/HAM TW10 ....157 F2
Richmond House School
HPTN TW12 ....172 E1
Richmond Magistrates Court
RCH/KEW TW9 ....136 E5
Richmond Park Golf Club
PUT/ROE SW15 ....158 B2
Richmond Park National Nature Reserve
RCHPK/HAM TW10 ....158 B4
Richmond Road Medical Centre
KUTN/CMB KT2 ....175 F3
Richmond Theatre
RCH/KEW TW9 ....136 E5
Richmond upon Thames College
WHTN TW2 ....155 K2
Ridge House Clinic
WCHMH N21 ....35 K2
Ridgeway Hotel
CHING E4 ....37 K4
Ridgeway Primary School
SAND/SEL CR2 ....212 A6
Rio Cinema
HACK E8 ....86 B3
Ripley Arts Centre
BMLY BR1 ....184 C4
Ripple Infant School
BARK IG11 ....90 E6
Risebridge Golf Club
ROM RM1 ....57 H5
Rise Park Primary School
ROM RM1 ....57 H4
Risley Avenue Primary School
TOTM N17 ....50 A4
The Ritz Hotel
WHALL SW1A 10 A7
Ritzy Cinema
BRXN/ST SW9 ....142 D5
Riverbank Park Plaza Hotel
STHWK SE1 ....17 G1
River Brent Business Park
HNWL W7 ....115 K3
River Gardens Business Centre
EBED/NFELT TW14 ....134 A5
River House Montessori School
POP/IOD E14 ....124 D1
River Mole Business Park
ESH/CLAY KT10 ....189 F5

River Place Health Centre
IS N1 ....85 J5
River Road Business Park
BARK IG11 ....108 E2
Riverdale Primary School
WAND/EARL SW18 ....159 K5
Riverside Business Centre
WAND/EARL SW18 ....160 A3
Riverside Business Park
WIM/MER SW19 ....178 B4
Riverside Community Health Care
WKENS W14 ....119 G3
Riverside Golf Club
THMD SE28 ....110 A5
Riverside Industrial Estate
BARK IG11 ....109 G2
DART DA1 ....151 H6
Riverside Primary School
BERM/RHTH SE16 ....123 H2
Riverside Quarter
WAND/EARL SW18 ....139 K5
Riverside Studios Cinema
BARN SW13 ....118 E5
Riverside Swimming Centre
ERITH DA8 ....130 B5
Riverside Wandle Trading Estate
MTCM CR4 ....194 E4
Riverston School
LEE/GVPK SE12 ....145 K6
Riverview CE Primary School
HOR/WEW KT19 ....206 E2
The RJ Mitchell Primary School
HCH RM12 ....93 K4
RNLI Lifeboat Station
TWRH EC3N 13 H7
Roan Industrial Estate
MTCM CR4 ....178 D4
Robert Blair Primary School
HOLWY N7 ....84 E4
Robert Browning Primary School
WALW SE17 ....122 E5
Robin Hood Infant School
SUT SM1 ....208 E3
Robin Hood Junior School
SUT SM1 ....209 F3
Robin Hood Lane Health Centre
SUT SM1 ....208 E3
Robin Hood Primary School
KUTN/CMB KT2 ....176 A1
Robinsfield Infant School
STJWD NW8 ....2 B2
The Roche School
WAND/EARL SW18 ....139 K6
Rockcliffe Manor Primary School
WOOL/PLUM SE18 ....128 A6
Rockmount Primary School
NRWD SE19 ....180 D2
Rockware Business Centre
GFD/PVL UB6 ....78 D6
Roding Primary School
BCTR RM8 ....91 J2
WFD IG8 ....53 J3
Roebuck Road Trading Estate
BARK/HLT IG6 ....55 H2
Roe Green J & I School
CDALE/KGS NW9 ....62 D1
Roehampton Church School
PUT/ROE SW15 ....158 E2
The Roehampton Priory Hospital
PUT/ROE SW15 ....138 C5
Roehampton Recreation Centre
PUT/ROE SW15 ....158 C2
Roehampton University
PUT/ROE SW15 ....159 H1
Roehampton University (Digby Stuart College)
PUT/ROE SW15 ....158 C6
Roehampton University (Froebel College)
PUT/ROE SW15 ....158 C1
Roehampton University (Southlands College)
PUT/ROE SW15 ....138 C6
Roger Ascham Primary School
WALTH E17 ....51 H4
Roger Bannister Sports Ground
KTN/HRWW/WS HA3 ....42 C2
Rokeby School
KUTN/CMB KT2 ....175 K3
SRTFD E15 ....88 B5
Rokesly Primary School
CEND/HSY/T N8 ....66 E2
Roman Bath
TPL/STR WC2R 11 H5
Roman Industrial Estate
CROY/NA CR0 ....197 F4
Roman Road Primary School
EHAM E6 ....107 H5
Roman Wall Remains
BARB EC2Y 12 C2
Romford Cemetery
ROMW/RG RM7 ....74 E4
Romford Clinic
ROM RM1 ....75 H1
Romford County Court
ROM RM1 ....75 H1
Romford Golf Club
GPK RM2 ....57 J6
Romford Ice Arena
ROMW/RG RM7 ....75 G2
Romford IT Learning Centre
ROM RM1 ....75 G2
Romford Shopping Hall
ROM RM1 ....75 G2
Ronald Rose Primary School
PUT/ROE SW15 ....159 G2

Rood Lane Medical Centre
FENCHST EC3M 13 G5
Rooks Heath High School
RYLN/HDSTN HA2 ....78 A1
Roosevelt Memorial
MYFR/PKLN W1K 9 H5
Ropery Business Park
CHARL SE7 ....126 B4
Rosary Priory High School
BUSH WD23 ....28 E1
Rosary RC Infant School
HEST TW5 ....114 E6
Rosary RC Primary School
HAMP NW3 ....83 J3
Rosebery Industrial Park
TOTM N17 ....50 D5
Rose Bruford College
BFN/LL DA15 ....168 C3
Roselands Clinic
NWMAL KT3 ....191 K1
Rose McAndrew Clinic
BRXN/ST SW9 ....142 A3
Rosemead Preparatory School
DUL SE21 ....162 D4
Rosendale Primary School
DUL SE21 ....162 D2
Rose of Kingston (Kingston Theatre)
KUT/HW KT1 ....174 E5
Rose Theatre Exhibition
STHWK SE1 ....12 E7
Rosetta Primary School
POP/IOD E14 ....107 F4
Rosewood Medical Centre
HCH RM12 ....93 K3
Rosh Pinah Primary School
EDGW HA8 ....30 D4
Rosslyn Park RFC
PUT/ROE SW15 ....138 C5
Rotherfield Primary School
IS N1 ....85 J6
Rotherhithe Primary School
BERM/RHTH SE16 ....123 K4
The Rotunda
KUT/HW KT1 ....175 F5
The Roundhouse Theatre
CAMTN NW1 ....84 A5
Roundshaw J & I School
WLGTN SM6 ....210 E5
Rowan Preparatory School
ESH/CLAY KT10 ....205 F5
Rowans School
RYNPK SW20 ....176 D3
Rowhill School
RDART DA2 ....171 F6
Rowley Industrial Park
ACT W3 ....117 J3
Roxbourne Medical Centre
RYLN/HDSTN HA2 ....60 B6
Roxbourne Middle School
RYLN/HDSTN HA2 ....59 H6
Roxeth First & Middle School
RYLN/HDSTN HA2 ....60 D6
Roxeth Manor First School
RYLN/HDSTN HA2 ....78 A1
Roxeth Mead School
RYLN/HDSTN HA2 ....60 D6
Roxwell Trading Park
LEY E10 ....69 G4
Royal Academy of Arts
MYFR/PICC W1J 10 A6
Royal Academy of Dance
BTSEA SW11 ....140 D2
Royal Academy of Dramatic Art
GWRST WC1E 10 C1
Royal Academy of Music
CAMTN NW1 ....3 H7
Royal Air Force Museum
CDALE/KGS NW9 ....45 J5
Royal Albert Hall
SKENS SW7 ....14 A3
Royal Arsenal
WOOL/PLUM SE18 ....127 G3
Royal Ballet School
COVGDN WC2E 11 F4
The Royal Ballet School
RCHPK/HAM TW10 ....158 A3
Royal Blackheath Golf Club
ELTH/MOT SE9 ....166 E2
Royal Botanic Gardens Kew School
RCH/KEW TW9 ....137 G3
Royal Brompton & National Heart Hospitals
CHEL SW3 ....120 C5
Royal Chace Hotel
ENC/FH EN2 ....23 F1
Royal College of Anaesthetists
RSQ WC1B 10 E1
Royal College of Art
SKENS SW7 ....120 B2
Royal College of Music
SHB W12 ....118 D3
SKENS SW7 ....14 A4
Royal College of Nursing
CAMTN NW1 ....4 B6
IS N1 ....6 A1
Royal College of Obstetricians & Gynaecologists
CAMTN NW1 ....2 E6
Royal College of Ophthalmologists
CAMTN NW1 ....3 G7
Royal College of Paediatrics & Child Health
GTPST W1W 3 J7
The Royal College of Pathology
STJS SW1Y 16 C1
Royal College of Physicians
CAMTN NW1 ....3 J6
Royal College of Surgeons
LINN WC2A 11 H3

Royal College of Veterinary
Surgeons
WEST SW1P 16 E6
Royal Courts of Justice
LINN WC2A 11 H4
Royal Court Theatre
BGVA SW1W 15 G7
Royal Court Young Peoples
Theatre
NKENS W10 ....100 C4
The Royal Dock Community
School
CAN/RD E16 ....107 G5
Royal Docks Medical Centre
EHAM E6 ....108 A5
Royal Epping Forest
Golf Club
CHING E4 ....38 C2
Royal Exchange
BANK EC3V 13 F4
Royal Festival Hall
STHWK SE1 ....17 G1
Royal Free Hospital School
of Medicine
HAMP NW3 ....83 J3
Royal Garden Hotel
KENS W8 ....120 A2
Royal Geographical Society
SKENS SW7 ....14 A3
The Royal Horseguards
Hotel
WHALL SW1A 17 F1
Royal Horticultural Society
New Hall
WEST SW1P 16 C5
Royal Horticultural Society
Old Hall
WEST SW1P 16 C6
Royal Hospital
RCH/KEW TW9 ....137 F4
Royal Hospital Chelsea
CHEL SW3 ....120 E5
Royal Hospital for
Neuro-Disability
PUT/ROE SW15 ....159 H1
Royal Hospital & Home
PUT/ROE SW15 ....158 E2
Royal Hospital Museum
CHEL SW3 ....121 F5
Royal Institute of British
Architects
REGST W1B 9 K1
Royal Institution's Faraday
Museum
MYFR/PICC W1J 9 K6
Royal Lancaster Hotel
BAY/PAD W2 ....8 B6
The Royal London Estate
TOTM N17 ....50 D3
Royal London Homeopathic
Hospital
BMSBY WC1N 11 F1
The Royal London
Hospital
WCHPL E1 ....104 D4
Royal Marsden Hospital
CHEL SW3 ....120 C5
The Royal Mews
BGVA SW1W 15 J4
Royal Mid-Surrey Golf Club
RCH/KEW TW9 ....136 E4
Royal Military School of Music
WHTN TW2 ....155 J1
Royal Mint Court
TWRH EC3N 13 K6
Royal National Orthopaedic
Hospital
GTPST W1W 3 K7
STAN HA7 ....29 H3
Royal National Theatre
CMBW SE5 ....142 B1
STHWK SE1 ....11 J7
Royal National Throat, Nose
& Ear Hospital
FSBYW WC1X 5 G4
Royal Opera House
COVGDN WC2E 11 F4
Royal Park Primary School
SCUP DA14 ....169 F5
Royal Russell School
CROY/NA CR0 ....212 D4
The Royal School
HAMP NW3 ....83 H2
Royal Society of Arts
CHCR WC2N 11 F6
Royal Society of Medicine
CAVSQ/HST W1G 9 J3
Royal Victoria College
CAMTN NW1 ....4 C1
Royal Victoria Docks
Watersports Centre
CAN/RD E16 ....106 E6
Royal Wimbledon Golf Club
WIM/MER SW19 ....176 E1
Royston Primary School
PGE/AN SE20 ....182 A4
RSPCA Animal Hospital
FSBYPK N4 ....67 F6
The Rubens at the Palace
Hotel
BGVA SW1W 15 K4
Rudolph Steiner Hall
CAMTN NW1 ....2 E6
Rufus Business Centre
WIM/MER SW19 ....160 A4
Ruislip Gardens Primary
School
RSLP HA4 ....76 C2
Ruislip Golf Club
HGDN/ICK UB10 ....58 A6
Ruislip Manor FC
RSLP HA4 ....58 D6
Ruislip RFC
RSLP HA4 ....58 C2
Ruislip Woods National
Nature Reserve
NTHWD HA6 ....40 A6

RSLP HA4 ....58 C2
Rush Croft School
CHING E4 ....51 K3
Rushey Green Primary
School
CAT SE6 ....164 E3
Rush Green Primary School
ROMW/RG RM7 ....75 F5
Rushmore Junior School
CLPT E5 ....86 E2
Ruskin House School
HNHL SE24 ....142 D6
The Russell JMI School
RCHPK/HAM TW10 ....156 E4
The Russell School
RCHPK/HAM TW10 ....156 E3
Russet House School
EN EN1 ....24 D2
Rutlish School
RYNPK SW20 ....177 J5
Ruxley Corner Industrial
Estate
SCUP DA14 ....186 E2
Ruxley Park Golf Centre
STMC/STPC BR5 ....186 E4
Ryefield Primary School
HGDN/ICK UB10 ....76 B6
Ryelands Primary School
SNWD SE25 ....197 J2
Rye Oak Primary School
PECK SE15 ....143 J4
Sacred Heart Catholic
Primary School
PUT/ROE SW15 ....138 D6
Sacred Heart High School
HMSMTH W6 ....119 F4
Sacred Heart Junior School
HMSMTH W6 ....119 G4
Sacred Heart Language
College
KTN/HRWW/WS HA3 ....42 E5
Sacred heart RC Infant
School
BTSEA SW11 ....140 D3
Sacred Heart RC Primary
School
NWMAL KT3 ....192 D1
OXHEY WD19 ....27 K1
RSLP HA4 ....58 C6
TEDD TW11 ....174 C3
TRDG/WHET N20 ....33 J4
Sacred heart RC School
CMBW SE5 ....142 D2
Sacred Heart School
HOLWY N7 ....85 F3
Saddlers Hall
CITYW EC2V 12 F4
Sadler's Wells Theatre
CLKNW EC1R 5 K4
SAE Institute
HOLWY N7 ....84 E3
Safari Cinema
CROY/NA CR0 ....196 C5
Safari Cinema & Bingo
HRW HA1 ....61 F2
Sai Medical Centre
POP/IOD E14 ....106 A6
St Agathas RC Primary
School
KUTN/CMB KT2 ....175 G2
St Agnes RC Primary School
BOW E3 ....105 J2
CRICK NW2 ....82 C1
St Aidans Primary School
FSBYPK N4 ....67 G4
St Aidans RC Primary School
IL IG1 ....72 D5
St Albans CE Primary School
HCIRC EC1N 11 J1
St Albans Health Clinic
HGT N6 ....84 A1
St Albans RC Aided Primary
School
E/WMO/HCT KT8 ....189 G2
St Albans RC Church & School
Presbytery
HCH RM12 ....93 J3
St Albans RC JMI School
HCH RM12 ....93 K5
St Albans Road Infant School
DART DA1 ....171 J1
St Alfege with St Peter CE
Primary School
GNWCH SE10 ....125 F6
St Aloysius College
HGT N6 ....66 C5
St Aloysius RC Infant School
CAMTN NW1 ....4 C4
St Aloysius RC Junior School
CAMTN NW1 ....4 B3
St Andrew & St Francis CE
JMI School
CRICK NW2 ....81 J4
St Andrews CE JMI School
TRDG/WHET N20 ....32 D4
St Andrews CE Primary School
EN EN1 ....23 K3
STHGT/OAK N14 ....34 C2
St Andrews CE School
CROY/NA CR0 ....211 H2
St Andrews Greek School
CAMTN NW1 ....84 B4
St Andrews Hospital
BOW E3 ....105 K3
St Andrews Primary School
BRXN/ST SW9 ....142 A3
IS N1 ....85 F6
St Andrews School
RYLN/HDSTN HA2 ....60 B2
WLSDN NW10 ....81 K5
St Angelas Ursuline Convent
School
FSTGT E7 ....89 F4
St Annes Catholic High School
for Girls
ENC/FH EN2 ....23 K5
PLMGR N13 ....35 G6

St Annes CE Primary School
WAND/EARL SW18 ....140 A6
St Annes CP School
STWL/WRAY TW19 ....152 B2
St Annes RC Primary School
LBTH SE11 ....122 A6
St Anne's Special School
MRDN SM4 ....193 K2
St Anne's Trading Estate
POP/IOD E14 ....105 H5
St Annes RC Primary School
SEVS/STOTM N15 ....67 K2
St Ann's General Hospital
FSBYPK N4 ....67 J2
St Anns School
HNWL W7 ....115 K1
St Ann's Shopping Centre
HRW HA1 ....60 E5
St Anselms RC Primary School
DART DA1 ....151 J6
HRW HA1 ....60 E4
NWDGN UB2 ....114 E3
St Anselms RC Primary School
TOOT SW17 ....161 F5
St Anthonys Hospital
WPK KT4 ....193 G5
St Anthonys RC Primary
School
EDUL SE22 ....163 H1
PGE/AN SE20 ....181 J4
St Anthony's School
(Junior House)
HAMP NW3 ....83 H3
St Anthony's School
(Senior House)
HAMP NW3 ....83 G3
St Antonys RC Primary School
FSTGT E7 ....88 E5
St Aubyns School
WFD IG8 ....52 D3
St Augustines CE High School
KIL/WHAMP NW6 ....100 E1
St Augustines Primary
School
BELV DA17 ....129 G3
KIL/WHAMP NW6 ....101 F1
St Augustines Priory School
EA W5 ....98 A4
St Augustines RC Infant
School
GNTH/NBYPK IG2 ....72 B2
St Augustines RC Primary
School
CAT SE6 ....182 E1
GNTH/NBYPK IG2 ....72 B2
HMSMTH W6 ....119 H6
St Barnabas & St Philip's CE
Primary School
KENS W8 ....119 K3
St Bartholomews CE Primary
School
SYD SE26 ....163 K6
St Bartholomews Hospital
STBT EC1A 12 B2
St Bartholomews Medical
School
FARR EC1M 6 B7
St Bartholomews & Royal
London School of Medicine
FARR EC1M 12 C1
St Bartholomew's the Great
STBT EC1A 12 B2
St Barts Hospital Sports
Ground
CHST BR7 ....185 J2
St Bedes RC Infant School
BAL SW12 ....161 J3
St Bedes RC Primary School
CHDH RM6 ....73 J2
St Benedicts Junior School
EA W5 ....97 J4
St Benedicts School
EA W5 ....97 K4
St Bernadette Catholic Junior
School
BAL SW12 ....161 H2
St Bernadettes RC First and
Middle School
KTN/HRWW/WS HA3 ....62 A1
St Bonaventures School
FSTGT E7 ....88 E5
St Boniface RC Primary
School
TOOT SW17 ....178 E1
St Catherines RC Girls School
BXLYHS DA6 ....149 J6
St Catherines RC J & I School
WDR/YW UB7 ....112 A2
St Catherines School
BAR EN5 ....20 D5
St Catherines School
TWK TW1 ....156 A4
St Cecilia's CE Primary School
WAND/EARL SW18 ....159 H2
St Cecilias RC Primary School
WPK KT4 ....193 G6
St Chads RC Primary School
SNWD SE25 ....197 F2
St Charles Hospital
NKENS W10 ....100 B4
St Charles RC Primary School
NKENS W10 ....100 B4
St Christinas Preparatory
School
STJWD NW8 ....2 D2
St Christophers School
BECK BR3 ....183 F5
HAMP NW3 ....83 H5
WBLY HA9 ....80 B1
St Clare Business Park
HPTN TW12 ....173 H2
St Clement Danes CE Primary
School
HOL/ALD WC2B 11 G4
St Clement & St James CE
Primary School
NTGHL W11 ....119 H1

St Clements Hospital
BOW E3 ....105 H2
St Clements Primary School
EW KT17 ....207 H6
St Columbas RC Boys School
BXLYHS DA6 ....149 J6
St Cuthbert With St Matthias
CE Primary School
ECT SW5 ....120 A5
St Cyprians Greek Orthodox
Primary School
THHTH CR7 ....180 D5
St Davids College
WWKM BR4 ....198 E4
St Davids Health Centre
STWL/WRAY TW19 ....152 A2
St Davids School
ASHF TW15 ....152 C5
St Dominics RC Primary
School
HAMP NW3 ....83 K3
St Dominics Sixth Form
College
HRW HA1 ....60 E6
St Dunstans CE Primary
School
CHEAM SM3 ....208 C4
St Dunstans College
CAT SE6 ....164 C3
St Ebba's Hospital
HOR/WEW KT19 ....206 E6
St Edmunds RC Primary
School
ED N9 ....36 D3
POP/IOD E14 ....124 D4
WHTN TW2 ....155 G2
St Edwards CE Comprehensive
School
CHDH RM6 ....74 C3
St Edwards CE Primary School
ROM RM1 ....75 F1
St Edwards RC JMI School
STJWD NW8 ....2 C1
St Elizabeths RC Primary
School
RCHPK/HAM TW10 ....157 G1
St Elpheges RC Primary
School
WLGTN SM6 ....210 E4
St Eugene de Mazenod RC
Primary School
KIL/WHAMP NW6 ....82 E5
St Faiths CE School
WAND/EARL SW18 ....140 A6
St Fidelis Catholic Primary
School
ERITH DA8 ....129 K6
St Francesca Cabrini Primary
School
FSTH SE23 ....163 K1
St Francis de Sales RC Junior
& Infant School
TOTM N17 ....50 A3
St Francis of Assisi Primary
School
NKENS W10 ....100 B6
St Francis RC Primary School
PECK SE15 ....123 H6
SRTFD E15 ....88 C3
St Francis Xavier College
BAL SW12 ....161 G1
St Gabriels CE Primary School
PIM SW1V 121 H5
St George's Cathedral
STHWK SE1 ....17 K4
St Georges CE Primary School
BMLY BR1 ....184 B5
CMBW SE5 ....143 F1
VX/NE SW8 ....141 H2
St Georges College
HOLWY N7 ....85 G1
St Georges Elizabethan
Theatre
HOLWY N7 ....84 D2
St Georges Hanover Square
CE Primary School
MYFR/PKLN W1K 9 H6
St Georges Industrial Estate
KUTN/CMB KT2 ....174 E1
PLMGR N13 ....49 H3
St Georges Medical Centre
HDN NW4 ....45 K6
St Georges RC Primary School
ENC/FH EN2 ....23 K3
HRW HA1 ....79 F1
St Georges RC School
MV/WKIL W9 ....101 F1
St Georges Shopping Centre
& Cinema
HRW HA1 ....60 D3
St George the Martyr CE
Primary School
BMSBY WC1N 5 G7
St Gildas RC Junior School
CEND/HSY/T N8 ....66 E4
St Giles College London
Central
RSQ WC1B 11 F1
St Giles School
SAND/SEL CR2 ....211 H4
St Gregorys High School
KTN/HRWW/WS HA3 ....61 K2
St Gregorys RC Primary
School
EA W5 ....97 J3
St Helens Catholic Infant
School
WALTH E17 ....70 A2
St Helens RC Primary School
BRXN/ST SW9 ....142 B4
CAN/RD E16 ....106 D3
St Helens School
NTHWD HA6 ....40 C1
St Helier Hospital
CAR SM5 ....194 B5

St Hildas School
BUSH WD23 ....28 B2
St Ignatius RC Primary
School
SEVS/STOTM N15 ....68 A3
St James CE J & I School
BERM/RHTH SE16 ....123 H1
St James CE Primary School
MUSWH N10 ....66 A1
NWCR SE14 ....144 B2
PEND EN3 ....24 E3
St James CE Junior School
FSTGT E7 ....88 D3
St James independent
School for Senior Boys
TWK TW1 ....156 B4
St James independent
School for Senior Girls
WKENS W14 ....119 H4
St James independent
Schools for Junior Boys &
Girls *WKENS* W14 ....119 H4
St James Medical Centre
CROY/NA CR0 ....196 E4
St James RC Primary School
HAYES BR2 ....201 G2
WHTN TW2 ....155 K5
St James & St Michaels CE
Primary School
BAY/PAD W2 ....101 G4
St James's Health Centre
WALTH E17 ....69 G2
St James's Palace
WHALL SW1A 16 B1
St James the Great RC
Primary School
PECK SE15 ....143 G2
THHTH CR7 ....180 C5
St Joachims RC Primary School
CAN/RD E16 ....107 G5
St Joan of Arc RC Primary
School
HBRY N5 ....85 H2
St John Fisher RC First &
Middle School
PIN HA5 ....60 A1
St John Fisher RC Primary
School
ERITH DA18 ....129 F3
GFD/PVL UB6 ....97 J2
RYNPK SW20 ....193 F2
St John of Jerusalem CE
Primary School
HOM E9 ....86 E5
St Johns and St James CE
School
UED N18 ....50 B1
St Johns Angell Town CE
Primary School
BRXN/ST SW9 ....142 C3
St Johns CE First School
STAN HA7 ....29 G6
St Johns CE Middle School
STAN HA7 ....29 G6
St Johns CE Primary School
BETH E2 ....104 E1
BKHH IG9 ....39 F3
CROY/NA CR0 ....213 H1
FBAR/BDGN N11 ....33 K6
KUT/HW KT1 ....175 F6
PGE/AN SE20 ....181 K3
TRDG/WHET N20 ....33 G4
St Johns CE School
CDALE/KGS NW9 ....63 G2
St John's CE Walham Green
School
FUL/PGN SW6 ....139 H1
St John's Concert Hall
WEST SW1P 16 E5
St Johns Highbury Vale CE
Primary School
HBRY N5 ....85 H1
St John's Hospital Day Centre
BTSEA SW11 ....140 C5
St John's Lodge
CAMTN NW1 ....3 G4
St Johns Preparatory & Senior
School
ENC/FH EN2 ....23 G2
St Johns Primary School
WEA W13 ....97 G6
St Johns Primary School
BERM/RHTH SE16 ....124 B2
St Johns RC Special School
WFD IG8 ....54 A1
St Johns & St Clements CE
J & I School
PECK SE15 ....143 H4
St Johns School
NTHWD HA6 ....41 F2
St Johns Upper Holloway CE
Primary School
ARCH N19 ....84 D1
St Johns Walworth CE
Primary School
WALW SE17 ....18 C7
St Johns Way Medical Centre
ARCH N19 ....66 D5
St Johns Wood Preparatory
School
STJWD NW8 ....2 C4
St John the Baptist CE Junior
School
KUT/HW KT1 ....174 E3
St John the Baptist CE
Primary School
BMLY BR1 ....165 H6
IS N1 ....7 G3
St John the Divine CE Primary
School
CMBW SE5 ....142 C1
St John the Evangelist RC
Primary School
IS N1 ....6 A2
St John Vianney RC Primary
School
SEVS/STOTM N15 ....67 H1

St Josephs Academic RC
School
BKHTH/KID SE3 ....**145** H4
St Joseph's Annexe
ABYW SE2 ....**128** D6
St Josephs Catholic Infant
School
LEY E10 ....**69** H5
St Josephs Catholic Junior
School
CMBW SE5 ....**142** D1
St Josephs Catholic Primary
School
BMLY BR1 ....**184** B3
St Josephs College
STRHM/NOR SW16 ....**180** C2
St Josephs Convent School
WAN E11 ....**70** E3
St Joseph's Primary School
HDN NW4 ....**63** K1
WAND/EARL SW18 ....**139** K6
St Joseph's RC College
HDN NW4 ....**31** H6
St Josephs RC First & Middle
School
KTN/HRWW/WS HA3 ....**43** C5
St Josephs RC Infant School
NRWD SE19 ....**180** D2
St Josephs RC Junior School
LEY E10 ....**69** J5
NRWD SE19 ....**180** D2
WBLY HA9 ....**80** B3
St Josephs RC Primary School
ARCH N19 ....**66** C6
BARK IG11 ....**90** C6
BERM/RHTH SE16 ....**123** K3
CHEL SW3 ....**14** E7
DAGW RM9 ....**92** B2
DART DA1 ....**150** A5
DEPT SE8 ....**144** D1
GNWCH SE10 ....**145** H5
HNWL W7 ....**115** K1
HOL/ALD WC2B **11** J3
KUT/HW KT1 ....**175** F5
OXHEY WD19 ....**27** F5
STHWK SE1 ....**18** D2
STHWK SE1 ....**123** H2
WLSDN NW10 ....**81** C5
St Judes CE Primary School
HNHL SE24 ....**162** C1
STHWK SE1 ....**18** A5
St Judes & St Pauls CE
Primary School
IS N1 ....**86** A3
St Katharine Pier
WAP E1W **13** K7
St Katherine
TPL/STR WC2R **11** H6
St Lawrence Business Centre
FELT TW13 ....**154** A4
St Lawrence Catholic School
FELT TW13 ....**154** A4
St Lawrence Junior School
E/WMO/HCT KT8 ....**173** J6
St Lawrence University
BMSBY WC1N **5** H1
St Leonards CE Primary School
STRHM/NOR SW16 ....**179** J1
St Leonards Hospital
IS N1 ....**7** H2
St Luke's Catholic Sixth Form
College
SCUP DA14 ....**186** A1
St Lukes CE Primary School
CAN/RD E16 ....**106** D5
FSBYE EC1V **6** D5
KUTN/CMB KT2 ....**175** C4
MV/WKIL W9 ....**100** D1
POP/IOD E14 ....**125** C4
WNWD SE27 ....**180** D1
St Lukes Health Centre
CAN/RD E16 ....**106** D5
St Lukes Hospital for
the Clergy
FITZ W1T **4** A7
St Lukes School
THHTH CR7 ....**196** B1
St Lukes Woodside Hospital
MUSWH N10 ....**66** A1
St Margaret Clitherow RC
Primary
THMD SE28 ....**128** C1
St Margaret Lee CE Primary
School
LEW SE13 ....**145** H5
St Margarets Business Centre
TWK TW1 ....**156** B2
St Margarets CE Primary
School
WOOL/PLUM SE18 ....**127** H6
St Margarets Clitherow RC
Primary School
WBLY HA9 ....**80** C1
St Margarets Primary School
BARK IG11 ....**90** B6
St Margarets School
BUSH WD23 ....**28** A2
HAMP NW3 ....**83** F2
St Marks Catholic School
HSLW TW3 ....**134** K4
St Marks CE Primary School
ARCH N19 ....**66** K6
HAYES BR2 ....**183** K6
LBTH SE11 ....**122** A6
SNWD SE25 ....**197** H1
St Marks Industrial Estate
CAN/RD E16 ....**126** C1
St Marks Primary School
HNWL W7 ....**115** K2
MTCM CR4 ....**178** E5
St Marthas Senior School
EBAR EN4 ....**20** E2
St Martin-in-the-Fields
CHCR WC2N **10** E6
St Martin in the Fields High
School
BRXS/STRHM SW2 ....**162** C4

St Martin of Porres Primary
School
FBAR/BDGN N11 ....**48** C2
St Martins Hospital
MYFR/PKLN W1K **9** G5
St Martins Medical Centre
RSLP HA4 ....**58** C4
St Martins School
MLHL NW7 ....**45** C1
St Martins School of Art
SOHO/SHAV W1D **10** D4
St Martins Theatre
LSQ/SEVD WC2H **10** D5
St Mary Abbots CE Primary
School
KENS W8 ....**120** A2
St Mary and St Pancras CE
Primary School
CAMTN NW1 ....**4** C3
The St Marylebone CE
School
MHST W1U **9** H1
St Marylebone Crematorium
FNCH N3 ....**47** F6
St Mary Magdalene CE
Primary School
MV/WKIL W9 ....**101** F4
WOOL/PLUM SE18 ....**126** E4
St Mary Magdalene Primary
School
HOLWY N7 ....**85** G4
St Mary Magdalen RC Junior
School
CRICK NW2 ....**81** K4
St Mary Magdalens Catholic
Primary School
BROCKY SE4 ....**144** B5
MORT/ESHN SW14 ....**138** A4
St Mary of the Angels RC
Primary School
NTGHL W11 ....**100** E5
St Marys Abbey
MLHL NW7 ....**31** J5
St Mary & St Joseph Catholic
School
SCUP DA14 ....**186** A1
St Mary & St Michael RC
Primary School
WCHPL E1 ....**104** E5
St Mary & St Peters CE
Primary School
TEDD TW11 ....**173** K1
St Marys Bryanston Square
CE Primary School
MBLAR W1H **8** D1
St Marys Catholic Primary
School
CHING E4 ....**38** B3
HCH RM12 ....**75** J5
St Marys CE Junior School
CEND/HSY/T N8 ....**66** E1
STWL/WRAY TW19 ....**152** B1
THDIT KT7 ....**190** C5
St Mary's Cemetery
BTSEA SW11 ....**140** D6
St Marys CE Primary School
EBAR EN4 ....**33** J1
FNCH N3 ....**46** D4
IS N1 ....**85** H5
LEW SE13 ....**144** E6
St Mary's CE Primary School
PUT/ROE SW15 ....**139** C4
St Marys CE Primary School
STNW/STAM N16 ....**67** K6
TWK TW1 ....**156** B2
WALTH E17 ....**69** K1
WLSDN NW10 ....**81** C4
St Marys Greek Cathedral
WDGN N22 ....**49** F4
St Marys High School
CROY/NA CR0 ....**196** D5
St Marys Hospital
BAY/PAD W2 ....**8** B3
St Marys Hospital Medical
School
BAY/PAD W2 ....**8** B3
St Mary's Infant School
CAR SM5 ....**209** J2
St Mary's Junior School
TWK TW1 ....**156** C2
St Marys Kilburn Primary
School
KIL/WHAMP NW6 ....**82** E6
St Marys Primary School
WKENS W14 ....**119** G3
St Marys RC Infant School
CAR SM5 ....**209** K3
St Marys RC J & I School
CROY/NA CR0 ....**196** E5
St Marys RC Junior School
WALTH E17 ....**52** A6
St Marys RC Primary School
BECK BR3 ....**183** F3
St Mary's RC Primary School
CHSWK W4 ....**118** B5
St Marys RC Primary School
CLAP SW4 ....**141** H6
ELTH/MOT SE9 ....**147** H6
St Marys RC Primary School
FSBYPK N4 ....**67** K2
St Marys RC Primary School
ISLW TW7 ....**136** B4
KIL/WHAMP NW6 ....**100** E1
NKENS W10 ....**100** C3
PEND EN3 ....**25** F5
VX/NE SW8 ....**141** G2
WIM/MER SW19 ....**177** K3
St Marys & St Johns CE
Primary School
HDN NW4 ....**63** K2
St Marys School
CEND/HSY/T N8 ....**67** F2
HAMP NW3 ....**83** G3
St Mary's University College
Twickenham
TWK TW1 ....**156** A5

St Matthews CE Primary
School
PEND EN3 ....**24** E6
RYNPK SW20 ....**176** D4
WDR/YW UB7 ....**112** B1
St Matthias CE Primary
School
BETH E2 ....**7** K6
STNW/STAM N16 ....**86** A3
St Meryl JMI School
OXHEY WD19 ....**27** J5
St Michael at Bowes CE Junior
School
PLMGR N13 ....**49** G2
St Michaels and St Martins RC
Primary School
HSLWW TW4 ....**134** E4
St Michaels Catholic
Grammar School
NFNCH/WDSPK N12 ....**47** F1
St Michaels CE Primary
School
ENC/FH EN2 ....**23** J2
HGT N6 ....**66** A4
WAND/EARL SW18 ....**159** J2
WDGN N22 ....**49** F4
St Michaels CE Aided Primary
School
WELL DA16 ....**148** D2
St Michaels RC Primary School
EHAM E6 ....**107** K1
St Michaels RC Secondary
School
BERM/RHTH SE16 ....**123** H2
St Michaels Sydenham CE
Primary School
SYD SE26 ....**164** B6
The St Michael Steiner School
WAND/EARL SW18 ....**139** K6
St Monicas RC Primary School
IS N1 ....**7** G4
St Monica's RC Primary School
IS N1 ....**7** G4
St Monicas RC Primary School
STHGT/OAK N14 ....**34** E5
St Nicholas Centre
SUT SM1 ....**209** F3
St Nicholas Preparatory
School
CDALE/KGS NW9 ....**62** E6
SKENS SW7 ....**14** B3
St Nicholas School
BORE WD6 ....**30** A1
CHST BR7 ....**185** H3
St Olaves Grammar School
ORP BR6 ....**217** H1
St Olaves Preparatory School
ELTH/MOT SE9 ....**167** G4
St Pancras Hospital
CAMTN NW1 ....**4** C1
St Pancras International
Youth Hostel
CAMTN NW1 ....**4** D4
St Pancras & Islington
Cemetery
EFNCH N2 ....**47** J4
St Patricks Church School
STHWK SE1 ....**17** J1
St Patricks Infants School
WAP E1W **123** J1
St Patricks International
School
SOHO/SHAV W1D **10** B3
St Patricks Primary School
KTTN NW5 ....**84** B4
St Patricks RC JMI School
ROMW/RG RM7 ....**56** D4
St Patricks RC Primary School
WALTH E17 ....**69** G1
WOOL/PLUM SE18 ....**127** J4
St Paulinus CE Primary School
DART DA1 ....**150** B5
St Pauls & All Hallows CE
Infant School
TOTM N17 ....**50** C3
St Pauls & All Hallows CE
Junior School
TOTM N17 ....**50** C3
St Paul's Cathedral
STP EC4M **12** C4
St Paul's Cathedral School
STP EC4M **12** C4
St Pauls CE Primary School
BTFD TW8 ....**116** E6
CHSGTN KT9 ....**206** A2
FBAR/BDGN N11 ....**48** A1
HAMP NW3 ....**83** J5
MLHL NW7 ....**31** K6
WALW SE17 ....**122** C5
WCHMH N21 ....**35** H2
WCHPL E1 ....**104** C6
St Pauls CE Junior School
KUTN/CMB KT2 ....**175** H3
St Pauls Cray CE Primary
School
STMC/STPC BR5 ....**186** D6
St Pauls Cray Health Clinic
STMC/STPC BR5 ....**186** B5
St Pauls Girls School
HMSMTH W6 ....**119** G4
St Pauls Primary School
HMSMTH W6 ....**119** G1
St Pauls RC Primary School
THDIT KT7 ....**189** K4
WDGN N22 ....**49** F5
St Pauls RC School
ABYW SE2 ....**128** B6
St Pauls Road Medical Centre
IS N1 ....**85** H4
St Pauls School
BARN SW13 ....**118** C5
St Pauls Steiner School
IS N1 ....**85** K4
St Pauls Way Community
School
BOW E3 ....**105** J4

St Pauls with St Lukes CE
Primary School
BOW E3 ....**105** H4
St Paul's with St Michael's CE
Primary School
HACK E8 ....**86** C6
St Peter Chanel RC Primary
School
SCUP DA14 ....**186** D1
St Peter & Paul RC Primary
School
STMC/STPC BR5 ....**185** K5
St Peter & St Pauls Primary
School
FSBYE EC1V **6** A6
St Peters Catholic Primary
School
ROM RM1 ....**57** F6
St Peters CE Primary School
HMSMTH W6 ....**118** D5
MLHL NW7 ....**100** E3
WALW SE17 ....**122** E5
WAP E1W **123** K1
St Peters Eaton Square CE
Primary School
BCVA SW1W **15** J5
St Peter's Hospital
COVGDN WC2E **11** F5
St Peters Primary School
SAND/SEL CR2 ....**211** K4
St Peters RC Primary School
DAGW RM9 ....**92** B6
WOOL/PLUM SE18 ....**127** C5
St Philips School
CHSGTN KT9 ....**205** K4
SKENS SW7 ....**120** B4
St Phillips Infant School
SYD SE26 ....**163** J6
St Philomenas Catholic High
School
CAR SM5 ....**209** J3
St Philomenas RC Primary
School
STMC/STPC BR5 ....**202** D4
St Quintins Health Centre
NKENS W10 ....**100** A4
St Raphaels Hospice
WPK KT4 ....**193** G6
St Raphaels RC Primary
School
NTHLT UB5 ....**95** F1
St Raphaels Way Medical
Centre
WLSDN NW10 ....**80** E3
St Richards with St Andrews
CE Primary School
RCHPK/HAM TW10 ....**156** C5
St Robert Southwell RC
Primary School
CDALE/KGS NW9 ....**62** E3
St Saviour & St Olaves School
STHWK SE1 ....**19** F5
St Saviours CE Primary
School
HNHL SE24 ....**142** D4
MV/WKIL W9 ....**101** F3
POP/IOD E14 ....**105** K4
WALTH E17 ....**69** H4
St Saviours CE Infant School
EA W5 ....**116** E1
St Saviours RC Primary
School
LEW SE13 ....**145** F5
St Scholasticas RC Primary
School
CLPT E5 ....**86** C1
St Stephens CE Junior School
TWK TW1 ....**156** B1
St Stephens CE Primary
School
BAY/PAD W2 ....**100** E4
DEPT SE8 ....**144** D3
SHB W12 ....**119** F1
St Stephens CE School
VX/NE SW8 ....**141** K1
St Stephens Primary
School
EHAM E6 ....**89** C6
St Stephens RC Primary
School
WELL DA16 ....**148** B4
St Swithun Wells RC Primary
School
RSLP HA4 ....**77** G1
St Teresa RC Primary School
BCTR RM8 ....**73** J1
St Teresas RC Primary School
KTN/HRWW/WS HA3 ....**42** C4
St Theresas RC Primary School
FNCH N3 ....**46** E6
St Thomas a' Becket RC
Primary School
ABYW SE2 ....**128** B3
St Thomas Becket RC Primary
School
SNWD SE25 ....**197** H3
St Thomas CE Primary School
NKENS W10 ....**100** C3
St Thomas' Hospital
STHWK SE1 ....**17** G4
St Thomas More RC Primary
School
BXLYHN DA7 ....**149** G3
ELTH/MOT SE9 ....**146** D4
St Thomas More RC School
CHEL SW3 ....**14** E6
ELTH/MOT SE9 ....**167** F1
WDGN N22 ....**49** F5
St Thomas of Canterbury
Primary School
MTCM CR4 ....**179** F6
St Thomas of Canterbury RC
Primary School
FUL/PGN SW6 ....**139** J1
St Thomas the Apostle
College
PECK SE15 ....**143** K2

St Ursulas Catholic Infant
School
HARH RM3 ....**57** K2
St Ursulas Convent School
GNWCH SE10 ....**145** G1
St Vincent de Paul RC
Primary School
WEST SW1P **16** A5
St Vincents Catholic Primary
School
ELTH/MOT SE9 ....**166** D6
St Vincents Hospital
PIN HA5 ....**40** C6
St Vincents RC Primary
School
ACT W3 ....**98** D6
BCTR RM8 ....**73** J6
St Vincent's RC Primary
School
MHST W1U **9** G2
St Vincents RC Primary
School
MLHL NW7 ....**31** K6
St Walter & St John Sports
Ground
TOOT SW17 ....**160** D3
St William of York Primary
School
FSTH SE23 ....**164** B2
St Winefrides Catholic Primary
School
MNPK E12 ....**89** K3
St Winifreds Catholic Junior
School
LEE/GVPK SE12 ....**165** J1
St Winifreds RC Infant School
LEW SE13 ....**145** H6
SS Angelas & Bonaventures
Sixth Form Centre
FSTGT E7 ....**89** F4
SS Peter & Paul RC Primary
School
MTCM CR4 ....**194** E1
SS Peter & Pauls Catholic
Primary School
IL IG1 ....**90** D1
Salcombe Preparatory School
(Infants)
STHGT/OAK N14 ....**34** B1
Salcombe Preparatory School
(Juniors)
STHGT/OAK N14 ....**34** B2
Salisbury Primary School
MNPK E12 ....**89** H3
Salisbury School
ED N9 ....**36** E2
Salters' Hall
BARB EC2Y **12** D2
Salisbury Primary School
KIL/WHAMP NW6 ....**82** C6
Salvatorian College
KTN/HRWW/WS HA3 ....**42** D5
Samaritan & Western
Ophthalmic Hospital
MBLAR W1H **8** E1
Samuel Jones Industrial
Estate
PECK SE15 ....**143** F1
Samuel Rhodes School
IS N1 ....**85** G6
Sanderstead Junior
School
SAND/SEL CR2 ....**211** K6
Sandgate Trading Estate
BERM/RHTH SE16 ....**123** J5
Sandhurst Primary School
CAT SE6 ....**165** H2
Sandown Golf Centre
ESH/CLAY KT10 ....**204** B1
Sandown Grandstand &
Exhibition Centre
ESH/CLAY KT10 ....**204** B1
Sandown Industrial Park
ESH/CLAY KT10 ....**189** F6
Sandown Park Racecourse
ESH/CLAY KT10 ....**204** B1
Sandown Sports Club &
Dry Ski Slope
ESH/CLAY KT10 ....**204** B1
Sandringham Primary School
FSTGT E7 ....**89** G4
Sandy Lodge Golf Club
NTHWD HA6 ....**26** B4
Sapcote Trading Centre
WLSDN NW10 ....**81** H3
Sarah Bonnell School
SRTFD E15 ....**88** C4
Sarum Hall School
HAMP NW3 ....**83** J5
Satmer Trust School
STNW/STAM N16 ....**68** C6
Savoy Pier
TPL/STR WC2R **11** G6
Savoy Theatre
TPL/STR WC2R **11** G6
Saxon Business Centre
WIM/MER SW19 ....**178** B5
Sayer Clinic
CROY/NA CR0 ....**211** F2
Sayer Clinics
MBLAR W1H **9** F4
Schomberg House
STJS SW1Y **16** B1
School of English
GLDGN NW11 ....**64** C5
School of Oriental & African
Studies
GWRST WC1E **4** D7
The School of Pharmacy
BMSBY WC1N **5** F6
The School of St David &
St Katharine
CEND/HSY/T N8 ....**66** E1
Science Museum
SKENS SW7 ....**14** B5
Science Museum IMAX Cinema
SKENS SW7 ....**14** A4

The Science Museum Library
SKENS SW7 ....14 A4
Scotts Park Primary School
BMLY BR1 ....184 B4
Scott Wilkie Primary School
CAN/RD E16 ....107 G5
Screen on Baker Street
Cinema
MHST W1U 9 F1
Screen on the Green Cinema
IS N1 ....6 A1
Screen on the Hill Cinema
HAMP NW3 ....83 J3
Sebright Primary School
BETH E2 ....104 C1
Secombe Centre
SUT SM1 ....209 F4
Sedgehill School
CAT SE6 ....182 E1
Sedgewick Centre
WCHPL E1 ....13 K3
Selborne Primary School
GFD/PVL UB6 ....97 F1
The Selfridge Hotel
MBLAR W1H 9 H4
Selhurst High School for Boys
CROY/NA CR0 ....196 E3
The Selhurst Medical Centre
SNWD SE25 ....197 F3
Sellincourt School
TOOT SW17 ....178 D2
Selsdon High School
SAND/SEL CR2 ....211 K5
Selsdon Primary School
SAND/SEL CR2 ....212 E6
Selsdon Road Industrial
Estate
SAND/SEL CR2 ....211 K5
Selwyn Primary School
CHING E4 ....52 A2
PLSTW E13 ....88 E6
Sergeant Industrial Estate
WAND/EARL SW18 ....160 A1
Serpentine Gallery
BAY/PAD W2 ....14 B1
Servite RC Primary School
WBPTN SW10 ....120 B6
Seven Islands Leisure Centre
BERM/RHTH SE16 ....123 K3
Seven Kings Health Centre
GDMY/SEVK IG3 ....72 E5
Seven Kings High School
ONTH/NBYPK IG2 ....72 D4
Seven Mills Primary School
POP/IOD E14 ....124 D2
Sevenoaks Way Industrial
Estate
STMC/STPC BR5 ....186 D6
Seven Sisters Primary School
SEVS/STOTM N15 ....67 K2
Seymour Gardens Medical
Centre
IL IG1 ....71 K5
Seymour Leisure Centre
MBLAR W1H 8 E2
Shaare Zedek Medical Centre
GLDGN NW11 ....64 D3
Shacklewell Primary School
HACK E8 ....86 B2
Shadwell Dock Stairs
WAP E1W 105 F6
Shaftesbury High School
KTN/HRWW/WS HA3 ....42 B4
Shaftesbury Hospital
LSQ/SEVD WC2H 10 E4
Shaftesbury Medical Centre
RYLN/HDSTN HA2 ....60 C5
Shaftesbury Park Primary
School
BTSEA SW11 ....141 H4
Shaftesbury Primary School
FSTGT E7 ....89 G5
Shaftesbury Theatre
LSQ/SEVD WC2H 10 E3
Shahjalal Medical Centre
WCHPL E1 ....104 C5
Shakespeare Business Centre
BRXN/ST SW9 ....142 C4
Shakespeare's Globe
Exhibition & Theatre
STHWK SE1 ....12 B6
The Shamrock Sports Club
ACT W3 ....98 E5
Shannon Corner Retail Park
NWMAL KT3 ....192 D1
Shapla J & I School
WCHPL E1 ....104 C6
Sharp Sports Centre
EDGW HA8 ....44 C2
Shawcroft School
STMC/STPC BR5 ....203 F2
Shepherd's Bush CC
ACT W3 ....99 G6
Shepherd's Bush Empire
SHB W12 ....119 F2
Sheraton Belgravia Hotel
KTBR SW1X 15 G5
Sheraton Business Centre
GFD/PVL UB6 ....97 J1

Sheraton Park Tower Hotel
KTBR SW1X 15 F2
Sheraton Skyline Hotel
HYS/HAR UB3 ....133 G1
Sheringdale Primary School
WAND/EARL SW18 ....159 J3
Sheringham Junior School
MNPK E12 ....89 K2
Sherington Primary School
CHARL SE7 ....126 A6
Sherlock Holmes Hotel
MHST W1U 9 F1
Sherlock Holmes Museum
CAMTN NW1 ....3 F7
Sherwood Park Primary
School
BFN/LL DA15 ....168 C1
Sherwood Park School
WLGTN SM6 ....210 D1
Sherwood School
MTCM CR4 ....195 H1
Shirley Clinic
CROY/NA CR0 ....197 K5
Shirley High School
CROY/NA CR0 ....213 F1
Shirley Oaks Hospital
CROY/NA CR0 ....197 K4
Shirley Park Golf Club
CROY/NA CR0 ....197 J6
Shirley Wanderers RFC
WWKM BR4 ....214 A2
Shooters Hill Golf Club
WOOL/PLUM SE18 ....147 H2
Shooters Hill Post 16 Campus
WOOL/PLUM SE18 ....147 F1
Shooting Star House
(Childrens Hospice)
HPTN TW12 ....172 E2
Shopping City
WDGN N22 ....49 F5
The Shopping Hall
EHAM E6 ....89 J6
Shore Business Centre
HOM E9 ....86 E5
Shoreditch Comprehensive
IS N1 ....7 H3
Shoreditch County Court
STLK EC1Y 7 F6
Shortlands Golf Club
HAYES BR2 ....183 H4
Shotfield Health Clinic
WLGTN SM6 ....210 B4
Showcase Cinema
WDGN N22 ....49 G5
Showcase Newham Cinema
BARK IG11 ....108 C2
Shrewsbury House School
SURB KT6 ....190 E6
Shrewsbury Road Health
Centre
FSTGT E7 ....89 H5
Sidcup Cemetery
BXLY DA5 ....168 E4
Sidcup Golf Club
BFN/LL DA15 ....168 B4
Sidcup Health Centre
SCUP DA14 ....168 B5
Sidcup Sports Club
SCUP DA14 ....168 A6
Sidney Russell School
DAGW RM9 ....92 A2
Silicon Business Centre
GFD/PVL UB6 ....97 J1
Silverdale Industrial Estate
HYS/HAR UB3 ....113 K1
Silver Industrial Estate
TOTM N17 ....50 B5
Silver Street Medical Centre
UED N18 ....36 A6
Silver Wing Industrial Estate
CROY/NA CR0 ....211 F4
Simon Marks Jewish Primary
School
STNW/STAM N16 ....68 B5
Singlegate Primary School
WIM/MER SW19 ....178 C3
Sion College
EMB EC4Y 11 K5
Sion Manning RC Girls School
NKENS W10 ....100 B4
Sir Francis Drake Primary
School
DEPT SE8 ....124 B5
Sir George Monoux College
WALTH E17 ....51 K5
Sir James Altham Swimming
Pool
OXHEY WD19 ....41 J1
Sir James Barrie School
VX/NE SW8 ....141 H2
Sir John Cass Foundation &
Redcoat CE Secondary
School *WCHPL* E1 ....105 F4
Sir John Cass Foundation
School
HDTCH EC3A 13 H4
Sir John Lillie Primary School
HMSMTH W6 ....119 H6
Sir John Soane's Museum
LINN WC2A 11 G3
Sir Thomas Abney Primary
School
STNW/STAM N16 ....67 K4
Sir Thomas Lipton Memorial
Hospital
STHGT/OAK N14 ....34 B2
Sir William Burrough Primary
School
POP/IOD E14 ....105 G5
Site of Greenwich Hospital
GNWCH SE10 ....125 J5
Six Bridges Trading Estate
STHWK SE1 ....123 H5
The Sixth Form College
CLPT E5 ....86 D1

Skillion Business Park
BARK IG11 ....109 F2
Skinners Companys Lower
Girls School
CLPT E5 ....68 D5
Skinners Companys School
for Girls
STNW/STAM N16 ....68 A4
Slade Green FC
ERITH DA8 ....150 E2
Slade Green Primary School
ERITH DA8 ....150 D1
Slade School of Fine Art
STPAN WC1H 4 C5
Sleaford Industrial Estate
VX/NE SW8 ....141 H1
Sloane Hospital
BECK BR3 ....183 G4
Smallberry Green Primary
School
ISLW TW7 ....156 B5
Smallwood Primary School
TOOT SW17 ....160 C6
SMA Medical Centre
LEY E10 ....69 K4
Smithy Street School
WCHPL E1 ....104 E4
Snaresbrook College
Preparatory School
SWFD E18 ....52 E5
Snaresbrook Crown Court
WAN E11 ....70 D2
Snaresbrook Primary
School
SWFD E18 ....70 E1
Snooker Club
WEA W13 ....116 C1
Snowsfields Primary School
STHWK SE1 ....19 G2
Sobell Leisure Centre
HOLWY N7 ....85 F1
Sobell Medical Centre
HOLWY N7 ....85 G2
Sofitel St James Hotel
STJS SW1Y 10 C7
Soho Parish CE Primary
School
SOHO/CST W1F 10 C5
Solent Road Health Centre
KIL/WHAMP NW6 ....82 E4
Somerset House
COVGDN WC2E 11 G5
Somers Town Community
Sports Centre
CAMTN NW1 ....4 B3
Sorsby Health Centre
CLPT E5 ....87 F2
Southall & West London
College
STHL UB1 ....114 D2
South Bank Business Centre
VX/NE SW8 ....121 J6
Southbank International
School Hampstead
HAMP NW3 ....83 G4
Southbank International
School Kensington
NTGHL W11 ....100 D6
South Bank University
STHWK SE1 ....18 A3
STHWK SE1 ....18 C4
Southborough Primary
School
HAYES BR2 ....201 F2
Southborough School
SURB KT6 ....206 A1
Southbury Primary School
PEND EN3 ....24 D5
South Camden Community
School
CAMTN NW1 ....4 B2
South Chelsea College
BRXN/ST SW9 ....142 A5
South Croydon Medical Centre
SAND/SEL CR2 ....211 J5
South Croydon Sports Club
CROY/NA CR0 ....212 A3
South Eastern University
HOLWY N7 ....85 F1
Southern Road Primary
School
PLSTW E13 ....107 F1
Southfield First & Middle
School
CHSWK W4 ....118 B2
Southfield Medical Centre
CHSWK W4 ....118 B2
The Southfields Clinic
WAND/EARL SW18 ....159 K1
Southfields Community
College
WAND/EARL SW18 ....159 K3
Southgate Cemetery
STHGT/OAK N14 ....34 C4
Southgate College
STHGT/OAK N14 ....34 C4
Southgate Compton CC
EBAR EN4 ....21 K5
Southgate Leisure Centre
STHGT/OAK N14 ....34 D2
Southgate Road Medical
Centre
IS N1 ....85 K5
Southgate School
EBAR EN4 ....22 B6
South Grove Primary School
WALTH E17 ....69 G3
South Hampstead CC
CRICK NW2 ....82 A5
South Hampstead High School
HAMP NW3 ....83 H4
South Haringay Infant School
SEVS/STOTM N15 ....67 H2
South Herts Golf Club
TRDG/WHET N20 ....32 E3
Southlake Primary School
ABYW SE2 ....128 E2

South Lewisham Health
Centre
CAT SE6 ....165 F6
South London Crematorium
MTCM CR4 ....179 H5
South London Gallery
CMBW SE5 ....143 F2
The South London Natural
Health Centre
CLAP SW4 ....141 H5
South London Tamil School
WIM/MER SW19 ....196 D4
Southmead Primary
School
WIM/MER SW19 ....159 H3
South Norwood Country
Park
SNWD SE25 ....197 K1
South Norwood Hill Medical
Centre
SNWD SE25 ....101 F5
South Norwood Medical
Centre
SNWD SE25 ....197 F1
South Norwood Pools &
Fitness Centre
SNWD SE25 ....197 K2
South Norwood Primary
School
SNWD SE25 ....197 H2
South Park Business Centre
IL IG1 ....72 E6
South Park Clinic
IL IG1 ....90 E7
South Park Hotel
SAND/SEL CR2 ....212 A2
South Park Primary School
GDMY/SEVK IG3 ....90 E1
South Quay Plaza
POP/IOD E14 ....124 E2
South Rise Primary School
WOOL/PLUM SE18 ....127 J5
Southside Industrial Estate
VX/NE SW8 ....141 H1
Southside Shopping Centre
WAND/EARL SW18 ....160 A1
South Thames College
PUT/ROE SW15 ....139 G6
PUT/ROE SW15 ....158 C1
TOOT SW17 ....178 D1
WAND/EARL SW18 ....140 A6
Southville Infant School
EBED/NFELT TW14 ....153 J3
Southwark Bridge Business
Centre
STHWK SE1 ....18 D1
Southwark Bridge Stairs
BLKFR EC4V 12 C6
Southwark Cathedral
STHWK SE1 ....12 E1
Southwark College
BERM/RHTH SE16 ....123 J3
CMBW SE5 ....143 F1
STHWK SE1 ....17 K2
STHWK SE1 ....19 H4
Southwark Crown Court
STHWK SE1 ....13 G7
Southwark Park Primary
School
BERM/RHTH SE16 ....123 K4
Southwark Park Sports
Centre
BERM/RHTH SE16 ....123 K4
Southwark Sports Ground
DUL SE21 ....163 G3
South West Middlesex
Crematorium
FELT TW13 ....154 D3
Southwold Primary School
CLPT E5 ....68 D6
South Woodford Health
Centre
SWFD E18 ....52 E4
Southwood Hospital
HGT N6 ....66 A4
Southwood Primary School
DAGW RM9 ....92 A2
Sovereign Business Centre
PEND EN3 ....25 H4
The Space Arts Centre Cinema
DEPT SE8 ....124 C4
Sparrow Farm Community
Junior School
EW KT17 ....207 K3
Sparrow Farm Infant School
EBED/NFELT TW14 ....154 B2
Sparrow Farm Junior School
EBED/NFELT TW14 ....154 A2
Spa School
STHWK SE1 ....19 K4
Speakers Corner
BAY/PAD W2 ....9 F5
The Speech & Language
Hearing Centre
CAMTN NW1 ....4 D4
Speedway Industrial Estate
HYS/HAR UB3 ....113 G2
Speke's Monument
BAY/PAD W2 ....120 B1
Spelthorne Sixth Form
College
ASHF TW15 ....152 C6
Spencer House
WHALL SW1A 16 A1
The Spires Shopping Centre
BAR EN5 ....20 C4
Spiritualist Temple
CAMTN NW1 ....84 C5
Spitalfields Community Farm
WCHPL E1 ....104 C3
Spitalfields Health Centre
WCHPL E1 ....104 B3
Spitfire Business Park
CROY/NA CR0 ....211 G4
Splashworld Swimming
Centre
BXLYHS DA6 ....148 E5

Springfield Christian School
CAT SE6 ....164 C5
Springfield Community
Primary School
SEVS/STOTM N15 ....68 C3
Springfield Hospital
TOOT SW17 ....160 D5
Springfield Primary School
VX/NE SW8 ....141 J1
Spring Grove Primary School
ISLW TW7 ....135 J3
Springhallow School
HNWL W7 ....97 F5
Spring Park Primary School
CROY/NA CR0 ....213 J1
Springvale Retail Park
STMC/STPC BR5 ....186 D6
Springwell Infant School
HEST TW5 ....134 D1
Springwell Junior School
HEST TW5 ....134 D1
Spurgeon's College
SNWD SE25 ....181 F5
Squirrels Heath Junior School
GPK RM2 ....75 K2
Squirrels Trading Estate
HYS/HAR UB3 ....113 J3
Sri Saddhatissa International
Buddhist Temple
CDALE/KGS NW9 ....62 G2
The Stables Gallery &
Art Centre
CRICK NW2 ....81 J2
Stadium Business Centre
WBLY HA9 ....80 C1
Stadium Industrial Estate
WBLY HA9 ....80 D3
Stadium Retail Park
WBLY HA9 ....80 C1
Stafford Cross Business Park
CROY/NA CR0 ....211 F3
The Stafford Hotel
WHALL SW1A 16 A1
Stag Lane Medical Centre
CDALE/KGS NW9 ....44 E6
Stag Lane Primary School
EDGW HA8 ....44 C5
Stamford Clinic
HMSMTH W6 ....118 D4
Stamford Hill Primary School
SEVS/STOTM N15 ....67 K3
Stanburn Middle School
STAN HA7 ....43 J3
Standard Industrial Estate
CAN/RD E16 ....126 C2
CAN/RD E16 ....126 E2
Stanford Primary School
STRHM/NOR SW16 ....179 J4
Stanhope Primary School
GFD/PVL UB6 ....96 C3
Stanley J & I School
TEDD TW11 ....155 K6
Stanley Park High School
CAR SM5 ....210 A4
Stanley Park Primary School
CAR SM5 ....209 K5
Stanley Technical High
School
SNWD SE25 ....181 G6
Stanmore College
STAN HA7 ....43 H2
Stanmore Golf Club
STAN HA7 ....43 H3
Stanton School of English
BAY/PAD W2 ....101 F5
Stanton Square Industrial
Estate
SYD SE26 ....164 C6
Staple Inn Buildings
HHOL WC1V 11 J2
Staples Corner Business
Park
CRICK NW2 ....63 J5
Star Business Centre
RAIN RM13 ....111 F4
Starksfield Primary School
ED N9 ....36 A3
Star Primary School
CAN/RD E16 ....106 C3
Stationers Hall
STP EC4M 12 B4
Stationery Office
HOL/ALD WC2B 11 G3
Stephen Hawking Primary
School
POP/IOD E14 ....105 H4
Stephen Hawking Primary
Special School
POP/IOD E14 ....105 G5
Stepney Day Hospital
WCHPL E1 ....104 E4
Stepney Greencoat CE
Primary School
POP/IOD E14 ....105 H5
Stepney Green College
WCHPL E1 ....105 F4
Sterling Industrial Estate
DAGE RM10 ....92 D2
Sterling Way Clinic
UED N18 ....50 B1
Stewart Fleming Primary
School
PGE/AN SE20 ....181 K6
Stewart Headlam Primary
School
WCHPL E1 ....104 D3
Stillness Primary School
FSTH SE23 ....164 B1
Stirling Retail Park
BORE WD6 ....31 F1
Stirling Way Industrial
Estates
CROY/NA CR0 ....195 K4
Stock Exchange
STBT EC1A 12 B3
Stockley Park Business
Centre
STKPK UB11 ....113 F1

Stockley Park Golf Club
 STKPK UB11 ....94 A6
Stockwell Park School
 BRXN/ST SW9 ....142 A2
Stockwell Primary School
 BRXN/ST SW9 ....142 A4
Stoke Newington School
 STNW/STAM N16 ....85 K1
The Stonebridge Primary
 School
 WLSDN NW10 ....80 E6
Stonebridge Shopping
 Centre
 WLSDN NW10 ....81 F6
Stonehill Business Centre
 UED N18 ....51 F2
Stonehill Business Park
 UED N18 ....51 F1
Stone Lake Retail Park
 CHARL SE7 ....126 B4
Stoneleigh First School
 EW KT17 ....207 K2
Stoneydown Park Primary
 School
 WALTH E17 ....69 G1
Stowford College
 BELMT SM2 ....209 G5
Strand on the Green J & I
 School
 CHSWK W4 ....117 H6
Strand Palace Hotel
 COVGDN WC2E 11 F5
Stratford College
 SRTFD E15 ....88 C5
Stratford Magistrates Court
 SRTFD E15 ....88 B5
Stratford School
 FSTGT E7 ....88 E5
Stratford Shopping Centre
 SRTFD E15 ....88 B5
Strathmore School
 RCHPK/HAM TW10 ....156 E3
Strawberry Fields School
 NTGHL W11 ....100 C6
Strawberry Hill Golf Club
 WHTN TW2 ....155 K5
Streatham Cemetery
 TOOT SW17 ....160 D5
Streatham & Clapham High
 School Junior Department
 BRXS/STRHM SW2 ....162 A3
Streatham & Clapham High
 School Senior Department
 STRHM/NOR SW16 ....161 H5
Streatham & Croydon RFC
 THHTH CR7 ....196 B2
Streatham Ice Rink
 STRHM/NOR SW16 ....179 K1
Streatham Leisure Centre
 STRHM/NOR SW16 ....161 K4
Streatham Modern School
 STRHM/NOR SW16 ....179 K2
Streatham Park Cemetery
 MTCM CR4 ....179 H5
Streatham Swimming Pool
 STRHM/NOR SW16 ....179 K1
Streatham Vale Sports Club
 STRHM/NOR SW16 ....179 H3
Streatham Wells Primary
 School
 BRXS/STRHM SW2 ....162 A4
Stroud Green Primary
 School
 FSBYPK N4 ....67 G5
Studholme Medical Centre
 ASHF TW15 ....152 C6
The Study Preparatory School
 WIM/MER SW19 ....177 G1
The Study School
 NWMAL KT3 ....192 B2
Sudbourne Primary School
 BRXS/STRHM SW2 ....142 A6
Sudbury Court Sports Club
 ALP/SUD HA0 ....79 J1
Sudbury Golf Club
 GFD/PVL UB6 ....79 J4
Sudbury Primary School
 ALP/SUD HA0 ....79 J4
Suffolks Primary School
 EN EN1 ....24 D3
Sulivan Primary School
 FUL/PGN SW6 ....139 K3
Summerside JMI School
 NFNCH/WDSPK N12 ....47 H2
Sunbury Court
 SUN TW16 ....172 C5
Sundridge Park Golf Club
 BMLY BR1 ....184 B2
Sun Life Trading Estate
 EBED/NFELT TW14 ....133 K4
Sunnyfields Primary School
 HDN NW4 ....45 K6
Sunnyhill Primary School
 STRHM/NOR SW16 ....162 A6
Sunshine House School
 NTHWD HA6 ....40 B2
Super Bowl
 BXLYHS DA6 ....149 G5
Surbiton Business Centre
 SURB KT6 ....190 E3
Surbiton Cemetery
 KUT/HW KT1 ....191 H1
Surbiton Golf Club
 CHSGTN KT9 ....205 H2
Surbiton High School
 KUT/HW KT1 ....191 F1
Surbiton Hospital
 SURB KT6 ....191 F3
Surbiton Natural Health
 Centre
 SURB KT6 ....191 F3
Surrey CCC (The Oval)
 LBTH SE11 ....122 A6
Surrey Docks Farm
 BERM/RHTH SE16 ....124 C2
Surrey Docks Health Centre
 BERM/RHTH SE16 ....124 B2

Surrey Docks Watersports
 Centre
 BERM/RHTH SE16 ....124 B3
Surrey Quays Leisure Park
 BERM/RHTH SE16 ....124 A3
Surrey Quays Shopping
 Centre
 BERM/RHTH SE16 ....124 A3
Surrey Square Primary
 School
 WALW SE17 ....123 F5
Susi Earnshaw Theatre
 School
 BAR EN5 ....20 D5
Sussex House School
 KTBR SW1X 14 E7
Sutcliffe Park Athletics Track
 LEE/GVPK SE12 ....146 A6
Sutton Alternative Health
 Centre
 SUT SM1 ....209 F3
Sutton Arena
 CAR SM5 ....194 C4
Sutton Bowling Club
 BELMT SM2 ....208 E6
Sutton Cemetery
 CHEAM SM3 ....193 J6
Sutton College of Learning
 for Adults
 SUT SM1 ....209 F3
Sutton Grammar School
 for Boys
 SUT SM1 ....209 G3
Sutton High Junior School
 SUT SM1 ....209 F4
Sutton High School
 for Girls GDST
 SUT SM1 ....209 G4
Sutton House
 HACK E8 ....86 E3
Suttons Business Park
 RAIN RM13 ....111 F2
Sutton Superbowl
 SUT SM1 ....209 F3
Sutton United FC
 SUT SM1 ....208 E2
Sutton West Centre
 SUT SM1 ....208 E3
Swaffield Primary School
 WAND/EARL SW18 ....160 B1
Swakeleys School
 HGDN/ICK UB10 ....94 A1
Swaminarayan School
 WLSDN NW10 ....81 F4
Swan Business Centre
 CHSWK W4 ....118 A4
Swan Business Park
 DART DA1 ....151 G5
Swan Lane Pier
 CANST EC4R 12 E6
Swanlea School
 WCHPL E1 ....104 D3
Swansmere School
 WOT/HER KT12 ....188 B5
Swedish School
 BARN SW13 ....118 D6
Swiss Cottage Leisure
 Centre
 HAMP NW3 ....83 H5
Swiss Cottage School
 STJWD NW8 ....83 H6
Swissotel the Howard
 TPL/STR WC2R 11 H5
Swiss Re-insurance Tower
 HDTCH EC3A 13 H4
Sybil Elgar School
 EA W5 ....98 A6
 NWDGN UB2 ....114 E3
Sybourn Infant School
 LEY E10 ....69 G5
The Sybourn Junior School
 WALTH E17 ....69 H4
Sydenham High Junior
 School
 SYD SE26 ....163 J5
Sydenham High Junior
 School
 SYD SE26 ....163 J6
Sydenham High School
 Sports Ground
 CAT SE6 ....182 D1
Sydenham High Senior
 School
 SYD SE26 ....181 J1
The Sydney Russell School
 DAGW RM9 ....91 K3
Syon House
 BTFD TW8 ....136 D2
Syon Park
 BTFD TW8 ....136 D3
Syon Park School
 ISLW TW7 ....136 C2
Syracuse University
 NTGHL W11 ....100 D6
Tabard Theatre
 CHSWK W4 ....118 B4
Taberner House
 CROY/NA CR0 ....211 J1
TA Centre
 EDGW HA8 ....44 D3
 HRW HA1 ....61 J1
 NFNCH/WDSPK N12 ....47 H4
Tait Road Industrial Estate
 CROY/NA CR0 ....197 F3
Talmud Torah School
 STNW/STAM N16 ....67 K4
Tamian Industrial Estate
 HSLWW TW4 ....134 B5
Tamworth Manor High School
 STRHM/NOR SW16 ....179 J6
Tandem Centre
 WIM/MER SW19 ....178 C2
Tate Britain
 WEST SW1P 16 E7
Tate Modern
 STHWK SE1 ....12 B7
Tavistock Clinic
 HAMP NW3 ....83 H4

TAVR Centre
 KUT/HW KT1 ....190 E1
Tavy Clinic
 ABYW SE2 ....128 D2
Tawhid Boys School
 STNW/STAM N16 ....68 B6
Teddington Business Park
 TEDD TW11 ....174 A1
Teddington Cemetery
 TEDD TW11 ....155 K6
Teddington Clinic
 TEDD TW11 ....173 K2
Teddington Memorial
 Hospital
 TEDD TW11 ....173 K2
Teddington Pool & Fitness
 Centre
 TEDD TW11 ....174 B1
Teddington School
 TEDD TW11 ....174 C2
The Teddington Theatre
 Club Ltd
 E/WMO/HCT KT8 ....189 J2
Telferscot Primary School
 BAL SW12 ....161 H3
Temperate House
 RCH/KEW TW9 ....137 G3
Temple Hill Primary School
 DART DA1 ....151 K6
Tenby Road Clinic
 DAGW HA8 ....44 B5
Tennis and Squash Club
 FNCH N3 ....46 C4
Tenterden Sports Ground
 KTN/HRWW/WS HA3 ....62 A4
Terence McMillan Stadium
 PLSTW E13 ....107 G3
Tetherdown Primary School
 MUSWH N10 ....66 A1
Thames Barrier
 CAN/RD E16 ....126 C2
Thames Barrier Information
 & Learning Centre
 CHARL SE7 ....126 C3
Thames Ditton & Esher
 GSH/CLAY KT10 ....189 J6
Thames Ditton Infant School
 THDIT KT7 ....190 A3
Thames Ditton Junior School
 THDIT KT7 ....190 A4
Thames House
 WEST SW1P 16 E6
Thameside Industrial Estate
 CAN/RD E16 ....126 C1
Thames Magistrates Court
 BOW E3 ....105 J2
Thamesmead Leisure Centre
 THMD SE28 ....109 G6
Thamesmead Shopping
 Centre
 THMD SE28 ....109 G6
Thames Valley University
 EA W5 ....97 J6
 EA W5 ....116 E1
Thamesview Business Centre
 RAIN RM13 ....111 G4
Thames View Clinic
 BARK IG11 ....109 F1
Thames View J & I School
 BARK IG11 ....109 G1
Thames Water Tower
 NTGHL W11 ....119 G2
Thatched House Hotel
 SUT SM1 ....208 D4
Theatre Centre
 BECK BR3 ....182 E5
Theatre for Mankind
 FSBYPK N4 ....67 F5
Theatre Museum Library &
 Archive
 COVGDN WC2E 11 F5
Theatre of the Dispossessed
 WIM/MER SW19 ....159 G3
Theatre Royal
 HOL/ALD WC2B 11 F4
 SRTFD E15 ....88 B4
Theatre Royal Haymarket
 STJS SW1Y 10 D6
Theodore McLeary Primary
 School
 EDUL SE22 ....143 G5
Therapia Trading Estate
 CROY/NA CR0 ....195 J4
Thistlebrook Industrial Estate
 ABYW SE2 ....128 D3
Thistle Hotel
 CAMTN NW1 ....4 B5
 CHCR WC2N 10 E6
 FSBYE EC1V 6 C5
 KENS W8 ....120 B2
Thistle Hyde Park Hotel
 BAY/PAD W2 ....101 G6
Thistle Kensington Gardens
 Hotel
 BAY/PAD W2 ....101 G6
Thistle Marble Arch Hotel
 MBLAR W1H 9 F4
Thistle Piccadilly Hotel
 SOHO/SHAV W1D 10 C6
Thistle Tower Hotel
 WAP E1W 13 J7
Thistle Westminster Hotel
 WESTW SW1E 15 K5
Thomas Arnold Primary School
 DAGW RM9 ....92 B5
Thomas Buxton Primary
 School
 WCHPL E1 ....104 C3
Thomas Fairchild Primary
 School
 IS N1 ....6 E2
Thomas Francis Academy
 BRXN/ST SW9 ....142 C5
Thomas Gamuel Primary
 School
 WALTH E17 ....69 J2

Thomas Jones Primary School
 NTGHL W11 ....100 C5
Thomas London Independent
 Day School
 KENS W8 ....120 A3
Thomas Road Industrial
 Estate
 POP/IOD E14 ....105 J4
Thomas's Preparatory School
 BTSEA SW11 ....140 C2
Thomas Tallis School
 BKHTH/KID SE3 ....146 A4
Thornhill Primary School
 IS N1 ....85 G5
Thornton Heath Health
 Centre
 THHTH CR7 ....196 D1
Thornton Heath Pools &
 Fitness Centre
 THHTH CR7 ....196 D1
Thornton Road Industrial
 Estate
 CROY/NA CR0 ....195 K3
Thorntree Primary School
 CHARL SE7 ....126 C5
Thorpe Hall Primary School
 WALTH E17 ....52 A4
Three Bridges Business
 Centre
 NWDGN UB2 ....115 H2
Three Bridges Primary School
 NWDGN UB2 ....115 G3
Three Mills Heritage Centre
 BOW E3 ....106 A2
Thurston Industrial Estate
 LEW SE13 ....144 E4
Tidemill Primary School
 DEPT SE8 ....144 D1
Tideway Industrial Estate
 VX/NE SW8 ....121 H6
Tiffin Girls School
 KUTN/CMB KT2 ....175 F2
Tiffin School & Sports Centre
 KUTN/CMB KT2 ....175 G5
Tiller Centre
 (Swimming Baths)
 POP/IOD E14 ....124 D3
Tiller Leisure Centre
 POP/IOD E14 ....124 D3
Timbercroft Primary School
 WOOL/PLUM SE18 ....147 K1
Timbers Clinic
 KTN/HRWW/WS HA3 ....42 D2
Times Square Shopping
 Centre
 SUT SM1 ....209 F3
Tiverton Primary School
 SEVS/STOTM N15 ....67 K3
Tobacco Dock
 WAP E1W 104 D6
Tokyngton Community
 Centre
 WBLY HA9 ....80 D3
Toldos School
 STNW/STAM N16 ....67 K5
Tollgate Primary School
 CROY/NA CR0 ....197 K3
 PLSTW E13 ....107 G3
Tolworth CP School
 SURB KT6 ....191 G5
Tolworth Girls School
 SURB KT6 ....206 B1
Tolworth Recreation Centre
 SURB KT6 ....206 B1
Tom Hood School
 WAN E11 ....88 D1
Tooting Bec Athletics Track
 TOOT SW17 ....161 G6
Tooting Bec Lido
 STRHM/NOR SW16 ....161 H5
Tooting Leisure Centre
 TOOT SW17 ....160 C6
Tooting & Mitcham United
 Football Club
 MTCM CR4 ....179 F4
Torah Temimah Primary
 School
 CRICK NW2 ....81 K2
Torah Vodaas
 GLDGN NW11 ....64 D6
Torriano Primary School
 KTTN NW5 ....84 C3
Torridon Primary School
 CAT SE6 ....165 G4
Torrington Clinic
 NFNCH/WDSPK N12 ....47 G1
Torrington Park Health
 Centre
 NFNCH/WDSPK N12 ....33 G6
Total Health Clinic
 SHB W12 ....118 E2
Tottenham Green Leisure
 Centre
 SEVS/STOTM N15 ....68 A1
Tottenham Hale Retail Park
 SEVS/STOTM N15 ....68 C1
Tottenham Hotspur FC
 (White Hart Lane)
 TOTM N17 ....50 B3
Tottenham Park Cemetery
 ED N9 ....36 D5
Tottenham Sports Centre
 TOTM N17 ....50 B4
Totteridge CC
 TRDG/WHET N20 ....32 E4
Tower 42
 OBST EC2N 13 G3
The Tower Bridge Exhibition
 STHWK SE1 ....19 J1
Tower Bridge Primary School
 STHWK SE1 ....19 J2
Tower Bridge Wharf
 WAP E1W 123 H1
Tower Hamlets College
 POP/IOD E14 ....105 K6
 WCHPL E1 ....104 E4

Tower House School
 MORT/ESHN SW14 ....137 K5
Tower Industrial Estate
 SNWD SE25 ....197 H1
Tower Medical Centre
 WCHPL E1 ....104 C5
Tower Millennium Pier
 TWRH EC3N 13 H7
Tower of London
 TWRH EC3N 13 J6
Tower Retail Park
 DART DA1 ....150 C6
Towers Business Park
 WBLY HA9 ....80 E2
Tower Stairs
 MON EC3R 13 G6
Town Farm Primary School
 STWL/WRAY TW19 ....152 A2
Townley Grammar School
 for Girls
 BXLYHS DA6 ....169 G1
Townmead Business
 Centre
 FUL/PGN SW6 ....140 B3
Townsend Industrial Estate
 WLSDN NW10 ....80 E6
Townsend Primary School
 WALTH E17 ....19 F6
Toynbee Hall & Curtain Theatre
 WCHPL E1 ....13 J2
Trade Union Congress
 NOXST/BSQ WC1A 10 D3
Trafalgar Business Centre
 BARK IG11 ....109 F3
Trafalgar Primary & Infant
 School
 WHTN TW2 ....155 J4
Trafalgar Square
 STJS SW1Y 10 D7
Trafalgar Trading Estate
 PEND EN3 ....25 H5
Tramshed Theatre
 WOOL/PLUM SE18 ....127 G4
Trans Atlantic College
 BETH E2 ....7 J2
Transport House
 WEST SW1P 16 E5
Travelodge
 ACT W3 ....98 C3
 BTFD TW8 ....117 F6
 BTSEA SW11 ....140 B4
 CAMTN NW1 ....8 D1
 CAN/RD E16 ....126 C1
 FSBYW WC1X 5 H4
 HEST TW5 ....114 B6
 IL IC1 ....90 B1
 KUTN/CMB KT2 ....175 F5
 LSQ/SEVD WC2H 10 E3
 POP/IOD E14 ....106 B5
 REDBR IG4 ....71 K3
 STPAN WC1H 5 F4
 SURB KT6 ....191 J5
 WCHPL E1 ....13 J3
 WLSDN NW10 ....98 C1
Treasury
 WHALL SW1A 16 E3
The Treaty Centre
 HSLW TW3 ....135 G4
Treehouse School
 MUSWH N10 ....66 A1
The Treehouse School
 BMSBY WC1N 5 G6
Trent CE Primary School
 EBAR EN4 ....21 K5
Trent Country Park
 EBAR EN4 ....22 A3
Trent Park Cemetery
 EBAR EN4 ....22 A4
Trent Park Golf Club
 STHGT/OAK N14 ....22 C5
Trevor Roberts School
 HAMP NW3 ....83 H5
Tricycle Theatre
 KIL/WHAMP NW6 ....82 D5
Trident Business Centre
 TOOT SW17 ....178 E1
Trinity Business Centre
 BERM/RHTH SE16 ....124 C2
Trinity Catholic Lower High
 School
 WFD IG8 ....38 E6
Trinity College Centre
 PECK SE15 ....143 F1
Trinity College London
 STHWK SE1 ....121 K5
Trinity College of Music
 GNWCH SE10 ....125 F6
 MHST W1U 9 H2
Trinity Hospital
 GNWCH SE10 ....125 G5
Trinity House
 TWRH EC3N 13 H5
Trinity RC High School (Upper)
 WFD IG8 ....38 E5
Trinity St Marys Primary
 School
 BAL SW12 ....161 F3
Trinity School
 CROY/NA CR0 ....197 K6
 DAGE RM10 ....92 C1
Trinity School Belvedere
 BELV DA17 ....129 K4
Trinity Trading Estate
 HYS/HAR UB3 ....113 K3
Tripcock Point Development
 Site
 THMD SE28 ....109 F6
Triumph Trading Estate
 TOTM N17 ....50 C2
Trocadero
 SOHO/SHAV W1D 10 C6
Trojan Business Centre
 WLSDN NW10 ....81 H4
Troy Industrial Estate
 HRW HA1 ....61 F2
True Buddha School
 IS N1 ....5 G1

TS Queen Mary
TPL/STR WC2R 11 G6
Tubbenden J & I Schools
ORP BR6 ....216 D2
Tudor Lodge Health Centre
WIM/MER SW19 ....159 G3
Tudor Lodge Hotel
PIN HA5 ....59 F3
Tudor Primary School
NFNCH/WDSPK N12 ....47 G3
STHL UB1 ....95 J6
Tufnell Park Primary School
HOLWY N7 ....84 D2
Tuke School
PECK SE15 ....143 J2
Tulloch Clinic
SHB W12 ....119 G1
Tunnel Avenue Trading Estate
GNWCH SE10 ....125 G2
Turney School
DUL SE21 ....162 D2
Turnham Primary School
BROCKY SE4 ....144 B5
Turtle Key Arts Centre
FUL/PGN SW6 ....119 K6
Tutorial College of West London
STHL UB1 ....115 F1
TV Studios
WBLY HA9 ....80 C1
Tweeddale Primary School
CAR SM5 ....194 C4
Twickenham Cemetery
WHTN TW2 ....155 G3
Twickenham Park Health Centre
TWK TW1 ....156 D1
Twickenham Preparatory School
HPTN TW12 ....173 G4
Twickenham Stadium
ISLW TW7 ....155 K1
Twickenham Trading Estate
TWK TW1 ....156 A1
Two Bridges Business Park
SAND/SEL CR2 ....211 K4
Twyford CE High School
ACT W3 ....117 H1
Twyford Sports Centre
ACT W3 ....117 J1
Tyburn Infant School
STJWD NW8 ....2 B6
Tynemouth Road Health Centre
SEVS/STOTM N15 ....68 B1
The Type Museum
BRXN/ST SW9 ....142 A2
Tyssen Primary School
STNW/STAM N16 ....68 C5
UCC Cinema
CRICK NW2 ....63 K5
UCI Cinema
ED N9 ....37 F2
SUT SM1 ....209 F3
UCI Empire Cinema
LSQ/SEVD WC2H 10 D6
UCI Filmworks Cinema
GNWCH SE10 ....125 J4
UGC Cinema
EA W5 ....97 K6
EN EN1 ....24 C5
HMSMTH W6 ....118 E4
SOHO/SHAV W1D 10 C5
WBPTN SW10 ....120 C5
UK Passport Office
PIM SW1V 15 K6
Underhill J & I School
BAR EN5 ....20 C6
Unicorn Primary School
BECK BR3 ....198 E2
Unicorn School
RCH/KEW TW9 ....137 G2
Unicorn Theatre
STHWK SE1 ....19 H2
United Medical & Dental Schools
STHWK SE1 ....17 G4
United Services Sports Ground
CHSWK W4 ....138 B2
Unity College
KTTN NW5 ....84 B2
Unity Trading Estate
WFD IG8 ....53 H6
University Church of Christ the King
STPAN NW1 ....4 C7
University College Hospital
CAMTN NW1 ....4 A6
HAMP NW3 ....83 H4
University College Junior School
HAMP NW3 ....83 G2
University College London
FITZ W1T 10 B1
STPAN WC1H 4 C6
University College London, Astor College
FITZ W1T 10 B1
University College London Medical School
FITZ W1T 10 A1
University College School
HAMP NW3 ....83 G3
University Hospital Lewisham
LEW SE13 ....144 E6
University of California
WHALL SW1A 16 A1
University of East London
BARK IG11 ....91 G2
CAN/RD E16 ....108 A6
PLSTW E13 ....107 F2
SRTFD E15 ....88 A6
SRTFD E15 ....88 C4
SRTFD E15 ....106 D1

University of Greenwich
DART DA1 ....171 J4
ELTH/MOT SE9 ....167 J1
GNWCH SE10 ....125 G5
WOOL/PLUM SE18 ....127 F3
University of Greenwich (Mansion Site)
ELTH/MOT SE9 ....167 H1
University of Greenwich Sports Ground
ELTH/MOT SE9 ....146 D5
ELTH/MOT SE9 ....167 H2
University of London
BAY/PAD W2 ....8 A4
BMSBY WC1N 5 F7
CLKNW EC1R 5 K6
FITZ W1T 10 C5
GWRST WC1E 10 D1
MBLAR W1H 8 D6
STPAN WC1H 4 D6
University of London Athletics Ground
NWMAL KT3 ....192 D2
University of the Arts London
MYFR/PKLN W1K 9 J4
University of Westminster
CAMTN NW1 ....4 A6
CAVSQ/HST W1G 9 K3
CHSWK W4 ....137 K2
FITZ W1T 10 A3
GTPST W1W 9 K1
HGT N6 ....66 B5
HRW HA1 ....61 G4
MHST W1U 9 G1
Uphall Primary School
IL IG1 ....90 B3
Upland Primary School
BXLYHN DA7 ....149 G4
Uplands Business Park
WALTH E17 ....51 F5
Upper Montagu Street Clinic
CAMTN NW1 ....8 E1
Upper Tooting Independent High School
TOOT SW17 ....160 D4
Upton Cross Primary School
PLSTW E13 ....89 F6
Upton Day Hospital
BXLYHS DA6 ....149 F5
Upton Lane Medical Centre
FSTGT E7 ....89 F4
Upton Primary School
BXLY DA5 ....149 F6
Upton Road School
BXLYHS DA6 ....149 F6
The Urdang Academy
LSQ/SEVD WC2H 10 E4
Ursuline High School
RYNPK SW20 ....177 G3
Ursuline Preparatory School
RYNPK SW20 ....177 G3
Uxbridge College
HYS/HAR UB3 ....94 E6
Uxbridge County Court
HYS/HAR UB3 ....94 C4
Uxendon Manor JMI School
ALP/SUD HA0 ....62 A2
Vale Farm Sports Centre
ALP/SUD HA0 ....79 H2
Vale Industrial Estate
WATW WD18 ....26 A3
The Vale Medical Centre
FSTH SE23 ....164 B4
Valence House Museum & Library
BCTR RM8 ....73 K6
Valence Junior School
BCTR RM8 ....73 K6
Valentine High School
GNTH/NBYPK IG2 ....72 A3
Valentines High Lower School
GNTH/NBYPK IG2 ....72 B2
Vale Park Industrial
ACT W3 ....118 B2
The Vale School
SKENS SW7 ....120 B3
Valley Link Business Centre
PEND EN3 ....37 G1
Valley Link Business Estate
PEND EN3 ....37 G1
Valley Primary School
HAYES BR2 ....183 J5
Valmar Trading Estate
CMBW SE5 ....142 D2
V & A Museum of Childhood
BETH E2 ....104 E2
Vanbrugh Theatre
GWRST WC1E 4 C7
Vanguard Trading Estate
SRTFD E15 ....88 A6
Vaudeville Theatre
COVGDN WC2E 11 F5
Vaughan First & Middle School
RYLN/HDSTN HA2 ....60 C3
Vauxhall Primary School
LBTH SE11 ....122 A5
Vernon House Special School
WLSDN NW10 ....80 E3
Vestry Hall
MTCM CR4 ....178 E6
Vestry House Museum
WALTH E17 ....69 K1
Vicarage Fields Health Clinic
BARK IG11 ....90 C5
The Vicarage Field Shopping Centre
BARK IG11 ....90 C5
Vicarage Primary School
EHAM E6 ....107 K2
Vicars Green Primary School
GFD/PVL UB6 ....97 J1
VI Components Industrial Park
ERITH DA8 ....130 B5
Victoria & Albert Museum
SKENS SW7 ....14 B5

Victoria Business Centre
WELL DA16 ....148 B3
Victoria Bus Station
PIM SW1V 15 K5
Victoria Chiropractic Clinic
SKENS SW7 ....14 E3
Victoria Coach Station
BCVA SW1W 15 J7
Victoria Hall
FNCH N3 ....46 D4
Victoria Industrial Estate
ACT W3 ....99 F4
Victoria Industrial Park
DART DA1 ....151 G6
Victoria Junior School
FELT TW13 ....154 A3
Victoria Medical Centre
PIM SW1V 16 B7
Victoria Palace Theatre
BGVA SW1W 15 K5
Victoria Park Industrial Centre
HOM E9 ....87 H5
Victoria Park Plaza Hotel
PIM SW1V 16 A6
Victoria Place Shopping Centre
PIM SW1V 15 K6
Victoria Rail/air Terminal
PIM SW1V 15 K6
Victoria Retail Park
RSLP HA4 ....77 H3
Victoria Wharf
POP/IOD E14 ....105 G6
Victoria Wharf Industrial Estate
DEPT SE8 ....124 B5
Victor Seymour Infant School
CAR SM5 ....209 K1
Victory Business Centre
ISLW TW7 ....136 A5
Victory Day School
BTSEA SW11 ....140 E2
Victory Primary School
WALW SE17 ....18 D6
Viking Business Centre
ROMW/RG RM7 ....74 E4
Viking Primary School
NTHLT UB5 ....95 H2
Village Infant School
DAGE RM10 ....92 C5
The Village School
HAMP NW3 ....83 K4
Villiers High School
STHL UB1 ....115 F1
The Vine Clinic
KUTN/CMB KT2 ....175 F2
Vine Medical Centre
E/WMO/HCT KT8 ....173 H6
The Vines School
BTSEA SW11 ....141 F5
The Vineyard Primary School
RCHPK/HAM TW10 ....157 F1
Vinopolis, City of Wine
STHWK SE1 ....12 D6
Vinters' Hall
BLKFR EC4V 12 D5
VIP Trading Estate
CHARL SE7 ....126 B4
Virginia Primary School
BETH E2 ....7 J5
Virgo Fidelis Convent Schools
NRWD SE19 ....180 D2
Vision College of Technology
HOM E9 ....87 J4
Vita et Pax School
STHGT/OAK N14 ....22 B6
Vittoria Primary School
IS N1 ....5 H1
Voyager Business Estate
BERM/RHTH SE16 ....123 H3
VUE Cinema
ACT W3 ....98 C3
CROY/NA CR0 ....196 A6
DAGW RM9 ....92 A6
FUL/PGN SW6 ....139 K1
HAMP NW3 ....83 G4
HRW HA1 ....61 G3
LSQ/SEVD WC2H 10 D5
NFNCH/WDSPK N12 ....47 H3
ROMW/RG RM7 ....75 G2
SHB W12 ....119 G2
Vulcan Business Centre
CROY/NA CR0 ....214 C6
Waddon Clinic
CROY/NA CR0 ....211 G3
Waddon Infant School
CROY/NA CR0 ....211 G3
Wadham Lodge Sports Centre
WALTH E17 ....51 K4
Wadsworth Business Centre
GFD/PVL UB6 ....97 J1
The Waldegrave Clinic
TEDD TW11 ....174 A1
Waldegrave Girls School
WHTN TW2 ....155 J5
Waldo Industrial Estate
BMLY BR1 ....184 B6
Waldorf School of SW London
BAL SW12 ....161 H4
Waldron Health Centre & Surgery
NWCR SE14 ....144 C1
Walgrove Primary School
STHGT/OAK N14 ....34 D4
The Wallace Centre
DEPT SE8 ....124 E6
The Wallace Collection
MHST W1U 9 G3
Wallbrook Business Centre
HSLWW TW4 ....134 A4
Wallington County Grammar School
WLGTN SM6 ....210 B1

Wallington High School for Girls
WLGTN SM6 ....210 B6
Walmer Road Clinic
NTCHL W11 ....100 C6
Walm Lane Clinic
CRICK NW2 ....82 B3
Walnuts Leisure Centre
ORP BR6 ....202 B5
Walnuts Shopping Centre
ORP BR6 ....202 B5
Walnut Tree Walk Primary School
LBTH SE11 ....17 J6
Waltham Forest College
WALTH E17 ....50 E6
WALTH E17 ....51 K6
Waltham Forest Magistrates Court
WALTH E17 ....51 K6
Waltham Forest Pool & Track
WALTH E17 ....51 K5
Waltham Forest Theatre
WALTH E17 ....51 H6
Walthamstow Business Centre
WALTH E17 ....52 A5
Walthamstow Greyhound Stadium
WALTH E17 ....51 K3
Walthamstow School for Girls
WALTH E17 ....69 K1
Walton Business Centre
WOT/HER KT12 ....188 A4
Walton Casuals FC
WOT/HER KT12 ....188 A2
Walton Community Hospital
WOT/HER KT12 ....188 A6
Walton Swimming Pool
WOT/HER KT12 ....188 A5
Walworth Lower School
WALW SE17 ....122 E5
Walworth Town Hall
WALW SE17 ....18 C7
Walworth Upper School
STHWK SE1 ....123 F5
Wandle Recreation Centre
WAND/EARL SW18 ....160 A1
Wandle Trading Estate
MTCM CR4 ....194 E4
Wandle Valley School
CAR SM5 ....194 D4
Wandsworth Adult College
BTSEA SW11 ....141 F2
TOOT SW17 ....160 D4
Wandsworth Cemetery
WAND/EARL SW18 ....160 B3
Wandsworth County Court
PUT/ROE SW15 ....139 H6
Wandsworth Trading Estate
WAND/EARL SW18 ....160 A2
Wanstead CC
WAN E11 ....71 F4
Wanstead CE Primary School
WAN E11 ....70 E2
Wanstead Golf Club
WAN E11 ....71 F4
Wanstead High School
WAN E11 ....71 G3
Wanstead Hospital
WAN E11 ....71 F1
Wanstead Leisure Centre
WAN E11 ....71 G3
Wapping Wharf
WAP E1W 123 K1
Warehouse Theatre
CROY/NA CR0 ....196 E6
War Memorial Sports Ground
SUT SM1 ....209 J2
Warnford Industrial Estate
HYS/HAR UB3 ....113 H2
Warren Comprehensive School
CHDH RM6 ....74 B2
Warren Dell Primary School
OXHEY WD19 ....27 G5
Warrender School
RSLP HA4 ....58 D4
Warren Junior School
CHDH RM6 ....74 B2
The Warren Medical Centre
WOT/HER KT12 ....95 F3
Warren Road Primary School
YEAD UB4 ....217 F2
Warren Sports Centre
CHDH RM6 ....74 B1
Warwick Dubbing Theatre
SOHO/CST W1F 10 C4
Warwick Estate
BAY/PAD W2 ....101 F3
Warwick Leadlay Gallery
GNWCH SE10 ....125 F6
Warwick School for Boys
WALTH E17 ....70 A1
The Washington Mayfair Hotel
MYFR/PICC W1J 9 K7
Waterfront Leisure Centre
WOOL/PLUM SE18 ....127 F3
Watergate School
CAT SE6 ....182 E1
LEW SE13 ....144 E5
Waterloo Health Centre
STHWK SE1 ....17 J5
Watermans Arts, Cinema & Theatre Centre
BTFD TW8 ....117 F6
The Watermans Hall
MON EC3R 13 G6
Watermeads High School
MRDN SM4 ....194 C3
Watermill Business Centre
PEND EN3 ....25 H3
Water Rats Theatre
STPAN WC1H 5 F4

Waterside Business Centre
ISLW TW7 ....136 C5
Waterside Primary School
WOOL/PLUM SE18 ....127 J5
The Waterside Trading Centre
HNWL W7 ....115 K3
Watersports Centre
FSBYPK N4 ....67 J5
Waterways Business Centre
PEND EN3 ....25 H1
Watling Clinic
EDGW HA8 ....45 F3
Watling Medical Centre
EDGW HA8 ....44 E4
Wavelengths Leisure Pool & Library
DEPT SE8 ....144 D1
Waverley Industrial Estate
HRW HA1 ....42 D6
Waverley Lower Secondary School
EDUL SE22 ....143 J6
Waverley School
EDUL SE22 ....143 K6
PEND EN3 ....24 E5
Waxchandlers' Hall
CITYW EC2V 13 F3
Weald First & Middle School
KTN/HRWW/WS HA3 ....43 F3
Webster Graduate Studies Center
CAMTN NW1 ....3 F6
Welbeck Clinic
CRICK NW2 ....82 E1
Welbourne Primary School
SEVS/STOTM N15 ....68 C1
Wellcome Institute
CAMTN NW1 ....4 C6
Welldon Park Middle School
RYLN/HDSTN HA2 ....78 C2
The Welling Clinic
WELL DA16 ....148 B3
Welling Medical Centre
WELL DA16 ....148 A5
Welling School
WELL DA16 ....148 C2
Wellington Arch
MYFR/PICC W1J 15 H2
Wellington Barracks
WESTW SW1E 16 B3
Wellington Primary School
BOW E3 ....105 J2
HSLW TW3 ....134 E3
Welling United FC
WELL DA16 ....148 D4
Wells Primary School
WFD IG8 ....39 F6
Wembley Arena
WBLY HA9 ....80 C2
Wembley Commercial Centre
WBLY HA9 ....61 K6
Wembley Conference Centre
WBLY HA9 ....80 B1
Wembley FC
ALP/SUD HA0 ....79 H2
Wembley High Technology College
ALP/SUD HA0 ....79 J1
Wembley Hospital
ALP/SUD HA0 ....79 K4
Wembley Manor Primary School
WBLY HA9 ....80 A1
Wembley Park Business Centre
WBLY HA9 ....80 D1
Wembley Stadium
WBLY HA9 ....80 C2
Wembley Stadium Industrial Estate
WBLY HA9 ....80 C1
WBLY HA9 ....80 E1
Wendell Park Primary School
SHB W12 ....118 C2
Wentworth Tutorial College
GLDGN NW11 ....64 B3
The Werner Collection at Ranger's House
GNWCH SE10 ....145 G2
Wesley's Chapel, House & Museum
STLK EC1Y 6 E6
Wessex Gardens Primary School
GLDGN NW11 ....64 C5
West Acton Primary School
ACT W3 ....98 D5
West Beckton Health Centre
CAN/RD E16 ....107 G4
Westbourne Green Sports Complex
BAY/PAD W2 ....100 E4
Westbourne Primary School
SUT SM1 ....208 E1
Westbridge College
BTSEA SW11 ....140 D2
Westbrooke School
WELL DA16 ....148 E4
The Westbury Hotel
CONDST W1S 9 K5
Westbury Medical Centre
WDGN N22 ....49 J5
Westcroft Leisure Centre
CAR SM5 ....210 A2
West Drayton Primary School
WDR/YW UB7 ....112 B2
West Ealing Business Centre
WEA W13 ....97 G6
Western Avenue Business Park
ACT W3 ....98 D3
Western International Market
NWDGN UB2 ....114 A4

Western Trading Estate
WLSDN NW10 ....98 E3
West Ewell Infant School
HOR/WEW KT19 ....207 F3
Westfields Primary School
BARN SW13 ....138 C3
Westgate Business Centre
NKENS W10 ....100 C3
Westgate Primary School
DART DA1 ....171 G2
West Green Primary School
SEVS/STOTM N15 ....67 J1
West Grove Primary School
STHGT/OAK N14 ....34 D2
West Ham Church Primary School
SRTFD E15 ....88 D6
West Ham Lane Clinic
SRTFD E15 ....88 C6
West Hampstead Clinic
KIL/WHAMP NW6 ....82 E5
West Ham United FC (Upton Park)
PLSTW E13 ....107 H1
West Hatch High School
WFD IG8 ....53 K1
West Hendon Clinic
CDALE/KGS NW9 ....63 H3
West Hill Primary School
DART DA1 ....171 H1
WAND/EARL SW18 ....139 K6
West India Pier
POP/IOD E14 ....124 C2
West India Shopping Centre
POP/IOD E14 ....124 D1
Westland Heliport
BTSEA SW11 ....140 C4
West Lea School
ED N9 ....36 A5
West Lodge Park Hotel
EBAR EN4 ....21 K1
West Lodge Preparatory School
BFN/LL DA15 ....168 A5
West Lodge Primary School
PIN HA5 ....59 H1
West London Academy
NTHLT UB5 ....77 H6
West London Academy Primary
NTHLT UB5 ....77 H5
West London County Court
WKENS W14 ....119 H4
West London Magistrates Court
HMSMTH W6 ....119 G5
West London Tamil School
WLSDN NW10 ....99 H1
West Mead Clinic
RSLP HA4 ....77 C1
West Middlesex Golf Club
STHL UB1 ....96 C6
West Middlesex University Hospital
ISLW TW7 ....136 B3
Westminster Abbey
WEST SW1P 16 E4
Westminster Abbey Choir School
WEST SW1P 16 D4
Westminster Business Square
LBTH SE11 ....122 A6
Westminster Cathedral
WESTW SW1E 16 A5
Westminster Cathedral Choir School
WEST SW1P 16 B3
Westminster Cathedral RC Primary School
PIM SW1V 121 J5
Westminster City Hall
WESTW SW1E 16 B5
Westminster City School
WESTW SW1E 16 B4
Westminster College
SOHO/CST W1F 10 B5
Westminster Hall
WHALL SW1A 17 F3
Westminster Industrial Estate
WOOL/PLUM SE18 ....126 C3
Westminster Kingsway College
CAMTN NW1 ....4 A5
WEST SW1P 16 B6
Westminster Natural Health Centre
PIM SW1V 16 A7
Westminster Pier
WHALL SW1A 17 F3
Westminster School
WEST SW1P 16 E4
Westminster Theatre
WESTW SW1E 16 A4
Westminster Under School
WEST SW1P 16 C7
Westmoor Community Clinic
PUT/ROE SW15 ....158 D2
West Norwood Clinic
WNWD SE27 ....162 D4
West Norwood Crematorium
WNWD SE27 ....162 D5
West One Shopping Centre
MYFR/PKLN W1K 9 H4
Weston Green School
THDIT KT7 ....189 K5
Weston Park Clinic
CEND/HSY/T N8 ....66 E2
Weston Park Primary School
CEND/HSY/T N8 ....67 F2
Westpoint Trading Estate
ACT W3 ....98 C4
West Ramp Coach Park
HTHAIR TW6 ....132 D2
West Ruislip Elementary School
HGDN/ICK UB10 ....76 A1

West 12 Shopping & Leisure Centre
SHB W12 ....119 G2
West Thames College
ISLW TW7 ....135 K2
West Thamesmead Business Park
THMD SE28 ....128 A3
West Thornton Primary School
CROY/NA CR0 ....196 A4
West Twyford Primary School
WLSDN NW10 ....98 C1
Westward Preparatory School
WOT/HER KT12 ....188 A6
Westway Business Centre
BAY/PAD W2 ....101 F4
Westway Sports Centre
NKENS W10 ....100 B5
West Wickham Swimming Baths
WWKM BR4 ....199 F5
West Wimbledon Primary School
RYNPK SW20 ....176 E6
Westwood College
WELL DA16 ....147 J5
Westwood Language College for Girls
NRWD SE19 ....180 D3
Westwood Primary School
WELL DA16 ....147 J3
Westwood School
BUSH WD23 ....28 D4
Wetherby Preparatory School
NTGHL W11 ....100 E6
Wetherby Pre-Preparatory School
BAY/PAD W2 ....100 E6
Whaddon House Clinic
CMBW SE5 ....143 F4
Whipps Cross Hospital
WAN E11 ....70 B3
White Bridge Primary School
LOU IG10 ....39 J2
Whitechapel Art Gallery
WCHPL E1 ....13 K3
Whitechapel Sports Centre
WCHPL E1 ....104 C4
Whitefield School
CRICK NW2 ....64 B4
Whitefield School & Leisure Centre
WALTH E17 ....52 B4
Whitefriars First & Middle School
KTN/HRWW/WS HA3 ....42 E5
Whitefriars Trading Estate
KTN/HRWW/WS HA3 ....42 D5
Whitehall Primary School
CHING E4 ....38 C4
Whitehall Theatre
WHALL SW1A 10 D7
White Hart Lane School
WDGN N22 ....49 H3
Whiteheath Junior School
RSLP HA4 ....58 A3
Whitehorse Manor Primary School
THHTH CR7 ....196 E2
The White House Preparatory School
BAL SW12 ....161 J3
Whitelands College
PUT/ROE SW15 ....158 C2
Whiteleys Shopping Centre
BAY/PAD W2 ....101 F5
Whiterose Trading Estate
EBAR EN4 ....33 J2
Whitgift Almshouses
CROY/NA CR0 ....196 D6
Whitgift School
SAND/SEL CR2 ....211 J3
Whitgift Shopping Centre
CROY/NA CR0 ....196 D6
Whiting Hill Primary School
BAR EN5 ....20 A6
Whitmore High School
RYLN/HDSTN HA2 ....60 C5
Whitmore Primary School
IS N1 ....7 F2
Whittingham Community Primary School
WALTH E17 ....51 G4
Whittington Hospital
ARCH N19 ....66 B6
Whitton Health Centre
WHTN TW2 ....155 H3
Whitton Health Clinic
WHTN TW2 ....155 G3
Whitton School
WHTN TW2 ....155 G3
Whitton Sports & Fitness Centre
WHTN TW2 ....155 G4
Whybridge Infant School
RAIN RM13 ....93 J6
Whybridge Junior School
RAIN RM13 ....93 H6
Wickham Court School
WWKM BR4 ....214 B2
Wickham Theatre
WWKM BR4 ....214 B1
Wide Way Health Clinic
MTCM CR4 ....179 J6
Widmore Centre
BMLY BR1 ....184 B5
Wigmore Hall
CAVSQ/HST W1G 9 J3
Wigram House (University of Westminster)
WEST SW1P 16 C5
Wilberforce Primary School
NKENS W10 ....100 C3

Wilbury Primary School
UED N18 ....49 K1
Willesden Centre for Health & Care
WLSDN NW10 ....81 J5
Willesden County Court
WLSDN NW10 ....99 G1
Willesden Medical Centre
CRICK NW2 ....81 K4
Willesden Sports Centre
WLSDN NW10 ....81 K6
Willesden Sports Stadium
WLSDN NW10 ....81 K6
William Bellamy J & I School
DAGE RM10 ....74 C3
William Byrd School
HYS/HAR UB3 ....113 F6
William C Harvey Special School
TOTM N17 ....49 K5
William Davies Primary School
FSTGT E7 ....89 H4
William Ellis School
KTTN NW5 ....84 A1
William Ellis Sports Ground
EDGW HA8 ....44 C4
William Ford CE Junior School
DAGE RM10 ....92 C5
William Hogarth School
CHSWK W4 ....118 B6
William Morris Academy
HMSMTH W6 ....119 G5
William Morris Gallery
WALTH E17 ....51 J6
William Morris School
MTCM CR4 ....179 J6
William Morris School
WALTH E17 ....51 G4
William Patten Primary School
STNW/STAM N16 ....68 B6
William Torbitt J & I School
GNTH/NBYPK IG2 ....72 E2
William Tyndale Primary School
IS N1 ....85 H5
Willington School
WIM/MER SW19 ....177 J2
Willow Business Centre
MTCM CR4 ....194 E2
Willow Business Park
SYD SE26 ....163 K5
Willowfield Adult Education Centre
WALTH E17 ....51 F6
Willowfield School
HNHL SE24 ....142 D5
Willowfield School
WALTH E17 ....51 G6
The Willows Clinic
CHST BR7 ....185 F2
The Willows School
YEAD UB4 ....95 H3
Willow Tree Primary School
NTHLT UB5 ....77 J4
Wilmington Boys Grammar School
RDART DA2 ....170 E5
Wilmington Grammar School for Girls
RDART DA2 ....170 E5
Wilmington Hall School
RDART DA2 ....170 D5
Wilmington Primary School
RDART DA2 ....170 E5
Wilson's School
WLGTN SM6 ....210 E4
Wimbledon Chase Primary School
RYNPK SW20 ....177 H4
Wimbledon Common Golf Club
WIM/MER SW19 ....176 E1
Wimbledon Common Pre-Preparatory School
WIM/MER SW19 ....177 F2
Wimbledon (Gap Road) Cemetery
WIM/MER SW19 ....160 A6
Wimbledon High School
WIM/MER SW19 ....177 H2
Wimbledon House School
WIM/MER SW19 ....177 J4
Wimbledon Lawn Tennis Museum
WIM/MER SW19 ....159 H5
Wimbledon Magistrates Court
WIM/MER SW19 ....177 K2
Wimbledon Park Athletics Track
WIM/MER SW19 ....159 J4
Wimbledon Park Golf Club
WIM/MER SW19 ....159 J5
Wimbledon Park Primary School
WIM/MER SW19 ....159 K4
Wimbledon Recreation Centre
WIM/MER SW19 ....178 A2
Wimbledon RFC
RYNPK SW20 ....176 C3
Wimbledon School of Art
WIM/MER SW19 ....177 H4
WIM/MER SW19 ....177 K3
Wimbledon Stadium
WIM/MER SW19 ....160 A4
Wimbledon Stadium Business Centre
WIM/MER SW19 ....160 A5
Wimbledon Theatre
WIM/MER SW19 ....177 K3
Winchcombe Business Centre
PECK SE15 ....123 F6
Winchmore Hill Clinic
WCHMH N21 ....35 H4

Winchmore Hill CC
WCHMH N21 ....35 J3
Winchmore School
WCHMH N21 ....35 J4
Windmill Business Centre
NWDGN UB2 ....115 H1
Windmill School
BRXS/STRHM SW2 ....161 K1
Windmill Trading Estate
MTCM CR4 ....195 H2
Windrush Primary School
THMD SE28 ....128 C1
Winfield House
CAMTN NW1 ....2 D4
Wingate & Finchley FC
NFNCH/WDSPK N12 ....47 H3
Wingate Trading Estate
TOTM N17 ....50 B3
Wingfield Primary School
BKHTH/KID SE3 ....145 K4
Winns Primary School
WALTH E17 ....51 H5
Winsor Primary School
EHAM E6 ....108 A5
Winston Churchill's Britain at War Experience
STHWK SE1 ....19 F1
Winterbourne Infant School
THHTH CR7 ....196 B1
Winton Primary School
IS N1 ....5 G3
Witley Industrial Estate
NWDGN UB2 ....114 E4
Wolf Fields Primary School
NWDGN UB2 ....114 E4
Wolfson Hillel Primary School
STHGT/OAK N14 ....34 D1
Wolfson Medical Centre
RYNPK SW20 ....176 D3
Wolsey Business Park
WATW WD18 ....26 B2
Wolsey Junior School
CROY/NA CR0 ....214 B5
The Women's Library
WCHPL E1 ....13 J3
The Woodberry Clinic
MUSWH N10 ....48 B6
Woodbridge High School & Language College
WFD IG8 ....53 F3
Woodbrook School
BECK BR3 ....182 C4
Woodbury Down Primary School
FSBYPK N4 ....67 J4
Woodcroft Primary School
EDGW HA8 ....45 F3
Wood End J & I Schools
GFD/PVL UB6 ....78 D3
Wood End Park Junior School
UX/CGN UB8 ....94 A6
Woodfield School
CDALE/KGS NW9 ....63 G5
Woodford County High School for Girls
WFD IG8 ....52 D2
Woodford Golf Club
WFD IG8 ....52 D1
Woodford Green Preparatory School
WFD IG8 ....52 E2
Woodford Green Primary School
WFD IG8 ....52 E2
Woodford Trading Estate
WFD IG8 ....53 G5
Woodgrange Infant School
FSTGT E7 ....89 F2
Woodgrange Park Cemetery
MNPK E12 ....89 H3
Wood Green Crown Court
WDGN N22 ....49 G4
Wood Green Shopping City
WDGN N22 ....49 F4
Wood Green Old Boys FC
WDGN N22 ....49 G3
Woodhall School
OXHEY WD19 ....27 J6
Woodhill Primary School
CHARL SE7 ....126 D4
Woodhouse College
NFNCH/WDSPK N12 ....47 H2
Woodlands F & M School
KTN/HRWW/WS HA3 ....42 C3
Woodlands J & I School
IL IG1 ....90 D2
Woodlands Medical Centre
LEW SE13 ....165 G1
Wood Lane Medical Centre
RSLP HA4 ....58 C5
Wood Lane School
FUL/PGN SW6 ....140 B2
Wood Lane Sports Centre
BCTR RM8 ....74 D5
Woodmansterne Primary School
STRHM/NOR SW16 ....179 J4
Woodridge Primary School
NFNCH/WDSPK N12 ....32 E5
Woodside Health Centre
SNWD SE25 ....197 J2
Woodside Infant School
CROY/NA CR0 ....197 H4
Woodside Junior School
WALTH E17 ....52 A6
Woodside Park Golf Club
NFNCH/WDSPK N12 ....32 E6
Woodside Park International School
FBAR/BDGN N11 ....47 K1
Woodside School
BELV DA17 ....129 J4

Wood Wharf
POP/IOD E14 ....124 E1
Wood Wharf Business Park
POP/IOD E14 ....125 F2
Woolmore Primary School
POP/IOD E14 ....106 A6
Woolwich County Court
WOOL/PLUM SE18 ....127 F3
Woolwich Crown Court
THMD SE28 ....127 K2
Woolwich Polytechnic School
THMD SE28 ....128 B1
Worcesters Primary School
ENC/FH EN2 ....24 B1
World Business Centre Heathrow
HTHAIR TW6 ....133 F2
Worlds End Place
WBPTN SW10 ....140 B1
World Spiritual University
WLSDN NW10 ....81 J5
World University Service
STLK EC1Y 6 E7
Wormholt Park Primary School
SHB W12 ....99 J6
Worple Primary School
ISLW TW7 ....136 B5
Worsley Bridge Junior School
BECK BR3 ....182 D3
Worton Hall Industrial Estate
ISLW TW7 ....135 K5
Wrencote
CROY/NA CR0 ....211 J1
Wyborne Primary School
ELTH/MOT SE9 ....167 G3
Wyke Green Golf Club
ISLW TW7 ....116 A6
Wykeham Primary School
HCH RM12 ....75 J5
Wyndhams Theatre
CHCR WC2N 10 D5
Wyvil Primary School
VX/NE SW8 ....141 K1
Yale University Press
HAMP NW3 ....83 J2
Yardley Primary School
CHING E4 ....37 K1
Yeading FC
YEAD UB4 ....114 B1
Yeading Medical Centre
NTHLT UB5 ....95 G2
Yeading Primary School
YEAD UB4 ....95 G4
Yerbury Primary School
ARCH N19 ....84 D1
Yeshivo Horomo Talmudical College
STNW/STAM N16 ....67 K5
Yesodey Hatorah Jewish School
STNW/STAM N16 ....68 A4
Yesodey Hatorah Senior Girls School
STNW/STAM N16 ....68 B4
Yetev Lev Day School for Boys
STNW/STAM N16 ....68 C5
Yiewsley Health Centre
WDR/YW UB7 ....112 B1
YMCA Leisure Centre
RSQ WC1B 10 D3
York Clinic
STHWK SE1 ....18 E1
York Hall
BETH E2 ....104 D1
York Rd Junior School & Language Unit
DART DA1 ....171 J2
York Water Gate
CHCR WC2N 11 F7
Young Actors Theatre
IS N1 ....5 J1
Young Vic Theatre
STHWK SE1 ....17 K2
Zennor Road Industrial Estate
BAL SW12 ....161 H3
Zephyr Business Centre
SEVS/STOTM N15 ....68 A1
Ziam Trading Estate
CLPT E5 ....68 E5

Schools address data provided by Education Direct

Petrol station information supplied by Johnsons

One-way street data provided by © Tele Atlas N.V. Tele Atlas

Garden centre information provided by

Garden Centre Association Britains best garden centres

Wyevale Garden Centres

The boundary of the London congestion charging zone supplied by Transport for London

The statement on the front cover of this atlas is sourced, selected and quoted from a reader comment and feedback form received in 2004

AA **Street by Street** QUESTIONNAIRE

Dear Atlas User
Your comments, opinions and recommendations are very important to us. So please help us to improve our street atlases by taking a few minutes to complete this simple questionnaire.

You do not need a stamp (unless posted outside the UK). If you do not want to remove this page from your street atlas, then photocopy it or write your answers on a plain sheet of paper.

Send to: Marketing Assistant, AA Publishing, 14th Floor Fanum House, FREEPOST SCE 4598, Basingstoke RG21 4GY

ABOUT THE ATLAS...

Please state which city / town / county street atlas you bought:

Where did you buy the atlas? (City, Town, County)

For what purpose? (please tick all applicable)

To use in your own local area ☐   **To use on business or at work** ☐

Visiting a strange place ☐   **In the car** ☐   **On foot** ☐

Other (please state)

Have you ever used any street atlases other than AA Street by Street?

Yes ☐   **No** ☐

If so, which ones?

Is there any aspect of our street atlases that could be improved?
(Please continue on a separate sheet if necessary)

continued overleaf

Please list the features you found most useful:

_____
_____
_____
_____

Please list the features you found least useful:

_____
_____
_____
_____

LOCAL KNOWLEDGE...

Local knowledge is invaluable. Whilst every attempt has been made to make the information contained in this atlas as accurate as possible, should you notice any inaccuracies, please detail them below (if necessary, use a blank piece of paper) or e-mail us at *streetbystreet@theAA.com*

_____
_____
_____

ABOUT YOU...

Name (Mr/Mrs/Ms)
_____
Address
_____
                                          Postcode
_____
Daytime tel no
_____
E-mail address
_____

Which age group are you in?

Under 25 ☐   **25-34** ☐   **35-44** ☐   **45-54** ☐   **55-64** ☐   **65+** ☐

Are you an AA member?   Yes ☐   No ☐

Do you have Internet access?   Yes ☐   No ☐

Thank you for taking the time to complete this questionnaire. Please send it to us as soon as possible, and remember, you do not need a stamp (unless posted outside the UK).

We may use information we hold about you to write to, telephone or email you about other products and services offered by the AA, we do NOT disclose this information to third parties.

Please tick here if you do not wish to hear about products and services from the AA. ☐